PAGE 46

ON THE ROAD

YOUR COMPLETE DESTINATION GUIDE
In-depth reviews, detailed listings and insider tips

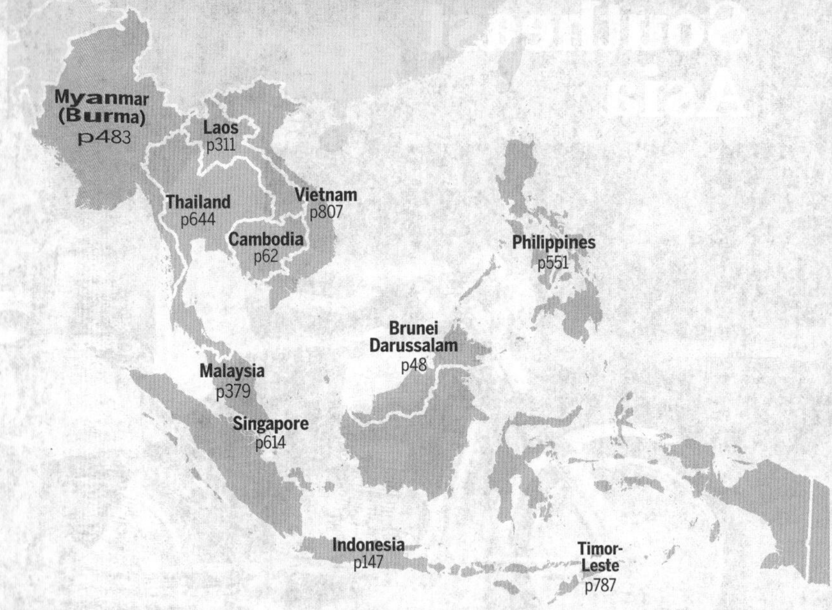

PAGE 925

SURVIVAL GUIDE

VITAL PRACTICAL INFORMATION TO HELP YOU HAVE A SMOOTH TRIP

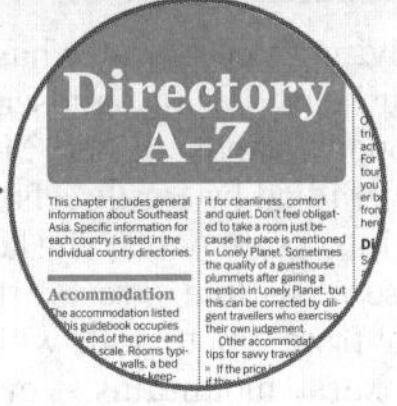

THIS EDITION WRITTEN AND RESEARCHED BY

China Williams

Greg Bloom, Celeste Brash, Stuart Butler, Jayne D'Arcy, Shawn Low, Brandon Presser, Nick Ray, Simon Richmond, Daniel Robinson, Adam Skolnick, Iain Stewart, Ryan Ver Berkmoes, Richard Waters

welcome to Southeast Asia

Elemental Forces

The life-giving force of water has sculpted many Southeast Asian landscapes. The jungle-topped islands of the Malay peninsula are cradled by coral reefs that tame the ocean into azure pools. The languorous Vietnamese coastline greets the South China Sea from tip to tail, while inland there are karst mountains – evidence of long-vanished oceans. And the muddy Mekong River lopes through tightly knit mountains to flat rice baskets. The traditional 'highways' of Borneo are tannin-stained rivers that slice through the wilderness. And the volcanoes of Indonesia and the Philippines provide a glimpse into the earth's blacksmithing core.

Spiritual Spaces

Southeast Asia bathes in spirituality. With the dawn, pots of rice come to a boil and religious supplications waft from earth to sky. Barefoot monks silently move through dull-lit streets collecting food alms from the faithful; prayers bellow from needle-tipped mosques calling the devotees to bend to earth in submission; family altars are tended like thirsty houseplants. And the region's great monuments have been built for the divine, from Angkor's heaven incarnate to Bagan's infinity-bending temple expanse. This is a region in close communication with the divine. Visitors can join in on the conversation on meditation retreats or by hiking into the mist

Exotic and tropical, friendly and hospitable, historic and devout, Southeast Asia offers a warm embrace, from its sun-kissed beaches and steamy jungles to its bustling modern cities and sleepy villages.

(left) Buddhist monks travelling by motorcycle taxi, Siem Reap
(below) Rice paddies in northern Vietnam

belt to visit a golden-spired temple or sacred mountain.

A Marriage of Old & New

Southeast Asian cities grabbed on to the future long before it became the present. Bangkok's masses zip between shopping malls aboard sky-suspended trains. Affluent Singapore shows off its multicultural heritage like a fashion show and Ho Chi Minh City is in a race to the top of the commercial heap. In between these modern marvels are rickety wooden villages filled with yawning dogs and napping grannies, where the agricultural clock measures out the rice planting and harvest seasons. These rural landscapes are best visited via human power: by cycling past sandal-clad villagers and curious children or trekking through high-altitude hill-tribe villages.

A Bountiful Harvest

In the absence of winter, the earth here is always pregnant with ambrosial fruits, spices once as prized as gold, and the staple, rice, which is concocted into three square meals and dessert. Grazing is a Southeast Asian art, cultivated in the hawker centres of Penang and Singapore or by itinerant vendors in Thailand and Vietnam. The cuisines – Indian curries, Chinese dim sum – reflect historic migrations, and the flavours flirt with the climate, balancing spicy, sweet, salty and sour.

Southeast Asia

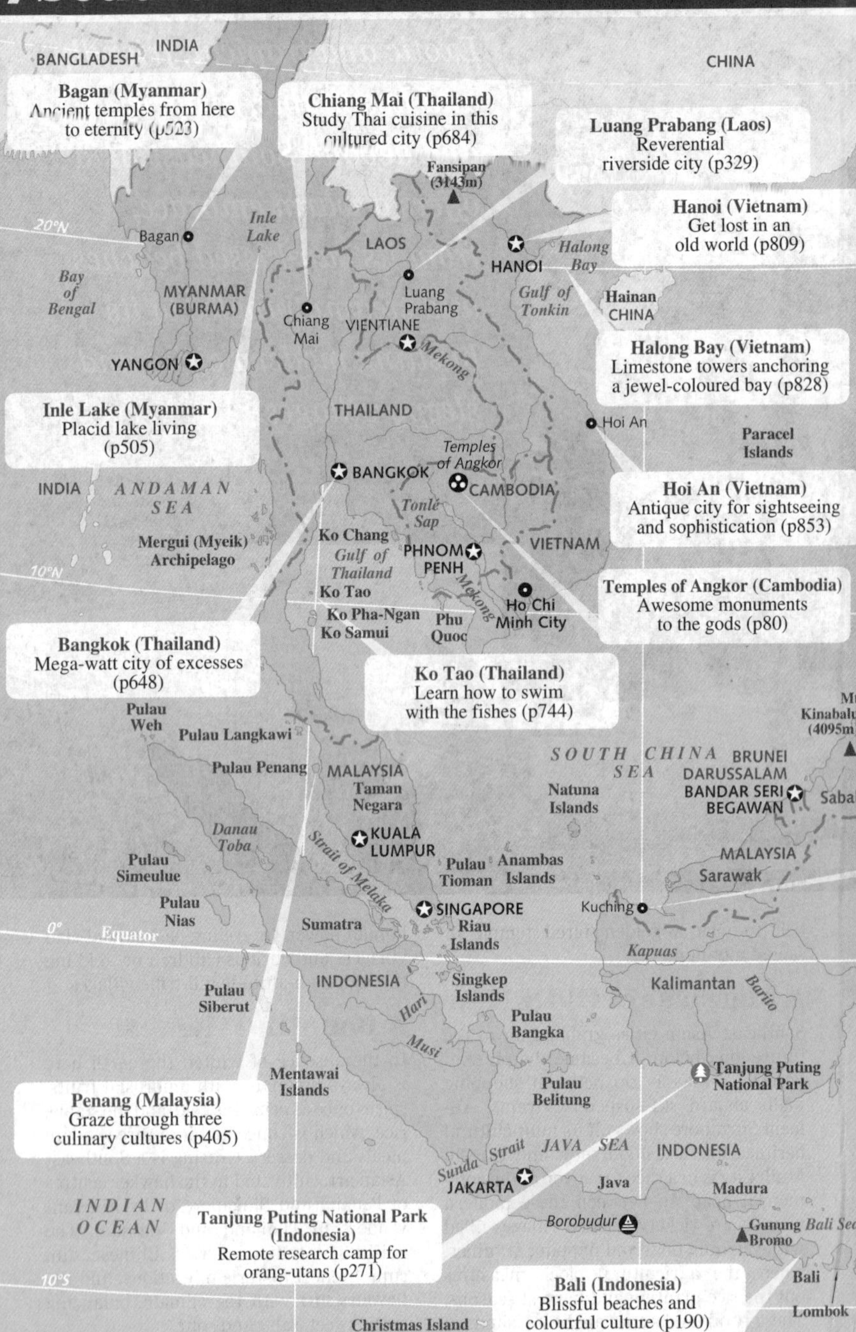

Bagan (Myanmar)
Ancient temples from here to eternity (p523)
Chiang Mai (Thailand)
Study Thai cuisine in this cultured city (p684)
Luang Prabang (Laos)
Reverential riverside city (p329)
Hanoi (Vietnam)
Get lost in an old world (p809)
Halong Bay (Vietnam)
Limestone towers anchoring a jewel-coloured bay (p828)
Inle Lake (Myanmar)
Placid lake living (p505)
Hoi An (Vietnam)
Antique city for sightseeing and sophistication (p853)
Temples of Angkor (Cambodia)
Awesome monuments to the gods (p80)
Bangkok (Thailand)
Mega-watt city of excesses (p648)
Ko Tao (Thailand)
Learn how to swim with the fishes (p744)
Penang (Malaysia)
Graze through three culinary cultures (p405)
Tanjung Puting National Park (Indonesia)
Remote research camp for orang-utans (p271)
Bali (Indonesia)
Blissful beaches and colourful culture (p190)
INDIA
BANGLADESH
CHINA
Fansipan (3143m)
20°N
Bagan
Inle Lake
LAOS
HANOI
Halong Bay
Bay of Bengal
MYANMAR (BURMA)
Luang Prabang
Gulf of Tonkin
Hainan CHINA
Chiang Mai
VIENTIANE
YANGON
Mekong
THAILAND
Hoi An
Paracel Islands
Temples of Angkor
BANGKOK
CAMBODIA
INDIA
ANDAMAN SEA
Tonlé Sap
Ko Chang
Mergui (Myeik) Archipelago
Gulf of Thailand
PHNOM PENH
VIETNAM
10°N
Ko Tao
Ko Pha-Ngan
Ko Samui
Phu Quoc
Ho Chi Minh City
Pulau Weh
Pulau Langkawi
Mt Kinabalu (4095m)
SOUTH CHINA SEA
BRUNEI DARUSSALAM
Pulau Penang
MALAYSIA
Taman Negara
Natuna Islands
BANDAR SERI BEGAWAN
Sabah
Danau Toba
KUALA LUMPUR
Strait of Melaka
Pulau Simeulue
Pulau Tioman
Anambas Islands
MALAYSIA
Sarawak
Pulau Nias
SINGAPORE
Riau Islands
Kuching
0°
Equator
Sumatra
Kapuas
INDONESIA
Pulau Siberut
Singkep Islands
Kalimantan
Bario
Hari
Pulau Bangka
Musi
Mentawai Islands
Tanjung Puting National Park
Pulau Belitung
Sunda Strait
JAVA SEA
INDONESIA
JAKARTA
Java
Madura
INDIAN OCEAN
Borobudur
Gunung Bromo
Bali Sea
10°S
Bali
Lombok
Christmas Island AUSTRALIA
100°E
110°E

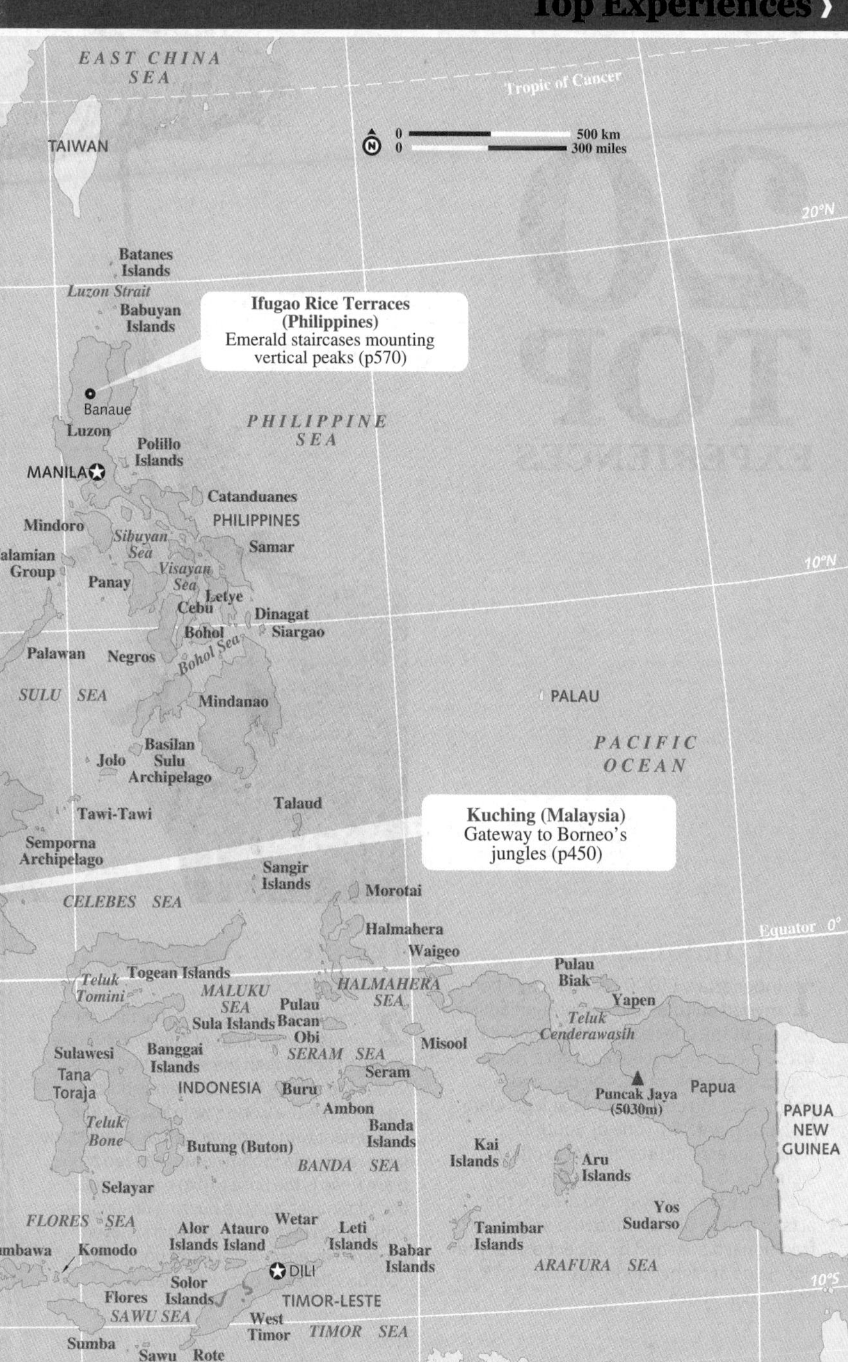
EAST CHINA SEA
Tropic of Cancer
0 500 km
0 300 miles
TAIWAN
20°N
Batanes Islands
Luzon Strait
Babuyan Islands
Ifugao Rice Terraces (Philippines)
Emerald staircases mounting vertical peaks (p570)
Banaue
Luzon
PHILIPPINE SEA
Polillo Islands
MANILA
Catanduanes
PHILIPPINES
Mindoro
Sibuyan Sea
Samar
Calamian Group
Visayan Sea
10°N
Panay
Leyte
Cebu
Dinagat
Bohol
Siargao
Palawan
Negros
Bohol Sea
SULU SEA
Mindanao
PALAU
PACIFIC OCEAN
Basilan
Jolo
Sulu Archipelago
Talaud
Tawi-Tawi
Kuching (Malaysia)
Gateway to Borneo's jungles (p450)
Semporna Archipelago
Sangir Islands
Morotai
CELEBES SEA
Halmahera
Equator 0°
Waigeo
Pulau Biak
Teluk Tomini
Togean Islands
MALUKU SEA
HALMAHERA SEA
Yapen
Pulau Bacan
Teluk Cenderawasih
Sula Islands
Obi
Misool
Sulawesi
Banggai Islands
SERAM SEA
Seram
Tana Toraja
INDONESIA
Buru
Puncak Jaya (5030m)
Papua
Ambon
PAPUA NEW GUINEA
Teluk Bone
Banda Islands
Butung (Buton)
Kai Islands
Aru Islands
BANDA SEA
Selayar
Yos Sudarso
FLORES SEA
Wetar
Alor Islands
Atauro Island
Leti Islands
Tanimbar Islands
Sumbawa
Komodo
Babar Islands
DILI
ARAFURA SEA
10°S
Flores
Solor Islands
TIMOR-LESTE
SAWU SEA
West Timor
TIMOR SEA
Sumba
Sawu
Rote
120°E
AUSTRALIA
140°E

20 TOP EXPERIENCES

Bali (Indonesia)

1 Indonesia's 17,000 islands may offer myriad cultural and exploration adventures, but the one island not to miss is Bali (p190). The original backpackers' haven, you can surf epic breaks by day and rub shoulders with supermodels at legendary clubs by night. With one of Southeast Asia's richest cultures, Bali also offers a chance to escape party glitz and stay in a family homestay in and around the arts centre of Ubud, where the sounds of traditional dance and music echo over the rice fields at night. Hindu ceremony on Kuta beach, Bali, above

Temples of Angkor (Cambodia)

2 One of the world's most magnificent sights, the temples of Angkor (p80) are so much better than the superlatives. Angkor Wat is the world's largest religious building; Bayon is the world's weirdest spiritual monument with its immense four-sided stone faces; and at Ta Prohm nature has run amok. Siem Reap is the base to explore this collection of temples and is a buzzing destination with superb restaurants and bars. Beyond the temples are cultural attractions, such as floating villages and cooking classes.

1

2

AUSTIN BUSH / LONELY PLANET IMAGES ©

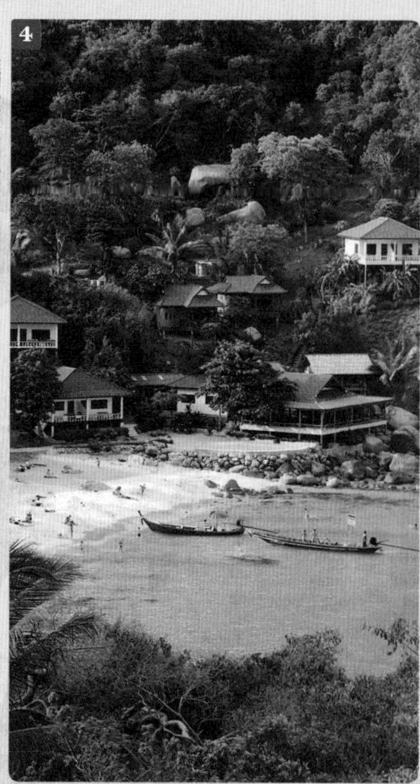

Bangkok (Thailand)

3 Southeast Asia's superstar city (p648) has it all in supersized proportions: food, shopping, fun and then some… It might be a pressure cooker for new arrivals but it will be a needed dose of civilisation after weeks of dusty back roads. Build in plenty of time to load up on souvenirs, refresh your wardrobe, be plucked and kneaded and recount tall tales over a sweaty bottle of beer. Don't forget a sunset river ferry ride, an evening noodle tour of Chinatown and one final round of temple spotting.

Ko Tao (Thailand)

4 The divemaster's island, Ko Tao (p744) is the cheapest and easiest spot to learn how to strap on a tank and dive into the deep. The water is warm and gentle and the underwater spectacles are not to be missed. Just offshore are rocky coves and coral reefs frequented by all manner of fish, providing a snorkelling aperitif. Its small size means that the island is something of a diving 'university', with a lively social scene after class. Ao Leuk beach, Ko Tao, above right

Halong Bay (Vietnam)

5 More than 3000 limestone-peaked islands sheltered by shimmering seas make Halong Bay (p828) one of Vietnam's top tourist draws as well as a Unesco World Heritage Site. An overnight cruise allows you to adore the scenery through the day's dramatic changes of light: rise early for an ethereal misty morn, kayak into the tidal-carved grottoes and lagoons and track the pastel parade of the sinking sun. If you're still hankering for more karst action, move on to less touristed Lan Ha Bay.

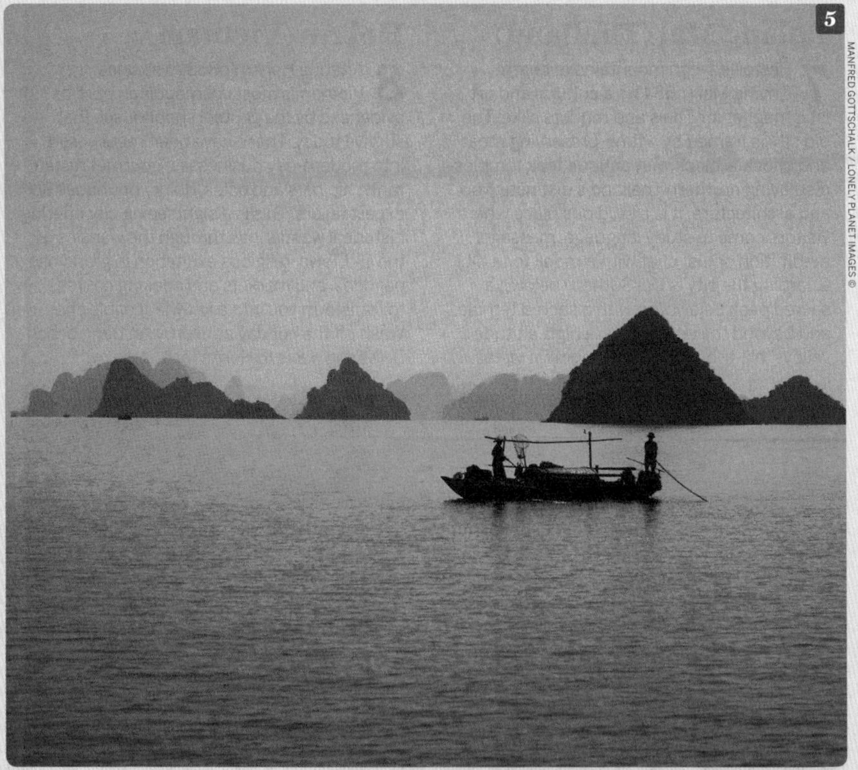

5

MANFRED GOTTSCHALK / LONELY PLANET IMAGES ©

Luang Prabang (Laos)

6 Hemmed in by the Mekong and Nam Khan rivers, this ancient city boasts history, religious devotion and natural beauty. Once a royal capital, Luang Prabang (p329) is populated by temples and Buddhist monks, best seen on their morning alms routes. In between are forested river views and world-class French cuisine. Hire a bike and explore the backstreets, take a cooking workshop or elephant trek, or just ease back with a restful massage at one of a dozen affordable spas. Prepare to adjust your timetable and stay a little longer than planned.

6

JERRY ALEXANDER / LONELY PLANET IMAGES ©

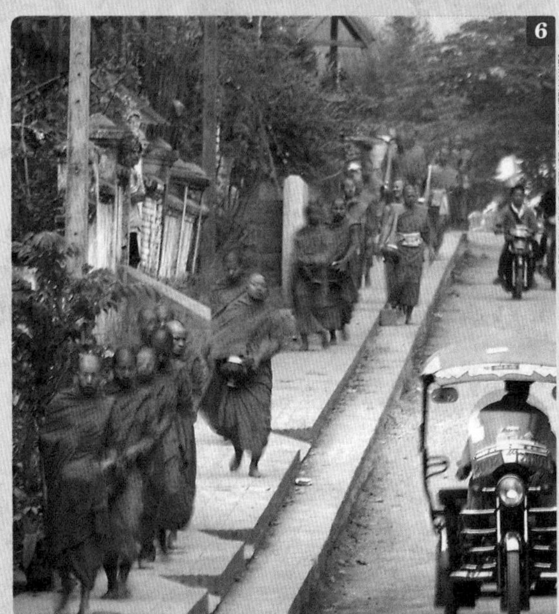

Chiang Mai (Thailand)

7 Bestowed with mountains of charm, Chiang Mai (p684) is a cultural and artistic magnet for Thais and tourists alike. The old city is framed by a time-preserving moat and chock-a-block with antique teak temples displaying northern Thailand's distinctive art and architecture. It is a studious place where visitors come to study language, massage, meditation or just chat with a monk for a bit. Guarding the city is Doi Suthep (below), a sacred peak bejewelled with a sacred temple, and beyond the city limits are high-altitude valleys, hill-tribe treks and mountain vistas.

Hoi An (Vietnam)

8 Antique Hoi An (p853) was once Vietnam's most cosmopolitan port, as evidenced by the genteel shophouses that survive today. These have been repurposed into modern-day businesses: gourmet restaurants, hip bars and cafes, quirky boutiques and expert tailors. This is a sightseeing city offering historical wanderings through the warrens of the Old Town, religious exultation in grandiose pagodas, and markets and cooking courses to transform you into a knowledgeable chef. Wash off the hot day at nearby An Bang beach.
Delivering wares to Hoi An market, below

SALLY DILLON / LONELY PLANET IMAGES ©

JOHN BANAGAN / LONELY PLANET IMAGES ©

PETER PTSCHELINZEW / LONELY PLANET IMAGES ©

Hanoi (Vietnam)

9 It is something of a sport to get decidedly lost in the Old Quarter of Hanoi (p809), a frantic commercial labyrinth where echoes of the past are filtered and framed by 21st-century energy. Eating and people-watching are other Hanoi-tailored pursuits. Enjoy the city's signature dishes – *pho bo* (beef noodle soup), *bun cha* (barbecued pork) and *banh cuon* (rice crepes) – while perched on a tiny chair claiming a small piece of the footpath. Later at night, join the socialising throngs enjoying refreshingly crisp *bia hoi* (draught beer) at makeshift street corner bars.

Penang (Malaysia)

10 The colonial Southeast Asian experience is still tangible on this steamy port island (p405) where Malaysian, Chinese, Indian and British cultures collide. The capital of Georgetown has been designated a Unesco World Heritage Site and the once-tumbledown Chinese shophouses, clan houses and colonial buildings are being painted and primped up. Wander a maze of streets where joss smoke and the call to prayer mingle with Bollywood tunes and fragrant street food on every corner. Outside the city are beaches, jungles and endless shopping malls. Kek Lok Si Temple, Penang, top right

Kuching (Malaysia)

11 Borneo's most sophisticated and stylish city (p450) brings together an atmospheric old town, a romantic waterfront, fine cuisine for all budgets and chic nightspots that would be right at home in London. But the city's biggest draw is what's nearby: some of Sarawak's finest natural sights that are easy to visit on day trips. You can spot orang-utans or search out a giant *Rafflesia* flower in the morning, or look for proboscis monkeys and wild crocs on a sundown cruise in the South China Sea. Finish off the evening by dining on fresh seafood or crunchy *midin* (jungle fern tips).

JOHNNY HAGLUND / LONELY PLANET IMAGES ©

Bagan (Myanmar)

12 More than 4000 Buddhist temples are scattered across the plains of Bagan (p523), the site of the first Burmese kingdom and an architectural complement to the temples of Angkor. Dating to between the 11th and 13th centuries, the vast majority have been renovated, as Bagan remains an active religious site and place of pilgrimage. Yes, there are tour buses and crowds at the most popular sunset-viewing spots, but they can be avoided. Pedal off on a bike and have your own adventure amid the not-so-ruined temples.

Singapore Food

13 This small city-state (p614) excels in the art of multi-culti cuisine served in the ever-approachable hawker centres. Over the generations, descendants from China, Malaysia, Indonesia and India joined their cooking pots into a communal conversation, importing, creating and tweaking dishes from their homelands. Now there's a wealth of edible options: steaming plates of chilli crab, *nasi biryani* and *char kway teow* to name just a few. Rarely is there a dish that is a pure breed but rather each boasts a hybrid ingredient that makes it uniquely Singaporean.

Temburong (Brunei)

14 From a low-flying Twin Otter turboprop (or on Google Earth), Brunei's Temburong District looks like all of Borneo once did: an unbroken carpet of primary rainforest unblemished by roads or logging gashes. On the ground, most of the sultanate's eastern sliver is off-limits except to scientists, but you can experience the primeval jungle at Ulu Temburong National Park (p57). The only way in is an exciting longboat ride. Once there you can climb into the jungle canopy and have wild fish nibble your feet in a cool stream. Bornean gibbon, above right

14

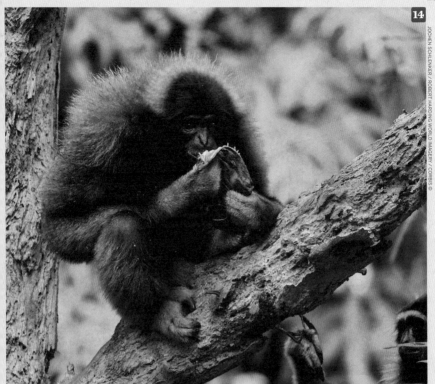

Inle Lake (Myanmar)

15 Surrounded by an enormous carpet of greenery, Inle Lake (p504) is so awe-inspiring and large that everybody comes away with a different experience. If you're counting days, you'll most likely be hitting the hot spots: water-bound temples, shore-bound markets and floating gardens. If you have more time, you can consider day hikes or exploring the more remote corners of the lake. The cool weather, friendly folks and that placid pool of ink-like water are bound to find a permanent place in your memory.

15

PETER STUCKINGS / LONELY PLANET IMAGES ©

DALLAS STRIBLEY / LONELY PLANET IMAGES ©

RICHARD I'ANSON / LONELY PLANET IMAGES ©

Phnom Penh (Cambodia)

16 The Cambodian capital (p66) is the 'phoenix risen' of modern-day history, signalled by the onset of urban chaos (a regional speciality) and influx of urbane businesses (watch out Bangkok). The city's beautiful riverfront is now an enclave for designer restaurants, funky bars and hip hotels ready to welcome the adventurous. Meanwhile the atrocities of the Khmer Rouge regime – remembered at the inspiring National Museum and the depressing Tuol Sleng Museum – require an emotional sense of adventure and historical civic duty. National Museum, Phnom Penh, above

Philippine Beaches

17 Nothing defines the Philippines (p551) better than a remote strip of pearly white sand. There's at least one beach for every one of the country's 7000-plus islands, and they are made-to-order. Want to be far away from everybody? Many a Visayan island is ringed by deserted beaches, while your own private island awaits in northern Palawan around El Nido and Coron. Seeking a good dive spot that's not just about diving? Dial up Malapascua or Sipalay. Want action with your beach experience? Kitesurf on Boracay or surf Siargao. Beach at El Nido, Palawan Island, top right

Ifugao Rice Terraces (Philippines)

18 These incredible terraces (p569) were hand-hewn centuries ago by the Ifugao tribe in the remote Cordillera mountains of the northern Philippines. The result was arable land where there had been only vertical impediments. Referred to as one of the wonders of the world, the rice terraces ring the towns of Banaue and Batad, but adventurous travellers will find terraces ribbing most of the spiny Cordillera. Trekking these emerald staircases – and sleeping among them in idyllic Batad – is an experience not to be missed. Rice terraces around Banaue, above

Atauro Island (Timor-Leste)

19 Get a group together, hire a dive boat and head to the incredible dive sites of Atauro (p794). The diving in Timor-Leste is world class, thanks to a perfect mix of cool, deep water, undamaged reefs, underfished marine life and its prime location in the Coral Triangle. Atauro, some 30km off the coast of Dili, has strong tides (you'll be drift diving) and is one of the few places you can dive and spot small reef-dwelling creatures as well as large pelagic creatures including turtles, hammer-head sharks, whales and dolphins.

Tanjung Puting National Park (Indonesia)

20 One of the best places to see orang-utans in their natural habitat is at Tanjung Puting National Park (p271). The journey is straight out of *Heart of Darkness* via *klotok* (traditional river boats), which double as floating hotels and put-put past the lush riverside of Sungai Sekonyer. Cruising gently between walls of pandanus fringing the river like spiky-haired stick figures, you may spot orang-utans perched on branches or macaques scurrying through a forest canopy shared with 200-plus bird species. Animal species abound.

19

MARK WEBSTER / LONELY PLANET IMAGES ©

20

THEO ALLOFS / CORBIS ©

need to know

Planes

» Affordable regional flights handy for Indonesian island-hopping or cutting out long-haul bus rides.

Buses

» The primary intra-country mode of travel in most of Southeast Asia though reliability and road conditions vary.

When to Go

High Season
(Dec–Feb)

» Dry, cool season

» Chilly in mountains

» Travel is difficult during Chinese New Year (Tet in Vietnam)

» Crowds for Christmas and New Year

» Height of Philippine festival season

» Rain in Indonesia

Shoulder Season
(Mar & Oct–Nov)

» Hot, dry season begins in March; crowds dissipate

» Dry season begins in Indonesia (Apr–May)

Low Season
(Apr–Sep)

» Hot, dry (Mar–Jun)

» Travel difficult for April's water festivals

» Wet season (Jul–Sep/Oct) , though unpredictable of late

» Easter festivities in Philippines

» Indonesia's high season (Jun–Aug)

Your Daily Budget

Budget less than
US$50

» Cheap guesthouse US$10–20

» Local meal or street eats US$1–5

» Local transport US$1–5

» Beer US$1–5

Midrange
US$50–100

» Hotel room US$21–75

» Restaurant meal US$6–10

» Motorcycle hire US$6–10

Top end over
US$100

» Boutique hotel or beach resort US$100+

» Dive trip US$50–100

» Car hire US$50

Trains

» Slow but scenic alternative to buses for a limited number of destinations.

Ferries

» Services link islands to the mainland and connect archipelago nations; quality and safety varies between countries.

Motorcycles/ Bicycles

» Easy and convenient get-abouts for in-town travel.

Cars

» Car hire is available in most tourist towns though road rules are confusing; better to hire a driver.

Websites

» **Lonely Planet** (www.lonelyplanet.com) Read country profiles, post questions to the traveller community on the Thorn Tree forum and make travel reservations.

» **Tales of Asia** (www.talesofasia.com) Handy website for traveller trip reports on overland border crossings, especially between Cambodia and Thailand.

» **Agoda** (www.agoda.com) Regional online hotel booking site.

» **Asia Times** (www.atimes.com) In-depth analysis of current events in Southeast Asia.

Money

Each country has its own currency; see the respective country chapter for details. ATMs are widely available in Cambodia, Thailand, Malaysia, Singapore, Philippines and Vietnam. Check with your bank and in each country's Money section to determine international withdrawal fees. ATMs are limited to major cities in Laos, Timor-Leste and Indonesia. There are no ATMs in Myanmar. In these countries, you should bring a supply of cash and travellers cheques.

Visas

» Most foreign nationals qualify for visas on arrival in Cambodia, Laos, Thailand, Indonesia, Philippines and Timor-Leste. Many of these arrival visas are valid for approximately a month, though there are some exceptions.

» You must arrange visas prior to arrival for Vietnam and Myanmar.

» See each country's Visas section for details on visa costs, duration, extensions and ports of entry. Be aware that overland border crossings are often fraught with minor rip-offs.

Arriving In...

» **Suvarnabhumi International Airport (Bangkok, Thailand)** Taxis (one hour) and rail (15 to 30 minutes) to the centre

» **Kuala Lumpur International Airport (Kuala Lumpur, Malaysia)** KLIA Ekspres rail (15 minutes) to centre

» **Soekarno-Hatta International Airport (Jakarta, Indonesia)** Taxis and buses (one hour) to centre

Staying in Touch

Most of Southeast Asia is globally wired with modern communication technologies. Tourist centres have more choices and more affordable rates than remote villages.

» **Mobile Phones** Local, pre-paid SIM cards and mobile phones are available throughout the region. International roaming is prohibitively expensive and not available in Myanmar.

» **Wi-fi & Internet Access** Internet cafes are common in tourist centres and wi-fi is often free in guesthouses in some countries.

» **Calling Home** International calling rates are fairly affordable. To call home on a mobile phone, dial an international access code + country code + subscriber number. Internet cafes are often equipped with headsets and Skype as an alternative. With mobile wireless capability, you can also make Skype calls from a mobile phone.

if you like...

Fabulous Food

Southeast Asian cuisine celebrates its tropical bounty with fresh and bold flavours. Thai chillies turn a meal into a head rush, Vietnamese food is so refreshing you won't need a beverage and exotic fruits are sweeter than desserts.

Bangkok (Thailand) Food glorious food! Fresh, tasty meals are everywhere in this 24-hour grazing city (p663)

Hanoi (Vietnam) Be an urban forager among Hanoi's rice and noodle stalls (p819)

Luang Prabang (Laos) Cafes and bakeries with a French flair preserve a delicious colonial connection (p334)

Chiang Mai (Thailand) Learn how to slice and dice like the Thai wok masters at a cooking school (p689)

Singapore Savour Asia old and new, from 50-year-old chicken-rice stalls to swish international outposts (p631)

Penang (Malaysia) Malaysia's multi-culti melting pot is an edible journey through Indian curries, Chinese dim sum and Malay desserts (p407)

Temples, Tombs & Towers

This is a holy land inundated with monuments to the divine. Empire builders achieved immortality with monuments that sprawl across mainland Southeast Asia. And modern altars testify to each country's artistic temperament, from modest mosques to flamboyant Buddhist temples.

Angkor (Cambodia) An architectural wonder of the world built by the great Khmer empire (p94)

Bagan (Myanmar) Hundreds of ancient temples stretch out towards the horizon like a grazing herd (p523)

Borobudur (Indonesia) A stunning stupa ringed by mist and mountains (p178)

Wat Phra Kaew (Thailand) A dazzling royal temple and home to the revered Emerald Buddha (p648)

Ho Chi Minh Mausoleum (Vietnam) Come face to face with history in Ho Chi Minh's austere mausoleum (p812)

Shwedagon Paya (Myanmar) A golden hilltop temple that gleams with heavenly splendour (p486)

Petronas Towers (Malaysia) For superlative seekers, this skyscraper still has the tallest 'twin' spires in the world (p383)

Spectacular Treks

Treks along mainland Southeast Asia's mountainous belt climb up forested mountains to remote hill-tribe villages. Further south, you'll find lush, critter-filled rainforests. And no trekking tour is complete without huffing and puffing up an Indonesian volcano.

Sapa (Vietnam) Dirt paths wind through verdant rice terraces tended by Hmong and other ethnic minorities (p838)

Nam Ha NPA (Laos) Eco-oriented treks through an old-growth forest and high-altitude hill-tribe villages (p346)

Cordillera Mountains (Philippines) Carved into jagged mountains are ancient rice terraces, hand-hewn thousands of years ago by tribal people (p566)

Gunung Bromo (Indonesia) An active volcano hiked up at night for a sunrise view of its moonscape summit (p186)

Taman Negara National Park (Malaysia) Old-growth rainforest conveniently close to civilisation (p430)

Mt Kinabalu (Malaysia) Borneo's highest mountain is a two-day march for a spiritual sunrise (p440)

CHRISTER FREDRIKSSON / LONELY PLANET IMAGES ©

» Couple walking along kitesurfing beach, Mui Ne (p865), Vietnam

Beautiful Beaches

From far-flung islands to long, leggy coastlines, Southeast Asia offers unofficial degrees in beachology. Do your 'research' on party beaches in Thailand and Indonesia, on the curvaceous Vietnam coast or on islands sprinkled throughout the region.

Ko Pha-Ngan (Thailand) Full-on Full Moon parties and hammock-hanging on the original beach-bum island (p738)

Bali (Indonesia) Justifiably famous for its beach bliss, lush volcanic interior and colourful culture (p190)

Krabi/Railay (Thailand) Rock-climbers scale the karst cliffs, while kayakers slice the jewel-hued waters (p763)

Sihanoukville (Cambodia) Good times rule at Cambodia's premier seaside hang-out (p111)

Nha Trang (Vietnam) Plenty of R&R is available at this mainland beach city (p859)

Mui Ne (Vietnam) Squeaky sands, towering dunes and kitesurfing galore (p865)

Boracay (Philippines) Paradise in a small package (p578)

Flores (Indonesia) The Catholic counterpart to Bali, with rustic living and nearby reefs (p233)

Diving & Snorkelling

Southeast Asia is one of the most affordable and rewarding places to dive. The shallow, clear waters of the Gulf of Thailand are a good place for beginners. From there, venture to the Andaman Sea's legendary sites and Indonesia's dramatic underwater landscapes.

Ko Tao (Thailand) Cheap dive certifications, shallow waters and year-round conditions (p744)

Pulau Sipadan (Malaysia) Legendary 'Coral Triangle' with visiting turtles and large pelagics (p448)

Surin & Similan Islands National Marine Parks (Thailand) These Andaman islands are global faves. They're visited on live-aboards, so start saving up (p755, p755)

Pulau Weh (Indonesia) Experience drift, wreck and drop-off dives on a relaxed island (p267)

Coron (Philippines) Dive down to sunken battleships (p601)

Togean Islands (Indonesia) Dive hot spot, with diverse reefs and fish aplenty (p282)

Pulau Perhentian (Malaysia) Low-key islands with near-shore pinnacle and shipwreck dives (p424)

Water Journeys

Southeast Asia is defined by water. The mighty Mekong snakes through former Indochina and Thailand, while the coastlines are petted and pounded by temperamental oceans. A boat journey offers unforgettable scenery and a slow-paced perspective on a liquid life.

Halong Bay (Vietnam) Prehistoric limestone mountains rise out of the aquamarine water at this Unesco World Heritage Site (p829)

Tonlé Sap Lake (Cambodia) Floating villages and slow-as-syrup pace unfold on Cambodia's Great Lake (p92)

Inle Lake (Myanmar) Tranquil floating gardens, stilted villages and country greenery (p505)

Luang Prabang (Laos) Take the slow boat along the Mekong for an unforgettable journey (p336)

Si Phan Don (Laos) These Mekong River islands surely invented relaxation (p364)

Batang Rejang (Malaysia) The Amazon of Borneo leads into the tribal Dayak culture of longhouses and communal living (p461)

month by month

Top Events

1. **Buddhist New Year/Water Festival**, April
2. **Deepavali**, November
3. **Rainforest World Music**, July
4. **Ork Phansaa**, October
5. **Festival of the Nine Emperor Gods**, October

January

Peak tourist season on mainland Southeast Asia coincides with the Christmas–New Year holidays and the dreary winter months for Europeans and North Americans. The weather is cool and dry and the beaches are packed. Most of the Philippines share this dry weather pattern. The northeast monsoon brings rain to parts of the east coast of the Malay peninsula (Samui Archipelago, Pulau Perhentian) and Indonesia; low season on Bali.

Tet

Vietnam's lunar New Year is the country's biggest holiday and coincides with Chinese New Year. The festival recognises the first day of spring and involves family reunions, ancestor worship, exchanges of presents and lots of all-night luck-inducing noise. Travel is difficult and many businesses close for about a week.

Chinese New Year

This lunar festival is celebrated in Chinese-dominated towns across Southeast Asia. In some towns, especially Penang, it is a family affair and businesses close for one to two weeks. But in Bangkok, Singapore, Phnom Penh and Kuching, there are dragon-dancing parades, food festivities and lots of night-time fireworks and noise.

Ati-Atihan

The mother of all Philippine fiestas, Ati-Atihan celebrates Santo Niño (Infant Jesus) with colourful, Mardi Gras–like indigenous costumes and displays in Kalibo on the island of Panay.

Islamic New Year

This lunar new year is celebrated throughout the Muslim world, including Indonesia and Malaysia.

Myanmar's Independence Day

The end of colonial rule in Burma is celebrated as a national holiday on 4 January.

Sultan of Brunei's Birthday

Colourful official ceremonies are held on 15 January to mark the birthday of Sultan Hassanal Bolkiah. In Bandar Seri Begawan, events include an elaborate military ceremony presided over by the supremo himself, smartly dressed in a medal-bedecked uniform.

February

Peak season continues on mainland Southeast Asia and the beaches are abuzz with snowbirds. In agricultural areas, the primary rice harvest is coming to a close. The east coast of the Malay peninsula starts to dry off as the rains move further east; still raining in Bali.

Bun Pha Wet

This Lao-Buddhist festival commemorates the story of the Buddha-to-be (Prince Vessantara or Pha Wet). It is considered an auspicious time to enter the monastery.

Makha Bucha

One of three holy days marking important

moments of Buddha's life, Makha Bucha falls on the full moon of the third lunar month and commemorates Buddha preaching to 1250 enlightened monks who came to hear him 'without prior summons'. It's a day for temple visits.

March

Mainland Southeast Asia is hot and dry and the beaches start to empty out. The winds kick up ushering in kiteboarding season. The northwest monsoon rains are subsiding to afternoon showers in Bali.

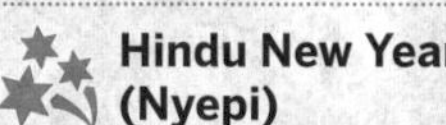

Hindu New Year (Nyepi)

In Bali and other Hindu communities, the new year is welcomed with lots of night-time racket. All of Bali shuts down for the day.

Prophet Mohammed's Birthday

The birthday of Islam's holy prophet is celebrated on the 12th day of the third month in the lunar-based Islamic calendar (usually March) with religious prayers and processions.

Easter Week

This Christian holiday (sometimes in April) is observed in the Philippines, Vietnam, Indonesia, Melaka and Timor-Leste. Holy Week (Semana Santa) in the Philippines starts on the Wednesday prior to Easter Sunday; businesses close or have limited hours. Spanish-influenced observances, such as fasting, rituals of penance and church attendance, ensue.

April

The hottest time of year on mainland Southeast Asia makes inland sightseeing a chore. Buddhist countries (except Vietnam) celebrate their traditional new year; make transport reservations in advance, as everyone is going somewhere else. Good shoulder season in Bali.

Buddhist New Year/ Water Festival

In mid-April, Thailand, Laos, Cambodia and Myanmar celebrate their lunar New Year with displays of religious devotion and symbolic water-throwing. In Thailand, it is called Songkran and it has morphed into water-warfare in Bangkok and Chiang Mai. Laos celebrates a more subdued version called Bun Pi Mai. Khmer New year is called Chaul Chnam and is mainly a family affair and a village homecoming for city dwellers.

Vietnamese Liberation Day

The day Saigon fell (30 April) to North Vietnamese forces is celebrated by the Communist Party as the country's national liberation day. Expect subdued celebrations in the south.

May

Still hot in mainland Southeast Asia but with an end in sight. May hosts preparations for the upcoming rainy season and festivals that encourage a bountiful harvest. There is spring-like weather in northern Vietnam, and Bali is not yet crowded.

Royal Ploughing Ceremonies

In Thailand and Cambodia, this royal ceremony employs astrology and ancient Brahman rituals to kick-off the rice-planting season.

Rocket Festival

Villagers craft bamboo rockets *(bang fai)* and fire them into the sky to provoke rainfall for a bountiful rice harvest. Mainly celebrated in northeastern Thailand and Laos; dates vary from village to village.

Visaka Bucha

This Buddhist holy day falls on the 15th day of the waxing moon in the sixth lunar month and commemorates Buddha's birth, enlightenment and *parinibbana* (passing away). Activities centre around the temple.

Independence Day (Timor-Leste)

One of the youngest nations celebrates Independence Day (20 May) with cultural events and sporting competitions.

June

The southwest monsoon brings rain, usually an afternoon downpour, to most of mainland Southeast Asia and most parts of the Philippines. As the European and North American summer approaches, there is another high season, especially on Bali.

Hue Festival (Biennial)

Vietnam's biggest cultural event (www.huefestival.com) is held every two years, including 2014. Art, theatre, music, circus and dance performances, include domestic and international acts, are held inside Hue's Citadel.

Gawai Dayak

The end of the rice harvest season is celebrated the first two days of June in the Malaysian Borneo state of Sarawak. City-dwelling Dayaks return to their longhouses to socialise, eat and down shots of *tuak* (rice wine).

July

Mainland Southeast Asia prepares for Buddhist Lent, a period of reflection and meditation that coincides with the rainy season (southwest monsoon). Despite the drizzle, this is an ideal time for rural sightseeing as rice planting begins and the formerly parched landscape becomes verdant. The Samui Archipelago often stays dry during the southwest monsoon.

Asanha Bucha

The full moon of the eighth lunar month commemorates Buddha's first sermon.

Khao Phansaa

Early in the monsoon rains, Buddhist monks retreat into monasteries. This is the traditional time for young men to enter the monkhood. Worshippers

(Above) Worshippers at Singapore's Sri Mariamman Temple (p619) during Deepavali festival (Below) Girls in hill-tribe costume for Buddhist New Year (Songkran) festivities in Chiang Mai (p684), Thailand

offer candles and donations to the temples.

Rainforest World Music

Sarawak (Malaysian Borneo) celebrates tribal music from around the world during this three-day music festival.

August

The region experiences a second high season during the northern hemisphere's summer holiday period. Indonesia's and especially Bali's weather is prime for its peak tourist season.

Independence Day (Indonesia)

The country celebrates its liberation on 17 August with large parades in Jakarta.

HM the Queen's Birthday

Thailand wishes its queen a happy birthday on 12 August with Bangkok-based festivities. The day is also recognised as Mother's Day.

September

This is the wettest part of the wet season for mainland Southeast Asia when flooding and boat cancellations are common. Occasional typhoons sweep in across Vietnam and the Philippines, wreaking havoc. Shoulder season in Bali.

Pchum Ben

In Cambodia, respects are paid to the dead through temple offerings. Many Khmers visit their home villages and try to pack in seven temples in seven days. Trung Nguyen is a similar festival celebrated in Vietnam, usually the preceding month.

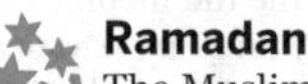

Ramadan

The Muslim fasting period is observed in Malaysia, Indonesia, Brunei and parts of southern Thailand. The holy period occurs in the ninth month of the Islamic calendar (usually August or September). Muslims are required to abstain from food, drink, cigarettes and sex between sunrise and sunset. Everyone comes out at night to celebrate the breaking of the fast. Idul Fitri marks the end of Ramadan. Advance travel arrangements are a must.

October

Mainland Southeast Asia prepares for the end of the rainy season and the end of Buddhist Lent. The northeast monsoon (which affects the east coast of the Malay peninsula and Indonesia) begins. Bali has occasional showers.

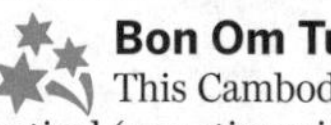

Bon Om Tuk

This Cambodian festival (sometimes in November) celebrates Jayavarman VII's victory over the Chams in 1177 and the reversal of the Tonlé Sap river. Boat races stir local patriotism, with huge crowds descending on Phnom Penh. A smaller event takes place in Siem Reap.

Festival of the Nine Emperor Gods

The Chinese Taoist deities of the nine emperor gods are believed to descend to earth from the stars. In Thailand, it is known as the Vegetarian Festival, during which the faithful abstain from meat, participate in temple meditation retreats and engage in other mind and body purification rituals. The most extreme version is Phuket's parade of entranced worshippers turning themselves into human shish kebabs. Variations occur in Singapore, Malaysia and Myanmar.

Ork Phansaa

The end of the Buddhist Lent (three lunar months after Khao Phansaa) is marked by the *gà·tĭn* ceremony, in which new robes are given to the monks by merit-makers. The peculiar natural phenomenon on the Mekong River known as the 'naga fireballs' coincides with Ork Phansaa. Localities in Thailand and Laos celebrate with traditional long-tail boat races.

November

This is a good shoulder season in mainland Southeast Asia, with cool, dry days and a lush landscape. In northern mainland Southeast Asia, this time is often called 'winter', because of the chilly nightly temperatures. The east coast of the Malay peninsula and Indonesia are in the midst of the rainy season.

Loi Krathong

During November's full moon, Thais launch banana-leaf boats decorated with candles in honour of the river goddess. In Chiang Mai, floating paper lanterns are made as offerings as well. A similar tradition is practised in the Shan State of Myanmar during the fire-balloon competitions in Taunggyi.

Deepavali

The most important festival in the Hindu calendar is this festival of lights that celebrates the triumph of good over evil. Tiny oil lamps are ceremoniously lit and friends and family are invited to a meal as a gesture of goodwill in Malaysia. Singapore's Little India hosts public festivities.

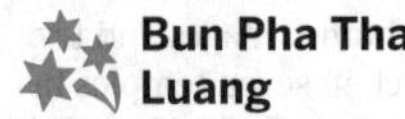

Bun Pha That Luang

Laos pays tribute to its iconic, gold-spired Pha That Luang in Vientiane with a weeklong festival coinciding with the full moon. Wax sculptures are paraded to the stupa, followed by other merit-making activities, traditional games and cultural displays.

December

Mainland Southeast Asia's peak tourism season is back and the weather is fine. Rain is tapering off on Samui Archipelago but still in effect in Bali.

Christmas

Most of the region has adopted Christmas in some form, but for Catholic communities in the Philippines, Timor-Leste, Indonesia and Vietnam, it is serious business with important religious services and ceremonies.

Lao National Day

This 2 December holiday celebrates the 1975 victory over the monarchy with parades and speeches. Lao national and Communist hammer-and-sickle flags are flown and celebration is mandatory.

HM the King's Birthday

This holiday (5 December) hosts parades and merit-making events; it is also recognised as Father's Day. Th Ratchadamnoen Klang in Bangkok is decorated with lights and regalia. Everyone wears pink shirts, the colour associated with the monarchy.

itineraries

Whether you've got six weeks or six months, these itineraries provide a starting point for the trip of a lifetime. Want more inspiration? Head online to lonelyplanet.com/thorntree to chat with other travellers.

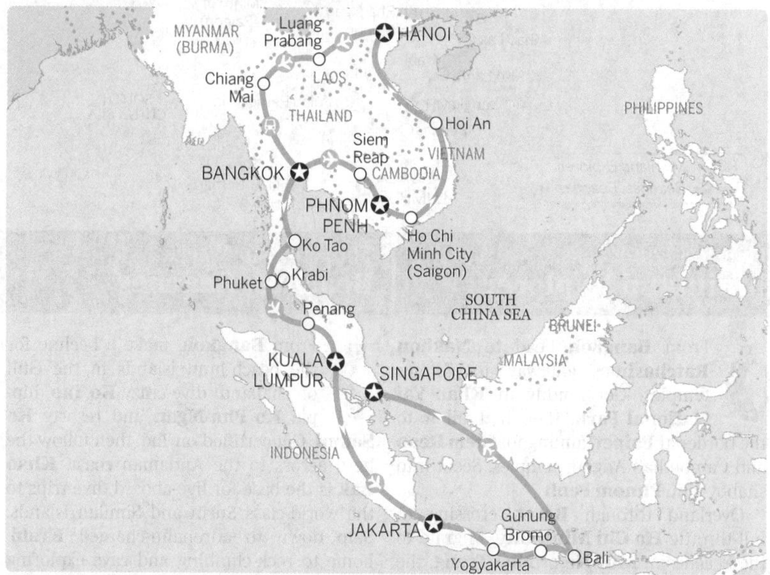

Eight Weeks

The Best of Southeast Asia

If you want a 'sampler plate' of Southeast Asia, then plan on jetting between countries to hit the highlights. Most international airlines fly to **Bangkok**, a chaotic but fantastic city. Fly to **Siem Reap** to see Angkor's magnificent temples. Bus to **Phnom Penh** and on to Vietnam's bustling **Ho Chi Minh City**. Work your way north with a stop in adorable **Hoi An** and on to **Hanoi**. Air-lift out of Vietnam to laid-back **Luang Prabang**, Laos' world heritage city, and then fly to chic **Chiang Mai**.

Return to Bangkok by overnight train and work your way south to **Ko Tao** to learn how to dive before hitting the beachy hot spots on Thailand's Andaman coast: **Phuket**, Ko Phi-Phi and **Krabi**.

Fly from polished Phuket to **Penang** and overland to Malaysia's multiethnic capital **Kuala Lumpur**. Catch a flight from Kuala Lumpur to **Jakarta** and soak up the culture in **Yogyakarta** and then bus to **Gunung Bromo**, an active volcano. Leapfrog to blessed **Bali** for sun, fun and culture. Then catch a cheap flight to sophisticated **Singapore**, which has air connections to everywhere else.

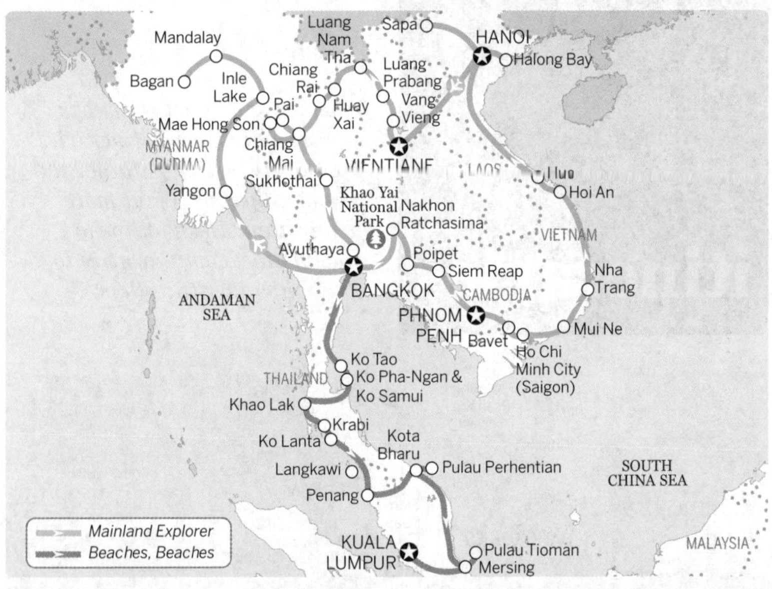

Four to Eight Weeks
Mainland Explorer

From **Bangkok** head to **Nakhon Ratchasima**, gateway to Khmer temples. Get muddy in **Khao Yai National Park**, then hightail it to the border at **Poipet**, aiming for **Siem Reap** and Cambodia's Angkor temples. Scoot into shabby-chic **Phnom Penh**.

Overland through **Bavet**, crossing to full-throttle **Ho Chi Minh City**. Migrate to the beaches of **Mui Ne** or **Nha Trang**, the antique city of **Hoi An** and imperial **Hue**. Rest in **Hanoi**, a mature, manicured capital. Cruise karst-filled **Halong Bay** and detour to **Sapa** and its highland communities. Return to Hanoi.

Fly to the Lao capital, **Vientiane**, bus to athletic **Vang Vieng** and on to **Luang Prabang**, a reverential riverside city. Continue to the trekking centre of **Luang Nam Tha**. Ride the Mekong River to the Laos–Thailand border at **Huay Xai**.

Slide into **Chiang Rai** for hill-tribe treks, or **Chiang Mai**. Escape to the mountains of **Pai** or **Mae Hong Son**. Pay homage to ancient capitals at **Sukhothai** and **Ayuthaya**.

Return to **Bangkok**. Fly to Myanmar's **Yangon** and continue to the island monasteries of **Inle Lake**, the ancient capital of **Mandalay** and the ruins of **Bagan**.

Three to Four Weeks
Beaches, Beaches

From **Bangkok**, make a beeline for the beach-bum islands in the Gulf of Thailand: dive-crazy **Ko Tao**, hippie **Ko Pha-Ngan** and resorty **Ko Samui**. Get certified on Tao, then follow the herd across to the Andaman coast. **Khao Lak** is the base for live-aboard dive trips to the world-class Surin and Similan islands. Skip down to adrenalin-charged **Krabi**, home to rock-climbing and cave exploring and then chill-out on laid-back **Ko Lanta**. Island-hop across the border at **Pulau Langkawi** to **Penang** to balance beaching with hawker-centre bingeing.

From Penang, bus to **Kota Bharu**, the jumping-off point for the fabulous jungle islands of **Pulau Perhentian**. Chase the coastline south to **Mersing**, the mainland port for sleepy **Pulau Tioman**, before returning to civilisation in **Kuala Lumpur**.

There are even more beaches to explore on even bigger islands. See our Indonesia to Timor-Leste itinerary.

» (above) Woman working the fields outside her home in Vietnam's far north
» (left) Worshipper praying at Wat Phra That Doi Suthep Buddhist temple (p685) in Chiang Mai, Thailand

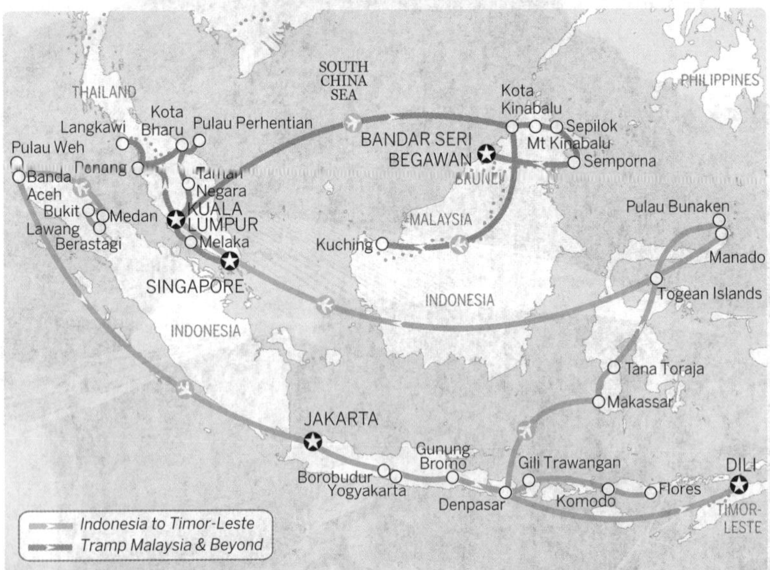

Four to Eight Weeks
Indonesia to Timor-Leste

Start at Indonesia's tip in **Medan** on the island of Sumatra, trundle to the orang-utan outpost of **Bukit Lawang** and go volcano hiking in **Berastagi**. Return to Medan and fly to lovely **Banda Aceh** and dive-tastic **Pulau Weh**.

Buzz to Java, touching down in **Jakarta**. Cruise **Yogyakarta's** culture trail. Day trip to the giant stupa of **Borobudur** or huff-and-puff up **Gunung Bromo**.

Leapfrog to **Denpasar**, in Bali, to nuzzle the sandy beaches of the Bukit Peninsula or get cultured in Ubud. Party in **Gili Trawangan**, spot dragons on **Komodo** and go rustic on the beaches of **Flores**. Check your visa and apply for an extension before flying to **Makassar** on the island of Sulawesi. Bus to **Tana Toraja**, where funeral rituals are ancient and bloody. (Stay tuned for a Tana Toraja airport in 2013.) Travel to the **Togean Islands** and the northern diving board of **Pulau Bunaken**. Fly from **Manado** to **Kuala Lumpur**.

Alternatively, from Denpasar hop over to Timor-Leste's capital of **Dili** to tour old colonial towns and uncrowded reefs.

Four Weeks
Tramp Malaysia & Beyond

Touchdown in **Kuala Lumpur**, an easy city for international arrivals. Bus to the tranquil Cameron Highlands and its glossy green tea plantations. Follow the northern migration to **Penang** for street eats and Malaysian fusion culture. Detour to the beaches of **Langkawi**. Return to Georgetown and bus to **Kota Bharu**, the jump-off point for car-free, carefree ambience on **Pulau Perhentian**. Pick up the Jungle Railway to **Taman Negara**, an ancient, accessible wilderness.

Return to **Kuala Lumpur** for a well-planned, well-funded tour of Malaysian Borneo. Fly to **Kota Kinabalu**, in Sabah, ascend Borneo's highest peak **Mt Kinabalu**. Head east to **Sepilok** and its orang-utan sanctuary. Swing over to **Semporna**, the gateway to dive sites. Culture vultures should detour to the oil-rich oddity of Brunei and its unassuming capital, **Bandar Seri Begawan (BSB)**, surrounded by pristine rainforests and water villages. Or fly from Kota Kinabalu to **Kuching** in Sarawak state, formerly known as the land of the headhunters.

If you're a city slicker, skip Borneo and cruise through **Melaka**, a colonial port of call, and then into **Singapore** for an immersion in modern Asia.

Six Months

The Whole Shebang

Start off in Bangkok and follow the eastern seaboard to forested **Ko Chang**, cross the Hat Lek–Cham Yeam border bound for **Sihanoukville's** collection of scruffy and sublime beaches. Stop in Franco-influenced **Kampot** and its nearby hill station. Turn inland to **Phnom Penh** to pay your respects at its genocide museums then bus to **Siem Reap** and the monumental splendour of Angkor.

Board a flight to **Pakse**, gateway to the easy river living of Si Phan Don. Bus to **Vientiane** and on to **Vang Vieng** then **Luang Prabang**. Trundle to Nong Khiaw for tribal trekking. Follow the rugged, revolutionaries' trail through the **Na Meo** border, a remote and adventurous crossing to **Hanoi**.

Work your way through Vietnam, sampling history, culture and beaches. Fly from **Ho Chi Minh City** to **Bangkok** and slide down the Malay Peninsula, swimming and diving around **Ko Pha-Ngan** in the Gulf of Thailand and around **Krabi** in the Andaman Sea.

Slip into Malaysia for the street eats of **Penang**. Cross the peninsula for the peaceful beach retreat of **Pulau Perhentian**. Pick up the Jungle Railway to **Taman Negara**, a wilderness preserve. Detour to the mist-shrouded hills of **Cameron Highlands** and then alight in **Kuala Lumpur**.

Fly to **Jakarta** (Java) and immerse yourself in the cultural city of **Yogyakarta** and the Unesco treasure of Borobudur. Bask on the beach in **Bali**, escape the beach crowds in **Flores**, and go dragon-spotting on **Komodo**. Return to Bali and catch a flight to **Dili** in Timor-Leste, a fledgling tourist nation.

Alternatively, from Jakarta fly to **Banjarmasin** (Kalimantan) for a jungle excursion into Borneo. Catch another flight to **Pangkalan Bun** with connections to the orang-utan research camps of **Tanjung Puting National Park**.

Fly from Banjarmasin to **Pontianak** and then bus to the Entikong–Tebedu border to Malaysia's **Kuching**, a gateway to more Borneo nature reserves and former headhunting cultures. After a cheap flight back to **Kuala Lumpur**, catch a connection to **Yangon** (Myanmar) and its Buddhist temples and isolated people, or to **Manila** (Philippines) and its Catholic population and volcanic setting. Bus to the mountains of **North Luzon**, then fly to **Cebu**, gateway to the Visayas beaches. If you opt for the Philippines route, you can then hop into East Asia (China or Japan) without having to backtrack.

Big Adventures, Small Budget

What's First: Planning Timeline

12 months before Calculate a trip budget and start saving.

6 months Pick which countries to visit, when and for how long.

6 to 4 weeks Get vaccinations and travel insurance.

4 weeks Start booking flights; make visa and passport arrangements.

2 weeks Reserve high-season transport and accommodation for popular destinations, live-aboard dive trips and Borneo trekking tours.

1 week Book accommodation for international arrival city; start packing.

How Much to Spend: Average Costs

Bottle of beer US$1 to US$3

Long-distance bus ticket US$15 to US$25

Food-stall meal US$1 to US$5

Guesthouse bed US$10 to US$20

Internet access per hour US$1 to US$6

Domestic flight US$50 to US$100

Admission to Angkor Wat US$20 to US$60

Cooking course in Chiang Mai US$35

When to Go

The monsoon rains and peak tourist season are two factors determining how to plot your trip. You might also want to plan a trip around famous festivals (see p20) or avoid public holidays when everything is closed (see individual country directories for a list of public holidays).

Monsoon Seasons

Southeast Asia is always hot and humid, but sometimes it is also hot, humid and wet. The region is affected by two monsoons. The southwest monsoon (June/July to September/October) brings rain to most of mainland Southeast Asia and the west coast of the Malay peninsula (Phuket and Langkawi). Most of the Philippines follows this same weather pattern. Following the rainy season, there is dry, cool weather (November to February) and then it turns hotter than usual (March to June).

The northeast monsoon starts in September, bringing rain to the east coast of the Malay peninsula (Ko Samui, Pulau Perhentian) and then migrating east through Indonesia, hitting Timor-Leste by December. In many parts of Indonesia, especially rainforest belts, it's a little rainy most of the year.

Beaches & Islands

It is a fine art to hit the right beach at the right time: nice weather and not too many topless European matrons. Shoulder seasons for the beaches usually bookend the rainy season (start and end), when there might be a short afternoon shower. Another shoulder season is the first few months of the hot, dry season when the natural air-conditioning of the ocean is a needed break from the harsh interior temperatures.

Best Times

» **March to May** Hot, dry season; good for mainland Southeast Asia's beaches and both coasts of the Malay peninsula; Bali gets some rain and dries out by April.

» **October to November** End of rainy season for mainland Southeast Asia and the west coast of the Malay peninsula (Phuket and friends); rainy on east coast of Malay peninsula and parts of Vietnamese coast.

» **September** Dry season for Bali; Ko Samui and the east coast of the Malay peninsula turn soggy. Whale migration begins in Timor-Leste.

Times to Avoid

» **June to August** High season on Bali and Ko Samui; great weather but crowded and expensive.

» **August to September** Wettest months for mainland Southeast Asia and the west coast of the Malay peninsula (Phuket and friends). On small islands hotels shut down and boat travel is interrupted by storms.

» **December to February** Peak tourist season for mainland Southeast Asia and west coast of Malay peninsula. Some showers on Bali.

Surfing & Kiteboarding

When the weather is too crummy for sunbathing, it is just right for hanging ten. May to September brings prime swells to Indonesia's Lombok and Sumbawa, while Bali always has a surfable spot somewhere. In the Philippines surf season coincides with the typhoons (August–November). Good for beginners, Phuket's surf season runs from April to September, and Cherating's goes from November to March.

Kiteboarding is catching on in Southeast Asia with reputable schools on Boracay (Philippines), the east and west coast of Thailand (Hua Hin and Phuket) and in Vietnam (Mui Ne). These beaches tend to have a long windy season through most of the year.

Diving

Diving depends on visibility and visibility depends on calm waters and storm-free days. This means that most diving locations have sub-par conditions during the rainy season. Luckily the double monsoon means that you'll find a dry spot in one corner while another is soggy. The Gulf of Thailand stays divable most of the year.

TOURIST SEASONS

» **High season** Ideal weather but crowded and prices are high.

» **Shoulder season** Iffy weather but affordable prices and fewer crowds.

» **Low season** Crummy weather, cheap prices, few visitors.

Trekking

Rain, not temperature, is the primary consideration when planning a trekking trip. When the rains come to the northern mountains of mainland Southeast Asia, the forests spring to life, the rivers transform from sluggish mud pits into watery bulldozers and remote roads are prone to flooding.

With a relatively short and concentrated rainy season, most of mainland Southeast Asia's forests are classified as deciduous, meaning they shed their leaves in an attempt to conserve water during the dry season. Trekking is obviously at its best in the months following the rainy season when the forest is lush and flooding is not a concern.

The Malay peninsula and Indonesia get two monsoon seasons that feed their dense canopies. These equatorial forests are classified as tropical rainforests because they have a longer rainy season of at least nine months. In some cases the differences in seasons varies between a little rain and a lot of rain.

Best Times: Mainland Southeast Asia

» **November to February** Just after the rainy season is ideal; in higher elevations frost is possible. December to January is high season for international and domestic tourists.

GREG ELMS / LONELY PLANET IMAGES ©

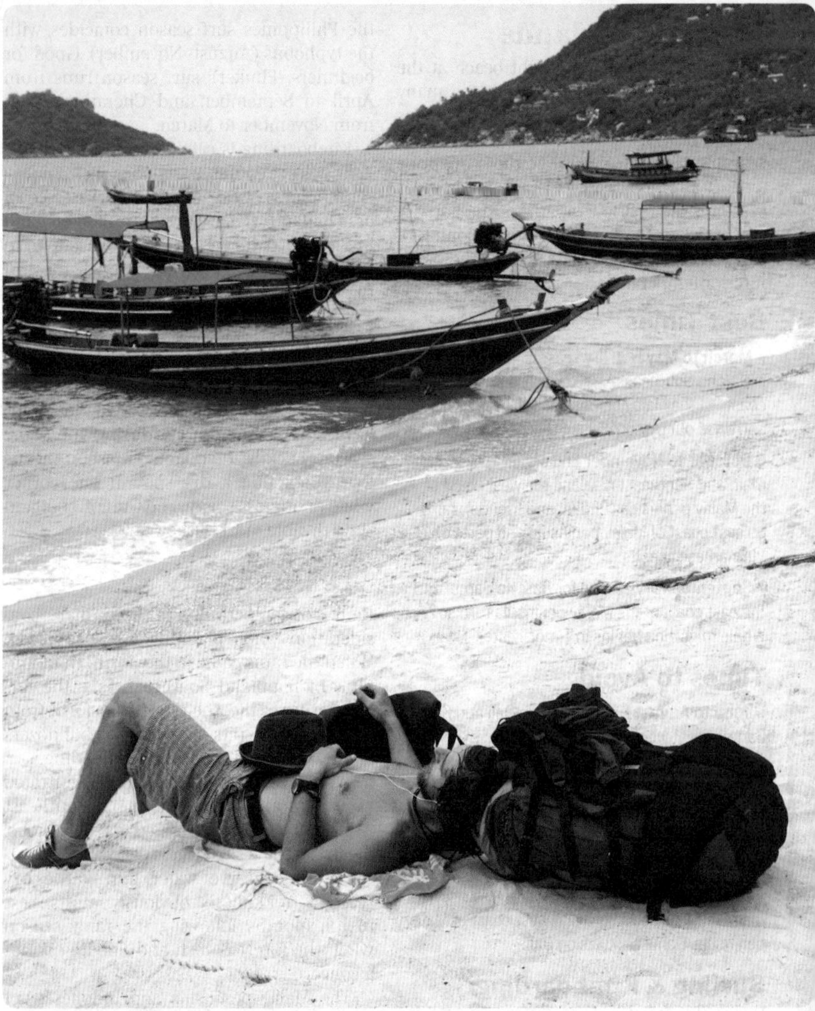

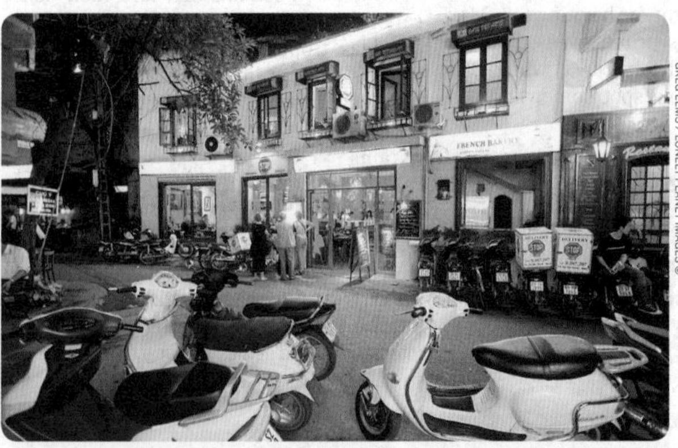

» (above) Backpacker lying on the beach, Ko Tao (p744), Thailand
» (left) Nightlife on Hang Hanh street, Hanoi (p809), Vietnam

WEATHER OR NOT? PICKING A BEACH BY SEASON

BEACH	JAN-FEB	MAR-APR	MAY-JUN	JUL-SEP	OCT-NOV	DEC
Ko Samui (Thailand)	dry, high season	dry, shoulder season	dry, shoulder season	dry until Sep, high season	rain, low season	end of rains, high season
Phuket (Thailand)	dry, high season	dry, shoulder season	start of rains, shoulder season	rain, low season	dry, shoulder season	dry, high season
Bali (Indonesia)	rain, low season	end of rains, shoulder season	dry, shoulder season	dry, high season	start of rains, shoulder season	rain, low season
Nha Trang (Vietnam)	dry, high season	dry, high season	dry, high season	dry, high season	rain, low season	end of rains, low season
Sihanoukville (Cambodia)	dry, high season	dry, shoulder season	start of rains, shoulder season	rain, low season	rain, shoulder season	end of rains, high season
Boracay (Philippines)	dry, high season	dry, high season	dry, shoulder season	rain, low season	end of rains, shoulder season	end of rains, high season
Timor-Leste	rain, low season	dry, high season	dry, high season	dry, high season	dry, high season	rain, low season

Times to Avoid

» **March to May** After four months without rain, the landscape turns brown, the trails are dusty and the air quality suffers as farmers burn rice paddies after the harvest.

» **June to October** Rainy season means the trails are muddy, downpours certain and flooding probable.

Best Times: Rainforests

» **May & September** The shoulder seasons of the European summer holiday period coincides with 'drier' weather.

Times to Avoid

» **January to February** The wettest months of the rainy season (October to April).

» **June to August** Peak tourist season.

Sightseeing

The ideal time to tour Southeast Asia's historic monuments and cities is when the weather is driest and coolest (relatively speaking). But the best weather also coincides with high season when hotel rates and crowds increase. The beginning of the rainy season is a recommendable shoulder season as rain is minimal and rural areas are busy with rice planting (a splendid sight). The hot months of the year, especially for mainland Southeast Asia, make sightseeing difficult, as temperatures can climb as high as 40°C and humidity is high.

Budget Guide

Western currencies enjoy a favourable exchange rate in Southeast Asia, meaning you have greater purchasing power. The cost of living is also cheaper in Southeast Asia and shoestringers can skimp their way to a daily budget of about US$25 a day. This covers the basics: food, shelter, local transport and a few beers. This budget will vary slightly by country, the popularity of the destination and the time of year (high versus low season).

In addition to this base rate, factor in the costs of long-distance travel – by bus, boat or air. Add any special activities, such as diving, rock-climbing, hill-tribe trekking or a sightseeing tour. Then allow for unexpected expenses, such as increased transport or accommodation costs due to holidays or needing to get somewhere in a hurry.

Accommodation costs occupy the largest portion of your budget and luckily the region is filled with simple guesthouses that charge simple prices. The more creature comforts (air-con, hot water, ensuite bathroom) you can forsake, the more money you'll save.

Public transport within each country is generally affordable. Costs rise with boat and air travel and wherever road conditions are rough. Local public transport won't stretch the budget but hiring private taxis is always pricey. Getting around individual islands can often be expensive because of price-fixing or lack of competition. You can save on local transport costs if you know how to ride a motorbike before arriving. Much cheaper is bicycle hire, which is a lovely way to tour the region's towns and countryside.

For more information on money matters, see individual country chapters.

Budget Tips

We posed the following question to our *Southeast Asia* authors: What is the cheapest place in which to have the best time in your country? Here are their answers:

Brunei Darussalam Tiny, oil-rich Brunei can be a great budget destination if you arrive by bus from Malaysian Borneo. Stay in a youth hostel (from US$7), dine in the open-air markets and tour the free cultural sights, national parks and opulent mosques.

Cambodia You can have a great, cheap time in Sihanoukville, where you can score dorm beds for US$3 to US$5.

Laos Muang Ngoi Neua is one of the best shoestring escapes in Southeast Asia. It has towering karst cliffs, sleepy riverine character, cheap digs and scenic country walks. Si Phan Don (Four Thousand Islands) is the quintessential lotus-eating country: hammock-hanging, a happening traveller scene, laid-back island life, tubing down the river and dolphin-spotting.

Indonesia Do Bali on the cheap by opting for an Ulu Watu homestay (US$15). You can enjoy a surfer-chic scene and epic views with enough spare cash to wash it all down with several Bintangs.

Malaysia Pulau Perhentian is an awesome deal and has some of the cheapest diving in Asia, comparable to Ko Tao. Cherating is another budget-friendly beach. In pricey Malaysian Borneo, Kuching could accommodate shoestringers with inexpensive dorms (US$5) and national parks and beaches accessible via public transport (instead of expensive charter taxis).

Myanmar It is a little bit of a schlep, but Mrauk U is one of the country's best value spots. It is an ancient capital of temples and carvings that doesn't cost a fortune to visit and has fewer package tourists than Bagan.

Philippines A proliferation of budget flights is opening up the Philippines to backpackers. North Luzon and Palawan are inexpensive, off-the-beaten-track options. Sleep amid Batad's rice terraces for US$5 per night or beach camp in Coron.

Singapore You can't afford to be a high-flyer in Singapore on a budget but you can soak up culture with the Singapore Symphony Orchestra's free concerts.

Thailand The budget impediments in Thailand are the beaches, which are decidedly upscale (starting at US$25). Ko Tao is still a cheap place for an Open Water diving certificate. The east side of Ko Pha Ngan remains a bargain. On the Andaman side, Khao Lak and Ko Lanta aren't the most beautiful beaches but they're good value.

Timor-Leste Getting to the beaches can be slow (on public transport) or expensive (in private transport). Instead catch a microlet heading to Liquica (US$1) and hop off at the rocky point near the Pope's monument. Welcome to Dili Rock West. There's no need for a boat, just jump in with your snorkel to see amazing coral and fish.

Vietnam With some of the cheapest beer in the region (around US$0.75), Vietnam might win the budget showdown. Nha Trang is the backpackers' beach with a rocking nightlife and affordable lodging.

STICKING TO A BUDGET

» Eat like a local at street stalls or markets.

» Opt for dorm rooms or share a room with a buddy.

» Stay in fan (non-air-con) rooms with shared bathroom.

» Travel overland instead of flying.

» Book air flights online rather than paying a travel agent's commission.

» Snorkel instead of dive.

» Hire a bicycle instead of a motorbike.

» Stick to small towns instead of big cities.

» Be discriminating about which national parks to visit.

» Avoid package deals (transport, lodging, touring).

Packing

Take as little as possible because you're going to have to carry it everywhere. Pack your bag once and then repack it with a third less stuff. Repeat until your pack is small enough to fit into the aircraft's overhead locker, which represents the average size of most stowage areas on Southeast Asia's buses and trains. The smaller your pack the

GOING WITH GADGETS

More and more travellers are taking multiple gadgets – phones, e-readers, laptops, cameras – with them on their trips, but the risk of theft or damage is high. Southeast Asia is hot and dusty, bags get dropped or tossed, thieves and pickpockets want what you have and you or your stuff could easily get caught in a rain storm long enough for a short-circuit.

Here are some tips for travelling smartly with technology:

» Limit yourself to one or two versatile devices: a tablet or iPad that can read books and check emails or a smartphone (like an iPhone) that can check emails and take pictures.

» Store your electronics in dry packs and separate the batteries in case of rain.

» Use a volt converter, as some destinations have power surges that can fry sensitive equipment.

» USB roaming sticks, available through local mobile phone providers, enable near-universal internet access from your computer.

easier it will be to climb on and off public transport (which doesn't always come to a complete stop), the easier it will be to walk if taxi drivers are asking too much money and you'll look like less of a target for touts and hustlers.

Money

In most places you can rely on your home bank's ATM card as your primary source of funds. Most ATM networks talk to overseas banks, so you can withdraw cash (in the local currency) directly from your home account.

But there will be towns and some countries (Myanmar, for example) where ATMs are not available. In this case take a mix of cash and travellers cheques. Currency exchanges at banks or private businesses are usually straightforward and usually accept US dollars, Australian dollars, British pounds and the euro. Travellers cheques are a bit antiquated but are a useful alternative if ATMs are scarce. They're also more secure than cash.

Here are some money tips we've often learned the hard way:

Keep your money in a safe place – in a money belt worn on your person – at all times; be careful about your valuables on overnight journeys and in communal dorms or rooms without lockable windows and doors.

Use your ATM card only when dealing with ATM cash machines, not for point-of-sale purchases.

Inform your bank (for both ATM and credit cards) that you'll be travelling overseas so that they won't reject foreign charges as suspicious activity.

Determine your bank's fee system (non-bank ATM surcharges, foreign-exchange rate charges)

Obtain a 24-hour international customer-service phone number for ATM and credit card companies in case of theft or loss.

Monitor credit-card activity to avoid missing payments and to protect against fraudulent charges.

Make sure your ATM and credit cards are not going to expire while you are away; contact your bank at least a month ahead of time to allow enough time for replacement cards to be issued.

When exchanging money, shop around for the best exchange rate.

Bring cash in crisp, untorn bills and a variety of denominations. Money changers in Myanmar and Indonesia will reject old or ripped bills.

Get your travellers cheques in large denominations of US dollars (US$100 or US$50) to avoid per-cheque commission fees.

Record which travellers cheques you've cashed, and keep this information separate from your money so that you can file a claim in the case of theft of loss.

Personal Belongings

☐ **Clothes** Southeast Asia is hot, very hot, so bring a week's worth of lightweight, light-coloured, breathable clothes that can be washed easily and match everything. No denim. If you're travelling to high-altitude areas, pack silk long johns and a fleece for chilly temperatures.

☐ **Rain gear** Even if it isn't the rainy season, it could still rain. Bring a lightweight rain jacket. Line your pack with a plastic bag to keep the contents dry.

☐ **Earplugs** Now you can sleep through your neighbours' drunken fight or the rooster's predawn alert.

☐ **Medicine** First-aid kit and any speciality medicines from home; see p940.

☐ **Odds and ends** A padlock, Swiss army knife, money belt, small torch (flashlight), travel adaptor and refillable water bottle.

☐ **Specialised gear** If you plan to do serious camping, trekking, snorkelling or diving, bring the equipment from home. For trekking, bring leech socks and rain gear for yourself and your pack.

☐ **Toiletries** Stock up on tampons and heavy-duty deodorant, which aren't so easy to come by. Also pack biodegradable soap.

☐ **Important documents** Make copies of your passport, tickets, travellers-cheque serial numbers and credit and ATM cards. Store this data online or on a password-protected USB drive.

☐ **USB drive** Handy storage device for photos and files.

Responsible Travel

Internet Resources

Responsible Travel (www.responsible-travel.org) General tips on how to be a 'better' tourist regarding environmental issues, begging and bargaining, as well as ethical holidays.

Mekong Responsible Tourism (www.mekongresponsibletourism.org) Online guide promoting community-based and socially responsible tourism in the Mekong region. Homestays, cultural attractions and eco-lodges are often featured.

WWF International (www.panda.org) Read up on WWF's environmental campaigns to protect Southeast Asia's threatened species and landscapes.

Mongabay (www.mongabay.com) Environmental science and conservation news site with a focus on tropical rainforests, including Indonesia.

Ecology Asia (www.ecologyasia.com) Facts and figures about Southeast Asia's flora and fauna.

Sealang Projects (http://sealang.net) Academic resource for learning Southeast Asian languages.

In Southeast Asia, tourism brings blessings and curses. Small-scale tourism fosters family-owned businesses that can propel communities into the middle class. Children of guesthouse owners often attend college and become professionals, accomplishments that would have been difficult to attain when subsistence agriculture or fishing was the primary industry. Tourism helps preserve cultural and environmental assets. From Cambodia's Angkor ruins to Borneo's forests, tourists' dollars make it more profitable to protect these treasures than to loot them. Tourism fosters one-on-one cultural exchanges that broaden people's understanding of the world and of humanity. It can create lifelong friendships or even spur-of-the-moment connections with someone you had previously regarded as foreign.

But tourism also puts pressures on the host country in a variety of ways, from environmental degradation to cultural and social confrontations. To ensure that your trip is a gift, not a burden, remember to mind your manners, be kind to the local environment, learn about the history, language and culture of your host country, and be a conscientious consumer.

Environmental Concerns

Southeast Asia is one of the planet's most biodiverse regions, containing biozone units that do not exist anywhere else and such mega-diverse countries as Indonesia, Malaysia and the Philippines. Southeast Asia's coral reefs are regarded as some of the world's most abundant and include a 6-million-sq-km area known as the Coral Triangle, which stretches all the way from Malaysia to the Solomon Islands. There are numerous bird species in Southeast Asia and natural areas serve as important flyover zones for migratory species, whose arrival heralds the approach of the monsoons. Many parts of the Indonesian jungle are so thick and remote that scientists have yet to explore and catalogue the resident flora and fauna.

Environmental degradation is immediately tangible here: smoke fills the air as the forests are cleared for beach bungalows, small-scale farms, palm oil plantations or logging; major cities are choked with smog and pollution; the waterways are clogged with plastic bags and soft-drink cans; and raw sewage is dumped into turquoise waters.

Southeast Asia's environmental superlatives include 75% of the world's coral species; the Mekong River, which rivals the Amazon's biodiversity; and the world's largest lizard (the komodo dragon).

Problems & Solutions

The final half of the 20th century saw massive deforestation in Southeast Asia. Borneo, for example, has one of the highest deforestation rates on earth. In the mid-1980s, about 75% of the island was covered in original forest; by 2005, this had dwindled to 50%. Due to deforestation and forest fires, Indonesia is the world's third-largest greenhouse gas emitter, according to national government statistics.

Another important forest feature long regarded as a wasteland are the mangrove forests that occupy the tidal flats and act as buffers from coastal storms and nurseries for marine species. Countries with long coastlines have cleared mangrove forests for prawn farming, often viewed as an economic development tool, and commercial tourism. Many scientists believe that the disastrous effects of the 2004 Boxing Day tsunami and 2008's Cyclone Nargis could have been reduced if the mangrove forests had been intact to absorb the tidal surges.

Water systems are suffering as well. Environmental degradation of coral reefs is caused by overfishing, sediment run-off from coastal development, as well as climate change. Along the Mekong River, hydroelectric dams are significantly altering the river's ecosystem, from sediment transport to fish migration, as well as water levels downstream.

Habitat loss is a serious threat to the region's indigenous wildlife, including such animal celebrities as tigers, elephants and monkeys. The few remaining natural areas are also subject to poaching, often by local people who augment subsistence farming with hunting for the lucrative wildlife trade. Thailand is one of the primary conduits through which live wildlife and harvested wildlife parts (which are often prized for perceived health and stamina benefits) travel to overseas markets in China, the USA and Europe. Favoured species include the sun bear, tigers and pangolins (a type of anteater). The number of plant species lost is probably higher, but precise figures are unavailable.

Though the problems are apparent, answers are not. Conserving wild lands lacks political will and is often undermined by moneyed industrial or commercial interests. Of all of the Southeast Asian nations, Brunei leads the conservationist charge with approximately 70% of its original forest cover still intact, but it is wealthy enough through its oil reserves to overlook the potential profit of undeveloped forests. In comparison, Thailand contains about 28% of natural forest cover, though deforestation has slowed to less than 1% since the mid-20th century. Indonesia has introduced a two-year ban on forest clearing and has entered into climate-protection pacts and conservation programs with wealthier nations and various UN agencies.

Environmental consciousness in Southeast Asia lags behind Western standards. Ecotourism is still in its infancy, lacking standardisation and subject to inflated marketing claims. There are, however, several promising efforts in Laos, Cambodia and Thailand that meet some of the ecotourism standards of providing funds for conservation, benefiting economic development and political empowerment of local communities, minimising tourism's impact on fragile environments and educating travellers. Throughout the book, activities and businesses that meet some of these standards are marked with a sustainable icon.

What You Can Do

Visitors should think about the power of tourism to provide economic value to undeveloped lands and marginalised local communities and the unintended consequences (namely waste production and

RESPONSIBLE DIVING

The popularity of Southeast Asia's diving industry places immense pressure on fragile coral sites. To help preserve the ecology, adhere to these simple rules. Please consider the following tips when diving to help preserve the reefs:

» Avoid touching living marine organisms, standing on coral or dragging equipment (such as fins) across the reef. Coral polyps can be damaged by even the gentlest contact.

» When treading water in shallow reef areas, be careful not to kick up clouds of sand, which can easily smother the delicate reef organisms.

» Reduce time in underwater caves where air bubbles can be caught within the roof and leave previously submerged organisms high and dry.

» Join a coral clean-up campaign, sponsored by dive shops.

» Don't feed the fish or allow your dive operator to dispose of excess food in the water. The fish become dependent on this food source and don't tend to the algae on the coral, causing harm to the reef.

» Don't collect souvenirs (corals, shells or shipwreck debris) from the sea.

resource consumption) of visiting fragile environments. Here are some modest ways to balance the positive and negative impacts of environmental tourism.

- ☐ Live like a local: opt for a fan instead of an air-con room; shower with cold water instead of hot.
- ☐ Use biodegradable soap to reduce water pollution.
- ☐ Eat locally sourced meals instead of imported products.
- ☐ Dispose of plastic packaging before leaving home so that it doesn't end up in overburdened refuse systems.
- ☐ Dispose of cigarette butts in rubbish bins not on the beach or into the water.
- ☐ Choose unplugged modes of transit (walking tour over minivan tour, bicycle over motorbike, kayak over jet ski).
- ☐ Volunteer with a local conservation or animal-welfare group.
- ☐ Be a responsible diver (see box above).
- ☐ Dispose of your rubbish in a proper receptacle, even if the locals don't.
- ☐ Don't eat or drink food products made from endangered animals or plants.
- ☐ Refill plastic bottles whenever possible.

Cultural & Social Concerns

Most Southeast Asians don't expect tourists to know very much about them and for this reason they overlook innocent breaches of social etiquette. But each culture has a host of taboos and sacred beliefs, and it can cause grave offence if they're disrespected. In addition to cultural ignorance, tourists often encounter problems when they show anger over money disputes or miscommunication and during drunken escapades. Patience is the key to these sometimes irritating social interactions.

Religious & Social Taboos

In every country or ethnic community you visit, determine what is sacred, what is off-limits and what constitutes a serious gaffe.

Though Southeast Asians are incredibly candid about topics that make Westerners blush, there are always a handful of subjects that are not discussed openly or critically. In Thailand, the monarchy is beyond reproach, and in Myanmar, political discussions can result in serious trouble for locals.

Because much of the region is very traditional, there are still many rules regarding women and their behaviour. In Buddhist countries, women aren't allowed to come into contact with monks; this means women can't sit or stand next to them on the bus, pass anything directly to them or touch their belongings. Most mosques have rules about where women can be and how they should be dressed.

To be a good guest, dress modestly, covering to elbows and knees (and always the belly). Showing too much skin makes locals feel embarrassed and disrespected.

Bargaining

Most Southeast Asian countries practise the art of bargaining. Remember that it is an art, not a test of wills, and the trick is to find a price that makes everyone happy. Bargaining is acceptable in markets and in shops where fixed prices aren't displayed. As a beginner, tread lightly by asking the price and then asking if the seller can offer a discount. The price may creep lower if you take your time and survey the object. If the discounted price isn't acceptable give a counter offer but be willing to accept something in the middle. Once you counter you can't name a lower price. Don't start haggling unless you're interested in actually buying it. If you become angry or visibly frustrated, you've lost the game.

What You Can Do

Here are some other pointers to keep you on everyone's good side.

- ☐ Always ask for permission before you take a picture of someone, especially during private moments; asking in the local language is even better.
- ☐ Know how much things cost; don't expect something for nothing, but don't let hustlers take advantage of you.
- ☐ Take a language course or at least learn to say 'thank you' and to count in every visited country.
- ☐ Observe local taboos and matters of etiquette.
- ☐ Treat religious objects, no matter how old or decrepit, with the utmost respect; don't clamber on temple ruins or pose behind headless Buddha statues.
- ☐ Learn about the country's history, current events and social problems.
- ☐ Take a gift when invited to someone's home.
- ☐ Share your snacks or cigarettes with your neighbour on long bus rides.
- ☐ Tip here and there as daily wages are pitifully small.
- ☐ Smile while bargaining; your beauty will distract them from opportunistic pricing.
- ☐ Keep a thick skin and a sense of humour.

Poverty & Economic Disparity

The disparity between rich and poor is one of Southeast Asia's most pressing social concerns. Few of the region's countries have well-developed social safety nets to catch people left homeless or jobless by debt mismanagement, rapid industrialisation or institutionalised discrimination.

Remote villagers, including ethnic minorities, often live precarious subsistence lives without access to health care, economic opportunity or basic education. In some cases, their traditional lifestyles are incompatible with the modern marketplace, and many villages lose their young people to jobs in the cities. Urban migrants often do menial labour for menial wages; some turn to more profitable enterprises, such as prostitution or other illicit ventures. When a family is financially compromised, children are often expected to work, either formally in a factory or informally as a street seller or tour guide. They often don't have the luxury of time or money to receive an education.

There is also an ongoing problem of human trafficking, mainly economic migrants who are lured to a neighbouring country for work to find that they are vulnerable to exploitation.

The attendant problems of marginalised people include drug abuse, HIV/AIDs, and unsanitary and dangerous living conditions.

INVASION OF PERSONAL SPACE SNATCHERS

Southeast Asia might be known for its easygoing nature but it is a pressure cooker when it comes to personal space. Tight quarters are everywhere – public transport, city streets and markets – and people are always squeezing into spaces that already seem filled to capacity. You might think that the minivan is full but the driver will shoehorn in three more sweaty bodies before he careens off towards the horizon. There are no queues. Customers crowd around the vendor, handing over money or barking orders. And they think Westerners are dim for standing around wide-eyed waiting for someone to pay attention to them. If you don't want to miss the proverbial boat, better master the art of fitting into small spaces, filling voids like flowing water and having a Zen-like calm on a cheek-to-jowl bus ride.

PROSTITUTION

Prostitution is technically illegal but common and tolerated in many parts of Southeast Asia. While some sex workers are adults, there are also minors who work in brothels and informal prostitution rings. They are sometimes sold or recruited by family members and are exploited by the business owner through intimidation and abuse. Unicef estimates that there are close to one million child prostitutes in all of Asia – one of the highest figures in the world.

Sex with minors is a serious offence that is enforced with severe penalties by Southeast Asian countries. Many Western countries also prosecute and punish citizens for paedophile offences committed abroad. For more information contact **End Child Prostitution & Trafficking** (Ecpat; www.ecpat.net), a global network that works to stop child prostitution, child pornography and the trafficking of children for sexual purposes. **Childsafe International** (www.childsafe-international.org), operating out of Cambodia, now covers Laos and Thailand as well, and aims to educate businesses and individuals to be on the lookout for children in vulnerable situations.

The World Bank estimates that one billion people in Southeast Asia live on less than $2 per day.

What You Can Do

☐ Volunteer as an English teacher at a local school or NGO; education is an important tool for economic success.

☐ Support businesses with a social-justice mission, such as fair-trade weaving cooperatives or job-skills development sites.

☐ Stay at village homestays to support traditional lifestyles.

☐ Discourage child labour by not patronising child vendors or hawkers.

☐ Make a donation to a local school or charity instead of handing out money or gifts to beggars, especially children.

☐ Hire local guides to encourage village-based employment opportunities.

☐ Avoid all-inclusive purchases (lodging, transport, tours, food); instead spread your spending so that more people benefit.

Volunteering & Voluntourism

Short-term volunteer positions and 'voluntourism' programs can be arranged throughout the region. There are many nongovernment aid groups in northern Thailand working with impoverished hill-tribe and Burmese communities. In Cambodia, volunteers can spend a little time or money to help orphans and street children. Malaysia has several environmental and wildlife conservation programs. Timor-Leste continues to rely on non-governmental agencies for poverty eradication and development programs.

Many government-funded organisations, such as the US Peace Corps and the British Voluntary Service Overseas, provide language training and development work for long-term commitments. For more information, see Volunteering in individual country chapters.

countries at a glance

Brunei Darussalam

Culture/History ✓
Outdoor Activities ✓✓
River Journeys ✓

Model Citizen

This oil-rich sultanate expertly balances Islamic devotion with modern sensibilities. Thanks to state subsidies, its citizens receive free pensions, schooling and medical care and enjoy one of the region's highest standards of living. Some describe it as a model for modern Islam and say it succeeds in supplying an 'abode of peace' (darussalam), as it is so named.

Between Earth & Sky

Brunei's rainforests are safeguarded as precious natural habitats rather than as potential profit centres. As a result, Borneo's diminishing forests are in pristine condition here and low-impact infrastructure allows visitors a bird's-eye view of the canopy.

Watery Veins

Glimpse Brunei's traditional culture in the world's largest stilt village built along the banks of Sungai Brunei, or experience a watery obstacle course aboard a longtail boat.

p48

Thailand

Culture/History ✓✓
Beaches ✓✓✓
Food ✓✓✓

Monarchs & Monuments

Though decidedly modern, the people of Thailand are devoted royalists and the country's architectural treasures are kingly creations. In the northeast of the country, the Khmer empire built mini-Angkors, while the Thais crafted their own versions of imperial might in the central plains. And Bangkok's glittering royal temples continue the tradition of fusing monarchy and religion.

Coastal Loafing

With their jewel-hued waters and blonde strands of sand, Thailand's southern beaches have tropical-island proportions complemented by a party personality. The Samui sisters are hang-out buddies, Krabi is a karst cathedral and diving abounds on both stunning coasts.

Curries & Chillies

A global culinary legend, Thai food combines four elemental flavours (spicy, sweet, sour and salty) into a phonebook-sized menu of cuisine. Curries gleam with fresh ingredients and radioactive-like colours, chillies are a building block of Thai flavours, not an accent, and traditional stir-fries are whipped up street-side with showmanship flair.

p644

Cambodia

Culture/History ✓✓✓
Outdoor Activities ✓✓
Beaches ✓

Mighty Empire

On par with Egypt's pyramids, the Temples of Angkor are a man-made wonder evoking the symbolism and symmetry of the divine. No journey to the region is complete without touring these great monuments and decoding the bas-relief Hindu-Buddhist stories.

Modern Nightmare

Extreme examples of human aggression are part of Cambodia's heartbreaking history, where an idealistic social experiment turned into genocide and social upheaval. Phnom Penh contains museums that document what happened, leaving us to contemplate why.

Traveller Be Good

Community-based tourism projects are turning former poachers into trekking guides in the Cardamom Mountains and creating rural Mekong River villages into affable hosts. Now you can interact, give back and do a little good while just being an ordinary tourist.

p62

Indonesia

Culture/History ✓✓
Outdoor Activities ✓✓✓
Beaches ✓✓✓

So Many Spice Islands

A huge archipelago spanning two great oceans, Indonesia is mythical and magical with smoking volcanoes, deep dark jungles, vibrant Javanese culture and tribal people that dominated Victorian tales of faraway places. Choose wisely among the options because arrival visas are only for 30 days.

Smoking Giants

A quintessential Indonesia experience is to huff and puff up a nearly vertical cone behind a local guide wearing flip-flops and with an always-lit cigarette. At the summit is a smouldering pot of foul-smelling gases that inspires a serious study of earth sciences.

Beach Buffet

Charming Bali is a cultured beach bum: a rare combination indeed. Just across the channel are the car-less diveable Gili islands, surfable Sumbawa, dragon-guarded Komodo and backpacker delight of Flores.

p147

Laos

Culture/History ✓✓
Outdoor Activities ✓✓✓
River Journeys ✓✓✓

Tribal Territory

More than 65 tribal groups (and still counting) call Laos home. In the rugged north, hill-tribe communities host village homestays that provide a face-to-face cultural (and economic) exchange.

Leafy Laos

With around 20 national protected areas, Laos has an abundance of undisturbed wilderness and several eco-oriented programs, such as the Gibbon Experience, where former poachers are trained as trekking guides. Glide on a zipline past the spray of a waterfall, sleep in a treehouse or rise with the dawn on a misty morn.

River Reverie

Almost every Lao attraction features a river and the easygoing pace of life fed by muddy waters. But when the waters run high, you can break up a nap with river rafting and kayaking, then return to hammock-hanging.

p311

Malaysia

Culture/History ✓✓
Beaches ✓✓
Outdoor Activities ✓✓✓

Laksa Luck

Malaysia is a multicultural success story: Chinese and Indian labourers arrived with little and built a lot, and local Malays intermarried with the new arrivals, mainly Chinese, to create a unique cultural offspring known as Babya Nonya. The diversity is evident at the hawker stalls where noodles and dumplings are served alongside coconut milk curries and steamed rice dishes.

Below the Surface

Diving in Borneo's Semporna archipelago or in Pulau Perhentian puts Malaysia on the scuba crowd's watchlist. Malaysia's beaches aren't as boozy as Thailand's, and for some that is a blessing.

Borneo Bound

The fabled jungles of Borneo sit just beyond the Malaysian gateway cities and are sliced open by tannin-coloured rivers. The granite spire of Mt Kinabalu is a two-day pilgrimage and orang-utan sanctuaries provide refuge for our hairier cousins.

p379

Myanmar

Culture/History ✓✓✓
Outdoor Activities ✓✓
Festivals ✓✓

Sacred Burma, Sequestered Myanmar

The country known by two names is a trip back in time when governments were as enigmatic as the immortals. Previous regimes, in crowns instead of military uniforms, built marvellous temples and the ancient cities around Mandalay, which have resisted gravity, colonialism and limited access to modernity.

Mountain Dew

The Shan State hugs an untamed landscape of mountains and Inle Lake where the Intha people have transformed the water's surface into fertile floating gardens. Boats are more important than shoes and the relaxing pace of puttering from place to place puts visitors in a peaceful state of mind.

Elemental Celebrations

Myanmar brightens up during its festival of lights (Tazaungdaing), and it douses the hot season during Burmese New Year (Thingyan).

p483

Philippines

Culture/History ✓✓
Outdoor Activities ✓✓✓
Beaches ✓✓✓

Maritime Madonna

Wandering mainlanders have long pointed their ships to Filipino shores. The Spanish reached across the globe and built colonial-era forts and towns and an ingrained reverence for Catholicism. The Americans marched behind leaving an inheritance of now-vintage US cars and English as a secondary language.

Coughing Cones

Volcanoes make fantastic landscapes – lush and statuesque – and the Philippines has a full collection, from still-smouldering specimens to dormant peaks. In the north these towers were carved into rice terraces thousands of years ago.

Coastal Jigsaw

The postcard promise of deserted palm-fringed beaches is a reality among the Philippines' 7000-plus islands. The interplay of sea and sand creates a huge playground for divers, kiteboarders and even surfers, as well as beachcombers and hammock hangers.

p551

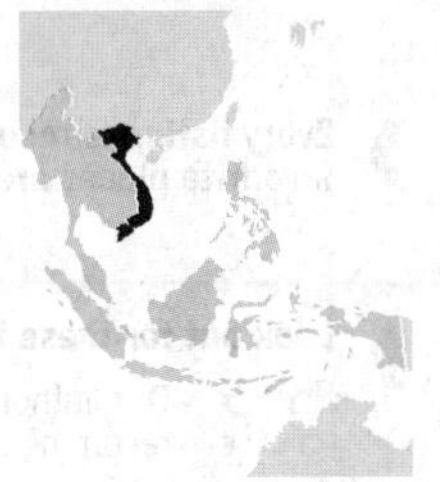

Singapore

Culture/History ✓✓
Food ✓✓✓
Urban Cool ✓✓

Singapore Super Powers

The best of East and West combine to form super-powered Singapore. It has a host of well-curated, well-funded museums, atmospheric colonial houses built during British rule and shopping malls and cinemas reflecting modern, air-conditioned Asia.

Hawk Me a Meal

Ever-efficient Singapore corralled its roaming vendors into popular hawker centres where appetites and meals could be happily united. These open-air pavilions are the centre of a community specialising in culinary traditions – Indian, Malay or Chinese – and meals that turn into nightcaps.

Malls & More

Shopping is more than just bargain- or fashion-hunting here. Malls and hawker centres (an inseparable duo) form the nucleus of every area. Orchard Road is a shopper's haunt of nearly two dozen malls, including modern ION Orchard Mall.

p614

Timor-Leste

Culture/History ✓✓
Outdoor Activities ✓
Beaches ✓

History in Motion

It might be one of the youngest nations in the world but Timor-Leste has lived many lives. Colonial-era architecture, hilltop crowning statues of Jesus Christ and habit-wearing nuns embody the Portuguese legacy, while Dili's cemeteries and museums memorialise the struggle for independence from Indonesia.

Vistas

Climb to the top of sacred Mt Ramelau for a sunrise view of the front and back of the island.

Coral Monogamy

Less than an hour away from the capital is a coral coast with more sea critters than scuba creatures. Not even a blip on the global dive radar, the Atauro Islands have healthy reefs mere steps from the shore. Nearby eco-resorts are powered by the sun and strive to lessen the visitors' load.

p787

Vietnam

Culture/History ✓✓
Beaches ✓✓✓
Food ✓✓✓

Small Country, Big History

Imperial powers couldn't keep their hands off Vietnam, be it neighbouring China, colonial France or anti-communist USA. There are epic tales of occupation and resistance coupled with its home-grown history of millennial-old Hanoi, emperors of Hue and the modern marketplace of Ho Chi Minh City.

Dunes, Dudes & Dudettes

Vietnam has a voluptuous coastline populated by a young, sociable vibe. If the party places are too loud, travel a few kilometres further for scenic solitude.

Nuoc Mam to You

Vietnam's cuisine is a global phenomenon thanks to the zesty dishes of the humid south and the hearty soups of the north. The legacy of colonialism has left behind a thriving coffee culture and crusty baguettes.

p807

Every listing is recommended by our authors, and their favourite places are listed first

Look out for these icons:

 Our author's top recommendation

 A green or sustainable option

 No payment required

See the Index for a full list of destinations covered in this book.

On the Road

Brunei Darussalam

Includes »

Best Regional Specialities

- » Ambuyat (p54)
- » Nasi Lemak (p54)
- » Satay (p54)
- » Tapai Nasi (p54)
- » Kuih Lenggang (p54)

Best Places for Cultural Connections

- » Kampung Ayer (p51)
- » Tamu Kianggeh (p54)
- » Omar Ali Saifuddien Mosque (p51)
- » Arts & Handicrafts Training Centre (p54)
- » Jerudong Park Playground (p56)

Why Go?

The tiny sultanate of Brunei, the last remnant of a naval empire that once ruled all of Borneo and much of the Philippines, is known for its unimaginable riches – it has some of the largest oil fields in Southeast Asia – but should be no less famous for having had the foresight and wisdom to preserve its rainforests. Today the country is blessed with some of the most pristine jungle habitats in all of Borneo – you can get a sense of their verdant vastness in Temburong District. If you take the time to slow down and talk with the locals, in the capital Bandar Seri Begawan (BSB) as well as in outlying towns and longhouses, you may find that there's more than first meets the eye in this quiet, verdant *darussalam* (Arabic for 'abode of peace').

When to Go

Bandar Seri Begawan

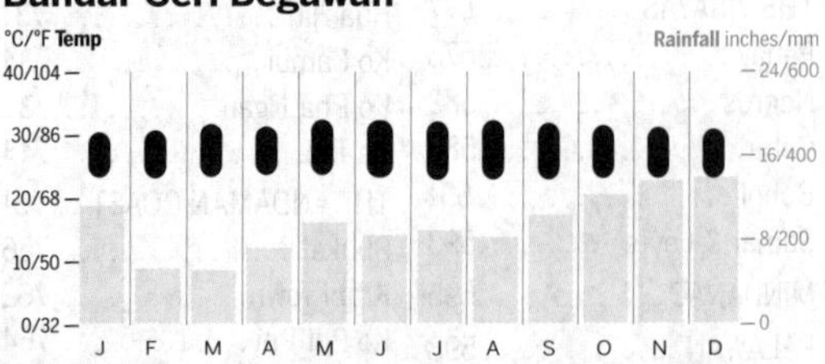

23 Feb Brunei National Day is celebrated with festive parades.

15 Jul Nationwide ceremonies mark the birthday of Sultan Hassanal Bolkiah.

Jul–Aug Sultan's palace open to public for Hari Raya Aidilfitri (last three days of Ramadan).

Don't Miss

Spending time surrounded by the rustling, buzzing, chirping rainforests of Ulu Temburong National Park is one of the highlights of a visit to Brunei Darussalam. After whizzing along *nipa*-lined waterways on a turbo-charged speedboat from BSB, you board a narrow Iban longboat, dodging submerged boulders and hanging vines as you make your way upriver through the early morning mist. A steep, slippery climb through virgin jungle takes you to a towering wall of scaffolding: the park's famous canopy walk. Held steady by guy wires, the structure creaks as you make your way up into the jungle canopy, passing bird's nest ferns, orchids and (if you're lucky) the flash of a hornbill's plumage.

ITINERARIES

Three Days

Spend your first day exploring BSB: visit the water village of Kampung Ayer in the morning, have lunch at Tamu Kianggeh market, and then head to the Twelve Roofs House and the Brunei Museum. Spend your second day on a tour of Ulu Temburong National Park, and your third back in BSB checking out Omar Ali Saifuddien Mosque, the Royal Regalia Museum and more excellent food stalls.

One Week

In addition to the three-day itinerary, spend another couple of days exploring BSB's culinary wonders and soaking up the gilded atmosphere of the Empire Hotel & Country Club; spend the night in Temburong District and do a bit of exploring; and add a day of beach relaxation (eg in Muara).

Essential Food & Drink

If there's one word you should learn during a visit to Brunei, it's *makan*, meaning 'eat' in Bahasa Malaysia. *Makan* isn't just a word, it's a way of life – because, the locals joke, there's nothing else to do!

BSB's hawker centres serve up some superb – and remarkably inexpensive – local dishes. In the city centre, Tamu Kianggeh has Malay-style chicken mains for just B$1 as well as mouthwatering desserts, while in the evening you can't beat Tamu Selera for BBQ specialities such as satay.

AT A GLANCE

» **Currencies** Brunei dollar (B$), Singapore dollar (S$)

» **Language** Bahasa Malaysia, English

» **Money** ATMs easy to find in towns, except in Temburong District

» **Mobile phones** Prepay local SIMs B$30

Fast Facts

» **Area** 5765 sq km

» **Capital** Bandar Seri Begawan (BSB)

» **Country Code** ☎673

» **Emergency** ambulance ☎991, police ☎993, fire ☎995

Exchange Rates

Australia	A$1	B$1.30
Canada	C$1	B$1.25
Euro zone	€1	B$1.65
Japan	¥100	B$1.50
New Zealand	NZ$1	B$1.05
UK	UK£1	B$2.00
USA	US$1	B$1.25

Set Your Budget

» **Dorm bed** B$10

» **Food stall meal** from B$1

» **Museum admission** free

» **Beer** fuhgeddaboudit!

Entering the Country

Daily buses link Sabah, Lawas and Limbang, and Miri with BSB and Temburong District. Ferries run to BSB from Pulau Labuan and – when they're running – from Lawas and Limbang.

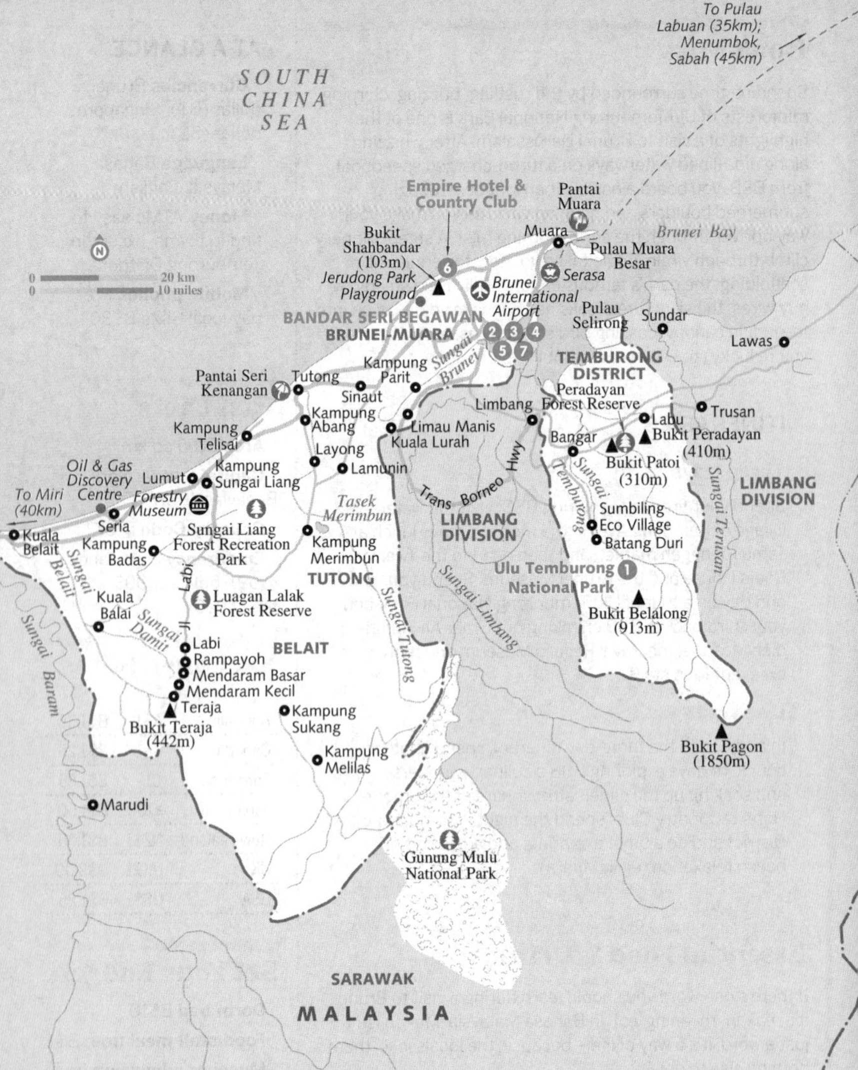

Brunei Darussalam Highlights

1 Climbing high into the rainforest canopy and swimming in a cool jungle river at **Ulu Temburong National Park** (p57).

2 Tearing along mangrove-lined waterways on a **speedboat** (p57) from Bandar Seri Begawan to Bangar.

3 Taking a water taxi to the water village of **Kampung Ayer** (p51) and then a boardwalk stroll.

4 Walking along Bandar Seri Begawan's newly refurbished **waterfront promenade** (p51).

5 Visiting the opulent **mosques** (p51) of Brunei's capital, Bandar Seri Begawan.

6 Marvelling at the over-the-top luxury of the **Empire Hotel & Country Club** (p57), a sparkling monument to world-class profligacy.

7 Enjoying a delicious lunch and scrumptious desserts at **Tamu Kianggeh** (p54), BSB's largest market.

BANDAR SERI BEGAWAN

POP 100,000

If you're expecting some kind of lavish mini-Dubai, think again – Brunei may be a super-rich oil state, but BSB (as the capital is known) has little nouveau riche ostentation. In fact, it's remarkably quiet and relaxed, with picturesque water villages, two opulent mosques, some great food stalls and a vibe as polite and unassuming as its people. Despite the almost total lack of nightlife, there's something quite alluring about BSB, whose mellow pace can definitely grow on you.

Sights & Activities

CENTRAL BSB

Kampung Ayer WATER VILLAGE

Home to an estimated 20,000 people, Kampung Ayer consists of 28 contiguous stilt villages – named after the crafts and occupations traditionally practised there – built along both (but especially the southern) banks of Sungai Brunei. Considered the largest stilt settlement in the world, it has its own schools, mosques, police stations and fire brigade. The houses, painted sun-bleached shades of green, blue, pink and yellow, have not been cutesified for tourists, so while it's far from squalid, be prepared for the rubbish that, at low tide, carpets the intertidal mud.

A good place to start a visit – and get acquainted with Brunei's pre-oil culture – is the new **Kampung Ayer Cultural & Tourism Gallery** (9am-5pm Sat-Thu, 9-11.30am & 2.30-5pm Fri), directly across the river from BSB's new **waterfront promenade** (Jl McArthur). A square, glass-enclosed **viewing tower** offers panoramic views of the bustling scene below.

Getting across the river from BSB's city centre is a breeze. Just stand somewhere that a motorboat – BSB's souped-up version of the gondola – can dock and flag down an empty one. The fare is supposed to be B$0.50 per person if you go straight across, more if you cross diagonally.

Omar Ali Saifuddien Mosque MOSQUE

(Jl Stoney; interior 8.30am-noon, 1.30-3pm & 4.30-5.30pm Sat-Wed, 4.30-5pm Fri, closed Thu, exterior compound 8am-8.30pm except prayer times) Built from 1954 to 1958, this lovely mosque – named after Brunei's 28th sultan (the late father of the current sultan) – is surrounded by an artificial lagoon that serves as a reflecting pool. Inside, the floor and walls are made from the finest Italian marble, the stained-glass windows and chandeliers were crafted in England, and the luxurious carpets were flown in from Saudi Arabia and Belgium. Jigsaw enthusiasts can admire the 3.5-million-piece Venetian mosaic inside the main dome.

The ceremonial stone boat sitting in the lagoon is a replica of a 16th-century *mahligai* (royal barge).

> **THE VIRTUE OF MODESTY**
>
> Bruneians are quite conservative when it comes to what they wear. Though visitors aren't expected to adopt Islamic standards, it is best to dress somewhat conservatively as a mark of respect to the locals. Sleeveless T-shirts and ripped jeans are inappropriate for men, bikini tops and shorts are unacceptable for women.

Royal Regalia Museum MUSEUM

(Jl Sultan; admission free; 9am-5pm Sun-Thu, 9-11.30am & 2.30-5pm Fri, 9.45am-5pm Sat, last entry 4.30pm) A celebration of the sultan and all the trappings of Bruneian royalty. The ground floor is dominated by a re-creation of the sultan's coronation day parade, while other sections feature medals bestowed upon the sultan and a selection of gifts presented by foreign leaders. Before entering, visitors must check cameras, mobile phones and bags, and remove their shoes.

Wild Monkeys MONKEYS

(just off Jl Tasek Lama) Long-tailed macaques and their adorable offspring often frolic in the trees along the road that heads up the hill (towards the radio tower) from the intersection just south of the Terrace Hotel.

A troupe of about 20 macaques, including babies, lives in the forested area behind (east of) **Tamu Kianggeh** and frequently comes down to the edge of the market (behind stall 49) in the morning (often from 6am to 8am) and in the afternoon (from about 2pm to 5pm).

EAST OF CENTRAL BSB

Brunei Museum MUSEUM

(Jl Kota Batu; 9am-5pm Sat-Thu, 9-11.30am & 2.30-5pm Fri, last entry 30min before closing) Brunei's national museum, officially opened by the queen of England in 1972, has galleries dedicated to **Islamic Art**, with pieces from as far back as the 9th century; **Brunei**

Traditional Culture, which spotlights Brunei's role in Southeast Asian history and commerce; **Natural History**, providing an excellent, if old-fashioned, introduction to Borneo's extraordinary biodiversity; and Brunei's **Independence**, one of whose displays features the words of Brunei's national anthem, 'Allah Save the King' (sound familiar?).

The museum is 4.5km east of central BSB along the coastal road, on a bluff overlooking Sungai Brunei. To get there, take bus 39 or a taxi (B$10 from the bus station).

Twelve Roofs House MUSEUM
(Bubungan Dua Belas; Jl Residency; ⌚9am-4.30pm Mon-Thu & Sat, 9-11.30am & 2.30-4.30pm Fri) The one-time residence of Britain's colonial-era High Commissioners is now a museum dedicated to the longstanding 'special relationship' between Brunei and the UK. The evocative photos include views of Brunei as it looked a century ago and many fine shots of the queen of England. Situated 1.5km southeast of Sungai Kianggeh, towards the Brunei Museum, on a hilltop dominating the river. To get there from the city centre, take bus 39, a taxi or a water taxi.

Bandar Seri Begawan

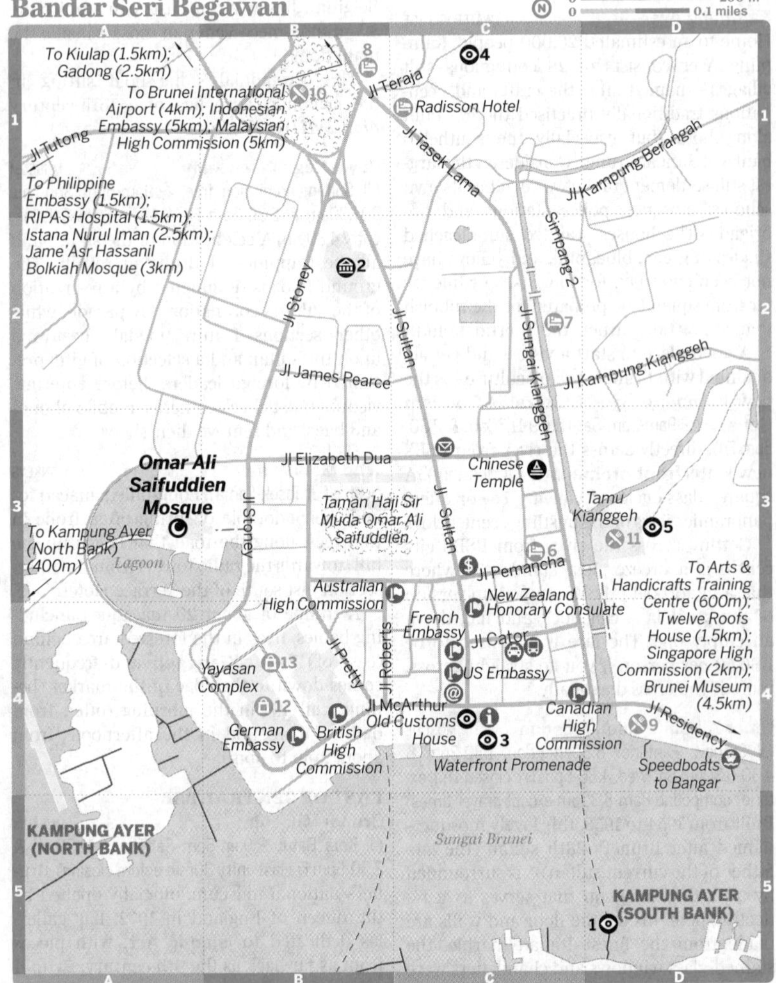

NORTH & WEST OF CENTRAL BSB

Jame'Asr Hassanil Bolkiah Mosque MOSQUE
(Sultan Hassanal Bolkiah Hwy, Kampung Kiarong; 8am-6pm Mon-Wed & Sat, 5-6pm Fri, 10.30am-6pm Sun, closed noon-2pm & 3-5pm daily) Built in 1992 to celebrate the 25th year of the current sultan's reign, Brunei's largest mosque and its four terrazzo-tiled minarets are a fantastic sight, especially when illuminated in the evening. The interior is jaw-dropping. It's 3km northwest of the city centre towards Gadong. To get there, take buses 01 or 22.

Istana Nurul Iman PALACE
(Jl Tutong) The best way to measure the grandeur of any residential structure is by counting the bathrooms. Istana Nurul Iman (Palace of the Light of the Faith), the official residence of the sultan, has 257! This 1788-room, 200,000-sq-metre behemoth – the largest dwelling of any sort in the world – is, if you can believe it, more than four times the size of the Palace of Versailles and three times larger than Buckingham Palace. It is open to the public only during the three-day Hari Raya Aidilfitri festivities at the end of Ramadan. The best way to check out the palace on the other 362 days of the year is to take a water taxi cruise.

Bandar Seri Begawan

Top Sights
Omar Ali Saifuddien Mosque A3

Sights
1 Kampung Ayer Cultural & Tourism Gallery D5
2 Royal Regalia Museum B2
3 Waterfront Promenade C4
4 Wild Monkeys C1
5 Wild Monkeys D3

Activities, Courses & Tours
Mona Florafauna Tours .... (see 6)

Sleeping
6 KH Soon Resthouse C3
7 Pusat Belia C2
8 Terrace Hotel B1

Eating
9 Gerai Makan Jalan Residency D4
Hua Ho Department Store .... (see 12)
10 Taman Selera B1
11 Tamu Kianggeh D3

Shopping
12 Hua Ho Department Store B4
Paul & Elizabeth Book Services .... (see 13)
Tamu Kianggeh .... (see 11)
13 Yayasan Complex B4

Information
DST Communications .... (see 13)
Paul & Elizabeth Cyber Café .... (see 13)

Tours

A number of local agencies offer tours of BSB and trips to nature sites around the sultanate, including Ulu Temburong National Park.

Borneo Guide ECOTOUR
(876 6796; www.borneoguide.com; Unit B1, 1st fl, Warisan Mata-Mata, Gadong) Excellent service, good prices and a variety of ecoprograms around Brunei and Borneo. A day trip to Ulu Temburong National Park costs B$98 from Bangar (9am to 3.30pm or 4pm) or B$110 from BSB (7.30am to 4.30 or 5pm).

Mona Florafauna Tours TOUR
(223 0761, 24hr 884 9110; mft.brunei@gmail.com; 209 1st fl, Kiaw Lian Bldg, 140 Jl Pemancha; 8.30am-5pm) Specialises in outdoor and wildlife tours. Situated a floor below KH Soon Resthouse.

Sleeping

Budget options are thin on the ground. Upscale places often offer big online discounts.

We've heard murmurs about homestays and B&B establishments starting up in Kampung Ayer – the Kampung Ayer Cultural & Tourism Gallery should have the latest info.

TOP CHOICE **Pusat Belia** HOSTEL $
(Youth Centre; 222 2900; Jl Sungai Kianggeh; dm B$10;) Gets rave reviews from backpackers despite the fact that couples can't stay together. The 28 spacious, strictly sex-segregated rooms, with four or 10 beds (all bunks), have functional furnishings, big windows, red cement floors and passable bathrooms. Situated at the southern end of the Youth Centre complex (behind the cylindrical staircase). Reception is supposed to be open from 7.45am to noon and 1.30pm to 4.30pm or later (often until 6pm or 6.30pm) but midday closure is longer on Friday and staffing can be intermittent on Sunday, in the evening and at night. If the office is locked, hang around and someone should find you. The adjacent swimming pool costs

B$1. May fill up with government guests on holidays and for sports events.

KH Soon Resthouse GUESTHOUSE $
(☎222 2052; http://khsoon-resthouse.tripod.com; 2nd fl, 140 Jl Pemancha; s/d B$35/39, without bathroom B$30/35; ❄) This matter-of-fact guesthouse, in a converted commercial space with floors the colour of a man-o-war's decks, offers a unique combination for Brunei: budget rates, huge but spartan rooms, and a super-central location. An extra bed costs B$17; a room for five is B$85. Staff can supply details on public transport to Miri and Kota Kinabalu.

Terrace Hotel HOTEL $$
(☎224 3554/5/6/7; www.terracebrunei.com; Jl Tasek Lama; d B$65-75; ❄@📶🏊) A classic tourist-class hotel whose 84 rooms are dowdy (think 1980s) but clean and come with marble bathrooms. Has a great little swimming pool. In a super location just 800m north of the waterfront, near a hawker centre. Excellent value for Brunei.

Eating

In the city centre, restaurants are sprinkled along the waterfront and on Jl Sultan (south of Jl Pemancha). The big shopping malls, including those out in Gadong, have food courts – at the Yayasan Complex, go to the 2nd floor of the northern end of the eastern building.

TOP CHOICE **Aminah Arif** AMBUYAT $$
(☎223 6198; Unit 2-3, Block B, Rahman Bldg, Spg 88, Kiulap; ambuyat for 2 B$16; ⏲9am-10pm) Aminah Arif is synonymous with *ambuyat*, Brunei's gloriously gluey signature dish that's made with the ground pith of the sago plant. If you're up for trying a generous serving of wiggly white goo, this is a very good place. Also serves rice and noodle dishes. Situated in Kiulap about 3km northwest of the city centre.

TOP CHOICE **Tamu Kianggeh** FOOD STALLS $
(Jl Sungai Kianggeh; mains from B$1; ⏲5am-5pm) The stalls here serve Brunei's cheapest meals, including *nasi lemak* (rice cooked in coconut milk and served with chicken, beef or prawn, egg and cucumber slices; B$1). A vegetarian-Chinese stall called **Tamu Chakoi** (stalls 49-51; ⏲8.30am-noon Tue-Sun; 🥬) offers a variety of inexpensive fried pastries and noodle dishes. For dessert, stop by **Hajjah Hasnah** (stall 214) for *tapai nasi* (half-fermented rice) – fermented for about three days, it packs a gentle but perceptible punch.

Taman Selera NIGHT MARKET $
(cnr Jl Tasek Lama & Jl Stoney; mains B$1-3.50; ⏲4pm-midnight) In a shady park, diners eat excellent, cheap Malay dishes under colourful tarps and ceiling fans. Options include satay (four skewers for B$1). Situated 1km north of the waterfront, across from the Terrace Hotel.

Gerai Makan Jalan Residency FOOD COURT $
(Jalan Residency Food Court; Jl Residency; mains B$2-5.50; ⏲24hr) Along the riverbank facing Kampung Ayer, this grouping of food stalls features satay (B$1 for four chicken or three lamb skewers), rice dishes and soups such as *soto* (noodle soup). Most places are open from 4pm to midnight but one will take care of the munchies round the clock.

TOP CHOICE **Hua Ho Department Store** SUPERMARKET $
(western bldg, Yayasan Complex, Jl Pretty; ⏲10am-10pm) Dozens of kinds of absolutely scrumptious Bruneian cookies and snacks (B$3 to B$5) can be found in the basement supermarket, in a case next to the fruit section. Some of the sweets are dusted with powdered sugar; many simply melt in your mouth. Among the highlights: *kuih lenggang*, a green, coconut-filled crepe.

Shopping

Shopping is Brunei's national sport. Locals bop through the shopping malls scouting out the best deals while bemoaning the fact that their micro-nation doesn't have as much variety as Singapore.

Escape the oppressive heat at the ritzy **Yayasan Complex** (Kompleks Yayasan Sultan Haji Hassanal Bolkiah; Jl Pretty), the city centre's main shopping mall, whose courtyard is aligned with Omar Ali Saifuddien Mosque. Don't miss the four-level **Hua Ho Department Store** (⏲10am-10pm), with its case of traditional Bruneian sweets in the basement. Woven crafts are sold along the river at **Tamu Kianggeh** (Jl Sungai Kianggeh), but prices are higher than in Malaysia.

The country's only traffic jam occurs nightly about 3km northwest of the city centre in **Gadong**, Brunei's main shopping district. The area features several air-conditioned bastions of commerce, including two huge malls, **Centrepoint** and **The Mall**.

Arts & Handicrafts Training Centre CRAFTS
(Jl Kota Batu; ⏲8am-5pm Sat-Thu, 8.30-11.30am & 2.30-5pm Fri) Sells pricey silverwork, carved wooden items, ornamental brass cannons

(from B$500) and ceremonial swords (about B$500) made by the centre's students and graduates. Not bad for window-shopping.

Paul & Elizabeth Book Services BOOKS
(☎222 0958; 2nd fl, eastern bldg, Yayasan Complex, Jl Pretty; ⏲9.30am-9pm) Stocks a few books on Brunei, English-language paperbacks and some ancient Lonely Planet guides.

Information

Internet Access

Amin & Sayeed Cyber Cafe (1st fl, cnr Jl Sultan & Jl McArthur; per hr B$1; ⏲9am-midnight)

Paul & Elizabeth Cyber Café (2nd fl, eastern bldg, Yayasan Complex, Jl Pretty; per hr B$1; ⏲9am-9pm) Overlooking the central atrium in the eastern building.

Medical Services

RIPAS Hospital (☎224 2424; Jl Tutong; ⏲24hr) Brunei's main hospital, with fully equipped, modern facilities. Situated about 2km west of the city centre (across the Edinburgh Bridge).

Money

Banks and international ATMs are sprinkled around the city centre, especially along Jl McArthur and Jl Sultan. The airport has ATMs, too.

HSBC (cnr Jl Sultan & Jl Pemancha; ⏲8.45am-4pm Mon-Fri, 8.45-11.30am Sat) Has a 24-hour ATM. You must have an HSBC account to change travellers cheques (B$25 fee).

Isman Money Changer (Ground fl, eastern bldg, Yayasan Complex, Jl Pretty; ⏲9.30am-7.30pm) Changes cash but not travellers cheques. Just off the central atrium.

Post

Main post office (cnr Jl Sultan & Jl Elizabeth Dua; ⏲8am-4.30pm Mon-Thu & Sat, 8-11am & 2-4pm Fri) Has a free internet computer. The Stamp Gallery displays some historic first-day covers and blow-ups of colonial-era stamps.

Telephone

International calling cards (for use in public phones) are sold at various shops around town, including several along Jl McArthur.

Amin & Sayeed Cyber Cafe (1st fl, cnr Jl Sultan & Jl McArthur; ⏲9am-midnight) Cheap overseas calls for B$0.25 to B$0.30 per minute.

DST Communications (www.dst-group.com; ground fl, western bldg, Yayasan Complex, Jl McArthur; ⏲9am-4pm Mon-Thu & Sat, 9am-11am & 2.30-4pm Fri, closed Sun) A prepay SIM card costs B$30, including B$5 worth of calls; registering (if you bought a SIM card elsewhere) is free. Bring your passport.

Tourist Information

Keep an eye out for the free **Borneo Insider's Guide** (BIG; www.borneoinsidersguide.com), a glossy magazine published four times a year.

Brunei Tourism (www.bruneitourism.travel), whose wonderful website has oodles of useful information, runs three tourist information counters that can supply the only decent maps of the sultanate:

Airport (Arrival hall; ⏲8am-noon & 1.30-5pm)

Kampung Ayer Cultural & Tourism Gallery (Kampung Ayer; ⏲9am-5pm Sat-Thu, 9-11am & 2.30-5pm Fri) Across the river from the city centre.

Old Customs House (Jl McArthur) Should be open by the time you read this.

Getting There & Away

For information about getting to/from Bandar Seri Begawan by air, boat and bus, see p60.

Getting Around

To/From the Airport

The airport, about 8km north of central BSB, is linked to the city centre, including the **bus terminal** (Jl Cator), by buses 23, 24, 36 and 38. A taxi to/from the airport costs B$20 to B$25 (B$35 after 10pm); taxis are unmetered so agree on a price before you get in. Some hotels offer airport pick-up.

Bus

Brunei's public bus system, run by several different companies, is rather chaotic, at least to the uninitiated, so getting around by public transport takes a bit of planning. Buses (B$1) operate daily from 6.30am to about 6.30pm (7pm on some lines); after that, your options are taking a taxi or hoofing it. If you're heading out of town and need to catch a bus back, ask the driver if and when he's coming back and what time the last bus back departs. Finding stops can be a challenge – some are marked by black-and-white striped uprights or a shelter, others by a yellow triangle painted on the pavement, and yet others by no discernable symbol whatsoever.

BSB's carbon-monoxide-choked **bus terminal** (Jl Cator), on the ground floor of a multistorey parking complex two blocks north of the waterfront, lacks an information office or a ticket counter. Next to each numbered berth, schematic signs (included in some tourist brochures) show the route of each line.

To get to the Serasa ferry terminal, take bus 37, 38 or 39 to Muara (B$1, at least twice an hour), from where it's a short ride on bus 33 to the ferry. Three express buses a day (B$2, 40 minutes) link BSB direct with the ferry; departures from BSB's bus terminal (from the berth for bus 39) are at 6.30am, 11.30am and 2.15pm.

Car

Brunei has Southeast Asia's cheapest fuel – petrol is just B$0.53 a litre and diesel goes for only B$0.30!

Hiring a car is a good way to explore Brunei's hinterland. Prices start at about B$80 a day. Surcharges may apply if the car is taken into Sarawak. Most agencies will bring the car to your hotel and pick it up when you've finished.

Among the rental companies (most of them local) with offices at the airport:

Avis (☎876 0642; www.avis.com)

Hertz (☎872 6000, 239 0300; www.hertz.com)

Taxi

Taxis are a convenient way of exploring BSB – if you can find one, that is: the entire country has fewer than 50 official taxis, all run by independent drivers. Unfortunately, there is no centralised taxi dispatcher and it's difficult or impossible to flag down a taxi on the street. Hotels can provide drivers' mobile phone numbers. Most taxis have yellow tops; a few serving the airport are all white.

BSB's only proper **taxi rank** (Jl Cator) is two blocks north of the waterfront at the bus terminal.

Taxis do not have meters so always agree on a price before getting in; fares go up by 50% after 10pm. Sample daytime taxi fares from the city centre include the Brunei Museum (B$10), Gadong (B$10 to B$15), the Serasa ferry terminal in Muara (B$30), the Empire Hotel & Country Club (B$30 to B$35) and the Jerudong Park Playground (B$35).

Water Taxi

If your destination is near the river, water taxis are a good way of getting there. You can hail one anywhere along the BSB waterfront that a boat can dock, as well as along Venice-themed **Sungai Kianggeh** (Jl Sungai Kianggeh). Crossing straight across the river is supposed to cost B$0.50 per person; diagonal crossings cost more. A river cruise to see Istana Nurul Iman – especially nice in the late afternoon – should cost about B$30.

AROUND BRUNEI

Jerudong

In its heyday, **Jerudong Park Playground** (Jerudong; admission free, 5/8 rides B$8/10; ⏲5-10.30pm Wed, Thu & Sun, 5pm-midnight Fri & Sat, closed Mon & Tue except during school holidays), a B$1 billion amusement park and Prince Jefri project opened in 1994, was hugely popular with local young people – as one Bruneian in his mid-20s put it, 'this was the highlight of our childhood'.

The concert hall hosted free concerts by the likes of Whitney Houston and Michael Jackson, the latter to celebrate the sultan's 50th birthday, and the many rides included a giant roller-coaster. That attraction, along with most of the others, was sold off to repay debts but 10 rides still operate, including a merry-go-round and junior bumper cars. Other family-friendly features include a clown show at 8pm and a musical fountain that does its thing at 8.30pm and 9.30pm.

There is no bus service to the park, which is near the coast about 20km northwest of BSB, so the only way to get there is by taxi (about B$35 from central BSB) or private car.

Muara

Not many people come to Brunei for a sun 'n' sand experience, but if you have some spare time to stretch out on the seashore, there are a couple of options about 25km northeast of BSB around the cargo, ferry and naval port of Muara, site of an Australian amphibious landing in April 1945.

Pantai Muara (Muara Beach), near the tip of the peninsula, is a popular weekend retreat, with food stalls, picnic tables and a children's playground. Muara's town centre is served by buses 37, 38 and 39 (B$1); bus 33 will take you from there to Pantai Muara.

Temburong District

Possibly the best-preserved tract of primary rainforest in all of Borneo covers much of Brunei's 1288-sq-km Temburong District (population 10,000), which is separated from the rest of the country by a strip of Malaysia's Limbang Division. The area's main draw is the brilliant Ulu Temburong National Park, accessible only by longboat.

The speedboat ride from BSB out to Bangar, the district capital, is the most fun you can possibly have for B$6. You roar down Sungai Brunei, slap through the *nipa*-lined waterways and then tilt and weave through mangroves into the mouth of Sungai Temburong.

BANGAR

Bangar, a three-street town on the banks of Sungai Temburong, is the gateway to (and administrative centre of) the Temburong

SPLURGE!

Dubaian in its proportions and opulence, the 523-room **Empire Hotel & Country Club** (☎241 8888; www.theempirehotel.com; Muara-Tutong Hwy, Kampung Jerudong; r incl breakfast from B$400, villa B$1300-2900;) was commissioned by Prince Jefri – get this – as lodging for guests of the royal family. To recoup some of the US$1.1 billion investment, the property was quickly transformed into an upscale resort, so now anyone with a thing for Las Vegas–style bling can hang out in the lobby and enjoy one of the US$500,000 lamps made of gold and Baccarat crystal (the other one lives in the Emperor Suite and can be appreciated privately for B$16,600 per night). Fun for an over-the-top honeymoon! Worth a visit just to take in the gilded spectacle; tea in the Lobby Lounge costs a mere B$5 a pot. To get there, take bus 57 from central BSB or Gadong (runs two or three times daily; on the way back, book at the hotel's Transport desk), or a taxi (B$30 to B$35).

district. It can be visited as a day trip from BSB if you catch an early speedboat.

Sleeping

Youth Hostel HOSTEL $
(Pusat Belia; ☎522 1694; dm B$10; office staffed 7.30am-4.30pm Sun-Thu) Part of a youth centre, this basic hostel sits in a fenced compound across the street from (west of) the Tourist Information Centre. Rooms, each with six beds (bunks), are clean and fan-cooled. If no one's around, try phoning.

Rumah Persinggahan Kerajaan Daerah Temburong GUESTHOUSE $
(☎522 1239; Jl Batang Duri; s/d/tr/q B$25/30/40/50, 4-person chalet B$80;) This government-run guesthouse has friendly, helpful staff and six spacious but slightly fraying rooms. Situated a few hundred metres west of the town centre, across the highway from the two mosques.

Information

3 in 1 Services (per hr B$1; 7.45am-9.30pm, closed Sun) Internet access on the 1st floor of the building next to the market (across the pedestrian bridge from the hawker centre). The shop number is A1-3.

Bank Islam Brunei Darussalam (8.45am-3.45pm Mon-Thu, 8.45-11am & 2.30-4pm Fri, 8.45-11.15am Sat) The only bank in town. The ATM does not take international cards.

Hock Guan Minimarket Exchanges Malaysian ringgits for Brunei dollars. In the second row of shops from the Tourist Information Centre.

Tourist Information Centre (☎876 6796) Run by Borneo Guide (www.borneoguide.com) but closed at the time of research.

Getting There & Away

By far the fastest way to/from BSB is by speedboat (adult/over 60 years B$6/5, 45 minutes, approximately hourly from 6am to at least 4.30pm, until as late as 6pm on Sunday and holidays). The crossing is handled by two companies, **Ampuan** (☎522 1985), whose boats are usually red and white, and **Koperasi** (☎522 628), whose vessels are usually blue and yellow. In BSB, the dock is on Jl Residency about 200m east of Sungai Kianggeh.

Buses run by **Jesselton** (☎in BSB 718 3838, 717 7755, 719 3835) pick up passengers heading towards Limbang and BSB in the early afternoon; its bus to Kota Kinabalu (B$20) and Lawas passes through town at about 10am.

To hire an unofficial taxi, ask around under the rain awning in front of the ferry terminal. Drivers may not speak much English.

ULU TEMBURONG NATIONAL PARK

One of the highlights of a visit to Brunei, **Ulu Temburong National Park** (admission B$5) is in the heart of the pristine rainforests covering most of southern Temburong. Only about 1 sq km of the park is accessible to tourists – in order to protect it for future generations, the rest is off-limits to *Homo sapiens* except scientists, who flock here from around the world.

Activities

Longboat Trip BOATING
One of the charms of Ulu Temburong National Park is that the only way to get there is by *temuai* (shallow-draft Iban longboat). The exhilarating trip, which takes 25 to 40 minutes from Batang Duri (16km south of Bangar), is challenging even for experienced skippers: submerged boulders have to be dodged, hanging vines evaded and the outboard must be taken out of the water at exactly the right moment. When it rains, the water level can quickly rise by up to 2m, but if the river is low you might have to get out and push.

Canopy Walk ADVENTURE TOUR

The park's main attraction is a delicate aluminium walkway, secured by guy ropes, that takes you through (or, more accurately, near) the jungle canopy up to 60m above the forest floor. In primary rainforests, only limited vegetation can grow on the ground because so little light penetrates, but up in the canopy all manner of life proliferates. Unfortunately, there are no explanatory signs here and some guides don't have the background to explain the importance of the canopy ecosystem and point out the huge variety of organisms that can live on a single tree: orchids; bird's nest ferns and other epiphytes; ants and myriad other insects; amphibians and snakes; and a huge selection of birds.

Sleeping

Ulu-Ulu Resort LODGE $$$

(www.uluuluresort.com; per person B$350; ❄) The park's only accommodation is an upscale riverside lodge built of hardwood, with 22 rooms, some 1920s Malay-style chalets. Prices include transport from BSB and board; activities tend to be expensive. In Malay, *ulu* (as in Ulu Temburong) means 'upriver' and *ulu-ulu* means, essentially, 'back of the beyond'.

Getting There & Away

For all intents and purposes, the only way to visit the park is by booking a tour. For details on BSB-based tour agencies that organise park visits (from B$98 for a day trip), see p53.

UNDERSTAND BRUNEI DARUSSALAM

Brunei Darussalam Today

Brunei's oil and gas wealth affords its citizens one of the highest standards of living in the world – per capita GDP is over US$50,000 and the government runs a budget *surplus* of 39%! Literacy stands at 93%, average life expectancy is 76 years, and there are pensions for all, free medical care, free schooling, free sport and leisure centres, cheap loans, subsidies for many purchases (including cars), short working weeks, no income tax and the highest minimum wages in the region. Economic diversification – including significant sovereign wealth investments overseas – and deep-sea exploration for oil aim to keep the cash rolling in and, as long as it does, the people of Brunei should stay happy (though in some cases slightly bored) with their felicitous lot.

Food

Brunei's delicious cuisine, much of it available for a song at market stalls, is similar to the Malay dishes popular in nearby Malaysia, though with local variations. One uniquely Bruneian speciality is *ambuyat,* an extraordinary white goo made from the pith of the sago plant (see p54).

In this chapter, restaurants are divided into three categories based on the price of their cheapest main dish: budget ($), up to B$3; midrange ($$), from B$3 to B$8; and top end ($$$), above B$8.

History

The earliest recorded references to Brunei concern China's trading connections with 'Pu-ni' in the 6th century, during the Tang dynasty. Prior to the region's embrace of Islam in the 1400s, Brunei was within the boundaries of the Sumatran Srivijaya Empire, then the Majapahit Empire of Java. By the late 15th and early 16th centuries, the so-called Golden Age of Sultan Bolkiah (the fifth sultan), Brunei Darussalam had become a considerable regional power, with its seafaring rule extending throughout Borneo and deep into the Philippines.

The Spanish and Portuguese were the first European visitors, arriving in the 16th century, but failed to make inroads by force. In the early 19th century, the more subtle approach of the British, in the guise of Sarawak's first White Rajah, James Brooke, spelled the end of Brunei's power. A series of treaties ceding land and power whittled away at the internally riven sultanate, which became a British protectorate in 1888. Two years later, with a final dash of absurdity, Limbang was lost to Sarawak, dividing Brunei into two parts.

In 1929, just as Brunei was about to be swallowed up entirely, oil was discovered, turning the tiny state into an economic power overnight. The present sultan's father, Sultan Omar Saifuddien, kept Brunei out of the Malayan confederacy and Malaysia, preferring that his country remain a British protectorate – and that oil revenues stay on home soil.

Saifuddien abdicated in 1967, leaving the throne to his popular son and heir, Sultan Hassanal Bolkiah. Early in 1984 he reluctantly led his tightly ruled country to complete independence from Britain. As a former public-school boy and graduate of the Royal Military Academy Sandhurst, the sultan rather enjoyed British patronage and the country still has very close political, economic and military ties to Britain.

After independence Brunei adopted a national ideology known as Melayu Islam Beraja (MIB; Malay Islamic Monarchy), which stresses Malay culture, Islam (the official religion) and the legitimacy of the sultan.

The Culture

Brunei is the most observant Islamic country in Southeast Asia. However, Bruneians embrace integration into the global economy, striving to strike a balance between international trends and local traditions.

Ethnic Malays (a category that includes the Belait, Bisayah, Dusun, Kedayan and Murut peoples) make up about two-thirds of the sultanate's 400,000 inhabitants. Iban, Kelabit and other tribes contribute around 3.4%, and people of Chinese heritage account for 11% of the population. Westerners, Thais, Filipinos, Indonesians, Indians and Bangladeshis – ie temporary workers – make up the rest.

Although the state religion is Islam and the Ministry of Religious Affairs actively promotes Islam (and, in some cases, limits the freedom of other religious groups, eg when it comes to building churches or Chinese temples), only 67% of the population is actually Muslim. Buddhists and Christians make up 13% and 10% respectively; about 10% of people have kept their indigenous beliefs.

Traditional crafts have almost disappeared in modern Brunei. In its heyday, the sultanate was a source of lost-wax brassware – gongs, kettles, betel containers and, most famously, ceremonial cannons – that was prized throughout Borneo and beyond. Brunei's silversmiths were also celebrated.

Jong sarat sarongs, still handwoven using gold thread, are still worn at formal ceremonial occasions.

Land & Environment

Brunei (5765 sq km) consists of two non-contiguous areas separated by the Limbang district of Sarawak. The larger, western part of the country contains the main towns: Bandar Seri Begawan (BSB); the oil town of Seria; and the commercial town of Kuala Belait. The eastern slice of the country, the hilly, mostly forested Temburong District, is much less developed.

Away from the coast, Brunei is mainly jungle, with about 75% of the country still covered by virtually untouched forests. As you can see if you fly over the sultanate (or connect to Google Earth), clear cutting, 'selective' logging, road building and palm oil plantations – the most serious threats to Borneo's incredibly rich ecosystems – stop dead at the sultanate's borders.

Brunei has several forest reserves as well as one national park, the superb Ulu Temburong National Park, a 500-sq-km swathe of protected primary rainforest.

SURVIVAL GUIDE

Directory A–Z

Accommodation

Accommodation in Brunei is significantly more expensive than in neighbouring Malaysia, but a handful of excellent budget options make shoestring travel possible. Accommodation prices in this chapter are divided into three categories: budget ($), for a place whose double rooms cost less than B$60; midrange ($$), for doubles that cost between B$60 and B$150; and top end ($$$), for doubles over B$150.

Business Hours

Shopping malls generally stay open from 9am or 10am until about 9.30pm. Most shops in central Bandar Seri Begawan open at around 10am and are closed by 6pm. Banks are generally open from 9am to about 3pm Monday to Friday and from 9am to 11am on Saturday. Government offices are open from 7.45am to 12.15pm and 1.30pm to 4.30pm (closed on Friday and Sunday). During Ramadan, business and office hours are shortened and Muslim-owned restaurants may close during daylight hours.

Embassies & Consulates

All of the following embassies, consulates and high commissions are located within Bandar Seri Begawan.

Australia High Commission (☎222 9435; www.bruneidarussalam.embassy.gov.au; 6th fl, Dar Takaful IBB Utama, Jl Pemancha)

Canada High Commission (☎222 0043; www.canadainternational.gc.ca/brunei_darussalam; 5th fl, Jl McArthur Bldg, 1 Jl McArthur)

France (☎222 0960; www.ambafrance-bn.org; Units 301-306, Kompleks Jl Sultan, Jl Sultan)

Germany (☎222 5547; www.bandar-seri-begawan.diplo.de; 2nd fl, Unit 2.01, Block A, Yayasan Complex, Jl Pretty)

Indonesia (☎233 0180; www.indonesia.org.bn; 4498 Simpang 528, Jl Muara, Kampung Sungai Hanching)

Malaysia High Commission (☎238 1095/6/7; www.kln.gov.my/web/brn_begawan; 61 Simpang 336, Jl Kebangsaan)

New Zealand Honorary Consulate (☎222 2422, 222 5880; c/o Deloitte & Touche, 5th fl, Wisma Hajjah Fatimah, 22-23 Jl Sultan)

Philippines (☎224 1465/6; www.philippineembassybrunei.net; 17 Simpang 126, Km 2, Jl Tutong)

Singapore High Commission (☎226 2741; www.mfa.gov.sg/brunei; 8 Simpang 74, Jl Subok)

UK High Commission (☎222 2231, 222 6001; http://ukinbrunei.fco.gov.uk/en; 2nd fl, Unit 2.01, Block D, Yayasan Complex, Jl Pretty)

USA (☎238 4616; http://brunei.usembassy.gov; Simpang 336-52-16-9, Diplomatic Enclave, Jl Kebangsaan) The new US embassy complex is about 5km northeast of the Terrace Hotel.

Gay & Lesbian Travellers

According to www.smartraveller.gov.au, 'consensual homosexual acts between adults (of either sex) are illegal and penalties include prison sentences'.

Internet Access

All upmarket hotels have internet connections and a veritable blanket of wi-fi has begun to cover central BSB.

Legal Matters

The sale and public consumption of alcohol is forbidden. When entering Brunei you'll see signs reading 'Warning: Death for drug traffickers under Brunei law'. Non-Muslim visitors over 17 years are allowed to import 12 cans of beer and two bottles of wine or spirits for personal consumption.

Media

The *Borneo Bulletin* (www.borneobulletin.com.bn; B$0.80) is filled with local and international news, most of it from news agencies, none of it locally controversial. News stories refer to the sultan as 'the benevolent ruler' so no prizes for guessing that the paper doesn't do hard-hitting investigative reporting.

Tourist Information

Brunei's national tourist body, **Brunei Tourism** (www.bruneitourism.travel), has a particularly useful website. By the time you read this, it should have three offices, including one at the airport.

KH Soon Resthouse in BSB can supply information on land transport to Miri (Sarawak) and Sabah.

Travellers with Disabilities

The streets of BSB are easier to negotiate than those of neighbouring Malaysia and most other countries of Southeast Asia, but ramps for wheelchairs and accessible public transport are unfortunately still lacking. On the plus side, most hotels in the capital have lifts.

Visas

Ninety-day visas are available to Americans, and 14- to 30-day visas are available for most other nationalities. Visas are free to most nationalities, except for Australians (B$20 or B$30), and three-day transit visas are available to almost everyone, except Israelis.

Women Travellers

Brunei is more devout and conservative than Sabah or Sarawak. Muslim women usually do not shake hands with men, thus a hand may not be extended to travellers of the opposite sex. Some women travellers have reported being the object of catcalls and come-ons, especially from passing motorists.

Getting There & Away

Brunei is a great rest stop if you are travelling between the Malaysian states of Sabah and Sarawak. Border crossings are generally open from 6am to 10pm.

Air

Brunei International Airport (☎flight enquiries 233 6767, 233 1747; www.civil-aviation.gov.bn) is about 8km north of central Bandar Seri Begawan. Short-haul flights, eg from Singapore, tend to be pricey.

Air Asia (www.airasia.com) Links BSB with Kuala Lumpur.

Cebu Pacific Air (www.cebupacificair.com) Flights to Manila.

Malaysia Airlines (www.malaysiaairlines.com) Goes to Kuala Lumpur.

Royal Brunei Airlines (www.bruneiair.com) Brunei's national carrier links BSB with London, Dubai, Australia and various cities in Asia. Sometimes offers good long-haul deals with a stopover in BSB.

Singapore Airlines (www.singaporeair.com) Flies to Singapore.

Boat

For details on the speedboats that (are supposed to) link BSB with Lawas and Limbang (in Sarawak's Limbang Division), see p469 and p470.

The car ferries from the Serasa ferry terminal in Muara, about 20km northeast of BSB, to Pulau Labuan (1½ hours) are run by **PKL Jaya Sendirian** (☎in Muara 277 1771, in Labuan 087 415 777; www.pkljaya.com; adult/car B$10/30 or RM25/60) departing from Muara at 8.45am and from Pulau Labuan at 11.30am. Daily ferries connect Pulau Labuan with Kota Kinabalu (115km by sea). There may also be passenger-only services between Serasa and Pulau Labuan. PKL Jaya Sendirian also operates a car ferry service from the Serasa ferry terminal to the Sabah port of Menumbok (2½ hours).

Bus

The only bus company authorised to transport passengers between Brunei and Malaysia is known by two names: Jesselton Express (for services eastward towards Kota Kinabalu) and PHLS (for services westward towards Miri).

Jesselton Express (☎in BSB 718 3838, 717 7755, 719 3835, for Danny 880 1180, in Kota Kinabalu 016 836 0009, 012 622 9722) sends a bus to Kota Kinabalu (B$45, eight to nine hours) via Limbang (B$10 or MR20), Bangar, Lawas (B$25 or RM50) and various towns in Sabah daily at 8am. In the other direction, the bus leaves Kota Kinabalu at 9.30am.

PHLS Express (☎in BSB 277 1668, 277 3818, 718 3838, for Danny 880 1180) links BSB with Miri (B$18 from BSB, RM40 from Miri, 3½ hours) twice daily. Departures from BSB's PGGMB building (Bangunan Guru-Guru) are at approximately 7am and 1pm, and from Miri's Pujut bus terminal at about 8am and 4pm. Tickets are sold on board.

Another option for travel between BSB and Miri is a 'private transfer' by a **seven-seater van** (☎in Malaysia 013 833 2331, 016 807 2893) run by a father-son team (RM60 per person). Departures from BSB are usually at 1pm or 2pm; departures from Miri are generally at 9am or 10am but may be earlier.

It may also be possible to hitch a ride with a **newspaper delivery van** (☎in BSB 876 0136, in Miri before 4pm 012 878 0136) for RM50 per person (3½ hours). Departure from Miri is at 5.30am; be prepared for an hour's delay at customs. For details, contact KH Soon Resthouse in BSB; the Dillenia (Mrs Lee), Minda and Highlands Guesthouses in Miri; or Miri's Visitors Information Centre.

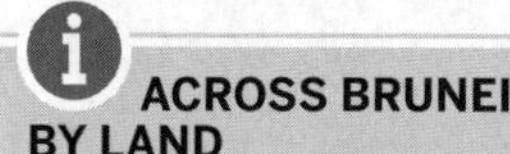

ACROSS BRUNEI BY LAND

Thanks to the Pan Borneo Hwy and some new bus links, it is now relatively easy, if time consuming, to travel from Sarawak to Sabah overland through Brunei. Make sure you've got empty pages in your passport – the traverse will add 10 chops!

Getting Around

For details on land and sea transport within Brunei, see p55, p57 and the box above.

Cambodia

Includes »

Best Temples

- Angkor Wat (p93)
- Bayon (p96)
- Ta Prohm (p97)
- Banteay Srei (p98)
- Beng Mealea (p98)

Best Places for Cultural Connections

- Ratanakiri (p127)
- Battambang (p99)
- Cooking Classes (p87)
- Mekong Discovery Trail (p126)
- National Museum (p67)

Why Go?

Ascend to the realm of the gods at Angkor Wat, a spectacular fusion of spirituality, symbolism and symmetry. Descend into the darkness of Tuol Sleng to witness the crimes of the Khmer Rouge. This is Cambodia, a country with a history both inspiring and depressing, a captivating destination that casts a spell on all those who visit.

Fringed by beautiful beaches and tropical islands, sustained by the mother waters of the Mekong River and cloaked in the some of the region's few remaining emerald wildernesses, Cambodia is an adventure as much as a holiday. This is the warm heart of Southeast Asia, with everything the region has to offer packed into one bite-sized chunk.

Despite the headline attractions, Cambodia's greatest treasure is its people. The Khmers have been to hell and back, but thanks to an unbreakable spirit and infectious optimism they have prevailed with their smiles and spirits largely intact.

When to Go

Phnom Penh

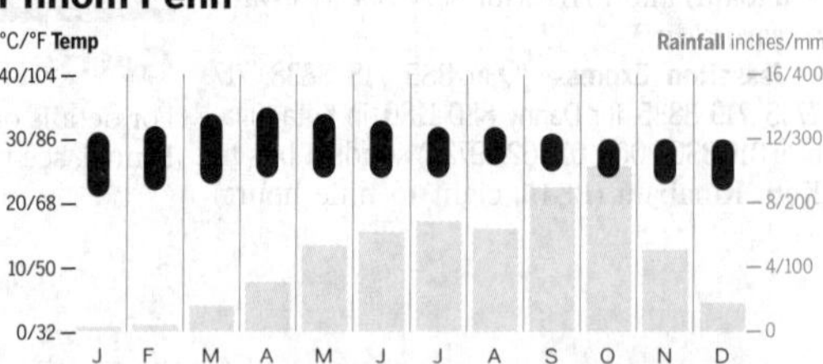

Nov–Feb The so-called windy season is the best all-round time to explore the country.

Apr–May Khmer New Year falls in mid-April and the mercury regularly hits 40°C.

Jul–Sep Green season, when rice paddies shimmer and downpours bring relief from the humidity.

Don't Miss

Cambodia's nightlife is the stuff of legend. While other cities in the region tuck themselves into bed for the night, thanks to curfews and closing times, Phnom Penh and Siem Reap rumble on from dusk till dawn.

Phnom Penh has a vibrant bar and club culture. The riverfront area is a good hunting ground for bars, but as the night wears on it is time to try other haunts such as popular St 278 or buzzin' St 51, home to **Pontoon** and the **Heart of Darkness**.

Up in sublime Siem Reap, one street boasts so many bars that it has earned itself the moniker 'Pub St'. There is no easier place for a crawl in the region and draft beer is almost a giveaway at US$0.50 a glass. Try alternative backpacker bars **Angkor What?** or the **Warehouse**, or try something a little more refined such as **Miss Wong**.

Oh yes, Cambodia rocks.

ITINERARIES

One Week

Soak up the sights, sounds and smells of Phnom Penh, Cambodia's dynamic and fast-changing capital. Travel by road to Siem Reap, gateway to the majestic temples of Angkor, passing by the pre-Angkorian temples of Sambor Prei Kuk or taking a longer detour via the charming colonial-era city of Battambang. Explore Angkor in depth, as nowhere does temples quite like Cambodia.

Two Weeks

Explore the ancient abode of the god kings, the incredible temples of Angkor, including a side trip to the water world of the Tonlé Sap Lake. Travel down to Phnom Penh to savour the dining and drinking scene. Head south to Cambodia's up-and-coming coastline, including the silvery sands of Sihanoukville. Finish up with the languid charms of Kampot and Kep if heading overland to Vietnam, or with the adrenalin adventures on offer around Krong Koh Kong if continuing to Thailand.

Essential Adventures

» **Elephant Valley Project** Experience 'walking with the herd' in the remote jungles of Mondulkiri Province.

» **Prasat Preah Vihear** Venture overland to the king of the mountain temples, Cambodia's other Unesco World Heritage Site.

» **Koh Rong** Beachcomb the deserted sands and shores of Koh Rong, a tropical island off the coast of Sihanoukville.

» **Chi Phat** Experience a local homestay in the jungle community of Chi Phat in the heart of the Cardamom Mountains.

» **Virachey National Park** Disappear for a week into the remote jungles of Ratanakiri Province.

AT A GLANCE

» **Currency** Riel

» **Language** Khmer

» **Money** ATMs common in major cities

» **Visas** Available on arrival for most nationalities

» **Mobile Phones** Prepay SIM cards are cheap, but passport needed to register

Fast Facts

» **Area** 181,035 sq km

» **Capital** Phnom Penh

» **Country Code** ☎855

» **Emergency** Police ☎117

Exchange Rates

Australia	A$1	4195r
Euro zone	€1	5305r
Thailand	1b	130r
UK	£1	6360r
US	US$1	4005r
Vietnam	1000d	190r

Set Your Budget

» **Budget guesthouse room** US$3–15

» **Local restaurant meal** US$1.50–3

» **Beer in backpacker bar** US$0.50–2

» **Moto ride** US$0.50–1

Entering the Country

» **Phnom Penh Airport** Taxi to centre, US$9, 30 minutes.

» **Siem Reap Airport** Taxi to centre, US$7, 15 minutes.

» **Land borders** With Laos, Thailand and Vietnam; visa on arrival.

Cambodia Highlights

1. Discover the eighth wonder of the world, **Angkor** (p92)
2. Enjoy the 'pearl of Asia', **Phnom Penh** (p66), with striking museums, a sublime riverside setting and happening nightlife
3. Explore the wild east of Cambodia, **Mondulkiri** (p130), a land of rolling hills, thundering waterfalls and indigenous minorities
4. Slip into the soporific pace of riverside **Kampot** (p118)
5. Bask on the brilliant beaches, scuba dive in uncharted waters, drink up the nightlife of **Sihanoukville** (p111)
6. Dine on grilled shrimp with crunchy-fresh Kampot pepper sprigs in **Kep** (p121)
7. Explore the lush **Battambang countryside** (p104), climbing hill-top temples and exploring caves
8. Float your boat down the mighty Mekong in search of the rare, freshwater Irrawaddy dolphins around **Kratie** (p124)
9. Explore the jungles, mangroves, waterfalls, islands and beaches of the **Koh Kong Conservation Corridor** (p110)

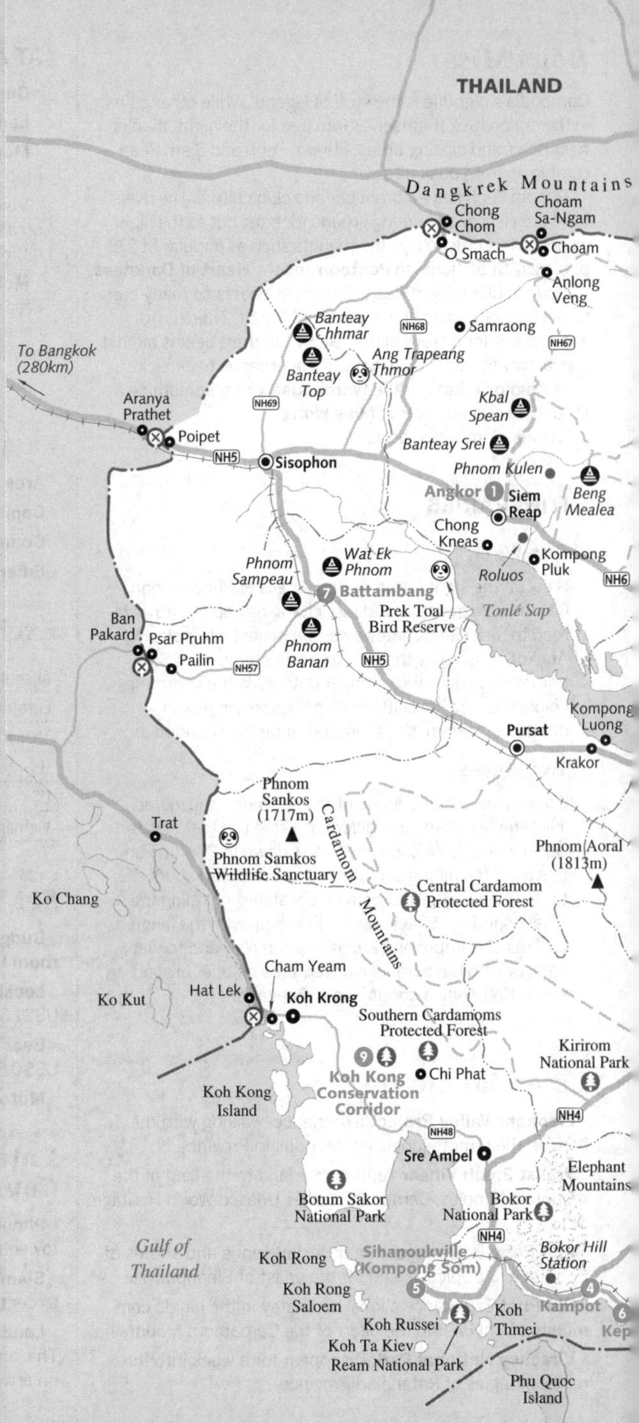

0 100 km
0 60 miles
LAOS
Prasat Preah Vihear
Sra Em
Koh Ker
Srayong
Tbeng Meanchey
Preah Khan
Eastern Highlands
Virachey National Park
Dong Kalaw
Trapeang Kriel
RATANAKIRI
Ban Lung
Le Thanh
Yadaw
Tonlé San
Lumphat
Tonlé Srepok
Stung Treng
Mekong River
Mekong Discovery Trail
Koh Nhek
3 Mondulkiri
Sambor Prei Kuk
Kompong Thom
Kakoah
Phnom Sontuk
Kampi
Kratie 8
Bou Sraa Falls
Sen Monorom
Tonlé Sap
Kompong Chhnang
Chhlong
Snuol
Trapaeng Sre
Loc Ninh
Skuon
Kompong Cham
Wat Maha Leap
Udong
Trapaeng Plong
Xa Mat
PHNOM PENH 2
Kompong Speu
Prey Veng
VIETNAM
Tonlé Bati
Phnom Tamao Wildlife Sanctuary
Phnom Chisor
Neak Luong Ferry
Tay Ninh
Moc Bai
Bavet
Angk Tasaom
Takeo
Kaam Samnor
Angkor Borei
Phnom Da
Vinh Xuong
Tonlé Bassac
Ho Chi Minh City (Saigon)
Kompong Trach
Phnom Den
Chau Doc
Tinh Bien
Prek Chak
Xa Xia
Ha Tien
Long Xuyen
My Tho
SOUTH CHINA SEA
NH1
NH2
NH3
NH5
NH6
NH7
NH11
NH64
NH78

PHNOM PENH

☎023 / POP 1.5 MILLION

Phnom Penh: the name can't help but conjure up an image of the exotic. This is the Asia that many dreamt of when first planning their adventures overseas. Phnom Penh is a crossroads of Asia's past and present, a city of extremes of poverty and excess, of charm and chaos, but one that never fails to captivate.

Once the 'Pearl of Asia', Phnom Penh's shine was tarnished by war and revolution. But that's history and Phnom Penh has risen from the ashes to take its place among the 'in' capitals of Asia. Delve into the ancient past at the National Museum or struggle to make sense of the more recent trauma at Tuol Sleng Museum. Browse the city's markets for a bargain or linger in the beautiful boutiques that are putting Phnom Penh on the style map. Street surf through local stalls for a snack or enjoy the refined surrounds of a designer restaurant. Whatever your flavour, no matter your taste, it's all here in Phnom Penh.

Sights

Phnom Penh's sights highlight the contradictions of Cambodia. The stunning legacy of the Angkorian god-kings at the National Museum and grandeur of the Royal Palace stand in stark contrast to the horrors of Tuol Sleng and Choeung Ek.

After exploring the shadowy depths of the city's markets (such as Psar Thmei and Psar Tuol Tom Pong), head to the thriving riverfront for a sunset stroll.

TOP CHOICE Royal Palace PALACE

(Map p70; Samdech Sothearos Blvd; admission 25,000r; ⌚8-11am & 2-5pm) The Royal Palace with its classic Khmer roofs and ornate gilding, dominates the diminutive skyline of the riverfront, where the Tonlé Sap meets the Mekong. Hidden away behind protective

Phnom Penh

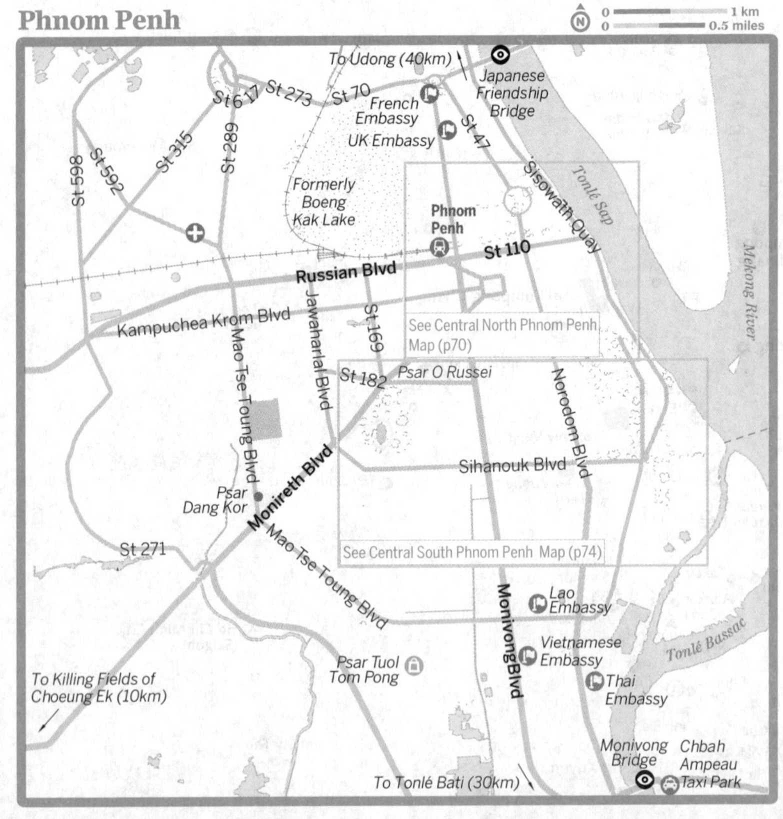

walls, it's an oasis of calm with lush gardens and leafy havens. Legs and upper arms must be covered while visiting the palace.

Inside the Royal Palace compound is the **Silver Pagoda**, so named because it's floored with 5000 silver tiles weighing 1kg each. It is also known as Wat Preah Keo (Pagoda of the Emerald Buddha) thanks to a Buddha statue made of Baccarat crystal. Check out the life-sized gold Buddha, weighing in at 90kg and decorated with 9584 diamonds.

TOP CHOICE National Museum MUSEUM

(Map p70; St 13; admission US$3, camera/video US$1/3; ⏲8am-5pm) The National Museum of Cambodia is home to the world's finest collection of Khmer sculpture, a millennium's worth and more of masterful Khmer design. Housed in a graceful, traditionally designed terracotta structure (built 1917–20), it provides the perfect backdrop to an outstanding array of delicate objects.

The Angkorian collection includes a giant pair of wrestling monkeys, an exquisite frieze from Banteay Srei, and a sublime statue of Jayavarman VII (r 1181–1219) meditating.

No photography is allowed except in the beautiful central courtyard.

TOP CHOICE Tuol Sleng Museum MUSEUM

(Map p74; St 113; admission US$2, video US$5; ⏲8-5pm) Once a centre of learning, Tuol Svay Prey High School was taken over in 1975 by Pol Pot's security forces, who transformed the classrooms into torture chambers and renamed the facility Security Prison 21 (S-21). At the height of its activity, some 100 victims were killed every day.

Like the Nazis, the Khmer Rouge leaders were meticulous in keeping records of their barbarism and each prisoner who passed through S-21 was photographed. When the Vietnamese army liberated Phnom Penh in early 1979, there were only seven prisoners alive at S-21, all of whom had used their skills – such as painting or photography – to stay alive. Today the long corridors of Tuol Sleng Museum display haunting photographs of the victims, their faces staring back eerily from the past.

For more information on Tuol Sleng and the Cambodian genocide, visit the websites of the **Documentation Center of Cambodia** (DC-Cam; www.dccam.org) or Yale University's **Cambodian Genocide Program** (www.yale.edu/cgp).

GETTING INTO PHNOM PENH

An official booth outside the airport arrivals area arranges taxis/*remorque-motos* (tuk-tuks) to anywhere in the city for a flat US$9/7. You can get a *remorque-moto* for $US5 and a moto (motorcycle taxi) for half that if you walk one minute out to the street. Heading to the airport from central Phnom Penh, a taxi/*remorque*/moto will cost about US$9/4/2.

If you arrive by bus, chances are you'll be dropped off near Psar Thmei (aka Central Market), a short ride from most hotels and guesthouses. Figure on US$0.50 to US$1 for a moto, and US$2 to US$3 for a *remorque*. Prices are about the same from the tourist boat dock on Sisowath Quay, where arriving boats from Vietnam and Siem Reap incite moto-madness.

Killing Fields of Choeung Ek MEMORIAL

(off Map p66; admission US$3; ⏲7am-5.30pm) Most of the 17,000 detainees held at the S-21 prison were executed at Choeung Ek, 14km southwest of Phnom Penh. Prisoners were often bludgeoned to death to avoid wasting precious bullets. When wandering through this peaceful, shady former orchard, it is hard to imagine the brutality that unfolded here, but the memorial stupa soon brings it home, displaying more than 8000 skulls of victims and their ragged clothes. See p135 for more on the Khmer Rouge.

Round-trip transport costs about US$5 by moto or about US$20 by taxi.

Wat Phnom TEMPLE

(Map p70; admission US$1) Wat Phnom, meaning Hill Temple, is appropriately set on the only hill (more like a mound at 27m) in Phnom Penh. The wat is revered by locals, who flock here to pray for good luck. Legend has it that in the year 1373 the first temple was built by a lady named Penh to house four Buddha statues that she found floating in the Mekong. Lady Penh's statue is in a shrine dedicated to her behind the *vihara* (temple sanctuary).

Beware of the monkeys around here, as they have been known to bite, necessitating rabies shots as a precaution.

Independence Monument MONUMENT

(Map p74; cnr Norodom & Sihanouk Blvds) Soaring over the city's largest roundabout is the grand

READING UP

For a greater insight into the methodical machine of death that was Tuol Sleng, pick up *Voices from S-21* by David Chandler, a chilling and incisive description of life in the prison, pieced together from accounts from the tortured and the torturers.

Independence Monument, built in 1958 to commemorate Cambodia's 1953 independence from France and now also a memorial to Cambodia's war dead. Modelled on the central tower of Angkor Wat, it was designed by leading Khmer architect Vann Molyvann.

Wat Ounalom TEMPLE
(Map p70; Samdech Sothearos Blvd) Wat Ounalom is the headquarters of Cambodian Buddhism. It is unexceptional, but might be worth visiting just for the one eyebrow hair of Buddha himself, preciously held in a stupa located behind the main building.

Activities

Stationed along Sisowath Quay are many private operators that offer boat cruises up and down the Mekong. Most offer a sunset cruise from US$10 per hour.

Most pool-equipped boutique hotels will let you swim if you buy a few bucks' worth of food or cocktails.

Cambodian Cooking Class COOKING COURSE
(Map p74; ☎012 524801; www.cambodian-cooking-class.com; booking office on 67 St 240, classes on St 19; half/full day US$12.50/20; ⏲Mon-Sat) Learn the art of Khmer cuisine at Frizz Restaurant. Reserve ahead.

Vicious Cycle CYCLING
(Map p70; ☎012 462165; www.grasshopperadventures.com; 29 St 130; bicycles per day US$4-8) This place runs great cycling tours to Mekong islands and Udong. Plenty of mountain and other bikes available.

Seeing Hands Massage MASSAGE
Riverside (Map p70; 12 St 13); St 108 (Map p70; 34 St 108) Helps you ease those aches and pains; helps blind masseurs stay self-sufficient. Massages average US$7 per hour.

Bodia Spa SPA
(Map p70; ☎226199; cnr Samdech Sothearos Blvd & St 178; massages from US$26) About the best rub-downs in town in a Zen-like setting (albeit with some street noise).

Nature Cambodia ADVENTURE TOURS
(☎012 676381; www.nature-cambodia.com; 1½hr/half-day US$15/35) Quad biking (ATV trips) in the beautiful countryside around Phnom Penh. The quads are automatic, so they're easy to handle for beginners. Follow the signs to Choeung Ek. It is about 300m before the entrance.

Himawari Hotel SWIMMING
(Map p74; ☎214555; 313 Sisowath Quay; admission weekend/weekday US$7/8) A larger pool fit for laps.

Sleeping

Against all odds, the few establishments that remain in Phnom Penh's traditional backpacker area around Boeung Kak Lake are somehow still thriving. Several miniature Khao San Rd backpacker colonies are lying in wait as potential heirs apparent to Boeung Kak: St 258, near the riverside; a strip on St 172; and the area south of Psar O Russei. St 278 – aka 'the Golden Mile' – is a flashpacker district of sorts. The riverfront is another smarter, if slightly more expensive, alternative.

MONIVONG WEST AREA

Narin Guesthouse GUESTHOUSE $
(Map p74; ☎982554; touchnarin@hotmail.com; 50 St 125; r US$8-10; ❄📶) One of the stalwarts of the Phnom Penh guesthouse scene, Narin has recently been given a makeover. Rooms are smart, bathrooms smarter still and the price is nice.

Spring Guesthouse GUESTHOUSE $
(Map p74; ☎222155; 34 St 111; r US$6-10; ❄@📶) This five-storey walk-up was the first of a new generation of smart guesthouses in this area. It offers bright, spotless rooms with cable TV.

Sunday Guesthouse GUESTHOUSE $
(Map p74; ☎211623; gech_sundayguesthouse@hotmail.com; 97 St 141; r US$8-12; ❄@📶) The rooms aren't quite as spiffy as at Spring, but the service is friendlier and staff can help with travel arrangements.

Smiley's Hotel GUESTHOUSE $
(Map p74; ☎012 365959; smileyhotel.pp@gmail.com; 37 St 125; r US$6-25; ❄@📶) A migrant from Siem Reap, Smiley's Hotel is a huge

new place with a choice of 40 spacious fan and air-con rooms. Includes an elevator.

Tat Guesthouse BACKPACKER $
(Map p74; ☎099 801000; tatguesthouse@yahoo.com; 52 St 125; s/d from US$3/6; ❄@🛜) A friendly, family-run place with cheap and cheerful rooms, plus a breezy rooftop hang-out area.

CENTRAL PHNOM PENH

One area that is worth seeking out for those wanting a modicum more comfort is the so-called 'Golden Mile', a strip of hotels on St 278 that all feature 'Golden' in their name. There is little to choose between them, as most offer air-con, cable TV, fridge, hot water and free laundry for US$13/15 a single/double.

TOP CHOICE **Top Banana Guesthouse** BACKPACKER $
(Map p74; ☎012 885572; www.topbanana.biz; 9 St 278; r US$6-15; ❄@🛜) A great location high above the street action, comfy open-air chill-out area and popular bar make it the Penh's top backpacker crash pad. Cheap rooms don't come with hot water, but the more expensive ones include brisk air-con. Book way ahead.

TOP CHOICE **Number 9 Guesthouse** GUESTHOUSE $$
(Map p74; ☎984999; www.number9hotel.com; 7C St 258; s/d/tr US$15/25/35; ❄@🛜≋) Oh, how times change. Rising from the lakeside ashes of backpackersville and propelling St 258 into flashpackersville, this is something. Smart and spacious rooms, flat-screen TVs, an ultra-trendy bar-restaurant and a rooftop jacuzzi.

Lazy Gecko Guest House BACKPACKER $
(Map p74; ☎078 786025; 1D St 258; d US$5-15; ❄@🛜) Well-known as a cafe in its lakeside days, it tacked on an equally appealing guesthouse upon moving to its new location on St 258. Arguably the best rooms in town in this price range.

Last Home BACKPACKER $
(Map p70; ☎6921009; www.lasthomecambodia.com; 21 St 172; d with fan/air-con from US$7/15; ❄@🛜) This was the first budget guesthouse to plant its flag on up-and-coming St 172. It has a loyal following among regulars, who appreciate extras like cable TV and newish bathrooms.

Hotel Indochine 2 GUESTHOUSE $$
(Map p70; ☎724239; indochinehtl@camnet.com.kh; 30 St 130; r US$10-25; ❄@🛜) A long-running guesthouse near the riverfront with a friendly management team. Aim for a street view. All rooms include TV, fridge and hot water.

Mad Monkey BACKPACKER $
(Map p74; ☎724239; www.monkeyhospitalitygroup.com; 26 St 302; dm US$5, r US$12-18; ❄@🛜) A popular new guesthouse in the Boeng Keng Kang (BKK) area of town. Rooms are homely enough and there are plans for more dorms. Popular bar-restaurant downstairs.

Me Mate's Place BACKPACKER $$
(Map p70; ☎5002497; www.matesplace.com; 5 St 90; r US$18-24; ❄🛜) Just north of Wat Phnom. The strip is not the most salubrious in town, but this is a smart little guesthouse-bar with wall murals, TV and fridge.

Encounters BACKPACKER $$
(Map p70; ☎012 753401; ppp.nomads@gmail.com; 30 St 108; dm US$4.50-6.50, r US$12; ❄@🛜) This budget crashpad specialises in cheap dorms that come with fan or air-con and include access to safety lockers. Reliable travel info available thanks to Cambo-experienced host Martin.

BOENG KAK AREA

11 Happy Guesthouse BACKPACKER $
(Map p70; ☎6301231; www.happy11ghcambodia.com; 4 St 93; r US$2-15; ❄@🛜) The friendly, informative staff put smiles on backpackers' faces with cheap laundry and good rooms at these prices.

Grand View Guesthouse BACKPACKER $
(Map p70; ☎430766; www.grandview.netfirms.com; 4 St 93; r US$4-10; ❄@🛜) This tall, skinny structure has unrivalled views of

STREET NUMBERS

Phnom Penh's sequentially numbered streets may be a paragon of logic, but when it comes to house numbering, utter chaos reigns. It's not uncommon to find a row of adjacent buildings numbered, say, 13A, 34, 7, 26. Worse, several buildings on the same street, blocks apart, may have adopted the same house number!

When you're given an address, try to get a cross-street, such as 'on St 240 near St 51'. In this guide, check the Phnom Penh maps for relevant cross-streets.

Central North Phnom Penh

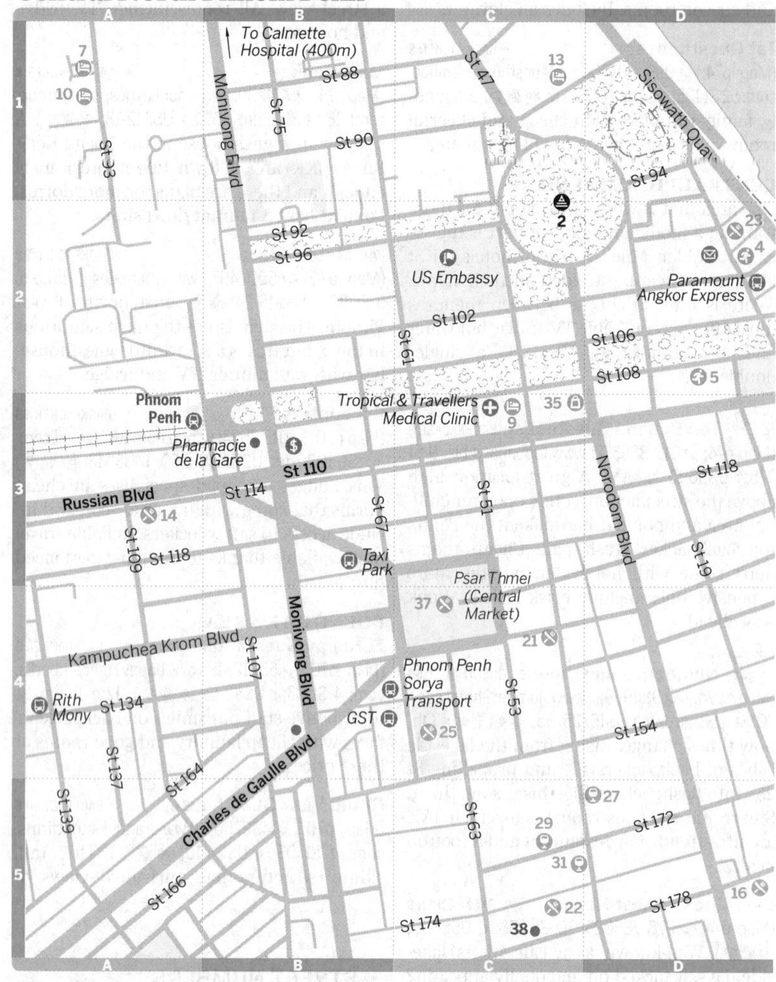

the sand dunes formerly known as Boeng Kak Lake.

Eating

Some travellers get into the habit of hunkering down on their guesthouse balcony, encouraged by proprietors who talk up the dangers of Phnom Penh. Don't do it. Phnom Penh is home to fantastic flavours, so make for the markets to dip into cheap Cambodian chow or delve into the city's impressive range of cosmopolitan eateries.

Unless stated otherwise, restaurants are open for breakfast, lunch and dinner.

TOP CHOICE Sleuk Chark CAMBODIAN $$
(Map p74; 165D St 51; mains US$3-10; ⏲11.30am-10.30pm; wi-fi) This place doesn't look much from the street, but venture inside for a dining experience that includes zesty frogs' legs and quails' eggs in sugar palm and black-pepper claypot or a fish-egg soup. Cushion seating on the floor.

Boddhi Tree Umma INTERNATIONAL $$
(Map p74; 50 St 113; mains US$1.50-6; ⏲7am-9pm; wi-fi) This eatery's lush garden is the perfect place to seek solace and silence after Tuol Sleng, across the road. Includes fusion

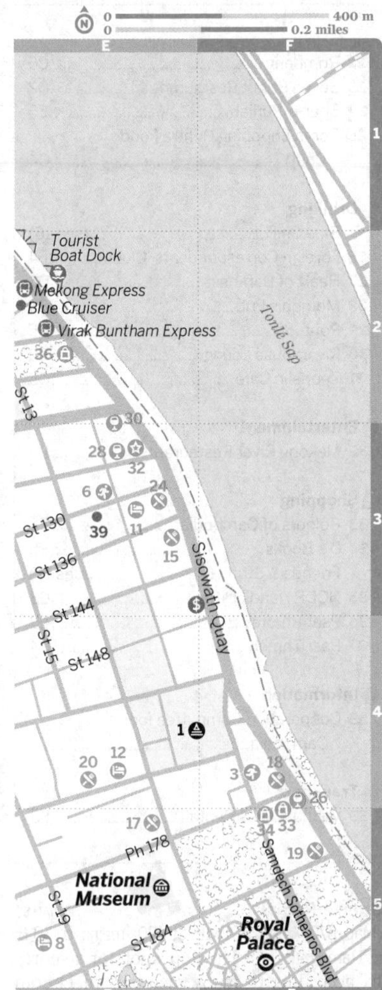

flavours, Asian dishes, innovative shakes and tempting desserts.

Boat Noodle Restaurant THAI, CAMBODIAN $
(Map p74; St 294; mains 8000-20,000r) This wooden house in a leafy garden brimming with water exudes old-school ambience and serves decent-value Thai and Cambodian food.

K'nyay CAMBODIAN $
(Map p74; 25K Suramarit Blvd; mains US$2-5; noon-9pm Mon-Fri, 7am-9pm Sat;) A stylish little Cambodian restaurant with a generous selection of vegetarian and vegan options, original health shakes and home-made ice cream such as ginger and honey.

Ebony Apsara Café CAMBODIAN $$
(Map p70; 42 St 178; mains US$3.50-6; 11am-midnight Mon-Fri, to 2am Sat & Sun;) A cool little cafe serving health shakes, vegetarian treats and Khmer food. Forty per cent of profits go to the Apsara Arts Association (p76).

Khmer Borane Restaurant CAMBODIAN $$
(Map p70; 389 Sisowath Quay; mains US$4-5.50; 7am-midnight) A great little restaurant for traditional Khmer recipes; choose from *trey kor* (steamed fish with sugar palm) or *lok lak* (fried diced beef with a salt, pepper and lemon dip).

Happy Herb Pizza ITALIAN $$
(Map p70; 362349; 345 Sisowath Quay; pizzas US$4-8; 8am-11pm;) No, happy doesn't mean it comes with free toppings, it means pizza *à la* ganja. The non-marijuana pizzas are also pretty good, but don't involve the free high. Delivery available.

Cantina MEXICAN $$
(Map p70; 347 Sisowath Quay; mains US$3-6; 2.30-11pm Sun-Fri) This is the spot for *tostadas*, fajitas and other Mexican favourites, all freshly prepared. It's also a journo hangout and a lively bar with professional margaritas and tequilas.

Laughing Fat Man CAFE $
(Map p70; St 172; mains US$2-4; 7.30am-11pm) Cheap food and big breakfasts at this welcoming place, formerly called Oh My Buddha. 'New name, same body', the jovial, corpulent owner joked.

Java Café CAFE $$
(Map p74; www.javaarts.org; 56 Sihanouk Blvd; mains US$3.50-7;) Consistently popular thanks to a breezy balcony and an

SPLURGE: PHNOM PENH

Blue Lime (Map p70; 222260; www.bluelime.asia; 42 St 19; r US$40-75;) is a popular boutique hotel offering smart, minimalist rooms and a leafy pool area done just right. The pricier rooms are true gems, with private plunge pools, four-poster beds and contemporary concrete love seats. No kids allowed.

Central North Phnom Penh

Top Sights
National Museum E5
Royal Palace F5

Sights
1 Wat Ounalom E1
2 Wat Phnom C2

Activities, Courses & Tours
3 Bodia Spa F4
4 Seeing Hands Massage D2
5 Seeing Hands Massage D2
6 Vicious Cycle E3

Sleeping
7 11 Happy Guesthouse A1
8 Blue Lime E5
9 Encounters C3
10 Grand View Guesthouse A1
11 Hotel Indochine 2 ..... E3
12 Last Home E4
13 Me Mate's Place C1

Eating
14 Bayon Supermarket A3
15 Blue Pumpkin E3
Cantina ..... (see 18)
16 Ebony Apsara Café D5
17 Friends E5
18 Happy Herb Pizza F4
19 Khmer Borane Restaurant F5
20 Laughing Fat Man E4
21 Psar Ta Pang C4
22 Romdeng C5
23 Seven Bright Restaurant D2
24 Sher-e-Punjab E3
25 Sorya Shopping Centre Food Court C4

Drinking
Blue Chilli ..... (see 16)
26 Foreign Correspondents' Club F4
27 Heart of Darkness D5
28 Memphis Pub E3
29 Pontoon C5
30 Riverhouse Lounge E2
31 Zeppelin Cafe C5

Entertainment
32 Mekong River Restaurant E3

Shopping
33 Colours of Cambodia F5
34 D's Books F5
Friends & Stuff ..... (see 17)
35 NCDP Handicrafts C3
36 Psar Reatrey E2
37 Psar Thmei C4

Information
38 Cooperation Committee for Cambodia C5

Transport
39 Vannak Bikes Rental E3

air-conditioned interior. The creative menu includes crisp salads, homemade sandwiches, towering burgers and daily specials, plus excellent coffee from several continents. Doubles as an art gallery.

Seven Bright Restaurant CAMBODIAN $
(Map p70; 6 St 13; mains US$1.50-5; 7am-10pm) This was once Gerard Depardieu's hotel lobby, at least in the Matt Dillon movie *City of Ghosts*. Good Khmer food, likeable location and occasional live music.

Café Yejj CAFE $$
(Map p66; 92A St 432; mains US$3.50-6;) An air-con escape from Psar Tuol Tom Pong (Russian Market), this bistro-style cafe specialises in pastas and salads. It promotes fair trade and responsible employment.

Sher-e-Punjab INDIAN $$
(Map p70; 992901; 16 St 130; mains US$3-6; 11am-11pm;) The top spot for a curry fix according to many members of Phnom Penh's Indian community; the tandoori dishes are particularly good.

Mama Restaurant CAFE $
(Map p74; 10C St 111; mains 6000-14,000r) The menu at this long-running hole-in-the-wall includes an affordable selection of Khmer, Thai, French and even African dishes served daily.

Self-Catering

Inexpensive restaurants are often cheaper than self-catering, but for midday snacks, supermarkets are perfect. Baguettes are widely available and the open-air markets have heaps of fresh fruit and vegetables.

Another trick is to call at the bakeries of five-star hotels after 6pm, when cakes are half price.

Bayon Supermarket SUPERMARKET $
(Map p70; 33 St 114; ⌚7am-9pm) Impressive supermarket on the airport road with a wide variety of imports.

Blue Pumpkin BAKERY $
(Map p70; Sisowath Quay; ⌚6am-11pm) New riverfront outpost of Siem Reap's best-loved cafe-bakery chain. Wholesome cakes, wholemeal breads and heavenly ice-cream.

Lucky Supermarket SUPERMARKET $
(Map p74; 160 Sihanouk Blvd; ⌚7am-9pm) The leading supermarket chain in town, with a professional deli counter.

Drinking

If it survives the developer's wrecking ball, the Boeng Kak lakeside is a great place for a sunset drink. Laze in a hammock and watch the sun burn red. But there is a whole lot more to Phnom Penh nightlife, including some tempting half-price happy hours.

There is quite a 'girlie bar' scene in Phnom Penh, with dozens of places dotted about town. They are pretty welcoming to both guys and girls, although 'I love you long time' should be taken with a pinch of salt.

TOP CHOICE **Foreign Correspondents' Club** BAR, RESTAURANT
(FCC; Map p70; www.fcccambodia.com; 363 Sisowath Quay; ⌚6.30am-midnight;) A Phnom Penh institution, the FCC is housed in a colonial gem with great views and cool breezes. One of those must-see places in Cambodia. Affordable happy hours run from 5pm to 7pm.

TOP CHOICE **Equinox** BAR
(Map p74; 3A St 278; ⌚7am-late) At the heart of the action on St 278, this is a popular place with a lively outdoor bar downstairs and excellent live music upstairs on any given night.

Elsewhere BAR
(Map p74; 2 St 278; ⌚8am-late) With ambient vibes, a great drinks menu and two plunge pools for punters, it's sedate by day but sexy by night.

Zeppelin Cafe BAR
(Map p70; 109 St 51; ⌚6.30pm-late) Who says vinyl is dead? It lives on here thanks to this old-school rock bar with a serious '60s and '70s music collection.

Heart of Darkness BAR, NIGHTCLUB
(Map p70; 26 St 51; ⌚8pm-late) This Phnom Penh institution with the alluring Angkor theme has evolved into a nightclub more

TOP FIVE: GOOD-CAUSE DINING

These fantastic eateries act as training centres for young staff and help fund worthy causes in the capital.

» **Romdeng** (Map p70; 74 St 174; mains US$4-7; ⌚11am-9pm;) Set in a gorgeous colonial villa with a small pool, the elegant Romdeng specialises in Cambodian country fare, including deep-fried spiders. Under the same management as Friends, it offers former street children a head start in the hospitality industry.

» **Friends** (Map p70; www.friends-international.org; 215 St 13; tapas US$2-5, mains from US$6; ⌚11am-9pm) One of Phnom Penh's best-loved restaurants, this place is a must, with tasty tapas bites, heavenly smoothies and creative cocktails.

» **Le Rit's** (Map p74; 71 St 240; mains US$2.50-7, set lunch US$6; ⌚7am-10pm;) The three-course lunch and dinners here are a relaxing experience in the well-groomed garden. Proceeds assist disadvantaged women to re-enter the workplace.

» **Hagar** (www.hagarcambodia.com) main restaurant (Map p74; 44 St 310); St 163 (9 St 163) The all-you-can-eat Asian fusion lunch buffet costs US$6.50 and all proceeds go towards assisting destitute or abused women. The St 163 branch charges only US$2.50 for a Cambodian buffet.

» **Lotus Blanc** (Map p74; 152 St 51; mains US$6; ⌚Mon-Sat) This suburban restaurant acts as a training centre for youths who previously scoured the city dump. Run by French NGO Pour un Sourire d'Enfant (For the Smile of a Child), it serves classy Western and Khmer cuisine.

Central South Phnom Penh

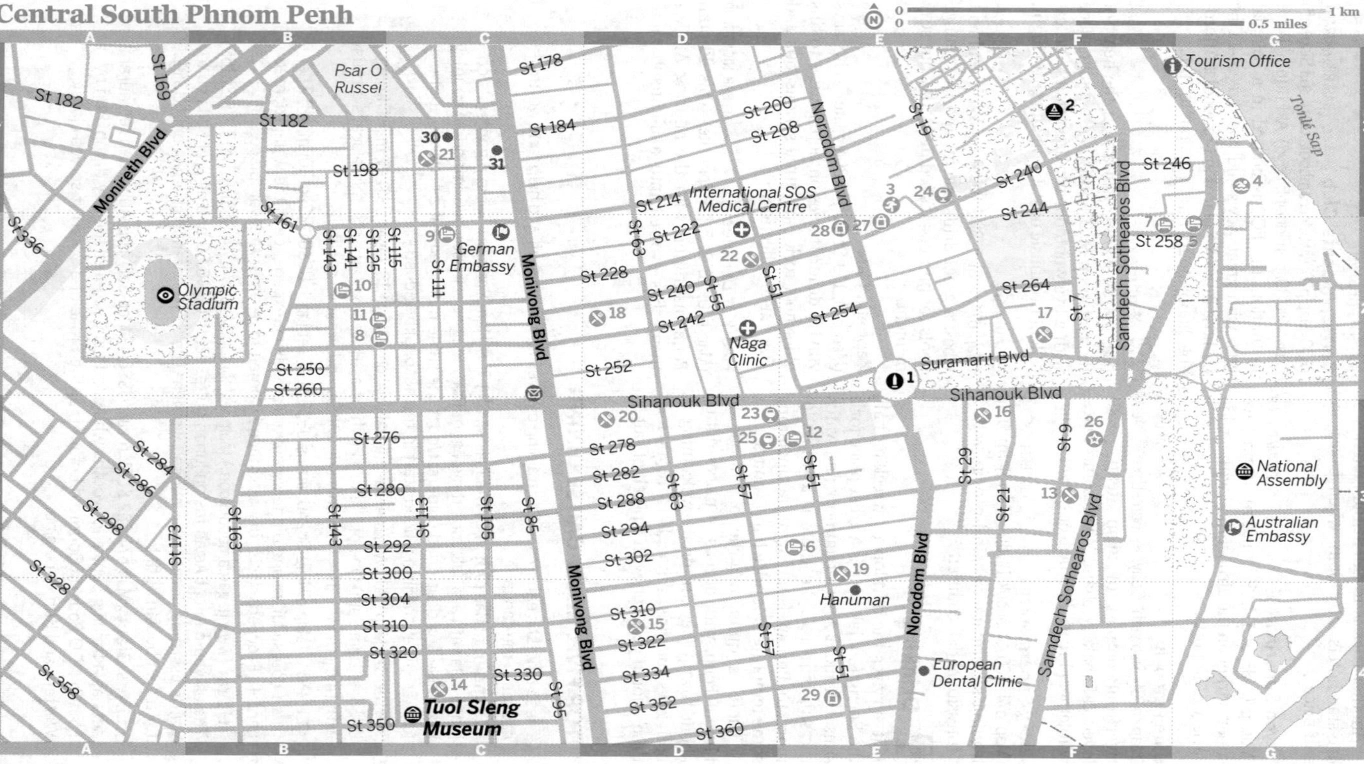

Central South Phnom Penh

Top Sights
Tuol Sleng Museum C4

Sights
1 Independence Monument E2
2 Silver Pagoda F1

Activities, Courses & Tours
3 Cambodian Cooking Class E1
4 Himawari Hotel Swimming Pool G1

Sleeping
5 Lazy Gecko Guest House G2
6 Mad Monkey E3
Narin Guesthouse .... (see 11)
7 Number 9 Guesthouse F2
8 Smiley's Hotel B2
9 Spring Guesthouse C2
10 Sunday Guesthouse B2
11 Tat Guesthouse B2
12 Top Banana Guesthouse E3

Eating
13 Boat Noodle Restaurant F3
14 Boddhi Tree Umma C4
15 Hagar D4
16 Java Café F3
17 K'nyay F2
18 Le Rit's D2
19 Lotus Blanc E3
20 Lucky Supermarket D3
21 Mama Restaurant C1
22 Sleuk Chark D2

Drinking
Elsewhere .... (see 12)
23 Equinox D3
24 Rubies E1
25 Score D3

Entertainment
26 Meta House F3

Shopping
27 D's Books E2
28 Monument Books E2
Nyemo .... (see 18)
29 Tabitha E4

Transport
30 Capitol Tour C1
31 Lucky! Lucky! C1
New! New! .... (see 31)

than a bar. It goes off every night of the week, attracting all sorts.

Pontoon NIGHTCLUB
(Map p70; www.pontoonclub.com; 80 St 172; admission Sat & Sun US$3-5, Mon-Fri free; 9.30pm-late) The city's premier nightclub often sees big foreign acts on the decks. Thursday is gay-friendly night, with a 1am lady-boy show.

Riverhouse Lounge LOUNGE
(Map p70; cnr St 110 & Sisowath Quay; 4pm-2am) Almost a club as much as a lounge, it has DJs and live music through the week. It's chic and cool with a minimalist bar-restaurant downstairs.

Rubies BAR
(Map p74; cnr St 240 & St 19; 5.30pm-late Tue-Sun) If you prefer the grape to the grain, then make for this small wine bar with a big personality. There are regular DJ nights and indie anthems aplenty.

Blue Chilli BAR
(Map p70; 36 St 178; 6pm-late) The owner of this gay-friendly bar stages his own drag show every Friday and Saturday at 10.30pm.

Score SPORTS BAR
(Map p74; 5 St 282; 8am-late) One of the most tasteful sports bars in town; watch the big-screen action or shoot some pool on the imported tables.

Entertainment

For the ins and outs of the entertainment scene, check the latest issues of **AsiaLIFE** (www.asialifecambodia.com) or **7 Days** (www.phnompenhpost.com), a Friday supplement in the popular *Phnom Penh Post*. Useful websites on events and live music include www.lengpleng.com for live music and www.ladypenh.com for the general Phnom Penh scene.

TOP CHOICE **Meta House** CINEMA
(Map p74; www.meta-house.com; 37 Samdech Sothearos Blvd; 6pm-midnight Tue-Sun) This multimedia arts centre has a diverse program of art-house films, documentaries and shorts from Cambodia and around the world. Films are sometimes followed by Q&As with those involved.

LOCAL FLAVOURS

Experience the real flavour of Phnom Penh with a meal at one of the city's many markets, where the food is fresh, tasty and cheap. **Psar Thmei** (Map p70; ⏲breakfast & lunch), **Psar Tuol Tom Pong** (Russian Market; Map p66; ⏲breakfast & lunch) and **Psar Reatrey** (Night Market; Map p70; ⏲Fri, Sat & Sun dinner) are three of the most popular places to combine some browsing with some bites. All have plenty of produce available for self caterers, plus dozens of food stalls with dishes from 4000r to 6000r. There are also several areas around the city with open-air food stalls during the early evening: try **Psar Ta Pang** (Map p70; cnr St 51 & St 136; ⏲dinner) for excellent *bobor* (rice porridge) and tasty desserts.

If the market stalls look a little raw and street surfing doesn't appeal, consider the air-conditioned alternative, **Sorya Shopping Centre Food Court** (Map p70; cnr St 63 & St 154; meals 4000-8000r), located on the 4th floor.

Also worthwhile for cheap BBQ fare washed down with cheap beer are any of the numerous open-air 'beer gardens' scattered around town – look for the illuminated Anchor or Angkor beer signs. For something a bit more upmarket, cross the Japanese Friendship Bridge, where there are plenty of big Cambodian restaurants built on stilts over the floodwaters.

Mekong River Restaurant CINEMA
(Map p70; ☎991150; cnr St 118 & Sisowath Quay; admission US$3; ⏲24hr) Screens two original films, one covering the Khmer Rouge and the other about landmines.

Apsara Arts Association DANCE
(☎012 979335, 011 857424; 71 St 598; tickets US$5) Hosts performances of classical dance and folk dance most Saturdays at 7pm (call to confirm). It's in Tuol Kork district, in the far northwest of the city.

Sovanna Phum Arts Association DANCE
(☎987564; 111 St 360; tickets US$5) Impressive traditional shadow-puppet performances and classical-dance shows are held here at 7.30pm on Friday and Saturday night. It's a few blocks west of Monivong Blvd.

Memphis Pub LIVE MUSIC
(Map p70; 3 St 118; ⏲5pm-1am Wed-Sun) The Penh's leading music venue, with live rock 'n' roll in a sound-proofed hideaway that can look deceptively closed even when it's open. Pricey drinks ensure there is no cover charge.

Shopping

An affirmation of identity, the *krama* (chequered scarf) is worn around the necks, shoulders and waists of nearly every Khmer. The scarves make superb souvenirs, as do Cambodia's sculptures and handicrafts.

Markets

Bargains galore can be found at Phnom Penh's vibrant markets. Navigating the labyrinths of shoes, clothing, bric-a-brac and food is one of the most enjoyable ways to earn a foot massage. Markets are open from 6.30am to 5.30pm.

Psar Thmei MARKET
(New Market; Map p70) Often referred to as Central Market, this art-deco landmark resembles a Babylonian ziggurat. It houses an array of stalls selling jewellery, clothing and curios. The food section is enormous, with produce spilling onto the streets.

Psar Tuol Tom Pong MARKET
(Map p66) Best known as Russian Market, this was the Russians' retail outlet of choice back in the 1980s. It includes designer clothing labels hot out of the factory, bootleg music and films, and carvings in wood, stone or bronze. It's a good location to practise your haggling skills and is the one market all visitors should explore during a trip to Phnom Penh. It is located in the far south of the city, about four blocks south of Mao Tse Tuong Blvd.

Psar Reatrey MARKET
(Map p70; St 106 & Sisowath Quay; ⏲4pm-midnight Fri-Sun) The Night Market is a cooler, al-fresco version of Psar Tuol Tom Pong and sells souvenirs, silks and knick-knacks. Bargain vigorously, as prices can be on the high side.

D's Books BOOKS
St 240 (Map p74; 79 St 240); St 178 (Map p70; 7 St 178) The largest chain of secondhand bookshops in the capital.

Monument Books BOOKS
(Map p74; 111 Norodom Blvd) The best-stocked bookshop in town, with every Cambodia-related book available. Also has an airport branch.

Information

The riverfront Sisowath Quay, lined with myriad restaurants and a brand-new promenade, is where most visitors gravitate. The city sprawls west from there. The main thoroughfares, Sihanouk Blvd and Norodom Blvd, intersect a few blocks east of the river at lotus-flower-like Independence Monument, a useful landmark.

Check out *Phnom Penh Drinking & Dining* (www.cambodiapocketguide.com) for the low-down on bars and restaurants. The *Phnom Penh Visitors' Guide* (www.canbypublications.com) is brimming with useful information on the capital, while *AsiaLife* (www.asialifecambodia.com) is a reliable read.

Dangers & Annoyances

Phnom Penh is a big bustling city, but in general it is no more dangerous than most capitals. Bag-snatching is a possibility in busy tourist areas; keep your valuables close or concealed and be prepared to let go rather than be dragged into the road. Keep shoulder bags in front of you when riding on motos. Be aware of traffic rules that seem to apply only to foreigners or you may have to pay some on-the-spot fines.

Emergency

Ambulance (☎119)
Fire (☎118)
Police (☎117)
Tourist police (☎724793)

Internet Access

Internet cafes are everywhere and usually charge US$0.50 to US$1 per hour. Many hotels, plus some cafes and restaurants, offer free wi-fi connections.

Medical Services

Calmette Hospital (off Map p70; ☎426948; 3 Monivong Blvd) A reputable hospital.

International SOS Medical Centre (Map p74; ☎216911; www.internationalsos.com; 161 St 51) International standards for health and teeth.

Pharmacie de la Gare (Map p70; ☎430205; 81 Monivong Blvd) Reliable French- and English-speaking pharmacists.

Tropical & Travellers Medical Clinic (Map p70; ☎366802; www.travellersmedicalclinic.com; 88 St 108) Well-regarded British-run clinic.

Money

Phnom Penh's airport has a few ATMs. The city has plenty of banks and exchange services, including the following:

ANZ Royal Bank (Map p70; 265 Sisowath Quay) With multiple locations, it offers cash advances and ATM withdrawals.

Canadia Bank (Map p70; 265 St 110) A city landmark, the Canadia Tower offers cash advances on MasterCard and Visa, plus ATMs.

TOP FIVE: GOOD-CAUSE SHOPPING

The stores here sell high-quality silk items and handicrafts to provide the disabled and disenfranchised with valuable training for future employment, plus a regular flow of income to improve lives.

» **Colours of Cambodia** (Map p70; 373 Sisowath Quay; ⌚9am-6pm) Tucked away underneath FCC, this is a popular fair-trade gift shop supporting NGO craft projects.

» **Friends & Stuff** (Map p70; 215 St 13; ⌚11am-9pm Mon-Sat) The closest thing to a charity shop or thrift store in Phnom Penh, with a good range of new and secondhand products sold to generate money to help street children.

» **Nyemo** (Map p74; 71 St 240; ⌚7am-5pm Mon-Sat) In Le Rit's restaurant and with a branch at Russian Market, Nyemo's focus is on quality silk and soft toys for children. It helps disadvantaged women return to work,

» **Rajana** (170 St 450; ⌚10am-6pm) Promoting fair wages and training, Rajana offers a beautiful selection of cards, some quirky metalware products, quality jewellery and bamboo crafts. Near the Russian Market.

» **Tabitha** (Map p74; 239 St 360; ⌚8am-6pm Mon-Sat) A leading NGO shop with a good collection of silk bags, tableware, bedroom decorations and children's toys. Proceeds go towards rural community development.

Post

Main post office (Map p70; St 13; ⏲7am-7pm) Located in a grand old building, this has increasingly reliable postal services.

Telephone

The cheapest local and domestic calls in Phnom Penh are found at private stalls with the mobile telephone prefixes displayed.

Many internet cafes offer low-cost international calls via the internet (or free via Skype).

Tourist Information

There is not much in the way of official tourist information in the Cambodian capital. Pick up the free listings mags and get up-to-date information from other travellers or guesthouses.

Travel Agencies

Reliable travel agencies include the following:

Hanuman (Map p74; ☎218396; www.hanuman.travel; 12 St 310)

VLK Tourism (Map p70; ☎723331; www.vlktravel.com; 195 Monivong Blvd)

Getting There & Away

Air

See p144 for a list of airlines that serve Phnom Penh.

Boat

Speedboats depart daily to Siem Reap (US$35, five to six hours) at 7.30am from the **tourist boat dock** (Map p70; Sisowath Quay) at the eastern end of St 104, but the tickets are overpriced compared with the bus.

Following the river to Chau Doc in Vietnam is a gorgeous way to go – see the boxed text opposite.

Bus

Phnom Penh is connected to all of the provincial capitals by bus. Healthy competition keeps transport prices reasonable and all the companies are similar in terms of comfort and price.

See the relevant sections for individual destinations and details on prices and journey times. Some of the leading companies:

Capitol Tour (Map p74; ☎011 601341; 14 St 182) Services to Battambang, Kep/Kampot, Poipet, Siem Reap and Sihanoukville, plus Ho Chi Minh City.

GST (Map p70; ☎007 607 0701; Psar Thmei) Services to Battambang, Poipet, Siem Reap, Kratie/Stung Treng, and Sihanoukville.

Mekong Express (Map p70; ☎427518; 87 Sisowath Quay) Upmarket services to Battambang, Siem Reap and Sihanoukville, plus Ho Chi Minh City.

Paramount Angkor Express (Map p70; ☎427567; 24 St 102) Double-decker buses to Battambang, Kampot, Krong Koh Kong, Kompong Cham, Kratie, Pailin, Pakse, Poipet, Siem Reap and Sihanoukville.

Phnom Penh Sorya Transport (Map p70; ☎210359; Psar Thmei) Long-running company serving most provincial destinations, plus Bangkok, Ho Chi Minh City and Pakse (Laos).

Virak Buntham Express (Map p70; ☎016 786270; St 106) Night buses to Siem Reap, plus buses to Battambang, Ha Tien (Vietnam), Ho Chi Minh City, Krong Koh Kong and Sihanoukville.

Car & Motorcycle

Guesthouses and travel agencies can arrange a car and driver for US$25 to US$60 a day, depending on the destination. See p80 for motorcycle rental details.

Share Taxi, Pick-up & Minibus

With buses so cheap, comfortable and safe, share taxis, pick-ups and minibuses offer few advantages besides flexible departure times. For Kampot, Krong Koh Kong and Sihanoukville minibuses, pick-ups and taxis leave from Psar Dang Kor (Map p66) in the far southwest of town on Monireth Blvd, while for most other places they leave from the northwest corner of Psar Thmei (Map p70). Vehicles travelling to the Vietnam border leave from Chbah Ampeau taxi park

TRANSPORT CONNECTIONS FROM PHNOM PENH

DESTINATION	CAR/ MOTORBIKE	BUS	BOAT	AIR
Siem Reap	5hr	6hr/US$11/frequent	5hr/US$35/7am	30 min/US$90/3 daily
Sihanoukville	3hr	4hr/US$4/frequent	N/A	N/A
Battambang	4hr	5hr/US$5/frequent	N/A	N/A
Kampot	3hr	4hr/US$5/frequent	N/A	N/A
Kratie	5hr	6hr/US$8/frequent	N/A	N/A

GETTING TO VIETNAM: MEKONG DELTA BORDERS

Bavet to Moc Bai

Getting to the border The most practical way of reaching and then crossing this border is on an international bus to Ho Chi Minh City (US$12, six hours). Several companies offer direct services, including Capitol Tour, Mekong Express and Phnom Penh Sorya Transport.

At the border There is no change required at the Bavet-Moc Bai border crossing (open from 7am to 10pm), 170km east of Phnom Penh. There are no border fees, but you must have a Vietnamese visa in advance.

Moving on Buses go right through, but if you arrive at the border independently, you can arrange a share taxi to Ho Chi Minh City for about US$25. See p883 for information on crossing this border in the other direction.

Kaam Samnor to Vinh Xuong

Getting to the border The most scenic way to reach Vietnam is to follow the Mekong to Kaam Samnor, about 100km south-southeast of Phnom Penh, cross the border to Vinh Xuong in Vietnam, and proceed to Chau Doc. Various companies do trips all the way through to Chau Doc using a single boat or some combination of bus and boat; prices vary according to speed and level of service. **Capitol Tour** (☎023 217 627; US$21) departs Phnom Penh at 8.30am and **Hang Chau** (☎017 336307; US$24) departs at noon. The more upmarket and slightly faster **Blue Cruiser** (Map p70; ☎016 868887; US$35) pulls out at 1pm. These companies take about four hours, including a slow border check, and use a single boat to Chau Doc. Backpacker guesthouses and tour companies in Phnom Penh offer the cheaper bus/boat combo trips. All boats depart from Phnom Penh's tourist dock.

At the border This border is open 7am to 5pm. Sometimes a small fee of US$1 to US$2 is requested on the Cambodian side. Possible overcharging for visa such as US$23 is also common. Visa is required in advance for Vietnam.

Moving on Chau Doc has land and river connections to points in the Mekong Delta and elsewhere in Vietnam. See p888 for information on crossing this border in the other direction.

Phnom Den to Tinh Bien

Getting to the border NH2 runs 58km from Takeo (linked to Phnom Penh by frequent buses) to the Phnom Den border crossing (⏲7am to 5pm). Transport options from Takeo include early morning minibuses (5000r), share taxis and motos (US$8). Phnom Penh Sorya Transport runs buses from Psar Thmei. It may be necessary (or quicker) to change to a moto or *remorque* at Kirivong, 8km from the frontier.

At the border This border is open 7am to 5pm. Sometimes a small fee of US$1 to US$2 is requested on the Cambodian side. Visa is required in advance for Vietnam.

Moving on After walking across the border, motos and taxis can take you to Chau Doc, though beware, as we've heard stories of overcharging and scams at bogus bus stations. See p888 for information on doing the trip in the opposite direction.

(Map p66), just east of the Monivong Bridge in far south of Phnom Penh.

 Getting Around

Bicycle

Simple bicycles can be hired from some guesthouses and hotels from US$1 a day, or contact Vicious Cycle (p68) for something more sophisticated.

Moto, Remorque & Cyclo

Motos are everywhere and those hanging out around tourist areas can generally speak good street English. Short rides around the city cost 2000r; it's US$1 to venture out a little further. At night these prices double. To charter one for a day, expect to pay around US$7 to US$10. *Remorques* usually charge double the price of a moto, possibly more if you pile on the passengers.

Cyclos aren't so common now that *remorques* have invaded the city. Cyclos cost about the same as motos. Arrange a cyclo tour through the **Cyclo Centre** (☎991178; www.cyclo.org.uk), dedicated to supporting cyclo drivers in Phnom Penh.

Motorcycle

Exploring Phnom Penh and the surrounding areas on a motorbike is a very liberating experience if you are used to chaotic traffic conditions. You get what you pay for when choosing a steel steed.

Lucky! Lucky! (Map p74; 413 Monivong Blvd) Has well-maintained trail bikes for US$13 per day.

New! New! (Map p74; 417 Monivong Blvd) Cheapest bikes.

Vannak Bikes Rental (Map p70; 46 St 130) Has good quality trail bikes up to 600cc from US$15 to US$30 per day.

Taxi

Taxis are cheap at 3000r per kilometre but don't expect to flag one down on the street. Call **Global Meter Taxi** (☎011 311888) or **Choice Taxi** (☎888023) for a pickup.

AROUND PHNOM PENH

There are several sites close to Phnom Penh that make for interesting excursions. Tonlé Bati, Phnom Tamao and Phnom Chisor are all near each other on NH2 and make a great full-day *remorque* excursion (US$20) or motorbike ride.

Tonlé Bati

Locals love to come to this **lake** (admission US$3) for picnics, as along the way they can stop off at two 12th-century temples: **Ta Prohm** and **Yeay Peau**. Ta Prohm is the more interesting of the two; it has some fine carvings in good condition, depicting scenes of birth, dishonour and damnation.

The well-marked turnoff to Tonlé Bati is on the right about 31km south of Phnom Penh. Buses going to Takeo (6000r) can drop you here; find a moto to the temples (about 2.5km from the highway).

Phnom Tamao Wildlife Sanctuary

(http://wildlifealliance.org; admission US$5) This sanctuary for rescued animals is home to gibbons, sun bears, elephants, tigers, deer and a bird enclosure. All were taken from poachers or abusive owners and receive care and shelter here as part of a sustainable breeding program.

Getting to Phnom Tamao, about 45km south of Phnom Penh, requires your own wheels or a moto (around US$8). Take NH2 for about [illegible]km, then turn right at the sign. The sanctuary is 5km from the highway on a dusty road often lined with elderly beggars.

Phnom Chisor

Some spectacular views of the countryside are on offer from the summit of Phnom Chisor, although the landscape screams Gobi Desert during the dry season. A laterite-and-brick **temple** (admission US$2; ⌚7am-6pm), dating from the 11th-century, with carved sandstone lintels, guards the hilltop's eastern face. From atop the temple's southern stairs, the sacred pool of **Tonlé Om** is visible below.

To get to Phnom Chisor, 57km south of Phnom Penh, follow the directions for Tonlé Bati (p80), but stay on the bus (8500r) until the signposted turn-off.

SIEM REAP & THE TEMPLES OF ANGKOR

☎063 / POP 119,500

Siem Reap is the life-support system for the temples of Angkor, the eighth wonder of the world. Although in a state of slumber from the late 1960s until a few years ago, the town has woken up with a jolt and is now one of the regional hot spots for wining and dining, shopping and schmoozing.

The ultimate fusion of creative ambition and spiritual devotion, the temples of Angkor are a source of inspiration and profound pride to all Khmers. No traveller to the region will want to miss their extravagant beauty and spine-tingling grandeur. One of the most impressive ancient sites on earth, Angkor has the epic proportions of the Great Wall of China, the detail and intricacy of the Taj Mahal and the symbolism and symmetry of the pyramids, all rolled into one.

Angkor is a place to be savoured, not rushed, and Siem Reap is the perfect base from which to plan your adventures.

ℹ Getting Around

There are endless options when it comes to exploring Angkor. Bicycles are a great way to get to and around the temples, which are linked by

WORTH A TRIP

KIRIROM NATIONAL PARK

You can really get away from it all at this lush elevated **park** (admission US$5) just a couple of hours' drive southwest of Phnom Penh. Winding walking trails lead to cascading wet-season waterfalls and cliffs with amazing views of the Cardamom Mountains, and there's some great mountain-biking to be done if you're adventurous. Or you could just relax and forget about the outside world for a few days at **Kirirom Hillside Resort** (016 590999; www.kiriromresort.com; r from US$50;), near the park entrance. With plastic dinosaurs, it's tacky at first glance, but scattered around the grounds are some great Scandinavian-style bungalows in various shapes and sizes. The pool has a lovely setting with the hills of Kirirom as a backdrop and is open to nonguests for US$5 per day. Nearby are camping and basic budget sleeping options, and a **Community-Based Ecotourism program** (www.geocities.com/chambokcbet; admission US$3) 10km from the park entrance in Chambok commune, where attractions include a 40m-high waterfall, traditional ox-cart rides and nature walks. **Homestays** (per person US$3, plus US$2 per home-cooked meal) are available and proceeds go back into the community. A taxi from Phnom Penh is about US$60 or chart your own course by motorbike.

flat roads in good shape. Just make sure you glug water at every opportunity. A **Grand Circuit** and a **Little Circuit** are marked on the Temples of Angkor map (p84). See p91 for details on bike rental.

Another environmentally friendly option is to explore on foot. There are obvious limitations, but exploring Angkor Thom's walls or walking to and from Angkor Wat are both feasible. Don't forget to buy an entrance ticket.

Motos (US$8 to US$10 per day, more for distant sites), zippy and inexpensive, are the most popular form of transport around the temples. Drivers accost visitors from the moment they set foot in Siem Reap, but they often end up being friendly and knowledgeable. Guesthouses are also a good source of experienced driver-guides.

Remorques (US$12 to US$15 a day, more for distant sites) take a little longer than motos but offer protection from the rain and sun.

Even more protection is offered by cars, though these tend to isolate you from the sights, sounds and smells. Hiring a car in Siem Reap costs about US$30 for a day cruising around Angkor; US$45 to Kbal Spean and Banteay Srei; US$70 to Beng Mealea; and US$90 out to Koh Ker.

As in days of old, it's possible to travel by elephant between the south gate of Angkor Thom and the Bayon (US$15; available 8am to 11am) and, for sunset, from the base to the summit of Phnom Bakheng (US$20; from about 4pm).

Siem Reap

Siem Reap is the comeback kid of Southeast Asia. It has reinvented itself as the epicentre of the new Cambodia, with more guesthouses and hotels than temples, world-class wining and dining and sumptuous spas.

At its heart, Siem Reap remains a charming town with rural qualities. Old French shophouses, shady tree-lined boulevards and a gentle winding river are attractive remnants of the past, while five-star hotels, air-conditioned buses and international restaurants point to a glitzy future.

Sights

TOP CHOICE **Angkor National Museum** MUSEUM
(Map p82; 966601; www.angkornationalmuseum.com; 968 Charles de Gaulle Blvd; admission US$12, audio guide US$3; 8.30am-6pm) A worthwhile introduction to the glories of the Khmer empire, the state-of-the-art Angkor National Museum will help clarify Angkor's history, religious significance, and cultural and political context. Displays include 1400 exquisite stone carvings and artefacts.

Les Chantiers Écoles HANDICRAFT WORKSHOP
(Map p82; 7am-5pm Mon-Fri & Sat morning) Tucked down a side road, Les Chantiers Écoles teaches traditional Khmer artisanship, including lacquer-making and wood- and stone-carving, to impoverished youngsters. Tours of the workshops are possible when school is in session. On the premises is an exquisite shop, Artisans d'Angkor.

To see the entire silk-making process, from mulberry trees to silk worms and spinning to weaving, visit Les Chantiers Écoles' **silk farm** (7.30am-5.30pm), 16km west of town. Shuttle buses leave the school at 9.30am and 1.30pm for a three-hour free tour.

Siem Reap

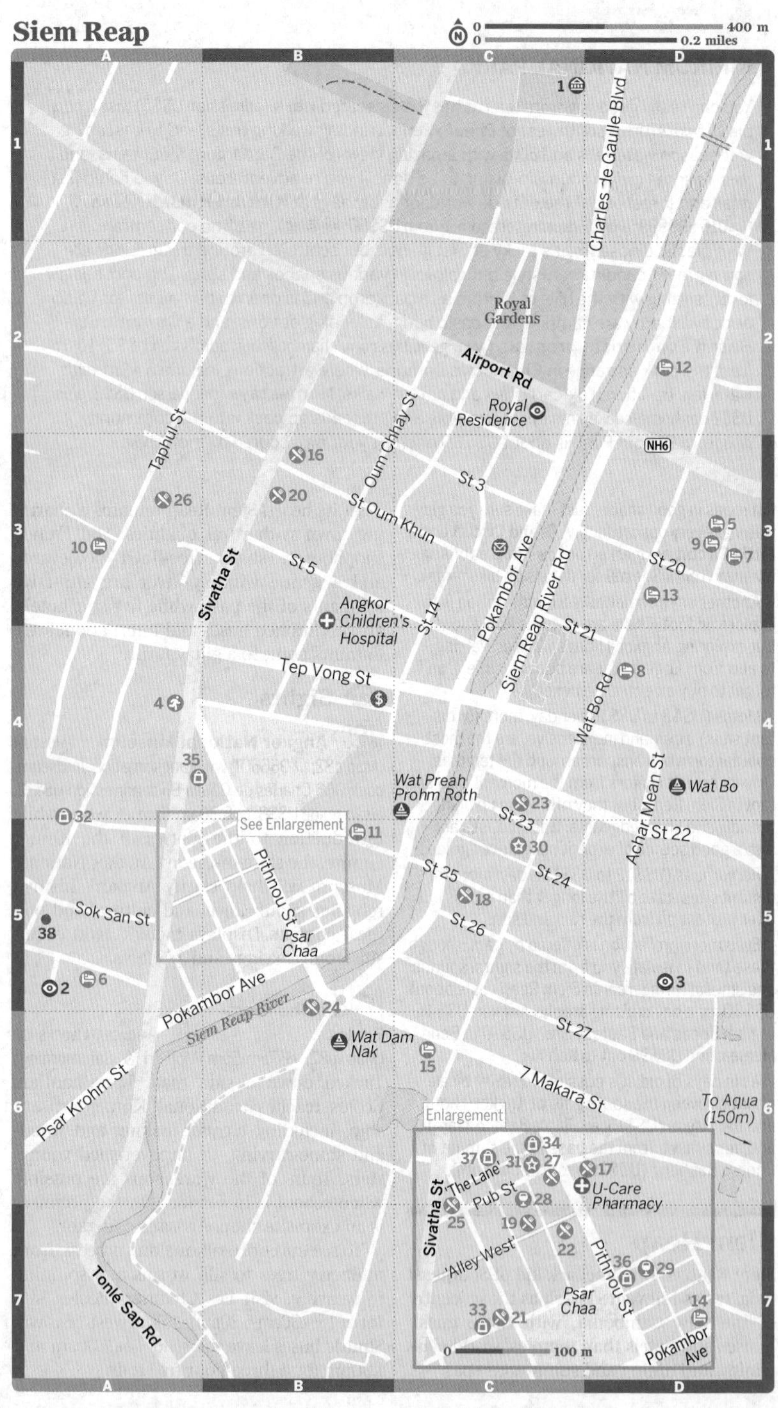

0 400 m
0 0.2 miles
Charles de Gaulle Blvd
Royal Gardens
Airport Rd
Royal Residence
NH6
Taphul St
Oum Chhay St
St 3
St Oum Khun
Sivatha St
St 5
Angkor Children's Hospital
St 14
Pokambor Ave
Siem Reap River Rd
St 20
St 21
Tep Vong St
Wat Bo Rd
Achar Mean St
Wat Bo
Wat Preah Prohm Roth
St 23
St 22
See Enlargement
Pithnou St
Psar Chaa
St 25
St 24
Sok San St
St 26
Pokambor Ave
Siem Reap River
St 27
Wat Dam Nak
Psar Krohm St
7 Makara St
To Aqua (150m)
Enlargement
The Lane
Pub St
U-Care Pharmacy
'Alley West'
Tonlé Sap Rd
0 100 m

Siem Reap

Sights
1 Angkor National Museum C1
2 Les Chantiers Écoles A5
3 Sam Veasna Center D5

Activities, Courses & Tours
Le Tigre de Papier .... (see 28)
4 Seeing Hands Massage 4 .... A4

Sleeping
5 Babel Guesthouse D3
6 EI8HT Rooms A5
7 European Guesthouse D3
8 Frangipani Villa Hotel D4
9 Happy Guesthouse D3
10 Mommy's Guesthouse A3
11 Prohm Roth Guesthouse B5
12 Rosy Guesthouse D2
13 Seven Candles Guesthouse D3
14 Shadow of Angkor Guesthouse D7
15 The Backpacker Hostel C6

Eating
16 Angkor Market B3
17 Blue Pumpkin D6
18 Butterflies Garden Restaurant C5
19 Cambodian BBQ C7
Chamkar .... (see 19)
20 Curry Walla B3
21 Joe-to-Go C7
22 Khmer Kitchen Restaurant C7
23 Le Café C4
Le Tigre de Papier .... (see 28)
24 Local Food Stalls B5
25 Local Food Stalls C7
26 Sala Bai A3
27 Soup Dragon C6

Drinking
28 Angkor What? C6
29 Laundry Bar D7
Miss Wong .... (see 31)
Warehouse .... (see 36)

Entertainment
30 Apsara Dances C5
31 Temple Club C6

Shopping
32 Angkor Night Market A4
Artisans d'Angkor .... (see 2)
33 Blue Aspara Bookshop C7
34 D's Books C6
35 Rajana A4
36 Senteurs d'Angkor D7
37 Three Seasons C6

Information
38 ConCERT A5

TOP CHOICE Cambodia Landmine Museum MUSEUM
(☎012 598951; www.cambodialandminemuseum.org; admission US$2; ⏰7.30am-5pm) Popular with travellers thanks to its informative displays on one of the country's postwar curses, the nonprofit Cambodia Landmine Museum has a mock minefield where visitors can search for deactivated mines. It's situated about 25km from Siem Reap and 6km south of Banteay Srei temple.

Banteay Srei Butterfly Centre BUTTERFLY CENTRE
(☎011 348460; www.angkorbutterfly.com; admission US$4; ⏰9am-5pm) This is a worthwhile place to include on a trip to Banteay Srei and the Landmine Museum. The largest fully enclosed butterfly centre in Southeast Asia, there are more than 30 species of Cambodian butterflies fluttering about. It is located about 7km before Banteay Srei on the right-hand side of the road.

Khmer Ceramics Centre POTTERY CENTRE
(Map p84; ☎017 843014; www.khmerceramics.com; Charles de Gaulle Blvd; ⏰8am-7.30pm) At this centre you can see ceramics being turned, decorated and fired using the traditional techniques that were almost lost because of the Khmer Rouge. Half-day courses are also available if you fancy taking the wheel. It's situated on the road to Angkor Wat.

Wat Thmei TEMPLE
(Map p84; ⏰6am-6.30pm) Modern-day pagodas offer an interesting contrast to the ancient sandstone structures of Angkor. On the left fork of the road to Angkor Wat, Wat Thmei, built in 1992, has a memorial stupa containing the skulls and bones of people killed here when the site served as a Khmer Rouge prison. Some of the young monks are keen to practise their English.

Temples of Angkor

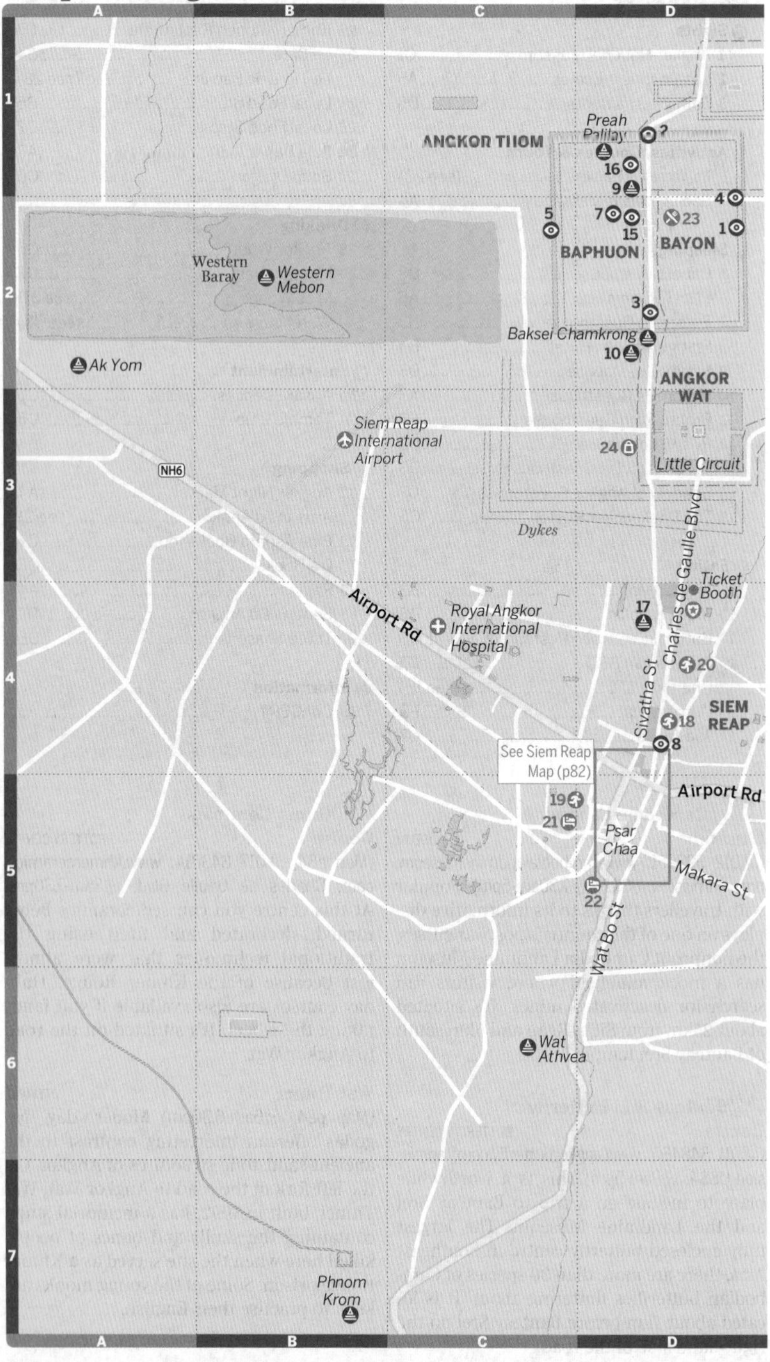

See Siem Reap Map (p82)

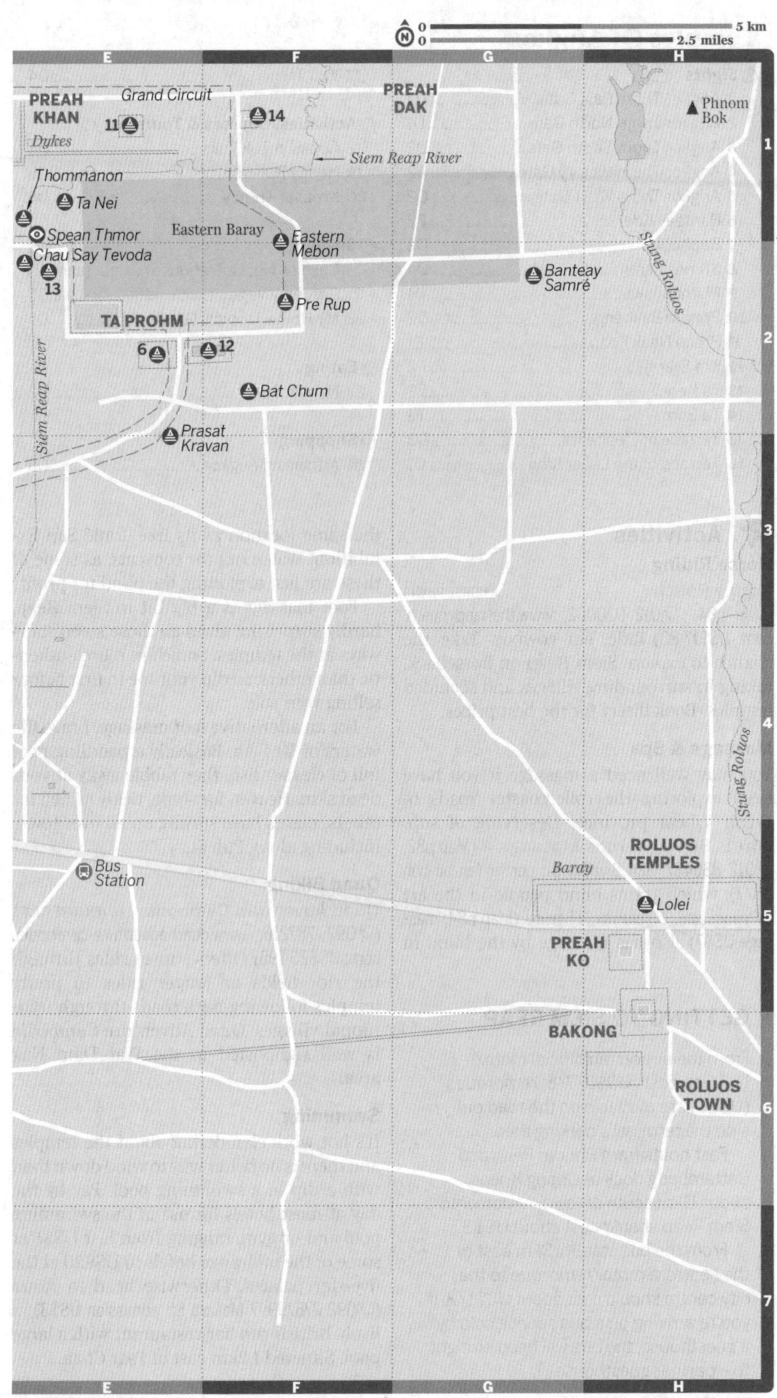

0 5 km
0 2.5 miles
E
F
G
H
PREAH KHAN
Grand Circuit
11
14
PREAH DAK
Phnom Bok
Dykes
Siem Reap River
Thommanon
Ta Nei
Spean Thmor
Eastern Baray
Eastern Mebon
Chau Say Tevoda
13
Banteay Samré
Stung Roluos
Pre Rup
TA PROHM
6
12
Bat Chum
Siem Reap River
Prasat Kravan
Stung Roluos
ROLUOS TEMPLES
Baray
Bus Station
Lolei
PREAH KO
BAKONG
ROLUOS TOWN
1
2
3
4
5
6
7

Temples Of Angkor

Sights
1 Angkor Thom East Gate D2
2 Angkor Thom North Gate D1
3 Angkor Thom South Gate D2
4 Angkor Thom Victory Gate D2
5 Angkor Thom West Gate C2
6 Banteay Kdei E2
7 Baphuon D2
8 Khmer Ceramics Centre D4
9 Phimeanakas D1
10 Phnom Bakheng D2
11 Preah Neak Poan E1
12 Sra Srang F2
13 Ta Keo E2
14 Ta Som F1
15 Terrace of Elephants D2
16 Terrace of the Leper King D1
17 Wat Thmei D4

Activities, Courses & Tours
18 Cooks in Tuk Tuks D4
19 Happy Ranch C5
20 Krousar Thmey D4

Sleeping
Cashew Nut Guesthouse .... (see 22)
21 Garden Village C5
22 My Home Tropical Garden Villa D5

Eating
23 Noodle Stalls D2

Shopping
24 Artisans d'Angkor D3

Activities

Horse Riding

Happy Ranch HORSE RIDING
(Map p84; ☎012 920002; www.thehappyranch.com; US$17-80) Ride 'em cowboy. Take the chance to explore Siem Reap on horseback, taking in surrounding villages and secluded temples. Book direct for the best prices.

Massage & Spa

You may well need a massage if you have been exploring the rollercoaster roads of Preah Vihear province. Deserving of support is **Seeing Hands Massage 4** (Map p82; ☎012 836487; 324 Sivatha St; per hr fan/air-con $5/7), which trains blind people in the art of massage. **Krousar Thmey** (Map p84; massage US$7) also has massage by the blind in the same location as its free Tonlé Sap Exhibition. Watch out for copycats, as some of these are just exploiting the blind for profit.

Foot massage is a big hit in Siem Reap, hardly surprising given all those steep stairways at the temples. Some are more authentic than others, so dip your toe in first before selling your sole.

For an alternative foot massage, brave the waters of **Dr Fish**. Basically a paddling pool full of cleaner fish, they nibble away at your dead skin. Heaven for some, tickly as hell for others, places have sprung up all over town, including along Pub St.

Quad Biking

Quad Adventure Cambodia ADVENTURE TOURS
(☎092 787216; www.quad-adventure-cambodia.com; US$25-195) Offers sunset rides through the rice fields or longer rides to pretty temples following back roads through traditional villages. Quad Adventure Cambodia is well signposted in the Wat Dam Nak area.

Swimming

It's hot work clambering about the temples and there is no better way to wind down than with a dip in a swimming pool. Pay by the day at most hotels for use of the swimming pool and/or gym, ranging from just US$5 at some of the midrange hotels to US$20 at the five-star palaces. Otherwise head to **Aqua** (☎092 276799; 7 Makara St; admission US$3), a lively British-run bar-restaurant with a large pool. Situated 1.2km east of Psar Chaa.

GETTING TO SIEM REAP

From the airport, an official moto/taxi/van costs US$2/7/8; *remorques* (US$5) are available on the road outside the terminal's parking area.

Fast boats from Phnom Penh and Battambang dock at Chong Kneas, about 11km south of town. A moto into Siem Reap should cost about US$3.

From the bus station, 3km east of the centre, a moto/*remorque* to the city centre should cost about US$1/2. If you're arriving on a bus service sold by a guesthouse, the bus will head straight to a partner guesthouse.

Courses

Cooks in Tuk Tuks COOKING

(Map p84; ☎963400; www.therivergarden.info; classes US$25; ⊙10am-1pm) The course starts at 10am daily with a visit to Psar Leu market, then returns to the peaceful River Garden boutique hotel for a professional class.

Le Tigre de Papier COOKING

(Map p82; ☎760930; www.letigredepapier.com; Pub St; classes US$12; ⊙10am-1pm) Starts at 10am daily and includes a visit to the market. Proceeds are used to support Sala Bai (p88).

Sleeping

There are now more guesthouses and hotels around Siem Reap than there are temples around Angkor – and that's a lot. While accommodation is spread throughout town, three areas hold the bulk of budget choices: the Psar Chaa area; the area to the west of Sivatha St; and the east bank of the river. Most of these places offer free pick-up from the airport, port or bus station: email or call ahead.

TOP CHOICE **My Home Tropical Garden Villa** HOTEL $$

(Map p84; ☎760035; www.myhomecambodia.com; r US$14-26; ❄@🛜🏊) Offering hotel standards at guesthouse prices, this is a fine place to rest your head. The decor includes some subtle silks and the furnishings are tasteful. And there's a swimming pool.

European Guesthouse BACKPACKER $

(Map p82; ☎012 582237; www.european-guesthouse.com; Wat Bo area; r US$8-18; ❄@🛜) Scandinavian-run, the European is a member of local NGO networks Childsafe and ConCERT and supports projects like the White Bicycles. Fun and friendly, the rooms are well-presented and the garden is a good place to relax.

Cashew Nut Guesthouse BACKPACKER $

(Map p84; ☎092 815975; thecashewnut.com; Wat Bo Rd; r US$9-20; ❄@🛜) A lively new place run by self-proclaimed 'nutters' who previously worked as tour leaders for Intrepid. Artful decoration and slick service propel this into boutique backpacker orbit.

Seven Candles Guesthouse GUESTHOUSE $

(Map p82; ☎963380; www.sevencandlesguesthouse.com; 307 Wat Bo Rd; r US$7-15; ❄@🛜) A likeable good-cause guesthouse, profits help a local foundation, which seeks to promote education to rural communities. Rooms include hot water, TV and fridge.

SUPPORTING RESPONSIBLE TOURISM IN SIEM REAP

Many travellers passing through Siem Reap are interested in contributing something to the communities they visit as they explore the temples and surrounding areas. **ConCERT** (Map p82; ☎963511; www.concertcambodia.org; 560 Phum Stoueng Thmey; ⊙9am-5pm Mon-Fri) is a Siem Reap–based organisation that is working to build bridges between tourists and good-cause projects in the Siem Reap-Angkor area. They offer information on anything from ecotourism initiatives to volunteering opportunities.

Prohm Roth Guesthouse GUESTHOUSE $

(Map p82; ☎012 466495; www.prohmroth-guesthouse.com; r US$9-25; ❄@🛜) Central, yet tucked away down a side street that runs parallel to Wat Preah Prohm Roth, this is a friendly place with a good range of rooms.

Babel Guesthouse BACKPACKER $$

(Map p82; ☎965474; www.babelsiemreap.hostel.com; Wat Bo area; r US$14-24; ❄@🛜) An upmarket guesthouse with a relaxing tropical garden. The service and presentation are a cut above the nearby budget places.

Shadow of Angkor Guesthouse GUESTHOUSE $$

(Map p82; ☎964774; www.shadowofangkor.com; 353 Pokambor Ave; r US$15-25; ❄@🛜) In a grand old French-era building overlooking the river, this friendly, 15-room place offers affordable air-con in a prime setting.

Mommy's Guesthouse GUESTHOUSE $

(Map p82; ☎012 941755; mommy_guesthouse@yahoo.com; r US$5-15; ❄@🛜) A warm and welcoming, family-run place, this 13-room villa has large rooms with air-con, as well as cheap digs with cold showers. Just off Taphul St.

The Backpacker Hostel BACKPACKER $

(Map p82; ☎012 313239; www.angkorbackpacker.com; St 7 Makara; r US$7-12; ❄@🛜) It may not be the 'original' backpacker hostel nearby, but it provides good value, clean rooms and free wi-fi.

SPLURGE: SIEM REAP

The Siem Reap outpost of the growing Frangipani empire, the **Frangipani Villa Hotel** (Map p82; ☎999930; www.frangipanihotel.com; Wat Bo Rd; r US$40-60; ❄@📶≋) is chic boutique on the cheap. Rooms include stylish touches such as flat-screen TVs. There's an inviting pool.

EI8HT Rooms GUESTHOUSE $$
(Map p82; ☎969788; www.ei8htrooms.com; r US$12-24; ❄@📶) A smart, gay-friendly guesthouse with boutique touches, bright silks, DVD players and free internet. So popular there are now 16 rooms set in two buildings.

Happy Guesthouse GUESTHOUSE $
(Map p82; ☎012 960879; http://www.angkorhotels.org/Happy_Guesthouse; Wat Bo area; r US$4-10; ❄@📶) This place will really make you happy thanks to welcoming owners, good-value rooms and free internet.

Garden Village BACKPACKER $
(Map p84; ☎012 217373; gardenvillage@asia.com; dm US$1, r US$3-12; ❄@📶) This old-fashioned backpacker hang-out offers some of the cheapest beds in town and is a good place to meet travellers. Options among its 70 rooms include eight-bed dorms and US$3 cubicles with shared bathroom.

Rosy Guesthouse GUESTHOUSE $
(Map p82; ☎965059; www.rosyguesthouse.com; Siem Reap River Rd; r US$8-30; ❄) A British-owned establishment whose 15 rooms come with TV and DVD, but the four cheapest are tiny and have shared bathrooms. Has a lively pub downstairs.

Eating

Worthy restaurants are sprinkled all around town but Siem Reap's culinary heart is the Psar Chaa area, whose focal point, The Alley, is literally lined with mellow eateries offering great atmosphere. It is wall-to-wall with good Cambodian restaurants, many family owned. Cheap eats can be found at the nearby **food stalls** (Pub St; mains 4000-8000r; ⏲4pm-3am), around Pub St's western end, or in the **small eateries** (mains 4000-8000r; ⏲4pm-3am) lining Psar Chaa.

For self-caterers, markets sell fruit and veg. **Angkor Market** (Map p82; Sivatha St; ⏲7.30am-10pm) can supply international treats.

TOP CHOICE **Blue Pumpkin** INTERNATIONAL $
(Map p82; Pithnou St; mains US$2-6; ⏲6am-10pm; ❄📶) Upstairs is a world of white minimalism with beds to lounge on and free wi-fi. Light bites, great sandwiches, divine shakes and superb cakes keep them coming.

Khmer Kitchen CAMBODIAN $
(Map p82; The Alley; mains US$2-5; ⏲11am-10pm) Can't get no (culinary) satisfaction? Then follow in the footsteps of Sir Mick Jagger and try this popular place, which offers an affordable selection of Khmer and Thai favourites.

Sala Bai INTERNATIONAL $$
(Map p82; www.salabai.com; Taphul St; set lunch US$8; ⏲7-9am, noon-2pm Mon-Fri) This school trains young Khmers in the art of hospitality and serves an affordable three-course lunch menu of Western and Cambodian cuisine.

Cambodian BBQ BARBECUE $$
(Map p82; ☎966052; The Alley; mains US$5-9; ⏲11am-11pm; 📶) Crocodile, snake, ostrich and kangaroo meat add an exotic twist to the traditional *phnom pleung* (hill of fire) grills. It has spawned a dozen copycats in the surrounding streets.

Le Tigre de Papier INTERNATIONAL $
(Map p82; Pub St; Khmer mains US$3-6.50; ⏲24hr; 📶) Established spot with a wood-fired oven and a great menu of Italian, French and Khmer food. Its 24-hour opening means it's a good place if the midnight munchies strike.

Butterflies Garden Restaurant INTERNATIONAL $$
(Map p82; St 25; mains US$3-7; ⏲8am-10pm; 📶) In a blooming garden aflutter with butterflies, this place serves Khmer flavours (including veggie and vegan) with an international touch. Supports good causes.

Le Café FRENCH $
(Map p82; Wat Bo area; mains US$4-5; ⏲7.30am-8pm; 📶) Brings five-star, Sofitel-inspired sandwiches, salads and shakes to the French Cultural Centre, where it serves as the in-house eatery.

Chamkar VEGETARIAN $
(Map p82; The Alley; mains US$3-5; ⏲11am-11pm; 📶) A creative menu of Asian vegetarian flavours includes stuffed pumpkin or vegetable kebabs in black pepper sauce.

Soup Dragon INTERNATIONAL $$
(Map p82; ☎964933; Pub St; mains US$2-10; ⏰6am-11pm; 📶) The ground floor serves up classic Asian breakfasts like *pho* (Vietnamese rice-noodle soup) for around US$1 – just the recipe for tackling the temples – while upstairs serves a diverse menu of Asian and international dishes.

Curry Walla INDIAN $
(Map p82; ☎965451; Sivatha St; mains US$2.75-6; ⏰10am-11pm) For good-value Indian food, this place is hard to beat. The *thalis* (set meals) are a bargain and the owner knows his share of spicy secrets from the subcontinent.

Drinking

Siem Reap is now firmly on the nightlife map of Southeast Asia. The Psar Chaa area is a good hunting ground, and one street is now known as 'Pub St': dive in, crawl out.

Angkor What? BAR
(Map p82; ☎012 490755; Pub St; ⏰6pm-late) Siem Reap's original bar is still serving up serious hangovers every night. The happy hour (to 8pm) lightens the mood for later when everyone's bouncing along to indie anthems, sometimes on the tables, sometimes under them.

Warehouse BAR
(Map p82; Pithnou St; ⏰10.30am-3am) A popular bar opposite Psar Chaa, offering indie anthems, table football, a pool table and devilish drinks.

Laundry Bar LOUNGE
(Map p82; Psar Chaa area; ⏰5pm-3am) One of the most alluring bars in town thanks to discerning decor, low lighting and a laid-back soundtrack. Happy hour is 5pm to 9pm.

Miss Wong COCKTAIL BAR
(Map p82; ☎092 428332; The Lane; ⏰6pm-1am or later) Miss Wong carries you back to the chic of 1920s Shanghai. The cocktails are the draw here. A gay-friendly bar.

Joe-To-Go CAFE
(Map p82; Psar Chaa; ⏰7am-9.30pm) If you need coffee to course through your veins to tackle the temples, then head here. Gourmet coffees, with proceeds supporting street children.

Entertainment

Classical dance shows take place all over the town, but only a few are worth considering. Children perform **apsara dances** at 7pm on Friday at the Soria Moria Hotel. The performance is free with a set menu (US$6/8 for Khmer/Western food).

Temple Club DANCE
(Map p82; Pub St; buffet incl dance show US$5) A very popular bar-restaurant that offers the best value classical dance show in town. Cultural performances upstairs, late-night mayhem downstairs.

Shopping

Siem Reap has an excellent selection of Cambodian-made handicrafts. **Psar Chaa** (Map p82) is well stocked. There are bargains to be had if you haggle patiently and humorously. **Angkor Night Market** (Map p82; www.angkornightmarket.com; near Sivatha St; ⏰4pm-midnight) is packed with silks, handicrafts and souvenirs. Up-and-coming **Alley West** is also a great strip to browse socially responsible fashion boutiques.

Several shops support Cambodia's disabled and disenfranchised:

Artisans d'Angkor HANDICRAFTS
(Map p82 & Map p84; www.artisansdangkor.com; ⏰7.30am-7.30pm) One of the best places in Cambodia for quality souvenirs and gifts, with everything from silk clothing to elegant reproductions of Angkorian-era statuary. Branches in town, opposite Angkor Wat, and at the airport.

Three Seasons FASHION
(Map p82; The Lane; ⏰10am-10pm) Three shops in one at this new place, including Elsewhere, Zoco and Keo Kjay, a fair-trade fashion enterprise helping HIV-positive women earn a living.

Rajana HANDICRAFTS
(Map p82; www.rajanacrafts.org; Sivatha St; ⏰8am-10pm Mon-Sat, 2-10pm Sun) Sells quirky wooden and metalware objects, silver jewellery and handmade cards. Rajana promotes fair trade and employment opportunities for Cambodians.

Senteurs d'Angkor BEAUTY
(Map p82; www.senteursdangkor.com; Pithnou St; ⏰7am-10pm) Has a wide-ranging collection of silk, stone carvings, beauty products, massage oils, spices, coffees and teas.

Blue Apsara Bookshop BOOKS
(Map p82; ⏰8am-11pm) Used books in several languages.

TRANSPORT CONNECTIONS FROM SIEM REAP

DESTINATION	CAR/ MOTORBIKE	BUS	BOAT	AIR
Phnom Penh	5hr	6hr/US$5-11/ frequent	5hr/US$35/ 7am	30 min/from US$90/3 daily
Kompong Thom	2hr	2½hr/US$5/ frequent	N/A	N/A
Battambang	3hr	4hr/US$4-5/ regular	7hr/US$20/ 7am	N/A
Poipet	3hr	4hr/US$4-5/ regular	N/A	N/A
Bangkok	8hr	10hr/US$12-15/ frequent	N/A	1hr/ from US$150/5 daily

D's Books BOOKS
(Map p82; Pithnou St; ⏲9am-10pm) The largest chain of second-hand bookshops in Cambodia. This is conveniently located for night browsing.

Information

Hotels, restaurants and bars can provide the free *Siem Reap Angkor Visitors Guide* (www.canby publications.com) and two handy booklets produced by *Pocket Guide Cambodia* (www.cambodiapocketguide.com).

There are ATMs at the airport and in banks and minimarts all over central Siem Reap, especially along Sivatha St. The greatest concentration of internet shops is along Sivatha St and around Psar Chaa. Free wi-fi is available at many of the leading cafes, restaurants and bars, not forgetting most guesthouses and hotels.

Angkor Hospital for Children (Map p82; ☎963409; Tep Vong St; ⏲24hr) A paediatric hospital supported by donors. It's free for anyone under 16, tourists included.

ANZ Royal Bank (Map p82; Achar Mean St) Plus ATMs conveniently dotted about town.

Main post office (Map p82; Pokambar Ave; ⏲7am-5.30pm) Offers EMS express international postal service.

Royal Angkor International Hospital (Map p84; ☎761888; NH6; ⏲24hr) A modern, international-standard facility affiliated with the Bangkok Hospital Medical Center.

Tourist police (Map p84; ☎012 969991) At the main Angkor ticket checkpoint.

U-Care Pharmacy (Map p82; Pithnou St; ⏲8am-9pm) Smart pharmacy and shop like Boots in Thailand (and the UK). English spoken.

Getting There & Away

Air

Siem Reap International Airport (Map p84; www.cambodia-airports.com) is a work of art set 7km west of the centre and offers regular connections to most neighbouring Asian cities. Domestic flights are limited to Phnom Penh, but it is hoped that direct flights will resume to Sihanoukville at some stage. For a list of airlines and contacts, see p144.

Boat

Boats for the trip to Battambang (US$20; p103) and the faster ride to Phnom Penh (US$35) depart at 7am from the tourist boat dock at Chong Kneas, 11km south of town. Tickets are sold at guesthouses, hotels and travel agencies, including pick-up from your hotel or guesthouse around 6am.

Bus

All buses depart from the bus station (Map p84), which is 3km east of town and about 200m south of NH6. Tickets are available at guesthouses, hotels, bus offices, travel agencies and ticket kiosks. Some bus companies send a minibus around to pick up passengers at their place of lodging. Most departures to Phnom Penh are between 7am and 1pm; buses to other destinations generally leave early in the morning. Upon arrival in Siem Reap, be prepared for a crowd of eager moto drivers greeting the bus.

Bus companies that serve Siem Reap:

Capitol Tours (☎963883)

GST (☎092 905016)

Mekong Express (☎963662)

Neak Kror Horm (☎964924)

Paramount Angkor Express (☎966469)

Phnom Penh Sorya (☎012 235618)

Rith Mony (☎012 344377)

Virak Buntham (015 958989) Tickets to Phnom Penh (six hours), via NH6, cost US$5 to US$11, depending on the level of service (air-con, comfy seats, a toilet, a hostess), whether foreigners pay more than locals and whether there's a hotel pick-up included. Many companies charge the same price to Kompong Thom as they do to Phnom Penh. Virak Buntham offers the only night bus services to Phnom Penh and through to Sihanoukville, departing between 8pm and midnight.

Several companies offer direct services to Kompong Cham (US$6, five or six hours), Battambang (US$5, four hours) and Poipet (US$5, four hours). GST has a bus to Anlong Veng (15,000r, three hours).

Share Taxi

Share taxis stop along NH6 just north of the bus station. Destinations include Phnom Penh (US$10, 4½ hours), Kompong Thom (US$5, two hours), Sisophon (US$5, 1½ hours) and Poipet (US$7, 2½ hours).

To get to Banteay Chhmar, head to Sisophon and catch transport from there.

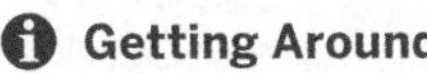

Getting Around

For details on ways to explore the temples of Angkor, see p145.

Short moto trips around the centre of town cost 2000r or 3000r, more at night. A *remorque* is double again, more with lots of people.

Most guesthouses and small hotels can usually help with bicycle rental for about US$2 per day. Look out for guesthouses and hotels supporting the **White Bicycles** (www.thewhitebicycles.org; per day US$2) project, whose proceeds go to local development projects.

Hiring a moto with a driver costs US$8 to US$10 for the whole day, while a *remorque* is about US$15. Motorbike hire is currently prohibited in Siem Reap.

GETTING TO THAILAND: REMOTE NORTHERN BORDERS

There are a couple of seldom-used crossings along Cambodia's northern border with Thailand.

Choam to Chong Sa Ngam

Getting to the border This crossing is 16km north of Anlong Veng (10,000r by moto) and 134km north of Siem Reap. From Anlong Veng, a modern sealed road heads up the Dangkrek escarpment to the border. Anlong Veng is located 118km north of Siem Reap (along the excellent NH67), 16km south of the Choam border crossing. Share taxis from Siem Reap (20,000r, two hours) are available; a private taxi is about US$40. **GST** (092-905026) has a 7am bus from Siem Reap to Anlong Veng (15,000r, three hours).

At the border This border is open from 7am to 5pm. Petty overcharging is possible on the Cambodian side, particularly for visas, as they often request payment at inflated Thai baht prices. No visa is required for Thailand for most nationalities. Cambodian visas are available on arrival.

Moving on On the Thai side, it should be possible to find a sŏrngtăaou (pick-up truck) to Phusing and from there a bus to Kantharalak. You might also suss out transport to Si Saket.

See p719 for information on doing the trip in the reverse direction.

O Smach to Chong Chom

Getting to the border This is not the easiest border crossing to reach. Share taxis (30,000r; four hours) link Siem Reap with Samraong, the backwater provincial capital, where you can hire a moto (US$10) or a private taxi (US$25) for the punishing drive to O Smach (nearly two hours, 40km) and its frontier casino zone.

At the border This border is open from 7am to 5pm. Petty overcharging is possible on the Cambodian side, particularly for visas, as they often request payment at inflated Thai baht prices. No visa is required for Thailand for most nationalities. Cambodian visas are available on arrival.

Moving on On the Thai side it's easy – sŏrngtăaou and motos take arrivals to the bus stop for Surin (1½ to two hours, 70km).

See p719 for information on crossing this border in the other direction.

Around Siem Reap

Sights

Chong Kneas FLOATING VILLAGE

This famous floating village is now so popular with visitors that it's become something of a floating cash cow, at least insofar as hiring a boat (US$11 per person plus US$2 entry fee) is concerned. Large tour groups tend to take over, and boats end up chugging up and down the channels in convoy. The small, floating **Gecko Environment Centre** (www.tsbr-ed.org; admission free; ⌚7am-4pm) has displays on the Tonlé Sap's remarkable annual cycle. **Tara Boat** (☎092 957765; www.taraboat.com) offers all-inclusive trips with a meal aboard a converted cargo boat. Prices include transfers, entry fees, local boats, a tour guide and a two-course meal, starting from US$27 for a trip with lunch.

To get to the floating village from Siem Reap costs US$2 by moto each way (more if the driver waits), or US$15 by taxi. The trip takes 20 minutes. Or rent a bicycle in town, as it's a leisurely 11km ride through pretty villages and ricefields.

Kompong Pluk STILTED VILLAGE

More memorable than Chong Kneas, but also harder to reach, is the friendly village of **Kompong Pluk**, an other-worldly place built on soaring stilts. Most of the houses are almost bamboo skyscrapers and the village looks as though it's straight out of a film set. In the wet season you can explore the nearby flooded forest by canoe. To get here, either catch a boat (US$55 return) at Chong Kneas or come via the small town of Roluos by a two-hour combination of road (about US$7 return by moto) and boat (US$8 per person). An all-weather elevated access road is under construction, which no doubt means a private company will start levying charges to visit Kompong Pluk.

Temples of Angkor

Where to begin with Angkor? There is no greater concentration of architectural riches anywhere on earth. Choose from the world's largest religious building, Angkor Wat, one of the world's weirdest, Bayon, or the riotous jungle of Ta Prohm. All are global icons and have helped put Cambodia on the map as the temple capital of Asia.

Beyond the big three are dozens more temples, each of which would be the star were it located anywhere else in the region: Banteay Srei, the art gallery of Angkor; Preah Khan, the ultimate fusion temple uniting Buddhism and Hinduism; or Beng Mealea, the Titanic of temples suffocating under the jungle. The most vexing part of a visit to Angkor is working out what to see, as there are simply so many spectacular sites. One day at Angkor? Sacrilege! Don't even consider it.

The hundreds of temples surviving today are but the sacred skeleton of the vast political, religious and social centre of the ancient Khmer empire. Angkor was a city that, at its zenith, boasted a population of one million when London was a small town of 50,000. The houses, public buildings and palaces of Angkor were constructed of wood – now long decayed – because the right to dwell in structures of brick or stone was reserved for the gods.

PREK TOAL BIRD RESERVE

Prek Toal Bird Reserve (210 sq km) is a seasonally inundated forest unmatched anywhere in Southeast Asia for its dry-season populations of endangered water birds. These include lesser and greater adjutant storks, milky storks and spot-billed pelicans. An all-day excursion to this ornithologist's fantasy land costs from US$98 per person, including land and lake transport, meals, fees and guides. Prek Toal lies on the northwestern tip of Tonlé Sap Lake, about 40km from Siem Reap.

Also accessible as a long day trip from Siem Reap is the **Ang Trapeang Thmor Reserve**, a wetland bird sanctuary 100km northwest of Siem Reap that's home to the extremely rare Sarus crane, depicted on bas-reliefs at Bayon, and 200 other bird species. Overnight stays are possible.

Sam Veasna Center for Wildlife Conservation (Map p82; ☎963710; www.samveasna.org; off Wat Bo Rd) runs birdwatching and ecotourism trips to these important sites, proceeds from which benefit local communities. Book at least three days ahead for overnight trips and 24 to 48 hours ahead for day trips.

EXPLORING THE TEMPLES

One Day

If you've got only one day to spend at Angkor, that's unfortunate, but a good itinerary would be Angkor Wat for sunrise, after which you can explore the mighty temple before the crowds arrive. From there, drop by Ta Prohm (p97) before breaking for lunch. In the afternoon, explore the temples within the walled city of Angkor Thom (p96) and the enigmatic faces of the Bayon (p96) in the late afternoon light. Biggest mistake: trying to pack in too much.

Three Days

With three days to explore the area, start with some of the smaller temples and build up to the big hitters. Visit the early Roluos group (p98) on the first day for some chronological consistency and try the stars of the Grand Circuit, including Preah Khan (p97) and Preah Neak Poan (p98). Day two might include Ta Prohm and the temples on the Small Circuit, plus the distant but stunning Banteay Srei (p98). Then the climax: Angkor Wat at dawn and the immense city of Angkor Thom in the afternoon.

One Week

Angkor is your oyster, so relax, enjoy and explore at will. Make sure you visit Beng Mealea (p98) and Kbal Spean (p98). For a change of pace, take boats to Prek Toal Bird Reserve (p92) and/or the floating village of Kompong Pluk (p92).

Tickets

The **Angkor ticket booth** (Map p84; 1-day/3-day/1-week tourist pass US$20/40/60; ⏲5am-5.30pm) is on the road from Siem Reap to Angkor. Three-day passes can be used on any three days over a one-week period, and one-week passes are valid over the course of a month. Tickets issued after 5pm (for sunset viewing) are valid the next day. Tickets are not valid for Phnom Kulen or Beng Mealea. Get caught ticketless in a temple and you'll be fined US$100.

Eating

There are dozens of local **noodle stalls** just near the Terrace of the Leper King, and a village with a cluster of **restaurants** opposite Sra Srang, the former royal bathing pond. Angkor Wat has full-blown cafes and restaurants.

Try to be patient with the hordes of children selling food, drinks and souvenirs, as they're only doing what their families have asked them to do to survive. You'll find that their ice-cold bottled water and fresh pineapples are heavenly in the heat.

For details on options for getting to and around the temples, see p145.

ANGKOR WAT

The traveller's first glimpse of **Angkor Wat** (Map p84), the ultimate expression of Khmer genius, is simply staggering and is matched by only a few select spots on earth such as Macchu Picchu or Petra.

Angkor is heaven on earth, namely the symbolic representation of Mt Meru, the Mt Olympus of the Hindu faith and abode of ancient gods. Angkor is the perfect fusion of creative ambition and spiritual devotion. The Cambodian 'god-kings' of old each strove to better their ancestors in size, scale and symmetry, culminating in the world's largest religious building, Angkor Wat.

Angkor Wat is the Khmers' national symbol, the epicentre of their civilisation and a source of fierce national pride. Unlike the other Angkor monuments, it was never abandoned to the elements and has been in virtually continuous use since it was built.

Angkor Wat is surrounded by a moat, 190m wide, which forms a giant rectangle measuring 1.5km by 1.3km. Stretching around the outside of the central temple complex is an 800m-long series of bas-reliefs, designed to be viewed in an anticlockwise direction. Rising 31m above the

Temples of Angkor

THREE-DAY EXPLORATION

The temple complex at Angkor is simply enormous and the superlatives don't do it justice. This is the site of the world's largest religious building, a multitude of temples and a vast, long-abandoned walled city that was arguably Southeast Asia's first metropolis, long before Bangkok and Singapore got in on the action.

Starting at the Roluos group of temples, one of the earliest capitals of Angkor, move on to the big circuit, which includes the Buddhist-Hindu fusion temple of 1 **Preah Khan** and the ornate water temple of 2 **Neak Poan**.

On the second day downsize to the small circuit, starting with an atmospheric dawn visit to 3 **Ta Prohm**, before continuing to the temple pyramid of Ta Keo, the Buddhist monastery of Banteay Kdei and the immense royal bathing pond of 4 **Sra Srang**.

Next venture further afield to Banteay Srei temple, the jewel in the crown of Angkorian art, and Beng Mealea, a remote jungle temple.

Saving the biggest and best until last, experience sunrise at 5 **Angkor Wat** and stick around for breakfast in the temple to discover its amazing architecture without the crowds. In the afternoon, explore 6 **Angkor Thom**, an immense complex that is home to the enigmatic 7 **Bayon**.

Three days around Angkor? That's just for starters.

TOP TIPS

» **Dodging the Crowds** Early morning at Ta Prohm, post sunrise at Angkor Wat and lunchtime at Banteay Srei does the trick.

» **Extended Explorations** Three-day passes can now be used on non-consecutive days over the period of a week but be sure to request this.

Bayon
The surreal state temple of legendary king Jayavarman VII, where 216 faces bear down on pilgrims, asserting religious and regal authority.

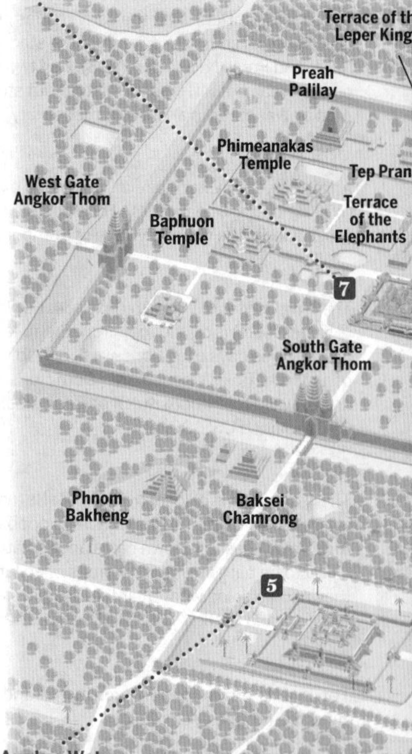

Angkor Wat
The world's largest religious building. Experience sunrise at the holiest of holies, then explore the beautiful bas-reliefs – devotion etched in stone.

CHRISTOPHER GROENHOUT / LPI ©

Angkor Thom

The last great capital of the Khmer empire conceals a wealth of temples and its epic proportions would have inspired and terrified in equal measure.

ANDERS BLOMQVIST / LPI ©

Preah Khan

A fusion temple dedicated to Buddha, Brahma, Shiva and Vishnu; the immense corridors are like an unending hall of mirrors.

ANDERS BLOMQVIST / LPI ©

Neak Poan

If Vegas ever adopts the Angkor theme, this will be the swimming pool, a petite tower set in a lake, surrounded by four smaller ponds.

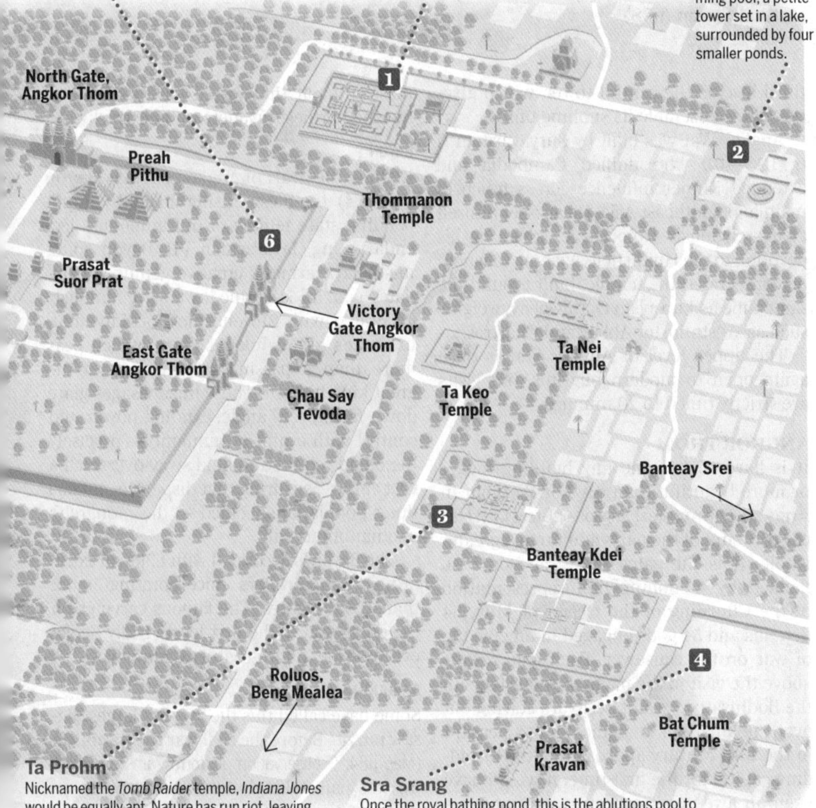

1
North Gate, Angkor Thom
2
Preah Pithu
Thommanon Temple
6
Prasat Suor Prat
Victory Gate Angkor Thom
East Gate Angkor Thom
Ta Nei Temple
Chau Say Tevoda
Ta Keo Temple
Banteay Srei
3
Banteay Kdei Temple
4
Roluos, Beng Mealea

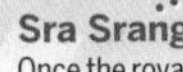

Bat Chum Temple
Prasat Kravan

Ta Prohm

Nicknamed the *Tomb Raider* temple, *Indiana Jones* would be equally apt. Nature has run riot, leaving iconic tree roots strangling the surviving stones.

Sra Srang

Once the royal bathing pond, this is the ablutions pool to beat all ablutions pools and makes a good stop for sunset.

ANDERS BLOMQVIST / LPI ©

ARIADNE VAN ZANDBERGEN / LPI ©

TOP ANGKOR EXPERIENCES

» See the sun rise over the holiest of holies, **Angkor Wat** (p93), the world's largest religious building

» Contemplate the serenity and splendour of the **Bayon** (p96), its 216 enigmatic faces staring out into the jungle

» Witness nature reclaiming the stones at the mysterious ruin of **Ta Prohm** (p97), the *Tomb Raider* temple

» Stare in wonder at the delicate carvings adorning **Banteay Srei** (p98), the finest seen at Angkor

» Trek deep into the jungle to discover the River of a Thousand Lingas at **Kbal Spean** (p98)

third level is the central tower, which gives the whole ensemble its sublime unity.

Angkor Wat was built by Suryavarman II (r 1113–40), who unified Cambodia and extended Khmer influence across much of mainland Southeast Asia. He also set himself apart religiously from earlier kings by his devotion to the Hindu deity Vishnu, to whom he consecrated the temple, built around the same time as European Gothic heavyweights such as Westminster Abbey and Chartres.

The upper level of Angkor Wat is once again open to modern pilgrims, but visits are strictly timed to 20 minutes.

ANGKOR THOM

It is hard to imagine any building bigger or more beautiful than Angkor Wat, but in **Angkor Thom** (Great Angkor, or Great City; Map p84) the sum of the parts add up to a greater whole. It is the gates that grab you first, flanked by a monumental representation of the Churning of the Ocean of Milk, 54 demons and 54 gods engaged in an epic tug of war on the causeway. Each gate towers above the visitor, the magnanimous faces of the Bodhisattva Avalokiteshvara staring out over the kingdom. Imagine being a peasant in the 13th century approaching the forbidding capital for the first time: it would have been an awe-inspiring yet unsettling experience to enter such a gateway and come face to face with the divine power of the god-kings.

The last great capital of the Khmer empire, Angkor Thom took monumental to a whole new level, set over 10 sq km. It was built in part as a reaction to the surprise sacking of Angkor by the Chams. Jayavarman VII (r 1181–1219) decided that his empire would never again be vulnerable at home. Beyond the formidable walls is a massive moat that would have stopped all but the hardiest invaders in their tracks.

BAYON

Right at the heart of Angkor Thom is **Bayon** (Map p84), the mesmerising if slightly mind-bending state temple of of Cambodia's legendary king, Jayavarman VII. Bayon epitomises Jayavarman's creative genius and inflated ego. Its 54 gothic towers are famously decorated with 216 enormous, coldly smiling **faces of Avalokiteshvara**, which bear more than a passing resemblance to the great king himself. These huge visages glare down from every angle, exuding power and control with a hint of humanity – precisely the blend required to hold sway over such a vast empire, ensuring that disparate and far-flung populations yielded to the monarch's magnanimous will.

The Bayon is decorated with 1.2km of extraordinary **bas-reliefs** incorporating more than 11,000 figures. The famous carvings on the outer wall of the first level vividly depict everyday life in 12th-century Cambodia.

BAPHUON

Some have called this the 'world's largest jigsaw puzzle'. Before the civil war the **Baphuon** (Map p84; ⏲observation platform 7am-3pm Mon-Fri) was painstakingly taken apart piece-by-piece by a team of archaeologists, but their meticulous records were destroyed during the Khmer Rouge madness. Now, after years of excruciating research, this temple is being restored. On the western side, the retaining wall of the second level was fashioned – apparently in the 15th or 16th century – into a reclining Buddha 60m in length.

TERRACE OF THE ELEPHANTS

The 350m-long **Terrace of the Elephants** (Map p84) – decorated with parading elephants towards both ends – was used as a giant viewing stand for public ceremonies and served as a base for the king's grand audience hall. As you stand here, try to imagine the pomp and grandeur of the Khmer empire at its height, with infantry, cavalry, horse-drawn chariots and, of course, elephants parading across the Central Square in a colourful procession, pennants and standards aloft.

TERRACE OF THE LEPER KING

This 7m-high **terrace** (Map p84), which once supported a pavilion made of lightweight materials, is topped by a (replica) statue once believed to be that of a leprous king. Researchers now believe it's Yama, the god of death, and that this site served as a royal crematorium.

The terrace's front retaining walls are decorated with at least five tiers of meticulously executed carvings of seated *apsaras* (celestial nymphs). At the base on the southern side, there is narrow access to a hidden terrace that was covered up (and thus protected from the elements) when the outer structure was built. The figures look as fresh as if they had been carved yesterday.

AROUND ANGKOR THOM

TA PROHM

If Angkor Wat and the Bayon are testimony to the genius of the ancient Khmers, the 12th-century Mahayana Buddhist temple of **Ta Prohm** (Map p84) reminds us equally of the awesome fecundity and power of the jungle. Looking much the way most Angkor monuments did when European explorers first set eyes upon them, this temple – built by Jayavarman VII from 1186 – is cloaked in dappled shadow, its crumbling towers and walls locked in the muscular embrace of centuries-old trees. Bas-reliefs on bulging walls are carpeted with moss and creeping plants, shrubs sprout from the roofs of monumental porches, and many of the corridors are impassable. Indiana Jones would feel right at home, and in fact Ta Prohm was used as a location for both *Tomb Raider* and *Two Brothers*.

BITTER RIVALRY

Much of Thailand's culture is linked to the Cambodian artisans, dancers, scholars and fighters with whom the Thais made off after they sacked Angkor in 1432. Have a peek at the bas-reliefs at Bayon and you'll see something that looks much like the 'Thai' kickboxing of today. The history of Angkor remains a seriously sensitive topic between the two cultures, fuelling a bitter rivalry that's lasted centuries.

PHNOM BAKHENG

The first of a succession of Angkor temples designed to represent mythical Mt Meru, this hill's main draw is the sunset view of Angkor Wat, although late afternoons here have turned into something of a circus, with hundreds of shutterbugs jockeying for space. Built by Yasovarman I (r 889–910), the **temple** (Map p84) has five tiers, with seven levels (including the base and the summit).

Phnom Bakheng is about 400m south of Angkor Thom. For information on elephant rides, see p132.

PREAH KHAN

One of the largest complexes at Angkor, **Preah Khan** (Sacred Sword; Map p84), constructed by Jayavarman VII, once housed

ON LOCATION WITH TOMB RAIDER

Several sequences for *Tomb Raider*, starring Angelina Jolie as Lara Croft, were shot around the temples of Angkor. The Cambodia shoot opened at Phnom Bakheng with Lara looking through binoculars for the mysterious temple. The baddies were already trying to break in through the East Gate of Angkor Thom by pulling down a giant polystyrene *apsara*. Reunited with her custom Landrover, Lara made a few laps around the Bayon before discovering a back way into the temple from Ta Prohm, where she plucked a sprig of jasmine and fell through into… Pinewood Studios. After battling a living statue and dodging Daniel Craig (aka 007) by diving off the waterfall at Phnom Kulen, she emerged in a floating market in front of Angkor Wat, as you do. She came ashore here before borrowing a mobile phone from a local monk and venturing in to the gallery of a thousand Buddhas, where she was healed by the abbot.

Nick Ray worked as Location Manager for Tomb Raider *in Cambodia*

FUSION TEMPLE

Preah Khan is a genuine fusion temple, the eastern entrance dedicated to Mahayana Buddhism with equal-sized doors, and the other cardinal directions dedicated to Shiva, Vishnu and Brahma with successively smaller doors, emphasising the unequal nature of Hinduism.

more than 1000 teachers and may have been a Buddhist university. The temple itself, a cruciform maze of vaulted corridors, fine carvings and lichen-clad stonework, is within a rectangular wall of around 700m by 800m. The southern corridor is a wonderfully atmospheric jumble of vines and stones, while near the eastern entrance stands a curious two-storey structure that would look more at home in Greece.

PREAH NEAK POAN

Another late-12th-century work of – no surprises here – Jayavarman VII, this petite **temple** (Map p84) has a large square pool surrounded by four smaller square pools, with a circular 'island' in the middle. Water once flowed into the four peripheral pools via four ornamental spouts in the form of an elephant's head, a horse's head, a lion's head and a human head.

ROLUOS TEMPLES

The monuments of Roluos, which served as the capital of Indravarman I (r 877–89), are among the earliest large, permanent temples built by the Khmers and mark the dawn of Khmer classical art. **Preah Ko**, dedicated to Shiva, has elaborate inscriptions in Sanskrit on the doorposts of each tower and some of the best surviving examples of Angkorian plasterwork. The city's central temple, **Bakong**, with its a five-tier central pyramid of sandstone, is a representation of Mt Meru.

Roluos is 13km east of Siem Reap along NH6 and can be easily combined with a visit to the stilted village of Kompong Pluk (p92).

FURTHER AFIELD

BANTEAY SREI

Considered by many to be the jewel in the crown of Angkorian art, **Banteay Srei** is cut from pinkish stone and includes some of the finest stone carving anywhere on earth. Begun in AD 967, it is one of the few temples around Angkor not to be commissioned by a king, but by a Brahman, perhaps a tutor to Jayavarman V.

Banteay Srei means 'Citadel of the Women' and it is said that it must have been built by women, as the elaborate carvings are too fine for the hand of a man.

Banteay Srei, 21km northeast of the Bayon and about 32km from Siem Reap, can be visited along with Kbal Spean and the Cambodia Landmine Museum (p83). Transport here will cost a little more than the prices quoted for the central temples of Angkor.

KBAL SPEAN

A spectacularly carved riverbed set deep in the jungle, **Kbal Spean** lies about 50km northeast of Siem Reap. More commonly referred to in English as the 'River of a Thousand Lingas', it's a 2km uphill walk to the carvings, which include phallic lingas and Hindu deities. From the carvings you can work your way back down to the waterfall to cool off. Carry plenty of water.

Kbal Spean was only 'discovered' in 1969, when EFEO ethnologist Jean Boulbet was shown the area by a local hermit; the area was soon off-limits due to the civil war, only becoming safe again in 1998.

At the nearby **Angkor Centre for Conservation of Biodiversity** (ACCB; www.accb-cambodia.org) trafficked animals are nursed back to health. Free tours generally begin at 1pm daily, except Sunday.

PHNOM KULEN

The most sacred mountain in Cambodia, the 487m **Phnom Kulen** is where Jayavarman II proclaimed himself a *devaraja* (god-king) in AD 802, giving birth to the Khmer empire. A popular place of pilgrimage during weekends and festivals, the views are spectacular. Attractions include a large waterfall, a reclining Buddha and riverbed carvings.

Phnom Kulen is 50km from Siem Reap and 15km from Banteay Srei. The private road charges a hefty US$20 toll per foreign visitor, but none of this goes towards preserving the site. It is possible to buy a cheaper entrance ticket to Phnom Kulen for US$12 from the City Angkor Hotel in Siem Reap.

BENG MEALEA

Built by Suryavarman II to the same floor plan as Angkor Wat, **Beng Mealea** (admission US$5) is Angkor's ultimate Indiana Jones experience. Nature has well and truly run riot here and jumbled stones lie like forgotten jewels swathed in lichen.

Beng Mealea is about 65km northeast of Siem Reap on a sealed toll road. It can be visited on the way to Koh Ker (p106).

NORTHWESTERN CAMBODIA

Offering highway accessibility and outback adventure in equal measure, northwestern Cambodia stretches from the Cardamom Mountains to the Dangkrek Mountains, with Tonlé Sap lake at its heart.

Battambang attracts the most visitors thanks to an alluring blend of mellowness, colonial-era architecture and excellent day tripping. Kompong Thom is also popular as gateway to the pre-Angkorian temples of Sambor Prei Kuk.

Northwestern Cambodia's remote plains and jungles conceal some of the country's most inspired temples, including spectacular Prasat Preah Vihear, declared a World Heritage Site in 2008, and Koh Ker, a rival capital to Angkor dating from the 10th century.

Battambang

053 / POP 140,000

The elegant riverside town of Battambang is home to Cambodia's best-preserved French-period architecture. The stunning boat trip from Siem Reap lures travellers here, but it's the remarkably chilled atmosphere that makes them linger. Battambang is an excellent base for exploring nearby temples (see p104) and villages that offer a real slice of rural Cambodia.

Sights

Colonial-Era Architecture NEIGHBOURHOOD

Much of Battambang's special charm lies in its early-20th-century French architecture. Some of the finest **colonial buildings** are along the waterfront (St 1), especially just south of **Psar Nat**, itself quite an impressive structure. The two-storey **Governor's Residence**, with its balconies and wooden shutters, is another handsome legacy of the early 20th century.

Battambang Museum MUSEUM

(St 1; admission US$1; 8-11am & 2-5pm Mon-Fri) This small museum displays Angkorian lintels and statuary from all over the province, including Phnom Banan.

Wats TEMPLES

A number of the monks at **Wat Phiphétaram**, **Wat Damrey Sar** and **Wat Kandal** speak English and are glad for a chance to practise; they're often around in the late afternoon.

Train Station TRAIN STATION

Here the time is always 8.02. Along the tracks just south of the station, you can explore a treasure trove of crumbling, French-era repair sheds, warehouses and rolling stock.

Activities

Sadly, Battambang's ingenious bamboo trains (*norry* or *nori*) are about to be run off the rails by a much-needed railway overhaul. The stuff of travel legend in Cambodia, the bamboo train was actually an ultralight bamboo frame powered by a 6HP gasoline engine and the whole contraption ran along the warped, French-era rail line.

WORTH A TRIP

BANTEAY CHHMAR

The temple complex of **Banteay Chhmar** (www.globalheritagefund.org; admission US$5) was constructed by Cambodia's most prolific builder, Jayavarman VII (r 1181–1219), on the site of a 9th-century temple. One of a handful of Angkorian sites to feature the towering heads of Avalokiteshvaras, with their enigmatic smiles, the 12th-century temple is also renowned for its intricate carvings.

A pioneering community-based **homestay project** (012 435660, cbtbanteaychhmar@yahoo.com; r US$7) makes it possible to stay in and around Banteay Chhmar. Rooms come with mosquito nets, fans that run when there's electricity (6pm to 10pm) and downstairs bathrooms. Bikes can be rented for US$1.50 a day.

Near the temple's eastern entrance, rustic **Banteay Chhmar Restaurant** (mains US$2-3) serves tasty Khmer food.

In Sisophon, share taxis to Banteay Chhmar (61km via a terrible road) leave from near Psar Thmei, on NH69 1km north of NH6. A moto from Sisophon to Banteay Chhmar should cost about US$12 return.

Battambang

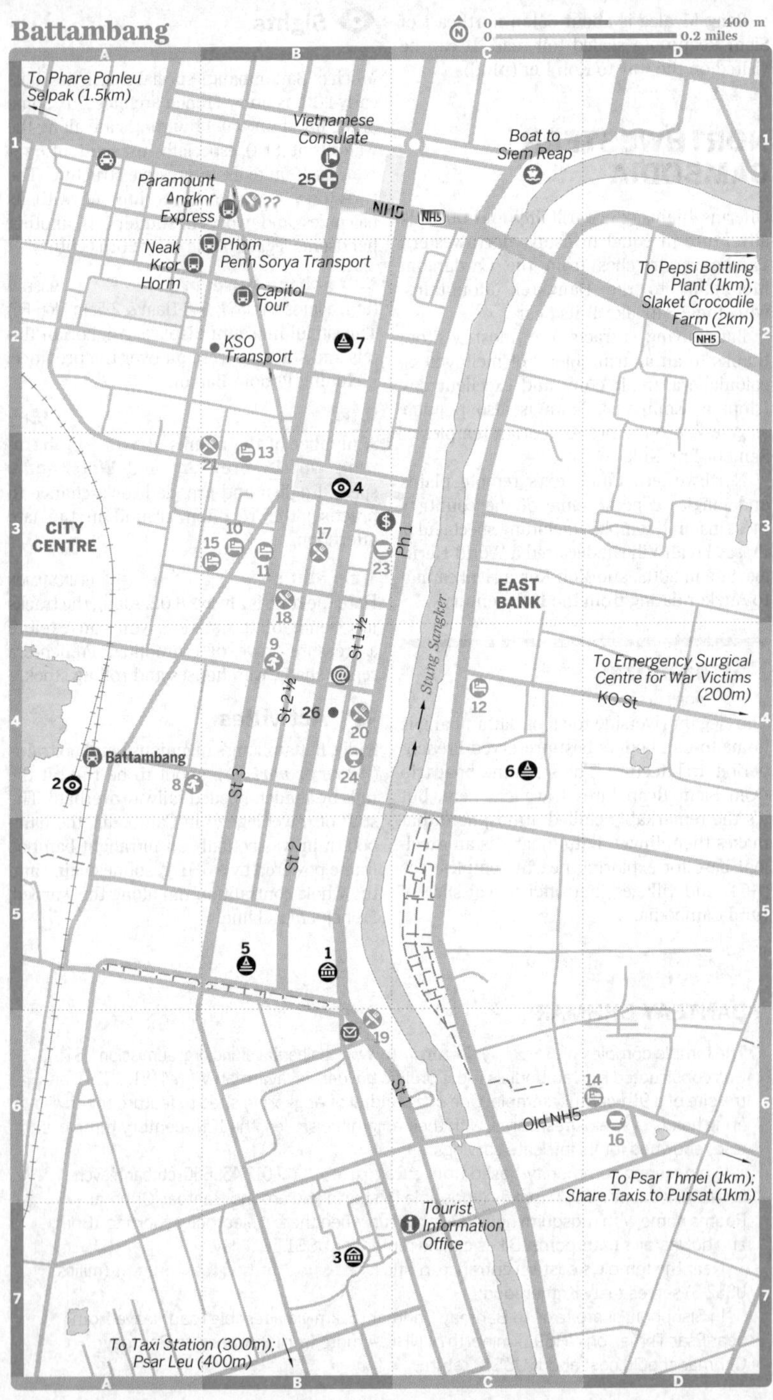

400 m
0.2 miles
To Phare Ponleu Selpak (1.5km)
Vietnamese Consulate
25
Boat to Siem Reap
Paramount Angkor Express
NH5
Neak Kror Horm
Phom Penh Sorya Transport
To Pepsi Bottling Plant (1km); Slaket Crocodile Farm (2km)
Capitol Tour
KSO Transport
7
21
13
4
CITY CENTRE
10
15
11
17
23
Ph 1
EAST BANK
18
St 1½
Stung Sangker
9
To Emergency Surgical Centre for War Victims (200m)
KO St
12
St 2½
26
20
24
Battambang
2
8
St 3
6
St 2
5
1
19
St 1
14
Old NH5
16
To Psar Thmei (1km); Share Taxis to Pursat (1km)
Tourist Information Office
3
To Taxi Station (300m); Psar Leu (400m)

FREE **Heritage Walking Tour** WALKING TOUR
(http://battambang-heritage.org/downloads.htm) Phnom Penh–based **KA Architecture Tours** (www.ka-tours.org) are highly regarded for their specialist tours in and around the capital and have collaborated with Battambang Municipality to create two heritage walks in the historic centre of Battambang. There are two downloadable PDFs including a colour map and numbered highlights.

Soksabike CYCLING
(☎012 542019; www.soksabike; ⏰7.30am departures daily) Based at 11/2 Street Cafe, Soksabike is a social enterprise aiming to connect visitors with the Cambodian countryside and its people. The half-day trip costs US$18 per person, covering about 30km, and the price includes a fresh coconut, seasonal fruits and a shot of rice wine.

Green Orange Kayaks KAYAKING
(☎077 204121; feda@online.com.kh; Ksach Poy Village; ⏰7am-5pm Mon-Fri) One- to three-person kayaks can be rented from Green Orange Kayaks, run by an NGO (www.fedacambodia.org) that offers free English classes. The half-day trip costs US$12 per person (including lifejackets); an optional guide is US$3.

PHARE PONLEU SELPAK CIRCUS SCHOOL

Roll up, roll up, the circus is now in town every Monday and Thursday. **Phare Ponleu Selpak** (☎952424; www.phareps.org) is a multi-arts centre for disadvantaged children that hosts internationally acclaimed circus (*cirque nouveau*) performances (admission US$8), often preceded by dinner (US$6; book a day ahead). Time your Battambang trip to catch the spectacle. To get here from the Vishnu Roundabout on NH5, head west for 900m and then turn right (north) and continue another 600m.

Seeing Hands Massage MASSAGE
(☎092 379903; St 3; per hr US$6; ⏰7am-10pm) Trained blind masseurs and masseuses offer soothing work-overs.

Courses

Australian Centres for Development LANGUAGE
(☎952370; acd@online.com.kh) Near the old train station. Offers well-regarded Khmer language classes.

Battambang

Sights
- 1 Battambang Museum B5
- 2 French-Era Train Repair Sheds A4
- 3 Governor's Residence B7
- 4 Psar Nat B3
- 5 Wat Damrey Sar B5
- 6 Wat Kandal C4
- 7 Wat Phiphétaram B2

Activities, Courses & Tours
- 8 Australian Centres for Development A4
- 9 Seeing Hands Massage B4
- Smokin' Pot Cooking Classes .... (see 20)
- Soksabike .... (see 23)

Sleeping
- 10 Chhaya Apartments B3
- 11 Chhaya Hotel B3
- 12 Golden Land Hotel C4
- 13 Royal Hotel B3
- 14 Spring Park Hotel D6
- 15 Tomato Guesthouse B3

Eating
- 16 Bamboo Train Cafe D6
- 17 Fresh Eats Café B3
- 18 Gecko Café B3
- 19 Night Market B6
- 20 Smokin' Pot B4
- 21 Sunrise Coffee House B3
- 22 Vegetarian Foods Restaurant B1

Drinking
- 23 1½ Street Cafe B3
- 24 Cafe Eden B4

Information
- 25 Polyclinique Visal Sokh B1
- 26 Smiling Sky Bookshop B4

Transport
- Gecko Moto .... (see 18)

Sleeping

TOP CHOICE **Chhaya Hotel & Apartments** HOTEL $
(☎952170; www.chhayahotel.com; 118 St 3; dm US$1, r US$3-12, apartments US$15-25; ❄@📶) One of the longest-running budget hotels in Battambang, it has the cheapest beds in town if you don't mind a dorm. The new serviced apartments are incredible value, offering tasteful decoration, acres of space and a kitchen for self-catering.

Golden Land Hotel HOTEL $
(Sovanphoom Hotel; ☎6903790; sovanphoom@yahoo.com; River Rd; d US$10-15; ❄@📶) Still looking brand spanking new during our visit, this riverfront pad offers excellent value for money. Be a VIP for the night and enjoy a swish bathroom.

Royal Hotel HOTEL $
(☎016 912034; www.asrhotel.com.kh; r with fan/air-con from US$8/10; ❄@📶) Deservedly popular with independent travellers, the 45-room Royal is clean, friendly and very central.

Tomato Guesthouse GUESTHOUSE $
(☎6907374; r from US$3) A new budget crash-pad with very few frills but the odd thrill. The friendly owners have opened a rooftop restaurant to relax after dark.

Spring Park Hotel HOTEL $
(☎730999; spparkhotel@yahoo.com; Old NH5; r US$6-35; ❄@📶) This place keeps on improving and now offers 78 rooms running from basic fan jobs through to deluxe minisuites.

Eating

Cheap dining is available in and around Psar Nat. There's a riverside **night market** (St 1; ⏲approx 3pm-midnight) opposite the Battambang Museum.

Fresh Eats Café INTERNATIONAL $
(St 2½; mains US$1.50-3; ⏲6am-9pm; 📶) Run by an NGO that helps children whose families have been affected by HIV/AIDS, this little place serves cheap, tasty food, including Western breakfasts, bagels, fried spring rolls and Khmer curry.

Smokin' Pot CAMBODIAN $
(☎012 821400; vannacksmokinpot@yahoo.com; mains US$2-3.50; ⏲7am-11pm) This cheery, laid-back restaurant serves good Khmer, Thai and Western food. Offers cooking classes (US$8) every morning.

Bamboo Train Cafe INTERNATIONAL $
(Old NH5; mains 4000-24,000r; ⏲7am-10pm) The affable owner ensures this place is always popular. As well as an eclectic menu with pizzas, pastas, curries and a delicious tofu *amoc*, there is a pool table and regular movie screenings.

Sunrise Coffee House INTERNATIONAL $
(mains 8000r-14,000r; ⏲6.30am-8pm Mon-Sat; 📶) Better than Starbucks, this is a great place for coffee, fresh-baked banana bread, California-style wraps, home-made tortillas, veggie or chicken quesadillas, and all-day breakfasts.

Gecko Café INTERNATIONAL $$
(www.geckocafecambodia.com; St 3; mains US$2.75-5; ⏲8am-1pm; 📶) This is Battambang's answer to the FCC thanks to the glorious setting in an old French shophouse. Mellow and atmospheric, it's a good place for some international bites or an evening drink.

Vegetarian Foods Restaurant VEGETARIAN $
(mains 1500-3000r; ⏲6am-11am; 🖉) Serves some of the most delicious vegetarian dishes in Cambodia, including rice soup and home-made soy milk. Open only for breakfast and brunch.

Drinking

Riverside Balcony Bar BAR
(cnr St 1 & NH57; mains US$3.50-7.50; ⏲4pm-midnight Tue-Sun) Set in a gorgeous wooden house high above the riverfront, this is Battambang's original bar and still the best spot in town. On the riverfront, about 500m south of Battambang Museum.

Cafe Eden BAR
(85 St 1; www.cafeedencambodia.com; ⏲8am-9pm, closed Tue) Located in an old colonial block on the riverfront, this is a social enterprise offering a relaxed space for an afternoon drink, great food and an original boutique out the back.

1½ Street Cafe CAFE
(1 St 1½; www.streetoneandahalf.com; ⏲7am-7pm) The home base of Soksabike, this tiny cafe offers a welcome refuge from the backstreets of Battambang. Choose from global coffees, infused teas and some homemade cakes.

Shopping

Smiling Sky Bookshop BOOKS
(113 St 2; ⏲8am-7.30pm) Used books in English, French and German.

Information

The focal point of Battambang's city centre, on the west bank of Stung Sangker, is Psar Nat (Meeting Market). There are lots of restaurants and bars dotting the old French-era streets between the riverfront and St 3. Look out for a copy of the free *Hello Battambang* listings magazine.

ANZ Royal (St 1) One of several banks facing Psar Nat. Has an ATM.

Emergency Surgical Centre for War Victims (☎370065; ⏲24hr for emergencies) This 106-bed surgical hospital *cannot* help with tropical diseases or routine illness, but may be able to save your life if you need emergency surgery.

KCT Internet Café (⏲7am to 9pm) Internet access.

Polyclinique Visal Sokh (☎952401; NH5; ⏲24hr) For minor medical problems.

Tourist Information Office (☎730217; www.battambang-town.gov.kh; St 1; ⏲7.30am-5.30pm) Brochures and maps for Battambang.

Vietnamese Consulate (☎952894; ⏲8-11am & 2-4pm Mon-Fri) Issues Vietnam visas in double-quick time.

Getting There & Away

Boat

The river boat to Siem Reap (US$20, five to nine or more hours; departure at 7am) squeezes through narrow waterways and passes by protected wetlands. It's a bird-watcher's paradise. It's operated on alternate days by **Angkor Express** (☎012 601287) and **Chann Na** (☎012 354344). In the dry season, passengers have to be driven to a navigable section of the river. Try to sit as far from the noisy motor as possible. These fast boats are not so popular with local communities along the way, as the wake has caused small boats to capsize and fishing nets are regularly snagged.

Bus

Battambang does not have a central bus station. Bus companies have offices on or near NH5. All companies serve Phnom Penh (293km, US$5 to US$8, five hours), Pursat (US$2.50, two hours), Sisophon (US$2 to US$3, one hour) and Poipet (US$3 to US$4, three hours). Capitol and Neak Kror Horm have buses to Bangkok (US$13 to US$15) and Siem Reap (US$5); Paramount Angkor Express also goes to Siem Reap (US$5). Phnom Penh Sorya has a service to Kompong Cham (US$9).

Bus companies include the following:

Capitol Tour (☎953040)

KSO Transport (☎012 320737)

Neak Kror Horm (☎953838)

Paramount Angkor Express (☎092 575572)

Phnom Penh Sorya (☎092 181804)

Ponleu Angkor Khmer (☎092 517792)

Rith Mony (☎012 823885)

Taxi

At the **taxi station** (NH5), share taxis to Poipet (20,000r), Sisophon (15,000r) and Siem Reap (30,000r) leave from the north side while taxis to Pursat (15,000r) and Phnom Penh (40,000r) leave from the southeast corner. Budget hotels can assist with arranging a private chartered taxi if you crave more space.

Getting Around

A moto ride in town costs 2000r to 3000r, plus a bit more at night. Hiring a moto driver who

GETTING TO THAILAND: PSAR PRUHM TO BAN PAKARD

Getting to the border This out-of-the-way crossing is 102km southwest of Battambang and 22km northwest of the town of Pailin. In Battambang, taxis leave from the west side of **Psar Leu**, at the southern end of St 3. A share taxi to Pailin town (two hours) costs 25,000r. An onward share taxi from Pailin to the frontier costs 10,000r. A private taxi from Battambang direct to the border (US$50) offers the option of stopping off at Phnom Sampeau.

At the border This border is open from 7am to 5pm. Petty overcharging is possible on the Cambodian side, particularly for visas, as they often request payment at inflated Thai baht prices. No visa is required for Thailand for most nationalities. Cambodian visas are available on arrival.

Moving on On the Thai side, you can avoid being overcharged for transport to Chanthaburi (150B by minibus; one hour) by hopping on a moto (50B) to the nearby sŏrngtăaou (pick-up) station. From Chanthaburi's bus station there are buses to Bangkok.

See p729 for information on crossing the border in the other direction.

WORTH A TRIP

KOMPONG LUONG

Kompong Luong has all the amenities you'd expect to find in a large fishing village – cafes, mobile-phone shops, chicken coops, ice-making factories, a pagoda, a church – except that here everything floats. The result is an ethnic-Vietnamese Venice without the dry land. In the dry season, when water levels drop and the Tonlé Sap shrinks, the entire aquapolis is towed, boat by boat, a few kilometres north. **Homestays** (US$6 per night) are available with local families and meals are available for US$1 to US$2 per person.

Kompong Luong is between 39km and 44km east of Pursat, depending on the time of year. From Pursat, transport options include moto (US$7 return) and private taxi (about US$30 return). At the dock, the official tourist rate to charter a four-passenger wooden motorboat around Kompong Luong is US$7 per hour for one to three passengers (US$10 for four to five). If there are enough takers for the large boat, it costs just US$2 per person.

Dozens of buses pass through Pursat daily, shuttling between Phnom Penh (US$5, three hours) and Battambang (10,000r, 1½ hours).

speaks English or French costs US$6 to US$8 for a half-day in and around town and US$12 for an all-day trip out of the city.

Gecko Moto (☎089 924260; www.geckocafecambodia.com; St 3; ⊙8am-7pm) rents out 100cc/250cc motorbikes for US$6/12 a day. The Chhaya Hotel charges US$5/7 a day for an old/new motorbike, while the Royal Hotel charges US$8.

Bicycles (US$2 a day at Gecko Moto or the Royal Hotel) are a great way to get around.

Around Battambang

Before you head out to see Battambang's surrounds, try to link up with an English-speaking moto driver, as it really adds to the experience. Admission to Phnom Sampeau, Phnom Banan and Wat Ek Phnom is US$2. If you purchase a ticket at any of the three locations, it's valid all day at the other two. Return travel by moto/*remorque* costs US$7/10 to Phnom Sampeau, US$8/12 to Phnom Banan and US$6/10 to Wat Ek Phnom; a full-day trip to several sights is about US$12/20.

PHNOM SAMPEAU

At the summit of this fabled limestone outcrop, 12km southwest of Battambang (towards Pailin), a complex of **temples** affords gorgeous views. Some of the macaques that live here, dining on bananas left as offerings, are pretty cantankerous.

Between the summit and the mobile-phone antenna, a deep canyon descends steeply through a natural arch to a 'lost world' of stalactites, creeping vines and bats. Nearby, two government artillery pieces still point west towards **Phnom Krapeu** (Crocodile Mountain), a one-time Khmer Rouge stronghold.

About halfway up the hill, a turn-off leads 250m up to the **Killing Caves of Phnom Sampeau**. An enchanted staircase, flanked by greenery, leads into a cavern where a golden reclining Buddha lies peacefully next to a glass-walled memorial filled with the bones and skulls of some of the people bludgeoned to death by Khmer Rouge cadres, before being thrown through the overhead skylight.

PHNOM BANAN

Exactly 358 stone steps lead up a shaded slope to 11th-century **Wat Banan**, 28km south of Battambang, whose five towers are reminiscent of the layout of Angkor Wat. The views are well worth the climb. From the temple, a narrow stone staircase leads south down the hill to three caves, two of which are not mined and can thus be visited with a torch-equipped local guide.

WAT EK PHNOM

This atmospheric, partly collapsed, 11th-century **temple** is 11km north of Battambang. A lintel showing the Churning of the Ocean of Milk can be seen above the east entrance to the central temple, whose upper flanks hold some fine bas-reliefs. This is a great place for a shady picnic.

On the way from Battambang by bicycle or moto, it's possible to visit a 1960s **Pepsi bottling plant** (1.2km north of Battambang's ferry landing), frozen in time since 1975 and, 1km further out, the **Slaket crocodile farm**.

Preah Vihear Province

Bordering Thailand and Laos to the north, vast Preah Vihear Province is home to several of Cambodia's most impressive legacies of the Angkorian era, including stunning Prasat Preah Vihear, high atop the Dangkrek escarpment. Much of this province was heavily forested and extremely remote, but it is now on the frontline of development thanks to the recent border conflict with Thailand.

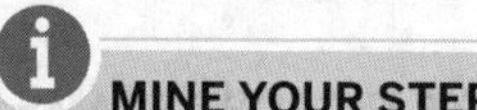

MINE YOUR STEP

Stick to well-marked paths, as the Khmer Rouge laid huge numbers of landmines around Prasat Preah Vihear as late as 1998.

TBENG MEANCHEY

☎064 / POP 22,000

Tbeng Meanchey, often referred to by locals as Preah Vihear (not to be confused with Prasat Preah Vihear), is sprawling and dusty-red (or muddy-red, depending on the season). The town makes a good staging post for the long trip to Prasat Preah Vihear, 110km north.

The centre of town is around the taxi park and the market. Acleda Bank, a block south of the market, has an ATM.

Prom Tep Guesthouse (☎012 964645; Koh Ker St; r with fan/air-con from US$6/16; ❄@) is large enough to be a hotel and offers 25 spacious rooms, all with cable TV and Western toilets.

The 10-room **Heng Heng Guesthouse** (☎012 900992; NH64; r with fan/air-con US$8/16; ❄), situated one block west and one block south of the taxi park, has the nicest rooms in town.

Dara Raksmey Restaurant (Mlou Prey St; mains 8000-20,000r; ⏲6.30am-9pm) is Tbeng Meanchey's fanciest eatery, with mirror-clad columns, massive wooden tables and Khmer favourites.

Getting There & Away

For details on public transport to/from Kompong Thom, 157km to the south via the execrable NH64, see p107. For details on transport to Prasat Preah Vihear, 110km to the north, see p106.

PRASAT PREAH VIHEAR

The most dramatically situated of all the Angkorian monuments, 800m-long **Prasat Preah Vihear** (elevation 625m; www.preahvihearauthority.org; admission free or US$5) consists of a series of four cruciform *gopura* (sanctuaries) decorated with exquisite carvings, including some striking lintels). Starting at the monumental stairway, a walk south takes you to the **Gopura of the Third Level**, with its early rendition of the Churning of the Ocean of Milk, and finally, perched at the edge of the cliff, the **Central Sanctuary**. The stupendous views of Cambodia's northern plains make this a fantastic spot for a picnic.

Before the armed stand-off between Thailand and Cambodia, visitors could visit Prasat Preah Vihear from Thailand, crossing into Cambodia with a special no-visa day pass (US$10). However, the border has now been closed since 2008, and the only way to visit is from the Cambodian side. Check on the latest situation in Phnom Penh, Siem Reap, Tbeng Meanchey or Sra Em before attempting to visit the temple.

The village of Kor Muy, at the base of the hill, was evacuated during the on-and-off fighting, so the nearest accommodation is in Sra Em, 27km away. Guesthouses are rudi-

GETTING TO THAILAND: POIPET TO ARANYA PRATHET

Getting to the border This is by far Cambodia's most popular land crossing with Thailand. There are regular buses from Siem Reap (US$5, four hours) and Battambang (US$4, three hours) or it is possible to charter a share taxi from either city to the Poipet border. Despite the claims in Siem Reap, there are no through buses to Bangkok and all travellers have to change vehicles at the border.

At the border From the roundabout at the western terminus of NH5, go through **passport control** (⏲7am-10pm), walk through the casino zone and cross the Friendship Bridge. Petty overcharging is possible on the Cambodian side, particularly for visas, as they often request payment at inflated Thai baht prices. No visa is required for Thailand for most nationalities. Cambodian visas are available on arrival.

Moving on On the Thai side you can catch a túk-túk (60B) for the 6km ride to Aranya Prathet, where buses can get you into Bangkok in about four hours. You can also catch the train to Hualamphong station in Bangkok (six hours). We've heard repeated reports of fake bus tickets being sold at the border.

See p669 for information on crossing this border in the other direction.

POIPET TRANSPORT SCAMS

Long the armpit of Cambodia, notorious for its squalor and sleaze, Poipet is Cambodia's Wild West, renowned for rip-offs and scams. Fear not, the rest of Cambodia does not carry on like this. Poipet is 48km west of Sisophon and 153km west of Siem Reap.

The moment you enter Cambodia at Poipet, whether you know it or not, you are the duly purchased client of a monopoly that has paid for the exclusive right to provide you with onward land transport.

Poipet now has two bus stations. The **Poipet Tourist Passenger International Terminal**, situated 9km east of town in the middle of nowhere, and the **International Tourist Terminal**, 1.5km east of the tourist zone. Posted fares at both these places are higher than the prices locals pay by up to 250%.

As you exit the immigration police office (where passports are stamped), fencing herds you into the 'Free Shuttle Bus Station', departure point for **OSP buses** (⏲7am-6pm) to the bus station. OSP's job is straightforward: to operate the bus terminals and make sure tourists get there.

Transport out of Poipet is orchestrated by three 'associations' that work out of the bus station on a rotational basis: each handles all buses and taxis for tourists on every third day. All charge the same fares, offering buses/four-passenger share taxis to Sisophon (US$5/5), Siem Reap (US$9/12), Battambang (US$10/10) and Phnom Penh (US$15/25).

For the cash-strapped traveller, the obvious solution is to find a taxi the way Cambodians do. The problem is that association enforcers, with police backing, often intervene to prevent independent taxi drivers from accepting foreign tourists.

If you can dodge the transport associations, there are some independent bus companies based in Poipet, including **Capitol Tour** (☎967350), **Phnom Penh Sorya** (☎092 181802) and **GST** (☎012 727771). Destinations include Sisophon (US$2 to US$3, 40 minutes), Siem Reap (US$5, 2½ hours to four hours), Battambang (US$3.75, two hours) and Phnom Penh (US$7.50, seven hours). Most departures are between 6.15am and 10.30am. Several companies, including Capitol, offer mid-afternoon services to Bangkok (300B).

Share taxis are available about 1.3km east of the roundabout if you can avoid the bus station associations. Destinations include Sisophon (100B, 40 minutes), Siem Reap (250B, three hours), Battambang (US$5 to 200B, two hours) and Phnom Penh (500B).

mentary, to say the least. The best of a bad bunch is **Tuol Monysophon Guesthouse** (☎099 620757; r without/with private bathroom US$7.50/10). It has 25 rooms with mosquito nets and wood-plank floors.

Pkay Prek Restaurant (mains 4000-15,000r; ⏲6am-10pm) serves delicious *phnom pleung* (hill of fire; $3.75), which you BBQ yourself.

Getting There & Away

Visiting Prasat Preah Vihear from the Cambodian side is much easier as the road has been fully sealed to ensure rapid access for Cambodian soldiers travelling to the border area.

Share taxis now link Sra Em with Siem Reap (30,000r, three hours), Anlong Veng (20,000r, two hours) and Tbeng Meanchey (25,000r, two hours).

For travel from Sra Em to Koh Muy (22km), a share taxi costs 10,000r per person while a moto is about 15,000r. From there, the return trip up to the temple (5km each way), past sandbagged machine-gun positions, costs US$5 by moto or US$25 by pick-up truck.

KOH KER

Abandoned to the forests of the north, **Koh Ker** (admission US$10), capital of the Khmer empire from AD 928 to AD 944, was long one of Cambodia's most inaccessible temple complexes. However, this has now changed thanks to a toll road from Dam Dek (via Beng Mealea) that puts Koh Ker within day-trip distance of Siem Reap.

Most visitors start at **Prasat Krahom** (Red Temple), the stone archways and galleries of which lean hither and thither; impressive stone carvings grace lintels, doorposts and slender window columns.

The principal monument is Mayan-looking **Prasat Thom** (Prasat Kompeng), a 55m-wide, 40m-high sandstone-faced pyramid whose seven tiers offer spectacular views across the forest. At press time, the upper level was closed for safety reasons.

Some of the largest Shiva *linga* (phallic symbols) in Cambodia can be seen inside four temples about 1km northeast of Prasat Thom.

In the quiet village of Srayong, 2km south of the toll plaza, the family-run **Ponloeu Preah Chan Guesthouse** (☎012 489058; r US$5) has 12 small rooms, only one of which has its own plumbing.

Koh Ker is 127km northeast of Siem Reap (2½ hours by car) and 72km west of Tbeng Meanchey (two hours). From Siem Reap, hiring a private car for a day trip to Koh Ker costs about US$90. From Tbeng Meanchey, a private taxi costs US$70 return, a moto about US$15 or so.

KOMPONG THOM

☎062 / POP 66,000

A bustling commercial centre, Kompong Thom is situated on NH6 midway between Phnom Penh and Siem Reap.

Sleeping & Eating

Arunras Hotel HOTEL $
(☎961294; 46 Sereipheap Blvd; r with fan/air-con US$6/15; ❄) Dominating the accommodation scene in Kompong Thom, this seven-storey corner establishment has 58 smart, good-value rooms, plus a very popular restaurant downstairs.

American Restaurant INTERNATIONAL $
(Prachea Thepatay St; mains US$3-7.50; ⏰7am-9pm; @) This outpost of culinary Americana specialises in thin-crust Neapolitan pizzas, spaghetti, sandwiches, burgers and home-made ice cream, as well as Khmer dishes.

Psar Kompong Thom Night Market CAMBODIAN $
(NH6; mains 2000-4000r; ⏰4pm-2am) Sit on a plastic chair at a neon-lit table and dig into chicken rice soup, chicken curry noodles, Khmer-style baguettes or a *tukalok* (fruit shake).

Information

Acleda Bank (NH6) Just north of the bridge. Has an ATM.

Internet pharmacy (NH6; per hr 4000r; ⏰6.30am-7pm) Internet access, one block north of the market.

Getting There & Around

Kompong Thom is on NH6, 165km north of Phnom Penh and 150km southeast of Siem Reap.

Dozens of buses on the Phnom Penh–Siem Reap (both US$5) route pass through Kompong Thom and can easily be flagged down near the Arunras Hotel. Share taxis, which leave from the taxi park (one block east of the Arunras Hotel), are faster and cost US$5 to either Phnom Penh (three hours), Siem Reap (two hours) or Kompong Cham (two hours); minibuses cost just 15,000r.

Heading north to Tbeng Meanchey (often referred to as Preah Vihear), pick-up trucks (20,000/15,000r inside/on the back, three to four hours) are the most common form of transport, although when NH64 is in decent condition share taxis also do the run.

Moto drivers can be found across from the Arunras Hotel on NH6. Count on paying about US$8 to US$10 per day.

THE FIGHT FOR PRASAT PREAH VIHEAR

For generations, Prasat Preah Vihear (Khao Phra Wiharn to the Thais) has been a source of tension between Cambodia and Thailand. This area was ruled by Thailand for several centuries but was returned to Cambodia during the French protectorate, under the treaty of 1907. In 1959 the Thai military seized the temple from Cambodia and then-Prime Minister Sihanouk took the dispute to the International Court of Justice in the Hague, gaining worldwide recognition of Cambodian sovereignty in a 1962 ruling.

Prasat Preah Vihear hit the headlines again in May 1998 because the Khmer Rouge regrouped here after the fall of Anlong Veng and staged a last stand that soon turned into a final surrender. The temple was heavily mined during these final battles and de-mining was ongoing up until the outbreak of the conflict with Thailand.

In July 2008 Prasat Preah Vihear was declared Cambodia's second Unesco World Heritage Site. The Thai government, which claims 4.6 sq km of territory right around the temple (some Thai nationalists even claim the temple itself), initially supported the bid, but the temple soon became a pawn in Thailand's chaotic domestic politics. In 2011 exchanges heated up once more and long-range shells were fired into civilian territory by both sides, including the controversial use of cluster munitions by the Thai army.

In July 2011, the International Court of Justice ruled that both sides should withdraw troops from the area to establish a demilitarised zone. It is to be hoped that with a pro-Thaksin (therefore possibly Hun Sen-friendly) government in Bangkok, the border dispute may finally come to an end.

Bicycles can be rented at **Piseth Bike Rental** (St 103; per day US$3; ⏲6am-5pm), a block north of the bridge.

AROUND KOMPONG THOM

SAMBOR PREI KUK

Cambodia's most impressive group of pre-Angkorian monuments, **Sambor Prei Kuk** (admission US$3) encompasses more than 100 brick temples scattered through the forest. Originally called Isanapura, it served as the capital of Chenla during the reign of the early-7th-century King Isanavarman.

Forested and shady, Sambor Prei Kuk has a serene and soothing atmosphere. The main temple area consists of three complexes, each enclosed by the remains of two concentric walls. The principal group, **Prasat Sambor**, is dedicated to Gambhireshvara, one of Shiva's many incarnations (the other groups are dedicated to Shiva himself). **Prasat Yeay Peau** (Prasat Yeai Poeun) feels lost in the forest, its eastern gateway both held up and torn asunder by an ancient tree.

Prasat Tao (Lion Temple), the largest of the Sambor Prei Kuk complexes, boasts excellent examples of Chenla carving in the form of two large, elaborately coiffed stone lions.

Just past the ticket booth, the **Isanborei Crafts Shop** sells a worthwhile English brochure (2000r) and high-quality craft items. Nearby are several **small eateries** offering a very basic selection of Khmer dishes. There are lots of children selling scarves around the complex, but there is no hard sell and they really want to practise their English.

From Kompong Thom, a day trip out here will cost about US$10.

SOUTH COAST

Cambodia's south coast is an alluring mix of clear blue water, castaway islands, pristine mangrove forests, time-worn colonial towns and jungle-clad mountains, where tigers and elephants lurk. Adventurers will find this region of Cambodia just as rewarding as sunseekers.

Krong Koh Kong

☎035 / POP 35,000

Once Cambodia's Wild West, its frontier economy dominated by smuggling, prostitution and gambling, Krong Koh Kong is striding towards respectability as ecotourists scare the sleaze away. The town serves as the gateway to the Koh Kong Conservation Corridor (p110).

Sights & Activities

Krong Koh Kong's main draw is for those seeking adventure in and around the Cardamom Mountains and the Koh Kong Conservation Corridor.

Peam Krasaop Wildlife Sanctuary MANGROVES

Anchored to alluvial islands – some no larger than a house – this 260-sq-km sanctuary's millions of magnificent mangroves protect the coast from erosion, serve as a vital breeding and feeding ground for fish, shrimp and shellfish, and provide a home to myriad birds (see www.ramsar.org).

To get a feel for the delicate mangrove ecosystem – and to understand how mangrove roots can stop a tsunami dead in its tracks – head to the 600m-long concrete **mangrove walk** (admission 5000r; ⏲6.30am-6pm), which wends its way above the briny waters to a 15m observation tower. The walk begins at the sanctuary entrance, about 5.5km south-east of the city centre. A moto/*remorque* costs US$5/10 return.

Tours

Boat tours are an excellent way to view Krong Koh Kong's many coastal attractions. If you speak some Khmer, you can try hiring open-top fibreglass outboards at the boat dock (cnr Sts 1 & 9), but it's easier and not much more expensive to take an organised tour. Most guesthouses can arrange these. Popular destinations include Koh Kong Island via Peam Krasaop Wildlife Sanctuary (full-day per person including lunch US$25), and Koh Por Waterfall (four-/eight-person speed boat US$45/60). There's a good chance of spotting endangered Irrawaddy dolphins early in the morning en route to Koh Kong Island. Bring sunscreen, a hat and plenty of bottled water.

Recommended operators for boat and other tours:

Koh Kong Eco Tour BOAT TOURS

(☎012 707719; oasisresort@netkhmer.com; St 3) Rithy's excursions include boat tours, birdwatching and guided mountain-biking odysseys (full-day per person incl food US$30).

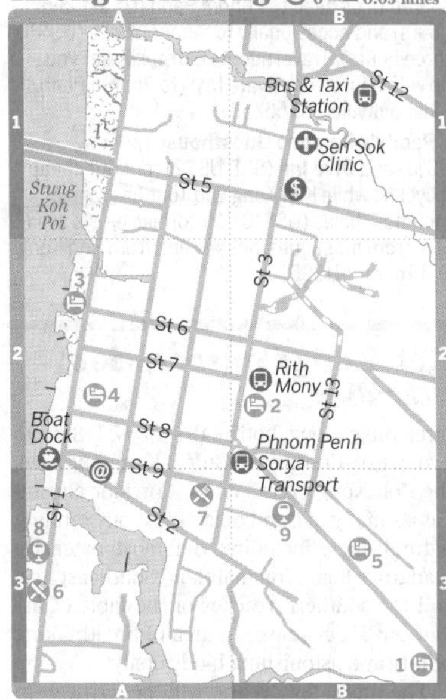

Krong Koh Kong

Blue Moon Guesthouse BOAT TOURS
(☎012 575741; bluemoonkohkong@yahoo.com) Mr Neat, a former park ranger, offers a range of boat trips (dry season only) and other tours.

Sleeping

Some places pay moto drivers a commission, leading to a whole lot of shenanigans.

Paddy's Bamboo Guesthouse GUESTHOUSE $
(☎015 533223; ppkohkong@gmail.com; dm US$2; r US$4-6;) Paddy's targets backpackers with a dormitory, basic rooms, a balcony for chillin', tours and a pool table. Shoot for the wood-floored rooms with shared bathrooms upstairs.

Koh Kong City Hotel HOTEL $$
(☎936777; http://kkcthotel.netkhmer.com; St 1; d US$15-20;) Ludicrous value for what you get: huge bathroom, two double beds, 50 TV channels, full complement of toiletries, free H2O and – in the US$20 rooms – glorious river views.

Dugout Hotel GUESTHOUSE $
(☎936220; thedugouthotel@yahoo.com; St 3; r with fan/air-con US$10/14;) Smack in the centre of town, five of the rooms here are arrayed around a small pool.

Koh Kong Guesthouse GUESTHOUSE $
(☎015 522005; St 1; d without/with bathroom US$5/6;) This great budget choice has woody rooms sharing a bathroom upstairs off an appealing common area with river views and floor pillows.

Blue Moon Guesthouse GUESTHOUSE $
(☎012 575741; bluemoonkohkong@yahoo.com; r with fan/air-con US$6/10;) Nine neat, clean rooms with spiffy furnishings and hot water line a long, narrow courtyard.

Eating & Drinking

The best cheap food stalls are in the south-east corner of Psar Leu, the main market. Riverfront food carts sell noodles and cans of beer for 2000r to 3000r.

Le Phnom CAMBODIAN $
(St1; meals US$2-4; 9am-10pm) *Banh chhayo* – meat, herbs and other goodies wrapped inside a pancake wrapped inside a lettuce leaf and hand-dipped in sweet sauce – is the speciality at this authentic Khmer eatery.

Café Laurent INTERNATIONAL $$
(St 1; mains US$4-7; 7am-midnight;) This chic, French-style restaurant has an old Citroën Deux Chevaux out front and refined Western and Khmer cuisine inside. Throw in seating in over-water pavilions and it's Krong Koh Kong's top restaurant.

Paddy's Bamboo Pub PUB $
(mains US$2-3) Paddy's angles for the backpacker market with US$1 beers and affordable Khmer food.

Aqua Sunset Bar PUB $
(St 1; snacks & sandwiches US$2-4) This bar is mystifyingly quiet given its attractive wood decor, pool table and breezy riverside locale. A worthy spot for a sundowner.

Information

Guesthouses, hotels and pubs are the best places to get the local low-down. Thai baht are widely used, so there's no urgent need to change baht into dollars or riels. Moto drivers who offer to help change money are probably setting you up for a rip-off.

Acleda Bank (cnr St 3 & St 5) ATM accepts Visa cards.

Canadia Bank (St 1) ATM accepts most Western plastic.

Mary Internet (St 2; per hr 40B; ⏲7am or 8am-9pm) Has five computers.

Sen Sok Clinic (kkpao@camintel.com; ☎012 555060; St 3 cnr St 5; ⏲24hr) Has doctors who speak English and French.

Getting There & Away

Rith Mony (☎015 558185; St 3), **Phnom Penh Sorya Transport** (☎012 308014; St 3) and **Virak Buntham** (☎6363900; St 3) each run two or three buses to Phnom Penh (US$7, five hours, last departure at 11.30am) and one or two trips to Sihanoukville (US$7, four hours). Trips to Kampot (four hours, US$12) and Kep (4½ hours, US$14) involve a change or two.

Most buses pick up passengers in town but may drop you off at Krong Koh Kong's unpaved **bus station** (St 12), where motos and *remorques* await, eager to overcharge tourists. Don't pay more than US$1/2 (preferably less) for a moto/*remorque* into the centre.

From the taxi lot next to the bus station, shared taxis head to Phnom Penh (US$11, 3½ hours) and occasionally to Sihanoukville (US$10, three hours). Travel agents can easily set you up with shared or private taxi (to Phnom Penh/Sihanoukville US$55/50).

Paddy's Bamboo Guesthouse (per day US$1) and **Dive Inn** (St 1; US$2) rent out cheap bicycles, while Koh Kong Eco Tour has fancier mountain bikes (US$10). Motorbike hire is available from most guesthouses and from Koh Kong Eco Tour for US$5.

Koh Kong Conservation Corridor

Stretching along both sides of NH48 from Krong Koh Kong to the Gulf of Kompong Som, the Koh Kong Conservation Corridor encompasses many of Cambodia's most outstanding natural sites, including the most extensive mangrove forests on mainland Southeast Asia and the southern reaches of the fabled **Cardamom Mountains**, an area of breathtaking beauty and astonishing biodiversity.

The next few years will be critical in determining the future of the Cardamom Mountains. NGOs such as **Conservation International** (www.conservation.org), **Flora & Fauna International** (www.fauna-flora.org) and **Wildlife Alliance** (www.wildlifealliance.org) are working to help protect the region's 16 distinct ecosystems from loggers and poachers. Ecotourism, too, can play a role in spurring sustainable development by generating income for local people. Wildlife Alliance is promoting several projects to transform the **Southern Cardamoms Protected Forest** (1443 sq km) into a world-class ecotourism destination.

BOTUM SAKOR NATIONAL PARK

Occupying almost the entirety of a 35km-wide peninsula, this 1834-sq-km national

GETTING TO THAILAND: CHAM YEAM TO HAT LEK

Getting to the border To travel the 8km from Krong Koh Kong to the Thai border, a private taxi costs about US$10, while a moto/*remorque* can be had for US$2/5.

At the border Petty overcharging is possible on the Cambodian side, particularly for visas, as they often request payment at inflated Thai baht prices. No visa is required for Thailand for most nationalities. Cambodian visas are available on arrival. Hours are 7am to 10pm thanks to the casino.

Moving on Change of transport is required. On the Thai side minibuses can take you to Trat, where you can connect to Ko Chang.

See p719 for information on crossing this border in the other direction.

CHI PHAT

Once notorious for its loggers and poachers, Chi Phat is now home to a pioneering **community-based ecotourism project** (CBET; www.ecoadventurecambodia.com) offering hardy travellers a unique opportunity to explore the Cardamoms ecosystem while contributing to its protection. Visitors can take day treks through the jungle, go sunrise birdwatching by boat, mountain bike to several sets of rapids, and look for monkeys and hornbills with a former poacher as a guide (US$6 to US$10 per day). Also possible are one- to five-night mountain-bike trips and jungle treks deep into the Cardamoms (US$30 per day, including guide and food). In the village, visitors can relax by playing volleyball, badminton or pool with the locals.

Basic accommodation options in Chi Phat include nine CBET-member guesthouses (US$5 per person) and eight homestays (US$3 per person). Reserve through the **CBET office** (☎092 720925; ecotourism@wildlifealliance.org) in Chi Phat.

Chi Phat is on the Preak Piphot River 21km upriver from Andoung Tuek, which is 98km east of Krong Koh Kong on the NH48. Any Krong Koh Kong–bound bus can drop you in Andoung Tuek. From Andoung Tuek to Chi Phat it's a two-hour boat ride or a one-hour motorbike ride on an unpaved but smooth road. Call the CBET office to arrange a boat (US$25 for a four-passenger boat) or moto (US$5 to US$7).

park, encircled by mangroves and beaches, is home to a profusion of wildlife, including elephants (about 20 of them, according to recent camera-trap evidence), tigers, deer, leopards and sun bears. It's not yet geared up for tourism but at the sleepy **park headquarters** (☎015 374797), on NH48 about 3.5km west of Andoung Tuek, it should be possible to arrange a hike with a ranger (per day US$5), or a boat excursion.

KOH KONG ISLAND

The west coast of Cambodia's largest island shelters seven pristine beaches fringed with coconut palms and lush vegetation, just as you'd expect in a true tropical paradise. At the sixth beach from the north, a narrow channel leads to a *Gilligan's Island*-style lagoon.

The island, about 25km south of Krong Koh Kong, is not part of any national park and thus has few protections against rampant development, which rumour has it will soon arrive. The best way to get here is on a tour from Krong Koh Kong (p108).

TATAI WATERFALL

About 18km east of Krong Koh Kong on the NH48, the Phun Daung (Tatai) Bridge spans the Tatai River. Nestled in a lushly forested gorge upstream from the bridge is the **Tatai Waterfall**, a thundering set of rapids in the wet season, plunging over a 4m rock shelf. Water levels drop in the dry season but you can swim year round in refreshing pools around the waterfall.

The turnoff to Tatai is about 15km southeast of Krong Koh Kong, or 2.8km northwest of the Tatai Bridge. From Krong Koh Kong, a half-day moto/*remorque* excursion to Tatai Waterfall costs US$10/15 return.

Sihanoukville

☎034 / POP 155,000

Surrounded by white-sand beaches and relatively undeveloped tropical islands, Sihanoukville (aka Kompong Som) is Cambodia's premier seaside resort. The city's lively bars and sands remain pretty laid-back, offering bliss and relaxation by day, drinking and chilling by night. Most of the action takes place not far from the scruffy city centre on busy Occheuteal Beach; for peace and quiet, venture south of town to Otres Beach or hit one of the islands.

Sights & Activities

Beaches

Sihanoukville's sandy beaches are in a state of flux as developers move in and leases are signed to cash in on the tourism boom. Most central is **Occheuteal Beach**, lined with ramshackle restaurants, whose northwestern end – a tiny, rocky strip – has emerged as a happy, easy-going travellers' hang-out known as **Serendipity Beach**.

South of Occheuteal, gloriously quiet **Otres Beach** is a seemingly infinite strip of almost-empty white sand, populated by casuarinas and a small colony of mellow resorts at the south end. Developers have long been eyeing Otres Beach, and in 2010 a stretch of resorts was forcibly removed. But at press time developers had yet to build on the land they claimed, which is sealed off by a fence.

Northwest of Serendipity, all but a tiny stretch of pretty 1.5km-long **Sokha Beach** now belongs to the exclusive Sokha Beach Resort. **Independence Beach** is a good stretch of clean sand but is being aggressively developed. A bit north of tiny, secluded **Koh Pos Beach**, a new bridge links the mainland with **Koh Pos** (Snake Island), where a Russian firm has plans to build an ambitious

Sihanoukville

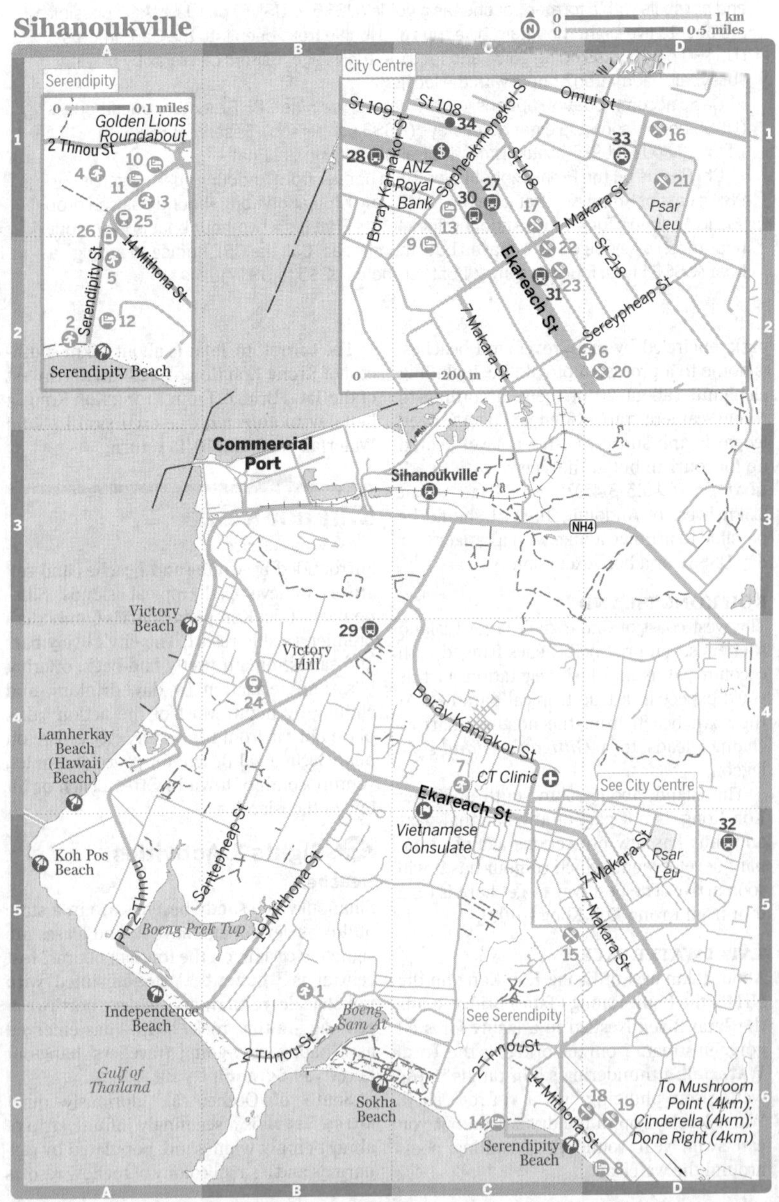

resort city. The original backpacker beach, **Victory Beach**, now under Russian management, is clean, orderly and devoid of buzz.

Diving

The diving near Sihanoukville isn't terrific. It gets better the further you go out, although you still shouldn't expect anything on a par with the western Gulf of Thailand or the Andaman Sea. Most serious trips will hit **Koh Rong Saloem**, while overnight trips target the distant islands of **Koh Tang** and **Koh Prins**. Overnight trips cost about US$85 per day including two daily dives, food, island accommodation and equipment. Two-tank dives out of Sihanoukville average US$70 including equipment.

Chez Claude DIVING
(☎934100; www.bestcambodia.com; above St 2 Thnou) Claude specialises in longer trips to distant reefs.

Dive Shop DIVING
(☎933664; www.diveshopcambodia.com; Rd to Serendipity) PADI five-star dive centre offering National Geographic Diver certification.

EcoSea Dive DIVING
(☎012 606646; 736949; www.ecoseadive.com; Rd to Serendipity) Offers PADI and cheaper SSI courses.

Scuba Nation Diving Center DIVING
(☎012 604680; www.divecambodia.com; Serendipity St) Cambodia's first PADI five-star dive centre. Four-day PADI open-water courses here include two days on Koh Rong Saloem.

Massage

NGO-trained blind and disabled masseurs deftly ease away the tension at **Seeing Hands Massage 3** (95 Ekareach St; per hr US$6; ⏲8am-9pm) and **Starfish Bakery & Café** (☎012 952011; 62 St 7 Makara, City Centre; per hr US$6-10; ⏲7am-6pm).

Courses

Traditional Khmer Cookery COOKING
(☎092 738615; http://cambodiacookeryclasses.com; 335 Ekareach St; half-/full-day course per person US$15/25; ⏲Mon-Sat) Teaches traditional culinary techniques in classes with no more than eight participants. Reserve a day ahead.

Sihanoukville

Activities, Courses & Tours

1 Chez Claude ... B5
2 Coasters ... A2
3 Dive Shop ... A1
4 EcoSea Dive ... A1
Eco-Trek Tours ... (see 10)
5 Scuba Nation Diving Center ... A2
6 Seeing Hands Massage 3 ... D2
Starfish Bakery & Café ... (see 23)
7 Traditional Khmer Cookery ... C4

Sleeping

8 Chiva's Shack ... D6
9 Geckozy Guesthouse ... C2
10 Mick & Craig's ... A1
11 Monkey Republic ... A1
12 New Sea View Villa ... A2
13 Small Hotel ... C1
14 The Cove ... C6
Utopia ... (see 25)

Eating

15 Cabbage Farm Restaurant ... C5
16 Food Stalls ... D1
17 Gelato Italiano ... C1
18 Grand Kampuchea ... D6
Happa ... (see 4)
19 Happy Herb Pizza ... D6
20 Holy Cow ... D2
New Sea View Villa ... (see 12)
21 Psar Leu ... D1
22 Samudera Supermarket ... C2
23 Starfish Bakery & Café ... C2

Drinking

JJ's Playground ... (see 2)
Monkey Republic ... (see 11)
24 Retox Bar ... B4
25 Utopia ... A1

Shopping

26 Cambodia Children's Painting Project ... A1
Casablanca Books ... (see 10)
M'lop Tapang Gift Shop ... (see 5)

Information

Ana Travel ... (see 11)

Transport

27 Capitol Tours ... C1
28 GST ... B1
29 New Bus Station ... B4
30 Paramount Angkor ... C1
31 Rith Mony ... C2
32 Taxi Station ... D5
33 Taxis to Kampot ... D1
34 Virak Buntham ... C1

Tours

Popular day tours go to some of the closer islands and to Ream National Park (p117).

Coasters BOAT TOURS
(☎933776; www.cambodia-beach.com; Serendipity St) A good bet for boat and snorkel trips. A daily trip to Koh Ta Kiev/Koh Russei (per person US$15/20) departs at 9am and includes breakfast and lunch, or hire a private boat (US$50).

Eco-Trek Tours TOURS
(☎012 987073; ecotrektourscambodia@yahoo.com; Rd to Serendipity; ⊗8am-10pm) Associated with the knowledgeable folks at Mick and Craig's, this travel agency has information on just about everything. Mountain bikes (US$2) available.

Sleeping

The area between Serendipity Beach and the Golden Lions Roundabout, including the road to Serendipity, is now the city's main travellers' hang-out. You pay a premium to stay right on the water, although Occheuteal Beach has some ultra-low-budget rooms for hard-core backpackers. Otres Beach is the up-and-coming backpacker hang-out. Away from the beaches, the town centre has a few good options, as does long-running Victory Hill. There are also lots of popular bungalow resorts popping up on the islands off Sihanoukville: see p117 for recommendations.

TOP CHOICE **Mushroom Point** GUESTHOUSE $
(☎078 509079; mushroompoint.otres@gmail.com; Otres Beach; dm US$5-7, bungalows US$25; 📶) The 'shroom-shaped open-air dorm over the restaurant wins the award for most awesome crashpad in Cambodia. Even those averse to communal living will be content in their mozzie-net-draped pods, good for two. The mushie-shaped private bungalows and food get high marks too.

Done Right GUESTHOUSE $
(☎088 6678668; Otres Beach; s/d without bathroom $5/9, bungalows US$15) Space-age, eco-friendly bungalows known as 'geodomes' are done right here – a bit like concrete yurts, with sky lights in lieu of windows. Above the restaurant are nine simple rooms with clapboard walls and lino floors. It's next to Mushroom Point.

Monkey Republic BACKPACKER $
(☎012 490290; http://monkeyrepublic.info; Rd to Serendipity; dm US$3, r US$10; @📶) A favourite of the young backpacker crowd, Monkey Republic has an eight-bed dorm and several dozen bright-blue bungalows set around two banana-shaded courtyards.

New Sea View Villa GUESTHOUSE $$
(☎092 759753; www.sihanoukville-hotel.com; Serendipity St; d with fan/air-con from US$15/20; ❄📶) Located very close to the beach, the 15 spacious, clean rooms are a favourite with in-the-know expats, as is the superb food at the restaurant.

Cinderella GUESTHOUSE $
(☎088 9907588; Otres Beach; s/d without bathroom $5/9, bungalows US$15) Way down at the far end of Otres Beach, this is the spot if you just want some private time. The A-frame cottages are basic, but you can't argue with the beachfront setting.

Mick & Craig's GUESTHOUSE $
(☎012 727740; www.mickandcraigs.com; Rd to Serendipity; r with fan/air-con from US$8/15; ❄📶) A popular restaurant and 17 simple concrete rooms in the heart of Serendipity's restaurant and bar strip.

Beach Road Hotel HOTEL $$
(☎017 827677; www.beachroad-hotel.com; Rd to Serendipity; r with fan/air-con from US$15/20; ❄📶🏊) Well-located and efficiently run, Beach Road has 76 modern rooms, some set around the pool.

Chiva's Shack BACKPACKER $
(☎012 360911; Occheuteal Beach; r US$2-6) One of the cheapest options right on the water, this aptly named party zone has 45 very basic rooms with thin plank walls, foam mattresses and shared bathrooms. Loud till late.

Geckozy Guesthouse GUESTHOUSE $
(☎012 495825; www.geckozy-guesthouse.com; City Centre; r US$5-7; 📶) Located on a quiet side street, this place has six basic rooms in an old wooden house, giving it the feel of a homestay.

Small Hotel HOTEL $$
(☎012 716385; www.thesmallhotel.info; City Centre; r US$13-18; ❄@📶) Neat and organised in the best Scandinavian tradition, this super-welcoming guesthouse has a cheerful lounge and 11 spotless rooms.

SPLURGE: SIHANOUKVILLE

The Cove (☎012 380296; www.thecovebeach.com; Serendipity Beach; r with fan incl breakfast US$24-29, with air-con US$33-35; ❄📶) is a hillside place with bungalows, balconies and a bar lapped by waves. Most bungalows face the sea and all have hammocks. Request a room high up for the best views.

Eating

Sihanoukville's centre of culinary gravity has shifted to the Serendipity area, but up on Victory Hill, the main drag still has a range of good-value restaurants. Unless stated otherwise, all restaurants listed here are open for breakfast, lunch and dinner.

SERENDIPITY AREA

For romance, nothing beats dining on the water, either at one of the resorts at Serendipity Beach or – more cheaply – in one of the shacks along adjacent Occheuteal Beach. Of the resorts, the best food is found at New Sea Villa (good for candlelight dinners) and Reef Resort.

Grand Kampuchea CAMBODIAN **$**
(23 Tola St; mains US$2.50-5) This popular outdoor eatery serves some of the best Amok in town, succulent grilled marlin and other sea beasties.

Kuren BARBECUE **$**
(Occheuteal Beach; mains US$2.50-3.50) Kuren's generous mixed seafood grill, fantastic value at US$3, separates it from the pack of BBQ shacks lining Occheuteul Beach.

Happy Herb Pizza PIZZA **$$**
(☎012 632198; 23 Tola St; small/medium/large from US$4/7/9.50) Serves Khmer dishes (US$1.50 to US$3) and 23 kinds of pizza, all available 'happy' (ie ganja-fortified). Free delivery.

Happa JAPANESE **$$**
(Rd to Serendipity; mains US$4-7; ⏲5pm-midnight) Authentic teppanyaki with a variety of sauce options is served amid tropical decor with Japanese touches.

AROUND THE CITY

For Sihanoukville's cheapest dining, head to the **food stalls** in and around **Psar Leu** (St 7 Makara; ⏲7am-9pm). The vendors across the street, next to the Kampot taxis, are open 24 hours.

Holy Cow ORGANIC **$$**
(83 Ekareach St; mains US$2.50-4.50; ⏲8.30am-11pm; 📶🖉) Options at this chic and funky cafe-restaurant include pasta, sandwiches on homemade bread and two vegan desserts, both involving chocolate.

Starfish Bakery & Café ORGANIC **$**
(www.starfishcambodia.org; behind 62 St 7 Makara; sandwiches US$3.50-4.50; ⏲7am-6pm; 🖉) This relaxing, NGO-run garden cafe specialises in filling Western breakfasts and healthy, innovative sandwiches heavy on Mexican and Middle Eastern flavours. Income goes to sustainable development projects.

Cabbage Farm Restaurant CAMBODIAN **$**
(small/large mains 8000/15,000r; ⏲11am-10pm) Known to locals as Chamkar Spey, it gets rave reviews for its seafood and spicy seasonings. An authentic Khmer dining experience.

Gelato Italiano ICE CREAM
(49 St 7 Makara; Italian ice per scoop $0.75; ⏲8am-9pm; ❄) Run by students from Sihanoukville's Don Bosco Hotel School, this Italian-style cafe specialises in gelatos (Italian ices) and serves coffee and light meals in a bright, airy space.

Samudera Supermarket SUPERMARKET **$**
(64 St 7 Makara; ⏲6am-10pm) Has a good selection of fruits, veggies and Western favourites, including cheese and wine.

Drinking

Many of Sihanoukville's liveliest nightspots are along Serendipity Beach and the road to Serendipity. Occheuteal Beach is lined with laid-back beach bars, some of which rock on until the early hours. Despite the arrival of girlie bars and the threat of demolition, Victory Hill's main drag still has some of its old-time backpacker vibe, as well as a certain French flair.

Among the nightspots that are worth a look:

JJ's Playground BAR
(Serendipity Beach) The scene changes frequently on Serendipity Beach, but for a while now JJ's has been the go-to spot for those seeking pure late-night debauchery.

Dolphin Shack BAR
(Occheuteal Beach) Like JJ's, it has a host of specials designed to get you drunk fast and

bevies of beautiful backpackers pouring drinks and passing out flyers.

Monkey Republic BAR
(Rd to Serendipity) The bar and upstairs chill-out area are ideal for meeting other travellers.

Utopia BAR
(cnr Rd to Serendipity & St 14 Mithona; ⏲24hr) The prime backpacker warm-up bar was starting to get a bit of a girlie-bar edge when we went. Then it wasn't, then it was again. One look will tell.

Retox Bar BAR
(Victory Hill; ⏲noon-1am or later) This pub, plastered with posters and album covers, often has live music (from 8.30pm) and jam sessions (instruments available).

Shopping

M'lop Tapang Gift Shop HANDICRAFTS
(www.mloptapang.org; Serendipity St) Run by a local NGO that works with at-risk children, this shop sells bags, scarves and good-quality T-shirts. Several other handicrafts shops are nearby.

Cambodia Children's Painting Project ART
(www.letuscreate.org; Serendipity St) Another NGO that works with underprivileged kids. You can buy small paintings here. The volunteer backpackers are happy to tell you more about the project.

Casablanca Books BOOKS
(Rd to Serendipity; ⏲8am-9pm, to 11pm in high season) Sells new and used English paperbacks.

Information

Details on local activities and businesses appear in two free brochures, the *Sihanoukville Visitors Guide* and the *Sihanoukville Advertiser*. Also see www.sihanoukville-cambodia.com.

Internet cafes (per hour 4000r) are sprinkled along the road to Serendipity and, in the city centre, along Ekareach St near Sophamongkol St.

Theft is a problem on Occheuteal Beach, so leave your valuables in your room. At night, both men and women should avoid walking alone along dark, isolated beaches and roads.

Ana Travel (☎016 499915; www.anatraveland tours.com; Rd to Serendipity; ⏲8am-10pm) Handles Cambodia visa extensions and Vietnam visas in one hour.

ANZ Royal Bank (215 Ekareach St) One of several ATM-equipped banks along Ekareach St.

CT Clinic (☎081 886666; 47 Boray Kamakor St; ⏲24hr for emergencies) The best medical clinic in town. Can administer rabies shots and snake anti-venin.

Vietnamese consulate (☎934039; 310 Ekareach St; ⏲8am-noon & 2-4pm Mon-Sat) Issues some of the world's speediest Vietnamese visas (US$45/90/120 for one/three/six months), often on the spot. Bring a passport photo.

Getting There & Away

All of the major bus companies have frequent connections with Phnom Penh (US$3.75 to US$6, four hours) from early morning until at least 2pm, after which trips are sporadic. The cheapest is **Capitol Tour** (☎934042; Ekareach St). **Virak Buntham** (☎011 558988; Ekareach St) runs the last trip at 8.30pm, while Capitol Tour, **GST** (☎6339666; Ekareach St) and **Paramount Angkor** (☎017 525366; Ekareach St) have late afternoon trips.

Virak Buntham and **Rith Mony** (☎012 644585; Ekareach St) have morning buses to Bangkok (US$25, change buses on the Thai side) via Krong Koh Kong (US$7, four hours). Paramount Angkor has daily services to Krong Koh Kong, Siem Reap, Battambang and Saigon. GST has a night bus to Siem Reap and day buses to Battambang and Saigon.

Virak Buntham and **Kampot Tours & Travel** (☎in Kampot 092 125556) run minibuses to Kampot (US$6, 1½ hours) that continue to Kep (US$10, 2½ hours) and Ha Tien in Vietnam (US$16, five hours). Travel agents can arrange hotel pickups. See p123 for details on crossing into Vietnam at Prek Chak.

Bus companies all have terminals downtown on Ekareach St. Most departures originate at these terminals and stop at the **new bus station** (St 19 Mithona) on the way out of town.

Cramped share taxis (US$6 per person, US$45 per car) and minibuses (15,000r) to Phnom Penh depart from the new bus station until about 8pm. Avoid the minibuses if you value things like comfort. Hotels can arrange taxis to Phnom Penh for US$50 or less.

Share taxis to Kampot (US$5, 1½ hours) leave mornings only from an open lot across St 7 Makara from Psar Leu. This lot and the new bus station are good places to look for rides to Krong Koh Kong or the Thai border. If nobody's sharing, expect to pay around US$50 to the Thai border.

Getting Around

Arriving in Sihanoukville, buses stop at the bus terminal, then most (but not all) continue to their central terminals. Prices to the Serendipity Beach area from the new bus station are fixed at a pricey US$2/6 for a moto/*remorque*, so continue to the centre if possible and get a cheaper, shorter *remorque* ride from there.

A moto/*remorque* should cost about US$1/2 from the centre to Serendipity, Occheuteal and Victory Beaches and Victory Hill. Serendipity to Victory Hill costs US$1.50/3.

Motorbikes can be rented from many guesthouses for US$5 to US$7 a day. For fund-raising purposes, the police sometimes 'crack down' on foreign drivers. Common violations: no driver's licence, no helmet, and no wing mirrors and driving with the lights on during the day.

Bicycles can be hired from many guesthouses for about US$1.50 a day.

Around Sihanoukville

More than a dozen tropical islands dot the waters off Sihanoukville. Developers have been drooling over the islands for years, but so far wide-scale development has been kept at bay.

The most appealing of the islands are neighbouring **Koh Rong** and **Koh Rong Saloem**, both about two hours offshore and ringed by white-sand beaches that count among Cambodia's best. Plans to turn Koh Rong into a Cambodian version of Thailand's Koh Samui, complete with ring road and airport, have stalled. Instead, the opening of several simple, extremely appealing beach resorts has turned Koh Rong into an ideal spot to escape civilisation. Koh Rong Saloem has a few lonely resorts of its own and some amazing wildlife, including macaques, black squirrels and sea eagles.

Closer to Sihanoukville, little **Koh Ta Kiev** has two resorts and a long white beach, while you can snorkel off **Koh Russei** (Bamboo Island), where development plans are forcing most resorts to shut down.

Sleeping

Most island resorts run their generators from about 6pm to midnight.

Monkey Island BUNGALOWS **$$**
(☎016 594177; Koh Rong; bungalow US$15-25) A cool spot on the southeast coast of Koh Rong, this one is run by Sihanoukville backpacker haven Monkey Republic. Most of the 19 bungalows share a bathroom.

Treehouse Bungalows BUNGALOWS **$$**
(☎081 830992; Koh Rong; beach/tree bungalow US$20/30) This backpacker pad has six beach bungalows and five treehouses on the southeast side of Koh Rong.

M'pay Bay Bungalows BUNGALOWS **$$**
(☎085 242257; Koh Rong Saloem; bungalow US$20) A cluster of simple bungalows in a fishing village on the north side of the island. The friendly owners bill it as a more ecofriendly option.

Koh Ta Kiev Island Resort BUNGALOWS **$$**
(☎011 708795; Koh Rong; bungalow US$20) Located on small Koh Ta Kiev island, this place is popular for a secluded getaway, with solid value-for-money bungalows.

Ten 103 Treehouse Bay BACKPACKER **$**
(☎017 662015; Koh Ta Kiev; dm US$7, bungalow US$20) The reincarnation of Jonty's Jungle Camp, this is a real getaway straight out of *The Beach*. Bungalows are finished in rustic driftwood and bathrooms are shared, but there is an impressive menu including homemade pizzas.

Getting There & Away

Island-hopping tours usually take in the closer islands such as Koh Ta Kiev and Koh Russei; book through a tour company or your guesthouse. For Koh Rong and Koh Rong Saloem, make arrangements through your resort.

WORTH A TRIP

REAM NATIONAL PARK

Also known as Preah Sihanouk National Park, this park – now seriously endangered by commercial development – comprises 150 sq km of primary forests and is an excellent place to see wildlife. Hiking unaccompanied is not allowed. However, fascinating two- to three-hour **jungle walks** (US$8 per person) led by rangers – most of whom speak English – are easy to arrange at the **park headquarters** (☎016 767686; ⏰7am-6pm), across the road from the Sihanoukville airport.

Ranger-led **boat trips** (1-5 people US$50) on the Prek Toeuk Sap Estuary and its mangrove channels are another option. Travel agencies in Sihanoukville offer day trips out to the park.

The park is 18km east of Sihanoukville. A return trip by moto should cost US$8 to US$12, depending on how long you stay.

Kampot

☎033 / POP 33,000

There is something about this little charmer that encourages visitors to linger. It might be the lovely riverside setting or the ageing French buildings, or it could be the great little guesthouses and burgeoning bar scene. Whatever the magic ingredient, this is the perfect base from which to explore nearby caves and tackle Bokor National Park.

Sights & Activities

This is not a town where you come and do, but a place to come and feel. Sit on the riverbank and watch the sun set beneath the mountains, or stroll among the town's fine **French shophouses** (in the triangle delineated by St 7 Makara, the central roundabout and the post office).

Kampot Traditional Music School MUSIC
(⏲6-9pm Mon-Fri) Visitors are welcome to observe training sessions and/or performances every evening at this school that trains orphaned and disabled children in traditional music and dance.

Seeing Hands Massage 5 MASSAGE
(per hr US$4; ⏲7am-11pm) Blind masseurs and masseuses offer soothing bliss.

Tours

One of the best ways to explore Kampot Province is on an organised day trip. Popular destinations include Kep and Bokor National Park (see p120), while various companies run sunset river cruises and countryside tours that include visits to pepper plantations. Try the following:

Kampot Dream Time Tours TOURS
(☎089 908417; www.kampotluxurytours.com) Runs upmarket countryside trips in air-con vans (per person US$35) and wine-and-cheese river cruises in a boat formerly owned by King Norodom Sihanouk.

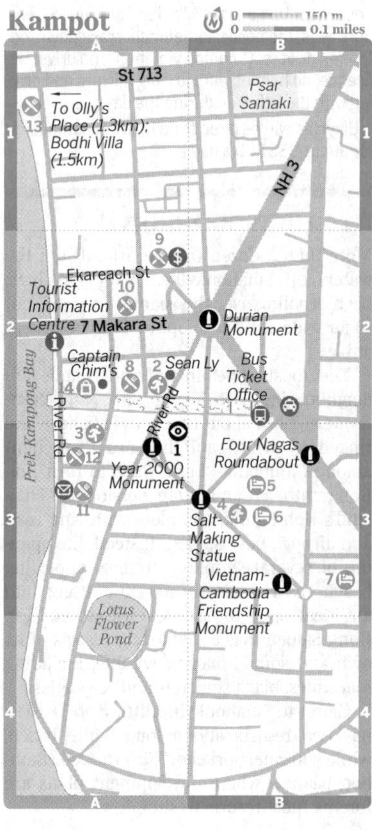

Kampot

Sights
1 Kampot Traditional Music School........ A3

Activities, Courses & Tours
2 Kampot Dreamtime Tours A2
3 Seeing Hands Massage 5..................... A3
4 Sok Lim Tours B3

Sleeping
5 Blissful Guesthouse............................ B3
6 Orchid Guest House B3
7 Ta Eng.. B3

Eating
8 Epic Arts Café A2
9 Fruit Stalls A2
10 Night Market A2
11 Rikitikitavi A3
12 Rusty Keyhole A3
13 Ta Ouv Restaurant A1

Shopping
14 Kepler's Kampot Books A2

Sok Lim Tours TOURS
(☎012 719872; www.soklimtours.com) Kampot's oldest and largest outfit, well regarded all around. Has trained pepper-plantation guides.

Captain Chim's BOAT TOURS
(☎012 321043) Sunset cruises on a traditional boat cost US$5 per head and include a cold beer.

Sleeping

Olly's Place BACKPACKER $
(☎092 605837; www.ollysplacekampot.com; r US$3-7; 📶) Windsurfers and paddle boards are both free on the other side of the river at Aussie-run Olly's. The thatched bungalows are ridiculous value considering the mellow vibe and top location.

Bodhi Villa BACKPACKER $
(☎012 728884; www.bodhivilla.com; dm US$2, r US$5-12; 📶) Situated 2km towards Tek Chhouu Falls from town, Boddhi is popular with Phnom Penh expats on weekends, when huge parties often erupt. At other times it's a peaceful hideaway across the river with a good bar.

Orchid Guest House GUESTHOUSE $
(☎092 226996; orchidguesthousekampot@yahoo.com; r with fan/air-con US$5/15, bungalow US$10; ❄@📶) Set in a manicured garden, this hostelry has comfortable air-con rooms, less comfortable fan rooms and three bungalows by a fish pond.

Blissful Guesthouse GUESTHOUSE $
(☎092 494331; www.blissfulguesthouse.com; 3-bed dm US$2, r without/with bathroom US$4/8) An old-time backpacker vibe lives on at this atmospheric wooden house. Has a popular bar-restaurant with a Sunday roast and slightly shabby rooms.

Ta Eng GUESTHOUSE $
(☎012 330058; r US$5-10; @📶) Ta Eng is the best of the Khmer-style high-rises thanks to squeaky clean rooms and friendly family ownership.

Eating

Quite a few restaurants line River Rd south of the old French bridge. There are **fruit stalls and little eateries** (⏲7am-10pm) next to the Canadia Bank and, nearby, a **night market** (St 7 Makara), with both mains and desserts.

KAMPOT PEPPER

In the years before the Cambodian civil war took its toll, no self-respecting French restaurant in Paris would be without Kampot pepper on the table. Pepper plantations are once again a common sight in the Kampot region and come in a variety of colours, including white, black, green and red.

Epic Arts Café CAFE $
(www.epicarts.org.uk; mains US$2-4; ⏲7am-6pm; 📶) A great place for breakfast, homemade cakes or tea, this mellow eatery is staffed by deaf and disabled young people. Profits fund arts workshops for disabled Cambodians.

Rikitikitavi INTERNATIONAL $$
(☎012 235102; www.rikitikitavi-kampot.com; River Rd; mains US$5-8; ⏲7am-10pm; 📶✎) Rikitikitavi's river-view restaurant, known for its Kampot pepper chicken, slow-cooked curry and salads, is a great place to sink a drink before sunset.

Ta Ouv Restaurant CAMBODIAN $$
(River Rd; mains US$5; ⏲10am-2pm & 6-10pm) Built on stilts over the river by the new bridge, it specialises in seafood (crab with peppercorns is a favourite), with plenty of other meat and veggie options.

Rusty Keyhole INTERNATIONAL $$
(☎092 758536; River Rd; sml/lge/x-lge ribs US$5/7.50/10; 📶) Popular riverfront bar-restaurant serves widely praised food. Order the famous ribs in advance or they may sell out.

Shopping

Kepler's Kampot Books BOOKS
(⏲8am-8pm) Secondhand books plus pepper, *kramas* (checked scarfs) and fine T-shirts.

Information

Guesthouses are the best source of travel information, and Bodhi Villa guesthouse can supply details on options for volunteering. There's a strip of copy shops with internet access southwest of the Durian monument on St 7 Makara.

Canadia Bank (Ekareach St) Has an ATM.

Tourist Information Center (☎6555541, 012 462286; lonelyguide@gmail.com; River Rd; ⏲7am-7pm) Kampot's new tourist office is the main point of contact for linking up with groups for Bokor National Park trips and information on caves and attractions in the surrounding area.

Getting There & Away

Kampot is 105km from Sihanoukville and 148km from Phnom Penh.

Paramount Angkor, Capitol Express, Phnom Penh Sorya Transport and Hua Lian sell tickets from offices opposite the Total petrol station near the Four Nagas Roundabout. All have two or three daily trips to Phnom Penh (US$3.50 to US$4.50, four hours), the last of which depart at 1pm; some go via Kep (US$2, 45 minutes). Across the street you can catch share taxis (US$6), packed-to-the-gills minibuses (16,000r) and private taxis (US$40) to Phnom Penh. Sorya also has daily trips to Siem Reap and Battambang.

Share taxis to Sihanoukville cost US$5 and a private taxi is US$30. Daily Kampot Tours & Travel and Virak Buntham minibuses go west to Sihanoukville (US$6, 1½ hours) and Krong Koh Kong (US$13, four hours with a bus transfer); and east to Ha Tien, Vietnam (US$10, 2½ hours). Guesthouses can arrange tickets and pick-ups.

A moto/*remorque*/taxi to Kep should cost about US$6/10/20.

Getting Around

Bicycles can be hired or borrowed for free from many guesthouses, which can also arrange motorbike hire, or try the following:

Captain Chim's Motorbike hire for US$4 per day.

Sean Ly (☎012 944687; ⏰7am-9pm) Rents 125cc bikes for US$3 a day (US$5 for a new one) and 250cc trail bikes for US$10.

Around Kampot

Picnic platforms, eateries and some refreshing rapids make **Tek Chhouu Falls**, 8km from Kampot, hugely popular with locals. A moto costs US$3 each way.

The limestone hills east towards Kep are honeycombed with fantastic caves, some of which can be explored with the help of local kids and a reliable torch (flashlight).

The temple cave of **Phnom Chhnork** (admission US$1), surrounded by blazingly beautiful countryside, is a real gem. Known for its 7th-century (Funan-era) brick temple, it is 8km from Kampot; for a return moto/*remorque* ride count on paying about US$5/10.

Also interesting is **Phnom Sorsia** (admission free), 15km southeast of Kampot on the road to Kep, which has several natural caves and a gaudily painted modern temple.

Bokor National Park

One of Cambodia's most spectacular protected areas, this 1581-sq-km **national park** (Preah Monivong National Park; admission US$5) is famed for its abandoned French hill station, refreshingly cool climate and lush primary rainforest. A massive resort project includes plans to restore the Bokor Palace to its former glory and even build a 36-hole golf course, although how golfers are supposed to make par – or even find the ball – in the fog is anyone's guess. A new road up to the hill station has been completed but is only opened to the public on selected holidays. Plans are to open it full-time in 2013.

At the park entrance, an informative **ranger station** has displays about Bokor's fauna. Threatened animals inhabiting the park include the leopard, Indian elephant, Asiatic black bear, Malayan sun bear, pileated gibbon, pig-tailed macaque, slow loris and pangolin. Don't expect to see much wildlife, however, as most of the animals survive by staying in more remote areas and, in addition, are nocturnal.

In the early 1920s the French (ever eager to escape the lowland heat) established **Bokor Hill Station** atop Phnom Bokor (1080m), known for its dramatic vistas of the coastal plain and for frequent pea-soup fogs. A grand, four-storey hotel, the **Bokor Palace**, opened in 1925, but the entire holiday village, including the **Catholic church** and the **post office**, was abandoned to the howling winds in the 1970s when Khmer Rouge forces infiltrated the area.

The hill station became a ghost town, its once-grand buildings turned into eerie, windowless shells. Over time they became carpeted with a bright-orange lichen that gives them an other-worldly cast. Other Phnom Bokor sights include lichen-caked **Wat Sampeau Moi Roi** (Five Boats Wat), from which an 11km trail (four or five hours) leads to two-tiered **Popokvil Falls**.

Sleeping

Bokor National Park Ranger Station HOSTEL $

(☎015 819666; bokornp@camintel.com; dm US$5, r US$20-30) Near the old hill station, Bokor Ranger Station has simply decorated rooms with hot water and up to four beds. Bring warm clothes and a torch (flashlight) as electricity goes off at 9pm.

Getting There & Away

Until the new road is finished, it is necessary to visit the park on an organised tour. The standard full-day tour takes you up to the hill station and involves a bit of on-road driving, a bit of off-road driving and a bit of trekking.

The standard tour costs US$25 per person (minimum four people) and includes all transport, food, an English-speaking guide, water and the park entry fee. Bring your own protection against mosquitoes, leeches, snakes and rain. It's usually easy to hook up with a group through the tourist information centre in Kampot or any travel agent or guesthouse.

Variations on the standard tour, including overnight trips, are possible. Walking the whole way up takes six to seven hours and costs US$40 to US$50 per person including overnight accommodation in a ranger station at the top.

Kep

☎036 / POP 13,300

The seaside resort of Kep-sur-Mer, famed for its spectacular sunsets and splendid seafood, was founded as a colonial retreat for the French elite in 1908. In the 1960s, Cambodian high rollers continued the tradition but Khmer Rouge rule brought evacuation followed by systematic looting. Today, scores of Kep's luxurious pre-war villas are still blackened shells, relics of a once-successful era that came to a sudden and violent end.

Sleepy Kep lacks a centre and its accommodation options are spread out all over the place. As a result, some find it a little soulless. Others revel in its sleepy vibe, content to relax at their resort, nibble on crab at the famed Crab Market and poke around the mildewed shells of modernist villas that speak of happier, carefree times.

Sights & Activities

Beaches BEACH

Most of Kep's beaches are too shallow and rocky to make for good swimming. The best is centrally located **Kep Beach**, but it's still somewhat pebbly and tends to fill up with locals on weekends. The best place for sunset viewing is the long wooden pier in front of Knai Bang Chat's **Sailing Club**, where there's also a small but shallow beach.

Kep National Park NATIONAL PARK

The interior of Kep peninsula is occupied by tiny Kep National Park, degraded in recent years by illegal logging, but finally guarded by a complement of rangers. An 8km circuit around the park, signposted in yellow, starts at the park entrance behind Veranda Natural Resort. Directly behind the Beach House guesthouse overlooking Kep Beach, the signposted Stairway to Heaven leads 800m up the hill to a pagoda, a nunnery and Sunset Rock, with superb views.

Koh Tonsay ISLAND

Offshore, rustic Koh Tonsay (Rabbit Island) has a lovely beach with several family-run clusters of rudimentary bungalows where you can overnight for US$5. Boats to the island (25 minutes) leave from a pier 2.7km east of the Kep Beach roundabout. Your guesthouse can arrange to get you on a boat for US$10 per person return, but make it clear which day you want to be picked up. A scheduled trip departs daily at 9am for the same price. A private boat arranged at the pier costs US$30 one-way for up to seven passengers.

Sleeping

Tree Top Bungalows BACKPACKER $

(☎012 515191; khmertreetop@hotmail.com; r US$4-25; @📶) The highlights here are the towering stilted bamboo bungalows with sea views; each pair shares a bathroom. Cool off at nearby Kep Lodge's pool.

Kukuluku Beach Club BACKPACKER $

(☎6300150; www.kukuluku-beachclub.com; dm US$3.50-5, d with fan/air-con US$10/20; 📶) The rooms are nothing special and the pool is tiny, but it's a great place to meet other travellers and party on weekends, when they sometimes import live music (and expat crowds) from Phnom Penh.

Kep Seaside Guesthouse HOTEL $

(☎012 684241; sengbunly@bnckh.com; r with fan/air-con from US$7/15; ❄📶) This three-storey place is a bit decrepit, but you can't argue with the location, right on the water (although lacking a beach).

Eating

Eating crab at the 'Crab Market', a row of wooden waterfront shacks next to a wet fish market, is a quintessential Kep experience. Most guesthouses also grill up eight-legged crustaceans.

Kimly Restaurant CRAB SHACK $$

(mains US$2.50-7; ⏲9am-10pm) The longest-running and still the best of the Crab Market eateries, it does crab every which way, 27 ways to be exact, all at US$6 to US$7.

SPLURGE: KEP

About 2.5km in from the Rabbit Island pier, **Jasmine Valley Eco-Resort** (☎097 7917635; www.jasminevalley.com; r US$24-64;) has funky bungalows raised dramatically amid dense jungle foliage. Green credits include solar power and a natural swimming pool complete with pond critters.

The Kampot pepper crab is truly mouth-watering.

Sailing Club INTERNATIONAL $$
(mains US$5-9; ⏰7am-10pm) Set in a traditional wooden fishermen's dwelling built on stilts over the sea, this is the affordable restaurant linked to exclusive boutique hotel Knai Bang Chatt. Fresh seafood, cool cocktails and slow-burn sunsets.

Breezes INTERNATIONAL $$
(mains US$5-8; ⏰9am-9pm) Nestled right on the water, this Dutch-owned restaurant boasts sleek furnishings, excellent food and fine views of Koh Tonsay.

Information

There are no banks or ATMs in Kep.

Kampot Information Center (☎097 7998777; pheng_say@yahoo.com; Kep Beach) Host Pheng is a font of information on buses and borders.

Rith Travel Center (☎016 789994; www.rithtravel.com; Crab Market) Specialises in island tours and handles bus tickets.

Getting There & Away

Kep is 25km from Kampot and 41km from the Prek Chak–Xa Xia border crossing to Vietnam. Phnom Penh Sorya Transport, Capitol Express and Hua Lian buses link the town with Kampot (US$2, 45 minutes) and Phnom Penh (US$4, four hours, last trips at 2pm). A private taxi to Phnom Penh (2½ hours) costs US$40 to US$45, to Kampot US$20.

See p123 for details on getting across the Vietnamese border to Ha Tien (Vietnam). Virak Buntham's Ha Tien-Sihanoukville bus rumbles through Kep, and Kampot Tours & Travel can also get you to Sihanoukville (US$10, 2½ hours). You can also board Virak Buntham's Kampot-Siem Reap night bus in Kep.

A moto/remorque to Kampot runs about US$6/10; private taxis are US$15 to US$20. Drivers hang out at the northern and Kep Beach roundabouts.

Motorbike rental averages US$7 per day, mountain bike rental is US$3 per day.

Around Kep

For an enchanting mixture of dramatic natural beauty and Buddhist piety, it's hard to beat **Wat Kiri Sela** (Phnom Kompong Trach, Wat Kirisan; admission US$1), 23km northeast of Kep. Built at the foot of a karst formation riddled with over 100 caverns and passageways, this Buddhist temple is linked by an underground passage to the centre of the hill, where the vine-draped cliffs of a hidden valley unfold before you. This is the sort of place where you'd hardly be surprised to see a dinosaur munching on foliage or, à la *Jurassic Park,* chewing on a lawyer. Friendly local kids with torches, eager to put their evening-school English to use, are happy to serve as guides; make sure your tip covers the cost of batteries.

To get to Wat Kiri Sela from Kep, take a moto/tuk-tuk (US$3/5) or grab a Phnom Penh–bound bus or minibus (both US$2). From the town of Kompong Trach, take the dirt road opposite the Acleda Bank for 2km.

NORTHEASTERN CAMBODIA

Eastern Cambodia is home to a diversity of landscapes and peoples, shattering the illusion that the country is all paddy fields and sugar palms. There are plenty of those in the lowland provinces, but in the northeast they yield to the forested mountains of Mondulkiri and Ratanakiri, both up-and-coming ecotourism areas.

If it is a walk on the wild side that fires your imagination, then the northeast is calling. It's home to rare forest elephants and freshwater dolphins, and peppering the area are thundering waterfalls, crater lakes and meandering rivers. Trekking, biking, kayaking and elephant adventures are all beginning to take off. The rolling hills and lush forests provide a home to many ethnic minority groups. Do the maths: it all adds up to an amazing experience.

Kompong Cham

☎042 / POP 45,400

This quiet Mekong city, an important trading post during the French period, serves as the gateway to Cambodia's northeast.

Sights & Activities

Koh Paen ISLAND

For a supremely relaxing bike ride, it's hard to beat Koh Paen, a rural, traffic-free island that's connected to the mainland about 600m south of the Mekong bridge by a motorised ferry in the wet season and an elaborate bamboo toll bridge – totally rebuilt from scratch each December – in the dry season.

Wat Nokor TEMPLE

The ultimate fusion temple, Wat Nokor (admission US$2) is a modern Buddhist pagoda squeezed into the walls of an 11th-century temple of sandstone and laterite. Located about 1km west of town.

Sleeping

There are several hotels along the riverfront.

Mekong Sunrise GUESTHOUSE $

(☎097 9129280; www.mekong-sunrise.com; Preah Bat Sihanouk St; r US$5-7; wi-fi) A new backpacker crashpad on the riverfront, Mekong Sunrise has spacious upper-floor rooms with access to a sprawling rooftop. Furnishings are sparse, but it's cheap enough.

Mekong Hotel HOTEL $

(☎941536; Preah Bat Sihanouk St; r with fan/air-con US$7/15; air-con, wi-fi) This old timer has been around for years and is still popular thanks to renovated rooms on the riverfront. The corridors are wide enough for an Ultimate Frisbee tournament.

Eating

Psar Thmei has **fruit stalls** in its northwest and southeast corners. After the sun goes down there's a **night market** along the river opposite the Mekong Hotel.

Destiny Coffee House CAFE $

(12 Vithei Pasteur St; mains US$2-5; ⏲7am-4.30pm Mon-Sat; wi-fi) An unexpected oasis, this stylish cafe has relaxing sofas and a contemporary look. The international menu includes some delicious hummus with dips and lip-smacking homemade cakes.

Smile Restaurant CAMBODIAN $

(Riverside St; www.bdsa-cambodia.org; mains US$2.50-4.50; wi-fi) This nonprofit restaurant run by the Buddhism and Society Development Association is a big hit with the NGO crowd for its big breakfasts, healthy menu and free wi-fi.

Lazy Mekong Daze INTERNATIONAL $

(Riverside St; mains US$2.50-4.50) With a pool table and a big screen for watching sports and movies, this is the place to be after dark. The menu parades a range of Khmer, Thai and Western food, and it has delicious Karem ice cream.

GETTING TO VIETNAM: PREK CHAK TO XA XIA

Getting to the border The easiest way to get to Prek Chak and on to Ha Tien, Vietnam, is on a direct bus from Phnom Penh (US$16, five hours), Sihanoukville (US$16, five hours), Kampot (US$10, two hours), or Kep (US$8, 1½ hours). Virak Buntham has a bus from Phnom Penh; Virak Buntham and two other companies ply the Sihanoukville–Kampot–Kep–Ha Tien route. A more flexible alternative from Phnom Penh or Kampot is to take any bus to Kompong Trach, then a moto (about US$3) for 15km, on a good gravel road, to the frontier. In Kep, tour agencies and guesthouses can arrange a direct moto (US$8, 40 minutes), *remorque* (US$13, one hour), or taxi (US$20, 30 minutes). Rates and times are almost double from Kampot.

At the border At **Prek Chak** (⏲6am-5.30pm), motos ask US$5 to take you to the Vietnamese border post 300m past the Cambodian one, and then all the way to Ha Tien (7km). You'll save money walking across no-man's land and picking up a moto on the other side for US$2 or so.

Moving on Travellers bound for Phu Quoc should arrive in Ha Tien no later than 12.30pm to secure a ticket on the 1pm ferry (230,000d; 1½ hours). Extremely early risers may be able to make it to Ha Tien in time to catch the (slower) 8.20am car ferry to Phu Quoc. Scheduled buses from Cambodia to Ha Tien arrive before the 1pm boat departs.

See p889 for information on crossing this border in the other direction.

Information

Preah Bat Sihanouk St, home to several hotels and eateries, runs along the riverfront. Psar Thmei (New Market) is a few blocks inland (west); Preah Monivong Blvd is one block further west.

ANZ Royal Bank (Preah Monivong Blvd) One of several banks with an ATM.

Sophary Internet (cnr Preah Bat Sihanouk St & Vithei Pasteur; per hr 3000r; ⏲7am-9pm) Check emails here.

Getting There & Around

Phnom Penh is 120km southwest. NH7 is in excellent shape all the way to the Lao border.

Phnom Penh Sorya and GST, with offices on Preah Monivong Blvd, run direct buses to Phnom Penh (13,000r, three hours). Rith Mony has two direct trips to Siem Reap per day (US$5, five hours). GST also has a daily trip to Battambang (30,000r, six hours).

Rith Mony buses from Phnom Penh to Sen Monorom (US$7.50), Ban Lung (US$10) and Stung Treng (US$7, six hours) pass through here, as do Sorya's buses to Stung Treng, and Pakse in Laos. Most buses come through around 10am. Most Stung Treng and Ban Lung buses take the long road via Snuol and stop in Kratie (US$4, three hours).

Faster share taxis to Phnom Penh (15,000r, two hours) leave from the northeast side of the market.

Several hotels and restaurants rent bicycles for US$1 to US$2 a day.

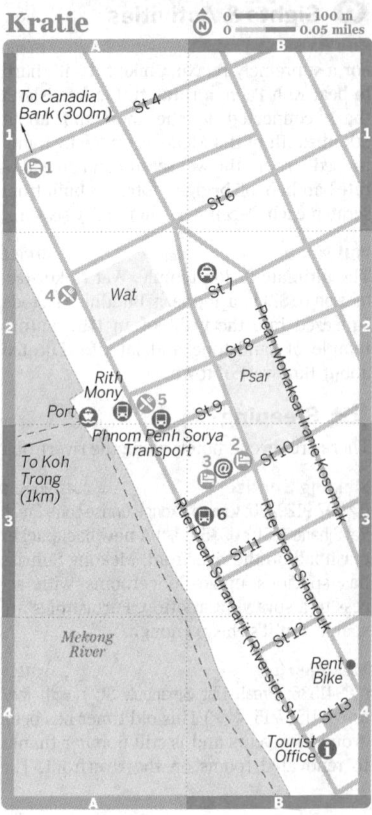

Kratie

☎072 / POP 30,000

The best place in Cambodia to glimpse Southeast Asia's remaining freshwater Irrawaddy dolphins, Kratie (pronounced 'kracheh') is a lively riverside town with a rich legacy of French-era architecture and some of the best Mekong sunsets in Cambodia. A thriving travel hub, it's the natural place to break the overland journey between Kompong Cham and Laos or to pick up the Mekong Discovery Trail (p126).

Kratie

Sleeping

1	Balcony Guesthouse	A1
2	Star Guesthouse	B3
3	You Hong Guesthouse II	B3

Eating

4	Food Stalls	A2
5	Red Sun Falling	A2

Transport

6	GST	B3

Sights & Activities

Dolphin Viewing WILDLIFE WATCHING

Approximately 75 critically endangered **freshwater Irrawaddy dolphins** (*trey pisaut*) live in the Mekong between Kratie and the Lao border. In the last few years, an alarming number of calves have been dying for reasons that are not clear to scientists. Groups working to ensure the survival of this rare creature and to promote sustainable dolphin-watching include the **WWF** (www.panda.org).

These gentle mammals can be seen at **Kampi**, about 15km north of Kratie (on the road to Sambor). A return moto/*remorque* ride costs about US$5/10, depending on how long the driver has to wait. Cycling is also an option.

Motorboats shuttle visitors out to the middle of the river to view the dolphins at close quarters. It costs US$9 per person for one to two persons and US$7 per person for groups of three or more. Encourage the boat driver to use the engine as little as possible once near the dolphins, as the noise is sure to disturb them.

Sleeping & Eating

As well as the guesthouses and hotels covered below, there are also homestays on the island of Koh Trong (p126) opposite Kratie town.

You Hong II Guesthouse GUESTHOUSE $
(☎085 885168; youhong _kratie@yahoo.com; 119 St 10; r US$5-13; ❄@) A great little guesthouse between the market and riverfront. As well as a good mix of rooms, there's a lively little bar-restaurant with travel info and internet access.

Balcony Guesthouse GUESTHOUSE $
(☎016 604036; balcony@y7mail.com; Rue Preah Suramarit; r US$5-12; ❄@) The sign proclaims it a Gust House, but don't be put off by the windbags, as this place attracts a crowd thanks to good-value rooms, a gay-friendly vibe and impressive food. Air-con costs an extra US$5.

Star Guesthouse GUESTHOUSE $
(☎017 491906; khmermao@yahoo.com; Rue Preah Sihanouk; r US$3-5; ❄) Back under the stewardship of the original family, this budget crashpad looks set to take off again thanks to cheap rooms and wholesome meals.

Red Sun Falling INTERNATIONAL $
(Rue Preah Suramarit; mains 6000-14,000r) One of the liveliest spots in town, with a relaxed cafe ambience, used books for sale and Asian and Western meals, including home-made brownies. By night it's a bar.

Along the riverfront, **food stalls** (Rue Preah Suramarit), sell two famous Kratie specialities: *krolan* (sticky rice, beans and coconut milk steamed inside a bamboo tube), displayed on tables that look like miniature church organs; and *nehm* (tangy, raw, spiced river fish wrapped in edible fresh leaves that are in turn wrapped in a cube of banana leaves).

GETTING TO VIETNAM: REMOTE EASTERN BORDERS

There are a couple of seldom-used remote border crossings in this part of Eastern Cambodia.

Trapaeng Plong to Xa Mat

Getting to the border Krek (Kraek), on NH7 55km southeast of Kompong Cham, is served by buses linking Kompong Cham with both Kratie and Sen Monorom. From there, take a moto 13km south along NH72 to snoozy Trapaeng Plong, marked by a candy-striped road barrier and a few tin shacks.

At the border The Trapaeng Plong border crossing is open from 7am to 5pm. Vietnamese visas must be arranged in advance via an embassy or consulate. Cambodian visas are available on arrival. There may be petty overcharging on either side, as with all remote borders. Transport change is necessary in both directions.

Moving on On the Vietnamese side, Xa Mat, motos and taxis go to Tay Ninh, 45km to the south.

Trapaeng Sre to Loc Ninh

Getting to the border To get to this crossing, seldom used by foreigners, catch a moto (US$5) in the much-maligned junction town of Snuol for an 18km trip southeast along NH74, which is little more than a rutted dirt track. Snuol, on nicely paved NH7, is linked by bus, share taxi and minibus with Sen Monorom, Kratie and Kompong Cham.

At the border The Trapaeng Sre border crossing is open 7am to 5pm. Vietnamese visas must be arranged in advance via an embassy or consulate. Cambodian visas are available on arrival. There may be petty overcharging on either side, as with all remote borders. Transport change is necessary in both directions.

Moving on On the Vietnamese side, the nearest town is Binh Long, 40km to the south – get there by moto or taxi.

These stalls are also a great place to sip a sunset beer or two.

Information

Kratie is laid out on a grid, with Rue Preah Suramarit running along the river and, at right angles, numbered streets heading inland. The market is one block inland between St 8 and St 10.

Cambodian Pride Tours (www.cambodianpridetours.com) Local tours website operated by two enthusiastic young guides from the Kratie area keen to promote real-life experiences.

Canadia Bank (cnr St 11 & Preah Mohaksat Iranie Kosomak) Includes an ATM.

CRDTours (099-834353; www.crdtours.org; Le Bungalow, Rue Preah Suramarit; 7.30-11am & 1.30-5pm daily) The best source of information on the Mekong Discovery Trail. Based at Le Bungalow boutique hotel, it is run to support local NGO the **Cambodian Rural Development Team** (CRDT; www.crdt.org).

Mekong Discovery Trail Office (cnr Rue Preah Suramarit & St 13) Supposedly located inside the Department of Tourism building, but rarely open.

Getting There & Away

Kratie is 348km northeast of Phnom Penh (250km via Chhlong) and 141km south of Stung Treng.

Express minivans, which pick you up from your guesthouse at 6am, are the fastest and most comfortable way to Phnom Penh (US$8, four hours). Buses depart from along the riverfront around St 8 and St 10. GST, Phnom Penh Sorya and Rith Mony operate buses to Phnom Penh (25,000r, six hours) via Snuol (US$2) and Kompong Cham (US$4, three hours); Stung Treng (20,000r, two hours); Ban Lung (US$10, six hours) in Ratanakiri; and Sen Monorom (25,000r) in Mondulkiri. There are also direct buses to Pakse (US$17; 12.30pm) in southern Laos.

Share taxis gather just north of the market, at St 7. Travelling via Chhlong (NH73) rather than along NH7, they can make it to Phnom Penh (US$10) in as little as four hours. Other destinations include Snuol (10,000r), Kompong Cham (30,000r) and Stung Treng (25,000r).

Hiring a moto driver costs about US$10 a day. Most guesthouses can arrange a motorbike (US$6 a day). Bicycles (6000r per day) are available from **Rent Bike** (124 Rue Preah Sihanouk; 6am-6pm), facing the post office.

Stung Treng

074 / POP 24,500

It may not be the most charming town in the country, but Stung Treng is back on the map thanks to the popular Cambodia–Laos border crossing just 60km north.

Tonlé Tourism Training Centre (973638; fieldco@tourismforhelp.org; s/d from US$6/8) is a guesthouse that doubles as a training centre to help underprivileged locals. Rooms are simple, but tasteful. The restaurant serves tasty Khmer dishes. **Riverside Guesthouse** (012 439454; riverside.tour@yahoo.com; r US$5-7; @) is a popular travellers' crossroads, with travel information and a popular bar-restaurant downstairs.

Eateries (mains around 4000r) with steaming pots of meat and fish for your perusal can be found in the southwest corner of the market.

Acleda Bank (half a block east of the market) has an ATM, and there are several internet places around the market.

THE MEKONG DISCOVERY TRAIL

The **Mekong Discovery Trail** (www.mekongdiscoverytrail.com) is a new initiative to open up stretches of the Mekong River around Stung Treng and Kratie to community-based tourism.

An excellent booklet outlining half-day to multi-day excursions around Kratie is available in Kratie and Stung Treng. Ideal for cycling, the trail is being signposted so that travellers interested in pedalling their way through a slice of rural life can follow the trail for a few hours or several days, overnighting in village **homestays** (US$3). Routes crisscross the Mekong frequently by ferry and traverse several Mekong islands, including **Koh Trong**, where there are two popular homestays and great cycling opportunities.

As well as homestays on Koh Trong, **CRDTours** (www.crdtours.org) can arrange homestays on **Koh Pdao**, an island 35km north of Kratie, and less popular **Koh Preah**, in southern Stung Treng province. Participants do some serious interacting with locals and even get their hands dirty on volunteer building or farming projects. Diversions include cycling and dolphin-spotting from the shore. It costs US$35/50 for one/two nights including all meals and transport.

GETTING TO LAOS: TRAPEANG KRIEL TO NONG NOK KHIENE

Getting to the border Minibuses link Kratie and Stung Treng (64km south of the frontier along smoothly paved NH7) with Trapeang Kriel and Laotian destinations further north. From Stung Treng there are minibuses (US$5) heading north to the border at around 7am and again after lunch (some continuing to Pakse).

At the border The Trapeang Kriel border post is open from 8am to 5pm. Cambodian (US$20) and Lao visas (US$30 to US$42 depending on nationality) are available at the border, but petty overcharging is common on both sides. The Laotians charge an 'overtime' fee if you pass through after 'working hours', ie on weekends, holidays or after 4pm.

Moving on Onward transport is not easily available at the border, so book a minibus at far as Don Det (US$9 from Stung Treng).

See p365 for information on crossing in the other direction.

Rith Mony, Phnom Penh Sorya and GST all have 7am buses to Phnom Penh (US$8 to US$10, nine hours) via Kratie (US$5, two hours) and Kompong Cham (US$7.50, six hours). Rith Mony has a 3pm bus to Ban Lung (US$5).

From the riverfront taxi park, share taxis and minibuses go to Phnom Penh (50,000r, eight hours) and Ban Lung (30,000r, four hours).

Ratanakiri Province

Up-and-coming Ratanakiri is making a name for itself as a diverse region of outstanding natural beauty that provides a remote home for a mosaic of minority peoples – Jarai, Tompuon, Brau and Kreung – with their own languages, traditions and customs.

Adrenalin activities abound. Swim in clear volcanic lakes, shower under waterfalls, or trek in the vast Virachey National Park, it's all here. Tourism is set to take off, but that is if the lowland politicians and generals don't plunder the place first. Ratanakiri is the frontline in the battle for land, and the slash-and-burn minorities are losing out thanks to their tradition of collective ownership. It is to be hoped someone wakes up and smells the coffee – there's plenty of that as well – before it's too late.

BAN LUNG

☎075 / POP 25,000

Affectionately known as '*dey krahorm*' (red earth) after its rust colour, Ban Lung provides a popular base for a range of Ratanakiri romps. It is one of the easiest places in Cambodia to arrange a jungle trek and has several beautiful lakes and waterfalls nearby (see p129).

Sights & Activities

Boeng Yeak Laom LAKE

(admission US$1) Boeng Yeak Laom is one of the most serene and sublimely beautiful sites in Cambodia. This clear blue crater lake, surrounded by dark-green jungle, is sacred to the indigenous minority peoples. It's a great place to take a dip, although Cambodians jump in fully clothed. The NGO-run **Cultural & Environmental Centre** (⌚8am-5.30pm), 500m around the lake, displays traditional Tompuon crafts. The adjacent kiosk sells authentic Tompuon crafts and rents innertubes (3000r).

Boeng Yeak Laom is 4km east of Ban Lung; turn right at the statue of the minority family. Motos cost about US$4 return, a bit more if the driver has to wait around.

Sleeping

TOP CHOICE **Tree Top Ecolodge** GUESTHOUSE $

(☎012 490333; www.treetop-ecolodge.com; r US$7-15; 📶) Setting the standard for budget digs in the northeast, rough-hewn walkways lead to all-wood bungalows with mosquito nets, thatch roofs and verandas with verdant valley views.

Lakeside Chheng Lok Hotel HOTEL $

(☎012 957422; lakeside-chhenglokhotel@yahoo.com; r US$5-20; ❄@📶) Overlooking Boeng Kansaign lake, this 65-room hotel has a choice of attractive garden bungalows or clean, spacious rooms, all with cable TV. Good all-rounder.

Prak Dara Guesthouse HOTEL $

(☎6666068; r with fan/air-con US$6/10; ❄@📶) Another new place above the lake, rooms here are cracking value given the cleanliness and comfort. Take advantage of the free wi-fi to plan your upcountry adventures.

Ban Lung

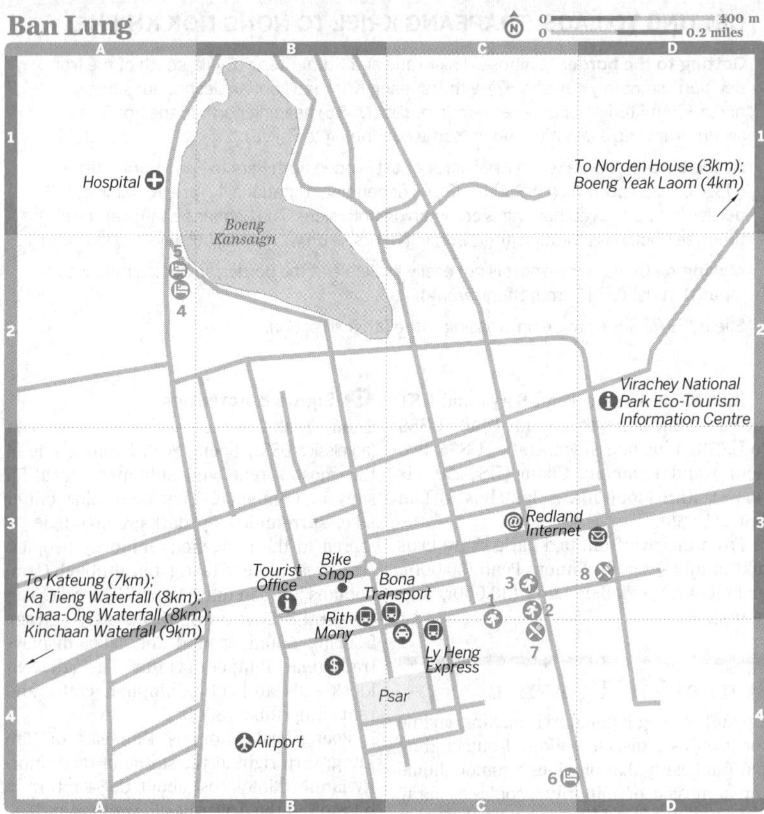

Ban Lung

Activities, Courses & Tours

1 Dutch Couple C3
2 Parrot Tours C3
3 Smiling Tours C3

Sleeping

4 Lakeside Chheng Lok Hotel A2
5 Prak Dara Guesthouse A2
6 Tree Top Ecolodge C4

Eating

7 A'Dam Restaurant C4
8 Gecko House D3
Rik's Café Cambodge .... (see 1)

Eating

Gecko House INTERNATIONAL $
(mains 6000-18,000r; ⏲10am-11pm) A charming little restaurant-bar with inviting sofas, soft lighting and famously frosty beer mugs, this is a great place by day or night. The menu features Thai, Khmer classics and some Western dishes.

Rik's Cafe Cambodge INTERNATIONAL $
(mains US$2-5) Run by the Dutch Couple, this relaxed cafe offers great valley views. Good for coffee and light bites by day and a spot of pre- or post-trek beer drinking by night.

A'Dam Restaurant INTERNATIONAL $
(mains US$2-4; ⏲11am-3pm & 5.30pm-midnight) An animated bar by night thanks to a pool table and dart board to tempt barflies, this mellow restaurant warmly welcomes locals, expats and travellers.

Information

For recommended tour companies, see the box opposite. Check out www.yaklom.com for ideas on what to do around Ratanakiri.

Acleda Bank Has an ATM.

Redland Internet Café (per hr US$2; ⏰7am-8pm)

Virachey National Park Eco-Tourism Information Centre (☎974125; ⏰7.30-11.30am & 2-5pm Mon-Fri) Has brochures on Ratanakiri.

Getting There & Away

Ban Lung is 588km northeast of Phnom Penh and 150km east of Stung Treng. The road between Ban Lung and O Pong Moan on NH7 was still under construction at the time of writing.

Buses to Phnom Penh (US$10, 11 hours) operate only in the dry season for now. Hong Ly, Rith Mony and Ly Heng Express make the trip, with early morning departures in either direction via Kratie, Snuol and Kompong Cham.

Speedy express minibus services offer guesthouse pick-ups at 6am and take the shortcut to Phnom Penh via Chhlong (US$12, nine hours). Try Ly Heng Express or **Bona Transport** (☎012 567161).

Share taxis go from the taxi park to Kratie (US$10 to US$12.50) and Phnom Penh (US$15 to US$17.50, seven hours). Pick-up trucks are slightly cheaper if you ride in the back.

Tree Top Guesthouse can arrange transport to Laos.

For details on the punishing overland trip to Sen Monorom, see p131.

Most guesthouses and hotels offer motorbike rentals from US$5 to US$7. Norden House rents out 250cc dirt bikes (US$25 per day). 4WDs start from US$50 and rise depending on the distance travelled.

Around Ratanakiri Province

WATERFALLS

Within 10km of Ban Lung you can visit spectacular **Chaa Ong**, set in a jungle gorge; **Ka Tieng** (Kateng), with a rock shelf you can clamber behind and vines to swing over the splashpool; and **Kinchaan** (Kachanh). Directions are signposted 3km west of town on the road to Stung Treng and admission to each is 2000r.

VOEN SAI

Situated 37km (1½ hours) northwest of Ban Lung, Voen Sai is on the banks of the Tonlé San about 15km south of Virachey National Park. A ferry (500r) links a cluster of eateries with the river's northern bank.

The Khmer Leu (Upper Khmer or ethnic minorities) of Ratanakiri bury their dead amid the ancient jungle, carving wooden effigies of the deceased – some holding sunglasses and mobile phones – to stand guard over the graves. In the village of **Kachon**, a 40-minute long-tailed motorboat ride upriver from Voen Sai, you can visit a **Tompuon cemetery** (admission US$1). The boat trip from Voen Sai costs US$15 for up to three people, including stops at an orderly **Chinese village**, five minutes downriver from Voen Sai, and a nearby Lao village.

RESPONSIBLE TREKKING AROUND RATANAKIRI

Overnight trekking has really started to take off around Ratanakiri, but make sure you link up with a guide who is culturally and ecologically sensitive and is clear about your expectations. Popular routes take in minority villages, including Kreung villages near the road to Ta Veng and Jarai villages up in Andong Meas district. Only official national-park rangers can take you into Virachey National Park. With deforestation continuing apace, last year's lush forest may be this year's barren expanse of tree stumps.

The association of **Tompuon guides** (yeak.loam@yahoo.com) is a good place to look for an indigenous guide. The association also runs an exclusive tour of several Tompuon villages around Boeng Yeak Laom.

Day hikes, elephant rides, kayaking and overnight treks are offered by a number of tour companies:

» **Dutch Couple** (☎097 679 2714; www.trekkingcambodia.com; ⏰closed Sep) One of the most experienced trekking operators in the province, run by – wait for it – a friendly Dutch couple.

» **Parrot Tours** (☎012 764714; www.jungletrek.blogspot.com) Sitha Nan is a national-park-trained guide with expert local knowledge.

» **Smiling Tours** (☎012 247713; smeyadventure@gmail.com) Smey often hangs out at Tree Top Ecolodge and offers a range of trips and treks.

TREKKING IN VIRACHEY NATIONAL PARK

One of Cambodia's most developed ecotourism programs takes visitors deep into 3325-sq-km **Virachey National Park** (admission US$5), an ecological gem in the country's far northeastern tip that's so remote it has yet to be fully explored. The park's forests and grasslands are home to elephants, gibbons and an amazing variety of birds, including hornbills and vultures. The area was once traversed by the Ho Chi Minh Trail and war relics are still lying around.

There are two treks available in Virachey. Prices listed are per-person for a group of two and include transport by moto to the trailhead, park admission, food, guides, porters, hammocks and boat transport where necessary. Prices rise for individuals.

» **Kalang Chhouy Sacred Mountain Trek** (two days/one night from US$59) This short trek starts from near Koklak village and includes a night by the Chai Chanang Waterfall. On the second day, continue to Phnom Gong, a sacred mountain for the Brau people, and swim at the Tju Preah rapids.

» **Phnom Veal Thom Wilderness Trek** (seven-day/eight-day from US$258/286) The longest trek starts from Ta Veng with an overnight homestay in a Brau village. The trek goes deep into the heart of the Phnom Veal Thom grasslands, an area rich in wildlife such as sambar deer, gibbon, langur, wild pig, bear and hornbill.

Bookings must be made at least a day or two ahead, via the park's official **Eco-Tourism Information Center** (☎075 974176, virachey@camintel.com; ⏰8-11.30am & 2-3pm Mon-Fri) in Ban Lung.

Voen Sai is 37km northwest of Ban Lung on an average-to-poor road, passable only by 4WD in the wet season.

Mondulkiri Province

Mondulkiri (Meeting of the Hills), the original Wild East of the country, is a world apart from the lowlands with not a rice paddy or palm tree in sight. Home to the hardy Bunong people and their noble elephants, this upland area is a seductive mix of grassy hills, pine groves and rainforests of jade green. Conservationists have grand plans for the sparsely populated province but are facing off against loggers, poachers, prospectors and well-connected speculators.

SEN MONOROM

☎073 / POP 10,000 / ELEV 800M

Sen Monorom, the best base for exploring Mondulkiri, has the feel of a remote outpost town. Many Bunong people from nearby villages come to Sen Monorom to trade; the distinctive baskets they carry on their backs makes them easy to spot.

Sights & Activities

Not much happens in Sen Monorom itself, but there's plenty to see and do nearby, including trips out to **Bunong villages** and **waterfalls**.

Head to the observation deck of **Phnom Bai Chuw** (Raw Rice Mountain), 6km northwest of Sen Monorom (accessible on foot or by moto), for a jaw-dropping view of the emerald forest, known to locals as **Samot Cheur** (Ocean of Trees).

GETTING TO VIETNAM: O YADAW TO LE THANH

Getting to the border Remote and rarely used by foreigners, this border crossing lies 64km from Ban Lung and 90km from Pleiku, Vietnam, for onward connections to Hoi An or Quy Nhon. From Ban Lung, take a through minibus (30,000r, 7.30am) to the O Yadaw border.

At the border The border crossing is open from 7am to 5pm. Vietnamese visas must be prearranged.

Moving on On the Vietnamese side of the frontier, *xe oms* (motos) await to take you to Duc Co (20km), where there are buses (20,000d) to Pleiku.

See p874 for information on crossing this border in the other direction.

Sleeping

TOP CHOICE Nature Lodge GUESTHOUSE $
(☎012 230272; www.naturelodgecambodia.com; r US$10-30) Located on a windswept hilltop near town, this quirky ecoresort has basic bungalow accommodation with hot showers and some incredible Swiss Family Robinson–style chalets. The inviting restaurant is decorated with abandoned tree trunks and has a good range of traveller fare, plus a pool table.

Phanyro Guesthouse GUESTHOUSE $
(☎017 770867; r US$8-12) This is a favourite with visiting volunteers and NGOs, offering a clutch of cottages perched on a ridge overlooking the river valley. Clean with a capital C.

Long Vibol Guesthouse GUESTHOUSE $
(☎012 944647; r US$5-20) An attractive wooden resort with 20 rooms set amid a lush garden. Staff here are knowledgeable about the area. Includes a restaurant popular with visiting Khmers.

Eating & Drinking

Greenhouse Restaurant INTERNATIONAL $
(mains US$1.50-3.50) As well as internet access and tour information, Greenhouse is a popular place for inexpensive Khmer and Western dishes. By night, this place draws the drinkers to sup beers and cocktails against a backdrop of ambient reggae beats.

Khmer Kitchen CAMBODIAN $
(mains US$2-4) This unassuming street-side eatery whips up some of the most flavoursome Khmer food in the hills. The *kari saik trey* (fish coconut curry) and other curries are particularly scrumptious.

Information

Acleda Bank An ATM located on the road to Phnom Penh.

Greenhouse (☎017 905659; www.greenhouse-tour.blogspot.com) Offers internet access and the most comprehensive tour progam around the province.

Bunong Place (☎012 474879; www.bunongcenter.org; ⏲6am-6pm) This NGO-run 'drop-in centre' for Bunong people is a good source of information on sustainable tourism, village homestays and elephant rides. Sells authentic Bunong textiles and local coffee, sodas and beers are available. Also provides trained Bunong guides for local tours, costing US$15/25 per half/full day, including motorbike.

THE OVERLAND TRAIL RUNS DRY

Glance at a map and it seems obvious: the best way to visit both Mondulkiri and Ratanakiri without backtracking is to make a grand loop via the remote villages of Koh Nhek and Lumphat. Alas, while the road from Sen Monorom to Koh Nhek (93km) is in good shape and takes just a couple of hours, north of there – until the Tonlé Srepok River – the road vanishes into a spider's web of ox-cart trails. Over the past few years, a handful of hardcore bikers have been using this route during the dry season (wet-season travel is close to impossible), but only attempt it if you have years of biking experience and an iron backside. A local guide who knows the route, spare parts for your bike, copious amounts of water and a compass should make for a smoother journey.

A few intrepid moto drivers in both Ban Lung and Sen Monorom ply this route. The journey takes about nine hours, with a few long breaks along the way, and costs a hefty US$50 or so. A cheaper option is to use a minibus between Sen Monorom and Koh Nhek (15,000r) and charter a moto driver from there to Lumphat for about US$25. In the reverse direction, make your way to Lumphat and negotiate a moto south to Koh Nhek. Cheaper again but a little less adventurous is a combination of two buses via Kratie.

Work has started on upgrading the road and a new overland trail should be up and running by 2013.

Getting There & Away

NH76 to Sen Monorom is now in fantastic shape, including some impressive bridges across the deep river valleys.

Rith Mony and Phnom Penh Sorya run morning buses to/from Phnom Penh (US$7.50, eight hours) via Snuol (US$3.75, three hours) and Kompong Cham (US$6.25, five hours). Faster morning share taxis (US$12.50) and minivans (US$10) to Phnom Penh are best reserved a day in advance.

Minivans are a good option for Kratie (30,000r, 4½ hours). Count on at least one early

WARNING

The Ho Chi Minh Trail once passed through the hills of Ratanakiri where it was nicknamed the Sihanouk Trail in reference to Cambodia's then head of state. This region was heavily bombed by the Americans and there is still some unexploded ordnance (UXO) around. Never touch anything that looks vaguely like UXO.

morning departure and two or three departures around lunchtime.

Getting Around

Motorbike rental (US$5 to US$10 a day) can be arranged through guesthouses and hotels in town. Greenhouse Restaurant has 250cc dirt bikes (US$15) for rent. 4WD or pick-up-truck rental starts from US$50 per day and up, depending on the destination.

AROUND SEN MONOROM

Monorom Falls, set in the forest a walkable 3km northwest of town, is the closest thing to a public swimming pool for Sen Monorom. Motos take people out here for about US$3 return.

Two-tiered **Bou Sraa Waterfall** (admission 5000r), 35km east of Sen Monorom along an unfinished toll road, is famous throughout the country. The toll is a little cheeky given the terrible state of the last part of the road. Hire a moto for the day (US$15) or charter a car (US$60) for a group.

UNDERSTAND CAMBODIA

Cambodia Today

Cambodia is at a crossroads in its road to recovery from the brutal years of Khmer Rouge rule. Compare Cambodia today with the dark abyss into which it plunged under the Khmer Rouge and the picture looks optimistic, but look to its more successful neighbours and it's easy to be pessimistic. Cambodia must choose its path: pluralism, progress and prosperity or intimidation, impunity and injustice. The jury is still very much out on which way things will go.

Another jury still out is that of the Khmer Rouge trial, sidelined by the politics of the Cold War for two decades, and then delayed by bureaucratic bickering at home and abroad. The Extraordinary Chambers in the Courts of Cambodia (ECCC) trial is finally under way, but it is by no means certain that the wheels of justice will turn fast enough to keep up with the rapid ageing of the surviving Khmer Rouge leaders. Military commander Ta Mok died in custody in 2006 and both Ieng Sary and Nuon Chea are suffering from health complications. However, the trial of Kaing Guek Eav, aka Comrade Duch, dominated headlines for much of 2010

THE ELEPHANT VALLEY PROJECT

For an original elephant experience, visit the **Elephant Valley Project** (☎099 696041; www.elephantvalleyproject.org). The project entices local mahouts to bring their often overworked and wounded elephants to this sanctuary, where, in the words of project coordinator Jack Highwood, 'they can learn how to act like elephants again'.

Most tour companies in Mondulkiri make a point to stress that their tours employ only humanely treated elephants. Highwood wonders whether it's possible to know the truth. 'Most elephants in Mondulkiri are in a highly abused state', he says. 'They are beaten on the head and made to do things they aren't meant to be doing. In Mondulkiri, the elephant is basically seen as a cheap tractor.'

Highwood no longer allows visitors to ride the elephants. Instead, you simply walk with the herd through the forest and observe them in their element. In the process you learn a lot about not only elephant behaviour but also Bunong culture and forest ecology.

A two-day stay, including all meals, transport to the site and a night's accommodation in exquisite bungalows tucked into the jungle on a ridge overlooking the valley, costs US$100 per person. A day trip costs US$50, but don't show up unannounced. **Bunong Place** in Sen Monorom can handle bookings. Short- and long-term volunteers who want to help the project while learning mahout skills are welcome, although volunteers must pay extra to cover training costs.

COMMUNITY HOMESTAYS IN MONDULKIRI

WWF (☎088 899 7060; www.mondulkiritourism.org) has recently helped two villages launch projects geared towards giving tourists a glimpse into traditional Bunong lifestyles. In **Krong Te**, about 25km east of Sen Monorom, you can ride elephants, view traditional dancing, learn to weave baskets and buy locally-produced honey, fruits and Bunong handicrafts. About 65km north of Sen Monorom on the road to Koh Nhek, the village of **Dei Ey** offers homestays, traditional meals, elephant rides and trekking in surrounding Mondulkiri Protected Forest. Choose from day trips to two-day and three-day experiences; prices start from US$19 for a day trip rising to the US$150 mark for three-day adventures, depending on group sizes. Portions of the proceeds from these initiatives go into a community fund designed to improve local livelihoods and protect the forest.

and an appeal verdict was anticipated in 2011. Many Cambodians were dismayed by the lenient sentence of 35 years (only 19 of which remain to be served) initially passed, given the magnitude of his crimes.

Cambodia remains one of the poorest countries in Asia, and it's a tough existence for much of the population. According to the UN Development Programme (UNDP; www.undp.org), Cambodia remains in worse shape than Congo and the Solomon Islands, just scraping in ahead of Myanmar, while Transparency International (www.transparency.org), the anticorruption watchdog, rates the country a lowly 158 out of the 180 countries ranked.

Cambodia is like the teen starlet who has just been discovered by an adoring public: everyone wants something from her but not everyone wants what is in her best interests. The government, long shunned by international big business, is keen to benefit from all these newfound opportunities. Contracts are being signed off like autographs and there are concerns for the long-term development of the country. The Chinese have come to the table to play for big stakes and have pledged US$1.1 billion in assistance in the last couple of years, considerably more than all the other donors put together– ostensibly with no burdensome strings attached.

There are two faces to Cambodia: one shiny and happy, the other dark and complex. For every illegal eviction of city dwellers or land grab by a general, there will be a new NGO school offering better education, or a new clean-water initiative to improve the lives of the average villager. Such is the yin and yang of Cambodia, a country that both inspires and confounds. Like an onion, the more layers you unravel, the more it makes you want to cry, but these are spontaneous tears, sometimes of sorrow, sometimes of joy.

The royal family has been a constant in contemporary Cambodian history and no-one more so than the mercurial monarch King Sihanouk, who once again surprised the world with his abdication in 2004. His relatively unknown son King Sihamoni assumed the throne and has brought renewed credibility to the monarchy, untainted as he is by the partisan politics of the past. Meanwhile, the political arm of the royal family, Funcinpec, has continued to haemorrhage.

But there's a new royal family in town, the Cambodian People's Party (CPP), and they are making plans for the future with dynastic alliances between their offspring. At the head of this elite is Prime Minister Hun Sen, who has proved himself a survivor, personally as well as politically, for he lost an eye during the battle for Phnom Penh in 1975. It would appear that for the time being at least, with a poorly educated electorate and a divided opposition, 'in the country of the blind, the one-eyed man is king'.

History

The good, the bad and the ugly is a simple way to sum up Cambodian history. Things were good in the early years, culminating in the vast Khmer empire, unrivalled in the region during four centuries of dominance. Then the bad set in, from the 13th century, as ascendant neighbours steadily chipped away at Cambodian territory. In the 20th century it turned downright ugly, as a brutal civil war culminated in the genocidal rule of the Khmer Rouge (1975–79), from which Cambodia is still recovering.

Funan & Chenla

The Indianisation of Cambodia began in the 1st century AD as traders plying the sea route from the Bay of Bengal to southern China brought Indian ideas and technologies to what is now southern Vietnam. The largest of the era's nascent kingdoms, known to the Chinese as Funan, embraced the worship of the Hindu deities Shiva and Vishnu and, at the same time, Buddhism, and was crucial in the transmission of Indian culture to the interior of Cambodia.

From the 6th to 8th centuries Cambodia seems to have been ruled by a collection of competing kingdoms. Chinese annals refer to 'Water Chenla', apparently the area around the modern-day town of Takeo, and 'Land Chenla', further north along the Mekong and around Sambor Prei Kuk.

The Rise & Fall of Angkor

The Angkorian era lasted from AD 802 to 1432, encompassing periods of conquest, turmoil and retreat, revival and decline, and fits of remarkable productivity.

In 802, Jayavarman II (reigned c 802–50) proclaimed himself a *devaraja* (god-king). He instigated an uprising against Javanese domination of southern Cambodia and, through alliances and conquests, brought the country under his control, becoming the first monarch to rule most of what we now call Cambodia.

The Khmer empire was made possible by *baray* (reservoirs) and irrigation works sophisticated and massive enough to support Angkor's huge population. The first records of such works date from the time of Indravarman I (r 877–89), whose rule was marked by the flourishing of Angkorian art, including the construction of temples in the Roluos area.

In the 9th century, Yasovarman I (r 889-910) moved the capital to Angkor, creating a new centre for worship, scholarship and the arts. After a period of turmoil and conflict, Suryavarman II (r 1113–1150) unified the kingdom and embarked on another phase of territorial expansion, waging successful but costly wars against both Vietnam and Champa (an Indianised kingdom that occupied what is now southern and central Vietnam). His devotion to the Hindu deity Vishnu inspired him to commission Angkor Wat.

The tables soon turned. Champa struck back in 1177 with a naval expedition up the Mekong, taking Angkor by surprise and putting the king to death. But the following year a cousin of Suryavarman II – soon crowned Jayavarman VII (r 1181 to c 1219) – rallied the Khmers and defeated the Chams in another epic naval battle. A devout follower of Mahayana Buddhism, it was he who built the city of Angkor Thom.

Scholars believe that Angkor's decline was already on the horizon when Angkor Wat was built – and that the reasons were partly environmental. The 1000-sq-km irrigation network had begun silting up due to deforestation and erosion, and the latest climate data from tree rings indicates that two prolonged droughts also played a role.

During the twilight years of the empire, religious conflict and internecine rivalries were rife. The Thais made repeated incursions into Angkor, sacking the city in 1351 and again in 1431, and from the royal court making off with thousands of intellectuals, artisans and dancers, whose profound impact on Thai culture can be seen to this day.

From 1600 until the arrival of the French, Cambodia was ruled by a series of weak kings whose intrigues often involved seeking the protection of either Thailand or Vietnam – granted, of course, at a price.

French Colonialism

The era of yo-yoing between Thai and Vietnamese masters came to a close in 1864, when French gunboats intimidated King Norodom I (r 1860–1904) into signing a treaty of protectorate. An exception in the annals of colonialism, the French presence really did protect the country at a time when it was in danger of being swallowed by its more powerful neighbours. In 1907 the French pressured Thailand into returning the northwest provinces of Battambang, Siem Reap and Sisophon, bringing Angkor under Cambodian control for the first time in more than a century.

Led by King Sihanouk (r 1941–55 and 1993–2004), Cambodia declared independence on 9 November 1953.

Independence & Civil War

The period after 1953 was one of peace and prosperity, and a time of creativity and optimism – Cambodia's golden years. Phnom Penh grew in size and stature and the temples of Angkor were the leading tourist destination in Southeast Asia. Dark clouds were circling, however, as the war in Vietnam began sucking in neighbouring countries.

As the 1960s drew to a close, the North Vietnamese and the Viet Cong were using Cambodian territory in their battle against South Vietnam and US forces, prompting devastating American bombing and a land invasion into eastern Cambodia.

MUST SEE

The Killing Fields (1984) is a poignant film about American journalist Sydney Schanberg and his Cambodian assistant both during and after the Khmer Rouge takeover.

In March 1970 Sihanouk, now serving as prime minister, was overthrown by General Lon Nol, and took up residence in Beijing. Here he set up a government-in-exile that allied itself with an indigenous Cambodian revolutionary movement that Sihanouk had dubbed the Khmer Rouge. Violence engulfed large parts of the country.

Khmer Rouge Rule

Upon taking Phnom Penh on 17 April 1975 – two weeks before the fall of Saigon (see p895) – the Khmer Rouge implemented one of the most radical and brutal restructurings of a society ever attempted. Its goal was to transform Cambodia – renamed Democratic Kampuchea – into a giant peasant-dominated agrarian cooperative, untainted by anything that had come before. Within days, the entire populations of Phnom Penh and provincial towns, including the sick, elderly and infirm, were forced to march into the countryside and work as slaves for 12 to 15 hours a day. Intellectuals were systematically wiped out – having glasses or speaking a foreign language was reason enough to be killed. The advent of Khmer Rouge rule was proclaimed Year Zero.

Leading the Khmer Rouge was Saloth Sar, better known as Pol Pot. As a young man, he won a scholarship to study in Paris, where he began developing the radical Marxist ideas that later metamorphosed into extreme Maoism. Under his rule, Cambodia became a vast slave labour camp. Meals consisted of little more than watery rice porridge twice a day, meant to sustain men, women and children through a back-breaking day in the fields. Disease stalked the work camps, malaria and dysentery striking down whole families.

Khmer Rouge rule was brought to an end by the Vietnamese, who liberated the almost-empty city of Phnom Penh on 7 January 1979. It is still not known exactly how many Cambodians died during the three years, eight months and 20 days of Khmer Rouge rule. The most accepted estimate is that at least 1.7 million people perished at the hands of Pol Pot and his followers. The **Documentation Center of Cambodia** (www.dccam.org) records the horrific events of the period.

A Sort of Peace

As Vietnamese tanks neared Phnom Penh in early 1979, the Khmer Rouge fled westward with as many civilians as it could seize, taking refuge in the mountains along the Thai border. The Vietnamese installed a new government led by several former Khmer Rouge officers, including current Prime Minister Hun Sen, who had defected to Vietnam in 1977. In the dislocation that followed liberation, little rice was planted or harvested, leading to a massive famine.

The civil war continued throughout the 1980s. In February 1991 all parties – including the Khmer Rouge – signed the Paris Peace Accords, according to which the UN Transitional Authority in Cambodia (UNTAC) would rule the country for two years. Although UNTAC is still heralded as one of the UN's success stories – elections with a 90% turnout were held in 1993 – the Khmer Rouge soon re-established a guerrilla network throughout Cambodia. UNTAC is also remembered for causing a significant increase in prostitution and AIDS.

The last Khmer Rouge hold-outs, including Ta Mok, were not defeated until the capture of Anlong Veng and Prasat Preah Vihear by government forces in the spring of 1998. Pol Pot cheated justice by dying a sorry death near Anlong Veng during that year, and was cremated on a pile of old tyres.

The Culture

People & Population

Nearly 15 million people live in Cambodia. With a rapid growth rate of about 2% a year, the population is predicted to reach 20 million by 2025. According to official statistics, around 96% of the people are ethnic Khmers, making the country the most homogeneous in Southeast Asia, but in reality anywhere between 10% and 20% of the population is of Cham, Chinese or Vietnamese origin.

MUST READ

First They Killed My Father (2001) was written by Luong Ung and covers the destruction of an urban Cambodian family through execution and disease during the Khmer Rouge period.

KHMER ROUGE & THE UN

The UN allowed the Khmer Rouge to occupy the Cambodian seat at the UN General Assembly until 1991, meaning the murderers represented their victims for 12 years. This was due to the politics of the Cold War at the time and China's insistence on protecting its Khmer Rouge allies.

Cambodia's diverse Khmer Leu (Upper Khmer) or Chunchiet (minorities), who live in the country's mountainous regions, probably number between 75,000 and 100,000.

The official language is Khmer, spoken by 95% of the population. English has taken over from French as the second language of choice, although Chinese is also growing in popularity. Life expectancy is currently 62 years.

Lifestyle

For untold centuries, life in Cambodia has centred on family, food and faith.

Extended families stick together, solving problems collectively, pooling resources and gathering to celebrate festivals and mourn deaths. Ties remain strong despite the fact that increasing numbers of young people are migrating to the cities in search of opportunity.

Food is extremely important to Cambodians as they have tasted what it is like to be without. Famine stalked the country in the late 1970s and, even today, there are serious food shortages in times of drought or inflation. For country folk – still the vast majority of the population – survival depends on what they can grow, and the harvest cycle dictates the rhythm of rural life.

Faith is a rock in the lives of many older Cambodians, and Buddhism helped them to survive the terrible years and then rebuild their lives after the Khmer Rouge.

Economy

Badly traumatised by decades of conflict, Cambodia's economy was long a gecko amid the neighbouring dragons. This has slowly started to change, as the economy has been liberalised and investors are circling to take advantage of the new opportunities.

Before the civil war, rubber was the leading industry and it's bouncing back with new plantations. Other plantation industries taking off include palm oil and paper pulp. Virgin forest is being cut down on the pretext of replanting, but the ecosystem never recovers.

The garment sector is important to the economy, with factories ringing the Cambodian capital. Cambodia is trying to carve a niche for itself as an ethical producer, with good labour relations and air-conditioned factories. It's no picnic in the factories, but the alternative is often the rice fields or the shadowy fringes of the entertainment industry, which is often a one-way ticket into prostitution.

Tourism is a big deal in Cambodia with more than two million visitors arriving in 2008, a doubling of numbers in just a few years. Thousands of jobs are being created every year and this is proving a great way to integrate the huge number of young people into the economy.

Foreign aid was long the mainstay of the Cambodian economy, supporting half the government's budget, and NGOs have done a lot to force important sociopolitical issues onto the agenda. However, with multibillion-dollar investments stacking up and the Chinese government loaning vast sums with no strings attached, it looks like their days in the sun could be numbered, and the government may no longer be influenced by their lobbying.

Corruption remains a way of life in Cambodia. It is a major element of the Cambodian economy and exists to some extent at all levels of government. Sometimes it is overt, but increasingly it is covert, with private companies often securing very favourable business deals on the basis of their connections. It seems everything has a price, including ancient temples, national parks and even genocide sites.

Religion

The majority of Khmers (95%) follow the Theravada branch of Buddhism. Buddhism in Cambodia draws heavily on its predecessors, incorporating many cultural traditions from Hinduism for ceremonies such as birth, marriage and death; as well as genies and spirits, such as Neak Ta, which link back to a pre-Indian animist past.

Under the Khmer Rouge, the majority of Cambodia's Buddhist monks were murdered and nearly all of the country's wats (more than 3000) were damaged or destroyed. In the late 1980s, Buddhism once again became the state religion.

Other religions found in Cambodia are Islam, practised by the Cham community;

animism, among the hill tribes; and Christianity, which is making inroads via missionaries and Christian NGOs.

Arts

The Khmer Rouge regime not only killed the living bearers of Khmer culture, it also destroyed cultural artefacts, statues, musical instruments, books and anything else that served as a reminder of a past it was trying to efface. The temples of Angkor were spared as a symbol of Khmer glory and empire, but little else survived. Despite this, Cambodia is witnessing a resurgence of traditional arts and a growing interest in cross-cultural fusion.

Cambodia's royal ballet is a tangible link with the glory of Angkor and includes a unique *apsara* (heavenly nymphs) dance. Cambodian music, too, goes back at least as far as Angkor. To get some sense of the music that Jayavarman VII used to like, check out the bas-reliefs at Angkor Wat.

In the mid-20th century a vibrant Cambodian pop music scene developed, but it was killed off by the Khmer Rouge. After the war, overseas Khmers established a pop industry in the USA and some Cambodian-Americans, raised on a diet of rap, are now returning to their homeland. The Los Angeles–based sextet Dengue Fever, inspired by 1960s Cambodian pop and psychedelic rock, is the ultimate fusion band.

The people of Cambodia were producing masterfully sensuous sculptures – much more than mere copies of Indian forms – in the age of Funan and Chenla. The Banteay Srei style of the late 10th century is regarded as a high point in the evolution of Southeast Asian art.

Environment

The Land

Modern-day Cambodia covers 181,035 sq km, making it a little more than half the size of Vietnam. It has 435km of coastline along the island-specked Gulf of Thailand.

Cambodia's two dominant geographical features are the mighty Mekong and Tonlé Sap, Southeast Asia's largest lake. The rich sediment deposited during the annual wet-season flooding has made central Cambodia incredibly fertile.

In Cambodia's southwest quadrant, much of the land mass is covered by the Cardamom Mountains and, near Kampot, the Elephant Mountains. Along Cambodia's northern border with Thailand, the plains collide with the Dangkrek Mountains, a striking sandstone escarpment more than 300km long and up to 550m high.

In the northeastern corner of the country, in the provinces of Ratanakiri and Mondulkiri, the plains give way to the Eastern Highlands, a remote region of densely forested mountains and high plateaus.

Wildlife

It's estimated that 212 species of mammal live in Cambodia. Creatures under serious threat include the Asian elephant, tiger, banteng (a wild ox), gaur, black gibbon, clouded leopard, fishing cat, marbled cat, sun bear, and pangolin.

A whopping 720 bird species find Cambodia a congenial home, thanks in large part to its year-round water resources, especially the marshes around Tonlé Sap. The Sam Veasna Center (p92) runs birdwatching trips.

Cambodia has some of the last remaining freshwater Irrawaddy dolphins (p124). The Mekong giant catfish, which can weigh up to 300kg, is critically endangered due to habitat loss and overfishing.

About 240 species of reptile can be found here. Four types of snake are especially dangerous: the cobra, king cobra, banded krait and Russell's viper.

The surest way to see Cambodian animals up close is to drop by the Phnom Tamao Wildlife Sanctuary (p80) near Phnom Penh or the Angkor Centre for Conservation of Biodiversity (ACCB; p98) near Siem Reap.

TONLÉ SAP: THE HEARTBEAT OF CAMBODIA

During the wet season (June to October), the Mekong River rises dramatically, forcing the Tonlé Sap river to flow northwest into Tonlé Sap (Great Lake). During this period, the lake swells from around 3000 sq km to almost 13,000 sq km, and from the air Cambodia looks like one almighty puddle. As the Mekong falls during dry season, the Tonlé Sap river reverses its flow, and the lake's floodwaters drain back into the Mekong. This unique process makes Tonlé Sap one of the world's richest sources of freshwater fish.

National Parks

The good news is that national parks, wildlife sanctuaries, protected landscapes and multiple-use areas now cover 43,000 sq km, or around 25% of Cambodia's surface area. The bad news is that the government does not have the resources – or, in some cases, the will – to actually protect these areas beyond drawing lines on a map.

Cambodia's most important national parks, all of them threatened by development and/or deforestation, are Bokor (p120), Botum Sakor (p110), Kirirom (p81), Ream (p117) and Virachey (p130).

Environmental Issues

The greatest threat to Cambodia's globally important ecosystems is illegal logging, carried out to provide charcoal and timber, and to clear land for cash-crop plantations. The environmental watchdog **Global Witness** (www.globalwitness.org) publishes meticulously documented exposés on corrupt military and civilian officials and their well-connected business partners.

In the short term, deforestation is contributing to worsening floods along the Mekong, but the long-term implications of deforestation are mind-boggling. Siltation, combined with overfishing and pollution, may lead to the eventual death of Tonlé Sap lake, a catastrophe for future generations of Cambodians.

A new challenge is oil, which has been discovered off Sihanoukville. Sloppy extraction could devastate Cambodia's lovely coast, including pristine mangrove forests and may inevitably add fuel to the fires of corruption that burn the Cambodian economy.

Detritus of all sorts, especially plastic bags and bottles, can be seen in distressing quantities all over the country.

Food & Drink

Some traditional Cambodian dishes are similar to those of neighbouring Laos and Thailand (though not as spicy), others closer to Chinese and Vietnamese cooking. The French left their mark, too.

Thanks to the Tonlé Sap, freshwater fish – often *ahng* (grilled) – are a huge part of the Cambodian diet. The legendary national dish, *amok*, is fish baked with coconut and lemon grass in banana leaves. *Prahoc* (fermented fish paste) is used to flavour foods, with coconut and lemongrass making regular cameos.

TRAVEL YOUR TASTE BUDS

You're going to encounter food that's unusual, strange, maybe even immoral – or just plain weird. The fiercely omnivorous Cambodians find nothing strange in eating insects, algae, offal or fish bladders. They'll dine on a duck embryo, brew up some brains or snack on some spiders. They'll peel live frogs to grill on a barbecue or down wine infused with cobra to increase their virility. To the Khmers, there's nothing 'strange' about anything that will sustain the body. They'll try anything once, even a burger.

For obvious reasons, please avoid eating endangered species.

We Dare You! The Top Five

Try these Cambodian treats:

- crickets
- duck embryo
- durian
- *prahoc* (fermented fish paste)
- grilled tarantulas

A proper Cambodian meal almost always includes *samlor* (soup), served at the same time as other courses. *Kyteow* is a rice-noodle soup that will keep you going all day. *Bobor* (rice porridge), eaten for breakfast, lunch or dinner, is best sampled with some fresh fish and a dash of ginger.

As an approximate guide, prices for main dishes when eating out are budget ($) US$1 to US$5, midrange ($$) US$5 to US$10 and top end ($$$) US$10 plus.

Tap water *must* be avoided, especially in rural areas. Bottled water is widely available but coconut milk, sold by machete-wielding street vendors, is more ecological and may be more sterile.

The beers of choice are Angkor, Anchor (pronounced An-Chore to differentiate it from Angkor), locally brewed Tiger, newcomer Kingdom Beer and many popular imports from Beerlao to Tsingtao. Rural folk drink palm wine, tapped from the sugar palms that dot the landscape. *Tukaloks* (fruit shakes) are mixed with milk, sugar and sometimes a raw egg.

SURVIVAL GUIDE

DIRECTORY A–Z

Accommodation

In popular tourist destinations, budget guesthouses generally charge US$5 to US$8 for a room with a cold-water bathroom. A few very basic places, some with shared showers, have rooms for US$3. In much of rural Cambodia, the standard rate for the cheapest room is US$5, usually with a bathroom and satellite TV.

Accommodation is busiest from mid-November to March. Discounts are possible during the wet season (June to October). All rooms quoted in this chapter have bathrooms unless stated otherwise.

Homestays, often part of a **community-based ecotourism project** (ww.ccben.org), are a good way to meet the local people and learn about Cambodian life.

Accommodation prices in this chapter are divided into three categories: budget ($), for a place whose double rooms cost less than US$20, midrange ($$) between US$210 and US$50, and top end ($$$) over US$50.

Activities

Cambodia is steadily emerging as an ecotourism destination and now offers rainforest trekking in the Cardamom Mountains and Ratanakiri (p129), walking with elephants in Mondulkiri (p132), scuba diving and snorkelling near Sihanoukville (p113), bird-watching in Siem Reap province and beyond (p92), and cycling along the Mekong Discovery Trail (p126) and around the temples of Angkor (p91). It's also a popular destination for adventurous dirt biking for those with some experience.

Business Hours

Most Cambodians get up very early and it's not unusual to see people out exercising at 5.30am when you're heading home – ahem, sorry, getting up.

Government offices, open from Monday to Friday and on Saturday mornings, theoretically begin the working day at 7.30am, break for a siesta from 11.30am to 2pm, and end the day at 5pm. However, it's a safe bet that few staffers will be around early in the morning or after 3.30pm or 4pm, as their real income is earned elsewhere. Government jobs are notoriously poorly paid and teachers, for instance, earn less than US$50 a month.

Local markets *(psar)* operate seven days a week and usually open and close with the sun, running from 6.30am to 5.30pm. Shops in cities and larger towns tend to be open from about 8am until 7pm Monday to Saturday, and most are open on Sundays too.

Banking hours vary slightly, but you can reckon on core weekday hours of between 8.30am and 3pm. Most are also open Saturday mornings.

Local restaurants are generally open from about 6.30am until 9pm and international restaurants until a little later.

Any exceptions to these hours are listed in individual reviews.

Customs

A 'reasonable amount' of duty-free items is allowed into the country. Travellers arriving by air might bear in mind that alcohol and cigarettes are on sale at well below duty-free prices on the streets of Phnom Penh. It is illegal to take antiquities out of the country.

Electricity

The usual voltage is 220V, 50 cycles, but power surges and power cuts are common, particularly in the provinces. Electrical sockets are usually two-prong, flat or round pin.

Embassies & Consulates

Some of the embassies located in Phnom Penh:

Australia (Map p74; ☎213413; 16 National Assembly St)

France (Map p66; ☎430020; 1 Monivong Blvd)

Germany (Map p74; ☎216381; 76-78 St 214)

BOTTOMS UP

When Cambodians propose a toast, they usually stipulate what percentage must be downed. If they are feeling generous, it might be just *ha-sip pea-roi* (50%), but more often than not it is *moi roi pea-roi* (100%). This is why they love ice in their beer, as they can pace themselves over the course of the night. Many a *barang* (foreigner) has ended up face down on the table at a Cambodian wedding when trying to outdrink the Khmers without the help of ice.

TOP FIVE READS ON CAMBODIA

A whole bookcase-worth of volumes examine Cambodia's recent history, including the French colonial period, the spillover of the war in Vietnam into Cambodia, the Khmer Rouge years and the wild 1990s. The best include the following:

» *A Dragon Apparent* by Norman Lewis (1951) is a classic account of the author's 1950 travels in Indochina.

» *First They Killed My Father* by Luong Ung (2001) is a personal memoir of Democratic Kampuchea. One of the best of many survivor accounts.

» *Golden Bones* by Siv Sichuan (2010) describes the author's remarkable story from Cambodian refugee in New York to US ambassador to the UN.

» *River of Time* by John Swain (1995) takes readers back to an old Indochina, lost to the madness of war.

» *The Gate* by Francois Bizot (2003) is a heartfelt account of the author's interrogation by Comrade Duch and his incarceration in the French Embassy after the fall of Phnom Penh on 17 April 1975.

Laos (Map p66; ☎982632; 15-17 Mao Tse Toung Blvd)

Thailand (Map p66; ☎726306; 196 Norodom Blvd)

UK (Map p66; ☎427124; 27-29 St 75)

USA (Map p70; ☎728000; 1 St 96)

Vietnam (Map p66; ☎362531; 436 Monivong Blvd)

For information on visas, see p143.

Gay & Lesbian Travellers

Cambodia is a very tolerant country when it comes to sexual orientation and the scene is slowly coming alive in the major cities. But as with heterosexual couples, displays of public affection are a basic no-no. Handy websites:

Cambodia Out (www.cambodiaout.com) Promoting the GLBT community in Cambodia and the gay-friendly Adore Cambodia campaign.

Sticky Rice (www.stickyrice.ws) Gay travel guide covering Cambodia and Asia.

Insurance

Make sure your medical insurance policy covers emergency evacuation: limited medical facilities mean that you may have to be airlifted to Bangkok for problems such as a traffic accident or dengue fever.

See p940 for information on health insurance and p934 for motorcycle and car hire insurance. Worldwide travel insurance is available at www.lonelyplanet.com/travel_services. You can buy, extend and claim online anytime, even if you're already on the road.

Internet Access

Internet access is widespread and there are internet shops in all but the most remote provincial capitals. Charges range from 2000r to US$2 per hour. In this chapter, guesthouses and hotels that offer access to an online computer are indicated by an internet icon: @.

Many hotels, guesthouses and cafes now offer wi-fi, although connections are easiest to find in Phnom Penh and Siem Reap. Places offering wi-fi are shown with the wi-fi icon: 📶.

Legal Matters

All narcotics, including marijuana, are illegal in Cambodia. However, marijuana is traditionally used in food preparation, so you may find it sprinkled across some pizzas.

Many Western countries have laws that make sex offences committed overseas punishable at home.

Maps

The best all-round map is Gecko's *Cambodia Road Map* at a 1:750,000 scale.

Money

Cambodia's currency is the riel, abbreviated here by a lower-case r written after the sum. Riel notes (there are no coins) come in denominations of 50r, 100r, 200r, 500r, 1000r, 2000r, 5000r, 10,000r, 20,000r, 50,000r and 100,000r, though you'll rarely see the highest-denomination bills. Cambodia's second currency (some would say its first) is the US dollar, which is accepted everywhere. In far western Cambodia, the Thai baht is also commonly used.

Throughout this chapter, prices are in the currency quoted to the average punter – so get ready to think in three currencies.

ATMs

ATMs that accept debit cards and credit cards are found in all major cities and a growing number of provincial towns and border crossings. Banks with ATMs include Acleda Bank in most provinces, ANZ Royal with good coverage in cities and Canadia for most major provincial towns.

Bargaining

Bargaining is expected in local markets, when travelling by share taxi or moto and, sometimes, when taking a cheap room. The Khmers are not ruthless hagglers, so a persuasive smile and a little friendly quibbling is usually enough to get a good price.

Cash

The US dollar is accepted everywhere in Cambodia and US cash is the currency of most ATMs, so there's no need to buy riel at the border (don't believe the touts). US$1 banknotes are particularly useful; banks can supply them if you run out. Avoid ripped banknotes, which Cambodians often refuse. Near the Thai border, many transactions are in Thai baht.

When paying in dollars or baht, change is often given in riel, which is handy since small-denomination riel notes can be useful when paying for things such as moto rides and drinks. When calculating change, the US dollar is usually rounded off to 4000r.

See www.xe.com for current exchange rates.

Credit Cards

Top-end hotels, airline offices and upmarket boutiques and restaurants generally accept most major credit cards (Visa, MasterCard, JCB, sometimes American Express), but they usually pass the charges on to the customer, meaning an extra 3% or more on the bill.

Travellers Cheques

Travellers cheques aren't much use when venturing beyond the main tourist centres. Most banks charge a commission of 2%, and dish out US dollars rather than riel. Some hotels and travel agents will cash travellers cheques after banking hours.

Photography

Many internet cafes will burn CDs from digital images using USB connections. Digital memory is widely available in Cambodia.

Post

The postal service is hit-and-miss, with Phnom Penh's main post office – where you'll find a poste restante service – the most reliable. At the counter, make sure postcards and letters are stamped to indicate that postage has been paid. Courier services include EMS, which has offices at all major post offices.

Public Holidays

Holidays may be rolled over if they fall on a weekend. Some people take off a day or two extra during major festivals (see p20). It is widely believed that Cambodia has more public holidays than any other country on earth.

International New Year's Day 1 January

Victory over Genocide Day 7 January

International Women's Day 8 March

International Labour Day 1 May

King's Birthday 13 to 15 May

International Children's Day 1 June

King Mother's Birthday 18 June

Constitution Day 24 September

Coronation Day 29 October

King Father's Birthday 31 October

Independence Day 9 November

International Human Rights Day 10 December

HOW TO AVOID A BAD TRIP

Watch out for *yama* (known as *yaba* in Thailand), which ominously shares its name with the Hindu god of death. Known as ice or crystal meth back home, it's not the usual diet pills but instead home-made methamphetamines often laced with toxic substances, such as mercury and lithium. It is more addictive than many users would like to admit, provoking reactions such as powerful hallucinations, sleep deprivation and psychosis.

Also note that most of what is sold as cocaine in Cambodia is actually pure heroin and far stronger than any smack you'll find on the streets back home. Bang this up your nose and you're in serious trouble – several backpackers die each year.

RESPONSIBLE TRIPPING IN CAMBODIA

Cambodia has been to hell and back and there are many ways in which you can put a little back into the country. Eating locally grown food is just one of many.

The looting of stone carvings from Cambodia's ancient temples has devastated many temples. Don't contribute to this cultural rape by buying antiquities of any sort – classy reproductions are available in Phnom Penh and Siem Reap, complete with export certificates.

Cambodians dress very modestly and are offended by skimpily dressed foreigners. Just look at the Cambodians frolicking in the sea – most are fully dressed. Wearing bikinis on the beach is fine but cover up elsewhere. Topless or nude bathing is a definite no-no.

The sexual exploitation of children is now taken very seriously in Cambodia. Report anything that looks like child-sex tourism to the **ChildSafe Hotline** (☎012 311112; www.childsafe-international.org) or to the national **police hotline** (☎023 997919). Tourism establishments that sport the ChildSafe logo have staff trained to protect vulnerable children and, where necessary, intervene.

Websites with lots of practical ideas for responsible travel:

» **Cambodia Community-Based Ecotourism Network** (www.ccben.org) The official website promoting community-based ecotourism in Cambodia. Browse here for more on projects and initiatives across the country.

» **ChildSafe** (www.childsafe-cambodia.org) Learn about the ChildSafe campaign, which aims to stop child-sex tourism and protect vulnerable children from all forms of exploitation.

» **ConCERT** (www.concertcambodia.org) Siem Reap–based organisation 'connecting communities, environment and responsible tourism'.

» **Mekong Discovery Trail** (www.mekongdiscoverytrail.org) The official website for the Mekong Discovery Trail, promoting community-based tourism initiatives.

» **Stay Another Day** (www.stay-another-day.org) Dedicated to tempting tourists into staying another day in Cambodia, packed with ideas on day trips, project visits and alternative things to see and do.

Safe Travel

Mines & Mortars

Cambodia is one of the most heavily mined countries in the world, especially in the northwest of the country near the Thai border. Many mined areas are unmarked, so *do not* stray from well-worn paths and *never, ever* touch any unexploded ordnance (UXO) you come across, including mortars and artillery shells. If you find yourself in a mined area, retrace your steps only if you can clearly see your footprints. If not, stay where you are and call for help. If someone is injured in a minefield, do not rush in to help even if they are crying out in pain – find someone who knows how to enter a mined area safely.

Traffic Accidents

Traffic in Cambodia is chaotic, with vehicles moving in both directions on both sides of the road. Get in a serious accident in a remote area and somehow you'll have to make it to Phnom Penh, Siem Reap or Battambang for treatment. The horn is used to alert other drivers to a vehicle's presence – when walking, cycling or on a motorbike, get out of the way if you hear one honking behind you.

Crime

Cambodia is now a generally safe place to travel as long as you exercise common sense. Hold-ups are rare but petty theft is still a problem in the major cities and at beaches. Late at night, walking alone in unlit areas is not advisable, particularly for unaccompanied women.

In the major cities, drive-by bag snatchings happen and are especially dangerous when you're riding a moto as you can fall and hit your head. Never put a bag or purse in the front basket of a motorbike. Shoulder bags are an attractive target, so on a moto hold them tightly in front of you so that thieves – approaching from behind – don't have a strap to slash.

Scams

Cambodia is legendary for its inventive (and often well-connected) scammers. No need to be alarmed, but it helps to arrive with an idea of their repertoire.

The scam action often starts right at the Cambodian frontier – or, in many cases (such as Poipet), before you even get there – with shameless overcharging for visas. In fact, you may encounter your first Cambodia-related scam in Bangkok – remember, if that bus fare to Siem Reap sounds too good to be true, it probably is and may involve arriving very late at night and being taken to a substandard, overpriced guesthouse.

Upon setting foot on Cambodian territory, you are likely to meet your first moto drivers' cartel. These seemingly aggressive fellows (usually quite friendly once you get to know them) are intent on convincing you (or forcing you, by making sure there's a dearth of other options) to pay over the odds to get to the nearest town.

Moto fares have been rising in recent years, in part because of the skyrocketing price of petrol – a fact oft-cited by moto drivers – but prices that are two or three times those quoted in this book are probably a gouge, not a cost-of-living adjustment.

If possible, frontier moto drivers would also like to help you 'change money', at rip-off rates. Remember, if you have US dollars (or, near Thailand, baht), there's absolutely no need to buy riel at the border. If you do want to exchange currency, never go to the exchange place 'recommended' by a moto driver, even if it bills itself as 'official'.

Both at borders and at inland bus stations, members of moto cartels with semi-official monopoly status will make a determined effort to overcharge for rides. In Sihanoukville, which is particularly notorious for this sort of thing, all you need to do to pay the usual price is walk out of the bus station to the main road.

In parallel, moto drivers will try to steer you to guesthouses and hotels that pay them fat commissions. Don't believe age-old lines such as 'that place is closed'. If you want to go to a specific establishment, insist on being taken there. Smiling also usually helps, as it does with everything in Cambodia.

We have also heard very occasional reports of local taxi drivers who stop midroute and ask for a higher fare.

Studying

Travellers can indulge in Khmer cooking lessons in Phnom Penh (p68), Siem Reap (p87), Sihanoukville (p113) and Battambang (p102).

Telephone

Landline area codes appear under the name of each city but in many areas service is spotty. Mobile phones, whose numbers start with 01, 07, 08 or 09, are hugely popular with both individuals and commercial enterprises. Foreigners need to present a valid passport to get a local sim card. For listings of businesses and government offices, check out www.yellowpages-cambodia.com.

Many internet shops offer cheap international calls for 100r to 1000r per minute, though in places with broadband speeds you can Skype for the price of an internet connection (usually 2000r to 4000r *per hour*). International calls from mobile phone shops cost about 1000r per minute.

Time

Cambodia, like Laos, Vietnam and Thailand, is seven hours ahead of Greenwich Mean Time or Universal Time Coordinated (GMT/UTC).

Travellers with Disabilities

Although Cambodia has one of the world's highest rates of limb loss (due to mines), the country is not designed for people with impaired mobility. Few buildings have lifts/elevators, footpaths and roads are riddled with potholes, and the staircases and rock jumbles of many Angkorian temples are daunting even for the able-bodied. Transport-wise, chartering is the way to go and is a fairly affordable option. Also affordable is hired help if you require it, and Khmers are generally very helpful should you need assistance.

Visas

For most nationalities, one-month tourist visas (US$20) are available on arrival at Phnom Penh and Siem Reap airports and all land border crossings. Unfortunately, except at the airports and the land crossings with Vietnam, overcharging is rampant, and uniformed Cambodian border officials – and touts who work with them – are often very creative in compelling travellers to pay more than official rates.

At the notorious Poipet-Aranya Prathet crossing and at Cham Yeam-Hat Lek, visitors are told they must pay in baht, with fees set at 1000B (US$34) to 1200B (US$40), plus 100B for a photo. A few valiant travellers insist on paying in US dollars, but you're unlikely to get away with less than US$25.

Avoid the Thai-side touts who will swear that visas are not issued at the frontier.

One-month tourist e-visas (US$20 plus a US$5 processing fee), which take three business days to issue and are valid for entry to Cambodia at the airports, Bavet, Poipet and Cham Yeam, are available from www.mfaic.gov.kh.

Tourist visas can only be extended once for one month, so if you're planning a longer stay, ask for a one-month business visa (US$25) when you arrive. Extensions for one/three/six/12 months cost about US$40/75/150/250 and take three or four business days; bring a passport photo. It may be cheaper to do a 'visa run' to Thailand, getting a fresh visa when you cross back into Cambodia. Overstayers are charged US$5 per day at the point of exit.

Thailand issues free 30-day visas to qualifying passport holders at all border crossings, but at least at Psar Pruhm-Ban Pakard (near Pailin) you'll have to show an onward ticket out of Thailand. Vietnamese visas are available in Phnom Penh, Sihanoukville and Battambang. Lao visas are issued in Phnom Penh or at the Trapeang Kriel-Dong Kalaw border post.

Volunteering

Cambodia hosts a huge number of NGOs, some of whom do require volunteers from time to time. The best way to find out who is represented in the country is to drop in on the **Cooperation Committee for Cambodia** (CCC; Map p70; ☎023-214152; 35 St 178) in Phnom Penh.

Professional Siem Reap–based organisations helping to place volunteers include **ConCERT** (Map p82; ☎063-963511; www.concertcambodia.org; 560 Phum Stoueng Thmey) and **Globalteer** (☎063-761802; www.globalteer.org), but their programs do involve a weekly charge.

Cambodian Children's Painting Project (www.artcambodia.org) Provides Sihanoukville beach children with a safe environment. Minimum volunteer period: one month.

Ockenden Cambodia (www.ockenden-cambodia.org) Works at grassroots level to empower communities and improve vulnerable people's quality of life.

Sustainable Cambodia (www.sustainablecambodia.org) Minimum commitment is five months.

Village Focus International (www.villagefocus.org) Can find placements for volunteers interested in helping vulnerable communities.

Volunteer in Cambodia (www.volunteerincambodia.org) English teaching.

Work

Job opportunities are limited in Cambodia, partly because Cambodians need the jobs more than foreigners and partly because the foreigners working here are usually professionals recruited overseas. The easiest option is teaching English in Phnom Penh, as experience isn't a prerequisite at the smaller schools. Places to look for work include the classifieds sections of the *Phnom Penh Post* and the *Cambodia Daily*, and the notice board at guesthouses and restaurants in Phnom Penh.

Getting There & Away

Air

Cambodia's two major international airports, Phnom Penh and Siem Reap, have frequent flights to destinations all over eastern Asia. International departure tax of US$25 is now included in the ticket price.

Air Asia (FD or AK; www.airasia.com) Flights from Phnom Penh and Siem Reap to Kuala Lumpur, plus Phnom Penh to Bangkok.

Air France (AF; www.airfrance.com) Flights from Phnom Penh to Paris via Bangkok.

Asiana Airlines (OZ; http://flyasiana.com/english) Flights to Seoul.

Bangkok Airways (PG; www.bangkokair.com) Flights from Phnom Penh and Siem Reap to Bangkok.

Cambodia Angkor Airways (K6; www.cambodiaangkorair.com) Daily connections from Phnom Penh and Siem Reap to Ho Chi Minh City (Saigon).

China Airlines (CI; www.china-airlines.com) Phnom Penh to Taipei.

China Eastern Airlines (MU; www.flychinaeastern.com) Links Siem Reap with Kunmíng.

China Southern Airlines (CZ; www.cs-air.com/en) Links Phnom Penh with Guangzhou.

Dragon Air (KA; www.dragonair.com) Phnom Penh and Siem Reap to Hong Kong.

Eva Air (BR; www.evaair.com) Phnom Penh to Taipei.

Jetstar Asia (3K; www.jetstarasia.com) Cheapest flights from Phnom Penh and Siem Reap to Singapore.

Korean Air (KE; www.koreanair.com) Phnom Penh and Siem Reap to Seoul.

Lao Airlines (QV; www.laos-airlines.com) Flights to Vientiane, Luang Prabang and Pakse.

Malaysia Airlines (MH; www.malaysia-airlines.com) Phnom Penh and Siem Reap to Kuala Lumpur.

Shanghai Airlines (FM; www.shanghai-air.com) Links Phnom Penh with Shanghai.

Silk Air (MI; www.silkair.com) Phnom Penh and Siem Reap to Singapore, plus Siem Reap to Danang in Vietnam.

Thai Airways International (TG; www.thaiair.com) Links Phnom Penh with Bangkok.

Vietnam Airlines (VN; www.vietnamairlines.com) Has flights to Ho Chi Minh City, Hanoi, Vientiane and Luang Prabang, and so offers useful Indochina loop options.

Border Crossings

For details on border crossings in the region, see p935. Cambodia shares land borders with Laos, Thailand and Vietnam.

Getting Around

It's highly advisable to avoid intercity travel at dusk and after dark as roads lack lighting, and blind overtaking/passing at high speeds is rampant. Come late afternoon, settle in for a mellow evening and prepare for an early getaway.

Air

The only scheduled domestic flights link Phnom Penh with Siem Reap (from US$90) and all are currently operated by Cambodia Angkor Airways, a monopolistic joint venture with Vietnam Airlines.

Bicycle

Cambodia is a great country for adventurous cyclists as travelling at gentle speeds allows for lots of interaction with locals. Cycling around Angkor is an awesome experience, as it really gives you a sense of the size and scale of the temple complex. Adventure mountain biking is likely to take off in the Cardamom Mountains and in Mondulkiri and Ratanakiri Provinces over the coming years.

AIRPORT TAXES

There's a tax of US$25 on all international flights out of Cambodia. The airport tax for domestic flights is US$6. Both are now included in the ticket price, so you do not need cash at the airport.

Much of Cambodia is pancake flat or only moderately hilly. Safety, however, is a considerable concern on paved roads as trucks, buses and cars barrel along at high speed.

Boat

For details on the fast boats from Phnom Penh to Siem Reap and the small boats linking Siem Reap with Battambang, see p145 and p103.

Bus

About a dozen bus companies serve all populated parts of the country. The largest and often least expensive is **Phnom Penh Sorya** (www.ppsoryatransport.com). Comfort levels and prices vary, and a few companies charge foreigners more than they do locals, so it pays to shop around. Booking bus tickets through guesthouses and hotels is convenient but incurs a commission.

Car & Motorcycle

Cambodia's main national highways (NH) are generally in good shape but can be quite dangerous due to the prevalence of high-speed overtaking/passing.

Guesthouses and hotels can arrange hire cars with a driver for US$25 to US$60 a day, plus petrol and lodging, and food for the driver.

While major national highways (NH) are too heavily trafficked for happy motorcycling, many of Cambodia's less travelled tracks are perfect for two-wheeled exploration. However, forays on motorcycles into the remote and diabolical roads of the northwest and northeast should only be attempted by experienced riders. In all cases, proceed cautiously, as outside Phnom Penh and Siem Reap medical facilities are as rudimentary as ambulances are rare.

Local Transport

A few *cyclos* (pedicabs) can still be seen on the streets of Phnom Penh and Battambang, but they have been almost completely replaced by

WARNING

Since singed flesh doesn't smell very nice and, in the tropical humidity, takes a long time to heal, get in the habit of climbing off a moto to your left, stepping clear of the scorching exhaust pipe.

motos (or *motodups*), unmarked motorbike taxis that you flag down and hop on.

It used to be that moto prices were rarely agreed to in advance, but with the increase in visitor numbers a lot of optimistic drivers have gotten into the habit of overcharging foreigners.

Chartering a moto for the day costs between US$7 and US$10, but can cost more if a greater distance is involved or the driver speaks English.

In many towns (Siem Reap is an exception), 100cc and 125cc motorbikes can be hired for US$5 to US$10 a day. 250cc bikes, where available, cost about double that. No one will ask you for a driver's licence except, occasionally, the police. Make sure you have a strong lock and always leave the bike in guarded parking where possible.

The vehicle known in Cambodia as a *remorque* (túk-túk) is, technically speaking, a *remorque-moto,* a roofed, two-wheeled trailer hitched to the back of a motorbike. Fares are roughly double those of motos, though in some places you pay per passenger. Still, for two or more people a *remorque* can be cheaper than a moto and much more comfortable if you've got luggage or it's raining.

Some guesthouses and hotels rent out bicycles for US$1 to US$2 per day. If you'll be doing lots of cycling, bring along a bike helmet, which can also provide some protection on a moto.

Local taxis can be ordered via guesthouses and hotels in Phnom Penh, Siem Reap and Sihanoukville.

Share Taxi, Minibus & Pick-up

Share taxis (usually jacked-up old Toyota Camrys) are faster, more flexible in terms of departure times and a bit more expensive than buses. They're also a lot more crowded. In addition to the driver, each one carries six or seven passengers – that's two in the front seat and four in the back, with a seventh passenger sometimes squished between the driver and his door! Pay double the regular fare and you get the front seat all to yourself; pay six fares and you've got yourself a private taxi. Haggle patiently, with a smile, to ensure fair prices.

Minibuses, which usually stick to sealed roads, are even more jam-packed, which is why they're a bit cheaper than share taxis. That and the fact that some are driven by maniacs.

Pick-up trucks, which are favoured by country folk with oversized luggage, some of it alive, continue to take on the worst roads in Cambodia. Squeeze in the air-con cab or, if you feel like a tan and a mouthful of dust, sit in the back. They leave when seriously full. Bring a *krama* (scarf), sun screen and, in the wet season, rain gear.

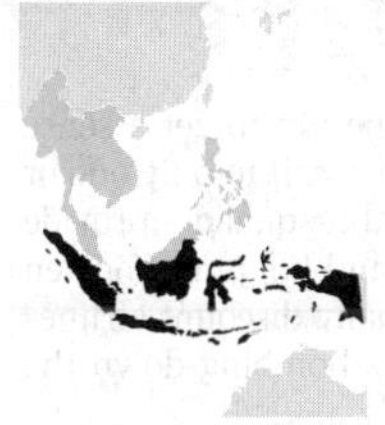

Indonesia

Includes »

Best Regional Specialities

- Spicy Padang food (p250)
- *Warung* (food-stalls) (p197)
- Grilled seafood (p199)
- Roast suckling pig (p209)
- Roast chilli sambal (p238)

Best Places for Cultural Connections

- National Museum (p153)
- Dance, Bali (p209)
- Funeral rites, Ubud (p281)
- Former spice islands (p285)
- Tribal culture, Papua (p291)

Why Go?

Indonesia defines adventure: the only limitation is how many of its 17,000 islands you can reach before your visa expires. Following the equator, Indonesia stretches between Malaysia and Australia in one long intoxicating sweep. The nation's natural diversity is staggering, alluring and inspiring, from the snow-capped peaks in Papua, sandalwood forests in Sumba, dense jungle in Borneo and impossibly green rice paddies in Bali and Java. Indonesian reefs are a diver's fantasy while the surf breaks above are the best anywhere.

But even as the diversity on land and sea run like a traveller's fantasy playlist, it's the mash-up of people and cultures that's the most appealing. Bali justifiably leads off, but there are also Papua's stone-age folk, the funeral-mad Toraja of Sulawesi, the artisans of Java, mall-rats of Jakarta and much more. Whether it's a dreamy remote beach, an orang-utan encounter or a Bali all-nighter, Indonesia scores.

When to Go

Jakarta

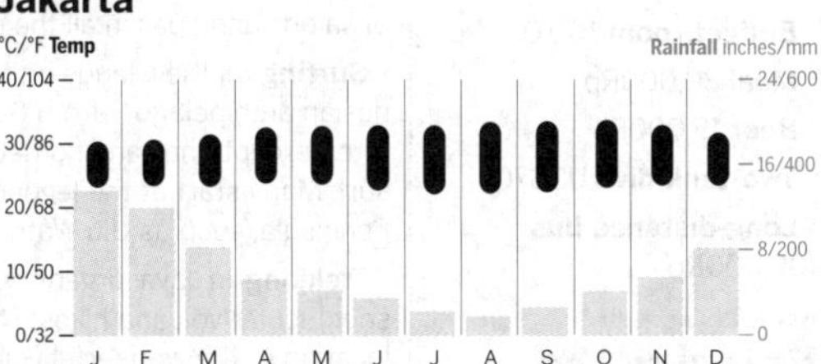

Sep-Mar Rainy season; starts later in the southeast. Rain everywhere in Jan & Feb.

Apr-Jun Dry days & highs that aren't withering. Hill towns like Bali's Ubud can be chilly at night.

Aug High season. Prices peak on Bali & the Gilis; book ahead. Remote spots may also fill up.

AT A GLANCE

» **Currency** Rupiah (Rp); 100,000Rp notes can be hard to break

» **Language** Bahasa Indonesia; English in tourist areas

» **Money** ATMs in major centres; carry rupiah for remote islands

» **Visas** Complicated! (see p307)

» **Mobile phones** SIMs (around 30,000Rp) sold everywhere; cheap call/text rates

Fast Facts

» **Area** 1.92 million sq km

» **Capital** Jakarta

» **Country code** ☎62

» **Emergency** Ask the nearest local for advice

Exchange Rates

Australia	A$1	9600Rp
Euro zone	€1	12,150Rp
UK	£1	14,600Rp
US	US$1	9200Rp

Set Your Budget

» **Budget room** 100,000Rp

» **Meal** 30,000Rp

» **Beer** 15,000Rp

» **Two-tank dive** US$70

» **Long-distance bus** 100,000Rp

Entering the Country

Fly into Jakarta or Bali; flights to Sulawesi, Lombok etc also available. Ferries to Sumatra from Malaysia and Singapore are popular.

Don't Miss

With 17,000 islands, it would be shame not to get a sense of this vast archipelago by limiting your visit to only one or two. Ferries – never luxurious, often a bit squalid – provide myriad links and truly adventurous island-hopping. Shorten distances with flights on any of the many discount airlines and connect overland dots with buses bombing down the middle of the road at breakneck speeds.

ITINERARIES

One Week

This is a tough one, but Bali is the obvious choice. Spend a couple of days in the south, possibly partying in Seminyak and/or surfing and chilling on the Bukit Peninsula. Head up to Ubud for rice-field walks and intoxicating culture. Catch a fast boat to/from the Gili Islands for a heaving travellers' scene.

One Month

Include your week on Bali and the Gilis, but start on Java and cross through the cultural city of Yogyakarta and the Unesco treasure of Borobudur. From Lombok catch ferries and buses across Sumbawa to Flores with stops at beaches and dragon-filled Komodo. Optionally finish your time following the spine of Sulawesi or head further east for Maluku's idyllic Banda Islands or track down orang-utans on Kalimantan or Sumatra.

Essential Outdoor Activities

» **Diving & Snorkelling** Diving highlights include western Flores and Komodo, the Gili Islands, Pulau Menjangan in Bali, Pulau Bunaken and the Togean Islands in Sulawesi, Pulau Weh in Sumatra, the Banda Islands in Maluku and the incredible Raja Ampat Islands in Papua.

» **Spas & Treatments** Bali leads the way, with a multitude of salons and spas in all the main travellers' centres.

» **Surfing** All the islands on the southern side of the Indonesian archipelago – from Sumatra to Timor – get reliable, often exceptional, and sometimes downright frightening surf. Many start at the legendary breaks of Bali's Bukit Peninsula, such as Ulu Watu. See p303 for more details.

» **Trekking** In Java, organised trekking centres on some spectacular volcano hikes. There's more variety in Bali, the location of the wonderful Gunung Batur region and the hills around Munduk, which offer walks amid cool hillside forests, spice plantations and waterfalls. Gunung Rinjani on Lombok is a dramatic and rewarding trek. The Baliem Valley in Papua is popular and Tana Toraja has fabulous trekking opportunities through Sulawesi's spectacular traditional villages.

JAVA

The heart of the nation, Java is an island of megacities and mesmerising natural beauty. It's the economic powerhouse of Indonesia, as well as the political epicentre, an island with complex, profound cultural traditions in art, dance, spiritualism and learning.

Many of the cities are pretty uninspiring; pollution levels are high and they're plagued by environmental issues. That said, the cities are where Javanese art and culture are at their most radiant and daring, and along with Bali, Javanese cities rock with vibrant nightlife and an exciting music scene.

Leaving the cities, you'll find a Java of bewitching landscapes – iridescent rice paddies, gurgling streams, villages of terracotta-tiled houses and patches of dense jungle-clad hills. Verdant and fecund, this is one of the most fertile parts of Earth, with three annual crops possible in some regions. And with over 40 volcanoes forming a spiky central backbone, it's safe to say almost every journey in Java passes a succession of giant, often smoking cones.

Getting There & Away

AIR Jakarta (p161) is Indonesia's busiest international arrival point and has numerous international connections on national and low-cost airlines to cities throughout Asia and beyond. Surabaya (p162) is the next busiest airport for international flights while Yogyakarta, Solo (Surakarta) and Badung all receive a few flights from other Southeast Asian cities.

BOAT Java is a major hub for shipping services. Jakarta (see p161) and Surabaya are the main ports for **Pelni ships** (www.pelni.co.id).

For information on ferries between Java and Bali, see p190 and for information on the Java to Sumatra boats, see p161.

Indonesia Highlights

1. Surfing by day, partying at night and absorbing amazing culture in **Bali** (p190)
2. Ascending the ancient Buddhist stupa of **Borobudur** (p178) before trawling the batik markets of bustling **Yogyakarta** (p175)
3. Peeking at komodo dragons at **Komodo** (p233) in Nusa Tenggara
4. Paying primate-to-primate respects to the 'man of the jungle', the **orang-utans** (p300) native to Sumatra and Kalimantan
5. Diving the pristine walls and coral canyons beneath seas of dimpled glass at **Pulau Bunaken** (p284) in Sulawesi
6. Exploring the lovely time capsule that is Maluku's **Banda Islands** (p287)
7. Hiking along raging rivers and scaling exposed ridges to reach interior Papua's remote tribal villages in the **Baliem Valley** (p291)

Java

Getting Around

AIR Domestic flight routes in Java are currently expanding rapidly and can be quite inexpensive. Surabaya and Yogyakarta to Jakarta is very popular and is covered by several airlines. Flight information is listed throughout this chapter and in the Transport chapter (p932).

BUS Travel is often slow and nerve-racking; night buses are a little faster and a little more dangerous! Trains are better for the long hauls, but bus departures are more frequent.

Public buses, 'cooled' by a flow of sooty air from an open window, are very frequent, but they also stop for passengers every five minutes. Better air-con buses also run the major routes and are well worth paying the 25% extra cost.

Small minibuses that cover shorter routes and back runs are commonly called *angkot* and shouldn't be confused with the door-to-door minibuses *(travel)*. The latter are air-con minibuses that travel all over Java and pick you up at your hotel and drop you off wherever you want to go in the destination city. These sound good in theory, but you can spend hours driving around the departure and arrival cities picking people up and dropping them off again.

LOCAL TRANSPORT Dream up a way of getting around and you will find it somewhere on the streets of Java. *Ojek* (motorcycle taxis) are very widely available. *Dokar* – brightly coloured, horse-drawn carts, awash with jingling bells and psychedelic motifs – are a highlight.

TRAIN Trains are usually quicker, more comfortable and more convenient than buses for getting between the main centres.

Ekonomi trains are dirt cheap, slow, crowded and often run late. Seats can be booked on the better *ekonomi plus* services. For a little extra, express trains with *bisnis* (business) and *eksekutif* (executive) sections are better and seating is guaranteed. For air-con and more comfort, go for the top-of-the-range *argo* (luxury) trains; don't expect anything luxurious – cracked windows and semi-swept aisles are the norm – though compared to bus travel they are heaven indeed. Meals are available on the better class of trains.

For basic *ekonomi* trains, tickets go on sale an hour before departure. *Bisnis* and *eksekutif* trains can be booked weeks ahead, and the main stations have efficient, computerised booking offices for *eksekutif* trains.

Try to book at least a day in advance, or several days beforehand, for travel on public holidays and long weekends.

The railway's **Train Information Service** (www.kereta-api.co.id) has more information (on the website, *Jadwal* means schedule).

Jakarta

021 / POP 8.9 MILLION

First impressions of Jakarta are not good. One of the world's greatest megalopolises, its grey, relentlessly urban sprawl spreads for tens of traffic-snarled kilometres across a flood-prone plain with barely a park to break the concrete monotony.

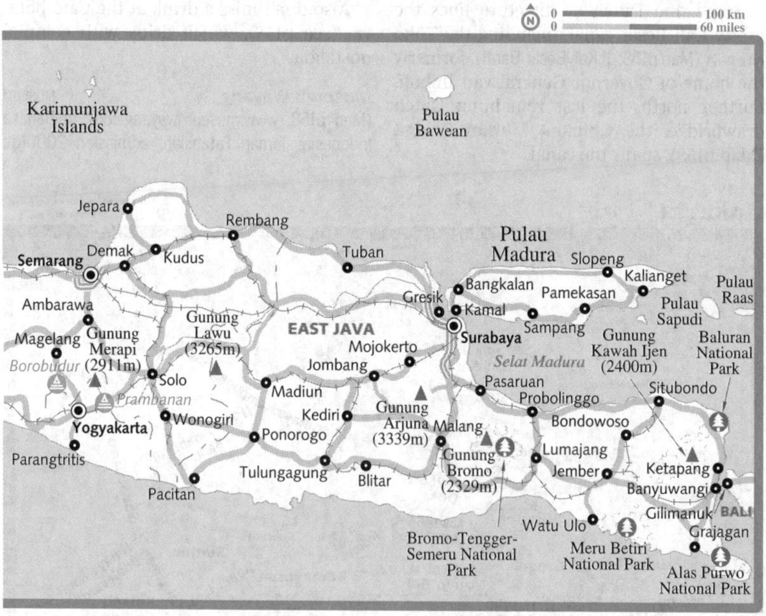

And yet beneath the unappealing facade of high-rises, slums and gridlocked streets, this is a city of surprises and many faces. From the steamy, richly scented streets of the old quarter to the city's riotous, decadent nightlife, Jakarta is filled with unexpected corners. Spend a Sunday on the pedestrianised streets of the old colonial Kota neighbourhood laughing over street performers, enjoying a *wayang* performance and mingling with locals and tourists at the venerable Café Batavia and you'll start to see that the 'Big Durian' is actually a highly cultured and artistic city with a huge amount going for it.

Metropolitan Jakarta sprawls 28km from the docks to the southern suburbs. Soekarno's national monument (Monas) in Lapangan Merdeka (Freedom Sq) is an excellent central landmark. North of the monument is the older part of Jakarta, which includes Chinatown, the former Dutch area of Kota and the old port of Sunda Kelapa. Tanjung Priok, the main harbour, is several kilometres further east. The sprawling modern suburbs of Jakarta are south of the monument.

Jl Thamrin is the main north–south street of the new city and has Jakarta's big hotels and banks. A couple of blocks east along Jl Kebon Sirih Raya is Jl Jaksa, the cheap accommodation centre of Jakarta.

Sights & Activities

KOTA

Jakarta's crumbling historic heart is Kota, home to the remnants of the Dutch capital of Batavia. **Taman Fatahillah**, the old town square, features cracked cobblestones, postcard vendors, fine colonial buildings, some ho-hum museums and, on weekends, masses of locals enjoying a carnival-like atmosphere. Trains from Gondangdia, near Jl Jaksa, run here. A taxi will cost around 30,000Rp from Jl Thamrin.

In and around Tamran Fatahillah are a number of interesting buildings and monuments including the **Gereja Sion** (Map p158; Jl Pangeran Jayakarta 1; ⌚dawn-dusk), which is the oldest remaining church in Jakarta. It was built in 1695 for the 'black Portuguese' brought to Batavia as slaves and given their freedom if they joined the Dutch Reformed Church.

The old Portuguese cannon **Si Jagur** (Mr Fertility; Map p158; Taman Fatahillah) was believed to be a cure for barrenness because of its suggestive clenched fist, and women sat astride it in the hope of bearing children.

Some fine Dutch architecture lines the grotty Kali Besar canal, including the **Toko Merah** (Map p158; Jl Kali Besar Barat), formerly the home of Governor General van Imhoff. Further north, the last remaining Dutch drawbridge, the **Chicken Market Bridge** (Map p158), spans the canal.

Also don't miss a drink at the Café Batavia (see p158), which drips with colonial nostalgia.

Museum Wayang MUSEUM
(Map p158; www.museumwayang.com, in Bahasa Indonesia; Taman Fatahillah; admission 2000Rp;

Jakarta

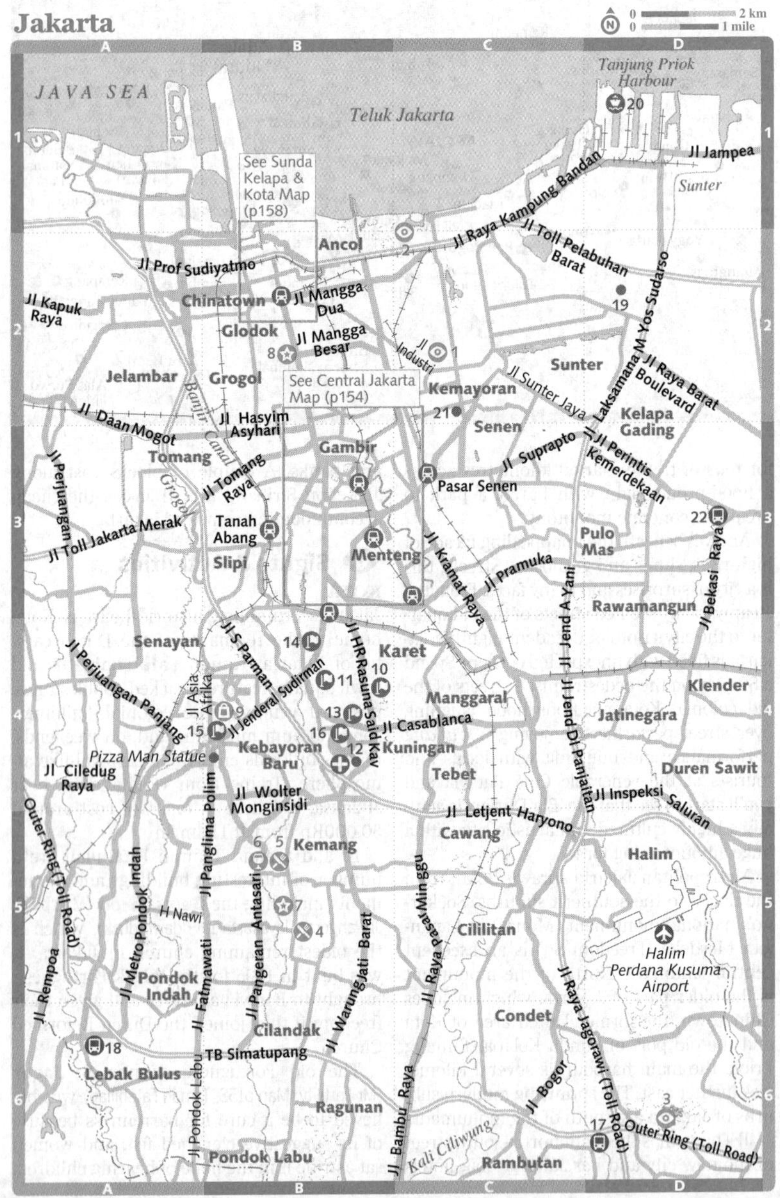

⌚9am-3pm Tue-Sun) This *wayang* (puppet) museum has one of the best collections of *wayang* puppets in the country and includes puppets not just from Indonesia but also from China, Vietnam, India, Cambodia and Europe, as well as masks used in dance performances. The best day to visit is Sunday when shadow-puppet performances take place at 10am, although do note that they occasionally skip a Sunday. The exact schedule is available on the website.

Jakarta History Museum MUSEUM
(Map p158; Taman Fatahillah 2; admission 2000Rp; ⌚9am-3pm Tue-Sun) At the Jakarta History Museum, there's little but colonial bric-a-brac; the fine old (1710) City Hall building, which houses the museum, is the real star.

Balai Seni Rupa MUSEUM
(Map p158; Taman Fatahillah; admission 2000Rp; ⌚9am-3pm Tue-Sun) The former Palace of Justice is now a fine-arts museum housing contemporary Indonesian works. There's also a ceramics museum.

SUNDA KELAPA

Among the hubbub, floating debris and oil slicks, the old Dutch **port** (admission 2000Rp) is still used by magnificent Buginese *pinisi* (fishing boats), their cargo unloaded by teams of porters walking along wobbly gangplanks. Someone can normally be found to take the old seadogs among you out onto the waters in a **rowing boat** (very negotiable 30,000Rp for 30min). Go at dawn or dusk when waterborne activity reaches the crest of a wave. The port is a 1km walk from Taman Fatahillah, or take one of the area's unique push-bike taxis known as *ojek sepeda* (2500Rp).

Museum Bahari MUSEUM
(Map p158; www.museumbahari.org; Jl Pasar Ikan; admission 2000Rp; ⌚9am-3pm Tue-Sun) Located in one of the old Dutch East India Company warehouses (1645), this maritime museum exhibits some fine photographs and sailing boats from across Indonesia.

Pasar Ikan MARKET
(Fish Market; Map p158; Jl Pasar Ikan; ⌚6am-2pm) The noisy, smelly and chaotic fish market, close to the Maritime Museum, is well worth a dawn visit.

LAPANGAN MERDEKA

TOP CHOICE **National Museum** MUSEUM
(Map p154; Jl Merdeka Barat; admission 10,000Rp; ⌚8.30am-4pm Tue-Thu, 8.30-11.30am & 1-4pm Fri, 8.30am-5pm Sat & Sun) The sensational National Museum has an excellent collection of ethnographic displays from across the archipelago, which, if nothing else, brings home just how utterly diverse this nation is. Upstairs is a glittering, jewel-encrusted treasure room while the impressive new wing houses displays related to prehistoric life in Indonesia and includes a tiny skull of a 'Flores Hobbit' – the tiny hominoid unearthed on Flores island in 2004. In addition the museum has fine exhibits of Han ceramics, ancient Hindu statuary and magnificent *kris* (traditional dagger) handles studded with rubies. This museum is also known as

Jakarta

Sights

1	Jakarta Fair Grounds	C2
	Purna Bhakti Pertiwi Museum	(see 3)
2	Taman Impian Jaya Ancol	C2
3	Taman Mini Indonesia Indah	D6

Eating

	Kemang Food Festival	(see 5)
4	Kinara	B5
5	Payon	B5

Drinking

6	Eastern Promise	B5

Entertainment

7	Nú China	B5
8	Stadium	B2

Shopping

	Pasar Seni	(see 2)
9	Periplus	B4

Information

10	Australian Embassy	B4
11	Canadian Embassy	B4
	Dutch Embassy	(see 12)
12	Erasmus Huis	B4
13	Malaysian Embassy	B4
14	New Zealand Embassy	B4
15	Papua New Guinean Embassy	B4
	Singaporean Embassy	(see 12)
16	Thailand Embassy	B4

Transport

17	Kampung Rambutan Bus Terminal	D6
18	Lebak Bulus Bus Terminal	A6
19	Merpati	D2
20	Pelni Passenger Terminal	D1
21	Pelni Ticket Office	C2
22	Pulo Gadung Bus Terminal	D3

Gedung Gajah (Elephant House) on account of the bronze elephant outside, which was donated by the king of Thailand in 1871.

National Monument MONUMENT
(Monas; Map p154; ☎384 0451; admission 7500Rp; ⏰8am-3pm) Soekarno attempted to tame Jakarta by giving it a central space, Lapangan Merdeka (Freedom Sq), and topping it with a gigantic monument to his machismo, the National Monument. The towering, 132m-high column, capped with a gilded flame, has been dubbed 'Soekarno's last erection' and one look at it and you'll see why – what was the archi-

Central Jakarta

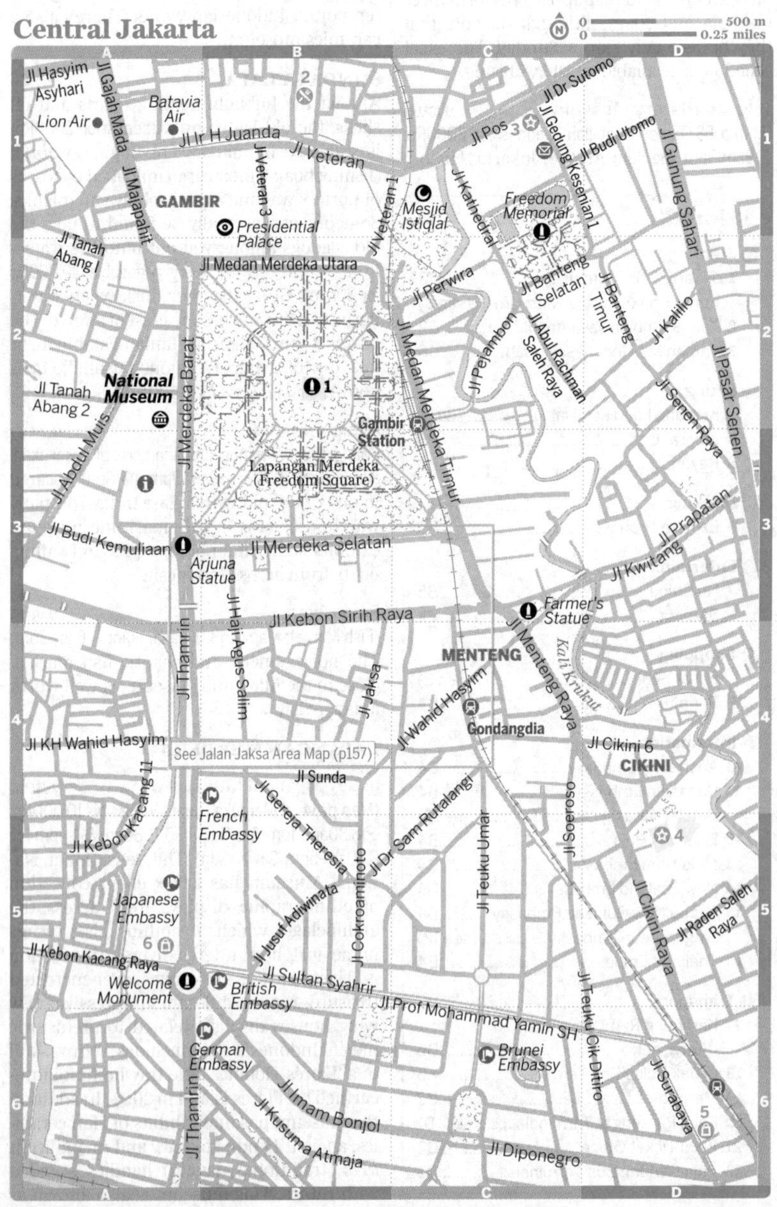

tect thinking? The price quoted above allows you to whiz up the 'shaft' for a shot of the city.

National History Museum MUSEUM
(Map p154; admission 2500Rp; ⌚8am-3pm) The National History Museum, in the base of 'Soekarno's erection', tells the story of Indonesia's independence struggle in 48 dramatic, overstated dioramas. Admission is also included in the entry fee for the monument.

OTHER AREAS

Taman Mini Indonesia Indah AMUSEMENT PARK
(Map p152; ☎545 4545; www.tamanmini.com; TMII Pintu 1; admission 9000Rp; ⌚9am-5pm) A 100-hectare theme park built to celebrate the nation, Taman Mini Indonesia Indah includes traditional houses from (most) Indonesian provinces set around a lagoon (boats are available to hire), an Imax theatre and a bird park. It's a great place to see traditional dance and costume from throughout the country. There's also an assortment of museums, including an insect house full of alarming-looking specimens, and, best of all, the air-conditioned **Purna Bhakti Pertiwi Museum** (Map p152; ⌚9am-5pm), which houses the stupendously opulent (and downright gaudy) gifts given to Soeharto, including a 5m ship carved entirely from jade.

To get there, take Koridor 7 bus to the Kampung Rambutan terminal and then a T15 metro-mini to the park entrance. A taxi from central Jakarta costs about 70,000Rp to 80,000Rp.

Taman Impian Jaya Ancol AMUSEMENT PARK
(Map p152; www.ancol.com, in Bahasa Indonesia; admission 15,000Rp; ⌚10am-10pm) A huge waterfront amusement complex with paintballing, waterslides, a beach, fairground rides, an Indonesian-style Disneyland (Dunia Fantasi, entrance an additional 80,000Rp) and much more. The highlight, though, is probably **Seaworld** (entrance an additional 60,000Rp), an impressive aquarium complex with sharks, turtles, coral reefs and even a sad-looking manatee. Should you be feeling brave it's even possible to go diving in the **shark tank** (200,000Rp). To get there, take bus 64, 65 or 125 or *angkot* 51 from Kota station. The complex is vast, but there are plenty of taxis available to run you between sights.

Festivals & Events

Jakarta has a packed calendar of festivals, fairs and other events. These are only some of the biggest or more tourist-friendly. For the full run-down get hold of a copy of the free *Jakarta Calendar of Events*, published annually and available from the tourist office.

Java Jazz Festival MUSIC FESTIVAL
(www.javajazzfestival.com) If you are here in early March, keep your eyes peeled for this festival.

Jl Jaksa Street Fair FESTIVAL
Features Betawi dance, theatre and music, as well as popular modern performances. It is held for one week in June and tourists are expected to get involved.

Jakarta Anniversary FESTIVAL
On 22 June, this festival marks the establishment of the city by Gunungjati back in 1527, and is celebrated with fireworks and the Jakarta Fair. The latter is held at the **Jakarta Fair Grounds** (Map p152), northeast of the city centre in Kemayoran, from late June until mid-July.

Independence Day FESTIVAL
Held on 17 August. The parades in Jakarta are the biggest in the country.

Sleeping

Jl Jaksa is Jakarta's budget-hotel enclave and there are plenty of cheap beds (and beers) on offer. There's a cosmopolitan atmosphere, as the area is also a popular place for Jakarta's young intelligentsia and artistic types to socialise. Jaksa is a short stroll from the main drag, Jl Thamrin, close to Gambir train station and even closer to Gondangdia train station, though not all trains stop there.

Central Jakarta

Top Sights
National Museum ... A2

Sights
National History Museum ... (see 1)
1 National Monument ... B2

Eating
2 Night Warung ... B1

Entertainment
3 Gedung Kesenian Jakarta ... C1
4 Taman Ismail Marzuki ... D5

Shopping
5 Flea Market ... D6
6 Plaza Indonesia ... A5

Hostel 35 GUESTHOUSE $$
(Map p157; ☎9824 1472; Jl Kebon Sirih Barat 1 35; r without/with air-con 150,000/250,000Rp; ❄) One of the better bets in the Jaksa area, this place has a large, slightly bizarre lobby bursting with tropical-style decor: bamboo and rattan furnishings and a fish pond. Offers a wide selection of clean rooms, all of which are well presented; most have attractive ensuite bathrooms. No telephone reservations.

Borneo Hostel GUESTHOUSE $
(Map p157; ☎314 0095; Jl Kebon Sirih Barat Dalam 37; s 70,000-110,000Rp, d 110,000-170,000Rp) A cheerful place with a warm, family atmosphere and polished rooms (see those bathrooms sparkle) set around a plant-filled courtyard. The tiny fans won't do much to keep you cool at night, though. It's on a peaceful side street.

Alinda Hotel HOTEL $$
(Map p157; ☎314 0373; www.alinda-hotel.com; Jl Jaksa 9; r with fan/air-con 165,000/235,000Rp; ❄@) This arrestingly blue hotel is tucked down a foliage-filled alleyway just off the main street and offers exceptionally clean and well-maintained rooms (though they are sadly less colourful than the hotel's exterior). Although it costs a little more than some other options, it's well worth the extra. At the time of research, it was still signed as the Hotel Yusran – its old name.

Istana Ratu Hotel HOTEL $$
(Map p157; ☎314 2464; Jl Jaksa 7-9; r incl breakfast from 300,000Rp; ❄P) With large, modern and stylish rooms boasting contemporary decor, bright duvets and soft pillows, this is more flashpacker than backpacker, but it's a perfect place to recharge the batteries for a night or two.

Bloem Steen Homestay GUESTHOUSE $
(Map p157; ☎3192 5389; Gang 1 173; s/d with fan 60,000/80,000Rp, d with air-con 130,000Rp; ❄@) This place has a nice little front terrace for chilling and a quiet location down a side alley. Cleanliness is taken seriously (shoes off at the door, folks!). The 18 rooms are super-spartan but tidy. Air-con rooms have tiny private bathrooms.

Wisma Delima GUESTHOUSE $
(Map p157; ☎3190 4157; Jl Jaksa 5; dm/s/d with shared mandi 35,000/55,000/75,000Rp) Ancient family-run place with cell-like rooms (with mosquito nets and fans), but it's extremely cheap and isn't dodgy – just read the rules above reception. No telephone reservations.

Eating

JL JAKSA AREA

Jl Jaksa is fine for no-nonsense, inexpensive Indonesian and Western fare, though many local dishes are toned down a notch to suit tourist tastes. For something more authentic, head to the night-hawker stalls grouped around the southern end of Jl Hagi Agus Salim (also known as Jl Sabang), which is famous for its street food (including satay).

KL Village ASIAN $
(Map p157; Jl Jaksa 21-23; mains from 15,000Rp; ⏲7am-11pm Sun-Wed, 24hr Thu-Sat;) Deservedly popular Malaysian place with pavement tables under a covered terrace. Offers great curries (try the *kambing masala*), Western food, terrific juices and fruit shakes (but no beer). Everything is cooked in full view, allowing you to watch the experts at work.

Restaurant Celebes INTERNATIONAL $
(Map p157; Jl Jaksa 37; mains 12,000-15,000Rp; ⏲8am-10pm;) A calm and friendly restaurant that's kept meticulously clean. It has a small selection of local Indonesian dishes as well as a range of pasta and steak options, and if all you're after is a caffeine rush, its huge range of coffee will keep you buzzing all night long. There's no sign board for it, but it's attached to the Hotel Tator.

Sate Khas Senayan INDONESIAN $
(Map p157; ☎3192 6238; Jl Kebon Sirih Raya 31A; mains from 25,000Rp; ⏲11.30am-10pm) Excellent two-storey air-con restaurant at the northern end of Jl Jaksa, renowned for its superb *sate* (satay), *rawon buntut* (oxtail stew) and other classic Indonesian dishes.

Memories INTERNATIONAL $
(Map p157; Jl Jaksa 17; mains 14,000Rp; ⏲24hr) A classic Jaksa haunt of fresh-in-town backpackers and seen-it-all expats. There are plenty of local dishes, lots of Chinese flavours and some ho-hum Western food, including popular set breakfasts. There's also a book exchange and lots of traveller talk.

OTHER AREAS

The upmarket suburb of Kemang, with plenty of stylish bars, clubs and restaurants, is popular with expats, but backpackers are a rare species here. It does, however, have a couple of food courts where you can chow down on the cheap before clubbing till dawn. A taxi (15,000Rp) from JL Jaksa area can easily take an hour thanks to the crazy

Jalan Jaksa Area

traffic, and Kemang doesn't sit on any handy TransJakarta Busway route.

Kemang Food Festival ASIAN $
(Map p152; Jl Kemang Raya; meals from 12,000Rp; ⏲11.30am-11pm) Fifty or so stalls rustle up *roti canai* (Indian-style flaky flat bread), Japanese noodles, and Iranian, Arabic and Indonesian food here. On weekend nights there's a real buzz and the place is packed.

Gedong Galangan CHINESE $
(Map p158; ☎6670981; Jl Kakap 1; mains 15,000-20,000Rp; ⏲10am-9pm) This Chinese cultural and arts centre close to the port has a very pleasant garden restaurant serving a variety of Chinese and Indonesian staples. If you're lucky, you might be able to catch a dance or music practise after lunch.

Night warung INDONESIAN $
(Map p154; Jl Pecenongan) Street food can be picked up at the night *warung* (food stalls), about 1km north of the National Monument.

Drinking

If you're expecting Jakarta, as the capital of the world's largest Muslim country, to be a pretty sober city with little in the way of drinking culture, think again. From expat pubs to gorgeous lounge bars with cocktail lists set at (near) London or New York prices, and far more beautiful people, Jakarta has it all. The bar zone on Jl Falatehan near Blok M (6km southwest of Jl Jaksa) is a good all-round bet, with everything from European-style pubs,

Jalan Jaksa Area

Activities, Courses & Tours
1 Divalina Tour & Travel C3
2 Robertur C2

Sleeping
3 Alinda Hotel C2
4 Bloem Steen Homestay C2
5 Borneo Hostel C2
6 Hostel 35 .... C2
7 Istana Ratu Hotel C2
8 Wisma Delima C2

Eating
9 KL Village C2
10 Memories C2
11 Night Hawker Stalls A3
12 Night Hawker Stalls B3
13 Restaurant Celebes C3
14 Sate Khas Senayan C2

Drinking
15 Melly's B3

Sunda Kelapa & Kota

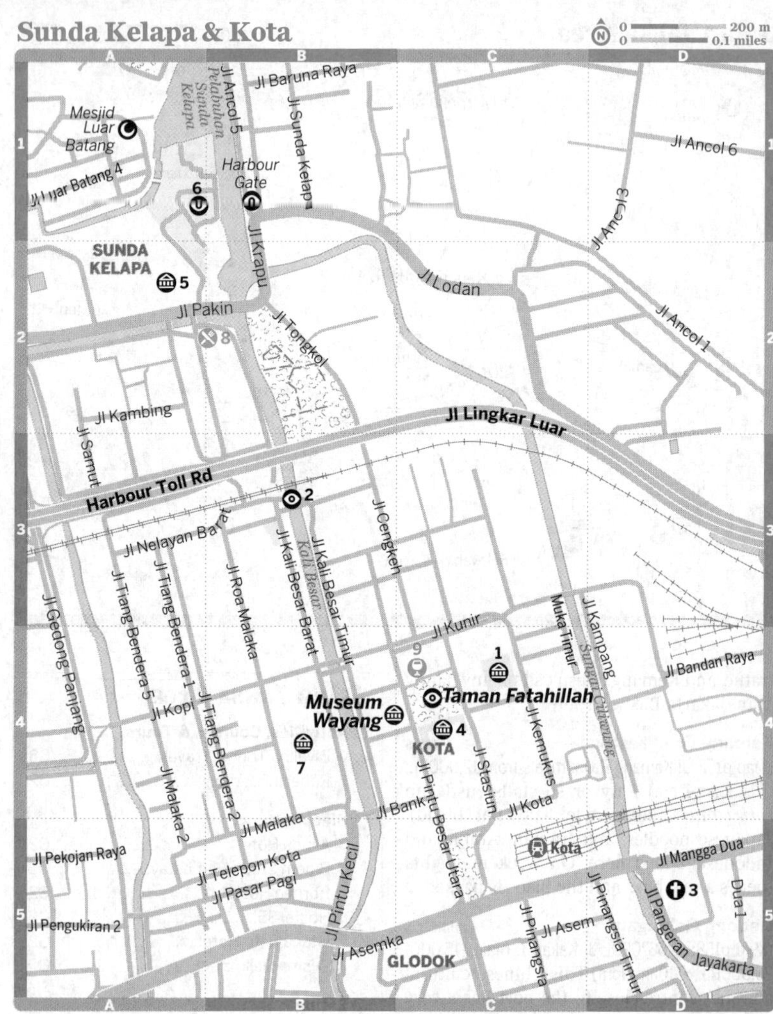

where you can shoot pool and sip wine, to raucous bar-clubs with heaving dance floors.

TOP CHOICE **Café Batavia** BAR

(Map p158; ☎691 5531; Jl Pintu Besar Utara 14) An essential visit if you're in Kota, this historic restaurant (mains 50,000Rp) and bar overlooks Taman Fatahillah. Its teak floors and art-deco furniture make for a richly atmospheric setting, though the menu is overly grandiose (and overly expensive – up to one million Rupiah for a set menu!) and seems to be stuck in 1970s nostalgia. Instead of eating, just kick back under a lazily spinning fan with a cold drink and relish the atmosphere.

Eastern Promise BAR

(Map p152; ☎7179 0151; Jl Kemang Raya 5; wi-fi) A classic British-style pub in the heart of Kemang, Eastern Promise has a pool table, a welcoming atmosphere, and filling Western and Indian grub. Service is prompt and friendly, the beer's cold and there's live music on weekends. It's a key expat hang-out.

Melly's BAR

(Map p157; Jl KH Wahid Hasyim 84; wi-fi) The best bet in the Jaksa area for a couple of drinks,

Sunda Kelapa & Kota

Top Sights

	Museum Wayang	B4
	Taman Fatahillah	C4

Sights

1	Balai Seni Rupa	C4
2	Chicken Market Bridge	B3
3	Gereja Sion	D5
4	Jakarta History Museum	C4
5	Museum Bahari	A2
6	Pasar Ikan	A1
	Si Jagur	(see 4)
7	Toko Merah	B4

Eating

8	Gedong Galangan	B2

Drinking

9	Café Batavia	C4

this quirky little place attracts a good mix of locals and Westerners, has cheap snacks and beer, and plenty of loungy sitting areas. It's open-sided (so it doesn't get too smoky) and there's a popular quiz here every Wednesday.

Entertainment

Check the entertainment pages of *Time Out Jakarta* or *Jakarta Kini* for films, concerts and special events.

Jakarta is the clubbing mecca of Southeast Asia. The city has some great venues (from dark 'n' sleazy to polished and pricey), internationally renowned DJs, world-class sound systems and some of the planet's longest party sessions (some clubs open around the clock for entire weekends). Entrance is typically 50,000Rp to 100,000Rp, but includes a free drink. Clubs open around 9pm, but don't really get going until midnight; most close around 4am.

If you're young enough to backpack but too old and sleepy to party the night away, Jakarta has plenty of more civilised nightlife options from theatre to dance and cinema.

Stadium NIGHTCLUB
(Map p152; www.stadiumjakarta.com; Jl KH Hayum Waruk 111 FF-JJ) The big daddy of Jakarta's scene, this club has the heritage (established in 1997), the reputation (DJs including Sasha and Dave Seaman have spun here), the capacity (around 4000), the sound system and the crowd. This ain't no disco and Stadium has a distinctly underground vibe. Its weekend session is totally hard-core – beginning on Thursday evening and running until Monday morning.

Taman Ismail Marzuki CULTURAL CENTRE
(TIM; Map p154; www.tamanismailmarzuki.com; Jl Cikini Raya 73) TIM is Jakarta's principal cultural centre, with a cinema, theatres (performances include Javanese dance, plays and *gamelan* – Javanese orchestra – concerts), two art galleries and several restaurants in the complex. The tourist office and listings magazines have program details.

Nú China NIGHTCLUB
(Map p152; Kemang Raya 23) New clubs are constantly opening (and closing!) in Jakarta and this one, which is really popular with a young, local student crowd, is the current flavour of the month.

Gedung Kesenian Jakarta CULTURAL CENTRE
(Map p154; ☎380 8282; Jl Gedung Kesenian 1) Hosts traditional dance and theatre, as well as European classical music and dance.

Shopping

Given the climate, it's not surprising that Jakartans love their air-conditioned malls – there are over 100 in the metropolitan area.

PAYON & KINARA

If a never-ending diet of *nasi goreng* is leaving you a little jaded, Jakarta is a great place to splash out on something that'll make your taste buds love you again. **Payon** (Map p152; ☎719 4826; Jl Kemang Raya 17; mains 40,000-110,000Rp; ⏰11.30am-11pm), where you dine under a delightful open pagoda surrounded by greenery, feels like a secret garden and is a very civilised setting for some superb authentic Javanese cuisine. For the spice girls (and boys) among you, **Kinara** (Map p152; ☎719 2677; Jl Kemang Raya 78B; mains 55,000-125,000Rp; ⏰11.30am-11pm), with its mock medieval doors and an opulent interior of grand arches, is an impressive setting for some of the finest Indian dishes in Jakarta – plump samosas, sublime chicken tikka and plenty of vegetarian choices.

Periplus BOOKS
(Map p152; Level 3, Plaza Senayan, Jl Asia Afrika; ⌚9am-7pm) One of the top bookshops in the city, Periplus stocks a wide range of English-language titles, including Lonely Planet guidebooks and Periplus maps.

Plaza Indonesia SHOPPING MALL
(Map p154; www.plazaindonesia.com; Jl Thamrin; 📶) Exclusive Plaza Indonesia tops Jakarta's A-list for shopping centres. There's a good, surprisingly inexpensive food court in the basement.

Pasar Seni MARKET
(Art Market; Map p152; Jl Raya Kampung Bandan; ⌚10am-10pm) For arts and crafts. Also check out Pasar Seni, at Taman Impian Jaya Ancol.

Flea market MARKET
(Map p154; Jl Surabaya; ⌚9am-6pm) Jakarta's famous flea market. Bargain like crazy – prices may be up to 10 times the value of the goods.

Information

Dangers & Annoyances

Considering its size and the scale of poverty, Jakarta is generally a safe city and security incidents are rare. That said, you should be careful late at night in Glodok and Kota – muggings do occasionally occur – and only use reputable taxi companies, such as the citywide Bluebird group. Keep your eyes open on buses and trains, which are a favourite haunt of pickpockets. It's wise to steer clear of political and religious demonstrations. In the past some high-profile Western chain hotels have been targeted by terrorists.

Dengue fever outbreaks occur in the wet season, so come armed with mosquito repellent. See p942 for more on dengue fever.

Emergency

Fire (☎113)

Police (☎110)

Medical help (☎118, 119)

Tourist Police (Map p157; ☎566000; Jl Wahid Hasyim) On the 2nd floor of the Jakarta Theatre.

Internet Access

Internet cafes are scattered all over Jakarta and generally charge between 4000Rp and 10,000Rp per hour. There are literally dozens of places in and around Jl Jaksa, and as names and details change by the month, we have avoided specifically naming any. For wi-fi access, most upmarket malls have free wireless connections, as do increasing numbers of cafes, bars and restaurants.

Medical Services

SOS Medika (Map p152; ☎5794 8600; www.sosindonesia.com; Menara Prima Building, Jl Lingkar Mega Kuningan) Offers English-speaking GP appointments, dental care and emergency, and specialist health-care services.

Money

There are banks all over the city, and you're never far from an ATM in Jakarta.

Post

Main post office (Map p154; Jl Gedung Kesenian 1; ⌚8am-7pm Mon-Fri, to 1pm Sat)

Telephone

Wartel Bhumi Bhakti (Map p157; Jl KH Wahid Hasyim; ⌚10am-10pm)

Tourist Information

Jakarta Visitor Information (Map p157; ☎3154094/3142067; www.jakarta-tourism.go.id; Jl KH Wahid Hasyim 9; ⌚9am-6.30pm Mon-Fri, 9am-1pm Sat) Inside the Jakarta Theatre building. A very helpful office; the staff here can answer many queries, though practical information is a little lacking. Has a good stock of leaflets and publications. There's also a desk at the airport.

Travel Agencies

Divalina Tour & Travel (Map p157; ☎3149330; Jl Jaksa 35) A professional agency with helpful English-speaking staff and a variety of Java- and Indonesia-wide tours.

Robertur (Map p157; ☎314 2926; Jl Jaksa 20B)

Getting There & Away

Jakarta is the main travel hub for Indonesia, with flights and ships to destinations all over the archipelago. Buses depart for cities across Java, and Bali and Sumatra, while trains are an excellent way to get across Java.

GETTING INTO THE CITY: JAKARTA

Soekarno-Hatta International Airport is 35km northwest of the city – an hour away via a toll road (up to two hours during rush hour).

Damri (☎460 3708, 550 1290) buses (20,000Rp, every 30 minutes, 5am to 7pm) run between the airport and Gambir train station (near Jl Jaksa) and to points in the city, including Blok M.

Taxis from the airport to Jl Thamrin/Jl Jaksa cost about 150,000Rp including tolls. Book via the official taxi desks to be safe, rather than using the unlicensed drivers outside.

Air

Soekarno-Hatta International Airport is 35km northwest of the city. See p307 for international airlines serving Jakarta.

Domestic airline offices in Jakarta include the following:

Air Asia (☎2927 0999; www.airasia.com; Terminal 3 & 2D Soekarno-Hatta International Airport)

Batavia Air (Map p154; ☎3899 9888; www.batavia-air.co.id; Jl Ir HJuanda 15)

Garuda Indonesia (Map p157; ☎2351 9999, 080 4180 7807; www.garuda-indonesia.com; Garuda Bldg, Jl Merdeka Selatan 13)

Lion Air (Map p154; ☎080 4177 8899; www.lionair.co.id; Jl Gajah Mada 7)

Merpati (Map p152; ☎654 8888; www.merpati.co.id; Jl Angkasa Blok B/15 Kav 2-3, Kemayoran)

Sriwijaya Air (☎2927 9777, 080 4177 7777; www.sriwijayaair.co.id; Terminal 1B Soekarno-Hatta International Airport)

Boat

The **Pelni ticket office** (Map p152; ☎421 1921; www.pelni.com; Jl Angkasa 18; ⏲8am-4pm Mon-Fri, to 1pm Sat) is 13km northeast of the city centre in Kemayoran. Tickets (plus commission) can be bought through numerous Pelni agents (many travel agents sell them).

Pelni ships all arrive at and depart from Pelabuhan Satu (Dock No 1) at Tanjung Priok (Map p152), 13km northeast of the city centre. When they are (eventually) completed, Busway Koridor 10 and 12 should provide the fastest connection to the port. A taxi from Jl Jaksa costs about 70,000Rp to 80,000Rp.

Bus

So many buses leave Jakarta's bus stations that you can usually just front up at the station and join the chaos, though it pays to book ahead. Travel agencies on Jl Jaksa sell tickets and usually include transport to the terminal, which saves a lot of hassle, though they'll charge a commission for this. Jakarta has four main bus stations, all well out of the city centre. There are buses that will take you to each station from the city centre; see the boxed text, p162.

Kalideres bus terminal Located 15km northwest of the city centre and has frequent buses to destinations west of Jakarta. Take a Koridor 3 TransJakarta bus to get here.

Kampung Rambutan bus terminal (Map p152) This terminal is 18km south of the city and primarily handles buses to destinations south and southeast of Jakarta, such as Bogor (normal/air-con 6000/7500Rp, one hour) and Cianjur (25,000Rp, three hours). Koridor 7 TransJakarta buses serve this terminal.

Pulo Gadung bus terminal (Map p152) Located 12km east of the city centre, serves central and eastern Java, Sumatra and Bali. Destinations include Yogyakarta (normal/air-con 100,000/175,000Rp, 12 hours). Koridor 4 or 2 TransJakarta buses serve here.

Lebak Bulus bus terminal (Map p152) Lebuk Bulus is 16km southwest of the city and also handles some deluxe buses to Yogyakarta, Surabaya and Bali. Most departures are in the late afternoon or evening. When completed Koridor 8 TransJakarta buses will whisk you out here.

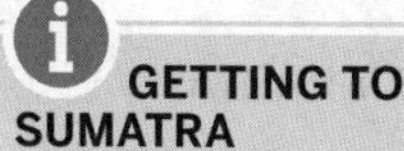

GETTING TO SUMATRA

Ferries to southern Sumatra leave from the small industrial town of Merak, three hours west of Jakarta. Buses to Merak cost 21,000Rp and leave from the Kalideres bus terminal. From Merak, fast ferries run every 30 minutes from 7am to 5pm (30,000Rp); the crossing takes 45 minutes. A slow ferry runs every 30 minutes, 24 hours a day and costs 11,500Rp for the two-hour trip. Damri buses sell a bus-boat-bus combination ticket from Jakarta to Bandarlampung (*bisnis/eksekutif* 115,000/150,000Rp, eight to 10 hours). See p247 for more.

Minibus

Door-to-door *travel* minibuses are not a good option in Jakarta because it can take hours to pick up or drop off passengers in the traffic jams. Some travel agencies book them, but you may have to go to a depot on the city outskirts.

Train

Jakarta's four main train stations are quite central, making trains the easiest way out of the city. The most convenient and important is Gambir train station (Map p154), on the eastern side of Merdeka Sq, a 15-minute walk from Jl Jaksa. Gambir handles express trains to Bogor, Bandung, Yogyakarta, Solo, Semarang and Surabaya. Some Gambir trains also stop at Kota train station (Map p158) in the north of the city. The Pasar Senen train station (Map p152) is to the east and mostly has *ekonomi*-class trains. Tanah Abang (Map p152) train station has *ekonomi* trains to the west.

There's a (slightly pricey) taxi booking desk inside Gambir train station; the fare to Jl Jaksa is 35,000Rp.

For express trains, tickets can be bought in advance at the booking offices at the northern end of Gambir train station, while the ticket windows at the southern end are only for tickets bought on the day of departure. Check timetables online at www.infoka.kereta-api.com (in Bahasa

TRANSJAKARTA BUSWAY

Jakarta has a new network of clean air-conditioned buses called TransJakarta that run on busways (designated lanes that are closed to all other traffic). Journey times have been slashed, and they now represent, by far, the quickest way to get around the city.

Most busways have been constructed in the centre of existing highways, and stations have been positioned (roughly) at 1km intervals. Access is via elevated walkways and each station has a shelter and many are manned, which means someone can normally point you towards your destination. Ten busway lines (called *koridor*) were up and running at the time of research, with a total of 15 planned, which should eventually form a network from Tanjung Priok south to Kampung Rambutan.

Tickets cost 3500Rp, payable before you board, which covers you to any destination in the network (regardless of how many *koridor* you use). Buses (5am to 10pm) are well maintained and not too crowded, as conductors (usually) ensure that maximum passenger numbers are not exceeded.

Indonesia), or consult the helpful staff at the station's **information office** (☎386 2363). For more information on these trains, see p308.

BOGOR Comfortable *Pakuan Express* trains (11,000Rp, one hour) leave from Juanda and Gambir train stations roughly every hour until early evening when they become more like bi-hourly. No-frills trains (4000Rp, 90 minutes) also run this route, about every 30 minutes, but can be horribly crowded during rush hours (watch your gear).

SURABAYA Most trains between Jakarta and Surabaya take the shorter northern route via Semarang, though a few take the longer southern route via Yogyakarta. *Eksekutif* class trains from Gambir leave at 9.30am, 5pm and 9.30pm (305,000Rp, eight to 10 hours).

YOGYAKARTA & SOLO The most luxurious trains are the *Argo Lawu* (270,000Rp, 8¼ hours) departing at 8pm, and the *Argo Dwipangga* (225,000Rp to 1,000,000Rp, 8¼ hours) departing at 8am. These trains go to Solo and stop at Yogyakarta, 45 minutes before Solo, but cost the same to either destination.

Getting Around

For details of Jakarta's excellent new TransJakarta busway network, see the boxed text. Other buses are not very useful for visitors, as they are much slower, hotter (they have no air-conditioning) and crowded (pickpockets can be a problem). Nevertheless, you may come across regular city buses, *patas* (express) buses and orange Metro minibuses from time to time; fares generally cost between 2000Rp and 3000Rp.

Local Transport

Bajaj (pronounced ba-jai) are Indonesian túk-túk. There are few about now in central Jakarta. If you hire one, it's worth remembering that they are not allowed on many major thoroughfares.

Taxi

Metered taxis cost 6000Rp for the first kilometre and 250Rp for each subsequent 100m. Make sure the *argo* (meter) is used.

Bluebird cabs (☎7917 1234; www.bluebirdgroup.com) can be booked ahead and have the best reputation; do *not* risk travelling with the less reputable firms.

Typical taxi fares from Jl Thamrin: to Kota (20,000Rp) or Blok M (30,000Rp). Any toll-road charges are extra and are paid by the passengers.

Bogor

☎0251 / POP 949,000

Known throughout Java as *kota hujan* (city of rain) for having over 300 storms a year, Bogor became a home away from home for Sir Stamford Raffles during the British interregnum, a respite for those mad dogs and Englishmen who preferred *not* to go out in the midday sun. These days, this once-quiet town is almost a suburb of Jakarta, with the traffic and hubbub to match. But while Bogor itself clogs up with bemo (three-wheeled pick-up truck) and mopeds, the real oasis remains untouched. Planted at the very hub of the city, with chaos all around to north, south, east and west, the town's world-class botanical gardens remain – in the words of one upstanding British visitor – 'a jolly fine day out'. They are a good day trip from Jakarta, one hour away by train.

Sights

TOP CHOICE **Kebun Raya** GARDENS

(Great Garden; www.bogor.indo.net.id/kri; Jl Otto Iskandardinata; admission 9500Rp; ⌚8am-5pm) A veritable 'green lung' in the heart of the city, Bogor's botanical gardens, the Kebun Raya,

Bogor

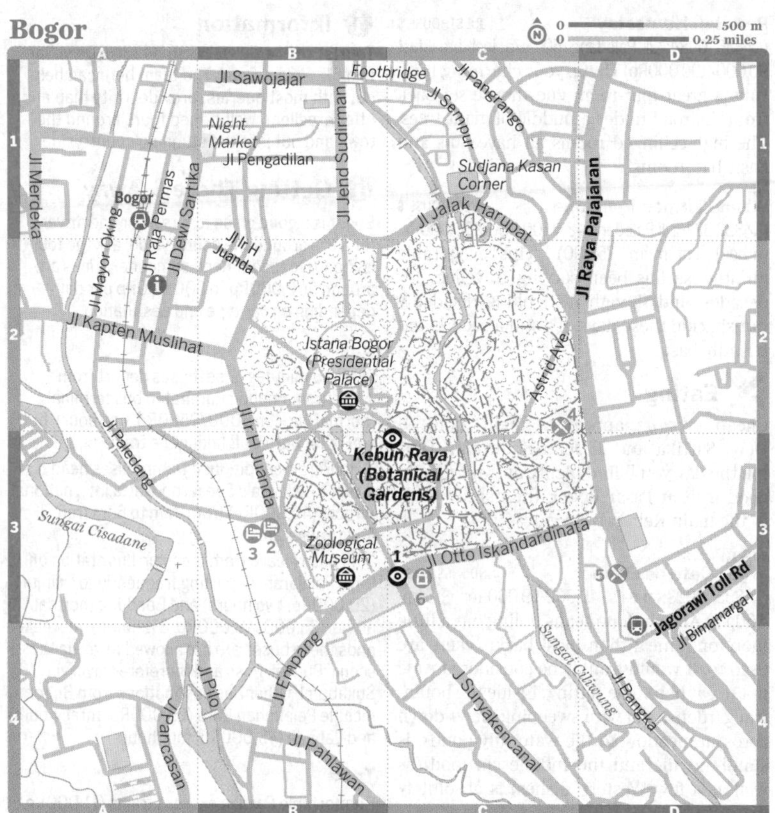

Bogor

Top Sights

Kebun Raya (Botanical Gardens) C3

Sights

1 Main Entrance to Kebun Raya C3

Sleeping

2 Puri Bali Homestay B3
3 Wisma Firman Pensione B3

Eating

4 Café de Daunen C2
5 Simpang Raya Bogor D3

Shopping

6 Pasar Bogor C3

are simply outstanding. British governor Sir Stamford Raffles first laid out a garden, but this was later expanded by Dutch botanists, including Johannes Teysmann, who planted and developed the garden over a 50-year period in the 19th century. Today the garden is an important research centre, and scientists based here are investigating new medical and agricultural uses for its many rare specimens. There are more than 15,000 species of trees and plants, including 400 types of magnificent palms.

Things can get hectic on Sundays, but during the week this is one of West Java's true oases (apart from the odd mosquito – bring some repellent). Highlights include the incredible collections of palms, the bizarre pandan trees with their 'spider leg' roots and the orchid house. Café de Daunen is a great cafe-restaurant in the grounds.

Sleeping

Most people just make a day trip from Jakarta, but if you choose to stay, Bogor has some good family-run places.

Puri Bali Homestay GUESTHOUSE $
(☎835 0984; Jl Paledang 50; s/d incl breakfast 90,000/100,000Rp) Danu, your charming host, runs a great four-room guesthouse set back from the road under a huddle of giant trees. The high-ceilinged rooms all have fans and basic bathrooms.

Wisma Firman Pensione GUESTHOUSE $
(☎832 3246; Jl Paledang 48; r 100,000-200,000Rp, without bathroom 75,000) This venerable guesthouse has been serving travellers for decades, and though it's looking decidedly ramshackle these days, it's still a secure and friendly base.

Eating

Cheap *warung* appear at night along Jl Dewi Sartika and Jl Jend Sudirman. During the day you'll find plenty of *warung* and good fruit at Pasar Bogor, the market close to the main Kebun Raya gates.

TOP CHOICE **Café de Daunen** INDONESIAN $$
(☎835 0023; meals 40,000-59,000Rp; ⏲8am-4.30pm) Although it means doling out a little more on a meal than most backpackers are used to, it would frankly be considered rude not to eat here. The setting, inside the botanical gardens, and with sweeping views down across a meadow to the water-lily ponds, is simply idyllic and the Indonesian food (as well as a few Western dishes) is absolutely first rate.

Simpang Raya Bogor INDONESIAN $
(Jl Raya Pajajaran; meals from 15,000Rp) A huge Padang restaurant serving up Sumatra's finest and spiciest. Heaves with customers by early evening; stroll in and find a seat wherever there is room.

Information

Tourist office (☎02 8836 3433; Jl Dewi Sartika 51; ⏲8am-5pm) The team here can help out with most queries, provide a city map and offer excellent, well-priced tours around the town and out into the stunning countryside.

Getting There & Away

Bogor is a good place to hire a car and driver for a trip around the countryside; ask the tourist board to recommend someone. Prices are around 500,000Rp to 800,000Rp per day depending on car type and destination.

Bus

Every 15 minutes or so, buses depart from Jakarta's Kampung Rambutan bus terminal (normal/air-con 6000/7500Rp, one hour), but you're far better off taking the train.

Hourly air-conditioned Damri buses head direct to Jakarta's Soekarno-Hatta International Airport (40,000Rp) from 4am to 6pm from Jl Raya Pajajaran.

All buses leave from the main bus station on JL Raya Pajajaran, departing frequently to Cianjur (20,000Rp, two hours) and Bandung (normal/air-con 25,000/40,000Rp, 3½ hours). At weekends these buses are not allowed to go via the scenic Puncak Pass and therefore travel via Sukabumi. Other bus destinations from Bogor include Pelabuhan Ratu (25,000Rp, three hours) and Labuan (45,000Rp, four hours).

Train

Comfortable *Pakuan* express trains (11,000Rp, one hour) leave Bogor from the station on Jl Raja Permas for the capital roughly every hour. *Ekonomi* trains (4500Rp, 1½ hours) run even more frequently, but are usually packed.

Getting Around

Angkot (minibuses; 2000Rp) make slow circuits of the gardens, taking in most central locations en route.

WORTH A TRIP

CIMAJA

This chapter covers just the highlights of Java, but of course on an island as diverse and large as Java there's plenty of scope for adventure beyond the pages of this book. One of our favourite off-the-beaten-track destinations in western Java is the small beach town of Cimaja close to the port of Pelabun Ratu. Cimaja is best known for being home to a number of quality surf spots, and as the closest real surf town to Jakarta, it's popular with landlocked expat wave riders as well as local rippers. But as well as expert-only waves, there are a number of good places for beginners to hit the surf, and the pretty beaches that hug the coastline west of town are starting to attract a trickle of adventurous backpackers. There's plenty of good-value accommodation in the area as well as surf lessons and board rental.

DON'T MISS

LIVE WITH THE LOCALS

The **Cianjur homestay programme** (☎0813 2110 1777/081 7085 6691; www.cianjuradventure.com) is a superb initiative set up by author Yudi Sujana, who lived for years in New Zealand, that allows travellers to experience life in a nontouristy town in Java. Yudi and his team all speak fluent English, so it's a wonderful opportunity to get to understand Sundanese and Indonesian culture. School visits, sightseeing trips and hikes (and occasionally some voluntary work opportunities for those with TEFL certificates) are offered at backpacking rates. Guests pay 175,000Rp per person per day, which includes family accommodation, three meals and even laundry; it's best to book a place a few days in advance. Airport pick-ups and drop-offs can also be arranged at very moderate rates, allowing you to bypass Jakarta completely.

Cibodas & Cianjur

☎0263 / POP CIBODAS 20,000, CIANJUR 156,000

Leaving Bogor you pass through the **Puncak Pass**, a once-lovely highland area destroyed by a rampant resort sprawl of hotels, weekend homes and factory shopping outlets. But continue east and you'll travel through some of Java's finest highland scenery: a bewitching landscape of plunging valleys, tea plantations and cool, misty mornings.

Sights & Activities

TOP CHOICE **Kebun Raya Botanical Gardens** GARDENS

(admission per person/car 3000/7500Rp; ⏱7am-6pm) Cibodas, 4km off the main road, is home to the stunning Kebun Raya Botanical Gardens, an incredible collection of over 5000 plants and trees from over 1000 species set in outrageously lush grounds of alpine forest, waterfalls and grasslands. The gardens, which we think are even better than those of Bogor, spread over the steep lower slopes of volcanoes Gunung Gede and Gunung Pangrango at an altitude of 1300m to 1440m, making them one of the dampest places in Java.

Gunung Gede HIKING

From April to October, you can climb Gunung Gede, a spectacular 2958m volcanic peak with a huge crater; from its summit it's possible to see the Indian Ocean and Java Sea on clear days. You must register for the climb and obtain a permit (6000Rp) one week in advance. This can either be done in person from the **PHKA office** (☎512776; ⏱8am-3.30pm Mon-Fri, 9am-2.30pm Sat & Sun) just outside the gardens' entrance or online (www.gedepangrango.org). It's seven hours to the summit, so start early (usually around 2am) or spend the night camping on the mountain (bring your own gear). Guides to the summit are compulsory and can be hired for around 400,000Rp at the office.

Sleeping & Eating

Accommodation tends to be expensive close to the Puncak Pass, as the area is popular with wealthy weekending Jakartans. The Cianjur homestay program (see box) is a good way to interact with local people.

Freddy's Homestay GUESTHOUSE $

(☎515473; r incl breakfast from 100,000Rp) Located down a narrow alleyway 500m before the gardens, Freddy's is *the* base in the area for birdwatchers. Rooms here are very simple and clean but overpriced. Nevertheless this homestay does offer good information and guides can be hired.

Getting There & Away

On weekdays, buses leave Jakarta's Kampung Rambutan bus terminal every 30 minutes to Cipanas (25,000Rp, two hours) and Cianjur (without/with air-con 21,000/26,000Rp, 2½ hours). At weekends (when traffic is terrible around Puncuk Pass) buses are routed via Sukabumi (add an extra hour to your journey time, and 5000Rp). Buses to/from Bandung (14,000/20,000Rp, 1¾ hours) run every half-hour.

There are buses to Bogor from Cianjur (without/with air-con 14,000/20,000Rp, two hours) and the highway by Cipanas every 20 minutes; *angkot* ply the route on Sundays.

Pangandaran

☎0265

Situated on a narrow isthmus, with a broad sweep of sand on either side and a thickly forested national park on the nearby headland, Pangandaran is Java's premier beach resort. Most of the year Pangandaran is

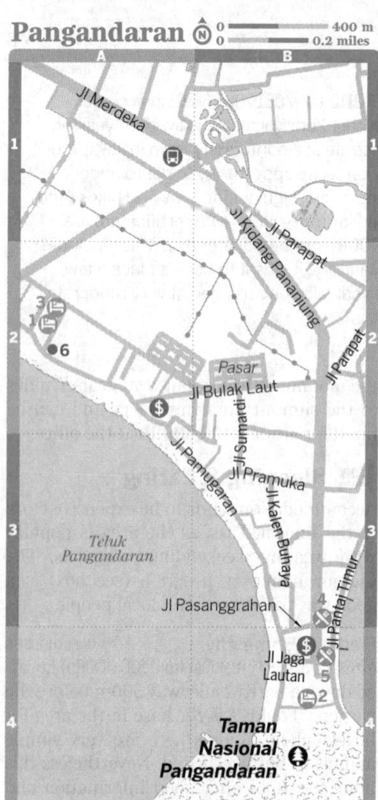

Pangandaran

Top Sights

Taman Nasional Pangandaran B4

Sleeping

1 Mini Tiga Homestay A2
2 Pondok Moris B4
3 Villa Angela A2

Eating

4 Green Garden Café B3
5 Sarimbit B4

Information

6 Din's Tourist Service & Money Changer A2

quiet, but the town fills up on holidays (and weekends). Swimming is dodgy, with heavy dumping surf and strong currents, but it's not a bad place to get out on a board, or to learn how, on small swells. When the waves are maxed out (which is often), head an hour up the coast to sheltered Batu Karas (p168).

Sights & Activities

Taman Nasional Pangandaran NATIONAL PARK
(Pangandaran National Park; admission 7000Rp; dawn-dusk) The Taman Nasional Pangandaran, which fringes the southern end of Pangandaran, is a stretch of untouched forest that's populated by barking deer, hornbills and Javan gibbons, and features some spectacular white-sand beaches. The Boundary Trail offers the best walk through the park, as it skirts the jungle. The park's other trails are somewhat vague; guides charge 75,000Rp to 150,000Rp (for a group of four), depending on the length of the walk. Numerous deer and monkeys gather next to the ticket offices and car parks, meaning that those with wallets sewn firmly shut can see some of the animals without actually entering the park.

Surf lessons SURFING
(per half-day incl board hire 150,000Rp) Surf lessons are offered at the northern end of the western beach. Pangandaran is a good place to learn, and local instructors have 'soft' boards ideal for beginners. The Mia Tiga Homestay can organise lessons.

Tours

For information on the popular Green Canyon tours, see p168.

Paradise Island BEACHES
There are tours available to Paradise Island, an uninhabited nearby island with good beaches and surfing. Day trips cost around 250,000Rp per person (minimum four persons) and overnight trips 400,000Rp. Many of the guesthouses or Din's Tourist Service & Money Changer are good sources for guides.

Sleeping

As Pangandaran has close to 100 hotels you should have no bother finding a bed, except during Christmas and Lebaran (the end of Ramadan) when half of Java seems to head here and prices skyrocket.

Many of Pangandaran's best homestays and *losmen* (basic accommodation) are crowded along the northern stretch of the town's western beach. None of the following have hot water.

WORTH A TRIP

BANDUNG

Big, burly Bandung is like a bat to the back of the head after the verdant mountains around Cibodas. Once dubbed the 'Paris of Java', this is one of Indonesia's megacities (the Bandung conurbation has over seven million inhabitants), with a city centre that's prone to Jakarta-style congestion. Few travellers make a concerted effort to come here, but rummage through the concrete sprawl and odd pockets of interest remain, including some Dutch art-deco monuments, the quirky fibreglass statues of Jeans St, and some cool cafes popular with the thousands of students who call this city home.

The main drag, Jl Asia Afrika, runs through the heart of the city centre past the *alun alun* (main public square). Many of Bandung's cheapest places are close to the train station on Jl Kebonjati and are looking quite run down these days, plus the area is very dark after nightfall. Backpackers should up their budgets in this prosperous city. The most popular hotel with travellers is **Guest House Pos Cihampelas** (☎423 5213; Jl Cihampelas 12; economy r from 90,000Rp, standard from 135,000Rp; ❄), which has a plethora of different rooms – from windowless economy options with shared bathroom facilities to smarter air-con doubles.

TOP CHOICE **Mini Tiga Homestay** GUESTHOUSE $
(☎639436; Jl Pamugaran; katmaja95@yahoo.fr; s/d incl breakfast 80,000/100,000Rp; @) The most popular place in town with backpackers and rightfully so. Mini Tiga has spacious rooms (all with en-suite bathrooms and Western toilets). Catherine, the French owner, has lived in Pangandaran for years and looks after her guests, offering cheap tours, transport and even home-made yoghurt.

Villa Angela GUESTHOUSE $
(☎639641; Jl Pamugaran; r 150,000Rp; ❄) Offering superb value, this guesthouse has spacious rooms (all with TV and bathroom) in two attractive villa-style houses. It's run by a welcoming family and has a nice little garden. Prices drop if you stay a few days.

Pondok Moris GUESTHOUSE $
(☎639490; Gang Moris 3; r 75,000Rp) Close to the national park this friendly little place has smallish rooms with character that are surrounded by greenery. It would be a veritable oasis, if it weren't so close to the mosque. It's a little hard to find, so use said mosque as a navigational aid.

Eating

Pangandaran is famous for its excellent seafood. For cheap Indonesian nosh, the town has many *warung*.

Green Garden Café INTERNATIONAL $
(Jl Kidang Pananjung 116; snacks/meals 10,000/20,000Rp) This excellent place has a relaxed boho vibe, with artwork on display and tables set back off the street. The menu is mainly Indonesian and has plenty of seafood, but some Western temptations slip in as well.

Sarimbit SEAFOOD $
(Jl Pantai Timor; meals around 25,000Rp) This simple place is one of several fresh-fish restaurants facing the east beach, and has tables looking out to the sea. Feast on red snapper or jumbo prawns cooked with a sauce of your choice.

Information

A 3500Rp admission charge is levied at the gates on entering Pangandaran. There's no tourist office in town. There are several internet cafes on Jl Kidang Pananjung.

BNI ATM (Jl Bulak Laut)

BRI bank (Jl Kidang Pananjung) Changes cash dollars and major brands of travellers cheques.

Din's Tourist Service & Money Changer (☎639262; denish_78@yahoo.com; Jl Pamugaran) Helpful travel agency selling onward tickets and a variety of local tours.

Getting There & Away

Pangandaran lies roughly halfway between Bandung and Yogyakarta. Most people get here by road, as there's no train station, but it's perfectly possible to arrive by rail and bus. Speak to staff at the Mini Tiga Homestay for impartial transport advice and possible routes, and you can book tickets there too.

Bus

Local buses run from Pangandaran's bus station, just north of town, to Sidareja (20,000Rp, 1¼ hours) and Cijulang (5000Rp, 40 minutes). Express buses also leave for Bandung

(38,000Rp, six hours) and Jakarta's Kampung Rambutan terminal (55,000Rp, 8½ hours).

Minibus

The most comfortable way to travel to Bandung (normal/air-con 100,000/130,000Rp) is aboard a door-to-door *travel* minibus. Minibuses also run to Jakarta's Kampung Rambutan terminal (normal/air-con 135,000/150,000Rp, nine hours) and to Yogyakatra (150,000Rp, seven hours). All of these can be reserved through Din's Tourist Services & Money Changer (see p167).

Train

To get to Yogyakarta by train you first need to get to Sidareja (by car costs 150,000Rp), from where there are train services to Yogya (*bisnis* class 50,000Rp); there's a fast train leaving Sidareja at noon, which takes 3½ hours.

Batu Karas

0265 / POP 3000

The idyllic fishing village and emerging surfing hot spot of Batu Karas, 32km west of Pangandaran, is one of the most enjoyable places at which to kick back in Java. It's a tiny one-lane settlement, bisected by a wooded promontory, and it has a low key, relaxed charm (except on weekends and holidays when it's jammed with Javanese visitors). There are two fine black-sand beaches, with sheltered sections that are usually calm enough for good swimming, but most visitors are here for the waves, and there's a lot of surf talk. The long right pointbreak here is a very mellow sand-bottom wave that's seriously sheltered from all but the biggest swells. This makes it one of the best places in Java to learn to surf. More experienced wave riders will probably rate the main pointbreak a fairly dull ride compared to most Indonesian waves, but 15 minutes' walk north of the village is a marginally more interesting, and consistent right reef. The locally run surf co-op charges 80,000Rp per person per day for lessons; board hire is extra (around 35,000Rp).

Sleeping & Eating

In addition to restaurants at the following hotels, there are a few cheap eating spots on the waterfront. Try **Kang Ayi** (mains 17,000-30,000Rp) and **Sederhana** (mains 15,000-25,000Rp). We probably don't need to tell you that you'll be eating seafood.

TOP CHOICE **Java Cove** HOTEL $$
(708 2020; www.javacovebeachhotel.com; r from 374,000Rp;) Gorgeous Australian-owned beachfront hotel that offers beautiful, contemporary-chic rooms as well as no-frills economy options. It might be expensive, but in this overpriced town it actually offers the best value for your Rupiah. It has a decked, surf-facing garden and a restaurant. Book online for 30% discounts.

Bonsai Bungalows BUNGALOWS $$
(709 3199; r from 200,000Rp) This would be a good choice if it were a little cheaper. It's well-constructed and very clean and has tidy thatched accommodation in neat little wooden rooms with fans and verandas. Breakfast is only included at weekends, so make sure you eat double portions to see you through the week.

Teratai BUNGALOWS $
(061 662 3372; r 150,000, bungalow 200,000-250,000Rp;) Somewhat overpriced, family-owned place with large rooms and clean *mandis* (a large water tank from which you scoop cool water with a dipper) scattered around a large grassy plot. The swimming pool was half empty (or was that half-full?) when we went past.

Getting There & Away

You have to pay a toll of 5000Rp to enter the village. Batu Karas can be reached from Pangandaran by taking a bus to Cijulang (5000Rp to 10,000Rp depending on bus type) and then an *ojek* (15,000Rp to 20,000Rp) on to Batu Karas. It's sometimes possible to charter a motorbike direct from Pangandaran for around 30,000Rp.

Around Batu Karas

About 6km inland from Batu Karas, pleasure boats run upriver to **Green Canyon**, a lush river valley where you can swim in surging emerald currents and take a natural power shower under the streams that tumble into the gorge (don't look up!). Boats cost 75,000Rp, and run between 7.30am and 4pm. Day trips can be organised from Pangandaran (see p166) for 150,000Rp, but it's easy enough to get here on a hired motorbike, as the route to the canyon is very well signposted.

Wonosobo

0286 / POP 110,000

Wonosobo is the main gateway to the Dieng Plateau. At 900m above sea level in the central mountain range, it has a comfortable climate and is a typical country town with a busy market.

TOP CHOICE **Wisma Duta Homestay** (☎321674; dutahomestay@yahoo.com; Jl Rumah Sakit 3; economy r 100,000Rp, standard s/d 200,000/300,000Rp) is one of the best homestays in the central mountains, occupying a lovely suburban house and garden. The basic rooms are a bit neglected while the sleek new rooms are exceptionally attractive. It's worth staying just to see the massive gold Harley Davidson that sits in pride of place in the front room!

If the Wisma Duta Homestay is full, alternative lodgings can be found at the large, concrete, motel-like **Hotel Sri Kencono** (☎321522; Jl A Yani 81; r from 200,000Rp), which has well-kept, spacious rooms with hot-water bathrooms and Western-style toilets. There are also a few basic economy options.

Shanti Rahayu (Jl A Yani 122; meals 8000-20,000Rp) is considered by locals to be among the best eateries in the town centre, and its chicken curry certainly made us believers.

Wonosobo's bus station is 4km out of town on the Magelang road. From Yogyakarta take a bus to Magelang (13,000Rp, 1½ hours) and then another bus to Wonosobo (15,000Rp, two hours). **Rahayu Travel** (☎321217; Jl A Yani 95) has door-to-door minibuses to Yogyakarta (40,000Rp, three hours).

Frequent buses to Dieng (8000Rp, one hour) leave from Jl Rumah Sakit.

Dieng Plateau

☎0286

A startling contrast from the heat and fecundity of the lowlands, the plateau of Dieng (Abode of Gods) is another world: a windswept volcanic landscape of swirling clouds, green hills, mist and damp punctuated with ancient ruins.

You can see all the main sights, including the temples, on foot in a morning or afternoon, though to really explore the plateau and its crater lakes, allow a couple of days.

Sights & Activities

Arjuna Temples RUINS

(admission 20,000Rp) On the swampy plain in front of Dieng village are the five Hindu temples of the **Arjuna Complex** that are thought to be the oldest in Java, dating back to AD 680. **Candi Gatutkaca**, a temple just to the south, has a small **museum** (⏲8am-4pm) containing statues and sculpture from the temples. Entrance to the museum and Candi Gatutkaca are included in the ticket price.

Natural Attractions LAKE, VOLCANO

The plateau's natural attractions and remote allure are as much a reason to visit as the temples. From the village, you can do a two-hour loop walk that takes in the turquoise lake of **Telaga Warna** (admission 9000Rp) and the steaming vents and frantically bubbling mud pools of **Kawah Sikidang** (admission incl in ticket for Arjuna temples) volcanic crater.

The walk to Sembungan village (2300m) to see the sunrise is heavily touted by the guesthouses, though having to pay to get up at 4.30am is a dubious privilege (particularly on cloudy mornings). All the guesthouses can arrange transport and **guides** (per person 65,000Rp) and hire out warm clothing.

Sleeping & Eating

Dieng's dozen or more guesthouses are notoriously poor value. Spartan conditions and draughty, semiclean rooms are the norm. Beware that hot water is not always forthcoming.

Hotel & Restaurant Bu Jono GUESTHOUSE $

(☎0853 1079 1967; Jl Raya Km 26; r 45,000-75,000Rp) This simple place does have a certain quirky, if ramshackle, charm. All rooms are small and there are three shared hot-water *mandis*. The restaurant is a good place to eat.

Homestay Bougenville GUESTHOUSE $

(Jl Pandawa; r 100,000Rp) Cool blue rooms are on offer in this friendly, family-run guesthouse, but not much English is spoken. The small bathrooms spurt forth hot H_2O. It's located very close to the entrance to the temple complex.

Getting There & Away

Dieng is 26km from Wonosobo, which is the usual access point. Buses run frequently (8000Rp, one hour).

Yogyakarta

☎0274 / POP 396,000

From an all-night shadow-puppet performance to the bold and socially aware graffiti that covers many a wall throughout the city, Yogyakarta is, above all else, a city of art and culture and a hotbed of Javanese intellectual and political thought. Although still headed by its sultan, whose *kraton* (palace) remains the hub of traditional life, contemporary

Yogyakarta

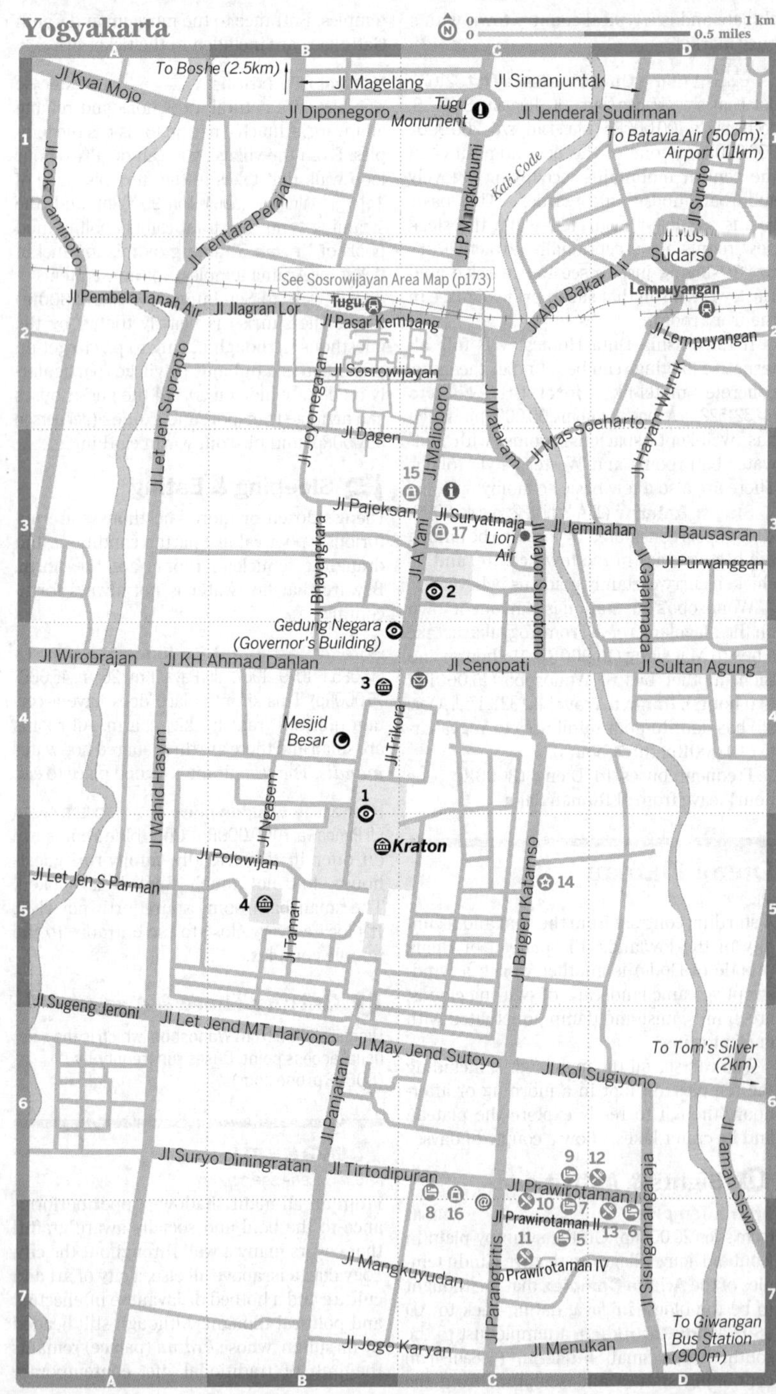
0 1 km
0 0.5 miles
To Boshe (2.5km)
Jl Magelang
Jl Simanjuntak
Jl Kyai Mojo
Jl Diponegoro
Tugu Monument
Jl Jenderal Sudirman
To Batavia Air (500m); Airport (11km)
Jl Cokroaminoto
Jl Tentara Pelajar
Kali Code
Jl P Mangkubumi
Jl Suroto
Jl Yos Sudarso
See Sosrowijayan Area Map (p173)
Jl Pembela Tanah Air
Jl Jlagran Lor
Tugu
Jl Pasar Kembang
Jl Abu Bakar Ali
Lempuyangan
Jl Lempuyangan
Jl Let Jen Suprapto
Jl Joyonegaran
Jl Sosrowijayan
Jl Mataram
Jl Hayam Wuruk
Jl Mas Soeharto
Jl Dagen
Jl Malioboro
Jl Pajeksan
Jl Suryatmaja
Lion Air
Jl Jeminahan
Jl Bausasran
Jl Bhayangkara
Jl A Yani
Jl Mayor Suryotomo
Jl Gajahmada
Jl Purwanggan
Gedung Negara (Governor's Building)
Jl Wirobrajan
Jl KH Ahmad Dahlan
Jl Senopati
Jl Sultan Agung
Mesjid Besar
Jl Trikora
Jl Wahid Hasym
Jl Ngasem
Kraton
Jl Polowijan
Jl Let Jen S Parman
Jl Brigjen Katamso
Jl Taman
Jl Sugeng Jeroni
Jl Let Jend MT Haryono
Jl May Jend Sutoyo
To Tom's Silver (2km)
Jl Kol Sugiyono
Jl Panjaitan
Jl Taman Siswa
Jl Suryo Diningratan
Jl Tirtodipuran
Jl Prawirotaman I
Jl Prawirotaman II
Prawirotaman IV
Jl Sisingamangaraja
Jl Mangkuyudan
Jl Parangtritis
To Giwangan Bus Station (900m)
Jl Jogo Karyan
Jl Menukan

Yogyakarta

Top Sights
Kraton ... B5

Sights
1 Kraton Entrance ... B4
2 Pasar Beringharjo ... C3
3 Sono-Budoyo Museum ... B4
4 Taman Sari ... B5

Sleeping
5 Delta Homestay ... C7
6 Kampoeng Djawa Guest House ... D7
7 Prambanan Guest House ... C7
8 Tulips Hotel & Restaurant ... C6
9 Via Via Guest House ... C6

Eating
Hanis Restaurant & Bakery ... (see 7)
10 Laba Laba Café ... C7
11 Milas ... C7
12 Ministry of Coffee ... D6
13 Via Via ... D7

Entertainment
14 Purawisata ... C5
Sono-Budoyo Museum ... (see 3)

Shopping
15 Batik Keris ... C3
16 Batik Plentong ... C6
Batik Winotosastro ... (see 16)
17 Terang Bulan ... C3

Transport
Dinda ... (see 7)

Yogya is as much a city of cybercafes, lounges and traffic jams as batik, *gamelan* and ritual.

But while the process of modernisation homogenises many of Java's cities, Yogya continues to juggle past and present with relative ease, sustaining a slower, more conservative way of life in the quiet *kampung* (villages) that thrive only a stone's throw from the throbbing main streets.

Yogya's potency has long outweighed its size, and it remains Java's premier tourist city, with countless hotels, restaurants and attractions of its own. The city is also an ideal base for exploring Borobudur and Prambanan.

Jl Malioboro is the main drag, running south from the train station to become Jl A Yani at its southern end (where you'll find the *kraton*). It's lined with stores, and you'll find the main budget accommodation enclave of Sosrowijayan just off it. A second swankier hotel and restaurant district lies to the south around Jl Prawirotaman.

Sights & Activities

Kraton PALACE

(Map p170; admission 12,500Rp, camera/video 1000/2000Rp, guided tour by donation; ⏲8am-2pm Sat-Thu, to 1pm Fri) Traditions hold firm in Yogya, and nowhere is this more evident than in the *kraton*, a walled royal enclave and the cultural and political heart of the city. Effectively a city within a city, over 25,000 people live within the compound. In all honesty, information about the glittering palaces, temples and treasures is a little lacking and not that well presented to the casual visitor, but that's partly because the *kraton* primarily remains the sultan's home and a centre of political power and influence, and only secondly a tourist attraction.

The golden pavilion, the official reception hall of the sultans, boasts a marble floor and showcases a host of free cultural events; see p175 for a rundown of these. Other highlights include the souvenir house, textile room and the small museum dedicated to Hamengkubuwono IX, the current sultan's father.

Try and visit the *kraton* during the week – at weekends the compound becomes a menagerie of tour buses, screeching kids, dripping ice creams and 'hello missterrrrs!'

Taman Sari & Pasar Ngasem PALACE, GARDENS

(Water Castle; Map p170; Jl Taman; admission 7000Rp, camera/video 1000/2000Rp; ⏲8am-3.30pm) The Taman Sari was a complex of canals, pools and palaces built within the *kraton* between 1758 and 1765 by a Portuguese architect who was allegedly later executed to keep the sultan's hidden 'pleasure rooms' secret. Damaged first by Diponegoro's Java War and then further by an earthquake, it is today a mass of ruins, crowded with small houses and batik galleries. The main bathing pools have been restored.

Sono-Budoyo Museum MUSEUM

(Map p170; JL Trikora 6; admission 5000Rp; ⏲8am-3.30pm Tue-Thu, Sat & Sun, 8am-2.30pm Fri) Close by the *kraton*, the Sono-Budoyo Museum is the best of Yogya's museums, with an astounding assortment of stone and gold Hindu statuary, Balinese carvings, *wayang kulit* puppets, *kris* and batik. There's even an entire Balinese temple in the courtyard. *Wayang kulit* performances are held here nightly at 8pm (see p174).

Bird Market MARKET

(Ring Rd Selatan; ⌚9am-4pm) On account of fears over bird flu, Yogya's bird market recently flapped its wings and flew from its city-centre location to a new, purpose-built market area on the southern outskirts of town. Despite the move, it remains a fascinating place in which to pick up a pet finch or owl. Or maybe you need a dark-as-night raven (traditionally used in black magic), a fluffy bunny, a smelly mongoose or a sweet terrapin? If you're not here to buy, the market is still an interesting place to explore.

Pasar Beringharjo MARKET

(Map p170; Jl A Yani; ⌚7.30am-4pm) Yogya's superb main market, Pasar Beringharjo, is a wonderful place to spend an hour or two. Buzzing with life, here you can shop for cheap batik, clothes, bags and sandals. On the upper floors there's a spice market and an area devoted to curios and antiques.

Affandi Museum ART GALLERY

(☎562 593; www.affandi.org; Jl Laksda Adisucipto 167; admission 20,000Rp, camera/video 10,000/20,000Rp; ⌚9am-4pm Mon-Sat) About 6km east of the city centre, the Affandi Museum, housed in a curious riverside tree house, exhibits the impressionist works of Affandi, Indonesia's best-known artist.

Festivals & Events

The three Gerebeg festivals – held each year at the end of January and April and the beginning of November – are Java's most colourful and grand processions.

Sleeping

Yogya has dozens of good guesthouses and hotels. Sosrowijayan is the main budget zone, while the Prawirotaman area, 2km south of the *kraton*, also has some cheap places as well as midrange options.

SOSROWIJAYAN AREA

Situated within a short walk of the Tugu train station, Sosrowijayan is a fascinating traditional neighbourhood of narrow *gang* (alleyways), lined with backpacker-geared accommodation, eateries, laundries and the like. Few of the guesthouses here include breakfast in their rates.

TOP CHOICE **Losmen Setia Kawan** GUESTHOUSE $

(Map p173; ☎512452; www.bedhots.com; s/d with cold water 100,000/120,000Rp, with hot water 150,000/200,000Rp; ❄@📶) One of the better choices in Sosrowijayan, this superb place is inviting and well run. It occupies a fine old artistically decorated house with rooms that are brushed up in trippy swirls of bright paint. It has a rooftop patio and a row of computers for internet access.

Bladok Losmen HOTEL $

(Map p173; ☎560452; Jl Sosrowijayan 76; s/d from 80,000/100,000Rp; ❄📶🏊) A great lodge of real character and charm, the Bladok feels much more sophisticated than any other guesthouse in this area, and its wide range of rooms and prices means it caters to both budget and midrange travellers. There's a decent in-house restaurant and the immaculate pool is sheer bliss at the end of a long, sticky day.

Dewi Homestay GUESTHOUSE $

(Map p173; ☎516014; Jl Sosrowijayan GT I 115; s/d 90,000/100,000Rp; ❄📶🏊) The Dewi Homestay breathes fresh air into the Sosrowijayan hotel scene. Set under a curtain of dense foliage the communal areas are rammed with old (and not so old) knick-knacks. The rooms are equally stuffed with Javanese character, including beautiful carved wooden doors.

Losmen Lucy GUESTHOUSE $

(Map p173; ☎513429; r from 90,000Rp) One of the best *losmen* in Yogya. The 12 fan-cooled rooms here are spick 'n' span and the beds still have some spring; all have en-suite *mandi* with squat toilets. Note that there's a nearby, and vastly inferior, *losmen* with the same name. The one you want has a big red-and-green mural on the exterior wall!

Tiffa Art Shop & Losmen GUESTHOUSE $

(Map p173; ☎512841; tiffaartshop@yahoo.com; s/d incl breakfast 90,000/100,000Rp) An excellent little *losmen* owned by a hospitable family with accommodation above an art shop. All the four rooms are smallish but have private *mandi*. A decent breakfast is also included.

JL PRAWIROTAMAN AREA

This area used to be the centre for midrange hotels in Yogya, but many have slashed their

Sosrowijayan Area

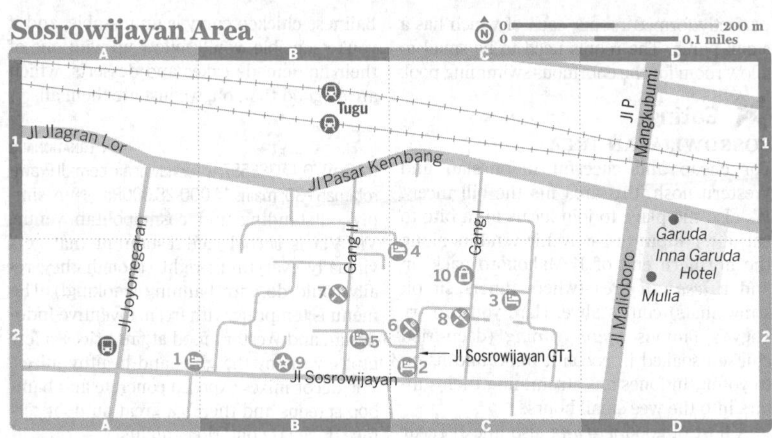

Sosrowijayan Area

Sleeping

1 Bladok Losmen ... A2
2 Dewi Homestay ... C2
3 Losmen Lucy ... C2
4 Losmen Setia Kawan ... C2
5 Tiffa Art Shop & Losmen ... B2

Eating

6 Atap ... C2
7 Bedhot Resto ... B2
FM Café ... (see 2)
8 New Superman's ... C2

Entertainment

9 Bintang Resto ... B2

Shopping

10 Lucky Boomerang ... C2

prices in recent years and there are bargains to be had. Breakfast is normally included in the hotel room rates.

Via Via Guest House BOUTIQUE HOTEL $
(Map p170; ☎374748; www.viaviajogja.com; Jl Prawirotaman mg 3; r without bathroom 150,000Rp, r with fan & bathroom 160,000Rp, r with air-con 200,000Rp;) This stylish little guesthouse down a quiet side street has immaculate whitewashed rooms adorned in superb photographic works of art. If you don't like one room, ask to see another, as they're all slightly different. Breakfast is eaten in the small courtyard.

Kampoeng Djawa Guest House BOUTIQUE HOTEL $
(Map p170; ☎378318; www.viaviajogja.com; Jl Prawirotaman I 40; r with fan/air-con 100,000/130,000Rp;) With exposed red-brick walls festooned in shadow puppets, old photos of Yogya court life and a jungle of foliage lining the hallways and courtyard, this superb place is something of a budget boutique hotel. But with just six well-maintained rooms, it fills up fast. Prices rise by 20% at weekends.

Prambanan Guest House HOTEL $$
(Map p170; ☎376167; www.prambanangh.be; Jl Prawirotaman I No 14; s/d with cold shower from 140,000/160,000Rp, s/d with air-con & hot water 260,000/300,000Rp;) An exceptionally well-run place with an attractive garden and attentive staff, Prambanan, with its plain but satisfactory rooms (better rooms have bathrooms with gallons of hot water), is a very good option. The swimming pool is just crying out for a pre-breakfast dip.

Tulips Hotel & Restaurant HOTEL $
(Map p170; ☎450137; www.hotel-tulips.com; Jl Tirtodipuran 42; r from 190,000Rp;) This hotel is a few minutes' walk from the main traveller scene, but its pristine colonial-style rooms, pretty gardens and one of the best swimming pools in town make the short walk well worthwhile.

Delta Homestay HOTEL $
(Map p170; ☎727 1047; www.dutagardenhotel.com; Jl Prawirotaman II 597A; s/d 95,000/110,000Rp, with bathroom & air-con 150,000/160,000Rp;) A decent little hotel with a selection of tiny yet

perfectly formed rooms, each of which has a small porch. The rooms need to be small to allow room for the enormous swimming pool.

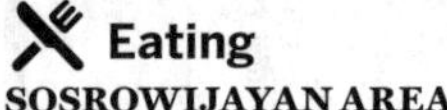

Eating

SOSROWIJAYAN AREA

For cheap and cheerful Indonesian and Western nosh, this area fits the bill nicely. It's also the place to join locals for a bite to eat; after 10pm the souvenir vendors along the northern end of Jl Malioboro pack up and a *lesahan* area (where diners sit on straw mats) comes alive. Here you can try Yogya's famous *ayam goreng* (deep-fried chicken soaked in coconut milk) and listen to young Indonesians strumming their guitars into the wee small hours.

A host of good *warung* also line Jl Pasar Kembang, beside the train line.

Bedhot Resto INTERNATIONAL $
(Map p173; Gang II; mains 20,000-40,000Rp) Bedhot means 'creative' in old Javanese and is perhaps the most stylish eatery in Sosrowijayan, with art on the walls and batik tablecloths. It has tasty Indonesian and Western food, good juices and internet access upstairs.

Atap INTERNATIONAL $
(Map p173; Jl Sosrowijayan GT 1/113; dishes from 10,000Rp; 5.30-10pm) Bohemian restaurant with tables made from car tyres and a great outdoor terrace. The menu has burgers and Indo favourites and a wicked sense of humour.

FM Café INTERNATIONAL $
(Map p173; Jl Sosrowijayan 14; mains around 20,000Rp) FM Café has a great courtyard setting and an eclectic menu ranging from *nasi goreng* to pizza. Happy hour is gloriously lengthy, lasting from 1pm to 8pm; bands perform here on Friday nights.

New Superman's INTERNATIONAL $
(Map p173; Jl Sosrowijayan, Gang 1; meals 15,000-25,000Rp) Huge, slightly charmless place that's nevertheless a key hang-out for travellers. It has a long, long menu of Western food – such as pizzas, jaffles and pancakes – and Chinese food.

JL PRAWIROTAMAN AREA

TOP CHOICE **Hanis Restaurant & Bakery** INTERNATIONAL $$
(Map p170; Jl Prawirotaman I 14; mains 40,000-50,000Rp) A cool, bright and modern cafe-restaurant with a fantastic range of perfectly prepared Indonesian and Italian dishes. The Balinese chicken curry is unmissable, and if you're sensible, you'll follow up with one of their homemade cakes and desserts, which are so good that, oh, we just ate them all.

TOP CHOICE **Via Via** INTERNATIONAL $
(Map p170; ☎386557; www.viaviacafe.com; Jl Prawirotaman I 30; mains 14,000-28,000Rp) A simply outstanding and cosmopolitan venue, Via Via is a cool cafe-restaurant that gets virtually everything right (though they really could do with banning smoking!). The menu is tempting with fresh, inventive Indonesian and Western food at fair prices, a few tapas, wine by the glass and healthy juices. The decor mixes exposed concrete and bamboo screens and there's a great outdoor terrace. Live jazz on Friday nights.

Milas VEGETARIAN $
(Map p170; ☎742 3399; Jl Prawirotaman IV 127; meals 15,000-19,000Rp; dinner only Mon-Fri, lunch & dinner Sat & Sun) This secret garden restaurant, located down a quiet side road, is a project centre for street youth. Offers tasty vegetarian cooking: healthy snacks, sandwiches, salads and organic coffee.

Laba Laba Café INTERNATIONAL $
(Map p170; Jl Prawirotaman I 2; mains 20,000Rp; Mon-Sat) Laba Laba (which means 'spider') has a great rear garden that's an ideal setting for some filling European or Indonesian food.

Ministry of Coffee INTERNATIONAL $
(Map p170; ☎747 3828; www.ministryofcoffee.com; Jl Prawirotaman I 15A; meals 20,000Rp) A landmark modernist structure, with a library (with English-language books and magazines) upstairs and a cafe below. It's ideal for an espresso or latte. The food (mainly snacks and cakes) is generally pretty average, but it earns points for the decent, and unusual, salads.

☆ Entertainment

Dance, *wayang* or *gamelan* are performed most mornings at the *kraton* (admission free). See box for more information.

Most dance performances in and around town are based on the Ramayana or at least billed as 'Ramayana ballet' because of the famed performances at Prambanan.

Wayang kulit performances can be seen at several places around Yogya every night of the week.

DON'T MISS

TODAY AT THE KRATON

The Kraton has a packed cultural calendar with something taking place every day of the week. The following were all correct at time of writing, but it's worth double checking times and performances with the tourist office or most hotels. Admission to the cultural events is included in the entrance ticket.

DAY	EVENT	TIME
Mon	*gamelan* performance	10am-noon
Tue	*gamelan* performance	10am-noon
Wed	*wayang gohek* (wooden puppets)	9am-1pm
Thu	*gamelan* orchestra	10am-noon
Fri	*macapat* singing	9am-noon
Sat	*wayang kulit* show	9.30am-1pm
Sun	classical dance	10am-noon

TOP CHOICE **Purawisata** DANCE
(Map p170; ☎375705; Jl B Katamso) This amusement park stages Ramayana performances every day at 8pm (tickets are 160,000Rp). If you can't get to see the outdoor extravaganza at Prambanan (see p177), this superb show, full of elaborate costumes, acrobatics and fireworks, is more than a mere consolation prize. You can also dine here.

Sono-Budoyo Museum PUPPET SHOW
(Map p170; JL Trikora 6; admission 5000Rp) Holds excellent two-hour shadow-puppet performances nightly from 8pm to 10pm (20,000Rp). Unless a tour group shows up the theatre is often virtually empty, thus giving you the benefit of an almost private performance.

Bintang Resto LIVE MUSIC
(Map p173; Jl Sosrowijayan 54; ⏲to 1am) This popular travellers cafe in Sosrowijayan has live blues, reggae or rock on Wednesday, Friday and Saturday nights from 9pm. It also serves a very standard menu of Indo classics and traveller favourites.

Boshe NIGHTCLUB
(off Map p170; ☎624 041; Jl Magelan, Km 6.5) The hottest club in town with a large central dance floor, pumping sound system and karaoke rooms on lower floors. Draws a young, up-for-it crowd with trance and tribal DJs, plus less impressive boy bands and dance troupes.

Shopping

Yogya is a great place to shop for crafts and artefacts; try the Beringharjo market first for bargains, or the Prawirotaman area, which has several fine antique stores.

Jl Malioboro is one great, long, throbbing bazaar of souvenir shops and stalls selling cheap cotton clothes, leatherwork, batik bags, *topeng* masks and *wayang golek* puppets.

Most of the batik workshops and several large showrooms are along Jl Tirtodipuran, south of the *kraton*. Many, such as **Batik Plentong** (Map p170; Jl Tirtodipuran 48) and **Batik Winotosastro** (Map p170; Jl Tirtodipuran 54), give free guided tours of the process. These places cater to tour groups, so prices are high. Batik is cheapest in the markets, especially Pasar Beringharjo, but quality is questionable. Jl Malioboro and Jl A Yani have good fixed-price places.

Fine filigree work is a Yogya speciality, but many styles and designs are available. Kota Gede, a couple of kilometres east of the city, has some very attractive jewellery, boxes, bowls, cutlery and miniatures, and there are dozens of smaller silver shops on Jl Kemesan and Jl Mondorakan, where you can get some good buys if you bargain.

Tom's Silver SILVER
(off Map p170; ☎525416; Jl Ngeski Gondo 60) You can get a guided tour to see the process of making silver jewellery, with no obligation to buy, at large factories like this: Tom's Silver has an extensive (and expensive) selection and some superb large pieces.

Batik Keris BATIK
(Map p170; ☎557893; Jl A Yani 71) Excellent quality batik. Best for traditional shirts; don't expect fashionable styles. Also see **Terang**

Bulan (Map p170; Jl A Yani 108), another nearby Batik store.

Lucky Boomerang BOOKS
(Map p173; Gang 1-67) Has used guidebooks and fiction, Periplus maps and books, plus souvenirs.

Information

Dangers & Annoyances

Yogya has more than its fair share of thieves. The Prambanan and Borobudur buses are favourites for pickpockets.

Wandering batik or art salesmen, posing as guides or instant friends, can be a pain, especially around the Taman Sari and the *kraton*.

Internet Access

Internet cafes can be found all over Yogyakarta, although many of the cheaper cafes (which charge around 3000Rp per hour) are located north of Jl Diponegoro.

11 Net (Map p170; Jl Parangtritis; per hr 5000Rp) Equipped with modern terminals, and speeds are quite respectable.

Internet Resources

The website www.yogyes.com is a useful portal to the city.

Medical Services

Ludira Husada Tama Hospital (☎620333; Jl Wiratama 4; ⏲24hr)

Money

There are numerous banks (and a few money changers) in the tourist areas. ATMs are widespread throughout the city.

Mulia (Map p173; Inna Garuda Hotel, Jl Malioboro 60) Some of the best exchange rates in Yogya.

Post

Main post office (Map p170; cnr Jl Senopati & Jl A Yani; ⏲7am-8pm Mon-Sat)

Tourist Information

Tourist information office (Map p170; ☎566000; Jl Malioboro 16; ⏲8am-7pm Mon-Thu, to 6pm Fri & Sat) A very helpful office; staff here can provide excellent information and tips. Tugu train station and the airport also have desks.

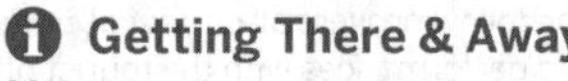

Getting There & Away

Air

Yogyakarta airport (code JOG) has international connections to Singapore and Kuala Lumpur (KL), plus frequent flights to Jakarta and Denpasar.

Air Asia (☎021-2927 0999; www.airasia.com) Flies to Jakarta, Singapore and KL.

Batavia Air (off Map p170; ☎547373; www.batavia-air.co.id; Ruko Mas Plaza, Jl Urip Sumohardjo) Has flights to Balikpapan, Batam, Denpasar, Jakarta, Medan, Pontianak and Surabaya.

Garuda (Map p173; ☎080 4180 7807; Inna Garuda Hotel, Jl Malioboro 60) Links Yogya with numerous domestic and international destinations but usually via a transit in Jakarta.

Lion Air (Map p170; ☎783 1919; Melia Purosani Hotel, Jl Mayor Suryotomo 31) Flies to Jakarta, Surabaya and Mataram.

Bus

Yogyakarta's **Giwangan bus station** (off Map p170; ☎410015; Jl Imogiri) is 5km southeast of the city centre, on the ring road.

Buses also operate regularly to towns in the immediate area, including Borobudur (15,000Rp, 1½ hours) and Kaliurang (10,000Rp, one hour).

For really long trips take a luxury bus. It's cheaper to buy tickets at the bus terminal, but it's less hassle to simply check fares and departures with the ticket agents along Jl Mangkubumi, Jl Sosrowijayan or Jl Prawirotaman.

Local bus 4 leaves from Jl Malioboro (2000Rp) for Giwangan.

Minibus

Door-to-door *travel* service all major cities from Yogyakarta, including Pangandaran (150,000Rp, eight hours), Semarang (30,000Rp, four hours), Surabaya (115,000Rp to 125,000Rp), Malang (100,000Rp) and Jakarta (175,000Rp, 12 hours). Most *travel* will pick you up from your hotel. Hotels and travel agencies

BUSES FROM YOGYAKARTA

DESTINATION	COST ECONOMY/AIR-CON (RP)	DURATION (HR)
Bandung	75,000/100,000	10
Jakarta	100,000/175,000	12
Semarang	25,000/35,000	4
Solo	10,000/20,000	2
Surabaya	75,000/100,000	8

BALI BOUND, BABY

Almost every hotel and travel agency in the city sells short tours that drop you in Bali. Direct minibuses costs 275,000Rp and pick you up from your hotel around 12.30pm. However, most people sensibly choose to break the journey up into several stages. There are a number of different possibilities, but the most popular is the three-day, two-night tour via Gunung Bromo (p186) and the Ijen plateau (p188). Prices start at 620,000Rp including accommodation. Many companies actually drop you at the ferry port between Java and Bali where you change to a larger bus for the journey onward to Denpasar.

There are also two-day, one-night tours running just to Gunung Bromo that will either drop you off in Bali, Surabaya or return you to Yogyakarta. These start at 310,000Rp including accommodation. Although most people seem to enjoy these tours, bear in mind that they are very rushed and that you'll be spending far more time on the road than out in the fresh air. The journey from Yogyakarta to Gunung Bromo alone takes a healthy 12 hours, and you only get an hour or so admiring the volcano the next day.

can arrange tickets for the minibuses, or you can book directly through **Dinda** (Map p170; ☎447015; Jl Prawirotaman 14).

Train

Yogya's main **Tugu train station** (Map p173; ☎514270) is conveniently central, although some *ekonomi* trains run to/from the Lempuyangan station (Map p170), 1km further east.

The comfortable *Taksaka* (from 230,000Rp, eight hours) departs twice daily for Jakarta at 10am and 8pm. The best train is the *eksekutif Argo Lawu* (from 270,000Rp, seven hours), which leaves at 8.53am.

Very regular trains run to Solo, including *Prameks* (10,000Rp to 15,000Rp, one hour), which depart six times daily from Tugu.

For Surabaya, the best option is the *eksekutif Argo Wilis* (from 170,000Rp, 5½ hours), which leaves at 2.22pm.

 Getting Around

Rent motorbikes from 30,000Rp to 35,000Rp a day, and bicycles for 15,000Rp a day. Yogya's airport is 10km east of the city centre. Buses 3A and 1A (3000Rp) serve Jl Malioboro. Taxis cost 55,000Rp to the city centre.

Bus

Yogya has a reliable new bus system called the TransJogja busway. These modern air-conditioned buses run from 6am to 10pm on six routes around the city to as far away as Prambanan. Tickets cost 3000Rp per journey, or 27,000Rp for a carnet of 10.

Bus 1A is a very useful service, running from Jl Malioboro as far as Jl Senopati, then northeast past the Affandi Museum, Ambarukmo Plaza and airport, to the ruins of Prambanan. Bus 3B connects Giwangan bus terminal with the airport and Prambanan before heading west to Jl Malioboro.

Local Transport

Becaks cost around 4000Rp minimum and the asking rate is a lot more. The trip from Jl Prawirotaman to Jl Malioboro costs at least 8000Rp.

Taxi

Taxis have meters and are quite efficient, costing 5500Rp for the first kilometre, then 2500Rp for each subsequent kilometre. A prepaid taxi from the airport to the city centre is 55,000Rp.

Prambanan

The grandest, most evocative Hindu temple complex in Java, **Prambanan** (www.borobudurpark.co.id; adult/student US$13/7; ⏲6am-6pm, last admission at 5.15pm) features some 50 temple sites. Many suffered extensive damage in the 2006 earthquake. Though the temples survived, hundreds of stone blocks collapsed or were cracked (479 in the Shiva temple alone). Parts of the complex are now fenced off (including the Shiva temple) and some temples are covered in scaffolding. It will take years to fully restore Prambanan. That said, Prambanan is certainly still well worth a visit, and you can get within a few metres of (if not enter) all the main monuments.

The **Shiva temple** is the largest and most lavish, towering 47 dizzy metres above the valley and decorated with an entire pantheon of carved deities. The statue of Shiva stands in the central chamber and statues of the goddess Durga, Shiva's elephant-headed son Ganesh, and Agastya the teacher stand in the other chapels in the upper part of the temple. The Shiva temple is flanked by the **Vishnu** and **Brahma temples**, the latter carrying further scenes from the Ramayana. In the small central temple, opposite the

Shiva temple, stands a statue of the bull Nandi, Shiva's mount.

Built in the 9th century AD, the complex at Prambanan was mysteriously abandoned soon after its completion. Many of the temples had collapsed by the 19th century and only in 1937 was any form of reconstruction attempted. A guide to the temple complex costs 75,000Rp.

TOP CHOICE **Ramayana ballet** (admission 75,000-250,000Rp; 7.30-9.30pm) is performed here from May to October several nights a week (hotels and tourist offices in Yogya can provide exact timetables). Based on the ancient Indian epic, one of the corner stones of traditional Indian culture and Hindu religion, the 250 dancers, elaborate costumes and extravagant dance routines, all set in front of a floodlit temple complex, make this one of the most memorable cultural shows in Indonesia. The smaller (50 dancers) **indoor version** (admission 75,000-175,000Rp; 7.30-9.30pm) is held year round – again check exact schedules with tourist offices and hotels.

Most backpacker hotels in Yogyakarta can organise transport to and from Prambanan for both a temple tour or for the ballet.

The main temples face Prambanan village on the highway, while others are scattered across the surrounding fields. The site is 17km east of Yogya on the Solo road. From Yogyakarta, take TransJogja bus 1A (3000Rp, 40 minutes) from Jl Malioboro. Solo-bound buses also stop here. A motorbike or bicycle is a good way to explore all the temples in the area via the back roads.

Borobudur

0293

The bustling little village of Borobudur, 42km northwest of Yogya, may at first seem to be nothing but a fairly inconsequential farming village, but looks deceive because it's actually home to one of the most important Buddhist sites in the world and one of the finest temple complexes in Southeast Asia.

Sights

Borobudur TEMPLE

(www.borobudurpark.co.id; admission to temple US$15; 6am-5pm) The breathtaking Borobudur temple complex is a stunning and poignant epitaph to Java's Buddhist heyday and a highlight of a visit to Indonesia.

The temple consists of six square bases topped by three circular ones, and it was constructed at roughly the same time as Prambanan in the early part of the 9th century AD. With the decline of Buddhism, Borobudur was abandoned, covered in volcanic ash by an eruption in 1006 and only rediscovered in 1814 when Raffles governed Java.

Nearly 1500 narrative relief panels on the terraces illustrate Buddhist teachings and tales, while 432 Buddha images sit in chambers on the terraces. On the upper circular terraces there are latticed stupas, which contain 72 more Buddha images (although at the time of research this upper level was closed for renovations).

Borobudur is best witnessed at sunrise, when morning mist hangs over the lush surrounding valley and distant hills. By 7am lots of tourists will have arrived: it is a popular school trip for students, so expect to get requests for pictures from giggling teenagers. If you really want to get the place pretty much to yourself, it's possible to enter at 5am if you're willing to pay 320,000Rp for the privilege.

Karmawibhangga archaeological museum & Samudraraksa museum

Admission to the temple includes entrance to Karmawibhangga archaeological museum, which contains 4000 original stones and carvings. Close by, the Samudraraksa museum is dedicated to the importance of the ocean and sea trade to Indonesia. There's an 18m wooden outrigger here, a replica of a boat depicted on one of Borobudur's panels. This boat was sailed to Africa in 2003, a voyage retracing Javanese trading links with the continent over 1000 years ago.

Knowledgeable guides for Borobudur can be hired (75,000Rp) at the ticket office for a 90-minute tour. For information about the Borobudur region, its villages and culture, contact Jaker (see the boxed text, p179).

Mendut Temple TEMPLE

(admission 3300Rp; 8am-4pm) This surprisingly little-visited temple, 3.5km east of Borobudur, is a rare delight. It has a magnificent 3m-high statue of Buddha seated with two disciples; the statues are often garlanded in flowers by pilgrims. This gives the temple a more 'lived-in' feel than Borobudur. It has been suggested that the Buddha here was originally intended to top Borobudur but proved impossible to raise to the summit. Tour buses from Yogya will stop here if you ask; otherwise a bemo is 2000Rp.

Sleeping & Eating

The Hotel Rajasa has a decent restaurant serving Javanese specialities for 20,000Rp to 30,000Rp. Otherwise there are plenty of cheap *warung* around the site's exit.

TOP CHOICE Lotus II GUESTHOUSE $
(788845; jackpriyana@yahoo.com.sg; Jl Balaputradewa 54; r incl breakfast from 175,000Rp;) Most of the artistically styled rooms here are exceptionally large, with bathrooms (some with tubs) bigger than most *losmen* rooms. There's also a wonderful rear balcony with views directly onto rice fields. There are only five rooms and demand is very high, so book as far ahead as you can.

Hotel Rajasa GUESTHOUSE $$
(788276; Jl Balaputradewa; r with fan 160,000Rp, s/d with air-con 300,000/350,000Rp;) A handful of large and well-cared-for rooms set around a quiet courtyard with views over the paddy fields. The more expensive rooms have hot-water showers. The fan rooms are a pretty good deal, but the air-con ones are about 100,000Rp too expensive. Breakfast included.

Pondok Tingal Hotel HOTEL $$
(788145; www.pondoktingal.com; Jl Balaputradewa 32; dm 25,000Rp, r with fan 145,000Rp, with air-con from 225,000Rp;) There's an excellent choice of inexpensive rooms around an attractive, peaceful garden, and even a couple of dorms here. However, it's a little forlorn and often half-empty.

Lotus Guest House GUESTHOUSE $
(788281; Jl Medang Kamulan 2; r incl breakfast 70,000-260,000Rp;) North of the temple, Lotus is one of the original guesthouses in Borobudur and it's still run by the same super-hospitable family. However, it's very basic and none too clean.

Getting There & Away

Most travellers get to Borobudur on a tour, which costs around 60,000Rp to 75,000Rp per person and includes door-to-door pick up/drop off at about 4am/noon. Direct buses between Borobudur and Yogyakarta cost 20,000Rp and the last one from Borobudur leaves around 6pm. If there are no direct buses, take a bus from Yogyakarta to Muntilan (10,000Rp), where you can change for Borobudur (10,000Rp).

DON'T MISS

MORE THAN A MONUMENT

Jaker (0293-788 845; jackpriyana@yahoo.com.sg) is a group of guides and local activists based in the small settlement of Borobudur.

If you want to explore the region around Borobudur, Jaker can provide expert local knowledge. Many guides speak fluent English. Backpacking rates are charged for trips to Selogriyo (towering rice terraces and a small Hindu temple), Tuksongo (a centre of glass-noodle production), tofu and pottery villages, and to Mahitan hill for sunrise over the Borobudur monument.

Solo (Surakarta)

0271 / POP 520,000

Arguably the epicentre of Javanese identity and tradition, Solo is one of the least Westernised cities on the island. An eternal rival to Yogyakarta, this conservative city hasn't gone out of its way to attract visitors. However, Solo rewards those with time on their hands who are willing to dig below the tourist gloss. The city has hidden, backstreet *kampung* and elegant *kraton,* traditional markets and gleaming malls, all of which more than warrant at least an overnight visit.

In many ways, Solo is also Java writ small, incorporating its vices and virtues and embodying much of its heritage. On the downside, the island's notoriously fickle temper tends to flare in Solo first – the city has been the backdrop for some of the worst riots in Java's recent history, especially in 1998. And Solo retains a reputation as a hotbed of radicalism. On the upside, most citizens are extremely hospitable and welcome visitors.

Sights & Activities

Kraton Surakarta PALACE
(Kraton Kasunanan; admission 15,000Rp; 9am-2pm Tue-Fri, to 3pm Sat & Sun) Once the hub of an empire, today the Kraton Surakarta is a faded memorial of a bygone era. It's still worth a visit, but it could be so much more if the authorities invested some of the money generated from visitor fees back into the complex. Much of the *kraton* was destroyed by fire in 1985, attributed by the Solonese to the *susuhunan*'s (the hereditary rulers of the city) lack of observance of tradition. Nevertheless,

Solo

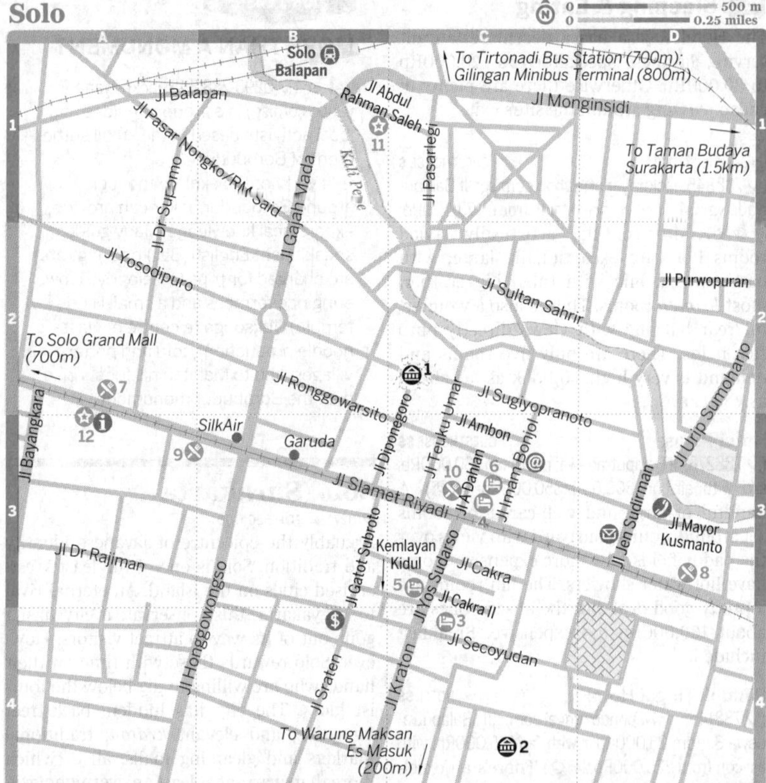

Solo

Sights

1 Istana Mangkunegaran C2
2 Kraton Surakarta C4

Sleeping

3 Cakra Homestay C4
4 Istaya Griya Homestay C3
5 Paradiso Guest House C3
6 Warung Baru Homestay C3

Eating

7 Adem Ayem A2
8 Galabo D3
9 O Solo Mio A3
10 Warung Baru C3

Entertainment

11 RRI Auditorium B1
12 Sriwedari Theatre A3

some fine silver and bronze Hindu-Javanese figures remain in the museum alongside dusty Javanese weapons, parasols and what must qualify as a near definitive horse-carriage collection. The distinctive pagoda-like tower, Panggung Songgo Buwono, built in 1782, is original and is used for meditation.

Dance shows take place with no real regularity on Sundays – children from 10am to noon and adults from 1pm to 3pm. However, even gate staff don't appear to know whether or not a show will take place nor the exact times!

Istana Mangkunegaran PALACE

(Jl Ronggowarsito; admission 10,000Rp, camera/video 1000/3000Rp; ⌚8.30am-2pm Mon-Sat, to 1pm Sun) Istana Mangkunegaran is a rival palace founded in 1757 by a dissident prince, Raden Mas Said. The weathered main structure itself, built in Javanese-European style with an extended front canopy, is in urgent need of restoration, but the museum rooms at the rear have some fascinating curios, including a diminutive gold genital cover, a tremendous mask collection and a wonderfully gaudy dining room complete with lashings of gild and a mirrored ceiling. One of Java's finest *gamelan* orchestras is based here.

The compulsory guided tours (included in the entrance fee but a tip is appreciated) arguably make this a more worthwhile visit than the Kraton Surakarta. At the pavilion, you can see excellent music, singing and dance practise sessions on Wednesday at 10am until 12.30pm and Friday from 4pm to 6pm.

Festivals & Events

Kirab Pusaka FESTIVAL

The Heirloom Procession has been held on the first day of the Javanese month of Suro (between March and May) since 1633. These colourful processions start at Istana Mangkunegaran in the early evening and continue late into the night.

Sleeping

Solo has plenty of budget hotels. In all of the following breakfast is included unless otherwise mentioned.

Cakra Homestay GUESTHOUSE $

(634743; Jl Cakra II/15; r with fan/air-con 100,000/175,000Rp;) With just a bit of effort, this could be one of the best guesthouses in Java. The rooms are set around a beautiful, traditional house and the charming gardens lead to a nice swimming pool. The staff are keen to promote Javanese arts and culture and there's often a free *gamelan* performance in the evening. Now, if they'd just add sinks, hot water and clean bed sheets to the rooms…

Warung Baru Homestay GUESTHOUSE $

(0815 6763 1000; Jl Ahmed Dahlan 23; r with fan/air-con from 75,000/100,000Rp;) This new guesthouse, run by the people of the restaurant with the same name, offers four great-value rooms set around a courtyard garden. The homely rooms are well cared for and

DON'T MISS

KALIURANG & GUNUNG MERAPI

On the flanks of Gunung Merapi, Kaliurang is a pleasant mountain resort, with crisp air and some spectacular views of one of Java's most boisterous volcanoes. It is 26km north of Yogya.

Gunung Merapi (Mountain of Fire) is Indonesia's most active volcano and has been in a near constant state of eruption for hundreds of years. People living on its conical flanks are regularly killed by pyroclastic flows. In 2006, 28,000 villagers had to be evacuated after intense seismic activity, and between October and December 2010 Merapi erupted again in spectacular fashion that resulted in 353 fatalities and thousands left homeless. Today some of these buried villages have turned into minor tourist attractions. This might sound like nothing more than gawking at other people's misfortune, which of course it is, but on the flip side it also allows survivors, who charge entrance fees and sell volcanic souvenirs, a way of making a little bit of money. If you want to visit the destroyed villages, you'll need to hire a car, as there's no public transport to these villages. It's also worth noting that just six months after the eruptions ceased a layer of vegetation was already starting to establish itself over the volcanic wasteland, and it's likely that within the lifetime of this book there will be very little left in the way of visible ruins.

Check the latest situation in Kaliurang, but at the time of writing the climb to the peak from Kaliurang had been strictly off limits since 1994 because of volcanic activity. However, you can hike to Kali Aden, a viewpoint that's about as close as most people would actually want to get to a bad tempered, fire-breathing volcano. Treks last around five hours, but in times of increased volcanic activity it might not be possible to do even this hike. Christian Awuy, owner of **Vogels Hostel** (895208, 0878 3829 0895; Jl Astamulya 76; dm 25,000Rp, r 50,000-125,000Rp, bungalows with hot-water bathroom from 100,000-150,000Rp), in Kaliurang, has organised climbs for years and is an essential first reference point. He charges US$15 per person with a departure time of 4.30am. The price includes a gut-busting breakfast. Vogels itself is a travellers' institution and has been serving up the same mixture of cheap, and very spartan, accommodation and hearty food for just as long.

Angkot from Yogyakarta's Terban station to Kaliurang cost 10,000Rp; the last leaves at 4pm. A taxi from Jl Malioboro will cost around 100,000Rp.

have colourful art on the walls. The more expensive rooms have hot water and bathtubs.

Istaya Griya Homestay GUESTHOUSE $
(☎632667; Jl A Dahlan 22; r with fan/air-con from 100,000/150,000Rp; ❄) Bright murals and textiles add character to what are otherwise ordinary rooms. More expensive rooms have hot water. It has lots of travel information and an in-house cafe.

Paradiso Guest House GUESTHOUSE $
(☎027154111; Kemlayan Kidul 1; r with fan/air-con from 55,000/110,000Rp) This is a fine place to stay, as you'll be lodging in a historic white residence of real character with ornate lighting and mirrors. All the rooms here are kept clean and tidy, and the location is quiet. Breakfast not included.

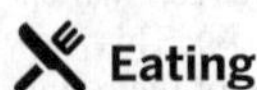

Eating

Solo has a superb street-food tradition and a fine traffic-free area called **Galabo** (Jl Slamet Riyadi; ⏲5-11pm), where you can sample it. Galabo is a kind of open-air food court with around 90 stalls – tuck into local specialities like *nasi gudeg* (unripe jackfruit served with rice, chicken and spices), *nasi liwet* (rice cooked in coconut milk and eaten with a host of side dishes) or the beef noodle soup *timlo solo* here. It's very sociable, though you'll have to bring your own Bintang.

Warung Maksan Es Masuk INDONESIAN $
(Jl Honggowongso 78; mains from 8000Rp) One of a couple of branches across the city, this is a 'posh' *warung* (no, we don't mean you need to wear a suit and tie or anything), and if the hectic crowds of locals who flock here are anything to go by, it's also one of the best *warung* in town. There's lots of excellent local specialities.

Warung Baru INDONESIAN $
(Jl Ahmad Dahlan 23; mains from 8500Rp; ⏲Mon-Sat) A long-time travellers' hang-out, the Baru bakes great bread, but the rest of the enormous menu can be pretty mediocre. Still, it does offer a variety of local specialities. The friendly owners arrange tours and batik classes.

Adem Ayem INDONESIAN $
(Jl Slamet Riyadi 342; meals around 15,000Rp) An ever-popular *rumah makan* (local restaurant), this place has a large dining room with swirling fans and photos of ye olde Surakarta. Everyone is here for the chicken – either fried or served up *gudeg*-style.

☆ Entertainment

Solo does offer a few opportunities to see traditional Javanese performing arts, although they're nowhere near as well advertised as similar events in Yogyakarta; contact the tourist board for the latest schedules.

Sriwedari Theatre DANCE SHOW
(admission 3000Rp; ⏲performances 8-10pm) At the back of Sriwedari Amusement Park, this theatre has a long-running *wayang orang* troupe – it's well worth dropping by to experience this masked dance-drama. You can come and go as you please.

RRI Auditorium THEATRE
(☎641178; Jl Abdul Rahman Saleh 51) RRI holds an eclectic program of cultural performances, including *wayang orang* and *ketoprak* performances.

Taman Budaya Surakarta PUPPET SHOW
(TBS; ☎635414; Jl Ir Sutami 57) Cultural centre that hosts all-night *wayang kulit* performances; private dance lessons are also available.

ℹ Information

BCA bank (cnr Jl Dr Rajiman & Jl Gatot Subroto) Has ATM and currency-exchange facilities.

Main post office (Jl Jenderal Sudirman)

Solo Grand Mall (Jl Jenderal Sudirman; 📶) Free wi-fi.

Speedy Net (Jl Ronggowarsito 4; per hr 6000Rp; ⏲24hr) Speedy connections and plenty of computers.

Telkom wartel (Jl Mayor Kusmanto) Near the post office.

Tourist office (☎711435; Jl Slamet Riyadi 275; ⏲8am-4pm Mon-Sat) Most staff are helpful here. They can provide a map of Solo and information on cultural events and places to visit. There are also desks at the bus and train stations, which can help with ticket bookings.

ℹ Getting There & Away

Air

A new terminal is scheduled to have opened at Solo's Adi Sumarmo airport (code SOC) by the time you read this. Currently there are just two international flights.

Air Asia (☎021 2927 0999; www.airasia.com) connects Solo to Kuala Lumpur daily. On Tuesday, Thursday and Saturday, **SilkAir** (☎724604/5; www.silkair.com; Novotel Hotel, Jl Slamet Riyadi 272) flies to/from Singapore.

Domestic services include frequent flights to Jakarta with **Garuda** (☎080 4180 7807; Hotel Cakra, Jl Slamet Riyadi 201) and **Sriwijaya Air-**

SPLURGE: O SOLO MIO

There are plenty of good reasons to come to Solo, but frankly **O Solo Mio** (727264; Jl Slamet Riyadi 253; mains around 50,000-60,000Rp; 10.30am-11pm), an authentic-to-the-last-olive Italian restaurant, is one of the best. In immensely civilised surroundings the waitresses serve up wood-flamed pizzas and homemade pasta dishes that are like another species altogether from the sloppy spaghetti of so many traveller cafes.

lines (723777; www.sriwijayaair-online.com; Adi Sumarmo airport).

Bus & Minibus

The Tirtonadi bus terminal is 3km from the centre of the city. Only economy buses leave from here to destinations such as Prambanan (13,000Rp, 1½ hours), Yogyakarta (from 13,000Rp, two hours) and Semarang (26,000Rp, 3¼ hours). Buses also travel to a number of destinations in East Java including Surabaya (52,000Rp, seven hours).

Near the bus terminal, the Gilingan minibus terminal has express air-con minibuses to almost as many destinations as the larger buses.

Travel minibus destinations include Yogyakarta (35,000Rp), Semarang (45,000Rp), Surayaba (100,000Rp) and Melang (110,000Rp). **Citra** (713684), based at Gilingan, runs *travel* minibuses to most main cities; call if you would like a pick-up. Homestays, cafes and travel agents also sell these tickets.

Train

Solo is on the main Jakarta–Yogyakarta–Surabaya train line and most trains stop at **Solo Balapan**, the main train station.

Seventeen daily trains connect Solo with Yogyakarta. The *pramek* (*bisnis* 10,000Rp, one hour) trains are reasonably comfortable but not air-conditioned.

Express trains to Jakarta include the 8am *Argo Lawu* (*eksekutif*, 320,000Rp, eight hours), which is the most luxurious day train.

The *Lodaya* (*bisnis/eksekutif* from 120,000/180,000Rp, nine hours) departs for Bandung at 8am and 8.30pm daily, while the *Sancaka* (*bisnis/eksekutif* 75,000/95,000Rp, five hours) heads for Surabaya twice daily.

Jebres train station in the northeast of Solo has a few very slow *ekonomi*-class services to Surabaya and Jakarta.

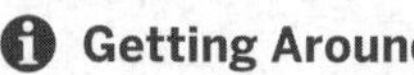

Getting Around

A taxi to/from Adi Sumarmo airport, located 10km northwest of the city centre, costs around 55,000Rp; otherwise you can take a bus to Kartosuro and then another to the airport. For a taxi, metered **Kosti Solo taxis** (856300) are reliable. Becak cost about 7000Rp from the train station or bus terminal into the centre. Public buses run up and down Jl Slamet Riyadi and cost 2000Rp. Motorcycles and bicycles (motorcycle/bicycle per day 70,000/15,000Rp) can be hired from homestays.

Around Solo

The fascinating and remote temple complex **Candi Sukuh** (admission 10,000Rp; 7am-4.30pm) on the slopes of Gunung Lawu (3265m), some 36km east of Solo, is well worth a visit. Dating from the 15th century, Sukuh was one of the last temples to be built in Java by Hindus, who were on the run from Muslims and forced to isolated mountain regions (and Bali). From the site, there are sweeping views across terraced fields.

The main pyramid resembles an Incan or Mayan monument, with steep sides and a central staircase; at its base are flat-backed turtles that may have been sacrificial altars. It's clear a fertility cult built up around the temple, as there are all manner of erotic carvings, including a *yoni-lingga* (vagina-phallus) representation and a figure clasping his erect penis.

Coming by public transport is very tricky. Take a bus bound for Tawangmangu from Solo as far as Karangpandan (6000Rp), then a Kemuning minibus (3000Rp) to the turn-off to Candi Sukuh; from here it's a steep 2km walk uphill to the site or a 10,000Rp *ojek* ride. For around 35,000Rp, *ojek* will take you to both Sukuh and Cetho. Hiring a motorbike and guide/driver in Solo costs around 200,000Rp, but it's a very long ride if you're not used to being on the back of a motorbike!

Malang

0341 / POP 760,000

With leafy, colonial-era boulevards and a breezy climate, Malang moves at a far more leisurely pace than the regional capital, Surabaya. It's a cultured city with several important universities and is home to a large student population.

City life revolves around the *alun alun* and the busy streets flowing into Jl Agus

SURABAYA

Surabaya's airport is the second busiest in the country and many travellers transit through the city. The airport is served by numerous airlines which link it to Singapore, Kuala Lumper, Penang, Hong Kong and destinations within Indonesia.

Surabaya is not an easy place to love. It's a big, noisy, polluted and commerce-driven city that's not well set up for visitors or pedestrians – just crossing the eight-lane highways that rampage through the centre is a challenge in itself. But though Surabaya's sheer size seems intimidating at first, it does have the odd curious attraction, including the **Qubah** – the city's labyrinthine Arab quarter. Centred upon the imposing **Mesjid Ampel** (Jl Ampel Suci), this fascinating quarter begs exploration. The mosque itself marks the burial place of Sunan Ampel, one of the *wali songo* (holy men) who brought Islam to Java; pilgrims chant and present rose-petal offerings at his grave behind the mosque. The warren of surrounding lanes are reminiscent of a Damascene souk, with stalls selling perfumes, sarongs, prayer beads, *peci* (black Muslim felt hats) and other religious paraphernalia.

Chinatown, just south of here, bursts into life at night when Jl Kembang Jepun becomes a huge street kitchen known as Kya Kya. Much of the food here is sourced from nearby at **Pasar Pabean** (Jl Panggung; ⏲8am-6pm) and the **fish market** (pasar ikan; Jl Panggung; ⏲from 8pm).

For accommodation some of the very cheapest, and roughest, hotels can be found near Kota train station, but it's best to spend a little extra. The **Sparkling Backpacker Hotel** (☎031 532 1338; www.sparklingbackpacker.com; Jl Kayoon 2A-B; r from 105,000Rp; ❄@📶) is probably the best base in town for backpackers. It's well organised and the staff are a good source of travel-related information. However, cleanliness isn't taken quite as seriously as the name would have you believe. If that's full, the **Hotel Paviljoen** (☎031 534 3449; Jl Genteng Besar 94; r from 100,000Rp; ❄) is a slightly shabby colonial villa that still has a twinkle of charm and grandeur. Rooms are plain but clean and have some lovely touches, including front porches with chairs.

Salim and Jl Pasar Besar near the central market. This is where you'll find the main shopping plazas, restaurants, cinemas and many of Malang's hotels. Banks are northwest of the *alun alun* along Jl Basuki Rahmat. Many of Malang's best restaurants are in the west of the city. For more historical wanderings, start with the circular Jl Tugu.

Sights

Hotel Tugu Malang MUSEUM
(www.tuguhotels.com; Jl Tugu 3) Just west of the Balai Kota, Malang's most impressive museum isn't actually a museum at all but a hotel – the five-star Hotel Tugu Malang (see box). Its culturally obsessed owners have amassed an astonishing collection of art, sculpture and treasures – 10th-century ceramics, ancient *wayang*, antique teak furniture, glassware and even the complete facade of a Chinese temple. Visitors are welcome to browse the collection, which is spread throughout the hotel premises (though you might consider it polite to buy a drink while you're here).

Colonial Architecture NOTABLE BUILDINGS
Malang has some wonderful colonial architecture. Just northwest of the centre, **Jl Besar Ijen** is Malang's millionaire's row, a boulevard lined with elegant whitewashed mansions from the Dutch era. Many have been substantially renovated, but there's still much to admire. If you're in town during late May, drop by for the **Malang Kembali festival** (p185).

Close to the city centre, the **Balai Kota** (Town Hall; Jl Tugu) is an immense Dutch administrative building, built in a hybrid of Dutch and Indonesian architectural styles with a tiered central roof that resembles a Javanese mosque.

Sleeping

There's some superb budget accommodation in Malang. Unless otherwise specified all of the following include breakfast.

Jona's Homestay GUESTHOUSE $
(☎324 678; Jl Sutomo 4; s/d from 66,000/82,000Rp) The sign here says 'home sweet home' and that's right on the money. Run by Anna, who speaks English and is a great source of infor-

mation, this homestay occupies a fine colonial villa with a pleasant front garden. Offers eight simple, functional economy rooms and has a selection of more spacious air-con options, some of which are huge. Good value Gunung Bromo (see p186) tours are available.

Hotel Helios HOTEL $
(☎362 741; www.hotelhelios-malang.com; Jl Pattimura 37; r with fan from 85,000Rp, with air-con from 198,000Rp; ❄📶) From the outside, Helios looks far too plush to accept scruffy road bums, but it actually bills itself as a backpackers' home and is true to its word. It has a wide selection of clean, comfortable rooms overlooking a garden; even the very cheapest are spartan but fine. Good travel information, bus bookings and tours are available. Breakfast is included in more expensive rooms.

Eating & Drinking

Malang's restaurants are spread throughout the city. For cheap eats head for Jl Agus Salim, which comes alive at night to the sights and smells of Malang's night food market. Local specialities *nasi rawon* (beef soup served with fried onion and rice) and *bakso malang* (meatball soup served with noodles and grilled fish) are always worth a try.

Agung INDONESIAN $
(Jl Basuki Rahmat 80; meals around 10,000Rp) A kind of fast food–style *warung*, this modern little place has tasty, inexpensive local food, including *martabak* (meat, egg and vegetable pancake-like dish), rice and fish dishes, plus great juices for 4000Rp.

Toko Oen INTERNATIONAL $$
(☎364 052; Jl Basuki Rahmat 5; mains 20,000-55,000Rp) An anachronism from colonial days, with rattan furniture and waiters in starched whites and peci hats. These days, the ambience is more English seaside than imperial grandeur. The Indonesian, Chinese and Western food is reasonably good, but it's the ice cream and sense of history that really draws the crowds.

DON'T MISS

MALANG KEMBALI

Held in late May, **Malang Kembali** is a colourful festival celebrating *ludruk*, an old-time music-hall tradition that was very popular in Java in the last century. Jl Ijen, home to many wonderful old Dutch villas, is closed to traffic for five days and there's street theatre, shows and actors in period costumes.

SPLURGE: HOTEL TUGU MALANG

If you're going to splash out in East Java, there's only one place to do so. The **Hotel Tugu Malang** (☎363 891; www.tuguhotels.com; Jl Tugu 3; r from US$105, ste US$140-1000; ❄@📶🏊) is so rich in Javanese character that we're struggling to find a single fault with it (the pool is small?). The premises are very grand indeed and the style mutates from fine-arts gallery to theatrical circus tent. It has a great spa, a bar, a superb cafe, and two fine restaurants, all decorated in the inimitable Tugu style. Nonsmoking; add 21% tax to room rates.

Information

Malang has plenty of banks with ATMs; most are congregated along Jl Basuki Rahmat, including BCA; or try Lippo Bank, opposite the *alun alun*.

Gunung Bromo National Park head office (☎490 885; Jl Raden Intan 6; ⏰8am-3pm Mon-Thu, to 11am Fri) For Bromo info.

Main post office (Jl Kauman Merdeka) Opposite the *alun alun*.

Prima Warung Internet (Jl Basuki Rahmat 33; per hr 3500Rp; ⏰24hr) Fast internet connections.

Tourist information kiosk (☎0857 5586 6599; alun alun; ⏰9am-3pm) This small kiosk is staffed by students. It's also open 'whenever there is demand' – whatever that might mean!

Tourist Information Office (☎558 919; Jl Gede 6; ⏰8am-4pm Mon-Fri) Helpful, but 3km northwest of the *alun alun*.

Getting There & Away

Bus

Malang has three bus terminals. **Arjosari**, 5km north of town, is the main one, with regular buses to destinations such as Surabaya (every 20 minutes, normal/air-con 7000/15,000Rp, two to three hours), Probolinggo (14,000/20,000Rp, 2½ hours) and Banyuwangi (45,000Rp, six hours). Luxury long-haul buses also run to Solo and Yogyakarta (from 80,000Rp) and Jakarta (around 180,000Rp), mostly leaving in the early evening. **Gadang bus terminal** is 5km south of the city centre, and has buses along the southern routes to destinations such as Blitar (13,000Rp, two hours). **Landungsari bus**

terminal, 5km northwest of the city, has buses to destinations west of the city, such as Batu (5000Rp, 30 minutes).

You can also book bus tickets at **Haryono Tours** (☎367 5000; www.haryonotours.com; Jl Kahuripan 22) and at guesthouses for a small commission.

Minibus

Plenty of door-to-door travel companies operate from Malang, and hotels and travel agencies can book them. Minibuses travel to Solo (95,000Rp), Yogyakarta (100,000Rp) and Probolinggo (45,000Rp), among other destinations.

Train

Malang train station is centrally located but not well connected to the main network. The best train to Surabaya is the Malang Ekspres (*eksekutif* 20,000Rp, two hours). For Jakarta, the executive-class Gajayana (from 335,000Rp, 15 hours) leaves Malang at 4.30pm bound for Jakarta's Gambir station and stopping at Blitar, Solo and Yogyakarta en route.

Getting Around

Mikrolet (small minibuses) run all over town. Most run between the bus terminals via the town centre. These are marked A-G (Arjosari to Gadung and return), A-L (Arjosari to Landungsari) or G-L (Gadang to Landungsari). Trips cost 2000Rp to 3000Rp.

Gunung Bromo

☎0335

A lunaresque landscape of epic proportions and surreal beauty, Gunung Bromo has always been one of Indonesia's most breathtaking sights. Right now, though, Bromo is erupting and is even more breathtaking than normal. Bromo is the Javanese translation of Brahma, the Hindu God of creation. It's an apt name because, as the volcano continues to chuck out thousands of tonnes of rock and sand, it's creating an entirely new landscape.

The exploding cone of Bromo is just one of three peaks to emerge from a vast caldera, the Tengger Massif (which stretches 10km across), its steep walls plunging down to a vast, flat sea of lava and sand. This desolate landscape has a distinctly end-of-the-world feeling, particularly at sunrise.

An even larger cone – Java's largest mountain, the fume-belching Gunung Semeru (3676m) – oversees Bromo's supernatural beauty, and the entire volcanic wonderland forms the Bromo-Tengger-Semeru National Park.

Bromo is an easy side trip from the main backpacking highway that runs between Bali and Yogyakarta, or it's about three hours from Surabaya. The usual jumping-off point is the town of Probolinggo, which is served by trains and buses from Surabaya and Banyuwangi.

Sights & Activities

Normally the best vantage point over this bewitching landscape is from the viewpoint known as **Gunung Penanjakan** (2770m). All the hotels, and several freelance guides, can put together 4WD trips (85,000Rp per person in a group of four to six people), leaving around 4am to catch the sunrise from Penanjakan. It's usually well worth the early start, as the views of Bromo, the Tengger crater and towards smoking Gunung Semeru are spellbinding – this is where those postcard shots are taken. However, at the time of research, thanks to the prevailing winds blowing a cloud of ash from the erupting Bromo over the viewpoint, the views were quite disappointing.

After you've seen the sunrise, you'll be driven back down the lip of the caldera and across the crater bed and the **Sand Sea** towards the squat grey cone of Gunung Bromo itself. Due to ash clouds from the current eruption, we considered the sunrise views from here superior to those of Gunung Penanjakan. Before the current eruption it was possible to climb to the summit and gaze into Bromo's steaming guts, however this will vary by the day depending on local wind directions and the amount of ash being thrown forth at the time.

If you don't want to pay for a jeep tour, it's a straightforward 3km hike (around an hour) from Cemoro Lawang to Gunung Penanjakan or just over a kilometre down onto the Sand Sea itself. The **Hindu temple** at the foot of Bromo and Gunung Bator is only open for religious ceremonies.

Though Probolinggo is the usual approach, Bromo can also be reached via **Tosari** from the northwest and **Ngadas** from the southwest.

Sleeping & Eating

CEMORO LAWANG

At the lip of the Tengger crater and right at the start of the walk to Bromo, Cemoro Lawang is the most popular place to stay and has plenty of cheap accommodation, although the vast majority of it is overpriced.

TOP CHOICE **Cafe Lava Hostel** HOTEL $$
(☎541020; r 162,000-456,000Rp) Tumbing down the side of the mountain, this is the best base in town for travellers, with a sociable vibe and English-speaking staff. Economy rooms have been renovated and are clean and neat if bare, while the smarter rooms are attractive (all have little porches with valley views) and have hot showers. The restaurant serves up filling, inexpensive Indonesian and Western grub, as well as the all important Bintang, and is the best place in town to get a group together for the jeep ride up Penanjakan. A filling buffet breakfast is included with the pricier rooms.

Cemara Indah Hotel HOTEL $
(☎541019; www.hotelcemaraindah.com; economy r 100,000Rp, with air-con, TV & hot water 350,000Rp; ❄) Enjoys a great position on the edge of the crater, but the staff can be a bit tour-pushy, the economy rooms are very avoidable and the other rooms have an optimistically high price tag!

NGADISARI

Another 3km back towards Probolinggo is the tiny village of Ngadisari.

Yoschi's Guest House GUESTHOUSE $$
(☎0335-541018; yoschi _bromo@telkom.net; r without/with shower 120,000/220,000Rp; @) A friendly, hospitable place with loads of character, this alpine chalet-style place has a good vibe, a peaceful garden and tasty food. Rooms are a little small, but with crazy mosaic-tiled bathrooms, hot water and eye-pleasing decorations, it's considerably better than anything in Cemoro Lawang. Tours and transport for the 4km to Bromo (50,000Rp per person) are offered.

PROBOLINGGO

On the highway between Surabaya and Banyuwangi, this is the jumping-off point for Gunung Bromo. Most travellers only see the bus or train station, but the town has hotels if you get stuck.

Hotel Bromo View HOTEL $
(☎43400; Jl Raya Bromo Km5; r with fan 95,000Rp, with air-con from 180,000Rp; ❄@) Ten minutes from the town centre but just a couple of minutes from the main bus station, this roadside motel-like place with its clean rooms (squat toilets only in the economy rooms) offers great value, though we beg to differ about the Bromo views.

BROMO ERUPTION

Bromo started erupting in late 2010 and continued on and off (but mainly on) right through the first half of 2011. It's expected to continue erupting for some time to come (the Thorn Tree forum on lonelyplanet.com has frequent updates on the current status of the volcano). At times the eruptions have been so fierce that a 2km or 3km restriction zone has been implemented around the volcano, which has made the view point, and the village of Cemero Lawang, out of bounds. At the time of research the restriction zone was down to 500m and sunrise tours were again operating.

ℹ Information

However you approach Bromo, a 25,000Rp park fee is payable at one of the many PHKA checkpoints.

PHKA post (☎541038; ⌚8am-3pm Tue-Sun) The PHKA post in Cemoro Lawang is opposite Hotel Bromo Permai, and has information about Bromo. Note that the Gunung Penanjakan viewpoint is outside the park and these fees are not applicable. The Sand Sea, though, is within the national park and you'll need to pay your fee at the park office on the edge of Cemero Lawang. Tickets are valid for the duration of your stay.

ℹ Getting There & Away

Probolinggo's bus station is 5km west of town on the road to Bromo; catch a yellow *angkot* from the main street or the train station for 2000Rp.

Shop around before you purchase a ticket. Normal/air-con buses travel to Surabaya (14,000/23,000Rp, two hours), Banyuwangi (30,000/50,000Rp, five hours), Yogyakarta (75,000/125,000Rp, nine hours) and Denpasar (100,000/135,000Rp, 11 hours). Economy buses also go to Malang (13,000Rp).

Gunung Bromo minibuses leave from Probolinggo's Bayuangga bus terminal and from the main bus station, heading for Cemoro Lawang (25,000Rp, two hours) via Ngadisari (12,000Rp, 1½ hours) until around 4pm. The late-afternoon buses charge more to Cemoro Lawang, when fewer passengers travel beyond Ngadisari. Make sure it goes all the way to Cemoro Lawang when you board. There are also special tourist shuttle minibuses, which charge 33,000Rp and take an hour.

About 2km north of town, the train station is 6km from the bus terminal. Probolinggo is on the Surabaya–Banyuwangi line. Most services are *ekonomi* class. The *Mutiara Timur* costs from 45,000/55,000Rp (*bisnis/eksekutif*) to Surabaya (two hours, departing at 2.07pm) or the same rate to Banyuwangi (*bisnis/eksekutif* 60,000/80,000Rp, five hours, departing at 10.57am).

Bondowoso

0332 / POP 70,000

Bondowoso is merely a transit point for nearby attractions such as Ijen, but it does have banks with ATMs and internet facilities. Tours to Ijen can be organised here.

Sleeping & Eating

Hotel Anugerah HOTEL $

(421870; Jl Sutoyo 12; r 100,000Rp, with TV & air-con 150,000Rp;) A friendly place run by a hospitable family, this hotel has a wide selection of rooms. All have slightly odd colour schemes, but they're clean and most are spacious. Good home-cooked meals (around 12,000Rp) are available and trips to Ijen (motorbike/car 175,000/600,000Rp) are offered.

Getting There & Away

There are many (cramped) minibuses to Ijen (12,500Rp), all leaving before noon for the 2½-hour trip. Other destinations from Bondowoso include Jember (5000Rp, 45 minutes), Probolinggo (14,000Rp, two hours) and Surabaya (28,0000Rp, five hours).

Ijen Plateau

The fabled Ijen Plateau is a vast volcanic region dominated by the three cones of Ijen (2368m), Merapi (2800m) and Raung (3332m). A beautiful and thickly forested alpine area, these thinly populated highlands harbour coffee plantations and a few isolated settlements.

The highlight of a visit here is without doubt the descent into the crater of Kawah Ijen, with its steaming, evil sulphurous lake, where an army of miners dig sulphur out of the crater floor in conditions that can only be described as a medieval vision of Hell.

Access roads to the plateau are poor, but despite that, visitor numbers are slowly starting to increase as word gets out that Ijen hides one of the most extraordinary sights in Java.

Sights & Activities

Kawah Ijen Hike HIKE

Bubbling and moody, the turquoise lake of Kawah Ijen lies at 2148m above sea level and is surrounded by sheer, and utterly sterile, crater walls. At the edge of the lake, noxious and sulphurous smoke billows from the volcano's vent, and the lake bubbles and boils when activity increases.

Ijen is a major sulphur-gathering centre (see box, p189), and you'll pass the collectors as you hike up the trail. Most now ask for a fee for photographs, though a cigarette will also usually be accepted as payment.

The starting point for the trek to the crater is the **PHKA post** (6am-5pm) at Pos Paltuding, which can be reached from Bondowoso or Banyuwangi. Sign in and pay the 15,000Rp entry fee here. The steep 3km path up to the sulphur-weighing point takes just over an hour. From here it's a further 45 minutes to the crater rim.

From the crater, a steep, gravelly path leads down to the lake and the sulphur deposits. Due to the extreme conditions, many people choose not to descend down into the crater and content themselves with a peak over the crater rim. If you do continue down to the lake, make sure you are suitably equipped: the sulphur gases are highly noxious and it's absolutely essential that you have some kind of face mask (if only basic surgical face masks are available, wear several at the same time and soak them before putting them on). People with any kind of respiratory problems, or those travelling with children, should not descend into the base of the crater. Bear in mind also that photographic equipment doesn't like the gases either. Keep your camera wrapped up as much as possible.

Sleeping & Eating

You'll find a couple of store-*warung* at the PHKA post, where you can get hot tea or a snack.

Cartimore GUESTHOUSE $

(0813 3619 9110; r from 135,000Rp, r in old wing from 275,000Rp) These rooms are located in the Kebun Balawan coffee plantation some 7km from Sempol. It's the most popular place with tour companies and travellers. The respectable, clean rooms are in a long row, or for a real (if very faded) colonial experience sleep in the original Dutch lodge, which dates back to 1894. There's a spring-fed hot tub; the swimming pool is chilly.

A HEAVY LOAD

The Ijen volcano produces a lot of sulphur, and around 300 collectors (all men) work here, getting up at between 2am and 4am to hike up the crater to hack out the yellow stuff by hand. For most the only protection against the cone's noxious fumes are the cotton scarves they tie around their noses. These DIY miners then spend the next six or so hours scurrying back down the volcano with loads of 60kg to 80kg on their backs. It's incredibly tough work that pays very little (around 600Rp per kilogram), and yet the physical exercise keeps the collectors incredibly fit – few report health problems, despite breathing great lungfuls of sulphurous fumes virtually every day of their lives. Ijen sulphur is used for cosmetics and medicine, and is added to fertiliser and insecticides. Historically, sulphur was commonly called brimstone.

Some of the miners achieved local celebrity status after appearing on the BBC's landmark *Human Planet* series.

Meals are served and tours are available. An *ojek* from Sempol is about 20,000Rp.

Arabika GUESTHOUSE $
(☎0811 350 5081; r incl breakfast from 140,000Rp) The Kebun Kalisat coffee plantation maintains this pleasant guesthouse 1km from the main road. There are three choices of rooms, ranging from bare but serviceable to spacious and comfortable; all have hot water. Service is friendly and meals are served. It's at Sempol, 13km before Pos Paltuding on the Bondowoso side.

Getting There & Away

It is possible to travel nearly all the way to Kawah Ijen by public transport, but most visitors charter transport.

From Bondowoso

From Wonosari, 8km from Bondowoso towards Situbondo, a badly potholed road runs via Sukosari and Sempol all the way to Pos Paltuding. It's in poor shape and is slow going, but a 4WD was not necessary at the time of research. Sign in at the coffee-plantation checkpoints (around 4500Rp) on the way. Several minibuses run from Bondowoso to Sempol (17,500Rp, 2½ hours), but only until noon. They will normally drop you at either of the two guesthouses mentioned above. You should be able to find someone in Sempol, or at either of the guesthouses, who will take you the 13km to Pos Paltuding by motorbike for around 120,000Rp return, including waiting time.

From Banyuwangi

The Banyuwangi–Ijen road is steep but paved and in pretty good condition, bar the odd dodgy stretch. Cars (600,000Rp per vehicle) can be set up through the **Banyuwangi Tourist Office** (☎424 172; Jl Ahmad Yani 78). There's no public transport all the way from Banyuwangi to Pos Paltuding. It may be possible to DIY using a minibus and an *ojek* or two, but don't count on it. From Banyuwangi's Blambangan terminal, take a Lin 3 *angkot* to Sasak Perot (2000Rp) on the eastern outskirts of town and then a minibus on to Jambu (8000Rp) at the turn-off to Kawah Ijen, a further 17km away. From Jambu, you might be able to persuade an *ojek* to take you via Sodong to Pos Paltuding for around 60,000Rp. If you're confident riding a scooter up steep mountains, hire one in Banyuwangi and head up yourself.

Banyuwangi

☎0333 / POP 110,000

The end of the line, Java's land's end is a pleasant enough town, but there's no reason to hang around here. Confusingly, the ferry terminus for Bali, bus terminal and train station are all some 8km north of town in the port of Ketapang, though all transport uses 'Banyuwangi' as a destination.

Sleeping & Eating

For cheap eats, there are *warung* on the corner of Jl MT Haryono and Jl Wahid Haysim.

Hotel Baru HOTEL $
(☎421369; Jl MT Haryono 82-84; r with fan/air-con from 40,000/90,000Rp; ❄) A short walk south of the *alun alun,* this is a clean little place with friendly staff, a choice of rooms (the air-con rooms are great value) and a cafe-restaurant.

Getting There & Away

Boat

Ferries from Ketapang depart roughly every 30 minutes around the clock for Gilimanuk in Bali. The ferry costs 6000Rp for passengers, 21,000Rp for a motorcycle and 80,000Rp for a car. Throughbuses between Bali and Java include the fare in the bus ticket and are by far the easiest option (if going from Java to Bali there are often no buses at all waiting at Gilimanuk).

Bus

Banyuwangi has two bus terminals. The Sri Tanjung terminal is 3km north of the Bali ferry terminal at Ketapang, and 11km north of town. Buses from this terminal travel to northern destinations, such as Probolinggo (normal/air-con 28,000/46,000Rp, five hours) and Surabaya (42,000/69,000Rp, seven hours). Buses also go right through to Denpasar (from 30,000Rp, five hours including the ferry trip). Brawijaya terminal (also known as Karang Ente), 4km south of town, has most of the buses to the south.

Train

The main Banyuwangi train station is just a few hundred metres north of the ferry terminal. The express *Mutiara Timur* leaves at 9am and 10.15pm for Probolinggo (4½ hours) and Surabaya (*bisnis/eksekutif* 85,000/110,000Rp, 6½ hours).

BALI

Impossibly green rice terraces, pulse-pounding surf, enchanting Hindu temple ceremonies, mesmerising dance performances, ribbons of beaches, charming people: there are as many images of Bali as there are flowers on the ubiquitous frangipani trees.

This small island – you can drive the entire coast in one day – looms large in any visit to Southeast Asia. No place is more visitor friendly. Hotels range from surfer dives where the fun never stops to hidden retreats in the lush mountains. You can dine on local foods bursting with flavours fresh from a market or snack on seafood from a beachside shack. From a cold Bintang at sunset to an epic night clubbing, your social whirl is limited only by your own fortitude. And when it comes time to relax, you can get a cheap beach massage or lose yourself in an all-day spa.

And small doesn't mean homogeneous. Manic Kuta segues into luxurious Seminyak. The artistic swirl of Ubud is a counterpoint to misty treks amid the volcanoes. Mellow beach towns like Amed, Lovina and Pemuteran are found right round the coast, and just offshore is the laid-back idyll of Nusa Lembongan.

As you stumble upon the exquisite little religious offerings that seem to materialise everywhere as if by magic, you'll see that their tiny tapestry of colours and textures is a metaphor for Bali itself.

History

Bali's first prehistoric tourists strolled out of the spume and onto the island's western beaches around 3000 BC. Perhaps distracted by primitive beach life, however, they got off to a relaxed start and it was only in the 9th century that an organised society began to develop around the cultivation of rice.

Hinduism followed hot on the heels of wider cultural development, and as Islam swept through neighbouring Java in the following centuries, the kings and courtiers of the embattled Hindu Majapahit kingdom began crossing the straits into Bali, making their final exodus in 1478. The priest Nirartha brought many of the complexities of the Balinese Hindu religion to the island.

In the 19th century the Dutch began to form alliances with local princes in northern Bali. A dispute over the ransacking of wrecked ships was the pretext for the 1906 Dutch invasion of the south, which climaxed in a suicidal *puputan* (fight to the death). The Denpasar nobility burnt their own palaces, dressed in their finest jewellery and, waving golden *kris*, marched straight into the Dutch guns.

In later years Bali's rich and complex culture was actually encouraged by many Dutch officials. International interest was aroused and the first Western tourists arrived in the 1930s.

The tourism boom, which started in the early 1970s, has brought many changes, and has helped pay for improvements in roads, telecommunications, education and health. Though tourism has had some marked adverse environmental and social effects, Bali's unique culture has proved to be remarkably resilient, even as visitor numbers top 2.3 million per year.

Dangers & Annoyances

Persistent hawkers are the bane of most visitors to Bali. The best way to deal with them is to ignore them from the first instance.

The beaches on the west side of the island, including Kuta and Seminyak, are subject to heavy surf and strong currents. The sea water near touristed areas is commonly contaminated by run-off from both built-up areas and surrounding farmland, especially after heavy rains. You can smell it.

Bali's economic and tourism boom means that traffic is now a huge problem across South Bali. It's also a menace: upwards of eight people die in traffic mishaps each day, a figure about eight times the rate in the US, Europe or Australia.

Bali

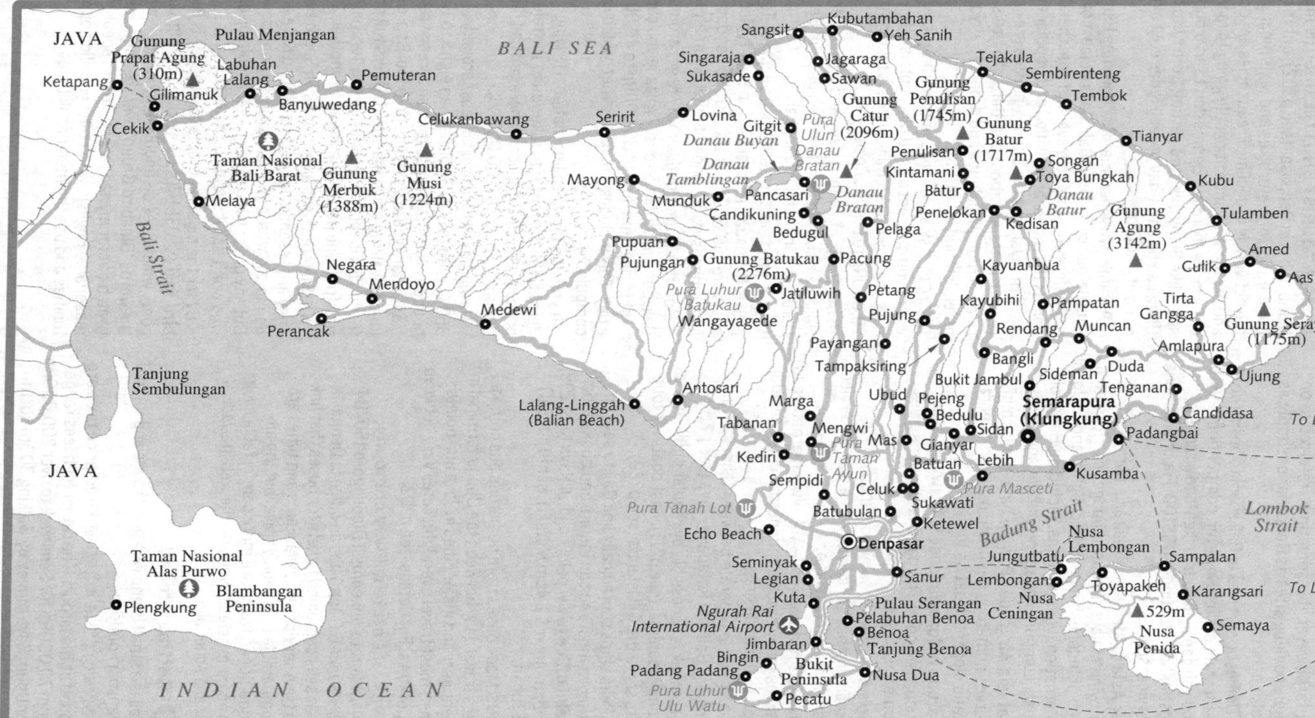

0 20 km
0 12 miles
JAVA
Gunung Prapat Agung (310m)
Pulau Menjangan
BALI SEA
Ketapang
Gilimanuk
Labuhan Lalang
Pemuteran
Banyuwedang
Cekik
Celukanbawang
Seririt
Lovina
Taman Nasional Bali Barat
Gunung Merbuk (1388m)
Gunung Musi (1224m)
Melaya
Bali Strait
Negara
Mendoyo
Perancak
Medewi
Tanjung Sembulungan
JAVA
Taman Nasional Alas Purwo
Blambangan Peninsula
Plengkung
INDIAN OCEAN
Sangsit
Kubutambahan
Yeh Sanih
Singaraja
Jagaraga
Sukasade
Sawan
Tejakula
Sembirenteng
Tembok
Gunung Penulisan (1745m)
Gunung Catur (2096m)
Gitgit
Pura Ulun Danau Bratan
Danau Buyan
Danau Tamblingan
Danau Bratan
Mayong
Munduk
Pancasari
Candikuning
Bedugul
Pelaga
Gunung Batur (1717m)
Penulisan
Kintamani
Batur
Songan
Toya Bungkah
Danau Batur
Penelokan
Kedisan
Tianyar
Kubu
Tulamben
Gunung Agung (3142m)
Amed
Culik
Aas
Pupuan
Pujungan
Gunung Batukau (2276m)
Pacung
Pura Luhur Batukau
Jatiluwih
Wangayagede
Petang
Pujung
Kayuanbua
Kayubihi
Pampatan
Rendang
Muncan
Tirta Gangga
Gunung Seraya (1175m)
Amlapura
Ujung
Payangan
Tampaksiring
Bangli
Sideman
Duda
Bukit Jambul
Tenganan
Antosari
Lalang-Linggah (Balian Beach)
Marga
Ubud
Pejeng
Bedulu
Semarapura (Klungkung)
Candidasa
Tabanan
Mengwi
Pura Taman Ayun
Mas
Gianyar
Sidan
Padangbai
To Lombok (25km)
Kediri
Batuan
Lebih
Kusamba
Sempidi
Celuk
Pura Masceti
Pura Tanah Lot
Sukawati
Lombok Strait
Batubulan
Ketewel
Badung Strait
Echo Beach
Denpasar
Nusa Lembongan
Jungutbatu
Sampalan
Seminyak
Legian
Sanur
Lembongan
Toyapakeh
Karangsari
To Lombok (25km)
Kuta
Pulau Serangan
Nusa Ceningan
Ngurah Rai International Airport
Pelabuhan Benoa
Benoa
529m
Semaya
Nusa Penida
Jimbaran
Tanjung Benoa
Bingin
Bukit Peninsula
Padang Padang
Nusa Dua
Pura Luhur Ulu Watu
Pecatu

Getting There & Away

AIR The only airport in Bali, Ngurah Rai International Airport (code DPS) is just south of Kuta; however, it is sometimes referred to on flight-booking sites as Denpasar or simply as Bali.

Domestic services in Bali seem to be in a constant state of flux. However, competition is fierce and you can usually find flights to a range of destinations for under US$100. For international service, see p307.

Air Asia (code AK; www.airasia.com) Fast-growing Malaysian-based budget carrier with a web of Indonesian domestic flights and regional international destinations, including Bangkok, Kuala Lumpur, Singapore, Darwin and Perth.

Batavia Air (code 7P; www.batavia-air.co.id) Serves numerous destinations; has the enigmatic slogan: 'Trust us to fly'.

Garuda Indonesia (code GA; www.garuda-indonesia.com) The national carrier serves numerous cities.

Lion Air (code JT; www.lionair.co.id) Fast-expanding budget carrier has a web of service across the archipelago.

Merpati Airlines (code MZ; www.merpati.co.id) Serves many smaller Indonesian cities, in addition to the main ones.

BOAT Ferries operate between Gilimanuk in western Bali and Ketapang, Java (see p215).

Lombok is accessible by regular public ferries from Padangbai (see p211). Fast boats for tourists serve the Gili Islands (see p229).

Pelni ships sporadically link Bali to several other islands. You can inquire and book at the **Pelni office** (www.pelni.co.id; Jl Raya Kuta 299; ⌚8am-noon & 1-4pm Mon-Fri, 8am-1pm Sat) in Tuban.

BUS Many buses from numerous bus companies travel daily between the Ubung terminal in Denpasar and major cities in Java and points east; most travel overnight. Fares vary between operators. For details, see p202.

TRAIN The **state railway company** (www.kereta-api.com; Jl Diponegoro 150/B4; ⌚8.30am-6.30pm) has an office in Denpasar that sells combined tickets for buses that link to train services on Java. Fares and times are comparable to bus-only travel but the air-conditioned trains are more comfortable even in economy class. Note: on the website *Jadwal* means schedule.

Getting Around

Bali is a small island with good roads and myriad transport options.

TO/FROM THE AIRPORT Fixed-price taxis are found at the airport. The rather high fees range from 70,000Rp for Seminyak to over 200,000Rp for Ubud. Save money by walking 300m north-east across the parking lot from the terminals to catch a metered Bluebird taxi outside the airport exit.

BEMO & TOURIST SHUTTLE BUS The main bemo hub is in Denpasar (see p202), but the proliferation of motorbikes and taxis means that the network is in decline. Frequencies are down and are mostly aimed at people going to market early in the morning. Bemos don't serve popular spots like Seminyak, and getting from Kuta to Ubud can be an all-day ordeal. Rides cost a minimum of 4000Rp.

Perama (www.peramatour.com) runs tourist shuttle-bus services in Bali. Book at least one day before you want to travel and note that like bemos the routes are ossified and popular areas like Seminyak and the Bukit Peninsula are not served. Rates are about one-third of a taxi's rates, although pick-ups and drop-offs at your hotels will add 20,000Rp.

BICYCLE Ask at your accommodation about where you can rent a good bike; hotels often have their own. Generally, prices range from 20,000Rp to 30,000Rp per day.

BOAT Boats of various sizes and speeds serve Nusa Lembongan and Nusa Penida from Benoa Harbour, Sanur and Padangbai.

CAR & MOTORCYCLE A small Suzuki or Toyota jeep is the usual rental vehicle in Bali. Typical costs are 150,000Rp to 180,000Rp per day, including insurance and unlimited kilometres.

Motorbikes are a popular way to get around Bali, but can be dangerous. Typically you can expect to pay from around 30,000Rp to 40,000Rp a day. This includes a flimsy helmet, which is compulsory.

If you don't have an International Driving Permit, ask the renter to take you to the relevant police station in Denpasar, where you can buy a temporary licence (200,000Rp).

Hiring a car with driver will cost around 350,000Rp to 600,000Rp for an eight- to 10-hour day (includes fuel). You can arrange rentals from where you are staying, or in tourist areas just by walking down the street. Offers will pour forth. This is the most common way for transferring from one part of the island to another.

TAXI Metered taxis are common in South Bali. They are essential for getting around Kuta and Seminyak, where you can easily flag one down. But any driver who claims meter problems or who won't use it should be avoided.

By far the most reputable taxi agency is **Bluebird Taxi** (☎0361-701111; www.bluebirdgroup.com), which uses distinctive blue vehicles with the words 'Bluebird Group' over the windshield (watch out for myriad fakes). Drivers speak reasonable English, won't offer you illicit opportunities and use the meter at all times.

Kuta & Seminyak

☎0361

The Kuta region is overwhelmingly Bali's largest tourist beach resort. Many budget visitors come here sooner or later because it's close to the airport and has the greatest range of cheap hotels, restaurants and tourist facilities. It is fashionable to disparage Kuta and its immediate neighbour to the north, Legian, for their rampant development, low-brow nightlife and crass commercialism, but the cosmopolitan mixture of beach-party hedonism and entrepreneurial energy can be fun in Kuta. At its worst, Legian is the vulgar Oz ghetto not actually found in Australia.

Seminyak may be immediately north of Kuta and Legian, but in many respects it feels like it's almost on another island. It's flash, brash and filled with bony models and expats. Think of it as the cool kids' section of Bali. It's beach is as deep and sandy as Kuta's, but less crowded. Kerobokan immediately north is more of the same.

Busy Jl Legian runs roughly parallel to the beach through Legian and Kuta. Jl Raya Seminyak is the continuation of Jl Legian and is lined with trendy shops.

Between Jl Legian and the beach is a tangle of narrow side streets, with an amazing hodgepodge of tiny hotels, souvenir stalls, *warung*, bars, construction sites and even a few remaining stands of coconut palms. A small lane or alley is known as a *gang*; the best known are called Poppies Gang I and II.

Sights & Activities

Much of your time in Kuta will centre on the famous beach, which stretches out of sight to the north and west. Hawkers will sell you sodas and beer, snacks and other treats, and you can rent lounge chairs and umbrellas (negotiable at 10,000Rp to 20,000Rp) or just crash on the sand.

Pura Petitenget — TEMPLE

(Map p196; Jl Pantai Kaya Aya) In Seminyak, north of the string of hotels on Jl Kaya Aya, Pura Petitenget is an important temple and a scene of many ceremonies. It is one of a string of sea temples that stretches from Pura Luhur Ulu Watu on the Bukit Peninsula north to Tanah Lot in western Bali.

Memorial Wall — MONUMENT

(Map p194; Jl Legian) Reflecting the international character of the 2002 bombings is the memorial wall, where people from many nationalities pay their respects.

Putri Bali — SPA

(Map p194; Jl Padma Utara; massage from 100,000Rp; ⏰10am-9pm) The delightfully relaxed spa at Putri Bali at the Wisata Beach Inn has very competitive prices.

Surfing

Kuta's famed beach is a mighty fine place to catch a wave or learn to catch one. Stalls on the side streets hire out surfboards (for a negotiable 30,000Rp per day) and boogie boards, repair dings and sell new and used boards. For a list of Bali's best surf breaks, see p303.

Pro Surf School — SURFING SCHOOL

(Map p194; www.prosurfschool.com; Jl Pantai Kuta; lessons from €45) Right along the classic stretch of Kuta Beach.

Rip Curl School of Surf — SURFING SCHOOL

(Map p194; ☎735858; www.ripcurlschoolofsurf.com; Jl Arjuna; lessons from 650,000Rp) On trendy Double Six beach.

Wave Hunter — BOARD RENTAL

(www.supwavehunter.com; Jl Sunset Rd 18X at Jl Imam Bonjol; rentals per day 250,000Rp; ⏰) Rents stand-up paddle boards, gives lessons.

Sleeping

Bali's tourist boom means that prices of even budget guesthouses have soared. Think US$20 per night as the median for a fan-cooled, cold-water room on a *gang* a few minutes from the beach in Kuta-Seminyak.

KUTA

Many cheap places line the tiny alleys and *gang* between Jl Legian and the beach in central Kuta. You'll be close to the beach, shops, nightlife and scores of other budget travellers.

TOP CHOICE **Berlian Inn** — HOTEL $

(Map p194; ☎751501; off Gang Sorga; r 120,000-250,000Rp; ❄) A stylish cut above other budget places, the 24 rooms in two-storey buildings here are pleasingly quiet and have ikat bedspreads and an unusual open-air bathroom design. Pricier rooms have air-con and hot water.

Bene Yasa I — HOTEL $

(Map p194; ☎754180; Jl Lebak Bene; r 90,000-200,000Rp; ❄🏊) The grounds at this 44-room hotel are large and open, with palms providing some shade. Three-storey blocks

Kuta & Legian

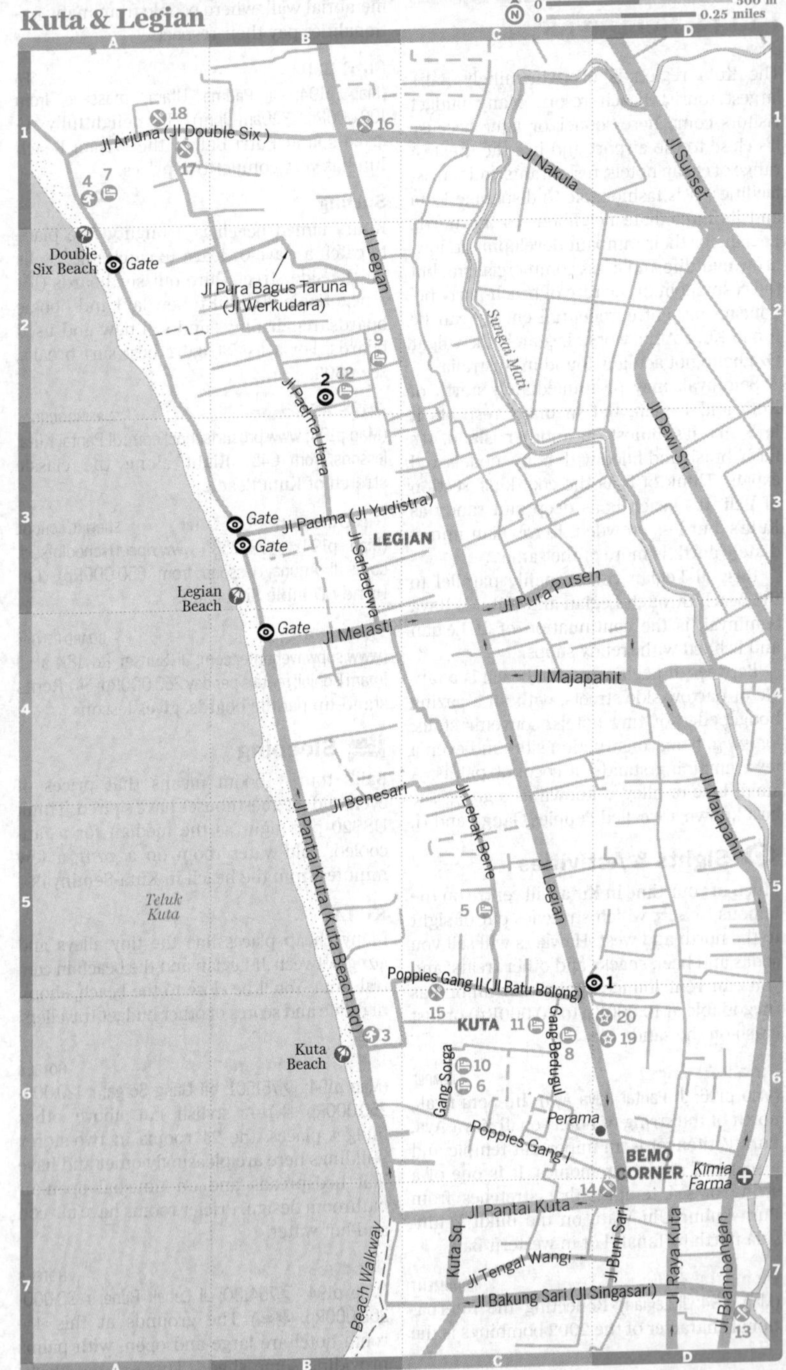
0 500 m
0 0.25 miles
Jl Arjuna (Jl Double Six)
18
17
16
4
7
Double Six Beach
Gate
Jl Pura Bagus Taruna (Jl Werkudara)
Jl Legian
Jl Nakula
Jl Sunset
Sungai Mati
Jl Dewi Sri
9
2
12
Jl Padma Utara
Jl Padma (Jl Yudistra)
Gate
Gate
Jl Sahadewa
LEGIAN
Legian Beach
Jl Pura Puseh
Gate
Jl Melasti
Jl Majapahit
Jl Benesari
Jl Pantai Kuta (Kuta Beach Rd)
Jl Lebak Bene
Jl Legian
Jl Majapahit
Teluk Kuta
5
Poppies Gang II (Jl Batu Bolong)
1
15
KUTA
11
Gang Bedugul
20
19
8
3
Kuta Beach
Gang Sorga
10
6
Perama
Poppies Gang I
BEMO CORNER
Kimia Farma
14
Jl Pantai Kuta
Jl Blambangan
Jl Buni Sari
Jl Raya Kuta
Kuta Sq
Jl Tengal Wangi
Jl Bakung Sari (Jl Singasari)
Beach Walkway
13
A
B
C
D
1
2
3
4
5
6
7

Kuta & Legian

Sights

1 Memorial Wall ... D5
2 Putri Bali ... B2

Activities, Courses & Tours

3 Pro Surf School ... B6
4 Rip Curl School of Surf ... A1

Sleeping

5 Bene Yasa I ... C5
6 Berlian Inn ... C6
7 Blue Ocean Bungalows ... A1
8 Gemini Star Hotel ... C6
9 Island ... B2
10 Mimpi Bungalows ... C6
11 Ronta Bungalows ... C6
12 Sri Beach Inn ... B2

Eating

13 Kuta Night Market ... D7
14 Made's Warung ... D7
15 Rainbow Cafe ... C6
16 Saleko ... B1
17 Warung Asia ... A1
18 Warung Murah ... A1

Entertainment

19 Bounty ... D6
20 Sky Garden Lounge ... D6

overlook the pool area, and the plethora of patios encourages a lively social scene.

Gemini Star Hotel HOTEL $

(Map p194; ☎750558; aquariushotel@yahoo.com; Gang Bedugal; r 140,000-300,000Rp; ❄☒) Only the monosyllabic mutterings of lounging surfers interrupt the peace at this 12-room hotel on a narrow alley. Two two-storey blocks shelter the sunny and surprisingly large pool area.

Mimpi Bungalows HOTEL $

(Map p194; ☎751848; kumimpi@yahoo.com.sg; Gang Sorga; r 150,000R-250,000Rp; ❄☒) The cheapest of the seven bungalow-style rooms here is the best value. Lush gardens boast orchids and shade, and the pool is a good size.

Ronta Bungalows HOTEL $

(Map p194; ☎754246; Gang Bedugal; r 130,000-230,000Rp; ❄) One of the best of the budget options, the rooms here are bungalow in name only – all 16 are in a two-storey block that is strenuously maintained.

LEGIAN

Leave the main streets with the touts and gaudy shabbiness for quieter *gang* inland.

Sri Beach Inn GUESTHOUSE $

(Map p194; ☎755897; Gang Legian Tewngah; r 150,000-300,000Rp; ❄) Follow a series of paths into the heart of old Legian. When you hear the rustle of palms overhead, you're close to this homestay with five rooms; more money gets you hot water, air-con and a fridge.

Island HOTEL $$

(Map p194; ☎762722; www.theislandhotelbali.com; Gang Abdi; dm 250,000Rp, r from 600,000Rp; ❄@☒) A real find, literally. Hidden in the attractive maze of tiny lanes west of Jl Legian, this flashpacker hang-out lies at the confluence of Gangs 19, 21 and Abdi. In a rarity for Bali, it has a very deluxe dorm room with eight beds.

Blue Ocean Bungalows HOTEL $

(Map p194; ☎730289; Jl Arjuna; r 200,000-350,000Rp; ❄☒) You can't get closer to popular Double Six Beach. The 24 rooms here are basic and slightly back off the action.

SEMINYAK & KEROBOKAN

The stylish surrounds mean that it can be hard to find a cheap sleep in these rarefied climes, but persistence pays off.

TOP CHOICE **Inada Losmen** GUESTHOUSE $

(Map p196; ☎732269; putuinada@hotmail.com; Gang Bima 9; r 120,000Rp) Buried in a *gang* behind Bintang Supermarket, this budget champ is a short walk from clubs, beach and other Seminyak joy. The 12 rooms are small and somewhat dark.

Sarinande Beach Inn HOTEL $

(Map p196; ☎730383; www.sarinandehotel.com; Jl Sarinande 15; r 350,000-500,000Rp; ❄☒) An excellent-value place. The 24 rooms are in older two-storey blocks around a small pool; the decor is older but everything is well-maintained. The beach is three minutes by foot.

Seminyak & Kerobokan

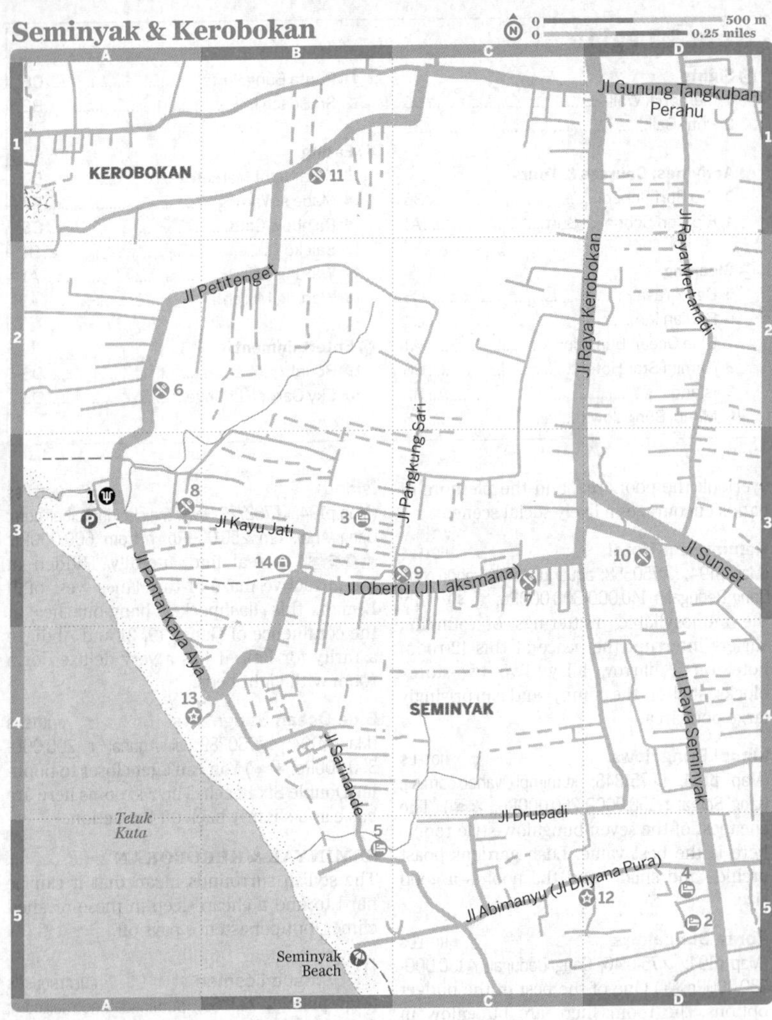

Seminyak & Kerobokan

Sights
1 Pura Petitenget A3

Sleeping
2 Inada Losmen D5
3 Mutiara Bali B3
4 Ned's Hide-Away D5
5 Sarinande Beach Inn B5

Eating
6 Biku A2
7 Café Zucchini C3
8 Ibu Mangku A3
9 Ultimo C3
10 Warung Ibu Made D3
11 Warung Sulawesi B1

Entertainment
12 Bali Jo D5
13 Ku De Ta A4

Shopping
14 Periplus Bookshop B3

Ned's Hide-Away GUESTHOUSE $
(Map p196; ☎731270; nedshide@dps.centrim.net.id; Gang Bima 3; r from 150,000Rp; ❄) Good-value basic rooms behind Bintang Supermarket. A new expansion should see some extra-cheap rooms added.

Eating

There's an incredible selection of restaurants in the Kuta area, from no-nonsense noodle bars to seriously swanky eateries in Seminyak. For excellent local fare, head north towards Kerobokan.

KUTA

Busy Jl Pantai Kuta keeps beachside businesses to a minimum in Kuta. Beach vendors are pretty much limited to drinks. Inland, traveller standards such as Indo classics, pasta, pizza and burgers are ubiquitous.

Made's Warung INDONESIAN $$
(Map p194; Jl Pantai Kuta; meals 60,000-200,000Rp) Made's was the original tourist *warung* in Kuta, and through the years the Westernised Indonesian menu has been much copied. Classic dishes such as *nasi campur* (rice served with side dishes) are served with colour and flair.

Kuta Night Market INDONESIAN $
(Map p194; Jl Blambangan; meals 15,000-25,000Rp; ⏲6pm-midnight) This enclave of stalls and plastic chairs bustles with locals and tourism workers chowing down on hot-off-the-wok treats, grilled goods and other fresh foods.

Rainbow Cafe GLOBAL $
(Map p194; Poppies Gang II; meals from 50,000Rp) Join generations of Kuta denizens munching the afternoon away. Many current customers are the offspring of backpackers who met at adjoining tables.

LEGIAN

The clutch of places at the end of Jl Arjuna (Jl Double Six) afford views of sandy action by day, strolling fun-seekers by night and sunsets in between.

Warung Murah INDONESIAN $
(Map p194; Jl Arjuna; meals from 20,000Rp) Lunch goes swimmingly at this authentic *warung* specialising in seafood. An array of grilled fish awaits; if you prefer fowl over fin, the *satay ayam* is succulent *and* a bargain. Hugely popular at lunch; try to arrive right before noon.

Warung Asia ASIAN $
(Map p194; off Jl Arjuna & Jl Pura Bagus Taruna; meals 20,000-50,000Rp; 📶) Look down a couple of little *gang* for this dollhouse of a cafe. Asian dishes like beef satay, fish curry and ginger chicken are paired with an authentic Italian espresso machine.

Saleko INDONESIAN $
(Map p194; Jl Nakula 4; meals from 15,000Rp) Just off the madness of Jl Legian, this modest open-front place draws the discerning for its simple Sumatran fare. Spicy grilled chicken and fish dare you to ladle on the volcanic sambal. Everything is cooked halal.

SEMINYAK & KEROBOKAN

Seminyak and Kerobokan have a great choice of inexpensive places alongside some of Asia's most remarkable restaurants.

TOP CHOICE **Warung Sulawesi** INDONESIAN $
(Map p196; Jl Petitenget; meals from 25,000Rp) Although seemingly upscale, Kerobokan is blessed with many a fine place for a local meal. Here you find a table in a quiet family compound and enjoy fresh Balinese and Indonesian food served in classic *warung* style. Choose a rice, then pick from a captivating array of dishes that are always at their peak at noon.

Biku FUSION $$
(Map p196; Jl Petitenget; meals 60,000-180,000Rp) Housed in an old antique shop, much-copied Biku retains the timeless vibe of its predecessor. But there's nothing old-fashioned about the food, which combines Indonesian, Asian and Western influences on a casual menu. Dishes, from the exquisite breakfasts to the elegant local choices to Bali's best burger, are artful and delicious.

SPLURGE: MUTIARA BALI

Although hidden on a small road behind Jl Laksmana, **Mutiara Bali** (Map p196; ☎708888; www.mutiarabali.com; Jl Karang Mas Sejahtera 88; r from US$85, villas from US$220; ❄@📶🏊) is close to everything: fine dining – two minutes; the beach – five minutes etc. There are 29 good-sized and nicely furnished rooms in two-storey blocks around a frangipani-draped pool area.

Ultimo ITALIAN $$

(Map p196; Jl Laksmana 104; meals 100,000-200,000Rp) *Uno:* find a table overlooking the throngs browsing the many restaurants here or in one of the gardens. *Due:* choose from the wide-ranging, authentic and tasty Italian fare. *Tre:* marvel at the efficient service from the army of servers. *Quattro:* smile at the reasonable bill.

Warung Ibu Made INDONESIAN $

(Map p196; Jl Raya Seminyak; meals 15,000Rp) The woks roar almost dawn to dusk amid the constant hubbub on this busy corner of Jl Raya Seminyak. It's one of a few simple stalls. The meals from this *warung* couldn't be fresher; they put to shame some of the Western fakery just down the road.

Ibu Mangku INDONESIAN $

(Map p196; Jl Kayu Jati; meals from 20,000Rp) Where your driver takes lunch. Look for the cabs in front of this bamboo place with a serene garden out back. The must-have is the superb minced-chicken satay redolent with lemongrass and other spices.

Cafe Zucchini ITALIAN, CAFE $

(Map p196; Jl Laksmana 49; dishes from 25,000Rp; wi-fi) Hidden behind trees, shrubs and vivid yellow-striped canopy, this Italian cafe is an ideal refuge from the surrounding retail pressures. Juices and various coffee drinks are the stars. There's a few more substantial Italian mains if you need real sustenance.

Drinking & Entertainment

The distinction between drinking and clubbing is blurry at best, with one morphing into another as the night wears on (or the morning comes up). Most bars are free to enter, and often have special drink promotions and 'happy hours' that run at various intervals until after midnight. Savvy partiers follow the specials from venue to venue and enjoy a massively discounted night out (club owners count on the drink specials to lure in punters who then can't be bothered to leave). It's also worth looking for cut-price drinks coupon fliers.

Bali club ambience ranges from the laid-back vibe of the surfer dives to high-concept nightclubs with long drink menus and hordes of prowling servers. Prostitutes have proliferated at some Kuta clubs.

With the closing of the legendary Double Six club in Legian, Bali's trendiest clubs cluster in about a 300m radius of the top-rated Sky Garden Lounge. You'll find many low-key boozers, amid their flashier brethren, along Jl Legian. In Seminyak numerous scenester spots line Jl Pantai Kaya Aya.

Sky Garden Lounge BAR

(Map p194; www.escbali.com; Jl Legian 61; 24hr) This multilevel palace of flash flirts with height restrictions from its rooftop bar where all of Kuta twinkles around you.

Bounty CLUB

(Map p194; Jl Legian; 10pm-6am) Set on a pirate ship amid a mini-mall of food and drink, the Bounty is a vast open-air disco that humps, thumps and pumps all night. Play seaman and get down on the poop deck to hip-hop, tribal, trance and anything else the DJs come up with. It's ground zero for Kuta's legendary party scene.

Bali Jo CLUB

(Map p196; Jl Abimanyu; 8pm-3am) Simply fun – albeit with falsies. Drag queens rock the house amid Bali's gay club strip.

Shopping

There are lots of local designers, crafts you won't find elsewhere, and more to be found just by wandering the main shopping streets to see what you can find. Kuta has a vast concentration of cheap places, as well as huge, flashy surf-gear emporiums on Kuta Sq and Jl Legian.

Seminyak has absolutely fabulous shopping along Jl Raya Seminyak. The retail wonderland splits off into the prime style country of Jl Laksmana while continuing north on Jl Raya Kerobokan.

DON'T MISS

BEACH BARS (& BEERS)

At the beach end of Jl Abimanyu (Jl Dhyana Pura) in Seminyak you have a choice: turn right for trendy, pricey beach lounges such as the over-hyped **Ku De Ta** (Map p196; www.kudeta.net; Jl Laksmana) or turn left for a much more purely Balinese experience. All manner of simple bars line the path along the sand. You'll discover mock-Moorish affairs with oodles of huge pillows for lounging, and as you go past Double Six into Legian, you'll find young local guys with simple chairs and cheap, cold beer (15,000Rp). The spectacular sunsets are free.

There are dozens of secondhand booksellers along the Poppies Gangs.

Periplus BOOKS
(Seminyak Sq, Jl Laksmana) Has the largest selection of new books in Bali.

Information

You'll find tourist information offices and tour-booking agencies every few metres along the main tourist streets of Kuta. There are scores of places to connect to the internet. ATMs abound and can be found everywhere, including in the ubiquitous convenience stores. Be careful with 'authorised' money changers. Extra fees may apply or, judging by readers' emails, they may be adeptly short-changing customers.

BIMC (☎761263; www.bimcbali.com; Jl Ngurah Rai 100X; ⏰24hr) Easily accessible from most of southern Bali, BIMC is a modern Western-style clinic that can do tests, hotel visits and arrange medical evacuation. Basic consultations cost 600,000Rp.

Kimia Farma (Map p194; ☎757483; Jl Raya Kuta 15; ⏰24hr) Part of a local chain of pharmacies, it's well stocked and carries hard-to-find items.

Getting There & Away

BEMO Bemos regularly travel between Kuta and the Tegal terminal in Denpasar – the fare should be 8000Rp. The route goes from Jl Raya Kuta near Jl Pantai Kuta, looping past the beach and then on Jl Melasti and back past Bemo Corner (Map p194) for the trip back to Denpasar.

TOURIST SHUTTLE BUS **Perama** (Map p194; ☎751551; www.peramatour.com; Jl Legian 39; ⏰7am-10pm) usually has at least one bus a day to all of its destinations.

Getting Around

Metered cabs from **Bali Taxi** (☎701111; www.bluebirdgroup.com) are easily hailed. A taxi to the heart of Kuta from Seminyak will be about 30,000Rp. You can beat the horrific traffic, save the ozone and have a good stroll by walking along the beach.

Canggu & Echo Beaches

Just up the coast from Kerobokan, Canggu Beach is a few kilometres along the sand northwest of Seminyak (but a long drive around). Just 500m northwest of Canggu Beach, Echo Beach (Batu Mejan) has trendy shops and beachside cafes. Both are popular with expats living in nearby villas and with surfers who come for the epic waves.

Sleeping

Green Room GUESTHOUSE $$
(☎923 2215; www.thegreenroombali.com; Jl Subak Catur, Canggu; r from €44;) Popular with surfers who groove to the hippie chic. Lounge on the 2nd-floor veranda and check out the waves (and villa construction) in the distance. The 14 rooms are comfy and breezy.

Canggu Mart GUESTHOUSE $
(☎824 7183; Jl P Batu Mejan 88; r 100,000-300,000Rp;) About 300m from Echo Beach, this basic place has simple new rooms behind a convenience store, a key resource for cheap, cold beer.

Bukit Peninsula

☎0361

Hot and arid, the southern peninsula is known as Bukit (*bukit* means 'hill' in Bahasa Indonesia). It's the centre of much tourism in Bali; backpackers will be especially interested in the rugged west coast running down to the important temple of Ulu Watu. It fronts some of the best surfing in the world. Little beach coves anchor an increasing number of hotels at places such as Balangan and Bingin.

Getting There & Away

Public transport is unheard of. Ride your rented motorbike or arrange for transport with your accommodation. Bluebird taxis from Kuta Jimbaran cost about 50,000Rp; to the remote beaches past Jimbaran it will average 80,000Rp.

JIMBARAN

Just south of Kuta and the airport, Teluk Jimbaran (Jimbaran Bay) is an alluring crescent of white sand and blue sea, fronted by a long string of popular seafood *warung*. These open-sided affairs are right on the beach and perfect for enjoying sea breezes and sunsets. The usual deal is to select your seafood fresh from iced displays or tanks, and to pay according to weight.

BALANGAN BEACH

Balangan Beach is a real find. A long and low strand at the base of the cliffs is covered with palm trees and fronted by a ribbon of near-white sand, picturesquely dotted with white sun umbrellas. Surfer bars (some with bare-bones sleeping rooms), cafes in shacks and even slightly more permanent guesthouses precariously line the shore where buffed first-world bods soak up rays amid third-world sanitation.

Balangan Beach is 6.5km off the main Ulu Watu road via Cenggiling.

Sleeping

Flower Bud Bungalows GUESTHOUSE $$
(0828 367 2772; www.flowerbudbalangan.com; r 350,000-500,000Rp;) Eight bamboo bungalows are set on spacious grounds near a classic kidney-shaped pool. There's a certain Crusoe-esque motif. Other choices are nearby.

BINGIN

An ever-evolving scene, Bingin comprises several funky lodgings scattered across cliffs and on the strip of white sand below. A 1km rocky road turns off the paved road (look for the thicket of accommodation signs), which in turn branches off the main Ulu Watu road at the small village of Pecatu.

An elderly resident collects 5000Rp at a T-junction, which is near parking for the trail down to the gorgeous **beach**. The surf is often savage, but the sands are calm and the roaring breakers mesmerising.

Sleeping

More than two dozen places to stay are scattered along and near the cliffs.

Bingin Garden GUESTHOUSE $
(Map p200; 0816 472 2002; tommybarrell76@yahoo.com; r from 250,000Rp) Six basic rooms in bungalows are set around tidy grounds back from the cliffs and 300m north of the toll gate. Each unit sleeps two and has cold water and a fan.

PADANG PADANG BEACH

Small but perfect, this little cove is near the main Ulu Watu road where a stream flows into the sea. Parking is easy and it is a short walk. Experienced surfers seeking tubes flock here.

Sleeping

Thomas Homestay GUESTHOUSE $
(Map p200; 0813 3803 4354; r from 200,000Rp) Stunning views up and down this spectacular coast. The seven simple rooms lie at the end of a very rough 400m track off the main road. A trail down the cliff leads to one of Bali's best almost-undiscovered beaches.

ULU WATU & AROUND

Ulu Watu has become the generic name for the southwestern tip of the Bukit Peninsula. It includes the much-revered temple and the nearby fabled surf breaks.

Sights & Activities

TOP CHOICE **Pura Luhur Ulu Watu** TEMPLE
(Map p200; admission 25,000Rp, parking 1000Rp; 8am-7pm) Pura Luhur Ulu Watu is perched precipitously on the southwestern tip of the peninsula, atop sheer cliffs that drop straight into the pounding surf. Watch out for monkeys, who like to snatch sunglasses and anything else within reach. The sunset **Kecak dance** (tickets 80,000Rp; 6-7pm) is one of the more delightful performances on the island.

Sleeping & Eating

The cliffs above the main Ulu Watu surf break are lined with a hodgepodge of cafes and guesthouses. Some cling to rocks over the waves. You can enter from the east (crowded) or from the south (a pretty walk).

Gong GUESTHOUSE $
(Map p200; 769976; thegongacc@yahoo.com; Jl Pantai Suluban; r from 150,000Rp) Few stay away long from the Gong. Tidy rooms surround a

Ulu Watu & Around

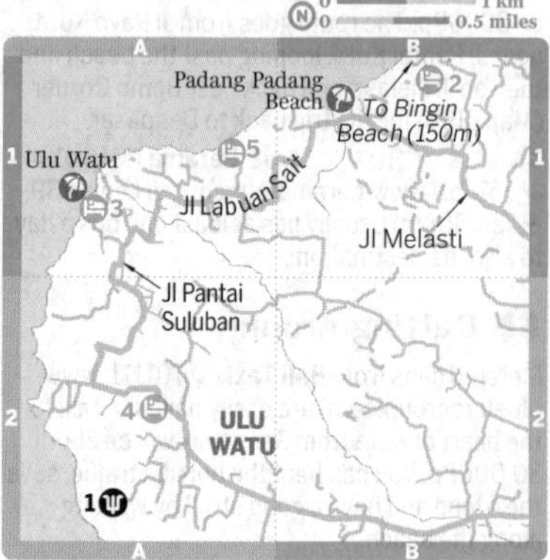

Ulu Watu & Around

Sights

1 Pura Luhur Ulu Watu A2

Sleeping

2 Bingin Garden B1
3 Delpi Uluwatu A1
4 Gong A2
5 Thomas Homestay A1

pool and have distant ocean views. It's about 500m back from the cliffs, amid a few other guesthouses.

Delpi Uluwatu GUESTHOUSE $
(Map p200; ☎0361 769863; r from 300,000Rp) Four basic cliffside rooms rattle to the beat of the surf day and night. Surfers' bars abound nearby.

NUSA DUA & TANJUNG BENOA

The peninsula of Tanjung Benoa extends about 4km north from the gated resort area of Nusa Dua to the fishing village of Benoa. The area caters to top-end travellers and those on package holidays.

Denpasar

☎0361 / POP 800,000

Sprawling, hectic and ever-growing, Bali's capital has been the focus of a lot of the island's growth and wealth over the last six decades. Denpasar can seem a little daunting and chaotic, but spend some time on the tree-lined streets in the relatively affluent government and business district of Renon and you will discover a more genteel side to the city.

Denpasar

Top Sights

Museum Negeri Propinsi Bali.............B2

Sleeping

1 Nakula Familar Inn.............A1

Eating

2 Ayam Goreng Kalasan.............D3

3 Cak Asm.............C4

Shopping

4 Pasar Badung.............A2

Denpasar

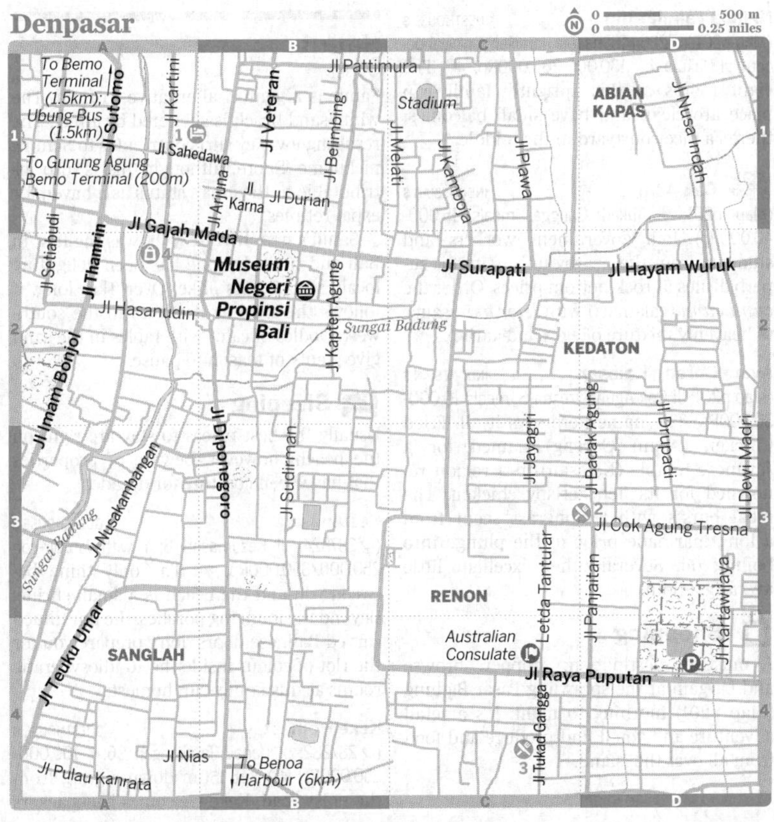

Sights

Museum Negeri Propinsi Bali MUSEUM

(Map p201; admission 5000Rp; ⏲8am-12.30pm Fri, 8am-4pm Sun-Thu) Denpasar's most important attraction, the Museum Negeri Propinsi Bali showcases a range of Balinese crafts, antiquities and cultural objects. This museum is quite well set up, and most displays are also labelled in English. Alongside the fine hand-spun textiles, you'll see some incredibly intricate drawings of the Ramayana, and startling *barong* costumes used for Balinese dance.

Sleeping & Eating

The only reason to stay in Denpasar is to be close to the bus stations or because you want to enjoy contemporary urban Balinese life. However, Denpasar has the island's best range of Indonesian and Balinese food. Savvy locals and expats each have their own favourite *warung* and restaurants.

Nakula Familar Inn GUESTHOUSE $

(Map p201; ☎226446; nakula_familiar_inn@yahoo.com; Jl Nakula 4; r 130,000-200,000Rp; ❄) The eight rooms at this sprightly family-run place are clean and have small balconies; there's a nice courtyard in the middle.

TOP CHOICE **Cak Asm** INDONESIAN $

(Map p201; Jl Tukad Gangga; meals 15,000-40,000Rp) Join government workers and students from the nearby university for superb dishes at rock-bottom prices. Order the *cumi cumi* (calamari) with *telor asin* sauce (a heavenly mixture of eggs and garlic).

Ayam Goreng Kalasan INDONESIAN $

(Map p201; Jl Cok Agung Tresna 6; meals 10,000-30,000Rp) The name here says it all. Fried Chicken (Ayam Goreng) named for a Javanese temple (Kalasan) in a region renowned for its fiery, crispy chicken. The meat bursts with lemongrass scent from a long marinade prior to the plunge into boiling oil. Several other excellent little *warung* adjoin.

Shopping

A must-see destination: shoppers browse and bargain at the sprawling Pasar Badung (Map p201) morning to night. It's a retail adventure and you'll find produce and food from all over the island.

Getting There & Around

Bemo & Bus

Denpasar is *the* hub for the creaky bemo network around Bali. The city has several bemo terminals – you'll often have to go via Denpasar and transfer from one terminal to another. Each terminal has regular bemo connections to the other terminals in Denpasar for 7000Rp. Ask around for which one is best.

The usual route to Java is a bus (get one with air-con) from Denpasar's Ubung terminal to Surabaya (145,000Rp, 10 hours), which includes the short ferry trip across the Bali Strait. Other buses go as far as Yogyakarta (215,000Rp, 16 hours) and Jakarta (370,000Rp, 24 hours), usually travelling overnight. Going east, combined bus and ferry tickets include Mataram on Lombok (150,000Rp, seven hours) and Sumbawa Besar (250,000Rp, 15 hours) on West Nusa Tenggara.

Book directly at offices in the Ubung terminal, 3km north of the city centre. To Surabaya or even Jakarta, you may get on a bus within an hour of arriving at Ubung, but at busy times you should buy your ticket at least one day ahead.

Sanur

☎0361

Sanur is a genteel alternative to Kuta. The white-sand beach is sheltered by a reef. The resulting low-key surf contributes to Sanur's nickname 'Snore', although this is also attributable to the area's status as a haven for expat retirees.

Sanur's **beachfront walk** was the first in Bali and from day one has been delighting locals and visitors alike. Over 4km long, it follows the sand as it curves to the southwest. Oodles of cafes with tables in the sand give plenty of reason to pause.

Sleeping

Usually the best places to stay are right on the beach; however, beware of properties that have been coasting for decades.

Kesumasari GUESTHOUSE $

(☎287824; Jl Kesumasari 6; r with fan/air-con 250,000/350,000Rp; ❄) The only thing between you and the beach is a small shrine. Beyond the lounging porches, the multihued carved Balinese doors don't prepare you for the riot of colour inside the 10 idiosyncratic rooms at this family-run homestay.

Keke Homestay GUESTHOUSE $

(☎287282; Jl Danau Tamblingan 96; r 100,000-250,000Rp; ❄) Set 150m down a *gang* from the noisy road, Keke welcomes backpackers into its genial family. The five quiet, clean rooms vary from fan-only to air-con cool.

Hotel Rita HOTEL $
(☎287969; ritabali2@yahoo.co.id; Jl Danau Tamblingan 152; r 300,000-350,000Rp; ❄) Lovely Rita is tailor-made for those who want a basic room in a nice garden. You've nothing to fear from meter maids at this secluded compound well off busy Jl Danau Tamblingan. The beach is 10 minutes east.

Eating & Drinking

The beach path offers restaurants, *warung* and bars where you can catch a meal, a drink or a sea breeze.

Bonsai Cafe CAFE $
(Jl Danau Tambligan 27; dishes 20,000-60,000Rp) Order from a long list of beach-cafe standards while chilling in comfy and shady wicker chairs. Then wander inland for a surprise: hundreds of the cafe's namesake plants growing small in a rather sensational formal garden.

Sari Bundo INDONESIAN $
(☎281389; Jl Danau Poso; dishes 5000-10,000Rp; ⏲24hr) Spotless and simple Padang-style joint serving the best curry chicken in Sanur.

Kalimantan BAR
(Jl Pantai Sindhu 11) Also known as Borneo Bob's, this veteran boozer is one of many casual joints on this street; enjoy cold ones under the huge trees.

Getting There & Around

The **Perama office** (☎285592; Jl Hang Tuah 39) is at Warung Pojok at the northern end of town. Shuttle destinations include Kuta (25,000Rp, 20 minutes), Ubud (40,000Rp, one hour) and Padangbai (60,000Rp, two hours).

Bemos go up and down Jl Danau Tamblingan and Jl Danau Poso for 4000Rp.

Nusa Lembongan

☎0366

Nusa Lembongan is one of three islands (along with Nusa Penida and Nusa Ceningan) that together comprise the Nusa Penida archipelago. It's the Bali many imagine but never find: rooms on the beach, cheap beers with incredible sunsets, days spent surfing and diving, and nights spent riffling through a favourite book or hanging with new friends.

Sights

Jungutbatu Beach BEACH
Jungutbatu beach, a lovely arc of white sand with clear blue water, has superb views across to Gunung Agung in Bali. The village itself is pleasant, with quiet lanes, no cars and a couple of temples.

Mushroom Bay BEACH
Gorgeous little Mushroom Bay, unofficially named for the mushroom corals offshore, has a perfect crescent of white-sand beach. The most pleasant way to get here from Jungutbatu is to walk along the trail that starts from the southern end of the main beach and follows the coastline for 1km or so past a couple of small beaches.

Activities

Most places will rent bicycles for 30,000Rp per day, surfboards for 50,000Rp and motorbikes for 30,000Rp per hour. Good snorkelling can be had just off Mushroom Bay as well as in areas off the north coast of the island. The diving at Nusa Penida is legendary and challenging.

World Diving DIVING
(☎081 2390 0686; www.world-diving.com) World Diving, based at Pondok Baruna on Jungutbatu beach, is well regarded. It offers various courses. Two-tank dives are from US$80; snorkelling trips are US$25.

Sleeping & Eating

Lembongan has become flashpacker central. The row of guesthouses (most with cafes) along Jungutbatu beach are continuously upgrading. As you follow the elevated coastal path west to Mushroom Bay, standards and prices generally elevate as well.

Puri Nusa Bungalows GUESTHOUSE $
(☎24482; r 150,000-450,000Rp; ❄) The 17 rooms here are clean and comfortable (some with hot water and air-con); the two upstairs in front have excellent views and there's a good cafe. Comfy loungers are scattered under trees on the manicured grounds.

Pondok Baruna GUESTHOUSE $
(☎0812 394 0992; www.world-diving.com; r from 260,000Rp; ❄@≋) Associated with World Diving, this place offers basic rooms with terraces facing the ocean. Other rooms with air-con surround a dive pool off the beach. The restaurant serves first-rate meals.

Lembongan Beach Retreat GUESTHOUSE $
(☎0878 6131 3468; r 150,000-400,000Rp) At the north end of the beach past the end of the breakwater, this little place lives up to its name. A retreat it is, with nothing stirring by day but the ripple of the surf.

Information

It's vital that you bring sufficient cash for your stay, as there's no ATM and few other services.

Getting There & Around

Boats anchor offshore, so be prepared to get your feet wet. And travel light – wheeled bags are comically inappropriate in the water and on the beach and dirt tracks. There are numerous ways of travelling between Nusa Lembongan and Sanur.

PUBLIC BOATS These leave from the northern end of Sanur beach at 7.45am (50,000Rp, 1¾ to two hours). This is the boat used for supplies, so you may have to share space with a melon.

PUBLIC SPEED BOAT These boats (180,000Rp, one hour) make the run in under an hour from same end of Sanur beach. Schedules vary.

PRIVATE SPEED BOAT For speed boats (30 to 40 minutes) that fly over and through the waves, **Scoot** (☎0361-285522; one-way/return 300,000Rp/500,000Rp) runs several returns daily.

There are also useful boat links between Nusa Lembongan and the Gilis.

The island is fairly small and you can easily walk most places. There are no cars. One-way rides on motorbikes or trucks cost 5000Rp.

Ubud

☎0361

Perched on the gentle slopes leading up towards the central mountains, Ubud is the other half of Bali's tourism duopoly. Unlike South Bali, however, Ubud's focus remains on the remarkable Balinese culture in its myriad forms.

It's not surprising that many people come to Ubud for a day or two and end up staying longer, drawn in by the rich culture and many activities. Besides the popular dance-and-music shows, there are numerous courses that allow you to become fully immersed in Balinese culture.

Ubud is home to chilled-out restaurants and cafes, plus artful and serene places to stay. Around Ubud are temples, ancient sites and whole villages producing handicrafts (albeit mostly for visitors). Although the growth of Ubud has engulfed several neighbouring villages, leading to an urban sprawl, parts of the surrounding countryside remain unspoiled, with lush rice paddies and towering coconut trees. You'd be remiss if you didn't walk one or more of the dozens of paths during your stay.

Sights

Spend time in the museums and walking the beautiful countryside. If you only visit for a brief time on a day trip you may wonder what the fuss is all about.

Sacred Monkey Forest Sanctuary FOREST
(Map p206; www.monkeyforestubud.com; Monkey Forest Rd; admission 20,000Rp; ⌚8am-6pm) This cool and dense swath of jungle, officially called Mandala Wisata Wanara Wana, houses three holy temples. The sanctuary is inhabited by a band of grey-haired, greedy long-tailed Balinese macaques who are nothing like the innocent-looking doe-eyed monkeys on the brochures.

Museum Puri Lukisan MUSEUM
(Palace of Fine Arts; Map p206; www.mpl-ubud.com; off Jl Raya Ubud; admission 20,000Rp; ⌚9am-5pm) The Museum Puri Lukisan, off Jl Raya Ubud, displays in a beautiful garden setting excellent examples of all schools of Balinese art.

Neka Art Museum MUSEUM
(Map p205; www.museumneka.com; Jl Raya Sanggingan; admission 40,000Rp; ⌚9am-5pm) Quite distinct from Neka Gallery, the Neka Art Museum is the creation of Suteja Neka, a private collector and dealer in Balinese art. It has an excellent and diverse collection and is the best place to learn about the development of painting in Bali.

Agung Rai Museum of Art MUSEUM
(ARMA; Map p205; www.armamuseum.com; Jl Raya Pengosekan; admission 30,000Rp; ⌚9am-6pm) This museum, gallery and cultural centre is the only place in Bali at which to see works by the influential German artist Walter Spies.

Activities

As well as visiting the museums and galleries, it is well worth exploring the natural beauty that inspires so much of it. There are wonderful walks around Ubud: east to Pejeng, across picturesque ravines south to Bedulu; north along the Campuan ridge; and west to Penestanan and Sayan, with views over the Sungai Ayung (Ayung River) gorge.

Ubud Area

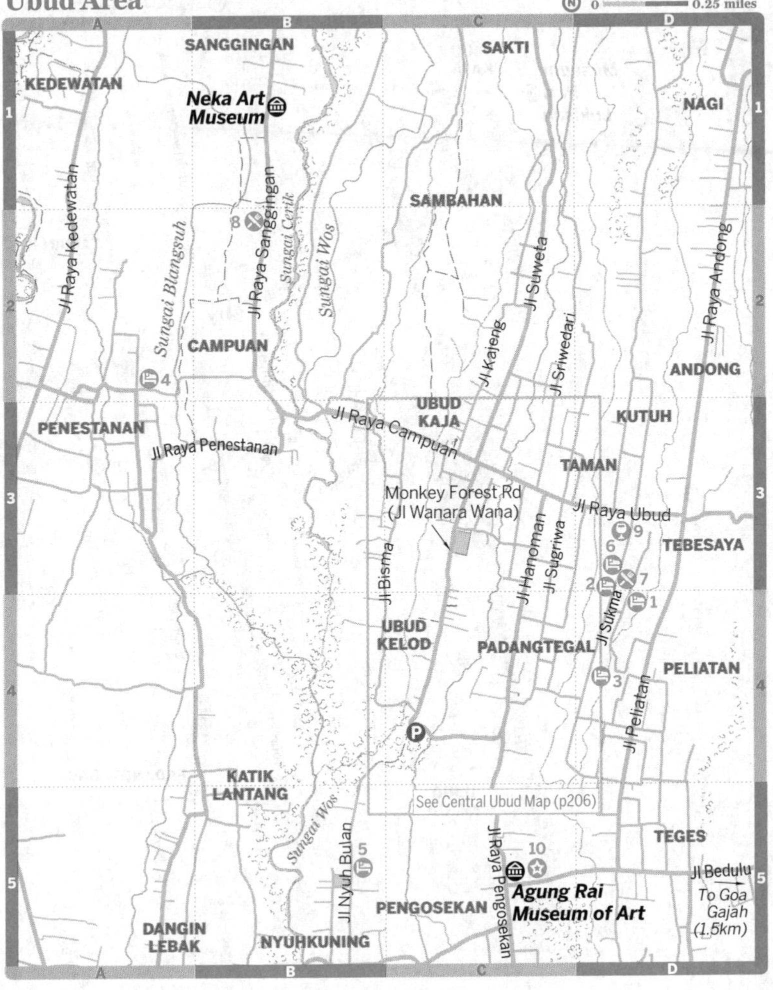

Ubud Area

Top Sights

Agung Rai Museum of Art C5
Neka Art Museum B1

Sleeping

1 Aji Lodge D4
2 Biangs D3
3 Puri Asri 2 .... D4
4 Santra Putra A2
5 Swasti Cottage B5
6 Yuliati House D3

Eating

7 Mama's Warung D3
8 Warung Pulau Kelapa B2

Drinking

9 Jazz Café D3

Entertainment

10 Arma Open Stage C5

Central Ubud

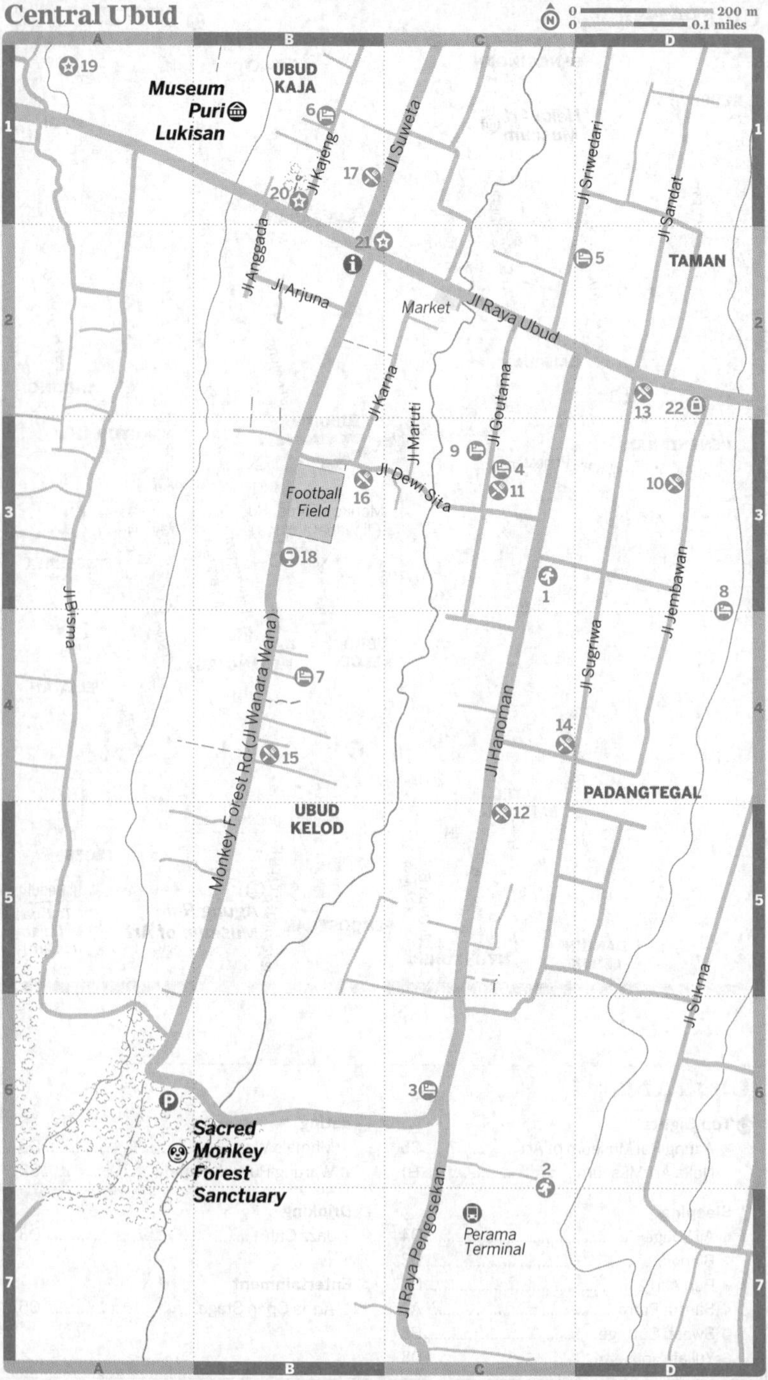

Central Ubud

Top Sights
- Museum Puri Lukisan ... B1
- Sacred Monkey Forest Sanctuary ... A6

Activities, Courses & Tours
- 1 Nur Salon ... C3
- 2 Yoga Barn ... C6

Sleeping
- 3 Dewi Sri Bungalows ... C6
- 4 Donald Homestay ... C3
- 5 Eka's Homestay ... D2
- 6 Lecuk Inn ... B1
- 7 Mandia Bungalows ... B4
- 8 Matahari Cottages ... D3
- 9 Nirvana Pension & Gallery ... C3

Eating
- 10 Bali Buddha ... D3
- 11 Dewa Warung ... C3
- 12 Kafe ... C5
- 13 Kué ... D2
- 14 Sopa ... C4
- 15 Three Monkeys ... B4
- 16 Tutmak Cafe ... B3
- 17 Warung Ibu Oka ... B1

Drinking
- 18 Lebong Café ... B3

Entertainment
- 19 Pura Dalem Ubud ... A1
- 20 Pura Taman Saraswati ... B1
- 21 Ubud Palace ... B2

Shopping
- 22 Ganesha Bookshop ... D2

Ubud is a nexus of pampering: spas, yoga and myriad New Age activities are on offer. Check the bulletin board outside **Bali Buddha** (Map p206; Jl Jembawan 1), a health-food cafe and shop, for listings. You can also find courses in Balinese arts.

TOP CHOICE Yoga Barn YOGA STUDIO
(Map p206; www.balispirit.com; off Jl Pengosekan; classes from 110,000Rp; 7am-9pm) A huge range of classes in yoga, Pilates, dance and life-affirming offshoots are held through the week.

Herb Walks NATURE WALKS
(975051; www.baliherbalwalk.com; walks US$20; 8.30am) Three-hour walks through lush Bali landscape; medicinal and cooking herbs and plants are identified and explained.

Nur Salon SPA
(Map p206; Jl Hanoman 28; 1hr massage 155,000Rp; 9am-8pm) In a traditional Balinese compound filled with labelled medicinal plants; offers a long menu of straight-forward spa and salon services.

Sleeping

There are hundreds of places to stay. Choices range from simple little *losmen* to world-class luxurious retreats. Inexpensive family lodgings are very small and tend to operate in clusters, so you can easily look at a few before choosing. There's no need to pay for air-con, as it's cool at night.

CENTRAL UBUD

Small streets east of Monkey Forest Rd, including Jl Karna and Jl Maruti, have numerous, family-style homestays, as does Jl Goutama. Don't settle for a room with road noise along Ubud's main drags.

TOP CHOICE Nirvana Pension & Gallery GUESTHOUSE $
(Map p206; 975415; www.nirvanaku.com; Jl Goutama 10; r 250,000-450,000Rp) There are *alang alang* (woven thatch) roofs, a plethora of paintings, ornate doorways and six rooms with modern bathrooms in a shady secluded locale. Batik courses are also held.

Lecuk Inn GUESTHOUSE $
(Map p205; 973445; bahula_lecuk@yahoo.com; Jl Kajeng 15; r 125,000-150,000Rp) On Jl Kajeng, which has many budget options, this six-room treat has ravine views. Rooms come with fridges, hot water and nice terraces.

Mandia Bungalows GUESTHOUSE $
(Map p206; 970965; Monkey Forest Rd; r 200,000-300,000Rp) It's heliconia heaven in the lush gardens. The four bungalow-style rooms are shaded by coconut palms and cooled by ceiling fans. Porches have comfy loungers, and the guys who run it are sweethearts.

Dewi Sri Bungalows GUESTHOUSE $
(Map p206; 975300; Jl Hanoman 69; r with fan/air-con 250,000/300,000Rp;) The best value here are the split-level fan-only rooms,

which have cute, open-air bathrooms below and a terrace with glimpses of rice above.

Eka's Homestay HOMESTAY $
(Map p206; ☎970550; Jl Sriwedari 8; r 100,000-150,000Rp) Follow your ears to this nice little family compound with seven basic hot-water rooms. Eka's is the home of Wayan Pasek Sucipta, a teacher of Balinese music.

Donald Homestay HOMESTAY $
(Map p206; ☎977156; Jl Goutama; r 200,000-250,000Rp;) The four rooms – some with hot water – are in a nice back corner of the family compound.

EAST OF CENTRAL UBUD

In Tebesaya, Jl Sukma and the *gang* that runs parallel just to the east are excellent hunting grounds for budget stays.

Puri Asri 2 GUESTHOUSE $
(Map p205; ☎973210; www.puriasrivilla.com; Jl Sukma 59; r 125,000-200,000Rp;) Work your way through a classic family compound and you'll find four bungalow-style rooms with views of a ravine. It's a fabulous deal and rooms come with hot water. Cool off in the nice pool.

Yuliati House HOMESTAY $
(Map p205; ☎974044; yuliahouse10@yahoo.com; Jl Sukma 10; s/d 125,000/250,000Rp) Some of the nine rooms here are cold-water only, others have tubs and some even have river-valley views. But the real draw is this talented-as-all-heck family that offers lessons in *gamelan*, dance and more.

Biangs HOMESTAY $
(Map p205; ☎976520; Jl Sukma 28; r 150,000Rp;) In a little garden, Biangs – meaning 'mama' – has six well-maintained rooms, with hot water. The best rooms have views of a small valley.

Aji Lodge HOMESTAY $
(Map p205; ☎973255; ajilodge11@yahoo.com; Tebesaya 11; s/d 100,000/150,000Rp) A passel of comfortable family compounds line a footpath east of Jl Sukma. Get a room down the hill by the river for the full bedtime symphony of birds, bugs and critters.

WEST OF CENTRAL UBUD

Penestanan is west of Ubud but still within walking distance. Out here, you can hear water coursing through the surrounding rice fields.

Santra Putra GUESTHOUSE $
(Map p205; ☎977810; karjabali@yahoo.com; off Jl Raya Campuan; r US$25-40;) Run by internationally exhibited abstract artist I Wayan Karja (whose studio/gallery is also on site), this place has nine big, open airy rooms with hot water. Enjoy paddy-field views from all vantage points.

Matahari Cottages GUESTHOUSE $$
(Map p206; ☎975459; www.matahariubud.com; Jl Jembawan; r US$25-85;) This idiosyncratic place has 10 flamboyant, themed rooms. The library is a vision out of a 1920s fantasy. It also boasts a self-proclaimed 'jungle Jacuzzi' and a multicourse breakfast and high tea elaborately served on silver.

Eating

CENTRAL UBUD

There are busy and tasty choices on Ubud's main street, Jl Raya Ubud.

TOP CHOICE **Three Monkeys** ASIAN $$
(Map p206; ☎974830; Monkey Forest Rd; mains 20,000-60,000Rp) Mellow music and artworks set a cultured mood. The tables overlooking the rice field out back make it magic and the place for romance. By day there are sandwiches, salads and gelato. At night there's a fusion menu of Asian classics; good for a lovely meal out.

Sopa VEGETARIAN $
(Map p206; Jl Sugriwa 36; meals 30,000-60,000Rp;) Open air and oh so groovy, this popular place captures the Ubud vibe. Look for specials of the day on display; the ever-changing *nasi campur* is a treat.

SPLURGE: SWASTI COTTAGE

One of Ubud's most inventive and appealing places to stay is **Swasti Cottage** (Map p206; ☎974079; www.baliswasti.com; Jl Nyuh Bulan; r 550,000-950,000Rp;), just five minutes' walk from the south entrance to the Monkey Forest. Run by a French-Balinese couple, this guesthouse has large, manicured grounds. Some rooms are in simple two-storey blocks; others are in vintage traditional bungalows brought here from across Bali.

Kafe INTERNATIONAL $
(Map p206; www.balispirit.com; Jl Hanoman 44; dishes 15,000-40,000Rp;) Kafe has an organic menu great for veggie grazing or just having a coffee, juice or house-made natural soda. One of *the* places to meet in Ubud. Always busy.

Dewa Warung INDONESIAN $
(Map p206; Jl Goutama; meals 15,000-20,000Rp) When it rains, the tin roof sounds like a tap-dance convention and the bare lightbulbs sway in the breeze. A little garden surrounds tables a few steps above the road where diners tuck into plates of sizzling fresh Indo fare.

Kué INTERNATIONAL $
(Map p206; Jl Raya Ubud; meals 30,000-80,000Rp;) A top-end organic bakery and chocolate shop; climb the side stairs to a lovely cafe that sits above the road chaos.

Warung Ibu Oka BALINESE $
(Map p206; Jl Suweta; meals 30,000Rp; 11am-3pm) Join the lunchtime lines opposite Ubud Palace waiting for one thing: the eponymous Balinese-style roast suckling pig.

Tutmak Cafe INTERNATIONAL $$
(Map p206; Jl Dewi Sita; meals 30,000-90,000Rp;) The breezy multilevel location here, facing both Jl Dewi Sita and the football field, is a popular place for a refreshing drink or a meal.

EAST OF CENTRAL UBUD

TOP CHOICE **Mama's Warung** INDONESIAN $
(Map p205; Jl Sukma; dishes 10,000-20,000Rp) A real budget find among the bargain homestays of Tebesaya. Mama herself cooks up Indo classics that are spicy and redolent with garlic (the avocado salad, yum!). The freshly made peanut sauce for the satay is silky smooth.

WEST OF CENTRAL UBUD

The restaurants and cafes west of the centre are dotted among rice fields, lanes and roads.

Warung Pulau Kelapa INDONESIAN $
(Map p205; Jl Raya Sanggingan; dishes 15,000-30,000Rp) A newish place along the road that climbs from Campuan to Sanggingan, Kelapa has stylish takes on local classics. The surrounds are stylish as well: plenty of whitewash and antiques. Terrace tables are best.

Drinking

No one comes to Ubud for wild nightlife. A few bars get lively around sunset and later in the night, but the venues certainly don't aspire to the club partying found in Kuta and Seminyak.

> **WRONG NUMBER?**
>
> Bali's landline phone numbers (those with area codes that include 0361, across the south and Ubud) are being changed on an ongoing basis through 2014. To accommodate increased demand for lines, a digit is being added to the start of the existing six- or seven-digit phone number. So 0361-761 xxxx might become 0361-4761 xxxx. The schedule and plans for the new numbers change regularly but usually you'll hear a recording first in Bahasa Indonesia and then in English telling you what digit to add to the changed number.

Jazz Cafe LOUNGE
(Map p205; www.jazzcafebali.com; Jl Sukma 2; 5pm-midnight) Always popular, Jazz Cafe has a relaxed vibe in a garden of coconut palms and ferns. Live music Tuesday to Saturday from 7.30pm. It provides transport around Ubud for patrons.

Lebong Café BAR
(Map p206; Monkey Forest Rd) Get up, stand up, stand up for your…reggae. This nightlife hub stays open at least until midnight, with live reggae and rock most nights. A few other places good for drinks are nearby.

☆ Entertainment

Few travel experiences can be more magical than experiencing a Balinese dance performance, especially in Ubud. Cultural entertainment keeps people returning and sets Bali apart from other tropical destinations. Get there a little early and buy a beer from the old women selling them out of ice-filled buckets.

Ubud Tourist Information has performance information and sells tickets (usually about 80,000Rp). For performances outside Ubud, transport is often included in the price. Tickets are also sold at the venues.

In a week in Ubud, you can see *kecak*, *legong* and *barong* dances, *wayang kulit* puppets, *gamelan* and more. For details on these dances, see p299. Top venues include the following:

ARMA Open Stage VENUE
(Map p206; ☎976659; Jl Raya Pengosekan) Some of the best troupes perform here.

Pura Dalem Ubud VENUE
(Map p206; Jl Raya Ubud) Perfect for the fire dance; one of the prettiest venues.

Pura Taman Saraswati VENUE
(Water Palace; Map p206; Jl Raya Ubud) A beautiful location.

Ubud Palace VENUE
(Map p206; Jl Raya Ubud) Near-nightly performances in a royal setting.

Shopping

In Ubud, Jl Hanoman and Jl Dewi Sita should be your starting points. Surrounding villages are hotbeds for arts and crafts – as you'll have noticed on your drive to Ubud.

Ganesha Bookshop BOOKS
(Map p206; www.ganeshabooksbali.com; Jl Raya Ubud) Bali's best bookshop has an amazing amount of stock. Excellent selection of titles on Indonesian studies, travel, arts, music and fiction (including secondhand titles).

Information

Along the main roads, you'll find most services you need.

Money

Ubud has numerous banks, ATMs and money changers along Jl Raya Ubud and Monkey Forest Rd.

Tourist Information

Ubud Tourist Information (Yaysan Bina Wisata; Map p206; Jl Raya Ubud; ⏰8am-8pm) The one really useful tourist office in Bali. It has a good range of information and a noticeboard listing current happenings and events.

Getting There & Around

Transport between South Bali and Ubud costs about 200,000Rp whether you take a metered taxi or arrange it with a guy on the street. There are no local metered taxis, but the ubiquitous drivers and motorbike owners will take you around town for a negotiable 10,000Rp to 40,000Rp depending on distance.

BEMO & BUS Ubud is on two bemo routes. Orange bemo travel from Gianyar to Ubud (8000Rp) and larger brown bemo from Batubulan terminal in Denpasar to Ubud (8000Rp). Perama buses run to Sanur (40,000Rp, one hour) and Kuta (50,000Rp, 90 minutes).

BICYCLE Shops renting bikes have their cycles on display along the main roads; your accommodation can always arrange bike rental.

Around Ubud

Two kilometres east of central Ubud, the cavern of **Goa Gajah** (Elephant Cave; off Map p205; admission 6000Rp, parking 2000Rp; ⏰8am-6pm) was discovered in the 1920s; the fountains and bathing pool were not unearthed until 1954. It is believed to have been a Buddhist hermitage.

In Tampaksiring, 18km northeast of Ubud, you'll find the most impressive ancient site in Bali, **Gunung Kawi** (admission 4100Rp; ⏰8am-5pm). This astonishing group of stone *candi* (shrines) cut into cliffs on either side of the plunging Pakrisan River valley is being considered for Unesco Heritage status. They stand in awe-inspiring, 8m-high sheltered niches cut into the sheer cliff face. From the end of the access road, a steep, stone stairway leads down to the river, at one point making a cutting through an embankment of solid rock.

East Coast Beaches

The main road that runs east from Sanur passes many black-sand beaches. One good stop is **Pura Masceti Beach**, 15km east of Sanur. Pura Masceti, one of Bali's nine directional temples, is right on the beach. It's architecturally significant and enlivened with gaudy statuary.

Semarapura (Klungkung)

☎0366

Once the centre of an important Balinese kingdom, Semarapura (also known as Klungkung) is the capital of Klungkung regency (a historical and present-day administrative area) and a great artistic and cultural focal point. Formerly the seat of the Dewa Agung dynasty, the **Semara Pura Complex** (admission 12,000Rp, parking 1000Rp; ⏰7am-6pm) has now largely crumbled away, but history and architecture buffs will enjoy a wander past the **Kertha Gosa** (Hall of Justice) and **Bale Kambang** (Floating Pavilion).

Padangbai

0363

There's a real backpacker vibe about this little beach town, which is also the port for the main public ferry connecting Bali with Lombok.

Padangbai is on the upswing. It sits on a small bay and has a nice little curve of beach. It has a whole compact seaside travellers' scene with cheap places to stay and some funky and fun cafes. The pace is slow, but should ambition strike there's good snorkelling and diving, plus some easy walks and a couple of great beaches.

Sleeping & Eating

Accommodation in Padangbai – like the town itself – is pretty laid-back. Prices are fairly cheap; simple cafes and *warung* are common.

Topi Inn GUESTHOUSE $
(41424; www.topiinn.com; Jl Silayukti; r from 100,000Rp;) Sitting at the end of the strip in a serene location, Topi has five pleasant rooms, some of which share bathrooms. The enthusiastic owners offer courses in cooking, among other diversions. The cafe is excellent.

Padangbai Billabong GUESTHOUSE $
(41399; Jl Silayukti; r 125,000-300,000Rp;) We prefer the bungalows right up front at this scrupulously tidy place, which has 12 rooms set amid immaculate gardens. It often seems to have rooms when others on the strip are full.

Kembar Inn GUESTHOUSE $
(41364; kembarinn@hotmail.com; r 150,000-350,000Rp;) There are 11 rooms (some with fans) at this inn linked by a steep and narrow staircase. The best awaits at the top and has a private terrace with views.

Information

Bank BRI (Jl Pelabuhan) Exchanges money and has an international ATM.

Getting There & Away

Padangbai is 2km south of the main Semarapura–Amlapura road.

Perama (Cafe Dona, Jl Pelabuhan; 7am-8pm) has a stop here for its services around the east coast; trips include Kuta (60,000Rp, three hours) and Ubud (50,000Rp, two hours).

Public ferries travel nonstop between Padangbai and Lembar on Lombok. There are also fast boats for travellers to the Gili Islands and Lombok. For details on these services, see p251.

EAST COAST TOUR

For a good day out, take a looping tour of east Bali. Start at a black-sand beach east of Sanur, then check out the old ruins at Semarapura. Lunch at Padangbai and then curve up into the hills through the picturesque rice fields around Tirta Gangga. Head west and then turn back south along the beautiful road through Sideman.

Candidasa

Candidasa is slouching into idle age, no longer the tourism darling it once was. The main drawback is the lack of a beach, which, except for the far eastern stretch, has eroded away as fast as hotels were built. It's a favourite place for sedate travellers to be, well, sedate.

Tirta Gangga

0363

Tirta Gangga (Water of the Ganges) is the site of a holy temple, some great water features and some of the best views of rice fields and the sea beyond in east Bali. High on a ridge, it is a relaxing place to stop for an hour or a longer period, which will allow for some treks through the surrounding terraced countryside, which ripples with coursing water.

Sights & Activities

Taman Tirta Gangga MONUMENT
(admission 5000Rp, parking 2000Rp; 24hr, ticket office 6am-6pm) Amlapura's water-loving raja, the last king of Karangasem, built the palace of his dreams at Taman Tirta Gangga. Originally built in 1948, the water palace was damaged in the 1963 eruption of Gunung Agung. The palace has several swimming pools and ornamental ponds, which serve as a fascinating reminder of the old days of the Balinese rajas.

Hiking in the surrounding hills is recommended. The rice terraces around Tirta Gangga are among the most beautiful in Bali. Back roads and walking paths take you to many picturesque traditional villages. Or you can ascend the side of **Gunung Agung**. Guides are a good idea. Ask at Homestay Rijasa, where the owner I Ketut Sarjana is an experienced guide.

Among the possible treks is a six-hour loop to Tenganan village, plus shorter ones across the local hills, which include visits to remote temples and all the stunning vistas you can handle. Rates average about 50,000Rp per hour for one or two people.

Sleeping & Eating

Most places to stay have cafes with mains under 20,000Rp.

Homestay Rijasa HOMESTAY $
(☎21873, 0813 5300 5080; r 100,000-200,000Rp) With elaborately planted grounds, this well-run nine-room homestay is opposite the water palace entrance. Better rooms have hot water, good for the large soaking tubs. The owner, I Ketut Sarjana, is an experienced trekking guide. Recommended.

Good Karma HOMESTAY $
(☎22445; r 200,000-250,000Rp) A classic homestay, Good Karma has four very clean and simple bungalows and a good vibe derived from the surrounding pastoral rice field. The good cafe's gazebos look towards the parking lot.

Getting There & Away

It's easiest to visit this region with your own transport.

Gunung Batur Area

☎0366

Volcanic Gunung Batur (1717m) is a major tourist magnet, offering treks to its summit and spectacular views of Danau Batur (Lake Batur), at the bottom of a huge caldera. Annoying touts and tourist buses detract from the experience around the rim of the vast crater, but the crater lake and cone of Batur are well worth exploring. Entry to the area costs 10,000Rp per person.

On a clear day, the village of **Penelokan** has superb views across to Gunung Batur and down to the lake at the bottom of the crater. It has numerous huge tourist restaurants catering to busloads of day trippers; avoid these.

The villages of Batur and Kintamani now virtually run together. Kintamani is famed for its large and colourful **market**, which is held every three days. If you don't want to go on a trek, the sunrise view from the road here is pretty good.

TOYA BUNGKAH

The main tourist centre is Toya Bungkah, which is scruffy but has a cute charm and a serene lakeside setting in the ancient caldera below the peaks.

The most popular local trek is from Toya Bungkah to the top of Gunung Batur for sunrise – a magnificent sight requiring a 4am start from the village. The **HPPGB** (Mt Batur Tour Guides Association; ☎52362; ⏰3am-noon) has a monopoly on guided climbs up Gunung Batur and charges about 400,000Rp for one to four people to hike Batur; breakfast is extra. Those attempting to trek Batur alone can expect hassle from the HPPGB.

Unless noted, hotels only have cold water, which can be a boon for waking up for a sunset climb. Most have restaurants, some of which serve *ikan mujair,* a delicious small lake fish, which is barbecued to a crisp with onion, garlic and bamboo shoots.

Lakeside Cottages & Restaurant (☎0813 386 0081; r from 250,000Rp; 🏊) serves home-style Japanese dishes. Its lakeside pool makes it a top pick. The owner can arrange all manner of treks.

With a lovely, quiet lakeside location opposite vegetable plots, **Under the Volcano III** (☎081 3386 0081; r 180,000Rp) has six clean and pretty rooms. Two other nearby inns are run by the same family.

Getting There & Around

There are two main roads in the Gunung Batur area. The caldera-rim road links Penulisan and Penelokan, and from Penelokan you drop down onto the inner-rim road. The latter is rough in parts, especially the western side of the circuit, but drivable for all vehicles.

This is a tough destination for public transport. Best to use – or arrange – your own transport. Day trips from south Bali and Ubud are popular.

Danau Bratan Area

Approaching from the south, you gradually leave the rice terraces behind and ascend into the cool, often misty mountain country around Danau Bratan. The name Bedugul is sometimes used to refer to the whole lakeside area, but strictly speaking, Bedugul is just the first place you reach at the top of the hill when coming up from South Bali. Candikuning and Munduk hold the star attractions in this area.

The big sight is **Pura Ulun Danau Bratan** (admission 10,000Rp, parking 5000Rp; ⏰tickets 7am-5pm, site 24hr), a graceful, very important Hindu-Buddhist lakeside temple. It dates to the 17th century.

WORTH A TRIP

AMED & THE FAR EAST COAST

Stretching from Amed to Bali's far eastern tip, this once-remote stretch of semi-arid coast draws visitors to a succession of small, scalloped, black-sand beaches and a relaxed atmosphere. The coast here is often called simply 'Amed', but this is a misnomer, as the coast is a series of seaside *dusun* (small villages) that start with the actual Amed in the north and then run southeast to Aas.

In nearby Tulamben (a 20-minute drive from Amed), the big attraction sank over 60 years ago. The WWII wreck of the US cargo ship *Liberty* is among the best and most popular dive sites in Bali, and this has given rise to an entire town based on scuba diving.

Snorkelling is excellent along the coast (in addition to the *Liberty*) and scuba diving is good. There are scores of dive operators in the area. **Euro Dive** (☎23469; www.eurodivebali.com; Lipah), in the heart of the Amed coast, and **Tauch Terminal** (☎0361-774504; www.tauch-terminal.com), in Tulamben, are both recommended. Expect to pay about €50 for a two-tank dive. Tauch also has an upscale hotel.

Every place to stay has at least a cafe. Driving the long road along the Amed coast you will find many options.

At chilled-out hideaway **Meditasi** (☎082 8372 2738; meditasi.8m.com; Aas; r 300,000-400,000Rp) you can take a break from the pressures of life. Meditation and yoga help you relax, and the four rooms are close to good swimming and snorkelling. Open-air baths allow you to count the colours of the bougainvillea and frangipani that grow in profusion.

Choose from a cold-water room with fan or something a scotch more posh (hot water) in a bungalow at **Sama Sama Bungalows** (☎0813 3738 2945; Jemeluk; r 150,000-300,000Rp), which is just across from the beach and has a good seafood cafe.

Alternatively, try **Galang Kangin Bungalows** (☎23480; bali_amed_gk@yahoo.co.jp; r 150,000Rp-600,000Rp; ❄), which is set on the hill side of the road amid a nice garden. The rooms here mix and match fans, cold water, hot water and air-con. Some are on the beach, as is the cafe.

Most people drive to the Amed area via the main road from Tirta Gangga to Culik. Public-transport options are limited. Many hotels rent bicycles for about 35,000Rp per day. At times you can get boats to/from the Gilis, which are just east on the horizon.

ℹ Getting There & Away

Danau Bratan is beside the main north–south road, so it's easy to reach from South Bali or Lovina using your own transport. Most minibuses running from Denpasar's Ubung terminal to Singaraja (for Lovina) will stop along the road near the temple.

Munduk

West from Danau Bratan, Munduk is a pretty, spread-out village perched high on a ridge. It's popular for its good trekking and hiking to coffee plantations, rice paddies, waterfalls and villages. Arrange a guide through your lodgings.

Puri Alam Bali GUESTHOUSE $
(☎0812 465 9815; www.purialambali.com; r from 250,000Rp) Perched on a precipice at the east end of the village, Puri Alam Bali's eight rooms (all hot-water) have better views the higher you go. The rooftop cafe is newly expanded and worth a visit. It surveys the local scene from on high. Think of the long concrete stairs down from the road as trekking practice.

Guru Ratna GUESTHOUSE $
(☎0813 3852 6092; r 150,000-300,000Rp) The cheapest place in the village has seven comfortable hot-water rooms in a colonial Dutch house. The best rooms have some style, carved wood details and nice porches. Ponder the distant ocean from the cafe.

Lovina & the North

☎0362

Relaxed is how people most often describe Lovina, and they are correct. This low-key, low-rise beach resort is the polar opposite of Kuta. Days are slow and so are the nights.

Almost merging into Singaraja, the regional capital to the west, the town is really a string of coastal villages – Pemaron, Tukad

Mungga, Anturan, Kalibukbuk (the main area), Kaliasem and Temukus – that have taken on this collective name.

Lovina is a convenient base for trips around the north coast or the central mountains. The beaches are made up of washed-out grey and black volcanic sand, and they are mostly clean near the hotel areas, but generally unspectacular. Reefs protect the shore, so the water is usually calm and clear.

Sights

Besides walking the modest beach path and not doing much of anything, the sights in Lovina are in the hills to the south, where waterfalls pour down into dense forest.

About 11km south of Singaraja, a well-signposted path goes 800m west from the main road to the touristy waterfall, **Air Terjun Gitgit** (admission 6000Rp). The path is lined with souvenir stalls and guides to nowhere. The 40m waterfalls pound away and the mists are more refreshing than any air-con. About 2km further up the hill, and roughly 600m off the western side of the main road, there's a multi-tiered **waterfall** (donation 5000Rp).

About 5km west of Lovina, a sign points to **Air Terjun Singsing** (Daybreak Waterfall). About 1km from the main road, there is a *warung* (food stall) on the left and a car park on the right. Walk past the *warung* and along the path for about 200m to the lower falls. The waterfall is not huge, but the pool underneath is ideal for swimming. Though not crystal clear, the water is cooler than the sea and very refreshing.

Sleeping

Hotels are spread out along the many side roads running off Jl Raya Lovina to the beach. There are decent places to stay in every price range.

A little over 10km from Singaraja, Kalibukbuk is the 'centre' of Lovina, with the biggest concentration of hotels.

Puri Bali Hotel HOTEL $
(☎41485; www.puribalilovina.com; Jl Ketapang, Kalibukbuk; r 180,000-350,000Rp; ❄🏊) The pool area is set deep in a lush garden – you could easily hang out here all day and let any cares wander off into the ether. The better of the 24 rooms, with hot water and air-con, are simple but comfortable. The cheapest, with fans and cold water, are merely simple.

Padang Lovina GUESTHOUSE $
(☎41302; padanglovina@yahoo.com; Gang Binaria, Kalibukbuk; r 150,000-350,000Rp; ❄🏊) Down a narrow lane in the very heart of Kalibukbuk. There's no pretension at all attached to the 14 comfortable bungalow-style rooms set around spacious grounds teeming with flowers. The best rooms have air-con and tubs.

Rini Hotel HOTEL $
(☎41386; rinihotel@telkom.net; Jl Ketapang, Kalibukbuk; r 180,000-500,000Rp; ❄🏊) This tidy 30-room place has a large saltwater pool. Cheaper rooms have fans and cold water, but the more expensive ones are huge, with air-con and hot water. In fact, should you come across a keg, you could have a party. A big one.

Puspa Rama GUESTHOUSE $
(☎42070; agungdayu@yahoo.com; Jl Kubu Gembong, Anturan; r 80,000-150,000Rp) In the small fishing village of Anturan, about 2km east of Kalibukbuk, Puspa Rama has grounds a few cuts above the others. The six rooms have hot water.

Eating & Drinking

Lovina's modest social scene centres on Kalibukbuk. Cafes by the beach are popular at sunset.

Khi Khi Restaurant CHINESE $
(meals 10,000-100,000Rp) Well off Jl Raya Lovina and behind the night market, this barn of a place specialises in Chinese food and grilled seafood, including lobster. It's always popular in a rub-elbows-with-your-neighbour kind of way.

Kantin 21 BAR
(Jl Raya Lovina; ⌚11am-1am) Funky open-air place where you can watch traffic by day and groove to acoustic guitar or garage-band rock by night. There's a long drinks list (jugs of Long Island iced tea for 75,000Rp), fresh juices and a few local snacks.

Information

There are ATMs plus internet places.

Getting There & Around

From South Bali by public transport, take a minibus from Denpasar (Ubung terminal, 35,000Rp) via Bedugul to Singaraja, where you connect to a blue bemo to Kalibukbuk (about 7000Rp).

Perama (☎41161; www.peramatour.com; Jl Raya Lovina, Anturan) links Lovina with Kuta

DON'T MISS

GUNUNG BATUKAU AREA

Often overlooked, Gunung Batukau is Bali's second-highest mountain (2276m), the third of Bali's three major mountains and the holy peak of the island's western end. Enjoy a magical visit to one of the island's holiest and most underrated temples, **Pura Luhur Batukau** (donation 10,000Rp). It has a seven-roofed *meru* (multiroofed shrine) dedicated to Maha Dewa, the mountain's guardian spirit. Mountain streams tumble down around the site.

At **Jatiluwih**, which means 'Truly Marvellous', you will be rewarded with vistas of centuries-old rice terraces that exhaust your ability to describe green. The locals will also be rewarded with your 'green', as there's a road toll for visitors (per person 10,000Rp, plus per car 5000Rp). The terraces have been nominated for Unesco status. You'll understand why just viewing the panorama from the narrow, twisting 18km road, but get out for a **rice-field walk**.

The only realistic way to explore the Gunung Batukau area is with your own transport.

(100,000Rp, four hours), Ubud (100,000Rp, three hours) and other destinations.

The Lovina strip is *very* spread out, but you can easily travel back and forth on bemo (4000Rp). Bikes are easily rented around town for about 30,000Rp per day.

Southwest Bali

From the busy western road along the south coast, turn north to **Mengwi**, where there's the impressive **Pura Taman Ayun** (admission 5000Rp; ⌚8am-5pm) water palace and temple.

A bit further west, and south of the main road, is **Pura Tanah Lot** (admission 30,000Rp; ⌚dawn-dusk), a reconstructed temple and major tourist trap, especially at sunset.

West Bali

BALIAN BEACH

Wild waves pounding an almost empty shore are driving the newfound popularity of this beach, which has a cool surfer's vibe and some funky, upscale hotels. It's 800m off the main road west at Lalang-Linggah.

Warung Ayu HOMESTAY $

(☎0812 399 353; r 150,000-250,000Rp) Like some vast surfer shack, the 11 rooms in this two-storey cold-water block look down the road to the surf, dude.

Made's Homestay HOMESTAY $

(☎0812 396 3335; r from 150,000Rp) Four basic bungalow-style units are surrounded by banana trees back from the beach. The rooms are basic, clean and large enough to hold numerous surfboards and have cold-water showers.

GILIMANUK

Gilimanuk is the terminus for the ferries to/from Banyuwangi just across the turbulent channel on Java.

Ferries from Gilimanuk depart roughly every 30 minutes around the clock. The ferry costs 6000Rp for passengers, 21,00Rp for a motorcycle, and 80,000Rp for a car. Through buses between Bali and Java include the fare in the bus ticket and are by far the easiest option.

TAMAN NASIONAL BALI BARAT

Visitors to Bali's only national park, Taman Nasional Bali Barat (West Bali National Park), can hike through bird-filled forests, enjoy the island's best diving at Pulau Menjangan and explore coastal mangroves.

The **park headquarters** (⌚7am-5pm) at Cekik displays a topographic model of the park and has some information about plants and wildlife. The **Labuhan Lalang visitors centre** (⌚7.30am-5pm) is in a hut located on the northern coast; snorkellers and dive boats launch here. At both places you can arrange for trekking guides.

Pemuteran

This oasis in the far northwest corner of Bali has a number of artful resorts set on a little bay and is the place to come for a real beach getaway. Most people dive or snorkel the underwater wonders at nearby Pulau Menjangan while here.

Activities

Reef Seen DIVING

(☎93001; www.reefseen.com) Right on the beach in a large compound, Reef Seen is ac-

DON'T MISS

PULAU MENJANGAN

Bali's most-rewarding dive area, **Pulau Menjangan**, has a dozen superb dive sites. The diving is excellent – iconic tropical fish, soft corals, great visibility (usually), caves and a spectacular drop-off. Most of the sites are close to shore and suitable for snorkellers or diving novices. Some decent snorkelling spots are not far from the jetty – ask the boatman where to go.

The most convenient place to stay for diving Menjangan is Pemuteran, where every hotel runs snorkelling trips and there are good dive shops. Day trips from other parts of Bali entail long, early-morning drives.

tive in local preservation efforts. It is a PADI dive centre and has a full complement of classes.

Sleeping & Eating

Pemuteran has many mellow midrange choices, all located on the bay, which has nice sand and is good for swimming. Cheaper options include the following:

TOP CHOICE **Taman Sari Bali Cottages** HOTEL $$
(☎93264; www.balitamansari.com; bungalows from US$70;) Thirty-one rooms are set in gorgeous bungalows (some quite grand), which feature intricate carvings and traditional artwork inside and out. It's located on a long stretch of quiet beach on the bay, and is part of the reef-restoration project.

Jubawa Home Stay HOTEL $
(☎94745; r 250,000-400,000Rp;) On the south (hill) side of the road, this clean hotel is a good budget choice. The best of the 12 rooms have hot water and air-con. The cafe serves Balinese and Thai food and there's a popular bar.

Rare Angon Homestay HOMESTAY $
(☎94747, 0813 3856 8000; rareangon@yahoo.co.id; r 200,000-400,000Rp;) Good basic rooms in a homestay located on the south side of the main road. K&K Dive Centre is here.

Getting There & Away

Pemuteran is served by any of the buses and bemo on the Gilimanuk–Lovina run. Labuhan Lalang and Taman Nasional Bali Barat are 12km west. It's a three- to four-hour drive from South Bali, either over the hills or around the west coast.

NUSA TENGGARA

An arc of islands extending from Bali towards northern Australia, Nusa Tenggara is lush and jungle green in the north, more arid savannah in the south, and in between a land of pink-sand beaches, schooling sharks and rays, and the world's largest lizard: the swaggering, spellbinding komodo dragon.

The Gili Islands see the bulk of the tourism, but those with a hunger for adventure head further east to Flores, charter boats to

Nusa Tenggara

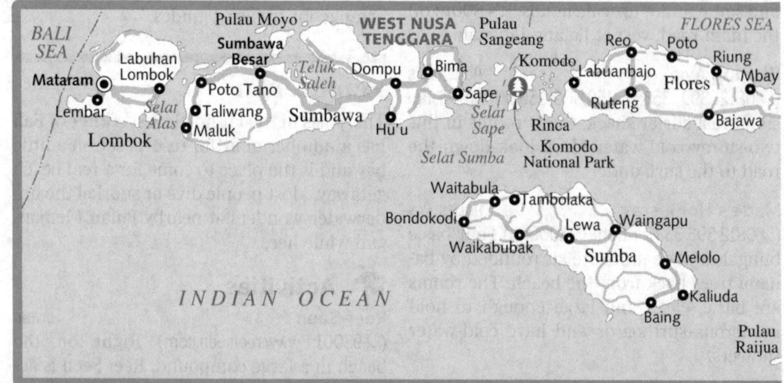

the Komodo Islands and back, then keep going south and east where the *bule* crowds and creature comforts are thin on the ground.

Getting There & Away

Most visitors use Bali as the international gateway to Nusa Tenggara. At research time, the only international flights to Nusa Tenggara were landing at Lombok's new airport, with connections to Singapore on SilkAir. International service with Air Asia was announced for 2012.

Getting Around

The easiest and most popular way to explore Nusa Tenggara is to fly from Bali to Labuanbajo (Flores) or Kupang (West Timor) and island hop from there.

AIR Merpati, Transnusa/Aviastar and Wings cover most destinations in Nusa Tenggara. Mataram, Kupang and Maumere are hubs. Sumbawa Besar, Bima (Sumbawa), Ende (Flores), Waikabubak and Tambolaka (Sumba) also have flights.

BOAT Regular vehicle/passenger ferries run Bali–Lombok, Lombok–Sumbawa, Flores–Sumbawa and Flores–Sumba. Perama makes the run from Lombok to Flores and back, taking in Komodo and Rinca, although Perama's safety has recently come into question due to a high-profile accident near Komodo (p234).

Pelni (www.pelni.com) has regular connections throughout Nusa Tenggara.

BUS Air-con coaches run across Lombok and Sumbawa, and from Kupang to Dili in Timor, but elsewhere small, slow minibuses are the norm.

CAR & MOTORCYCLE A motorcycle is an ideal way to explore Nusa Tenggara, but hiring one is not always easy outside Lombok. You can rent one in Bali or Lombok, and portage across by ferry. Bring an extra petrol can. For groups, cars with driver/guides are a great option. They cost 500,000Rp to 800,000Rp per day, depending upon the season.

Lombok

Lombok is an easy hop from Bali, and is the most popular spot in Nusa Tenggara. It has a spectacular, mostly deserted coastline with palm coves, Balinese Hindu temples, looming cliffs and epic surf. The majestic and sacred Gunung Rinjani rises from its centre – a challenging and rewarding climb. The Gilis, a carless collection of islands infused with a sun-drenched party vibe, are Lombok's biggest draw.

Getting There & Away

AIR The island's new airport, Lombok International Airport (LOP), opened in October 2011. It is 40km south of Mataram and replaces the old Selaparang airport. While it is convenient to Kuta, it is now a much longer haul to the main resorts of Senggigi. Roads are not entirely finished, so the going can be slow and transport links were still being refined at time of research. The airport is served by taxis.

Air Asia has announced plans for international service starting in 2012 and local boosters hope for much more new service. Airlines include the following:

Garuda Indonesia (www.garuda-indonesia.com) Flies twice daily to Jakarta, and once daily to Denpasar.

Lion/Wings Air (www.lionair.co.id) Flies direct to Jakarta and Bali several times daily.

Merpati Airlines (www.merpati.co.id)

SilkAir (www.silkair.com) Serves Singapore four times weekly.

Transnusa/Aviastar Airlines (www.transnusa.co.id) Well connected throughout Nusa

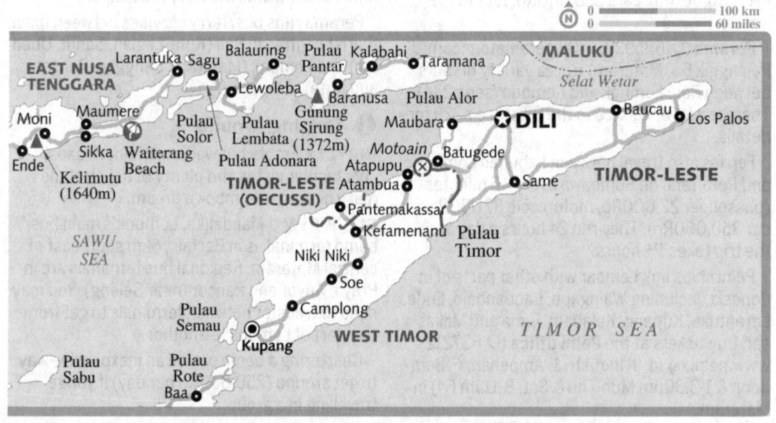

Lombok

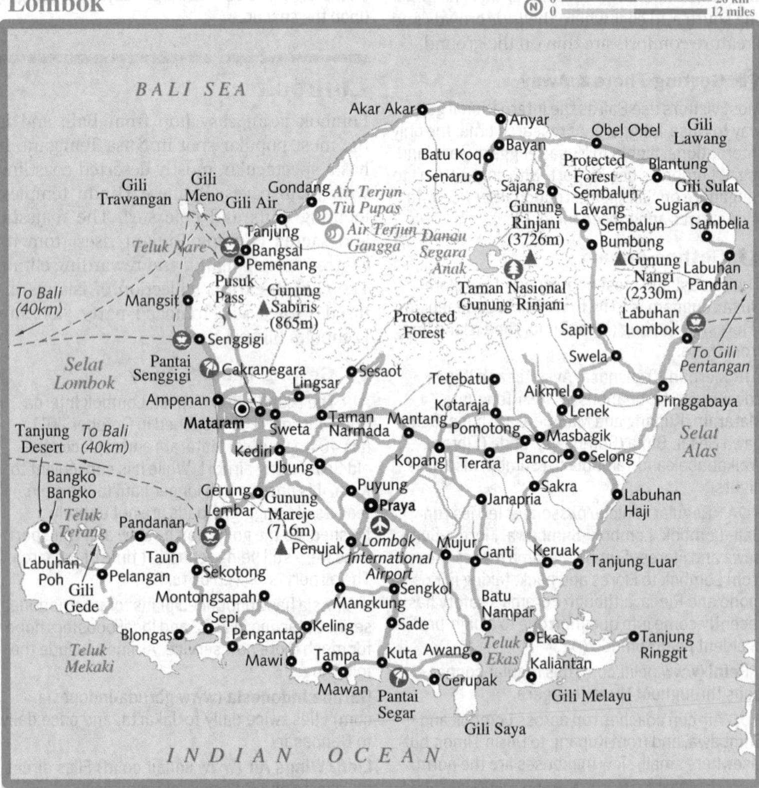

Tenggara, it has frequent flights between Mataram and Denpasar.

BOAT Large car ferries travel from Bali's Padangbai port to Lombok's Lembar harbour every two hours (passenger 36,000Rp, motorcycle 86,000Rp, cars 555,000Rp; four to five hours).

Perama (☎635928; www.peramatour.com; Jl Pejanggik 66, Mataram) runs a variety of tours between Bali, Lombok and Komodo (see p234). There is a lot of service to the Gilis; see p229 for details.

Ferries also travel between Labuhan Lombok and Poto Tano on Sumbawa every 45 minutes (passenger 22,000Rp, motorcycle 87,000Rp, car 350,000Rp). They run 24 hours a day and the trip takes 1½ hours.

Pelni ships link Lembar with other parts of Indonesia, including Waingapu, Labuanbajo, Ende, Larantuka, Kupang, Kalabahi, Bima and Makassar. Buy tickets at the **Pelni office** (☎637212; www.pelni.co.id; Jl Industri 1, Ampenan; ⏲8am-noon & 1-3.30pm Mon-Thu & Sat, 8-11am Fri) in Mataram.

BUS Long-distance public buses depart daily from Mataram's Mandalika terminal for major cities in Bali and Java in the west, and to Sumbawa in the east. Purchase tickets in advance from travel agencies along Jl Pejanggik in Mataram. Fares include the ferry crossings.

Perama runs bus/ferry services between main tourist centres in Bali (Kuta-Legian, Sanur, Ubud etc) and Lombok (Mataram, Senggigi, Bangsal and Kuta).

Getting Around

BICYCLE Empty but well-maintained roads, spectacular vistas and plenty of flat stretches make cycling in Lombok a dream.

BUS & BEMO Mandalika, Lombok's main bus/bemo terminal, is in Bertais, 6km southeast of central Mataram. Regional bus terminals are in Praya, Anyar and Pancor (near Selong). You may need to transfer between terminals to get from one part of Lombok to another.

Chartering a bemo can be an inexpensive way to get around (250,000Rp per day) if you're travelling in a group.

CAR & MOTORCYCLE Senggigi is the best place to rent wheels. Elsewhere, prices skyrocket and selection suffers. Suzuki Jimmies cost 150,000Rp per day, *kijangs* are 225,000Rp. Motorcycles can be rented in Senggigi for 90,000Rp per day. Scooters are cheaper.

LEMBAR

0370

Hassle-filled Lembar, Lombok's main port, is where Bali ferries and Pelni ships dock. Bus connections are abundant, and bemos run regularly to the Mandalika bus/bemo terminal (5000Rp), so there's no reason to linger. Taxis cost 65,000Rp to Mataram, and 125,000Rp to Senggigi.

MATARAM

0370 / POP 330,000

Lombok's sprawling capital, actually a cluster of four towns – Ampenan (port), Mataram (administrative centre), Cakranegara (commercial centre) and Sweta (bus terminal) – has some charms. There are ample trees, decent restaurants and a few cultural sights, but few travellers spend any time here.

Sights & Activities

Pura Meru TEMPLE

(Jl Selaparang; admission by donation; 8am-5pm) Everyone loves the Balinese, but did you know that they colonised Lombok for 100 years before the Dutch arrived? The proof is in the relics. Pura Meru, built in 1720, is a Hindu temple that has 33 shrines, and wooden drums that are thumped to call believers to ceremony.

Mayura Water Palace PALACE

(Jl Selaparang; admission by donation; 7am-7.30pm) Near Pura Mera, this palace was built in 1744 for the Balinese royal court.

Sleeping

A handful of good budget options are hidden among the quiet streets off Jl Pejanggik/Selaparang, east of Mataram Mall.

Mataram

Sights

1 Mayura Water Palace D2
2 Pura Meru D2

Sleeping

3 Hotel Melati Viktor I B2
4 Hotel Melati Viktor II B2
5 Oka Homestay B2

Eating

6 Aroma A2
7 Bakmi Raos A2

Mataram

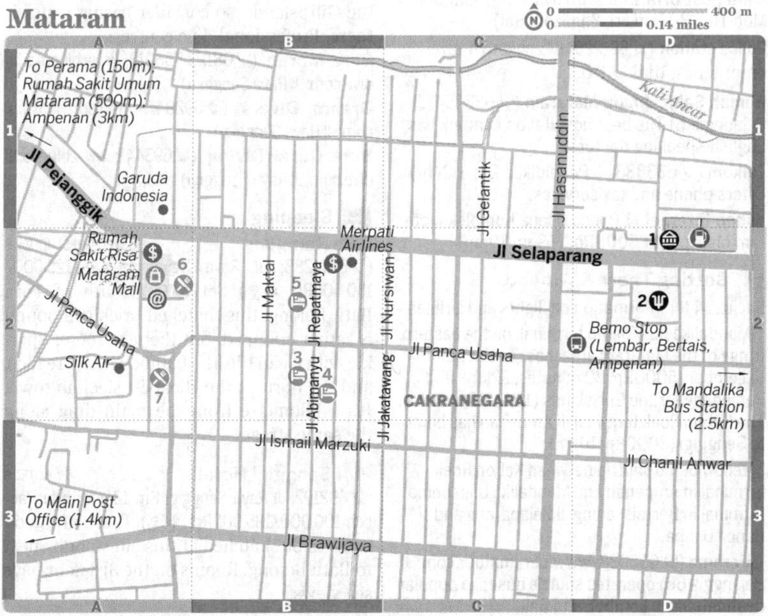

TOP CHOICE **Oka Homestay** GUESTHOUSE $
(☎622406; Jl Repatmaya 5; r from 100,000Rp) Balinese owned, this garden compound, patrolled by three friendly poodles, is a great deal. Rooms just got a good sprucing up, and are fan cooled and quite clean.

Hotel Melati Viktor 1 HOTEL $
(☎633830; Jl Abimanyu 1; d with fan/air-con 100,000/150,000Rp; ❄) The high ceilings, clean rooms and Balinese-style courtyard, complete with Hindu statues, make this one of the best-value hotels in town. If it's full, head to Viktor II across the street, where the wood-panelled ceilings are high and everything is brand new.

Eating

TOP CHOICE **Aroma** SEAFOOD $
(Jl Pejanggik; meals from 15,000Rp) Popular among Mataram's Chinese-Indonesians, it serves an outstanding fried *gurami* fish (35,000Rp) accompanied by a fiery sweet-chilli sauce.

Bakmi Raos NOODLES $
(Jl Panca Usaha; dishes 9000-20,000Rp) An authentic, modern noodle joint that attracts Mataram's hip, young and beautiful.

Information

Banks on Jl Selaparang and Jl Pejanggik have ATMs. Most change foreign cash and travellers cheques.

Main post office (Jl Sriwijaya 37; ⏲8am-5pm Mon-Thu, 8-11am Fri, 8am-1pm Sat)

Police station (☎631225; Jl Langko) In an emergency, dial ☎110.

Rumah Sakit Umum Mataram (☎622254; Jl Pejanggik 6) The best hospital on Lombok has English-speaking doctors.

Telkom (☎633333; Jl Pendidikan 23; ⏲24hr) Offers phone and fax services.

Yahoo Internet (1 Panca Usaha Komplek Mataram Mall; per hr 5000Rp; ⏲9am-10pm)

Getting There & Around

See p234 for information on flights and airlines.

Mandalika bus/bemo terminal, on the eastern fringe of the Mataram area, has regular bemo to Lembar (5000Rp, 30 minutes, 22km), and Pemenang for the Gili Islands (10,000Rp, 31km). The Kebon Roek terminal in Ampenan has bemo to Senggigi (3000Rp, 10km).

Yellow bemo shuttle between Kebon Roek terminal in Ampenan and Mandalika bus/bemo terminal in Bertais, along Jl Selaparang and Jl Panca Usaha.

Perama (☎635928; www.peramatour.com; Jl Pejanggik 66) operates shuttle buses to popular destinations in Lombok and Bali.

SENGGIGI

☎0370

You can spend a lifetime searching for the perfect beach, and it would be hard to top those around Senggigi. Think: a series of sweeping bays with white-sand beaches, coconut palms, cliff and mountain backdrops, and blood-red sunset views of Bali's Gunung Agung. Of course, there's also a flourishing naughty karaoke industry geared to the midlife-crisis set.

Senggigi spans nearly 10km of coast. Hotels, shops, banks, ATMs and restaurants are clustered along a central strip starting 6km north of Ampenan.

Sights & Activities

Pura Batu Bolong TEMPLE
(admission by donation; ⏲dawn-dusk) Pura Batu Bolong is a small Balinese-Hindu temple set on a rocky volcanic outcrop that spills into the sea, 2km south of central Senggigi. The detailed pagodas are oriented towards Gunung Agung, Bali's holiest mountain. Wear a sash to explore the temple.

Snorkelling & Diving WATER SPORTS
There's decent snorkelling off the rocky point that bisects Senggigi's sheltered bay in front of Windy Cottages; many hotels and restaurants in central Senggigi hire out mask-snorkel-fin sets for 25,000Rp per day. Diving trips from Senggigi normally visit the Gili Islands, so consider basing yourself there. Professional dive centres:

Blue Marlin (☎08123 756012; www.bluemarlindive.com; Jl Raya Senggigi)

Dream Divers (☎692047; www.dreamdivers.com; Jl Raya Senggigi)

Blue Coral Diving (☎693441; www.bluecoraldive.com; Jl Raya Senggigi)

Sleeping

Bale Kampung HOSTEL, GUESTHOUSE $
(☎6194288; Jl Raya Senggigi; s/d 125,000/150,000Rp; ❄📶) Set 300m south of Pura Batu Bolong, this thatched brick compound is rather cramped, but the new rooms sparkle with clean tile, the bamboo beds are nice, and the dorm is the cheapest sleep in town. It's a kilometre from the main drag along the same street.

Puri Senggigi Hotel HOTEL $
(☎692192; Jl Raya Senggigi Km 12; r with fan/air-con 100,000/185,000Rp; ❄📶) There are good deals to be snatched at this old standby next to Batu Bolong. Rooms on the 3rd floor have sea views.

Senggigi

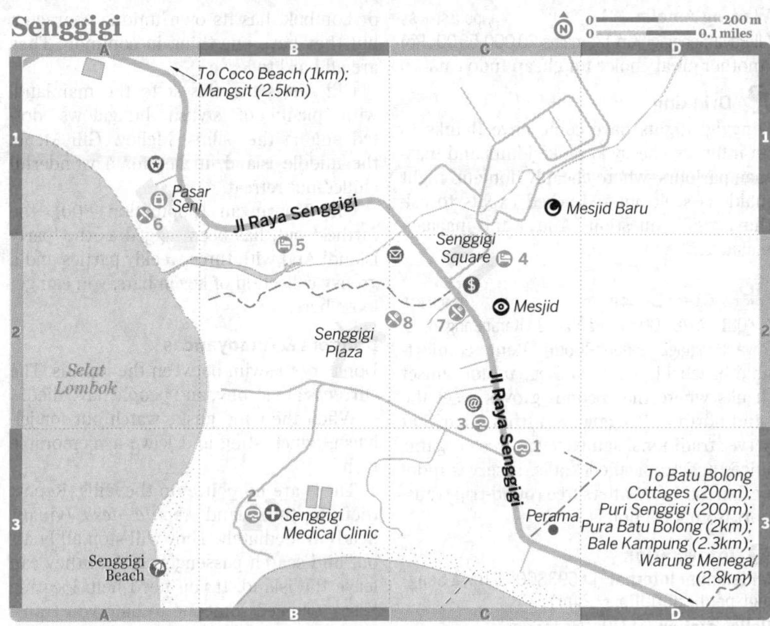

Senggigi

Activities, Courses & Tours

Sleeping

Eating

Batu Bolong Cottages COTTAGES $$
(☎693065; Jl Raya Senggigi; r from 300,000Rp; ❄) Bamboo is the operative term at this charming bungalow-style hotel set on both sides of the road south of the centre. Beachfront rooms open onto a manicured lawn that fades into white sand.

Hotel Elen HOTEL $
(☎693077; Jl Raya Senggigi; r 100,000Rp; ❄) Elen has long been a backpacker mainstay. Rooms are basic, but those facing the koi pond come with spacious tiled patios.

Sonya Homestay HOMESTAY $
(☎0813 3989 9878; Jl Raya Senggigi 54; d from 50,000Rp) A family-run enclave of six cramped rooms with patios. The real reason to stay is to eat Ibu Maria's cooking.

Eating

For authentic street food, head to the hillside *warung* on the route north to Mangsit where *sate* sizzles, pots of noodles bubble and corn roasts at dusk.

TOP CHOICE **Warung Menega** SEAFOOD $$
(Jl Raya Senggigi 6; meals 75,000-250,000Rp) If you fled Bali before experiencing the spectacular Jimbaran fish grills, you can make up for it at this sister restaurant to one of Jimbaran's finest, where fresh daily catch are grilled over smouldering coconut husks.

Coco Loco SEAFOOD $$
(☎693396; Pasar Seni, Jl Raya Senggigi; mains 25,000-60,000Rp) The best and cheapest of the Pasar Seni feed stations. Succulent seafood dishes are served with sweet bay views.

Warung Kangen INDONESIAN $
(☎6194109; Senggigi Plaza; mains 10,000-25,000Rp) This stylish *warung* has good Sasak grub and a tasty *soto ayam* (chicken soup) too. It's tucked among the karaoke cafes.

Warung Amelia INDONESIAN $$
(Jl Raya Senggigi Km 12; mains 20,000-55,000Rp) Another great choice for cheap Indo eats.

Drinking

Senggigi nights have come alive thanks to an influx of cheesy karaoke joints and massage parlours, where cheaply done-up night maidens seek out red-nosed expats to ask the age-old question, 'You want maaaaassaaaage?'

TOP CHOICE **Coco Beach** BEACH BAR
(081 7578 0055; Pantai 2 Kerandangan, Jl Raya Senggigi; noon-10pm) Rent comfortable beachside bamboo *berugas* for sunset drinks where the coconut groves meet the sand north of Senggigi. Sip from a bar that serves traditional Jamu tonics, fresh organic juices and tropical cocktails. It serves Indonesian food, and offers free round-trip transport from local hotels.

Information

Millennium Internet (693860; Jl Raya Senggigi; per hr 8000Rp; 24hr)
Police station (110) Pasar Seni.
Senggigi Medical Clinic (673210) Based at the Senggigi Beach Hotel.

Getting There & Around

Regular bemo travel between Senggigi and Ampenan's Kebon Roek terminal (3000Rp, 20 minutes, 10km).

Headed to the Gilis? Organise a group of up to six people and charter a bemo to Bangsal harbour (100,000Rp, one hour).

Perama (693007; www.peramatour.com; Jl Raya Senggigi) operates daily boat services from Padangbai (p251), in Bali, to Senggigi (ferry/fast boat 100,000/400,000Rp), and from Senggigi to the Gili Islands (200,000Rp, 60 to 90 minutes), which enables you to avoid Bangsal.

Scooters rent for 50,000Rp per day plus petrol. Motorcycles go for 90,000Rp.

GILI ISLANDS

0370

For decades, travellers have made the hop from Bali for a dip in the turquoise-tinted, bathtub-warm waters of the irresistible Gili Islands and stayed longer than anticipated. Perhaps it's the deepwater coral reefs teeming with sharks, rays and reasonably friendly turtles? Maybe it's the serenity that comes with no motorised traffic? Or it could be the beachfront bungalows, white sand and friendly locals. Each of these pearls, located just off the northwestern tip of Lombok, has its own unique character, but they have one thing in common. They are all hard to leave.

Gili Air is the closest to the mainland, with plenty of stylish bungalows dotted among the palms. Mellow Gili Meno, the middle island, makes for a wonderful chilled-out retreat.

Gili Trawangan (population 800), the furthest out, has been tagged as the 'party island'. And with three weekly parties and a groovy collection of beach bars, you can get loose here.

Dangers & Annoyances

Don't try to swim between the islands. The currents are strong, and people have died.

When the wind gusts, watch out for jellyfish, which sting and leave a memorable rash.

There are no police on the Gilis. Report theft to the island *kepala desa* (village head) immediately. They will stop all boats out and search passengers before they can leave the island. If you need help locating them, or need someone to help you translate, the dive schools are a good point of contact. If you are on Gili Trawangan, notify Satgas, the community organisation that runs island affairs. Satgas uses its community contacts to resolve problems or track down stolen property with a minimum of fuss.

Incidents are very rare, but some foreign women have experienced sexual harassment and even assault while on the Gilis – it's best to walk home in pairs to the dark corners of the islands.

Activities

Diving is the best reason to get wet. Marine life is plentiful and varied. Turtles and black- and white-tip reef sharks are common, and the macro life (small stuff) is excellent, with seahorses, pipefish and lots of crustaceans. Around full moon, large schools of bumphead parrot fish appear to feast on coral spawns, while at other times of year, mantas soar.

Safety standards are generally high in the Gilis despite the modest dive costs. Rates are fixed (no matter who you dive with) at 370,000Rp a dive, with discounts for packages of five dives or more. A PADI open-water course costs 3,400,000Rp, the advanced course is 2,700,000Rp. Divemaster starts at 7,350,000Rp.

Snorkelling is fun and the fish are plentiful on all the beach reefs. Gear can be hired for 25,000Rp to 30,000Rp per day.

Walking and cycling are the best land activities. Bikes can be hired for 30,000Rp per day. On Trawangan, time your circumnavigation (2½ hours on foot) with the sunset, and watch it from the hill on the southwest corner where you'll have a tremendous view of Bali's Gunung Agung.

Blue Marlin Dive Centre DIVING
(Maps p226, p223 & p228; ☎632424; www.bluemarlindive.com) On Gili Air, Gili Meno and Gili T.

Dream Divers DIVING
(Map p226, Map p223; ☎634547; www.dreamdivers.com) Gili Air and Gili T.

Manta Dive DIVING
(Map p226, Map p223; ☎643649; www.manta-dive.com, www.manta-dive-giliair.com) Gili Air and Gili T.

Trawangan Dive DIVING
(Map p226; ☎649220; www.trawangandive.com) Gili T.

Big Bubble DIVING
(Map p226; ☎625020; www.bigbubblediving.com) Gili T.

Gili Air

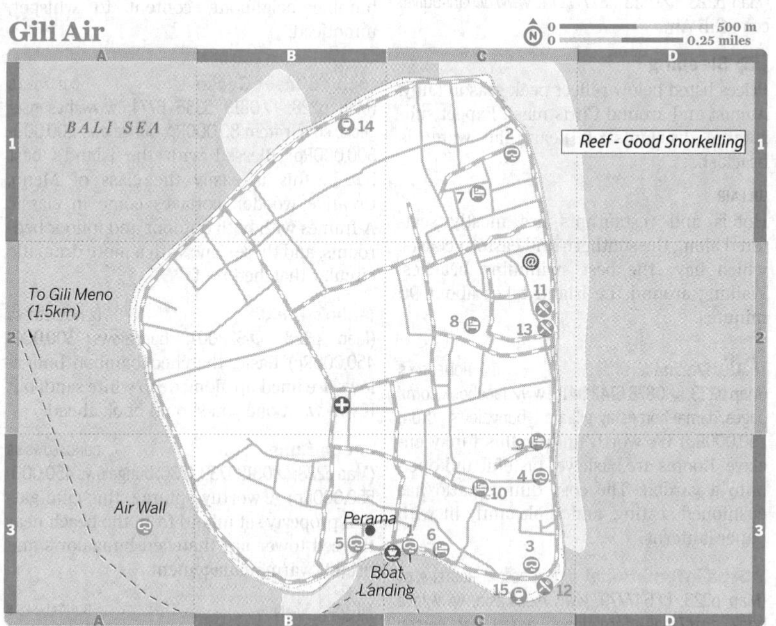

Gili Air

Activities, Courses & Tours
1 7 Seas International C3
2 Blue Marlin Dive Centre C1
3 Dream Divers C3
4 Manta Dive C3
5 Oceans 5 .... B3

Sleeping
6 7 Seas International Hostel C3
7 Damai C1
8 Gili Air Santay C2
9 Gita Gili C3
10 Nina Cottages C3

Eating
11 Biba Beach Cafe C2
Paradiso 2 .... (see 12)
12 Scallywags C3
13 Warung Sasak C2

Drinking
14 Mirage B1
15 Zipp Bar C3

Freedive Gili DIVING, YOGA
(Map p226; ☎640503; www.freedivegili.com, www.giliyoga.com) The Gili's only free-diving centre. It also offers strenuous but stress-relieving yoga classes (per class 90,000Rp) in its sweet studio.

Gili Divers DIVING
(Map p226; ☎0813 7246 8234; www.gilidivers.com) Gili T.

7 Seas International DIVING
(Map p223; ☎647779; www.7seas.asia, www.facebook.com/7seas.international) Gili Air.

Oceans 5 DIVING
(Map p223; ☎0813 3877 7144; www.oceans5dive.com) Gili Air.

Sleeping

Prices listed below reflect peak season (July, August and around Christmas). Expect substantial discounts off peak. Tap water is brackish.

GILI AIR

Hotels and restaurants are mostly scattered along the southern and eastern coasts, which have the best swimming beaches. Walking around the island takes about 90 minutes.

TOP CHOICE **Damai** HOMESTAY $
(Map p223; ☎0878 6142 0416; www.facebook.com/pages/damai-homestay-gili-air; bungalows from 250,000Rp) It's worth finding this funky enclave. Rooms are basic yet tasteful and open onto a garden. The cosy dining patio has cushioned seating, and is elegantly lit with paper lanterns.

7 Seas International DIVE RESORT, HOSTEL $, $$
(Map p223; ☎647779; www.7seas.asia, www.facebook.com/7seas.international; hostel per person 70,000Rp, bungalows from 500,000Rp; ❄📶) The plush Lumbung-style cottages are nice, but that bamboo barn behind them is the hostel, where you can score the Gilis' cheapest sleep. Hostel rooms come with just two beds, and the communal bathroom is huge and sparkling.

Gili Air Santay BUNGALOWS $$
(Map p223; ☎0818 0375 8695; www.giliair-santay.com; bungalows 350,000Rp) Set back from the beach in a quiet coconut grove, these spacious bamboo-and-timber huts are a good choice and conveniently sleep up to three people.

Gita Gili BUNGALOWS $
(Map p223; ☎0878 6452 2124; bungalows with fan/air-con 250,000/400,000Rp) A chilled-out bungalow property just off the harbour. The concrete and bamboo bungalows are fan-cooled, clean and decent value.

Nina Cottages BUNGALOWS $$
(Map p223; bungalows from 200,000Rp) Cute bungalows tucked away inland from the harbour. All are reasonably clean, and set in a blooming garden.

GILI MENO

While Trawangan continues to boom and Air develops a buzz, Meno remains the humble neighbour, content to whisper, unnoticed.

TOP CHOICE **Sunset Gecko** COTTAGES $
(Map p228; ☎0813 5356 6774; www.thesunsetgecko.com; r from 80,000Rp, bungalows 200,000-500,000Rp) Blessed with the island's best beach, this is easily the class of Meno. Creative wooden cottages come in classic A-frames with both outdoor and indoor bedrooms, and there's one with a more dramatic circular thatched roof.

Malia's Child BUNGALOWS $$
(Map p228; ☎622007; bungalows 300,000-450,000Rp) Basic, thatched bamboo bungalows are lined up along deep white sand, but if you want one you should book ahead.

Jepun Bungalows BUNGALOWS $$
(Map p228; ☎0819 1739 4736; bungalows 450,000-550,000Rp) A worthy splurge, this cute garden property set inland from the beach near the cell tower has thatched bungalows and bright, warm management.

Mimpi Manis BUNGALOWS $
(Map p228; ☎642324; s/d 100,000/200,000Rp) Basic bamboo bungalows set back from the beach with more cottages on the way.

GILI TRAWANGAN

Social but not trashy, relaxed but not boring, all natural, yet wired, and sprinkled with great restaurants and bars that would satisfy any devout cosmopolitan, Gili T is the road-weary backpacker's fantasy incarnate. Cheap sleeps are inland. Book ahead whenever possible.

Tanah Qita BUNGALOWS $$
(Map p226; ☎639159; bungalows 250,000-500,000Rp; ❄) One of our favourite places on the island. Bungalows have high arched

ceilings and private patios. Those funkified, fan-cooled bamboo nests are a steal.

Paradise Bungalows BUNGALOWS $
(Map p226; ☎0812 3779 3533; s/d 200,000/250,000Rp) A terrific new compound of five wooden cottages with stylish outdoor bathrooms. Service is superb.

Black Sand Homestay HOMESTAY $
(Map p226; ☎081 2372 0353; r from 150,000Rp) One- and two-storey wooden bungalows nestled in a sweet garden with views of the hill. Two-storey jobs come with TV and an outdoor bathroom.

Beach Café and Bungalows 2 BUNGALOWS $
(Map p226; ☎0819 1728 2578; bungalows 250,000-300,000Rp) Four thatched wooden bungalows with outdoor bathrooms and a lovely stretch of beach out front.

Gili Ran-Ta BUNGALOWS $
(Map p226; ☎0819 1797 8090; r from 300,000Rp) Three stylish Lumbung bungalows mere steps from the sand; owned and operated by a lovely young mother.

Gerald Homestay HOMESTAY $
(Map p226; ☎0878 6425 6988; r 125,000Rp) These four simple but spotless tiled rooms, just 150m from the art market, are among the best value in the Gilis. Look for the hand-scrawled signage.

Pondok Gili Gecko GUESTHOUSE $
(Map p226; ☎0818 0573 2814; r 250,000-300,000Rp) An inviting new guesthouse with a charming gecko motif. Rooms are super clean, and have ceiling fans and private tiled patios overlooking the garden.

Lumbung Cottages 2 BUNGALOWS $
(Map p226; ☎0878 6503 1795; www.lumbungcottage.com; s/d 250,000/300,000Rp; ❄) New Lumbung-style cottages, set deep in the village, tucked up against the hillside.

Koi Gili HOMESTAY $
(Map p226; ☎0819 599 5760; s/d 200,000/250,000Rp) The young and hip gravitate to this groovy new guesthouse with a daybed in the garden and a mod colour scheme on the facade.

Trawangan Dive HOSTEL $
(Map p226; ☎649220; www.trawangadive.com; per person 100,000-150,000Rp) Gili T's only hostel, it has 11 dorm rooms, each with two beds, and 11 more on the way.

Midnight Star Cottage HOMESTAY $
(Map p226; ☎0819 1645 4123; r from 160,000Rp) New and clean, steps from the harbour, and a laid-back vibe.

Pondok Wahyu GUESTHOUSE $
(Map p226; ☎0819 1794 4039; r 150,000Rp) Really good value, fan-cooled budget rooms set around a charming garden.

Eating

GILI AIR

TOP CHOICE **Scallywags** INTERNATIONAL $$
(Map p223; www.scallywagsresort.com; mains 46,000-95,000Rp; 📶) Set on Gili Air's softest and widest beach, and more a groovy hippie-chic beach club than a mere restaurant, you can make any number of excuses to spend the day here. Chief among them is the tuna sashimi drizzled with olive oil and sprinkled with rock salt.

Biba Beach Cafe ITALIAN $$
(Map p223; www.bibabeach.com; mains 40,000-70,000Rp; ⊙dinner) A beachside trattoria that serves excellent homemade pasta (think: gnocchi with mussels and clams or tagliatelle arrabiata) and wood-fired pizza.

Paradiso 2 INDONESIAN $
(Map p223; mains 25,000-60,000Rp) Next door to Scallywags, on that same fabulous stretch of sand, it has beachside bamboo lounges and Indonesian food all day.

Warung Sasak INDONESIAN $
(Map p223; mains 25,000-35,000Rp) A local *warung* with thatched dining *berugas* set on an exquisite turquoise shore. It specialises in Sasak dishes.

GILI MENO

Rust Warung INDONESIAN $$
(Map p228; mains 8000-75,000Rp; ⊙7am-10am, 11am-3.30pm & 6pm-late) This restaurant has beachfront *berugas* and a terrific assortment of fresh daily catch.

GILI TRAWANGAN

TOP CHOICE **Kikinovi** INDONESIAN $
(Map p226; mains 15,000-25,000Rp) Set in the art market, Kikinovi is beloved for its tasty home cooking, which yields one hell of a pick-and-mix *nasi campur*. Dishes usually come out fresh at 11:30am, just before the dive-master lunch rush.

Pasar Malam NIGHT MARKET $
(Map p226; mains 12,000-25,000Rp; ⊙6pm-midnight) Blooming nightly in front of the art

Gili Trawangan

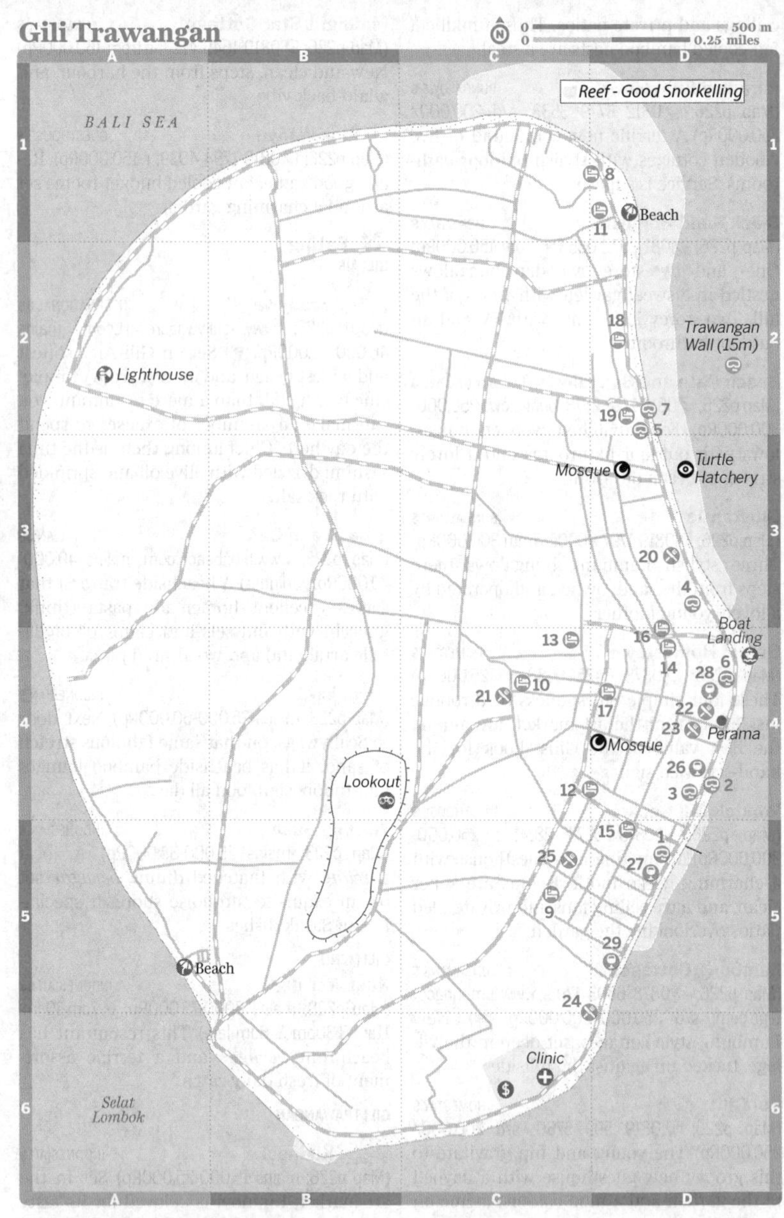

market, this market is the place to indulge in ample local eats, including tangy noodle soup, savoury *mie goreng* (fried noodles), scrumptious *ayam goreng* (fried chicken) and grilled fresh catch.

Cafe Gili INTERNATIONAL **$$**

(Map p226; www.facebook.com/cafegilitrawangan; mains 32,000-75,000Rp;) Simple, elegant and nourishing, Gili T's most endearing new kitchen spills from a shabby-chic whitewashed dining room and rambles across the street to

Gili Trawangan

Activities, Courses & Tours

1 Big Bubble D5
2 Blue Marlin Dive Centre D4
3 Dream Divers D4
4 Freedive Gili D3
5 Gili Divers D2
6 Manta Dive D4
7 Trawangan Dive D2

Sleeping

8 Beach Café & Bungalows 2 ..... D1
9 Black Sand Homestay C5
10 Gerald Homestay C4
11 Gili Ran-Ta D1
12 Koi Gili C4
13 Lumbung Cottages 2 ..... C4
14 Midnight Star Cottage D4
15 Paradise Bungalows D5
16 Pondok Gili Gecko D4
17 Pondok Wahyu D4
18 Tanah Qita D2
19 Trawangan Dive D2

Eating

20 Cafe Gili D3
Extrablatt ..... (see 20)
21 Ibu Gado Gado C4
22 Kikinovi D4
23 Pasar Malam D4
24 Scallywags C5
25 Warung Indonesia C5

Drinking

26 Blue Marlin D4
27 Rudy's Pub D5
28 Sama Sama D4
29 Tir na Nog D5

the shore. Think cushioned seating, candlelight, and maybe a bit too much Jack Johnson (an island-wide sin, we assure you). The menu meanders from eggs Florentine and breakfast baguettes to deli sandwiches and salads, to terrific pasta and seafood dishes.

Scallywags INTERNATIONAL **$$**
(Map p226; mains from 45,000; wi-fi) Its open, shabby-chic decor and plush patio seating help make this spot a major draw at all hours. It has tender steaks, a daily selection of fresh fish and Aussie pies, and an organic ethos.

Extrablatt GERMAN, INDONESIAN **$$**
(Map p226; mains 27,000-75,000Rp; wi-fi) This place has garnered recent buzz, less for its love of all things sausage and more for its epic fish grill and lovely beachside setting under trees dangling with lanterns. The red snapper on display when we rolled through was downright biblical.

Warung Indonesia INDONESIAN **$**
(Map p226; mains 15,000-20,000Rp; 8am-9pm; wi-fi) A new *warung* with a tasty pick-and-mix bar, and a menu of Indo staples like oxtail soup, *soto ayam* (chicken soup) and *ikan goreng* (fried fish). Its lofted thatched dining room is lit with vintage lanterns, and is wired.

Ibu Gado Gado INDONESIAN **$**
(Map p226; gado gado 7000Rp; 8am-4pm; vegetarian) Veggie budgeteers, rejoice! On the corner, beside Gerald Homestay, Ibu Ella turns out fresh and tasty *gado gado* that is nourishing and filling. She'll adjust the fiery sambal to taste.

Drinking

Official party nights on Gili Trawangan are Monday, Wednesday and Friday – although given the amount of contraband on offer, and the scattering of stylish bars to investigate, each and every night can be a party.

GILI AIR

TOP CHOICE **Mirage** BAR
(Map p223; drinks 40,000-55,000Rp) A terrific beach bar on Air's rustic west coast. It's on a sublime stretch of beach with technicolor sunsets. It hosts live bands on Friday nights.

Zipp Bar BEACH BAR
(Map p223) This teak bar, set on a sandy beach perfect for swimming, has bamboo beach lounges, an excellent booze selection and decent pub grub. It throws full-moon beach parties.

GILI MENO

Diana Café BEACH BAR
(Map p228) A hippie bar deluxe, and your ice-cold-Bintang stop at sunset. The stilted *berugas* have cushions, coffee tables and ideal sunset views. There's great snorkelling nearby.

GILI TRAWANGAN

Tir na Nog PUB
(Map p226; www.tirnanogbar.com; to 4am Wed) Known simply and affectionately as 'The

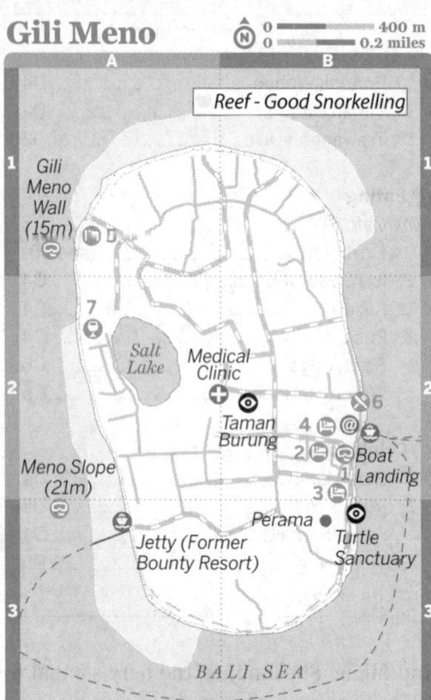

Gili Meno

Activities, Courses & Tours

1 Blue Marlin Dive Centre B2

Sleeping

2 Jepun Bungalows B2
3 Malia's Child B2
4 Mimpi Manis B2
5 Sunset Gecko A1

Eating

6 Rust Warung B2

Drinking

7 Diana Café A2

Irish', it has a barnlike, sports-bar interior and a brilliant outdoor bar with a live DJ that draws the biggest crowds in town. Wednesday is its party night.

Rudy's Pub BAR

(Map p226; ⏲to 4am Fri) Rudy's has as much to do with Gili T's party-hard reputation as all the other bars combined – mostly due to its weekly debaucherous Friday-night throw downs and a preponderance of drinks and dishes involving a certain fungus.

Sama Sama BAR

(Map p226) Locally owned and easily the best reggae bar in Indonesia. It has a top-end sound system, a killer live band at least six nights a week and great barmen who mix tasty mojitos. It throws a full-moon party too.

Blue Marlin BAR

(Map p226; ⏲to 3am Mon) Of all the party bars, this upper-level venue has the largest dance floor and the meanest sound system – which pumps out trance and tribal sounds on Monday.

Information

All islands have internet cafes and wired restaurants and hotels. Trawangan offers the best connection.

There are a few ATMs on Trawangan. Although Air and Meno have shops and hotels that change money and arrange cash advances, the rates are appalling. Bring rupiah instead.

Getting There & Away

PRIVATE BOATS The fast-boat industry has exploded in the last 18 months. More companies than ever buzz guests from Bali and mainland Lombok direct to the Gilis. The good part: there are always seats available, even last minute in the high season, when some companies offer two and even three crossings per day. Less good: safety standards on some boats are problematic, and boats have sunk. See p309 for details on choosing a safe operator.

Our advice is to stick with the old standards that charge a bit more, but know what they're doing.

Gili Cat (☎0361-271680; www.gilicat.com) Leaves from Padangbai (550,000Rp; 2½ hours) at 9am daily.

Blue Water Express (☎0361-3104558; www.bwsbali.com) Leaves from Benoa harbour (590,000Rp; 2½ hours).

Scoot (☎0361-285522; www.scootcruise.com) The one stand-out newcomer. Leaves from Sanur (600,000-650,000Rp; three hours) and travels to Gili Trawangan via Bali's Nusa Lembongan. Book your seats on www.gilibookings.com.

Perama buses and its (painfully) slow boat head to the Gilis via Padangbai (see p218) and Senggigi (200,000Rp).

PUBLIC BOATS Coming from other parts of Lombok, you can travel via Senggigi, or via the public boats that leave from Bangsal harbour (the cheapest route), or charter your own boat from Bangsal (235,000Rp).

Coming by public transport via Mataram, catch a bus or bemo to Pemenang, from which it's 1km by *cidomo* (horse-drawn cart; 3000Rp) to Bangsal harbour. Boat tickets at Bangsal harbour are sold at the Koperasi harbour office on the beach.

Buy a ticket elsewhere and you're getting played. Public boats run from roughly 8am to 5pm, but don't leave until full (about 20 people). The one-way fares at the time of research were 8000Rp to Gili Air, 9000Rp to Gili Meno and 10,000Rp to Gili Trawangan. The first boat of the day returning from Gili Trawangan offers a shuttle service to Senggigi (75,000Rp).

Boats pull up on the beach when they get to Gili Air and Gili Meno. Prepare to wade ashore.

Getting Around

The Gilis are flat and easy enough to get around by foot or bicycle. A torch (flashlight) is useful at night. Hiring a *cidomo* for a clip-clop around an island is a great way to explore; a short trip costs between 35,000Rp and 50,000Rp.

There's a twice-daily island-hopping boat service that loops between all three islands (20,000Rp to 23,000Rp). Check the latest timetable at each island's dock. You can also charter your own island-hopping boat (220,000Rp to 250,000Rp).

GUNUNG RINJANI

Lombok's highest peak, and the second-highest volcano in Indonesia (3726m), supports a smattering of villages, and is of great climatic importance to Lombok. The Balinese call Gunung Rinjani 'the seat of the Gods' and place it alongside Gunung Agung in spiritual lore. Lombok's Sasaks also revere it, and make biannual pilgrimages to honour the mountain spirit. It sure is one hell of a climb. Reach the summit and look down upon a 6km-wide caldera with a crescent-shaped cobalt lake, hot springs and smaller volcanic cones. The stunning sunrise view from the rim takes in north Lombok, Bali's Gunung Agung and the Indian Ocean, drenched in an unforgettable pink hue.

SENARU

POP 1330

With sweeping views and an eternal spring climate, the mountain villages of Senaru and nearby **Batu Koq** are the best bases for Rinjani climbs. Be sure to make the 30-minute walk to the spectacular **Air Terjun Sendang Gila waterfalls** (admission 2000Rp; dawn-dusk), and visit the traditional village, **Dusun Senaru** (admission by donation).

Many *losmen* along the main road have basic rooms with breakfast. **Bukit Senaru Cottages** (r 100,000Rp), shortly before Dusun Senaru, has four decent semidetached bungalows nestled in a sweet flower garden.

Pondok Senaru & Restaurant (081 0363 0668; r from 200,000Rp) is a class act, with lovely little terracotta-tiled cottages, and comfortable suites. Or just grab a table (dishes 20,000Rp to 35,000Rp), and eat perched on the edge of a rice-terraced valley.

From Mandalika terminal in Mataram catch a bus to Anyar (20,000Rp, 2½ hours).

TREKKING GUNUNG RINJANI

Agencies in Mataram and Senggigi arrange all-inclusive treks, but you can make your own, cheaper, arrangements. Seek out the **Rinjani Trek Centre** (RTC; 086 8121 04132; www.info2lombok.com) in Senaru. It has great maps, and rotates local guides and porters for trekking tours. June to August is the best trekking season. During the wet season (November to April), tracks can be slippery and dangerous.

The most common trek is to climb from Senaru to Pos III (2300m) on the first day (about five hours of steep walking), camp there and climb to Pelawangan I, on the crater rim (2600m), for sunrise the next morning (about two hours). From the rim, descend into the crater and walk around to the **hot springs** (two hours) on a very exposed track. The hot springs, revered by locals for their healing properties, are a good place to relax and camp for the second night.

Or continue east from the hot springs, and camp at Pelawangan II (about 2900m). From there a track branches off to the summit. It's a heroic climb (three or four hours) over loose footing to the top (3726m). Start at 3am so that you can glimpse the sunrise on the summit.

The most popular package is the three-day, two-night trek from Senaru to Sembalun Lawang via the summit. It includes food, equipment, guide, porters, park fee and transport back to Senaru. This costs about 1,750,000Rp per person.

Bring several layers of clothing, solid footwear, rain gear, extra water (do not depend on your guide for your water supply, or you may suffer) and a torch (flashlight). Buy food and supplies in Mataram or Senggigi. People die every year on the mountain; it shouldn't be approached lightly.

Bemo leave Anyar for Senaru (7000Rp) every 20 minutes until 4.30pm.

KUTA

0370

They may share a name, but Lombok's Kuta is languid and stunningly gorgeous, with white-sand beaches, rugged hills and world-class surf. And now that the long-planned Dubai-sponsored development deal has fallen apart, the only real action Kuta sees is during the August high season, around the *nyale* (sea worm) fishing festival in February or March, and in all those illegal gold mines grinding away in plain sight.

Kuta Bay has a wide golden beach with stunning headlands on both ends, and exposed turquoise shallows at low tide. Rollers crash on a reef 300m from shore. Seek out **Tanjung Aan**, an empty horseshoe bay with looming headlands. **Pantai Seeger** is likewise gorgeous.

Activities

For surfing, stellar lefts and rights break on the reefs off Kuta Bay and east of Tanjung Aan. Boatmen will take you out for around 70,000Rp. Seven kilometres east of Kuta is the fishing village of **Gerupak**, where there's a series of reef breaks, both close to the shore and further out, but they require a boat, at a negotiable 200,000Rp per day. Wise surfers buzz past Gerupak, take the road to Awang, and hire a boat (300,000Rp for up to six people) to **Ekas**, where crowds are thin and 6ft faces plentiful.

West of Kuta you'll find **Mawan**, a stunning swimming beach (the first left after Astari), and **Mawi**, a popular surf paradise with world-class swells and a strong riptide.

Kimen Surf SURFING

(655064; www.kuta-lombok.net) Drop in to Kimen Surf, just west of the junction, for swell forecasts, tips and information. Boards can be rented here (50,000Rp per day).

Kuta Reef Surf Shop SURFING

(087864 741986; Jl Pantai Kuta; 7am-10pm) Set among the beach *warung*, it rents boards (50,000Rp) and offers lessons (250,000Rp) that include all-day motorbike and board rental.

Sleeping & Eating

Accommodation is on or within walking distance of the beach. The law of Kuta grub: keep it simple, and keep it local.

TOP CHOICE **Hey Hey Homestay** HOMESTAY $

(081805 228822; r 100,000Rp) An outstanding new homestay, with clean, spacious rooms and sea views from private patios. Try to score the bamboo room on the top floor – the view is amazing. Take the dirt road south from the intersection.

Kuta Baru Homestay HOMESTAY $

(08185 48357; Jl Pariswata Kuta; r 125,000Rp; wi-fi) One of Kuta's two best homestays. It has a cute patio strung with the obligatory hammock, daily coffee breaks, free wi-fi, sparkling tiles and an all-around good vibe. Located 110m east of the intersection.

Together Homestay HOMESTAY $

(087864 023551; Jl Pariswata Kuta; r 100,000Rp) Great spot with clean tile rooms in a family's garden compound. The owner can organise motorbike rental and transport. It's 100m east of the intersection.

TOP CHOICE **Lombok Lounge** CHILI CRAB $$

(chilli crab per kg 150,000Rp) You're here for the scintillating, finger-licking chilli crab, a Chinese-Indonesian classic. Wash it down with icy Bintang. One kilogram feeds two to three people. Located 80m east of the intersection.

Astari ORGANIC, INTERNATIONAL $

(Jl ke Mawan; dishes 18,000-38,000Rp; 8am-6pm Tue-Sun) Australian-owned Astari (3km west of town) has a jaw-dropping setting: high above town with stunning vistas of the ocean rollers and a succession of beaches and bays. The menu raids Italy, the Middle East, India and Indonesia with samosas, focaccias and stupendous desserts.

Coffee House GREEK $

(mains 25,000-47,000Rp; wi-fi) Because laws (see earlier) are made to be broken, and because this slick, Aussie-owned joint on the intersection is decorated with Indonesian antiques, and offers a tasty Greek menu (think: souvlaki, kebabs, tzatziki and hummus) at a reasonable price. It has espresso, too.

Warung Jawa 1 INDONESIAN $

(Jl ke Mawan; meals 10,000Rp) On the Mawan road about 50m east of the intersection, this little bamboo shack has a cheap and mean *nasi campur*. Munch and watch buffalo graze against an ocean backdrop. It's 120m east of the intersection

Drinking

Shore Beach Bar BAR $
(10am-late) If you're in town on a Saturday night, you'll probably wind up here on the breezy sea-front terrace or in the dance hall grooving to a live band. It's on the beach road.

Information

Dheril Cell (8am-9pm) has speedy internet access with a hot spot for laptop and smartphone addicts. It rents bicycles (per day 30,000Rp) too. Virtually everything in Kuta is on a single road that parallels the beach and intersects the road from Praya. There's a Mandiri ATM opposite the beach in the Tastura Beach Resort complex.

Getting There & Away

How many bemo does it take to get to Kuta? Three. Take one from Mataram's Mandalika terminal to Praya (5000Rp), another to Sengkol (3000Rp) and a third to Kuta (2000Rp).

Perama (654846; www.peramatour.com) runs tourist buses to Mataram (110,000Rp, two hours), with connections to Senggigi (120,000Rp), and the Gilis (180,000Rp).

If you're travelling with two or more and need a ride to the airport, consider hiring a driver (250,000Rp).

LABUHAN LOMBOK

You're here to catch a Sumbawa-bound ferry. Frequent buses and bemo travel between Labuhan Lombok and Mandalika terminal (14,000Rp, two hours) in Mataram. Boats run 24 hours. Some buses drop you at the port entrance road. If they do, catch another bemo to the ferry terminal. It's too far to walk.

Sumbawa

Beautifully contorted and sprawling, Sumbawa is all volcanic ridges, terraced rice fields, jungled peninsulas and sheltered bays. The southeast coast is the most accessible playground, which explains why Lakey Peak has become a year-round surf magnet.

Though well connected to Bali and Lombok, Sumbawa is a very different sort of place. It's far less developed, much poorer and extremely conservative. Transport connections off the cross-island road are infrequent and uncomfortable, and most overland travellers don't even get off the bus as they roll from Lombok to Flores. For now, it's the domain of surfers, miners and mullahs.

Getting There & Away

AIR Bima is the main hub, with direct flights to Denpasar (five times per week). You can also connect to Mataram and Maumere. There are a few weekly flights between Mataram and Sumbawa Besar.

BOAT Ferries run every 45 minutes, 24 hours a day, between Labuhan Lombok and Poto Tano (22,000Rp, 1½ hours). In the east, Sape is the departure point for daily ferries to Labuanbajo, Flores. Pelni ships dock at Bima.

BUS Night buses run in a convoy from Mataram via the ferry to Bima, where they hook up with smaller shuttles to the Flores ferry at Sape.

POTO TANO & AROUND

Poto Tano is the Lombok-bound ferry port, but there's no reason to linger. Most travellers pass straight through to Sumbawa Besar. You can also venture south of Taliwang to the superb surf at **Maluk**, a contemporary boomtown thanks to a nearby copper mine. **Santai Bungalows** (087863 935758; Rantung; s/d 80,000Rp/100,000Rp) attracts surfers to its basic rooms. Fifteen kilometres further south is another gorgeous surf beach, **Sengkongkang**.

Ferries run regularly to/from Lombok. The through buses from Mataram to Bima include the ferry fare, but you'll move faster if you stay indie, and hop on one of the buses that meet the Poto Tano ferry and go to Taliwang (15,000Rp, one hour) and Sumbawa Besar (30,000Rp, three hours). Bemo link Taliwang to Maluk (20,000Rp; 30 minutes)

There is also a twice-daily **ferry** (100,000Rp, Mon-Sat) between Benete Harbour near Maluk and Labuhan Lombok, which is ideal for the surf set.

SUMBAWA BESAR

0371 / POP 57,000

Sumbawa Besar, nestled in a lush, sunkissed breadbasket, is the main town on the western half of the island. Horse carts outnumber bemo here.

Sleeping & Eating

Hotels congregate on Jl Hasanuddin. The nearby mosque provides free wake-up calls.

TOP CHOICE **Hotel Suci** HOTEL $
(21589; Jl Hasanuddin 57; d with fan 100,000Rp, with air-con 150,000-200,000Rp;) Located right next to the mosque, this is the top of the local lodging heap. Economy rooms are not to be trusted, but the air-con rooms in the new building are large and airy with high ceilings.

Warung Kita 2 INDONESIAN $
(☎23065; Jl Setia Budi 13; dishes 9000-17,000Rp) A bright, delicious pick-and-mix diner with trays of broiled chicken, tasty fried prawns and curried green beans.

Information

At research time there were no longer any internet cafes in the town centre, though a few were sprinkled along the highway near the bus terminal. Many businesses close around midday on weekends. Restaurants and some shops re-open at night.

BNI bank (Bank Negara Indonesia; Jl Kartini 10; ⌚8am-2.30pm Mon-Fri, 8am-noon Sat) Currency exchange and an ATM.

Sub-post office (Jl Yos Sudarso)

Telkom office (Jl Yos Sudarso; ⌚24hr)

Getting There & Away

Transnusa/Aviastar (☎21565; Jl Hasanuddin 110) is the only active carrier, with regular flights from Bima to Denpasar via Mataram.

The long-distance bus station is Terminal Sumur Payung, 5.5km northwest of town on the highway, where seven bus lines run air-con coaches to Bima (80,000Rp, six hours via Dompu). Routes also include Poto Tano (30,000Rp, three hours, hourly from 8am to midnight) and Mataram (100,000Rp, six hours).

HU'U & LAKEY BEACH

Lakey Beach, a gentle crescent of golden sand 3km south of Hu'u, is where Sumbawa's tourist pulse beats year-round, thanks to seven world-class surf breaks that curl and crash in one massive bay.

There are several decent budget places to stay, and one midrange spot. **Puma Bungalow** (r with fan 70,000-110,000Rp, with air-con 110,000-160,000Rp; ❄) has colourful concrete bungalows with tiled roofs, shady front porches, and leafy grounds with fabulous views.

Lakey Beach Inn (mains 25,000-40,000Rp) has the beach's best kitchen. Dine on tasty home-style fish dinners, roast chicken, burritos and pizza as you screen your own daily surf exploits shot by shore-side cinematographers.

Aman Gati and Blue Lagoon both offer **internet service** (per 10 min 5000Rp; ⌚8am-noon, 1-5pm & 6-10pm).

From Dompu take a bemo (2000Rp) to the Lepardi local terminal on the southern outskirts. There are two (slow) buses per day as far as Hu'u (25,000Rp, 1½ hours), where you can hire an *ojek* (20,000Rp) to Lakey Beach. Most visitors come here by chartered taxi from Bima airport (400,000Rp).

A round-trip *ojek* ride from Lakey to the breaks costs 50,000Rp.

BIMA & RABA

☎0374 / POP 273,000

These twin cities – grubby but lively Bima and orderly but dull Raba – form Sumbawa's main port and commercial hot spot, but there's no good reason to nest here.

Sleeping & Eating

Most hotels are in central Bima, near the market.

Hotel La'mbitu HOTEL $
(☎42222; Jl Sumbawa 4; r with fan/air-con 132,000/200,000Rp; ❄) Bima's best, with several clean, bright, airy rooms to choose from.

TOP CHOICE **Rumah Makan Sabar Subur** SEAFOOD $
(☎646236; Jl Salahudin, Bandara; meals 15,000Rp; ⌚7am-6pm) Just down the road and opposite the airport, these long wooden tables are always crowded with locals who come to grind *bandeng goreng*, a flash-fried freshwater fish.

Getting There & Away

Bima's airport is 17km out of town; 60,000Rp by taxi. At research time, **Merpati** (☎44221; www.merpati.co.id) flew daily to Denpasar and Mataram, **Transnusa/Aviatsar** (☎Kupang 0380-822 555; www.transnusa.co.id) flew daily to Denpasar, and **Lion/Wings Air** (☎Jakarta 021-6379 8000; www.lionair.co.id) flew to Denpasar four times weekly. Bima departures require a 21,000Rp airport tax.

Pelni (☎42625; www.pelni.co.id) sails twice monthly from Bima to Ende, Waingapu and Kupang and back to Benoa in Bali.

Buses to points west of Bima leave from the central bus station, south of town. Express night-bus agencies near the station sell tickets to Sumbawa Besar (80,000Rp, six hours) and Mataram (180,000Rp, 11 hours). Most buses heading west leave around 7pm.

Buses to Sape (9000Rp, two hours) depart from Kumbe in Raba, a 20-minute bemo ride (2000Rp) east of Bima, but they can't be relied upon to meet the early morning ferry to Flores. Charter a car (250,000Rp, 1½ hours) to Sape to make the 8am ferry.

SAPE

☎0374

The ferry to Labuanbajo, Flores, shoves off from tumbledown Pelabuhan Sape. The small port, perfumed with the conspicuous scent of drying cuttlefish, is 3km from town.

There's a **PHKA Komodo Information Office** (⌚8am-2pm Mon-Sat) 500m inland from the port, with a few brochures and maps.

Express buses with service to Lombok and Bali meet arriving ferries.

Buses leave every half-hour for Raba (9000Rp, two hours) until around 5pm.

Always double-check the latest ferry schedules in Bima or Sape. **Cabang Sape** (☎71075; Jl Yos Sudarso, Pelabuhan Penye Berangan Sape) operates the daily ferry to Labuanbajo (per person 46,000Rp, motorcycle 122,000Rp, eight to nine hours).

Komodo & Rinca

Parched, desolate, beautiful Komodo and Rinca rise from waters that churn with riptides and whirlpools, and are patrolled by lizard royalty, the komodo dragon.

Komodo National Park (www.komodonationalpark.org) encompasses both islands and several neighbouring isles. A three-day visitor permit issued on arrival by rangers includes your park entrance fee (20,000Rp) and the conservation fee (US$15 for adults). There's an additional fee (50,000Rp) for photographers.

A short, guided dragon-spotting trek is included with your entrance fee. For a longer, hour-long trek on Rinca you'll pay an additional 50,000Rp. On Komodo, where the hiking is superb, you can pay between 50,000Rp and 250,000Rp for guided treks.

Sights & Activities

Dragons lurk year-round at the dry riverbed Banu Nggulung. A half-hour walk from Loh Liang, it's the most accessible place to see dragons on Komodo and was once set up like a theatre, though the curtain has fallen on the gruesome ritual of feeding live goats to the reptiles. Most tourists seldom venture further afield on Pulau Komodo. Big mistake.

TOP CHOICE **Loh Sebita via Poreng Valley** HIKING
(Pulau Komodo; per person 150,000Rp) Here's where you track dragons on foot (9km, five hours) through primordial Poreng Valley, up and over Bukit Randolph, a memorial to the 79 year-old Randolph Von Reding who disappeared on Komodo in 1979, before descending towards the marsh at Loh Sebita where you can organise your boat to scoop you up. You'll likely spot a couple of dragons, wild water buffalo, deer and boar.

Gunung Ara HIKING
(Pulau Komodo; per person 200,000Rp) The chances of seeing dragons are slim on this hike (9km, five hours), but there are expansive views from the top of this 538m peak.

Pantai Merah BEACH
(Pulau Lasa) A gorgeous pink sand beach (thanks to the abundance of red coral offshore) with fantastic snorkelling. The park headquarters rents snorkel gear (per day 50,000Rp).

Sleeping & Eating

PHKA Camp LODGE $$
(r 350,000Rp) Komodo's PHKA camp is an overpriced version of a basic Indonesian hotel. New wooden bungalows are available on Rinca, but most folks opt to sleep on the decks of their chartered boats.

Getting There & Away

The only way here is by tour or charter. Labuanbajo is the best jumping-off point for Komodo and Rinca.

Chartering a boat to Rinca costs about 950,000Rp return from Labuanbajo. Boats usually leave at about 8am for the two-hour journey to the island and then return via snorkelling spots. You can book through your hotel, an agency or freelance agents in Labuanbajo, or speak directly to the captains at the harbour, which will allow you to size up the boat, and check that the vessel has a radio and life jackets. Day trips to Rinca cost 450,000Rp.

Two-day Komodo trips cost a standard 1,500,000Rp from Labuanbajo for up to six people. Price includes landings on Rinca and Komodo, meals and snorkelling gear.

Flores

Flores is the kind of gorgeous that grabs hold of you tightly. There are empty white- and black-sand beaches and bay islands; exceptional diving and snorkelling near Labuanbajo; an interior skyline of perfectly shaped volcanoes; and hip-high, luminescent rice fields that undulate in the wind next to swaying palms in spectacular river canyons. The serpentine, potholed east–west Trans-Flores Hwy is long and slow, but never boring. It skirts waterfalls, conquers mountains, brushes by traditional villages in Bajawa, leads to the incredible multicoloured volcanic lakes of Kelimutu and kisses three coastlines. The Portuguese named it 'Flowers' when they colonised Flores in the 16th century. The name stuck (so did Catholicism) because of its sheer, wild beauty.

BOAT TOURS BETWEEN LOMBOK & FLORES

Travelling by sea between Lombok and Labuanbajo is a popular way to get to Flores, as you get to see more of the region's spectacular coastline and dodge some painfully long bus journeys. Typical itineraries from Lombok take in snorkelling at Pulau Satonda off the coast of Sumbawa and a dragon-spotting hike on Komodo. From Labuanbajo, boats usually stop at Rinca and Pulau Moyo.

Be warned, this is no luxury cruise. Some shifty operators have reneged on 'all-inclusive' deals en route, and others, including the long-running Perama tour, which had a well-documented sinking in March 2011, have been known to operate old vessels without enough life jackets or working lifeboats. This crossing is especially hazardous during the monsoon, when seas are rough.

Getting There & Away

AIR Labuanbajo has become Flores' primary gateway because scores of tourists funnel in to see the dragons and dive the reefs of Komodo National Park. Maumere and Ende are also serviced by frequent flights.

BOAT Daily ferries connect Labuanbajo with Sape, Sumbawa. From Larantuka, ferries go to Kupang (West Timor). From Ende and Aimere, boats will take you to Waingapu on Sumba.

Getting Around

The Trans-Flores Hwy twists and tumbles for 700 (often) paved, tremendously scenic kilometres from Labuanbajo to Larantuka. Cheap, cramped public buses run when full. Many tourists hire a car and driver. Trans-Flores trips run from 550,000Rp to 850,000Rp a day, including petrol. You can arrange trips with hotels and agents in Labuanbajo, but you'll get a better deal if you start from Maumere.

The flat, coastal 'Trans-Northern Hwy' runs from Maumere to Riung.

LABUANBAJO

☎0385 / POP 15,000

Welcome to Indonesia's newest hot spot. A steady stream of Komodo-bound package tourists and young backpackers are descending on this gorgeous, ramshackle bay harbour, freckled with islands and blessed with surrealist sunsets. A recent influx of foreign-flagged dive boats escort giddy divers to Komodo National Park's world-class reefs. There are sweet beach bungalows on empty islands closer to shore and an expanding collection of hotels and restaurants with a view in town.

Activities

The pristine reefs and preponderance of underwater life in Komodo National Park is one of the big draws to Labuanbajo. Currents are strong and unpredictable with cold up-swellings and dangerous down currents thanks to the convergence of the warm Flores Sea and the cooler *Selat Sumba* (Sumba Strait). These conditions nourish a rich plankton soup that attracts whales, mantas, dolphins, turtles, four species of shark, and clouds of colourful fish. It's challenging diving, and you'll have the most fun if you've been certified for Advanced Open Water.

Local dive operators have virtually uniform prices. At research time the price was around 800,000Rp for two dives in Komodo National Park, plus a 250,000Rp surcharge to stop and see the dragons.

Dive offices are strung along or just off the seafront road:

Dive Komodo (☎41862; www.divekomodo.com)
Divine Diving (☎41948; www.divinediving.info; Jl Soekarno Pelabuhan 1)
Wicked Diving(☎082146 116553; www.wicked diving.com)

Tours

Labuanbajo is the main jumping-off point for tours to Komodo and Rinca; see box for details.

Sleeping

Prices listed here reflect those charged during the July to August peak season, when reservations are advisable.

TOP CHOICE **Bayview Gardens** GUESTHOUSE $$
(☎41549; www.bayview-gardens.com; Jl Ande Bole; d from 450,000Rp; ❄📶) A hillside property with five sweet cottages outfitted with queen beds and private terraces with massive bay views. It also has an ecological soul, as it funnels rainwater into showers and uses grey water to irrigate its blooming garden.

Golo Hilltop HOTEL $$
(☎41337; www.golohilltop.com; Jl Binoko; d with fan/air-con 200,000/350,000Rp; ❄📶) Modern,

super-clean concrete bungalows in a hilltop garden setting with magnificent bay views.

Gardena Hotel BUNGALOWS $

(☎41258; Jl Soekarno Hatta; bungalows 150,000-165,000Rp) A collection of basic bamboo huts on a rambling hillside, overlooking the gorgeous bay harbour and distant islands. The restaurant is solid.

Kanawa Beach Bungalows BUNGALOWS $$

(☎085857 043197; www.kanawaresort.com; Jl Soekarno Hatta; bungalows from 220,000Rp) Perched on a small bay island with Komodo and Rinca views, this is the place to spend a few days relaxing, diving and sunbathing. The solar-powered bungalows aren't fancy, but they are romantic. Make arrangements at the office on the main drag.

Eating & Drinking

TOP CHOICE **Mediterano** ITALIAN $$

(Jl Soekarno Hatta; dishes 38,000-82,000Rp; Wi-Fi) A happening spot with excellent Italian food. We love the pastas and the pizzas, and there's an excellent barracuda carpaccio. The groovy interior extends beneath whitewashed rafters dangling with woven rattan lanterns. The restaurant grows its own fresh herbs, and on Sundays you can buy drinks and dine for free at a large buffet.

The Lounge INTERNATIONAL $$

(Jl Yos Sudarso; tapas from 20,000Rp, mains 25,000-60,000Rp; ⏲8am-10pm; Wi-Fi) A sleek dining room with red lounges, Balinese art and (of course) amazing views. Tapas are good, so are the pizzas and homemade ravioli.

Pesona SEAFOOD $

(Jl Soekarno Hatta; meals 20,000-50,000Rp) Cute, ramshackle wooden restaurant perched above the harbour, specialising in fresh seafood.

Tree Top SEAFOOD $

(Jl Soekarno Hatta; meals 25,000-59,000Rp) This fun, double-decker art cafe offers harbour and island views, and tasty, spicy Indonesian seafood.

Paradise Bar & Restaurant BAR $

(Jl Binoko; meals 20,000-45,000Rp; ⏲11am-late) Once it was the only flicker of nightlife in town, and we still love it because of the expansive 180-degree sea views, the all-you-can-eat 50,000Rp Indonesian buffet on Wednesday night and the live band.

Information

The Telkom office is near the tourist office.

BNI bank (Jl Yos Sudarso) Changes money and has an ATM.

PHKA information booth (☎41005; Jl Yos Sudarso; ⏲8am-2.30pm Mon-Thu, to 11am Fri) PHKA administers the Komodo National Park and provides information for Komodo and Rinca islands.

Post office (Jl Yos Sudarso)

Tourist office (Dinas Pariwisata; ☎41170; ⏲7am-2pm Mon-Thu & Sat, to 11am Fri) About 1km out of town on the road to the airport.

Getting There & Away

AIR Labuanbajo's Bandar Udara Komodo has a short runway, but plenty of flights.

Lion/Wings Air (☎Jakarta 021 6379 8000; www.lionair.co.id) Flies to Denpasar and Kupang three times weekly.

Merpati (☎41177) Flies to Denpasar daily and to Kupang three times weekly

Transnusa/Aviastar (☎41800; Jl Soekarno Hatta) Flies daily to Denpasar and Kupang, via Ende.

BOAT The daily ferry from Labuanbajo to Sape (46,000Rp to 66,000Rp, eight to nine hours) leaves at 7am or 8am depending upon the day. Tickets can be purchased at the harbour master's office (in front of the pier) one hour before the vessel's departure. To be safe, get here just before 7am.

BUS Buses leave for Bajawa (80,000Rp, eight hours) and Ende (150,000Rp, 15 hours) from the Garantolo bus terminal 10km outside town. Buy your tickets in advance and buses will pick you up in town.

Bajo Express (☎42068) runs regular minibus routes to Bajawa (120,000Rp), Ende (180,000Rp), Moni (250,000Rp) and Maumere (300,000Rp) without making endless loops searching for passengers.

BAJAWA

☎0384

With a pleasant climate, and surrounded by forested volcanoes, Bajawa is a great base from which to explore dozens of traditional villages that are home to the Ngada people. Their fascinating architecture features *ngadhu* (carved poles supporting a conical thatched roof).

Sights & Activities

Bajawa's top attractions are the traditional villages. Guides linger around hotels and arrange day trips for 400,000Rp per person with motorbike transport, village entry fees and lunch. Trips cost 900,000Rp with a car. **Bena**, 19km south of Bajawa on the flank of Gunung Inerie, is the best village in the area with several megalith tombs and soaring thatched roofs. **Nage** is likewise fascinating.

Sleeping & Eating

TOP CHOICE Edelweis HOTEL **$$**
(☎21345; Jl Ahmad Yani 76; r 150,000-250,000Rp) Great volcano views, reasonably clean VIP rooms and friendly management, who will gladly boil water for a welcome hot-water morning *mandi*.

Hotel Korina HOTEL **$**
(☎21162; Jl Ahmad Yani 81; r 100,000-300,000) The bottom of the Bajawa barrel in terms of room size and cleanliness, but the staff is friendly and it will do for a night.

Dito's INDONESIAN **$**
(Jl Ahmad Yani; mains 17,000-50,000Rp) Twinkling with Christmas lights, Dito's does a brisk business serving pork satay and fresh tuna *bakar*, which it gets from nearby Aimere and grills to perfection.

Information

BNI bank (Jl Pierre Tendean) Has an ATM.
Telkom office (☎21218; Jl Soekarno Hatta)
Warnet 31 (Jl Ahmad Yani 12; per hr 5000Rp; ⌚8am-midnight)

Getting There & Away

Merpati has resumed flights between Bajawa and Kupang in West Timor. Contact its office in Kupang (see p241).

The Watujaji bus station is 3km south of town, but hotels arrange tickets and pick-ups. Buses to Labuanbajo (110,000Rp, 10 hours) leave at 6am; buses to Ende (50,000Rp, five hours) depart at 7am, 8am and 12.30pm.

Bemo and trucks to surrounding villages depart from the Jl Basuki Rahmat terminal.

ENDE

☎0381 / POP 89,000

Muggy, dusty and crowded, this south-coast port's ultimate saving grace is its spectacular setting. The eye-catching cones of Gunung Meja and Gunung Iya loom over the city, while barrels roll in continuously from the Sawu Sea and crash over a coastline of black sand and blue stones.

Soekarno was exiled here during the 1930s, where he reinvented himself as a truly horrid playwright. Fortunately the revolutionary-hero thing worked out.

Sights

Musium Bung Karno MUSEUM
(Jl Perwira; admission by donation; ⌚7am-noon Mon-Sat) History buffs can visit Soekarno's house of exile, where he penned the epic Frankenstein-inspired *Doctor Satan*.

Sleeping & Eating

Accommodation is spread all over town, but frequent bemo make it easy to get around.

Hotel Safari HOTEL **$**
(☎21997; Jl Ahmad Yani 65; economy r from 65,000, with air-con s/d 200,000/250,000Rp; ❄) Right next door to Hotel Ikhlas, rooms are large and clean and open onto a courtyard garden. Air-con rooms should be booked in advance.

Hotel Ikhlas HOTEL **$**
(☎21695; Jl Ahmad Yani 69; s/d without bathroom 40,000/60,000Rp, s/d with bathroom 70,000/90,000Rp, s/d with air-con 150,000/200,000Rp; ❄) This well-run place has plenty of basic but neat little rooms at good prices.

Rumah Makan Istana Bambu INDONESIAN **$**
(Jl Kemakmuran 30A; dishes 15,000-35,000Rp) Here's a classic, delicious, funkified fish house run by the matriarch.

THE NGADA

Over 60,000 Ngada people inhabit the upland Bajawa plateau and the slopes around Gunung Inerie. Older animistic beliefs remain strong, and most Ngada practise a fusion of animism and Christianity. They worship Gae Dewa, a god who unites Dewa Zeta (the heavens) and Nitu Sale (the earth).

The most evident symbols of continuing Ngada tradition are pairs of *ngadhu* and *bhaga*. The *ngadhu* is a parasol-like structure about 3m high, consisting of a carved wooden pole and thatched 'roof', and the *bhaga* is a miniature thatched-roof house.

The *ngadhu* is 'male' and the *bhaga* is 'female', and each pair is associated with a particular family group within a village. Some were built over 100 years ago to commemorate ancestors killed in long-past battles.

WORTH A TRIP

RIUNG

Fans of laid-back coastal mangrove villages will love Riung, which has garnered a hearty backpacker buzz in recent months. But the 24 offshore islands of the **Seventeen Islands Marine Park** (strangely named in honour of Indonesia's 17 August Independence Day), with luscious white-sand beaches and excellent snorkelling, are the real attraction. The park entrance fee is 20,000Rp per person plus 25,000Rp per boat. Day charters (350,000Rp for up to six people, not including guide) are easily arranged in Riung.

Pondok SVD (081339 341572; r 120,000-350,000Rp;) has spotless rooms with desks, reading lights and Western toilets, while **Rumah Makan Murah Muriah** (mains from 30,000Rp, large beer 15,000Rp) serves delicious, fresh grilled fish and icy Bintang.

From Ndao terminal in Ende (40,000Rp, four hours), a bus leaves every afternoon at 1pm. Two buses from Bajawa (30,000Rp to 50,000Rp, three hours) leave at 8am and 1pm. The Bajawa road is a mess and is 4WD only. Buses to Bajawa depart at 6am.

Information

BNI bank (Bank Negara Indonesia; Jl Gatot Subroto) Near the airport, this bank offers the best exchange rates and has an ATM.

Tourism office (21303; Jl Soekarno 4; 8am-1pm Mon-Sat)

Zyma Internet (24697; Jl Sudarso 3; per hr 3000Rp; 11am-10pm) Good connection in the cathedral's shadow.

Getting There & Away

AIR **Transnusa** (24222; Jl Kelimutu 37) offers flights to Denpasar via Labuanbajo on Monday, Wednesday and Saturday. It flies to Kupang daily.

BOAT **ASDP** (22007) operates twice-weekly ferries to Waingapu (85,000Rp, six hours, departing 6.30am Wednesday and Saturday) and weekly crossings to Kupang (75,000Rp, seven hours, departing 6.30am Monday).

Pelni (630 1249; www.pelni.co.id; Jl Kathedral 2; 8am-noon & 2-4pm Mon-Sat) sails west to Waingapu, Bima, Benoa and Surabaya, and east to Kupang.

BUS It's about 5km from town to Wolowana terminal, where you catch eastbound buses for Moni (20,000Rp, two hours) and Maumere (50,000Rp, five hours), leaving almost hourly from 6am to 2pm. You can also hop on an *ojek* (20,000Rp) to Moni.

Westbound buses leave from the Ndao terminal, 2km north of town, for Bajawa (50,000Rp, five hours) at 7am and 11am.

KELIMUTU

There aren't many better ways to wake up than to sip ginger coffee as the sun crests Mt Kelimutu's western rim, filtering through mist and revealing three deep, volcanic lakes, each one a different, striking shade. Minerals in the water account for the chameleonic colour scheme – although the turquoise lake never changes, the others fluctuate between yellow, orange and red.

Most visitors glimpse them at dawn, leaving nearby Moni at 4am, but afternoons are usually empty and peaceful at the top of Mt Kelimutu, and when the sun is high the colours sparkle. Clouds are your only obstacles, and they can drift in at anytime.

To get there, hire an *ojek* (one way/return 35,000/60,000Rp), or charter a bemo (one way/return 150,000/250,000Rp, maximum six people) or car (400,000Rp return, maximum five people) from Moni. The park entry post, halfway up the road, charges a 20,000Rp entry fee.

You can walk the 13.5km down through the forest and back to Moni in about 2½ hours.

MONI

Moni, the gateway to Kelimutu, is a picturesque village sprinkled with rice fields, ringed by soaring volcanic peaks, with distant sea views. The cool, comfortable climate invites long walks and a few extra days, but there are no banks and only one telephone. About 2km west of Moni is the turn-off to Kelimutu. The Monday market, on the soccer pitch, is a major local draw and a good place to snare *ikat*.

Sleeping & Eating

Moni has a cluster of mostly forgettable cheapies to choose from. Prices peak in July and August. The only notable kitchen is listed below. The rest serve differing versions of the same depressing tourist fare.

TOP CHOICE **Bintang Bungalows and Lodge** GUESTHOUSE $$
(085237 906259; r 150,000-350,000Rp; @) Just four tidy rooms and two of Moni's best

bungalows, all with little garden patios out front and views of the valley below.

Palm Bungalows BUNGALOWS $
(☎081227 320223; bungalows 100,000Rp) Set down a narrow path and nestled in a lush garden, the bungalows are rickety yet romantic.

Bambu Restaurant MONI $$
(meals 40,000-70,000Rp; ⊙dinner served at 7pm; ☑) Attached to Maria's Inn, this is where enterprising local chef Eran Iwan serves traditional Moni cuisine. Meals include mountain rice, smoky vegetable soup, wild banana flower, and chicken cooked in bamboo. It also offers vegetarian meals and is only open for dinner. Head to Maria's and order before 5pm.

Getting There & Away

Ende-bound buses (20,000Rp, two hours) roll through town from 7am. Buses to Maumere (35,000Rp, four hours) stop here at about 9am or 10am, and later at around 7pm.

MAUMERE

☎0382 / POP 52,000

Maumere has the second busiest airport on the island, and you'll probably do some time here. Fortunately you can escape from the neglected city centre to some truly excellent beach bungalows lining the coast nearby.

Sleeping

TOP CHOICE **Gardena Hotel** HOTEL $
(☎22644; Jl Patirangga 28; r with fan/air-con 100,000/150,000Rp; ❄) A terrific budget spot on a quiet residential street east of the harbour crush.

Hotel Sylvia HOTEL $$
(☎21829; Jl Gajah Mada 88; r from 300,000Rp; ❄📶🏊) A brand-new hotel 3km from downtown near the bus station. Expect wood floors, all the mod cons and a rather inviting pool out back.

Eating

The harbour doubles as restaurant row, with a string of inexpensive seafood and Indonesian kitchens.

TOP CHOICE **Rumah Makan Ikan Bakar Jakarta** SEAFOOD $
(Jl Pelabuhan; dishes 10,000-20,000Rp) The popular choice among seamen and local families for the fish – fresh and perfectly prepared and served almost instantly with a sensational roasted chilli sambal that will make you sweat.

Layar Resto CHINESE $
(Jl Pelabuhan; dishes 10,000-35,000Rp) Next door to Rumah Makan Ikan Bakar Jakarta, this popular option does all the familiar Chinese-Indonesian dishes, featuring shrimp, squid, chicken and fish, with more dining-room grace and much less grill smoke. The soups and noodles look particularly good.

Information

BNI bank (Jl Soekarno Hatta 4) Best rates in town; ATM.

Comtel (☎22132; Jl Bandeng 1; per hr 12,000Rp; ⊙9am-9pm) High-speed internet access.

Post office (Jl Pos; ⊙8am-2pm Mon-Sat)

Telkom office (Jl Soekarno Hatta 5)

Getting There & Around

AIR **Merpati** (☎21342; Jl Raya Don Tomas) has daily flights to/from Kupang, Labuanbajo and Makassar. **Transnusa/Aviastar** (☎21393; Bandara) flies regularly to Kupang, Denpasar, Labuanbajo, Alor, and Waingapu or Tambolaka in Sumba. **Lion/Wings Air** (☎22993; Bandara) serves Denpasar.

Hop on an *ojek* to the airport for 10,000Rp. Departure tax is 11,000Rp.

BOAT **Pelni** (☎21013; www.pelni.co.id; Jl M Sugiyo Pranoto 4) sails fortnightly to Kupang and Makassar.

BUS Buses to Larantuka (50,000Rp, four hours) leave from the Lokaria (or Timur) terminal, 3km east of town, at 7.30am and 3pm. Buses west to Moni (30,000Rp, three hours) and Ende (50,000Rp, five hours) leave from the Ende terminal 1.5km southwest of town.

LOCAL TRANSPORT Bemo around town cost 2000Rp. *Ojeks* charge 3000Rp.

AROUND MAUMERE

A small army of expert artisans lies in wait in the weaving village of Sikka, 26km south of Maumere. Along the north coast, east of Maumere, is where you'll find the best beaches and healthiest reefs.

The beaches of Ahuwair and Waiterang, 24km and 26km east of Maumere, ooze tranquillity. Lena House 1 and 2 (☎081339 407733; d 95,000Rp) offer five clean bamboo bungalows set on two pristine coves, also 26km and 24km from Maumere respectively. The newer bungalows at Lena 2 are more comfortable and quieter.

TOP CHOICE **Ankermi** (☎08124 669667; www.ankermi-happydive.com; bungalows s/d incl breakfast & dinner 225,000/390,000Rp), located 29km from Maumere, has cute, thatched concrete and bamboo bungalows with squat toilets, showers and front decks with ocean views. Meals are included in the price. Its dive shop is Maumere's best. Come via a Larantuka-bound bus or bemo from Maumere's Lokaria terminal (3000Rp, 35 minutes).

LARANTUKA

0383

This busy little port, and former Portuguese enclave, is nestled at the base of Gunung Ili Mandiri on the eastern tip of Flores, separated from the Solor and Alor archipelagos by a narrow strait. Most people come here simply to hop on a ferry.

Sleeping & Eating

TOP CHOICE **Hotel Rulies** GUESTHOUSE $

(21198; Jl Yos Sudarso 40; r without bathrooms 75,000, r with bathrooms 80,000-120,000Rp) This funky spot near the harbour has the cleanest and best rooms in town.

Rumah Makan Nirwana INDONESIAN $

(Jl Yos Sudarso; dishes 5000-24,000Rp) Larantuka's first choice. The Chinese and Indonesian dishes come in filling portions.

Informationy

Telkom Warnet (per hr 10,000Rp; 24hr;) has solid internet access. **BNI** (Jl Fernandez 93) has an ATM.

Getting There & Away

All boats depart from the main pier in the centre of town. Double-check departure times.

Wooden boats to Lewoleba on Lembata (30,000Rp, four hours), all via Waiwerang on Adonara (20,000Rp) and Lamalera on Solor (16,000Rp), depart from the pier in the centre of town at 7.30am, 11.30am and 12.30pm. There is no early boat on Monday mornings.

The new Fantasi Fast Boat, leaves once daily at 8.30am and runs nonstop to Leloweba (75,000Rp, one hour).

Pelni (www.pelni.co.id) ships serve Kalabahi, Kupang and Makassar.

Regular buses run between Maumere and Larantuka (50,000Rp, five hours). The main bus station is 5km west of town (3000Rp by bemo), but you can pick buses up in the town centre.

West Timor

With rugged countryside and scores of traditional villages, West Timor is an undiscovered gem. Deep within its lontar palm-studded interior, animist traditions persist alongside 14 tribal dialects, while Kupang, its coastal capital and East Nusa Tenggara's top metropolis and transport hub, buzzes to a typical Indonesian beat.

Getting There & Away

AIR A good way to explore eastern Nusa Tenggara is to fly directly from Bali to Kupang and island hop from there. For details on flights, see p241.

BOAT **ASDP** (0380 890420; Bolok) has regular car-and-passenger ferries linking Bolok, 14km southwest of Kupang, to numerous East Nusa Tenggara destinations.

WORTH A TRIP

ALOR

Alor, the final link in an island chain that extends east of Java, is as remote, rugged and beautiful as it gets. Thanks to impenetrable terrain, the 170,000 inhabitants are fractured into 50 tribes with 14 languages, and they were still taking heads into the 1950s. Alor is also famous for its strange, bronze *moko* drums.

Superb diving can be arranged through **La Petite Kepa** (0813 5370 9719; www.la-petite-kepa.com; bungalows incl meals per person 150,000-600,000Rp) on Pulau Kepa. **Alor Dive** (222 2663; www.alor-dive.com; Jl Gatot Subroto 33, Kalabahi) also arranges trips.

Kalabahi, located on a sweeping, palm-fringed bay, is the main port. There are banks and ATMs. **Hotel Pelangi Indah** (21251; Jl Diponegoro 100; r 75,000-250,000Rp;), on the main drag, has reasonably clean rooms flanking a flower garden.

The airport is 9km from town, and offers one of the most dramatic approaches in the country. **Susi Air** (081 1381 3801; www.susiair.com) flies to and from Kupang three to four times weekly.

To Kupang, ferries leave on Tuesday and Sunday (80,000Rp, around 18 hours). A weekly ferry departs from Kalabahi for Lewoleba (80,000Rp) on Sunday, where you can connect to Larantuka.

Pelni passenger ships serve several ports infrequently.

Getting Around

The good main highway is surfaced all the way from Kupang to East Timor, though the buses that ply it are of the crowded, thumping-disco variety. Away from the highway, roads are improving but can be impassable in the wet season.

KUPANG

0380 / POP 362,000

Kupang, the capital of Nusa Tenggara Timur (NTT), is noisy, energetic, scruffy, bustling with commerce, and a fun place to hang around for a few days. Captain Bligh did, after his mutiny issues in 1789.

Kupang sprawls. You'll need to take bemo (2000Rp) or *ojek* (5000Rp) to get around. The waterfront district, which stretches along Jl Sumba and rambles inland with Jl Ahmad Yani, has the bulk of the budget lodging options.

Kupang

Sleeping

1 Hotel Maliana ... C1
2 Lavalon B&B ... B1
3 Pantai Timor Hotel ... C1

Eating

4 Pasar Malam ... B1
5 Rumah Makan Wahyu Putra Solo ... C1

Drinking

6 Lavalon ... B1

Sights

East Nusa Tenggara Museum MUSEUM
(Jl Raya El Tari; admission 750Rp; 8am-noon & 1.30-3pm Mon-Fri) Although under renovation at research time, this museum has a collection of crafts and artefacts worth exploring.

Sleeping

TOP CHOICE **Lavalon B&B** HOSTEL $
(832236; www.lavalontouristinfo.com; Jl Sumatera I 8; dm 40,000Rp, r without bathroom 55,000Rp) The best value in town, with clean, ceramic-tiled rooms, all with shared bathrooms.

Hotel Maliana HOTEL $
(821879; Jl Sumatera 35; r with fan/air-con 100,000/170,000Rp;) These basic yet comfy motel rooms are a popular budget choice. Rooms are clean and have ocean views from the front porch.

Pantai Timor Hotel HOTEL $$
(831651; Jl Sumatera 31; s/d 140,000/160,000Rp;) A decent choice; rooms on the 3rd floor (220,000Rp) have air-con and sea views. Be choosy.

Eating

TOP CHOICE **Rumah Makan Wahyu Putra Solo** INDONESIAN $
(Jl Gunung Mutis 31; meals 15,000-40,000Rp) Kupang's best pick-and-mix *warung* offers beef, chicken, fish, potatoes and greens deep- and stir-fried, stewed in coconut sauce, and chilli-rubbed and roasted.

Pasar Malam NIGHT MARKET $
(Jl Garuda; dishes from 6000Rp; 6-10pm) Kupang was never considered a good eat-

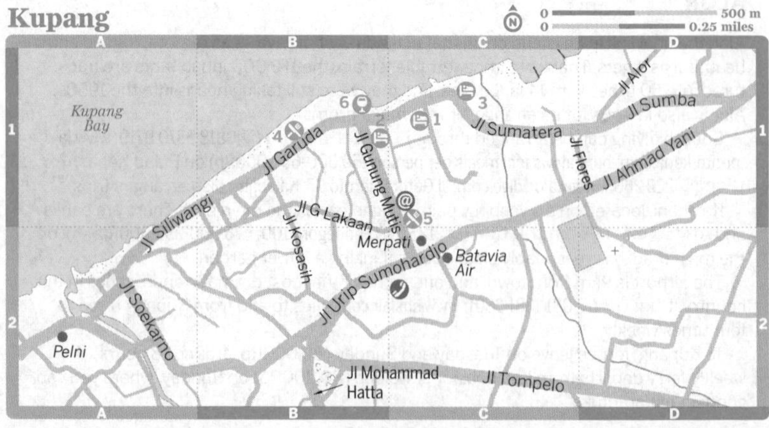

GETTING TO TIMOR-LESTE

From Kupang, direct minibuses (175,0000Rp to 185,000Rp one way, 10 hours) to Dili are operated by **Timor Tour & Travel** (☎881543), **Paradise Tours & Travel** (☎830414) and **Livau** (☎821892). Call for a hotel pick-up. This is the easiest and most cost-effective way to cross the border, but before making the trek you will need to apply for an East Timor visa ($30) at the Kupang consulate, which takes three business days.

Still, it's the cheapest way to renew your Indonesian visa from Nusa Tenggara. Once in East Timor, you can get another 30-day visa at the Indonesian embassy.

There is also a new fast ferry (economy/VIP US$35/45, 12 hours) running from Kupang to Dili every Sunday, Monday, Thursday and Friday and from Dili to Kupang every Friday, Tuesday and Wednesday, with visas issued upon arrival. Ask at Lavalon in Kupang for details about departure times and dock information.

See the boxed text, p806, for information on doing the trip in the reverse direction.

ing town until this wonderful, lamp-lit market launched and turned Jl Garuda over to street-side grill and wok chefs, who expertly prepare inexpensive dishes.

Drinking

Lavalon BAR
(www.lavalontouristinfo.com; Jl Sumatera 44; @ wi-fi) This romantic, open-air, tin-roofed watering hole, with spectacular sea views, is an absolute must.

Information

The NTT Tourist Office is out in the sticks near the bus station – it's not worth the trip. Kupang has scores of banks and ample ATMs at both ends of town.

Lavalon (www.lavalontouristinfo.com; Jl Sumatera 44; wi-fi) Internet access. Edwin Lerrick, the proprietor, is a vital source for the latest transport information, as well as interesting cultural attractions throughout NTT.

Main post office (Jl Palapa 1) Take bemo 5.

Plasa Telkom (Jl Urip Sumohardjo 11; ⏲8am-4pm Mon-Fri, 8am-noon Sat; wi-fi) Offers international calls and wi-fi.

Ratunet (2nd fl, Jl Gunung Mutis 31; per hr 4000Rp; ⏲24hr) Internet.

Getting There & Around

AIR Kupang's El Tari airport (code KOE) is 15km east of town and the most important hub in East Nusa Tenggara. Taxi fare into town is fixed at 60,000Rp.

Batavia Air (☎830555; Jl Ahmad Yani 73) Serves Waingapu and Surabaya.

Garuda (☎827333; Jl Palapa 7) Flies to Denpasar and Jakarta.

Lion Air (☎882119; El Tari airport) Serves Surabaya and Jakarta.

Merpati (☎833833; Jl Timor Timur Km 5) Departures include Denpasar, Waingapu, Tambolaka, Maumere, Ende, Lewoleba and Atambua.

Susi Air (☎08113 813801; www.susiair.com) Flies to Kupang three to four times weekly.

Transnusa/Aviastar (☎822555; Palapa 7, Oebobo-Kupang) Flies to Ende, Maumere, Waingapu, and Tambolaka.

BOAT **ASDP** (☎890420) Ferries leave from Bolok, 14km southwest of Kupang, for Larantuka (Sunday and Thursday), Waingapu (Monday), Kalabahi (Tuesday) and Ende (Friday).

Pelni (☎824357; www.pelni.co.id; Jl Pahlawan 3; ⏲8.30am-3pm Mon-Sat, 9-11am Sun) Near the waterfront. Several ships dock here with weekly departures for Waingapu, Bima, Ambon, Larantuka, Aimere, Ende, Makassar and Bali.

BUS Long-distance buses depart from Oebobo terminal on the eastern side of town – catch bemo 10. Daily departures include Soe (20,000Rp, 2½ hours) and Niki Niki (25,000Rp, four hours). Buses leave hourly from 6am to 8pm.

See the boxed text for information on getting to East Timor.

SOE

☎0368 / ELEV 800M / POP 30,000

Traditional, beehive-like *lopo* (hut) villages and the indigenous Dawan people who live in them are the attraction of this modernising market town 800m above sea level. The government has deemed the *lopo* a health hazard (they're smoky and lack ventilation) and is in the process of replacing them with modern homes. Once received, the Dawan simply build new *lopo* behind them and live there. Village tours are easily arranged in Soe.

The **tourist information centre** (☎21149; Jl Diponegoro) can arrange guides. **BNI** (Jl Diponegoro) and **BRI** (Jl Hatta) branches have ATMs.

Hotel Gajah Mada (☎21997; Jl Gajah Mada; standard/VIP 250,000/400,000Rp) has basic rooms with new-ish tile and wood furnishings, while **Hotel Bahagia II**

(☎21095; Jl Gajah Mada 55; d 145,000Rp, cottages 225,000-495,000Rp; @) has plenty of spacious rooms with queen-sized beds.

The Haumeni bus terminal is 4km west of town (2000Rp by bemo). Regular buses go to Kupang (20,000Rp, three hours) and Oinlasi (10,000Rp, 1½ hours), while bemo serve Niki Niki (5000Rp).

AROUND SOE

Market days attract villagers from miles in every direction; they arrive wearing traditional dress and sell exquisite hand-woven *ikat*, carvings and masks. This is why you travel. The Tuesday market at **Oinlasi**, 51km from Soe, is one of the biggest and best in West Timor, and the Wednesday market at **Niki Niki**, 34km east of Soe, is a lively, more accessible, second choice.

The main attraction around Soe is **Boti**, a traditional village presided over by a self-styled raja, who is something of a fundamentalist animist. Traditional dress code and hairstyle is enforced, and locals maintain strict adherence to *adat* (customary law), a devotion that has proven immune to Christian missionaries.

It's possible to stay with the raja in his house, with all meals provided, for 75,000Rp per person. It'll cost another 100,000Rp to see a traditional dance performance. Day-trippers are expected to make a donation (25,000Rp should work); bring from Soe a guide conversant with local *adat*.

From Niki Niki, there is a new turn-off to Boti. It's a 20km trip on a rocky, hilly road that's passable by motorcycle or 4WD.

Sumba

According to local legend, humankind first made landfall on earth by climbing down a huge celestial ladder from heaven to Sumba – a dry limestone isle swathed in grasslands. Plate tectonics broke Sumba off the Indonesian archipelago's southeastern arc in the Sawu Sea, and it has kept to itself ever since, and although Christianity has seeped in, tribal traditions – such as *marapu*, a religious belief system that revolves around ancestral spirits, bloody sacrificial funeral rites, hand-carved tombs, divine *ikat* weaving, and the use of horses for status, wealth and to score a hot wife – remain strong. Generational tribal tensions also simmer beneath the surface, and are recalled every year during western Sumba's Pasola festivals (see the boxed text, p243), when mock battles between mounted warriors sometimes descend into actual violence.

Most of the 540,000 residents live in comparatively moist and fertile West Sumba, and though some Bahasa Indonesia is spoken throughout the island, six tribal languages are more prevalent. Note that, as international aid has poured in, remote villagers expect larger and larger donations from visitors – whether they are government officials, NGO staff or tourists.

Getting There & Away

AIR Waingapu and Tambolaka both offer frequent flights.

BOAT Waingapu has weekly ASDP ferries to Ende (and on to Kupang) and Aimere on Flores. Pelni has useful services from Waingapu to Ende, and beyond.

WAINGAPU

☎0387 / POP 53,000

Sumba's gateway town has grown up from a dusty trading post to an urbanising commercial centre. But just like in the old days, business revolves around dyewoods, timber and the island's prized horses. You're here to explore the surrounding villages.

Waingapu spreads from the harbour in the north, 1.5km southeast to the main market and bus station.

Sleeping & Eating

Most hotels are in the new part of Waingapu, near the bus station. The best dinner option is the *pasar malam* (night market) at the old wharf.

Hotel Sandle Wood HOTEL $
(☎61887; Jl Panjaitan 23; s/d with fan 99,000/143,000Rp, with air-con 187,000/209,000Rp; ❄) Decent-value rooms set around a bright courtyard on a quiet street. Management can hook you up with cars (with drivers) or motorbikes.

Hotel Merlin HOTEL $
(☎61300; Jl Panjaitan 25; standard/VIP 132,000/154,000Rp; ❄) This longstanding travellers' favourite has a decent assortment of rooms on three floors. Top-floor fan rooms are nicer and cleaner than the VIP rooms on the 1st floor.

Warung Enjoy Aja SEAFOOD $
(Pelabuhan; mains 15,000-40,000Rp; ⏲6-10pm) The last night-market *warung* before the pier on the east side. The fish and squid are

PASOLA FESTIVAL – SUMBA AT WAR

The thrilling, often gruesome mock battles between spear-hurling horsemen during Sumba's Pasola festival are a must for travellers passing through Nusa Tenggara in February or March. The high-energy pageant aims to placate the spirits and restore harmony with the spilling of blood. Happily, though, blunt spears have been used in recent decades to make the affair less lethal. The ritualistic war kicks off when a sea worm called *nyale* washes up on shore, a phenomenon that also starts the planting season. Call hotels in Waingapu or Waikabubak to find out the latest schedules. The festival is generally held in the Lamboya and Kodi districts in February, and at Wanokaka and Gaura in March.

expertly grilled and served with three types of sambal and a sea-salt garnish.

Warung Kedau Etnik INDONESIAN **$**
(Jl Ahmad Yani 67; mains 15,000-50,000Rp) A cute, new bamboo *warung,* with classy glass sandbox tables and the usual Indo flavours in the kitchen.

Information

BNI bank (Bank Negara Indonesia; Jl Ampera) ATM accepts Visa/Plus cards. It usually has the best exchange rates.

Post office (Jl Hasanuddin; 8am-4pm Mon-Fri)

Telkom office (Jl Tjut Nya Dien; 24hr)

Warnet Hamu Eti (Jl Panjaitan 92; per 36 min 4000Rp; 24hr)

Getting There & Around

AIR The airport is 6km south on the Melolo road. Hotels offer free pick-up and drop-off service for guests. **Merpati** (61323; Jl Ahmad Yani 75) serves Kupang and Denpasar twice weekly.

Transnusa/Aviastar and Batavia also serve Kupang and Denpasar three or four times weekly. Contact **TX Waingapu** (61534; www.txtravel.com; Jl Beringin 12).

BOAT Waingapu is served by weekly **ASDP ferries** (61533; Jl Wanggameti 3) departing for Ende and Kupang from the old pier.

Pelni (www.pelni.co.id) ships serve Ende, Benoa in Bali, and Surabaya from the newer Darmaga dock west of town. It's too far to walk. Bemo charge 5000Rp per person.

BUS Eastbound buses to Melolo and Rende leave from the bus station near the market. Buses to Waikabubak (25,000Rp, five hours) leave from the West Sumba terminal, 5km west of town, at 7am, 8am, noon and 3pm. Book at your hotel or through an agency opposite the bus station.

AROUND WAINGAPU

Several traditional villages in the southeast can be visited from Waingapu by bus and bemo. The stone tombs are impressive and the area produces some of Sumba's best *ikat*. Small donations are expected.

Located about 7km away from unspectacular **Melolo** – accessible by bus from Waingapu (15,000Rp, 1½ hours) – is **Praiyawang**, the ceremonial centre of **Rende** (15,000Rp, 1½ hours), with its traditional Sumbanese compound and stone-slab tombs. The massive one belongs to a former raja.

There's epic surf at **Tarimbang**, a palm-draped cove south of Lewa. The reef break is superb, the snorkelling decent and either of the two homestays, which don't offer advanced booking but will accommodate you upon arrival, will do just fine. Both charge from per person 50,000Rp, all-inclusive. Daily trucks to Tarimbang leave Waingapu in the morning (35,000Rp, 3½ hours).

WAIKABUBAK

0387 / POP 19,000

A conglomeration of thatched clan houses, ancient tombs, concrete office buildings and satellite dishes, Waikabubak is strange but appealing. Interesting traditional villages such as **Kampung Tarung**, up a path next to Tarung Wisata Hotel, are right within town. One of the spectacular attractions of West Sumba is the **Pasola**, the mock battle held near Waikabubak each February or March.

Sleeping & Eating

Warung congregate opposite the mosque on the main strip.

Karanu Hotel GUESTHOUSE **$**
(21645; Jl Sudirman 43; r 80,000-200,000Rp;) A bright garden hotel east of the downtown swirl, and within view of nearby rice fields. Rooms are clean, with new tiles and crisp sheets.

Aloha Hotel HOTEL **$$**
(22563; Jl Sudirman 26; r 125,000-225,000Rp;) Bright, cosy, basic fan rooms are set around a courtyard blooming with…satellite dishes?

Rumah Makan Gloria INDONESIAN $
(☎21389; Jl Bhayangkara 46; dishes 10,000-45,000Rp) Cute and cheerful, it rolls out all the Indonesian hits, including an absolutely sensational *soto ayam*.

Information

BNI bank (Bank Negara Indonesia; Jl Ahmad Yani; ⌚8am-3.30pm Mon-Fri) Has an ATM and offers fair exchange rates.

Tourist office (☎21240; Jl Teratai 1; ⌚8am-2pm Mon-Fri) Non-English-speaking staff offer limited tips on local funerals and cultural events in the area.

Telkom Plasa (per hr 5000Rp; ⌚24hr) A swift web portal.

Getting There & Away

Taxis to the Tambolaka airport, 42km north, cost 150,000Rp. **Merpati** (☎21051; Jl Bhayangkara 20) and **Transnusa/Aviastar** (☎Kupang 0380 822555) serve Kupang and Denpasar.

Buses run to Waingapu (30,000Rp, five hours) throughout the day. Frequent bemo rattle to Anakalang.

AROUND WAIKABUBAK

Set in a lush valley 22km east of Waikabubak, **Anakalang** sports some of Sumba's most captivating megalith tombs. More interesting villages are south of town past the market. **Kabonduk** has Sumba's heaviest tomb. It took 2000 workers more than three years to carve it.

Located south of Waikabubak is Wanokaka district, which is a centre for the Pasola festival (see p243). **Praigoli** is a somewhat isolated village and deeply traditional.

Our favourite place in all of West Sumba, **Pantai Oro** (☎081339 110068; info@oro-beachbungalows.com; r 400,000Rp, bungalow 450,000Rp), is but a 15 minute drive from Tambolaka airport along a mostly rutted dirt road. Think: three wild beachfront acres owned by a special family (she runs an NGO, he's an architect with a disaster-relief background). The simple house has stunning touches, like that sundial of coconut timbers in the up-lit eaves. They offer excellent seafood meals, mountain biking and snorkelling just off shore. They can also get you into the local villages.

SUMATRA

Lush, enormous and intriguing, Sumatra stretches for 2000km across the equator. Happily, there is a payoff for every pothole along the Trans-Sumatran Hwy: Steaming volcanoes brew and bluster while standing guard over lakes that sleepily lap the edges of craters created by Jurassic-era lava; orang-utans swing through rainforests; and long, white beaches offer world-class surf breaks on the surface and stunning coral reefs below.

Besides natural beauty, the world's sixth-largest island boasts a wealth of resources, particularly oil, gas and timber. These earn Indonesia the bulk of its badly needed export dollars, even as their extraction devastates habitats.

When Mother Nature is this majestic and bountiful, there is usually a flip side, and Sumatra has seen more than its share of her fury. Eruptions, earthquakes, floods and tsunamis are regular headline grabbers and the steep cost of living in one of the richest ecosystems in the world.

Getting There & Away

The international airports at Medan, Padang, Banda Aceh and Pekanbaru are visa free (for more on visas, see p307), as are the seaports of Sekupang (Pulau Batam), Belawan (Medan), Dumai, Padang and Sibolga.

AIR Medan is Sumatra's primary international airport, with frequent flights to mainland Southeast Asian cities such as Singapore, Kuala Lumpur and Penang. In West Sumatra, Padang receives flights from Singapore and Kuala Lumpur.

You can also hop on a plane from Jakarta to every major Sumatran city aboard a range of airlines. Flights from Sumatra to other parts of Indonesia often connect through Jakarta.

BOAT Despite cheap airfares, a handful of travellers still heed the call of the sea and enter Sumatra by ferry from Malaysia. The only ferry route commonly used by backpackers is the inconvenient Melaka (Malaysia) to Dumai (Indonesia) crossing. Dumai is on Sumatra's east coast and is a 10-hour bus ride from Bukittinggi; see p269 for more information. There are also several daily departures to Batam (one-way RM69; 1½ hours) and Tanjung Pinang on Bintan (one-way RM86; 2½ hours) from Johor Bahru in Malaysia (on the Singapore–Malaysia border). Additional boats also depart from Kukup, southwest of Johor Bahru, and Batu Bahat to Yanjung Balai (also in Sumatra).

From Singapore, ferries make the quick hop to Pulau Batam and Bintan, the primary islands in the Riau archipelago.

From Batam, boats serve the following mainland Sumatran ports: Dumai, Palembang and Pekanbaru. Again, once you hit Indonesian soil it's a long old bus ride to any postcard-worthy spots. See p269 for more information.

Ferries cross the narrow Sunda Strait linking the southeastern tip of Sumatra at Bakauheni

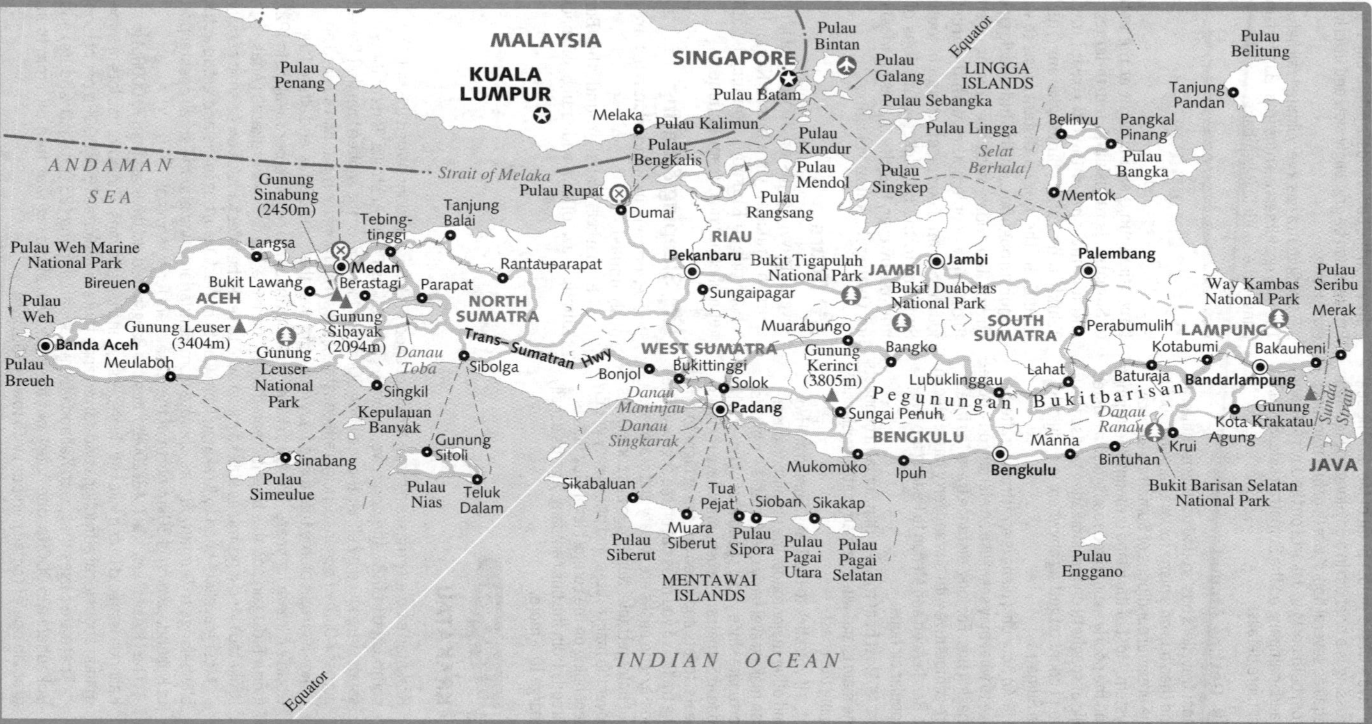
Sumatra
0 200 km
0 120 miles
MALAYSIA
KUALA LUMPUR
SINGAPORE
ANDAMAN SEA
Strait of Melaka
Equator
Pulau Penang
Pulau Bintan
Pulau Galang
Pulau Batam
LINGGA ISLANDS
Pulau Sebangka
Pulau Lingga
Pulau Belitung
Tanjung Pandan
Melaka
Pulau Kalimun
Pulau Bengkalis
Pulau Kundur
Pulau Mendol
Pulau Singkep
Selat Berhala
Belinyu
Pangkal Pinang
Pulau Bangka
Mentok
Pulau Rupat
Dumai
Pulau Rangsang
Gunung Sinabung (2450m)
Tanjung Balai
Tebing-tinggi
Langsa
Pulau Weh Marine National Park
Medan
Rantauparapat
RIAU
Pekanbaru
Bukit Tigapuluh National Park
JAMBI
Jambi
Palembang
Bireuen
Bukit Lawang
Berastagi
Parapat
ACEH
NORTH SUMATRA
Sungaipagar
Bukit Duabelas National Park
Pulau Seribu
Way Kambas National Park
Merak
Pulau Weh
Gunung Leuser (3404m)
Gunung Sibayak (2094m)
Muarabungo
SOUTH SUMATRA
Perabumulih
LAMPUNG
Banda Aceh
Gunung Leuser National Park
Danau Toba
Trans-Sumatran Hwy
WEST SUMATRA
Gunung Kerinci (3805m)
Bangko
Kotabumi
Bakauheni
Pulau Breueh
Meulaboh
Sibolga
Bonjol
Bukittinggi
Solok
Lubuklinggau
Lahat
Baturaja
Bandarlampung
Singkil
Danau Maninjau
Padang
Pegunungan Bukitbarisan
Danau Singkarak
Sungai Penuh
Danau Ranau
Gunung Krakatau
Kota Agung
Sunda Strait
Kepulauan Banyak
Gunung Sitoli
BENGKULU
Manna
Krui
Sinabang
Pulau Simeulue
Pulau Nias
Teluk Dalam
Mukomuko
Ipuh
Bengkulu
Bintuhan
JAVA
Sikabaluan
Tua Pejat
Sioban
Sikakap
Bukit Barisan Selatan National Park
Pulau Siberut
Muara Siberut
Pulau Sipora
Pulau Pagai Utara
Pulau Pagai Selatan
Pulau Enggano
MENTAWAI ISLANDS
INDIAN OCEAN

to Java's westernmost point of Merak. The sea crossing is a brief dip in a day-long voyage that requires several hours' worth of bus transport from both ports to Jakarta on the Java side and Bandarlampung on the Sumatran side. See p247 for more details.

Getting Around

Most travellers bus around northern Sumatra and then hop on a plane to Java, largely avoiding the dreadful conditions of Sumatra's highway system. Most of the island is mountainous jungle and the poorly maintained roads form a twisted pile of spaghetti on the undulating landscape. Don't count on getting anywhere very quickly on Sumatra.

AIR An hour on a plane is an attractive alternative to what may seem like an eternity on a bone-shaking bus. For long-distance travel, airfares are competitive with bus and ferry fares. Medan to Banda Aceh and Medan to Padang are two popular air hops.

BOAT Most boat travel within Sumatra connects the main island with the many satellite islands lining the coast.

BUS If you stick to the Trans-Sumatran Hwy and other major roads, the big air-con buses can make travel fairly comfortable – which is fortunate since you'll spend a lot of time on the road in Sumatra. The best ones have reclining seats, toilets and video but run at night to avoid the traffic, so you miss out on the scenery. The non-air-con buses are sweaty and cramped, but unforgettable. Numerous bus companies cover the main routes, and prices vary greatly, depending on the comfort level. Buy tickets directly from the bus company. Agents usually charge 10% more.

Travel on the back roads is a different story. Progress can be grindingly slow and utterly exhausting.

TRAIN Sumatra has a very limited rail network. The only useful service runs from Bandarlampung in the south to Palembang.

Bandarlampung

0721 / POP 859,000

Bandarlampung, sitting right at the bottom of Sumatra, is the island's fourth-largest city and an amalgam of the old coastal town of Telukbetung and Tanjungkarang further inland. In the not so distant past, it was a major throughfare on the Indo-backpacking circuit, but today, with the advent of cheap flights, few people bother with the gruelling journey from Jakarta up through southern Sumatra to the big ticket attractions of the north. However, the city makes an ideal base for visiting Krakatau volcano.

Tours

Several travel agents on Jl Monginsidi offer tours to Krakatau via a bus to Kalianda and a boat ride to Krakatau. You may be able to get a cheaper deal from Kalianda.

Sleeping & Eating

Budget options in Bandarlampung are seriously limited.

The market stalls around the Bambu Kuning Plaza offer a wide range of snacks.

DON'T MISS

KRAKATAU

Krakatau's beauty masks a mean streak of apocalyptic proportions. When this volcano combusted in 1883, the boom was heard as far away as Perth, Australia. Tens of thousands were killed by either the resulting 30m-high tsunami or the molten lava that flowed across 40km of ocean to incinerate coastal villages. The monster mountain spewed an 80km-high ash plume that turned day into night over the Sunda Strait and altered the world's climate for years. The earth kept rumbling under the remains of Krakatau. In 1927 it erupted again and this time it created an evil mini-me, the Child of Krakatau (Anak Krakatau). And it grumbles still, so make sure to seek the latest advice on seismic activity.

Most travellers head to Krakatau from Carita in West Java, but the island group actually belongs to Sumatra. Tours operate from Bandarlampung and the small coastal port of Kalianda, which is 30km north of the Bakauheni ferry terminal.

The **Hotel Beringin** (322008; Jl Kesuma Bangsa 75; d incl breakfast from 70,000Rp) in Kalianda is an old Dutch villa with high ceilings and languid fans. The hotel has lots of information about local attractions and can arrange tours to Krakatau (690,000Rp per person).

There are buses that go to Kalianda from Bandarlampung (25,000Rp, 1½ hours) and Bakauheni (25,000Rp, one hour), but they drop you at the highway turn-off. From there, grab an *opelet* (small minibus) into town (3000Rp).

WORTH A TRIP

SOUTHERN SUMATRA

Aside from Krakatau and the ferry crossing to Java, southern Sumatra is something of a blank on the backpacker map but the region hides plenty of enticing little secrets. Chief among these are the wild forests and swamps of the **Way Kambas National Park** to the northeast of Bandarlampung. The highlight of a visit to this park is the elephant-back safari rides.

If sun, sand and surf is more your thing, the laid-back village of **Krui** has your name all over it. Five hours' drive from Bandarlampung, Krui has recently gained a serious name for itself among travelling surfers thanks to the coastline being littered with world-class spots (many of them not beginner-friendly). Backpackers are still a rare sight, but if the backpack trail ever takes off in South Sumatra, Krui, with its sublime beaches, will quite rightly become every beach bum's favourite hang-out.

Hotel Grande HOTEL **$$**
(☎261448; Jl Raden Intan 77; d incl breakfast from 215,000Rp; ❄📶) The best option in this price range. It is well managed and maintained, with big, comfortable rooms.

Hotel Lusy HOTEL **$**
(☎471020; Jl Diponegoro 186; r with fan/air-con 80,000/120,000Rp; ❄) One of the very few budget hotels in town. However, it's dirty, overpriced and a 50,000Rp taxi ride from the centre.

ℹ Getting There & Away

Air

The airport is 24km north of the city. Both **Garuda** (www.garuda-indonesia.com) and **Sriwijaya Air** (www.sriwijayaair-online.com) operate daily flights to Jakarta.

Bus

There are two bus terminals in Bandarlampung. The city's sprawling Rajabasa bus terminal is 10km north of town and serves long-distance destinations. Panjang bus terminal is 6km southeast of town along the Lampung Bay road and serves local and provincial destinations.

From Rajabasa, buses run to Bukittinggi (regular/air-con 190,000/300,000Rp, 22 hours) as well as many other large Sumatran towns and cities.

You've got several bus options for getting to the Bakauheni pier, from which boats go to Java. The most convenient option is the Damri bus-boat-bus combination ticket to Jakarta (*bisnis/eksekutif* 115,000/150,000Rp, eight to 10 hours). Buses leave from Bandarlampung's train station at 10am, 9pm and 10pm. Damri's office is in front of Bandarlampung's train station.

Train

The train station is in the town centre at the northern mouth of Jl Raden Intan. Sumatra's only convenient rail service connects Bandarlampung with Palembang (*ekonomi/bisnis* 15,000/55,000, 10 hours) and then beyond to Lubuklinggau.

ℹ Getting Around

Taxis charge 80,000Rp to 100,000Rp for the ride from the airport to town. Take the green *opelet* (minibus) from the town centre to the Rajabasa bus terminal for 2000Rp.

Bakauheni

Bakauheni is the departure point for ferries to Merak, Java. Fast ferries run every 30 minutes from 7am to 5pm (30,000Rp); the crossing takes 45 minutes. A slow ferry runs every 30 minutes, 24 hours a day and the two-hour trip costs 11,500Rp.

Frequent buses depart from outside Bakauheni's ferry terminal and travel the 90km to Bandarlampung (25,000Rp, two hours). If you're planning to stay the night in Bandarlampung, pay 30,000Rp for a private taxi, which will take you to the hotel of your choice.

Padang

☎0751 / POP 833,584

Most backpackers fly into Padang only to catch the first bus to Bukittinggi. Big mistake. Despite a devastating earthquake in September 2009 that left around 5000 people dead and destroyed large sections of Padang, Sumatra's largest west-coast city has a gorgeous waterfront setting, with Minangkabau roofs soaring from modern public buildings and a leafy old quarter dominated by a narrow, brackish river harbour crowded with colourful fishing boats, yachts and lux Bugis schooners. The coastline south of

Padang

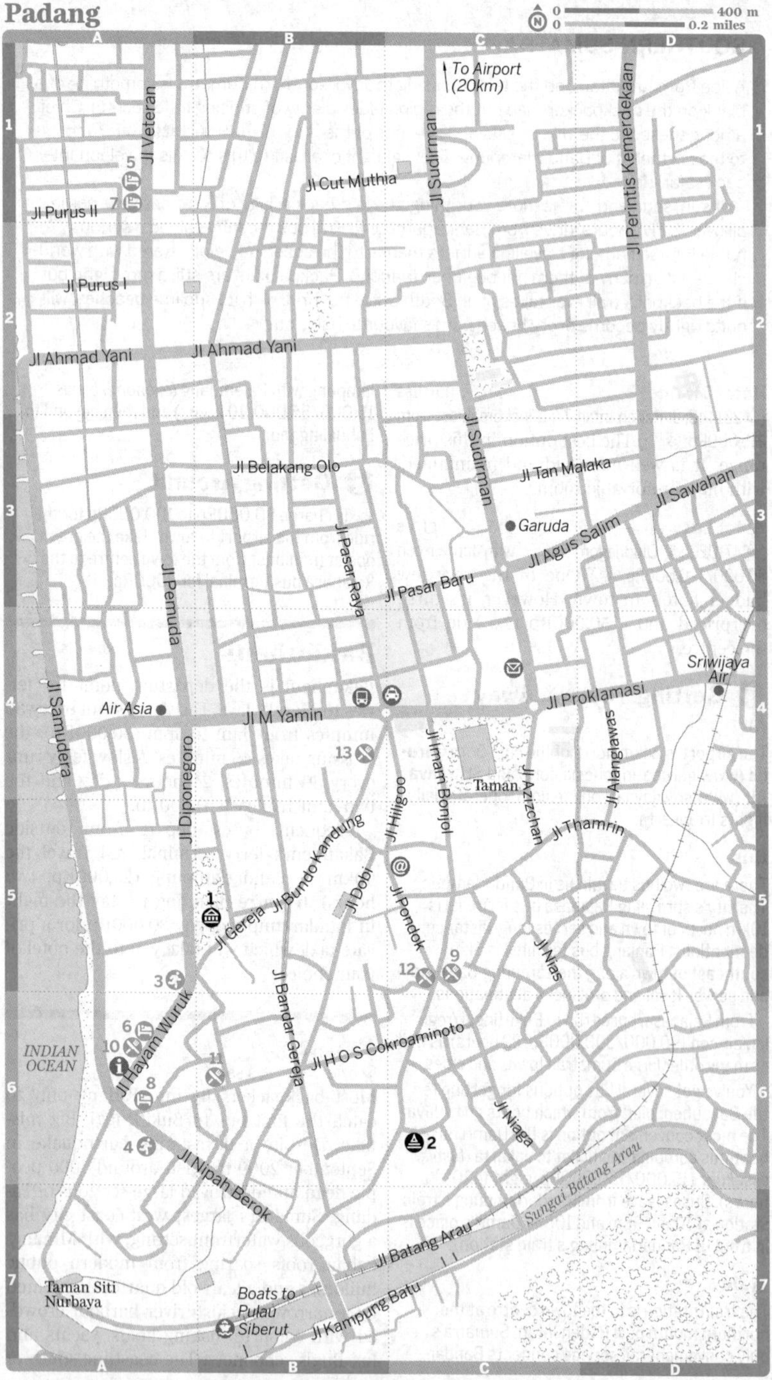

0 400 m
0 0.2 miles

To Airport (20km)

Jl Veteran
Jl Purus II
Jl Purus I
Jl Cut Muthia
Jl Sudirman
Jl Perintis Kemerdekaan
Jl Ahmad Yani
Jl Belakang Olo
Jl Tan Malaka
Jl Sawahan
Garuda
Jl Agus Salim
Jl Pasar Raya
Jl Pasar Baru
Jl Pemuda
Sriwijaya Air
Jl Proklamasi
Jl Samudera
Air Asia
Jl M Yamin
Jl Imam Bonjol
Jl Diponegoro
Taman
Jl Azizchan
Jl Alanglawas
Jl Thamrin
Jl Hiligoo
Jl Bundo Kandung
Jl Dobi
Jl Pondok
Jl Gereja
Jl Nias
Jl Bandar Gereja
Jl Hayam Wuruk
INDIAN OCEAN
Jl H O S Cokroaminoto
Jl Niaga
Jl Nipah Berok
Sungai Batang Arau
Jl Batang Arau
Taman Siti Nurbaya
Boats to Pulau Siberut
Jl Kampung Batu

Padang

Sights

Activities, Courses & Tours

Sleeping

Eating

town is magnificent too, and the city beach is edged by a popular promenade, which is where you'll want to be when the sun drops.

The Teluk Bayur port is 8km east of the centre, the shiny new airport is located 20km to the north, and the Bengkuang bus terminal is inconveniently located in Aie Pacah, about 12km from town.

Sights & Activities

Locals converge on the beach promenade at sunset for snacks, cool drinks and football games on the sand.

Colonial Quarter HISTORIC MONUMENT
Many of the city's fading colonial buildings were destroyed in the 2009 earthquake, but enough survive to make worthwhile a stroll among antiquated Dutch and Chinese warehouses in the colonial quarter along Jl Batang Arau. While you're in this area, don't pass up the opportunity to sit quietly on the waterfront watching the fishing boats ease into dock after a night's work. The nearby incense-perfumed, candlelit **Chinese Temple** is an evocative homage to the Confucian age.

Adityawarman Museum MUSEUM
(Jl Diponegoro; admission 1500Rp; 8am-4pm Tue-Sun) The Adityawarman Museum is beautifully built in a traditional Minangkabau architectural style with two rice barns out front. It has a bland collection, but lovely grounds. Enter from Jl Gereja.

Tours

Bevys Sumatra/ Sumatran Surfariis SURF TOUR
(34878; www.sumatrasurfariis.com; Jl Pondok 121) Long-standing Mentawi surf charter-boat operator that trades under two names.

East West Tour & Travel SURF TOUR
(36370; Jl Nipah Berok 1) A respected Indonesian-run charter-boat company offering 12-day Mentawai surf trips from US$2200 per person.

Sleeping

Much of the accommodation in Padang was destroyed in the earthquake. While many of the midrange places have been rebuilt or new ones have opened up, many budget (and, strangely, top-end) places remain closed. The few budget places that do still exist have hoisted their prices by so much that price wise, if not quality wise, there's little to differentiate between budget and midrange digs. Therefore in Padang, more than anywhere else in Sumatra, we'd recommend spending a little bit more in order to get a whole lot more.

TOP CHOICE **Spice Homestay** GUESTHOUSE $$
(25982; spicehomey@yahoo.com; Jl HOS Cokroaminoto 104; dm/r incl breakfast 155,000/ 280,000Rp;) After the original Spice Homestay was flattened in the earthquake, the owners have rebuilt it bigger, better and spicier just around the corner. The cool and stylish rooms are often taken over by masses of surfers in transit to the Mentawai Islands, but it's also the city's number-one traveller centre.

Meruit Hotel HOTEL $$
(34034; hotelmeruit@gmail.com; Jl Purus II 6; r incl breakfast without/with bathroom from 275,000/360,000Rp;) Just north of the centre, this new hotel might cost a bit more than you're used to paying, but in an expensive town such as Padang it offers some of the best-value accommodation you'll find. The small rooms are modern and well designed and have deliciously comfortable beds.

Immanuel Hotel HOTEL $
(28560; Jl Hayam Wuruk 43; s/d incl breakfast 151,000/181,000Rp;) This is one of the few remaining budget places in the city centre, though you'd hardly describe it as good value. On the plus side, the tiny, tiled rooms have attached bathrooms and the staff are friendly.

Hotel Tiga Tiga HOTEL $
(☎22173; Jl Veteran 33; r from 150,000Rp; ❄) North of the centre, this old travellers' dosser has cheap (by Padang standards), simple rooms only five minutes' walk from the sea. However, it's noisy and has zero character. Grab any white *opelet* heading up Jl Permuda (20,000Rp).

Eating

The city is famous as the home of *nasi Padang* (Padang food), the spicy Minangkabau cooking that's found throughout Indonesia, and is served quicker than fast food. Try **Pagi Sore** (Jl Pondok 143; dishes 8000Rp) and **Simpang Raya** (Jl Bundo Kandung; dishes 8000Rp).

Jl Sumadera and Jl Batang Arau are full of cheap *warungs* that spring to life at night, while discerning foodies head for Jl Pondok and Jl HOSCokroaminoto. Juice wagons loiter near the beach end of Jl Hayam Wuruk. Grab a snack from the carts at the *opelet* station opposite the market.

TOP CHOICE **Ikan Bakar 'Pak Agus'** SEAFOOD $$
(Jl HOSCokroaminoto 91; set meals from 50,000Rp) Standing proud above the ruins of the earthquake, Pak Agus flames his sea creatures to perfection. The seafood is delivered fresh every day. A set meal contains a whole barbecued fish, sides, rice and a drink, but the price depends on the size and type of fish you choose.

Fellas INTERNATIONAL $
(Jl Hayam Wuruk 47; mains 20,000-25,000Rp; 📶) A cool, fashion-conscious cafe (with wi-fi) by day, Fellas fills with a cosmopolitan mix of young locals, surfers and tourists in the evenings. The food is a melange of Indonesian, Chinese and Western flavours that'll make your taste buds very happy indeed.

Bakmi Raos INDONESIAN $
(Jl Niaga 122; mains 15,000-18,000Rp) This is something a little different. The cuisine is spicy Padang food with a few other Indonesian dishes thrown in for good measure. The setting is a bright, clean, European-style coffee shop.

Information

Padang has branches of all the major Indonesian banks. There are ATMs all over town, including a string on Jl Pondok.

Caroline Street Internet (Jl Pondok 5F; per hr 6000Rp; ⌚9am-9pm)

Post office (Jl Azizchan 7; internet per hr 6000Rp)

Rumah Sakit Yos Sudarso (☎33230; Jl Situjuh 1) Privately owned health clinic.

Tourism Padang (Dinas Kebudayaan Dan Pariwisata; ☎34186; www.tourism.padang.go.id; Jl Samudera 1; ⌚7.30am-4pm Mon-Fri, 8am-4pm Sat & Sun) Its website has a handy list of events.

Getting There & Away

Air

Bandara Internasional Minangkabau airport (code BIM) is 20km north, off Jl Adinegoro. The following airlines operate international and domestic flights. There is a 100,000Rp departure tax on international flights.

Air Asia (☎021 5050 5088; Hotel Huangtuah, Jl Pemuda 1) Flies twice daily to Kuala Lumpur, Malaysia.

Batavia (☎446600; www.batavia-air.co.id; Jl Khatib Sulaiman No 63C) Flies to Jakarta, Medan and Batam.

Garuda (☎080 4180 7807; www.garuda-indonesia.com; Jl Sudirman 2) Operates four flights daily to Jakarta.

Lion Air (☎080 4177 8899; www.lionair.co.id; airport) Flies to Jakarta seven times daily.

Sriwijaya Air (☎811777; www.sriwijayaair-online.com; Jl Proklamasi No 39 Terandam) Daily flights to Jakarta and Medan.

Boat

Padang has three commonly used ports. Depending on the tide, boats to Siberut and other Mentawai islands will leave from either the river mouth (Sungai Muara) on Sungai Batang Arau, just south of Padang's city centre, or from Teluk Kabung port at Bungus, 20km (45 minutes) away. Check the boat's departure point with your travel agent on sailing day.

Teluk Bayur is the commercial freight port 8km from town and receives a monthly **Pelni** (www.pelni.co.id) ship to/from Nias (*ekonomi*/1st class 117,000/449,000Rp, 20 hours).

Bus

The days of heading 12km out of town to the Bengkuang terminal at Aie Pacah are over. Most locals prefer to take minibuses directly from Padang.

Buses and minibuses will often pick you up (or drop you off) outside your hotel of choice. Ask your hotel to call in advance to organise this. Tranex has a depot 2km north of the Pangeran Beach Hotel, opposite the Indah Theatre. Catch any white *opelet* (2000Rp) heading north on Jl Permuda and ask for 'Tranex'.

For Medan and Jakarta, it's cheaper and faster to fly.

Getting Around

Airport taxis start from 120,000Rp. Tranex buses (25,000Rp) are a cheaper alternative and loop through Padang. Tell the conductor your street and they'll drop you at the right stop. Heading to the airport, they pass by Bumiminang Hotel and Jl Pemuda/Veteran. From Bukittinggi alight at the motorway overpass and take an *ojek* to the terminal.

There are numerous *opelet* around town, operating out of the Pasar Raya terminal off Jl M Yamin. The standard fare is 2000Rp.

Bukittinggi

☎0752 / ELEV 930M / POP 91,000

Early on a bright clear morning, the market town of Bukittinggi sits high above the valley mists as three sentinels – fire-breathing Merapi, benign Singgalang and distant Sago – all look on impassively. Modern life seems far removed until 9am. Then the traffic starts up, and soon there's a mile-long jam around the bus terminal, and the air turns the colour of diesel. The mosques counter the traffic by cranking their amps up to 11.

Such is the incongruity of modern Bukittinggi, blessed by nature, choked by mortals. Lush. Fertile. Busy. And at 930m above sea level, deliciously temperate all year round.

Bukittinggi was once a mainstay of the banana-pancake tourist trail, but regional instability, shorter visas and the rise of low-cost air-carriers have seen the traveller tide reduced to a low ebb.

Sights & Activities

Taman Panorama PARK

(Jl Panorama; admission 3000Rp) Taman Panorama, on the southern edge of town, overlooks the deep Ngarai Sianok (Sianok Canyon), where fruit bats swoop at sunset.

Friendly guides will approach visitors – settle on a price (around 20,000Rp) before continuing to avoid misunderstandings

WORTH A TRIP

MENTAWAI ISLANDS

It was surfing that put the Mentawais on the tourism radar; nowhere else on earth has such a dense concentration of world-class surf spots in such a small area. Today, dozens of wave-hunting live-aboards run from Padang harbour year-round and a growing number of dedicated surf camps populate the banner spots. Surfing is big business here year-round, but the season peaks between April and October. Like many Indonesian surf areas, the Mentawais are not suitable for learners. The waves, which break over shallow reefs, tend to be fast, hollow, heavy and unforgiving, and many of the spots are not even suitable for intermediate surfers.

But it's not just surfers who come out here; more and more ecotourists are also braving the rugged ocean crossing and muddy malarial jungle of this remote archipelago to trek, glimpse traditional tribal culture and spot endemic primates. Many consider it the highlight of their trip through Southeast Asia.

The economic, and culturally responsible, choice for touring is to take a public boat to Siberut and seek out a Mentawai guide. You pay less and directly benefit the community you've come to experience.

As far as surfing tours go the vast majority of surfers pre-arrange boat charters or surf camp accommodation with a surf travel company in their home country. These are ideal if all you want to do is get off a plane and surf your guts out. However, it's a real bubble-like existence and the only Indonesians you're actually likely to meet will be your boat crew. If you've got lots of time then it's perfectly possible, and much closer to the true spirit of old-school surf travel, to take the public ferry out to the islands and once there arrange local boat transport and accommodation in one of the cheap and simple *losmens* that can be found close to many of the breaks.

As there is no longer a public speedboat (or flights) to the islands, all ferries to Mentawai charge the same price (deck/cabin 85,000/100,000Rp) and usually take 10 hours. Pay the extra for the cabin, as the deck sucks. All boats run overnight, and usually return the following evening (unless continuing). The ferry schedules are changing constantly so always check what's available on arrival in Padang.

Tickets can be bought directly at the **port** (☎0850 5333, Jl Batang Arau) in Padang.

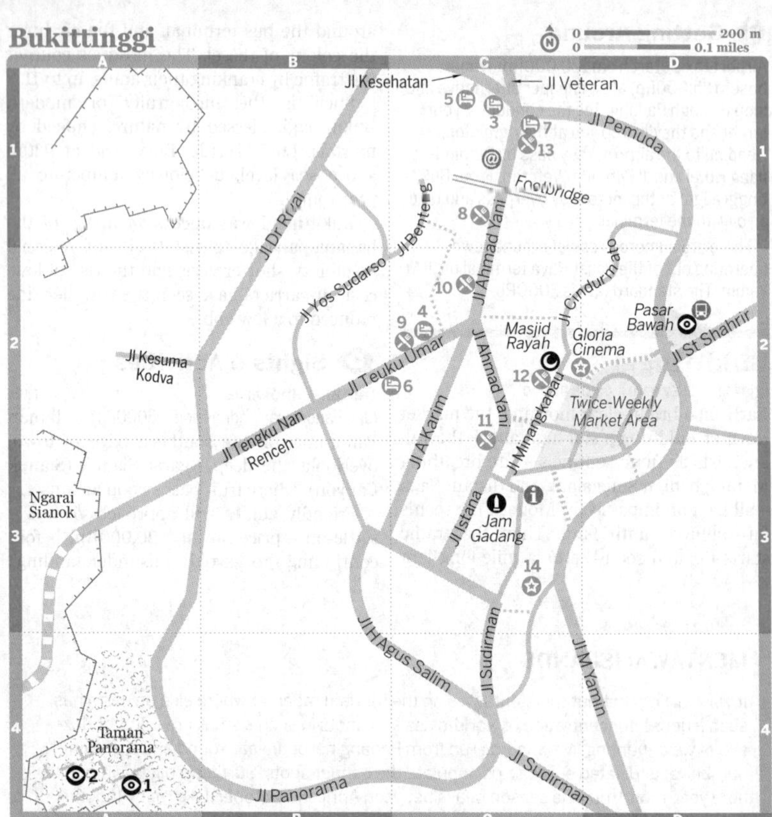

Bukittinggi

Sights

1 Gua Jepang....A4
2 Taman Panorama....A4

Sleeping

3 Hotel Asia....C1
4 Hotel Kartini....C2
5 Lima's Hotel....C1
6 Orchid Hotel....C2
7 Raja Wali Homestay....C1

Eating

8 Bedudal Café....C1
9 Canyon Cafe....C2
10 Gon Raya....C2
11 Selamat....C2
12 Simpang Raya....C2
13 Turret Cafe....C1

Entertainment

14 Medan Nan Balinduang....C3

later – to lead you through **Gua Jepang** (Japanese Caves), tunnels built by Indonesian slave labour for the occupying Japanese.

Sleeping

Most hotels include a simple breakfast. On holidays, rooms fill quickly with Indonesian visitors. In Bukittinggi's temperate climate, hot water is more desirable than air-con.

Orchid Hotel HOTEL $
(☎32634; roni_orchid@hotmail.com; Jl Teuku Umar 11; r cold/hot water 90,000/120,000Rp) Roni runs this popular backpacker inn, which has clean rooms, squat toilets and a friend-

ly atmosphere, and he can tailor a tour to almost anywhere in the vicinity.

Raja Wali Homestay GUESTHOUSE $
(☎26113; Jl Ahmad Yani 152; r 60,000Rp) Basic rooms in this incredibly popular German-run homestay right in the centre of all the action (and noise!). The irrepressible Ulrich has been here forever and is a font of local knowledge and has detailed maps and advice on the area's attractions.

Hotel Kartini HOTEL $
(☎22885; Jl Teuku Umar 6; r from 175,000Rp) This place looks like an old family home, which indeed it once was. Today it's been reincarnated as a budget hotel, everything about the place is kept ship-shape and it would be hard to deny that it has the most comfortable cheap beds in town.

Lima's Hotel HOTEL $$
(☎22641; Jl Kesehatan 34; r incl breakfast 250,000-400,000Rp, plus 10% tax; wi-fi) This is a great-value midrange option, whose cosy rooms have polished wooden furniture and a slightly old-fashioned feel. Some have memorable views down the valley. Choose your room wisely, though, because some are much better than others.

Hotel Asia HOTEL $
(☎625277; Jl Kesehatan 38; r incl breakfast from 120,000Rp; air-con) Centrally located, the Asia, which is filled with giant Chinese-style vases, offers spotless and spacious rooms for a bargain price. The airy common balconies evoke a Himalayan vibe. The orchestra of road noise can be a pain, though.

Eating & Drinking

Bukittinggi has always been the one place in Sumatra that weary road-bums can give their poor chilli-nuked organs a chance to recover with lashings of loveably bland *makan Amerika*.

Jl Ahmad Yani comes alive at night with food stalls doing excellent satay and *nasi/mie goreng*. For *nasi Padang*, try **Selamat** (upper Jl Ahmad Yani; mains from 8000Rp), **Gon Raya** (Jl Ahmad Yani; mains from 8000Rp) or **Simpang Raya** (Jl Minangkabau; mains from 8000Rp), which all offer classic Indonesian dishes in settings just one step up from a street food cart.

Turret Cafe INTERNATIONAL $
(Jl Ahmad Yani 140-142; mains from 12,000Rp; @) Good food (think pasta, pizzas and toned-down Indo dishes), relaxed outdoor lounges, internet and a crowd of other backpackers. What more can a traveller want? A hearty breakfast menu? OK, it can do that too.

Bedudal Café INTERNATIONAL $
(Jl Ahmad Yani; mains from 20,000Rp) Has all the old traveller favourites dished up with a dose of the Rasta vibe. The waiters often launch into impromptu jam sessions.

Canyon Cafe INTERNATIONAL $
(Jl Teuku Umar 8; mains from 15,000Rp) Still playing Creedence and waiting for the tide to change, though the food's always good.

Entertainment

Medan Nan Balinduang DANCE
(Jl Lenggogeni; tickets 40,000Rp; ⏲8.30pm) Offers Minangkabau dance/theatre shows featuring graceful dancing, colourful costumes and a martial-arts demonstration. Check with the tourist office for the latest schedule.

Information

Banks with ATMs, and money changers are clustered along Jl Ahmad Yani, home also to dozens of travel agents and many more services.

DON'T MISS

OUT & ABOUT IN BUKITTINGGI

A vast array of local tours can be arranged in Bukittinggi. Generally these fall into two categories: culture or nature, and can range from a half-day meander through neighbouring villages to a three-day jungle trek to Danau Maninjau, or an overnight assault on Gunung Merapi.

Half-/full-day tours start at around 100,000/175,000Rp and multiday trekking is roughly 200,000Rp per day.

Guides hang out in all the cafes. Be clear about what you want and what is and isn't included. If going solo, make sure somebody knows who's guiding you.

There's also a healthy climbing scene. A day on the cliffs costs around US$35, but if you can find some locals and avoid the entrepreneurs, it'll work out cheaper.

BUSES FROM BUKITTINGGI

DESTINATION	PRICE ECONOMY/AIR-CON (RP)	DURATION (HRS)
Medan	130,000/180,000	20
Jakarta	270,000/350,000	30-35
Parapat	130,000/180,000	16
Sibolga	100,000	10-12

One Stop Internet Place (Jl Ahmad Yani; per hr 4000Rp) Internet access.

Post office (Jl Sudirman; internet per hr 6000Rp) South of town near the bus terminal.

Tourist office (Jl Sudirman; ⌚7am-4pm) Opposite the clock tower (Jam Gadang); it's got maps, tours and tickets to cultural events.

Turret Cafe (Jl Ahmad Yani 140-142; per hr 6000Rp) Internet access.

Getting There & Away

The chaos of the Aur Kuning bus terminal 2km south is easily reached by *opelet* (2000Rp). Ask for 'terminal'.

Minibuses run regularly to Padang (17,000Rp, two hours) and Solok (16,000Rp, two hours). A full-sized bus to Padang is 20,000Rp. Decrepit buses make the Danau Maninjau run (13,000Rp, 1½ hours) while a taxi starts at 160,000Rp.

Trans-Sumatran buses also stop here, though only masochists sign up for the really long-haul trips (Jakarta, Medan etc). Still, if you get off on being bounced about for hour upon hour in a hot bus the table 'Buses from Bukittinggi' might be useful.

Minibuses head to Pekanbaru (70,000Rp to 100,000Rp depending on demand; 5-6 hours).

Getting Around

Opelet cost 2000Rp. *Bendi* start from 20,000Rp. An *ojek* from the bus terminal to the hotels costs 7000Rp and a taxi costs 25,000Rp. Transfers direct to Padang airport can be arranged from any travel agent for 35,000Rp.

Danau Maninjau

☎0752

Maninjau, 38km west of Bukittinggi, is one of Sumatra's most spectacularly peaceful crater lakes. The unforgettable final descent includes 44 hair-pin turns that offer stunning views over the shimmering sky-blue lake (17km long, 8km wide) and the 600m crater walls. Maninjau is well set up for travellers (even if low numbers mean that locals have turned to fishing), and should be considered an alternative to Bukittinggi as a place to stay. Life travels slowly here, making it the ideal place to kick back and do nothing. On the other hand, the rainforests and waterfalls of the caldera are just waiting to be explored.

Activities

The Lake SWIMMING, BOATING

This is an outstanding swimming lake. Though it's 480m deep in some places, the water is warmer than Danau Toba, and outside town, the water becomes pure as liquid crystal. Some guesthouses rent dug-out canoes or truck inner tubes to float upon.

When relaxation becomes too much, many visitors tackle the 70km sealed road that circles the lake. It's about six hours by mountain bike or 2½ hours by moped.

Sakura Hill HIKING

There's a strenuous two-hour trek to Sakura Hill and the stunning lookout of **Puncak Lawang**. Catch a Bukittinggi-bound bus to Matur and climb 5km to the viewpoint; from there descend to the lake on foot.

Sleeping

Aquaculture has transformed the Maninjau foreshore. *Losmen* with sublime views now look over fishponds and jetties, although there are still beautiful spots.

Outside Maninjau village, most *losmen* are reached by walking along rice-paddy paths, so look for the sign by the roadside.

Distances indicated with listings are from the Maninjau intersection.

MANINJAU

The majority of the town options front onto aquaculture.

TOP CHOICE **Muaro Beach Bungalows** BUNGALOWS $
(☎61189; Jl Muaro Pisang 53, 300m NW; r 60,000Rp) Down a maze of footpaths on a delightful stretch of private beach somehow

free of fish ponds, these clean bungalows are the best value of the village group. The owners are friendly and can organise a wealth of tours and actitivies, and when they're not entertaining you, the squawking hens and lazy cats that hang around here will.

House of Annisa HISTORIC HOTEL $$
(☎085 7660 41558; 300m S; r 200,000Rp) This wonderful old Dutch villa has been lovingly restored by the great-grandchildren of the original owners. There are just three rooms (one with a stunning brass four-poster bed festooned with mirrors) and it's shared bathrooms only. It's impeccably clean and well-maintained and there is a gorgeous balcony filled with antique benches and chairs.

BAYUR

The following are beyond Bayur village.

Beach Inn BUNGALOWS $
(☎081 3740 80485; 4km N; r 60,000Rp) Outstanding value for money is to be found at this rickety little place right on a private patch of beach. It offers accommodation in either rooms or private bungalows (prices are the same) and it gets our vote as one of the friendliest places in the area. It's a 300m walk through the rice paddies from the road.

'Arlen' Nova's Paradise BUNGALOWS $
(☎26471; novaf@hotmail.com; Sungai-Rangeh, 5.5km N; r 150,000Rp) Walk through rice paddies to these simple bungalows on a private beach with nary a fishpond in sight. It has snagged what is easily the nicest location on the lake.

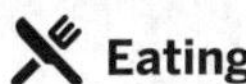

Eating

Most of the guesthouses serve standards such as *nasi/mie goreng*, some Western favourites and freshly caught fish.

Rama Cafe INDONESIAN $
(mains 20,000-30,000Rp) Share a *martabark* (20,000Rp) before hooking into a plate of *ikan panggang* (baked fish; 30,000Rp) while lazing on cushions among kites and drums. Look out for the extraordinary weaver-bird nests hanging from the rafters.

Getting There & Around

Buses run hourly between Maninjau and Bukittinggi (10,000Rp, 1½ hours). Taxis from Bukittinggi start from 150,000Rp. There is also an economy bus to/from Dumai (50,000Rp).

Several places rent out mountain bikes (per day 15,000Rp), motorcycles (80,000Rp) and canoes (15,000Rp).

Minibuses plod around the lake road during daylight hours (from 2000Rp). Alternatively, an *ojek* from the Maninjau intersection to Bayur will cost around 7000Rp.

Danau Toba

☎0625 / POP 550,000

There's no denying the beauty of Danau Toba (Lake Toba), home of the fun-loving Batak people. This 1707-sq-km, 450m-deep lake, set in the collapsed caldera of an extinct volcano, is surrounded by mountains ribboned with waterfalls and terraced with rice fields. Its pale-blue magnificence hits you on the

DON'T MISS

PULAU NIAS

Sitting off the west coast of Sumatra, the lonely island of Nias is home to one of the world's best surf spots – the legendary righthander of Lagundri Bay. For non-surfers the island also has much to offer: the traditional hill villages, such as **Tundrumbaho** and **Bawomataluo**, will captivate even casual cultural tourists as well as ethno-architectural buffs.

The waves of Lagundri (or more correctly Pantai Sorake) on the southwest corner of the island, are best between April and October. On smaller days it's a fairly accessible wave for all but total beginners, but as soon as the swell starts to pick up, it becomes an experts-only barrel machine. The point here is lined by a string of very basic and almost identical *losmen*. The going rate is between 50,000Rp and 100,000Rp per night, but you are expected to eat at your *losmen* too. And that'll cost you. A plate of chicken or fish can fetch 50,000Rp.

To get to Nias you have the option of flying from Medan once or twice a day with **Merpati** (www.merpati.co.id). The more romantic way of reaching the island is by ferry from the seedy mainland port of Sibolga. Daily fast ferries run from Sibolga to Gunung Sitoli, the 'capital' of Nias. Slower, overnight boats run once a week from Sibolga to Teluk Dalam in the south of Nias and much closer to the surf.

Danau Toba

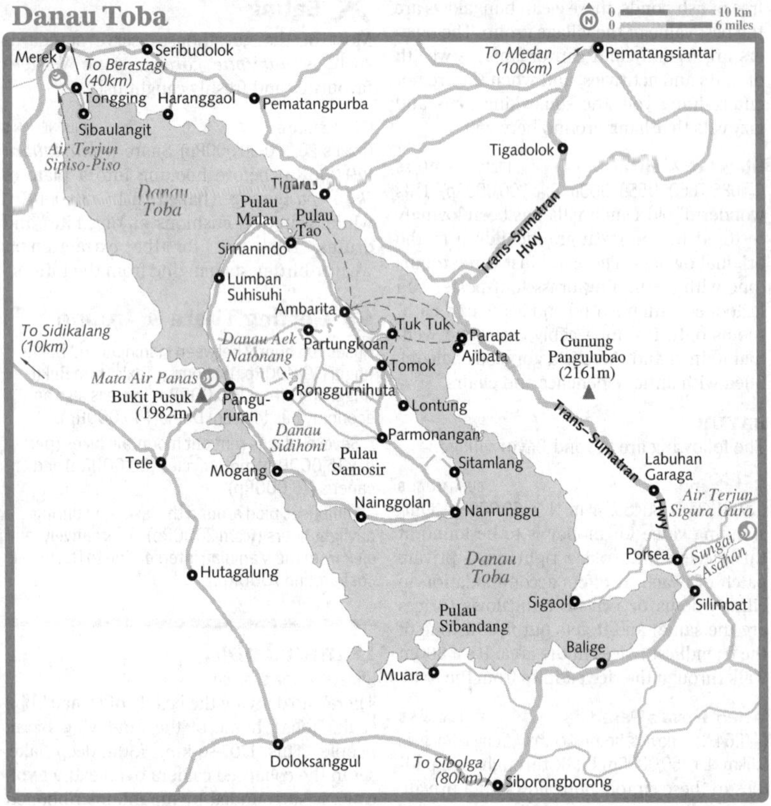

bus ride into Parapat, when you'll also spot in the middle of the lake Pulau Samosir – a Singapore-sized island of blissful greenery and chilled-out vibes. When there's a touch of mist in the air, and the horizon is obscured, the water seems to blend perfectly with the sky. Combine the climate, scenery, sights and friendly locals with some great food and an impressive array of cheap accommodation and you'll see why Lake Toba is Sumatra's backpacker hang-out par excellence.

PARAPAT

☎0625

The mainland departure point for Danau Toba, Parapat has everything a transiting tourist needs: transport, lodging and supplies.

The commercial sector of the town clumps together along the Trans-Sumatran Hwy (Jl SM Raja). Branching southwest towards the pier, Jl Pulau Samosir passes most of Parapat's hotels. After 1km, a right fork (Jl Haranggaol) leads to the pier, another 1km southwest. The bus terminal is 2km east of town, but most buses pick up and drop off passengers from ticket agents along the highway or at the pier.

Getting There & Away

The **bus terminal** (Trans-Sumatran Hwy) is about 2km east of town on the way to Bukittinggi, but is not frequently used (so say the travel agents). Prices are highly negotiable, so shop around at the different ticket agents.

Buses to Medan (22,000Rp, five hours) are frequent, although services taper off in the afternoon. There are also minibuses (70,000Rp) that deliver passengers to Jl SM Raya in Medan. Buses to Bukkitiggi are 130,000 to 180,000Rp and buses to Sibolga cost 70,000Rp.

PULAU SAMOSIR

☎0625 / ELEV 900M / POP 120,000

Trek, swim, explore traditional Batak villages, soak in hot springs, party or just chill with cool local people in Pulau Samosir. Your bus-beaten body will begin to unwind on the slow, 8km ferry cruise over to this volcanic isle (it's actually connected to the mainland by a narrow isthmus, but why quibble?). **Tuk Tuk**, the island's resort town, has seen busier times, which means low prices, high value and tranquillity.

Sights

The following sights are located around Danau Toba (Map p256).

Simanindo VILLAGE

At the northern tip of the island, in Simanindo, there's a fine old traditional house that has been restored and now functions as a **museum** (admission 30,000Rp; ⏲10am-5pm). It was formerly the home of Raja Simalungun, a Batak king, and his 14 wives. Displays of traditional **Batak dancing** are performed at 10.30am from Monday to Saturday if enough tourists show up.

The village of Simanindo is 15km from Tuk Tuk and is accessible with a hired motorbike.

Pangururan VILLAGE

The road that follows the northern rind of Samosir between Simanindo and the town of Pangururan is a scenic ride through the Bataks' embrace of life and death. Amid fertile rice fields are large **multistorey graves** decorated with the distinctive Batak-style house and a simple white cross. Typical Christian holidays, such as Christmas, dictate special attention to the graves. Crossing the island back to Tuk Tuk from here, you can dip into hill-top **hot springs** (admission 10,000Rp) and enjoy spectacular views.

Tomb of King Sidabutar MONUMENT

(admission by donation; ⏲dawn-dusk) **Tomok**, 2km southeast of Tuk Tuk, is the main village on the east coast of Samosir and the souvenir-stall capital of the island. Tucked away among them, 500m up a path from the road, is the ancient Tomb of King Sidabutar, one of the last pre-Christian animist kings. The grave's hand-carved details are intriguing, but the grounds need some love. Close by are some well-preserved traditional Batak houses, which some people might find more interesting than the tomb itself.

Stone Chairs HISTORIC SITE

(admission 2000Rp; ⏲8am-6pm) About 5km north of the Tuk Tuk peninsula, the village of **Ambarita** has a group of 300-year-old stone chairs where important matters were discussed among village elders, and where wrong-doers were tried – then apparently led to a further group of stone furnishings where they were beheaded.

Sleeping

The best sleeping options are along the north and south coasts, where little guesthouses are tucked in between village chores: washing the laundry on the rocks and collecting the news from neighbours.

Liberta Homestay COTTAGES $

(Map p258; ☎451035; liberta_homestay@yahoo.com.co.id; r without/with bathroom 25,000/40,000Rp; @) It may have only limited lake views, but a chill

DON'T MISS

MASTER CHEF CLASS

Sign up for **Heddy's Cooking Class** (Map p258; class 250,000Rp; ⏲1-4pm) held at Juwita Café in Tuk Tuk and you can learn to cook an Indonesian banquet to impress the folks back home. The three-hour course covers a vegetarian, chicken and fish dish and a dessert of your choice. You need to reserve in person the day before.

DON'T MISS

STRIDING OVER SAMOSIR

If you really want to get into the rural beat of the island, then this two-day village-to-village trek from Ambarita to Pangururan will do the job nicely. The jungle is long gone, but the paths are challenging and interesting as they wind past coffee and clove plantations. Get a map in Tuk Tuk because paths are not well marked.

The trek starts opposite the bank in Ambarita. Continue along, walking straight at the escarpment and take the path to the right of the graveyard. The climb to the top is hard and steep, taking about three hours, longer in the wet season when it becomes slippery and a bit hazardous. The path then leads to the village of **Partungkoan (Dolok)**, where you can stay at **Jenny's Guest House** (r 5000Rp) or **John's Losmen** (r 5000Rp). From Partungkoan, it takes about five hours to walk to Pangururan via **Danau Sidihoni**.

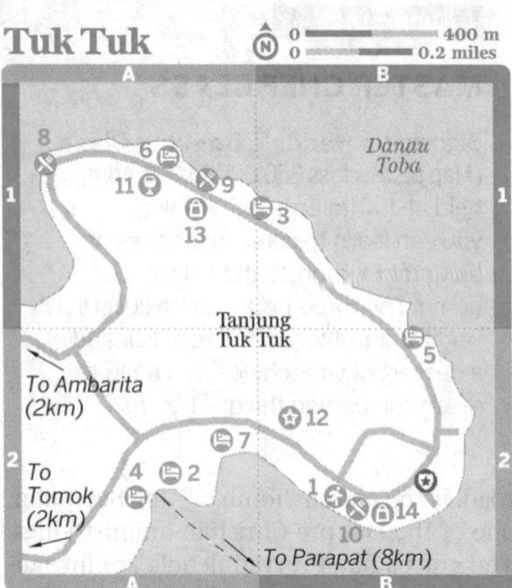

Tuk Tuk

Activities, Courses & Tours
1 Heddy's Cooking Class B2

Sleeping
2 Bagus Bay Homestay A2
3 Harriara Guesthouse B1
4 Liberta Homestay A2
5 Merlyn Guesthouse B2
6 Samosir Cottages A1
7 Tabo Cottages A2

Eating
8 Bamboo Restaurant & Bar A1
9 Jenny's Restaurant A1
10 Today's Cafe B2

Drinking
11 Brando's Blues Bar A1

Entertainment
12 Roy's Pub B2

Shopping
13 Gokhan Library A1
14 Penny's Bookstore B2

universe is created here by a lazy-day garden and arty versions of traditional Batak houses. The popular Mr Moon is a great source of travel information. The downside is that it seems to be as popular with mosquitoes as it is with backpackers!

Bagus Bay Homestay GUESTHOUSE $
(Map p258; ☎451287; www.bagus-bay.page.tl; r without/with bathroom from 30,000/75,000Rp; @) Rooms in the traditional Batak houses overlook avocado trees, a children's playground and a volleyball court. The cheaper rooms are more like prison cells, but the more expensive ones come with great bathrooms (complete with hot water – a rarity for a cheap hotel in these parts). At night its restaurant, which has frequent film evenings, is a lively spot for travellers to congregate.

Samosir Cottages HOTEL $
(Map p258; ☎451170; www.samosircottages.com; r from 80,000Rp; @) A good choice for travellers who want to hang out with young like-minded folk and boisterous young staff, plus the lake swimming is pretty good here. The rooms are a bit dated but well maintained.

Harriara Guesthouse GUESTHOUSE $
(Map p258; ☎451183; r 70,000Rp) This great-value guesthouse has a top-notch lakeside setting, riotous tropical flower gardens and rooms that are so sparkling clean you'd never guess they were nearly 25 years old! If there's nobody at reception, enquire in the nearby restaurants.

Merlyn Guesthouse GUESTHOUSE $
(Map p258; ☎451057; r from 45,000Rp; @) Situated right on the lake, Merlyn has rooms in traditional Batak-style houses (some with tiny dollhouse-sized doors). It's as cheap and charming as you'll find.

Eating & Drinking

The guesthouses tend to mix eating and entertainment in the evening. Most restaurants serve the Batak speciality of barbecued carp (most from fish farms). Magic or 'special' omelettes are commonly seen on restaurant menus. We probably don't need to warn you that the mushrooms contained in these are not the sort that you can buy at your local supermarket.

> **SPLURGE: TABO COTTAGES**
>
> The swankiest accommodation on the island, **Tabo Cottages** (Map p258; ☎451318; www.tabocottages.com; r from 215,000Rp; @)is a German-run lakeside place with beautiful traditional-style Batak houses, which come with huge bathrooms and hammocks swinging lazily on the terrace. The home-made cakes are worthy of mention as well. A great place for a splurge.

INDONESIA DANAU TOBA

TOP CHOICE **Jenny's Restaurant** FISH & CHIPS $$

(Map p258; mains 30,000-50,000Rp) Although there are lots of different options on the menu at Jenny's, there's only really one thing to eat – grilled or fried lake fish with chips and salad. Follow it up with the fruit pancake, which is almost embarrassingly well proportioned. We enjoyed few meals in Sumatra more than this one.

Today's Cafe INTERNATIONAL $

(Map p258; mains 25,000-40,000Rp) This is a great new restaurant, with a laid-back vibe just in keeping with Tuk Tuk life. It's run by a couple of friendly ladies who whip up a mean pasta as well as all the Indo staples – all served with a dollop of easy chit-chat.

Bamboo Restaurant & Bar INTERNATIONAL $

(Map p258; mains 20,000-40,000Rp) With incredible lake views, Bamboo is a stylish place to watch the sun slink away, with cosy cushion seating, a down-tempo mood and a reliable menu. Does good cocktails too.

Drinking & Entertainment

On most nights, music and spirits fill the air with the kind of camaraderie that only grows in small villages. The parties are all local – celebrating a wedding, new addition on a house or the return of a Toba expat. Invitations are gladly given and should be cordially accepted.

Brando's Blues Bar BAR

(Map p258; ☎451084) There are a handful of foreigner-oriented bars, such as this one, in between the local jungle-juice cafes. Happy hour is from 6pm to 10pm.

Batak Music & Dance TRADITIONAL DANCE

Bagus Bay Homestay and Samosir Cottages both have traditional Batak music and dance performances on Wednesday and Saturday evenings at 8.15pm.

Roy's Pub LIVE MUSIC

(Map p258; ⏲9pm-1am) Roy's has live music (normally local rock bands) several nights a week (Tuesday, Thursday and Saturday) in a graffiti-splattered building. The over-the-top sports car parked outside is pretty memorable.

Information

There is a small police station (Map p258). Load up on reading material in Toba, because the rest of Sumatra is a desert for the printed word. Penny's Bookstore (Map p258) and Gokhan Library (Map p258) have both used and rental books.

Internet access (10,000Rp per hour) is available at many of the guesthouses and restaurants. Change your money before you get to Samosir. Exchange rates at the island's hotels and money changers are pretty awful. The only post office is in Ambarita.

Getting There & Away

BOAT Ferries between Parapat and Tuk Tuk (7000Rp) operate about every hour from 7am to 7pm. The ferries stop at near Bagus Bay Homestay (35 minutes); other stops are by request. When leaving for Parapat, stand on your hotel jetty and wave a ferry down.

Five ferries a day (passenger/car 4000/75,000Rp, 7am to 9pm) shuttle vehicles and people between Ajibata, just south of Parapat, and Tomok.

BUS See Parapat (p257), the mainland transit point, for information on bus travel to/from Danau Toba.

On Samosir, to get to Berastagi, you'll have to catch a bus from Tomok to Pangururan (12,000Rp, 45 minutes), from where you take another bus to Berastagi (30,000Rp to 35,000Rp, three hours). This bus goes via Sidikalang, and the price depends on demand and bus type.

Getting Around

Local buses serve the whole of Samosir except Tuk Tuk. You can rent motorcycles in Tuk Tuk for 75,000Rp a day, which includes petrol and helmet. Bicycle hire costs from 25,000Rp per day.

Minibuses run between Tomok and Ambarita (2000Rp), continuing to Simanindo (6000Rp) and Pangururan (12,000Rp). The road along the neck of the peninsula is a good spot to flag down these minibuses. Services dry up after 5pm.

Berastagi

☎0628 / POP 600,000

Escaping from the infernal heat of sea-level Medan, the colonial Dutch traders climbed high into the lush, cool volcanic hills, took one look at the stunningly verdant, undulating landscape and decided to set up camp and build a rural retreat where Berastagi (also called Brastagi) now stands.

Beyond the town are the green fields of the Karo Highlands, dominated by two volcanoes: Gunung Sinabung to the west and the smoking Gunung Sibayak to the north. Each is a day hike, making them two of Sumatra's most accessible volcanoes and the primary reason why tourists get off the bus in the first place.

Sights & Activities

Gunung Sibayak VOLCANO, WALKING

Gunung Sibayak (2094m) offers summit views straight out of a tourist brochure, especially during the June to August dry season. Try to avoid weekends, when Medan day trippers are out in force. If you're with a friend, you could probably do without a guide, but don't hike alone as a number of tourists have gone missing on the mountain over the years. Guides charge from 150,000Rp, depending on the route. You'll need good walking shoes, warm clothes, food and drink.

The easiest route starts northwest of town, 10 minutes' walk past the Sibayak Multinational Guesthouse. Take the left track beside the entrance hut (2000Rp). From here it's 7km, and three hours (one-way), to the top.

On the way down, stop and soak in the **hot springs** (admission 3000-5000Rp), a short ride from Semangat Gunung on the road back to Berastagi.

Alternatively, you can catch a local bus (5000Rp) to **Semangat Gunung** at the base of the volcano, from where it's a two-hour climb to the top; there are steps part of the way, but the trail is narrow and in worse condition than the one from Berastagi.

A longer option is to trek through the jungle from the **Air Terjun Panorama**, the waterfall on the Medan road, 5km north of Berastagi. This five-hour walk demands a local guide.

Gunung Sinabung VOLCANO, WALKING

Gunung Sinabung (2450m) is Sibayak's taller, better-looking (meaning the views) and far more difficult sister. It takes around 10 hours return, and should only be tackled with a guide (from 200,000Rp). Solo hikers have perished here. Sinabung is shy, often hiding behind thick cloudbanks that obscure views.

Berastagi

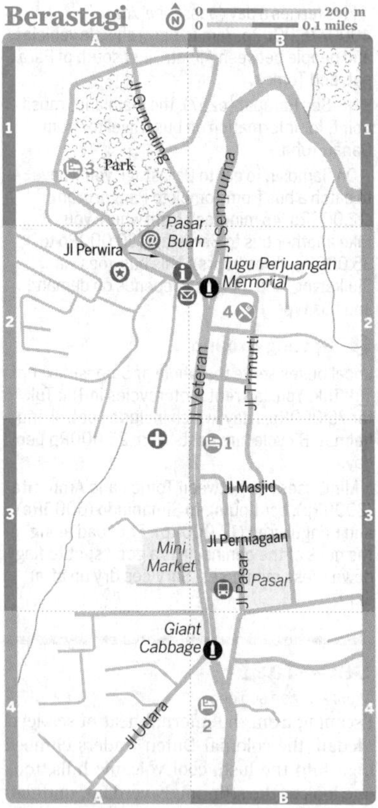

Berastagi

Sleeping

1 Sibayak Losmen Guesthouse............B3
2 Wisma Sibayak............B4
3 Wisma Sunrise View............A1

Eating

4 Café Raymond............B2

Sleeping

TOP CHOICE **Sibayak Multinational Resthouse** GUESTHOUSE $$

(☎91031; Jl Pendidikan 93; r incl breakfast 250,000Rp) If you want a treat, this fantastic family-run guesthouse is the place to do it. Set in immaculate gardens and surrounded by nothing but peace and quiet, the vast, modern rooms here virtually sparkle, so vigorously have they been attacked with a mop and brush. There's hot water in the bathrooms and breakfast is included. The hotel is a short *opelet* ride north of town on the road to Gunung Sibayak.

Wisma Sibayak GUESTHOUSE $

(☎91104; Jl Udara 1; r without/with bathroom 50,000/100,000Rp; @) Tidy and spacious rooms that are quiet and comfortable, but have cold-water showers only. It offers lots of excellent travel information, a friendly family feel and a decent restaurant. If you can't live without a hot shower, you can pay 10,000Rp extra and sing away to your heart's content under a stream of steaming hot water.

Wisma Sunrise View GUESTHOUSE $

(☎081 974 06784; Jl Kaliaga; r 60,000Rp) With a setting – five minutes' walk from town – of utter peace and tranquillity, and lime-green rooms off-set with dark wood panelling, this is an enjoyable budget guesthouse.

Sibayak Losmen Guesthouse HOTEL $

(☎91122; dicksonpe lawi@yahoo.com; Jl Veteran 119; r without/with bathroom 65,000/75,000Rp; @ 🛜) You wouldn't describe the small clapboard-style rooms here as luxurious, but you would describe the staff as warm and helpful.

Eating

The rich volcanic soils of the surrounding countryside supply much of North Sumatra's produce, which passes through Berastagi's colourful produce and fruit markets.

Most of the budget hotels have restaurants, but head into town for more diversity. Along Jl Veteran there is a variety of evening food stalls, as well as simple restaurants specialising in *tionghoa* (Chinese food).

Café Raymond INTERNATIONAL $

(Jl Trimurti 49; mains 8000-20,000Rp; ⏲7am-midnight; @) Berastagi's local bohemians hang out at Café Raymond, which serves fruit juices, beer and Western food such as steak and pasta. Oh, and don't forget all your favourite Indonesian staples.

Information

Berastagi is essentially a one-street town spread along Jl Veteran. Banks have ATMs.

D'Z@S Net (Jl Perwira; ⏲7am-midnight) Decent-speed internet.

Post office (Jl Veteran) Near the memorial at the northern end of the street.

Sibayak Trans Tour & Travel (☎91122; dicksonpelawi@yahoo.com; Jl Veteran 119) Books plane tickets and has information on local and onward travel. Same building as the Sibayak Losmen Guesthouse.

Tourist Information Centre (☎91084; Jl Gundaling 1; ⏲8am-5pm Mon-Fri) Has maps and can arrange guides, but staff were vague about whether it opened on weekends or not, with half the staff thinking they did and half thinking they didn't!

Getting There & Away

The **bus terminal** (Jl Veteran) is conveniently located near the centre of town. You can also catch buses to Padang Bulan in Medan (10,000Rp, 2½ hours) anywhere along the main street, Jl Veteran.

To reach Danau Toba without backtracking through Medan, catch an *opelet* to Kabanjahe (3000Rp, 15 minutes) and change to a bus for Pematangsiantar (16,000Rp, three hours), then connect with a Parapat-bound bus (8000Rp to 10,000Rp, 1½ hours).

Medan

☎061 / POP 2,109,000

Sumatra's major metropolis, and Indonesia's third-largest city, has a dubious legend in travellers' circles, regularly taking honours in 'What's the worst place you've ever visited?' conversations. The pollution, poverty and persistent cat calls of 'Hello Mister!' can be an unnerving jolt of dirt-under-your-fingernails Asia. However, if you've worked your way north through Sumatra and have a little more resistance to the culture shock, it's easier to see past the grime and discover an amenity-filled, leafy and modern town with more than a hint of crumbling, Dutch colonial charm.

A taxi ride from the airport to the nearby centre should cost 40,000Rp. From the southern bus terminal, the giant Amplas, it's a 6.5km bemo ride (5000Rp) into town.

Sights & Activities

Ghosts of Medan's colonial mercantile past are still visible along Jl Ahmad Yani from Jl Palang Merah north to Lapangan Merdeka. Some are still stately relics, while others have been gutted and turned into parking garages.

Mesjid Raya MOSQUE

(Grand Mosque; cnr Jl Mesjid Raya & Jl SM Raja; admission by donation; ⏲9am-5pm except prayer times) The black-domed Mesjid Raya is breathtaking, especially when people stream in for Friday prayers. It was commissioned by the sultan in 1906 and built in the Moroccan style with Italian marble and Chinese stained glass.

Sleeping

The majority of accommodation is on or near Jl SM Raja. Most budget options have cold water only.

Pondok Wisata Angel GUESTHOUSE $

(Hotel Angel; ☎732 0702; Jl SM Raja 70; s with fan without/with bathroom 50,000/70,000Rp, s/d with air-con 120,000/150,000Rp; ❄ 🛜) The best backpacker option in town, Angel's clean rooms are a swirl of vivid blues and yellows, a colour scheme that almost succeeds in offsetting the noisy traffic. It has a sociable streetfront cafe.

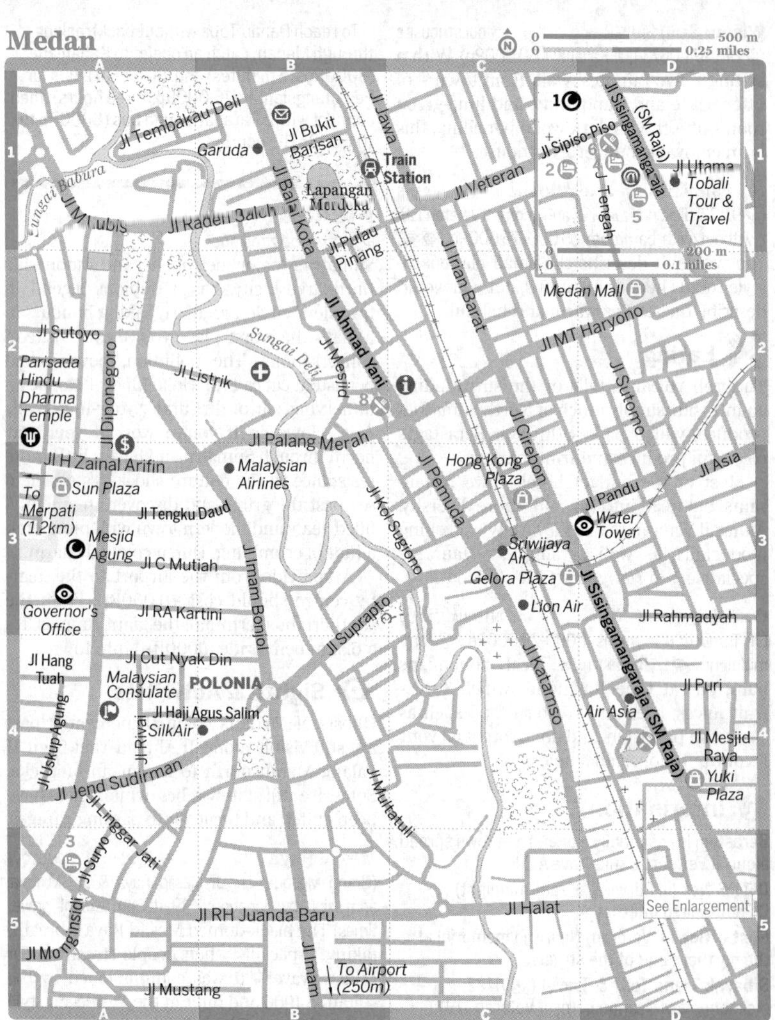

Medan

Sights

1 Mesjid Raya C1

Sleeping

2 Hotel Zakia C1
3 JJ's Guesthouse Medan A5
4 Pondok Wisata Angel D1
5 Trav-Fella Homestay D1

Eating

6 Corner Café Raya D1
7 Taman Rekreasi Seri Deli D4
8 Tip Top Restaurant B2

JJ's Guesthouse Medan GUESTHOUSE $
(☎457 8411; www.guesthousemedan.com; Jl Suryo 18; s/d incl breakfast 150,000/180,000Rp; ❄) In an old Dutch villa, JJ's has tidy boarding house-style rooms run by a mannerly Dutch-speaking Indonesian woman. Opposite the KFC, its lack of signage makes it tricky to find (look for the sticker on the gate reading 'Find us on Facebook'. Said gates are normally locked, so you'll need to ring the doorbell tucked inside the left side of the gate and be patient – it takes time for the elderly owner to get to you!

Hotel Zakia GUESTHOUSE $
(☎732 2413; Jl Sisiso 10-12; r without bathroom 50,000Rp, with bathroom from 55,000Rp) Tucked away down a quiet side street (well, OK, it's quiet until the adjacent mosque rocks the casbah at 5am!), these dirt-cheap rooms are surprisingly dirt free and also very spacious. Add it all up and it spells good deal.

Trav-Fella Homestay GUESTHOUSE $
(☎732 1494; Jl SM Raja 66; r 35,000-100,000Rp) The colourful rooms here are presided over by keen-to-please management, but it's slightly let down by the fact that most rooms share common bathrooms.

Eating

Medan has the most varied selection of cuisines in Sumatra, from basic Malay-style *mie* (noodle) and *nasi* (rice) joints to top-class hotel restaurants.

Tip Top Restaurant INTERNATIONAL $$
(Jl Ahmad Yani 92; www.tiptop-medan.com; dishes 25,000-50,000Rp; ❄📶) Only the prices have changed at this old colonial relic, great for a drink of bygone imperialism. It offers tasty Indonesian, Chinese and Western dishes, including a good steak menu.

Taman Rekreasi Seri Deli MALAYSIAN $
(Jl SM Raja; dishes from 8000Rp; ⊙dinner) For basic Malay food, this venue, opposite the Mesjid Raya, is a slightly upmarket approach to stall dining. But the *kerupuk* (prawn cracker) sellers, blind beggars and spoon players might find you more of an oddity than vice versa.

Corner Café Raya INTERNATIONAL $
(cnr Jl SM Raja & Jl Sipiso Piso 1; dishes 15,000-30,000Rp; ⊙24hr) Western-Indo fare plus cold beer and satellite sports in a heady mix of seedy sex-pats and fresh-faced backpackers, which makes its location directly opposite the Mesjid Raya mosque a little puzzling.

Information

Internet Access

Medan has speedy *warnets* (public internet) across the city, and internet is also available at most of the large shopping plazas. Prices range from 3000Rp to 5000Rp per hour.

X-Net (Jl SM Raja; ⊙24hr) In the middle of the cheap-hotel strip.

Medical Services

Rumah Sakit Gleneagles (☎456 6368; Jl Listrik 6) English-speaking doctors.

Money

ATMs are everywhere, with a string on Jl Pemuda.

BCA Bank (cnr Jl Diponegoro & Jl H Zainal Arifin) Exchanges money.

Post

Main post office (Jl Bukit Barisan; ⊙8am-6pm)

Tourist Information

There is a basic tourist information office immediately to the right as you exit the international airport terminal.

North Sumatra Tourist Office (☎453 8101; www.northsumatratravel.net; Jl Ahmad Yani 107; ⊙8am-4pm Mon-Fri) Provides excellent information, brochures and maps. Also has displays of traditional North Sumatran costumes.

Travel Agencies

Jl Katamso is packed with travel agencies that handle air tickets and ferry tickets.

Tobali Tour & Travel (☎732 4471; Jl SM Raja 79C) For tourist buses to Danau Toba (100,000Rp, four hours).

Getting There & Away

Air

There's a departure tax of 75,000Rp. The following airlines have offices in Medan and serve the destinations as listed:

Air Asia (☎021 2927 0999; www.airasia.com; Jl SM Raja 18) Inside Garuda Plaza Hotel; has flights to Bandung, Surabaya, Kuala Lumpur, Penang, Johor Bahru, Bangkok and Hong Kong, as well as some longer-haul destinations.

Garuda Jl Monginsidi (☎0804 180 7807; Jl Monginsidi 340); Jl Balai Kota 2 (☎453 7844; Inna Dharma Deli, Jl Balai Kota 2) Flies to Jakarta and Banda Aceh.

Lion Air (☎080 4177 8899; Jl Katamso 41) Flies to Jakarta, Banda Aceh and Penang.

Malaysian Airlines (☎075 135888; www.malaysiaairlines.com; Hotel Danau Toba International, Jl Imam Bonjol 17) Flies to Kuala Lumpur.

Merpati (☎4551888; www.merpati.co.id/EN; Jl Iskandar Muda 54) Flies to Batam, Dumai, Sibolga, Gunung Sitoli (Nias) and several other off-the-beaten-track destinations.

SilkAir (☎453 7744; www.silkair.com; Hotel Polonia, Jl Sudirman 14) Flies to Singapore.

Sriwijaya Air (☎455 2111; www.sriwijayaair-online.com; Jl Katamso 29) Flies to Jakarta, Banda Aceh, Batam, Padang and Pekanbaru.

Boat

Due to the growth in budget airlines the ferries connecting Medan to Penang in Malaysia that were once such a popular way of entering and exiting

Sumatra no longer operate. Infrequent Pelni ships sail to Jakarta and Batam. The **Pelni office** (☎662 2526; Jl Krakatau 17A) is 8km north of the city centre, but it is much easier to buy tickets and check schedules from the agencies on Jl Katamso.

Bus

There are two main bus stations. Buses south to Parapat (22,000Rp, four hours), Bukittinggi (economy/air-con 130,000/180,000Rp; 22 hours) and beyond leave from the **Amplas bus terminal** (Jl SM Raja), 6.5km south of downtown. Almost any *opelet* heading south on Jl SM Raja will get you to Amplas.

Buses to the north leave from **Pinang Baris bus terminal** (Jl Gatot Subroto), 10km west of the city centre. Get there by taxi (around 40,000Rp) or by *opelet* down Jl Gatot Subroto. There are public buses to both Bukit Lawang (20,000Rp, three hours) and Berastagi (10,000Rp, 2½ hours) every half-hour between 5.30am and 6pm. A fleet of 'tourist' minibuses also set off daily to Bukit Lawang (75,000Rp to 100,000Rp, depending on bus type). They will pick you up from your hotel in Medan.

Tobali Tour & Travel (☎732 4472; Jl SM Raja 79C) also runs a 'tourist' minibus to Parapat (100,000Rp, four hours).

Getting Around

Becak drivers fetch about 8000Rp for most destinations in town, and *opelets* (3000Rp) are omnipresent. *Opelets* run along colour-coded routes: the white line hits Kesawan Sq, Merdeka Walk and the train station; yellows will take you to Little India and Sun Plaza. They cost 2500Rp per ride. Bargain hard with taxi drivers.

Bukit Lawang

☎061 / POP 30,000

Lost in the depths of the Sumatran jungle is this sweet little tourist town built around an orang-utan viewing centre. While orang-utan spotting is easily the highlight of a visit to Bukit Lawang, the town has much more to offer beyond our red-haired cousins. (For more on orang-utans, see p300.) It's very easy to while away a few days lounging in the many riverside hammocks, listening to the mating calls (mainly those of the orang-utans!) over the gushing river and watching the jungle life swing and sing around you. It's also an ideal base for jungle treks into Taman Nasional Gunung Leuser, where you will see wild and semiwild orang-utans.

The bus station is 1km east of the river-side tourist district. Minibuses may go a bit further to the small square at the end of the road, where a rickety hanging bridge crosses the river to the hotels.

Sights & Activities

Bohorok Orang-Utan Viewing Centre — WILDLIFE RESERVE

Twice a day (8.30am and 3pm) visitors can watch rangers feed nearly a dozen semiwild orang-utan, who are being rehabilitated from captivity or sudden habitat displacement due to logging. The bland fare of bananas and milk encourages the apes to forage on their own. So far, 200 have been successfully re-released into the jungle, mating with communities of wild apes.

The feeding platform is located on the west bank of Sungai Bohorok within the park boundaries, about a 20-minute walk up from the village. The river crossing to the park office is made by dug-out canoe. Permits are required to enter the park (20,000Rp) and are available from the **office** (⌚8am-10am & 3-4pm) at the foot of the trail to the platform. There's a camera fee of 50,000Rp.

Jungle Trekking — HIKING

Trekking in **Taman Nasional Gunung Leuser** is an absolute must. Guides are mandatory in the national park and prices are fixed. See the table opposite for the various price options. The most popular choice is a two-day, one-night jungle trek combined with 'tubing' back down river to Bukit Lawang. Spending the night in the jungle vastly increases your chances of spotting wild orang-utan. Remember, not all guides are sensitive to the environment. Check your guide's licence, talk to the park rangers and ask other travellers before signing up.

Tubing — RAFTING

A shed along the river en route to the orang-utan centre rents inflated truck inner tubes (10,000Rp per day), which can be used to ride the at-times-dangerous Sungai Bohorok rapids. Avoid the very last section as you approach the town centre.

Sleeping & Eating

The further up river you go the more likely you are to ogle the swinging monkeys and apes from your porch hammock. You won't find hot water or air-con at any of the guesthouses, but all serve food.

Jungle Inn — GUESTHOUSE $

(☎013 7016 0172; r 100,000-200,000Rp) The last guesthouse along the strip near the park en-

JUNGLE TREKKING FEES

TREK DURATION	PER PERSON – 1-2 PEOPLE	PER PERSON – 3 PEOPLE +
Half-day	200,000Rp	180,000Rp
1 day	360,000Rp	300,000Rp
2 days	720,000Rp	600,000Rp
3 days	1,200,000Rp	900,000Rp

trance, Jungle Inn is an old favourite of many a reader. One room overlooks a virtually private waterfall, while another incorporates the hill's rock face, and the bathroom sprouts a shower from living ferns. Its only downside is the sometimes unreliable information provided by guides and overpriced treks.

On the Rocks BUNGALOWS $
(☎0812 6303 1119; r 100,000-200,000Rp) More on the hill than on the rocks, the handful of 'tribal' huts here verge on being luxurious in an ethnic kind of way. Each hut has a veranda and sunken bathroom and all are shrouded in peace and with beautiful views. The downside to all this tranquillity is that it is a fair hike from all the action.

Green Hill GUESTHOUSE $
(☎081 3 703 4 9124; www.greenhill-bukitlawang.com; r without/with bathroom incl breakfast 60,000/150,000Rp) For a few more rupiah, you get a lot more than most of the competition. Run by an English conservation scientist, Andrea, and her Sumatran husband, Green Hill has two lovely stilt-high rooms ideal for couples, where the en-suite bamboo-shoot showers afford stunning jungle views while you wash. The food in the restaurant is good but service can be surly and woefully slow (we've waited two hours for a meal before).

Sam's Bungalows GUESTHOUSE $$
(☎0813 7009 3597; r 150,000-250,000Rp) Here you'll find an excellent range of wooden treehouses, as well as more solidly built rooms painted in sunny Mediterranean colours with huge bathrooms and Italian rain showers.

Nora's Homestay GUESTHOUSE $
(☎081 3620 70656; r without bathroom 30,000-40,000Rp, r with bathroom 50,000Rp) Nora's cluster of wooden rooms between the rice fields and the main road equals backpacker bliss. The rooms are kept clean, there's a friendly dining area (with Western meals like pasta, burgers and all the rest) and it's a super place to hook up with other travellers. It also goes by the name Rainforest.

Plain Stone Inn HUTS $
(☎0821 6596 4047; r 50,000Rp) A couple of great-value huts with attached bathrooms (squat toilets only) set in a chicken-filled garden on the calmer side of the river.

Information

The **Bukit Lawang Visitors Centre** (⏲8am-3pm) has displays of flora and fauna found in Taman Nasional Gunung Leuser, plus a book of medicinal plants and their uses. Past visitors often record reviews of guides in the sign-in book.

A fee of 15,000Rp is charged for entrance to Bukit Lawang.

Getting There & Away

Buses leave from the edge of the village about a 30-minute walk from the feeding station. There are direct buses to Medan's Pinang Baris bus terminal every half-hour between 5.30am and 5pm (20,000Rp, four hours). 'Tourist' minibuses depart daily for Medan (75,000Rp to 100,000Rp), Parapat (150,000Rp to 220,000Rp) and Berastagi (100,000Rp to 185,000Rp).

Banda Aceh

☎0651 / POP 210,000

Indonesian cities are rarely coupled with pleasant descriptions, but Banda Aceh breaks the mould. The sleepy provincial capital is a pleasant spot to spend a few days. The village-like atmosphere and dusty, unobtrusive streets make for an easy-to-explore and laid-back town filled with cheery faces. The proud folk rarely betray the tragedy experienced during the Boxing Day tsunami (which killed 61,000 here), and it's impossible to correlate the reconstructed city with the distraught images of 2004.

Banda Aceh is a fiercely religious city, and the ornate mosques are at the centre of daily life. In this devoutly Muslim city, religion and respect are everything. The hassles are few and the people are easygoing and extremely hospitable to visitors.

Sights

Tsunami Museum MUSEUM
(Jl Iskandar Muda) Costing a whopping US$5.0 million to build, Banda Aceh's impressive Tsunami Museum would be the highlight (in a very sad and depressing kind of way) of a visit to Banda Aceh. The museum contains a virtual simulation of the earthquake, walls of water and a powerful set of images from the aftermath of the tsunami. Unfortunately, the museum appears to be on the brink of turning into a white elephant and, despite only opening in 2010, it was closed for 'renovations' by early 2011. Prior to that, it was only open intermittently.

Tsunami Sights MONUMENTS
Aside from the Tsunami Museum, the most famous of the tsunami sights are the **boat in the house** in Lampulo, and the 2500-tonne **power generator vessel** that was carried 4km inland by a wave.

Mesjid Raya Baiturrahman MOSQUE
(Jl Mohammed Jam; admission by donation; ⏲7-11am & 1.30-4pm) With its brilliant white walls and liquorice black domes, the Mesjid Raya Baiturrahman somehow survived the tsunami intact, which, despite the rampant loss of life, has been interpreted by fundamentalists as evidence of a merciful God.

Museum Negeri Banda Aceh MUSEUM
(Jl Alauddin Mahmudsyah 12; admission 1000Rp; ⏲8.30am-noon & 2-4.30pm Tue-Fri, 9am-noon & 2.30-4.30pm Sat & Sun) The Museum Negeri Banda Aceh is the site of the Rumah Aceh, a traditional stilt home built without nails. On weekends it's sometimes possible to see traditional dance and music sessions here.

Sleeping

The influx of international aid workers jacked up the prices but not the standards of the few hotels left in town since the tsunami, and there is very little for budget travellers.

Hotel Medan HOTEL $
(☎21501; Jl Ahmad Yani 17; r with breakfast from 175,000Rp; ❄@📶) This business-class hotel has comfortable and spotless rooms. It's probably the most popular hotel in town with both foreign and Indonesian visitors and is certainly the best value.

Hotel Prapat HOTEL $$
(☎22159; Jl Ahmad Yani 19; d with fan/air-con 100,000/200,000Rp; ❄) One of the more affordable spots, Prapat from the outside has the feel of a cheap rundown motel, though rooms are good value, with Western toilets and clean sheets.

Eating

The square at the junction of Jl Ahmad Yani and Jl Khairil Anwar is usually the setting for the Pasar Malam Rek, Banda Aceh's lively night food market. Many night food stalls are found on Jl SM Raja.

Rumah Makan Asia INDONESIAN $
(Jl Cut Meutia 37/39; mains 10,000Rp) Aceh's version of *masakan Padang* (Padang dish) has an array of zesty seafood dishes that waiters plonk on your table, such as *ikan panggang* (baked fish).

Tropicana Seafood CHINESE $
(Jl SM Raja; mains from 20,000Rp; ❄) Chinese restaurant serving delicious seafood dishes and cold Bintang. Vegetarians beware: even the 'mixed vegetables' contains chicken and prawns.

Information

There are plenty of ATMs and internet cafes around town.

Post office (Jl Bendahara 33; ⏲8am-4pm Mon-Fri; @) A short walk from the centre; also has internet.

Getting There & Away

There are several flights a day from Banda Aceh to Medan and Jakarta on Garuda, Sriwiyaya and Lion Air. Air Asia flies daily to Kuala Lumpur, and Firefly to Penang in Malaysia.

South of the city centre you'll find the new **Terminal Bus Bathoh** (Jl Mohammed Hasan), which has numerous buses to Medan. Economy buses (150,000Rp, 14 hours) depart at 4pm, while 'deluxe' buses leave all day (200,000Rp, 12 hours).

Getting Around

Airport taxis charge a set rate of 70,000Rp for the 16km ride into town. A taxi from the airport to Uleh-leh port will cost 100,000Rp; from town to Uleh-leh is 50,000Rp

Labi labi (minibuses) are the main form of transport around town and cost 1500Rp. The **labi-labi terminal** (Jl Diponegoro) is that special breed of Indonesian mayhem. For Uleh-leh (5000Rp, 30 minutes), take the blue *labi labi* signed 'Uleh-leh'.

From the bus station, a becak into town will cost around 15,000Rp. A becak around town should cost between 5000Rp and 10,000Rp.

Pulau Weh

☎0652 / POP 25,000

A tiny tropical rock off the tip of Sumatra, Weh is a little slice of peaceful living that rewards travellers who've journeyed up through the turbulent greater mainland below. After hiking around the jungles, volcanoes and lakes of the mainland, it's time to jump into the languid waters of the Indian Ocean. Snorkellers and divers bubble through the great walls of swaying sea fans, deep canyons and rock pinnacles, while marvelling at the prehistorically gargantuan fish. This is one of the finest underwater sites you'll find. Both figuratively and geographically, Pulah Weh is the cherry on top for many visitors' trip to Sumatra.

Most people pass through Sabang fairly quickly en route to the tourist beaches, but return to town for provisions.

Sights & Activities

Beaches BEACH

It's all about fun in the sun on this blessed island, and there are some mighty fine patches of sand on which to frolic, as well as even finer underwater landscapes to explore with a mask strapped to your face. About a 2km walk from Sabang town, **Pantai Kasih** (Lover's Beach), is a palm-fringed crescent of white sand. Popular with a mixture of domestic and international tourists is **Gapang Beach**, which offers terrific swimming, with frequent turtle sightings. Just over the headland from Gapang Beach is **Iboih Beach**, which is saturated in a castaway vibe that makes it pretty much irresistible to backpackers. The forested slopes above the turquoise waters here hide lots of cheap, bungalow-style accommodation. Opposite Iboih, and 100m offshore, is **Pulau Rubiah**, surrounded by epic coral reefs known as the **Sea Garden**.

Rubiah Tirta Divers DIVING

(☎332 4555; www.rubiahdivers.com; introductory dive €45, dive with rental equipment €25, courses from €200) There are several dive operators on the island. At Iboih, Rubiah Tirta Divers is the oldest dive operation on the island.

Lumba Lumba Diving Centre DIVING

(☎332 4133; 081 168 2787; www.lumbalumba.com; introductory dive €45, dive with rental equipment €27, PADI Open Water course €290) At Gapang, Lumba Lumba Diving Centre is the centre of activity.

Sleeping & Eating

Iboih, with its simple palm-thatch bungalows, many built on stilts and overhanging crystal-clear water, is Pulau Weh's backpacker hang-out par excellence. Virtually next door, and occupying a sandy cove, Gapang is a lazy stretch of beach lined with shack restaurants and simple guesthouses. In Iboih in particular there are dozens of different places to stay with almost nothing whatsoever to differentiate them from each other. In fact, it's often hard to know where one place ends and another begins. Wherever you choose to hang your flip-flops, if you stay for several days, you can normally negotiate a discount on the daily rates quoted below.

Rates and visitors double on weekends.

Lumba Lumba Diving Centre HOTEL $$

(☎332 4133; 081 168 2787; www.lumbalumba.com; Gapang Beach; r €12-29; @📶) As well as helping you feel at home under the waves, the Lumba Lumba Diving Centre will also make you feel quite at home on land with the most luxurious rooms on the island. However, it's often booked out by dive-school students.

Yulia's HUTS $

(☎0852 7070 6003; Iboih Beach; r without bathroom 80,000Rp) A 500m trudge over the cliffs rewards you with the best of Iboih's huts, some excellent front-door snorkelling and a good restaurant.

Mama Jungle HUTS $

(Gapang Beach; r without bathroom from 50,000Rp) Rickety, but clean, wooden bungalows set under the palms a hundred metres back from the beach.

Green House HUTS $

(☎0852 7748 3299; Iboih Beach; r 100,000Rp) One of the first places you come to and no different to any of the others except that you needn't carry your bags far.

Information

There are a couple of internet places in Iboih and a bank or two (with ATMs) in Sabang.

Getting There & Away

Fast ferries to Pulau Weh (60,000Rp, one hour) leave from Uleh-leh, 15km northwest of Banda. Slow ferries (16,000, two hours) also leave daily. Check schedules at the port.

Getting Around

From the port, there are regular minibuses to Gapang and Iboih (35,000Rp, 40 minutes). A lift on the back of a motorbike costs 50,000Rp. Allow at least an hour to travel from the port to Iboih.

Pekanbaru

0761 / POP 793,000

Pekanbaru was once little more than a sleepy river port on Sungai Siak. Today it is Indonesia's oil capital, with all the hustle and bustle of a modern city. It used to be a key transit stop for backpackers travelling overland from Singapore or Malaysia to Sumatra, but with the advent of cheap flights very few budget travellers pass through nowadays.

Airport taxis charge 60,000Rp for the 10km trip into town. Most banks, ATMs and hotels are on Jl Sudirman. The bus station is 7km west of town. There are plenty of travel agencies around town that can book plane and bus tickets as well as tours of the local area.

Sleeping & Eating

If this is your first night in Indo, take an evening food-stall crawl on Jl Sudirman, at the junction with Jl Imam Bonjol. There are dozens of good-value midrange hotels throughout the town, but pitifully few budget options that will accept foreign tourists.

Poppie's Homestay GUESTHOUSE $
(988 4265; Jl Cempedak III 11A; d 90,000Rp) About the only budget hotel left in town that will gladly accept foreigners, this friendly homestay offers basic rooms in the family home. There's no way you'll find it without some local help!

Wisma Permata HOTEL $
(23549; Jl Sudirman 290; r from 115,000Rp; ❄) Staff here aren't at all sure what to do with foreign tourists, but they speak a little English, smile a lot and if they're not full (which they seem to be most of the time), they'll rent you a room. Road noise is ear-drum busting.

Information

There are internet cafes and banks with ATMs throughout the city centre.

Getting There & Away

Simpang Tiga airport is a visa-free entry point.

Air Asia (www.airasia.com) Flies direct to/from Kuala Lumpur.

Fire Fly (www.fireflyz.com) Flies direct to/from Kuala Lumpur.

Garuda (www.garuda-indonesia.com) Flies direct to/from Jakarta.

Lion Air (www.lionair.co.id) Flies direct to/from Jakarta and Surabaya.

Frequent buses go to Bukittinggi (70,000Rp, five hours) from the uncharacteristically organised and modern Terminal Akap. 'Tourist' minibuses also ply the same route for the same price.

If you've traipsed all the way out to Pekanbaru, we're guessing you want to know about boats onward to Singapore or Malaysia.

For Singapore hop on one of the daily boats to Pulau Batam, where you change boats for the short ride to Singapore. For Melaka in Malaysia take a bus to Dumai (60,000Rp), where boats glide across to Malaysia each morning. But note that by the time you add up all the different fares it's cheaper (though less romantic) to fly.

KALIMANTAN

With its dense jungles, hothouse biodiversity and indigenous peoples, Kalimantan is one of the world's last great wildernesses. As mysterious as it is vast, it covers some two thirds of Borneo and 30% of Indonesia's total landmass. Formerly headhunting country, this is a land of longhouses and superstitious Dayak villages where, despite incursions of 21st-century technology, the drum-roll of the shaman effortlessly coalesces with the trill of mobile phones. Given Kalimantan's ongoing environmental struggles, particularly with palm-oil plantations, there has never been a more vital time to visit.

History & Culture

Kalimantan's riches drew Chinese and Indian traders as far back as AD 400. Dutch and English imperialists began sparring over Kalimantan in the early 17th century; Holland won and England took Sarawak and Sabah. Global industrialisation and expanding wealth spurred demand for traditional commodities and new ones: coal and oil. Petroleum drew Japan's attention during WWII. It also spelled the end of white man's rule, for the war's end brought independence to Indonesia. Over the past six decades, Kalimantan has struggled to find its place in Indonesia. Economic opportunity increasingly attracts outsiders; with a cast of crusading missionaries and imams, loggers, palm-oil planters and conservationists, government administrators and traditional leaders, the

Kalimantan

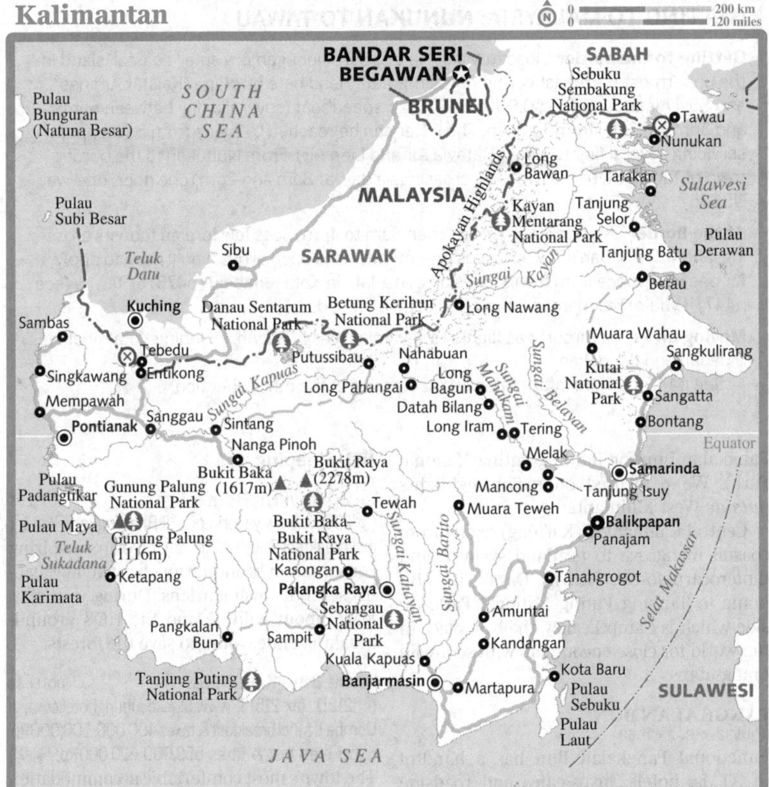

struggle for Kalimantan's soul continues. Joseph Conrad would be busy, indeed.

Getting There & Away

Balikpapan's Seppingan Airport is Kalimantan's only entry point offering visa on arrival (VOA; see p307). All other entry from outside Indonesia – by land, sea or air – requires a visa in advance.

AIR **SilkAir** (www.silkair.net) flies between Balikpapan and Singapore. **Batavia Air** (www.batavia-air.co.id) flies between Pontianak and Kuching in Sarawak, plus Batam near Singapore. **Garuda** (www.garuda-indonesia.com) and Batavia fly the most routes to the rest of Indonesia.

BOAT Boats depart daily (except Sunday) from Tarakan and more frequently from Nunukan in East Kalimantan to Tawau in Sabah.

Pelni (www.pelni.co.id) connects to Jakarta, Semarang and Surabaya on Java, and Makassar, Pare Pare, Mamuju and Toli Toli on Sulawesi.

BUS Air-con buses link Pontianak and Kuching (140,000Rp to 200,000Rp, 10 hours).

Getting Around

As an alternative to riding infernally hot buses, *kijangs,* Kalimantan's ubiquitous taxi, can be chartered between cities. Short journeys can be taken in a *colt,* a hop-on hop-off minibus, usually blue, green and orange, which operate on given routes.

Catching internal flights is the only way to see Kalimantan's scattered highlights. **Lion Air** (www2.lionair.co.id/), **Kal-Star** (www.kalstaronline.com), **Batavia** (www.batavia-air.co.id) and **Garuda** (www.garuda-indonesia.com) are but a few of the many airlines.

Klotoks (wooden boats with covered passenger cabins converted into accommodation) are best for exploring the jungle.

West & Central Kalimantan

Entering Kalimantan from Sarawak, your first destination will be Pontianak, which has plenty of accommodation and forward flights to the rest of the country (including

GETTING TO MALAYSIA: NUNUKAN TO TAWAU

Getting to the border Close to Malaysia's Sabah, Nunukan is a small coastal island in the uppermost northeast corner of Kalimantan. Head here by plane (Kalstar Airlines and Susi Air, around Rp250.000/US$28) or speedboat (several a day between 6am and 3pm; US$20) from Tarakan. The latter can be reached by plane from Balikpapan, servicing several flights a day (Batavia Air and Lion Air). From Nunukan to the border town of Tawau there are two ferry crossings a day, at 8am and 2pm (one hour; one-way US$35).

At the border This border crossing (open 8am to 4pm) sees few foreign tourists crossing, and while Sabah's Tawau issues one-month visas upon arrival you'll need to apply for one in advance from the Indonesian consulate in Kota Kinabalu (p475) or Tawau (see p447) if you're Kalimantan bound (it can take three days).

Moving on Tawau Airport has flights to several places in Sabah, including Kota Kinabalu, Sipadan and Sandakan.

See p447 for more information about crossing in the other direction.

Pangkalan Bun for Tanjung Puting National Park). We've focused on major highlights *outside* West Kalimantan.

Central Kalimantan (KalTeng) segues from coastal mangrove to peatland swamps and dipterocarp forest. Heavily Dayak, it's also home to Tanjung Puting National Park, inside which is Camp Leakey, the best place in the world for close encounters with semiwild orang-utans.

PANGKALAN BUN

☎0532 / POP 43,168

Functional Pangkalan Bun has a handful of ATMs, hotels, tasty cafes and roadside *warung*. Serviced by a nearby airport, it's the easiest place to stay if you're en route to Tanjung Puting National Park to see orang-utans up close.

Tours

The following tour operators will happily visit your hotel lobby to consult with you on your trip.

Borneo Orangutan Adventure Tour TOURS
(☎0062 852 745600; www.orangutantravel.com) Run by the excellent Ahmad Yani, head of the Guide Association, and the first official guide in Pangkalan Bun. He's honest and can sort your trip to Tanjung Puting and beyond.

Borneo Holidays TOURS
(☎29673, 081 2500 0508; borneoholidays@planet-save.com) Owner Harry Purwanto offers personalised tours of Tanjung Puting and the interior. Harry's slick, English-speaking and a nice guy.

Sleeping

TOP CHOICE **Yayorin Homestay** HOTEL $$
(☎29057; www.yayorin.org; Jl Bhayangkara, Km 1; r incl breakfast 300,000Rp; ❄) Yayorin's inspiring conservation headquarters has two new cabins set in its lush gardens. During your stay, learn about wildlife and the HQ's groundbreaking endeavours to save the forests.

Hotel Blue Kecubung HOTEL $$
(☎21211; fax 21513; www.bluekecubunghotel.com; Jl Domba 1; s incl breakfast & taxes 400,000-500,000Rp, d incl breakfast & taxes 550,000-620,000Rp; ❄📶) The town's most comfortable accommodation sits on a hill 10 minutes' walk from the centre. Rooms have en suites and TVs and are decorated with an international flair.

Hotel Andika HOTEL $
(☎21218; fax 21923; Jl Hasanudin 20A; r incl breakfast 70,000-110,000Rp; ❄) Andika has 17 ensuite rooms fronting a verdant courtyard. Its restaurant (mains 15,000Rp; open 8am to 9pm) features Indonesian favourites.

Eating

In addition to the eateries reviewed, you will find more *warung* on Jl Kasumayuda and Jl P Antasari.

TOP CHOICE **Pranbanan Fish Restaurant** INDONESIAN $
(Jl Hasanuddin; mains from 5000Rp; ⌚8am-10pm) Down the road from KalStar, this semi-alfresco resto is a real gem renowned by locals and expats for its grilled and fried *bakar* (fish), chicken and duck. Low-key vibe.

Warung Amara Ini STREET VENDOR $
(cnr Gang Addullah Machmud & Jl Kasumayuda; meals 3000-7000Rp; ⏲7am-2pm; ✎) Vegetarians' delight, with at least four home-cooked varieties, plus fish and chicken choices dished out cafeteria style. Take away or join the family at a low table.

Iduna Bakery & Café CAFE $$
(☎24007; Jl Rangga Santrek 5; mains 15,000-32,000Rp; ⏲9am-9pm) Ambiently lit Iduna is perfect for cappuccinos, burgers and sandwiches, not to mention great doughnuts next door at its sister bakery.

Information

Apotik Pondok Sehat (☎21276; Jl P Antasari 86) Well-stocked pharmacy with doctor's offices.

BNI bank (Jl PAntasari) Exchanges travellers cheques and cash.

Pahala Internet Café (Jl Kasumayuda; per hr 5000Rp) Quick connection, no smoking and cool.

Post office (Jl Kasumayuda 29)

RS Sultan Imanudin (Jl Sutlan Syaharir) Hospital.

Getting There & Away

Kal-Star (☎28765; Jl Hasanuddin 39) has daily flights to Banjarmasin (from where you can pick up flights to Jakarta, Pontianak, Ketapang and Semarang), while **Avia Star** (☎25144; Jl Dah Hamzah 2) offers flights to Central Kalimantan's capital, Palangka Raya.

Getting Around

Taxis to/from the airport (5km) cost 40,000Rp. *Opelet* (minibuses) around town cost 3000Rp. Minibuses to Kumai (20,000Rp, 20 minutes) and *ojek* leave from the roundabout at the end of Jl Kasumayuda. Taxis to Kumai cost 150,000Rp.

KUMAI

☎0532 / POP 23,000

Kumai is the departure point for Tanjung Puting National Park; come here to choose your *klotok* (boat) and acquire a permit from the **PHKA Office** (National Park Office) – situated next to your departure point. Note: there are no ATMs here, so stock up on cash in Pangkalan Bun, 20 minutes away.

Getting There & Away

Reach Kumai by minibus from Pangkalan Bun (20,00Rp, 20 minutes). Taxis from Pangkalan Bun airport to Kumai cost 150,000Rp, including all stops for visiting Tanjung Puting National Park.

TANJUNG PUTING NATIONAL PARK

Possibly *the* highlight of Borneo, this unforgettable adventure takes you puttering up Sungai (river) Sekonyer to **Camp Leakey**. Established in 1971 by eminent primatologist Dr Biruté Galdikas, a visit here almost guarantees you intimate encounters with orang-utans. Ninja-quiet and brilliantly camouflaged, an orang-utan's distinctly orange fur only lights up when there's sun behind it; as such you may find yourself a few feet away from one without even realising. En route you'll see macaques, pot-bellied proboscis monkeys, kingfishers, majestic hornbills and – if you're lucky – false gharial crocodiles (best seen at low tide). Around the camp you may also spot sun bears, porcupines, gibbons and Sambar deer.

Part of the rehabilitation process here is the daily feeding of orang-utans at jungle platforms, where you'll go and view them. Rangers, armed with panniers of bananas whoop to empty trees and gradually our distant cousins appear. If you're lucky enough to see the current alpha male, Tom, be careful not to engage in a staring match (cheek pads signify an increased level of aggression).

Feedings take place at three camps: **Tanjung Harapan** at 3pm, **Pondok Tangui** at 9am and **Camp Leakey** at 2pm (check for schedule changes). Reaching feeding-stations requires a short, sometimes slippery walk (about 15 minutes) from the dock. Bring rain protection and vats of insect repellent!

For more on orang-utans, see p300.

Guides

Taking a guide is vital for facilitating a smooth trip: purchasing food, communicating with your *klotok* driver and getting you to the feeding platform at the right time, as well as taking you trekking. Guide fees range from 150,000Rp to 250,000Rp per day. We recommend the following licensed guides (it's worth emailing them in advance):

Purwadi (purwadi2010@gmail.com)

Ahmad Yani (☎0062 852 4930 9250; yaniguideteam@lycos.com)

Fery Candra (☎0062 813 4961 6480; librarysclub@yahoo.com)

Rustam Efendy (☎ 0062 856 5110 7442; rusty2010@gmail.com)

Andy Arysad: (☎0062 813 529 50891; andijaka2010@gmail.com)

Rules & Conduct

Many of the orang-utans are unafraid of humans, so under no circumstances approach them; they're semiwild and some are prone to biting visitors. If a female is with her baby, be especially vigilant. Resist the temptation to swim in rivers – large saltwater crocodiles still lurk; several years ago a British volunteer was killed swimming just off the dock at Camp Leakey.

Klotok Hire

Two-tiered *klotoks* are the most romantic way to visit Tanjung Puting and serve as your restaurant, watchtower and home, accommodating up to four guests. Come twilight, moor up beside the jungle, your *klotok* aflicker with candlelight. You usually bed down early – the upper deck transformed with mattress and mozzie net – then at dawn wake to the gibbon's mellow call and myriad animal sounds... pure epiphany material.

Boat demand peaks in July and August. Daily rates fluctuate from 400,000Rp to 450,000Rp for a boat and captain, including fuel. Cooks and food generally costs 100,000Rp per person per day. It's considered normal to provide the crew's food. So, when you add up your guide, food and boat, you shouldn't be shelling out more than around 900,000Rp for two people (per day).

Advance book a *klotok* with tour agencies in Pangkalan Bun (see p271) and throughout Kalimantan.

Sleeping

Only visitors that absolutely must bed down on terra firma should miss sleeping on a *klotok*. Some alternate nights on water and land.

Rimba Lodge HOTEL $$$
(☎0532-671 0589; www.ecolodgesindonesia.com; r incl breakfast 500,000-1,500,000Rp; ❄) Riverside Rimba has comfortable cabanas, offering en suites, warm showers and traditional decor. Its restaurant (mains 20,000Rp to 40,000Rp; open 7am to 9pm) serves Chinese and Indonesian food.

Information

Visiting Tanjung Puting starts with registration at Pangkalan Bun police station. Bring photocopies of your passport and visa. This can be organised by your guide.

Next stop is the **PHKA office** (☎23832; Jl HM Rafi'I Km 1.5; ⏰7am-2pm Mon-Thu, 7am-11am Fri, 7am-1pm Sat) on the way into Pangkalan Bun from the airport. Registration costs 50,000Rp per day per person, and 5000Rp per day for a *klotok* (15,000Rp for a speedboat). Provide a copy of your police letter from Pangkalan Bun and another photocopy of your passport. Then head to Kumai. When the park office is closed, it may be possible to arrange entry at the park's entry checkpoint.

Orangutan Foundation International (OFI; ☎1-323-938-6046; www.orangutan.org; 4201 Wilshire Blvd, Ste 407, Los Angeles, CA, USA 90010) runs Camp Leakey, while **Orangutan Foundation UK** (☎44-207-724-2912; www.orangutan.org.uk; 7 Kent Terrace, London, NW1 4RP) works tirelessly to secure safe 'reintroduction' for orang-utans in the nearby Lamandau Reserve.

The dry season runs May to September when reduced rainfall makes journeys more enjoyable. Note: March is prime time for an abundance of fruit in the forest, during which time orang-utans may be absent from the feeding platforms – a bummer if you've come this far to see them.

East Kalimantan

East Kalimantan (KalTim) may have been long exposed to logging and oil extraction, but it can still boast vast unpenetrated jungle, the mighty Mahakam River and some of the best off-coast diving in Borneo.

BERAU

☎0554 / POP 52,000

Riverbound Berau, your pit-stop before paradisical Sangalaki Archipelago, comes into its own by night, with a carnivalesque atmosphere of fairy-lit *warung* on Jl Yani.

PALM OIL: A DOUBLE-EDGED SWORD

Found in hundreds of products in Western supermarkets, this high-yield 'miracle crop' is the single biggest threat to Kalimantan's forests. Despite the considerable local employment its plantations create, the real loser is the planet; huge swaths of rainforest have been indiscriminately destroyed, critically endangering Kalimantan's unique biodiversity.

A two-year moratorium, beginning in 2011, on clearing forests has given conservationists a chance to establish the argument for 'REDD+ programs', where standing, preserved forests can be monetised with local people financially rewarded for preserving their vital function as global carbon silos. Perhaps then *carbon sequestration* can finally compete economically with palm oil.

WORTH A TRIP

ISLANDS OFF KALIMANTAN

Uninhabited **Sangalaki Island** boasts deserted beaches, turquoise water and white sand spits. Plankton-rich waters attract giant manta rays; there are a couple of their 'cleaning stations' north of the island, where they sweep up the micro-organisms they live on. Amid underwater coral formations resembling Venusian landscapes you may see them. More likely, you'll bump into giant green turtles, which lay their eggs on Sangalaki's beaches. To learn more, visit www.turtle-foundation.org.

Nearby **Kakaban Island** has thousands of evolutionary anomalies – jellyfish minus their sting. Swimming among them in the murky waters of Kakaban's lagoon is unforgettable. But the real high is back at the jetty where your boatman moors, as here the most preserved 'upper reef' in the Celebes Sea drops vertiginously into the abyss. Freedive past colonies of parrot, bat and clown fish.

Berau's Kalimarau international air terminal is nearing completion (future flights from Kuala Lumpur, Singapore and Jakarta), so by the time you read this the islands of Derawan and the Sangalaki Archipelago will be more accessible.

Sleeping

TOP CHOICE **Hotel Derawan Indah** HOTEL $$
(☎24255; Jl Panglima Batur 396; r incl buffet breakfast 300,000-400,000Rp plus 21% tax; ❄☒) This huge edifice offers the best digs in Berau as well as a swimming pool. The cavernous restaurant has an Indo menu. It can also do airport pick-ups. There's a 10% discount on request.

Hotel Sederhana HOTEL $$
(☎24041; fax 21534; Jl P Antasari 471; r incl breakfast 280,000-365,000Rp; ❄) Close to the river, Sederhana has large, well-appointed rooms set around a riad-style inner courtyard. There's free wi-fi in the eternally empty cafe. Nearby is useful **LIA Tours** (☎270 7879), which can help with booking flights, and water taxis to Derawan and Sangalaki.

Eating & Drinking

Sari Ponti Restaurant CHINESE $$
(☎21388; Jl Durian 2 35; mains from 20,000Rp; ⏲8am-9pm) This popular Chinese restaurant has a seafood-leaning menu featuring squid, *tiram* (oysters), frog and *ketapang* (crab), served up a myriad ways.

Warung Asri INDONESIAN $
(Jl A Yani; mains 15,000-20,000Rp; ⏲7am-9pm) Overlooking the riverfront, this friendly nook serves fresh eats ranging from *ikan bakar* (grilled fish) to delicious *nasi goreng*. It also serves heavenly chicken satay glazed in peanut sauce.

Information

Find ATMs along Jl P Antasari and Jl Maulana.

BNI bank (Jl Maulana) Foreign exchange.

LIA Tours (☎2707879; fax 2707283; Hotel Sederhana, Jl P Antasari) Flight bookings.

H2O Net Palace (Jl A Yani; per hr 6000Rp; ⏲24hr) No-smoking riverfront internet with private cubicles and quick connection. Sporadically closed.

THM Travel (☎21238; Jl Niaga II) English-speaking staff here can help you with flights and getting to Derawan and Sangalaki Archipelago by boat and taxi.

Getting There & Away

AIR **Trigana** (☎Jl Haji Asa; ☎0062 554 2027 885; fax 20279; Jl Maulana 45) flies from Berau to Samarinda (580,000Rp), Balikpapan (749,000Rp) and Tarakan (330,000Rp). **Kal-Star** (☎21007; Jl Maulana 45) offers daily flights (except Sunday) to Balikpapan (699,000Rp) and Samarinda (600,000Rp).

BOAT Speedboats to Pulau Derawan (three hours) wait off Jl A Yani. Negotiations may start at 2,000,000Rp one-way, but 1,500,000Rp is more realistic. Far cheaper Derawan transport goes via *kijang* (75,000Rp, minimum five persons) to Tanjung Batu, or KM Tasmania I, from where it's a short trip by speedboat to the islands.

Getting Around

Taxis to the airport (9km) cost 40,000Rp while *angkot* cost (3000Rp).

Pulau Derawan

☎0551

Fringed by coral-blue water and powder-fine beaches, this tear-shaped fishing island is a traveller's dream and one of the richest dive spots in Southeast Asia. Where else can you step off your *losmen* jetty and be gliding

NABUCCO ISLAND RESORT: PARADISE BOTTLED

As close to a Robinson Crusoe idyll as possible, **Nabucco Island Resort** (☎0542-593 635; www.nabuccoislandresort.com; info@nabuccoislandresort.com; Nabucco Island, Maratua atoll; r per person incl breakfast s/d 1,140,000/800,000Rp) has Asian Fusion cuisine and beautiful Dayak-Bagao–inspired cabanas that are well worth the journey. However, it's the setting that takes your breath away, for the water, occasionally broken by trippy sandbars, is so perfectly turquoise you feel as if it's been 'Photoshopped'. Guests dive with reef shark, giant green turtle, barracuda, tuna, eagle ray and manta. From Derawan Island charter a speedboat (850,000Rp) to get here or call the hotel to catch their speedy taxi boat from Berau (145km).

with giant green turtles, clown fish, scorpion fish, moray eel and parrot fish a moment later? By night Derawan is a sleepy affair, braziers glowing on street corners as the Celebes Sea incandesces with fishing boats.

Among the 30-odd islands in the archipelago, **Nabucco** and **Maratua** also have accommodation; however, booking is essential and digs here are vastly more upmarket and expensive.

Activities

Pulau Derawan's underwater activities are conducted from upmarket **Derawan Dive Resort** (☎081-257 411 988; www.divederawan.com; Pulau Derawan) and earthy **Losmen Danakan** (☎086-8121 6143; Pulau Derawan). Individual local dives cost around 250,000Rp, including tank and equipment hire; snorkelling gear costs 55,000Rp to hire per day. Dive trips to Pulau Sangalaki and Kakaban cost around 800,000Rp – expect to see shark and barracuda. Village boats to dive sites cost around 700,000Rp per boat, exclusive of equipment. If that sounds too expensive and you're staying at Pelangi Guesthouse, speak to Tony about borrowing snorkelling equipment and sourcing a boat and driver. Manta ray sightings are down at the moment; however, the best place to see them is off Pulau Sangalaki.

Sleeping & Eating

Stilted *losmen* here are cosy and offer the sea as your back garden. Cafes along Main St serve up fresh seafood.

TOP CHOICE **Pelangi Guesthouse** GUESTHOUSE $
(☎081-347 807 078; Pulau Derawan; r 150,000-250,000Rp; ❄) Crayola-coloured Pelangi (Rainbow) is fresh, with a basic cafe, free snorkel gear, private verandas and en suites. Look out for giant green turtles that pop up like periscopes beside the jetty.

Derawan Dive Resort RESORT $$
(☎081-257 411 988; www.divederawan.com; Pulau Derawan; r 300,000-450,000Rp; ❄) Patronised by divers, this resort's high luxe cabanas have wood floors, Western en suites and fresh linen but are somewhat overpriced. The generator-driven restaurant serves mercifully cool beer.

April's Restaurant RESTAURANT $$
(☎081-350 582 483; Pulau Derawan; mains 25,000Rp; ⏲7am-8pm) Halfway down Main St, guacamole-green April's dishes up mouth-watering *ikan bakar* (barbecued fish) as well as fried rice and chicken. We were greeted by a 4ft-long monitor lizard on arrival.

Getting There & Away

From Berau, the economy route to Derawan is a *kijang* (75,000Rp, at least two hours) to Tanjung Batu, and a boat from there. *Kijangs* wait along the riverfront from 9am, but won't leave with fewer than five passengers, which often means departing midafternoon while you wait in a cafe on Jl A Yani. At Tanjung Batu, hire a speedboat (400,000Rp to 600,000Rp depending on number of passengers, one hour) to Pulau Derawan. Be prepared to haggle.

A direct speedboat from Berau can cost up to 2,000,000Rp (three hours, 140km). Derawan *losmen* can arrange a village boat back to Tanjung Batu (400,000Rp, two hours). Leave early: *kijangs* depart here for Berau at 8am sharp.

SULAWESI

Looking like the remains of blanket shredded by a pack of mad jackals, Sulawesi is as wild in reality as it appears on a map. The massive island's many-limbed coastline is drawn with sandy beaches, fringing coral reefs and a mind-boggling variety of fish. Meanwhile the interior is shaded in with impenetrable mountains and jungles thick with wildlife, such as rare nocturnal tarsiers and flamboyantly colourful maleo birds. Just exploring this ink-blot of an island can gobble up a 30-day visa before you know it, so be sure to leave time for the diving around Pulau Bunaken; it's reached by the legendary travellers' trail along Sulawesi's spine: from bustling Makassar to Tana Toraja, on to the chilled Togean Islands and finally Manado and Bunaken.

Getting There & Away

AIR The three transport hubs are Makassar and Manado, which are well connected with the rest

Sulawesi

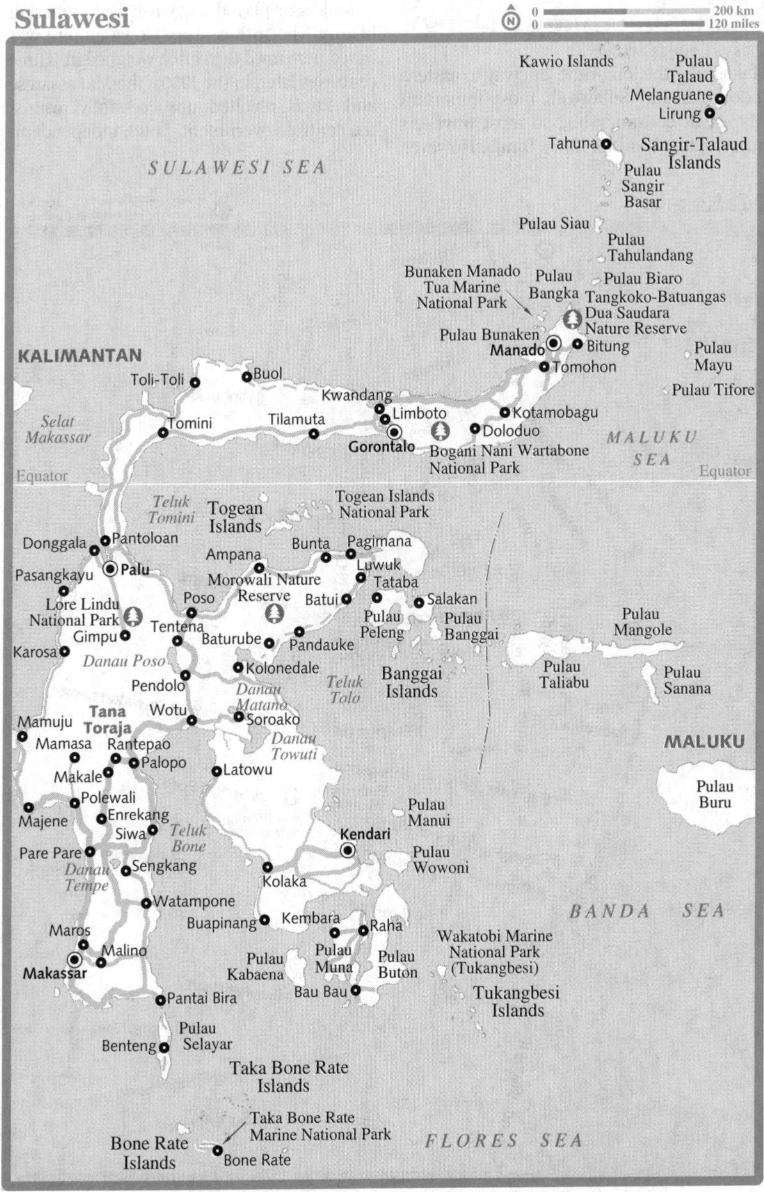

of Indonesia, and Palu, which offers connections to Balikpapan in Kalimantan. SilkAir flies to Manado from Singapore several times a week.

BOAT Sulawesi is well connected, with more than half Pelni's fleet calling at Makassar and Bitung (the seaport for Manado), as well as a few other towns.

Makassar (Ujung Padang)

0411 / POP 1.6 MILLION

Makassar – the long-time gateway to eastern Indonesia, and Sulawesi's most important city – can be unnerving, so most travellers immediately head for Tana Toraja. However, you're likely to spend at least one night here, so check out the busy harbour stacked and packed with Bugis schooners, and the neighbourhood surrounding, which is accented by children playing football on dry docks as huge trucks are loaded with endless bananas and a windfall of rice. Otherwise the shopping is good as are the seafood restaurants.

Makassar played a key role in Indonesian history. The 16th-century Gowa empire was based here until the Dutch weighed in. Three centuries later, in the 1950s, the Makassarese and Bugis revolted unsuccessfully against the central government. Loud, independent-

Makassar

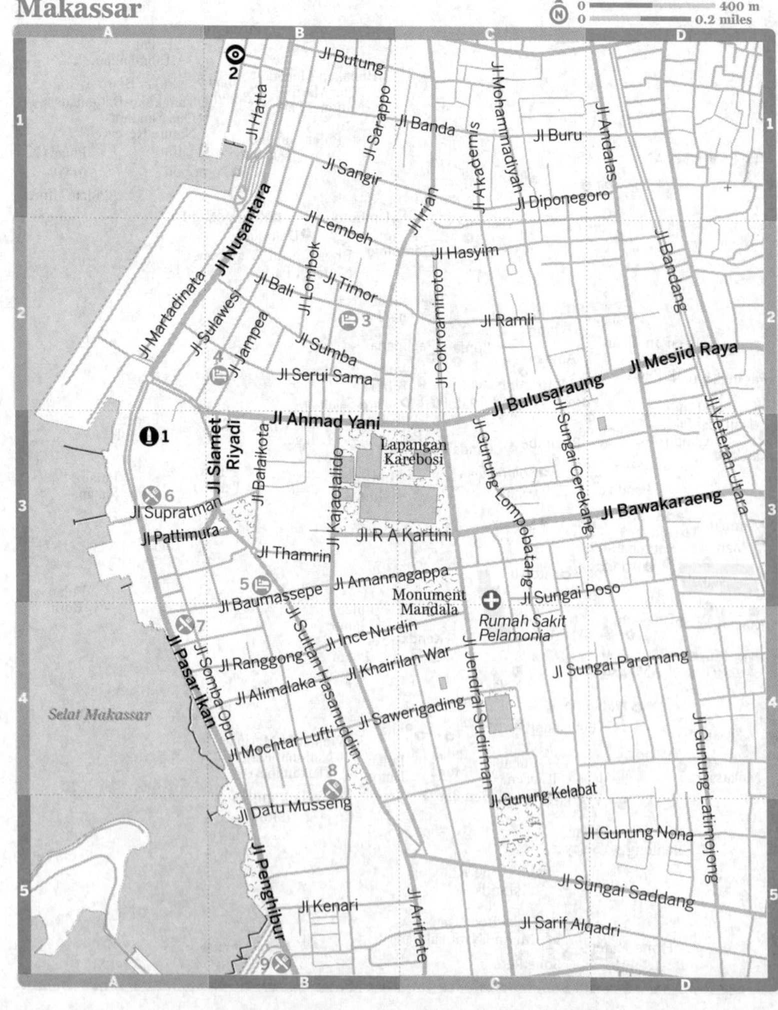

minded, intense and proud, Makassar is a shot of Red Bull to jump-start your trip.

Sights & Activities

Most of the action takes place in the west, near the sea. The port is in the northwest; Fort Rotterdam is in the centre of the older commercial hub.

Fort Rotterdam HISTORIC BUILDING
(Jl Pasar Ikan; suggested donation 10,000Rp; 7.30am-6pm) Fort Rotterdam dates from 1545. First a Gowanese fort, usurped by Dutch forces in 1667, this is one of the best-preserved examples of colonial Dutch architecture in Indonesia, although renovations have been fanciful. Two museums are set to reopen in 2012.

Pelabuhan Paotere HARBOUR
(Paotere Harbour; admission 500Rp) Bugis schooners dock at Pelabuhan Paotere, a 15-minute becak ride north from the city centre. This place is captivating. You can spend hours wandering the sweltering alleyways.

Sleeping

Pondok Suada Indah HOTEL $$
(361 7179; Jl Sultan Hasanuddin 12; r from 190,000Rp;) Set in an old colonial-era house that feels far from the city's hubbub, which is just out the front door. Rooms are huge and are decorated with a tatty mix of heavy antiques and cheap modern furniture; some have age-worn bathtubs.

New Legend Hostel GUESTHOUSE $
(313777, 361 3777; www.newlegendhostel.com; Jl Jampea 5G; dm 75,000, r 95,000-135,000Rp; @) Catering to backpackers, this clean and very helpful place has rooms and dorms, but most are small, windowless and boxlike.

Hotel Lestari HOTEL $
(362 7337; Jl Savu 16; r 162,000-265,000Rp;) Thirty clean rooms all with satellite TV and minibar are among the best deals in Makassar. Only the most expensive have windows.

Eating

For many it's the food that makes Makassar a great destination. There's an abundance of seafood, Chinese dishes and local 'specialities' such as *coto makassar* (soup made from buffalo innards).

Hundreds of night *warung* just off Jl Metro Tanjung Bunga serve up fresh and cheap Indonesian and Chinese meals. Just as good is the string of makeshift seafood *warung* set up every night on the foreshore opposite Fort Rotterdam.

TOP CHOICE **Lae Lae** SEAFOOD $
(Jl Datu Musseng 8; mains from 20,000Rp) A very basic dining hall packed with food-frenzied locals, this place is as social as the seafood is good. Servers lead you to the icebox where you choose your fish, which gets grilled out front. Other good options are close by.

Kafe Kareba CAFE $
(Jl Penghibur; meals from 20,000Rp) At this outdoor beer garden on the corner opposite the Losari Beach Hotel live bands play and the beer flows. The menu is extensive and the sea breeze cooling.

Cafe Dapoer Sulawesi CAFE $
(cnr Jl Pasar Ikan & Jl Supratman; meals from 20,000Rp;) Slightly stylish corner cafe has excellent coffees, sandwiches, a shady wrap-around terrace and free wi-fi.

Information

Countless banks with ATMs are found on the main streets.

Rumah Sakit Pelamonia (324710; Jl J Sudirman 27) Well-equipped hospital.

Getting There & Away

Air

Makassar's slick and modern airport (code: UPG) is well connected to the rest of Indonesia.

The following airlines all have offices located at the airport:

Batavia Air (www.batavia-air.com) Flies to Jakarta, Surabaya and Balikpapan.

Makassar

Sights
1 Fort Rotterdam ... A3
2 Pelabuhan Paotere Port Entrance ... B1

Sleeping
3 Hotel Lestari ... B2
4 New Legend Hostel ... B2
5 Pondok Suada Indah ... B3

Eating
6 Cafe Dapoer Sulawesi ... A3
7 Kafe Kareba ... A4
8 Lae Lae ... B4
9 Night Warung ... B5

Garuda (www.garuda-indonesia.com) Flies to Manado, Denpasar and Jakarta.

Lion Air (www.lionair.co.id) Flies to Manado, Gorontalo, Palu, Ambon, Jakarta, Surabaya and Denpasar.

Merpati (www.merpati.co.id) Flies to Jakarta, Manado and Yogyakarta.

Boat

Pelni (www.pelni.co.id; Jl Sam Ratulangi; ⌚8am-2pm Mon-Sat) has connections to countless destinations across Indonesia, including Surabaya, Jakarta, East Kalimantan, Ambon and Papua.

Bus

Buses heading north leave from Terminal Panaikang, aka Terminal Daya, in the eastern suburbs. There are numerous services to Rantepao (from 60,000Rp) in Tana Toraja. Get to the terminal with a blue *pete-pete* (minibus) from Makassar Mall (3000Rp, 30 minutes).

Getting Around

Hasanuddin airport is 22km east of the city centre, 100,000Rp by taxi or 5000Rp by *pete-pete*. The main *pete-pete* station is at Makassar Mall, and the base fare is 2000Rp. Becak drivers/hawkers can be charming and exhausting all at once. Their shortest fare is 3000Rp. Taxis are metered.

Tana Toraja

Get ready for a dizzying cocktail of stunningly serene beauty, elaborate, brutal and captivating funeral rites, exquisite traditional architecture and a profoundly peculiar fascination with the dead. It comes garnished with a pinch of Indiana Jones intrigue, and is served by some of the warmest and toughest people you'll ever meet: the Torajans. Life for the Torajans revolves around death and their days are spent earning the money to send away their dead properly. During funeral season, in July and August, the tourist numbers swell and prices soar, but the rest of the year it's empty and starved for visitors, which means grateful hosts, good deals and a frontierlike appeal.

The capital, Makale, and Rantepao, the largest town and tourist magnet, are the main centres. Bemo link them to surrounding villages, where you'll find cultural hot spots tucked into spectacular countryside (see the boxed text, p281).

RANTEPAO

☎0423 / POP 49,000

With a variety of lodgings, Rantepao is the best base for exploring Tana Toraja. There is one unforgettable sight: **Pasar Bolu**, the market 2km northeast of town. It peaks every six days, overflowing with livestock. The main market is a very big, social occasion that draws crowds from all over Tana Toraja.

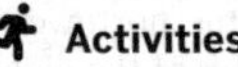

Activities

Plan on spending your days exploring this captivating region. Guides charge 250,000Rp to 350,000Rp per day. In addition, motorbikes cost about 70,000Rp per day; a guide with a car for up to four people costs 600,000Rp per day. You'll get to some of the most interesting places by foot or motorbike, although improving roads have made much accessible by car.

The best place to find a guide is Mart's Cafe. Be sure to hire a Torajan guide, as interlopers from elsewhere won't have the same access and sensitivity to funerals and other cultural events. A good contact for guides is **Elda Tato** (☎0813 5523 9856), who speaks excellent English.

To fully immerse yourself in Toraja land, trek off the main roads. Good footwear is vital, and so is ample food, water, a torch (flashlight; some villages lack electricity) and rain gear. If you desire a professional trekking outfitter, contact **Indo' Sella** (☎0423-25210; www.sellatours.com; Jl Andi Mappanyukki 111), which also organises white-water rafting trips (750,000Rp for two people).

For a brilliant day trek, take a morning bemo to Deri, then veer off-road and traverse the incredible cascading rice fields all the way to Tikala. Farmers and villagers will help point the way, but a guide would be a wise decision for this trek.

Another good day trek starts in the hills at Batutumonga and follows rice fields back to Rantepao. Popular multiday treks include the following:

» **Batumonga–Lokomata–Pangala–Baruppu–Pulu Pulu–Sapan** Three days.

» **Bittuang–Mamasa** Three days.

» **Pangala–Bolokan–Bittuang** Two days on a well-marked trail.

Sleeping

TOP CHOICE **Hotel Indra Toraja** HOTEL $

(☎21163; indratorajahotel.com; Jl Landorundun 63; r 300,000-500,000Rp; 📶) Right in the centre of Rantepao, the Indra has rooms on two floors around a small courtyard. Everything is well run, the breakfast is good and the rooms are comfortable. You can refill your water bottles here.

Tana Toraja

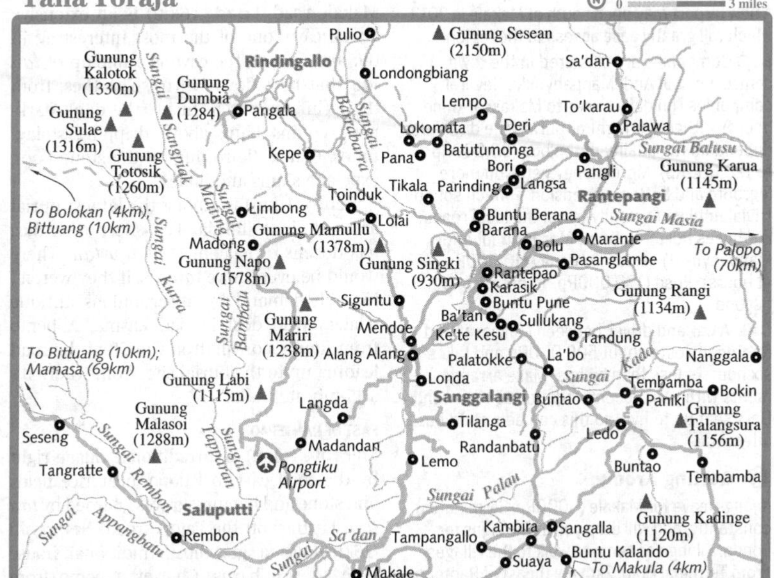

Pia's Poppies Hotel HOTEL $
(☎21121; r 130,000-200,000Rp) Rooms have some quirky details like stone bathrooms, and each terrace overlooks a languorous garden. There's hot water; it's a 10-minute walk from the centre.

Hotel Pison HOTEL $
(☎21344; s/d 120,000/130,000Rp; 📶) Opposite Pia's, the bland but good-value Pison has 32 rooms, each with a clean bathroom and minibalcony with mountain views. All the rooms come with hot water.

Wisma Maria I GUESTHOUSE $
(☎21165; adespasakal1@yahoo.com; Jl Sam Ratulangi 23; r 60,000-120,000Rp) A fine 21-room cheapie in the town centre; rooms are plain but good sized.

Wisma Monika GUESTHOUSE $
(☎21216; Jl Sam Ratulangi 36; r 100,000-200,000Rp) A very friendly, family-run central spot with 20 rooms in a newish building. Inspect a few to find a bright one.

✕ Eating

The best-known dish is *pa'piong* (meat stuffed into bamboo tubes along with vegetables and coconut). Order in advance and enjoy it with black rice.

TOP CHOICE **Mart's Cafe** CAFE $
(Jl Sam Ratulangi 44; dishes 15,000-45,000Rp) With good local food, Mart's gets lively in the evenings when the resident guides start crooning and strumming their guitars. The Bintang flows...

Rimiko Restoran INDONESIAN $
(Jl Andi Mappanyukki; dishes from 25,000Rp) This place attracts a convivial crowd of travellers and has a few Torajan specialities on the menu that don't require ordering in advance.

Riman Restoran INDONESIAN $
(Jl Andi Mappanyukki; dishes from 25,000Rp) Fronting Indo' Sella and next to Rimiko, Riman has a menu that features Torajan standards. Another good place to meet a guide.

Information

Jl Diponegoro has banks, internet places and ATMs. Bring sunscreen, as none is sold locally.

Government Tourist Office (Jl Ahmad Yani 62A; ⏲9am-2pm Mon-Sat) Provides information about local ceremonies, festivals and other activities; good for ping-pong, which occupies much of the staff's time. Just south of the hospital.

Rumah Sakit Elim (☎21258; Jl Ahmad Yani) The main hospital in town. If anything serious should befall you in Toraja, make for Makassar, as facilities here are basic.

Getting There & Away

A new airport may open south of Makale in 2013, which will greatly ease access to the region.

BUS Companies are clustered in the town centre along Jl Andi Mappanyukki. Several companies run daily buses to Makassar (nine hours), either overnight or during the day. Fares depend on the quality of the bus (80,000Rp to 120,000Rp). More money gets you more legroom and better suspension – which sounds trivial until you actually travel the local roads. For buses north, **Rappan Marannu** (Jl Andi Mappanyukki) serves Tentena (110,000Rp, 11 hours), Poso (130,000Rp, 14 hours) and beyond.

CAR A car and driver between Makassar and Rantepao costs about 500,000Rp and takes six hours – less than by bus. Make arrangements with your accommodation at either end. Cars seat up to five, so this can be a good bus alternative.

Getting Around

Kijangs leave for Makale (5000Rp, 30 minutes) constantly, and will drop you at the signs for Londa, Tilanga or Lemo to walk to the villages. From Terminal Bolu, 2km northeast of Rantepao, frequent vehicles go east to Palopo, and regular bemo and *kijangs* go to all the major villages, such as Lempo (near Batutumonga).

Motorbikes can be rented from hotels and tour agencies for 70,000Rp per day.

AROUND RANTEPAO

On day trips from Rantepao there's the beautiful: stunning panoramas, magical bamboo forests and rice terraces, shaped by natural boulders and fed by waterfalls, that drop for 2000m. There's the strange: *tau tau* (wooden effigies) of long-lost relatives guarding graves carved out of vertical limestone rock faces or hung from the roof of deep caves. And there's the intermingling of the two: incredibly festive and colourful four-day funerals where buffalo are slaughtered and stewed, palm wine is swilled from bamboo carafes and a spirit soars to the afterlife.

SOUTH OF RANTEPAO

Karasik (1km from Rantepao) is on the outskirts of town, just off the road leading to Makale. The traditional houses were erected years ago for a funeral.

Just off the main road, southeast of Rantepao, **Ke'te Kesu** (6km) is famed for its woodcarving. On the cliff face behind the village are cave graves and some very old hanging graves – the rotting coffins are suspended from an overhang.

Located about 2km off the Rantepao–Makale road, **Londa** (6km) is an extensive burial cave, one of the most interesting in the area. Above the cave is a line-up of *tau tau* that peer down, in fresh clothes, from their cliffside perch. Inside the dank darkness, coffins hang above dripping stalagmites. Others lie rotting on the stone floor, exposing skulls and bones.

Lemo (11km) is among the largest burial areas in Tana Toraja. The sheer rock face has dozens of balconies for *tau tau*. There would be even more *tau tau* if they weren't in such demand by unscrupulous antique dealers who deal in bad karma. A bemo from Rantepao will drop you off at the road leading up to the burial site, from where it's a 15-minute walk.

EAST OF RANTEPAO

Marante (6km) is a traditional village right by the road east to Palopo, near rice fields and stone and hanging graves guarded by *tau tau*. Further off the Palopo road, **Nanggala** (16km) has a grandiose traditional house with 14 rice barns. Charter a bemo from Rantepao, and you can be taken straight here, or take a public one, and walk 7km from the Palopo road.

NORTH & WEST OF RANTEPAO

This is where you'll find the finest scenery in Tana Toraja. **Batutumonga** (20km) has an ideal panoramic perch, sensational sunrise views and a few homestays. The best is **Mentirotiku** (☎081 142 2260; r 75,000-220,000Rp). The views are even more stunning from the summit of **Gunung Sesean**, a 2150m peak towering above the village. Most bemo stop at **Lempo**, an easy walk from Batutumonga.

There are more cave graves and beautiful scenery at **Lokomata** (26km), just a few kilometres west past Batutumonga.

The return to Rantepao is an interesting and easy trek down the slopes through tiny villages to **Pana**, with its ancient hanging graves, and baby graves in the trees. The path ends at **Tikala**, where regular bemo go to Rantepao.

The three-day, 59km trek from **Mamasa** in the west to Bittuang is popular, and there are plenty of villages en route with food and accommodation (remember to bring gifts). There's no direct transport from Rantepao to Mamasa because the roads are appalling. Currently, jeeps are running from Mamasa to Ponding for 80,000Rp every day, where

TORAJA CULTURE

The local culture in Tana Toraja is among the world's most unique and distinctive. That the people are genuinely welcoming of visitors makes it unmissable.

Architecture

Traditional *tongkonan* houses – shaped like boats or buffalo horns, with the roof rearing up at the front and back – are the enduring image of Tana Toraja. They are similar to the Batak houses of Sumatra's Danau Toba and are always aligned north–south, with small rice barns facing them.

A number of villages are still composed entirely of these traditional houses, but most now have corrugated-iron roofs. The houses are painted and carved with animal motifs, and buffalo skulls often decorate the front, symbolising wealth and prestige.

Burial Customs

The Toraja generally have two funerals, one immediately after the death, and a second, more elaborate, four-day ceremony after enough cash has been raised. Between the two ceremonies, the dead will live at home in the best room of the house and visitors will be obliged to sit, chat and have coffee with them. Regularly. This all ends once buffalo are sacrificed (one for a commoner, as many as 24 for a high-ranking figure) and the spirit soars to the afterlife.

The expenses associated with funerals are *the* major expense for locals. People keep careful track of who brings what to ceremonies (gifts are often announced to the funeral throngs over a loudspeaker) and an offering considered 'cheap' is cause for great shame. A run-of-the-mill buffalo costs 25 million rupiah, while the most prized animals (with white heads and perfect hides) cost 80 million rupiah – about the same as a new house. A local joke uttered at funerals when an animal is sacrificed is 'there goes another Toyota'.

To deter the plundering of generous burial offerings, the Toraja started to hide their dead in caves or on rocky cliff faces. You can often see *tau tau* – life-sized, carved wooden effigies of the dead – sitting in balconies on rock faces, guarding the coffins. Descendents are obliged to change and update their fake deceased relatives clothing. Also regularly.

Funeral ceremonies are the region's main tourist attraction. Visitors are welcomed to the multiday affairs and are shown great hospitality, including tea and snacks. In return your guide will advise you on what modest gifts to bring (cigarettes and snacks in lieu of, say, a buffalo). The ritual slaughter of buffalo, pigs and other animals can be quite grisly and is disturbing to many.

Ceremonies & Festivals

The end of the rice harvest, from around May onwards, is ceremony time in Tana Toraja. These festivities involve feasting and dancing, buffalo fights and *sisemba* kick-boxing. Guides will also take you to these ceremonies.

you can hook up with a horse on to Bittuang for about 150,000Rp.

MAKALE & AROUND

The **Makale Market**, held every six days, is one of the region's best.

One of the most stunning sights in Tana Toraja is the *tau tau* at **Tampangallo**, between Sangalla and Suaya, which is 6km east of Makale. The graves belong to the chiefs of Sangalla, descendants of the mythical divine being Tamborolangiq, who is believed to have introduced the caste system, death rituals and agricultural techniques into Torajan society. Take a *kijang* from Makale to Sangalla, get off about 1km after the turn-off to Suaya, and walk a short distance (less than a kilometre) through the rice fields to Tampangallo.

Tentena

☎0458 / POP 12,000

This lakeside town of white picket fences and churches is a good place to break your bus journey north from Rantepao. Surrounded by clove-covered hills, it's a peaceful and very easy-to-manage town.

The price is right, service is good and the rooms are clean at **Hotel Victori** (☎21392; Jl Diponegoro 18; r from 140,000Rp; ❄). Only the higher-end rooms have air-con. This is a good spot to meet guides. Good meals are served.

Buses make the run to Poso (20,000Rp, two to three hours) throughout the day.

Poso

☎0452 / POP 48,000

Poso is the main town, port and terminal for road transport on the northern coast of Central Sulawesi. It's a spread out, noisy place and there's little reason to stay besides to hit up an ATM, change money, shop or change buses. Services are few until Manado.

Losmen Alugoro (☎21336; Jl Sumatera 20; d 40,000-175,000Rp; ❄) is a reliably decent but characterless place that's central to the bus offices and restaurants.

Buses leave the terminal, 800m north of the post office, for Tentena (20,000Rp, two to three hours), Ampana (minibus 75,000Rp, five hours) and Rantepao (130,000Rp, 14 hours).

Ampana

☎0464

Ampana is the gateway to the Togeans. Given bus and ferry schedules, you will likely spend a night here.

Oasis Hotel (☎21058; Jl Kartini; r from 100,000Rp; ❄) has clean rooms and dorms, but don't expect to sleep till the karaoke shuts down at 11pm. The most expensive rooms include air-con and hot water. It's near the Togean Islands boat dock.

Minibuses travel each day to Luwuk (100,000Rp, six hours) and Poso (75,000Rp, five hours).

Togean Islands

Yes, it does take some determination to get to the Togean Islands, but believe us, it takes much more determination to leave. Island hop from one forested golden-beach beauty to the next, where hammocks are plentiful, the fish is fresh and the welcome is homey. There are lost lagoons and forgotten coves, and arguably the best diving in Sulawesi (which ranks it near the top worldwide). Plunge into crystal-clear, bottomless seas to explore all three major reef systems – atoll, barrier and fringing. Colours absolutely pop. Fish are everywhere.

ℹ Getting There & Away

Getting boat information in advance of a trip to the Togeans can be a challenge. Your best option is to contact the place you intend to stay at and let them advise you. If you are travelling the length of Sulawesi, try to go from Ampana to the Togeans to Gorontolo (or the reverse), which will save you the endless land journey via Palu.

FROM THE SOUTH

Boats depart most days from Ampana to Wakai, the Togeans' hub (about 50,000Rp, three hours) and usually make other stops in the islands.

FROM THE NORTH

The quickest way to get to the Togeans is to fly from Manado to Luwuk on **Merpati** (www.merpati.co.id). Service is a few times per week and the flight takes an hour. Travel by road from there to Ampana (minibus 100,000Rp, hired car 500,000Rp, six hours).

Boats from Gorontalo to various islands run two times per week (120,000Rp, 13 hours).

ℹ Getting Around

Charters around the Togeans are easily arranged in Wakai, Bomba and Kadidiri (300,000Rp).

WORTH A TRIP

TANGKOKO-BATUANGAS DUA SAUDARA NATURE RESERVE

With 8800 hectares of forest bordered by a sandy coastline and offshore coral gardens, Tangkoko is one of the most impressive and accessible nature reserves in Indonesia. The park is home to black macaques, cuscus and tarsiers, maleo birds and endemic red-knobbed hornbills, among other fauna, and rare types of rainforest flora. Tangkoko is also home to a plethora of midges, called *gonones*, which bite and leave victims furiously scratching for days afterwards. Always wear long trousers, tucked into thick socks, and take covered shoes and plenty of insect repellent. Sadly, parts of the park are falling victim to encroachment by local communities, but money generated from visitors might help stave that off.

To get to nearby Batuputih from Manado, take a bus to Bitung, get off at Girian and catch a *mikrolet* or pick-up truck to Batuputih.

PULAU KADIDIRI

This is definitely the island to go to if you're feeling social, but during the low season you could potentially wind up on your own here. Just a short boat trip from Wakai, the three lodging options (all right next to each other) are on a perfect strip of sand with OK snorkelling and swimming, and superb diving beyond.

Sleeping & Eating

Hotels usually provide transport from Wakai. Rates usually include all meals.

Pondok Lestari GUESTHOUSE $
(www.lestari.ladz.de; cottages 90,000Rp) Stay with a charming Bajo family who take their guests on daily free snorkelling trips. The older bamboo bungalows are very rustic and share a rudimentary bathroom. The owner usually meets the ferries at Wakai.

Black Marlin Cottages RESORT $$
(☎0856 5720 2004; www.blackmarlindiving.com; cottages from 200,000Rp) This is arguably the most lively place on Kadidiri and is home to Black Marlin Dive. The 15 cottages are large, wooden, well decorated and have good bathrooms. Travellers amass on the pontoon here for sunsets.

TOGEAN ISLAND & AROUND

The main settlement on Togean Island is the very relaxed Katupat village, which has a small market and a couple of shops.

Around the island there are magical **beaches**, and some decent **hikes** for anyone sick of swimming, snorkelling and diving.

Fadhila Cottages GUESTHOUSE $
(☎0813 4117 9990; fadhilacottages.free.fr; cottages per person 150,000-170,000Rp) Across from Katupat village on private Pagempa Island, this relaxed and welcoming place offers wooden cottages with superb beaches and snorkelling.

PULAU BATU DAKA

BOMBA

This tiny outpost at the southeastern end of Pulau Batu Daka has nearby reefs and exquisite beaches.

Island Retreat (☎0852 4115 8853; www.togian-island-retreat.com; r per person US$15-28) is run by an expat Californian woman and her band of friendly dogs. Set on the beautiful beach at Pasir Putih, the 20 cottages are well cared for and the food is great. There's a dive centre here; staff are good at arranging transport from afar.

WAKAI

The Togeans' largest settlement is a departure point for ferries to Ampana and Gorontalo and for charters to Pulau Kadidiri and beyond. There are a few general stores, if you need supplies, but there's no reason to stay the night.

Gorontalo

☎0435 / POP 150,000

The port of Gorontalo has the feel of an overgrown country town, where all the locals seem to know each other. The town features some of the best-preserved Dutch houses in Sulawesi; it offers the best services north of Poso.

Melati Hotel (☎822934; avelberg@hotmail.com; Jl Gajah Mada 33; r 80,000-200,000Rp; ❄@) is a longtime traveller favourite. It's based around a lovely home, built in the early 1900s. The rooms in the original house are basic but atmospheric; the newer rooms are set around a pretty garden. This is a good place to stay while sorting Togean ferry options.

Getting There & Away

Lion Air (www.lionair.co.id) has daily flights from Manado (40 minutes) and Makassar (90 minutes).

The main bus terminal is 3km north of town. There are direct buses to Manado (from 80,000Rp, 10 hours); minibuses are more comfortable and cost 150,000Rp.

Manado

☎0431 / POP 485,000

Once described by anthropologist Alfred Russel Wallace as 'one of the prettiest [cities] in the East', Manado has sold its soul to commerce. However, it remains a necessary base for exploring North Sulawesi.

Along Jl Sam Ratulangi, the main north-south artery, you'll find restaurants, hotels and supermarkets. The shopping-mall blitz dominates parallel Jl Piere Tendean (aka 'The Boulevard') closer to the waterfront, which is one vast construction site – though even the new sidewalks are perilous!

Sleeping

TOP CHOICE **Hotel Minahasa** HOTEL $$
(☎862559; www.hotelminahasa.com; Jl Sam Ratulangi 199; r with fan/air-con from 200,000/340,000Rp;

) Flower-filled grounds stretch up the hill to a luxurious pool and fitness centre with city views. Fan rooms are basic and OK value, but you'll be tempted to upgrade to a superior room with a terrace and a view.

Hotel Regina HOTEL $
(850091; Jl Sugiono 1; r from 200,000Rp;) Five storeys of bland but big rooms here are spotless and plush for the price. The hearty Indonesian breakfasts are another perk.

New Angkasa Hotel HOTEL $
(864062; Jl Sugiono 10; r with fan/air-con from 80,000/150,000Rp;) This place is always full because of its 17 good-value though basic rooms.

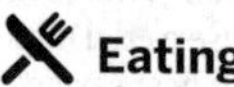

Eating

Adventurous diners migrate to the night *warung* along Jl Piere Tendean. Regional delights include *kawaok* (fried 'forest rat') and *rintek wuuk* (spicy dog meat).

Hidden behind the massive Mega Mall on Jl Piere Tendean are good seafood *warung*. Across the street, the IT Centre Mall has a food court on the top floor with fresh local dishes under 15,000Rp.

Singapura Bakery BAKERY $
(Jl Sam Ratulangi 22; pastries from 5000Rp) Has a mind-boggling array of baked goods, fresh juices and shakes, plus a popular cheap cafe next door serving yummy Javanese fare. It's always thronged with locals.

Information

You're never far from a bank, ATM or internet place.

Main post office (Jl Sam Ratulangi 23; 8am-7.30pm Mon-Fri, 8am-6pm Sat & Sun)

Rumah Sakit Umum (853191; Jl Monginsidi; Malalayang) The general hospital is about 4.5km from town and includes a decompression chamber.

Getting There & Around

Air

Mikrolet (minibus) from Sam Ratulangi International Airport go to Terminal Paal 2 (4000Rp), where you can change to a *mikrolet* heading to Pasar 45 or elsewhere in the city for a flat fee of 2500Rp. Fixed-price taxis cost 100,000Rp for the trip from the airport to the city (13km).

Manado is well connected by air. Airlines have offices at the airport.

Air Asia (www.airasia.com) Flies to Kuala Lumpur.

Batavia Air (www.batavia-air.com) Flies to Balikpapan, Surabaya and Jakarta.

Garuda (www.garuda-indonesia.com) Flies to Makassar, Balikpapan and Denpasar.

Lion Air (www.lionair.co.id) Flies to Makassar, Jakarta and Surabaya

Merpati (www.merpati.co.id) Flies to Luwuk, Jakarta and Makassar.

SilkAir (www.silkair.com) Flies to Singapore.

Boat

Pelni (www.pelni.co.id) ships use the deep-water port of Bitung, 55km from Manado. Service includes Ternate, Ambon, Sorong, Luwuk and other ports along the southeastern coast.

Bus

From Karombasan terminal, 5km south of the city, buses go to Gorontolo (from 80,000Rp, 10 hours); minibuses are more comfortable and cost 150,000Rp.

Public Transport

There's no *mikrolet* shortage in Manado. Destinations are shown on a card in the front windscreen. There are various bus stations around town for destinations outside Manado; get to any of them from Pasar 45, the main traffic circle near the harbour. Bluebird taxis use their metres.

Pulau Bunaken

Pulau Bunaken is Sulawesi's top destination: 300 varieties of pristine coral and 3000 species of fish in Bunaken Manado Tua Marine National Park draw acolytes from around the globe. Tourist accommodation is spread out along two beaches and there is a delightful island vibe, thanks especially to the lovely locals. When not on the water, you can wander the lush paths alongside the mangroves.

Activities

Snorkellers are rewarded with rich reefs close to the surface; divers have a menu of choices from muck to drop-offs. The Bunaken park fee is 50,000Rp per day or 150,000Rp for an annual pass. Trips around Bunaken and nearby islands will cost from US$70 for two dives. Whole schools of dive operators are at the resorts and most people usually go with the outfit native to where they're staying.

Sleeping & Eating

Pantai Liang, to the west, is remote from the rest of the island and has a beautiful stretch of sand. Pantai Pangalisang, near Bunaken village, is the eco-choice. There's no beach to lie on, but it overlooks an armada of stately mangrove trees closer to Bunaken village, and the nearby reef is ideal for snorkelling. Most hotels quote rates per person for full board.

PANTAI PANGALISANG

TOP CHOICE **Seabreeze Resort** RESORT $$

(☎081 143 9558; www.bunakendivers.com; cottages per person from €20; 📶) A large, sprawling resort with quite a few different types of bungalows here; beers are cold thanks to the Aussie owner, and it is the only place with wi-fi. The common area is as delightful a place to hang out and meet other travellers as you can imagine. The dive operation, Bunaken Divers, is excellent.

Daniel's Homestay GUESTHOUSE $

(☎081 143 3829; daniels@indostat.net.id; bungalows from 200,000Rp) Wood cottages are very basic but spacious. Pay a little more for a seafront cottage.

Lorenso's Beach Garden GUESTHOUSE $

(☎0852 5697 3345; www.lorenso-bunaken.com; r 150,000-350,000Rp) A 15-minute walk north from the village, Lorenso has an affable owner and a variety of bungalows and rooms amid a beach and mangroves.

PANTAI LIANG

Panorama GUESTHOUSE $

(☎0813 4021 7306; ester_kasehung@hotmail.com; cottages per person from 150,000Rp) Tucked up in a corner on a hillside, the basic wood bungalows here with terraces and commanding views are the best budget deal on the island.

Froggies RESORT $$

(☎081 2430 1356; www.divefroggies.com; cottages per person €25-35) Good beachfront location, rooms are well decorated and spotless, and the interesting restaurant area feels a bit like the bat cave. Nondivers not welcome.

ℹ Getting There & Away

Every day at about 3pm, except Sunday, a public boat leaves Manado harbour, near Pasar Jengki fish market, for Bunaken village and Pulau Siladen (50,000Rp, one hour). A charter speedboat costs at least 250,000Rp to 350,000Rp one way (bargain hard). Many places to stay will also arrange transport. Avoid the over-priced charter boats that leave Manado from Marina Plaza.

Tomohon

Pleasantly cool and lush, this popular weekend escape from Manado rests at the foot of Gunung Lokon in the Minahasa Highlands. It is renowned for its beauty and its **market**, which reaches its lurid peak on Saturdays when all manner of species are sold for food.

There's frequent *mikrolet* travel to Tomohon (6000Rp, 40 minutes) from Manado's Karombasan terminal.

MALUKU

Welcome to the original 'spice islands'. Back in the 16th century when nutmeg, cloves and mace were global commodities that grew nowhere else, Maluku was a place where money really did grow on trees. Today the spices have minimal economic clout and Maluku (formerly known as 'the Moluccas') has dropped out of global consciousness. The region is protected from mass tourism by distance, unpredictable transport and memories of a brief if tragically destructive period of ethnic conflict between 1999 and 2002 (with occasional echoes even today).

While transport can prove infuriatingly inconvenient, given flexibility and patience you can visit the amazing Bandas, with their beaches, nutmeg forests and ruined Dutch fortresses.

ℹ Getting There & Around

Ambon is the region's air hub. There are flights daily to Jakarta and Makassar, which is a good place to transfer for other points on Sulawesi and Bali. There are also connections to Papua.

Ambon is a hub for Pelni service.

Pulau Ambon

Pulau Ambon is ribboned with villages, dressed in shimmering foliage and defined by two great bays. This is your launch pad to the Bandas, but also a charming retreat and diving base in its own right. Although at times a source of friction, the close proximity of Christian churches – often filled with hymn-singing parishioners – and mosques is an interesting study of Indonesian multiculturalism.

KOTA AMBON

☎0911 / POP 385,000

By the region's dreamy tropical standards, Maluku's capital, commercial centre and transport hub is a busy, regional centre.

Maluku

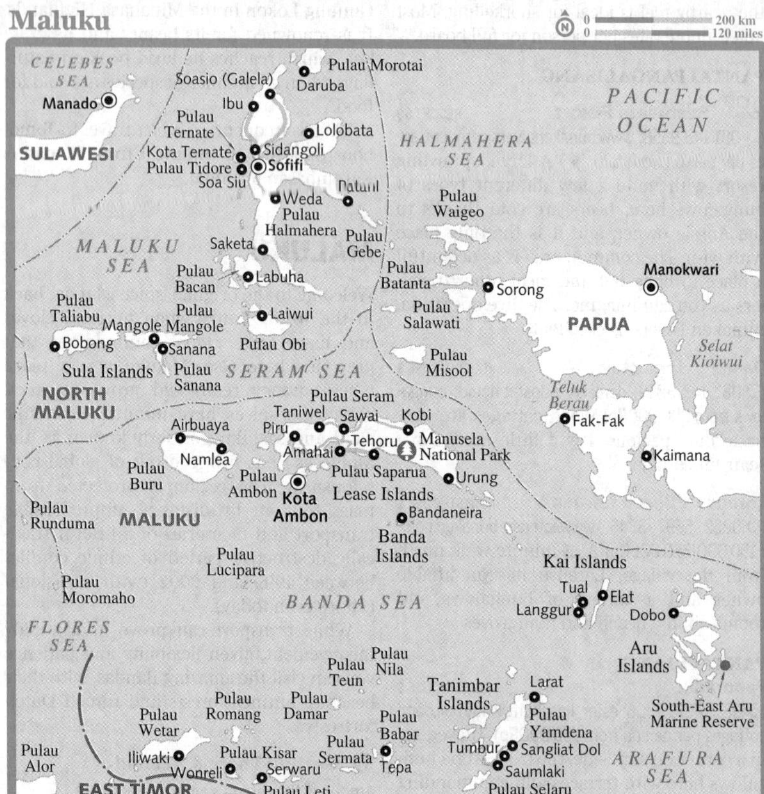

Sights are minimal and architecture wins no prizes, but compared to cities elsewhere, Kota Ambon retains a languid charm. And its waterfront location can't be beaten.

Sleeping & Eating

For good cheap eats, there are *warung* near the Batu Merah market and on Jl Ahmad Yani.

Hotel Jamilah HOTEL $
(353626; Jl Soabali; d 125,000-170,000Rp;) Behind a grotto of fake golden rocks, this 20-room family hotel is clean and has a peaceful, homely charm. It's well located in the centre.

Hotel Mutiara HOTEL $
(353873; www.hotelmutiaraambon.com; Jl Raya Pattimura; r from 300,000Rp;) Behind a dainty curtain of tropical foliage, this cosy, tastefully executed 26-room hotel has rooms that are dead quiet. Just the refuge needed if your travel plans go awry.

Pondok Wisata 'Avema' Lestari GUESTHOUSE $
(355596, 0813 4303 3842; Jl WR Supratman 18; r from 170,000Rp;) This welcoming family homestay has neat, clean rooms and airy communal spaces. The helpful – if elusive – owner speaks fluent Dutch and English.

Foodmart SUPERMARKET $
(Ambon Plaza Mall, Jl Dr Sam Ratulangi) Best place in the region to stock up on food and supplies.

Information

Change or withdraw enough money in Kota Ambon for trips to outlying islands where there are no exchange facilities whatsoever.

Michael Erenst (0813 4302 8872) Highly helpful fixer, usually found working the info desk at the airport. Works with Banda guesthouses on transport logistics for guests. Can arrange very basic homestays near the airport (about 80,000Rp).

Tourist office (Jl Jenderal Sudirman, Tantui; ⏲8am-4pm Mon-Fri) Offers fistfuls of colourful free brochures.

www.virtualtourist.com Filled with info for travellers to Maluku.

ℹ Getting There & Away

Pattimura airport (code: AMQ) is 30km round the bay from central Kota Ambon. Bemos are the cheapest link (5000Rp, 90 minutes) while taxis are the easiest (150,000Rp, 50 minutes).

Batavia (www.batavia-air.com) Daily Jakarta flights.

Lion Air/Wings Air (www.lionair.co.id) Daily flights include Makassar and Sorong.

Pelni (www.pelni.co.id) Has an office opposite the Pattimura Memorial. Boats depart for much of the region from Yos Sudarso harbour.

WORTH A TRIP

LEIHITU

The portion of land across the bay from Ambon, Leihitu, is much more than just the location of the airport. It has beaches and historic places of genuine interest, especially if you are having transport challenges and need to kill time. Chartering a car and driver will cost about 300,000Rp for a half day's touring of Ambon's most picturesque and archetypal coastal villages. In **Hila** the 1649 **Benteng Amsterdam** (10,000Rp donation expected) retains hefty ramparts and a three-storey keep.

Banda Islands

☎0910 / POP 15,000

This tiny yet historically fascinating cluster of 10 picturesque islands is Maluku's most inviting travel destination: a gathering of epic tropical gems, with deserted stretches of white sand and crescent bays. In the 1990s they briefly blipped onto the backpacker radar and have now faded back into glorious anonymity. Which means you'll have the beaches and those stark undersea drop-offs draped in technicolour coral gardens to yourself.

The Dutch and the English wrestled for control of these islands for several centuries beginning in the 1600s all because of nutmeg, which is native to the islands and once commanded extravagant prices in Europe. The legacy of this era is everywhere, with ruined forts, evocative colonial buildings and still-thriving plantations scattered about.

Snorkelling – often from various deserted beaches – is richly rewarding. While you can fill your tanks and rent gear at Bandaneira, the lack of a pro shop means that scuba divers are on their own.

BANDANEIRA

The main port of the Banda Islands, situated on Pulau Neira, is a friendly, pleasantly sleepy town. It's streets are lined with a stunning array of colonial buildings.

Stop by the impressive **Benteng Belgica**, built on the hill above Bandaneira in 1611. The fort's upper reaches have incredible views of **Gunung Api**. Several historic Dutch houses have been restored. Down in the flats, **Benteng Nassau** is a moody ruin.

🛏 Sleeping

Most accommodation is here in the Banda's main town. Three guesthouses stand out.

TOP CHOICE **Mutiara Guesthouse** GUESTHOUSE $

(☎0813 3034 3377; banda_mutiara@yahoo.com; r fan/air-con from 110,000/150,000; ❄@) Superb-value rooms and sturdy, classically styled furniture highlight this homestay run by the fantastically helpful Abba. Delicious and convivial dinners (60,000Rp) feature local foods and attract visitors from other guesthouses.

Vita Guesthouse GUESTHOUSE $

(☎21332; allandarman@gmail.com; Jl Pasar; r fan/air-con 100,000/125,000Rp; ❄) Seven comfortable rooms form a colonnaded L around a waterfront palm garden whose wonderful wooden jetty area is an ideal perch from which to gaze at Gunung Api. There's a useful communal kitchen and fridge.

Delfika I & II GUESTHOUSE $

(☎21027; delfika1@yahoo.com; r 80,000-200,000Rp; ❄@) There are two locations. For great water views, upstairs rooms at Delfika II are hard to beat. Meanwhile the original, Delfika I, has colonial charm with an atmospheric garden courtyard. The cafe is a pleasure.

OTHER ISLANDS

Pulau Banda Besar is the largest of the Banda islands, and the most important historical source of nutmeg. You can explore nutmeg groves at the **Kelly Plantation** or explore the ruins of fort **Benteng Hollandia** (c 1624).

Pulau Hatta has crystal waters and a mind-expanding, coral-encrusted vertical drop-off near Lama village.

Pulau Ai is also blessed with rich coral walls and postcard beaches. It has a few very simple homestays, from which you can explore the perfectly empty white-sand beaches. **Green Coconut** (Jl Patalima; r per person 125,000Rp) has a fine seafront location with wonderful views.

Furthest west, **Pulau Run** is mostly notable as the island the Dutch received from the English in return for Manhattan – guess who got the better deal?

Getting There & Around

The biggest problem when visiting the Bandas is transport. Fortunately the recommended guesthouses are adept at making arrangements.

AIR NBA flies from Ambon once or twice a week. However the flights are prone to cancellation and you may have to wait a week for another chance. Tickets are obtained in advance through your Banda guesthouse but are quite cheap (320,000Rp, one hour).

BUS **Pelni** (www.pelni.co.id) has various ships that pass through sporadically. The run to/from Ambon takes upwards of 12 hours. Ships are usually over-crowded (try to reserve a cabin) and, in the case of the *Kelimutu*, quite dirty.

Passenger longboats buzz between Bandaneira and Pulau Banda Besar (5000Rp) and Pulau Ai (20,000Rp). Guesthouses can arrange tours and boat charters.

PAPUA (IRIAN JAYA)

Even a country as full of adventure travel as Indonesia has to have its final frontier, and here it is – Papua, half of the world's second-biggest island, New Guinea. A land where numberless rivers rush down from 5km-high mountains to snake across sweating jungles populated by rainbow-hued birds of paradise and kangaroos that climb trees. Peaks are frosted with glaciers and snowfields, and slopes and valleys are home to an array of exotic cultures (250 and counting), like the gourd-wearing Dani, wood carving Asmat warriors and tree house-dwelling Korowai. The coast is more modern, and more Indonesian feeling, unless you venture to the Raja Ampats, a remote archipelago where you can find empty beaches and, according to experts, the world's richest reefs.

Papua's history is no slouch either. The battle for the Pacific was decided here – with memorials and WWII wrecks to prove it. Indonesia didn't inherit Papua until 1963, when they named it Irian Jaya and immediately began capitalising on its abundant resources. This did not sit well with the Papuans, whose Free Papua Organisation (OPM) remains active. Many Papuans want to be free of Indonesian rule, but their chances of that seem slim now that Papua is home to over one million non-Papuans.

Getting There & Around

AIR Papua is well connected with the rest of Indonesia, and with so few viable roads, flying is the

WORTH A TRIP

PULAU TERNATE & TIDORE

The perfect volcanic cone of Ternate is an unforgettable sight. Pulau Tidore, Ternate's age-old, next-door rival, is a laid-back island of charming villages and empty beaches.

The dramatic volcanic cone of 1721m Gamalama *is* Pulau Ternate. Settlements are sprinkled around its lower coastal slopes, with villages on the east coast coalescing into North Maluku's biggest town, Kota Ternate. The city makes a useful transport gateway for the region, and neighbouring volcano islands look particularly photogenic viewed from the few remaining stilt-house neighbourhoods, colourful boats in the harbour or hillside restaurant terraces. It has three 17th-century Dutch forts that have been over-restored.

Gently charming Tidore makes a refreshing day-trip escape from the bustle of Ternate, its neighbour and implacable historical enemy. An independent Islamic sultanate from 1109, Tidore's sultanate was abolished in the Soekarno era, but the 36th sultan was reinstated in 1999. The island's proud volcanic profile looks especially magnificent viewed from Bastiong on Ternate.

Ternate has places to stay for all budgets strung out along its encircling, volcano-hugging ring road. It can be reached with **Wings Air** (www.lionair.co.id) from Manado and Ambon or by various Pelni ships.

Papua (Irian Jaya)

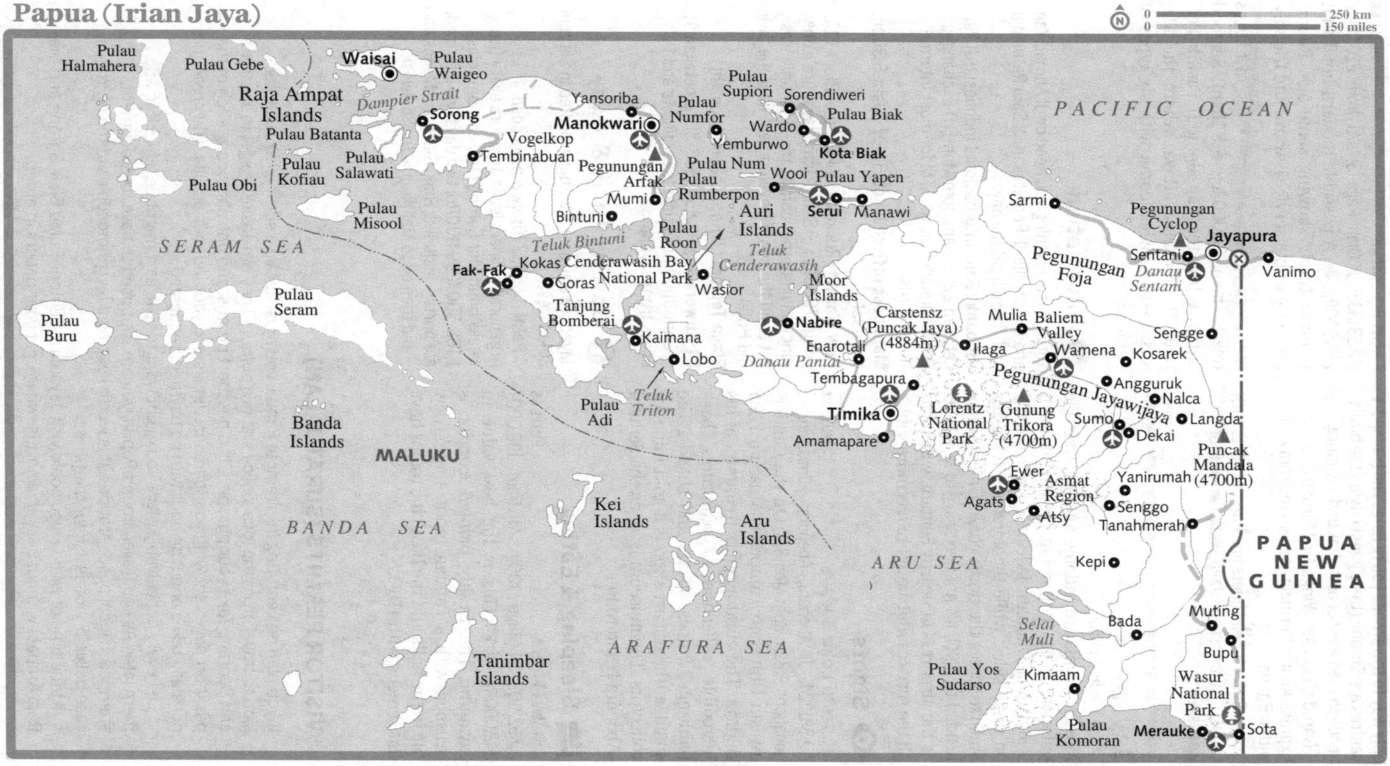

only way to travel once you're here. The transport centres are Sorong (the biggest city on the bird's head–shaped west coast), Biak and Jayapura.

Garuda, Lion Air/Wings Air, Merpati and Express Air are the main carriers to, from and within Papua.

BOAT Several Pelni liners link Papuan ports with Maluku, Sulawesi and Java every two or four weeks.

Jayapura

0967 / POP 149,000

Most residents are Indonesian and street life pulses to their rhythm, but the environment is all Papua. Dramatic jade hills cradle the city on three sides, while the gorgeous Teluk Yos Sudarso kisses the north coast. Unless you're headed to PNG, it's not necessary to stay here, as the airport is in nearby Sentani, which has all the services. But Jayapura has more soul.

Sights

Museum Loka Budaya MUSEUM

(581224; Jl Abepura, Abepura; admission by donation; 8am-3pm Mon-Sat) On the Cenderawasih University campus is Museum Loka Budaya. The curator offers free tours of his incredible collection of sculptures, bark paintings, canoes, spears and shields. The small, authentic art shop is a gold mine for collectors. The museum is along the Sentani -Abepura bemo route.

Sleeping & Eating

Amabel Hotel HOTEL $$

(522102; Jl Tugu 100; s/d from 198,000/ 242,000Rp;) This is the best value in Jayapura. The freshly painted exterior is brushed with a Papuan motif, there's new tile in the halls and the Ikea-chic rooms have flat screens with HBO.

Permata Hotel HOTEL $$

(531333; Jl Olah Raga 3; s/d from 220,000/ 295,000Rp;) A passable modern hotel that is prematurely showing some age. Rooms aren't huge, but service is warm and friendly.

Makassar Raya FOOD STALL $

(meals from 30,000Rp; 6-11pm) Seafood *warung* line the bay along Jl Pasifik Permai. Try Makassar Raya, where the Makassar-style dishes come with six types of *sambal.*

Information

You'll find everything you need on Jl Ahmad Yani and the parallel Jl Percetakan. Jl Sam Ratulangi and Jl Koti front the bay.

BII bank (Bank Internasional Indonesia; Jl Percetakan 22; 8am-3pm Mon-Fri) Exchanges US dollars and has an ATM for most international cards.

Main post office (Jl Koti 3; 7.30am-6.30pm Mon-Sat)

New Warnet (Rusko Pasifik Permai Block F12; per hr 7000Rp; 8am-10pm) Jayapura's only functional internet cafe at research time was set amid the newer development near the Swiss Bel Hotel.

Plasa Telkom (Jl Koti; 8am-midnight)

PT Kuwera Jaya (533333; Jl Percetakan 96; 8am-9pm) Sells tickets for flights and Pelni boats from Jayapura.

Getting There & Away

Jayapura's airport is actually located in Sentani 36km west.

Pelni (533270; www.pelni.co.id; Jl Argapura 15) liners leave Jayapura every two weeks bound for Sorong (1st/economy class 1,168,500/299,000Rp; two days) via intermediate ports – including Biak, Serui and Manokwari – and then on to Maluku and/or Sulawesi.

VISITOR PERMITS (SURAT JALAN)

If you plan on venturing into remote Papua, you must obtain a *surat jalan,* a permission to travel, from the local police station *(polres)*. They are easiest to get in Jayapura and Sentani. Take your passport, two passport photos, and one photocopy each of the passport pages showing your personal details and your Indonesian visa. The procedure normally takes about an hour with no payment requested.

List every conceivable place you might want to visit, as it might be difficult to add them later. As you travel around Papua, you are supposed to have the document stamped in local police stations. It is worth keeping a few photocopies of the permit in case police or hotels ask for them.

At the time of writing, you could visit Jayapura, Sentani, Pulau Biak, Sorong and the Raja Ampats without a *surat jalan*. Elsewhere, get your papers in order.

GETTING TO PAPUA NEW GUINEA: JAYAPURA TO VANIMO

Getting to the border There are no flights between Papua and Papua New Guinea, and the only route across the border that is open to foreigners is between Jayapura (north-east Papua) and Vanimo (northwest PNG, about 65km from Jayapura).

At the border Most visitors to PNG need a visa; the standard 60-day tourist visa (225,000Rp) can be obtained (after a two- to five-day wait) at the **Papua New Guinea Consulate** (☎0967-531250; congenpng_id@yahoo.com; Jl Raya Argapura; ⏰9am-noon & 1-3pm Mon-Thu, variable hr Fri), 3km south of downtown Jayapura. You can charter a *taksi* from the market at Abepura (called Pasar Abepura or Pasar Yotefa), 13km south of downtown Jayapura, to the border at Wutung (1½ hours) for 200,000Rp to 400,000Rp.

Moving on Cross the border itself on foot then hire a car to Vanimo for about 10 kina (US$3.50). Air Niugini links Vanimo with Port Moresby three times weekly.

Sentani

☎0967

Sentani, the growing airport town 36km west of Jayapura, is set between the forested Pegunungan Cyclop and beautiful Danau Sentani. It's quieter, cooler and more convenient than Jayapura. Don't miss the soul-soothing views of Danau Sentani from **Tugu MacArthur**. Most facilities are on Jl Kemiri Sentani Kota.

Sleeping & Eating

Rasen Hotel HOTEL $$
(☎594455; Jl Kelutahan 2; s 230,000Rp, d 290,000-365,000Rp, all incl breakfast; ❄📶) This new and very green hotel is a stone's throw from the airport and the best value in town. Which, frankly, isn't saying much.

Hotel Semeru Anaron HOTEL $
(☎591447; Jl Yabaso 10; d with fan/air-con 165,000/220,000Rp; ❄) A fresh coat of paint doesn't quite mute the shabby here, but it's clean enough and remains Sentani's cheapest option.

Manna House CHINESE, INDONESIAN $$
(Jl Kemiri-Sentani; mains 25,000-80,000Rp) One Surabaya-born, Sanur-trained chef operates the two best kitchens in town. This one is set two traffic lights north of the hotel cluster and serves tasty Indo and Chinese dishes. American missionaries pack the joint on Sunday nights. His new offering **Warung Sate Bandara** (Jl Bandara) does mixed-grill satay.

Getting There & Away

Jayapura airport (☎591809) is actually at Sentani. Airlines, most with Jayapura offices, include the following:

Batavia (☎532199; www.batavia-air.com) Flies to Makassar and Jakarta.

Expressair (☎550444; www.expressair.biz; Blok G 10/2, Jl Pasifik Permai, Jayapura) Flies to Sorong, Manokwari, Makassar and Jakarta.

Garuda (☎522221/2; www.garuda-indonesia.com; Jl Yani 5-7, Jayapura) Flies to Biak, Timika, Denpasar, Makassar and Jakarta.

Lion/Wings Air (☎594042/3; www.lionair.co.id) To Makassar and Jakarta.

Merpati (☎533111; www.merpati.co.id; Jl Yani 15, Jayapura) Flies to Biak, Timika, Merauke, Makassar, Jakarta and Manado.

Getting to Sentani from Jayapura via public transport demands three different bemo, and 90 minutes. Taxis are pricey (200,000Rp, half-price outside the airport) but more direct.

Baliem Valley

The Baliem Valley is the most accessible gateway to tribal Papua. It's a place where *koteka* (penis gourds) are not yet out of fashion, pigs can buy love, sex or both, and the hills bloom with flowers and deep-purple sweet-potato fields. Unless you land here during the August high season, when Wamena and nearby villages host a festival with pig feasts, mock wars and traditional dancing to attract the tourism buck, you will be outnumbered by Christian missionaries (a constant presence since the valley's 'discovery' in 1938) and Javanese *transmigrasi* (migrants through a resettling program). You may also be startled by evidence of Indonesia's neocolonisation of Papua, but mostly you will marvel at the mountain views, roaring rivers, tribal villages and at the tough but sweet spirit of the warm Dani people.

WAMENA

☎0969 / POP 8500

The commercial centre in the Baliem Valley, Wamena is dusty and sprawling, but the air is cool, purple mountains peek through billowy white clouds and local markets are enthralling. It's also a base from which to explore nearby tribal villages. It's expensive – a consequence of having to fly everything in from Jayapura.

Sleeping & Eating

TOP CHOICE **Putri Dani Inn** INN $$
(☎31685; Jl Irian 40; s 400,000-450,000Rp, d 495,000-575,000Rp) About 600m west of Jl Trikora, this family-run place offers spotless rooms with hot showers. Book ahead.

Baliem Pilamo HOTEL $$
(☎31214; Jl Patimura 32; r from 283,000Rp) A long-running Wamena staple, this place just opened its fresh modern wing, which has rooms that feel downright urbane and somewhat out of place in dusty Wamena. But they are comfortable if a bit spendy. The hotel still has clean budget rooms too.

Hotel Mas Budi HOTEL $$
(☎31214; Jl Patimura 32; r from 348,000Rp) This well-run place has 12 reasonably clean rooms. All except the cheapest have hot showers in ample bathrooms. The restaurant is Wamena's best (mains 30,000Rp to 75,000Rp).

Shopping

Possible souvenirs include *noken* (string bags), *suale* (head decorations made from cassowary feathers), the inevitable *koteka* (price depends on, ahem, size) and *mikak* (necklaces made of cowrie shells, feathers and bone). Prepare to bargain.

Information

No banks exchange foreign cash or travellers cheques, but two ATMs accept international cards. *Wartel* dot Jl Trikora.

Papua.com (☎34488, 0813 4461 0699; fuj0627@yahoo.co.jp; Jl Yani 49; per hr 9000Rp; ⏰9am-8.30pm) Busy, efficient internet cafe that also functions as a highly useful tourist information centre.

Police Station (☎31972; Jl Safri Darwin; ⏰9am-3pm Mon-Sat, 3-5pm Sun) For reporting on arrival or to apply for a *surat jalan* (visitor permit).

Getting There & Around

The main carriers between Jayapura (Sentani) and Wamena are **Trigana Air** (☎31611; airport) and **Transnusa/Aviastar** (☎34872; airport). Both normally fly three times daily each way, charging about 440,000Rp to Jayapura and 790,000Rp to 850,000Rp from Jayapura.

AROUND WAMENA

Trekking is the best way to taste traditional life, and considering lodging prices in Wamena, the cost isn't prohibitive.

Getting Around

From Wamena, hopelessly overcrowded bemo go as far south as Sugokmo (15,000Rp, 30 minutes), as far north, on the western side of the valley, as Pyramid (20,000Rp, one hour), and as far north on the eastern side as Tagime. They gather at the **'Misi' taksi terminal** (Jl Ahmad Yani).

SOUTH BALIEM VALLEY

The road south through Baliem Valley stops a few kilometres short of **Kurima**, a village bursting with flowers, divided by the river and fed by cascading streams. This is the land of eternal spring. The walk here and around will take you through sweet-potato terraces to the best panoramas in the valley. You can rent a room in Kurima at the missionary house, but the best plan is to keep walking up the ridge to **Kilise**, where you'll want to bed down at **Kilise Guest House** (per person 120,000Rp) on clean bamboo mats in a traditional Dani grass hut with sweeping views that will immobilise you. Bring your own food.

EAST BALIEM VALLEY

Near **Pikhe**, the northern road crosses mighty Sungai Baliem and passes **Aikima**, the resting place of a 270-year-old **Werapak Elosak mummy** (admission 30,000Rp; ⏰daylight hr). **Jiwika** is the best base from which to explore the east. **Sumpaima**, 300m north of Jiwika, is home to the 280-year-old **Wimontok Mabel mummy** (admission 30,000Rp; ⏰daylight hr), the best of its kind near Wamena.

At the turn-off to Iluwe in Jiwika, you'll find **Lauk Inn** (r 100,000Rp), a pleasant spot with basic but clean rooms.

In **Wosilimo**, the incredible cave **Gua Wikuda** (admission 10,000Rp; ⏰8am-4pm Mon-Sat) is 900m long and has stalagmites that are 1000 years old. Stay in a hut and fish well at **Danau Ane-gerak**, an hour's walk west of Wosilimo. From Wosilimo, a trekking trail continues beyond Pass Valley.

Sorong

☎0951 / POP 144,000

Papua's second-biggest city, Sorong, sits at the northwest tip of the Vogelkop. It's a busy port and a base for oil and logging opera-

WORTH A TRIP

PASS VALLEY

If you crave a trip of a lifetime, and don't mind bushwhacking your way through undergrowth (like, literally bushwhacking… with a machete) and hiking for a week just to win the opportunity to climb one of three massive, pristine, jungled peaks, then you should find your way from Wamena to this massive jade, roadless valley. Those three peaks – **Mt Galet**, **Mt Tobi** and **Mt Elite** – rise from lowland rainforest into cloud forest before finally peeking out above the clouds. You'll need to be well-prepared and well-supplied, and you should definitely hire a guide and porter (per day porter 60,000Rp, guide 350,000Rp to 500,000Rp), which will cost you. But you'll be in virgin territory out here, explorers among mere travellers. Begin at the **Papua.com** (see p293) office, where you can peruse countless maps and get the most up to date, objective and thorough trekking information in Wamena.

tions in the region. Few travellers stay longer than it takes to book passage to the epic Raja Ampat Islands.

Sleeping & Eating

The best rooms book up fast.

Hotel Royal Membramo HOTEL $$
(☎325666; www.royalmembramo.com; Jl Sam Ratulangi; standard/superior 300,000/490,000Rp; ❄📶) Sorong's newest offering has plenty of style and comfort and it's walking distance to the waterfront.

Hotel Tanjung HOTEL $$
(☎323782; Jl Yos Sudarso; r from 200,000Rp; ❄) Situated on the Pantai Lido waterfront, popular Hotel Tanjung has a range of acceptable rooms, all with air-con.

TOP CHOICE **Lido Kuring** SEAFOOD $
(Jl Yos Sudarso; mains 25,000-50,000Rp) Chinese Indonesian seafood doesn't get much better or less frilly than what you'll find in this plain, cavernous dining hall on the Lido pier next to Hotel Tanjung.

Information

Raja Ampat Tourism Office (☎0812 483 5115; www.gorajaampat.com, www.diverajaampat.org; JE Meridien Hotel, Jl Basuki Rahmat Km 7; ⏲9am-4pm Mon-Fri) Helpful office has maps and printed information in English. It also runs a booth in the airport arrivals hall. Pay your 500,000Rp fee to visit the islands at one of these places.

Getting There & Around

Official airport taxis charge 70,000Rp to hotels in town; out on the street you can charter a public *taksi* for half that. Airport departure tax is 13,000Rp.

Expressair (☎328200; JE Meridien Hotel, Jl Basuki Rahmat Km 7) flies to Jakarta, Jayapura and Makassar.

Pelni (☎0821 9874 5555; www.pelni.co.id; Jl Yani 13), near the west end of Jl Yani, posts its schedule in front of this ticket office. Seven ships dock here once or twice monthly between trips east to Jayapura and west to Maluku, Sulawesi and Java.

The town sprawls, so taxis, *ojek* and chartered *angkot* are the best way to visit banks, airline offices, the main port or government offices.

Raja Ampat Islands

POP 40,000

This archipelago of approximately 1500 stunning, mostly uninhabited limestone islands off the coast of Sorong are sheltered by some of the world's richest and most diverse coral reefs. Though not geared to travellers on tight budgets, here you'll explore dense jungle, thick mangroves, pristine white-sand beaches and hidden lagoons.

The four biggest islands are Waigeo in the north, with the fast-growing new regional capital, Waisai; Salawati, just southwest of Sorong; Batanta, off northern Salawati; and Misool to the southwest. The Dampier Strait between Waigeo and Batanta has many of the best dive sites.

Visitors to the islands must pay an entry fee (Indonesian citizens/visitors 250,000/500,000Rp) at the Raja Ampat Tourism Office in Sorong.

Sleeping & Eating

There are several dive resorts and dozens of village homestays scattered among the islands.

TOP CHOICE Papua Paradise RESORT $$

(www.papuaparadise.com; Pulau Birie; per night per person €135;) Nowhere else on earth will you find such elegant overwater bungalows on such a pristine island with such spectacular views at this price. Here, you can take a sunrise trek through a teeming jungle past waterfalls in search of the mythical *cenderwasih* (bird of paradise) and enjoy three epic dives per day and unlimited sunset snoozes in your hammock.

Pulau Wai HOMESTAY $$

(0812 4879 1985; full board per person 300,000Rp) A clean and basic four-room lodge, with shared *mandi* and toilet, built over the water on sweet Pulau Wai, a dollop of white sand opposite Pulau Birie. You could happily burn weeks here. Guests are welcome to dive at Papua Paradise.

Harapan Jaya Homestay HOMESTAY $$

(0813 4435 3030; Kampung Harapan Jaya, Pulau Misool; full board per person 350,000Rp) The only homestay on consistently spectacular Misool, which offers the Raja Ampats at their most remote. Guided hikes to hidden caves and waterfalls are easily arranged (guides per day 100,000Rp).

Mangkur Kodon HOMESTAY $$

(0853 9504 0888; full board s/d 400,000/600,000Rp) A homestay and dive centre in Yenbuba Village on the south tip of Pulau Mansuar. Transport from Wisai (per person 300,000Rp) is available.

Getting There & Around

Marina Express (economy/VIP 120,000/150,000Rp, two hours) operates fast passenger boats with airline-style seating to Waisai from Sorong's Pelabuhan Rakiat harbour. A larger, slow ferry (economy/VIP 100,000/120,000Rp, 3½ hours) also makes the crossing every day except Saturday. Dive resorts include boat transfers to and from Sorong. Smaller places will usually collect you at Waisai if you contact them ahead.

UNDERSTAND INDONESIA

Indonesia Today

Indonesia is a land of good news and bad news. First the good.

Economically, Indonesia has bucked global economic trends with growth averaging 5% to 6% a year. More than a decade after the fall of Soeharto, the consensus is that the nation has established itself as a workable democracy. And on the terrorism front there have been steady gains. In September 2009 police raided a house near Solo and killed Noordin Mohamed Top, the alleged mastermind of a decade's worth of terrorism, including bombings in Bali and Jakarta.

On the bad news front there are the regular ferry sinkings and plane crashes that emphasise the nation's decrepit infrastructure. Other challenges include corruption, the destruction of the environment, poverty, fundamentalism and taxation reform. Sectarian violence, while on the decline overall, is never far from the surface, as seen by outbreaks in Ambon in 2011.

And the good news is often tempered by the bad. Even as Bali enjoys record tourism and growth that is spurring the creation of a new middle class, there are growing pollution and congestion woes that threaten to tarnish the island's shine. Still, most observers would say Indonesia is doing better than many expected.

History

Beginnings

Until the last few years it was widely believed that the first humanoids *(Homo erectus)* lived in Central Java around 500,000 years ago, having reached Indonesia across land bridges from Africa, before either dying off or being wiped out by the arrival of *Homo sapiens*.

But the discovery in 2003 of the remains of a tiny islander, dubbed the 'hobbit', seems to indicate that *Homo erectus* survived much longer than was previously thought, and that previously accepted timelines of Indonesia's evolutionary history need to be re-examined (though many scientists continue to challenge the hobbit theory).

Most Indonesians are descendents of Malay people who began migrating around 4000 BC from Cambodia, Vietnam and southern China. They steadily developed small kingdoms, and by 700 BC these settlers had developed skilful rice-farming techniques.

Hinduism & Buddhism

The growing prosperity of these early kingdoms soon caught the attention of Indian and Chinese merchants, and along with silks

INDONESIAN SUPERLATIVES

Biggest archipelago Covering an area of 1.92 million sq km, Indonesia's 17,000 (some say 20,000) islands make up the world's largest archipelago.

Biggest lizard The komodo dragon *(Varanus komodoensis)* is the biggest lizard in the world. The largest authenticated specimen was a gift from the Sultan of Bima to a US scientist and measured 3.1m.

Largest flower The world's biggest flower, *Rafflesia arnoldi,* often blooms in the thick Sumatran forests near Bukittinggi between August and November.

Longest snake The reticulated python, native to Indonesia, is the world's longest snake. A specimen killed in Sulawesi in 1912 measured 9.85m.

Most diverse Kalimantan is one of the most biologically diverse places on earth, with twice as many plant species as the whole of Africa.

Most populous Java has the largest population of any island in the world, with an estimated 140 million inhabitants.

and spices came the dawn of Hinduism and Buddhism in Indonesia.

These religions quickly gained a foothold in the archipelago and soon became central to the great kingdoms of the 1st millennium AD. The Buddhist Srivijaya empire held sway over the Malay peninsula and southern Sumatra, extracting wealth from its dominion over the strategic Straits of Melaka. The Hindu Mataram and Buddhist Sailendra kingdoms dominated Central Java, raising their grandiose monuments, Borobudur and Prambanan, over the fertile farmland that brought them their prosperity.

When Mataram slipped into mysterious decline around the 10th century AD, it was fast replaced with an even more powerful Hindu kingdom. Founded in 1294, the Majapahit empire made extensive territorial gains under its ruler, Hayam Wuruk, and prime minister, Gajah Mada, and while claims that they controlled much of Sulawesi, Sumatra and Borneo now seem fanciful, most of Java, Madura and Bali certainly fell within their realm.

But things would soon change. Despite the Majapahit empire's massive power and influence, greater fault lines were opening up across Indonesia, and Hinduism's golden age was swiftly drawing to a close.

Rise of Islam

With the arrival of Islam came the power, the reason and the will to oppose the hegemony of the Majapahits, and satellite kingdoms soon took up arms against the Hindu kings. In the 15th century the Majapahits fled to Bali, where Hindu culture continues to flourish, leaving Java to the increasingly powerful Islamic sultanates. Meanwhile, the influential trading kingdoms of Melaka (on the Malay peninsula) and Makassar (in southern Sulawesi) were also embracing Islam, sowing the seeds that would later make modern Indonesia the most populous Muslim nation on earth.

European Expansion

Melaka fell to the Portuguese in 1511 and European eyes were soon settling on the archipelago's riches, prompting two centuries of unrest as the Portuguese, Spanish, Dutch and British wrestled for control. By 1700 the Dutch held most of the trump cards, with the Dutch East India Company (VOC) controlling the region's lucrative spice trade and becoming the world's first multinational company. Following the VOC's bankruptcy, however, the British governed Java under Sir Stamford Raffles between 1811 and 1816, only to relinquish control again to the Dutch after the end of the Napoleonic wars, who then held control of Indonesia until its independence 129 years later.

It was not, however, a trouble-free tenancy and the Dutch had to face numerous rebellions: Javan Prince Diponegoro's five-year guerrilla war was finally put down in 1830, costing the lives of 8000 Dutch troops.

Road to Independence

By the beginning of the 20th century, the Dutch had brought most of the archipelago under their control, but the revolutionary tradition of Diponegoro was never truly quashed, bubbling beneath the surface of Dutch rule and finding a voice in the young Soekarno. The debate was sidelined as the

Japanese swept through Indonesia during WWII, but with their departure came the opportunity for Soekarno to declare Indonesian independence, which he did from his Jakarta home on 17 August 1945.

The Dutch, however, were unwilling to relinquish their hold over Indonesia and – supported by the British, who had entered Indonesia to accept the Japanese surrender – moved quickly to reassert their authority over the country. Resistance was stiff and for four bitter years the Indonesian resistance fought a guerrilla war. But American and UN opposition to the reimposition of colonialism and the mounting casualty toll eventually forced the Dutch to pack it in, and the Indonesian flag – the *sang merah putih* (red and white) – was finally hoisted over Jakarta's Istana Merdeka (Freedom Palace) on 27 December 1949.

Depression, Disunity & Dictatorship

Unity in war quickly became division in peace, as religious fundamentalists and nationalist separatists challenged the fledgling central government. After almost a decade of political impasse and economic depression, Soekarno made his move in 1957, declaring Guided Democracy (a euphemism for dictatorship) with army backing and leading Indonesia into nearly four decades of authoritarian rule.

Despite moves towards the one-party state, Indonesia's 3 million–strong Communist Party (Partai Komunis Indonesia; PKI) was the biggest in the world by 1965 and Soekarno had long realised the importance of winning its backing. But as the PKI's influence in government grew, so did tensions with the armed forces. Things came to a head on the night of 30 September 1965, when elements of the palace guard launched an attempted coup. Quickly put down by General Soeharto, the coup was blamed – perhaps unfairly – on the PKI and became the pretext for an army-led purge that left as many as 500,000 communist sympathisers dead. Strong evidence later emerged from declassified documents that both the US (opposed to communism) and the UK (seeking to protect its interests in Malaysia) aided and abetted Soeharto's purge by drawing up hit lists of communist agitators. By 1968 Soeharto had ousted Soekarno and was installed as president.

Soeharto brought unity through repression, annexing Irian Jaya (Papua) in 1969, and reacting to insurgency with an iron fist. In 1975 Portuguese Timor was invaded, leading to tens of thousands of deaths, and separatist ambitions in Aceh and Papua were also met with a ferocious military response. But despite endemic corruption, the 1980s and 1990s were Indonesia's boom years, with meteoric economic growth and a starburst of opulent building ventures transforming the face of the capital.

Soeharto's Fall

As Asia's economy went into freefall during the closing years of the 1990s, Soeharto's house of cards began to tumble. Indonesia went bankrupt overnight and the country found an obvious scapegoat in the cronyism and corruption endemic in the dictator's regime. Protests erupted across Indonesia in 1998, and the May riots in Jakarta left thousands, many of them Chinese, dead. After three decades of dictatorial rule, Soeharto resigned on 21 May 1998.

Passions cooled when Vice President BJ Habibie took power on a reform ticket, but ambitious promises were slow to materialise, and in November of the same year riots again rocked many Indonesian cities. Promises of forthcoming elections succeeded in closing the floodgates, but separatist groups took advantage of the weakened central government and violence erupted in Maluku, Irian Jaya, East Timor and Aceh. East Timor won its independence after a referendum in August 1999, but only after Indonesian-backed militias had destroyed its infrastructure and left thousands dead.

Democracy & Reform

Against this unsettled backdrop, the June 1999 legislative elections passed surprisingly smoothly, leaving Megawati Soekarnoputri (Soekarno's daughter) and her reformist Indonesian Democratic Party for Struggle (PDI-P) as the largest party with 33% of the vote. But months later the separate presidential election was narrowly won by Abdurrahman Wahid (Gus Dur), whose efforts to undo corruption met with stiff resistance. Megawati was eventually sworn in as president in 2001, but her term proved a disappointment for many Indonesians, as corrupt infrastructures were left in place, the military's power remained intact, poverty levels remained high and there were high-profile terrorism attacks such as the 2002 Bali bombings.

Megawati lost the 2004 presidential elections to Susilo Bambang Yudhoyono (or 'SBY'), an ex-army officer who served in East

Timor but who also has an MBA. Dubbed the 'thinking general', his successes have included cracking down on Islamic militants, pumping more money into education and health, and introducing basic social-security payments.

SBY's term has also been marked by a series of disasters, beginning with the 2004 Boxing Day tsunami that ravaged Aceh in northern Sumatra. In 2006, a quake shook Yogyakarta, killing 6800 people, and in 2009 a quake devastated Padang in Sumatra.

Elections in 2009 went off more smoothly than many had predicted, with SBY cruising to re-election on a platform of continuing moderate policies. During parliamentary elections earlier in the year, extremist Islamic parties – who had predicted major gains – ended up with only 8% of the vote. Moderates, including the party of SBY, won the day.

The Culture

The old Javanese saying *'bhinneka tunggal ika'* (they are many; they are one) is said to be Indonesia's national dictum, but with a population of over 240 million, 300-plus languages and 17,000 islands it's not surprising that many from the outer islands resent Java, where power is centralised. Indonesia is loosely bound together by a single flag (which is increasingly flown with pride during national holidays) and a single language (Bahasa Indonesia), but in some ways can be compared to the EU – a richly diverse confederacy of peoples.

The world's most populous Muslim nation is no hardline Islamic state. Indonesians have traditionally practised a relaxed form of Islam, and though there's no desire to imitate the West, most see no conflict in catching a Hollywood movie in an American-style shopping mall after prayers at the mosque. The country is becoming more cosmopolitan; Facebook usage is epic. Millions of Indonesians now work overseas – mainly in the Gulf, Hong Kong and Malaysia – bringing back extraneous influences to their villages when they return. A boom in low-cost air travel has enabled a generation of Indonesians to travel internally and overseas conveniently and cheaply for the first time, while personal mobility is much easier today – it's possible to buy a motorbike on hire purchase with as little as a 500,000Rp deposit.

But not everyone has the cash or time for overseas jaunts and there remains a yawning gulf between the haves and the have-nots. Indonesia is much poorer than many of its Asian neighbours, with almost 50% surviving on US$2 a day, and in many rural areas opportunities are few and far between.

Population

Indonesia's population is the fourth-biggest in the world, with over 240 million people. Over half this number live on the island of Java, one of the most crowded places on earth with a population density of 940 people per square kilometre. But while Java (and Bali and Lombok) teem with people, large parts of the archipelago are very sparsely populated, particularly Papua (under 10 per square kilometre) and Kalimantan.

Birth rates have fallen considerably in recent years (from an average of 3.4 children per woman in 1987 to 2.4 today) thanks to successful family-planning campaigns and increasing prosperity levels.

Religion

If Indonesia has a soundtrack, it is the muezzin's call to prayer. Wake up to it once and it won't come as a surprise that Indonesia is the largest Islamic nation on earth, with over 220 million Muslims (88% of the total population).

But while Islam has a near monopoly on religious life, many of the country's most impressive historical monuments, such as the temples of Borobudur and Prambanan, hark back to when Hindu and Buddhist kingdoms dominated Java. These religions maintain important communities, with Hinduism (2% of the population) continuing to flourish in Bali, while Buddhists (1%) are scattered throughout the country. Christians make up nearly 9% of the nation, forming the majority in Papua, on several islands of Nusa Tenggara and Maluku, and in parts of Sumatra. Animist traditions also survive below the surface in many rural areas.

Official Faiths

Alongside commitments to democracy and humanity, the Pancasila (Indonesia's five principles of nationhood) enshrines the principle that all citizens must have an official state religion and that it should be 'based in the belief in the one and only God'. This has meant that Indonesia's many practitioners of indigenous religions, particularly remote tribal communities, have been pressured to adopt one of six state-sanctioned religions

INDONESIAN FESTIVALS & EVENTS

Religious events and official holidays are a vital part of Indonesian life. There are many through the year and they're often cause for celebrations and festivals. With such a diversity of people in the archipelago, there are many local holidays, festivals and cultural events. This is especially true on Bali where religious events can easily occupy a third of the typical person's calendar.

The Muslim fasting month of Ramadan requires that Muslims abstain from food, drink, cigarettes and sex between sunrise and sunset. Many bars and restaurants close and it is important to avoid eating or drinking publicly in Muslim areas during this time. For the week before and after Lebaran (Idul Fitri), the festival to mark the end of the fast, transport is often fully booked and travelling becomes a nightmare – plan to stay put at this time. Ramadan, Idul Fitri and Idul Adha (Muslim day of sacrifice) move back 10 days or so every year, according to the Muslim calendar.

Although some public holidays have a fixed date, the dates for many events vary each year depending on Muslim, Buddhist or Hindu calendars.

January/February

» **New Year's Day** Celebrated on 1 January.

» **Imlek (Chinese New Year)** Special food is prepared, decorations adorn stores and homes, and *barongasai* (lion dances) are performed; held in January/February.

» **Muharram (Islamic New Year)** The date varies each year, but is usually in late January.

» **Mohammed's Birthday** Celebrated in January in 2013 and 2014; prayers are held in mosques throughout the country, and there are street parades in Solo and Yogyakarta.

March/April

» **Hindu New Year (Nyepi)** Held in March/April; in Bali and other Hindu communities, villagers make as much noise as possible to scare away devils. Virtually all of Bali shuts down.

» **Good Friday** Occurs in March or April.

April/May

» **Waisak (Buddha's Birthday)** Mass prayers are said at the main Buddhist temples, including Borobudur.

May/June

» **Ascension of Christ** Occurs in May/June.

» **Ascension of Mohammed** Special prayers are held in mosques.

August

» **Independence Day** Celebrated on 17 August with plenty of pomp and circumstance; government buildings are draped in huge red-and-white flags and banners, and there are endless marches.

» **Lebaran (Idul Fitri)** Everyone returns to their home village for special prayers and gift giving, and it's a time for charity donations.

October

» **Idul Adha** The end of the Haj is celebrated with animal sacrifices, the meat of which is given to the poor.

November/December

» **Christmas Day** Marked by gift giving and special church services in Christian areas; the celebration falls on 25 December.

(Islam, Protestantism, Catholicism, Hinduism, Buddhism and Confucianism). Even the Balinese had to tweak their belief system so that a supreme deity could emerge from a pantheon of gods, and Hinduism could be declared an officially recognised faith.

Arts

Dance

Indonesia has a rich heritage of traditional dances. In Yogyakarta there's the Ramayana ballet, a spectacular dance drama; Lombok has a mask dance called the *kayak sando* and war dances; Malaku's *lenso* is a handkerchief dance; while Bali has a multitude of elaborate dances (see box).

Music

There's much more to the Indonesian music scene than the saccharine-sweet pop and *dangdut* (Indonesian dance music with strong Arabic and Hindi influences) that dominates the airwaves. Alongside a vibrant punk scene, led by bands such as Bali's Superman is Dead and Yogya's Black Boots, there's social invective from hip-hoppers Homicide and Iwa K, while house and techno DJs like Romy play to thousands in Jakartan clubs and around Asia.

Gamelan is the best-known traditional Indonesian music: besides Bali, Java has orchestras composed mainly of percussion instruments, including drums, gongs and *angklung* (shake-drums), along with flutes and xylophones.

Environment

Indonesia has lost more tropical forest than anywhere else in the world, bar Brazil, in the last few decades. That said, some incredible national parks and landscapes remain virtually untouched, mainly in remote areas away from the main centres of population.

The Land

At 1.92 million sq km, Indonesia is an island colossus, incorporating 10% of the world's forest cover and 11,508 uninhabited islands (6000 more have human populations). From the low-lying coastal areas, the country rises through no fewer than 129 active volcanoes – more than any country in the world – to the snow-covered summit

DON'T MISS

BALINESE DANCE & MUSIC

Enjoying a Balinese dance performance is for many a highlight of a visit to Bali. The haunting sounds, elaborate costumes, careful choreography and even light-hearted comic routines add up to great entertainment. Swept up in the spectacle, you'll soon understand why Balinese culture is among the world's most developed.

Balinese music is based around an ensemble known as a *gamelan,* also called a *gong*. This melodic, sometimes upbeat and sometimes haunting percussion that often accompanies traditional dance is one of the most lasting impressions for tourists to Bali.

You can catch a quality dance performance anywhere there's a festival or celebration, and you'll find exceptional performances in and around Ubud (see p209).

There are more than a dozen different basic dances in Bali and myriad variations. The most important:

» **Kecak** Probably the best-known dance for its spell-binding, hair-raising atmosphere, the Kecak features a 'choir' of men and boys who sit in concentric circles and slip into a trance as they chant and sing the 'chak-a-chak-a-chak', imitating a troupe of monkeys.

» **Barong and Rangda** Features the good, a mischievous and fun-loving shaggy dog-lion called a Barong, battling the bad, an evil widow-witch called Rangda. One or more monkeys attend the Barong and these characters often steal the show.

» **Legong** Characterised by flashing eyes and quivering hands, this most graceful of Balinese dances is performed by young girls. Their talent is so revered that in old age, a classic dancer will be remembered as a 'great Legong'.

» **Kekac Fire Dances** These dances were developed to drive out evil spirits from a village. Two young girls dance a dream-like Legong in perfect symmetry and a boy in a trance dances around and through a fire of coconut husks.

ORANG-UTANS

Orang-utans, the world's largest arboreal mammal, once swung through the forest canopy throughout all of Southeast Asia, but are now found only in Sumatra and Borneo. Researchers fear that the few that do remain will not survive the continued loss of habitat to logging and agriculture.

While orang-utans are extremely intelligent animals, their way of life isn't compatible with a shrinking forest. Orang-utans are mostly vegetarians; they get big and strong (some males weigh up to 90kg) from a diet that would make a Californian hippie proud: fruit, shoots, leaves, nuts and tree bark, which they grind up with their powerful jaws and teeth. They occasionally also eat insects, eggs and small mammals.

The 'orang hutan' (a Malay word for 'person of the forest') has an extremely expressive face that has often suggested a very close kinship with the hairless ape (humans). But of all the great apes, the orang-utans are considered to be the most distantly related to humans.

Mothers rear their young for seven years – the longest nursery time in the animal kingdom. During this intensely intimate period, they teach them everything, for example how to climb through the canopy by *brachiation* (travelling from branch to branch), how to identify the medicinal qualities of plants and the poisonousness of certain nuts, and how to mentally map the forest. The rehabilitation of orphans involves as close an approximation of this as possible.

The two classic places to view orang-utans in Indonesia are Bukit Lawang (p264) on Sumatra and Tanjung Puting National Park on Kalimantan (p271).

of Puncak Jaya (4884m) in Papua. Despite the incredible diversity of its landscapes, it is worth remembering that Indonesia is predominantly water; Indonesians refer to the country as Tanah Air Kita (literally 'Our Earth and Water').

Wildlife

In his classic study, *The Malay Archipelago,* British naturalist Alfred Russel Wallace divided Indonesia into two zones. To the west of the so-called Wallace Line (which runs between Kalimantan and Sulawesi and south through the straits between Bali and Lombok) the flora and fauna resemble that of the rest of Asia, while the species and environments to the east become increasingly like those of Australia. Scientists have since fine-tuned Wallace's findings, but while western Indonesia is known for its orang-utan, rhinos and tigers, as well as spectacular *Rafflesia* flowers, eastern Indonesia boasts fauna such as the komodo dragon and marsupials, including Papuan tree kangaroos.

National Parks

There are officially 50 *taman nasional* (national parks) in Indonesia. Most are in remote areas and have basic visitor facilities, but they are remarkable in their ecological diversity and wildlife. Some of the finest include Tanjung Puting in Kalimantan for its orang-utans and wetland birds, and Komodo for its dragons and astonishing coral reefs.

Environmental Issues

From the perspective of a Jakarta-based bureaucrat, Indonesia has full environmental-responsibility credentials, with stringent land-use and environmental-impact regulations, and large tracts of forest lands set aside for conservation. In the field, the picture is markedly different, as a wilful disregard of regulations – generally with the collusion of the newly empowered regional authorities – make official environmental policies mere words on paper.

Forest continues to be cleared at a horrific rate, both through illegal logging and conversion to palm-oil plantations. Greenpeace estimates that 50% of Indonesia's 150 million hectares of forests have been cleared and the government itself allows an average 1.8 million hectares a year in additional clearance. Furthermore upwards of 70% of Indonesia's mangrove forests have been damaged according to the US-based Mangrove Action Project.

The side effects of deforestation are felt across the nation and beyond: floods and landslides wash away valuable topsoil, rivers become sluggish and fetid, and haze from clearing fires blankets Malaysia and

Singapore every dry season. The problems flow right through to Indonesia's coastline and seas, where over 80% of reef habitat is considered to be at risk by the UN.

The rampant consumerism of the burgeoning middle class is straining the nation's wholly inadequate infrastructure: private vehicles clog urban streets creating massive air pollution; waste removal services have difficulty coping with household and industrial garbage; and a total lack of sewerage -disposal systems makes water from most sources undrinkable without boiling, putting further pressure on kerosene and firewood supplies.

Food & Drink

By eating in Indonesia you savour the essence of the country, as few nations are so well represented by their cuisine. The abundance of rice reflects Indonesia's fertile landscape, the spices are reminiscent of a time of trade and invasion, and the fiery chilli echoes the passion of the people. Indonesian cuisine is really one big food swap. Chinese, Portuguese, colonists and traders have all influenced the ingredients that appear at the Indonesian table, and the cuisine has been shaped over time by the archipelago's diverse landscape, people and culture.

Coriander, cumin, chilli, lemon grass, coconut, soy sauce and palm sugar are all important flavourings; *sambal* is a crucial condiment. Fish is a favourite and the seafood restaurants are common in this island nation. Indonesians traditionally eat with their fingers, hence the stickiness of the rice. Satay (skewered meat), *nasi goreng* (fried rice) and *gado gado* (vegetables with peanut sauce) are some of Indonesia's most famous dishes. *Nasi campur* (mixed rice) is the national dish and includes a sampling of dishes served in myriad variations.

Regional Variations

Popular dishes are not surprisingly diverse in this land of over 300 languages.

JAVA

The cuisine of the Betawi (original inhabitants of the Jakarta region) is known for its richness. *Gado gado* is a Betawi original, as is *ketoprak* (noodles, bean sprouts and tofu with soy and peanut sauce). *Soto Betawi* (beef soup) is made creamy with coconut milk. There's also *nasi uduk* (rice cooked in coconut milk, served with meat, tofu and/or vegetables).

Central Javan food is sweet, even the curries, such as *gudeg* (jackfruit curry). Yogyakarta specialities include *ayam goreng* (fried chicken) and *kelepon* (green rice-flour balls with a palm-sugar filling).

BALI

High-quality *warung* popular with visitors can be found across Bali. Many are listed in this chapter. *Babi guling* (spit-roast pig stuffed with chilli, turmeric, garlic and ginger) is widely sold as is *bebek betutu* (duck stuffed with spices, wrapped in banana leaves and coconut husks and cooked in embers). The local satay, *sate lilit,* is made with minced, spiced meat pressed onto skewers.

MARKET LIFE

There's no better place to get acquainted with Indonesian cuisine than the local market. But it's not for late sleepers. The best time to go is around 6am to 7am. If you're any later than 10am, the prime selections have been snapped up. Any town and city will have markets, although often they are only at their best on certain days of the week.

Markets offer a glimpse of the variety and freshness of local produce, often brought in within a day or two of being harvested, sometimes sooner. The atmosphere is lively and colourful with baskets loaded with fresh fruits, vegetables, flowers, spices, and varieties of red, black and white rice. There are trays of live chickens, dead chickens, freshly slaughtered pigs, sardines, eggs, colourful cakes, ready-made offerings and *base* (spice paste), and stalls selling *es cendol* (colourful iced coconut drink) and other foods ready to eat. There are small packets of coffee, noodles and cleaning detergents, and cooking utensils made from natural materials, such as a stone spice grinder, coconut-wood spoons, coconut-shell ladles and bamboo steaming pots. Local specialities abound.

SNACK TIME

Jajanan (snacks) are sold everywhere – there are thousands of varieties of sweet and savoury snacks made from almost anything and everything: peanuts, coconuts, bananas, sweet potato etc. You'll find them sold at cafes and roadside rest areas, usually in neatly packed little plastic bags. Try a few to find your favourites (we like the roasted peanuts with chilli).

NUSA TENGGARA

In dry East Nusa Tenggara you'll eat less rice and more sago, corn, cassava and taro. Fish remains popular and one local dish is Sumbawa's *sepat* (shredded fish in coconut and mango sauce).

The Sasak people of Lombok like spicy *ayam Taliwang* (roasted chicken served with a peanut, tomato, chilli and lime dip) and *pelecing* (sauce made with chilli, shrimp paste and tomato). In fact, Lombok-style chicken is popular across the nation.

SUMATRA

In West Sumatra, beef is used in *rendang* (beef coconut curry). Padang food is famed for its rich, chilli-heavy sauces, and is popular throughout Indonesia. It's usually delicious, though not cooked fresh – dishes are displayed for hours (days even) in the restaurant window. Padang restaurant *(masakan Padang)* food is served one of two ways. Usually a bowl of rice is plonked in front of you, followed by a whole collection of small bowls of vegetables, meat and fish. Or you approach the window display and pick a few dishes yourself.

KALIMANTAN

Dayak food varies, but you may sample *rembang,* a sour fruit that's made into *sayur asem rembang* (sour vegetable soup). The regional soup, *soto banjar,* is a chicken broth made creamy by mashing boiled eggs into the stock. Chicken also goes into *ayam masak habang,* cooked with large red chillies.

SULAWESI

South Sulawesi locals love seafood, especially *ikan bakar* (grilled fish). For sugar cravers, there's *es pallubutun* (coconut custard and banana in coconut milk and syrup). The Toraja people have their own distinct cuisine. The best-known dish is *pa'piong* (meat stuffed into bamboo tubes along with vegetables and coconut).

MALUKU

A typical Maluku meal is tuna and *dabu-dabu* (raw vegetables with a chilli and fish-paste sauce). Sometimes fish is made into *kohu-kohu* (fish salad with citrus fruit and chilli).

PAPUA

In the highlands of Papua the sweet potato is king. Other plants, such as sago palms, are also cultivated. The locals eat the pith of the sago palm and also leave the plant to rot so that they can collect and eat beetle grubs. On special occasions, chickens and pigs are cooked in earth ovens.

Drink

Bottled water and soft drinks are available everywhere, and many hotels and restaurants provide *air putih* (boiled water) for guests. The iced juice drinks can be good, but take care that the water/ice has been purified or is bottled. (Ice in Jakarta and Bali is usually fine.)

Indonesian tea is fine and coffee can be excellent; for a strong local brew ask for *kopi java* or *kopi flores,* depending on where you are of course. Beer is quite good: Bintang is one of Asia's finest lagers and costs 15,000Rp to 25,000Rp for a large bottle in most places. Bali Brem rice wine is really potent, and the more you drink the nicer it tastes. *Es buah,* or *es campur,* is a strange concoction of fruit salad, jelly cubes, syrup, crushed rice and condensed milk. And it tastes absolutely *enak* (delicious).

Price Indicators

In this chapter, price indicators for a main course or meal are separated into two price bands.

BALI & GILI ISLANDS	COST (RP)
$ budget	less than 50,000
$$ midrange	50,000-200,000
$$$ top end	more than 200,000

REST OF INDONESIA	COST
$ budget	less than 30,000
$$ midrange	30,000-100,000
$$$ top end	more than 100,000

WHERE TO SURF

New surf spots are being discovered all the time in Indonesia, the choices simply never end.

Java

Batu Karas (p168), with fine breaks, is one of the most enjoyable places to kick back in Java. **Pangandaran** (p165) is also popular.

Bali

It really is a surfer's paradise in Bali. Breaks are found right around the south side of the island and there's a large infrastructure of schools, board-rental places, cheap surfer dives and more that cater to the crowds.

Five famous spots you won't want to miss:

» **Kuta Beach** (Map p194) Where surfing came to Asia. This is a good place for beginners, with long, steady breaks.

» **Bingin** (Map p200) A white-sand beach backed by funky accommodation makes this a natural.

» **Ulu Watu** (Map p200) Some of the largest sets in Bali.

» **Medewi** (Map p191) Famous point break with a ride right into a river mouth.

» **Nusa Lembongan** (Map p191) The island is a mellow scene for surfers and nonsurfers. The breaks are right in front of the places to stay. See p203.

Nusa Tenggara

Lombok's **Kuta** (p230) has world-class waves and turquoise water. Sumbawa has superb surf at isolated **Maluk** (p231).

Sumatra

Northern Sumatra's **Pulau Nias** (p255) is the most visited surfing destination in the province.

The **Mentawai Islands** have good surf camps and draw charters (p251).

SURVIVAL GUIDE

Directory A–Z

Accommodation

Hotel, *losmen*, *penginapan* (simple lodging house), *wisma* (guesthouse): there are several words for somewhere to lay a weary head, and options to suit every budget in most Indonesian towns.

Cheap hotels are usually pretty basic, but a simple breakfast is often included. In-room, Western-style toilets are nearly standard in tourist areas. Traditional washing facilities consist of a usually private *mandi*, a large water tank from which you scoop cool water with a dipper. Climbing into the tank is very bad form! The air-con symbol (❄) denotes whether air-con rooms are available; otherwise rooms are assumed to come with a fan.

Accommodation prices in tourist areas peak in August, and during Easter and the Christmas period, though at the budget end of the market, price hikes are marginal. Elsewhere in the country, rates increase during Idul Fitri (the period following Ramadan).

PRACTICALITIES

» Videos you buy or watch are based on the PAL system, also used in Australia, New Zealand, the UK and most of Europe. Pirated DVDs are abundant and you usually get what you pay for.

» Smoking is common and cigarettes are relatively cheap.

» Tap water is never safe to drink.

» For electrical plug information see p927.

Generally, budget rooms are plain and purely functional rooms. But along the main travelling trail, in Yogyakarta and in parts of Lombok and Sumatra, budget places can be very attractive and decorated with artistic touches, and often come with a veranda. Bali is in a league of its own in terms of quality: for 200,000Rp a night there are some wonderful places, some with pools.

In this chapter, price indicators are separated into two price bands.

BALI & GILI ISLANDS	COST
$ budget	less than 300,000Rp
$$ midrange	300,000Rp-US$150
$$$ top end	more than US$150

REST OF INDONESIA	COST
$ budget	less than 200,000Rp
$$ midrange	200,000Rp-US$100
$$$ top end	more than US$100

Business Hours

In this chapter it is assumed that standard hours are as follows. Significant variations are noted in listings.

Banks 8am to 2pm Monday to Thursday, 8am to noon Friday, 8am to 11am Saturday

Government offices 8am to 3pm Monday to Thursday, 8am to noon on Friday, but they are not standardised

Post offices 8am to 2pm Monday to Friday; longer in tourist centres

Restaurants and cafes 8am to 9pm daily

Shops and services catering to visitors 9am to 8pm

Customs

Indonesia has the usual list of prohibited imports, including drugs, weapons, fresh fruit and anything remotely pornographic.

Items allowed include the following:

» 200 cigarettes (or 50 cigars or 100g of tobacco)

» a 'reasonable amount' of perfume

» 1L of alcohol

Embassies & Consulates

BALI

Australia (Map p201; ☎0361-241118; www.bali.indonesia.embassy.gov.au; Jl Tantular 32, Denpasar) The Australian consulate has a consular-sharing agreement with Canada.

USA (☎0361-233605; amcobali@indo.net.id; Jl Hayam Wuruk 188, Renon, Denpasar)

JAKARTA

Australia (Map p152; ☎021-2550 5555; www.indonesia.embassy.gov.au; Jl HR Rasuna Said Kav 15-16)

Brunei (☎021-3190 6080; Jl Teuku Umar 9, Menteng)

Canada (Map p152; ☎021-2550 7800; www.canadainternational.gc.ca/indonesia-indonesie/; World Trade Centre, 6th fl, Jl Jenderal Sudirman Kav 29-31)

France (Map p154; ☎021-2355 7600; www.ambafrance-id.org; Jl Thamrin 20)

Germany (Map p154; ☎021-3985 5000; www.jakarta.diplo.de; Jl Thamrin 1)

Malaysia (Map p152; ☎021-522 4947; www.kln.gov.my/web/idn_jakarta/home; Jl HR Rasuna Said Kav X/6 No 1)

Netherlands (Map p152; ☎021-524 8200; indonesia.nlembassy.org; Jl HR Rasuna Said Kav S-3)

INDONESIAN READS

Lonely Planet's *Bali & Lombok, Borneo* and *Indonesia* guides explore the country in more detail, while Lonely Planet's *Indonesian Phrasebook* is the perfect guide to the language. Read *Healthy Travel: Asia & India* for the lowdown on keeping healthy during your travels.

Krakatoa – The Day the World Exploded is Simon Winchester's highly readable account centred on the 1888 eruption of Krakatau – the world's biggest bang.

The Year of Living Dangerously by Christopher J Koch is the harrowing tale of a journalist in Soekarno's Indonesia of 1965. Many have seen the movie with a young Mel Gibson and Linda Hunt. The book is more harrowing.

Rimbaud in Java: The Lost Voyage by Bali writer Jamie James is a quixotic account of the famous poet's mysterious 19th-century visit.

Eat, Pray, Love by Elizabeth Gilbert is a famously successful book (and less than successful movie). Fans of the lurid, self-absorbed prose flock to Ubud looking for love.

New Zealand (Map p152; ☎021-2995 5800; www.nzembassy.com/indonesia; 10th fl, Sentral Senayan 2, Jl Asia Afrika No 8)

Papua New Guinea (Map p152; ☎021-725 1218; 6th fl, Panin Bank Centre, Jl Jenderal Sudirman 1)

Singapore (Map p152; ☎021-2995 0400; www.mfa.gov.sg/jkt/; Jl HR Rasuna Said, Block X/4 Kav 2)

Thailand (Map p152; ☎021-2932 8190; www.mfa.go.th/web/2712.php; Jl Mega Kunignan kav E3.3, No 3)

UK (Map p154; ☎021-2356 5220; ukinindonesia.fco.gov.uk; Jl Thamrin 75)

USA (Map p157; ☎021-3435 9000; jakarta.usembassy.gov; Jl Merdeka Selatan 3-5)

MEDAN

Malaysia (☎061-453 1342; www.kln.gov.my/web/idn_medan/home; Jl Diponegoro 43)

Gay & Lesbian Travellers

Gay travellers in Indonesia will experience few problems, especially in Bali. Physical contact between same-sex couples is acceptable (Indonesian boys and girls often hold hands or link arms in public). Homosexual behaviour is not illegal – the age of consent is 16. Immigration officials may restrict entry to people who reveal HIV-positive status. Gay men in Indonesia are referred to as *homo* or *gay;* lesbians are *lesbi*.

Indonesia's transvestite and transsexual *waria* – from *wanita* (woman) and *pria* (man) – community has always had a public profile.

Internet Access

Internet places are found in most towns and tourist centres (and wi-fi is common at hotels and cafes in popular destinations). Speeds are usually pedestrian, though. Expect to pay between 5000Rp and 12,000Rp per hour.

Legal Matters

The government takes the smuggling, using and selling of drugs very, *very* seriously. Once caught, you may have to wait for up to six months in jail before trial. Gambling is illegal (although it's common, especially at cockfights), as is pornography.

Generally, you are unlikely to have any encounters with the police unless you are driving a rented car or motorcycle, in which case you may be stopped for a dubious reason and asked to pay an impromptu 'fine' of about 50,000Rp.

The age of consent is 18.

CULTURAL CONSIDERATIONS

Generally Indonesians are a relaxed lot, but that's no reason to go rudely trampling their sensibilities.

» Indonesia is a conservative, largely Muslim country, and while bikinis and Speedos are tolerated in the beach resorts of Bali, try to respect local clothing traditions wherever possible. This is particularly true near a mosque.

» Couples should avoid canoodling or kissing in public.

» You have to haggle in Indonesia, but it's important to do so respectfully and learn when to draw the line. It's very bad form to shout or lose your temper. Remember that a few extra rupiah may make a great deal of difference to the other party.

» A little Bahasa Indonesia, which is very easy to pick up, will get you a long way. Not only will you delight the locals, but it'll save you cash when it comes to dealing with stall owners, hoteliers and becak drivers.

Post

The postal service in Indonesia is generally good.

Public Holidays

Official holidays and religious events are intertwined in the Indonesian calendar, with the result being a plethora of days when much of the nation shuts down or has the day off. See p298 for details.

Safe Travel

If you've never been before, Indonesia might seem like one of the world's most dodgy nations: accident-prone, and cursed by natural disasters and terrorist outrages.

But while transport safety standards are dodgy, earthquakes are frequent and there has been a number of highly publicised incidents of terrorism and sectarian violence, Indonesia is actually a very safe nation for travellers, unless you're very unlucky.

Personal safety, even in the big cities, is not usually a major concern. Keep your wits about you, yes, but violent crime (and even petty theft) is rare in Indonesia. Be mindful of your valuables and take the usual precautions and the chances of getting into trouble are tiny.

It *is* important to keep abreast of current political developments, however, and maybe give political or religious demos a wide berth. At the time of writing, most of the country was peaceful.

Drug penalties can be severe. Beware of noncommercial *arak*, the potent rice or palm hootch; there have been incidents of poisoning. And on Bali, beware of dogs, as there is a major rabies epidemic.

But most importantly, go and enjoy yourself.

Time

Indonesia has three time zones. Western Indonesia time (Sumatra, Java, West and Central Kalimantan) is seven hours ahead of GMT, Central Indonesia time (Bali, South and East Kalimantan, Sulawesi and Nusa Tenggara) is eight hours ahead, and East Indonesia time (Maluku and Irian Jaya) is nine hours ahead.

Toilets

Public toilets are extremely rare except in bus and train stations. Expect to have to dive into restaurants and hotels frequently.

Indonesian toilets are holes in the ground with footrests on either side (although Western toilets are common in tourist areas). To flush, reach for that plastic scooper, take water from the tank *(mandi)* and flush it away.

Visas

Most visitors obtain a 30-day visa on arrival (VOA) at recognised entry points in Indonesia, which comprise 15 airports and 21 sea ports. These include ferry ports to/from Sumatra: Penang-Belawan, Melaka-Dumai and Singapore-Batam/Bintan. All major international airports are covered. For land border crossings you'll need to arrange a visa in advance.

At the time of writing, citizens of over 60 countries were eligible for a VOA, including those from Australia, Canada, much – but not all – of the EU including Ireland, the Netherlands and the UK, plus New Zealand and the USA. The cost is US$25 and it is best to have exact change. In 2010 it became possible to renew a 30-day VOA for another 30 days. To do so you must go to a local immigration office at least one week before your VOA expires. The process can be complex.

To get a much-prized 60-day visa you have to apply through an embassy or consulate before you arrive in Indonesia.

Indonesia requires that your passport is valid for six months following your date of arrival.

Travel Permits

Technically, if you're heading to Papua you should obtain a *surat jalan* (visitor permit; see the boxed text, p290).

Volunteering

There are excellent opportunities for aspiring volunteers in Indonesia.

Bali is a hub for many charitable groups and NGOs, including the following:

East Bali Poverty Project (www.eastbalipovertyproject.org; Denpasar) Works to help children in the impoverished mountain villages of East Bali.

IDEP (Indonesian Development of Education & Permaculture; www.idepfoundation.org; Ubud) Has projects across Indonesia; works on environmental projects, disaster planning and community improvement.

ProFauna (www.profauna.or.id) A large non-profit animal-protection organisation operating across Indonesia; the Bali office has been aggressive in protecting sea turtles. Volunteers needed to help with hatchery releases and editing publications.

Smile Foundation of Bali (Yayasan Senyum; www.senyumbali.org) Organises surgery to correct facial deformities.

SOS (Sumatran Orangutan Society; www.orangutans-sos.org) An Ubud-based group that works to save endangered species throughout Indonesia.

Yakkum Bali (Yayasan Rama Sesana; www.yrsbali.org; Denpasar) Dedicated to improving reproductive health for women across Bali.

Yayasan Bumi Sehat (www.bumisehatbali.org; Ubud) Operates a clinic and gives reproductive services to poor women in Ubud; accepts donated time from medical professionals; also has a clinic in Aceh.

Two animal-welfare groups outside Bali:

Borneo Orangutan Survival Foundation (BOSF; www.orangutan.or.id) Accepts volunteers for its orang-utan and sun bear rehabilitation and reforestation programs at Samboja Lestari between Balikpapan and Samarinda.

Kalaweit Care Centre (www.kalaweit.org) Works to rehabilitate ex-captive gibbons on Sumatra and Borneo.

Getting There & Away

Entering Indonesia

The main bureaucratic consideration for entering Indonesia involves visas. See p307 for details.

Air

Jakarta (p307) and Bali (p307) are the main hubs, but other useful international connections include Balikpapan (Kalimantan), Mataram (Lombok), Manado (Sulawesi), Medan (Sumatra), Palembang (Sumatra), Padang (Sumatra), Solo (Java) and Surabaya (Java).

The following are some major international airlines with services to Indonesia:

Air Asia (code AK; www.airasia.com) Serves a wide range of Indonesian destinations from Kuala Lumpur, plus Bali and Jakarta from Bangkok and Singapore.

Emirates (code EK; www.emirates.com) Serves Jakarta from Dubai.

Firefly (code FY; www.fireflyz.com.my) Serves major cities on Sumatra from Kuala Lumpur and Penang in Malaysia.

Garuda Indonesia (code GA; www.garuda-indonesia.com) Indonesia's national airline serves Bali and Jakarta from Australia and points across Asia.

Jetstar/Qantas Airways (code QF; www.qantas.com.au) Serves Bali and Jakarta from Australia.

KLM (code KL; www.klm.com) Serves Jakarta and Bali from Amsterdam.

Lion Air (code JT; www.lionair.co.id) Fast-growing budget airline serves airports across Indonesia from major Asian cities.

Lufthansa (code LH; www.lufthansa.com) Serves Jakarta from Frankfurt.

Malaysia Airlines (code MH; ☎0361-764995; www.mas.com.my) Serves Bali and Jakarta from Kuala Lumpur.

Merpati Airlines (code MZ; www.merpati.co.id) Serves Dili in East Timor from Bali.

> **DEPARTURE TAX**
>
> Indonesian airports typically charge a departure tax. This charge varies by airport – as high as 150,000Rp for international flights – and is payable in cash.

Pacific Blue (code DJ; www.flypacificblue.com) Offshoot of Virgin Australia; serves Bali from several Australian cities.

SilkAir (code MI; www.silkair.com) Serves numerous Indonesian destinations from Singapore, including Balikpapan and Lombok.

Singapore Airlines (code SQ; www.singaporeair.com) Numerous flights to Bali and Jakarta daily.

Thai Airways International (code TG; www.thaiair.com) Serves Bali and Jakarta from Bangkok.

Tiger Airways (code TR; www.tigerairways.com) Budget carrier based in Singapore; serves Jakarta.

Land

There are three land links between Indonesia and neighbouring countries. Buses link Pontianak and Kuching on Borneo. See p241 for information on crossing into East Timor. And you can cross from Jayapura to Vanimo in Papua New Guinea.

Sea

Malaysia and Singapore are linked to Sumatra by boats and ferries, although the links are inconvenient and most travellers fly. Boats make the Melaka (Malaysia) to Dumai (Indonesia) crossing. From Singapore, ferries make the quick hop to Pulau Batam and Bintan, the primary islands in the Riau archipelago.

There is a link on Borneo from Nunukan in East Kalimantan to Tawau in Malaysian Sabah. There is currently no sea travel between the Philippines and Indonesia.

Getting Around

Air

The domestic-flight network in Indonesia continues to grow; schedules and rates are in a constant state of flux. Local carriers servicing small routes often operate

RELIABLE TRANSPORT INFO

In a country where accurate info for ferries, airlines and buses can at best be elusive, guesthouses, hotels and resorts are good sources of information, especially for more obscure destinations. They need you to reach them to stay in business and often can give you all the up-to-date details needed.

cramped and dated aircrafts, whereas flights to Jakarta, Bali and other major destinations are usually on larger, newer crafts.

Depending on the size of the airlines and where they fly, timetables will vary from accurate, national schedules to hand-adjusted printouts of localised areas or provinces on specific islands. Website information is useful for the bigger carriers but nonexistent for the smaller ones. The best option is to check with local airline offices and travel agents (see regional transport information within this chapter for contact details) to see what's available.

Individual airlines and contacts are listed in the relevant city coverage.

Tickets

The larger Indonesian-based carriers have websites listing fares; however, it may be hard if not impossible to purchase tickets over the internet from outside Indonesia (Air Asia and Garuda are possible exceptions). You may have to call the airline in Indonesia – or better, if the option exists, an office outside Indonesia. Note that you may not reach anyone on the phone who speaks English.

Another option is to enlist the services of one of the many travel agents listed in major cities in this book. Sometimes the best way to get a ticket for travel within Indonesia is to simply go to the airport and compare prices at the various airline offices. Many airlines are strictly cash-based, and offer last-minute deals if there are empty seats.

It is *essential* to reconfirm. Overbooking is a problem, and if you don't reconfirm at least a few days before departure, you may well get bumped. Expect problems in the outer islands, where flights are limited, communications poor and booking procedures haphazard – you should reconfirm and reconfirm again.

Bicycle

Bicycles can be hired in all major centres for 15,000Rp to 50,000Rp per day from hotels, travel agents and shops. The tropical heat, heavy traffic and poor road conditions make long-distance travel a challenge, but some hardy souls manage it.

Boat

Sumatra, Java, Bali and Nusa Tenggara are connected by ferries. Pelni, the national passenger line, covers the archipelago, albeit infrequently.

Pelni Ships

Pelni (www.pelni.co.id) has a fleet of large vessels linking all of Indonesia's major ports and the majority of the archipelago's outlying areas. Pelni's website is a good resource, showing arrivals and departures about a month in advance.

Pelni ships have four cabin classes, plus *kelas ekonomi*. Class I has two beds per cabin (and is often more expensive than using a low-cost airline); Class IV has eight beds to a cabin. *Ekonomi* is extremely basic, with mattresses that can be rented. However, these designations are often meaningless on the many boats that are both filthy and over-crowded. By all means book the best class of service you can afford, noting that the bathroom may be unworkable, decks impassable with throngs of stoic passengers and food unpalatable.

You can book tickets up to two weeks ahead; it's best to book at least a few days in advance.

Other Boats

Sumatra, Java, Bali, Nusa Tenggara and Sulawesi are all connected by regular ferries, and you can use them to island hop all the way from Sumatra to Timor. These ferries run either daily or several times a week, so there's no need to spend days in sleepy little port towns. Check with shipping companies, the harbour office or travel agents for current schedules and fares.

DOMESTIC DEPARTURES TAX

Indonesian airports typically charge a departure tax. This charge varies by airport – it averages 40,000Rp for domestic flights – and is payable in cash.

TRAVELLING SAFELY BY BOAT

Boat safety is an important consideration across Indonesia, where boats that barely seem seaworthy may be your only option to visit that idyllic little island. In many cases these services are accidents waiting to happen, as safety regulation is not even spotty.

This is especially true on the busy routes linking Bali, Nusa Lembongan, Lombok and the Gilis. In 2010 a boat between Lombok and Gili T capsized killing three. Two fast boats between Gili T and Bali have sunk recently, and in each case, the tourists and crew aboard were lucky to survive by swimming to shore or being rescued by other boats that happened to be passing by.

Conditions are often rough in Indonesia's waters. Although the islands are in close proximity and are easily seen, the ocean between can get more turbulent than is safe for small speedboats zipping across the heavy seas.

With these facts in mind, it is essential that you take responsibility for your own safety, as no one else will. Consider the following points:

» **Bigger is better** It may take you 30 minutes or more longer, but a larger boat will simply deal with the open ocean better than the over-powered small speedboats.

» **Check for safety equipment** Make certain your boat has life preservers and that you know how to locate and use them. In an emergency, don't expect a panicked crew to hand them out. Also, check for life boats.

» **Avoid over-crowding** Travellers report boats leaving with more people than seats and with aisles jammed with stacked luggage.

» **Look for exits** Cabins may only have one narrow entrance making them death traps in an accident.

» **Avoid fly-by-nighters** Taking a fishing boat and jamming too many engines on the rear in order to cash in on booming tourism is a recipe for disaster.

However, schedules are often very vague, so be prepared to hang around until something turns up. Be warned that because vessels may be ancient and routinely overcrowded, safety standards are at times poor – though most people make it across the archipelago in one piece.

It's also possible to make some more unusual sea trips. Old Makassar schooners still ply Indonesian waters, and it may be possible to travel on them from Sulawesi to other islands. Tourist boats travelling between Lombok and Flores with a stop on Komodo are also popular. See the boxed text, p234, for details.

Bus

Most Indonesians use buses to get around, so there is a huge variety of services, with everything from air-con deluxe buses with blaring TVs, toilets and karaoke that speed across the major islands, to *trek* (trucks) with wooden seats that rumble along the dirt roads of Flores. Local buses are the cheapest; they leave when full and stop on request – on the outer islands this is often your only choice.

Minibuses often do shorter runs.

Car & Motorcycle

Self-drive jeeps can be hired for as little as 80,000Rp to 150,000Rp a day with limited insurance in Bali, but become increasingly expensive and hard to come by the further you get from tourist areas. If you're not happy negotiating Indonesia's chaotic roads, a vehicle with driver can usually be hired for between 350,000Rp and 600,000Rp per day; the more remote areas tend to be the most expensive.

Motorcycles and scooters can be hired across Indonesia for 25,000Rp to 50,000Rp per day. Be sure to get a crash helmet, as wearing one is supposed to be compulsory.

Hitching

Hitching is possible, but cannot be advised. Drivers may well ask for as much as the bus would cost – maybe more – and safety is obviously a concern.

Local Transport

Public minibuses (most commonly called bemo, but also known as *colt, opelet, mikrolet, angkot, angkudes* and *pete-pete*) are everywhere. Bemos run standard routes (fares average 3000Rp to 5000Rp), but can also be chartered like a taxi.

Cycle rickshaws are called becak, while *bajaj* are Indonesian túk-túk: three-wheelers that carry two passengers (three at a squeeze) and are powered by rasping two-stroke engines. In quieter towns, you may find horse-drawn carts, variously called *dokar, cidomo, andong* and *ben hur*.

An extremely handy form of transport is the *ojek* (motorcycle taxi); expect to pay about 2500Rp to 10,000Rp for a short ride. Most towns have taxis, which require careful negotiations. In major cities (Jakarta, South Bali etc) look for Bluebird taxis, which are reliable and use their meters.

Train

Java has a good railway service running the length of the island (see p310). There is also an extremely limited rail service in Sumatra.

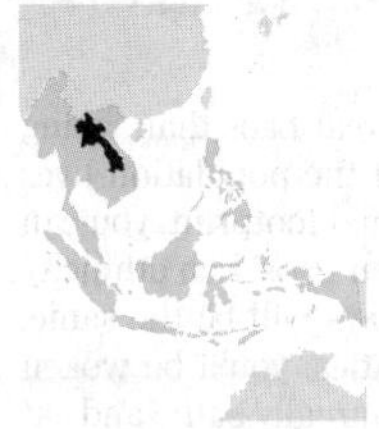

Laos

Includes »

Best Regional Specialities

- Làap (p328)
- Fǒe (p361)
- Baguettes with pâté (p357)
- Mok pa (p332)
- Tạm màak hung (p320)

Best Places for Cultural Connections

- Handicraft Night Market (p332)
- Minority villages (p346)
- Fishing with locals (p367)
- Luang Prabang's temples (p329)

Why Go?

Beneath the tourist radar for decades, Laos has finally exfoliated her Marxist scales, repainted herself in ecogreen colours and opened her arms to the world. This is a country oozing authenticity, a destination that makes you feel you've really escaped: glimmering rice paddies, towering karsts, apricot-robed monks, Indochinese villas and a richly ethnic population...pure magic. For the traveller who wants shoestring digs and organised adventure, Laos delivers. Ecotreks through 'Lost World' jungles, elephant rides and vertiginous zip-lines; homestays with ethnic tribes and creepy boat trips through subterranean rivers – your choices are myriad. And when your limbs are weary with adventure head to the travellers' legend that is Luang Prabang, for its affordable spas, Indochinese chic and fantastically eclectic range of cuisine.

China's high-speed train links from Beijing and Kunming (currently under construction) will shortly pass through Vientiane and Luang Prabang, perhaps changing them forever. Now really is the time to visit.

When to Go

Vientiane

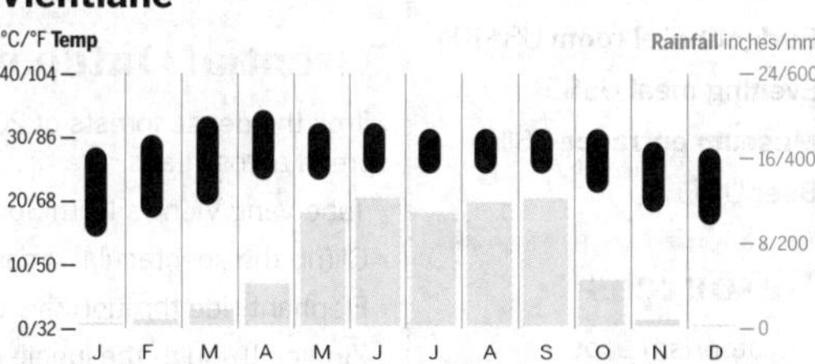

Jan Cool-season breezes and even the infernal south is pleasant.

Oct Cool weather; locals celebrate the full moon and boat racing festivals.

Nov & Dec Carnivalesque celebrations for Bun Pha That in Nov. Cool weather but peak prices in Dec.

AT A GLANCE

Currency Kip

Language Lao

Money ATMs in major centres. Credit cards accepted in Luang Prabang and Vientiane.

Visas On arrival (30-day; US$30–42 depending on which passport you hold).

Mobile phones Pre-pay SIMs available for as little as 10,000K. Decent connections.

Fast Facts

Area 236,000 sq km

Capital Vientiane

Country code ☎856

Emergency police ☎191

Exchange Rates

Australia	A$1	8350K
Canada	C$1	8050K
Japan	¥100	9550K
New Zealand	NZ$1	6500K
UK	UK£1	12,650K
USA	US$1	8000K

Set Your Budget

Budget hotel room US$10

Evening meal US$5

Museum entrance US$2

Beer US$1

Resources

» Ecotourism Laos (www.ecotourismlaos.com)

» Lonely Planet (www.lonelyplanet.com)

» Lao Bumpkin (www.laobumpkin.blogspot.com)

Don't Miss

There's no better way to discover the real Laos than trying a homestay. Beyond the cities, 80% of the population lives in rural villages and now, with a minimal footprint, you can experience an evening with them. Given Laos' rich ethnicity and varied geography no two homestays will be the same, but you can rely on a few commonalities: you'll be woken by children and the local rooster, communally bathe and eat by the fire, and be guaranteed one of your most memorable nights in this country. Take a Lao phrasebook, photos of your family and, most of all, a sense of humour!

ITINERARIES

One Week

After spending a few days in riverside Vientiane sampling its Soviet-Franco architecture, sophisticated bars and Asian-fusion cuisine, travel north to the unforgettable ancient city of Luang Prabang (p329) to experience its temples, crumbling villas, pampering spas, elephant treks and Gallic cuisine.

Two Weeks

Fly to Vientiane, imbibe its cafes, bars and cuisine for a few days, then head north to Vang Vieng (p325) for climbing, kayaking and tubing in serene karst scenery. Move on to enchanting Luang Prabang (p329), so bedecked with bakeries, temples, boutiques and restaurants you may not want to leave. After a few days here take a two-day slowboat up the Mekong River to Huay Xai (p349), having already booked yourself in for the memorable Gibbon Experience (see the boxed text, p350), and their overnight stays in jungle treehouses. If you've got time, head up to Luang Nam Tha (p346) for an ecoconscious trek in the wild Nam Ha National Protected Area. From here you can fly back to Vientiane to catch your flight out.

Essential Outdoor Activities

» Trek the dense forests of 20 national protected areas spread across Laos.

» Tube Vang Vieng's Nam Song River, a Lao rite of passage.

» Climb the spectacular limestone karsts in Vang Vieng.

» Elephant ride through rivers in Luang Prabang.

» Zip-line through the jungle canopy with The Gibbon Experience or Treetop Explorer.

VIENTIANE

☎021 / POP 237,000

Vientiane has been steadily prettified with boutique hotels morphing from formerly crumbling colonial villas, and restaurants of almost every cuisine – particularly Gallic – competing with the cosmopolitan mix of Soviet-, Sino- and Franco-styled architecture. Whether wandering by the Mekong River, browsing shops on temple-bordered Th (Street) Setthathirat or taking in historical sights between having a cheap spa and chilling at one of Vientiane's French bakeries, a few days here are a delight.

The three main streets parallel to the Mekong – Th Fa Ngum, Th Setthathirat and Th Samsenthai – form the central inner city of Vientiane and are where most of the budget guesthouses, bars and restaurants are located. Nam Phu is the best central landmark if you're catching a taxi or túk-túk into town. Heading northeast at a 90-degree angle to Th Setthathirat is the boulevard of Th Lan Xang, where you'll find the Talat Sao, Patuxai monument and Pha That Luang, Laos' most distinctive structure.

History

Vientiane was first settled as an early Lao fiefdom. Through 10 centuries of history it was variously controlled, ravaged and looted by the Vietnamese, Burmese, Siamese and Khmer. When Laos became a French protectorate at the end of the 19th century, it was renamed as the capital, was rebuilt and became one of the classic Indochinese cities, along with Phnom Penh and Saigon (Ho Chi Minh City). By the early 1960s and the onset of the war in Vietnam, the city was teeming with CIA agents, madcap Ravens (maverick US Special Ops pilots) and Russian spies.

In 2009 the city hosted the Southeast Asian Games, a major illustration of the country's new profile. And while the newly constructed trainline from Thailand to within a few klicks of Laos is still largely useless, China's Kunming to Vientiane express route (part of a multibillion dollar investment) will be completed in 2014.

Sights

Pha That Luang TEMPLE

(Great Sacred Reliquary or Great Stupa; off Map p316; Th That Luang; admission 5000K; ⌚8am-noon & 1-4pm Tue-Sun) Svelte and golden Pha That Luang is the most important national monument in Laos; a symbol of Buddhist religion and Lao sovereignty. Legend has it that Ashokan missionaries from India erected a *tâht* (stupa) here to enclose a piece of Buddha's breastbone as early as the 3rd century BC.

Pha That Luang is about 4km northeast of the city centre at the end of Th That Luang.

Wat Si Saket & Haw Pha Kaew TEMPLE

Built in 1818 by King Anouvong (Chao Anou), **Wat Si Saket** (Map p318; cnr Th Lan Xang & Th Setthathirat; admission 5000K; ⌚8am-noon & 1-4pm, closed public holidays) is the oldest temple in Vientiane and well worth a visit even if you've overdosed on temples. Uniquely, the interior walls of the cloister are riddled with niches containing more than 2000 silver and ceramic Buddha images. Over 300 seated and standing Buddhas of varying age, size and material (wood, stone and bronze) rest on long shelves below the niches. A Khmer-style Naga Buddha is also on display.

Diagonally opposite is **Haw Pha Kaew** (Map p318; Th Setthathirat; admission 5000K; ⌚8am-noon & 1-4pm), a royal temple built specifically to house the famed Emerald Buddha, but today used as a national museum of religious art; it has the best collection of Buddha images in Laos.

Patuxai MONUMENT

(Victory Monument; Map p316; Th Lan Xang; admission 3000K; ⌚8am-5pm) Vientiane's Arc de Triomphe replica is a slightly incongruous sight, dominating the commercial district around Th Lan Xang. Officially called Patuxai and commemorating the Lao who died in prerevolutionary wars, it was built in 1969 with cement donated by the USA intended for the construction of a new airport; hence expats refer to it as 'the vertical runway'. Climb to the summit for panoramic views over Vientiane.

Xieng Khuan (Buddha Park) MUSEUM

(Buddha Park or Suan Phut; off Map p316; admission 5000K, camera 3000K; ⌚8am-4.30pm, sometimes later) Located 25km southeast of Vientiane, eccentric Xieng Khuan thrills with otherworldly Buddhist and Hindu sculptures, and was designed and built in 1958 by Luang Pu; a yogi-priest-shaman who merged Hindu and Buddhist philosophy, mythology and iconography into a cryptic whole.

Bus 14 (8000K, one hour, 24km) leaves the Talat Sao bus station every 15 or 20 minutes throughout the day and goes all the way to Xieng Khuan. Alternatively, charter a túk-túk (145,000K return).

Laos Highlights

1. **Luang Prabang** (p329) This ancient city of temples is a traveller's dream: royal history, Indochinese chic, colourful monks, stunning river views and world-class French cuisine
2. **Kong Lo Cave** (p352) Take a boat ride through this exhilarating yet spooky 7.5km cave, home to fist-sized spiders and stalactite woods
3. **The Gibbon Experience, Huay Xai** (p350) An adrenalin rush with an eco-conscience; trek and zip across the forest by day, guided by ex poachers turned forest rangers, who lead you to your bed for the night in cosy treehouses
4. **Nam Ha National Protected Area** (p346) Eco-responsible treks to some of the wildest, densest jungle in the country, home to tigers and a rich variety of ethnic tribes
5. **Si Phan Don** (p364) The hammock capital of Laos, otherwise known as Four Thousand Islands; a steamy traveller's idyll where the Mekong turns turquoise and your pulse palpably drops

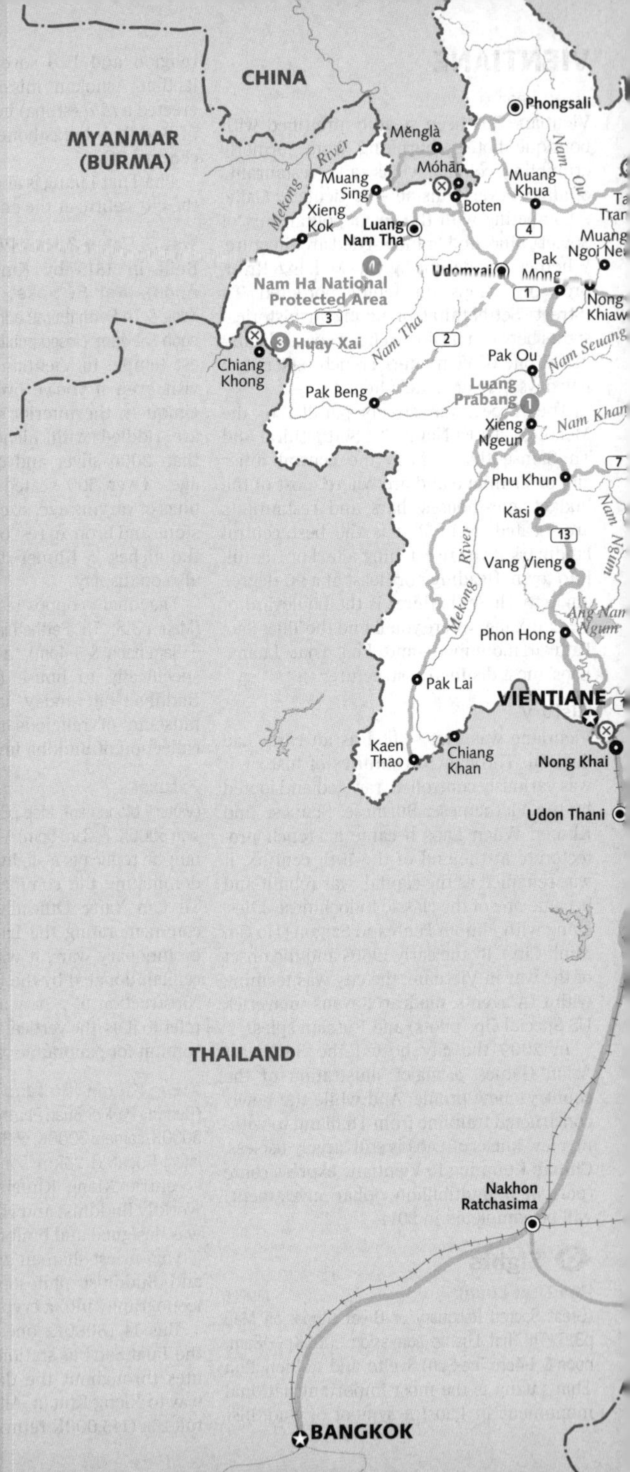

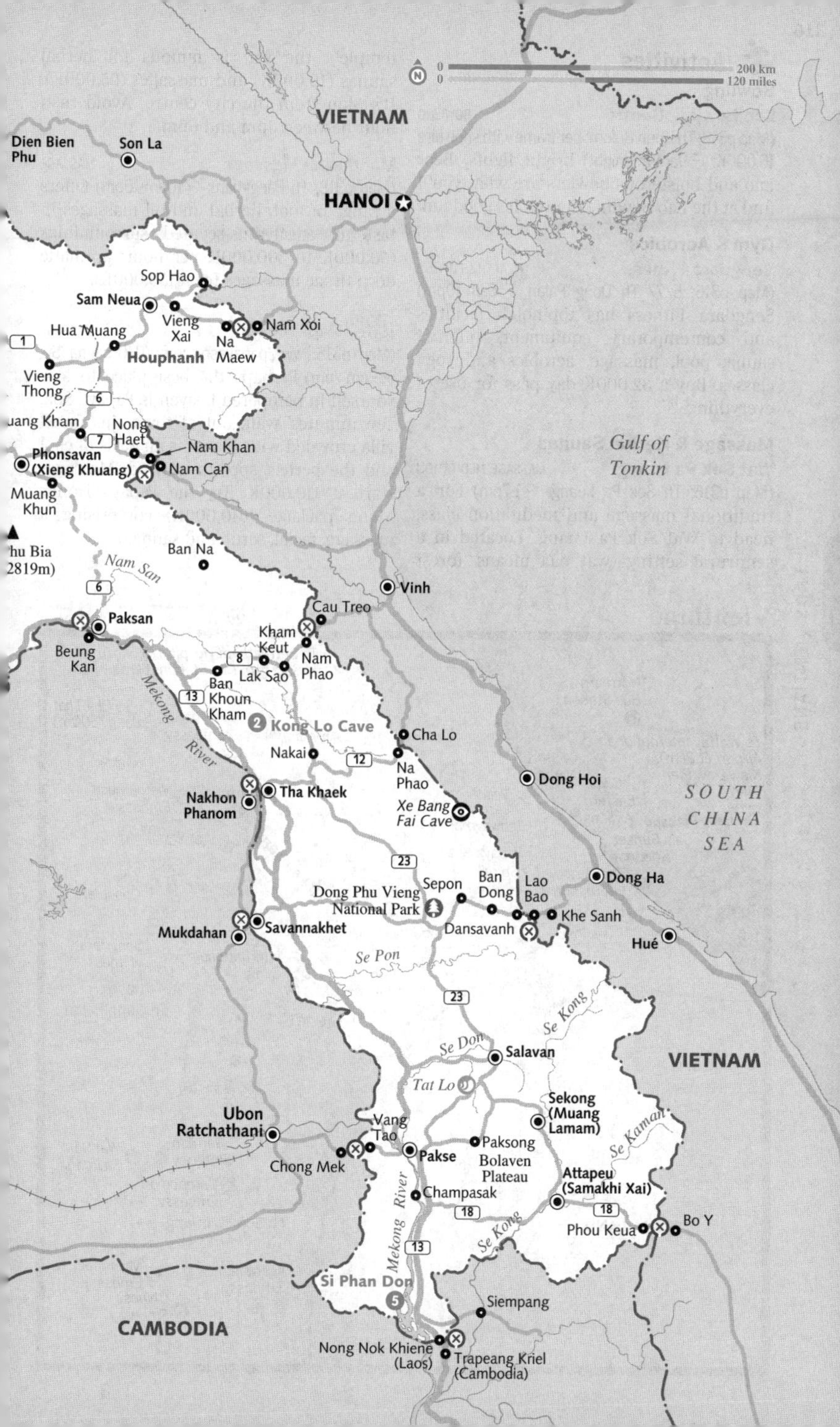
0
0
200 km
120 miles
VIETNAM
Dien Bien Phu
Son La
HANOI
Sop Hao
Sam Neua
Vieng Xai
Na Maew
Nam Xoi
Hua Muang
1
Houphanh
Vieng Thong
6
uang Kham
Nong Haet
7
Nam Khan
Phonsavan (Xieng Khuang)
Nam Can
Muang Khun
Gulf of Tonkin
hu Bia (2819m)
Ban Na
Nam San
6
Vinh
Paksan
Cau Treo
Beung Kan
Kham Keut
8
Lak Sao
Nam Phao
Ban Khoun Kham
13
Mekong River
Kong Lo Cave
Cha Lo
Nakai
12
Na Phao
Dong Hoi
Nakhon Phanom
Tha Khaek
Xe Bang Fai Cave
SOUTH CHINA SEA
23
Dong Phu Vieng National Park
Sepon
Ban Dong
Lao Bao
Dong Ha
Khe Sanh
Mukdahan
Savannakhet
Dansavanh
Hué
Se Pon
23
Se Kong
Se Don
Salavan
VIETNAM
Tat Lo
Sekong (Muang Lamam)
Ubon Ratchathani
Vang Tao
Se Kaman
Chong Mek
Pakse
Paksong
Bolaven Plateau
Attapeu (Samakhi Xai)
Mekong River
Champasak
18
18
Phou Keua
Bo Y
Se Kong
13
Si Phan Don
Siempang
CAMBODIA
Nong Nok Khiene (Laos)
Trapeang Kriel (Cambodia)

Activities

Bowling

Lao Bowling Centre BOWLING

(Map p318; Th Khun Bulom; per frame with shoe hire 16,000K; ⌚9am-midnight) Bright lights, Beer Lao and boisterous bowlers are what you'll find at the Lao Bowling Centre. It's good fun.

Gym & Aerobics

Sengdara Fitness HEALTH & FITNESS

(Map p316; 5/77 Th Dong Palan; ⌚6am-10pm) Sengdara Fitness has top-notch facilities and contemporary equipment, offering sauna, pool, massage, aerobics and yoga classes. Buy a 32,000K day pass for use of everything.

Massage & Herbal Saunas

Wat Sok Pa Luang MASSAGE, MEDITATION

(Map p316; Th Sok Pa Luang; ⌚1-7pm) For a traditional massage and meditation class, head to Wat Sok Pa Luang. Located in a semirural setting (wat pàa means 'forest temple'), the wat is famous for herbal saunas (10,000K) and massages (25,000K). It's 3km from the city centre. Avoid rush hour between 3pm and 6pm.

Mandarina Massage MASSAGE

(Map p318; Th Pangkham; ⌚10am-10pm) Offers a range of foot, herbal and oil massages in tasteful, eucalyptus-scented surroundings (50,000K to 300,000K per hour; aromatic deep tissue massages from 150,000K).

TOP CHOICE **Papaya Spa** MASSAGE

(Map p316; www.papayaspa.com; Th Phagna Sy; ⌚9am-7pm) Perhaps the best place to lose yourself in pampered heaven is Papaya Spa. Ten minutes' walk out of town this faded villa crowded with plants is an oasis of cool and the perfect spot to unwind. Massages start at 110,000K. Try the Papaya Honey Moon package (810,000K) comprising a massage, facial, scrub and sauna.

Vientiane

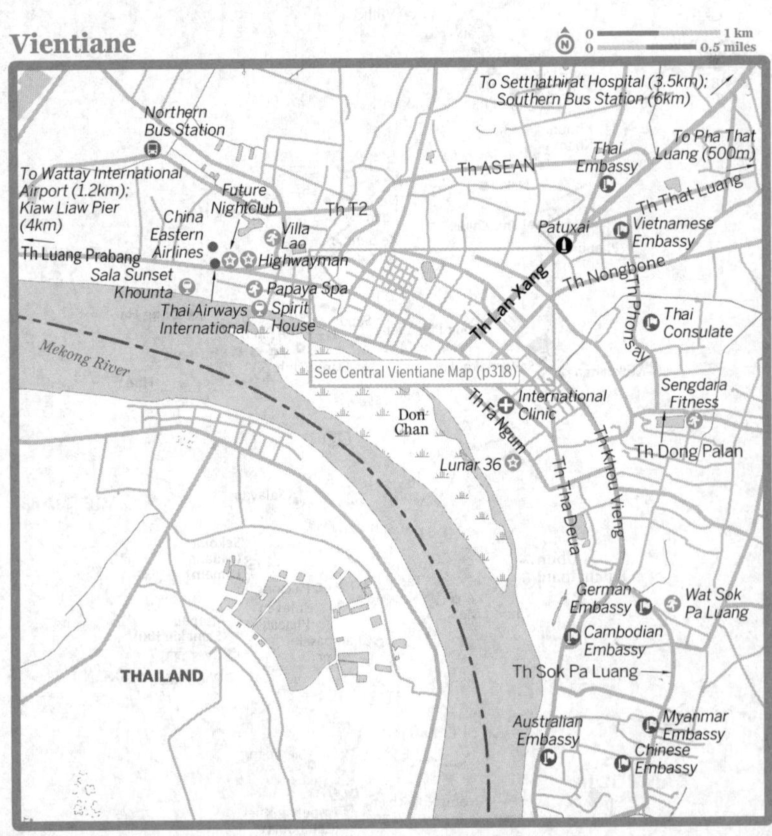

DON'T MISS

COPE CENTRE

Since the end of the war over 12,000 people have fallen victim to unexploded ordnance (UXO) – many of them children. A 10-minute bike ride from the city centre, the excellent **Cope Centre** (Map p318; www.copelaos.org; Th Khou Vieng; admission free; ⏲9am-6pm) is an inspiring not-for-profit organisation dedicated to supporting victims; providing clinical mentoring and training programs for local staff in the manufacture of artificial limbs and related rehabilitation activities. COPE makes high-tech but low-cost artificial limbs, transforming the lives of people who've had to make do with their own improvised limbs.

The recently updated UXO exhibition is fascinating, with photographs portraying the salvaged lives of victims, as well as 'The Cave cinema', a bunker-style screening room showing a number of documentaries. Take a free tour around the centre accompanied by an English-speaking guide; purchase a funky COPE T-shirt and, of course, donations are more than welcome.

Swimming

The **Vientiane Swimming Pool** (Map p318; Th Ki Huong; admission 10,000K; ⏲8am-7pm) is a 25m alfresco delight, but buy some goggles (25,000K) – there's enough chlorine in there to strip the barnacles off Davy Jones. The **Australian Embassy Recreation Club** (AERC; Map p316; Km 3, Th Tha Deua; ⏲9am-8pm) is another option, but for Hollywood glamour sample the kidney-shaped pool at the **Settha Palace Hotel** (Map p318; 6 Th Pangkham; admission 50,000K).

Courses

Lao-language courses are held at the Centre Culturel et de Coopération Linguistique. For details, see p322.

Cooking

Villa Lao COOKING

(Map p316; ☎242 292; www.villa-lao-guesthouse.com; off Th Nong Douang; half-day class 125,000K) Courses at beautiful Thongbay Guesthouse are organised on demand (maximum 10 people) and start at 9am, finishing at 4pm. The price includes a trip to the market for ingredients.

Meditation

Foreigners are welcome at a regular Saturday afternoon sitting at Wat Sok Pa Luang. The session runs from 4pm until 5.30pm with an opportunity to ask questions afterwards.

Festivals & Events

Pii Mai FESTIVAL

Lao New Year is celebrated once more in mid-April for this mass water fight. Be warned – drunk driving and theft go through the roof at these times so remain vigilant of your driver and wallet!

Awk Phansa & Bun Nam FESTIVAL

In October, Awk Phansa celebrates the end of Buddhist Lent and the rain's retreat, when monks make *heua fai* (little bamboo boats) in which candles are lit then floated downstream. Thousands flock to river cities to launch their own. Bun Nam (River Festival), following directly after, sees boat races held on the Mekong River, with rowing teams from across the country competing. Three nights of partying by Vientiane's riverbank.

That Luang Festival FESTIVAL

Held in early November, Bun Pha That Luang is the largest temple fair in Laos, incandescent with fireworks and a colourful procession between Pha That Luang (p313) and Wat Si Muang.

Sleeping

The old days of shadowy flophouses are out the window. Up have gone the prices but with them an improvement in taste and what you can expect for your money.

TOP CHOICE **Lao Heritage Hotel** GUESTHOUSE $$

(Map p318; ☎265093; Th Phnom Penh; s/d US$20/25; ❄@📶) This stunning midranger is a cut above the rest thanks to its lovely outside terraced gardens and tasteful rooms with boutique flourishes: white walls, stained-wood floors and cable TV. Rooms 1 and 2 were our favourites.

Syri 1 Guesthouse GUESTHOUSE $

(Map p318; ☎212682; Th Saigon; r 70,000-150,000K; ❄) This backpackers' favourite

Central Vientiane

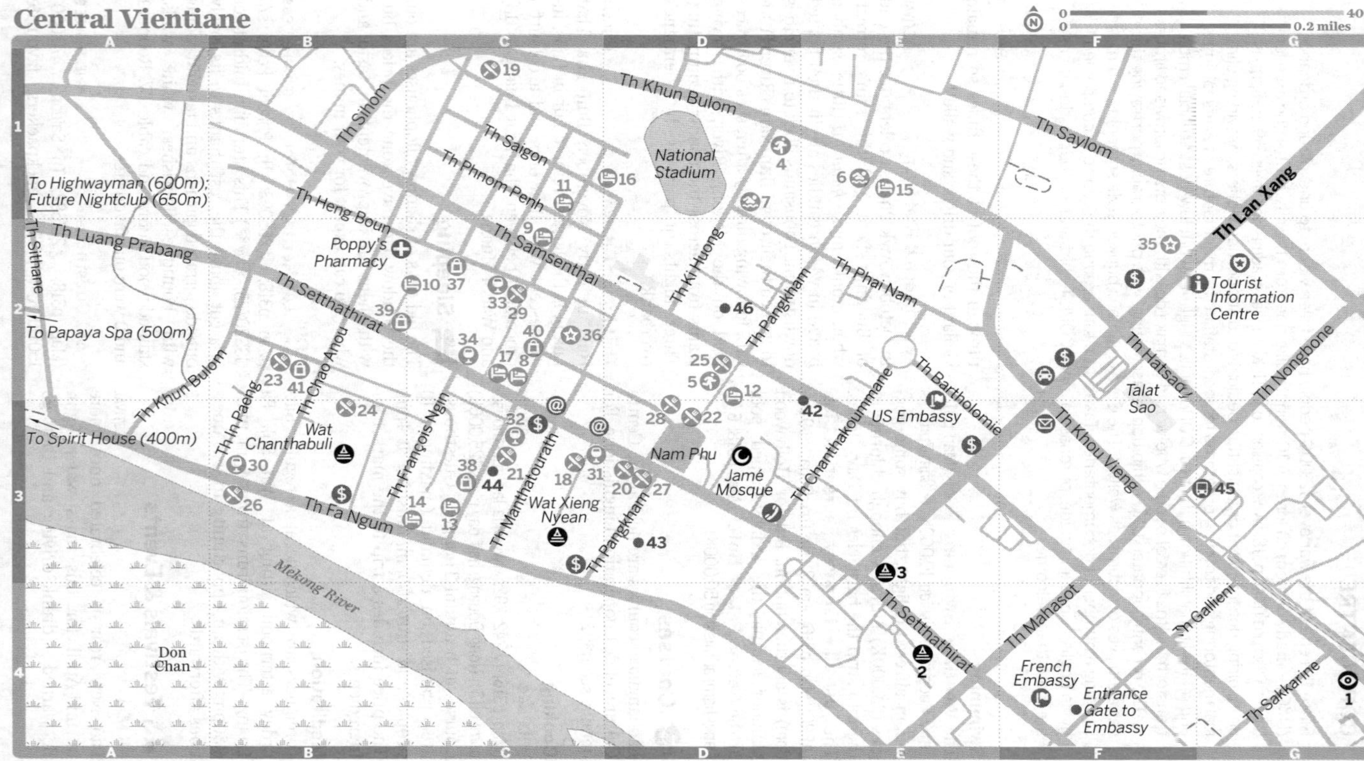

Central Vientiane

Sights

1	COPE Centre	G4
2	Haw Pha Kaew	E4
3	Wat Si Saket	E3

Activities, Courses & Tours

4	Lao Bowling Centre	D1
5	Mandarina Massage	D2
6	Settha Palace Hotel	E1
7	Vientiane Swimming Pool	D1

Sleeping

8	Chanta Guest House	C2
9	Dragon Lodge	C2
10	Lani Guest House	C2
11	Lao Heritage Hotel	C1
12	Mali Namphu Guest House	D2
13	Mixay Guest House	C3
14	Orchid Guesthouse	C3
15	Soukxana Guest House	E1
16	Syri 1 Guest House	D1
17	Vayakorn House	C2

Eating

18	Amphone	C3
19	Ban Anou Night Market	C1
20	JoMa Bakery Café	D3
21	Le Banneton	C3
22	Le Provencal	D3
23	Le Vendôme	B2
24	Makphet	B3
25	Nam Phu Café	D2
26	Open-air Riverside Food Vendors	B3
27	PhimPhone Market	D3
28	Scandinavian Bakery	D3
29	YuLaLa	C2

Drinking

30	Bor Pennyang	B3
31	Jazzy Brick	C3
32	Martini Bar	C3
33	Noy's Fruit Heaven	C2
34	Samlo Pub	C2

Entertainment

35	Centre Culturel et de Coopération Linguistique	F2
36	Lao Traditional Show	C2

Shopping

37	Book Café	C2
38	Camacrafts	C3
39	Indochina's Handicrafts	B2
40	Monument Books	C2
41	T'Shop Lai Gallery	B2

Transport

42	Europcar	E3
43	Lao Airlines	D3
44	PVO	C3
45	Talat Sao Bus Station	G3
	Thai-Lao International Bus	(see 45)
46	Vietnam Airlines	D2

is a great place to meet other travellers. Generously sized rooms and bikes for rent. The owner, Air, can take you on a tailored bike tour of the city.

Lani Guesthouse GUESTHOUSE $$
(Map p318; ☎214919; www.laniguesthouse.com; Th Setthathirat; r US$33-38; ❄) Located down a quiet street, Lani Guesthouse's Art Deco building has traditional rooms boasting handicrafts, mozzie nets and bamboo-framed beds. Atmospheric lobby crammed with stuffed animals.

Mixay Guest House GUESTHOUSE $
(Map p318; ☎262210; 39 Th Nokeo Khumman; dm 50,000K, s/d without bathroom 70,000/85,000K, r with air-con 110,000K; ❄) Great value, fan-cooled rooms. Some have hot-water bathrooms, while others are bereft of windows. Also has a left-luggage facility.

Vayakorn House HOTEL $$
(Map p318; ☎241911; 91 Th Nokeo Khumman; s/d/tr 140,000/220,000/280,000K; ❄📶) Long a stalwart for no-nonsense comfort, popular Vayakorn has 21 rooms with fresh linen, private bathrooms, TV and air-con. Accepts credit cards.

Mali Namphu Guest House GUESTHOUSE $$
(Map p318; ☎215093; 114 Th Pangkham; r incl breakfast 170,000-250,000K; ❄📶) A lush courtyard forms the centrepiece to this lovely midranger with fragrant rooms decked in Lao handicrafts, and enjoying impeccably clean bathrooms. There's also cable TV.

Orchid Guesthouse HOTEL $$
(Map p318; ☎252825; Th Fa Ngum; r 90,000-160,000K; ❄@) Teetering into the sky like some lantern-festooned Jenga tower, Chinese-owned Orchid is short on charm but its maze of rooms – many windowless –

boast private bathrooms and a great sundown terrace overlooking the Mekong.

Chantha Guest House GUESTHOUSE $

(Map p318; ☎243204; Th Setthathirat; standard/deluxe 75,000/120,000K; ❄) Its eight rooms are boxy but clean. Ask for one overlooking the street. There's also a Japanese restaurant next door.

Soukxana Guesthouse GUESTHOUSE $$

(Map p318; ☎264114; soukxana_guest_house@yahoo.com; 13 Th Pangkham; r 100,000-150,000K; ❄) Opposite Settha Palace, rooms here are houseproud even if the walls are a little tired. The staff are friendly, and there's a free computer and coffee-making facilities. Prices depend on the number of people in the room and whether it's air-con or overhead fan.

Dragon Lodge GUESTHOUSE $$

(Map p318; ☎250112; dragonlodge2002@yahoo.com; Th Samsenthai; r 130,000-180,000K; ❄) Contemporary-looking Dragon has terracotta-coloured walls, a swish bar and restaurant festooned in lanterns, and small but welcoming rooms. Check out its useful noticeboard.

Eating

Eat your way round a global route from Japan to France – with just about everything in between – in a vast selection of affordable, classy restaurants as well as informal cafes, juice bars and delicious roadside vendors.

TOP CHOICE **Makphet** LAO $

(Map p318; Th Setthathirat; mains 40,000K; ⏲11am-9pm Mon, Wed, Thu, Fri & Sat, 6-9pm Tue) Makphet helps disadvantaged kids build a future as chefs and waiters, while reviving the country's traditional cuisine. Guacamole-green walls and hardwood furnishings add style to delicious dishes like *tąm màak hung* (spicy green papaya salad). Note that this restaurant isn't actually on Th Setthathirat but two streets behind it on a small alley behind a temple.

YuLaLa JAPANESE $

(Map p318; Th Heng Boun; meals 40,000K; ⏲11.30am-2pm & 6-9pm Tue-Sun; ❄) Cosy interior with hardwood floors and scatter cushions, the menu features veggie delights such as 'Fried tofu dumpling with radish sauce', accompanied by jazz music.

Le Provencal FRENCH $

(Map p318; Nam Phu; mains 40,000K; ⏲lunch Mon-Sat, dinner daily; ❄) This seasoned trusty has an old-world ambience with its shadowy, wooden interior. The menu excels with wood-fired pizzas and succulent steaks.

Amphone LAO $$

(Map p318; 10/3 Th Wat Xieng Nyean; mains 20,000-65,000K; ⏲11am-2pm & 5.30-10pm; ❄) Amphone replicates traditional Lao dishes based on owner, Mook's grandmother's creations. 'Luang Prabang sausage' and 'fish citronella' are but a few.

La Vendôme FRENCH $$

(Map p318; 39 Th In Paeng; mains 75,000K; ⏲5-10pm Tue-Sun) Hidden behind a cascade of ivy, it's almost as if this vintage restaurant is in hiding. Candlelit ambience accompanies very reasonably priced soufflés, pâtés, salads and wood-fired pizzas, plus a good wine selection.

JoMa Bakery Café BAKERY $

(Map p318; Th Setthathirat; mains 28,000K; ⏲7am-9pm Mon-Sat; ❄📶) Vientiane's busiest bakery is thick with the tang of Arabica and its comfy couches, free wi-fi, American breakfasts, cinnamon buns, bagels and bespoke subs will keep you coming back for more.

Le Banneton BAKERY $

(Map p318; Th Nokeo Khumman; breakfast 45,000K; ⏲7am-9pm; ❄) Creating the city's best croissants, Banneton's Doisneau-spattered interior makes a nice place to read a paper over a tart, salad, panini or tasty omelette.

Scandinavian Bakery BAKERY $

(Map p318; Nam Phu; mains 10,000-30,000K; ⏲7am-7pm; ❄) Having had more facelifts than a Hollywood starlet, Vientiane's oldest bakery has an expanded upstairs lounge with BBC News and an alfresco balcony. Its pastries, donuts, éclairs, gateaux, sandwiches and brownies are life affirming.

Phimphone Market SELF-CATERING $

(Map p318; 94/6 Th Setthathirat; mains 10,000-30,000K; ⏲7am-9pm Mon-Sat; 📶) Self-catering oasis stocking everything from Western magazines to ice cream; salami, bread, biscuits and chocolate, as well as Western toiletries. Don't miss its cafe serving great coffees, juices and tasty baguette sandwiches.

Nam Phu Café LAO $

(Map p318; Th Pangkham; mains 20,000K; ⏲11am-10pm) Hidden next to a tailor's on the corner of Th Pangkham and Th Samsenthai, this local favourite has been creating tasty Lao grub for years. Try the 'Drunken Fish'.

GETTING TO THAILAND: VIENTIANE TO NONG KHAI

Getting to the border The Thai–Lao Friendship Bridge is 22km southeast of Vientiane. The easiest way to cross is on the comfortable Thai–Lao International bus (100,000k, 90 minutes), which leaves Vientiane's Talat Sao bus station roughly every two hours from 7.30am till 6pm. Alternatively catch a taxi (500B) or jumbo (four-wheeled túk-túk, seating 12; 200B), or public bus 14 from Talat Sao (15,000K) between 6am and 5.30pm.

At the border If entering Laos you'll need to obtain a 30-day visa, available on arrival at the Lao border post (open 6am to 10pm), US$30–42, depending on your nationality. Bring some photo ID and extra cash (approx US$5) for administrative costs charged on weekends and holidays. If you're entering Laos don't accept the offer of help from a túk-túk driver to get your visa, it's quicker to do it yourself. If entering Thailand you'll be given a free 15-day visa.

Moving on From the Thai border catch a túk-túk (20B) to Nong Khai train station where a sleeper train leaves for Bangkok at 6.30pm (fan/air-con 490B/1220B). For information on crossing this border in the other direction see p724.

Ban Anou Night Market LAO $
(Map p318; meals 10,000-15,000K; ⏲5-10pm) Setting up on a small street off the north end of Th Chao Anou every evening, this atmospheric open-air market dishes up Lao cuisine from grilled meats to chilli-based dips with vegetables and sticky rice.

Open-Air Riverside Food Vendors STREET FOOD $
(Map p318; Th Fa Ngum; meals 10,000-30,000K; ⏲5-11pm) Numerous stands serve up fresh Lao- and Chinese-influenced dishes and fresh grilled fish and seafood.

Drinking

The river plays host to a parade of American-style bars. For more chic refinement comb the backstreets radiating from Th Setthathirat.

Noy's Fruit Heaven JUICE BAR
(Map p318; Th Heng Boun; fruit shakes 7000K; ⏲7am-9pm) This juice bar-cum-snack cafe turns out mouth-watering salads, and Noy's vitamin-bursting shakes are a great antidote to Beerlao headaches.

Spirit House COCKTAIL BAR
(Map p316; Th Fa Ngum; ⏲7am-11pm) This sensual riverside bar pipes chillsome tunes to complement the dark woods and comfy couches. Even Richard Burton would be excited by its expansive drinks menu.

Sala Sunset Khounta BAR
(Map p316; Th Fa Ngum; ⏲11am-11pm) Shipwrecked against the banks of the Mekong, this serene sunset institution is in danger of closure due to riverfront redevelopment. Beerlao in hand, sit back and watch the sky turn a burnt peach.

Bor Pennyang BAR
(Map p318; Th Fa Ngum; ⏲10am-midnight) A friendly cast of locals, expats, bar girls and travellers. The setting is a rooftop bar overlooking the river with pool tables, pumping cheesy rock, cheap beer and sports on TV.

Martini Bar BAR
(Map p318; Th Nokeo Khumman; ⏲7pm-late) This sleek watering hole has myriad cocktails, ochre walls and a vibe as chilled as the resident fish tank. Indie films shown at 8pm Monday to Wednesday in the lounge upstairs.

Samlo Pub BAR
(Map p318; Th Setthathirat; ⏲7pm-late) A seasoned haunt with a roguish cast of hookers, lady-boys and shady expats patronising the darkness. Duck in for a beer but don't hang around!

Jazzy Brick BAR
(Map p318; Th Setthathirat; ⏲7pm-late) Stylish, low-lit, exposed brick interior adorned with old jazz posters. Great mojitos and Bloody Marys – if a little pricey – and occasional live music, typically Latin and Bossa Nova.

Entertainment

By law entertainment venues close at 11.30pm, though a number of places push the envelope. Vientiane has movies, cultural shows, a circus, Lao boxing and a clutch of nightclubs to keep you busy, as well as music concerts. Conveniently, two of Vientiane's better nightclubs – **Future Nightclub** (Map p316; Th Luang Prabang;

⊙8pm-1am) and **Highwayman** (Map p316; Th Luang Prabang; ⊙8pm-midnight) are near each other on the airport road. Expect a lot of noise and a very up-for-it Lao crowd.

Lao Traditional Show LIVE MUSIC
(Map p318; Th Manthatulat; admission US$7) Traditional music and dancing performed by the Laos National Theatre is aimed directly at tourists, and plays Monday to Saturday at 5.30pm.

Centre Culturel et de Coopération Linguistique CINEMA
(French Cultural Centre; Map p318; www.ambafrance-laos.org/centre; Th Lan Xang; ⊙9.30am-6.30pm Mon-Fri, to noon Sat) Dance, art exhibitions, literary discussions and live music in this Gallic hive of cultural activity. As well as cult French films (shown 7.30pm Tuesday, Thursday and Saturday; 10,000K), the centre also offers French and Lao lessons.

Lunar 36 CLUB
(Map p316; Don Chan Palace Hotel; ⊙6pm-3am Wed, Fri & Sat) Lunar 36, off Th Fa Ngum, is Vientiane's official late-night altar to hedonism, with a decent disco, outside veranda and cosmo cast of working ladies and expats.

Shopping

Numerous handicraft and souvenir boutiques are dotted around streets radiating from Nam Phu, particularly Th Pangkham and Th Setthathirat.

TOP CHOICE **T'Shop Lai Gallery** BEAUTY, HOMEWARES
(Map p318; www.laococo.com/tshoplai.htm; off Th In Paeng; ⊙8am-8pm Mon-Sat, 10am-6pm Sun) Exquisite furniture recycled from eggshell, coconut, bamboo and rattan. Check out its divine soaps and aromatic oils, all made from locally sourced materials, while enjoying a coffee in the gallery's beautiful surroundings.

Camacrafts HANDICRAFTS
(Map p318; www.camacrafts.org; Th Nokeo Khumman; ⊙10am-6pm Mon-Sat) Nonprofit Camacrafts markets handicrafts created by Hmong women using traditional skills, with a range of silk pashminas, quilts and wall hangings. Your purchase goes directly to help the artisans' families.

Indochina's Handicrafts HANDICRAFTS
(Map p318; Th Setthathirat; ⊙9am-8pm) This cave of a place would have kept Aladdin quiet with its antique Russian watches, waxed gold and wooden Buddhas, opium pipes, Hmong earrings and bracelets. Upstairs there's a bijou cafe.

Book Café BOOKS
(☎020 689 3741; Th Heng Boun; ⊙8am-8pm Mon-Fri) Good range of thrillers and general fiction, plus works by Lao-based authors.

Monument Books BOOKS
(☎243708; 124 Th Nokeo Khumman; ⊙9am-8pm Mon-Fri, to 6pm Sat & Sun) Glossy travel pictorials, thrillers and magazines.

Information

Emergency

Ambulance (☎195)

Fire (☎190)

Police (☎191)

Tourist Police (Map p318; ☎251128; Th Lan Xang)

Internet Access

There are several internet cafes on Th Samsenthai and Th Setthathirat. Rates are around 7000K per hour, with a decent broadband speed. Most have international telephone facilities.

Apollo Net (Map p318; Th Setthathirat; ⊙8.30am-11pm) Broadband (6000K per hour) and telephone kiosk (3000K per minute for calls to Australia, the UK and US).

True Coffee Internet (Map p318; Th Setthathirat; ⊙9am-9pm) This swish, cool cafe makes writing home a pleasure. Enjoy a posh latte or delicious home-made yoghurt as you Skype, email (8000K per hour) or use its wi-fi outside on your laptop (10,000K per hour).

Media

Your only option for local news and upcoming events is state-censored *Vientiane Times*. *Bangkok Post*, the *Economist*, *Newsweek* and *Time* can also be found in minimarts.

Medical Services

Vientiane's medical facilities will do for broken bones and the diagnosis of dengue fever and malaria, but for anything more serious we strongly recommend you cross to Thailand for the **Aek Udon International Hospital** (☎0066-4234 2555; www.aekudon.com; Posri Rd, Amphur Muang, Udon Thani Province), which can dispatch an ambulance, or in critical situations an airlift, to take you to Udon Thani. The Friendship Bridge is closed between 10pm and 6am, but Thai/Lao immigration will open for ambulances.

In Vientiane try the following:

Australian Embassy Clinic (Map p316; ☎353840; ⊙8.30am-5pm Mon-Fri) For nationals of Australia, Britain, Canada, Papua New Guinea and New Zealand only. This clinic's Australian doctor treats minor problems by appointment; it doesn't have emergency facilities. Accepts cash or credit cards.

International Clinic (Map p316; ☎214021/2; Th Fa Ngum; ⊙24hr) Part of the Mahasot Hospital; probably the best place for not-too-complex emergencies. Some English-speaking doctors. Take ID and cash.

Poppy's Pharmacy (Map p318; ☎030-981 0108;Th Heng Boun ⊙8am-9pm) Fully stocked apothecary with English-speaking staff, selling malaria pills, diarrhoea and headache pills, as well as Western-brand toiletries.

Money

There are plenty of ATMs, especially along Th Setthathirat. Several banks change cash and travellers cheques and will do cash advances against credit cards for a commission. The unofficial moneychangers near Talat Sao have good rates and keep longish hours.

Banque pour le Commerce Extérieur Lao (BCL; Map p318; cnr Th Pangkham & Th Fa Ngum; ⊙8.30am-7pm Mon-Fri, to 3pm Sat & Sun) Best rates; longest hours. Exchange booth on Th Fa Ngum and three ATMs attached to the main building.

Joint Development Bank (Map p318; 75/1-5 Th Lan Xang) Usually charges the lowest commission on cash advances. Also has an ATM.

Lao Development Bank (Map p318; Th Setthathirat;⊙8.30-11.30am & 2-4pm Mon-Fri)

Siam Commercial Bank (Map p318; 117 Th Lan Xang) ATM and cash advances on Visa.

Post

Post, Telephone & Telegraph (PTT; Map p318; cnr Th Lan Xang & Th Khu Vieng; ⊙8am-noon & 1-5pm Mon-Fri, 8am-noon Sat) Stamps, poste restante and (slow) internet services available.

Telephone

Lao Telecom Numphu Centre (Map p318; Th Setthathirat; ⊙9am-7pm) International fax, and domestic and international calls. For cheaper local calls have your mobile unlocked and buy a pay-as-you-go SIM card. Tigo and M-Phone top-up cards are widely available.

Tourist Information

Tourist Information Centre (NTAL; Map p318; www.ecotourismlaos.com; Th Lan Xang; ⊙8.30am-noon & 1.30-4pm) With bags of informative visual displays detailing provincial attractions, there are helpful English-speaking staff, brochures and regional maps. Staff can arrange trips to Phu Khao Khuay NPA for no charge.

FIND A FRIEND

Activities with companies like Green Discovery become vastly cheaper when there are larger numbers in your group.

Travel Agencies

A-Rasa Tours (☎213633; Th Francois Ngin; ⊙8.30am-5pm Mon-Fri, 8.30am-noon Sat) Run by Mrs Inthavong, dependable A-Rasa organises tours to Phongsali, books international and domestic plane tickets and sleeper trains to Bangkok.

Green Discovery (☎218373; www.greendiscoverylaos.com; Th Setthathirat) Offers three-day motorbike trips on the Ho Chi Minh Trail (two-person group US$330 per person), as well as kayaking, trekking and zip-lining two-day packages staying in a jungle campsite by the Nam Lik River (three-person group US$167 per person). One-day's zip-lining there costs US$100 per person for a group of two people.

Lasi Ticketing (☎222851; www.lasiglobal.com; Th Francois Ngin; ⊙8.30am-5pm Mon-Fri, 8.30am-noon Sat) Helpful, English-speaking staff, Lasi sells air, VIP bus and train tickets.

Getting There & Away

Air

Wattay International Airport is the main transport hub for the rest of the country (for more details and info on international flights, see p377). Beside it is the rickety Domestic Terminal. The following airlines offer domestic flights:

Lao Airlines (Map p318; ☎212051; www.laoairlines.com; Th Pangkham, Vientiane; ⊙8am-noon & 1-4pm Mon-Sat, till noon Sun) Also based at Wattay International Airport, has daily flights to Luang Prabang (US$87) and Pakse (US$131). Offers five flights per week to Phonsovan (US$87), and three flights per week to Udomxai, Huay Xai, Savannakhet and Luang Namtha (US$112).

Lao Capricorn Air (☎513009; www.lao.capricornair.net; Wattay International Airport, Domestic Terminal; ⊙8am-5pm) Operates twice-weekly flights to Sam Neua (US$105) and once weekly to Phongsali and Sainyabuli (US$80).

Boat

Rare, no-frills cargo boats head upstream to Luang Prabang (taking four days to one week) from Kiaw Liaw Pier (off Map p316), 3.5km west of the fork in the road where Rte 13 heads north in Ban Kao Liaw. During the dry season (November to April) it's out of the question.

Bus & Sŏrngtăaou

Buses use three different stations in Vientiane.

Northern bus station (Map p316; ☎260255; Th Asiane) About 2km northwest of the city centre, serves all points north of Vang Vieng, including China, and has some buses to Vietnam.

Southern bus station (off Map p316; ☎740521; Rte 13 South) Commonly known as Dong Dok bus station or just *khíw lot lák kâo* (Km 9 bus station), it's 9km from the city centre and serves everywhere south. Buses to Vietnam stop here.

Talat Sao bus station (Map p318; ☎216507) International VIP buses to Thailand's Udon Thani (100,000K) leave here at 10.30am and 11.30am. A VIP bus for Bangkok also leaves from here; see the table below.

For buses to China, contact **Tong Li Bus Company** (☎242657) at the Northern Bus Station. For Vietnam, **SDT** (☎720175) has buses leaving daily from the Southern Bus Station: Hanoi (US$25, 24 hours, 6pm), via Vinh (US$30, 16 hours), Hué (US$23, 19 hours, midnight), Danang (US$25, 19 hours, 6pm) and Ho Chi Minh City (US$60, up to 48 hours, 8am).

Getting Around

Central Vientiane is all accessible on foot.

To/From the Airport

Wattay International Airport is about 4km northwest of the city centre. Taxis cost 50,000K into town. Alternatively, walk 500m to the airport gate where you can get a túk-túk for about 30,000K.

Bicycle, Motorcycle & Car

Bicycles can be rented for 8000K per day from tour agencies and guesthouses. Scooters are a great way to get about town, but remember to keep your helmet on.

PVO (Map p318; ☎254354; Th Nokeo Khumman; ⏲8am-6pm Mon-Sat) Rents scooters (70,000K per day) or Honda Baja motorcross (250,000K per day) on a flexible 24-hour basis. It's also possible to drop the bike off in Pakse for an extra 400,000K – perfect if you're head-

BUS SERVICES FROM VIENTIANE

Talat Sao Bus Station

DESTINATION	COST (K)	DURATION (HR)	DISTANCE (KM)
Vang Vieng	40,000	4	153
Nong Khai	15,000	1½	95
Udon Thani	22,000	2	76

Northern Bus Station

DESTINATION	COST (K)	DURATION (HR)	DISTANCE (KM)
Huay Xai	210,000	30-35	869
Kunming	610,000	30	781
Luang Nam Tha	180,000	18	676
Luang Prabang	110,000	11	384
Udomxai	130,000-150,000	13-15	578
Phonsavan	110,000-130,000	9-11	374
Sam Neua	170,000-190,000	15-17	612

Southern Bus Station

DESTINATION	COST (K)	DURATION (HR)	DISTANCE (KM)
Attapeu	140,000	22-24	812
Lak Sao	35,000	7-9	334
Pakse	110,000	14-16	677
Savannakhet	75,000	8-11	457
Tha Khaek	40,000	7	332

MINDFUL TRAVELLER

Reefer on tap, thumping house music, painted ravers in bikinis – sounds like every young man's fantasy. Except this is Laos, where for centuries people have covered their bodies out of religious observation. And the drugs and pounding beat are a new phenomenon too. Get caught with a joint and it's a US$600 fine and your passport is confiscated until the payment is made. Get sprung with crystal meth and you're talking US$1500, while the dealer who sold it you will be taken away and shot. Plainclothes cops are everywhere, so be conscious of the law and be considerate.

ing to Cambodia – freeing you up from sweaty, cramped buses.

Túk-Túk

Many túk-túk have a laminated list of vastly inflated tourist prices, and won't budge for less than the price already agreed upon with the other drivers (starting at 15,000K). You can also flag down shared, fixed-route túk-túk (with passengers already in them), which cost 2000K to 5000K, depending on your destination.

NORTHERN LAOS

Whether you're here to trek, ride an elephant, zip-line, kayak, cycle or try a homestay, a visit to the mountainous north is unforgettable. Hemmed in by China to the far north, Vietnam to the east and Myanmar (Burma) to the west, there's a fascinating cast of ethnic peoples here. Hidden amid this rugged simplicity is Southeast Asia's premier Shangri La, Luang Prabang and beyond it unfettered, dense forests still home to a cornucopia of animals. East of here, rugged Xieng Khuang province holds the mysterious Plain of Jars and is still cratered by the heavy US bombing from the American Vietnam War (1964–73), while distant Hua Phan Province in the northeast is home to gothic karst scenery, serene mountains and the caves of Viengxai.

Vang Vieng

☎023 / POP 30,000

With its hedonistic lads' mag atmosphere running amok in a riverine landscape of black karsts and sleepy ricefields, Vang Vieng is a bizarre contradiction. For many this is an example of what happens when Laos tries too hard to please foreigners, and there's a palpable sense of loss for its old bucolic way of life.

There are two camps in town: the outdoor, tranquillity-seeking crowd that heads to guesthouses downstream of the Nam Ou, and the younger hedonists flouting Lao modesty and burning the midnight oil on Don Khang (aka 'Party Island'). If you want to come here and just tune out in video bars and take the 'rites of passage' tube down the river, that's fine, but don't miss the excellent climbing, kayaking, caving, cycling and hot air ballooning. And should you partake of the odd joint, keep your third eye active for plainclothes cops (see the boxed text).

Dangers & Annoyances

The Nam Song is lethal when it runs high after the wet season. And while it might be *de rigueur* here to imbibe, pot and beer combined make for a purple haze that will find you flailing for your life if you flip and the current takes you. Never hire a tube on your own, nor attempt to return after dark.

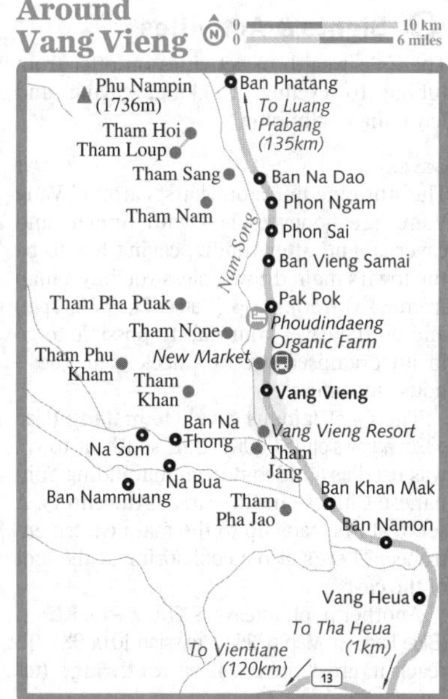

Vang Vieng

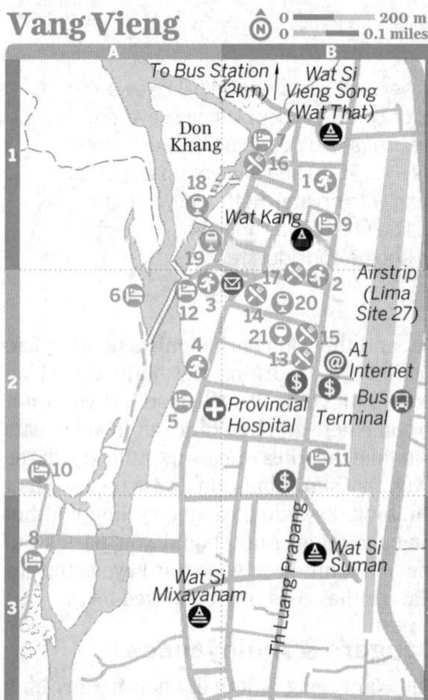

Vang Vieng

Activities, Courses & Tours

1 Adam's Rock Climbing School............B1
2 Green Discovery............B2
3 Tubing Operators............A2
4 V.L.T. Natural Tours............A2

Sleeping

5 Ban Sabai Bungalows............A2
6 Banana Bungalows............A2
7 Champa Lao............B1
8 Chez Mango............A3
9 Chillao Hostel............B1
10 Maylyn Guest House............A2
11 Pan's Place............B2
12 Phoubane Guesthouse............A2

Eating

13 Babylon Restaurant............B2
14 Nokeo............B2
15 Organic Mulberry Farm Cafe............B2
16 Phad Thai Restaurant............B1
17 Restaurant Luang Prabang Bakery............B2

Drinking

18 Bucket Bar............A1
19 Jaidee's............A1
20 Rising Sun............B2
21 Sakura............B2
Smile Bar............(see 18)

There's been a series of burglaries in a couple of budget guesthouses, which seemingly implicate the staff. Stash your valuables carefully and be subtle when airing your Western gadgetry.

Sights & Activities

There's a wealth of activities on offer from tubing to cycling, trekking, caving and kayaking to climbing.

Caves CAVE

The stunning limestone karsts around Vang Vieng are honeycombed with tunnels and caverns, and after tubing, caving has to be the town's main draw. Unless you buy a map from **BKC bookshop** (Market St; 7am-7pm) and do the caves yourself, it's possible to go in an organised group. Check your guesthouse for info.

The most famous cave, **Tham Jang** (Map p325; admission 15,000K), 1km south of town, was used as a hideout from marauding Yunnanese Chinese in the early 19th century. A set of stairs leads up to the main cavern entrance. There's also a cool spring at the foot of the cave.

Another popular cave is **Tham Phu Kham** (Blue Lagoon; Map p325; admission 10,000K). To reach it, cross the **bamboo footbridge** (toll walking/cycling 4000/6000K), then walk or pedal 7km along a scenic, unsealed road to Ban Na Thong, from where you have to walk 1km to a hill on the northern side of the village. It's a tough final 200m climb but worth it for a dip in the blue stream afterwards.

Tham Sang (Map p325; admission 5000K), 13km north along Rte 13, is a small cavern containing a few Buddha images and a Buddha 'footprint', plus the elephant-shaped stalactite that gives the cave its name.

Kayaking KAYAKING

Kayaking is popular, with day trips (100,000K per person) typically taking you down a few rapids and stopping at caves and villages. Before using an operator, check guides' credentials and that they issue life jackets and have medical kits.

Tubing ADVENTURE TOUR

Hire an inner tube from the operators by the old market (50,000K rental, 20,000K deposit, US$7 fine if not returned on time) who will take you 3km upriver and leave you to drift

TREAT YOURSELF

Best enjoyed first thing in the morning, hot air ballooning is the perfect way to take in the jaw-dropping scenery. Flights with **Travel With Your Eyes** (☎020 9691 82222) take place at 6.30am, 7.30am & 4pm (admission US$70) and last approximately 40 minutes. Call to book a flight.

back in your own time. Stop for a dance and refreshment at the many riverside bars en route. Be warned though, the 10m-high zip-lines over the river are dangerous in the dry season; one *falang* (foreigner) recently broke his neck landing in perilously shallow water.

Tours

Adam's Rock Climbing School ADVENTURE TOUR
(Map p326; ☎020 5501 0832; www.laos-climbing.com; Th Luang Prabang) The only dedicated climbing outfit in town, with experienced guides and sturdy kit.

Green Discovery ADVENTURE TOUR
(Map p326; ☎511230; www.greendiscoverylaos.com; Th Luang Prabang; ⏲7am-7pm) Runs half-day climbing courses on moderate to easy climbs as well as offering caving and trekking. All climbs for a half/full day cost US$16/22. It also runs half-day kayaking excursions for as little as US$24 per person if there are at least four of you.

VLT Natural Tours ADVENTURE TOUR
(Map p326; ☎511369; www.vangviengtour.com) Charges US$18 for kayaking trips and has good kit.

Sleeping

At the last count there were 120 guesthouses in Vang Vieng! Avoid the ugly town and head downriver. Super-cheap digs are found on Party Island.

Chez Mango GUESTHOUSE $
(Map p326; ☎020 7758 9733; r 40,000-60,000K; ❄) Located over the bridge, Mango is new, scrupulously clean and has seven colourful cabanas (some with private bathroom) in its flowery gardens. Head to the market with owner Mango to choose the ingredients for the Lao dinner she can teach you to make, or play *boules* with her French husband, Noah.

Maylyn Guest House GUESTHOUSE $
(Map p326; ☎020 560 4095; jophus _foley@hotmail.com; r 50,000-80,000K; ❄) Over the bridge, Maylyn is a stalwart of peace with cabana huts set in gardens bursting with butterflies and lantana flowers, affording possibly the most dramatic view of the karsts. There's a new building with immaculate rooms with private bathroom, plus a natty little café.

Ban Sabai Bungalows GUESTHOUSE $$$
(Map p326; Xayoh Riverside Bungalows; ☎511088; r US$34-58; ❄) Next to Elephant Crossing, Sabai has 13 rustically finished bungalow rooms with exposed brick walls and elevated verandas, from where you can take in the panorama of the river. Great looking elevated bar and restaurant terrace for sundowners.

Champa Lao GUESTHOUSE $
(Map p326; ☎020 501 8501; www.thelongwander.com; r 40,000-100,000K; 📶) Champa has an ambient-lit garden restaurant casting off heavenly aromas, and comfortable rooms in the main building or in bungalows down the bank by the river. Fan-only rooms with or without private bathroom.

Pan's Place GUESTHOUSE $
(Map p326; ☎511484; neilenolix@hotmail.com; Th Luang Prabang; r 60,000-90,000K) Basic rooms with private bathroom, plus cosy bungalows out the back with shared bathroom. There's an internet cafe and a restaurant with a tasty Western-leaning menu, plus a TV room with a choice of 400 films.

Organic Mulberry Farm GUESTHOUSE $
(Map p325; ☎511220; www.laofarm.org; r 50,000-90,000K) Known locally as Phoudindaeng Mulberry Farm, this organic farm a few kilometres out of town has simple accommodation and a great restaurant – try the mulberry pancakes or mulberry mojitos! Sadly someone's selfishly built a rave bar nearby on the river, so bring earplugs.

Phoubane Guest House BUNGALOWS $
(Map p326; ☎511306; s/d/tr with fan 50,000/60,000/100,000K, deluxe with air-con 160,000-215,000K; ❄) Just west of the post office, Phoubane has cool, river-facing bungalows with tiled floors and clean bathrooms with hot water. Its original wooden bungalows are fan cooled, well maintained and a 10th of the price of the new ones.

Banana Bungalows BUNGALOWS $
(Map p326; r with bathroom & air-con 100,000K, with fan & shared bathroom 30,000K) Banana never sleeps and is at the heart of Party Island. Rooms, though weary as the hedonists who choose not to sleep in them, are functional and do the job.

Chillao Hostel HOSTEL $
(Map p326; Th Luang Prabang; s/d/dm 40,000/50,000/20,000K) You get what you pay for – namely very little – but staying here will stretch your kip a bit longer. There's a noisy Chinese restaurant next door, and rooms are fan-only with shared bathroom.

Eating

It's easy to forget you're in Laos given Vang Vieng's plethora of try-hard Western-style joints, but look around and you'll see there's a number of authentic Lao eateries.

TOP CHOICE **Organic Mulberry Farm Cafe** LAO $
(Map p326; meals 20,000-30,000K) Down the quieter, southern end of Th Luang Prabang, this is a real find for vegetarians and carnivores alike, with fresh produce directly from its farm a few kilometres away. Stir-fries, curries and seafood.

Nokeo LAO $
(Map p326; meals 8000-20,000K; ⏲8am-8pm) This authentic Lao eatery has almost been subsumed by the development around it, but if you're tiring of burgers and fries, try its delicious variations of *làap* (spicy salad of minced meat, poultry or vegetables).

Babylon Restaurant LAO $
(Map p326; Th Luang Prabang; meals 25,000K) With its cushioned lounging areas and rattan furnishing, Babylon feels like a slice of Ko Pha-Ngan. Salads, tofu, sandwiches and soups complement a laid-back atmosphere. And guess what, they don't screen *Friends*. Yippee!

Phad Thai Restaurant THAI $
(Map p326; Th Luang Prabang; meals 25,000K) Next to Nam Song Guesthouse, and strung with green lanterns and bags of atmosphere, this juicy little joint features the usual suspects of Thai cuisine and, when we passed, a very satisfied crowd.

Restaurant Luang Prabang Bakery BAKERY $
(Map p326; meals 7000-30,000K; ⏲breakfast, lunch & dinner) Hansel and Gretel sanctuary of fruit shakes, brownies, cakes, juicy subs and nightly films on demand. Munchies heaven!

Drinking

Choose between relaxed chilling bars and anything-goes haunts on Party Island, such as the Bucket Bar and Smile Bar, which don't close until 4am.

Jaidee's BAR
(Map p326; ⏲9am-1am) Hendrix would have dug this low-lit, riverside cave piping out '60s and '70s classics. Owner Jaidee is friendly and there's a nightly fire pit.

Sakura BAR
(Map p326; ⏲5-11.30pm) Sakura is still packed to the gills thanks to a plasma widescreen tuned to sports channels, an attractive bamboo interior and upbeat sounds.

Rising Sun BAR
(Map p326; ⏲5-noon) Another option – especially for homesick Brits – is this bar with its blokey atmosphere, Guinness, Britpop and pool table.

Information

Banque pour le Commerce Extérieur Lao (Map p326; ⏲8.30am-3.30pm Mon-Sun) Just west of Xayoh Café, does exchanges and cash advances and has a 24-hour ATM.

A1 Internet (per hr 6000K; ⏲8am-11pm) Internet access, CD burning, international internet phone calls. Organises onward visas.

Post office (Map p326; ⏲8.30am-3.30pm Mon-Fri) Beside the old market.

Provincial Hospital (Map p326; ☎511604) This flash new hospital has X-ray facilities and is fine for broken bones, cuts and malaria.

Getting There & Away

From the **bus station** (Map p325; Rte 13), 2km north of town, buses leave for Luang Prabang (85,000K, seven to 11 hours, 168km, several daily), Vientiane (35,000K, 3½ to 4½ hours, 156km, four times daily) and Phonsavan (85,000K, six to seven hours, 219km, daily at about 9am). For Vientiane, pick-ups (30,000K, 3½ to 4½ hours) leave every 20 minutes from 5am until 4pm.

Tickets for minibuses and VIP buses with air-con travelling direct to Vientiane (60,000K, three hours) or Luang Prabang (105,000K, six to eight hours) are sold at guesthouses, tour agencies and internet cafes in town. There is no VIP bus to Phonsavan.

DOS & DON'TS IN LAOS

» Always ask permission before taking photos.

» Don't prop your feet on chairs or tables while sitting.

» Never touch any part of someone else's body with your foot.

» Refrain from touching people on the head.

» Remove your shoes before entering homes or temple buildings.

Getting Around

The township is small enough to walk around with ease. Bicycles can be rented for around 10,000K a day. Motorcycles are sadly off-limits due to drunken accidents. A túk-túk up to the Organic Mulberry Farm or Tham Sang costs around 10,000K per person.

Luang Prabang

☎071 / POP 62,000

This glittering Shangri La of affordable top-class cuisine and colonial buildings is so achingly pretty it has you reaching for your camera at every turn. With its Unesco-protected peninsula of 33 Buddhist temples there are few places in Southeast Asia that lay claim to such a special mix of chic refinement and ancient charm.

The good news is there are still bags of great-value digs and the best things are still cheap, hiring a bike to explore, chilling by the riverbank with a sundowner, shopping in the night market and visiting the menthol-blue Kuang Si cascades; temple-hopping, ecotrekking, elephant riding, taking a cooking course – your choices are myriad.

Spas have really taken off and between lounging in cafes you can enjoy a full-body massage for a few dollars. The stamp of the French lives on as freshly baked croissants send out aromas from Gallic-style cafes, and old Indochinese mansions are reborn as boutique hotels.

Most of the tourist sights are in the Old Quarter on the peninsula bounded by the Mekong and Nam Khan Rivers. The majority of restaurants, accommodation, tour companies and internet cafes line and radiate from central Th Sisavangvong, while additional bars are to be found on Th Kingkitsarat.

Sights

Royal Palace Museum MUSEUM

(☎212470; Th Sisavangvong; admission US$2; ⊙8.30-10.30am & 2-4pm Wed-Mon, last entry 3.30pm) Known to locals as Haw Kham (Golden Hall), the Royal Palace Museum was constructed in 1904 for King Sisavangvong and his family. When the king died in 1959, his son, Savang Vattana, inherited the throne, but after the 1975 revolution the palace was converted into a museum.

Various royal religious objects are on display in the large entry hall; however, the museum's most prized artwork is the **Pha Bang**, the gold standing Buddha after which the city is named.

Take a look at the **Royal Palace Car Collection** in a new exhibition, including a Concours Lincoln Continental, dilapidated Citroën DS and an old wooden speedboat. Footwear can't be worn inside the museum, no photography is permitted and you must leave bags with the attendants. **Floating Buddha** (admission free; ⊙8-11.30am & 1.30-4pm Wed-Mon), a photographic study of Buddhist meditation, can currently be seen in an outbuilding in the royal palace grounds.

Wat Xieng Thong TEMPLE

(off Th Sakkarin; admission 20,000K; ⊙8am-5pm) Wat Xieng Thong is the jewel in the crown of Luang Prabang's temples. Built by King Setthathirat in 1560, it remained under royal patronage until 1975. The *sĭm* (chapel) represents classic Luang Prabang temple architecture, with roofs sweeping low to the ground. The rear wall features an impressive tree-of-life mosaic, and inside, richly decorated wooden columns support a ceiling that's vested with *dhammacakka* (dharma wheels). Near the compound's eastern gate stands the royal funeral chapel; inside is an impressive 12m-high funeral chariot. The exterior of the chapel features gilt panels depicting erotic episodes from the Ramayana.

Wat Wisunarat TEMPLE

(Wat Visoun; Th Wisunarat; admission 20,000K; ⊙8am-5pm) The oldest continually operating temple in Luang Prabang (constructed in 1513), Wat Wisunarat was burnt down by marauding Haw Chinese in 1887 then rebuilt in 1898. Inside the high-ceilinged *sĭm* is a collection of wooden Calling for Rain Buddhas and 15th- to 16th-century Luang Prabang *sima* (ordination stones). In front of the *sĭm* is **That Pathum** (Lotus Stupa), which was built in 1514.

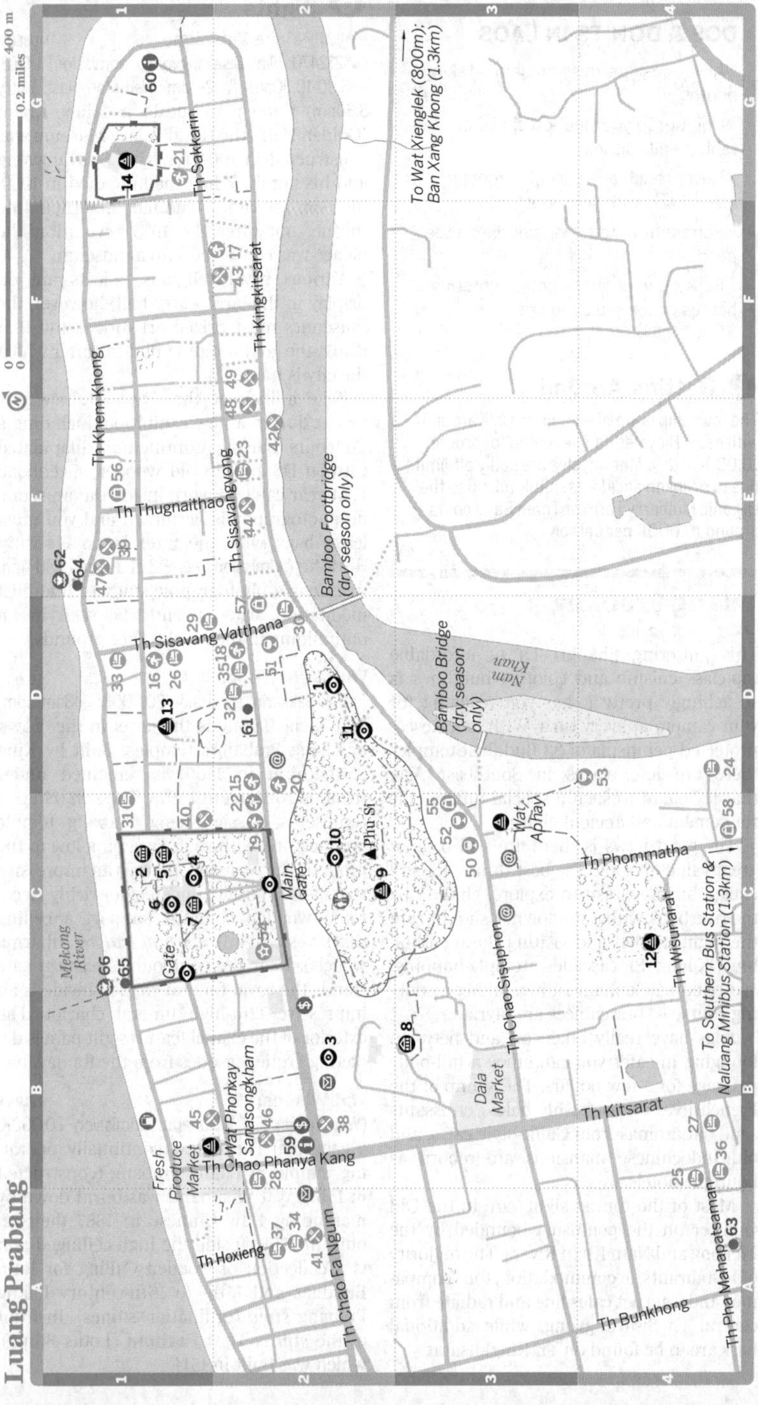

Luang Prabang

0 400 m
0 0.2 miles
Mekong River
Fresh Produce Market
Wat Phonxay Sanasongkham
Th Hoxieng
Th Chao Phanya Kang
Th Chao Fa Ngum
Gate
Main Gate
Phu Si
Th Khem Khong
Th Sisavang Vatthana
Th Thugnaithao
Th Sisavangvong
Th Kingkitsarat
Th Sakkarin
Bamboo Footbridge (dry season only)
Bamboo Bridge (dry season only)
Nam Khan
To Wat Xienglek (800m); Ban Xang Khong (1.3km)
Dala Market
Th Chao Sisuphon
Wat Aphay
Th Phommatha
Th Wisunarat
Th Kitsarat
Th Bunkhong
Th Pha Mahapatsaman
To Southern Bus Station & Naluang Minibus Station (1.3km)
1 2 3 4 5 6 7 8 9 10 11 12 13 14 15 16 17 18 19 20 21 22 23 24 25 26 27 28 29 30 31 32 33 34 35 36 37 38 39 40 41 42 43 44 45 46 47 48 49 50 51 52 53 54 55 56 57 58 59 60 61 62 63 64 65 66

Phu Si TEMPLE
(admission 20,000K; ⌚8am-6pm) One-hundred-metre-high Phu Si justifies the heady climb to its summit with its serene sunset views. **That Chomsi**, the temple at the summit, is backed by a small cave-shrine sometimes referred to as **Wat Tham Phu Si**. Around the northeast flank are the ruins of **Wat Pha Phutthabaht**, which was originally constructed in 1395 during the reign of Phaya Samsenthai on the site of a Buddha footprint.

Other Temples TEMPLE
In the Old Quarter, the ceiling of **Wat Xieng Muan** (⌚8am-5pm) is painted with gold *naga* (mythical serpent-being) and the elaborate *háang thien* (candle rail) has *naga* at either

Luang Prabang

Sights

1 Buddha Footprint ... D2
2 'Floating Buddha' Photographs ... C1
3 Handicraft Night Market ... B2
4 Pha Bang ... C1
5 Royal Palace Car Collection ... C1
6 Royal Palace Exhibition Halls ... C1
7 Royal Palace Museum ... C1
8 TAEC ... B3
9 That Chomsi ... C2
10 That Chomsi Ticket Booth ... C2
11 That Chomsi Ticket Booth ... D2
12 Wat Wisunarat ... C4
13 Wat Xieng Muan ... D1
14 Wat Xieng Thong ... G1

Activities, Courses & Tours

15 All Lao Service (Elephant Camp) ... D2
All Lao Travel ... (see 15)
16 Big Brother Mouse ... D1
17 Hibiscus ... F2
18 Lotus Du Lao Massage ... D2
Tamarind ... (see 49)
19 Tiger Trail ... C2
20 Treasure Travel ... D2
21 Tum Tum Cheng Cooking School ... G1
22 White Elephant ... C2

Sleeping

23 Chittana Guesthouse ... E2
24 Cold River Guest House ... D4
25 Jaliya Guest House ... B4
26 Kinnaly Guest House ... D1
27 Mano Guest House ... B4
28 Oudomphone Guest House 2 ... B2
29 Paphai Guest House ... D1
30 Pathoumphone Guest House ... D2
31 Phousi Guesthouse 2 ... C1
32 Sackarinh Guest House ... D2
33 Silichit Guest House ... D1
34 Souksavath Guesthouse ... A2
35 Thanaboun Guesthouse ... D2
36 Thavisouk Guest House ... B4
37 Xayana Guesthouse ... A2

Eating

38 Baguette Stalls ... B2
39 Big Tree Café ... E1
40 Blue Lagoon ... C1
41 JoMa Bakery Café ... A2
42 Kon Kai ... E2
43 Le Banneton ... F2
44 Le Café Ban Vat Sene ... E2
45 Morning Market ... B1
46 Night Food Stalls ... B2
47 Saffron Café ... E1
48 Sala Café ... E2
49 Tamarind ... F2

Drinking

50 Hive Bar ... C3
51 Ikon Club ... D2
52 Lao Lao Garden ... C3
53 Utopia ... D4

Entertainment

54 Royal Theatre ... C2

Shopping

Big Tree Gallery ... (see 39)
55 L'Etranger Books & Tea ... C3
56 OckPopTok (Ban Wat Nong) ... E1
57 OckPopTok (Ban Xieng Mouane) ... D2
58 Pathana Boupha Antique House ... C4

Information

59 Provincial Tourism Department ... B2
60 Unesco World Heritage Information ... G1

Transport

61 Bangkok Airways ... D2
62 Boats to Pak Ou Caves and Nong Khiaw ... E1
63 Laos Airlines ... A4
64 Long-Tail Boat Ticket Office ... E1
65 Navigation Office ... C1
66 Slow Boat Landing ... C1

end. With backing from Unesco and New Zealand, the monks' quarters have been restored as a classroom for training young novices and monks in the artistic skills needed to maintain and preserve Luang Prabang's temples. Among these skills are woodcarving, painting and Buddha-casting, all of which came to a virtual halt after 1975.

Handicraft Night Market MARKET
(Th Sisavangvong; ⏲5.30-10pm) Come sundown a visit to this central market is magical. A seemingly endless ribbon of colourful textiles, paper lanterns, T-shirts and weavings adorn the candle-lit street. Be it locally designed jewellery, the finest Sam Neua pashminas or paintings by local artists, you're sure to find something to commemorate your trip.

TAEC ARTS CENTRE
(www.teaclaos.org; admission 20,000K; ⏲9am-6pm Tue-Sun) Learn to distinguish between the Hmong, Akha and Khmu tribes through the differences in their ethnic garb and jewellery. This clear and visually descriptive exhibition is based in a 1920's building up the hill by Dala market. There's also a shop and pleasant cafe (mains 25,000K).

Activities

The best way to explore the city is by **bike**, meandering through the peninsula past scenes of monastic life and children playing. Basic/mountain bikes cost 20,000/50,000K per day and can be hired along Th Sisavangvong. For easier journeys, automatic one-gear scooters cost around US$20 to US$25 per day.

Massage

Luang Prabang is all about pampering, and what better way to ease those trekked-out muscles than sampling the city's affordable **spa parlours**; try a basic herbal sauna, traditional Lao massage, Swedish massage or hot stones massage (to name a few). A few of the best:

Hibiscus MASSAGE
(Th Sakkarin; ⏲10am-10pm) Set in a former gallery in an old French building, Hibiscus wafts chillsome tunes through its silk-draped walls while you get pummelled to perfection. Traditional massage from 60,000K.

Lotus du Lao Massage MASSAGE
(Th Sisavangvong; ⏲9am-10.30pm) This central spa has years of experience and air choking essential oils. Choose from a range of massage, facials and reflexology. Prices start at 60,000K.

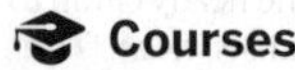

Courses

Cooking

Tamarind LAO COOKING
(☎020 770484; www.tamarindlaos.com; Ban Wat Nong; 1-day course 250,000K, ⏲9am-3pm Mon-Sat) Join Tamarind at its lakeside pavilion for a day's tuition in the art of Lao cuisine, meeting first at its restaurant before heading to the market for ingredients for classic dishes such as *mok pa* (steamed fish in banana leaves). For its restaurant, see p334.

Tum Tum Cheng Cooking School LAO COOKING
(☎253388; 29/2 Th Sakkarin; 1-day course 250,000K, incl free cook book) Celebrated chef Chandra teaches you the secrets of his alchemy. Includes a visit to the market to select your veg. The day usually starts at the school on the peninsula at 8.30am and finishes at 2pm.

Tours

If you have a few days, whimsical Kuang Si waterfalls (p337) and Pak Ou Caves (p337) are well worth a visit. There's a plethora of tour companies down Th Sisavangvong. We recommend **All Lao Travel** (☎253522; Th Sisavangvong; ⏲8am-10pm) as a one-stop shop for flights, boat and VIP bus tickets, and visa extensions, while **Treasure Travel** (☎254682; www.treasuretravellaos.com; Th Sisavangvong; ⏲8am-9pm) can also arrange these services as well as organising trips to Pak Ou (80,000K per person) and Kuang Si (300,000K). The following options are good for trekking, rafting, elephant riding and cycling excursions:

All Lao Service (Elephant Camp) ADVENTURE TOUR
(☎253522; www.mahoutecolodge.com; Th Sisavangvong) Based in the same office as All Lao Travel, elephant treks cost US$45 for one-day's trekking (with a minimum of two people).

> **SPLURGE: DREAM WEAVERS**
>
> Learn to weave your own scarf and dye your own textiles with the excellent one-day course at **Ock PopTok** (☎212597; www.ockpoptok.com; US$59; ⏲8.45am-4pm Mon-Sat). Teachers are master craftsmen, you get to keep your handiwork and lunch is included. Situated 2km past Phousy market, a free túk-túk will pick you up and bring you back.

White Elephant ADVENTURE TOUR

(☎020 254481; www.white-elephant-adventures-laos.com; Th Sisavangvong) White Elephant is hailed for its relationships with remote Hmong and Khmu villages, allowing you a deeper insight into ethnic life without bumping into another *falang*. You can do this on a trek or by mountain bike in solid two- and three-day tours.

Tiger Trail ADVENTURE TOUR

(☎252655; www.laos-adventures.com; Th Sisavangvong; ⏲8.30am-9pm) Focusing on socially responsible tours benefitting local people, Tiger Trail offers intimate treks through Hmong and Khmu villages. All tours can be tailored to include kayaking, elephant riding, rafting and mountain biking. Prices range from 350,000K, with elephant rides costing from US$40 to US$75.

Festivals & Events

The two most important annual events in Luang Prabang are **Pii Mai** (Lao or Lunar New Year) in April, when Luang Prabang is packed to the gills with locals armed with water pistols (book accommodation well in advance), and boat races during **Bun Awk Phansa** (End of the Rains Retreat) in October.

Sleeping

The most memorable area to stay is the Old Quarter on the historic peninsula. There are also decent guesthouses near the Mekong, a few blocks southwest of the Hmong handicraft night market.

OLD QUARTER

Thanaboun Guesthouse GUESTHOUSE $$

(☎260606; Th Sisavangvong; r US$25; ❄@) In the heart of town, Thanaboun excels with clean, tastefully finished rooms. Rooms out the back backing on to the temple grounds are quieter. There's also an internet cafe (8000K per hour).

Paphai Guest House GUESTHOUSE $

(☎212752; Th Sisavang Vatthana; r without bathroom 30,000-60,000K, f 90,000K) Super-basic digs in a traditional wooden house near the action of Th Sisavangvong. All rooms are fan-cooled, rattan-walled, have padlocks on doors and shared bathroom.

Chittana Guesthouse GUESTHOUSE $$

(☎212552; off Th Sakkarin; r without bathroom 150,000K) Atmospheric wood-varnished, fan-only rooms with basic toilets and house-proud touches. The room by the street on the 1st floor is the best.

Sackarinh Guest House GUESTHOUSE $$

(☎254412; Th Sisavangvong; r 130,000-150,000K) Hidden down a sidestreet choking on flowers, this is a colourful option for your first night while you get your bearings. Right in the centre of town, rooms are basic (if overpriced) and spacious.

Pathoumphone Guest House GUESTHOUSE $

(☎212946; Th Kingkitsarat; r 60,000-90,000K) This unpretentious guesthouse has paint-weary rooms, with serene views of the peaceful Nam Khan River. With rattan ceilings and lino floors, these are basic cells. Nice cafe outside to chill.

Silichit Guest House GUESTHOUSE $

(☎212758; Th Sisavang Vatthana; r 70,000-95,000K; ❄) Boxy, basic rooms with a trad-Lao style. The walls are thirsty but it's the location that wins you over. Try for rooms 4 and 6 upstairs.

Phousi Guesthouse 2 GUESTHOUSE $

(☎253717; Th Khem Khong; r 100,000K, without bathroom 80,000K; ❄@) Small but house-proud rooms finished with conch shells on white walls. Rooms out the back are shadowy, so opt for one facing the Mekong. There's also an internet cafe.

Kinnaly Guest House GUESTHOUSE $$

(☎212416; Th Sisavang Vatthana; r with/without air-con 130,000/150,000K; ❄) Perched next to Café Toui, Kinnaly has a range of rooms – all of which are clean and functional – two with air-con and one with a balcony. All rooms with fan and bathroom.

BIG BROTHER MOUSE

If you want to get involved in improving local literacy, seek out **Big Brother Mouse** (BBM; www.bigbrothermouse.com; Th Sothikuman, Luang Prabang), a home-grown initiative that brings the delights of the written word to infants in remote villages who, for lack of materials, rarely get the chance to read. If you sponsor a book party (2,135,000K), you can go with them. Alternatively, hang out at your local BBM for a couple of hours and read to the kids who attend. Look out for Big Brother Mouse's offices in Luang Prabang and Vientiane.

LUANG PRABANG

Oudomphone Guest House 2 GUESTHOUSE $
(☎252419; r 100,000K, without bathroom 60,000K; 📶) Backpacker favourite run by a pleasant family with fan-cooled, tile-floored rooms. The owners also run cooking classes and rent scooters.

Souksavath Guesthouse GUESTHOUSE $$
(☎212043; Th Hoxieng; r 150,000-180,000K; ❄📶) Souksavath has houseproud rooms with fresh paint, bureaus and wall-mounted flatscreens. Good value, pleasant staff and just around the corner from JoMa Bakery.

Xayana Guesthouse GUESTHOUSE $
(☎260680; www.mylaohome.com; Th Hoxieng; dm 35,000K, r 80,000-160,000K) Next to Souksavath Guesthouse, this place has immaculately clean dorms, plus fresh private bathrooms. There's a nice space out the front to read, drink coffee and meet other travellers.

Thavisouk Guest House GUESTHOUSE $
(☎252022; Th Pha Mahapatsaman; r 70,000-100,000K; ❄@) Basic digs with a few sticks of furniture and peppermint-hued bed linen complementing wood floors. Nice chill-out veranda plus internet cafe.

Mano Guest House GUESTHOUSE $
(☎253112; mano sotsay@hotmail.com; Th Pha Mahapatsaman; r 80,000-120,000K; ❄📶) Slightly musty yet homey rooms with large TV, tiled bathrooms, iris-stemmed lights and wall hangings. Directly in the flight path, it's favoured by Lao Airlines pilots.

Jaliya Guest House GUESTHOUSE $
(☎252154; Th Pha Mahapatsaman; r 70,000-120,000K; ❄) Jaliya has pleasant motel-style bungalows in its garden out the back – perfect for a bit of sun worshipping – as well as decent rooms in the old house itself. Aircon or fan rooms with private bathroom.

EAST OF PHU SI

More budget options are found 300m east of Phu Si down a lane running to the Nam Khan River.

TOP CHOICE **Cold River Guest House** GUESTHOUSE $
(☎252810; off Th Phommatha; r 120,000K, without bathroom 60,000K, incl breakfast; 📶) Bags of atmosphere in this old house overlooking the Nam Khan River; higgledy-piggledy corridors and a communal chill-out area. Rooms vary but the newish ones with balconies are cosy. Snacks available all day and owner Silvan is a charm.

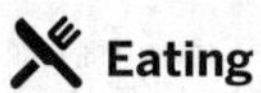

Eating

The city's bakeries and French restaurants could give Paris' Left Bank a run for its money. Quick, cheap eats are found at baguette stalls opposite the tourist office from early morning till sunset. After this the adjacent night market is packed with interesting barbecued food (keep an eye out for exotica like lizards, frogs, eels and snakes).

TOP CHOICE **Tamarind** LAO $
(www.tamarindlaos.com; Th Kingkitsarat; mains 40,000K; ⏰11am-10pm) Chic Tamarind's à la carte menu boasts delicious sampling platters with bamboo dip, stuffed lemongrass and *meuyang* (DIY parcels of noodles, herbs, fish and chilli pastes, and vegetables). Its cooking courses are recommended (p332).

TOP CHOICE **Le Banneton** BAKERY $
(Th Sakkarin; meals 35,000K; ⏰6.30am-6pm; 📶) Easily the best croissants in Laos, this peaceful peninsula cafe has a sweet-toothed menu of *pain au chocolat,* fruit shakes, sandwiches, quiches and home-made sorbets.

Big Tree Café KOREAN $
(www.bigtreecafe.com; Th Khem Khong; mains 30,000K; ⏰9am-9pm) Terrific Korean food made by a genuine Korean! Eat in the cafe or outside on its sun terrace overlooking the Mekong. There's also a choice of Western and Japanese dishes.

Le Café Ban Vat Sene FRENCH $
(Th Sakkarin; mains 30,000K; ⏰6.30am-10pm; 📶) Retro fans whirr over an Indochinese scene of flower-shaded lights and stylish refinement. This is the place to sip an afternoon *pastis* and read a paper. French wine, salads, quiche, pasta and pizza...*parfait*!

Sala Café FRENCH $$
(☎254738; Th Kingkitsarat; mains 60,000K; ⏰7.30am-9.30am) With its Parisian-inspired interior, Sala is perfect for watching the afternoon light golden the opposite banks of the Nam Khan. Heavily French menu with dishes such as duck breast in honey sauce.

Saffron Café WESTERN $
(Th Khem Khong; mains 30,000K; ⏰7am-9pm; 📶) This stylish cafe turns out great pasta dishes, has excellent coffee and warm service, as well as a choice of interior and alfresco dining.

SPLURGE: AUBERGE LES 3 NAGAS

If you're thinking of proposing, this is the place to do it. Get your glad rags on and head down the peninsula to **Auberge les 3 Nagas** (☎253888; www.alilahotels.com/3nagas; Th Sakkarin), Luang Prabang's original boutique hotel where Indo-chic was minted. The 100-year-old Lao-style building shaded in mango trees brims with old world atmosphere and romance. Its classy restaurant features an exquisite Asian fusion menu – and perhaps the best *làap* in the city – all served with French flair.

JoMa Bakery Café BAKERY $
(Th Chao Fa Ngum; mains 10,000-30,000K; ⏰7am-9pm; ❄📶) A haven of cool with comfy chairs and a contemporary vibe, JoMa is the city's busiest bakery. Tasty muffins, sandwiches and salads.

Kon Kai LAO $
(Th Kingkitsarat; mains 35,000K; ⏰8am-10pm) With unbroken views of the Nam Khan, Kon Kai has a heavily Lao and Chinese menu, brick floors and alfresco tables shaded by tamarind trees. Tasty spring rolls and delicious *oh pa daek* (Luang Prabang pork casserole). Late lunch onwards for the best light.

Blue Lagoon WESTERN $$
(www.blue-lagoon-restaurant.com; next to Royal Palace; mains 70,000K; ⏰10am-10pm) A favourite with expats for its lantern-festooned walls, leafy patio and jazz-infused atmosphere. The menu features Luang Prabang sausage, pasta, salads and very tasty *làap*.

Drinking

The following do their best to squeeze as much hedonistic juice as possible before the 11.30pm curfew.

TOP CHOICE **Utopia** BAR
(Take the turn-off at the top of Th Phommatha) Utopia is all recliner cushions, low-slung tables and hookah pipes with celestial views of the Nam Khan River. Sounds wrong but it works. Chill over a fruit shake, play volleyball or lose yourself in a sea of candles come sunset. Bar snacks too (mains 25,000K).

Hive Bar BAR
(Th Kingkitsarat) A stylish den of hidden coves. Out the back in the garden there's a dance floor, projector wall and more tables. Check out the excellent ethnic fashion show nightly at 7pm. Tapas, happy hour and cocktails.

Ikon Klub BAR
(Th Sisavang Vatthana) Less a club and more of a boudoir, there's something deliciously subversive about this boho bar; the lights are low, the decor tinged with elements of the 1930s plus a room upstairs with hidden potential. Tom Waits croaking through the speakers finishes it off perfectly.

Lao Lao Garden BAR
(Th Kingkitsarat) Lit up like a jungle Vegas, this garden bar on the skirts of Phu Si calls you to relax by candlelight, listen to easy sounds and warm your cockles by the fire pit. Happy hour all day for cocktails.

Entertainment

Royal Theatre THEATRE
(Th Sisavangvong; admission US$8-20; ⏰shows 6pm Mon, Wed, Fri & Sat) Inside the Royal Palace Museum compound, local performers put on a show that includes a *bąsĭ* ceremony, traditional dance and folk music. There are also traditional dances of Lao ethnic minorities, such as the Phoo Noi and Hmong people.

L'Etranger Books & Tea CINEMA
(booksinlaos@yahoo.com; Th Kingkitsarat) Screens blockbusters nightly at 7pm.

Shopping

Handicraft Night Market MARKET
(Th Sisavangvong; ⏰5.30-10pm) The first visit to Luang Prabang's Handicraft Night Market is magical. A seemingly endless ribbon of colourful textiles, paper lanterns, T-shirts and weavings adorn the candle-lit street.

TOP CHOICE **Big Tree Gallery** GALLERY
(29/4 Th Khem Khong; ⏰9am-10pm) Photographer Adri Berger's compositions of rural Lao capture Laos' honeyed afternoon light like no one else. His prints start at US$100.

Pathana Boupha Antique House ANTIQUES
(29/4 Ban Visoun; ⏰8.30am-5.30pm) Follow the sweeping stairs in the garden to this Aladdin's cave of antique Buddhas, golden *naga*, silver betel nut pots, Akha-style bracelets and Hmong necklaces.

OckPopTok CLOTHING

Ban Wat Nong (www.ockpoptok.com; 73/5 Ban Wat Nong; ⌚8am-9pm); Ban Xieng Mouane (Th Sisavangvong; ⌚8am-9pm) OckPopTok works with 16 tribes, helping to preserve their handicraft traditions. Fine silk and cotton scarves, chemises, dresses, wall hangings and cushion covers make perfect presents.

L'Etranger Books & Tea BOOKS

(booksinlaos@yahoo.com; Th Kingkitsarat; ⌚8am-10pm Mon-Sat, 10am-10pm Sun) The city's best loved bookshop and the cheapest spot for secondhand travel books and thrillers – you can also exchange old novels here. Upstairs there's a comfy lizard-lounge with walls plastered in *National Geographic* covers and a decent cafe to read in. Mainstream films shown nightly at 7pm.

Information

Internet Access & Telephone

Most internet cafes in Luang Prabang town have Skype, and offer international calls for 3000K and mobile calls for 4000K per minute, charging 4000K per hour for internet use. For free wi-fi access try Le Café Ban Vat Sene or JoMa Bakery Café. Internet cafes are peppered along Th Sisavangvong.

Medical Services

Luang Prabang's **Provincial Hospital** (☎254025; Ban Naxang; consultation 100,000K) is OK for minor problems but for any serious illnesses consider flying to Bangkok or returning to Vientiane for **Aek Udon International** (☎0066-4234 2555; www.aekudon.com; Posri Rd, Amphur Muang, Udon Thani) just over the Thai border. Note the Provincial Hospital charges double for consultations on weekends or anytime after 4pm. There are plenty of pharmacies in the centre of town.

Pharmacie (Th Sakkarin; ⌚8.30am-8pm) Stocks basic medicines. Weekend hours are variable.

Money

BCEL (Th Sisavangvong; ⌚8.30am-3.30pm Mon-Sat) Changes major currencies in cash or travellers cheques, has a 24-hour ATM, and allows you to make cash advances against Visa and MasterCard.

Lao Development Bank (65 Th Sisavangvong; ⌚8.30am-3.30pm Mon-Sat) Has a 24-hour ATM.

Post

Post office (Th Chao Fa Ngum; ⌚8.30am-3.30pm Mon-Fri, to noon Sat) Phone calls and Western Union facilities too.

Tourist Information

Provincial Tourism Department (☎212487; www.tourismlaos.com; Th Sisavangvong; ⌚8am-4pm Mon-Fri) General info brochure pitstop on festivals and ethnic groups, as well as selling Hobo maps. Pointlessly, its staff speak no English.

Unesco World Heritage Information (www.unesco.org; Villa Xiengmouane, Th Sakkarin; ⌚9am-6pm Mon-Fri) Situated in an old French customs house, visit to learn more about Unesco's valuable work.

Getting There & Away

Air

By the time you read this there could well be international flights to Hong Kong, Kuala Lumpur, Singapore and Tokyo from **Luang Prabang International Airport** (☎212173), which is currently undergoing expansion (for more details and info on international flights, see p377). **Lao Airlines** (☎212172; www.laoairlines.com; Th Pha Mahapatsaman) flies from Luang Prabang to Vientiane (one way US$88, three times daily) and Pakse (one way US$320, three times weekly). A route may be operating from Luang Prabang to Phonsavan and also to Huay Xai by this book's publication.

Boat

PAK BENG & HUAY XAI

Slow boats motor northwest daily to Huay Xai (200,000K), departing at 8am by the **Navigation Office** (⌚8-11am & 2-4pm) located behind the Royal Palace. You can buy tickets direct from there or from a travel agent. The trip takes two days with an overnight stop in Pak Beng (100,000K, nine hours). From Pak Beng it's also possible to take the bus northeast to Udomxai.

White-knuckle speedboats up the Mekong leave at 8.30am daily from Ban Don pier, a 7km, 10,000K shared túk-túk ride north of the town centre. Compared to the slow boat, they rocket to Pak Beng (190,000K, three hours) and Huay Xai (300,000K, six hours) in a fraction of the time but with 10 times the danger. Are you really in such a hurry that you'd place your life in their hands?

Bus & Sŏrngtăaou

Most inter-provincial buses and sŏrngtăaou heading north depart from the Northern bus station, while southbound vehicles use the Southern bus station, 3km south of town. On all these routes the durations can vary wildly during monsoonal weather).

A better option is the Naluang minibus station – opposite the Southern bus station – that runs new minibuses to Nong Khiaw (55,000K, 9.30am), Vang Vieng (95,000K, 8.30am), Phonsavan (95,000K, 9am), Luang Namtha (105,000K, 8.30am), Hanoi (320,000K, 6pm)

MEKONG COWBOYS

Beware Luang Prabang's boatmen scam claiming they can't leave until the boat is full. You and the other *falangs* (foreigners) end up clubbing together for the 'ghost' fare and then magically the last person appears stage left. Don't leave until you get your cash back.

and Kunming (sleeper bus 420,000K, 7am). If you've got sufficient numbers, it's possible to charter a bus; short journeys like Phonsavan and Vang Vieng will cost around US$120.

VIENTIANE & VANG VIENG

Several local buses leave the Southern bus station for Vientiane (110,000K, 10 to 14 hours) at 6.30am, 11am, 4pm & 6.30pm. VIP buses en route to Vientiane (130,000K, about 10 hours, 8am, 9am & 7.30pm) stop in Vang Vieng (100,000K, six to nine hours).

UDOMXAI, LUANG NAM THA, NONG KHIAW & SAM NEUA

From the Northern bus station, daily sŏrngtăaou and local buses go to Udomxai (60,000K, four hours, four daily), Luang Nam Tha (100,000K, nine hours, 9am), Nong Khiaw (40,000K, four hours, two to five daily), Sam Neua (130,000K, 16 hours, 9am and 5pm), Huay Xai (local bus 120,000K, 5.30pm; VIP bus, 140,000K, 7pm) and Phongsali (120,000K, 13 hours, 5.30pm).

PHONSAVAN & SAIYABOULI

From the Southern bus station local buses leave daily to Phonsavan (95,000K, eight hours, 8.30am) and Saiyabouli (60,000K, five hours, 9am and 2pm).

Getting Around

From the airport into town, 4km away, jumbos or minitrucks charge a uniform 50,000K per vehicle, and up to six can share the ride. In the reverse direction you can usually charter an entire jumbo for 30,000K to 40,000K.

Most of the town is accessible on foot. Jumbos usually ask foreigners for 15,000K a ride. Scooters cost US$18 to US$25 per day, mountain/ordinary bikes cost 50,000/20,000K per day.

Around Luang Prabang

Caves CAVES

About 25km upstream on the Mekong and at the mouth of the Nam Ou, the dramatic **Pak Ou Caves** (admission 20,000K) are set into limestone cliffs and are crammed with hundreds of Buddha images; a kind of statue's graveyard where unwanted images are placed. This pantheon of statuary is split into two levels with the lower being more impressive. Bring a torch.

Most boat trips stop at small villages along the way, especially **Ban Xang Hai**. Boatmen call this tourist-dominated place 'Whisky Village', as it's known for its free-flowing *lào-láo* (rice whisky).

You can hire long-tail boats to Pak Ou from Luang Prabang's charter boat landing at 130,000K for one to three people or 170,000K for four to five people, including petrol. The trip takes two hours upriver and one hour down, plus stops. Túk-túk make the trip for about half the price.

Public Park PARK

Kuang Si falls, 32km from the city, are a tonic for sore eyes, with a multi-tiered cascade tumbling over limestone formations into menthol-green pools. The waterfall is set in a lush, well-manicured **public park** (admission 16,000K), and there's nothing more Eden-like than plunging into the icy water to cool off. Near the entrance are enclosures housing sun bears rescued from poachers.

Some visitors come by hired bicycle. Freelance guides proliferate down Th Sisavangvong in Luang Prabang and offer trips by jumbo, or boat and jumbo (both for about 100,000K per person).

Nong Khiaw

☎071

Nestled along the cherry blossom riverbank of the Nam Ou and towered over by forest-clad karsts, pretty Nong Khiaw is a haven of cafes, guesthouses and, thanks to the arrival of Green Discovery and Tiger Trail, it now has plenty of activities to keep you busy. Watch a cult film at the video lounge or eat at a couple of tasty restaurants. Note: the opposite side of the river where most guesthouses are based is called Ban Sop Houn.

Sights & Activities

Trekking & Cycling

You can walk to **Tham Pha Tok**, an enormous many-levelled cave where villagers hid out during the Second Indochina War. Head 2.5km east of the bridge then look for a clearly visible cave mouth in the limestone cliff on the right.

Tiger Trail TREKKING

(☎252655; info@laos-adventures.com; Delilah's Place, Nong Khiaw) Offers treks around the

TONY POE: THE HORROR, THE HORROR

CIA special ops agent, Anthony Poe was infamous for going native a la Colonel Kurtz, collecting Pathet Lao ears and dropping heads on his enemy's porch from a Cessna plane. In 1961 Poe was sent to the mountainous north to repel North Vietnamese forces from Laos (see p370) with the aid of 10,000 Hmong warriors. Poe won the loyalty of his hardy, communist-averse soldiers (and the trade of their opium), contravening his paymasters' orders by fighting beside them and intrepidly attacking enemy-infested strongholds on the Chinese border (risking China's intervention in the Secret War). Pathet Lao ears were stapled by Poe to progress reports and sent to the CIA 'Bubble' in Bangkok. As far as he was concerned: 'War is hell, if you're gonna do it you've gotta do it with gusto.'

The partial inspiration for Francis Ford Coppola's Colonel Kurtz in *Apocalypse Now*, cinema's most enduring icon of the war in Vietnam, Poe died in 2003.

local area, including one-day trips to the '100 waterfalls' (270,000K per person, group of four). A two-day trek through Hmong villages incorporating a homestay costs 410,000K per person. Tiger Trail rents mountain bikes for 30,000K per day.

Green Discovery TREKKING, CYCLING
(☎020 336 6110; www.nongkiau.com; Nong Kiau Riverside Resort, Ban Sop Houn) Offers overnight camping treks near the summit of Phou Nang None (450,000K per person, group of four). Cycling through Khamu, Thai Lu and Hmong villages is recommended and for a group of four costs 390,000K per person. Green Discovery charges 50,000K for superior bikes.

Kayaking, Tubing, Fishing & Climbing

As well as tubing and kayaking (210,000K per person, group of four) on the Nam Ou, Tiger Trail also organises fishing classes with local fishermen, while Green Discovery runs one- and three-day kayaking excursions to Luang Prabang. Run by the able Mr Somneuk, Green Discovery is also the one to scale the karsts with. Climbs for a group of four cost 150,000K per person.

Sleeping & Eating

Guesthouses in Nong Khiaw are near the bridge on the west side of the river, and in the more popular village of Ban Sop Houn, on the east side.

Sunset Guest House GUESTHOUSE $
(☎020 559 7103; sunsetgh@hotmail.com; Ban Sop Houn; r 100,000-150,000K) Ever-evolving Sunset has an excellent new roof cafe and along with its cheaper offerings, two lovely new cabanas isolated in a little meadow. The owner speaks English and French.

Sengdao Chittavong Guest House GUESTHOUSE $
(Nong Khiaw; r 80,000-100,000K) Sizeable cabanas located in gardens of cherry blossom by the river. Rooms are rattan-walled, with simple decoration, fresh flowers, clean linen and balconies.

Bamboo Paradise Guest House GUESTHOUSE $
(☎020 555 45286; Ban Sop Houn; r 80,000K) Clean wood-floored cells with patchy walls, comfy beds and hot showers in a peach-coloured block. Its cabanas have better river views.

Sunrise Guest House GUESTHOUSE $
(☎020 2207 9587; Ban Sop Houn; r 60,000-100,000K) Overlooking the bridge, the view of the river from Sunrise's basic new cabanas is blissful. Rooms are spartan with shower and squat toilet. Verandas save the day with cool-breeze hammocks.

Delilah's Place WESTERN, LAO $
(Nong Khiaw; mains 30,000K; ⏲7am-10pm) Strung with creeper vines, this tasteful eatery offers an eclectic selection ranging from delicious pancakes, bagels, salads, spring rolls and Lao green curries to hamburgers and Western breakfasts. You can even get a proper latte.

Deen INDIAN $
(Ban Sop Houn; mains 25,000K; ⏲8.30am-10pm) Recently migrated from Huay Xai, with its wood-fired naan bread, moreish tandoori dishes, zesty curries and homey atmosphere, it's always packed. There's also a bank of computers (internet costs 15,000K per hour, wi-fi free).

CT Restaurant & Bakery WESTERN, LAO $
(Ban Sop Houn; mains 20,000K; ⏲7am-10pm) At the end of the bridge lit up like a beacon of doughy smells and good cheer, CT has a

Western-friendly menu of pancakes, breakfasts, sandwiches and staple Lao dishes. Decent cakes and take-away sarnies for trekking.

Getting There & Away

Boat

In the high season, boats heading up the Nam Ou to Muang Ngoi Neua (one way 20,000K, one hour) leave at 11am and 2pm. Tickets are bought at an office at the bus station. Boats sometimes continue to Muang Khua (88,000K, seven hours) from Muang Ngoi Neua.

Public boats make the six- to nine-hour trip through striking karst scenery to Luang Prabang. With a minimum of 10 people tickets cost 100,000K per person. If this is not happening you can charter the boat for 1,500,000K. See p336 for information on boat travel from Luang Prabang.

Bus & Sŏrngtăaou

Sŏrngtăaou and small local buses to Luang Prabang (50,000K, three hours) depart every two hours between 8.30am and 1.30pm. If the bus is full, gather 10 of you and charter one for 50,000K.

If you're heading east towards Houaphanh or Xieng Khuang (Phonsavan), you can get a bus to Sam Neua (120,000K, 13 hours, daily at 11.30am), or catch the local bus stopping briefly at the Ban Sop Houn side of the bridge every night between 6pm and 7pm.

Muang Ngoi Neua

Street stalls fry up pancakes in the morning and mist hangs on the pyramid-shaped karsts as river life in Muang Ngoi Neua crackles to life. Chill in your hammock and take in the jaw-dropping views of the karsts, or stir yourself for trekking, caving and kayaking. Unlike in Vang Vieng, a recent crackdown on drugs means this village hasn't become a stoner casualty, and thankfully, locals are still welcoming.

Generators provide electricity from 6pm to around 10pm. There are no banks here and barely a mobile phone signal, so bring sufficient cash to get back.

Tours

Lao Youth Travel TOUR
(030-514 0046; www.laoyouthtravel.com; 7.30-10.30am & 1.30-6pm) Offering kayaking (group of four costs US$28 per person), trekking (group of two costs US$28), cookery classes, homestays and boat trips.

Muang Ngoi Tour Office TOUR
(020 213 6219; top of the boat landing stairs; 8am-9pm) Run by friendly Chang and offering similar and slightly cheaper offerings to Lao Youth Travel.

Kongkeo Tours ADVENTURE TOUR
(020 2386 3648; kongkeoteacher@yahoo.com) An affable English-speaking teacher, Mr Kongkeo has long been taking travellers on his one- to five-day treks to the caves and Khamu and Hmong villages.

Sleeping & Eating

With 'budget' tattooed over its dip-and-pour, hammock-slung cabanas, you're in traveller territory. Restaurants are generally tagged on to guesthouses.

TOP CHOICE **Bungalows Ecolodge** GUESTHOUSE $
(020 2338 88163; off main street; r 80,000K) Hidden down a side street, cabanas have sliding shutters that allow you to lie in bed and watch the sky turn amber over the karsts. Tasteful linen, solar-heated showers,

GETTING TO VIETNAM: SOP HUN TO TAY TRANG

Getting to the border The border at Sop Hun in Phongsali Province has now opened as an international entry point to Tay Trang in Vietnam. There are three buses a week bound for Dien Bien Phu leaving from the Lao village of Muang Khua (50,000K, 6.30am, five to six hours). Get there early for a decent seat.

At the border Note, there are no facilities or waiting vehicles at either Lao or Viet borders (open 8am to 5pm). The nearest ATM in Laos is in Udomxai so bring plenty of dollars. You'll need to organise a Vietnamese visa in advance. Lao visas are available on arrival for US$30 to US$42, depending on your nationality. Bring some photo ID and some extra cash (approx US$5) for administrative costs charged on weekends and holidays.

Moving On Once through the Vietnamese border it's a further 35km to Dien Bien Phu. For information on crossing this border in the other direction see p840.

mozzie nets and locally sourced food elevate it above the crowd.

Aloune Mai Guest House GUESTHOUSE $
(r 70,000K) Found down a dirt track (over the road from the river) and reached by a bridge, Aloune Mai sits beside a meadow and has 10 fresh rooms in a handsome rattan building with heated showers. Better still, there are stunning views of the cliffs.

Lattanavongsa Guest House GUESTHOUSE $
(☎030-514 0770; r 100,000K) In a palm-filled garden, these cabanas positioned towards karsts/sunset are tasteful with houseproud flourishes, including gas-fired showers.

Ning Ning Guest House GUESTHOUSE $$
(☎020 386 3306, r incl breakfast US$17-20) Nestled around a peaceful garden, immaculate wood cabanas have mozzie nets, verandas, fresh private bathrooms and bed linen, with walls ornamented with ethnic tapestries.

Saylom Guest House GUESTHOUSE $
(r 40,000-50,000K) Close to the boat ramp this powder-blue guesthouse has clean, tiled-floor rooms, an adjoining restaurant and verandas with hammocks.

Rainbow Guest House GUESTHOUSE $
(☎020 2295 7880; r 50,000K) Close to the boat ramp this newly constructed house has clean if charmless rooms. Fragrant linen, large private bathrooms and communal veranda. There's also a sunset-facing cafe.

Eating

The best food is served up on the street.

Riverside Restaurant LAO $
(meals 35,000K; ⏲7.30am-10pm) Shaded by a mango tree festooned with lanterns, this traveller magnet has lovely views of the Nam Ou River and a menu encompassing noodles, fried dishes and *làap*.

Phetdavanh Street Buffet LAO $
(⏲from 7pm) Phetdavanh runs an excellent nightly buffet drawing in locals and travellers. BBQ pork, chicken, fish, sticky rice and vegetables. Lip smacking.

Lao Friend Coffeeshop LAO $
(☎020 389 1827; meals 25,000K; ⏲noon-10pm) New chilling bar with a garden strewn with bomb casings repurposed as flowerpots. Cocktails, lounging chairs, glowing lanterns by night, and a menu including steaks and fresh fish.

Information

Generators provide electricity from 6pm to 10pm. A couple of pharmacies sell basic medicines; for anything serious get yourself back to Luang Prabang.

Getting There & Away

Boats to Nong Khiaw leave at 9am (or when full) and cost 20,000K. Heading north, a boat goes most days to Muang Khua (minimum 10 persons, 100,000K, seven hours) for those headed for the Sop Hun–Tay Trang border crossing. Buy tickets at the boat office, halfway up the boat landing stairs next to Lattanavongsa Restaurant. There's a boat to Nong Khiaw from Muang Khua that stops in Muang Ngoi Neua at 1.30pm.

Phonsavan

☎061 / POP 60,000

Phonsavan bears its cratered war scars like an acne-ridden pensioner, while stoic locals make the most of decommissioned unexploded ordnance (UXO), using it to decorate houses and hotel foyers. Touchingly, while other areas of Laos erupt in pockets of sophistication, Phonsavan, like some retro-leaning Muscovite, barely changes. Often mist-shrouded, this dusty old town (latterly known as Xieng Khuang) has heaps of charm if you look past its nondescript, Soviet facade – blame that on its hasty rebuild after it was decimated.

Its two main streets are peopled by an intriguing cosmopolitan cast of Chinese, Vietnamese, Lao and Hmong, thanks to its location as a trade hub. The town is well serviced by an airport, a handful of OK guesthouses and restaurants, plus a wet and dry goods market.

Sights

Most come here to witness the mysterious Plain of Jars, considered to be funeral urns dating back to the Stone Age. It's possible you're also here to learn more about the Secret War, so pop into the **Mines Advisory Group** (MAG; www.mag.org.uk; Rte 7; ⏲4-8pm), whose tireless detection, detonation and diffusion of unexploded ordnance is helping to make Laos a safer place. To deepen your understanding, watch the harrowing documentaries, *Bombies* and *On War*, screened daily at 4.30pm, 5.45pm and 6.30pm. Two doors down, **Xieng Khouang UXO-survivors' Information Centre** (☎213349; www.laos.worlded.org; ⏲8am-8pm) displays prosthetic

AN ENDURING LEGACY

Between 1964 and 1973, the USA conducted one of the largest sustained aerial bombardments in history, flying 580,344 missions over Laos and dropping two million tonnes of bombs, costing US$2.2 million a day. Around 30% of the bombs dropped on Laos failed to detonate, leaving the country littered with unexploded ordnance (UXO).

For people all over eastern Laos (the most contaminated provinces being Xieng Khuang, Salavan and Savannakhet), living with this appalling legacy has become an intrinsic part of daily life. Since the British **Mines Advisory Group** (MAG; www.mag.org.uk; Rte 7; ⏲4-8pm), began clearance work in 1994, only a tiny percentage of the quarter of a million pieces in Xieng Khuang and Salavan has been removed. At the current rate of clearance it will take more than 100 years to make the country safe.

limbs and UXO, adding additional grim insight.

Sleeping

Phonsavan digs are hardly up there with Luang Prabang, but the following are OK.

Kong Keo Guesthouse GUESTHOUSE $
(☎211354; www.kongkeojar.com; r 60,000-80,000K) With an open-pit barbeque, cabins with private bathroom and a block of more comfortable rooms, this is a cool place to pitch up. Likeable owner Mr Keo runs excellent tours to the jars.

Auberge De La Plaine Des Jarres CABINS $$$
(☎020 5599 9192; r US$60) Hillside elevation, Scotch pines and Swiss-style interiors give these inviting hobbit holes an incongruously alpine feel. There's a great restaurant with a nightly fire, and walls decked in animal horns like some hunter's eyrie. Expensive…a credit card treat?

Maly Hotel GUESTHOUSE $$
(☎312031; www.malyht.laotel.com; r incl breakfast 230,000-260,000K; ❄@) Maly excels with wooden beams and candlelit ambience. Rooms beckon with private bathroom, TV and hot water. Cosy.

Nice Guest House GUESTHOUSE $
(☎312454; r 70,000-110,000K) Fresh and fragrant rooms, Nice shows no signs of ageing with clean private bathrooms, spotless rooms and firm beds. Chinese lanterns cast a ruby glow into the chill.

Nam Chai Guest House GUESTHOUSE $
(☎312095; r 80,000K) Still smelling pine-fresh, this nondescript new guesthouse is functional with clean rooms with fan, TV and private bathroom.

White Orchid Guesthouse GUESTHOUSE $$
(☎312403; r incl breakfast 80,000-200,000K; ❄📶) Average-looking rooms with menthol-green walls, clean private bathrooms and appealing blankets. The higher you go, the better the views.

Eating

The **fresh food market** (⏲6am-5pm) sells everything from fruit to Korean, Indian and Lao fare at its many stalls. The following are clustered around the central area of Rte 7:

Nisha Restaurant INDIAN $
(meals 12,000K; ⏲breakfast, lunch & dinner) Tasty and value for money, Nisha has a wide range of vegetarian options and makes lovely *dosa* (flat bread), tikka masala and rogan josh, as well as great lassis.

Jars Café WESTERN $
(mains 30,000K; ⏲7am-10pm; 📶) Finally – somewhere in Phonsavan you can get a great cup of coffee! This homey cafe has cakes, spring rolls, sandwiches, pancakes and omelettes. Comfy leather couches and wi-fi make it a cool place to go online.

Simmaly Restaurant LAO $
(meals 15,000-20,000K; ⏲breakfast, lunch & dinner) Dishes up a tasty line of rice dishes, noodles and spicy meats. The pork with ginger is lovely.

Maly Hotel LAO $
(meals 25,000K; ⏲breakfast, lunch & dinner) Maly serves Lao, Thai food and wholesome soups, and is a great place to warm those chilly pinkies after the jars sites.

Craters Bar & Restaurant WESTERN $
(meals 30,000K; ⏲breakfast, lunch & dinner) A mainstay of NGOs, Craters has CNN on the tube as you munch through toasties, soups, burgers, fried chicken, steaks and pizzas.

GETTING TO VIETNAM: NONG HAET TO NAM CAN

Getting to the border Direct buses to Vinh (on the Vietnamese side) leave Phonsavan three times per week (150,000K) crossing at the lonely Nam Can/Nam Khan border (open 8am to noon and 1.30pm to 5pm). The nearest town on the Lao side is Nong Haet.

At the border If entering Vietnam, you'll need to have organised a Vietnamese visa in advance. If entering Laos a 30-day visa is available on arrival, costing between US$30 and US$40 depending on your nationality.

Moving on The first town en route to Vinh, 403 km away, is Muong Xen where there's a basic hotel. From here there's also a 4pm bus to Vinh. For information on crossing this border in the other direction, see p829.

Drinking

Barview BAR
(☎020 234 5581; ⏰8am-11pm) For sunset beers over the rice-paddy fields try simple Barview.

☆ Entertainment

Sousath Travel CINEMA
(☎312031; Rte 7; ⏰8am-9pm) At 7pm every evening, this place pulls down the drapes and surreptitiously screens an insightful documentary (currently banned in Laos) called *The Most Secret Place on Earth*; essential viewing for a revelatory perspective on the US involvement during the war.

ℹ Information

Amazing Lao Travel (☎020 234 0005; www.amazinglao.com; Rte 7) Runs treks to the Plain of Jars sites and two-day treks in the mountains, including a homestay in a Hmong village. As ever the more the merrier, with prices falling for larger groups. Three jar sites including food and driver will cost around 120,000K per person. It also books minibuses and bus tickets and has a bank of internet terminals.

BCEL (Rte 7) Located past the dry goods market. Has a 24-hour ATM.

Lao Development Bank (Rte 7) Currency exchange.

Lao-Mongolian Friendship Hospital (☎312166) Good for minor needs, but medical emergencies will need to be taken to Thailand.

Post office (⏰8am-4pm Mon-Fri, to noon Sat) Domestic phone service.

Provincial tourist office (☎312217) Now organising treks, it also produces a great two-page document called 'Do-it yourself activities around Phonsavan', detailing how to invite yourself to a local wedding, info on war memorials, local lakes and more.

Sousath Travel (☎312031; Rte 7) Rasa runs reliable tours to the Plain of Jars and Ho Chi Minh Trail. By the time you read this he'll be able to take you to the formerly forbidden Long Tien air base (a former CIA landing strip during the Secret War) in the infamous Special Zone.

ℹ Getting There & Away

Lao Airlines (☎212027) flies to/from Vientiane (one way US$87, daily except Tuesday, Thursday and Saturday). Jumbos to the airport cost around 8500K per person.

Buses leave from the bus station 4km west of town, while minibuses leave from the centre of town behind Sousath Travel. Most long-distance buses depart between 7am and 8am. Buses run to Sam Neua (80,000K, eight hours, two daily), Vientiane (local bus/VIP 110,000/130,000K, 11 hours, several daily commencing 7am, one VIP ride at 8pm), Vang Vieng (local bus 80,000K, six hours, daily at 7.30am; minibus 100,000K, daily at 8am) and Luang Prabang (local bus 85,000K, 10 hours, daily at 8.30am; minibus 100,000K, daily at 8.30am). For Paksan (local bus 100,000K, daily at 7.30am) the road is improved but still unsealed in parts and the trip takes 10 hours.

There are public buses and sǒrngtǎaou to Muang Kham (30,000K, two hours, four daily), Muang Sui (30,000K, one hour, three daily) and Nong Haet (40,000K, four hours, four daily).

Other destinations include Lat Khai (Plain of Jars Site 3; 20,000K, 30 minutes, one daily) and Muang Khoun (20,000K, 30 minutes, six daily). Buses also go all the way through to Vinh in Vietnam (138,000K, 11 hours, 6.30am Tuesday, Thursday and Sunday).

Plain of Jars

The Plain of Jars represents a huge area of Xieng Khuang, scattered with thousands of limestone jars of undetermined age. Thought to be funerary urns after bones were discovered within them, the jars have been divided into 160 sites, three of which represent the greatest concentration. These are the designated UXO-cleared tourist areas you should visit.

Site 1 (Thong Hai Hin; admission 10,000K), the biggest and most accessible site, is 15km southwest of Phonsavan and features 250 jars, most of which weigh from 600kg to 1 tonne each. The largest jar weighs as much as 6 tonnes and is said to have been the victory cup of mythical King Jeuam, and so is called Hai Jeuam.

Two other jar sites are readily accessible by road from Phonsavan. **Site 2** (Hai Hin Phu Salato; admission 10,000K), about 25km south of town, features 90 jars spread across two adjacent hillsides. Vehicles can reach the base of the hills, then it's a short, steep walk to the jars.

More impressive is 150-jar **Site 3** (Hai Hin Lat Khai; admission 10,000K). It's about 10km south of Site 2 (or 35km from Phonsavan) on a scenic hilltop near the charming village of **Ban Xieng Di**, where there's a small monastery containing the remains of Buddha images damaged in the war. The site is a 2km hike through rice paddies and up a hill.

Getting There & Away

It's possible to charter a sŏrngtăaou to Site 1 for about 85,000K return, including waiting time, for up to six people. All three sites are reachable by bike or motorcycle (per day 160,000K through guesthouses). **Happy Motorbikes** (Rte 7; 8am-6pm) rents out bicycles (40,000K per day) and scooters (90,000K per day).

Otherwise, you're on a tour. Guesthouses and a number of travel agents (see p342) offer tours for 120,000K to 200,000K per person in a minibus with around eight passengers. **Sousath Travel** (312031; Rte 7; 8am-9pm) and **Kong Keo Tours** (061-211354; www.kongkeojar.com; off Rte 7) receive consistently good reports.

Tours are often extended to include other interesting sites, including a crashed US F-105 Thunderchief, a Russian tank, Viet Cong bunkers, the US Lima Site 108 airstrip supposedly used for drug running, and hot springs.

Sam Neua

064 / POP 40,168

Isolated, riverside Sam Neua is back on the map thanks to the reintroduction of flights from Vientiane. Your efforts to come here are rewarded by a serene landscape of lush green rice paddies bookended by pine-carpeted hills. There's a palpable Soviet influence here with a communist-era memorial and the Russian hats worn by old boys in the market. It's cold too, so button up and wander through the dry and wet goods markets – keeping an eye out for the country's best silk pashminas. While the town itself has little to offer, it's a good place to stay en route to the fascinating Vieng Xai Caves.

Sleeping & Eating

Sam Neua's digs are unspectacular but reasonable value. They're found beside the Nam Sam River. For cheap *fŏe* (rice-noodle soup), samosas, spring rolls and fried sweet potato, the **market** (6am-6pm) is the place to go.

Kheamxam Guest House GUESTHOUSE $
(312111; r 40,000-70,000K) Rooms vary from basic to larger ones with immaculate private bathrooms and TV. Free airport pickup/drop off by arrangement.

Shuliyo Guest House GUESTHOUSE $
(312462; r 70,000K) The beds could be comfier, but the water is hot, the sheets clean and travellers seem to like it. The nearest you'll get to a smile might be Ho Chi Minh's picture in the lobby, but Shuliyo is good value for money.

Dan Nao Restaurant LAO $
(mains 15,000K; breakfast, lunch & dinner) Fronting the main road by the bridge this diminutive hole in the wall has a few tables to eat basic fare, like noodles, grilled chicken, fried eggs, tender beef salad and egg fried rice.

Sokdee Restaurant LAO $
(mains 15,000K breakfast, lunch & dinner) Given the Lao proclivity for eating anything with fur it's no surprise Sokdee is a favourite with locals but repellent among vegetarians. Come here for fried intestines and other exotic carnivorous fare.

Information

Agricultural Promotion Bank (8am-noon & 1.30-4pm Mon-Fri) On the main road north out of town, this bank exchanges Thai baht and Vietnamese dong, though you'll get better exchange rates at the fabric stalls in the dry goods market.

Lao Development Bank (8am-4pm Mon-Fri) On the main road 400m north of the bus station on the left; exchanges cash and travellers cheques.

Post office (8am-4pm Mon-Fri) In a large building directly opposite the bus station. A telephone office at its rear offers international calls.

Provincial tourist office (☎312567; ⏰8am-noon & 1.30-4pm Mon-Fri) An excellent tourist office with English-speaking staff eager to help.

Getting There & Away

Capricorn Air (☎020 448 8771; www.laocapricornair.net) flies to Vientiane on Wednesday and Saturday (850,000K, 1¼ hours) at 11.20am. The airport is 3km from town and a motorcycle taxi costs about 85,000K.

Sam Neua's bus station is roughly 1.2km away (túk-túk 8500K). There are two buses a day to Phonsavan (80,000K, eight to 10 hours, 9am and noon). It's a sinuous but beautiful hike through the mountains. The bus then continues on to Vientiane (from Sam Neua 130,000K, 20 to 24 hours). A VIP bus also runs to Vientiane (150,000K, 18 hours, noon).

A daily bus heads west to Nong Khiaw (80,000K, 12 hours, 8am) and continues on to Luang Prabang (from Sam Neua 110,000K, 16 hours, 7.30am). If you're heading for Udomxai, take this bus and change at Pak Mong (120,000K). **Nathong bus station** is 1km to the east heading for Vieng Xai. Sŏrngtăaou run from here to Vieng Xai (8000K, 50 minutes, 29km) at 8am, 10am, 11am, 2.30pm and 4pm; the scenery is among the most stunning in Laos. The 8am bus to Thanh Hoa in Vietnam (180,000K, 11 hours) stops here. Ensure you buy a ticket from the kiosk to avoid being overcharged once on the bus.

Vieng Xai

☎064 / POP 32,800

Set amid valleys glistening with wet rice paddies and towered over by dramatic karsts, beautiful Vieng Xai seems an unlikely place to have suffered a decade's worth of American air assaults. Its 450 limestone caves provided sanctuary for more than 23,000 people during the Secret War, playing host to bakeries, a hospital, school, a metalwork factory and, more importantly, the political headquarters of the communist Pathet Lao party. As the bombs fell near the virtually unassailable caves, President Kaysone Phomvihane plotted the transformation of his country in a dank grotto, undecorated but for a framed photo of Che Guevara and a few other keepsakes.

Today the most historically significant caves are open to tourists. Vieng Xai is a fascinating and peaceful place to spend a day or two. A wooden board in front of the market features a map of the town.

Sights & Activities

The Caves CAVES

Fringed with frangipani trees, the beautiful gardens that now adorn the caves can easily make you forget what their inhabitants had to endure. Perhaps the most atmospheric, as it housed the long-reigning president himself and hosted his politburo meetings, is Phomvihane's eponymous **Tham Than Kaysone**. The electricity is often out so you'll most likely be exploring by candlelight, your flame falling on his meagre library, a Russian oxygen machine poised for a chemical attack, a bust of Lenin…

Tham Than Souphanouvong, named after the communist-leaning 'Red Prince', has a crater from a 230kg bomb near the entrance, while **Tham Than Khamtay**, where up to 3000 Pathet Lao hid, is the most spectacular of the caves.

The best way to visit the caves is by **bicycle** (per tour/day 10,000/20,000K), available to rent from the **Vieng Xai Cave Tourist Office** (admission 50,000K; ⏰8-11.30am & 1-4.30pm); which allows you to see more caves in less time. Admission to the four major caves includes the mandatory guide. Two-hour tours leave the office between 9am and 11am and 1pm and 4pm and take in three or four caves. At other times you will need to pay an additional fee of 40,000K per tour to cover staff costs. Getting to the tourist office involves a 2km walk from the bus station by the market.

Sleeping & Eating

Naxay Guest House GUESTHOUSE $

(☎314336; r 50,000K) Naxay has six fan-only cabanas with private bathroom, wooden interior and tidy linen. You may need to wear an extra jumper to bed.

Thavisay Hotel GUESTHOUSE $

(☎020 571 2392; r 90,000K) Hands-down the best accommodation in town, it's nicer than anything Sam Neua has to offer. With its quiet lakeside setting, hot-water private bathrooms, comfy beds and TV, you'll be glad you stayed. There's also a restaurant selling basic Lao grub (meals 20,000K).

Getting There & Away

Sŏrngtăaou run regularly between Sam Neua's Nathong bus station and Vieng Xai (10,000K, 50 minutes, 29km, 6.20am to 5.20pm). From Vieng Xai market to Sam Neua, sŏrngtăaou run at 7am, 10am, 1pm, 2.30pm and 4pm.

GETTING TO VIETNAM: NAM XOI TO NA MEO

Getting to the border If you're crossing the Na Meo–Nam Xoi border (open 7.30am to 11.30am and 1.30pm to 4.30pm), take the daily bus from Sam Neua's Nathong bus station bound for Thanh Hoa (180,000K, 11 hours, 8am). Buy your ticket at the bus station itself to avoid being overcharged on the bus.

At the border Heading into Vietnam you'll need to have prearranged a visa. Lao visas are available on arrival from Vietnam, for US$30 to US$40 depending on nationality. Remember to bring ID and a passport photo too. There are no ATM facilities at this remote border crossing. On the Lao side there are a couple of restaurants, while at Na Meo on the Vietnamese side there's a relatively new hotel, **Yen Trang Hotel** (☎37-359 2511, in Vietnam).

Moving on If you've bought a ticket from Sam Neua heading through Thanh Hoa to Hanoi (290,000K) you'll have to change buses at Thanh Hoa. There's also a night train from Thanh Hoa to Hanoi departing at 11.30pm and arriving inconveniently at 4am. For information on crossing this border in the other direction see p828.

Udomxai

☎081 / POP 80,000

Udomxai Province is home to some of northern Laos' thickest forests, making it a great place to trek and visit Hmong and Khmu villages. Close to China's Yunnan province, you'll find 15 ethnic minorities in the area but the dominant group is increasingly the Yunnanese, working in construction and plantation operations. That said, it's hard to be positive about the town of Udomxai, with its dust devils, prostitutes and Chinese truck drivers, as gruffly inexpressive as the ugly Soviet buildings. Recently a few decent eateries and guesthouses have tried their luck, while the tourism office continues to do an excellent job of promoting treks in the ethnically rich, forest-abundant hills. Arrange a trip with staff in advance and give the town a body swerve.

Sleeping & Eating

Most places are along – or just off – Rte 1.

Villa Keoseumsack GUESTHOUSE $$
(☎312170; r 120,000-140,000K; wi-fi) Has the town's best rooms, with private bathroom, TV, wi-fi and a reading balcony.

Lithavixay Guest House GUESTHOUSE $
(☎212175; Rte 1; r 60,000-120,000K; air-con, internet) Traveller fave Lithavixay Guest House has a welcoming lobby, internet cafe and large rooms.

Xayxana Guest House GUESTHOUSE $
(☎020 578 0429; off Rte 1; r 60,000-80,000K; air-con) The fresh-looking Xayxana Guest House offers immaculate rooms, tiled floors and comfortable beds.

Meuang Neua Restaurant LAO $
(meals 30,000K; 7am-11pm) This restaurant has walls decorated with arabesques and there's an equally imaginative menu ranging from salads through to pumpkin soup, curry, fish and stir-fries.

Sinphet Restaurant LAO $
(mains 20,000K; breakfast, lunch & dinner) Almost falling down with age and dust from the road, Sinphet Restaurant, near the bridge, has noodle dishes, steak and salads.

Siso Bakery LAO $
(sandwiches 10,000K; 7am-9pm) Head here for cookies, burgers, banana fritters and cake (as well as internet, 6000K per hour).

Information

Air Computer (Rte 1; per min 200K; 8am-7pm) Speedy connection.

BCEL (☎211260; Rte 1) Changes foreign currency into kip; 24-hour ATM.

Udomxai provincial tourism office (☎212483; Rte 1; 8am-noon & 1.30-6.30pm) Just west of the bridge, this well-run office conducts ecotreks to Khmu villages, forests and the recently discovered Chom Ong Cave. There are six different packages to choose from. Speak to Mr Sikounavong.

Getting There & Away

Lao Airlines (☎312047; airport) flies to Vientiane (one way 695,000K) every Tuesday, Thursday and Saturday.

The **bus station** (☎212218) at the southwestern edge of town has buses to Luang Prabang (all VIP buses, 60,000K, five hours, 8.30am, 11.30am and 3pm daily), Nong Khiaw

(30,000K, four hours, four daily), Pak Beng (45,000K, five hours, 8am and 10am daily), Pakmong (30,000K, 9am and 2pm daily), Luang Nam Tha (40,000K, four hours, 8am, noon and 3pm daily), Muang Khua (35,000K, four hours, 8.30am, noon and 3pm daily), Boten (35,000K, four hours, 8am daily), Phongsali (75,000K, eight to 12 hours, 8.30am daily) and Vientiane (ordinary bus 100,000K, 16 hours, two daily; VIP bus 140,000K, 11 hours, 11am and 2pm daily).

Luang Nam Tha

☎086 / POP 18,000

Thanks to its location next to the Nam Ha National Protected Area (NPA), Luang Nam Tha is one of the best bases in the country for jungle junkies to head to, with more trekking companies per sq metre than anywhere else in Laos. There are bags of cheap guesthouses, restaurants serving tasty food and a lively market, as well as a couple of banks, internet cafes and cycle-hire and scooter shops. The town also invites exotic appearances from Hmong tribeswomen in rainbow garb at the candlelit night market. Many travellers spend a day pedalling around local waterfalls and temples before setting out into the wilds of Nam Ha.

Sights & Activities

The dense jungle of the **Nam Ha National Protected Area** is home to clouded leopards, gaur and elephants. Visiting it involves going on a tour with an experienced guide (there are still tigers in there and it's easy to get lost). Guides also offer **rafting**, **canoeing** and **mountain biking** along the Nam Tha River, as well as **homestays**.

Places of interest within easy cycling or motorbiking distance include **Wat Ban Vieng Tai** and **Wat Ban Luang Khon**, near the airfield; a hilltop stupa, **That Phum Phuk**, about 4km west of the airfield; a small **waterfall** about 6km northeast of town past **Ban Nam Dee**; plus a host of Khmu, Lenten, Thai Dam and Thai Lü villages dotted along dirt roads through ricefields. Pick up a map and brochures at the provincial tourism office before setting off.

Luang Nam Tha Museum MUSEUM
(admission 5000K; 8.30-11.30am & 1.30-3.30pm Mon-Thu, 8.30-11.30am Fri) Pop in to this museum to see its varied collection of hunting weapons, ceramics, bronze drums, Buddha images and tribal wear.

> **TIMBER!**
>
> Increasingly, China is turning to imports and illegal logging to slake its thirst for timber, and Laos, hungry for the income, is willing to oblige. Added to this, the Environmental Investigation Agency (EIA) claims that the furniture industry in Vietnam has grown tenfold since 2000, with Laos facilitating the flow of its timber to enable this. An estimated 500,000 cu metres of logs find their way over the border every year. While an outwardly hard-line approach has been taken against mass logging by the government, it's the self-funded military and local officials in remote areas who can fall prey to bribes.

Tours

Jungle Eco-Guide Services ADVENTURE TOUR
(☎212025; www.thejungle-ecotour.com; 8am-9pm) Offers 11 different trips ranging from one-day treks in Nam Ha NPA (group of two persons, 280,000K per person), to Khmu homestay and trekking (group of two persons, 590,000K per person). It also runs three-day treks (staying at jungle camps) that take you deeper into the interior.

Green Discovery ADVENTURE TOUR
(☎211484; www.greendiscoverylaos.com; 8am-9pm) Runs a panoply of activities ranging from one- to three-day treks, involving a combo of kayaking and trekking in the Nam Ha NPA, as well as cycling trips to ethnic villages. Larger groups keep the prices down.

Namtha River Experience ADVENTURE TOUR
(☎212047; www.namtha-river-experience-laos.com; 8am-9pm) Specialising in kayaking and rafting trips through Khamu and Lanten villages, it also facilitates homestays. Typically a group of two persons costs US$30 per person for a one-day trip.

Sleeping

In the high season (December to March) the town gets busy, so it's worth calling ahead to book a room.

TOP CHOICE **Zuela Guest House & Restaurant** GUESTHOUSE $
(☎312183; r 70,000-120,000K) Located in a leafy courtyard, Zuela has a welcoming restaurant serving pancakes, salads and chilli-

based Akha dishes, while its spotless rooms have wood floors, fans and fresh linen. It also rents out scooters.

Khamking Guest House GUESTHOUSE $
(☎312238; r 70,000K) Fresh and colourful with flourishes like bedside lights, attractive curtains and bed covers. Be warned though – you're in the chicken zone with a coop just behind you, so earplugs are essential!

Manychan Guest House-Restaurant GUESTHOUSE $
(☎312209; r 60,000-120,000K) Justifiably the town's best-loved traveller magnet, Manychan's cafe, with walls spattered in ethnic photography, covers the bases with salads, steaks and breakfasts. Rooms are adequate with hot-water showers and TV.

Adounsiri Guest House GUESTHOUSE $
(☎020 299 1898; s 50,000-60,000K, d & f 90,000K) Located down a quiet street behind the central drag, this newly built Lao villa has scrupulously clean rooms with white walls draped in handicrafts, fresh bed linen and tiled floors. TV in every room.

Thoulasith Guest House GUESTHOUSE $
(☎212166; r 70,000-90,000K; wi-fi) An injection of taste and value, rooms are spotless with bedside lamps and there's a wi-fi enabled balcony.

Eating

TOP CHOICE **Boat Landing Restaurant** LAO $$
(www.theboatlanding.laopdr.com; meals 42,000K) Laos' premier ecolodge has a vaulted longhouse serving award-winning pot roasts, *làap* and Western food. Located 7km south of the new town. Catch a shared jumbo here for 15,000K per person.

Aysha Restaurant INDIAN $
(mains 30,000K; ⏱7am-10pm) Delicious Madras cuisine dished up with flair and spice. Home-made naan, veggie options galore and chicken korma that could make you weep for joy after a day out in the wilds.

Minority Restaurant LAO $
(mains 10,000-15,000K; ⏱7am-10.30pm) Inviting, wood-beamed restaurant giving you a chance to sample Khamu, Tai Dam and Akha dishes, as well as generic stir-fries.

Panda Restaurant WESTERN, LAO $
(☎606549; mains 15,000K; ⏱6.30am-noon) Wooden beams are quirkily strung with bees' nests and buffalo horns. The menu is equally random, with dishes like fish 'n' chips and spaghetti carbonara, plus a few veg options.

Information

BCEL (⏱8.30am-3.30pm Mon-Fri) Changes US-dollar travellers cheques and cash; gives cash advances on credit cards. ATM.

Lao Telecom Long-distance phone calls.

Post office (⏱8am-noon & 1-4pm Mon-Fri)

Provincial Hospital (⏱24hr) Adequately equipped for X-rays, dealing with broken limbs and dishing out antibiotics. Ask for English-speaking Dr Veokham.

Provincial tourism office (☎211534; ⏱8am-noon & 2-5pm) English-speaking staff can help you with treks in the nearby Nam Ha NPA and have a wealth of maps and photocopied brochures on local flora and fauna and ethnic minorities.

Smile Internet Cafe (per hr 12,000K; ⏱8.30am-9pm)

Getting There & Away

Air

For now, **Lao Airlines** (☎312180; www.laoairlines.com) has regular flights to/from Vientiane (one way US$112, one hour, Tuesday, Thursday and Saturday) but there are plans to expand the flights servicing Luang Nam Tha. See the website for updates on new routes.

Boat

Charter boats make the wonderful trip along the Nam Tha through remote country to Pak Tha on the Mekong, or all the way to Huay Xai. They leave from the boat landing, 7km south of town on the Nam Tha, at 9.30am (between June and October) and cost 1,800,000K to Pak Tha, or 1,900,000K to Huay Xai. Sign up before your departure to share the charter costs for this two-day trip in an open longtail boat. In the high season a boat leaves almost every day. An additional 50,000K covers food and lodgings with the boatman's family. Bring sun protection, plus plenty of water and snacks. Go to the boat landing office opposite the Boat Landing Guest House to sign up for the trip.

Bus & Sŏrngtăaou

The bus terminal is 11km south of Luang Nam Tha's new town, beyond the airport. A sŏrngtăaou should cost 20,000K to/from there. Buses run to Udomxai (40,000K, five hours, 8.30am, 12.30pm and 2.30pm). A VIP bus leaves for Vientiane at 8.30am (190,000K, eight hours) followed by a local bus at 2.30pm (170,000K, 19 hours). There's only one bus to Luang Prabang (90,000K, eight hours, 9am) and Muengla (55,000K, 8am), while two buses run daily to Huay Xai – marked as Bokeo – (55,000K, 9am and 12.30pm). Finally, there's one daily service to Phonsavan (100,000K, 8am).

The local bus station is about 500m south on the outskirts of town. Sŏrngtăaou travel daily to Vieng Phoukha (20,000K, four hours, 9am and noon). About six sŏrngtăaou run to Muang Sing daily (22,000K, two hours); one daily bus goes to Muang Long (40,000K, five hours, 8.30am) and Boten (45,000K, two hours, 8am) on the Laos–China border.

Getting Around

Jumbos from the main street to the airport, 7km away, cost 10,000K per person for a minimum of three people. To the Nam Tha boat landing, or the nearby Boat Landing Guest House, figure on 15,000K per person on a shared jumbo.

Mountain/one-speed bicycles cost 15,000/10,000K per day from the **bicycle shop** (9am-6pm) on the main street, which also rents out motorcycles for 70,000K for a decent Honda – avoid cheap Chinese models for long journeys. Luang Nam Tha to Muang Sing by scooter is an exhilarating experience, giving you a chance to pass through Nam Ha NPA. It takes about two to three hours. Bring a jumper as it gets mighty cold up there.

Muang Sing

081 / POP 8000

At the heart of the infamous 'Golden Triangle' and rubbing shoulders with Myanmar and China, Muang Sing's wilting houses and air thick with wood smoke seem to hark back to a simpler time. Although tribeswomen are likely to offer you a rock of opium – Hmong, Thai Lü, Akha, Thai Dam and Yao are all seen here in traditional dress – trekking has overtaken smuggling contraband. In fact there's a glut of new tour providers itching to take you on adventures in the nearby Nam Ha NPA. Visitors who venture here from Luang Nam Tha are rewarded by beautiful countryside and Southeast Asia's most ethnically rich area (45% of Muang Sing's population is Akha).

Sights & Activities

The main draw for Muang Sing is its proximity to tribal villages and trekking in Nam Ha NPA. If you're just here to cycle, grab a map (Wolfgang Kom's excellent *Muang Sing Valley* map) from Muang Sing Tourism Information, hire a bike and make your own explorations.

Tribal Museum MUSEUM
(admission 5000K; 8.30am-4.30pm Mon-Fri, 8-11am Sat) Set in a delightful old wooden building, the museum has an interesting display of traditional textiles, woven baskets, handicrafts, amulets and cymbals, as well as photographic exhibitions and a documentary on the Akha (40,000K extra).

Muang Sing Tourism Information ECOTOUR
(020 239 3534; msnamhaecotrek@hotmail.com; 8-11am & 1.30-5pm Mon-Fri, 8-10am & 3-5pm Sat & Sun) An excellent government-run resource for travellers keen to explore the natural wonders and ethnological diversity of the area. Plenty of visual information and maps.

Tours

Tour operators to look out for include the following:

Nam Ha Eco Trek Service Center ECOTOUR
(030-511404; 8am-5pm Mon-Fri) Operates one- to four-day treks in the Nam Ha NPA, visiting Akha villages, with forest camping and homestays. Talk to English-speaking Mr Sendy.

GETTING TO CHINA: BOTEN TO MÓHĀN

Getting to the border The easiest place in Laos from which to reach China is the small town of Muang Sing, some 55km from the Lao border post of Boten (open 7.30am to 4.30pm). Buses leave by Muang Sing's market at 8am and 1pm (40,000K) every day. A daily bus (marked Muengla) also leaves Luang Nam Tha at 8am (55,000K).

At the border Lao visas are available on entry, costing between US$30 and US$40 depending on your nationality. When heading into China, some travellers have managed to buy a 14-day pass on the spot (though it's safer to prearrange). Túk-túk shuttle across no man's land from the Lao side to the Chinese immigration post in Móhān. Buses depart from Móhān's bus stand (on the main street) bound for Mengla (RMB15, 80 minutes) every 20 minutes or so till early afternoon.

Moving on Once you reach Mengla's 'bus station 2', head across the city to the 'northern bus' station to catch forward buses to Jinghong or Kunming.

Exotissimo ADVENTURE TOUR
(020 239 3534 8am-5pm Mon-Fri, 8-10am & 3-5pm Sat & Sun) Based at Muang Sing Tourism Information. Its 'Akha Experience' involves a three-day, two-night trek and homestay with the eponymous tribe.

Saophoudoy Tours ADVENTURE TOUR
(086-400 012; www.laosexploretravel.com; 7am-7.30pm) Gets decent reviews for its one- to seven-day treks and homestays to remote Hmong and Akha villages on the Burmese border.

Tiger Man ADVENTURE TOUR
(020 5546 7833; 8am-6pm) Run by friendly Mr Tong Mua and specialising in caving trips in the Nam Ha NPA.

Sleeping & Eating

Most of Muang Sing's extremely basic guesthouses and attached restaurants are on the town's main strip.

TOP CHOICE **Pho Lu 2 Guest House** GUESTHOUSE $$
(030-511 0326; r US$15-45) In a lush oasis chequered with mangos and palms, its 22 bamboo cabanas are finished with Hmong handicrafts and fresh linen. There's a choice of small, double or family rooms. The nicest digs in Muang Sing.

Stupa Mountain Lodge & Restaurant GUESTHOUSE $
(020 286 0819; stupamtn@laotel.com; r 50,000K) Vertiginously perched on stilts on a hill overlooking ricefields and distant China, cabanas here are cosy, with rattan walls and wood terraces to chill on. Edible food, but the place is spooky if you're travelling solo.

Thai Lü Guest House & Restaurant GUESTHOUSE $
(212375; r 30,000-40,000K) This creaky wooden building has rattan-walled rooms with squat toilets. The restaurant downstairs (meals 8000K to 12,000K; breakfast, lunch and dinner) serves Lao and Western dishes.

Sengduan Bungalows GUESTHOUSE $
(r 45,000K) Colourful cabanas in a back garden; rooms have brick and rattan walls and private bathrooms, and terraces that catch the afternoon light.

Information

Lao Development Bank (8am-noon & 2-3.30pm Mon-Fri) Changes cash but no ATM.
Post office (8am-4pm Mon-Fri)

BAD TRIPS

Muang Sing was once at the heart of the infamous Golden Triangle, and though Lao government programs to eradicate poppy fields have been largely successful, opium is still grown here and you may well be offered some. Not long ago a *falang* imbibed more than he could handle and ran naked and screaming into a *ban* (village) in the middle of the night – he was badly beaten by villagers who presumed he was an evil spirit!

Getting There & Around

Sŏrngtăaou ply back and forth between Muang Sing and Luang Nam Tha (20,000K, two hours, 8am, 9.30am, 11am, 12.30pm, 2pm and 3.30pm), and the Chinese border (15,000K, 8am), and Muengla in China (40,000K, 8am and 1pm). There are also about four sŏrngtăaou a day to Xieng Kok (30,000K, three to four hours) on the Myanmar border, from where speedboats race down to Huay Xai. Most passenger vehicles depart from the bus terminal opposite the market on the northwestern edge of town. Buy your tickets at the kiosk and get here a little early to ensure your seat. You can rent bikes from shops and guesthouses.

Huay Xai

084 / POP 17,800

Allegedly a US heroin processing plant was based here during the Secret War – these days the only things spirited through Huay Xai are travellers en route to Luang Prabang. Separated from Thailand by the cocoa-brown Mekong River, it is for many their first impression of Laos (don't worry, it gets better!). By night its central drag dons fairy lights and fires up roadside food vendors. There are some welcoming guesthouses and cafes, and Huay Xai is also the HQ of the fabled Gibbon Experience (see the boxed text, p350), Laos' most talked about jungle adventure.

Sleeping & Eating

Budget sleeping and eating haunts are going strong, with a wealth of choice on the main street.

TOP CHOICE **Sabaydee Guest House** GUESTHOUSE $
(212252; Th Saykhong; r incl breakfast 90,000-130,000K; @) Unfailingly clean rooms with comfy beds, TV, fan, optional air-con and private bathroom. Decked in bright colours

THE GIBBON EXPERIENCE

Essentially a series of navigable 'zip-lines' criss-crossing the canopy of some of Laos' most pristine forest, **The Gibbon Experience** (☎212021; www.gibbonx.org; Th Saykhong, Huay Xai; Classic & Waterfall 3-day trek/Gibbon Spa US$290/340) traverses the home of tigers, clouded leopards, black bears and the eponymous black-crested gibbon.

Seven years ago poaching was threatening the extinction of the black crested gibbon. Cue Animo is a conservation-based tour group that convinced the hunters of Bokeo Nature Reserve to become the forest's guardians. As guides, they now make more for their families than in their old predatory days.

You'll stay in fantastical tree houses complete with cooking facilities and running rain-water showers, 200ft up in the trees! In between scouting for wildlife, you'll be zipping. Your safety harness with a wheel on the end of a cable is attached to a zip-line; all you need then is a little faith and an adventurous spirit. It's a heart-stopping, superhero experience.

Your day also involves a serious amount of trekking. Bring a pair of hiking boots and long socks to deter the ever-persistent leeches, plus a torch and earplugs. The guides are helpful, though be vigilant with the knots in your harness.

There are three options to choose from: the 'Classic', which gives you more time to ponder the jungle and less time trekking; the 'Waterfall', with an increased amount of slog balanced by a wonderful dip in a cascade pool; and 'The Gibbon Spa' incorporating the best of the former but with gourmet food, improved lodgings and massages. Fees include transport to and from the park, plus all food and refreshments. All options are for two nights.

and pleasant furnishings, some rooms overlook the river.

Oudomphone 2 Guest House GUESTHOUSE $
(☎211308; Th Saykhong; r 80,000-120,000K; ❄) Decent-sized rooms and a bijou cafe make this a worthwhile place to stay – but for the resident rooster out the back with the faulty body clock.

Gateway Villa Guest House GUESTHOUSE $$
(☎212180; Th Saykhong; r 80,000-190,000K; ❄) Close to the boat landing, these are tastefully furnished rooms with hardwood floors, wicker chairs, TVs and contemporary looking linen. Some rooms are more prettified than others. Singles, doubles and triples.

Kaupjai Guest House GUESTHOUSE $$
(☎020 5568 3164; Th Saykhong; r 130,000K; ❄) Super fresh rooms with private bathrooms, vivid-white walls and cool tiled floors.

BAP Guest House GUESTHOUSE $$
(☎211083; bapbiz@live.com; Th Saykhong; r 60,000-160,000K; ❄) Run by English-speaking Mrs Changpeng, this wayfarer's fave has a pleasant restaurant dishing up snacks, veggie dishes and Lao staples (mains 14,000K). Rooms vary wildly with the best ones facing the river (air-con and TV come as extras).

TOP CHOICE **Gecko Bar** LAO, WESTERN $
(aka Muang Ner Café; Th Saykhong; meals 30,000K; ⏲6.30am-11pm) With its worn turquoise walls adorned in animal horns, Gecko is still the best traveller magnet in town. Mouthwatering *làap,* Western breakfasts and wood-fired pizzas all complement the welcoming vibe.

Nut Pop Restaurant LAO, VIETNAMESE $
(Th Saykhong; meals 30,000K; ⏲4.30-10pm) Reached via a bridge and by night alluringly lit with ropes of golden light, this treehouse-style restaurant makes for a romantic dinner. Tasty Lao and Vietnamese food.

Drinking

Bar How BAR
(Th Saykhong; ⏲6am-11.30pm; 📶) Perfect for chilling, with its walls suspended with muskets and coolie hats, funky How makes a mean Western breakfast, tasty Lao fare and sandwiches (mains 25,000K). Free wi-fi.

Information

BCEL (⏲8.30am-4.30pm Mon-Fri) Opposite BAP Guest House; 24-hour ATM, exchange facility and Western Union. Bring plenty of cash if you're going on The Gibbon Experience in case the ATM is out of order.

Lao Airlines (☎211471; Th Saykhong; ⏲8am-4.30pm) South of the boat ramp.

Luang Prabang Travel (☎211095; Th Saykhong; ⏲8am-4.30pm) Government-sanctioned tour company offering homestays, rafting, kayaking and treks. Speak to Mr Loon.

Post office (Th Saykhong) Contains a telephone office (open from 8am to 10pm).

Yon Computer Internet Cafe (Th Saykhong; per hr 15,000K; ⌚9am-9pm) Decent connection with Skype, also fixes laptops. Next door to Bar How.

Getting There & Away

Air

Huay Xai's airport lies a few kilometres south of town. **Lao Airlines** (☎211026; www.laoairlines.com) flies to/from Vientiane (one way 895,000K, Tuesday, Thursday and Saturday).

Boat

Slow boats headed down the Mekong River to Luang Prabang (200,000K per person, two days) hold about 70 people, but captains try to cram in more than 100. Refuse en masse and a second boat might be drafted in. Even better, try and charter your own boat and captain for around 4,250,000K and enjoy the trip with plenty of space.

Boats leave from the boat landing at the north end of town at 10.30am and stop for one night in Pak Beng (100,000K, six to eight hours). Tickets are available from the boat landing the afternoon before you travel, or from guesthouses.

Speedboats (see the boxed text 'Mekong Cowboys', p337) to Pak Beng (190,000K, three hours) and Luang Prabang (300,000K, six hours) leave from a landing about 2km south of town at 9.30am daily, though only when full. Buy your ticket at any one of the guesthouses or on arrival at the kiosk above the boat landing. Deaths are not uncommon given the recklessness of the drivers. Bring earplugs, close your eyes and sit at the stern.

Slow boats also run to Luang Nam Tha (1,530,000K to 1,700,000K per boat split between passengers, plus 40,000K each for food and accommodation) via Ban Na Lae. Ask at BAP Guest House (p350) for more information.

For any journey take plenty of water, food supplies and padding for your back.

Bus & Sŏrngtăaou

Buses and large sŏrngtăaou ply the road daily northeast to Vieng Phoukha (50,000K, five hours, three to four daily), Luang Nam Tha (60,000K, four hours, 9am and noon) and Udomxai (85,000K, six hours, 8.30am). There are daily local buses to Luang Prabang (120,000K, eight hours, 9am and 2pm). VIP buses run to Luang Prabang (145,000K, 5pm) and Vientiane (230,000K, 18 hours, 11.30am) and there's also a bus to Muangla in China (120,000K, 8.30am).

Travel companies operate on the main drag and boat ramp. They can arrange daily minibuses to Chiang Mai, Thailand (average price 95,000K, five hours, 10.30am and 6.30pm).

CENTRAL & SOUTHERN LAOS

Steamy rice plains, gothic karst formations, vast forests, coffee-growing plantations and authentic riverine life: all of this beckons those en route to and from Cambodia. Mekong-bound Pakse and Savannakhet have recently finessed their trekking options, giving you reasons to stop for a day or two. And rush straight to the lotus-eater charms of Four Thousand Islands at your peril, for in between are the likes of charming Tha Khaek and the mysterious 7.5km Kong Lo cave, and sleepy Champasak with its beautiful Khmer ruins.

GETTING TO THAILAND: HUAY XAI TO CHIANG KHONG

Getting to the border Longtail boats (one-way 10,000K, five minutes, 8am to 6pm) run across the Mekong between the immigration post of Huay Xai in Laos (open 8am to 6pm) and Thailand's Chiang Khong. A huge vehicle ferry (per car 1000B) also makes the trip.

At the border Huay Xai abounds with accommodation. Thirty-day Lao visas are available on arrival at the immigration office at the bottom of the boat ramp for between US$30 and US$40 depending on your nationality. Bring a passport photo if you're headed into Laos, otherwise pay an extra 40B. A 15-day Thai visa is automatically granted when entering Thailand. Arriving in Chiang Khong, pay the 30B port fee and catch a 30B túk-túk to take you to the bus station. The nearest ATM on the Thai side is 2km south.

Moving on Many leave Huay Xai bound for Chiang Mai (300B, four hours) with buses typically leaving from the Thai side at 10am. Organise this at a number of Huay Xai's independent tour companies based on the main street. For information on crossing this border in the other direction see p703.

Route 8 to Lak Sao

Wind your way through a lost world of jungle and dreamlike rock formations in some of the country's trippiest landscape. The first major stop is **Ban Khoun Kham** (also known as Ban Na Hin), 41km east of Rte 13, in the lush Hin Bun valley. The village makes a base from which to explore Phu Hin Bun National Protected Area. You can also catch your forward bus to the extraordinary **Kong Lo cave**. Community-based treks gear up at the **tourist information centre** (Rte 8) just south of the Tat Namsanam entrance.

Sights

Kong Lo Cave CAVE

If you were to realise the ancient Greek underworld (minus the spirits), you might end up with Kong Lo cave. Situated in the 1580-sq-km wilderness of **Phu Hin Bun National Protected Area**, this 7.5km tunnel running beneath an immense limestone mountain is unearthly. In the words of Aussie traveller Megan: 'I've done loads of caves, but this is the creepiest and the best I've ever seen.'

Puttering upriver (longtail boat is the only means to enter the subterranean caves) you witness the gaping mouth of the cave, your breath stolen before you've even entered the eerie, black cavern. Passing into the church-high darkness (100m in some places) and watching the light of the cave mouth recede, is a spooky experience. As you moor up to the riverbank, strolling through a stalactite wood, you feel like you've wandered onto an old *Star Trek* set.

Remember to bring a decent torch, plus rubber sandals. You can make a day trip to Kong Lo cave from Ban Khoun Kham, but it's more fun to overnight near the cave. Kong Lo village (about 1km downstream of the cave mouth), in response to the growing number of visitors, has recently started to develop.

Sleeping & Eating

Ban Khoun Kham

Digs in Ban Khoun Kham are basic but do the job, with warm showers and private bathrooms.

Xok Xai Guesthouse GUESTHOUSE $

(☎051-233 629; Rte 8; r 50,000-100,000K; ❄) To reach this guesthouse walk 400m north from the market and you'll find a couple of timber buildings with fan-only rooms. Motorbikes for rent at US$10 make for an easy DIY trip to Kong Lo cave.

Mi Thuna Restaurant Guesthouse GUESTHOUSE $

(☎020 224 0182; Rte 8; r 50,000-100,000K; ❄) Mi Thuna has TV, air-con, modern bedrooms and quirky management. The restaurant serves Lao food. It's 800m south of the market, past the Shell fuel stop, and it also rents scooters (100,000K per day).

Kong Lo Village

Not as comfortable as Chantha Guest House but definitely memorable are the **homestay options** (per person incl breakfast & dinner 50,000K) in Kong Lo village. Simply ask around and a family will take you in.

Chantha Guest House GUESTHOUSE $

(☎020 210 0002; r 80,000K) Should you arrive too late to do the cave and want to stay the night, head for the Swiss-style chalet of Chantha Guest House, which has 16 comfortable rooms.

Mithuna Restaurant

(Kong Lo village; mains 30,000K; ⏲7am-8pm) For dinner head here for Western breakfasts and snacks and well-cooked Lao cuisine.

GETTING TO THAILAND: PAKSAN TO BUENG KAN

Getting to the border In Paksan head past Manolom Guest House and follow a sign to the port and Lao border post (open 8am to noon & 1.30pm to 4.30pm). Best caught at its busiest time in the morning – it won't leave until there are seven passengers – the boat across the Mekong to Bueng Kan takes a few minutes and costs 60B per person or charter for 480B.

At the border Fifteen-day Thai visas are granted on arrival but check in advance as this is a remote spot seldom used by travellers. Thirty-day Lao visas are granted on arrival and cost between US$30 and US$40, depending on your passport.

Moving on Buses leave Beung Kan in Thailand for Udon Thani and Bangkok. For information on crossing this border in the other direction see p722.

GETTING TO VIETNAM: NAM PHAO TO CAU TREO

Getting to the border The border crossing (open 7am to 4.30pm) at Nam Phao (Laos) and Cau Treo (Vietnam) is 32km from Lak Sao. Sŏrngtăaou leave (20,000K, 45 minutes) leave every hour or so from Lak Sao market. Alternatively, direct buses from Lak Sao to Vinh (120,000K, five hours) leave several times a day between noon and 2pm (you may have to change buses at the border).

At the border Laos issues 30-day visas (costing between US$30 and US$40) on arrival, though you'll need to prearrange a visa if heading into Vietnam. There's an exchange booth on the Laos side with ungenerous rates and, inconveniently, the Vietnam border post is another 1km up the road.

Moving on On the Vietnamese side beware an assortment of characters who'll offer to take you to Vinh by minibus for US$30 – it should cost US$5 per person. A metered taxi costs around US$40 while a motorbike fare is 200,000D. Hook up with other travellers to improve bargaining power. These woes can be avoided by taking the direct bus from Lak Sao to Vinh. Once in Vinh take the sleeper train, Reunification Express, direct to Hanoi. For information on crossing this border in the other direction see p841.

Getting There & Away

All transport along Rte 8 stops at Ban Khoun Kham. Buses for Vientiane (70,000K) usually stop between 7am and 10.30am. For Tha Khaek (50,000K, three hours, 143km), there are a couple of buses in the morning; for Lak Sao take any passing bus or sŏrngtăaou (25,000K).

From Ban Khoun Kham to Ban Kong Lo, it's an easy and picturesque 20-minute journey by scooter or sŏrngtăaou (25,000K).

In Ban Kong Lo boatmen charge 120,000K per boat, as well as a 5000K entrance fee for the return trip through the cave (about 2½ hours, maximum three people). If you're travelling solo, you'll have to stump the entire 120,000K fee. If you're doing 'the loop' (p355) and returning to Tha Khaek, ask the ever-helpful Mr Somkiad at Tha Khaek's tourist information centre (p354) for more details.

Tha Khaek

☎051 / POP 30,000

Predictions that somnolent Tha Khaek was heading into fresh territory as a boutique destination were misplaced, for this riverside town, despite its crumbling Indochinese charm, is still to be developed. That said, the new bridge linking Tha Khaek with nearby Thailand looks set to bring a healthy dose of investment and increased trade. Presently there are a couple of decent places to eat and stay if you're making your way south or are headed to Kong Lo Cave. Catch a riverside sundowner or wander along its atmospheric streets as dusk's amber light kicks in and douses the old buildings in charm. With its centrepiece fountain and tree-shaded boulevards glowing with braziers, Tha Khaek is reminiscent of Vientiane 10 years ago.

Sleeping

TOP CHOICE **Tha Khek Travel Lodge** GUESTHOUSE $
(☎212931; travell@laotel.com; dm 25,000K, r 50,000-110,000K; ❄@📶) This traveller's oasis excels with 17 immaculate rooms varying in luxury (as well as a dorm). And with the courtyard's sociable, nightly fire pit, this is the perfect place to swap stories about doing 'the Loop' (see p355) by scooter (85,000K per day, ask for details at reception). It also runs one-day trips to Kong Lo cave by minibus (group of four, 550,000K per person, leaves 8am).

Mekong Hotel HOTEL $$
(☎250777; Th Setthathirat; r 100,000-170,000K; 📶) Pleasant rooms in this elephant-grey, Soviet-style monolith. Parquet floors, cupboards, fresh walls and fridge; TV, spotless bathrooms and fine river views of the Mekong through a column of acacia trees. Good value.

Tha Khek Mai Guest House GUESTHOUSE $
(☎212551; Th Vientiane; r 120,000K) Beside its cavernous restaurant this large house has 16 rooms. The ones on the 1st floor away from the road are preferable; with mint-coloured walls, private bathroom, TV, wooden floors and fresh linen.

Eating & Drinking

Several *khào jįi* (baguette) vendors can be found on or near Fountain Sq in the morning, and the adjacent riverfront is good for a cheap meal any time.

Duc Restaurant LAO $
(meals 10,000K; ⏲6am-10pm) Unnamed but for an ETL sign, Duc Restaurant looks like someone's front room (hung with family photos and portraits of Ho Chi Minh) and serves delicious *fŏe hàeng* (rice noodle soup with broth).

Smile Restaurant LAO $
(meals 25,000K; ⏲noon-11.30pm) Smile pleases with its old wooden building and decked veranda overlooking the river. Fried food galore: fish, chicken, squid and (sorry, Jiminy) crickets!

Inthira Restaurant FUSION $
(Th Chao Annou; mains 30,000K; ❄) Complimenting the Lao/international theme of the hotel, its Asian Fusion menu features spicy salads, *steak au frites*, Thai stir-fries and steamed fish. With its open range kitchen and adjacent bar it's perfect for breakfast or evening dinner.

Sabaidee Thakhaek LAO $
(Th Chao Annou; mains 30,000K; ⏲7.30am-10pm) A welcoming traveller's haunt in the centre of town, it has chequered table cloths, Western-style grub, tasty Lao curries, memorable *tom yum* (prawn and vegetable soup), and curiously, amid the secondhand thrillers, gay porn DVDs.

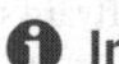

Information

BCEL (☎212686; Th Vientiane) Changes major currencies and travellers cheques, and makes cash advances on Visa. Including the ATM in Fountain Sq there are three ATMs in town, plus one at the bus station.

Green Discovery (☎251390; Inthira Hotel, Th Chao Annou; ⏲8am-9pm) Has a desk at the Inthira Hotel and runs a range of treks and kayaking excursions in the lush Phou Hin Boun NPA including Kong Lo cave. Cycling, kayaking and a homestay can also be combined.

Lao Development Bank (☎212089; Th Kuvoravong) Cash only.

Post office (Th Kuvoravong) Also offers expensive international phone calls.

Tha Khaek Hospital (cnr Th Chao Anou & Th Champasak) Tha Khaek Hospital is fine for minor ailments or commonly seen problems, including malaria and dengue. Seek out English-speaking Dr Bounthavi.

Tourist information centre (☎212512; Th Vientiane; ⏲8.30-9pm) This excellent tourist office is one of the best in the country with exciting one and two-day treks in Phou Hin Boun NPA, including a homestay with a local village (group of four, 590,000K per person). There are also treks to the awe-inspiring and remote Xe Bang Fai cave.

Tourist police (☎250610; Fountain Sq)

Wangwang Internet (Fountain Sq; per hr 7000K; ⏲7.30am-9.30pm) Opposite Inthira Hotel.

Getting There & Away

Tha Khaek's **bus station** (Rte 13) is about 3.5km from the centre of town. For Vientiane (60,000K, six hours, 332km, one VIP), buses leave every hour or so between 5.30am and noon. There's also a VIP bus (80,000K, six hours, 9.15am). Any buses going north stop at at Vieng Kham (Thang Beng; 30,000K, 90 minutes, 102km) and Paksan (40,000K, three to four hours, 193km). There are daily services to Attapeu (85,000K, 10 hours, 3.30pm), Salavan (85,000K, 11pm) and Sekong (75,000K, 10am and 3.30pm).

Southward buses to Savannakhet depart at 10.30am, noon and then every half-hour till 3pm, and there's a VIP bus (60,000K, six hours) to Pakse that leaves at 8.15am. For Vietnam, buses leave at 8am for Hué (100,000K), 8pm for Danang (100,000K) and 8.30pm for Hanoi (160,000K, 17 hours), as well as Dong Hoi (85,000K, 10 hours, 7am, every other day).

If you're headed direct to Don Khong (80,000K, 15 hours, 452km) in the Four Thousand Islands, a bus from Vientiane stops around 5.30pm.

Sŏrngtăaou heading east along Rte 12 depart every hour or so from the main bus terminal, Talat Lak Sam bus terminal (aka Sooksomboon bus terminal), between 7am and 3pm for

GETTING TO THAILAND: THA KHAEK TO NAKHON PHANOM

Getting to the border As we were going to print a new Friendship bridge had just opened with new immigration offices. The boat that used to run is now closed to foreigners and only runs for Lao and Thai nationals. The bridge is some 7km from Tha Khaek and a túk-túk over the bridge carrying two people will cost you 30,000K per person.

At the border In Tha Khaek Laos immigration issues 30-day visas for between US$30 and US$40 depending on your nationality. A free 15-day visa is granted on entry to Thailand.

Moving on From Nakon Phanom buses leave regularly for Udon Thani and also Bangkok (at 7.30am and from 7pm to 8pm). For information on crossing this border in the other direction, see p722.

GETTING TO VIETNAM: NA PHAO TO CHA LO

Getting to the border This border (open 7am to 4pm) is so out of the way it might be better to opt for an easier crossing elsewhere. Transport on either side is slow and scarce, though there are two daily sŏrngtăaou from Tha Khaek (45,000K, 3½ hours, 142km) at 8.15am and noon bound for Lang Khang, 18km short of the border. Catch the early sŏrngtăaou as you'll need to organise your own forward transport to the border.

At the border This is a small, sleepy border post. On the Vietnamese side the nearest sizeable city is Dong Hoi.

Moving on A direct bus from Tha Khaek to Dong Hoi (130,000K, 10 to 14 hours) leaves four times a week at 7pm, making this the easiest way to cross this border. For information on crossing this border in the opposite direction, see p847.

Mahaxai (15,000K, 1½ hours, 50km), Nyommalat (30,000K, two to three hours, 63km), Nakai (35,000K, 2½ to 3½ hours, 80km) and Na Phao (for the Vietnam border; 45,000K, five to seven hours, 142km).

There's also a daily bus from here to Ban Khoun Kham (50,000K, 7.30am), for those of you headed to Kong Lo cave. If you miss this, catch an hourly bus from the main bus terminal to Vieng Kham (30,000K, 90 minutes), from where you can catch a túk-túk to Kong Lo village.

Getting Around

Chartered jumbos cost about 15,000K to the bus terminal out of town. **Mr Ku's Motorbike rental** (Tha Khaek Travel Lodge; ⏲7.30am-4.30pm) at Tha Khek Travel Lodge rents scooters for 90,000K a day. The tourist information centre can arrange bicycle hire.

Around Tha Khaek

Travellers often rent motorbikes and take on the **The Loop**, a three- or four-day motorbike trip through the province via Nakai, Lak Sao, Khoun Kham (Na Hin) and Kong Lo cave; for details look at the travellers' log at Tha Khek Travel Lodge (p353). The new buzz is about **Xe Bang Fai cave**; located at the edge of Hin Namno NPA, and even longer than Kong Lo, this 9.5km subterranea boasts some of the tallest caverns and stalagmites (not to mention 25cm spiders) of any river cave on earth. Two-day trips are in their infancy but involve a homestay in a nearby Ban Nong Ping village (group of four, 1,800,000K per person). Talk to English-speaking Mr Somkiad at Tha Khaek's **tourist information centre** (☎051-212512; Th Vientiane).

Savannakhet

☎041 / POP 77,000

With its honey-coloured French villas, their facades crumbling in the unrelenting sun, Savannakhet evokes a sense of grand nostalgia. There's little to do but wander by old boys busy with their *pétanque,* past vendors cooking up grilled prawns by the slow rolling Mekong. This is a sleepy city, at least in its desirable 'old town area'. A recent tourist drive has seen local activities being remarketed, with improved signage for cultural highlights and a fresh trekking drive. Beyond its old town, Savannakhet is a busy, unpretentious city retaining some of its industry experienced in former days as a crucial Indochinese trading centre. Don't expect Luang Prabang, but do expect to be charmed by its languid authenticity.

Sights & Activities

Your best bet is to hire a bicycle and pedal through the cracked streets and along the riverfront, or take a trek in the neighbouring protected areas with Savannakhet's Eco Guide Unit (p357).

Savannakhet Provincial Museum MUSEUM
(Th Khanthabuli; admission 5000K; ⏲8-11.30am & 1-4pm Mon-Sat) The Savannakhet Provincial Museum is a good place to see war relics, artillery pieces and inactive examples of the deadly UXO that has claimed the lives of over 12,000 Lao since the end of the Secret War.

Musee Des Dinosaures MUSEUM
(Th Khanthabuli; admission 5000K; ⏲8am-noon & 1-4pm) The enthusiastically run Dinosaur Museum is an interesting place to divert yourself for an hour or so. Savannakhet Province is home to five dinosaur sites.

Wat Sainyaphum TEMPLE

(Th Tha He) The oldest and largest monastery in southern Laos, its grounds includes a workshop near the river entrance that's a veritable golden-Buddha production line.

Sleeping

There are some decent options in town; the following are our favourites:

Saisouk Guesthouse GUESTHOUSE $

(☎212207; Th Phetsalat; r 30,000-70,000K; ❄) For sheer value, this atmospheric villa with its shadowy corridors hung with coolie hats, buffalo horns and curios, is unbeatable. Rooms are basic with a pleasant communal chilling balcony.

Leena Guesthouse GUESTHOUSE $

(☎212404; Th Chao Kim; r 40,000-80,000K; ❄📶) Fairy-lit Leena is something of a motel with kitsch decor in comfortable clean rooms, hot water showers, TV and a pleasant breakfast area. Air-con rooms are bigger.

Sayamungkhun Guest House GUESTHOUSE $

(☎212426; Th Ratsavongseuk; r 50,000-70,000K; ❄) Rambling accommodation in an atmospheric colonial era building, rooms in the main house are preferable to the faded bungalows out back. Ask for one away from the busy road.

Salsavan Guest House GUESTHOUSE $$

(☎212371; Th Kuvoravong; r incl breakfast US$20-25; ❄📶) Salsavan has banana-hued rooms with high ceilings and wooden floors evoking a scent of old Indochine. Located in the former Thai consulate the villa has a nice garden to read in, but feels overpriced.

Souannavong Guest House GUESTHOUSE $

(Th Saenna; ☎212600; r 60,000-80,000K) A welcoming spot to stay; rooms have hot water, bathroom and TV, plus there's a communal lounge with a modest library. Located down a peaceful bougainvillea-bordered street.

Savannakhet

Sights

1 Musee des Dinosaures A2
2 Savannakhet Provincial Museum A4
3 Wat Sainyaphum A3

Sleeping

4 Leena Guesthouse B3
5 Saisouk Guesthouse A4
6 Salasavan Guest House A3
7 Sayamungkhun Guest House B4
8 Souannavong Guest House B3

Eating

9 Café Anakot B3
10 Café Chez Boune B2
11 Dao Savanh Restaurant A3
12 Friendship Bakery A4
13 Riverside Snack & Drink Vendors A3
14 Xokxay A3

Information

15 Eco Guide Unit A4

GETTING TO THAILAND: SAVANNAKHET TO MUKDAHAN

Getting to the border Regular buses (13,000K, 45 minutes) leave Savannakhet's bus station for Thailand's Mukdahan between 8.15am and 7pm.

At the border This is a well organised, busy border (open 9am to 4.30pm). Only Thai and Lao nationals can still use the ferry crossing. If entering Laos a 30-day tourist visa is granted for between US$30 and US$40 depending on your nationality, while a free 15-day tourist visa is given on entering Thailand. Note that to obtain a 30-day Thai visa, you'll need to arrive in the country by air.

Moving on Head to Nakon Phanom bus station to catch local (330B) and VIP buses (760B) to Bangkok and regular buses to Ubon Ratchathani (air-con 144B). For information on crossing this border in the other direction, see p721.

Eating & Drinking

For cheap *páa-tê* (meat paste) baguettes head to the vendors on the corners of Th Ratsavongseuk and Th Phagnapui. Akin to its French-era buildings, there's some great Gallic cuisine here, as well as Lao, Japanese and Thai restaurants.

TOP CHOICE Café Anakot JAPANESE $
(Th Ratsavongseuk; mains 20,000K; ⌚8.30am-9pm) We dig this place for its Japanese cuisine and hip vibe. The menu features homemade yoghurt, fruit, veggie spring rolls and terrific shakes. It also sells a good range of secondhand books, cool T-shirts and handicrafts.

Dao Savanh Restaurant FRENCH $$
(Th Si Muang; snacks 40,000K, mains 100,000-150,000K; ⌚7am-10pm; @ 📶) This elegant plaza-facing villa is perfect for light lunch downstairs, with a menu of salads, sandwiches and croque monsieur. Upstairs the decor is classier with another menu boasting grilled duck breast, tenderloin steak and lamb chops *Provencale*. There are also a couple of internet terminals here (5000K per hour).

Friendship Bakery BAKERY $
(Th Tha Dan; mains 15,000K; ⌚9am-10pm) This welcoming house of pastry, and all things bad for the waistline, creates a range of brownies, fudge cake, apple or blueberry pie and decent coffees, as well as ice lollies (you'll need them!).

Xokxay LAO $
(Th Si Muang; mains 15,000K; ⌚9am-9pm) Authentic Lao food at this friendly hole in the wall is renowned for its noodle dishes, fried rice and salads. The crispy fried shrimp is lovely.

Café Chez Boune WESTERN $$
(Th Ratsavongseuk; mains 60,000K; ⌚7am-10pm) Cuisine to please French tastes, we found the *fillet mignon* with pepper sauce absolutely perfect. Other dishes include pasta and pizza. Opposite Wat Sainyaphum, the riverside **snack and drink vendors** (⌚afternoon & evening) are great for sundowners.

Information

BCEL Bank (Th Ratsavongseuk; ⌚8.30am-4pm) Cash exchange and credit-card advances. ATM.

Dao Savanh Restaurant (Th Si Muang; per hr 5000K; ⌚7am-10pm; @ 📶) It's the perfect place to catch up on emails over a glass of vino.

Eco Guide Unit (☎214203; www.savannakhet-trekking.com; Th Ratsaphanith; ⌚8-11.30am & 1.30-5pm closed Sunday) This excellent office provides free city maps and one-day tours to Turtle Lake and the Ho Chi Minh Trail. It also arranges homestays, camping, cycling tours in Dong Natad NPA and cooking classes (50,000K per person). Finally, it rents bikes (15,000K) and books flights and VIP bus tickets.

Lao Development Bank (Th Udomsin; ⌚8.30-11.30am & 1.30-3.30pm) Same services as BCEL.

Police (☎212069; Th Ratsaphanith)

Post office (☎212205; Th Khanthabuli)

Provincial hospital (☎212051; Th Khanthabuli)

Savannakhet provincial tourism office (☎212755; Th Muang sing; ⌚8-11.30am & 1.30-4.30pm) With helpful city maps and English-speaking staff with suggestions of things to do, from food to local sights.

Getting There & Away

Savannakhet's airport fields flights to and from Vientiane (US$62, Wednesday, Friday and Sunday) and Pakse (US$62, Wednesday, Friday and Sunday). They also fly to Bangkok (US$135) on the same days.

Savannakhet's **bus terminal** (☎212143) is 2km north of town on Th Makkasavan. Buses leave for Vientiane (70,000K, nine hours, 470km) hourly from 6am to 11.30am. Thereafter you'll have to catch buses headed to Pakse that pass through Tha Khaek (30,000K, 2½ to four hours, 125km) until 10pm. A sleeper VIP bus to Vientiane (120,000K, six to seven hours) leaves at 9.30pm.

Heading south, at least nine buses start here or pass through from Vientiane for Pakse (40,000K, five to six hours, 230km) and Don Khong (70,000K, six to eight hours) between 7am and 10pm. Buses for Dansavanh (40,000K, five to seven hours) on the Lao/Viet border leave at 7am and noon, stopping at Sepon (40,000K, four to six hours). A local bus to Hue (80,000K) and Danang (110,000K) leaves daily at 10pm, continuing to Hanoi (200,000K, 24 hours, 650km). Sŏrngtăaou leave more frequently for local destinations such as Tha Khaek (25,000K).

Getting Around

A túk-túk to the bus terminal will cost about 20,000K; prices double after dark. The town is fairly sprawled out so it might be a good idea to rent a bicycle/scooter for 15,000/70,000K per day from Eco Guide Unit.

Pakse

☎031 / POP 119,000

If you're moving north from the Four Thousand Islands or headed south to Cambodia, you'll be stopping in the former Indochinese capital of Pakse. Until recently you might have stayed a night before moving on, but thanks to Green Discovery's newly opened Tree Top Explorer (zip-lining adventure) and a more active 'eco' drive from the tourist office, the city is now worth staying in longer. Pakse is close to the Khmer ruins of Wat Phu and the Bolaven Plateau coffee-growing region and its Edenic waterfalls.

Central Pakse is bound by the Mekong to the south and by the Se Don River to the north and west. On and below Rte 13 towards the Mekong are most of Pakse's guesthouses,

Pakse

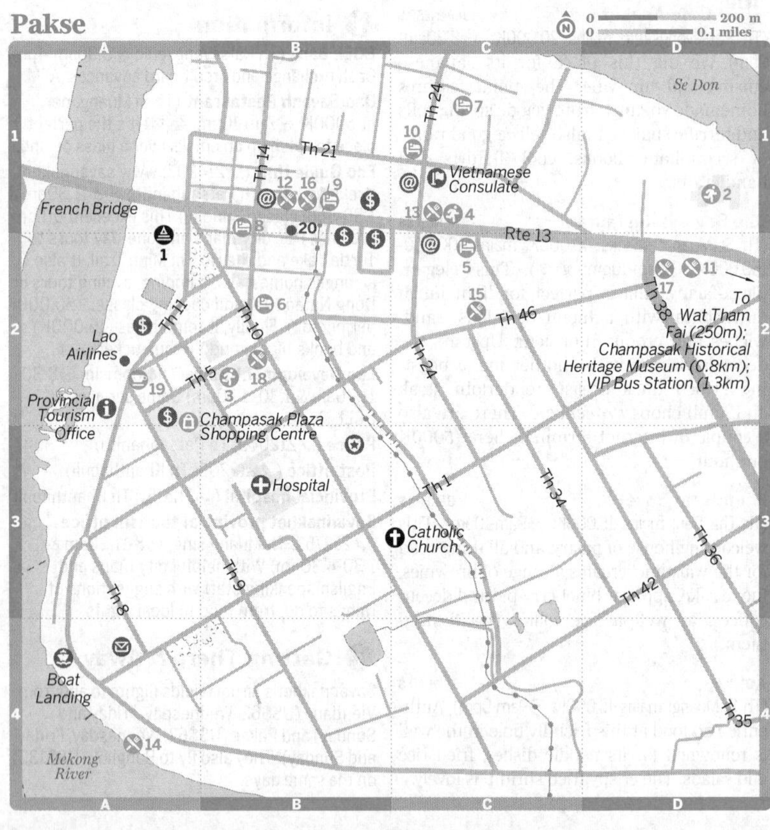

GETTING TO VIETNAM: DANSAVANH TO LAO BAO

Getting to the border Buses for the Dansavanh–Lao Bao border (open 8am to 5pm) leave from Savannakhet (40,000K, five to seven hours) at 7am and noon, and regularly from Sepon (12,000K, one hour, 45km).

At the border It's a 1km walk between the two border posts (hop on a motorbike taxi on the Vietnamese side for 10,000D). Formalities don't take long if you have a prearranged Vietnam tourist visa. Laos 30-day visas are granted on entry and cost between US$30 and US$40 depending on your nationality. There is simple accommodation on both sides of the border.

Moving on A daily 8am bus runs from Savannakhet to Dong Ha (US$12, about eight hours, 329km), while a 10am and 10pm bus also run from Savannakhet to Hue (local/VIP 80,000/110,000K, about 12 hours, 409km). The same VIP bus continues to Danang (11,000K, about 14hrs, 508km). No matter what you hear, you will have to change buses at the border. For information on crossing this border in the other direction see p848.

shops and restaurants. Heading west across Se Don takes you to the northern bus terminal. The southern bus terminal and market are 8km in the opposite direction.

Sights & Activities

Wats TEMPLE

There are 20 wats in town; the largest are **Wat Luang**, featuring ornate concrete pillars and carved wooden doors and murals, and **Wat Tham Fai**, which has a small Buddha footprint shrine in its grounds.

Champasak Historical Heritage Museum MUSEUM

(Rte 13; admission 5000K; ⏲8-11.30am & 1-4pm) Champasak Historical Heritage Museum documents the history of the province, with historical photos and ethnological displays.

Clinic Keo Ou Done MASSAGE

(Traditional Medicine Hospice; 1hr massage 20,000K; ⏲4-9pm Mon-Fri, 10am-9pm Sat & Sun) This is a real Lao experience. Go east on Rte 13, turn right about 100m before the Km 3 marker and follow the 'Massage Sauna' signs another 800m.

Dok Champa Massage MASSAGE

(Th 5; 1hr massage 35,000-60,000K; ⏲9am-9pm) Based in town and offering a range of traditional, oil and herbal massage.

Champasak Palace Hotel Gym HEALTH & FITNESS

(Gym visitors 7000K; ⏲2-10pm) The Champasak Palace Hotel has a decent gym, massages, sauna and Jacuzzi.

Pakse

Sights

1 Wat Luang ... A2

Activities, Courses & Tours

2 Champasak Palace Hotel Gym ... D1
3 Dok Champa Massage ... B2
4 Green Discovery ... C1
Xplore-Asia ... (see 8)

Sleeping

5 Daovieng 2 Hotel ... C2
6 Hotel Salachampa ... B2
7 Sabaidy 2 Guesthouse ... C1
8 Saigon Champasak Hotel ... B1
9 Sang Aroun Hotel ... B1
10 Thalaung Hotel ... C1

Eating

11 Delta Coffee ... D2
12 Jasmine Restaurant ... B1
13 Katuad Café ... C1
14 Khem Khong Restaurant ... A4
15 Local Restaurants ... C2
16 Mengky Noodle Shop ... B1
17 Oulayvan Minimart ... D2
18 Xuan Mai Restaurant ... B2

Drinking

19 Sinouk Coffee Shop ... A2

Transport

20 Lankham Hotel ... B1

Tours

Most hotels and guesthouses can arrange day trips to the Bolaven Plateau, Wat Phu Champasak and Si Phan Don (Four Thousand Islands).

Green Discovery ADVENTURE TOUR
(☎252908; www.greendiscoverylaos.com; Rte 13) As well as the excellent new Treetop Explorer zip-line adventure, GD operates one- and two-day treks in Phou Xieng Thong NPA as well as three-day elephant treks in Xe Pian NPA (group of four costs US$172 per person); also, cycling and kayaking combo trips (group of four costs US$195 per person, including food, guide, accommodation and transport) to Si Phan Don.

Xplore-Asia ADVENTURE TOUR
(☎251983; www.xplore-laos.com; Th 14) One- and two-day treks to Xe Pian NPA as well as one-day treks to Tad Lo (170,000K per person), Tad Fane and Katang ethnic villages. There's also a two-day kayaking trip to Don Dhet (4K islands; US$75 per person), overnighting on Don Khon.

Provincial Tourism Office ADVENTURE TOUR
(☎212021; Th 11; ⊙8am-noon & 1.30-4pm Mon-Fri) Two- or three-day treks in Xe Pian NPA and Phu Xieng Thong NPAs, involving kayaking, camping and homestay combos taking in Wat Phu (a group of four, US$65 per person). It also now runs two-day elephant treks up Phou Asa (a group of four, US$65 per person).

Sleeping

Affordable, traveller-magnet digs abound in Pakse.

Sabaidy 2 Guesthouse GUESTHOUSE $
(☎/fax 212992; www.sabaidy2laos.com; Th 24; dm 30,000 K, s & d 45,000-85,000K; ❄) The benefits of staying in this traditional wooden house are its leafy courtyard bar and the chance to meet other travellers and swap stories. Another draw is the gregarious owner, Mr Vong, who runs treks to the Bolaven Plateau. Rooms are pretty basic, a few enjoy private bathrooms.

Hotel Salachampa GUESTHOUSE $$
(☎212273; fax 212646; Th 14; r US$20-48; ❄) Pakse's oldest French villa, with a range of solid bungalow accommodation. But the real stars are the romantic rooms in the old house furnished with period furniture. Attached is a pleasant cafe serving a mix of Lao and Western fare (mains 20,000K).

Daovieng 2 Hotel HOTEL $
(☎214331; Rte 13; r incl breakfast 100,000-130,000K; ❄📶) Rooms vary from cramped singles to attractive fresh doubles with private bathroom, comfy beds, sparkling linen and TV. Choose one away from the road.

Saigon Champasak Hotel GUESTHOUSE $
(☎254181; Th 14; s/d 120,000/160,000K; ❄) These Vietnamese-run digs need a freshen up with threadbare stairwells and thirsty walls. The rooms, however, are spacious and clean with private bathroom, fridge and TV.

Thaluang Hotel GUESTHOUSE $
(☎251399; Th 21; r 60,000-70,000K; ❄) Well-run Thaluang has a range of ordinary bungalow rooms and nicer ones in the house itself, with ochre walls, fantasy art, TV and private bathroom. A myna bird hails your arrival.

Sang Aroun Hotel HOTEL $$
(☎252111; Rte 13; r 140,000-250,000K; ❄📶) Don't be put off by the nondescript exterior. This place is immaculate, with spacious, sugar-white rooms, plush furniture and even an inhouse masseuse. A nice family option, extra beds cost 50,000K.

Eating

There are baguette vendors near Jasmine Restaurant, and by night braziers crackle to life on Rte 13 selling barbecued chicken

SUPER FLY GUY

Pakse's **Green Discovery** (☎252908; www.greendiscoverylaos.com; Rte 13) runs exhilarating excursions to the recently opened **Tree Top Explorer**, a series of 11 zip-lines in the Bolaven Plateau that looks set to rival The Gibbon Experience for its sheer adrenalin rush. The longest ride is 450m but the most dramatic cable is that which crosses directly in the spray of a huge waterfall. Trek through jungle and stay in eco-conscious 20m-high treehouses in the semi-evergreen forests of Don Hua Sao NPA – on two-day, one-night excursions (a group of two costs US$187 per person). Thanks to safety-conscious guides and controlled visitor numbers, current reviews are excellent.

and pork. For late-night munchies head to Oulayvan minimart.

TOP CHOICE **Delta Coffee** ITALIAN $
(Rte 13; mains 20,000K; ⌚7am-10pm) Carb-heavy menu of tasty Italian fare and numerous steaks (though avoid the uninspiring pizza). Delta sells its own coffee and sets up schools for plantation workers' children. Make a donation in the box out the front.

Xuan Mai Restaurant LAO, VIETNAMESE $
(Th 4; mains 20,000K; ⌚6am-11.30pm) On the corner opposite the Pakse Hotel, Vietnamese-run Xuan Mai serves top-notch *fŏe* (8000K) and *khào pûn* (white flour noodles with sweet-spicy sauce). The house *làap* is full of zing.

Katuad Café WESTERN $
(Rte 13; mains 30,000K; ⌚7am-9pm; wi-fi) This new modern cafe does a decent trade with Western breakfasts, sandwiches, hamburgers and ice cream, as well as stir-fries and spicy salads. Great coffee, fruit shakes and there's a quick wi-fi connection, too.

Jasmine Restaurant INDIAN $
(Rte 13; mains 20,000-30,000K; ⌚8am-10pm) Delicious curries and tasty Malayan dishes such as nasi goreng with mutton. It lays claim to the best service in town and possibly the tastiest chicken tikka masala in Laos – you'll be wiping it up with pillow-soft naan.

Khem Khong Restaurant SEAFOOD $
(Th 11; mains 24,000K; ⌚9am-11pm) Set upon pontoons on the Mekong, you'll need decent sea legs as you tuck into a seafood-focused menu of beer-grilled prawns, crab meat, spicy prawn *làap* and *pîing paa* (grilled fish). Pleasantly rowdy and fairy lit.

Mengky Noodle Shop LAO $
(Rte 13; meals 8000-15,000K; ⌚7am-10pm) Visit during the morning rush hour and you can tuck into noodle broths from a huge cauldron with the locals.

Drinking

Wander down the Mekong riverfront and stop at a terrace bar for a beer. Alternatively nurse a Bloody Mary on the Parisien-style rooftop bar at the Pakse Hotel.

Sinouk Coffee Shop CAFE
(Cnr Th 9 & Th 11; mains 20,000K; ⌚7am-8pm; wi-fi) In addition to posh lattes and cappuccinos, stylish Sinouk is stuffed to the gills with temptations: apple pie, chocolate or sponge cake, *pain au chocolat*, juices and breakfast. Mmm!

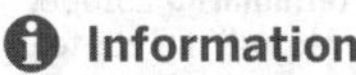

Information

There are now plenty of 24-hour ATMs clustered in the centre of town on Rte 13. There are several internet places on Rte 13 with decent broadband connections, which can also burn CDs.

BCEL (Th 11; ⌚8.30am-3.30pm Mon-Fri, to 10am Sat) South of Wat Luang, this has the best rates for cash and travellers cheques. Cash advances against Visa and MasterCard. Plus ATM.

Hospital (☎212018; cnr Th 10 & Th 46)

Lao Development Bank (Rte 13; ⌚8am-4pm Mon-Fri, to 3pm Sat & Sun) Changes cash and travellers cheques in the smaller exchange office; cash advances (Monday to Friday only) in the main building. Also houses a Western Union (money transfers only available weekdays). There's an ATM on the opposite side of the road.

Lankham Internet (Rte 13; per hr 5000K; ⌚7.30am-10pm) Also has free wi-fi.

Police (☎212145; Th 10)

Post office (cnr Th 1 & Th 8; ⌚8am-noon & 1-5pm)

Provincial tourism office (☎212021; Th 11; ⌚8am-noon & 1.30-4pm Mon-Fri)

SK Internet (Rte 13; per hr 5000K; ⌚8am-10pm)

Getting There & Away

Air

Lao Airlines (☎212252; www.laoairlines.com; Th 11; ⌚8-11.30am & 1.30-4.30pm Mon-Fri) flies between Pakse and Vientiane daily (one way US$131, 70 minutes), and usually three times a week to Luang Prabang (US$168, one hour 40 minutes).

The airport has a BCEL exchange office. Note: you can't buy tickets at the airport, so purchase them at the Lao Airlines office.

Boat

Speak to Joe at Pakse's Provincial tourism office to book a seat on a boat to Champasak (100,000K, 8.30am, daily). If there are 10 of you, it's possible to charter a boat to the Four Thousand Islands for as little as US$20 per person (six hours).

Bus & Sŏrngtăaou

Pakse has several bus and sŏrngtăaou terminals. 'Sleeper' VIP buses leave from the **VIP bus station** (Km 2 bus station; ☎212228), off Rte 13, for Vientiane (170,000K, eight to 10 hours, 677km) every evening. The handy Thai–Lao International Bus headed to Bangkok (210,000K, 8.30am and 3.30pm) and Ubon (55,000K, same bus) also departs from here; for details see the boxed text below. Finally there's a bus to Phnom Penh (230,000K, 7.30am).

From the **northern bus terminal** (☎251508; Rte 13) sometimes referred to as 'Km 7 bus terminal', agonisingly sweltering local buses crawl north every 40 minutes or so between 6.30am and 4pm for Savannakhet (40,000K, four to five hours, 277km), Tha Khaek (60,000K, eight to nine hours) and, for those with a masochistic streak, Vientiane (110,000K, 16 to 18 hours).

For buses or sŏrngtăaou anywhere south or east, head to the **southern bus terminal** (Rte 13), also known as 'Km 8 bus terminal'. The terminal is 8km south of town and costs 15,000K on a túk-túk. For Si Phan Don, transport departs for Muang Khong on Don Khong island (including ferry 40,000K, three hours, 120km) between 8.30am and 3pm, and for Ban Nakasang (for Don Det and Don Khon; 35,000K, three to four hours) hourly between 7.30am and 4pm. A sŏrngtăaou runs to Kiet Ngong (Xe Pian NPA) and Ban Phapho (20,000K, two to three hours) at 1pm.

To the Bolaven Plateau, transport leaves for Paksong (25,000K, 90 minutes) hourly between 7am and 4pm, stopping at Tat Fan if you ask.

Regular buses and sŏrngtăaou leave Talat Dao Heung (New Market) for Champasak (20,000K, one to two hours) and Ban Saphai (for Don Kho; 8000K, about 40 minutes).

Mai Linh Express (☎254149) operates a daily minibus service from outside the Saigon Champasak Hotel to Lao Bao (140,000K, 6.30am) on the Vietnam border, Hue (180,000K, 7am) and Danang (220,000K, 7am).

Getting Around

A jumbo to the airport, 3km northwest of town, should cost about 10,000K. Pakse's main attractions are accessible by foot. Bicycles/scooters (around 15,000/70,000K per day) can be hired from **Lankham Hotel** (☎213314; latchan@laotel.com; Rte 13), which also has some decent Honda Bajas for 230,000K a day, excellent for super-swift day trips to the Bolaven Plateau.

Bolaven Plateau

Laos' principal coffee-growing region, the Bolaven Plateau (Phu Phieng Bolaven in Lao) is home to dense jungles and celebrated by travellers for its handful of refreshing waterfalls and cooler climate. Surging 1500m above the Mekong valley, the claw-shaped plateau is home to several Mon Khomer ethnic groups, including the Alak, Laven (Bolaven means 'land of the Laven'), Ta-oy, Suay and Katu. You're probably here for the rustic serenity of Tat Lo, which is an excellent place to hire a bike, take an elephant trek or explore the nearby waterfalls.

Tat Lo

☎034

Secluded Tat Lo is an oasis of menthol-green waterfalls with deliciously cool pools to swim in. On the Salavan road (Rte 20), 90km from Pakse, it's well worth the effort to get here. There are decent digs at affordable prices and a couple of places to eat, but the real charm of the place is its paradise-like setting and chilled vibe.

The nearest cascade to the village is **Tat Hang**, which can be seen from the bridge, while **Tat Lo** itself is about 700m upriver via a path leading through Saise Guesthouse. The spectacular third cascade is **Tat Suong**, about 10km from town and best reached by motorbike or bicycle – get directions from Bah at Palamy Guesthouse. For **elephant treks** (leaving at 8am, 10am, 1pm and 3pm (100,000K per person) head to Tad Lo Lodge.

Sleeping & Eating

The village is a one-street affair, with most accommodation either side of the bridge

GETTING TO THAILAND: VANG TAO TO CHONG MEK

Getting to the border Heading to the busy border (open 5am to 6pm) of Vang Tao (Laos) and Chong Mek (Thailand) is straightforward if catching a sŏrngtăaou from Pakse (10,000Kper person, 75 minutes, 37km), or taxi (per person 20,000K, 45 minutes).

At the border This is a busy, well-organised trade route. There are ATMs on the Thai side, a market and restaurants. You have to walk a bit between the two posts but in general it's hassle free. Thirty-day visas for Laos are granted on arrival for between US$30 and US$40 depending on nationality. Free 15-day visas are granted on arrival in Thailand.

Moving on Easier than taking a taxi to the border is the Thai-Lao International bus that leaves from Pakse's VIP bus station headed to Ubon Ratchathani at 7am, 8.30am, 2.30pm and 3.30pm. The same bus continues on to Bangkok (210,000K). For details on crossing the border in the other direction, see p720.

GETTING TO VIETNAM: PHOU KEUA TO BO Y

Getting to the border In far southeastern Attapeu province, a border with Vietnam links Phou Keua (Laos) to Bo Y (Vietnam). It's 113km southeast of Attapeu town. Three buses per week (9am, Mon, Wed and Fri) leave here headed for Pleiku via Kon Tum (118,000K, 12 hours). Tickets are sold in the Thi Thi restaurant west of the bridge in Attapeu. Minibuses to Bo Y cost 80,000K per person and leave between 7am and 10am from the same spot by Thi Thi restaurant.

At the border Thirty-day visas are granted on arrival in Laos and cost between US$30 and US$40 depending on your nationality. Vietnamese visas must be arranged in advance.

Moving on Once on the Vietnamese side minibuses continue to Ngoc Hoi, 18km away. There are places to stay here and morning departures for a wide range of destinations. For information on crossing this border in the other direction see p859.

(budget places are concentrated on the east side). The best cuisine is found at Tad Lo Lodge, up the hill.

Palamy Guest House & Restaurant GUESTHOUSE $
(r 30,000-60,000K) Overlooking a meadow, Palamy's better rooms have mozzie nets, terraces and, in some cases, fridges. The cheaper cabanas have shared bathrooms. The friendly management rents out scooters (70,000K per day) and bikes (15,000K per day), and there's also communal dinner.

Saise Guest House & Restaurant HOTEL $
(☎/fax 211886; r 60,000-150,000K) Well situated at the base of the falls, there's a range of bungalows (the cheapest being the older ones at the back), all of which are comfortable. Its restaurant has a simple menu of stir-fries, salads and various fish incarnations (mains 40,000K).

Tad Lo Lodge RESTAURANT $$
(mains 45,000K; @) Situated above the falls with a view of the teal-green river, the stylish Lao restaurant cooks up dishes such as fried pork chop, grilled Mekong fish and steaks. Cosy, well appointed rooms close to the falls cost US$40 to US$57.

Champasak

☎031 / POP 14,000

This serene riverside town drips with charm thanks to its silkscreen-style mountain fringed by emerald rice paddies and the easy manner of its locals. Among faded colonial villas there's a sprinkling of high-end style with a boutique hotel and a couple of upscale restaurants, but the real highpoint is the picturesque ruins of Wat Phu Champasak.

The town stirs once a year when pilgrims gravitate here for **Bun Wat Phu Champasak**, a three-day Buddhist festival (usually held in February) of praying, offerings, traditional music, Thai boxing, comedy shows and cockfights. Guesthouses are mainly found near the fountain south of Champasak's only roundabout.

Sights

Wat Phu Champasak TEMPLE
(admission 30,000K; ⏲8am-4.30pm) Overlooking the Mekong valley, Wat Phu Champasak, while not being in the same league as Angkor Wat, is one of the most impressive archaeological sites in Laos and well worth visiting. It's divided into lower and upper parts and joined by a steep, flower-bordered stone stairway.

The lower part consists of two ruined palace buildings at the edge of a large square pond, itself split in two by a causeway, used for ritual ablutions. The upper section is the temple sanctuary itself, which once enclosed a large Shiva phallus. Some time later the sanctuary was converted into a Buddhist temple, but original Hindu sculpture remains in the lintels. Just north of the Shiva-lingam sanctuary you'll find the elephant stone and the enigmatic crocodile stone (if you can locate it!). The *naga* stairway leading to the sanctuary is lined with *dok jampa* (frangipani) trees. The upper platform affords spectacular views of the Mekong valley below.

Sleeping & Eating

Anouxa Guest House GUESTHOUSE $
(☎511006; r 100,000-150,000K; ❄) Friendly Anouxa Guest House has homey bungalows (including some that face the river),

CHAMPASAK EXPRESS

A new 28km road from Pakse allows you to avoid taking the ferry from Ban Muang to Champasak, and makes for an easy hour's ride by scooter. Head from Pakse over the Lao–Japanese Bridge, and after almost exactly 2km there's a turn-off on your left at the 'Welcome to Champasak' billboard. From here it's a straight ride.

with peach interiors with immaculately clean bathrooms and linen. Add to this its pleasant gardens and tempting restaurant to sit with a sundowner Beerlao and it's a winner.

Thavisab Guest House GUESTHOUSE $
(☎020 535 4972; r with/without air-con 100,000/50,000K; ❄) Pleasant rooms with mint-coloured curtains and clean linen in an airy old house set back from the river. To save even more money ask for a room with cold-water shower.

Frice and Lujane Restaurant ITALIAN $
(mains 40,000K) Offering cuisine from the Friulian alpine region of Italy, this atmospheric restaurant based in a renovated villa has a menu encompassing gnocchi, marinated pork ribs and goulash. Owner Marco is especially proud of his homemade sausage!

Inthira Hotel & Restaurant SOUTHEAST ASIAN $
(mains 35,000K; 📶) The belle of the river, Inthira's sumptuous low-lit restaurant gives us yet another reason to stay another day in Champasak. Based in a beautifully renovated Chinese shophouse.

Getting There & Around

Regular buses and sŏrngtăaou run between Champasak and Pakse (20,000K, one hour) from about 6.30am until 3pm; early morning is busiest.

If you're heading south to Ban Nakasang (for Don Det) or Muang Khong (on Don Khong), get to Ban Lak 30 (on Rte 13), where you can flag down anything going south.

Bicycles (per day 10,000K to 15,000K) and scooters (per half/full day 50,000/80,000K) can be hired from guesthouses. A return túk-túk to Wat Phu costs from 80,000K, including waiting time.

Si Phan Don (Four Thousand Islands)

☎031

This beguiling archipelago of islets is the emerald jewel near the end of the Mekong's 4350km journey. In the cool and dry season (after and before monsoon) the river is at its most perfect, passing around thousands of sandbars sprouting with betel trees and sugar palms, its colour a rich peacock green. At night the waters are dotted with the lights of fishing boats and fireflies, the soundtrack provided by braying buffalo and cicadas. Between tubing, kayaking and cycling around the three main islands – Don Khong, and sister islands Don Det and Don Khon – spotting the rare Irrawaddy dolphin or visiting waterfalls, there's little to do but hammock dwell, listening to the putter of fishermen's longtails. Islands Det and Khon are popular with the younger crowd, while neighbour Don Khong has less of a traveller scene.

DON KHONG

POP 13,000

Less claustrophobic than islands Det and Khon, Don Khong (18km long, 8km wide) is sleepy to say the least. On arrival in its main settlement, Muang Khong – a one-street affair with a couple of guesthouses and restaurants – you'll be struck by the friendliness of the locals. If you want to get off the 'traveller circuit' for a day or two, this is a nice place to visit. Wander past fishing nets drying in the sun or take a sunset boat ride to Cambodian waters; read by the river or hire a bike to explore the island.

Sleeping & Eating

There are a couple of great-value oases at which to rest your bones. You'll find all these guesthouses located in Muang Khong.

TOP CHOICE **Villa Kang Khong** GUESTHOUSE $
(☎213539; r 50,000-60,000K) The most romantic budget digs in town, this stalwart teak house creaks with uneven floors and nostalgic furnishings. Rooms are basic, fan cooled and, with their colourful wood interiors, remind vaguely of Romany gypsy caravans.

Pon's River Guest House & Restaurant GUESTHOUSE $
(☎214037, 020 227 0037; r 80,000-150,000K; ❄) Eighteen cosy rooms decked in carved wooden lights, fresh linen and immaculate private bathrooms. The river-facing rooms

upstairs are lovely. Accepts Visa and Mastercard. The restaurant (mains 40,000K) is shaded by mature trees and serves *làap*, grilled fish, steamed fish and fish, fish, fish!

Done Khong Guesthouse & Restaurant GUESTHOUSE $
(☎214010; r 80,000-100,00K; ❄) Welcoming, fresh rooms with tiled floors, sugar-white linen and homey furnishings in an old house run by a French-speaking lady. Try to bag a river-facing room. Its restaurant (mains from 30,000K) features a wide range of Western dishes as well as Lao fare like grilled pork with honey.

Mekong Guesthouse & Restaurant GUESTHOUSE $
(r 40,000-150,000K) Set around a pretty flower garden close to the river, the accommodation here varies from the original wooden affairs out the back – which are cheaper and more atmospheric with wooden floors, verandas and shared bathroom – to the newer ones in the remodelled house.

Souksabai Guest House GUESTHOUSE $
(☎214122; r with/without air-con 100,000/66,000K ❄) Set back from the road, Souksabai has roomy digs in a new block with fresh private bathrooms. And though the walls are already patched with humidity the place is clean. There's also a restaurant with a shaded sun terrace. Ask for discount in low season.

Lattana Guesthouse GUESTHOUSE $
(☎213673; r 50,000-100,000K; ❄@) Recently renovated with comfortable river-facing rooms (avoid the drab originals out the back) enjoying origami-lotus folded towels, marble floors, Siberian air-con and handsome furnishings. Ground-floor rooms have enormous windows close to the road – ever felt like a goldfish? – so get one upstairs.

ℹ Information

One road back from the river, 400m south of Wat Phuang Kaew, the **Agricultural Promotion Bank** (⏲8.30am-3.30pm Mon-Fri) exchanges travellers cheques and cash (no sterling) at poor rates. There's no ATM on the island but you can get cash advances on your card at Pon's River Guesthouse & Restaurant, which charges a 5% commission. For medical complaints, the **hospital** is a little further south of the bank; ask for English- and French-speaking Dr Souban.

The **telephone office** (⏲8am-noon & 2-4pm Mon-Fri) is west of the boat landing, while the **post office** (⏲8am-noon & 2-4pm Mon-Fri) is just south of the bridge. **Lattana Guesthouse** (☎213673; per min 500K; ⏲8am-7.30pm) has mediocre-speed internet connection. **Khong Island Travel** (☎213011; www.khongisland travel.com), based at Villa Muong Khong, can organise boat trips to Don Det and Don Khon, and forward travel/visas to Cambodia.

ℹ Getting There & Away

From Don Khong to Pakse, buses (50,000K, 2½ to three hours, 128km) and sŏrngtǎaou leave from outside Wat Phuang Kaew between 6am and 10am. After that, head over to Rte 13 and wait for anything going north.

For the Cambodian border there's usually a 9am connection that costs US$10 to Stung Treng, US$13 to Kratie, US$20 to Ban Lung, and US$20 to Siem Reap and Phnom Penh.

There are regular boats between Hat Xai Khun and Don Khong's Muang Khong town – 27,000K per boat for one to three people, or 10,000K per person for more.

Boats for Don Det and Don Khon (130,000K, 1½ hours) leave when you stump up the cash

GETTING TO CAMBODIA: NONG NOK KHIENE TO TRAPEANG KRIEL

Getting to the border The days of crossing this once complicated border (open 8am to 5pm) are gladly over. Although it's still possible to charter a boat to make the crossing, given the glitzy new land border it's really not worth the hassle. Now called the Nong Nok Khiene–Trapeang Kriel border crossing, you'll likely hear it referred to by its former name, Voen Kham–Dom Kralor. Many travellers from the Four Thousand Islands take a minibus and pass through here en route to Cambodia's Stung Treng (US$8, three hours), Kratie (US$13, five hours), Ban Lung (US$11, six hours), or Phnom Penh (US$18, 11 hours). From Pakse it costs 120,000K to Stung Treng or 230,000K to Phnom Penh.

At the border Despite rumours to the contrary, 30-day tourist visas are definitely granted in Laos on arrival and cost US$30 to US$40 depending on the passport you hold. Thirty-day tourist visas for Cambodia are also available and cost around US$30.

Moving on If you're not on a direct bus, head to Stung Treng to catch a bus to Phnom Penh, Siem Reap and Banlung. There are ATMs here as well as a wealth of restaurants and guesthouses. See p127 for information on crossing in the other direction.

– boatmen are under the tree near the bridge (40,000K per person). For the same price dependable Mr Pon's (p364) boat leaves at 8.30am.

Getting Around

Bicycles/motorbikes (10,000/80,000K per day) can be hired from guesthouses and elsewhere along the main street.

DON DET & DON KHON

While many choose to hammock-flop here there's loads of inexpensive activities to busy yourself with in one of Southeast Asia's most talked about traveller legends, be it cycling, tubing and kayaking by day, or relaxing in the river bars come sunset. Expect to see

Si Phan Don

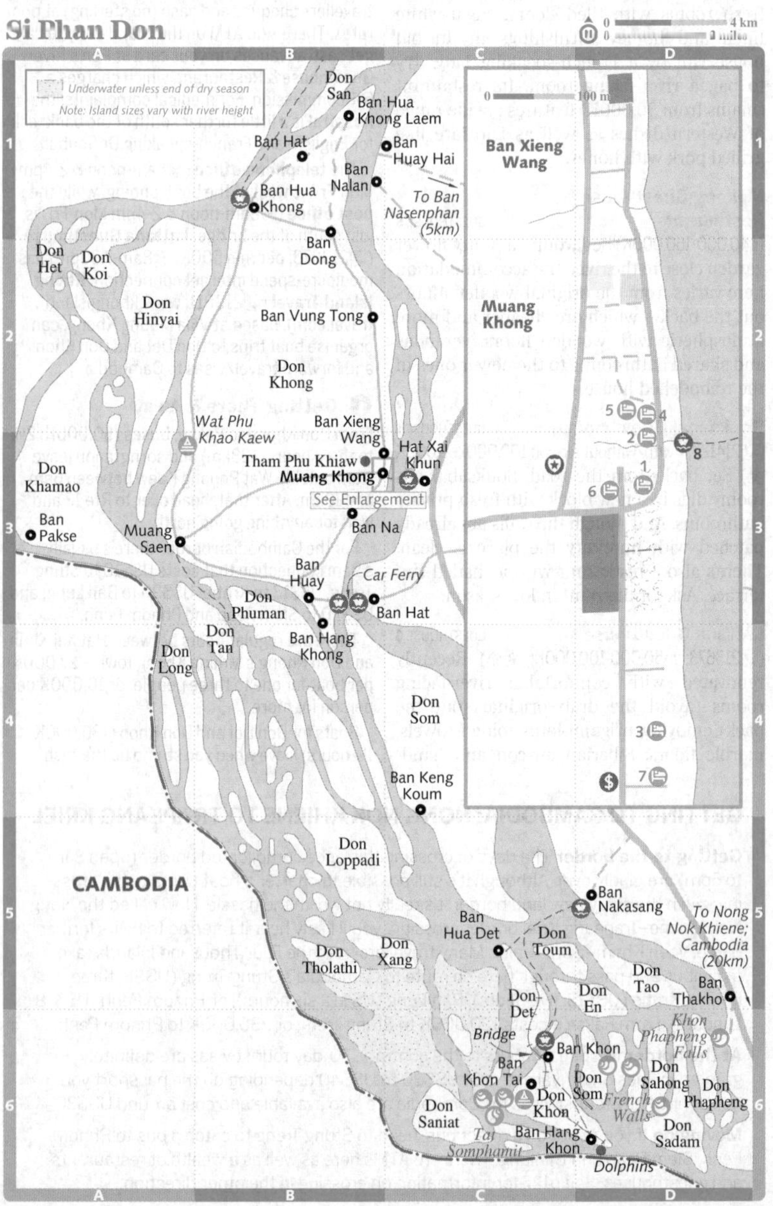

fishermen in pirogues, doe-eyed buffalo in the shallows and villagers taking morning ablutions. By night, campfires burn on the beach and conversation flows.

A tropical *yin* and *yang*, Don Det is overcrowded with *falang* – particularly by the ferry point of **Ban Hua Det** (known as 'Sunrise' boulevard) – while sultry Don Khon is quieter. Villagers are glad for the new electricity lines that have been connected, as will you come nighttime in your fan-cooled room.

Sights & Activities

Tat Somphamit & Khone Phapheng WATERFALL
Admirers of thundering waterfalls will like Tat Somphamit (cross the French bridge to Don Khon; 19,000K) and Khone Phapheng – considered the largest (by volume) in Southeast Asia. Entry is 9000K and the falls are often included in the itinerary of dolphin-viewing day trips (see p367).

WATER SPORTS

Xplore-Asia KAYAKING, RAFTING
(www.xplore-asia.com; Ban Hua Det, Don Det) Kayaking and rafting can be organised with Xplore-Asia, which also offers forward travel to Pakse as well as Cambodian destinations (Kratie, Stung Treng, Phnom Penh and Siem Reap). Kayaking costs 250,000K per person for a group of two people.

Happy Island Tours KAYAKING
(☎020 267 7698; Ban Hua Det) Run by Boun, this outfit takes its kayaking seriously, with solid kit and one-day trips down Grade-2 to Grade-3 rapids. For two people this typically costs 200,000K per person, but the price becomes cheaper the larger your group.

Si Phan Don

Sleeping

1 Done Khong Guesthouse & Restaurant D3
2 Lattana Guesthouse D3
3 Mekong Guesthouse & Restaurant D4
4 Pon's River Guest House & Restaurant D2
5 Souksabai Guest House D2
6 Villa Kang Khong D3
7 Villa Muong Khong D4

Transport

8 Boats to Hat Xai Khun D3

PARADISE RETAINED!

Don Det has distanced itself from its stoner image by cultivating a range of activities like cycling and kayaking, and you're more likely to see travellers fishing with locals than buying joints off them. Villagers are grateful for your trade and there are a few things you can do to keep your footprint positive. If partaking a little spliff, be subtle. And a word to women travellers: the village chief has asked that you keep more than just a bikini on around the island. It's a pain because it's hot, but the Lao find it culturally offensive.

FISHING

Souksan Guest House FISHING
(Sunrise Blvd, Ban Hua Det, Don Det) One-day fishing trips (a two-person outing costs 100,000K per person) with locals using traditional nets can be organised at Souksan Guest House. You get to barbecue your catch on a beach and enjoy a swim.

Tours

Irrawaddy Dolphin BOAT TOUR
Dolphin numbers are around 20 in this area. See them early evening and first thing in the morning off the southern tip of Don Khon, where they congregate in a 50m-deep pool. Boats are chartered (42,500K, maximum three people) from the old French pier. Alternatively, walk or ride to the beach at Ban Hang Khon and ask the boatman to take you from there.

Sleeping

Don Det's 'Sunrise Boulevard' on the northern tip is claustrophobic, crowded and noisy, but if you want to keep the party going (at least till the 11pm curfew) head here. Increasingly, digs are becoming more upscale further south and over on sedate Don Khon. Boatmen will drop you near your chosen guesthouse – saving you a walk – if you insist.

TOP CHOICE **Little Eden Guest House** GUESTHOUSE $$
(☎020 7773 9045; www.littleedenguesthouse-dondet.com; Ban Hua Det, Don Det; bungalows 220,000-260,000K; ❄📶) Little Eden is set in lush gardens on the northern tip of the island and boasts fragrant rooms, tiled floors and modern furnishings. The restaurant is perfect for sunset dinners. You can also get cash

advances on your credit card for a 5% commission charge.

Seng Ahloune Guest House & Restaurant GUESTHOUSE $$
(☎260934; Don Khon; r US$35-50) Beautifully appointed bungalows next to the bridge, with rattan walls, mozzie nets, wooden floors and ornate lamps. Its restaurant, Mekong De Fleur (meals 30,000K), is a fine place for a sundowner. Salads, fried fish, chicken and ginger are but a few of the dishes.

Don Dhet Bungalows GUESTHOUSE $
(020 7772 1572; Sunrise Blvd, Ban Hua Det, Don Det; bungalows 130,000K) Vastly superior new bungalows set back from the river with unimpaired sunrise views. The floors are varnished wood, the bedspreads fragrant and there's a lively restaurant with reclining cushions.

Souksan Guest House GUESTHOUSE $
(☎020 5469 0168; Sunrise Blvd, Ban Hua Det, Don Det; bungalows 60,000-70,000K) Nestled around a leafy courtyard, Souksan's basic bungalows are immaculate and fan cooled. The restaurant may have diminished but the helpful manager can assist you with forward travel.

Pan's Guesthouse & Restaurant GUESTHOUSE $$
(☎020 4463 1437; Don Khon; r 100,000-250,000K; @❄) A range of bungalows finished with wooden interiors, pebble-floor showers, immaculate private bathrooms and balconies slung with hammocks. All rooms have fans or air-con. Try for a new one fronting the river, then sample its excellent cafe (mains 20,000K) over the road.

Santiphab Guesthouse GUESTHOUSE $
(☎020 5461 4231; Don Det; r 40,000-80,000K) This old trusty by the bridge has much-improved bungalows with basic interiors and private bathrooms but the real draw is the unbroken view of the bridge and river. The homey cafe offers everything from fried Western breakfasts to *làap.*

Sengthavan Guesthouse & Restaurant GUESTHOUSE $
(☎020 5613 2696; Sunset Blvd, Ban Hua Det, Don Det; r 80,000K) The best 'Sunset' side guesthouse, its rooms are fastidiously clean, with private bathroom, and enjoy uncluttered views of Cambodia. Its low-key cafe has recliner cushions, chequered-clothed tables and a Lao menu.

River Garden GUESTHOUSE $
(☎020 7770 1860; near old bridge, Don Det; r 50,000-80,000K) Gay-friendly River is house-proud, its pristine cabanas enjoying fine river views. There's also a Western and Lao restaurant (mains 35,000K) hung with Buddha paintings, plus a shaded sun terrace that's perfect for reading.

Mekong Dream Guesthouse GUESTHOUSE $
(near old bridge; Don Det; r 40,000-60,000K) Four basic rooms with fan and private bathroom, the hammock lounge facing the French bridge is the perfect statement of relaxation. Its Lao-accented menu is pretty attractive too, with fried or barbecued fish (mains 25,000K)

Eating & Drinking

Establishments open for breakfast early, and close anytime around 11pm – some a little later.

TOP CHOICE **Little Eden Restaurant** WESTERN $$
(www.littleedenguesthouse-dondet.com; Ban Hua Det, Don Det; mains 60,000K; ❄📶) Little Eden is arguably the best place to eat upscale Lao and Western cuisine on all the islands. Owner Matt Verborg is a professional chef and his eclectic menu, added to the restaurant's breezy riverside location, never fails to delight.

Jasmine Restaurant INDIAN $
(Sunrise Blvd, Ban Hua Det, Don Det; meals 25,000K) Lesser sister of the excellent Jasmine's in Pakse, this fan-cooled eatery is hugely popular thanks to its central location and excellent Malayan and Indian grub. All the usual suspects on offer but with sluggish service.

Chanthounma's Restaurant LAO $
(Don Khon; mains 20,000K) This tumbledown long-timer has dished up its tasty spring rolls, papaya salads and veggie options to happy travellers for years. Fastidiously clean and friendly service thanks to Mama Chanthounma.

Streetview Café Bar BAR $
(Sunrise Blvd, Ban Hua Det, Don Det; mains 25,000K) Piping out decent rock 'n' roll, this shadowy hole-in-the-wall turns out shooters, beer and cocktails. Thanks to its baker owner there are some scrumptious munchies antidotes such as cinnamon buns, doughnuts and chocolate and carrot cakes.

Pool Bar BAR
(Ban Hua Det, Don Det) Near the boat landing and Souksan Guest House, this traveller magnet is a cool place to meet others, play

pool (surprise, surprise) and find a second-hand book to read. About as busy as it gets.

Information

You'll find internet services by the boat landing in Ban Hua Det (400K per minute). There's no post or bank here, so stock up on funds before you leave Pakse or else head to Little Eden Guest House on Don Det and ask for a cash advance on your card (5% commission charge).

Getting There & Around

Boats regularly leave Don Det for Ban Nakasang (per person/boat 15,000/30,000K). Boats for Don Khong leave according to demand, though you're looking at an extortionate price of 200,000K per boat. For the same price, Little Eden Guest House (p367) will also bring you back. Boats can be hired to go anywhere in the immediate islands for about 100,000K an hour.

For Pakse (60,000K, 2½ to three hours, 148km), buses or sŏrngtăaou leave Ban Nakasang at 6am, 8am, 9am and 10am. For buses from Pakse, see p361. **Wonderfull Tours** (☎020 5570 5173; Ban Hua Det, Don Det) organises daily VIP buses to Stung Treng (US$6), Ban Lung (US$6), Kratie (US$13), Phnom Penh (US$13) and Siem Reap (US$20) in Cambodia, all of which leave at 9am from the other side of the river. Buses to Vietnam leave at 11.30am and include Dong Ha (260,000K), Hue (220,000K) and Danang (260,000K)

UNDERSTAND LAOS

Laos Today

Up until early 2008 it was all going extremely well for Laos, with record figures of foreign visitors. Not to mention the hydro-electric power dams, newly built and ready to roll; the copper and gold mining concessions and the largely foreign investors keen to climb into bed with Laos' natural resources. Then the economic axe fell on the US and those subprime mortgages started impacting every aspect of Laos' attempt to escape its hated status as one of the 20 poorest nations by 2020. Suddenly the foreign investors pulled out because of their own lack of liquidity, and mining concessions collapsed as the price of copper was slashed. There were fewer travellers coming, too. Through no fault of its own Laos looked to be heading back to the dark days of stagnation.

Times haven't been easy, but they could have been worse – despite global gloom, by 2010 Laos was back on track with a GDP of 7.7%. And now, as China flourishes, Laos is reaping the rewards of their close association. And China, ever the opportunist, has moved in with celerity to grab what it can in return for improving Laos' transport infrastructure. Beijing's multibillion dollar rail investment in a Southeast Asian rail network, due to be finished in 2015, will connect the red giant with countries as far afield as Pakistan, India and Singapore, and to achieve this they'll pass directly through Laos. Route 3, from Kunming to Vientiane, via Luang Prabang, should be ready by 2014. In the next 10 years it's predicted you'll be able to travel at speeds of up to 400km/h through this beautiful green country. How this will impact on this sleepy paradise is anyone's guess, but it's all the more reason for your well-timed visit right now.

History

The Kingdom of Lan Xang

Before the French, British, Chinese and Siamese drew a line around it, Laos was a collection of disparate principalities subject to an ever-revolving cycle of war, invasion, prosperity and decay. Laos' earliest brush with nationhood was in the 14th century, when Khmer-backed Lao warlord Fa Ngum conquered Wieng Chan (Vientiane). It was Fa Ngum who gave his kingdom the title still favoured by travel romantics and businesses – Lan Xang, or (Land of a) Million Elephants. He also made Theravada Buddhism the state religion and adopted the symbol of Lao sovereignty that remains in use today, the Pha Bang Buddha image, after which Luang Prabang is named. Lan Xang reached its peak in the 17th century, when it was the dominant force in Southeast Asia.

French Rule

By the 18th century the nation had crumbled, falling under the control of the Siamese, who coveted much of modern-day Laos as a buffer zone against the expansionist French. It was to no effect. Soon after taking over Annam and Tonkin (modern-day Vietnam), the French negotiated with Siam to relinquish its territory east of the Mekong, and Laos was born.

The first nationalist movement, the Lao Issara (Free Lao), was created to prevent the country's return to French rule after the invading Japanese left at the end of WWII. In 1953, without any regard for the Lao Issara, sovereignty was granted to Laos by the French.

Internecine struggles followed with the Pathet Lao (Country of the Lao) Army forming an alliance with the Vietnamese Viet Minh (which opposed French rule in their own country). Laos was set to become a chessboard on which the clash of communist ambition and US anxiety over the perceived Southeast Asian 'domino effect' played itself out.

The Secret War

In 1954 at the Geneva Conference Laos was declared a neutral nation – as such neither Vietnamese nor US forces could cross its borders. Thus began a game of cat and mouse as a multitude of CIA operatives secretly entered the country to train anticommunist Hmong fighters in the jungle. From 1965 to 1973, the US, in response to the Viet Minh funnelling massive amounts of war munitions down the Ho Chi Minh Trail, devastated eastern and northeastern Laos with nonstop carpet-bombing (a reported plane load of ordnance dropped every eight minutes). The intensive campaign exacerbated the war between the Pathet Lao and the Royal Lao armies and, if anything, increased domestic support for the communists.

The US withdrawal in 1973 saw Laos divided up between Pathet Lao and non-Pathet Lao, but within two years the communists had taken over and the Lao People's Democratic Republic (PDR) was created under the leadership of Kaysone Phomvihane. Around 10% of Laos' population fled, mostly to Thailand. The remaining opponents of the government – notably tribes of Hmong (highland dwellers) who had fought with and been funded by the CIA – were suppressed, often brutally, or sent to re-education camps for indeterminate periods.

A New Beginning

Laos entered the political family of Southeast Asian countries known as Asean in 1997, two years after Vietnam. In 2004 the USA promoted Laos to Normal Trade Relations, cementing the end to a trade embargo in place since the communists took power in 1975. Politically, the Party remains firmly in control. And with patrons like one-party China and Vietnam, there seems little incentive for Laos to move towards any meaningful form of democracy. While still heavily reliant on foreign aid, Laos has committed to income-generating projects in recent years in a bid to increase its prosperity. Ecotourism is flourishing and the country is enjoying more Western visitors every year.

The 35-year-long Hmong 'insurgency' has seen thousands of guerrillas reduced to a few hundred and forced into the upper reaches of Xaisomboun District. Most have now surrendered, emerging from the jungle as ragged protagonists in a war almost forgotten.

The Culture

National Psyche

Trying to homogenise the people and psyche of Laos is difficult, for the country is really a patchwork of different beliefs, ranging from animism to the prevailing presence of Thervada Bhuddism – and often both combined. But certainly there's a commonality in the laid-back attitude you'll encounter. Some of this can be ascribed to Buddhism and its emphasis on controlling extreme emotions by keeping *jai yen* (cool heart) and making merit; doing good in order to receive good. But the rest is a Lao phenomenon. Thus you'll rarely hear a heated argument, and can expect a level of kindness that you don't see to the same extent in other neighbouring countries.

Lifestyle

Laos' strongest cultural and linguistic links are with Thailand, with Thai music and TV an almost ubiquitous presence in the country.

Touching another person's head is taboo, as is pointing your feet at another person or at a Buddha image. Strong displays of emotion are also discouraged. The traditional greeting gesture is the *nop* or *wâi*, a prayer-like placing together of the palms in front of the face or chest, although in urban areas the handshake is becoming more commonplace.

For all temple visits, dress neatly. In general you won't see many shirtless Lao; to their credit, *falang* are generally respectful of this rule.

Population

The government has been at pains to encourage national pride and a unifying 'Lao' identity, despite the fact that 132 ethnic groups comprise the people of Laos. Around 60% of these are Lao Loum (lowland Lao), who have the most in common with their Thai neighbours, and it's their cultural beliefs and way of life that are known as 'Lao culture'. The remainder is labelled according to the altitude at which the groups live: Lao Theung (midlevel mountain group including Khmu, Lamet and Alak), Lao Thai (upland valleys), Lao Theung (upland Lao) and Lao Soung (1000m or more above sea level, including Hmong, Mien and Akha).

Religion

Most lowland Lao are Theravada Buddhists and many Lao males choose to be ordained temporarily as monks, typically spending anywhere from a month to three years at a wat (temple). Indeed, a young man is not considered 'ripe' until he has completed his spiritual term. After the 1975 communist victory, Buddhism was suppressed, but by 1992 the government had relented and it was back in full swing, with a few alterations. Monks are still forbidden to promote *phî* (spirit) worship, which has been officially banned in Laos along with *sâiyasaat* (folk magic).

Despite the ban, *phî* worship remains the dominant non-Buddhist belief system. Even in Vientiane, Lao citizens openly perform the ceremony called *sukhwăn* or *bąsî,* in which the 32 *khwăn* (guardian spirits of the body) are bound to the guest of honour by white strings tied around the wrists (you'll see many Lao people wearing these).

Outside the Mekong River valley, the *phî* cult is particularly strong among tribal Thai, especially among the Thai Dam. The Khamu and Hmong-Mien tribes also practise animism.

Arts

The true expression of Lao art is found in its religious sculpture, temples, handicrafts and architecture. Distinctively Lao is the Calling for Rain Buddha, a standing image with hands held rigidly at his sides. Similarly widespread is the Contemplating the Bodhi Tree Buddha, with crossed hands at the front.

Wat in Luang Prabang feature *sĭm* (chapels), with steep, low roofs. The typical Lao *tâht* is a four-sided, curvilinear, spire-like structure. There are also hints of classical architectural motifs entering modern architecture, as with Vientiane's Wattay International Airport. Many of the beautiful villas from the days of Indochina were torn down by the new regime in favour of harsh Soviet designs, though fortunately there are plenty of villas left, with their distinctive shuttered windows and classic French provincial style.

Upland crafts include gold- and silversmithing among the Hmong and Mien tribes, and tribal Thai weaving (especially among the Thai Dam and Thai Lü). Classical music and dance have all but evaporated, partly due to the vapid tentacles of Thai pop and the itinerant nature of Laos' young workforce.

Food & Drink

Food

Budget eating in this chapter is defined as a main course costing less than 40,000K (US$5), midrange as 40,000K (US$5) to 80,000K (US$10), and top end as more than 80,000K (US$10).

The standard Lao breakfast is *fŏe* (rice noodles), usually served in a broth with vegetables and meat of your choice. The trick is in the seasoning, and Lao people will stir in some fish sauce, lime juice, dried chillies, mint leaves, basil or chilli, testing it along the way. *Làap* is the most distinctively Lao dish, a delicious spicy salad made from minced beef, pork, duck, fish or chicken, mixed with fish sauce, small shallots, mint leaves, lime juice, roasted ground rice and lots and lots of chillies. Another famous Lao speciality is *tąm màak hung* (known as *som tam* in Thailand), a salad of shredded green papaya mixed with

SPIRITS, ARE YOU THERE?

The life of a Lao person involves a complex appeasement of spirits through a carousel of sacrifices and rituals designed to protect the supplicant. The *phĭi héuan* (good spirits) represent both the guardian spirits of the house and ancestral spirits. In order to promote domestic happiness they're fed with Pepsi, and come crisis time it's their job to recalibrate the troubled household.

In the backyard or garden, you'll often see what look like miniature ornamental temples, the *pha phum* (spirits of the land). Their task is to protect the grounds from any malignant spirits – for in Laos the air is thick with them. Before anything is built within their grounds, offerings must be made and permission granted. The same goes for a tree that must be knocked down to make way for a bridge, a field before a harvest…and so on. It's an endless animistic communion between the seen and unseen, the prosaic and the spiritual.

garlic, lime juice, fish sauce, sometimes tomatoes, palm sugar, land crab or dried prawns and, of course, chillies by the handful.

In lowland Laos almost every dish is eaten with *khào nĭaw* (sticky rice), which is served in a small basket. Take a small amount of rice and, using one hand, work it into a walnut-sized ball before dipping it into the food.

Drink

Beerlao remains a firm favourite with 90% of the nation, while officially illegal *Lào-láo* (Lao liquor, or rice whisky) is a popular drink among lowland Lao. It's usually taken neat and offered in villages as a welcoming gesture. Water purified for drinking purposes is simply called *nâam deum* (drinking water), whether it's boiled or filtered. All water offered to customers in restaurants or hotels will be purified, and purified water is sold everywhere. Having said that, do be careful of the water you drink – there was an outbreak of E coli in 2008, so check that the ice in your drink originated from a bottle.

Juice bars and cafes proliferate around Vientiane and Luang Prabang and smoothies and cappuccinos are usually on the menu in most Western-leaning places. Lao coffee is usually served strong and sweet. Chinese-style green tea is the usual ingredient in *nâam sáa* or *sáa láo* – the weak, refreshing tea traditionally served free in restaurants.

Environment

The Land

With a landmass of 236,800 sq km, Laos is a little larger than the UK and, thanks to its relatively small population and mountainous terrain, one of the least altered environments in Southeast Asia. Unmanaged vegetation covers an estimated 85% of the country, and 10% of Laos is original-growth forest. A hundred years ago this last statistic was nearer 75%, which provides a clear idea of the detrimental effects of relentless logging and slash-and-burn farming. Nonetheless, most Lao still live at or just above subsistence level, consuming far fewer of their own natural resources than the people of any developed country.

In 1993 the government set up 18 National Protected Areas (NPAs) comprising a total of 24,600 sq km, just over 10% of the land. An additional two were added in 1995 (taking the total coverage to 14% of Laos). International consulting agencies have also recommended another nine sites, but these have yet to materialise. Despite these conservation efforts, illegal timber felling and the smuggling of exotic wildlife are still significant threats to Laos' natural resources.

Wildlife

Laos is home to Asian elephants, jackals, Asiatic black bears, black-crested gibbons, langurs, leopards, tigers, pythons, king cobras, 437 kinds of bird and the rare Irrawaddy dolphin – to name a few! Driven by neighbours – particularly China – who seek body parts of endangered animals for traditional medicine and aphrodisiac purposes, the illegal wildlife trade is flourishing. Compared with Vietnam and Thailand though – much of which are now deforested, urbanised and farmed – Laos is an enviable hothouse of biodiversity.

Almost two-thirds of Lao people live in rural areas and rely on wildlife as a source of protein to supplement their diet.

SURVIVAL GUIDE

Directory A–Z

Accommodation

Budget digs – usually a room with a fan and sometimes private bathroom – are getting better every year. Even though guesthouse prices are rising, particularly in the cities, they're still unbeatable value when compared with the West. At less than US$10 (85,000K) a night, who can argue?

Accommodation prices listed in this chapter are for the high season. An icon is included to indicate if air-con is available (❄); otherwise assume a fan will be provided. In this book, accommodation is listed in order of merit rather than price.

Budget is defined as accommodation costing less than 120,000K (US$15), midrange as 120,000K (US$15) to 280,000K (US$35), and top end as more than 280,000K (US$35).

Homestays

For more than 75% of Laotians, the 'real Laos' is life in a village. Minority people in villages across the country now welcome travellers into their homes to experience life Lao-style. This means sleeping, eating and washing as they do. It's not luxury – the mattress will be on the floor and you'll 'shower' by pouring water over yourself from a 170L (44-gallon) drum while standing in the middle of the

WILD THING

Here's a guide to some of Laos' endangered animals, a few of which you may encounter during your travels.

» **Asian tiger** The National Protected Areas (NPAs) in northeastern Laos, with their deep, intractable forests, are thought to harbour the densest populations of tigers.

» **Mekong catfish** Growing up to 3m in length and weighing in at 300kg, the world's largest freshwater fish is unique to the Mekong River.

» **Irrawaddy dolphin** Estimates suggest between 64 and 76 dolphins still exist in the Lao Mekong River. The best place to see them in Laos is off the southern tip of Don Khon.

» **Black-crested gibbon** Males are black, females golden, and in Laos these soulful tree athletes only exist in Bokeo Province (home of The Gibbon Experience; p350).

yard (men and women should take a sarong). But it's exactly this level of immersion that makes a homestay so worthwhile. It's also good to know that the 50,000K you'll pay for bed, dinner and breakfast is going directly to those who need it most.

Activities

Cycling

Laos' uncluttered, peaceful roads are a haven for cyclists with a head for heights and a decent set of gears. Many roads are now sealed, though if you're visiting straight after the monsoon you'll find them potholed or, in the case of the Bolaven Plateau, mired in mud. In Vientiane be careful about leaving bags in the front basket, as passing motorcyclists have been known to lift them. Laos' main towns all have bicycle-rental shops. Several companies offer mountain-bike tours, particularly from Luang Nam Tha, Nong Khiaw and Luang Prabang.

Kayaking & Rafting

Laos has several world-class rapids, as well as lots of beautiful, less challenging waterways. The industry remains dangerously unregulated and you should not go out on rapids during the wet season unless you are completely confident about your guides and equipment. Vang Vieng has the most options. **Green Discovery** (☎023-511230; www.greendiscoverylaos.com; Vang Vieng) has a good reputation, as does **Happy Island Tours** (☎020 267 7698; Ban Hua Det, Don Det) on Don Det.

Rock Climbing

Organised rock-climbing operations are run by **Green Discovery** (www.greendiscoverylaos.com) and **Adam's Rock Climbing School** (www.laos-climbing.com; Th Luang Prabang) in the karst cliffs around Vang Vieng, while Green Discovery is the only real operator in Nong Khiaw. Vang Vieng has the most established scene, with dozens of climbs ranging from beginner to expert.

Trekking

Where else can you wander through forests past ethnic hill tribes and rare wildlife with a triple canopy towering above you? Several environmentally and culturally sustainable tours allow you to enter these pristine areas and experience the lives of the indigenous people without exploiting them. These treks are available in several provinces and are detailed on www.ecotourismlaos.com. You can trek from Luang Nam Tha, Muang Sing, Udomxai, Luang Prabang, Vientiane, Tha Khaek, Savannakhet and Pakse. Treks organised through the provincial tourism offices are the cheapest, while companies such as **Green Discovery** (www.greendiscoverylaos.com) offer more expensive and professional operations.

Tubing

Tubing involves inserting yourself into an enormous tractor inner tube and floating down a river. Vang Vieng, Muang Ngoi Neua and Si Phan Don are all hot spots to do this. Just keep an eye on reefer intake and how much you drink; the two combined can be lethal, especially in the dark if you take a tumble in a rogue current.

Books

Lonely Planet's *Laos* has all the information you'll need for extended travel in Laos, with more detailed descriptions of sights and wider coverage to help get you off the beaten track. The following offer further insights:

» *A Dragon Apparent* (1951) Sees Norman Lewis travelling through the twilight of French Indochina.

» *The Lao* (2008) Robert Cooper's locally published book (available in Vientiane) offers a penetrating insight into Lao culture and its psyche.

» *The Ravens: Pilots of the Secret War of Laos* (1987) Christopher Robbins' page-turning account of the 'Secret War' and the role of American pilots and the Hmong is an excellent read.

» *Shooting at the Moon: The Story of America's Clandestine War in Laos* (1998) Roger Warner's well-respected book exposes the 'Secret War' against the Ho Chi Minh Trail, and the CIA and Hmong role in it.

Business Hours

Government offices are typically open from 8am to noon and 1pm to 4pm Monday to Friday. Banking hours are generally 8.30am to 4pm Monday to Friday. Shops have longer hours and are often open on weekends. Restaurants typically close by 10pm and bars stay open until around 11.30pm, sometimes later.

Customs

You can expect borders to be fairly sleepy affairs, and customs officers are equally chilled – so long as you're not carrying more than 500 cigarettes and 1L of spirits, drugs, knives or guns on your person.

Dangers & Annoyances

Urban Laos is generally very safe thanks to the gentle, nonconfrontational nature of its people. You should still exercise reasonable vigilance at night in Vientiane (thanks to more widespread drug taking and bag snatching), while Vang Vieng suffers from theft – usually in budget accommodation – as well as 'soft' muggings after dark.

Since the 1975 revolution, there have been occasional shootings by Hmong guerrillas on Rte 13 between Vang Vieng and Luang Prabang. Given that their numbers are now depleted, their insurrection is unlikely to reignite. Finally, in the eastern provinces, particularly Xieng Khuang, Salavan and Savannakhet, UXO is a hazard. *Never* walk off well-used paths.

Embassies & Consulates

Australia (Map p316; ☎021-353800; www.laos.embassy.gov.au; Th Tha Deua, Ban Wat Nak, Vientiane) Also represents nationals of Britain, Canada and New Zealand.

Cambodia (Map p316; ☎021-314952; fax 021-314951; Km 3, Th Tha Deua, Ban That Khao, Vientiane) Issues visas for US$20.

China (Map p316; ☎021-315105; fax 021-315104; Th Wat Nak Nyai, Ban Wat Nak, Vientiane) Issues visas in four working days.

France (Map p318; ☎021-215258, 215259; www.ambafrance-laos.org; Th Setthathirat, Ban Si Saket, Vientiane)

Germany (Map p316; ☎021-312111, 312110; Th Sok Pa Luang, Vientiane)

Myanmar (Map p316; ☎021-314910; Th Sok Pa Luang, Vientiane) Issues tourist visas in three days for US$20.

Thailand Vientiane embassy (Map p316; ☎021-214581; www.thaiembassy.org/vientiane; Th Kaysone Pomvihane; ⏰8.30am-noon & 1-3.30pm Mon-Fri); Vientiane consulate (Map p316; ☎021-214581; 15 Th Bourichane; ⏰8am-noon & 1-4.30pm); Savannakhet consulate (Map p356; ☎041-212373; cnr Th Tha He & Th Chaimeuang) Head to the Vientiane consulate for visa renewals.

USA (Map p318; ☎021-267000; www.laos.usembassy.gov; Th Bartholomie)

Vietnam Vientiane embassy (Map p316; ☎021-413400; Th That Luang); Savannakhet consulate (Map p356; ☎041-212418; Th Sisavangvong) The embassy in Vientiane issues tourist visas in three working days for US$45 or while you wait for US$60. The consulate in Savannakhet issues a one-month/three-month tourist visa for US$50/60 (one photo, three working days).

Festivals & Events

Festivals are mostly linked to agricultural seasons or historic Buddhist holidays. Dates change with the lunar calendar and even from village to village, but www.tourismlaos.gov.la has more accurate dates for some major festivals, known as *bun* in Lao.

Makha Busa (Magha Puja or Bun Khao Chi, Full Moon) Held in February, this commemorates a speech given by Buddha to 1250 enlightened monks. Chanting and offerings mark the festival, culminating in candlelit circumambulation of wats throughout the country.

Vietnamese Tet & Chinese New Year (Tut Jiin) Celebrated in Vientiane, Pakse and Savannakhet in February with parties, fireworks and visits to Vietnamese and Chinese temples.

Pii Mai (Lao Lunar New Year) Practically the whole country celebrates the Lao New Year, held 14 to 16 April. Houses are cleaned and Buddha images washed with lustral water. Later, people douse one another (and random tourists) with water. This festival is particularly picturesque in Luang Prabang, where it includes elephant processions and traditional costuming. The 14th to 16th are public holidays.

Bun Bang Fai (Rocket Festival) One of the wildest festivals in Laos, this pre-Buddhist rain ceremony is celebrated alongside Visakha Busa. It involves homemade rockets, music, dance, drunkenness, cross-dressing, large wooden phalluses and the occasional incinerated house... great fun. Held in May.

Visakha Busa (Visakha Puja, Full Moon) Falling on the 15th day of the sixth lunar month (usually in May), this is considered the day of Buddha's birth, enlightenment and *parinibbana* (passing into nirvana). Activities are centred on the wat.

Bun Khao Phansa (Khao Watsa, Full Moon) Late July is the beginning of the traditional three-month-rains retreat, when Buddhist monks are expected to station themselves in a single monastery.

Bun Awk Phansa (Ok Watsa, Full Moon) Celebrating the end of the three-month-rains retreat, in September/October.

Bun Nam (Bun Suang Héua, Boat Racing Festival) Held the day after Awk Phansa in September/October. Boat races are held in most riverside towns, though in smaller towns they're often postponed until National Day (2 December).

Bun Pha That Luang (That Luang Festival, Full Moon) Takes place at Pha That Luang in Vientiane in early November. Hundreds of monks assemble to receive alms and floral votives early on the first day. There is a colourful procession between Pha That Luang and Wat Si Muang. Elsewhere, it's all fireworks, music and drinking.

Lao National Day Held on 2 December, this public holiday celebrates the 1975 victory of the proletariat over the Royal Lao with parades and speeches.

Gay & Lesbian Travellers

Laos has a liberal attitude towards homosexuality, but a very conservative attitude towards public displays of affection. Gay couples are unlikely to be given frosty treatment anywhere. Laos doesn't have an obvious gay scene, though Luang Prabang has Laos' first openly gay bar, Khob Chai (opposite Hive Bar), and has the rainbow-coloured gay pride flag flying in a few places around town.

Lesbians won't be bothered, but do expect some strange looks from Lao men.

Legal Matters

There is virtually nothing in the way of legal services in Laos. If you get yourself in legal strife, contact your embassy in Vientiane, though the assistance it can provide may be limited. For Brits, contact your embassy in Bangkok or the Australian embassy.

It's against the law for foreigners and Lao to have sexual relations unless they're married. Be aware that a holiday romance could result in being arrested and deported.

Maps

The best all-purpose country map available is *Laos* by **GT-Rider** (http://gt-rider.com), a sturdy laminated affair with several city maps. Look for editions dated from 2005 onwards.

Hobo Maps has produced a series of decent maps for Vientiane, Luang Prabang and Vang Vieng. These maps are widely available in the relevant destinations.

Media

The government-run *Vientiane Times* is a bland, censored sketch of improving Sino-Lao relations and reveals very little. The *Bangkok Post, Economist, Newsweek* and *Time* can be found in minimarts and bookshops. BBC and CNN are widely available on satellite TV.

Money

Bargaining

With the exception of túk-túk drivers in Vientiane (who are a law unto themselves), most Lao are not looking to rip you off. Take your time when haggling: start lower and gradually meet in the middle. And always keep in perspective you're a comparatively rich person in a very poor country – is it really that important to screw them for that precious fifty cents?

Exchanging Money & Travellers Cheques

US dollars and Thai baht can be exchanged all over the country. Banks in Vientiane and Luang Prabang change UK pounds, euro,

Thai baht, Japanese yen, and Canadian, US and Australian dollars. The best overall exchange rate is usually offered by BCL.

Banks in all provincial centres will exchange US dollar travellers cheques. If you are changing cheques into kip, there is usually no commission, but changing into dollars attracts a minimum 2% charge.

Post

Postal services from Vientiane are painfully slow but generally reliable, the provinces less so. If you have valuable items or presents to post home, there is a **Federal Express** (⌚8am-noon & 1-5pm Mon-Fri, 9am-noon Sat) office inside the main post office compound in Vientiane.

Public Holidays

Aside from government offices, banks and post offices, many Lao businesses do not trouble themselves with weekends and public holidays. Most Chinese- and Vietnamese-run businesses close for three days during Vietnamese Tet and Chinese New Year in February. International Women's Day is a holiday for women only.

International New Year 1 January

Army Day 20 January

International Women's Day 8 March

Lao New Year 14 to 16 April

International Labour Day 1 May

International Children's Day 1 June

Lao National Day 2 December

Studying

There are no formal opportunities to study in Laos. Short courses in cooking are available in the capital and Luang Prabang (p317) and informal Lao-language lessons are advertised in Vientiane.

Telephone

Laos' country code is ☎856. To dial out of the country press ☎00 first. As a guide, all mobile phone numbers have the prefix ☎020, while the newer WIN Phones (fixed phones without a landline) begin with ☎030.

Toilets

Unlike Thailand, the hole-in-the-floor toilet is not common in Laos. The exception is if you're visiting destinations such as hill-tribe villages.

Tourist Information

The Lao National Tourism Administration (NTAL) and provincial tourism authorities have offices throughout Laos. The offices in Tha Khaek, Savannakhet, Pakse, Luang Nam Tha, Sainyabouli, Phongsali and Sam Neua are excellent, with well-trained staff and plenty of brochures.

NTAL also has three good websites:

Central Laos Trekking (www.trekkingcentrallaos.com)

Ecotourism Laos (www.ecotourismlaos.com)

Lao National Tourism Administration (www.tourismlaos.gov.la)

Travellers with Disabilities

Laos is woefully unprepared for people with physical special needs; however, its main cities such as Vientiane, Savannakhet and Luang Prabang have decent pavements (generally) and disabled toilets in most international hotels. Transport is a no-no with cramped conditions on most buses. Contact hotels in advance to see what facilities they have.

Volunteering

It's not easy to find short-term volunteer work in Laos. The Organic Mulberry Farm in Vang Vieng (p327) needs volunteers occasionally, as does Big Brother Mouse (see the boxed text, p333). If you're an orthopaedic surgeon, physio or an IT and graphic designer, you may be able to work at the Cope Centre (see the boxed text, p317).

Women Travellers

Stories of women being hassled are few. Much of the time any attention will be no more than curiosity, as Western women are generally so physically different to Lao women.

Remember, you're in a strictly Buddhist country so the revealing of flesh, despite the heat, is seen as cheap and disrespectful. Sarongs and long-sleeved T-shirts are a good idea – wearing a bikini is no different to wandering around in your underwear in Lao people's eyes.

Working

English teaching is the most common first job for foreigners working in Laos, and schools in Vientiane are often hiring. There are also an inordinate number of development organisations – see www.directoryofngos.org for a full list – where foreigners with technical skills and volunteer experience can look for employment. Ask around.

Getting There & Away

Air

With over a dozen border crossings into Laos, visiting the country has never been easier. Also, the newly improved Lao Airlines is servicing most corners of the country and neighbouring countries with frequent flights. The following airlines fly to and from Laos. All fares are one way.

Bangkok Airways (Map p330; ☎071-253334; www.bangkokair.com; 57/6 Th Sisavangvong, Ban Xiengmuan, Luang Prabang)

China Eastern Airlines (Map p316; ☎021-212300; www.ce-air.com; Th Luang Prabang, Vientiane)

Lao Airlines (Map p318; ☎021-212051; www.laoairlines.com; Th Pangkham, Vientiane)

Thai Airways International (Map p316; ☎021-222527; www.thaiair.com; Th Luang Prabang, Vientiane)

Vietnam Airlines (Map p318; ☎021-217562; www.vietnamairlines.com; 1st fl, Lao Plaza Hotel, Th Samsenthai, Vientiane)

CAMBODIA

There are daily flights with Lao Airlines between Phnom Penh and Vientiane (one-way US$165, 1½ hours) and a daily direct flight with Vietnam Airlines. Lao Airlines flies daily between Siem Reap and Vientiane (one-way US$175, two hours) and between Vientiane and Pakse (one way US$131, 1½ hours).

CHINA

Lao Airlines has daily services between Kunming and Vientiane (US$180, three hours). China Eastern Airlines flies daily to Kunming and Na Ning (US$209).

THAILAND

Lao Airlines and Thai Airways International have regular daily flights between Bangkok and Vientiane (US$149). Bangkok Airways flies daily between Bangkok and Luang Prabang (US$215, two hours). Lao Airlines also has daily flights between Vientiane and Chiang Mai (US$160, 2½ hours), via Luang Prabang (US$87, one hour). Lao Airlines also flies from Luang Prabang to Chiang Mai (one-way US$120, daily) and to Bangkok (one-way US$160), and from Pakse to Bangkok (US$150, 1¼ hours).

VIETNAM

Lao Airlines flies daily between Vientiane and Hanoi (US$130, one hour), and Vientiane and Ho Chi Minh City (US$172, three hours). There are also daily services between Luang Prabang and Hanoi (US$144) and regular flights from Pakse to Ho Chi Minh City (US$150).

MALAYSIA

Between Vientiane and Kuala Lumpur (US$126, 1½ hours) there are now regular flights with Air Asia.

Land

Laos has open land borders with Cambodia, China, Thailand and Vietnam, but not Myanmar. Under current rules, 30-day tourist visas are available on arrival at several (but not all) international checkpoints. We also recommend checking the **Thorn Tree** (lonelyplanet.com/thorntree) for other travellers' accounts, as things change frequently.

Getting Around

Air

Lao Airlines (www.laoairlines.com) handles all domestic flights in Laos. Fortunately, its revamped new fleet has slick MA60s, with the airline rapidly improving its safety record. Check the Lao calendar for public festivals before you fly, as it can be difficult getting a seat. In provincial Lao Airlines offices you'll be expected to pay in cash.

Always reconfirm your flights a day before departing, as undersubscribed flights may be cancelled or you could get bumped off the passenger list.

Bicycle

The light and relatively slow traffic in most Lao towns makes for favourable cycling conditions. Bicycles are available for rent in major tourist destinations, costing around 10,000K per day for a cheap Thai or Chinese model.

Boat

Given Laos' much improved trade roads, the days of mass river transport are almost over. The most popular river trip in Laos – the slow boat between Huay Xai and Luang Prabang – remains a daily event. Other popular journeys – between Pakse and Si Phan Don, or between Nong Khiaw and Luang Prabang – are all recommended if you have time.

River ferries are basic affairs and passengers usually sit, eat and sleep on the wooden decks; it's worth bringing some padding. The toilet (if there is one) is an enclosed hole in the deck at the back of the boat. For shorter river trips, such as Luang Prabang to the Pak Ou Caves, you can easily hire a river taxi.

Between Luang Prabang and Huay Xai and between Xieng Kok and Huay Xai, deafeningly loud and painfully uncomfortable speedboats operate, covering the same distance in six hours as that of a river ferry in two days. They kill and injure people every year when they disintegrate on contact with floating debris, or flip when they hit a standing wave.

Bus & Sŏrngtăaou

Long-distance public transport in Laos is either by bus or sŏrngtăaou (literally 'two rows'), which are converted trucks or pickups with benches down either side. Buses are more frequent and go further than ever. Privately run VIP buses operate on some busier routes, but slow, simple standard buses (occasionally with air-con) remain the norm.

Sŏrngtăaou usually service shorter routes within a given province. Most decent-sized villages have at least one sŏrngtăaou, which will run to the provincial capital daily except Sunday, stopping wherever you want.

Car & Motorcycle

Second-rate Chinese and sturdier Japanese-made 100cc scooters can be rented for 50,000K to 90,000K a day in Vientiane, Tha Khaek, Savannakhet, Pakse and Luang Nam Tha. Try to get a Japanese bike if you're travelling any distance out of town (or across mountains). In Vientiane and Pakse it's also possible to rent dirt bikes for around 250,000K per day. Three-day motorcycle tours of the Ho Chi Minh Trail are newly offered by **Green Discovery** (☎021-218373; www.greendiscoverylaos.com; Th Setthathirat, Vientiane). Meanwhile, **Jules' Classic Rental** (☎020 760 0813; www.bike-rental-laos.com; Th Setthathirat, Vientiane; per day 85,000-255,000K) and **PVO** (Map p318; ☎254354; Th Nokeo Khumman, Vientiane; ⏰8am-6pm Mon-Sat) have a range of performance bikes and the option to rent in Vientiane and drop off in Luang Prabang or Pakse for an additional charge.

Car rental in Laos is a great if relatively costly way of reaching remote places. **Europcar** (Map p318; ☎223867; www.europcarlaos.com; Th Samsenthai; ⏰8am-6pm Mon-Sat) offers vehicles from US$59 per day, charging US$20 extra for a driver.

Hitching

Hitching is possible in Laos, if not common. It's never entirely safe and not recommended, especially for women, as the act of standing beside a road and waving at cars might be misinterpreted.

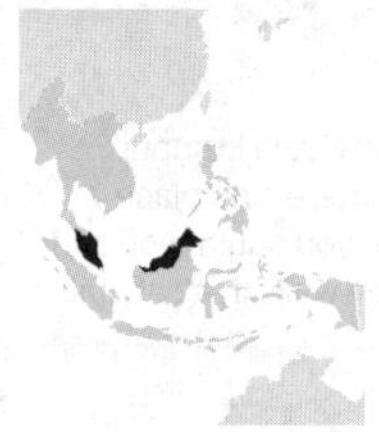

Malaysia

Includes »

Best Regional Specialties

- Laksa asam (p407)
- Ikan bakar (p425)
- Satay celup (p399)
- Roti canai (p473)
- Sarawak laksa (p454)

Best Places for Cultural Connections

- Batu Caves (p385)
- Khoo Kongsi (p406)
- Gelanggang Seni (p426)
- Borneo longhouses (p462)

Why Go?

Malaysia is like two countries in one, cleaved in half by the South China Sea. The multicultural peninsula flaunts Malay, Chinese and Indian influences, while Borneo hosts a wild jungle of orang-utans, granite peaks and remote tribes. Throughout these two regions is an impressive variety of microcosms ranging from the space-age high-rises of Kuala Lumpur to the smiling longhouse villages of Sarawak. And then there's the food. Malaysia (particularly along the peninsular west coast) has one of the best assortments of cuisines in the world. Start with Chinese-Malay 'Nonya' fare, move on to Indian curries, Chinese buffets, Malay food stalls and even impressive Western food. Yet despite all the pockets of ethnicities, religions, landscapes and the sometimes-great distances between them, the beauty of Malaysia lies in the fusion of it all, into a country that is one of the safest, most stable and manageable in Southeast Asia.

When to Go

Kuala Lumpur

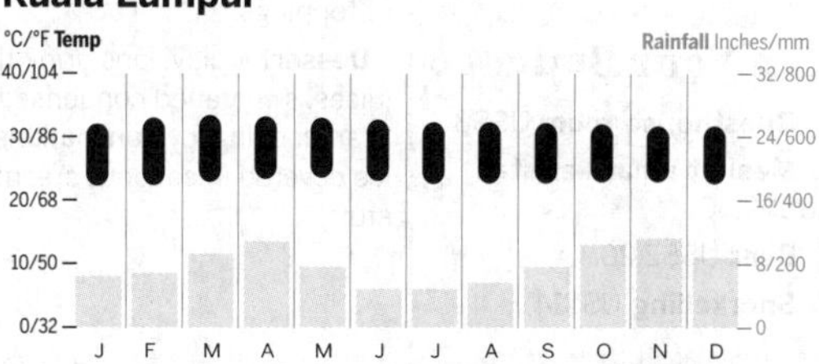

Dec-Feb High season: school holidays and Chinese New Year. Prices rise; bookings essential.

Nov-Mar Monsoon season sees many east-coast peninsular islands shut; Cherating fills with surfers.

Jul-Aug Many restaurants close during the day for Ramadan. Food bazaars open at night.

AT A GLANCE

» **Currency** Malaysian ringitt (RM)

» **Language** Bahasa Malaysia, Chinese (Hakka & Hokkien), Tamil, English

» **Money** ATMs in large towns

» **Visas** Most nationalities get a 30- to 90-day visa on arrival

» **Mobile Phones** Local SIMs are RM16, calls are 30 sen per minute. Data 3G plans are RM15 per week

Fast Facts

» **Area** 328,600 sq km

» **Capital** Kuala Lumpur

» **Country code** ☎60

» **Emergency** ☎999

Exchange Rates

Australia	A$1	RM3.20
Canada	C$1	RM3.10
Euro zone	€1	RM4.05
Japan	¥100	RM3.70
New Zealand	NZ$1	RM2.50
UK	UK£1	RM4.85
USA	US$1	RM3.10

Set Your Budget

» **Guesthouse room** US$8

» **Meal at a hawker stall** US$2.50

» **Beer** US$2.20

» **Snorkelling** US$14

Entering the Country

Thailand and Singapore border Peninsular Malaysia. Indonesia and Brunei border Malaysian Borneo.

Don't Miss

The Petronas Towers observation deck in Kuala Lumpur (KL). Yeah it's a pain getting a ticket but there's no place more iconic of modern Malaysia – plus if you squint you can imagine Catherine Zeta-Jones scaling the walls in a cat suit.

ITINERARIES

One Week

Gorge on endless street food in **Penang** then cool off in the **Cameron Highlands** by exploring mossy forests and tea plantations. Hop over to the **Perhentian Islands** for snorkelling, diving and beachside revelry.

Two Weeks

Follow the one-week itinerary backwards then catch a flight to **Kota Kinabalu** and spend the next week trekking the **wild jungles** of Borneo, perhaps ascending **Mt Kinabalu**, one of the highest mountains in Southeast Asia.

Essential Food & Drink

» **Breakfast** *Nasi lemak* (coconut rice served with a variety of accompaniments), *roti canai* (Indian flat bread), *won ton mee* (egg noodles and wontons), dim sum or rice congee (savoury rice porridge).

» **Barbecue** Fish, lobster, prawns, squid, cockles and stingray. Point to it then watch it get slathered in sambal and grilled in a banana leaf.

» **Noodles** Fried or in soup. The best include *char kway teow* (fried noodles with egg, soy sauce, chilli and a variety of additions), laksa, *curry mee* (curry noodles), *Hokkein mee* (fried noodles with chicken, pork and other additions) and *won ton mee*.

» **Rice** *Nasi campur* is a lunch favourite of rice and a buffet of toppings.

» **Dessert** Malaysians *drink* their sweets via sugared fruit juices, sweetened condensed milk in hot beverages and scary looking icy concoctions like *cendol* and ABC (shave ice covered in coconut cream, jellies, beans and other crazy stuff).

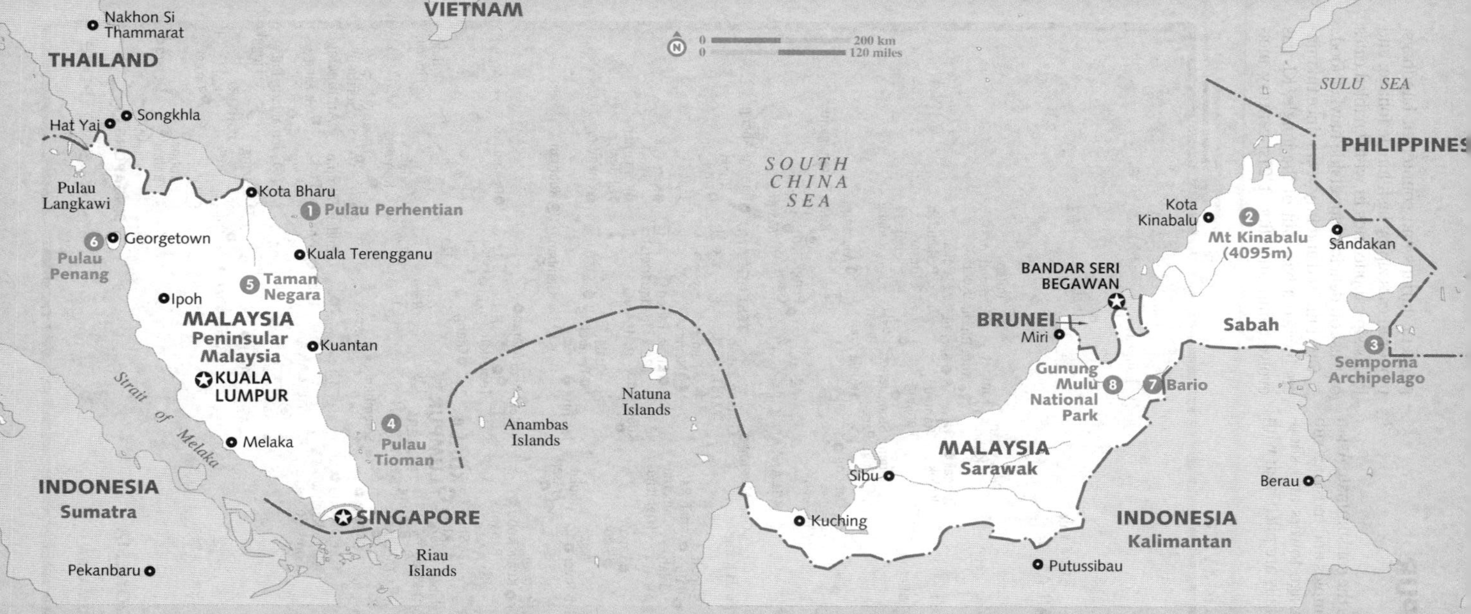

Malaysia Highlights

1 Waking up, swimming, lying on the beach, snorkelling, eating and snoozing on **Pulau Perhentian** (p424)

2 Hoofing it over pitcher plants and moonscapes for sunrise atop the granite spire of **Mt Kinabalu** (p440)

3 Smiling in your scuba mask as you pass turtles, sharks and technicolour coral in the **Semporna Archipelago** (p448)

4 Hopping between perfect beach villages, diving reefs and wrecks, and spotting monkeys on **Pulau Tioman** (p418)

5 Getting wet, muddy and covered in leeches but loving every swashbuckling minute of it in **Taman Negara** (p430)

6 Gorging on hawker food, breathing incense and exploring Georgetown's rickety alleyways on **Penang** (p405)

7 Sipping wild teas at a wobbly longhouse in **Bario** (p467)

8 Climbing the crags of the Pinnacles at **Gunung Mulu National Park** (p465)

KUALA LUMPUR

03 / POP 1.5 MILLION

Kuala Lumpur (KL) is the consummate Asian cyber-city: historic temples and mosques rub shoulders with space-age towers and shopping malls; traders' stalls are piled high with pungent durians and counterfeit handbags; monorail cars zip by lush jungle foliage; and locals sip cappuccinos in wi-fi–enabled cafes or feast on delicious streetside hawker food.

One hundred and fifty years since tin miners hacked a base out of the jungle, KL has evolved into an affluent 21st-century met-

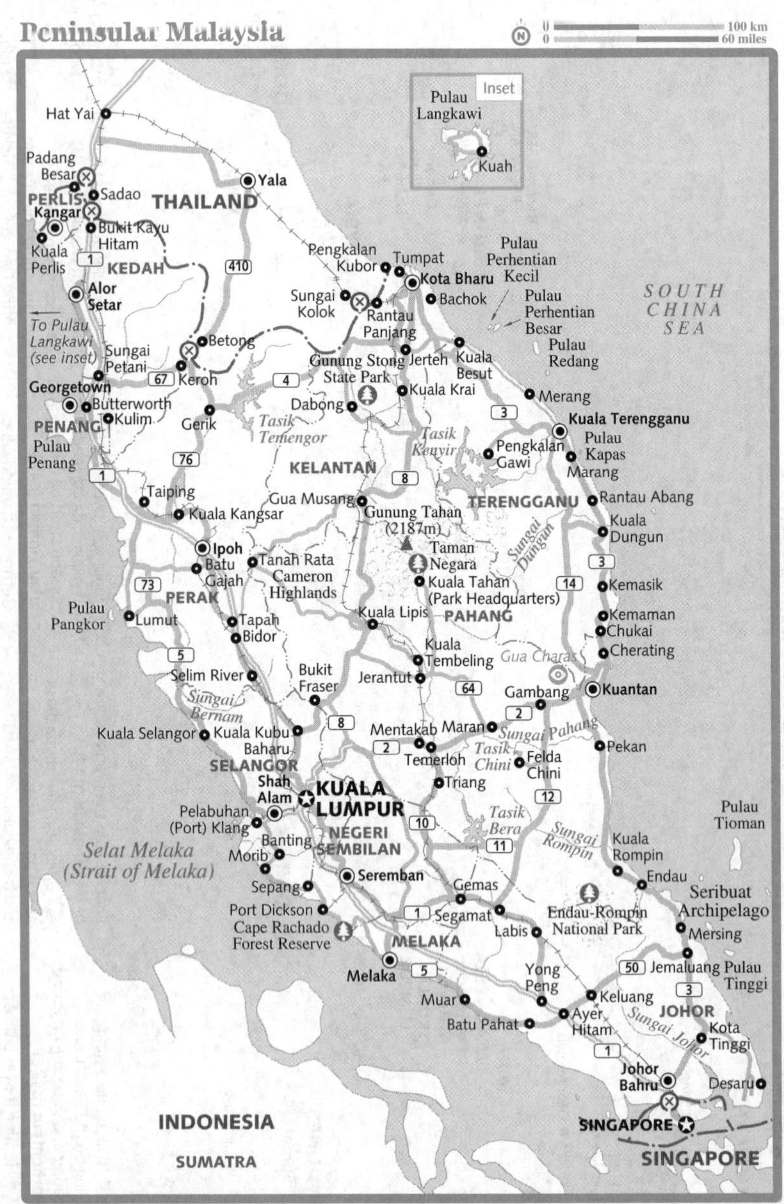

ropolis remarkable for its cultural diversity. Ethnic Malays, Chinese prospectors, Indian immigrants and British colonials all helped shape the city, and each group has left its indelible physical mark as well as a fascinating assortment of cultural traditions.

Merdeka Sq is the traditional heart of KL. Southeast across the river, the banking district merges into Chinatown, popular with travellers for its budget accommodation and lively night market.

To the east of Puduraya bus station, around Jln Sultan Ismail, the Golden Triangle is the modern, upmarket heart of the new KL.

Sights

Six-lane highways and flyovers may slice up the city but the best way to get a feel for KL's atmosphere is to walk.

CHINATOWN & MERDEKA SQUARE

Circuitous streets and cramped chaos create a pressure cooker of sights and sounds in Chinatown. **Jln Petaling** is a bustling street market selling souvenirs, such as 'authentic' Levis and cheap Crocs; it opens around 10am and shuts late at night. Chinatown is reached on the Putra LRT to Pasar Seni station or on the KL Monorail to Maharajalela station. Chinese coffee shops are along Jln Panggong and Jln Balai Polis (Map p386).

Merdeka Square SQUARE

(Map p386; Jln Raja Laut) The one-time cricket field formerly known as the Padang, Merdeka Square is where Malaysia's independence (Merdeka) was proclaimed in 1957. Today it's a choice spot to see some fetching colonial architecture.

Masjid Negara MOSQUE

(National Mosque; Map p386; Jln Perdana; ⌚9am-noon, 3-4pm & 5.30-6.30pm, closed Fri morning) One of Southeast Asia's largest mosques. The main dome is an 18-point star that symbolises the 13 states of Malaysia and the five pillars of Islam.

Sri Mahamariamman Temple TEMPLE

(Map p386; Jln Tun HS Lee) The oldest in Malaysia, founded by migrant workers in 1873. Flower-garland vendors crowd the entrance and the temple is crowned by a huge *gopuram* (temple tower) covered in statues of Hindu deities.

Sze Ya Temple TEMPLE

(Map p386; Jln Tun HS Lee; ⌚7am-5pm) The most atmospheric Chinese Taoist temple in KL, constructed in 1864. Enter the temple through the stucco gatehouse on Jln Tun HS Lee or the back gate on the next alley west.

Old Railway Station HERITAGE BUILDING

(Map p386; Jln Sultan Hishamuddin) South is the old railway station, a fanciful castle of Islamic arches and spires.

LITTLE INDIA & AROUND

Little India has the feel of a bazaar. The sari shops and the women shopping along **Jln Masjid India**, the district's main street, are swathed in vibrant sherbets, turquoise and vermilions. Meanwhile Indian pop blasts through tinny speakers, and musky incense and delicious spices flavour the air. The district swings into a full spectacle during the Saturday *pasar malam* (night market). On the first and third weekends of every month **CapSquare** (off Map p386; www.capsquare.com.my) hosts a bazaar that features food and fashion as well as some interesting knick-knacks.

Little India is best reached on the Star or Putra LRT to Masjid Jamek station.

Masjid Jamek MOSQUE

(Friday Mosque; Map p386; off Jln Tun Perak; ⌚8.30am-12.30pm & 2.30-4pm, closed Fri 11am-2.30pm) Masjid Jamek, set in a grove of palm trees, is KL's most delightful mosque. Built in 1907, the mosque is a creation of onion domes and minarets of layered pink and cream bricks.

Bank Negara Malaysia Museum & Art Gallery MUSEUM

(Map p384; http://museum.bnm.gov.my) With a few galleries starting to open since late 2011, the Bank Negara Malaysia Museum and Art Gallery is set in a futuristic, metal-clad complex west of Jln Kuching.

GOLDEN TRIANGLE

A forest of high-rises, the Golden Triangle is central KL's business, shopping and entertainment district. To get here, take the Putra LRT to KLCC station.

Petronas Towers TOWER

(Map p390; www.petronas.com.my/petronas; Jln Ampang; admission RM10; ⌚9am-7pm Tue-Sun, closed Mon & 1-2.30pm Fri) Formerly the world's tallest skyscrapers (until Taipei 101 took the title in 2004), the twin Petronas Towers serve as the elegant headquarters of the national petroleum company. There are three packages for going up the towers, all purchased from the ticket counter in the basement. The cheapest deal accesses the 41st-floor **Skybridge**, 170m above

Kuala Lumpur

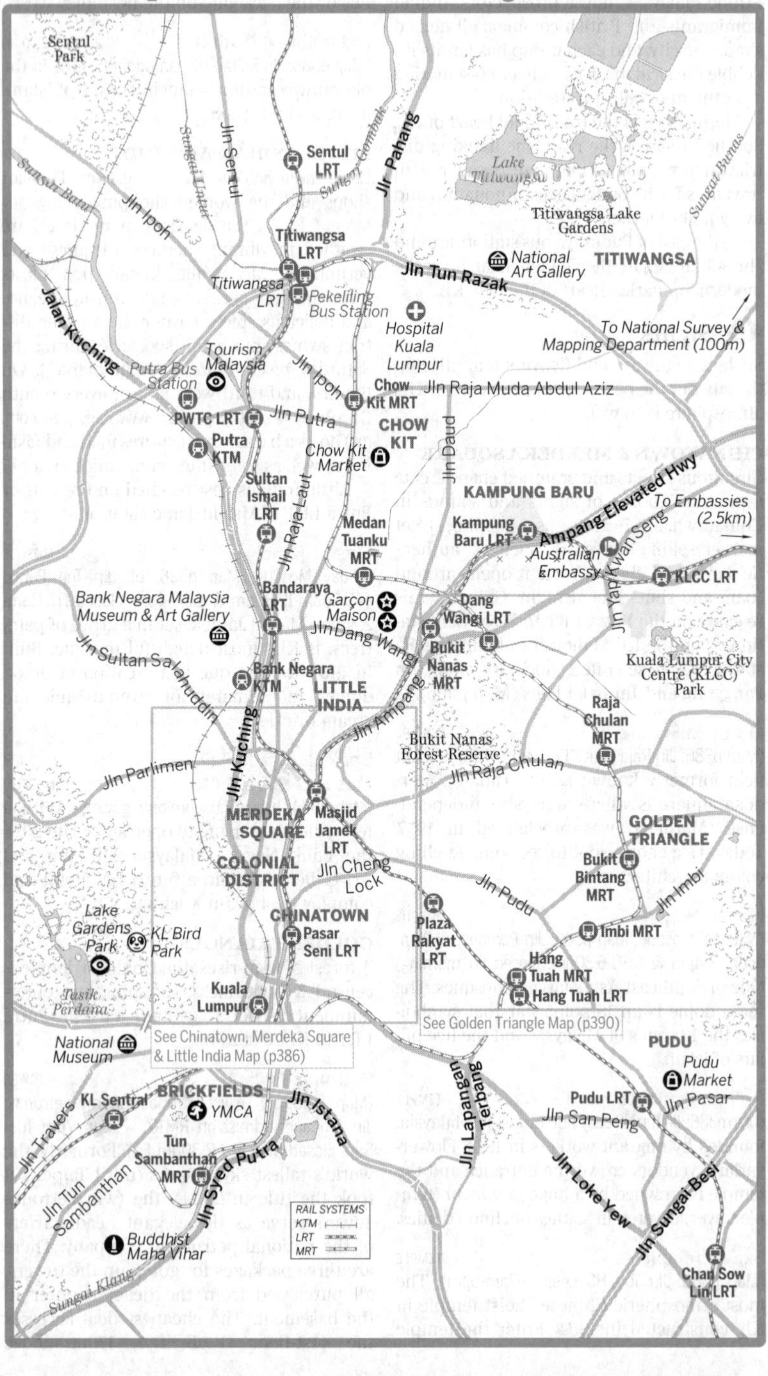

0 — 1 km
0 — 0.5 miles

Sentul Park
Jln Sentul
Sungai Untut
Sungai Gombak
Jln Pahang
Sentul LRT
Sungai Batu
Jln Ipoh
Lake Titiwangsa
Titiwangsa Lake Gardens
Sungai Bunus
Titiwangsa LRT
Titiwangsa LRT
Pekeliling Bus Station
Jln Tun Razak
National Art Gallery
TITIWANGSA
Jalan Kuching
Hospital Kuala Lumpur
To National Survey & Mapping Department (100m)
Tourism Malaysia
Putra Bus Station
Jln Ipoh
Chow Kit MRT
Jln Raja Muda Abdul Aziz
PWTC LRT
Jln Putra
CHOW KIT
Putra KTM
Chow Kit Market
Jln Daud
Sultan Ismail LRT
Jln Raja Laut
KAMPUNG BARU
Ampang Elevated Hwy
To Embassies (2.5km)
Medan Tuanku MRT
Kampung Baru LRT
Jln Yap Kwan Seng
Australian Embassy
KLCC LRT
Bandaraya LRT
Garçon
Maison
Bank Negara Malaysia Museum & Art Gallery
Jln Dang Wangi
Dang Wangi LRT
Jln Sultan Salahuddin
Bukit Nanas MRT
Kuala Lumpur City Centre (KLCC) Park
Bank Negara KTM
LITTLE INDIA
Jln Ampang
Raja Chulan MRT
Jln Kuching
Bukit Nanas Forest Reserve
Jln Parlimen
Jln Raja Chulan
MERDEKA SQUARE
Masjid Jamek LRT
GOLDEN TRIANGLE
COLONIAL DISTRICT
Jln Cheng Lock
Bukit Bintang MRT
Jln Imbi
Jln Pudu
Lake Gardens Park
KL Bird Park
CHINATOWN
Pasar Seni LRT
Plaza Rakyat LRT
Imbi MRT
Tasik Perdana
Kuala Lumpur
Hang Tuah MRT
Hang Tuah LRT
See Chinatown, Merdeka Square & Little India Map (p386)
See Golden Triangle Map (p390)
National Museum
PUDU
Pudu Market
BRICKFIELDS
KL Sentral
YMCA
Jln Istana
Jln Lapangan Terbang
Pudu LRT
Jln Pasar
Jln San Peng
Jln Travers
Tun Sambanthan MRT
Jln Syed Putra
Jln Tun Sambanthan
Jln Loke Yew
Jln Sungai Besi
RAIL SYSTEMS
KTM
LRT
MRT
Buddhist Maha Vihar
Sungai Klang
Chan Sow Lin LRT

ground. For RM40 you can continue up to the 88th-floor observation deck in Tower 2, while a premium package (including lunch/dinner RM200/350) gains you access to the members-only Malaysian Petroleum Club for a meal.

Menara Kuala Lumpur TOWER
(KL Tower; Map p390; ☎2020 5448; www.menarakl.com.my; 2 Jln Punchak; admission RM38; ⏲9am-10pm; last tickets up 9.30pm) Sitting on a forested hill, Menara Kuala Lumpur easily trumps the Petronas Towers when it comes to the view. The tower's bulbous pinnacle is inspired by a Malaysian spinning top and the 276m-high **viewing deck** is over 100m higher than the Petronas Towers' Skybridge.

A free **shuttle bus** (every 15 min; ⏲9am-9.30pm) runs to the tower from the gate on Jln Punchak opposite the PanGlobal building. Alternatively, get a workout climbing the short nature trails that run through the forest reserve, which you can explore alone or on a free guided tour starting from the entrance to the tower at 11am, 12.30pm, 2.30pm and 4.30pm daily and lasting about 45 minutes.

LAKE GARDENS & AROUND

Escape from the heat and concrete to this inner-city garden district at the western edge of central KL. From Chinatown, Intrakota Bus 21C from the Jln Sultan Mohammed bus stop, or buses 21B, 22, 48C and F3, will take you there. It is also a 20-minute walk from Masjid Jamek.

National Museum MUSEUM
(Muzium Negara; Map p384; ☎2282 6255; www.muziumnegara.gov.my; Jln Damansara; admission RM2; ⏲9am-6pm) At the edge of the Lake Gardens, the recently renovated National Museum boasts colourful displays on Malaysia's history, economy, arts, crafts and culture. Free guided tours in English are held at 11am Tuesday, Thursday and Saturday and in French at 9am and noon Thursday.

KL Bird Park AVIARY
(Map p384; ☎2272 1010; www.klbirdpark.com; Jln Cenderawasih; admission RM45; ⏲9am-6pm) This fabulous aviary brings together some 200 species of (mostly) Asian birds flying around beneath an enormous canopy.

Islamic Arts Museum MUSEUM
(Muzium Kesenian Islam Malaysia; Map p386; ☎2274 2020; www.iamm.org.my; Jln Lembah Perdana; admission RM12; ⏲10am-6pm) One of best collections of Islamic decorative arts in the world, including carpets, jewellery and calligraphy-inscribed pottery housed in a building decorated with domes and glazed tilework.

Lake Gardens Park PARK
(Taman Tasik Perdana; Map p384; Jln Tembusu; ⏲daylight hr) A vast park planted with native plants, trees and shrubs. Rent boats in the lake for RM6 per hour and watch t'ai chi practitioners in the early morning.

NORTHERN KL

National Art Gallery MUSEUM
(Balai Seni Lukis Negara; Map p384; ☎4026 7000; www.artgallery.org.my; 2 Jln Temerloh, off Jln Tun Razak; admission free; ⏲10am-6pm) Further north near Lake Titiwangsa, the National Art Gallery displays works by contemporary Malaysian and international artists. Take any Len Seng bus from Lebuh Ampang (north of

WORTH A TRIP

BATU CAVES

Get closer to KL's Indian culture by visiting the **Batu Caves** (admission free; ⏲8am-8pm), a system of three caves 13km northwest of the capital. The most famous is Temple Cave, because it contains a Hindu shrine reached by a straight flight of 272 steps, guarded by a 43m-high Murga statue, the highest in the world. **Dark Cave** (www.darkcave.com.my; admission RM35) lets you explore some limestone passageways via guided tour, and **Cave Villa** (admission RM15; ⏲9am-6pm) has Hindu paintings and a dance show every half-hour. About a million pilgrims visit the Batu Caves every year during Thaipusam (January/February) to engage in or watch the spectacularly masochistic feats of the devotees.

To get here take Bus 11 (RM2, 45 minutes) from where Jln Tun HS Lee meets Jln Petaling, just south of Medan Pasar in KL. The bus also stops along Jln Raja Laut in the Chow Kit area. A taxi costs around RM20.

Chinatown, Merdeka Square & Little India

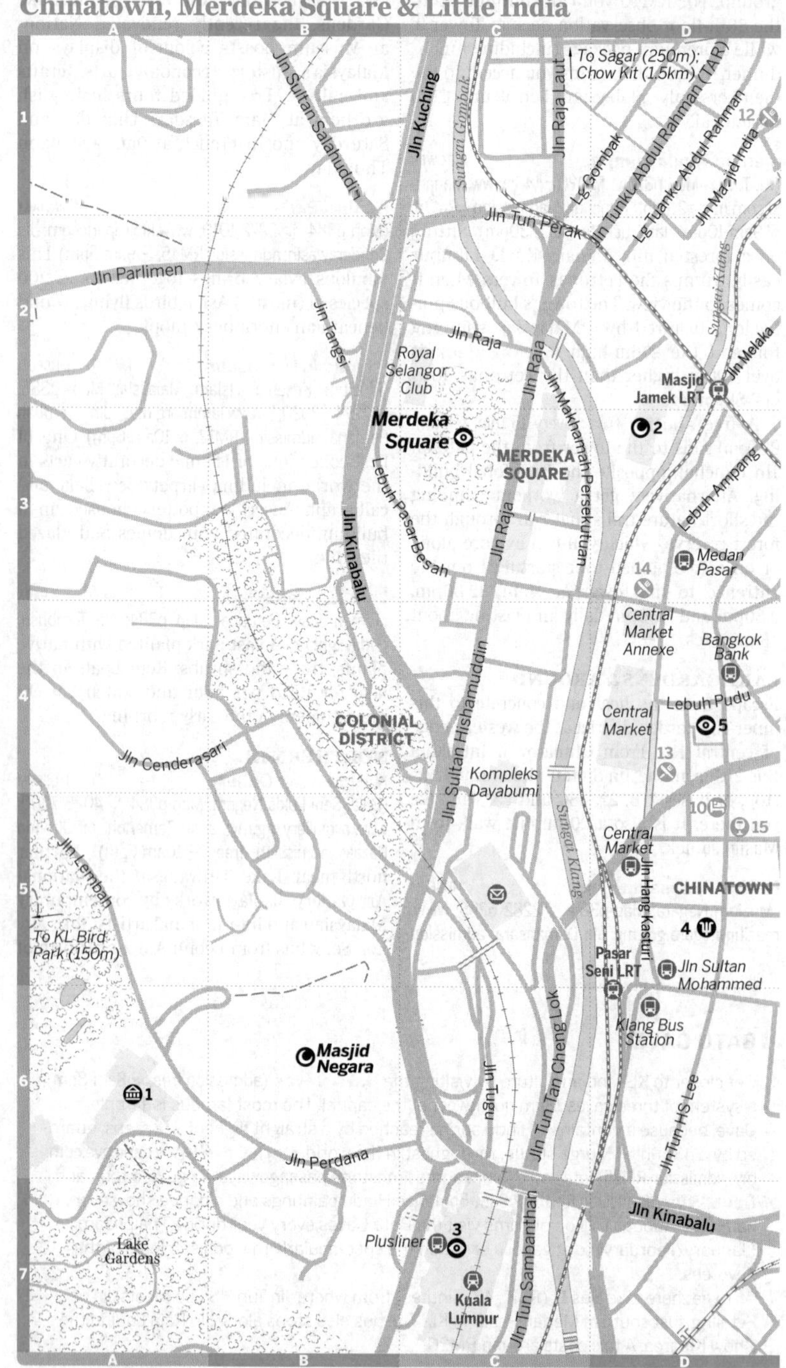

A
B
C
D
1
2
3
4
5
6
7
To Sagar (250m); Chow Kit (1.5km)
Jln Sultan Salahuddin
Jln Kuching
Sungai Gombak
Jln Raja Laut
Lg Gombak
Jln Tunku Abdul Rahman (TAR)
Lg Tuanku Abdul Rahman
Jln Masjid India
12
Jln Tun Perak
Jln Parlimen
Jln Tangsi
Jln Raja
Sungai Klang
Jln Melaka
Royal Selangor Club
Masjid Jamek LRT
Merdeka Square
2
MERDEKA SQUARE
Jln Makhamah Persekutuan
Lebuh Pasar Besah
Jln Kinabalu
Lebuh Ampang
Medan Pasar
14
Central Market Annexe
Bangkok Bank
Jln Sultan Hishamuddin
COLONIAL DISTRICT
Central Market
Lebuh Pudu
5
13
Jln Cenderasari
Kompleks Dayabumi
10
15
Jln Lembah
Central Market
Jln Hang Kasturi
CHINATOWN
To KL Bird Park (150m)
4
Pasar Seni LRT
Jln Sultan Mohammed
Klang Bus Station
Masjid Negara
Jln Tugu
Jln Tun Tan Cheng Lok
1
Jln Tun HS Lee
Jln Perdana
Jln Kinabalu
Jln Tun Sambanthan
Plusliner
3
Lake Gardens
Kuala Lumpur

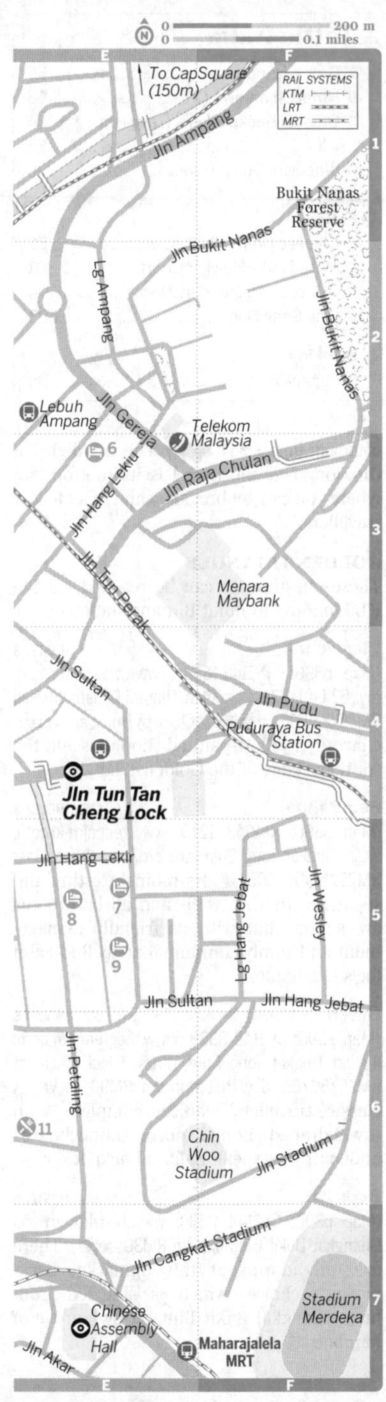

Central Market) in Chinatown or from along Jln Raja Laut; get off at the hospital stop.

Chow Kit Market MARKET
(Map p384; 469-473 Jln TAR; ⏲8am-9pm) It's sensory overload at the Chow Kit Market, where tightly jammed stalls sell clothes; toys; spices; meat; live, flapping fish; and weird and wonderful tropical fruit.

Activities

Spa & Massage

There's a concentration of Chinese massage and reflexology places along Jln Bukit Bintang, south of BB Plaza. The going price is usually RM75 for a one-hour full-body massage. Expect to pay about RM30 for 30 minutes of foot reflexology.

Alternatively, fish spas are the hip, new thing: live fish nibble the dead skin off your feet for up to 30 minutes for around RM30.

Foot Master Dr Fish Spa FISH SPA
(Map p390; ☎2141 6651; Level 5, Pavillion KL; ⏲10am-10pm) You can also have a full body fish feed here – we dare you – for RM108.

Old Asia MASSAGE
(Map p390; ☎2143 9888; 14 Jln Bukit Bintang; ⏲10am-10pm) One of the more reliable and pleasantly designed places.

Courses

Buddhist Maha Vihar MEDITATION
(Map p384; ☎2274 1141; www.buddhistmahavihara.com; 123 Jln Berhala) This Brickfields landmark offers a variety of courses. Meditation and chanting classes are held daily.

YMCA LANGUAGE & DANCE CLASSES
(Map p384; ☎2274 1439; www.ymcakl.com; 95 Jln Padang Belia, Brickfields) Offers Bahasa Malaysia classes as well as Thai, Mandarin/Cantonese and Japanese. You can also study martial arts and different types of dancing.

Sleeping

Vibrant Chinatown is your best hunting ground for rock-bottom crash pads and is an easy walk from the Puduraya bus station. The Golden Triangle area's budget options are pricier but cleaner and in a more low-key (and arguably less exciting) neighbourhood. Unless otherwise noted, all the options listed share bathrooms.

CHINATOWN & LITTLE INDIA

If you're arriving from the airport or a long-distance bus station other than Puduraya,

Chinatown, Merdeka Square & Little India

these guesthouses can be reached via the Star LRT to Plaza Rakyat, Putra LRT to Pasar Seni or the KL Monorail to Maharajalela station.

TOP CHOICE BackHome HOSTEL $
(Map p386; ☎2078 7188; www.backhome.com.my; 30 Jln Tun HS Lee; dm/d with breakfast from RM42/100; ❄@📶) This new hostel is a chic pit stop for flashpackers with its polished concrete finishes, Zen simple decoration, fab rain showers and a blissful central courtyard sprouting spindly trees.

Hotel Chinatown (2) HOTEL $
(Map p386; ☎2072 9933; www.hotelchinatown2.com; 70-72 Jln Petaling; s/d from RM69/90; ❄@📶) The slightly cheaper and more appealing of the two Hotel Chinatowns pleases with a lobby equipped with comfy lounge area, water feature and piano.

Wheelers Guest House GUESTHOUSE $
(Map p386; ☎2070 1386; www.backpackerskl.com/wheelers.htm; Lvl 2, 131-133 Jln Tun HS Lee; dm/r R13/30, r with bathroom RM60; ❄@) With its mini-aquarium, potted plants and murals, Wheelers is one of KL's quirkier hostels.

Grocer's Inn GUESTHOUSE $
(Map p386; ☎2078 7906; www.grocersinn.com.my; 78 Jln Sultan; dm/s/d from RM15/35/45; ❄@) In a century-old building this backpackers has good fan and air-con rooms as well as rooftop dorm and balconies overlooking Chinatown. The entrance is in an alley just off Jln Sultan.

Original Backpackers Travellers Inn HOSTEL $
(Map p386; ☎2078 2473; www.backpackerskl.com; 60B Jln Sultan; dm/s/d RM11/28/30, r with bathroom from RM54; ❄@) The highlight of this long-running hostel is its rooftop bar, where you can get breakfast and meet fellow travellers.

GOLDEN TRIANGLE

These guesthouses can be reached via the KL Monorail to Bukit Bintang station.

Classic Inn HOSTEL $
(Map p390; ☎2148 8648; www.classicinn.com.my; 52 Lg 1/77A, Changkat Thambi Dollah; dm/s/d RM35/88/118; ❄@) Occupying a retro-charming, yellow-painted shophouse on the southern edge of the Golden Triangle.

Red Palm GUESTHOUSE $
(Map p390; ☎2143 1279; www.redpalm-kl.com; 5 Jln Tingkat Tong Shin; dm/s/d/tr incl breakfast RM30/50/70/105; @) Its rooms are tiny and separated by thin walls and all bathrooms are shared, but with its friendly management and comfy communal areas Red Palm feels like home.

Green Hut Lodge GUESTHOUSE $
(Map p390; ☎2142 3339; www.thegreenhut.com; 48 Jln Tingkat Tong Shin; dm/s/d incl breakfast RM25/50/65, d with bathroom RM90; ❄@) A classic travellers' choice, complete with towel-draped 12-bed dorm, noticeboards and staff who speak Bahasa Backpacker.

Bedz KL HOSTEL $
(Map p390; ☎2144 2339; www.bedzkl.com; 58 Changkat Bukit Bintang; dm RM30; ❄@) There are only dorms at this upmarket backpacker's choice, which is shielded from busy Changkat Bukit Bintang by a grove of bamboo.

SPLURGE IN KL!

KL can be taxing so if you're going to spend a little more on a place to stay in Malaysia, this is where to do it.

Sahabat Guest House (Map p390; ☎2142 0689; www.sahabatguesthouse.com; 41 Jln Sahabat; d with breakfast from RM96; ❄@📶) An adorable eight-room guesthouse tucked away off Tingkat Tong Shin.

Fraser Place Kuala Lumpur (Map p390; ☎2118 6288; http://kualalumpur.frasershospitality.com; Lot 163, 10 Jln Perak; apt with breakfast from RM350; ❄@📶🏊) These serviced, self-catering studios and apartments are superstylish and can be booked for as little as one night.

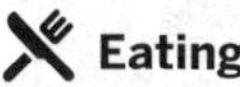

Eating

All the food groups – including Indian, Chinese, Malay and Western fast food – abound in the Malaysian capital.

CHINATOWN & LITTLE INDIA

In the morning, grab a marble-topped table in one of the neighbourhood's *kedai kopi* (coffee shops) for a jolt of coffee spiked with condensed milk. The midday meal can be slurped down at the stalls that line Jln Sultan serving all the you-name-it noodles, from prawn or *won ton mee* (Chinese-style egg noodles served with stuffed wontons) to *laksa lemak* (white rounded noodles served with coconut milk, also called curry laksa). Jln Petaling market is closed to traffic in the evenings and Chinese restaurants set up tables beside all the action.

Little India is your best hunting ground for a slap-up Indian curry sopped up with flaky *roti canai* (Indian-style flaky flat bread, also known as 'flying dough').

Sing Seng Nam COFFEE SHOP $
(Map p386; Medan Pasar; ⏲7am-5pm Mon-Sat) A genuine *kopitiam* (coffee shop), busy with lawyers from the nearby courts who come to enjoy a breakfast of *kaya* toast and runny boiled egg or a *kopi peng* (iced coffee with milk).

Restoran Yusoof dan Zakhir INDIAN MUSLIM $
(Map p386; Jln Hang Kasturi; roti RM2; ⏲24hr) This huge canteen opposite Central Market serves huge portions of delicious *mamak* food; perfect for a roti and curry sauce snack.

Masjid India Hawker Court HAWKER STALLS $
(Map p386; Jln Masjid India; meals RM2-10; ⏲8am-9pm) A bustling covered hawker court serving all the usual Malay, Indian and Chinese favourites.

GOLDEN TRIANGLE & KLCC

Jln Nagansari, off Changkat Bukit Bintang, is lined with Malay food stalls and open-air restaurants. Jln Alor, two streets northwest of Jln Bukit Bintang, has a carnival-like night market of Chinese hawker stalls. When it's hot outside, head to central KL's air-con shopping centres for international and local food. Take the KL Monorail to Bukit Bintang to reach the following listings.

TOP CHOICE **Imbi Market** MALAYSIAN, CHINESE $
(Map p384; Jln Kampung; meals RM10; ⏲6.30am-12.30pm Tue-Sun) Breakfast is almost like a party here with locals happily recommending their favourite stalls.

GAY & LESBIAN KUALA LUMPUR

Check out www.utopia-asia.com and www.fridae.com for the latest on KL's small but friendly gay scene. **Prince World KL** (www.princeworldkl.com) organises big gay dance parties several times a year.

Garçon (Map p384; ☎2381 2088; 8 Jln Yap Ah Shak; cover RM30; ⏲9pm-3am Sun) For Sunday nightclubbers this boy-friendly dance event at the glam Maison is the place to be seen.

Blue Boy (Map p390; ☎2142 1067; 54 Jln Sultan Ismail; ⏲5pm-3am) Malaysia's oldest gay club is a gritty pick-up joint with karaoke-singing lady boys.

Golden Triangle

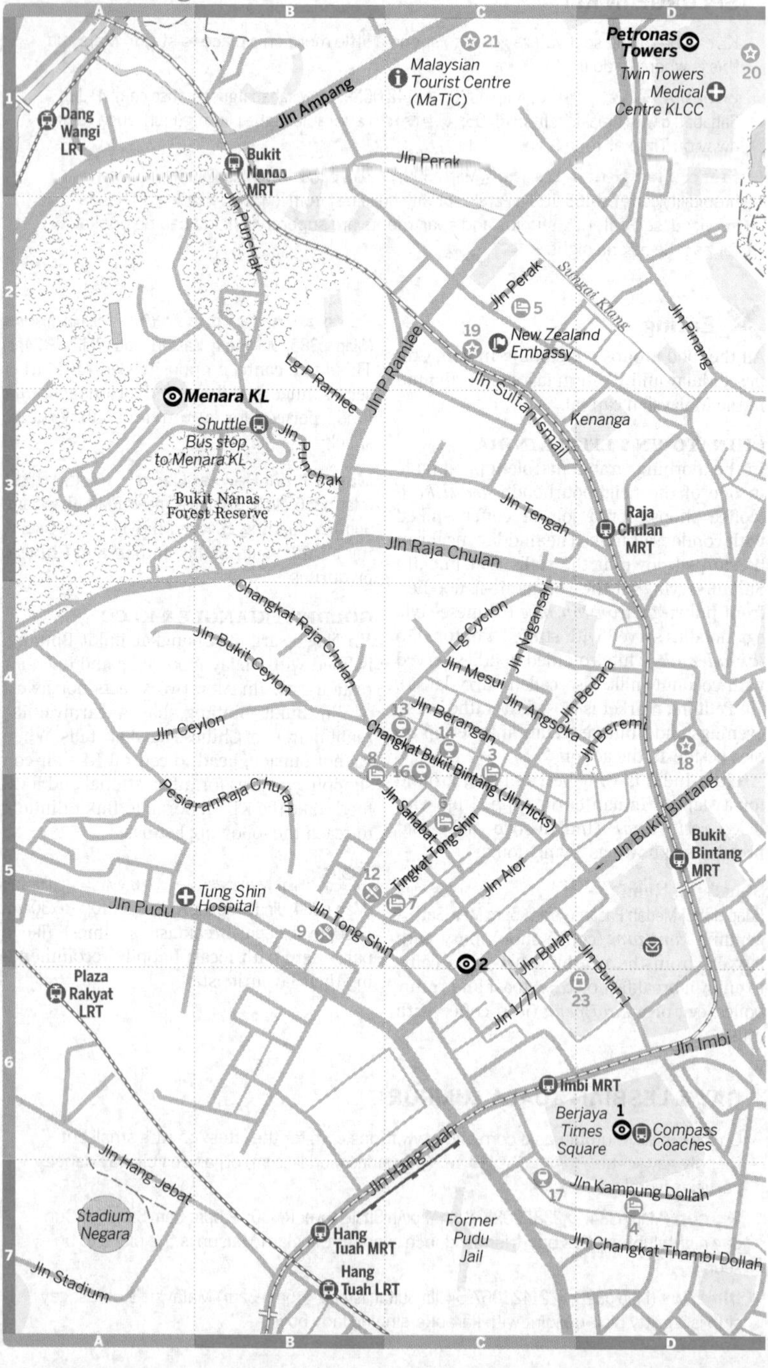

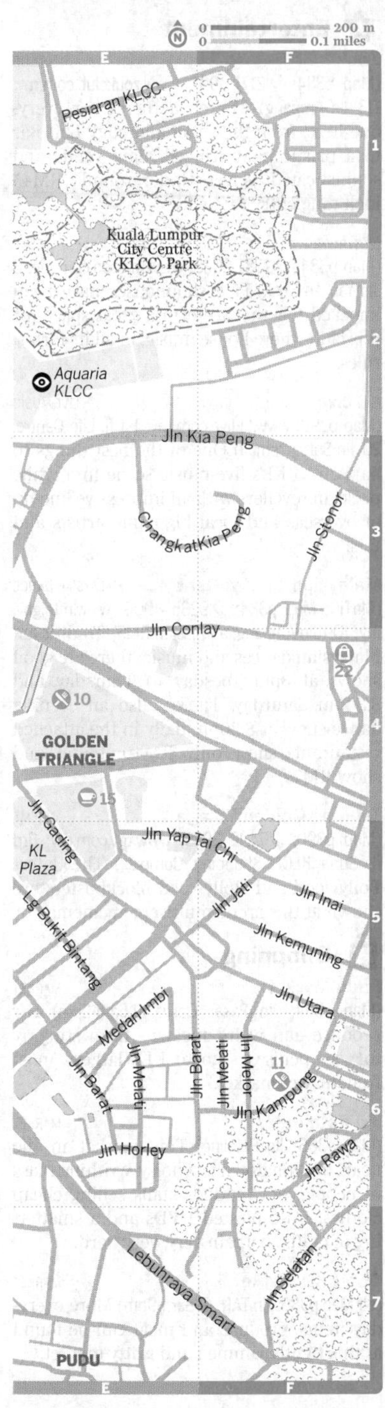

Blue Boy Vegetarian Food Centre VEGETARIAN $
(Map p390; ☎2144 9011; Jln Tong Shin; meals RM5-10; ⏰7.30am-9.30pm; 🌿) Get all your meat and fish substitutes prepared local style at this spotless, backstreet eatery.

Sagar INDIAN $
(off Map p386; ☎2691 3088; Semua House, Jln Masjid India; meals RM10; ⏰8am-8pm; 🌿) Enjoy *thali* meals (rice or bread served with assorted vegetables and curries) at this sidewalk cafe, and soak up the street life of Little India.

Ngau Kee Beef Ball Noodles CHINESE $
(Map p390; Tingkat Tong Shin; noodles RM5; ⏰24hr) Serves a two-part dish: dry, steamed

Golden Triangle

noodles topped with a thick soy-sauce mince, and chunky beef balls in a clear soup.

Food Republic FOOD COURT $$
(Map p390; Level 1, Pavilion KL, 168 Jln Bukit Bintang; meals RM10-20; ⏲10am-10pm) Outstanding choice and slick design make this probably the best shopping-mall food court in KL. It's also surrounded by scores of proper restaurants.

Drinking

Drinking in Malaysia is definitely no budget activity and drinks at 'proper' bars are nearly double in price. The cheapest places to imbibe are Chinese eateries or open-air hawker stalls.

Meat-market bars congregate along Jln P Ramlee while sophisticates and the indie-inclined heat up at nearby CapSquare. Head to Bangsar for classy expat bars and cafes.

Check out the latest club news in **KLue** (www.klue.com.my; RM5). Clubs are typically open Wednesday to Sunday and usually charge a cover (including one drink) of RM20 to RM40 Thursday to Saturday.

Ceylon Bar BAR
(Map p390; 20-2 Changkat Bukit Bintang; ⏲4pm-1am, from 11am Sun) Big, comfy lounges, inexpensive drinks and a genuinely convivial mood make this one of the friendliest drinking holes in KL.

Reggae Bar BAR
(www.reggaebarkl.com; ⏲noon-late) Chinatown (Map p386; 158 Jln Tun HS Lee) Golden Triangle (Map p390; 31 Changat Bukit Bintang) Travellers gather in droves at these pumping bars, one in the thick of Chinatown and the other in Bukit Bintang. The one in Chinatown has outdoor seats if you'd like to catch the passing parade.

Green Man PUB
(Map p390; www.greenman.com.my; 40 Changkat Bukit Bintang; ⏲noon-1am, to 2am Fri-Sun) KL's original Irish pub has a very loyal crowd.

Sixty Nine Bistro CAFE
(off Map p390; ☎2144 3369; 14 Jln Kampung Dollah; ⏲noon-midnight) Worth checking out for its eclectic junk shop–chic furnishings, milk and fruit shakes and resident fortune tellers and tarot-card readers.

Luk Yu Tea House TEAHOUSE
(Map p390; Feast fl, Starhill Gallery, 181 Jln Bukit Bintang; ⏲10am-1am) Enjoy a premium brew inside a charming traditional Chinese teahouse along with dim sum and other dainty snacks.

Entertainment

Zouk CLUB
(Map p384; ☎2171 1997; www.zoukclub.com.my; 113 Jln Ampang) There's a theme for everyone here, from the small and edgy Loft Bar to a plastic palm-fringed main venue and sophisticated Velvet Underground (RM45 including entry to Zouk).

Maison CLUB
(Map p384; ☎2381 2088; www.maison.com.my; 8 Jln Yap Ah Shak) Five shophouses have been knocked together to form a great space for this club where house music, in all its forms, rules.

KL Live LIVE MUSIC
(Map p390; www.kl-live.com.my; 1st fl, Life Centre, 20 Jln Sultan Ismail) One of the best things to happen to KL's live-music scene in a while packs in revellers with an impressive line-up of overseas and local big-name artists and DJs.

Malaysian Tourist Centre MALAYSIAN DANCE
(MaTiC; Map p384; ☎9235 4900; www.mtc.gov.my; 109 Jln Ampang; admission RM5) Traditional Malaysian dances and music; there are good shows at 3pm Tuesday to Thursday and 8.30pm Saturday. There's also an evening dance show at 8.30pm daily in the attached restaurant (show only RM40; buffet and show RM75).

Tanjung Golden Village CINEMA
(Map p390; ☎7492 2929; www.tgv.com.my; 3rd fl, Suria KLCC Shopping Complex) The latest Bollywood and Hollywood blockbusters are shown at this arctic multiscreen cinema.

Shopping

Pudu Market MARKET
(Map p384; Jln Pasar Baru; ⏲6am-2pm) For produce and weird meats – from stingray to pig's penises – go to KL's largest, most frenetic wet market.

Jln Petaling MARKET
(Map p386; Jln Petaling) This market in the heart of Chinatown is a noisy, writhing mass of people and outdoor stalls selling cheap clothes, fruit, pirated DVDs and a smattering of crafts; bargain very, very hard.

Chow Kit Market MARKET
(off Map p386; Jln TAR; ⏲8am-9pm) More everyday items, produce and meat can be found at this tightly jammed and gritty market.

Low Yat Plaza ELECTRONICS
(Map p390; ☎2148 3651; 7 Jln 1/77 off Bukit Bintang) Go here for all your digital and electronic needs.

Kompleks Budaya Kraf ARTS & CRAFTS
(Map p390; ☎2162 7459; Jln Conlay; ⊙9am-8pm Mon-Fri, to 7pm Sat & Sun) This place has a large selection of handicrafts.

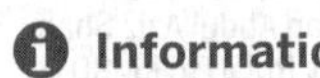

Information

Bookshops

Kinokuniya (☎2164 8133; 4th fl, Suria KLCC Shopping Complex)

Immigration Offices

Immigration Office (☎2095 5077; Block I, Pusat Bandar Damansara) It's 2km west of the Lake Gardens; handles visa extensions.

Internet Access

Internet cafes are everywhere; the going rate per hour is RM3. If you're travelling with a wi-fi-enabled device, you can get online at hundreds of cafes, restaurants, bars and many hotels for free; sign up for an account with **Wireless@KL** (www.wirelesskl.com).

Media

KLue (www.klue.com.my; RM5) An excellent local-listings magazine, with features about what's going on in and around the city.

Medical Services

Hospital Kuala Lumpur (Map p384; ☎2615 5555; www.hkl.gov.my; Jln Pahang)

Twin Towers Medical Centre KLCC (Map p384; ☎2382 3500; Lot 401 F&G, 4th fl, Suria KLCC Shopping Complex)

Money

You'll seldom be far from a bank or ATM. Money changers offer better rates than banks for changing cash and (at times) travellers cheques; they are usually open later hours and on weekends and are found in shopping malls.

Post

Main post office (Map p386; Jln Raja Laut; ⊙8.30am-6pm Mon-Sat) The office is closed on the first Saturday of the month.

Telephone

Payphones abound in the capital and most take coins, credit cards and phonecards (available from convenience stores). Most internet cafes offer Skype and other net-phone services.

Telekom Malaysia (Map p386; Jln Raja Chulan; ⊙8.30am-4.30pm Mon-Fri, to 12.30pm Sat) You can make international calls and send faxes.

Tourist Information

Malaysian Tourist Centre (MaTiC; Map p384; ☎9235 4900; www.mtc.gov.my; 109 Jln Ampang; ⊙8am-10pm) Almost a tourist attraction in its own right, this is Kuala Lumpur's most useful tourist information office. It also hosts good cultural performances (see p393).

Tourism Malaysia (www.tourismmalaysia.gov.my) KL Sentral (☎2274 5823; ⊙9am-6pm); Kuala Lumpur International Airport (KLIA; ☎8776 5651; International Arrival Hall, Sepang); Putra World Trade Centre (Map p384; ☎2615 8188; Level 17, 45 Jln Tun Ismail; ⊙9am-6pm Mon-Sat)

Getting There & Away

Kuala Lumpur is Malaysia's principal international arrival gateway and it forms the crossroads for domestic bus, train and taxi travel.

Air

For details of international airlines, see p479.

Kuala Lumpur International Airport (KLIA; ☎8777 8888; www.klia.com.my; Pengrus Besar) is the main airport, 75km south of the city centre at Sepang. **AirAsia** (☎8775 4000; www.airasia.com) flights arrive and depart from the nearby

WORTH A TRIP

FORESTRY RESEARCH INSTITUTE OF MALAYSIA (FRIM)

Birdsong and wall-to-wall greenery replaces the drone of traffic and air-conditioning at the **Forestry Research Institute of Malaysia** (FRIM; ☎6279 7525; www.frim.gov.my; admission RM1, cars RM5; ⊙8am-6.30pm), 16km northwest of KL. The highlight of this 600-hectare jungle park is its 200m-long, 30m-high **Canopy Walkway** (admission RM5; ⊙9.30am-2.30pm Tue-Thu, Sat & Sun).

The walkway is reached by a steep trail from FRIM's **information centre** (⊙8am-5pm Mon-Fri, 9am-4pm Sat & Sun). Heading down from the walkway the trail picks its way through the jungle to a shady picnic area where you can cool off in a series of shallow waterfalls. The return hike incorporating the walkway takes around two hours.

Take a KTM Komuter train to Kepong (RM1.30) and then a taxi (RM5); arrange for the taxi to pick you up again later.

Low Cost Carrier Terminal (LCCT; ☎8777 8888; www.lcct.com.my), while **Firefly** (☎03-7845 4543; www.fireflyz.com.my) and **Berjaya Air** (☎2145 2828; www.berjaya-air.com) flights use **Sultan Abdul Aziz Shah Airport** (☎7845 8382) in Subang, about 20km west of the city centre.

Boat

Ferries sail to Tanjung Balai on Sumatra (one way RM145, 3½ hours, 11am Monday to Saturday) in Indonesia from Pelabuhan Klang (Port Klang), accessible by KTM Komuter train from KL Sentral or by public bus (RM3.50) from Klang bus stand by Pasar Seni LRT station.

Bus

KL's main bus station is **Puduraya** (Map p386; Jln Pudu) just east of Chinatown. The only long-distance destinations that Puduraya doesn't handle are Kuala Lipis and Jerantut (for access to Taman Negara) – buses to these places leave from **Pekeliling bus station** (Map p384; ☎4042 7256; Jln Tun Razak); and Kota Bharu and Kuala Terengganu, buses for which leave from **Putra bus station** (Map p384; ☎4042 9530; Jln Putra).

Taxi

Shared-taxi fares from the depot on the 2nd floor of the **Puduraya bus station** (Map p386; Jln Pudu) include Melaka (RM300), Penang (RM600), Johor Bahru (RM500), Ipoh (RM300) and the Cameron Highlands (RM350). Toll charges are normally included, though some unscrupulous drivers make passengers pay extra.

Train

KL Sentral station is the national hub of the **KTM** (☎1300 88 5862; www.ktmb.com.my; ⏲info office 9am-9pm, ticket office 7am-10pm) railway system. There are daily departures for Butterworth, Wakaf Baharu (for Kota Bharu and Jerantut), Johor Bahru, Thailand and Singapore; fares are cheap, especially if you opt for a seat rather than a berth (for which there are extra charges), but journey times are slow.

Not to be confused with the intercity long-distance line is the KTM Komuter, which runs from KL Sentral, linking central KL with the Klang Valley and Seremban.

Getting Around

KL has an extensive public transport system. The only transport option to Sultan Abdul Aziz Shah Airport is a taxi; expect to pay RM50 to RM80.

Bus

Most buses in KL are provided by either **Rapid KL** (☎1800 388 228; www.rapidkl.com.my) or **Metrobus** (☎5635 3070). Local buses leave from many of the bus terminals around the city, including **Puduraya bus station** (Map p386; Jln Pudu), near Plaza Rakyat LRT station, and **Klang bus station** (Map p386), near Pasar Seni LRT station. The fare is RM1 to RM 4; have the correct change ready when you board.

Taxi

KL's taxis are cheap, starting at RM3 for the first two minutes, with an additional 20 sen for each 45 seconds. From midnight to 6am there's a surcharge of 50% on the metered fare, and extra passengers (more than two) are charged 20 sen each. Luggage placed in the boot is an extra RM1 and there's a RM12 surcharge for taxis to KLIA.

Although required to use the meter by law, taxi drivers often don't, and tend to overcharge tourists. It should cost no more than RM10 to go right across the central city area, even in moderate traffic. Note that taxis will often only stop at the numerous officially signposted taxi stands.

Train

The user-friendly **Light Rail Transit** (LRT; ☎1800 388 288; www.rapidkl.com.my) system

SAMPLE BUS FARES FROM KL

DESTINATION	FARE (RM)	DURATION (HR)
Alor Setar	39.10	5
Butterworth	31.30	5
Cameron Highlands	30	4
Ipoh	17.40	2½
Johor Bahru	31.20	5
Kuantan	22	4
Melaka	12.40	2
Penang	35	5
Singapore	46.20	5½

GETTING INTO TOWN

Kuala Lumpur International Airport (KLIA)

The efficient KLIA Ekspres (adult one way/return RM35/70, 28 minutes, every 15 to 20 minutes from 5am to 1am) spirits you to/from the international airport (KLIA) to the KL City Air Terminal, located in KL Sentral train station. This is without doubt the easiest way to travel to/from the airport.

If you have more time than money, catch the **Airport Coach** (☎8787 3894; www.airportcoach.com.my; one way/return RM10/18) to KL Sentral (one hour); it can also take you onwards to any central KL hotel from KLIA and pick up for the return journey for a round-trip total of RM25. The bus stand is clearly signposted inside the terminal.

Taxis from KLIA operate on a fixed-fare coupon system. Purchase a coupon from a counter at the arrival hall and use it to pay the driver. Standard taxis cost RM67.10.

Low Cost Carrier Terminal (LCCT)

Skybus (www.skybus.com.my; one-way RM9) and Aerobus (one-way RM8) depart every 15 minutes from 4.30am to 12.45am and take an hour. From LCCT, prepaid taxis charge RM62 to Chinatown or Jln Bukit Bintang (50% more from midnight to 6am). Buy your coupon at the desk near the arrivals hall exit. A taxi from the city to LCCT will cost around RM65. There's also a shuttle bus to and from the LCCT to Salak Tinggi station where you can pick up the KL Transit Train into the city.

is composed of the Ampang/Sentul Timur, Sri Petaling/Sentul Timur and Kelana Jaya/Terminal Putra lines. Fares range from RM1 to RM2.80 and trains run every six to 10 minutes from 6am to 11.50pm (11.30pm Sunday and holidays).

KL's zippy **monorail** (☎2273 1888; www.klmonorail.com.my; RM1.20-2.50; ⊙6am-midnight) runs between KL Sentral in the south to Titiwangsa in the north. It's a handy service linking up many of the city's sightseeing areas and providing a cheap air-con tour as you go.

KTM Komuter (☎2272 2828; tickets from RM1), not to be confused with the long-distance KTM service (see p482), links Kuala Lumpur with outlying suburbs and the historic railway station.

KL Sentral station, in the Brickfields area, is the central transit station for all train travel in KL.

PENINSULAR MALAYSIA – WEST COAST

Malaysia's multiculturalism is best viewed along the west coast. Nestled against the Straits of Melaka, the convenient shipping route has, over the centuries, created a cosmopolitan populace, well schooled in English. Besides Pulau Langkawi, the islands of this coast don't compare to those in the east or in Thailand, but they are always host to great seafood and an array of cultural adventures.

Melaka

☎06 / POP 648,500

Melaka has all the advantages of a metropolis: seemingly hundreds of cheap, fantastic places to eat and stay; artistic and tolerant locals; diverse entertainment; and nightlife and a colourful history that you can nearly touch. Yet it's a small, manageable place that exudes a calm that's only a notch more stressful than a tropical beach. Melt into the daily grind of dim-sum breakfasts, the call to prayer followed by church bells, laksa lunches, rides in crazy and gaudy trishaws, tandoori dinners and late-night drinks at balmy bars. It's hard not to like this town.

Melaka was founded in the 14th century by Parameswara, a Hindu prince from Sumatra, became protected by the Chinese in 1405, then dominated by the Portuguese in 1511, then the Dutch in 1641 and then finally ceded to the British in 1795. The intermingling of peoples created the Peranakan people (also called Baba Nonya), who are descended from Chinese settlers (see p472); the Chitties, who are of mixed Indian and Malay heritage; and Eurasians born of Malay and Portuguese love affairs.

Chinatown is Melaka's most interesting and scenic area. Town Sq, also known as Dutch Sq, is the centre of a well-preserved museum district. Further northeast is Melaka's tiny Little India. Backpacker guesthouses

Melaka

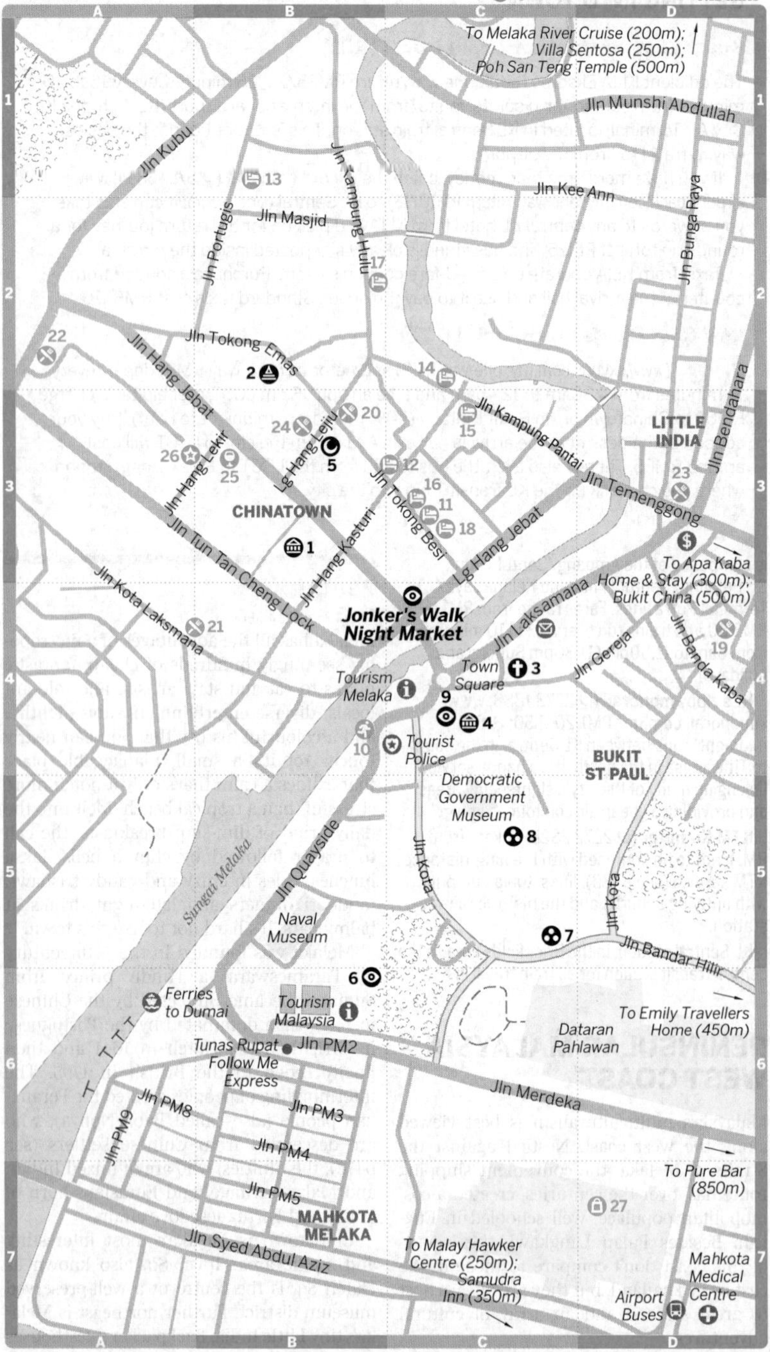

0 200 m
0 0.12 miles

To Melaka River Cruise (200m); Villa Sentosa (250m); Poh San Teng Temple (500m)

Jln Munshi Abdullah

Jln Kubu

13

Jln Kampung Hulu

Jln Kee Ann

Jln Bunga Raya

Jln Masjid

Jln Portugis

17

22

Jln Tokong Emas

Jln Hang Jebat

2

14

Jln Bendahara

20

24

15

Jln Kampung Pantai

LITTLE INDIA

Lg Hang Lekir

26

25

5

12

Jln Temenggong

Jln Hang Lekir

16

23

CHINATOWN

11

18

Jln Tokong Besi

Lg Hang Jebat

Jln Tun Tan Cheng Lock

1

Jln Hang Kasturi

To Apa Kaba Home & Stay (300m); Bukit China (500m)

Jln Kota Laksmana

Jln Laksamana

Jonker's Walk Night Market

21

Jln Gereja

Jln Banda Kaba

19

Town Square

3

Tourism Melaka

9

4

10

Tourist Police

BUKIT ST PAUL

Democratic Government Museum

8

Jln Kota

Sungai Melaka

Jln Quayside

Jln Kota

Naval Museum

7

Jln Bandar Hilir

6

Ferries to Dumai

Tourism Malaysia

To Emily Travellers Home (450m)

Dataran Pahlawan

Tunas Rupat Follow Me Express

Jln PM2

Jln Merdeka

Jln PM8

Jln PM3

Jln PM9

Jln PM4

To Pure Bar (850m)

Jln PM5

27

MAHKOTA MELAKA

Jln Syed Abdul Aziz

To Malay Hawker Centre (250m); Samudra Inn (350m)

Mahkota Medical Centre

Airport Buses

are found in Chinatown and around the nearby, less scenic Jln Melaka Raya.

Sights & Activities

TOWN SQUARE & BUKIT ST PAUL

Melaka River Cruise CRUISE
(☎286 5468; RM10, minimum 8 people; ⌚9-12am on demand) Riverboat cruises along Sungai Melaka (Melaka River) leave from two locations: the 'Spice Garden' on the corner of Jln Tun Mutahii and Jln Tun Sri Lanang in the north of town, and the quay behind the Maritime Museum. Cruises go 9km upriver and take around 40 minutes).

Stadthuys MUSEUM
(Town Sq; adult RM5; ⌚9am-5.30pm Sat-Thu, 9am-12.15pm & 2.45-5.30pm Fri) The most imposing relic of the Dutch period in Melaka is Stadthuys, the massive red town hall and governors' residence. Believed to be the oldest Dutch building in the East, it houses the **Historical, Ethnographic & Literature Museums**, which are included in the admission price and exhaustively recount Malaysian history and literary development. Facing the square is the bright-red **Christ Church** (1753).

St Paul's Church RUINS
From Stadthuys, steps lead up Bukit St Paul, which is a hill topped by the breezy ruins of St Paul's Church, built in 1521 by a Portuguese sea captain, and overlooking the famous Straits of Melaka.

DISCOUNT COUPONS

Get 20% off many local attractions by picking up coupons at the Tourism Melaka office across from the Stadthuys.

Menara Taming Sari TOWER
(admission RM20; ⌚10am-10pm) Within the park across from Jln Kota you won't be able to miss the 80m-high Menara Taming Sari, a revolving tower that's a bit tourist-tacky, but is the most fun way to get great views over the city.

Porta de Santiago FORT
A quick photo stop, Porta de Santiago was built by the Portuguese as a fortress in 1511.

CHINATOWN

Chinatown is the heart of Melaka. Stroll along **Jln Tun Tan Cheng Lock**, formerly called Heeren St, which was the preferred address for wealthy Baba (Straits-born Chinese) traders who were most active during the early 20th century. The centre street of Chinatown is **Jln Hang Jebat**, formerly known as Jonker St (or Junk St), which was once famed for its antique shops but is now

Melaka

Top Sights

Jonker's Walk Night Market C4

Sights

1 Baba-Nonya Heritage Museum B3
2 Cheng Hoon Teng B2
3 Christ Church C4
4 Historical, Ethnographic & Literature Museums C4
5 Masjid Kampung Kling B3
6 Menara Taming Sari B6
7 Porta de Santiago C5
8 St Paul's Church C5
9 Stadthuys C4

Activities, Courses & Tours

10 Melaka River Cruise B4

Sleeping

11 Jalan Jalan Besi C3
12 Jalan Jalan Guesthouse C3
13 Ringo's Foyer B1
14 River View Guesthouse C2
15 Roof Top C3
16 Sama-Sama Guest House C3
17 Sayung Sayung B2
18 Voyage Guesthouse C3

Eating

19 Capitol Satay D4
20 Low Yong Mow B3
21 Pak Putra Restaurant B4
22 Po Piah Lwee A2
23 Selvam D3
24 Vegetarian Restaurant B3

Drinking

25 Geographér Cafe B3

Entertainment

26 Eleven Club A3

Shopping

27 Mahkota Parade Shopping Complex D7

BIKE MELAKA'S COUNTRYSIDE

Alias leads three-hour **Eco bike tours** (☎019 652 5029; www.melakaonbike.com; RM100 per person, minimum 2 people) through 20km of oil-palm and rubber-tree plantations and delightful *kampung* (village) communities surrounding town. Escort to and from your hotel is included and the tour can leave at 8.30am, 3pm or 7pm for night cycling any day of the week.

more of a collection of clothing and crafts outlets and restaurants. On Friday, Saturday and Sunday nights the street is transformed into the **Jonker's Walk Night Market**, a lively market of food and trinket stalls. The northern section of quiet **Jln Tukang** (also known as Harmony St) has a handful of authentic Chinese shops.

Baba-Nonya Heritage Museum MUSEUM
(☎283 1273; 48-50 Jln Tun Tan Cheng Lock; adult RM8; ⏲10am-12.30pm & 2-4.30pm Wed-Mon) A captivating museum of the Nonya culture set in a traditional Peranakan town house in Chinatown.

Cheng Hoon Teng TEMPLE
(Qing Yun Ting, Green Clouds Temple; Jln Tukang) Chinatown's most famous temple, dating back to 1646. It's Malaysia's oldest Chinese temple and all materials used in its building were imported from China.

Masjid Kampung Kling MOSQUE
(Jln Tokong) This mosque has a pagoda-like multitiered, stacked *meru* roof that owes its inspiration to Hindu temples, and a Moorish watchtower minaret typical of early mosques in Sumatra.

ELSEWHERE

Villa Sentosa MUSEUM
(☎282 3988; www.travel.to/villasentosa; 138 Kampong Morten; admission by donation; ⏲9am-1pm & 2-5pm Sat-Thu, 2.45-5pm Fri) In Kampung Morten, tours of this ancestral *kampung* home are led by family members; it's filled with Malay handicrafts and architecture.

Bukit China CEMETERY
(Jln Puteri Hang Li Poh & Jln Laksmana Cheng Ho) More than 12,500 graves, including about 20 Muslim tombs, cover the 25 grassy hectares of this serene hill. **Poh San Teng Temple** sits at the base of the hill and was built in 1795. To the right of the temple is the **King's Well**, a 15th-century well built by Sultan Mansur Shah.

Sleeping

JLN TAMAN MELAKA RAYA & AROUND

A clutch of guesthouses congregate along charmless Jln Taman Melaka Raya (Jln TMR) about five- to 10-minutes' walk from Chinatown while a few other guesthouses have opened up around town closer to the river and Chinatown.

TOP CHOICE **Apa Kaba Home & Stay** GUESTHOUSE $
(☎283 8196; apakaba28@gmail.com; 28 Kg Banda Kaba; r incl breakfast RM40-70; ❄📶) Nestled in a quiet Malay *kampung* that seems to magically float in a bubble in the heart of town, this homestay-style guesthouse is in a beautiful old Malay house complete with creaky wood floors, louvred shutters and bright paint.

Emily Travellers Home GUESTHOUSE $
(☎012 301 8524; 71 Jln Parameswara; dm/s RM16/24, d RM32-48) Sleeping options range from funky cottages with semi-outdoor 'jungle showers', to simple wooden rooms in the house – the dorm rooms have two beds apiece.

Samudra Inn GUESTHOUSE $
(☎282 7441; samudrainn@hotmail.com; 348B Jln Melaka Raya 3; dm/d from RM12/30; ❄) The owners at the very quiet Samudra run a tight ship and go above and beyond standard service to make sure guests are comfortable. It's a homestay atmosphere with chirping birds and satellite telly at night.

CHINATOWN & AROUND

Melaka's most scenic section of town is a really fun place to stay. Because of preservation restrictions, however, most places only have shared bathrooms. Take town Bus 17 (RM1.40) from Melaka Sentral to Town Sq.

River View Guesthouse GUESTHOUSE $
(☎012 327 7746; riverviewguesthouse@yahoo.com; 94 & 96 Jln Kampung Pantai; r RM45-60; ❄@📶) Bordering the riverfront promenade, this immaculate guesthouse is set in a large heritage building. If it's full, its sister property **Roof Top** is just down the road.

Jalan Jalan Guesthouse GUESTHOUSE $
(☎283 3937; www.jalanjalanguesthouse.com; 8 Jln Tukang Emas; dm/s/d RM12/23/34; @📶) In a

restored periwinkle-blue shophouse, fan-cooled rooms with one shared bathroom are spread out over a tranquil inner courtyard garden. Their overflow property is **Jalan Jalan Besi** just down the street.

Sama-Sama Guest House GUESTHOUSE **$**
(☎305 1980; 26 Jln Tukang Besi; dm RM12, d RM20-40) Big creaky rooms are arranged around an interior courtyard of water lilies and cool breezes. Downstairs lazy cats and the odd human snooze to a soundtrack of reggae.

Ringo's Foyer GUESTHOUSE **$**
(☎016 354 2223; www.ringosfoyer.com; 46-A Jln Portugis; dm/s/d/tr RM13/30/35/50; 📶) Just far enough out of central Chinatown to be quiet, but close enough to be convenient, Ringo's is plain and clean, has friendly staff and a relaxing rooftop chill-out area.

Sayung Sayung HOSTEL **$**
(☎012 250 5138; 16 Jln Kampung Hulu; dm/r RM9/38; 📶@) Ingenious closet-like rooms have a platform loft sleeping area and Ikea-style couches below that can sleep a third person. The big dorm has every bunk separated by curtains.

Voyage Guesthouse HOSTEL **$**
(☎281 5216; Jln Tukang Besi; dm RM12) Clean, industrial-sized dorm rooms and common areas are decorated with a nouveau-heritage lounge look.

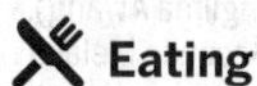

Eating

Melaka's most famous cuisine is Nonya food. In Melaka the Portuguese might have wreaked havoc on civic order, but they built up a tradition for cakes and seafood, which is most obvious in the Eurasian dish of devil's curry. Then there are the immigrant contributions of Indian curries and the ever-versatile Chinese noodle dishes.

TOP CHOICE **Pak Putra Restaurant** PAKISTANI **$**
(56 Jln Taman Kota Laksamana; tandoori from RM5; ⏲dinner, closed every other Mon) This Pakistani place cooks up a variety of meats and seafood in clay tandoori ovens perched on the sidewalk. Side dishes of veg are around RM5 and a mango lassi costs RM4.

Capitol Satay SATAY CELUP **$**
(☎283 5508; 41 Lg Bukit China; meals RM5-10; ⏲Tue-Sun) Stainless-steel tables have a bubbling vat of satay sauce in the middle in which you boil skewers of okra (ladies' finger) stuffed with fish, tofu, Chinese sausage, chicken, pork, prawns and bok choy.

Selvam INDIAN **$**
(☎281 9223; 3 Jln Temenggong; meals RM7; ⏲breakfast, lunch & dinner; 🖉) Melakans love this Indian banana-leaf smorgasbord. There's a choice range of tasty curries and roti, plus a Friday afternoon vegetarian special with 10 tasty dishes for only RM7.50.

Low Yong Mow DIM SUM **$**
(32 Jln Tukang Emas; dim sum RM1-3; ⏲5am-noon Wed-Mon) A bustling Chinese favourite for a traditional dim-sum breakfast and famed for its giant *pao* (pork buns).

Vegetarian Restaurant VEGETARIAN **$**
(43 Jln Hang Lekui; mains around RM3; ⏲7.30am-2.30pm Mon-Sat; 🖉) All the local specialities from laksa to 'fish balls' are here but made completely meat-free.

Poh Piah Lwee NONYA **$**
(Jln Kubu; ⏲9am-5pm) One specialist cook makes Hokkien-style *popiah* (fresh spring rolls; RM2), another makes near-perfect *rojak* (a fruit and vegie salad topped with a sweet-and-spicy gravy; RM3), while the third whips up a fantastic laksa (RM3).

DON'T LEAVE MELAKA WITHOUT TRYING...

» **Cendol** Shaved-ice treat with jellies, coconut milk and Melaka's famous cane syrup.

» **Laksa** The regional version is distinguished by its coconut milk and lemongrass-infused broth.

» **Nonya pineapple tarts** Buttery pastries with a chewy pineapple-jam filling.

» **Popiah** An uber-spring roll stuffed with shredded carrots, prawns, chilli, garlic, palm sugar and much, much more.

» **Satay celup** Like fondue but better; dunk tofu, prawns and more into bubbling soup to cook it to your liking.

Drinking & Entertainment

During the weekend night market on Jonker St, the happening bar strip on Jln Hang Lekir turns into a street party closed off to traffic. The alleys in the backpacker area off Jln TMR have lots of watering troughs.

Eleven Club BAR
(11 Jln Hang Lekir) This is *the* place to go if you want to get your groove on in Chinatown. Head here after around 11pm (weekends in particular) when resident DJs spin their best and the dance floor fills.

Geographér Cafe BAR
(☎281 6813; www.geographer.com.my; 83 Jln Hang Jebat; ⏲10am-1am Wed-Sun) This ventilated, breezy bar with outside seating and late hours, in a prewar corner shophouse, is a godsend. A tasty choice of local and Western dishes and laid-back but professional service round it all off.

Pure Bar CLUB
(591-A Jln Taman Melaka Rayal; ⏲5pm-2am) This has become Melaka's most fun bar-nightclub; it's popular with locals.

Shopping

A wander through Chinatown, with its quality assortment of clothing, trinket and antique shops, will have you wishing for more room in your pack. **Dataran Pahlawan** (Jln Merdeka) and **Mahkota Parade Shopping Complex** (Jln Merdeka) are Melaka's two megamalls, the former being the larger and more fashion-conscious and the latter being better for practical needs such as a pharmacy or camera shop.

Jonker's Walk Night Market (Jln Hang Jebat; ⏲6-11pm Fri, Sat & Sun) is Melaka's weekly shopping extravaganza and keeps the shops along Jln Hang Jebat open late while trinket sellers, food hawkers and the occasional fortune teller close the street to traffic.

Information

Money changers are scattered about town, especially near the guesthouses off Jln TMR and Chinatown.

Fenix Internet Centre (Fenix Hotel, 156 Jln Taman Melaka Raya; per hr RM3) Also has fax and full business services.

Immigration office (☎282 4958; 2nd fl, Wisma Persekutuan, Jln Hang Tuah)

Mahkota Medical Centre (☎281 4426/442; www.mahkotamedical.com; No 3, Mahkota Melaka, Jln Merdeka)

HSBC (Jln Hang Tuah) With 24-hour ATMs that accept international cards.

Post office (Jln Laksamana) This small post office can be found off Town Sq.

Tourism Malaysia (☎283 6220; ⏲9am-10pm) At the Menara Taming Sari; has very knowledgeable, helpful staff.

Tourism Melaka (☎281 4803, 1800 889 483; www.melaka.gov.my; Jln Kota; ⏲9am-1pm & 2-5.30pm)

Tourist Police (☎285 4114; Jln Kota)

Getting There & Away

Melaka is 144km southeast of KL.

Melaka's local bus station, express bus station and taxi station are all combined into the massive **Melaka Sentral** (Jln Panglima Awang), roughly 5km north of Town Sq. Because Melaka is a popular weekend destination, make advance bus reservations for Singapore and Kuala Lumpur.

Transnational airport buses (RM22; departs 5am, 8am, 12.30pm and 2.30pm; 2¾ hours) run to the KL International Airport from the Mahkota Medical Centre. Check schedules at the Tourism Malaysia office near the Menara Tamin Sari.

MELAKA BUS FARES

Buses run to most destinations on the peninsula.

DESTINATION	FARE (RM)	DURATION (HR)
Jerantut	23	5
Johor Bahru	19	3
Kota Bharu	51	10
Kuala Lumpur	12	2
Mersing	23	4½
Singapore	22	4½

GETTING TO INDONESIA: MELAKA TO DUMAI, PEKANBARU & PULAU BENGKALIS

Getting to the border High-speed ferries (one-way/return RM119/179, 1¾ hours) make the trip from Melaka to Dumai in Sumatra, Indonesia, daily at 10am. The quay is walking distance or a short túk-túk ride from most hotels and guesthouses and tickets are available at the **Tunas Rupat Follow Me Express** (☎283 2505; 310 Taman Melaka Raya).

At the border Most visitors can obtain a 30-day visa on arrival (VOA) in Indonesia, depending on nationality.

Moving on Dumai is on Sumatra's east coast and is a 10-hour bus ride from Bukittinggi.

Getting Around

Bus 17 runs frequently from Melaka Sentral bus station to Town Sq, Mahkota Parade Shopping Complex and Jln Taman Melaka Raya (RM1.40).

Melaka is a walking city. Bicycles can be hired at some guesthouses and hotels for around RM10 a day.

Taking to Melaka's streets by trishaw is a fun option; they should cost about RM40 per hour, but you'll have to bargain.

Taxis should cost around RM15 for a trip anywhere around town with a 50% surcharge between 1am and 6am.

Cameron Highlands

☎05

If you've been sweating through jungles and beaches for weeks and another sticky day will make your clothes unwearable, we grant you a reprieve: the Cameron Highlands. This alpine-scape of blue peaks, green humps, fuzzy tea plantations and white waterfalls has a temperature that rarely drops below 10°C or climbs above 21°C. Trekking, tea tasting and visiting local agritourism sites are all on the to-do list. Unfortunately, development, erosion and poorly planned agriculture have taken their toll on the highlands, and landslips and floods have been the environmental by-product.

The Cameron Highlands stretches along the road from the town of Ringlet, through to the main highland towns of Tanah Rata, Brinchang and beyond to smaller villages in the northeast. Most guesthouses offer free internet and there are two ATMs in the tourist centre at Tanah Rata.

Sights & Activities

There are over a dozen numbered trekking trails in the hills surrounding Tanah Rata and maps are available at most guesthouses and tour offices – ask about trail conditions before you set out as not all routes are maintained, and in recent years several people have become lost. Single women have also been attacked in remote areas, although this is very uncommon. Taking in a jungle stroll is often the best way to reach some of the area's other tourist attractions as well. Most walks and sights can be accessed by the local bus, a rattler that chugs up and down the main highway.

FREE Sungai Palas Boh Tea Estate TEA ESTATE
(Gunung Brinchang Rd, Brinchang; ⏰9am-4.30pm Tue-Sun) Sungai Palas Boh Tea Estate is the easiest plantation to visit on your own. Tours are free and the tea rooms out the back offer grand vistas. Take the local bus north from the main (Tanah Rata) bus station, past Brinchang towards Kampung Raja. In between is a tourist strip of strawberry and butterfly farms; hop off the bus at the roadside vegetable stalls and follow the intersecting road.

Sam Poh Temple TEMPLE
(Brinchang; admission by donation) Sam Poh Temple is a typically Chinese kaleidoscope of Buddha statues, stone lions and incense burners. It's accessible from Tanah Rata – take Trail 3, near the golf course, and then connect to Trail 2.

Tours

Tour operators in Tanah Rata offer a variety of day trips that include visits to a tea plantation, strawberry farm, flower and cactus nursery, honey farm and butterfly farm for around RM25 per person. Tours operating out of Father's Guest House include a good jungle-flora trip perfect for plant nerds.

Sleeping

Book early during peak holiday periods (April, August and December) and weekends.

Cameron Highlands

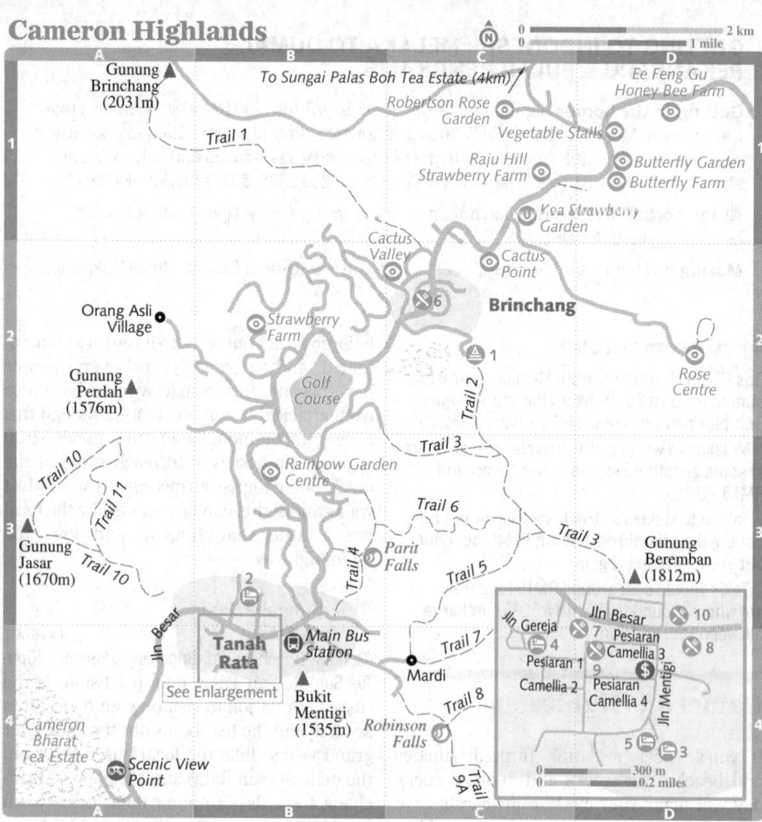

Cameron Highlands

Sights

1 Sam Poh Temple.......C2

Sleeping

2 Daniel's (Kang's) Lodge.......B3
3 Eight Mentigi.......D4
4 Father's Guest House.......C4
5 Twin Pines Chalet.......D4

Eating

6 Brinchang Night Market.......C2
7 Malay Food Stalls.......D3
8 Malay Food Stalls.......D4
9 Restaurant Bunga Suria.......D4
10 Rosedale Bistro.......D3

Most guesthouses have a mix of rooms with shared and private bathrooms, and all have hot water. Many also have libraries, video lounges, laundry, internet access and trekking information.

Father's Guest House GUESTHOUSE $
(☎491 2484; off Jln Gereja; http://fathers.cameronhighlands.com; dm/r from RM15/90; @☎) Perched on a flower-bedecked butte, Father's excellent reputation is earned from its tip-top management and cheerful setting. Gardenside rooms have doors that open onto a flower-filled patio, and the big, bright dorm has a summer-camp camaraderie. It's a couple of minutes' walk from Jln Besar.

Daniel's (Kang's) Lodge GUESTHOUSE $
(☎491 5823; www.daniels.cameronhighlands.com; 9 Lg Perdah; dm/r from RM8/28; @☎) Its 'Fuck the Lonely Planet' whiteboard has been up for years – and it's now framed – but sticks and stones don't break our bones, we like this place! French guys roll cigarettes, British gap-years get drunk in the back garden and

German hikers compare boots. Rooms are clean and the management is helpful.

Eight Mentigi GUESTHOUSE $
(☎491 5988; www.eightmentigi.com; 8 Jln Mentigi; dm/r from RM15/50; @☎) A new, relatively quiet and very clean place behind Twin Pines with an outdoor patio area and indoor lounge area with big sofas.

Twin Pines Chalet GUESTHOUSE $
(☎491 2169; http://twinpines.cameronhighlands.com; 2 Jln Mentigi; s/d from RM15/25; @☎) A social place where nights are spent around a bonfire, watching films in the lounge or sipping tea with other travellers on the patio.

Eating & Drinking

Tanah Rata has some great food and the cheapest places are the mainly **Malay food stalls** stretching down Jln Besar towards the bus and taxi stations – for a splurge in the same area try the steamboat (a Chinese-style fondue where you cook your meat and veg in bubbling vats of soup; RM30 for two people).

Restaurant Bunga Suria INDIAN $
(☎491 4666; 66A Pesiaran Camellia 3; set meals RM5-9; ⏰breakfast, lunch & dinner) The best value in town is to be had at this truly excellent South Indian joint.

Brinchang Night Market MARKET $
(☎491 5188; Brinchang; ⏰6.30-10pm) Snack on everything from savoury fried tidbits to chocolate-dipped strawberries on skewers.

Rosedale Bistro INTERNATIONAL $$
(☎491 1419; 42-A Jln Besar; mains RM5-18; ⏰breakfast, lunch & dinner; ☎) Very popular with travellers foreign and domestic, the Rosedale's menu spans several cuisine genres (Chinese, Malay, European, Indian).

Getting There & Around

From Tanah Rata, buses go to/from KL (RM30, four hours, six daily between 8am and 4.30pm). Another bus leaves Tanah Rata bound for Ipoh (RM10, two hours, four daily) and Georgetown (RM32, five hours, two daily). Buses also go to Singapore (RM105, eight hours, one daily). Book tickets at the bus station. For east-coast destinations, connect through Ipoh.

Kang Tours (☎491 5828; 47 Jln Besar) sells tickets for daily minibuses to Kuala Besut (RM60, six hours) to catch a boat to Pulau Perhentian or Kuala Tahan (Taman Negara; RM85, eight hours). You can also take these minibuses partway and get off at Gua Musang to catch the Jungle Railway (see p429).

Local buses run from Tanah Rata to Brinchang (RM1, every 1½ hours from 6.30am to 6.30pm) and less frequently on to Kampung Raja (RM3), passing butterfly attractions and the turn-off to Sungai Palas Boh.

Taxi services from Tanah Rata include Ringlet (RM20), Brinchang (RM9), Sungai Palas Boh Tea Estate (RM24) and Boh Tea Estate (RM28). For touring around, a taxi costs RM28 per hour, or you can go up to Gunung Brinchang and back for RM90.

While we never recommend hitch-hiking, many travellers do so here to get between Tanah Rata and Brinchang and the tea plantations beyond.

Ipoh

☎05 / POP 710,800

Ipoh (ee-po) is a gritty, frenetic city of faded tropical mansions, a lively central *padang* (field) and food so good folks from Penang rave about it. It also has a reputation for prostitution and feels a little less wholesome than most Malaysian cities. The mellow **Old Town** showcases elegant colonial architecture and the magnificent **train station** (known locally as the 'Taj Mahal'). Traffic-clogged, charmless New Town east of the river is home to most of the hotels and restaurants.

The city is a transport hub to many travellers on their way to the Cameron Highlands. Luckily, the local bus station is only about 400m from the most interesting part of town.

Sleeping & Eating

Ipoh's culinary specialities include *kway teow* (rice-noodle soup) and Ipoh white coffee, made with palm-oil margarine and served with condensed milk. Many Penang specialties are found here and, some say, are done better.

CAVE TEMPLES

Ipoh's jungle-clad limestone hills are riddled with caves that locals believe to be a great source of spiritual power. There are Buddhist cave temples on the outskirts of town, including the beautiful mural-heavy **Perak Tong** (⏰8am-5pm), 6km north on the road to Kuala Kangsar, and **Sam Poh Tong** (⏰8am-5pm), a few kilometres to the south, which is the largest cave temple in Malaysia and has an ornamental garden in front. Both are easily accessible by local bus.

IPOH LONG-DISTANCE BUS FARES

Buses run to most destinations on the peninsula.

DESTINATION	FARE (RM)	DURATION (HR)
Alor Setar	18	4
Butterworth	16	3
Kota Bharu	27	7
Kuala Lumpur	16	3
Lumut	7	2
Melaka	24	5
Hat Yai, Thailand	68	9

Steer clear of some of the city's cheap dingy 'hotels' that are actually brothels.

Sun Golden Inn HOTEL $
(☎243 6255; 17 Jln Che Tak; r RM40-90; ❄) One of Ipoh's better budget choices, the Sun Golden Inn is a clean and friendly Chinese hotel, with good management who is used to dealing with Westerners.

MBI Terrace MALAY $
(off Jln Sultan Abdul Jalil; ⏲7pm-midnight) Essentially attached to the city's municipal sports complex, many Ipoh residents will tell you the best *kway teow* in town is served here.

Medan Selera Dato Tawhil Azar MALAY $
(Jln Raja Musa Aziz; ⏲dinner) This large open-air food stall around a small square is a good spot for a Malay meal.

Information

HSBC (Jln Tun Sambathan) This bank is near the clocktower.

Tourist Information Centre (☎241 2959; Jln Tun Sambathan; ⏲8am-5pm Mon-Fri) Near the *padang*.

Getting There & Away

The **long-distance bus station** (Medan Gopeng) is south of the train station and the city centre; frequent shuttle buses to the city bus station cost RM1.50.

The local bus station is near Old Town about 400m from the train station. Local buses depart from here for outlying regions close to Ipoh, such as Kuala Kangsar (RM6) and Tanah Rata in the Cameron Highlands (RM10).

Ipoh's **train station** (☎254 0481; Jln Panglima Bukit Gantang Wahab) is on the main Singapore–Butterworth line. There are daily trains to both KL (RM12, 4½ hours) and Butterworth (RM17, five hours), the latter continuing to Hat Yai in Thailand (RM30, 10 hours).

Lumut

☎05

Lumut is the departure point for Pulau Pangkor. **Tourism Malaysia** (☎683 4057; Jln Sultan Idris Shah; ⏲9am-5pm Mon-Fri, 9am-1.45pm Sat) is midway between the jetty and the bus station. Next door you'll find a money changer offering better rates than on Pulau Pangkor, and Maybank further down the street.

Direct buses run to/from KL (RM25, four hours, eight daily), Butterworth (RM20, five hours, three daily) and Melaka (RM38, six hours, two daily). There are no direct buses from Lumut to the Cameron Highlands; take a bus to Ipoh (RM8, two hours, hourly), then transfer to Tanah Rata.

The Pulau Pangkor pier is an easy walk from the bus station. Boats run every 30 to 45 minutes and cost RM10.

Pulau Pangkor

☎05 / POP 25,000

Pulau Pangkor is more of a girl-next-door island as opposed to the supermodels of the east coast and Langkawi. That said, it feels good to get away from the glitz and settle into an honest *kampung* with a lazy island atmosphere. The jungle is swarming with monkeys and hornbills, the beaches are dazzling and you can dine nightly on fresh fish while watching the sunset.

Teluk Nipa is a nice white-sand beach near most backpacker accommodation but walk five minutes north over a headland to find the isle's prettiest beach, Coral Bay.

Ferries from Lumut first stop on the eastern side of the island at Sungai Pinang Kecil (SPK) and then go to Pangkor Town, where you'll find banks, restaurants and shops.

Sights & Activities

Snorkel gear and boats can be hired at hotels or on the beach. The main beaches are on the west coast. Travellers, especially women, should take care on empty stretches at the island's northeastern side and south of Pangkor Town. There's also good walking here, arguably better than on any other Malaysian island; most guesthouses have lots of information and can organise a guide.

Sleeping & Eating

All these options are on Teluk Nipah on roads running inland from the beach. There are several restaurants along the main road and most serve alcohol.

Nazri Nipah Camp GUESTHOUSE $
(☎685 2014, 012-576 0267; rozie1982@hotmail.com; dm/r from RM10/40) Located at the edge of the jungle, there's (surprise) a chilled-out reggae theme going on here. Accommodation ranges from simple A-frames to more comfortable chalets with bathrooms.

Ombak Inn GUESTHOUSE $
(☎685 5223; www.ombakinnchalet.com; r from RM70; ❄@) Wood chalets with air-con and terraces are ageing but still comfortable.

Purnama Beach Resort GUESTHOUSE $
(☎685 3530; www.purnama.com.my; chalets from RM85; ❄@≋) This spiffy complex of chalets includes some fairly simple (and lovely) fan huts and neat, motel-style doubles.

Getting There & Around

In the high season, ferries run to and from Lumut and Pangkor Town (return RM10, 30 minutes, departing every 30 to 45 minutes from 6.30am to 8.30pm).

There are no public buses, but pink minibus taxis operate between 6.30am and 9pm. Fares are set for the entire vehicle to/from the jetty in Pangkor Town and go to Teluk Nipah (RM12) and around the island (RM48).

Motorcycles (RM35) and bicycles (RM15) can be rented in Pangkor Town and at main beaches.

Butterworth

This mainland town is a major transport hub for Penang, and it's not a place worth lingering. The Butterworth–Penang ferry jetty (RM1.20, every 15 to 20 minutes from 5.30am to 12.30am) is conveniently located next to the train and bus stations. Fares for the ferry are charged only for the journey from Butterworth to Georgetown (on Penang); returning to Butterworth is free.

There are three daily trains to KL (from RM31) from the **train station** (☎323 7962). Heading north, there are three daily trains to Hat Yai, Thailand (economy/berth RM34/97); the afternoon service continues to Bangkok, arriving the next day.

Penang

'Pearl of the Orient' conjures romantic images of trishaws pedalling past Chinese shophouses, blue joss smoke and a sting of chilli in the air. Or maybe it's ornate Chinese temples around the corner from grand white mosques sending a call to the midday prayer. But really, whatever you're imagining, chances are that Penang *is* that reality. Add some slick cafes, shopping malls, jungle and a few (mediocre) beaches and you'll have an even clearer picture.

Historically, Penang was the waterway between Asia's two halves and the outlet to

BUTTERWORTH BUS FARES

Buses run to most destinations on the peninsula.

DESTINATION	FARE (RM)	DURATION (HR)
Ipoh	16	3
Johor Bahru	53	12
Kota Bharu	31	7
Kuala Lumpur	28	5
Melaka	36	12
Singapore	53	9

Penang

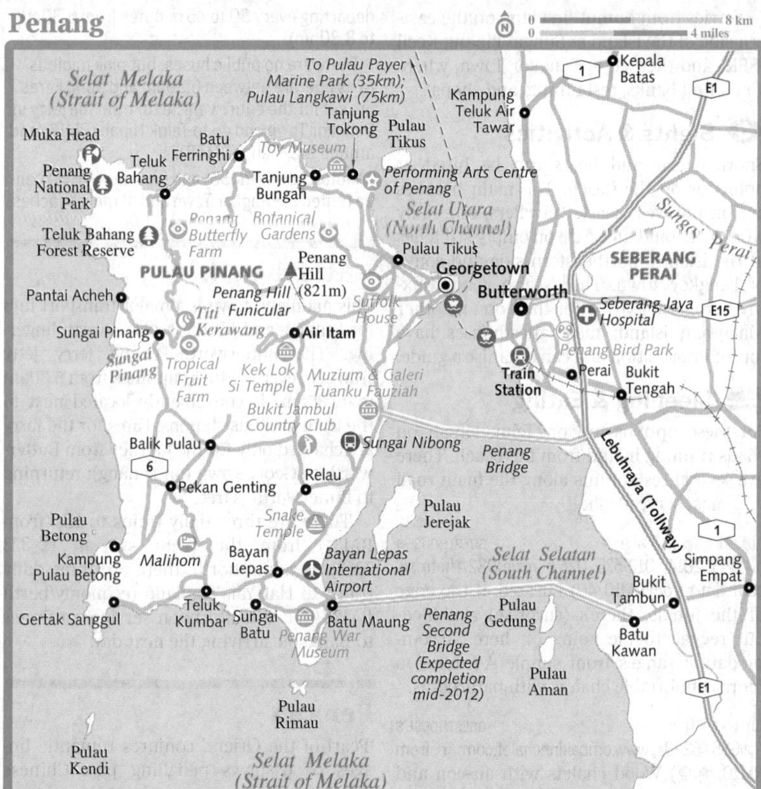

the markets of Europe and the Middle East. Today the culture of this region, forged over decades of colonialism, commercial activity and hosting tourists, is one of Malaysia's most tolerant, cosmopolitan and exciting – particularly when it comes to the food.

GEORGETOWN

☎04 / POP 178,304

It's full of car exhaust and has a marked lack of sidewalks, but Georgetown is able to woo even the most acute cityphobe with its explosive cultural mishmash. Dodge traffic while strolling past Chinese shophouses where people might be roasting coffee over a fire or sculpting giant incense sticks for a ceremony. Trishaws, pedalling tourists and the occasional local cruise around the maze of chaotic streets and narrow lanes, past British Raj-era architecture, strings of paper lanterns and retro-chic pubs, boutiques and cafes. Outside the historic centre, soaring skyscrapers and massive shopping complexes gleam high above.

Arrive on an empty stomach and graze at will. Between the city's outrageous hawker food and fine restaurants this is the food capital of Malaysia.

Sights & Activities

Khoo Kongsi CHINESE CLANHOUSE
(Lebuh Cannon; adult RM10; ⌚9am-5pm) This is Penang's finest *kongsi* (clan house), decorated with a colourful mix of dragons, statues, paintings, lamps, coloured tiles and carvings. A *kongsi* is a building that's used partly as a temple and partly as a meeting hall for Chinese people of the same clan or surname.

Pinang Peranakan Mansion MUSEUM
(☎264 2929; www.pinangperanakanmansion.com.my; 29 Lebuh Gereja; admission RM10; ⌚9.30am-5pm Mon-Sat) Every door, wall and archway of this stunning building is carved and often painted in gold leaf.

Cheong Fatt Tze Mansion HISTORIC BUILDING
(☎262 5289; www.cheongfatttzemansion.com; Lebuh Leith; adult RM12; ⏲tours 11am & 3pm Mon-Fri, 11am Sat & Sun) The periwinkle-blue Cheong Fatt Tze Mansion was built in the 1880s by Cheong Fatt Tze, the 'Rockefeller of the East'. The mansion doubles as a luxurious bed and breakfast (rooms from RM250).

Kuan Yin Teng CHINESE TEMPLE
(Lebuh Pitt; admission by donation; ⏲9am-5pm) In honour of the goddess of mercy, good fortune, peace and fertility, the Kuan Yin Teng was built in the early 19th century by the first Hokkien and Cantonese settlers in Penang.

Kapitan Keling Mosque MOSQUE
(Lebuh Pitt) Built by Penang's first Indian-Muslim settlers, the yellow Kapitan Keling Mosque has a single minaret in an Indian-influenced Islamic style.

Sri Mariamman Temple HINDU TEMPLE
(Lebuh Pitt; ⏲8am-noon & 4-9pm) Sri Mariamman Temple is where local Tamils pay homage to Tamil Nadu by worshipping Mariamman, a mother goddess popular with diaspora Indians. Built in 1883, this is Georgetown's oldest Hindu house of worship.

Penang Museum MUSEUM
(☎261 3144; Lebuh Farquhar; adult RM1; ⏲9am-5pm Sat-Thu) Excellent exhibits on the ground floor illustrate the customs and traditions of Penang's various ethnic groups with impressive appreciation for diversity.

Fort Cornwallis BRITISH FORT
(Lebuh Light; adult RM3; ⏲9am-7pm) Fort Cornwallis was built on Georgetown's cape, the historic landing of the city's founder Captain Francis Light in 1786. A visit involves lots of panel reading.

WALK ABOUT

The best way to see Penang is on a DIY walking tour. Head to **Penang Heritage Trust** (☎264 2631; www.pht.org.my; 26 Lebuh Gereja; ⏲9.30am-12.30pm & 2.30-4.30pm Mon-Fri) for free brochures with details of self-guided walks, such as the Endangered Trades Walk and Historic Georgetown Trails. Another highly recommended walk is Global Ethic Penang's World Religions Walk, which takes you past the iconography and houses of worship of Christians, Muslims, Hindus, Sikhs, Buddhists and Confucians and even to a Jewish cemetery. Details and a map are available at www.globalethicpenang.net/webpages/act_02b.htm.

Sleeping

Georgetown has plenty of cheap accommodation, mainly clustered in Chinatown along bustling Lebuh Chulia and quieter Love Lane. During holidays, most notably Chinese New Year (January/February), hotels fill up very quickly and prices soar. Cheaper rooms have shared bathrooms.

Red Inn GUESTHOUSE $
(☎261 3931; www.redinnpenang.com; 55 Love Lane; dm/d incl breakfast from RM30/70; ❄📶) Upping the Love Lane ante, the Red Inn offers decent-sized rooms with plenty of retro flair including built-in bookcases and designer colour schemes. Dorm rooms have only three beds.

Hutton Lodge GUESTHOUSE $
(☎263 6003; www.huttonlodge.com; 175 Lg Hutton; dm/s/d incl breakfast RM30/50/65; ❄@📶)

PENANG MUST EATS

Penang is known as the hawker capital of Malaysia and most of the city's specialities – claiming mixed Malay and Chinese extraction – are best fetched from a portable cart or food centre. Don't leave without trying:

» **Cendol** Garishly coloured green strands (made from sweetened pea flour) are layered with crushed ice, coconut milk and brown-sugar syrup.

» **Char kway teow** Medium-width rice noodles are stir-fried with egg, vegetables, shrimp and Chinese sausage in a dark soy sauce.

» **Laksa asam** Also known as Penang laksa, this is a fish-broth soup spiked with a sour tang from tamarind paste *(asam)* and a mint garnish; it's served with thick, white rice noodles (laksa).

» **Rojak** A fruit-and-vegetable salad tossed in a sweet tamarind and palm sugar sauce and garnished with crushed peanuts, sesame seeds and chillies.

Georgetown

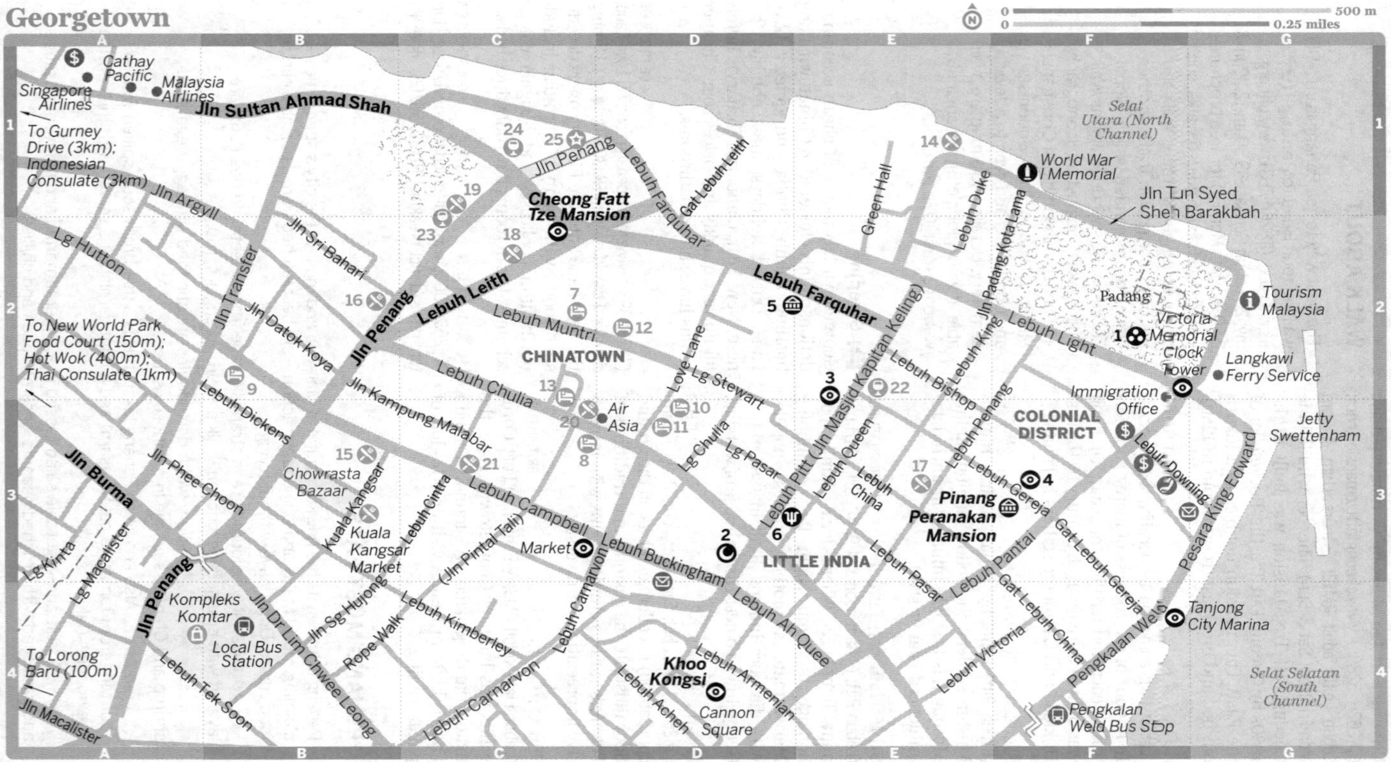

0 500 m
0 0.25 miles
Cathay Pacific
Malaysia Airlines
Singapore Airlines
Jln Sultan Ahmad Shah
To Gurney Drive (3km); Indonesian Consulate (3km)
Jln Argyll
Lg Hutton
Jln Transfer
Jln Sri Bahari
Jln Datok Koya
Jln Penang
Lebuh Leith
Cheong Fatt Tze Mansion
Jln Penang
Lebuh Farquhar
Gat Lebuh Leith
Green Hall
Lebuh Duke
Jln Padang Kota Lama
World War I Memorial
Selat Utara (North Channel)
Jln Tun Syed Sheh Barakbah
Padang
Tourism Malaysia
Victoria Memorial Clock Tower
Langkawi Ferry Service
Immigration Office
Jetty Swettenham
Lebuh Light
Lebuh King
Lebuh Bishop
Lebuh Farquhar
Jln Masjid Kapitan Keling
Lebuh Pitt
CHINATOWN
Lebuh Muntri
Love Lane
Lg Stewart
Lebuh Chulia
Air Asia
To New World Park Food Court (150m); Hot Wok (400m); Thai Consulate (1km)
Lebuh Dickens
Jln Kampung Malabar
Lg Chulia
Lg Pasar
Lebuh Queen
Lebuh China
Lebuh Penang
COLONIAL DISTRICT
Lebuh Downing
Pesara King Edward
Lebuh Gereja
Pinang Peranakan Mansion
Jln Burma
Jln Phee Choon
Chowrasta Bazaar
Kuala Kangsar
Kuala Kangsar Market
Lebuh Cintra
Lebuh Campbell
(Jln Pintal Tali)
Market
Lebuh Buckingham
LITTLE INDIA
Lebuh Pasar
Lebuh Pantai
Gat Lebuh Gereja
Tanjong City Marina
Lg Kinta
Lg Macalister
Jln Penang
Kompleks Komtar
Local Bus Station
Jln Dr Lim Chwee Leong
Jln Sg Hujong
Rope Walk
Lebuh Kimberley
Lebuh Carnarvon
Lebuh Ah Quee
Gat Lebuh China
Pengkalan Weld
Lebuh Victoria
To Lorong Baru (100m)
Lebuh Tek Soon
Jln Macalister
Lebuh Carnarvon
Khoo Kongsi
Lebuh Armenian
Lebuh Acheh
Cannon Square
Pengkalan Weld Bus Stop
Selat Selatan (South Channel)

Heritage outside, Ikea on the inside, this is a quiet, clean place with good management and a free, light breakfast.

Old Penang Guest House GUESTHOUSE $
(☎263 8805; 53 Love Lane; dm/s/d from RM23/45/65; ❄@📶) Hardwood floors, white walls, high ceilings and splashes of red paint add a hip vibe to this hostel set in a restored pre-WWII house.

Banana Guest House GUESTHOUSE $
(☎262 6171; www.banananewguesthouse.com; 355 Lebuh Chulia; r RM25-100; ❄@) The backpacker route lands firmly at this all-purpose hostel–bar–travel agency. Rooms are OK, and the best are in the new wing above the travel agency office.

Ryokan HOSTEL $
(☎250 0287; www.myryokan.com; 62 Lebuh Muntri; dm RM33-40; ❄@📶) A sharp, professional flashpacker hostel with solid bunks equipped with locker and reading lights.

Stardust GUESTHOUSE $
(☎263 5723; 370 Lebuh Chulia; r RM25-40; ❄@) Despite the name that sounds like an ABBA album, Stardust is several cuts above the average Chulia hotel or Love Lane flophouse.

75 Travellers Lodge GUESTHOUSE $
(☎262 3378; 75 Lebuh Muntri; dm/r from RM10/18; ❄@) The cheapest place in town is an old-school backpacker crash pad with half-naked hippie dudes passed out in the dorm rooms most of the day.

Eating

Penang cuisine is legendary: Indian, Chinese and Malay purveyors jostle with one another for affection from a constantly snacking populace. Along with Melaka, Penang boasts the indigenous fusion of Baba Nonya cuisine. Lebuh Cintra is lined with bustling Chinese noodle and dim-sum joints. Lg Baru, just off Jln Macalister, has a row of food stalls whipping up satay; however, things don't start sizzling until nightfall. Little India is replete with cheap eating places, especially along Lebuh Pasar and Lebuh Penang, serving up curries, roti, tandoori and biryani.

Tho Yuen Restaurant DIM SUM $
(☎261 4672; 92 Lebuh Campbell; dim sum RM1-5; ⊙6am-3pm Wed-Mon) It's packed with newspaper-reading loners and chattering groups of locals all morning long, but you can usually squeeze in somewhere.

Hot Wok NONYA $
(☎227 3368; 124 Jln Burma; mains from RM9; ⊙lunch & dinner Wed-Mon; ❄) Located in a grand Nonya mansion filled with latticework and beautiful, distracting details, this restaurant feels upscale but is reasonably priced. Try the *sambal sotong* (chilli squid).

Madras New Woodlands Restaurant INDIAN $
(☎263 9764; 60 Lebuh Penang; mains from RM3; ⊙breakfast, lunch & dinner; ✎) One of the best bets for vegetarians offers tasty banana-leaf meals and North Indian specialities, including lots of traditional sweets.

Georgetown

Top Sights
- Cheong Fatt Tze Mansion....C2
- Khoo Kongsi....D4
- Pinang Peranakan Mansion....F3

Sights
- 1 Fort Cornwallis....F2
- 2 Kapitan Keling Mosque....D3
- 3 Kuan Yin Teng....E2
- 4 Penang Heritage Trust....F3
- 5 Penang Museum....D2
- 6 Sri Mariamman Temple....D3

Sleeping
- 7 75 Travellers Lodge....C2
- 8 Banana Guest House....C3
- 9 Hutton Lodge....B2
- 10 Old Penang Guest House....D3
- 11 Red Inn....D3
- 12 Ryokan....D2
- 13 Stardust....C2

Eating
- 14 Esplanade Food Centre....E1
- 15 Hammediyah....B3
- 16 Kheng Pin....B2
- 17 Madras New Woodlands Restaurant....E3
- 18 Red Garden Food Paradise & Night Market....C2
- 19 Restoran Sup Hameed....C1
- 20 Sky Hotel....C3
- 21 Tho Yuen Restaurant....C3

Drinking
- 22 Pitt Street Corner....E2
- 23 Soho Free House....C2
- 24 Uptown Bistro....C1

Entertainment
- 25 Slippery Senoritas....C1

HAWKER-STALL HEAVEN

Not eating at a stall in Penang is like missing the Louvre in Paris – you simply have to do it. Prices are cheap and most serve beer as well.

» **Gurney Drive** (Gurney Dr; ⏰dinner) Penang's most famous food area sits amid modern high-rises bordered by the sea. Try Laksa stall 11.

» **Lorong Baru** (New Lane; Lg Baru, off Jln Macalister; ⏰dinner) You'll find all the standard faves along with a few more adventurous choices like the Chee Chong Chook stall, which serves 'pig spare parts porridge'.

» **Esplanade Food Centre** (Jln Tun Syed Sheh Barakbah; ⏰dinner) You can't beat the seaside setting of this food centre, nestled right in the heart of Penang's colonial district.

» **New World Park Food Court** (Lg Swanton; ⏰lunch & dinner) Every stall serves something different at this ultramodern, covered food court with mist-blowing fans and shiny industrial decor.

» **Red Garden Food Paradise & Night Market** (Lebuh Leith; ⏰breakfast, lunch & dinner) Excellent location in the heart of Chinatown with a wide selection including most local specialities, dim sum, pizza and even sushi.

Kheng Pin CHICKEN RICE $
(80 Jln Penang; mains from RM4; ⏰7am-3pm Tue-Sun) Locals swear by the *lorbak* (spiced ground pork wrapped in bean curd dipped in black gravy) and Hainan chicken rice served at this stall.

Sky Hotel PORK & DUCK RICE $
(☎262 2322; 348 Lebuh Chulia; around RM6; ⏰11.30am-2.30pm) Don't miss the pork and roast duck here. Order your pork *'pun fei sau'* (half-fat, half-lean) to get that proper combination of slightly wet and firm roasted goodness.

Hammediyah INDIAN $
(164 Lebuh Campbell; mains from RM3; ⏰lunch & dinner) Line up for the *murtabak*, a crepe-esque dish filled with beef and minced onions.

Restoran Sup Hameed MALAYSIAN $
(☎261 8007; 48 Jln Penang; mains from RM3; ⏰24hr) This ultrapopular smorgasbord has everything from spicy *sup* (soup!) and *nasi kandar* to *roti canai*. Curried squid is the house speciality.

Drinking & Entertainment

The cheapest beer is found at the hawker stalls.

Slippery Senoritas LIVE MUSIC
(Garage, 2 Jln Penang; ⏰happy hour 5-9pm) Come to this see-and-be-seen club for surprisingly good cover bands, lots of drinking and a Tom Cruise *Cocktail*-esque juggling show put on by the bar staff.

Uptown Bistro BAR
(Cnr Jln Penang & Jln Sultan Ahmad Shah; ⏰7pm-3am) The waitresses wear tacky sequined minis and the band isn't the best but many start the night here for the buy-one-get-one-free drinks between 5pm and 8pm, and the free dim sum and beer buckets for RM75.

Soho Free House PUB
(50A Jln Penang; midday-midnight) This place starts rocking out early (1980s music anyone?) with a mostly Chinese clientele who nosh bangers and mash (RM14) and swill pints like good Brits.

Pitt Street Corner BAR
(94 Lebuh Pitt; 24hrs) Sit back with a beer to the sounds of Bollywood at this very friendly Wild West–style saloon in Little India.

Information

Branches of major banks and 24-hour ATMs are concentrated around Kompleks Komtar and around Lebuh Pantai and Lebuh Downing. Almost every guesthouse has internet access, and it's easy to pick up on a wi-fi signal around town. You can stock up on reading supplies at a host of secondhand bookshops.

The monthly *Penang Tourist Newspaper* (RM3) has comprehensive listings of shops, tourist attractions and hotel promotions, as well as detailed pull-out maps. It's usually available free from tourist offices and some hotels.

General Hospital (☎229 3333; Jln Residensi) About 2km west of Kompleks Komtar.

Immigration Office (☎261 5122; 29A Lebuh Pantai)

Tourism Malaysia (☎262 0066; 10 Jln Tun Syed Sheh Barakbah; ⌚8am-5pm Mon-Fri)

DANGERS & ANNOYANCES

While generally a safe place to wander around, Georgetown has its seamy side. Travellers have been mugged along dimly lit side streets, so take care if you're out late. Motorcycle snatch thieves are also a problem so keep bags and purses strapped across your chest.

ℹ Getting There & Away

See p405 for information about reaching Pulau Pinang from the mainland, and for long-distance train and bus travel from the mainland.

AIR Airlines with services to Pulau Pinang:

AirAsia (☎644 8701; www.airasia.com; Ground fl, Kompleks Komtar)

Cathay Pacific (☎226 0411; www.cathaypacific.com; Menara Boustead, 39 Jln Sultan Ahmad Shah)

Jetstar (☎1800 81 3090; www.jetstar.com; Bayan Lepas International Airport)

Malaysia Airlines (☎262 0011; www.malaysiaairlines.com; Menara KWSP, Jln Sultan Ahmad Shah)

Singapore Airlines (☎226 6211; www.singaporeair.com; Wisma Penang Gardens, Jln Sultan Ahmad Shah)

Thai Airways International (☎226 6000; www.thaiair.com; Wisma Central, 41 Jln Macalister)

BOAT There are daily ferries from Georgetown to Langkawi (one way/return RM60/115, 2½ hours). Boats leave at 8.30am (direct) and 8.45am (one stop at Pulau Payar), returning from Langkawi at 2.30pm and 5.30pm. Check the times the day before, as schedules vary.

GETTING INTO GEORGETOWN

Penang's **Bayan Lepas International Airport** (☎643 4411) is 18km south of Georgetown.

Taxis take about 45 minutes from the centre of town, while the bus takes at least an hour. Bus 401 runs to and from the airport (RM3) every half hour between 6am and 11pm daily and stops at Komtar and Weld Quay. A taxi is RM50.

If arriving via the Butterworth–Penang ferry, exit towards Pengkalan Weld and catch the MPPP Free Shuttle or any Kompleks Komtar–bound bus (RM1.50, 15 minutes) to reach accommodation in Chinatown.

TOO BIG FOR ITS BRIDGES

Today an average of 70,000 people cross the 13.5km **Penang Bridge**, one of the longest bridges in the world – but this isn't expected to meet Penang's rapid development needs. Construction is underway on a second bridge linking Batu Maung at the southeastern tip of the island to Batu Kawan on the mainland. It's expected to be completed by mid-2012.

BUS Buses to all major towns on the southern peninsula leave from Komtar or Penang's main long distance bus station in Sungai Nibong. For destinations in the north you'll have to transfer in Butterworth. Buy tickets direct from the bus companies – we've received letters and talked to travellers whose agent-bought tickets from Georgetown only got them part-way to where they were meant to go.

There are also bus and minibus services to Thailand: Hat Yai (RM35, four hours), Phuket (RM61 to RM70, 12 hours) and Surat Thani (RM65, nine hours). The minibuses usually don't go directly to some destinations so there are significant waiting times. The train from Butterworth is usually quicker and more comfortable.

ℹ Getting Around

Penang has a good public transport system that connects Georgetown with the rest of the island.

BUS There are several local bus stops in Georgetown. Kompleks Komtar and Pengkalan Weld, in front of the Butterworth–Penang jetty, are two of the largest stops. Most of the buses also have stops along Lebuh Chulia. Fares within Georgetown are RM1.50 to RM4; points beyond are RM1 to RM4 depending on the destination (exact change required).

For around RM7 you can do a circuit of the island by public transport.

MOTORCYCLE & BICYCLE You can hire bicycles from shops at Lebuh Chulia, Batu Ferringhi (13km northwest of Georgetown) and some guesthouses. Bicycles cost RM10, and motorcycles start at RM40 per day. Remember that if you don't have a motorcycle licence, your travel insurance probably won't cover you in the case of an accident.

TAXI Penang's taxis all have meters, which many drivers flatly refuse to use, so negotiate the fare before you set off. Typical fares around town cost around RM6 to RM15. Other fares include Batu Ferringhi (RM45), Penang Hill/Kek Lok Si Temple (RM30) and Bayan Lepas airport (RM38).

PENANG BUS FARES

Typical one-way fares from Sungai Nibong include the following:

DESTINATION	FARE (RM)	DURATION (HR)
Cameron Highlands	23.50-28	6
Ipoh	10.70	2½
Johor Bahru	49	9½
Kuala Lumpur	27-60	5
Melaka	36.20	7

TRISHAW Bicycle rickshaws are an ideal way to negotiate Georgetown's backstreets and cost around RM30 per hour but, as with taxis, agree on the fare before departure. From the ferry terminals, a trishaw to the hotel area around Lebuh Chulia should cost RM10.

PENANG HILL & AROUND

Once a fashionable retreat for the city's elite, Penang Hill (821m) provides cool temperatures and spectacular views. There are pretty gardens, an old-fashioned kiosk, a restaurant and a hotel, as well as a lavishly decorated Hindu temple and a mosque at the top.

From Kompleks Komtar or at Lebuh Chulia in Georgetown, you can catch one of the frequent local buses (204) to the funicular railway (RM30, every 15 to 30 minutes from 6.30am to 9.30pm). Those who feel energetic can get to the top by an interesting three-hour trek, starting from the Moon Gate at the Botanical Gardens, or, if you're really fit, hike through the forest from the upper funicular station to Teluk Bahang, 6.6km away (around five hours).

Kek Lok Si Temple (⏲9am-6pm), the largest Buddhist temple in Malaysia, stands on a hilltop at Air Itam. Construction started in 1890, took more than 20 years and was largely funded by donations. To reach the entrance, walk through the souvenir stalls until you reach the seven-tier, 30m-high **Ban Po Thar** (Ten Thousand Buddhas Pagoda; admission RM2). There are several other temples here, as well as shops and an excellent **vegetarian restaurant** (☎828 8142; mains from RM5; ⏲lunch & dinner Tue-Sun), while a **cable-car** (one way/return RM4/2) whisks you to the highest level, presided over by an awesome 36.5m-high bronze statue of **Kuan Yin**, goddess of mercy.

BATU FERRINGHI

☎04

Following the coastal road east will lead you to Batu Ferringhi, Penang's best beach area, which is lined with resorts at one end and guesthouses at the other. While it doesn't compare with Malaysia's east-coast beaches or those on Langkawi, the sleepy village ambience at the eastern end of the beach is a lovely respite.

Low-key guesthouses are clustered together opposite the beach, and most will give discounts for multiday stays.

Baba Guest House (☎881 1686; babaguesthouse2000@yahoo.com; 52 Batu Ferringhi; r RM45-80; ❄) is a large Chinese family home with plain rooms (most of which have shared bathrooms).

Bus 101 or 102 from Kompleks Komtar takes around 40 minutes to reach Batu Ferringhi and costs RM3.

TELUK BAHANG

☎04

There's not enough beach at the sleepy fishing village of Teluk Bahang for any resorts to crop up, so the main thing to do here is tool around the 2300-hectare **Penang National Park** (Taman Negara Pulau Pinang).

The area encompasses white, sparkling beaches that are devoid of humans but popular with monkeys, and has some challenging trails through the jungle. Start at the **Penang National Park Office** (☎881 3500; end of Jln Hassan Abbas; ⏲8am-4.30pm Mon-Fri, 8am-noon & 2-4pm Sat & Sun) for maps and suggestions.

If you want to stay the night, stop at **Miss Loh's Guest House** (☎885 1227; off Jln Teluk Bahang; dm/s/d from RM8/15/30; ❄), a ramshackle throwback to the good ol' days of long-term backpacking. To find the guesthouse, look for a store on Teluk Bahang's main street that says 'GH Information.'

Bus 101 runs from Georgetown every half-hour all the way along the north coast of the island to just beyond the roundabout in Teluk Bahang.

Alor Setar

☎04

Most travellers use strongly Islamic Alor Setar as a hopping-off point to Thailand, Langkawi or southern Malaysia, but there's enough of interest here to keep you exploring for a few hours. The city's long association with Thailand is evident in Thai temples scattered around town, while its small Chinese population lives in an atmospheric, compact Chinatown.

Flora Inn (☎732 2375; http://florainn.tripod.com; 8 Kompleks Medan Raja, Jln Pengkalan Kapal; r RM13-75; ❄) overlooks the Sungai Kedah river, which is little more than algal green gloop. Rooms are clean and cheap, and the management is bend-over-backwards friendly.

To reach Langkawi from Alor Setar, take one of the frequent local Kuala Kedah buses (RM1.20, 15 minutes) to the ferry jetty. A shuttle bus (RM1) connects the town centre with the bus station, 3.5km away; a taxi will cost RM10. Between April and October, from about 7am to 7pm, ferries operate roughly every half-hour in either direction between Kuala Kedah and Kuah on Langkawi (RM23, 1½ hours).

Buses from Alor Setar include Ipoh (RM28, four hours, three daily), Kota Bharu (RM35, two daily, six hours) and Kuala Lumpur (RM39, hourly, six hours).

The **train station** (☎731 4045; Jln Stesyen) is a 15-minute walk southeast of town. There is one daily north-bound train to Hat Yai, Thailand (from RM9, three hours), and one south-bound to KL (seat/berth from RM22/45, 11½ hours).

Kuala Perlis

☎04

This small port town in the extreme northwest of the peninsula is a departure point for ferries to Pulau Langkawi. Your least-grotty sleeping option if you stop to sample the region's special laksa is **Pens Hotel** (☎985 4122; Jln Kuala Perlis; r from RM75; ❄).

Ferries (RM18) depart for Kuah, on Pulau Langkawi, every hour between 7am and 7pm.

The bus and taxi stations are behind the row of shophouses across from the jetty. From here infrequent buses go to Butterworth, Alor Setar and KL, and Padang. A greater selection of bus services can be found at Kangar; the frequent Bus 56 to/from Kangar (RM1.60) swings by the jetty before terminating at the station.

Pulau Langkawi

☎04

You'd think these 99 islands, dominated by 478.5-sq-kmPulau Langkawi, would have been overdeveloped past recognition by now – the district's been duty-free since 1986 and was roping in tourists long before that. Yet the knife-edged peaks floating in dark vegetation and the colour contrast of the ocean blues make this island an undisputed tropical paradise despite the resort buildup. Just a little way off the main (quite lovely) beaches

GETTING TO THAILAND

Bukit Kayu Hitam to Sadao

Frequent buses go from Alor Setar to the Bukit Kayu Hitam–Sadao border crossing (RM4), which is open from 7am to 7pm daily. You'll have to take a minibus on the Thai side of the border to the transport hub of Hat Yai.

Kangar to Padang Besar

Trains travelling south and north pass through the border towns of Padang Besar and Kangar, linking the towns along the train line (including Penang–Butterworth) to the border. Trains leave Alor Setar and arrive at the currently dodgy transport hub town of Hat Yai (from RM9) three hours later; travellers can also catch an international express that leaves Alor Setar for Bangkok, also via Hat Yai. The border is open 7am to 10pm daily.

Kuala Perlis to Satun

Large longtail boats run from Kuala Perlis to Tammalang Pier in Satun, Thailand (RM30, one hour) from 9.30am to 4.30pm daily. From Tammalang Pier there are direct air-con minivans to Hat Yai for 90B or sŏrngtăaou (pick-up truck) go to central Satun for 40B.

See p751 for details on travelling from Thailand to Malaysia.

GETTING TO THAILAND: PULAU LANGKAWI TO SATUN OR KO LIPE

There are five daily ferries from Kuah on Pulau Langkawi to Satun (one way RM20, 1¼ hours) on the Thai mainland from where there are more bus and boat connections. From 1 November to 15 May **Tigerline** (www.tigerlinetravel.com) and **Telaga Harbour** (www.telagaharbour.com/Lipeshuttle) run two ferries apiece each way between Langkawi and Ko Lipe (one way RM128, 1½ hours) in Thailand with onward service available to as far as Ko Lanta.

See p771 and p413 for information on doing the border crossing in the opposite directions.

is idyllic rural Malaysia, all *kampungs* and oil lamps.

Plus Langkawi is fun. You'll see all sorts of wholesome Malaysian revelry going on (hundreds of Malays line dancing on a beach is unforgettable), but come night, there's plenty of Western-style booze-fuelled fun about – and the beer is cheaper here than anywhere else in Malaysia.

The Langkawi archipelago sits 30km off the coast from Kuala Perlis and 45km from the border town of Satun. In the southeast corner of Langkawi is Kuah, the major town and the arrival point for ferries. On the west coast are Pantai Cenang (cha-*nang*), a lively beach strip with shops and restaurants, and adjacent Pantai Tengah, which is a bit quieter and a short walk to Pantai Cenang.

Sleeping

During peak tourist times (November to February) Langkawi's rooms fill quickly but at other times of the year supply far outstrips demand.

PANTAI CENANG

The gorgeous 2km-long strip of sand at Pantai Cenang has the biggest concentration of hotels, and is popular with everyone from 20-something backpackers to package tourists. The water is good for swimming, but jellyfish are common.

Several backpacker places are clustered together near Gecko Guesthouse so it's easy to shop around.

Gecko Guesthouse GUESTHOUSE $
(019 428 3801; rebeccafiott@hotmail.com; dm RM15, r RM35-80;) This is the most backpacker of fun backpacker joints. There's a jungly collection of bungalows, chalets and dorms, lots of dreadlocked folk in the common area and very good chocolate milkshakes behind the bar – book early but do lock up your belongings as we've had complaints about security here.

Palms Guest House GUESTHOUSE $
(017 631 0121; r from RM65;) Run by a friendly English couple, rooms here feel like the guest suite in a family cottage by the sea. They're clean and centred around a gravel-strewn courtyard shaded by palms, and there's free wi-fi.

Daddy's Guest House GUESTHOUSE $
(www.daddysguesthouse.blogspot.com;dm/rRM15/50) Daddy's consists of a room block that's draped with hammocks and eclectic touches such as bright paint, Thai cushions and Chinese lanterns.

Rainbow Lodge GUESTHOUSE $
(955 8103; www.rainbowlodgelangkawi.com; dm RM15, r from RM40) Set a little way back from the beach, this is a cheap place to rest. The dorm looks like a barracks, but it's a good spot for meeting folks.

PANTAI TENGAH

Pantai Tengah is less built-up and is popular with Malay families. Its main drag is stuffed with more upscale eateries and bars.

Zackry Guest House GUESTHOUSE $
(www.zackryguesthouse.langkawinetworks.com; r RM35-90;) Zackry Guest House is a friendly, sprawling guesthouse inhabited by happy travellers boozing it up in the common area, and Irish owner Neve and her Malaysian boyfriend Chaz. Rooms are clean and cosy.

Eating

Langkawi's proximity to Thailand means that the Thai penchant for fiery chillies has found its way into local dishes. There's a *pasar malam* north of Pantai Cenang held once or twice a week; it's a good place to get authentic Malay food on the cheap.

Champor-Champor MALAYSIAN, INDIAN $$
(☎955 1449; mains from RM18; ⏰7-10.30pm) Dine on imaginative regional cuisine such as pan-fried *bamakoise* (a local fish) with banana, tofu satay and coconut-crusted calamari.

Red Tomato ITALIAN $$
(☎955 9118; mains from RM18; ⏰8am-3pm & 6-11pm Sat-Thu) Run by expats, this place cranks out some of the best pizza and pasta on the island but they're certainly not giving it away.

Tomato MALAYSIAN, INDIAN $
(☎955 5853; mains from RM4; ⏰24hr) Not red or anything like its pizza-slinging counterpart, this cluster of stalls under one restaurant name serves excellent rotis as well as yummy tandoori and an Indian/Malay menu at all hours.

Boom Boom Corner MALAYSIAN, PAKISTANI $
(☎012 473 7167; mains from RM4; ⏰5pm-late) At Pantai Tengah try Boom Boom Corner, a bustling Malay and Pakistani food court at the northern end of the strip.

Drinking

Langkawi is arguably the best (and cheapest) spot for a drink in Malaysia. Most bars open around 5pm and close late.

You can start at Bob Marley Bar, which pops up right on Pantai Cenang around lunchtime. There are beach mats, posters of the great dreaded one, a predictable soundtrack and very good vibe. If you head south along Pantai Cenang, you'll hit the 1812 Bar, run by a friendly northern Englishman who is one of the best barmen on the island.

Reggae Bar BAR
(⏰noon-2am Sat-Thu) As the evening wears on lots of folks end up in Pantai Tengah at Reggae Bar, a beachside affair.

Sunba Retro Bar BAR
(Pantai Tengah; ⏰evening-3am) On the main drag of Pantai Tengah, this place turns into a dancey megaclub.

Little Lylia's Chill Out Bar BAR
(Pantai Cenang; ⏰afternoon-late) As the name suggests, a laid-back spot that stays open till – wow, is that sunrise?

Information

The only banks are at Kuah, although there are ATMs at the airport and Telaga Harbour Park and moneychangers tucked into and around duty-free shops and at Pantai Cenang.

Tourism Malaysia (☎966 7789; Jln Persiaran Putra, Kuah; ⏰9am-1pm & 2-6pm) offers comprehensive information and advice about the island.

Getting There & Away

Air

Check prices online – during off-season and promotions flying can cost the same as the ferry. **Malaysia Airlines** (☎955 6322; www.malaysiaairlines.com), **AirAsia** (☎32-171 9333; www.airasia.com) and **Firefly** (☎37-845 4543; www.fireflyz.com.my) all have two or three flights daily between Langkawi and KL. Malaysia Airlines and Firefly fly to Penang and **Tiger Airways** (www.tigerairways.com) and **SilkAir** (☎955 9771; www.silkair.com) fly to Singapore.

Boat

All passenger ferries to/from Langkawi operate out of Kuah. From about 8am to 6.30pm, ferries operate roughly every hour to/from the mainland port of Kuala Perlis (RM18, one hour) and every 30 minutes to/from Kuala Kedah (RM23, 1½ hours).

Langkawi Ferry Services (LFS; ☎966 9439) and **Ekspres Bahagia** (☎966 5784) operate two daily ferries between Kuah and Georgetown on Penang (RM60/115 one way/return, 2½ hours). Boats depart from Georgetown at 8.15am and 8.30am and leave Kuah at 2.30pm and 5.30pm.

Getting Around

There is no public transport. Car hire is excellent value starting at RM60 per day for a Kancil or RM35 for a motorbike. A few places also rent mountain bikes for RM15 per day.

Otherwise, taxis are the main way of getting around. Fixed fares for the entire vehicle (which can be split between passengers) include the following from the Kuah jetty: Kuah town (RM6), Pantai Cenang (RM24) and Pantai Tengah (RM24).

PENINSULAR MALAYSIA – EAST COAST

Refreshingly Malay, the peninsula's east coast is an entirely different experience from the mobile phone–obsessed, traffic-clogged west coast. Headscarves, skullcaps and the hauntingly melodious call to prayer are as ubiquitous here as the white-sand beaches that fringe the sunrise-drenched coasts and jewel-like islands.

GETTING TO SINGAPORE: JOHOR BAHRU TO SINGAPORE

Getting to the border There are frequent buses between JB's Larkin bus station, 5km north of the city, and Singapore's Queen St bus station. Most convenient is the Singapore–Johor Bahru Express (RM2.50, one hour, every 20 minutes from 6.30am to midnight). Alternatively, there's the slower city Bus 170 (RM1.80).

At the border All buses stop at Malaysian immigration. Disembark from the bus with your luggage and go through immigration then reboard your bus (keep your ticket). The bus then brings you to Singapore immigration where you get off the bus with your luggage once more, clear Singapore customs then get back on your bus (again keep your ticket), which will take you to Singapore's Queen St bus station.

Moving on After clearing Singapore immigration, there are buses from Queen St, taxis and an MRT station that can take you anywhere you need to go in the city. There are ATMs at Singapore immigration and at the Queen St bus station if you need Singapore dollars.

See p642 for details on doing the trip in the opposite direction.

Johor Bahru

07

The frenetic border town of Johor Bahru (known as JB) is connected to Singapore by the 1038m-long Causeway bridge. The city has been cleaned up over the years but it still has plenty of beggars, a lack of smiles and a petty crime problem. Still, watching suit-clad Singaporeans buy knock-off watches from Malays in gangster wear and Indian women hawking gold bracelets on the sidewalk as incense wafts from Chinese shops gives the walkable heritage downtown area a unique, edgy vibe. To check it out walk west from the Customs, Immigration and Quarantine complex and keep alert for motorcycle snatch thieves.

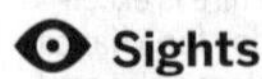

Sights

Muzium Diraja Abu Bakar MUSEUM
(223 0555; adult US$7; 9am-5pm Sat-Thu) The finest museum of its kind in Malaysia, Muzium Diraja Abu Bakar conveys the wealth and privilege of the sultans. Tickets are payable in ringgit at a bad exchange rate; the ticket counter closes at 4pm.

Sleeping & Eating

If you're on a tight budget hop on any bus and leave town – JB has some of the priciest rooms in Malaysia. Most budget hotels ask for a room deposit of around RM30 that's returned to you when you check out. The food, however, is cheap and tasty.

Meldrum Hotel HOTEL $
(227 8988; www.meldrumhotel.com; 1 Jln Siu Nam; dm/s/d RM40/70/80;) Air-conditioned, clean, spacious and freshly painted rooms with TVs, free drinking water and kettles.

JB Hotel HOTEL $
(223 4989; 80-A Jln Wong Ah Fook; s/d RM54/60;) Small air-con rooms come with TV, tiled floor and sinks but bathrooms are shared.

JOHOR BAHRU BUS FARES

Johor Bahru's long-distance bus station is Larkin station, located 5km north of the centre. Buses run to and from Larkin to most parts of the country.

DESTINATION	FARE (RM)	DURATION (HR)
Butterworth	65	12
Ipoh	48	7
Kota Bharu	49	10
Kuala Lumpur	31	4
Kuala Terengganu	44	9
Kuantan	27	5
Melaka	19	3
Mersing	12	3

GETTING TO INDONESIA: JOHOR BAHRU TO PULAU BATAM & PULAU BINTAN (RIAU ISLANDS)

Getting to the border There are several daily departures to Batam (one way RM69, 1½ hours) and Tanjung Pinang on Bintan (one way RM86, 2½ hours), both islands (part of Indonesia's Riau Islands) with connections to Sumatra, Indonesia. Ferries depart from the ZON Ferry Terminal (for schedule details see www.zon.com.my/ferry.html) that's serviced by buses 10A, SS, 22, 123, 507A from downtown Johor Bahru. You'll be charged a RM10 seaport tax and stamped out of Malaysia before you board the boat.

Additional boats depart from Kukup, southwest of JB, to Tanjung Balai on Karimun (three times daily, RM45) and to Sekupang, Batam (twice daily, RM60) also in Indonesia; see www.ferrytuah.comoj.com for schedules and reservations. Port fees are RM25 per person and you'll get stamped out of Malaysia before departure. Buses travel to Kukup from Johor Bahru (RM6, 45 minutes) and KL (RM26, 3½ hours).

Moving on From Batam, boats serve the mainland Sumatran ports of Dumai, Palembang and Pekanbaru, which are serviced by buses.

Medan Selera Meldrum Walk MALAYSIAN $
(meals from RM3; ⌚dinner) Yummy food stalls selling the local laksa and grilled fish are crammed along the alley that runs parallel to Jln Meldrum

Information

There's a **Tourism Malaysia** (⌚8am-4.30pm Mon-Thu, 8am-12.15pm & 2.45-4.30pm Fri, 8am-12.45pm Sat) in the Customs, Immigration and Quarantine complex just as you clear Singapore immigration that has some handy maps.

Getting There & Away

Air

JB is served by **Malaysia Airlines** (☎334 1011; www.malaysiaairlines.com.my), **Firefly** (☎603 7845 4543; www.fireflyz.com.my) and **AirAsia** (☎1300 889 933; www.airasia.com). Most domestic flights connect through KL, a four-hour bus ride away. Larkin bus station is 2.5km north of the city centre.

JB's airport is 32km northwest of town at Senai.

Boat

Ferries leave Johor Bahru for islands in Indonesia; see p417 for details.

Bus & Taxi

Most people travel from Johor Bahru to Singapore by bus; see p416 for more.

Long-distance taxis also leave from Larkin (there's a price list at the stand). A local taxi from central JB to the bus station should cost RM8. Metered taxis are found just beyond the bus station gate past berth 33.

Train

Daily express trains depart Johor Bahru three times per day for Kuala Lumpur (from RM33). It is also possible to change at Gemas (from RM21) and hop aboard the Jungle Railway for connections to Jerantut (if you're headed for Taman Negara) and Kota Bharu. See p429 for further information on the Jungle Railway.

Mersing

☎07

The jumping-off point for Pulau Tioman, Mersing is busy and compact, and has everything that travellers might need: cheap internet, good sleeping options, grocery stores, cold beer and a pharmacy. The river is clogged with colourful fishing boats but beyond the riverfront there's not much to explore.

Sleeping & Eating

There are several places around town for *roti canai* and *kopi* (coffee) and seafood stalls open up nightly along Jln Endau by the river.

Hotel Embassy HOTEL $
(☎798 2864; 2 Jln Ismail; r with bathroom RM55; ❄📶) This is a fabulously posh-feeling choice compared to the other cheapies in town: all rooms are huge, and have cable TV, air-con and bathrooms.

Hotel Golden City HOTEL $
(☎799 5028; 23 Jln Abu Bakar; r RM20-50; ❄) Bare-bones rooms have cement floors and saggy mattresses but it's clean and friendly here. Singles have shared bathrooms and only the most expensive options have air-conditioning.

Information

There are a few ATMs in the main part of town.

Mersing Tourist Information Centre (Mon-Sat 8am-5pm) is on the road to the pier; this place is helpful and has all the bus schedules.

Getting There & Away

Most buses depart from the station near the bridge on the river although a few leave from bus company offices near the pier (which can be convenient if it's brutally hot or raining). Some buses will also drop you at the pier when you arrive at Mersing if you ask nicely. Destinations include Kuala Lumpur (RM40, six hours, five daily), Johor Bahru (RM12, three hours, two daily), Kuantan (RM17, five hours, two daily), Kuala Terengganu (RM34, nine hours, two daily) and Singapore (RM16, three hours, two daily).

See p420 for information on ferries to/from Pulau Tioman.

Pulau Tioman

09

From late nights at Salang bars to days of trekking through the wild jungles, surfing the beaches at Juara or diving the reefs and wrecks off the coast, Tioman has as much action or nonaction as anyone could hope for. The proximity to Singapore and the availability of upscale digs has made Tioman particularly popular with Singaporean and domestic tourists but the island is so big and the locals are so mellow that the weekend crowds are absorbed without affecting the island's laid-back vibe.

During the east-coast monsoon, from about November to March, boat services to the island are infrequent or suspended. If you plan to visit Tioman during this time be prepared to get stuck in Mersing overnight or longer.

Most budget accommodation is clustered in Air Batang (ABC) and Salang on the northern end of the west coast. Salang has wider stretches of sand and the mood is decidedly 'spring break', while ABC has a more Malay, chill-out-with-your-friends kind of vibe. Other small beaches reachable only by boat run south along the west coast.

On the east coast of the island, Juara has a stunning beach, surfing during the monsoon and affordable accommodation.

Sights & Activities

Diving

Most places rent snorkelling gear and you can join day trips to Pulau Tulai, better known as Coral Island, where you can swim with fish and sometimes sharks.

Open-water dive courses cost around RM1200, and fun dives are around RM100. There are nearly more dive shops than accommodation options so shop around for the best deal.

Hiking

There's a fantastic 7km hike that crosses the island's waist from Tekek to Juara (carry plenty of water). It takes around 2½ hours, is steep in parts and starts near the jetty in Tekek. Over the hill on the Juara side there's a small, hidden waterfall (look for a trail next to an abandoned cement house off the paved jeep road), and the jungle is awesome. There are also several other trails on the island connecting beaches and climbing to more waterfalls.

Sleeping & Eating

In late July through August, accommodation becomes tight on weekends. Either side of these months it's a buyer's market. Budget digs around the island are nearly identical and are of low standard – think old mattresses and saggy floors – but most do have private bathrooms, fans and mosquito nets.

Restaurants, with similar menus, are usually attached to chalet operations. ABC,

Tekek and Salang all have small convenience stores.

AIR BATANG (ABC)

The far northern and southern ends of the beach here have the best sand while some in-between areas are rocky and marshy. At night the whole beach ends up drinking at **Sunset Corner** (three beers for RM10 during happy hour from 5pm to 7pm) at the southern end of the beach.

Mokhtar's Place GUESTHOUSE $

(s RM25, d RM30-50, tr RM60-65; ❄@) Cheaper bungalows are set back from the beach under pleasant shady trees and all rooms are spacious and clean, though ageing. Internet is available (when it's working) for RM10 per hour.

My Friend's Place GUESTHOUSE $

(☎419 1150; r RM25) Busy, social and priced a hair lower than the competition, this is a clean place with all rooms facing the garden.

Johan's Resort GUESTHOUSE $

(☎419 1359; dm/chalets/f RM15/30/130) The two good, clean four-bed dorms here are up on the hillside and some of the chalets face the sea.

SALANG

The small bay at the south of Salang has a beautiful beach and swimming area backed by a murky river that's teeming with giant monitor lizards.

TOP CHOICE **Ella's Place** GUESTHOUSE $

(☎419 5004; chalets RM50-100; ❄) There's usually a loungeable patch of sand here at this cute-as-a-button family-run place at the coconut palm–shaded, quiet northern end of the beach. There are 10 clean chalets (some with air-con) but you'll have to reserve in advance to nab one.

Salang Indah Resort GUESTHOUSE $

(☎419 5015; d/longhouse tw RM35/60, chalets hillside/sea view RM85/100, q RM130; ❄@) The expanse of chalets sprawl on seemingly forever. The mosque-looking restaurant serves everything from cheeseburgers to local-style seafood (dishes around RM8). There's also a bar, a shop and internet access (per hour RM10).

Pak Long Island Chalet GUESTHOUSE $

(☎419 5000; enquiry@paklongislandchalet.com.my; chalets with fan/air-con RM50/60; ❄@) Has wooden chalets with peeling plastic flooring and OK verandahs, the more expensive of which face the sea.

JUARA

There's little to do in Juara except swim, surf (between November and April), snooze under the swaying palms (but beware of sand flies) or take a gander into the jungle. It's actually two connected beaches and both are wide and white.

TOP CHOICE **Beach Hut** GUESTHOUSE $

(☎012 696 1093; camp sites with tent for 2 people RM15, dm/chalets from RM15/45) A bona fide surf shack, chalets here (on the southern beach) are decorated with shell mobiles, driftwood, fishing nets and colourful fabrics. Budget warriors can get a tent (which come with sleeping bags) or stay in the five-bed dorm.

Bushman GUESTHOUSE $

(☎419 3109; matbushman@hotmail.com; chalets RM50-80) Nabbing one of Bushman's comfy beachfront wood chalets is like winning the Juara lottery – reserve in advance! It's right up against the boulder outcrop and a stunning flat knuckle of white sand.

Rainbow Chalets GUESTHOUSE $

(☎419 3140; d RM50, tr RM60-70) These fittingly colourful beachfront chalets have an excellent reputation and so are always full. It's right before Bushman at the southern end of the northern bay.

Information

You'll be charged a RM5 national park entry fee before you board the ferry in Mersing.

Connected to ABC by a footpath over a rocky headland, Tekek is the island's main village, where you'll find a bank, the island's only ATM, telephones and a post office. The duty-free shop at the airport in town sells beer cheaper than water – seriously.

TIOMAN SCAMS

Bus and taxi drivers might try to take you to agents around town who sell accommodation on Tioman. Rates from these agencies are sometimes doubled, turning what would otherwise be a great budget hut into an overpriced disappointment. If you're worried about finding accommodation, call the guesthouse yourself to reserve a room.

Getting There & Away

Berjaya Air (code J8; ☎419 1303; www.berjaya-air.com), has daily flights to/from KL and Singapore.

Mersing is the ferry port for Tioman (RM35, two to three hours). There are usually four to six ferry departures throughout the day between 7am and 5pm, but specific departure times vary with the tides. Ferries drop off passengers in south-to-north order on the island.

Getting Around

You can walk from ABC to Tekek in about 10 minutes. But you'll need to charter a boat through a guesthouse or restaurant to travel between ABC and Salang (RM30).

To get to Juara hire a 4WD taxi (RM25 to RM30 for up to four people) in Tekek – better is to book your room in advance so your host can pick you up at the Tekek pier. Alternatively, you can walk through the jungle to Juara from Tekek (7km).

Kuantan

☎09

Many travellers find themselves on an overnight stopover in Kuantan, the pious and functional state capital, as it's the main transit point between Taman Negara and Pulau Tioman. Kuantan's star attraction is **Masjid Negeri**, one of the east coast's most impressive mosques. At night it's a magical sight with its spires and lit turrets.

Sleeping & Eating

Kuantan has some seriously dismal budget options and the following are the only ones we found worth mentioning.

Classic Hotel HOTEL $
(☎516 4500; chotel@tm.net.my; 7 Jln Besar; d incl breakfast RM98; ❄📶) It's fading and not great value unless you can nab a river-view room, but this place is clean and equipped with tea-making facilities, TVs and air-con. Add the central location and Malay-style breakfast and it's worth the splurge.

Hotel Makmur HOTEL $
(☎514 1363; 1st & 2nd fl, B 14 & 16 Lg Pasar Baru 1; r RM30-70; ❄) Totally boring and functional but it's clean, reception is friendly and it's an easy pack haul to the long-distance bus station.

Central Market MARKET $
(Jln Bukit Ubi) Food stalls can be found along the riverbank across from Hotel Baru Raya, and at the central market.

Information

Banks are clustered at Jln Bank and there are plenty of ATMs around Jln Haji Abdul Aziz (the continuation of Jln Mahkota).

Tourist information centre (☎516 1007; Jln Mahkota; ⌚9am-10pm Mon-Thu, 2.45-5pm Fri, 9am-1pm & 2-5pm Sat) One of Malaysia's most helpful.

Getting There & Away

Air

Kuantan airport (Lapangan Terbang Sultan Ahmad Shah; ☎538 2923) is 15km from the city centre; take a taxi (RM30). **Malaysia Airlines** (☎531 2123; www.malaysiaairlines.com.my) has direct flights to KL (three daily), and **Firefly** (☎03-7845 4543; www.fireflyz.com.my) also has two daily flights to/from KL's Subang Airport.

Bus & Taxi

At the time of writing all buses were arriving and departing from **Terminal Makmur** (Jln Stadium) but the **local bus station** (Jln Besar; services to Cherating & Merang) near the river was not going to re-open until an undesignated time in the future.

There are two long-distance taxi stands in town – one on Jln Stadium in front of the long-distance bus station, and the other on Jln Mahkota, just near the local bus station. Destinations and costs (per car) include Mers-

KUANTAN BUS FARES

DESTINATION	FARE (RM)	DURATION (HR)
Butterworth	53	8
Cherating	4.50	1½
Jerantut	18	3½
Kota Bharu	31	7
Kuala Lumpur	26	4½
Kuala Terengganu	24	3
Kota Bharu	31	7
Marang	10	3

ing (RM220), Cherating (RM50) and Jerantut (RM200).

Cherating

09

Back when there were no direct transport links between Taman Negara and the Perhentian Islands, Cherating was a major backpacker stop. Nowadays only dedicated wanderers, surfers and a few intrepid backpackers make it out this way but most who do find that there's something special about this place.

The village itself is just a strip of guesthouses and shops with more monkeys, monitor lizards and cats walking around than humans, but between the cracks are a resident band of hipster Malay surfers, artists and *kampung* folk who genuinely want to hang out over a beer and share in the holiday spirit.

Activities

There's an exceptional amount to do in Cherating.

Surfing & Kitesurfing

During the monsoon season (November to March) storms kick up surfable waves, especially good for beginners. Several places in town rent out surfboards for around RM20 per hour and you can get surf lessons at **Satu Saku** (Main Rd; Nov-Mar). **Don't Tell Mama** (9.30am-11pm), on the beach, rents out windsurfing and kitesurfing equipment from around RM50 per hour and offers classes.

Batik-Making

Matahari Chalets (p421) and Limbong Art (a shop on the Main Rd) both offer courses (from RM25) where you can make your own batik handkerchief or sarong.

Tours

Myriad adventures such as **firefly-spotting** (per person RM20, one hour) and **wildlife watching** (RM20, 1½ hours) are available on the river, offered by Payung Guesthouse and other agents around town. For wildlife, expect to see mostly snakes and monkeys – the fireflies are magical.

There are also **snorkelling trips** (per person RM50, two hours) and **fishing adventures** (three-hour boat hire RM300). **Sea turtle watching** (RM45, three to four hours) is at night during the nesting season – from March to October.

Sleeping & Eating

Cherating has a 'strip' where most of the restaurants and guesthouses congregate. Book in advance during the monsoon surf season from November through January.

Payung Guesthouse GUESTHOUSE $

(581 9658; chalets RM50-80;) Backs onto the river, with the town's neatest rows of clean chalets in the garden. The friendly attached tour office offers bike and surfboard rentals and mangrove or snorkelling tours.

Matahari Chalets GUESTHOUSE $

(581 9835; chalets from RM35) Chalets in an open garden are clean and equipped with a fridge, windows, mosquito nets and spacious verandahs. It's popular and a good place to meet other travellers.

Nabil's Cafe RESTAURANT $

(seafood barbecue from RM8; dinner) This is where the locals go (just across from Payung Guesthouse). Choose your seafood from the ice boat (from fish to squid); it then gets slathered in a very tasty sambal, wrapped in a banana leaf and cooked on the grill.

Drinking

TOP CHOICE Don't Tell Mama BAR
(till late) The hippest bar in town is right on the beach and is a great place to stop by day or night to make friends over a cold beer. Impromptu barbecues and parties are the norm.

Information

There are no banks in Cherating.

Tourist Information Centre (hwy at Cherating turn-off) Rarely open.

Travelpost (581 9796; 9am-11pm) Organises bus tickets to just about anywhere (takes a commission), has bike hire (per hour RM3), internet access (per hour RM4) and tourist information, and exchanges money at a poor rate.

Getting There & Away

Cherating doesn't have a bus station, but any Kuantan–Terengganu bus will drop off passengers at the turn-off to the village road, which will involve a short stroll. To go south from Cherating you'll need to wave down the local bus bound for Kuantan that runs every 30 minutes (RM4.50, 1¼ hours); for Kuala Terengganu book long-distance bus tickets (RM17, three hours, frequent) through Payung Guesthouse (p421) or **Travelpost** (581 9796; 9am-11pm).

Marang

09

Marang is the jump-off point for ferries to Pulau Kapas and a quiet fishing town, a little overbuilt by the highway but still pleasant in a rural way. If you're around on Sunday, check out the excellent **Sunday Market**, which starts at 3pm near the town's jetties.

There are regular local buses to/from Kuala Terengganu (RM2). Buy long-distance bus tickets at the Kapas boat agents near the pier. There are buses to/from Kuala Lumpur (RM35, two daily, eight hours), Johor Bahru (RM37, two daily, nine hours), and Kuantan (RM25, four hours, five daily) via Cherating.

Pulau Kapas

09

There's not much action on tiny Pulau Kapas, but that's the beauty of the place. Outside July, August and a few holiday weekends expect to have the white beaches, aquamarine waters and wild jungle trails to yourself. Climb into a hammock with a good book and you may see several days go by before you're able to climb out.

All accommodation, the few restaurants and handful of dive shops are clustered together on two small beaches on the west coast, but you can walk around the headlands to quieter beaches. The diving, run by **Dive Kapas** (019 379 6808, 019 983 5879; www.divekapas.com; two dives RM180, PADI open-water courses RM1100), is excellent, with prices similar to those in the Perhentian Islands.

Note that accommodation on the island shuts down during monsoon season (November to March).

The most budget-oriented option on Kapas is **Capt's Longhouse** (012 377 0241; www.captslonghouse.blogspot.com; dm/d RM30/60), a rustic but lovely elevated jungle longhouse with oil paintings by the owner, hammocks and mellow tunes on the sound system. Otherwise snazzy and popular **Kapas Island Resort** (631 6468; www.kapasislandresort.com; dm RM35, r RM130-200;), set among pretty landscaped gardens, is a good choice.

Six kilometres offshore from Marang, Kapas is reached by boats in 15 minutes from Marang's main jetty. Tickets (RM40 return) can be purchased from any of the agents nearby and boats depart when four or more people show up. Be sure to arrange a pick-up time when you purchase your ticket. You can usually count on morning departures from 8.30am.

Kuala Terengganu

09

Kuala Terengganu is a made-for-the-movies Southeast Asian success story: fishing village finds oil, money flows in, modernity ensues. Here and there you'll find an old *kampung* house seemingly hiding among the high-rises, and these glimpses, plus a seafood-heavy local cuisine and a slew of beautiful mosques, make Kuala Terengganu worth a day or two of exploration.

Note that Kuala Terengganu is very, very Islamic and official business is closed on Friday and Saturday.

Sights

Central market MARKET
(cnr Jln Kampung Cina & Jln Banggol; 8am-5pm Sat-Thu) The central market is a lively place to graze on exotic snacks, and the floor above the fish section has a wide collection of batik and *kain songket* (handwoven fabric). Across from the market is a flight of stairs leading up to **Bukit Puteri** (Princess

Kuala Terengganu

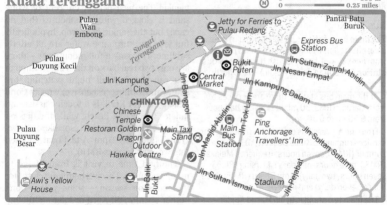

Hill), a 200m hill with city vistas and the remains of a fort.

Chinatown NEIGHBOURHOOD
Kuala Terengganu's compact Chinatown is situated along Jln Kampung Cina (also called Jln Bandar).

Kompleks Muzium Negeri Terengganu MUSEUM
(Terengganu State Museum; ☎622 1444; adult RM5; ⌚9am-5pm) This place claims to be the largest museum in the region, and it attractively sprawls over landscaped gardens along the banks of the Sungai Terengganu. Traditional architecture, fishing boats and textiles comprise the bulk of the collection. The museum is 5km south of Terengganu; to get there take minibus 10 (RM1).

Pulau Duyung Besar ISLAND
In the middle of Sungai Terengganu, Pulau Duyung Besar carries on the ancient boatbuilding tradition handed down for generations. The village is good for a day of wandering and snacking. Take the local ferry (60 sen) from the jetty near the Immigration Office across from Bukit Puteri.

Sleeping & Eating

Ping Anchorage Travellers' Inn HOTEL $
(☎626 2020; www.pinganchorage.com.my; 77A Jln Sultan Sulaiman; r RM25-65; ❄) Spread over two floors above the travel agency of the same name, Ping's rooms are reasonably clean, but it doesn't have much going for it besides the fact that it's the only traveller-oriented place in town.

Awi's Yellow House GUESTHOUSE $
(☎624 7363, 622 2080; r RM18-25) Built over the Sungai Terengganu river on Pulau Duyung, Awi's welcomes you with the smell of fish paste, salt and chilli, no air-con and nights that stick to you like a wet kiss. Don't come here if you don't like roughing it a little.

Restoran Golden Dragon CHINESE $
(☎622 3034; 198 Jln Kampung Cina; mains from RM5; ⌚lunch & dinner) The Golden Dragon is constantly packed, serves beer and has one of the finest menus of Chinese seafood in town.

Hawker centres MALAYSIAN & CHINESE $
(off Jln Kampung Cina) There are cheap food stalls inside the main bus station and a night market along the beachfront every Friday evening; the latter is a great place to sample *kerepok*, satay and sweets. Chinatown's outdoor hawker centre is divided into Chinese and Malay sections.

Information

Jln Sultan Ismail is the commercial hub and home to most banks, which are open 9.30am to 3.30pm, except Friday.

Tourist Information Office (☎617 1553; Jln Sultan Zainal Abidin; ⌚9am-5pm Sat-Thu) Brochures on Terengganu.

Getting There & Away

Air

Malaysia Airlines (☎662 6600; Airport) and **AirAsia** (☎32-171 9333; Airport) have direct flights to KL, and **Firefly** (☎03-7845 4543) has flights to/from Singapore four times per week. A taxi to/from the **airport** (☎666 3666), located

13km northeast of the town centre, costs around RM35.

Bus & Taxi

The **main bus station** (Jln Masjid Abidin) is for local buses. Some long-distance buses depart from here as well, but most use the **express bus station** (Jln Sultan Zainal Abidin), in the north of town.

At the main bus station, there are services to/from Marang (RM2, 30 minutes, every half-hour from 6.30am to 6.30pm).

From the express bus station, there are regular services running to Kuala Besut (RM11), Kuala Lumpur (RM40, seven hours, frequent), Melaka (RM33, nine hours, one daily), Mersing (RM33, seven hours, two daily), Kota Bharu (RM15, three hours, seven daily) and more.

The main taxi stand is at Jln Masjid Abidin across from the main bus station.

Kuala Besut

The primary jetty town for boats to Pulau Perhentian is Kuala Besut (bee-su), south of Kota Bharu. It is a sleepy fishing village with a minimall of collaborating boat-company tour offices.

Some taxi drivers get paid commission to take travellers to the jetty of **Tok Bali**, just across the river. Ferries here are nearly as frequent as Kuala Besut–based boats so this shouldn't pose a problem for you. For details of ferries between Kuala Besut and Pulau Perhentian see p426.

There are five daily direct buses from Kota Bharu (RM7) but the trip takes two hours so it makes more sense to take a minibus (RM20 per person) or share a taxi (RM60 for the whole taxi; to Tok Bali it's also about RM60). From the south, you can go to/from Kuala Terengganu by bus (RM11) or taxi (RM90 per car). There are also two daily buses to/from KL (RM42, nine hours).

The agents at Kuala Besut's jetty also sell minibus tickets to the Cameron Highlands (RM45, six hours), Taman Negara (RM55, eight hours), Penang (RM65, 10 hours) and the Kota Bharu airport (RM25, one hour).

Pulau Perhentian

☎09

Long Beach on Pulau Kecil of the Perhentian Islands is not only one of Malaysia's most popular backpacker spots, it's also one of the cheapest places on the planet to get your PADI open-water dive certification (from around RM1000) – and the diving is spectacular. The near-perfect crescent of white sand is clogged with guesthouses (but no cars!) but the jungle backdrop, hypnotically fun vibe and turquoise water are all utterly sublime. This isn't a full-moon party – there are only two real bars on the sand – although you can stay out all night watching fire shows and swilling (expensive) whisky. Coral Beach, also on Kecil, is a touch classier and quieter than Long Beach, while the digs on Pulau Besar verge on the resortlike and everyone's in bed by 11pm. A taxi boat between the two islands costs RM10.

The best time to visit is from March to mid-November. The Perhentians close for the monsoon season – some places don't bother opening till April or later – although some hotels remain open for hardier tourists. Some diving outfits stay open year-round but off-season there's often low visibility and the sea is rough.

There are no banks on the Perhentians. Generators are the source of power and are run during limited hours. There are no public phones but mobile phones work. Internet is scarce and costs around RM20 per hour.

Also please, please note: this is still Malaysia, and topless sunbathing is rude. Locals are too polite to tell people to their face, but baring your breasts insults their sense of modesty.

Activities

A four-day open-water course costs RM1000 to RM1200 and fun dives cost between RM70 and RM90. For the surface skimmers, guesthouses arrange excellent snorkelling trips around the island (around RM40).

Sleeping & Eating

On Pulau Kecil (Small Island), Long Beach has the biggest range of budget chalets and 'nightlife'. In the high season (usually from late May to early September), finding accommodation here can be tough, so book ahead or arrive early. Accommodation on Pulau Besar (Big Island) is more upmarket and usually includes air-con and a private bathroom.

Alcohol is available in a few bars and hotel restaurants on both islands. The best hunting grounds for a beer are the more popular Long Beach cafes and Watercolours Resort on Pulau Besar. At the time of writing the cheapest beer (RM7) was available from a guy carting a big cooler along the beaches of Pulau Kecil.

For dinner, the restaurants at Coral Bay on Pulau Kecil have the best prices for *ikan bakar* (barbecued fish) with choices of several types of fish and seafood, and sauces in which to slather them.

PULAU KECIL

A trail over the narrow waist of the island leads from Long Beach to smaller Coral Bay (sometimes known as Aur Bay) on the western side of the island. It's a five- to 10-minute walk along a footpath through the quickly developing jungle interior.

LONG BEACH

The surf can get big on Long Beach and several places along the beach rent boogie boards and old clunky surfboards. Take care when swimming here as there have been several near tragedies.

Perhantian Tropicana Inn GUESTHOUSE $
(☎016 266 1333; www.perhentiantropicana.com; dm/r RM20/60; wi-fi) Inland on the trail to Coral Bay, this new, well-run place has clean dorm and private rooms that are in better shape than anything else in this price range.

Matahari Chalets GUESTHOUSE $
(☎019 956 5756; www.matahrichalets.com; chalets RM30-130; air-con) Ageing longhouse rooms and A-frame huts ramble around a well-kept but shadeless garden off the beach. All have attached bathrooms except the cheapest A-frame huts and there's an attached dive centre.

Panorama Chalets GUESTHOUSE $
(☎691 1590; www.panoramaperhentianisland.com; chalet RM35-150) Offers a similar set up to Matahari next door. While the rooms here are shabbier, the dive centre is more professional and has better gear.

Lemon Grass GUESTHOUSE $
(☎012 956 2393; chalet RM35) At the scenic, southern tip of Long Beach, Lemon Grass has tiny brown huts with a shared bathroom lined up close together in a charming, shady garden.

Chempaka Chalets GUESTHOUSE $
(☎010 985 7329; r RM25-50) Very colourful but small and rickety A-frames chalets with shared bathroom sit in the cutest garden ever.

CORAL BAY

Coral Bay faces the west for brilliant sunsets and calm swimming. Seafood barbecue on the beach offers a nightly feast and many people head over here from Long Beach for better deals on meals.

Fatima GUESTHOUSE $
(chalet RM35-45; @ wi-fi) Big but rustic wood bungalows with attached bathrooms nab a prime location on the beach, and are in slightly better shape than the competition (though that's not saying much). The wi-fi and internet work sometimes and cost RM20 per hour.

Butterfly Chalets GUESTHOUSE $
(r RM45-60) Ageing huts look out over Coral Bay, picking up sea breezes, and are tucked in by hibiscus flowers. They are nearly always full.

Aur Bay Chalets GUESTHOUSE $
(r RM35-45) This fading place right on the beach next to Fatima feels like a mini *kampung*, with its sweet Malay owners and kids skipping in the sand.

OTHER BEACHES

There are also a number of small bays around the island, each with one set of chalets, and often only accessible by boat.

Mira Chalets GUESTHOUSE $
(☎016 647 6406; www.mirabeach.com; r RM30-75) Mira, on the west coast, has sea-weathered, rustic huts with mosquito nets perched over a perfect, deserted beach; the snorkelling is phenomenal. There are dorms, chalets with or without attached bathrooms and a restaurant. It's a 20-minute walk from Coral Bay or a taxi boat costs about RM10.

D' Lagoon Chalets GUESTHOUSE $
(☎019 985 7089; www.dlagoonperhentian.net; dm RM20, r RM30-60) Only accessible by boat, this place fronts a gorgeous but often agitated bay on the northeastern side of the island. There are longhouse rooms and chalets. Diving is also available.

PULAU BESAR

Pulau Besar has two busy main beaches facing Pulau Kecil that offer skinny but shady stretches of white sand. Teluk Dalam (also called Flora Bay), over the hill, is a silken secluded bay with good snorkelling and more peace and quiet. An easily missed track leads from behind the second jetty over the hill to Teluk Dalam (a 40-minute walk) – or a five-minute taxi boat to Teluk Dalam costs RM10.

Samudra Beach Chalet GUESTHOUSE $
(☎691 1677; Teluk Dalam; www.samudrabeachchalet.com; d RM40-75, f RM60) Clean, fan-cooled

bungalows on gorgeous Teluk Dalam in the shade of coconut palms.

Mama's Place GUESTHOUSE $
(☎019 985 3359; www.mamaschalet.com.my; r RM65-300;) The best budget option on Pulau Besar's main beach, the chalets here are spacious, well-maintained and are lined up in a big garden.

Fauna Beach Chalet GUESTHOUSE $
(☎691 1607; Teluk Dalam; r RM55, chalets RM70-175) Solid, good-value rooms and wooden bungalows with a friendly, local ambience.

Watercolours Resort GUESTHOUSE $$
(☎691 1111; www.watercoloursworld.com; r RM70-130;) Rooms are basic for the price but the service is excellent and the flowery garden and beachfront location lovely.

Getting There & Around

Speedboats (RM70 return, 35 minutes) run several times a day from Kuala Besut to the Perhentians from 8.30am to 5.30pm. The boats will drop you off at any of the beaches. In the other direction, speedboats depart from the islands daily at around 8am, noon and 4pm. You'll pay a RM5 park entry fee when you buy your ferry ticket.

When the waves are high on Long Beach, you'll be dropped off or picked up on the other side of the island at Coral Bay. Also, guesthouse operators on Long Beach charge RM3 per person for ferry pick-ups and drop-offs.

The easiest way to island (or beach) hop is by boat (RM10 to RM25). Posted fares and boat operators usually camp out under a shady coconut tree. From island to island, the trip costs RM10 per boat.

Kota Bharu

☎09

Very Islamic but supremely mellow Kota Bharu has the energy of a midsized city, the compact feel and friendly vibe of a small town, superb food and a good spread of accommodation. It's the logical overnight stop between Thailand and the Perhentians, but you'd be wise to give Kota Bharu more time than a pit stop.

Sights

TOP CHOICE **Gelanggang Seni** CULTURAL SHOW
(☎744 3124; Jln Mahmud; admission free; ⏲3.30-5.30pm & 9-11pm Mon, Wed & Sat Feb-Sep) For a dose of Malay tradition, the cultural centre, Gelanggang Seni, has top-spinning, *seni silat* (martial arts), shadow puppetry, kite-making etc. Check with the tourist information centre, as opening and performance times vary.

Central Market MARKET
(Pasar Besar Siti Khadijah; Jln Hulu; ⏲6am-6pm) Kota Bharu's Central Market is one of the most colourful and active in Malaysia and is at its busiest first thing in the morning – it's usually packed up by early afternoon. Downstairs is the produce section, while upstairs stalls sell spices, brassware and batik.

Istana Jahar MUSEUM
(Royal Customs Museum; ☎748 2266; Jln Hilir Kota; adult RM3; ⏲8.30am-4.45pm Sat-Thu) Exhibits royal rites of passage and traditional ceremonies, such as circumcision and engagement, from birth to death; the scenic building gives a glimpse into Malay Muslim architecture.

Muzium Negeri Kelantan MUSEUM
(State Museum; ☎748 2266; Jln Hospital; adult RM2; ⏲8.30am-4.45pm Sat-Thu) The Muzium Negeri Kelantan has interesting exhibits about the state's history and culture, but the accompanying signage is poor.

Sleeping

The backpacker places listed here are all great, and have both shared-bathroom and private-bathroom (read: pricier) options.

Zeck's Travellers' Inn GUESTHOUSE $
(☎743 1613; www.zeck-traveller.com; 7088G Jln Sri Cemerlang; dm/s/d RM10/18/25; @) An oasis just 10 minutes' walk from the city, Zeck's is relaxed, clean and over-the-top hospitable. The turn-off from Jln Sri Cemerlang is easy to miss.

Ideal Travellers' Guest House GUESTHOUSE $
(☎744 2246; www.ugoideal.com; 3954F Jln Kebun Sultan; r RM12-40; @) Down an alley off Jln Pintu Pong, the Ideal is a long-running, friendly place with spacious, airy rooms with lots of natural light.

KB Backpackers GUESTHOUSE $
(☎748 8841, 019 944 5222; www.kb-backpackers.com.my; 1872-D Jln Padang Garong; dm/r from RM8/20; @) KB's rooms are only so-so but the owner Pawi is so helpful, and the vibe at his hostel is so internationally chilled out, that we can't help but declare our love of KB.

Denai Lodge GUESTHOUSE $
(☎017 370 7781, 019 963 2324; denai_lodge@yahoo.sg; 2984-F Jln Parit Dalam; dm/r from RM13/20; @) Run by former trekking guides, Denai

Kota Bharu

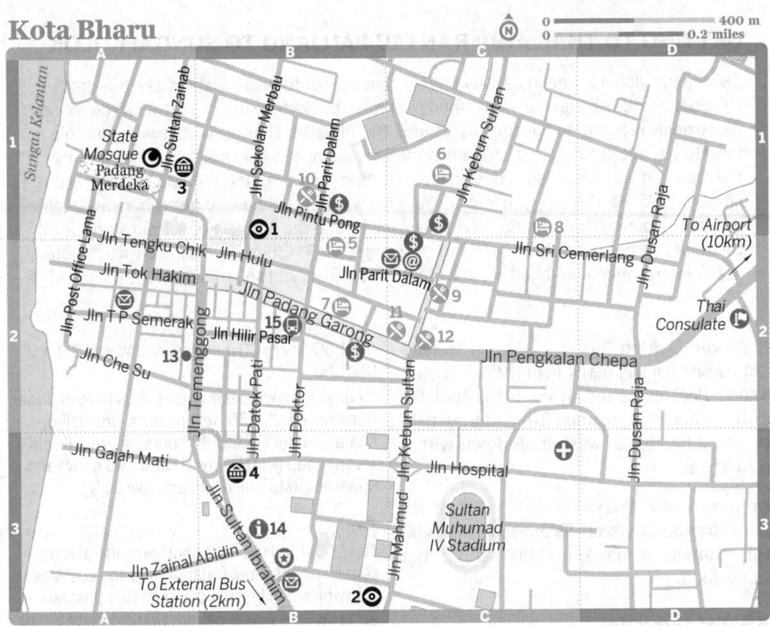

has friendly owners and clean digs. It's a sociable, easy-going spot with a quiet reading room, TV-centred common room etc.

Eating

Kota Bharu is a conservative Muslim city so alcohol is not widely available; head to Chinese restaurants if you're hankering for a beer.

TOP CHOICE Night Market MALAYSIAN $
(cnr Jln Datok Pati & Jln Pintu Pong; dinner) For a bonanza of regional Malay and Indian specialities at hawker prices, head to this vibrant market. Here you will find *ayam percik* (marinated chicken on bamboo skewers), *nasi kerabu* (rice tinted blue with herbs, mixed with coconut, fish, vegetables and spices), savoury *murtabak* (thick Indian pancake stuffed with onion, egg, chicken, mutton or vegetables), and a bewildering array of cakes. Prayer always pulls rank over food and at prayer time (roughly between 7pm and 7.45pm) everyone is chased out of the market.

Restoran Sri Devi INDIAN $
(746 2980; 4213F Jln Kebun Sultan; dishes RM3-6; breakfast, lunch & dinner;) As popular with locals as with tourists, this is a great place for banana-leaf curry, *roti canai* and mango lassi. There are also plenty of vegetarian options.

Kota Bharu

Sights
- 1 Central Market ... B1
- 2 Gelanggang Seni ... B3
- 3 Istana Jahar ... A1
- 4 Muzium Negeri Kelantan ... B3

Sleeping
- 5 Denai Lodge ... B2
- 6 Ideal Travellers' Guest House ... C1
- 7 KB Backpackers ... B2
- 8 Zeck's Traveller's Inn ... C1

Eating
- 9 Chinese Night Market ... C2
- 10 Night Market ... B1
- 11 Restoran Golden City ... C2
- 12 Restoran Sri Devi ... C2

Information
- 13 Immigration Office ... A2
- 14 Tourist Information Centre ... B3

Transport
- 15 Central Bus Station ... B2
- Taxi Stand ... (see 15)

GETTING TO THAILAND: RANTAU PANJANG TO SUNGAI KOLOK

Continuing violence and instability on this coast of southern Thailand make this crossing a dangerous endeavour, and although some travellers do still cross the border here we strongly recommend against it. Attacks are unpredictable, and with many possible targets you could easily find yourself in the wrong place at the wrong time by entering the region. If you must risk it, buses depart on the hour from the Kota Bharu central bus station (RM5.20, 1½ hours) to Rantau Panjang where you'll have to disembark and walk across the border; it's about a kilometre from here to the Sungai Kolok train station. Share taxis from Kota Bharu to Rantau Panjang cost RM38 per car and take 45 minutes.

For information about getting to Malaysia from Thailand see p785.

Restoran Golden City CHINESE $
(Jln Padang Garong; mains from RM5; ⏲lunch & dinner) Besides being an excellent spot for Chinese noodles, steamed fish and tofu dishes, you'll be able to wash it all down with a cold Tiger.

Chinese Night Market CHINESE $
(Jln Kebun Sultan; meals RM3; ⏲6pm-midnight) Has numerous hawker stalls selling hot snack food.

Information

Banks and ATMs are scattered around town; **Maybank** (Jln Pintu Pong), near the night market, is usually open till 7pm. Internet shops can be found in the alleys around Jln Doktor and Jln Kebun Sultan.

Immigration office (☎748 212; Jln Temenggong)

Tourist Information Centre (☎748 5534; Jln Sultan Ibrahim; ⏲8am-1pm & 2-4.30pm Sun-Wed)

Getting There & Away

Air

AirAsia (☎746 1671) and **Firefly** (☎037-845 4543) have direct daily flights to KL.

Bus

There are three bus stations in Kota Bharu. Local buses depart from the **central bus station** (Jln Padang Garong), also known as the state-run SKMK bus station. Most long-distance buses will drop off passengers near here, but do not depart from here. When buying your ticket, verify which long-distance terminal the bus departs from. Most Transnacional long-distance buses depart from **Langgar bus station** (☎748 3807; Jln Pasir Puteh), in the south of the city. All the other long-distance bus companies operate from the **external bus station** (Jln Hamzah).

A few handy local buses include the ones to Pasir Puteh (RM5) and Kuala Besut (RM7) – for the ferry to the Perhentians, Kota Bharu airport (RM1.50, every 20 minutes) and Wakaf Baharu (RM1.50).

Long-distance destinations from here include Butterworth (RM35, seven hours, one daily), Kuala Lumpur (RM38, 10 hours, hourly), Kuala Terengganu (RM11, three hours, two daily) and Kuantan (RM31, seven hours, five daily).

Taxi

The taxi stand is on the southern side of the central bus station. Destinations and costs per car (which can be split between four passengers) include Wakaf Baharu (RM25), Kota Besut (RM60) and Tok Bali (RM60). Taxi drivers in Kota Bharu are uncharacteristically aggressive; do your homework on fares. Most guesthouses arrange shared taxis, especially for early morning departures.

Train

The nearest **train station** (☎719 6986) to Kota Bharu is at Wakaf Baharu, on the Jungle Railway line. A line also runs to Bangkok, although services have been suspended for some time due to violence in southern Thailand.

PENINSULAR INTERIOR

A thick band of jungle buffers the two peninsular coasts from one another. Within the middle is Taman Negara, the peninsula's most famous national park, and the Jungle Railway, an engineering feat.

Jerantut

☎09

Jerantut is the first of several stepping stones to Taman Negara. It's a dingy yet easy town, where you can pick up supplies, change money or stay overnight to break up your trip.

There are two ATMs, both near the bus station, where you can cash up before heading to the jungle.

Sleeping & Eating

A food court specialising in *tom yam* (spicy Thai-style) seafood is on Jln Pasar Besar. Chinese liquor stores line up along Jln Diwangsa hoping you'll want to stock up on booze before heading to dry Kuala Tahan.

NKS Hostel HOSTEL $
(21-22 Jln Besar; d incl breakfast with/without shower RM50/35) Run by the same folks as Sri Emas, NKS has clean, tiled rooms, and all the NKS buses to Kuala Tahan and Kuala Tembeling (for the boat) stop right outside the restaurant and internet cafe on the ground floor.

Hotel Sri Emas HOSTEL $
(266 4499; tamannegara@hotmail.com; 46 Jln Besar; dm RM8, d with shower RM38, without shower RM15-35, tr/f RM21/64; @) Many people get herded here by the handy NKS minivan that picks up at the bus and train station and it's not a bad place to end up. Fan doubles with shared hot-water bathrooms have saggy mattresses but are clean and excellent value (RM15).

Hotel Chet Fatt GUESTHOUSE $
(266 5805; 177 Jln Diwangsa; dm/d RM10/20; @) Stumble across the street from the bus station if you arrive late at night to this place with window-lit rooms, internet terminals and free filtered water.

Greenleaf Traveller's Inn GUESTHOUSE $
(267 2131; 3 Jln Diwangsa; dm RM10, d RM20-30;) Run by a sweet lady and her family, this is a quiet choice with simple, clean rooms and dorms.

Getting There & Away

Boat

Motor-run canoes make the scenic journey between Kuala Tembeling and Kuala Tahan. Travel agents sell combination tickets that include transfer from Jerantut to the jetty and ferry to Kuala Tahan.

For more information on boats to Kuala Tahan, see p433.

Bus & Taxi

The bus station and taxi stand are in the centre of town.

Most people arriving in Jerantut want to head directly to the Kuala Tembeling jetty (where boats leave for Taman Negara). To do this, follow the NKS representative, who meets arriving buses and trains and organises minibus transfers (RM5) from Jerantut to Kuala Tembeling.

You can also skip the boat journey and hop on a Kuala Tahan–bound bus (signed as 'Latif'; RM7, one to two hours, four daily); Kuala Tahan is the base-camp village for Taman Negara. You save money by doing this, although many travellers cite the voyage upriver from Kuala Tembeling as a highlight of visiting Taman Negara.

Alternatively, you can hire a taxi to Kuala Tembeling (RM24 for the entire car) or to Kuala Tahan (RM70) or an NKS minibus to Kuala Tahan costs RM110 for up to six people.

When you are ready to get the hell out of Jerantut, there are several daily buses to/from KL's Pekeliling bus station (RM19, 3 hours) via Temerloh (last bus to/from Jerantut 5/4pm). If you miss the bus to KL, buses go every hour to Temerloh (RM5, one hour, last bus 6.30pm),

WORTH A TRIP

JUNGLE RAILWAY

The name 'Jungle Railway' conjures images of forest people hunting tigers with blow pipes – but you're not going to find any of that here. Nowadays this clean, air-conditioned train trundles through the mountainous, oil palm–clad interior, stopping at *kampung*, letting on a few schoolchildren and headscarfed women lugging over-sized bundles of produce. Enjoy views of misty jungle, cave-studded karst cliff faces and a few brightly painted railside Indian temples. It's not super adventurous, but this is one of the more pleasant ways to get from Pulau Perhentian to Taman Negara.

The northern terminus is Tumpat, but most travellers start/end at Wakaf Baharu, the closest station to the transport hub of Kota Bharu. The train departs from Wakaf Baharu on its southbound journey around 7am and it reaches Jerantut, the jumping-off point for Taman Negara, around eight hours later (RM25). The journey continues south to Gemas (RM34), meeting the Singapore–KL train line.

There are also express trains that travel at night, but that would defeat the purpose of seeing the jungle. The train's schedule changes every six months, so it pays to double-check departure times locally.

from where there are more connections to KL and other destinations. Three daily buses run to/from Kuantan (RM18, 3½ hours). One bus runs daily to Johor Bahru (RM43).

NKS arranges minibuses and buses to a variety of destinations, including KL (RM50), Perhentian Islands jetty (RM85), Kota Bharu (RM80) and Cameron Highlands (RM80), all of which leave from the NKS cafe.

Long-distance taxis go to Temerloh (RM60) KL (RM220) and Kuantan (RM200).

Train

Jerantut is on the Jungle Railway (Tumpat–Gemas line; see p429). The train station is off Jln Besar, just behind Hotel Sri Emas. For the famed jungle view, catch the northbound local train at around 12.30pm to Wakaf Bahru (RM25). If you opt to skip the view, two daily northbound express trains leave Jerantut in the middle of the night (seat/berth RM17/31, four hours).

Two express trains run daily to Singapore (2am and 12.30pm), via Johor Bahru. For KL Sentral, take the 12.30am express. For an up-to-date timetable and list of fares, consult **KTM** (www.ktmb.com.my).

Taman Negara

☎09

Taman Negara blankets 4343 sq km in shadowy, damp, impenetrable jungle. Inside this tangle, trees with gargantuan buttressed root systems dwarf luminescent fungi, orchids and even the giant *Rafflesia* (which is the world's largest flower). Trudge along muggy trails in search of elusive wildlife (tigers, elephants and rhinos can hide much better than you'd think), balance on the creaky canopy walk or spend the night in a 'hide' where jungle sounds make you feel like you've gone back to the caveman days.

The best time to visit the park is in the dry season between February and September. During the wet season, or even after one good rainfall, leeches come out in force.

Kuala Tahan is the base camp for Taman Negara and has accommodation, minimarkets and floating-barge restaurants. It's a scruffy place and standards are low but it's pleasant enough. Directly opposite Kuala Tahan, across Sungai Tembeling, is the entrance to the national park, Mutiara Taman Negara Resort and the park headquarters located at the Wildlife Department.

Most people purchase permits (park entrance/camera RM1/5) when they buy their bus and/or boat tickets to Kuala Tahan in Jerantut. Otherwise you'll need to get your permits at the **Wildlife Department** (☎266 1122; ⊙8am-10pm Sat-Thu, 8am-noon & 3-10pm Fri). The reception desk also provides basic maps, guide services and advice.

Activities

Trekking

There are treks to suit all levels of motivation, from a half-hour jaunt to a steep nine-day tussle up and down Gunung Tahan (2187m). It's unanimous that the guides are excellent.

Popular do-it-yourself treks, from one to five hours, include the following.

Canopy Walkway TREKKING

(admission RM5; ⊙10am-3.30pm Sat-Thu, 9am-noon Fri) Anyone who says walking isn't an adrenalin sport has never been suspended on a hanging rope bridge constructed of wooden planks and ladders elevated 45m above the ground; come early to avoid long waits in line.

Bukit Teresik TREKKING

From behind the Canopy Walkway a trail leads to the top of this hill, from which there are fine views across the forest. It's steep and slippery in parts. The return trip is about one hour.

PLANNING FOR TAMAN NEGARA

Stock up on essentials in Jerantut. If it's been raining, leeches will be unavoidable. Tobacco, salt, toothpaste and soap can be used to deter them, with varying degrees of success. A liberal coating of insect spray over shoes and socks works best. Tuck pant legs into socks; long sleeves and long pants will protect you from insects and brambles. Even on short walks, take more water than you think you'll ever need, and on longer walks take water-purifying tablets.

Camping, hiking and fishing gear can be hired at the Mutiara Taman Negara Resort shop or at several shops and guesthouses on the Kampung Kuala Tahan side. Asking prices per day are around RM8 for a sleeping bag, RM10 for a rucksack, RM25 for a tent, RM20 for a fishing rod, RM5 for a sleeping pad, RM8 for a stove and RM8 for boots. Prices can be negotiated and it's good to shop around for bargains as well as quality.

DON'T MISS

HIDES & SALT LICKS

Animal-observation hides *(bumbun)* are built overlooking salt licks and grassy clearings, which attract feeding nocturnal animals. You'll need to spend the night in order to see any real action but staying in the heart of the jungle is what the Taman Negara experience is all about. There are several hides close to Kuala Tahan and Kuala Trenggan that are too close to human habitation to attract the shy animals, but even if you don't see any wildlife, the jungle sounds are well worth it – the 'symphony' is best at dusk and dawn.

Hides (per person per night RM5) need to be reserved at the Wildlife Department and they are very rustic with pit toilets. Some travellers hike independently in the day to the hides, then camp overnight and return the next day, while others go to more far-flung hides that require some form of transport and a guide; the Wildlife Department can steer you in the right direction. For overnight trips you'll need food, water and a sleeping bag. Rats on the hunt for tucker are problematic, so hang food high out of reach.

Some of the following hides can be reached by popular treks (see p430):

» **Bumbun Blau & Bumbun Yong** On Sungai Yong. From the park headquarters it's roughly 1½ hours' walk to Bumbun Blau (3.1km), which sleeps 12 people and has water nearby, and two hours to Bumbun Yong (4km). Both hides can also be reached by the riverbus service (see p433).

» **Bumbun Cegar Anjing** Once an airstrip, this is now an artificial salt lick, established to attract wild cattle and deer. A clear river runs a few metres from the hide. It's 1½ hours' walk from Kuala Tahan; after rain Bumbun Cegar Anjing may only be accessible by boat (four-person boat RM40). The hide sleeps eight people.

» **Bumbun Kumbang** From the park headquarters it's roughly five hours' walk to Bumbun Kumbang. Alternatively, take the riverbus service from Kuala Tahan up Sungai Tembeling to Kuala Trenggan (four-person boat RM90, 35 minutes), then walk 45 minutes to the hide. Tapirs, monkeys and gibbons are rarely seen here and elephant sightings are even rarer. The hide has bunks for 12 people.

» **Bumbun Tahan** Roughly five minutes' walk from the park headquarters. There's little chance of seeing any animals at this artificial salt lick but ya never know.

» **Tabing Hide** About 1½ hours' walk (3.1km) from park headquarters, this hide is near the river so it's also accessible by the riverbus service. The best animal-watching (mostly tapir and squirrels) here is at nightfall and daybreak.

Lubok Simpon TREKKING

This is a popular swimming hole. Near the Canopy Walkway, take the branch trail that leads across to a swimming area on Sungai Tahan.

Kuala Trenggan TREKKING

The well-marked main trail along the bank of Sungai Tembeling leads 9km to Kuala Trenggan. This is a popular trail for those heading to Bumbun Kumbang.

Longer treks, which require a guide, include the following:

Gunung Tahan TREKKING

For the gung-ho, Gunung Tahan, 55km from the park headquarters, is Peninsular Malaysia's highest peak (2187m). The return trek takes nine days at a steady pace, although it can be done in seven. Guides are compulsory (RM550 per person for nine days if there are four people; prices vary depending on how many are in the group). Try to organise this trek in advance through the Wildlife Department.

Rentis Tenor TREKKING

(Tenor Trail) From Kuala Tahan, this trek takes roughly three days via Yong camping ground, the Rentis camping ground and across Sungai Tahan (up to waist deep) to Kuala Tahan – or you can stop at the Lameh camping ground, about halfway.

Fishing

The sport fish known locally as *ikan kelah* (Malaysian mahseer) is a cousin of India's king of the Himalayan rivers and is a prized catch. You'll need a fishing licence, transport and a guide to fish along the river; head to the Wildlife Department (☎266 1122; ⏰8am-10pm Sat-Thu, 8am-noon & 3pm-10pm Fri) for more information.

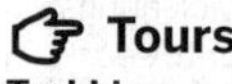

Tours

Trekking

You really don't need a guide or tour for day trips – or even overnight trips – to the hides if you're prepared to organise your own gear, food and water. You'll need one for longer treks, however, and the going rate is RM150 per day (one guide can lead up to 12 people), plus a RM100 fee for each night spent out on the trail. Guides who are licensed by the Wildlife Department have completed coursework in forest flora, fauna and safety and are registered with the department. Often the Kuala Tahan tour operators offer cheaper prices than the Wildlife Department, although there is no guarantee that the guide is licensed.

Wildlife & Rapids

Everyone in Kuala Tahan wants to take you on a wildlife or boat tour (RM35) where you motor down the rapids. There are popular night tours (RM35) on foot or by 4WD. You're more likely to see animals (such as slow loris, snakes, civets and flying squirrels) on the drives, which go through palm-oil plantations outside the park, but even these don't guarantee sightings.

Orang Asli

Many travellers sign up for tours to an Orang Asli settlement where you'll be shown how to use a long blowpipe and start a fire. While local guides insist that these tours provide essential income for the Orang Asli, most of your tour money will go to the tour company. A small handicraft purchase in the village will help spread the wealth.

Sleeping & Eating

Arrive early in the day or book in advance (although many places never answer their phones) since the better places fill up quickly and there's invariably a nightly collection of lost souls searching for rooms in the rain. For details on staying at a hide, see p431.

Kuala Tahan is no culinary centre – unexciting Malaysian and Western fare can be found at a collection of floating restaurants on the river.

Tahan Guesthouse GUESTHOUSE $
(☎266 7752; r RM50) Tahan Guesthouse has excellent four-bed dorms and colourfully painted bright rooms upstairs all with attached bathrooms. The whole place feels like a happy preschool with giant murals of insects and flowers all over the place.

Durian Chalet GUESTHOUSE $
(☎266 8940; A-frames RM25, r RM40-50) About 800m outside the village between rubber and durian plantations, this hideaway has microscopic, rustic A-frame huts and large doubles and family rooms. All options have fans, attached bathrooms and mosquito nets.

Yellow Guesthouse GUESTHOUSE $
(☎266 4243; r RM40-80; ❄@📶) Up and over the top of the hill from the NKS floating restaurant (behind the school), this quiet place is cleaner and in better shape than most of the others, plus there's air-con, wi-fi and hot-water showers.

Tembeling Riverview Hostel GUESTHOUSE $
(☎266 6766; rosnahtrv@hotmail.com; dm RM10, r RM35-50) Straddling the thoroughfare footpath, folks stay here to be close to the action, not for privacy. Rooms are lodge-basic.

Liana Hostel GUESTHOUSE $
(☎266 9322; dm RM10) Has popular barracks-like, four-bed dorm rooms and nonexistent service.

Drinking

Mutiara Taman Negara Resort RESTAURANT/BAR
Kuala Tahan is dry, so if you're after a beer you'll have to cross over to Mutiara Taman Negara Resort for the most expensive beer in Malaysia (RM19). Pricey Western food is also available (RM17 to RM55).

Information

Internet access is unreliable and slow at the best of times and costs RM5 to RM6 per hour. There are a handful of terminals at Agoh Chalets and a few more at an unnamed shop across from Teresek View Motel. There are no banks in Taman Negara.

Getting There & Away

Most people reach Taman Negara by taking a bus from Jenatut to the jetty at Kuala Tembeling then a river boat from there to the park, but there are also popular private minibus services that go directly to/from several tourist destinations around Malaysia directly to/from Kampung Kuala Tahan. You can also take a bus from Jerantut direct to Kampung Kuala Tahan, but by doing this you miss the scenic boat trip.

Boat

The river jetty for Taman Negara–bound boats is in Kuala Tembeling, 18km north of Jerantut.

Boats (one way RM35) depart Kuala Tembeling daily at 9am and 2pm (9am and 2.30pm on Friday). On the return journey, boats leave Kuala Tahan at 9am and 2pm (and 2.30pm on Friday). The journey takes three hours upstream and two hours downstream. Note that the boat service is irregular during the November-to-February wet season.

Bus & Taxi

For details on buses and taxis from Jerantut to Kuala Tembeling, see p429. A public bus from Kampung Kuala Tahan goes to KL (RM29) every day at 8am via Jerantut. **NKS** (☎03-2072 0336; www.taman-negara.com) and **Banana Travel & Tours** (☎017 902 5952; Information Centre, Kampung Kuala Tahan) run several useful private services including daily buses to KL (RM35) and minibuses to Penang (RM120), the Perhentian Islands (RM165 including boat) and the Cameron Highlands (RM80). These minibuses can also drop you off en route anywhere in between.

Getting Around

There is a frequent cross-river ferry (RM1) that shuttles passengers across the river from Kuala Tahan to the park entrance and Mutiara Taman Negara Resort.

Nusa Camp's floating information centre in Kuala Tahan runs scheduled riverboat (also called riverbus) services along the river to Bumbun Blau/Bumbun Yong (one-way RM15, three daily), the Canopy Walkway (one-way RM10, two daily), Gua Telinga (one-way RM10, four daily), Kuala Tembeling (one-way RM25, one daily) and Kuala Trenggan (one-way RM30, two daily). Check with the information desk for times and prices, as these services may be dropped entirely during the wet season. You can arrange for the boats to pick you up again for the return trip on their schedule, and there's a slight discount for a round-trip fare.

In addition to the riverbus, you can also charter a boat for considerably more – Bumbun Blau (RM75) and Kuala Trenggan (RM110). You can arrange private boat trips at the Wildlife Department, at the resort or at the restaurants in Kuala Tahan (the latter are usually 10% cheaper).

MALAYSIAN BORNEO – SABAH

Sabah's coastal waters – green, blue, teal and every shade of tropical cool in between – are inhabited by sea life so fantastical and surreal it looks like lost footage from the *Star Trek* cutting-room floor. Where water hits land, waves lap golden sand and the sea filters into estuaries where crocodiles and monitor lizards lurk, meeting tropical rivers that sustain pygmy elephants, bearded pigs and of course the great ginger man himself: the orang-utan. Sabah's incredibly diverse wildlife can be spotted hopping, grunting, hunting, squealing, squawking, preying and playing along the banks of the chocolate-brown Sungai Kinabatangan, below the starlight fireflies of Sungai Klias and in the state's deep, ancient rainforests. Topping it all is Mt Kinabalu, the tallest mountain in Borneo, home of spirits, snow, an 'iron road' and some of the most magnificent sunrises anywhere.

Kota Kinabalu

☎088 / POP 436,100

Kota Kinabalu – everyone calls it 'KK' – is probably not going to be the sleeper hit of your Southeast Asian odyssey, but as mid-sized Malaysian provincial capitals go, it's pretty cool. The centre is compact and walkable, there's a lovely waterfront packed with atmospheric markets, and you'll find some garish malls, a surprisingly popping nightlife scene (relative to Malaysia) and some damn fine food. Right, we realise you almost certainly didn't come to Sabah for the urban scene, but you gotta book permits somewhere, you gotta sleep after climbing Mt Kinabalu/diving off Pulau Sipadan/exploring the jungle, and you need someplace to connect to onward travel. KK is a good place (sometimes the only place) to do all of the above.

Sights

CITY CENTRE

Central Market MARKET

(Jln Tun Fuad Stephens; ⌚6.30am-6pm) A colorful spot to watch as locals go about their daily business.

Sunday Market MARKET

(Jln Gaya; ⌚7am-3pm) On Sundays, a lively Chinese street fair takes over the entire length of Jln Gaya.

BEYOND THE CITY CENTRE

Some of KK's best attractions are located outside KK's city centre, and it's well worth putting in the effort to check them out.

Sabah State Museum MUSEUM

(☎253199; www.museum.sabah.gov.my; Jln Kebajikan; RM15; ⌚9am-5pm Sat-Thu) The best place

Malaysian Borneo

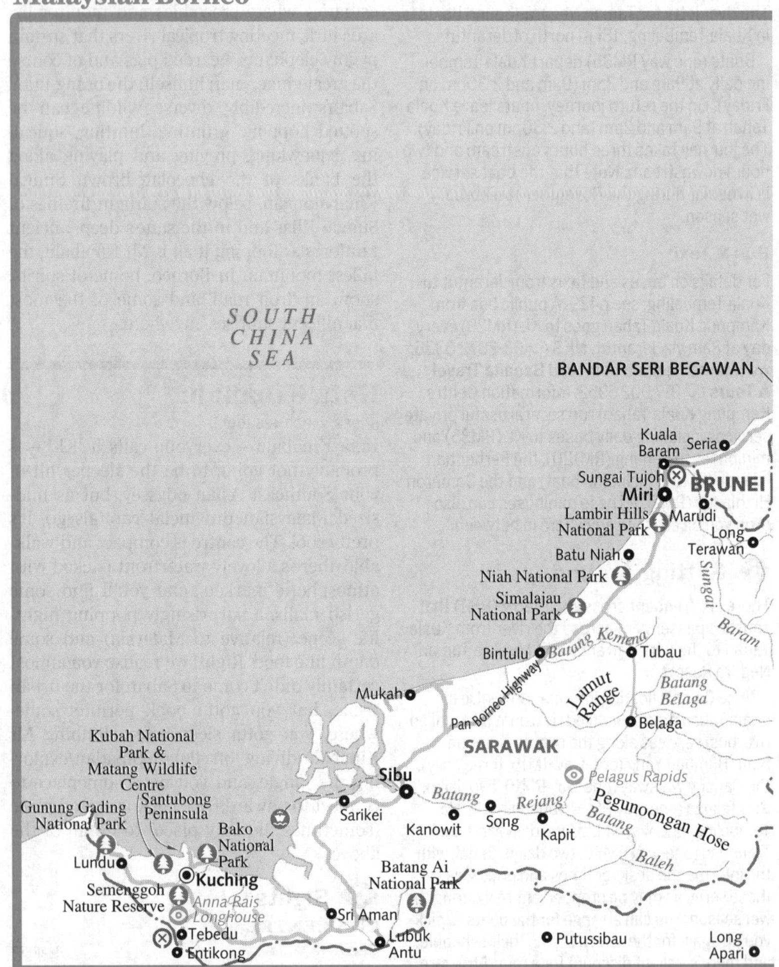

in KK for an introduction to Sabah's ethnic groups and ecology – and, at the adjoining **Science & Education Centre**, the local petroleum industry.

The complex includes the **Museum of Islamic Civilisation**, which has five domes representing the Five Pillars of Islam and six galleries devoted to Islamic culture and history. It's situated about 2km south of the city centre very near the corner of Jln Penampang and Jln Kebajikan. To get here, catch a bus (RM1) along Jln Tunku Abdul Rahman and get off just before the **Sabah State Mosque** (Jln Tunku Abdul Rahman), a modernist structure that holds 5000 and whose gold-chevronned dome can be seen on the way from the airport.

Kota Kinabalu Wetland Centre MUSEUM
(☎246955; www.sabahwetlands.org; Jln Bukit Bendera Upper; admission RM10; ⏰8am-6pm Tue-Sun) This lovely spot encompasses the last 24 hectares of a mangrove swamp that once stretched across what was KK. A series of wooden walkways leads into a lovely wetland. By road, the entrance is 4km northeast of the centre (take Jln Tun Fuad Stephens).

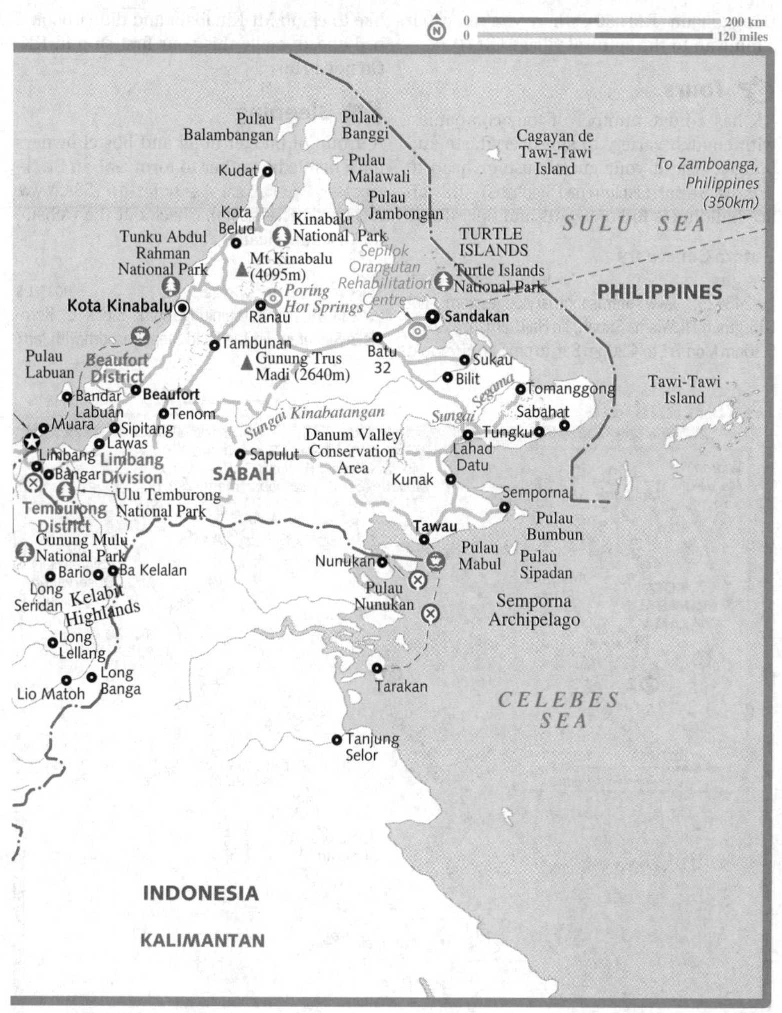

Lok Kawi Wildlife Park ZOO
(☎765710; www.lokkawiwildlifepark.com; Jln Penampang, Papar Lama; admission RM20; ⏱9.30am-5.30pm) A good place to check out the orang-utans if you can't make it out to Sepilok. It's best to arrive by 9.50am at the latest – feedings take place throughout the park at 10am. Situated about 25km southeast of KK; served by minibus 17B (RM2).

Tunku Abdul Rahman National Park NATIONAL PARK
(www.sabahparks.org.my; admission RM10) Just west of KK, the five islands of Manukan, Gaya, Sapi, Mamutik and Sulug, and their beaches and the reefs in between make up this 49 sq km national park. Ideal day-trip material for anyone in the mood for an ex-urban unwind. Situated a short boat ride from Jesselton Point, which is about 500m northeast of Wisma Sabah.

Monsopiad Cultural Village LIVING MUSEUM
(☎761336; www.monsopiad.com; RM65; ⏱9am-5pm) A privately run heritage centre that focuses on Kadazan-Dusun culture. The highlight is the House of Skulls. Located about 16km south of the city centre. To get there, take a bus from central KK to

Donggongon (RM1.50), where you can catch a minivan to the cultural village (RM1).

Tours

KK has a huge number of tour companies, with enough variety to suit every taste and budget. Ask at your guesthouse or head to **Wisma Sabah** (Jln Tun Fuad Stephens) – this office building is full of agents and operators.

Sutera Sanctuary Lodges KINABALU ACCOMMODATION
(☎243629; www.suterasanctuarylodges.com; Lot G15, ground fl, Wisma Sabah, Jln Haji Saman; ⊙9am-6.30pm Mon-Fri, to 4.30pm Sat, to pm Sun) If you'd like to climb Mt Kinabalu and didn't book a bed ahead, make this your first stop in KK. Go now! Hurry!

Sleeping

A group of budget hotel and hostel owners have banded together to form **Sabah Backpacker Operators Association** (SBA; www.sabahbackpackers.com). Check out the website for discount deals.

TOP CHOICE **Step-In Lodge** HOSTEL $
(☎233519; www.stepinlodge.com; Block L, Kompleks Sinsuran, Jln Tun Fuad Stephens; dm with fan/

Kota Kinabalu

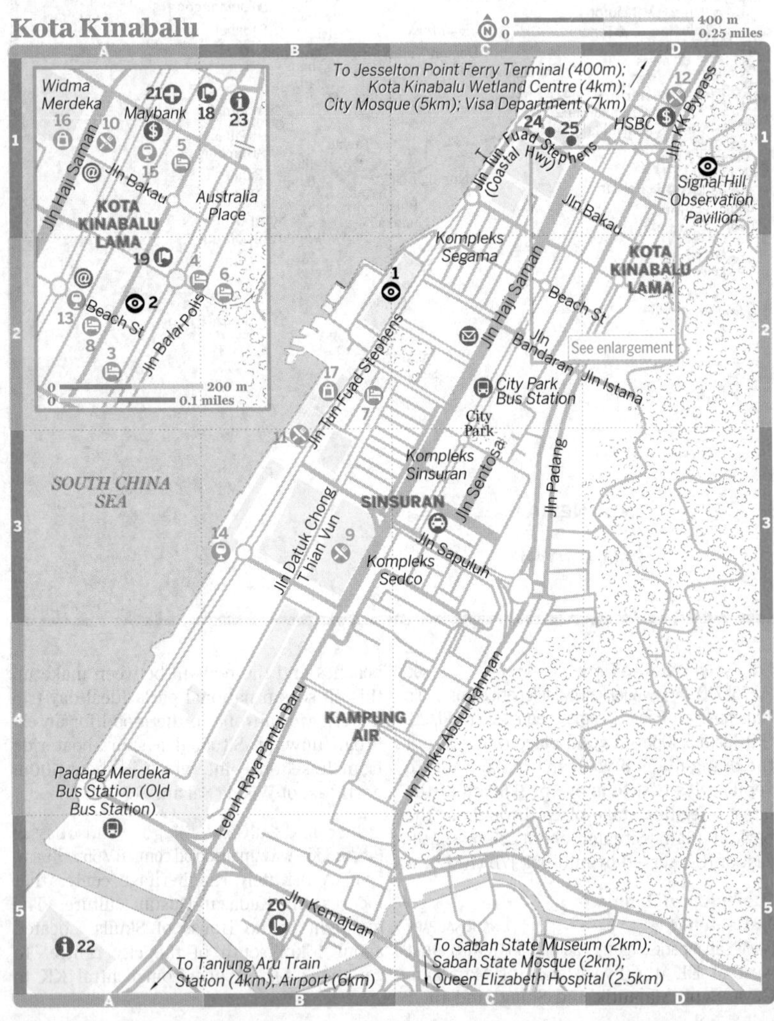

air-con RM28/38, d with fan/air-con RM70/90; ❄📶) KK's smartest hostel, with larger-than-usual bunk beds, comfy mattresses, real coffee at breakfast and an excellent (not to mention knowledgeable) staff.

Summer Lodge HOSTEL $
(☎244499; www.summerlodge.com.my; Lot 120, Jln Gaya; dm/d RM28/70; ❄📶) Feels a bit like a bed factory, but with that social vibe many backpackers adore. Owners are very friendly and helpful.

Lucy's Homestay GUESTHOUSE $
(Backpacker's Lodge; ☎088-261495; http://lucyhomestay.go-2.net; Lot 25, Lg Dewan, Australia Pl; dm/s/d incl breakfast RM20/45/50; 📶) Has loads of charm, with wooden walls smothered in stickers, business cards and crinkled photographs.

Akinabalu Youth Hostel HOSTEL $
(☎272188; www.akinabaluy.com; Lot 133, Jln Gaya; dm/r incl breakfast from RM20/56; ❄📶) Friendly staff, fuchsia-accent walls and trickling Zen fountains make this a solid option. Accommodation is mostly in basic four-bed rooms, with windows facing an interior hallway.

Borneo Gaya Lodge HOSTEL $
(☎242477; www.borneogayalodge.com; No 78, Jln Gaya; dm/d from RM25/69; ❄📶) A typical high-guest volume hostel. Staff are a peach, and will help organise damn near anything, and you're as centrally located in KK as can be.

Borneo Backpackers HOSTEL $
(☎234009; www.borneobackpackers.com; 24 Lg Dewan, Australia Pl; dm/s/d incl breakfast from RM20/40/60; ❄📶) This long-running place is a bit cramped, but it's very popular, especially with younger travellers.

Eating

KK is one of the few cities in Borneo with an eating scene diverse enough to refresh the noodle-jaded palate. Besides the ubiquitous Chinese *kedai kopi* and Malay halal restaurants, you'll find plenty of interesting options around the city centre. Head to the suburbs if you're looking for some truly unique local fare.

Night Market HAWKER $
(off Jln Tun Fuad Stephens; meals from RM2; ⏲5-11pm; 🖉) The best, cheapest and most interesting place in KK for dinner.

Kedai Kopi Fatt Kee CHINESE $
(28 Jln Bakau; mains from RM5; ⏲noon-10pm Mon-Sat) The woks are always sizzlin' at this popular Chinese place next to Ang's Hotel. Their *sayur manis* cooked in *belacan* (shrimp paste) is a classic, and the salt-and-pepper prawns are wonderful.

Centre Point Basement Food Court HAWKER $
(Basement fl, Centre Point Shopping Centre, Jln Pasar Baru; mains RM3-10; ⏲11am-10pm) Your ringgit will go a long way at this popular and

Kota Kinabalu

Sights
1 Central Market C2
2 Sunday Market A2

Sleeping
3 Akinabalu Youth Hostel A2
4 Borneo Backpackers A2
5 Borneo Gaya Lodge A1
6 Lucy's Homestay B2
7 Step-In Lodge B2
8 Summer Lodge A2

Eating
9 Centre Point Basement Food Court B3
10 Kedai Kopi Fatt Kee A1
11 Night Market B3
12 Tong Hing Supermarket D1

Drinking
13 Beach Street A2
14 Bed B3
15 Hunter's A1

Shopping
16 Borneo Books A1
17 Handicraft Market (Filipino Market) B2

Information
18 Australian Consulate B1
19 British Consulate A2
20 Indonesian Consulate B5
21 Permai Polyclinic A1
22 Sabah Parks A5
23 Sabah Tourism Board B1
24 Sutera Sanctuary Lodges C1
25 Wisma Sabah C1

PLAN AHEAD!

Mt Kinabalu and the Semporna Archipelago (Pulau Sipadan) are the two most popular spots in Sabah that have stringent visitation regulations imposed by the Malaysian government. As we researched our way across the island, we encountered scores of vacationers lamenting booked-out beds, or bemoaning being barred from national parks. So, we're coming right out and saying it – plan ahead or you may find yourself ensnared by thick coils of red tape!

Sabah rewards, and sometimes requires, prior planning and deeper pockets than the rest of Southeast Asia. Yes, you can explore Sabah without any advance planning – just be prepared for a fair number of little annoyances, and for these to coalesce into one blindingly frustrating ball of hassle.

Swarms of travel agents in KK will try to convince you that Sabah can only be discovered while on a tour. This is simply not true. Yes, there are places like the Danum Valley that cannot be accessed by private vehicle, but hot spots like Sepilok, Sandakan or Sungai Kinabatangan can easily be explored under your own steam.

Here are our tips for some of Sabah's most visited sites:

Mt Kinabalu

Book as far in advance as possible – a month is ideal, but if you want your pick of lodging, six months is more like it. If you did not organise your climb before leaving home, here's the drill: head directly to the Sutera Sanctuary Lodges office in KK (p436) – sitting in front of the booking agents will increase your chances of finding a cancellation. If this doesn't work, find a travel agency around town that has a bed available (at a much higher price, unfortunately – you'll be paying both Sutera and the agency's commission).

Pulau Sipadan

For a scuba session, divers must obtain a permit, which usually comes with booking a dive package and/or accommodation in the Semporna Archipelago. If you extend your stay on the islands, your hotel/lodge should be able to get you extra days. If you're on a tight, inflexible schedule, book well in advance (two weeks at least).

Sungai Kinabatangan

If you want to stay at a meals-inclusive lodge on the Kinabatangan River, it's best to book at least a few days ahead as there are a limited number of chalets at each lodge. If you'd like to do a homestay, you can probably just show up to Sukau or Bilit, but we'd strongly advise that you book ahead by at least a few days; it's both polite and practical.

varied basement foodcourt in the Centre Point mall.

Tong Hing Supermarket SUPERMARKET $
(Jln Gaya) For picnic supplies.

Drinking & Entertainment

If you're up for a quiet drink, your best bet may be to grab a beer in a Chinese restaurant. Otherwise, get ready for loads of karaoke bars and big, booming nightclubs such as those clustered around the **Waterfront Esplanade** (Jln Tun Fuad Stephens); **KK Times Square** (Coastal Highway), at the southern edge of the city centre, where the newest hot spots are congregating; or semi-pedestrian **Beach St**, three blocks south of Wisma Sabah, which is cluttered with bars and eateries. Live music is the name of the game – local bars and clubs provide employment for a whole flotilla of local and Filipino cover bands.

Bed NIGHTCLUB
(☎251901; Waterfront Esplanade) It's big, it's crowded, it's cheesy – chances are you'll end up in Bed on one of your KK nights. Yes, get those bed puns ready, as well as your dancing shoes and patience for a *lot* of hip locals in outfits that are often shiny, skimpy and slinky. Bands play from 9pm, followed by DJs til closing.

Hunter's BAR
(☎016-825 7085; Kinabalu Daya Hotel, Jln Pantai) A favourite of local guides and expats,

Hunter's offers up karaoke, sport on a plasma TV and balmy outdoor seating in the heart of the city.

Shopping

Handicraft Market MARKET
(Filipino Market; Jln Tun Fuad Stephens; ⏰10am-6pm) A good place for inexpensive souvenirs, including pearls, textiles, seashell crafts, jewellery and bamboo goods, some from the Philippines, some from Malaysia and some from other parts of Asia. Needless to say, bargaining is a must!

Borneo Books BOOKS
(☎538077/241050; www.borneobooks.com; ground fl, Phase 1, Wisma Merdeka, Jln Tun Razak; ⏰10am-7pm) Carries a brilliant selection of Borneo-related books and maps, and a small used-book section.

Information

For details on the Indonesian consulate and the honorary consulates of Australia and the UK, see p475.

Emergency

Ambulance (☎999 or 218166)
Fire (☎994 or 214822)
Police (☎999, 212092; Jln Dewan)

Internet Access

Every sleeping spot we list has some form of internet connection.

Borneo Net (Jln Haji Saman; per hr RM3; ⏰9am-midnight) Twenty terminals, fast connections and loud music.

Net Access (Jln Pantai; per hr RM3; ⏰9am-2am) Plenty of connections, less noise.

Medical Services

Permai Polyclinic (☎232100; 4 Jln Pantai) Excellent private outpatient clinic.

Queen Elizabeth Hospital (☎218166; Jln Penampang) A few hundred metres past the Sabah State Museum.

Money

Central KK is chock-a-block with 24-hour ATMs.

HSBC (☎212622; 56 Jln Gaya; ⏰9am-4.30pm Mon-Thu, 9am-4pm Fri)

Maybank (☎254295; 9 Jln Pantai; ⏰9am-4.30pm Mon-Thu, 9am-4pm Fri)

Post

Main Post Office (☎210855; Jln Tun Razak; ⏰8am-5pm Mon-Fri) Cashes Western Union cheques and money orders.

Tourist Information

Sabah Parks (☎486430/2; www.sabahparks.org.my; Lot 45 & 46, Lvl 1-5, Block H, Signature Office, KK Times Sq, Coastal Highway; ⏰8am-1pm & 2-4.30pm Mon-Thu, 8-11.30am & 2-4.30pm Fri, 8am-12.50pm Sat) Good source for information on the state's parks. Situated 1.6km southwest of Wisma Sabah.

Sabah Tourism Board (☎212121; www.sabahtourism.com; 51 Jln Gaya; ⏰8am-5pm Mon-Fri, 8am-4pm Sat, 9am-4pm Sun) Housed in the historic post-office building. Has helpful staff and a wide range of brochures. Ask about its homestay program.

Visa Department (☎488700; Kompleks Persekutuan Pentadbiran Kerajaan, Jln UMS; ⏰8am-1pm & 2-5pm Mon-Thu, 8-11.30am & 2-5pm Fri) Situated 7km northeast of Wisma Sabah.

Getting There & Away

Air

Malaysia Airlines (MAS; ☎1-300 883 000, 088-515555; www.malaysiaairlines.com; 1st fl, Departure Hall, Kota Kinabalu International Airport; ⏰5.30am-7.30pm) and **AirAsia** (☎03-2171 9333; www.airasia.com; ground fl, Wisma Sabah, Jln Gaya) offer international flights to/from Brunei, Shenzhen, Jakarta, Manila, Singapore and Tapei. Within Malaysia, you can fly to/from Johor Bahru, Kuala Lumpur and Penang in Peninsular Malaysia, and Kuching, Labuan, Miri, Sandakan and Tawau in Borneo. **JetStar** (www.jetstar.com) and **Tiger Airways** (www.tigerairways.com) both have flights to Singapore.

MASwings (www.maswings.com.my) serves Bornean destinations such as Sandakan, Lahad Datu, Tawau, Labuan, Mulu, Miri, Sibu and Bintulu.

Boat

Passenger boats connect Jesselton Point Ferry Terminal (500m northeast of Wisma Sabah) to Pulau Labuan twice daily (economy class RM31, 3¼ hours), with onward service to Brunei.

Tunku Abdul Rahman National Park is linked to Jesselton Point by a 20-minute speedboat ride. Boats leave when full from 7am to 6pm. Return fares are about RM30; a two-island ticket is an extra RM10 or so.

Bus & Minivan

In general, land transport heading east departs from Inanam (Utara Terminal; 9km north of the city), while vehicles heading north and south along the west coast leave from Padang Merdeka Bus Station (also called Wawasan or 'old bus station'; at the south end of the city centre). Local buses (RM1.80) from Wawasan can take tourists to Inanam if you don't want to splurge on the RM20 taxi.

It's a good idea to have your hotel call the relevant bus station to book you a seat in advance.

MAIN BUS DESTINATIONS FROM KK

The following bus and minivan transport information was provided to us by the Sabah Tourism Board and should be used as an estimate only – transport times can fluctuate due to weather, prices may change and the transport authority has been known to alter departure points.

DESTINATION	DURATION (HR)	PRICE (RM)	BUS STATION	DEPARTURES
Beaufort	2	10	Padang Merdeka	7am-5pm (frequent)
Lahad Datu	8	40	Inanam	7am, 8.30am, 9am, 8pm
Lawas (Sarawak)	4	20	Padang Merdeka	8.30am & 1.30pm
Mt Kinabalu NP	2	15	Inanam & Padang Merdeka	7am-8pm (very frequent)
Sandakan	6	33	Inanam	7.30am-2pm (frequent) & 8pm
Semporna	9	50	Inanam	7am, 8.30am, 9am, 8pm
Tawau	9	55	Inanam	7.30am, 2pm, 8pm

Same-day bookings are usually fine, although weekends are busier than weekdays.

Train

Borneo's only railway line, run by the **Sabah State Railway** (www.sabah.gov.my/railway), runs two or three trains a day from Tanjung Aru, 4km southwest of central KK, south to Beaufort and Tenom, a distance of 134km. Inaugurated in 1896, this scenic line was recently renovated.

Getting Around

To/From the Aiport

Kota Kinabalu's international airport is in Tanjung Aru, located 7km south of the city centre. Its two terminals are not connected – in fact, they feel like two different airports. Most airlines operate out of Terminal 1, while AirAsia, Tiger Airways and charter flights use Terminal 2.

City bus 2 and bus 16A (RM1) service Terminal 2 and can be boarded in the city centre at the City Park Bus Station. Minibuses (RM3) leave from City Park for Terminal 1; bus 1 may access this terminal in the future. Public transport runs from 6am to 7pm daily.

Taxis *from* the airport to the city operate on a voucher system (RM30). Taxis heading *to* the airport should not charge over RM35 if you catch one in the city centre. Between 9pm and 6am airport cabs cost RM40.

Taxis

Most of KK's taxis have meters, but few drivers will agree to use them. Set prices rule the roost, but you should always negotiate a fare before heading off.

Mt Kinabalu & Kinabalu National Park

The 4095m peak of **Mt Kinabalu** (Gunung Kinabalu; www.sabahparks.org.my; park fee RM15) may not be as wow-inducing as, say, a Himalayan sky-poker, but Malaysia's first Unesco World Heritage Site is by no means an easy climb. Around 60,000 visitors of every ilk make the gruelling trek up Borneo's ultimate thighmaster each year, returning to the bottom with stories of triumph, pictures of sunlit moonscapes, and *really* sore legs.

Climbing the great Kinabalu – the highest peak in Maritime Southeast Asia outside of Papua – is a heart-pounding two-day adventure that you won't soon forget. After checking in at park headquarters (1520m) around 9am, trekkers ascend for four to seven hours to Laban Rata (3273m), where they spend the night. Usually, they hit the trail again at about 2.30am the next morning in order to reach the summit for a breathtaking sunrise.

The ascent of Kinabalu is unrelenting as almost every step you take will be uphill – or downhill. You'll have to negotiate a variety of obstacles along the way, including slippery rocks, blinding fog, frigid winds and slow-paced Japanese 50-somethings decked out in Chanel tracksuits.

Virtually every tour operator in KK can hook you up with a trip to the mountain, but some of these go for as much as RM1200. It's possible, and often cheaper, to do it on your own – just make sure you plan ahead.

Sights & Activities

Although there are some nice walks around the base of the mountain, most visitors come with one goal in mind: sunrise from the summit. If this is your plan, you'll need a climbing permit (admission RM100) and climbing insurance (per person RM7). Guide fees for the summit trek are RM100 (RM10 to RM20 more for the Mesilau trail). Permits and guides must be arranged at the **Sabah Parks office** (7am-7pm), which is immediately on your right after you pass through the main gate of the park (next door to the Sutera Sanctuary Lodges office).

Your guide will be assigned to you on the morning you begin your hike. If you ask, park staff will try to attach individual travellers to a group so that guiding fees can be shared. Couples can expect to be given their own guide. Guides are mostly Kadazan from a village nearby and many of them have been up to the summit several hundred times. Try to ask for a guide who speaks English – he or she (usually he) might point out a few interesting specimens of plant life. The guides walk behind the slowest member of the group, so think of them as safety supervisors rather than trailblazers.

Remember that the above-mentioned fees do not include at least RM385 per person for room-and-board on the mountain at Laban Rata.

Sleeping

Access to the summit is essentially rationed by access to the huts on the mountain at Laban Rata (3273m) so advance accommodation bookings are essential.

LABAN RATA

Sutera Sanctuary Lodges MOUNTAIN LODGE $$$
(303917; http://suterasanctuarylodges.com.my; Lot G15, ground flr, Wisma Sabah, Kota Kinabalu; dm without/with heat RM385/435, d with heat RM920) Prices include bedding and three meals. Yes, the inflated prices feel monopolistic and are patently ridiculous. Many travellers report frustration with the booking system, saying it's disorganised and inefficient and that it's difficult to get a confirmed booking. Reservations can be made online, in person or over the phone – our experience was that it is best to try to book at Sutera's offices in KK.

Pendant Hut MOUNTAIN LODGE $$$
(www.mountaintorq.com) The other option at Laban Rata. Owned and operated by Mountain Torq, all guests are required to participate in (or at least pay for) the *via ferrata* (iron road) circuit. Pendant Hut is slightly more basic than Sutera (no heat – though climbers sleep in uberwarm sleeping bags), but there's a bit of a summer-camp vibe here while Laban Rata feels more like a Himalayan orphanage. Prices are comparable to Sutera.

EQUIPMENT & CLOTHING

No special equipment is required to summit Kinabalu. However, a headlamp is strongly advised for the predawn jaunt to the top – you'll need your hands free to negotiate the ropes on the summit massif. Expect freezing temperatures near the summit, not to mention strong winds and the occasional rainstorm, so it's a good idea to bring along a quick-drying fleece jacket and a waterproof shell to go over it.

PARK HEADQUARTERS

The options listed below are operated by Sutera Sanctuary Lodges and are overpriced compared to the free-market sleeping spots outside the park (see p442).

Grace Hostel HOSTEL $$
(303917; http://suterasanctuarylodges.com.my; dm RM145) A clean, comfortable 20-bed dorm with fireplace and drink-making area.

Rock Hostel HOSTEL $$
(303917; http://suterasanctuarylodges.com.my; dm RM145) Another somewhat institutional 20-bed hostel. Twin-share rooms are available for RM420 per room.

Getting There & Away

Park headquarters is 88km by road northeast of KK. Express buses (RM25) leave KK from the city bus station every hour on the hour from 7am to 10am and at 12.30pm, 2pm and 3pm; departures in the other direction are at the same times.

A shuttle bus (RM40) runs from the Pacific Sutera (9am), the Magellan Sutera (9.10am) and Wisma Sabah (9.20am) to Kinabalu National Park HQ, arriving at 11.30am – much too late to begin a hike. In the reverse direction, the shuttle leaves Kinabalu National Park HQ at 3.30pm. There is also a shuttle bus from park HQ to Poring Hot Springs at noon (RM25) and another at 3.30pm (RM25) to Mesilau Nature Resort.

Express buses and minivans travelling between KK and Ranau (and Sandakan) pass the park turn-off, 100m uphill from the park entrance.

DON'T MISS

VIA FERRATA

The Kinabalu climbing experience changed dramatically a few years back when a *via ferrata* ('iron road' in Italian) – a permanent network of mountaineering cables, rungs and rails – was attached to the mountain's dramatic granite walls. After ascending Kinabalu in the traditional fashion, climbers can use the *via ferrata*, managed by **Mountain Torq** (www.mountaintorq.com), to return to the Laban Rata rest camp. The star attraction, the **Low's Peak Circuit** (minimum age 17; RM550), is a four- to five-hour scramble down metre-upon-metre of sheer rock face. The route's thread-like tightrope walks and swinging planks will have you convinced that the course designers are sadistic, but that's what makes it so darn fun – testing your limits without putting your safety in jeopardy. Those who don't want to feel their heart leaping out of their chest should try the **Walk the Torq route** (minimum age 10; RM400), a two- to three-hour initiation into the world of *via ferrata* offering dramatic mountain vistas with fewer knee-shaking moments.

You can head to Sandakan (RM40) if the bus has room.

It is advised that summit seekers check in at the park headquarters by 9am, which means that if you're coming from KK, you should plan to leave by 7am – or consider spending the night somewhere near the base of the mountain.

Around Kinabalu

Kinabalu National Park is home to Borneo's highest mountain and some of the island's best-preserved rainforest. Most travellers make a beeline for the mountain and the main park headquarters area, but the following spots are also worth exploring.

Sights & Activities

Kundasang War Memorial MEMORIAL
(Kundasang; admission RM10; ⊙8am-5.30pm) Has bucolic English and Anzac gardens commemorating the WWII POWsS who died on the Sandakan Death March. Situated on the KK–Ranau highway 10km east of Kinabalu National Park headquarters; take the turn-off for Mesilau Nature Resort.

Poring Hot Springs HOT SPRINGS
(admission RM15) Steaming, sulphurous water is channelled into manmade pools and tubs where visitors can relax their tired muscles after summiting Mt Kinabalu. Don't forget a towel and your swimming trunks.

The highlight here is the **Canopy Walkway** (RM15; ⊙9am-4pm), a series of walkways suspended from trees up to 40m above the jungle floor that provides unique views of the rainforest canopy. Get here early if you want to see birds or other wildlife. You can also visit the **Tropical Garden** (admission RM3; ⊙9am-4pm), **Butterfly Farm** (admission RM4; ⊙9am-4pm Tue-Sun) and **Orchid Garden** (admission RM10; ⊙9am-4pm). Giant *Rafflesia* flowers sometimes bloom in the area; keep an eye out for signs in the visitors centre and along the road.

Poring Hot Springs are officially part of Kinabalu National Park, whose HQ is 43km away.

Sleeping

If you've got time, it's worth spending a night around the base of Kinabalu before your ascent.

The accommodation at Mesilau and Poring – like that at park HQ – is run by Sutera Sanctuary Lodges, so brace yourself for bed rates as high as Mt Kinabalu. Fortunately, there are also plenty of privately owned sleeping options looping around Kinabalu's base. Most of these are located along the road between the park headquarters and Kundasang (ie east of the park's entrance).

Mountain Guest House LODGE $
(☎016-837 4040, 888632; dm/s/d incl breakfast from RM20/60/70) A good choice if you're on a tight budget, with clean rooms and some shocking pink bedspreads.

D'Villa Rina Ria Lodge LODGE $$
(☎889282; www.dvillalodge.com.my; dm/r RM30/120; @) A charming lodge run by exceptionally friendly staff. Has cute, cosy rooms and a dining area with a lovely mountain view.

Strawberry Garden Hotel LODGE $$
(☎889309, 019-842 4015; bs_tours@streamyx.com; Kundasang; r RM70-140) Looks a bit institutional from the highway but interior rooms are good value for money, with clean tile floors and comfy beds.

Getting There & Around

Buses to/from KK stop in front of park headquarters and in Ranau (RM15, two hours) from 7am to 8pm.

In Ranau, minivans (RM5) serving nearby attractions (park HQ, Poring etc) operate from a blue-roofed shelter.

The national park operates a van service between the headquarters and Poring (RM25) at noon.

Sandakan

089 / POP 450,400

With a colourful history of slow boats and fast women, Sandakan has been a dot on many a trader's map for centuries. After the nearby natural wonders – Sepilok and an idyllic tropical archipelago – the city's biggest draw is its turbulent history, retold through religious relics, haunting cemeteries and stunning colonial mansions. Modern Sandakan has plenty of character and even a certain grubby charm, though once the shop shutters come down in the evening the centre can feel a bit deserted. Nights are best spent singing karaoke, clinking cocktails at sunset and devouring fresh seafood.

Sights

Central Sandakan is light on attractions, although history buffs will appreciate the *Sandakan Heritage Trail* brochure available at the tourist office. See also www.sandakan-deathmarch.com.

Agnes Keith House HISTORIC HOUSE
(Jln Istana; RM15; 9am-5pm) On the hill above town, this two-storey wooden house shelters a museum dedicated to Agnes Keith, an American who came to Sandakan with her husband in the 1930s and ended up writing several books about her experiences, including the famous *Land Below the Wind*. To get here, follow Jln Singapura from the city centre and turn right up the hill, or head up the Tangga Seribu (100 Steps) to Jln Residensi Drive and turn left.

TOP CHOICE **Sandakan Memorial Park** MEMORIAL
(Taman Peringatan; admission free; 9am-5pm) Now just a quiet patch of woods, this was the site of a Japanese POW camp and the starting point of the infamous Death Marches to Ranau. Of the 1800 Australian and 600 British troops imprisoned here, by July 1945 the only survivors were six Australian escapees. To reach the park, take any Batu 8 (or higher-numbered) bus from the local bus terminal in the city centre (RM1.80), get off at the 'Taman Rimba' signpost and walk down Jln Rimba. A taxi from downtown costs about RM20 one way.

Sleeping

If you're only passing through Sandakan on your way to see the orang-utans, you're better off staying at Sepilok, about 25km from town.

Sandakan Backpackers HOSTEL $
(221104; www.sandakanbackpackers.com; Lot 108, Block SH-11, Harbour Sq Complex; dm/s/d RM25/40/60; @) Clean, well lit, affordable and a decent place to meet other citizens of Backpackistan.

Sandakan Harbour Square B&B HOTEL $
(223582; www.shsbnb.com; HS10, Harbour Sq Complex; dm RM20, d with/without bathroom RM45/40; @) A modern, somewhat cookie-cutter budget spot for crashing out. Service is friendly and personable, and fan dorms are dirt cheap (but not dirty). Next to the KFC.

Eating

For an authentic Malay meal, head to the KFC in the waterfront Harbour Sq Complex – but don't eat there! Head to the nearby restaurants, which are cheap and flavourful. Most are standard Malay *kedai kopi*, with prices that rarely top RM6 per main dish; all are open from roughly 9am to 9pm.

New Market MARKET $
(Jln Pryor; 7am-2pm) The upstairs food stalls (Chinese, Malay, Indonesian and Filipino) are the best place in town for a cheap breakfast or lunch.

Drinking

If you're wondering where everyone goes in the evening, just hop in a taxi to Bandar Indah, commonly known as Mile 4 or Batu 4. This buzzing grid of two-storey shophouses is the playground of choice for locals and expats alike, packed with restaurants, bars, karaoke lounges and nightclubs.

TOP CHOICE **Balin** LOUNGE
(272988; www.nakhotel.com; Jln Pelabuhan Lama; drinks from RM7, mains from RM15; lunch & dinner) Bringing a certain LA rooftop sexiness to Sandakan, Balin is your best bet for nightlife in the city centre. The three tiers of uberchill lounge space are accented by a

factory's worth of pillows and some genuinely classy cocktails that any boutique 'mixologist' bar in London or New York would be justifiably jealous of.

Information

Cyber Cafe (3rd fl, Wisma Sandakan, Lebuh Empat; per hr RM3; ⏲9am-9pm)

Duchess of Kent Hospital (☎219460; Mile 2, Jln Utara)

MayBank (Lebuh Tiga) Has a full-service bank, an ATM and a sidewalk currency-exchange window (open daily from 9am to 5pm).

Tourist Information Centre (☎229751; Wisma Warisan; ⏲8am-12.30pm & 1.30-4.30pm Mon-Thu, 8-11.30am & 2-4.30pm Friday) Located opposite the municipal offices (known as MPS) and up the stairs from Lebuh Tiga.

Getting There & Away

Air

Malaysia Airlines (☎1-300-883000; www.malaysiaairlines.com; cnr Jln Pelabuhan Lama & Lebuh Dua) has daily flights to/from KK and KL; it's subsidiary, **MASwings**, in the same office, has one daily flight to/from Tawau and two to/from KK. **AirAsia** (☎222737; 1st & 2nd fl, Airport) serves KL and KK.

Bus

Buses and minibuses to KK, Lahad Datu, Semporna and Tawau leave from the long-distance bus station, situated in a large parking lot at Batu 2.5, 4km north of town. Most express buses to KK (RM33 to RM40, six hours) leave between 7am and 2pm. All pass the turn-off to Kinabalu National Park headquarters.

Buses depart regularly for Lahad Datu (RM20, 2½ hours) and Tawau (RM35, 5½ hours). There's also a bus to Semporna (RM30, 5½ hours) at 8am; if you miss it, head to Lahad Datu, then catch a minivan to Semporna.

Minivans depart throughout the morning from Batu 2.5 for Ranau (RM26, four hours) and Lahad Datu (some of those continuing to Tawau). Minivans for Sukau (RM15) leave from a lot behind Centre Point Mall in town.

Getting Around

The airport is 11km from the city centre. Batu 7 Airport bus (RM1.80) stops on the main road about 500m from the terminal. A coupon taxi to the town centre costs RM30; going the other way expect to pay about RM25.

Buses run from 6am to 6pm on the main road to the north, Jln Utara, designated by how far from town they go, eg Batu (mile) 8. Fares range from RM1 to RM4.

GETTING TO THE PHILIPPINES: SANDAKAN TO ZAMBOANGA

Getting to the border **Weesam Express** (☎212872; ground fl, Hotel New Sabah, Jln Singapura, Sandakan) links Sandakan with Zamboanga (2nd/1st class RM200/280), on the Philippine island of Mindanao. Ferries depart Sandakan harbour at 6am on Tuesday and Friday, arriving in Zamboanga at 7.30pm the same day.

At the border Travellers we spoke to said you don't need an onward ticket to enter the Philippines, but the Filipino government says otherwise; it may be wise to have one just in case. Because of lawlessness and an Islamist insurgency, Western embassies warn against travel to or through western Mindanao, including Zamboanga, so check local conditions before taking this ferry.

Local minivans wait behind Centre Point Mall; fares cost from RM2. Use for the Pasir Putih seafood restaurants and the harbour area.

To reach the long-distance bus station, catch a local bus (RM1.50, 20 minutes) from the stand at the waterfront.

Taxis cruise the town centre and park near main hotels. Many hotels will steer you toward a preferred driver – not a bad thing. It's RM12 to Bandar Indah and RM40 for a lift to Sepilok.

Sepilok

☎089

Sepilok's Orangutan Rehabilitation Centre (SORC) is the most popular place on earth to see Asia's great ginger ape in its native habitat. Those with time to stick around can also take scenic nature walks, visit a sanctuary for the elusive proboscis monkey and find a couple of great places to call home for a night or two.

Sights & Activities

TOP CHOICE **Sepilok Orangutan Rehabilitation Centre** PRIMATE SANCTUARY (SORC; ☎531180; soutan@po.jaring.my; admission RM30, camera RM10; ⏲9-11am & 2-3.30pm) One of only four orang-utan sanctuaries in the world, Sepilok is about 25km north of Sandakan. Established in 1964, it now covers 40 sq km and has become one of Sabah's top tourist attractions, second only to Mt Kinabalu.

Feedings – to supplement the orang-utans' natural diet of forest fruits – are at 10am and 3pm and last 30 to 50 minutes. Tickets are valid for the whole day, so if the apes don't show in the morning you can come back in the afternoon. Tour groups tend to be most numerous in the morning. A worthwhile 20-minute video about Sepilok's work is shown five times daily (9am, 11am, noon, 2.10pm and 3.30pm) in the auditorium opposite reception.

Several walking trails, ranging from 250m to 4km, lead into the forest; register at the visitor reception centre to use them.

Rainforest Discovery Centre OUTDOOR MUSEUM
(RDC; ☎533780; www.forest.sabah.gov.my/rdc; admission RM10; ⌚8am-5pm) About 1.5km from SORC, the RDC and its botanical garden offer an engaging introduction to tropical flora and fauna. A series of eight canopy towers are being built, and you can book night walks. It's best to get here either at 8am or 4pm, as wildlife tends to hide away during the sweltering hours in the middle of the day.

Labuk Bay Proboscis Monkey Sanctuary PRIMATE RESERVE
(☎672133; www.sabahtourism.com; RM60, camera RM10, video RM20) Named for their long bulbous noses, proboscis monkeys are pot-bellied and red-faced, and males are constantly, unmistakably…aroused. A local palm plantation owner has created a 6 sq-km sanctuary, attracting the floppy-schnozzed creatures with sugar-free pancakes at 11.40am and 4.30pm; there's often a third feeding at 2.30pm as part of a ranger-led hike deeper in the sanctuary. A half-day visit costs RM150 from Sepilok and RM160 from Sandakan, including transfers. Overnight trips with meals and a night walk start at RM250.

If you're going to be in Kuching, it's cheaper and easier to see proboscis monkeys at Bako National Park.

Sleeping

Most accommodation options are scattered along Jln Sepilok, the 2.5km-long access road to the rehabilitation centre.

TOP CHOICE **Paganakan Dii** LODGE $$
(☎532005; www.paganakandii.com; dm/chalet RM30/150; ❄📶) A quiet, welcoming retreat deep within a deer preserve, just past a public park. Chic design details made from recycled materials and a ridiculously friendly staff will have you convinced the owners left a zero off the price tag.

Sepilok Forest Edge Resort RESORT $$
(☎533190, 533245; www.sepilokforestedge.com; dm/d/chalet from RM30/70/180; ❄🏊) The serviceable dorm beds and double rooms are located in a pretty longhouse, while the comfortable cabins are scattered across obsessively maintained acreage (think golf course).

Sepilok B&B LODGE $
(☎534050, 019-8330901; www.sepilokbednbreakfast.com; Jln Arboretum; dm/s/d RM23/40/60) Stark and simple yet cosy, with something of a summer-camp vibe. Crooked picnic tables and varnished lounge chairs offer plenty of room to chill out after a sweaty day of orang-utanning. Situated opposite the forest research centre, about 250m off Jln Sepilok and 1km short of the SORC entrance.

Uncle Tan's LODGE $
(☎531639, 535784; www.uncletan.com; dm/tw incl all meals RM38/100; ❄@) A couple of decent thatch-roofed gazebos and a stack of backpacker shacks.

Information

There's an ATM at the Petronas Station on the road between Sandakan and Sepilok. The next closest ATM is at Sandakan Airport.

Getting There & Away

Sepilok is located at 'Batu 14' – that is, it's 14 miles (23km) from Sandakan.

From Sandakan's city centre, bus 14 (RM3) departs hourly. If you're coming from KK, take a Sandakan-bound bus and ask the driver to let you off at 'Batu 14'.

Taxi 'pirates', as they're known, wait at Batu 14 to give tourists a ride into Sepilok. It's RM3 per person for a lift. Travellers spending the night can arrange a lift with their accommodation if they book ahead of time. Walking to the SORC is also an option – it's only 2.5km.

If you are planning to head to Sungai Kinabatangan in the afternoon, you can usually organise transport from Sepilok after the morning orang-utan feeding.

Sungai Kinabatangan

The Kinabatangan River is Sabah's longest: 560km of water so chocolate-y brown it would pose a serious safety risk to Augustus Gloop.

DON'T MISS

HOMESTAYS ON THE KINABATANGAN

Great little homestay programs are popping up with increasing frequency in Sukau, Bilit and other Kinabatangan villages, giving tourists a unique opportunity to stay with local Orang Sungai – and inject money almost directly into the local economy. The contacts below are for homestay program coordinators who will place you with individual families.

» **Bali Kito Homestay** (☎013-869 9026; http://sukauhomestay.com; sukauhomestay@yahoo.com; r from RM50) In Sukau.

» **Bilit Village Homestay** (☎013-891 3078, 019-537 0843, 019-853-4997; http://bilithomestay.wordpress.com; bilit2002@hotmail.com; r from RM55) In tiny Bilit, we often wondered which houses *weren't* homestays.

» **Mescot/Miso Walai Homestay** (☎089-551064, 551070; www.misowalaihomestay.com; r RM70) Located near Batu Pulih, the village adjacent to the Batu Tulug caves. One of the oldest and best-run community ecotourism initiatives in the area.

Rainforest lines the river bank, swarming with wild creatures, some of them fleeing ever-encroaching palm-oil plantations. Dozens of tin boats putter along the shores offering tourists the opportunity to have a close encounter with a rhinoceros hornbill or perhaps a doe-eyed orang-utan.

River cruises are exceedingly popular and these days dozens of lodges are vying for your precious ringgit. A 'three-day/two-night' stint usually involves the following: arrive in the afternoon on day one for a cruise at dusk, two boat rides (or a boat/hike combo) on day two, and an early morning departure on day three after breakfast and a sunrise cruise. When booking ask about the cost of pick-up and drop-off – this is usually extra.

Sleeping

If you are planning to visit Sungai Kinabatangan on your own, Sukau is your best option for lodging and river tours.

Sukau Greenview B&B LODGE $
(☎013-869 6922, 089-565266; sukau_greenview@yahoo.com; s/tw RM45/60, meals RM10) Basic but comfy enough for the price, with nine rooms (with twin beds) in a small cottage-style lodge. River cruises cost RM35, night rides are RM45 and trips to Oxbow Lake are RM45 per person.

Barefoot Sukau Lodge LODGE $
(☎089-235525; www.barefootsukau.com; r per person RM80, meals RM25) The best budget option in Sukau outside of the homestays.

Sukau B&B LODGE $
(☎019-583 5580, 089-565269; dm/s/tw incl breakfast RM20/40/40) This is as budget as the Kinabatangan gets. The road leading into Sukau ends here: a grassy knoll with longhouse-style accommodation and a small cottage in the back.

Information

There's an **internet cafe** (per hr RM1.50; ⏲9am-6pm) in the cream building on the main road.

Getting There & Away

Taking a public bus instead of tour-operated transport to – or at least near – Sungai Kinabatangan can save you quite a bit of cash.

To reach Sungai Kinabatangan by bus from KK, board a Tawau- or Lahad Datu–bound bus (RM35) and ask the driver to let you off at 'Sukau Junction,' also known as 'Meeting Point' – the turnoff road to Sukau. If you're on a Sandakan-bound bus, make sure your driver remembers to stop at the Tawau–Sandakan junction – it's called 'Batu 32' or 'Checkpoint' (sometimes it's also known as Sandakan Mile 32).

From Sepilok or Sandakan, expect to pay around RM15 to reach 'Batu 32', and around RM20 if you're on a Sandakan–Tawau bus and want to alight at 'Meeting Point'.

You can arrange transport from these drop-off points with your tour operator or with a local minivan.

Danum Valley Conservation Area

At any given time, more than a hundred scientists are conducting research in the Danum Valley, a steaming, primary rainforest teeming with orang-utans, tarsiers, sambar deer, bearded pigs, flying squirrels, proboscis monkeys, gibbons and pygmy elephants (to name a few). For visitors, the main activities are walking 50km of marked, meandering trails. Birdwatchers from around the world flock here to spot rare rainforest species, including several types of hornbill.

Sleeping & Eating

The only two places to stay are a very luxurious resort and a budget-priced research centre where the main priority is accommodating scientists as opposed to, well, you. You must have accommodation arranged with one of them before you visit.

Danum Valley Field Centre LODGE $$
(DVFC; ☎089-8841100/1, 088-881688; camping RM30, resthouse r & board from RM160; ❄) An outpost for scientists and researchers, the field centre also welcomes tourists to its hostel, resthouse, VIP accommodation and camping spots (no tent needed but bug spray recommended). Tourists take their meals in the cafeteria-style canteen (vegie friendly).

Getting There & Away

The Danum Valley is accessible only by authorised private vehicle. Tourists staying at the Danum Valley Field Centre must board one of two jungle-bound vans (per person RM100) that leave the booking office in Lahad Datu at 3.30pm on Monday, Wednesday and Friday. Vans return to Lahad Datu at 8.30am on the same days. Chartering a private vehicle into the park costs at least RM300.

Semporna

☎089 / POP 140,000

Semporna (the town) on the mainland is a lacklustre layover that may snag you for a night on your way to Semporna (the archipelago) and all your diving/snorkelling fantasies. Due to large numbers of tough-looking young men hanging around, this is one of the few places in Sabah where we felt a bit uncomfortable at night.

Scuba is the town's lifeline, and there's no shortage of places to sign up for some serious bubble blowing. Operators are clustered around the 'Semporna Seafront', while other companies have offices in KK. It's highly recommended to do your homework and book ahead – diving at Pulau Sipadan is limited to 120 people per day.

Sleeping

If you have to overnight in Semporna, your options are limited – but not dire. If you've already signed up with a scuba operator, ask them about sleeping discounts – and don't be shy about trying to finagle a good deal.

Dragon Inn HOTEL $
(Rumah Rehat Naga; ☎781088; www.dragoninnfloating.com.my; 1 Jln Kastam; dm RM15-20, r incl breakfast RM70-99; ❄@) The tiki tropical decor is a bit tacky but in an endearing way.

Scuba Junkie HOSTEL $
(☎785372; www.scuba-junkie.com; Lot 36, Block B, Semporna Seafront; dm/r RM40/100; ❄@) A sociable, clean and basic spot.

Borneo Global Sipadan HOSTEL $
(☎785088; borneogb@gmail.com; Jln Causeway; dm/tr incl breakfast RM22/90; ❄) Cheap and cheerful, if rather lacking in character.

GETTING TO INDONESIA: TAWAU TO NUNUKAN & TARAKAN

Getting to the border Ferries (Tawindo Express, ☎089-774277; Indomaya Express, ☎089-772559) link Tawau, in Sabah's southeastern corner, with the Kalimantan islands of Nunukan (RM65, one hour, departures 10am and 3pm Monday to Saturday) and Tarakan (RM130, three or four hours, departures 11.30am Monday, Wednesday and Friday, and 10.30am Tuesday, Thursday and Saturday).

At the border Tawau is the only crossing point between Sabah and Kalimantan where foreigners can get a visa to enter Indonesia. The Indonesian consulate (☎089-772052, 089-752969; Jln Sinn Onn, Tuwau; ⌚9am-noon & 1-3pm) is known for being fast and efficient – many travellers are in and out in an hour.

Moving on From Tarakan, eight boats run daily to Tanjung Selor (200,000Rp, 1½ hours), on the mainland, from Pelabuhan Tengkayu on Jln Yos Sudarso, opposite the post office. Pelni (☎51169; Jln Yos Sudarso) ships steam to Makassar and Pare Pare (both on Sulawesi) and Surabaya (Java) from Pelabuhan Malundung, the main harbour at the south end of Jln Yos Sudarso. Travel agents are generally more helpful than Pelni's office.

See p270 for information about crossing in the other direction.

Getting There & Away

Flights to Tawau from KK and KL land at Tawau airport, roughly 28km from town. A private taxi from Tawau airport to Semporna costs RM90, but Tawau–Semporna buses (RM15) will stop at the airport if you ask the driver nicely. Remember that flying less than 24 hours after diving can cause serious health issues, even death.

The bus terminal hovers around the Milimewa supermarket, not too far from the mosque's looming minaret. Destinations include Kota Kinabalu (RM50, nine hours, departures at about 7am and 7pm) and, from early morning until 4pm, Tawau (RM15, 1½ hours), Lahad Datu (RM20 to RM25, 2½ hours) and Sandakan (RM35 to RM40, 5½ hours).

Semporna Archipelago

Take the word 'blue' and mentally turn it over through all of its possibilities, from the deepest, richest shades to the robin egg tones of the sky at noon: this is the rippled waterscape of the Semporna Archipelago, accented with rainbow-coloured boats, swaying palms and white sand. But no one comes this way just for the island beaches – it's the ocean and everything in it that appeals because, first and foremost, this is a diving destination, one of the best in the world.

Activities

Located 36km off Sabah's southeast coast, **Sipadan** (Pulau Sipidan; www.sabahparks.org.my) is the shining star in the archipelago's constellation of shimmering islands. The macrodiving around **Mabul** (Pulau Mabul), too, is world-famous. In fact, the term 'muck diving' was invented here. The submerged sites around **Kapalai**, **Mataking** and **Sibuan** are also of note.

The following dive operators are among the growing list of companies serving the area. It is *highly* recommended that you book in advance.

Billabong Scuba (☎089-781866; www.billabongscuba.com; Lot 28, Block E, Semporna Seafront) Semporna-based outfit with reasonable prices.

Blue Sea Divers (☎089-781322; www.blueseadivers-sabah.com; Semporna Seafront) Reputable day-trip operator in Semporna.

Borneo Divers (☎088-222226; www.borneodivers.info; 9th fl, Menara Jubili, 53 Jalan Gaya, Kota Kinabalu) The original operators in the area, Borneo Divers unveiled Sipadan to an awestruck Jacques Cousteau.

DECOMPRESSION

The closest **decompression chamber** (☎089-783100) is at the naval base in Semporna.

Scuba Junkie (☎089-785372; www.scuba-junkie.com; Lot 36, Block B, Semporna Seafront) Popular with the young backpacker crowd, Scuba Junkie invented the hard sell in Semporna.

Scuba Jeff (☎019-5855125, 017-8690218; www.scubajeffsipadan.com) Based in the fishing village in Mabul. Good option for the budget crowd.

Sipadan Scuba (☎089-784788, 089-919128; www.sipadanscuba.com; Lot 23, Block D, Semporna Seafront) The only PADI 5 Star Instructor Development Centre in Semporna.

Uncle Chang's (Borneo Jungle River Island Tours; ☎089-785372; 36 Semporna Seafront) Offers diving and snorkelling day trips, plus stays on Mabul or Maiga (RM80 per person).

Sleeping

Sleeping spots – generally with all meals included – are sprinkled across the archipelago, with the majority of options clustered on the peach-fringed island of Mabul. (Sleepovers are banned on Sipidan itself.) Divers and snorkellers can also opt to stay in the town of Semporna, which offers slightly more bang for your buck, but you'll miss out on post-dive chill sessions along flaxen strips of sand.

A pretty little speck of land, Mabul is blessed with one very small, white-sand beach, fantastically blue waters and two small settlements: a camp of Bajau sea gypsies and a Malaysian stilt village.

Mabul Beach Resort LODGE **$$**
(☎089-785372; www.scuba-junkie.com; dm RM80, r RM150-270; ❄📶) All the rage with the flashpacker crowd. Chalets come with en suite bathrooms, porches and polished wood floors.

Scuba Jeff LODGE **$**
(☎019-5855125, 017-8690218; www.scubajeffsipadan.com; r RM60-80) A tatty place that's great for meeting random folks on a budget (including quite a few backpacking Malays).

Arung Hayat Resort LODGE **$**
(☎089-782526; www.arunghayat.com; per person r/ste RM70/90) A friendly homestay with low-

slung beds, baby-blue walls and plenty of smiles. In a stilthouse over the water.

Uncle Chang's LODGE $
(☎017-895002, 089-786988; www.ucsipadan.com; per person dm/s/d RM60/80/90, per person d with air-con & private bathroom RM90; ❄) A fun, sociable spot that periodically throws kicking little parties. The air-con rooms are good value for money.

Billabong LODGE $
(☎089-781866; www.billabongscuba.com; per person r RM70) Chill with fishermen, watch the sunset over the plank boards and set out for some diving adventures with associated Billabong Scuba.

Lai's Homestay LODGE $
(per person r RM70) Features a large, wood-planked verandah stretching over the sea. The rooms are clean and breezy.

Getting There & Around

All transport to the marine park is funnelled through the town of Semporna. Your accommodation (book ahead!) will take care of your transport needs, usually for an extra fee.

Beaufort District

This shield-shaped peninsula on Sabah's southwestern coast is a marshy plain marked with curling rivers and fringed by golden dunes. Tourists with tight travel schedules should consider doing a wildlife river cruise here if they don't have time to reach Sungai Kinabatangan. You can book trips to Beaufort's rivers in any of the travel agencies on the ground floor of Wisma Sabah in KK (p436), or through any KK guesthouse.

Sights & Activities

The tea-brown **Sungai Klias** looks somewhat similar to the mighty Kinabatangan, offering short-stay visitors the chance to spend an evening observing free-range primates. Several companies offer two-hour river cruises, including **Borneo Authentic** (☎088-773066; www.borneo-authentic.com; package trip RM150; ⏲5pm), whose trips include a large buffet dinner and a short night walk to view swarms of fireflies.

Narrower than the Klias, **Sungai Garama** is another popular river for buffet dinner cruises from KK. **Only In Borneo** (☎088-260506; www.oibtours.com; package tour RM190; ⏲5pm) has a well-maintained facility along the shores of Sungai Garama and offers an overnight option in dorms or doubles.

Getting There & Away

Express buses to KK (RM10, 1½ hours, four daily) and Sipitang (RM4.50, 1½ hours, four daily) stop near the old train station at the south end of Jln Masjid.

Minivans to KK (RM10, two hours), and less frequently to Sipitang (RM12, 1½ hours), Lawas (RM15, 1¾ hours) and Menumbok (for Labuan; RM8, one hour), stop across from the mosque at the north end of Jln Masjid.

Pulau Labuan

☎087 / POP 95,000

Pulau Labuan is Sabah's version of Vegas, but if you're expecting shmancy hotels and prostitutes you're only half-right... The island doesn't feel seedy though; in fact, think of Labuan as a giant airport terminal – everything is duty-free because politically the island is a federal territory governed directly from KL. The main town, Bandar Labuan, is the transit point for ferries linking Kota Kinabalu and Brunei. WWII buffs will find several sights of interest, including the **Labuan War Cemetery** (Jln OKK Abdullah).

Sleeping

TOP CHOICE **Labuan's Homestay Program** HOMESTAY $
(☎422622; www.labuantourism.com.my; 1-/2-day stay incl full board RM65/140) This excellent service matches visitors with friendly locals in one of three villages around the island. If you want to be near Bandar Labuan, ask for accommodation at Patau Patau 2 – it's a charming stilt village out on the bay. Stay a bit longer and learn how to make *ambuyat*, a surprising Bruneian dish.

ASV Backpackers HOSTEL $
(☎413728; asvjau@yahoo.com; Lot U0101, Jln Merdeka; r with shared bathroom RM35; ❄) Cheap but cleaner and more comfortable than most of the dingy midrangers around town.

Getting There & Away

Malaysia Airlines (☎1300-883000; www.malaysiaairlines.com.my) has flights to/from KK and KL, while **AirAsia** (☎087-480401; www.airasia.com) flies to KL.

Passenger ferries (1st/economy class RM39/31, 3¼ hours) leave KK for Labuan from Monday to Saturday at 8am and 1.30pm (3pm on Sunday). In the opposite direction, they depart Labuan from Monday to Saturday at 8am and 1pm (10.30am and 3pm on Sunday).

For details on car ferries to/from Brunei's Serasa Ferry Terminal in Muara, see p61. For information on the somewhat irregular speedboats to Limbang and Lawas in Sarawak's Limbang Division, see p469.

MALAYSIAN BORNEO – SARAWAK

Sarawak makes access to Borneo's natural wonders and cultural riches a breeze. Base yourself in Kuching, Borneo's most sophisticated and dynamic city. From here you can make day trips to pristine rainforests, where you can spot orang-utans, proboscis monkeys, killer crocodiles and the world's largest flower, the *Rafflesia*, with plenty of time in the evening for a delicious meal and a drink in a chic bar back in town. More adventurous travellers can take a 'flying coffin' riverboat up the Batang Rejang, 'the Amazon of Borneo', to seek out remote longhouses, or fly to the spectacular bat caves and extraordinary rock formations of Gunung Mulu National Park, a Unesco World Heritage Site. Everywhere you go, you'll encounter the warmth, unforced friendliness and sense of humour that make the people of Sarawak such delightful hosts.

Kuching

☎082 / POP 600,000

The capital of Sarawak brings together a kaleidoscope of cultures, crafts and cuisines. The old Chinatown and bustling markets amply reward visitors with a penchant for aimless ambling. Chinese temples decorated with dragons abut shophouses dating from the time of the White Rajas; a South Indian mosque is a five-minute walk from stalls selling half a dozen Asian cuisines; and a landscaped riverfront park attracts families out for a stroll and a quick bite.

Kuching's other huge asset is its day-trip proximity to a dozen first-rate nature sites.

Sights & Activities

While Kuching ('cat' in Bahasa Malaysia) has some great museums, colourful temples and historic sites to keep you occupied, the main attraction here is the city itself. Leave plenty of time to wander aimlessly and soak up the relaxed vibe and charming cityscapes of areas such as Chinatown, Jln India, the Waterfront Promenade and Jln Padungan.

Sarawak's museums, which are free, are open every day of the year, except on the first day of two-day public holidays.

TOP CHOICE Waterfront Promenade PARK
(along Main Bazaar & Jln Gambier) The south bank of Sungai Sarawak has been turned into a watery promenade offering great views of the **Astana** (official residence of the governor of Sarawak since 1869), Fort Margherita and the **Sarawak State Assembly**, with its golden, pointy roof. Great for a stroll anytime a cool breeze blows off the river, especially at sunset.

Jalan Carpenter STREET
Lined with evocative, colonial-era shophouses and home to several colourful Chinese temples, Jln Carpenter – Kuching's old-time Chinatown – stretches from ornamental **Harmony Arch** (cnr Jln Tun Abang Haji Openg) eastward to **Hong San Si Temple** (cnr Jln Wayang), also known by its Hokkien name, Say Ong Kong.

Jalan India PEDESTRIAN STREET
Many of the shops along this exuberant commercial thoroughfare are run by Indian Muslims. Turn off Jln India (between Nos 37 and 39A) or Jln Gambier (between Nos 24 and 25A) onto tiny **Indian Mosque Lane** (Jln Sempit) and you enter another world, anchored by Kuching's oldest **mosque** (Indian Mosque Lane; ⏲6am-8.30pm except during prayers), built in 1863 by Muslim traders from Tamil Nadu.

TOP CHOICE Sarawak Museum MUSEUM
(☎244232; www.museum.sarawak.gov.my; Jln Tun Abang Haji Openg; ⏲9am-4.30pm) Has a first-rate collection of cultural artefacts and is a must-visit for anyone interested in Borneo's peoples and habitats. In the **Old Building** (west side of Jln Tun Abang Haji Openg), on the top of the hill, the upstairs ethnography section has superb exhibits on Dayak crafts, customs and longhouses. Downstairs is an old-fashioned natural history museum whose highlight, some say, is a hairball taken from the stomach of a man-eating crocodile. Across the street (and linked by a footbridge), **Dewan Tun Abdul Razak** (New Bldg; west side of Jln Tun Abang Haji Openg) has exhibits on Sarawakian history and archaeology.

Chinese History Museum MUSEUM
(cnr Main Bazaar & Jln Wayang; ⏲9am-4.30pm) Provides an excellent introduction to the

LAND OF THE HEADHUNTERS

Headhunting has been relegated to the realm of Dayaks' self-deprecating witticisms, but for over 500 years it was an important element of Borneo's indigenous culture.

Many of the rites, rituals and beliefs surrounding this gruesome tradition remain shrouded in mystery, but we know that one aspect was unchanging: the act of taking heads was always treated with the utmost seriousness.

The hunters of heads bore no personal animosity to their victims. After a successful hunt, the warrior would wander the jungle, wrestling with the taken spirit rather than letting down his guard for a nap. In the morning, he would return to his longhouse where the head would be smoked and strung up for the others to see and honour. Heads were worshipped and revered, and food offerings were not uncommon. A longhouse with many heads was feared and respected by the neighbouring clans.

The tradition began its gradual decline in 1841 when James Brooke, at the behest of Brunei's sultan, started quashing the hunt for heads, in part to attract foreign traders, who had tended to keep their distance due to the island's fearsome reputation for harbouring ferocious cranium-nabbing natives.

During WWII, British commandos found headhunting useful for the war effort – so long as the victims were Japanese troops. Many of the heads that now adorn longhouses date from this period.

As Borneo's indigenous people embraced Christianity and rejected traditional animistic superstitions, many longhouses dismantled their dangling skulls. Though if you ask around, you'll quickly learn that the heads haven't actually been tossed away – that would just be bad luck!

nine Chinese communities – each with its own dialect, cuisine and temples – who began settling in Sarawak around 1830. The entrance is on the river side of the building.

Fort Margherita FORT
(north bank of Sungai Sarawak, Kampung Boyan; ⏲9am-4.30pm) Inspired by an English Renaissance castle, whitewashed Fort Margherita (1879) manages to feel medieval European and tropical. A steep spiral staircase leads up three flights of stairs to the crenellated roof. To get here, take a *tambang* (boat; 50 sen) from the Waterfront Promenade to Kampung Boyan and then follow the signs for 500m.

Satok Weekend Market MARKET
(Pasar Minggu; Jln Satok; ⏲about noon-10pm Sat, 6am-1pm or 2pm Sun) At Kuching's biggest and liveliest market, rural folk, some from area longhouses, arrive with their fruits, vegies, fish and spices. Situated about 1km west of the Sarawak Museum – from the centre, walk south on Jln Tun Abang Haji Openg and turn west at Jln Satok (under the flyover).

Sleeping

Kuching's accommodation options range from international-standard suites with high-rise views to musty, windowless cells deep inside converted Chinese shophouses. Most of the budget places are in or near Chinatown, while the top-end spots are a bit to the east, on or near Jln Tunku Abdul Rahman. There's a cluster of small, cheap hotels in the ugly commercial blocks along L-shaped Jln Green Hill. In most budget guesthouses, the majority of the rooms – especially those under RM50 – have shared bathrooms. Prices at some guesthouses rise in July, or from June to September.

TOP CHOICE **Singgahsana Lodge** GUESTHOUSE $
(☎429277; www.singgahsana.com; 1 Jln Temple; dm RM30, d with share/private bathroom RM88/98; ❄@☜) This hugely popular guesthouse, decked out with stylish Dayak crafts, has an unbeatable location, a great chill-out lobby and a tropical rooftop bar. Organises group trips to Kuching-area nature sites.

Diocesan Centre GUESTHOUSE $
(☎381442, 016-525-0468; bishopk@streamyx.com; Jln McDougall; s/d with share bathroom RM20/25, apt with bathroom & kitchen RM30-50; ⏲office 8.30am-approx 5pm Mon-Fri; ❄) The best ultra-budget deal in town, with 36 very basic but gloriously ventilated rooms. Has a bathroom on the ground floor and a night toilet on the 2nd floor. Enter from Jln McDougall. On weekdays after 5pm and on the weekend, call ☎016-5250468.

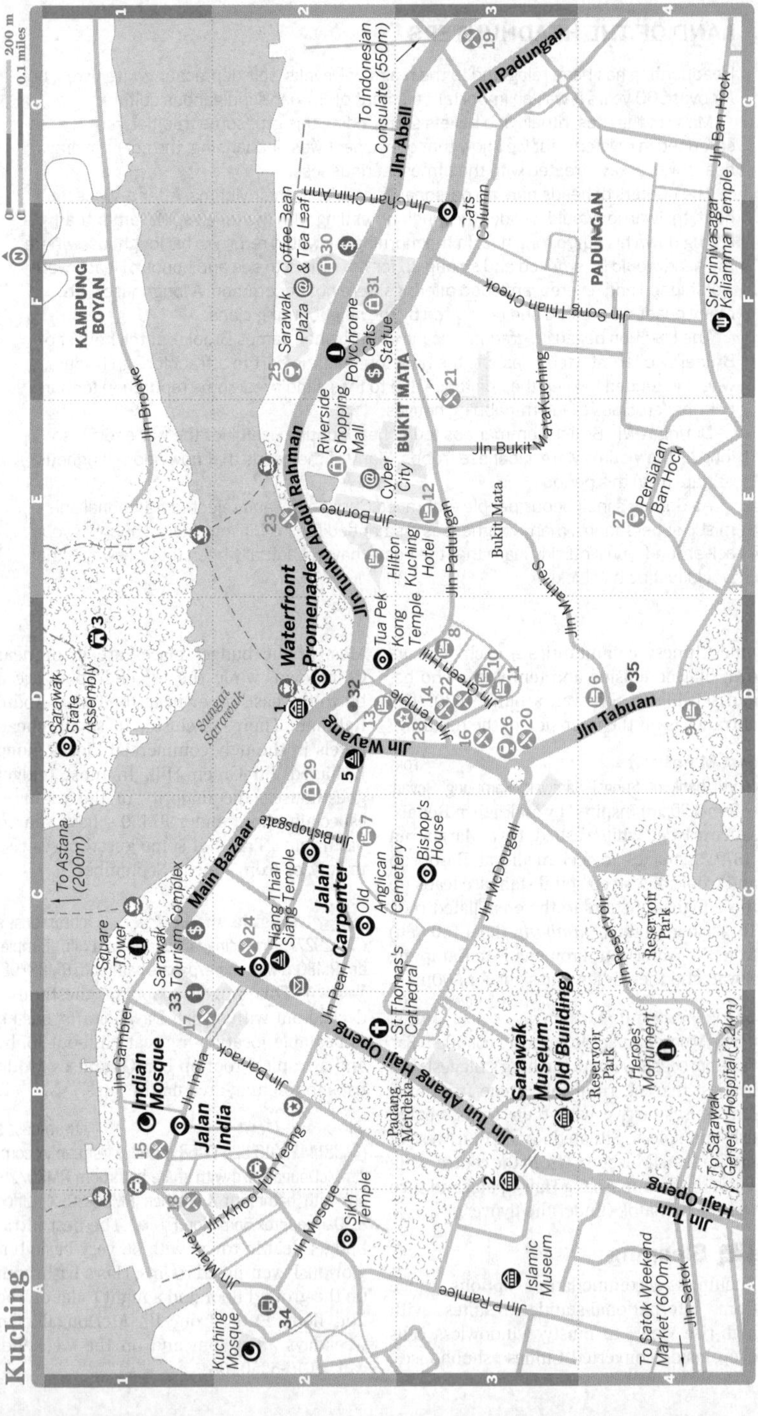

Kuching

0 200 m
0 0.1 miles

KAMPUNG BOYAN
Jln Brooke
Sarawak State Assembly
3
To Astana (200m)
Square Tower
Jln Gambier
Indian Mosque
15
18
Jalan India
Jln India
Jln Market
Jln Khoo Hun Yeang
Kuching Mosque
34
33
Sarawak Tourism Complex
17
Main Bazaar
Sungai Sarawak
4
24
Hiang Thian Siang Temple
Jln Barrack
Jln Mosque
Sikh Temple
Jln Pearl
Jalan Carpenter
Jln Bishopsgate
29
1
Waterfront Promenade
Jln Tunku Abdul Rahman
23
25
Sarawak Plaza
Coffee Bean & Tea Leaf
30
Jln Chan Chin Ann
To Indonesian Consulate (550m)
Jln Abell
Riverside Shopping Mall
Polychrome Cats Statue
31
Jln Borneo
Cyber City
BUKIT MATA
Hilton Kuching Hotel
12
Tua Pek Kong Temple
5
32
Jln Wayang
13
Old Anglican Cemetery
7
St Thomas's Cathedral
Padang Merdeka
Bishop's House
Jln Tun Abang Haji Openg
28
14
Jln Temple
22
Jln Green Hill
8
Jln Padungan
21
Cats Column
19
Jln Padungan
16
10
11
26
20
Jln McDougall
Bukit Mata
Jln Bukit MataKuching
Jln Song Thian Cheok
PADUNGAN
Jln P Ramlee
2
Islamic Museum
Sarawak Museum (Old Building)
Jln MathieS
6
Jln Tabuan
35
27
Persiaran Ban Hock
Reservoir Park
Jln Reservoir
Heroes' Monument
Reservoir Park
To Satok Weekend Market (600m)
Jln Satok
Jln Tun Haji Openg
To Sarawak General Hospital (1.2km)
9
Sri Srinivasagar Kaliamman Temple
Jln Ban Hock

Kuching

Top Sights

- Indian Mosque ... B1
- Jalan Carpenter ... C2
- Jalan India ... B1
- Sarawak Museum (Old Building) ... B3
- Waterfront Promenade ... D2

Sights

- 1 Chinese History Museum ... D2
- 2 Dewan Tun Abdul Razak ... B3
- 3 Fort Margherita ... D1
- 4 Harmony Arch ... C2
- 5 Hong San Si Temple ... D2

Sleeping

- 6 B&B Inn ... D4
- 7 Diocesan Centre ... C2
- 8 John's Place ... D3
- 9 Lodge 121 ... D4
- 10 Mandarin Hotel ... D3
- 11 Nomad Borneo B&B ... D3
- 12 Pinnacles ... E3
- 13 Singgahsana Lodge ... D2
- Tracks B& B ... (see 11)

Eating

- 14 Green Hill Corner ... D3
- 15 Jubilee Restaurant ... B1
- 16 Junk ... D3
- 17 Little Lebanon ... B1
- 18 Open-Air Market ... A1
- 19 Popular Vegetarian ... G3
- 20 Ting & Ting ... D3
- 21 Top Spot Food Court ... F3
- 22 Vegetarian Food ... D3
- 23 Waterfront Promenade ... E2
- 24 Yang Choon Tai Hawker Centre ... C2

Drinking

- 25 Funky Gibbon ... F2
- 26 Living Room ... D3
- 27 Ruai ... E4

Entertainment

- 28 Star Cineplex ... D3

Shopping

- 29 Main Bazaar ... D2
- 30 Mohamed Yahia & Sons ... F2
- 31 Tun Jugah Shopping Centre ... F2

Information

- 32 Klinik Chan ... D2
- Maridon Treks ... (see 32)
- Mr Clean ... (see 10)
- National Park Booking Office ... (see 33)
- 33 Visitors Information Centre ... B1

Transport

- An Hui Motor ... (see 20)
- 34 Saujana Bus Station ... A2
- 35 Tek Hua Motor ... D4

Lodge 121 HOSTEL $
(☎428121; www.lodge121.com; 1st fl, Lot 121, Jln Tabuan; dm/s/d/tr/q with share bath RM24/49/69/89/119, d/tr with bathroom RM99/129; ❄@📶) Polished concrete abounds at this mod charmer, whose owners have transformed a commercial space into a sleek, spotless and low-key hang-out for flashpackers.

Nomad Borneo B&B HOSTEL $
(☎237831; www.borneobnb.com; 3 Jln Green Hill; dm/s/d/f RM18/40/50/90; ❄@📶) There's a buzzing backpacker vibe at this Iban-run favourite. The dorm rooms have windows but the cell-like singles and doubles make do with exhaust fans.

Tracks B&B HOSTEL $
(☎019-6407372; www.tracksbnb.com; 5 Jln Green Hill; dm/d incl breakfast RM15/40; ❄@📶) Has a laid-back local ambience, graffiti testimonials on the stairwell walls, a washing machine and all-you-can-drink tea and coffee. All but two rooms have windows; none have private bathrooms.

Mandarin Hotel HOTEL $
(☎418269; 6 Jln Green Hill; d from RM55; ❄) This old-time Chinese hotel is head and shoulders above half a dozen similarly priced joints nearby.

Pinnacles HOSTEL $
(☎419100; www.pinnacleskuching.com; 1st fl, Lot 21, Block G, Jln Borneo; dm/d with share bathroom RM30/80, d/q with bathroom RM110/135; ❄@📶) A bright orange lobby leads to 10 well kept but unromantic rooms, all of them clean, some with airwell-view windows. Prices include breakfast.

B&B Inn HOSTEL $
(☎237366; bnbswk@streamyx.com; 30-1 Jln Tabuan; dm RM16, s/d/tr with share bathroom RM25/35/45, d with bathroom RM70; ❄@📶) Clean, simple and low-key, this 12-room establishment has a lived-in, old-fashioned

feel. Women and men have separate dorm rooms.

John's Place GUESTHOUSE $
(☎258329; 5 Jln Green Hill; d RM55-60, tr 80;) Hidden away in a commercial building, John's is a neat but rather unexciting spot to lay your head. The cheaper doubles look out onto the hallway.

Eating

Kuching is a great place to work your way through the entire range of Sarawak-style Malay cooking and the cuisines of the city's nine Chinese dialect groups. Jln Padungan is undergoing something of a restaurant, cafe and bar boom.

TOP CHOICE **Top Spot Food Court** SEAFOOD $$
(Jln Padungan; fish per kilo RM35-70, veg dishes RM8-12; noon-11pm) A perennial favourite, this lively, neon-lit courtyard and its half a dozen seafooderies sit, rather improbably, on the roof of a concrete parking garage – look for the giant backlit lobster.

Open-Air Market HAWKER $
(Jln Khoo Hun Yeang; mains from RM2.50-4) Possibly the best hawker centre in the town centre, with Malay and Chinese sections separated by a parking area. Dishes to look for include *Sarawak laksa,* Chinese-style *mee sapi* (beef noodle soup) and red *kolo mee* (noodles with sweet barbecue sauce).

Yang Choon Tai Hawker Centre HAWKER $
(23 Jln Carpenter; mains RM3.50-6; 6am-1am) The stalls here serve up an eclectic assortment of native bites, including *kolo mee* (flash-boiled egg noodles) with seafood and *char siew* (barbecue pork).

TOP CHOICE **Popular Vegetarian** VEGETARIAN $
(Lot 105, Section 50, Jln Abell; 3-course lunch RM5; 9.30am-2pm & 5.30-9.30pm;) Serves superb vegie versions of Chinese, Malay and assorted Asian dishes made with soy, mushrooms and oats instead of meat. Situated four buildings south of the Lime Tree Hotel.

DON'T MISS

LAKSA LUCK

Borneo's luckiest visitors start the day with a breakfast of Sarawak-style *laksa*, noodle soup made with coconut milk, lemon grass, sour tamarind and fiery *sambal belacan* (shrimp paste sauce), with fresh calamansi lime juice squeezed on top. Unbelievably *lazat* ('delicious' in Bahasa Malaysia)!

Jubilee Restaurant INDIAN $$
(49 Jln India; 6.30am-6pm) A veteran halal Indian restaurant in the heart of Kuching's Indian Muslim district.

Waterfront Promenade FOOD STALLS $
(Jln Tunku Abdul Rahman; meals from RM5; evening) What could be better than an evening stroll along the river accompanied by fresh fruit juice and a few sticks of satay? Opposite the Hilton Kuching Hotel.

Green Hill Corner HAWKER $
(cnr Jln Temple & Jln Green Hill; meals RM2.50-6) Several stalls here crank out porridge, *laksa,* chicken rice and noodle dishes.

Vegetarian Food VEGETARIAN $
(Jln Green Hill; mains RM3.50-5; 6am-3.30pm;) Situated on the outside corner of Viva Cafe, a mini-hawkers centre, this stall does cheap, tasty vegie versions of all the local favourites.

Little Lebanon LEBANESE $$
(Japanese Bldg, Jln Barrack; mains RM5-15) Borneo's only Levantine restaurant sits in an elegant archway overlooking the eastern end of colourful Jln India. Swing by after 6pm for flavourful puffs on a *sheesha* pipe (RM12 to RM21).

Ting & Ting SUPERMARKET $
(30A Jln Tabuan; h9am-9pm, closed Sun & holidays) Self-catering.

Drinking & Entertainment

Cosmopolitan Kuching has a clutch of spirited drinking spots, including a number along Jln Padungan (around No 62). Most stay open until about 1am, although live music can blare on until later (especially on Friday and Saturday nights). Just for the record, Fort Margherita does not serve cocktails.

Ruai BAR
(off Persiaran Ban Hock; 4pm-1am or 2am) A welcoming, Iban-owned open-air bar with a laid-back cool all its own. Situated behind the Telang Usan Hotel.

Funky Gibbon BAR
(Jln Tunku Abdul Rahman, ground fl, Riverbank Suites; 5pm-2am) A favourite with locals and expats alike. The verandah has superb river views.

Living Room WINE BAR
(23 Jln Wayang; 6pm-midnight Wed-Mon) At this impossibly cool wine bar you may find yourself wondering where you are: is this Borneo, Bali or Barcelona?

Star Cineplex CINEMA
(www.starcineplex.com.my; 9th fl, parking garage, Jln Temple; ticket RM5-9) Most movies are in English; the rest have English subtitles. A great escape, especially when it's raining. Screenings start at 11.30am (last screening 12.45am).

Shopping

Kuching is probably the best place in Borneo to purchase the island's traditional arts and crafts, including hand-woven textiles and baskets, masks, drums, beaded headdresses, painted shields and Bruneian miniature cannons. Don't be afraid to negotiate a bit – there's plenty to choose from, and the quality varies as much as the price. Overpricing and dubiously 'aged' items are common, so be sure to spend some time browsing to familiarise yourself with prices and range.

TOP CHOICE **Main Bazaar** DAYAK CRAFTS
(Main Bazaar; approx 10am-6.30pm, some shops closed Sun) Shops range from upscale art galleries to chaotic establishments with a 'garage sale' appeal.

Mohamed Yahia & Sons BOOKS
(416928; http://sites.google.com/site/mohdyahiasons; basement, Sarawak Plaza, Jln Tunku Abdul Rahman; 10am-9pm) Specialises in English-language books about Borneo.

Information

For details on the Indonesian consulate and the honorary consulates of Australia and the UK, see p475.

Mr Clean (246424; Jln Green Hill; per kg RM7, 4hr service RM10.50; 8am-6pm Mon-Sat, to 4pm Sun & holidays) is a reliable laundrette on a commercial backstreet a block northeast of the Mandarin Hotel.

Dangers & Annoyances

There have recently been incidents of bag snatching from tourists (mainly women) by motorbike-mounted miscreants. Exercise reasonable caution when walking along deserted stretches of road, especially after dark.

Emergency

Police, Ambulance & Fire (999)

SPLURGE: JUNK

(259450; 80 Jln Wayang, Kuching; mains RM20-50; 6-11pm, closed Tue) Filled to the brim with antiques, this chic complex of dining rooms (three) and bars (two) – housed in three 1920s shophouses – is a favourite among Malaysian celebs, who also love the lounge, amply supplied with pillows and provocatively decorated with Pop Art. The food is Western and fusion, with an Italian bias. Pasta costs RM24 to RM32, pizzas are RM20 to RM38.

Internet Access

Cyber City (ground fl, Block D, Taman Sri Sarawak; 1st/2nd hr RM4/3; 10am-11pm Mon-Sat, 11am-11pm Sun & holidays) Hidden away behind the Riverside Shopping Mall (Jln Tunku Abdul Rahman) – to get there, exit the mall on the '2nd floor' and walk up the hill.

Maridon Treks (1st fl, 96 Main Bazaar; 10am-5.30pm) Free internet computers, wi-fi, tea and coffee.

Coffee Bean & Tea Leaf (ground fl, Sarawak Plaza, Jln Tunku Abdul Rahman; per hr RM3; 8.30am-11.30pm Sun-Thu, 8.30am-12.30am Fri & Sat) A Starbucks-style cafe with internet computers.

Medical Services

Normah Medical Specialist Centre (440055, emergency 311-999; www.normah.com.my; Jln Tun Abdul Rahman, Petra Jaya; emergency 24hr, clinic 8.30am-4.30pm Mon-Fri, to 1pm Sat) Considered Kuching's best private hospital by many expats. Situated north of the river, about 6km by road from the centre. Served by the same buses as Bako National Park.

Klinik Chan (240307; 98 Main Bazaar; 8am-noon & 2-5pm Mon-Fri, 9am-noon Sat, Sun & holidays) Conveniently central. Great for minor ailments.

Sarawak General Hospital (Hospital Umum Sarawak; 276666; http://hus.moh.gov.my/v3, in Malay; Jln Hospital; 24hr) Has good facilities and reasonable rates but is often overcrowded. Situated about 2km south of the centre along Jln Tun Abang Haji Openg; served by buses K6, K8, K9 and K18.

Money

Most of Kuching's banks and ATMs are on or near Jln Tunku Abdul Rahman.

Airport Exchange Counter (RHB Bank; 8.30am-7.30pm) Cash only. The terminal also has ATMs.

Mohamed Yahia & Sons (basement, Sarawak Plaza, Jln Tunku Abdul Rahman; 10am-9pm)

GETTING TO INDONESIA: TEBEDU TO ENTIKONG

Getting to the border Bus companies including Bus Asia and SJS ply the route between Kuching (and other cities along the Sarawak coast) and the West Kalimantan city of Pontianak (RM55 to RM80, eight to nine hours), passing through the Tebedu–Entikong crossing 80km south of Kuching.

At the border Travellers from 64 countries can get an Indonesian visa on arrival at the road crossing between Tededu (Malaysia) and Entikong (Indonesia), the only official land border between Sarawak and Kalimantan. A number of semiofficial crossings make it possible to cross briefly into East Kalimantan from the Kelabit Highlands.

Moving on Pontianak isn't very interesting so we don't cover it in this book. The city is linked to other parts of Indonesia and Singapore by airlines such as Batavia Air (www.batavia-air.com).

No commission, good rates, accepts US$100 bills and travellers cheques in six currencies. Inside the bookshop.

Tourist Information

Visitors Information Centre (☎410944/2; www.sarawaktourism.com; Sarawak Tourism Complex, northern end of Jln Tun Abang Haji Openg; ⏲8am-6pm Mon-Fri, 9am-3pm Sat, Sun & public holidays) Located in the atmospheric old courthouse complex (built 1887), this office has helpful and well-informed staff, free maps and brochures, and oodles of travel information, much of it on bulletin boards.

National Park Booking Office (☎248088; www.sarawakforestry.com; Sarawak Tourism Complex, northern end of Jln Tun Haji Openg; ⏲8am-5pm Mon-Fri) Next door to the Visitors Information Centre. Staff can book overnight stays at Bako, Gunung Gading and Kubah National Parks and the Matang Wildlife Centre (you can also book via http://ebooking.com.my) and have the latest news flashes on *Rafflesia* sightings (posted in the window for 24-hour viewing). Telephone enquires are patiently answered.

Maridon Treks (☎421346; 1st fl, 96 Main Bazaar; ⏲10am-5.30pm; @📶) A great place to relax, meet other travellers and assemble groups for tours or treks. Has an informative bulletin board, internet computers, free wi-fi, free tea and coffee and a clean toilet.

Visa Extensions

Visa Department (Bahagian Visa; ☎245661; www.imi.gov.my; 2nd fl, Bangunan Sultan Iskandar, Kompleks Pejabat Persekutuan, cnr Jln Tun Razak & Jln Simpang Tiga; ⏲8am-5pm Mon-Thu, 8-11.45am & 2.15-5pm Fri) Situated in a 17-storey federal office building about 3km south of the centre. From the Saujana Bus Station, take City Public Link buses K8 or K11 or Sarawak Transport Company buses 8G1, 8G2 and 8G3 (all RM1).

Getting There & Away

Bako National Park and Semenggoh Nature Reserve are served by public buses, but the only way to get to most other nature sites in western Sarawak is to hire a taxi or join a tour group (guesthouses can make arrangements).

Air

Kuching International Airport is 12km south of the centre. **AirAsia** (www.airasia.com) links Kuching with Kuala Lumpur, Johor Bahru, Penang and Singapore; and, within Borneo, with Kota Kinabalu, Sibu, Bintulu and Miri. **Malaysia Airlines** (www.malaysiaairlines.com) has flights to/from Singapore, Kota Kinabalu and Kuala Lumpur. **MASwings** (www.maswings.com.my) serves 16 destinations in Sarawak and Sabah.

Boat

For details on the ferry to Sibu – much faster and a lot more fun than the bus – see p460. Ferries depart from the **Express Wharf**, 6km east of the centre; a taxi from town costs RM25.

Bus

Long-distance buses depart from the **Regional Express Bus Terminal** (Third Mile Bus Terminal; Jln Penrissen), which is about 5km south of the centre. A taxi from the centre costs RM20 or RM25; from about 6am to 6.30pm, buses run every half-hour or so to/from central Kuching's **Saujana Bus Station**.

A dozen different companies send buses along Sarawak's northern coast to Miri (RM90, 15 hours), with stops at Sibu (RM50, eight hours), Bintulu (RM70, 12 hours), Batu Niah Junction (jumping-off point for Niah National Park) and Lambir Hills National Park. To get to Brunei or Sabah, you have to change buses in Miri.

A **new long-distance bus terminal** (Sixth Mile Bus Terminal; cnr Jln Penrissen & Jln Airport) is being built 10km south of the city centre, near the airport. It's likely to come on line during the life of this guide.

Getting Around

To/From the Airport

The price of a coupon taxi into Kuching is fixed at RM26. Buses no longer serve the airport but it may be possible to find a local bus on a nearby highway – exit the terminal, turn left, walk to the T-junction, turn right and the bus station should be on your left. Rumour has it that Rapid Kuching is looking into adding an airport bus line.

Motorcycle

Two motorcycle-repair shops on Jln Tabuan hire out motorbikes (including a helmet) for RM25 to RM40 a day, plus a deposit of RM100. Insurance covers the bike but not the driver and may be valid only within a 60km radius of Kuching.

An Hui Motor (☎412419, 016-8863328; 29 Jln Tabuan; ⏰8am-6pm Mon-Sat, to noon Sun)

Tek Hua Motor (☎233957, 019-8876848; 68B Jln Tabuan; ⏰8am-6pm Mon-Sat)

Taxi

Taxis can be hailed on the street or at taxi queues (eg at the larger hotels). All Kuching taxis – except those on the flat-fare run to/from the airport (RM26) – are required to use meters; flag fall is RM10.

Around Kuching

Kuching's biggest asset is its proximity to a cornucopia of natural wonders. The city is a great base for trips to the coast and the jungle.

BAKO NATIONAL PARK

Occupying a jagged peninsula that juts out into the South China Sea, **Bako National Park** (☎478011; www.sarawakforestry.com; admission RM10), Sarawak's oldest, is just 37km northeast of downtown Kuching but feels like worlds and eons away. Many visitors cite this park as one of their favourite Borneo experiences.

The coast of this 27-sq-km peninsula consists of lovely pocket beaches tucked into secret bays and interspersed with wind-sculpted cliffs, forested bluffs and stretches of brilliant mangrove swamp. The interior of the park is home to streams, waterfalls and a range of distinct ecosystems, including classic lowland rainforest (mixed dipterocarp forest) and *kerangas* (heath forest).

Bako provides a protected home for incredible natural diversity. Scientists estimate that the park is home to about 190 kinds of bird, 24 reptile species and 37 species of mammal. Surprisingly, the area around park HQ is one of the best places to spot wildlife, including reddish-brown proboscis monkeys, the males' pendulous noses flopping as they chew on tender young leaves.

> **DON'T FEED THE CROCODILES!**
>
> The muddy, tannin-stained waters of Bako National Park's rivers shelter ferocious saltwater crocodiles, so forget about swimming – or even dipping your toe in. A few years ago a schoolboy was eaten by a croc a bit upriver from Bako Bazaar; his body was never found.

Sights & Activities

Bako's 17 **hiking trails** – colour-coded and clearly marked with stripes of paint – are suitable for all levels of fitness and motivation, with routes ranging from short walks around park headquarters to strenuous all-day treks to the far (eastern) end of the peninsula. Aim to be back at Telok Assam before dark, ie by about 6pm at the latest. At park HQ it's possible to hire a boat to one of the far beaches and then hike back, or to hike to one of the beaches and arrange for a boat to meet you there.

Sleeping

In-park accommodation often fills up, especially from June to August, so if you'd like to stay over – highly recommended! – book ahead online via http://ebooking.com.my, stop by the National Park Booking Office in Kuching, or phone the park. By the time you read this, a new hostel should be open and some of the chalets upgraded. The designated **camping zone** (per person RM5) at park headquarters has only three spots.

Getting There & Away

Getting from Kuching to Bako National Park is a cinch. Bright red bus 1 run by **Rapid Kuching** (☎012-883-3866; http://rapidkuching.com; RM3) starts its bumpy run to Bako Bazaar at 6 Jln Khoo Hun Yeang, in front of a buffet restaurant called Toko Minuman Jumbo (and across the street from a brilliant hawker centre perfect for breakfast). There are departures from Kuching every hour on the hour from 7am to 5pm, and from Bako Bazaar every hour on the half-hour from 6.30am to (usually) 5.30pm or 6pm.

Hiring a motorboat from the Bako Bazaar dock, where visitors pay their park entry fee, to park headquarters costs RM47. Since each vessel can carry up to five people, it makes sense to assemble a quintet to optimise cost-sharing.

CHEEKY MACAQUES

The long-tailed macaques that hang about the park headquarters are great to watch, but they are mischievous and cunning opportunists who will make running leaps at anything potentially edible they think they can carry off. Lock your doors, close your bags and do not leave valuables, food or drink – or anything in a plastic bag – unattended, especially on the beaches or on the chalet verandahs.

Take note of the boat's number (or ask for the boatman's mobile phone number) and be sincere when you agree to a pick-up time. If you prefer to share a different boat back, give park headquarters your boat number – staff are happy to call and cancel your original boat.

A cab from Kuching to Bako Bazaar (45 minutes) costs RM40.

SANTUBONG PENINSULA

The Santubong Peninsula (also known as Damai) is a 10km-long finger of land jutting out into the South China Sea. The main drawcards are the Sarawak Cultural Village, some beaches and **Gunung Santubong** (880m), which can be climbed from a point about 1km south of the Sarawak Cultural Village (look for the Green Paradise Cafe). Santubong is the best place in Sarawak for a lazy, pampered beach holiday.

Sights & Activities

Sarawak Cultural Village ECO-MUSEUM
(SCV; ☎846411; www.scv.com.my; admission RM60; ⏲9am-5.15pm, last entry 4pm) A living museum featuring seven traditional dwellings (including four Dayak longhouses) and demonstrations of traditional crafts. It sounds hokey, but the intent is sincere and even travellers who have been to Borneo's interior are generally impressed by the opportunity to see truly traditional longhouses.

A twice-daily **cultural show** (45 min; ⏲11.30am & 4pm) showcases the traditional music and dances of the various tribes. It's all quite touristy, of course, but most visitors – 60% of whom are Sarawakians, including school groups – generally enjoy the performances.

Sleeping

Permai Rainforest Resort RESORT $$
(☎846487/90; www.permairainforest.com; Damai Beach; campsite RM14, 6-bed longhouse RM220, 6-bed cabins RM250, 2-bed treehouse RM260; @📶) Set on a lushly forested hillside with sea views, this is just one of several resort complexes on the peninsula.

Getting There & Away

The minibuses that link Kuching with the Santubong Peninsula (45 minutes) are operated by two companies:

Damai Beach Resort (☎846999, 082-380-970; one-way RM12, return RM20) Has departures from Kuching's Grand Margherita Hotel and Riverside Majestic Hotel every two hours from 7.15am to 10pm.

Setia Kawan (☎019-8251619; tickets RM10) Has departures from Kuching's waterfront (Singgahsana Lodge, the Harbour View Hotel and the Hilton) every two or three hours from 7.15am to 10pm.

SEMENGGOH NATURE RESERVE

One of the best places in the world to sneak a peek at our ginger-haired cousins in their natural habitat, the **Semenggoh Wildlife Centre** (☎618325; www.sarawakforestry.com; admission RM3; ⏲8am-5pm) is home to 27 semi-wild orang-utans. Hour-long feedings begin at 9am and 3pm but orang-utans often turn up at park HQ so don't rush off straight away if everything seems quiet.

Semenggoh Nature Reserve has two beautiful rainforest trails: the **Masing Trail** (Main Trail; red trail markings; 30 minutes), which links the HQ with the highway; and the **Brooke's Pool Trail** (yellow and red trail markings), a 2km loop from headquarters. A guide can be hired at the Information Centre for RM20 (for up to five people).

Getting There & Away

Semenggoh, 24km south of Kuching, is easily accessible on a half-day trip from Kuching. From Kuching's Saujana Bus Station, take City Public Link bus K6 (RM2.50), which departs at 7am, 9.30am, 1pm, 3pm and 5pm, or Sarawak Transport Company bus 6 (RM2.50) at about 7.20am and 1.20pm. At Semenggoh, the stop is 1.3km down the hill from park HQ.

A taxi from Kuching costs RM40 one-way or RM90 round-trip, including wait time. Most Kuching guesthouses offer half-day tours but these don't leave any time to hike.

ANNAH RAIS LONGHOUSE

Although this 97-door **Bidayuh longhouse** (adult/student RM8/4) has been on the tourist circuit for decades, it's still an excellent place to get a sense of what a longhouse is and what longhouse life is like. Once you pay your entry fee (in a pavilion next to the parking lot), you're free to explore Annah

Rais' three longhouses, with a guide or on your own. The most important feature is the *awah,* a long, covered common verandah – with a springy bamboo floor – used for economic activities, socialising and celebrations. A dozen smoke-blackened human skulls still have pride of place – suspended over an 18th-century Dutch cannon – in the headhouse.

Sleeping

Edward Homestay HOMESTAY
(www.longhouseadventure.com; 2 days & 1 night per person RM98, incl activities RM298) Offers a wide range of rainforest activities.

Macheree's Homestay HOMESTAY
(www.mdrlonghousehomestay.com; 2 days & 1 night per person RM298) Jungle activities start at 10am.

Getting There & Away

The only way to get to Annah Rais, 60km south of Kuching, is by taxi. From Kuching, expect to pay RM80 one-way or RM160 return, including wait time.

In Kuching, a variety of tour agencies and guesthouses offer four-hour group tours to Annah Rais for RM80 per person.

KUBAH NATIONAL PARK & MATANG WILDLIFE CENTRE

A super destination for true lovers of the rainforest, 22-sq-km **Kubah National Park** (☎845033; www.sarawakforestry.com; admission incl Matang Wildlife Centre RM10) is a haven for mixed dipterocarp forest, among the lushest and most threatened habitats in Borneo.

When you pay your entry fee, you'll receive a schematic map of the park's six trails, all of which are interconnected (except the Belian Trail). They're well marked so a guide isn't necessary.

A 15km drive (or three-hour walk) beyond Kubah National Park, the **Matang Wildlife Centre** (☎374869, 375163; www.sarawakforestry.com; admission incl Kubah National Park RM10; ⏲8am-5pm, last entry 3.30pm) has had remarkable success rehabilitating jungle animals rescued from captivity, especially orang-utans and sun bears. The highly professional staff do their best to provide their abused charges with natural living conditions on a limited budget, but there's no denying that the centre looks like a low-budget zoo plopped down in the jungle. Because of the centre's unique role, there are endangered animals here that you cannot see anywhere else in Sarawak.

Sleeping & Eating

Kubah and Matang's attractive, inexpensive chalets can be booked by phone, online via http://ebooking.com.my or at the National Park Booking Office in Kuching.

Matang is supposed to get a cafeteria at some point but for now you'll need to bring your own food. At Kubah, cooking is allowed in the chalets but there's nowhere to buy food so bring everything you'll need.

Getting There & Away

Kubah National Park is 22km from downtown Kuching. A taxi from Kuching costs RM50 one-way or RM100 return, including wait time. If you'd like to see both Kubah and the Matang Wildlife Centre, you can arrange to be dropped off at one and picked up at the other – they're linked by the Rayu Trail (three hours).

GUNUNG GADING NATIONAL PARK

The best place in Sarawak to see the world's largest flower, the renowned *Rafflesia*, **Gunung Gading National Park** (☎735144; www.sarawakforestry.com; admission RM10; ⏲8am-5pm or later) makes a fine day trip from Kuching. Its old-growth rainforest covers the slopes of four mountains (*gunung*) – Gading, Lundu, Perigi and Sebuloh – traversed by well-marked walking trails that are great for day hikes.

To find out if a *Rafflesia* is in bloom – something that happens only 30 to 50 times a year – and how long it will stay that way (never more than five days), call the park or the National Park Booking Office in Kuching.

Sleeping

The park has a **hostel** (dm/r RM15/40) with four fan rooms and two three-bedroom **chalets** (chalet RM150; ❄) for up to six people. **Camping** (per person RM5) is possible at park HQ.

Getting There & Away

Four public buses a day link Kuching's Regional Express Bus Terminal with Lundu, but from there you'll either have to walk north 3km to the park or hire an unofficial taxi (RM5 per person). Kuching guesthouses can arrange day trips.

Sibu

☎084 / POP 255,000

Gateway to the Batang Rejang, Sibu has been a busy centre for trade with the upriver hinterland since the time of James Brooke. These days, it's a major transit point for travellers, and while the 'swan city' is no rival to Kuching in terms of charm, it's not a bad place to spend a day or two before or after a waterborne trip to the interior.

Sights

Tua Pek Kong Temple CHINESE TEMPLE
(Jln Temple; ⏲6am-8pm) A colourful Buddhist and Taoist temple established in the early 1870s. For a brilliant view up and down the muddy Batang Rejang, climb the seven-storey Kuan Yin Pagoda; ask for a key at the ground-floor desk.

TOP CHOICE **Sibu Heritage Centre** MUSEUM
(Jln Central; ⏲9am-5pm Tue-Sun) Opened in 2010, the well-presented exhibits – rich in evocative photographs – explore the captivating history of Sarawak and Sibu.

Sleeping

Some of Sibu's ultrabudget places (ie those below RM30 a room) are of a very low standard. We recently heard of some Japanese tourists who were bitten by rats!

TOP CHOICE **Li Hua Hotel** HOTEL $
(☎324000; www.lihua.com.my, sibu@lihua.com.my; Lg Lanang 2; s/d/ste from RM50/60/150; ❄📶) Sibu's best-value hotel is very convenient if you'll be arriving or leaving by ferry.

River Park Hotel HOTEL $
(☎316688, 016-578-2820; siewling1983@hotmail.com; 51-53 Jln Maju; d/q from RM50/100; ❄📶) An unexceptional but well-run hotel with friendly staff and a pleasant riverside location. All 30 rooms have windows (except the very cheapest).

Eating

Sibu is a great spot for local eats, especially Foochow-style Chinese. Try *kam pua mee,* the city's signature dish – thin noodle strands soaked in pork fat and served with a side of roast pork.

TOP CHOICE **Night Market** FOOD STALLS $
(Pasar Malam; Jln Market; ⏲5.30-11pm) Chinese stalls are at the eastern end of the lot, while Malay stalls (with superb satay and scrumptious barbecue chicken) are to the west, on the other side of the clothing stalls. Also has a few Iban places.

Islamic Nyonya Kafé PERANAKAN $$
(141 Kampung Nyabor Rd; mains RM10-13; ⏲10am-11pm) Serves the deliciously spicy dishes of the Straits Chinese (as interpreted by the Indian chef), including *ayam halia* (ginger chicken) and *kari kambing* (mutton curry). Has great lunch deals (11am to 2pm).

Pasar Sentral Sibu MARKET $
(PSS; ⏲4am or 5am-7pm) One of Malaysia's largest fruit and vegie markets. Upstairs, Chinese, Malay and Iban food stalls serve food until 9pm.

Giant Supermarket SUPERMARKET $
(ground fl, Wisma Sanyan, Jln Sanyan; ⏲9am-10pm) Near McDonald's.

Information

Email Centre (ground fl, Sarawak House Complex, cnr Jln Centre & Jln Kampung Nyabor; per hr RM3; ⏲9am-9pm Mon-Sat, to 3pm Sun) Internet access near McDonald's.

Rejang Medical Centre (☎330733; www.rejang.com.my; 29 Jln Pedada) Twenty-four-hour emergency services. Situated about 1km northeast of the Sibu Gateway.

Visitors Information Centre (☎340980; www.sarawaktourism.com; 32 Jln Tukang Besi; ⏲8am-5pm Mon-Fri, closed public holidays) Has plenty of maps, brochures and bus and ferry schedules. May move down the block to the Sibu Heritage Centre.

Getting There & Around

Boat

By far the quickest way to get from Sibu to Kuching is by boat. **Ekspress Bahagia** (☎in Sibu 084-319228, 016-8005891, in Kuching 082-412246, 082-429242, 016-8893013; ⏲from Sibu 11.30am, from Kuching 8.30am) runs a daily express ferry from Sibu's **express ferry terminal** (Terminal Penumpang Sibu; Jln Kho Peng Long) to Kuching's Express Wharf (RM45; five hours).

'Flying coffins' (narrow, fast passenger ferries) run by six companies head to Kapit (140km; 2nd/business/1st class RM20/25/30, 2¼ to three hours) once or twice an hour from 5.45am to 2.30pm. From Kapit, boats heading down to Sibu depart between 6.40am and 3.30pm.

If the water level at the Pelagus Rapids is high enough (verify that it is before you book), one daily **boat** (☎084-337004, 013-8061333; ⏲5.45am from Sibu, 7.30am from Belaga) continues up to Belaga (about 300km from Sibu; RM55, 11 hours).

Bus

Sibu's **long-distance bus station** (Jln Pahlawan) is about 3.5km northeast of the centre. A variety of companies send buses to Kuching (RM40, eight hours, regular departures between 7am and 4am), Miri (RM40, 6½ hours, roughly hourly from 6am to 3.30am) and Bintulu (RM20, 3¼ hours, roughly hourly from 6am to 3.30am).

Getting Around

The airport is 23km from the centre. Buses run by Panduan Hemat link the airport junction (RM2.70; hourly from 6am to 6pm), five minutes on foot from the terminal, with the city centre. It may also be possible to take a yellow-roof minibus. A taxi to/from the airport costs RM35.

To get from the local bus station (in front of the express ferry terminal) to the long-distance bus station, take Lanang Bus 20 or 21 (RM1, 10 minutes, once or twice an hour from 6.30am to 5.15pm).

Batang Rejang

A trip up the tan, churning waters of Batang Rejang (Rejang River) – the 'Amazon of Borneo' – is one of Southeast Asia's great river journeys. Though the area is no longer the jungle-lined wilderness it was in the days before Malaysian independence, it still retains a frontier, *ulu-ulu* (upriver, ie back-of-the-beyond) vibe, especially in towns and longhouses accessible only by boat.

KAPIT

084 / POP 19,500

The main upriver settlement on the Batang Rejang, Kapit is a bustling trading and transport centre dating back to the days of the White Rajas. Its lively markets, including **Pasar Teresang** (5am-6pm), are an important commerce hub for the longhouse communities hidden in the nearby jungle.

An antiquated permit system is in place for those wishing to travel from Kapit to Belaga or up the Batang Baleh. Although the Resident's Office continues to issue permits, we've never heard of any authority actually checking if travellers have them. Strangely, a permit is not required for travel in the other direction.

Sights & Activities

Fort Sylvia MUSEUM
(Jln Kubu; 10am-noon & 2-5pm, closed Mon & public holidays) Offers a pretty good intro to the traditional lifestyles of the Batang Rejang Dayaks. Housed in a fort built by Charles Brooke in 1880.

Longhouse Visits LONGHOUSES
Longhouses, many of them quite modern and some accessible by road (longboat travel is both slower and pricier than going by van), can be found along the Batang Baleh, which conflows with the Batang Rejang 9km upstream from Kapit, and the Sungai Sut, a tributary of the Batang Baleh.

At the time of research, Kapit had only two guides licensed by the **Sarawak Tourism Board** (STB; www.sarawaktourism.com), **Alice Chua** (019-8593126; atta_kpt@yahoo.com) and her partner **Christina Yek Leh Mee** (013-8466133). A day trip to a nearby longhouse costs RM280/330/380 for two/three/four people.

There have been reports that some other guides overcharge tourists.

Sleeping & Eating

New Rejang Inn HOTEL $
(796600; 104 Jln Teo Chow Beng; d RM60;) The best-value accommodation in town.

Night Market FOOD STALLS $
(Taman Selera Empaurau; mains from RM2.50; 5pm-midnight) The mainly Malay stalls are situated half a block up the slope from the town square.

Information

Kapit has several banks with ATMs.

Good Time Cyber Centre (1st fl, 354 Jln Yong Moo Chai; per hr RM3; 8.30am-10.30pm or 11pm) Internet access. Hugely popular with young gamers.

Resident's Office (796230; www.kapitro.sarawak.gov.my; 9th fl, Kompleks Kerajaan Negeri Bahagian Kapit, Jln Bleteh; 8am-1pm & 2-5pm Mon-Thu, 8-11.45am & 2.15-5pm Fri) Issues permits for upriver travel in just a few minutes. Situated 2km west of the centre; to get there, take a minibus (RM1.50) from the southeast corner of Pasar Teresang.

Getting There & Away

For details on the 'flying coffin' boats that link the **Kapit Passenger Terminal** (Jln Panglima Balang) with Sibu, see p460.

When the water is high enough for the Pelagus Rapids (32km upriver from Kapit) to be navigable, one 77-seat express boat a day links the jetty at Kapit's town square (two blocks north of the Kapit Passenger Terminal) with Belaga (RM35; 4½ hours). Boats depart from Kapit at about 9.30am and from Belaga at 7.30am or 8am. When the river is too low, the only way to get to Belaga is overland via Bintulu.

BELAGA

086 / POP 2500

By the time you pull into Belaga after the long journey up the Batang Rejang, you may feel like you've arrived at the very heart of Borneo – in reality you're only about 100km (as the crow flies) from the coastal

THE BORNEO LONGHOUSE

Longhouses are the traditional dwellings of Dayaks, the indigenous people of Borneo. Raised on stilts above the damp forest floor, these large communal dwellings can contain more than a hundred individual family 'apartments' beneath one long roof. The most important part of every longhouse is the covered common verandah, which serves as a social area, 'town hall' and sleeping space.

Like the rest of us, Dayaks love their mod-cons, so over time most longhouse communities have upgraded their building materials from thatch and bamboo to corrugated iron and linoleum.

Visiting a Longhouse

According to longstanding Dayak tradition, anyone who shows up at a longhouse must be welcomed and given accommodation. Generations of jungle travellers knew the routine: upon arrival they would present themselves to the headman (known as a *ketua kaum* in Malay, a *tuai rumah* in Iban and *maren uman* in Kayan), who would arrange for very basic sleeping quarters. But in the last decade or two, as transport has become easier and tourist numbers have soared, this tradition has come under strain, and these days turning up at a longhouse unannounced may be an unwelcome imposition on longhouse residents – in short, bad manners.

The upshot is that in many areas, the days when anyone could turn up unannounced and stay at a longhouse are largely over. Even if you make your own way to a longhouse that's happy to have you, you are likely to face communication and cultural barriers. Interacting spontaneously with locals isn't always easy, as the elders usually don't speak English, and the younger people have often moved to the 'big city' to pursue careers.

Finding a Guide

The way to avoid these pitfalls is to hire a guide who can coordinate your visit with longhouse residents and make introductions. Guesthouses can recommend guides, and the **Sarawak Tourism Board** (STB; www.sarawaktourism.com) has an online listing of registered tour operators (click 'Directory'). Some of the best guides work for tour operators, which saves them from having to go through the rigmarole of getting their own STB licence. Some unlicensed freelance guides are friendly and knowledgeable but, alas, some are not; in any case, neither type can be held accountable if something goes wrong.

When choosing a guide, do not hesitate to be upfront about your preferences and concerns. Do you require a certain level of sleeping comfort? How important is it that you be able to communicate with your hosts in English? Do you want to be the only traveller at the longhouse, or would you prefer it if there were others? Finding the right guide – and, through them, the right longhouse – can mean the difference between spending a sleepless night with other sweaty, bored tourists, and having a spirited evening (double entendre intended) swapping smiles, stories and shots of rice wine with the locals.

What to Expect

When you arrive at a longhouse, don't be surprised to find that it wouldn't make a very good film set for a period drama about headhunters. The Dayaks have moved – for the most part willingly – into the 21st century and so have their dwellings. Remember, though, that a longhouse, more than being a building, is a way of life embodying a communal lifestyle and a very real sense of mutual reliance and responsibility. It is this spirit rather than the physical building that makes a visit special.

Every longhouse is led by a headman. Depending on the tribe, he (it's almost always a he) may be appointed by his predecessor or elected. Either way, heredity often plays a key role in selection.

Do your best to engage with the inhabitants of any community you enter, rather than just wandering around snapping photographs. A good guide can act as a translator, and he or she will keep you abreast of any cultural norms – like when and where to take off your shoes – so you won't have to worry too much about saying or doing the wrong thing.

city of Bintulu. There's not much to do in the town itself except soak up the frontier outpost vibe, but nearby rivers are home to quite a few Kayan/Kenyah and Orang Ulu longhouses.

Sight & Activities

The main reason that tourists visit Belaga is to venture deep into the jungle in search of hidden longhouses and secret waterfalls. But before you can share shots of rice wine with smiling locals, you'll have to find a tour guide. Try tracking down **Hamdani** (☎019-8865770) at the Hotel Belaga or **Hasbee** (☎461240; freeland_blg@yahoo.com; 4 Main Bazaar) at the Belaga B&B.

Unfortunately, we have received reports of overcharging, so network with other travellers and make sure you know what your trip does and does not include.

Sleeping

Most of Belaga's accommodation is of the cheap and shabby variety.

Daniel Levoh's Guesthouse GUESTHOUSE $
(☎461997, 013-8486351; daniellevoh@hotmail.com; Jln Teh Ah Kiong; dm RM10-15, d/tr RM25/35; wifi) Run by a veteran guide. Rooms, a backpackers' chill-out balcony and bathrooms are all on the 2nd floor.

Hotel Belaga HOTEL $
(☎461244; 14 Main Bazaar; d RM30-35; air-con) A convenient location makes up for the less-than-perfect standards. The air-con works, which is more than can be said of the plumbing.

Belaga B&B HOTEL $
(☎461512, 013-8429767; Main Bazaar; r RM20-25; air-con) Has seven very basic but clean rooms. Run by Hasbie, a longtime longhouse guide.

Information

The nearest banks and ATMs are in Kapit and Bintulu.

Hasbee Enterprises (☎461514, 013-8429767; 4 Main Bazaar) Local travel services and internet.

Getting There & Away

When the Batang Rejang is high enough for the Pelagus Rapids to be navigable, one daily express boat links Belaga with Kapit (155km) and Sibu – for details, see p461 and p460.

A bone-jarring (and, in the rain, fiendishly slippery) logging road links Belaga with Bintulu (160km), passing through a heartbreaking landscape of devastated jungle. On most days, 4WD Toyota LandCruisers (per person RM50, four hours) depart Belaga at about 7.30am and from Bintulu in the early afternoon (approximately 2pm). In Belaga, 4WDs to Bintulu congregate in front of Belaga B&B at about 7am. Finding a vehicle in the bustle of Bintulu is a bit more complicated – try calling **Ah Kiat** (☎013-8075598) or **Ah Kian** (☎086-461-392).

Bintulu

☎086 / POP 120,000

Roughly midway between Sibu and Miri (about 200km from each), Bintulu is a bustling coastal town that owes its wealth to huge offshore natural gas fields. Each autumn, it hosts the **Borneo International Kite Festival** (www.borneokite.com).

Bintulu makes a convenient stopover on the way from Sibu to Niah National Park or Miri – or inland to Belaga.

Sleeping

Bintulu's ultrabudget lodgings can be dodgy so you may be better off paying a bit more for peace of mind.

Kintown Inn HOTEL $
(☎333666; kintowninn@yahoo.com; 93 Jln Keppel; s/d RM80/86; air-con wifi) Delivers the best value for your buck (K)in town.

Information

Fi Wee Internet Centre (1st fl, 133 Jln Masjid; per hr RM2.50; ⏲9am-1am) Has 30 internet computers.

Getting There & Away

For details on travelling overland to Belaga, see p463.

Bintulu's long-distance bus station is 5km northeast of the centre (AKA Bintulu Town) at Medan Jaya. A bunch of companies run buses approximately hourly to Kuching (RM60 to RM70, 10 hours) via Sibu (RM20 to RM27, 3½ hours), and to Miri (RM20 to RM27, 4½ hours) via Niah Junction.

Niah National Park

Near the coast about 115km south of Miri, the 31-sq-km **Niah National Park** (☎085-737-454/0; www.sarawakforestry.com; admission RM10; ⏲park office 8am-5pm) is home to one of Borneo's gems, the Niah Caves. In addition to lots of bats, they shelter some of the oldest evidence of human habitation in Southeast Asia.

Sights & Activities

Niah Archaeology Museum MUSEUM

(⏲9am-4.30pm Tue-Sun) Across the river from park HQ; houses rather old-fashioned displays on Niah Caves' geology, ecology and prehistoric archaeology.

TOP CHOICE **Great Cave** CAVE

A vast cavern approximately 2km long, up to 250m across and up to 60m high. Reached along a 3.1km plankwalk through the rainforest.

Painted Cave CAVE

A short walk from the Great Cave. It's easy to miss the small fenced-off area by the entrance that protects the (now empty) death ships and the ancient paintings. Many of the red hematite figures have faded beyond recognition.

Sleeping

Bookings for **dorm beds** and **chalets** (1/2 r with fan RM105/157, with air-con RM236/157) can be made at park HQ or through one of the **National Park Booking Offices** (☎in Miri 085-434184, in Kuching 082-248088) – but *not* through the Sarawak Forestry's website. **Camping** (per person RM5) is permitted near the park HQ.

Getting There & Away

Park headquarters is not on the main (inland) Miri–Bintulu highway but rather 15km north of the highway's lively Batu Niah Junction. This makes getting to the park by public transport a bit tricky. The good news is that all the long-haul buses that link Miri with Bintulu, Sibu and Kuching pass by here. The bad news is that the only way to get from the junction to Batu Niah Town (11km) or the park itself is to hire a private car – the price should be RM25 to RM30. National park staff (or, after hours, park security personnel) can help arrange a car (RM30) back to the junction.

Guesthouses in Miri offer reasonably priced day trips.

Lambir Hills National Park

The closest protected rainforest to Miri, the 69-sq-km **Lambir Hills National Park** (☎085-471609; www.sarawakforestry.com; admission RM10; ⏲park office 8am-5pm) offers jungle waterfalls, cool pools where you can take a dip, and a bunch of great, colour-coded walking trails that branch off four primary routes and lead to 14 destinations. Rangers can supply you with a map and are happy to make suggestions.

Sleeping

The park's reasonably comfortable **chalets** (d/q with fan RM50/75, with air-con RM100/150) have two bedrooms, each with two beds. **Camping** (per person RM5) is permitted near the park HQ. Book by calling the park or through Miri's National Park Booking Office.

Getting There & Away

Park headquarters is 32km south of Miri on the main highway. All the buses linking Miri's Pujut Bus Terminal with Bintulu pass by park headquarters (RM10 from Miri).

Miri

☎085 / POP 295,000

An oil-rich boomtown, Miri (www.mirireso rtcity.com) serves as a major transport hub – if you're travelling to/from Brunei, Sabah, the Kelabit Highlands or the national parks of Gunung Mulu, Niah or Lambir Hills, chances are you'll pass this way. The city itself is busy and modern – not much about it is Borneo – but there's plenty of money sloshing around so the eating is good and the broad avenues brightly lit.

Sights

Canada Hill MUSEUM

Malaysia's first oil derrick, dating from 1910, still stands right outside the **Petroleum Museum** (Jln Canada Hill; ⏲9am-4.30pm Tue-Sun), whose interactive exhibits are a good introduction to the hugely lucrative industry that made Miri – from the earnest, cheery perspective of Shell, Petronas and the government, of course.

Miri City Fan PARK

(Jln Kipas) An expanse of nicely landscaped, themed gardens that boasts an indoor stadium and an Olympic-sized swimming pool (RM1).

Sleeping

Miri has some excellent backpackers' guesthouses.

Minda Guesthouse GUESTHOUSE $

(☎411422; www.mindaguesthouse.com; 1st & 2nd fl, Lot 637, Jln North Yu Seng; per person dm/d RM20/50; ❄@📶) In the heart of Miri's liveliest dining district, this spotless, modern establishment offers a rooftop sundeck and great value for money.

Dillenia Guesthouse GUESTHOUSE $
(☎0434204; dillenia.guesthouse@gmail.com; 1st fl, 846 Jln Sida; dm/s/d/q incl breakfast RM30/50/80/110; ❄@📶) In the northwest corner of a commercial area, this super-welcoming hostel lives up to its motto, 'a home away from home'.

Highlands Guesthouse GUESTHOUSE $
(☎0422327; 3rd fl, 1271 Jln Sri Dagang; dm/d RM25/50; ❄@) Miri's original backpacker guesthouse still serves as a 'budget tourist and travel information centre'.

Eating

TOP CHOICE **Summit Cafe** KELABIT $
(Centre Point Commercial Centre, Jln Melayu; mains from RM3; ⏰6am-3.30pm Mon-Sat) If you've never tried Kelabit cuisine, this place will open up whole new worlds for your taste-buds. Come early for lunch – once the food runs out they close!

Apollo Seafood Centre SEAFOOD $
(4 Jln South Yu Seng; mains from RM6; ⏰10.30am-11.30pm) Hugely and deservedly popular among locals and expats alike.

Khan's Restaurant Islamic INDIAN $
(229 Jln Malu; mains RM4-8; ⏰6.30am-8.30pm) This simple canteen is one of Miri's best North Indian eateries.

Tamu Muhibbah MARKET
(Jln Padang; ⏰2am-7pm) Fruits and vegies.

Information

ATMs can be found at Miri airport and are sprinkled all over town.

Internet Shop (1st fl, Soon Hup Tower, cnr Jln Bendahara & Jln Merbau; per hr RM2; ⏰8am-8pm)

IT Cyber Station (top fl, western end, Bintang Plaza, Jln Miri Pujut; per hr RM2.50; ⏰10am-10pm) Has 70 internet computers.

Maybank Bureau de Change (1271 Centre Point Commercial Centre; ⏰9am-5pm) Changes cash and travellers cheques and does cash advances.

Miri City Medical Centre (☎426622; www.mcmcmiri.com; 916-920 & 1203 Jln Hokkien) Has various private clinics and a 24-hour accident and emergency department.

National Park Booking Office (☎434184; www.sarawakforestry.com; 452 Jln Melayu; ⏰8am-5pm Mon-Fri) Inside the Visitors Information Centre. Has details on Sarawak's national parks and can book beds and rooms at Niah and Lambir Hills (but not at Gunung Mulu or Similajau).

Visitors Information Centre (☎434181; www.sarawaktourism.com; 452 Jln Melayu; ⏰8am-6pm Mon-Fri, 9am-3pm Sat & Sun) Helpful staff can provide maps, information on accommodation and a list of guides.

Getting There & Away

Air

Miri is the main hub of the Malaysia Airlines subsidiary **MASwings** (www.maswings.com.my), whose 16 destinations around Malaysian Borneo include Bario, Bintulu, Gunung Mulu National Park (Mulu), Lawas, Limbang, Kota Kinabalu, Kuching and Sibu.

The discount airline **AirAsia** (www.airasia.com) can get you to Kuching, Kota Kinabalu, Kuala Lumpur, Johor Bahru and Singapore.

Bus

Long-distance buses use the **Pujut Bus Terminal**, about 4km northeast of the centre, which is linked to the centre by MTC bus 33A.

There are frequent buses to Kuching (RM90, 14 hours, departures from 6am to 10pm) via Batu Niah Junction (15km south of Niah National Park), Bintulu (RM25, 3½ hours) and Sibu (RM50, eight hours).

For details on getting to destinations in Brunei, including Bandar Seri Begawan, see p61.

Gunung Mulu National Park

Few national parks anywhere in the world pack so many natural marvels into such a small area. From some of the world's most incredible (and accessible) **caves** (www.mulucaves.org) to brilliant old-growth rainforest to natural oddities such as the Pinnacles formation, **Gunung Mulu National Park** (☎085-792300; www.mulupark.com; per day RM10; ⏰park headquarters 8am-5pm) is truly one of the world's wonders.

Sights & Activities

When you register, helpful park staff will give you a placemat-sized schematic map of the park on which you can plan out your daily itinerary. Ask about jungle trails that can be explored without a guide.

Mulu's 'show caves' (caves that can be visited without special training or equipment) are its most popular attractions and for good reason: they are awesome. Cave routes that require special equipment and a degree of caving experience are known as 'adventure caves'. Bring a torch/flashlight.

The park also offers some of the best and most accessible jungle trekking in Borneo.

Mulu Discovery Centre MUSEUM

(7.30am-9pm) A good introduction to the park as a 'biodiversity hot spot' – and to its extraordinary geology.

TOP CHOICE **Nightwalk** GUIDED WALK

(per person RM10; 7pm except if raining) On this 2km, two-hour walk, creatures you're likely to see – but only after the guide points them out – include tiny tree frogs, enormous spiders, vine snakes and stick insects (phasmids) up to 20cm long.

Mulu Canopy Skywalk CANOPY WALK

(per person RM30) Climbing up into the forest canopy is the only way to see what a tropical rainforest is all about, since most of the flora and fauna do their thing high above the ground.

TOP CHOICE **Deer Cave & Lang's Cave** CAVES

(per person RM20; departures 2pm & 2.30pm) Over 2km in length and 174m in height, Deer Cave is the world's largest cave passage open to the public. (It was considered the world's largest cave passage, full stop, until an even larger one was discovered in Vietnam in 2009.) Every evening around dusk (unless it's raining), millions of bats (see www.muluparkbatcam.com) fly off in search of insects in spiralling, twirling clouds – an awe-inspiring sight. Their corkscrew trajectories are designed to foil the dinner plans of bat hawks perched nearby on the cliffs.

TOP CHOICE **Wind Cave** CAVES

(per person incl boat ride RM40; departures 8.45am & 9.15am) Named for its deliciously cool breezes, Wind Cave has several chambers filled with phantasmagorical forests of stalactites and stalagmites.

Lagang Cave CAVE

(per person incl boat RM55; 1pm) Opened in 2010, this cave gets rave reviews thanks to its extraordinary stalactites and stalagmites and its state-of-the-art light show.

The Pinnacles TREK

(3 days/2 nights per person RM325) Getting to a viewpoint overlooking the Pinnacles – an incredible formation of 45m-high stone spires – involves a boat ride and, between two overnights, an unrelentingly steep 2.4km ascent. The trail passes through some gorgeous jungle.

Gunung Mulu Summit TREK

(4 days/3 nights per person RM405) If you're very fit and looking for real adventure, the 24km ascent to the summit of Gunung Mulu (2376m) may be for you. Bring a sleeping bag, rain gear and enough food for four days.

Headhunters' Trail TREK

Linking the park with Limbang, this route (two days/one night) is named after the Kayan war parties that used to make their way up the Sungai Melinau. You can do it on your own (park HQ has details) but a simpler option is to join a group organised by the park (per person RM395; including the Pinnacles RM550).

GETTING TO BRUNEI: MIRI TO BANDAR SERI BEGAWAN (BSB)

Getting to the border **PHLS Express** (BSB 277 1668, 277 3818, 718 3838, for Danny 880 1180) links Miri with BSB (B$18 from BSB, RM40 from Miri, 3½ hours) twice daily. Departures are from Miri's Pujut bus terminal at about 8am and 4pm. Tickets are sold on board.

Another option for travel between Miri and BSB is a 'private transfer' by a **seven-seater van** (in Malaysia 013 833 2331, 016 807 2893) run by a father-son team (RM60 per person). Departures from Miri are generally at 9am or 10am but may be earlier. It may also be possible to hitch a ride with a **newspaper delivery van** (012 878 0136, in Miri before 4pm) for RM50 per person (3½ hours). Departure from Miri is at 5.30am. For details, contact the Dillenia (Mrs Lee), Minda ord Highlands Guesthouses in Miri or Miri's Visitors Information Centre.

At the border Make sure you have enough pages in your passport for two more chops.

Moving on There is no public transport on the Brunei side of the Miri-Kuala Belait border crossing.

GUIDES, FEES & RESERVATIONS

Almost all of the caves and rainforest treks in Gunung Mulu National Park require that visitors be accompanied by a guide. Advance reservations are a must, especially if you've got your heart set on adventure caving, or on trekking up to the Pinnacles or the summit of Gunung Mulu. July and August are the park's busiest months.

Sleeping

Options at park headquarters include a **hostel** (dm incl breakfast RM40) with 19 beds in a clean, spacious dormitory-style room with ceiling fans, **longhouse rooms** (s/d/tr/q incl breakfast RM170/180/215/250; ❄), **chalets** (s/d/tr/q incl breakfast RM170/180/215/250; ❄) and **garden bungalows** (s/d/tr incl breakfast RM200/230/250; ❄). All private rooms have attached bath; prices include a delicious breakfast. Book at least a few days in advance, especially from June to August – just call ☎085-792300 or visit www.mulupark.com.

Several ultrabudget places are located outside the park, across the bridge from park HQ along the banks of the river.

Mulu River Lodge HOSTEL $
(Edward Nyipa Homestay; ☎012-8527471; dm incl hot breakfast RM35) Has 30 beds in a giant hall.

Gunung Mulu Homestay GUESTHOUSE $
(☎012-8753517; per person camping RM5, bed RM20) Rooms are fanless but clean.

Mulu Homestay GUESTHOUSE $
(☎Anthony 017-8959370; per person camping RM5, bed RM15) Has 20 beds.

If you've got a tent, you can pitch it at some of the private guesthouses across the bridge from park HQ.

Eating

Cooking is not allowed at park accommodation. Some of the guesthouses across the bridge from park HQ serve inexpensive curries, fried rice and noodle dishes.

TOP CHOICE **Wild Mulu Café** ORANG ULU $$
(mains RM8-20; ⌚7.30am-9.30pm, last order 9pm) Serves excellent local dishes such as *Mulu laksa*. A beer or a glass of surprisingly good wine costs RM8. Staff are happy to prepare packed lunches.

Information

Gunung Mulu National Park is truly in the middle of nowhere so there are no ATMs, no pharmacy and only a few poorly-stocked shops. Internet computers are available at park headquarters (per hr RM10).

Getting There & Away

MASwings (www.maswings.com.my) flies 68-seat ATR-72 turboprops from/to Miri, with onward flights to KK and other destinations.

It's possible to travel from Miri to Mulu by river (via Marudi and Long Terawan), but it's a long, long journey and it actually costs more than flying.

Kelabit Highlands

Nestled in Sarawak's northeastern corner, the upland rainforests of the Kelabit (keh-*lah*-bit) Highlands are sandwiched between Gunung Mulu National Park and the Indonesian frontier. The main activity here, other than enjoying the clean, cool air, is trekking from longhouse to longhouse on mountain trails. Unfortunately, logging roads are encroaching and some of the Highlands' primary forests have already succumbed to the chainsaw.

The area is home to the Kelabits, a particularly well-educated Dayak group who number only about 6500, as well as the Penan, a seminomadic group whose members have fared much less well in modern Malaysia.

BARIO

The 'capital' of the highlands, Bario consists of about a dozen 'villages' spread over a beautiful valley, much of it given over to rice growing. Some of the appeal lies in the mountain climate (the valley is 1500m above sea level) and splendid isolation (the only access is by air and torturous 4WD track), but above all it's the unforced hospitality of the Kelabit people that will quickly win you over.

Sights & Activities

TOP CHOICE **Bario Asal Longhouse** LONGHOUSE
This friendly, 19-door longhouse has the traditional Kelabit layout. On the *dapur* (enclosed front verandah) each family has a hearth, while on the other side of the family units is the *tawa'*, a long, wide hallway used for weddings, funerals and celebrations and decorated with historic family photos.

TREKKING GUIDES

With very few exceptions, the only way to explore the Kelabit Highlands is to hire a local guide. Fortunately this could hardly be easier. Any of the guesthouses in Bario can organise a wide variety of short walks and longer treks (eg to Batu Lawi or Gunung Murud) led by guides they know and rely on. If you link up with other travellers in Bario or Miri, the cost of a guide can be shared.

The going rate for guides is RM80 per day (for either a Bario-based day trip or a longer trek), plus an additional RM20 per day if overnighting en route (except in Pa' Lungan). If you're trekking in one direction only (eg Bario to Ba Kelalan), you will be expected to continue paying the guiding fee while your guide returns home.

If you are connecting the dots between rural longhouses, expect to pay RM40 per person (RM55 to RM70 in Pa' Lungan) for a night's sleep plus three meals (you can opt out of lunch and save RM10).

Junglebluesdream Art Gallery ART GALLERY
(☎019-884 9892; junglebluesdream@gmail.com; ⏰daylight hrs) Kelabit artist Stephen Baya displays his renowned paintings, many of which have traditional Kelabit motifs.

Prayer Mountain HALF-DAY HIKE
From the Bario Asal Longhouse, it's a steep, slippery ascent (two hours) up to the summit of Prayer Mountain, which has amazing views of the Bario Valley. Two-thirds of the way up is what may be the world's least pretentious church.

Megalith Trails HIKING
Hidden deep in the jungle around Bario are scores of mysterious megaliths and other 'cultural sites'. Short-haul options include the Pa' Umur Route (1½ hours), which passes a salt spring, and the Pa' Lungan Route (3½ or four hours from Bario to Pa' Lungan, where you'll find longhouse homestays). At research time, trails for megalith treks lasting two, three and five days were being marked. For background, ask your guide for a copy of *Stone Culture of the Northern Highlands of Sarawak, Malaysia* (RM20).

Bario to Ba Kelalan HIKING
The three-day trek from Bario to Ba Kelalan covers a variety of mostly gentle terrain – some of it inside Indonesia – and gives a good overview of the Kelabit Highlands.

To avoid doubling back, you can trek from Bario to Ba Kelalan and then fly down to Miri or Lawas.

Sleeping & Eating

Laid-back Bario is a great place to base yourself during a visit to the Highlands. There are several cosy options, most offering bed-and-board services for a flat per-person rate. En suite bathrooms are in short supply. Some of the most relaxing establishments are a bit out of town (up to 5km).

No need to book ahead – available rooms outstrip the space available on flights and guesthouse owners meet incoming flights at the airport. Check out www.ebario.com (click 'Rooms') for a longer list of homestays and online booking. The places below – a mere sampling of what's available – are listed alphabetically.

Bario Asal Longhouse HOMESTAY $
(☎for Peter 014-8931139; paranmatu@yahoo.com; bed RM20, per person incl 3 meals RM86) This friendly Kelabit longhouse has Bario's only 24-hour electricity.

De Plateau Lodge GUESTHOUSE $
(☎019-8559458; deplateau@gmail.com; bed/full board RM20/70; 📶) A two-storey wooden chalet with a homey living room. Situated about 2km east of the centre (bear left at the fork).

Gem's Lodge GUESTHOUSE $
(☎013-8280507; gems_lodge@yahoo.com; dm RM25, per person incl 3 meals RM60) Tranquillity incarnate, with five pleasant rooms, a two-room chalet (per person RM80), a cosy common area and solar power. Situated 5km southeast of town (bear right at the fork) near the longhouse village of Pa' Umor. Transport to/from the airport by 4WD costs RM25 per person.

Junglebluesdream GUESTHOUSE $
(☎019-8849892; junglebluesdream@gmail.com; per person incl board RM70; 📶) Owned by local artist (and one-time guide), this lodge-cum-gallery has four mural-decorated rooms, quality beds and quilts, and fantastic Kelabit food.

Raja View Inn GUESTHOUSE $
(☎Seluma 019-5940039, Stuart 014-8777322; rajaviewbario@gmail.com; per person incl board RM85) A very welcoming five-room place opened in 2010. The food is Penan-Kelabit fusion.

Information

There are no banks, ATMs or credit-card facilities anywhere in the Kelabit Highlands so bring plenty of small-denomination banknotes for accommodation, food and guides, plus some extra in case you get stranded. There's no pharmacy, either, so bring any medications you might need.

The airport has wi-fi, as do several guesthouses.

eBario Telecentre (☎010-5984170, 013-8099583; www.ebario.com; per hr RM10; ⏲10am-4pm Mon-Fri, to 2pm Sat) Solar powered internet access in 'downtown' Bario.

Getting There & Away

Bario is linked with Miri twice a day by Twin Otters operated by **MASwings** (www.maswings.com.my); checked baggage is limited to 10kg. Weather sometimes causes delays and cancellations.

The people of Bario treat the air link to Miri almost like their own private airline and absolutely love dropping by the wifi-equipped airport terminal to meet flights. Lodging operators often swing by to scoop up trekkers when the planes land.

It is now possible to travel to Bario by 4WD (to/from Miri per person RM150/200, 12 to 14 hours) along rough logging roads.

Limbang Division

Shaped like a crab claw, the Limbang Division slices Brunei in two and separates the diminutive sultanate from Sabah. There is little of interest to travellers.

LIMBANG

A prosperous and bustling river port, Limbang is the northern terminus of the Headhunters Trail to/from Gunung Mulu National Park.

Sights & Activities

Limbang Regional Museum MUSEUM
(www.museum.sarawak.gov.my; Jln Kubu; ⏲9am-4.30pm Tue-Sun) Showcases the area's archaeology, culture and crafts. Situated in one of Charles Brooke's forts 1km south of the centre.

Weekly Market MARKET
(Jln Talap; ⏲Fri) Attracts Bisayah villagers from all around the district.

Sleeping & Eating

Continental Hotel HOTEL $
(☎085-215600; cnr Jln Wong Tsap En & Jln Wayang; d old/new RM45/68; ❄) Has 29 clean, comfy rooms, some with river views.

Tamu Limbang HAWKER $
(Jln Wong Tsap En; mains RM3.50-5; ⏲6.30am-5.30pm) Has food stalls on the 1st floor.

Night Market HAWKER $
(riverfront) For a cheap, tasty dinner.

Information

Golden Cyber World (Jln Pandaruan; per hr RM2.50; ⏲9am-11pm) Has eight internet computers.

Getting There & Around

MASwings (www.maswings.com.my) links Limbang's airport, 7km south of the centre, with Miri.

The fastest way to get to BSB is by **speedboat** (☎012-8522050; RM20 or BSB B$10; ⏲from Limbang 11.30am, from BSB 8am).

Jesselton Express (☎in Limbang 085-212990, 016-8550222, in Brunei +673-718-3838, 717-7755, 719-3835, in KK 016-8360009) has a bus to BSB at 2pm or 3pm and to Bangar, Lawas (RM30), and various towns in Sabah and KK (RM50) at 9.30am.

Ferries to Pulau Labuan (RM30, two hours, departure at 8am) are run by two companies on alternate days, **Lim Pertama** (☎019-805-1260, 019-823-8337) and **Royal Limbang** (☎013-882-3736). Boats depart from Limbang's immigration hall daily at 8am.

LAWAS

Lawas is a transit point in the sliver of Sarawak pinched between Sabah and the Temburong district of Brunei.

GETTING TO BRUNEI: LAWAS TO BANGAR & BANDAR SERI BEGAWAN

Getting to the border The fastest way to get to Brunei (to the Serasa Ferry Terminal, 20km northeast of BSB) is to take the daily **express boat** (☎013-5721413; RM25 or B$22, 1hr). **Jesselton Express** (☎in Lawas 016-8326722) has a 12.30pm bus to Bangar and BSB.

At the border Make sure you have enough pages in your passport for two more chops.

Moving on There is no local transport from the Lawas–Sipitang border crossing into Brunei's Temburong District.

GETTING TO BRUNEI: LIMBANG TO BANDAR SERI BEGAWAN (BSB) & BANGAR

Getting to the border The fastest way to get to BSB is to take a 12-seat **speedboat** (012-8522050; RM20 or BSB B$10; from Limbang 11.30am, from BSB 8am) – if it's running, that is.

Jesselton Express Limbang (085-212-990, 016-855-0222), Brunei (+673-718-3838, 717-7755, 719-3835), KK (016-836-0009) has a bus to BSB at 2pm or 3pm and to Bangar (Temburong District, Brunei) at 9.30am. Tickets are sold at **Wan Wan Cafe & Restaurant** (Jln Pandaruan, Limbang). Taking a taxi from Limbang to the Kuala Lurah border crossing (towards BSB) costs RM40 to RM60 (more from 6pm to 9pm).

At the border Make sure you have enough pages in your passport for two more chops.

Moving on Local buses link the Kuala Lurah border crossing with BSB. In the other direction, there are no buses or taxis from the Limbang–Bangar border crossing to Bangar.

See p61 for details on making this crossing in the other direction.

Sleeping

Borneo Hotel HOTEL $
(085-285700; 1st fl, Lot 437, Jln Masjid Baru; s/d RM58/77;) Offers the best accommodation deals in town.

Getting There & Away

MASwings (www.maswings.com.my) flies Twin Otters from Lawas' airport, 2km from the centre, to Miri and Ba Kelalan.

If there are enough passengers, **ferries** (019-8146868) also go to Pulau Labuan (RM30, 2½ hours, from Lawas 7.30am, from Labuan 12.30pm) daily except Tuesday and Thursday.

Several other companies send daily buses to Miri (without stops in Brunei) and KK (RM20, four hours).

UNDERSTAND MALAYSIA

Malaysia Today

Malaysia has been ruled by the same coalition of major political parties (called the BN: National Front) since the 1970s and, from the time of the country's independence in 1956, the country has been ruled by the same interest groups under different titles. Opposition parties have claimed for years that the BN have manipulated elections and that there have been restrictions put on opposing parties. The BN maintains that it has created a stable government that rightfully retains its popularity. Meanwhile Malaysia was ranked 143rd out of 196 countries in the 2011 Freedom of the Press survey, equal to Angola and Madagascar.

In 2007 and 2011 Bersih (Coalition for Clean and Fair Elections), a group of non-government organisations, staged rallies in KL demanding that the electoral commitee clean up the electoral list, reform absentee voting, use indelible ink, introduce a minimum 21-day campaign period, allow all parties free access to the media, and put an end to electoral fraud. The group was not granted a license to rally – the police claimed the mid-city gatherings would create chaos and traffic problems. Despite this, up to 50,000 people in 2007 and over 20,000 in 2011 marched in KL for electoral reform. On the days of the rallies, the police shot water cannons and tear gas and arrested thousands of people.

The rally in 2007 is said to have greatly aided opposition parties in the 2008 election, when Penang became the first and only state with an opposition majority. With elections set for 2013 pundits are expecting that the ill-fated Bersih rally of 2011 will once again lead to sweeping gains against the BN.

History

Early Influences

The earliest evidence of human life in the region is a 40,000-year-old skull found in Sarawak's Niah Caves. But it was only around 10,000 years ago that the aboriginal Malays, the Orang Asli, began moving down the peninsula from a probable starting point in southwestern China.

By the 2nd century AD, Europeans were familiar with Malaya, and Indian traders had made regular visits in their search for gold, tin and jungle woods. Within the next century Malaya was ruled by the Funan empire, centred in what's now Cambodia, but more significant was the domination of the Sumatra-based Srivijayan empire between the 7th and 13th centuries.

In 1405 Chinese admiral Cheng Ho arrived in Melaka with promises to the locals of protection from the Siamese encroaching from the north. With Chinese support, the power of Melaka extended to include most of the Malay Peninsula. Islam arrived in Melaka around this time and soon spread through Malaya.

European Influence

Melaka's wealth and prosperity attracted European interest and it was taken over by the Portuguese in 1511, then the Dutch in 1641 and the British in 1795.

In 1838 James Brooke, a British adventurer, arrived to find the Brunei sultanate fending off rebellion from inland tribes. Brooke quashed the rebellion and in reward was granted power over part of Sarawak. Appointing himself Raja Brooke, he founded a dynasty that lasted 100 years. By 1881 Sabah was controlled by the British government, which eventually acquired Sarawak after WWII when the third Raja Brooke realised he couldn't afford the area's upkeep. In the early 20th century the British brought in Chinese and Indians, which radically changed the country's racial make-up.

Independence to the Current Day

Malaya achieved *merdeka* (independence) in 1957, but it was followed by a period of instability due to an internal Communist uprising and an external confrontation with neighbouring Indonesia. In 1963 the north Borneo states of Sabah and Sarawak, along with Singapore, joined Malaya to create Malaysia. In 1969 violent interracial riots broke out, particularly in Kuala Lumpur, and hundreds of people were killed. The government moved to dissipate the tensions, which existed mainly between the Malays and the Chinese. Present-day Malaysian society is relatively peaceful and cooperative.

Led from 1981 by outspoken Prime Minister Dr Mahathir Mohamad, Malaysia's economy grew at a rate of over 8% per year until mid-1997, when a currency crisis in neighbouring Thailand plunged the whole of Southeast Asia into recession. After 22 momentous years, Dr Mahathir Mohamad retired on 31 October 2003. He handed power to his anointed successor, Abdullah bin Ahmad Badawi, who went on to convincingly win a general election in March 2004. Since this win, the new prime minister has increasingly been criticised by Mahathir for scrapping many of the former prime minister's projects.

The Culture

The National Psyche

From the ashes of the interracial riots of 1969 the country has forged a more tolerant multicultural society, exemplified by the coexistence in many cities and towns of mosques, Christian churches and Chinese temples. Though ethnic loyalties remain strong and there are undeniable tensions, the concept of a much-discussed single 'Malaysian' identity is gaining credence and for the most part everyone coexists harmoniously. The friendliness and hospitality of Malaysians is what most visitors see and experience.

Moving from the cities to the more rural parts of the country, the laid-back ethos becomes stronger and Islamic culture comes more to the fore, particularly on the peninsula's east coast. In Malaysian Borneo you'll be fascinated by the communal lifestyle of the tribes who still live in jungle longhouses (enormous wooden structures on stilts that house tribal communities under one roof; see p462). In longhouses, hospitality is a key part of the social framework.

Lifestyle

The *kampung* (village) is at the heart of the Malay world and operates according to a system of *adat* (customary law) that emphasises collective rather than individual responsibility. Devout worship of Islam and older spiritual beliefs go hand in hand with this. However, despite the mutually supportive nature of the *kampung* environment, and growing Westernisation across Malaysia, some very conservative interpretations of Islam continue in certain areas, particularly along the peninsula's east coast.

The rapid modernisation of Malaysian life has led to some incongruous scenes. In Sarawak, some ramshackle longhouses and huts sport satellite dishes and have recent-vintage cars parked on the rutted driveways out front. And almost everywhere you go people incessantly finger mobile phones as if they're simply unable to switch them off.

DID YOU KNOW?

Malaysia is obsessed with world records and publishes its own *Malaysia Book of World Records* once a year. Successes include the most days spent inside a box with 6069 scorpions and creating the highest stack of cans in 15 minutes.

Population

Malaysians come from a number of different ethnic groups: Malays, Chinese, Indians, the indigenous Orang Asli (literally, 'Original People') of the peninsula, and the various tribes of Sarawak and Sabah in Malaysian Borneo. The mixing of these groups has created the colourful cultures and delicious cuisine that makes Malaysia such a fabulous destination.

It's reasonable to generalise that the Malays control the government while the Chinese dominate the economy. Approximately 85% of the country's population of nearly 25 million people lives in Peninsular Malaysia and the other 15% in Sabah and Sarawak on Borneo.

There are still small, scattered groups of Orang Asli in Peninsular Malaysia. Although most of these people have given up their nomadic or shifting-agriculture techniques and have been absorbed into modern Malay society, a few such groups still live in the forests.

Dayak is the term used for the non-Muslim people of Borneo. It is estimated there are more than 200 Dayak tribes in Borneo, including the Iban and Bidayuh in Sarawak and the Kadazan in Sabah. Smaller groups include the Kenyah, Kayan and Penan, whose way of life and traditional lands are rapidly disappearing.

Religion

The Malays are almost all Muslims. But despite Islam being the state religion, freedom of religion is guaranteed. The Chinese are predominantly followers of Taoism and Buddhism, though some are Christians. The majority of the region's Indian population comes from the south of India and are Hindu and Christian, although a sizeable percentage are Muslim.

While Christianity has made no great inroads into Peninsular Malaysia, it has had a much greater impact in Malaysian Borneo, where many indigenous people have been converted and carry Christian as well as traditional names. Others still follow animist traditions.

Arts

It's along the predominantly Malay east coast of Peninsular Malaysia that you'll find Malay arts and crafts, culture and games at their liveliest. Malaysian Borneo is replete with the arts and crafts of the country's indigenous peoples.

Arts & Crafts

A famous Malaysian Bornean art is *pua kumbu,* a colourful weaving technique used to produce both everyday and ceremonial items.

The most skilled woodcarvers are generally held to be the Kenyah and Kayan peoples, who used to carve enormous, finely detailed *kelirieng* (burial columns) from tree trunks.

Originally an Indonesian craft, the production of batik cloth is popular in Malaysia and has its home in Kelantan. A speciality of Kelantan and Terengganu, *kain songket* is a handwoven fabric with gold and silver

THE PERANAKANS

One of Peninsular Malaysia's most celebrated cultures is that of the Peranakans, descendants of Chinese immigrants who, from the 16th century onwards, settled in Singapore, Melaka and Penang. While these arrivals often married Malay women, others imported their wives from China; all of them like to refer to themselves as Straits-born or Straits Chinese to distinguish themselves from later arrivals from China. Another name you may hear for these people is Baba-Nonyas, after the Peranakan words for males *(baba)* and females *(nonya)*.

The Peranakans took the religion of the Chinese, but the customs, language and dress of the Malays. The Peranakans were often wealthy traders who could afford to indulge their passion for sumptuous furnishings, jewellery and brocades. Today they are most famous for their delicious fusion cooking that's best experienced in Melaka (see p399).

threads through the material. *Mengkuang* is a far more prosaic form of weaving using pandanus leaves and strips of bamboo to make baskets, bags and mats.

Dance

Menora is a dance-drama of Thai origin performed by an all-male cast in grotesque masks; *mak yong* is the female version. The upbeat *joget* (better known around Melaka as *chakuncha*) is Malaysia's most popular traditional dance, often performed at Malay weddings by professional dancers.

Rebana kercing is a dance performed by young men to the accompaniment of tambourines. The *rodat* is a dance from Terengganu and is accompanied by the *tar* drum.

Music

Traditional Malay music is based largely on the *gendang* (drum), of which there are more than a dozen types. Other percussion instruments include the gong, *cerucap* (made of shells), *raurau* (coconut shells), *kertuk* and *pertuang* (both made from bamboo), and the wooden *celampang*.

Wind instruments include a number of types of flute (such as the *seruling* and *serunai*) and the trumpet-like *nafiri*, while stringed instruments include the *biola*, *gambus* and *sundatang*.

The *gamelan*, a traditional Indonesian gong-orchestra, is also found in the state of Kelantan, where a typical ensemble will comprise four different gongs, two xylophones and a large drum.

> **MUST SEE**
>
> Highly recommended viewing is anything starring P Ramlee, who was the king of Malaysian cinema in the 1950s and acted in some 70 films. He remains a national icon; a road is named after him in KL.

Food & Drink

Food

Mealtime in Malaysia is a highly social event and the food strongly reflects the country's Malay, Chinese and Indian influences. As an approximate guide to the cost of a main dish, three pricing categories are used in this guide: budget ($) is up to RM10; midrange ($$) is from RM10 to RM20; and top end ($$$) is RM20 or over.

There are fewer culinary choices outside the cities, where staple meals of *mee goreng* (fried noodles) and *nasi goreng* (fried rice) predominate. Vegetarian dishes are usually available at both Malay and Indian cafes, but are hardly sighted at *kedai kopi* (coffee shops). You can also find an excellent selection of fruits and vegetables at markets.

Roti canai (flaky flat bread dipped in a small amount of dhal and potato curry) is probably the cheapest meal (around RM1.50) in Malaysia. But really everything, from seafood laksa to the freshly caught and cooked wild cat or mouse deer you may be offered at a longhouse, is good and often cheap.

Halfway between a drink and a dessert is *ais kacang*, something similar to an old-fashioned snow-cone, except that the shaved ice is topped with syrups and condensed milk, and it's all piled on top of a foundation of beans and jellies (sometimes corn kernels). It sounds and looks gross but tastes terrific.

Drink

Tap water is safe to drink in many cities but check with locals if you're unsure.

With the aid of a blender and crushed ice, simple and delicious juice concoctions are whipped up in seconds. Lurid soybean drinks are sold at street stalls and soybean milk is also available in soft-drink bottles. Medicinal teas are a big hit with the health-conscious Chinese.

Alcohol isn't popular with the Muslim population and incurs incredibly high taxes. A mug of beer at a *kedai kopi* will cost around RM7, and around RM12 to RM15 at bars and clubs. Anchor and Tiger beers are popular, as are locally brewed Carlsberg and Guinness. Indigenous people have a soft spot for *tuak* (rice wine), which tends to revolt first-timers but is apparently an acquired taste. Another rural favourite is the dark-coloured spirit *arak*, which is smooth and potent.

Environment

The Land

Malaysia covers 329,758 sq km and consists of two distinct regions. Peninsular Malaysia is the long finger of land extending south from Asia and though the mountainous northern half has some dense jungle coverage, unprotected forests are getting cut down at an alarming rate, mostly to create palm oil plantations. The peninsula's western side has a large fertile plain running to the sea, while the eastern side is fringed with sandy beaches. Malaysian Borneo consists of Sarawak and Sabah; both states are covered in thick jungle and have extensive river systems. Sabah is crowned by Mt Kinabalu (4095m), the highest mountain between the Himalaya and New Guinea.

Wildlife

Malaysia's ancient rainforests are endowed with a cornucopia of life forms. In Peninsular Malaysia alone there are over 8000 species of flowering plants, including the world's tallest tropical tree species, the *tualang*. In Malaysian Borneo, where hundreds of new species have been discovered since the 1990s, you'll find the world's largest flower, the *Rafflesia*, measuring up to 1m across, as well as the world's biggest cockroach. Mammals include elephants, rhinos (extremely rare), tapirs, tigers, leopards, honey bears, *tempadau* (forest cattle), gibbons and monkeys (including, in Borneo, the bizarre proboscis monkey), orang-utans and pangolins (scaly anteaters). Bird species include spectacular pheasants, sacred hornbills and many groups of colourful birds such as kingfishers, sunbirds, woodpeckers and barbets. Snakes include cobras, vipers and pythons. Once a favourite nesting ground for leatherback turtles, recorded landings now hover around 10 per year.

National Parks

Malaysia's 19 national parks cover barely 5% of the country's landmass. The country's major national park is Taman Negara, on the peninsula, while Gunung Mulu and Kinabalu are the two main parks in Sarawak and Sabah, respectively. Especially on Borneo, the rarity and uniqueness of local flora and fauna is such that scientists – from dragonfly experts to palm-tree specialists – are regular visitors and vocal proponents of new parks and reserves both on land and in the surrounding waters. There are also 13 marine parks in Malaysia, notably around Pulau Perhentian, Tioman and Sipadan, although enforcement of protection measures is very loose.

Environmental Issues

When it comes to environmental faux pas, Malaysia has done it all. Logging is believed to have destroyed more than 60% of the country's rainforests and generates some US$4.5 billion per year for big business. Another growing phenomenon is palm-tree plantations, where vast swathes of land are razed and planted with trees that yield lucrative palm oil. But the crown of eco and social irresponsibility goes to Bakun Dam in Sarawak which began to flood some 690 sq km of some of the world's most diverse rainforest in late 2010 and forced up to 10,000 indigenous peoples from their homes. The dam been criticised as being corrupt, ill-planned and unnecessary but the state already has plans to build more dams in the region. In equally bad environmental news, much of the power generated at Bakun looks likely to go to a giant aluminium smelter in Sarawak.

Responsible ecotourism is the traveller's best weapon in a country where cold cash is fiercer than tigers; see p478 for information.

SURVIVAL GUIDE

Directory A–Z

Accommodation

In this book accommodation costing up to RM100 per night is considered budget ($), from RM100 to RM400 is midrange ($$), and above RM400 is top end ($$$).

Books

Lonely Planet's *Malaysia, Singapore & Brunei* has all the information you'll need for extended travel to these countries while *Kuala Lumpur, Melaka & Penang* focuses on those three cities. Lonely Planet also publishes the *Malay Phrasebook*, an introduction to the Malay language.

Budding explorers should read *Stranger in the Forest*, Eric Hansen's account of a remarkable half-year journey across Borneo on foot, and Redmond O'Hanlon's marvellous *Into the Heart of Borneo*. Essential reading for anyone intending to do a lot of local mountain walking is *Mountains of Malaysia – A Practical Guide and Manual*, by John Briggs.

Ghost Train to the Eastern Star by the forever opinionated Paul Theroux sees the writer get laid low by a tummy bug in Penang. For an inside, modern view of the country read *Urban Odysseys*, edited by Janet Tay and Eric Forbes, which is a mixed bag of short stories set in Kuala Lumpur that capture the city's flavour.

TRAVEL HINTS

» Malaysia is a Muslim country so dress appropriately by covering everything to the knees and over the shoulders.

» Airfares can be so cheap around Borneo that flying is sometimes cheaper than bussing.

Business Hours

Banks are open from 10am to 3pm Monday to Friday, and 9.30am to 11.30am Saturday. Department stores open from 10am to 8pm. Government offices open 8am to 12.45pm and 2pm to 4.15pm Monday to Thursday, and 8am to 12.15pm and 2.45pm to 4.15pm Friday. Shopping malls are open from 10am to 9pm, while shops open 9am to 6pm Monday to Saturday.

In the more Islamic-minded states of Kedah, Perlis, Kelantan and Terengganu, government offices, banks and many shops close on Friday and on Saturday afternoon.

Exceptions to these hours are noted in individual reviews.

Customs

When arriving in Malaysia, note that you are legally entitled to carry 1L of alcohol and 200 cigarettes. Cameras, portable radios, perfume, cosmetics and watches do not incur duty. Trafficking of illegal substances can result in the death penalty – don't do it.

Dangers & Annoyances

In general Malaysia is very safe, with violent attacks being uncommon. However, the usual travel precautions apply, such as restraining your urge to go wandering around seedy areas alone late at night. Credit-card fraud is a growing problem so only use your cards at established businesses and guard your credit-card numbers. The snatching of bags by thieves on motorcycles is a recurring crime in KL, Johor Bahru and Penang's Georgetown, so keep bags away from the roadside in these areas. In seedy areas such as Ipoh and KL's Golden Triangle, male travellers may be harassed to buy pirated porn DVDs, drugs or the services of prostitutes.

A disturbingly high incidence of theft occurs in guesthouse dorms. Sometimes this involves an outsider sneaking in and other times it involves fellow travellers. Don't leave valuables or important documents unattended, and carry a small padlock.

See p479 for issues specific to women travellers.

Rabies is an ever-present problem in Malaysia – you should treat any animal bite very seriously. Leeches can be a nuisance after heavy rain on jungle walks; see p430 for tips on discouraging them.

Driving Licence

A valid overseas driving licence is required for vehicle rental.

Embassies & Consulates

Unless otherwise specified, all the following foreign embassies are in Kuala Lumpur and are generally open 8am to 12.30pm and 1.30pm to 4.30pm Monday to Friday. A full list of embassies and consulates in Malaysia can be found at www.mycen.com.my/malaysia/embassy.html.

Australia (Map p384; ☎03-2146 5555; www.australia.org.my; 6 Jln Yap Kwan Seng)

Brunei (off Map p384; ☎03-2161 2800; Level 19, Menara Tan & Tan, 207 Jln Tun Razak)

Canada (off Map p384; ☎03-2718 3333; Level 18, Menara Tan & Tan, 207 Jln Tun Razak)

France (off Map p384; ☎03-2053 5500; 196 Jln Ampang)

Germany (off Map p384; ☎03-2142 9666; www.kuala-lumpur.diplo.de; Level 26, Menara Tan & Tan, 207 Jln Tun Razak)

Indonesia Georgetown (off Map p408; ☎04-227 5141; 467 Jln Burma, Georgetown, Penang); Kota Kinabalu (Map p436; ☎088-219110; Jln Kemajuan; ⏲8am-1pm Mon-Fri); Kuala Lumpur (off Map p384; ☎03-2116 4100; 233 Jln Tun Razak; visa R170, ready in one day); Kuching (off Map p452; ☎082-241734; 111 Jln Tun Haji Openg, Kuching, Sarawak; ⏲8.30am-noon & 2-4pm Mon-Fri); Tawau (☎089-772052; Jln Apas, Tawau, Sabah)

Ireland (off Map p384; ☎03-2161 2963; Ireland House, the Amp Walk, 218 Jln Ampang)

Netherlands (off Map p384; ☎03-2168 6200; www.netherlands.org.my; 7th fl, the Amp Walk, 218 Jln Ampang)

MUST READ

The Harmony Silk Factory, by Malaysian author Tash Aw, is set deep in the heart of Peninsular Malaysia partly during WWII and won the 2005 Whitbread First Novel award.

New Zealand (Map p384; ☎03-2078 2533; Level 21, Menara IMC, 8 Jln Sultan Ismail)

Singapore (off Map p384; ☎03-2161 6277; 209 Jln Tun Razak)

Thailand Georgetown (off Map p408; ☎04-226 8029; 1 Jln Tunku Abdul Rahman, Georgetown, Penang); Kota Bharu (Map p427; ☎09-744 0867; 4426 Jln Pengkalan Chepa, Kota Bharu, Kelantan); Kuala Lumpur (off Map p384; ☎03-2148 8222; 206 Jln Ampang)

UK (off Map p384; ☎03-2148 2122; www.britain.org.my; 185 Jln Ampang)

USA (off Map p384; ☎03-2168 5000; http://malaysia.usembassy.gov; 376 Jln Tun Razak)

Festivals & Events

There are many cultures and religions coexisting in Malaysia, which means there are many occasions for celebration throughout the year.

Ramadan is the major annual Muslim event, connected with the 30 days during which Muslims cannot eat, drink, smoke or have sex from sunrise to sunset. The dates of Ramadan change every year; in 2012 it begins on 20 July, and in 2013 it begins on 9 July.

Thaipusam (January/February) One of the most dramatic Hindu festivals, in which devotees honour Lord Subramaniam with acts of amazing physical resilience. Self-mutilating worshippers make the procession to the Batu Caves outside KL.

Malaysian Grand Prix (March/April) Formula One's big outing in Southeast Asia is held at the Sepang International Circuit in Selangor either at the end of March or early April.

Gawai Dayak (late May/early June) Festival of the Dayaks in Sarawak, marking the end of the rice season. War dances, cock fights and blowpipe events take place.

Festa de San Pedro (June) Christian celebration on 29 June in honour of the patron saint of the fishing community; notably celebrated by the Eurasian-Portuguese community of Melaka.

Dragon Boat Festival (June to August) Celebrated in Penang.

Rainforest World Music Festival (July/August) Held for three days at the Sarawak Cultural Village (p458), this music and arts festival features musicians from around the world and highlights indigenous music from Borneo.

National Day (Hari Kebangsaan) (August) Malaysia celebrates its independence on 31 August with events all over the country, but particularly in KL where there are parades and a variety of performances in the Lake Gardens.

Moon Cake Festival (September) Chinese festival celebrating the overthrow of Mongol warlords in ancient China with the eating of moon cakes and the lighting of colourful paper lanterns.

Festival of the Nine Emperor Gods (October) Involves nine days of Chinese operas, processions and other events honouring the nine emperor gods.

Deepavali (November) The Festival of Lights, in which tiny oil lamps are lit outside Hindu homes, celebrates Rama's victory over the demon King Ravana.

Gay & Lesbian Travellers

Conservative political parties and religious groups make a regular habit of denouncing gays and lesbians in Malaysia, a country where Muslim homosexuality is punishable by imprisonment and caning. Fortunately, these groups remain on the fringe and outright persecution of gays and lesbians in the country is rare. Nonetheless, while in Malaysia, gay and lesbian travellers (particularly the former) should avoid any behaviour that attracts unwanted attention. Visit www.utopia-asia.com or www.fridae.com, both of which provide good coverage of gay and lesbian events and activities right across Southeast Asia.

Internet Access

Internet access is widespread and available at numerous internet cafes, backpacker hang-outs and shopping malls, generally on fast broadband connections. In cities, rates range from RM2 to RM4 per hour; on islands and in remote areas, rates skyrocket (and speed plummets) to around RM6 to RM20 per hour. Wi-fi is easily found in cities, sparingly in medium-sized towns and often not at all in the countryside.

Internet Resources

Lonely Planet (lonelyplanet.com) Succinct summaries on travelling to Southeast Asia, and the Thorn Tree bulletin board and other useful travel resources.

Malaysiakini (www.malaysiakini.com) Find out what's really going on in the country at Malaysia's best online news site.

Tourism Malaysia (www.tourismmalaysia.gov.my) The official government site for tourist information has events calendars, regional links, background information, and listings of domestic and international tourist offices.

Legal Matters

In any of your dealings with the local police it pays to be deferential. Minor misdemeanours may be overlooked, but don't count on it and don't offer anyone a bribe.

It's simply not worth having anything to do with drugs in Malaysia: drug trafficking carries a mandatory death penalty, and even the possession of tiny amounts of drugs for personal use can bring about a lengthy jail sentence and a beating with the *rotan* (cane).

Maps

Periplus (https://peripluspublishinggroup.com) has maps covering Malaysia, Peninsular Malaysia and KL. Tourism Malaysia's free *Map of Malaysia* has useful distance charts, facts about the country and inset maps of many of the major cities.

For accurate maps of rural areas contact the **National Survey & Mapping Department** (off Map p384; Ibu Pejabat Ukur & Pemetaan Malaysia; ☎03-2617 0800; www.jupem.gov.my; Jln Semarak, Kuala Lumpur; ⏰7.30am-5.30pm Mon-Fri).

Media

The government tightly controls the main media outlets, and will often pursue its critics through the courts. The main newspapers tend to parrot the official line and the less said about news on Malaysian TV channels, the better.

NEWSPAPERS

Malaysia has newspapers in English, Malay, Chinese and Tamil. The *New Straits Times* is the main English-language publication, while *Borneo Post* focuses more on issues relevant to Sabah and Sarawak. Foreign magazines are widely available.

RADIO

There's a variety of radio stations in Malaysia broadcasting in Bahasa Malaysia, English and various Chinese and Indian languages and dialects. The number of English stations is highest around KL, while radio-wave pickings are scarce in Malaysian Borneo.

TV

Malaysia has two government TV channels (RTM 1 and 2) and two commercial stations. Programs range from local productions in various languages to Western imports.

Money

Bargaining is not usually required for everyday goods in Malaysia, but feel free to bargain when purchasing souvenirs, antiques and other tourist items, even when the prices are displayed. Transport prices are generally fixed, but negotiation is required for trishaws and taxis around town or for charter.

Tipping is not common in Malaysia.

Post

There are poste restante services at all major post offices, which are open from 8am to 5pm daily except Sundays and public holidays (also closed on Fridays in Kedah, Kelantan and Terengganu districts).

Aerograms and postcards cost 50 sen to send to any destination. Letters weighing 20g or less cost 90 sen to Asia, RM1.40 to Australia or New Zealand, RM1.50 to the UK and Europe, and RM1.80 to North America.

You can send parcels from any major post office, although the rates are fairly high (from RM20 to RM60 for a 1kg parcel, depending on the destination).

Public Holidays

Although some public holidays have a fixed annual date, Hindus, Muslims and Chinese follow a lunar calendar, which means the dates for many events vary each year.

Chinese New Year is the most important celebration for the Chinese community and is marked with dragon dances and street parades. The major holiday of the Muslim calendar, Hari Raya Puasa marks the end of the month-long fast of Ramadan with three days of joyful celebration. During Hari Raya Puasa and Chinese New Year, accommodation may be difficult to obtain. At these times, many businesses may also be closed and transport can be fully booked.

In addition to national public holidays, each state has its own holidays, usually associated with the sultan's birthday or a Muslim celebration.

National holidays:

New Year's Day 1 January

Chinese New Year January/February

Birth of the Prophet March

Wesak Day April/May

Labour Day 1 May

Agong's (King's) Birthday 1st Saturday in June

National Day 31 August

Hari Raya Puasa September/October

Deepavali November

Hari Raya Haji December

Awal Muharam December

Christmas Day 25 December

Responsible Travel

Malaysia has a serious rubbish problem, so try to create as little waste as possible by avoiding packaged drinks and eating locally grown food; if possible, bring your own water filter to avoid buying water in plastic bottles. When diving and snorkelling never touch or walk on coral and avoid tour operators who practise poor ecological habits such as dropping anchor on coral. Try to buy local handicrafts and souvenirs in preference to mass-produced items, so that the money goes back to local communities. It might seem obvious, but never buy butterflies or any products made from endangered species.

Studying

Kota Bharu and Cherating are the best places to get a hands-on feel for batik, while Kuala Lumpur is the place to study Bahasa Malaysia. Cooking courses are occasionally offered in Kuala Lumpur and Penang.

Ask at local tourist offices to see what's on offer when you're in town.

Telephone

If you have your mobile phone with you, once you've sorted out a local SIM (buy one for RM8.50) you should have no problem dialling overseas. If you're sticking to Peninsula Malaysia any of the major mobile phone service providers are fine, but if you're heading into the remoter parts of Malaysian Borneo then get **Celcom** (www.celcom.com.my), which has the largest coverage. Rates for a local call are around 40 sen per minute and an SMS is 10 to 15 sen. Top-up cards for prepaid SIM cards are available at all 7-Elevens and, if you're planning on calling overseas a lot, it's probably worthwhile getting a calling card too; a good one is TM's **iTalk** (www.i-talk.com.my).

International direct dial (IDD) phone calls and operator-assisted calls can be made from any private phone. The access code for making international calls to most countries is ☎00. For information on international calls, dial ☎103.

To call Malaysia from outside the country, dial ☎60, drop the 0 before the Malaysian area code, then dial the number you want.

Toilets

Although there are still some places with Asian squat-style toilets in Malaysia, you'll most often find Western-style ones these days. At public facilities toilet paper is not usually provided. Instead, you will find a hose which you are supposed to use as a bidet or, in cheaper places, a bucket of water and a tap.

Public toilets in shopping malls and at transport depots are usually staffed by attendants and cost 10 sen to 30 sen to use; an extra 10 sen often gets you a dozen sheets of toilet paper.

Tourist Information

Tourism Malaysia (www.tourismmalaysia.gov.my) has a network of overseas offices, which are useful for predeparture planning. Its domestic offices range from extremely helpful to hardly ever open, depending on the region. All stock some decent brochures as well as the excellent *Map of Malaysia*.

Travellers With Disabilities

For the mobility impaired, Malaysia can be a nightmare. In most cities and towns there are often no footpaths, kerbs are very high and pedestrian crossings are few and far between. Budget hotels almost never have lifts. On the upside, KL's modern urban railway lines are reasonably wheelchair-accessible.

Malaysia Airlines and Keretapi Tanah Melayu (the national railway service) offer 50% discounts for travellers with disabilities.

Visas

Visitors must have a passport valid for at least six months beyond the date of entry into Malaysia. Nationals of most countries are given a 30- to 60-day visa on arrival. The following gives a brief overview of other requirements – full details of visa regulations are available on the website www.kln.gov.my.

Commonwealth citizens (except those from India, Bangladesh, Sri Lanka and Pakistan) and citizens of the Republic of Ireland, Switzerland, the Netherlands, San Marino and Liechtenstein do not require a visa to visit Malaysia.

Citizens of Austria, Belgium, the Czech Republic, Denmark, Finland, France,

Germany, Hungary, Iceland, Italy, Japan, Luxembourg, Norway, Slovak Republic, South Korea, Sweden, the United States and most Arab countries do not require a visa for a visit not exceeding three months.

Citizens of Greece, South Africa and many South American and African countries do not require a visa for a visit not exceeding one month. Most other nationalities are given a shorter stay-period or require a visa.

Citizens of Israel cannot enter Malaysia.

Sarawak is semi-autonomous. If you travel from Peninsular Malaysia or Sabah into Sarawak, your passport will be checked on arrival and a new stay-permit issued, usually for 30 days. Travelling from either Sabah or Sarawak back to Peninsular Malaysia there are no formalities and you do not start a new entry period, so your 30-day permit from Sabah or Sarawak remains valid. You can then extend your initial 30-day permit, though it can be difficult to get an extension in Sarawak.

Volunteering

Opportunities include the following:

LASSie (www.langkawilassie.org.my) Dog and cat lovers may want to help out at the Langkawi Animal Shelter & Sanctuary Foundation, next to Bon Ton Resort.

Ma Daerah turtle sanctuary (http://madaerah.org) About 70km south of Terengganu, you can help work to protect turtle populations along the east coast.

Malaysian AIDS Council (www.mac.org.my) Assist in its campaigning work.

Miso Walai homestay program (http://misowalaihomestay.com) Gets travellers involved with local wetlands restoration projects.

Regional Environmental Awareness Cameron Highlands (Reach; www.reach.org.my) Take part in reforestation and recycling programs in the Cameron Highlands.

Sepilok Orang-utan Centre Has one of the best established volunteer centres (p444).

Wild Asia (www.wildasia.net) Options are generally connected with the environment and sustainable tourism in the region.

Women Travellers

Foreign women travelling in Malaysia can expect some attention, though most of it will just involve stares from locals unfamiliar with (or curious about) Westerners. It helps, and is much more respectful of the culture, if you dress conservatively by wearing long pants or skirts and loose tops that cover the shoulders. Western women are not expected to cover their heads with scarves (outside mosques, that is). In resort areas you can wear shorts, sleeveless tops and swimwear, but it isn't appropriate anywhere in the country to sunbathe topless. On more remote beaches you're better off doing like the locals do and swimming fully clothed. Keep a watch out for sleazy local beach boys in Langkawi, Cherating and the Perhentians.

Tampons and pads are widely available, especially in big cities, and over-the-counter medications are also fairly easy to find.

Getting There & Away

Air

Airports & Airlines

The gateway to Peninsular Malaysia is the city of Kuala Lumpur, although Penang and Johor Bahru (JB) also have international connections. Singapore is a handy arrival/departure point, since it's just a short trip across the Causeway from JB. Malaysia Airlines is the country's main airline carrier; although AirAsia and Firefly flights are much cheaper. AirAsia connects KL to Europe, Australia, India, Indonesia, Thailand and China.

The following are some airlines servicing Malaysia; numbers beginning with ☎03 are for Kuala Lumpur.

AirAsia (code AK; ☎03-8775 4000; www.airasia.com)

Air India (code AI; ☎03-2142 0166; www.airindia.com)

Cathay Pacific Airways (code CX; ☎03-2035 2788; www.cathaypacific.com)

China Airlines (code CI; ☎03-2142 7344; www.china-airlines.com)

Garuda Indonesian Airlines (code GA; ☎03-2162 2811; www.garuda-indonesia.com)

Japan Airlines (code JL; ☎03-2161 1722; www.jal.com)

Lufthansa (code LH; ☎03-2161 4666; www.lufthansa.com)

Malaysia Airlines (code MH; ☎1300 883 000, 03-2161 0555; www.malaysiaairlines.com)

Royal Brunei Airlines (code BI; ☎03-2070 7166; www.bruneiair.com)

Singapore Airlines (code SQ; ☎03-2692 3122; www.singaporeair.com)

Thai Airways International (code TG; ☎03-2031 2900; www.thaiairways.com)

Vietnam Airlines (code VN; www.vietnamairlines.com)

Tickets

Brunei Malaysia Airlines and AirAsia have direct flights between Bandar Seri Begawan and KL.

Cambodia Flights between KL and Phnom Penh are available with Malaysia Airlines and AirAsia. AirAsia also flies from KL to Siem Reap.

Indonesia AirAsia and Firefly have connections between KL and numerous destinations in Indonesia. **Kartika Airlines** (www.kartika-airlines.com) flies between Medan in Sumatra and Penang. From Kuching **Batavia Air** (www.batavia-air.co.id) flies to Pontianak.

Philippines You can fly with Malaysia Airlines or AirAsia from KL to Cebu/Manila. AirAsia also has flights to Manila from Kota Kinabalu.

Singapore AirAsia, Firefly, Malaysia Airlines and Singapore Airlines operate frequent flights between Singapore and KL as well as several other destinations in Malaysia.

Thailand AirAsia has flights from Bangkok and a dozen other Thai cities to KL. Firefly connects KL (Subang) with Ko Samui and Penang with Phuket.

Vietnam Malaysia Airlines and Vietnam Airlines operate flights from KL to Ho Chi Minh City and Hanoi. AirAsia runs flights from KL to Hanoi.

Land

BRUNEI

Only a few of the buses that pass through Brunei are allowed to let passengers off inside the sultanate. See p466 for more details on both crossings.

INDONESIA

Frequent buses link Pontianak in Kalimantan with Kuching and Miri in Sarawak, and Kota Kinabulu in Sabah. The buses cross at the Tebedu/Entikong border (see p456)

SINGAPORE

At the southern tip of Peninsular Malaysia you can cross into Singapore via Johor Bahru by bus (see p416). Taking the train from JB is less convenient.

THAILAND

From western Peninsular Malaysia, you can travel by bus from Alor Setar to the border crossing at Bukit Kayu Hitam (p110) and on to the transit town of Hat Yai in Thailand, via Sadao.

There are trains passing through Alor Setar to Padang Besar and then continuing north into Thailand (see p413).

Though there is a border crossing at Rantau Panjang on the eastern peninsula that is geographically convenient to Kota Bharu, all travel through this section of southern Thailand should be avoided until the security situation vastly improves.

There is also a border crossing between Keroh (Malaysia) and Betong (Thailand), but at the time of writing it was inadvisable to travel here due to the violence in Yala Province, Thailand.

Sea

BRUNEI

Boats connect Brunei to Lawas and Limbang in Sarawak, and to Pulau Labuan, from where boats go to Sabah. With the exception of speedboats for Limbang, all international boats depart from Muara, 25km northeast of Bandar Seri Begawan.

See p469 for more information on boat services.

INDONESIA

The following are the main ferry routes between Indonesia and Malaysia:

- Pulau Bengkalis, Sumatra to Melaka (see p401)
- Dumai, Sumatra to Melaka (see p401)
- Pekanbaru, Sumatra to Melaka (see p401)
- Tanjung Pinang on Pulau Bintan (Riau Islands) to JB (p417)
- Pulau Batam (Riau Islands) to JB (p417)
- Tarakan, Kalimantan to Tawau (see p447).

THAILAND

Regular ferries run between Pulau Langkawi and Satun in Thailand and to Ko Lipe in Thailand with onward service as far as Ko Lanta (see p414).

Getting Around

Air

The main domestic operators are **Malaysia Airlines** (code MAS; ☎1300 883 000, outside Malaysia ☎03-2161 0555; www.malaysia-airlines.com.my), MAS subsidiary **Firefly** (☎03-7845 4543; www.fireflyz.com.my) and **AirAsia** (☎1300 889 933, outside Malaysia ☎603 8660 4343; www.airasia.com).

Berjaya Air (☎03-7847 8228; www.berjaya-air.com) flies between KL (Subang), Pulau Tioman and Pulau Redang, as well as Singapore and Koh Samui in Thailand.

In Malaysian Borneo, **MASwings** (☎1300 883 000, outside Malaysia 603 7843 3000; www.maswings.com.my) offers domestic flights within and between Sarawak and Sabah. These services often book up during school holidays.

Bicycle

The main road system in Malaysia has good surfaces, making the country good for bike touring, but the secondary road system is limited. Mountain bikes are recommended for forays off the beaten track.

KL Bike Hash (www.klmbh.org) has a whole load of useful information and links to other cycling-connected sites in Malaysia. Also see **David's Cycling Adventure** (www.bicycletouringmalaysia.com).

Boat

There are no ferry services between Malaysian Borneo and the peninsula. On a local level, there are boats and ferries between the peninsula and offshore islands, and along the rivers of Sabah and Sarawak – see the relevant sections for details. If a boat looks overloaded or otherwise unsafe, do not board it.

Bus

Peninsular Malaysia has an excellent bus system. In larger towns there may be several bus stations. Local and regional buses often operate from one station and long-distance buses from another; in other cases, KL for example, bus stations are differentiated by the destinations they serve.

On major runs you can usually just turn up and get on the next bus. On many routes there are air-conditioned buses – but take your arctic gear, the air-con is usually pumped up to the max! *Ekspres,* in the Malaysian context, often means indeterminate stops.

In Sabah, daily express buses, minivans and share taxis follow the paved arc from Kota Kinabalu to Tawau, passing most of the tourism hot spots. Circling back to Kota Kinabalu through the south (via Sapulut) is a more difficult task, as there's no public transport. It's important to note that many of Sabah's natural gems are managed by private organisations, so you may find yourself on a tour more times than not.

In Sarawak, the Pan Borneo Highway from Kuching to Sabah via Miri and Brunei is in great shape. Express buses ply the Kuching–Miri route all the time, although it should be noted that the ferry from Kuching to Sibu is significantly faster than the bus (see p460 for details).

Car & Motorcycle

Roads in Malaysia are generally high quality and driving standards aren't too hair-raising. Road rules are basically the same as in Britain and Australia. Driving in KL and some of the bigger cities can be a nightmare, however, and you'll always have to keep an eye out for motorcyclists and animals. Cars are right-hand drive and you drive on the left side of the road. The speed limit is officially 110km per hour.

Unlimited-distance car-rental costs from around RM180/1155 per day/week, including insurance and collision-damage waiver.

Be aware that insurance companies will most likely wash their hands of you if you injure yourself driving a motorcycle without a licence.

Hitching

Malaysia has long had a reputation for being an excellent place to hitchhike but, with the ease of bus travel, most travellers don't bother. On the west coast hitching is quite easy but it's not possible on the main *lebuhraya* (highway). On the east coast traffic is lighter and there may be long waits between rides. Of course hitching is never entirely safe and you do so at your own risk.

Local Transport

Local transport varies but almost always includes local buses and taxis. In a few Peninsular Malaysia towns there are also bicycle rickshaws but in general these are dying out. The best towns for rickshaws are Georgetown and Melaka.

In the bigger cities across Malaysian Borneo you'll find taxis, buses and minibuses. Once you're out of the big cities, though, you're basically on your own and must either walk or hitch. If you're really in the bush your alternatives are riverboats, aeroplanes or lengthy jungle treks.

Taxi

Drivers are legally required to use meters if they exist – you can try insisting that they do so, but more often than not you'll just have to negotiate the fare before you get in.

Compared to buses, long-distance (or share) taxis are expensive. The taxis work on fixed fares for the entire car and between major towns you'll have a reasonable chance of finding other passengers without having to wait around too long; otherwise, you'll probably have to charter a whole taxi.

Train

There are two main types of rail services: express and local trains. Express trains are air-conditioned and have 'premier' (1st class), 'superior' (2nd class) and sometimes 'economy' seats (3rd class). Similarly on overnight trains you'll find 'premier night deluxe' cabins (upper/lower berth RM50/70 extra), 'premier night standard' cabins (RM18/26), and 'standard night' cabins (RM12/17). Local trains are usually economy class only, but some have superior seats. Express trains stop only at main stations, while local services stop everywhere, including the middle of the jungle.

PENINSULAR MALAYSIA

Malaysia's privatised national railway company is **Keretapi Tanah Melayu** (KTM, ☎03-2267 1200; www.ktmb.com.my). It runs a modern, comfortable and economical railway service, although for the most part services are slow.

One line runs up the west coast from Singapore, through KL, Butterworth and on into Thailand. The other branches off from this line at Gemas and runs through Kuala Lipis up to the northeastern corner of the country near Kota Bharu in Kelantan. Often referred to as the 'Jungle Railway', this line is properly known as the 'East Coast Railway'.

MALAYSIAN BORNEO

In Sabah there is the **Sabah State Railway** (www.sabah.gov.my/railway/indexeng.html), a narrow-gauge railway line that runs from Sembulan south to Beaufort and then through Sungai Pegas gorge to Tenom.

Myanmar (Burma)

Includes »

Best Regional Specialities

- Mohinga (p489)
- Leq-p'eq thouq (p484)
- Shan-style noodle soup (p489)
- Tamarind flakes (p527)

Best Places for Cultural Connections

- Hsipaw (p522)
- Myitkyina (p530)
- Mrauk U (p534)
- Moustache Brothers (p518)

Why Go?

Turn back the clock in this time-warped country that's a world apart from the rest of Southeast Asia. Travelling in Myanmar is a chance to swap the hubbub and electronic demands of modern life for the calm of gilded temples and ancient monasteries. Enjoy slowly unfolding journeys through serene landscapes including meandering rivers, lush jungles, ethnic minority villages and pristine palm-fringed beaches.

Democracy champion Aung San Suu Kyi is free from house arrest and the tourism boycott has been lifted. Myanmar remains a troubled land and it's up to you to decide whether to visit or not (see the boxed text, p488). Keep in mind that the long-suffering people are gentle, humorous, engaging, considerate, inquisitive and passionate; they want to play a part in the world and to know what you make of their world. Come with your mind open and you'll leave with your heart full.

When to Go

Yangon

°C/°F **Temp** — **Rainfall** inches/mm

40/104 – 30/86 – 20/68 – 10/50 – 0/32 — 12/300 – 8/200 – 4/100 – 0

J F M A M J J A S O N D

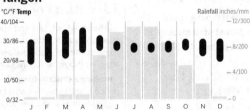

Jan Independence day (4 Jan), celebrating the end of British rule, is marked by nationwide fairs.

Apr The Water Festival (Thingyan) can be fun, but it's also one of the hottest times in Myanmar.

Dec Peak season with many visitors heading to the country over the Christmas–New Year break.

AT A GLANCE

» **Currency** Burmese kyat (K)

» **Language** Burmese

» **Money** Cash only. See p488 for more information.

» **Visas** Maximum 28 days, nonextendable. For details, see p548.

» **Mobile phones** No international roaming. Prepaid SIMs available for local phones.

Fast Facts

» **Area** 243 sq km

» **Capital** Nay Pyi Taw

» **Country code** ☎95

» **Emergency** Police (Yangon) ☎199

Exchange Rates

Australia	A$1	K750
Canada	C$1	K750
Euro zone	€1	K990
Japan	¥100	K9
New Zealand	NZ$1	K740
UK	UK£1	K1155
USA	US$1	K770

Set Your Budget

» **Guesthouse** US$10–20

» **Street stall meal** US$1–2

» **Large beer** US$1.50

Entering the Country

Land borders are closed to foreigners. Limited access via the following:

» **Mae Sai, Thailand**

» **Ranong, Thailand**

» **Ruili, China**

Don't Miss

Myanmar is one of the most devout Buddhist countries in the world. Yangon's **Shwedagon Paya** (p493), Mandalay's **Mahamuni Paya** (p514) and **Bagan's plain of temples** (p526) are all must-see locations, but there are also many other less internationally famous Buddhist religious sites that will impress you with their beauty and spirituality. A 10-storey tall seated buddha watches over Pyay's hill-top **Shwesandaw Paya** providing sweeping views of the town (p501). The old Rakhaing capital of **Mrauk U** (p535) is dotted with scores of ruined and functioning temples and monasteries, while in **Mount Kyaiktiyo** (p502) you can join the pilgrims as they fix gold leaf squares on this incredible balancing boulder.

ITINERARIES

One Week

In Yangon, visit the Shwedagon Paya and shop for handicrafts at Bogyoke Aung San Market. Overnight on a bus to Mandalay, climb Mandalay Hill, see the famed Mahamuni Paya and Moustache Brothers. Take a morning boat to Mingun, home to a giant earthquake-cracked stupa, following up with a sunset boat ride past U Bein's Bridge at Amarapura. Connect by bus or boat to Bagan, allowing a couple of days to explore the thousands of temples there.

Three Weeks

In addition to the above venture east to beautiful Inle Lake; consider trekking there from Kalaw (minimum two days). From Bago head to Mt Kyaiktiyo to view the amazing Golden Rock, then to Mawlamyine for a taste of tropical Myanmar and the chance to ride a slow boat to the Kayin State capital, Hpa-an. Return to Yangon then fly to Sittwe where you can take another boat to the amazing temple ruins of Mrauk U (minimum five days).

Essential Food & Drink

» **ăthouq** – light, tart and spicy salads made with raw vegetables or fruit tossed with lime juice, onions, peanuts, roasted chickpea powder and chillies. A common one is leq-p'eq thouq, which includes fermented tea leaves.

» **mohinga ('moun-hinga')** – a popular breakfast dish this is rice noodles served with fish soup and as many other ingredients as there are cooks.

» **Shan khauk-swe** – Shan-style noodle soup; thin wheat noodles in a light broth with meat or tofu, available across the country but most common in Mandalay and Shan State.

» **htamin chin** – literally sour rice, this turmeric-coloured rice salad also hails from Shan State.

» **black tea** – brewed in the Indian style with lots of milk and sugar.

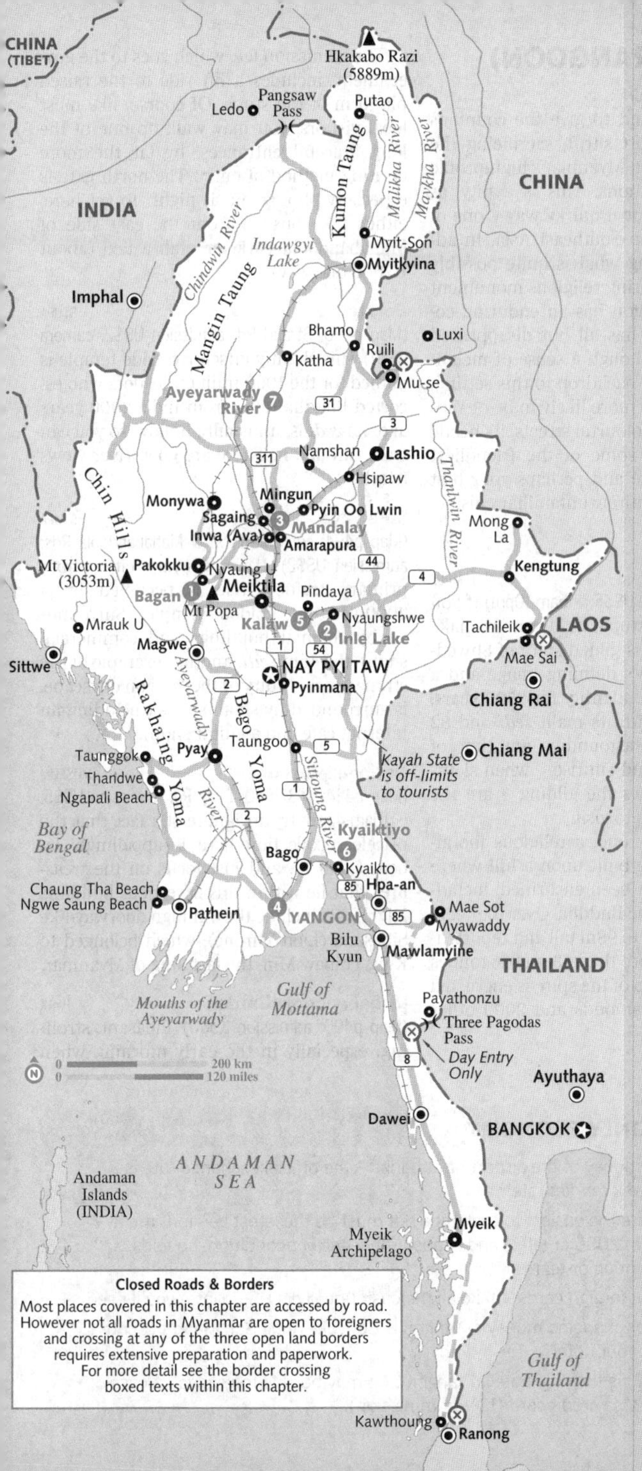

Myanmar (Burma) Highlights

1 Climb a quiet temple and witness the beauty of a misty dawn breaking over 4000 Buddhist temples on the plains of **Bagan** (p524)

2 Spend longer than you planned at pristine **Inle Lake** (p505), a mythical landscape of floating villages, stilted monasteries and aquatic gardens

3 Myanmar's former capital, **Mandalay** (p510), is the gateway to the intriguing old cities of Amarapura, with its famed teak bridge, and some stupa-pendous views from Sagaing

4 The social and economic capital of the country, if no longer the political capital, **Yangon** (p486) is home to the dazzling Shwedagon Paya

5 **Kalaw** (p508) is Myanmar's trekking HQ and the place to begin a walk through forested hills and fascinating, friendly minority villages to Inle Lake

6 Test your mettle by making the full 11km uphill pilgrimage to this sacred and gravity-defying **Kyaiktiyo** (p502), the Golden Rock

7 Way off the beaten track, embrace the concept of journey as destination by taking a series of boats along the **Ayeyarwady** (p530) from Myitkyina to Mandalay

YANGON (RANGOON)

☎01 / POP 4.35 MILLION

Many travellers tend to give the country's former capital short shrift, sacrificing the city for extra time in Myanmar's high-profile upcountry destinations. This is a pity, as the city is – in its own quirky way – one of the more unique in Southeast Asia. In addition to possessing what is quite possibly the most awe-inspiring religious monument in the region, Yangon has an enduring colonial charm that has all but disappeared elsewhere. And although a sense of melancholy is a frequent backdrop to this setting, your memories are more likely to be of Yangon's vibrant and colourful streets, its hectic open-air markets, some of the friendliest urbanites anywhere and perhaps your first experience of an entirely unfamiliar cuisine.

Sights

Shwedagon Paya TEMPLE

(Map p496; admission US$5; ⊙5am-10pm) If you only see one *zedi* (stupa) in Myanmar, make sure it's the glorious gilded spire of Shwedagon Paya, the city's defining image and a symbol of Burmese identity for 2500 years. The compound, with its main *zedi* and 82 other buildings, is astounding any time of day, but evening and sunrise – when slanting light illuminates the gilding – are the most magical times to visit.

The *paya* ('holy one', a religious monument) is said to be built upon a hill where Buddha relics have been enshrined, including eight hairs of the Buddha. Over the years the *zedi* has grown to 98m tall and reportedly accumulated more than 53 metric tonnes of gold leaf. The top of the spire is encrusted with over 5000 diamonds and 2000 other stones.

The admission fee, which goes to the government, includes a lift ride to the raised platform of the stupa. Of course, like most local visitors, you may walk up one of the long graceful entrances, by far the more exciting method of entry. The north gate is especially photogenic at night. To get here, either take bus 43 from the east side of Mahabandoola Park, or grab a taxi (about K2000 one way).

Botataung Paya STUPA

(Map p490; Strand Rd; admission US$2, camera US$1) This slightly kitsch riverside temple is named for the 1000 military leaders who escorted Buddha relics from India 2000 years ago. Its *zedi* is, unusually, hollow, so you can walk through it. There are good river views nearby.

Sule Paya STUPA

(Map p494; cnr Sule Paya & Mahabandoola Rds; admission US$2) It's not every city whose primary traffic circle is occupied by a 2000-year-old golden temple. Surrounded by colonial buildings and commercial shops, the 46m *zedi*, another example of the strange incongruity of the Yangon cityscape, is surrounded by small shops (including an internet cafe and a guitar shop).

National Museum MUSEUM

(Map p494; ☎371540; Pyay Rd; admission US$5; ⊙10am-4pm) Try to ignore the fact that the priceless collection here is appallingly labelled and lit, and just focus on the treasures that lie within this cavernous building. Highlights include the 8m-high doorway-like Sihasana (Lion Throne), which belonged to King Thibaw Min, the last king of Myanmar.

Mahabandoola Garden PARK

(Map p490; admission K500) Pleasant strolling, especially in the early morning when

CASH-ONLY ECONOMY

- Do not change money at the airport or at banks – the official exchange rate is a fraction of the black market rate.
- US dollar bills are the easiest to exchange but must be the latest version (multi-coloured bills from 2006 or later) and in *absolutely perfect* condition: no folds, stamps, stains, writing or tears.
- No ATMs accept foreign cards – take all the cash (ideally in US dollars) you'll need.
- Your best bet for changing money in Yangon is Bogyoke Aung San Market (Scott Market; p491) or your hotel.
- Parkroyal (p492) is the only hotel in Yangon that may be able to give you a cash advance on your Visa credit card (12% commission).

Yangon

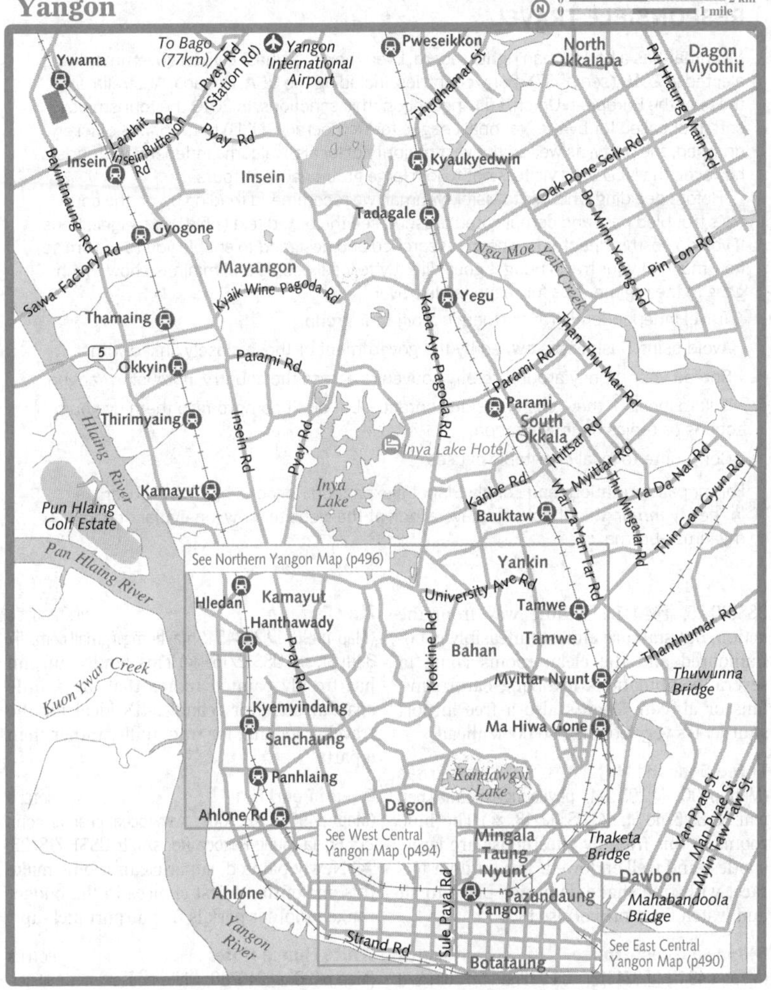

the air hasn't yet filled with traffic fumes. Here you'll also find the **Independence Monument**.

Kheng Hock Keong TEMPLE
(Map p494; Strand Rd; admission free; 24hr) Yangon's largest Chinese temple is most lively from around 6am to 9am when it's thronged with worshippers.

Moseah Yeshua Synagogue SYNAGOGUE
(Map p494; 85 26th St) Founded in 1894 it has a lovingly maintained interior for the city's now tiny congregation of Jews.

Chaukhtatgyi Paya TEMPLE
(Map p496; Shwe Gone Daing St) If you don't make it to Bago, the reclining Buddha at Chaukhtatgyi Paya is nearly as impressive.

Sleeping

The central Yangon is by far the liveliest part of the city and staying here will save you a small fortune in taxi fares. All prices include breakfast.

TOP CHOICE **Mother Land Inn 2** HOTEL $
(Map p490; 291343; www.myanmarmotherlandinn.com; 433 Lower Pazundaung Rd; dm US$8, r

RESPONSIBLE TRAVEL

Myanmar has a bad human rights record. Even though a quasi-civilian government was elected in 2010 (see p537) many countries, including the USA, Canada, Australia and those of the European Union, still apply economic sanctions. In 2010 the tourism boycott, first called for by the National League for Democracy (NLD) in 1995, was officially dropped; the party, as well as the vast majority of locals, welcome independent tourists; however, the NLD asks visitors not to join large group package tours.

Before deciding whether to visit Myanmar, we recommend reading up on the country's troubled past and complicated present; see the boxed text (p539) for suggestions. If you do go, this chapter has been researched and designed to enable you to maximise how much of your travel budget goes directly to local people and minimise how much goes to the regime. Tips for responsible travel:

» Travel independently rather than in a big tour group.

» Avoid using businesses owned by the government or those closely linked with it.

» Spread your money around, ie buy souvenirs across the country, not just in Yangon.

» Talk to locals – they relish outside contact – but don't compromise them by your actions or topics of conversation.

» Contribute to local charitable causes.

For more information read Lonely Planet's expanded Responsible Travel coverage in the *Myanmar* guidebook and have a look at the website www.lonelyplanet.com/myanmar-burma.

US$810-25; ❄@) It's a little way from the action, but staff are almost unfeasibly good-humoured and the clean rooms come in several combinations involving bathrooms, fans or air-con. There's also a free airport shuttle. It's very popular, so book ahead.

Three Seasons Hotel GUESTHOUSE $
(Map p490; ☎293304; phyuaung@mptmail.net.mm; 83-85 52nd St; s/d US$12/18; ❄) The nine rooms in this friendly guesthouse are large, spotless and well endowed. The outdoor terrace, with tree shade, is a nice place to sit and watch the world cruise by.

Okinawa Guest House HOTEL $
(Map p494; ☎374318; 64 32nd St; dm/s/d US$5/14/18; ❄) Down a potholed street one-minute's walk from Sule Paya, this bougainvillea-fronted old A-frame houses a hotchpotch of rooms in wood, bamboo and faux-brick. The atmosphere is invariably relaxed; the attic dorm has character.

Beautyland Hotel II HOTEL $
(Map p490; ☎240054; www.goldenlandpages.com/beauty; 188-192 33rd St; r US$8-24; ❄) A convenient location and exceedingly tidy rooms with friendly and confident service make this one of the better budget choices in central Yangon.

May Fair Inn GUESTHOUSE $
(Map p490; ☎253454; maytinmg@gmail.com; 57 38th St; s/d US$12/15; ❄) This family-run inn has freshly painted rooms that are a little spartan but ever reliable. It's ideal for the traveller looking for tranquillity rather than a party.

Ocean Pearl Inn HOTEL $
(Map p490; ☎297007; www.oceanpearlinn.com; 215 Bo Ta Taung Pagoda Rd; s/d/tr US$13/18/23; ❄) Newly painted, super-clean rooms make this one of the tidiest choices in the budget range. Another perk is free airport pick-up.

White House Hotel HOTEL $
(Map p490; ☎240780; white house@mptmail.net.mm; 69/71 Kon Zay Dan St; s US$8-15, d US$14-20; ❄) Pluses include generous breakfasts, rooftop hammocks, cold beer, expansive views and useful travel desk. Negatives are a thigh-burning number of stairs, small and sometimes windowless rooms, and basic bathrooms (shared and private).

Eating

Yangon has Myanmar's best range of restaurants. Central Yangon is packed with street-side stalls selling a dizzying array of cheap snacks, and many inexpensive Bamar, Shan, Chinese and Indian restaurants. Smarter places are found in the more affluent, expat-occupied north. While most restaurants are open from about 7am until 9pm daily, it can be hard to find a meal anywhere after 9pm.

Along Anawrahta Rd, west of Sule Paya Rd, there are many super-cheap Indian biryani shops (*keyettha dan bauk* in Burmese). All-you-can-eat thali meals or biryani cost from about K800.

TOP CHOICE Aung Thukha BURMESE $
(Map p496; Dhamazedi St; meals from K2000) Handy for Swedagon Paya, this longstanding, eternally busy place offers heaps of choice, with everything from rich, meaty curries to light, freshly made salads, and the flavours are more subtle here than elsewhere. Friendly service and a palpable old-school atmosphere make the experience akin to eating at someone's home.

Nilar Biryani & Cold Drink INDIAN $
(Map p494; 216 Anawrahta Rd; meals from K800) Giant cauldrons full of spices, broths and rice bubble away at the front of this bright and brash Indian joint. It's never less than packed, and for good reason: the biryanis are probably among the best that your lips will ever embrace.

Danuphyu Daw Saw Yee Myanmar Restaurant BURMESE $
(Map p494; 175/177 29th St; meals from K2000; ⌚lunch & dinner) The local's choice for Burmese food in central Yangon is this longstanding shophouse restaurant. There's a brief English-language menu, but your best bet is to pick from the selection of curries behind the counter.

999 Shan Noodle Shop SHAN $
(Map p490; 130B 34th St; noodle dishes from K500; ⌚breakfast & lunch) A handful of tables are crammed into this tiny, brightly coloured eatery serving a range of tasty noodle and non-noodle dishes, such as Shan tofu (made from chickpea flour) and the delicious Shan yellow rice with tomato.

Feel Myanmar Food BURMESE $$
(Map p494; 124 Pyidaungsu Yeiktha St; meals from K3000; ⌚lunch & dinner) A superb place to get your fingers dirty experimenting with the huge range of tasty Burmese dishes, which are laid out in little trays that you can just point to. It's very popular at lunchtime with local businesspeople and foreign embassy staff.

New Delhi Restaurant INDIAN $
(Map p494; Anawrahta Rd; mains from K500) This grubby place serves tasty Muslim-influenced South Indian dishes such as an insanely rich mutton curry, as well as meat-free options including *puris* (puffy breads), *idli* (rice ball in broth), various *dosai* and banana-leaf *thalis*.

Aung Mingalar Shan Noodle Restaurant SHAN $
(Map p494; Bo Yar Nyunt St; mains from K1000; ⌚breakfast & lunch) An excellent place to indulge simultaneously in people-watching and noodle sipping. It's simple and fun with trendy city cafe overtones.

YANGON'S STREET EATS

Yangon's street-food options can be both overwhelming and challenging (pork offal on a skewer, anyone?). Some of our favourites and the best places to eat them:

» **Samusa thoke** During the day a line of **vendors** (Map p490; Mahabandoola Garden St; per serve K500) near Mahabandoola Park sell this 'salad' of sliced samosas served with a thin lentil gravy.

» **Bein moun & moun pyar thalet** These delicious 'Burmese pancakes' (K200), served sweet *(bein moun)* or savoury *(moun pyar thalet)*, can be found at most Yangon corners day and night.

» **Dosai** At night along Anawratha St several street-side vendors sell this thin southern Indian crepe (from K500), known in Burmese as *to-shay*.

» **Mohinga** This soup of thin rice noodles and fish broth is just about everywhere but our favourite is from **Myaung Mya Daw Cho** (Map p490; 158 51st St; soup from K500; ⌚4.30-9am). There's no English sign here; look for the green sign near some trees.

» **Grilled food** Every night, the strip of 19th St between Mahabandoola and Anawrahta Rds hosts dozens of stalls and open-air restaurants serving **grilled snacks** (Map p493; meals from K5000; ⌚5-11pm) and draught beer.

East Central Yangon

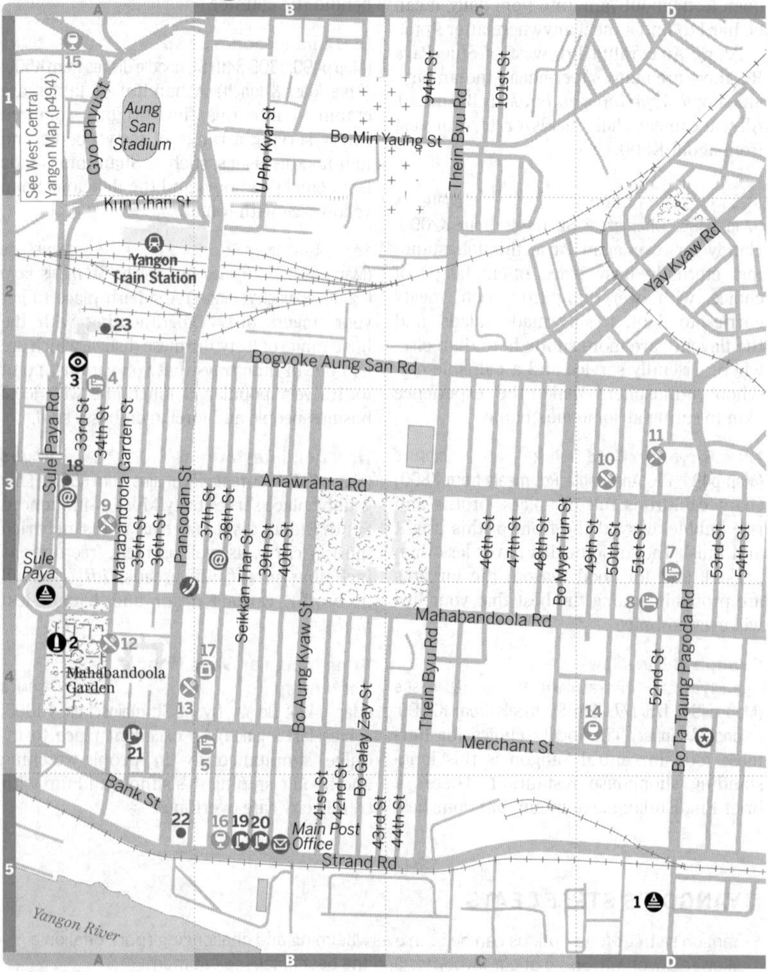

Coffee Circles INTERNATIONAL $$
(Map p496; 107 Dhama Zedi Rd; mains from K3000; ❄📶) This chic restaurant-cafe is the place to go if you want to forget you're in Yangon. In addition to real coffee, it offers a menu ranging from Thai to burgers, and fast wi-fi to boot.

Drinking

We hope you had your fun in Bangkok, because things are quiet here… Most places close by 10pm and the main form of local nightlife is hanging out in beer gardens, teashops or 'cold drink' shops.

Mr Guitar Café LIVE MUSIC
(Map p496; 22 Sayasan St; ⏲6pm-midnight; ❄) Founded by famous Myanmar vocalist Nay Myo Say, this cafe-bar features live folk music from about 7pm to midnight nightly. There's food, and the clientele is a mix of locals and expats.

50th Street Bar & Grill BAR
(Map p490; 9-13 50th St; ⏲11am-2.30pm & 5pm-late Mon-Fri, 10.30am-late Sat & Sun; ❄📶) Decorated in teak and heavy leather furniture this place is popular with locals and expats on Wednesday nights, when it has US$6 pizzas to soften the drinking.

British Club Bar BAR
(Map p490; off Gyo Phyu St; ⌚1st Fri evening of month until midnight) Once a month the ever-so-prim British Club throws open its doors and discussion moves from world peace to beer consumption. Expats (of all nationalities) rate this as the social event of the month. Bring your passport.

Zero Zone Rock Restaurant BAR
(Map p494; 4th fl, 2 Theingyi Zei market) This breezy rooftop bar offers live karaoke-like music from 7pm and cheap draught beer.

Sky Bistro BAR
(Map p490; 20th fl, Sakura Tower, cnr Sule Paya & Bogyoke Aung San Rds; ⌚9am-10pm; ❄) The views from the 20th floor are pretty impressive and there's a generous happy hour from 4pm to 10pm.

Strand Bar BAR
(Map p490; 92 Strand Rd; ⌚until 11pm; ❄📶) Your budget might not stretch to a room at the classic colonial Strand Hotel but there's nothing to stop you dropping by its bar on Friday afternoon and early evening when there's a two-for-one happy hour. A standard happy hour runs all other days from 5pm to 7pm.

☆ Entertainment

Yangon's handful of dance clubs, full of local quirks, are more appropriate for anthropological investigation than a night on the town.

JJ City CLUB
(Map p496; Mingala Zei; admission K3000; ⌚8pm-2am) Ostensibly a disco, but most punters appear to come for the truly bizarre 10pm fashion show, in which the 'JJ Queen' is chosen on a nightly basis. Your admission fee gets you a beer.

Pioneer CLUB
(Map p496; Ahlone Rd; admission K6000; ⌚7pm-3am) This disco sees a relative mix of people, from upper-class locals to profit-seeking 'dancing girls'.

YGN Bar CLUB
(Map p496; Ahlone Rd; free admission; ⌚7pm-3am) There's no admission fee, so you can do as the locals do and sip a beer while staring at the handful of girls who dare to dance. On Saturday nights the place has a distinctly gay vibe.

Shopping

Bogyoke Aung San Market MARKET
(Map p494; Bogyoke Aung San Rd; ⌚10am-5pm Tue-Sun) A half-day could easily be spent wandering around this 70-year-old sprawling market (sometimes called by its old British name, Scott Market). It has over 2000 shops and the largest selection of Myanmar handicrafts you'll find under several roofs. Moneychangers are located on the main aisle and are relatively reliable.

Theingyi Zei MARKET
(Map p494; Shwedagon Pagoda Rd) The local market for everyday homewares and textiles. It extends four blocks east–west from Kon Zay Dan to 24th Sts, and north–south

East Central Yangon

Sights
1 Botataung Paya D5
2 Independence Monument A4
3 Sakura Tower A2

Sleeping
4 Beautyland Hotel II A2
5 May Fair Inn D4
6 Mother Land Inn 2 .... E3
7 Ocean Pearl Inn D3
8 Three Seasons Hotel D4

Eating
9 999 Shan Noodle Shop A3
10 Lucky Seven Teashop D3
11 Myaung Mya Daw Cho D3
12 Samusa Thoke vendors A4
13 Shwe We Htun A4

Drinking
14 50th Street Bar & Grill D4
15 British Club Bar A1
Sky Bistro .... (see 3)
16 Strand Bar B5

Shopping
17 Bagan Book House B4

Information
18 AA Pharmacy A3
19 Australian Embassy B5
20 British Embassy B5
Columbus Travels & Tours .... (see 3)
21 Indian Embassy A4
New Zealand Embassy .... (see 20)

Transport
22 Myanmar Airways A5
23 Myanmar Railways Booking Office A2

from Anawrahta to Mahabandoola Rds. Theingyi Zei is also renowned for its traditional Burmese herbs and medicines.

Bagan Book House BOOKS
(Map p490; ☎377227; 100 37th St) Has the most complete selection of English-language books on Myanmar and Southeast Asia.

Information

Emergency

Your embassy may also be able to assist in an emergency.

Ambulance (☎192)
Fire (☎191)
Police (☎199)
Red Cross (☎383 680)

Internet Access

Wi-fi is available at a handful of hotels, restaurants and bars. In the hotel lobbies it's generally free (or you're at least expected to buy a drink or snack), otherwise it costs about US$1 per hour. Internet shops can be found in just about every corner of central Yangon, including the following:

Castle Internet & Café (Map p490; 2nd fl, 142-146 Sule Paya Rd; per hr K400; ⏰7am-11pm)

Click Me Quick (Map p490; 97 38th St; per hr K400; ⏰8am-11pm) This quiet and relatively fast internet cafe also provides wi-fi (per hr K4000).

YANGON'S CAFE CULTURE

Yangon's numerous teashops are not just places to have cups of milk tea and coffee or tiny pots of Chinese tea. They're also places to hang out with locals, grab a snack or a better breakfast than provided at your guesthouse. The following are our top three Yangon teashops. All are open approximately 6am to 4pm, a cup of tea costs about K250, and snacks and light meals start at about K400.

» **Lucky Seven** (Map p490; 49th St) Our all-around favourite – tidy, lively and with excellent food. The *mohinga* (soup of thin rice noodles and fish broth) is outstanding, as are most other Burmese-style noodle dishes.

» **Shwe We Htun** (Map p490; 81 37th St) A buzzing old-school teashop that serves better quality food than most. There's no English sign, but you'll know it by the crowds.

» **Thone Pan Hla** (Map p493; 454 Mahabandoola Rd) This centrally located teashop features an English-language menu of teashop staples.

Medical Services

AA Pharmacy (Map p490; 142-146 Sule Paya Rd; ⏰9am-10pm) Just north of Sule Paya.

International SOS Clinic (off Map p496; ☎667879; www.internationalsos.com; Inya Lake Hotel, 37 Kaba Aye Pagoda Rd; ⏰8.30am-5.30pm Mon-Fri, 8.30am-12.30pm Sat) Your best bet for emergencies.

Money

Yangon offers the best exchange rates in the country. Reputable dealers loiter in the main aisle of Bogyoke Aung San Market, or try your hotel or guesthouse. Don't change money at the airport. **Parkroyal** (Map p494; ☎250388; 33 Ah Lan Paya Pagoda Rd) is the only hotel in Yangon that may be able to give you a cash advance on your Visa credit card (12% commission).

Post

DHL (Off Map p490; ☎664434; Parkroyal, 33 Ah Lan Paya Pagoda Rd; ⏰8am-6pm Mon-Fri)

Main post office (Map p490; Strand Rd; ⏰7.30am-6pm Mon-Fri) Stamps are sold on the ground floor; go to the 1st floor to send mail.

Telephone

Central Telephone & Telegraph office (CTT; Map p490; cnr Pansodan St & Mahabandoola Rd) A government-run place.

Tourist Information

Myanmar Travels & Tours (MTT; Map p494; ☎374281; 118 Mahabandoola Garden St; ⏰8.30am-5pm) Once you wake them up from their nap, the people at this government-run information centre are actually quite friendly and helpful, although their resources are very limited.

Travel Agencies

Yangon's privately run travel agencies are the best place in the country for hiring a car or guide, booking an air ticket and checking on the latest travel restrictions.

Asian Trails (Map p494; ☎211212; www.asiantrails.info; 73 Pyay Rd) This outfit can arrange specific-interest tours of Myanmar, including cycling and mountaineering, and can facilitate visits to far northern Myanmar and other remote areas.

Columbus Travels & Tours (Map p490; ☎255123; www.travelmyanmar.com; 3rd fl, Sakura Tower, cnr Bogyoke Aung San & Sule Paya Rds)

Good News Travels (Map p494; ☎375050, 09-511 6256; www.myanmargoodnewstravel.com; 4th fl, FMI Centre, 380 Bogyoke Aung San Rd; ⏰9am-5pm Mon-Sat) The owner, William Myatwunna, is extremely personable and knowledgeable, and can help arrange visits to remote parts of Myanmar.

 Getting There & Away

Air

For information on international air services, see p547. Domestic flights leave from the same

BUSES FROM YANGON

Aung Mingalar Bus Station (Highway Bus Centre)

DESTINATION	COST (K)	DURATION (HR)	FREQUENCY
Bagan	18,000 (air-con)	13	4pm
Bago	6000 (air-con)	4	every 30min 6am-6pm
Kalaw	11,000 (air-con)	12	4pm
Kyaiktiyo/Kinpun (for Golden Rock)	7000 (air-con)	5	7-10.30am
Mandalay	11,000 (air-con)	12-15	7am & 5-7pm
Mawlamyine	8600-10,000 (air-con)	8-10	6-8am
Pyay	4000 (air-con)	6	hourly 7.30am-8pm
Taunggyi (for Inle Lake)	11,000-18,000 (air-con)	15-17	5-7pm

Hlaing Thar Yar Bus Station

DESTINATION	COST (K)	DURATION (HR)	FREQUENCY
Chaung Tha Beach	8000 (air-con)	6-8	6am
Ngwe Saung Beach	8000 (air-con)	5-7	6am
Pathein	6000 (no air-con)	4	5.30am-2pm

West Central Yangon

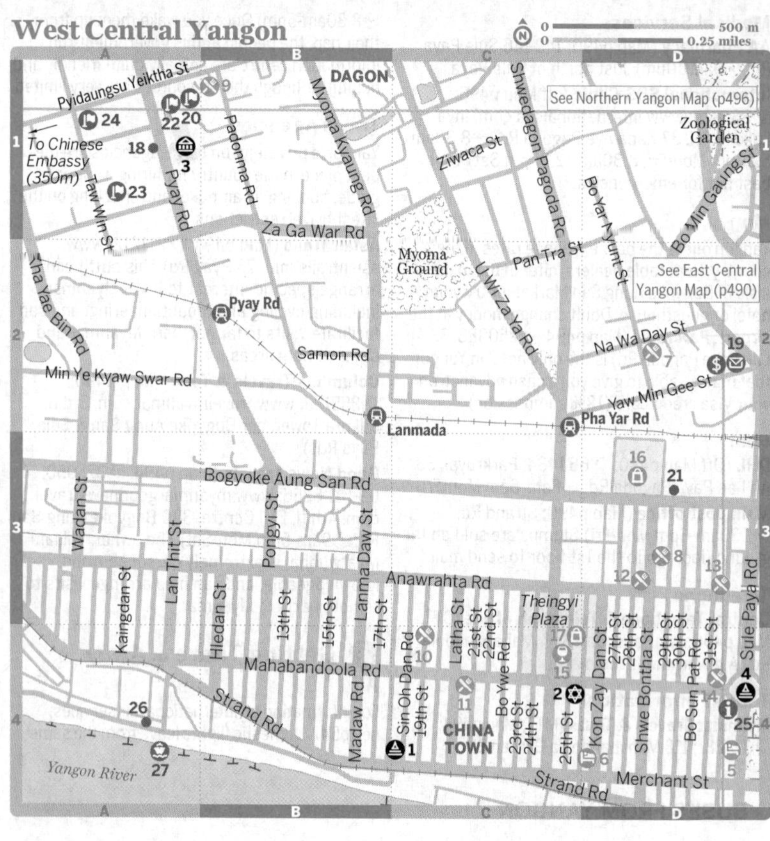

West Central Yangon

Sights
1 Kheng Hock Keong ... C4
2 Moseah Yeshua Synagogue ... C4
3 National Museum ... A1
4 Sule Paya ... D4

Sleeping
5 Okinawa Guest House ... D4
6 White House Hotel ... D4

Eating
7 Aung Mingalar Shan Noodle Shop ... D2
8 Danuphyu Daw Saw Yee Myanmar Restaurant ... D3
9 Feel Myanmar Food ... B1
10 Grilled Snack Vendors ... C4
11 Indian Street Stalls ... C4
12 New Delhi Restaurant ... D3
13 Nilar Biryani & Cold Drink ... D3
14 Thone Pan Hla ... D4

Drinking
15 Zero Zone Rock Restaurant ... C4

Shopping
16 Bogyoke Aung San Market ... D3
17 Theingyi Zei (Market) ... C4

Information
18 Asian Trails ... A1
19 DHL Worldwide Express ... D2
20 French Embassy ... A1
21 Good News Travel ... D3
22 Indonesian Embassy ... A1
23 Lao Embassy ... A1
24 Malaysian Embassy ... A1
25 Myanmar Travels & Tours (MTT) ... D4

Transport
26 Inland Water Transport Office ... A4
27 Lan Thit Jetty ... A4

airport as international flights, Yangon (Rangoon) airport, and include daily services to Nyaung U (for Bagan, around US$91), Mandalay (US$97) and Heho (for Inle Lake and Kalaw, US$91) and Sittwe (US$107).

Boat

Lan Thit jetty (Map p494) is where **Inland Water Transport** (IWT; Map p494; ☎381912, 380764; Lan Thit jetty) runs ferries to Pathein daily at 5pm (deck class/private cabin US$7/42, 17 hours). Foreigners must buy tickets from the deputy division manager's office next to Building 63 on Lan Thit jetty.

Bus

Guesthouses can assist with purchasing tickets for a small additional fee. Several larger companies have convenient bus-ticket offices opposite Yangon train station.

Aung Mingalar Bus Station (Highway Bus Centre), located about 5km northeast of the airport, is the only official bus terminal for all 150 bus lines leaving for the northern part of Myanmar, as well as for Kyaiktiyo (Golden Rock), Mawlamyine and destinations to the south. A taxi here costs US$7.

Hlaing Thar Yar Bus Station is for travel to the delta region (often called Ayeyarwady Division) and to destinations west of Yangon. It's 45 minutes to an hour away by taxi (K7000) west of the city centre.

For bus departures, see the table (p493).

Train

Yangons train station (Map p490; ☎202178; ⏲6am-4pm) is located a short walk north of Sule Paya, although advance tickets must be purchased at the adjacent **Myanmar Railways Booking Office** (Map p490; Bogyoke Aung San Rd; ⏲7am-3pm).

For more information on rail travel within Myanmar using the government's Myanmar Railways, see p550. For train services from Yangon, see the table, p495.

GETTING INTO YANGON

Walk past the taxi stands in the airport terminal (about 15km north of the city centre) and negotiate with the drivers outside. It will cost you about US$7 to central Yangon; make sure you have small bills handy. All airport taxi drivers can arrange money exchanges at reasonable (if not great) rates. Most buses arrive at the Aung Mingalar bus station (Highway Bus Centre), a few kilometres northeast of the airport; a taxi to town will cost about the same as the airport run, or follow the locals to a city bus.

Getting Around

Bus

Buses are impossibly crowded, the conductors rarely have change, the routes are confusing and there's virtually no English spoken or written – you'd really have to be pinching pennies to rely on them as a way of getting around. The typical fare within central Yangon is K100. Prices often double at night. Some useful bus routes from the Sule Paya stop:

Shwedagon Paya Bus 43

Yangon airport Bus 51, 53, 132, 136 and 231 all go to 10th Mile bus stop, from where it's possible to transfer to a pick-up to the airport

Aung Mingalar bus station Bus 43

Taxi

Licensed taxis carry red licence plates, though there is often little else to distinguish a taxi from any other vehicle in Yangon. The most expensive are the *car-taxis* (beaten-up old Japanese cars). Breakdowns are not exactly unknown. Fares are highly negotiable; trips around the central area cost about K1000 to K1500. Sule Paya to Shwedagon Paya runs to about K2000. Late at night, expect to pay more. A taxi for the day is US$40 to US$60. For all types of taxis the

TRAINS FROM YANGON

DESTINATION	COST ORDINARY/ UPPER/SLEEPER (US$)	DURATION (HR)	DEPARTURE
Bago	2/4/-	3	5am, 5.30am, 6am
Kyaikto	3-4/8-10/-	4-5	2am, 6.30am, 7.15am
Mandalay	11-15/30-35/33-40	4	5am, 5.30am, 6am, 12.15pm
Mawlamyine	5-7/14/-	9-11	2am, 6.30am, 7.15am
Pyay	5/13/-	7-8	1pm
Taungoo	5/13/-	6	5am, 5.30am, 6am, 8am, 11am

Northern Yangon

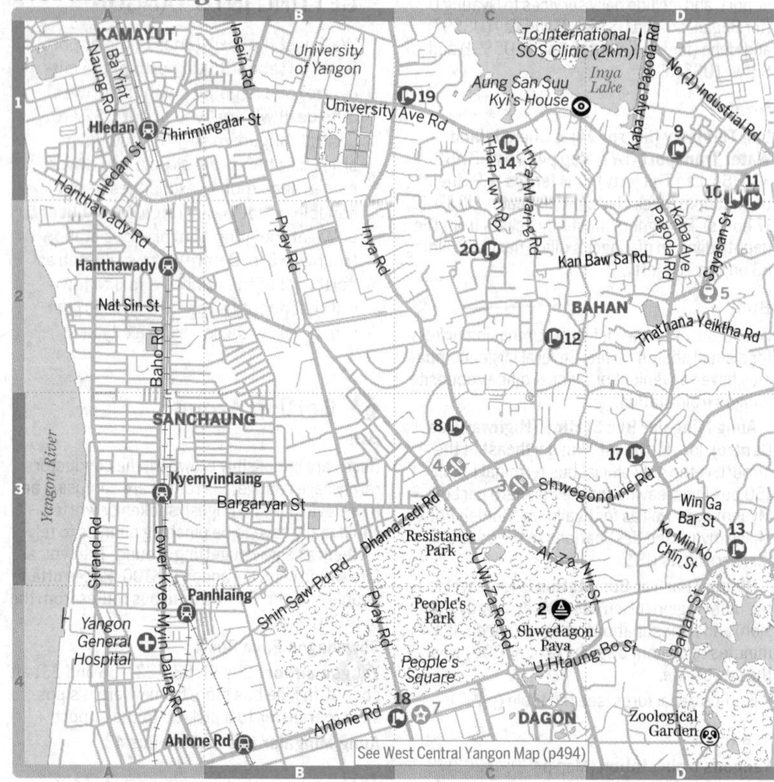

asking fares usually leap by 30% or so after sunset and on weekends.

Trishaw

Useful for getting around central Yangon, but they aren't allowed near Sule Paya. Rides across the city centre cost about K500.

THE DELTA, WEST COAST BEACHES & NORTH OF YANGON

Unlike the teeming beaches in neighbouring Thailand, Myanmar's are virtually empty except on weekends. Ngapali Beach in the south of Rakhaing State is the finest, but the long and/or expensive trip and lack of budget accommodation means most shoestringers skip it; for details see Lonely Planet's *Myanmar (Burma)*. Instead, head from Yangon through the Ayeyarwady Delta to sleepy Pathein and on to serendipitous Ngwe Saung or scruffy Chuang Tha beaches. Avoid during the monsoon season (mid-May to mid-September).

North of Yangon the main roads pass through a few interesting towns that are worth a look or stopover en route to Bagan, Mandalay and Inle Lake.

Pathein (Bassein)

☎042 / POP 300,000

A good staging post on the way to Chaung Tha or Ngwe Saung beaches, Pathein, 180km west of Yangon, is Myanmar's fourth-largest city. Despite being the commercial and administrative heart of the Ayeyarwady Delta, Pathein has a languid, easygoing ambience. It's known primarily for its parasol industry and fragrant rice, but much of the appeal comes from the wide, scenic Pathein River flowing through town.

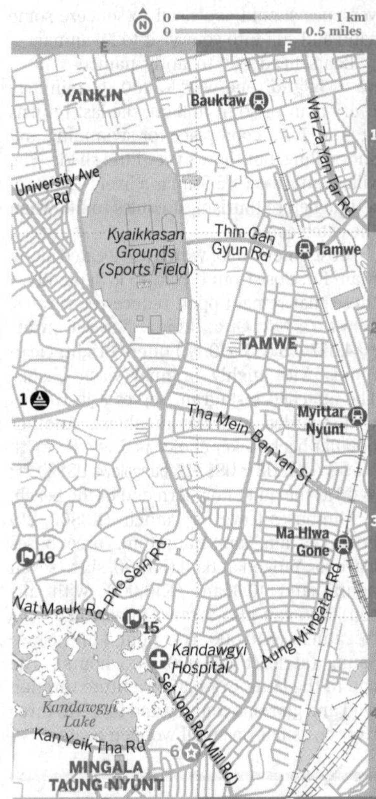

Northern Yangon

Sights

1 Chaukhtatgyi Paya E2
2 Shwedagon Paya C4

Eating

3 Aung Thuka C3
4 Coffee Circles C3

Drinking

5 Mr Guitar Café D2

Entertainment

6 JJ City E4
7 Pioneer & YGN Bar C4

Information

8 Bangladeshi Embassy C3
9 Cambodian Embassy D1
10 German Embassy E3
11 Israeli Embassy D1
12 Italian Embassy C2
13 Japanese Embassy D3
14 Korean Embassy C1
15 Nepalese Embassy E4
16 Philippines Embassy D1
17 Singaporean Embassy D3
18 Thai Embassy C4
19 US Embassy C1
20 Vietnamese Embassy C2

Sights

Shwe Sar Umbrella Workshop HANDICRAFTS
(☎25127; 653 Tawya Kyaung Rd; ⏰8am-5pm) Sun shades are made in workshops scattered across the northern part of the city, particularly around the Twenty-Eight Paya, off Mahabandoola Rd. It's fun to wander the area, sticking your head into a workshop here and there to see how they're made. They're cheap, and the saffron-coloured ones, made for monks, actually are waterproof. This workshop is particularly welcoming.

Shwemokhtaw Paya TEMPLE
This large complex, unusually well layered in legend, is found in the centre of Pathein near the riverfront. The huge bell-shaped *zedi* consists of a top tier made from 6.3kg of solid gold, a middle tier of pure silver and a bottom tier of bronze – the Olympic pagoda, perhaps? The seated Buddha in the southern shrine apparently floated here on a raft from Sri Lanka.

Settayaw Paya TEMPLE
This charming *paya,* in the northeast of town and wrapped over a couple of green hillocks, is dedicated to a mythical Buddha footprint left by the Enlightened One during his legendary perambulations through Southeast Asia.

Sleeping & Eating

Taan Taan Ta Guest House HOTEL $
(☎22290; 7 Merchant St; r US$6-10; ❄) Popular, with tidy and colourful rooms and friendly staff, but the secret's out and it fills up quickly.

Paradise Hotel HOTEL $
(☎25055; 14 Zegyaung St; s/d US$14/15; ❄) Fronting a canal, a short walk from the central market, this place features unremarkable rooms in a large modern building.

Shwe Zin Yaw Restaurant BURMESE $
(24/25 Shwezedi Rd; meals from K1500; ⏰lunch & dinner) Oh you lucky, lucky taste buds, finally you're going to get something different,

including goat curry and sardine salad! A handy place for lunch before hopping on a bus out of here.

Getting There & Away

Boat

For boats from Yangon, see p548. To Yangon, boats leave daily at 5.30pm, arriving the next day at noon. Tickets (deck/cabin class US$7/42) are available in the morning at the **IWT Office** (Mahabandoola Rd; ⏲10am-noon), located in a wooden colonial-era building near the jetty, or from 3pm onward at the jetty itself.

Bus

For Yangon (K6000, four hours, 3.30am, 5.30am, 6.30am and 1.30pm), head to the informal **bus company offices** (Shwezedi Rd) directly east of Shwe Zin Yaw Restaurant. Arrive early and a shuttle truck will transport you to the main bus station and your bus.

Insanely uncomfortable minibuses ply the route from Pathein to Chaung Tha beach (K2500, 2½ hours, 7am, 11am, 1pm and 3pm), departing from an informal **bus station** (Yadayagone St) a couple of blocks northeast of the clock tower. To Ngwe Saung beach (K4000, two hours, 9am, 11am and 3pm) buses leave from yet another **bus station** (Strand Rd).

Chaung Tha Beach

☎042

A place of holiday excess for the Myanmar middle class, Chaung Tha, 40km west of Pathein, is far from the most awe-inspiring piece of coastline you'll ever encounter (Ngwe Saung is much nicer). On the plus side it offers cheap accommodation and convenience should you need to squeeze some sand and sun into your visit to Myanmar.

Boats head out to aptly named **White-sand Island** (one way K3000, 15 minutes) every hour or so from 8am; the last returns at 5pm. It's a good place for swimming and snorkelling, but there's very little shade. The village **market** (⏲6-9am) is a lively vestige of a time before tourism; it comes to life when the catch comes in.

Most hotels, all of which are located along Main Rd, close from 15 May to 15 September; those that remain open reduce room rates. **Shwe Ya Min Guesthouse & Restaurant** (☎42127; s/d US$5/10; ❄) offers bright, clean rooms with highly original wash basins. The attached restaurant serves a justifiably well-regarded pancake breakfast. Another popular backpacker choice is **Shwe Hin Tha Hotel** (☎42118; r US$7-12, bungalows US$20-25; ❄@) at the quiet northern end of the beach.

Minibuses leave for Pathein (K3800, 2½ hours) at 7am, 9am, 11am, 1pm. Direct buses leave for Yangon at 6am (K7000, six to seven hours) and 10.30am (K10,000, with air-con). You can also arrange motorbike taxis to Pathein (K10,000, two hours) and Ngwe Saung (at least K15,000, two hours). The trip to the latter is a real adventure through wild and glorious country and involves three river crossings on small wooden boats.

Bago (Pegu)

☎052 / POP 200,000

Founded in AD 573 by the Mon, this one-time capital probably contains a greater density of blissed-out buddhas and treasure-

WORTH A TRIP

NGWE SAUNG BEACH

Although it has gentrified significantly in the last few years, the 13km of wide, white-sand beach at Ngwe Saung, 46km west of Pathein, seldom gets busy. The water here is deeper and clearer than that at Chuang Tha, and a small forested island off the southern end of the beach is perfect for leisurely snorkelling and fishing.

The best of the increasingly rare breed of budget accommodation options is **Shwe Hin Tha Hotel** (☎042-40340; bungalows US$15-35; ❄), offering cheap and simple bamboo huts or more solid and luxurious bungalows. For inexpensive, good eats locals recommend **Golden Myanmar Restaurant** (mains from K1000), a seafood shack in the middle of the village.

A daily bus leaves for Yangon at 6.30am (K8000, six hours) from the crossroads between the village and the beach resorts. Minibuses from Pathein (K3000, two hours) stop first at the intersection between the beginning of the village and the Treasure Beach Resort. If staying further south, the bus should be able to drop you at your resort; conversely, you should be able to catch the bus leaving Ngwe Saung (7am, 8am, 9am, 11am and 3pm) by waiting by the side of the road.

filled temples than any other similar-sized town in southern Myanmar. All this makes Bago a superb and simple day trip from Yangon, or the ideal first stop when you leave the city behind.

Sights & Activities

Many of Bago's monuments are actually centuries old, but don't look it, due to extensive restorations. This is an excellent place to explore by bicycle, as most attractions are near each other. Bikes are available for rent at **Bago Star Hotel** (☎30066; http://bagostarhotel.googlepages.com; 11-13 Kyaikpon Pagoda Rd).

Shwethalyaung Buddha MONUMENT
This 55m reclining Buddha image, which extends 9m longer than the famous one at Wat Pho in Bangkok, has a sweet, life-like face. A mural tells the temple's melodramatic story, which began in 994.

Just before the Shwethalyaung is the reconstructed **Maha Kalyani Sima** (Hall of Ordination) and another, hastily reconstructed, reclining Buddha image.

Mahazedi Paya STUPA
The design of this 'Great Stupa', with its white-washed stairways leading almost to the stupa's summit, is unusual for this part of Myanmar and certainly one of the more attractive religious buildings in Bago.

Shwemawdaw Paya STUPA
Rebuilt after an earthquake in 1930, the Shwemawdaw Paya is 14m higher than Shwedagon Paya in Yangon. Look out for the large chunk of the *zedi's* spire, toppled by an earthquake in 1917, resting at the north-eastern corner of the *paya*. The busy stupa draws plenty of pilgrims during the **full-moon festival** at Tagu (March/April).

Kha Khat Wain Kyaung MONASTERY
One of Myanmar's three biggest Buddhist monasteries, this is a bustling hive of several hundred monks – a welcoming place. Tourists come to watch the 10.30am lunch, but it's more relaxed at other times.

Kanbawzathadi Palace PALACE
The original site of Hanthawady, which surrounded Kanbawzathadi Palace, a former Mon palace, was excavated just south of the huge Shwemawdaw Paya. Walled in the Mon style, the square city measured 1.6km along each side and had 20 gates.

ENTRANCE FEES & OPENING HOURS

Though foreigners can visit the town for free, officially they must buy an entrance ticket valid for all the town's sights for US$10. During our visit, this could only be purchased at the Shwemawdaw Paya, but should also be available at the Shwethalyaung Buddha. Nearly all of the sights charge an additional 300K for camera and 500K for video cameras. All of the sights are open from just before sunrise until well after dark.

Sleeping & Eating

Bago has some good-value rooms, but few travellers spend the night. Main Rd is deafeningly noisy – ask for a room at the back.

Emperor Hotel HOTEL $
(☎21349; Main Rd; s & d US$6-14; ❄) This place is the best of the central budget lot. Rooms have recently been repainted and the more expensive have a bit of light and space. The rooftop offers great views of the surrounding religious monuments.

San Francisco Motel HOTEL $
(☎22265; 14 Main Rd; r US$4-10; ❄) Rough and ready but an excellent budget hang-out in the true sense of the word. The knowledgeable guys who run it organise excellent motorbike tours of Bago's sights.

Hanthawaddy CHINESE, BURMESE $$
(192 Hintha St; mains K2000-8000; ⌚lunch & dinner) The food here isn't amazing, but it's the only restaurant in Bago with a bit of atmosphere. The open-air upper level is breezy and offers great views of Shwemawdaw Paya.

Hadaya Café CAFE $
(⌚breakfast & lunch) Opposite the Emperor Hotel, this is a popular teashop with a nice selection of pastries, and good quality tea and coffee.

Getting There & Away

Buses

Buses to Yangon (K1500, two hours) depart approximately every 45 minutes from 6.45am to 5.15pm. Going south, buses to Kinpun, the starting point for Mt Kyaiktiyo (Golden Rock) leave every hour or so during the day (K5000, three hours). During the rainy season (May to October), buses only go as far as Kyaikto, 16km

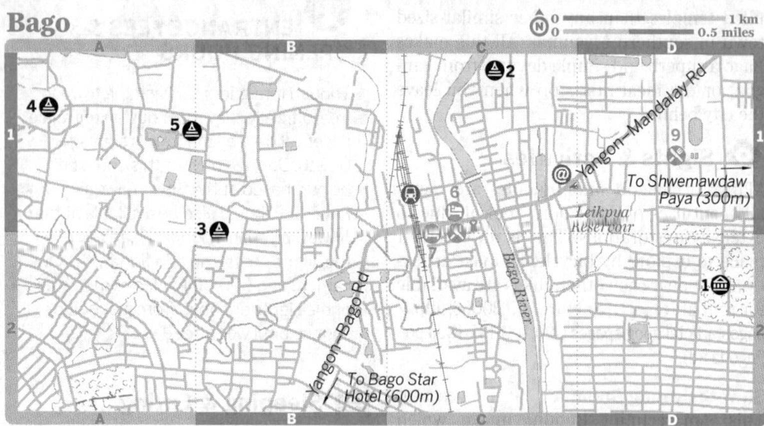

Bago

Sights

1 Kanbawzathadi Palace........................D2
2 Kha Khat Wain Kyaung........................C1
3 Maha Kalyani Sima (Maha Kalyani Thein)........................B1
4 Mahazedi Paya........................A1
5 Shwethalyaung Buddha........................A1

Sleeping

6 Emperor Hotel........................C1
7 San Francisco Motel........................C2

Eating

8 Hadaya Café........................C1
9 Hanthawaddy........................D1

from Kinpun. To Mawlamyine departures are at 7.45am, 8am and 9am (K8000, seven hours).

Heading north, to Mandalay there are departures at 5.30pm and 8pm (K11,500). It's also possible to hop on one of the buses coming from Yangon – try to book ahead and ask your hotel to help. For Taungoo and Inle Lake, you might be able to grab a seat on one of the buses originating in Yangon between 1.30pm and 4pm (K14,000 to K16,000, 12 hours).

Taxi

Some travellers make a day trip out of Bago with a hired car from Yangon. It costs around US$60, but it does give you the advantage of having transport between sites once you get to Bago and saves traipsing all the way out to the bus station in Yangon. One-way taxis back from Bago straight to your hotel in Yangon cost about K40,000.

A guide and driver to Mt Kyaiktiyo can be hired for around US$55 return. For any of these options, you can inquire at the town's **taxi stand** (Yangon–Mandalay Rd) or through any of the central Bago hotels.

Train

For train services from Bago, see opposite page.

Getting Around

Trishaw is the main form of local transport. A one-way trip in the central area should cost no more than K500. Hiring a trishaw or motorcycle for the day should cost about K6000.

Taungoo

054 / POP 120,000

Just under halfway from Yangon to Mandalay, it's hard to imagine Taungoo was once the nerve centre of a powerful kingdom. Today it's a sleepy place that most people see from a bus or train window. However, it gets the 'real-deal experience' thumbs up from those who do stop and it's home to one of Myanmar's more memorable guesthouses.

On the town's west side **Shwesandaw Paya** (built 1597) is the main pilgrimage site. Nearby, pretty Kandawgyi Lake is pleasant to stroll or cycle around.

At the south end of town **Myanmar Beauty Guest House II, III & IV** (23270, 23527; fourdoctors@mptmail.net.mm; Pauk Hla Gyi St; r in III US$10-15, s/d in IV US$15/25;) consists of three teak houses with four-poster beds, hot showers and wide-open views of the rice paddies and hills that loom beyond. Rates include a gut-busting local breakfast.

Heading north or south on air-con buses you'll pay full fare. Most stop near the hospital, in the town centre. Local buses to Yangon (K3500 to K4300, six hours) leave at 7am and 7pm. Mandalay buses (K6500) pass about 6.30pm. Trains between Yangon and Mandalay stop here too.

Pyay (Prome)

053 / POP 95,000

With a breezy location on the Ayeyarwady, Pyay is the most interesting stop on the Yangon–Bagan Hwy. Soak up its lively atmosphere along the riverfront and the roundabout, at the centre of which is a gilded equestrian statue of Aung San.

The city's glory days date back to the ancient Pyu capital of Thayekhittaya, the partially excavated remains of which lay 8km east of Pyay's main attraction: the dazzling **Shwesandaw Paya**. Perched atop a central hill, this attractive temple is actually 1m taller than Shwedagon Paya in Yangon, and apparently dates from 589 BC. Facing the *paya* from the east is **Sehtatgyi Paya** (Big Ten Storey), a giant seated Buddha.

Follow Strand Rd north during the morning to catch all the action at the lively and colourful **central market**, which spreads over several blocks.

About 14km south of Pyay, **Shwemyetman Paya** is home to a large, white-faced, seated Buddha – sporting a pair of giant gold-plated glasses! Hop on a local Yangon-bound bus or southbound pick-up, and get off in Shwedaung town.

Sleeping & Eating

Myat Lodging House HOTEL $
(25695; 222 Bazaar St; r US$6-12; ❄) Two blocks north of Aung San, and two in from the river, this family-run guesthouse has simple, well-loved rooms. Shared bathrooms are clean, but only the top-priced rooms have private bathrooms. Pyay maps are available.

Smile Motel HOTEL $
(22523, 25169; 10-11 Bogyoke Rd; r US$18; ❄) The long corridor leading to the simply furnished rooms may have a shabby carpet and remind you of *The Shining* but it's all pretty clean and the staff are nice.

The **night market** on Mya Zay Tann St between the Aung San statue and the river is well worth browsing for cheap eats.

Getting There & Away

Ferries run along the Ayeyarwady from Pyay, but schedules are notoriously variable. At research time, a ferry left at 5.30am on Wednesday for Mandalay (about five days), and another cargo boat left Tuesday night for Yangon (deck/cabin class US$9/18; about three days). The **IWT office** (24503; Strand Rd; 9am-5pm Mon-Fri) has details.

The highway bus station, 2km east of the town centre, sends frequent buses to Yangon (K4100, seven hours). No direct buses go to Bagan; either jump on a Yangon–Bagan bus (for full fare) or take the 8.30am bus to Magwe (K4100, six to seven hours), from where a 6am bus leaves for Bagan.

A daily train leaves Pyay's central train station at 11.30pm for Yangon (ordinary/1st/upper/sleeper class US$5/10/13/14, 8½ hours). From Shwethekar station, 5km east of the city, you can also board the Bagan–Yangon bound train as it makes a three-minute pause at 10pm (sleeper/upper/1st class US$28/26/23); Yangon departures are at 2.30am.

SOUTHEASTERN MYANMAR

Teetering on a cliff edge, the Golden Rock of Kyaiktiyo draws a few visitors off the main trail for a tough-but-rewarding pilgrimage. Further south, Mawlamyine offers glimpses of old Burma and is the launching pad for the scenic boat ride upriver to Hpa-an,

TRAIN SERVICES FROM BAGO

DESTINATION	COST (ORDINARY/UPPER)	DURATION (HR)	FREQUENCY
Mandalay	US$10/US$27	14	6.11am, 6.51am, 7.21am, 7.50am, 1.50pm
Mawlamyine	US$5/US$12	8	8.18am, 9.07am
Yangon	US$2/US$5	3	6am-8pm

CLIMBING MT KYAIKTIYO

There are two ways to the rock: hiking 11km uphill from Kinpun (four to six hours one way), or trucking (K1500 to K2000, 45 minutes, 6am to 6pm) and then walking 45 minutes to an hour up the remaining steep, paved switchback path. Those with accessibility concerns, or royal fantasies, might want to be carried the rest of the way in a sedan chair (US$5 to US$7 one way). Walking down to Kinpun takes from three to four hours and should not be attempted in the dark, even with a torch; it's too easy to stumble.

There is a US$6 government entrance fee and US$2 camera fee, payable at the checkpoint near the top, just after the Mountain Top Hotel. Men shouldn't wear shorts at the shrine and women should wear long skirts only – no trousers, miniskirts or skimpy tops.

the way-off-the-beaten-track, way-welcoming capital of Kayin (Karen) State.

Kyaiktiyo (Golden Rock)

☎057

The gravity-defying golden rock Kyaiktiyo is one of Myanmar's most enigmatic and intriguing sights. Perched on the very edge of a cliff on Mt Kyaiktiyo, this giant, gold-leaf-covered boulder is topped by a stupa containing a Buddha hair donated by a hermit in the 11th century. Apparently, the hair was salvaged from the bottom of the sea and brought here by boat. The boat subsequently turned to stone and is visible a few hundred metres away.

Kyaiktiyo has a mystical aura; it's a place of miracles, not least of which is how the boulder has managed to hang on, withstanding several earthquakes, for all these years. Pilgrims come in their thousands and the experience is more interesting because of them. That said, on weekends especially the mountaintop can feel like a theme park.

Since the rock is especially beautiful illuminated in the evening, plan on spending a night in the 'base camp' of **Kinpun**, a collection of restaurants and guesthouses 11km from the summit of Mt Kyaiktiyo. Kyaikto, where trains and long-distance buses stop, has several guesthouses, none of them very appealing, and there really is no reason to stay here rather than in Kinpun.

Sleeping & Eating

The following include breakfast in their rates:

TOP CHOICE **Golden Sunrise Hotel** HOTEL $$
(☎in Yangon 01-701027; gsunrise@myanmar.com.mm; s US$20, d US$30-35; ❄) A few minutes' walk outside the centre of Kinpun village in the direction of the highway, this great-value hotel has eight bamboo-heavy bungalows with a touch of class. The private verandas overlooking the secluded gardens are the perfect place to relax at the end of the day with a drink.

Mountain Top Hotel HOTEL $$$
(☎01-502479 in Yangon; grtt@goldenrock.com.mm; r US$50-78; ❄) Overpriced, but clean and well maintained with good service, and situated right on the summit of the mountain only a couple of moments' stroll to the shrine complex. If you want to catch the best light and most enchanting atmosphere at the shrine, it's worth the splurge.

Sea Sar Guest House HOTEL $
(☎60367; r US$5-15; ❄) In the heart of Kinpun but set in spacious gardens, the more expensive rooms here are memorable for all the right reasons. The cheaper rooms look like a crime scene, though. The staff are dialled into travellers' needs. The attached restaurant has all the staples for K1500 to K2000.

Pann Myo Thu Inn GUESTHOUSE $
(☎60285; r US$5-20; ❄) The cheap rooms at this lush, green place are better value than those at the Sea Sar. It has a friendly home-away-from-home feel – probably because it is in fact the owners' home.

Mya Yeik Nyo BURMESE $
(meals from K2000) The pick of Kinpun's so-so Chinese and Bamar restaurants is very close to where the trucks depart for the mountain.

Getting There & Away

Bus

Win Express runs air-con buses from Kyaikto to Bago (three hours) and Yangon (five hours) at 8.30am, 10am, 12.30pm and 2pm. Despite where you're getting off, you'll have to pay the full fare to Yangon (K7000). Tickets, purchased in Kinpun across from Sea Sar Guest House, include the truck fare to Kyaikto, where you'll board the bus.

TRAINS FROM KYAIKTO

DESTINATION	COST (ORDINARY/UPPER)	DURATION (HR)	FREQUENCY
Mawlamyine	US$3/$US$7	4	6.20am, 10.40am, 12.30pm
Yangon	US$4/US$9	5	10am, 1.20pm, 3.40pm

Similar air-con buses also run to Mawlamyine (K7000, 4½ hours, 5am, 6am, 7.30am, 8.30am and 10.30am).

Small pick-ups leave from Kinpun to Hpa-An (K5000, five hours) from 6am to 1pm, or there is a more comfortable bus (K7000, 1.30pm).

Pick-ups cruise the road between Kyaikto and Kinpun every half an hour or so (K500).

Train

For trains from Yangon, see p550. For trains from Kyaikto, see the table above.

Mawlamyine (Moulmein)

☎057 / POP 300,000

Known as Moulmein to George Orwell during his time as a policeman here, and also to Rudyard Kipling who wrote about it after spending just three days, Myanmar's third-largest city is the quintessential go-slow tropical town. With a ridge of stupa-capped hills on one side, the sea on the other and a centre filled with mildewed mosques, Mawlamyine has an attractive urban setting, made more charming by the general air of melancholy. There's enough here and around town to keep you amused for a day or two, as well as all the traveller life-support systems, including several internet places on the main street.

Government-run **Mon Cultural Museum** (cnr Baho & Dawei Jetty Rds; admission US$2; ⏲9.30am-4.30pm Sun-Fri) has a modest, poorly lit selection of Mon pieces. For a cityscape and peaceful ramble, climb the tallest stupa, **Kyaikthanlan Paya**, or nearby pagodas.

Picturesque **Gaungse Kyun** (Shampoo Island) is a pleasant diversion for an hour or two. It's reached by boat (2000K return) from near the Mawlamyine Hotel, at the north end of town.

About 14km south of Mawlamyine is **Pa-Auk-Taw-Ya Monastery** (☎22853; www.paauk.org), one of the largest meditation centres in Myanmar. Foreigners can stay the night or several days; sleeping and eating is gratis.

Sleeping & Eating

Most of Mawlamyine's accommodation is a K1000 motorcycle taxi ride from the train station, bus station or boat pier.

Cinderella Hotel HOTEL $$
(☎24411; www.cinderellahotel.com; 21 Baho Rd; s/d/tr US$18/30/40; ❄@📶) Worth the extra dosh for its capable staff who look after huge rooms with heaps of amenities.

Breeze Guest House HOTEL $
(Lay Hnyin Tha; ☎21450; breeze.guesthouse@gmail.com; 6 Strand Rd; s US$6-12, d US$16; ❄) The rooms aren't much but the priceless staff are an endless source of information, pleasant conversation and superb guiding skills.

Beer Garden 2 BEER GARDEN $
(58 Strand Rd; meals from K3000; ⏲dinner) Ignore the misleading English-language menu and head straight for the barbecued snacks: these guys are truly talented grillers. Couple your skewers with a glass of what must be the coldest draught beer in Myanmar and you've got Mawlamyine's best meal.

WORTH A TRIP

BILU KYUN

Fascinating Bilu Kyun (Ogre Island), east of Mawlamyine, is peppered with villages involved in the production of coconut fibre-mats and even coconut-inspired and created cutlery and teapots. Spend an interesting day exploring by taking the daily ferry (US$1) at 9.45am and 10.45am from the pier at the northern end of Strand Rd. On the island, transport is mainly by horse and cart. The final ferry back to Mawlamyine leaves Nut-Maw village at 3pm. A guide is recommended: Mr Antony or Mr Khaing at Breeze Rest House charge US$12 for an eight-hour tour.

TRAVEL TIPS

» If you're bound for Mawlamyine, consider taking the train – it's a slow but scenic journey.

» If you're planning on taking the scenic ferry between Mawlamyine and Hpa-an, departures are on Monday and Friday only.

» Overnight buses from Yangon pause at the bridge linking Mawlamyine with the north until dawn before being allowed to cross – anything up to five hours!

Getting There & Away

Boat

Ferries depart the Kyaik Hpa Nai jetty at 12.30pm on Monday and Friday for the trip up the Thanlwin River to Hpa-an (US$2, at least five hours) cruising through stunning scenery of limestone mountains and sugarcane fields. Bring your own food and drinks.

Bus & Train

For bus and train services from Mawlamyine, see the tables, below and opposite.

Hpa-An

058

Verdant, village-like Hpa-an is hemmed in by higgledy-piggledy hills rising abruptly from fields of rice and sugarcane. There are the inevitable golden stupas and a vibrant market, but the best activities are outside town.

Take a boat across the Thanlwin River from Hpa-an (K500, every half-hour from 7am to 5pm) to reach **Hpan Pu Mountain**, a craggy pagoda-topped peak that can be scaled in one sweaty morning. Another demanding two-hour climb is up **Mt Zwegabin** (722m), 11km south of town, for gods'-eye views, an 11am monkey-feeding session and free monastery lunch at noon. Around 27km southeast of Hpa-an, vast **Saddar Cave**, aka the Gates of Hell, is full of Buddhist iconography and stalagmites.

Budget accommodation pickings are slim. **Soe Brothers Guest House** (21372; 2/146 Thitsar St; s/d US$10/14, without bathroom US$5/10), near the market, is the backpacker fave due mainly to the owners, who have handy maps of town and can arrange tours. Rooms range from tiny wooden cells to slightly larger spaces with modest private bathrooms; either way, you can forget about swinging cats. Larger better-appointed rooms can be found at the **Golden Sky** (21510; 2 Thitsar St; s/d US$15/20;), mere steps from the jetty.

A friendly and popular place serving an almost overwhelming variety of excellent curries, soups and stir-fries, **San Ma Tau Myanmar Restaurant** (1/290 Bogyoke St; meals from K2000; lunch & dinner) also doubles as an internet cafe.

Getting There & Away

Boats leave Hpa-an at 5.30am on Monday and Friday (US$2, four hours). The predawn departure means that you will actually miss the best of the scenery, so though the journey from Mawlamyine is longer, it's better to travel from there to Hpa-an by boat.

Hpa-an's bus station is inconveniently located about 6.5km north of the clock tower, but tickets can be bought and buses boarded at a few centrally located **ticket stalls** (clock tower). Staff at Soe Brothers can also arrange tickets.

Services to Yangon (K4000 to K8000, seven hours, 7am, 8am and 7pm) stop in Kyaikto (four hours) and Bago (six hours); even if you're getting off in these towns, you're expected to pay the full fare. To Mawlamyine (K1100, two hours), buses leave hourly from 6am to 4pm.

INLE LAKE & SHAN STATE

With rebel groups, warlords and drug dealers living in its mysterious mountains, Shan

BUSES FROM MAWLAMYINE

DESTINATION	COST (K)	DURATION (HR)	FREQUENCY
Bago	5100 (air-con)	6	8am, 9am, 7pm, 7.30pm
Hpa-an	1050 (no air-con)	2	6am-4pm
Kyaikto	5100 (air-con)	4	8am, 9am, 7pm, 7.30pm
Yangon	5100 (air-con)	8	8am, 9am, 7pm, 7.30pm

TRAINS FROM MAWLAMYINE

DESTINATION	COST (ORDINARY/UPPER)	DURATION (HR)	FREQUENCY
Bago	US$8/US$10	6	6am, 8.15am, 11.25am
Kyaikto	US$5/US$7	4-5	6am, 8.15am, 11.25am
Yangon	US$7/US$16	9	6am, 8.15am, 11.25am

State is largely unexplored by and off-limits to foreigners. Of the places you can go, Inle Lake is the main attraction, a beautiful body of water hemmed in by mountains and populated by floating communities. Trekking is hugely popular around here and Kalaw is the affordable base for adventure. Homestays are possible and the Shan are some of the friendliest folk in the country.

Inle Lake & Nyaungshwe

☎081 / POP 10,000

A wonderful watery world of floating gardens, stilted villages and crumbling stupas, Inle Lake is one of those few places that are a tonic for the soul. While away the days canoeing, cycling and walking through the lush countryside.

In September and October the **Phaung Daw U festival** runs for nearly three weeks, and is followed by the **Thadingyut festival**. Always cooler than the rest of the country, Inle gets downright chilly at night in January and February – bring warm clothes.

The village of Nyaungshwe, at the lake's north end, is home to all the budget accommodation and traveller services, including internet, and is easily navigated by foot or bicycle.

Sights & Activities

Motorboats Trips BOAT TOUR

Every hotel in town can arrange boat trips around the lake, and freelance boat drivers will approach you in the street. A whole-day trip around the lake starts at K12,000, or K15,000 if you include a stop at **Inthein**, where the weather-beaten pagodas on the hilltop are incredibly atmospheric despite the crowds. Other popular stops include the monastery **Nga Phe Kyaung**, on the eastern side of the lake, which is famous for its cats trained to leap through hoops by the monks; **floating gardens**, where Intha farmers raise flowers, fruit and vegetables on long wooden trellises supported on floating mats of vegetation; and **village markets** and **artisans' shops**, where weaving, blacksmithing and jewellery-making go on. There's no

BORDER CROSSING: KAWTHOUNG–RANONG

Kawthoung (also known as Victoria Point), at the far southern end of Myanmar, is a legal crossing point for foreign tourists coming from Thailand, but lacks transport links with the rest of Myanmar. As with all Myanmar's land crossings (or in this case, water crossings), visits are restricted to a limited number of days within a limited area, you have to leave your passport at the border and you're generally expected to return the same way you came in.

Though it's not possible for travellers already in Myanmar to exit the country via this crossing, you can visit Kawthoung on a 'visa trip' from Thailand. Several travel agencies in Ranong offer these trips for about 400B, but it is easy enough to do unassisted. Boats to Kawthoung leave the Saphan Pla pier, located about 10km from Ranong, regularly from around 8am till 4pm (200B, 40 minutes). After getting your passport stamped by Thai immigration, board one of the boats near the immigration office and you'll be taken to the Myanmar immigration office, where you must surrender your passport and pay a fee of US$10 or 500B for a permit that allows you to stay in Kawthoung for up to 14 days. If you decide to stay – sights include the town's busy **waterfront** (Strand Rd) and a hilltop temple **Pyi Taw Aye Paya** – there's the centrally located but overpriced **Honey Bear Hotel** (☎592 1352; Strand Rd; s/d US$36/48; ❄).

Note, if you're crossing at Ranong to get a fresh Thai tourist visa, they're now limited to only 14 days.

obligation to buy anything. Cloth is one of the better buys around Inle Lake.

Yadana Man Aung Paya TEMPLE
(Phaung Daw Seiq Rd; ⏲6am-10pm) The oldest and most important Buddhist shrine in Nyaungshwe, this handsome gilded stupa is hidden away inside a square compound south of the market. The stepped stupa is unique in Myanmar, and the surrounding pavilion contains a museum of treasures amassed by the monks over the centuries.

Buddha Museum MUSEUM
(Museum Rd; admission US$2; ⏲9.30am-4pm Tue-Sun) It's worth coming to this boring government-run museum to see the stately brick-and-teak *haw* (palace) of the 33rd and last Shan *sao pha*, Sao Shwe Thaike.

Mingala Market MARKET
Flooded with locals every morning, when traders from the lake bring in fresh fish and produce from the floating gardens. A few stalls sell local handicrafts.

Sleeping

Nyaungshwe is teeming with good budget rooms, so if the below options are all full there are plenty of decent alternatives. All include breakfast and most rent out bicycles.

Teakwood Guest House GUESTHOUSE $
(☎209250; teakwood.htl@gmail.com; Kyaung Taw Anouk Rd; r US$10-25; @) At this attractive guesthouse, popular with older independent travellers, the best rooms are in the new block – big windows let in lots of light and the bathrooms are finished with small pebbles. The communal areas are great, but be ready for some assertive sales pitches from the owner for boat trips and excursions.

Aquarius Inn GUESTHOUSE $
(☎209352; aquarius352@gmail.com; 2 Phaung Daw Pyan Rd; s/d US$7/12) Charming owners make this small, family-run guesthouse a real home away from home. The cosy rooms contain an intriguing collection of local bric-a-brac and there's a plant-filled yard where you can sit and chat in the evenings.

Nawng Kham – Little Inn GUESTHOUSE $
(☎209195; Phaung Daw Pyan Rd; s/d US$6/12) This small but perfectly formed guesthouse has just seven rooms with fans, private bathrooms and hot showers, set in a peaceful garden.

GOVERNMENT FEE

There is a US$5 government fee to enter the Inle Lake area, which you must pay on arrival at the **permit booth** (⏲6am-9pm) by the bridge at the entrance to Nyaungshwe. We cruised into town on an extremely packed bus from Taunggyi and circumvented paying the fee, and we weren't asked to show proof of payment later, suggesting the authorities may not take it very seriously.

May Guest House GUESTHOUSE $
(☎209417; 85 Myawady Rd; s/d/tr US$7/12/16) Wagon wheels mounted in the front wall set the tone at this village-style guesthouse in the monastery quarter. The simple square rooms have fans and private bathrooms, and the breakfast is said to be one of the best in town.

Queen Inn GUESTHOUSE $
(☎209544; queen.ine@gmail.com; Win Quarter; r US$7-20) Located on the opposite side of the canal, if it wasn't for the noise of boats, this would be a budget dream. Rooms are simple, but the highlight is the family feel, emphasised in the nightly family-style dinners for only K2000.

Eating

TOP CHOICE Lin Htett Myanmar Traditional Food BURMESE $$
(Yone Gyi Rd; meals from K4000; ⏲lunch & dinner) As friendly as its food is delicious, this place offers authentic Myanmar dining.

Lotus Restaurant INTERNATIONAL, BURMESE $
(Museum Rd; mains from K1000; ⏲all day) With only five tables, this family-run place is as small as its menu is short. Go for the family-style dinner that includes soup, salad, curry and a generous fruit plate for only K3500. Host Pyone Cho is also an excellent trekking guide.

Thu Kha Coffee TEASHOP $
(cnr Main & Yone Gyi Rds; snacks from K200; ⏲5am-4pm) This tidy place serves good tea and, in the mornings, tasty *pakoda* (deep-fried vegetable dumplings). Come later in the afternoon for sweets such as roti (deep-fried dough).

Inle Pancake Kingdom PANCAKES $
(off Phaung Daw Seiq Rd; mains from K800) Choose from a huge range of filled pancakes and

Nyaungshwe

toasted sandwiches at this cute little cabin on a narrow alley north of the sports field. For authentic local eats, check out the **food stalls** (breakfast & lunch) in Mingala Market. Every evening there's also a basic **night market** (Gyi Rd; 5-9pm), with dishes such as Shan noodles and tofu, hot pot, roti and murtabak.

Getting There & Away

Air

Inle's airport is at Heho, 26km northwest of Nyaungshwe on the way to Kalaw. Both Air Mandalay and Air Bagan offer three daily services to Yangon (US$86 to US$95, one to three hours), with their afternoon flights routing through Mandalay (US$42 to US$53, 25 minutes) and Nyaung U (Bagan; US$68 to US$75, one hour). Hotels and private travel agents in Nyaungshwe can make bookings.

Either take a taxi from the airport to Nyaungshwe (K25,000, one hour) or hike 1km to the highway and wait for a pick-up or bus bound for Taunggyi (K2000, 1½ hours); ask to be let off at Shwenyaung, from where you can change for Nyaungshwe. Bear in mind that you might face a long wait.

Bus & Pick-up

Any bus travelling from Mandalay or Yangon to Taunggyi can drop you at Shwenyaung for the full Taunggyi fare.

Nyaungshwe

Sights
1 Buddha Museum D1
2 Mingala Market C1
3 Yadana Man Aung Paya B2

Sleeping
4 Aquarius Inn B3
5 May Guest House C2
6 Nawng Kham – Little Inn B2
7 Queen Inn A2
8 Teakwood Guest House B2

Eating
9 Food Stalls C1
10 Inle Pancake Kingdom A2
11 Lin Htett Myanmar Traditional Food C2
12 Lotus Restaurant C1
13 Night Market B2
14 Thu Kha Coffee B2

To Yangon, overnight buses originating in Taunggyi reach Shwenyaung at about 3pm (K14,000, 16 to 20 hours). Similarly, the Mandalay-bound bus arrives at Shwenyaung at around 6pm (K10,000, 12 hours) and the bus to Nyaung U (Bagan) at around 5am (K10,000, eight hours). Hotels and travel agents in Nyaungshwe can book seats on these buses but be sure to be

BIKE RIDE TO HOT SPRINGS

Rent a bike and pedal through beautiful countryside to **Kaung Daing**, a quiet Intha village on Inle's northwestern shore, about 8km from Nyaungshwe. Here take a dip in the **hot springs** (swimming pool K3000, private bathhouse K5000, mixed hot pool K5000; ⏲6am-6pm), which are also the start or end point of several trekking routes between Kalaw and Inle Lake. If you don't feel like pedalling all the way back, load your bike onto a boat and motor across to Maing Thauk (K5000) before cycling home, starting on a long wooden bridge.

at the junction in Shwenyaung early so you don't miss your bus.

To reach Kalaw (K3000, four hours), first take a pick-up or taxi to Shwenyaung. Once you reach the highway junction, you can flag down local buses and pick-ups heading west.

Getting Around

Shops on Yone Gyi and Phaung Daw Pyan Rds rent bicycles (K1000 per day). Motorcycle taxis at the stand near the market can take you to Kaung Daing hot springs for K5000 return.

From Nyaungshwe, pick-ups run to Shwenyaung (K500, 30 minutes) and Taunggyi (K1000, one hour) from 7am to around 5pm.

Kalaw

☎081 / POP ABOUT 25,000

Welcome to Myanmar's trekking heartland, combining cool mountain climbs and a chilled vibe beloved by backpackers. Located at 1320m on the rolling, pine-clad hills of the Shan Plateau, Kalaw is the beginning point for treks heading west to Inle Lake (about 45km), over mountains dotted with Palaung, Pa-O, Intha and Shan villages.

Kalaw is easy to navigate on foot. **Cyber World Internet Café** (Aung Chan Thar St; per hr K1000; ⏲8am-11pm) is just uphill from **Aung Chan Thar Zedi**, a glittery stupa covered in gold- and silver-coloured glass mosaics.

Activities

Trekking

During high season (November to February) it can get pretty busy on the more popular routes, while in the wet season paths get miserably muddy and few tourists head this way.

The most popular trek is undoubtedly the two- to four-day trek to Inle Lake. A less common route is the multiday trek to Pindaya, via Taung Ni. It's worth requesting a route via the villages of several different ethnic groups. Have good shoes and warm clothing for the cool evenings. Guesthouses can transport your unneeded bags for a small charge.

Trekking without a guide is not recommended – the trails are confusing, the terrain challenging and few people in the hills speak English. The going rate for a guided day walk ranges from US$5 to US$7 per person in groups of three or more, US$8 to US$12 for overnight treks. Recommended guides include **JP Barua** (☎50549), Kalaw-based with good reviews; Pyone Cho at Lotus Restaurant in Nyaungshwe (p506); Than Htay and Ko Htwe at **Sunny Day Tour Services** (htwe.sunny@yahoo.com; cnr Main & Yone Gyi Rds, Nyaungshwe); Naing Naing at **Ever Smile** (☎50683; Yuzana St, Kalaw); Harri and Rambo at the Golden Lily Guest House; and **Sam Trekking Guide** (☎50377; Union Hwy, Kalaw).

Sleeping

Electricity is especially temperamental here, but you won't need air-con (or even a fan) to sleep. All rates include breakfast.

Eastern Paradise Motel HOTEL $
(☎50315; 5 Thirimingalar St; r US$7-15) There's no need to be suspicious of the unintentionally self-deprecating moniker; large homey rooms and gracious service make this one of the best deals in town.

Honey Pine Hotel HOTEL $
(☎50728; 44 Zatila St; s/d/tr US$10/20/30) Of the handful of new hotels going up in Kalaw, this was the only one finished at research time. The budget-priced rooms here include midrange amenities such as TV and fridge, although the single rooms lack windows and feel a bit tight.

Golden Lily Guest House HOTEL $
(☎50108; goldenlily@mandalay.net.mm; 5/88 Natsin Rd; r US$3-10; @) The more expensive rooms share a wide balcony that looks over the town and are substantially nicer than the cheaper rooms, the shared bathrooms of which could really use some work. Trekking can be arranged here, although it comes with an annoying hard sell.

Kalaw

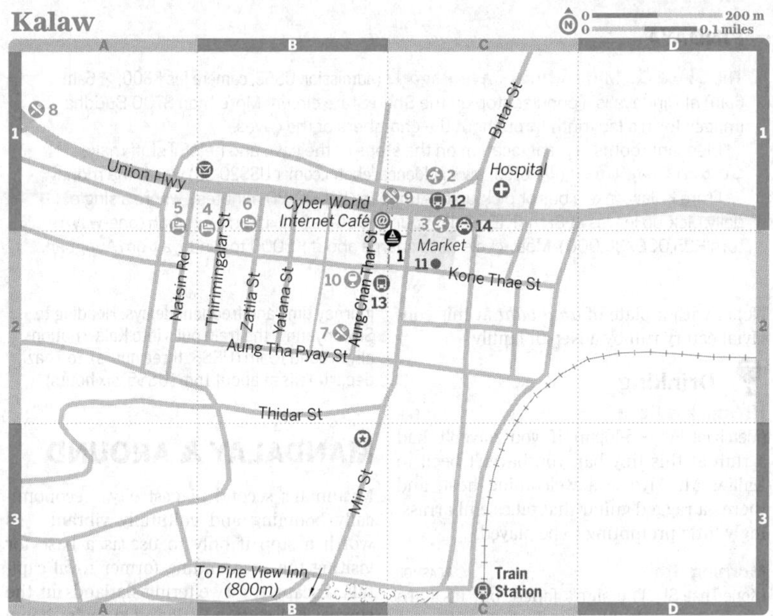

Pine View Inn HOTEL $

(☎50185; University Rd; s/d US$10/15) If you'd rather stay in the leafy part of town, this quiet hotel offers plain but tidy rooms in a new bungalow block or an older wooden house.

Eating

Thu Maung Restaurant BURMESE $

(Union Hwy; meals from K2500; ⊙lunch & dinner) Probably the best Burmese restaurant in town, serving tasty chicken, pork and fish curries with all the usual Myanmar salads, pickles and trimmings.

Pyae Pyae Shan Noodle SHAN $

(Union Hwy; noodles from K500) Slurp delicious bowls of the eponymous noodle, or choose from a short menu of rice-based dishes.

Sam's Family Restaurant INTERNATIONAL, BURMESE $

(Aung Chan Thar St; mains from K1000) Run by the same family as Sam Trekking Guide, this cosy little place serves Indian, Myanmar and Chinese standards and old-fashioned backpacker breakfasts.

Everest Nepali Food Centre NEPALI $

(Aung Chan Thar St; set meals from K2000; ⊙lunch & dinner) Relive memories of trekking in

Kalaw

Sights

1 Aung Chan Tha Zedi C2

Activities, Courses & Tours

2 Ever Smile C1
Harri & Rambo Trekking Guides. (see 5)
3 Sam Trekking Guide C1

Sleeping

4 Eastern Paradise Motel B1
5 Golden Lily Guest House A1
6 Honey Pine Hotel B1

Eating

7 Everest Nepali Food Centre B2
8 Pyae Pyae Shan Noodle A1
Sam's Family Restaurant .... (see 7)
9 Thu Maung Restaurant C1

Drinking

10 Hi Snack & Drink B2
Morning Star .... (see 10)

Transport

11 Bus Ticket Offices C2
12 Buses to Bagan, Yangon & Mandalay C1
13 Buses to Taunggyi B2
14 Motorcycle Taxis C1

WORTH A TRIP

PINDAYA

The **Shwe Oo Min Natural Cave Pagoda** (admission US$3, camera fee K300; 6am-6pm) at Pindaya is a popular stop on the Shan State circuit. More than 8700 Buddha images form a labyrinth throughout the chambers of the caves.

Pleasant rooms, a great location on the steps of the cave and helpful staff make **Golden Cave Hotel** (66166; www.goldencavehotel.com; r US$20-35) worth the money.

From Kalaw, take a bus or pick-up to Aungban (K1000, 20 minutes), where a single daily pick-up leaves at 8am (K1000, 1½ hours). Or take a taxi from Aungban (one-way/return K25,000/30,000). Motorcycle taxis charge about K6000 to Pindaya from Aungban.

Nepal with a plate of *dhal baht* at this convivial eatery run by a Nepali family.

Drinking

Hi Snack & Drink BAR

(Merchant Rd; 5-10pm) If you haven't had a rum at this tiny bar, you haven't been to Kalaw. Mr Myo is a welcoming host, and there's a ragged guitar that takes embarrassingly little prompting to be played.

Morning Star TEASHOP

(Kone Thae St) The sign's faded, but it's hard to miss this tidy, blue teashop. Couple your sweet tea with equally sweet Indian sweets.

Getting There & Away

Air

Kalaw is about 16km from Heho airport and a taxi there costs K30,000 (for more on flights, see p507). Coming from Heho by taxi, it's hard to find people to share with, as most passengers head to Inle Lake. Consider negotiating to Heho village and boarding a pick-up (K3000) from there.

Bus

Several bus ticket offices across from the market book seats on the long-distance buses between Yangon and Mandalay and Taunggyi. These buses stop on the main road, in front of the market.

Small local buses bound for Taunggyi depart from a stop behind the Aung Chang Tha Zedi. Buses, minivans and pick-ups bound for Thazi will drop you in Shwenyaung (Inle Lake; two hours) for the same fare.

Buses, minivans and pick-ups to Thazi (K2500, four hours) stop periodically on the highway – fares for foreigners are routinely doubled along this route.

For more info on bus services from Kalaw, see the table opposite.

Train

A single daily train departs from either end of the winding line that links Thazi and Shwenyaung. Stunning scenery makes up for the slow journey time and frequent delays. Heading to Shwenyaung, the train pulls into Kalaw notionally around 10am (US$3, three hours); to Thazi, departure is at about 1pm (US$5, six hours).

MANDALAY & AROUND

Myanmar's second biggest city – economically booming and culturally vibrant – is worth a stop if only to use as a base for visiting the surrounding former royal capitals. Escape the sweltering flatlands in the surreal hill station of Pyin Oo Lwin, home to brilliant old colonial buildings, horse-drawn carriage taxis and good restaurants catering for an influx of Myanmar's nouveau riche. Further north, charming little Hsipaw makes a great alternative base for easy treks into fascinating minority villages.

Mandalay

02 / POP 950,000

For those who haven't been – and that includes *The Road to Mandalay* author Rudyard Kipling – the mention of 'Mandalay' typically conjures up images of Asia at its most traditional and timeless. The reality is instead a sprawling city where dusty streets teem with traffic and there's a construction project on every block. In spite of this, it's impossible not to be impressed by the golden Buddha of Mahamuni Paya, or the sunset views across the flat landscape from stupa-studded Mandalay Hill.

Mandalay became the capital of the Burmese empire in 1861, an entity that by 1885 had been exiled into history by the British. Prior to Mandalay, several other places within a short distance also served as capitals, and it's these ancient cities that are the real attractions.

Unlike Yangon, Mandalay is booming – thanks largely to Chinese investment.

BUSES FROM KALAW

DESTINATION	COST (K)	DURATION (HR)	FREQUENCY
Bagan	12,000-13,000 (air-con)	8	7am
Mandalay	8000-10,000 (air-con)	9	8am, 9pm
Taunggyi	2000 (no air-con/pick-up)	3	6am, 6.30am, 7am
Thazi	2500 (pick-up)	4	6am-2pm
Yangon	14,000 (air-con)	12-15	4pm-5.30pm

Beneath the bustling bravado and low-slung Chinese jeeps, Mandalay is also the nation's cultural capital and a fine place to delve into many Burmese arts.

Sights

The government collects a flat US$10 fee for a ticket that covers the main sights in Mandalay. Tickets are checked at the palace, Kuthodaw Paya, Shwenandaw Kyaung and Shwe Ta Bin Kyaung. The same ticket is also valid for Amarapura (p519) and Inwa (Ava; p520). Sometimes collection desks don't operate before 8am or after 4.30pm, and alternative entrances bypass ticket checkers.

Mandalay Hill VIEWPOINT

(Map p514) It's around a 45-minute, barefoot and sweaty climb to the top of Mandalay Hill, but what a view. Two hundred and thirty metres above the plain, you can rest your eyes on the Shan hills, the Ayeyarwady and the vast palace grounds, and imagine that they might one day be to Mandalay what Central Park is to New York.

The most common starting point is at the south, either between **two giant chinthe** (guardian lion-dog creatures) or by another stairway starting further southeast where the **Bobokyi Nat** (Spirit Statue) watches over the entrance. The routes converge a little south of a large **standing buddha** (Map p514) that points down at Mandalay.

GETTING TO THAILAND: TACHILEIK TO MAE SAI

Getting to the border At the time of writing, we'd received reports of a few travellers who had been permitted to cross into Thailand at the seedy frontier smuggling town of Tachileik with advance permission from MTT in Yangon. Permits are issued in around two weeks and cost at least $50, but you may be required to book your flights and a taxi to the border through MTT.

Starting from Mae Sai, in Thailand, it's straightforward to cross to Tachileik for the day and slightly more complicated to get a two-week visa and permission to visit Kengtung where you can visit myriad tribal groups living in the surrounding hills.

At the border The Thai immigration office is officially open from 6.30am to 6.30pm. After taking care of the usual formalities, cross the bridge and head to the Myanmar immigration office. Here you pay 500B and have your picture taken for a temporary ID card that allows you to stay in town for the day; your passport will be kept at the office.

If you'd like to stay longer, or visit Kengtung, you'll be directed to the adjacent tourist information office. You'll need three photos, US$10 and 50B to process a border pass valid for 14 days; your passport will be kept at the border.

For budget accommodation in Tachileik try **River Side Hotel** (☎51161; r 600B; ❄) a block from the bridge connecting Myanmar and Thailand. It's also obligatory to hire a guide for the duration of your stay. Guides cost 1000B per day (400B of this goes to MTT), and if you haven't already arranged for a Kengtung-based guide to meet you at the border, you'll be assigned one by MTT and will also have to pay for your guide's food and accommodation during your stay.

Moving on On entry into Thailand, the Thai authorities will issue you a 14-day visa on arrival, or you can enter with a visa obtained overseas.

Greater Mandalay

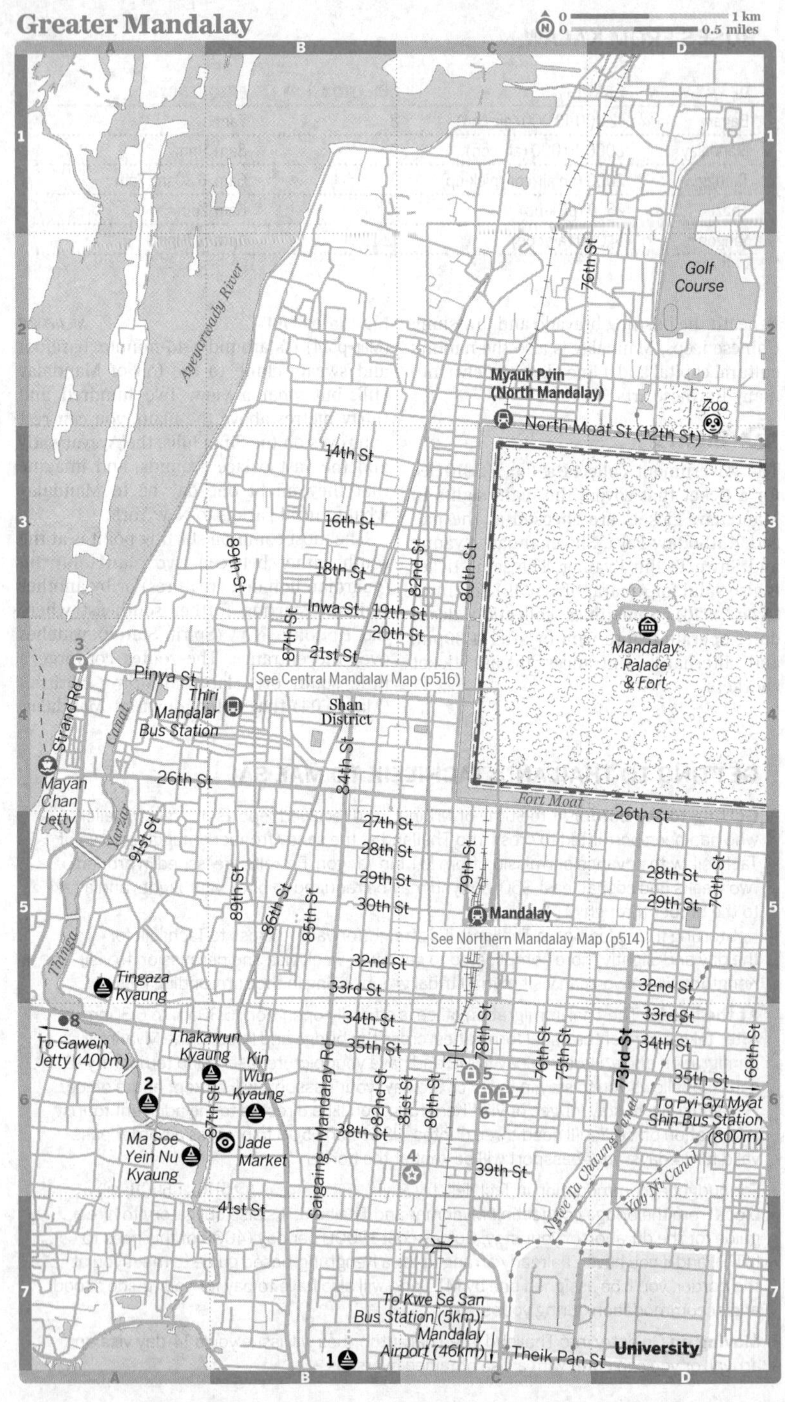

0 1 km
0 0.5 miles
Ayeyarwady River
Golf Course
Zoo
Myauk Pyin (North Mandalay)
North Moat St (12th St)
76th St
14th St
16th St
18th St
89th St
82nd St
80th St
Inwa St
19th St
20th St
21st St
87th St
Mandalay Palace & Fort
Pinya St
See Central Mandalay Map (p516)
Thiri Mandalar Bus Station
Shan District
Strand Rd
Canal
84th St
Mayan Chan Jetty
26th St
Fort Moat
26th St
Yarzar
91st St
27th St
28th St
29th St
30th St
79th St
28th St
29th St
70th St
89th St
86th St
85th St
Mandalay
See Northern Mandalay Map (p514)
Thinga
Tingaza Kyaung
32nd St
33rd St
34th St
32nd St
33rd St
To Gawein Jetty (400m)
Thakawun Kyaung
35th St
78th St
76th St
75th St
73rd St
34th St
68th St
Kin Wun Kyaung
35th St
87th St
Saigaing–Mandalay Rd
82nd St
81st St
80th St
To Pyi Gyi Myat Shin Bus Station (800m)
Ma Soe Yein Nu Kyaung
Jade Market
38th St
39th St
Ngwe Ta Chaung Canal
Yay Ni Canal
41st St
To Kwe Se San Bus Station (5km); Mandalay Airport (46km)
Theik Pan St
University

According to legend, Buddha, accompanied by his disciple Ananda, climbed Mandalay Hill and prophesied that, in the 2400th year of his faith (1857), a great city would be founded below the hill; this was the year that King Mindon did indeed decree the capital's move from Amarapura to Mandalay.

If you aren't up to walking, it's possible to take a taxi (blue/normal taxi K8000/10,000) using a long switchback road (allegedly built with forced labour) that brings you within an escalator ride of the summit. Along the same route there are also very occasional shared pick-up shuttles charging K1000 per person that leave from near the giant chinthe entrance.

Mahamuni Paya TEMPLE

(Map p512) The central 4m-tall Buddha image of this temple was seized from Rakhaing State in 1784 and is so highly venerated that it's covered in around 15cm of gold leaf. It might have been cast as early as the 1st century AD. Every morning at 4am a team of monks lovingly washes the image's face and the soupy run-off is bottled as holy water. Women are not allowed to touch the image. In the northwest corner of the surrounding pavilion are six intricate bronze Khmer figures, war booty from Angkor Wat via Thailand.

Lots of new Buddha images are being hewn from stone at workshops to the west of the *paya*.

Shwe In Bin Kyaung MONASTERY

(Map p512; cnr 89th & 38th Sts) Meaning 'teak monastery', this elegant building dates from 1895, when wealthy Chinese jade merchants funded its construction. It's lovely, and off the tourist trail. Shwe In Bin Kyaung is at the heart of the city's 'monks' district'; come early and just wander from monastery to monastery, among hundreds of monks walking to and fro along the leafy lanes.

Kuthodaw Paya TEMPLE

(Map p514) A number of pagodas draw visitors and worshippers to the south and southeast of Mandalay Hill. Kuthodaw Paya, aka the 'world's biggest book', draws tour buses for its 729 slabs that retell the Tripitaka canon. It's included in the US$10 ticket, but after around 4.40pm ticket checkers tend to slope off. Nearby, the **Sandamuni Paya** (Map p514) has more such slabs and is free to enter.

Shwenandaw Kyaung MONASTERY

(Map p514) This intricately carved wooden monastery, the only surviving part of the original Mandalay Palace, was moved outside the palace walls following King Mindon's death. It's also included in the US$10 ticket.

Mandalay Palace & Fort PALACE

(Map p514; ⌚7.30am-5pm) On the advice of their celestial advisers, the kings of old moved their palaces every generation or two. Mindon Min, one of the last kings of Myanmar, ordered the old palace in Amarapura dismantled and relocated to this sprawling, moated complex. Thibaw Min occupied it until the Brits drove him out.

During WWII, fierce fighting between occupying Japanese forces and advancing British and Indian troops resulted in fires that burned the original to the ground. This reconstruction, built using concrete, aluminium and, allegedly, forced labour, is impressive for its scale (over 40 timber buildings) but less so for artistry and upkeep. If you don't want to pay the US$10 ticket fee imposed at the east entrance (the only entrance open to foreigners), walk along a shady promenade on the south of the surrounding fort, near central Mandalay, to admire the original walls close up for free.

Sleeping

The nearest thing to a 'backpacker zone' is the three-block area around the Nylon Hotel. Many budget places fill up quickly in the high season from October to March. Breakfast is included at all listed places.

Greater Mandalay

Sights
- 1 Mahamuni Paya B7
- 2 Shwe In Bin Kyaung A6

Drinking
- 3 View Point A4

Entertainment
- 4 Moustache Brothers C6

Shopping
- 5 Aurora C6
- 6 Gold Leaf Pounding Workshops C6
- 7 Soe Moe C6

Transport
- 8 IWT Office A6

Northern Mandalay

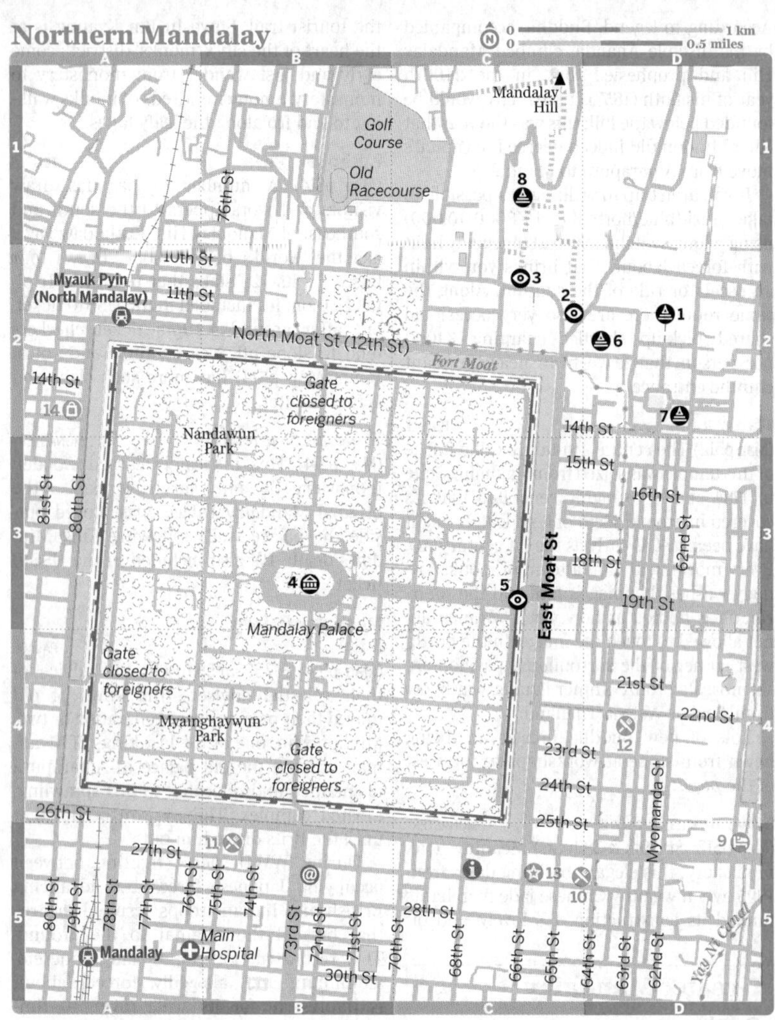

TOP CHOICE **Royal Guest House** GUESTHOUSE $
(Map p516; ☎31400, 65697; 25th St, 82/83; s/d US$10/15, with shared bathroom US$5/10; ❄) Gloss paints in multiple pastel colours, little carved panels and a frontage of pot plants and foliage all help set this popular place apart, though bed quality is inconsistent and cheap rooms can be seriously small.

ET Hotel HOTEL $
(Map p516; ☎65006, 66547; tmchomdy@mandalay.net.mm; 129A 83rd St; s/d US$14/18, without bathroom US$6/12; ❄@) The only thing extra-terrestrial here is the glow of the lone fluorescent bulb against the mint-green walls in clean but dated rooms. However, beds are comfy, showers hot and the helpful staff understand travellers' needs.

Nylon Hotel HOTEL $
(Map p516; ☎33460; 25th at 83rd St; s/d with fan US$7/12, with air-con US$10/15; ❄@) A no-nonsense 25-room, five-floor tower (no lift). Decently tiled rooms come with solar-heated showers and are more likely to have windows than at the similarly priced Garden Hotel next door.

Northern Mandalay

Sights

1 Kuthodaw Paya ... D2
2 Mandalay Hill Entrance ... C2
3 Mandalay Hill Entrance ... C2
4 Mandalay Palace & Fort ... B3
5 Mandalay Palace East Gate ... C3
6 Sandamuni Paya ... D2
7 Shwenandaw Kyaung ... D2
8 Standing Buddha ... C1

Sleeping

9 Peacock Lodge ... D5

Eating

10 Green Elephant ... C5
11 Marie-Min ... B5
12 Spice Garden ... D4

Entertainment

13 Mandalay Marionettes ... C5

Shopping

14 Garuda ... A2
Sunflower ... (see 11)

Silver Star Hotel HOTEL $$
(Map p516; ☎33394, 66786; www.silverstarhotelmandalay.com; 27th at 83rd St; s/d US$25/28, cnr room US$27/30; ❄@) A vast step up from most of Mandalay's dreary midrange hotels, the Silver Star isn't particularly stylish but it's spotlessly clean, with pine furniture and creamy yellow walls. The lift works and the rooms are bright, especially corner rooms.

Eating & Drinking

Mandalay has plenty of inexpensive Asian restaurants. However, there is definitely not a lively night scene, particularly when you consider this is a city of almost one million inhabitants. Leave your dancing shoes in Yangon.

V Café/Skybar INTERNATIONAL $$
(Map p516; 25th at 80th St; espresso/draft beer/cocktails K800/1000/3000, mains/burgers K5000/2000; ⏲9am-10.30pm; ❄) One of Mandalay's new breed of air-con Western cafe-bars, V offers vaguely 1970s retro decor and a menu including pasta, Mexican stir-fry, tempura, burgers and pizza. Its rooftop bar has views across the walled fort towards distant Mandalay Hill.

Green Elephant BURMESE, THAI, CHINESE $$
(Map p514; ☎61237; 27th, 64/65; mains/extras/rice 6000/2400/1200K, set menu per person K8000; ⏲8.30am-3pm & 5-9.30pm; ❄) Consistently recommended for regional cuisine, a few tables are within a colonial-era building and full of period relics. Others spill out into a bamboo-tufted garden.

Spice Garden INDIAN, BURMESE, EUROPEAN $$
(Map p514; ☎61177; Hotel on the Red Canal, 22nd at 63rd St; mains US$3-8, beer US$4; ⏲6am-10.30pm) Serves some of Mandalay's most authentic Indian food, along with set-menu European and Burmese dinners (US$10 to US$15). Fair value, though the drinks can get pricey. Appealing garden seating also available.

Marie-Min VEGETARIAN $$
(Map p514; off 27th St, 74/75; dishes K1300-2000, rice K300; ⏲8.30am-9pm, closed Jun; ✍) Above an antiques shop on a residential alley, the friendly English-speaking owners have tailored a short menu of vegie delights, including all-day breakfasts, stomach-safe lassis and delicious eggplant (aubergine) dip.

View Point BEER GARDEN $
(Map p512; Strand Rd; draught beer K600; ⏲9am-11pm) The river views to the west are magnificent, while south there's an endlessly fascinating mayhem of loading and unloading riverboats. From 7pm loud karaoke performers change the atmosphere completely. Open air, very limited food.

SPLURGE: PEACOCK LODGE

At homestay-style **Peacock Lodge** (Map p515; ☎61429, 09 204 2059; www.pyinoolwin.info/peacock.htm; 5 60th St, 25/26; s/d US$18/24; ❄), the engaging owners treat you like part of the family. Expect lively conversation over breakfast, and chilled hours reading in the quiet garden where delicious Burmese set dinners (K8000, order 24 hours in advance) are served. It's a fair way from central Mandalay, but it's easy enough to cycle into town. Get here by taking 26th St east, then turning north at a sign to 'Hotel Treasure'.

Central Mandalay

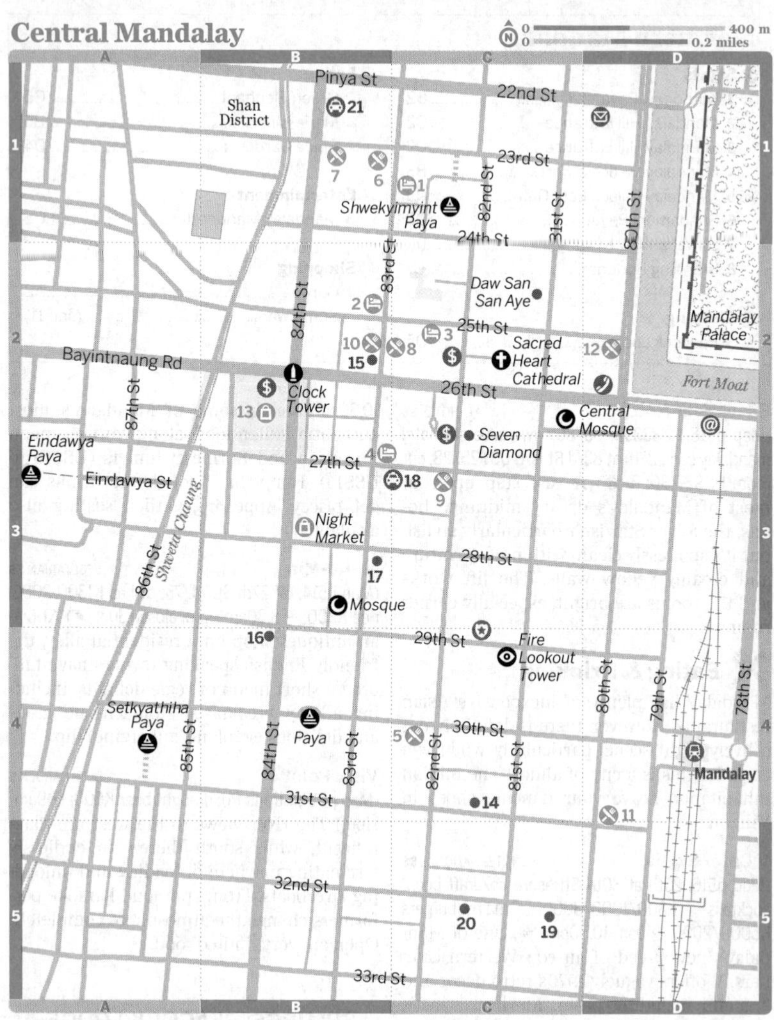

☆ Entertainment

Mandalay Marionettes PUPPET SHOW
(Map p514; www.mandalaymarionettes.com; 66th St, 26/27; admission K10,000; ⊙8.30pm) On a tiny stage, colourful marionettes expressively re-create tales based on the Buddhist texts. Occasionally a sub-curtain is lifted so you can briefly admire the skill of the puppeteers' deft hand movements. The troupe has travelled and performed internationally.

Shopping

Mandalay is a major crafts centre, and probably the best place in the country for traditional puppets and hand-woven embroidered tapestries. Virtually nothing you see will be 'antique'; items are often scuffed up or weathered to look much older than they are. Handicraft specialists include **Aurora** (Map p512; 78th St, 35/36), **Garuda** (Map p514; 80th at 15th St), **Soe Moe** (Map p512; 36th St, 77/78) and **Sunflower** (Map p514; Marie-Min restaurant, 27th St, 74/75).

There are numerous **silk workshop-shops** and a couple more handicraft emporia along main Sagaing road in Amarapura (p519). Puppets are sold at Moustache Brothers and Mandalay Marionettes. There

Central Mandalay

Sleeping

1	ET Hotel	C1
2	Nylon Hotel	B2
3	Royal Guest House	C2
4	Silver Star Hotel	B3

Eating

5	Gold Medal	C4
	Golden Shan	(see 6)
6	Karaweik	B1
7	Lashio Lay	B1
8	Mann	C2
9	Nay	C3
10	Nylon Ice Cream Bar	B2
11	SB	D4
12	V Café/Skybar	D2

Shopping

13	Zeigyo	B2

Transport

14	Duhtawadi	C4
15	Mr Jerry	B2
16	Pick-ups to Amarapura, Inwa (Ava), Sagaing & Mingun	B4
17	Pick-ups to Pyin Oo Lwin	B3
	Pick-ups to the Highway Bus Station	(see 16)
18	Pyin Oo Lwin Share Taxis	C3
19	Share Taxis to Hsipaw & Lashio	C5
20	Shwe Li Oo	C5
21	Shwe Li Shan	B1

are also several interesting shops on 36th St beside the **gold leaf pounding workshops** (Map p512), where you can buy square gold leaf sheets.

Zeigyo MARKET

(Map p516; 84th St, 26/28) Spread over two large modern buildings, this central market is packed with plenty of Myanmar-made items (including handicrafts) that spill onto the surrounding footpaths. This market will be replaced in a few years by a vast 25-storey tower mall, currently under construction.

Information

Internet Access

Internet cafes are fairly common along 27th St and are scattered widely around the city centre but most are appallingly slow.

Acme-Net (Map p516; 26th St, 78/79; per hr K500; ⏲9am-9pm) Better connection than most and adept with proxy servers.

Dream Land (Map p514; 27th St, 72/73; per hr K400; ⏲9.30am-11pm; ❄) Good connection and free drinking water.

Money

Most guesthouses will change pristine US dollars cash, but for better rates ask at certain gold

DINING DOWNTOWN

In the central traveller zone (Map p516) there's a disappointing lack of inspirational dining. If you lack the transport to head further afield, try the following options. But don't expect anything very special. For something more interesting, get on your bike.

Nay (27th at 82nd St; ⏲5-11.30pm) has roadside tables and serves curry snacks (K250 to K1000) with fresh chapattis (K150 each). **Nylon Ice Cream Bar** (83rd St, 25/26; ice cream K500-1500, beer K1700; ⏲8am-10pm) is another ultra-simple pavement-table meeting place, open all day and offering shakes, lassis and beer as well as ice cream.

Crusty shop-restaurant **Mann** (83rd St, 25/26; dishes K1500-2000, rice K300, beer K1600; ⏲10am-10pm) is an eternally popular foreigner meeting place for its location more than for its very average Chinese fare. Bakeries **Gold Medal** (30th St, 81/82) and **SB** (80th at 31st St) sell bagged-up super-soft bread and sticky cakes Japanese style.

There's a gaggle of Shan restaurants around the 83rd/23rd St corner, where **Karaweik** (83rd at 23rd St) teashop (unsigned in English) whips up Shan noodles (K600) and semi-sweet tandoori-naan bread (K100) that's ideal for tea dipping. **Golden Shan** (83rd at 23rd St) charges K3000 for an all-you-can-eat buffet, while **Lashio Lay** (83rd at 23rd St) charges per plate (K500 to K900 plus K300 rice) from a pre-cooked spread.

THE MOUSTACHE BROTHERS

The **Moustache Brothers** (Map p513; 39th St, 80/81; donation K8000; ⏲8.30pm) has earned its reputation as Myanmar's best-known dissident comedy troupe the hard way. Two members of the comedy trio, Par Par Lay and Lu Zaw, served six years hard labour after joking about the government during a performance at Aung San Suu Kyi's house in 1996; English-speaking Lu Maw had been 'holding the fort' back home at the time. Their detention became a cause célèbre among foreign comedians and Par Par Lay was mentioned in the Hugh Grant film *About a Boy*.

They were eventually released in 2002. Before long, however, they were banned from performing their *a-nyeint pwes* (traditional folk operas), a blend of in-yer-face slapstick, dancing and painted signs, by a government fearful of their influence. But they refused to be silenced. The shows went on as 'demonstrations' in their tiny home theatre in the Mandalay backstreets. Despite a further arrest in 2007, they continue to take the mickey out of the government, so long as they only perform at home and, most depressing for the two non-English-speakers, not in Burmese.

As one of the few openly dissenting voices in a nation silenced by fear, it's well worth supporting their performance. These days the shows include a slightly indulgent level of self-parody, but remain one of Mandalay's greatest talking points for Western visitors.

shops such as **Shwe Hinn Thar** (Map p516; 26th St, 84/85; ⏲10am-4pm), or travel agencies such as Seven Diamond Express. Marie-Min restaurant also offers decent rates.

Post

Main post office (Map p516; 22nd St, 80/81; ⏲10.30am-4pm)

Telephone

Local/national calls cost K100/200 per minute from PCO street stands. Royal Guest House offers international calls for US$2 per minute.

Tourist Information & Travel Agencies

Daw San San Aye (Map p516; ☎31799; Hotel dynasty, 81st St, 24/25; ⏲7.30am-8pm) Very obliging, fair-priced air-ticket sales booth.

Seven Diamond (Map p516; ☎30128, 72828; 82nd St, 26/27; ⏲8am-9pm) Helpful agency. Henry speaks great English.

MTT (Map p514; ☎60356; 68th at 27th St; ⏲9am-5pm) The government-run travel company doubles as tourist office selling city maps (K200), as well as transport tickets and permit-needing tours.

ℹ Getting There & Away

For details on pick-ups and other transport to Amarapura, Inwa, Sagaing and Mingun, see p519.

Air

Mandalay's air connections include Yangon (US$92, several daily), Nyaung U (for Bagan; US$42, several daily), Heho (for Inle Lake; US$42, several daily) and Myitkyina (US$95, Monday, Tuesday, Thursday, Friday and Sunday). Domestic fares are slightly cheaper from travel agents.

Boat

The **IWT office** (Map p512; ☎36035; 35th St; ⏲sales 10am-2pm) sells tickets for slow government-run ferries on the Ayeyarwady, including trips to Bagan (deck/cabin class US$12/33, 13 to 15 hours, 5.30am Wednesday and Sunday), and Bhamo (deck/cabin US$9/54, three to five days, 6am Monday, Thursday and Saturday). Boats depart from Gawein jetty a little further to the west of the IWT office.

From about September to March two private 'express' boats run to Bagan; of the two the more reliable service is *Malikha* (US$36, nine hours). Your hotel or travel agent can arrange tickets.

NAVIGATING MANDALAY

Mandalay city streets are laid out on a grid system and numbered from east to west (up to 49th) and from north to south (over 50th). A street address that reads 66th, 26/27 means the place is located on 66th St between 26th and 27th Sts. Corner addresses are given in the form 26th at 82nd St. Some of the longer east–west streets can also take names once they cross the Shweta Chaung (Shweta Canal) heading west.

The 'downtown' area runs roughly from 21st to 35th St between 80th and 88th Sts. Major east–west thoroughfares include 26th and 35th Sts, plus 19th St east of the moat.

Bus

Mandalay's **Kwe Se Kan bus station** (off Map p512), 7km south of town, farewells buses to destinations across the country. Schedules are flexible and expect fewer services to places like Bagan in low season. You can buy tickets at the station, but most travellers save the trip and get them through their guesthouse or city-centre agents.

Buses to Monywa (K2000, three hours) leave from **Thiri Mandalar bus station** (Map p512; 89th St, 21/22), while those to Hsipaw go from **Pyi Gyi Myat Shin bus station** (off Map p512; 60th St, 35/37), 3km east of the city centre.

For details of bus services from Mandalay, see the table below.

Taxi

The easiest way to Pyin Oo Lwin (Maymyo) is via share taxi (back/front seat K5000/6000, 1½ hours). They depart from a **taxi stand** (Map p516; 27th at 83rd St), but your guesthouse can usually arrange to have you picked up.

Duhtawadi (Map p516; ☎61938; 31st St, 81/82) arranges share taxis to Hsipaw (K15,000, five to six hours) departing from its city office most days around 8.30am. If there is no Hsipaw car, take one bound for Lashio, operated by **Shwe Li Oo** (Map p516; ☎33280; 32nd St, 81/80) for K15,000/17,000 (back/front seat) at 6.30am, 8am and 9am, and **Shwe Li Shan** (Map p516; 84th St, 22/23) for K18,000/21,000 (back/front seat) when full.

Train

Mandalay's gargantuan, butt-ugly **train station** (Map p516; 30th St, 78/79) is in the city centre. For train services from Mandalay, see the table, p520.

Getting Around

Try not to shop with a driver, as you'll end up paying over the odds thanks to commission deals drivers arrange with shop owners.

Bicycle & Motorcycle

Rent a bicycle for around K1500 per day from ET Hotel, a shop opposite the Royal Guest House and from **Mr Jerry** (Map p516; 83rd St, 25/26; ⏲8am-6.30pm), who also rents drive-your-own motorcycles at K10,000 per day.

Taxi

White taxis and 'blue taxis' – ancient Mazda 600cc pick-ups – and motorbike taxis whisk folks around Mandalay; prices are negotiable. Reckon around K2000 to the Gawein jetty from central Mandalay. Charter all day for about K15,000/20,000 in town/to the ancient cities (Amarapura, Inwa and Sagaing). Guesthouses can help you find a reliable taxi or motorcycle driver.

Trishaw

Traditionally the main form of city transport, the trishaws are steadily disappearing from the city centre; rumour has it that they might be phased out altogether by the time you read this. From the city centre to Thiri Mandalar bus station is K500, to the base of Mandalay Hill K1500. All-day hire is from around K8000. English-speaking drivers include eloquent **Ko Re** (koore6070@gmail.com), and Mr 'Take it Easy', who waits outside the Central Hotel (27th St, 80/81).

Around Mandalay

From Mandalay it's easy to day trip to four old cities nearby. Although it is possible to use **pick-ups** (Map p516; cnr 29th & 84th Sts) from Mandalay to visit the cities, it's a major hassle; its far easier and more convenient to rent a 'blue taxi' (K18,000 per day for four people). If you're fit and sun-proof, consider using a rental bike.

AMARAPURA

The 'City of Immortality', a short-lived capital 11km south of Mandalay, is famed for **U Bein's Bridge**, the world's longest teak bridge at 1.2km. At 200 years old, the bridge sees lots of life along its 1060 teak posts, with monks and fishers commuting to and fro. It leads to **Kyauktawgyi Paya** and small **Taungthaman** village, with tea and toddy shops. A popular sunset activity is renting a **boat** (about K2500) to drift along as the

BUSES FROM MANDALAY

DESTINATION	COST (K)	DURATION (HR)	FREQUENCY
Bagan	8500-9000 (local bus)	8	8am, 8.30am, 4.40pm, 9pm
Hsipaw	4000 (local bus)	7	5.30am, 3pm
Taunggyi (Inle Lake)	10,000-11,000 (air-con)	11	6pm, 6.30pm
Yangon	10,400-12,000 (air-con)	10	many from 5-8.30pm

TRAINS FROM MANDALAY

DESTINATION	COST ORDINARY/ UPPER/SLEEPER (US$)	DURATION (HR)	FREQUENCY
Hsipaw	4/7/-	10	4am
Monywa	3/-/-	5¼	6.15am
Myitkyina	10/27/30	22+	noon, 4.15pm
	14/31/36	10-20	4.30am
Naba (for Katha)	6/13/16	11¾	noon, 4.15pm
Nyaung U (Bagan)	4/10/-	8	9pm
Yangon	15/35/40	15¼	9.45pm
	11/30/33	16	5am, 5.30am, 6am

skies turn orange, or watching life go by from a waterside beer station.

Just west is the **Ganayon Kyaung**, where hundreds of monks breakfast at 10.30am. Resist the temptation to thrust a camera in their faces, as some travellers do.

It's possible to cycle here from Mandalay in about 45 minutes.

INWA (AVA)

Cut off by rivers and canals, Inwa (called Ava by the British) served as the Burmese capital for nearly four centuries. **Horse carts** (K5000 for one or two people) lead a three-hour loop around Inwa's beaten track; if you're lucky you may get them to stop at other crumbling sights sans vendors, or to allow you to rest your butt.

The finest sight is the atmospheric **Bagaya Kyaung**, an 1834 teak monastery supported by 267 posts. A US$10 Mandalay ticket will get in here and into the **Maha Aungmye Bonzan** (aka Ok Kyaung), which is a brick-and-stucco monastery dating from 1822. The 27m **Nanmyin** watchtower leans precariously.

GETTING INTO MANDALAY

Most visitors arrive at the dusty Main (Kwe Se Kan) bus station, 7km south of central Mandalay. A taxi to town is about K3000, or take a pick-up. The train station is downtown, south of Mandalay Palace; take a trishaw to most accommodation (around K200). Mandalay airport is a staggering 45km southwest of central Mandalay. Taxis are the only option; pay K10,000 to town if you use one of the counters on the arrivals floor, more if you opt for a freelance taxi.

SAGAING

Across the Ava Bridge from the Inwa junction and 18km from Mandalay, the stupa-studded hilltops of Sagaing loom over the Ayeyarwady. With 500 stupas and monasteries galore, Sagaing is where Burmese Buddhists come to relax and meditate. Sagaing is also known for **silver shops** and **guitars**.

Sagaing Hill (Sagaing/Mingun ticket US$3) is the big attraction. Trees hang over stone steps leading past monasteries to the top. **Tilawkaguru**, near the southwest base, is a mural-filled cave temple dating from 1672 (closed to the public). There are great views above, and pathways lead all the way to the water for the adventurer. The hill is 1km north of the market.

Sagaing is spread out. Take a motorbike taxi here from Mandalay, then rent a trishaw for the day.

MINGUN

Home to a trio of unique pagodas, **Mingun** (admission Sagaing/Mingun US$3 ticket) is a compact riverside village site that's a great half-day excursion from Mandalay. The journey is part of the attraction, whether puttering up the wide Ayeyarwady or rollercoasting from Sagaing along a rural lane through timeless hamlets of bamboo-weave homes.

The **Mingun Paya** is actually the remains of a planned 150m stupa, surely a candidate for the world's largest pile of bricks. It is still possible to climb up. Just to the north is the **Mingun Bell**, which holds the record for the world's largest uncracked bell. It's worth pressing on 200m north to the white, wavy-terraced **Hsinbyume Paya**.

There's a daily riverboat service from the western end of 26th St in Mandalay departing at 9am (K5000 return, one hour). These boats return from Mingun at 1pm. If there are fewer than five passengers or if you want different departure times, you can rent a whole small/larger boat for K25,000/40,000. Now that the road is mostly asphalt, it is increasingly popular to ride to Mingun by motorbike (around 25 minutes from Sagaing) as part of an ancient cities loop.

Pyin Oo Lwin (Maymyo)

☎085 / POP 80,000

Set in the foothills of northern Shan State, this colonial hill station was established by British Captain May as a retreat from the stifling heat of Mandalay, and was subsequently named for him (*myo* means town). Under the British it served as a summer capital and domestic tourists still flock here during the hottest months (March to May).

The main activity is cycling through history, passing faded English-style country mansions and cute pony-led miniature wagons, straight out of the Wells Fargo days of the American West (actually India, 1914, as one driver told us), that serve as local transport. You will no doubt also notice a lot of green uniforms around here as Pyin Oo Lwin is home to the Defence Services Academy.

Pyin Oo Lwin is very spread out. The Mandalay–Lashio Rd doubles as the main road. Bicycle is the best way to get around.

Sights

National Kandawgyi Gardens PARK

(☎22130; admission/camera US$5/1; ⏲8am-6pm) Modelled on the famous Kew Gardens of London, this 176-hectare little Eden is now owned by Tay Za, a crony of the government. It's a scenic cycle south of town, via a series of big, old and sometimes abandoned British-era mansions.

Anisakan Falls WATERFALL

About 1km north of Anisakan village (9km south of Pyin Oo Lwin), the plateau disappears into an impressively deep wooded amphitheatre, its sides ribboned with several waterfalls. Pick-ups run to Anisakan (around K500) from the main road in Pyin Oo Lwin. In Anisakan, take the second asphalted turn right (signposted) and keep right past the first large pagoda. At the end of this road a pair of basic shack-restaurants marks the start of a forest trail along which the falls' base is reached by a 45-minute trek. Sales kids act as guides (K1000) and can prove helpful, especially if taking the 'alternative' very steep route back.

Central Market MARKET

(Zeigyo Rd; ⏲7am-5pm) Sample Pyin Oo Lwin's famous (if seasonal) strawberries, damsons, plums, passion fruit and other fruit, fresh, dried or as jams and wine.

Purcell Tower CLOCK TOWER

Still chimes to the tune of Big Ben, while other colonial relics are all around, and particularly along Multi-Office, Forest and Circular Rds.

Sleeping & Eating

Many of Pin Oo Lwin's cheaper hotels aren't licensed to accommodate foreigners. Those listed here are all in or within walking distance of the town centre and include breakfast. Decent Shan, Burmese, Chinese and Indian food is available on or just off the main road; eat early or miss out.

Golden Dream Hotel HOTEL $

(☎21302; 42/43 Mandalay–Lashio Rd; s/d US$6/12, without bathroom US$5/10) For the price this is about the best you'll find – it's reasonably clean and the beds are not unbearably saggy. There are even windows in most rooms, unlike similarly priced Grace 2 Hotel next door.

Grace Hotel 1 GUESTHOUSE $

(☎21230; 114A Nan Myaing Rd; s/d/tr US$12/24/36) The major attraction here is the lovely garden. The rooms aren't sophisticated but they're large with high ceilings and are good value for single travellers. Bicycles/motorbikes are available for rent at K3000/8000 per day.

Golden Triangle Café BAKERY, CAFE $

(Mandalay–Lashio Rd; cakes, sandwiches & pizzas K500-2000; ⏲7am-10pm) This upbeat Western-flavoured cafe, occupying a column-fronted late-colonial building, serves a range of coffees (K500 to K1800), juices, cakes, sandwiches, pizzas and burgers.

Family Restaurant INDO-BURMESE, THAI $

(off Mandalay–Lashio Rd; meals K1500-5000; ⏲9.30am-9pm) Its delicious curry spread (K1500 to K2500) comes with complimentary rice, soup, pappadams and a 10-dish smorgasbord of salad vegies, side dishes, chutneys and dips.

Information

Pyin Online (www.pyinoolwin.info)

Skynet (4th St; per hr K500; ⌚9am-10pm) Unusually fast internet...sometimes.

TKY Internet (per hr K500; ⌚9am-8pm) Handy for Grace Hotel 1.

Getting There & Away

Yangon-bound buses (K11,500 to K15,000, 13½ to 16 hours) depart between 2pm and 5pm from the main bus station **Thiri Mandala** (☎22633), 3km east of the Shan market (K1500 by motorbike taxi). Pick-ups to Mandalay (back/front seat K2000/3000) also depart frequently from here from 5am, becoming rarer in the later afternoon.

From the main bus station, 600m back to the Lashio road and outside the Shi May clothing shop there's a bus stand for minibuses to Hsipaw (K4000, 7am and 4pm). At around 7.30am shared taxis to Hsipaw (back/front seat K14,000/16,000) also depart from here.

For Mandalay some pick-ups start from the petrol pump roundabout and a few start near the train station. At least three companies offer shared taxis (back/front seat K6000/6500). **Win Yadana** (☎22490) and **Soe Moe Aung** (☎21500) cars start across from 4th St. **Lwin Man** (☎21709) starts near the Central Market.

Trains to Mandalay are much slower and rarely run to schedule.

Getting Around

BICYCLE The unmarked **bike shop** (Mandalay–Lashio Rd; ⌚7am-6pm) beside Grace 2 Hotel rents bicycles for K3000/4000 per day/24 hours.

MOTORCYCLE TAXIS Easiest to find beside Hotel Bravo; around K2000 to Kandawgyi Gardens.

THREE-WHEEL PICK-UPS Congregate outside the market.

WAGON Reckon around K1500 for a short trip across town, K12,000 for an all-day tour in one of Pyin Oo Lwin's signature horse-drawn buggies.

Hsipaw

☎082 / POP 54,000

Travellers come to this laid-back highland town for a couple of days and before they know it a week has passed. Trekking is the main draw, but Hsipaw is not without charms, including a bustling riverside market, good food and, in season, lively guesthouses.

Guesthouses can arrange guides (around K10,000 per day) to take you on fascinating treks into the hills above town visiting Shan, Palaung and Lisu villages. Mr Charles Guest House is especially well organised.

Sights

Produce Market — MARKET

Most interesting before dawn when the road outside is jammed with hill-villagers selling their wares: all will have cleared away by 7am, though the market continues until 1pm.

Mahamyatmuni Paya — PAGODA

(Namtu Rd) South of the central area, this is Hsipaw's biggest and grandest pagoda.

Myauk Myo — NEIGHBOURHOOD

Towards the northern edge of town, Hsipaw's oldest section today has a village-like atmosphere and two delightful old teak monasteries. Around and behind lie a few clumps of ancient brick stupas (hence the nickname 'Little Bagan').

Sunset Hill — VIEWPOINT

For sweeping views across the river and town, climb to **Thein Daung Pagoda**, also known as Five Buddha Hill or, most popularly, Sunset Hill. Find it behind the Lashio road, around 2.5km south of Hsipaw.

Sleeping

TOP CHOICE **Mr Charles Guest House** — TRAVELLER HUB $

(☎80105; 105 Auba St; s/d from K10,000/15,000, without bathroom K4500/9000, rooms with air-con from K22,000; ❄) Has a wide range of rooms in a wooden house or concrete annexe. Staff can arrange transport, treks and tours, and change US dollars (at poor rates). Breakfast is included but served in the yard (bring a blanket!)

Golden Doll/Mr Kid — GUESTHOUSE $

(☎80066; 124 Bogyoke Rd; s/d US$6/10, without bathroom US$5/8) The obliging if laid-back family welcome makes this feel like an overgrown homestay. Conditions are basic.

Eating & Drinking

The market stalls offer Hsipaw's best cheap eats.

San — SHAN, CHINESE $

(Namtu Rd; meals K1000-2500, BBQ items from K100) Cosier than many alternatives, the barbecue is well stocked, large Dali beers cost only K800 and there's a bilingual picture menu of other options.

Best Place — TEASHOP $

(Aung Tha Paya St; shakes K500-800; ⌚7am-10pm) In this archetypal part-timbered teashop 'Mr Shake' speaks English while his wife whizzes up scrumptious lassis using grated coconut and Pyin Oo Lwin strawberries (seasonal).

Law Chun ('Mr Food') CHINESE $$
(Mr Food; Namtu Rd; mains K1000-4000) 'Mr Food' stands out very obviously from the pack due to its bright white if far from atmospheric interior. The Chinese food is reliable and there's draught Dagon beer on tap.

Information

A remarkable source of local information is Ko Zaw Tun (aka Mr Book), who runs a small **bookstall** (Namtu Rd; 7am-8.15pm) opposite the entrance to the Central Pagoda.

There are several internet cafes but connection breaks down frequently.

Getting There & Away

Bus services often involve unscheduled stops, known as breakdowns. Buses leave Hsipaw at 5.30am for Mandalay via Pyin Oo Lwin (K5000 to either).

Share taxis run to and from Mandalay (back/front seat K11,000/13,000, five hours), leaving about 7am. Pick-ups are also an option.

The train to Pyin Oo Lwin (ordinary/upper class US$3/6, six hours) and Mandalay (US$4/9, 11 hours) crosses the creaking, British-era Gokteik Gorge and is revered as one of Myanmar's top rail journeys. It's supposed to leave Hsipaw at 9.40am daily but is often late.

BAGAN (PAGAN) & AROUND

Bagan

061

The Bagan Archaeological Zone stretches 41 sq km across central Myanmar. Despite centuries of neglect, looting, erosion, regular earthquakes, including a massive one in 1975, not to mention dodgy restoration, this temple-studded plain remains a remarkably impressive and unforgettable vision.

In a 230-year building frenzy up until 1287 and the Mongol invasions, Bagan's kings commissioned over 4000 Buddhist temples. These brick-and-stucco religious structures are all that remain of their grand city, since the wooden 11th to 13th century buildings have long gone.

Many restoration projects have resulted in a compromised archaeological site that can barely be described as ruined. Still, Bagan remains a wonder. Working temples such as Ananda Pahto give a sense of what the place was like at its zenith, while others conceal colourful murals and hidden stairways that lead to exterior platforms and jaw-dropping views across the plain.

Sights

Plan your daily temple viewing around a dawn/dusk visit, building in a leisurely lunch/siesta/poolside lounging period from around 12.30pm to 4pm. Temperatures will be more pleasant and the light is better for photographs.

OLD BAGAN

This 2km circuit within the old city walls is manageable on foot or by bicycle.

North of the government-run **Archaeological Museum** (Map p524; Bagan-Chauk Rd; admission US$5; 9am-4.30pm), the 60m-high **Gawdawpalin Pahto** (Map p524) is one of Bagan's most imposing temples. About 200m south of here, a dirt road leads past **Mimalaung Kyaung** (Map p524; note the *chinthe*, a half-lion, half-guardian deity) and **Nathlaung Kyaung** (Map p524; the only remaining Hindu temple at Bagan) to the 63m-tall **Thatbyinnyu Pahto** (Map p524). Built

BAGAN ORIENTATION

Bounded by the Ayeyarwady on its northern and western flanks, Bagan is a vast plain dotted with settlements. Most independent travellers stay in Nyaung U, home to the bus station, and 5km northwest of the airport and train station. Old Bagan, about 4km southwest and atmospherically located amid the bulk of the temples, is an enclave of expensive hotels. Between here and New Bagan, about 4km further south, is the village of Myinkaba. Well-paved roads connect these centres, crisscrossed by dirt trails leading to the temples.

In Nyaung U, 'Main Rd' is used (locally and in text) to refer to the main strip, which runs along the north–south Bagan–Nyaung U Rd, and along the Anawrahta Rd from the market to the Sapada Paya. Just east of the bus station is Yarkinnthar Hotel Rd, more popularly known as 'restaurant row', with lots of eating options.

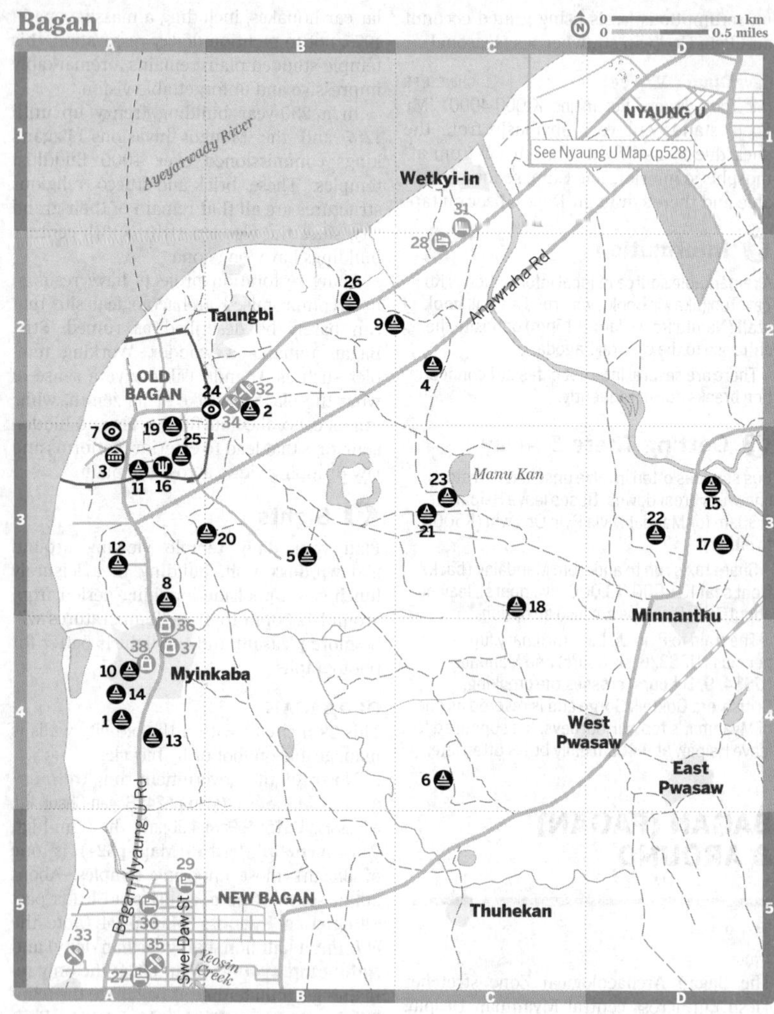

in 1144, it has a square base, surrounded by diminishing terraces, rimmed with spires.

Another 200m north of Thatbyinnyu is **Shwegugyi** (Map p524), a temple dating from 1131 with lotus *sikhara* (Indian-style temple finial) atop and stucco carvings inside. Back on the main Nyaung U–Old Bagan Rd continue to the 9th-century **Tharabar Gate** (Map p524), the former eastern entry to the walled city.

NORTH PLAIN

About half a kilometre east of Thatbyinnyu, the 520m-high **Ananda Pahto** (Map p524), with its golden *sikhara* top and gilded spires, is probably Bagan's top draw. Finished in 1105, the temple has giant teak Buddha images facing each of the four entranceways. On the full moon of the month of Pyatho (between mid-December and mid-January), a three-day *paya* festival attracts thousands of pilgrims.

Just northwest is **Ananda Ok Kyaung** (Map p524), with colourful murals detailing 18th-century life, some showing Portuguese traders. No photos allowed.

Midway between Old Bagan and Nyaung U, **Upali Thein** (Map p524) features large, brightly painted murals from the early 18th

Bagan

Sights

1	Abeyadana Pahto	A4
2	Ananda Ok Kyaung	B2
	Ananda Pahto	(see 2)
3	Archaeological Museum	A3
4	Buledi	C2
5	Dhammayangyi Pahto	B3
6	Dhammayazika Paya	C4
7	Gawdawpalin Pahto	A3
8	Gubyaukgyi	A3
9	Htilominlo Pahto	B2
	Kyat Kan Kyaung	(see 15)
10	Manuha Paya	A4
11	Mimalaung Kyaung	A3
12	Mingalazedi Paya	A3
13	Nagayon	A4
14	Nan Paya	A4
15	Nandamannya Pahto	D3
16	Nathlaung Kyaung	A3
17	Payathonzu	D3
18	Pyathada Paya	C3
19	Shwegugyi	A3
20	Shwesandaw Paya	B3
21	Sulamani Pahto	C3
22	Tayok Pye Paya	D3
23	Thabeik Hmauk	C3
24	Tharabar Gate	B2
25	Thatbyinnyu Pahto	A3
26	Upali Thein	B2

Sleeping

27	Bagan Central Hotel	A5
28	Golden Express Hotel	C2
29	Kumudara Hotel	A5
30	Thiri Marlar Hotel	A5
31	Winner Guest House	C1

Eating

32	Be Kind to Animals the Moon	B2
33	Green Elephant	A5
34	Sarahba III/Gyi Gyi's	B2
	Scoopy's	(see 32)
35	Silver House	A5

Shopping

36	Art Gallery of Bagan	A4
37	Family Lacquerware Work Shop	A4
38	Golden Cuckoo	A4

century. Across the road, the location for the terraced 46m-high **Htilominlo Pahto** (Map p524) was picked in 1218 by King Nantaungmya, using a 'leaning umbrella'. Just south of Anawrahta Rd, **Buledi** (Map p524) is a good sunrise/sunset viewing spot and useful for getting your bearings.

CENTRAL PLAIN

South of Anawrahta Rd the 11th-century, five-terraced **Shwesandaw Paya** (Map p524) is a graceful white pyramid-style pagoda with 360-degree views of Bagan's temples. It's packed for sunset, but pretty empty during the day. Note the original *hti* (decorated top of a *stupa*) lying to the south – it was toppled by the quake.

About 500m east, monumental **Dhammayangyi Pahto** (Map p524) has two encircling passageways, the inner one of which has been intentionally filled. It's said that King Narathu, who commissioned the temple, was so cruel that the workers ruined it after his assassination in 1170.

About 800m east, the broad two-storeyed **Sulamani Pahto** (Map p524; 1181) is one of the area's prettiest temples, with lush grounds and carved stucco. Just 150m east, **Thabeik Hmauk** (Map p524) looks like a mini Sulamani, but without the hawkers – *and* you can climb to the top. And at sunset, don't miss the broad viewing platform at **Pyathada Paya** (Map p524), about 1km southeast.

AROUND MYINKABA

Just north of Myinkaba, **Mingalazedi Paya** (Map p524; 1274) has three receding terraces lined with 561 glazed tiles and tasty views of the nearby river and temples.

On the north edge of town, **Gubyaukgyi** (Map p524; 1113) sees a lot of visitors thanks to its richly coloured interior paintings. In the village, the modern-looking **Manuha Paya** (Map p524; 1059) was named for the Mon king who was held captive here. Note the four giant Buddha images that are seemingly too large for the enclosure, symbolic of Manuha's discontent with his prison life. Stairs at the rear lead above the reclining Buddha.

Just south, **Nan Paya** (Map p524), from the same era, is a cave-style shrine; Nan Paya was possibly once Hindu, as suggested by the three-faced Brahma situated on the pillars.

About 500m south of Myinkaba, the 11th-century **Abeyadana Pahto** (Map p524) was likely to have been commissioned by King Kyanzittha's Bengali wife and features original frescoes. Across the road, **Nagayon**

TOP TEMPLES

» **Ananda Pahto** One of the best-preserved and most revered of all the Bagan temples.

» **Dhammayangyi Pahto** An absolute colossus, this red-brick temple is visible from all over Bagan.

» **Sulamani Pahto** This late-period beauty is known as Crowning Jewel, and with good reason.

» **Pyathada Paya** Super sunset (or sunrise) spot and typically less crowded.

» **Thatbyinnyu Pahto** Bagan's tallest temple, topped with a golden spire.

(Map p524) has some tight stairs leading up to the roof. Its corncob *sikhara* (finial) was possibly a prototype for Ananda.

SOUTH PLAIN

About 3km east of New Bagan, **Dhammayazika Paya** (Map p524; 1196) is unusual for its five-sided design. It's very well tended with lush grounds and lavish attention from worshippers. A dirt road leads a mile north to Dhammayangyi.

An excellent cluster of sites is about 3km east. North of the road, **Tayok Pye Paya** (Map p524) has good westward views of Bagan. To the south, 13th-century **Payathonzu**, a small complex of three interconnected shrines, draws visitors to its murals.

About 200m north, **Nandamannya Pahto** (Map p524), from the same period, features the 'temptation of Mura' murals – in the form of topless women reaping no response from a meditating Buddha. It's often locked; ask at Payathonzu for the 'key master'. Just behind, **Kyat Kan Kyaung** (Map p524) has been a cave-style monastery for nearly 1000 years.

AROUND NYAUNG U

In town, the gilded bell of **Shwezigon Paya** (Map p528; 1102) is considered by many to be the prototype for many Burmese pagodas. A yellow compound on the east side (called '37 Nats' in English) features figures of each of the animist spirits.

Sleeping

Bagan accommodation can be loosely categorised as: Nyaung U for budget travellers; New Bagan for good-value midrange rooms; and Old Bagan's mostly joint-venture hotels for bigger wallets. The last are not covered here, so sneak a look at someone's Lonely Planet *Myanmar* guide if you feel like indulging.

NYAUNG U

TOP CHOICE **New Park Hotel** HOTEL $
(Map p528; ☎60322, 60484, in Yangon 01-290073; www.newparkmyanmar.com; 4 Thiripyitsaya; s US$10-20, d US$14-30; ❄@) Best of the bunch on the leafy backstreets off Restaurant Row. Its older rooms, with bungalow-style front decks, are comfortable, with spic-and-span bathrooms. The newer wing gets you more space, a fridge and a TV.

Golden Express Hotel HOTEL $$
(Map p524; ☎02-60034, 02-60381; www.goldenexpresstours.com; Main Rd; s US$21-35, d US$25-44; ❄@≋) The best value of the four classes at this out-of-town complex, with its cartoon colours and pagodas next door, are the superior single/double rooms (US$29/34), with wooden floors, a bit more space and bathtubs. There's a nice pool and a big buffet breakfast served on the grounds.

Thante Hotel HOTEL $$
(Map p528; ☎60315, in Yangon 01-664 424; nyaungu thante@gmail.com; Anawrahta Rd; s/d US$30/40; ❄≋) For a pool right in Nyaung U, the Thante's comfy, somewhat worn bungalows are an option. Or just visit for a swim (US$3). There's also a good bakery cafe on site.

May Kha Lar Guest House GUESTHOUSE $
(Map p528; ☎60304, 60907; Main Rd; s US$8-14, d US$12-18; ❄) The best kept of the main-road budget choices, with lots of handy traveller info and a shrine room! On the ground floor the cheap, gaudy-tile rooms are compact, with air-con, fan and private bathroom. Nicer upstairs options have wooden floors and TV.

New Heaven GUESTHOUSE $
(Map p528; ☎60921; off Yarkinnthar Hotel Rd; s US$10-12, d US$15-18; ❄) Offers clean, compact rooms with small decks looking over the peaceful lawn. The bigger more pricey rooms include TV.

Eden Motel GUESTHOUSE $
(Map p528; ☎60815, 60812; Anawrahta Rd; s/d from US$8/15; ❄) Split in two by the busy road towards the airport, Eden isn't exactly a garden party. The rooms in the newer Eden Motel II have bigger, tiled rooms and an over-touted bathtub, but we prefer the

ones in the original – particularly those with all-bamboo walls and hardwood floors.

Inn Wa Guest House GUESTHOUSE $
(Map p528; ☎60902, 60849; Main Rd; s US$8-10, d US$13-15; ❄) If you just need a cheap bed, this place works. Rooms 206 or 306 have more window light (and less street noise). Advance booking gets you a free transfer from your point of arrival.

Winner Guest House GUESTHOUSE $
(Map p524; ☎61069; Main Rd, Wetkyi-in village; s US$5-7, d US$7-10; ❄) If money's tight, opt for this little family-run guesthouse on the road to Old Bagan. The cheapest rooms share the common bathroom.

NEW BAGAN

TOP CHOICE **Kumudara Hotel** HOTEL $$
(Map p524; ☎65142, in Yangon 01-295 472; www.kumudara-bagan.com; s/d superior US$18/22, junior ste US$26/30, ste US$40; P❄@≋) No hotel boasts better balcony views of the mighty sprawl of red-brick temples than Kumudura. Opt for the chic junior suites or the suites in a green geometrical building that fits well with the arid, desert-like setting.

Thiri Marlar Hotel HOTEL $$
(Map p524; ☎65050, 65229; thirimarlar@mptmail.net.mm; s/d US$23/25; ❄) Teak walkways lead to the 15 spotless rooms, which are compact but inviting, with shiny wooden floors, small rugs and views of bougainvillea draping over the wall outside.

Bagan Central Hotel HOTEL $
(Map p524; ☎65057, 65265; Main Rd; s/d from US$15/20; ❄) These good-value bamboo-style rooms with pebble-stone-style facades are compact and clean and set around a courtyard shaded by trees. For rooms with bathtubs add US$5 to the rates.

Eating & Drinking

NYAUNG U

Nyaung U's Yarkinnthar Hotel Rd (aka Restaurant Row) is touristy, but easily the hub(bub) of Bagan action. Many of the restaurants are copycats, with similar 'everything goes' menus (Chinese, Burmese, Thai, Indian, pizza, 'Western' options).

TOP CHOICE **Aroma 2** INDIAN $$
(Map p528; Yarkinnthar Hotel Rd; dishes K2000-7000; ⏲11am-10pm) 'No good – no pay' is the mantra of this justifiably confident operation serving delish vegie and meat curries on banana leaves (or plates) with an endless stream of hot chapattis and five dollops of condiments (including tamarind and mint sauces).

TOP CHOICE **Black Bamboo** EUROPEAN $$
(Map p528; ☎09-650 1444; off Yarkinnthar Hotel Rd; dishes K3500-6000; ⏲9am-9.30pm) Run by a French woman and her Burmese husband, this garden-set cafe and restaurant is a lovely place to relax over a decent steak and chips, a well-made espresso or delicious home-made ice cream. Service is friendly but leisurely.

San Kabar Restaurant & Pub ITALIAN $$
(Map p528; Main Rd; pizza K4000-6000, salads K1500-2700; ⏲7am-10pm) Famous as the birthplace of Bagan pizza, the San Kabar's streetside candlelit courtyard is all about its thin-crusted pizza and well-prepared salads.

Shwe Ya Su BAMAR, INTERNATIONAL $$
(Map p528; Yarkinnthar Hotel Rd; dishes K1500-3000; ⏲7am-10.30pm) Since this place started selling draught Myanmar Beer (look for the illuminated sign outside) it's become quite the local hang-out. It's a pleasant spot to revive with twinkling fairy lights hanging from the trees and tasty snacks, such as bits of barbecued pork.

OLD BAGAN

Save yourself the schlep back to Nyaung U by having lunch in Old Bagan.

TOP CHOICE **Be Kind to Animals The Moon** VEGETARIAN, BAMAR $$
(Map p524; off Bagan-Nyaung U Rd; dishes K1500-3000; ⏲7am-10pm; 🖉) Offers a friendly welcome and delicious food, including pumpkin and ginger soup, eggplant curry, and a lime and ginger tea recommended for stomach upsets.

Sarahba III/Gyi Gyi's VEGETARIAN, BAMAR $
(Map p524; off Bagan-Nyaung U Rd; dishes from K300; ⏲6am-6pm) Join the crowds under a shady tree squatting on low chairs at green-painted tables and tucking into some of Bagan's best tucker, all freshly prepared and supremely tasty. There's no sign – the name is what local's jokingly call the place.

Scoopys ICE CREAM $
(Map p524; off Bagan-Nyaung U Rd; dishes from K300; ⏲11am-6pm) This relaxed cafe and ice-cream parlour serves toasted sandwiches, home-made muffins and treats such as

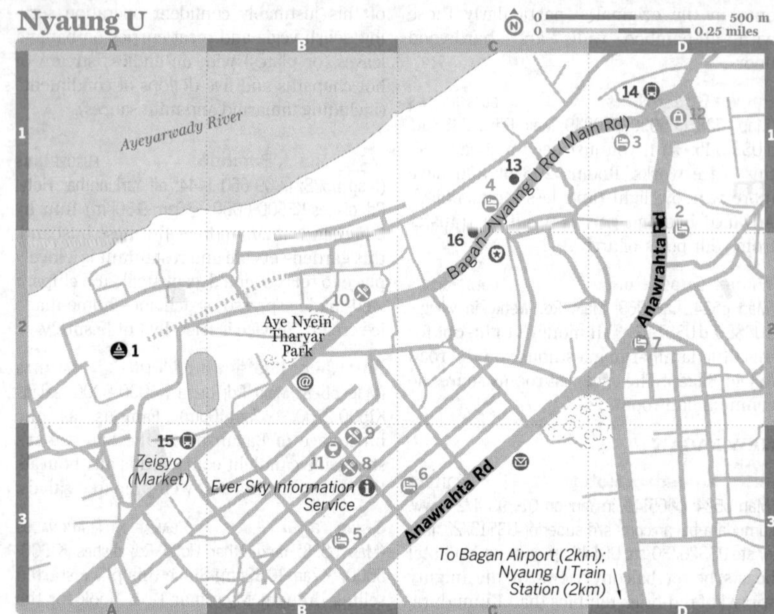

Nyaung U

Sights

1 Shwezigon Paya ... A2

Sleeping

2 Eden Motel ... D1
3 Inn Wa Guest House ... D1
4 May Kha Lar Guest House ... C1
5 New Heaven ... B3
6 New Park Hotel ... C3
7 Thante Hotel ... D2

Eating

8 Aroma 2 ... B3
9 Black Bamboo ... B3
10 San Kabar Restaurant & Pub ... B2

Drinking

11 Shwe Ya Su ... B3

Shopping

12 Mani-Sithu Market ... D1

Transport

13 Blue Sea (Train Ticket Office) ... C1
14 Buses to Old Bagan ... D1
15 Nyaung U Bus Station ... A3
16 Seven Diamond ... C2
Sun Far ... (see 16)

Western chocolate bars – all great for picnic snacks while touring the temples.

NEW BAGAN

Main Rd is lined with several inexpensive Chinese and Burmese restaurants.

Green Elephant BAMAR, ASIAN $$
(Map p524; Main Rd; mains K7000-9000; ⏲11am-4pm & 6-10pm) This appealing riverside operation serving a good-value, tasty set meal (K8000) can get busy with tour groups.

Silver House BAMAR, ASIAN $$
(Map p524; Main Rd; mains K5000; ⏲7am-10pm) Welcoming family-run restaurant that offers large, tasty portions of dishes such as traditional Myanmar chicken curry and tomato salad.

Shopping

Bagan is the lacquerware capital of Myanmar. Head to Myinkaba, where several family-run workshops produce high-quality traditional pieces – look for earthy colours. Reliable places include the following:

Art Gallery of Bagan LACQUERWARE
(Map p524) English-speaking Maung Aung Myin has two rooms and a busy workshop. They also sell puppets (US$20 to US$150).

Family Lacquerware Work Shop LACQUERWARE
(Map p524) Smaller workshop with a few more modern styles with fewer layers of lacquer and nontraditional colours such as blue and yellow.

Golden Cuckoo LACQUERWARE
(Map p524) This family-run workshop spans four generations and focuses on 'traditional' designs.

Mani-Sithu Market MARKET
(Map p528; Main Rd, Nyaung U; ⏲6am-5pm Mon-Sat) This busy market is best visited early in the day to see it at its liveliest. Traveller-oriented doodahs (woodcarvings, T-shirts, antique pieces) are found at its northern end.

Information

All foreign visitors to the Bagan Archaeological Zone are required to pay a US$10 entrance fee, which goes to the government.

Nyaung U is home to most traveller life-support systems, including a post office, several internet cafes and pricey international calls.

Ever Sky Information Service (Map p528; ☎60895; Yarkinnthar Hotel Rd; ⏲7.30am-9.30pm) Very friendly place with travel and transport information and a used bookshop.

Internet (Map p528; Thanakar Complex, Yarkinnthar Hotel Rd; K600 per hr; ⏲9am-9pm)

Getting There & Away

Most travel services operate from Nyaung U. Ask at Ever Sky Information Service or your guest-house about air tickets or hiring a share taxi. A charter to Inle Lake is about US$170, Mandalay US$80.

Air

Airlines connect Bagan daily with Mandalay (US$38 to US$40, half-hour), Heho (US$60 to US$62, 40 minutes) and Yangon (US$82 to US$85, one hour 10 minutes). **Seven Diamond** (Map p528; ☎60883; Main Rd) and **Sun Far** (Map p528 ☎60901; Golden Myanmar Guest House, Main Rd) can arrange tickets.

Boat

Boats to Mandalay go from either Nyaung U or Old Bagan, depending on water levels. The Nyaung U jetty is about 800m northeast of the market.

The government-run IWT ferry (aka 'slow boat') heads to Mandalay on Monday and Thursday at 5am (US$10, two days) and over-nights near Pakokku. The southbound service leaves weekly to Magwe (US$5, two days) and Pyay (US$9, three days). If open (unlikely!) the IWT office, about 250m inland from the jetty, sells tickets. Alternatively book a ticket through your hotel or one of the travel agencies listed earlier who can also secure tickets for the faster *Malikha 2* (US$32, 11 hours) boat to Mandalay.

From the Nyaung U jetty, small local boats leave for Pakokku (K4000, 2½ hours) a few times daily (6am, 9am and noon), the last re-turning to Nyaung U at 2pm. Chartering a boat to Pakokku costs about K10,000 one way.

Bus

Local buses to Mandalay (K6500, eight hours) leave at 4am, 7am, 8.30am, 9am and 7pm from Nyaung U bus station (Map p528). Here you can catch a 3pm air-con bus to Yangon (K15,000, 11 hours) via Pyay (nine hours), or a 4am bus (or minibus) to Taunggyi (K10,500, about 10 hours) via Kalaw (nine hours). Book tickets well in ad-vance in peak season.

Train

The Bagan train station is about 3km southeast of Nyaung U. The shop **Blue Sea** (Map p528; Main Rd) sells tickets with a US$2 commission. For train services from Bagan, see the table, p530.

Getting Around

BICYCLES The going rate is K1500 to K2000 per day in Nyaung U, double that in New Bagan. Carry water, though, as some temples don't have vendors.

HORSE CART Good way to get to grips with Bagan on day one. It's K10,000 for the whole day, but there is only really sufficient space for two people. Arrange one with a foam cushion, as they can get pretty uncomfortable after a few hours.

PICK-UPS Between Nyaung U, Old Bagan and New Bagan, pick-ups run along the main street, starting from the roundabout outside the Nyaung U market. A ride costs K200.

TAXI Costs about $25 for the day. A taxi from the airport costs K5000/6000/7000 to Nyaung U/Old Bagan/New Bagan.

Pakokku

☎062

An alternative route between Bagan and Monywa goes by this slow-paced, authentic town on the west bank of the Ayeyarwady. Stay at the ultra-basic but super-friendly **Mya Yatanar Inn** (☎21457; 75 Lanmataw St; r per person K5000-6000), where English-speaking grandma Mya Mya, her daughter and four granddaughters, will welcome you to their 100-year-old home on the river. They can rustle up a delicious meal for under

TRAINS FROM BAGAN

DESTINATION	COST ORDINARY/ UPPER/SLEEPER (US$)	DURATION (HR)	FREQUENCY
Mandalay	5/10/-	8	7am
Yangon	30/40/50	16	4.30pm

K1000 and help you get a taxi deal to see the sights.

Minibuses to Monywa (K1300, three hours) leave at 6am, 9am, 11am and 2pm from the corner of Tinda and Aung Taw Mu Sts. From the main bus station on Myoma Rd there are three services daily to Mandalay (K3000, seven hours). Ferries to Nyaung U (K3400, two hours) leave at 5am, 10am and 1.30pm.

Monywa

☎071 / POP 180,000

This engaging if slightly scrappy trade town is a sensible stopping point if you're looping between Mandalay and Bagan via Pakokku. About 20km south, **Thanboddhay Paya** (admission $3; ⊙6am-5pm) bursts with carnival shades of pink, orange, yellow and blue. Inside are more than half a million Buddhas filling nooks and crannies.

About 4km east of the *paya* is **Bodhi Tataung**, a Buddha frenzy in the foothills, including, at 130m, the world's second-tallest **standing Buddha**. The easiest way to visit is by taxi.

Across the Chindwin River and 24km west, the 492 **Hpo Win Daung Caves** (admission US$2) were carved into a limestone hillside between the 14th and 18th centuries. None of the 'caves' are more than a few metres deep, and many are just big enough for a single buddha image but a few of the best (notably caves 478 and 480) have retained some colourfully well-executed murals. To get here, rent a chauffeured motorbike in Monywa for the day (around K8000) and catch a boat from the Monywa jetty (each way K2500 for up to five people, plus K700 per motorbike).

In central Monywa, the facade of the **Shwe Taung Tarn** (☎21478; 70 Station Rd; r per person $8-12; ❄) looks unkempt, and the front building's US$8 rooms unappealing, but behind is an unexpectedly pleasant little garden and a pair of newer two-storey buildings with nicer rooms. There's also a restaurant, with a chic roof-top dining area, that cooks fine Chinese food.

Getting There & Away

The bus station is 2km southeast of the clock tower down Bogyoke St, hidden behind the Great Hotel.

MANDALAY Several companies operate hourly buses from 5am to 4pm (K1700, 3¼ to four hours).

PAKOKKU AGB buses (K1300, 4½ hours) leave at 6.30am, 8.30am, 12.30pm and 3pm. Other companies leave at 8am, 10.30am and 1.15pm. Take a morning bus if you want to connect with a same-day ferry to Nyaung U from Pakokku.

UPPER AYEYARWADY

Drifting down the Ayeyarwady, past friendly villagers for whom the river and its traffic are a lifeline to the outside world, is a memorable experience. Most travellers fly north or take the train to Myitkyina or Bhamo before enjoying life in the slow lane on the return journey. Which, in this case, is as much the destination as towns along the way.

Most of the area away from the river is closed to foreigners.

Myitkyina

☎074 / POP 40,000

The capital of Kachin State, Myitkyina lacks much in the way of real sights but it's an engaging multicultural place, home to Kachin, Lisu, Chinese and Burmese, as well as a popular embarkation point for a river trip south. Internet is available.

The town's best sight is its colourful riverside **produce market** (⊙5am-5pm). It's also worth timing your trip to coincide with the **Manao Festival** (Kachin State Day; 10 Jan) and celebrations for the **Lisu New Year** (before Feb full moon).

Snowland Tours (☎23499; snowland@mptmail.net.mm; Wai Maw St), southwest of the market, may be able to help with trekking tours to Kachin villages. The YMCA has maps of town and can help arrange motorbikes (K10,000 to K15,000) for the scenic 90-minute ride north to **Myit-son**, where the Ayeyarwady begins at the confluence of the Malikha and Maykha Rivers.

Sleeping & Eating

YMCA GUESTHOUSE $
(☎23010; mka-ymca@myanmar.com.mm; YMCA St; s/d/ste US$12/16/20, s/d without bathroom US$8/13; ❄@) The 'Y' is an ageing, basic place whose main attractions are low prices and the very helpful English-speaking staff who are a font of information.

TOP CHOICE **Kiss Me** BURMESE $
(Zaw John Rd; snacks K500-1500; ⏱6am-9pm) This simple stilted riverside pavilion with low wooden stalls, quite unexpectedly, turns out some of Myanmar's very best snack food.

Getting There & Away

Air

Your best bet is Air Bagan, which has services to Mandalay (US$95) and Yangon (US$125), both on Monday, Tuesday, Thursday, Friday and Sunday.

Boat

A daily express boat departs for Bhamo via Sinbo around 8.30am (foreigner K8000, five hours) from Talawgyi pier, a 20-minute, three-wheeler ride (K5000) from town. In Sinbo you'll usually need to stay the night in the ultra-simple guesthouse before continuing next morning to Bhamo.

Bus

The only bus route open to foreigners is Myitkyina–Bhamo (K12,000, six hours) leaving Myitkyina at 7.30am from just north of the centre of Tha Khin Net Phay Rd. Before getting aboard it's essential to prepare five photocopies of the visa and ID pages from your passport to hand out at the various checkpoints en route. Attractive scenery.

Train

There are three daily trains to Mandalay (ordinary/upper class/sleeper US$10/27/30, 16 to 40 hours). Bring a blanket for the cold nights and motion sickness pills for the incredible bouncing over warped rails.

Bhamo

☎074 / POP 25,000

More of a charmer than Myitkyina, the riverside town of Bhamo has a bustling daily market, drawing Lisu, Kachin and Shan folk from surrounding villages. Worth searching out is the awesome seasonal **bamboo bridge** (return toll K300 with bicycle), near the **Shwe Kyina Pagoda**, 5km north of Bhamo, that allows you to make your precarious way across the wide Tapin River.

Interesting **Kachin villages** can be explored if you hire a guide; try helicopter improviser (he'll tell you) **Sein Win** (☎0086-692 927 8557; per day K15,000 without transport). Ask for him at the **Friendship Hotel** (☎50095; Letwet Thondaya Rd; s/d/tr without bathroom US$7/14/21, s/d with air-con US$20/25; ❄@), one of the better provincial pads, with good-value rooms, luxury and otherwise, useful transport information and a handy map.

MT OLYMPUS OF MYANMAR

If you're in the Bagan area for more than a couple of days, consider a trip to Mt Popa, the spiritual HQ to Myanmar's infamous '37 *nat*' and thus a premier venue for worship of these pre-Buddhist spirits.

Mt Popa proper is the 1517m extinct volcano covered in lush forests protected within the Popa Mountain Park; on the mountain's lower flank is Popa Taung Kalat, a tower-like 737m volcanic plug crowned with a gilded Buddhist temple accessed by 777 steps. The 20-minute climb up goes past devout pilgrims, cheeky monkeys and, occasionally, slow-stepping hermit monks called *yeti*. The **Mahagiri shrine**, at the foot of Popa Taung Kalat, features a display of the 37 *nat*.

A pick-up (K3000 each way) leaves Nyaung U bus station at 8.30am, often with a change in Kyaukpadaung. Far easier is a slot in a share taxi (US$35 split between four passengers). Ask the driver to point out remnants of the petrified forest along the way and to pause at toddy palm plantations where you can sample the home-made alcohol and jaggery (palm sugar).

Getting There & Away

Boat

IWT FERRIES

Southbound dry-season departures (approximately 7am on Monday, Wednesday and Friday) for Katha (US$4, 10 to 12 hours) and Mandalay (deck/cabin class US$9/54, 30 to 50 hours) are from a jetty 4km south of central Bhamo.

FAST BOATS

Fast boats for Katha (K15,000, around eight hours) via Shwegu (K7500, 2½ hours) depart at 8.30am from the northern end of the central waterfront.

For Myitkyina (two days) start with the 9.30am boat to Sinbo (see p531; K7000, six hours) that departs from the middle of the central waterfront.

In the rainy season most boats are faster and there may be a direct seasonal fast boat to Mandalay departing at dawn.

Bus & Pick-up

For Myitkyina a bus leaves at 7am (K12,000, six hours) from Bawdi St, around 400m south of Friendship Hotel. Book one evening ahead (hotels can help) and prepare five photocopies of the visa and ID pages from your passport for checkpoints.

Katha

074 / POP 12,000

Fans of George Orwell's *Burmese Days* will enjoy foraging around this sleepy town on the Ayeyarwady. Eric Blair (Orwell's real name) was stationed here in 1926–27 and based his novel on this setting. Several Orwell-related buildings that featured in the book are still standing but none are marked as such and none are commercialised tourist attractions, so ask politely before trying to barge in.

The better of Katha's two basic accommodation options **Ayeyarwady Guest House** (25140; Strand Rd; r per person K5000-7000) has rooms overlooking the river near the ferry landing.

Getting There & Away

Take a bus from Katha to the rail junction 26km west at Naba (K1000, one hour), where trains between Mandalay and Myitkyina stop.

The IWT ferry leaves for Mandalay (deck/cabin class US$7/42, around 40 hours in the dry season) departs around 5pm Monday, Wednesday and Friday, and for Bhamo (US$4) Monday, Thursday and Saturday; timings unpredictable. The fast boat to Mandalay (K36,000, 13½ hours) departs every second day at 5am and to Bhamo (K15,000, eight hours) daily at 8am. Timings can vary significantly.

WESTERN MYANMAR

Western Myanmar, home to the proud Rakhaing people, is a land unto itself. Isolated from the rest of the country by the Arakan Mountains, this enigmatic region is in many ways closer to Bangladesh than Myanmar. For foreign travellers Sittwe is only accessible by air or water and 'baby Bagan', the atmospheric temple city of Mrauk U, is reached by a further boat ride inland. If you're here, you're really travelling.

The Rakhaing people are dubbed 'Burmese' by the government but are passionate about their distinct language and culture. The Mahumuni Buddha remains a sensitive subject and locals love telling the story of how it was stolen by the Burmese and moved to Mandalay in 1784.

Sittwe (Aykab)

43 / POP 200,000

For most people, a trip to Mrauk U will include a stay in Sittwe, a port town where the wide Kaladan River meets the Bay of Bengal. The British moved the regional capital here from Mrauk U in the 1820s and there's no denying Sittwe has seen better days. Still, it retains a lively yet laid-back atmosphere and has sufficient sights to fill a day while you wait for a boat.

Sights

Most of Sittwe's action runs along the almost north–south Main Rd, which parallels the Kaladan River.

Central Market MARKET

Focused around the 1956 municipal market building, there's lots going on here from dawn up to noon and beyond. Head straight past *longyi* (wraparound garment worn by women and men), fishing net and vegetable stands to the fish and meat area, where stingrays and gutted eels and drying sharks make quite a scene. In the bay, small boats jostle for space to unload their catch.

View Point VIEWPOINT, BEACH

The riverside Strand Rd leads about 2km south to this great spot where you can eat or sip on a beer or fresh coconut juice as the

GETTING TO CHINA: MU-SE TO RUILI

Entering or leaving Myanmar from this border with China needs to be done on a package in both directions. Coming from Kunming you should book a multiday 'visa-and-package trip' – you can't go on your own – to cross the border at Mu-Se and on to Lashio. It's about Y1400 (US$200). Ruili is about 20 hours from Kunming by road, and Lashio is a five-hour trip from the border, but you can stay in Mu-Se if necessary.

Heading in the other direction, MTT in Yangon and Mandalay quoted us deals from Lashio to the border, including a permit, guide, car and driver for 1/2/3 passengers at US$170/220/255. Once across the border, onward connections to Kunming or Dali are straightforward.

sun sets over the Bay of Bengal. The nearby broad grey-brown-sand **beach** has a tricky undertow, where a few swimmers lose their lives each year.

Lokananda Paya TEMPLE
You can't miss this big golden pagoda between the airport and the town centre. Its gilded, cavernous worship hall held aloft by decorated pillars is pretty spectacular. Rakhaing State Day (a Saturday in mid-December) is staged here.

Rakhaing State Cultural Museum MUSEUM
(Main Rd; admission US$2; ⌚10am-4pm Tue-Sat) This government-run museum features two floors of Rakhaing cultural goodies that benefit from just enough English subtitles.

Jama Mosque MOSQUE
(Main Rd) Next to the museum, this impressive 1859 building could have been ripped from the pages of *Arabian Nights*.

Sleeping & Eating

TOP CHOICE **Mya Guest House** GUESTHOUSE $$
(☎22358, 23315; 51/6 Bowdhi Rd; s/d US$20/30) A bit off Main Rd, this guesthouse and excellent teahouse with a garden has a new brick building offering simple, spacious tiled rooms, fan and private bath (no hot water).

Prince Guest House GUESTHOUSE $
(☎22539, in Yangon 09-503 4780; www.mraukuprincehotel.com; 27 Main Rd; s/d US$6/12) English-speaking staff and a bit of travellers' advice make up for the rather dingy rooms (small, with fan and mosquito net and coil) and shared bathrooms you'll want to wear sandals in.

TOP CHOICE **Mondi stand** RAKHAING $
(soup K200; ⌚6am-6pm) *Mondi* is the Rakhaing-style fish noodle soup downed by locals for breakfast. Sittwe's best – many claim – is served at the tiny stand facing the city hall.

Utingdameer INDIAN $
(Main Rd; meals K1000; ⌚10am-3pm) At the back of the compound in which the Jama Mosque sits is this family-run canteen dishing up a bargain lunch of several tasty curries and vegetable dishes with rice.

Moe Plearl TEAHOUSE, BAKERY $
(80 Main Rd; cakes K100-200; ⌚6am-7pm) Smart little bakery and cafe that's a good spot to stock up on biscuits, cakes and savouries for journeys, or to rest and enjoy a tea (K200) or coffee (K100).

Information

A pudgy tout, at the time of research going by the name Mr Learn, *will* meet you however you arrive and try to get commissions on whatever you do (eg boats to Mrauk U, hotels in Sittwe); his rates for boat transfers are not above the norm. He's harmless, but persitent enough to annoy some travellers.

KISS (Main Rd; K500 per hr; ⌚noon-9pm) Has webcams and plenty of terminals, though connections can be slooow.

Getting There & Away

Overland routes between Sittwe, Yangon and Mrauk U are closed to foreigners. The airport is about 2.5km southwest of the town centre; the main boat jetty is about 3km north.

Note that schedules change from season to season and from year to year, so double-check everything well in advance.

Air

In peak season **Air Mandalay** (☎21638) and **Air Bagan** (☎23113) fly daily to Yangon (US$108, one hour 25 minutes). Schedules are erratic. Before leaving Sittwe, you must reconfirm your booking – your guesthouse will help.

SITTWE BY LAND & SEA

Adventurous travellers can access Sittwe without flying by using the following route. From Pyay catch the 5pm minibus for Taunggok (K10,000, 11 hours). In Taunggok, the very basic **Royal Guest House** (043-61088; r K6000), near the bus station, takes foreigners. The **Mallkha Express** (043-60127) boat to Sittwe leaves at 7am on Monday, Wednesday and Saturday (US$40, nine hours), stopping at the island of Kyaukpyu for 30 or 40 minutes for lunch.

Boat

For details of boats to and from Mrauk U, see p535. If you arrive in Sittwe in the afternoon, don't expect to be able to leave on such boats until early the next day.

Mrauk U (Myohaung)

043 / POP 50,000

'Little Bagan?' Not by a long shot. Mrauk U (mraw-oo) was the Rakhaing capital from 1430 to 1826, during which time hundreds of temples were built. Unlike in Bagan, goat shepherds and vegetable farmers live around the ruins and still functioning temples sited amid gorgeous lush scenery of rounded hillocks. Think laid-back smiles, no hassle, almost no motorised transport and very few tourists. Internet is available at the Mrauk U Princess hotel.

Sights

The original site of Mrauk U is spread over 28 sq km, though the town today and bulk of the 700 or so temples to visit cover a 7-sq-km area. With a bike, a packed lunch and the heart for exploration, you could take any path for DIY adventures.

For foreign visitors there's an archaeological site 'entry fee' of US$5 usually collected at the Shittaung Paya or at the boat jetty; on the government ferry you'll be asked to show proof of payment before leaving. However, many people arriving and leaving by private boats manage to avoid paying the fee with little consequence. The palace site museum also charges US$5 for entry.

Shittaung Paya TEMPLE
(archaeological sites admission US$5) The usual starting point is at Mrauk U's most complex temple. Built in 1535, the pagoda has a maze-like floor plan. An outer passage, accessible via two doors from the entry hall to the east side, passes 1000 sculptures; the inner chamber coils to a dead end via a 'Buddha footprint'. Keep an eye out for the (fenced-off) relief of a frisky couple with their, erm, hands full.

Just north is the sublime 16th century **Andaw Paya**, and beyond is the **Ratanabon Paya**, a stupa dating from 1612 that survived a WWII bomb.

Dukkanthein Paya TEMPLE
Dating from 1571, this bunker-like pagoda's interior features spiralling cloisters lined with images of buddhas and common people (eg landlords, governors, officials and their spouses) sporting 64 different traditional hairstyles. The passageway nearly encircles the centre three times before reaching the sun-drenched Buddha image lit by Christmas-style lights.

Mahabodhi Shwegu TEMPLE
This squat hilltop temple (built in 1448) is decorated with 280 Jataka scenes, depicting Buddhist visions of heaven, earth and hell, including acrobats, worshippers, and animal love scenes (!) engraved onto either side of the arched entry walls.

Kothaung Paya TEMPLE
About 2km east of the remains of the palace walls, the massive 'Shrine of the 90,000 Images' was named by King Minbun's son to beat daddy's 80,000 Buddha images at Shittaung. The outer passageway is lined with thousands of bas reliefs on the walls and Buddha images (some headless). Stairways lead up to a top terrace, once dotted with 108 stupas.

Sleeping & Eating

TOP CHOICE **Golden Star Guest House** GUESTHOUSE $
(24200, ext 50175, 09-850 1664; 116 Min Bar Gree Rd; r per person US$5-15) Mrauk U's best cheap deal, with little Rakhaing-style figurines and cold-water bathrooms in most of the 13 basic rooms. Two 'traditional house' rooms at the back (US$15) look out into a palm forest.

Prince Hotel GUESTHOUSE $
(24200, ext 50174, Yangon 09-501 9114; www.mraukuprince.com; r US$15 & 25) About 1km southeast of the market, this leafy complex

Mrauk U

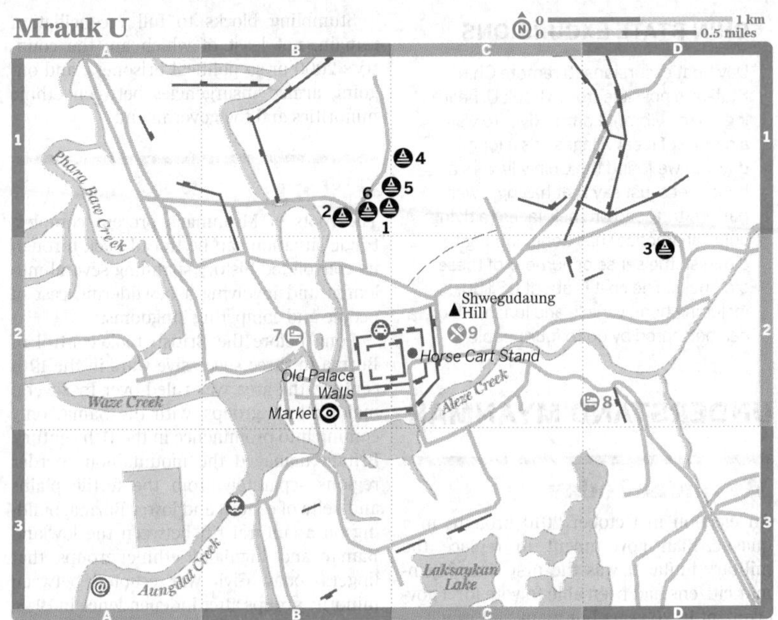

of nine bungalows sits below a hill in a leafy garden. The family who run it are extremely hospitable, the wife being an excellent cook. They can also arrange good trips to nearby Chin villages.

Moe Cherry BAMAR, RAKHAING $$
(☎24200, ext 50177; dishes K1000-2000, beer K1500) This travellers' favourite has a range of Rakhaing-style curries, a couple of vegie options, an airy balcony setting and a larger-than-life woman owner. It can also arrange car and boat rental.

Getting There & Around

The only way to/from Mrauk U for foreigners is by boat. You will have offers for a private boat (from US$120, five to six hours) – a simple tarp-covered boat with flat deck, a few plastic chairs and a very basic toilet – before you can get out of Sittwe airport. Generally a boat can fit four to six people. The driver will wait for you for two or three nights but ask ahead about the cost if you decide to stay another day in Mrauk U.

The IWT double-decker ferry (US$4, six to seven hours) departs Sittwe on Tuesday and Friday, and returns from Mrauk U on Wednesday and Saturday usually around 7am. Deck chairs are available (K500) and there's a stall serving basic food. We're told there's also a similar private ferry service (US$10) leaving Sittwe on Monday and returning on Tuesday.

The fastest boat is the **Shwe Pyi Tan** (☎09-862 8145) leaving Sittwe at 3pm on Monday and Wednesday and Mrauk U at 7am on Tuesday and Thursday (US$15, two hours).

A horse cart around the temples is around K10,000 per day. Bicycle rental is K2000 to K3000 per day. The taxi stand (for jeeps, from K20,000 a day) is on the north side of the palace.

Mrauk U

Sights

1 Andaw Paya ... B1
2 Dukkanthein Paya ... B1
3 Kothaung Paya ... D2
4 Mahabodhi Shwegu ... C1
5 Ratanabon Paya ... C1
6 Shittaung Paya ... B1

Sleeping

7 Golden Star Guest House ... B2
8 Prince Hotel ... D2

Eating

9 Moe Cherry ... C2

CHIN STATE EXCURSIONS

Day boat excursions to remote Chin State are possible from Mrauk U, heading up the vibrant Lamro River to visit a couple of local villages. It's a long day, but we found the Chin villagers a hoot – let's just say that having a web pattern tattooed on their faces (a dying cultural practice) has done nothing to diminish the sense of humour of these old ducks. The cost is about US$80, including boat, vehicle and lunch, which can be shared by up to four people.

UNDERSTAND MYANMAR

Myanmar Today

An election in October 2010 brought in a quasi-civilian government to replace the military junta. It was the first time Myanmar citizens had been able to vote for a government in 20 years but many just saw it as new wine in old bottles; the UN called the election 'deeply flawed'. Former general and old prime minister Thein Sein was 'chosen' by the elected reps to take over from Senior General Than Shwe, Myanmar's supreme ruler for the past two decades.

Since then, however, there have been several promising developments. Aung San Suu Kyi, leader of the National League for Democracy (NLD), was released in November 2010: she had spent 15 out of the 21 years since 1989 shut away from the public as a prisoner of conscience.

She has been permitted to leave Yangon to meet supporters, and many international journalists and politicians have been allowed to meet with her, including US Secretary of State Hillary Clinton.

In August 2011 Aung San Suu Kyi had talks with Thein Sein in the capital Nay Pyi Taw. The government lifted restrictions on previously banned media, including allowing access to websites critical of the government, and has appealed to dissidents to return to Myanmar and help rebuild the country.

In November 2011 Aung San Suu Kyi announced she intends to stand in upcoming by-elections for the parliament and in December 2011 the NLD officially registered as a political party (it had been declared illegal after it boycotted the 2010 elections).

Stumbling blocks to full reconciliation remain, not least of which are the country's 2000 or so political prisoners, and ongoing armed insurgencies between ethnic minorities and the government.

History

The roots of Myanmar's present complex, tragic situation can be traced back through its convoluted history spanning several millennia and involving a bewildering cast of people and competing kingdoms.

Long before the British took control of Burma in three successive wars in the 19th century, the area was ruled over by several major ethnic groups, with the Bamar only coming into prominence in the 11th century. Britain managed the mountainous border regions separately from the fertile plains and delta of central and lower Burma, building on a cultural rift between the lowland Bamar and highland ethnic groups that lingers today. Civil war erupted between minority groups after independence in 1948, and in pockets of the country continues still.

General Ne Win wrested control from the elected government in 1962 and began the world's longest-running military dictatorship, which pursued xenophobic policies leading Burma to full isolation. State socialism ruined the economy, necessitating several major currency devaluations, the last of which sparked massive, yet peaceful, street protests in 1988.

The prodemocracy marches saw Aung San Suu Kyi, daughter of independence hero General Aung San, emerge as the leader of the NLD. The military used violence to stop the marches, then, to everyone's surprise, called a national election. It thought it couldn't lose. However, at the 1990 election, the NLD won 82% of the assembly seats. The military simply refused to transfer power and threw many elected politicians into jail.

In the years since, trade with its neighbours (particularly Thailand and China) and Myanmar's membership of Asean have enabled the government to withstand increased international scorn and Western sanctions. The military's brutal reaction to the 2007 protests (the failed 'Saffron Revolution') and its breathtaking inaction following Cyclone Nargis in 2008, the worst natural disaster ever to befall the nation, caused it to become even more despised and feared.

BURMA OR MYANMAR?

What to call the Republic of the Union of Myanmar (the country's official name as of 2011) has, since 1989, been a political flashpoint. That was the year in which the military junta dumped Burma, the name commonly used since the mid-19th century, into the rubbish bin, along with a slew of other British colonial-era place names such as Rangoon, Pagan, Bassein and Arakan.

The UN recognises Myanmar as the nation's official name; Myanmar is more inclusive than Burma for a population that isn't by any means 100% Burman. However, nearly all opposition groups (including the NLD), many ethnic groups and several key nations including the USA and UK continue to refer to it as Burma.

In this book, we go with Myanmar, with Burma used for periods before 1989. 'Burmese' refers to the Bamar people, the food and the language.

The Culture

Although isolated, subjugated and poor, the Myanmar people are as proud of their country and culture as any nationality on earth. Locals gush over ancient kings, *pwe* (festivals), *mohinga* (noodles with chicken or fish) breakfasts, great temples and their religion. A typical Burmese Buddhist values meditation, gives alms freely and sees his or her lot as the consequence of sin or merit in a past life. The social ideal for most Burmese is a standard of behaviour commonly termed *bamahsan chin* (Burmese-ness). The hallmarks of *bamahsan chin* include showing respect for elders, acquaintance with Buddhist scriptures and discretion in behaviour towards the opposite sex. Most importantly, *bamahsan chin* values the quiet, subtle and indirect over the loud, obvious and direct.

Lifestyle

Outside the cities, families are generally big and several generations may share one roof. Electricity remains in short supply and even running water is uncommon in the countryside, where farming is the backbone of life. Visitors find it easy to engage with city folk, particularly the older generation, who often speak English well.

Beneath the smiles, life is one long struggle for survival for many in Myanmar, thanks in no small part to a government that rules in the interests of a small military elite and their supporters and not the wider nation. Higher education is disrupted every time there's a hint of unrest, as the government shuts the universities. The banks are under government control, so savings can be and have been wiped out at the whim of the rulers.

Nominally, Myanmar citizens have relative economic freedom, but just about any business opportunity requires bribes or connections. The small elite has modern conveniences, good medical treatment, fancy, well-fortified homes and speedy cars. Peaceful political assembly is banned and citizens are fearful of discussing politics with foreigners – although many relish doing so if they're sure potential informers aren't listening.

Population

Exactly how many people live in Myanmar is a mystery (see the boxed text, p538). The government recognises 135 distinct ethnic groups that make up eight official 'major national ethnic races': Bamar, Shan, Mon, Kayin, Kayah, Chin, Kachin and Rakhaing. The 1983 census records 69% of the population as Bamar, 8.5% Shan, 6.2% Karen, 4.5% Rakhine, 2.4% Mon, 2.2% Chin, 1.4% Kachin and 1% Wa.

Under the 2008 constitution Myanmar is divided into seven regions (they used to be called divisions; these are where the Bamar are in the majority) and seven states (minority regions, namely Chin, Kachin, Kayah, Kayin, Mon, Rakhaing and Shan States). In addition there are six ethnic enclaves (Danu, Kokang, Naga, Palaung, Pa-O and Wa) with a degree of self-governance.

The relatively large numbers of Indians and Chinese you'll encounter in Myanmar are a legacy of colonial times and ongoing economic co-operation.

Religion

About 87% of Myanmar's citizens are Theravada Buddhists, but this is blended with a strong belief in *nat* (guardian spirit beings).

MYANMAR READING LIST

Even more than with most countries, it's worth reading up before arriving in Myanmar to gain a grasp of the country's political and social complexities. Pick up Lonely Planet's *Myanmar (Burma)* for more comprehensive coverage, and the helpful *Burmese Phrasebook*. The following are some other recommended titles:

» *River of Lost Footsteps* by Thant Myint U is a must-read historical review that recounts kings' blunders and successes, while adding occasional family anecdotes of Burma's early days of independence.

» *Everything is Broken* by Emma Larkin is an eye-opening account of the callousness of the regime in the face of the worst natural disaster to befall Myanmar in modern history.

» *Burma/Myanmar: What Everyone Needs to Know* by David Steinberg sheds light on many aspects of the country's complex situation via a series of concise and understandable Q&As on history and culture.

» *Burma Chronicles* by Guy Delisle is an amusing and horrifyingly graphic account of a year in Myanmar by the Canadian cartoonist who travelled with his wife, an administrator for Medecins Sans Frontières (MSF).

» *Nowhere To Be Home*, edited by Maggie Lemere and Zoë West, presents 22 oral histories of Myanmar citizens gathered both from those living in the country and those in exile.

Remember, when they're read, these books and others also become priceless gifts in a country so starved of intellectual perspective.

Many hill tribes are Christian, and smaller Hindu and Muslim communities are dotted throughout the country.

Buddhism

For the average Burmese Buddhist much of life revolves around the merit (*kutho*, from the Pali *kusala*, meaning 'wholesome') that is accumulated through rituals and good deeds. One of the more common rituals performed by individuals visiting a stupa is to pour water over the Buddha image at their astrological post (determined by the day of the week they were born) – one glassful for every year of their current age plus one extra to ensure a long life.

Every Burmese male is expected to take up temporary monastic residence twice in his life: once as a *samanera* (novice monk), between the ages of five and 15, and again as a *pongyi* (fully ordained monk), some time after the age of 20. Almost all men or boys under 20 years of age participate in the *shinpyu* (initiation ceremony), through which their family earns great merit.

While there is little social expectation that they should do so, a number of women live monastic lives as *dasasila* ('ten-precept' nuns). Burmese nuns shave their heads, wear pink robes and take vows in an ordination procedure similar to that undertaken by monks.

THE FICTION OF MYANMAR STATISTICS

That famous quip about lies, damn lies and statistics rings particularly true in Myanmar. Even a basic figure such as Myanmar's population is elusive. The Chinese news agency Xinhua quotes the government's 2009 official figure as 59.12 million, while the Asian Development Bank has it as 58.84 million and the CIA World Factbook as 54 million.

Sean Turnell, an expert in Myanmar's economy at Sydney's Macquarie University, isn't surprised by this 10% spread. 'The last full census was back in 1913', he says, pointing out that all subsequent attempts at a head count, including the oft-quoted census from 1983, have been compromised by lack of data from parts of the country experiencing rebellions and unrest.

Population figures in this chapter are not to be taken as wholly accurate but more as a way to gauge the relative size of different towns and cities.

DOS & DON'TS

» Don't touch anyone's head, as it's considered the spiritual pinnacle of the body.

» Don't point feet at people if you can help it, and avoid stepping over people.

» Burmese women don't ride atop pick-ups as it can be insulting to men beneath them.

» Hand things – food, gifts, money – with your right hand, tucking your left under your right elbow.

» Dress modestly when visiting religious sites – avoid above-the-knee shorts, tight clothes or sleeveless shirts.

» Take off your shoes when entering temple precincts, usually including the long steps up to a hilltop pagoda.

Nat Worship

Buddhism in Myanmar has overtaken, but never entirely replaced, the pre-Buddhist practice of *nat* worship. The 37 *nat* figures are often found side by side with Buddhist images. The Burmese *nats* are spirits that can inhabit natural features, trees or even people. They can be mischievous or beneficent.

The *nat* cult is strong. Mt Popa (see the boxed text, p531) is an important centre. The Burmese divide their devotions and offerings according to the sphere of influence: Buddha for future lives, and the *nat* – both Hindu and Bamar – for problems in this life. A misdeed might be redressed with offerings to the *nat* Thagyamin, who annually records the names of those who perform good deeds in a book made of gold leaves. Those who commit evil are recorded in a book made of dog skin.

Arts

For centuries the arts in Myanmar were sponsored by the royal courts, mainly through the construction of major religious buildings that required the skills of architects, sculptors, painters and a variety of craftspeople. Such patronage was cut short during British colonial rule and has not been a priority since independence. This said, there are plenty of examples of traditional art to be viewed in Myanmar, mainly in the temples that are an ever-present feature of town and countryside.

Marionette Theatre

Yok-thei pwe (Burmese marionette theatre) was the forerunner of Burmese classical dance. Marionette theatre declined following WWII and is now mostly confined to tourist venues in Yangon, Mandalay and Bagan.

Music

Traditional Burmese music relies heavily on rhythm and is short on harmony, at least to the Western ear. Younger Burmese listen to heavily Western-influenced sounds – you will often hear Burmese-language covers of classic oldies, usually sappy love or pop tunes. A number of Burmese rock musicians, such as Lay Phyu of the band Iron Cross, produce serious songs of their own, but the country's censors keep a lid on anything remotely rebellious.

Pwe

The *pwe* (show) is everyday Burmese theatre. A religious festival, wedding, funeral, celebration, fair, sporting event – almost any gathering – is a good excuse for a *pwe*. Once underway, a *pwe* traditionally goes on all night. If an audience member is flaking at some point during the performance, they simply fall asleep. Ask a trishaw driver if a *pwe* is on nearby.

Myanmar's truly indigenous dance forms are those that pay homage to the *nat*. In a special *nat pwe*, one or more *nat* are invited to possess the body and mind of a medium. Sometimes members of the audience seem to be possessed instead, an event greatly feared by most Burmese.

Environment & Wildlife

Myanmar covers an area of 671,000 sq km, which is roughly the size of Texas or France. From the snowcapped Himalaya in the north to the coral-fringed Myeik (Mergui) Archipelago in the south, Myanmar's 2000km length crosses three distinct ecological regions, producing what is probably the richest biodiversity in Southeast Asia.

Unfortunately, that wildlife – which includes a third of the world's Asiatic elephants, more venomous snakes than any other country and the largest tiger reserve on the planet – is threatened by habitat loss. Rampant deforestation by the timber industry, which occurs in order to feed demand in Thailand and China, is a primary cause, as is destructive slash and burn agriculture. Optimistically, about 7% of the country is protected in national parks and other protected areas, but most of these are just lines on maps. Wildlife laws in Myanmar are seldom enforced, due to a desperate lack of funding, and in recent years some wildlife reserves that date back to the colonial era have been un-reserved to allow logging.

For travellers, seeing wildlife will be more a matter of luck than design. And without some serious cash, forget about visiting national parks.

Food & Drink

Food

As an approximate guide, prices for main dishes when eating out are budget ($) US$1 to US$3; midrange ($$) US$4 to US$10; and top end ($$$) over US$10.

Mainstream Burmese cuisine represents a blend of Bamar, Mon, Indian and Chinese influences. A typical meal has *htamin* (rice) as its core, eaten with a choice of *hin* (curry dishes), most commonly fish, chicken, pork, prawns or mutton. Soup is always served, along with a table full of condiments (including pickled vegies as spicy dipping sauces). Most meals include free refills, so come hungry.

Outside of Rakhaing State (near Bangladesh), most Burmese food is pretty mild on the chilli front. Most cooks opt for a simple masala of turmeric, ginger, garlic, salt and onions, plus plenty (and we mean loads!) of peanut oil and shrimp paste. *Balachaung* (chillies, tamarind and dried shrimp pounded together) or the pungent *ngapi kyaw* (spicy shrimp paste with garlic) is always nearby to add some kick. Almost everything in Burmese cooking is flavoured with *ngapi* (a salty paste concocted from dried and fermented shrimp or fish).

Noodle dishes are often eaten for breakfast or as light snacks between meals. The seafood served along the coasts is some of the best and cheapest you'll find in the entire region.

Drink

Non-alcoholic drinks

Teashops, a national institution, are good places to meet people over a drink and inexpensive snacks such as *nam-bya* and *palata* (flat breads) or Chinese fried pastries. Burmese tea (about K250 a cup), brewed Indian-style with lots of condensed milk and sugar, is the national drink. Ask for *lahpeq ye* (tea with a dollop of condensed milk); *cho bouk* is less sweet, and *kyauk padaung* is very sweet. Most restaurants will provide as much free Chinese tea as you can handle. Real coffee is limited to a handful of modern, Western-style cafes in Yangon and other large cities. Sugarcane juice is a very popular streetside drink.

Alcohol

Partly owned by the government, Myanmar Beer is a bit lighter in flavour and alcohol than other Southeast Asian beers. A more watery beer is Mandalay Beer. Mandalay Brewery, in Yangon, also produces the New

'MOUTH-WATERING SNACKS'

Fancy yourself as an adventurous eater? Seek out *tha yei za* (mouth-watering snack) at night markets in Yangon and street stalls around the country. Desserts are common, and come in the form of multicoloured sticky-rice sweets, poppyseed cakes, banana puddings and the like. Others test local claims that 'anything that walks on the ground can be eaten' – not to mention any claims you might have to 'hardcore traveller' status – and are definitely in the unidentified frying object category:

- **wek thaa douk htoe (barbecue stands)** Footpath stalls selling graphic, sliced-up pig
- **pa-yit kyaw (fried cricket)** Sold on skewers or in a 10-pack for about K500
- **bi-laar (beetle)** Prepared like crickets; locals suggest 'suck the stomach out, then chew the head part'
- **thin baun poe (larva)** Insect larva, culled from bamboo, are lightly grilled and served still wriggling

Mandalay Export label, which is the best-tasting local beer.

Very popular in Shan State is an orange brandy called *shwe leinmaw*, a pleasant-tasting liqueur that packs quite a punch. There's a couple of vineyards making wine, and in Pyin Oo Lwin there are several sweet strawberry-based wines.

There are also a variety of stronger liquors, including rum in Mandalay, and the fermented palm juice known as toddy.

DRINKING WATER

Only drink purified water. Be wary of ice in remote areas, though it is usually factory-produced in towns and cities. Bottled water costs from K300 a litre and is widely available. Consider sterilising your water, and saving dozens of PET bottles, by using a UV sterilising wand.

SURVIVAL GUIDE

Directory A–Z

Accommodation

Listings in this book are ordered by author preference and divided into three groups with regard to price for a double room: budget ($) under US$20; midrange ($$) US$20 to US$60; and top end ($$$) over US$60. Note that most hotels charge one price for foreigners and another for locals.

Hotels and guesthouses are a touch more expensive in Myanmar than in neighbouring countries. The cheapest places (around US$8 for a double room) are very plain; think concrete floors, squashed mosquitoes on the walls, a fan (usually) and a shared bathroom down the hall, with a basic breakfast if you're lucky. For a few dollars more you get air-con, hot water and even TV. These, however, will be of limited value unless your lodging has a generator, because electricity supplies are sketchy right across Myanmar. Unless stated otherwise, prices include private bathroom.

Nearly all hotels and guesthouses quote prices in US dollars. Most accept kyat at a slightly disadvantageous rate. Prices listed in this chapter are for peak season, roughly October to March. Discounts may be available in the low season; don't be afraid to haggle gently if planning a longer stay. Passport and visa details are required at check-in, but hotels don't need to hold your passport.

All accommodation supposedly must be licensed to accept foreign guests, meaning the cheapest places are usually off-limits. In out-of-the-way towns, some unlicensed guesthouses will accept weary travellers.

Business Hours

Most government offices – including post offices and official telephone centres – are open from 9.30am to 4.30pm Monday to Friday.

Shops are generally open Monday to Saturday, from 9am or 9.30am to 6pm or later, but sometimes for a half-day on Saturday. Most cafes and restaurants open at 7am or 8am and close at 9pm or 10pm. Internet shops tend to open from noon to 10pm. Exceptions to these opening hours are noted in this chapter's listings.

PRACTICALITIES

» Connect (when it's working) to the electricity supply (230V, 50Hz AC). Power outlets can have three-pronged, two-pronged round or flat sockets – bring an all-purpose adaptor. Many hotels have generators (some run at night only). Local power sources in many towns are scheduled for night hours only.

» Read the English-language newspapers *Myanmar Times*, which offers some useful travel and entertainment information, and the government mouthpiece *New Light of Myanmar*.

» Bring a shortwave radio and listen, like many locals, to BBC and VOA broadcasts.

» Watch satellite TV rather than the state-controlled broadcast channels – you'll often find CNN, BBC World and other news and entertainment channels at hotels.

» Petrol is sold by the gallon; distances are in miles, not kilometres. 1 Burmese *viss* or 100 *ticals* = 3.5lb; 1 *gaig* = 36in.

AVOIDING GOVERNMENT HOTELS

Small-time guesthouses and hotels are practically all private enterprises; the only full-on government hotels are often named after the destination (eg Sittwe Hotel in Sittwe). Generally 10% of what you spend at any guesthouse or hotel goes to the government.

Customs

Any foreign currency in excess of US$2000 is supposed to be declared upon entry (we, and other travellers we've met, have failed to declare larger amounts and have not had problems). Genuine antiques cannot be taken out of the country.

Embassies & Consulates

Most foreign embassies and consulates are in Yangon. Check the government's **Ministry of Foreign Affairs** (www.mofa.gov.mm) for more information.

Australia (Map p490; ☎01-251810, 251809; fax 01-246159; 88 Strand Rd, Yangon)

Bangladesh (Map p496; ☎01-515275; 11B Thanlwin Rd, Kamaryut Township, Yangon)

Cambodia (Map p496; ☎01-549609; 25 New University Ave Rd, B3/4B, Yangon)

Canada (☎662-636-0540) Affairs handled by Australian embassy or Canadian embassy in Bangkok.

China (off Map p494; ☎01-221281; 1 Pyidaungsu Yeiktha Rd, Dagon, Yangon)

France (Map p494; ☎01-212178; fax 01-212527; 102 Pyidaungsu Yeiktha Rd, Dagon, Yangon)

Germany (Map p496; ☎01-548951; fax 01-548899; 9 Bogyoke Aung San Museum Rd, Yangon)

India (Map p490; ☎01-243972, 01-391219; 545-547 Merchant St, Yangon)

Indonesia (Map p494; ☎01-254465, 254469; 100 Pyidaungsu Yeiktha Rd, Yangon)

Israel (Map p496; ☎01-515155; fax 01-515116; 15 Kabaung Rd, Hlaing Township, Yangon)

Italy (Map p496; ☎01-527100; 3 Inya Myaing Rd, Yangon)

Japan (Map p496; ☎01-549644; 100 Nat Mauk Rd, Yangon)

Korea (Map p496; ☎01-510205; 97 University Ave Rd, Bahan, Yangon)

Laos (Map p494; ☎01-222482; A1 Diplomatic Quarters, Taw Win St, Yangon)

Malaysia (Map p494; ☎01-220249; 82 Pyidaungsu Yeiktha Rd, Yangon)

Nepal (Map p496; ☎01-545880; fax 01-549803; 16 Nat Mauk Rd, Yangon)

Netherlands (☎662-309-5200) Affairs handled by German embassy or Netherlands embassy in Bangkok.

New Zealand (Map p490; ☎01-256438, 370863; fax 01-380322; 80 Strand Rd, Yangon) Affairs handled by UK embassy.

Philippines (Map p496; ☎01-558149; 50 Sayasan St, Yangon)

Singapore (Map p496; ☎01-559001; 238 Dhama Zedi Rd, Yangon)

Thailand (Map p496; ☎01-226721; 94 Pyay Rd, Dagon, Yangon)

UK (Map p490; ☎01-256438, 370863; fax 01-380 322; 80 Strand Rd, Yangon)

USA (Map p496; ☎01-536509, 535756; fax 01-650306; 110 University Ave, Kamayut, Yangon)

Vietnam (Map p496; ☎01-511305; 72 Thanlwin Rd, Bahan, Yangon)

Gay & Lesbian Travellers

Gay and transgendered people in Myanmar are rarely 'out', except for 'third sex' spirit mediums who channel the energies of *nat* spirits. As elsewhere, it can be seen as a bit of a cultural taboo, though most of Myanmar's ethnic groups are known to be tolerant of homosexuality, both male and female. A local woman walking with a foreign man will raise more eyebrows than two same-sex travellers sharing a room. Public displays of affection, whether heterosexual or homosexual, are frowned upon. **Utopia-Asia** (www.utopia-asia.com) has some Yangon scene reports.

Internet Access

There are plenty of internet cafes in the big cities and wi-fi connections at cafes and several hotels. During research for this chapter, we even found internet access in relatively remote locations such as Mrauk U.

However, with sometimes tightly squeezed bandwidth, blocked sites and power outages, it can be a frustrating and fruitless exercise to send and receive emails or check websites. Also, in March 2011, Skype and other VoIP (Voice Over Internet Protocol) calls were banned by the authorities at internet cafes – businesses that continue to offer such services are in danger of losing their licences.

Ingenious locals have come up with ways around government censorship of sites; typing https:// before the site URL can sometimes give you access. However, proceed cautiously as internet shop owners can get into big trouble if they're found to be allowing access to prohibited sites.

Internet Resources

Democratic Voice of Burma (www.dvb.no) Norway-based media organisation.

Irrawaddy (www.irrawaddy.org) Thailand-based news and features site.

Mizzima (www.mizzima.com) A nonprofit news service organised by Burmese journalists in exile.

Myanmar Image Gallery (www.myanmar-image.com) Pictures and text on myriad Myanmar-related subjects.

Online Burma/Myanmar Library (www.burmalibrary.org) Database of books and past articles on Myanmar.

Legal Matters

Myanmar does not have an independent judiciary. If you engage in political activism (eg handing out pro-democracy leaflets as some Westerners have), illegally cross the border into the country, or get caught with drugs, you have no legal recourse. Drug trafficking crimes are punishable by death. Political activists, or those entering illegally from Thailand are more likely to be locked up than deported (unless you're Rambo, of course).

Maps

Periplus Editions (scale 1:2,000,000), ITMB (1:1,350,0000) and Nelles (1:1,500,000) all make dedicated maps of Myanmar. Design Printing Services' (DPS; www.dpsmap.com) *Myanmar Guide Map* is free at the MTT office, travel agents and (sometimes) the airport in Yangon. DPS also makes maps of Yangon, Mandalay and Bagan.

Money

ATMs, Credit Cards & Travellers Cheques

Forget your plastic – none of Myanmar's few ATMs accept overseas cards. Credit cards and travellers cheques are also useless.

Banks

There are no international banks. National banks are of little use to travellers, as official exchange rates massively overvalue the kyat.

Moneychangers

Avoid the official exchange counters, which undercut black-market rates substantially (K7 per dollar, rather than K850).

You will be asked to 'change money' many times on your trip. Technically, the only reasonable way to buy kyat is through the 'black market' – meaning from shops, hotels, travel agents, restaurants or less reliable guys on the street. You can change US dollars, euros and some other currencies in Yangon, but generally only US dollars elsewhere.

The US$100 bill gets the best exchange rate, and rates are usually marginally better early in the week (Monday or Tuesday).

It's safest to change money in hotels or shops, rather than on the street. The moneychangers standing around just east of the Mahabandoola Garden in Yangon have a reputation for short-changing new arrivals of several thousand kyat.

Never hand over your money until you've received the kyat and counted them. Honest moneychangers will expect you to do this. Considering that K5000 is the highest denomination, you'll get a lot of notes. Moneychangers give ready-made, rubber-banded stacks of a hundred K1000 bills. It's a good idea to check each note individually. Often you'll find one or two (or more) with a cut corner or taped together, neither of which anyone will accept. We heard from some travellers that Yangon moneychangers have asked for a 'commission'.

Many travellers do the bulk of their exchanging in Yangon, where you can get about K100 more per dollar than elsewhere, then carry the stacks of kyat for a couple of weeks around the country. Considering the relative safety from theft, it's not a bad idea, but you *can* exchange money elsewhere.

KYAT & DOLLARS

Prices in this chapter alternate between kyat (K) and US dollars (US$), depending on the currency in which prices are quoted.

Also, when paying for rooms and services in US dollars, check your change carefully. Locals like to unload slightly torn bills that will be worthless for the rest of your trip in Myanmar.

FECs

Some government businesses may still quote prices in Foreign Exchange Certificates (FECs). Since one FEC is equal to US$1 there is absolutely no value in you acquiring them (the requirement that visitors had to change US$200 into FECs on arrival in the country was scrapped in 2003).

Tipping

Tipping is not customary, though little extra 'presents' are sometimes expected (even if they're not asked for) in exchange for a service (such as unlocking a locked temple at Bagan, helping move a bag at the airport or showing you around the 'sights' of a village).

Have small notes (K50, K100, K200) handy when visiting a temple or monastery for donations.

Photography & Video

Most internet cafes can burn digital photos onto a CD for about K1000. Some sights, including some pagodas, charge small camera fees. Avoid taking photos of military facilities, uniformed individuals, road blocks, bridges and NLD offices.

Post

Myanmar is the place to get retro with postcards at just K30 to anywhere in the world. That's US$0.03! And it's likely to get there. **DHL Worldwide Express** (Map p494; ☎01-664423; www.fastforward.dhl.com; 7A Kaba Aye Pagoda Rd, Yangon; ⏰8am-6pm Mon-Sat) is a more reliable way of sending out bigger packages (though you can send only documents to the USA because of sanctions). Packages begin at US$80 (0.5kg/1.1lb), while documents start at US$72.

Public Holidays

Major public holidays include the following:

Independence Day (4 January)

Union Day (12 February)

Peasants' Day (2 March)

Armed Forces Day (27 March)

Workers' Day (1 May)

National Day (October or November)

Christmas Day (25 December)

> **BRING NEW BILLS!**
>
> We cannot stress enough the need to bring pristine 'new' US dollar bills to Myanmar – that means no folds, creases, tears and pen or other marks on the notes, and that they should be the ones with the larger full frame heads. Anything else risks being rejected by moneychangers, hotels, restaurants, shops and museums.

Safe Travel

Usually the only time a local will be running with your money or belongings is if they're chasing you down the road with something you've dropped. For now theft remains quite rare, but don't tempt fate in this poor country by flashing valuables or leaving them unguarded. The only real scams are dodgy moneychangers short-changing you, and drivers or guides getting a commission for purchases at any shops you visit.

Areas around the Myanmar–Thai border, home to the country's notorious drug trade, can be dangerous (and off-limits) to explore.

Power outages are highly annoying and commonplace everywhere except the surreal capital, Nay Pyi Taw. Many businesses have their own generators, but check with your guesthouse whether the power will be on all night, especially in the hot season.

The poor state of road and rail infrastructure, plus lax safety standards and procedures for flights and boats, means that travelling can sometimes be dangerous.

Telephone

Local Calls

Most business cards purposely list a couple of phone numbers, and often a mobile (cell) phone number, as lines frequently go dead and calls just don't go through.

Local call stands – as part of a shop, or sometimes just a table with a phone or two on a pavement – can be found all over Myanmar. A local call should be K100 per minute.

To dial long distance within Myanmar, dial the area code (including the '0') and the number.

International Calls

Official telephone (call) centres are sometimes the only way to call overseas, though sometimes this can be done on the street too, through vendors offering use of their mobile phones.

Generally, it costs about US$5 per minute to call Australia or Europe and US$6 per minute to phone North America. You'll usually be asked to pay in US dollars. In March 2011 the authorities banned Skype and other internet-based call services at internet cafes, as the lower rates charged for such calls was impacting the revenue made at government call centres.

FESTIVAL CALENDAR

Myanmar follows a 12-month lunar calendar, and most festivals are on the full moon of the Burmese month in which they occur – hence shifting dates. The build-up to festivals can go on for days.

February/March

Shwedagon Festival Myanmar's largest *paya* festival takes place in Yangon.

March/April

Full-Moon Festival Biggest event of the year at Shwemawdaw Paya in Bago.

April/May

Buddha's Birthday The full moon also marks the day of Buddha's enlightenment and his entry to nirvana. One of the best places to observe this ceremony is at Yangon's Shwedagon Paya.

Thingyan (Water Festival) The Burmese New Year is the biggest holiday of the year, celebrated with a raucous nationwide water fight. It is impossible to go outside without getting drenched so just join the fun. Businesses close and some transport – especially buses – stops running for around a week.

June/July

» **Buddhist Lent** Start of the Buddhist Rains Retreat. Laypeople present monasteries with new robes, because during the three-month Lent period monks are restricted to their monasteries.

July/August

» **Wagaung Festival** Nationwide exercise in alms-giving.

September/October

» **Boat Races** This is the height of the wet season, so boat races are held in rivers, lakes and even ponds all over Myanmar. Inle Lake is best.

» **Thadingyut** Celebrates Buddha's return from a period of preaching.

October/November

» **Tazaungdaing** The biggest 'festival of lights' sees all Myanmar lit by oil lamps, fire balloons, candles and even mundane electric lamps.

» **Kathein** A one-month period at the end of Buddhist Lent during which new monastic robes and requisites are offered to the monastic community.

December/January

» **Rakhaing State Day** A Saturday in mid-December sees traditional sports such as wrestling and bamboo pole climbing held in Sittwe.

» **Kayin New Year** Karen communities throughout Myanmar celebrate by wearing their traditional dress and by hosting folk-dancing and singing performances. Big celebrations are held in the Karen suburb of Insein, just north of Yangon, and in Hpa-an.

» **Ananda Festival** Held at the Ananda Pahto in Bagan at the full moon.

To call Myanmar from abroad, dial your country's international access code, then ☎95 (Myanmar's country code), the area code (minus the '0') and the five- or six-digit number. Area codes are listed below town headings throughout this chapter.

Mobile Phones

Mobile-phone numbers begin with ☎09. There's no international roaming in Myanmar, so in most cases your mobile phone will be useless here. You'll see plenty of them in use, though. This is a serious status symbol (even without a Beyoncé ringtone), considering the SIM card alone officially costs K1.5 million (around US$1685) and much more on the black market.

During our research US$50 cards (with credit expiring in three months) were widely on sale for use in CDMA phones. You can find a CDMA 450 phone for as little as US$50 in Yangon.

Time

The local Myanmar Standard Time (MST) is 6½ hours ahead of Greenwich Mean Time (GMT/UTC). When coming in from Thailand, turn your watch back half an hour; coming from India, put your watch forward an hour.

Toilets

In many out-of-the-way places, Burmese toilets are often squat jobs, generally in a cobweb-filled outhouse that is reached by a dirt path behind a restaurant. In guesthouses and hotels you will usually find Western-style thrones. Toilet paper is widely available but as Confucius might have said: 'The wise traveller carries an emergency TP stash, the unwise traveller uses this page'. Either way, don't flush it.

Tourist Information

Government-operated **Myanmar Travels & Tours** (MTT; http://myanmartravelsandtours.com), with offices in Yangon, Mandalay, New Bagan and Inle Lake, is the main 'tourist information' service. Other than at Yangon, these offices are pretty quiet, and often the staff have sketchy knowledge on restricted areas. We don't recommend using its services, but it does have brochures and maps, arranges permits to travel in restricted areas and knows the latest news on border crossings. There are no MTT offices abroad.

Much of the tourist industry in Myanmar is privatised. Travellers who want to arrange a driver, or have hotel reservations awaiting them, would do well to arrange a trip with the help of private travel agents in Yangon. Many Myanmar 'travel agents' outside Yangon only sell air tickets.

Travellers with Disabilities

Myanmar is a tricky country for mobility-impaired travellers. Wheelchair ramps are virtually unheard of and public transport is crowded and can be difficult, even for the fully ambulatory.

Visas

Everyone requires a visa to visit Mynamar. If you're applying for a tourist visa (US$20, valid 28 days) at home, you should start the process no later than three weeks before your trip, or a month before to be safe.

If you're already travelling, it's usually possible to get a tourist visa at the **Myanmar embassy in Bangkok** (☎662-233-2237; 132 Sathorn Nua Rd) within 24 hours if you apply in person; the cost for this service is 1010B.

Applications

All visas are valid for up to three months from the date of issue and most embassies and consulates need at least two weeks to process an application.

There are slight differences between the application procedures at Myanmar embassies in different countries. Some require two forms to be filled out – the general application and a work history form, others just the general application. Some require two passport photos, others only one. Postal applications are usually OK, but it's best to check first with your nearest embassy about their specific application rules.

When applying for a tourist visa it's unwise to list your occupation as any of the following: journalist, photographer, editor, publisher, motion-picture director or producer, cameraperson, videographer or writer. Of course, plenty of media professionals do get into the country – usually by declaring a different profession on their visa application; we've found 'consultant' works.

Myanmar foreign missions may also be suspicious of anyone whose passport shows two or more previous visits to Myanmar in a five-year period. Obviously the government can't believe anyone would want to visit Myanmar more than once or twice! In cases such as these you'll need more of a reason than simply 'tourism' for receiving another visa. Be creative.

Visa Extensions & Overstaying

Tourist visas cannot be extended and you can run into problems if you choose to stay longer than the allotted 28 days. Hotels are obliged to report travellers whose visas have expired to the authorities and, if found to have not done so, will be in trouble themselves.

Also you may have difficulties with airport immigration if you're planning domestic flights, particularly in far-flung airports (like Sittwe or Myitkyina). If you do overstay, it's wise to stick with land routes and places within easy access of Yangon as we've heard stories of such tourists being instructed to leave the country immediately when discovered by the authorities.

All said, overstaying your visa a few days – even a week or so – is possible. At research time, Yangon airport's immigration charged US$3 per day, plus a US$3 'registration fee' for visitors who go over the allotted 28 days. Have exact change ready (they're not likely to change your US$100 bill and they won't take kyat) and arrive early enough to fill out the few forms necessary.

Volunteering

Official opportunities to volunteer are greatly limited. A list of NGOs that may have volunteering opportunities can be found on www.ngoinmyanmar.org, although mostly the postings are for specific experienced workers (often in medicine). Don't let this sway you. Everyone in Myanmar wants to learn English, and few can afford to. Ask in towns or villages to sit in at an English class.

VISA ON ARRIVAL?

In 2010 Myanmar test-ran a 'tourist visa on arrival' system for flights into Yangon, but at the time of our research it didn't appear to be operating, despite many websites indicating that it still did.

It now appears that 'visas on arrival' are once again available at Yangon airport but only in very specific circumstances. To get one you need to enter Myanmar on the scheduled Myanmar Airways International flights from either Guangzhou, China, or Siem Reap, Cambodia.

The following are able to accept both skilled and unskilled volunteers, but give them as much advance notice as possible.

Eden Centre for Disabled Children (☎640399; www.edencentre.org) The first Myanmar-run NGO working to better the lives of disabled children in the city.

Growing Together School (gt.camp@gmail.com) Swiss-run project with two schools based in and around Yangon. It generally requires volunteer trained and untrained teachers and builders and handypeople for at least six weeks.

Myanmar Charity Group (www.myanmarcharitygroup.org) Provides assistance for the education and general welfare of disabled and orphaned children.

Unicef (www.unicef.org/myanmar/index.html) Runs various programs to protect children and improve public health.

Women Travellers

Women travelling alone are more likely to be helped than harassed. In some areas you'll be regarded with friendly curiosity – and asked, with sad-eyed sympathy, 'Are you only one?' – because Burmese women tend to prefer to travel en masse. At remote religious sites, a single foreign woman may be 'adopted' by a Burmese woman, who will take you and show you the highlights. At some sites, such as Mandalay's Mahamuni Paya and Golden Rock, 'ladies' are not permitted to the central shrine; signs will indicate if this is the case.

Tampons are available only at upmarket shops in Yangon and Mandalay.

Getting There & Away

Air

Practically all international flights arrive at Yangon (Rangoon) airport (RGN); there's also a connection to Kunming in China from Mandalay airport (MDL). The most common route to Yangon is via Bangkok, though there are direct flights with several other regional cities such as Singapore and Kuala Lumpur.

Airlines with regular international links include the following. For a list of domestic carriers, see p548.

Air Asia (☎01-251885; www.airasia.com) Twice daily to/from Bangkok and Kuala Lumpur.

Air China (☎01-505024; www.airchina.com) Five times weekly to/from Beijing and Kunming.

DEPARTURE TAX

Foreigners pay US$10 departure tax, not included with your air ticket. Have the US dollars in hand when leaving the country. You pay at the window in the entrance hall, before you check-in. Kyat are not accepted. There is no departure tax for domestic flights

Air India (☎01-253601; http://home.airindia.in) To/from Kolkata (Calcutta) on Monday and Friday.

Bangkok Airways (☎01-255122; www.bangkokair.com) Four times weekly to/from Bangkok.

China Airlines (www.china-airlines.com) Three times weekly to/from Taipei.

Malaysia Airlines (☎01-2410 0720; www.malaysiaairlines.com) Daily to/from Kuala Lumpur.

Myanmar Airways International (☎01-255260; www.maiair.com) Unaffiliated with the government's Myanma Airways. Flies to/from Bangkok, Gaya, Guangzhou, Kuala Lumpur, Siem Reap and Singapore. There are plans to add Delhi, Hong Kong, Kunming, Seoul and Tokyo flights to its schedule.

Silk Air (☎01-255287; www.silkair.com) Daily to/from Singapore.

Thai Airways (☎01-255499; www.thaiair.com) Daily to/from Bangkok.

Vietnam Airlines (☎01-255066; www.vietnamairlines.com) Five times weekly to/from Hanoi and twice weekly to/from Ho Chi Minh.

Getting Around

Unless you fly, all travel in Myanmar takes time. Often lots of time. Large areas of the country are off-limits, or accessible only with permission. Securing such permission:

» Takes time – a minimum of at least two weeks but more commonly around a month.

» Requires the help of an experienced travel agency: for a list of reputable Yangon-based agencies, see p493.

» Always involves paying fees to the government, usually via the government-owned travel agency MTT, even if you're dealing with another agency.

» Usually means dancing to MTT's tune when it comes to how you visit the area in question and who you go with.

Sometimes areas that were possible to visit with or without a permit suddenly become off-limits: that's how it is in Myanmar.

Exiting Myanmar by a land border (only three possible) will require permits and 'guide' fees and plenty of advanced notice.

Air

Five airlines ply Myanmar's skyways. Schedules are approximate at best, and can change right up to the departure time; recheck all bookings. Although only one of the domestic airlines is owned outright by the government (Myanma Airways), the other four have known or suspected links. At the very least, all pay hefty government licence and administration fees.

Air Bagan (☎01-513322, 513422; www.airbagan.com) Has the largest fleet with six planes.

Air Kanbawza (☎01-255260) Owned by the same Kanbawza Bank tycoon who owns Myanmar Airways International, this two-plane operation started up in April 2011.

Asian Wings (☎01-516654; www.asianwingsairways.com) Rumoured to be a subsidiary of Air Bagan, this two-plane operation started in January 2011.

Air Mandalay (☎01-525488; www.airmandalay.com) A Singapore–Malaysia joint venture with three planes.

Myanma Airways (☎01-374874, 373828; www.mot.gov.mm/ma) Government airline.

One-way tickets are half the return fare and should be bought at least a day ahead. You'll need your passport and US dollars. Travel agencies sell air tickets for slightly less than airline offices. There's no domestic departure tax.

Boat

There are 8000km of navigable river in Myanmar and, unlike elsewhere in Asia, slow boats remain a vital transport link here. Even in the dry season, boats can travel on the Ayeyarwady (Irrawaddy) from the delta to Bhamo, with small boats continuing to Myitkyina. Other important rivers include the Twante Canal, which links the Ayeyarwady to Yangon, and the Chindwin, which joins the Ayeyarwady a little north of Bagan. Most ferries are operated by the government's **Inland Water Transport** (IWT; www.iwt.gov.mm).

The Mandalay–Bagan service is popular among travellers. A government ferry runs at least twice a week, and in season there's also the faster, more comfortable private service *Malikha 2;* buy tickets from travel agencies. Some slower local boats continue to Pyay (Prome) and even Yangon. The best long-haul river trip – in season – is drifting south from Myitkyina or Bhamo. For something shorter, take the boat from Mawlamyine (Moulmein) to Hpa-an.

Bus

Almost always faster and cheaper than trains, Myanmar buses range from luxury air-con express buses, less luxurious but nice buses (without air-con), local buses and mini 32-seaters. Most are operated by private companies.

Breakdowns are frequent and roads are so bad in most places that two vehicles travelling in opposite directions can't pass without pulling off the road. On the other hand, bus travel is cheap and reasonably frequent, and it's easy to meet local people during the regular food stops.

Buying tickets in advance is recommended, lest you get stuck sitting on a sack in the aisle. On minibuses, beware of the back seat – on Myanmar's rough roads you'll be bouncing around like popcorn. Keep some warm clothing handy for air-con or trips through mountains.

You can pay kyat for all bus fares. Note, foreigners will pay more than locals – and on occasion the price is 'set' on the spot. For sample foreigner fares and trip times, see the table, p550.

Car & Motorcycle

The cost of hiring a car and driver is tied to the fluctuating price of black-market petrol. Older cars without air-con cost about US$50 per day (including driver and petrol) from Yangon.

Many locals remain reluctant to rent motorcycles to foreigners, but it is possible in some places, including Mandalay and Myitkyina, for around K10,000 per day.

Local Transport

In most places, horse carts *(myint hlei),* vintage taxis *(taxi),* tiny four-wheeled Mazdas (*lei bein,* meaning 'four wheels', or blue taxi) and, for those with Burmese-size arses (they make Kate Moss look hefty), bicycle rickshaws or trishaws (*sai-kaa* – that's pidgin for sidecar) double as public transport. We indicate some sample rates in this chapter, but prices are usually negotiable.

Larger cities – including Yangon, Mandalay, Pathein (Bassein) and Mawlamyine – have dirt-cheap public buses that ply the main streets.

Bicycles are widely available to hire for K500 to K3000 per day.

Pick-Up

You can get almost anywhere in Myanmar on the ubiquitous trucks with bench seats known variously as pick-ups (also called *kaa*), *lain-ka* (linecar) or *hi-lux*. They leave when full and stop pretty much everywhere. Sitting up the back is cheaper than a bus, while a seat at the front costs double for

GOVERNMENT-OWNED TRANSPORT

The government profits from the use of transport services that it owns and/or operates. Foreigners pay multiples of local fares on the ferry and train. Depending on who you believe, the extra money goes either straight into the general's pockets or towards wages and upkeep of seriously creaky infrastructure. Government-owned transport includes the following:

» **Inland Water Transport** (IWT) Foreigners are charged at least five times the local price.

» **Myanma Airways** (domestic) Not recommended, as much for its safety record as its ownership.

» **Myanma Five Star Line** (MFSL; ships) Finding accurate schedules is so difficult that few travellers bother.

» **Myanmar Railways** Foreigners are charged 10 times the local fare.

BUSES IN MYANMAR

FROM	TO	COST (K)	DURATION (HR)
Bagan	Taunggyi	10,500	10
Mandalay	Bagan	6500	8
Mandalay	Hsipaw	5000	6
Mandalay	Taunggyi	6000	12
Yangon	Bagan	15,000	15
Yangon	Bago (Pegu)	6000	2
Yangon	Chaung Tha Beach	8000	7
Yangon	Kyaiktiyo	7000	4½
Yangon	Mandalay	11,000	12-15
Yangon	Pyay	4000	7
Yangon	Taunggyi	11,000	17

little more room. Journey times are wildly elastic.

Train

Myanmar Railways is government owned and operated. Foreigners pay up to 10 times the local rate, always in crisp US dollar bills that disappear into the government coffers. The British-era railways are much-maligned in Myanmar, and services often run late. Though as one local said: 'It's not as bad as some people say, not as good as you hope.'

If you do decide to take the train, it's worth trying to find a local to buy your ticket (then acting dumb once you get on board). Otherwise, in many places foreigners are only allowed to buy expensive upper-class seats. Upper class involves international-style reclining seats and (in theory) air-con, 1st class is hard-backed seats with some cushioning, and ordinary class involves stiff wooden seats. The Pyin Oo Lwin–Hsipaw line is the most scenic, particularly around the Gokteik Gorge.

Reservations and ticketing can be done at train stations and English-language information is available through MTT. Note that express trains are much more comfortable than the average Burmese train. Reserve sleepers (ie anything that contains sleeping berths, including some day trains) several days in advance. Try to have exact US dollar change, as ticket offices often won't have any dollars and refuse to pay change in kyat.

Philippines

Includes »

Best Beaches

» Boracay (p578)
» Malapascua (p590)
» Sabang (p599)
» Sipalay (p583)
» Alona Beach (p592)

Best Places for Cultural Connections

» Bontoc (p569)
» Vigan (p570)
» Quiapo (p553)
» Baguio (p567)
» Siquijor (p584)

Why Go?

Just when you thought you had Asia figured out, you get to the Philippines. Instead of monks you have priests; instead of túk-túk you have tricycles; instead of *pho* you have *adobo*. At first glance the Philippines will disarm you more than charm you, but peel back the country's skin and there are treasures to be found – aplenty. Just for starters, you can swim with whale sharks, scale volcanoes, explore desert islands, gawk at ancient rice terraces, submerge at world-class dive sites and venture into rainforests to visit remote hill tribes.

Beyond its obvious physical assets, the Philippines possesses a quirky streak that takes a bit longer to appreciate. There are secret potions and healing lotions, guys named Bong and girls named Bing, grinning hustlers, deafening cock farms, wheezing *bangkas* (outrigger boats), crooked politicians, fuzzy carabao (water buffalo), graffiti-splashed jeepneys and cheap beer to enjoy as you take it all in.

When to Go

Manila

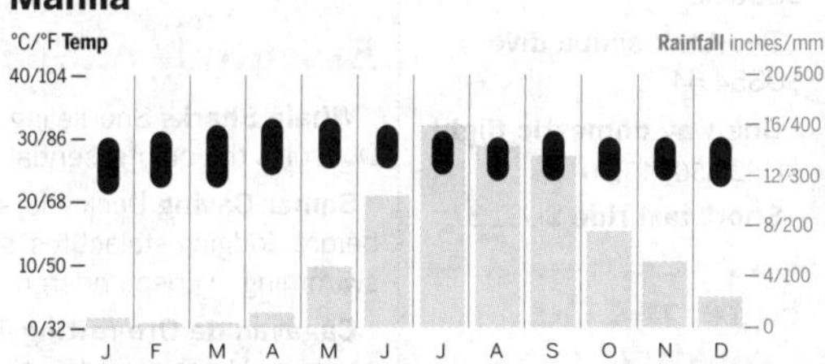

Jan–Feb Cool, pleasant weather & height of the festival season.

Apr Easter festivals; best time for whale-shark-spotting in Donsol.

Sep Typhoons are a surfer's delight; low-season deals on beaches.

AT A GLANCE

» **Currency** Peso (P)

» **Languages** Tagalog (Pilipino), English

» **Money** ATMs abound in cities, scarce in remote areas

» **Visas** Visas on arrival (21-days) the norm

» **Mobile Phones** Local SIM cards essentially free

Fast Facts

» **Area** 300,000 sq km

» **Capital** Manila

» **Country Code** ☎63

» **Emergency** ☎117

Exchange Rates

Australia	A$1	45P
Euro zone	€1	55P
Japan	¥100	50P
Thailand	B1	1.40P
UK	UK£1	70P
US	US$1	45P

Set Your Budget

» **Budget hotel room** $US11.38

» **Litre of bottled water** $US0.68

» **Two-tank scuba dive** $US54.64

» **One-way domestic flight** $US22.50–45.50

» **Short taxi ride** $US1.37

Entering the Country

Entering the country is straightforward and usually done by air through Manila, Cebu or Clark Airport.

Don't Miss

Filipinos revel in colourful **fiestas**, and it's worth scheduling your travels around one. The granddaddy of them all is the **Ati-Atihan** (p578) festival in Kalibo. At Bacolod's (p582) **MassKara** festival, mischievous masked men stir the masses into a dancing frenzy every October. The Easter **crucifixion ceremony** in San Fernando, north of Manila, produces a more macabre tableau, with Catholic devotees being physically nailed to crosses. Every little town holds a fiesta, so your odds of seeing one are pretty good.

The Filipino joie de vivre manifests itself in other ways – namely, singing. A **karaoke** night out in Manila is essential. Or pay homage to Filipino cover bands worldwide with some **live music**. Cover-band shows in Malate can be lively, or head up to Quezon City or Makati for more original fare.

ITINERARIES

One Week

Beach bums and divers should select a Visayan island and go. Popular, easy-to-reach picks include Bohol, with its mix of marine and terrestrial attractions; well-rounded Southern Negros; and adventure-laden Northeast Mindanao. Kitesurfers and hedonists should plot a course towards Boracay. If mountains are your thing, do the spectacular North Luzon overland loop from Baguio to Sagada to Banaue and back to Manila.

Two Weeks

Spend a day exploring Manila, then complete the North Luzon loop. Fly from Manila to Coron in northern Palawan for some island hopping, then make the stunning eight-hour sea journey to El Nido, gateway to cliff-addled Bacuit Bay. Travel overland to Puerto Princesa, taking maximum time to linger on lonely beaches along Palawan's west coast. From Puerto, fly back to Manila or Cebu to catch your onward flight.

Essential Outdoor Activities

» **Whale Sharks** Snorkeling with the gentle *butanding* of Donsol is the quintessential Philippine adventure.

» **Samar Caving** Deck yourself out in full caving regalia before dodging stalactites, slithering through crevasses and swimming in crisp underground pools.

» **Cagayan de Oro rafting** The whitewater around this northern Mindanao adventure hotbed is surprisingly brisk and can be paddled year round.

» **Boracay Kitesurfing** Bulabog Beach's shallow lagoon is perfect for learning, while stiff winds from December to March challenge experts.

» **Siargao Surfing** Tackle the Philippines' ultimate wave, Cloud Nine.

MANILA

02 / POP 11.5 MILLION

Manila's moniker, the 'Pearl of the Orient', couldn't be more apt – its cantankerous shell reveals its jewel only to those resolute enough to pry. No stranger to hardship, the city has endured every disaster both man and nature could throw at it, and yet today the chaotic 600-sq-km metropolis thrives as a true Asian megacity. Skyscrapers pierce the hazy sky, mushrooming from the grinding poverty of expansive shantytowns, while gleaming malls foreshadow Manila's brave new air-conditioned world. The congested roads snarl with traffic, but like the overworked arteries of a sweating giant, they are what keep this modern metropolis alive.

The determined will discover Manila's tender soul, perhaps among the leafy courtyards and cobbled streets of serene Intramuros, where little has changed since the Spanish left. Or it may be in the eddy of repose arising from the generosity of one of the city's 11 million residents.

Metro Manila is composed of 16 cities. From a tourist perspective, the important ones are the City of Manila ('downtown'), which includes the touristy districts of Malate, Ermita and Intramuros; Makati, which is the business, restaurant and nightlife hub; and pleasant, youthful Quezon City, the country's most populous city with almost three million residents.

History

The Spanish brushed aside a Muslim fort here in 1571 and founded the modern city as the capital of their realm. They named it Isigne y Siempre Leal Ciudad (Distinguished and Ever Loyal City), but the name Manila (from Maynilad, derived from a local term for a mangrove plant) soon became established. Spanish residents were concentrated around the walled city of Intramuros until 1898, when the Spanish governor surrendered to the Filipinos at San Agustin Church. After being razed to the ground during WWII, the city grew exponentially during the postwar years as migrants left the countryside in search of new opportunities. President Ferdinand Marcos consolidated 17 towns and villages into Metro Manila in 1976.

Sights

The main sights are downtown in the old walled city of Intramuros, which lies just south of the Pasig River, and south of Intramuros around Rizal Park (Luneta). You can walk to both of these easily enough from Malate and Ermita.

WORTH A TRIP

BINONDO & QUIAPO MARKETS

Lovers of markets and utter chaos are advised to make DIY trips over the Pasig River to **Binondo** (Manila's old Chinatown) and **Quiapo**, where every manner of product is sold to a throng of humanity. Around **Quiapo Church** look for the apothecary vendors. They sell herbal potions, folk medicines and amulets that are said to ward off evil spirits. Take the LRT-1 to the Carriedo stop to get to the heart of the action.

Intramuros HISTORIC DISTRICT

(Map p558) A spacious borough of wide streets, leafy plazas and lovely colonial houses, the old walled city of Intramuros was the centrepiece of Spanish Manila. The Spanish replaced the original wooden fort with stone in 1590, and these walls stand much as they were 400 years ago. They're still studded with bastions and pierced with gates *(puertas)*.

At the mouth of the Pasig River you'll find Manila's premier tourist attraction, **Fort Santiago** (Map p558; admission P65; 8am-6pm), fronted by a pretty lily pond and the **Intramuros Visitors Center** (8am-5pm). During WWII the fort was used as a prisoner-of-war camp by the Japanese. Within the fort grounds you'll find the **Rizal Shrine** (8am-5pm) in the building where national hero José Rizal was incarcerated as he awaited execution. It contains Rizal's personal effects and an original copy of his last poem, 'Mi Ultimo Adios' (My Last Farewell).

The most interesting building to survive the Battle of Manila is the church and monastery of **San Agustin** (Map p558; General Luna St). The interior is truly opulent and the ceiling, painted in 3-D relief, will make you question your vision. You must visit during a mass, or access it through the interesting **San Agustin Museum** (admission P100; 8am-noon & 1-6pm).

Opposite the church, **Casa Manila** (Map p558; General Luna St; admission P70; 9am-6pm Tue-Sun) is a beautiful reproduction of a

Philippines Highlights

1. Drift among the limestone cathedrals and azure lagoons of the Bacuit Archipelago around **El Nido** (p600)
2. Trek through the skyscraping **rice terraces** around Banaue (p569) and Bontoc (p569) in North Luzon's Cordillera Mountains
3. Have a night out in **Manila** (p562), a city that never sleeps
4. Explore sunken WWII wrecks and kayak amid the myriad islands around **Coron** (p601)
5. Sun, sea sports and dancing till dawn on the stunning beaches of **Boracay** (p578)

6 Hop from natural spring to coral reef, to volcano, to waterfall around lush **Camiguin Island** (p597)

7 Discover unheralded **Dumaguete** (p583), in range of an enviable mix of adventures and getaways

8 Take **Cebu** (p585) by storm: partying in Cebu City, then detoxing on idyllic Malapascua Island

Metro Manila

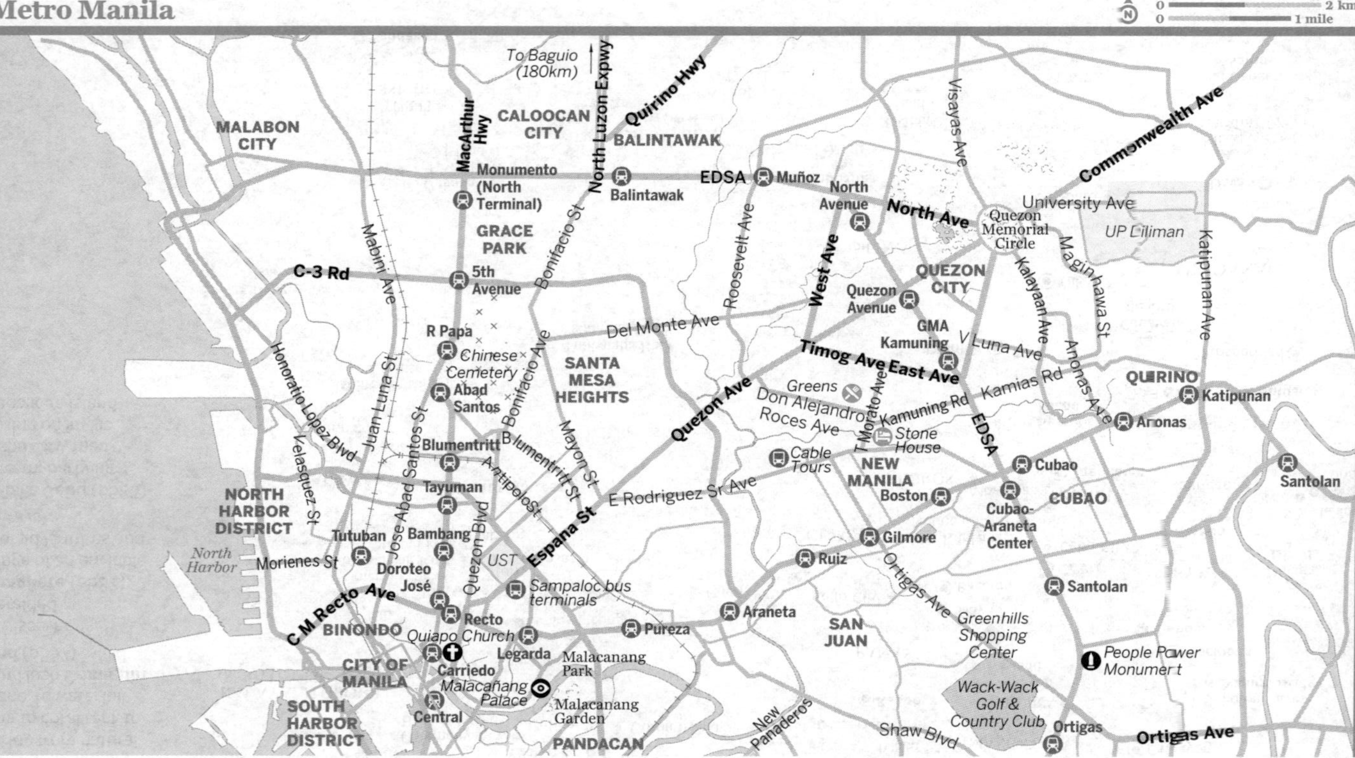

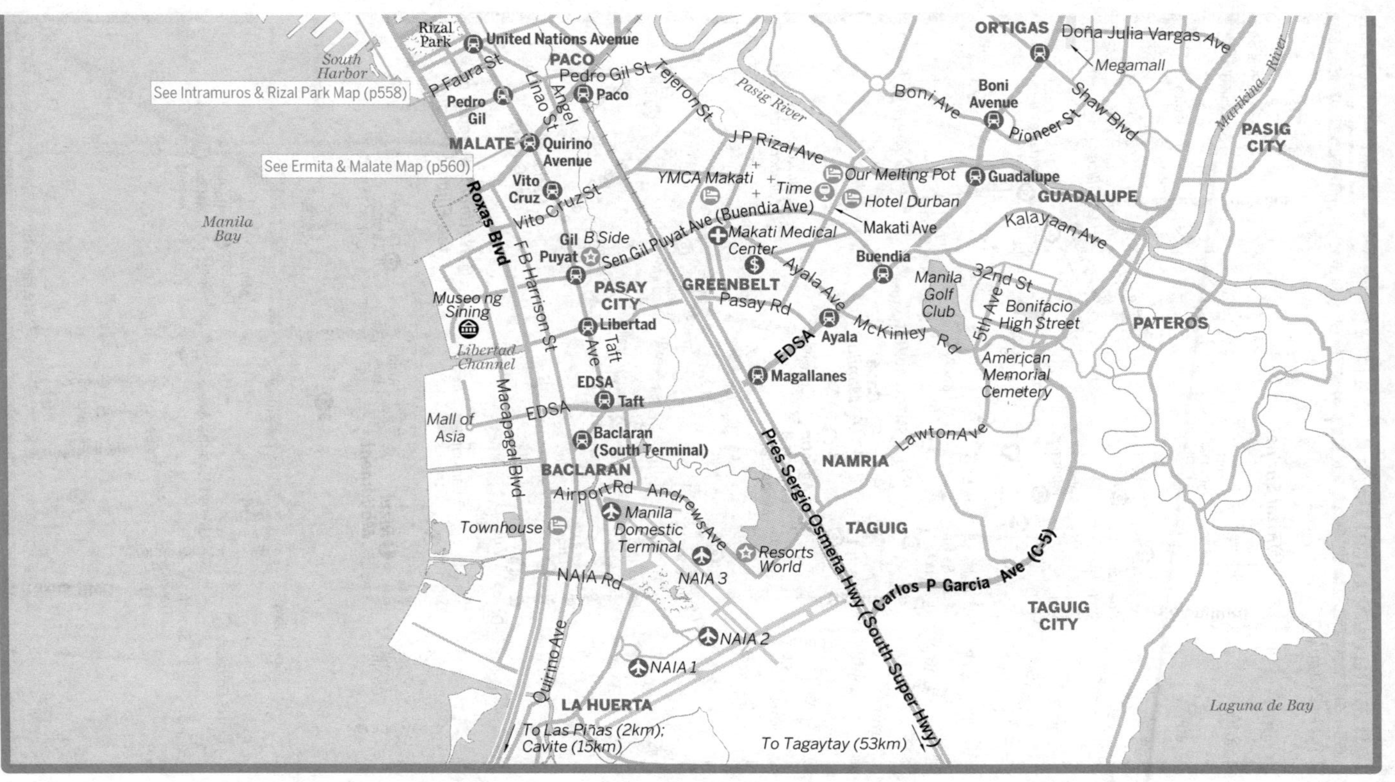

See Intramuros & Rizal Park Map (p558)

See Ermita & Malate Map (p560)

Intramuros & Rizal Park

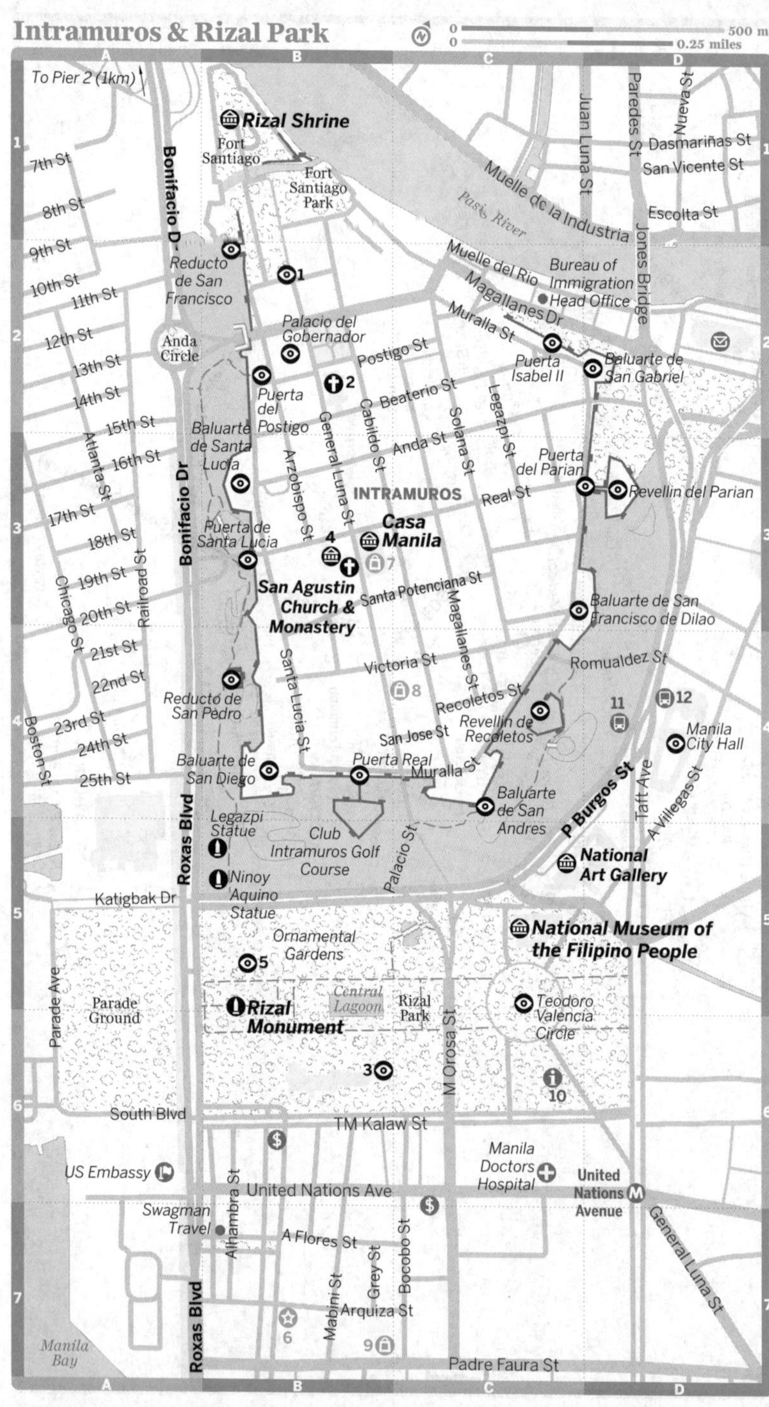

0 500 m
0 0.25 miles
To Pier 2 (1km)
Rizal Shrine
Fort Santiago
Fort Santiago Park
Pasig River
Muelle de la Industria
Muelle del Rio
Magallanes Dr
Muralla St
Bureau of Immigration Head Office
Juan Luna St
Paredes St
Nueva St
Dasmariñas St
San Vicente St
Escolta St
Jones Bridge
Bonifacio Dr
Reducto de San Francisco
Anda Circle
Palacio del Gobernador
Postigo St
Puerta del Postigo
Puerta Isabel II
Baluarte de San Gabriel
Beaterio St
Baluarte de Santa Lucia
Arzobispo St
General Luna St
Cabildo St
Anda St
Solana St
Legazpi St
Puerta del Parian
Revellin del Parian
INTRAMUROS
Real St
Casa Manila
Puerta de Santa Lucia
San Agustin Church & Monastery
Santa Potenciana St
Magallanes St
Baluarte de San Francisco de Dilao
Romualdez St
Victoria St
Santa Lucia St
Reducto de San Pedro
Recoletos St
Revellin de Recoletos
San Jose St
Baluarte de San Diego
Puerta Real
Muralla St
Baluarte de San Andres
P Burgos St
Taft Ave
A Villegas St
Manila City Hall
Legazpi Statue
Club Intramuros Golf Course
Palacio St
National Art Gallery
Ninoy Aquino Statue
Roxas Blvd
Katigbak Dr
National Museum of the Filipino People
Ornamental Gardens
Central Lagoon
Rizal Park
Rizal Monument
Parade Ave
Parade Ground
M Orosa St
Teodoro Valencia Circle
South Blvd
TM Kalaw St
US Embassy
Manila Doctors Hospital
United Nations Avenue
United Nations Ave
General Luna St
Swagman Travel
Alhambra St
A Flores St
Mabini St
Grey St
Bocobo St
Arquiza St
Manila Bay
Padre Faura St
7th St
8th St
9th St
10th St
11th St
12th St
13th St
14th St
15th St
16th St
17th St
18th St
19th St
20th St
21st St
22nd St
23rd St
24th St
25th St
Atlanta St
Chicago St
Railroad St
Boston St
A
B
C
D
1
2
3
4
5
6
7
8
9
10
11
12

three-storey Spanish colonial mansion, filled with priceless antiques.

Rizal Park PARK

One of the precious few bits of green in Manila, the 60-hectare Rizal Park (also known as Luneta; Map p558) offers urbanites a place to decelerate among ornamental gardens and a whole pantheon of Filipino heroes. Located at the bay end of the park are the **Rizal Monument** (Map p558) and the moving **site of Rizal's execution** (Map p558; admission P10; ⏲8am-5pm Wed-Sun).

National Museum of the Filipino People MUSEUM

(Map p558; T Valencia Circle, Rizal Park; adult/student P100/70, Sun free; ⏲10am-5pm Tue-Sun) The splendid National Museum of the Filipino People has interesting displays on the wreck of the *San Diego*, a Spanish galleon from 1600, plus plenty of artefacts and comprehensive exhibits on the various Filipino ethnic groups.

National Art Gallery MUSEUM

(Map p558; adult/student P100/70, Sun free; ⏲10am-4.30pm Wed-Sun) Kitty-corner to the National Museum, the art gallery contains many works of Filipino masters, including Juan Luna's impressive signature work, *Spoliarium*.

Chinese Cemetery CEMETERY

(Map p556; Rizal Ave Extension; ⏲7.30am-7pm) Boldly challenging the idea that you can't take it with you, the mausoleums of wealthy Chinese in the Chinese Cemetery, north of Binondo, are fitted with flushing toilets and crystal chandeliers. Hire a bicycle (per hour P100) to get around the sprawling grounds, and consider hiring a guide (P350) for access to the best tombs. To get here take the LRT to Abad Santos then walk or take a tricycle (P25) to the south entrance.

Ayala Museum MUSEUM

(Greenbelt 4; foreigner/resident P425/225; ⏲9am-6pm Tue-Fri, 10am-7pm Sat & Sun) Here brilliant dioramas tell the story of the Filipino quest for independence. It also houses the Philippines' best contemporary art collection.

FREE **Museo ng Sining** MUSEUM

(Museum of Art; Map p556; GSIS Bldg, CCP Complex, Pasay; ⏲9am-noon & 1-4pm Tue-Sat) More contemporary art is on display here.

Tours

Carlos Celdran WALKING TOURS

(☎0920 909 2021; http://celdrantours.blogspot.com; tours P1000-1100) If you're in Manila over a weekend, don't miss out on the flamboyant tours of Intramuros and other destinations by Carlos Celdran.

Old Manila Walks WALKING TOURS

(☎0918 962 6452; www.oldmanilawalks.com; tours P650-1100) Tour leader Ivan Man Dy has a deep knowledge of Manila and its history and culture.

Sleeping

Manila's budget accommodation is downtown around Ermita and Malate. Those looking to spend more usually stay uptown in Makati, although the downtown area also has scores of midrange and top-end

Intramuros & Rizal Park

Top Sights

- Casa Manila ... B3
- National Art Gallery ... C5
- National Museum of the Filipino People ... C5
- Rizal Monument ... B5
- Rizal Shrine ... B1
- San Agustin Church & Monastery ... B3

Sights

1. Fort Santiago Entrance ... B2
2. Manila Cathedral ... B2
3. Rizal Park ... B6
4. San Agustin Museum ... B3
5. Site of Rizal's Execution ... B5

Entertainment

6. Hobbit House ... B7

Shopping

7. La Monja Loca ... B3
8. Silahis Arts & Artifacts ... C4
9. Solidaridad Bookshop ... B7

Information

10. Department of Tourism Information Centre ... C6
- Intramuros Visitors Center ... (see 1)

Transport

11. Jeepneys to Ermita, Malate & Baclaran ... D4
12. Jeepneys to Quiapo, Sampaloc & Cubao ... D4

places that mainly cater to Asian business travellers.

MALATE & PASAY

TOP CHOICE **Malate Pensionne** INN $
(Map p560; ☎523 8304; www.mpensionne.com.ph; 1771 Adriatico St, Malate; fan dm P350, r P750-P1700; ❄@📶) This beautifully maintained and grandly atmospheric travellers' centre with hardwood detail throughout is justifiably popular. It has a three-bed men's dorm and a bigger women's dorm. It draws a mellow crowd and has a useful traveller message board. Wi-fi is paid.

Friendly's Guesthouse HOSTEL $
(Map p560; ☎489 8897, 0917 333 1418; www.friendlysguesthouse.com; 1750 Adriatico St, Malate; dm with/without air-con P375/325, s/d from P500/675; ❄@📶) Captained by the suitably friendly Benjie, this is backpacker HQ, with an air-con dorm, a great balcony-lounge area and free coffee.

Pension Natividad HOSTEL $
(Map p560; ☎521 0524; 1690 MH del Pilar St, Malate; dm P400, d P1000-1500; ❄📶) Set around a private courtyard, this popular Peace Corps volunteer roost features

Ermita & Malate

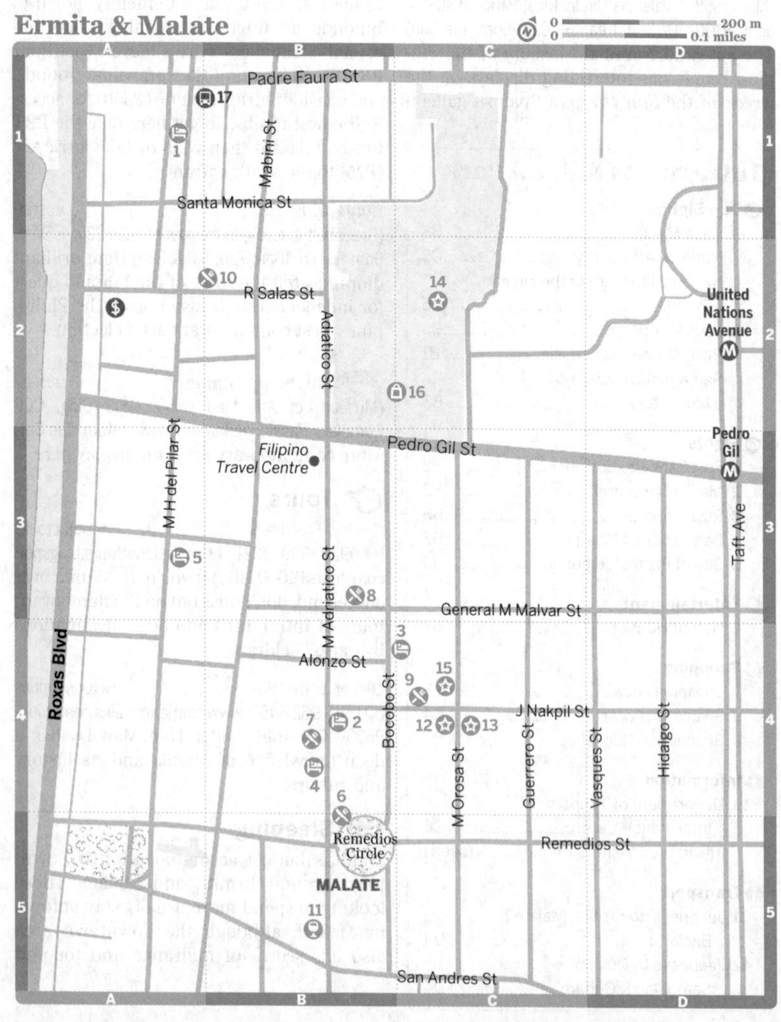

low-priced munchies and large single-sex dorms. Stay elsewhere if you want to party.

Chill-Out Guesthouse HOSTEL $
(Map p560; 450 8023; 1288 MH Del Pilar St, Ermita; dm P350, r P800-1340;) New hostel passes the eye test, with lovely and blissfully air-conditioned dorms. Location is gritty, however.

Townhouse INN $
(Map p556; 854 3826; bill_lorna@yahoo.com; 31 Bayview Dr, Parañaque; dm P180, r P300-950;) Creaky shoestring option near the airport.

Lovely Moon Pension Inn INN $
(Map p560; 524 9974; 1718 J Bocobo St, Malate; d P400-850;) Sweltering old-school Southeast Asian dive draws a mix of diehard backpackers and colourful locals.

MAKATI & QUEZON CITY

TOP CHOICE Our Melting Pot HOSTEL $$
(Map p556; 659 5443; ourmeltingpotbackpackers@gmail.com; Makati Ave cnr Gen Luna St, Makati; 2-/4-/6-bed dm incl breakfast P850/800/750, r incl breakfast P1000-1600;) Occupying an apartment within swanky A Venue Suites, OMP delivers on minimalist style (lovely beds), yet remains down-to-earth and welcoming. The place to be if you want to save pesos yet be near Makati's nightlife. Private rooms are in an annexe nearby on Kalayaan Ave.

Hotel Durban HOTEL $$
(Map p556; 897 1866; www.durbaninn.com; 4875 Durban St, Makati; r P1100-1700;) Makati's best midrange value is a tightly run ship. The immaculate rooms, with faux-wood panelling, are more than adequate for the price. It's popular, so book ahead.

YMCA Makati HOSTEL $
(Map p556; 899 6379; www.ymcamakati.com; 7 Sacred Heart St; air-con men's dm P400, r from P1100;) The tidy Makati 'Y' is in a quiet *barangay* within walking distance of the Makati business district. Such prices are rare in this zipcode.

Stone House HOTEL $$
(724 7551; www.stonehouse.ph; 1315 E Rodriguez Ave, Quezon City; r P1100-2500;) If you want to dwell in hip Quezon City during your time in Manila, this place is your best bet, with stylish rooms to suit many budgets. It's within easy walking distance of restaurant-laden Tomas Morato St.

Eating

Every style of Asian food is well represented in Manila and there are some solid French, German and Middle Eastern restaurants as well.

For vegetarian food try the dozens of Korean and Chinese restaurants in Malate and Quiapo. And note that mall food courts are always a good bet for affordable sustenance.

The city's best restaurants have mostly moved uptown to Makati's Greenbelt area and Fort Bonifacio, where a large chunk of Manila's expat community lives.

MALATE & ERMITA

For simple street fare, try Santa Monica St in Ermita or the barbecue shacks near San Andres Market in Malate. Drinking opportunities abound down here. You can quaff cheap suds curbside just west of Remedios Circle on Remedios St – dubbed the 'Monoblock Republic' because of the preponderance of brittle plastic furniture.

Ermita & Malate

Sleeping
1 Chill-Out Guesthouse A1
2 Friendly's Guesthouse B4
3 Lovely Moon Pension Inn C4
4 Malate Pensionne B4
5 Pension Natividad A3

Eating
6 Café Adriatico B5
7 Erra's Place B4
8 Hap Chan Tea House B3
9 Kuwagos Grill C4
Robinsons Place .... (see 16)
10 Shawarma Snack Center B2

Drinking
11 1951 (Penguin Cafe) B5

Entertainment
12 Bed C4
13 O Bar C4
14 Robinsons Movieworld C2
15 The Library C4

Shopping
16 Robinsons Place C2

Transport
17 Cagsawa B1
RSL .... (see 17)

TOP CHOICE Shawarma Snack Center MIDDLE EASTERN $
(p560; 485 R Salas St; pita shawarma P55, meals P100-250; 24hr;) With freshly grilled kebabs and delectable appetisers such as falafel, *muttabal,* and hummus, this street-side eatery is a gastronomic delight. Hookah pipes round out the effect.

Café Adriatico INTERNATIONAL $$
(Map p560; 1790 M Adriatico St, Malate; meals P250-500; 7am-5am;) This corner bistro is worth a splurge for the original Spanish fare with English, American and Italian effects, and for the people-watching on Remedios Circle.

Hap Chan Tea House CHINESE $$
(Map p560; 561 General M Malvar St; mains P120-250; 24hr;) Delicious, steaming platters of Hong Kong specialities are the name of the game here. It's popular for a reason.

Kuwagos Grill FILIPINO $$
(Map p560; 615 J Nakpil St, Malate; mains P100-200; 4pm-8am) This 2nd-floor open-air joint under a thatched roof is an ideal place to grab a drink and some bar food while watching the action on busy J Nakpil St.

Erra's Place BAR $
(Map p560; M Adriatico St) Cheap snacks and P29 (!!) San Miguel in a perfectly located open-air setting make Erra's a logical warm-up – or warm-down – spot.

Robinsons Place FOOD COURT $
(Map p560; Pedro Gil St, Ermita) Ermita's main mall has scores of eating options, including a food court and the always-reliable Mexicali (burritos P125) on the 2nd floor near the Pedro Gil entrance.

MAKATI & QUEZON CITY

TOP CHOICE Greens VEGETARIAN $
(92 Scout Castor St, Quezon City; 11am-10pm;) It's almost worth the long slog up to Quezon City just to sample the wonderful vego fare here. Try the 'beef' and broccoli.

Ziggurat MIDDLE EASTERN $$
(897 5179; just off Makati Ave; mains from P200; 24hr;) Don't let its location just off girlie-bar-laden P Burgos St fool you: this open-air gem is one of Makati's best-kept secrets, with an encyclopedic menu bearing Indian, Middle Eastern and African influence.

Som's Noodle House THAI $$
(5921 A Alger St, Makati; mains P150-220; 10.30am-10pm;) Filipinos generally struggle with Thai food but not Som's, which spices staples like red curry and tom yam to your liking. It's roughly behind Grilla Bar & Grill.

Grilla Bar & Grill BARBECUE $$
(cnr Kalayaan Ave & Rockwell Dr, Makati; mains P150-300) Classic Filipino 'restobar' a short walk from P Burgos St along Kalayaan Ave.

Drinking & Entertainment

You name it, it's there. That about sums up Manila nightlife. As a rule, Malate has cover bands and gay bars, Makati and the new Resorts World (Map p556) in Parañaque are where the nightclubs are, and Quezon City has the best original live music. Movies are in the malls (mostly imported blockbusters, in English, tickets P120 to P170), and theatres and performing arts troupes, including tranny shows, are scattered all over the metropolis.

Manila sadly lacks a *Time Out*-style weekly entertainment guide, but the website www.clickthecity.com fills the gap, with extensive movie and entertainment listings, as well as shopping and eating listings.

MALATE & PARAÑAQUE

The trendy nightclubs migrated from Malate long ago. What's left are a few uni clubs and lounges behind the street bars of the Monoblock Republic (aka Remedios St), live music all around, and a clutch of gay bars and clubs near the corner of J Nakpil St and M Orosa St. Scattered liberally among it all are various 'karaoke' bars, which are denser in seedy Ermita.

TOP CHOICE 1951 (Penguin Café) CAFE
(Map p560; 1951 Adriatico St; from 6pm Tue-Sat;) This legendary bar-cum-gallery has reopened in Malate after a failed move to Makati. It's a magnet for bohemian types and on Fridays and Saturdays squeezes in some of the finest musical talent in the Philippines, including, on occasion, Kalayo (see p605).

Hobbit House LIVE MUSIC
(Map p558; 521 7604; 1212 MH del Pilar St, Ermita; admission P125-150; 5pm-2am) Often forgotten amid the vertically challenged waiters is that Hobbit House consistently draws Manila's best live blues acts.

Republiq CLUB
(www.republiqclub.com; Resorts World, opposite NAIA Terminal 3, Pasay; admission varies; Wed, Fri & Sat) Metro Manila's 'it' club at the time

of research, along with neighbouring Opus Lounge.

The gay bars and clubs at the corner of J Nakpil and M Orosa Sts in Malate spill out into the streets until the wee hours on weekends and sometimes on weekdays. Popular places include tiny **O Bar** (Map p560; ⌚6pm-late), the infamous **Bed** (Map p560; ⌚Thu-Sat) and **The Library** (Map p560; www.thelibrary.com.ph; 1139 M Orosa St; admission P100-500; ⌚Thu-Sat), with comedy shows most nights.

MAKATI

Along with nearby Resorts World's two chichi clubs, the key targets for clubbers are all up in Makati. **Time** (http://timeinmanila.com; 7840 Makati Ave), opposite A Venue shopping centre, and **Palladium** (New World Hotel, Esperanza St; admission incl drink P500; ⌚Wed-Sat), behind Greenbelt 3, were pick of the litter at the time of research.

B-Side LIVE MUSIC
(Map p556; The Collective, Malugay St) Bands play most nights outside B-Side in the open-air courtyard of 'The Collective,' a conglomeration of arty-farty shops and bars. Reggae bands kick off at 4.20pm on Sundays.

SaGuijo LIVE MUSIC
(☎897 8629; www.saguijo.com; 7612 Guijo St; ⌚6pm-2am Tue-Sat) It styles itself as in indie-rock club, but it's really a cool and down-to-earth little bar where the live music is just part of the attraction.

Shopping

With a hulking shopping centre seemingly around every corner, Manila is a mall rat's fantasy. Robinsons Place (Map p560) and the mammoth **Mall of Asia** (Map p556) are the closest to the tourist belt in Malate. **Greenbelt** (Map p556; Makati Ave) is an oasis of calm in the centre of Makati.

Away from these air-conditioned temples, the masses shop in vast flea markets like Greenhills in Ortigas, or on the frenzied streets of Quiapo.

Worthy souvenir items include wood-carved Ifugao *bulol* (rice guards), *barong* (traditional Filipino shirts), lacquered coconut-shell trinkets and indigenous textiles.

Silahis Arts & Artifacts ARTEFACTS
(Map p558; 744 General Luna St, Intramuros; ⌚10am-7pm) It's almost more cultural centre than store here. Intricately woven baskets, *bulol* and textiles from North Luzon and Mindanao are some of the specialities.

La Monja Loca SOUVENIRS
(Map p558; cnr Real & General Luna Sts; ⌚9am-6pm Tue-Sun) Great selection of creative souvenirs at 'The Crazy Nun', run by celebrated tour guide Carlos Celdran.

Fully Booked BOOKS
(Mall of Asia, Pasay) Comprehensive bookstore with outstanding travel section. Located in Mall of Asia (Map p556).

Solidaridad BOOKS
(Map p558; 531 Padre Faura St, Ermita; ⌚9am-6pm) Leftie bookshop particularly good for books and documentaries on local history and politics.

Information

Dangers & Annoyances

Manila is probably no more dangerous than the next city, but it can still be dodgy, particularly after dark. The district of Tondo, particularly around the north ports, is one area to avoid walking around solo after dark. The sheltered malls of Makati are pretty darn safe, as is most of Makati's CBD. The tourist belt in Malate and especially Ermita are rife with street dwellers and destitution. They are considered relatively safe, but they don't always feel safe at night.

Traffic is the big annoyance in Manila; you'll probably spend half your time either stuck in it or talking about it. Leave extra time to get to airports, bus stations and dinner dates.

Pickpocketing is rampant on the MRT, and on major bar strips, where drunk tourists present easy prey.

Internet Access

There are internet cafes all over the place; malls such as Robinsons Place (Map p560) often have several. Rates vary from P30 to P60 per hour.

Medical Services

Makati Medical Center (Map p556; ☎888 8999; 2 Amorsolo St, Makati)

Manila Doctors Hospital (Map p558; ☎524 3011; 677 United Nations Ave, Ermita)

Money

Malate, Ermita and Makati are littered with ATMs. For cash transactions, there are numerous money changers along Mabini and Adriatico Sts but, as always, be careful when using these services.

The following are particularly useful:

American Express (☎524 8681; Ground fl Eurovilla 1, Rufino St cnr Legazpi St, Makati; ⌚9am-5pm Mon-Fri) For US-dollar travellers cheques.

HSBC main office (Map p556; 6766 Ayala Avenue, Makati) Allows P40,000 withdrawals.

SCAM CITY

Manila is notorious for scams that target tourists. The most common scam involves confidence tricksters posing as a group of friends or a family and befriending (usually solo) travellers. They eventually invite them home or on a short excursion. The situation ends with the traveller being drugged and robbed. If you feel that a stranger is acting overly friendly, walk away. Also, beware of people who claim to have met you before or claim to be staying in your hotel.

Be wary of the money changers along MH del Pilar and Mabini Sts in Ermita. Some have been known to use amateur-magician card tricks to cheat you.

Rigged taxi meters are becoming more common. If you see the meter changing within the first 500m and/or racing up suddenly, you're being had. Ten minutes in a properly metered taxi in normal Manila traffic should bring you to P50 to P80.

Post

Manila Central Post Office (Map p558; Magallanes Dr; ⌚6am-6.30pm Mon-Fri, 8am-noon Sat) A landmark, offers full services.

Tourist Information

Department of Tourism Information Centre (DOT; Map p558; ☎524 2384; www.visitmyphilippines.com; TM Kalaw St; ⌚7am-6pm Mon-Sat) This large, friendly office is in a beautiful pre-WWII building at the Taft Ave end of Rizal Park. Hands out maps and some interesting walking tours. There are also smaller DOT offices at the various NAIA terminals.

Travel Agencies

Malate and Ermita are filled with travel agencies that can help with domestic air and bus tickets (for a fee).

Filipino Travel Center (Map p560; ☎528 4507-9; www.filipinotravel.com.ph; cnr M Adriatico & Pedro Gil Sts; ⌚8am-6pm Mon-Fri, 9am-5pm Sat) Catering to foreign tourists, this agency organises a wide variety of tours; can buy Banaue bus tickets.

Getting There & Away

Train

Philippine National Railways (PNR; ☎319 0041) runs from Tutuban Station in Tondo (Map p556) to Naga (seat/sleeper/executive P548/950/1425, 10 hours) in Southeast Luzon with five quick stopovers in Lucena, Hondagua, Tagkawayan, Cagay and Sipocot. Trains leave at 6:30pm from both stations.

Air

Ninoy Aquino International Airport (NAIA; code MNL; Map p556) is about 6km south of Malate, in Parañaque. It has four separate terminals – see the boxed text 'Terminal Chaos' on p611 for information on which terminal to use. See p611 and p612 for details on international and domestic routes and airlines flying in and out of NAIA. Airlines have offices at the terminal where they are based, and some also have satellite offices in Makati.

Boat

Manila's port is divided into two sections, South Harbor and the hardscrabble, hard-to-reach North Harbor. The following are the two main lines operating long-haul ferries out of Manila to most major cities in the Visayas, Mindanao and Palawan. Full schedules are on their websites.

Negros Navigation (☎554 8777; www.negrosnavigation.ph; Pier 2, North Harbor)

SuperFerry (☎528 7000; www.superferry.com.ph; Pier 15, South Harbor) Also has a ticket office on Level 1 of Robinsons Place in Ermita.

Bus

Confusingly there's no single long-distance bus station in Manila. The terminals are mainly strung along EDSA, with a cluster near the intersection of Taft Ave in Pasay City to the south, and in Cubao (part of Quezon City) to the north. Another cluster is north of Quiapo in Sampaloc. If you're confused, just tell a taxi driver which station you want in which city (eg 'the Victory Liner terminal in Cubao'), and they should know where it is. Buses heading into Manila will usually just have 'Cubao', 'Pasay' or 'Sampaloc' on the signboard.

Comfortable 27-seat 'deluxe' express buses – usually overnight – are available to Legazpi via Naga in southeast Luzon, and to Vigan and Baguio in North Luzon. It's recommended to book these, and the direct night bus to Banaue, a day or more ahead.

NORTH LUZON Useful bus companies:

Cable Tours (Map p556; St Luke's Medical Center, E Rodriquez St, Quezon City) Nightly bus to Bontoc (P650, 12 hours).

Florida Bus Line (☎743 3809; cnr Extremadura & Earnshaw Sts, Sampaloc) Buses to Solano (hourly) and on-and-off buses to Banaue (P450, eight hours).

Ohayami (☎516 0501; Loyola St cnr Cayco St, Sampaloc) Nightly bus to Banaue (P450, eight hours).

Partas Pasay Terminal (☎851 4025; EDSA cnr Tramu St) Hourly buses to Vigan (air-con/deluxe P700/820, 8½ hours).

Victory Liner Cubao (☎727 4534; cnr EDSA & New York Ave); Pasay (☎833 5020; cnr EDSA & Taft Ave) Hourly buses to Baguio (air-con/deluxe P450/715; 6/4½ hours) and Solano (frequent).

CLARK AIRPORT Philtranco runs a convenient shuttle service to Clark airport, with four trips daily from its Pasay station (P450, 1¾ hours), stopping to pick up passengers at Megamall (Map p556; P400, 1½ hours) in Ortigas. Partas runs two daily trips to Clark from its Pasay terminal. Another option is to take any northbound bus north to Dau (near Angeles), a short taxi ride from Clark.

BATANGAS, PUERTO GALERA & TAGAYTAY For Puerto Galera on Mindoro, two companies run bus/boat services, leaving around 8am from Ermita. These take about four hours and cost roughly P350 more than fending for yourself:

Swagman Travel (Map p558; ☎523 8541; www.swaggy.com; 411 A Flores St, Ermita) Tickets P850.

Si-Kat (☎521 3344; Citystate Tower Hotel, 1315 Mabini St, Ermita) Tickets P700.

Air-con buses to Batangas pier cost P180 and take about 1½ hours. Companies leaving roughly every 20 minutes throughout the day include the following:

JAM Transit (cnr Taft & Sen Gil Puyat Aves, Pasay)

DLTB (cnr Taft & Sen Gil Puyat Aves, Pasay)

For Tagaytay take a bus bound for Nasugbu or Matabungkay from the 'Pasay Rotunda' terminal at the corner of Taft Ave and EDSA in Pasay. BSC/Batman has frequent trips.

SOUTHEAST LUZON The hub for Bicol-bound buses is the newly relocated **Araneta Bus Terminal** (Btwn Times Sq Ave & Gen Romulo Ave, Cubao, Quezon City). RSL and Cagsawa have overnight buses straight from Ermita. Expect to pay about P680 for air-con buses to Naga (eight hours) and P800 to Legazpi (10 hours). 'Deluxe' services are quicker and cost more. To save money, take one of the myriad 'ordinary' (non-air-con) buses that leave from the Araneta Bus Terminal.

Cagsawa (Map p560; ☎525 9756; Padre Faura St, Ermita) Has two night trips to Naga/Legazpi.

Isarog Bus Lines (☎482 1600; Araneta Bus Terminal, Cubao) Runs super-comfortable deluxe and air-con buses to Naga (six daily) and Legazpi (six daily).

Philtranco Pasay Terminal (☎851 8078/9; cnr EDSA & Apelo Cruz St) Buses head to Naga (twice daily) and Legazpi (twice daily).

RSL (Map p560; ☎525 7077; Padre Faura St, Ermita) Has a nightly bus to Legazpi via Naga.

Getting Around

Epifanio de los Santos Ave (EDSA; Map p556) is the main artery that links downtown Manila with Makati, Ortigas and Quezon City. The MRT line conveniently runs right along EDSA, and links with the LRT at Taft Ave.

For tips on taxi travel, see p613 and p565.

Bus

Buses that run along EDSA are a decent alternative to the packed MRT at rush hour. There are also buses to Makati from Malate via Sen Gil Puyat Ave (Buendia Ave). Destinations are displayed in the bus window. Fares are from P8 on regular buses, and P10 on air-con services.

Jeepney

Heading south from Ermita/Malate along M H del Pilar St, 'Baclaran' jeepneys end up on EDSA just west of the Pasay bus terminals and just east of Mall of Asia. Going north from Ermita/Malate along Mabini St, jeepneys (Map p558) go to Rizal Park before heading off in various directions:

GETTING INTO TOWN: MANILA

Manila's airport situation is a mess (see the boxed text, p611). Since there are no direct public transport routes from either of the four terminals to the tourist belt in Malate, bite the bullet and take a taxi, especially if you have a lot of luggage. Avoid the white, prepaid 'coupon' taxis that charge set rates of more than P400, and look for the yellow airport metered taxis. These have a flagfall of P70 (taxis on the street have a P40 flagfall). Your total bill to Malate should be about P170. To save a few pesos you can walk upstairs to the arrivals area of any of the terminals and angle for a regular metered taxi on a drop-off run. The Domestic terminal does still have a rank of white regular metered taxis.

If you arrive in Manila by boat, you're also better off catching a taxi into town, as the harbour is a pretty rough area and public transport routes are complicated.

With the number of different bus stations in Manila, if you arrive by bus you could end up pretty much anywhere. Luckily, most terminals are located on or near Manila's major artery, Epifanio de los Santos Ave (EDSA), linked to the tourist belt in Malate by MRT and LRT (see p566 for tips on using Manila's metro).

'Santa Cruz' and 'Monumento' jeepneys take the MacArthur Bridge, passing the main post office, while 'Cubao' and 'Espana' jeepneys (Map p558) traverse the Quezon Bridge to Quiapo church before peeling off to, respectively, the Cubao and Sampaloc bus terminals.

Train

There are three elevated railway lines in Manila. The most useful, if you are staying in the Malate/Ermita tourist belt, is the LRT-1, which runs south along Taft Ave to the MRT interchange at EDSA near the Pasay bus terminals, and north to Quiapo. From the EDSA interchange, the MRT runs north to Makati and Cubao. The Metro Manila map (p556) shows all metro routes. Prices start from P12, and trains run between 4am and midnight. During rush hour, these trains can get mosh-pit crowded.

AROUND MANILA

Several worthy excursions offer opportunities to escape the oppressive heat and traffic of Manila. Aside from the following, there's good wreck diving and hiking north of Manila at Subic Bay, or you can climb Mt Pinatubo, site of a cataclysmic volcanic eruption in 1991. The latter is easiest as an organised tour through Filipino Travel Center (p564); departure is pre-dawn from Manila or slightly later from Angeles.

Tagaytay

046 / POP 61,500 / ELEV 640M

Views just don't come much better than those served up in Tagaytay, a popular weekend retreat located 60km south of Manila. From the town's 15km-long ridge you peer right down into the maw of eerie **Taal Volcano**, which rises out of **Taal Lake** 600m below. There are dozens of *inahaw* (barbecue) eateries situated along the ridge, from where you can kick back with a beer and a stick of meat, and just enjoy the vista.

If you wish to get closer to the action, charter a *bangka* (P1500) to 'Volcano Island' from **Talisay**, on the lake's northeast shore, and do the sweltering walk up to Taal Volcano's crater (45 minutes).

Accommodation in Tagaytay and Talisay is rather expensive, so consider a day trip from Manila or visit on your way to Puerto Galera. If you want to stay a night, your best budget bet is **Java Jazz B&B** (860 2699; http://javajazzcoffee.blogspot.com; 442 Calamba Rd; r incl breakfast P980-1400; ❄) on Tagaytay's long ridge road.

From Manila, **BSC/Batman** (Pasay Rotunda Bus Terminal, cnr EDSA & Taft Ave, Pasay) has frequent buses to Nasugbu, which rumble through Tagaytay (P80, 1½ hours). Talisay is a 25-minute jeepney (P35, infrequent) or tricycle (P200) ride straight downhill from Tagaytay.

Batangas

043 / POP 295,000

Batangas is an industrial city that is the jumping-off point to Puerto Galera on Mindoro (see p585 for information on boats heading to Puerto Galera). Frequent buses from Manila go straight to Batangas pier along the newly extended STAR Expressway. See p565 for bus companies.

NORTH LUZON

Luzon's north is a vast expanse of misty mountains, sprawling plains and endless coastline. The region's trophy piece is the central mountainous area known as the Cordillera, where the Ifugao built their world-famous rice terraces in and around Banaue more than 2000 years ago. Elsewhere, historic Vigan boasts a colonial hub that is the country's best-preserved vestige of its Spanish heritage. Explorers can continue north of Vigan to Luzon's wild northern tip, where remote white-sand beaches embrace the coastline and rarely visited islands lurk offshore.

The Cordillera

Most who venture into North Luzon set their sights squarely on the Cordillera, a river-sliced hinterland of lush green forests covering hectare after hectare of jagged earth. The amazing rice terraces near Banaue are perhaps the Philippines' most iconic site, yet they receive relatively few tourists. Lesser known but no less spectacular terraces exist throughout the Cordillera, most notably around Bontoc. Hippie-esque Sagada has a few terraces of its own, although the main attractions there are caving, hiking and the laid-back ambience.

The tribespeople of the Cordillera, collectively known as the Igorot, are as compelling as the landscape, and it's worth studying their culture if you're heading up this way.

In remote areas you may observe *cañao* (sacrificial ceremonies) and see elders wearing indigenous garb such as G-strings (loin cloths).

Throw a poncho in your bag, as the Cordillera can get chilly at night. There are no functioning ATMs outside of Baguio so bring cash, but not too much because you'll only need about P1000 a day.

Getting There & Around

The usual way into the Cordillera is via Baguio or Banaue, although more obscure routes exist. Rainy season landslides often close the Cordillera's twisting roads, so pack patience. The Halsema 'highway' linking Banaue with Bontoc is mostly sealed. A real engineering feat when it was built in the 1920s, the Halsema snakes along a narrow ridge at altitudes up to 2255m, offering great views of precipitous valleys, green rice terraces and the Philippines' third-highest peak, Mt Pulag (2922m).

BAGUIO

074 / POP 302,000 / ELEV 1450M

Vibrant, woodsy and cool by Philippine standards, Baguio (*bah*-gee-oh) is the Cordillera's nerve centre. The Philippines' 'summer capital' was founded as a hill station for the US military in the early 1900s. A university town, Baguio is known for live-music bars, artist colonies, faith healers and funky restaurants. Unfortunately, even without tricycles (which can't make it up the hills), Baguio has major air- and noise-pollution problems. The city's charm lies well outside the centre, in pine-forested parks such as Camp John Hay.

Sights

City Market MARKET

Baguio is a shopping mecca where you can find all manner of handicrafts, including basketwork, textiles, Ifugao woodcarvings and jewellery (silver is a local speciality). Bargain hunters might check out the lively city market near the west end of Session Rd – it's an infinite warren of stalls selling everything from knock-off handicrafts to fresh-grilled chicken foetus.

Tam-Awan Village CULTURAL CENTRE

(446 2949; www.tam-awanvillage.com; Long-Long Rd, Pinsao; admission P50) Eight traditional Ifugao homes and two rare Kalinga huts were taken apart and then reassembled on the side of a hill at the artist colony Tam-awan Village. Spending the night in one of these huts is a rare treat. You can participate in art workshops, learn dream-catcher making and see indigenous music and dance demonstrations. On clear days there are wonderful views of the South China Sea. To get here, take a Quezon Hill-Tam-awan or Tam-awan-Long-Long jeepney from the corner of Kayang and Shagem Sts.

Sleeping

The most unique choice is **Tam-awan Village** (s/d P500/900), but note it's at least a 15-minute ride from the centre.

Blue Mountain Hotel HOTEL $

(443 8411; Marcos Hwy; d from P600; P) The well-furnished rooms here are kept obsessively clean and represent some of the best bang for your buck in Baguio.

Baguio Village Inn INN $

(442 3901; 355 Magsaysay Ave; s P300, d P600-1500) This warm and inviting backpacker special is reminiscent of the cosy pinewood guesthouses in Sagada. Only the noisy location, beyond the Slaughterhouse Bus Terminal, spoils the illusion.

Burnham Hotel INN $$

(442 2331; www.burnhamhotelbaguio.com; 21 Calderon St; d from P985;) This graceful place off Session Rd is beautifully adorned with local handicrafts, although some rooms are in need of TLC and we've heard animals frolicking in the ceilings.

Mile Hi-Inn HOSTEL $$

(446 6141; Mile Hi Center; dm/d P600/1800) Immaculate four-bed dorms within peaceful Camp John Hay, a 10-minute FX van ride from Session Rd.

Eating

Baguio has some truly unique eateries that are worthy of a few extra pesos – think funky, earthy and often vegetarian.

SPLURGE: VILLA CORDILLERA

A woodsy lodge overlooking Baguio Country Club on the city outskirts, **Villa Cordillera** (619 2062; www.villacordillera.com; 6 Outlook Dr; d/tr/q P1600/2400/3200;) is so quiet you'll hardly realise you're in Baguio. Rooms are spiffy with wood floors and tightly made single beds. Sample the home-baked raisin bread.

TOP CHOICE Cafe by the Ruins FUSION $$
(25 Chuntug St; mains P150-325;) The 'ruins' in this case are merely the former residence of an ex-governor, but the effect is still sublime, and the organic, Cordillera-inspired Filipino food as original as the ambience.

Bliss Cafe VEGETARIAN $$
(www.blissnbaguio.multiply.com; Elizabeth Hotel lobby, 1 J Felipe St; mains P150-250; 11am-9pm;) Owner-chef Shanti home cooks delectable vegetarian pasta and a few Indian dishes. Art-house flicks are shown every Sunday evening.

Oh My Gulay VEGETARIAN $$
(La Azotea Bldg, Session Rd; mains P150-250; 11am-8.30pm;) Baguio's most creative interior is five storeys up under a vast atrium. The mercifully compact all-vegetarian menu is equally creative.

Flying Gecko FILIPINO $$
(444 9372; 102 Session Rd; sandwiches P145-220) Tranquil oasis on Session Rd that does decent Filipino fusion fare.

Drinking

Worthy watering holes include the following:

Red Lion Pub/Inn PUB
(92 Upper General Luna Rd) Expat fave.

Rumours BAR
(56 Session Rd) Peace Corps volunteer hang-out.

City Tavern PUB
(cnr Abanao & Chuntug Sts; 8am-3am) Atmospheric live-music establishment.

18 BC BAR
(16 Legarda Rd; 6.30pm-late) Another good place for live music, especially reggae

Nevada Square BARS, CLUBS
(Loakan Rd off Military Circle) Collection of bars and clubs with a raucous, fraternity-party atmosphere

Information

Session Rd hosts a number of internet cafes, banks and telephone offices. **Cordillera Regional Tourist Office** (442 6708; Governor Pack Rd) has information on tours throughout the Cordillera.

Getting There & Away

Sky Pasada (in Manila 02-912 3333; www.skypasada.com) operates flights to and from Manila, Batanes and other North Luzon destinations.

Victory Liner (619 0000; Upper Session Rd) has express buses to/from Manila along the Subic–Clark–Tarlac Expressway (P715, 4½ hours, five daily). Otherwise you are looking at a six-hour trip with one of several bus companies that operate from Governor Pack Rd.

GL Lizardo has hourly buses until 1pm to Sagada (P230, 6½ hours) from the **Dangwa Terminal** (Magsaysay Ave), a five-minute walk north of Session Rd. **D'Rising Sun** buses to Bontoc (P220, six hours) leave hourly until 4pm from the **Slaughterhouse Terminal** (Magsaysay Ave), five minutes by jeepney beyond the Dangwa Terminal. Both routes follow the Halsema Hwy.

KMS and **Ohayami** have several buses to Banaue (P465, 8½ hours) each day along the sealed, southern route via Solano. Their terminals are near each other on Shanum St, west of Burnham Park.

SAGADA

POP 1550 / ELEV 1547M

The epitome of mountain cool, Sagada (1477m) is where you go if you want to escape from civilisation for a few days – or months. **Caves**, **peaks**, **waterfalls** and **hanging coffins** beckon the active traveller, while more sedate types can just kick back with a hot drink and a book and revel in Sagada's delightfully earthy ambience. Try to time your visit for a *begnas* (traditional community celebration), when the hearty Kankanay locals gather in *dap-ay* (meeting places) to bang gongs, smoke pipes, swill brandy and sacrifice chickens.

Take a guide for any trekking or caving you do around here or you'll almost surely get lost; grab one (per day P600 to P1000) at the tourist information centre, where you can also snag a map (P10) and hire a private jeepney if need be. Our favourite excursion is the thrilling half-day **cave connection**.

Sleeping

Sagada's basic but charming guesthouses, featuring cosy linens and buckets of hot water (P50), are a delight.

Sagada Homestay GUESTHOUSE $
(0919 702 8380; s/d P250/500;) It's not really a homestay, but it's nonetheless friendly, eminently affordable and loaded with character born of polished pine. It also boasts righteous views.

George Guesthouse GUESTHOUSE $
(0918 548 0406; s/d from P200/400;) The George offers exceptional value rooms, friendly service, clean sheets and reliable wi-fi. A large double room with a TV costs P600 – a veritable splurge in Sagada.

WORTH A TRIP

THE MUMMIES OF KABAYAN

A road heading north out of Baguio for 50 winding kilometres leads to picturesque **Kabayan**, the site of several caves containing eerie mummies entombed centuries ago by the Ibaloi people. Some of these caves can be visited, while others are known only to Ibaloi elders. After exploring Kabayan for a day or two, you can walk back to the Halsema Hwy (about five hours, straight uphill) via the **Timbac Caves**, the spot where the best-preserved mummies lurk. The keys are with a caretaker who lives up the hill from the caves. From the caves, it's about a 45-minute walk out to the Halsema Hwy.

Sagada Guesthouse GUESTHOUSE $
The rustic, cheerful doubles here, overlooking the central square, are perhaps the best value in town.

Eating

Sagada has a few surprisingly good eating options.

TOP CHOICE **Log Cabin** FUSION $$
(0920 520 0463; mains P150-250; dinner) The fireplace dining here hits the spot on those chilly Sagada evenings. On Saturdays there's a wonderful buffet (P350; prepaid reservations only) prepared by a French chef.

Yoghurt House FUSION $
(breakfasts P60-140, mains P85-160) Fuel up here with mountain coffee and the trademark yoghurt muesli breakfasts before a long day of hiking or caving. Also has a book exchange.

Bana's Cafe CAFE $
(breakfasts P100, mains P130-150;) This artsy place specialises in coffee and breakfast (great omelettes). Its narrow balcony overlooks a gorge and catches the morning sun.

Information

Golinsan Internet Café (per hr P40; 8am-8.30pm) Below Alfredo's Cabin.

Getting There & Away

There are jeepneys to Bontoc every hour until 1pm (P40, one hour). The last bus to Baguio leaves at 1pm (see p568 for details). For Manila, you must transfer in Baguio, Bontoc or Banaue.

BONTOC

074 / POP 3300

This Wild West frontier town is the central Cordillera's transport and market hub. You can still see tribal elders with full-body tattoos and G-strings strolling the streets, especially on Sunday when people descend from the surrounding villages to sell their wares at Bontoc's bustling market. Make a point of visiting the **Bontoc Museum** (admission P50; 8am-noon & 1-5pm), which has fascinating exhibits on each of the region's main tribes. Check out the grisly photos of head-hunters and their booty.

There's some mint trekking to be done around Bontoc, most notably to the stone-walled **rice terraces of Maligcong**, which rival those in Batad. To really get off the beaten track, head even further north into Kalinga Province, where you can hike to remote villages and meet aged former head-hunters. Ask around the hotels for **Kinad** (0929 384 1745) for treks around Bontoc, or Francis Pa-In for Kalinga treks. Guides cost about P1000 per day.

If you are staying a night, **Churya-a Hotel & Restaurant** (0906 430 0853; darwin_churyaa@yahoo.com; s/d/tr P250/400/700) has clean if unspectacular rooms, and a pleasant balcony over Bontoc's main street.

Cable Tours has the only direct bus to/from Manila, leaving Bontoc daily at 3pm (P650, 12 hours) and leaving Manila nightly at 8.30pm. It goes via Banaue (P120, two hours). Also to Banaue there is a jeepney around noon and several morning buses. Jeepneys to Sagada (P40, one hour) leave hourly until 5.30pm. For buses to Baguio, see p568.

BANAUE & THE RICE TERRACES

074 / POP 2600

Banaue is synonymous with the Unesco World Heritage-listed Ifugao rice terraces, hewn out of the hillsides using primitive tools and an ingenious irrigation system some 2000 years ago. Legend has it that the god Kabunyan used the steps to visit his people on earth.

The Ifugao by no means had a monopoly on rice terraces in the Cordillera, but they were arguably the best sculptors, as the mesmerising display above Banaue suggests. Banaue proper – a ragged collection of tin-roofed edifices along a ridge – often spoils things for those looking for a perfect first ooh-and-aah moment. But you can't argue with the setting. Meanwhile, that perfect ooh-and-aah moment is not too far away, in Batad.

Two kilometres north of town you can ogle rice terraces to your heart's content at the **viewpoint**; a tricycle there and back costs P200. If your heart's still not content, there are similarly impressive specimens lurking in nearby Bangaan, Hapao, Kiangan and of course Batad.

The weather tends to be a bit more volatile in Banaue than in more western parts of the Cordillera. Incessant fog and rain can ruin the view for weeks. Call the Tourism Information Centre to get a weather update before setting out.

Sleeping & Eating

Uyami's Greenview Lodge GUESTHOUSE $
(☎386 4021; www.ugreenview.wordpress.com; s P250, d P500-1500;) It's the busiest place in town so it must be doing something right. The rooms are cosy and clean, with shiny parquet floors, and there's a rustic restaurant downstairs.

Sanafe Lodge & Restaurant GUESTHOUSE $
(☎386 4085; www.sanafelodge.com; s/d/ste P400/700/1200) Has the best-looking rooms in the centre and the best terrace views, but lacks the convivial ambience of Greenview.

People's Lodge GUESTHOUSE $
(☎386 4014; s/d from P250/500;) Service couldn't be friendlier at this sweet-value spot, with fine views and a popular if ugly restaurant.

Stairway Lodge & Restaurant GUESTHOUSE $
(r per person P250) Acceptable rooms for the price. It's a little past Greenview.

Information

The **Tourist Information Centre** (☎386 4010; ⏲6am-7pm) adjacent to the plaza arranges accredited guides (full day P1200) and private transport according to a remarkably transparent list of prices. Good little maps of the main hiking routes are widely available for P15. You can change dollars at poor rates at Greenview or People's Lodge.

Getting There & Away

For bus companies making the overnight trip from Manila, see p564). If you prefer daytime travel, take a bus to Solano (P375, seven hours) and continue by jeepney to Banaue (P110, 2¼ hours with a change in Lagawe).

For bus companies serving Baguio, see p568. Buses to Baguio ply the lowland route via Solano. To take the scenic highland route (ie via Bontoc and the Halsema Hwy), you must transfer in Bontoc. There's an early-morning jeepney to Bontoc, and a handful of Bontoc-bound buses pass through Banaue throughout the day (about P150, two hours).

BATAD

POP 1100

To really see the **Ifugao rice terraces** in all their glory, you'll need to trek to Batad (900m), which sits at the foot of a truly mesmerising amphitheatre of rice fields. Most of the inhabitants still practise traditional tribal customs in what must be one of the most serene, picture-perfect villages to grace the earth.

A slippery 40-minute walk beyond the village itself is the gorgeous 30m-high **Tappiya Waterfall** and swimming hole. To escape tourists altogether, hike 1½ hours to the remote village of **Cambulo**, which has several simple guesthouses.

Most guesthouses are in *sitio* (small village) Chung Chung, perched on a spectacular hill facing Batad village and the amphitheatre. Hillside Inn, Batad Pension, Rita's and Simon's Inn all have restaurants and rooms for P150 to P200 per head. They're all simple, clean and rustic, but Hillside wins our hearts with its all-round charm.

From Banaue, it's 12km over a rocky road to Batad junction, where a 4WD track leads three bone-jarring kilometres up to the 'saddle' high above Batad. From the saddle it's a 45-minute hike to Batad.

From Banaue, a few (mostly afternoon) jeepneys/buses pass by Batad junction (P50, one hour). From there you'll have to walk to the saddle. Alternatively, you can team up with other travellers and hire a private jeepney to the saddle (return P2500). Tricycles can get you to the junction (return P700). Motorcycle taxis can go all the way to the saddle (return P800).

If you are overnighting in Batad, get out to the junction early the next morning to catch jeepneys heading to Banaue.

Vigan

☎077 / POP 49,000

Spanish-era mansions, cobblestone streets and *kalesa* (two-wheeled horse carriages) are the hallmarks of Unesco World Heritage site Vigan. Miraculously spared bombing in WWII, the city is considered the finest surviving example of a Spanish colonial town. Two of Vigan's finer mansions are the **Crisologo Museum** (Liberation Blvd; admission free; ⏲8.30-11.30am & 1.30-4.30pm Tue-Sat) and

WILD ABOUT WWOOFING

You can do more than just eat the many wonderful vegetables plucked from the earth in the Cordillera Mountains. Fulfil your farming fantasies as a volunteer on one of two organic farms certified by **Willing Workers on Organic Farms** (WWOOF; www.wwoof.org).

In Pula, a *barangay* (village) of Asipulo in Ifugao Province, there's a WWOOF project run out of the **Julia Campbell Agroforest Memorial Park** (☎0905 732 2942; http://juliacampbellpark.wordpress.com, jcamgerald@yahoo.com). Julia Campbell was a US Peace Corps volunteer whose murder at the hands of a local man on the main trail to Batad in April 2007 shocked the country. The park dedicated to her is a working organic coffee farm that produces a rare type of coffee derived from the excrement of the coffee bean-eating **civet**. The park accepts both volunteers and regular tourists to enjoy electricity-free life in a small Ifugao village surrounded by natural forest. Accommodation is in basic Ifugao huts. The cost is P150 per night, or free if you're volunteering.

Closer to Baguio, the Cosalan family's organic **Enca Farm** (☎0919 834 4542; www.encaorganicfarm.com) is in Acop, Benguet, an hour north of Baguio on the Halsema Hwy. Their farm grows beans, lettuces, broccoli, carrots, radishes and coffee. Volunteers usually do about eight hours of farm work per day and sleep in rustic but cosy cottages (P250). There are caves to explore and hiking to be done on off days. Contact the farm or the **Benguet Provincial Tourism Office** (☎422 1116) in La Trinidad for help getting to the farm.

the **Syquia Mansion Museum** (Quirino Blvd; admission P20; ⏲9am-noon &1.30-5pm).

The **Vigan Town Fiesta** is in the third week of January, while the **Viva Vigan Festival of the Arts** takes place in early May.

Sleeping & Eating

It's worth paying a little extra to stay in one of Vigan's charismatic colonial homes. Prices drop from June to October.

Grandpa's Inn HOTEL **$$**
(☎722 2118; 1 Bonifacio St; d incl breakfast from P750; ❄📶) With a great restaurant, top-notch service and an impressive array of rooms in a rustic old house, this is Vigan's best value.

Hem Apartelle GUESTHOUSE **$**
(☎722 2173; 32 Gov A Reyes St; r from P600; ❄) No heritage-style lodging here: the Hem is just an air-conditioned guesthouse that's the best budget deal in town.

SPLURGE: VILLA ANGELA

A magnificent 130-year-old mansion, **Villa Angela** (☎722 2914; www.villangela.com; 26 Quirino Blvd; d/q incl breakfast from P1500/2800; ❄) has a giant *sala* (living room) festooned with fabulous antique furniture and four huge bedrooms looking much as they would have in the 18th century. One of the Philippines' true gems.

Cafe Leona FILIPINO **$$**
(Crisologo St; meals P100-300) Serves terrific Ilocano food and passable Japanese specials on the cobbled street.

Street Stalls STREET FOOD **$**
(Plaza Burgos) Evening street stalls peddle local snacks such as *empanadas* (deep-fried tortillas with shrimp, cabbage and egg) and *okoy* (shrimp omelettes).

Uno Grille BARBECUE **$**
(Bonifacio St; mains P100-180) This and coffee-shop Cafe Uno across the street are sister restaurants run by neighbouring Grandpa's Inn.

Getting There & Away

There are many companies serving Manila (p564). The three nightly 'deluxe' buses run by **Partas** (☎722 3369; Alcantara St) are the most comfortable. Partas also has about 10 daily trips to Baguio (P375, five hours).

SOUTHEAST LUZON

Fiery food, fierce typhoons and furious volcanoes characterise the adventure wonderland known as Bicol. The region's most famous peak, Mt Mayon, may just be the world's most perfect volcano. And it's no sleeping beauty, either. A steady stream of noxious fumes leaks out of its maw, and minor eruptions are frequent. Underwater, Bicol is home to one of the Philippines' top attractions: the gentle, graceful *butanding* (whale sharks) of Donsol.

You'll want to pay extra attention to the news before heading to Bicol, lest you waltz into one of the region's patented typhoons. The Pan-Philippine or Maharlika Hwy runs right through Bicol down to Matnog, where ferries cross to Samar.

Naga

054 / POP 160,516

Naga, the capital of Camarines Sur (CamSur) province, is relatively cosmopolitan by Philippine standards, with a vibrant student population and a burgeoning reputation as an adventure-sports mecca. The city centres on a pleasant double plaza that often hosts large concerts or festivals after sundown. In September the immensely popular **Peñafrancia Festival** kicks off, packing hotels to the gills. Be sure to sample the spicy local Bicol cuisine, as well as *pili* nuts (a local favourite).

Activities

CamSur Watersports Complex WAKEBOARDING
(475 0689; www.cwcwake.com; 8.30am-7pm Mon-Thu, to 9pm Fri-Sun;) The CamSur Watersports Complex, 12km south of Naga in the town of Pili, is an impressively modern cable wakeboarding centre, complete with surfer-dude music, restaurants, wi-fi and a range of accommodation. It's heaps of fun for experienced riders and beginners alike. The ever-growing list of activities on offer includes a waterpark, a go-cart track and a downhill mountain-bike facility on nearby Mt Isarog (1966m).

Mt Isarog National Park NATIONAL PARK
(admission P100) Superb hiking is available in Mt Isarog National Park, 20km east of Naga. You can launch an assault on the summit or embark on shorter hikes through the jungle lower down. Access to the national park is from the town of Panicuason, where you can find guides.

Kadlagan Outdoor Shop & Climbing Wall ROCK CLIMBING
(472 3305; http://kadlagan.i.ph; 16 Dimasalang St; 9am-7pm) The Kadlagan Outdoor Shop & Climbing Wall hires out tents and other camping gear, and guides day and overnight excursions on Mt Isarog. Jojo Villareal knows all the local rocks and routes and is usually here in the evenings. Guides cost P600 to P900 per day, excluding meals and equipment.

Sleeping

Sampaguita Tourist Inn HOTEL $
(478 7171; Panganiban Dr; s/d/tr from P350/500/1100;) Flanking the river, this is the best budget option in town, but rooms vary wildly in size and location; check some out before checking in. Several other budget hotels are nearby

Ecovillage HUTS $
(477 5636; d/q from P350/850,) The cheapest accommodation option at the Camsur Watersports Complex. The 14 basic tin shacks are set in a quiet garden and share a large, clean, locker room-style bathroom.

CBD Plaza Hotel HOTEL $$
(472 0318; www.cbdplazahotel.com; Ninoy & Cory Ave; s/d from P600/1000;) A good midrange selection, painted in bright colours. Rooms are plain but very clean and comfortable.

Eating & Drinking

'Magsaysay' jeepneys along Peñafrancia Ave lead to bar- and restaurant-loaded Avenue Sq on Magsaysay Ave. Beyond this mall is a huddle of slightly upscale restaurants and bars around Beanbag Coffee.

Geewan FILIPINO $
(Burgos St; dishes from P70; lunch & dinner;) This is a great place to sample fiery Bicol dishes such as *pinangat* (taro leaves wrapped around minced fish or pork), 'Bicol *exprés*' (spicy minced pork dish) and *ginataang pusit* (squid cooked in coconut milk).

Beanbag Coffee CAFE $
(Magsaysay Ave; 9am-midnight;) Does a great imitation of Seattle's best, only much cheaper and quite artsy. The cakes are delicious.

Lolo's Music Bar BAR $
(Avenue Sq, Magsaysay Ave; 4pm-1am;) A cool bar with plenty of room to breathe and live music from 9pm. It frowns on shorts and sandals.

Getting There & Away

Cebu Pacific and Airphil Express have frequent flights to Manila.

The bus station is over Panganiban Bridge next to brand-new SM Mall. **RSL** (472 6885) and **Cagsawa** (811 2541) go directly to Ermita in Manila, while several others go to Cubao (see p565). The deluxe night buses to/from Manila fill up fast, so book a few days ahead.

The fastest way to Legazpi is by minivan (P150, two hours) from the van terminal, opposite SM Mall. They leave when full, usually every 30 minutes, until 7pm. Air-con buses to Legazpi take much longer and cost P120, while ordinary (no air-con) buses sometimes take six hours!

Infrequent jeepneys to Panicuason depart from just off Caceres St, near the Naga City Market (P25, 30 minutes). Alternatively, take a frequent jeepney to nearby Carolina and transfer to a tricycle.

Legazpi

☎052 / POP 179,481

Charm is in short supply in the city of Legazpi, but with the towering cone of Mt Mayon hogging the horizon no one seems to notice. The city is divided into Albay District, where the provincial government offices and airport are located, and commercial Legazpi City. A steady stream of jeepneys connects the two districts along the National Hwy (Rizal St). Make the vigorous 30-minute climb up **Liñgon Hill**, north of the city near the airport, for the best views of Mt Mayon. The **Magayon Festival** in Albay District lasts the entire month of April, packing all hotels to the gills.

Sleeping

Legazpi Tourist Inn INN $
(☎820 4880; V&O Bldg, Quezon Ave, Legazpi City; s/d from P550/600; ❄📶) The best midrange option, this modern place has clean, well-kept rooms, quality TVs and lots of mirrors.

Dreams Inn & Cafe INN $
(☎820 0885; F Imperial St; s/d from P350/700; ❄) Pick what you want – TV, hot water, air-con, private bathroom, window, etc. – and adjust the price. Don't plan on throwing a party in the singles.

Sampaguita Tourist Inn HOTEL $
(☎480 6258; Rizal St, Legazpi City; s/d from P250/500; ❄) There are a ton of rooms here in case everything else is booked out. Even the simplest rooms are clean and bright, if nothing else.

Eating

Try the nightly street stalls along Quezon Ave near the Trylon Monument in Legazpi City for budget Bicol fare.

TOP CHOICE **Small Talk** FUSION $$
(Doña Aurora St near National Hwy, Albay District; mains P75-155; ⏲lunch & dinner) This delightful little eatery adds Bicol touches to its Italian fare. Try the pasta *pinangat* or 'Bicol express' pasta.

WayWay Restaurant FILIPINO $
(Peñaranda St; dishes around P100; ⏲lunch & dinner, closed Sun) Just north of Legazpi City, this is a great place to try Bicol food. A surprisingly palatable choice for the adventurous eater is *candingga* (diced pig liver and carrots sweetened and cooked in vinegar).

Information

The **Provincial Tourism Office** (☎820 6314; http://tourism.albay.gov.ph; Astrodome Complex, Aquende Dr, Albay District) hands out the excellent *EZ Map* of the city for free.

Getting There & Away

Cebu Pacific, Airphil Express and Zest Air each fly at least once daily to/from Manila.

The main bus terminal is at the Satellite Market, just west of Pacific Mall in Legazpi City. Cagsawa and RSL bus lines have night buses that go directly to Ermita in Manila, while several others go to Cubao (p565).

For options to Naga, see p572. Air-con minivans zip to Donsol roughly hourly until 5pm or so (P80, 1¼ hours) and to Sorsogon (P70, 1¼ hours, frequent), where you can pick up a jeepney to Matnog, gateway to Samar.

Around Legazpi

MT MAYON

Bicolanos sure hit the nail on the head when they named this monolith – *magayon* is the local word for 'beautiful'. The impossibly perfect slopes of the volcano's cone rise to a height of 2462m above sea level, and emit a constant plume of smoke across the flat plains and over the surrounding coconut plantations.

The spirit of the mountain is an old king whose beloved niece ran away with a young buck. The grumpy old man's pride still erupts frequently. In February 1993, an eruption killed 77 people. Shortly after lava flows subsided in 2006, a biblical typhoon triggered mudslides on Mt Mayon that killed more than 1000 people.

The mountain's 'knife edge' – the highest point to which you can climb, at about 2200m – closes from time to time but was open at the time of writing. For most people it's a 1½-day climb with an overnight at 'Camp 2' (1600m), but fit climbers can do it in a day. Guides are mandatory. The 1½-day trek costs about P7000 for one person plus about P1500 per additional person, and includes transport from Legazpi, camping equipment, porters, food etc.

The best time of year to climb Mt Mayon is February to April. From May to August it's unbearably hot; from September to January it's wet. The following organise Mt Mayon climbs: **Bicol Adventure** (☎480 2266; www.bicoladventure.com; V&O Bldg, Quezon Ave, Legazpi City) and **Mayon Outdoor Guides Association** (☎0915 422 4508; pinangat2001@yahoo.com).

DONSOL

POP 4200

Every year, between December and early June, large numbers of whale sharks *(butanding)* frolic in the waters off this sleepy fishing village about 50km from Legazpi. It's truly an exhilarating experience swimming along with these silver-spotted marine leviathans, which can reach 14m in length. In the peak months of February to May sightings are virtually guaranteed, although bad weather can make sightings more difficult. Check the forecast and contact the **regional tourism office** (☎052-482 0712, 0927 233 0364; donsoltravel@yahoo.com) in Legazpi before you visit to see if the whale sharks are in town.

When you arrive in town, head to the **Donsol Visitors Center** (⏲7.30am-5pm) to pay your registration fee (P500) and arrange a boat (P5000, good for seven people) for your three-hour tour. The Visitors Center does its best to ensure each boat is full. Each boat has a spotter and a *Butanding* Interaction Officer on board – tip them a couple hundred pesos, especially if you've had a good day. Snorkelling equipment is available for hire (P300). Scuba diving is prohibited.

Sleeping & Eating

Amor Farm Beach Resort RESORT $$
(☎0921 245 4028; amorfarmbeachresort@gmail.com; r with fan/air-con from P800/2200; ❄) A peaceful resort with cottages scattered around a garden. The fan rooms are the best value in the Visitors Center area.

Giddy's Place RESORT $
(☎0917 848 8881; www.giddysplace.com; d P600-2500; ❄📶≋) With a good bar and restaurant, a pool and a range of amenities, Giddy's has significantly upped the ante in Donsol lodging. It's opposite the market proper, 2km south of the Visitors Center.

Santiago Lodging House HOMESTAY
(Main Rd, town proper; r P700) Basically a homestay with three good, clean rooms in a beaten-up wooden house.

Hernandez Guesthouse GUESTHOUSE
(☎0906 431 4173; Main Rd, town proper; r P700-1200; ❄) Opposite Santiago, it has a handful of simple rooms.

Getting There & Away

Air-con minivans leave for Legazpi every hour until about 3pm (P80, 1¼ hours).

MINDORO

There are two sides to this large island just south of Luzon: Puerto Galera, and the rest of Mindoro. The thriving dive centre of Puerto Galera is in the heart of the Verde Island Passage – one of the world's most biologically diverse underwater environments. It's essentially an extension of Luzon.

Then there's the rest of Mindoro – an untamed hinterland of virtually impenetrable mountains populated by one of one of Asia's most primitive tribes, the Mangyan. Those who like to get *way* off the beaten track need look no further. Off the west coast, accessible from the towns of Calintaan and Sablayan, dive wonderland **Apo Reef** is populated by sharks and stingrays.

Getting There & Away

The way to Puerto Galera is by fast *bangka* ferry from Batangas on Luzon. From Batangas you'll also find frequent 'ROROs' (roll-on-roll-off, or car ferries; P192, 2½ hours) and speedy 'fastcraft' boats (P300, one hour) to Calapan in northern Mindoro, along with ferries to Abra de Ilog (P260, 2½ hours), gateway to Sablayan and Apo Reef.

Regular car ferries to Caticlan (for Boracay) depart from Roxas in southern Mindoro.

Puerto Galera

☎043 / POP 28,035

It lacks the beautiful beach, classy resorts and hip nightlife of Boracay, but this diving hot spot on the northern tip of Mindoro is conveniently located just a hop, skip and a *bangka* ride from Manila. The name Puerto Galera (PG) typically refers to the town of Puerto Galera and the resort areas surrounding it – namely Sabang, 7km to the east, and White Beach, 7km to the west. The town proper has a breathtakingly beautiful harbour, but otherwise is of little interest.

Puerto Galera finally has ATMs – an Allied Bank in PG town, and a Max Bank in Sabang.

Getting There & Around

Speedy *bangka* ferries to Puerto Galera town, Sabang Beach and White Beach leave regularly throughout the day from Batangas pier until about 4.30pm (P250, one hour). The last trip back to Batangas from Sabang leaves at 1pm or 2pm (on Sundays and in peak periods there's a later boat); from White Beach it's 3pm, and from Puerto Galera town it's 3.30pm. Be prepared for a rough crossing.

To reach Roxas, where ferries depart for Caticlan (Boracay), take a jeepney to Calapan from the Petron station in PG town (P100, 1½ hours, every 45 minutes), then transfer to a Roxas-bound van (P180, three hours).

Regular jeepneys connect Sabang and PG town during daylight hours (P15, 20 minutes); a tricycle between the two costs P100 (more at night); from Sabang to Talipanan it's P300. Motorcycle taxis are cheaper.

SABANG

Sabang is where most of the hotels, restaurants and bars are concentrated. Drinking and underwater pursuits are the activities of choice, with plenty of establishments offering variations on these themes.

Sabang's 'beach' is a narrow sliver of brown sand traversed by rivulets of sewage, and its late-night entertainment scene is less than wholesome. To escape, walk around the headland to cleaner, more laid-back **Small La Laguna Beach**, where several resorts front a brown strip of sand. Beyond that is **Big La Laguna Beach**.

Activities

Dive prices vary wildly, so shop around. **Blue Ribbon** (☎0920 823 5452; www.blueribbondivers.com; Small La Laguna Beach) and **Dive VIP** (☎287 3140; www.divevip.com) charge P1000 per dive, including equipment. An open-water course will set you back P15,000 to P20,000, with Blue Ribbon and Dive VIP offering the best rates.

Sleeping

Expect big discounts off these prices in the June-to-October low season. You'll find some great prices down at the far eastern end of Sabang Beach.

TOP CHOICE **Reynaldo's Upstairs** GUESTHOUSE $
(☎0917 489 5609; rey_purie@yahoo.com; r incl breakfast P500-1200; ❄☎) Run by a nice family, Reynaldo's has a splendid mix of more-than-passable budget fan rooms and large 'view' rooms with kitchenettes and private balconies on a hillside.

Capt'n Gregg's Dive Resort LODGE $$
(☎287 3070; www.captngreggs.com; r P800-1800; ❄@☎) This Sabang institution recently expanded after 24 years in business. The compact but cosy wood-lined 'old' rooms, right over the water, still have the most charm.

Steps Garden Resort COTTAGES $$
(☎287 3046; www.stepsgarden.com; d P1200-1900); ❄☎≋) Boasts a lovely new pool, and hillside cottages with private balconies and superb views.

Big Apple Dive Resort RESORT $
(☎287 3134; www.divebigapple.com; r P500-2000; ❄☎≋) In the middle of Sabang Beach, this is party central, with some noisy and tatty fan rooms to go with swankier digs around the pool out back.

Dive VIP INN $
(☎287 3140; www.divevip.com; r P500) The four rooms are basic but in fine shape, with patios, hot water and TVs.

Eating & Drinking

Restaurants in Sabang are, in a single word, expensive.

Tina's FILIPINO $$
(mains P155-400) Tina's has some of the best food on the beachfront, although prices have gone up recently. Do try the schnitzel.

McJim's FAST FOOD $
(sandwiches P30, fried rice P60; ⊙24hr) This basic fast-food shack next to Big Apple Dive Resort is a hit with peso pinchers.

Teo's Native Sizzling House FILIPINO $
(mains P150-300; ⊙24hr) Low-key place with a comprehensive menu of sizzling dishes, Filipino classics and steaks.

Drinking

Point Bar BAR
(El Galleon Resort) With a plum spot on the point between Sabang and Small La Laguna Beach, this is the best spot for a sundowner. The CD collection is as colourful as the cocktails.

PUERTO GALERA TOWN

The town proper boasts a row of restaurants that front the gorgeous harbour. **Badladz** (☎0927 268 9095; www.badladz-adventure-divers.com; r with P800-1200; ❄☎) has a well-regarded

Puerto Galera & Around

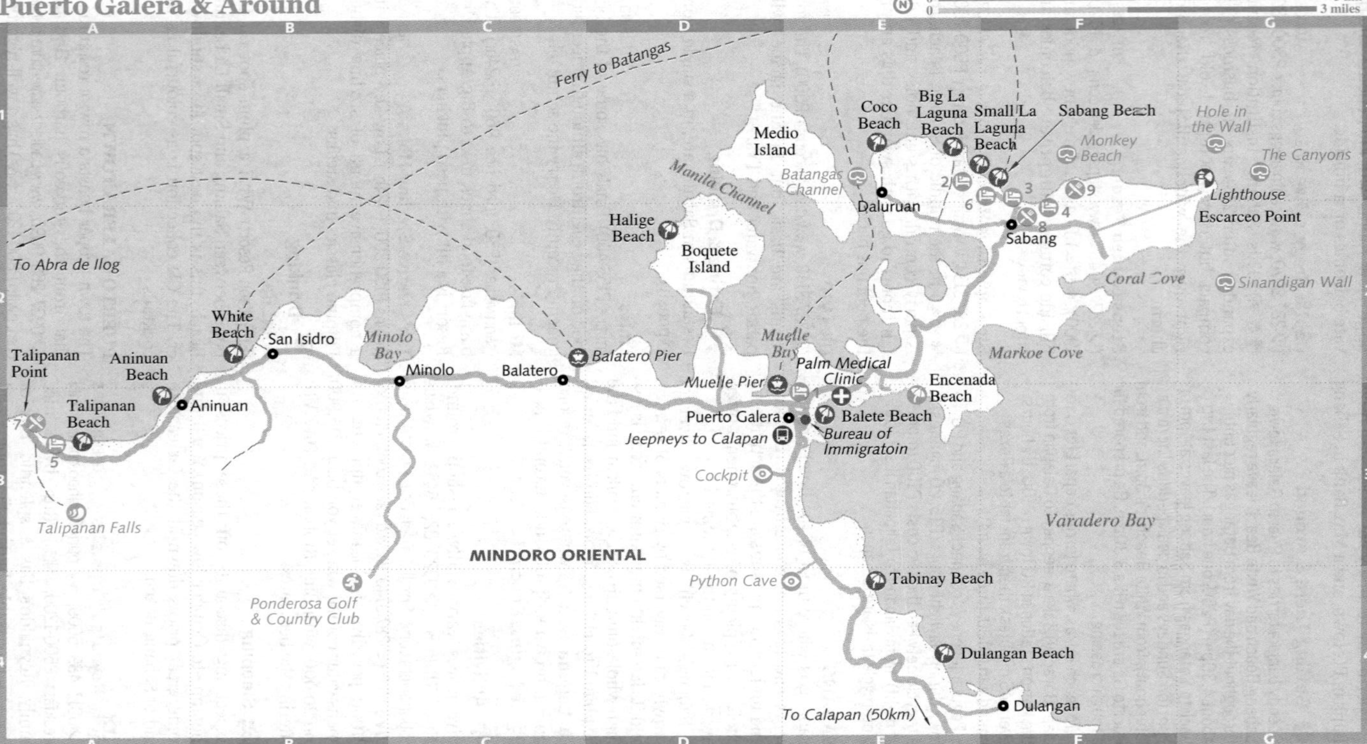

dive shop, functional if unspectacular rooms, and tasty Mexican faves like *huevos rancheros*. **Hangout Bar** (mains P150-250;) has pub grub and computers with internet access.

WEST BEACHES

About 7km west of Puerto Galera are three neighbouring beaches. First up is **White Beach**. It has a much better beach than Sabang, but accommodation is overpriced and it fills up with mobs of Manileños on weekends and in the March to May 'summer' season. During non-summer weekdays, it can be quiet and pleasant.

Next up is mellow, clean **Aninuan Beach**, but to escape the girlie bars of Sabang, a better option is attractive **Talipanan Beach**, at the end of the road in the shadow of Mt Malasimbo (860m). It's worth the trip here just to eat at **Luca's Cucina Italiana & Lodge** (0916 417 5125; info@lucaphilippines.com; mains from P180-280), ideally positioned at the isolated west end of the beach. The food is delicious, especially the pizzas, which are cooked in an outdoor brick oven.

There are a few places to stay in Talipanan, but none with rooms for under P1000 in the high season. The best are Luca's (rooms from P1500) and, next door, **El Canonero** (0915 845 4399; www.divingresortelcanonero.com; r P1300-2500;), another Italian-owned place with a dive centre and nice pool.

Puerto Galera & Around

Activities, Courses & Tours

	Blue Ribbon	(see 2)
	Dive VIP	(see 4)

Sleeping

1	Badladz	E3
	Big Apple Dive Resort	(see 6)
2	Blue Ribbon	E1
3	Capt'n Gregg's Dive Resort	F1
4	Dive VIP	F2
5	El Canonero	A3
	Reynaldo's Upstairs	(see 9)
6	Steps Garden Resort	F1

Eating

	Hangout Bar	(see 1)
7	Luca's Cucina Italiana & Lodge	A3
	McJim's	(see 6)
8	Teo's Native Sizzling House	F2
9	Tina's	F1

Drinking

	Point Bar	(see 2)

SPLURGE: BLUE RIBBON

Rooms at the newly renovated **Blue Ribbon** (0920 823 5452; www.blueribbondivers.com; Small La Laguna Beach; r P1400-2300;) are terrific value. It has a gym, pool and lovely restaurant. Divers can net room discounts.

Roxas

043 / POP 10,000

Roxas is a dusty little spot with ferry connections to Caticlan. **Roxas Villa Hotel & Restaurant** (289 2026; roxasvillahotel@yahoo.com; Administration St; s/d from P350/450;) has basic rooms in the town centre.

If you are heading to Caticlan (P400, four hours), call the **Ports Authority** (289 2813) at Roxas' Dangay pier, about 3km from the centre, to check the schedule, as departures are infrequent during the day. At the time of research **Montenegro Lines** (0932 461 9096) had a 2pm departure, a 4pm departure and several night trips; other companies had night trips only.

Vans to Calapan (P180, three hours) leave from Dangay pier and from several points in the town centre.

THE VISAYAS

If it's white sand, rum and coconuts you're after, look no further than the jigsaw puzzle of central islands known as the Visayas. From party-mad Boracay and Cebu to mountainous Leyte and Negros, to dreamy Siquijor and Malapascua, the Visayas has about everything an island nut could ask for. Hopping among paradisiacal, palm-fringed isles, you'll inevitably wonder why you can't go on doing this forever. Indeed, many foreigners *do* give it all up and live out their years managing this resort or that dive centre on some exquisite patch of white sand. Others merely end up extending their trip for weeks – or months. This is one area of the country where you can dispense with advance planning. Just board that first ferry and follow your nose.

Getting There & Around

All the major cities in the Visayas are well connected to Manila by both air and sea. Cebu City

The Visayas

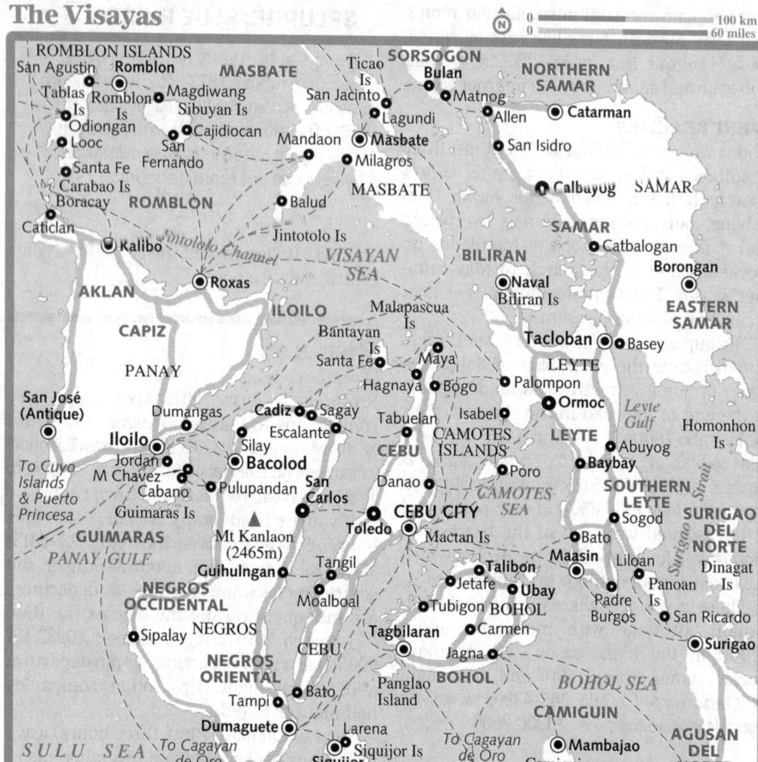

and ports in the southern Visayas have ferry connections to Mindanao.

To enter the Visayas overland from Luzon, head to Matnog on the southern tip of southeast Luzon, which is just a short ferry hop from Allen in northern Samar. Alternatively, take a bus to Batangas in southern Luzon, then a ferry to Calapan, Mindoro, a van to Roxas, and a ferry to Caticlan, Panay.

Cebu City is the Visayas' main ferry hub, and is linked to all major and minor Visayan ports by a veritable armada of zippy fastcraft and slower RORO ferries.

Panay

The large, triangular island of Panay is where you'll enter the Visayas if taking the ferry from Mindoro. To most travellers, mainland Panay is just a large planet around which orbits the diminutive party satellite Boracay island. Yet Panay has plenty to offer plucky independent travellers, including decaying forts, Spanish churches, remote thatch-hut fishing villages and the mother of all Philippine fiestas, Kalibo's Mardi Gras-like **Ati-Atihan**, which peaks in the third week of January. Panay's capital and gateway to the rest of the Visayas is Iloilo, a six-hour bus ride south of Boracay.

BORACAY

☎036 / POP 9800

With a postcard-perfect, 3km-long white beach and the country's best island nightlife, it's not hard to figure out why Boracay is the country's top tourist draw. Overdevelopment has made some old-timers long for the halcyon days of no electricity, but the debate about whether it's better now or was better then won't worry you too much when you're digging your feet into the sand on White Beach and taking in the Philippines' most famous sunset. Parasails, seabirds, frisbees and *paraw* (small *bangka* sailboats) cut across the Technicolor horizon, while palm trees whisper in the breeze and reggae wafts through the air. Oh yeah, and you're in a beachfront bar that's generously serving you two-for-one cocktails. Yes, even 'developed' Boracay remains a master mixologist of that mellow island vibe.

Most of the action is on White Beach, where three out-of-service 'boat stations' orient visitors. The area south of Station 3, known as Angol, most resembles the less-developed 'old Boracay' and is where most of the budget accommodation is located. The stretch between Station 1 and Station 3 is busy and commercial. Most top-end accommodation is on an incredible stretch of beach north of Station 1.

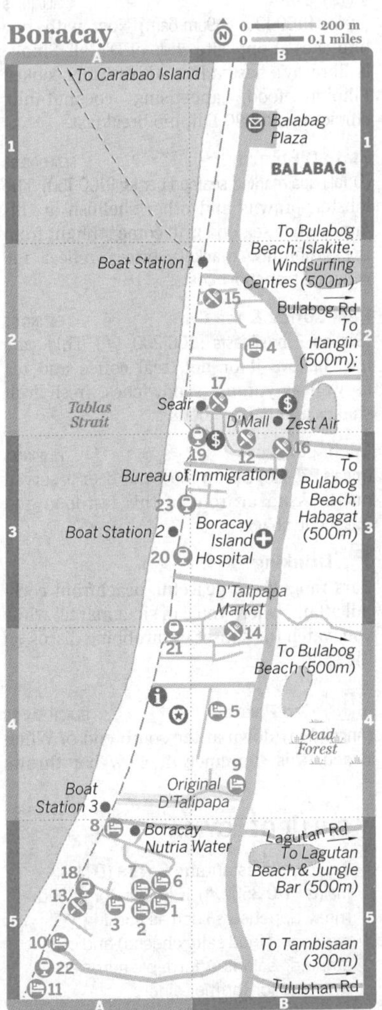

Activities

On Boracay you can try your hand at a stupendous array of sporting pursuits, including **paraw rides** (per hour P600), **diving**, **windsurfing** and **parasailing**. Daily games of **football**, **volleyball** and **ultimate frisbee** kick off in the late afternoon on White Beach.

Kitesurfing KITESURFING

From December to March, consistent winds, shallow water and rapidly inflating but still decent prices (about US$450 for a 12-hour certification course) make Bulabog Beach on the east side of the island the perfect place to learn kitesurfing. The action shifts to White Beach during the less consistent May-to-October southwest monsoon.

Operators include **Hangin** (www.kite-asia.com), **Islakite** (www.islakite.com) and **Habagat** (www.kiteboracay.com).

Sleeping

Head south of Station 3 (aka Angol) for the lower prices and mellow island vibe of yesteryear. Rates everywhere drop 20% to 50% in the low season (June to October). Bargaining might bear fruit at any time of year.

Boracay

Sleeping

1 Bora Bora Inn ... A5
2 Dave's Straw Hat Inn ... A5
3 Escurel ... A5
4 Frendz Resort ... B2
5 Jung's House Resort ... B4
6 Ocean Breeze Inn ... A5
7 Orchids ... A5
8 Sulu-Plaza ... A5
9 Trafalgar Garden & Cottages ... B4
10 Tree House ... A5
11 White Beach Divers Hostel ... A5

Eating

12 Cyma ... B3
13 Michaella's ... A5
14 Plato D'Boracay ... B4
15 Real Coffee & Tea Cafe ... B2
16 Smoke ... B3
17 Smoke ... B2

Drinking

18 Arwana ... A5
19 Epic ... B3
20 Juice ... A3
21 Nigi Nigi Nu Noos ... A4
22 Red Pirates ... A5
23 Summer Place ... A3

SPLURGE: SULU-PLAZA

At **Sulu-Plaza** (☎288 3400; www.sulu-plaza.com; r P1600-2000; ❄📶), for a very reasonable price, you get a stylish room filled with two bamboo chairs, comfy thick beds and attractive art, plus a beachfront location right at Station 3.

SOUTH OF STATION 3

White Beach Divers Hostel BACKPACKER $
(☎288 3809; www.whitebeachdivers.com; r P500-600; 📶) A stellar deal, especially if you get the spacious bamboo loft at the back, which sleeps three. Other rooms are more basic. The owner is a receptacle of knowledge about tours in the area.

Tree House RESORT $
(☎288 3601; treehouse_damario@yahoo.com.ph; dm P200, d P1000-3500; ❄) Proprietor Mario offers a wide variety of rooms spread across two complexes. The four-bed dorm rooms, behind Da Mario's tasty Italian restaurant, are the island's cheapest crash pads.

Walk-in guests are advised to walk beyond Station 3 to a cluster of about 10 resorts located up a path behind Arwana Resort. The best deal is **Ocean Breeze Inn** (www.oceanbreezeinn.info; r P900-1500; ❄), where a couple of elegant rattan-swathed garden cottages complement air-conditioned concrete rooms. Cheapest (and furthest from the beach) is **Bora Bora Inn** (☎288 3186; r P800-1800; ❄), while **Dave's Straw Hat Inn** (☎288 5465; www.davesstrawhatinn.com; r P1200-2200; ❄@📶) is cosiest and most stylish.

Other good options here are the **Orchids** (☎288 3313; www.orchidsboracay.com; r P915-2000; ❄📶) and **Escurel** (☎288 3611, 0928 341 1911; s/d from P1300/1500; ❄@📶). Haggle hard at all of the above.

NORTH OF STATION 3

Trafalgar Garden & Cottages GUESTHOUSE $
(☎288 3711; trafalgarboracay@hotmail.com; 'Original' D'Talipapa; r P650-1700; ❄) It's close to the main road yet seals off the noise well and the P650 stand-alone budget cottages with small hammocks out front are super value.

Jung's House Resort HOTEL $$
(☎288 5420; Station 2; r with fan/air-con P800/1000; ❄) The Korean owner offers up the island's cheapest air-con rooms at this tidy spot about 150m in from the beach.

Frendz Resort BACKPACKER $
(☎288 3803; frendzresort@hotmail.com; Station 1; dm P700, r P2800-3800; @📶) Frendz' dorm rooms are overpriced but much cosier than those at Tree House.

Eating

You'll find the best deals on Filipino food near two wet markets: D'Palengke in the southeast corner of D'Mall, and D'Talipapa near Station 2. Of course, it's worth paying a bit more for the ambience of White Beach – just stroll along until you see something that takes your fancy.

TOP CHOICE **Smoke** FILIPINO $
(mains P100-120; ⏲9am-6am) Now with two branches at opposite ends of D'Mall, Smoke is Boracay's best value, with freshly cooked Filipino food, appetising coconut-milk curries and a P80 Filipino breakfast.

Plato D'Boracay SEAFOOD $$
(D'Talipapa market; seafood per kg P100-150) The lobster, prawns and other shellfish at this family-style seafood grill come straight from the adjoining market; prices reflect the reduced transport costs.

Real Coffee & Tea Cafe EATING $$
(Station 1; breakfasts P100-200; 🖉) This cafe has, believe it or not, real coffee and tea as well as yummy sandwiches, fresh fruit shakes and baked goods.

Michaella's FILIPINO $
(meals P75-110) Cheap food and beer is served on the sand in front of this fast-food and barbecue shack.

Drinking

Bars range from peaceful, beachfront cocktail affairs where you can sip a mai tai while you watch the sunset to throbbing discos on the sand.

TOP CHOICE **Red Pirates** BEACH BAR $$
(Angol) Way down at the south end of White Beach, this supremely mellow bar throws

SPLURGE: CYMA

The Greek restaurant, **Cyma** (D'Mall; mains P170-350; 🖉), is known for grilled meat, appetisers such as flaming *saganaki* (fried salty cheese) and outstanding salads. Affordable gyros are available for thriftier diners.

funky driftwood furniture onto the sand and best captures the spirit of 'old Boracay'.

Nigi Nigi Nu Noos BEACH BAR $$
(Station 2; happy hour 5-7pm) The legendary mason jars of Long Island iced tea – they're two-for-one during happy hour – more than capably kick-start any evening.

Jungle BEACH BAR $$
(Lagutan Beach) Isolated on a cove at the back side of the island, hippie, trippy Jungle bar is known for three-day full-moon parties and its notorious 'F*** you Archie' cocktail. Often quiet or dead; just as often raucous.

Arwana BEACH BAR $
(happy hour 1-10pm) All-day happy hour means Boracay's cheapest San Miguel (P30) on demand.

Follow thumping beats to find the discos; about five or six of them carry momentum into the wee hours, even in the low season. **Summer Place** is rowdiest, **Epic** is most chichi, and **Juice** is the smallest and most down-to-earth.

Information

BPI (D'mall) ATMs, and there are a few others along the main road.

Metrobank (D'mall) ATMs.

Tourist Center (9am-11pm; Station 3) Offers a range of services, including internet access, postal services and money-changing facilities (including Amex travellers cheques). Also sells plane tickets and posts ferry schedules.

Getting There & Away

To get to Boracay, you must first travel to Caticlan. From Caticlan small *bangka* ferries shuttle you to Boracay's Cagban pier (P150 including terminal and environmental fee, 15 minutes). Tricycles from Cagban pier cost P150 per tricycle, or P25 per person, for central White Beach destinations.

AIR Cebu Pacific, Airphil Express, **Seair** (D'Mall) and **Zest Air** (D'Mall) have multiple flights per day from Manila to Caticlan until 4.30pm or so, while Cebu Pacific (two daily) and Airphil Express (daily) ply the Cebu–Caticlan route.

Flights to nearby Kalibo are a cheaper alternative to flying to Caticlan. Air-con vans meet flights in Kalibo and run to Caticlan pier (P160, 1½ hours).

From Caticlan airport to Caticlan pier is a five-minute walk or a one-minute tricycle ride (P50).

BOAT Caticlan is well connected by ferry to Roxas (p577), Mindoro.

BUS Ceres Lines has hourly buses to Iloilo via Kalibo from Caticlan pier, the last one departing at 4pm (P313, six hours). Speedier air-conditioned vans to Iloilo (P350) usually depart in the morning only.

SAVINGS IN A BOTTLE

Save the environment – and plenty of money – by refilling plastic water bottles at filling stations dotted along Boracay's main road. Closer to the beach, near Station 3, is **Boracay Nutria Water** (1L refill P7).

Getting Around

To get from one end of White Beach to the other, either walk or flag down a tricycle along the main road. These cost only P7 provided you steer clear of the disingenuously named 'special trips' offered by stationary tricycles, which cost a not-so-special P40 to P60.

ILOILO

033 / POP 419,000

Panay's bustling capital offers doses of culture and nightlife, and is a pleasant enough stopover on the Boracay–Negros route. For ideas try the informative **tourist office** (337 5411; Bonifacio Dr) next to Museo Iloilo.

Sights & Activities

Museo Iloilo MUSEUM
(Bonifacio Dr; admission P25; 8-11am & 2-5pm Mon-Sat) It has a worthwhile display on Panay's indigenous *ati* (negrito) people and a collection of old *piña* (pineapple fibre) weavings, for which the area is famous.

Tours

Panay Adventures ADVENTURE TOURS
(321 4329, 0917 717 1348; panay_adventures@yahoo.com.ph) Anthropologist Daisy organises ecocultural tours to visit tribal groups around Panay, mountain-bike trips on nearby Guimaras Island and climbing and caving in Bulabog Puti-An National Park.

Sleeping & Eating

Pensionne del Carmen HOMESTAY $
(0926 578 2057; 24-26 General Luna St; s/d/tr P500/550/700;) Essentially a homestay, and a brilliant one at that. Quiet and right on the river.

Highway 21 HOTEL $$
(335 1839; General Luna St; s/d from P750/875;) Terrific midrange deal.

Family Pension House PENSION HOUSE $
(335 0070; familypension@yahoo.com; General Luna St; s/d from P325/450;) Old backpacker

fave going to seed a bit, but still cheap and popular.

Bluejay Coffee & Delicatessen CAFE $$
(Gen Luna St; sandwiches/mains from P85/150;) This dreamy cafe combines the best elements of a Starbucks coffeeshop and a German deli.

Drinking & Entertainment

Smallville Complex BARS, CLUBS
(Diversion Rd) No reason to look any further for bars and nightlife, most of the action is here. Flow (admission weekends/weekdays P150/free) is the king of clubs.

Getting There & Around

There are frequent flights to Manila with Zest Air, Cebu Pacific, Airphil Express and PAL. The latter three have daily flights to/from Cebu. The airport is 15km north of town in Santa Barbara. Take a jeepney or shuttle van from the Travellers Lounge at SM City Mall.

Fastcraft operators Sea Jet, Oceanjet and Weesam Express, based at Iloilo's central Muelle Pier, take on the rough crossing between Iloilo and Bacolod (P300, one hour, 20 daily).

From the La Paz Norte Pier, **Milagrosa Shipping** (337 3040) sails twice weekly and **Montenegro Lines** (708 1322; www.montenegrolines.com.ph) weekly from Iloilo to Puerto Princesa (from P950, 25 to 30 hours) on Palawan.

From the Fort San Pedro Pier, Negros Navigation (two weekly) and SuperFerry (weekly) have ferries to Manila (from P1000, 20 hours). For boats to Cebu, see p589.

Ceres buses to Caticlan (P313, six hours) leave every 30 minutes until 4pm from the **Tagbac Bus Terminal**, about 7km north of the centre, while a few speedier vans (P350, 4½ hours) leave in the morning from the Travellers Lounge.

Negros

If any Visayan island can boast to have it all, it is surely Negros. Here you'll find one of the country's top dive spots (Apo Island), one of the top remote beaches (Sipalay) and one of the top treks (volcanic Mt Kanlaon). The heavily forested interior, besides being a major biodiversity hotbed, provides a stunning backdrop for drives around the island. Along the west coast, sprawling, bright-green sugarcane fields abut the shimmering waters of the Sulu Sea. Lovely, laid-back Dumaguete makes a fine base for exploring it all.

BACOLOD

034 / POP 500,000

Bacolod is a little too large and intractable to be of much appeal. The city boomed in the 19th century when Iloilo's clothing industry collapsed and the textile barons migrated across the Panay Gulf to try their luck at sugar. Locals masquerade in grinning masks for October's MassKara Festival.

Activities

The main reason to stay in Bacolod is to get permits for the protected areas around Negros. The main attraction is Mt Kanlaon Natural Park where the Visayas' highest peak (2645m) lurks. Permits (P300) can be obtained at the Office of the Park Superintendent (0917 301 1410; eioibibar@yahoo.com; Porras & Abad-Santos Sts, Barangay 39; from 8am Mon-Fri). Access to the mountain is tightly controlled and guides (P500 per day) are mandatory, so reserve ahead. There are three routes to the top, one of which can be done by fit climbers in a day. The climbing seasons are March to May and October to December.

The trekking is at least as good in bird-infested Northern Negros Natural Park, accessible from Patag, a small town 32km east of Silay. The Silay Tourist Office (495 5553) can help you get a guide and a permit (required). The Biodiversity Conservation Center (433 9234; South Capitol Rd, Bacolod; 9am-5pm Mon-Sat) has information on the natural park and also runs a small zoo.

Sleeping

Pension Bacolod GUESTHOUSE $
(433 3377; 27 11th St; s P150-430, d P200-520;) For a place to lay your head, look no further than this professionally run bargain, with a diverse array of rooms on a quiet side street near the Ceres north bus terminal. Mice reportedly like it here too.

Eating & Drinking

Art District ENTERTAINMENT COMPLEX
(Lacson St, Mandalagan) A complex of artsy-fartsy bars, restaurants and galleries. Students smoke sheeshas and guzzle cocktails in Gypsy Bar Tea Room, while creative types prefer outdoor Café Joint (4pm-late).

Goldenfield's Commercial Complex ENTERTAINMENT COMPLEX
About 3km south of the centre, the city's nightlife centres around the once-blighted, now-flashy Goldenfield's Commercial Complex, where you'll find a gaggle of bars, restaurants, nightclubs and a casino.

Getting There & Away

PAL, Cebu Pacific and Airphil Express all have frequent flights to both Cebu City and Manila. Zest Air flies just to Manila.

For info on fastcraft ferries to Iloilo, see p582. Iloilo-bound ferries call in at the Bredco Port, near SM Mall about 1km west of the centre.

From the **Ceres north bus terminal** (☎433 4993; cnr Lopez Jaena St & IV Ferrer Ave) there are frequent buses to San Carlos (P140, 3½ hours), where six daily ferries depart for Toledo, Cebu. Morning buses to Cebu (P650, seven hours) also take this ferry.

From the **Ceres south bus terminal** (☎434 2386/7; cnr Lopez Jaena & San Sebastian Sts), buses run hourly until 7pm to Dumaguete (P310, six hours) via Kabankalan, and until mid-evening to Sipalay (P170, five hours).

SIPALAY

☎034 / POP 11,275

You could get stuck for days – make that months – in this remote fishing town on Negros' southwest edge. At delicious Sugar Beach a small outcrop of resorts caters to those looking to achieve the full Robinson Crusoe effect. The town proper has an endless beach where every morning fishermen unload their catch, which can include several-hundred-pound tuna. Divers should head 6km south of Sipalay to the pricier resorts of *barangay* (village) Punta Ballo.

Sleeping

The following are all on Sugar Beach.

TOP CHOICE Driftwood Village RESORT $

(☎920 900 3663; www.driftwood-village.com; dm P280, d from P400; wi-fi) Hosts Daisy and Peter (he's Swiss) are a lot of fun, and so is their resort, which features a dozen cosy *nipa* huts (traditional thatched Filipino hut), good Thai food and a range of bar sports.

Sulu Sunset RESORT $

(☎0919 716 7182; www.sulusunset.com; r P450-1000) The cheapest rooms here are open-air 'tree-houses' – lofts actually – accessible by ladder. The bigger cottages are great value. It's at the less-appealing far end of the beach.

Getting There & Away

Ceres buses to/from Bacolod (P170, 4½ hours) leave every half-hour until evening. For Dumaguete, see p584.

Sugar Beach is about 5km north of Sipalay proper, across two rivers. Arrange a boat transfer to your resort from Sipalay proper (P350, 15 minutes), or disembark from the Bacolod–Sipalay bus in *barangay* Montilla and take a tricycle to *barangay* Nauhang (P100, 15 minutes), where small paddleboats bring you across the river to Sugar Beach for P15.

> **COCKSURE GAMBLERS**
>
> Heavy male drinking and bonding occur over gambling – on anything from *sabong* (cockfights) to horse racing. But *sabong* are what Filipino men get most excited about. All over the country, every Sunday and public holiday, irritable and expensive fighting birds are let loose on one another. The cockpits are full to bursting and the audience is high with excitement – as much as P100,000 may be wagered on a big fight. All this plus cheap booze, lots of guns, pimps, players and prostitutes make for an interesting life for police.

DUMAGUETE

☎035 / POP 116,000

There are only a few Philippine provincial cities worth more than a day of your time, and Dumaguete (doo-ma-*get*-ay) is one of them. A huge college campus engulfs much of its centre, saturating the city with youthful energy and attitude. The location – in the shadow of twin-peaked Cuernos de Negros (1903m) and just a few clicks from some marvellous hiking, beaches and diving – takes care of the rest.

Perdices St is the main commercial drag, but most dining, drinking and strolling happens on and around the attractive waterfront promenade flanking Rizal Blvd.

Activities

The Dumaguete area boasts top-notch diving, hiking, caving and many other adventures. Nearby Apo Island is the big draw for underwater breathers. Back on terra firma you'll find caving, rock climbing and trekking on Cuernos de Negros and around the **Twin Lakes**, north of Dumaguete near Bais.

Recommended operators:

Scuba Ventures DIVING

(☎225 7716; www.dumaguetedive.com; Hibbard Ave) Under Harold's Mansion, it offers open-water dive certification courses for a very reasonable P15,000.

Dumaguete Outdoors HIKING, TOURS

(☎226 2110; www.dumagueteoutdoors.com; 3 Noblefranca St) Michelle and Chad dispense advice and arrange tours – including regular group climbs up Mt Kanlaon that dispense with the red tape.

Sleeping

TOP CHOICE **Harold's Mansion** BACKPACKER $
(☎225 8000; www.haroldsmansion.com; 205 Hibbard Ave; dm/s/d from P250/350/500; ❄@☜) With free coffee, a roomy six-bed dorm room and a down-to-earth owner who runs cool tours, Harold's deserves its popularity among independent travellers.

Vintage Inn INN $
(☎225 1076; Surban St; s/d from P300/400; ❄☜) Cheap is the name of the game at this central option opposite the market. Rooms are simple and mostly windowless.

Bethel Guesthouse HOTEL $$
(☎225 2000; www.bethelguesthouse.com; Rizal Blvd; s/d from P850/1000; ❄@☜) Big, bright, sea-facing property with spacious rooms, giant TVs and all the mod-cons.

Eating & Drinking

BBQ stalls set up along Rizal Blvd in the evening.

Qyosko FILIPINO $
(cnr Santa Rosa & Perdices Sts; mains P60-100; ⏲24hr; ☜) A budget traveller's dream, this spot serves up hot Filipino dishes and free wi-fi, and delicious shakes and coffee from its adjoining coffee shop.

Persian Kebab Tandoori MIDDLE EASTERN $$
(San Juan St; mains P95-350; ⏲11am-11pm Mon-Sat; ✎) Just west of Rizal Blvd, Persian Kebab has plenty of vegetarian options among its line-up of Middle Eastern and Indian staples.

Hayahay FILIPINO
(Flores St; mains P100-250; ⏲4pm-late) In a cluster of bars and restaurants on the waterfront 2km north of Bethel Guesthouse, Hayahay is known for delicious fresh seafood and rockin' reggae Wednesdays.

Café Antonio FILIPINO $
(cnr San Juan & Catalina Sts; mains P40-80) Student favourite grills meat and slings coffee upstairs in an exquisite Spanish-era building.

Getting There & Away

Cebu Pacific and PAL have a few daily flights to Manila. Cebu Pacific has a daily flight to Cebu.

Oceanjet fastcraft go to/from Cebu (P970, four hours, twice daily) via Tagbilaran (P680, two hours) on Bohol. There are also RORO ferries to Cebu (see p589).

From the nearby port of Sibulan, frequent fastcraft (P62) and *bangkas* (P45) alternate trips to Lilo-an on Cebu island (25 minutes), from where there are buses to Cebu City and Moalboal.

Ceres Bus Lines (Perdices St) connects Dumaguete and Bacolod (P310, six hours, hourly until 7pm).

Getting to Sipalay requires three separate Ceres buses: Dumaguete to Bayawan (two hours), Bayawan to Hinoba-an (1½ hours) and Hinoba-an to Sipalay (45 minutes). Connections are easy. The entire trip costs P200 and takes 4½ to 5½ hours.

APO ISLAND

☎035 / POP 745

For a taste of small-village life on an isolated island, it's hard to beat this coral-fringed charmer off the coast of southern Negros. It's also one of the Philippines' best snorkelling spots.

Most people visit on day trips from Dauin or Dumaguete (diving/snorkelling trips about P2900/1600 per person including two dives), but thrifty souls will fare better staying in one of the island's two resorts. **Liberty's Community Lodge** (☎424 0888; www.apoisland.com; dm/s/d incl full board from P800/1300/1950; @☜) has well-designed rooms and a laid-back atmosphere, and transfers guests to the island for P300 per person. Around the point from Liberty's, the more stylish **Apo Island Beach Resort** (☎225 5490; www.apoislandresort.com; dm P800, cottages from P2500) has a lovely secret cove all to itself. You'll really feel like you're away from it all here. Both resorts offer diving. There are also homestays available on the island for P500.

A couple of *bangkas* depart the island for Malatapay, 18km south of Dumaguete, around 6.30am and return around 3pm (P300, 45 minutes). Chartering a five-passenger *bangka* costs P1700.

Siquijor

☎035 / POP 87,700

Spooky Siquijor is renowned for its witches and healers, but don't be scared away. This is backpacker paradise, with breathtaking scenery and some of the best-value accommodation in the Philippines. With your own transport you can travel around the island in a day and explore beaches, colonial relics, waterfalls, caves and charming villages.

A good strategy is to arrange for motorbike hire (per day P350) at the pier in Siquijor town when you arrive and investigate accommodation options on your own. The best budget places are in **Sandugan**, 15km northeast of Siquijor town. The best beaches and a few good midrange lodging options are along the west coast at **Solangon**, 9km southwest of Siquijor town.

Sleeping

TOP CHOICE JJ's Backpackers Village and Cafe BACKPACKER $
(☎0918 670 0310; jiesa26@yahoo.com; tent/dm/d P150/300/400; @) Laid-back JJ's is a throwback to the carefree days when you could camp and cook your own food on a beach without any worries. It also serves cheap, tasty food.

Guiwanon Spring Park Resort BUNGALOW $
(☎0926 978 6012; cottages P300-350) The three cottages here are essentially overwater tree houses in the middle of a mangrove reserve. They are very basic, but two of them directly face the ocean. Certainly one of the quirkiest lodging experiences you'll ever have. Look for the hard-to-spot sign on the left about 5km east of Siquijor town.

Coral Cay Resort RESORT $$
(☎019 269 1269; www.coralcayresort.com; d P850-2600; ❄≋) This fine resort has lavish rooms on a perfect stretch of white-sand beach at Solangon. The beachfront cottage suites are practically lapped by waves and at P1600 are a steal.

Kiwi Dive Resort RESORT $
(☎424 0534; www.kiwidiveresort.com; r P450-990; ❄@🛜) Well-situated resort in Sandugan with a dive centre and free pickups from either pier.

Swiss Stars Guesthouse GUESTHOUSE $
(☎480 5583; National Hwy; r P380-850; @) A good budget option just east of Siquijor town if you don't mind being off the beach; also has an incredibly affordable restaurant.

Getting There & Around

The vast majority of visitors arrive at the pier in Siquijor town via diminutive fastcraft from Dumaguete. Delta Fast and Oceanjet ply the route (P160, one hour, about five total trips daily). GL Shipping and Montenegro Lines follow with slower ROROs (P100); Montenegro and Delta Fast each add an early morning trip to Larena, 9km northeast of Siquijor town. Lite Shipping has a daily 5pm trip from Larena to Cebu City via Tagbilaran, while Palacio Shipping sails thrice weekly to Tagbilaran (P180 to P280, 3½ hours).

Tricycles are the favoured transport mode. From the pier in Siquijor town, figure on P120 to Solangon or Larena, P170 to Sandugan.

Cebu

Surrounded on all sides by the Philippine isles and dotted with tranquil fishing villages, Cebu is the island heart of the Visayas. Cebuanos are proud of their heritage – it is here that Magellan sowed the seed of Christianity and was pruned for his efforts at the hands of the mighty chief Lapu-Lapu. The island's booming metropolis, Cebu City, is a transport hub to pretty much anywhere you may wish to go. Pescador Island, near the laid-back town of Moalboal, placed Philippine diving on the world map, while the Malapascua marine scene boasts close encounters of the thresher-shark kind.

CEBU CITY

☎032 / POP 799,000

The island capital is much more laid-back than Manila as a place to arrive in or leave the Philippines. One of the first stops on Spain's conquest agenda, Cebu lays claim to everything old – including the oldest street (Colon St), the oldest university and the oldest fort. By night Cebu turns decidedly hedonistic.

Cebu's downtown district (Map p586) is its mercantile nucleus. Most of the sights are here, but you must wade through exhaust fumes, beggars, prostitutes and block after block of downmarket retail madness to get to them. Uptown (Map p588) is much more pleasant and has better accommodation, mostly near the central Fuente Osmeña roundabout. **Mactan Island**, where Magellan came a distant second in a fight with

GETTING INTO CEBU

Airport taxis at Mactan International Airport have a slightly inflated P70 flagfall and cost under P400 to the city centre, or you can cross the street outside the arrivals area, climb the stairs and grab a regular metered taxis (P40 flagfall). Taking public transport is complicated but possible; ask the tourist desk in the arrival hall for directions.

To get uptown from the ports, catch one of the jeepneys that pass by the piers to Pres Osmeña Blvd, then transfer to a jeepney going uptown.

Downtown Cebu City

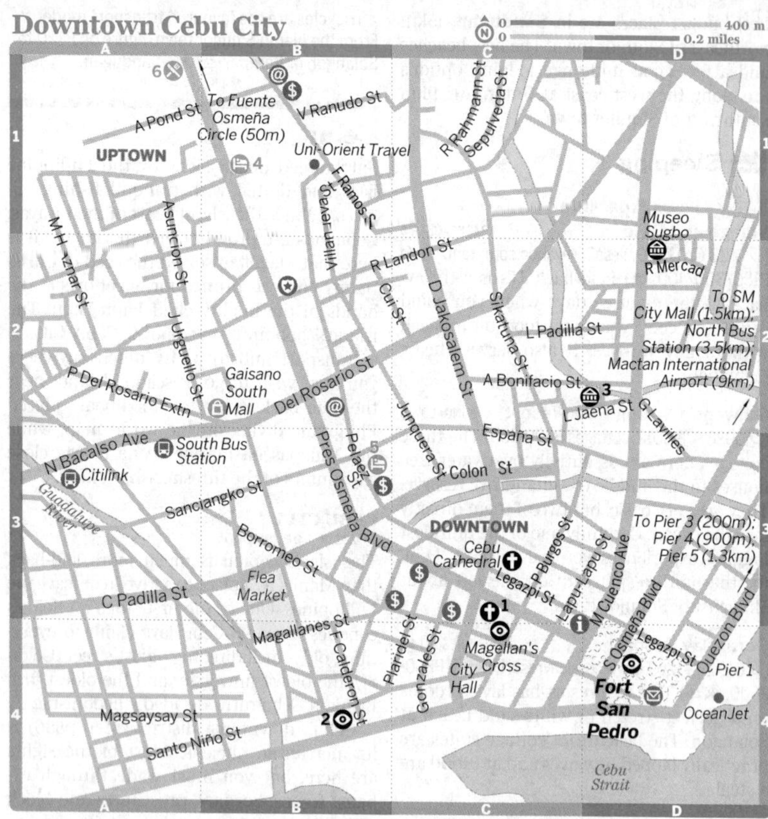

Downtown Cebu City

Top Sights
- Fort San Pedro D4

Sights
- 1 Basilica Minore del Santo Niño C3
- 2 Carbon Market B4
- 3 Casa Gorordo Museum D2

Sleeping
- 4 Arbel's Pension House B1
- 5 Hotel de Mercedes B3

Eating
- 6 Food Stalls A1

Chief Lapu-Lapu, is now the site of Cebu's airport and is joined to the city by a bridge.

Sights

Most sights worth seeing are downtown within walking distance of Fort San Pedro.

Fort San Pedro FORT
(Map p586; S Osmeña Blvd; admission P30; ⊙8am-7.30pm) This gently crumbling ruin, built by Miguel Legazpi in 1565, is the oldest Spanish fort in the country.

Basilica Minore del Santo Niño CHURCH
(Map p586; Pres Osmeña Blvd) Built in 1740, Cebu's holiest church houses a revered Flemish statuette of the Christ child (Santo Niño). People line up for hours to pray in front of the icon, which dates to Magellan's time.

Casa Gorordo Museum MUSEUM
(Map p586; 35 L Jaena St; admission P70; ⊙9am-6pm Tue-Sun) North of the church, the Casa Gorordo Museum, in an astonishingly beautiful ancestral house, offers a glimpse into upper-class life in Cebu in the 19th century.

Tops Lookout VIEWPOINT
(admission P100) Make your way to JY Square Mall (off Map p588), where motorcycle

taxis depart for the thrilling 30-minute ride (round trip P300) to the Tops lookout point 600m above Cebu.

Carbon Market BAZAAR
(Map p586) West of Fort San Pedro, the sprawling Carbon Market is a boisterous, cacophonous frenzy that seemingly never sleeps. It's a must for market lovers.

Sleeping

Passable super-budget rooms are practically nonexistent in Cebu. Snoop around downtown in the commercial district and you might turn up a double for P200 to P300, but it won't be pretty. It's worth spending extra to be uptown.

TOP CHOICE **Mayflower Inn** HOTEL $$
(Map p588; ☎255 2800; www.mayflowerinn.multiply.com; Villalon Dr; s/d/tr P900/1250/1600; ❄📶) The rooms are spacious, the soundproofing is tight and the earthy-toned paint is meticulously applied at this clean and modern gem.

Kukuk's Nest Pension House GUESTHOUSE $
(Map p588; ☎231 5180; 124 Gorordo Ave; 3-bed fan dm P400, d P600-700; ❄@📶) This eclectic backpacker standby defines 'quirky', with contemporary art hanging about, a resident armless charcoal sketcher and a 24-hour restobar that draws all types.

Premiere Citi Suites HOTEL $$
(Map p588; ☎266 0442; www.premierecitisuites.webs.com; 62 M Cristina St; r P995-1895; ❄📶) Incredible value, top central location, friendly staff – no surprise this stylish, fresh new kid on the block books out in advance.

Arbel's Pension House GUESTHOUSE $
(Map p586; ☎253 5303; 57 Pres Osmeña Blvd; s/d from P375/500; ❄) This is the rare Cebu cheapie that doesn't venture into 'disgusting' territory. Rooms are predictably basic but at least have windows, and the location is relatively quiet.

Myra's Pensionne GUESTHOUSE $
(Map p588; ☎231 5557; 12 N Escario St; dm/d from P336/896; ❄) Myra's adds dorms in an annexe near JY Mall to decidedly homey digs in the main house.

Hotel de Mercedes HOTEL $
(Map p586; ☎253 1105; www.hoteldemercedes.com; 7 Pelaez St; s/d from P500/670; ❄📶) Good downtown choice with wide range of rooms.

Travelbee Pension GUESTHOUSE $
(Map p588; ☎253 1005; travelbee-pension@yahoo.com; 294 DG Garcia St; d P400-900; ❄) No-frills option with mostly windowless rooms.

Eating

TOP CHOICE **STK ta Bay! Sa Paolito's Seafood House** SEAFOOD $$
(Map p588; ☎256 2700; 6 Orchid St, Capitol Site; meals P95-300; ⏲9am-2.30pm & 5-10pm) Ask a Cebuano where to dine and those in the know will point you to this large ancestral home turned restaurant. Don't miss the hot 'n' spicy *calamares*.

Cofifi Café CAFE
(Map p588; R Aboitiz Street; coffee P50-75; ⏲7.30am-midnight; 📶) Polished concrete floors, good coffee and funky furniture – there's nothin' Starbucks about this cool little hideaway. Good breakfasts.

Ayala Center FOOD COURT $
(Map p588; Lahug district) As is the case in Manila, many of the best restaurants are in the malls, particularly the Ayala Center. There is a food court on the 3rd floor for budget meals. For finer dining, you should consider one of the eateries at **The Terraces** on the north side of the mall.

Belly Idol BAR & GRILL $
(Map p588; Gen Maxilom Ave) How can you not love a place called Belly Idol? There's occasional live music, cheap San Miguel and a simple menu of Filipino bar food, including 'The pork belly that rock' (sic).

Food Stalls STREET FOOD $
(Map p586; Pres Osmeña Blvd; dishes P30-50) Opposite the Crown Regency Hotel on Pres Osmeña Blvd you'll find outdoor food stalls that serve exotic dishes like *sinagaang bakasi* (sea-snake soup) and more-familiar Filipino dishes.

Joven's Grill BUFFET $$
(Map p588; cnr Pres Osmeña Blvd & Jasmine St; all-you-can-eat buffet P178-199; ⏲lunch & dinner) The best place to gorge after an extended boat journey.

Drinking

Mango Square CLUBS
(Map p588; Mango Square Mall, Mango Ave; admission per club P50-100) This gaggle of clubs and bars in one central location attracts a fun, lively crowd. Check out college fave the

Uptown Cebu City

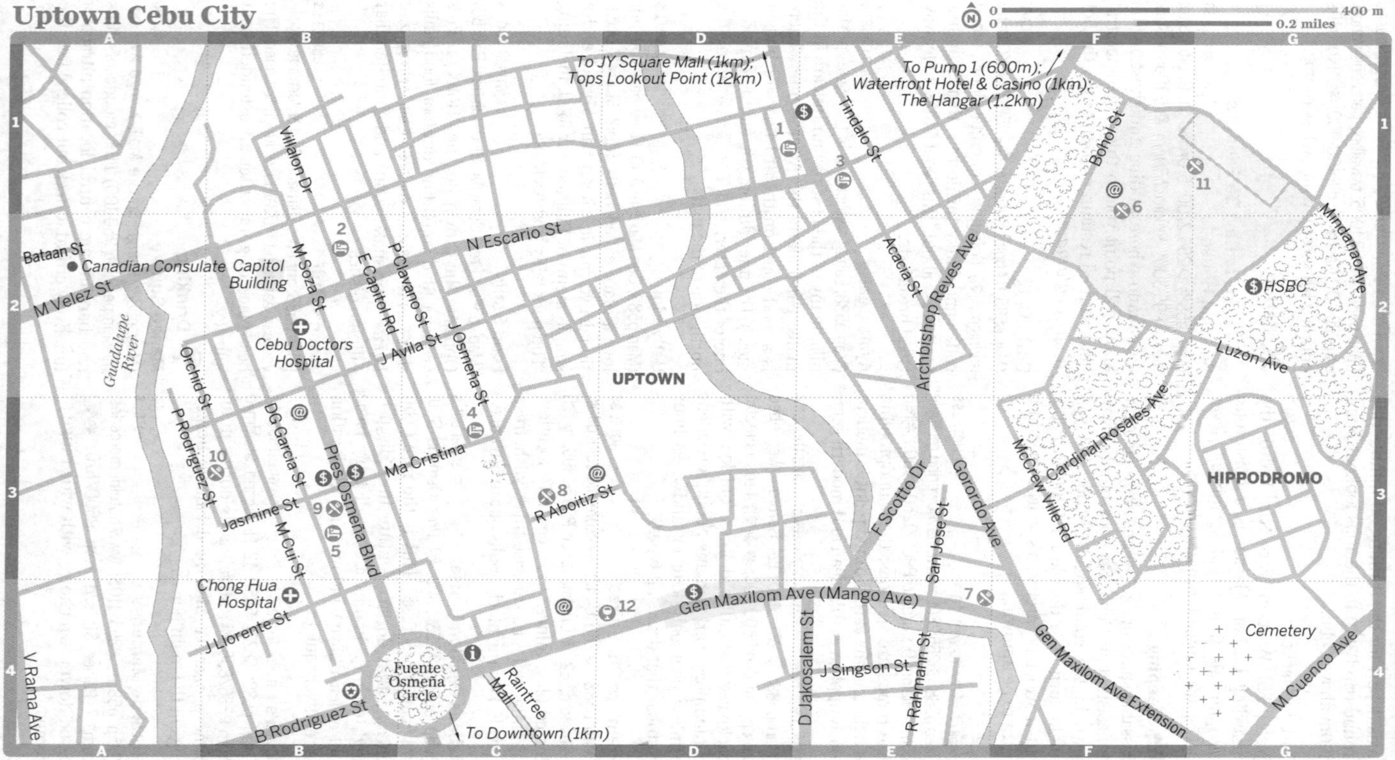

Uptown Cebu City

Sleeping

1	Kukuk's Nest Pension House	D1
2	Mayflower Inn	B2
3	Myra's Pensionne	E1
4	Premiere Citi Suites	C3
5	Travelbee Pension	B3

Eating

6	Ayala Center	F1
7	Belly Idol	E4
8	Cofifi Café	C3
9	Joven's Grill	B3
10	STK ta Bay! Sa Paolito's Seafood House	B3
11	The Terraces	G1

Drinking

	Beat	(see 12)
	Juliana's	(see 12)
12	Mango Square	D4
	Numero Doce	(see 12)

Shopping

	Fully Booked	(see 11)

Beat, gay-friendly **Numero Doce** and the latest in-spot, **Juliana's**.

Hangar CLUB
(off Map p588; Salinas Drive, Lahug) Sometimes referred to as Sunflower City (referring to the average club towards the back), this is a semi-outdoor space with various bars and clubs competing for attention. It's near Waterfront Hotel & Casino.

Pump 1 CLUB
(off Map p588; ☎232 3637; Archbishop Reyes, Lahug) Long-running club near the Hangar is a rare stayer in the fickle Cebu City club scene.

Shopping

Fully Booked BOOKS
(Map p588; the Terraces, Ayala Center) Excellent bookstore.

Information

There are plenty of internet cafes and ATMs around Fuente Osmeña Circle (Map p588).

Cebu Doctors Hospital (Map p588; ☎253 7511; Pres Osmeña Blvd)

Central post office (Map p586; Quezon Blvd)

Department of Tourism Region VII Office (Map p586; ☎254 2811; LDM Bldg, Legazpi St; ⏲7am-5pm Mon-Fri) Informative office has great maps of Cebu City and other Visayan locales.

HSBC Bank (Map p588; Cardinal Rosales Ave) Allows P40,000 ATM withdrawals and cashes travellers cheques; opposite Ayala Center.

Getting There & Away

AIR For international flights into Cebu's Mactan International Airport, see p611. Airphil Express, Cebu Pacific, PAL and Zest Air have regular connections to Manila and a number of regional destinations. Newcomer **Mid-Sea Express** (☎032-495 6976; www.midseaexpress.com) hops a few times per week to a handful of not-so-distant destinations, including Siquijor, Camiguin and Tagbilaran.

BOAT There's no need to purchase tickets ahead for the popular fastcraft to Tagbilaran (Bohol), Ormoc (Leyte) and Dumaguete. The *Sun Star* daily newspaper runs up-to-date schedules.

You can buy ferry tickets for many ferries at the handy **Travellers Lounge** (☎232 0291; ⏲8am-8pm) just outside SM City Mall (off Map p586). You can also buy tickets at the piers.

Useful shipping companies in Cebu City include the following:

Cokaliong Shipping (☎232 7211-18; Pier 1) ROROs to Surigao (P537, 13 hours, daily except Sunday); Maasin, Leyte (P320, five hours, four weekly); Dumaguete (P300, six hours, daily); Calbayog, Samar (P690, 11 hours, three weekly); Larena, Siquijor (P280, eight hours); and Iloilo (P550, 12 hours, three weekly).

Lite Shipping Corporation (☎416 6462; www.lite-shipping.com; Pier 1) ROROs to Tagbilaran (P220, four hours, three daily), Tubigon (P150, two hours, three daily) and Ormoc (P400, five hours, almost daily).

Oceanjet (Map p586; ☎255 7560; www.oceanjet.net; Pier 1) Oceanjet has fastcraft to Tagbilaran (P520, two hours, five daily) and Dumaguete (P970, four hours, two daily).

Negros Navigation (off Map p586; ☎02-554 8777, 231 1004; Pier 4) Services Manila (P1128, 21 hours, weekly).

Palacio Shipping (Map p586; ☎255 4538; Pier 1) Serves Tagbilaran (P220, four hours, three weekly) and Calbayog, Samar (P780, 12 hours, three weekly).

Roble Shipping Lines (off Map p586; ☎232 2236; Pier 3) ROROs to Hilongos (P250, five hours, daily) and Catbalogan (P650, 12 hours, weekly).

Supercat (off Map p586; ☎233 7000; www.supercat.com.ph; Pier 4) Supercat has fastcraft to Ormoc (P895, 2¾ hours, three daily) and Tagbilaran (P520, 1¾ hours, three daily).

SuperFerry (off Map p586; ☎233 7000; www.superferry.com.ph; Pier 4) Four boats weekly to Manila (P1600, 23 hours) and five weekly to Cagayan de Oro (P980, eight hours).

Super Shuttle Ferry (☎233 5733; www.supershuttleferry.com; Pier 8) ROROs to Camiguin (P880, 11 hours, weekly).

Trans Asia Shipping Lines (off Map p586; ☎254 6491; www.transasiashipping.com; Pier 5) Serves Cagayan de Oro (P615, 12 hours, daily) and Iloilo (P710, 12 hours, six weekly).

Weesam Express (off Map p586; ☎412 9562; Pier 4) Fastcraft to Tagbilaran (P500, 1¾ hours, three daily) and Ormoc (P550, 2¼ hours, twice daily).

BUS There are two bus stations in Cebu. **Ceres Bus Lines** (☎345 8650) services southern and central destinations, such as Bato (P170, four hours, frequent) via Moalboal (P115, three hours) or via Oslob, from the **South Bus Station** (Map p586; Bacalso Ave). Quicker air-con vans ('V-hires') leave for Moalboal/Bato (P100/150) from the **Citilink Station** (Map p586; Bacalso Ave), near the South Bus Station.

The **North Bus Station** (M Logarta Ave) is beyond SM City Mall. From here Ceres has buses to Hagnaya (P132, 3½ hours, hourly) for Bantayan Island, and Maya (P163, four hours, frequent) for Malapascua Island.

MOALBOAL

☎032 / POP 27,400

The Philippines' original diving hotbed, Moalboal remains a throwback to the days when diving came cheap and minus the attitude. **Panagsama Beach**, where the resorts are, meanders lazily along a sea wall within rock-skipping distance of a stunning diving wall (which can also be snorkelled). While the beach itself is hardly worthy of the name, Moalboal's mellow vibe and mischievous weekend nightlife attract divers and nondivers alike.

Sights & Activities

White Beach BEACH
Beach lovers can take a tricycle (P150) 5km north to lovely White Beach.

Scuba Diving DIVING
Divers can paddle out to the coral-studded wall off Panagsama Beach, or take a 10-minute *bangka* ride to **Pescador Island**, which swarms with marine life. A single-tank dive shouldn't exceed US$25.

Tours

Planet Action ADVENTURE TOURS
(☎474 3016; www.action-philippines.com) Run by the wry and affable Jochen, Planet Action runs mountain biking, canyoning and other mountain tours, including a trip across the Tañon Strait to climb Mt Kanlaon on Negros (2½ days, per person P9500).

Sleeping

TOP CHOICE **Sumisid Lodge** RESORT $$
(☎474 0005; www.seaquestdivecenter.ph; s/d from P700/1000; ❄☎) The tidy fan rooms at this gem in central Panagsama share clean bathrooms over an attractive, immaculately kept restaurant-lounge area. Out front, wicker *chaises longues* are perched on a stone wall over Panagsama's lone strip of white sand.

Quo Vadis RESORT $$
(☎474 0018; www.moalboal.com; d from P850; ❄@☎≋) Moalboal's best all-round resort has something to suit every taste, from tidy 'economy' rooms to tasteful deluxe digs facing the sea.

Moalboal Backpacker Lodge HOSTEL $
(☎0905 227 8096; www.moalboal-backpackerlodge.com; dm/s/d from P220/350/450; ☎) This newish hostel has an airy dorm and a couple of semiprivate rooms over a coffee shop.

Eating & Drinking

Drinking is the national sport of the Moalboal Republic, and there are dozens of eateries where you can secure food to soak up the deluge of beer. Saturday-night discos at Pacita's Resort are famous – or infamous, depending on your point of view.

Last Filling Station RESTAURANT $$
(meals from P180; ✎) We love its protein-heavy shakes and breakfasts.

Chilli Bar BAR-RESTAURANT $
(dishes from P80) A Panagsama institution with a lethal cocktail menu.

Getting There & Around

Frequent Ceres buses pass through town heading south to Bato (P60, two hours) and north to Cebu's South Bus Station (P110, three hours). To Cebu, there are also air-con vans driven by sadistic drivers (P100, two hours).

Motorbikes to Panagsama Beach from Moalboal cost about P30, tricycles up to five times that.

MALAPASCUA ISLAND

POP 3500

Blessed with a long ribbon of pearly white sand, this sleepy little dive mecca off the northern tip of Cebu has long been touted as the 'next Boracay'. With a walking path set back from the beach and a few restaurants offering seaside seating in the sand, signature **Bounty Beach** does resemble Boracay in parts, but Boracay-like crowds are probably a long way off.

Activities

Thresher sharks are the big attraction here. Divers head out at 5.30am to **Monad Shoal**, where they park on the seabed at 35m hoping to catch a glimpse of these critters. The chances are pretty good – about 70%. By day Monad Shoal attracts manta rays.

Sleeping

Malapascua's electricity grid functions only from 6pm to midnight, so make sure your resort has a generator to avoid sweltering to death.

Cocobana Beach Resort RESORT $$
(☎437 1040; www.cocobana.ch; s/d incl breakfast from P800/1000; ❄) Smack bang in the middle of Bounty Beach, Malapascua's original resort has comfy cottages and 24-hour electricity.

BB's GUESTHOUSE $
(☎0916 756 6018; r from P300) The fan rooms here are serviceable and friendly on the wallet but get hot when the power cuts out at midnight. It's off the beach, next to Ging-Ging's restaurant.

Mike & Josie's Beach Cottages RESORT $
(☎0905 263 2914; r from P500) Backpacker special at the far east end of Bounty Beach has a few basic cottages facing the beach.

Mr Kwiz GUESTHOUSE $
(☎0906 620 5475; r P500) Good cheapie in the village has basic concrete and very pink rooms.

Eating

Expect anything on Bounty Beach to cost more than you want to pay.

La Isla Bonita Restaurant INTERNATIONAL $$
(mains P200-280) Hidden off the beach near Ging-Ging's, this was the best restaurant on the island until Angelina opened in 2009. It's still recommended for its range of lovingly cooked Continental and Thai offerings.

> **SPLURGE: ANGELINA**
>
> The eponymous chef at **Angelina** (mains P320-400), on Poblacion Beach, around the point from Bounty Beach, cooks up heavenly creations that will have you craving Italian food for weeks. The homemade *tagliatelle asparagi* is *al dente* bliss.

Ging-Ging's Flower Garden FILIPINO $
(mains P40-100; 🖉) Inland from the beach, Ging-Ging's serves tasty, cheap, filling vegetarian food and curries.

Getting There & Away

Bangkas from Maya (P50, 30 minutes) to Malapascua leave when full, roughly every hour until 5pm or so. If you miss the last boat, you'll have to charter a *bangka* for P500 to P800. At low tide you must pay a barge operator P20 to shuttle you to/from the *bangka*.

Frequent Ceres buses leave Cebu's North Bus Station for Maya (P163, four hours).

Bohol

It's difficult to reconcile Bohol's bloody history with the relaxed isle of today. It's here that Francisco Dagohoy led the longest revolt in the country against the Spaniards, from 1744 to 1829. The Chocolate Hills, rounded mounds resembling chocolate drops, are the big tourist magnet. Bohol also has endearing little primates, coral cathedrals off Panglao Island and lush jungle, ripe for exploration, around the town of Loboc.

Getting There & Away

Tagbilaran is the main gateway, but there are also ferries between Cebu and Tubigon in northwest Bohol; between Bato (Leyte) and Ubay in northeast Bohol; and between Jagna in southeast Bohol and Cagayan de Oro and Camiguin (Mindanao).

TAGBILARAN

☎038 / POP 92,000

There's no reason to waste much time in traffic-snarled Tagbilaran. Your first port of call should be the **tourist office** (⊙8am-6pm) at the ferry dock, which can help with transport arrangements.

If you do need to stay the night, your best bets are **Charisma Lodge** (☎412 3094; CPG Ave; s/d from P150/300; ❄) and across the street at the homier **Nisa Travelers Inn** (☎411 3731; CPG Ave; s/d incl breakfast from P550/700; ❄). Both are susceptible to street noise, so request rooms at the back. Eat, cool off and escape the tricycle madness at the food court in BQ Mall, opposite Nisa Travellers Inn.

The main domestic airlines all serve Tagbilaran from Manila.

Various fastcraft and slow craft head to Cebu (see p589). Oceanjet operates two daily fastcraft to/from Dumaguete (P680, two hours). Negros Navigation has a weekly trip to/from Manila (P1300, 30 hours). Trans Asia has three trips weekly to/from Cagayan de Oro (P655, 10 hours).

The main bus terminal is next to Island City Mall in Dao, 3km north of the centre.

To avoid expensive van rides and slow public transport, consider hiring your own motorbike in Tagbilaran (P500 to P600 per day) to explore the rest of Bohol.

AROUND TAGBILARAN

It's just a short drive north of Tagbilaran to two of the Philippines' signature attractions – the Chocolate Hills and that lovable palm-sized primate, the tarsier.

You can visit both in a single day on an excursion from Tagbilaran, but you're much better off basing yourself in Loboc at **Nuts Huts** (☎0920 846 1559; www.nutshuts.com; dm P300, s P400, d P600-1000), a backpacker Shangri-la in the middle of the jungle. With a sublime location overlooking the emerald-tinged Loboc River, Nuts Huts provides at least as much reason to visit inland Bohol as brown loam lumps or miniature monkeys. The Belgian hosts can tell you everything you need to know about exploring the area, and you can hike and mountain bike on a network of trails in the immediate vicinity.

To get to Nuts Huts from Tagbilaran, catch a Carmen-bound bus and get off at the Nuts Huts sign. It's a 15-minute walk from the road. Alternatively, take a bus to Loboc and then a *habal-habal* (motorcycle taxi; P50) or shuttle boat up the river from the Sarimanok landing (per person P200).

Near Nuts Huts is the **Loboc Ecotourism Adventure Park** with an exciting head-first 500m zipline (P350) running over the Loboc River gorge.

You are unlikely to spot the nocturnal tarsier in the wild, so head to the **Philippine Tarsier Sanctuary** (www.tarsierfoundation.org; admission P50; ⏲9am-4pm) in *barangay* Canapnapan, between the towns of Corella and Sikatuna. About 10 saucer-eyed tarsiers hang out in the immediate vicinity of the centre – the guides will bring you right to them. This is a much more humane and ecofriendly way to appreciate the tarsier than visiting the animals kept in cages by tourist operators in Loboc.

From Nuts Huts the sanctuary is a 30- to 45-minute motorbike ride, or take a jeepney from Loboc (P25, 45 minutes). From Tagbilaran catch a bus to Sikatuna (P25, one hour) from the Dao terminal and ask to be dropped off at the centre.

An interesting quirk of nature, the **Chocolate Hills** consist of over 1200 conical hills, up to 120m high. They were supposedly formed over time by the uplift of coral deposits and the effects of rainwater and erosion. Since this explanation cannot be confirmed, the local belief that they are the tears of a heartbroken giant may one day prove to be correct. In the dry season, when the vegetation turns brown, the hills are at their most chocolate-y.

From Nuts Huts, the Chocolate Hills are a 45-minute motorbike ride; alternatively, flag down a bus bound for Carmen (4km north of the Chocolate Hills) and hop off at the Chocolate Hills viewpoint turn-off, where *habal-habal* (P20) await to whisk you up to the **viewpoint** (admission P50). A more invigorating method of seeing the hills is to take a *habal-habal* in and around the hills; a one-hour ride costs P250.

From Tagbilaran there are regular buses from the Dao terminal to Carmen (P60, two hours).

PANGLAO ISLAND

☎038

Linked by two bridges to Bohol, Panglao is where divers head to take advantage of the spectacular coral formations and teeming marine life on the nearby islands of Balicasag and Pamilacan. Ground zero for divers is **Alona Beach**, which is sort of like a mini Boracay, minus the stunning beach and nightlife. Alona Beach has gone upscale in recent years, but determined deal-hunters can still find bargains on diving and accommodation.

Activities

Diving & Snorkelling DIVING

Dive prices average P1200 per dive, not including equipment. Rates vary wildly so shop around. Most dive trips go to **Balicasag Island**, which is also suitable for **snorkelling**. There's also good snorkelling about 75m offshore from Alona Beach.

Tours

Dolphin-Watching TOURS

You can arrange early-morning dolphin-watching tours near Pamilacan Island through most resorts and dive centres. Figure on paying P1500 for a four-person boat.

Sleeping & Eating

Beachfront dining opportunities on Alona Beach are ample but come at a price. Most affordable eateries and bars are north of the beach, towards Citadel Alona.

ALL CREATURES SMALL & GREAT

Contrary to popular belief, the lovable tarsier is *not* the world's smallest primate. That distinction belongs to the pygmy mouse lemur of Madagascar. However, the Philippines can still proudly lay claim to the world's smallest hoofed mammal – the rare Philippine mouse deer of Palawan. Meanwhile, the Philippines' 24mm *Hippocampus bargibanti* recently lost the title of world's smallest seahorse to a newly discovered rival in Indonesia: the 16mm *Hippocampus denise*.

Casa-Nova Garden RESORT $
(☎502 9101; s/d from P300/500; ❄✉) True shoestring accommodation survives in Alona thanks to this cosy oasis. It's a bit out of the way, however. The turn-off is 700m beyond (west of) Helmut's Place.

Bohol Divers Resort RESORT $$
(☎502 9047; www.boholdiversresortph.com; s P500, d P800-4000; ❄@☎✉) This sprawling complex is one of the few places on the beach still offering budget rooms. Accommodation runs the gamut from basic fan rooms to upscale villas.

Citadel Alona Inn GUESTHOUSE $
(☎502 9424; www.citadelalona.com; d P600-800; ❄) Inland from the beach is this appealing, artsy house where all rooms share squeaky-clean bathrooms. There's a big kitchen for self-caterers.

Trudi's Place FILIPINO $
(mains P90-210) Rare cheap tucker on the beach.

Getting There & Around

From Tagbilaran, buses with 'Tawala Alona' signboards head to Alona Beach roughly hourly until 3pm from the corner of Hontanosas and F Rocha Sts (P25, 45 minutes). An easier option is to hire a *habal-habal* (P150), tricycle (P200) or taxi (P350).

Samar & Leyte

'Rugged' is usually the word you hear associated with these two eastern Visayan provinces, separated from each other by the narrowest of straits near Leyte's capital, Tacloban. It's an apt tag. The interior of both islands is consumed by virtually impenetrable forest. This naturally creates opportunities for adventure, although you'll need a guide to take advantage of it.

The coastlines of both islands serve up a few gems of their own, most notably great diving – and possible whale shark sightings – in tourist-free Southern Leyte. There's history here too – in 1521 Magellan first stepped ashore on what would become Philippine soil on the island of Homonhon, off Samar. In October 1944, General MacArthur fulfilled his pledge to return to the Philippines on Red Beach south of Tacloban.

CATBALOGAN

☎055 / POP 92,454

Catbalogan is the preferred base for exploring the interior of Samar. A ban on motorised tricycles in the city centre also makes it a pleasant stopover on the road from Allen to Tacloban. From the pier you can spot about 30 different islands offshore, plus some giant peaks on Biliran Island off Leyte.

Sights & Activities

Spelunking, climbing, scrambling, birdwatching, mountain biking – you name it, Samar's got it.

Spelunking CAVING
A spelunking tour of the **Jiabong Caves**, close to Catbalogan, is one of the Visayas' top one-day adventures. The tour is run by **Trexplore** (☎251 2301; www.bonifaciojoni.blogspot.com; Allen Ave), headed by North Face-clad Joni Bonifacio. Check out his website for some ideas for adventure. One-third of the six-hour tour is spent swimming underground in full spelunking kit. The tour ends outdoors with a late-afternoon 45-minute paddle downriver in a dugout canoe. Joni's tours of the huge **Langub–Gobingob Cave** near Calbiga, 50km south of Catbalogan, involve a night camping underground.

Sleeping & Eating

Fortune Hotel HOTEL $
(☎251 2147; 555 Del Rosario St; s/d from P290/390) Even the budget rooms are fastidiously cared for at this central option. Downstairs is a bustling Chinese restaurant.

First Choice Hotel HOTEL $
(☎251 2688; hotelfirstchoice@yahoo.com; Del Rosario St; s/d from P300/400; ❄☎) The obscene pink colour scheme does it no favours, but rooms here are cheap, clean and decent value.

THE BALANGIGA MASSACRE

On 28 September 1901, Filipino guerrillas masquerading as women massacred 59 members of the US garrison stationed at Balangiga in Eastern Samar. For the Americans it was the bloodiest day of the Filipino–American War, and the massacre triggered a massive retributive campaign, which was led by General Jacob 'Howling Mad' Smith, who killed scores of innocent civilians while fulfilling his vow to turn Samar into a 'howling wilderness'. There is an annual re-enactment and commemoration on that date.

Flaming Hat FILIPINO $
(meals P60-210;) By far the best eating option in town.

Getting There & Away

The main domestic airlines fly regularly to Calbayog, 72km north of Catbalogan.

To get to Allen (P180, four hours), departure point for ferries to Matnog in southeast Luzon (P120, 1¼ hours, at least every two hours), hail a Manila-bound bus on the National Hwy, or take a more frequent bus (P80) or van (P90) to Calbayog (1½ hours) and connect to onward transport there.

There are buses (P100, 2¾ hours) and air-con vans (P120, two hours) south to Tacloban. Buses leave from the bus station by the wharf and vans leave from company terminals in the centre of town.

TACLOBAN

053 / POP 217,199

The birthplace of Imelda Marcos – the 'Rose of Tacloban' – is a busy commercial centre and transport hub. It's hardly chic, but it does have a strip of decent restaurants where you can escape the rat race and cool off with an iced latte and air-con. Northwest of Tacloban, volcanic **Biliran Island** has some splendid beaches and waterfalls.

Sleeping & Eating

Steer clear of the noisy, congested city centre and stay closer to the internet cafes, restaurants and bars around Burgos and MH del Pilar Sts. For trendy restaurants, clubs and bars, the drinking precinct known as Club 65 Hundred is where you want to be.

Rosvenil Pensione GUESTHOUSE $
(321 2676; Burgos St; r from P600;) Located in a great rambling house, Rosvenil offers an enticing mix of rooms, including some truly swanky digs in its new wing.

Welcome Home Pension GUESTHOUSE $
(321 2739; 161 Santo Niño St; r from P350;) This quiet place set off the street has a mix of simple rooms with shared bathrooms (some windowless) and bigger, brighter digs that sleep three or four.

Libro CAFE $
(cnr Santo Niño & Gomez Sts; sandwiches from P50; noon-8pm) A fantastic second-hand bookstore that serves real coffee, sandwiches and a great selection of cakes.

Getting There & Away

The big domestic airlines all serve Manila and/or Cebu.

Duptours (cnr Ave Veteranos & Santo Niño St) runs speedy vans to Ormoc (P120, two hours), Naval on Biliran Island (P140, 2½ hours) and Catbalogan (P120, 2¼ hours). At the New Bus Terminal, about 3km west of the centre, you'll find more buses and vans to these and many other destinations, including Sogod (bus/van P120/150, 3½/2½ hours), where there are connections to Padre Burgos and Pintuyan.

ORMOC

053 / POP 177,524

Ormoc is mainly a springboard for boats to Cebu. If you arrive late, stay in the hulking **Don Felipe Hotel** (255 2460; I Larrazabal St; s/d from P400/480;) on the waterfront opposite the pier. Pricier rooms have wonderful views.

Supercat and Weesam Express have several fastcraft per day to Cebu (from P675, 2¼ hours). For slower, cheaper options see Boat on p589). Conveniently, the bus terminal is opposite the port, with connections to Tacloban and all points south.

DON'T MISS

LEYTE LANDING MEMORIAL

General Douglas Macarthur made his famous return to the Philippines on Red Beach in Palo, 6km south of Tacloban, now the site of a unique memorial. Take a 'Tacloban-Gov't Center-Baras' jeepney from the plaza next to McDonald's on Trece Martirez St to get there (P15, 15 minutes).

SOUTHERN LEYTE

☎053

Leyte's bowlegged rump straddles heavenly Sogod Bay in the remote province of Southern Leyte. **Whale sharks** have been known to frolic from November to April on the east side of the bay around Pintuyan. However, sightings are much more sporadic here than at Donsol – one year it's great, the next year there's nothing. Before going, get the low-down from **Moncher Bardos** (☎0916 952 3354; moncher64bardos@yahoo.com), who assists with a community-based tourism project to snorkel with the *tiki-tiki,* as they are known in the local dialect.

On the west side of the bay, the town of **Padre Burgos** gets divers' tails wagging, but most travellers passing through Southern Leyte are on their way to/from Surigao. A new port in Benit, San Ricardo, 10km south of Pintuyan, sends car ferries to Lipata, near Surigao (P120, 1½ hours, five daily). The boat trip is longer, but the bus trip shorter, from the still-functioning old port in Liloan (P300, 3½ hours, four daily). Buses to either port from points north usually involve a transfer in Sogod.

If you're heading to Padre Burgos from Cebu, take a ferry to Maasin, Bato or Hilongos or Ormoc, and continue to Burgos by bus or multicab (mini-jeepney). Boats also go between Southern Leyte and Ubay, Bohol.

MINDANAO

Sprawling Mindanao, the world's 19th-largest island, is known for dazzling scenery, primitive hill tribes and an almost complete lack of tourists because of political unrest and occasional fighting between the government and Muslim separatists. What most don't realise is that the lovely coastal stretch of northern Mindanao between Cagayan de Oro and Siargao Island is Catholic, Cebuano (Visayan) speaking – and quite safe. The area is known for first-rate surfing on Siargao and a peaceful island-life existence on Camiguin. Elsewhere, Mindanao offers up plenty of cherries for the intrepid traveller, including the Philippines' highest mountain, Mt Apo (2954m), accessible from Davao in southern Mindanao. Exercise caution if you are heading south or west of Cagayan de Oro (see the boxed text, p595).

Getting There & Away

Domestic airlines service most major cities in Mindanao from Manila and/or Cebu. Popular jumping-off points for ferries from the Visayas include Cebu City, Southern Leyte and Jagna (Bohol).

> **WARNING**
>
> Most embassies strongly warn tourists against travelling to potential conflict zones such as Maguindanao province (and its notoriously violent capital, Cotabato), Zamboanga and the entire Sulu Archipelago. While embassies tend to be a bit alarmist, it pays to exercise considerable caution when travelling to these areas. Check local news sources to make sure your destination and travel route are safe. See p604 for more on the conflict in Mindanao.

Surigao

☎086 / POP 132,000

Congested Surigao is a key transport hub and the gateway to Siargao Island. If you need to stay the night, **Dexter Pension House** (☎232 7526; cnr San Nicolas & Magallanes Sts; s/d from P200/350; ❄) has a central location and small but passable rooms – many windowless – in an antique house. Expat fave **EY Tourist Pension** (☎826 5440; Navarro St; s/d from P780/900; ❄📶) is your minor splurge.

Getting There & Away

Airphil Express, PAL and Cebu Pacific fly daily to/from Manila; Cebu Pacific also has several flights a week to Cebu.

Speedy, super-sized *bangka* ferries head to Dapa on Siargao from in front of the Tavern Hotel (P250, 2¼ hours, three daily, last trip around 11.30am). In bad weather, opt for the daily RORO (P144, 3¼ hours, noon) from the **main pier** (Borromeo St).

For ferries to Liloan and Benit (San Ricardo) in Southern Leyte, see p595; these call in at the port of Lipata, 10km northwest of Surigao, accessible by tricycle (P200). For services to Cebu, see p589.

Bachelor buses run regularly from Surigao to Butuan (P195, 2½ hours). Change in Butuan for Cagayan de Oro. The bus terminal is near the airport, 5km west of the city centre.

Siargao

☎086 / POP 70,000

It's best known for having one of the world's great surf breaks, but the island of Siargao is no one-trick pony. Surrounded by idyllic

GETTING TO MALAYSIA BY SEA

At the time of writing, the only sea route to Malaysia was Zamboanga to Sandakan, Sabah. **Aleson Shipping Lines** (☎062-991 2687; Veterans Ave, Zamboanga) has boats that leave Zamboanga on Monday and Thursday, and depart Sandakan on Tuesday and Friday (economy/cabin P2900/3300, 20 hours). However, travel in the Zamboanga region is considered risky (see p595).

islands and sprinkled with coves and quaint fishing villages, it has plenty to offer non-surfers too.

CLOUD NINE & GENERAL LUNA

The legendary **Cloud Nine break** off Tuazon Point is what put Siargao on the map. While it's now dubbed 'Crowd Nine' by locals, that's probably an exaggeration – although the sleepy village of Cloud Nine does get overrun in October for the **Siargao International Surfing Cup**. The breaks around here are reef breaks, but it's a soft, spongy reef and there are some moderate swells around for beginners, especially in the flat season (May to July). Lessons cost about P500 per hour including board rental – inquire at Ocean 101 or Sagana Beach Resort. Peak season for waves is late August to November.

Hippie's Surf Shop (www.surfshopsiargao.com) just before the Ocean 101 Beach Resort, rents boards (P300 half-day) and holds yoga classes (P200).

Most of the resorts are in Cloud Nine, a bumpy 10-minute *habal-habal* ride north of General Luna ('GL'). All resorts can organise island-hopping trips. In GL you'll find cheap eateries and a couple of bars frequented by local surfer dudes and chicks.

Sleeping & Eating

Prices mushroom and rooms fill up fast from August to October. Some resorts shut down during the rainy low season (December to March in these parts).

Ocean 101 Beach Resort HOTEL $
(☎0910 848 0893; www.ocean101cloud9.com; r P660-1100; ❄@📶) This is surfing HQ, with a mix of well-maintained budget rooms and pricier beachfront quarters distributed among two ugly blue concrete edifices.

Boardwalk at Cloud 9 HOTEL $$
(☎762 7690; www.surfingsiargao.com; r from P1350; ❄📶) It stares straight at Cloud Nine and offers a mix of basic rooms and downright elegant cottages. Can also teach stand-up paddle boarding and kitesurfing. Better than Kesa Cloud 9 in the same courtyard.

Point 303 HOTEL $
(☎0946 261 4316; r P600) Ocean 101's sister property, opposite Sagana, targets budget-minded surfers.

Kawayan INTERNATIONAL $$
(mains P250; ⏲6am-2pm & 6pm-11pm) Exotic North Africa-inspired cuisine.

Drinking

Nine Bar BAR $
Located between Cloud Nine & GL, Nine Bar is where you go to swill beer and swap swell tales.

Getting There & Away

Cebu Pacific has two weekly flights from Cebu to Siargao's small airport in Del Carmen. Otherwise you'll need to arrive by boat from Surigao.

From the pier in Dapa, a *habal-habal* should cost P200 to GL (20 minutes) or P250 to Cloud Nine (30 minutes). Tricycles cost the same but are much slower.

Sporadic jeepneys run from Dapa to GL and points north. To explore the island, you're better off hiring a motorcycle (per day P500).

Cagayan de Oro

☎088 / POP 554,000

It may not be the world's most cosmopolitan city, but every Friday and Saturday night the good people of this city descend on the central thoroughfare and engage in a giant, boozy street party. Take that, Rio! 'CDO' also has some kickin' nightclubs.

Activities

White-Water Rafting RAFTING
Situated on the banks of the Cagayan River, CDO is the one place in the Philippines that has good rapids for rafting year-round. Among the six rafting companies are highly recommended **Kagay CDO Rafting** (☎856 3972; www.cdorafting-map.com) and **CDO Bugsay River Rafting** (☎309 1991; www.bugsayrafting.com; Apolinar Velez St).

Sleeping

Nature's Pensionne HOTEL $
(☎857 2274; T Chavez St; r P680-1380; ❄) This hotel, located in the concrete jungle of downtown CDO, is the best midrange option, with clean, tastefully decorated rooms.

Victoria Suites HOTEL $$
(☎857 4447; www.victoriasuitesonline.com; Tirso Neri St; s/d incl breakfast P650/850; ❄📶) The two four-storey Romanesque pillars and awnings belie its austere interior, but there's security, a coffee shop and an in-house masseuse.

Hotel Ramon HOTEL $
(☎857 4804; cnr Burgos & Tirso Neri Sts; r P550-950; ❄📶) Rooms here are nothing special, but the quiet, riverside location is. Alas, river-view rooms lack balconies, although the restaurant has one.

Eating

The weekend street party on the central boulevard known as Divisoria – dubbed 'Night Cafe' – is a wallet-friendly culinary fiesta. There's a buzzing restaurant and bar scene northeast of the centre at flashy Rosario Arcade, next to Limketkai Mall.

TOP CHOICE **Karachi** PAKISTANI $
(Hayes St; mains P100) Feels like a hole in the wall, but has absolutely fabulous curries, kebabs and other Pakistani food. Top it off with a flavoured hookah (P100). Get here early before the evening karaoke begins.

Butcher's Best Barbeque BARBECUE $
(cnr Corrales & Hayes Sts; meat skewers P15) CDO is awash in cheap barbecue places. This one is preferred by the city's expats.

Drinking

The bar and club action is centred on Tiano Brothers St between Hayes and Gaerlan Sts.

Tilt CLUB
(cnr Apolinar Velez & Hayes Sts) DJs hold court here; shorts and flip-flops are frowned upon.

Club Mojo LIVE MUSIC
(Tiano Brothers St) Live music most nights.

Getting There & Around

Between Cebu Pacific, PAL and Airphil Express there are many daily flights to both Manila and Cebu. The airport is about 10km west of town. From Divisoria take a Carmen jeepney, then transfer to a Lumbia jeepney. Taxis cost an inflated P250. A new airport 30km west of Cagayan was scheduled to open by 2013.

At Macabalan Pier, 5km north of the city centre, various ferry companies serve Cebu (see p589), while Negros Navigation sails to Iloilo (P1995, 14 hours, weekly), Trans Asia goes to Tagbilaran, Bohol (P655, 10 hours, three weekly), and several companies serve Jagna, Bohol (P650, seven hours, most days).

Bachelor Tours buses head up the coast to Butuan (air-con P325, 4½ hours) via Balingoan (P145, two hours). Change buses in Butuan for Surigao. The main bus terminal is located on the edge of town, just beside the Agora Market.

Camiguin

☎088 / POP 81,000

With seven volcanoes, various waterfalls, hot springs, cold springs, deserted islands offshore and underwater diversions aplenty, Camiguin is developing a reputation as a top adventure-tourism destination. The dramatic landscape makes it a great place to strike out on your own and explore, preferably by motorbike (per day P400 to P500), mountain bike (per day P250) or on foot.

Adventure lovers should head to Camiguin Action Geckos (see p598) or **Johnny's Dive N' Fun** (☎387 9588; www.johnnysdive.com; Caves Dive Resort). They both offer a range of trekking, rappelling, mountain biking and diving tours, and are happy to dispense advice to do-it-yourselfers.

Getting There & Around

The most reliable way to Camiguin is to catch a ferry from Balingoan on mainland Mindanao to Benoni, 17km southeast of Mambajao (P170, one hour, roughly hourly until 4pm) on Camiguin. The on-again, off-again fastcraft direct from CDO (2½ hours) was off again when we visited.

From the Balbagon pier near Mambajao, Super Shuttle Ferry has a daily 8am car ferry (P425, 3½ hours) to Jagna on Bohol and a Sunday evening car ferry to Cebu (P880, 11 hours). Oceanjet has a daily fastcraft from Benoni to Jagna (P550, two hours, 2.20pm).

Multicabs circle the island mostly counterclockwise, passing any given point roughly every hour until about 5pm. A special trip in a tricycle/multicab from Benoni to Mambajao costs P150/400.

MAMBAJAO

In this shady capital of Camiguin, life rarely gets out of first gear. Mambajao is a good place to observe ornate *okkil* architecture. The best example is the Landbank building along the National Hwy in the town centre.

Notice the intricate patterns cut into the wooden awning.

TOP CHOICE **Enigmata Treehouse Ecolodge** (0918 230 4184; http://camiguinecolodge.com; dm P200-250, ste from P950;) is a hippie-esque artist hang-out in the woods, and is more a way of life than a resort. Most rooms are in a fantastic house built around a towering hardwood tree and swathed in wooden furniture, murals and artwork. Head honcho Ros does much to promote Camiguin arts and is a fine artist in her own right. The dirt road here turns off the highway at the Tarzan statue about 2km east of Mambajao.

There are a couple of Filipino eateries on the waterfront in Mambajao.

AROUND MAMBAJAO

Most of Camiguin's resorts are on the black-sand beaches in *barangay* Bug-Ong, about 4km west of Mambajao. A tricycle to Bug-Ong costs P75 to P100 from Mambajao.

TOP CHOICE **Camiguin Action Geckos** (387 9146; www.camiguinaction.com; r without bathroom P600, cottages with bathroom P1500) has truly exceptional beachfront cottages, which define rustic sophistication. The cosy budget rooms flank an exquisite chill-out deck above the restaurant.

The big bungalows at **Seascape** (0910 920 6512; Bug-Ong; r P500-700), all bamboo and native materials, are barren inside but have big balconies boasting hammocks and prime views of the ocean. Cheaper rooms are concrete with inlaid bamboo.

Choose between garden cottages and breezy rooms in a big beachfront house at **Caves Dive Resort** (0918 807 6888; www.cavesdiveresort.com; r P700-2500;). It stares at a marooned slick of sand known as White Island.

PALAWAN

Palawan is veritable haven for nature buffs and intrepid adventurers. Drifting on the Philippines' western edge, this long sliver of jungle is one of the country's last ecological frontiers. The Amazonian interior of the main island is barely connected by a few snaking roads that will make your fillings jingle, and the convoluted coast is comprised of one breathtaking bay after another leading up to the limestone cliffs of El Nido and Bacuit Bay in the north. Eight hours north of mainland Palawan, the Calamian group of islands offers beaches, unbeatable wreck diving and a number of El Nido–esque cliffs of their own.

Getting There & Around

Cebu Pacific has daily flights to Puerto Princesa from both Manila and Cebu, while Airphil Express and Zest Air fly from Manila only. Cebu Pacific, Airphil Express and Zest Air have frequent flights daily between Manila and Coron. Seair has on-again, off-again flights to El Nido (they were on again as of this writing). The other option to El Nido from Manila is with pricey **ITI** (in Manila 02-851 5674; www.islandtransvoyager.com; tickets P7500; 3 daily).

SuperFerry (048-434 5734; Rizal Ave, Puerto Princesa) has a weekly vessel to Puerto Princesa from Manila (from P800, 28 hours) via Coron. **Milagrosa Shipping** (048-433 4806; Rizal Ave) and **Montenegro Lines** (048-434 9344; www.montenegrolines.com.ph; Puerto Princesa Pier) sail weekly between Puerto Princesa and Iloilo (P950, 30 hours) via the Cuyo Islands.

Airphil Express has twice weekly flights between Puerto and Coron.

Puerto Princesa

048 / POP 210,500

If only all Philippine cities could be a little more like earthy Puerto Princesa. Strictly enforced fines for littering (P200) keep the streets clean (we're not kidding!), while the municipal government actively promotes the city as an eco- and adventure-tourism hub. Scattered around town is a handful of funky restaurants and guesthouses, where the design motif is part ethnic Filipino, part tripped-out '60s hippie. Yes, there's the usual stream of tricycles down the main commercial drag, Rizal Ave. But even the tricycles seem quieter than in most other provincial centres. In short, 'Puerto' makes a great launching pad for checking out the myriad natural attractions in the surrounding area.

Sights

Palawan Museum MUSEUM
(Mendoza Park, Rizal Ave; admission P20; 9am-noon & 1.30-5pm Mon-Sat) If you're in town, give the small Palawan Museum a gander.

Sleeping

TOP CHOICE **Banwa Art House** BACKPACKER $
(434 8963; www.banwa.com; Liwanag St; dm P350, s/d from P550/750;) This back-

MALARIA WARNING

Malaria is an issue in rural areas. Use the mosquito nets provided by most guesthouses and coat yourself with insect repellent at dusk. Minuscule, stinging sandflies (aptly named *nik-niks*) delight in biting exposed skin and can be a curse on some western beaches.

packer oasis oozes charm from every artisan craft adorning its walls. There's a groovy lounge, surrounded by a waterfall of vines, which has cool tunes wafting from the house CD player.

Manny's Guesthouse GUESTHOUSE $
(☎723 3615; www.mannysguesthouse.com; 2B Mendoza St; r P400-600; ❄📶) Another appealing choice near Banwa, Manny's has spacious rooms in an attractive house with sweeping views of Puerto Bay.

Badjao Inn HOTEL $
(☎433 2761; badjao_inn@yahoo.com; 350 Rizal Ave; r P500-1000; ❄@) To be closer to the airport and the bars, Badjao isn't a bad choice. It has a wide variety of rooms in an ugly edifice surrounding a pleasant interior garden courtyard and restaurant.

Ancieto's Pension GUESTHOUSE $
(☎434 6667; arc_tess@yahoo.com.ph; cnr Mabini & Roxas Sts; s/d from P250/400; ❄📶) Another good choice near Banwa is this family-run bargain. Rooms are basic and susceptible to some street noise, but there's a cosy sitting area with a TV.

Eating & Drinking

TOP CHOICE **Kalui Restaurant** FILIPINO $$
(369 Rizal Ave; mains from P200; ⏱lunch & dinner Mon-Sat) This seafood specialist in a funky *nipa* (traditional hut) complex thoroughly deserves its reputation as one of the finest restaurants in the country. It's a splurge only by the standards of Puerto, where delicious food at low prices is the norm.

Ima's Vegetarian VEGETARIAN $
(Fernandez St; dishes P60-80; ⏱11am-9pm Sun-Thu, to 3pm Fri) A decidedly healthy – and delicious and remarkably cheap – option run by a warm husband-and-wife team. Try the spicy black-bean burger or tofu burger for *merienda* (daytime snack).

Neva's Place PIZZERIA $
(Taft St; mains P70-200) Great budget Filipino and Thai food, as well as pizzas, all served in a blissful garden.

Kinabuch Grill & Bar BAR, GRILL $$
(Rizal Ave; mains P100-150; ⏱5pm-2am) Sprawling 'KGB' has two pool tables and is the watering hole of choice for the thirsty masses.

Cafe Itoy's CAFE $$
(Rizal Ave; ⏱6am-11pm; 📶) Starbucks-style coffee joint on main drag.

Information

Internet cafes line busy Rizal Ave. Metrobank, BDO and BPI, all on Rizal Ave, have mainland Palawan's only working ATMs.

Pasyar Developmental Tourism (☎723 1075; www.pasyarpalawan.tripod.com; Rizal Ave) Genuinely dedicated to conservation and community-based tourism, Pasyar is a great choice for day tours like Honda Bay and dolphin-watching as well as longer adventures.

Tourist Information & Assistance Counter (☎434 4211; airport arrivals hall; ⏱7am-6pm) Run by City Tourism Office, which has an office next door, it distributes a city map and can help with hotel bookings.

Subterranean River National Park Office (☎434 2509; www.puerto-undergroundriver.com; Badjao Inn, 350 Rizal Ave) Issues Subterranean River permits (see p599).

Getting There & Around

The main bus terminal is at the San Jose market 6km north of town; to get there grab a multicab (mini-jeepney) from anywhere along Rizal Ave (P15). Buses and/or vans serve El Nido, Port Barton and Sabang – see those sections for details.

Sabang

☎048

Tiny Sabang has a heavenly expanse of beach and is famed for the navigable **Puerto Princesa Subterranean River National Park** (admission P200), which winds through a spectacular cave before emptying into the sea. Tourist paddleboats are allowed to go 1.5km upstream into the cave (45 minutes return). At certain times of the year it's possible to proceed further upstream with a permit (P400) from the national park office in Puerto (see p599). From the beach in Sabang it's a thrilling 5km walk through the jungle to the mouth of the river, or you can book a boat (P700 for up to six people, 15 minutes) through the Sabang Information Office at the pier.

Sleeping & Eating

Most places run their generators from 6pm to 10pm or 11pm.

Dab Dab Resort BUNGALOW $
(☎0910 924 1673; cottages P400-800) The most appealing budget option in Sabang, Dab Dab has tasteful dark-wood and bamboo cottages, great food and a glorious common area under a soaring octagonal canopy. Unfortunately, it lacks a good beach. It's 200m south of the pier.

Blue Bamboo Cottages BUNGALOW $
(☎0910 582 2589; cottages P300-800) Walk south past Dab Dab, through a small village and find Sabang's cheapest quarters in an eclectic compound. The simple raised cottages have private porches and shaggy thatched roofs.

Mary's Cottages BUNGALOW $
(☎0910 384 1705; cottages P350-700) Mary's occupies the peaceful north end of Sabang Beach, a 10-minute walk from the pier. Expect simplicity and you will not be let down.

Getting There & Away

Vans ply the sealed road between Sabang and Puerto Princesa, departing at 7am, 2pm and 4pm in either direction (P300, two hours). Slower, cheaper jumbo jeepneys and buses make a few trips as well. If you're heading to Port Barton or El Nido, backtrack by road to Salvacion and flag down a northbound bus from the highway.

High-season *bangkas* chug up to El Nido (P2000, seven hours) almost daily, with drop-offs, but not pick-ups, in Port Barton (P1200, 3½ hours).

Port Barton

☎048 / POP 4400

People find themselves unable to leave Port Barton, and only partly because of the town's poor transport links. Set on a small, attractive cove, the area has some fine islands in the bay and good snorkelling. **Island-hopping excursions** (P1500 for up to 4 people) can be easily arranged.

Sleeping & Eating

TOP CHOICE **Greenviews Resort** BUNGALOW $$
(☎0929 268 5333; www.palawan-greenviews.com; r from P900) The last place on the north end of the beach is the best all-round choice and also has the finest restaurant – try the shrimp omelette (P150). The standard rooms are more than acceptable, and the more luxurious cottages are set around a garden.

Summer Homes Beach Resort HOTEL $
(☎0921 401 6906; www.portbarton.info/summerhomes; d P550-1200; ❄@🛜) Summer Homes spurns the native look with well-kept concrete cottages set on a manicured lawn.

El Dorado Sunset Cottages BUNGALOW $
(☎0920 329 9049; d P400-800) Just short of Greenviews at the northern end of town, El Dorado has nine clean cottages set amid gardens behind a beachfront bar.

Getting There & Away

There's one morning jumbo jeepney to Roxas (P100, 1½ hours) and another one to Puerto Princesa (P200, four hours). To get to El Nido, make your way to Roxas and flag down a northbound jeepney.

From Puerto, you can take a more frequent Roxas-bound jeepney as far as San Jose, 2km south of Roxas, and transfer to a motorcycle taxi (P400, one hour). Heavy rains occasionally close this road.

The Port Barton boatman's association bans the high-season Sabang–El Nido *bangkas* from picking up passengers in Port Barton. Hiring a private three-passenger boat costs P6000 to El Nido, P3500 to Sabang.

El Nido

☎048 / POP 5600

El Nido is the primary base for exploring Palawan's star attraction, the stunning **Bacuit Archipelago** (10-day admission P200). Tiny swiftlets build edible nests out of saliva in the immense limestone cliffs that surround the ramshackle town – hence the name, El Nido (nest in Spanish). The town feels touristy by Philippine standards, but sporadic electricity (it cuts off from 6am to 2pm each day), rugged access roads and adventure opportunities galore are firm reminders that you are still in Palawan.

Activities

Island Hopping BOAT TOUR
All-day island-hopping trips in the Bacuit Archipelago cost about P700 to P900 per person, including lunch. Miniloc Island's **Big Lagoon** and **Small Lagoon** are not to be missed; for full effect get there at dawn when you'll have them to yourself. There are several dive operators in town. Art Café has

a list of short hiking expeditions you can do on your own.

Sleeping

There's remarkably little to differentiate the resorts lining El Nido's beach in terms of price (P500 to P800 for a fan room) or quality (mediocre), so consider strolling the beach until you find something you like. Prices drop substantially in the low season – negotiate hard.

TOP CHOICE Alternative Centre BACKPACKER $
(0917 595 5952; beckygordon8@yahoo.com; dm/d from P200/500;) The beach-facing rooms here are beyond creative. Enter through the garage-style front doors into a tangle of intricately carved wooden furniture, cascading streamers and vinelike plants. The cheaper rooms upstairs have octagonal mattresses among other design liberties, and adjoin an equally funky, vegetarian-friendly restaurant.

Makulay Lodge & Villas GUESTHOUSE $$
(0917 257 3851; makulayelnido@yahoo.com; r/apt from P1000/2700;) Just a short walk around the point east of town, Makulay on Caalan Beach feels light years removed from El Nido. It has decent rooms with good views and snazzier hilltop apartments.

Chislyk Cottages BUNGALOW $
(0919 879 9333; ana.bacsa@yahoo.com; cottages P500) Several small bamboo cottages share a stamp-sized beachfront; each has its own porch.

Ogie's Beach Pension HOTEL $
(0916 707 0393; r with fan/air-con incl breakfast from P800/1600;) Has enough rooms (15) that there's a good chance of something being available. The rooms are good value to boot – especially the luscious triples.

Eating & Drinking

Balay Tubay FUSION $
(Real St; mains P120) Tribal-infused live music sets a perfect vibe at this welcome addition to the El Nido nightlife scene, and the food isn't half bad either.

Seaslug's SEAFOOD $
(Hama St; mains P100-220) One of several establishments near Ogie's that will satisfy fans of grilled seafood and suds in the sand.

Pukka Restobar FILIPINO $
(mains P80-150) Good-value breakfasts and local fare on the east side of the beach.

Information

Run like clockwork by the Swiss owner, the **El Nido Boutique & Art Café** (0920 902 6317; www.elnidoboutiqueandartcafe.com;), near the wharf, is a repository for information about El Nido. You can buy plane tickets here, check boat and bus schedules, get cash advances on credit cards (with an 8% surcharge), browse the library, buy art, eat good food and drink real coffee. It's also as good a place as any to arrange boat or sea kayaking excursions into Bacuit Bay.

Getting There & Around

Seair and ITI fly from El Nido to Manila (see p599). The only way to the airport is by tricycle for P150.

For boats to Coron, see p602. Atienza Shipping Lines has a trip to Manila via Coron every Friday.

High-season *bangkas* plow down to Sabang (P2000, seven hours) roughly every other day, stopping in Port Barton (P1500, four hours) by request.

Six vans (P600, about 5½ hours, last trip at 1pm) and a few morning buses (P380, about eight hours) make the journey to Puerto Princesa.

Coron

POP 10,000

Divers know it as a wreck-diving hot spot, but the area known as Coron also has untouched beaches, crystal-clear lagoons and brooding limestone cliffs to tempt nondivers. Coron itself is actually just the sleepy main town of Busuanga Island – not to be confused with Coron Island to the south. Both Busuanga Island and Coron Island are part of the Calamian Group, located about halfway between Mindoro and mainland Palawan.

Activities

Wreck Diving DIVING
Fifteen Japanese ships sunk by US fighter planes roost on the floor of Coron Bay around Busuanga. Getting to the wrecks from Coron involves a one- to four-hour boat

THE PERFECT BEACH

There's a rumour that the island described in Alex Garland's backpacker classic *The Beach* was somewhere in the Calamian Group. Garland set the book in Thailand, but admits that the real island was somewhere in the Philippines. He lived in the Philippines for a spell and set his second novel, *The Tesseract*, in Manila.

ride, but diving is still affordable, averaging about US$40 for a two-tank dive. Most of the wrecks are for advanced divers, although there are a few in less than 25m that are suitable for beginners.

Island Hopping BOAT TOUR
Coron town lacks a beach, but you can hire a boat (four-/eight-person boat per day about P1500/2500) to explore the seemingly infinite supply of islands nearby. **Coron Island**, with its towering spires of stratified limestone, is the star attraction. You can paddle around on a bamboo raft and swim in Coron Island's unspoiled **Lake Cayangan** (admission P250), or go diving in **Barracuda Lake** (admission P100), where the clear water gets scorching hot as you descend.

Sleeping & Eating

The following are in Coron town; the hotels hire out boats for island hopping.

Krystal Lodge BUNGALOW $
(0949 333 0429; pretty_kryz23@yahoo.com; r P400-800, cottages P1200;) Like much of Coron, this bamboo complex is built on stilts over the water. It's a maze of shady walkways ending in rooms that range from passable boxes to utterly unique overwater 'apartments'.

Sea Dive Resort HOTEL $
(0920 945 8714; www.seadiveresort.com.ph; d P400-1200;) A three-storey monolith on the sea accessed by a long walkway, this place has it all: decent rooms, restaurant, bar, internet and busy dive shop.

TOP CHOICE **Bistro Coron** FRENCH $$
(meals P175-500) A mouth-watering French bistro on one of the Philippines' most isolated islands? It works for us. Consider splurging for the tiger prawns, one of the best meals we've had in the Philippines.

SPLURGE: SANGAT ISLAND DIVE RESORT

If you really want to treat yourself – and be much closer to the wrecks – the superb **Sangat Island Dive Resort** (0920 954 4328; www.sangat.com.ph; cottages per person incl 3 meals from P4000) is on its own island, about a 45-minute boat ride from Coron (free transfer for guests). Perfect for R&R or action.

Getting There & Away

For air connections, see p599. Coron's YKR airport is a smooth 35-minute ride north of Coron town; vans (P150) meet the flights.

The weekly SuperFerry vessel between Manila and Puerto Princesa passes through Coron town (see p612).

Atienza Shipping Lines (0919 377 9751) runs a weekly cargo boat from Manila with space for 80 to 100 passengers (P850, 22 hours). It continues to El Nido (P950, 10 hours) every Wednesday evening. The pricier options to El Nido are 15-passenger *bangka* (motorised outriggers), which depart most mornings (P2200, eight hours).

UNDERSTAND PHILIPPINES

Philippines Today

In the 2010 presidential elections, the country found the fresh face it was looking for in the form of Benigno Aquino III, the squeaky clean son of Corazon Aquino, hero of the first People Power revolution in 1986. Riding a wave of national grief after his mother's death in 2009, Aquino emerged from a crowded pack and won in a landslide.

The early returns on Aquino's first six-year term have been positive. Analysts have lauded his willingness to tackle corruption and face down interest groups. But two crucial issues promise to test Aquino's-political will.

In the run-up to the 2010 gubernatorial elections in Maguindanao, Mindanao, 58 people were gunned down at a campaign event for an opposition candidate. Thirty-four of the victims were members of the media. President Aquino has vowed to achieve justice in the case. Ultimately, the success of his presidency may rest on doing just that.

Meanwhile, the Philippines' population surpassed 100 million in 2011, up from just 76.5 million in 2000. In 2008, Congress introduced the Reproductive Health Bill – a national family-planning program that encourages contraceptives and birth-control pills. The powerful Catholic Church opposes the bill, which failed to pass during the last two years in office of Aquino's predecessor, President Arroyo. Aquino supports the bill, and all eyes are on its fate in 2012.

OFF THE BEATEN TRACK IN CORON

Looking to get off the beaten track? Hire a boat or sea kayak and wade around the untouched beaches and islands off the west coast of Busuanga. Or tackle the rough coastal road to Busuanga's northwest tip by motorcycle (P500 to P700), taking pit stops at beaches along the way.

Highlights of the area include **Calumbuyan Island** and **Banana Island**, both of which have world-class snorkelling. Off the northwest tip is **Calauit Island**, home to the **Calauit Safari Park** (admission P350), where the descendents of giraffes, zebras and gazelles brought over from Kenya by Ferdinand Marcos in the 1970s roam. Boats to Calauit leave from Macalachao, 7km north of Buluang (P350, 10 minutes).

Some off-road experience is advised if you go the motorcycle route (the author's riding partner suffered two broken ribs in a fall near Buluang).

History

In a Nutshell

Ancient Filipinos stuck to their own islands and social groups until the 16th century, when Ferdinand Magellan claimed the islands for Spain and began the bloody process of Christianisation. Filipinos' waning acceptance of Spanish rule evaporated after the Spaniards executed national hero José Rizal in 1896. They revolted and won, only to have the Americans take over, whereupon they revolted again and lost. WWII brought much bloodshed, but out of the war's ashes rose an independent republic, albeit one that would soon elect hardliner Ferdinand Marcos as president. Marcos' declaration of martial law in 1972 and the 1986 'People Power' revolution that led to his overthrow are the two defining moments of modern Filipino history. Since 'People Power' the country has remained democratic but its fortunes have improved little under a string of leaders who have done little to eradicate the paralysing corruption and cronyism of the Marcos years.

Spanish Colonialists

In the early 16th century all signs pointed to the archipelago universally adopting Islam, but in 1521 Portuguese explorer Ferdinand Magellan changed the course of Filipino history by landing at Samar and claiming the islands for Spain. Magellan set about converting the islanders to Catholicism and winning over various tribal chiefs before he was killed by Chief Lapu-Lapu on Mactan Island near Cebu City.

In 1565 Miguel de Legazpi returned to the Philippines and, after conquering the local tribes one by one, declared Manila the capital of the new Spanish colony. But outside Manila real power rested with the Catholic friars – the notoriously unenlightened *friarocracia* (friarocracy), who acted as sole rulers over what were essentially rural fiefdoms.

The Philippine Revolution

At the end of the 18th century, Spain was weakened by the Seven Years War, which briefly saw Great Britain take over Manila. As Spain grew weaker, and as the friars grew ever more repressive, the indigenous people started to resist. The Spanish sealed their fate in 1896 by executing the writer José Rizal for inciting revolution. A brilliant scholar and poet, Rizal had worked for independence by peaceful means. His death galvanised the revolutionary movement.

With aid from the USA, already at war with Spain over Cuba, General Emilio Aguinaldo's revolutionary army drove the Spanish back to Manila. American warships defeated the Spanish fleet in Manila Bay in May 1898, and independence was declared on 12 June 1898.

American Rule

Alas, the Americans had other ideas. They acquired the islands from Spain and decided to make the Philippines an American colony. War inevitably broke out in February 1899. But the expected swift American victory didn't materialise, and as the Philippine–American War dragged on, public opposition mounted in the US. The character of the American home-front debate, and the ensuing drawn-out guerrilla war, would have eerie parallels to the Vietnam and Iraq wars many decades later. It was only on 4 July 1902, that the US finally declared victory in the campaign.

The Americans quickly set about healing the significant wounds their victory

RIZAL'S TOWER OF BABEL

The Philippines' answer to Gandhi, writer and gentle revolutionary Dr José Rizal, could read and write at the age of two. He grew up to speak more than 20 languages, 18 of them fluently, including English, Sanskrit, Latin, French, German, Greek, Hebrew, Russian, Japanese, Chinese and Arabic. His last words were *consummatum est!* (it is done!).

had wrought, instituting reforms aimed at improving Filipinos' lot and promising eventual independence. The first Philippine national government was formed in 1935 with full independence pencilled in for 10 years later.

This schedule was set aside when Japan invaded the islands in WWII. For three years the country endured a brutal Japanese military regime before the Americans defeated the Japanese in the Battle for Manila in February 1945. The battle destroyed a city that had been one of the finest in Asia and resulted in the deaths of over 100,000 civilians.

People Power

The 1983 assassination of Ferdinand Marcos' opponent Benigno 'Ninoy' Aquino pushed opposition to Marcos to new heights. Marcos called elections for early 1986 and the opposition united to support Aquino's widow, Corazon 'Cory' Aquino. Both Marcos and Aquino claimed to have won the election, but 'people power' rallied behind Cory Aquino, and within days Ferdinand and his profligate wife, Imelda, were packed off by the Americans to Hawaii, where the former dictator later died.

Cory Aquino failed to win the backing of the army but managed to hang on through numerous coup attempts. She was followed by Fidel Ramos, Ferdinand Marcos' second cousin. In 1998 Ramos was replaced by B-grade movie actor Joseph 'Erap' Estrada, who promised to redirect government funding towards rural and poor Filipinos. Estrada lasted only 2½ years in office before being ousted over corruption allegations in a second 'people power' revolt and replaced by his diminutive vice-president, Gloria Macapagal Arroyo, who would somehow serve nine years, battling her own corruption allegations and threats of a third people-power revolt.

The Moro Problem

Muslim dissent emanating out of Mindanao has been the one constant in the Philippines' roughly 450 years of history as a loosely united territory. The country's largest separatist Muslim group is the 12,500-strong Moro Islamic Liberation Front (MILF), but the group that grabs all the headlines is Abu Sayyaf, which was responsible for a highly publicised kidnapping in 2001 that became the basis of the acclaimed *Atlantic Monthly* piece 'Jihadists in Paradise'.

The MILF signed a ceasefire with the government in 2001, but periodic violence and bombings continued to occur in Mindanao's predominantly Muslim Autonomous Region in Muslim Mindanao (ARMM) until the ceasefire collapsed in August 2008. Fighting intensified and continued until a truce was signed about a year later. Peace negotiations resumed in Malaysia in late 2009, but had borne little fruit at the time of research.

People & Culture

Lifestyle

It's impossible to deny it: Filipinos have a zest for life that may be unrivalled on our planet. The national symbol, the jeepney, is an apt metaphor for the nation. Splashed with colour, laden with religious icons and festooned with sanguine scribblings, the jeepney flaunts the fact that, at heart, it's a dilapidated pile of scrap metal. Like the jeepney, Filipinos face their often dim prospects in life with a laugh and a wink. Whatever happens...'so be it'. This fatalism has a name: *bahala na,* a phrase that expresses the idea that all things shall pass and in the meantime life is to be lived.

For centuries the two most important influences on the lives of Filipinos have been family and religion. The Filipino family unit extends to distant cousins, multiple godparents and one's *barkada* (gang of friends). Filipino families, especially poor ones, tend to be large. It's not uncommon for a dozen family members to live together in a tiny apartment, shanty or *nipa* hut.

Filipinos are a superstitious lot. In the hinterland, a villager might be possessed by a wandering spirit, causing them to commit strange acts. In urban areas, faith healers, psychics, fortune-tellers, tribal shamans, self-help books and evangelical crusaders can all help cast away ill-fortune.

CULTURE HINTS

» Don't lose your temper – Filipinos will think you're *loco loco* (crazy).

» When engaged in karaoke (and trust us, you will be), don't insult the guy who sounds like a chicken getting strangled, lest it be taken the wrong way.

» Abstain from grabbing that last morsel on the communal food platter – your hosts might think you're a pauper.

Another vital thread in the fabric of Filipino society is the overseas worker. At any given time more than one million Filipinos are working abroad. Combined, they send home more than US$15 billion a year, according to official figures (the real figure is likely much higher). The Overseas Filipino Worker (OFW) – the nurse in Canada, the construction worker in Qatar, the entertainer in Japan, the cleaner in Singapore – has become a national hero.

Population

A journey from the northern tip of Luzon to the southern tip of the Sulu islands reveals a range of ethnic groups speaking some 170 different dialects. Filipinos are mainly of the Malay race, although there's a sizeable and economically dominant Chinese minority and a fair number of *mestizos* (Filipinos of mixed descent).

The country's population is thought to be about 100 million and expanding at a rapid clip of about 2% per year – one of the fastest growth rates in Asia. As the population grows it's becoming younger and more urban: the median age is only 22.5 and almost a quarter of the population lives in or around metro Manila.

Arts

Cinema

The Philippines has historically been Southeast Asia's most prolific film-making nation. The movie industry's 'golden age' was the 1950s, when Filipino films won countless awards. In the 1980s and '90s the industry surged again thanks to a genre called 'bold' – think sex, violence and dudes with great hair in romantic roles. Today the mainstream studios are in decline, but the quality of films is improving with the proliferation of independent films such as *Kubrador* (see the boxed text, p606) and the international success of indy directors like Brillante Mendoza, who won Best Director at the 2009 Cannes Film Festival for his graphic, controversial film *Kinatay* (Slaughtered).

Music

Filipinos are best-known for their ubiquitous cover bands and their love of karaoke, but they need not be in imitation mode to show off their innate musical talent. 'OPM' (Original Pinoy Music – 'Pinoy' is what Filipinos call themselves) encompasses a wide spectrum of rock, folk and new age genres – plus a subset that includes all three.

Embodying the latter subset is the band Kalayo (formerly Pinikpikan), which performs a sometimes frantic fusion of tribal styles and modern jam-band rock. The 11-piece band uses bamboo-reed pipes, flutes and percussion instruments and sings in languages as diverse as Visayan, French and Bicol.

The big three of Pinoy rock are slightly grungy eponymous band Bamboo, agreeable trio Rivermaya (formerly fronted by Bamboo), and sometimes sweet, sometimes surly diva Kitchie Nadal, who regularly tours internationally. All of the above sing in both Filipino and English.

MUST READ

» Rafe Bartholomew's *Pacific Rims: Beermen Ballin' in Flip-Flops and the Philippines' Unlikely Love Affair with Basketball* (2010) explores the Philippines' national pastime. It's as riotous as the title implies.

» *Playing with Water – Passion and Solitude on a Philippine Island* is James Hamilton-Paterson's account of life on a remote islet off Marinduque. It sheds light on many aspects of Philippine culture.

» Alex Garland's *The Tessaract* (1999), a thrilling romp through Manila's dark side, was the second novel penned by the author of the 1996 cult backpacker hit, *The Beach*.

VIEWING LIST

» *Imelda* (2004) – Filipina American Ramona Diaz directs this fascinating look into the psyche of Imelda Marcos.

» *Kubrador* (2006) – Top actress Gina Pareño stars in this superb film about the illegal numbers game *juetang*.

» *Serbis* (2008) – Pareño also stars in Brillante Mendoza's film about life in a family-run porn-movie house in the Philippines' prostitution capital, Angeles.

» *Manila 1945: The Forgotten Atrocities* (2007) – Damning documentary about the Japanese role in the destruction of Manila, available at Manila's Solidaridad bookshop (p563).

» *Paper Dolls* (2006) – Interesting film about the lives of transvestite overseas Filipino workers (OFWs) in Tel Aviv.

Food & Drink

Food

As an approximate guide, prices for main dishes when eating out are budget ($) US$1 to US$5, midrange ($$) US$5 to US$10 and top end ($$$) US$10 plus.

Kain na tayo – 'let's eat'. It's the Filipino invitation to eat, and if you travel here, you will hear it over and over again. The phrase reveals two essential aspects of Filipino people: one, that they are hospitable, and two, that they love to, well, eat. Three meals a day isn't enough, so they've added two *merienda*. The term means 'snack', but don't let that fool you – the afternoon *merienda* can include filling *goto* (Filipino congee) or *bibingka* (fluffy rice cakes topped with cheese).

Other favourite Filipino snacks and dishes:

Adobo Chicken, pork or fish in a dark tangy sauce.

Balut Half-developed duck embryo, boiled in the shell.

Crispy pata Deep-fried pork hock or knuckles.

Halo-halo A tall, cold glass of milky crushed ice with fresh fruit and ice cream.

Kare-kare Meat (usually oxtail) cooked in peanut sauce.

Kinilaw Delicious Filipino-style *ceviche*.

Lechon Spit-roast suckling pig.

Lumpia Spring rolls filled with meat or vegetables.

Mami Noodle soup, like *mee* soup in Malaysia or Indonesia.

Pancit Stir-fried *bihon* (white) or *canton* (yellow) noodles with meat and vegetables.

Pinakbet Vegetables with shrimp paste, garlic, onions and ginger.

Sisig Crispy fried pork ears and jowl.

Drink

The national brew, San Miguel, is very palatable and despite being a monopolist is eminently affordable at around P20 (P30 to P55 in bars). Tanduay rum is the national drink, and amazingly cheap at around P75 per litre. It's usually served with coke. Popular nonalcoholic drinks include *buko* juice (young coconut juice with floating pieces of jelly-like flesh) and sweetened *calamansi* juice (*calamansi* are small local limes).

Environment & Wildlife

An assemblage of 7107 tropical isles scattered about like pieces of a giant jigsaw puzzle, the Philippines stubbornly defies geographic generalisation. The typical island boasts a jungle-clad, critter-infested interior and a sandy coastline flanked by aquamarine waters and the requisite coral reef. More-populated islands have less jungle and more farmland.

The Philippines' flora includes well over 10,000 species of trees, bushes and ferns, including 900 types of orchid. About 25% of the Philippines is forested, but only a small percentage of that is primary tropical rainforest.

Endangered animal species include the mouse deer (see the boxed text, p593), the tamaráw (a species of dwarf buffalo) of Mindoro, the Philippine crocodile of Northeast Luzon, the Palawan bearcat and the flying lemur. As for the country's national bird, there are thought to be about 500 pairs of *haribon*, or Philippine eagles, remaining in the rainforests of Mindanao, Luzon, Samar and Leyte.

There's an unbelievable array of fish, shells and corals, as well as dwindling numbers of the *duyong* (dugong, or sea cow). If your timing's just right, you can spot *butanding* (whale sharks) in Donsol and Southern Leyte.

National Parks

The Philippines' national parks, natural parks and other protected areas comprise about 10% of the country's total area, but most lack services such as park offices, huts, trail maps and sometimes even trails. The most popular national park is surely Palawan's Subterranean River National Park (p599).

Environmental Issues

The Philippines has strict environmental laws on its books, but they just aren't enforced. Only 1% of the reefs are in a pristine state, according to the World Bank, while more than 50% are unhealthy.

The biggest culprit of reef damage is silt, which is washed down from hills and valleys indiscriminately – and often illegally – cleared of their original forest cover. Illegal logging also exacerbates flooding and is the cause of landslides, such as the one in February 2006 that killed more than 1000 people in St Bernard, Southern Leyte. Some lip service is given to the issue by the government, but little is done to combat illegal logging. Incredibly short-sighted techniques for making a few extra bucks include dynamite and cyanide fishing.

SURVIVAL GUIDE

DIRECTORY A–Z

Accommodation

Budget Ranges

In this chapter a hotel qualifies as 'budget' if it has double rooms for P700 or less and/or dorm rooms for no more than P400 per bed.

What to Expect

Rooms in the P200 to P450 range are generally fan-cooled with a shared bathroom, and rooms in the P500 to P700 range usually have fan and private bathroom. Anything higher should have air-conditioning. Prices are higher in Manila and in trendy resort areas such as Boracay and Alona Beach, although reasonable dorm beds can be had in Manila for about P400.

Seasonal Price Fluctuations

This chapter lists high-season (November to May) rates. Prices in tourist hot spots go down by up to 50% in the low season, but may triple or even quadruple during Holy Week (Easter) and around New Year's.

Activities

Popular outdoor activities (see individual sections in this chapter for details):

Cycling & Mountain Biking See www.bugoybikers.com.

Diving The best dive hot spots include Puerto Galera (Mindoro), Apo Island (Negros), Panglao Island (Bohol), and Moalboal and Malapascua Island (Cebu). Generally, it costs certified divers US$23 to US$30 for a single-tank dive with equipment. PADI open-water certification courses vary widely from resort to resort and can cost from US$300 to US$450.

Kayaking & Whitewater Rafting Besides Cagayan de Oro (p596), there's seasonal (September to December) whitewater on the upper Chico River around Bontoc (p569). For advice on kayaking and rafting countrywide, contact **Raft Sagada** (☎0919 698 8361; www.luzonoutdoors.com), also runs trips on the upper Chico.

Rock Climbing www.climbphilippines.com.

Surfing The top surfing destination in the Philippines is Siargao Island (p596). Other good breaks can be found all along the Philippines' eastern border, although many of the best breaks are virtually inaccessible and must be reached by boat. The season on the east coast generally coincides with typhoon season, roughly August to November. There is smaller but more consistent surf to be had from November to early March in San Juan, near San Fernando (La Union) on the west coast of Luzon. See www.surfpinoy.com for a rundown of surf spots in the Philippines.

Trekking See the wonderful website www.pinoymountaineer.com for comprehensive profiles of all the major peaks.

Business Hours

Banks 9am to 4pm Monday to Friday.

Bars 6pm to late.

Restaurants 7am or 8am to 10pm or 11pm.

Shopping malls 10am to 9.30pm.

Supermarkets 9am to 7pm or 8pm.

Climate

The Philippines is hot throughout the year, with brief respites possible from December to February. For most of the country, the dry season is during the *amihan* (northeast monsoon), roughly November to May. Rains start once the *habagat* (southwest monsoon) arrives in June, peak in August, and start tapering off in October. Typhoons are common from June to early December.

But in parts of the country the seasons are flipped. Eastern Mindanao, Southern Leyte, Samar and Southeast Luzon are rainy from December to March and relatively dry when the rest of the country is sopping (although the Eastern seaboard north of Mindanao is highly vulnerable to typhoons).

Use the website of **PAGASA** (www.pagasa.dost.gov.ph) or www.typhoon2000.ph to avoid meteorological trouble spots.

Embassies & Consulates

The **Philippines Department of Foreign Affairs** (DFA; www.dfa.gov.ph) website lists all Philippine embassies and consulates abroad, and all foreign embassies and consulates in the Philippines.

The following are located in Manila:

Australia (☎02-757 8100/8102; 23rd fl, Tower 2, RCBC Plaza, 6819 Ayala Ave, Makati)

Brunei (☎02-816 2836; 11th fl, BPI Bldg, cnr Ayala Ave & Paseo de Roxas, Makati)

Canada (☎02-857 9000; Levels 6-8, Tower 2, RCBC Plaza, 6819 Ayala Ave, Makati)

France (☎02-857 6900; 16th fl, Pacific Star Bldg, cnr Gil Puyat Ave & Makati Ave, Makati)

Germany (☎02-702 3000; 25/F Tower 2, RCBC Plaza, 6819 Ayala Ave, Makati)

Indonesia (☎02-892 5061; 185 Salcedo St, Makati)

Laos (☎02-852 5759; 34 Lapu-Lapu Ave, Magallanes, Makati)

Malaysia (☎02-864 0761-68; 330 Sen Gil Puyat Ave, Makati)

Myanmar (☎02-893 1944; Gervasia Bldg, 152 Amorsolo St, Makati)

New Zealand (☎02-891 5358-67; 23rd fl, BPI Buendia Centre, Gil Puyat Ave, Makati)

Singapore (☎02-856 9922; 505 Rizal Drive, Fort Bonifacio)

Thailand (☎02-815 4220; 107 Rada St, Makati)

UK (☎02-858 2200; 120 Upper McKinley Rd, McKinley Hill, Taguig City)

USA (Map p558; ☎02-301 2000; 1201 Roxas Blvd, Ermita)

Vietnam (☎02-524 0364; 670 Pablo Ocampo St, Malate)

Gay & Lesbian Travellers

Bakla (gay men) and *binalaki* or *tomboy* (lesbians) are almost universally accepted in the Philippines. There are well-established gay centres in major cities, but foreigners should be wary of hustlers and police harassment. Remedios Circle in Malate, Manila, is the site of a June gay-pride parade and the centre for nightlife.

Online gay and lesbian resources for the Philippines include **Utopia Asian Gay & Lesbian Resources** (www.utopia-asia.com).

Internet Access

Internet cafes are all over the Philippines. Speedy connections are readily available in all cities for P25 to P60 per hour. Wi-fi is now the rule rather than the exception in hotels and coffee shops in large cities and touristy areas.

Maps

The Nelles Verlag *Philippines* map is a good map of the islands at a scale of 1:1,500,000. For local travel, E-Z Maps and Accu-Map (www.accu-map.com) produce excellent maps covering most major islands, large cities and tourist areas. They are widely

PRACTICALITIES

» **Newspapers** The best broadsheets are the national papers *Philippine Daily Inquirer, Business World* and *Business Mirror.*

» **TV** About seven major channels broadcast from Manila (in English or Tagalog). Most midrange hotels have cable with up to 120 channels, including obscure regional channels, Filipino and international movies and news and sports channels such as BBC and ESPN.

» **Radio** Manila stations worth listening to are Jam 88.3 and, for Filipino Rock, Win Radio 107.5.

» **Video** NTSC video system.

» **Weights & Measures** Metric system; weights quoted in kilograms, distances in kilometres.

available at hotels, airports, bookshops and gas stations for P99 to P150.

Money

The unit of currency is the peso, divided into 100 centavos.

ATMs

Getting crisp P500 and P1000 peso bills out of the myriad ATM machines that line the streets of any decent-sized provincial city usually isn't a problem. Where a region covered in this chapter does not have ATMs (such as most of Palawan), it is noted in that section.

The Maestro-Cirrus network is most readily accepted, followed by Visa/Plus cards, then by American Express (Amex). The most prevalent ATMs that accept most Western bank cards belong to Banco de Oro (BDO), Bank of the Philippine Islands (BPI) and Metrobank.

Most ATMs charge P200 per withdrawal and have a P10,000-per-transaction withdrawal limit; the HSBC ATMs in Manila and Cebu let you take out P40,000 per transaction.

Cash

Emergency cash in US dollars is a good thing to have in case you get stuck in an area with no working ATM. Other currencies, such as the euro or UK pound, are more difficult to change outside the bigger cities.

'Sorry, no change' becomes a very familiar line. Stock up on P20, P50 and P100 notes at every opportunity.

Credit Cards

Major credit cards are accepted by many hotels, restaurants and businesses. Outside Manila, businesses sometimes charge a bit extra (about 4%) for credit-card transactions. Most Philippine banks will let you take a cash advance on your card.

Public Holidays

Offices and banks are closed on public holidays, although shops and department stores stay open. Maundy Thursday and Good Friday are the only days when the entire country closes down – even most public transport and some airlines stop running. Public holidays:

New Year's Day 1 January

People Power Day 25 February

Maundy Thursday, Good Friday & Easter Sunday March/April

Araw ng Kagitingan (Bataan Day) 9 April

Labour Day 1 May

Independence Day 12 June

Ninoy Aquino Day 21 August

National Heroes Day Last Sunday in August

All Saints' Day 1 November

End of Ramadan Varies; depends on Islamic calendar

Bonifacio Day (National Heroes Day) 30 November

Christmas Day 25 December

Rizal Day 30 December

New Year's Eve 31 December

PROSTITUTION

Prostitution and its most insidious form, child prostitution, is unfortunately prevalent in the Philippines. The Asia-Pacific office of the **Coalition Against Trafficking in Women** (☎02-426 9873; www.catw-ap.org) is based in Quezon City. Its website has information about prostitution in the Philippines and several useful links. **ECPAT Philippines** (☎02-920 8151; ecpatphil@gmail.com) in Quezon City works to promote child-safe tourism and end the commercial sexual exploitation of children.

For more information on prostitution in the SE Asia, see p41.

Safe Travel

The Philippines certainly has more than its share of dangers. Typhoons, earthquakes, volcano eruptions, landslides and other natural disasters can wreak havoc with your travel plans – or worse if you happen to be in the wrong place at the wrong time. Keep an eye on the news and be prepared to alter travel plans to avoid weather trouble spots.

Mindanao (the central and southwest regions in particular) and the Sulu Archipelago are the scenes of clashes between the army on one side and Muslim separatist groups on the other (see p604 and p595).

Manila in particular is known for a few common scams (see p564).

Telephone

The Philippine Long Distance Telephone Company (PLDT) operates the Philippines' fixed-line network. Local calls cost almost nothing; long-distance domestic calls are also very reasonable.

International calls can be made from any PLDT office. PLDT offers flat rates of US$0.40 per minute for international calls (operator-assisted calls are much more expensive).

Dialling Codes

For domestic long-distance calls or calls to mobile numbers, dial ☎0 followed by the city code (or mobile prefix) then the seven-digit number.

Useful dialling codes from land lines:

Philippines country code ☎63.

International dialling code ☎00.

PLDT directory ☎187 nationwide

International operator ☎108

Domestic operator ☎109

Mobile Phones

Mobile phones are ubiquitous, and half the country spends much of the time furiously texting the other half. For travellers, cellphones are also useful for booking rooms (often accomplished by text message) and texting newly made Filipino friends. Prepaid SIM cards cost as little as P40 and come preloaded with about the same amount of text credits. The two companies with the best national coverage are **Globe** (www.globe.com.ph) and **Smart** (www.smart.com.ph).

Text messages on both networks cost P1 to P2 per message, while local calls cost P7.50 per minute (less if calling within a mobile network). International text messages cost P15, and international calls cost US$0.40 per minute.

Philippine mobile-phone numbers begin with ☎09. If a number listed in this book has 10 digits and begins with ☎09, assume it's a mobile number.

Phonecards

Use the PLDT 'Budget' card to call the US for only P3 per minute (other international destinations slightly more). These cards are available at phone kiosks in malls.

Toilets

Toilets are commonly called a 'CR', an abbreviation of the delightfully euphemistic 'comfort room'. Public toilets are virtually nonexistent, so aim for one of the ubiquitous fast-food restaurants should you need a room of comfort.

Travellers with Disabilities

Steps up to hotels, tiny cramped toilets and narrow doors are the norm apart from at four-star hotels in Manila, Cebu and a handful of larger provincial cities. Elevators are often out of order, and boarding any form of rural transport is likely to be fraught with difficulty. On the other hand, most Filipinos are more than willing to lend a helping hand, and the cost of hiring a taxi for a day, and possibly an assistant as well, is not excessive.

Visas

Citizens of nearly all countries do not need a visa to enter the Philippines for stays of less than 22 days. When you arrive, you'll receive a 21-day visa free of charge. If you overstay your visa, you face fines and airport immigration officials may not let you pass through immigration.

Avoid this inconvenience by extending your 21-day visa to 59 days before it expires. Extensions cost P3030 and are a breeze at most provincial Bureau of Immigration (BOI) offices. The process is infinitely more painful at the **BOI head office** (Map p558; ☎02-338 4536; Magallanes Dr, Intramuros, Manila; ⏲7.30am-5pm Mon-Fri).

Another option is to secure a three-month visa before you arrive in the Philippines. These cost US$30 to US$45 depending on where you apply.

For a full list of provincial immigration offices, hit the 'BI-Subport Offices' link at http://immigration.gov.ph. Useful provincial offices include the following:

Baguio (☎074-447 0805; 38 Military Cut Off Rd)

Boracay (Map p579; ☎036-288 5267; Nirvana Resort, Main Rd; ⏲7.30am-5.30pm Mon & Tue)

Cebu City (☎032-345 6442; cnr Burgos St & Mandaue Ave, Mandaue)

Puerto Galera (Map p576; ☎043-288 2245; 2nd Fl, Public Mkt; ⏲9am-5pm Mon & Tue, to 12.30pm Wed)

Puerto Princesa (☎048-433 2248; 2nd fl, Servando Bldg, Rizal Ave)

Onward Tickets

Be prepared to show the airline at your point of departure to the Philippines a ticket for onward travel within three weeks of your arrival date if you want a 21-day visa on arrival. If you don't have one, the airline will more often than not make you buy one on the spot. BOI offices also sometimes ask to see onward tickets before they process visa extensions.

Volunteering

As might be expected in an overwhelmingly Christian country, the Philippines has loads of voluntourism opportunities:

Gawad Kalinga (www.gk1world.com/ph) GK's mission is building entire communities for the poor and homeless. Volunteers can build houses, teach children or get involved in a host of other activities.

Habitat for Humanity (☎02-846 2177; www.habitat.org.ph) Builds houses for the poor all over the country, concentrating on disaster-affected areas.

Hands on Manila (☎02-386 6521; www.handsonmanila.org) This organisation is always looking for eager volunteers to help with disaster assistance and other projects.

Volunteer for the Visayas (☎053-325 2462; www.visayans.org) Runs various volunteer programs around Tacloban, Leyte.

DEPARTURE TAX

International departure tax is P750 at NAIA and Clark, and P550 at Cebu.

Getting There & Away

Most people enter the Philippines via one of the three main international airports in Manila, Cebu and Clark. A handful of international flights also go straight to Davao, Mindanao, and to Kalibo near Boracay.

The only feasible non-flight option is by ferry to Zamboanga (Mindanao) from Sandakan in the Malaysian state of Sabah.

Flights, tours and train tickets can be booked online at lonelyplanet.com/bookings.

Air

Airports & Airlines

Ninoy Aquino International Airport (NAIA; Code MNL; ☎02-877 1109) The country's recently upgraded flagship airport is in flux – see the boxed text below for important arrival/departure information regarding terminals.

The Philippines' primary low-cost carrier, Cebu Pacific, serves an ever-growing list of Southeast Asian cities, including Bangkok, Brunei, Jakarta, Kota Kinabalu, Kuala Lumpur, Saigon and Singapore. The other low-cost airlines flying to/from NAIA are local carrier Zest Air, Singapore's Jetstar Asia and Tiger Airways. The country's flagship carrier, Philippine Airlines (PAL), also serves many Southeast Asian destinations.

Diosdado Macapagal International Airport (Clark Airport; code DMIA; www.clarkairport.com) Clark Airport is near Angeles, a two-hour bus ride north of downtown Manila. It has become a hot destination for Asian low-cost airlines. Cebu Pacific serves a host of Southeast Asian destinations from here, while Tiger Airways flies from Bangkok, Hong Kong, Macau and Singapore. Air Asia serves Kuala Lumpur and Kota Kinabalu.

Mactan International Airport (Code CEB; ☎032-340 2486; www.mactan-cebuairport.com.ph) If you're heading to the Visayas, consider flying into Cebu City. Cebu Pacific flies direct to Cebu from Singapore and Seoul. Cathay Pacific and PAL have direct flights to/from Hong Kong, while Silk

TERMINAL CHAOS

Plans are in place at Manila's Ninoy Aquino International Airport (NAIA) to eventually shift all international flights from the airport's dismal, antiquated Terminal 1 to the new Terminal 3. However, questions remain about the technical soundness of Terminal 3, which was built in 2002 but stood idle for six years as a dispute simmered between the builders and the Philippine government.

For now, Airphil Express and Cebu Pacific are the only airlines using Terminal 3. All Philippine Airlines (PAL) flights use yet another terminal, the relatively modern Centennial Terminal 2, while other international carriers use Terminal 1. Smaller domestic carriers Zest Air and Seair use the old Manila Domestic Terminal, located down the road from Terminal 3.

The four NAIA terminals share runways, but they are not particularly close to each other and are linked only by busy public roads. Allow plenty of time between connecting flights if you have to switch terminals.

A **shuttle bus** (P20; ⏲7am-10pm) links the four terminals.

Air and PAL service Singapore. Zest Air services Seoul and Shanghai.

Kalibo International Airport (Code KLO) Domestic carrier Zest Air has launched flights to/from Chengdu, Pusan, Seoul, Shanghai and Taipei, and one can see that list expanding.

The following are the main airlines serving Southeast Asia from the Philippines:

Air Asia (code AXM; www.airasia.com)

Cathay Pacific (code CX; ☎02-757 0888; www.cathaypacific.com)

Cebu Pacific (code 5J; ☎02-702 0888; www.cebupacificair.com)

Jetstar (code 3K; ☎1-800 1611 0280; www.jetstar.com)

Malaysia Airlines (code MH; ☎02-887 3215; www.malaysiaairlines.com)

Philippine Airlines (code PR; ☎02-855 8888; www.philippineairlines.com)

Thai Airways International (code TG; ☎02-812 4744; www.thaiairways.com)

Tiger Airways (code TGW; ☎02-884 1524; www.tigerairways.com)

Silk Air (☎02-239 2871; www.silkair.com.sg)

Singapore Airlines (code SQ; ☎02-756 8888; www.singaporeairlines.com)

Vietnam Airlines (code VN; ☎02-830 2335; www.vietnamairlines.com)

Zest Air (code 6K; ☎02-855 3333; www.zestair.com.ph)

Sea

Although there are plenty of shipping routes within the Philippines, international services are scarce. The only route open to foreigners, as of this writing, was Zamboanga to Sandakan in the Malaysian state of Sabah. See p596 for further details.

Getting Around

Air

The main domestic carriers are PAL and low-cost carrier Cebu Pacific. Together they serve most main cities out of Manila and/or Cebu.

PAL's budget subsidiary, Airphil Express (formerly Air Philippines), competes with rapidly expanding Cebu Pacific in the low-cost domestic market. Smaller carriers include ITI, Mid-Sea Express, Sky Pasada, Seair and Zest Air. The latter two fly from Manila to Caticlan (Boracay) and a few other cities. ITI flies exclusively from Manila to El Nido, Palawan. Mid-Sea Express does short hops from Cebu, while Sky Pasada does the same from Baguio.

We do not list domestic flight prices in this chapter, but one-way flights on Cebu Pacific, Airphil Express and Zest Air only cost P1000 to P2000 (including taxes) on most routes provided you book in advance. PAL is slightly more expensive. Seair and ITI are pricier 'boutique' airlines.

Flight times range from 45 minutes for short hops such as Manila to Caticlan to 1½ hours for flights from Manila to southern Mindanao.

Airline details:

Cebu Pacific (code 5J; ☎02-702 0888; www.cebupacificair.com; NAIA Terminal 3)

ITI (☎815 5674; www.islandtransvoyager.com; Andrews Ave, Pasay City)

Airphil Express (code 2P; ☎02-855 9000; www.airphilexpress.com; NAIA Terminal 3)

Mid-Sea Express (☎032-495 6976; www.midseaexpress.com; General Aviaton Rd, Mactan Island, Cebu)

Philippine Airlines (code PR; ☎02-855 8888; www.philippineairlines.com; NAIA Terminal 2)

Seair (code DG; ☎02-849 0100; www.flyseair.com; 2nd fl Doña Concepcion Bldg, A Arnaiz Ave, Makati)

Sky Pasada (WCC; code SP; (☎074-912 3333; www.skypasada.com; NAIA Domestic Terminal)

Zest Air (code 6K; ☎02-855 3333; www.zestair.com.ph; Domestic Rd cnr Andrews Ave, Pasay City)

Boat

If boats are your thing, this is the place for you. The islands of the Philippines are linked by an incredible network of ferry routes and prices are generally affordable. Ferries usually take the form of motorised outriggers (known locally as *bangka,* also called pumpboats), speedy 'fastcraft' vessels, car ferries (dubbed RORO, or 'roll-on-roll-off' ferries) and, for long-haul journeys, vast multidecked ships. Fastcraft services are passenger-only and are popular on shorter routes. They can cut travel times by half but usually cost twice as much as slower RORO ferries. Some shipping lines give 20% to 30% off for students.

Bangkas are also available for hire for diving, island-hopping or getting around. The engines on these boats can be deafeningly loud, and they aren't the most stable in rough seas, but on islands with poor inland infrastructure the *bangka* can be preferable to travelling overland.

MOVING ON FROM CLARK AIRPORT

Several bus companies run trips directly from Clark to Manila (see p565 for a list of companies).

For points north of Clark, take the airport shuttle van (P45) or a fixed-rate taxi (P500) to Angeles' Dau bus terminal, where you'll find plenty of buses going to Baguio, Vigan and elsewhere.

Getting to Banaue is trickier. If you're comfortable changing buses, the recommended route is Dau–Tarlac–San Jose (or Cabanatuan)–Solano–Lagawe–Banaue. The alternative is to backtrack to Manila and get the direct night bus to Banaue.

Booking ahead is essential for long-haul liners and can be done at ticket offices or travel agents in most cities. For fastcraft and *bangka* ferries, tickets can usually be bought at the pier before departure.

For the most part, ferries are an easy, enjoyable way to island hop, but accidents are not unknown. In May 2008 a Sulpicio Lines ferry went down off Romblon in Typhoon Frank; less than 60 passengers survived and more than 800 perished. In May 2009 an overloaded *bangka* ferry sank en route to Puerto Galera from Batangas. Twelve of the 60 passengers drowned. A large SuperFerry vessel went down off Mindanao in September 2009. Miraculously all but nine of the 900 passengers were rescued.

Bus & Van

Philippine buses come in all shapes and sizes, from rusty boxes on wheels to luxury air-con coaches. Depots are dotted throughout towns and the countryside, and most buses will stop if you wave them down.

Generally, more services run in the morning – buses on unsealed roads may run only in the morning, especially in remote areas. Most buses follow a fixed schedule but may leave early if they're full. Night services are common between Manila and major provincial hubs in Luzon.

Air-con minivans shadow bus routes in many parts of the Philippines and in some cases have replaced buses altogether. However, you may have to play a waiting game until the vehicles are full. Minivans are a lot quicker than buses, but they are also more expensive and more cramped.

Local Transport

HABAL-HABAL

Common in many Visayan islands and northern Mindanao, these are simply motorcycle taxis with extended seats (literally translated as 'pigs copulating', after the level of intimacy attained when sharing a seat with four people). *Habal-habal* function like tricycles, only they are a little bit cheaper. Outside of the Visayas (and in the north Visayas) they're known as 'motorcycle taxis' or 'singles'.

JEEPNEY

The first jeepneys were modified army jeeps left behind by the Americans after WWII. They have been customised with Filipino touches such as chrome horses, banks of coloured headlights, radio antennae, paintings of the Virgin Mary and neon-coloured scenes from action comic books.

Jeepneys form the main urban transport in most cities and complement the bus services between regional centres. Within towns, the starting fare is usually P8, rising modestly for trips outside of town. Routes are clearly written on the side of the jeepney.

TAXI

Metered taxis are common in Manila and most major provincial hubs. Flag fall is a mere P40, and a 15-minute trip rarely costs more than P150.

Most taxi drivers will turn on the meter; if they don't, politely request that they do. If the meter is 'broken' or your taxi driver says the fare is 'up to you', the best strategy is to get out and find another cab (or offer a low-ball price).

TRICYCLE

Found in most cities and towns, the tricycle is the Philippine rickshaw – a little, roofed sidecar bolted to a motorcycle. The standard fare for local trips in most provincial towns is P8. Tricycles that wait around in front of malls, restaurants and hotels will attempt to charge five to 10 times that for a 'special trip'. Avoid these by standing roadside and flagging down a passing P8 tricycle. You can also charter tricycles for about P300 per hour or P150 per 10km if you're heading out of town.

Many towns also have nonmotorised push tricycles, alternately known as pedicabs, *put-put* or *podyak,* for shorter trips.

Singapore

Includes »

Best Regional Specialities

» Hawker food at Gluttons Bay (p632)

» Hawker food at Singapore Food Trail (p631)

» *Kaya* (coconut jam) toast and sweetened coffee at Ya Kun Kaya Toast (p632)

Best Places for Cultural Connections

» Straits Chinese culture at Peranakan Museum (p618)

» Learn all about Asia at the Asian Civilisations Museum (p618)

» Soaking up the buzz in Little India (p619)

Why Go?

One of Asia's success stories, tiny little Singapore's GDP consistently ranks it as one of the wealthiest countries in the world. Along with that wealth comes a rich culture borne of a multiracial population. Get lost in the mad swirl of skyscrapers in the central business district (CBD), be transfixed by the Bolly beats in the streets of ramshackle Little India, hike a dense patch of rainforest in Bukit Timah or just give yourself up to the retail mayhem of Orchard Rd.

It's affluent, high tech and occasionally a little snobbish, but Singapore's great leveller is the hawker centre, the ubiquitous and raucous food markets where everyone mucks in together to indulge the local mania for cheap eating and drinking. In short, Singapore makes for a perfect pit stop to recover from the rough-and-tumble of the rest of Southeast Asia.

When to Go

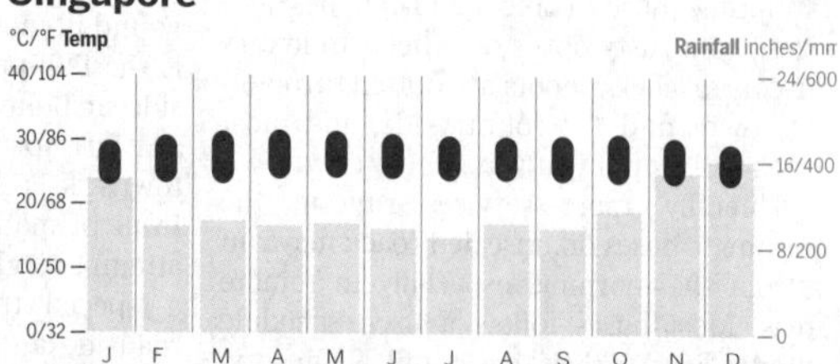

Feb Chinese New Year and Chingay are the events to catch.

Apr–May Lots of events and just before the local school holidays start.

Dec The north-east monsoons bring lashing rains, but they also cool Singapore down.

Don't Miss

The **Colonial District**. This is the heart of Singapore and the former seat of British power. It also connects up the modern, fast-changing Singapore. You can't avoid the Marina Bay and CBD cityscape. Get to a rooftop bar or up on the Singapore Flyer for a bird's eye view of the entire area.

Of course, Singapore is famous for its **cuisine**. Find a hawker centre or food court (there's one in every mall) and follow your nose or join the longest queues for gastronomic delights.

ITINERARIES

Day One

Start in the Colonial District. Take in the architectural glory and wander along the Singapore River through the Quays towards Marina Bay. The museums here are perfect for dodging the searing humidity while taking in some culture. Go for dinner at Gluttons Bay before hitting Clark Quay to drink and party.

Day Two

Start the morning with a stroll in the Botanic Gardens before indulging in retail therapy along Orchard Rd. If malls aren't your thing, get to Little India for a slice of grubby, authentic Singapore. Finish the night with food, drinks and *sheesha* (waterpipe) in Kampong Glam.

Day Three

Spend the day either checking out the zoo and night safari or out on an island. Pick Sentosa for beaches and kitschy theme parks or Pulau Ubin for a rustic getaway. If you have energy left, head to any neighbourhood in Eastern Singapore for dinner and Tiger beer.

Essential Food & Drink

» **Char kway teow** Flat rice noodles wok-fried with bean sprouts, cockles, prawns and Chinese sausage in dark soy sauce and chilli sauce.

» **Chilli crab** Fresh crab cooked in thick, piquant tomato and egg-based chilli gravy.

» **Nasi padang** Steamed white rice served with your choice of meats and vegetables. Lots of curries available. Just choose and point.

» **Murtabak** Pan-fried pancake stuffed with spiced mince meat (chicken, beef or mutton), garlic, egg and onion.

» **Hainanese chicken rice** Tender poached chicken served on a bed of fragrant rice (cooked in chicken stock) with accompanying garlic chilli sauce.

» **Tiger beer** While not the national drink, Singapore's local brew is a pale lager that goes down a treat.

AT A GLANCE

» **Currency** Singapore dollar (S$)

» **Language** English (primary), Mandarin, Bahasa Malay, Tamil

» **Money** ATMs widely available. Credit cards accepted most places.

» **Visas** On arrival. Generally not needed for stays up to 90 days.

Fast Facts

» **Area** 694 sq km

» **Population** 4.98 million

» **Country code** ☎65

» **Emergency** ☎999

Exchange Rates

Australia	A$1	S$1.30
Canada	C$1	S$1.25
Euro zone	€1	S$1.65
Japan	¥100	S$1.50
Malaysia	RM10	S$4.10
UK	UK£1	S$2.00
USA	US$1	S$1.25

Set Your Budget

» **Dorm Bed** US$14–21

» **Hawker meal** US$3.50

» **Bottle of Tiger** US$4.25

Getting into Town

» **Public Bus** 36; S$2, every 10min, 6am-midnight

» **MRT (Metro)** S$2.70, every 7min, 6am-11.45pm change at Tanah Merah

» **Taxi** S$20 approx; S$3-5 surcharge applies, 50% extra from midnight-6am

» **Airport Shuttle** S$9, every 15-30min, 6am-midnight

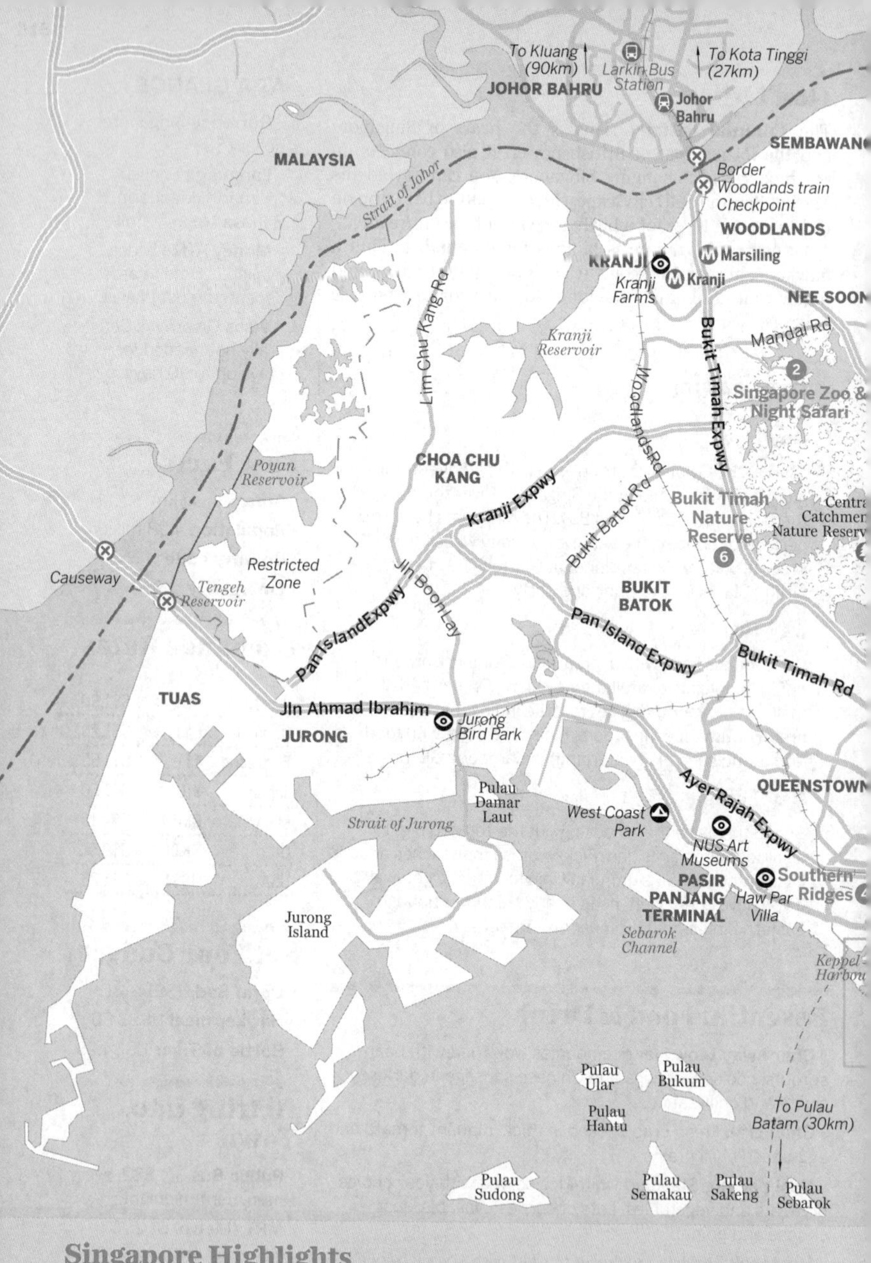

Singapore Highlights

1 Navigate **Little India** (p619), a jumble of gold, textiles, temples and cheap eats

2 Experience the animal magnetism of **Singapore Zoo** (p625) and **Night Safari** (p625), two outstanding open-concept zoos

3 Book the detailed tour through **Baba House** (p619), a gorgeous restored Peranakan house

4 Pack lots of water and walk along **Southern Ridges** (p627), Singapore's best urban trail

5 Hark back to the days of the empire as you stroll through the **colonial architecture** (p618) in the Colonial District

6 Hike through one of the world's only patches of urban primary rainforest at **Bukit Timah** (p628), or over a treetop walk at **MacRitchie Reservoir** (p629)

7 Time travel back to a Singapore stuck in the dusty, slow-paced village days at **Pulau Ubin** (p628)

Sights

After dealing with the in-your-faceness of Ho Chi Minh City and slumming it with the masses in polluted Bangkok, you'll find sweet blessed (and often air-conditioned) relief in Singapore.

The Singapore River cuts the city in two: south is the CBD and Chinatown, and to the north is the Colonial District. The trendy Clarke and Robertson Quays, and the popular Boat Quay dining areas, hug the riverbanks.

Further north from the Colonial District are Little India and Kampong Glam, the Muslim quarter. Northwest of the Colonial District is Orchard Rd, Singapore's premier shopping strip.

To the west of the island, the predominantly industrial area of Jurong contains a number of tourist attractions. Heading south you'll find the recreational islands of Sentosa, Kusu and St John's.

Eastern Singapore has some historical (and sleazy) suburbs such as Geylang and Katong, and East Coast Park and Changi Airport. The central north of the island has much of Singapore's remaining forest and the zoo.

COLONIAL DISTRICT

To the north of Singapore River is the Colonial District (Map p620 and Map p622), where you'll find many imposing remnants of British rule, including **Victoria Concert Hall & Theatre**, **Old Parliament House** (now an arts centre), **St Andrew's Cathedral**, **City Hall** and the **Old Supreme Court**, which are arranged around the **Padang**, a cricket pitch. Rising above them is the spaceship of the Norman Foster–designed **Supreme Court** building.

Asian Civilisations Museum MUSEUM
(Map p622; 6332 7798; www.acm.org.sg; 1 Empress Pl; admission S$8, half price after 7pm Fri; 1-7pm Mon, 9am-7pm Tue-Thu, Sat & Sun, Fri 9am-9pm; Raffles Place) Features 10 thematic galleries that explore different aspects of Asian culture, from the Islamic world to the history of the Singapore River. Get a joint ticket with the Peranakan Museum to save some bucks.

Peranakan Museum MUSEUM
(Map p620; 6332 7591; 39 Armenian St; admission S$6; 1-7pm Mon, 9.30am-7pm Tue-Sun, to 9pm Fri; City Hall) Stands as a testament to the Peranakan (Straits-born locals) cultural revival in the Lion City and is a must-visit for anyone who wants to understand local culture.

DON'T MISS

RAFFLES HOTEL

A Singaporean icon that should not be missed, **Raffles Hotel** (Map p620; 6337 1886; www.raffleshotel.com; 1 Beach Rd; City Hall) is open to non-guests, though shorts and flip-flops will make you unwelcome. Most tourists head to the famous Long Bar (p634) to sit under the ceiling fans and chuck peanut shells on the floor.

National Museum of Singapore MUSEUM
(Map p620; 6332 5642; www.nationalmuseum.sg; 93 Stamford Rd; admission S$10, Living Gallery free 6-9pm; History Galleries 10am-6pm, Living Galleries 10am-9pm; Dhoby Ghaut) The sparkling white Victorian splendour of the National Museum of Singapore, with its architecturally brilliant modern annex and interactive historical displays, is well worth a look.

Fort Canning Park PARK
(Map p620) Pop out the back of the National Museum into Fort Canning Park, the former seat of colonial power, today a wonderfully peaceful, leafy retreat from the broiling masses below.

FREE **Raffles Hotel Museum** MUSEUM
(Map p620; 3rd fl, Raffles Hotel Arcade; 10am-7pm) Located in the Raffles Hotel, this museum could easily be dismissed as an exercise in self-aggrandisement, but it has interesting historical narrative, photos and artefacts.

Singapore Art Museum ART GALLERY
(SAM; Map p620; 6332 3222; www.singaporeartmuseum.com; 71 Bras Basah Rd; admission S$10; 10am-7pm Sat-Thu, to 9pm Fri; Bras Basah) Three blocks west of Raffles Hotel, the Singapore Art Museum showcases local and Southeast Asian art. Check out **8Q SAM** (free with SAM ticket), the experimental wing across the road.

Singapore Flyer OBSERVATION WHEEL
(off Map p620; 6333 3311; www.singaporeflyer.com,sg; 30 Raffles Ave; tickets S$30; 8.30am-10.30pm; Promenade) The Singapore Flyer currently holds the title as the world's largest 'observation wheel' – the 30-minute ride offers views towards the Colonial District, CBD, Marina Bay, high-rise housing landscape to the east and out to the South China Sea.

CBD, MARINA BAY & THE QUAYS

Marina Bay Sands INTEGRATED RESORT

(Map p622; 1 Bayfront Ave; M Promenade) Across the Marina Bay is the large 'fish slapped on top of three towers' building that is the Marina Bay Sands integrated resort. It houses a casino, loads of top-end shops and the moderately interesting **Artscience Museum** (admission S$15-28). A 10-minute walk south of Promenade MRT station.

Merlion LANDMARK

(Map p622) At the river mouth is the freakish Merlion statue, a bizarre hybrid lion/fish creature cooked up in the 1960s as a tourism icon for the Singapore Tourism Board. And you thought they'd banned drugs.

Clarke Quay NEIGHBOURHOOD

(Map p622) The latest darling among Singapore's fickle night-trippers is Clarke Quay, a strip of former warehouses dating back to the river's days as a trading hub and now home to bars, restaurants and clubs.

Boat Quay & Robertson Quay NEIGHBOURHOOD

(Map p622) Boat Quay and Robertson Quay are known for their eateries and bars, the latter being quiet and sans restaurant touts.

CHINATOWN

Bustling Chinatown is crammed with small shops, eateries and tradition, though some of the tradition has disappeared behind a wave of renovation. Some of the renovation is good (the restored shophouses); some of it is not (the Pagoda St tourist market).

Chinatown Heritage Centre MUSEUM

(Map p622; www.chinatownheritage.com.sg; 48 Pagoda St; admission S$10; ⌚9am-6.30pm; M Chinatown) Housed across three floors of a converted shophouse, the moving Chinatown Heritage Centre focuses on the squalid living conditions that early Chinese immigrants once endured.

Buddha Tooth Relic Temple & Museum TEMPLE

(Map p622; www.btrts.org.sg; 288 South Bridge Rd; ⌚7am-7pm; M Chinatown) This huge, eye-catching, five-storey, southern Chinese–style Buddhist temple's main drawcard is what is believed to be a sacred tooth of Buddha (dental experts have expressed doubts over its authenticity).

Baba House MUSEUM

(off Map p622; ☎6227 5731; http://nus.edu.sg/museum/baba; 157 Neil Rd; ⌚2-3.30pm Mon, 10-11.30am Thu; M Outram) The one- to two-hour guided tour of this prewar terrace house built in the elaborate Peranakan style is top notch. Knowledgeable tour guides weave tales of Peranakan life with every detail. Book online or via phone. Ten minutes' walk south of Outram MRT.

Sri Mariamman Temple TEMPLE

(Map p622; ☎6223 4064; 244 South Bridge Rd; ⌚7.30am-8.30pm; M Chinatown) Chinatown's most recognised and photographed icon, ironically, is the colourful Sri Mariamman Temple, Singapore's oldest Hindu house of worship.

Thian Hock Keng Temple TEMPLE

(Map p622; ☎6423 4616; 158 Telok Ayer St; ⌚7.30am-5.30pm; M Raffles Place) This is Singapore's oldest Hokkien building, with elaborately carved and painted beams and panels.

LITTLE INDIA

Disorderly and pungent, Little India is a world away from the rest of Singapore. Weekends are truly an eye-opener for locals and tourists alike. Produce, spices and other trinkets spill onto the streets and crowd the five-foot ways. Many businesses operate late into the night (some run 24 hours) and traffic slows to a messy crawl.

SINGAPORE: A WORK IN PROGRESS

Gardens by the Bay (www.gardensbythebay.org.sg), across from Marina Bay Sands, will be Singapore's third botanic gardens (after Fort Canning and the Botanic Gardens at the end of Orchard Rd). The 101-hectare garden will house state-of-the-art greenhouses, large structures powered by solar energy and, of course, loads of flora. ETA for completion is 2012. It will connect the Colonial District to the Marina Bay Sands and across to the Marina Barrage. Talk about civic planning!

The old Supreme Court and City Hall along St Andrew's Rd are being converted into Singapore's next major **National Art Gallery** (www.nationalartgallery.sg) due to open in 2015. The collection will focus on 19th and 20th century Southeast Asian art.

Colonial District

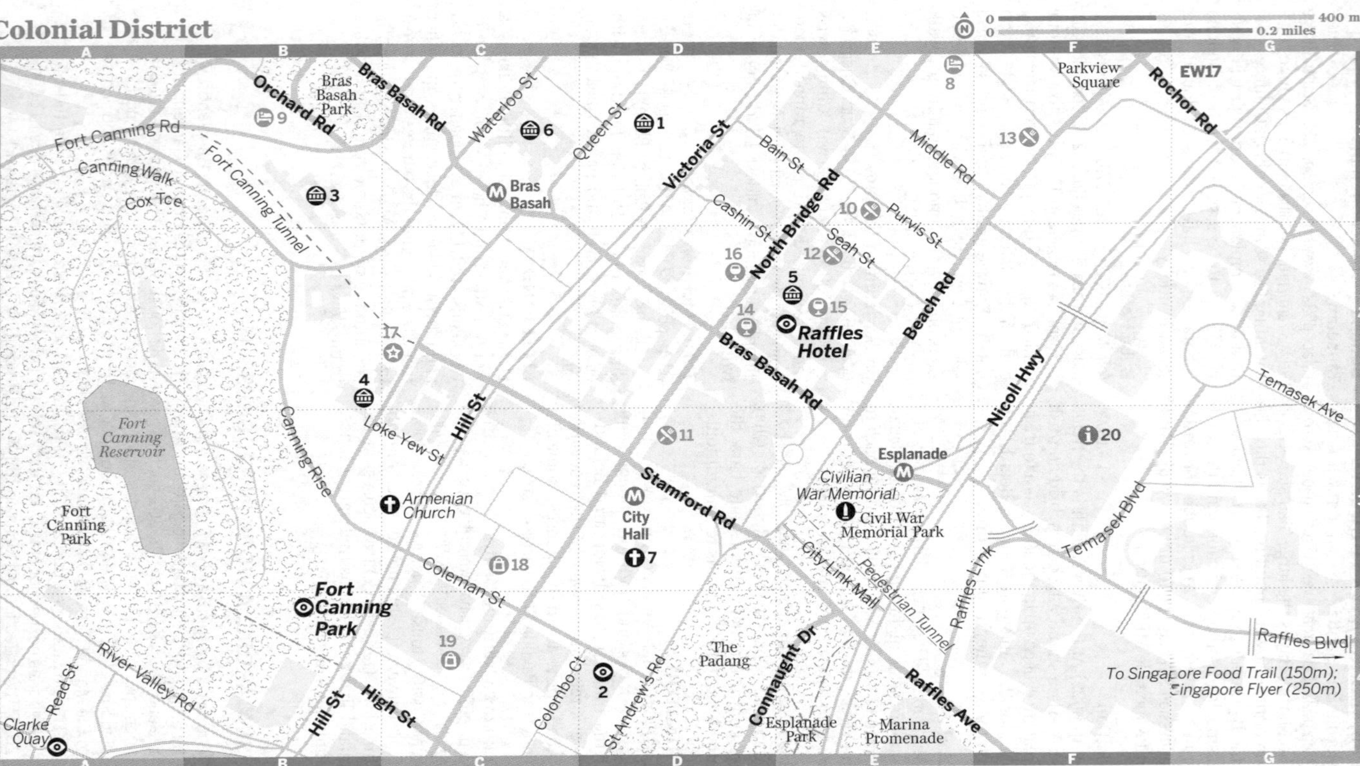

Colonial District

Top Sights

Fort Canning Park B4
Raffles Hotel E2

Sights

1 8Q SAM D1
2 City Hall D4
3 National Museum of Singapore B1
4 Peranakan Museum B2
5 Raffles Hotel Museum E2
6 Singapore Art Museum C1
7 St Andrew's Cathedral D3

Activities, Courses & Tours

Duck Tours ..... (see 20)

Sleeping

8 Backpackers Cozy Corner E1
9 YMCA International House B1

Eating

Food for Thought ..... (see 1)
10 Purvis St Food Outlets E1
11 Raffles City Food Outlets D3
12 Seah St Food Outlets E2
13 Steamboat Restaurants F1

Drinking

14 Bar & Billiard Room D2
15 Long Bar E2
16 Loof D2

Entertainment

17 Timbre@Substation C2

Shopping

18 Cathay Photo C3
19 Funan DigitaLife Mall C4

Information

20 Singapore Tourism Board (Suntec City) F3

Sri Veeramakaliamman Temple TEMPLE
(Map p624; ☎6293 4634; 141 Serangoon Rd; ⊙8am-noon & 4-8.30pm) For temple hounds there is the Sri Veeramakaliamman Temple, dedicated to the goddess Kali.

Sakaya Muni Buddha Gaya Temple TEMPLE
(Map p624; ☎6294 0714; 366 Race Course Rd; ⊙8am-4.30pm) Further out is the Thai Buddhist Sakaya Muni Buddha Gaya Temple, popularly known as the Temple of 1000 Lights. It houses a 15m-high seated Buddha.

KAMPONG GLAM

Southeast of Little India is Kampong Glam, Singapore's Muslim quarter. Here you'll find shops selling clothing, raw cloth and dry goods. This is also home to the Sultan Mosque.

Malay Heritage Centre MUSEUM
(Map p624; ☎6391 0450; www.malayheritage.org.sg; 85 Sultan Gate; admission S$3; ⊙10am-6pm Tue-Sun, 1-6pm Mon) Istana Kampong Glam is the former palace of the last Sultan of Singapore, restored and turned into the Malay Heritage Centre. The museum was undergoing renovations at the time of research, and is due to open in June 2012.

Sultan Mosque MOSQUE
(Map p624; 3 Muscat St; ⊙5am-8.30pm) This golden-domed structure is the biggest and most active mosque in Singapore.

SINGAPORE ON THE CHEAP

» Always eat at hawker centres or food courts.

» Each neighbourhood tends to radiate out from a mall and a food centre or two – great places to people watch, have cheap meals and order large S$6 bottles of Tiger beer.

» If you drink at a bar, go during happy hours (for discounted booze and/or one-for-one specials).

» Visit the museums for free (or cheap) after 6pm, and catch free concerts at the Esplanade or Singapore Botanic Gardens.

» Pack a picnic and spend a day at the beach in East Coast Park or Sentosa.

» Hike in Bukit Timah Nature Reserve, around the MacRitchie Reservoir or along the Southern Ridges.

Chinatown, the CBD & the Quays

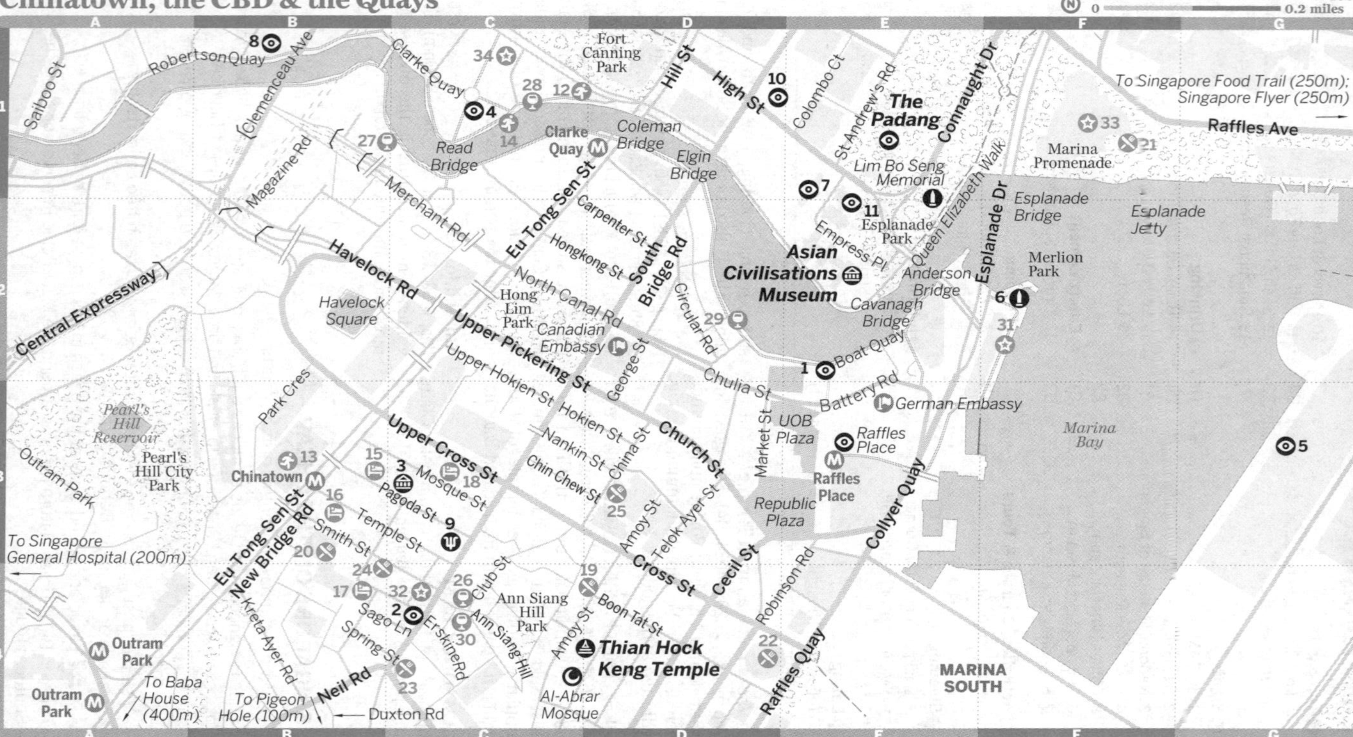

Chinatown, the CBD & the Quays

Top Sights

Asian Civilisations Museum......E2
The Padang......E1
Thian Hock Keng Temple......D4

Sights

1 Boat Quay......E2
2 Buddha Tooth Relic Temple & Museum......C4
3 Chinatown Heritage Centre......C3
4 Clarke Quay......C1
5 Marina Bay Sands......G3
6 Merlion......F2
7 Old Parliament House......E1
8 Robertson Quay......B1
9 Sri Mariamman Temple......C3
10 Supreme Court......D1
11 Victoria Concert Hall & Theatre......E2

Activities, Courses & Tours

12 Hippo River Pass......C1
13 People's Park Complex......B3
14 Singapore Explorer......C1
Singapore River Cruises......(see 6)

Sleeping

15 Beary Good Hostel (Pagoda St)......B3
16 Beary Good Hostel (Smith St)......B3
17 Fernloft......B4
18 Pillows & Toast......C3

Eating

19 Annalakshmi Janatha......D4
20 Chinatown Complex......B3
21 Gluttons Bay......F1
22 Lau Pa Sat......D4
23 Maxwell Road Food Centre......C4
24 Smith Street Hawker Stalls......B4
25 Ya Kun Kaya Toast......D3

Drinking

26 Beaujolais......C4
27 Brewerkz......B1
28 Crazy Elephant......C1
Harry's Bar......(see 29)
29 Penny Black......D2
30 Screening Room......C4

Entertainment

31 Butter Factory......F2
32 Chinese Theatre Circle......C4
33 Esplanade – Theatres on the Bay......F1
34 Zirca Mega Club......C1

ORCHARD ROAD

No one visits Orchard Rd for the sights, though the Christmas light displays are breathtaking. The only major historical site is the President's digs, the **Istana** (Map p626; ☎6737 5522; www.istana.gov.sg; Orchard Rd), but it's only open on selected public holidays. Check the website for details.

Emerald Hill Road Houses ARCHITECTURE

Take some time out to wander through the pedestrianised Peranakan Pl to residential Emerald Hill Rd (Map p626), where original Peranakan terrace houses totter between glamorous decay and immaculate restoration.

Singapore Botanic Gardens GARDENS

(Map p626; ☎6471 7361; www.sbg.org.sg; 1 Cluny Rd; ⏰5am-midnight; Ⓜ Botanic Gardens) When you're about to lose your mind from retail overload, the expansive, serene Singapore Botanic Gardens is a beautiful spot to rest and revive. The gardens host free open-air music concerts on the last Sunday of the month at the Shaw Foundation Symphony Stage – check the website for details.

HARRY LEE KUAN YEW'S HUMBLE ABODE

If you're planning a jaunt down Orchard Rd, make a short detour and head along Oxley Rd. The house (off Map p626) of the father of modern Singapore, Harry Lee Kuan Yew, is on this street. Lee Kuan Yew was the leader of the People's Action Party in Singapore, and it was under his leadership that Singapore transformed itself into one of the most prosperous nations in Asia. In order to keep out the plebs and crazies, car gantries are installed at either end of the road. Pedestrians are free to walk through, but expect to be hurried along by heavily armed Ghurkhas. Go on, walk on the side of the guards for a closer look – we dare you.

Cathay Gallery MUSEUM
(Map p626; ☎6737 5522; www.thecathaygallery.com.sg; 02-16 the Cathay, 2 Handy Rd; admission free; ⏰noon-8pm Mon-Sat; Ⓜ Dhoby Ghaut) Film buffs will go ga-ga at the Cathay Gallery, chock-a-block with local movie memorabilia, and housed in Singapore's first high-rise building.

EASTERN SINGAPORE

Geylang NEIGHBOURHOOD
(Ⓜ Kallang, Aljunied) Nowhere else is Singapore's mishmash of food, commerce, religion, culture and sleaze more at ease than in the Geylang area. Come nightfall, you might see a crowd spill out onto the streets from evening prayer at a mosque, rubbing shoulders with prostitutes. Join hordes of people sweating over plates of local food. To get here, take the MRT to Kallang, then cross the road and head south towards all the action.

Katong NEIGHBOURHOOD
This former Peranakan enclave is rife with food outlets and beautiful shophouse architecture, and so is worth strolling through. Bus 12 or 32 from North Bridge Rd and stop along East Coast Rd.

Little India & Kampong Glam

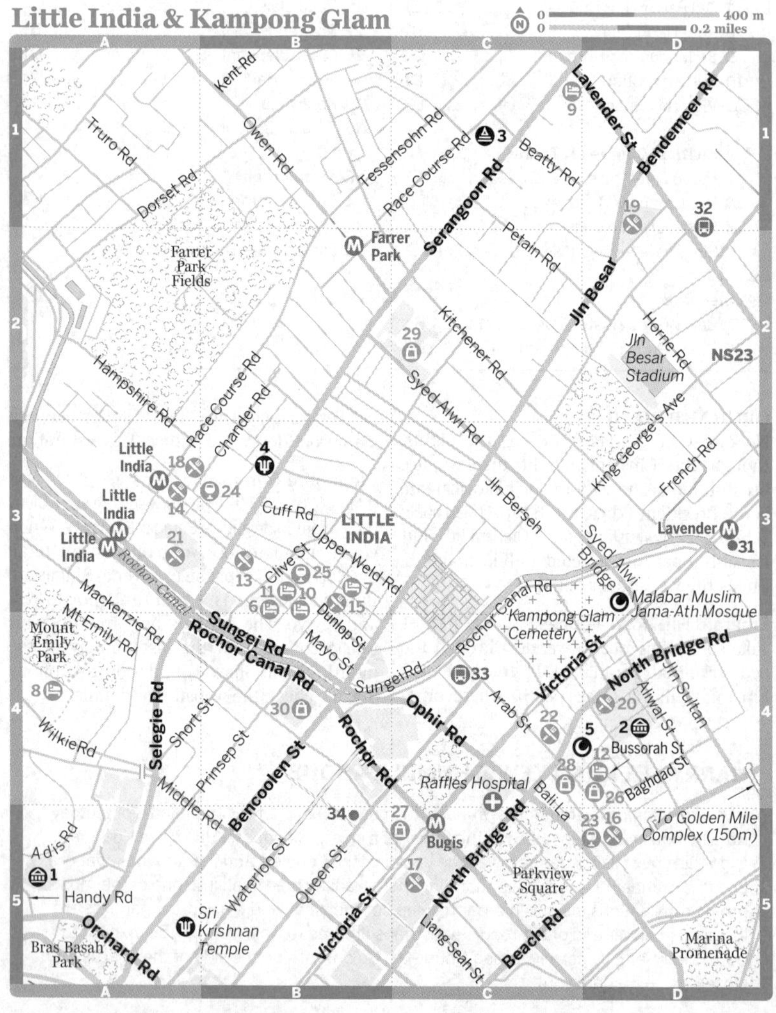

East Coast Park PARK

Stretching for 10km along East Coast Parkway (ECP), East Coast Park is where Singaporeans come to take a dip in the soupy Strait of Singapore, windsurf, cable-ski, eat, cycle, in-line skate, and chill out on the sand. Bus 401 runs from Bedok MRT station to here on weekends, or take 197 and walk through the underpass from Marine Parade Rd.

Changi Village NEIGHBOURHOOD

On the northeastern coast, Changi has a village atmosphere, with the lively and renowned hawker centre next to the bus terminus being a focal point. Across from the bus terminal is Changi Beach, where thousands of Singaporean civilians were executed during WWII. Changi Village is the jumping-off point for the rural retreat of Pulau Ubin (p628). Bus 2 from Tanah Merah MRT.

NORTHERN & CENTRAL SINGAPORE

Night Safari ZOO

(☎6269 3411; www.nightsafari.com.sg; 80 Mandai Lake Rd; admission S$32; ⏰7.30pm-midnight) Next door to the zoo is the Night Safari, a 40-hectare forested park where you can view nocturnal animals, including tigers, lions and leopards. Come early. The tram ride is a must.

DON'T MISS

SINGAPORE ZOO

Set on a peninsula jutting into the Upper Seletar Reservoir, this **zoo** (☎6269 3411; www.zoo.com.sg; 80 Mandai Lake Rd; admission S$20; ⏰8.30am-6pm) is world class. Its 28 landscaped hectares and open design (no cages) houses 2530 residents. You can save money by buying a combined ticket for the zoo, the night safari and Jurong Bird Park (p627). Go to Ang Mo Kio MRT, then catch bus 138.

Kong Meng San Phor Kark See Monastery TEMPLE

(☎6453 5300; www.kmspks.org; 88 Bright Hill Rd; ⏰gates 6am-9pm, halls 8am-4pm) Singapore's largest and most stunning monastery has 12 buildings. Expect dragon-topped pagodas, shrines, plazas and lawns linked by

Little India & Kampong Glam

Sights

1 Cathay Gallery A5
2 Malay Heritage Centre D4
3 Sakaya Muni Buddha Gaya Temple (Temple of 1000 Lights) C1
4 Sri Veeramakaliamman Temple B3
5 Sultan Mosque D4

Sleeping

6 Checkers Inn B3
7 Footprints B3
8 hangout @ mt emily A4
9 Hive C1
10 Inn Crowd B3
11 Prince of Wales B3
12 Sleepy Sam's D4

Eating

13 Ananda Bhavan B3
14 Andhra Curry A3
15 Bismillah Biryani B3
16 Cafe Le Caire D5
17 Cold Storage C5
18 Gandhi Restaurant A3
19 Lavender Food Square D1
20 Pariaman Warong Nasi D4
21 Tekka Centre A3
22 Zam Zam C4

Drinking

23 BluJaz Cafe D5
24 Kerbau Road Beer Garden B3
Prince of Wales .... (see 11)
25 Zsofi Tappas Bar B3

Shopping

26 Arab St Shops D4
27 Bugis Village C5
Bussorah St Shops .... (see 12)
28 Haji Lane Shops C4
29 Mustafa Shopping Centre C2
30 Sim Lim Square B4

Information

31 Immigration & Checkpoints Authority D3

Transport

32 Lavender Street Bus Terminal D1
33 Queen Street Bus Terminal C4
Transnational Bus Service .... (see 32)
34 Trishaw Uncle B5

Orchard Road

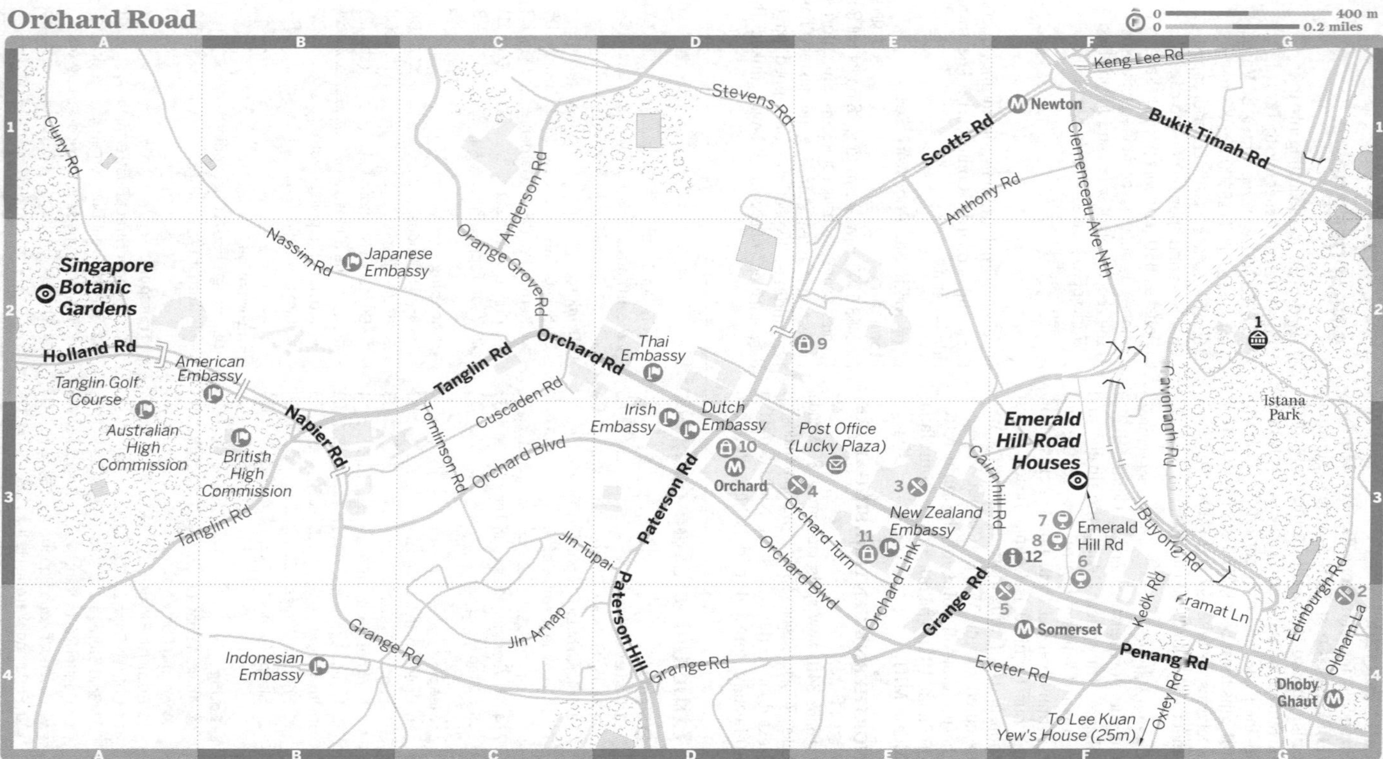

Orchard Road

Top Sights
- Emerald Hill Road Houses F3
- Singapore Botanic Gardens A2

Sights
- 1 Istana G2

Eating
- 2 Carrefour G4
- 3 Din Tai Fung E3
- 4 Food Republic E3
- 5 Oriole Cafe & Bar F4
- Takashimaya Food Village .... (see 11)

Drinking
- 6 Alley Bar F3
- 7 Ice Cold Beer F3
- 8 No 5 .... F3

Entertainment
- Sistic .... (see 4)

Shopping
- 9 Far East Plaza E2
- 10 Ion Orchard D3
- Kinokuniya .... (see 11)
- 11 Ngee Ann City E3

Information
- 12 Singapore Visitors Centre@Orchard F3
- Singapore Visitors@ION Orchard .... (see 10)

Escher-like staircases. Finish your visit by reflecting under a bodhi tree. Buses 52 and 410 (white plate) run here from Bishan MRT station.

SOUTHERN & WESTERN SINGAPORE

For a beautiful view, walk up 116m **Mt Faber**, then catch the **cable car** (☎6270 8855; www.mountfaber.com.sg; one-way/return S$24/26; ⏰8.30am-9.30pm) to the Harbour-Front Centre or across to Sentosa Island. Mt Faber is connected to Kent Ridge Park via HortPark in a 9km-long chain known as the **Southern Ridges**, arguably Singapore's best walking trail. The walk takes visitors along shady forested paths and across bridges which pass through forest canopy.

NUS Art Museums ART GALLERY
(☎6516 4617; www.nus.edu.sg/museum; 50 Kent Ridge Cres; admission free; ⏰10am-7.30pm Tue-Sat, 10am-6pm Sun) The art museums in the National University of Singapore (NUS) campus are top-notch and worth a look. Catch bus 95 from Buona Vista MRT.

Haw Par Villa CULTURAL SITE
(☎6872 2780; 262 Pasir Panjang Rd; admission free; ⏰9am-7pm; MHaw Par Villa) 'That which is derived from society should be returned to society', said Aw Boon Haw, creator of the Tiger Balm miracle salve. A million dollars later, what he returned was the Haw Par Villa, an unbelievably weird and undoubtedly kitsch theme park showcasing Chinese culture.

Jurong Bird Park ZOO
(☎6265 0022; www.birdpark.com.sg; 2 Jurong Hill; admission S$18; ⏰8am-6pm) Offers impressive enclosures and beautifully landscaped gardens for over 8000 birds (all enveloped in the inescapable scent of bird poop). Get here on bus 194 or 251 from Boon Lay MRT station.

SENTOSA ISLAND

Epitomised by its star attraction, Universal Studios, Sentosa is essentially a giant theme park. And as such, kids love it. In addition to Universal Studios, the island itself is packed with rides, activities and shows, most of which cost extra.

The island's beaches, of course, are completely free and very popular with locals and tourists alike.

TOTO, WE'RE NOT IN ORCHARD RD ANYMORE...

Farm owners in Kranji have formed a collective, **Kranji Countryside Association** (www.kranjicountryside.com), to promote awareness of their existence. Thus far, they've done a great job, considering they don't have the multimillion-dollar advertising budgets of retail heavies, and hey, anyone who decides to make a living selling goats' milk deserves special mention.

A daily minibus service, the **Kranji Express** (Kranji MRT Station; tickets S$3; duration 90mins; ⏰9am, 10.30am, noon, 1.30pm, 3pm & 4.30pm) does a loop to and from Kranji MRT Station, visiting the best farms en route. Look out for organic veggies and fruit, pottery, frogs, wheat grass, cafes and restaurants. And yes, sample some goats' milk too.

Get to VivoCity (Harbourfront MRT) and walk across (S$1) or take the Sentosa Express monorail (return S$3). For a more spectacular ride, take the cable car (one-way S$18.90) from the HarbourFront centre. All Sentosa-crossing options are signposted at the MRT station.

Universal Studios THEME PARK
(Map p629; www.rwsentosa.com; Resorts World; admission S$72; ⏲10am-7pm, sometimes 10am-9pm during peak summer months) Universal Studios is the top-draw attraction in Resorts World. Shops, shows, restaurants, rides and roller coasters all neatly packaged into fantasy-world themes based on your favourite Hollywood films. One of the highlights is the pair of 'duelling roller coasters' in Sci-fi City, said to be the tallest of their kind in the world.

Underwater World AQUARIUM
(Map p629; ☎6275 0030; www.underwaterworld.com.sg; behind Siloso Beach; admission S$25.90; ⏲9am-9pm) Stingrays and 10ft sharks cruise inches from your face as the travellator takes you through the Ocean Colony's submerged glass tubes in Underwater World.

Fort Siloso MUSEUM
(Map p629; Siloso Point; admission S$8; ⏲10am-6pm) A former military base, Fort Siloso recreates the Japanese invasion and occupation.

Images of Singapore MUSEUM
(Map p629; Imbiah Lookout; admission S$10; ⏲9am-7pm) History buffs might also enjoy the visual displays of Singapore's past at Images of Singapore.

SINGAPORE'S OTHER ISLANDS

Pulau Ubin ISLAND
A rural, unkempt expanse of jungle full of fast-moving lizards, strange shrines and cacophonic birdlife. Tin-roofed buildings bake in the sun, chickens squawk and panting dogs slump in the dust, while in the forest, families of wild pig run for cover as visitors pedal past on squeaky rented bicycles (S$5 to S$10, depending on condition). Get to Tanah Merah MRT, then take bus 2 to Changi Village Ferry Terminal. There boats (one way S$2.50, 10 minutes; ⏲5.30am to 9pm) depart for the island whenever there are 12 people aboard.

Southern Islands ISLAND
Three other islands popular with castaway-fantasising locals are **St John's**, **Lazarus** and **Kusu**. They're quiet and great for fishing, swimming, picnics and guzzling BYO six packs. The islands have changing rooms and toilets. You can camp for free. Kusu Island is culturally interesting; devotees come to pray for health, wealth and fertility at its Taoist temple and Malay *kramat* (shrine).

Facilities are almost non-existent: You can stay the night on St John's, and there are toilets on St John's and Kusu, but there is nowhere to buy food or drink on any of the islands, so come prepared. Catch a ferry from the **Marina South Pier** (☎6534 9339; www.islandcruise.com.sg; 31 Marina Coastal Drive; return S$15; ⏲10am & 2pm Mon-Fri, 9am, noon & 3pm Sat, 9am, 11am, 1pm, 3pm & 5pm Sun). To get to Marina South Pier, take bus 402 from outside the Marina Bay MRT station.

Activities

Though the national pastimes are probably shopping and eating, there are opportunities for athletic, outdoorsy types. The best spot for **cycling** is definitely East Coast Park (p625). Pulau Ubin (p628) has dedicated mountain-biking trails. For **swimming** there are reasonable beaches on Sentosa, the Southern Islands and East Coast Park. To find out more about sports and activities in Singapore, check out www.ssc.gov.sg.

Spas in Singapore tend to be of the upmarket variety. **Massages**, however, are cheap and readily available. Foot reflexology is a major trade. For a good foot rub, look for places with wizened old men, with their years of expertise. Check out **People's Park Complex** (Map p622; Eu Tong Sen St) for foot reflexology. Most malls have at least one reflexology place. For Thai massage, try **Golden Mile Complex** (off Map p624; Beach Rd). Prices should be displayed on the doors, but if you aren't sure, shop around. Expect to pay roughly S$22 for a 45-minute massage.

Bukit Timah Nature Reserve OUTDOORS
(☎1800 468 5736; www.nparks.gov.sg; ⏲8.30am-6pm) There are good trails in Bukit Timah Nature Reserve, the only large area of primary rainforest left in Singapore. Hike one of four trails including the one to the peak, at 163m, the highest natural point in Singapore. Look out for Rock Path, which will leave you clambering on your hands and knees in places, over rocks and tree roots; it all adds to the adventure. Watch out for troops of monkeys (long-tailed macaques)! Catch Bus 171 from Orchard MRT Station. Get off at Bukit Timah Shopping Centre and follow the road till you see Hindehede Dr to your right.

Sentosa Island

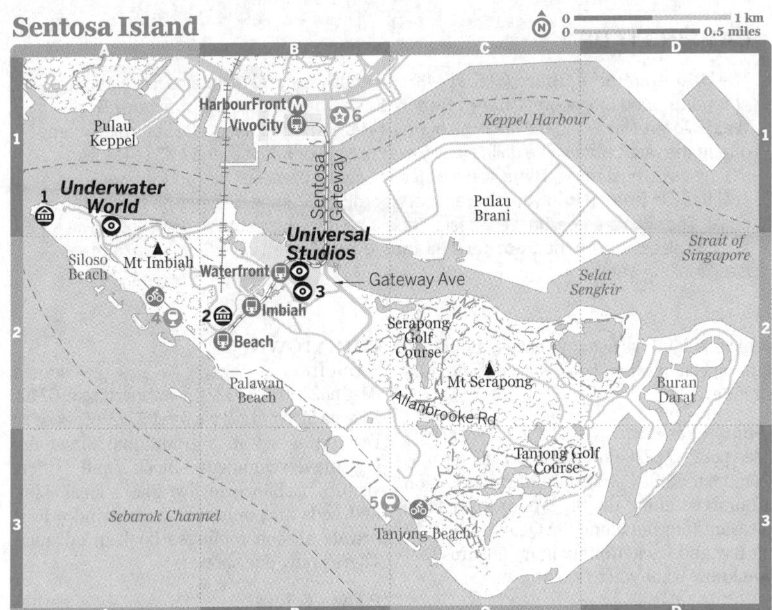

SINGAPORE COURSES

MacRitchie Reservoir OUTDOORS

(☎6256 4248; www.nparks.gov.sg; Lornie Rd; ⏰8.30am-6pm) MacRitchie Reservoir has a hiking trail up to a fantastic **treetop walk**, a 250m-long suspension bridge perched 25m up in the forest canopy. Trails then continue through the forest and around the reservoir, sometimes on dirt tracks, sometimes on wooden boardwalks. Take Bus 157 from Toa Payoh MRT station.

Ski360° ADVENTURE SPORTS

(☎6442 7318; www.ski360degree.com; 1206A East Coast Parkway; per hr weekdays/weekends S$32/42; ⏰10am-9.45pm Mon-Thu, to 11.45pm Fri, 9am-11.45pm Sat, to 9.45pm Sun) Wakeboarders and water-skiers should check out the tethered Ski360° circuit at East Coast Park Lagoon.

Courses

Cookery Magic COOKING

(☎6348 9667; www.cookerymagic.com; 117 Fidelio St; classes S$65-130; Ⓜ Paya Lebar) Ruqxana conducts standout Asian cooking classes in her own home. She also conducts classes on an eco-farm (harvest your own veggies before cooking!) and on Pulau Ubin (in an old *kampong* home).

Sentosa Island

Top Sights

Sights

Drinking

Entertainment

Tours

Original Singapore Walks WALKING TOUR

(☎6325 1631; www.singaporewalks.com; half-day from S$30) Conducts insightful tours of Chinatown, Little India, Kampong Glam, the Colonial District and Singapore's battlefields.

Duck Tours BUS TOUR

(Map p620; ☎6228 6877; www.ducktours.com.sg; Suntec City, 1 Raffles Blvd; tours from S$33) This city tour in a WWII amphibious

CAMPING IT UP

The **National Parks Board** (☎6391 4488; www.nparks.gov.sg) maintains five camping grounds around Singapore: **Changi Beach**, **East Coast Park**, **Sembawang Park**, **West Coast Park**, and the east end of **Pasir Ris Park**. You need a S$1 permit to camp during the week, obtainable online (www.axs.com.sg) or from several AXS (ATM-like) machines in most malls. There's a small fee to use the barbecue pits and shower facilities. On **Pulau Ubin** you can camp at Noordin or Maman Beaches on the north coast. The sites are free, but very basic. There's no drinking water, so bring your own. You can also camp on the **Southern Islands** (Kusu, Lazarus and St John's) for free. BYO drinking water.

vehicle is loud, garish and cheesy but oh-so fun, especially when it splashes out into Marina Bay.

Hippo River Pass RIVER CRUISE
(Map p622; ☎6228 6877; www.ducktours.com.sg; tours from S$18; ⏰8.30am-10.30pm) Jump on a bumboat along the Singapore River for a pleasant tour out along the Quays into Marina Bay and back. Commentary ensures that you know what you're looking at.

Singapore River Cruises RIVER CRUISE
(Map p622; ☎6336 6111; www.rivercruise.com.sg; tours from S$15) Another cruise operator with similar launching locations to Hippo.

Sleeping

Once, budget-room hunters in Singapore were limited to flea-bitten flophouses (they still exist!), but thankfully these days there are decent hostels and guesthouses even in the more expensive parts of the city. Unless otherwise stated, prices are for shared bathrooms.

COLONIAL DISTRICT

Backpackers Cozy Corner HOSTEL $
(Map p620; ☎6339 6128; www.cozycornerguest.com; 490 North Bridge Rd; dm S$12-17, d incl breakfast S$36-60; ❄@) This place can get a li'l *too* cosy when it's busy (and it usually is). The location is a huge plus, though rooms are dark and a little cramped. Ask for a dorm facing away from busy North Bridge Rd.

YMCA International House HOSTEL $
(Map p620; ☎6336 6000; www.ymcaih.com.sg; 1 Orchard Rd; dm/d/f incl breakfast S$47/210/250; ❄@≋) Even after you add on the S$3 temporary membership, the Y's roomy four-bed dorms (attached bathroom) are good value. It has a pool, it's centrally located, and hotel-quality rooms can be had cheaply online.

CHINATOWN

Fernloft HOSTEL $
(Map p622; ☎6323 3221, www.fernloft.com; 02-82, 5 Banda St; dm/d incl breakfast S$22/65; ❄@ᯤ) Fernloft is set in a traditional Singapore housing-development block and offers visitors a chance to live like a local. Limited beds and only two large (windowless) private air-con rooms so book in advance. There's only one shower.

Pillows & Toast HOSTEL $
(Map p622; ☎6220 4653; www.pillowsntoast.com; 40 Mosque St; dm S$26-33; Ⓜ Chinatown; @ᯤ) Bright, clean and friendly with comfortable wood-framed bunk beds and well-looked after common areas.

Beary Good Hostel HOSTEL $
(www.abearygoodhostel.com) 66 Pagoda St (Map p622; ☎6222 4955; dm S$26; Ⓜ Chinatown; @ᯤ); 46 Smith St (Map p622; dm S$26; Ⓜ Chinatown; @ᯤ) So popular it opened another branch, called Beary Nice Hostel, a stone's throw away in Smith St. Both are fun, brightly painted affairs, and have separate bathrooms for boys and girls; a beary nice touch.

LITTLE INDIA & KAMPONG GLAM

Inn Crowd HOSTEL $
(Map p624; ☎6296 9169; www.the-inncrowd.com; 73 Dunlop St; dm/d/tr incl breakfast S$20/48/68; Ⓜ Little India; ❄@ᯤ) Ground Zero for Singapore's backpackers. Clean accommodation, living areas where travellers like to hang and saccharine-sweet staff. The atmosphere's decidedly convivial, with free lockers and internet, discounted tickets to sights, laundry and cheap Tiger draught beer on tap.

Prince of Wales HOSTEL $
(Map p624; ☎6299 0130; www.pow.com.sg; 101 Dunlop St; dm/d S$20/60; Ⓜ Little India; ❄@ᯤ) This Australian-style pub and hostel has a

raucous beer-and-sawdust rock bar downstairs and clean, high-ceilinged dorms upstairs. The two private rooms share a bathroom. Not everyone wants to rock out, but it's a lively place in an ace location.

Hive HOSTEL $
(Map p624; ☎6341 5041; www.thehivebackpackers.com; 269A Lavender St; dm/s/d/tr from S$20/35/50/85; Ⓜ Boon Keng; @📶) The Hive's friendliness and cleanliness go a long way towards making up for its slightly inconvenient location at the junction of Lavender St and Serangoon Rd. Dorms are fairly standard, but bright, colourful private rooms are excellent value. Five minutes' walk south from Boon Keng MRT Station.

Hangout@Mt Emily HOSTEL $$
(Map p624; ☎6438 5588; www.hangouthotels.com; 10A Upper Wilkie Rd, dm/d incl breakfast S$41/117; Ⓜ Little India; ❄@📶🏊) Prices for the comfy seven-bed (not bunk) dorms are a relative bargain considering the location: walking distance to Orchard Rd, the Colonial District and Little India (though it's quite a hike up to the hotel itself). Lovely rooftop terrace with a 'standing pool', a library, a cafe, free internet and cosy lounge areas with a large plasma TV.

Footprints HOSTEL $
(Map p624; ☎6295 5134; www.footprintshostel.com.sg; 25A Perak Rd; dm S$21-28; Ⓜ Little India; @📶) Well run, with comfortable communal areas for lounging, eating and laptopping. Shared bathrooms are huge. Female-only dorms also available.

Checkers Inn HOSTEL $
(Map p624; ☎6392 0693; www.checkersinn.com.sg; 46-50 Campbell Lane; dm S$30; Ⓜ Little India; @📶) Bright, spacious and fabulously funky. Female-only dorms also available.

KAMPONG GLAM

Sleepy Sam's HOSTEL $
(Map p624; ☎9277 4988; www.sleepysams.com; 55 Bussorah St; dm/s/d/tr S$28/59/89/99; Ⓜ Bugis; ❄@📶) Prices at this budget-hostel mainstay have gone upwards and staff attitudes downwards. It's saved by its laid-back ambience, pier-and-beam ceilings, book-filled common area-cafe and well-furnished dorm rooms. Book ahead.

Eating

Singaporean life is best epitomised by the ubiquitous (but wholly unique) hawker centre. Grab a seat, order a super-sweet coffee or a S$6 Tiger beer, join the queue for a local meal and listen to people talk about politics, English Premier League, Hollywood diets and maids. Dishes rarely cost more than S$5 (unless you're eating seafood), and each centre has a huge variety of cuisines, including Malay, South Indian, Cantonese, Hokkien, Teochew and Indonesian. There are also countless excellent restaurants, though costs are going to spiral up to at least S$12 per plate.

COLONIAL DISTRICT

Singapore Food Trail HAWKER CENTRE $$
(off Map p620; Singapore Flyer; 30 Raffles Ave; dishes S$5-15; ⏰10.30am-10.30pm; Ⓜ Promenade) Retro-inspired recreation of the hawker stalls from 1960s Singapore, except with air-conditioning. A good alternative to Gluttons Bay, located under the shadow of the Singapore Flyer.

Seah St Food Outlets LOCAL $$
(Map p620; Seah St; Ⓜ City Hall) This short street next to the impeccable Raffles Hotel has a couple of good eating options. Standouts include Hock Lam Beef Noodles (piquant thick sauce coats strips of beef and rice noodles) and chicken rice at Sin Swee Kee and Swee Kee (no relation to each other). Order the Hainanese pork chop at Swee Kee: fried battered pork cutlet slathered with a spiced tomato-based sauce. YUM!

Purvis St Food Outlets LOCAL $$
(Map p620; Purvis St; Ⓜ City Hall) Purvis St packs in a whole heap of restaurants. The chicken rice at old-school, 50-odd year old Yet Con is superb and you can shovel Thai food at Jai Thai. If you're in the area for brekkie, drop by Killiney Kopitiam or YY Kafei Dian for some *kaya* toast and thick coffee that'll knock your socks off.

Raffles City Food Outlets INTERNATIONAL $$
(Map p620; ☎6338 7766; www.rafflescity.com; Basement, 252 North Bridge Rd; Ⓜ City Hall) Handburger makes yummy (but somewhat small) burgers, Skinny Pizza is popular for its gourmet-topped pizzas made with flat cracker bread, punters queue out the door at Din Tai Fung for it's divine *xiao long pao* (pork dumplings), or guzzle German beer and sausages at Brotzeit. Check out the deli counters at the basement Marketplace supermarket for a picnic basket.

Food for Thought FUSION $$
(Map p620; ☎6338 9887; 8 Queen St; mains from S$10; Ⓜ Bras Basah) We admire the philosophy behind the restaurant – a portion of the proceeds go to aid projects. The food itself is a mix of familiar favourites: pastas, grilled meats and sandwiches…with a twist. The chicken chop is coated in a lightly curried batter for example. It's popular, so expect to wait during peak times.

Steamboat Restaurants STEAMBOAT $$
(Map p620; cnr Beach Rd & Liang Seah St; ⊙dinner) For an ultracheap feed, pull up a table at one of several steamboat restaurants where S$17 to S$20 will buy you an 'all you can eat' spread of meats, seafood and vegies.

CBD & THE QUAYS

Ya Kun Kaya Toast BREAKFAST $
(Map p622; 01-01 Far East Sq, 18 China St; ⊙7.30am-7pm Mon-Fri, 8.30am-5.30pm Sat & Sun) Though a chain of outlets have mushroomed across Singapore, this outlet most closely matches the original 1940s stall, selling strong coffee, runny eggs and the *kaya* toast that so many Singaporeans love.

Lau Pa Sat HAWKER CENTRE $
(Map p622; 18 Raffles Quay; ⊙24hr) Famous for its renovated Victorian market building, Lau Pa Sat hawker centre is chock-a-block with food.

CHINATOWN

Gluttons Bay HAWKER CENTRE $$
(Map p622; ☎6336 7025; 01-15 Esplanade Mall; dishes S$5-25; ⊙6pm-3am; Ⓜ Esplanade) This bayside collection of the best hawkers (or street-food masters, as they call them) have been selected by the author of the local food bible, *Makansutra*. It's a great place to start your exploration of the island's food culture. Try the oyster omelette, satay and barbecue stingray and the *kaya* (coconut jam) fondue.

Annalakshmi Janatha INDIAN $
(Map p622; ☎6223 0809; 104 Amoy St; meals S$5-10; ⊙11am-3pm Mon-Sat) A real gem, serving up Indian vegetarian buffets on an 'eat as you like, pay as you feel' basis (S$5 to S$10 per head is acceptable). It's run by volunteers and profits help support various charities.

Chinatown Complex HAWKER CENTRE $
(Map p622; 11 New Bridge Rd; ⊙8am-9.30pm) Join the locals for some Hainanese chicken rice at this no-nonsense hawker centre smack bang in the middle of Chinatown.

Maxwell Road Food Centre HAWKER CENTRE $
(Map p622; cnr Maxwell & Neil Rds; ⊙24hr) Esteemed as one of Singapore's best hawker centres, this is in an open-sided food barn with over 100 stalls under the roof.

Smith Street Hawker Stalls STREET HAWKERS $
(Map p622; Smith St; ⊙4-11pm) Completely touristy but popular open-air street market serving Singapore favourites.

LITTLE INDIA

Bismillah Biryani INDIAN $
(Map p624; 50 Dunlop St; kebabs from S$4, biryani from S$6; ⊙noon-8pm) A banner proclaims that Google lists this place as the 'best biryani in Singapore'. We have to agree. The mutton biryani is special, so is the mutton shish kebab, which is melt-in-the-mouth good. Most of the best dishes are long gone before 8pm.

Gandhi Restaurant SOUTH INDIAN $
(Map p624; 29 Chander Rd; dishes from S$2, set meals from S$4; ⊙11am-11pm) Canteen-style restaurant hits the spot with delicious set-meal *thali* (traditional 'all-you-can-eat' meals), *dosa* (paper-thin lentil-flour pancake) or *uttapam* (thick, savoury South Indian rice pancake with finely chopped onions, green chillies, coriander and coconut).

Ananda Bhavan SOUTH INDIAN VEGETARIAN $
(Map p624; ☎6297 9522; 58 Serangoon Rd; mains from S$4; ⊙7.30am-10pm) There are several branches of this superlative South Indian vegetarian eatery, which serves up excellent *idli* (rice dumplings), *thali*, *dosa* and lots of Indian sweets.

Andhra Curry SOUTH INDIAN $$
(Map p624;41 Kerbau Rd; set meals from S$8; ⊙11am-11pm; ☑) No-frills restaurant that prides itself on fiery recipes from the Indian state of Andhra Pradesh. Order up some Hyderabadi biryani (oven-baked rice with vegetables and meat), or a vegetarian set-meal *thali*. Masala tea helps quell the fire in your belly.

Tekka Centre HAWKER CENTRE $
(Map p624; cnr Serangoon & Buffalo Rds; ⊙10am-10pm) Serves most everything but with a focus on Indian food. Look out for Al-Rahman Royal Prata (01-248) for its divine *murtabak* (stuffed savoury pancake).

Lavender Food Square HAWKER CENTRE $
(Map p624; cnr Jln Besar & Foch Rd; ⊙24hr) People queue for ages to get the wonton noodles.

KAMPONG GLAM

Zam Zam MUSLIM $$

(Map p624; 699 North Bridge Rd; dishes S$4-8; ⏲8am-11pm) These guys have been here since 1908, so we figure they know what they're doing. Longevity hasn't bred complacency – the touts try to herd passers-by through the door as frenetic chefs whip up *murtabaks* (mutton-, chicken- or vegetable-filled flaky, flat bread).

Pariaman Warong Nasi MUSLIM $$

(Map p624; ☎6292 2374; 738 North Bridge Rd; meals S$6-10; ⏲7.30am-3.30pm) You'll smell the food before you see the crowd waiting to order the *nasi padang* dishes at this corner coffee shop where cars roll up for quick take-aways at lunchtime. The *beef rendang* (dry beef curry) and *sambal goreng* (long beans, tempeh and fried bean curd) are yummy.

Cafe Le Caire EGYPTIAN $$

(Map p624; ☎6292 0979; 39 Arab St; mains S$8-17, shisha S$15; ⏲10am-3.30am) This casual Egyptian hole-in-the-wall comes to life at night and attracts a multinational crowd. For a filling budget meal, you can't go past the mezze platter, washed down with an iced mint tea and a relaxing puff on a water pipe.

Golden Mile Food Centre HAWKER CENTRE $

(off Map p624; 505 Beach Rd; ⏲10am-10pm) The famous *tulang* (bone marrow) soup from basement stalls 4, 15 and 28 are messily good. Also try the famous *ah balling* (glutinous rice balls with sweet fillings) and *char kway teow* on the 2nd floor.

Cold Storage SUPERMARKET $

(Map p624; www.coldstorage.com.sg; B1-16, Bugis Junction, 200 Victoria St) This supermarket is great for picking up make-your-own lunch items.

Golden Mile Complex THAI $

(off Map p624; ⏲10am-10pm) Here you'll find many cheap Thai food stalls sitting next to seedy discos.

ORCHARD ROAD

Din Tai Fung CHINESE $$$

(Map p626; ☎6836 8336; B1-03 Paragon, 290 Orchard Rd; mains S$6-17; ⏲lunch & dinner) While waiting, watch chefs at work through 'fishbowl' windows; they painstakingly make 18 folds in the dough used for the *xiao long pao* (steamed pork dumplings). Delicate dumplings are served steaming in bamboo baskets and explode with flavour in your mouth.

> **SPLURGE: ORIOLE CAFE & BAR**
>
> The modern bistro menu at Oriole (Map p626; ☎6238 8348; 01-01 Pan Pacific Serviced Suites, 96 Somerset Rd; mains S$10-18; ⏲lunch & dinner) is guaranteed to induce dining indecision. Do you go with the beef-cheek tagliatelle, fish and chips or a Philly steak and cheese? Staff pull perfect espressos behind the impressive La Marzocco machine.

Food Republic FOOD COURT $$

(Map p626; Wisma Atria, 435 Orchard Rd; ⏲10am-10pm) Slightly upmarket food court, with views along Orchard Rd to match the yummy local dishes.

Takashimaya Food Village FOOD COURT $

(Map p626; Takashimaya, Ngee Ann City, 391 Orchard Rd; ⏲10am-10pm) Get your fill of Japanese food and goodies in this basement food court.

Carrefour SUPERMARKET $

(Map p626; Plaza Singapura, 68 Orchard Rd) An outlet of the French hypermarket chain, perfect for self-catering.

Drinking

Drinking in Singapore is expensive. The cheapest way to drink is to park yourself in a hawker centre, where beers cost S$6 to S$8 for a large bottle. If you're hitting the bars and clubs, start early: happy hours (one for one and discounted drinks) generally finish at 9pm. The main drinking places include Clarke and Boat Quays, and Emerald Hill Rd off Orchard Rd. Most bars open from 5pm daily until at least midnight Sunday to Thursday, and until 2am on Fridays and Saturdays.

COLONIAL DISTRICT

Loof BAR

(Map p620; 6338 8035; 03-07 Odeon Towers Bldg, 331 North Bridge Rd; ⏲5pm-1.30am Sun-Thu, to 3am Fri & Sat) This breezy bar is situated on the 'loof'top of a building across from Raffles Hotel. Chilled-out vibes, comfy couches and good happy-hour specials make it stand out.

CBD & THE QUAYS

Falling into disrepair a few years ago, Clarke Quay has been revamped, and is now far and away the most popular (though very gaudy) nightspot in Singapore.

SPLURGE: RAFFLES HOTEL

It's a compulsory and costly cliché to sink a Singapore Sling (S$25) in the Long Bar (open 11am to 12.30am) at **Raffles Hotel** (Map p620; ☎6337 1886; 1 Beach Rd). For a less touristy experience head for the century-old snooker tables at the Bar & Billiard Room (open 11.30am to 12.30am), where you can almost hear Somerset Maugham clacking away on his typewriter in the courtyard.

Brewerkz BAR
(Map p622; ☎6438 7438; 01-05 Riverside Point, 30 Merchant Rd; ⊙noon-midnight Sun-Thu, to 1am Fri & Sat) Across the river from Clarke Quay, this large microbrewery (the irony doesn't escape us) brews eight beers on site. Happy hours run from opening to 9pm, with prices escalating throughout the day (pints S$4 to S$15, jugs S$10 to S$37).

Crazy Elephant BAR
(Map p622; ☎6337 7859; www.crazyelephant.com; 01-03/04 Clarke Quay; ⊙5pm-1am Sun-Thu, to 2am Fri & Sat) Anywhere that bills itself as 'crazy' should set the alarm bells ringing, but you won't hear them once you're inside. This touristy rock bar is beery, blokey, loud, graffiti-covered and testosterone-heavy – rock on!

Boat Quay BARS
(Map p622) Boat Quay is a popular boozing haunt for expat city workers. The British-style **Penny Black** (26 Boat Quay) gets very busy, as does **Harry's Bar** next door.

CHINATOWN

Tanjong Pagar Rd has an active gay and lesbian bar scene but welcomes drinkers regardless of their sexuality. The sophisticated bars of Club St are housed in attractive, restored shophouses (many are closed Sunday).

Pigeon Hole CAFE
(off Map p622; www.thepigeonhole.com.sg; 52-53 Duxton Rd; coffee from S$2.50, beer from S$10; ⊙10am-11pm Tue-Thu, 10am-1am Fri, 11.30am-1am Sat, 11.30am-8pm Sun) Arty cafe with friendly staff, great coffee, live music (some weekends) and fun open-mic evenings a couple of times a month (check the website). Located 200m northwest of Tanjong Pagar MRT.

Beaujolais BAR
(Map p624; 1 Ann Siang Hill; wine & beer from S$10; ⊙noon-1am) Get here early, grab a table on the terrace and watch this ultra-chic corner of Chinatown cruise by as you enjoy a glass or two of fine French wine.

Screening Room BAR
(Map p624; www.screeningroom.com.sg; 12 Ann Siang Rd; cocktails from S$15; ⊙6pm-2am) Best known for its sofa-strewn mini-cinema, Screening Room also has a hugely popular, extremely swanky rooftop bar. Sip cocktails or chug beer while admiring views of heritage buildings and the CBD.

LITTLE INDIA & KAMPONG GLAM

Zsofi Tapas Bar BAR
(Map p624; ☎6297 5875; 68 Dunlop St; beer from S$12; ⊙4pm-1am Mon-Thu, 4pm-2am Fri & Sat) Inspired by their travels through Spain, two mates decided to open a tapas bar named after a travelling companion. All drinks come with a tapas of choice. Now that's choice!

Prince of Wales PUB
(Map p624; ☎6299 0130; www.pow.com.sg; cnr Dunlop & Madras Sts; beer from S$10; ⊙9am-1am) This knockabout Australian drinking den, which doubles as a backpacker hostel, is friendly and very popular and has live music pretty much every night (from 9pm).

Kerbau Road Beer Garden DRINKS STALL
(Map p624; Kerbau Rd; beer from S$3; ⊙10am-11pm) Little more than a couple of drinks stalls with plastic tables and chairs, this 'beer garden' is packed every night with Indian drinkers who come for the Bollywood movies shown on the small TV as much as for the cheap booze.

BluJaz Cafe BAR
(Map p624; ☎6292 3800; www.blujaz.net; 11 Bali Lane; beer from S$6; ⊙noon-midnight Mon-Thu, noon-2am Fri, 4pm-2am Sat) This ultrabusy bar-restaurant next to an artists' studio is as close as you'll get to a bohemian hang-out in Singapore. There's live music (not always jazz) at weekends.

ORCHARD ROAD AREA

Emerald Hill Bars BARS
(Map p626; Emerald Hill Rd) Emerald Hill has a collection of bars in the renovated shophouses just off Orchard Rd, including the cool **Alley Bar** (2 Emerald Hill Rd) and even cooler **No 5** (5 Emerald Hill Rd). At the end of the strip, **Ice Cold Beer** (9 Emerald Hill Rd) is a raucous spot with indie/rock music at high decibels and a range of chilled brews.

SENTOSA ISLAND

Cafe del Mar BAR
(Map p629; Siloso Beach; beer from S$10, cocktails from S$14, coffee from S$5; ⌚10am-11pm Mon-Fri, to 2am Sat & Sun) Ibiza-style beach bar with loungers, a small pool and chill-out music.

Tanjong Beach Club BAR
(Map p629; Tanjong Beach; beer from S$12, cocktails from S$15; ⌚9am-11pm Mon-Fri, to 1am Sat & Sun) The beautiful flock here to sip cocktails and stretch out on deck chairs. If you don't fancy swimming in the beach, there's a pool for a dip.

Wave House BAR
(Map p629; Siloso Beach; beer from S$10, cocktails from S$15; ⌚11am-11pm Mon-Fri, to 2am Sat & Sun) Surfer-friendly beach bar with its own ordinary pool as well as two 'flowriders': wave pools that you can pay to surf in.

☆ Entertainment

Singaporeans love the cinema (a cheap way to dodge the tropical heat, tickets cost S$10 or so). The *Straits Times, I-S Magazine* and *Time Out* have listings for movies, theatre and music. Tickets for most events are available through **Sistic** (Map p626; ☎6348 5555; www.sistic.com.sg; Wisma Atria, 435 Orchard Rd) or **Tickets.com** (☎6296 2929; www.tdc.com.sg). Sistic also has agencies at Bugis Junction, Raffles City and the Singapore Visitors Centres that are located on Orchard Rd (Map p626).

St James Power Station CLUB
(Map p629; ☎6270 7676; www.stjamespowerstation.com; 3 Sentosa Gateway; admission men/women S$12/10, men Wed S$30) An entertainment complex housed in a 1920s coal-fired power station. All the bars and clubs are interconnected, so one cover charge gets access to all of them. Some bars have no cover charge. There's **Dragonfly** (⌚6pm-6am), a Mando- and Canto-pop club, **Movida** (⌚6pm-3am), a Latin live-band dance club, **Powerhouse** (⌚8pm-4am Wed, Fri & Sat), a large dance club aimed at the younger crowd, and the **Boiler Room** (⌚8.45pm-3am Mon-Sat), a mainstream rock club featuring live bands. Minimum age is 18 for women and 23 for men at all except Powerhouse, where the age is 18 for both.

FREE CONCERTS

The **Esplanade – Theatres on the Bay** (Map p622; www.esplanade.com; 1 Esplanade Dr) has free outdoor gigs on Fridays, Saturdays and Sundays that kick off around 7pm. The **Singapore Symphony Orchestra** (www.sso.org.sg) performs free at the Singapore Botanic Gardens monthly. Check the websites for details.

Zouk CLUB
(☎6738 2988; www.zoukclub.com.sg; 17 Jiak Kim St; men/women incl 2 drinks S$45/38, before 10pm S$25) This stayer of the Singaporean club scene still nabs top-name DJs. It's actually three clubs in one, plus a wine bar, so go the whole hog and pay the full entrance. It's just northeast of Chinatown; taxi is the easiest way there.

Butter Factory CLUB
(Map p622; ☎6333 8243; www.thebutterfactory.com; 02-02 One Fullerton, 1 Fullerton Rd; admission incl 2 drinks from S$21; ⌚7pm-1am Tue, 7pm-3am Thu, 8pm-3am Wed & Fri, Sat 8pm-4am) The 8000 sq ft Butter Factory is slick as hell. Street art on the walls of Bump, the hip-hop and R&B room, appeals to the younger crowds.

Zirca Mega Club CLUB
(Map p622; ☎6235 2292; www.zirca.sg; 01-02 Block 3C River Valley Rd, the Cannery, Clarke Quay; admission incl 2 drinks men S$25-28, women S$20-25; ⌚9.30pm till late Wed-Sat) Located in the premises of the former Ministry of Sound. Mash with the mainly 20-somethings in Zirca (dance club), Rebel (hip-hop arena) or Yellow Jello (retro disco).

Chinese Theatre Circle OPERA
(Map p622; ☎6323 4862; www.ctcopera.com.sg; 5 Smith St; 1-/2-hr show S$20/35, tickets through Sistic) Get into Chinese opera at a teahouse session organised by this nonprofit company. Friday and Saturday shows start at 7pm and 8pm with a brief talk (in English) on Chinese opera, followed by an excerpt from a Cantonese opera.

Timbre@Substation LIVE MUSIC
(Map p620; ☎6337 7800; 45 Armenian St; ⌚6pm-midnight) At night, groups of art-school types hang out and bob heads to live alt-rock sets while downing pints of Erdinger, hands oily from one too many buffalo wings.

Shopping

Once renowned as a bargain paradise, Singapore has been overtaken by other cities in the region, but there are still bargains to be had on items such as clothing, electronics, IT gear and books. Prices are usually fixed except at markets and in smaller non-chain stores (don't start bargaining if you don't have any real interest in purchasing). Most shops open at 10am or 11am and close around 9pm or 10pm.

ORCHARD ROAD

Ngee Ann City MALL

(Map p626; ☎6733 0337; 391 Orchard Rd) Packed with high-end brands and Kinokuniya, the best bookshop in the city.

Ion Orchard MALL

(Map p626; 430 Orchard Rd) Next to Orchard MRT is the new Ion Orchard, with a shimmery 21st-century media wall, an art space and a wide range of stores.

Far East Plaza MALL

Map p626; ☎6235 2411; 14 Scotts Rd) Great for cheap clothes and shoes, and getting inked.

COLONIAL DISTRICT

Funan DigitaLife Mall MALL

(Map p620; ☎6337 4235; 109 North Bridge Rd) IT greenhorns rejoice. Computers, software, camera gear and MP3 players are priced and labelled. Family-run **John 3:16** (05-46) is a popular camera shop. **Challenger** (06-01) is open 24 hours.

Cathay Photo CAMERA

(Map p620; ☎6337 4274; 01-11 Peninsula Plaza, 111 North Bridge Rd) All the pros (and wannabes) shop at the extensively stocked Cathay Photo. Several secondhand camera stores next door.

LITTLE INDIA & KAMPONG GLAM

Little India bursts with handicrafts, gold, saris, incense, Bollywood music and DVDs. In Kampong Glam, for handicrafts, raw cloth and tourists trinkets, wander along **Bussorah St** (Map p624) and **Arab St** (Map p624). **Haji Lane** (Map p624) has a series of stores selling up-to-the-minute fashion… assuming they haven't shut down because of soaring rent.

Mustafa Shopping Centre MALL

(Map p624; ☎6294 7742; www.mustafa.com.sg; 145 Syed Alwi Rd; ⏰24hr) Has all manner of goods (electronics, jewellery, household items, toys, shoes etc). A new extension has a supermarket with a wide range of Indian foodstuffs and a rooftop restaurant.

Bugis Village MALL

(Map p624; Victoria St) This warren, opposite Bugis Junction, is good hunting ground for cheap clothes, shoes and accessories.

Sim Lim Square MALL

(Map p624; 1 Rochor Canal Rd) This is a geek paradise, overflowing with cheap IT gear and electronics. We'd only advise going if you know your stuff however, because novices will be fleeced.

ℹ Information

Emergency

Ambulance & Fire (☎995)

Police (☎999)

SOS Helpline (☎1800 211 4444)

Internet Access

Hostels offer free internet via PCs or wi-fi. Travellers with laptops or phones with wi-fi should sign up for free wireless internet, Wireless@SG. Wireless@SG hot spots are located in most malls and many public buildings in Singapore. You need a mobile phone with a working SIM (local or global roaming) to register.

Medical Services

Raffles Hospital (Map p624; ☎6311 1111; www.raffleshospital.com; 585 North Bridge Rd; ⏰24hr)

Singapore General Hospital (off Map p622; ☎6222 3322; www.sgh.com.sg; Level 2, Block 1, Outram Rd; ⏰24hr)

Money

Money changers can be found in every shopping centre and don't charge fees on foreign money or travellers cheques. Many shops accept foreign cash and travellers cheques at poorer rates than you'd get from a money changer.

Post

Tourist information centres sell stamps and post letters. Changi Airport Terminal 2 has a post-office counter. Post offices:

Lucky Plaza (Map p626; 02-29 Lucky Plaza, Orchard Rd)

Ion Orchard (Map p626; B2-62 ION Orchard, 2 Orchard Turn; Ⓜ Orchard).

Tourist Information

Singapore Tourism Board (STB; www.visitsingapore.com) Most STB offices provide a wide range of services, including tour bookings and event ticketing.

Singapore Visitors Centre@ION Orchard (Map p626; Lvl 1 ION Orchard, 2 Orchard Turn; ⏰10am-10pm)

Singapore Visitors Centre@Orchard (Map p626; ☎1800 736 2000; cnr Orchard & Cairnhill Rds; ⏰9.30am-10.30pm)

Websites

Visit Singapore (www.visitsingapore.com) Official tourism board website.

Sistic (www.sistic.com.sg) Comprehensive events calendar and ticket bookings.

UNDERSTAND SINGAPORE

Singapore Today

Singapore is undergoing a development boom, gearing up to boost its population to 6.5 million and reposition itself as a centre for everything from biomedical research to tourism. Two huge casino resorts on Sentosa Island and at Marina South were completed in 2011 while the entire Marina Bay area around the futuristic Esplanade theatre is being turned into an upmarket commercial, residential, leisure, botanic gardens and water-sports centre (talk about a Swiss army knife of civic planning!).

Singapore quickly shrugged off the effects of the financial crisis and in 2010 had the third-highest growing GDP in the world with S$100 billion in reserve. While the incumbent People's Action Party might have faced its greatest political election loss since independence in 2011, it seems like they've at least set the foundation stone for Singapore's continued prosperity.

History

Lion City

Singapore was originally a tiny sea town squeezed between powerful neighbours Sumatra and Melaka. According to Malay legend, a Sumatran prince spotted a lion while visiting the island of Temasek, and on the basis of this good omen he founded a city there called Singapura (Lion City).

Raffles

Sir Thomas Stamford Raffles arrived in 1819 on a mission to secure a strategic base for the British Empire in the Strait of Melaka. He decided to transform the sparsely populated, swampy island into a free-trade port. The layout of central Singapore is still as Raffles drew it.

World War II

The glory days of the empire came to an abrupt end on 15 February 1942, when the Japanese invaded Singapore. For the rest of WWII the Japanese ruled the island harshly, jailing Allied prisoners of war (POWs) at Changi Prison and killing thousands of locals. Although the British were welcomed back after the war, the empire's days in the region were numbered.

Foundation for the Future

The socialist People's Action Party (PAP) was founded in 1954, with Lee Kuan Yew as its secretary general. Lee led the PAP to victory in elections held in 1959, and hung onto power for over 30 years. Singapore was kicked out of the Malay Federation in 1965, but Lee pushed through an ambitious, strict and successful industrialisation program.

His successor in 1990 was Goh Chok Tong, who loosened things up a little, but maintained Singapore on the path Lee had forged.

In 2004 Goh stepped down to make way for Lee's son, Lee Hsien Loong.

Lee the Younger faces the huge challenge of positioning Singapore to succeed in the modern, globalised economy. As manufacturing bleeds away to cheaper competitors, the government is focused on boosting its population, attracting more 'foreign talent' and developing industries such as tourism, financial services, digital media and biomedical research.

The Culture

The National Psyche

Affluent Singaporeans live in an apparently constant state of transition, continuously urged by their ever-present government to upgrade, improve and reinvent. On the surface, these are thoroughly modernised people, but many lives are still ruled by old beliefs and customs. There is also a sharp divide between the older generation, who experienced the huge upheavals and relentless graft that built modern Singapore, and the pampered younger generation, who enjoy the fruits of that labour.

Lifestyle

While family and tradition are important, many young people live their lives outside of home, working long hours and staying out late after work.

The majority of the population lives in Housing Development Board flats (you can't miss them). These flats are heavily subsidised by the government (which even dictates the ratio of races living in each block). These subsidies favour married couples, while singles and gay and lesbian couples have to tough it out on the private real-estate market.

Women have equal access to education and employment. Likewise, despite the oft-touted anti-homosexual stance of the government, gay men and lesbians are a visible part of everyday life in Singapore.

Population

The majority of the 4.48 million people are Chinese (75.2% of the population). Next come the Malays (13.6%), Indians (8.8%) and Eurasians and 'others' (2.4%). Western expats are a very visible group. Also visible is the large population of domestic maids and foreign labourers. Contrary to popular belief, English is the first language of Singapore. Many Singaporeans speak a second language or dialect (usually Mandarin, Malay or Tamil).

Religion

The Chinese majority are usually Buddhists or Taoists, and Chinese customs, superstitions and festivals dominate social life.

The Malays embrace Islam as a religion and a way of life. *Adat* (customary law) guides important ceremonies and events, including birth, circumcision and marriage.

Over half the Indians are Hindus and worship the pantheon of gods in various temples across Singapore.

Christianity, including Catholicism, is also popular in Singapore, with both Chinese and Indians pledging their faith to this religion.

Environment

Singapore's chief environmental issue is rubbish disposal. The government has recognised the need to encourage recycling, both industrial and domestic. However, massive government effort doesn't necessarily translate to environmental awareness on the ground level. Locals still love their plastic bags when shopping, and get domestic helpers to wash their cars daily. Singaporeans are encouraged to recycle but aren't provided with easy means to do so (all waste in Housing Development Board flats still goes into one central bin).

Air quality is generally much better than in most large Southeast Asian metropolises, but the annual haze that descends on the island around September and October, generated by slash-and-burn fires in Indonesia, is a serious concern.

Much of Singapore's fresh water is imported from Malaysia but, with large reservoirs, desalination plants and a huge waste-water recycling project called Newater, Singapore hopes to become self-sufficient within the next few decades. Tap water is safe to drink.

Singapore has a proud and well-deserved reputation as a garden city. Parks, often beautifully landscaped, are abundant and the entire centre of the island is a green oasis.

SURVIVAL GUIDE

Directory A–Z

Accommodation

Hostels offer competitive prices (S$20 to S$40 for a dorm bed) and facilities such as free internet, breakfast and laundry use. Cheaper hotel rooms (S$50 to S$100) are cramped and often windowless, with shared facilities. Most places offer air-con rooms, with cheaper fan rooms. Establishments usually quote nett prices, which include all taxes. If you see ++ after a price, you'll need to add a 10% service charge and 7% GST. Room prices quoted in this chapter include all taxes and are divided into three categories: budget ($), for a place where rooms cost less than S$40, midrange ($$) between S$41 and S$100, and top end ($$$) over S$100.

Business Hours

Opening hours throughout the book are only listed if they differ from those listed below.

Banks Monday to Friday: 9.30am to 4.30pm. Some branches close at 6pm. Saturday: 9.30am to 11.30am.

Government & post offices Monday to Friday: between 8am and 9.30am to between 4pm and 6pm. Saturday: between 8am and 9.30am to between 11.30am and 2pm.

Restaurants & bars Top restaurants generally open between 12pm and 2pm for lunch and between 6pm and 10pm for dinner. Casual restaurants and food courts open all day (some 24 hours). Bars usually open 5pm till midnight, later on weekends.

Shops Monday to Sunday: 10am to 6pm, malls and larger shops open until 9.30pm or 10pm. Some smaller shops in Chinatown and Arab St close on Sunday. It's busiest in Little India on Sundays.

Climate

There are no seasons in Singapore. The weather is uniformly hot and humid all year round. November to January are considered slightly wetter months, though rain is common throughout.

Customs

You can bring in 1L each of wine, beer and spirits duty free, but no unopened packets of cigarettes. Electronic goods, cosmetics, watches, cameras, jewellery, footwear, toys, arts and crafts are not dutiable. Duty-free concessions are not available if you are arriving from Malaysia or if you've been out of Singapore for less than 48 hours.

Obscene or seditious material, gun-shaped cigarette lighters, pirated recordings and publications, and chewing gum are prohibited.

Dangers & Annoyances

Short-term visitors are unlikely to be troubled by Singapore's notoriously tough laws, which have turned the city into one of the safest in Asia. Street crime is minimal, though pickpockets have been known to operate in Chinatown, Little India and other tourist areas. See also Legal Matters, p640.

Driving Licence

To drive in Singapore you'll need your home driver's licence and an international permit from a motoring association in your country.

Embassies & Consulates

For a list of Singaporean missions abroad, check out www.visitsingapore.com, where you'll also find a full list of foreign embassies and consulates in Singapore.

Australia (Map p626; ☎6836 4100; www.australia.org.sg; 25 Napier Rd)

Canada (Map p622; ☎6854 5900; www.cic.gc.ca; 11-01, One George St)

France (☎6880 7800; www.ambafrance-sg.org; 101-103 Cluny Park Rd)

Germany (Map p622; ☎6533 6002; www.singapur.diplo.de; 12-00 Singapore Land Tower, 50 Raffles Pl)

Indonesia (Map p626; ☎6737 7422; www.kbrisingapura.com; 7 Chatsworth Rd)

Ireland (Map p626; ☎6238 7616; www.embassyofireland.sg; 08-00 Liat Towers, 541 Orchard Rd)

Italy (☎6250 6022; www.ambsingapore.esteri.it; 27-02 United Square, 101 Thomson Rd)

Japan (Map p626; ☎6235 8855; www.sg.emb-japan.go.jp; 16 Nassim Rd)

Netherlands (Map p626; ☎6737 1155; www.mfa.nl/sin; 13-01 Liat Towers, 541 Orchard Rd)

New Zealand (Map p626; ☎6235 9966; www.nzembassy.com; 15-06/10 Ngee Ann City, 391A Orchard Rd)

Thailand (Map p626; ☎6737 2475; www.thaiembassy.sg; 370 Orchard Rd)

UK (Map p626; ☎6424 4200; www.ukinsingapore.fco.giv.uk; 100 Tanglin Rd)

USA (Map p626; ☎6476 9100; http://singapore.usembassy.gov; 27 Napier Rd)

For information on visas, see p641.

Festivals & Events

Singapore's multicultural population celebrates an amazing number of festivals and events. For details on public holidays in Singapore, see p640.

Chinese New Year The major festival, held in January/February. Look out for parades throughout Chinatown and festive foods in shops.

Singapore Food Festival This month-long festival (www.singaporefoodfestival.com) in March and April celebrates eating, and is held at hawker centres and gourmet restaurants.

Great Singapore Sale In June and July, merchants drop prices to boost Singapore's image as a shopping destination.

Food & Drink

Singapore has food outlets to suit every budget. For this book, we've used the following price ranges:

$ S$3 to S$15

$$ S$16 to S$30

$$$ from S$30

Gay & Lesbian Travellers

Male homosexuality is still technically illegal, but the city is slowly opening up and the laws have not prevented the emergence of a thriving gay scene. Check out www.utopia-asia.com and www.fridae.com for coverage of venues and events.

Legal Matters

The law is extremely tough in Singapore, but also relatively free from corruption. Possession and trafficking of drugs is punishable by death. Smoking in all public places, including bars, restaurants and hawker centres, is banned unless there's an official smoking 'area'.

Maps

The Official Map of Singapore, available free from the STB and hotels, is excellent.

Media

Magazines

Free publications with events information, such as *Where Singapore, Juice* and *I-S Magazine* are available at tourist offices, most major hotels and several restaurants, cafes and bars. The international listings magazine *Time Out* now has a Singapore edition, too.

Newspapers

English dailies include the progovernment spin sheet *Straits,* the *Business Times* and the tabloid-style *New Paper. Straits Times* has decent coverage of Asia. *New Paper* is best for a flavour of 'real life' Singapore and sports. *Today* and *Mypaper,* are freebie tabloids that you can pick up at MRT stations in the mornings and afternoons.

Money

The Singaporean dollar is made up of 100 cents. Singapore uses 5c, 10c, 20c, 50c and S$1 coins, while notes come in denominations of S$2, S$5, S$10, S$50, S$100, S$500 and S$1000.

Banks and ATMs are everywhere. Money changers are easily found in most malls and busy locations. You don't get charged any fees and you can haggle a little if you're changing a largeish quantity.

Contact details for credit-card companies in Singapore:

American Express (☎6396 6000)

Diners Club (☎6571 0128)

MasterCard (☎1800 1100 113)

Visa (☎6437 5800, 1800 1100 344)

Post

Post in Singapore is among the most reliable in Southeast Asia. Postcards cost S$0.50 to anywhere in the world, and a letter costs S$0.65 to S$2.50 depending on where it's going. Call ☎1605 to find the nearest post office branch, or check www.singpost.com.sg. Letters addressed to 'Poste Restante' are held at the **Singapore Post Centre** (☎6841 2000; 10 Eunos Rd), next to the Paya Lebar MRT.

Public Holidays

The following days are public holidays. Many are based on the lunar calendar, and their dates are variable.

New Year's Day 1 January

Chinese New Year January/February (three days)

Good Friday March/April

Vesak Day May

Labour Day 1 May

National Day 9 August

Deepavali October

Hari Raya Puasa October/November

Christmas Day 25 December

Hari Raya Haji December/January

Responsible Travel

Modern and cosmopolitan though it appears, Singapore is a little sensitive when it comes to brash behaviour by foreigners – quiet, polite behaviour will win you more respect. Public transport is efficient and you can even call hybrid-fuel taxis.

Telephone

Mobile Phones

Mobile-phone numbers in Singapore start with 8 or 9. If you have global roaming, your GSM phone will lock into one of Singapore's three networks, MI-GSM, ST-GSM or Starhub.

You can buy a SIM card (usually S$18) or a 'disposable' mobile from most post offices and 7-Eleven stores, though you need to show your passport.

Phone Codes

Singapore's country code is ☎65. There are no area codes in Singapore; telephone numbers are eight digits unless you are calling toll free (☎1800). Malaysia's access code is

☎20, followed by the area code of the town in Malaysia that you wish to call (minus the leading zero) and then the number.

Toilets

Toilets in Singapore are clean and well maintained, though they might vary between the sit-down and rarer squatting types. In some hawker centres you may have to pay S$0.10. You can usually find a toilet in malls, fast-food outlets and large hotels.

Tourist Information

See p637 for branches of the Singapore Tourist Board (STB).

Travellers with Disabilities

Travellers using wheelchairs can find Singapore difficult, though a massive accessibility project to improve life for the elderly and those with disabilities has seen things improve. The pavements in the city are nearly all immaculate, MRT stations all have lifts and there some buses and taxis equipped with wheelchair-friendly equipment.

The **Disabled People's Association** (☎6899 1220; www.dpa.org.sg) has an online accessibility guide to the country.

Visas

Citizens of most countries are granted 30-day visas upon arrival in Singapore whether by air or overland. The exceptions are citizens of the Commonwealth of Independent States (former Soviet republics), India, Myanmar, China and most Middle Eastern countries. Visitors must have a valid passport or internationally recognised travel document valid for at least six months beyond the date of entry into Singapore. Extensions can be applied for at the **Immigration & Checkpoints Authority** (Map p624; ☎6391 6100; www.ica.gov.sg; 10 Kallang Rd). This can also be done online. Applications take at least a day to process.

For details of embassies and consulates, see p639.

Volunteering

The **National Volunteer & Philanthropy Centre** (www.nvpc.org.sg) coordinates a number of community groups, including grassroots projects in areas such as education, the environment and multiculturalism.

Women Travellers

There are few problems for women travelling in Singapore. In Kampong Glam and Little India skimpy clothing may attract unwanted stares. Tampons and pads are widely available across the island, as are over-the-counter medications.

Getting There & Away

Air

Singapore is a great hub for any Southeast Asian journey. The budget air-travel boom connects Changi Airport cheaply with dozens of regional destinations.

Budget airlines operating out of Changi include the following:

Air Asia (☎6307 76883; www.airasia.com)

Berjaya-Air (☎6227 3688; www.berjaya-air.com) Daily flights to Tioman and Redang islands in Malaysia.

Cebu Pacific (☎agents 6735 7155, 6737 9231, 6220 5966; www.cebupacificair.com)

Jetstar (☎800 6161 977; www.jetstar.com)

Tiger Airways (☎6808 4437; www.tigerairways.com)

Bus

Malaysia

For Johor Bahru (JB), the Causeway Express air-con buses (S$2.40) and the public SBS bus 170 (S$1.70) depart every 15 minutes between 6.30am and 11pm from the **Queen Street bus terminal** (Map p624; cnr Queen & Arab Sts). From JB to Singapore, take a bus from Larkin bus station. The buses stop at the Singapore checkpoint; keep your ticket and hop on the next bus that comes along after you've cleared immigration. The process is the same when heading into Malaysia from Singapore. Share taxis (S$12) to JB leave from the Queen St bus terminal. From JB, there's a taxi (RM12) terminal opposite the Puteri Pan Pacific Hotel.

Arriving from Malaysia, you'll be dropped either at the **Lavender St bus terminal** (Map p624; cnr Lavender St & Kallang Bahru), a 500m walk north of Lavender MRT station, or outside the **Golden Mile Complex** (off Map p624; Beach Rd).

Numerous private companies run comfortable bus services to many destinations in Malaysia, including Melaka and Kuala Lumpur. The buses depart from various points in Singapore. If you're stumped, head to the Golden Mile Complex, where there are many bus agencies selling tickets. You can also book online at www.busonlineticket.com.

GETTING TO/FROM

Malaysia

The 1km-long Causeway bridge in the north, at Woodlands, connects Singapore with Johor Bahru in Malaysia. To the west, the Second Link bridge connects Tuas to Tanjung Kupang in Malaysia. Immigration procedures on both sides of the bridges are straightforward. See p641 for details of buses and trains heading across the border.

Indonesia

Ferries and speedboats run between Singapore and the Riau archipelago (Pulau Bintan and Pulau Batam) in Indonesia. Immigration in Singapore is straightforward, though you should expect to pay for an Indonesian visa (US$20 for three days) when heading into Indonesia.

Grassland Express (☎6293 1166; www.grassland.com.sg; 5001 Beach Rd, 01-26 Golden Mile Complex)

Transnasional Bus Service (Map p624; ☎6294 7035; www.transnasional.com.my; Lavender Street Bus Terminal, cnr Lavender St & Kallang Bahru)

Transtar Travel (☎6299 9009; www.transtar.travel; 5001 Beach Rd, 01-15 Golden Mile Complex)

Thailand

The main terminal for buses to and from Thailand is at the **Golden Mile Complex** (off Map p624; Beach Rd). Buses go to Hat Yai and beyond. Most leave around 6pm and travel overnight.

Grassland Express (☎6293 1166; www.grassland.com.sg)

Phya Travel (☎6294 5415; www.phyatravel.com)

Train

Malaysian company **Keretapi Tanah Melayu Berhad** (☎6222 5165; www.ktmb.com.my) operates three air-con express trains daily (1st/2nd/3rd class S$68/34/19), for the seven-hour run from Singapore to Kuala Lumpur, with connections on to Thailand. Trains depart from the **Woodlands Train Checkpoint** (☎6767 5885; 11 Woodlands Crossing; 🚌170, Causeway Link from Queen St). You can book tickets at the station or via the KTM website.

Sea

There are several main ferry terminals with services to Malaysia and Indonesia:

Changi Point Ferry Terminal (☎6546 8518; Ⓜ Tanah Merah, then Ⓢ2)

Harbourfront Ferry Terminal (www.singaporecruise.com; ☎6513 2200)

Tanah Merah Ferry Terminal (www.singaporecruise.com; ☎6513 2200; Ⓜ Tanah Merah, then Ⓢ35)

MALAYSIA

From the Changi Point Ferry Terminal, ferries depart for Tanjung Belungkor, east of Johor Bahru. The 11km journey takes 45 minutes and costs S$18/22 one way/return. From the Tanjung Belungkor jetty, buses operate to Desaru and Kota Tinggi. Ferries also sail from Pengerang (one-way S$6), across the Straits of Johor in Malaysia. There's no fixed schedule; ferries leave between 7am and 4pm when full (12 people).

INDONESIA

Direct ferries run between Singapore and the Riau Archipelago islands (including Pulau Batam, Pulau Bintan, Tanjung Balai and Tanjung Batu). Batam ferries dock at Sekupang, where you can take a boat to Tanjung Buton on the Sumatran mainland. From there it's a three-hour bus ride to Palembang.

The ferries are modern, fast and air-conditioned. Expect to pay around S$16 for a one-way ticket to Batam, S$24 to S$36 to Bintan, Balai or Batu.

These are the main ferry operators:

BatamFast (☎6270 0311; www.batamfast.com) Ferries to Batam Centre, Sekupang, and Waterfront City depart from Harbourfront Ferry Terminal. Ferries to Nongsapura depart from the Tanah Merah Ferry Terminal.

Berlian Ferries (☎6546 8830) Ferries to Pulau Batam depart from Harbourfront Ferry Terminal.

Bintan Resort Ferries (☎6542 4369; www.brf.com.sg) Ferries to Bandar Bintan Telani depart from Tanah Merah Ferry Terminal.

Indo Falcon (☎6275 7393; www.indofalcon.com.sg) Ferries to all four destinations depart from Harbourfront Ferry Terminal.

Penguin Ferries (☎6271 4866; www.penguin.com.sg) Ferries to Batam Centre, Sekupang, and Tanjung Balai depart from Harbourfront Ferry Terminal. Ferries to Tanjung Pinang depart from the Tanah Merah Ferry Terminal.

TRANSPORT MADE EZ

If you're going to be using the MRT and buses a lot, it's cheaper and more convenient to buy a S$15 Ez-Link card from any MRT station (S$5 nonrefundable deposit and S$10 credit). Fares using this card are 20% cheaper than cash fares.

Alternatively, a **Singapore Tourist Pass** (www.thesingaporetouristpass.com) offers unlimited train and bus travel for S$8 daily plus a S$10 refundable deposit.

Getting Around

Bicycle

There is an ever-expanding network of bike paths connecting Singapore's many parks. Search 'Park Connectors' on the website of the **National Parks Board** (www.nparks.gov.sg) for a map of the bike paths.

The 12km bike path along East Coast Park makes for a good ride. Hire a decent mountain bike from S$6 at one of the numerous booths at East Coast Park. You can also get in-line skates here.

Boat

See p630 for a list of boat tours along the Singapore River. Bumboats also leave the Changi Point Ferry Terminal for Pulau Ubin.

Bus

Public buses run between 6am and midnight. Each bus stop has information on bus numbers and routes. Fares cost S$1 to S$2.10. When you board the bus, tell the driver where you're going, drop the exact money into the fare box (no change given) and collect your ticket.

Use Ez-Link cards on all buses for discounted fares. You'll need to tap the card on the card reader when boarding the bus and again when leaving.

Mass Rapid Transit

The MRT subway system is the easiest, quickest and most comfortable way to get around. The system operates from 6am to midnight, with trains at peak times running every three minutes, and off-peak every six minutes.

Single-trip tickets cost S$1 to S$2.70, with a S$1 refundable deposit for every ticket.

Taxi

The major cab companies are **City Cab** (☎6552 1111) and **Comfort** (☎6552 1111) and **SMRT** (☎6555 8888).

Fares start from S$2.80 to S$3.20 for the first kilometre, then 20c for each additional 385m. There are a raft of surcharges, ie late-night services (50%), peak-hour charges (30%), restricted-zone charges, airport pickups and bookings. All taxis are metered. Extra charges are always shown on the meter except for that of going into a restricted zone during peak hours. You can flag down a taxi any time or use a taxi rank outside hotels and malls.

Trishaw

Bicycle trishaws congregate at popular tourist places, such as Raffles Hotel and outside Chinatown Complex. Agree on the fare beforehand. Expect to pay around S$40 for half an hour. There's also a fixed-price system at **Trishaw Uncle** (Map p624; ☎9012 1233; Queen St btwn Fu Lu Shou Complex & Albert Centre Market; rides from S$39).

Thailand

Includes »

Best Regional Specialities

» Kài yâang (p715)

» Southern-style curries (p750)

» Kà·nŏm jeen nám ngée·o (p698)

Best Places for Cultural Connections

» Meditation Retreats (p689)

» Elephant Study Centre (p717)

» Kham Pia Homestay (p723)

» Salak Kok Kayak Station (p729)

Why Go?

Lustrous Thailand radiates a hospitality that makes it one of the most accessibly exotic destinations on earth. Its natural landscape is part of the allure: the blonde beaches are lapped at by cerulean seas, while the northern mountains cascade into the misty horizon. In between are emerald-coloured rice fields and busy, prosperous cities. It is a bountiful land where the markets are piled high with pyramids of colourful fruits and the *rót khēn* (vendor cart) is an integral piece of a city's infrastructure.

The new millennium has brought Thailand into a new era of prosperity. Bangkok reigns as an Asian superstar, and once rustic islands are now international package resorts. It is easy and cheap to hop around by plane and domestic tourists are just as likely to hit the tourist trail as foreigners.

You'll suffer few travelling hardships and be rewarded with fodder for the mind and spirit, from fiery curries to meditating Buddhas.

When to Go

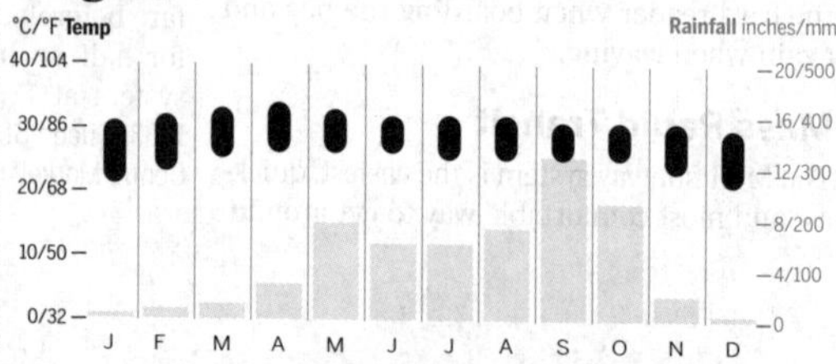

Nov–Feb Cool and dry season; peak tourist season is December to January.

Mar–Jun Hot season is hot but a good shoulder season for the beaches.

Jul–Oct Rainy season begins with a drizzle and ends with a downpour.

Don't Miss

Seeing the early morning alms route – when barefoot, orange-robed monks walk the streets collecting food from the faithful – is one of the great highlights (made easy when suffering from jet-lag) in Thailand. The silent procession transforms Thailand's otherwise deafening cities into calm, meditative spaces.

ITINERARIES

One Week

Get tussled about by Bangkok's chaos, then cruise up to Sukhothai to tour the quiet old ruins. Continue north to Chiang Mai, an easy, breezy cultural city. Climb up the mountain range to Pai for mountain scenery and bluesy late-nighters.

Two Weeks

From Bangkok, head south to the Samui islands (Ko Samui, Ko Pha-Ngan, Ko Tao) to become a certified beachaholic and diver. Then hop the peninsula to the Andaman beaches of Krabi/Railay, Ko Phi-Phi, Ko Lanta and Trang Islands.

Essential Food

» **kài phàt bai kà-phrao kài** – fiery stir-fry of chopped chicken, chillies, garlic and fresh basil.

» **khâo phàt** – fried rice, you never knew it could be so good; garnish it with ground chillies, sugar, fish sauce and a squirt of lime.

» **phàt phrík thai krà-thiam kài/mŏo** – stir-fried chicken or pork with black pepper and garlic.

» **phàt thai** – Thailand's oh-so-famous dish of rice noodles fried with egg and prawns garnished with bean sprouts, peanuts and chillies; eaten with chopsticks.

» **phàt phàk khanáa** – stir-fried Chinese greens, often fried with a meat (upon request), served over rice; simple but delicious.

AT A GLANCE

» **Currency** Baht (B)

» **Language** Thai

» **Money** ATMs widespread; 150B fee on foreign accounts

» **Visas** 30-day free visa for air arrivals; 15-day free visa for land arrivals; pre-arrange 30-day tourist visas

» **Mobile phones** Prepay SIMs from 150B

Fast Facts

» **Area** 513,000 sq km

» **Capital** Bangkok

» **Country code** ☎66

» **Emergency** ☎191

Exchange Rates

Australia	A$1	32B
Canada	C$1	31B
China	Y10	49B
Euro zone	€1	41B
Japan	¥100	37B
New Zealand	NZ$1	25B
Russia	Ruble10	10B
UK	£1	49B
US	US$1	31B

Set Your Budget

» **Basic room** US$6–25

» **Market meals** US$1–2

» **Beer** US$1.30–2.50

Entering the Country

» **International flights** Arrive at Suvarnabhumi Airport, Bangkok.

» **Popular border crossings** Poipet–Aranya Prathet (Cambodia); Huay Xai–Chiang Khong (Laos); Ko Lipe–Langkawi (Malaysia)

Thailand Highlights

1. Joining the urban orbit in **Bangkok** (p648), a rowdy metropolis that never sleeps, always eats and knows how to party
2. Ogling the perfect beach paradise proportions. of **Ko Phi-Phi** (p764)
3. Soaking up the cool and cultured vibe in **Chiang Mai** (p684)
4. Learning to swim the ocean deep in **Ko Tao** (p744)
5. Partying like a day-glo rock-star on **Ko Pha-Ngan** (p738)
6. Peddling around the ruined capital of **Sukhothai** (p680)
7. Going wild in **Khao Yai National Park** (p716)
8. Trekking to the hill-tribe villages around **Chiang Rai** (p696)

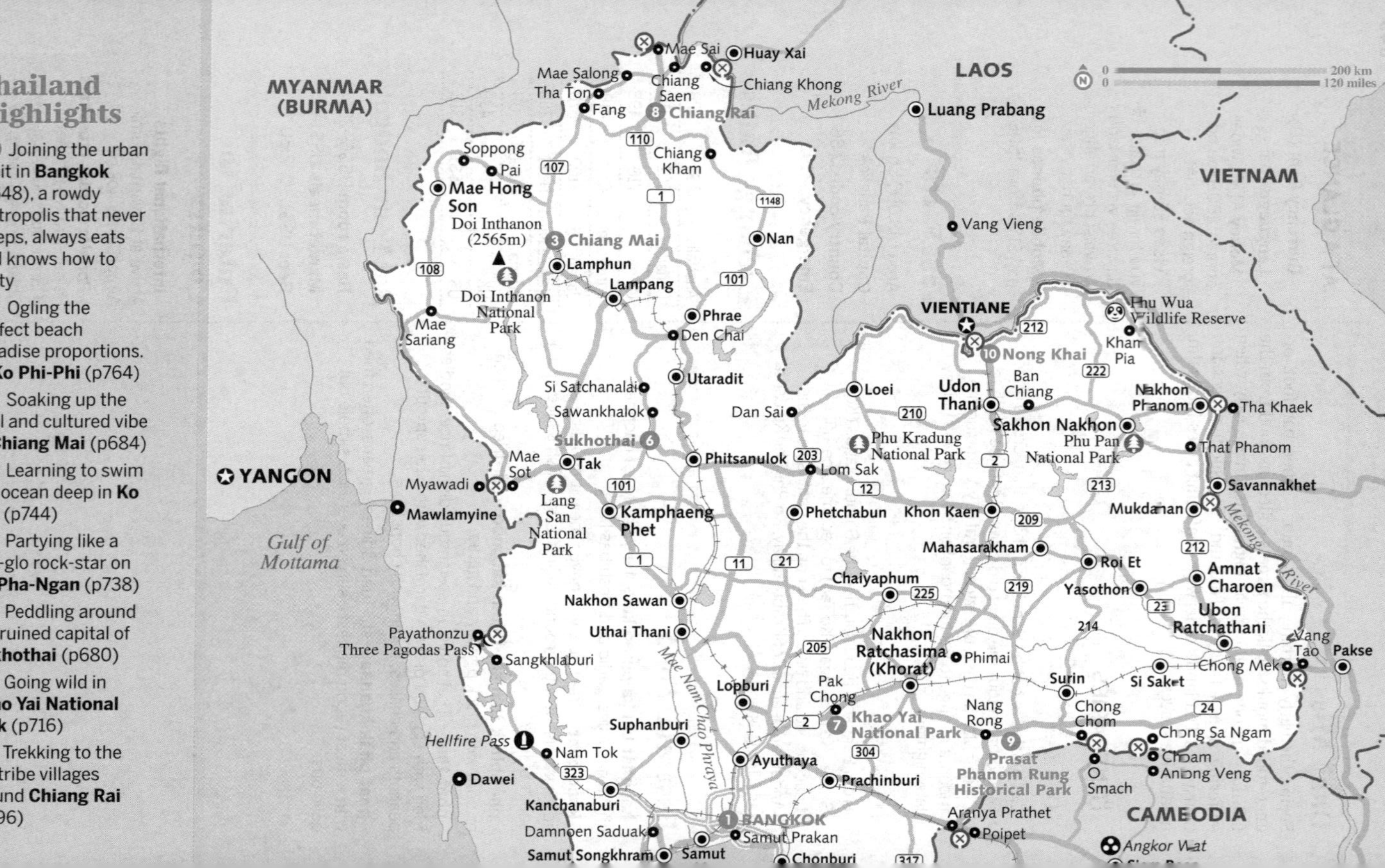

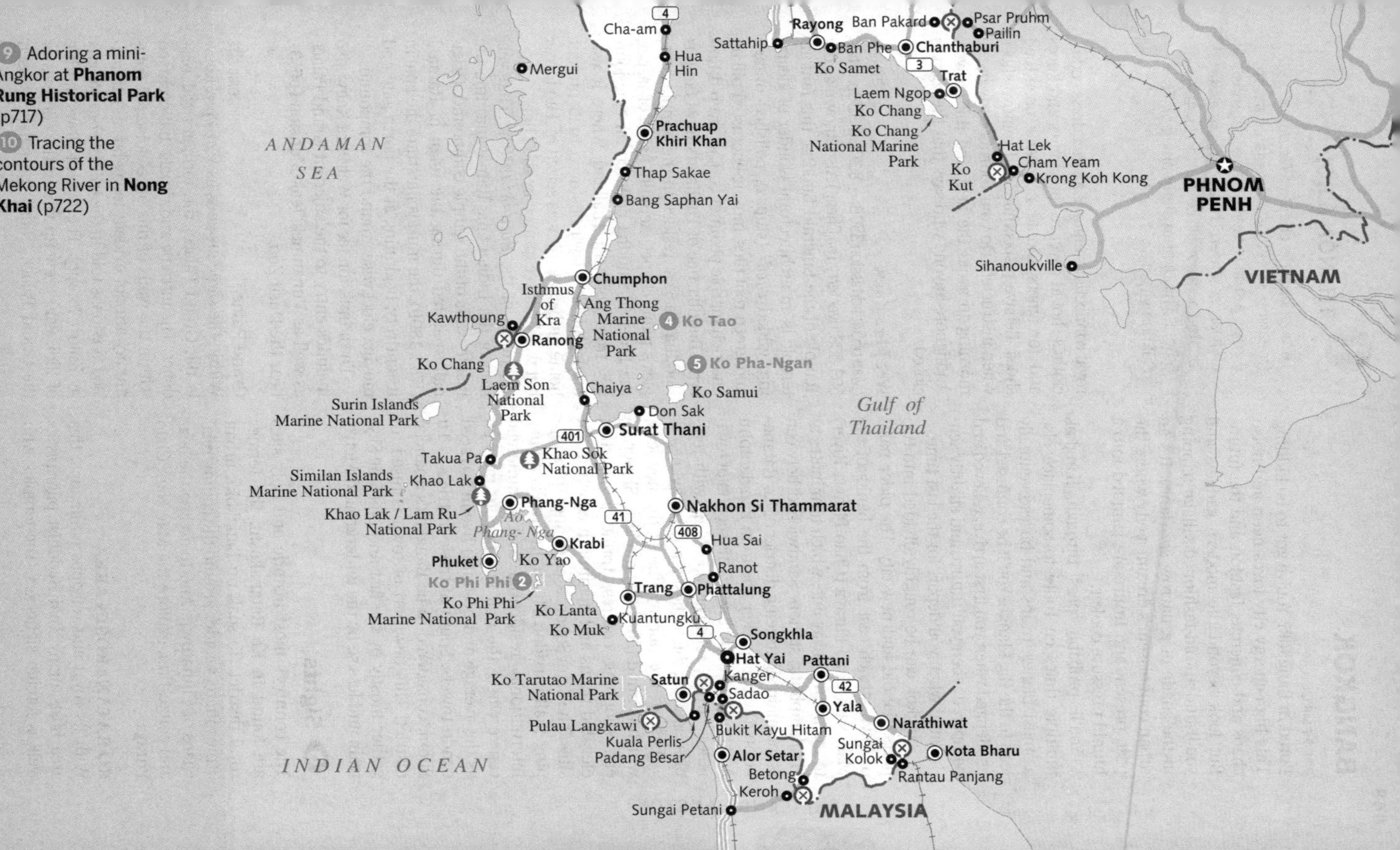
9 Adoring a mini-Angkor at **Phanom Rung Historical Park** (p717)
10 Tracing the contours of the Mekong River in **Nong Khai** (p722)
ANDAMAN SEA
INDIAN OCEAN
Gulf of Thailand
Cha-am
Hua Hin
Mergui
Prachuap Khiri Khan
Thap Sakae
Bang Saphan Yai
Chumphon
Isthmus of Kra
Kawthoung
Ranong
Ko Chang
Laem Son National Park
Surin Islands Marine National Park
Ang Thong Marine National Park
4 Ko Tao
5 Ko Pha-Ngan
Ko Samui
Chaiya
Don Sak
Surat Thani
Takua Pa
Khao Sok National Park
Similan Islands Marine National Park
Khao Lak
Khao Lak / Lam Ru National Park
Phang-Nga
Ao Phang-Nga
Krabi
Phuket
Ko Yao
Ko Phi Phi 2
Ko Phi Phi Marine National Park
Ko Lanta
Ko Muk
Kuantungku
Trang
Phattalung
Nakhon Si Thammarat
Hua Sai
Ranot
Songkhla
Hat Yai
Pattani
Ko Tarutao Marine National Park
Satun
Kanger
Sadao
Pulau Langkawi
Kuala Perlis
Padang Besar
Bukit Kayu Hitam
Yala
Narathiwat
Sungai Kolok
Kota Bharu
Rantau Panjang
Alor Setar
Betong
Keroh
Sungai Petani
MALAYSIA
Sattahip
Rayong
Ban Pakard
Psar Pruhm
Pailin
Ban Phe
Chanthaburi
Ko Samet
Trat
Laem Ngop
Ko Chang
Ko Chang National Marine Park
Hat Lek
Cham Yeam
Krong Koh Kong
Ko Kut
PHNOM PENH
Sihanoukville
VIETNAM
4
3
401
41
408
4
42

BANGKOK

POP 7.7 MILLION

Bored in Bangkok? You've got to be kidding. This high-energy city loves neon and noise, chaos and concrete, fashion and the future. But look beyond the modern gadgets and you'll find an old-fashioned village napping in the shade of a narrow *soi* (lane). It's an urban connoisseur's dream: a city where the past, present and future are jammed into a humid pressure cooker.

You'll probably pass through Bangkok multiple times en route to someplace else as most planes, trains and buses eventually lead to the Big Mango. You'll be confused and challenged when you first arrive, relieved and pampered when you return, and slightly sentimental when you depart for the last time.

Bangkok can be roughly divided into two parts: the old and new city. The older parts of town stretch east from the banks of the Mae Nam Chao Phraya (Chao Phraya River) to the main railway line, which terminates at Hualamphong station. Sandwiched between is the main sightseeing district of Ko Ratanakosin, the backpacker ghetto in Banglamphu and bustling Chinatown. This section of town is less urban, relatively speaking, with temples claiming the highest strata of skyline.

East of the railway line is the new city, which is mind-blowingly modern. Skyscrapers, shopping centres, traffic jams, slick elevated trams and mammoth construction sites. The Siam Square area defines the shopping mall corridor. Th Sukhumvit is a busy international residential and commercial centre where the rich and famous (as well as the average and ho-hum) live in terraced condo towers. South of these districts is Th Silom, considered to be Bangkok's financial district. This new part of town is fused together mostly by the fast and efficient Skytrain and less so by the underground Metro.

THÀNŎN & SOI

Throughout this chapter, *Thànŏn* (meaning 'street') is abbreviated as 'Th'. A *soi* is a small street or lane that runs off a larger street. The address of a site located on a *soi* will be written as 48/3-5 Soi 1, Th Sukhumvit, meaning off Th Sukhumvit on Soi 1.

Sights

The country's most historic and holy sites are found in Ko Ratanakosin, the former royal district. To soak up Bangkok's urban atmosphere, wander around the commercial chaos of Chinatown. And to escape the heat and congestion, explore the Mae Nam Chao Phraya.

KO RATANAKOSIN AREA

With its royal and religious affiliations, this area hosts many Thai Buddhist pilgrims as well as foreign sightseers. The temples with royal connections enforce a strict dress code – clothes should cover to the elbows and knees and foreigners should not wear open-toed shoes. Behave respectfully and remove shoes when instructed. Do your touring early in the morning to avoid the heat and the crowds. And ignore anyone who says that the sight is closed.

Wat Phra Kaew TEMPLE

(Map p654; admission 350B; ⏲8.30am-3.30pm; bus 503, 508, river ferry Tha Chang) Also known as the Temple of the Emerald Buddha, this famous temple is an architectural wonder of gleaming, gilded *chedi* (stupas), polished orange and green roof tiles, mosaic-encrusted pillars and rich marble pediments. The revered Emerald Buddha, one of Thailand's most famous Buddha images, resides in the temple complex's main chapel. Actually made of jasper, the Emerald Buddha endured an epic journey from northern Thailand, where it was hidden inside a layer of stucco, to its present home. In between it was seized by Lao forces but was later recaptured by the Thais.

Murals of the *Ramakian* (the Thai version of the Indian epic Ramayana) line the inside walls of the temple compound. Originally painted during the reign of Rama I (1782–1809), the murals illustrate the epic in its entirety, beginning at the north gate and moving clockwise around the compound.

The admission fee for Wat Phra Kaew also includes entry to the adjacent Grand Palace as well as Vimanmek Teak Mansion (p653), near the Dusit Zoo.

Grand Palace HISTORIC SITE

Within the same grounds as Wat Phra Kaew is the Grand Palace, the former royal residence. The intrigue and rituals that occurred within the walls of this once-cloistered community are not evident today but a fictionalised version is told in the trilogy *Four Reigns* by Kukrit Pramoj. The book follows the life of Ploi, who grew up within the confines of the Grand Palace. Today the palace is used for certain ceremonial occasions, such as Coronation Day; the royal family's Bangkok residence has long since moved elsewhere (presently they reside at Chitlada Palace in the northern part of the city). The exteriors of the four Grand Palace buildings are worth a swift perusal for their royal bombast, but their interiors are usually closed to the public.

Wat Pho TEMPLE

(Map p654; Wat Phra Chetuphon; Th Sanamchai; admission 50B; ⏲8am-9pm; bus 508, 512, river ferry Tha Tien) Wat Pho sweeps the awards for superlatives: it's the oldest and largest temple in Bangkok, dating from the 16th century; it houses the country's largest reclining Buddha; and it has the biggest collection of Buddha images in the country. The *big* attraction of course is the biggest Buddha, a stunning reclining image measuring 46m long and 15m high; the pose illustrates the passing of Buddha into final nirvana. The figure is modelled out of plaster around a brick core and finished in gold leaf. Mother-of-pearl inlay ornaments the eyes and feet, and the feet display 108 different auspicious *lák̀sànà* (characteristics of a Buddha).

Wat Pho is also the national headquarters for the teaching and preservation of traditional Thai medicine, including Thai massage. The temple's famous massage school has massage pavilions within the temple grounds as well as air-con facilities within the training school (see p691).

Museum of Siam MUSEUM

(Map p654; www.museumsiam.com; Th Maha Rat; admission 300B; ⏲10am-6pm Tue-Sun; bus 32, 524, river ferry Tha Tien) This fun museum employs a variety of media to explore the origins and culture of the Thai people. Housed in a Rama III–era palace, the exhibits are superinteractive, well balanced and entertaining. Highlights include the informative and engaging narrated videos in each exhibition room, and an interactive Ayuthaya-era battle game.

National Museum MUSEUM

(Map p654; 4 Th Na Phra That; admission 200B; ⏲9am-3.30pm Wed-Sun; bus 32, 123, 503, river ferry Tha Chang) This museum is reportedly the largest in Southeast Asia and offers an overview of Thai art and culture, a useful stepping stone to exploring the ancient capitals of Ayuthaya and Sukhothai. The history wing boasts modern curatorial aesthetics with a succinct chronology of prehistoric, Sukhothai-, Ayuthaya- and Bangkok-era events. But the labelling in the art wing, which contains a must-see overview of Buddhist iconography, isn't exactly illuminating so try one of the free **guided tours** (⏲9.30am Wed & Thu).

Wat Arun TEMPLE

(Map p654; Th Arun Amarin; admission 50B; ⏲8.30am-4.30pm; cross-river ferry from Tha Tien) Named after the Indian god of dawn (Aruna), Wat Arun looms large on the Thonburi side of the Mae Nam Chao Phraya, looking as if it were carved from granite. Closer inspection reveals a mosaic of porcelain tiles covering the imposing 82m Khmer-style *praang* (spire). The tiles were left behind by Chinese merchant ships no longer needing them as ballast. After the fall of Ayuthaya, King Taksin ceremoniously clinched control of the country here on the site of a local shrine (formerly known as Wat Jaeng) and established a royal palace and a temple to house the Emerald Buddha.

CHINATOWN & PHAHURAT

Cramped and crowded Chinatown is a beehive of commercial activity. The main thoroughfare is lined with gleaming gold shops, towering neon signs bearing Chinese characters and bisected by serpentine lanes with shopfronts spilling out onto the footpath. The neighbourhood's energy is at once exhilarating and exhausting. Th Yaowarat is fun to explore at night when it is lit up like a Christmas tree and filled with food vendors.

Talat Mai MARKET

(Map p650; Soi 16/Trok Itsaranuphap, Th Yaowarat; bus 73, 159, 507, MRT Hua Lamphong, river ferry Tha Ratchawong) Talat Mai is a nearly three-block-long market selling exotic food stuffs and Chinese Buddhist religious paraphernalia.

Wat Traimit TEMPLE

(Map p650; cnr Th Yaowarat & Th Charoen Krung; admission 40B; ⏲8am-5pm Tue-Sun; MRT Hua Lamphong, river ferry Tha Ratchawong) Wat Traimit shelters a 3m-tall, 5.5-tonne solid-gold Buddha image – an impressive sight, even in the land of a million Buddhas. Like many treasured Buddhas, this figure was once covered in stucco, a common measure to deter looters during periods of unrest. Donations and a constant flow of tourists have proven profitable, and the statue is now housed in a brand-new four-storey marble structure. The 2nd floor of the building is home to the **Phra Buddha Maha Suwanna Patimakorn Exhibition** (admission 100B; ⏲8am-5pm Tue-Sun), which has exhibits on how the statue was made,

Central Bangkok

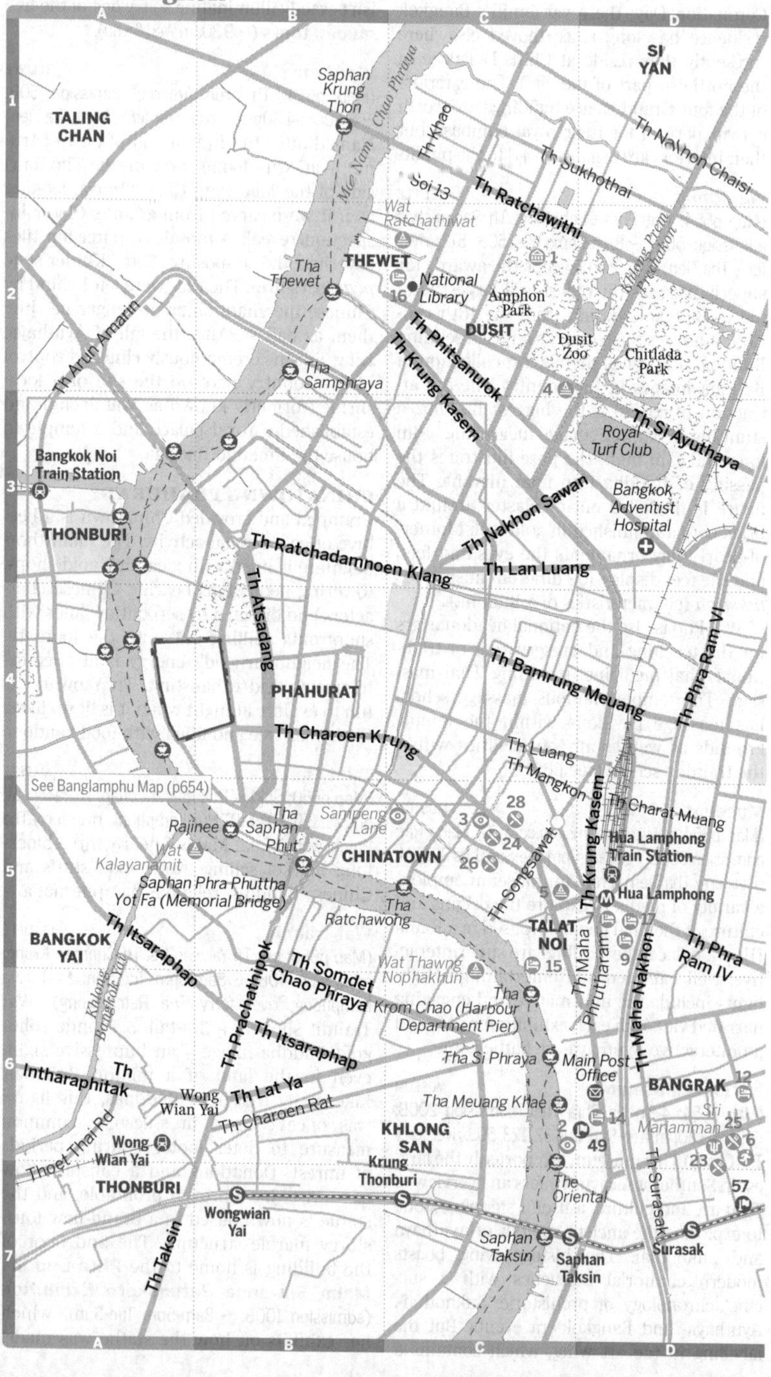

A B C D
1 2 3 4 5 6 7

TALING CHAN
Saphan Krung Thon
Mae Nam Chao Phraya
Th Khao
Soi 13
Wat Ratchathiwat
Th Sukhothai
Th Nakhon Chaisi
Th Ratchawithi
SI YAN
Khlong Prem Prachakon
1
THEWET
Tha Thewet
16
National Library
Amphon Park
DUSIT
Dusit Zoo
Chitlada Park
Th Arun Amarin
Th Phitsanulok
Th Krung Kasem
Tha Samphraya
4
Royal Turf Club
Th Si Ayuthaya
Bangkok Noi Train Station
THONBURI
Th Nakhon Sawan
Bangkok Adventist Hospital
Th Ratchadamnoen Klang
Th Lan Luang
Th Atsadang
Th Bamrung Meuang
PHAHURAT
Th Phra Ram VI
Th Charoen Krung
Th Luang
Th Mangkon
See Banglamphu Map (p654)
Tha Saphan Phut
Rajinee
Sampeng Lane
28
3
24
26
Th Charat Muang
Hua Lamphong Train Station
Wat Kalayanamit
CHINATOWN
Saphan Phra Phuttha Yot Fa (Memorial Bridge)
Tha Ratchawong
Th Songsawat
5
Hua Lamphong
Th Krung Kasem
7
17
TALAT NOI
9
Th Phra Ram IV
Th Itsaraphap
BANGKOK YAI
Khlong Bangkok Yai
Th Somdet Chao Phraya
Wat Thawng Nophakhun
15
Th Maha Phrutharam
Th Maha Nakhon
Tha Krom Chao (Harbour Department Pier)
Th Prachathipok
Th Itsaraphap
Tha Si Phraya
Main Post Office
Th Intharaphitak
Wong Wian Yai
Th Lat Ya
BANGRAK
12
Th Charoen Rat
Tha Meuang Khae
KHLONG SAN
14
Sri Mariamman
25
6
Wong Wian Yai
2
49
23
Thoet Thai Rd
Krung Thonburi
The Oriental
Th Surasak
57
THONBURI
Wongwian Yai
Surasak
Saphan Taksin
Saphan Taksin
Th Taksin

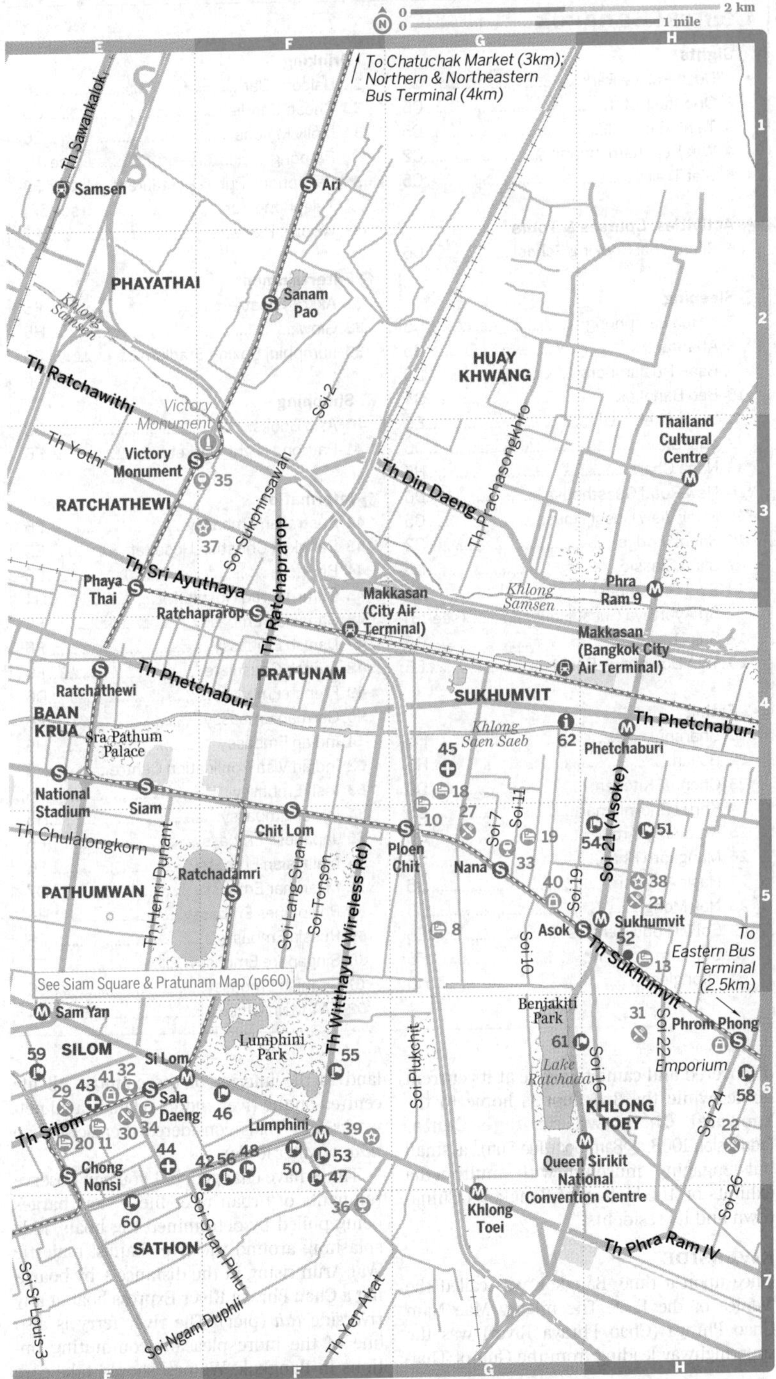

0 2 km
0 1 mile
To Chatuchak Market (3km); Northern & Northeastern Bus Terminal (4km)
Th Sawankalok
Samsen
Ari
PHAYATHAI
Khlong Samsen
Sanam Pao
HUAY KHWANG
Th Ratchawithi
Victory Monument
Soi 2
Th Yothi
Victory Monument
Thailand Cultural Centre
RATCHATHEWI
Th Din Daeng
Th Prachasongkhro
Soi Sukhphinsawan
Th Ratchaprarop
Th Sri Ayuthaya
Phaya Thai
Ratchaprarop
Makkasan (City Air Terminal)
Khlong Samsen
Phra Ram 9
Makkasan (Bangkok City Air Terminal)
Ratchathewi
Th Phetchaburi
PRATUNAM
BAAN KRUA
SUKHUMVIT
Sra Pathum Palace
Khlong Saen Saeb
Th Phetchaburi
Phetchaburi
National Stadium
Siam
Chit Lom
Ploen Chit
Nana
Soi 7
Soi 11
Soi 21 (Asoke)
Th Chulalongkorn
Th Henri Dunant
Ratchadamri
PATHUMWAN
Soi Lang Suan
Soi Tonson
Th Witthayu (Wireless Rd)
Soi 19
Asok
Sukhumvit
Soi 10
Th Sukhumvit
To Eastern Bus Terminal (2.5km)
See Siam Square & Pratunam Map (p660)
Sam Yan
Benjakiti Park
Lumphini Park
Soi Plukchit
Phrom Phong
SILOM
Si Lom
Lake Ratchada
Soi 16
Soi 22
Emporium
Sala Daeng
KHLONG TOEY
Th Silom
Lumphini
Soi 24
Chong Nonsi
Queen Sirikit National Convention Centre
Khlong Toei
Soi 26
SATHON
Soi Suan Phlu
Th Phra Ram IV
Soi St Louis 3
Soi Ngam Duphli
Th Yen Akat
THAILAND BANGKOK

Central Bangkok

Sights

1 Dusit Palace Park ... C2
2 Oriental Hotel ... C6
3 Talat Mai ... C5
4 Wat Benchamabophit ... C2
5 Wat Traimit ... C5

Activities, Courses & Tours

6 Silom Thai Cooking School ... D6

Sleeping

7 @Hua Lamphong ... D5
8 Atlanta ... G5
9 Baan Hualampong ... D5
10 Bed Bangkok ... G4
11 HQ Hostel ... E6
12 Lub*d ... D6
13 Nana Chart ... H5
14 New Road Guesthouse ... D6
15 River View Guest House ... C5
16 Shanti Lodge ... C2
17 Siam Classic ... D5
18 Soi 1 Guesthouse ... G4
Sri Ayuttaya Guest House ... (see 16)
19 Suk 11 ... G5
20 YHA Downtown Bangkok ... E6

Eating

21 Bharani ... H5
22 Bo.lan ... H6
23 Chennai Kitchen ... D6
24 Khrua Phornlamai ... C5
25 Krua Aroy-Aroy ... D6
26 Mangkorn Khao ... C5
27 Nasir Al-Masri ... G5
28 Nay Mong ... C5
29 Soi 10 Food Centres ... E6
30 Somtam Convent ... E6
31 Thonglee ... H6

Drinking

32 Balcony Bar ... E6
33 Cheap Charlie's ... G5
34 Molly Malone's ... E6
Patpong ... (see 41)
35 Saxophone Pub & Restaurant ... F3
Telephone Bar ... (see 32)
36 Wong's Place ... F7

Entertainment

37 Aksra Theatre ... F3
38 Glow ... H5
39 Lumphini Boxing Stadium ... F6

Shopping

40 Asia Books ... G5
41 Patpong Night Market ... E6

Information

42 Australian Embassy ... F6
43 Bangkok Christian Hospital ... E6
44 BNH ... E6
45 Bumrungrad Hospital ... G4
46 Canadian Embassy ... F6
47 Danish Embassy ... F6
48 French Consulate ... F6
49 French Embassy ... D6
50 German Embassy ... F6
51 Indian Embassy ... H5
52 Indian Visa Application Centre ... H5
53 Irish Embassy ... F6
54 Israeli Embassy ... H5
55 Japanese Embassy ... F6
56 Malaysian Embassy ... F6
57 Myanmar Embassy ... D7
58 Philippines Embassy ... H6
59 Russia Embassy ... E6
60 Singapore Embassy ... E7
61 Spanish Embassy ... G6
62 TAT Main Office ... G4

discovered and came to arrive at its current home, while the 3rd floor is home to the **Yaowarat Chinatown Heritage Center** (admission 100B; 8am-5pm Tue-Sun), a small but engaging museum with multimedia exhibits on the history of Bangkok's Chinatown and its residents.

RIVERSIDE

Once upon a time, Bangkok was called the 'Venice of the East'. The mighty Mae Nam Chao Phraya (Chao Phraya River) was the superhighway leading from the Gulf of Thailand to the interior of the country. All life centred on the river and its related canal networks and Thais considered themselves *jâo náam* (water lords).

Times have changed, but you can observe remnants of urban river life – slow barges being pulled by determined tug boats, kids splashing around the river banks, majestic Wat Arun rising in the distance – by boarding a Chao Phraya River Express boat at any riverside *tâh* (pier). The river ferry is also one of the more pleasant commuting options in Bangkok. Women should take care

OUT-SMARTING THE SCAMS

Commit these classic rip-offs to memory and join us in our ongoing crusade to outsmart Bangkok's crafty scam artists.

» **Closed today** Ignore any 'friendly' local who tells you that an attraction is closed for a Buddhist holiday or for cleaning. These are set-ups for trips to a bogus gem sale or shopping.

» **Túk-túk rides for 10B** Say goodbye to your day's itinerary if you climb aboard this ubiquitous scam. These 'tours' bypass the sights and instead cruise to the overpriced tailor and gem shops that pay commissions.

» **Flat-fare taxi ride** Flatly refuse any driver who quotes a flat fare, which will usually be three times more than the meter rate. Head out to the street and flag down a cab. If the driver 'forgets' to turn on the meter, just say, 'Meter, kha/khap'.

» **Long-distance tourist buses** Buy your long-distance bus tickets from the government-run bus stations instead of tourist-centre agents selling private tourist bus tickets. Sometimes agents will inflate their commission fees or charge for VIP service but deliver cut-rate vehicles. Readers have consistently reported thefts from personal bags and stowed luggage from private buses.

» **Bus-boat combination tickets** A popular way for getting to the islands is to buy one of these combo tickets; just double check that you've got both a bus and boat ticket as you'll be left on dry land without proof of payment for the second leg of the journey. Also buy from a reputable company.

» **Friendly strangers** Be wary of smartly dressed locals who approach you asking where you're from and where you're going. Their opening gambit is usually followed with: 'Ah, my son/daughter is studying at university in (your city)'. This sort of behaviour is out of character for Thais and is usually a prelude for the notorious gem scam.

» **Unset Gems** Bangkok is no place to be an amateur gem trader. Never accept an invitation to visit a gem shop and refuse to purchase unset stones that can supposedly be resold in your home country.

not to accidentally bump into a monk and should not sit next to them or stand in the same area of the boat. For more information about the river ferry, see p785.

You can also charter a longtail boat to explore Khlong Bangkok Noi and other scenic canals in Thonburi. Longtail boats can be arranged from any river pier, including Tha Chang. Just remember to negotiate a price before departure.

Oriental Hotel HISTORIC SITE

(Map p650; ☎0 2659 9000; 48 Soi Oriental/Soi 38, Th Charoen Krung; river ferry Tha Oriental or Tha Sathon) Foreign traders established their Bangkok outposts along the river during the heyday of the shipping era. Two Dutch sea captains built the majestic Oriental Hotel, an attraction in its own right. Somerset Maugham and Joseph Conrad were among the Oriental's famous guests. You can toast those literary giants in the hotel's Author Wing cafe or the riverside bar; dress smartly, though.

OTHER AREAS

Dusit Palace Park MUSEUM

(Map p650; ☎0 2628 6300; admission 100B, free with Grand Palace ticket; ⌚9.30am-4pm; bus 70, 510) Dusit Palace Park is an atmospheric example of Thailand's flirtation with the Victorian period. In the early 20th century King Chulalongkorn (Rama V) returned from his European tour with exotic ideas for establishing a new and modern royal residence. He moved the royal family to this leafy compound and set up house in the **Vimanmek Teak Mansion**, reputedly the world's largest golden teak building. Compulsory tours of the interior by poorly proficient English-speaking guides are given and visitors must dress modestly (cover to the elbows and the ankles). Other ornate buildings decorate the compound and contain small craft and art museums supported by the royal family.

Jim Thompson's House MUSEUM

(Map p660; www.jimthompsonhouse.com; 6 Soi Kasem San 2; admission 100B; ⌚9am-5pm, compulsory tours in English & French every 20min;

Banglamphu

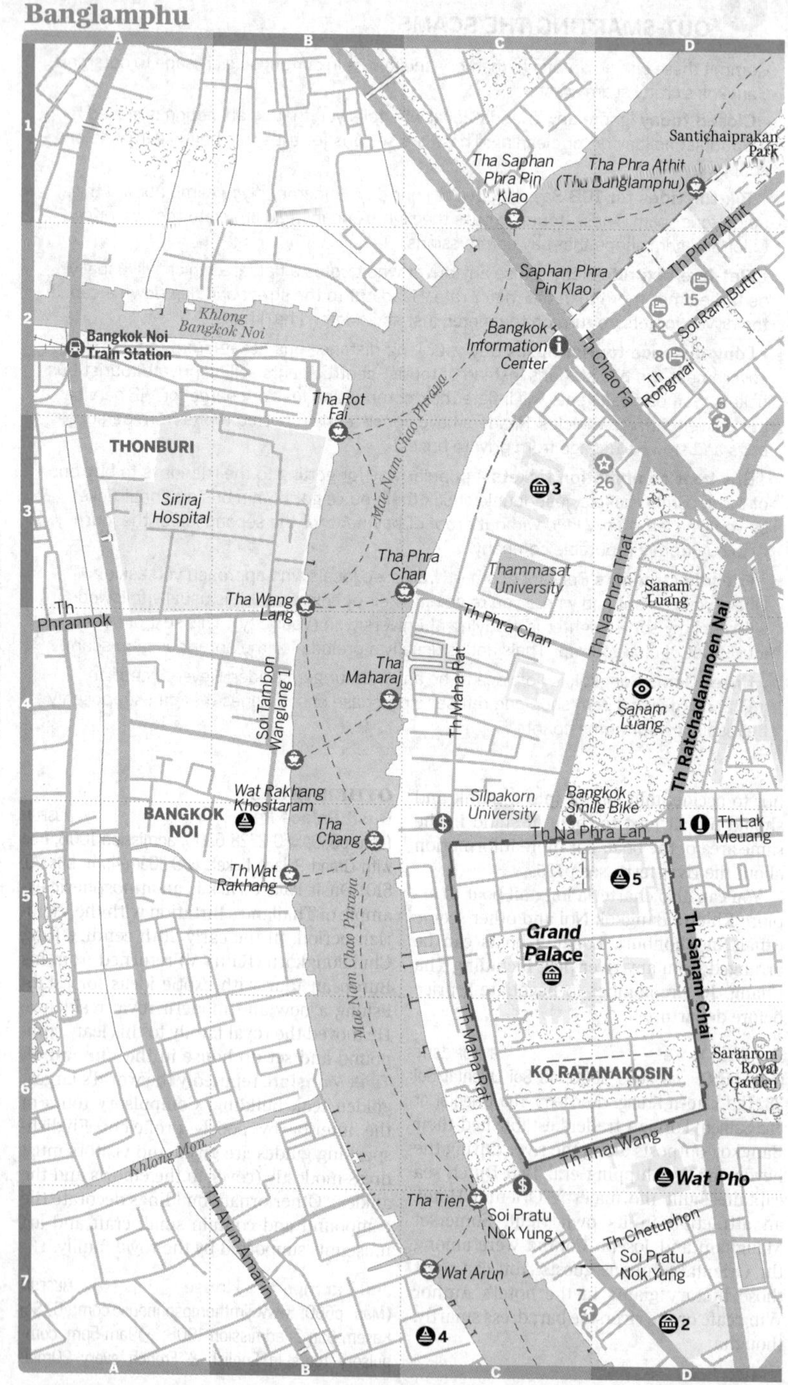

Santichaiprakan Park
Tha Saphan Phra Pin Klao
Tha Phra Athit (Tha Banglamphu)
Th Phra Athit
Saphan Phra Pin Klao
15
12
Soi Ram Buttri
Khlong Bangkok Noi
Bangkok Noi Train Station
Bangkok Information Center
Th Chao Fa
8
Th Rongmai
6
Tha Rot Fai
Mae Nam Chao Phraya
THONBURI
26
3
Siriraj Hospital
Tha Phra Chan
Thammasat University
Th Na Phra That
Sanam Luang
Th Phrannok
Tha Wang Lang
Th Phra Chan
Th Ratchadamnoen Nai
Tha Maharaj
Soi Tambon Wanglang 1
Th Maha Rat
Sanam Luang
Wat Rakhang Khositaram
Silpakorn University
Bangkok Smile Bike
BANGKOK NOI
Tha Chang
Th Na Phra Lan
1
Th Lak Meuang
Th Wat Rakhang
5
Th Sanam Chai
Grand Palace
Mae Nam Chao Phraya
Saranrom Royal Garden
KO RATANAKOSIN
Th Maha Rat
Khlong Mon
Th Thai Wang
Wat Pho
Tha Tien
Soi Pratu Nok Yung
Th Chetuphon
Th Arun Amarin
Soi Pratu Nok Yung
Wat Arun
7
2
4

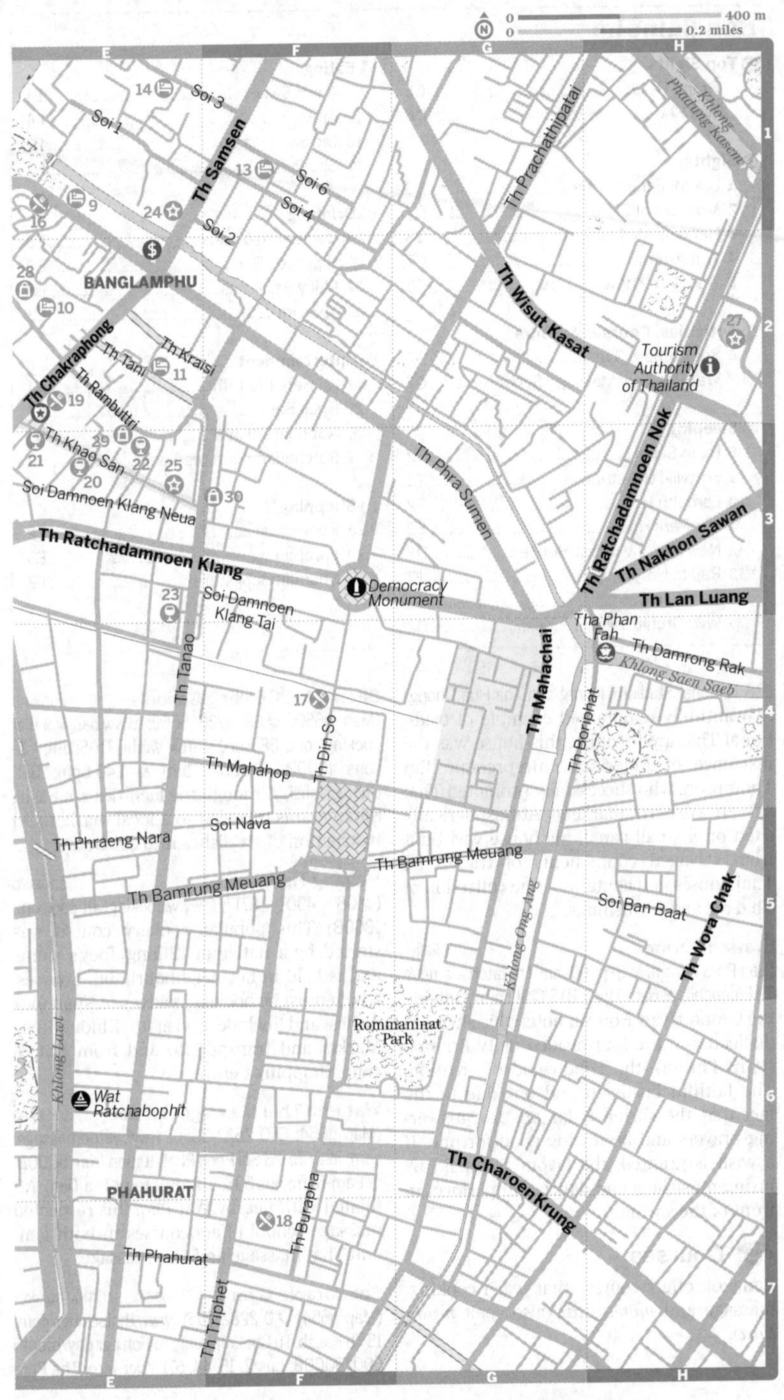
0
400 m
0
0.2 miles
Khlong Phadung Kasem
Soi 3
Soi 1
Th Samsen
Soi 6
Soi 4
Soi 2
Th Prachathipatai
BANGLAMPHU
Th Wisut Kasat
Th Chakraphong
Th Tani
Th Kraisi
Th Rambuttri
Tourism Authority of Thailand
Th Khao San
Soi Damnoen Klang Neua
Th Phra Sumen
Th Ratchadamnoen Nok
Th Nakhon Sawan
Th Ratchadamnoen Klang
Democracy Monument
Th Lan Luang
Soi Damnoen Klang Tai
Tha Phan Fah
Th Damrong Rak
Khlong Saen Saeb
Th Mahachai
Th Tanao
Th Din So
Th Boriphat
Th Mahahop
Soi Nava
Th Phraeng Nara
Th Bamrung Meuang
Th Bamrung Meuang
Soi Ban Baat
Khlong Ong Ang
Th Wora Chak
Rommaninat Park
Khlong Lawt
Wat Ratchabophit
Th Charoen Krung
PHAHURAT
Th Burapha
Th Phahurat
Th Triphet

Banglamphu

Top Sights

	Grand Palace	C5
	Wat Pho	D6

Sights

1	Lak Meuang Shrine	D5
2	Museum of Siam	D7
3	National Museum	C3
4	Wat Arun	C7
5	Wat Phra Kaew	D5

Activities, Courses & Tours

6	Sor Vorapin Gym	D2
7	Wat Pho Thai Massage School	C7

Sleeping

8	Baan Sabai	D2
9	Fortville Guesthouse	E1
10	Lamphu House	E2
11	NapPark Hostel	E2
12	New Merry V Guest House	D2
13	Rajata Hotel	F1
14	Sam Sen Sam	E1
15	Wild Orchid Villa	D2

Eating

16	Ann's Sweet	E1
17	Arawy	F4
18	Old Siam Plaza	F7
19	Shoshana	E2

Drinking

20	Center Khao San	E3
21	Hippie de Bar	E3
22	Molly Bar	E3
23	Taksura	E3

Entertainment

24	Ad Here the 13th	E1
25	Brick Bar	E3
26	National Theatre	D3
27	Ratchadamnoen Stadium	H2

Shopping

28	Book Lover	E2
29	Saraban	E3
30	Shaman Bookstore	F3

BTS National Stadium, klorng taxi Tha Hua Chang) A beautifully maintained example of traditional Thai architecture, this house was the residence of American entrepreneur Jim Thompson, who successfully promoted Thai silk to Western markets. Atmospherically sited on a small canal, his house was built from salvaged components of traditional Thai houses and contains a fine collection of Thai art and furnishings.

Erawan Shrine SHRINE

(San Phra Phrom; Map p660; cnr Th Ratchadamri & Th Ploenchit; ⏲6am-11pm; BTS Chit Lom) Outside the Grand Hyatt Erawan hotel, this shrine is dedicated to the four-headed deity Brahma (Phra Phrom), the Hindu god of creation. The faithful bustle in and out due to the fact that the shrine is famous for answering prayers and bestowing good fortune. If a wish is granted, the favour is repaid by hiring musicians and dancers to perform in front of the shrine.

Courses

Bangkok offers courses that teach cooking, massage and *moo·ay tai* (also spelt *muay thai*).

Silom Thai Cooking School COOKING

(Map p650; ☎08 4726 5669; www.bangkokthaicooking.com; 68 Soi 13/Trok Vaithi, Th Silom; lessons 1000B; ⏲9.30am-1pm & 1.40-6pm; BTS Chong Nonsi) Although the facilities are basic, Silom crams in a visit to a local market and instruction of six dishes into 3½ hours.

Helping Hands COOKING

(☎08 4901 8717; www.cookingwithpoo.com; 1000B) This popular cookery course was started by a native of Khlong Toey's slums and is held in her neighbourhood. Courses, which must be booked in advance, span four dishes and include a visit to Khlong Toey Market and transport to and from Emporium Shopping Centre.

Wat Pho Thai Massage School MASSAGE

(Map p654; ☎0 2622 3550; www.watpomassage.com; 392/25-28 Soi Phen Phat; tuition from 5000B; ⏲8am-6pm; bus 508, 512, river ferry Tha Tien) Affiliated with nearby Wat Pho, this respected massage school offers courses in both general Thai massage and foot massage.

Sor Vorapin Gym MUAY THAI (THAI BOXING)

(Map p654; ☎0 2282 3551; www.thaiboxings.com; 13 Th Kasab, Th Chakraphong; tuition per day/month 500/9000B; bus 2, 15, 44, 511, river ferry Tha Phra

Athit) Specialises in training foreign students of both genders. The gym is sweating distance from Th Khao San, but more serious training is held outside the city.

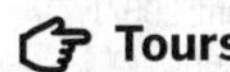

Tours

ABC Amazing Bangkok Cyclists BICYCLE TOUR
(☎0 2665 6364; www.realasia.net; 10/5-7 Soi 26, Th Sukhumvit; tours from 1000B; ⊙daily tours depart at 8am, 10am or 1pm; BTS Phrom Phong) Discover the rural aspects of the city on a cycling tour.

Grasshopper Adventures BICYCLE TOURS
(☎0 2280 0832; www.grasshopperadventures.com; 57 Th Ratchadamnoen Klang; tours from 750B; ⊙8.30am-6.30pm Mon-Fri; bus 2, 15, 44, 511, klorng taxi Phan Fah) This lauded outfit runs a variety of unique bicycle tours in and around Bangkok, including a night tour and a tour of the city's green zones.

Festivals & Events

Chinese New Year CULTURAL
(February/March) Thai-Chinese celebrate the lunar new year with a week of house-cleaning, lion dances and fireworks. Festivities centre on Chinatown.

Songkran CULTURAL/RELIGIOUS
(mid April) Bangkok's celebration of the Thai New Year has morphed into water warfare centred around Th Khao San. Prepare to be soaked.

Royal Ploughing Ceremony CULTURAL/RELIGIOUS
(early May) The Crown Prince commences rice-planting season with a royal-religious ceremony at Sanam Luang.

Queen's Birthday CULTURAL
(12 August) The queen's birthday is recognised as the national Mother's Day and celebrated in Bangkok with festivities centred around Th Ratchadamnoen and the Grand Palace.

Vegetarian Festival FOOD
(September/October) This 10-day Chinese-Buddhist festival strives for religious perfection by consuming meatless meals. Look for yellow-flagged vegetarian vendors in Chinatown.

King Chulalongkorn Day CULTURAL
(23 October) Rama V is honoured on the anniversary of his death in front of his statue in Dusit.

Loi Krathong CULTURAL
(early November) The Mae Nam Chao Phraya receives huge devotional crowds who float small lotus-shaped boats throughout this river-honouring festival.

King's Birthday CULTURAL
(5 December) Locals celebrate their monarch's birthday with parades and festivities on the royal avenue of Th Ratchadamnoen.

Sleeping

Because the city has legendary traffic jams, narrow your search first by the geographic area that best suits your needs. If you're in the city for a layover, stay as close to your next mode of transport as possible.

TH KHAO SAN, BANGLAMPHU & THEWET

If you're returning to 'civilisation' and need traveller amenities, then the backpacker ghetto of Th Khao San and surrounding

HIGH CULTURE, LOW COST

Thai classical dance is typically promoted among package tourists as a dinner theatre experience but baht-minded travellers can see performances in free, or nearly free, venues.

» **Lak Meuang Shrine** (Map p654; cnr Th Ratchadamnoen Nai & Th Lak Meuang), near Wat Phra Kaew, showcases shrine dances commissioned to perform for the guardian spirits by merit-makers whose wishes were granted.

» **Erawan Shrine** (p656), next to Grand Hyatt Erawan hotel, also features shrine dancers.

» **Dusit Palace Park** (p653) hosts daily classical dance performances at 10am and 2pm.

» **National Theatre** (Map p654; 2 Th Rachini; tickets 60-100B; river ferry Tha Chang) hosts traditional dance performances on the first and second Sundays of the month and on the first Friday of the month, while Thai musical performances are held on the third Friday of the month.

WORTH A TRIP

MINIATURE WONDERS

The industrial town of Samut Prakan is an unlikely place for the open-air architectural museum of the **Ancient City** (Meuang Boran; ☎0 2709 1644; www.ancientcity.com; 296/1 Th Sukhumvit; admission 300B; ⏰8am-5pm), a unique intersection of entertainment, artistry and curatorship. One hundred scaled-down models of Thailand's famous architectural monuments were re-created in an attempt to preserve traditional craftsmanship skills and create beautiful things to look at. The museum is 12km south of Samut Prakan (also known as Pak Nam). From Bangkok take air-con bus 511 from the eastern side of Th Sukhumvit to Samut Prakan's bus station. From there board minibus 36 (25B), which will pass the entrance of the Ancient City.

Banglamphu is cheap and convenient. The area is packed with guesthouses and hotels. Most of the cheapies have been replaced with more upscale options but you can still hunt for a few holdouts on Th Khao San and the nearby *soi*. Quieter and more charming enclaves are on Th Ram Buttri and on the numbered *soi* off Th Samsen. Th Si Ayuthaya, in Thewet, the district north of Banglamphu near the National Library, is a pleasant backpacker enclave, particularly popular with families and the over-30 crowd. It is a lovely leafy area, but during the rainy season it can be prone to flooding.

NapPark Hostel HOSTEL $
(Map p654; ☎0 2282 2324; www.nappark.com; 8 Th Tani; dm 550-750B; river ferry Tha Tien; ❄@📶) This exceedingly well-done hostel features dorm rooms of various sizes, the smallest and most expensive of which boasts six pod-like beds outfitted with power points, mini-TV, reading lamp and wi-fi. Daily cultural-based activities, including bike trips and volunteer opportunities, ensure that you may not actually get the chance to plug in.

Fortville Guesthouse GUESTHOUSE $
(Map p654; ☎0 2282 3932; www.fortvilleguesthouse.com; 9 Th Phra Sumen; r 650-970B; bus 32, 33, 64, 82, river ferry Tha Phra Athit; ❄@📶) The design concept of this unique new hotel is a bit hard to pin down: is it a fort, a castle or a modern masterpiece? Regardless, rooms are stylishly minimal, and the more expensive include perks such as fridge, balcony and free wi-fi.

Baan Sabai GUESTHOUSE $
(Map p654; ☎0 2629 1599; baansabai@hotmail.com; 12 Soi Rongmai; r 190-600B; bus 53, 516, river ferry Tha Phra Athit; ❄@) Truly living up to its name (Comfortable House), this rambling old building holds dozens of plain but comfy rooms at a variety of prices. There's a palpable old-school atmosphere here, particularly at the inviting open-air restaurant/bar area downstairs.

Wild Orchid Villa GUESTHOUSE $
(Map p654; ☎0 2629 4378; www.wildorchidvilla.com; 8 Soi Chana Songkhram; r 280-1800B; bus 32, 33, 64, 82, river ferry Tha Phra Athit; ❄@📶) The cheapies here are some of the tiniest we've seen anywhere, but all rooms are clean and neat, and come in a bright, friendly package. This place is exceedingly popular, so it's best to book ahead.

TOP CHOICE **Lamphu House** GUESTHOUSE $
(Map p654; ☎0 2629 5861; www.lamphuhouse.com; 75-77 Soi Ram Buttri; r 200-950B; river ferry Tha Phra Athit; ❄@📶) Tucked off Soi Ram Buttri, you'll forget how close to Th Khao San you are in this quiet, homey budget hotel. Rooms are simple but clean, with the cheapies cooled by fan and sharing bathrooms.

Sam Sen Sam GUESTHOUSE $
(Map p654; ☎0 2628 7067; www.samsensam.com; 48 Soi 3, Th Samsen; r 590-2400B; river ferry Tha Phra Athit; ❄@📶) One of the homiest places around, this bright, refurbished villa gets good reports about its friendly service and quiet location.

Rajata Hotel HOTEL $
(Map p654; ☎0 2628 8084; www.rajatahotel.com; 46 Soi 6, Th Samsen; r 650-850B; bus 53, 516, river ferry Tha Phra Athit; ❄@📶) This old-fashioned hotel is a plain but comfortable choice for those who want to be near but not close to Th Khao San.

New Merry V Guest House GUESTHOUSE $
(Map p654; ☎0 2280 3315; newmerry@gmail.com; 18-20 Th Phra Athit; r 150-700B; bus 32, 33, 64, 82, river ferry Tha Phra Athit; ❄@) The cheap rooms here are as bare as they come, but are spotless and have ample natural light.

Sri Ayuttaya Guest House GUESTHOUSE $

(Map p650; ☎0 2282 5942; 23/11 Th Si Ayuthaya, Thewet; r 400-1000B; bus 32, 516, river ferry Tha Thewet; ❄@📶) Nice design, low-key location; some rooms share bathrooms.

Shanti Lodge GUESTHOUSE $

(Map p650; ☎0 2281 2497; 37 Th Si Ayuthaya; dm 250B, r 400-1950B; bus 32, 516, river ferry Tha Thewet; ❄@📶) The maven of Thewet; walls are bamboo-thin in the cheap rooms, but there's a huge variety of accommodation so check out a few before making a decision.

HUALAMPHONG & CHINATOWN

Hotels near the Hualamphong train station are cheap but not especially interesting and the traffic along Th Phra Ram IV has to be heard to be believed. The surrounding neighbourhood of Chinatown makes for interesting walks but is not especially geared for tourists.

Baan Hualampong GUESTHOUSE $

(Map p650; ☎0 2639 8054; www.baanhualampong.com; 336/20-21 Trok Chalong Krung; dm/r incl breakfast 250/290-800B; MRT Hua Lamphong; ❄@📶) Repeat visitors rave about the homey setting and warm, personal service at this guesthouse. Located a short walk from Hualamphong train station, kitchen and laundry facilities are also available, and there are lots of chill-out areas and computers.

Siam Classic HOSTEL $

(Map p650; ☎0 2639 6363; www.siamclassic-hostel.com; 336/10 Trok Chalong Krung; r 450-1400B; MRT Hua Lamphong, river ferry Tha Ratchawong; ❄@📶) Good budget option near the train station.

@Hua Lamphong GUESTHOUSE $

(Map p650; ☎0 2639 1925; www.at-hualamphong.com; 326/1 Th Phra Ram IV; dm 200, r 690-1000B; MRT Hua Lamphong, river ferry Tha Ratchawong; ❄@📶) Another budget chic choice near the train station.

SIAM SQUARE

If you need to be centrally located, then opt for Siam Square, which is on both BTS (Skytrain) lines. Accommodation in Siam Square is more expensive than Banglamphu but you'll save in cab fare. Unofficially known as the 'secret *soi*', San Kasem San 1 has a low-key personality and traveller-friendly facilities. You can also bypass rush hour traffic between here and Th Khao San by hopping on the *klorng* taxi at Tha Ratchethewi.

TOP CHOICE **Lub*d** HOSTEL $

(Map p660; ☎0 2634 7999; www.lubd.com; Th Pha Ram I; dm/r 550/1350-1800B; BTS National Stadium; ❄@📶) The title is a play on the Thai word *làp dee,* meaning 'sleep well', but the fun atmosphere at this backpacker hostel might make you stay up all night. There are 24 dorms (including ladies-only dorms), each with only four beds, and a few private rooms with and without bathrooms. If this one's full, there's another **branch** (Map p650; ☎0 2634 7999; www.lubd.com; 4 Th Decho; dm/r 400/1050-1400B; BTS Chong Nonsi; ❄@📶) just south of Th Silom.

A-One Inn GUESTHOUSE $

(Map p660; ☎0 2215 3029; www.aoneinn.com; 25/13-15 Soi Kasem San 1; s/d/tr 600/750/950B; BTS National Stadium, klorng taxi to Tha Ratchathewi; ❄@📶) The rooms here are tight and simple, but the wealth of backpacker amenities (computers, luggage storage, free ice and water) makes up for this.

Wendy House GUESTHOUSE $$

(Map p660; ☎0 2214 1149; www.wendyguesthouse.com; 36/2 Soi Kasem San 1; r incl breakfast 900-1200B; BTS National Stadium, klorng taxi to Tha Ratchathewi; ❄@📶) The rooms here are small and basic, but well stocked (TV, fridge) for this price range.

Bed & Breakfast Inn GUESTHOUSE $

(Map p660; ☎0 2215 3004; Soi Kasem San 1; r incl breakfast 500-700B; BTS National Stadium, klorng taxi to Tha Ratchathewi; ❄📶) This maze-like guesthouse has standard but comfortable rooms.

SUKHUMVIT

The closest option to the airport is Th Sukhumvit, a high-end neighbourhood. It is also near the Eastern (Ekamai) bus station and on the BTS and MRT (underground metro) lines; the MRT links to the Hualamphong train station. Be warned that the lower numbered *sois* attract sex tourists visiting the nearby go-go bars.

Suk 11 GUESTHOUSE $

(Map p650; ☎0 2253 5927; www.suk11.com; 1/33 Soi 11, Th Sukhumvit; s/d/tr incl breakfast 535-695/749-963/963-1284B; BTS Nana; ❄@📶) Extremely well run and equally popular, this guesthouse is an oasis of woods and greenery in an urban jungle. The cheaper rooms have shared bathrooms, and although they've somehow managed to stuff nearly 100 rooms in, you'll still need to book at least two weeks ahead.

Siam Square & Pratunam

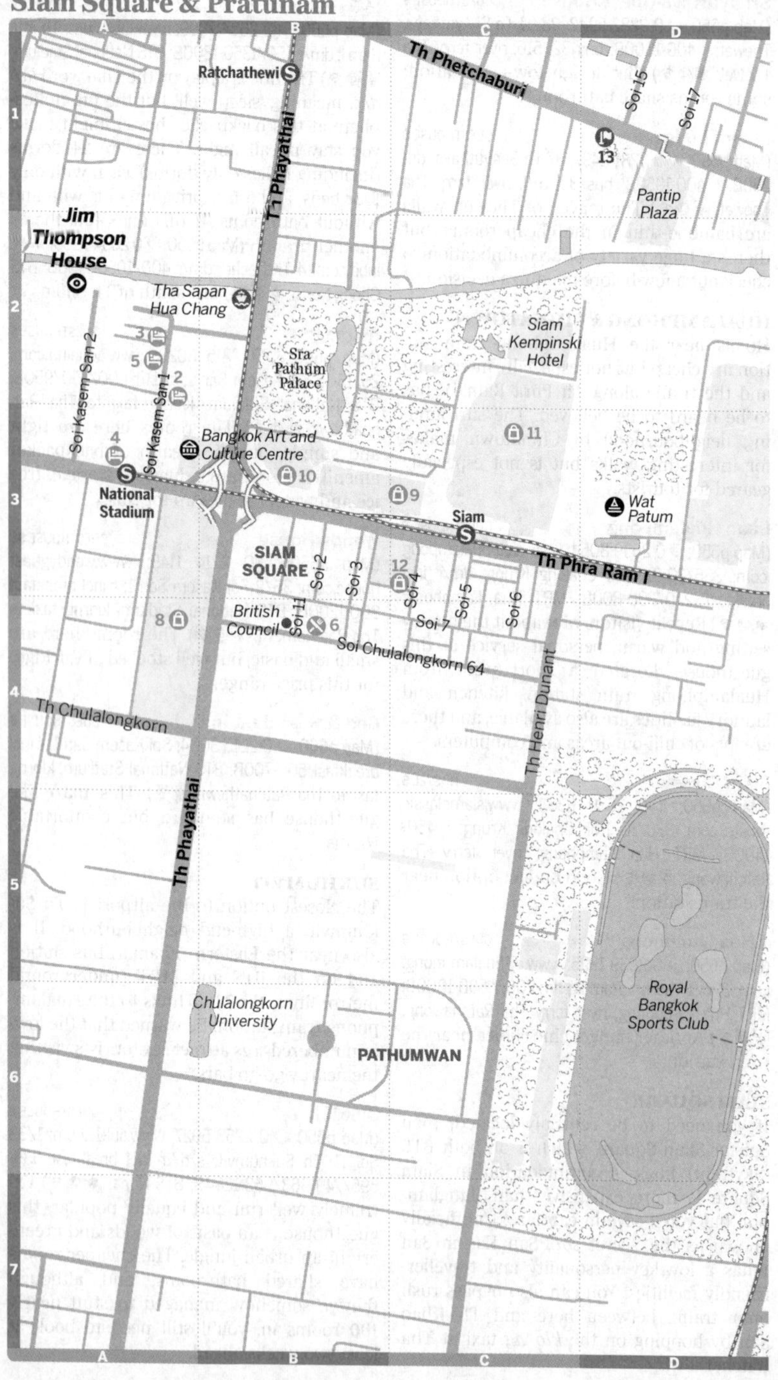

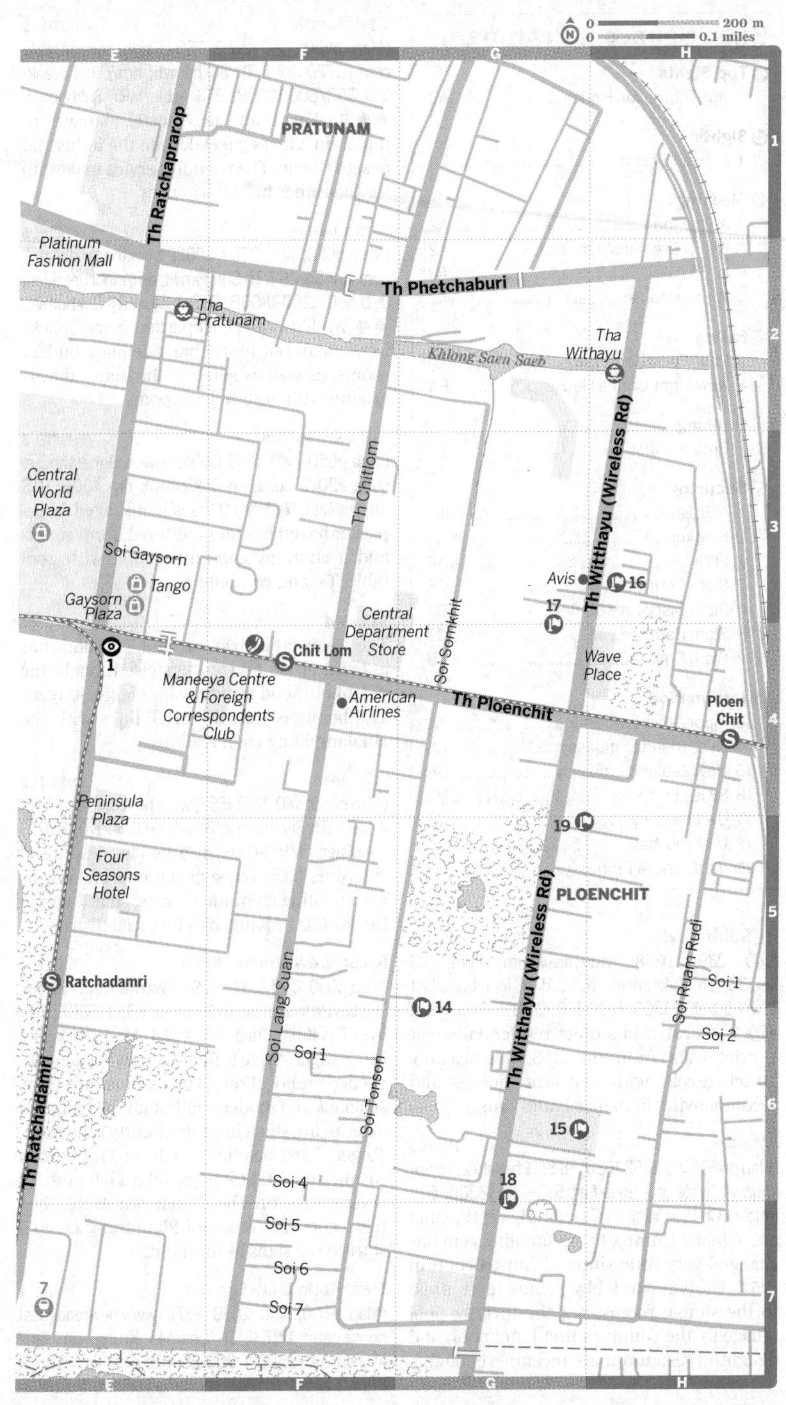

0 200 m
0 0.1 miles
E
F
G
H
PRATUNAM
Th Ratchaprarop
Platinum Fashion Mall
Th Phetchaburi
Tha Pratunam
Khlong Saen Saeb
Tha Withayu
Central World Plaza
Th Chitlom
Soi Gaysorn
Tango
Gaysorn Plaza
Central Department Store
1
Chit Lom
Maneeya Centre & Foreign Correspondents Club
American Airlines
Th Ploenchit
Soi Somkhit
Th Witthayu (Wireless Rd)
Avis
16
17
Wave Place
Ploen Chit
19
Peninsula Plaza
Four Seasons Hotel
PLOENCHIT
Ratchadamri
Soi Ruam Rudi
Soi 1
Soi 2
14
Soi Lang Suan
Soi 1
Soi Tonson
15
Th Ratchadamri
18
Soi 4
Soi 5
Soi 6
Soi 7
7
1
2
3
4
5
6
7

Siam Square & Pratunam

Top Sights
- Jim Thompson House A2

Sights
- 1 Erawan Shrine E4

Sleeping
- 2 A-One Inn A2
- 3 Bed & Breakfast Inn A2
- 4 Lub*d A3
- 5 Wendy House A2

Eating
- MBK Food Court .... (see 8)
- 6 New Light Coffee House B4

Drinking
- 7 Brown Sugar E7

Shopping
- Asia Books .... (see 10)
- Kinokuniya .... (see 11)
- 8 MBK A4
- 9 Siam Center C3
- 10 Siam Discovery Center B3
- 11 Siam Paragon C3
- 12 Siam Square C3

Information
- 13 Indonesian Embassy D1
- 14 Netherlands Embassy G5
- 15 New Zealand Embassy G6
- 16 Swiss Embassy H3
- 17 UK Embassy G3
- 18 US Embassy G6
- 19 Vietnamese Embassy G5

HI-Sukhumvit HOSTEL $
(☎0 2391 9338; www.hisukhumvit.com; 23 Soi 38, Th Sukhumvit; dm/s/d/tr incl breakfast 320/650/900-1300/1200-1500B; BTS Thong Lo; ❄@📶) Located in a quiet residential street a brief walk from the BTS, this friendly hostel excels with its neat dorms and accompanying immense bathrooms.

Atlanta HOTEL $
(Map p650; ☎0 2252 1650; 78 Soi Phasak/2, Th Sukhumvit; r/ste incl breakfast 535-650/1820B; BTS Phloen Chit; ❄@📶🏊) Defiantly antiquated and equally frumpy, this crumbling gem has changed very little since its construction in 1952. The vintage lobby stands in contrast to the simple rooms, but the inviting pool (allegedly the country's first hotel pool) and delightful restaurant are incentive enough.

Bed Bangkok HOSTEL $
(Map p650; ☎0 2655 7604; www.bedbangkok.com; 11/20 Soi 1, Th Sukhumvit; dm/r incl breakfast 390/800-1200B; BTS Asok, MRT Sukhumvit; ❄@📶) This brand new hostel manages to maintain a homey feel despite the industrial design theme. The friendly service makes up for the rather hard dorm beds.

Nana Chart HOSTEL $
(Map p650; ☎0 2259 6908; www.thailandhostel.com; cnr Soi 25 & Th Sukhumvit; dm/r incl breakfast 390-550/1200-1800B; BTS Asok, MRT Sukhumvit; ❄@📶) This tidy backpacker hostel packs in 68 plain but more-than-adequate budget rooms, as well as some of the better dorms around with ensuite bathrooms.

Soi 1 Guesthouse HOSTEL $
(Map p650; ☎0 2655 0604; www.soi1guesthouse.com; 220/7 Soi 1, Th Sukhumvit; dm 400B; BTS Phloen Chit; ❄@📶) This slightly aged backpacker haven has four cluttered dorm rooms and a chummy communal area with pool table, TV and computers.

SILOM

The financial district around Th Silom has a handful of budget hostels, though the neighbourhood is mainly for bigger budgets. The bonus is that the MRT links with the Hualamphong train station.

HQ Hostel HOSTEL $
(Map p650; ☎0 2233 1598; www.hqhostel.com; 5/3-4 Soi 3, Th Silom; dm/r 380-599/1300-1700B; BTS Sala Daeng, MRT Si Lom; ❄@📶) This new hostel combines basic but stylish rooms and dorms with inviting communal areas, smack dab in the middle of Bangkok's financial district.

River View Guest House HOTEL $
(Map p650; ☎0 2234 5429; www.riverviewbkk.com; 768 Soi Phanurangsi, Th Songwat; r 350-1500B; river ferry Tha Krom Chao Tha; ❄📶) After 20 years, this budget staple is finally receiving a much-needed renovation. The rooms are now spacious and modern, although the halls and exterior are stuck in a rather gritty time warp. To get there, heading north on Th Charoen Krung from Th Si Phraya, take a left onto Th Songwat (before the Chinatown Arch), then the second left onto Soi Phanurangsi. You'll start to see signs at this point.

New Road Guesthouse HOSTEL $
(Map p650; ☎0 2630 9371; www.newroadguesthouse.com; 1216/1 Th Charoen Krung; dm fan/air-con 160/250B, r 900-2500B; river ferry Tha Si Phraya; ❄@📶) For those on tight budgets,

the clean fan dorms are among the cheapest accommodation in all of Bangkok.

YHA Downtown Bangkok HOSTEL $
(Map p650; ☎0 2266 4443; 395/4 Th Silom; dm/r 299/699-1129B; BTS Chong Nonsi; ❄@📶) Another tidy and conveniently located backpacker hostel.

Eating

No matter where you go in Bangkok, food is never far away. Surfing the street stalls is the cheapest and tastiest culinary pursuit, but don't neglect the city's mall food courts that combine the variety of an outdoor market without the noise and heat.

Bangkok also offers an international menu thanks to its many immigrant communities. Chinatown is naturally good for Chinese food; Middle Eastern fare can be found in Little Arabia, off Th Sukhumvit; Indian hangs out near the Hindu temple on Th Silom; and Western cuisine dominates Th Sukhumvit.

Do note that food vendors do not set up on Mondays, ostensibly for citywide street cleaning.

TH KHAO SAN & BANGLAMPHU

Th Khao San is lined with restaurants, but the prices tend to be higher and the quality incredibly inauthentic. Serial snackers can survive by venturing off Khao San and into the *soi* around Th Samsen or the old district of Phra Nakhon.

Ann's Sweet BAKERY $
(Map p654; 138 Th Phra Athit; mains 75-150B; ⊙lunch & dinner; bus 32, 33, 64, 82, river ferry Tha Phra Athit; ❄) Ann, a native of Bangkok and a graduate of the Cordon Bleu cooking program, makes some of the most authentic Western-style cakes you'll find anywhere in town.

TOP CHOICE **Arawy** VEGETARIAN $
(Map p654; 152 Th Din So; dishes 20-40B; ⊙breakfast, lunch & dinner; bus 15, klorng taxi Tha Phan Fah; 🖉) A Thai greasy spoon, Arawy's idea of decor is old boxes piled up beside a TV set. But the pre-made point-and-eat dishes are delicious and authentic. The restaurant was inspired by ex-Bangkok governor Chamlong Srimuang's strict vegetarianism. The roman-script sign reads 'Alloy'; it's opposite the Municipal Hall.

Shoshana ISRAELI $$
(Map p654; 88 Th Chakraphong; mains 90-220B; ⊙lunch & dinner; bus 32, 516, river ferry Tha Phra Athit; ❄) Although prices have gone up slightly since it began back in 1982, Shoshana still puts together a cheap and tasty Israeli meal. Feel safe ordering anything deep-fried and don't miss the eggplant dip.

HUALAMPHONG & CHINATOWN

Old Siam Plaza THAI $
(Map p650; ground fl, Old Siam Plaza, cnr Th Phahurat & Th Triphet; mains 15-50B; ⊙9am-6.30pm; river ferry Tha Saphan Phut) Sugar junkies, be sure to include this stop on your Bangkok eating itinerary. The ground floor of this shopping centre is a candyland of traditional Thai sweets and snacks, most made right before your eyes.

SLEEPING NEAR THE AIRPORT

If you're still in transit and don't want to bed in central Bangkok, there are more and more options on the eastern outskirts of town within striking distance of the Survarnabhumi International Airport.

» **Refill Now!** (☎0 2713 2044; www.refillnow.co.th; 191 Soi Pridi Bhanom Yong 42, Soi 71, Th Sukhumvit, Phra Khanong; dm/s/d 480/928/1215B; BTS Phra Khanong & access by taxi; ❄@📶🏊) The closest, cheapest option near the airport, this hip hostel blends the Habitat catalogue with the '60s chic of a Kubrick movie, making you a dorm convert.

» **Grand Inn Come Hotel** (☎0 2738 8189-99; www.grandinncome-hotel.com; 99 Moo 6, Th Kingkaew, Bangpli; r incl breakfast from 1800B; ❄@📶) Solid midranger 10km from the airport, with airport shuttle and 'lively' karaoke bar.

» **All Seasons Bangkok Huamark** (☎0 2308 7888; 5 Soi 15, Th Ramkhamhaeng; r 1366-2195B; ❄@📶🏊) Less than 20km from the airport, this midranger has 268 rooms to choose from.

» **Novotel Suvarnabhumi Airport Hotel** (☎0 2131 1111; www.novotel.com; r incl breakfast from 7146B; ❄@📶) With 600-plus luxurious rooms in the airport compound.

SOY, OH JOY!

During the annual Vegetarian Festival in September/October, Bangkok's Chinatown becomes a virtual orgy of nonmeat cuisine. The festivities centre on Chinatown's main street, Th Yaowarat, but food shops and stalls all over the city post yellow flags to announce their meat-free status.

Standard Thai dishes, like *đôm yam* and *gaang kĕe·o wăhn*, are transformed into vegetarian versions, while festival specific Hokkien-style yellow noodles are stir-fried with meaty mushrooms and big chunks of vegetables. Don't cut those long noodles as they represent good luck.

Mangkorn Khao THAI $
(Map p650; cnr Th Yaowarat & Th Yaowaphanit; dishes 30B; ⏲7-11pm; bus 73, MRT Hualamphong) This streetside stall is a lauded vendor of *bà·mèe* (Chinese-style wheat noodles) served with handmade wontons in a subtle broth. Note that there is no roman-script sign.

Khrua Phornlamai THAI $
(Map p650; Th Plaeng Nam; dishes 40-60B; ⏲dinner; bus 73, MRT Hualamphong) A modest street stall across the street from Burapa Birds Nest restaurant, this is a great place for greasy but delicious stir-fried faves such as *pàt kêe mow* – wide rice noodles stir-fried with Thai basil and so many chillies you might feel drunk, as the name implies.

Nay Mong THAI $
(Map p650; 539 Th Phlap Phla Chai; dishes 40-60B; ⏲dinner; bus 73, MRT Hualamphong) This minuscule restaurant is renowned for its delicious *hŏy tôrt* (a crepe-like shellfish omelette). It is about 50m on the right-hand side from the intersection of Th Charoen Krung.

SIAM SQUARE

Food vendors on Soi Kasem San 1 do a brisk business of feeding hungry clockwatchers and lounging *faràng* (foreigners); they are masters at communicating with hand gestures.

TOP CHOICE **MBK Food Court** THAI $
(Map p660; 6th fl, MBK, cnr Th Phra Ram I & Th Phayathai; dishes 40-60B; ⏲lunch & dinner; BTS National Stadium) The best introduction to street food a roving stomach could find. This mall food court has helpful English menus, cool air-con and all the standard dishes you'll need to know in order to conquer the menu-less street stalls.

New Light Coffee House INTERNATIONAL $$
(Map p660; 426/1-4 Siam Sq; dishes 60-200B; ⏲11am-2pm & 6-10pm; BTS Siam; ❄) Travel back to the near past at this vintage diner popular with Chulalongkorn University students. Try old-school Western dishes, accompanied by a roll and green salad, or choose from the extensive Thai menu.

SUKHUMVIT

Fine dining is Sukhumvit's strong suit but you can find a few modest places too.

Soul Food Mahanakorn THAI $$
(www.soulfoodmahanakorn.com; 56/10 Soi 55/ Thong Lor, Th Sukhumvit; mains 120-250B; ⏲dinner; BTS Thong Lo) Started up by a US expat, this cosy bar/restaurant does upscale takes on rustic Thai dishes such as southern-style fried chicken and northern-style pork curry alongside cocktails, of course.

Nasir Al-Masri MIDDLE EASTERN $$
(Map p650; 4/6 Soi 3/1, Th Sukhumvit; mains 80-350B; ⏲24hr; BTS Nana) One of several similar Middle Eastern restaurants in Little Arabia, Nasir Al-Masri is easily recognisable by its genuinely impressive floor-to-ceiling stainless steel 'theme'. Middle Eastern food generally means meat, meat and more meat, but there are also several delicious veggie-based mezze.

Bharani THAI $
(Sansab Boat Noodle; Map p650; 96/14 Soi 23, Th Sukhumvit; mains 50-200B; ⏲10am-10pm; BTS Asok, MRT Sukhumvit) This cosy Thai restaurant dabbles in a bit of everything, from ox-tongue stew to fried rice with shrimp paste, but the real reason to come is for the rich, meaty 'boat noodles', a homage to the ancient Ayuthaya tradition of floating noodle vendors.

Thonglee THAI $
(Map p650; Soi 20, Th Sukhumvit; mains 40-100B; ⏲lunch & dinner, closed 3rd Sun of the month; BTS Asok, MRT Sukhumvit) One of the few remaining homestyle Thai places on Th Sukhumvit, this tiny kitchen offers a few dishes you won't find elsewhere, like *mŏo pàt gà·pì* (pork fried with shrimp paste) and *mèe gròrp* (sweet-and-spicy crispy fried noodles).

Soi 38 Night Market THAI $

(Soi 38, Th Sukhumvit; dishes 30-60B; ⊙8pm-3am; BTS Thong Lo) For budget noshing in an expensive part of town, this nightly collection of Thai-Chinese stalls is something of an oasis. It is also open late for post-clubbing chowing.

Bo.lan THAI $$$

(Map p650; ☎0 2260 2962; www.bolan.co.th; 42 Soi 26/Rongnarong Phichai Songkhram, Th Sukhumvit; set meal 1500B; ⊙lunch & dinner) If you're going to do one upscale Thai meal in Bangkok, do it here. Started up by two former chefs of London's Michelin-starred Nahm, the emphasis is on set meals featuring full-flavoured regional Thai dishes.

SILOM

Bangkok's financial district does a bustling lunchtime business, and the Muslim and Indian restaurants, offshoots of their respective ethnic enclaves, are worth an evening outing.

Chennai Kitchen INDIAN $

(Map p650; 10 Th Pan; mains 50-150B; ⊙10am-3pm & 6-9.30pm; BTS Surasak; ❄) This thimble-sized restaurant delivers southern Indian vegetarian without ever straying into 'blah'. For the determined, there's the arm-length *dosa* (a parchment-thin crepe) or a thali set for the indecisive.

Somtam Convent THAI $

(Map p650; 2/4-5 Th Convent; mains 20-120B; ⊙10.30am-9pm; BTS Sala Daeng, MRT Si Lom) Northeastern Thai food is usually relegated to gritty street stalls but this well-lighted place offers a less intimidating introduction to *lâhp* (a minced meat 'salad'), *sôm·đam* (papaya salad) and other Isan delights.

Soi 10 Food Centres THAI $

(Map p650; Soi 10, Th Silom; mains 20-60B; ⊙lunch Mon-Fri; BTS Sala Daeng, MRT Si Lom) These two food barns tucked behind Soi 10 are the main lunchtime fuelling stations for this area's office staff. Choices range from southern-style *kôw gaang* (point-and-choose curries ladled over rice) to virtually every form of Thai noodle.

TOP CHOICE **Krua Aroy-Aroy** THAI $

(Map p650; Th Pan; mains 30-70B; ⊙8am-8.30pm, closed 2nd & 4th Sun of each month; BTS Surasak) It can be crowded and hot, but Krua Aroy-Aroy ('Delicious Kitchen') lives up to its name. Stop by for some of Bangkok's richest curries, as well as a revolving menu of daily specials.

Drinking

Bangkok's curfew (midnight to 1am for bars) is strictly enforced, though there are always loopholes. Smoking has been successfully banned from all indoor bars and clubs and some open-air places as well.

Most backpackers are pleased to find that the party finds them on Th Khao San, where night-time equals the right time for a drink. Beer and cocktails are sold from every corner and a tonne of hip Thais have carved out a local scene too.

Center Khao San BAR

(Map p654; Th Khao San) A classic Khao San watering hole, this long-running spot has a front-row view of the street's human parade as well as late-night bands.

Molly Bar BAR

(Map p654; Th Rambutri) Packed on weekends for live music, this off-Khao San bar has a more mellow vibe on weekdays with outdoor seating amongst fairy lights.

Hippie de Bar BAR

(Map p654; 46 Th Khao San) Despite the name, you'll be hard-pressed to find dreadlocks or a yoga mat at this boozer shack, popular with local university students. Regardless, everybody's welcome, and there's food, pool tables and a rockin' soundtrack.

Taksura BAR

(Map p654; 156/1 Th TanaoTanao) Part of the adventure is actually locating this seemingly abandoned, century-old house. Reward your discovery with some spicy nibbles and a whisky set (a bottle of Thai whiskey mixed with soda water, Coke and ice).

Molly Malone's BAR

(Map p650; 1/5-6 Th Convent, Th Silom; ⊙11am-1am; BTS Sala Daeng, MRT Si Lom) A recent makeover has this longstanding pub leaning perilously towards Irish kitsch, but it still pulls a fun crowd and the service is friendly and fast.

Cheap Charlie's BAR

(Map p650; Soi 11, Th Sukhumvit; ⊙Mon-Sat; BTS Nana) A veteran of the bar world, this outdoor beer stall is decorated with novelty trinkets and other wooden curiosities. As the name suggests, drinks are easy on the wallet, attracting expats and front-loaders (drinkers heading elsewhere after cheap drinks here). It is located on a sub-*soi* off Soi 11, look for the 'Sabai Sabai Massage' sign.

Wong's Place BAR
(Map p650; 27/3 Soi Sri Bumphen, off Soi Ngam Duphli, Th Phra Ram IV; ⏲8pm until late; MRT Lumphini) Enforced curfew laws have sobered up Bangkok's reputation but there are still a few after-hours joints should sleeping seem out of the question. This late-night hovel is beloved by backpackers who stayed so long they're now expats; don't show up until after midnight.

☆ Entertainment

Most dance clubs charge a cover fee ranging from 200B to 500B.

Brick Bar LIVE MUSIC
(Map p654; ☎0 2629 4477; basement, Buddy Lodge, 265 Th Khao San; river ferry Tha Phra Athit) This underground pub hosts a revolving cast of live Thai bands slotted for an almost exclusively domestic crowd. If this all sounds a bit too foreign, come just before midnight for Teddy Ska's reggae beats.

Ad Here the 13th LIVE MUSIC
(Map p654; 13 Th Samsen; river ferry Tha Phra Athit) Just over Khlong Banglamphu bridge, this cosy hole-in-the-wall is packed with regulars, cold beer, good cheer and a brilliant blues band.

Brown Sugar LIVE MUSIC
(Map p660; 231/20 Th Sarasin; BTS Ratchadamri) Jazz it up with a visit to this intimate club dedicated to brass and blues.

Saxophone Pub & Restaurant LIVE MUSIC
(Map p650; 3/8 Th Phayathai; BTS Victory Monument) A Bangkok live-music legend, Saxophone fills its beer-cellar bar with jazz, blues, reggae and rock, and big groups of partying friends.

RCA DANCE CLUBS
(Royal City Ave; Th Phra Ram IX) This suburban strip of megaclubs packs in barely legal Thais, professional drunks of every nationality (including a few dirty old 'uncles') and enthusiastic backpackers. The club venues change but at the moment you'll find the crowds at 808 Club, Flix/Slim and Cosmic Cafe.

Glow DANCE CLUB
(Map p650; www.glowbkk.com; 96/4-5 Soi 23, Th Sukhumvit; admission from 200B; BTS Asoke, MRT Sukhumvit) This tiny club packs 'em in with a menu of music ranging from hip-hop to electronica and just about everything in between.

Aksra Theatre TRADTIONAL ARTS
(Map p650; ☎0 2677 8888 ext 5730; www.aksratheatre.com; King Power Complex, 8/1 Th Rang Nam, Th Phayathai; tickets 400-600B; ⏲shows 7.30-8.30pm Mon-Wed, dinner shows 6.30-7pm Thu-Sun; BTS Victory Monument) The descendants of the famous Joe Louis Puppet Troupe perform scenes from *Ramakian* with traditional knee-high puppets requiring three puppeteers to strike humanlike poses.

Lumphini Boxing Stadium MUAY THAI
(Map p650; Th Phra Ram IV; tickets 1000-2000B; ⏲6.30pm Tue, Fri, Sat; MRT Lumphini) The country's best *muay thai* fighters bubble up from the temple fair rings to the big-league in Bangkok. Aficionados say the best-matched bouts are reserved for Tuesday nights at Lumphini. Tickets aren't cheap for foreigners but bargaining isn't an option.

Ratchadamnoen Stadium MUAY THAI
(Map p654; Th Ratchadamnoen Nok; tickets 1000-2000B; ⏲bouts 6.30pm Mon, Wed, Thu & Sun; bus 503 & 70) Thursday nights at Ratchadamnoen typically features the sport's leading contenders.

🛍 Shopping

Thailand is a great shopping destination but smart travellers opt for a shopping spree right before their return flight to avoid hauling extra cargo across Southeast Asia. If

GAY & LESBIAN BANGKOK

Bangkok's gay community is loud, proud and knows how to party. A newcomer might want to visit the websites **Utopia** (www.utopia-asia.com), **Dreaded Ned** (www.dreadedned.com), **Fridae** (www.fridae.com) and **Lesbian Guide to Bangkok** (www.bangkoklesbian.com) for nightlife tips.

Bangkok's 'pink alleys' branch off Th Silom. Reliable standards include **Balcony Bar** (Map p650; 86-88 Soi 4, Th Silom; BTS Sala Daeng, MRT Silom) and **Telephone Bar** (Map p650; ☎0 2234 3279; 114/11-13 Soi 4, Th Silom; BTS Sala Daeng, MRT Silom), while dance clubs cluster on Soi 2, Th Silom. The lesbian hang-out is at **Zeta** (Phra Ram IX), a low-key club in RCA (Royal City Avenue).

PINNING DOWN THE PARTY

Bangkok's party people are fickle and dance clubs are used up like tissues. To chase down the crowds check out **Dude Sweet** (www.dudesweet.org), which organises popular monthly parties, and **Bangkok Recorder** (www.bangkokrecorder.com), which promotes various club theme nights and visiting celeb DJs. Other sources of info include **BK** (http://bk.asia-city.com/nightlife) or **Thonglor Ekamai** (www.thonglor-ekamai.com), which profiles upper Sukhumvit's expanding nightlife.

there isn't a posted price, then you should bargain for it.

Chatuchak Market MARKET
(Th Phahonyothin; www.chatuchak.org; ⌚9am-6pm Sat & Sun; BTS Mo Chit, MRT Chatuchak Park & Kamphaeng Phet) Chatuchak is the mother of all markets. On weekends it sprawls over a huge area with tens of thousands of stalls and hundreds of thousands of visitors a day. From handicrafts and antiques to second-hand clothes and housewares, Chatuchak has evolved from a utilitarian wholesaler to creative design supplier. Everyone leaves thoroughly exhausted, totally dehydrated and overloaded with armfuls of plastic bags – it's great fun. To navigate the market like a pro, pick up a copy of *Nancy Chandler's Map of Bangkok*. The market is north of central Bangkok.

MBK MALL
(Mahboonkhrong; Map p660; cnr Th Phayathai & Th Phra Ram I; BTS National Stadium & Siam) Bangkok's most hyperactive mall, MBK is an air-conditioned playground for average folks, trendy Thai teenagers, escalator-shy grannies and sunburned Europeans. Small, inexpensive stalls and shops sell mobile phones and accessories, cheap clothes and toiletries.

Siam Center & Siam Discovery Center MALL
(Map p660; cnr Th Phayathai & Th Phra Ram I; BTS National Stadium & Siam) Thailand's first shopping centre, Siam Center opened its doors in 1976 and has refashioned itself for the fashion-conscious teens. The attached Siam Discovery Center is the leading lady of home decor. Peruse the 3rd-floor stores for an idea of what a Bangkok socialite's sky-high apartment might look like. There is also an **Asia Books** branch here.

Siam Paragon MALL
(Map p660; Th Phra Ram I; BTS Siam) Touted as Southeast Asia's biggest mall, Paragon is a humongous homage to luxury, a seemingly frivolous venture in today's downgraded economy. On the third floor, **Kinokuniya**, Thailand's largest English-language bookstore, is the mall's most useful and busiest store. Most locals hang around the main lobby as if it were an urban park, or they venture to the basement-level food court for dressed-up Thai meals. Often the attached courtyard hosts Thai bands, fashion shows and other excessively amplified events.

Patpong Night Market MARKET
(Map p650; Patpong Soi 2, Th Silom; ⌚7pm-1am; BTS Sala Daeng, MRT Silom) Knock-off designer bags and watches are the speciality amid Bangkok's red light district.

Asia Books BOOKS
(Map p650; www.asiabook.com; Soi 15, 221 Th Sukhumvit; ⌚8am-9pm; BTS Asok, MRT Sukhumvit) Also a branch in Siam Discovery Center.

Book Lover BOOKS
(Map p654; Soi Ram Buttri; ⌚noon-10.30pm Tue-Sun; bus 2, 15, 44, 511, river ferry Tha Phra Athit) Well-stocked used bookstore.

Kinokuniya BOOKS
(Map p660; www.kinokuniya.com; Siam Paragon 3rd fl, Th Phra Ram I; ⌚10am-10pm; BTS Siam) The country's largest book store.

Saraban BOOKS
(Map p654; 106/1 Th Rambuttri; ⌚9.30am-10.30pm; bus 2, 15, 44, 511, river ferry Tha Phra Athit) Stocking the largest selection of international newspapers and new Lonely Planet guides on Th Khao San.

Shaman Bookstore BOOKS
Susie Walking Street (Map p654; Susie Walking Street, off Th Khao San; ⌚9am-11pm) Th Khao San (Map p654; Th Khao San; ⌚9am-11pm) With two locations on Th Khao San, Shaman has the area's largest selection of used books.

Information

Dangers & Annoyances

Bangkok's most heavily touristed areas – Wat Phra Kaew, Th Khao San, Jim Thompson's House, Siam Square – are favourite hunting grounds for professional con artists. See the boxed text Out-smarting the Scams (p653).

DENOMINATING MONEY

The Thai *baht* (B) is divided into colour-coded notes as well as coins of various sizes.

Coins come in 1B, 2B (gold-coloured), 5B and 10B denominations. There are 100 *satang* to 1B and occasionally you'll see 25 and 50 satang coins at department stores or supermarkets.

Notes are in 20B (green), 50B (blue), 100B (red), 500B (purple) and 1000B (beige) denominations of varying shades and sizes. In the dark it can be easy to mix up a 50B note with a 500B note so take care to segregate your bills by denomination. ATM withdrawals dispense cash in 1000B notes, which can be impossible for a taxi driver or market vendor to change. Break your big bills at 7-Elevens.

Emergency

If you have a medical emergency and need an ambulance, contact the hospitals with English-speaking staff (listed under Medical Services.

Fire (☎199)

Police & Emergency (☎191)

Tourist police (☎1155; ⊙24hr) An English-speaking unit that investigates criminal activity involving tourists, including gem scams. It can also act as a bilingual liaison with the regular police.

Internet Access

Internet cafes are ubiquitous and most are equipped with Skype and headsets for inexpensive overseas calls. The cheapest access is found around Th Khao San, where it starts at around 20B an hour. Siam Square is the next best bet, while the Th Sukhumvit and Silom areas are more expensive.

Wi-fi is mostly free of charge and is becoming increasingly available at hotels, guesthouses and public hot spots.

Internet Resources

Austin Bush Food Blog (www.austinbushphotography.com/category/foodblog) Food blog by Bangkok-based Lonely Planet author.

Greg To Differ (www.gregtodiffer.com) Stories, rants and observations on expat life in Bangkok.

Media

The two English-language dailies, the *Bangkok Post* and the *Nation*, are available at streetside newsagents near hotels or tourist areas. Monthly magazines are available in bookstores.

Bangkok 101 (www.bangkok101.com) A monthly city primer with photo essays and reviews of attractions.

Bangkok Post (www.bangkokpost.net) Leading English-language daily.

BK (http://bk.asia-city.com) Free weekly listings mag for the young and hip.

CNN Go (www.cnngo.com/bangkok) Online magazine covering hot spots, food trends and lifestyle news.

The Nation (www.nationmultimedia.com) English-language daily with a heavy focus on business.

Medical Services

There are several outstanding hospitals in Bangkok with English-speaking staff.

Bangkok Christian Hospital (Map p650; ☎0 2235 1000; 124 Th Silom; BTS Sala Daeng, MRT Si Lom)

BNH (Map p650; ☎0 2686 2700; 9 Th Convent; BTS Sala Daeng, MRT Si Lom)

Bumrungrad Hospital (Map p650; ☎0 2667 1000; 33 Soi 3, Th Sukhumvit; BTS Phloen Chit)

Money

Thai banks have currency exchange kiosks that have extended hours (usually 8am to 8pm) in many parts of Bangkok, especially tourist areas. ATMs are conveniently located. Go to 7-Eleven shops or other reputable places to break 1000B bills; don't expect a vendor or taxi to able to make change on a note 500B or larger.

Post

Main post office (Map p650; Th Charoen Krung; ⊙8am-8pm Mon-Fri, 8am-1pm Sat & Sun) Poste restante and a packing service for parcels. Branch post offices also offer similar services.

Tourist Information

Bangkok Information Center (Map p654; ☎0 2225 7612-4; www.bangkoktourist.com; ⊙8am-7pm Mon-Fri & 9am-5pm Sat & Sun; bus 32, 33, 64, 82, river ferry Tha Phra Athit)

Tourism Authority of Thailand (TAT; www.tourismthailand.org) Main office (Map p650; ☎0 2250 5500; 1600 Th Phetchaburi Tat Mai; ⊙8.30am-4.30pm; MRT Phetchaburi); Banglamphu (Map p650; ☎0 2283 1500; Th Ratchadamnoen Nok; ⊙8.30am-4.30pm); Suvarnabhumi International Airport (☎0 2134 0040; 2nd fl, btwn Gates 2 & 5; ⊙24hr).

Getting There & Away

Air

Bangkok is the air-travel hub for Thailand and mainland Southeast Asia. **Suvarnabhumi**

GETTING TO CAMBODIA: ARANYA PRATHET TO POIPET

Many travellers undertaking the Angkor pilgrimage start this epic journey in Bangkok and cross the border at Aranya Prathet-Poipet. Resist the urge to book this trip through Th Khao San's guesthouses and travel agencies as the scams are numerous, annoying and time-consuming. The border is fraught with minor scams and hassles. Read up on the tricks and tricksters on **Tales of Asia** (www.talesofasia.com/cambodia-overland.htm).

The crossing can be done in one day but if you get delayed in Aranya Prathet, there are a string of guesthouses along the road to the border that are happy to have you.

Getting to the border Buses leave from Bangkok's Northern and Northeastern (Mo Chit) bus terminal (207B, 4½ hours), Eastern (Ekamai) station (200B, four hours) and Suvarnabhumi (Airport) bus station (187-190B; three hours) directly to the border. Minivans also leave from Bangkok's Victory Monument (230B, four hours, every half-hour).

Two daily trains leave Bangkok's Hualamphong station (3rd-class 48B, six hours) to Aranya Prathet town, where sŏrngtăaou (15B), motorcycle taxi (60B) or túk-túk (80B) can take you the final 6km to the border.

Aranya Prathet is also accessible by bus from Chanthaburi (150B, four hours, hourly) and Khorat (190B, four hours, six daily).

At the border It is advisable to reach the border as early as possible, especially on weekends when casino-bound Thais and guest workers clog the immigration lines. Cambodia visas are available on arrival with the usual formalities (passport photo and US$20 visa fee). Ignore any touts or money exchange services and watch out for pickpockets.

Moving on The best way to continue to Siem Reap is by taxi.

See p105 for information on crossing from Cambodia into Thailand.

International Airport (☎0 2132 1888; www.bangkokairportonline.com), 30km east of Bangkok, handles all international air traffic and most domestic routes. The airport name is pronounced '*sù·wan·ná·poom*,' and its airport code is BKK.

Don Muang airport (☎0 2535 1111; www.airportthai.co.th), 25km north of central Bangkok, handles domestic routes with Nok Air, Orient Thai and Solar Air.

For a list of international and domestic airlines in Bangkok, see p783.

Bus

Buses departing from the government bus station are recommended over those departing from Th Khao San and other tourist areas, due to a lower incidence of theft and greater reliability. The Bangkok bus terminals (all with left-luggage facilities) are as follows:

Eastern bus terminal (Ekamai; ☎0 2391 2504; Soi 40/Soi Ekamai, Th Sukhumvit; BTS Ekamai) Serves southeastern cities such as Rayong, Ban Phe (for Ko Samet), Chanthaburi, Trat and Laem Ngop (for Ko Chang).

Northern & Northeastern bus terminal (Mo Chit; northern routes ☎0 2936 2841, ext 311/442, northeastern routes ☎0 2936 2852, ext 611/448; Th Kamphaeng Phet) These terminals serve all northern and northeastern cities, including Chiang Mai, Nakhon Ratchasima (Khorat), Ayuthaya, Lopburi and Aranya Prathet (near the Cambodian border). From the Mo Chit Skytrain station take bus 3, 77 or 509.

Southern bus terminal (Sai Tai Mai; ☎0 2435 1199; Th Bromaratchachonanee, Thonburi) Serves southern and western cities like Nakhon Pathom, Kanchanaburi, Hua Hin, Surat Thani, Phuket and Hat Yai. Accessible by bus 79, 159, 201 or 516 from Th Ratchadamnoen (near Khao San) or bus 40 from Victory Monument.

Suvarnabhumi public transport centre (☎0 2132 1888; Suvarnabhumi Airport) Located 3km from Suvarnabhumi International Airport, this terminal serves various points east and northeast including Aranya Prathet (for the Cambodian border), Chanthaburi, Ko Chang, Nong Khai (for the Lao border), Rayong (for Ko Samet), Trat and Udon Thani. It can be reached from Suvarnabhumi Airport by a free shuttle bus.

TRAVEL HINTS

Skip the bus services that originate out of Bangkok's Th Khao San; these often have hidden costs, commission-generating hassles and a high-rate of theft from stowed luggage.

GETTING INTO TOWN

Suvarnabhumi International Airport

Airport Rail Link A rail line linking Suvarnabhumi airport to central Bangkok opened in 2010. If you arrive at the Bangkok City Air Terminal (Makkasan station) at least three hours before your departure, there are check-in facilities for three airlines (Thai Airways, Bangkok Airways and Lufthansa).

» **Local service** (30 minutes, 45B, ⊙6am-midnight) Six stops between airport and Phaya Thai station, which is connected to BTS Phaya Thai. Disembark at Phaya Thai and flag a cab to Khao San; BTS links to Siam Square area.

» **Express service** (15 minutes, 150B, ⊙6am-midnight) Nonstop between airport and Makkasan/Bangkok City Air Terminal, accessible to MRT Phetchaburi. The MRT links to Silom and Sukhumvit.

Local Bus Local buses travel between central Bangkok and the airport's public transport centre, a 3km ride on a free shuttle bus from the airport. Bus fares start at 25B and run roughly from 6am to 9pm. Useful routes include the following:

» Bus 551 (Victory Monument)

» Bus 554 (Don Muang)

» Bus 556 (Th Khao San)

» Minivan 552 (On Nut BTS station)

Intercity Bus The airport's public transport centre has services to other eastern cities within Thailand; see Getting There & Away (p669) for more information.

Taxi Public meter taxis (not the 'official airport taxis') queue outside of baggage claim. Taxi lines tend to be long; you can always dodge the line by flagging a cab from the arrivals hall.

Minivan

Privately run minivans *(rót đôo)* are increasingly replacing buses for fast and comfortable service between Bangkok and its neighbouring provinces as they travel directly into town (usually the central market) instead of the out-of-town bus stations. In Bangkok, Victory Monument (Map p650) is surrounded by various minivan depots with services to the following:

Ayuthaya (60B, one hour, from 5am to 8.30pm)

Aranya Prathet (for the Cambodian border; 230B, 3½ hours, from 6am to 6pm)

Ban Phe (for Ko Samet; 200B, 2½ hours, from 6am to 9pm)

Muak Lek (for Khao Yai; 120B, 2½ hours, from 8am to 8pm)

Southern bus terminal (35B, one hour, 6.30am to 9pm)

Suvarnabhumi International Airport (40B, one hour, from 5am to 10.30pm).

Train

Hualamphong station (Map p650; ☎0 2220 4334, general information & advance booking 1690; Th Phra Ram IV; MRT Hua Lamphong) Bangkok's central train station; from Sukhumvit and Silom, take the MRT, from Banglamphu (Khao San) take bus 53. See p786 for information on train routes and stops.

Bangkok Noi station (Thonburi; cross-river ferry Tha Rot Fai) A minor commuter line with service to Nakhon Phanom and Kanchanaburi.

Getting Around

Bangkok is nearly always choked with traffic, but it can be especially impossible to travel down Th Sukhumvit or Th Ratchadamnoen during rush hour. You will need a good map and a lot of patience to get around. If you plan to use Bangkok's economical bus system, purchase Roadway's *Bangkok Bus Map*. Check out *Nancy Chandler's Map of Bangkok* for a schematic representation of attractions, restaurants and other tips.

Boat

Chao Phraya River Express (☎0 2623 6001) is a scenic and efficient way of exploring the sights in Ko Ratanakosin, Banglamphu and parts of Silom. The boats ply a regular route along the Mae Nam Chao Phraya between Tha Wat Ratchasingkhon in the south to Nonthaburi

Touts often offer flat fares (usually inflated), but you can try to bargain for a fare closer to the meter rate. For meter taxis you must also pay a 50B airport surcharge to the driver and toll charges (usually about 60B). Politely insist that the meter is used ('Meter, na kha/khrap') if the driver suggests otherwise. Depending on traffic, meter rates should be as follows:

- Banglamphu/Khao San: 350B to 425B
- Th Sukhumvit: 200B to 250B
- Th Silom: 300B to 350B

Don Muang Airport

Bus The following useful air-con buses stop on the highway in front of the airport:

- Bus 510 (Victory Monument and Southern bus terminal)
- Bus 513 (Th Sukhumvit and Eastern bus terminal)
- Bus 29 (Northern bus terminal, Victory Monument, Siam Square and Hualamphong train station)

Taxi There is a 50B airport surcharge added to the meter fare and tolls are paid by the passenger. Sample fares:

- Banglamphu/Th Khao San: 400B
- Sukhumvit or Silom: 300-350B

Train Exit Terminal 1 towards the Amari Airport Hotel to connect to Don Muang train station with service to Hualamphong train station (5-10B, one hour, roughly every hour from 4am 9.30pm).

in the north and overlaps with the Saphan Taksin Skytrain station at Tha Sathon. During rush hour pay close attention to the boat's colour-coded flags to avoid boarding an express line. The company operates the following services:

Express – Indicated by an orange, yellow or yellow-and-green flag, 14B to 32B, morning and evening rush hour till 7pm.

Local – Without a flag, 9B to 13B, morning and evening rush hour till 6pm)

Tourist – Larger boat; 19B, one-day pass 150B, 9.30am to 3.30pm.

Klorng taxis (tickets 7B to 20B, 6am to 7pm) zip up and down Khlong Saen Saep, a narrow waterway connecting eastern and western Bangkok. The canals are something akin to an open sewer so try not to get splashed and take care when boarding and disembarking as the boats stop for mere seconds. Useful piers include the following:

Tha Phan Fah – Eastern terminus, Banglamphu.

Tha Hua Chang – Siam Square area.

Tha Pratunam Interchange pier, BTS Chitlom.

BTS (Skytrain)

The elevated **Bangkok Mass Transit System** (BTS; ☎0 2617 7300; www.bts.co.th) is a slick ride through the modern parts of town. There are two lines: the Sukhumvit and Silom lines. Trains run frequently from 6am to midnight; fares vary from 15B to 40B. Ticket machines operate on a zone system: select your destination's zone number and deposit the required coins (5B and 10B denominations). Staffed booths provide change but do not sell single fare tickets. You can buy value-stored tickets from the booths.

Trains are labelled with the line and the terminal station (indicating the direction the train is travelling). The Sukhumvit line heading east terminates at On Nut; west at National Stadium. The Silom line heading north terminates at Mo Chit; south, Wongwian Yai. Silom is the interchange station between the two lines.

There are also interchange stations with MRT (Metro); see the MRT entry for more information.

Bus

The Bangkok bus service is frequent and frantic and is operated by **Bangkok Mass Transit Authority** (☎0 2246 4262; www.bmta.co.th). Fares for ordinary buses start at 6.50B and air-con buses at 11B. Most buses operate between 5am and 10pm or 11pm; a few run all night.

Bangkok Bus Guide, by thinknet, is the most up-to-date route map available. The following bus lines are useful:

Bus 15 Sanam Luang (accessible to Wat Phra Kaew), Th Ratchadamnoen Klang (accessible to Th Khao San), MBK (connect to BTS).

Bus 47 Sanam Luang, Th Ratchadamnoen, MBK.

MRT (Metro)

Bangkok's subway or underground (depending on your nationality) is operated by the **Metropolitan Rapid Transit Authority** (MRTA; www.mrta.co.th). For visitors the MRT is most useful if travelling from Silom or Sukhumvit to the Hualamphong train station. Trains operate from 6am to midnight and cost 16B to 41B, depending on distance. The following MRT stations provide interchange to BTS (Skytrain):

Chatuchak (BTS Chatuchak)

Sukhumvit (BTS Asoke)

Silom (BTS Sala Daeng).

Taxi

Most taxis in Bangkok are meter taxis, though some drivers 'forget' to use their meters or prefer to quote a flat (and grossly inflated) fare to tourists. Many of the taxis that park near tourist haunts operate under an informal no-meter policy. We suggest skipping these cabs and instead flagging down a roving cab on one of the main streets. Unless it is a rainy rush hour, there is usually no problem finding an available cab. Fares should generally run from 60B to 100B, depending on distance.

In most large cities, the taxi drivers are seasoned navigators familiar with every nook and cranny, but this is not the case in Bangkok where many an upcountry farmer moonlights while his fields rest. To ensure that you'll be able to return home, grab your hotel's business card, which will have directions in Thai.

Motorcycle taxis camp out at the mouth of a *soi* to shuttle people from the main road to their destinations down the lane. *Soi* trips cost 10B; don't ask the price, just pay them as you disembark.

Túk-Túk

The Thai version of a go-kart is Bangkok's most iconic vehicle and its most enduring hassle. They chatter like a chainsaw, take corners at an angle and are relentless in drumming up business. There are so many túk-túk scams that you really need some tenure in the city to know how much your trip should cost before bargaining for a ride and when a túk-túk is handier and cheaper than a cab. If you climb aboard just for the fun of it, you might end up being taken for a ride, literally. Beware of túk-túk drivers who offer to take you on a sightseeing tour for 10B or 20B – it's a touting scheme designed to pressure you into purchasing overpriced goods. You must fix fares in advance for all túk-túk rides.

AROUND BANGKOK

Floating Markets

The photographs of Thailand's floating markets – wooden canoes laden with multi-coloured fruits and vegetables, paddled by women wearing indigo-hued clothes and wide-brimmed straw hats – have become an iconic and alluring image for the kingdom. They are also a sentimental piece of history. Like all good nations do, Thailand has modernised, replacing canals with roads, and boats with motorcycles and cars. The floating markets, which were once lively trading posts for produce farmers and local housewives, have crawled ashore.

The most heavily promoted floating market is **Damnoen Saduak** (⌚7am-4pm Sat & Sun), 104km southwest of Bangkok between Nakhon Pathom and Samut Songkhram. It is little more than a souvenir market catering to foreign tourists. If you don't expect authenticity, then the unique shopping setting makes for a good story back home.

Air-con buses 78 and 996 go direct from the Southern bus terminal in Thonburi to Damnoen Saduak (80B, two hours, every 20 minutes from 6am to 9pm). Most buses will drop tourists off directly at the piers. The going rate for boat hire is about 300B per person per hour. A yellow sŏrngtăaou (5B) does a frequent loop between the floating market and the bus stop in town.

The **Amphawa Floating Market** (see p673) is the Thai counterpart to Damnoen Saduak, focusing more on food than factory-made souvenirs.

CENTRAL THAILAND

Thailand's heartland, the central region is a fertile river plain that birthed the country's history-shaping kingdoms of Ayuthaya and Sukhothai and crafted the culture and language that defines the mainstream Thai identity. The nationally revered river, the Mae Nam Chao Phraya is the lifeblood of the region and connects the country's interior with the Gulf of Thailand. Geographically, central Thailand is a necessary thorough-

WORTH A TRIP

A JOURNEY OF RAILS & RUDDERS

The riverine character of central Thailand is still alive and well in the quaint canalside village of Amphawa in Samut Songkhram province, less than 100km from Bangkok. City slickers often make the weekend journey for the Amphawa Floating Market.

Sights & Activities

The **floating market** (⌚4-9pm Fri-Sun) is popular with nostalgic Bangkokians who have only read about old Siam's boat-based commerce in books. Floating noodle vendors paddle around looking for appetites. Many visitors spend the night to enjoy the country setting and zip through the canals on **long-tail boat tours** (60B per person Fri-Sun; 500B charter Mon-Thu) to see fireflies *(hìng hôy)* illuminate the darkness; best viewed during the wet season.

Sleeping

Many of the canalside houses offer **homestays** (fan/air-con 200/1000B). Accommodation can be either a mattress on the floor or upscale guesthouse-style rooms. You'll see signs around the market for accommodation offerings.

Getting There & Away

The scenic route to Amphawa is via the Mahachai short-line train from Bangkok. The ride travels the back lots of Bangkok's urban grid and the marshy landscape along the Gulf of Thailand. Catch a train from Wong Wian Yai train station (located in Thonburi and accessible from central Bangkok via Skytrain) to Samut Sakhon (Mahachai; 10B, one hour, hourly departures), where you'll transfer to another nearby line to Samut Songkhram (Mae Klang).

At the end of the first leg (in Samut Sakhon), work your way through the fresh market to the river pier and across by ferry to Ban Laem (3B), where you'll find the train station for the second leg of the journey. Trains depart this sleepy station at 10.10am, 1.30pm and 4.40pm bound for Samut Songkhram (10B).

The train pulls right into the middle of a bustling day market, with vendors moving goods and sunshades minutes before the train's arrival. It is such a spectacle that it even appears on a YouTube clip.

From the market, charter a boat (800B) or hop in a nearby sŏrngtăaou (8B) for the 10-minute ride to Amphawa.

To return, catch a minivan from Amphawa (weekend service only) or Samut Songkhram to Bangkok's Victory Monument (70B, one hour).

fare for any Chiang Mai-bound traveller, but culturally it is a worthwhile stop.

Ayuthaya

POP 137,550

The fabled city, the fallen city: Ayuthaya crowned the pinnacle of ancient Thai history and defined the country's ascendance to regional domination. It was built at the confluence of three rivers (Mae Nam Lopburi, Chao Phraya and Pa Sak) on a unique island of land and was auspiciously named after the home of Rama in the Indian epic *Ramayana*.

The rivers formed both a natural barrier to invasion and an invitation to trade, allowing the city-state to flourish into a fully-fledged nation from 1350 to 1767. Though the Thai kings outmanoeuvred Western power plays, it was the repeated attempts by the Burmese that eventually sacked the city and ended Ayuthaya's reign. After two years of war the capital fell in 1767; the Burmese looted the city and the Thais re-established their power centre near present-day Bangkok.

Today the ruins of the old city survive with many battle scars amid a modern provincial town, a slight distraction for imagining what Ayuthaya once was. To its credit, the kingdom's history was better preserved and more accessible than previous kingdoms.

The modern town still clings to the old ways of the river, which acts as transport, bath and kitchen sink for its residents. The holiday of **Loi Krathong**, when tiny votive boats are floated on rivers as a tribute to the River Goddess, is celebrated with great fanfare in Ayuthaya.

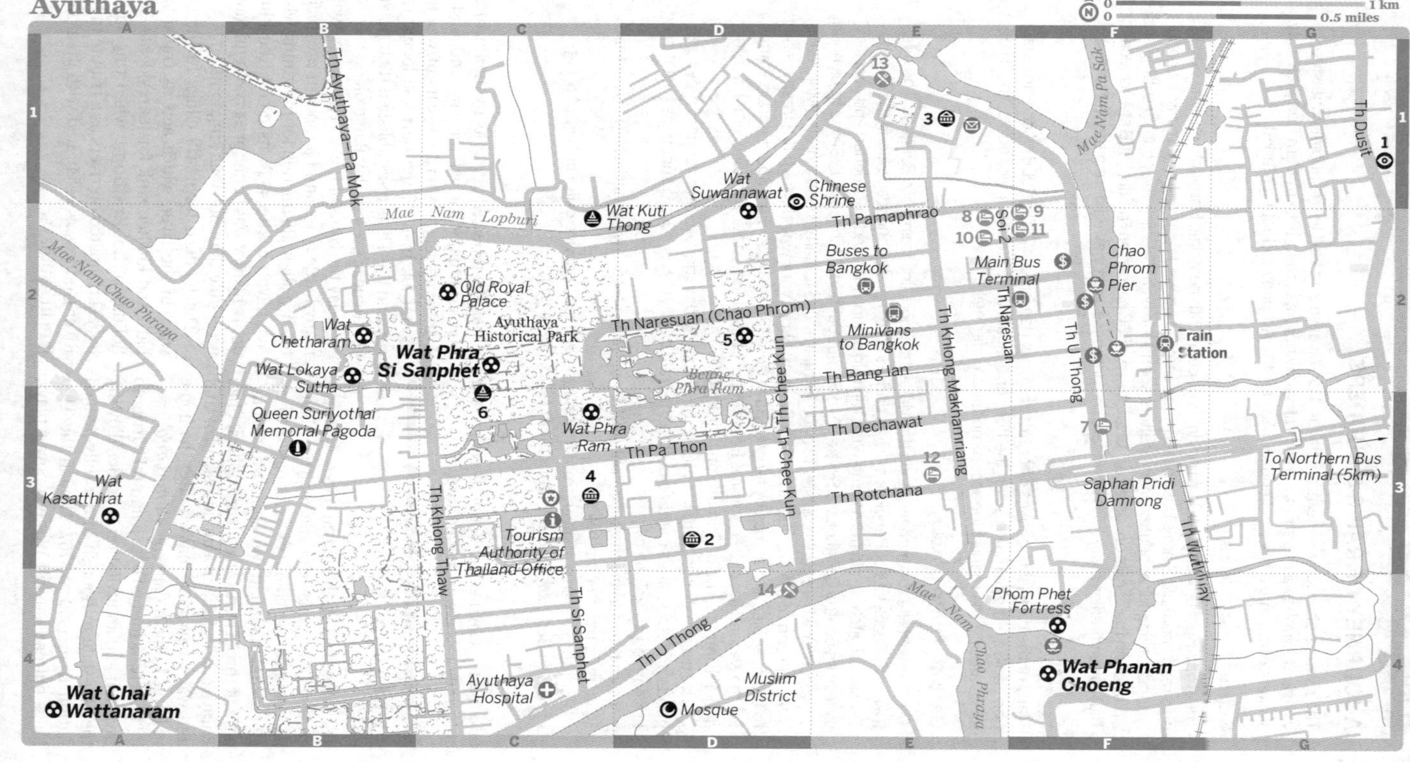
Ayuthaya
0 1 km
0 0.5 miles
Th Dusit
Th Ayuthaya–Pa Mok
Mae Nam Lopburi
Mae Nam Chao Phraya
Mae Nam Pa Sak
Wat Kuti Thong
Wat Suwannawat
Chinese Shrine
Th Pamaphrao
Soi 2
Buses to Bangkok
Main Bus Terminal
Chao Phrom Pier
Train Station
Old Royal Palace
Ayuthaya Historical Park
Th Naresuan (Chao Phrom)
Minivans to Bangkok
Th Khlong Makhamriang
Th Naresuan
Th U Thong
Wat Chetharam
Wat Phra Si Sanphet
Wat Lokaya Sutha
Beung Phra Ram
Th Bang Ian
Th Chee Kun
Queen Suriyothai Memorial Pagoda
Wat Phra Ram
Th Dechawat
Th Pa Thon
To Northern Bus Terminal (5km)
Saphan Pridi Damrong
Th Rotchana
Wat Kasatthirat
Th Khlong Thaw
Tourism Authority of Thailand Office
Th Si Sanphet
Th Wutthiay
Phom Phet Fortress
Mae Nam Chao Phraya
Th U Thong
Ayuthaya Hospital
Muslim District
Mosque
Wat Phanan Choeng
Wat Chai Wattanaram
1
2
3
4
5
6
7
8
9
10
11
12
13
14
A
B
C
D
E
F
G

Sights

A Unesco World Heritage Site, Ayuthaya's historic temples are scattered throughout the city and along the encircling rivers. The ruins are divided into two geographical areas: ruins 'on the island', in the central part of town between Th Chee Kun and the western end of Th U Thong, which are best visited by bicycle; and those 'off the island' on the other side of the river, which are best visited on an evening boat tour or by motorbike.

Most temple ruins are open from 8am to 4pm; the more famous sites charge an entrance fee. A one-day pass for most sites on the island is available for 220B and can be bought at the museums or ruins.

ON THE ISLAND

Wat Phra Si Sanphet TEMPLE

(admission 50B) The most distinctive example of Ayuthaya architecture is Wat Phra Si Sanphet, thanks to its three bell-shaped *chedi* that taper off into descending rings. This site served as the royal palace from the city's founding until the mid-15th century, when it was converted into a temple.

KNOW MORE

The English-language audio guides (150B) – available at Wat Phra Si Sanphet, Wat Phra Mahathat and Wat Chai Wattanaram – provide excellent information and vivid details.

Although the grounds are now well tended, these efforts cannot hide the ravages of war and time. The surrounding buildings are worn through to their orange bricks, leaning to one side as gravity takes its toll. The complex once contained a 16m-high standing Buddha covered with 250kg of gold, which was melted down by the Burmese conquerors.

The adjacent **Wihaan Phra Mongkhon Bophit** houses a huge bronze seated Buddha. In 1955 the Burmese prime minister visited and donated 200,000B to help restore the building, an act of belated atonement for his country's sacking of the city 200 years before.

Wat Phra Mahathat TEMPLE

(admission 50B) Wat Phra Mahathat has one of the first Khmer-style *praang* built in the capital. One of the most iconic images in Ayuthaya is Buddha's head engulfed by tentacle-like tree roots.

Ayuthaya Historical Study Centre MUSEUM

(☎0 3524 5124; Th Rotchana; adult/student 100/50B; ⏲9am-4.30pm Mon-Fri, to 5pm Sat & Sun) Getting a handle on the religious and historical importance of the temples is difficult to do without some preliminary tutoring. Ayuthaya Historical Study Centre has informative, professional displays about the ancient city.

Chantharakasem National Museum MUSEUM

(Th U Thong; admission 100B; ⏲9am-4pm Wed-Sun) This national museum contains a collection of Buddhist art, sculpture and antique weapons. The museum is housed within a former palace built in 1577.

Chao Sam Phraya National Museum MUSEUM

(cnr Th Rotchana & Th Si Sanphet; admission 150B; ⏲9am-4pm Wed-Sun) The less charming but larger Chao Sam Phraya National Museum protects the few surviving artefacts and treasures of Ayuthaya's golden period.

Ayuthaya

Top Sights

- Wat Chai Wattanaram A4
- Wat Phanan Choeng F4
- Wat Phra Si Sanphet C2

Sights

1. Ayothaya Floating Market G1
2. Ayuthaya Historical Study Centre D3
3. Chantharakasem National Museum E1
4. Chao Sam Phraya National Museum C3
5. Wat Phra Mahathat D2
6. Wihaan Mongkhon Bophit C3

Sleeping

7. Baan Khun Phra F3
8. Baan Lotus Guest House E2
9. Chantana Guest House F2
10. PU Inn Ubonpon E2
11. Tony's Place F2
12. Wiang Fa Hotel E3

Eating

13. Hua Raw Night Market E1
14. Sai Thong D4

PARTS OF A WAT

Planning to conquer Thailand's temples and ruins? With this handy guide, you'll be able to sort out your wats (Thai temple complex) from your what's that:

» **chedi** – large bell-shaped tower usually containing five structural elements symbolising (from bottom to top) earth, water, fire, wind and void; relics of Buddha or a Thai king are housed inside the *chedi;* also known as a stupa.

» **praang (prang)** – towering phallic spire of Khmer origin serving the same religious purpose as a *chedi.*

» **wihaan** – main sanctuary for the temple's Buddha sculpture and where laypeople come to make offerings; sometimes it is translated as the 'assembly hall'; typically the building has a three-tiered roofline representing the triple gems (Buddha, the teacher; Dharma, the teaching; and Brotherhood, the followers).

OFF THE ISLAND

Wat Phanan Choeng TEMPLE
(admission 20B) Wat Phanan Choeng contains a 19m-high sitting Buddha image, which reportedly wept when the Burmese sacked Ayuthaya. The temple is dedicated to Chinese seafarers and on weekends is crowded with Buddhist pilgrims from Bangkok. The best way to get here is to take the cross-river ferry (5B) from the pier near Phom Phet Fortress.

Wat Chai Wattanaram TEMPLE
(admission 50B) A popular stop for shutterbugs, this is Ayuthaya's most photogenic temple with its proud central *praang* and riverside setting. It was built in 1630 and reclaimed from the jungle a mere 40 years ago.

Ayothaya Floating Market MARKET
(⌚9am-8pm) This replica of a floating market breaks up the monotony of temple-spotting with a mix of commerce and snacking. Thais adore these purpose-built floating markets, which are far from authentic but popular enough for good people-watching. The market is to the east of the old city off Th Dusit, near Wat Kudi Dao.

Sleeping

Budget travellers can walk from the bus stop to the guesthouses, most of which are located on Soi 2, Th Naresuan.

Baan Lotus Guest House GUESTHOUSE $
(☎0 3525 1988; 20 Th Pamaphrao; r 200-600B; ❄📶) Set in a shady garden, this converted teak house offers a calm respite for road-weary travellers. Staff are as charmingly old-school as the building itself.

Tony's Place GUESTHOUSE $
(☎0 3525 2578; www.tonyplace-ayutthaya.com; 12/18 Soi 2, Th Naresuan; r 200-1200B; ❄📶) Budget rooms still offer just the basics, but renovated rooms cater to the flashpackers with almost palatial trimmings.

PU Inn Ubonpon GUESTHOUSE $
(☎0 3525 1213; www.puguesthouse.com; 20/1 Soi Thaw Kaw Saw; r 200-900B; ❄@📶) The upbeat staff are always a friend indeed when arranging trips or sorting out travel details. Rooms are bright and clean.

Chantana Guest House GUESTHOUSE $
(☎0 3532 3200; chantanahouse@yahoo.com; 12/22 Soi 2, Th Naresuan; r 400-500B;❄) Standing out from the nearby tumbledown spots, Chantana has helpful staff and clean rooms. A balcony room is well worth the extra 50B.

Baan Khun Phra GUESTHOUSE $
(☎0 3524 1978; www.bannkunpra.com; 48/2 Th U Thong; dm/d 250/600B; 📶) With a charming riverside location, this century old home could have gone upscale a long time ago but it remains delightfully shabby chic. Rooms are simple, though some are adorned with antiques. Dorms sleep up to four.

Wiang Fa Hotel GUESTHOUSE $
(☎0 3524 3252; 1/8 Th Rotchana; r 500B; ❄📶) Rooms are small in this two-storey guesthouse. But an outdoor patio extends the living space and a laid-back ambience pervades.

Eating

The range of restaurants in Ayuthaya can come as a disappointment after living it up in Bangkok.

Hua Raw Night Market THAI $
(Th U Thong; dishes 30-40B) This evening market offers a simple riverside setting and a range of Thai and Muslim dishes; for the latter look for the green star and crescent.

Sai Thong THAI $
(Th U Thong; dishes 90-150B; ⌚9.30am-10pm) With 180 items on the menu, live music and spectacular food, this old-school restaurant is the best place to eat on the island. As well as the regular fare, there are interesting variations, such as chicken marinated in whiskey.

Information

Dangers & Annoyances

Traffic lights are often absent from road junctions so take care when crossing intersections. Remember Thailand's unofficial road rules: if you're faster and larger, you have right of way. When cycling, put bags around your body, not in baskets where they could be snatched.

At night packs of dogs roam the streets. Avoid eye contact and keep your distance.

Main post office (Th U Thong)

Ayuthaya Hospital (☎1669, 0 3532 2555; cnr Th U Thong & Th Si Sanphet)

TAT office (☎0 3524 6076; 108/22 Th Si Sanphet; ⌚8.30am-4.30pm) Distributes tourist information and maps.

Tourist police (☎emergency 1155; Th Si Sanphet)

Getting There & Away

Bus

Ayuthaya has two bus terminals. The provincial bus stop is on Th Naresuan, a short walk from the guesthouse area. Services include:

Lopburi 40B; two hours; every 45 minutes.

Suphanburi 60B; two hours; every 30 minutes. Suphanburi is a transfer town for buses to Kanchanaburi.

Bangkok buses and minivans leave from stops on Th Naresuan to the following areas of the city:

Victory Monument 60B; 1½ hours; departing hourly from 5.30am to 7pm.

Southern (Sai Tai Mai) station 70B; one hour; frequent departues from 4.30am to 7pm.

Northern (Mo Chit) station 50B; 1½ hours; frequent departures. These buses also stop at Don Muang airport.

For long-distance travel to the north, the terminal is 5km east of the centre on the Asia Hwy.

Sukhothai From 255B to 328B; six hours; departures every two hours.

Phitsanulok From 224B to 227B; five hours; frequent departures.

Chiang Mai From 403B to 806B; nine hours; frequent.

Train

Ayuthaya's train station is on the eastern banks of the Mae Nam Pa Sak and is an easy walk from the centre city via a short ferry ride (5B). Sŏrngtăaou to the guesthouse area should cost 50B. Services include the following:

Bangkok's Hualamphong station Ordinary, rapid and express trains, 15B, 20B and 315B; around 1½ hours; frequent morning and night departures.

Bangkok's Bang Sue station Ordinary, rapid and express trains, 15B, 20B and 315B; around 1½ hours; frequent morning and night departures. Convenient for the Th Khao San area.

Chiang Mai Ordinary, rapid and express trains, 586B, 856 and 1198B; six departures a day.

Pak Chong Ordinary, rapid and express trains, 23B, 73B and 130B; frequent. The nearest station to Khao Yai National Park.

Khon Kaen Ordinary, rapid and express trains, 173B, 265B and 375B; six hours; four daily.

Getting Around

Bikes can be rented at most guesthouses (50B). Túk-túk can be hired for the day to tour the sites (around 200B per hour); a trip within the city should be about 30B or 40B.

Lopburi

POP 26,500

This small, low-key town is a delightful respite from the rigours of the tourist trail. No aggressive túk-túk drivers, no grumpy guesthouse staff and few foreigners making you feel that you flew a long way to be with familiar faces. Lopburi is an ancient town with plenty of old ruins to prove its former occupation by almost every Southeast Asian kingdom: Dvaravati, Khmer and Ayuthaya. The old city is presently occupied by ordinary Thai life: noodle stands, motorcycle stores and, most importantly, a gang of monkeys. The city celebrates its resident monkeys with an annual festival during the last week of November.

Sights

Lopburi's old ruins are easy to walk to from the town centre and a 150B day pass (available at Phra Narai Ratchaniwet) allows entry to all sights.

Phra Narai Ratchaniwet MUSEUM
(Th Sorasak; admission 150B; ⌚museum 8.30am-4pm Wed-Sun, grounds 8am-5.30pm) This

former palace now museum is a good place to begin a tour of Lopburi. Built between 1665 and 1677, the palace was designed by French and Italian architects, creating an unusual blend of styles. Inside the grounds is the **Lopburi National Museum**, which contains an excellent collection of Lopburi period sculpture, as well as an assortment of Khmer, Dvaravati, U Thong and Ayuthaya art, plus traditional farm implements.

Prang Sam Yot TEMPLE
(Sacred Three Spires; Th Wichayen; admission 50B; ⌚8am-6pm) The most distinctive of Lopburi's ruins is Prang Sam Yot, which comprises three linked towers symbolising the Hindu Trimurti of Shiva, Vishnu and Brahma. Like any good Hindu shrine in this region, it was successfully converted to Buddhism with the addition of a few Lopburi-style Buddha images. This is also the resident monkeys' favourite hang-out place.

Wat Phra Si Ratana Mahathat TEMPLE
(Th Na Phra Kan; admission 50B; ⌚7am-5pm) Directly across from the train station, Wat Phra Si Ratana Mahathat is a large 13th-century Khmer temple that's worth a look.

Sleeping

Budget guesthouses are about all there is in Lopburi. In the old town most are old and basic, but they are within walking distance of the ruins.

TOP CHOICE **Noom Guest House** GUESTHOUSE $
(☎0 3642 7693; www.noomguesthouse.com; Th Phraya Kamjat; r 150-300B; ❄📶) Bamboo-roofed bungalows facing a leafy garden make this one of the more pleasant places to stay. Upstairs rooms have shared bathrooms. A sister guesthouse is around the corner.

Nett Hotel GUESTHOUSE $
(☎0 3641 1738; netthotel@hotmail.com; 17/1-2 Th Ratchadamnoen; r 300-550B; ❄📶) Still one of the best-value spots, the renovated rooms are clean and the location couldn't be more central. Cheaper rooms are fan-only and have cold-water showers.

Eating

Khao Tom Hor THAI
(cnr Th Na Phra Kan & Th Ratchadamnoen, dishes 30-80B) The busiest place in town offers excellent stir-fried dishes, including *pàd gàprow gài* (chicken stir-fried with basil). Service is speedy and efficient.

Teu THAI
(Th Pratoo Chai; dishes 40-70B; ⌚3pm-12.30am) To eat with the locals, pull up a plastic stool and sup on fantastic *gaang Ƃàh nêua* (spicy jungle curry with beef) and a slushy frozen beer. Seating is opposite the restaurant or inside, next to the chaotic kitchen. No roman script sign so look out for the big red sign.

Central Market MARKET
(off Th Ratchadamnoen & Th Surasongkhram; ⌚6am-5pm) Wander through the narrow alleyways and take in the sights and smells of this local market. Blood-red strawberries, orange prawns and silver fish are laid out alongside *kôw đom mùd* (rice wrapped in coconut leaves), *đa·go peu·ak* (taro custard with coconut milk), and *gài tôrt* (fried chicken). In the centre is a vegetarian pavilion.

Drinking

When it comes to drinking, options in the old town are limited to **Noom Guesthouse** (Th Phraya Kamjat), where expats cradle their Changs and Leos, or around the corner there is **Sahai Phanta** (Th Sorasak), a popular venue with its 'songs-for-life' house band. There's no English sign, so look for the giant 'Benmore' banner on the roof.

Information

Muang Narai Hospital (☎0 3661 6300 Th Pahonyohtin)

Post office (Th Phra Narai Maharat)

TAT office (☎0 3642 2768; Th Phra Narai Maharat; ⌚8.30am-4.30pm) An inconvenient 5km from the old town.

Getting There & Away

Lopburi's **bus station** (Th Naresuan) is nearly 2km outside of the old town. Services include:

Ayuthaya 40B; two hours; frequent departures.

Bangkok's Northern & Northeastern (Mo Chit) station 80B; three hours, frequent departures.

Suphanburi 65B; three hours; departures every 1½ hours. Head here for bus connections to Kanchanaburi.

Minivans leave from Th Na Phra Kan to Bangkok's **Victory Monument** (110B, frequent).

Lopburi's **train station** (Th Na Phra Kan) is in the old town. The train station has a left-luggage facility and some savvy travellers arrive early from Ayuthaya, stow their luggage for a few hour's visit and then hop on the train northward. There are frequent morning and early afternoon departures.

Services include:

Ayuthaya Ordinary, rapid and express trains, 13B, 20B and 310B; two hours.

Bangkok's Hualamphong station Ordinary, rapid and express trains, 28B, 50B and 344B; three to four hours.

Phitsanulok Ordinary, rapid and express trains, 49B, 99B and 393B.

Getting Around

Săhmlór go anywhere in old Lopburi for 30B. Sŏrngtăaou run a regular route between the old and new towns for 10B per person and can be used to travel between the bus station and the old town.

Phitsanulok

POP 84,000

Because of its convenient location on an important train route, many travellers use Phitsanulok as a base for visiting the ancient city of Sukhothai. As an attraction in itself, Phitsanulok (often abbreviated as 'Philok') boasts a famous Buddha and a few minor curiosities.

Sights

Wat Phra Si Ratana Mahathat TEMPLE

(6am-9pm) Known locally as Wat Yai, this famous temple contains the Phra Phuttha Chinnarat, regarded as one of the most beautiful and revered Buddha images in all of Thailand. This stunning bronze Buddha was cast in the 14th century in classic Sukhothai style, except for a unique detail: the flamelike halo that stretches from head to torso.

Sergeant Major Thawee Folk Museum MUSEUM

(26/43 Th Wisut Kasat; admission 50B; 8.30am-4.30pm) The Sergeant Major Thawee Folk Museum displays a remarkable collection of tools, textiles and photographs from the province. It is spread throughout five traditional-style buildings with well-groomed gardens. Nearby is the founder's other hobbies: a small Buddha-casting foundry and an aviary. The museum is located south of central Phitsanulok; a túk-túk here should cost about 60B.

Sleeping

Lithai Guest House GUESTHOUSE $

(0 5521 9626; 73 Th Phayalithai; r incl breakfast 220-460B;) These airy rooms don't have much character but they don't cost much either. Most have large en suite bathrooms with hot water, cable TV, plentiful furniture and a fridge. As well as breakfast, rates include free bottled water.

Kraisaeng Place HOTEL $

(0 5521 0509; 45 Th Thammabucha; r 350-450B;) An apartment-block hotel, Kraisaeng is a value find with well-equipped rooms, though a fair bit of traffic noise.

Eating

Night Bazaar THAI $

(mains 40-80B; 5pm-3am) The city is particularly obsessive about night markets - there are no fewer than three dotted throughout town. This is the most famous because of the riverfront restaurants specialising in *pàk bûng loy fáh* (literally 'floating-in-the-sky morning glory vine'). Cooks fire up a batch of *pàk bûng* in the wok and then fling it through the air to a waiting server who catches it on a plate. If you're lucky, you'll be here when a tour group is attempting the routine.

Rim Nan THAI $

(5/4 Th Phaya Sua; mains 20-35B; 9am-4pm) North of Wat Phra Si Ratana Mahathat, this is one of a few similar restaurants serving the Phitsanulok speciality *gŏoay·đĕe·o hôy kăh* (literally, 'legs-hanging' noodles). The name comes from the way customers sit on the floor facing the river, with their legs dangling below. There's no roman-script sign.

Ban Mai THAI $$

(93/30 Th Authong; mains 60-150B; 11am-2pm & 5-10pm;) Dinner at this local favourite is like a meal at your grandparents': opinionated conversation, frumpy furniture, and an overfed Siamese cat. Don't expect home cooking though: Ban Mai specialises in unusual dishes like *gaang pèt pèt yâhng* (curry of smoked duck) or *yam đà·krái* (lemongrass salad).

Drinking

Wood Stock BAR

(08 1785 1958; 148/22-23 Th Wisut Kasat; dishes 35-70B; 5pm-midnight) Combines funky 1960s- and '70s-era furniture, live music, and a cheap menu of *gàp glâam* (Thai-style nibbles).

Information

Internet shops dot the streets around the railway station and on the western bank of the river.

Krung Thai Bank (35 Th Naresuan; to 8pm) An after-hours exchange window.

Post office (Th Phuttha Bucha)

BUS SERVICES FROM PHITSANULOK

DESTINATION	FARE (B)	DURATION (HR)	FREQUENCY
Bangkok	224-380	5	hourly 7am-midnight
Chiang Rai	249-320	5	hourly 8am-midnight
Mae Sai	280-456	6	hourly 5.30am-midnight
Nan	238	6	two nightly departures
Mae Sot	210	5	two nightly departures
Chiang Mai	211-317	6	hourly 8am-midnight
Lampang	155-265	4	hourly 8am-midnight
Sukhothai	28-50	1	hourly 5.40am-6pm
Kamphaeng Phet	53-74	3	hourly 5am-6pm

TAT (☎0 5525 2742; 209/7-8 Th Borom Trailokanat; ⊙8.30am-4.30pm) Distributes a walking-tour map.

 Getting There & Away

Transport options out of Phitsanulok are good as it's a junction for several bus routes. Phitsanulok's **bus station** (☎0 5521 2090) is 2km east of town on Hwy 12. Minivans also depart from the bus terminal.

The **train station** (Th Ekathotsarot & Th Naresuan) is in the centre of town within walking distance of accommodation. Destinations include:

Bangkok 80B to 1164B; five to seven hours; 11 times daily.

Chiang Mai 143B to 1145B, seven to nine hours; six times daily.

 Getting Around

Rides on the town's Darth Vader-like săhmlór start at about 60B.

Sukhothai

POP 37,000

The Cambodians get irritated by such claims, but the ruins of Sukhothai are a mini version of the architectural styles found in Angkor. Considered the first independent Thai kingdom, Sukhothai emerged as the Khmer empire was crumbling in the 13th century and subsequently ruled over parts of the empire's western frontier for 150 years. The new Thai kingdom took artistic inspiration from its former overseers and the resulting city of temples is now a compact and pleasant collection of gravity-warped columns, serene Buddha figures and weed-sprouting towers.

Though Ayuthaya has a more interesting historical narrative, Sukhothai's ancient city is better preserved and architecturally more engaging. No surprise since Sukhothai (meaning 'Rising Happiness') is regarded as the blossoming of a Thai artistic sensibility.

The modern town of Sukhothai (often referred to as New Sukhothai; 12km from the ruins) is a standard, somewhat bland, provincial town but it is close and convenient.

Sights & Activities

SUKHOTHAI HISTORICAL PARK

Ranked as a World Heritage Site, the Sukhothai Historical Park (known in Thai as *'meuang kào'* or 'old city') comprises most of the ancient kingdom, which was surrounded by three concentric ramparts and two moats bridged by four gateways – important celestial geometry. Inside the old walls are the remains of 21 historical buildings; there are an additional 70 sites within a 5km radius. The ruins are divided into five geographic zones, each of which charges a 100B admission fee.

The historical park also hosts a beautiful version of Thailand's popular **Loi Krathong** festival in November.

CENTRAL ZONE

This is the historical park's main **zone** (admission 100B; ⊙6.30am-8pm, plus per bicycle/motorcycle 10/30B) and is home to what are arguably some of the park's most well-preserved and impressive ruins. An audio tour can be rented at the ticket booth for 150B. This zone is best reached from town by sŏrngtăaou. Once at the park, renting a bicycle is ideal; shops nearby rent bikes for 30B per day.

Ramkhamhaeng National Museum MUSEUM

(☎0 5561 2167; ⏲9am-4pm) This national museum is a good place to start an exploration of Sukhothai history and culture. The most impressive display is a replica of the famous Ramkhamhaeng inscription, said to be the earliest example of Thai writing.

Wat Mahathat TEMPLE

Wat Mahathat is the crown jewel of the old city and is one of the best examples of Sukhothai architecture, typified by the classic lotus-bud stupa that features a conical spire topping a square-sided structure on a three-tiered base. This vast assemblage, the largest in the city, once contained 198 *chedi,* as well as various chapels and sanctuaries. Some of the original Buddha images remain, including a 9m standing Buddha among the broken columns.

Wat Si Sawai TEMPLE

Wat Si Sawai, just south of Wat Mahathat, has three Khmer-style *praang* and a moat. From images found in the *chedi,* this was originally a Hindu temple, later retrofitted for Buddhism.

Wat Sa Si TEMPLE

Wat Sa Si is a classically simple Sukhothai-style temple set on an island.

Wat Trapang Thong TEMPLE

Wat Trapang Thong, next to the museum, is reached by a footbridge crossing a large, lotus-filled pond. It remains in use today as a temple.

NORTHERN ZONE

This **zone** (admission 100B, plus per bicycle/motorcycle 10/30B; ⏲7.30am-5.30pm) is located 500m north of the old city walls and is easily reached by bicycle.

Wat Si Chum TEMPLE

This wat is northwest of the old city and contains an impressive 15m-high brick-and-stucco seated Buddha. This Buddha's elegant, tapered fingers are much photographed.

Wat Phra Phai Luang TEMPLE

Somewhat isolated to the north of the old city, Wat Phra Pai Luang is similar in style to Wat Si Sawai.

WESTERN ZONE

This **zone** (admission 100B, plus bicycle/motorcycle 10/30B; ⏲7.30am-5.30pm) is 2km east of the old city walls but contains largely featureless ruins. A bicycle or motorcycle is necessary to explore this zone.

Wat Saphan Hin TEMPLE

Located on the crest of a hill, Stone Bridge Temple offers a fine view of the Sukhothai

Sukhothai Historical Park

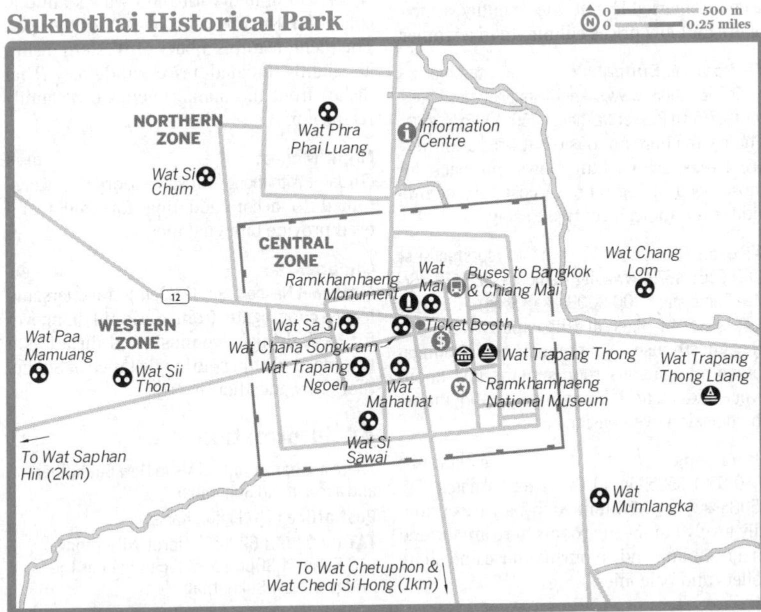

ruins to the southeast and the mountains to the north and south. All that remains of the original temple are a few *chedi* and the ruined *wíhăhn,* consisting of two rows of laterite columns flanking a 12.5m-high standing Buddha image on a brick terrace.

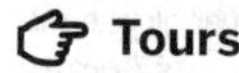 Tours

Cycling Sukhothai BICYCLE TOURS
(☎0 5561 2519; www.cycling-sukhothai.com; half/full day 600/750B, sunset tour 300B) A Belgian cycling enthusiast offers a variety of fun and educational bicycle tours of the area.

Sleeping

At Home Sukhothai GUESTHOUSE $
(☎0 5561 0172; www.athomesukhothai.com; 184/1 Th Vichien Chamnong; r incl breakfast 400-800B; ❄@🛜) Located in the 50-year-old childhood home of the proprietor, this attractive structure could easily pass as a newborn after recent renovations. The simple but comfortable rooms really do feel like home. There's a lotus pond out back, and virtually every other service, from food to Thai massage, in front.

Ban Thai BUDGET HOTEL $
(☎0 5561 0163; banthai_guesthouse@yahoo.com; 38 Th Prawet Nakhon; r 200-500B; ❄@🛜) Centred around a garden, this mish-mash of rooms and tiny bungalows is among the more popular budget places in town. Rooms aren't remarkable but the friendly atmosphere and low prices culminate in a winner.

TR Room & Bungalow GUESTHOUSE $
(☎0 5561 1663; www.sukhothaibudgetguesthouse.com; 27/5 Th Prawet Nakhon; r 250-400B; ❄@🛜) The rooms here are basic but tidy, and there are five spacious bungalows out back for those needing leg room. A cosy terrace provides even more incentive to stay.

4T Guesthouse GUESTHOUSE $$
(☎0 5561 4679; www.4tguesthouse.ob.tc; 122 Soi Mae Ramphan; r 300-900B; ❄@🛜≋) Hardly a leaf is out of place at this expansive resort-like guesthouse. A smorgasbord of bungalows and spacious rooms spans just about every budget, and the swimming pool makes the decision even easier.

Hung Jeng GUESTHOUSE $
(☎0 5561 0585; 44/10 Th Prawet Nakhon; r 150-350B; ❄@🛜) Maintained by an exceptionally lovely family, the rooms here are located in a rambling and colourful house and share toilets and balconies.

J&J Guest House GUESTHOUSE $
(☎0 5562 0095; www.jjguest-house.com; 12 Th Kuhasuwan; r 500-600B; ❄@🛜) Located in a tidy garden by the river, the eight bungalows are new, cool and relatively spacious.

Sabaidee House GUESTHOUSE $
(☎0 5561 6303; www.sabaideehouse.com; 81/7 Moo 1 Tambol Banklouy; r 200-600B; ❄@🛜) Having graduated from homestay status, this cheery guesthouse boasts five attractive bungalows and cheaper accommodation in the main house. Free bicycles and transport from the bus station. Sabaidee is located 1.5km west of the Mae Nam Yom, on a side street about 200m before the intersection with Rte 101 – look for the sign.

Eating & Drinking

Thai towns love to claim a signature dish and Sukhothai weighs in with its own version of *kŭaytĭaw* (noodle soup), featuring a sweet broth, pork, ground peanuts and thinly sliced green beans. The dish is available at **Jayhae** (Th Jarot Withithong; dishes 25-40B; ⏰7am-4pm) and **Ta Pui** (Th Jarot Withithong; dishes 25-35B; ⏰7am-3pm), located across from each other on Th Jarot Withithong, about 1.3km west of the Mae Nam Yom.

Dream Cafe THAI $$
(86/1 Th Singhawat; dishes 80-150B; ⏰lunch & dinner) Decorated with the owner's antique collection, Dream Cafe is a feast for the eyes. The menu features a bevy of Western dishes at slightly inflated prices and tasty Thai dishes from the management's own family recipe box.

Night Market THAI $
(Th Jarot Withithong) Most vendors are accustomed to accommodating foreigners and even provide bilingual menus.

Chopper Bar BAR
(Th Prawet Nakhon; ⏰5-12.30pm) Travellers and locals congregate from dusk till hangover for food, drinks, live music and flirtation at this place, within spitting distance of Sukhothai's tiny guesthouse strip.

Information

There are banks with ATMs in New Sukhothai and a few in Old Sukhothai.

Post office (Th Nikhon Kasem)

TAT (☎0 5561 6228; Th Jarot Withithong; ⏰8.30am-4.30pm) New location near the bridge in New Sukhothai.

WORTH A TRIP

THE EMPIRE'S SUBURBS

The Sukhothai empire expanded its administrative centre and monument-building efforts to Si Satchanalai and Chaliang, two satellite cities about 70km away. Today the historic park containing the remaining temple ruins is set amidst rolling hills and offers a more pastoral experience than Old Sukhothai. An all-inclusive admission fee (220B) allows entry to Si Satchananalai, Chaliang's Wat Chao Chan and the Si Satchanalai Centre for Study & Preservation of Sangkalok Kilns.

Si Satchanalai

This historic **zone** (admission 100B; ⏲8.30am-5pm) covers roughly 720 hectares and is surrounded by a 12m-wide moat along the banks of Mae Nam Yom. An information centre distributes useful maps, and bicycles can be rented (20B) near the entrance gate. **Wat Chang Lom** has a *chedi* surrounded by Buddha statues set in niches and guarded by the remains of well-preserved elephant buttresses. Climb to the top of the hill supporting **Wat Khao Phanom Phloeng** for a view over the town and river. **Wat Chedi Jet Thaew** has a group of stupas in classic Sukhothai style.

Chaliang

Chaliang is an older city site, dating to the 11th century, and sits 1km from Si Satchanalai. **Wat Phra Si Ratana Mahathat** (admission 20B) contains a classic walking Buddha, a hallmark of the Sukhothai era. **Wat Chao Chan** (admission 100B; ⏲8am-5pm) has a large Khmer-style tower probably constructed during the reign of Khmer King Jayavarman VII (1181-1217). The roofless *wíhăhn* contains the laterite outlines of a large standing Buddha that has all but melted away from exposure.

The Kilns

The Si Satchanalai-Chaliang area was famous for its beautiful pottery, much of which was exported. The Chinese and Indonesians were once keen collectors, and some fine specimens can still be seen in the National Museum in Jakarta, Indonesia. **Si Satchanalai Centre for Study & Preservation of Sangkhalok Kilns** (admission 100B; ⏲9am-4pm), 5km northwest of Si Satchanalai, has large excavated kilns and intact pottery samples documenting the area's historical pottery traditions.

Getting There & Away

Si Satchanalai-Chaliang Historical Park is off Rte 101 between Sawankhalok and new Si Satchanalai. From Sukhothai, take a Si Satchanalai bus (46B, two hours, 11am) and ask to get off at *'meuang gòw'* (old city). The last bus back to New Sukhothai leaves at 4.30pm.

Tourist police (☎1155; Sukhothai Historical Park)

ℹ Getting There & Away

The bus station is 1km northwest of the town centre on Hwy 101. Services include the following:

Bangkok 255B to 380B; seven hours; frequent.

Chiang Mai 218B; six hours; frequent.

Phitsanulok 28B to 39B; one hour; frequent.

Sawankhalok 19B to 27B; one hour; every hour.

Si Satchanalai 46B; 1½ hours; one morning departure.

Mae Sot Minivan departures 130B; three hours; every two hours 9am-4pm.

Alternatively, if you're staying near the historical park, buses for Bangkok (262B to 380B, six hours, 9am and 8.20pm) and Chiang Mai (300B, five hours, frequent departures from 7.30am to 8.30pm) can be boarded near Vitoon Guesthouse.

ℹ Getting Around

Sŏrngtăaou run between New Sukhothai and Sukhothai Historical Park (20B, 30 minutes, 6am to 5.30pm), leaving from Th Jarot Withithong near Poo Restaurant.

Transport from the bus terminal into New Sukhothai costs 60B by charter. Motorbike taxis charge 40B. If going directly to Old Sukhothai, sŏrngtăaou charge 180B and motorcycle taxis 150B. A ride by săhmlór around New Sukhothai should cost no more than 40B.

Kamphaeng Phet

POP 30,000

An easy detour from the tourist trail, Kamphaeng Phet (Diamond Wall) is a peaceful provincial town known for its whitewashed city walls. Historically it played a protective role on the front lines of defence for the Sukhothai kingdom. It's a nice place to spend a day or so wandering around the ruins and experiencing daily Thai life.

Sights

Kamphaeng Phet Historical Park HISTORIC SITE
(☎0 5571 1921; admission 100-150B, plus bicycle/motorbike 10/20B; ⊙8am-5pm) A Unesco World Heritage Site, this historical park contains a number of temple ruins dating back to the 14th century. One sector of the historical park is the old city, sheltered within the town's namesake 'Diamond Wall'. Wat Phra Kaew is the dominant but subdued feature here.

The majority of ruins are 1.5km north of the city. Noteworthy is **Wat Phra Sri Iriyabot**, which features the shattered remains of standing, sitting, walking and reclining Buddha images.

Kamphaeng Phet National Museum MUSEUM
(☎0 5571 1570; Th Pindramri; admission 100B; ⊙9am-noon & 1-4pm Wed-Sun) This national museum has the usual survey of Thai art periods. Upstairs is a collection of artefacts from the Kamphaeng Phet area including an immense Shiva statue that is the largest bronze Hindu sculpture in the country.

Sleeping & Eating

A busy night market sets up every evening near the river, just north of the Navarat Hotel, and there are some cheap restaurants near the roundabout.

Three J Guest House GUESTHOUSE $
(☎0 5571 3129; 79 Th Rachavitee; r 300-700B;) Mr Charin is the congenial host of this backpackers' lodge. Each of the bungalows is different, and the cheaper ones share a clean bathroom. Bicycles and motorbikes are available for rent.

Bamee Chakangrao THAI $
(Th Ratchadamnoen; dishes 25-30B ⊙8.30am-3pm) This restaurant is famous for its freshly made *bàmèe* (wheat-and-egg noodles), a speciality of Kamphaeng Phet. No English sign.

Getting There & Away

The bus station is 1km west of Mae Nam Ping and serves the following destinations:

Bangkok Air-conditioned buses 210B to 315B; five hours; hourly.

Sukhothai 70B; 1½ hours; hourly.

Phitsanulok 56 to 78B; 2½ hours; hourly.

Mae Sot 140B; 2½ hours; 8am to 6pm.

If coming from Sukhothai or Phitsanulok ask to be let off in the old city or at the roundabout on Th Tesa to save a sŏrngtăaou back to town.

Red sŏrngtăaou (15B per person) go from the bus station to the roundabout across the river. From there take a săhmlór anywhere in town for 20B to 30B. Motorcycle taxis from the bus station to most hotels downtown cost 40B.

NORTHERN THAILAND

Forming the crown of the country is a mountainous region loved for its lush forest and unique cultural and natural attractions. This cascade of peaks and valleys unites northern Thailand with the peoples and the cultures of neighbouring Myanmar, Laos and southwestern China. The region's ancient kingdom, known as Lanna Thai (Million Thai Rice Fields), established its capital in Chiang Mai, which retains it connection to the past. Other wanderers, such as the autonomous hill-tribe peoples, traversed the range, limited only by altitude rather than political boundaries.

Chiang Mai

POP 174,000

Chiang Mai is a cultural darling: it is a cool place to kick back and relax, the streets of the old city are filled with monks and motorcycle-driving housewives, bookshops outnumber glitzy shopping centres and the region's Lanna heritage is worn with pride. For culture vultures, Chiang Mai is a vibrant classroom to study Thai language, cooking, meditation and massage.

The old city of Chiang Mai is a neat square bounded by a moat and remnants of a medieval-style wall built 700 years ago to defend against Burmese invaders. A furious stream of traffic flows around the old city, but inside the old district narrow *soi* lead to a quiet world of family-run guesthouses and leafy gardens.

Th Moon Muang, along the east moat, is the main traveller centre. Intersecting with Th Moon Muang, Th Tha Phae runs east from the exterior of the moat towards the Mae Nam Ping. Once it crosses the river, the road is renamed Th Charoen Muang and eventually arrives at the main post office and train station.

Finding your way around Chiang Mai is fairly simple. A copy of Nancy Chandler's *Map Guide to Chiang Mai* is a good investment; pick up a copy at bookshops or guesthouses.

Sights

Chiang Mai's primary attractions are the old city's historic and holy temples that show off distinctive northern Thai architecture. A few stand-out features include intricate carved gables, colourful exterior mosaics, Singha lions guarding the entrances and octagonal high-based *chedi*.

Wat Phra Singh TEMPLE

(Th Singharat; donations appreciated; ⏲6am-6pm) Wat Phra Singh is the star amid the old city's famous temples and is a perfect example of Lanna architecture. Established in 1345, it houses the city's revered Buddha image, Phra Singh, which is the focal point for the religious festivities of Songkran (Thai New Year) in mid-April.

Wat Chedi Luang TEMPLE

(Th Phra Pokklao; donations appreciated; ⏲6am-6pm) Wat Chedi Luang contains the ruins of a huge *chedi* dating from 1441 that was believed to be one of the tallest structures in Chiang Mai at the time. Little is known about its destruction: either by an earthquake or cannon fire in the 16th or 18th century. A partial restoration has preserved the 'ruined' look. The venerable Emerald Buddha, now housed in Bangkok's Wat Phra Kaew, occupied the eastern niche here in 1475. The temple's other attraction is the *làk meuang* (city pillar, believed to house the city's guardian deity) enshrined in a small building to the left of the compound's main entrance. In May, the building is opened to the public for merit-making.

Wat Phan Tao TEMPLE

(Th Phra Pokklao; donations appreciated) Near Wat Chedi Luang, this small temple is hardly historic but immensely pretty with its old teak *wíhăhn* constructed entirely of moulded teak panels fitted together and supported by 28 gargantuan teak pillars. The *wíhăhn* also features *naga* (mythical serpent-being) bargeboards inset with coloured mirror mosaic.

Wat Chiang Man TEMPLE

(Th Ratchaphakhinai; donations appreciated) Wat Chiang Man is considered to be the oldest wat within the city walls and was erected by King Mengrai, Chiang Mai's founder, in 1296. Two famous Buddha images (Phra Sila and Phra Satang Kamanee, or the Crystal Buddha) are kept here in the *wíhăhn* to the right of the main *bòht* (central sanctuary) The Crystal Buddha is believed to have the power to bring seasonal rains.

Wat Suan Dok TEMPLE

(Th Suthep; donations appreciated) West of the old city, Wat Suan Dok is not Chiang Mai's most beautiful temple but its collection of whitewashed *chedi* framed by the nearby mountains of Doi Suthep and Doi Pui are a favourite photographic subject. The temple also hosts a Buddhist university and conducts popular meditation retreats (see the boxed text, p689).

Chiang Mai City Arts & Cultural Centre MUSEUM

(Th Ratwithi; admission 90B; ⏲8.30am-5.30pm Tue-Sun) Conveniently located in the old city, the Chiang Mai City Arts & Cultural Centre is a municipally funded introduction to the city's history with surprisingly engaging displays.

Chiang Mai National Museum MUSEUM

(☎0 5322 1308; www.thailandmuseum.com; off Rte 11/Th Superhighway; admission 100B; ⏲9am-4pm Wed-Sun) Less modern but more academically important is the Chiang Mai National Museum, northwest of the old city. The best curated exhibits are the Lanna art sections, which display Buddha images in all styles and periods.

Wat Phra That Doi Suthep TEMPLE

(admission 30B) Perched on a hilltop 16km northwest of town, Wat Phra That Doi Suthep is one of the north's most sacred temples. The site was 'chosen' by an honoured Buddha relic mounted on the back of a white elephant; the animal wandered until it stopped (and died) on Doi Suthep, making this the relic's new home. A snaking road

SERVING TIME IN THE MASSAGE CHAIR

When you tire of sightseeing in the old city, just duck into the women's prison for a massage. Seriously. The **Chiang Mai Women's Prison Massage Centre** (100 Th Ratwithi; foot/traditional massage 150-180B; ⏲8am-4.30pm) offers body and foot massages by inmates participating in a job-training program.

Chiang Mai

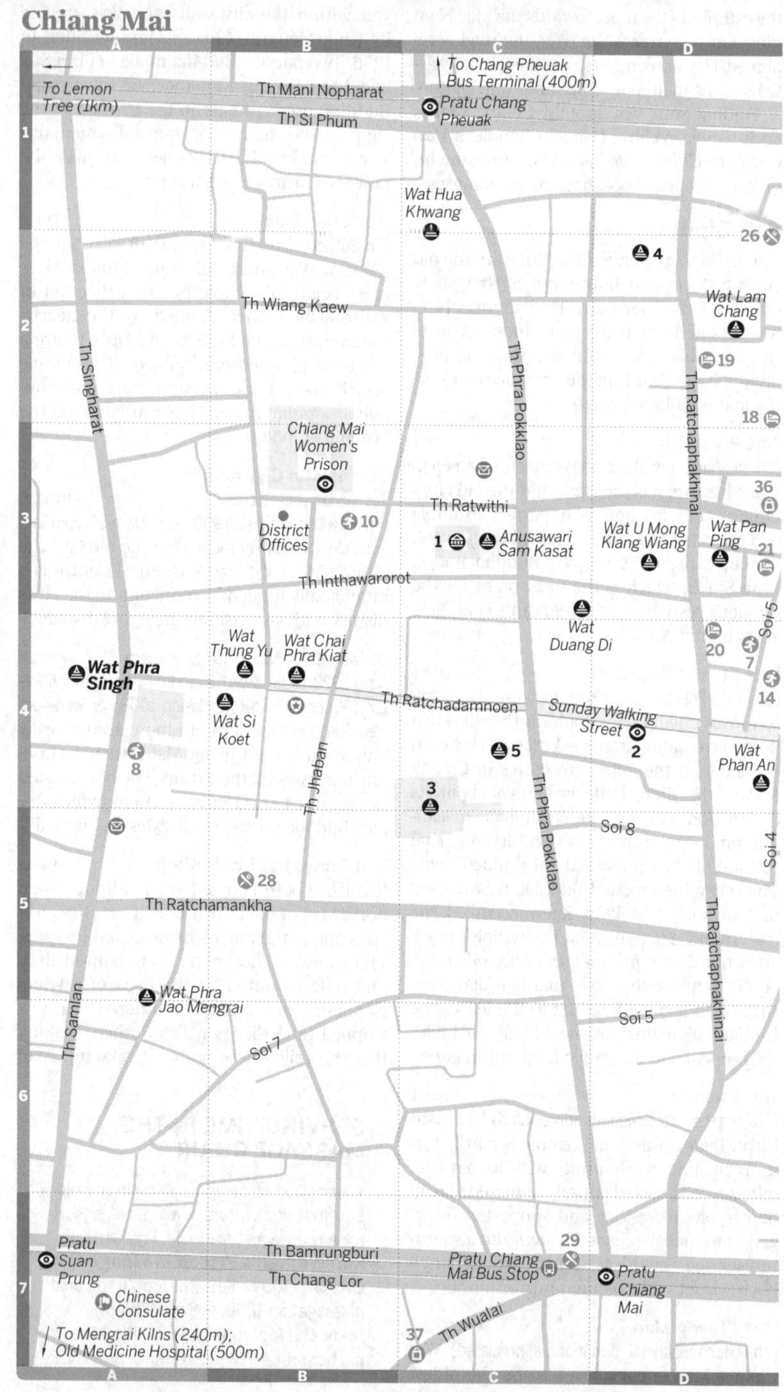

To Lemon Tree (1km)
Th Mani Nopharat
Th Si Phum
To Chang Pheuak Bus Terminal (400m)
Pratu Chang Pheuak
Wat Hua Khwang
26
4
Wat Lam Chang
19
18
Th Wiang Kaew
Th Singharat
Th Phra Pokklao
Th Ratchaphakhinai
Chiang Mai Women's Prison
Th Ratwithi
36
District Offices
10
1
Anusawari Sam Kasat
Wat U Mong Klang Wiang
Wat Pan Ping
21
Th Inthawarorot
Wat Duang Di
20
Soi 5
7
14
Wat Thung Yu
Wat Chai Phra Kiat
Wat Phra Singh
Th Ratchadamnoen
Sunday Walking Street
2
Wat Si Koet
5
Wat Phan An
8
3
Th Jhaban
Soi 8
Soi 4
28
Th Ratchamankha
Wat Phra Jao Mengrai
Th Samlan
Soi 7
Soi 5
29
Pratu Suan Prung
Th Bamrungburi
Th Chang Lor
Pratu Chiang Mai Bus Stop
Pratu Chiang Mai
Chinese Consulate
To Mengrai Kilns (240m); Old Medicine Hospital (500m)
37
Th Wualai

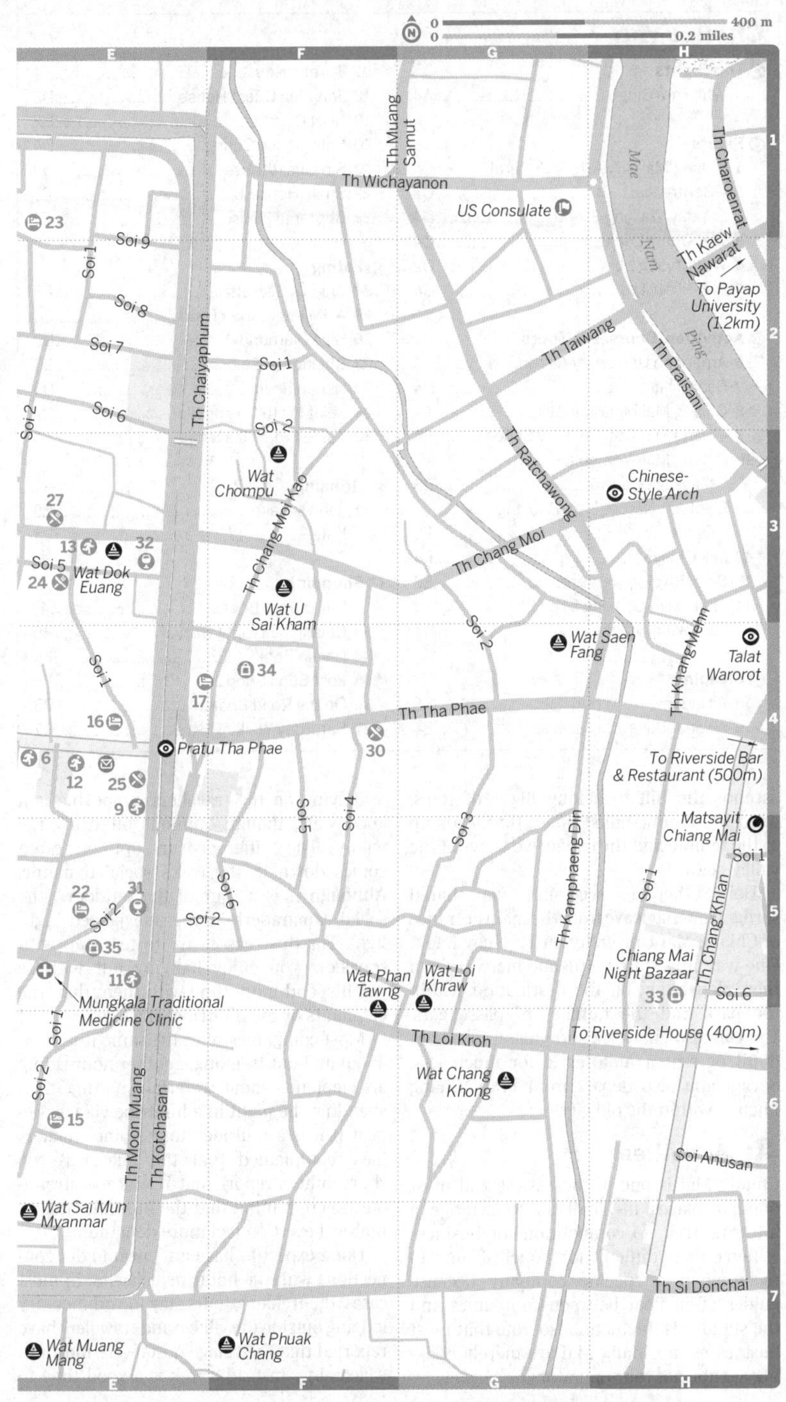

0
400 m
0
0.2 miles
E
F
G
H
Th Muang Samut
Th Wichayanon
US Consulate
Mae
Nam
Ping
Th Charoenrat
Th Kaew Nawarat
To Payap University (1.2km)
23
Soi 9
Soi 1
Soi 8
Soi 7
Th Chaiyaphum
Soi 1
Th Taiwang
Th Praisani
Soi 2
Soi 6
Soi 2
Wat Chompu
Th Ratchawong
Chinese-Style Arch
27
13
32
Soi 5
24
Wat Dok Euang
Th Chang Moi Kao
Th Chang Moi
Wat U Sai Kham
Soi 2
Wat Saen Fang
Th Khang Mehn
Talat Warorot
Soi 1
34
17
16
Th Tha Phae
Pratu Tha Phae
6
12
25
9
30
To Riverside Bar & Restaurant (500m)
Soi 5
Soi 4
Soi 3
Matsayit Chiang Mai
Soi 1
22
31
Soi 2
Soi 6
Soi 2
Th Kamphaeng Din
Soi 1
35
11
Wat Phan Tawng
Wat Loi Khraw
Chiang Mai Night Bazaar
Th Chang Khlan
33
Soi 6
Mungkala Traditional Medicine Clinic
Soi 1
Th Loi Kroh
To Riverside House (400m)
Soi 2
Wat Chang Khong
15
Th Moon Muang
Th Kotchasan
Soi Anusan
Wat Sai Mun Myanmar
Th Si Donchai
Wat Muang Mang
Wat Phuak Chang
1
2
3
4
5
6
7

Chiang Mai

Top Sights

Wat Phra Singh ... A4

Sights

1 Chiang Mai City Arts & Cultural Centre ... C3
2 Sunday Walking Street ... D4
3 Wat Chedi Luang ... C4
4 Wat Chiang Man ... D2
5 Wat Phan Tao ... C4

Activities, Courses & Tours

6 American University Alumni ... E4
7 Baan Thai ... D4
8 Chiang Mai Mountain Biking ... A4
9 Chiang Mai Thai Cookery School ... E4
10 Chiang Mai Women's Prison Massage Centre ... B3
11 Elephant Nature Park Booking Office ... E5
12 Lek Chaiya ... E4
13 Siam River Adventures ... E3
14 Thai Farm Cooking School Booking Office ... D4

Sleeping

15 All in 1 ... E6
16 Awanahouse ... E4
17 Daret's House ... E4
18 Jonadda Guest House ... D2
19 RCN Court ... D2
20 Safe House Court ... D4
21 Siri Guesthouse ... D3
22 Smile House 1 ... E5
23 Supreme House ... E1

Eating

24 Angel's Secrets ... E3
25 AUM Vegetarian Food ... E4
26 Blue Diamond ... D2
27 Chiangmai Saloon ... E3
28 Heuan Phen ... B5
29 Talat Pratu Chiang Mai ... C7
30 Taste From Heaven ... F4

Drinking

31 John's Place ... E5
32 Kafe ... E3

Shopping

Backstreet Books ... (see 34)
33 Chiang Mai Night Bazaar ... H5
34 Gecko Books ... F4
35 Lost Book Shop ... E5
36 On the Road Books ... D3
37 Saturday Walking Street ... C7

ascends the hill to a long flight of steps, lined by ceramic-tailed *naga,* that leads up to the temple and the expansive views of the valley below.

Doi Suthep is accessible via shared sŏrngtăaou that leave from the main entrance of Chiang Mai University on Th Huay Kaew. One-way fares start at 40B and increase from there depending on the destination within the park and the number of passengers. You can also charter a sŏrngtăaou for about 600B or rent a motorcycle for much less. Sŏrngtăaou also depart from Pratu Chang Pheuak within the old city.

Activities

Chiang Mai is one of the easiest and most popular places in Thailand to arrange a hill-tribe trek, so competition for business is fierce. It is difficult for Lonely Planet to recommend a specific company because guides often float between companies and the standards fluctuate. Also note that most businesses in Chiang Mai are merely booking agents, not tour operators.

Relying on the travellers' grapevine is a good start, though opinions often diverge wildly. The difference in opinion often comes down to the trek's social dynamic. Although it is a tour of the outdoors, the social camaraderie is the unexpected highlight. For this reason, try to team up with travellers you enjoy hanging out with as you'll spend more time with them than the elephants or the hill-tribe villagers.

Most companies offer the same itinerary: about an hour trekking, another hour riding an elephant, some waterfall-spotting then spending the night in a hill-tribe village. Repeat if it is a multiday tour. Some trekkers have complained that the hike was too short, others report that it was too strenuous. Keep in mind that the humidity makes physical exertion feel more demanding.

Don't expect to have any meaningful connections with the hill-tribe villagers; in most cases, the trekking tours stay in rudimentary lodging outside the village and travellers have reported that the village hosts were most unwelcoming. Instead a trek is a good time to get to know Thailand through the Thai guide, who is usually young and charismatic. If you want meaningful interaction with hill-tribe villagers, donate your time to one of the non-profits working with these communities; see Volunteering (p783) for more information.

We don't advise prebooking in Bangkok as the potential for rip-off is too great. Instead shop around locally to find the lowest commission rates.

It is also possible to go trekking in Mae Hong Son and Chiang Rai; the latter has trekking companies with an economic and educational development component.

Chiang Mai has developed a fairly sophisticated soft-adventure scene for travellers looking for more of a workout than the hill-tribe treks.

Chiang Mai Mountain Biking MOUNTAIN BIKING
(☎08 1024 7046; www.mountainbikingchiangmai.com; 1 Th Samlan; tours 1450-2700B) Guided mountain-biking tours through Doi Suthep National Park.

Click & Travel CYCLING
(☎0 5328 1553; www.clickandtravelonline.com; tours 950-1300B) Bicycle tours of cultural sights in Chiang Mai.

Elephant Nature Park ELEPHANT SANCTUARY
(☎0 5320 8246; www.elephantnaturepark.org; 1 Soi 1, Th Ratchamankha; full-day tour 2500B) Semi-wild sanctuary for abused or retired elephants; tours include watching the herd and bathing the animals.

Peak ADVENTURE TOURS
(☎0 5380 0567; www.thepeakadventure.com; tours 1500-2500B) Variety adventure tours, from white-water rafting and trekking to rock climbing and abseiling.

Siam River Adventures RAFTING
(☎08 9515 1917; www.siamrivers.com; Kona Café, 17 Th Ratwithi; tours from 1800B) White-water rafting and kayaking on Mae Nam Taeng.

Courses

Cooking

Cooking classes typically include a tour of a local market, hands-on cooking instruction and a recipe booklet. Classes start at 1000B and are held at either an in-town location for those with limited time or at an out-of-town garden setting for more ambience. There are dozens of schools.

Baan Thai COOKING
(☎0 5335 7339; www.baanthaicookery.com; 11 Soi 5, Th Ratchadamnoen)

Chiang Mai Thai Cookery School COOKING
(☎0 5320 6388; www.thaicookeryschool.com; booking office 47/2 Th Moon Muang)

MEDITATION COURSES & RETREATS

The seekers and the curious often come to Thailand to explore the spiritual discipline of meditation.

Bangkok's **Wat Mahathat** (Map p654; ☎0 2222 6011; Th Maharat; ⊙courses 7am, 1pm & 6pm, three hours; donations appreciated) offers meditation instruction as a religious complement to a sight-seeing tour of Ko Ratanakosin's famous temples.

The sacred city of Chiang Mai is home to **Wat Suan Dok** (see p685), which conducts monthly meditation retreats.

Female nuns are the primary residents at **Daen Maha Mongkol Meditation Centre** (Hwy 323, Sai Yok district, Kanchanaburi), a forest temple outside of Kanchanaburi. A British woman runs English-language meditation sessions (4am & 6pm; two hours; donations appreciated). The centre is off Hwy 323, 12km from the Tiger Temple, and is well signposted. By train, get off at Maha Mongkol station.

Wat Pa Nanachat (www.watpahnanachat.org), in the northeastern town Ubon Ratchathani, was founded by renowned forest monk Phra Ajan Chah. The temple is geared toward serious monastic trainees who are non-Thai Buddhists and English is the primary language.

Thailand's most famous retreat is run by **Wat Suanmok** (Wat Suan Mokkhaphalaram; www.suanmokkh-idh.org), near the southern town of Chaiya. It is a forest temple founded by Ajahn Buddhadasa Bhikkhu.

You can merge your beach needs with your spiritual needs at Ko Pha-Ngan's **Wat Khao Tham** (www.watkowtahm.org). Periodic meditation retreats are held by an American-Australian couple.

THAILAND'S HILL-TRIBE COMMUNITIES

Thailand's hill-tribe communities (referred to in Thai as *chao khao*, literally 'mountain people') are ethnic minorities who have traditionally lived in the country's mountainous frontier. Most tribes migrated from Tibet and parts of China some 200 years ago and settled along Southeast Asia's mountain belt from Myanmar to Vietnam. The Tribal Research Institute in Chiang Mai recognises 10 different hill tribes, but there may be up to 20 in Thailand.

Hill-Tribe Groups

The **Karen** is the largest hill-tribe group in Thailand and number about 47% of the total tribal population. They tend to live in lowland valleys and practise crop rotation rather than swidden agriculture. Their numbers and proximity to the mainstream society has made them the most integrated and financially successful of the hill-tribe groups. Thickly woven V-neck tunics of various colours are typically worn. There are four distinct Karen groups – the Skaw (White), Pwo, Pa-O (Black) and Kayah (Red).

The **Hmong** are Thailand's second-largest hill-tribe group and are especially numerous in Chiang Mai province, with smaller enclaves in the other northern Thai provinces. They usually live on mountain peaks or plateaus above 1000m. Tribespeople wear simple black jackets and indigo or black baggy trousers (White Hmong) with striped borders or indigo skirts (Blue Hmong) and silver jewellery. Sashes may be worn around the waist, and embroidered aprons draped front and back.

The **Akha** are among the poorest of Thailand's ethnic minorities and live mainly in Chiang Mai and Chiang Rai provinces, along mountain ridges or steep slopes 1000m to 1400m in altitude. They are regarded as skilled farmers but are often displaced from arable land by government intervention. Their traditional garb is a headdress of beads, feathers and dangling silver ornaments.

Other minority groups include the Lisu, Lahu and Mien.

Village Etiquette

The minority tribes have managed to maintain their own distinct cultural identity despite increased interaction with the majority culture, conversion to Christianity or Buddhism and adoption of second-hand clothing instead of traditional garb. If you're planning on visiting hill-tribe villages, talk to your guide about dos and don'ts.

» Always ask permission before taking photos, especially at private moments inside dwellings. Many traditional belief systems view photography with suspicion.

» Show respect for religious symbols and rituals. Don't touch totems at village entrances or sacred items. Don't participate in ceremonies unless invited to join.

» Avoid cultivating a tradition of begging, especially among children. Instead talk to your guide about donating to a local school.

» Avoid public nudity and be careful not to undress near an open window where village children might be able to peep in.

» Don't flirt with members of the opposite sex unless you plan to marry them. Don't drink or do drugs with the villagers; altered states sometimes lead to culture clashes.

» Smile at villagers even if they stare at you; ask your guide how to say 'hello' in the tribal language.

» Avoid public displays of affection, which in some traditional systems is viewed as offensive to the spirit world.

» Don't interact with the villagers' livestock; these creatures are valuable possessions not curiosities. Also avoid interacting with jungle animals, which may be viewed as visiting spirits.

» Don't litter.

» Adhere to the same feet taboos of Thai culture (see the boxed text on p775).

Thai Farm Cooking School COOKING
(☎08 7174 9285; www.thaifarmcooking.com; booking office, 2/2 Soi 5, Th Ratchadamnoen)

Language

Being a university town, Chiang Mai fosters continuing education opportunities in Thai language.

Payap University LANGUAGE
(http://ic.payap.ac.th; Th Kaew Nawarat; course from 7500B) Intensive Thai language courses and academic culture studies.

American University Alumni LANGUAGE
(AUA; ☎0 5327 8407; www.learnthaiinchiangmai.com; 73 Th Ratchadamnoen; course 4200B) Six weeks of structured Thai-language coursework at different fluency levels.

Massage

Lek Chaiya TRADITIONAL MASSAGE
(☎0 5327 8325; www.nervetouch.com; 27-29 Th Ratchadamnoen; course from 5000B) Specialises in *jàp sên* (similar to acupressure) and the use of medicinal herbs.

Old Medicine Hospital TRADITIONAL MASSAGE
(OMH; ☎0 5327 5085; www.thaimassageschool.ac.th; 78/1 Soi Siwaka Komarat, Th Wualai; courses 6000B) A traditional northern Thai program with two 10-day courses a month. Classes tend to be large during the months of December to February.

Muay Thai (Thai Boxing)

Lanna Muay Thai MUAY THAI
(Kiatbusaba; ☎0 5389 2102; www.lannamuaythai.com; 161 Soi Chiang Khian; day/month courses 400/8000B) A boxing camp northwest of town that offers authentic *muay thai* instruction to foreigners as well as Thais. 1998 Lumphini champion boxer Parinya Kiatbusaba (also a *kàter·i*, or transvestite) trained here.

Festivals & Events

Flower Festival CULTURAL
(early February) Celebrating Chiang Mai's agricultural bounty, this festival features a parade of flower-covered floats, beauty contest and dance performances.

Songkran CULTURAL
(mid-April) Celebrate the Thai New Year in wet and wild Chiang Mai.

Loi Krathong CULTURAL
(late October to early November) In Chiang Mai this national festival is known as Yi Peng and is celebrated by launching cylindrical hot-air balloons as well as candle-lit miniature boats.

Sleeping

A concentration of guesthouses can be found in the northeastern corner of the old city on Soi 7 and Soi 9 off Th Moon Muang. Most guesthouses make their 'rice and curry' from booking trekking tours and reserve rooms for those customers. Some guesthouses will arrange free transport from the bus/train station with advance warning and most have free wi-fi.

TOP CHOICE **Awanahouse** GUESTHOUSE $
(☎0 5341 9005; www.awanahouse.com; 7 Soi 1, Th Ratchadamnoen; r 225-850B; ❄@≋) What started out as a small guesthouse has grown into a multi-storey apartment-style building on a quiet *soi*. Awana is a bit institutional, but has large and bright rooms. The cheapest rooms have fans and shared bathrooms.

Safe House Court GUESTHOUSE $
(☎0 5341 8955; www.safehousecourt.com; 178 Th Ratchaphakhinai; r 350-550B; ❄@ᯤ) A cut above the other cheapies, Safe House Court has a leafy location, bright rooms and friendly service.

Smile House 1 GUESTHOUSE $
(☎0 5320 8661; www.smileguesthouse.com; 5 Soi 2, Th Ratchamankha; r 300-1000B; ❄≋) A little backpacker village flourishes around an old Thai house here. It's tucked away in a small nook of the old city. It's popular with backpackers for lounging around the pool with cold drink in hand.

RCN Court GUESTHOUSE $
(☎0 5341 8280-2; www.rcnguesthouse.com; 35 Soi 7, Th Moon Muang; r 350-500B; ❄@ᯤ) This basic place is well known for its affordable monthly rates (from 6300B) and central location. Rooms (either fan or air-con) are nothing special but have cable TV and fridge. There is an outdoor kitchen for guests, a small front patio and a fitness room.

Siri Guesthouse GUESTHOUSE $
(☎0 5332 6550; 31/3 Soi 5, Th Moon Muang; r 350-450B; ❄) Go for one of the upstairs rooms that have more light and space. The cheaper rooms are fine, although boxy and small on the ground floor. It's a quiet old city location.

Daret's House GUESTHOUSE $
(☎0 5323 5440; 4/5 Th Chaiyaphum; s/d 160/220B) A long-time backpackers' fave

with stacks of well-worn rooms, Daret's looks like many of Th Khao San's backpacker flops. But because this is Lanna-land, amiable Khun Daret is often found in the cafe downstairs. You pay more for the luxury of hot water.

Riverside House GUESTHOUSE $
(☎0 5324 1860; www.riversidehousechiangmai.com; 101 Th Chiang Mai-Lamphun; r 500-800B;) Be an adventurer on the east bank of the river at this modest abode. Reception is via the attached travel agency and the quietest rooms are deeper into the property.

International Hotel Chiangmai HOSTEL $
(☎0 5322 1819; www.ymcachiangmai.org; 11 Soi Sermsak, Th Hutsadisawee; r 600-1800B;) Quite possibly the ugliest building in a country where the competition is fierce, this local branch of the YMCA redeems itself with some excellent bargains for rooms with a view of Doi Suthep. Skip their overpriced dorm beds though.

All In 1 GUESTHOUSE $
(☎0 5320 7133; www.allin1gh.com; 31 Soi 2, Th Moon Muang; r 400-700B;) Clean rooms with cable TV, plus outdoor garden bar.

Supreme House GUESTHOUSE $
(☎0 5322 2480; 44/1 Soi 9, Th Moon Muang; r 150B) Relaxed atmosphere and bar-hopping access.

Jonadda Guest House GUESTHOUSE $
(☎0 5322 7281; 23/1 Soi 2, Th Ratwithi; r 250-450B;) Spotless, basic rooms.

Eating

Dining in Chiang Mai is homey and healthy with an emphasis on vegetarianism. The city is also well known for its covered markets. **Talat Pratu Chiang Mai** (Th Bamrungburi) is a busy morning market selling fresh fruit, piles of fried food and fistfuls of sticky rice. After its midday siesta, the market caters to the dinner crowd.

The weekend walking streets (see boxed text, p694) have great eats, especially when it comes to northern Thai specialities like *khâo sawy*. More northern Thai specialities can be found near the Night Bazaar at the string of restaurants around **Ban Haw Mosque** (Matsayit Chiang Mai; Soi 1, Th Charoen Prathet), the anchor for Chiang Mai's Yunnanese Muslim community. But honestly, the atmosphere is way better than the food.

TOP CHOICE **Khun Churn** VEGETARIAN $
(Soi 17, Th Nimmanhaemin; buffet 100B; lunch;) It's all-you-can-eat at this stylish vegetarian restaurant popular with health-minded Thais and international NGO workers.

Angel's Secrets VEGETARIAN $
(cnr Soi 1 & 5, Th Ratchadamoen; dishes 60-90B; breakfast, lunch Tue-Sun;) Shielded by a fence of greenery, this outdoor eatery exudes a touchy-feely goodness through its tasty and freshly prepared vegetarian dishes.

Heuan Phen NORTHERN THAI $$
(☎0 5327 7103; 112 Th Ratchamankha; dishes 60-150B; lunch & dinner) Chiang Mai's purveyor of northern Thai cuisine serves dinner in an antique-cluttered room that attracts visiting appetites, both Thai and foreign. The food is a tad lacklustre but the ambience is a treat. Daytime meals are served in a large canteen.

AUM Vegetarian Food VEGETARIAN $
(66 Th Moon Muang; dishes 50-120B; lunch & dinner;) An easygoing place filled with used paperbacks and newspaper-thumbing expats, AUM does respectable vegetarian Thai food, healthy juices and organic coffee.

Blue Diamond INTERNATIONAL $
(35/1 Soi 9, Th Moon Muang; dishes 50-100B; breakfast, lunch & dinner Mon-Sat) This relaxed garden cafe bakes its own bread, brews eye-opening coffee and Thai veggie fare. Breakfast is its speciality.

Taste From Heaven VEGETARIAN $
(237-239 Th Tha Phae; dishes 60-110B; lunch & dinner;) Affiliated with the Elephant Nature Park, this vegetarian restaurant makes delectable curries and Thai-Indian fusion dishes. The pleasant courtyard garden offers a cool evening retreat.

Burmese Restaurant BURMESE $
(cnr Th Nimmanhaemin & Soi 14; dishes 30B; lunch & dinner) This basic eatery sells delicious Burmese food attesting to Chiang Mai's increasing population of economic migrants. The food comes quick, goes down even quicker and is easy on the wallet.

Lemon Tree THAI $
(26/1-2 Th Huay Kaew; dishes 40-100B; lunch & dinner) Near Kad Suan Kaew shopping mall, this cheery place does an exhaustive list of Thai dishes, like *kaeng paa lûuk thûng kài* (spicy jungle curry with free-range chicken).

NORTHERN CUISINE

Thanks to northern Thailand's cooler climate, familiar vegetables such as broccoli and cauliflower might make an appearance in a stir-fry. Untranslatable herbs and leaves from the dense forests are also incorporated into regional dishes, imparting a distinct flavour of mist-shrouded hills. Even coffee grows here. Day-market vendors sell blue sticky rice, which is dyed by a morning glory-like flower and topped with an egg custard.

Showing its Burmese, Chinese and Shan influences, the north prefers curries that are milder and more stewlike than the coconut milk-based curries of southern and central Thailand. Sour notes are enhanced with the addition of pickled cabbage and lime. The most famous example is *khâo sawy*, a mild chicken curry with flat egg noodles. A Burmese expat, *kaeng hang-leh* is another example of a northern-style curry. Like the Chinese, northern Thais love pork and vendors everywhere sell *kâap mŭu* (deep-fried pork crackling) as a snack and side dish.

Chiangmai Saloon INTERNATIONAL $$

(30 Th Ratwithi; mains 120-200B; ⏰breakfast, lunch, dinner; @) Welcome to the Wild West, Thai style. A travellers' standby, this friendly old joint mixes Aussie beef with southern American know-how. Come for a meal that devolves into a drinking session.

Drinking & Entertainment

The ale flows fast and furious at the bars along Th Moon Muang near Pratu Tha Phae. West of the old city, Th Nimmanhaemin is where Thai uni students go bar-hopping.

John's Place BAR

(Th Moon Muang) An old-school backpacker spot, John's dominates the corner wedge with neon and beer bellies. Climb the stairs to the roof deck where a cold beer is good company at sunset and beyond.

Kafe BAR

(Th Moon Muang) A cute wooden affair with a couple of sunny, outdoor tables snuggled in beside Soi 5, Kafe is often crowded with Thais and backpackers when every other place is empty. It offers a simple formula: cheap cold beer and efficient service.

Dayli BAR

(Soi 11, Th Nimmanhaemin) This ginormous outdoor bar-restaurant won't win any hygiene awards but it does excel in the medal-worthy category of cheap, cold beer. Late Friday and Saturday nights everyone becomes a Dayli convert.

Riverside Bar & Restaurant LIVE MUSIC

(Th Charoenrat) Chiang Mai's version of the Hard Rock Café, Riverside has been serving meals and music on the banks of the Mae Nam Ping for more than two decades. On weekends, the Riverside knits together *faràng* and Thais into sing-along parties.

Bridge Bar LIVE MUSIC

(Soi 11, Th Nimmanhaemin) This cosy club hosts local bands that are loud enough to drown out your chattering travelling companion. Outside seating allows for mingling with local Thais.

Warm-Up CLUB

(40 Th Nimmanhaemin) The hippest spot in town, Warm-Up has been going steady with the young and beautiful for years now. Variety keeps this marriage alive: hip-hop, house and live bands occupy different corners of the club for attention-deficit dancers. Arrive late and dressed in your coolest duds: you'll be competing with spiked wolf hair-dos and pointy heels.

Shopping

Chiang Mai has long been an important centre for handicrafts. Th Tha Phae is filled with interesting antique and textile stores. Soi 1, Th Nimmanhaemin is Chiang Mai's nascent boutique scene with arts and decor suited to handsome budgets.

Backstreet Books BOOKS

(0 5387 4143; 2/8 Th Chang Moi Kao) A local chain for used books.

Gecko Books BOOKS

(0 5387 4066; Th Chiang Moi Kao) Another local chain for used books.

Lost Book Shop BOOKS

(0 5320 6656; 34/3 Th Ratchamankha) Secondhand books free of plastic wrap for easy browsing; same owner as Backstreet Books.

PEDESTRIAN COMMERCE

Once upon a time Chiang Mai was a destination for itinerant Yunnanese merchants trading goods along an ancient route from China all the way to Burma. Today the city's pedestrian markets tap into this tradition and expertly merge commerce and culture.

» **Sunday Walking Street** (Th Ratchadamnoen; ⏲4pm-midnight Sun) is a festive night bazaar that takes over the old city. Chiang Mai lets down its hippie hair with lots of ethnic chic accessories (many are handmade locally) and undyed cotton T-shirts for sale. The temples along the way host food stalls selling northern Thai cuisine and other shopping-stamina boosts. The market is extremely popular and gets very crowded.

» **Saturday Walking Street** (Th Wualai; ⏲4pm-midnight Sat) is a smaller version that unfolds along the traditional silver-smithing neighbourhood south of the old city. Vendors peddling many of the same wares and Thai snacks give everyone a reason to wander, nibble and shop.

» **Chiang Mai Night Bazaar** (Th Chang Khlan; ⏲7pm-midnight) is the leading night-time tourist attraction occupying an old Yunnanese trading post. The market offers a huge variety of ordinary souvenirs, some northern Thai handicrafts, and lots of people-watching and people-dodging on the congested footpaths.

On the Road Books BOOKS
(☎05341 8169; 38/1 Th Ratwithi) Small selection of good quality reads.

 Information

Dangers & Annoyances

The majority of guesthouses in town subsidise their cheap room rates through commissions on booking trekking tours. For this reason, they might limit nontrekkers to a three-day stay, but ask at check-in.

Avoid the private bus and minivan services from Bangkok's Th Khao San to Chiang Mai because they are full of commission-generating schemes to subsidise the cut-rate fares.

Emergency

Tourist police (☎0 5324 7318, 24hr emergency ☎1155; Th Faham; ⏲6am-midnight)

Internet access

Internet cafes are everywhere and most guesthouses include wi-fi for free.

Media

1 Stop Chiang Mai (www.1stopchiangmai.com) City attractions with an emphasis on day trips and outdoor activities.

City Life (www.chiangmainews.com) Monthly lifestyle magazine.

Chiangmai Mail (www.chiangmai-mail.com) Weekly English-language newspaper.

Irrawaddy News Magazine (www.irrawaddy.org) Respected journal covering Myanmar, northern Thailand and other parts of Southeast Asia.

Medical Services

Chiang Mai Ram Hospital (☎0 5322 4880; Th Bunreuangrit) Internationally savvy hospital.

Malaria Centre (☎0 5322 1529; 18 Th Bunreuangrit) Does blood checks for malaria.

McCormick Hospital (☎0 5392 1777; Th Kaew Nawarat) Best-value place for minor treatments.

Money

All major Thai banks have branches and ATMs throughout Chiang Mai; many are along Th Tha Phae and Th Moon Muang.

Post

Main post office (Th Charoen Muang) Inconveniently east of town; handy branches on Th Singarat/Samlan, Th Praisani and the airport.

Telephone

Many internet cafes have headsets for Skype calls. Overseas calls can also be made from one of the private offices along Th Moon Muang.

CAT office (Th Charoen Muang; ⏲7am-10pm) Behind the main post office.

Tourist Information

TAT (☎0 5324 8604; 105/1 Th Chiang Mai-Lamphun; ⏲8.30am-4.30pm) Provides maps and brochures and answers basic tourist questions; does not make travel or accommodation bookings.

 Getting There & Away

Air

Regularly scheduled international and domestic flights arrive at **Chiang Mai International**

Airport (www.chiangmaiairportonline.com). Destinations include the following:

Kuala Lumpur (from 2500B, daily flights) Via Air Asia.

Bangkok (from 1600B, daily flights) via Bangkok Airways (Suvarnabhumi Airport), THAI (Suvarnabhumi Airport), Orient Thai (Don Muang Airport) and Nok Air (Don Muang Airport).

Luang Prabang (from 4000B, three times weekly) Via Lao Airlines.

Pai (from 1890B, daily) Via Kan Air.

Mae Hong Son (from 1250B, daily) Via Nok Air and Kan Air.

Singapore (from 10,000B; four times weekly) Via Silk Air.

Seoul (16,000B, twice weekly) Via Korean Air.

Bus

There are two bus stations in Chiang Mai. The **Arcade bus station** (Th Kaew Nawarat), 3km northeast of town, covers long-distance destinations. For Bangkok travel, purchase tickets directly from bus station agents rather than tourist centre agents to ensure that you're travelling with a reputable company. From the town centre, a túk-túk or chartered sŏrngtăaou to the Arcade bus station should cost about 50B to 60B.

Chang Pheuak bus station (Th Chang Pheuak), north of the old city, handles buses to nearby provincial towns; to reach the Chang Pheuak bus station get a sŏrngtăaou at the normal 20B rate. Destinations include Fang (80B, three hours, frequent) and Tha Ton (90B, four hours, five daily).

Train

The **train station** (☎0 5324 5364; Th Charoen Muang) is 2.5km east of the old city. There are six daily departures between Chiang Mai and Bangkok and the journey takes 12 to 15 hours. Most trains leave in the early evening or late afternoon and arrive in the morning. Fares vary depending on the type of train (express, rapid and sprinter), the type of car (1st, 2nd and 3rd class; the latter have either fan or air-con) and the type of seat (seat or sleeping berth, either upper or lower). Sample 2nd-class fares to Bangkok are as follows:

Seats (fan 391-431B, air-con 541-611B)

Sleeping berths (fan 491-541B, air-con 751-821B)

Advance bookings need to be made in person at the station and are recommended for securing air-con sleepers, particularly around public holidays or peak tourist season (November to March). Transport to the station via sŏrngtăaou should cost 40B to 60B.

Getting Around

Airport taxis cost a flat 150B. If you aren't in a hurry, you can also walk out to the main road and flag down a túk-túk or red sŏrngtăaou, which should cost 60B or 80B to your hotel.

Red sŏrngtăaou circulate around the city operating as shared taxis. Flag one down and tell them your destination; if they are going that way, they'll nod and maybe pick up other passengers along the way. The starting fare is 20B, with longer trips 40B. Túk-túk rides around town cost about 40B to 60B; negotiate the fare beforehand.

You can rent bicycles (60B a day) or 100cc motorcycles (from 150B to 200B) to explore

BUS SERVICES FROM CHIANG MAI'S ARCADE BUS STATION

DESTINATION	PRICE	DURATION (HR)	FREQUENCY
Bangkok	605-810B	9½	frequently from 6.30am-9.30pm
Chiang Khong	215-275B	6½	three daily
Chiang Rai	215-275B	6½	frequently from 5.30-5pm
Chiang Saen	165-220B	3-4	two daily
Khon Kaen	505B	12	10 daily
Lampang	20-100B	2	hourly from 6.30am-9.30pm
Mae Hong Son	145-340B	7-8	eight daily
Mae Sariang	100-200B	4-5	six daily
Mae Sot	240-310B	6½	two daily
Nan	150-420B	6	11 daily
Pai	75-150B	4	12 daily
Phitsanulok	210-320B	5-6	frequent
Sukhothai	220B	5-6	frequent

Chiang Mai. Bicycles are a great way to get around the city.

Around Chiang Mai

DOI INTHANON NATIONAL PARK

The highest peak in the country, Doi Inthanon (2565m), and the surrounding **national park** (admission 200B) have hiking trails, waterfalls and two monumental stupas erected in honour of the king and queen. It's a popular day trip from Chiang Mai for tourists and locals, especially during the New Year's holiday when there's the rarely seen phenomenon of frost.

Most visitors come on a tour from Chiang Mai but the park is accessible via public transport. Buses leave from Chang Pheuak terminal and yellow sŏrngtăaou leave from Pratu Chiang Mai for Chom Thong (70B), 58km from Chiang Mai and the closest town to the park. Some buses go directly to the park's entrance gate near Nam Tok Mae Klang, and some are bound for Hot and will drop you off in Chom Thong.

From Chom Thong there are regular sŏrngtăaou to the park's entrance gate (30B), about 8km north. Sŏrngtăaou from Mae Klang to the summit of Doi Inthanon (90B) leave almost hourly until late afternoon.

MAE SA VALLEY LOOP

One of the easiest mountain escapes, the Mae Sa Valley loop travels from the lowland's concrete expanse into the highlands' forested frontier. The 100km route makes a good day trip with private transport. Golden Triangle Rider (www.gt-rider.com) publishes a detailed map of the area.

Head north of Chiang Mai on Rte 107 (Th Chang Pheuak) toward Mae Rim, then left onto Rte 1096. The road becomes more rural but there's a steady supply of tour-bus attractions: orchid farms, butterfly parks, snake farms, you name it.

The road eventually starts to climb and twist into the fertile **Mae Sa Valley**, once a high-altitude basin for growing opium poppies. Now the valley's hill-tribe farmers have re-seeded their terraced fields with sweet peppers, cabbage, flowers and fruits – which are then sold to the royal agriculture projects under the Doi Kham label.

On the outskirts of the valley, the road swings around the mountain ridge and starts to rise and dip until it reaches the conifer zone. Beyond, the landscape unfolds in a cascade of mountains and eventually the road spirals down into **Samoeng**, a pretty Thai town, and then arcs back into Chiang Mai.

Chiang Rai

POP 62,000

Leafy and well groomed, Chiang Rai is more liveable than visitable. The town itself is a convenient base for touring the Golden Triangle and an alternative to Chiang Mai for arranging hill-tribe treks. Don't assume you'll be the only foreigner in town; Chiang Rai is well-loved by well-heeled package tourists.

Sights

Wat Phra Kaew TEMPLE

(cnr Th Trairat & Th Reuang Nakhon) This temple's claim to fame is its role in the discovery of the country's highly revered Emerald Buddha (presently residing in Bangkok's Wat Phra Kaew). In the mid-14th century, lightning struck open the *chedi* here, thus revealing the Emerald Buddha within. The figure made a long and politically fraught journey across the country, to Laos and eventually was settled in Bangkok.

Oub Kham Museum MUSEUM

(☎0 5371 3349; www.oubkhammuseum.com; 81/1 Military Front Rd; admission 300B; ⊗8am-6pm) This museum houses an impressive collection of Lanna-era paraphernalia along with an odd assortment of Thai kitsch. Guided tours are obligatory. It is 2km outside town.

Hilltribe Museum & Education Center MUSEUM

(☎0 5374 0088; www.pda.org; 3rd fl, 620/25 Th Thanalai; admission 50B; ⊗9am-6pm Mon-Fri, 10am-6pm Sat & Sun) Run by the nonprofit Population & Community Development Association (PDA), this museum covers the history of Thailand's major hill tribes with clothing displays, slide shows and a knowledgeable curator. PDA also organises hill-tribe treks.

Activities

Trekking is big business in Chiang Rai. Most tours (starting at 1200B) typically cover the areas of Doi Tung, Doi Mae Salong or Chiang Khong. The following are primarily nonprofit community development organisations working in hill-tribe communities

SLOW BOATS TO CHIANG RAI

Escape the daredevil highway antics of Thailand's bus drivers with a slow ride on the Mae Nam Kok departing from the small town of Tha Ton, north of Chiang Mai. The river ride is a big hit with tourists and includes stops at hill-tribe villages that specialise in Coca-Colas and souvenirs. This isn't unchartered territory but it is relaxing.

Chiang Rai-bound boats (☎0 5305 3727; 350B; departs 12.30pm) carrying 12 passengers, leave from Tha Ton and stop at Mae Salak (90B), a large Lahu village, and Ban Ruammit (300B), a Karen village. The trip takes three to five hours and both stops are well touristed, but you can get off the path by joining a **hill-tribe trek** from here. You can also do the trip in reverse (from Chiang Rai to Tha Ton), a less popular direction affording you more leg room, but it also takes longer. Go to **CR Pier** (☎0 5375 0009) in the northwest corner of Chiang Rai. Passenger boats embark daily at 10.30am.

If you overnight in Tha Ton, check out **Apple Resort** (☎0 5337 3144; Tha Ton; r fan/aircon 350/500B; ❄), which is a pleasant riverside place with stylishly decorated garden bungalows.

Slow, local buses to Tha Ton (90B, four hours) leave from Chiang Mai's Chang Pheuak station. You can skip an overnight in Tha Ton if you catch the first morning bus, though you might have to transit through Fang, 23km to the south.

Adding to your indecision, you could skip the river and backdoor to Chiang Rai via the ridgetop village of Mae Salong (p700). Yellow sŏrngtăaou make the scenic journey to Mae Salong (70B, 1½ hours, mornings only).

that use trekking as an awareness campaign and fundraiser.

Mirror Foundation TREKKING
(☎0 5373 7416; www.themirrorfoundation.org) This NGO sponsors educational workshops, advocates for Thai citizenship, works to prevent human trafficking as well as offers treks led by local guides; there are also village volunteer programs.

PDA Tours & Travel TREKKING
(☎0 5374 0088; www.pda.or.th/chiangrai) Culturally sensitive tours led by PDA-trained hill-tribe members. Profits are recycled back into the community for HIV/AIDS education, health clinics and educational scholarships.

Akha Hill House TREKKING
(☎08 9997 5505; www.akhahill.com; Akha River House) A portion of the profits from their guesthouse and trekking tours go into a local school.

Sleeping

Jansom House GUESTHOUSE $
(☎0 5371 4552; 897/2 Th Jet Yod; r incl breakfast 450-500B; ❄@📶) This three-storey hotel offers spotless, spacious rooms set around a small plant-filled courtyard. Plus there are frills like cable TV, well-designed bathrooms and tiled floors.

The North GUESTHOUSE $
(☎0 5371 9873; www.thenorth.co.th; 612/100-101 Sirikon Market; r 350-450; ❄@📶) Located steps away from the bus station, this place has provided a bit of colour to a drab area. The 18 rooms combine Thai and modern design with a common chill-out area.

Lek House GUESTHOUSE $
(☎0 5371 1550; cnr Th Ratyotha & Th Baanpa Pragarn; r incl breakfast 350-550B; ❄@📶🏊) This purple compound is home to a collection of simple fan-cooled rooms. Lek House is located near the corner of Th Thanalai and Th Baanpa Pragarn.

Baan Bua Guest House GUESTHOUSE $
(☎0 5371 8880; www.baanbuaguesthouse.com; 879/2 Th Jet Yot; r 300-500B; ❄@📶) This quiet guesthouse consists of 17 bright green rooms surrounding a garden. Rooms are simple, but clean and cosy.

Orchids Guest House GUESTHOUSE $
(☎0 5371 8361; www.orchidsguesthouse.com; 1012/3 Th Jet Yod; r 400B; ❄@📶) This collection of spotless rooms in a residential compound is a good budget catch.

Jitaree Guest House GUESTHOUSE $
(☎0 5371 9348; Soi Flat Tamruat; r 200B; 📶) Cool fan rooms in an apartment-like complex. Jitaree is located in the tiny backpacker enclave off Th Singhaclai, near the new bridge.

Chiang Rai

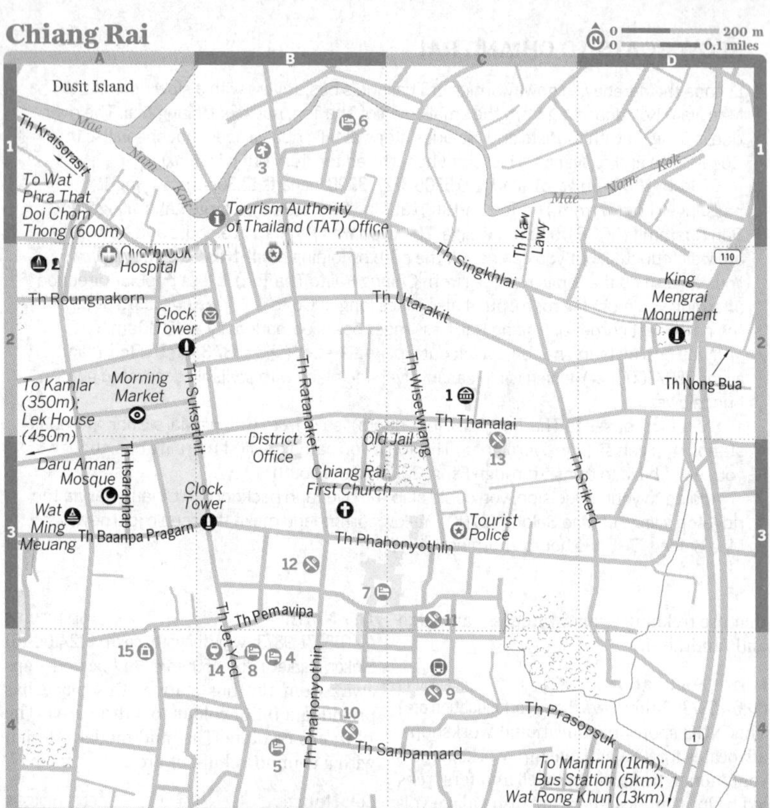

Eating

The **night market** has a decent collection of food stalls offering snacks and meals as well as post-noshing shopping.

BaanChivitMai Bakery BAKERY $
(Th Prasopsuk; dishes 20-100B; 7am-9pm Mon-Sat, 2-9pm Sun) Locally grown coffee makes an appearance here along with Swedish-style sweets and the self-satisfaction of supporting a local NGO project.

TOP CHOICE **Nam Ngiaw Paa Nuan** VIETNAMESE, NORTHERN THAI $
(Th Sanpannard; mains 10-100B; 9am-5pm) This understated place serves a delicious mix of Vietnamese and northern Thai dishes.

Paa Suk NORTHERN THAI $
(Th Sankhongnoi; mains 10-25B; 8am-3pm Mon-Sat) This immensely popular third-generation restaurant specialises in the local dish *kà·nŏm jeen nám ngée·o*, a thin broth of pork or beef and tomatoes served over fresh rice noodles. The restaurant is located between Soi 4 and Soi 5 of Th Sankhong-noi (the street is called Th Sathanpayabarn where it intersects with Th Phahonyothin); look for the yellow sign.

Phu-Lae NORTHERN THAI $$
(673/1 Th Thanalai; mains 80-320B; lunch & dinner;) This air-conditioned restaurant is exceedingly popular among Thai tourists for its tasty, but slightly gentrified northern Thai fare. Recommended dishes include the *gaang hang·lair* (a Burmese-style pork curry) served with pickled garlic, and *sâi òo·a* (herb-packed sausages).

Old Dutch INTERNATIONAL $$
(541 Th Phahonyothin; mains 150-300B;) This cosy, foreigner-friendly restaurant is a good choice if you're tired of rice. There's a variety

Chiang Rai

of well-done Dutch and other Western dishes as well as baked goods.

Drinking

Cat Bar BAR
(1013/1 Th Jet Yot; ⏲5pm-1am) Among the bars on Th Jet Yot, this spot mixes pool tables with live nightly music (from 10.30pm).

Shopping

Orn's Bookshop BOOKS
(off Soi 1, Th Jet Yot; ⏲8am-8pm) Great used bookstore.

Information

Banks can be found along Th Thanalai and along Th Utarakit. Internet access is readily available.

Overbrook Hospital (☎0 5371 1366; www.overbrookhospital.com; Th Singkhlai) Modern, English-speaking hospital.

Post office (Th Utarakit) South of Wat Phra Singh.

TAT (☎0 5374 4674; 448/16 Th Singkhlai; ⏲8.30am-4.30pm)

Tourist police (☎0 5371 1779, 1155; Th Phahonyothin)

Getting There & Away

Air

Chiang Rai airport (☎0 5379 8000; Superhighway 110) is 8km north of town. Destinations include:

Bangkok's Don Muang Airport (1550B, 1¼ hours, twice daily) Via Orient Thai

Bangkok's Suvarnabhumi Airport (2164B to3120B, 1¼ hours, six times daily) Via Air Asia and THAI

Chiang Mai (1399B, 40 minutes, twice daily) Via Kan Air.

Bus

Chiang Rai's **provincial bus station** (Th Prasopsuk) is in the heart of town; it also serves ordinary (fan) buses to nearby provinces. Destinations include:

Chiang Khong 65B; 2½ hours; hourly.

Chiang Mai 142B; seven hours; every 45 minutes from 6.30am to noon.

Chiang Saen 32B; 1½ hours, frequent.

Mae Sai 39B; 1½ hours; frequent.

If you're heading beyond Chiang Rai province (or are in a hurry), you'll have to go to the **new bus station** (☎0 5377 3989), 5km south of town on Hwy 1. Sŏrngtăaou linking it and the old station run from 5am to 9pm (10B, 20 minutes). Minivans also depart from here:

Bangkok's Northern (Mo Chit) bus terminal Air-con buses 546B to 706B, VIP 733B; 11 hours.

Chiang Mai Ordinary buses 106B, air-con 191B; four hours; hourly.

Boat

Chiang Rai is accessible by boat along Mae Nam Kok from the northern tip of Chiang Mai province (see the boxed text, p697).

Golden Triangle

The three-country border between Thailand, Myanmar and Laos forms the legendary Golden Triangle, once a mountainous frontier where the opium poppy was a cash crop for the region's ethnic minorities. Thailand has successfully stamped out its cultivation through infrastructure projects, crop-substitution programs and aggressive law enforcement. But the porous border and lawless areas of the neighbouring countries have switched production to the next generation's drug of choice: methamphetamine and, to a lesser extent, heroin. Much of this illicit activity is invisible to the average visitor and the region's heyday as the

Golden Triangle & Around

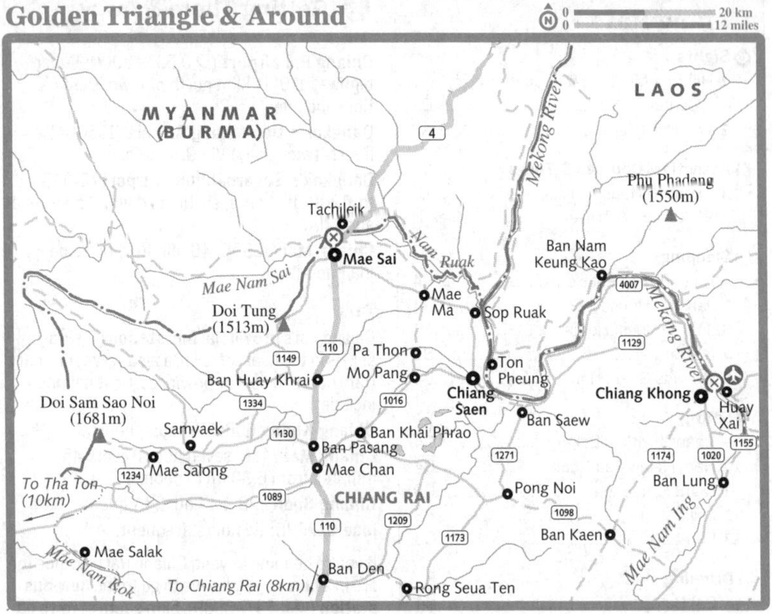

leading opium producer is now marketed as a tourist attraction.

MAE SALONG

POP 25,400

Built along the spine of a mountain, Mae Salong is more like a remote Chinese village in Yúnnán than a Thai town. It was originally settled by the 93rd Regiment of the Kuomintang Nationalist Party (KMT), which fled from China after the 1949 revolution. The ex-soldiers and political exiles initially settled in Myanmar but later were forced to Thailand, where they supported themselves as middlemen between the opium growers and the opium warlords. The modern-day descendants still carry on the language and traditions (minus the profession) of their forefathers: Chinese is more frequently spoken here than Thai and the land's severe incline boasts tidy terraces of tea and coffee plantations.

An interesting **morning market** (⏲6-8am) convenes at the T-junction near Shin Sane Guest House. The market attracts town residents and tribespeople from the surrounding districts. Most of the guesthouses in town can arrange **treks** to nearby hill-tribe villages, though the surrounding area has been significantly denuded over the years.

Shin Sane Guest House (☎0 5376 5026; 32/3 Th Mae Salong; s/d from 50/100B, bungalow 300B; @) is Mae Salong's original guesthouse, boasting the standards and prices of decades past. **Little Home Guesthouse** (☎0 5376 5389; www.maesalonglittlehome.com; 31 Moo 1, Th Mae Salong; s/d from 50/100B, bungalow 600B; @), next door to Shin Sane, is a delightful wooden house with basic rooms and spiffy bungalows. The friendly owner has produced an accurate map of the area.

Getting to Mae Salong is an adventure in transport: take a Chiang Rai-Mae Sai bus and get off at Ban Basang (ordinary 20B, 30 minutes, frequent). From there, sŏrngtăaou climb the mountain to Mae Salong (500B per vehicle split between passengers, one hour). You can also approach Mae Salong from the scenic western road via Fang or Tha Ton (50B).

MAE SAI

POP 21,800

Thailand's northernmost town is a busy trading post for gems, jewellery, cashews and lacquerware, and is also a legal border crossing into Myanmar. Many travellers make the trek here to extend their Thai visa or to dip their toes into Myanmar.

Most guesthouses line the street along the Mae Nam Sai to the left of the border checkpoint. **Bamboo Guesthouse** (☎08 6916 1895; 135/3 Th Sailomjoi; r 150-200B) has bare-bones shelters. **Top North Hotel** (☎0 5373

1955; 306 Th Phahonyothin; d 400-600B, tr 900B; ❄@), located along the main strip, is a short walk to the border bridge; it is an older hotel with spacious rooms.

Mae Sai has a **night market** (Th Phahonyothin) with an excellent mix of Thai and Chinese dishes. **Khrua Bismillah** (☎08 1530 8198; Soi 4, Th Phahonyothin; dishes 25-40B; ⏰6am-6pm) is run by Burmese Muslims and does an excellent biryani; look for the green halal sign.

The **bus station** (☎0 5364 6437) is 4km from the immigration office. Destinations include Bangkok (air-con 582B to 749B, VIP 874B, 15 hours, six departures), Chiang Mai (air-con/VIP 241/375B, four to five hours, five departures) and Chiang Rai (ordinary 38B, 1½ hours, frequent). The bus to Tha Ton (51B) and Fang (71B) leaves at 7am and takes two hours.

On Th Phahonyothin by Soi 8 there's a 'bus stop' sign, from which sŏrngtăaou run to Sop Ruak (45B, frequent) and terminate in Chiang Saen (50B).

CHIANG SAEN

POP 10,800

A sedate river town, **Chiang Saen** is famous in the Thai history books as the 7th-century birthplace of the Lanna kingdom, which later moved to Chiang Mai. You can wander around the kingdoms' ruins at **Wat Pa Sak** (admission 50B), about 200m from Pratu Chiang Saen, or survey the artefacts at **Chiang Saen National Museum** (☎0 5377 7102; 702 Th Phahonyothin; admission 100B; ⏰8.30am-4.30pm Wed-Sun). Today, huge river barges from China moor in town, heralding the expanding and sanctioned interior Asian trade.

An easy day trip from Chiang Saen is the so-called 'official' centre of the Golden Triangle, **Sop Ruak**, an odd souvenir and museum stop for package tourists. The **House of Opium** (Baan Phin; ☎0 5378 4060; www.houseofopium.com; admission 50B; ⏰7am-8pm), across from Phra Chiang Saen Si Phaendin, has historical displays pertaining to opium culture. Another drug-themed museum is the **Hall of Opium** (☎0 5378 4444; www.goldentrianglepark.com; admission 300B; ⏰10am-3.30pm), 1km south of town opposite the Anantara Resort & Spa. Run by royally sponsored Mah Fah Luang Foundation, the facility includes a fascinating history of opium and examines the effects of abuse on individuals and society.

Sleeping options in Chiang Saen include **Chiang Saen Guest House** (☎0 5365 0196; 45/2 Th Rimkhong; r 150-300B), opposite the river and night stalls, and **Gin's Guest House** (☎0 5365 0847; 71 Mu 8; r 300-700B, bungalows 200B), on the north side of town (about 1.5km north of the bus terminal) with views of the Mekong River. A night market sets up each evening along the bank of the Mekong River.

Chiang Saen has an informal bus terminal at the eastern end of Th Phahonyothin. Destinations include Chiang Rai (ordinary 70B, two hours, frequent) and Chiang Mai (ordinary/air-con 126/227B, five hours, two daily).

You can also travel directly to the Chinese town of Jinghong from Chiang Saen via **passenger ferry** (3500B one-way, 15hr) but departures are dependent on river conditions and service is usually suspended during the dry season of March to May. Further complicating the trip is the fact that you'll need a pre-arranged Chinese visa (the nearest consulate is in Chiang Mai; see p780). Call **Chiang Saen Tour and Travel** (☎0 5377 7051; 64 Th Rimkhong;

GETTING TO MYANMAR: MAE SAI TO TACHILEIK

In peaceful times, foreigners may cross from Mae Sai into Tachileik, Myanmar. On occasion and without notice, the border may close temporarily. Ask about current conditions before making the trip to Mae Sai.

At the border The **Thai immigration office** (⏰7am-6.30pm) is just before the bridge over the Mae Nam Sai in the centre of town. On the other side is the Myanmarese immigration office, which charges 500B for a temporary ID card allowing a one-day pass; your passport is held as a deposit. The border town of Tachileik looks a lot like Mae Sai, except with more teashops and Burmese restaurants (go figure).

Moving on You're allowed to venture as far into Myanmar as Kengtung (the capital of the Shan state), but you'll need certain permits and permissions. The **Tourist Information office** can prepare the documents (three photos required) and the 14-day pass (US$10 or 500B)it's also obligatory to hire a guide for the duration of your stay.

For information on this border crossing in the other direction, see the boxed text, p511.

⏰8am-6pm) to determine current schedules before arranging a visa.

To Chiang Mai be sure to take the *săi mài* (new route), which is more direct. There are frequent sŏrngtăaou between Chiang Saen and Sop Ruak (20B, every 20 minutes from 7am to 5pm). Six-passenger speedboats also shuttle between the two towns (one way/return 500/600B, 35 minutes).

CHIANG KHONG

POP 12,000

Remote yet lively Chiang Khong is historically important as a market town for local hill tribes and for trade with northern Laos. Travellers pass through en route to Laos and southern China.

Sleeping

Baanrimtaling GUESTHOUSE $
(☎0 5379 1613; maleewan_th@yahoo.com; 99/2 Moo 3; dm/r 100-120/150-450B; @📶) The rooms here are pretty run-of-the-mill but the homey atmosphere and river views add pizzaz.

Portside Hotel HOTEL $
(☎0 5365 5238; portsidehotel@hotmail.com; 546 Th Sai Klang; r with fan/air-con 300/500B; ❄@📶) This good value hotel features two floors of tidy but slightly cramped rooms. There are no river views, but a communal rooftop area makes up for this.

PP Home GUESTHOUSE $
(Baan Pak Pon; ☎0 5365 5092; baanpakpon@hotmail.co.th; r 350-600B; ❄@📶) One of a dwindling number of locally owned accommodation, this attractive wooden house features large rooms with private balcony looking over the river.

Baan-Fai Guest House GUESTHOUSE $
(☎0 5379 1394; 108 Th Sai Klang; r 100-200B; 📶) Located in an attractive wooden Thai home, the basic rooms are a budget find.

Boom House BUDGET HOTEL $
(☎0 5365 5136; www.boomhouseresort.com, in Thai; 406/1 Th Sai Klang; dm/r 100/250-400B; ❄📶) This multilevel place has a variety of plain but tidy rooms, the more expensive of which have air-con, TV and fridge.

Eating

Khao Soi Pa Orn NORTHERN THAI $
(Soi 6; mains 15-30B; ⏰8am-4pm) Chiang Khong's version of *kôw soy* forgoes the coconut milk and replaces it with a rich minced pork and tomato mixture. There's no English-language sign here; look for the gigantic highway pillar at the eastern end of Soi 6.

Bamboo Mexican House INTERNATIONAL $
(Th Sai Klang; mains 30-180B; ⏰7am-8pm) Run by the manager of a now-defunct guesthouse, this tiny restaurant/bakery opens early and can prepare boxed lunches for the boat ride.

Pai

POP 2000

This cool corner of the northern mountains started out as a hippie enclave for Chiang Mai bohos who would come to hang out beside the rambling river and strum out blues tunes at night. Word spread and the dusty little town now does a thriving trade in mountain scenery and laid-back living. Urban Thais have joined the Pai altar for its stress-reducing setting and the oddity of 'winter' (from December to January). The town itself – a modest mixture of Shan, Thai and Muslim Chinese residents – can be explored in a matter of minutes, but the real adventure lies along the paths in the hills beyond. Some might sniff that Pai is played out, but remember folks this isn't a race.

Sights & Activities

Since Pai is more of a 'state of mind', it is lean on full-fledged tourist attractions. If you need an outing, head to **Wat Phra That Mae Yen**, 1km east of town, for its hilltop vista. The other main contender is **Tha Pai Hot Springs** (admission 200B; ⏰6am-7pm), a well-kept park featuring a scenic stream and pleasant hot-spring bathing pools. The park is 7km southeast of town across Mae Nam Pai.

The rest of your time will be spent on various wanderings or pamperings. All the guesthouses in town can provide information on **trekking** (from 700B per day). Treks should include a maximum of 10 people.

Thai Adventure Rafting RAFTING
(☎0 5369 9111; www.thairafting.com; Th Chaisongkhram; from 2500B) Folks rave about rafting on the Mae Nam Pai, available during the wet season only (July to December). Rafting trips last from one to two days.

Pai Kayak KAYAKING
(☎0 5306 4426; www.paikayak.com; Pai Let's Go Tour, Th Rangsiyanon) Two-hour kayaking excursions tackle the Mae Nam Pai.

GETTING TO LAOS: CHIANG KHONG TO HUAY XAI

This is the most popular crossing for Chiang Mai-Luang Prabang (Laos) travellers.

Getting to the border The Mekong River village of Chiang Khong is where you can catch longtail boats to the Lao village of Huay Xai (30B, frequently from 8am-6pm). The pier is at the northern end of town.

At the border Foreigners can purchase a 30-day Lao visa upon arrival in Huay Xai for US$30 to $42, depending on nationality. There is an extra US$1 charge after 4pm and on weekends; bring a passport photo or get one at the border for 40B.

Moving on From Huay Xai, there are boats to Luang Prabang. You can also continue by bus to Udomxai or Luang Nam Tha. Huay Xai also has transit connections to China (though Chinese visas need to be arranged beforehand). Buses from Huay Xai go directly to the Xishuangbanna town of Mengla.

For information on entering Thailand from Laos at this crossing, see p351.

Pai Traditional Massage MASSAGE
(☎0 5369 9121; 68/3 Soi 1, Th Wiang Tai; massage from 180B, sauna 80B; ⏲9am-9pm) Northern Thai massage, *sàmŭn phrai* (medicinal herb) sauna and even massage courses.

Thom's Pai Elephant Camp Tours ELEPHANT RIDES
(☎0 5369 9286; www.thomelephant.com; 4 Th Rangsiyanon; rides 500-1500B) Jungle elephant rides through the forest to waterfalls and hot springs.

Mam Yoga House YOGA
(☎08 9954 4981; www.mamyoga.paiexplorer.com; Th Rangsiyanon; 1-day course from 200B; ⏲10am-noon & 3-5pm) Just north of the police station, Mam offers Hatha yoga classes

Sleeping

Pai's accommodation upgraded after the 2005 flood and now very few cheapies remain. There are still some budget spots outside of town, which is more idyllically rural. During the cool season (November to April) it can be difficult to find a room and prices increase with demand.

Breeze of Pai Guesthouse GUESTHOUSE $
(☎08 1998 4597; Soi Wat Pa Kham; r 400-800B; ❄📶) This well-groomed compound near the river consists of nine attractive and spacious rooms and six large A-frame bungalows (with fan and air-con). It's close to the action without the noise pollution, and the friendly English owner can provide local advice.

Pai Country Hut GUESTHOUSE $
(☎08 4046 4458; Ban Mae Hi; r 500B; 📶) The bamboo bungalows here are utterly simple, but are tidy and have bathrooms and porch hammocks. Although it's not exactly riverside, it's the most appealing of several similar places in the area.

TOP CHOICE **Amy's Earth House** GUESTHOUSE $$
(☎08 6190 2394; www.amyshouse.net; Ban Mae Khong; bungalows 600B; 📶) Claiming to be Pai's adobe pioneer, Amy's simple mud huts overlook the valley and have open-air showers. The hotel is located about 3.5km outside town off the road to Mae Hong Song.

Charlie's House GUESTHOUSE $
(☎0 5369 9039; Th Rangsiyanon; r 200-600B; ❄) This long-standing and locally run place offers a range of options in a suburban compound.

Mr Jan's Guest House GUESTHOUSE $
(☎0 5369 9554; Soi Wanchaloem 18; r 300-2000B; 📶) Owned by a Pai native, the plain and dark rooms are set around a medicinal herb garden.

Eating

During the day there's takeaway food at **Saengthongaram Market** (Th Khetkelang). For tasty local eats, try the **evening market** (gàht láang; Th Raddamrong; ⏲3pm-sunset). Night vendors turn Th Chaisongkhram and Th Rangsiyanon into an open-air buffet, hawking all manner of food and drink from stalls and refurbished VW vans.

Mama Falafel ISRAELI $
(Soi Wanchaloem; set meals 80-90B; ⏲11am-8pm) This friendly native of Pai has been cooking up tasty falafel, hummus and other Israeli faves since 2002. Come on Friday and

WORTH A TRIP

CAVE HOUNDS

The insides of northern Thailand's vast mountains have been carved and sculpted for millennia by water as it obeys gravity's pull. One of the most dramatic underground landscapes is Tham Lot (pronounced '*tâm lôrt*'), a large limestone cave about 70km from Mae Hong Son outside of the town of Soppong. It is one of the largest known caves in Thailand, stretching 1600m. There are impressive stalagmites, 'coffin caves' (an ancient and little-understood burial ritual) and a stream that runs through it. The tourism infrastructure is also applauded as a local ecotourism model. Local guides from nearby Shan villages must be hired to tour the caverns. You can base your stay at nearby **Cave Lodge** (☎0 5361 7203; www.cavelodge.com; dm 90-120B, r 250-2000B), which is run by an unofficial spelunking expert.

Tham Lot can be reached by motorcycle taxi (80B) from Soppong, which is accessible by bus from Pai (ordinary 40B, minivan 100B; 1 hour to 1½ hours) or Mae Hong Son (ordinary 40B, minivan 150B; two hours).

Saturday when she does hamin, the Jewish stew, accompanied by challah bread.

Je-In Pai VEGETARIAN $
(Pure Vegetarian Food; Th Raddamrong; mains 40-80B; 10am-8pm;) Opposite the District Office, this simple open-air place serves tasty and cheap vegan and vegetarian Thai food.

Good Life INTERNATIONAL $
(Th Wiang Tai; dishes 60-140B;) Wheat grass and secondhand New-Age books function as interior design at this eclectic and popular cafe. The menu is mainly liquid – teas, coffees, 'juice joints' – but it also does breakfasts and vegetarian Thai dishes.

TOP CHOICE **Laap Khom Huay Pu** NORTHERN THAI $
(Ban Huay Pu; mains 35-60B; 9am-10pm) Escape the tofu junkies to this local carnivore eatery. The house special is *lâhp kôoa*, minced meat (beef or pork) fried with local herbs and spices. The restaurant is on the road to Mae Hong Son, about 1km north of town, just past the turn-off to Belle Villa and Baan Krating (no English sign).

Yunnanese Restaurant CHINESE $$
(Ban Santichon; mains 25-200B; 8am-8pm) This open-air place in Ban Santichon serves the traditional dishes of the town's Yunnanese residents. Standouts include *màntŏ* (steamed buns), served with stewed pork leg. Or you could always go for the excellent noodles, made by hand and topped with a mixture of minced pork, garlic and sesame. The restaurant is the giant rock in Ban Santichon, about 4km west of Pai.

Drinking

Bebop LIVE MUSIC
(Th Rangsiyanon; 6pm-1am) If you want to become a card-carrying member of the Pai night-crawlers, hang your hat at Bebop. Live R&B and rock nightly.

Information

Several places around town offer internet services (20B to 30B per hour). Banks and ATMs can be found along Pai's two main streets, Th Rangsiyanon and Th Chaisongkhram.

Siam Books (☎0 5369 9075; Th Chaisongkhram) Boasts the town's largest selection of new and used books.

Getting There & Around

Pai's airport is 1.5km north of town and offers a daily connection to Chiang Mai (1890B, 25 minutes) on **Kan Air** (☎0 5369 9955; www.kanairlines.com).

The **bus stop** (Th Chaisongkhram) is in a dirt lot in the centre of town. The road from Chiang Mai to Pai and on to Mae Hong Son is savagely steep. Destinations include:

Chiang Mai 72B to 150B; three to four hours; frequent from 8am to 4pm.

Mae Hong Son 70B; 4½ hours; 11am and 1pm.

Minivans also depart from Pai's bus terminal. Bookings can be made at **aYa Service** (☎0 5369 9940; www.ayaservice.com; 22/1 Moo 3 Th Chaisongkhram). Destinations include:

Chiang Mai 150B; three hours; hourly from 7am to 4.30pm.

Mae Hong Son 150B; 2½ hours; hourly from 8.30am to 5.30pm.

Most of Pai is accessible on foot. For local excursions you can rent bicycles or motorcycles around town.

Mae Hong Son

POP 6000

Northern Thai aficionados prefer the far-flung border feel of Mae Hong Son to that of Pai. Mae Hong Son is a quiet provincial capital that practically peers into Myanmar and is skirted by forested mountains. The local trekking scene in Mae Hong Son is the primary draw but the daily market and local eats further impress its fan base.

Sights & Activities

Mae Hong Son's temples are surviving monuments to their Burmese and Shan artisans and benefactors and hint at the town's past as a logging and elephant-training centre. **Wat Jong Klang** and **Wat Jong Kham** boast whitewashed stupas and glittering zinc fretwork. The temples are often lit at night, reflecting in the still waters of Nong Jong Kham (Jong Kham Lake).

Glimpse the misty morning fog from **Wat Phra That Doi Kong Mu**, which sits on a hilltop west of town.

The **Poi Sang Long Festival** in March takes place at Wat Jong Klang and Wat Jong Kham. It's a surviving Shan custom in which young boys entering the monastery as novice monks are dressed in ornate costumes and paraded around the temple under festive parasols.

Treks to nearby hill-tribe villages, as well as **white-water rafting** and **longtail boat trips** on the Mae Nam Pai are all popular pastimes. Guesthouses can handle bookings for outdoor trips, which start at around 1000B for the day.

Friend Tour TREKKING

(☎0 5361 1647; 21 Th Pradit Jong Kham) With nearly 20 years experience, this recommended outfit offers trekking, elephant riding and rafting, as well as day tours.

Nature Walks TREKKING

(☎0 5361 1040, 08 9552 6899; www.trekkingthailand.com; from 1000B) Treks range from one-day nature walks to multiday journeys.

Sleeping

Coffee Morning GUESTHOUSE $

(☎0 5361 2234; 78 Th Singhanat Bamrung; r 300-500B; @ wi-fi) This old wooden house unites an attractive cafe-bookshop and four basic but cosy rooms. This isn't the best bargain around since bathrooms are shared but the atmosphere tips the scales.

Friend House GUESTHOUSE $

(☎0 5362 0119; 20 Th Pradit Jong Kham; r 150-400B; wi-fi) Clean and efficient, this guesthouse complex covers all the bases and a few rooms overlook the lake.

Palm House Guest House GUESTHOUSE $

(☎0 5361 4022; 22/1 Th Chamnanshtit; r 300-600B; air-con) Slightly sterile, Palm House is clean and predictable with a few flourishes.

Eating & Drinking

Mae Hong Son's **morning market** is a cultural and culinary adventure. Several vendors at the north end of the market sell *tòoa òon,* a Burmese noodle dish with thick chickpea porridge. Others sell a local version of *kà·nŏm jeen nám ngée·o* (thin white noodles) topped with Shan-style deep-fried vegetables.

There are two **night markets**: the one near the airport is mostly takeaway northern Thai food, while the market near Nong Jong Kham has seating and serves standard Thai food.

Mae Si Bua NORTHERN THAI $

(51 Th Singhanat Bamrung; dishes 20-30B ⏰lunch) For authentic local eats, try this restaurant specialising in Shan curries, soups and dips. Auntie Bua doesn't speak English, but the universal language of pointing should work.

Ban Phleng NORTHERN THAI $

(108 Th Khunlum Praphat; mains 45-100B; ⏰lunch & dinner Mon-Sat) A popular open-air restaurant, Ban Phleng does tasty local dishes, indicated as 'Maehongson style' on the English-language menu. It is located south of town – look for the white banners at the side of the road.

La Tasca ITALIAN $$

(Th Khunlum Praphat; mains 89-209B; ⏰lunch & dinner) This cosy place has been serving homemade pasta, pizza and calzone for as long as we can remember.

Sunflower Café BAR

(Th Pradit Jong Kham; ⏰7am-midnight) This open-air place combines draught beer, live lounge music and views of the lake. Sunflower also does meals and runs tours.

Information

Most of the banks on Th Khunlum Praphat have ATMs. A few internet shops can be found around the southern end of Th Khunlum Praphat.

Post office (Th Khunlum Praphat)

Srisangwarn Hospital (☎0 5361 1378; Th Singhanat Bamrung)

TAT (☎0 5361 2982; Th Khunlum Praphat; ⏰8.30am-4.30pm Mon-Fri) Across from the post office.

Tourist police (☎0 5361 1812, emergencies 1155; Th Singhanat Bamrung; ⏰8.30am-4.30pm) Report thefts or lodge complaints here.

Getting There & Around

Mae Hong Son is 368km from Chiang Mai, but the terrain is so rugged that the trip takes at least eight long, but scenic, hours. For this reason, many people opt for the 35 minute flight to/from Chiang Mai (1590-1890B, 35 minutes, four flights daily) with **Kan Air** (☎0 5361 3188; www.kanairlines.com) and **Nok Air** (☎1318; www.nokair.co.th). The airport is near the centre of town.

Mae Hong Son's bus station is 1km south of the city. Destinations include:

Bangkok 718B to 838B; 15 hours; three departures from 2pm to 4pm.

Chiang Mai Northern route 127B; eight hours; 8.30am and 12.30pm. Southern route 178B; nine hours; frequent departures from 6am to 9pm.

Mae Sariang 95B; four hours; frequent departures from 6am to 9pm.

Pai (70B; 4½ hours 8.30am and 12.30pm.

Minivans also depart from the bus station. Destinations include:

Chiang Mai 250B; six hours; every hour from 7am to 3pm.

Pai 150B; 2½ hours; every hour from 7am to 4pm.

The centre of Mae Hong Son can be covered on foot. Motorbike rental is available from **PA Motorbike** (☎0 5361 1647; 21 Th Pradit Jong Kham; ⏰7.30am-7.30pm), opposite Friend House.

Mae Sariang

Little-visited Mae Sariang is gaining a low-key buzz for its attractive riverside setting and emerging eco-trekking tours. There's natural beauty, ethnic and cultural diversity as well as a new breed of community-based trekking outfits.

Dragon Sabai Tours (☎08 548 0884; www.thailandhilltribeholidays.com; Th Mongkolchai); **Mae Sariang Tours** (☎08 2032 4790, 08 8404 8402; www.maesariangtravel.multiply.com); and **Salawin Tour & Trekking** (☎08 1024 6146; Th Laeng Phanit; 800B per person per day) are all recommended for their eco-conscious and culturally sensitive tours.

Sleeping

Northwest Guest House GUESTHOUSE $
(☎08 9700 9928; www.northwestgh.blogspot.com; 81 Th Laeng Phanit; r 250-450B; ❄@📶) The rooms in this cosy wooden house have simple mattresses on the floor, but it offers helpful local tour advice.

Mitaree Hotel GUESTHOUSE $
(☎0 5368 1110; www.mitareehotel.com; 256 Moo 2, Th Mae Sariang; r 250-500B; ❄) This is Mae Sariang's oldest hostelry. It has fan-cooled rooms in the old wooden wing or air-con rooms with hot-water shower in the new wing.

Eating & Drinking

Inthira Restaurant THAI $
(Th Wiang Mai; mains 30-150B; ⏰8am-10pm) Probably the town's best restaurant, this place features a strong menu of dishes using unique ingredients such as locally-grown shiitake mushrooms and fish from the Mae Nam Moei.

Leelawadee THAI $
(cnr Th Wiang Mai & Th Mae Sariang; mains 40-180B; ⏰7am-9pm; 📶) This cosy and friendly place has an English-language menu of both one-dish meals and mains, as well as real coffee and free wi-fi.

Getting There & Away

Bus destinations from Mae Sariang:

Bangkok 444B to 571B; 13 hours; four departures from 4pm to 7.30pm.

Chiang Mai 95B to 171B; four to five hours; five departures from 7am to 3pm.

Mae Hong Son 95B to 171B, three to four hours, six departures from 7am to 1am.

WESTERN THAILAND

Tall rugged mountains rise up from the central plains to meet Thailand's western border with Myanmar. Though the distances from population centres are minor, much of the region remains remote and undeveloped with an undercurrent of border intrigue. Displaced ethnic minorities seek safe haven from military persecution in Myanmar, while the untamed forests provide much-needed animal habitats in an increasingly industrialised region. Kanchanaburi, just a few hours' bus ride from Bangkok, is a convenient and historical gateway to the region.

Kanchanaburi

POP 47,147

If you don't have time for Chiang Mai and its surrounding mountain scenery, head to Kanchanaburi, west of Bangkok, quietly lounging alongside Mae Nam Khwae (Kwai River). The town has a healthy soft adventure scene – elephant rides and bamboo rafting – and is a peaceful place to relax if Bangkok made you dizzy. It also has an unlikely claim on WWII history as the site of a Japanese-operated WWII prisoner-of-war camp made famous by the movie *The Bridge Over the River Kwai*. Today visitors come to pay their respects to fallen Allied soldiers or to learn more about this chapter of the war.

Sights

Death Railway Bridge (Kwai River Bridge) HISTORICAL SITE

History often memorialises otherwise unremarkable places. Such is the case with this ho-hum bridge that provides a tangible hook to a compelling historical story.

Starting in 1942 during the Japanese occupation of Thailand, captured Allied soldiers and Burmese and Malay conscripts were transported to the jungles of Kanchanaburi to build 415km of rail – known today as the Death Railway because of the many lives (more than 100,000 men) lost. The railway was intended to link Thailand and Burma (Myanmar) in order to secure an alternative supply route for future Japanese conquests in Southeast Asia. The Japanese completed the Thai portion of the rail line in an astonishing 16 months – a construction feat considering the rough terrain, rudimentary equipment and harsh working conditions. The rails were joined 37km south of Three Pagodas Pass and in use for 20 months before Allied planes destroyed the bridge in 1945. Bomb damage on the now-reconstructed span is still apparent on the pylons closest to the riverbank.

The bridge is 2.5km from the town centre and is best reached via rented bicycle. Surrounding the bridge are tacky souvenir shops and other businesses that lack the gravitas the site should garner. At certain times you can walk across the span to the other side of the river where there are riverfront cafes and a more sylvan setting.

A **mini train** (20B, 15 mins, frequent departures from 8am-10am & noon-3pm) does a quick trip over the bridge from a nearby station. You can also ride along a longer portion of the POW-constructed line aboard trains that depart from Kanchanaburi's train station, across the bridge to the Nam Tok station north of town. This **historic line** (100B, two hr, 5.30am, 10.30am & 4pm departures) capitalises on the appeal to foreign tourists and charges them an inflated price for the one-way privilege.

During the first week of December there's a sound-and-light show put on at the bridge. The town gets a lot of tourists during this week, so book early.

Thailand-Burma Railway Centre MUSEUM

(☎0 3451 0067; www.tbrconline.com; 73 Th Chaokanen; admission 100B; ⏰9am-5pm) So you know that there was a bridge, a war and a catchy movie song but that's all you know about Kanchanaburi's role in WWII. Before you head out to see the Kwai River Bridge, get a little history at this museum. Professional exhibits outline Japan's military endeavours in Southeast Asia during WWII and its plan to connect Yangon (in Burma) with Bangkok via rail for transport of military supplies.

Allied War Cemetery CEMETERY

(Th Saengchuto; ⏰8am-6pm) Across the street from the Thailand-Burma Railway Centre is this immaculately maintained cemetery providing final shelter for the POWs who died here. The cemetery is maintained by the War Graves Commission. Of the 6982 POWs buried here, nearly half were British; the rest came mainly from Australia and the Netherlands. It is estimated that at least 100,000 people died while working on the railway, the majority being labourers from nearby Asian countries, though not one of these has an identifiable grave. If you are looking for the resting place of a relative or loved one, a small office to the side has lists of names and their locations within the cemetery.

World War II Museum MUSEUM

(Th Mae Nam Khwae; admission 40B; ⏰8am-6.30pm) Just southeast of the bridge is a privately owned museum, sometimes also called the JEATH War Museum to capitalise on the popularity of another museum by the same name in town. The collection might be the oddest assortment of memorabilia under one roof, but the building does afford picture-postcard views of the bridge.

Kanchanaburi

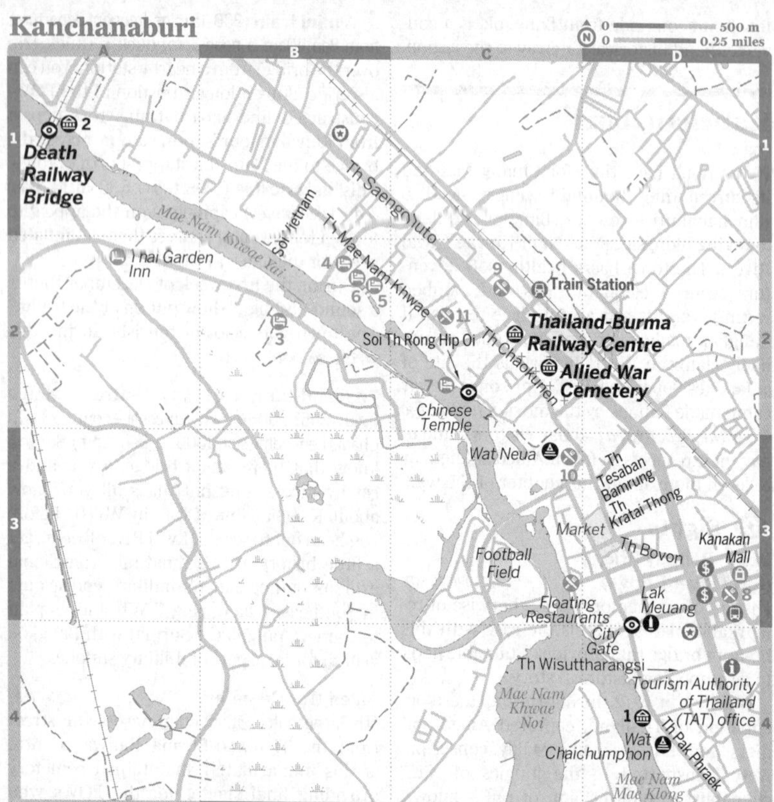

Jeath War Museum MUSEUM

(Th Wisuttharangsi; admission 30B; ⌚8am-6pm) This outdoor museum is hosted by Wat Chaichumphon (Wat Tai) and built to resemble the bamboo shelters where the POWs were housed. More a photo gallery than museum, it isn't very informative, but it is heartfelt, especially the fading pictures of surviving POWs who returned to Thailand for a memorial service. Jeath is an acronym of the countries involved in the railway: Japan, England, Australia/America, Thailand and Holland.

Chung Kai Allied War Cemetery CEMETERY

Chung Kai, 4km south of town, was the site of a major prisoner camp during WWII. Allied POWs built their own hospital and church close to here. Today relatively few people come to see this remote cemetery, which is the final resting place of 1700 soldiers, mostly Dutch, British, French and Australian. Most graves have short, touching epitaphs.

The cemetery is across the Mae Nam Khwae Noi and can be easily reached by bicycle or motorcycle.

Wat Tham Seua & Wat Tham Khao Noi TEMPLE

No visit to a Thai town is complete without seeing at least one temple. Here you can see two. These neighbouring hilltop monasteries, 14km south of town, offer almost panoramic views of the countryside. **Wat Tham Khao Noi** (Little Hill Cave Monastery) has an intricately designed Chinese-style pagoda while the larger **Wat Tham Seua** (Tiger Cave Monastery) boasts an 18m-tall Buddha covered in a golden mosaic. In front of the Buddha there is a conveyor belt with small silver trays into which donations are made and then tipped into a central pot. You can walk to the top or take the easy option and go by cable car (10B).

You'll need a motorbike to get out here; it's near Kheuan Meuang (City Dam).

Kanchanaburi

Top Sights

Allied War Cemetery C2
Death Railway Bridge A1
Thailand-Burma Railway Centre C2

Sights

1 Jeath War Museum D4
2 World War II Museum A1

Sleeping

3 Apple's Retreat B2
4 Blue Star Guest House B2
5 Pong Phen B2
6 Sam's House B2
7 VN Guest House C2

Eating

Blue Rice .... (see 3)
8 Night Market D3
9 Night Market C2
10 Saisowo C3
11 Sri Rung Rueng C2

Sleeping

The most atmospheric places to stay are built along the river. The once noisy karaoke barges are now limited to weekend evening merriment.

TOP CHOICE **Apple's Retreat** GUESTHOUSE $
(0 3451 2017; www.applenoi-kanchanaburi.com; 153/4 M.4 Bahn Tamakahm; r 490-690B;) With the welcoming smiles, this long-running guesthouse has friendly and knowledgeable staff and compact, clean rooms in a well-maintained garden. In a bid to be ecofriendly, the rooms lack a TV and fridge.

Sam's House GUESTHOUSE $
(0 3451 5956; www.samsguesthouse.com; Th Mae Nam Khwae; d 400-800B;) Bright and airy from reception to terrace, rooms are basic but come with fine views of the hyacinth-covered water.

Blue Star Guest House GUESTHOUSE $
(0 3451 2161; 241 Th Mae Nam Khwae; r 150-650B;) Set in a leafy garden, this is one laid-back crash pad with a variety of options.

Pong Phen GUESTHOUSE $
(0 3451 2981; www.pongphen.com; Th Mae Nam Khwae; r 150-1000B;) Score a cheapie here and you'll have pool access at a serious bargain.

VN Guest House GUESTHOUSE $
(0 3451 4082; www.vnguesthouse.net; 44 Soi Th Rong Hip Oi; r 280-450B;) One of the best of the older floating raft guesthouses; prepare for a few passing karaoke rafts if you stay at the weekend.

Eating

The **night market** (Th Saengchuto), near the bus station, is well-known for *hŏy tôrt* (fried mussels in an egg batter). Another **night market** (Th Saengchuto; Thu-Tue) sets up near the train station and serves fried treats and blended drinks.

Blue Rice THAI $
(153/4 M.4 Bahn Tamakahm; dishes 50-100B) Along with standard Thai dishes, chef Apple imports other regional dishes, such as blue rice and refreshing *yam sôm oh* (pomelo salad).

Saisowo THAI $
(Th Chaokunen; dishes 20-30B; 8am-4pm) This long-running noodle emporium has some of the finest *kŭaytĭaw mŭu* (pork noodles) in town. No English sign.

Sri Rung Reung INTERNATIONAL $
(Th Mae Nam Khwae; dishes 60-150B) The food is reasonably authentic but you'd best ask if you want some kick to your *sôm-tam* (papaya salad).

Information

Several major Thai banks can be found along Th Saengchuto near the market and bus terminal. Internet cafes can be found along Th Mae Nam Khwae. Check out www.kanchanaburi-info.com for general information.

Post office (Th Saengchuto)

TAT (0 3451 2500; Th Saengchuto; 8.30am-4.30pm) Near the bus terminal, it provides information on trips beyond Kanchanaburi.

Thanakarn Hospital (0 3462 2366) Best-equipped hospital for foreigners.

Tourist police (0 3451 2668; Th Saengchuto)

Getting There & Away

Bus

Kanchanaburi's **bus station** (Th Saengchuto) is near Th Lak Meuang and the TAT office. Services:

Bangkok's Southern (Sai Tai Mai) bus terminal (84B to 99B, two hours, frequent)

Bangkok's Northern (Mo Chit) bus terminal (94B to 122B, two hours, frequent) Transfer station for buses to northern Thailand.

Bangkok's Victory Monument (110B, two hours, frequent)

Sangkhlaburi (180B to 192B, four hours, frequent)

Suphanburi (47B, two hours, frequent) Connections to Ayuthaya.

Ratchaburi (47B to 65B, two hours, frequent) Connections to Hua Hin or Phetchaburi.

Train

Kanchanaburi's **train station** (Th Saengchuto) is 500m from the river, near the guesthouse area. Kanchanaburi is on the Bangkok Noi-Nam Tok rail line, which includes a portion of the historic Death Railway. The SRT promotes this as a historic route, and charges foreigners 100B for any one-way journey, regardless of the distance. Destinations include:

Bangkok Noi station (Three hours, departs 7.19am and 2.44pm) Located in Thonburi, across the river from Bangkok; trains depart for Kanchanaburi at 7.44am and 1.55pm.

Nam Tok (Two hours, departs 5.30am, 10.30am & 4.19pm) Returns to Kanchanaburi at 5.20am, 12.55pm and 3.15pm.

Getting Around

Săhmlór within the city cost 50B a trip. Regular sŏrngtăaou ply Th Saengchuto for 10B, but be careful you don't accidentally 'charter' one. There are plenty of places hiring motorbikes along Th Mae Nam Khwae. The going rate is 150B per day and it's a good way of getting to the rather scattered attractions around Kanchanaburi. Bicycles can be hired from most guesthouses for around 50B a day.

Around Kanchanaburi

Head out of town to explore Kanchanaburi's forests and rivers. Most of the guesthouses will book minivan tours that do a little bit of everything in a hurry.

Erawan National Park (☎0 3457 4222; admission 200B; ⌚8am-4pm) is the home of the seven-tiered **Erawan Falls**, which makes for a refreshing day swimming in pools and climbing around the trails. Go early as this is a popular tour spot. Buses from Kanchanaburi stop at the entrance to the falls (50B, 1½ hours, hourly from 8am to 5.20pm) The last bus back to Kanchanaburi leaves at 4pm.

Hellfire Pass Memorial (admission by donation; ⌚9am-4pm) curates a section of the Death Railway that was carved out of unforgiving mountain terrain under breakneck speed. The pass was so named for the fire-light shadows cast by the night-labouring POWs. Today a walking trail follows the old railbed. Located near the Km 66 marker on the Sai Yok-Thong Pha Phum road, Hellfire Pass can be reached by a Sangkhlaburi-bound or Thong Pha Phum-bound bus (60B, 1½ hours, last bus back at 4.45pm). Inform the attendant of your destination so that the bus stops en route.

Sangkhlaburi

Few tourists know the scenic but small town of Sangkhlaburi, but for international aid workers this is one of many remote outposts for refugee relief work. Many displaced people, whether they be Mon, Karen or Burmese, arrive in Thailand with few belongings and fewer rights. The town itself consists of just a few paved roads overlooking the enormous Kheuan Khao Laem (Khao Laem Dam). The surrounding wilderness is an underappreciated natural attraction boasting one of the largest conservation areas in Southeast Asia. Guesthouses in town can arrange outdoor outings.

P Guest House (☎0 3459 5061; www.pguesthouse.com; 8/1 Mu 1; r 250-950B; ❄) has English-speaking staff and rooms with lake views. Fan rooms are plain and have shared bathrooms. If you're interested in volunteer opportunities or visits to nearby forest sanctuaries, enquire here.

Burmese Inn (☎0 3459 5146; www.sangkhlaburi.com; 52/3 Mu 3; r 400-800B; ❄) has been renovated from flimsy to comfortable.

Travellers tend to eat at the main guesthouses, which all have lakefront restaurants. The **day market** is across from the bus stop and is good for sampling Mon-style curries (look for the large metal pots). **Baan Unrak**

THE END OF THE ROAD

If you've come this far, you might as well follow the road all the way to the end: to the border crossing of **Three Pagodas Pass**, 28km north of Sangkhlaburi. The pass hosts a market on both sides of the border and has long been a notorious smuggling route for contraband (though it isn't obvious, you can always pretend). For many years now the entrance to the Burmese town of Payathonzu has been closed to foreigners, but things could always change and when this border is open you can usually obtain a day pass (500B or US$10) to the Burmese market. Border formalities can be arranged at the checkpoint.

OF MIGRANTS & MISFORTUNE

Burmese refugees first crossed into Thailand in 1984, when the Myanmarese army penetrated the ethnic Karen state and began a campaign of forced relocation of the ethnic minority populations. Today there are three refugee camps around Mae Sot, and the UN High Commissioner for Refugees (UNHCR) estimates that 140,000 Burmese, mainly ethnic Karen, live in nine camps that line the border between Thailand and Myanmar. Within the camps, the refugees are assured of protection from the military, but have little opportunities to gain an education, employment or an independent life because the Thai government does not recognise them as citizens or residents. Some have lived in this limbo state for decades.

Bakery (snacks 25B to 90B) is a meat-less cafe with excellent pastries and Thai dishes and is run by a local charitable organisation.

The bus stop is across from the day market; destinations include:

Bangkok's Northern (Mo Chit) terminal 228B to 293B; seven hours; four daily departures.

Kanchanaburi 175B; 3½ hours; frequent.

Three Pagodas Pass 30B; 45minutes; frequent.

Mae Sot

POP 120,569

Mae Sot is a scruffy border town preoccupied with trading and cross-border traffic. But it's the population's diversity that is most striking – Indo-Burmese, Chinese, Karen, Hmong and Thai – an ethnic mix that makes border towns so intriguing. The town also hosts a relatively large population of foreign doctors and NGO aid workers, whose presence attests to the human cost of Myanmar's failed government.

There aren't a lot of official sights to lure tourists this far west, but a few come for a visa run and stay longer, realising that they can tap into the charitable spirit through a variety of volunteer organisations or escape the tourist crowds of northern Thailand with visits to the nearby underdeveloped nature preserves and hill-tribe communities.

Sights & Activities

Border Market MARKET

There is an expansive covered market alongside the Mae Nam Moei on the Thai side of the border that sells a mixture of workaday Burmese goods and cheap Chinese electronics. However the real reason most come here is to cross to Myawadi in Myanmar (see p712). The border was closed at the time of writing, though that status could change.

Sŏrngtăaou go to the border (20B, frequent departures from 6.30am to 5.30pm), 5km west of Mae Sot; ask to be let off at *'rim moei'* (Moei River bank). The last sŏrngtăaou going back to Mae Sot leaves at 5.30pm.

Herbal Sauna SAUNA

(Wat Mani; admission 20B; ⏲3-7pm) Many a rural Thai temples once boasted herbal saunas, a relaxing past-time. Gender specific facilities are located towards the back of the monastery grounds, past the *gù·dì* (the monk's living quarters).

Borderline Shop HANDICRAFTS

(☎0 5554 6584; www.borderlinecollective.org; 674/14 Th Intharakhiri; ⏲10am-6pm Tue-Sat, 2-6pm Sun) This shop has a bit of everything: it's a cafe, cooking school and craft collective, selling work by refugee women.

Sleeping

TOP CHOICE **Ban Thai Guest House** GUESTHOUSE $

(☎0 5553 1590; 740 Th Intharakhiri; r 250-950B; ❄@🛜) Mae Sot's best budget spot is also a favourite among visiting volunteers. Five converted Thai houses sit atop a well-manicured lawn, and the common area is conducive to meeting someone doing something interesting.

Green Guest House GUESTHOUSE $

(☎0 5553 3207; 406/8 Th Intarahakhiri; dm 100B, r 120-250B) Run by a teacher and her husband, this peaceful guesthouse offers a variety of good-sized rooms with TV. It is a great value, centrally located place.

Bai Fern Guesthouse GUESTHOUSE $

(☎0 5553 1349; www.bai-fern.com; 660 Th Inthara-khiri; r 150-300; ❄@) Set just off the road in a large house, the rooms here are tidy, but plain. All have well-equipped shared bathrooms. The service is very friendly with the use of a kitchen, fridge and wireless internet in the communal area.

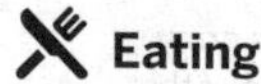

Eating

Mae Sot is a culinary crossroads. For breakfast head to the area south of the mosque where several Muslim restaurants serve sweet tea, roti and *nanbya* (a tandoori-style bread). The town's vibrant day market is the place to try Burmese dishes such as *mohinga*, a popular noodle dish. And Mae Sot's night market, at the eastern end of Th Prasat Withi, features mostly Thai-Chinese dishes.

Khrua Canadian INTERNATIONAL **$$**
(3 Th Sri Phanit; dishes 40-280B; ⏲breakfast, lunch & dinner) This is the place to go to get away from Asia for awhile. The servings are large, the menu is varied and local information is plentiful.

Lucky Tea Garden BURMESE **$**
(Th Bun Khun; mains 10-50B; ⏲5.30am-9pm) For the Burmese teashop experience without a border crossing, visit this friendly cafe equipped with sweet tea, tasty snacks, and of course, bad Burmese pop music.

Aiya BURMESE **$**
(533 Th Intharakhiri; dishes 45-80B; ⏲lunch & dinner Tue-Sun) Opposite Bai Fern Guest House, Aiya does Burmese and vegetarian.

Drinking

For a night on the town, head to the bars at the western end of Th Intharakhiri.

Mali Bar BAR
(Th Intharakhiri; ⏲6pm-midnight) Staffed by Burmese and popular with the NGO set, this rather dark bar has a pool table and a world music soundtrack.

Information

There are several banks with ATMs in the town centre.

Tourist police (☎1155; 738/1 Th Intharakhiri) East of the town centre at the border market.

Getting There & Away

Se Southeast Express (522/3 Th Intharakhiri) is a helpful travel agent. The bus station is 1.5km west of town. Destinations from Mae Sot include the following:

Bangkok (307B to 613B, eight hours, frequent)

Chiang Mai (253B to 326B, six hours, two morning departures)

Phitsanulok (157B, four hours, frequent) By minivan.

Sukhothai (125B, three hours, frequent) By minivan.

Orange sŏrngtăaou bound for Mae Sariang (200B, six hours, six departures from 6.20am to 12.20pm) depart from the old bus station near the centre of town.

NORTHEASTERN THAILAND

Thailand's other regions have natural beauty, but the northeast has soul. The main event in this undervisited region is the people, friendly folks who might invite you over to share their picnic under a shade tree.

That's not to say that there isn't beauty in the flat, sun-beaten landscape of rice fields punctuated by shade trees and lonely water buffaloes. Indeed, you've never seen such a vivid green until you've trundled through in the wet season when rice shoots are newly born.

GETTING TO MYANMAR: MAE SOT TO MYAWADI

This border has been closed since 2010. In the event it reopens, the following information applies. Mae Sot is a legal crossing point into the Myanmarese town of Myawadi for a one-day stay. Since this border doesn't grant entry into all of Myanmar, most travellers use it to renew an expiring Thai visa.

Getting to the border The border is 5km west of Mae Sot; sŏrngtăaou make the trip to the border (20B, frequent departures from 6.30am to 5.30pm).

At the border Mae Sot's **Thai immigration booth** (☎0 5556 3000; ⏲6.30am-6.30pm) can verify the border's open/closed situation. When open, you are required to pay US$10 (or 500B) for a day pass into Myanmar and your passport is left as a deposit. Then you're free to wander around Myawadi as long as you're back at the bridge by 5.30pm Myanmar time (which is a half-hour behind Thai time). On your return to Thailand, you will receive a new 15-day visa.

Also referred to as Isan, the northeast is one of Thailand's most rural and agricultural regions. It is a tapestry of Lao, Thai and Khmer traditional cultures, which meandered across the shifting borders much like the mighty Mekong River. The Mekong defines a wide arc across the northern reaches of the region passing small riverfront towns. Local festivals display the region's unique fusion of cultures, and magnificent mini-Angkor Wats were left behind by the Khmer empire.

There's little in the way of guesthouse culture and few English speakers. Indeed, this is the end of the tourist trail and the beginning of the Thailand trail.

Nakhon Ratchasima (Khorat)

POP 2 MILLION

To most shoestringers, Nakhon Ratchasima (or more commonly known as 'Khorat') is just a transit hub. Bland concrete development has buried much of its history, and its status as Thailand's second-largest city makes Bangkok look exponentially more interesting. But if you're curious, Khorat is a part of the urban Isan puzzle, where village kids grew up to be educated bureaucrats living comfortable middle-class lives – an economic success story.

Sights

Thao Suranari Memorial HISTORIC SITE

(Khun Ying Mo Memorial; Th Ratchadamnoen) In the city centre is the defiant statue of Thao Suranari, a local heroine who led the inhabitants against Lao invaders during the reign of Rama III (r 1824–51). A holy shrine, the statue receives visitors offering gifts and prayers or hired singers to perform Khorat folk songs. The annual Thao Suranari Festival is held 23 March to 3 April.

Dan Kwian HANDICRAFTS VILLAGE

Just a quick trip out of town, Dan Kwian has been producing pottery for hundreds of years and is something of a magnet for Thailand's artistic hippies. The ceramic creations are famous for their rough texture and rust-like hue derived from local kaolin sources. The village is essentially a row of art-gallery shops lining the highway. To get here, hop on a bus (14B, 30 minutes) from Khorat's southern city gate, the eastern gate or Bus Station 2.

Sleeping

Doctor's House GUESTHOUSE $

(08 5632 3396; 78 Soi 4, Th Seup Siri; r 200-350B;) The only backpacker abode in town, this old wooden house has simple but clean rooms with shared bathroom. It's not for party animals as the gate is locked at 10pm.

Sansabai House HOTEL $

(0 4425 5144; www.sansabai-korat.com; 335 Th Suranari; r 270-600B;) Though the lobby might dampen your spirits, even the cheapest rooms are bright and spotless and come with minifridge and little balconies.

Sri Ratna Hotel HOTEL $

(0 4424 3116; 7 Th Suranaree; r 180-300B;) Sri Ratna trades the Doctor's House's homey vibe for a central location. It has the ambience of an insane asylum, but the owners run it with care and efficiency.

Eating

Khorat is famous for *pàt mèe khorâht,* a local twist on the ubiquitous *phàt thai.*

Rabieng-Pa THAI $$

(0 4424 3137; 284 Th Yommarat; dishes 60-330B; dinner) The leafiest and loveliest restaurant on this busy stretch of Th Yommarat has a massive picture menu ensuring a tasty meal.

Wat Boon Night Bazaar THAI $

(Th Chumphon; 6-10pm) Head east to the Wat Boon Night Bazaar where you can sample all the market specialities: deep-fried crickets, pork sausages and other Isan delights.

Ming Ter VEGETARIAN $

(Th Rajadamnern; dishes 30-80B; breakfast & lunch;) This homey vegetarian affair does mock-meat versions of Thai and Chinese standards (though the menu is in Thai). Avoid communication confusion by pointing to something in the buffet tray.

Gai Yang Saang Thai NORTHEASTERN THAI $

(Th Rajadamnern; whole free-range chicken 150B; breakfast, lunch & dinner) Some of the best *gài yâhng* in Khorat for over 40 years. No English sign.

Information

There are banks galore in central Nakhon Ratchasima, all with ATMs and some with exchange services.

Post office (Th Jomsurangyat)

Bangkok Hospital (0 4426 9999; Th Mittaphap)

Nakhon Ratchasima (Khorat)

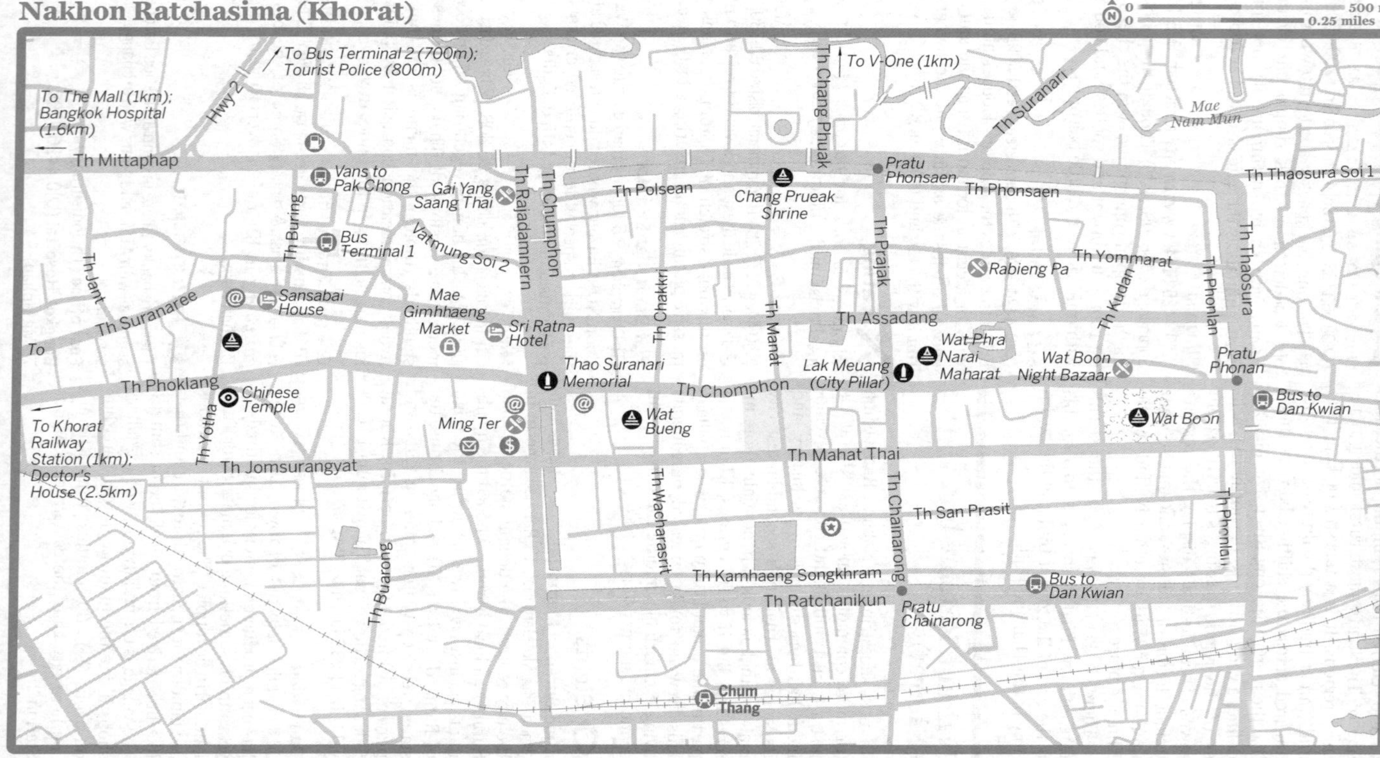

ISAN CUISINE: PUTTING THE FIRE IN SPICY

The holy trinity of Isan cuisine – *kài yâang* (grilled chicken), *sôm-tam* (papaya salad) and *khâo niaw* (sticky rice) – are integral to the identity of hard-working farmers. The Isan diaspora has been so widespread that their cuisine has now been adopted as mainstream.

Every Isan town wakes to a veritable chicken massacre, in which side-of-the-road grills are cluttered with marinated carcasses, and wafts of smoke lure appetites. Beside the grill is an earthenware *khrók* (mortar) and wooden *sàak* (pestle) beating out the ancient rhythm of *sôm-tam* preparation: in go grated papaya, sliced limes, a fistful of peppers, sugar and a host of preferential ingredients. People taste the contents and call out adjustments: more *náam plaa* (fish sauce) or *plaa ráa* (fermented fish sauce, which looks like rotten mud). Everything is eaten with the hands, using sticky rice as a 'spoon', and a plate of fresh, chalky-tasting vegetables help offset the chilli burn.

TAT (☎0 4421 3666; Th Mittaphap; ⏰8.30am-4.30pm) Next to Sima Thani Hotel.

Tourist police (☎0 4434 1777, ☎1155) Opposite Bus Station 2, north of the city centre.

ℹ Getting There & Away

Bus

Nakhon Ratchasima has two bus stations: **Bus Station No 1** (☎0 4424 2899; Th Burin) in the city centre serves Bangkok and towns within Nakhon Ratchasima province. Destinations include Bangkok's Northern & Northeastern (Mo Chit) bus station (154B to 250B, three hours) and **Pak Chong** (60B, one hour), the access point for Khao Yai National Park.

Bus Station No 2 (☎0 4425 6006; Hwy 2) serves all other destinations and also has minivan service. The white No 15 sŏrngtăaou with purple stripes and the blue-and-white No 7 go to Bus Terminal 2 *(bor kŏr sŏr sŏrng)*. Destinations include:

Aranya Prathet (190B, four hours)

Ayuthaya (132B, four hours)

Chiang Mai (435B to 653B, 12 to 13 hours)

Khon Kaen (118B to 230B, three hours)

Lopburi (120B, 3½ hours)

Nang Rong (66B to 85B, two hours) Access point for Phanom Rung.

Nong Khai (210B to 420B, six hours)

Surin (90B to 157B, four hours)

Trat (324B, eight hours) Transfer town for Ko Chang.

Ubon Ratchathani (203B to 330B, five to six hours)

Train

The **train station** (☎0 4424 2044; Th Mukkhamontri) is on the western side of the city. There are frequent services between Bangkok and the two terminal stations of Nong Khai and Ubon Ratchathani, though buses to most destinations are faster. Destinations:

Bangkok's Hualamphong train station (3rd class 100B, 2nd class 243B to 325B, five hours)

Ubon Ratchathani (3rd-class 168B, 2nd-class fan 243B, air-con 423B, five to six hours)

Nong Khai (3rd-class 214B, 2nd-class air-con 368B, 5½ hours)

ℹ Getting Around

Sŏrngtăaou (8B) run fixed routes through the city, but even locals complain about how difficult it is to figure out the numbers and colours assigned to the routes. Most pass down Th Suranari near the market, which is a good place to start. Heading west on Th Suranaree, the yellow sŏrngtăaou No 1 with white and green stripes will take you past the train station, near the Doctor's House.

Túk-túk and motorcycle taxis cost between 30B and 70B around town.

Phimai

Of the many Khmer temples that pepper Isan, **Phimai Historical Park** (☎0 4447 1568; Th Anantajinda; admission 100B; ⏰7.30am-6pm) is an easy day trip from Khorat, making it an ideal ruin for those pressed for time. Tourist infrastructure is further augmented by English-speaking guides, a valuable resource in these parts.

The temple was built a century before its strikingly similar cousin Angkor Wat and marked one of the westernmost outposts of the Khmer empire's holy highway of laterite temples. The site was originally started by King Jayavarman V in the late 10th century and finished by King Suryavarman I (r 1002-49). The majestic structure boasts a 28m-tall main shrine of cruciform design and made of white sandstone, while the adjunct shrines are of pink sandstone and laterite. The sculptures over the doorways to the main shrine depict Hindu gods and scenes from the Ramayana.

Phimai National Museum (Th Songkhran; admission 100B; ⏲9am-4pm Wed-Sun), outside the main complex, has a fine collection of Khmer sculpture, including temple lintels and other architectural ruins.

If Khorat is too busy for you, consider overnighting in Phimai town. Options include **Old Phimai Guesthouse** (☎08 0159 5363; www.phimaigh.com; Th Chomsudasadet; dm/s/d 100/170/200-370B; ❄📶), an old wooden house tucked down a quiet *soi*. The friendly hosts are a great source of information and run day trips to Phanom Rung.

Sai Ngam (Beautiful Banyan; admission free; ⏲daylight hr) is a 350-plus years old tree that blankets an island east of town where food vendors serve *pàt phimai,* which is basically *pàt mèe khorâht,* which is basically *phàt thai.*

All buses to Phimai leave from Khorat's Bus Station 2 (36B to 50B, 1¼ hours, half-hourly departures until 10pm).

Khao Yai National Park

Thailand's oldest and most remarkable national park, **Khao Yai** (☎08 6092 6529; admission 400B) is a vast wilderness astonishingly close to the country's major population centres. This is one of the largest intact monsoon forests in mainland Asia and, along with neighbouring forest complexes, it is now a Unesco World Heritage Site.

The park is centred around a 1351m-high mountain on the western edge of the Dangrek range, which forms a natural boundary between Thailand and Cambodia. There are more than 50km of trekking trails (many of them formed by the movement of wildlife), some wild elephant herds, majestic waterfalls (for part of the year) and impressive bird life.

The most beautiful time to visit is just after the monsoon rains in November through to the start of the hot season (around April) when the landscape is green and the waterfalls are full. But this is also when leeches are at their fiercest.

The park headquarters has some general trail information but doesn't have an accurate trail map. For the major highlights it is easy enough to visit on your own but you'll need a guide for minor trails and to spot wildlife. The guesthouses in Pak Chong can arrange transport and day tours. **Greenleaf Guesthouse** has long earned enthusiastic praise and a new player, **Bobby's Jungle Tours** (☎0 4432 8177; www.bobbysjungletourskhaoyai.com) looks promising.

Sleeping & Eating

Staying within the park cuts out your commute, though access to food and transport are limited. Park restaurants at the visitor centre close at 7pm. Most backpackers base themselves in the nearby town of Pak Chong.

TOP CHOICE **Greenleaf Guesthouse** GUESTHOUSE $
(☎0 4436 5073; www.greenleaftour.com; Th Thanarat, Km7.5; r 200-300B; 📶) Step past the slightly chaotic common areas to find good-value rooms (with cold-water private bathrooms) at this long-running family-owned place. Note that in high season they might be 'full' if you don't book a tour.

Park Accommodation CAMPING $
(☎0 2562 0760; www.dnp.go.th/parkreserve; camping 30B, r from 800B) Within the park there are campsites and a variety of rooms and bungalows, which require advance reservation through the central park's system. Camping gear is also available for rent.

Khao Yai Garden Lodge HOTEL $$
(☎0 4436 5178; www.khaoyaigardenlodgekm7.com; Th Thanarat, Km 7; r 250-2500B; ❄@📶🏊) This lodge is mainly an upscale resort but there are a few shared-bath cheapies for the hoi polloi.

Getting There & Around

All 2nd-class Bangkok-Khorat buses stop in Pak Chong (from Bangkok 108B to 139B, two hours; from Khorat 60B to 74B, one hour). From Bangkok, use the Northern & Northeastern bus terminal. There are also minivans to Bangkok's Victory Monument (160B, 2½ hours; hourly) that depart from the traffic light, and to Khorat (60B, one hour, every 20 minutes) from the market. Minivans departing from Khorat stop in Ayuthaya (90B) and Lopburi (70B) and accept Pak Chong passengers if there are empty seats.

Sŏrngtăaou travel the 30km from Pak Chong to the park's northern gate (40B, 45 minutes, every half-hour from 6am to 5pm); hop aboard on Th Thanarat in front of the 7-Eleven store and hop off at the ticket gate. From here it is another 14km to the visitor centre; hitchhiking this stretch is quite common. There are also motorcycle rentals at the gate and in Pak Chong town (300B).

Pak Chong is also on the rail line, but this is only a good option if you're coming from Ayuthaya (3rd class 53B, 2nd-class 83B to 173B, two hours, frequent), which saves you from backtracking into Bangkok.

Phanom Rung Historical Park

Spectacularly located atop an extinct volcano, **Prasat Phanom Rung** (☎0 4463 1746; admission 100B; ⏰6am-6pm) is the largest and best restored of the ancient Khmer sanctuaries in Thailand. Dating from the 10th to 13th centuries, the complex faces east towards the sacred capital of Angkor in Cambodia. It was first built as a Hindu monument and features sculpture relating to Vishnu and Shiva. Later it was converted into a Buddhist temple.

The craftsmanship at Phanom Rung represents the pinnacle of Khmer artistic achievement, on a par with the bas-reliefs at Angkor Wat in Cambodia. One of the most striking design features is the promenade, an avenue sealed with laterite and sandstone blocks and flanked by sandstone pillars with lotus-bud tops. It leads to the first and largest of three *naga* bridges, which are the only surviving architectural features of their kind in Thailand.

The central *prasat* (tower) has a gallery on each of its four sides, and the entrance to each gallery is itself a smaller incarnation of the main tower. The galleries have curvilinear roofs and windows with false balustrades. Once inside the temple walls, check out the galleries and the *gopura* (entrance pavilion), paying particular attention to the lintels over the doors.

If you can, plan your visit for one of the four times of the year when the sun shines through all 15 sanctuary doorways. This solar alignment happens during sunrise on 3 to 5 April and 8 to 10 September and sunset on 5 to 7 March and 5 to 7 October (one day earlier in leap years).

Several English-speaking guides (fees are negotiable) are available at the information centre.

Sleeping

Phanom Rung is a day trip from Nakhon Ratchasima (Khorat) and Surin, but some people spend the night in Nang Rong, the nearest town to the temple.

P California Inter Hostel GUESTHOUSE $
(☎08 1808 3347; www.pcaliforniananangrong.webs.com; Th Sangkakrit; r 250-700B; ❄@📶) On the east side of town, this guesthouse has bright, good-value rooms. The friendly, English-speaking owners are full of advice about the area and can arrange Phanom Rung tours as well as bike and motorcycle hire.

A 'RUIN'ED NEIGHBOURHOOD

Surrounding Phanom Rung are other minor Khmer ruins worth visiting for their remote ambience. **Prasat Muang Tam** (admission 100B; ⏰6am-6pm) was once a shrine to Shiva and dates to the 10th or 11th century. A 150B combo ticket allows entry to both Phanom Rung and Muang Tam. Motorcycle taxis will make the trip from Phanom Rung for another 150B.

Honey Inn GUESTHOUSE $
(☎0 4462 2825; www.honeyinn.com; 8/1 Soi Si Kun; r 250-350B; ❄@📶) This place, 1km from the bus station, has simple rooms.

Getting There & Away

For day-trippers from Khorat (Nakhon Ratchasima) or Surin, take a bus to Ban Tako (60B to 85B, two hours, hourly), a well-marked turn-off 14km east of Nang Rong, the closet village to the historic site. From here the easiest option is to hire a motorcycle taxi (300B to 400B roundtrip).

If you're overnighting in Nang Rong, buses pass through from Khorat (70B to 80B, two hours, hourly) and Pak Chong (1st class 140B, 2½ hours, hourly). From Nang Rong there's a sŏrngtăaou that leaves from the old market at the east end of town to the parking lot at the foot of Phanom Rung. You'll need to hire transport up the mountain.

Surin & Around

POP 41,200

There's not a lot to see in sleepy Surin until the annual Elephant Roundup comes to town in November. The rest of the year, a few travellers trickle through en route to the Khmer temple of Phanom Rung and other minor temples that line the Cambodian border. Culturally, Surin has a strong Khmer influence, and the province is renowned for its silk-weaving villages.

Surin is also a launching point for a little-used border-crossing point for Siem Reap-bound travellers (see p719).

Sights

Elephant Study Centre ELEPHANT VILLAGE
(☎0 4414 5050; Ban Ta Klang; admission 100B; ⏰shows 10am & 2pm) To see Surin's elephants on their home turf, head to this village, about 50km north of Surin. The Suay people are a minority ethnic group who traditionally

herded and trained elephants. Twice daily elephant shows include the usual tusker tricks. There are also elephant rides and a homestay program. Sŏrngtăaou run here from Surin's bus terminal (50B, two hours, hourly), with the last one returning at 4pm.

Craft Villages HANDICRAFT CENTRES

There are many silk and silvercraft villages within easy striking distance of Surin town. These villages' traditional arts display Khmer influences and are not widely available in the rest of the country. **Ban Tha Sawang**, 8km from Surin, is one of the most renowned silk villages in Thailand, known for its exquisite brocade fabrics *(pâh yók torng)*. Sŏrngtăaou (15B, 20 minutes) run regularly from Surin's day market, and a túk-túk should cost about 150B to 200B.

Ban Khwao Sinarin and **Ban Chok**, about 18km north of Surin, are known for silk and silver respectively. Khun Manee, who runs **Phra Dab Suk** (08 9865 8720; Ban Khwao Sinarin) on the main drag takes visitors to see silk being woven; call in advance. Big blue sŏrngtăaou to Ban Khwao Sinarin (25B, 1½ hours, hourly) leave from Surin's train station.

Volunteering

Surin has a volunteer scene thanks to **Starfish Ventures** (08 1723 1403; www.starfishvolunteers.com) and **LemonGrass Volunteering** (0819775300; www.lemongrass-volunteering.com). If you'd like to spend some quality time with elephants, the **Surin Project** (08 4482 1210; www.surinproject.org; 12,000B), run by the Elephant Nature Park, helps educate villagers about ecotourism opportunities as a revenue alternative to street begging.

Festivals

The annual **Elephant Round-up** (November) showcases the elephants in mock battles and various feats of strength and dexterity, and all of the hotels fill up with foreigners – an astonishing feat in itself.

WEIRD & WONDERFUL ISAN

From ghouls to gunpowder, Isan dominates in the bizarre attractions category.

Dan Sai's Spirit Festival

The raucous **Phi Ta Khon Festival** is a cross between the revelry of Carnival and the ghoulishness of Halloween. The festival coincides with a subdued Buddhist holy day of Bun Phra Wet (Phra Wet Festival), honouring the penultimate life of Buddha, Phra Wessandara (often shortened in Thai to Phra Wet). But in Dan Sai the main event is a rice-whisky-fuelled parade in which villagers don masks to transform themselves into the spirits who welcomed Phra Wet's return. The shop **Kawinthip Hattakham** (08 9077 2080; phitakhon@yahoo.com; 70/1 Th Kaew Asa; 6.30am-8pm) can help arrange homestay accommodation. Dan Sai sits between Loei (60B, 1½ hours) and Phitsanulok (94B, three hours) and the festival usually occurs in June.

Yasothon's Kaboom Fest

Rocket Festivals *(Bun Bâng Fai)* are held across Isan in May and June to tell Phaya Thaen, a pre-Buddhist rain god, that it's time for him to send down the wet stuff; but no place celebrates as fervently as Yasothon, where the largest rockets, called *bâng fai síp láhn*, are 3m long and packed with 500kg of gunpowder. There are homestays available and Yasothon can be reached by bus from Nakhon Ratchasima (158B to 205B, four hours) and Ubon Ratchathani (66B to 85B, 1½ hours) and by minivan from Mukdahan (76B, two hours, every half-hour).

Si Saket's Glass Temple

Before recycling was in vogue, the idea for the **Million Bottle Temple** (Wat Lan Khuat; daylight hr) was born from a religious vision. In 1982, the abbot dreamt of a sanctuary in heaven made of diamonds and gems. Wishing to replicate this divine splendour he set about covering the temple buildings in the most sparkly material he could find: green bottles. And today the temple shines *sort of* gem-like. The temple sits outside of Si Saket in Khun Han, 11km south of Hwy 24 via Rte 2111. Public transport is limited so you'll have to rent a motorbike in Surin.

GETTING TO CAMBODIA

If you find yourself in this remote corner of Thailand, you're surprisingly close to Cambodia's Angkor temples. The following are little-used crossings that can get you to Siem Reap.

Chong Chom to O Smach

Getting to the border Minibuses leave from Surin's bus terminal to the border (60B, 1½ hours, frequent).

At the border Travellers have reported Thai officials charging unnecessary fees (politely decline this opportunity). Cambodian visas (US$20; bring a passport photo) are available at the border.

Moving on Transport is tricky on the Cambodian side; share taxis go to Samraong and moto or private taxis do the remainder to Siem Reap, though the road is in poor condition.

See p93 for information on doing the trip in the opposite direction.

Chong Sa Ngam to Choam

This remote crossing provides access to the former Khmer Rouge stronghold of Anlong Veng and on to Siem Reap.

Getting to the border There is no direct public transport from Surin or Si Saket to the border so it is easiest (though not cheapest) to hire transport.

At the border Cambodian visas are available at the border with the usual formalities (US$20, passport photo).

Moving on Once across, travellers have reported hiring motos to tour Khmer Rouge sites, like Pol Pot's grave, and the road to Siem Reap is in good condition.

See p91 for information on doing the trip in the opposite direction.

Sleeping & Eating

During the elephant roundup, every hotel in town is booked and rates can triple; reserve well in advance.

Pirom-Aree's House GUESTHOUSE $
(☎0 4451 5140; Soi Arunee, Th Thungpo; s/d 120/200B) This guesthouse is 1km west of the city in a peaceful but somewhat far-flung location. Still, Pirom is a knowledgeable asset for tourism in Isan and can arrange tours to Khmer ruins. The wooden, shared bathrooms back onto a shady garden and rice paddy.

Ban Donmai GUESTHOUSE $
(☎08 9948 4181; Rte 226; r 300-500B; ❄) The 'Treehouse' is a combination of Gilligan's Island and a dishevelled basement. It's 3km from downtown, along the highway. Boonyai and Nan, the cheerful owners, prefer that guests book at least a day in advance; in return, there's free pick-up.

Night Bazaar THAI $
(Th Krungsri Nai; ⊙5-10pm) Everybody in town turns up for the pedestrian-only market to shop, eat dinner and watch each other.

Petmanee 2 NORTHEASTERN THAI $
(☎08 4451 6024; Th Murasart; dishes 20-60B; ⊙lunch) Surin's most famous purveyor of *sôm-tam* and *kài yâang* is down a small *soi* south of Ruampaet Hospital and next to Wat Salaloi. There's no English spoken or written here and no English sign, but the food is so good it's worth the hassle.

Getting There & Away

The **bus terminal** (Th Jit Bamrung) is one block from the train station. Destinations include the following:

Aranya Prathet 137B; six hours; three daily.

Bangkok 250B to 320B; seven hours.

Nakhon Ratchasima 90B to 157B; four hours; every half-hour.

Ubon Ratchathani 105B to 200B; three hours.

The **train station** (Th Nong Toom & Th Thawasan) is centrally located. Destinations:

Bangkok 3rd class 73B, 2nd class 279B to 399B; three hours.

Ubon Ratchathani 3rd class 81B, 2nd class 122-150B; seven hours.

GETTING TO LAOS: CHONG MEK TO VANG TAO

This busy border crossing connects to Laos' Si Phan Don (Four Thousand Islands) region via Pakse; it is also the only Thai-Lao border where you don't have to cross the Mekong.

Getting to the border Minivans from Ubon Ratchathani go to Chong Mek (100B, 1¼ hours, every half hour). There are also direct buses from Ubon to Pakse that stop at the border for visa formalities.

At the border The crossing is largely hassle-free, save for the occassional practice of a 50B 'stamping' levy by Lao officials. Lao visas are available on the spot for US$30 to US$42, depending on nationality; a passport photo is also needed.

Moving on The southern Lao city of Pakse is about 45 minutes away.

For information on crossing this border in the opposite direction, see p362.

Ubon Ratchathani

POP 115,000

Although it is one of the bigger cities in the region, Ubon still retains a small-town feel thanks to the relaxing nature of the Mae Nam Mun, Thailand's second-longest river, and its palpable Lao heritage. It is easily traversed by foot and easily appreciated by aimless wandering.

Ubon doesn't see a lot of foreign visitors because it is in an odd corner of the country, but there is a nearby Thai-Lao border crossing that provides an alternative route into southern Laos.

Sights

Wat Si Ubon Rattanaram TEMPLE

(Th Uparat) Wat Si Ubon Rattanaram houses the 7cm-tall Topaz Buddha (Phra Kaew Butsarakham), which was reportedly brought here from Vientiane at Ubon's founding and is the city's holiest possession.

Ubon Ratchathani National Museum MUSEUM

(Th Kheuan Thani; admission 100B; 9am-4pm Wed-Sun) Housed in a former palace of the Rama VI era, Ubon National Museum is a good place to delve into local history and culture.

Festivals

Candle Parade FESTIVAL

Ubon is most famous for its Candle Parade, when huge wax sculptures are paraded to the temples. It marks the beginning of the Buddhist rains retreat in July.

Sleeping & Eating

Rates shoot up and availability goes down during the Candle Festival.

TOP CHOICE **Sri Isan Hotel** HOTEL $

(0 4526 1011; www.sriisanhotel.com; Th Ratchabut; r 380-800B;) The exception to Isan's low-grade hotels is this cheerful place.

Thongcome Mansion HOTEL $

(08 1579 3629; Th Suriyat; r 350B;) This little family-run place has some of Ubon's spiffiest rooms in this price range.

River Moon Guesthouse GUESTHOUSE $

(0 4528 6093; 21 Th Sisaket 2; r 150-200B;) A crumbling old place with cheap rooms, 300m from the train station.

TOP CHOICE **Jumpa-Hom** THAI $$

(Th Phichit Rangsan; dishes 55-1500B; dinner;) Lovely and delicious, Jumpa-Hon does a little of everything.

Night Market THAI $

(Th Kheuan Thani; 4pm-midnight) Over the past few years, Ubon's city centre night market has grown into an excellent dining destination.

Porntip Gai Yang Wat Jaeng NORTHEASTERN THAI $

(Th Saphasit; dishes 20-130B; breakfast, lunch & dinner) It looks like a tornado whipped through this no-frills spot, but the chefs cook up a storm of their own. This is considered by many to be Ubon's premier purveyor of *gài yâhng, sôm·đam,* sausages and other Isan foods.

Information

Main post office (Th Luang; 8.30am-4.30pm Mon-Fri, 9am-noon Sat, Sun & holidays)

Ubonrak Thonburi Hospital (0 4526 0285; Th Phalorangrit)

TAT (☎0 4524 3770; www.tatubon.org; 264/1 Th Kheuan Thani; ⊙8.30am-4.30pm)

Tourist police (☎0 4524 5505, emergency ☎1155; Th Suriyat)

Getting There & Around

Ubon's **bus terminal** (☎0 4531 6085; Th Chayangkun) is located at the far northern end of town, 3km from the centre. It is accessible via sŏrngtăaou No 2, 3 or 10. Destinations include:

Bangkok's Northern & Northeastern (Mo Chit) bus terminal 385B to 473B, eight hours.

Nakhon Ratchasima 203B to 330B, five to six hours.

Mukdahan 75B to 135B, 3½ hours.

Surin 105B to 200B, three hours.

The **train station** (☎0 4532 1588; Th Sathani) is located in Warin Chamrap, south of central Ubon, accessible via sŏrngtăaou No 2. There are a couple of night trains in either direction connecting Ubon and Bangkok (3rd class 245B, 2nd class 371B to 551B).

Numbered sŏrngtăaou (10B) run throughout town. A túk-túk trip will cost at least 40B.

Mukdahan

POP 34,300

Mukdahan is a well-oiled revolving door between Thailand and Savannakhet in Laos, thanks to the Thai-Lao Friendship Bridge 2, an infrastructure link brought about by the ambitious Trans-Asia Highway project that continues by road all the way to the Vietnamese port town of Danang. Though the world has arrived at Mukdahan's doorstep, the town provides little distraction between arrival and departure.

If you need to overnight here, **Ban Rim Suan** (☎0 4263 2980; Th Samut Sakdarak; r 330B; ❄@📶) is the best budget deal in the city. **Wine Wild Why?** (11 Th Samron Chaikhongthi; dishes 40-150B; ⊙lunch & dinner) is an atmospheric eatery for Thai and Isan food. **Goodmook** (414/1 Th Song Nang Sathit; dishes 70-380B; ⊙breakfast, lunch & dinner; 📶) has all the ingredients of a travellers' cafe: an international menu, free wi-fi and actual decor. The **night market** (Th Song Nang Sathit; ⊙4-10pm) provides plenty of Vietnamese food along with the usual suspects.

Mukdahan's bus terminal is on Rte 212, west of town. Take a yellow sŏrngtăaou (10B) from Th Phitak Phanomkhet near the fountain. Destinations include:

Bangkok's Northern & Northeastern bus terminal 390B to 502B, 10 hours, evening departures.

Nakhon Phanom 52B to 88B, 2½ hours, frequent.

That Phanom 28B to 45B, one hour.

Khon Kaen 155B to 187B, 4½ hours, frequent.

Ubon Ratchathani (75B to 135B, 3½ hours, frequent).

That Phanom

This drowsy hamlet is a little piece of Laos on the wrong side of the Mekong River. It is not a place you'd chart a course to on purpose but if you're headed to Nong Khai from the Mukdahan border crossing, That Phanom is a lovely detour. The highlight in town is **Wat Phra That Phanom** (Th Chayangkun), crowned by an iconic *tâht,* a needle-like Lao-style *chedi*. A lively **Thai-Lao market** (⊙7am-noon Mon & Thu) gathers by the river north of the pier where Lao merchants sell herbal medicines, forest roots and river crabs. During the **That Phanom Festival** (late January or early February) visitors come for a boisterous temple fair including *mŏr lam* (Isan traditional music).

Kritsada Rimkhong Hotel (☎08 1262 4111; www.ksdrimkhong-resort.com; 90 Th Rim-

GETTING TO LAOS: MUKDAHAN TO SAVANNAKHET

The Thai-Lao Friendship Bridge 2 links Mukdahan and Savannakhet, where onward transport continues to the Vietnamese coast.

Getting to the border From Mukdahan, buses (45B, 45 minutes, hourly from 7.30am to 7pm) make the crossing.

At the border Border formalities are handled on the bridge. A 30-day Lao visa is available for US$30 to $42, depending on nationality; bring a passport photo.

Moving on On the Lao side there are long-distance buses to Vietnam, a journey of about seven hours.

For information on crossing from Laos into Thailand, see p357.

khong; r 350-500B; ❄@📶) has rooms that range from plain to attractive.

There's a small **night market** (🕐4-10pm) and **riverside eateries** (Th Rimkhong) for dinner.

That Phanom's bus station is west of town with services to Ubon Ratchathani (95B to 167B, 4½ hours, hourly), Mukdahan (26B to 45B, one hour), Udon Thani (109B to 167B, four hours, five daily) and Nakhon Phanom (27B to 47B, one hour, five daily). You can also take one of the frequent sŏrngtăaou (35B, 90 minutes) that park in town.

Nakhon Phanom

POP 31,700

This tidy provincial capital has a picturesque setting beside the Mekong River overlooking the asymmetrical peaks of Laos. With its French colonial buildings and Vietnamese influences, this is a little piece of Indochina on the far northeastern fringes of Siam. There's also a legal border crossing into Laos should you be looking for an escape hatch.

The **TAT Office** (☎4251 3490; Th Sunthon Wijit; 🕐8.30am-4.30pm) has a map pointing out several heritage buildings. The neighbouring village of Ban Na Chok, 3km west of town, gave refuge to Vietnamese liberator Ho Chi Minh. He planned the resistance movement in what is now called **Uncle Ho's House** (admission 50B), which served as his residence from 1928-29. More Uncle Ho memories are kept at the **community centre** (donations appreciated; 🕐8am-5pm).

The city runs an hour-long **sunset cruise** (☎08 6230 5560; 50B; departs 5pm) along the Mekong on *Thesaban 1,* which docks across from the Indochina Market.

Nakhon Phanom is famous for its October **Illuminated Boat Procession**, a modern twist on the ancient tradition of floating offerings to the Mekong *naga,* a mythical serpent that appears in Buddhist art and iconography.

Winter Hotel (☎0 4251 1946; 272 Th Bamrung Meuang; r 250-400B; ❄@📶) has clean if elderly rooms. **Nakhon Phanom Design Center Hostel** (NDC; ☎08 5668 1780; Th Goobahtwai; dm incl breakfast & bicycle 350B; ❄📶) is an outpost of cool occupying a converted shophouse with loads of character.

The outdoor terrace at the **Indochina Market** (Th Sunthon Wijit; 🕐breakfast, lunch & dinner) has choice seats that frame the mountain views. The **night market** (Th Fuang Nakhon; 🕐4-9pm) cooks up a variety of take-away food. **Luk Tan** (☎0 4251 1456; 83 Th Bamrung Meuang; buffet 89B; 🕐dinner), in the centre of town, is a quirky spot featuring international dishes.

The **bus terminal** (Th Fuang Nakhon) is east of the town centre. Destinations include Nong Khai (210B, six hours, six daily departures), Udon Thani (155B to 195B, five hours, frequent), Mukdahan (52B to 88B, two hours, hourly), That Phanom (27B to 49B, one hour, five daily) and Bangkok (450B to 592B, 12 hours, morning and evening departures).

Nong Khai

POP 61,500

Adorable Nong Khai has a winning recipe: a sleepy setting beside the Mekong River, enough tourist amenities to dispel isolation

GETTING TO LAOS: REMOTE BORDERS

Nakhon Phanom To Tha Khaek

Though not the most convenient crossing, Nakhon Phanom feeds into the Lao town of Tha Khaek.

At the border The new Thai-Lao Friendship bridge opened in 2011 and the crossing is now made by bus. Lao visas are available at the border for US$30 to US$42, depending on nationality; bring a passport photo.

Moving on Savannakhet is a two-hour bus ride from Tha Khaek.

See p354 for information on doing the trip in the reverse direction.

Bueng Kan to Paksan

Although it's very rarely done, you can cross the border here to Paksan, but only if you already have your Lao visa. The boat costs 60B per person and goes when there are eight passengers. Buses to Bueng Kan leave from Nong Khai (100B, 2½ hours, six daily), Nakhon Phanom (130B, three hours, six daily) and Udon Thani (150B, 4½ hours, 12 daily).

AT HOME WITH THE HERD

Thailand's rural northeast is flush with village homestay programs, mainly aimed at urban Thais who didn't grow up beside a rice paddy. Of the few that can accommodate English-speaking visitors is **Kham Pia Homestay** (☎0 4241 3578, 08 7861 0601; www.thailandwildelephanttrekking.com; per person 200B, meals 50-90B), which is located within walking distance of the 186-sq-km Phu Wua Wildlife Reserve. The reserve has nature trails and a resident herd of elephants. Kham Pia is 190km east of Nong Khai, just 3km off Hwy 212. Buses from Nong Khai (140B, 3½ hours) will drop you at Ban Don Chik, 3km away.

and enough local attractions to fill a day with sightseeing, snacking and wandering. It's an easy overnight train ride from Bangkok and sits right on a convenient border crossing into Vientiane, Laos.

Sights

Sala Kaew Ku SCULPTURE PARK
(Wat Khaek; admission 20B; ⏲8am-6pm) A curious, must-see attraction, Sala Kaew Ku is a sculpture park that was born from a spiritual vision by a Brahmanic yogi-priest-shaman who emigrated from Laos. The statues are a potpourri of the Hindu and Buddhist pantheon, and the immense statues offer some freaky photo opportunities. While the motivations for its 20-year construction were undoubtedly spiritual, the end result is a masterpiece of modern religious art. The sculpture park is 5km southeast of town. It is easily reached by bicycle from Nong Khai; Mut Mee Guest House distributes maps.

Talat Tha Sadet MARKET
(Th Rimkhong; ⏲8.30am-6pm) Talat Tha Sadet follows the river, obscuring the view with stalls selling crusty French baguettes, salted and grilled river fish, silks, souvenirs, and, if you look really hard, possibly the kitchen sink.

Volunteering

Nong Khai has sprouted a volunteer scene. **Isara** (www.isara.org) and **Open Mind Projects** (www.openmindprojects.org) place volunteers.

Festivals

Like many other northeastern towns, Nong Khai has a **Rocket Festival** *(Bun Bâng Fai),* which begins on Visakha Bucha day in late May/early June.

The end of Buddhist Lent *(Ork Phansaa)* in late October/early November ushers in a variety of river-based events, including **long-tail boat races** and the mysterious **naga fireballs** (when illuminated seemingly gaseous balls rise out of the river on the night of the full moon).

Sleeping

Nong Khai is the only Isan town with a full-fledged backpacker scene, so enjoy it while you can.

Mut Mee Garden Guesthouse GUESTHOUSE $
(☎0 4246 0717; www.mutmee.com; Soi Mutmee, Th Kaew Worawut; r 150-1200B; ❄📶) Overlooking the mighty Mekong, the Mut Mee is a destination in itself. The rooms are good value, the garden is *soooo* relaxing and the friendly English owner is a great storyteller.

Ruan Thai Guesthouse GUESTHOUSE $
(☎0 4241 2519; 1126/2 Th Rimkhong; r 200-400B, f 1200B; ❄@📶) Once little more than a small private home, this pleasant spot has grown with the boom times and now boasts a variety of quality rooms and a flower-filled garden.

E-San Guesthouse GUESTHOUSE $
(☎08 5010 2540; 419/1 Th Khun Muang; r 200-700B; ❄📶) This quiet place east of Talat Tha Sadet has simple rooms in a beautifully restored wooden house. There's also a modern air-con wing as well.

Sawasdee Guesthouse GUESTHOUSE $
(☎0 4241 2502; www.sawasdeeguesthouse.com; 402 Th Meechai; s/d 160/200-450B; ❄@📶) This Franco-Chinese shophouse has tidy rooms (the fan options share bathrooms) that are rich in history though lacking in decor. The owner is quite a character.

Eating

TOP CHOICE **Nagarina** THAI $
☎0 4241 2211; Th Rimkhong; dishes 40-250B; ⏲lunch & dinner; 📶🖉) Associated with Mut Mee Guesthouse, this floating restaurant turns out real-deal Thai without turning

GETTING TO LAOS: NONG KHAI TO VIENTIANE

Nong Khai to Vientiane is one of the most popular Thai-Lao border crossings.

Getting to the border Túk-túk from central Nong Khai go to the Thai-Lao Friendship Bridge (100B for two people), where border formalities are handled.

At the border After getting stamped out of Thailand, you can take a minibus (20B) across the bridge to the Lao immigration checkpoint, where visas are available (US$32 to US$42, depending on nationality; bring a passport photo).

Moving on From the bridge it's 22km to Vientiane, via buses, túk-túk and taxis. If you already have a Lao visa, there are also direct buses to Vientiane from Nong Khai's bus terminal (55B, one hour).

For information on making this crossing in the opposite direction, see p321.

down the spicy, fishy flavours. There's a sunset cruise (100B) most nights around 5pm.

TOP CHOICE **Dee Dee Pohchanah** THAI $
(Th Prajak; dishes 40-230B; ⏲lunch & dinner) Dee Dee means 'really good' in Thai and you can tell from the crowd.

Daeng Namnuang VIETNAMESE $
(Th Rimkhong; dishes 45-180B; ⏲breakfast, lunch & dinner; 📶) This massive Vietnamese restaurant has grown into an Isan institution known throughout the country for its *nǎam neu·ang* (pork spring rolls).

Saap Lah NORTHEASTERN THAI $
(897/2 Th Meechai; dishes 25-60B; ⏲breakfast, lunch & dinner) For excellent *gài yâhng, sôm·đam* and other Isan foods, follow your nose to this no-frills food shop. No English sign.

Drinking

There are several pubs along Th Rimkhong, the riverfront road. Two standouts are **Gaia** (⏲7pm-late Wed-Mon) and **Warm Up** (476/4 Th Rimkhong; ⏲7pm-2am), which has a pool table and is popular with Thais and travellers.

Shopping

Hornbill Bookshop BOOKS
(☎0 4246 0272; Soi Mut Mee, Th Kaew Worawut; ⏲10am-7pm Mon-Sat) Best used English-language bookstore in Isan.

Information

There is no shortage of banks with ATMs in town. For a wealth of information on Nong Khai and the surrounding area, visit www.mutmee.com.

Immigration (☎0 4242 3963; ⏲8.30am-noon & 1-4.30pm Mon-Fri) South of the Friendship Bridge; does Thai visa extensions.

Nong Khai Hospital (☎0 4241 1504; Th Meechai)

Post office (Th Meechai)

TAT (☎0 4242 1326; Hwy 2; ⏲8.30am-4.30pm Mon-Fri)

Getting There & Away

Nong Khai's main **bus terminal** (☎0 4241 1612) is just off Th Prajak, by the Pho Chai market, about 1.5km from the riverfront guesthouses. Nearby is Udon Thani, a major bus hub with more transport options. Destinations include:

Bangkok's Northern & Northeastern (Mo Chit) station 2nd class 350B, 1st class 450B, VIP 700B; 11 hours; afternoon and evening departures.

Bangkok's Suvarnabhumi (Airport) bus station 454B; nine hours; departs 8pm.

Udon Thani Ordinary 25B, 1st class 47B, one hour; frequent departures.

Nakhon Phanom Ordinary 175B, 2nd class 220B; six hours; six daily.

The **train station** (☎0 4241 1592; Hwy 212) is 2km west of town. Two express trains connect to **Bangkok** (2nd-class air-con 498B; 11 to 12 hours; one morning and one afternoon departure).

Udon Thani

POP 227,200

Sprawling Udon Thani is too big to be charming and too conservative to be cultured. It boomed on the back of the Vietnam War when it hosted a US air base. Today it sees relatively few foreigners other than a large number of former sex tourists now married to Thai women.

The rest of us might roll through to visit **Ban Chiang**, one of the earliest prehistoric cultures known in Southeast Asia. The affiliated **museum** (☎0 4220 8340; admission 150B;

Ko Samet

0 1 km
0 0.5 miles
To Ban Phe (7km)
Laem Noi Na
Laem Phra
Ao Wiang Wan
Ao Kham
Ao Noi Na
Ferry Terminal
Na Dan Pier
Sŏrngtăaou Stop
Na Dan
Ko Samet Health Centre
Ao Prao
Khao Laem Ya/Ko Samet National Park
National Parks Main Office
Prince & Mermaid Statues
Laem Yai Hut Resort
Laem Yai
Jep's Bungalows
Hat Sai Kaew
Ao Hin Khok
Ao Phai
Ao Phutsa (Ao Tub Tim)
Laem Rua Taek
Ao Nuan
Sŏrngtăaou Stop
Ao Cho
GULF OF THAILAND
Ao Wong Deuan
Candlelight Beach
Tonhard Bungalow
Ao Thian
Ao Wai
GULF OF THAILAND
Ao Kiu Na Nai
Ao Kiu Na Nok
Laem Khut
Ao Karang

⌚8.30am-4.30pm) displays pottery and tools from the civilisation and includes an excavation pit used as a burial ground dating to 300 BC. Ban Chiang is 50km from Udon Thani and accessible from bus terminal 1 via Sakhon Nakhon- or Nakhon Phanom-bound buses; get off at Ban Nong Mek (40B, 45 minutes) and hire a túk-túk (60B) for the remainder.

Simple but friendly guesthouses in town include **P & Mo Guesthouse** (☎08 4031 8337; 39 Th Rung Sun; r 300-400B; ❄@📶), near the bus station, and **Udon Backpackers** (☎08 9620 8684; www.udonbackpacker.com; 299/5 Soi Fairach 1; 150B; 📶). In Ban Chiang, **Lakeside Sunrise Guesthouse** (☎0 4220 8167; Ban Chiang; r 250B; @) has a countryside setting near the museum and a helpful English-speaking owner who rents out bikes (50B per day) and motorcycles (250B per day).

Udon has two bus stations, connected by the yellow city bus. **Bus Terminal No 1** (☎0 4222 2916; Th Sai Uthit) serves Bangkok's Northern and Northeastern (Mo Chit) bus station (550B to 641B, eight hours, eight daily), Suvarnabhumi airport (418B, eight hours, 9pm) and Khorat (181B to 258B, 4½ hours, half-hourly). **Bus Terminal No 2** is on the Ring Rd west of the city. Destinations include Loei (66B to 92B, three hours, frequent) and Chiang Mai (409B to 613B, 12 hours, six daily). For Nong Khai (35B to 47B, one hour, frequent) you can use either terminal, but the most frequent departures are from Rangsina Market, reached by the No 6 sŏrngtăaou.

Udon Thani is on the Bangkok–Nong Khai rail line. Destinations include Bangkok (2nd class 479B, 10 to 11 hours, two daily departures) and Nong Khai (3rd class 11B, 2nd class 55B to 85B; one hour; three daily departures).

EASTERN GULF COAST

Thailand's east coast isn't as stunning as the postcard-famous southern coast, but it is an ideal beach jaunt from jostling Bangkok if you're pinched for time or travelling overland to/from Cambodia. While your friends are still packed into buses en route to Ko Pha-Ngan, you'll be sun-kissed and sandy-toed.

Ko Samet

Bangkok's beachy backyard, Ko Samet is close enough for a weekend escape, yet worlds away from the urban bustle. Traffic-weary Thais, foreign expats and beach-hopping backpackers are Samet's steady clientele – and everyone squeezes into the petite east-coast beaches. It's been a **national park** (admission 200B) since 1981 and is still surprisingly rustic considering Thailand's penchant for urban makeovers of its seaside parks. Walking trails connect the beaches and the rocky headlands, the interior road isn't paved and coconut trees tower over the buildings.

The northeast part of the island has the most popular and populated areas. **Hat Sai Kaew** is the widest swathe of sand popular with Russian and domestic package tourists. The beach is beautiful but busy by day with speedboats and at night with karaoke and discos.

More subdued than its northern neighbour, **Ao Hin Khok** and **Ao Phai** are two gorgeous bays separated by rocky headlands. The crowd here tends to be younger and more stylish than the middle-aged crew in Hat Sai Kaew and the parties are late-nighters. These two beaches are the traditional backpacker party centres of the island.

Ao Thian (Candlelight Beach) is punctuated by big boulders that shelter small sandy spots ideal for castaways. It is one of Samet's most casual, easygoing beaches and is deliciously lonely on weekdays. On weekends, Bangkok university students serenade the stars with all-night guitar sessions.

The cove 'caboose' is **Ao Wai**, a lovely beach far removed from everything else (in reality it is 1km from Ao Thian).

Bring along mosquito spray as the forested island is home to everyone's favourite blood suckers.

Sleeping & Eating

Most bungalows have restaurants offering mixed menus of Thai and traveller food. Weekday rates don't rank well on the value scale (fan rooms start at 800B) but look incredibly attractive considering that weekend and holidays rates increase by as much as 100%. Eat locally at the noodle bars and stir-fry joints in Na Dan, the small village next to the pier.

Laem Yai Hut Resort GUESTHOUSE $
(☎0 38644282; Hat Sai Kaew; r 800-1000B; ❄) A colourful collection of weather-worn huts camp out in a shady garden on the north end of the beach. The laid-back vibe creates an alternate backpacker universe in a firmly rooted package-tour beach.

Jep's Bungalows GUESTHOUSE $
(☎0 3864 4112; www.jepbungalow.com; Ao Hin Khok; r 500-1600B; ❄@) Good old Jep's still has cheapie fan huts clambering up a forested hillside, just like the old days (a mere five years ago).

Candlelight Beach GUESTHOUSE $
(☎08 1762 9387; Ao Thian; r 700-1200B; ❄) On the beach, these fan and air-con bungalows with sea-facing porches have a natural, woody ambience.

Tonhard Bungalow GUESTHOUSE $
(☎08 1435 8900; Ao Thian; r 700-1500B; ❄) On a wooded part of the beach, this place has bungalows that vary from basic to less basic. But in return you get a friendly and relaxing setting.

Information

ATMs and internet cafes can be found in Na Dan and Ao Wong Deuan.

Ko Samet Health Centre (☎0 3861 1123; ⊙8.30am-9pm Mon-Fri, to 4.30pm Sat & Sun) For minor medical problems; on the main road between Na Dan pier and Hat Sai Kaew.

Getting There & Around

Ko Samet is reached by boat from the mainland town of Ban Phe. Services include:

Ferry to Na Dan One-way 50B, return 100B, 45 minutes, hourly 8am to 4pm) Easiest access to Samet.

Ferry to Ao Wong Deuan (One-way 50B, one hour, two daily departures) Service varies with the season.

Speedboat charter (250B for 10 passengers, 2500B for the boat) Disembarks at requested beach.

Ban Phe's **bus station** (near Tha Thetsaban) serves the following destinations:

Bangkok's Eastern (Ekamai) station (157B, four hours, hourly 6am to 6pm)

Bangkok's Victory Monument (250B, hourly 7am to 6pm, four hours)

Laem Ngop (350B, two daily departures, four to five hours) Mainland pier for boats to Ko Chang.

The nearby town of Rayong has more transport options, including Bangkok's Suvarnabhumi (Airport) bus station (165B, 2½ hours, eight daily departures); sŏrngtăaou make the trip between Ban Phe and Rayong (25B, frequent).

Sŏrngtăaou on the island cost from 20B to 80B, depending on your destination and the number of passengers. Most drivers charge between 200B to 500B for the vehicle if there aren't enough people to split the cost.

Chanthaburi & Trat

Surrounded by palm trees and fruit plantations, Chanthaburi and Trat are mainly transit transfers for travellers headed to Ko Chang or the Cambodian border. If you stop to catch your breath, you'll find that Chanthaburi dazzles with its weekend gem market, and sleepy Trat is filled with old teak shophouses and genuine small-town living.

Sleeping & Eating

CHANTHABURI

You're unlikely to need a bed in Chanthaburi, but just in case...

River Guest House HOTEL $
(☎0 3932 8211; 3/5-8 Th Si Chan; r 150-400B; ❄@) Standard hotel boxes aren't much to get excited about but this is as good as it gets in the budget range. There's a fair bit of highway noise, so request a room on the opposite side of the building.

Seafood Noodle Shop THAI $
(Th Sukhaphiban; dishes 25-50B; ⊙lunch & dinner) The old city, along Mae Nam Chanthaburi, is where you'll find most sightseeing Thais eating this Chanthaburi variation of the basic rice-noodle theme; nearby are other homemade snacks.

TRAT

You're more likely to overnight in Trat and the town has a small but charming guesthouse scene.

Ban Jaidee Guest House GUESTHOUSE $
(☎0 3952 0678; 6 Th Chaimongkol; r 200B; 📶) This relaxed Thai-style home decorated with artistic flourishes has simple rooms with shared bathrooms. It's very popular, so book ahead.

Residang House GUESTHOUSE $
(☎0 3953 0103; www.trat-guesthouse.com; 87/1-2 Th Thana Charoen; r 260-500B; ❄📶) Big beds with thick mattresses, good bathrooms with hot showers – what more do you need? Fan rooms come with breezes and balconies.

TOP CHOICE **Cool Corner** CAFE $
(☎08 4159 2030; 49-51 Th Thana Charoen; dishes 50-150B; ⊙breakfast, lunch & dinner) Though it's no longer on the corner, this cafe is as cool as ever and the artist/owner still serves up great vibes, good beats and darn good mango lassies.

Kluarimklong Cafe THAI $
(☎0 3952 4919; cnr Th Thana Charoen & Soi Rimklong; dishes 70-90B; ⊙lunch & dinner) The winning combination here is delicious Thai food served in modern air-conditioned surroundings. The dishes are surprisingly affordable given the slick decor.

Information

Bangkok Trat Hospital (☎0 3953 2735; Th Sukhumvit; ⊙24hr) Best health care in the region. It's 400m north of the town centre.

Tratosphere Bookshop (23 Rimklong Soi, Trat; ⊙8am-10pm) Load up on beach reading or get travel tips on the area.

Trat Map (www.tratmap.com) An online directory of businesses and attractions in Trat.

Getting There & Away

Most buses originating in Bangkok stop in Chanthaburi and Trat.

Chanthaburi

For travellers heading to/from the northeast, Chanthaburi is the transfer station. Chanthaburi's **bus station** (Th Saritidet) serves the following:

Bangkok's Eastern (Ekamai) station (187B, 3½ hours, hourly 6am to 11.30pm)

Bangkok's Northern (Mo Chit) station (187B; four hours; two daily departures)

Trat (70B, 1½ hours; every 1½ hour; 6.30am to 11.30pm)

Khorat (266B; hourly 6am to 6pm) Gateway to the northeast.

Sa Kaew (106B to 137B; hourly 6am to 10pm) Transfer point for buses to Aranya Prathet border crossing.

Chanthaburi's minivans leave from a stop near the market and go to Trat (80B), Rayong (100B) and Ban Phe (120B; for Ko Samet).

Trat

The bus station is outside of town; local sŏrngtăaou leave from Th Sukhumvit near the market to the bus station (20B to 60B, depending on number of passengers). Destinations:

Bangkok's Eastern (Ekamai) station (248B, 4½ hours, hourly 6am to 11.30pm)

Bangkok's Northern (Mo Chit) station (248B; 5½ hours; two morning departures)

Bangkok's Suvarnabhumi (Airport) station (248B; 4 to 4½ hours; five daily departures)

Chanthaburi (70B; 1½ hours; every 1½ hour 6.30am to 11.30pm)

Hat Lek (120B to 150B; one hour) Minivans depart when full; morning departures are more frequent.

Minivans to Chanthaburi (80B) leave when full from a stop on Th Sukhumvit north of the indoor market. **Family Tour** (☎08 1996 2216; Th Sukhumvit cnr Th Lak Meuang) runs minivans to Bangkok's Victory Monument (300B, five hours, hourly 8am to 5pm) and continue on to Th Khao San (350B).

To Laem Ngop Piers

Ko Chang-bound travellers have several bus options to reach the mainland pier of Laem Ngop. From Bangkok's Eastern (Ekamai) station buses go all the way to Laem Ngop's Tha Centrepoint (250B, five hours, three morning departures). This route includes a stop at Suvarnabhumi (Airport) bus station as well as Trat's bus station. In the reverse direction, there are two afternoon departures from Laem Ngop. There are also bus and minivan options directly to Ko Chang (see p733).

From Trat town, shared sŏrngtăaou leave from a stop on Th Sukhumvit to Laem Ngop's Tha Centrepoint (50B per person for six passengers; 45 minutes). If departing from Laem Ngop's other piers, inquire about land transfer when you purchase your boat tickets.

Ko Chang

Jungle-clad Ko Chang used to sit on the forgotten eastern frontier but these days it has been lassoed into Thailand's package tourism industry, with an assortment of sophisticated resorts, tonnes of bars and daily flights from the capital to nearby Trat. Plenty of backpackers still make the Ko Chang-Cambodia tour. Though it is no longer a castaway's idyll, Ko Chang has a way with hyperactive visitors: diving and snorkelling spots are nearby, the forested interior can be explored by foot or by elephant, and kayaks can survey sea coves and mangrove bays. Ko Chang is part of a larger **national park** that includes neighbouring islands.

Sights & Activities

Mainly the west coast has been developed for tourism. In the northwest is **Hat Sai Khao**, by far the biggest, busiest and brashest beach. The backpacker fave is **Lonely Beach**, which is lonely no more, especially at night. An old-fashioned fishing community in **Bang Bao** has become a bustling tourist market. The **east coast** is largely undeveloped with only a few low-key spots, like Hat Yao (Long Beach).

In a forested setting in the northern interior, **Ban Kwan Chang** (☎08 1919 3995; Khlong Son; ⊙8.30am-5pm; 900B) offers a quiet experience with its nine resident elephants.

Ko Chang cuts an impressive and heroic profile when viewed from the sea aboard a kayak. Most hotels rent open-top kayaks (from 300B per day) that are convenient for near-shore outings and non-committal kayakers. For more serious paddlers, **Kayak Chang** (☎08 7673 1923; www.kayakchang.com; Amari Emerald Cove Resort, Khlong Phrao) rents closed-top kayaks (from 1000B per day) and leads day and multiday trips.

On the east side of the island, explore the mangrove swamps of Ao Salak Kok while supporting an award-winning eco-tour program. The **Salak Kok Kayak Station** (☎08 1919 3995; kayak rentals 100B per hr) rents self-guided kayaks and is a village-work project designed to protect the traditional way of life. The kayak station can also arrange hiking tours.

The **dive sites** near Ko Chang offer a variety of coral, fish and beginner-friendly shallow waters on par with other Gulf of Thailand dive sites.

Sleeping

Accommodation prices on Ko Chang are higher than quality because of the package-tour industry. Prices and crowds increase around the Christmas holiday period.

Independent Bo's GUESTHOUSE $
(☎08 5283 5581; Hat Sai Khao; r 350-550B) A colourful place that clambers up the jungle hillside, Bo's keeps the northern end of Hat Sai Khao firmly rooted in backpacker ways – lots of cheap chillaxin; first come, first served.

Blue Lagoon Resort GUESTHOUSE $
(☎08 6330 0094; Ao Khlong Prao; r 600-1000B; ❄) Rustic bungalows overlook a serene lagoon in this shady grove of a guesthouse. A wooden walkway leads to the beach. There are also exceedingly friendly Thai cooking classes.

Tiger Huts GUESTHOUSE $
(☎08 1762 3710; Ao Khlong Prao; r 600B) The only thing that separates these wooden huts from labourer shanties is indoor plumbing. They are low on comfort and hospitality, but high on location, claiming the widest and prettiest part of the beach. The neighbouring resorts must be very jealous.

GETTING TO CAMBODIA: COASTAL BORDERS

Hat Lek to Cham Yeam

This is the most convenient border crossing between Ko Chang and Sihanoukville in coastal Cambodia.

Getting to the border Take a minivan from Trat's bus station to the border at Hat Lek (120B to 150B, one hour, departs when full, more frequently in the morning).

At the border Cambodian tourist visas are available at the border for 1200B; payment is only accepted in baht at this border. Bring a passport photo and avoid the runner boys who want to issue a health certificate or other 'medical' paperwork.

Moving on From the Cambodian border, take a taxi (US$10) or moto (US$3) to Koh Kong where you can catch onward transport to Sihanoukville and Phnom Penh; arriving in the morning ensures more onward transport options.

For information on making this crossing in the other direction, see p110.

Ban Pakard to Psar Pruhm

If you're heading to Siem Reap (or Battambang) from Ko Chang, you don't have to schlep up to Aranya Prathet-Poipet border crossing. This crossing isn't crowded and shaves off some travel time.

Getting to the border Take a minibus from Chanthaburi to Ban Pakard/Pong Nam Ron (150B, one to two hours; three times daily); the Chanthaburi minibus stop is across the river from River Guesthouse.

At the border Cross the border with the usual formalities (a passport photo and US$20 visa fee) to Psar Pruhm.

Moving on From the border, arrange a share taxi to Pailin, which has connections to Battambang and from there to Siem Reap.

See p103 for information on crossing in the other direction.

Buzza's Bungalows GUESTHOUSE $
(☎08 7823 6674; Hat Kaibae; r from 400B; ❄@) Solid concrete bungalows with porches create a laid-back travellers ambience. It's a short and hassle-free stroll to the beach.

Porn's Bungalows GUESTHOUSE $
(☎08 9251 9233; Hat Kaibae; www.pornsbungalows-kohchang.com; r from 800-900B) Kaibae's resident rasta scene hangs out in a shady coconut grove beside the beach; wooden fan bungalows with hot-water showers. First come, first served.

Oasis Bungalows GUESTHOUSE $
(☎08 1721 2547; Lonely Beach; www.oasis-khochang.com; r from 350B;) Sitting at the end of an interior *soi*, Oasis has basic wooden bungalows in a pretty fruit and flower garden. You'll have to walk through the village and down the main road to get to the beach. If Oasis is full, this *soi* is filled with comparable options.

Jungle Way GUESTHOUSE $
(☎08 9247 3161; Khlong Son Valley; www.jungleway.com; r 200-400B) Ko Chang's unsung attribute is its jungle interior and the English-speaking guides who grew up playing in it. Lek, a local guide, and his family run this friendly guesthouse, deep in the woods and beside a babbling brook. Bungalows are simple but adequate and the on-site restaurant will keep you well fed. Free pier pick-up.

Treehouse Lodge GUESTHOUSE $
(☎08 1847 8215; Hat Yao; r 300B) The namesake of a once great backpacker crash pad, the new Treehouse resides on remote Hat Yao (Long Beach), in the far southeastern peninsula. Basic huts (with basic bathrooms) chill along a hillside, looking down to a softly sanded slice of beach. The road to Hat Yao is well-sealed to the lookout point but poorly maintained past that, so plan on staying awhile. Inquire in Trat about a taxi service that goes all the way to Long Beach.

Eating

KaTi Culinary THAI $
(☎08 1903 0408; Ao Khlong Prao; dishes 60-150B; ⊙lunch & dinner) Across the road from Blue Lagoon Resort, KaTi is a popular Thai kitchen and cooking school.

Nid's Kitchen THAI $
(Hat Kaibae; dishes 30-80B; ⊙lunch & dinner) A sweaty little restaurant north of GajaPuri Resort, Auntie Nid's does all the Thai standards like a wok wizard. Plus the beers are cold.

Magic Garden THAI $$
(☎0 3955 8027; Lonely Beach; dishes 60-120B; ⊙dinner) Magic Garden is a pagoda to Lonely Beach's special variety of relaxing. Grab some grub, polish off some Beer Changs and then wander down to the beach for some DJ beats.

Ruan Thai SEAFOOD $$
(☎08 7000 162; Ban Bang Bao; dishes 100-300B; ⊙lunch & dinner) It's about as fresh as it gets (note your future dinner greeting you in tanks as you enter) and the portions are large. The doting service is beyond excellent – they'll even help you crack your crabs.

Information

Internet cafes and banks with ATMs are plentiful on the island, especially in Hat Sai Khao.

Ko Chang Hospital (☎0 3952 1657; Ban Dan Mai) Near the police headquarters.

Police (☎0 3958 6191; Ban Dan Mai)

Post office (☎0 3955 1240; Hat Sai Khao)

Tourist police office (☎1155) Based north of Ban Khlong Prao. Also has smaller police boxes in Hat Sai Khao and Hat Kaibae.

Getting There & Around

Beware of the cheap minibus tickets from Siem Reap to Ko Chang; these usually involve some sort of time- and money-wasting commission scam.

Ko Chang-bound boats depart from the mainland piers collectively referred to as Laem Ngop, southwest of Trat. You'll arrive in Ko Chang at either Tha Sapparot or Tha Centrepoint, depending on which pier and boat company you used on the mainland.

Tha Sapparot is the closest to the west coast beaches and receives vehicle ferries from the mainland pier of Tha Thammachat. **Koh Chang Ferry** (☎0 3955 5188; one way 80B; 30 min; ⊙hourly 6.30am-7pm) runs this service.

At the time of writing, the car ferry associated with Tha Centrepoint was competing aggressively for business by offering cheaper prices, more commissions and a Bangkok-Laem Ngop bus service. You cut out some of the land transfers with the new bus service but Tha Centrepoint (on Ko Chang) is further from the west coast beaches, so the time-saving is negligible. **Centrepoint Ferry** (☎0 3953 8196; one way/return 80/100B; 45 min; ⊙hourly 6am-7.30pm) runs this service. Weekend service in high season runs until 9pm.

There is also a new bus route directly from Bangkok's Suvarnabhumi (airport) station to Ko Chang (308B, six hours) via the car ferry with stops on the mainland at Trat and Chanthaburi. The bus leaves Suvarnabhumi at 7.30am and departs from Khlong San area of Ko Chang at 1.30pm.

Another option is a minivan service from Bangkok's Victory Monument that goes all the way to Ko Chang's Tha Sapparot (one-way 300B; four hours; hourly departures).

Sŏrngtăaou on the island will shuttle you from the pier to the various beaches (50B to 200B). It is not recommended to drive a motorcycle between Ban Khlong Son south to Hat Sai Khao as the road is steep and treacherous with several hairpin turns and occassional mudslides during storms. If you do rent a motorbike, stick to the west coast beaches. Wear protective clothing when riding a motorcycle to reduce injury.

SOUTHERN GULF COAST

Palm-fringed beaches, warm lazy days, jewel-toned seas: the southern gulf coast pours an intoxicating draught of paradise that attracts a steady crowd of sun worshippers. Most are bound for one or more of the offshore islands: resorty Ko Samui, hippie Ko Pha-Ngan and dive-centric Ko Tao.

If the Vitamin D treatments have you recharged, stop off en route at a few of the mild-mannered provincial capitals that live and work by the sea for a glimpse at the rhythms of coastal Thailand. Even further south, Thailand starts to merge with Malaysia: onion-domed mosques peep over the treeline; the diction is fast and furious as southern Thais are legendary speed talkers; and a roti seller can be found on every corner.

The best time to visit Thailand's southern reaches is from March to May, when the rest of the country is practically melting from the angry sun.

Hua Hin

POP 42,000

Within reach of Bangkok, Hua Hin is considered the elegant alternative to seedy Pattaya. It is a city by the sea long favoured by older Europeans and hi-so Bangkok Thais, and oft neglected by backpackers searching for rustic island living. But as the bamboo beach hut goes the way of the do-do bird, it is time to reconsider Hua Hin and its old fishing port charm, lively seafood night market and long silky sand beaches.

Hua Hin's best **beaches** are south of town heading towards Khao Takiab (Chopstick Mountain; accessible by green sŏrngtăaou leaving from the market) and Khao Tao (Turtle Mountain; accessible by Pranburi bus, transfer to motorcycle taxi).

Sleeping

Most of the budget options are in town, an atmospheric location but you'll have to 'commute' to the beach.

Pattana Guest House GUESTHOUSE $
(☎0 3251 3393; 52 Th Naresdamri; r 350-550B; ❄) Tucked away down a *soi*, this simple teak house has a lovely nook-filled garden. The rooms are small and basic but adequate and the family who runs it is friendly and artistic.

Tong-Mee House GUESTHOUSE $
(☎0 3253 0725; 1 Soi Raumpown, Th Naebkehardt; r 450-550B; ❄@) Down a quiet residential *soi*, this smart guesthouse is the best value in town. The rooms are small but well kept and have balconies.

Euro-Hua Hin City Hotel YHA HOSTEL $
(☎0 3251 3130; 5/15 Th Sasong; r 250-800B; ❄) Just like any large hostel, this place feels both comfortable and institutional. All rooms have air-con, even the somewhat cramped dormitories. Add 50B to these prices if you don't belong to HI.

Rahmahyah Hotel GUESTHOUSE $$
(☎0 3253 2106; 113/10 Soi Hua Hin 67, Th Phetkasem, South Hua Hin; r from 1000B; ❄📶≋) Across the street from Market Village, about 1km south of town, is a small guesthouse enclave tucked between the high-end resorts and with beach access. Rahmahyah is the best of the bunch, with professional staff and clean, functional rooms.

Eating

Night Market SEAFOOD $$
(Th Dechanuchit btwn Th Phetkasem & Th Sasong; dishes from 60B; ⌚5pm-midnight) An attraction that rivals the beach, Hua Hin's night market tops locals' lists of favourite spots to eat. Ice-packed displays of spiny lobsters and king prawns appeal to the big-spenders but the simple stir-fry stalls are just as tasty.

Th Chomsin Food Stalls THAI $
(cnr Th Chomsin & Th Naebkhardt; dishes from 30B; ⌚lunch & dinner) If you're after authentic eats, check out the food stalls that congregate at this popular lunch corner.

Chatchai Market THAI $
(Th Phetkasem; ⌚dishes from 30B; daylight hours) The city's day market resides in an

historic building. There are the usual market refreshments: morning vendors selling *þah·tôrng·gŏh* (Chinese-style doughnuts) and *gah·faa boran* (ancient-style coffee spiked with sweetened condensed milk); as well as all-day noodles with freshly made wontons; and the full assortment of tropical fruit.

Information

Hospital San Paolo (☎0 3253 2576; 222 Th Phetkasem) Just south of town with emergency facilities.

Municipal Tourist Information Office (☎0 3251 1047; cnr Th Phetkasem & Th Damnoen Kasem; ⊙8.30am-4.30pm Mon-Fri) Provides maps and information about Hua Hin. There's another branch (☎0 3252 2797; Th Naebkehardt; 9am-7.30pm Mon-Fri, 9.30am-5pm Sat & Sun) near the clock tower.

Tourist police (☎0 3251 5995; Th Damnoen Kasem)

Getting There & Around

Hua Hin's long-distance **bus station** (Th Phetkasem btw Soi Hua Hin 94 & 98) is south of town and serves the following destinations:

Prachuap Khiri Khan 65B; 1½ hours.

Phuket 856B; nine hours; one nightly departure.

Surat Thani 480B; seven hours; two daily departures.

Ubon Ratchathani 1200B; 13 hours; one daily departure.

Chiang Mai 785B; 12 hours; three daily departures.

Bangkok buses (160B, three hours, every two hours from 8am-9pm) leave from an in-town **office** (Th Sasong), near the Night Market. Minivans to Bangkok's Sai Tai Mai (Southern) bus station and Victory Monument (180B, three hours, every 30 minutes from 4am-8pm) leave from an office on Th Naebkehardt.

Lomprayah (☎0 3253 3739; Th Narasdamri) offers a bus-boat combination from Hua Hin to Ko Tao (1000B, 8½ hours; one morning and night departure).

There are frequent **trains** running to/from Bangkok's Hualamphong station (2nd class 212B to 302B, 3rd class 94B to 154B, four hours) and other stations on the southern railway line.

Green sŏrngtăaou depart from the corner of Th Sasong and Th Dechanuchit, near the Night Market and travel south on Th Phetkasem to Khao Takiab (20B). Pranburi-bound buses depart from the same stop. Túk-túk fares in Hua Hin are outrageous (starting at 100B). Motorcycle taxis are much more reasonable (40B to 50B) for short hops.

Prachuap Khiri Khan

POP 86,870

A prettier-than-average seaside town, Prachuap Khiri Khan is relaxed and untouristed with only a few minor attractions, a draw in itself if you're looking to escape 'Khao San' culture.

The bus dumps you off in the centre of town – not a pushy motorcycle taxi in sight. At the base of town is a sparkling blue bay sprinkled with brightly coloured fishing boats. To the north is **Khao Chong Krajok** (Mirror Tunnel Mountain), topped by a wat with spectacular views; the hill is claimed by a clan of monkeys who supposedly hitched a ride into town on a bus from Bangkok to pick up some mangoes. There isn't much else to do except walk along the waterfront promenade or rent a motorcycle and explore the northern bays, fishing villages and the cave temple at **Wat Ao Noi**. You'll find a swimming beach at **Ao Manao**, 6km south of the city within the grounds of a Thai air-force base. It is popular with local Thais who swim fully clothed.

Sleeping & Eating

You can always find a place to stay near the sea as many of the oceanfront residences rent out rooms. In recent years, Prachuap has gained a small guesthouse scene.

Maggie's Homestay GUESTHOUSE $

(☎08 7597 9720; 5 Soi Tampramuk; r 150-600B; ❄@) In the old-fashioned backpacker tradition, lovely owner Maggie oversees an eclectic collection of travellers who call her house home. Simple rooms occupy a converted house with a shady garden and shared kitchen facilities.

Yuttichai Hotel GUESTHOUSE $

(☎0 3261 1055; 115 Th Kong Kiat; r 160-400B; ❄@) One of Prachuap's original guesthouses, Yuttichai has simple budget rooms (cold-water showers) close to the train station. The cheapest rooms share baths. If you don't stay here, at least stop by their old-style Thai-Chinese café, popular with the 'men in brown' (police).

Happy Inn GUESTHOUSE $

(☎0 3260 2082; 149-151 Th Suanson; r 250-500B) North of town, these simple bungalows (with cold-water showers) face each other along a brick drive that ends next to a pleasant forested canal. You are right across the road from Ao Prachuap's beach and the staff are sweet and soft spoken.

BEACH TIME MACHINE

Bang Saphan Yai, 100km south of Prachuap Khiri Khan, fits that most famous beach cliché: it is Thailand 15 years ago before pool villas and package tourists pushed out all the beach bums. Once you settle into a simple beachfront hut, you probably won't need shoes and the days will just melt away.

The easiest way to get to Bang Saphan Yai is by train. There are several daily options but the sprinter train (special express No 43) is one of the fastest. It leaves Bangkok's Hualamphong station at 8am and arrives in Bang Saphan Yai (450B) at 1pm. When you decide to leave, you can hop on an afternoon train to Chumphon with plenty of time to spare before the ferry to Ko Tao. From the train station, take a motorcycle taxi to the beach (70B).

Ma Prow INTERNATIONAL **$$**
(48 Th Chai Thaleh; dishes 80-200B; ⌚lunch & dinner) An airy wooden pavilion across from the beach, Ma Prow cooks up excellent *plah săm·lee dàat dee·o* (a local speciality of whole sun-dried cotton fish that is fried and served with mango salad). The tamarind fish dish is another favourite.

Suan Krua VEGETARIAN **$**
(Soi Tampramuk; dishes 30-60B; ⌚lunch; ✍) Next door to Maggie's Homestay, this vegetarian restaurant cooks fast and furiously for a limited time only and then it closes until the next day. Be here promptly and hungrily.

Night market THAI **$**
(Th Kong Kiat; ⌚5-9pm) Smallish market serving standard evening meals.

ℹ Getting There & Away

There are hourly air-con buses that leave from Th Phitak Chat to the following destinations:

BANGKOK (170B, five hours)

HUA HIN (100B, 1½ hours)

Minivans leave from the corner of Th Thetsaban Bamrung and Th Phitak Chat to the following destinations:

BANGKOK (250B)

HUA HIN (80B)

BANG SAPHAN YAI (80B, 1½ hours)

CHUMPHON (180B, 3½ hours)

Long-distance buses to southern destinations (like Phuket and Krabi) stop at the new bus station, 2km northwest of town on the main highway; motorcycle taxis will take you for 40B to 50B.

The train station is on Th Maharat; there are frequent services to/from Bangkok (1st class 768B, 2nd class 210B to 425B, 3rd class 168B; six hours).

Chumphon

POP 55,835

Chumphon is a jumping-off point for boats to Ko Tao. The transition from bus to boat is fairly painless and travel agencies can help with onward travel to the Andaman coast. The tourist businesses are used to people hanging around waiting to leave and provide all sorts of day-use amenities (such as luggage storage, shower and toilet).

Suda Guest House (☎0 7750 4366; 8 Soi Bangkok Bank; r 230-500B; ❄) keeps prices low but standards high. If Suda is full, try **San Tavee New Rest House** (☎0 7750 2147; 4 Soi Bangkok Bank; r 200-300B) two doors down. The four rooms are small but clean and have fans and shared bathroom.

You can stock up on food supplies for the slow boat at the small **night market** (Th Krom Luang Chumphon). **Fame Restaurant** (188/20 Th Sala Daeng; dishes 80-220B; ⌚breakfast, lunch & dinner) is a long-running *faràng* depot that does a little bit of everything: cooks up Western breakfasts, books ferry tickets and rents out day-use showers.

ℹ Getting There & Away

Boat

You have many boat options to Ko Tao, though departure times are limited to mainly morning and night. Most ticket prices include pier transfer. If you buy a combination ticket, make sure you have a ticket for both the bus and the boat.

SLOW BOAT (250B, six hours, departs midnight) The cheapest, slowest and most romantic option as everyone stretches out on the open deck of the fishing boat with the stars twinkling overhead. This boat doesn't run in rough seas or inclement weather.

CAR FERRY (350B, six hours, departs 11pm daily) A more comfortable ride with bunk or mattress options available on board.

SONGSERM EXPRESS BOAT (450B, three hours, departs 7am) Faster, morning option leaving from Tha Talaysub, 10km from town.

LOMPRAYAH CATAMARAN (600B, 1¾ hours, departs 7am and 1pm) A popular bus-boat combination leaving from Tha Tummakam, 25km from town; ticket office is beside Chumphon train station.

Bus

The main **bus terminal** is on the highway, an inconvenient 16km from Chumphon. To get there you can catch a sŏrngtăaou (50B) from Th Nawamin Ruamjai. You'll have to haggle with the taxi drivers for night transit to/from the station; it shouldn't cost more than 200B.

There are several in-town bus stops. **Choke Anan Tour** (☎0 7751 1757; soi off Th Pracha Uthit), in the centre of town, has departures to the following destinations:

Bangkok's Southern (Sai Tai Mai) station 375B to 550B; eight hours; five daily.

Hat Yai 370B; seven hours; four departures.

Phuket 320B; 3½ hours; four departures.

Suwannatee Tour (☎0 7750 4901), 700m southeast of train station road, serves the following destinations:

Bangkok's Southern (Sai Tai Mai) station 2nd class and VIP buses; 270B to 405B; three daily.

Prachuap Khiri Khan 120B.

Hua Hin 170B.

Minivan companies are numerous and depart from individual offices throughout town:

Surat Thani (170B, three hours, hourly), departs from an unnamed *soi* on Th Krom Luang Chumphon; the *soi* is east of an optical shop.

Bang Saphan Yai (120B, two hours, two afternoon departures) departs from Th Poramin Mankha, near the hospital.

Train

The **train station** (Th Krom Luang Chumphon) is within walking distance of the centre of town. There are frequent services to/from Bangkok (2nd class 292B to 382B, 3rd class 235B, 7½ hours). Overnight sleepers range from 440B to 770B. Southbound rapid and express trains – the only trains with 1st and 2nd class cars – are less frequent and can be difficult to book out of Chumphon from November to February.

Ko Samui

POP 40,230

One of the original islands that started the backpacker migration to Thailand, Ko Samui has matured into an all-purpose beach resort. The hotels have international standards, the guests are mainly package tourists and the transition from home to deck chair involves little culture shock. Families and honeymooners put Ko Samui at the top of their lists for its conveniences and impressive stoles of sand.

But for all the 'too-touristy' talk, Samui is underappreciated for its size and variety of beaches: with one cab ride you can travel from brash and beautiful to sleepy and rustic. Plus there is a thriving Thai community on the island where you can nosh at roadside curry shacks or grab a cup of thick coffee at the morning market with the gossiping vendors. Samui is a unique hybrid for beach people who also want to see Thailand.

Sights

Ko Samui is quite large – the island's ring road is almost 100km in total. **Chaweng** is the most popular spot – it's the longest and most beautiful beach on the island. At the south end of **Lamai**, the second-largest beach, you'll find the infamous **Hin-Ta** and **Hin-Yai** stone formations providing endless mirth to giggling Thai tourists. **Hua Thanon**, just beyond, is home to a vibrant Muslim community, and their anchorage of high-bowed fishing vessels is a veritable gallery of intricate designs.

Although the **northern beaches** have coarser sand and aren't as striking as the beaches in the east, they have a laid-back vibe and stellar views of Ko Pha-Ngan. **Bo Phut** stands out with its charming Fisherman's Village.

At 30m, **Nam Tok Na Muang** is the tallest waterfall on Samui. It lies in the centre of the island about 12km from Na Thon. For temple enthusiasts, **Wat Laem Sor**, at the southern end of Samui near Ban Phang Ka, has an interesting, highly venerated old Srivijaya-style stupa. At Samui's northern end, on a small rocky island linked by a causeway, is **Wat Phra Yai** (Temple of the Big Buddha). Nearby, a new temple, **Wat Plai Laem**, features an enormous 18-armed Buddha.

Courses

Samui Institute of Thai Culinary Arts COOKING

(SITCA; ☎0 7741 3434; www.sitca.net; Hat Chaweng) Lunchtime classes begin at 11am, while dinner starts at 4pm; both cost 1950B for a three-hour course with three or more dishes. Included is an excellent tutorial about procuring ingredients in your home country.

Ko Samui

Sleeping

CHAWENG

TOP CHOICE Jungle Club BUNGALOWS $$
(☎08 1894 2327; www.jungleclubsamui.com/ bungalows 800-4500B; ❄@☜≋) The perilous drive up the slithering dirt road is totally worthwhile once you get a load of the incredible views from the top. There's a relaxed back-to-nature vibe – guests chill around the stunning horizon pool or tuck themselves away for a catnap under the canopied roofs of an open-air *săh·lah* (shelter). Call ahead for a pick up.

Ark Bar RESORT $$
(☎0 7742 2047; www.ark-bar.com; bungalows 1500B; ❄☜≋) You'll find two of every creature at Ark Bar – hardcore partiers, chilled hippies, teenagers, forty-somethings, even Canadians. Lately, the perennially popular resort has started to shift gears – higher-end digs is now the name of the game.

Loft Samui HOSTEL $
(☎0 7741 3420; www.theloftsamui.com; r from 590B; ❄@☜) A newer budget operation in Chaweng, the Loft is giving has-beens like Wave a run for their money with cheap digs furnished by a couple of quirky details like adobe styling and savvy built-ins.

Akwa GUESTHOUSE $
(☎08 4660 0551; www.akwaguesthouse.com; r from 700B; ❄@☜) A charming B&B-style sleeping spot, Akwa has a few funky rooms decorated with bright colours. Expect teddy bears adorning each bed, quirky bookshelves stocked with DVDs and cartoon paintings all over.

Samui Hostel HOSTEL $
(☎08 9874 3737; dm 180B; ❄@) It doesn't look like much from the front, but the dorm rooms here are surprisingly spic and span. It's a great place for solo travellers on a tight budget.

DON'T MISS: ANG THONG MARINE NATIONAL PARK

The 40-some jagged jungle islands of Ang Thong Marine National Park stretch across the cerulean sea like a shattered emerald necklace – each piece a virgin realm featuring sheer limestone cliffs, hidden lagoons and perfect peach-coloured sands. These dream-inducing islets inspired Alex Garland's cult classic *The Beach*, about dope-dabbling backpackers.

The best way to reach the park is to catch a private day-tour from Ko Samui, like **Blue Stars** (☎0 7741 3231; www.bluestars.info; trips 2600B). Although the islands sit between Samui and the mainland pier at Don Sak, there are no ferries that stop off along the way. The park officially has an admission fee (400B), although it should be included in the price of every tour (ask your operator if you are unsure). Private boat charters are another possibility, although high gas prices will make the trip quite expensive.

February, March and April are the best months to visit this ethereal preserve of greens and blues; crashing monsoon waves means that the park is almost always closed during November and December.

LAMAI

Pinch-a-penny digs can be scouted at **Beer's House** (☎0 7723 0467; Lamai North; bungalows 200-550B) and **New Hut** (☎0 7723 0437; newhut@hotmail.com; Lamai North; huts 200-500B) in North Lamai.

Spa Resort BUNGALOWS **$$**
(☎0 7723 0855; www.spasamui.com; Lamai North; bungalows 800-2800B; ❄📶) This health spa has a bevy of therapeutic programs on offer, and no one seems to mind that the lodging is cheap by Lamai's standards. Programs include colonics, massage, aqua detox, hypnotherapy and yoga, just to name a few. The bathrooms leave a bit to be desired, but who needs a toilet when you're doing a weeklong fast?

iBed HOSTEL **$**
(☎0 7745 8760; www.ibedsamui.com; dm/s 550/1100B) The sleekest hostel on the island (if not all of Thailand), iBed has all the accoutrements of an Apple-sponsored space station: personal TVs at each bed, smooth coats of paint, bleach-white linens, and plenty of polished concrete. The wide verandas and mod kitchen foster a sociable vibe during the busier months.

Amarina Residence GUESTHOUSE **$**
(www.amarinaresidence.com; r 900-1200B) Although the lobby is unusually dark compared to most tropical foyers, the rooms upstairs are sun-drenched and sport tasteful light wood furnishing.

NORTHERN BEACHES

BIG BUDDHA BEACH (BANG RAK)

Samui Mermaid RESORT **$**
(☎0 7742 7547; www.samui-mermaid.info; r 400-2500B; ❄@📶🏊) Samui Mermaid is a great choice in the budget category because it feels like a full-fledged resort. There are two large swimming pools, copious beach chairs, two lively restaurants and every room has cable TV. The landing strip at Samui's airport is only a couple of kilometres away, so sometimes there's noise, but free airport transfers sweeten the deal.

Shambala BUNGALOWS **$**
(☎0 7742 5330; www.samui-shambala.com; bungalows 600-1000B; ❄📶) While surrounding establishments answer the call of upmarket travellers, this laid-back, English-run place is a backpacking stalwart with a subtle hippie feel. There's plenty of communal cushion seating, a great wooden sun-deck, and the bungalows are bright and roomy. Staff dole out travel tips and smiles in equal measure.

BO PHUT & MAE NAM

TOP CHOICE **L'Hacienda** GUESTHOUSE **$$**
(☎0 7724 5943; www.samui-hacienda.com; r 1400-3500B; ❄📶🏊) Polished terracotta and rounded archways give the entrance a Spanish mission motif. Similar decor permeates the eight adorable rooms, which sport loads of personal touches such as pebbled bathroom walls and translucent bamboo lamps. There's a charming surprise waiting for you on the roof, and we're pretty sure you'll love it as much as we did.

Shangrilah BUNGALOWS **$**
(☎0 7742 5189; bungalows 300-2000B; ❄) A backpackers' Shangri La indeed – these are some of the cheapest huts around and they're in decent condition.

Khuntai GUESTHOUSE $
(☎0 7724 5118; r 400-850B; ❄) This clunky orange guesthouse is as cheap as decent rooms get on Samui. A block away from the beach, on the outskirts of Fisherman's Village, Khuntai's 2nd-floor rooms are drenched in afternoon sunshine and feature outdoor lounging spots.

Eating & Drinking

CHAWENG

Dozens of the restaurants on the 'strip' serve a mixed bag of local bites, international cuisine and greasy fast food. For the best ambience, get off the road and head to the beach, where many bungalow operators set up tables on the sand and have glittery fairy lights at night. Market oglers should not miss the opportunity to check out **Laem Din** (dishes from 30B; ⏲4am-6pm, night market 6pm-2am).

Gringo's Cantina MEXICAN $$
(dishes 140-280B; ⏲dinner) Wash down a Tex-Mex classic with a jug of sangria or a frozen margarita. We liked the *chimichangas* (mostly because we like saying '*chimichanga*'). There are burgers, pizzas and vegie options too, for those who don't want to go 'south of the border'.

Wave Samui INTERNATIONAL $
(dishes from 60B; ⏲breakfast, lunch & dinner) Everyone says that Samui is going upmarket, but the most crowded restaurants at dinnertime are still the old-fashioned budget spots, like this one. This jack-of-all trades (guesthouse-bar-restaurant) serves honest food at honest prices and fosters a travellers ambience with an in-house library and a popular happy hour (3pm to 7pm).

Bar Solo BAR
(Hat Chaweng) A sign of things to come, Bar Solo has future-fitted Chaweng's outdoor beer halls into an urban setting with sleek cubist decor and a cocktail list that doesn't scream holiday hayseed. The evening drink specials lure in the front-loaders preparing for a late, late night at the dance clubs on Soi Solo and Soi Green Mango.

Green Mango BAR
(Hat Chaweng) This place is so popular it has an entire *soi* named after it. Samui's favourite power drinking house is very big, very loud and very *faràng*. Green Mango has blazing lights, expensive drinks and masses of sweaty bodies swaying to dance music.

Reggae Pub BAR
(Hat Chaweng) This fortress of fun sports an open-air dance floor with music spun by foreign DJs. It's a towering two-storey affair with long bars, pool tables, and a live-music stage. The whole place doubles as a shrine to Bob Marley.

LAMAI

Most visitors dine wherever they're staying. The **Tesco Lotus** is a great place to pick up snacks for a beachside picnic, or try the Thai equivalent of a grocery store at the **Lamai Day Market** (dishes from 30B; ⏲6am-8pm) or the Muslim **Hua Thanon Market** (dishes from 30B; ⏲6am-6pm). Class things up at **Beach Republic** (www.beachrepublic.com), which is recognised by the yawning thatch-patched awnings. There's an inviting wading pool, comfy lounge chairs and an endless cocktail list.

NORTHERN BEACHES

Karma Sutra INTERNATIONAL $$
(Bo Phut; mains 130-260B; ⏲breakfast, lunch & dinner) A haze of purples and pillows, this charming chow spot in the heart of Bo Phut's Fisherman's Village serves up international and Thai eats listed on colourful chalkboards. Karma Sutra doubles as a clothing boutique.

Starfish & Coffee THAI $$
(Bo Phut; mains 130-180B; ⏲breakfast, lunch & dinner) This streamer-clad eatery was probably named after the Prince song, since we couldn't find any starfish on the menu (there's loads of coffee though). Evenings feature standard Thai fare and sunset views of rugged Ko Pha-Ngan.

Woo Bar LOUNGE
(Mae Nam) The W Retreat's signature lobby bar gives the word 'swish' a whole new meaning with cushion-clad pods of seating plunked in the middle of an expansive infinity pool that stretches out over the infinite horizon. This is, without a doubt, the best place on Samui for a sunset cocktail.

WEST COAST

The quiet west coast features some of the best seafood on Samui. Na Thon has a giant **day market** on Th Thawi Ratchaphakdi – it's worth stopping by to grab some snacks before your ferry ride.

About Art & Craft Café VEGETARIAN $$
(Na Thon; dishes 80-180B; ⏲breakfast & lunch; 🖉) An artistic oasis in the midst of hurried Na Thon, this cafe serves an eclectic assortment of healthy and wholesome food, gourmet

SPLURGE: FIVE ISLANDS

(www.thefiveislands.com; Taling Ngam; dishes 150-500B, tours 3000-6500B; ⏲lunch & dinner) Five Islands offers the most unique eating experience on the island. Before your meal, a traditional longtail boat will take you out into the turquoise sea to visit the haunting Five Sister Islands where you'll learn about the ancient and little-known art of harvesting bird nests to make bird's nest soup, a Chinese delicacy. The lunch tour departs around 10am, and the dinner program leaves around 3pm.

coffee, and, as the name states, art and craft, made by the owner and her friends. Relaxed and friendly, this is also a gathering place for Samui's dwindling population of bohemians and artists.

Nikki Beach LOUNGE
(www.nikkibeach.com/kohsamui; Lipa Noi) The acclaimed luxury brand has brought their international *savoir faire* to the secluded west coast of Ko Samui. Expect everything you would from a chic address in St Barts or St Tropez: haute cuisine, chic decor and gaggles of jetsetters. Themed brunch and dinner specials keep the masses coming throughout the week.

Information

Bangkok Samui Hospital (☎0 7742 9500, emergency 0 7742 9555) Your best bet for just about any medical problem.

Hyperbaric Chamber (☎0 7742 7427; Big Buddha Beach) The island's dive medicine specialists.

Immigration Office (☎0 7742 1069; Na Thon; ⏲8.30am-noon & 1-4.30pm Mon-Fri) Expect extensions to take the entire afternoon.

Main post office (Na Thon) Near the TAT office.

TAT office (☎0 7742 0504; Na Thon; ⏲8.30am-4.30pm) At the northern end of Na Thon; this office is friendly, helpful and has handy brochures and maps – although travel agents throughout the island can provide similar information.

Tourist police (☎0 7742 1281, emergency 1155) Based at the south end of Na Thon.

Getting There & Away

Air

Samui's airport is located in the northeast of the island near Big Buddha Beach. **Bangkok Airways** (www.bangkokair.com) operates flights roughly every 30 minutes between Samui and Bangkok's Suvarnabhumi Airport (50 minutes). Bangkok Air also flies direct from Samui to Phuket, Chiang Mai, Singapore and Hong Kong. **Firefly** (www.fireflyz.com.my) operates direct flights from Samui to Kuala Lumpur's Subang airport.

Boat

To reach Samui, of the four main piers on the mainland, Tha Thong (in central Surat) and Don Sak are the most common. On Samui, the three oft-used ports are Na Thon, Mae Nam and Big Buddha. Expect complimentary taxi transfers with high-speed ferry services.

There are frequent boat departures between Samui and Surat Thani. The hourly Seatran ferry is a common option. The slow night boat to Samui leaves from central Surat Thani at 11pm, reaching Na Thon around 5am. It returns from Na Thon at 9pm, arriving at around 3am.

There are almost a dozen daily departures between Samui and Ko Pha-Ngan. These leave either from the Na Thon, Mae Nam or Big Buddha piers and take from 20 minutes to one hour. Most boats continue on to Ko Tao.

Bus & Train

A bus/ferry combo is more convenient than a train/ferry package for getting to Ko Samui because you don't have to switch transport in Phun Phin. However, the trains are much more comfortable and spacious – especially at night. If you prefer the train, you can get off at Chumphon and catch the Lomprayah catamaran service the rest of the way.

Getting Around

MOTORBIKES You can rent motorcycles (and bicycles) from almost every resort on the island. The going rate is 200B per day.

SŎRNGTĂAOU These vehicles run regularly during daylight hours. It's about 50B to travel between beaches, and no more than 100B to travel halfway across the island.

TAXIS Taxis typically charge around 500B for an airport transfer. Some Chaweng travel agencies can arrange minibus taxis for less.

Ko Pha-Ngan

POP 11,000

Swaying coconut trees, brooding mountains, ribbons of turquoise water: Ko Pha-Ngan has held fast to its title as favourite backpacker idyll. Despite some modernisation during the upscale push of the early 2000s, Ko Pha-Ngan is still rustic and remote, it doesn't have an airport (yet) and there are still some cheap beachfront bungalows intended for hammock-hanging and simple living.

Every sunburnt face you meet in Khao San's bars will tell you all about the most brilliant beaches on Ko Pha-Ngan, which means you won't be alone in paradise, but nobody really wants a lonely planet.

Activities

Diving & Snorkelling

With Ko Tao, the high-energy diving behemoth, just a few kilometres away, Ko Pha-Ngan enjoys a much quieter, more laid-back diving scene focused on fun diving rather than certifications. The favourite snorkelling spot is **Ko Ma**, a small island in the northwest connected to Ko Pha-Ngan by a charming sandbar.

A major perk of diving from Ko Pha-Ngan is the proximity to **Sail Rock** (Hin Bai), the best dive site in the Gulf of Thailand and a veritable beacon for whale sharks.

Three-dive day trips cost around 3650B to 3800B.

Reefers DIVING
(08 6471 4045; www.reefersdiving.com; Hat Yao) Based at Shiralea, Reefers is one of the newer outfits on the island.

Lotus Diving DIVING
(0 7737 4142; www.lotusdiving.net; Chalok Lam) This dive centre has top-notch instructors, and owns two beautiful boats.

Other Activities

Wake Up WAKEBOARDING
(08 7283 6755; www.wakeupwakeboarding.com; Jan-Oct) Jamie passes along his infinite wakeboarding wisdom to eager wannabes at his small water sports school in Chalok Lam. Fifteen minutes of 'air time' will set you back 1500B (2500B for 30 minutes). Kite-boarding, wake-skating and water-skiing sessions are also available.

Ko Pha-Ngan

Eco Nature Tour TOUR
(☎08 4850 6273) The exceedingly popular 'best of' tour includes elephant trekking, snorkelling, a visit to the Chinese temple, and a stop at a stunning viewpoint. The day trip, which costs 1500B, departs at 9am and returns around 3pm. Bookings can be made at its office in Thong Sala or at the Backpackers Information Centre.

Sleeping

HAT RIN

During Full Moon events, bungalow operations expect you to stay for a minimum number of days (around four or five). We strongly suggest booking a room in advance.

Pha-Ngan Bayshore Resort RESORT $$
(☎0 7737 5227; www.phanganbayshore.com; Hat Rin Nok; r 1700-3200B;) After a much-needed overhaul in 2009, this hotel-style operation has primed itself for the ever-increasing influx of flashpackers in Hat Rin. Sweeping beach views and a giant swimming pool make Pha-Ngan Bayshore one of the top addresses on Sunrise Beach.

Seaview Sunrise BUNGALOWS $
(www.seaviewsunrise.com; Hat Rin Nok; r 500-800B;) As far as budget digs are concerned, this is the only solid option for Full Moon revellers who want a sleeping spot within inches of the tide. Huts are sturdy and perfectly utilitarian. The polished wooden interiors are splashed with the occasional burst of neon paint from the ghosts of parties past.

Coral Bungalows RESORT $
(☎0 7737 5023; www.coralhaadrin.com; Hat Rin Nai; bungalows 500-1000B;) This party-centric paradise has firmly planted its flag in 'Backpackerland' as the go-to spot for a booze-addled rompfest. By day, sun-worshippers straddle beachside chaises. Then, by night, like a vampire, Coral transforms into a sinister pool party machine fuelled by one too many vodka Red Bulls.

Paradise Bungalows BUNGALOWS $
(☎0 7737 5244; Hat Rin Nok; bungalows 300-1200B;) The world-famous Full Moon Party was hatched at this scruffy batch of bungalows, and the place has been living on its name fame ever since. The backpackers keep on coming to wax nostalgic, although the grounds are starting to look more like a junkyard now that the family has divvied up the land into several small 'resorts'. Paradise lost.

THE TEN COMMANDMENTS OF FULL MOON FUN

On the eve of every full moon, thousands of bodies converge on the kerosene-soaked sands of Sunrise Beach for an epic trance-a-thon fuelled by adrenaline and a couple other substances.

Some critics claim that the party is losing its carefree flavour, especially since the island's government is trying to charge a 100B entrance fee to partygoers. Despite the disheartening schemes hatched by money-hungry locals, the night of the Full Moon is still the ultimate partying experience, so long as one follows the unofficial Ten Commandments of Full Moon fun:

» Thou shalt arrive in Hat Rin at least three days early to nail down accommodation during the pre-Full Moon rush of backpackers.

» Thou shalt double-check the party dates as sometimes they coincide with Buddhist holidays and are rescheduled.

» Thou shalt secure all valuables, especially when staying in budget bungalows.

» Thou shalt savour some delicious fried fare in Chicken Corner before the revelry begins.

» Thou shalt wear protective shoes during the sandy celebration, unless ye want a tetanus shot.

» Thou shalt cover thyself with swirling patterns of neon body paint.

» Thou shalt visit Magic Mountain or The Rock for killer views of the heathens below.

» Thou shalt not sample the drug buffet, nor shalt thou swim in the ocean under the influence of alcohol.

» Thou shalt stay in a group of two or more people, especially if thou art a woman.

» Thou shalt party until the sun comes up and have a great time.

SPLURGE: SARIKANTANG

(☎0 7737 5055; www.sarikantang.com; Hat Seekantang; bungalows 1400-6200B; ❄📶🏊) Don't get too strung out over trying to pronounce the resort's name – you can simply call this place 'heaven'. Cream-coloured cabins, framed with teak posts and lintels, are sprinkled among swaying palms and crumbling winged statuettes. Inside, the rooms look like the set of a photo shoot for an interior design magazine.

SOUTHERN BEACHES

The waters along the south coast tend to be shallow and opaque, especially during low season, but lodging options are well-priced compared to other parts of the island, and you're not too far from Hat Rin.

TOP CHOICE Coco Garden BUNGALOWS $
(☎0 7737 7721, 08 6073 1147; www.cocogardens.com; bungalows 450-1250B; ❄📶) The best budget spot along the southern coast, Coco Garden one-ups the nearby resorts with well-manicured grounds and sparkling bungalows that are almost pathologically clean.

Boom's Cafe Bungalows BUNGALOWS $
(☎0 7723 8318; www.boomscafe.com; bungalows 400-1000B;❄) Staying at Boom's is like visiting the Thai family you never knew you had. The friendly owners lovingly tend their sandy acreage and dote on the contented clientele. No one seems to mind that there's no swimming pool, since the curling tide rolls right up to your doorstep. Boom's is located at the far eastern corner of Ban Khai, near Hat Rin.

WEST COAST BEACHES

Now that there are two smooth roads between Thong Sala and Chalok Lam, the west coast has seen more development. The atmosphere is a pleasant mix between the east coast's quiet seclusion and Hat Rin's sociable vibe.

TOP CHOICE Chills Resort RESORT $$
(☎08 9875 2100; www.chillsresort.com; Ao Srithanu; r from 1200B; ❄📶🏊) Set along a stunning and secluded stretch of stony outcrops, Chills' cluster of delightfully simple-but-modern rooms all have peaceful ocean views letting in plenty of sunlight and sea breezes. The natural rock-pool perched along the breakers is the perfect place to swig an afternoon cocktail while watching the sunset.

TOP CHOICE Shambhala Bungalow Village BUNGALOWS $
(☎08 9875 2100; www.shambhala-phangan.com; Ao Nai Wok; bungalows 600-1200B; ❄📶) Rather than bulldozing tired old beachside bungalows, the owners of Shambhala have lovingly restored a batch of huts and added loads of personal touches that make this not only a memorable place to stay, but also a very comfortable one for those with small coffers. Expect fresh linen, carved wood, artistic lighting, and neatly designed bathrooms.

Cookies Salad RESORT $$
(☎0 7734 9125, 08 3181 7125; www.cookies-phangan.com; bungalows 1500-3000B; 🏊) The resort with a tasty name has delicious Balinese-styled bungalows orbiting a two-tiered lap pool tiled in various shades of blue. Shaggy thatching and dense tropical foliage gives the realm a certain rustic quality, although you won't want for creature comforts.

Shiralea BUNGALOWS $
(☎08 0719 9256; www.shiralea.com; Hat Yao; bungalows 500B; ❄📶🏊) Although this batch of fresh-faced poolside bungalows is not right on the beach (about 100m away), you'll be hard-pressed to find a better deal on the island. Reefers, the on-site dive outfit offers world-class diving at your doorstep, and don't forget to ask the friendly owner where the name Shiralea comes from – we're pretty sure you'll be quite surprised.

NORTHERN BEACHES

Stretching from Chalok Lam to Thong Nai Pan, the dramatic northern coast is a wild jungle with several stunning and secluded beaches – it's the most scenic coast on the island.

Bottle Beach II BUNGALOWS $
(☎0 7744 5156; Hat Khuat; bungalows 350-500B) At the far eastern corner of the beach, this is the spot where penny pinchers can live out their castaway fantasies. Grab a long-tail taxi boat from Chalok Lam for 50B to 120B (depending on the boat's occupancy).

Dolphin BUNGALOWS $
(Thong Nai Pan; bungalows 500-1400B; ❄📶) This hidden retreat gives yuppie travellers a chance to rough it in style, while granola-types will soak up every inch of the laid-back charm. Quiet afternoons are spent lounging on comfy cushions in one of the

small pagodas hidden throughout the jungle. Lodging is available on a first-come basis.

Longtail Beach Resort BUNGALOWS $
(☎0 7744 5018; www.longtailbeachresort.com; Thong Nai Pan; 390-1150B; ❄📶) Effortlessly adorable, and one of the last remaining batches of beach bungalows in the area, Longtail offers backpackers a taste of Pha-Ngan's past with its charming thatch-and-bamboo abodes.

EAST COAST BEACHES

Robinson Crusoe, eat your heart out! For the most part, you'll have to hire a boat to get to these beaches; water taxis are available in Hat Rin and Chalok Lam.

TOP CHOICE **Sanctuary** BUNGALOWS $$
(☎08 1271 3614; www.thesanctuarythailand.com; Hat Thian; dm 200B, bungalows 450-5450B) If you're looking for Alex Garland's mythical beach, this is about as close as it gets. A friendly enclave promoting relaxation, The Sanctuary is an inviting haven offering splendid lodging while also functioning as a holistic retreat (think yoga classes to detox sessions). Accommodation, in various manifestations of twigs, is scattered around the resort, married to the natural surroundings.

Mai Pen Rai BUNGALOWS $
(☎0 7744 5090; www.thansadet.com; Than Sadet; bungalows 600B; @) *'Mai pen rai'* is the Thai equivalent of 'don't worry, be happy', which isn't too surprising since this bay elicits nothing but sedate smiles. Bungalows sit on the hilly headland, and sport panels of straw weaving with gabled roofs.

Eating

Ko Pha-Ngan is no culinary capital, especially since most visitors quickly absorb the lazy lifestyle and wind up eating at their accommodation.

HAT RIN

The infamous **Chicken Corner** is a popular intersection stocked with several faves such as **Mr K Thai Food** (Ban Hat Rin; dishes 30-80B) and **Mama Schnitzel** (Ban Hat Rin; dishes 40-100B) who promise to cure any case of the munchies, be it noon or midnight.

Lazy House INTERNATIONAL $$
(Hat Rin Nai; dishes 90-270B; ⏲lunch & dinner) Back in the day, this joint was the owner's apartment – everyone liked his cooking so much that he decided to turn the place into a restaurant and hang-out spot. Today, Lazy House is easily one of Hat Rin's best places to veg out in front of a movie with a shepherd's pie.

Little Home THAI $
(Ban Hat Rin; mains from 40B; ⏲breakfast, lunch & dinner) With no design aesthetic whatsoever, Little Home woos the masses with cheap, flavourful Thai grub that's gobbled up with alacrity among wooden tables and flimsy plastic chairs.

SOUTHERN BEACHES

Night Market MARKET $
(Thong Sala; dishes 25-180B; ⏲dinner) A heady mix of steam and snacking locals, Thong Sala's night market is a must for those looking for a dose of culture while nibbling on a low-priced snack. Banana pancakes and fruit smoothies abound for dessert.

Kaito JAPANESE $$
(Thong Sala; dishes from 130B; ⏲dinner Thu-Mon) Authentic Japanese imports are the speciality here – slurp an Asahi while savouring your tangy seaweed salad and *tonkatsu* (pork cutlet). The upstairs level has cosy cushion sitting while the main sitting area is flanked with *manga* and pocket-sized Japanese novels.

OTHER BEACHES

TOP CHOICE **Sanctuary** HEALTH FOOD $$
(Hat Thian; mains from 130B) Forget what you know about health food – sanctuary's restaurant proves that wholesome eats can also be delicious. Enjoy a tasty parade of plates – from Indian pakoras to crunchy Vietnamese spring rolls – as an endless playlist of music (undoubtedly the island's best) wafts overhead.

Cucina Italiana ITALIAN $$
(Jenny's; Chalok Lam; pizza 180B; ⏲dinner) Cucina Italiana has a cult following on Ko Pha-Ngan. The friendly Italian chef is passionate about his food, and creates all of his dishes from scratch. On Thursday and Sunday, you can order unlimited toppings on your oven-roasted pizza for only 180B.

Drinking

Hat Rin is the beating heart of the legendary Full Moon fun, and the area can get pretty wound up even without the influence of lunar phases. The following party venues flank Hat Rin's infamous Sunrise Beach from south to north:

Rock BAR/CLUB

(Hat Rin Nok) Great views of the party from the elevated terrace on the far south side of the beach.

Club Paradise BAR/CLUB

(Hat Rin Nok) Paradise basks in its celebrity status as the genesis of the lunar *loco*-motion.

Drop-In Bar BAR/CLUB

(Hat Rin Nok) This dance shack blasts the chart toppers that we all secretly love. The other nights of the year are equally as boisterous.

Zoom/Vinyl BAR/CLUB

(Hat Rin Nok) An ear-popping trance venue.

Cactus Bar BAR/CLUB

(Hat Rin Nok) Smack in the centre of Hat Rin Nok, Cactus pumps out a healthy mix of old school tunes, hip hop and R&B.

Sunrise BAR/CLUB

(Hat Rin Nok) A newer spot on the sand where trance beats shake the graffiti-ed walls.

Tommy BAR/CLUB

(Hat Rin Nok) One of Hat Rin's largest venues lures the masses with black lights and trance music blaring on the sound system. Drinks are dispensed from a large ark-like bar.

Mellow Mountain BAR/CLUB

(Hat Rin Nok) Also called 'Mushy Mountain' (you'll know why when you get there), this trippy hang-out sits at the northern edge of Hat Rin Nok delivering stellar views of the shenanigans below.

Information

Check out the pocket-sized **Phangan Info** (www.phangan.info) for comprehensive information about the island.

Main police station (☎0 7737 7114, 191) Located about 2km north of Thong Sala. The police station in Hat Rin (near Hat Rin school) will not let you file a report; to do so you must go to Thong Sala.

Backpackers Information Centre (☎0 7737 5535; www.backpackersthailand.com; Hat Rin) A must for travellers looking to book high-quality tours (diving, live-aboards, jungle safaris etc) and transport. Run by friendly expats.

Ko Pha-Ngan Hospital (☎0 7737 7034; Thong Sala; ⊙24hr) About 2.5km north of Thong Sala; offers 24-hour emergency services.

Main post office (⊙8.30am-4.30pm Mon-Fri, 9am-noon Sat) In Thong Sala; there's a smaller office right near the pier in Hat Rin.

Dangers & Annoyances

As tempting as it may be to dabble with local herb we strongly suggest that you abstain. Local police are not shy about tossing drug users in jail. Also note that your travel insurance does not cover any drug-related injury or treatment.

Solo female travellers should be extra careful. We've received many reports about drug- and alcohol-related rape (and these situations are not limited to Full Moon parties).

Ko Pha-Ngan has more motorcycle accidents than injuries incurred from Full-Moon tomfoolery. Simply put: don't rent a bike.

Getting There & Away

Bangkok, Hua Hin & Chumphon

The Lomprayah and Seatran services have bus/boat combination packages that depart from Bangkok and pass through Hua Hin and Chumphon. It is also quite hassle-free to take the train from Bangkok to Chumphon and switch to a ferry service.

Ko Samui & Ko Tao

There are around a dozen daily departures between Ko Pha-Ngan and Ko Samui. These boats leave throughout the day from 7am to 6pm and take from 20 minutes to an hour. Most boats leave from Thong Sala. The *Haad Rin Queen* goes back and forth between Hat Rin and Big Buddha Beach on Samui.

All boats to Ko Tao leave from Thong Sala. Lomprayah ferries depart at 8.30am and 1pm (arriving at 9.45am and 2.15pm respectively). Seatran operates on a similar schedule. The cheaper-but-slower Songserm leaves Ko Pha-Ngan at 12.30pm and alights at 2.30pm.

Surat Thani & The Andaman Coast

Combination boat/bus tickets are available at any travel agency; simply tell them your desired destination and they will sell you the necessary links in the transport chain. Most travellers will pass through Surat Thani as they swap coasts. There are approximately six daily departures from Ko Pha-Ngan on the Raja Car Ferry, Songserm or Seatran. These boats leave from Thong Sala throughout the day from 7am to 8pm. Every evening a night boat runs from Surat, departing at 11pm. Boats in the opposite direction leave Ko Pha-Ngan at 10pm.

Getting Around

MOTORBIKE You can rent motorcycles all over the island for 150B to 250B per day. Always wear a helmet – it's the law on Ko Pha-Ngan, and local policemen enforce it.

SŎRNGTĂAOU Pick-up trucks and sŏrngtăaou chug along the island's major roads and the riding rates double after sunset. Ask your accommodation about free or discount transfers when you leave the island. The trip from Thong Sala to Hat Rin is 100B.

WATER TAXI Long-tail boats depart from Thong Sala, Chalok Lam and Hat Rin, heading to a variety of far-flung destinations such as Hat Khuat (Bottle Beach). Expect to pay anywhere from 50B to 300B.

Ko Tao

POP 1382

First there was Ko Samui, then Ko Pha-Ngan; now, the cult of Ko Tao ('Ko Taoism' perhaps?) has emerged along Thailand's crystalline gulf coast. Today, thousands of visitors come to worship the turquoise waters offshore, and quite often they stay.

Many years have passed since the first backpacker came to the scrubby island and planted a flag in the name of self-respecting shoestring scuba-holics everywhere (hello pizza parlours and ladyboy shows), but fret not, there's still plenty of time to join the tribe.

Sights & Activities

Diving

Never been diving before? Ko Tao is *the* place to lose your scuba virginity. The shallow bays scalloping the island are the perfect spot for newbie divers to take their first stab at scuba. On shore, over 40 dive centres are ready to saddle you up with some gear and teach you the ropes in a three-and-a-half-day Open Water certification course. We know, we know, homework on a holiday sucks, but the intense competition among scuba schools means that certification prices are unbeatably low, and the standards of service are top notch, as dozens of dive shops vie for your baht.

A **PADI** (www.padi.com) Open Water certification course costs 9800B; an **SSI** (www.ssithailand.com) Open Water Certification is slightly less (9000B, because you do not have to pay for instructional materials). An Advanced Open Water certification will set you back 8500B. Fun divers should expect to pay roughly 1000B per dive, or around 7000B for a 10-dive package. Discounts are usually given if you bring your own equipment.

Expect large crowds and booked-out beds throughout the months of December, January, June, July and August, and a monthly glut of wannabe divers after every Full Moon Party on Ko Pha-Ngan next door.

Ban's Diving School DIVING
(Map p746; ☎0 7745 6466; www.amazingkohtao.com; Sairee Beach) A well-oiled diving machine and relentlessly expanding conglomerate, Ban's certifies more divers per year than any other scuba school in the world and refurbishments in 2009 have given it a five-star feel.

Big Blue Diving DIVING
(Map p746; ☎0 7745 6415, 0 7745 6772; www.bigbluediving.com; Sairee Beach) If Goldilocks were picking a dive school, she'd probably pick Big Blue – not too big, not too small, this operation gets props for fostering a sociable vibe while maintaining a high standard of service.

Buddha View DIVING
(Map p745; ☎0 7745 6074; www.buddhaview-diving.com; Chalok Ban Kao) Another big dive operation on Ko Tao, Buddha View offers the standard fare of certification and special programs for technical diving (venturing beyond the usual parameters of recreational underwater exploration).

Crystal DIVING
(Map p746; ☎0 7745 6107; www.crystaldive.com; Mae Hat) Crystal is the Meryl Streep of dive operators, winning all the awards for best performance. It's one of the largest schools on the island (and around the world), although high-quality instructors and intimate classes keep the school feeling quite personal.

Snorkelling

Most snorkel enthusiasts opt for the do-it-yourself approach on Ko Tao, which involves swimming out into the offshore bays or hiring a longtail boat to putter around further out. Orchestrating your own snorkelling adventure is simple, since the bays on the east coast have small bungalow operations offering equipment rental for 100B to 200B per day.

Freediving

Over the last couple of years freediving (exploring the sea using breath-holding techniques rather than scuba gear) has grown rapidly in popularity.

Freediving prices are standardised across the island as well – a two-and-a-half-day SSI beginner course costs 5500B.

Apnea Total FREEDIVING
(Map p746; ☎08 7183 2321; www.apnea-total.com; Sairee Beach)

Blue Immersion FREEDIVING
(Map p746; ☎08 7682 1886; www.blue-immersion.com; Sairee Beach)

Other Activities

TOP CHOICE **Flying Trapeze Adventures** ACROBATICS
(Map p746; FTA; ☎08 0696 9269; www.flyingtrapezeadventure.com; Sairee Beach; ⊙4-8pm) Find out if you're a great catch while donning a pair of hot pink tights during a one-hour group trapeze lesson (950B).

Goodtime Adventures TOURS
(Map p746; ☎08 7275 3604; www.gtadventures.com; Sairee Beach, ⊙noon-late) Goodtime offers a wide variety of land- and sea-based activities

Ko Tao

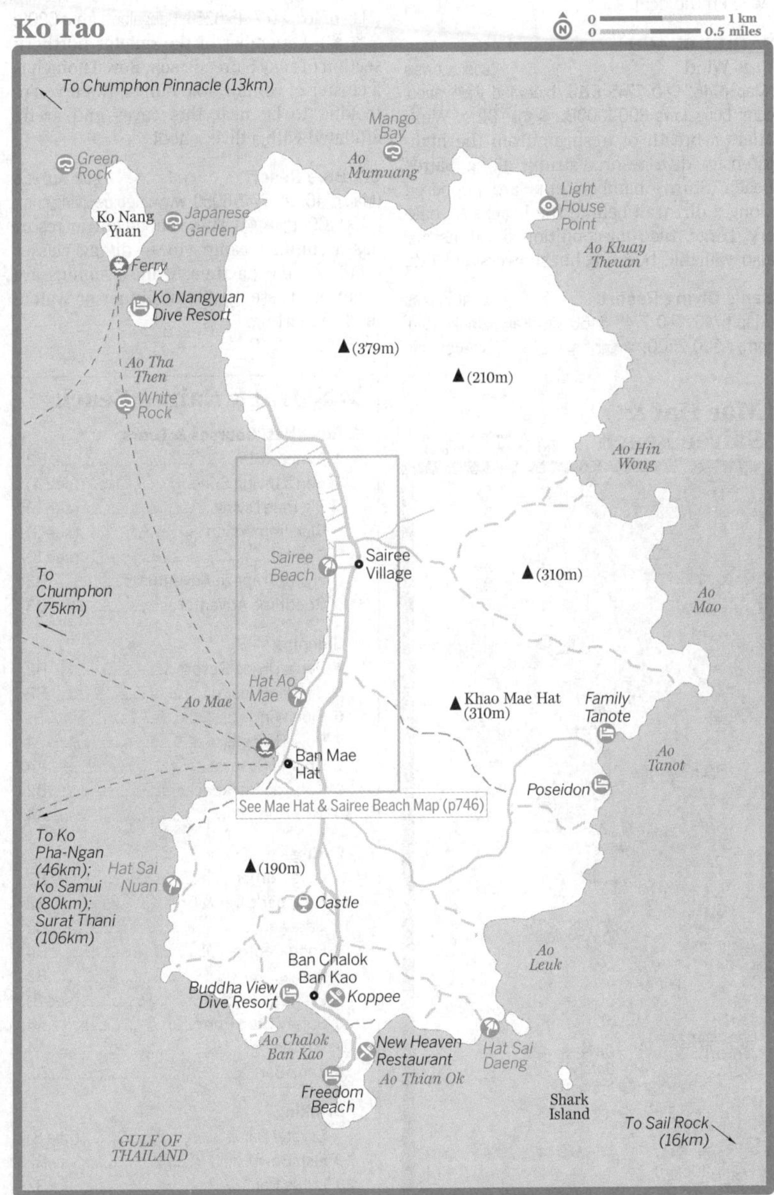

to get the adrenaline pumping, like abseiling, rockclimbing and cliff jumping.

Sleeping

If you are planning to dive while visiting Ko Tao, your scuba operator will probably offer you free or discounted accommodation to sweeten the deal.

SAIREE BEACH

Blue Wind BUNGALOWS $

(Map p746; ☎0 7745 6116; bluewind_wa@yahoo.com; bungalows 300-1000B;) Blue Wind offers a breath of fresh air from the high-intensity dive resorts strung along Sairee Beach. Sturdy bamboo huts are peppered along a dirt trail behind the beachside bakery. Large, tiled air-conditioned cabins are also available, boasting hot showers and TVs.

Ban's Diving Resort RESORT $$

(Map p746; ☎0 7745 6466; www.amazingkohtao.com; r 500-2500;) This dive-centric party palace offers a wide range of quality accommodation from basic backpacker digs to sleek hillside villas. Post-scuba chill sessions happen on Ban's prime slice of beach, or at one of the swimming pools out back.

Bow Thong BUNGALOWS $

(Map p746; ☎0 7745 6266; bungalows from 600B;) A member of the quieter northern section of silky Sairee Beach, Bow Thong has a cluster of comfortable bungalows if you're looking to be near the waves and aren't affiliated with a dive school.

Big Blue Resort BUNGALOWS $

(Map p746; ☎0 7745 6050; www.bigbluediving.com; r 400-1000B;) This scuba-centric resort has a summer camp vibe – diving classes dominate the daytime, while evenings are spent en masse, grabbing dinner or watching fire twirling.

Mae Hat & Sairee Beach

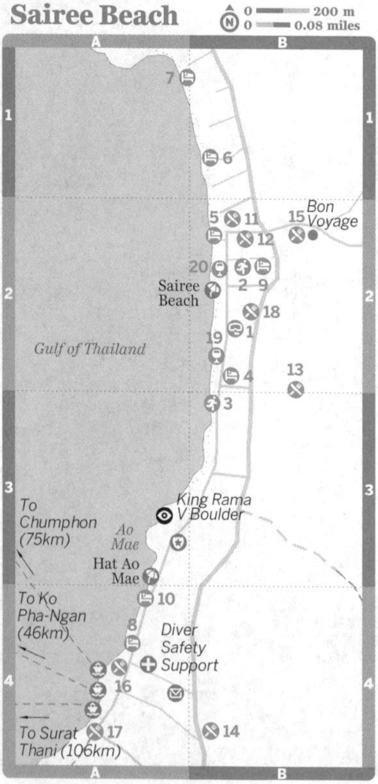

0 — 200 m
0 — 0.08 miles

Mae Hat & Sairee Beach

Activities, Courses & Tours

1 Apnea Total B2
Ban's Diving School .... (see 4)
Big Blue Diving .... (see 5)
Blue Immersion .... (see 3)
Crystal .... (see 8)
2 Flying Trapeze Adventures B2
3 Goodtime Adventures B3

Sleeping

4 Ban's Diving Resort B2
5 Big Blue Resort B2
6 Blue Wind B1
7 Bow Thong A1
8 Crystal Resort A4
9 Koh Tao Backpackers B2
10 Mr J Bungalow A4

Eating

11 Café Corner B2
12 Chopper's Bar & Grill B2
13 Darawan B2
14 Food Centre B4
15 Kanya B2
Pranee's Kitchen .... (see 8)
16 Safety Stop Pub A4
17 Whitening A4
18 ZanziBar B2

Drinking

Crystal Bar .... (see 8)
19 Fish Bowl B2
20 Lotus Bar B2

Koh Tao Backpackers HOSTEL $
(Map p746; ☎08 8447 7921; www.kohtaobackpackers.com; dm 300B; ❄📶) No frills bunk beds for serious penny pinchers.

MAE HAT

Crystal Resort BUNGALOWS $
(Map p746; ☎0 7745 6107; www.crystaldive.com; bungalows 800-1500B; ❄🏊) The bungalow and motel-style accommodation at Crystal is reserved for its divers, and prices drop significantly for those taking courses. Guests can take a dip in the refreshing pool when it isn't overflowing with bubble-blowing newbie divers.

Mr J Bungalow BUNGALOWS $
(Map p746; ☎0 7745 6066; bungalows 250-1000B) Even though Mr J tried to charge us 50B for his business card, we still think he's well worth the visit. The eccentric owner entangles guests in a philosophical web while tending to his flock of decent bungalows.

CHALOK BAN KAO

Buddha View Dive Resort BUNGALOWS $
(Map p745; ☎0 7745 6074; www.buddhaview-diving.com; r 300-1500B; ❄) Like the other large diving operations on the island, Buddha View offers its divers discounted on-site digs in a super-social atmosphere. If you plan on staying a while, ask about the 'Divers Village' across the street, which offers basic accommodation from around 4000B per month.

Freedom Beach BUNGALOWS $
(Map p745; ☎0 7745 6596; bungalows 400-1500B; ❄) On its own secluded beach at the eastern end of Ao Chalok, Freedom feels like a classic backpacker haunt, although there's a variety of accommodation to suit various humble budgets. The string of bungalows (from wooden shacks to sturdier huts with air-con) links the breezy seaside bar to the resort's restaurant high on the cliff.

EAST COAST BEACHES

Poseidon BUNGALOWS $
(Map p745; ☎0 7745 6735; poseidonkohtao@hotmail.com; Tanote Bay; bungalows from 300B) Poseidon keeps the tradition of the budget bamboo bungalow alive with a dozen basic-but-sleepable huts scattered near the sand.

Family Tanote BUNGALOWS $$
(Map p745; ☎0 7745 6757; Tanote Bay; bungalows 700-3500B) As the name suggests, this scatter of hillside bungalows is run by a local family who take pride in providing comfy digs to solitude seekers. Strap on a snorkel mask and swim around with the fish at your doorstep, or climb up to the restaurant for a tasty meal and pleasant views of the bay.

KO NANG YUAN

Photogenic Ko Nang Yuan, just off the coast of Ko Tao, is easily accessible by the Lomprayah catamaran, and by water taxis that depart from Mae Hat and Sairee.

Ko Nangyuan Dive Resort BUNGALOWS $$$
(Map p745; ☎0 7745 6088; www.nangyuan.com; bungalows 1200-9000B; ❄📶) Although the obligatory 100B tax to access the island is a bit off-putting, Nangyuan Dive Resort is nonetheless a charming place. The rugged collection of wood and aluminium bungalows winds its way across three coolie-hat-like islands connected by an idyllic sandbar.

Eating

SAIREE BEACH

Darawan INTERNATIONAL $$
(Map p746; mains 160-400B; ⏰lunch & dinner) Like a top-end dining venue plucked from the posh shores of nearby Samui, regal Darawan is the island's newest place to take a date. Designer lighting, efficient waiters and a tasty 'wagyu' burger seal the deal.

ZanziBar SANDWICHES $
(Map p746; sandwiches 90-140B; ⏰breakfast, lunch & dinner) The island's outpost of sandwich yuppie-dom slathers a mix of unpronounceable condiments betwixt two slices of wholegrain bread.

Chopper's Bar & Grill INTERNATIONAL $$
(Map p746; dishes 60-200B; ⏰breakfast, lunch & dinner) So popular that it's become a local landmark, Chopper's is a two-storey hangout where divers and tourists can widen their beer belly. There's live music, sports on the big-screen TVs, billiards and a cinema room.

Kanya THAI $
(Map p746; mains 60-130B; ⏰breakfast, lunch & dinner) Tucked at back of Sairee Village on the road to Hin Wong, four-table Kanya serves an assortment of international dishes, but you'll be missing out if you stray from the delectable array of homecooked Thai classics – the *tom yam plaa* is divine.

Café Corner CAFE $
(Map p746; snacks & mains 30-120B; ⏰breakfast & lunch) Prime real estate, mod furnishings, and tasty iced coffees have made Café

Corner a Sairee staple over the last few years. Scrumptious baked breads are buy-one-get-one-free before being tossed at sunset.

MAE HAT

TOP CHOICE **Whitening** INTERNATIONAL $$
(Map p746; mains 160-300B; ⊙dinner) Although it looks like a pile of forgotten driftwood during the day, this beachy spot falls somewhere between a restaurant and chic seaside bar. Dine amid dangling white Christmas lights while keeping your bare feet tucked into the sand.

Safety Stop Pub INTERNATIONAL $
(Map p746; mains 60-250B; ⊙breakfast, lunch & dinner;) A haven for homesick Brits, this pier-side restaurant and bar feels like a tropical beer garden. Stop by on Sundays to stuff your face with an endless supply of barbecued goodness, and surprisingly the Thai dishes aren't half bad!

Pranee's Kitchen THAI $
(Map p746; mains 50-120B; ⊙breakfast, lunch & dinner;) An old Mae Hat fave, Pranee's serves scrumptious curries and other Thai treats in an open-air pavilion sprinkled with lounging pillows, wooden tables and TVs. English movies (with hilariously incorrect subtitles) are shown nightly at 6pm.

Food Centre THAI $
(Map p746; mains from 30B; ⊙breakfast, lunch & dinner) An unceremonious gathering of hot tin food stalls, Food Centre – as it's come to be known – lures lunching locals with veritable smoke signals rising up from the concrete parking lot abutting Mae Hat's petrol station. You'll find some of the island's best papaya salad here.

CHALOK BAN KAO

New Heaven Restaurant INTERNATIONAL $$
(Map p745; mains 60-350B; ⊙lunch & dinner) The best part about New Heaven Restaurant is the awe-inducing view of Shark Bay (Ao Thian Ok) under the lazy afternoon moon. The menu is largely international, and there are nap-worthy cushions tucked under each low-rise table.

Koppee CAFE $$
(Map p745; mains 60-180B; ⊙breakfast, lunch & dinner) A clone of some of the sleeker cafes in Mae Hat and Sairee, white-washed Koppee serves scrumptious international fare including a variety of home-baked desserts.

Drinking & Entertainment

After diving, Ko Tao's favourite pastime is drinking, and there's definitely no shortage of places to get tanked. In fact, the island's three biggest dive centres each have bumpin' bars – **Fish Bowl** (Map p746) in Sairee, **Crystal Bar** (Map p746) in Mae Hat and **Buddha On The Beach** (Map p745) in Chalok Ban Kao – that attract swarms of travellers and expats alike. It's well worth stopping by even if you aren't a diver.

Castle CLUB
(Map p745; www.thecastlekohtao.com; Mae Hat) Located along the main road between Mae Hat and Chalok Ban Kao, the Castle has quickly positioned itself at the most loved party venue on the island, luring an array of local and international DJs to its triad of parties each month.

Lotus Bar BAR
(Map p746; Sairee Beach) Lotus is the de facto late-night hang-out spot along the northern end of Sairee. Muscular fire twirlers toss around flaming batons, and the drinks are so large there should be a lifeguard on duty.

Information

The ubiquitous **Koh Tao Info** (www.kohtaoonline.com) booklet lists loads of businesses on the island and goes into some detail about the island's history, culture and social issues.

Bon Voyage (Map p746; Sairee Beach) Run by the kind Ms Jai, a native Ko Taoian, Bon Voyage is a great place to make your transport connections. It's located along the road connecting Sairee Beach and Hin Wong.

Diver Safety Support (Map p746; Mae Hat; ⊙on call 24hr) Has a temporary hyperbaric chamber and offers emergency evacuation services.

Police station (Map p746; ☎0 7745 6631) Between Mae Hat and Sairee Beach along the rutty portion of the beachside road.

Post office (Map p746; ☎0 7745 6170; ⊙9am-5pm Mon-Fri, 9am-noon Sat) A 10- to 15-minute walk from the pier; at the corner of Ko Tao's main inner-island road and Mae Hat's 'down road'.

Getting There & Away

Bangkok, Hua Hin & Chumphon

Lomprayah's new air service – **Solar Air** (www.lomprayah.com) jets passengers from Bangkok's Don Mueang airport to Chumphon once daily in each direction from Monday to Saturday. Upon arriving in Chumphon, travellers can make a seamless transfer to the catamaran service bound for Ko Tao. Buses from Bangkok and Hua Hin follow the same route on the ground.

If you are planning to travel through the night, the train's couchettes are a much more comfortable option than the bus.

From Ko Tao, the high-speed catamaran departs for Chumphon at 10.15am and 2.45pm (1½ hours), the Seatran leaves the island at 4pm (two hours), and a Songserm boat makes the same journey at 2.30pm (three hours). There's also a midnight boat from Chumphon arriving early in the morning. It returns from Ko Tao at 11pm.

Ko Pha-Ngan & Ko Samui

The Lomprayah Catamaran offers twice daily service, leaving Ko Tao at 9.30am and 3pm and arriving on Ko Pha-Ngan around 10.50am and 4.10pm, and Ko Samui at 11.30am and 4.40pm. The Seatran Discovery Ferry offers an identical service. The Songserm Express Boat departs daily at 10am and arrives on Ko Pan-Ngan at 11.30am and Ko Samui at 12.45pm. Hotel pick-ups are included in the price.

Surat Thani & The Andaman Coast

There are two direct routes form Ko Tao to the Andaman coast. The first is through Surat Thani – board any Surat-bound boat then transfer to a bus upon arrival. The night boat leaves Ko Tao at 8.30pm.

The second option is to take a ferry to Chumphon on the mainland and then switch to a bus or train bound for the provinces further south.

Getting Around

SŎRNGTĂAOU Sŏrngtăaou, pick-up trucks and motorbikes crowd around the pier in Mae Hat as passengers alight. If you're a solo traveller, you will pay 100B to get to Sairee Beach or Chalok Ban Kao. Groups of two or more will pay 50B each. These prices are rarely negotiable. Many dive schools offer free pick ups and transfers as well.

MOTORBIKE Renting a motorcycle is a dangerous endeavour if you're not sticking to the main, well-paved roads. Daily rental rates begin at 150B for a scooter.

WATER TAXI Boat taxis depart from Mae Hat, Chalok Ban Kao and the northern part of Sairee Beach. Long-tail boats can be chartered for around 1500B per day.

Surat Thani

POP 128,990

Known in Thai as 'City of Good People', Surat Thani was once the seat of the ancient Srivijaya empire. Today, this busy junction has become a transport hub that indiscriminately moves cargo and people around the country. Travellers rarely linger here as they make their way to the deservedly popular islands of Ko Samui, Ko Pha-Ngan and Ko Tao.

If you need to spend the night in Surat, hop on a sŏrngtăaou heading towards the Phang-Nga district. Tell the driver 'Tesco-Lotus', and you'll be taken about 3km out of town to a large shopping centre. A handful of reasonable hotel options orbit the mall including **100 Islands Resort & Spa** (☎0 7720 1150; www.roikoh.com; 19/6 Moo 3, Bypass Rd; r 590-1200B; ❄@📶🏊) – this is as good as it gets in Thailand for under 600B.

Go to the **night market** (Sarn Chao Ma; Th Ton Pho) for fried, steamed, grilled or sautéed delicacies. There are additional evening food stalls near the departure docks for the daily night boats to the islands, a seafood market at **Pak Nam Tapi**, and an afternoon **Sunday market** (⏲4-9pm) near the TAT office. During the day many food stalls near the downtown bus terminal sell *kôw gài òp* (marinated baked chicken on rice).

Information

Th Na Meuang has a bank on virtually every corner in the heart of downtown. If you're staying near the 'suburbs', the Tesco-Lotus has ATMs as well.

Boss Computer (per hr 20B; ⏲9am-midnight) The cheapest internet connection around. Located near the post office.

Siam City Bank (Th Chonkasem) Has a Western Union office.

Taksin Hospital (☎0 7727 3239; Th Talat Mai) The most professional of Surat's three hospitals. Just beyond the Talat Mai Market in the northeast part of downtown.

TAT office (☎0 7728 8817; tatsurat@samart.co.th; 5 Th Talat Mai; ⏲8.30am-4.30pm) Friendly office southwest of town. Distributes plenty of useful brochures and maps, and staff speak English very well.

Getting There & Away

In general, if you are departing Bangkok or Hua Hin for Ko Pha-Ngan or Ko Tao, consider taking the train or a bus/boat package that goes through Chumphon rather than Surat. If you require any travel services, try **Holiday Travel** (Th Na Meuang) or **Pranthip Co** (Th Talat Mai) – both are reliable and English is spoken.

Air

Although flights from Bangkok to Surat Thani are cheaper than the flights to Samui, it takes a significant amount of time to reach the gulf islands from the airport. If you want to fly through Surat, there are daily shuttles to Bangkok on

Thai Airways International (THAI; ☎0 7727 2610; 3/27-28 Th Karunarat).

Boat

Most boats – such as the Raja and Seatran services – leave from Don Sak (about one hour from Surat; bus transfers are included in the ferry ticket) although the Songserm leaves from the heart of Surat town. The boat trip usually takes around 90 minutes to Ko Samui and 2½ hours to Ko Pha-Ngan, although oftentimes the captain will cut the engines to half propulsion, slowing the journey down.

From the centre of Surat there are nightly ferries to Ko Tao (eight hours, departs 10pm), Ko Pha-Ngan (seven hours, departs 10pm) and Ko Samui (six hours, departs 11pm). These are cargo ships, not luxury boats, so bring food and water and watch your bags.

Bus & Minivan

The most convenient way to travel around the south, frequent buses and minivans depart from two main locations in town. Talat Kaset 1, on the north side of Th Talat Mai (the city's main drag) offers speedy service to Nakhon. At Talat Kaset 2, on the south side of Th Talat Mai, you'll find frequent transport to Hat Yai and minibuses to Nakhon, Trang, Khanom and Krabi. Andaman-bound buses (usually destined for Phuket) depart every hour from 7am to 3.30pm. The 'new' bus terminal (which is actually a few years old now, but still referred to as 'new' by locals) is located 7km south of town.

Train

When arriving by train you'll actually pull into Phun Phin, 14km west of Surat. From Phun Phin, it is possible to reach Phuket, Phang-Nga and Krabi by bus – some via Takua Pa, the stopping point for Khao Sok National Park.

Trains passing through Surat stop in Chumphon and Hua Hin on their way up to the capital, and in the other direction you'll call at Trang, Hat Yai and Sungai Kolok before hopping the border.

Getting Around

Air-conditioned vans to/from the Surat Thani airport cost around 70B per person and they'll drop you off at your hotel.

To travel around town, sŏrngtăaou cost 10B to 30B (it's 15B to reach Tesco-Lotus from the city centre), while săhmlór (three-wheeled vehicles) charge 20B to 40B.

Fan-cooled orange buses run from Phun Phin train station to Surat Thani every 10 minutes (15B, 25 minutes). For this ride, taxis charge 200B for a maximum of four people, while share-taxis charge 100B per person.

Hat Yai

POP 157,400

Welcome to backcountry Thailand's version of big city livin'. Songkhla Province's liveliest town has long been a favourite stop for Malaysian men on their weekend hooker tours. These days Hat Yai gladly shakes hands with globalisation – Western-style shopping malls stretch across the city, providing local teenagers with a spot to loiter and middle-aged ladies with a place to do their cardio.

Hat Yai has dozens of hotels within walking distance of the train station. The city is the unofficial capital of southern Thailand's cuisine, offering Muslim roti and curries, Chinese noodles and dim sum, and fresh Thai-style seafood from both the Gulf and Andaman coasts.

Information

Immigration Office (Th Phetkasem) Near the railway bridge, it handles visa extensions.

TAT Office (tatsgkhla@tat.or.th; 1/1 Soi 2, Th Niphat Uthit 3) Very helpful staff here speak excellent English and have loads of info on the entire region.

Tourist police (Th Niphat Uthit 3; 24hr) Near the TAT office.

Getting There & Away

Air

Thai Airways International (THAI; 182 Th Niphat Uthit 1) operates eight flights daily between Hat Yai and Bangkok.

Nearly all of the low-cost airlines now operate flights to/from Bangkok:

Air Asia (www.airasia.com) Daily flights from Hat Yai to Bangkok and Kuala Lumpur.

Nok Air (www.nokair.com) Daily flights between Hat Yai and Bangkok's Don Meuang Airport.

Bus

Most inter-provincial buses and south-bound minivans leave from the bus terminal 2km south-east of the town centre, while most northbound minivans now leave from a minivan terminal 5km west of town at Talat Kaset, a 60B túk-túk ride from the centre of town. Buses link Hat Yai to almost any location in southern Thailand.

Prasert Tour (Th Niphat Uthit 1) has minibuses to Surat Thani (4½ hours, 8am to 5pm), and **Cathay Tour** (93/1 Th Niphat Uthit 2) can also arrange minivans to many destinations in the south.

Train

There are four overnight trains to/from Bangkok each day, and the trip takes at least 16 hours. There are also seven trains daily that run along the east coast to Sungai Kolok and two daily trains running west to Butterworth and Padang Besar, both in Malaysia.

Getting Around

Airport Taxi Service (0 7423 8452; 182 Th Niphat Uthit 1) makes the run to the airport four times daily (80B per person). A private taxi for this run costs 280B.

Sŏrngtăaou run along Th Phetkasem (10B per person). Túk-túk and motorcycle taxis around town cost 20B to 40B per person.

THE ANDAMAN COAST

The Andaman is Thailand's turquoise coast, that place on a 'Travel to Paradise' poster that makes you want to leave your job and live in flipflops...forever. And for once, the beauty exceeds the hype. White beaches, cathedral-like limestone cliffs, neon corals and hundreds of jungle-covered isles extend down the Andaman Sea from the border of Myanmar to Malaysia. Photographs haven't yet fully captured the array of blues and greens, let alone the soft fingers of humidity on the skin or the feel of the world's softest sands between your toes. For this, you'll need to visit.

Ranong

POP 24,500

On the eastern bank of the Sompaen River's turbid, tea-brown estuary, the frontier town of Ranong is a short boat ride – or a filthy swim – from Myanmar. This border town *par excellence* (shabby, frenetic, slightly seedy) has a thriving Burmese population (keep an eye out for men wearing traditional *longyi;* Burmese sarong), a clutch of **hot springs** (Th Petchkasem; admission free; 8am-5pm) and some tremendous street food.

Today the town is basking in the transit tourism to Ko Phayam more than the visa runs it was once known for (visas given at the border are only valid for two weeks now). Meanwhile, more and more dive operators specialising in live-aboard trips to the Surin or Similan Islands and Burma Banks are establishing themselves here, adding a pinch of an expat feel. Try **A-One-Diving** (0 7783 2984; www.a-one-diving.com; 256 Th Ruangrat; 4-night packages from 15,900B) or **Andaman International Dive Center** (0 7783 4824; www.aidcdive.com; Th Petchkasem), located at the bus station.

Sleeping & Eating

If you are doing a visa run through an agency, they'll ship you in and out of town without having to sleep over. If you decide to spend the night, try **Dhala House** (0 7781 2959; http://dahla.siam2web.com; 323/5 Th Ruangrat; r 400-500B;), which has cute, concrete bungalows with tiled floors and pebbled tile bathrooms; the bungalows line a garden and are set off the main drag.

For some grub, there's a **night market** not far from Hwy 4 that sells great Thai dishes at low prices. The **day market** on Th Ruangrat offers inexpensive Thai and Burmese meals. Expats hang out at **Sophon's Hideaway** (0 7783 2730; Th Ruangrat; mains 80-250B; lunch & dinner;), which has a bit

GETTING TO MALAYSIA: KANGAR TO PADANG BESAR OR SADAO TO BUKIT KAYU HITAM

Getting to the border The best way to get to Malaysia from the Gulf is to pop over the border at Sadao (road crossing) or Kangar (road and rail crossing), which are a stone's throw from the southern hub of Hat Yai. There is a well-trodden taxi route from Hat Yai down to the border crossing at Sadao for around 2000B in a private taxi (one hour). Share minivans ply this route as well. There's also a bus that takes passengers from Hat Yai to Penang, Malaysia – any travel agent in Hat Yai can make this booking. If you are on the train from Hat Yai, you will cross the border at the Kangar–Padang Besar border crossing and continue on to Butterworth. The road crossing at Kangar–Padang Besar is not recommended as it is a less fluid border crossing than Sadao and has fewer transfers available.

At the border Most tourists come here to extend their visas. Running the border by yourself is rare and ill-advised, but 'tour' visa runs can be sorted from Hat Yai and this is the most stress-free solution. You'll be paying about the same if you were to do it solo.

Moving on Once through the border, you can take a bus to Alor Setar. Keep in mind that Malaysia is one hour ahead of Thai time. See p413 for details on doing the trip in reverse.

of everything, including a free pool table, a pizza oven and rattan furnishings aplenty.

Information

Internet can be found along Th Ruangrat for 20B per hour and there's a cluster of ATMs at the Th Tha Meuang and Th Ruangrat intersection.

Main post office (Th Chonrau; ⊙9am-4pm Mon-Fri, to noon Sat)

Pon's Place (☎08 1597 4549; www.ponplace-ranong.com; Th Ruangrat; ⊙7.30am-midnight) The go-to spot in Ranong for transportation tickets and local info.

Getting There & Away

Air

Ranong Air (☎0 7783 2222; www.ranongair.com) runs four flights per week between Ranong and Bangkok (one way 2800B), Phuket (one way 2300B) and Hat Yai (one way 2800B).

Bus

The bus terminal is on Th Petchkasem 1km from town, though some Bangkok-bound buses stop at the main market.

Minivans head to Surat Thani (250B, 3½ hours, four times daily) and Chumphon (120B, three hours, hourly from 6am to 5pm).

Getting Around

Motorcycle taxis will take you almost anywhere in town for 20B, to the hotels along Th Petchkasem for 25B and to the pier (for 50B) for boats to Ko Chang, Ko Phayam and Myanmar.

Ko Chang

If you're looking for the big Ko Chang, you've come to the wrong place. But if your suitcase is overflowing with novels and you're seeking a silent stretch of sand on which to read them, then welcome! Unlike most of the Andaman's islands, Ko Chang enjoys its back-to-basics lifestyle – there are no ATMs here.

Aladdin Dive Cruise (☎0 7782 0472; www.aladdindivecruise.de) runs PADI courses and offers a range of live-aboard dive safaris.

Sleeping & Eating

Crocodile Rock GUESTHOUSE $
(☎08 0533 4138; tonn1970@yahoo.com; Ao Yai; bungalows 250-450B) Outstanding bamboo bungalows hover on Ao Yai's serene southern headland with superb bay views through gentle foliage. Its classy kitchen turns out homemade yoghurt, breads, cookies, good espresso and a variety of veggie and seafood dishes.

Sawasdee GUESTHOUSE $
(☎08 6906 0900; www.sawadeekohchang.com; Ao Yai; bungalows 350-600B) The A-frame wooden bungalows have vented walls to keep things cool. Every option has sunken bathrooms painted bright colours, and hammocks on the terraces.

Getting There & Away

From central Ranong Town, take a sŏrngtăaou (25B) or a shuttle run by most guesthouses (50B) to Saphan Plaa. Three long-tail boats (150B) and two speedboats (350B) leave daily from mid-October to May. All stop on the island's west coast beaches.

A taxi boat service connecting Ko Chang and Ko Phayam runs on weekdays from Koh Chang Resort on Ao Yai (150B, one hour).

Ko Phayam

Technically part of Laem Son National Park, little Ko Phayam is a beach-laden isle that – for now – is managing to go mainstream while still holding onto its soul. Spectacular beaches are dotted with beach bungalows

BUSES FROM RANONG

DESTINATION	PRICE	DURATION (HR)
Bangkok	240-680B	10
Chumphon	100B	3
Hat Yai	410B	5
Khao Lak	150B	3½
Krabi	200-300B	6
Phuket	240B	5-6
Surat Thani	100-180B	4-5

GETTING TO MYANMAR: RANONG TO KAWTHOUNG (VICTORIA POINT)

The dusty, tumbledown port at the southernmost tip of mainland Myanmar is known as Kawthoung. The easiest way to renew your Thai visa is to opt for one of the 'visa trips' (from 1000B per person including visa fees) offered by travel agencies in Ranong. All-inclusive trips from Phuket or Ko Samui are also a possibility.

If you perform the renewal yourself you can take a boat from Saphan Plaa, 5km from Ranong. Stop at the immigration window at the pier to stamp out, then take a boat (per person one way/return 100/200B) over to Myanmar. At the checkpoint, you must inform the authorities that you're a day visitor – in which case you will pay a fee of US$10 (or 500B) with a new, unblemished bill.

The whole process will take a minimum of two hours. Bear in mind when you are returning to Thailand that Myanmar's time is 30 minutes behind Thailand's, so leave plenty of time to return to Thailand before 4.30pm when the border closes.

For more information about Kawthoung, see p505.

and the wooded interior has some rudimentary concrete motorbike paths.

The main drawback of Ko Phayam is that the snorkelling isn't great, but the Surin Islands are relatively close by. For dive trips and PADI courses try **Phayam Divers** (08 6995 2598; www.phayamlodge.com; Ao Yai).

Sleeping & Eating

TOP CHOICE **PP Land** HOTEL $
(08 1678 4310; www.payampplandbeach.com; Ao Hin-Khow; bungalows 650B) This is a stunning ecolodge, north of the pier on the little-visited windward side of the island. The stylish concrete bungalows are powered by the wind and sun, and have terraces that overlook the sea.

Starlight Bungalows GUESTHOUSE $
(08 1978 5301; http://sites.google.com/site/starlightbungalows; Ao Khao Kwai; bungalows 500-650B) American-Thai run, choose from high-ceiling spacious wooden huts or small bamboo ones further back in the trees. The social vibe here is as fab as the food – Pom the cook regularly wins local Thai food cook-offs.

Getting There & Around

There are daily ferries from Ranong's Saphan Plaa to Ko Phayam's main pier (150B, 1½ to two hours) at 9am and 2pm, and speedboats (350B, 45 minutes) at 10am and 2.30pm. From Ko Phayam back to Ranong the boats run at 9am and 1pm. Long-tail boat charters to Ko Chang are 1200B, or you can take the taxi boat (150B, one hour) that departs from the main pier at 4pm on weekdays only.

A motorcycle taxi from the pier to the main beaches costs 50B to 80B per person each way depending on the beach. Motorbike and bicycle rentals are available in the village, and from most of the larger resorts.

Khao Sok National Park

If your leg muscles have atrophied after one too many days of beach-bumming, consider venturing inland to the wondrous Khao Sok National Park. Many believe this lowland jungle – the wettest spot in Thailand – to be over 160 million years old, making it one of the oldest rainforests on the globe. It features dramatic limestone formations and waterfalls that cascade through juicy thickets drenched with rain. A network of dirt trails snakes through the quiet park, allowing visitors to spy on the exciting array of indigenous creatures.

Sleeping

We recommend the two-day, one-night trips (2500B per person) to Chiaw Lan, where you sleep in floating huts on the lake and go on a variety of canoeing excursions.

Art's Riverview Jungle Lodge GUESTHOUSE $
(08 6470 3234; http://krabidir.com/artsriverviewlodge; bungalows 650B) In a monkey-filled jungle bordering a river with a natural limestone cliff-framed swimming hole, this is the prettiest location in Khao Sok. Wood bungalows are simple but big; all have river views.

Jungle Huts GUESTHOUSE $
(0 7739 5160; www.khao-sok-junglehuts.com; huts 300-1200B) Basic but good-value huts sit in a forest of fruit trees near a river or high up on stilts connected by a vertiginous walkway.

Information

The **park headquarters** (☎0 7739 5025; www.khaosok.com; park admission 200B) and visitors centre are 1.8km off Rte 401, close to the Km 109 marker.

There's an ATM outside the Morning Mist Mini-Mart and internet is available near the park entrance for 2B per minute.

Getting There & Around

Minivans to/from Surat Thani (250B, one hour), Krabi (300B, two hours) and a handful of other destinations leave daily from the park. Otherwise, from Surat catch a bus going towards Takua Pa, or from the Andaman coast take a Surat Thani-bound bus. Buses drop you off along the highway (Rte 401), 1.8km from the visitors centre. If guesthouse touts don't meet you, you'll have to walk to your chosen nest (from 50m to 2km).

To explore Chiaw Lan lake on your own, charter a long-tail (2000B per day) at the dam's entrance.

Khao Lak & Around

Hat Khao Lak is a beach for folks who shun the glitz of Phuket's bigger resort towns, but still crave comfort, shopping and plenty of facilities. With warm waves to frolic in, long stretches of golden sand backed by forested hills, and easy day trips to the Similan and Surin Islands, Khao Sok and Khao Lak/Lam Ru National Parks or even Phuket, the area is a central base for exploring the North Andaman – above and below the water.

Activities

Diving & Snorkelling

Diving or snorkelling day excursions to the Similan and Surin islands are immensely popular, but if you can, opt for a live-aboard trip. Since the islands are around 60km from the mainland (about three hours by boat), if you do opt for a live-aboard you'll have a more relaxing trip and experience the islands sans day-trippers. All dive shops offer live-aboard trips from around 10,000/19,000B for two-/three-day packages and day trips for 4900B to 6500B.

Similan Diving Safaris DIVING
(☎0 7648 5470; www.similan-diving-safaris.com) The speciality here is the high-quality four-day live-aboard that regularly attracts return customers – this is the best bang for your baht. Day trips are also available.

Wicked Diving DIVING
(☎0 7648 5868; www.wickeddiving.com) An exceptionally well-run and environmentally conscious outfit that offers a wide range of diving and snorkelling live-aboard trips in conjunction with **Ecocean** (www.whaleshark.org).

Sea Dragon Dive Centre DIVING
(☎0 7648 5420; www.seadragondivecenter.com; Th Phetkasem) One of the older operations in Khao Lak, Sea Dragon has maintained high standards throughout the years.

Sleeping

For the cheapest sleeps in town, head to Sea Dragon Dive Center and ask about the dorm beds at Tiffy's Café, which go for 180B per night.

Greenbeach HOTEL $$
(☎0 7648 5845; greenbeach_th@yahoo.com; bungalows 1300-2300B; ❄) On an excellent stretch of Khao Lak beach and extending back into a garden, this place has a warm, family-style soul. The wooden bungalows have glass doors, air-con and fan, shady terraces and views of a towering, ancient banyan tree.

Fasai House GUESTHOUSE $
(☎0 7648 5867; r 500-700B; ❄@) The best budget choice in Khao Lak, Fasai has immaculate motel-style rooms and smiling staff members.

Khaolak Banana Bungalows BUNGALOWS $
(☎0 7648 5889; www.khaolakbanana.com; r 500-1200B; ❄≋) These adorable little bungalows have swirls painted on the cement floors and sun-filled indoor-outdoor bathrooms. A cute pool with deckchairs sweetens the deal.

Eating & Drinking

Early-morning divers will be hard-pressed to find a place to grab a bite before 8.30am.

Mama's Restaurant SEAFOOD $
(Th Petchkasem; dishes 60-300B) Nobody does seafood better than Mama's, across from Boat 813.

Phu Khao Lak THAI $
(Th Petchkasem; dishes 80-240B; ⊙breakfast, lunch & dinner) This is place for a tasty assortment of Thai and international faves.

Happy Snapper BAR
(Th Petchkasem) Happy Snapper has a fully stocked bar and a house band during high season.

Information

For diving-related emergencies, call the **SSS Ambulance** (08 1081 9444), which rushes injured persons down to Phuket.

There are numerous travel agencies scattered about – the best is **Khao Lak Land Discoveries** (0 7648 5411; www.khaolaklanddicovery.com; Th Phetkasem).

Getting There & Away

Any bus running along Hwy 4 between Takua Pa (50B, 45 minutes) and Phuket (100B, two hours) will stop at Hat Khao Lak if you ask the driver.

Khao Lak Discoveries runs hourly minibuses to/from Phuket International Airport (600B, 1¼ hours). Alternatively you can take a taxi (1200B) or tell a Phuket-bound bus driver to let you off at the 'airport' – you'll get let off at an intersection where motorcycle taxis to the airport (10 minutes) cost 100B.

Surin Islands Marine National Park

The five gorgeous islands that make up this **national park** (www.dnp.go.th; admission 400B; mid-Nov–mid-May) sit about 60km offshore, a measly 5km from the Thai-Burma marine border. Healthy rainforest, pockets of white-sand beach in sheltered bays and rocky headlands that jut into the ocean characterise these granite-outcrop islands. The clearest of water makes for great marine life, with underwater visibility often up to 35m. Park headquarters and all visitor facilities are at Ao Chong Khad on Ko Surin Nuea, near the jetty.

Khuraburi, on the mainland, is the jumping-off point for the park. The pier is 9km north of town, as is the **national park office** (0 7649 1378; 8am-5pm), with good information, maps and helpful staff.

Sights & Activities

Dive sites in the park include **Ko Surin Tai** and **HQ Channel** between the two main islands. **Richelieu Rock** (a seamount 14km southeast) is also technically in the park and happens to be one of the best, if not the best, dive sites on the Andaman coast. There's no dive facility in the park itself, so dive trips (four-day live-aboards around 20,000B) must be booked from the mainland.

Ban Moken at Ao Bon on the South Island welcomes visitors. Post-tsunami, Moken have settled in this one sheltered bay where a major ancestral worship ceremony (Loi Reua) takes place in April. The national park offers a **Moken Village Tour** (per person 300B).

Sleeping & Eating

Park accommodation is decent, but because of the island's short, narrow beaches it can feel seriously crowded when full (around 300 people). Book online at www.dnp.go.th or with the mainland **national park office** (0 7649 1378; 8am-5pm) in Khuraburi.

Getting There & Away

Tour operators use speedboats (return 1600B, one hour) that leave around 9am.

Several tour operators run day trips from Khao Lak and Khuruburi (2900B including food and park lodging) to the park; try **Greenview** (0 7640 1400; Khuraburi pier). The Surin Islands are also accessible via live-aboard; the best of which depart from Khao Lak.

Similan Islands Marine National Park

Known to divers the world over, beautiful **Similan Islands Marine National Park** (www.dnp.go.th; admission 400B; Nov-May) is 60km offshore. Its smooth granite islands are as impressive above water as below, topped with rainforest, edged with white-sand beaches and fringed with coral reefs.

Two of the nine islands, Island 4 (Ko Miang) and Island 8 (Ko Similan), have ranger stations and accommodation; park headquarters and most visitor activity centres are on Island 4. Recently, the park was expanded to include Ko Bon and Ko Tachai.

Khao Lak is the jumping-off point for the park. The pier is at Thap Lamu, about 10km south of town.

Sights & Activities

The Similans offer diving for all levels of experience, at depths from 2m to 30m. There are dive sites at each of the six islands north of Ko Miang; the southern part of the park (Islands 1, 2 and 3) is off-limits to divers and is a turtle nesting ground. No facilities for divers exist in the national park itself, so you'll need to take a dive tour.

You can hire snorkelling gear (per day 100B) from the park headquarters. Day trippers from Khao Lak usually visit three or four different snorkelling sites (trips from 3000B).

The islands also have some lovely walking trails where you can spot a variety of bird life.

Sleeping & Eating

Book online at www.dnp.go.th or with the mainland **national park office** (☎0 7645 3272) at Khao Lak. Tour agents in Khao Lak also arrange overnight to multiday trips that include transport, food and lodging at the park. Longhouse and bungalow accommodation is available on Ko Miang from 1000B. There's electricity from 6pm to 6am.

Getting There & Away

There's no public transport to the park but theoretically independent travellers can book a speedboat transfer (return 1700B, 1½ hours one way) with a Khao Lak snorkelling operator, though they much prefer that you join the snorkelling tour and generally discourage independent travel. The most common way to visit is on a multiday live-aboard trip from Khao Lak.

Phuket

POP 83,800

The island of Phuket has long been misunderstood. First of all, the 'h' is silent. Ahem. And second, Phuket doesn't feel like an island at all. It's so huge (the biggest in the country) that one can never really get the sense that they're surrounded by water, which is probably the reason why the 'Ko' (meaning 'island') was dropped from its name. Dubbed the 'pearl of the Andaman' by savvy marketing execs, this is Thailand's original flavour of tailor-made fun in the sun.

Phuket's beating heart can be found in Patong. Located halfway down the western coast, Thailand's 'sin city' is the ultimate gong show where podgy beachaholics sizzle like rotisserie chickens and gogo girls play ping-pong – without paddles...

These days, however, Phuket's affinity for luxury far outshines any of the island's other stereotypes; jetsetters come through in droves, getting pummelled during swanky spa sessions, and swigging sundowners at one of the many fashion-forward nightspots. But you don't have to be an heiress or an Oscar-winner to tap into Phuket's trendy to-do list. There's deep-sea diving, high-end dining, soda-white beaches that beckon your book and blanket – whatever your heart desires. Visitors never say *ph*uket to *P*huket.

Sights

Phuket's stunning west coast, scalloped by sandy bays, faces the crystal Andaman Sea. **Patong** is the eye of the tourist storm, with **Kata** and **Karon** – Patong's little brothers – to the south. The island's quieter east coast features gnarled mangroves rather than silky sand. **Phuket Town**, in the southeast, is the provincial capital and home to most of the island's locals.

Big Buddha SHRINE

Set on a hilltop just northwest of Chalong circle and visible from almost half of the island, Big Buddha sits at the best viewpoint in Phuket. To get here follow the red signs from the main highway (Hwy 402) and wind up a country road, passing terraced banana groves, and tangles of jungle. Of course, you'll be forgiven if you disregard the view for a few minutes to watch local craftsmen put the finishing touches on their 60 million baht Buddha, dressed in Burmese alabaster.

Phuket Town NEIGHBOURHOOD

Phuket has an interest collection of Sino-Portuguese architecture. The most magnificent examples are the **Standard Chartered Bank** (Th Phang-Nga), the **THAI office** (Th Ranong); and the **old post office building**, which now houses the **Phuket Philatelic Museum** (Th Montri; admission free; ⌚9.30am-5.30pm). Check out the **Shrine of the Serene Light** (Saan Jao Sang Tham; ⌚8.30am-noon & 1.30-5.30pm), which injects some added colour to the neighbourhood.

Phuket Gibbon Rehabilitation Centre ANIMAL SHELTER

(☎0 7626 0492; www.gibbonproject.org; Khao Phra Taew Royal Wildlife & Forest Reserve; donations encouraged; ⌚9am-4pm) Financed by donations, the centre adopts gibbons that have been kept in captivity in the hopes they can be re-introduced to the wild. The centre also has volunteer opportunities.

Cable Jungle Adventure Phuket ZIP LINES

(☎08 1977 4904; 232/17 Moo 8, Th Bansuanneramit, Khao Phra Taew Royal Wildlife & Forest Reserve; per person 1950B; ⌚9am-6pm) If you're the thrill-seeking sort, harness up at this maze of eight zip lines, linking cliffs to ancient trees tucked away in hills.

Thalang District NEIGHBOURHOOD

A few hundred metres northeast of the famous **Heroines Monument** is **Thalang National Museum** (☎0 7631 1426; admission 30B; ⌚8.30am-4pm). The museum contains five exhibition halls chronicling southern themes such as the history of Thalang-

Phuket

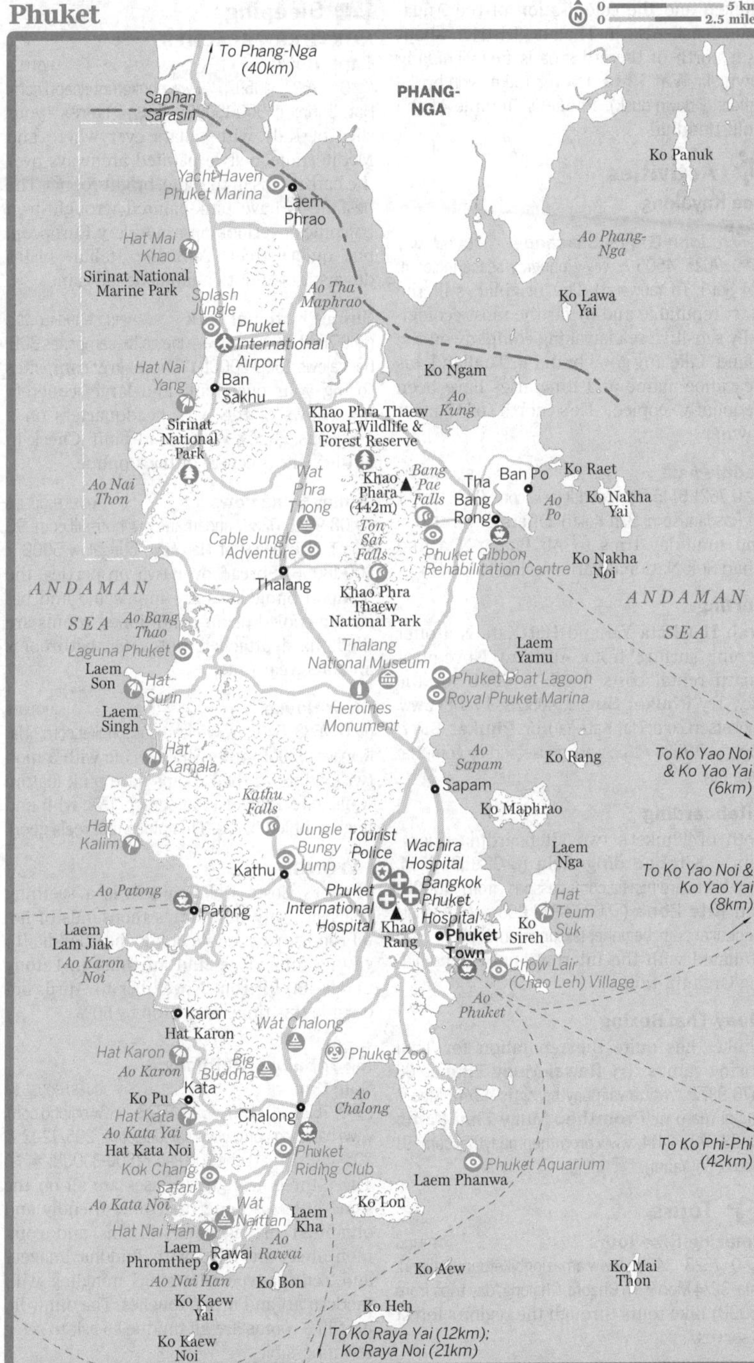
0 5 km
0 2.5 miles
To Phang-Nga (40km)
PHANG-NGA
Saphan Sarasin
Ko Panuk
Yacht Haven Phuket Marina
Laem Phrao
Hat Mai Khao
Ao Phang-Nga
Sirinat National Marine Park
Splash Jungle
Ao Tha Maphrao
Ko Lawa Yai
Phuket International Airport
Hat Nai Yang
Ban Sakhu
Ko Ngam
Ao Kung
Khao Phra Thaew Royal Wildlife & Forest Reserve
Sirinat National Park
Ao Nai Thon
Wat Phra Thong
Khao Phara (442m)
Bang Pae Falls
Tha Bang Rong
Ban Po
Ko Raet
Ao Po
Ko Nakha Yai
Ton Sai Falls
Cable Jungle Adventure
Phuket Gibbon Rehabilitation Centre
Ko Nakha Noi
Thalang
ANDAMAN SEA
Khao Phra Thaew National Park
ANDAMAN SEA
Ao Bang Thao
Laguna Phuket
Thalang National Museum
Laem Yamu
Laem Son
Hat Surin
Phuket Boat Lagoon
Royal Phuket Marina
Heroines Monument
Laem Singh
Hat Kamala
Ao Sapam
Ko Rang
To Ko Yao Noi & Ko Yao Yai (6km)
Sapam
Ko Maphrao
Kathu Falls
Hat Kalim
Jungle Bungy Jump
Tourist Police
Wachira Hospital
Laem Nga
To Ko Yao Noi & Ko Yao Yai (8km)
Kathu
Bangkok Phuket Hospital
Ao Patong
Phuket International Hospital
Patong
Khao Rang
Hat Teum Suk
Laem Lam Jiak
Ko Sireh
Phuket Town
Ao Karon Noi
Chow Lair (Chao Leh) Village
Ao Phuket
Karon
Hat Karon
Wat Chalong
Hat Karon
Phuket Zoo
Ao Karon
Big Buddha
Ko Pu
Kata
Hat Kata
Ao Chalong
Chalong
Ao Kata Yai
Hat Kata Noi
Phuket Riding Club
To Ko Phi-Phi (42km)
Kok Chang Safari
Phuket Aquarium
Laem Phanwa
Ao Kata Noi
Wat Naittan
Ko Lon
Laem Kha
Hat Nai Han
Laem Phromthep
Rawai
Ao Rawai
Ao Nai Han
Ko Bon
Ko Aew
Ko Mai Thon
Ko Kaew Yai
Ko Heh
To Ko Raya Yai (12km); Ko Raya Noi (21km)
Ko Kaew Noi

Phuket, and the colonisation of the Andaman Coast. Also in Thalang District, about 5km north of the crossroads near Thalang town, is **Wat Phra Thong** (admission by donation; ⏲dawn-dusk), Phuket's 'Temple of the Gold Buddha'.

Activities

Sea Kayaking

TOP CHOICE John Gray's Seacanoe SEA KAYAKING
(☎0 7625 4505-7; www.johngray-seacanoe.com; 124 Soi 1, Th Yaowarat) The original, still the most reputable and by far the most ecologically sensitive sea kayaking company on the island. Like any good brand in Thailand, his 'Seacanoe' name and itineraries have been frequently copied. He's north of Phuket Town.

Paddle Asia SEA KAYAKING
(☎0 7621 6145; www.paddleasia.com; 9/71 Moo 3, Th Rasdanusorn, Ban Kuku) Offers several day and multiday trips to Ao Phang-Nga and Khao Sok National Park on classic kayaks.

Surfing

Both Hat Kata Yai and Hat Kata Noi offer decent surfing from April to November. Board rental costs 300B to 600B for the day. Try **Phuket Surf** (☎08 7889 7308; www.phuketsurf.com; Hat Kata Yai) or **Phuket Surfing** (☎0 7628 4183; www.phuketsurfing.com; Hat Kata Yai).

Kiteboarding

Both of Phuket's two kiteboarding operators – **Kiteboarding Asia** (☎08 1591 4594; www.kiteboardingasia.com; lessons from 4000B) and **Kite Zone** (☎0833 952 005; www.kitesurfingphuket.com; beginner lessons from 1100B) – are affiliated with the International Kiteboarding Organization.

Muay Thai Boxing

Phuket has quite the reputation for Thai boxing camps. Try **Rawai Muay Thai** (☎08 1476 9377; www.rawaimuaythai.com; 43/42 Moo 7, Th Sai Yuan) or **Promthep Muay Thai Camp** (☎08 5786 2414; www.promthepmuaythai.com; 91 Moo 6, Soi Yanui).

Tours

Amazing Bike Tours CYCLING
(☎0 7628 3436; www.amazingbiketoursthailand.asia; 32/4 Moo 9, Th Chaofa, Chalong; day trips from 1600B) Bike tours through the region's forest reserves.

Sleeping

NORTHERN BEACHES

Capri Hotel HOTEL $
(☎0 7627 0597; www.phukethotelcapri.com; Hat Surin; r 900-1500B; ❄📶) Here's your slice of Italy with pillars everywhere and Mediterranean-style painted archways over the bathrooms in the cute, bright rooms. The best nests have pink painted wrought-iron balconies overlooking a not-very-European, but quiet street. Add the Italian bistro downstairs and it's a fantastic bargain.

Sirinat National Park CAMPING, BUNGALOWS $
(☎0 7632 7152; reserve@dnp.go.th; campsites 30B, bungalows 1000-2000B) There are campsites (bring your own tent) and large, concrete bungalows at the park headquarters on a gorgeous, shady, white-sand bluff. Check in at the visitors centre or book online.

Rimlay Bungalows GUESTHOUSE $
(☎08 9646 0239; andaman-car@hotmail.com; 90 Moo 5 Nai Yang, Hat Nai Yang; bungalow 500B, r 800-1800B) Spread over two properties, the bamboo bungalows are minuscule and basic fan-cooled or air-conditioned rooms are tiled, have attached hot-water bathrooms and are great value.

Clear House HOTEL $
(☎0 7638 5401; www.clearhousephuket.com; Hat Kamala; r 1300B; ❄📶) Shabby chic with a mod twist, white-washed rooms have pink feature walls, plush duvets, flat screen TVs, wi-fi and huge pebbled baths. This place just feels good.

PATONG

Phuket's Costa Del Soul-less is a seething beachside city that crams thousands of hotel rooms between its craggy headlands. It's getting difficult to find anything in Patong under 1000B from November to April, but outside this time rates drop by 50%.

TOP CHOICE Baipho, Baithong & Sala Dee GUESTHOUSE $$
(☎0 7629 2074, 0 7629 2738; www.baipho.com, www.baithong.com, www.saladee.com; 205/12-13 & 205/14-15 Th Rat Uthit 200 Pee; r 1800-3300B; ❄📶) These three arty guesthouses are all on the same little *soi* under the same friendly and organised management. Rooms and common areas are filled with Buddha imagery and Zen-spa-type trimmings mingling with modern art and urban touches. The dimly lit, nest-like rooms are all unique so ask to see a few if possible.

Baan Pronphateep HOTEL $$
(☎0 7634 3037; baanpronphateep.com; 168/1 Th Thawiwong; r 1600-2100B; ❄) Banyan tree shaded and nestled down a secluded little *soi*, this is a quiet and simple three-star choice. Rooms are spacious and come with a full-sized fridge and a private patio.

Casa Jip GUESTHOUSE $
(☎0 7634 3019; www.casajip.com; 207/10 Th Rat Uthit; r from 700B; ❄) Italian run and great value, this place has very big, if simple, rooms with comfy beds and a taste of Thai style. You get cable TV and there's even a breakfast room service.

Patong Backpacker Hostel HOSTEL $
(☎0 7625 6680; www.phuketbackpacker.com; 167 Th Ranong; dm 300-450B, r 1200B; ❄📶) This is a great location near the beach and the owner offers info on all the best, cheapest places to eat in town. Dorm prices vary depending on the number of beds in the room (three to 10). The top floor is the brightest but dorm rooms on the lower floors each have their own attached bathrooms.

SOUTHERN BEACHES

Caffe@Caffe GUESTHOUSE $$
(☎0 7628 4005; www.caffeatcaffe.com; 100/60-61 Th Kata, Kata; r 1800B; ❄📶) Tiled rooms with gold-coloured wallpaper alternated with white painted walls, striped duvets, mini-balconies, fridges and TVs make this place as comfy as it is hip. It's in a three-storey building with a modern cafe downstairs.

Ao Sane Bungalows BUNGALOW $
(☎0 7628 8306; 11/2 Moo 1, Th Viset, Hat Nai Han; bungalows 600-850B; ❄) The rickety cold-water, fan-cooled wooden bungalows are on a secluded beach, with million-dollar views of Ao Sane and Ao Nai Han. There's a beachside restaurant, dive centre and an old-hippie vibe. To reach the 'resort', follow the narrow road past the yacht club.

Fantasy Hill Bungalow HOTEL $
(☎0 7633 0106; fantasyhill@hotmail.com; 8/1 Th Patak, Kata; r with fan/air-con 450/800B; ❄) Sitting in a lush garden on a hill, the older but well-maintained bungalows here are great value. The place is peaceful but central and the staff super sweet. Angle for a corner room with air-con and a view.

Kangaroo Guesthouse GUESTHOUSE $
(☎0 7639 6517; 269/6-9 Karon Plaza, Karon; r 800B; ❄📶) Basic, but very clean, sunny tiled rooms with hot water, air-con, a cute breakfast nook, and balconies overlooking a narrow, slightly seedy *soi*.

PHUKET TOWN

Phuket Town has a healthy assortment of budget-friendly lodging options, but it's nowhere near the beach.

Phuket 346 GUESTHOUSE $
(☎08 7281 1898; www.phuket346.com; 15 Soi Romanee; r 1300B; ❄) On charming Soi Romanee, this romantic old shophouse has been exquisitely restored to look like a cosy art gallery. Rooms have white-patterned wallpaper and the occassional bright-coloured wall decorated with modern art.

Casa 104 GUESTHOUSE $$
(☎0 7622 1268; 104 Th Yaowarat; r from 1000B; ❄📶) This is a stunning renovation of a 100-year-old shophouse with burgundy walls, dangling chandeliers, bouquets of bamboo and peacock feathers, and early days swing on the sound system. And that's just the lobby bar. Guestrooms are more sparse and windowless, but still elegant with white concrete floors, rain showers and original art nouveau fixtures.

Sleep Sheep Phuket Hostel HOSTEL $
(☎0 7621 6464; www.sleepsheepphuket.com; 243-245 Soi Dtac Shop; r 650B; ❄@📶) In an alleyway off Th Thalang, this relatively modern place has big, brightly painted rooms with hot-water bathrooms and uncommonly friendly staff; plus it smells like freshly laundered sheets.

Eating

NORTHERN BEACHES

TOP CHOICE **Taste** FUSION $$
(Hat Surin; tapas 160-225B) The best of a new breed of urban-meets-surf eateries along the beach. Dine indoors or al fresco on meal-sized salads, perfectly cooked fillet mignon or a variety of Thai-Mediterranean starters and mains. Service is outstanding and there's an enticing attached gallery selling Tibetan, Nepali and local jewellery and art.

Rockfish FUSION $$
(33/6 Th Kamala Beach, Hat Kamala; dishes 150-1000B; ⏱breakfast, lunch & dinner) Perched above the river mouth and the bobbing longtails, with beach, bay and mountain views, is Kamala's best dining room. It rolls out gems such as braised duck breast with kale, and prosciutto-wrapped scallops.

PATONG

Bargain seafood and noodle stalls pop up across town at night – try the lanes on and around Th Bangla, or venture over to the **Patong Food Park** (Th Rat Uthit; ⊙4pm-midnight) once the sun drops.

Mengrai Seafood SEAFOOD $$
(Soi Tun; meals 120-300B) Located down a sweaty, dark *soi* off Th Bangla is a wonderful food court serving fresh, local food. The stalls towards the end of the *soi* serve daily curries that local expats swear by. This restaurant specialises in (very) fresh fish, prawns and mussels.

Chicken Rice Briley THAI $
(Patong Food Park, Th Rat Uthit; meals 35-45B; ⊙breakfast & lunch) The only diner in the Patong Food Park to offer sustenance when the sun shines. Steamed chicken breast is served on a bed of rice with a bowl of chicken broth with crumbled bits of meat and bone, along with roast pork. Dip in the fantastic chilli sauce. There's a reason it's forever packed with locals.

SOUTHERN BEACHES

TOP CHOICE **Pad Thai Shop** THAI $
(Th Patak East; dishes 40B; ⊙breakfast, lunch & dinner) On the busy main road behind Karon, just north of the tacky Ping Pong Bar, is this glorified food stand where you can find rich and savoury chicken stew (worthy of rave reviews in its own right), and the best *pàt tai* on planet earth. Spicy and sweet, packed with prawns, tofu, egg and peanuts, and wrapped in a fresh banana leaf, you will be grateful. It closes at around 7pm.

Capannina ITALIAN $$
(☎0 7628 4318; capannina@fastmail.fm; 30/9 Moo 2, Th Kata; mains 200-700B) Everything here – from the pastas to the sauces – are made fresh and you can taste it. The ravioli and gnocchi are memorable, the risotto comes highly recommended, and it does great pizzas, calzones and veal Milanese, too. It gets crowded during the high season, so you may want to reserve ahead.

Thai Kitchen THAI $
(Th Thai Na; meals 80B; ⊙breakfast, lunch & dinner) Good rule of thumb: if a humble, roadside cafe is packed with Thai people, you can be certain that the food will rock. Its green curry (warning: your nose will run) and glass-noodle dishes are superb. It's just down the road from, ahem, 'Pussy Bar'.

PHUKET TOWN

There's good food in Phuket Town, and meals here cost a lot less than those at the beach.

TOP CHOICE **Cook** ITALIAN THAI $
(101 Th Phang-Nga; dishes 60-120B) The Thai owner-chef used to cook Italian at a mega-resort, so when he opened this ludicrously inexpensive Old Town cafe he fused the two cultures. So, order the sensational green curry pizza with chicken, or the pork curry coconut-milk pizza, and fall in love.

China Inn THAI FUSION $$
(Th Thalang; dishes 80-250B) The organics movement meets Phuket cuisine at this turn-of-the-century shophouse. There's red curry with crab, a host of veggie options, homemade yoghurt and fruit smoothies with organic honey. There's also a gallery here with textiles, carvings and clothes from Myanmar and Laos.

Uptown Restaurant THAI $
(Th Tilok Uthit; dishes 30-60B; ⊙10am-9pm) This classic, breezy Chinese-style cafe may not look fancy, but look around and you'll notice mounted photos of Thai celebrities who have stopped by to slurp the spectacular noodles.

Drinking & Entertainment

Th Bangla is Patong's beer and bar-girl mecca and features a number of spectacular go-go extravaganzas, where you can expect the usual mix of gyrating Thai girls and often red-faced Western men. There are plenty of more subdued options in Phuket Town.

Two Black Sheep PUB
(www.twoblacksheep.net; 172 Th Rat Uthit, Patong; ⊙11am-2am) Owned by a fun Aussie couple (he's a musician, she's a chef), this old-school pub is a great find. It has good grub and live music nightly. From 8pm to 10pm there's an acoustic set, then Chilli Jam, the house band, gets up and rocks till the last call.

Sound Phuket CLUB
(www.soundphuket.com; Jung Ceylon complex, Unit 2303, 193 Th Rat Uthit, Patong; ⊙10pm-4am) When internationally renowned DJs come to Phuket these days, they are usually gigging amid the rounded, futuristic environs of Patong's hottest (and least sleazy) nightclub. If top-shelf DJs are on the decks, expect to pay up to 300B entry fee.

Phuket Simon Cabaret CABARET

(www.phuket-simoncabaret.com; Th Sirirach, Patong; admission 700-800B; ⏲performances 7.30 & 9.30pm nightly) About 300m south of town, this cabaret offers entertaining transvestite shows. The 600-seat theatre is grand, the costumes are gorgeous and the ladyboys *(gà·teu·i)* are convincing. The house is often full – book ahead.

Bangla Boxing Stadium THAI BOXING

(Th Phisit Karani, Patong; tickets 1000-1500B; ⏲9-11.30pm Tue, Wed, Fri & Sun) Old name, new stadium, same game: a packed line-up of competitive *muay thai* (Thai boxing) bouts.

Information

The weekly English-language *Phuket Gazette* (www.phuketgazette.net) publishes information on activities, events, dining and entertainment around the island, as well as the latest scandals.

Main post office (Th Montri, Phuket Town; ⏲8.30am-4pm Mon-Fri, 9am-noon Sat)

Phuket International Hospital (☎0 7624 9400; www.phuketinternationalhospital.com; Th Chalermprakiat) International doctors rate this hospital as the best on the island.

TAT office (☎0 7621 2213; www.tat.or.th; 73-75 Th Phuket, Phuket Town; ⏲8.30am-4.30pm) Has maps, information brochures, a list of standard sŏrngtăaou fares out to the various beaches, and the recommended charter costs for a vehicle.

Tourist police (☎1699; cnr Th Thawiwong & Th Bangla, Patong)

Getting There & Away

Air

Phuket International Airport (☎0 7632 7230) is 30km northwest of Phuket Town; it takes around 45 minutes to an hour to reach the southern beaches from here.

Some regional airline carriers:

Air Asia (www.airasia.com) In addition to several daily flights to Bangkok (around 1480B), it also flies direct to Hong Kong (5000B), Chiang Mai (1600B), Singapore (1400B), Bali (2730B) and other destinations.

Bangkok Airways (☎0 7622 5033; www.bangkokair.com; 58/2-3 Th Yaowarat) Daily flights to Ko Samui, Bangkok and more.

Nok Air (www.nokair.com) Links Phuket to Bangkok.

THAI (☎0 7621 1195; www.thaiairways.com; 78/1 Th Ranong, Phuket Town) Operates around seven daily flights to Bangkok with connections to/from several other destinations.

Boat

Tha Rasada, north of Phuket Town, is the main pier for boats to Ko Phi-Phi with connections to Krabi, Ko Lanta, the Trang Islands, Ko Lipe and even as far as Langkawi Island in Malaysia (where there are further ferry connections to Penang). For quicker service to Krabi and Ao Nang via the Ko Yao Islands, boats leave from Tha Bang Bong north of Tha Rasada.

Bus

You'll find the **bus terminal** (☎0 7621 1977) just to the east of Phuket Town's centre, within walking distance of the many hotels. Services from here are shown in the table below.

Getting Around

A bright orange **government airport bus** (www.airportbusphuket.com; tickets 85B) runs between the airport and Phuket Town via the Heroines Monument about every hour between 6am and 7pm. Services to Patong, Kata and Karon beaches cost 180B if there are enough passengers.

Local transport around Phuket can be frustrating. Large bus-sized sŏrngtăaou run regularly from Th Ranong near Phuket Town's day market to the various west coast beaches (25B to 40B per person) These run from around 7am to 5pm.

BUSES FROM PHUKET

DESTINATION	BUS TYPE	FARE	DURATION (HR)
Bangkok	2nd class	487B	15
	VIP	974B	13
Hat Yai	air-con	556B	6-7
Ko Samui	air-con	430B	8 (bus/boat)
Krabi	ordinary	95B	4
Ranong	ordinary	209B	6
Surat Thani	ordinary	195B	6
Trang	air-con	240B	5

Túk-túk circulate around Patong for 50B to 100B per ride. There are numerous places to rent 125cc motorbikes and jeeps.

Krabi Town

POP 27,500

Krabi Town is majestically situated among impossibly angular limestone karsts jutting from the mangroves, but midcity you're more likely to be awe-struck by the sheer volume of guesthouses and travel agencies packed into this compact, quirky little town.

Wat Tham Seua (Tiger Cave Temple) is a sprawling hill and cave temple complex 8km northwest of Krabi that's a worthwhile day trip from town.

For local sea-kayaking tours, try **Sea Kayak Krabi** (☎0 7563 0270; www.seakayak-krabi.com; 40 Th Ruen Rudee).

Sleeping

Krabi has an exceptional and ever-improving guesthouse scene; flashpackers should head to Ao Nang.

Pak-up Hostel HOSTEL $
(☎0 5611 955; www.pakuphostel.com; 87 Th Utarakit; dm 180-200B, d 600B; ❄📶) This snazzy hostel features several uberhip 10-bed dorms with big wooden bunks built into the wall, each equipped with personal lockers. Modern shared bathrooms have cold-water stalls as well as a few hot-water rain showers.

Chan Cha Lay GUESTHOUSE $
(☎0 7562 0952; www.chanchalay.com; 55 Th Utarakit; r 400-700B, r without bathroom 250B; ❄) The rooms here, with en suite and decorated in gorgeous Mediterranean blues with polished-concrete semi-outdoor bathrooms, are Krabi's most stylish and comfortable. The shared-bathroom, fan-only rooms are plain, but spotless with firm beds.

Eating

Krabi Town offers a great opportunity for market eats. Try the **night market** (Th Khong Kha; meals 20-50B) near the Khong Kha pier for authentic papaya salad, fried noodles, *đôm yam gûng* (prawn and lemon grass soup) and sweet milky Thai desserts. The **day market** (Th Sukhon; meals 20-60B) serves up a bounty of tropical fruits, simmering curry pots, and banquet trays of steaming noodles.

Information

Immigration office (☎0 7561 1350; Th Chamai Anuson; ⊙8.30am-4pm Mon-Fri) Handles visa extensions.

Krabi Hospital (☎0 7561 1210; Th Utarakit) About 1km north of town.

Post office (Th Utarakit) Just south of the turn-off to Khong Kha pier.

Getting There & Away

Air

Most domestic carriers offer flights between Bangkok and Krabi International Airport (one way around 4400B, 1¼ hours). **Bangkok Air** (www.bangkokair.com) has a daily service to Ko Samui for around 3800B.

Boat

Boats to Ko Phi-Phi and Ko Lanta leave from the passenger pier at Khlong Chilat, about 4km southwest of Krabi. Travel agencies will arrange free transfers.

The largest boat operator is **PP Family Co** (☎0 7561 2463; www.phiphifamily.com; Th Khong Kha), which has a ticket office right beside the pier in town. In high season there are boats to Ko Phi-Phi (300B, 1½ hours) at 9am, 10.30am, 1.30pm and 3pm while in low season the schedule is reduced to two boats per day.

From November to May, there is daily boat service to Ko Lanta (350B, two hours) leaving Krabi's Khlon Chilat pier at 11.30am.

For Railay, take a long-tail boat from Krabi's Khong Kha pier (150B, 45 minutes) from 7.45am to 6pm.

Bus

The **Krabi bus terminal** (☎0 7561 1804; cnr Th Utarakit & Hwy 4) is in nearby Talat Kao, about 4km north of Krabi. Air-conditioned government buses leave for Bangkok (720B, 12 hours) at 7am, 4pm and 5.30pm. The VIP bus to Bangkok (1100B) leaves at 5.30pm daily. Regular, air-conditioned government buses from Talat Kao also service Hat Yai (170B, three hours), Phuket (145B, 3½ hours), Surat Thani (140B, 2½ hours) and Trang (90B, two hours).

Minivan

Minivans are booked through travel agencies in town. Some sample fares are Ko Lanta (350B, 1½ hours) and Phuket (350B, three hours).

Sŏrngtăaou

Sŏrngtăaou run from the bus station to central Krabi and on to Hat Noppharat Thara (40B), Ao Nang (60B) and the Shell Cemetery at Ao Nam Mao. There are services from 6am to 6.30pm. In the high season there are more frequent services until 10pm for a 10B surcharge.

Getting Around

Central Krabi is easy to explore on foot, but the bus terminal and airport are both a long way from the town centre. A taxi from the airport to town will cost 400B. In the reverse direction, taxis cost 350B. Agencies in town can arrange seats on the airport bus for 120B. Sŏrngtăaou between the bus terminal and central Krabi cost 40B.

Motorbikes are available at most guesthouses for around 200B per day.

Ao Nang

POP 12,400

Ao Nang provides 'civilisation' instead of scenery. It's convenient for a 'night out' but not the tropical hideaway that most people are looking for.

Activities and tours abound – from mangrove kayaking trips to bike trips – and travel agents are very willing to saddle you up with a variety of options. For the popular island tours try **Ao Nang Long-tail Boat Service** (☎0 7569 5313; www.aonangboatco-op.com). Day trips to Ko Phi-Phi on the **Ao Nang Princess** (tickets 1400B) are also possible.

Budgetarians should try **Dream Garden** (☎0 7563 7338; r 950-1200B; ❄@) or **J Hotel** (☎0 7563 7878; j_hotelo@hotmail.com; r from 800B; ❄@) for a place to crash. If you want to class things up a bit go for **Somkiet Buri Resort** (☎0 7563 7320; www.somkietburi.com; r 1700-6200B; ❄🛜🏊).

Ao Nang is full of mediocre fare. Walk along **Soi Sunset** (☎0 7569 5260; Soi Sunset; dishes 60-400B; ⊙lunch & dinner) – a narrow pedestrian-only alley housing several seafood joints – to find the best catch of the day.

If you get tired of the beach bars and video movies on the strip, the **Aonang Krabi Muay Thai Stadium** (☎0 7562 1042; admission 800B, ringside 1200B) has boisterous *muay thai* bouts two days a week.

Getting There & Around

Bus, Car & Minivan

Sŏrngtăaou run to/from Krabi (50B, 20 minutes). Airport buses to and from Ao Nang cost 80B to 100B. Minibuses go to Phuket (350B, 3½ hours), Pak Bara (300B, 3½ hours) and Ko Lanta (400B, two hours)

Boat

The 15-minute boat ride to Railay's Hat Railay West is run by **Ao Nang Long-tail Boat Service** (☎0 7569 5313; www.aonangboatco-op.com). Rates are 80B per person from 7.30am to 6pm.

Railay

Krabi's fairytale limestone crags come to a dramatic climax at Railay, the ultimate jungle gym for rock-climbing fanatics. This quiet slice of paradise fills in the sandy gaps between each craggy flourish, and although it's just around the bend from chaotic tourist hustle in Ao Nang, the atmosphere here is nothing short of laid-back, Rasta-Thai heaven.

Sights

At the eastern end of Hat Phra Nang is **Tham Phra Nang** (Princess Cave), an important shrine for local fishermen. About halfway along the path from Hat Railay East to Hat Phra Nang, a crude path leads up the jungle-cloaked cliff wall to a hidden lagoon known as **Sa Phra Nang** (Holy Princess Pool) with a killer viewpoint.

Activities

With nearly 500 bolted routes, ranging from beginner to challenging advanced climbs, all with unparalleled cliff-top vistas, it's no surprise that Railay is among the top rock climbing spots in the world.

The going rate for climbing courses is 800B to 1000B for a half-day and 1500B to 2000B for a full day. Recommended climbing shops:

Highland Rock Climbing ROCK CLIMBING
(☎08 0693 0374; chaow_9@yahoo.com; Hat Railay East)

Hot Rock ROCK CLIMBING
(☎0 7562 1771; www.railayadventure.com; Hat Railay West)

King Climbers ROCK CLIMBING
(☎0 7563 7125; www.railay.com; Hat Railay East)

Wee's Climbing School ROCK CLIMBING
(☎08 1149 9745; www.tonsai basecamp; Hat Ton Sai)

Sleeping & Eating

RAILAY

Railay West is beautiful and developers know it – you'll only find midrange and top-end resorts around here. Rates drop by 30% in the low season. You can't go wrong with any of the resorts' restaurants.

TOP CHOICE **Railay Phutawan Resort** HOTEL $$
(☎08 4060 0550, 0 7581 9478; www.phuritvalleyresort.com; Railay Highlands; bungalows 1140-1940B, r 1640B; @❄) The best options here are the super-spacious polished cement bungalows highlighted with creamy yellow walls, big rain shower bathrooms and all the trimmings of a high-end resort.

Railay Cabana GUESTHOUSE $
(☎0 7562 1733, 08 4057 7167; Railay Highlands; bungalows 350-600B) Superbly located high in the hills in a bowl of karst cliffs, this is your hippie tropical mountain hideaway. Simple, clean thatched-bamboo bungalows are surrounded by mango, mangosteen, banana and guava groves.

HAT TON SAI

Paasook HOTEL $
(☎08 9645 3013; bungalows 300-800B) The most stylish budget establishment on Ton Sai: wooden bungalows have elongated floor-to-ceiling windows and concrete floors. The gardens are lush, management is friendly and there's a rustic-chic outdoor restaurant, perfect for steamy evenings.

Countryside Resort HOTEL $
(☎08 5473 9648; countryside-resort.com; cabins 850B; ❄@) This is a UK-owned property with attractive solar-powered cabins. There are high ceilings, lace curtains and ceiling fans. Top-row nests have insane karst views, and you'll love Ewok-faced Ollie, the property mascot.

Drinking

There's a bunch of places on the beaches where you can unwind and get nicely inebriated, including **Chillout Bar** (Hat Ton Sai), **Highland Rock Climbing** (Railay Headlands) and **Ya-ya Bar** (Railay Headlands).

Getting There & Around

Long-tail boats to Railay run from Khong Kha pier in Krabi and from the seafronts of Ao Nang and Ao Nam Mao. Boats between Krabi and Hat Railay East leave every 1½ hours from 7.45am to 6pm (150B, 45 minutes).

Boats to Hat Railay West or Hat Ton Sai from Ao Nang cost 80B (15 minutes) from 7.30am to 6pm or 150B at other times.

From October to May the *Ao Nang Princess* runs from Hat Noppharat Thara National Park headquarters to Ko Phi-Phi with a stop at Hat Railay West.

The fare to Ko Phi-Phi from Railay is 350B.

Ko Phi-Phi

Oh, how beauty can be a burden. Like Marilyn Monroe, Phi-Phi Don's stunning looks have become its own demise. Everyone wants a piece of her. This is Thailand's Shangri-la: a hedonistic paradise where tourists cavort in azure seas and snap pictures of long-tails puttering between craggy cliffs.

With its flashy, curvy, blonde beaches and bodacious jungles it's no wonder that Phi-Phi has become the darling of the Andaman coast. And, like any good starlet, this island can party hard all night and still look like a million bucks the next morning.

Diving

Crystal-clear Andaman water and abundant marine life make the perfect recipe for top-notch scuba. An Open Water certification course costs around 12,900B, while the standard two-dive trips cost from 3200B.

Adventure Club DIVING
(Map p766; ☎08 1970 0314; www.phi-phi-adventures.com) Our favourite diving operation on the island runs an excellent assortment of educational, ecofocused diving, hiking and snorkelling tours.

Blue View Divers DIVING
(Map p765; ☎0 7581 9395; www.blueviewdivers.com) Focuses on community involvement and beach clean-ups (its latest effort cleared up 700 tonnes of rubbish) and is the only shop to offer dives from a long-tail.

Snorkelling

A popular snorkelling destination is **Ko Mai Phai** (Bamboo Island), located just 5km north of Phi-Phi Don. There's a shallow area here where you may be able to see small sharks.

Snorkelling trips cost between 600B and 2400B, depending on whether you travel by long-tail or motorboat. Most bungalows and resorts rent out equipment for 150B to 200B per day.

Rock Climbing

There are some good rock climbing outfitters on the island, with most places charging around 1000B for a half-day of climbing.

Try **Spider Monkey** (Map p766; ☎0 7581 9384; www.spidermonkeyclimbing.com) or **Cat's Climbing Shop** (Map p766; ☎08 1787 5101; www.catclimbingshop.com).

Ko Phi-Phi

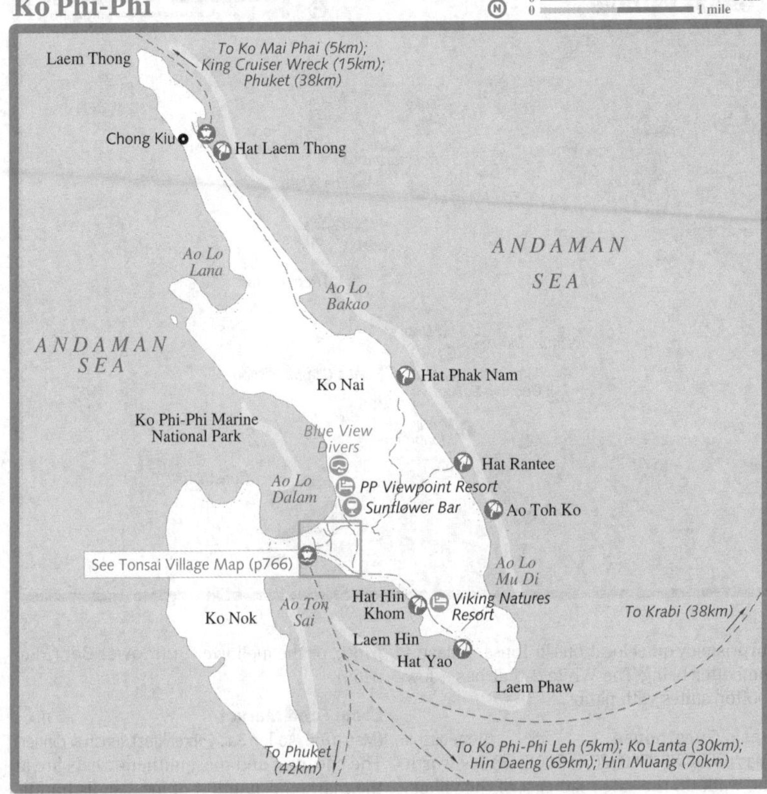

Courses

Pum Restaurant & Cooking School COOKING
(Map p766; ☎08 1521 8904; www.pumthaifoodchain.com; classes 450-4650B) Try a cooking class with Pum Restaurant in the tourist village. You'll learn to make some of the excellent dishes that are served in its restaurant and go home with a great cookbook.

Tours

Ever since Leo smoked a spliff in Alex Garland's *The Beach,* **Ko Phi-Phi Leh** has become somewhat of a pilgrimage site. Tours last about half a day and include snorkelling stops at various points around the island, with detours to Viking Cave and Ao Maya. Long-tail trips cost 800B; by motorboat you'll pay around 2400B. Expect to pay a 400B national-park day-use fee upon landing. It is possible to camp on Phi-Phi Leh through **Maya Bay Camping** (☎08 6944 1623; www.mayabaycamping.com; per person 2100B).

Sleeping

Simply put: Phi Phi's prices are higher than the surrounding islands. Be sure to book your room in advance. The following options are in and around Ton Sai Village.

PP Viewpoint Resort HOTEL **$$**
(Map p765; ☎0 7560 1200, 0 7561 8111; www.phiphiviewpoint.com; bungalows 1700-3500B; ❄🏊) At the far northeastern end of Ao Lo Dalam, wooden bungalows sit high on stilts and enjoy awesome views. There is a small swimming pool that practically drops into the ocean below and a glass-walled tower with 360-degree views.

The White GUESTHOUSE **$$**
(Map p766; ☎0 7560 1300; www.whitephiphi.com; r 1500-1800B; ❄@📶) Geared towards the 'flashpacker' crowd, The White has two comfy and

Tonsai Village

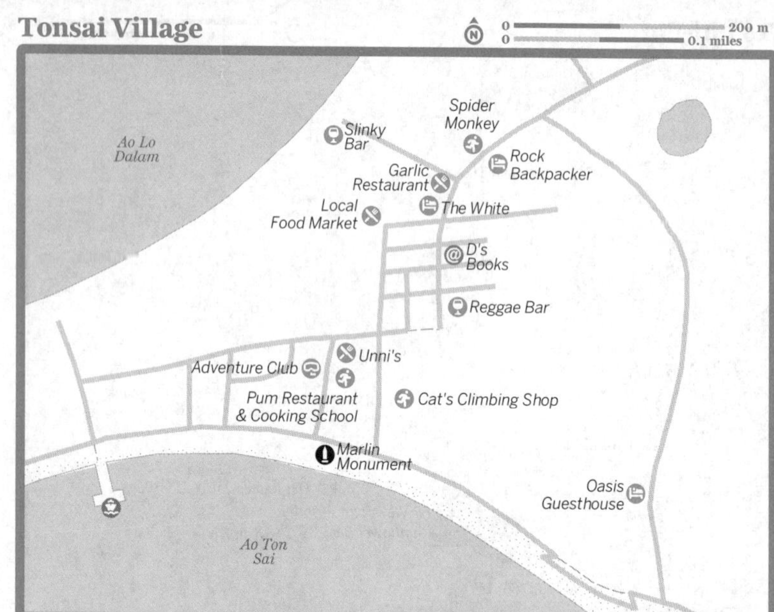

surprisingly quiet locations in Tonsai Village – the better being The White 2 that has a few rooftop suites with patios.

Oasis Guesthouse GUESTHOUSE $
(Map p766; ☎0 7560 1207; r 900B; ❄) It's worth the walk up the side road east of the village centre to find this cute guesthouse with wooden shutters and surrounded by trees. The innkeeper can be surly, but freshly painted rooms have sparkling bathrooms. It's first come, first served only.

Viking Natures Resort HOTEL $$
(Map p765; ☎08 3649 9492; www.vikingnaturesresort.com; bungalows 1000-6500B;) OK it's funky, but the wood, thatch and bamboo bungalows here are dreamily creative and stylish with lots of driftwood, shell mobiles and hammock-decked lounging spaces with outrageous views of Ko Phi-Phi Leh.

Rock Backpacker HOSTEL $
(Map p766; ☎08 1607 3897; dm 300B, r 400-600B) A proper hostel on the village hill, with clean dorms lined with bunk beds, tiny private rooms, and an inviting restaurant-bar.

Eating & Drinking

All of your partying needs will be met at **Reggae Bar** (Map p766), **Slinky Bar** (Map p766), or the mellower **Sunflower Bar** (Map p765).

Local Food Market THAI $
(Map p766; Ao Ton Sai; breakfast, lunch & dinner) The cheapest and most authentic eats are at the market. A handful of local stalls huddle on the narrowest sliver of the isthmus and serve up scrumptious *pàt tai*, fried rice, *sôm·đam* (spicy green papaya salad) and smoked catfish.

Unni's INTERNATIONAL $$
(Map p766; mains around 120B; breakfast, lunch & dinner) Come here for lunch to dine on homemade bagels topped with everything from smoked salmon to meatballs. There are also massive salads, Mexican food, tapas, cocktails and more.

Garlic Restaurant THAI $
(Map p766; ☎08 3502 1426; dishes 45-95B; breakfast, lunch & dinner) A bright shack-like place that's always packed with happy travellers chowing terrific, not-too-spicy Thai food.

Getting There & Away

Ko Phi-Phi can be reached from Krabi, Phuket, Ao Nang, Railay and Ko Lanta. Most boats moor at Ao Ton Sai. The Phuket and Krabi boats operate year-round, while the Ko Lanta and Ao Nang boats only run between October to April.

Boats depart from Krabi for Ko Phi-Phi (300B, 1½ hours) at 9am and 3.30pm, while from Ao Nang (350B, 1½ hours) there's one boat at 3.30pm each day. From Phuket, boats leave at 9am, 2.30pm and 3pm and return from Ko Phi-Phi at 9am, 1.30pm and 3pm (400B, 1¾ to two hours). Boats to Ko Lanta leave Phi-Phi at 11.30am and 2pm and return from Ko Lanta at 8am and 1pm (300B, 1½ hours).

Getting Around

There are no roads on Phi-Phi Don so transport on the island is mostly by foot. Long-tails can be chartered from Ao Ton Sai pier to Hat Yao (100B to 150B), Laem Thong (800B) and Hat Rantee (500B).

Ko Lanta

POP 20,000

Long and thin, and covered in bleach-blond tresses, Ko Lanta is Krabi's sexy beach babe. The largest of the 50-plus islands in the local archipelago, this relaxing paradise effortlessly caters to all budget types with its west-coast parade of peach sand. Ko Lanta is relatively flat compared to the karst formations of its neighbours, so the island can be easily explored by motorbike. A quick trip around reveals a colourful crucible of cultures – fried-chicken stalls sit below slender minarets, creaking *chow lair* villages dangle off the island's side, and small Thai wat hide within green-brown tangles of curling mangroves.

Don't miss a visit to **Ban Ko Lanta** (Old Town), which was the original port and commercial centre for the island. Stop by **Hammock House** (☎0 4847 2012; www.jumbohammock.com; ⏲10am-5pm) and pick up their fabulous *Lanta Biker's Map*, full of off-the-beaten-path recommendations.

Also worth a look is **Ko Lanta Marine National Park** (admission 400B) – which protects 15 islands in the Ko Lanta group – and the **Tham Khao Maikaeo** cave hidden deep within the interior jungle.

Activities

Some of Thailand's top diving and snorkelling spots are within arm's reach of Ko Lanta. The best diving can be found at the undersea pinnacles called **Hin Muang** and **Hin Daeng**, about 45 minutes away by speedboat.

The sites around **Ko Haa** have consistently good visibility, with depths of 18m to 34m, plenty of marine life and a cave known as 'the Cathedral'.

Trips out to Hin Daeng/Hin Muang cost around 5000B to 6000B, while trips to Ko Haa tend to be around 3500B to 4500B.

Scubafish DIVING
(☎0 7566 5095; www.scuba-fish.com) One of the best dive operations on the island is located at Baan Laanta Resort on Ao Kantiang. A 'Liquid Lense' underwater photography program is available as well.

Courses

Time for Lime COOKING
(☎0 7568 4590; www.timeforlime.net) On Hat Khlong Dao, this place has a huge, professional kitchen with plenty of room to run amok. It offers cooking courses with a slightly more exciting selection of dishes than most cookery schools in Thailand; five-hour courses cost 1800B.

Sleeping

Some resorts close down for the May-to-October low season, while others drop their rates by 50% or more.

TOP CHOICE **Bee Bee Bungalows** GUESTHOUSE $
(☎08 1537 9932; www.beebeebungalows; Hat Khlong Khong; bungalows 400-800B; ❄@≋) One of the best budget spots on the island, Bee Bee's super-friendly staff care for a dozen creative bamboo cabins – every one is unique and a few are up on stilts in the trees.

Relax Bay HOTEL $$
(☎0 7568 4194; www.relaxbay.com; Ao Phra Ae; bungalows 1200-2500B; ❄≋) This gorgeous French-run place is spread out over a tree-covered headland near a small beach. Its wooden bungalows sit on stilts with large decks, or for a more unique experience, sleep in a seaview luxury tent.

Sanctuary GUESTHOUSE $
(☎08 1891 3055; sanctuary_93@yahoo.com; Ao Phra Ae; bungalows 600-1200B) The original Phra Ae resort is still a delightful place to stay. There are artistically designed wood-and-thatch bungalows with lots of grass and a hippie-ish atmosphere that's low-key and friendly.

Lanta Darawadee HOTEL $
(☎0 7566 7094; www.lantadarawadee.com; Hat Khlong Khong; bungalows 1000-1600B; ❄📶≋) If you're digging the Hat Khlong Khong scene but can't live without air-con, here's

a great-value option right on the beach. It's bland but the new, clean rooms have good beds, terraces, minifridges and TVs.

Mu Ko Lanta Marine National Park Headquarters CAMPING $
(☎in Bangkok 0 2561 4292; Laem Tanod; camping with own tent per person 30B, with tent hire 300-400B) The secluded jungle grounds of the national park headquarters are a wonderfully serene and wild place to camp. There are toilets and running water, but you should bring your own food.

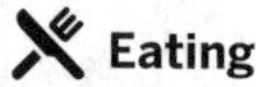

Eating

Ban Sala Dan has plenty of restaurants and minimarts. Don't miss the seafood restaurants along the northern edge of the village, like **Lanta Seafood** (☎0 7566 8411; Ban Sala Dan). With tables on verandahs over water, they offer fresh seafood sold by weight (which includes cooking costs). In Old Town try **Beautiful Restaurant** (☎0 7569 7062; Ban Ko Lanta; mains 100-200B). Tables are scattered on four piers that extend into the sea. The fish is fresh and exquisitely prepared.

Drinking & Entertainment

If you're looking for roaring discotheques, pick another island. If you want a more low-key bar scene with music wafting well into the night, then head to Ao Phra Ae, where you'll find a cluster of fun spots such as **Opium**, **Earth Bar** and **Reggae House**.

Information

Ban Sala Dan village has a number of internet cafes (1B per minute), travel agencies, dive shops and motorcycle rental joints. There are five 7-Elevens spread along the island's west coast – each one has an ATM.

Ko Lanta Hospital (☎0 7569 7085) It's 1km south of Ban Ko Lanta (Old Town).

Police station (☎0 7569 7017) North of Ban Ko Lanta.

Getting There & Away

Boat

There are two piers at Ban Sala Dan. The passenger jetty is about 300m from the main strip of shops; vehicle ferries leave from a second jetty several kilometres further east.

There is one passenger ferry connecting Krabi's Khlong Chilat pier with Ko Lanta, departing from Ko Lanta at 8am (400B, two hours).

Boats between Ko Lanta and Ko Phi-Phi technically run year-round, although service can peter out in the low season if there are too few passengers. Ferries usually leave Ko Lanta at 8am and 1pm (300B, 1½ hours).

Tigerline (☎08 1092 8800; www.tigerlinetravel.com), a high-speed ferry, runs between Ban Sala Dan and Ko Lipe (1400B, four to five hours), stopping in the Trang Islands. The service leaves at 1pm. The next day the same boat makes the return trip from Ko Lipe departing at 9am. The **Satun-Pak Bara Speedboat Club** (☎0 7475 0389, 08 2433 0114; www.tarutaolipeisland.com) runs a similar service.

Minivan

Minivans run year-round and are your best option from the mainland. Daily minivans to Krabi airport (280B, 1½ hours) and Krabi Town (250B, 1½ hours) leave hourly between 7am and 3.30pm. From Krabi, minivans depart hourly from 8am till 4pm. Minivans to Phuket (350B, four hours) leave Ko Lanta every two hours or so, but are more frequent in the high season. There are also several daily air-conditioned minivans to Trang (250B, 2½ hours) and less frequent services to Khao Lak (650B, six hours) and Ko Samui (650B including boat ticket).

Getting Around

Most resorts send vehicles to meet the ferries – a free ride *to* your resort. In the opposite direction expect to pay 80B to 250B. Alternatively, you can take a motorcycle taxi from opposite the 7-Eleven in Ban Sala Dan; fares vary from 50B to 250B depending on distance.

Motorcycles (250B per day) can be rented all over the island.

Trang

POP 64,700

Most visitors to Trang are in transit to nearby islands, but if you're an aficionado of culture, Thai food or markets, plan to stay a day or more. It's an easy-to-manage town where you can get lost in wet markets by day and hawker markets and late-night Chinese coffee shops by night; at nearly any time of the year, there's likely to be some minor festival that oozes local colour.

Most of the tourist facilities lie along the main drag, Th Praram VI, between the clock tower and the train station. For a place to crash, try the renovated **Sri Trang Hotel** (☎0 7521 8122; www.sritrang.com; 22-26 Th Praram VI; r 450-690B; ❄📶).

Don't miss the best **night market** (btwn Th Praram VI & Th Ratchadamnoen; meals around 30B; ⊙dinner) on the Andaman coast – it will have you salivating over bubbling curries, fried chicken and fish, *pàt tai* and an array of Thai desserts. Go with an empty stomach and a sense of adventure.

Information

You'll find several internet cafes and various banks with ATMs and foreign-exchange booths on Th Praram VI.

My Friend (☎0 7522 5984; 25/17-20 Th Sathani; per hr 30B) Has the best 24hr internet cafe in town.

Post office (cnr Th Praram VI & Th Kantang) Also sells CAT cards for international phone calls.

Getting There & Away

Air

Nok Air (www.nokair.com) and **Orient Thai Airways** (www.orient-thai.com) operate daily flights from Bangkok (Don Muang airport) to Trang (around 1500B one-way). The airport is 4km south of Trang.

Bus

Buses leave from the Trang **bus terminal** (Th Huay Yot). Air-conditioned buses from Trang to Bangkok cost 600B to 680B (12 hours, morning and afternoon). VIP 24-seater buses leave at 5pm and 5.30pm (1050B).

Other services:

Hat Yai 110B, three hours, frequent departures.

Krabi 115B, two hours, frequent departures.

Phang-Nga 180B, 3½ hours, hourly.

Phuket 240B, five hours, hourly.

Minivan & Share Taxi

Hourly vans heading to Surat Thani (180B, 2½ hours), with connections to Ko Samui and Ko Pha-Ngan, leave from a **depot** (Th Tha Klang) just before Th Tha Klang crosses the railway tracks. Several daily air-conditioned minivans between Trang and Ko Lanta (250B, 2½ hours) leave from the travel agents across from the train station. There are shared taxis to Krabi (180B, two hours) and air-conditioned minivans to Hat Yai (160B, two hours) from offices just west of the Trang bus terminal.

Minivans leave regularly from the depot on Th Tha Klang for Pak Meng (70B, 45 minutes), Hat Chao Mai (80B, one hour) and Kuantungku pier (100B, one hour) for onward boat travel.

Train

Only two trains go all the way from Bangkok to Trang: the express 83 and the rapid 167, which both leave from Bangkok's Hua Lamphong station in the afternoon and arrive in Trang the next morning. From Trang, trains leave in the early and late afternoon.

Trang Islands

The mythical Trang Islands are the last iteration of the Andaman's iconic limestone peaks before they tumble into the sea like sleeping giants. Shrouded in mystery and steeped in local legend, these stunning island Edens are home to roving *chow lair* (sea gypsies) and technicolour reefs.

Ko Ngai (often called Ko Hai) is the northernmost island, offering shallow sandy bays that end at reef drop-offs with excellent snorkelling. **Ko Muk**, to the south, is perhaps the most famous for its Emerald Cave – a limestone tunnel that leads 80m to a mint-green lagoon at the centre of the island (pirates once hid treasure here). The island also features a sugary white sandbar known as Hat Sivalai dotted with spiky palms. **Ko Kradan**, next door, features bathtub-warm shallows and jaw-dropping limestone karst views. Mangroves – home to the rare sea dugong – cloak the shores of **Ko Libong**, and a large Muslim settlement sits atop of the quiet crag of **Ko Sukorn**.

Sleeping

KO NGAI

The boat pier is at Koh Ngai Resort, but if you book ahead resorts on the other beaches will arrange transfers.

Ko Hai Seafood GUESTHOUSE $
(☎08 1367 8497; r 1200B; ❄@🏊) These solid bamboo bungalows are easily the most charming budget choice on the beach. The owners are happy, fun and laid-back, plus they have one of the best kitchens on the island.

Ko Hai Camping CAMPING $
(☎08 1970 9804; seamoth2004@yahoo.com; tents 600B) Big, clean fan-cooled tentalos on the beach have shared bathrooms and are run by friendly Tu, who also manages the adjacent Sea Moth Dive Center.

KO MUK

Sawasdee Resort GUESTHOUSE $
(☎08 1508 0432; www.kohmook-sawadeeresort.com; Hat Faràng; bungalows 800B) Unremarkable wooden bungalows with terraces are right on the quiet shady north end of Hat Faràng. You're paying for the location – which is sublime.

Ko Mook Garden Resort GUESTHOUSE $
(☎08 1748 384; Hat Lodung; bungalows 300B, r 500B) The wooden rooms here are large

while the bamboo bungalows are small and basic. Staying here means you're with a local family who take guests snorkelling, lend out bikes and give out detailed maps of all the island's secret spots.

OTHER ISLANDS

Sukorn Beach Bungalows HOTEL $$
(☎0 7520 7707, 08 1647 5550; www.sukorn-island-trang.com; Ko Sukorn; bungalows 1000-2500B; ❄📶) Easily the most professionally run place on Ko Sukorn, the concrete-and-wood bungalows all have comfy verandahs and a long swimming beach out the front from which you can watch the sun set over outlying islands. Oh, and the food (mains 180B to 300B) is the best in the Trang Islands.

Libong Beach Resort HOTEL $
(☎0 7522 5205; www.libongbeachresort.com; Ko Libong; bungalows 500-800B; ❄@) This is the only place on Ko Libong that's open year-round – rates drop considerably in the low season. There are several options from bland slap-up shacks behind a murky stream to beachfront – and very comfortable – varnished wood-and-thatch chalets.

Paradise Lost GUESTHOUSE $
(☎08 9587 2409; www.kokradan.wordpress.com; Ko Kradan; dm 250B, bungalows 900-1600B, with shared bathrooms 700B) One of the first places built on Kradan and still one of the best, this groovy, inland US-owned bungalow property has easy access to the island's more remote beaches.

Getting There & Away

In the high season, the **Tigerline** (☎08 1092 8800; www.tigerlinetravel.com) high-speed ferry runs between Ko Lanta and Ko Lipe, stopping at Ko Muk, Ko Kradan, Hat Yao (on the mainland) and Ko Lao Liang. The entire journey takes five hours. **Satun Pakbara Speed Boat Club** (☎0 7475 0389; www.tarutaolipeisland.com) follows a similar route between Ko Lanta and Ko Lipe, stopping on Ko Ngai and Ko Muk only. Prices range from 750B to 1400B depending on the length of your journey.

Boats from Kuantungku on the mainland depart every other hour throughout the morning and early afternoon for Ko Muk and Ko Kradan (100B to 450B; 30 minutes to one hour). Chartered longtails from Kuantungku cost 600B to 800B. Daily boats from Hat Pak Meng stop on Ko Ngai (400B, 1½ hours). Chartered longtails from Hat Pak Meng cost 1200B to Ko Ngai, and 1500B to Ko Kradan. Visitors to Ko Sukorn can charter a boat (1750B) from Ko Lao Liang after taking one of the speed ferries, or hire a longtail from the mainland (around 1000B).

Longtails between the islands can also be arranged. The journey from Ko Muk to Ko Kradan, for example, costs 600B and takes roughly 30 minutes.

Ko Lipe

Ko Lipe is this decade's poster child for untamed development in the Thai Islands. Blessed with two wide white-sand beaches separated by jungled hills, and within spitting distance of protected coral reefs, the island was once only spoken about in secretive whispers. The whispers quickly became gossip, which turned into a roar – you know, the kind generally associated with bulldozers. Although the island may be going the way of Ko Phi-Phi there's still plenty to love about little Lipe.

GETTING TO MALAYSIA: SATUN TO KUALA PERLIS OR PULAU LANGKAWI

Getting to the border An interprovincial bus services the route from Hat Yai to Satun route. The mainland town of Satun provides boat links to Malaysia's mainland and to the island resort of Langkawi. Boats to Malaysia leave from Tammalang pier, 7km south of Satun. Large longtail boats run to Kuala Perlis in Malaysia (300B one-way, one hour), mainly for travellers on visa tours. For Pulau Langkawi boats (300B, 1½ hours) leave at 9.30am, 1.30pm and 4.30pm daily in high season or 9.30am/12pm/4pm during the low season. If you're island-hopping it is easier to make the leap from Ko Lipe.

At the border Boats only run when the immigration offices are open, so there shouldn't be any problems as all passengers are funnelled through border control.

Moving on Onward transport from Kuala Perlis is not efficient, meaning this crossing is best suited to short visa runs. Onward transport is easier from Langkawi.

See p413 and p414 for details on making the crossing in the opposite direction. Keep in mind that Malaysia is one hour ahead of Thai time.

GETTING TO MALAYSIA: KO LIPE TO PULAU LANGKAWI

This is a popular west coast crossing for Andaman island hoppers.

Getting to the border Both of Ko Lipe's speedboat companies offer daily trips to Pulau Langkawi (1200B, one hour) in Malaysia; departures are at 7.30am, 10.30am and 4pm.

At the border Be at the immigration office at the Bundhaya Resort early to get stamped out.

Moving on See p414 for travel from Langkawi to other parts of Malaysia. Note that Thailand and Malaysia are in different time zones.

There are no banks or ATMs on the island, though several of the bigger resorts can change travellers cheques, cash or give advances on credit cards – all for a hefty fee.

Activities

There's good coral all along the southern coast and around **Ko Kra**. Most resorts rent out mask and snorkel sets and fins for 50B each, and can arrange four-point longtail snorkel trips to must-see **Ko Adang** and other coral-fringed islands for around 1500B.

Diving is also an option, though visibility can be pretty hit-and-miss. Figure 2700B for a two-dive excursion.

Forra Diving DIVING
(☎08 4407 5691; www.forradiving.com) Friendly French-run school with an office on both Sunrise and Pattaya beaches. Offers good accommodation too.

Ocean Pro DIVING
(☎08 9733 8068; www.oceanprodivers.net) Professional and knowledgeable staff run a seamless operation.

Sleeping

Most, but not all, resorts on Ko Lipe close from May to October. For ultra-cheap digs, try **South Sea** (☎08 0544 0063; Sunset Beach; bungalows 350B) just inland from Sunset Beach.

Daya Resort HOTEL $
(☎0 7472 8030; Hat Pattaya; bungalows 500-1000B) One of the few places that's still locally run, the striped bungalows here are your standard slap-up wooden affairs but the beach is fantastic, the flowery back garden charming, and the restaurant has the absolute best and cheapest seafood grill on the island…and that's saying something.

Blue Tribes HOTEL $$
(☎08 6285 2153; www.bluetribeslipe.com; Hat Pattaya; bungalows 1200-1700B; ❄@) One of Pattaya's more attractive small resorts, its best nests are the two-storey thatched wooden bungalows with downstairs living rooms and top-floor bedrooms that have sliding doors opening to sea views.

Eating & Drinking

Hat Pattaya's resorts put on nightly fresh seafood barbecues and Daya's is arguably the best.

Nong Bank Restaurant RESTAURANT $$
(Hat Pattaya; dishes 80-120B; ⏰breakfast, lunch & dinner) This place serves point-and-grill seafood and a superb yellow curry with crab (120B), with a half-dozen tables scattered beneath a tree on the white sand.

Pooh's Bar RESTAURANT, BAR $
(☎0 7472 8019; www.poohlipe.com) This massive complex was built by a Lipe pioneer and includes bungalows, a dive shop and several restaurants. It's a very popular local expat hang-out, especially in the low season. Each night it projects films onto its big screen.

Getting There & Away

From 21 October through the end of May, speedboats run from Pak Bara to Ko Lipe at 9.30am, 11am, 12.30pm and 2pm (550B to 650B, 1½ hours). A boat charter to Ko Lipe from Pak Bara is a hefty 4000B each way.

Tigerline (☎08 1092 8800; www.tigerlinetravel.com) offers the cheapest high-speed ferry service to Ko Lanta (1500B, 5½ hours), stopping at Ko Muk (1400B, 3½ hours), Ko Kradan (1400B, four hours) and Ko Ngai (1400B, 4½ hours). It departs from Ko Lipe's Pattaya Beach at 9.30am. The **Satun-Pak Bara Speedboat Club** (☎0 7475 0389, 08 2433 0114; www.tarutaolipeisland.com) offers similar service.

Pak Bara

The small fishing community of Pak Bara is the main jumping-off point for the islands in the Ko Tarutao Marine National Park (including Ko Lipe). The main road from La-Ngu terminates at the pier where there are several travel agencies, internet cafes, cheap restaurants and shops selling beach gear.

Travellers planning to visit the quieter islands of the Ko Tarutao National Park should stop by the **park headquarters** (☎0 7478 3485) just behind the pier, where you can book accommodation and obtain permission for camping. Travel agencies at the pier will gladly sell you a ticket to wherever you want to go, and many of these businesses also offer kayaking and snorkelling day trips (from 1500B).

Getting There & Away

There are hourly buses between 7am and 4pm from Hat Yai to the pier at Pak Bara (90B, 2½ hours).

Air-conditioned minivans leave hourly for Hat Yai (150B, two hours) from travel agencies near Pak Bara pier. There are also minivans to Trang (200B, 1½ hours), which connect to numerous destinations such as Krabi (450B, four hours) and Phuket (650B, six hours).

UNDERSTAND THAILAND

Thailand Today

After a five-year period of political instability initiated by the 2006 coup d'état, Thailand has reached a political plateau with the 2011 general election. Ousted prime minister Thaksin Shinawatra's politically allied party, Puea Thai, won a clear majority of parliamentary seats, and his sister Yingluck Shinawatra, a political novice, was elected prime minister. She is Thailand's first female prime minister and this is the fifth straight win for a Thaksin-backed political party.

Prime minister Yingluck's first days in office set about raising the national minimum wage to 300B per hour (a 30% increase), extending symbolic olive branches to the monarchy and the military and pledging to work towards national reconciliation.

The next question mark in Yingluck's administration is when there will be a pardon for her brother, allowing him to return from exile. He was barred from politics until 2012 and is evading a two year prison term. Thaksin has publicly stated that he has no plans to return to Thailand, though this statement contradicts campaign speeches in which he described his sister as his 'clone' and spoke of an unspecified time when he would return.

It is unclear if the military would allow a Thaksin return as allegiances within that institution are divided and subject to change based on behind-the-scenes negotiations. Presently the monarchy and the military are aligned against Thaksin, though they have cooperated with the outcome of the general election and have not interfered with the new government's assumption of power.

Thais in general seem fatigued from the previous years' political distress, which undermines a deep-seated sense of a unified 'Thai-ness' and a cultural aversion to violence and anger. Bangkokians, especially, are exhausted by the hassles of traffic jams and road closures that accommodate the exercise of freedom of assembly.

History

Rise of Thai Kingdoms

It is believed that the first Thais migrated southwest from modern-day Yúnnán and Guangxi, China, to what is today known as Thailand. They settled along river valleys and formed small farming communities that eventually fell under the dominion of the expansionist Khmer empire of present-day Cambodia. What is now southern Thailand, along the Malay peninsula, was under the sway of the Srivijaya empire based in Sumatra.

By the 13th and 14th centuries, what is considered to be the first Thai kingdom – Sukhothai (meaning 'Rising Happiness') – emerged and began to chip away at the crumbling Khmer empire. The Sukhothai kingdom is regarded as the cultural and artistic kernel of the modern state.

Sukhothai was soon eclipsed by another Thai power, Ayuthaya, established by Prince U Thong in 1350. This new centre developed into a cosmopolitan port on the Asian trade route, courted by various European nations. The small nation managed to thwart foreign takeovers, including one orchestrated by a Thai court official, a Greek man named Constantine Phaulkon, to advance French interests. For 400 years and 34 successive reigns, Ayuthaya dominated Thailand until the Burmese led a successful invasion in 1765, ousting the monarch and destroying the capital.

The Thais eventually rebuilt their capital in present-day Bangkok, established by the

Chakri dynasty, which continues to occupy the throne today. As Western imperialism marched across the region, King Mongkut (Rama IV, r 1851-68) and his son and successor, King Chulalongkorn (Rama V, r 1868-1910), successfully steered the country into the modern age without becoming a colonial vassal. In return for the country's continued independence, King Chulalongkorn ceded huge tracts of Laos and Cambodia to French-controlled Indochina – an unprecedented territorial loss in Thai history.

A Struggling Democracy

In 1932 a peaceful coup converted the country into a constitutional monarchy, loosely based on the British model. What has followed has been a near-continuous cycle of power struggles among three factions – the elected government, military leaders and the monarchy backed by the aristocrats. These groups occasionally form tenuous allegiances based on mutual dislike for the opposition and the resulting power grab is often a peaceful military takeover sometimes dubbed 'smooth as silk' coups.

During the mid-20th century, the military dominated the political sphere with an anticommunist tenure that is widely regarded as being ineffectual except in the suppression of democratic representation and civil rights. In 1973, student activists staged demonstrations calling for a real constitution and the release of political dissidents. A brief respite came, with reinstated voting rights and relaxed censorship. But in October 1976, a demonstration on the campus of Thammasat University in Bangkok was brutally quashed, resulting in hundreds of casualties and the reinstatement of authoritarian rule. Many activists went underground to join armed communist insurgency groups hiding in the northeast.

In the 1980s, as the regional threat of communism subsided, the military-backed Prime Minister Prem Tinsulanonda stabilised the country and moved towards a representative democracy. The military reemerged in 1991 to overthrow the democratically elected government; this was the country's 10th successful coup since 1932. In May 1992 huge demonstrations led by Bangkok's charismatic governor Chamlong Srimuang erupted throughout the city and the larger provincial capitals. The bloodiest confrontation occurred at Bangkok's Democracy Monument, resulting in nearly 50 deaths, but it eventually led to the reinstatement of a civilian government.

Same, Same but Different

Through the turn of this century, Thailand's era of coups seemed to have ended. Democratically elected governments oversaw the 1997 enactment of Thailand's 16th constitution, commonly called the 'people's constitution' because it was the first charter in the nation's history not written under military order. The country pulled through the 1997 Asian currency crisis and entered a stable period of prosperity in the early 2000s. Telecommunications tycoon Thaksin Shinawatra

COLOURS: MORE THAN MEETS THE EYE

Colours in Thailand have always had meaning. Each day of the week is associated with a colour, which in turn symbolises a person's birth day. (Thai astrology is based on the day of the week not the month or date of a person's birth.)

Starting in 2006 anti-Thaksin demonstrators donned yellow shirts showing their allegiance to the king (Thaksin was viewed as having designs on the crown); yellow is the colour associated with the present king because of his birth day. This group was dubbed 'Yellow Shirts' and soon the colour became entwined with the political movement. Yellow Shirts were primarily Bangkok urban elites, aristocrats and some middle class.

The pro-Thaksin camp adopted the colour red as a symbol of democracy and they became known as the 'Red Shirts'. Red Shirts were primarily working class or rural class hailing originally from the north and northeast.

To some degree the ongoing political crisis is a class struggle, though there are left-leaning intellectuals and pro-democracy advocates within the ranks of the Red Shirts, as well as avid anti-Thaksin Yellow Shirts from humble backgrounds. In the middle of the extremes are the un-colour-coded Thais who have sympathies with both sides. The ambivalent middle avoids wearing either colour lest they offend a zealous neighbour or friend.

For the monarchy fans with no political intentions, there are now abandoned drawers of yellow shirts. But luckily this group thought of a solution: pink is the new yellow.

and his populist Thai Rak Thai party were elected into power in 2001 and over the next five years effectively engineered one-party rule. With little political opposition, Thaksin consolidated power in all ranks of government, stifling press criticism and scrutiny of his administration.

In 2006 Thaksin was accused of abusing his powers and conflicts of interest, most notably in his family's sale of their Shin Corporation to the Singaporean government for 73 billion baht (US$1.88 billion), a tax-free gain thanks to telecommunications legislation that he helped craft. Meanwhile Thaksin's working-class and rural base rallied behind him, spotlighting longstanding class divides within Thai society.

Behind the scenes the military and the aristocrats forged an allegiance that resulted in the 2006 coup of the Thaksin government, forcing the charismatic prime minister into exile. At first the military takeover was heralded as a necessary step in ridding the country of an elected dictator and cleptocracy. The military spent the next year attempting to 'clean house' of Thaksin's political party (Thai Rak Thai) only to have the regenerated (and re-christened) party win the 2007 reinstatement of democratic elections. In response, the aristocrats, organised under the group calling itself the People's Alliance for Democracy (PAD) but often dubbed 'Yellow Shirts', were unhappy with the return of Thaksin's political proxies and staged massive protests in Bangkok that took over the parliament building and closed down the city's two airports for a week in November 2008. This dealt a blow to Thailand's economy just as the US financial crisis was morphing into a global recession.

The Constitutional Court sided with PAD's demands and dissolved the ruling (and popularly elected) party due to a technicality. A new coalition was formed in December 2008, led by Oxford-educated Abhisit Vejjajiva, leader of the Democrat party and Thailand's fourth prime minister of the year. It was viewed by pro-Thaksin factions as a silent coup.

The pro-Thaksin faction (known as 'Red Shirts') retaliated with a crippling demonstration after Thailand's Supreme Court ordered the seizure of US$46 billion of Thaksin's assets and charged him with abusing his powers as prime minister. Starting in March 2010, thousands of Red Shirts occupied Bangkok's central shopping district for two months. Protest leaders demanded the dissolution of the government and reinstatement of elections. In May 2010 the military used forced to evict the protestors, resulting in bloody clashes (91 people were killed) and a smouldering central city (US$1.5 billion of crackdown-related arson damage was estimated). In an effort to avoid future civilian-military showdowns, elections were held in 2011 and Thaksin's politically allied party won a clear majority.

The Monarchy

Further complicating matters is the ailing health of the revered King Bhumibol Adulyadej (Rama IX, r 1946-), who defined a new political role for the monarchy as a paternal figure who acted with perceived wisdom in times of political crisis. Now 83 years old, the king is the world's longest-serving monarch but as his health has declined, his role in the society at large has diminished. During the most recent political struggle, the monarchy and the military were clearly aligned against the outcome of democracy and the now-deposed Thaksin government, whose consolidation of power was viewed as a threat to the smooth transfer of the crown from father to son, Crown Prince Vajiralongkorn.

The Culture

Thais are laid-back, good-natured people whose legendary hospitality has earned their country a permanent place on the global travel map.

The National Psyche

Paramount to the Thai philosophy of life is *sànùk* (fun) – each day is celebrated with food and conversation, foreign festivals are readily adopted as an excuse for a party and every task is measured on the *sànùk* meter.

The social dynamics of Thai culture can be perplexing. The ideals of the culture are based on Buddhist principles and include humility, gratitude and filial piety. These golden rules are translated into such social conventions as saving face *(nâa)*, in which confrontation is avoided and people endeavour not to embarrass themselves or other people.

An important component of saving face is knowing one's place in society: all relationships in Thai society are governed by conventions of social rank defined by age, wealth, status and personal and political power. Thais 'size up' a Westerner's social status with a list of common questions: Where are you from? How old are you? Are you married? These questions to a Thai

DON'T GET TIED-UP BY THAI ETIQUETTE

Master this simple list of dos and don'ts (mainly don'ts) and you'll be an honoured guest.

» The king's anthem is played before every movie in a theatre and the national anthem is played twice a day (in the morning and evening) in public places like bus and train stations. You are expected to stand respectfully during both.

» Thailand is a nonconfrontational culture. Don't get angry, yell or get physically violent; keep your cool and things will work out.

» Feet are the lowest and 'dirtiest' part of the body. Keep your feet on the floor, not on a chair; never touch anyone or point with your foot; never step over someone (or something) sitting on the ground; and take your shoes off when you enter a home or temple.

» Dress modestly (cover shoulders and knees) and don't sunbathe topless.

» Women aren't allowed to touch or sit next to a monk or his belongings. The very back seat of the bus and the last row on public boats are reserved for monks.

» A neat and clean appearance complements Thais' persistent regard for beauty. Frequent daily showers provide natural air-conditioning and a pleasing scent to your neighbours.

» Traditionally, Thais greet each other with a *wâi,* a prayerlike gesture. In general, if someone *wâi*s you, then return the *wâi* (unless *wâi*-ed by a child or a service person). The placement of the fingertips in relation to the facial features varies with the recipient's social rank and age. The safest, least offensive spot is to place the tips of your fingers to nose level and slightly bow your head.

» It is illegal to step on money in Thailand, as the king's image is on all coins and notes; all images of the king are treated like holy objects.

are matters of public record and aren't considered impolite.

Religion and the monarchy, which is still regarded by many as divine, are the culture's sacred cows. Whatever you do, don't insult the king or disrespect his image, especially in this new era of ultra-sensitivity towards the institution.

Lifestyle

Thailand straddles the divide between the highly Westernised urban life in major cities and the traditional rhythms of rural, agricultural life. But several persisting customs offer a rough snapshot of daily life. Thais wake up early, thanks in part to the roosters that start crowing sometime after sunset. In the grey stillness of early morning, barefoot monks carrying large round bowls travel through the town to collect their daily meals from the faithful. The housewives are already awake steaming rice and sweeping their front porches with stiff bristled brooms. Soon business is in full swing: the vendors have arrived at their favourite corner to feed the uniformed masses, be they khaki-clad civil servants or white-and-black wearing university students.

Eating appears to make up the rest of the day. Notice the shop girls, ticket vendors or even the office workers: they can be found in a tight circle swapping gossip and snacking (or *gin lên,* literally 'eat for fun'). Then there is dinner and after-dinner and the whole seemingly chaotic, yet highly ordered, affair starts all over again.

Population

About 75% of citizens are ethnic Thais, further divided by geography (north, central, south and northeast). Each group speaks its own Thai dialect and to a certain extent practises customs unique to its region or influenced by neighbouring countries. Politically and economically the central Thais are the dominant group. People of Chinese ancestry make up roughly 14% of the population, many of whom have been in Thailand for generations. Ethnic Chinese probably enjoy better relations with the majority population here than in any other country in Southeast Asia. Other large minority groups include the Malays in the far south, the Khmers in the northeast and the Lao, spread throughout the north and east. Smaller non-Thai-speaking groups include the hill tribes living in the northern mountains.

Sport

Thailand is obsessed with football (soccer), like the rest of the world, but there are some home-grown sports worth watching.

Muay Thai (Thai Boxing)

Enjoying a global appreciation, *muay thai* is a martial sport akin to boxing but all surfaces of the body are fair targets and everything but the head can deliver a blow. Many foreigners come to Thailand to study the sport or to watch the skilled boxers in their home setting, where matches are accompanied by wild musical orchestration and frenzied betting. You'll know when a match is on because all the taxi and motorcycle drivers will be huddled around a communal TV, cheering in unison.

The most famous matches are at the major stadiums in Bangkok (see p666). There are also 'tourist' matches held at stadiums throughout the country.

Tàkrâw

Sometimes called Siamese football, *tàkrâw* is best described as volleyball for the feet. This sport does not enjoy much commercial success but it is a popular pastime, often played in school yards or as informal pick-up games in empty lots. In its most formal variation, players assemble on either side of a net and volley a *lûuk tàkrâw* (rattan ball) using their feet or head to touch the ball. Like gymnasts, the players perform aerial pirouettes to spike the ball. But the most common variation is for players to stand in a circle and simply try to keep the ball airborne.

Religion

Alongside the Thai national flag flies the yellow flag of Buddhism – Theravada Buddhism (as opposed to the Mahayana schools found in East Asia and the Himalaya). Country, family and daily life are all married to religion. Every Thai male is expected to become a monk for a short period in his life, since a family earns great merit when a son 'takes robe and bowl'.

More evident than the philosophical aspects of Buddhism is the everyday fusion with animist rituals. Monks are consulted to determine an auspicious date for a wedding or the likelihood of success for a business. Spirit houses *(phrá phuum)* are constructed outside buildings and homes to encourage the spirits to live independently from the family but to remain comfortable so as to bring good fortune to the site.

Roughly 95% of the population practises Buddhism, but in southern Thailand there is a significant Muslim minority community.

Arts

Music

Classical Thai music was developed for the royal court as an accompaniment to classical dance-drama and other forms of theatre. Traditional instruments have more pedestrian applications and can often be heard at temple fairs or provincial festivals. Whether used in the high or low arts, traditional Thai music has an incredible array of textures and subtleties, hair-raising tempos and pastoral melodies.

In the north and northeast there are several popular wind instruments with multiple reed pipes, which function like a mouth organ. Chief among these is the *khaen,* which originated in Laos; when played by an adept musician it sounds like a calliope organ. It is used chiefly in *măw lam* music, a rural folk tradition often likened to the American blues. A near cousin to *măw lam* is *lûuk thûng* (literally, 'children of the fields'), which enjoys a working-class fan base much like country music does in the US.

Popular Thai music has borrowed rock-and-roll's instruments to create perky teenybop hits to hippie protest ballads and even urban indie anthems. It is an easy courtship with Thai classic rock, like the decades-old group Carabao and the folk style known as *phleng phêua chii-wít* (songs for life). Alternative rock groups like Modern Dog and Aparment Khunpa, have defined Thailand's new millennial sound.

Sculpture & Architecture

Thailand's most famous sculptural output has been its bronze Buddha images, coveted the world over for their originality and grace. Traditional architecture is more visible as it is applied to simple homes and famous temples. Ancient Thai homes consisted of a single-room teak structure raised on stilts, since most Thais once lived along river banks or canals. The space underneath also served as the living room, kitchen, garage and barn. Rooflines in Thailand are steeply pitched and often decorated at the corners or along the gables with motifs related to the *naga* (mythical sea serpent), long believed to be a spiritual protector. Temple buildings demonstrate more formal aspects of traditional architecture and artistic styles.

Theatre & Dance

Traditional Thai theatre consists of six dramatic forms, including *khŏhn,* a formal masked dance-drama depicting scenes from the *Ramakian* (the Thai version of India's Ramayana) that were originally performed only for the royal court. Popular in rural villages, *lí-gair* is a partly improvised, often bawdy folk play featuring dancing, comedy, melodrama and music. The southern Thai equivalent is *mánohraa,* which is based on a 2000-year-old Indian story. Shadow puppet plays (*năng*) found in southern Thailand demonstrate that region's cultural heritage with Malaysia and Indonesia.

Environment

Thailand's shape on the map has been likened to the head of an elephant, with its trunk extending down the Malay peninsula. The country covers 517,000 sq km, which is slightly smaller than the US state of Texas. The centre of the country, Bangkok, sits at about 14° north latitude – level with Madras, Manila, Guatemala and Khartoum. Because the north-south reach spans roughly 16 latitudinal degrees, Thailand has perhaps the most diverse climate in Southeast Asia.

The Land

The country stretches from dense mountain jungles in the north to the flat central plains to the southern tropical rainforests. Covering the majority of the country, monsoon forests are filled with a sparse canopy of deciduous trees that shed their leaves during the dry season to conserve water. The landscape becomes dusty and brown until the rains (from July to November) transform everything into a fecund green. As the rains cease, Thailand enters its 'winter', a period of cooler temperatures, virtually unnoticeable to a recent arrival except in the north where night-time temperatures can drop to 13°C. By March, the hot season begins and the mercury climbs to 40°C or more at its highest, plus humidity.

In the south, the wet season lasts until January, with months of unrelenting showers and floods. Thanks to the rains, the south supports the dense rainforests more indicative of a 'tropical' region. Along the coastline, mangrove forests anchor themselves wherever water dominates.

Thailand's national flower, the orchid, is one of the world's most beloved parasites, producing such exotic flowers that even its host is charmed.

Wildlife

Thailand is particularly rich in bird life: more than 1000 resident and migrating species have been recorded and approximately 10% of all world bird species dwell here. Thailand's most revered indigenous mammal, the elephant, once ran wild in the country's dense virgin forests. Since ancient times, annual parties led by the king would round up young elephants from the wild to train them as workers and fighters. Integral to Thai culture, the elephant symbolises wisdom, strength and good fortune. White elephants are even more auspicious and by tradition are donated to the king. Sadly, elephants are now endangered, having lost their traditional role in society and much of their habitat.

Environmental Issues

Like all countries with a high population density, there is enormous pressure on Thailand's ecosystems: in the middle of last century about 70% of the countryside was forest; by 2000 an estimated 20% of the natural forest cover remained.

In response to environmental degradation, the Thai government created protected natural areas and outlawed logging. Thailand designated its first national park (Khao Yai) in the 1960s and has added over 100 parks, including marine environments, to the list since. Together these cover 15% of the country's land and sea area, one of the highest ratios of protected to unprotected areas of any nation in the world. Since the turn of the millennium, forest loss has slowed to about 0.2% per year according to the World Bank.

Though the conservation efforts are laudable, Thailand's national parks are poorly funded and poorly protected from commercial development, illegal hunting and logging, or swidden agriculture. The passing of the 1992 Environmental Act was an encouraging move by the government, but standards still lag behind Western nations. Thailand is a signatory to the UN Convention on International Trade in Endangered Species (CITES). Forty of Thailand's 300 mammal species are on the International Union for Conservation of Nature (IUCN) list of endangered species.

Food & Drink

Food

Restaurants reviewed in this guide are organised into the following categories: budget $ (up to 150B), midrange $$ (151B to 350B) and top-end $$$ (more than 350B).

Thai food is a complex balance of spicy, salty, sweet and sour. The ingredients are fresh and light with lots of lemongrass, basil, coriander and mint. Chilli peppers pack a slow, nose-running, tongue-searing burn. And pungent *náam plaa* (fish sauce; generally made from anchovies) adds a touch of the salty sea. Throw in a little zest of lime and a pinch of sugar and the ingredients make a symphony of flavours that becomes more interesting with each bite.

Thailand is a country where it is cheaper and tastier to eat out than to cook at home. Day and night markets, pushcart vendors, makeshift stalls, open-air restaurants – prices stay low because of few or no overheads, and cooks become famous in all walks of life for a particular dish. No self-respecting shoestringer would shy away from the pushcarts in Thailand for fear of stomach troubles. The hygiene standards are some of the best in the region, and sitting next to the wok you can see all the action, unlike some of the guesthouses where food is assembled in a darkened hovel.

For breakfast and late-night snacks, Thais nosh on *kŭaytĭaw,* a noodle soup with chicken or pork and vegetables. There are two major types of noodles you can choose from: *sên lek* (thin) and *sên yài* (wide and flat). Before you dig into your steaming bowl, first use the chopsticks (or a spoon) to cut the noodles into smaller segments so they are easier to pick up. Then add to taste a few teaspoonfuls of the provided spices: dried red chilli, sugar, fish sauce and vinegar. Now you have the true taste of Thailand in front of you. The weapons of choice when eating noodles (either *kŭaytĭaw* or *phàt thai*) are chopsticks and a rounded soup spoon.

Thais are social eaters: meals are rarely taken alone and dishes are meant to be shared. Usually a small army of plates will be placed in the centre of the table, with individual servings of rice in front of each diner. The protocol goes like this – ladle a spoonful of food at a time on to your plate of rice. Dishes aren't passed in Thailand; instead you reach across the table to the different items. Using the spoon like a fork and your fork like a knife, steer the food (with the fork) onto your spoon, which enters your mouth. To the Thais placing a fork in the mouth is just plain weird. When you are full, leave a little rice on your plate (an empty plate is a silent request for more rice) and place your fork so that it is cradled by the spoon in the centre of the plate.

Even when eating with a gang of *faràng,* it is still wise to order 'family style', as dishes are rarely synchronised. Ordering individually will leave one person staring politely at a piping hot plate and another staring wistfully at the kitchen.

Drink

Water purified for drinking is simply called *náam dèum* (drinking water), whether boiled or filtered. All water offered in restaurants, offices or homes will be purified. Ice is generally safe in Thailand. *Chaa* (tea) and *kaa-fae* (coffee) are prepared strong, milky and sweet – an instant morning buzz.

Thanks to the tropical bounty, exotic fruit juices are sold on every corner. Thais prefer a little salt to cut the sweetness of the juice; the salt also has some mystical power to make a hot day tolerable.

Cheap beer appears hand-in-hand with backpacker ghettos. Beer Chang and Beer Singha (pronounced 'sing', not 'sing-ha') are a couple of local brands. Thais have created yet another innovative method for beating the heat; they drink their beer with ice to keep the beverage cool and crisp.

More of a ritual than a beverage, Thai whisky usually runs with a distinct crowd – soda water, Coke and ice. Fill the short glass with ice cubes, two-thirds whisky, one-third soda and a splash of Coke. Thai tradition dictates the youngest in the crowd is responsible for filling the other drinkers' glasses. Many travellers prefer to go straight to the ice bucket with shared straws, not forgetting a dash of Red Bull for a cocktail to keep them going.

SURVIVAL GUIDE

DIRECTORY A–Z

Accommodation

A tiered pricing system has been used in this book to determine budget category. In big cities and beach resorts, rate under 1000B are indicated as budget ($), 1500B to 3000B as midrange ($$) and over 3000B as top end ($$$). For small towns, rates under 600B are budget ($), 600B to 1500B are midrange ($$) and over 1500B are top end ($$$). There is a healthy selection of budget accommodation in Thailand, starting at around 200B to 350B for a dorm bed or a bed-in-a-box single with fan and shared (cold water) bathroom. In the small towns, 400B and higher should get you a private (hot water) bathroom and air-con. In the big cities and beach resorts, such amenities cost around 700B.

Guesthouses are the primary budget options. Many started out as converted family homes, and sometimes have graduated into multi-storey apartment-style towers. Guesthouses usually subsidise their low room rates with an attached restaurant, which cultivates a sense of community accompanied by lots of travel advice and cultural conversation.

More impersonal are the Thai-Chinese hotels that cater to a local clientele and are sometimes the only option in non-touristed places. The amenities and rates tend to be higher (usually around the 500B-plus range).

During Thailand's peak season (December to February), prices increase and availability decreases, especially on the island and beach resorts.

Unless otherwise noted, reservations at the guesthouses are not recommended as standards vary from room to room and year to year. It is imperative for a traveller to inspect the room beforehand since refunds are not a common practice in Thailand. Advance payment to secure a reservation is also discouraged.

In this chapter, high-season prices have been quoted. Enquiries for discounts can be made during off-tourist seasons.

Customs

Thailand allows the following items to enter duty free:

» reasonable amount of personal effects (clothing and toiletries)
» professional instruments
» 200 cigarettes
» 1L of wine or spirits

Thailand prohibits import of the following:

» firearms and ammunition (unless preregistered with the police department)
» illegal drugs
» pornographic media

When leaving Thailand, you must obtain an export licence for any antique reproductions or newly cast Buddha images (except personal amulets). Submit two front-view photos of the object(s), a photocopy of your passport, the purchase receipt and the object(s) in question, to the **Department of Fine Arts** (☎0 2628 5032). Allow four days

BUSINESS HOURS

The following are standard business hours in Thailand. Reviews in this book list only variations from these. Government offices and banks are closed public holidays (see p781).

TYPE OF BUSINESS	BUSINESS HOURS	EXCEPTIONS
Bars	6pm-midnight (officially)	Closing times vary due to local enforcement of curfew laws; bars close during elections and certain religious public holidays.
Banks	9.30am-3.30pm, Mon-Fri	ATMs accessible 24 hours
Clubs (discos)	8pm-2am	Closing times vary due to local enforcement of curfew laws; clubs close during elections and certain religious public holidays.
Government offices	8.30am-4.30pm, Mon-Fri	Some close for lunch (noon-1pm), while others are open Saturday (9am-3pm).
Live-music venues	6pm-1am	Closing times vary due to local enforcement of curfew laws; clubs close during elections and certain religious public holidays.
Restaurants	10am-10pm	Some shops specialise in morning meals and close by 3pm.
Stores	local stores: 10am-6pm, department stores: 10am-8pm.	In some small towns, local stores close on Sunday.

for the application and inspection process to be completed.

Dangers & Annoyances

Although Thailand is not a dangerous country, it's wise to be cautious, particularly if travelling alone. Most tourist-oriented towns will have a **tourist police office** (☎1155), with officers who can speak English and liaise with the Thai police. The tourist police can also issue official documentation for insurance purposes if valuables are stolen.

It is not recommended to travel into Thailand's southernmost provinces of Yala, Narathiwat, Pattani and remote corners of Songkhla.

Here are a few pointers to avoid problems:

» Avoid arguments with Thais (especially about money or matters of the heart), who might react inexplicably violently when they feel a 'loss of face' (public embarrassment or humiliation).

» Don't wander around alone at night intoxicated, especially women and especially on Ko Samui and Ko Pha-Ngan.

» Don't buy, sell or possess drugs (opium, heroin, amphetamines, hallucinogenic mushrooms and marijuana); there are strict punishments for drug possession and trafficking that are not relaxed for foreigners.

» Don't accept an invitation to go shopping or play cards with a stranger you've met on the street. This is the lead up to a well-rehearsed scam.

» Carry your personal effects (money, credit cards, passport) on your person to avoid theft or loss, especially during long-distance travel when stowed luggage can be accessed by thieves.

Driving Licence

An International Driving Permit is necessary to drive vehicles in Thailand, but this is rarely enforced for motorcycle hire.

Electricity

Thailand uses 220V AC electricity; power outlets most commonly feature two-prong round or flat sockets. See p927 for details.

Embassies & Consulates

Most foreign embassies are located in Bangkok; a few have consulates in Chiang Mai or Phuket.

Australia (Map p650; ☎0 2344 6300; www.thailand.embassy.gov.au; 37 Th Sathon Tai, Bangkok)

Cambodia (☎0 2957 5851-2; 518/4 Pracha Uthit/Soi Ramkamhaeng 39, Bangkok)

Canada Bangkok (Map p650; ☎0 2636 0540; www.thailand.gc.ca; 15th fl, Abdulrahim Bldg, 990 Th Phra Ram IV); Chiang Mai Consulate (Map p686; ☎0 5385-0147; 151 Superhighway, Tambon Tahsala)

China Bangkok (☎0 2245 7044; www.china embassy.or.th; 57 Th Ratchadaphisek); Chiang Mai Consulate (Map p686; ☎0 5327 6125; 111 Th Chang Lor, Tambon Haiya)

Denmark (Map p650; ☎0 2343 1100; www.ambbangkok.um.dk; 10 Soi 1, Th Sathon Tai; Bangkok) Consulates in Phuket and Pattaya.

France (Map p650; ☎0 2657 5100; www.ambafrance-th.org; 35 Soi 36, Th Charoen Krung); Bangkok Visa & Culture Services (Map p650; ☎0 2627 2150; 29 Th Sathon Tai); Chiang Mai Consulate (Map p686; ☎0 5328 1466; 138 Th Charoen Prathet) Consulates in Phuket & Surat Thani.

Germany (Map p650; ☎0 2287 9000; www.bangkok.diplo.de; 9 Th Sathon Tai, Bangkok)

India (Map p650; ☎0 2258 0300-6; indianembassy.in.th; 46 Soi Prasanmit/Soi 23, Th Sukhumvit); Bangkok Visa Application Centre (Map p650; ☎02 6652 9681; www.ivac-th.com; Glass Haus Bldg,15th fl, ste 1503, Th Sukhumvit) Chiang Mai Consulate (Map p686; ☎0 5324 3066; 33/1 Th Thung Hotel, Wat Gate)

Indonesia (Map p660; ☎0 2252 3135; www.kemlu.go.id/bangkok; 600-602 Th Phetchaburi, Bangkok)

Ireland (Map p650; ☎0 2677 7500; www.irelandinthailand.com; 28th fl, Q House, Th Sathon Tai, Bangkok) Consulate only; the nearest Irish embassy is in Kuala Lumpur.

Israel (Map p650; ☎0 2204 9200; bangkok.mfa.gov.il; Ocean Tower 2, 25th fl, 25 Soi 19, Th Sukhumvit, Bangkok)

Japan Bangkok (Map p650; ☎0 2207 8500; www.th.emb-japan.go.jp; 177 Th Withayu); Chiang Mai Consulate (Map p686;☎0 5320 3367; 104-107 Airport Business Park, Th Mahidon)

Laos (☎0 2539 6678; www.bkklaoembassy.com; 502/1-3 Soi Sahakarnpramoon, Pracha Uthit/Soi 39, Th Ramakamhaeng)

Malaysia (Map p650; ☎0 2629 6800; 35 Th Sathon Tai, Bangkok) Consulate in Songkhla.

Myanmar (Burma; Map p650; ☎0 2233 2237; www.mofa.gov.mm; 132 Th Sathon Neua, Bangkok)

Nepal (☎0 2391 7240; www.immi.gov.np; 189 Soi 71, Th Sukhumvit, Bangkok)

PRACTICALITIES

» *Bangkok Post* and the *Nation* are Thailand's English-language news dailies.

» The main video format is PAL.

» Thailand follows the international metric system.

» Thailand measures its year from the beginning of the Buddhist Era (in 543 BC); meaning that 2012 is 2555 in Thailand.

Netherlands (Map p660; ☎0 2309 5200; www.netherlandsembassy.in.th; 15 Soi Tonson, Th Ploenchit, Bangkok)

New Zealand (Map p660; ☎0 2254 2530; www.nzembassy.com; 14th fl, M Thai Tower, All Seasons Pl, 87 Th Withayu, Bangkok)

Philippines (Map p650; ☎0 2259 0139; www.philembassy-bangkok.net; 760 Th Sukhumvit, Bangkok)

Russia (Map p650; ☎2234 9824 www.thailand.mid.ru; 78 Soi Sap, Th Surawong) Consulates in Pattaya & Phuket.

Singapore (Map p650; ☎0 2286 2111; www.mfa.gov.sg/bangkok; 129 Th Sathon Tai, Bangkok)

Spain (Map p650; ☎0 2661 8284; es.embassyinformation.com; 23 fl, Lake Ratchada Office Complex, 193 Th Ratchadaphisek)

Switzerland (Map p660; ☎0 2674 6900; www.eda.admin.ch/bangkok; 35 Th Withayu Neua)

UK Bangkok (Map p660; ☎0 2305 8333; ukinthailand.fco.gov.uk; 14 Th Withayu); Chiang Mai Consulate (Map p686; ☎0 5326 3015; British Council, 198 Th Bamrungrat) Consulate also in Pattaya.

USA Bangkok (Map p660; ☎0 2205 4049; http://bangkok.usembassy.gov; 95 Th Withayu); Chiang Mai Consulate (Map p686; ☎0 5310 7777; 387 Th Wichayanon)

Vietnam (Map p660; ☎0 2251 5836-8; www.vietnamembassy-thailand.org; 83/1 Th Withayu, Bangkok)

Festivals & Events

Many Thai festivals are linked to Buddhist holy days and follow the lunar calendar. Thus they fall on different dates each year. Many provinces hold annual festivals or fairs to promote their agricultural specialities. A complete, up-to-date schedule of events around the country is available from TAT.

Businesses typically close and transport becomes difficult preceding any public holiday or national festivals. The following are popular national festivals:

Songkran Festival From 12 to 14 April, Buddha images are 'bathed', monks and elders have their hands respectfully sprinkled with water and a lot of water is wildly tossed about on everyone else for fun. Bangkok and Chiang Mai are major battlegrounds.

Loi Krathong On the night of the full moon in November, small lotus-shaped boats made of banana leaves and decorated with flowers and candles are floated on waterways in honour of the river goddess.

Gay & Lesbian Travellers

Gays and lesbians won't have a problem travelling through Thailand as long as they are respectful of the culture and remain somewhat discreet. Prominent gay communities exist in large cities such as Bangkok and Chiang Mai, and gay-pride events are celebrated in Bangkok, Pattaya and Phuket. Although public displays of affection are common (and are usually platonic) between members of the same sex, you should refrain from anything beyond friendly hand holding.

Gay, lesbian and transsexual Thais are generally tolerated in day-to-day life, though they face institutional discrimination and are often labelled as 'sexual deviants' and barred from studying to become teachers or from joining the military.

Utopia (www.utopia-asia.com) is a good starting point for more information on Thailand for gay or lesbian travellers.

Internet Access

You'll find plenty of internet cafes in most towns and cities. The going rate is anywhere from 40B to 80B an hour. Connections tend to be pretty fast. At many guesthouses, free wi-fi is available though downed service is common and staff are poorly trained to fix it. Wi-fi signals can also be weak if your room is located too far from the router.

Legal Matters

In general, Thai police don't hassle foreigners, especially tourists. One major exception is in regard to drugs.

If you are arrested for any offence, the police will allow you the opportunity to make a phone call to your embassy or consulate in Thailand, if you have one, or to a friend or relative if not. Thai law does not presume an indicted detainee to be either 'guilty' or 'innocent' but rather a 'suspect', whose guilt or innocence will be decided in court. Trials are usually speedy.

Post

The Thai postal system is relatively efficient and few travellers complain about undelivered mail or lost parcels. Never send cash or small valuable objects through the postal system, even if the items are insured. Poste restante can be received at any town that has a post office.

Public Holidays

Government offices and banks close on the following days; also see p781 for details on national festivals and Buddhist holy days.

New Year's Day January 1

Makha Bucha Day, Buddhist holy day February (date varies)

Chakri Day, commemoratess founder of the Chakri dynasty, Rama I April 6

Songkran Festival, traditional Thai New Year and water festival April 13-14

Coronation Day, commemorating the 1946 coronation of HM the King and HM the Queen May 5

Labour Day May 1

Visaka Bucha, Buddhist holy day May/June (date varies)

Asahna Bucha, Buddhist holy day July (date varies)

Queen's Birthday August 12

Chulalongkorn Day October 23

Ork Phansaa, the end of Buddhist 'lent' October/November (date varies)

King's Birthday December 5

Constitution Day December 10

New Year's Eve December 31

Telephone

The telephone numbers listed in this chapter are written for domestic dialling; to call a Thai telephone number from outside the country, omit the initial '0'.

If you want to call an international number from Thailand, dial an international access code then the country code then the subscriber number. There are various international access codes with different rates per minute. The standard is ☎001; it is the most expensive with the best sound quality. Economy rates are available with ☎007, ☎008 and ☎009.

Here's an example of how to call the US from Thailand: ☎ 007 (international access code) + 1 (country code) + 415 776 8322 (subscriber number).

Many expats use **DeeDial** (www.deedial.com), a direct-dial service that requires a prepaid account managed through the internet. The cheapest service it offers is the 'ring-back' feature, which circumvents local charges on your mobile phone.

There are also a variety of international phonecards available through **CAT** (www.cthai.com).

Toilets

Increasingly, the Asian-style squat toilet is less of the norm in Thailand. There are still specimens in provincial bus stations, older homes and modest restaurants. Some modern toilets also come with a small spray hose – Thailand's version of the bidet. For info on how to use a squat toilet, see p930.

Tourist Information

The **Tourist Authority of Thailand** (TAT; www.tourismthailand.org) has offices throughout the country that distribute maps and sightseeing advice. TAT offices do not book accommodation, transport or tours. Contact information for regional offices is listed under each town.

Travellers With Disabilities

Thailand presents one large, ongoing obstacle course for the mobility-impaired. The book *Exotic Destinations for Wheelchair Travelers* by Ed Hansen and Bruce Gordon contains a useful chapter on seven locations in Thailand. See p930 for organisations that promote travel for special-needs individuals.

Visas

The Ministry of Foreign Affairs oversees immigration and visas issues. Check the Thai embassy or consulate for application procedures and costs. Changes to visa requirements are often monitored by **Thaivisa** (www.thaivisa.com).

VISA EXEMPTIONS & TOURIST VISAS

The Thai government allows citizens from most of Europe, Australia, New Zealand and the USA to enter the country without a prearranged visa. Arrivals by air receive a 30-day visa and arrivals by land receive 15-day visa (no fee is charged in either case).

Technically, without proof of an onward ticket and sufficient funds, any visitor can be denied entry but this is rarely enforced.

If you plan to stay in Thailand longer than your arrival visa allows, you should apply for the 60-day tourist visa from a Thai consulate or embassy before entering the country.

VISA EXTENSIONS

If you wish to stay in the country longer than your visa allows, you have two options for extension. You can cross a land border and receive a new 15-day visa upon reentry (at no charge); or you can apply for a visa extension at a Thai immigration office and receive seven to 10 days with a fee.

The fee for a visa extension is 1900B and the number of days (seven to 10) depends on the discretion of the immigration officer. Bring two passport-sized photos and one copy each of the photo and visa pages of your passport. Dress neatly and do not hire a third party proxy.

If you overstay your visa, the penalty is 500B per day, with a 20,000B limit. Fines can be paid at the airport or in advance at an immigration office. If you've overstayed only one day, you don't have to pay.

The following are immigration offices where visa extensions can be handled:

Bangkok (☎0 2141 9889; Bldg B, Bangkok Government Center, Th Chaeng Wattana; ⏰9am-noon & 1-4.30pm Mon-Fri)

Chiang Mai (☎0 5320 1755-6; Th Mahidon; ⏰8.30am-4.30pm Mon-Fri)

Krabi (☎0 7561 1097; Th Utarakit, Krabi Town; ⏰8.30am-4.30pm Mon-Fri)

Ko Samui (☎0 7742 1069; Th Thaweerat-phakdee; Nathon; ⏰8.30am-4.30pm Mon-Fri)

Phuket (☎0 7622 1905; 482 Th Phuket, Phuket Town; ⏰8.30am-4.30pm Mon-Fri)

Volunteering

Voluntary and paid positions with charitable organisations can be found in the education, development or public-health sectors. Volunteers typically work with marginalised communities – like Burmese migrants, hill-tribe villagers or rural northeastern Thais. There are also opportunities to work at animal sanctuaries or on environmental issues.

The following are volunteering organisations:

Akha Association for Education and Culture in Thailand (Afect; www.akhathai.org; Chiang Rai) A hill-tribe-run NGO that operates schools and public information programs in northern Thai villages.

Andaman Discoveries (☎08 7917 7165; www.andamandiscoveries.com; Phang Nga) A learning centre for children of Burmese migrants, an orphanage and a school for disabled children in southern Thailand.

Cultural Canvas Thailand (☎08 6920 2451; www.culturalcanvas.com; Chiang Mai) A placement organisation working with migrant learning centres and other social-justice projects in northern Thailand.

Isara (☎0 4246 0827; www.isara.org; Nong Khai) Free program for English and computer teachers in underprivileged schools around Thailand.

LemonGrass Volunteering (☎08 1977 5300; www.lemongrass-volunteering.com; Surin) A program for English teaching positions around the northeastern town of Surin.

Open Mind Projects (☎0 4241 3578; www.openmindprojects.org; Nong Khai) Volunteer positions in IT, health care, education and community-based ecotourism throughout Thailand.

Working

Teaching English is one of the easiest ways to immerse yourself into a Thai community. Those with academic credentials, such as teaching certificates or degrees in English as a second language (ESL) or English as a foreign language (EFL), get first crack at the better-paying jobs at universities and international schools. But there are hundreds of language schools for every variety of native English speaker. **Ajarn.com** (www.ajarn.com) has job listings and tips on teaching.

Getting There & Away

Air

Thailand has one primary international airport in Bangkok, while Chiang Mai, Phuket and Ko Samui receive some international flights from nearby countries.

The following airlines fly to and from Bangkok:

Air Asia (☎0 2515 9999; www.airasia.com)

Air Berlin (☎0 2236 9779; www.airberlin.com)

Air Canada (☎0 2670 0400; www.aircanada.com)

Air China (☎0 2634 8991; www.fly-airchina.com)

Air France (☎0 2610 0808; www.airfrance.fr)

Air New Zealand (☎0 2235 8280; www.airnewzealand.com)

Bangkok Airways (☎1771; www.bangkokair.com)

British Airways (☎0 2627 1701; www.britishairways.com)

Cathay Pacific Airways (☎0 2263 0606; www.cathaypacific.com)

China Airlines (☎0 2250 9898; www.china-airlines.com)

Delta Airlines (☎0 2660 6900; www.delta.com)

Emirates (☎0 2664 1040; www.emirates.com)

Eva Air (☎0 2269 6288; www.evaair.com)

Garuda Indonesia (☎0 2679 7371; www.garuda-indonesia.com)

Gulf Air (☎0 2254 7931; www.gulfairco.com)

Japan Airlines (☎0 2649 9520; www.jal.co.jp)

Jetstar Airways (☎0 2267 5125; www.jetstar.com)

KLM-Royal Dutch Airlines (☎0 2610 0800; www.klm.com)

Korean Air (☎0 2620 6900; www.koreanair.com)

Lao Airlines (☎0 2236 9822; www.laoairlines.com)

Lufthansa Airlines (☎0 2264 2400; www.lufthansa.com)

Malaysia Airlines (☎0 2263 0565; www.mas.com.my)

Myanmar Airways International (☎0 2261 5060; www.maiair.com)

Nepal Airlines (☎0 2266 7146; www.nepalairlines.com.np)

Orient Thai (☎1126; www.flyorientthai.com)

Philippine Airlines (☎0 2263 0565; www.philippineairlines.com)

Qantas Airways (☎0 2236 2800; www.qantas.com.au)

Royal Brunei Airlines (☎0 2637 5151; www.bruneiair.com)

Scandinavian Airlines (☎0 2645 8200; www.flysas.com)

Singapore Airlines (☎0 2353 6000; www.singaporeair.com)

South African Airways (☎0 2635 1410; www.flysaa.com)

Thai Airways International (☎0 2288 7000; www.thaiair.com)

United Airlines (☎0 2353 3939; www.ual.com)

Vietnam Airlines (☎0 2655 4137; www.vietnamair.com.vn)

Land

Thailand enjoys open and safe border relations with Cambodia, Laos and Malaysia. Myanmar's internal conflicts require a restricted border that is subject to frequent closings and shifting regulations.

CAMBODIA

Cambodian tourist visas are available at the border for US$20, though some borders charge 1200B. Bring a passport photo and avoid the runner boys who want to issue a health certificate or exchange money.

Aranya Prathet to Poipet (p669) The most direct land route between Bangkok and Angkor Wat.

Hat Lek to Cham Yeam (p729) The coastal crossing for travellers heading to/from Ko Chang/Sihanoukville.

Ban Pakard to Psar Pruhm (p729) A backdoor route from Ko Chang (via Chanthaburi) to Battambang and Angkor Wat.

Several little-used crossings include Chong Chom-O Smach and Chong Sa-Ngam-Choam (p719).

LAOS

It is fairly hassle-free to cross into Laos. Lao visas (US$30 to US$42) can be obtained on arrival and applications require a passport photo.

Nong Khai to Vientiane (p724) The main gateway between the two countries. Nong Khai is easily reached by train or bus from Bangkok.

Chiang Khong to Huay Xai (p703) A popular crossing linking Chiang Mai with Luang Prabang.

Mukdahan to Savannakhet (p721) Trilateral link between Thailand, Laos and Vietnam.

Nakhon Phanom to Tha Khaek (p722) The third Thai-Lao Friendship Bridge opened in 2011.

Chong Mek to Vang Tao (p720) Links Ubon Ratchathani to Pakse in Laos.

Remote crossings include Bueng Kan to Paksan (Lao visas must be arranged in advance), Tha Li-Kaen Thao and Ban Huay Kon-Muang Ngeun, though they aren't recommended because of difficulty or expense of onward transport.

MALAYSIA

Malaysia, especially the west coast, is easy to reach via bus, train and even boat.

Kangar to Padang Besar (p751) Trains pass through this border crossing from Hat Yai (originating in Bangkok) to Malaysia's Butterworth, the mainland transfer point to Penang.

Sadao to Bukit Kayu Hitam (p751) Buses from Hat Yai to Malaysia's west coast pass through here.

Ko Lipe-Langkawi (p771) Boats provide a convenient high-season link between these two Andaman islands.

Satun-Langkawi/Kuala Perlis (p772) Boats shuttle from this mainland port to Malaysia.

Sungai Kolok to Kota Bahru Due to continued violence in Thailand's Deep South, we do not recommend this overland route.

MYANMAR

Most of the land crossings into Myanmar have restrictions that don't allow full access to the country; in most cases these borders are used for a visa run. Border points are also subject to unannounced closures, which can last anywhere from a day to years.

Mae Sai-Tachileik (p701) The only crossing through which foreigners can travel beyond the border town, though travel is limited and subject to regulations.

Ranong-Kawthoung (p753) This is a popular visa-renewal point in the southern part of Thailand.

Mae Sot to Myawadi (p712) This border was closed at the time of research. If it reopens, this is only a day-trip crossing useful for visa runs.

Three Pagodas Pass (p710) This crossing has been closed to foreigners since 2006. Prior to its closure, the border was open for day trips only and did not issue Thai visa renewals.

Getting Around

Air

Thailand's major domestic carrier is Thai Airways International (THAI), with Bangkok Airways running a close second. There are several budget airlines making air travel a price-competitive option over long-distance buses. The most useful routes are Bangkok to Chiang Mai, Ko Samui or Phuket. Book your tickets in advance. When researching domestic flights, compare fares on www.domesticflightsthailand.com or talk to a travel agent.

Bicycle

Bicycles can be rented in most towns for about 50B to 150B per day. Bikes are an ideal form of local transport because they're cheap, nonpolluting and keep you moving slowly enough to see everything. Carefully note the condition of the bike before hiring; most have dodgy brakes.

Boat

Being a riverine people, Thais have colourful boats of traditional design. With a long graceful breast that barely skims the water and an elongated propeller, longtail boats are used as island-hoppers, canal coasters and river ferries. Small wooden fishing boats, brilliantly painted, sometimes shuttle tourists out to nearby islands. Cargo boats and high-speed ferries make the island voyage as well. Boat services are often suspended during rainy season and schedules are subject to weather conditions.

Bus & Minivans

The Thai bus service is widespread, convenient and phenomenally fast – nail-bitingly so. Reputable companies operate out of the government bus stations not the tourist centres. Starting at the top, VIP buses are the closest you will come to a rock star's tour bus. The seats recline, the air-con is frosty and an 'air hostess' dispenses refreshments and snacks. Various diminishing classes of air-con buses begin to strip away the extras until you're left with a fairly beat-up bus with an asthmatic cooling system.

For trips to nearby cities, minivans are a convenient option. They depart from the market instead of an out-of-town bus station and, in some cases, offer hotel drop-off.

For long-distance trips, check out schedules and/or purchase tickets the day before.

Car & Motorcycle

Cars and motorcycles can be rented in most tourist towns. Inspect the vehicle beforehand as fleets are often poorly maintained. Always verify that the vehicle is insured for liability before signing a rental contract, and ask to see the dated insurance documents.

Motorcycle travel is a popular way to get around Thailand. Motorcycle rental usually requires that you leave your passport as a deposit. Be sure to wear a helmet, especially on the islands where this law is enforced. Also wear protective clothing to reduce injury in the event of an accident. Drive slowly in wet conditions or on uneven pavement.

Thais drive on the left-hand side of the road – most of the time. Every two-lane road has an invisible third lane in the middle that all drivers use as a passing lane. The main rule to be aware of is that 'might makes right' and smaller vehicles always yield to bigger ones. Drivers usually use their horns to indicate that they are passing.

Hitching

It is uncommon to see people hitching, since bus travel is inexpensive and reliable. Hitching becomes an option where public transport isn't available. In this case you can usually catch a ride, but remember to use the Asian style of beckoning: hold your arm out towards the road, palm-side down and wave towards the ground.

That said, hitching is never entirely safe, and travellers who do so should understand that they are taking a small but potentially serious risk.

Local Transport

Săhmlór & Túk-Túk

Săhmlór (also written 'samlor'), meaning 'three wheels', are pedal rickshaws found mainly in small towns for short hops. Their modern replacements are the motorised túk-túk, named for the throaty cough of their two-stroke engines. In Bangkok, túk-túk drivers give all local transport a bad name. In other towns they tend to be more reliable.

You must bargain and agree on a fare before accepting a ride.

Sŏrngtăaou

Sŏrngtăaou (literally, 'two benches') are small pick-up trucks with a row of seats down each side. In some towns, sŏrngtăaou serve as public buses running regular, fixed-fare routes. But in tourist towns, sŏrngtăaou act as shared taxis or private charter; in this case agree on a fare beforehand.

Train

The **State Railway of Thailand** (SRT; www.railway.co.th) operates comfortable and moderately priced, but rather slow, services. All rail travel originates in Bangkok and radiates north, south and northeast. Trains are convenient for overnight travel between Bangkok and Chiang Mai and south to Chumphon or Surat Thani. The train can also dodge Bangkok traffic to Ayuthaya.

The SRT operates passenger trains in three classes – 1st, 2nd and 3rd – but each class varies depending on the train type (ordinary, rapid or express). Rapid and express trains make fewer stops than ordinary trains.

Fares are calculated from a base price with surcharges added for distance, class and train type. Extra charges are added for air-con and for sleeping berths (either upper or lower).

Advance bookings can be made from one to 60 days before your intended date of departure. You can make bookings in person from any train station. Train tickets can also be purchased at travel agencies, which usually add a service charge to the ticket price. If you are planning long-distance train travel from outside the country, you should email the **State Railway of Thailand** (passenger-ser@railway.co.th) at least two weeks before your journey. You will receive an email confirming the booking. Pick up and pay for tickets an hour before leaving at the scheduled departure train station.

Timor-Leste

Includes »

Best Colonial Relics

» Pousada de Maubisse (p797)

» Pousada de Baucau (p795)

» Maubara's fort (p797)

» Balibo's fort (p797)

» Fatusuba Fort (p798)

Best Places for Cultural Connections

» Australia Flag House (p797)

» Resistance Museum (p791)

» Santa Cruz Cemetery (p791)

» Chega! Exhibition (p790)

» Lospalos (p797)

Why Go?

With mountains to climb and untouched reefs to dive, Asia's newest country, Timor-Leste, is a winner. It's home to a youthful population and a diverse international presence that adds just the right amount of spice. Its capital, Dili, has all the bright lights, but venture out for wild cultural experiences. Stay in a grand Portuguese *pousada* on a misty hilltop, or at a quiet island ecolodge. Get rowdy dancing the night away at a Timorese wedding, journey down roads alongside herds of buffalo, then wind up through rainforests dotted with coffee plants. Keep an eye out for whales as you grip the cliffs along the north-coast road. Photogenic white sand beaches with aqua waters tempt swimmers, and for those who want to delve deeper, Dili-based dive companies have spent the past decade discovering world-class dive sites. Trailblaze your way through this amazing country; it's adventure with a smile.

When to Go

Dili

°C/°F **Temp** — **Rainfall** inches/mm

40/104 – 30/86 – 20/68 – 10/50 – 0/32 — 6/150 – 4/100 – 2/50 – 0

J F M A M J J A S O N D

May–Nov (Dry Season) There's little rainfall and good weather (though Dili gets a little dusty).

Sep The sun is bearing down during the excitement of the Tour de Timor bike race.

May The country is drying out as the Dili Marathon takes centre place.

DON'T MISS

Even if you're not a scuba diver, getting under the water in Timor-Leste is a must. Grab a snorkel and ask around for the best spot for **snorkelling**. You won't believe your eyes.

Fast Facts

» **Area** 15,007 sq km

» **Capital** Dili

» **Country Code** ☎670

» **Emergency** police ☎121, 723 0365; ambulance ☎723 3212; fire ☎723 0686

Exchange Rates

Australia	A$1	US$1.03
Canada	C$1	US$1.00
Euro zone	€1	US$1.32
Indonesia	1000Rp	US$0.11
Japan	¥100	US$1.20
NZ	NZ$1	US$0.81
UK	£1	US$1.58

Set Your Budget

» **Dorm bed** US$15–20

» **Local restaurant meal** US$3–$10

» **Snorkelling** US$10

Entering the Country

» **Nicolau Lobato International Airport** Taxi to centre US$10, airport transfer $18 (five minutes). Microlet (local bus) from main road US$0.25.

» **Dili Seaport** In central Dili, taxis around the city US$2.

At a Glance

» **Currency** US dollars. Anything under US$1 can be paid for in East Timorese Centavos (cv).

» **Language** Portuguese (official language), Bahasa Indonesia, Tetun and other local languages

» **Money** ATMs in Dili and Baucau. Major supermarkets and more expensive hotels take credit cards.

» **Visas** Visa on arrival at Dili airport or seaport; US$30 for 30 days. Most nationalities need a visa in advance for land border arrivals.

» **Mobile Phones** Good coverage throughout major population centres. Timor Telecom SIM cards can be used in unlocked phones.

ITINERARIES

One Week

From Dili it's off to the eastern end of the island, stopping along the spectacular coast before overnighting in Baucau. Use Baucau as a base for multinight trips to the colonial relic of Venilale and the Timor Village Hotel ecoresort at Loi Hunu. Then explore Com, the stunning views at Tutuala, and the stunning beach at Jaco Island. Return to Dili and cap off your trip by heading out to Atauro Island for a few nights.

One Month

As above, then head west to Batugade, close to the Indonesian border. Turn inland to Balibo for a slice of history, and on to Maliana, overlooking the verdant Nanura Plains. The next day head south via Bobonaro to Suai, with its pretty villages and beach, then turn east and head back into the mountains via either Ainaro or Same to Hatubuilico to climb Mt Ramelau. Next stop is Maubisse with its old Portuguese *pousada*, then back to Dili.

Essential Outdoor Activities

» **Diving and snorkelling, Dili** At the western end of Av de Portugal, the Pertamina Pier's pylons provide a habitat for countless sea creatures. Just west of the airport, an amazing array of sea critters at Tasitolu continues to amaze divers.

» **Trekking, Mt Ramelau** Watch the sunrise from Timor-Leste's highest peak: on a clear day you can see both coasts.

Timor-Leste Highlights

1 Go diving in **Dili** (p792) and enjoy being in one of the few cities in the world where the reef is just steps away from the urban centre

2 Snorkel and relax daytrip-style on **Atauro Island** (p794), or stay awhile at **Tua Kóin Eco-Village** (p794), a true ecoresort

3 See coffee plantations and misty valleys give way to views of the coast near **Maubisse** (p797) or **Mt Ramelau** (p797)

4 Chill out at **Oecussi** (p798), a barely visited laid-back enclave wedged between Indonesia and stunning reefs

5 Peek over at Jaco Island from open-air thatched rooms on Walu beach, **Tutuala** (p796)

6 Make the pilgrimage to Australia Flag House in **Balibo** (p797), near where five Australian-based journalists were killed in 1975

7 Cheer on the fit and adventurous during the **Dili Marathon** or **Tour de Timor** (p792)

DILI

POP 234,000

Dili is a city undergoing a rapid transformation, and while some changes seem at odds with common sense (oversized embassies lining prime beachfront land, for instance), most changes capture the essence of reconstruction in Timor-Leste. Burnt-out buildings still form a small part of the scenery, as do century-old banyan trees on the foreshore.

Dili is a good place to recharge batteries (literally) and base yourself for jaunts into the regions; it's a chance to indulge in international food, buy supplies and meet some of the locals and expats. Dili itself spreads from the airport, along the waterfront and all the way to the Jesus statue in the east. Most of the action occurs on the waterfront, or one or two blocks north of it. You'll find travellers' hubs at East Timor Backpackers (p792) and Castaway Bar (p793).

Sights

Waterfront WATERFRONT

From children covered in seaweed to serious boatmen reading the weather conditions opposite the grand **Palácio do Governo** (Government Palace), Dili has a waterfront with a distinctive Timorese personality. It stretches for kilometres in a quasi-boomerang shape, with **Farol lighthouse** beaming at one end, and Lita Supermarket at the other. Further west is an esplanade dotted with gigantic 'look at me' embassies, which front vibrant evening **fish & chicken stalls**.

FREE **Chega! Exhibition** MUSEUM

(331 0315; Estrada de Balide; 9am-noon & 2-5pm Mon-Fri) This must-see exhibition is housed in a prison where countless human rights violations occurred and hundreds of resistance figures were interned by the Indonesian military. *Chega!* ('no more/stop/enough' in Portuguese) is the title of the report of the Timor-Leste Commission for Reception, Truth and Reconciliation (CAVR) and the focus of the well-researched and presented displays. The exhibition, set in the prison buildings and cells, gives visitors a glimpse of the realities of the notorious prison. There is a public library and coffee shop on site. Bookings are essential and can be made by phone.

Cape Fatucama & the Jesus Statue STATUE

Around 7km east of town on Cape Fatucama is the hard-to-miss **Jesus statue**, a popular morning and evening exercise spot for locals and expats. Expect calm beaches, and bars where you sink into the sand while sipping beers and watching beach volleyball.

Dili

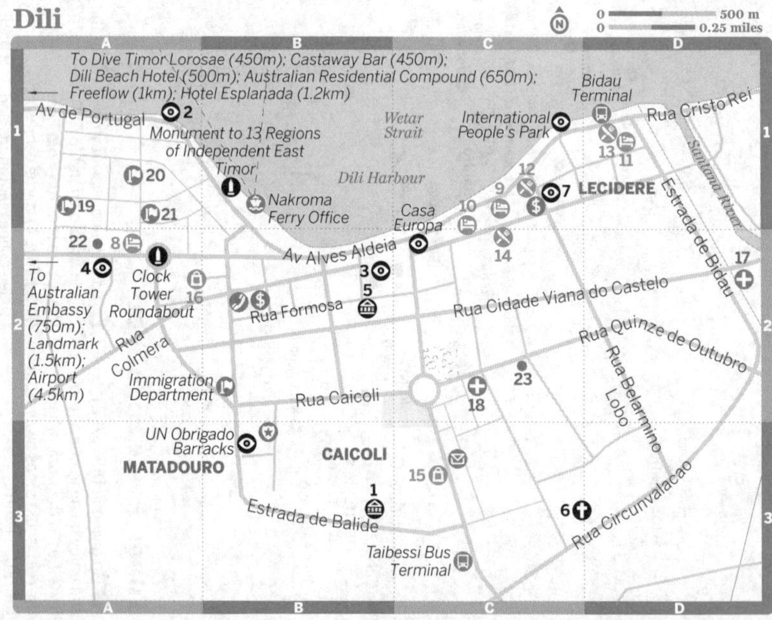

From the cape, the views of turquoise bays and green-covered mountains are stunning. As you climb the well-marked path up to Jesus, look for a little path after the last of 14 grottoes. It leads down to an often-deserted beach, known as **Jesus Backside beach**. A taxi to the statue from town should cost US$5, though it can be difficult getting back.

Arte Moris ART GALLERY
(Av dos Mártires de Pátria, Comoro; admission free; ⏲9am-6pm Mon-Sat) There's a distinct Bob Marley/boho feel to Arte Moris, a residential art gallery in what was Dili's domed Indonesian-era museum. Downstairs the collection features creative woodcarvings and paintings sprayed onto *tais* (woven cloth). Those with artistic bones and a yearning to hang around are welcome to impart knowledge, and you'll get to hang out with the esteemed theatrical troupe Bibi Bulak, which calls the centre home. Travelling west from town, the compound is over the Comoro bridge, just before the airport.

DON'T MISS

TRIVIA NIGHTS

Dili's social event of the week is Trivia Night. Test your knowledge each Tuesday at 7.30pm at Dili Beach Hotel and profits go to a local medical clinic.

Dili

Sights

1	Chega! Exhibition	B3
2	Farol Lighthouse	A1
3	Palácio do Governo	B2
4	Presidential Palace	A2
5	Resistance Museum	B2
6	Santa Cruz Cemetery	C3
7	Xanana Gusmão Museum, Art Gallery & Reading Room	C1

Activities, Courses & Tours

	Compass Charters	(see 22)

Sleeping

8	East Timor Backpackers	A2
9	Hotel Dili	C1
10	Rocella	C1
11	Venture Hotel	D1

Eating

12	Kebab Club	C1
13	Lita Supermarket	D1
14	Starco	C2

Shopping

15	Alola Foundation	C3
16	Tais Market	A2

Information

17	Dili Nacional Hospital	D2
18	Foho Osan Mean Farmacia	C2
19	Indonesian Embassy	A1
20	Irish Embassy	A1
21	New Zealand Embassy	A1

Transport

22	Tiger Fuel	A2
23	Timor Tour & Travel	C2

Santa Cruz Cemetery CEMETERY
On 12 November 1991, Indonesian soldiers fired on a peaceful memorial procession at the Santa Cruz Cemetery. Although exact figures aren't known, it's estimated by experts that at least 280 civilians died, many of them after they were rounded up and trucked away by the military. British journalist Max Stahl filmed the bloody attack, and his footage features in the documentary *In Cold Blood*. The massacre at the Santa Cruz Cemetery is cited as a turning point in the independence struggle.

Xanana Gusmão Museum, Art Gallery & Reading Room MUSEUM
(☎332 2831; Rua Belarmino Lobo; admission free; ⏲10am-6pm Mon-Fri, to 4pm Sat) Housing loads of memorabilia from its namesake, the Xanana Reading Room is a small and busy library with a book-swap facility and souvenirs. The adjoining internet facility charges US$3 per hour.

Resistance Museum MUSEUM
(Rua Formosa; admission US$1; ⏲9.30am-5.30pm Tue-Sat, 1.30-5.30pm Sun) This museum commemorates the 24-year struggle against the Indonesians. The story of Falintil's resistance is brought to life with a timeline, photos, and exhibits of the weapons and tools of communication the East Timorese used in their fight for independence.

Presidential Palace NOTABLE BUILDING
(Av dos Mártires de Pátria) During construction of his palace, President José Ramos-Horta thought that such a large compound was a waste for one man. He wanted to share his palace with his people so there are no large walls or gun-toting soldiers. Instead he recruited spear-wielding warriors in traditional dress, installed a children's pool and

LANGUAGE? WHICH LANGUAGE?

Most Timorese are multilingual and not only speak their own dialect (Tetun; also known as Tetum) and their regional dialect (one of 16), but also, for the older folk, Portuguese (the official language), and, for those who were educated or working between 1976 and 1999, Bahasa Indonesia. A few Tetun words go a long way, and certainly any attempt to communicate in Tetun will be appreciated. Lonely Planet's *East Timor Phrasebook* is a handy (and compact) introduction.

playground and constructed a dozen open-air bungalows with around-the-clock free wireless internet for all. There's also a Tyrannosaurus Rex skeleton in the foyer.

Activities

The reef fringing the entire north coast of Timor-Leste provides spectacular **diving** and **snorkelling** opportunities. Many sites, including the legendary K41 east of town, are easily accessed by walking in from the beach, with dramatic drop-offs just 10m offshore in parts.

FreeFlow DIVING
(☎723 4614; www.freeflowdiving.blogspot.com; Av de Portugal) FreeFlow offers guided shore dives for US$40 per dive, including transport and gear. Safari trips include delicious lunches. There's also a full range of PADI courses from US$350.

Dive Timor Lorosae DIVING
(☎723 7092; www.divetimor.com; Av de Portugal) This dive centre offers shore dives (US$45) and day-trip diving around Atauro Island, including two dives from US$165 per person. It also has a well-stocked gear shop, training pool and runs the full range of PADI courses.

Compass Charters WHALE-WATCHING/DIVING
(☎723 0966; info@compassadventuretours.com; Av dos Mártires de Pátria) Compass specialises in boat dives to the premier Atauro Island and north coast sites starting at US$50 per person with a group of six to eight divers. It's next to Tiger Fuel.

Dili City of Peace Marathon RUNNING
(www.dilimarathon.com) This full (42km) and half (21km) marathon is held each May, beginning at the Palicio Governu. It's not for the faint hearted, though there is a 7 km fun run.

Tour de Timor CYCLING
(www.tourdetimor.com; registration US$1000) Each September up to 300 cyclists make their way along the roads of Timor-Leste. Cheer them on or join in the rugged five-day challenge.

Sleeping

Dili doesn't have many cheap beds, and until the influx of UN and NGO staff wanes, prices will remain high.

East Timor Backpackers HOSTEL $
(☎755 7578; info@easttimorbackpackers.com; Av dos Mártires de Pátria; dm US$12; ❄) While it doesn't have the best beds in town, this is *the* meeting place for backpackers. There's a bar and kitchen out the back. It also rents bikes (guests/nonguests US$3/5).

Rocella HOTEL $$
(☎723 7993; Rua Presidente Nicolau Lobato 18; incl breakfast & internet r US$35; ❄@) Rooms here are comfortable and clean. The ostentatiously lit bar actually has a pleasant atmosphere and the family who run the place can cook up a Portuguese storm (meals US$7 to US$20).

Vila Harmonia GUESTHOUSE $
(☎725 8265; vilaharmonia@hotmail.com; Av Liberdade Emprensa 418, Becora; per person US$10) About 3km from town, this mishmash of rooms – including an *uma adat* (traditional house) – is worth staying at for the unusual sculptures that pay tribute to Timor-Leste's long-time supporters.

Venture Hotel HOTEL $$
(☎331 3276; venture_hotel@hotmail.com; Rua Filomena de Camera; r US$23-33; ❄≋) Stick a bunch of portable rooms together, insert air conditioners and this is what you get. There's nothing fancy about this place, especially the shared bathrooms, though the pool's a welcome addition and there are good views from the upstairs gym.

Hotel Dili HOTEL $$
(☎331 3958; www.hoteldili.com; Av dos Direitos Humanos; incl breakfast & internet r US$45-140; ❄@) Hotel Dili offers chilled, air-conditioned rooms, good tropical-fruit breakfasts and a waterfront location. The cheapest rooms share bathrooms; all rooms have high-speed internet and satellite TV.

SPLURGE: HOTEL ESPLANADA

The **Esplanada** (☎331 3088; www.hotelesplanada.com; Ave de Portugal; r incl breakfast US$120; ❄@≋) has a great location right on the water and a restaurant that makes the most of the views. Two-storey blocks surround a pleasant pool oasis at this modern and vaguely stylish compound. After lounging about the spacious grounds, head up to the bar-restaurant for a cool drink as the sun sets over the sea.

Eating

TOP CHOICE **Castaway Bar** INTERNATIONAL $
(Av de Portugal; mains US$6-16; ⏲breakfast, lunch & dinner) A very popular two-storey joint overlooking the western waterfront. Crowds enjoy pizzas, steaks, burgers and Asian fare while taking in the cool breezes. Open all day; be sure to have a look at the lunch and dinner specials. This is one of the best places in the west of Dili for a drink.

Fish & chicken stalls MARKET $
(opposite the Australian Residential Compound; ⏲dinner) After sunset this stretch of road is a-smokin' (literally); fill up on delicious and simple chicken and fish dishes from the various stalls for US$0.25 to US$3.

Kebab Club TURKISH $
(Rua Belarmino Lobo; mains US$4-7) Darn authentic Turkish fare, including delicious kebabs, velvety hummus and perfect baklava. The charming owner serves it all up with a smile.

Starco INDONESIAN, CHINESE $
(Rua Presidente Nicolau Lobato; meals US$4-5; ⏲lunch & dinner) You'll find tasty and fresh Indonesian and Chinese fare at good prices. It is easy to find and centrally located next to the Plaza Hotel.

Lita SUPERMARKET $
(Av dos Direitos Humanos) Sells everything from Tim Tams to bug repellent to fishing tackle.

Drinking

Caz Bar BAR
(Area Branca) Sink back in your chair on the beach at this popular place that tops the line-up of beachside joints east of town. At sunset, it's a toss-up between a beer and a US$1 fresh coconut milk.

Shopping

Alola Foundation HANDICRAFTS
(www.alolafoundation.org; Av Bispo de Medeiros) Alola sells *tais,* sculptures, soaps and other crafts from around the country to support its work with the women and children of Timor-Leste.

Tais Market HANDICRAFTS
(Rua Sebastiao da Costa) A *tais* is a piece of East Timorese woven cloth and each region possesses its own distinctive style. This market has *tais* of varying quality from all over the country.

Information

As yet there's no tourist office, however hotel staff are always a good source of info.

CAST OF CHARACTERS

Two men form the face of modern-day Timor-Leste.

Xanana Gusmão is Timor-Leste's charismatic prime minister. Gusmão was a leader of guerrilla forces from 1978 until 1992, when he was captured and imprisoned in Jakarta. He became the first president of the country, and earned the enmity of many of his old Fretilin brethren by breaking with the party after independence. Following the troubled 2007 parliamentary elections, Gusmão was named prime minister. He led the National Congress for Timorese Reconstruction (CNRT) party, which favours a pragmatic approach to relations with neighbours such as Australia and Indonesia. His wife is Australian-born Kirsty Sword Gusmão, who runs the prominent charity the Alola Foundation.

Jośe Ramos-Horta is the magnetic Nobel Prize winner who spent 20 years in exile during the Indonesian occupation. He took over as prime minister after Alkatiri was forced from office in 2006, and was elected president in 2007 with a huge margin, despite the fact that he disassociates himself from any political party. In 2008 he was shot during an alleged assassination attempt and recovered in Darwin, Australia. Single and known for his courtly ways, Ramos-Horta has said that all the nation's women are his first ladies.

Dangers & Annoyances

Be aware that violent outbreaks can and do occur quickly, so stay clear of simmering trouble. Theft can be a problem. The city is all but deserted after dark, when you should take extra care. See p804 for general information on safety.

Internet Access

Try Timor Telecom or Xanana Gusmão Museum, Art Gallery & Reading Room for internet access ($3 per hour). Those staying in Timor-Leste longer may want to purchase a 3G USB dongle (which Timor Telecom calls a 'NetBoot 3G pen'). It's US$90; prepaid access starts at US$59 for 1GB.

Medical Services

Medical services in Timor-Leste are limited; serious cases may require evacuation to Darwin. Check with your embassy for other options.

Australian Residential Compound (☎331 1555; Av de Portugal, Marconi) You don't have to be Australian to see the doctor here.

Dili Nacional Hospital (☎331 1008; Rua Cidade Viana do Castelo) A cadre of Western volunteers assists locals at this busy place just east of Estrada de Bidau.

Foho Osan Mean Farmacia (☎725 6978; Rua Quinze de Outubro; ⌚8am-9pm Mon-Sat, 8am-1pm Sun) Offers consultations (from US$3 to US$10) and pharmaceuticals.

Money

Banks are generally open between 9am and 3.30pm Monday to Friday.

ANZ (☎332 4800; www.anz.com/timorleste; cnr Rua Presidente Nicolau Lobato & Belarmino Lobo) The ATM dispenses US dollars. Also has ATMs at the airport, Lita and Tiger Fuel.

Western Union (☎332 1586; Rua José Maria Marques) Transfers funds internationally.

Post & Telephone

Post office (Av Bishop de Medeiros; ⌚8am-5pm Mon-Fri) This new central post office is opposite the Alola Foundation.

Timor Telecom (☎332 2245; www.timortelecom.tp; Rua Presidente Nicolau Lobato; ⌚8am-6.30pm Mon-Fri, 8am-6pm Sat) Has phone and internet services.

Getting There & Away

For details of getting in and out of Dili by air see p805.

The **Nakroma ferry office** (Av de Portugal; ⌚8.30am-5.30pm) is in the large building at the port. Buy your tickets one day in advance. Ferries for Oecussi (12 hours) leave at around 5pm Monday and Thursday, returning Tuesday and Friday (see p806). The Atauro Island service (US$5, two hours) departs Saturdays at 9am. See p806 for more details.

Dili's bus 'terminals' (which are actually more like shabby shelters) are served by taxis and *mikrolet* (small minibuses). Buses are more frequent in the morning.

Tasitolu Terminal, west of the airport, is the hub for destinations to the west of the country (Ermera, Maliana and Liquiçá). Buses travelling to the east (Baucau, Lospalos, Viqueque etc) leave from Bidau Terminal, on the waterfront near Santana River. The Taibessi Terminal, at the huge Taibessi market, is the stop for transport to Maubisse, Same and Suai.

Getting Around

Mikrolet (US$0.25) buzz about on designated routes during daylight hours. They stop frequently over relatively short distances, so choosing a taxi might be quicker.

See p806 for car-hire options. Cars are useful for night travel, but walking and using taxis should suffice otherwise.

Smart yellow (unmetered) taxis abound in Dili, and if you negotiate before you get in, most trips cost US$1. If you find, or hear of a good driver, ask for their mobile number and see if they'll be your night driver, as streets are usually taxi-free by 9pm.

ATAURO ISLAND

After busy Dili, Atauro Island seems positively deserted. Its sandy beaches are gateways to broad fringing reefs and there's great snorkelling off the pier at Beloi and in front of Tua Kóin. Walking trails lead through savannah and remnants of tropical forest.

Atauro Island's location, 30km from Dili over a section of sea 3km deep in parts, made it perfect for use as a jail by both the Portuguese and Indonesian governments. Dili's dive shops (p792) arrange underwater tours; you can arrange snorkelling trips with local fishing boats from US$15, or swim out. Ask the locals about the many hiking possibilities.

Sleeping

Tua Kóin Eco-Village GUESTHOUSE **$$**
(☎723 6085; www.atauroisland.com; Vila; per person incl meals r US$25) This Timorese-owned and operated ecovillage holds true to its name. Pad over from your solar-powered thatched-roof cabin to the composting toilet and open-roof shower room. Friendly staff can organise everything from a massage

LOCAL KNOWLEDGE

WHY DIVE TIMOR-LESTE?

Expat Kym Smithies has been diving Timor-Leste's sites since 2002.

What's so good about diving in Timor-Leste? Only 40 minutes from Dili you can dive pristine reefs filled with small colourful marine life. Healthy, colourful coral, small shoals of fish, the occasional reef shark and turtle, and a wonderful variety of macro-life are guaranteed. Nudibranch lovers will enjoy spotting a large variety of different species as well as frogfish, seahorses, mimic octopus and more.

Any particular highlights? Atauro Island is one of the few places where you may see large pelagic creatures like turtles, hammerhead sharks, whales and dolphins (mostly from the boat). Strong currents mean that most dives are drift dives.

to transport to the island and back. Book ahead.

Barry's Eco-Lodge GUESTHOUSE $$
(☎723 6084; boyhinton@yahoo.com.au; per person incl meals r US$30) Just north of the ferry dock in Beloi, this lodge is run by an Australian (Barry) and his family. The sun-drenched thatched cabins are right on the beach; the one Barry calls his writer's cabin has mesmerising views from an upper level. Book ahead.

Getting There & Around

Compass Charters (☎723 0966; info@compassadventuretours.com; Av dos Mártires de Pátria, next to Tiger Fuel, Dili) runs a daily water-taxi service to Atauro Island (US$30 one way, 90 minutes). This is by far the best and most reliable way to get to the island.

The **Nakroma ferry** (☎728 09638; Av de Portugal, Dili) departs from Dili every Saturday at 9am and returns at 4pm, taking two hours each way. Fares for foreigners are US$5 each way. Fishing boats and outriggers also makes the run between Vila and Dili (up to US$15, three hours) several days a week, depending on the tides. It is not regular, nor especially safe.

EAST OF DILI

With your own wheels (or on painfully slow public transport) you'll stumble across lime-green rice paddies, mangroves and idyllic beaches where buffalos (and the occasional crocodile) roam. Some of the best diving in the country is found just off shore.

Baucau

While Baucau is best known for its beach, it's actually a long way down (5km) to the water from the Old Town, and even further from the bland, Indonesian-built New Town *(Kota Baru)*. The Old Town boasts a Portuguese-era **mercado municipal** (municipal market) and roadside **town market** where pyramid-shaped piles of potatoes, neat bunches of greens and mounds of maize form a colourful patchwork on the pavement. Head down through the market and take a left to spot the pink **Pousada**. A right turn at the roundabout takes you towards Lospalos, or keep travelling down the lush ravine to find the delightful palm-fringed beach of **Osolata**.

Sleeping & Eating

Pousada de Baucau HOTEL $$
(☎724 1111; Rua de Catedral, Old Town; incl breakfast r US$65; ❄@) Despite its eerie history as a torture centre during Indonesian times, this large, salmon-pink building is still one of Timor-Leste's nicest hotels, with *tais* bedheads, timber floorboards and air con. The restaurant has good Portuguese food (meals from US$5).

Melita Guesthouse GUESTHOUSE $
(☎725 0267; Rua Vao Redi Bahu, Old Town; r per person US$15) Enjoy clean rooms with bathrooms and fans (and air-con if you need it). There is a palm-tree-and-sea view from the common area. To find it take a left at the Pousada roundabout.

Baucau Beach Bungalows BUNGALOWS $
(☎730 4371; Osolata; r per person US$15) Choose from a simple thatched bungalow that sleeps six, or one of three rooms in a neighbouring Indonesian-style house (with shared kitchen and lounge). Meals can be arranged for US$6, with fish sourced from the local fishing boats.

Restaurante Amalia PORTUGUESE $
(☎726 2330; Old Town; mains US$4-6; ⏲noon-10pm) Take a shady spot on the outdoor terrace and enjoy the sea views, along with

delicious Portuguese-style meals served with a smile.

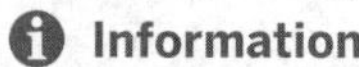

Information

The characterless New Town overlooks the Old Town. On the road linking the two, **Timor Telecom** (9am-5pm; US$1 per hr) has internet access, and there's currency exchange and an ANZ ATM next door.

Getting There & Away

Numerous buses each day drive the 123km between Dili and Baucau (US$3, three hours). Buses also head to Viqueque (US$2, two hours) and Lospalos (US$4, 3½ hours). Ask to be dropped off in the Old Town.

South of Baucau

South of Baucau are the lush hills where Fretilin members hid during the Indonesian occupation.

After 28km of rugged road you come to the large and impressive buildings of **Venilale**, a town wedged between Mt Matebian in the east and Mt Mundo Perdido (Lost World; 1775m) in the west. The road deteriorates along the 16km to the misty village of **Ossu**. Some 9km south of here take a sharp left at the sign for **Timor Village Hotel** (Loi Hunu; 331 0616; www.tvh.tl; incl breakfast d US$20/35), a spotless hydro-powered hotel set on a hillside near a surging river and waterfall. The meals are good and you can arrange hiking guides here. Travel past roadside waterfalls and white cliffs to the sprawling town of **Viqueque**, 63km from Baucau. The new town has a market and an abundance of Indonesian monuments. **Finlos Restaurant and Guesthouse** (725 2827; incl breakfast r US$10) is a spotless place to stay about 2km north of the centre.

Buses and *mikrolet* run daily between Viqueque and Baucau (US$2, two hours) and on to Dili (US$8, three hours).

Around Baucau

South of Baucau is **Mt Matebian** (2315m). Topped with a statue of Christ and known as 'Mountain of the Souls', this holy place attracts thousands of pilgrims annually for All Souls Day (2 November). About 15km from Baucau is **Molia**, turn-off point for the end-of-the-road village of **Quelicai**. On the right-hand side of the road between the market and the church is the green **Matebian Guesthouse** (726 8812; whitehead.simon@ymail.com; per person incl meals US$25), a family-run guesthouse that offers walking tours to Matebian and the family's *uma adat* (traditional house).

One or two *mikrolet* make the 33km journey from Baucau to Quelicai in the mornings and early afternoons (US$1, 1½ hours), or you can charter one from Baucau for US$17.

COM

You're literally at the end of the road in Com, a town focused on fishing and tourism. There's excellent snorkelling and a good, long beach (although it's beaten by the one at the 171km marker to the west).

Guesthouses line this stretch, as does the very average shell-studded **Com Beach Resort** (728 3311; r US$25-120;). The best is the beachside, *uma adat*–styled **Kati Guesthouse** (732 4294; r US$20), which has nine small rooms (with shared bathrooms) and meals.

You'll be eating at the resort's **Ocean View Restaurant** (mains US$5-15) unless you book ahead at a guesthouse.

There are regular *mikrolet* from Lospalos to Com (US$2, one hour).

TUTUALA & JACO ISLAND

The 50km of road from Lautem to Tutuala ventures past the shimmering waters of Lake Ira Lalaro, a few stilted Fataluku houses and through Nino Konis Santana National Park (p802). The road ends on a bluff in Tutuala village, where there are sweeping views out to sea and a practically deserted Portuguese *pousada*. Push on and tackle the steep 8km track down to **Walu**, a stunning white-sand beach. Turn left after the descent and you'll find thatched cabins at the community-run **Walu Sere** (729 9076; r US$15). Fall asleep listening to waves lapping and wake to the stunning vision of Jaco Island, just offshore across the turquoise waters. Jaco has a sacred meaning to the Timorese, and was once the hiding place of Xanana Gusmão. No one lives there (or stays overnight), however, fisherfolk can zoom you over on their outriggers for US$8. In the two minutes the trip takes you'll be transported to an island paradise where amazing white sands circle a forested centre.

Staff at Walu Sere can organise tours of the local rock-art caves.

You can take a daily *mikrolet* to/from Lospalos (US$2, three hours), or you can charter one from Com for about US$20.

LOSPALOS

Lospalos, home to the Fataluku-language speakers, is mostly of interest for its market, nearby caves and Fataluku houses. A good budget choice for accommodation is **27@** (☎766 9115; r per person US$15). Look for the traditional roof behind the office of the Plan children's charity. The five clean rooms have mosquito nets and a shared bathroom. The name derives from the day in August 1999 when the owner's husband was among scores of locals killed by the retreating Indonesians.

Buses and *mikrolet* run between Lospalos and Baucau (US$4, 3½ hours).

WEST OF DILI

The border with Indonesian West Timor is four hours west of Dili along a coast-gripping road punctuated by small villages selling differing wares.

Liquiçá has some grand Portuguese-era buildings, and its bustling market is a few kilometres east of the main town.

At beachside **Maubara**, 40km from Dili, there's a Portuguese restaurant in the rejuvenated 17th century Dutch **fort** and a handicraft market. There's accommodation at a **retreat** (☎725 1767; per person incl meals US$30) run by Carmelite nuns 3km west of town. Look for the 'Maubara–Fatubessi' sign and follow the track up. *Mikrolets* depart Dili and stop at both villages (US$1, one hour). Buses from Dili pass through the skimpy border town of **Batugade** (111km from Dili); see p806 for details on the border crossing into West Timor.

WORTH A TRIP

BALIBO

Inland from Batugade is the mountain town of **Balibo**, where five Australia-based journalists were killed by Indonesian soldiers in 1975.

The Australian flag the journalists painted for protection is still visible on **Australia Flag House**, which is now a community centre with a memorial inside.

An early 18th-century Portuguese fort stands high on the hill, and from 2012/2013 this should be open as Balibo Fort House Hotel (http://balibo forthotel.com).

The hills of West Timor are in plain view over the rice fields adjoining **Maliana**, 26km inland from Balibo. The place to stay here is Timorese-owned **Tansos** (r US$20), which has clean rooms with shared bathrooms and great views of the plains. Off the road to **Bobonaro** is the rebuilt swimming pool, aka **Be Manis** (Hot Springs). Continue on to **Suai** (though roads can be diabolical during the wet season). You can also do a round trip to **Same** and **Maubisse** from here.

SOUTH OF DILI

From bare winding passes to rainforest canopies that shade coffee beans, the area south of Dili shows how diverse this country is. Coffee-country grabs you in **Aileu** before you hit the true cloud-dwelling town of Maubisse.

Maubisse

ELEV 1400M

Waking up in chilly Maubisse, 70km from Dili, and watching clouds rising, uncovering the village below, is a highlight of travelling in Timor-Leste. Do this from the best bed in town at the historic, hilltop **Pousada de Maubisse** (☎724 9567; per person r Mon-Thu US$17, Fri & Sat US$56, Sun US$22), formerly the governor's residence. Great food (mains US$6) and gorgeous grounds make for great-value weekdays. A cheaper weekend option is the sparkling **Café Maubisse** (☎727 4756; per person US$10) opposite Maubisse's elaborate church. There are several restaurants near the buzzing **market** on the southern side of town.

Buses depart from Dili for Maubisse (US$3, three hours) each morning.

Hatubuilico & Mt Ramelau

Wild roses grow by the road and mountain streams trickle through the teeny town of **Hatubuilico**, located at the base of Mt Ramelau (2963m). Stay at the eight-room **Pousada Alecrim Namrau** (☎730 4366; Rua Gruta Ramelau Hun 1; per person r US$10), where meals can be arranged for US$2.50. The uniquely decorated guesthouse is run by the village chief, who can arrange a guide (US$10) to get you up the mountain – and up at 3am in time to reach the peak for sunrise.

Hiking from the village to the Virgin Mary statue at the top of Mt Ramelau takes around three hours; with a 4WD you can

GETTING TO INDONESIA

Getting to the border: Catch a direct Dili–Kupang bus through **Timor Tour & Travel** (☎333 1014; Rua Quinze de Outubro 17, Dili); if booking from Kupang, call +62 0380 881 543. **Paradise Tour & Travel** (☎728 6673, 723 5678; Rua Mártires da Pátria, Dili) offers the same service; if booking from Kupang, call +62 0394 471543. Services depart each morning (US$20, 12 hours); book in advance.

It's slightly cheaper but harder work to catch a local bus to Batugade (US$5). Walk through both border checkpoints and catch local transport on the other side (US$3 to Atambua, then US$7 Kupang; 8 hours).

At the border: You'll need an Indonesian visa, available from the Indonesian Embassy in Dili (p804). Usual business hours apply.

drive 2.5km to a meadow from where it's a two-hour walk to the top. The trail is a wide walking path, with plenty of evidence of use by horses, and is very easy to follow. An open-air church sits on a plateau at the 2700m mark. From the peak the south and north coast is visible. Sunrise will give you chills, both down your spine and up your arms (temperatures average 5°C).

From Maubisse, the Hatubuilico turn-off is at the 81km post; you'll reach the village after 18km. If the road is passable, *angguna* (tray trucks) travel from Maubisse to Hatubuilico on Wednesdays and Saturdays. The price depends on the number of passengers, but the trip should cost around US$2 and take three hours.

Same & Betano

Same (Sar-may), 43km south of Maubisse, is a lush town at the base of a picturesque valley. There's a great little **handicrafts market** in the centre and a couple of good places to stay.

Samata Backpackers (☎741 5215; samatabackpackers@hotmail.com; per person incl breakfast US$15) can organise treks ($US5 per person) and a bed. If you've got this far, it is worth making the simple 45-minute journey to the quiet black-sand beach at Betano (27km). From here, in dry season, you can journey east over narrow tracks through crocodile-infested mangroves to Viqueque (this takes six or more hours).

Angguna run frequently between Maubisse and Same (US$3, two hours), and between Same and Betano (US$1, one hour).

Suai

Suai, the south coast's main town, sprawls 5km inland and is a confusing collection of villages. The main town, Debos, is dominated by a recently rebuilt cathedral, where, in September 1999, East Timorese were pushed to their deaths from the balcony. The now-demolished Our Lady of Fatima Church, also the scene of a massacre, is today the site of a memorial to 'Black September'. Sleep at the **Fronteria Guesthouse** (per person US$10) and dine on Malaysian at chic **Kamenasa Restaurant** (meals US$10).

Angguna run between Suai and Maubisse (around US$2, at least four hours), via Ainaro (with its colourful church) or Same. You can also get here via Maliana.

OECUSSI

POP 63,000

There are reasons to feel sorry for Oecussi: it's part of Timor-Leste yet it's surrounded on three sides by Indonesian West Timor; its only direct link with Dili is a twice-weekly ferry and it often seems to be forgotten by international NGOs and even, occasionally, by its own government. However, Oecussi is a Cinderella-in-waiting. It's fronted by long stretches of beach and reef, is the source of some of the most beautiful *tais* in the country and even has pools of hot mud bubbling in its southernmost region.

Pantemakassar, aka Oecussi town, is (literally) a one-taxi town. It's a flat, spread-out town with so little going on that any movement seems surprising. There are frequent sightings of dugong in the waters here, and the sheer coral drop-off about 20m offshore augurs well for **snorkelling**, though a 'croc watch' is essential. Just 1.5km to its south you can climb up to the old Portuguese fort **Fatusuba**, which is a whisper of its former self. Travel 5km along the coast west of Pantemakassar and you'll find **Lifau**, the site of the original Portuguese settlement. A rock-studded monument commemorates the first landing. The best beach begins 2km east of town on **Pantai Mahata**, which ends at a stunning red-rock headland.

Hot mud (for bathing in!) is found near the southern town of **Passabe**.

The cleanest digs are at **Rao Homestay & Restaurant** (☎738 9352; s/d US$15/20). Beachfront **Apartment Lifau** (☎728 3777; rooms US$10) has potential and sea views. **Restaurant Aries** does a filling *nasi rendang* for US$1.25. Internet is available at **Timor Telecom** (Rua Francisco Mousino; ⊙8am-3pm Mon-Fri) east of the traffic circle. The **Nakroma ferry** (☎728 0963; Av de Portugal, Dili; economy/business class US$4/14; ⊙9am-5pm) travels from Dili to Oecussi (12 hours) on Monday and Thursday nights. The return departure is around 5.30pm the following evening. In Pantemakassar the office is opposite the dock.

You'll need an Indonesian visa to get from Oecussi to West Timor overland (available in Dili). *Ojeks* (boys on motorbikes) can give you a lift from the border to town for a few dollars.

UNDERSTAND TIMOR-LESTE

Timor-Leste Today

Life after independence was turbulent, with a series of violent events (communal conflict, violence between the army and police and an assumed attempted coup) leaving many wondering: when do the good times start?

Well, finally, for many, the good times *have* started. The nation is playing host to international events and petroleum revenues are flowing from the Timor Sea. Timorese-owned businesses are in operation. The international presence is still here and newcomers arrive daily.

Fretilin, which led the struggle for independence during the Indonesian occupation, suffered from divisions in 2005. Prime Minister Mari Alkatiri sacked one third of the army in March 2006 and, in the ensuing months of rioting, more than 150,000 people fled their homes. Relative peace only returned after public demonstrations forced Alkatiri to resign, and the UN force was beefed up again. In 2007, after a year as acting prime minister, José Ramos-Horta was elected president of Timor-Leste with 70% of the vote. The vote for prime minister was not as clear-cut. Xanana Gusmão's National Congress for Timorese Reconstruction (CNRT) came second to Fretilin, winning 24% of the votes to Fretilin's 29%. However, CNRT quickly formed a coalition with other parties and Gusmão was sworn in as prime minister. Angry Fretilin supporters rioted, causing damage around the country and boosting the numbers of the more than 100,000 people already living in crowded internally displaced persons camps.In February 2008, Ramos-Horta was shot and injured near his home during an alleged attempted coup led by former naval commander and Timor-Leste Defence Force (F-FDTL) Major Alfreido Reinado. Reinado, who had been playing a cat-and-mouse game with Australian forces since escaping from jail in 2006, was killed at the scene by Ramos-Horta's security. Since 2008 Timor-Leste has been a safer and more stable country. The UN and International Stabilisation Force (Australian and New Zealand forces) will remain in the country until (at least) the presidential and parliamentary elections in 2012.

History

Portugal Settles In

Little is known of Timor before AD 1500, although Chinese and Javanese traders visited the island from at least the 13th century, and possibly as early as the 7th century. These traders searched the coastal settlements for aromatic sandalwood and beeswax. Portuguese traders arrived between 1509 and 1511, but it wasn't until 1642 that the Topasses (descendents of Dominicans from nearby islands) established the first Portuguese settlement at Lifau in Oecussi and set about converting the Timorese to Catholicism.

To counter the Portuguese, the Dutch established a base at Kupang in western Timor in 1653. The Portuguese appointed an administrator to Lifau in 1656, but the Topasses went on to become a law unto themselves, driving out the Portuguese governor in 1705.

By 1749 the Topasses controlled central Timor and marched on Kupang, but the Dutch won the ensuing battle, expanding their control of western Timor in the process. On the Portuguese side, after more attacks from the Topasses in Lifau, the colonial base was moved east to Dili in 1769.

The 1859 Treaty of Lisbon divided Timor, giving Portugal the eastern half, together with the north-coast pocket of Oecussi; this was formalised in 1904. Portuguese Timor was a sleepy and neglected outpost ruled through a traditional system of *liurai* (local chiefs).

Control outside Dili was limited and it wasn't until the 20th century that the Portuguese intervened in a major way in the interior.

World War II

In 1941, Australia sent a small commando force into Portuguese Timor to counter the Japanese, deliberately breaching the colony's neutral status. Although the military initiative angered neutral Portugal and dragged Portuguese Timor into the Pacific War, it slowed the Japanese expansion. Australia's success was largely due to the support it received from the locals, including young *creados* (young Timorese boys who assisted Australian servicemen during WWII). In 1942 the Portuguese handed control of Portuguese Timor to the Japanese. Japanese soldiers razed villages, seized food and killed Timorese in areas where Australians were operating. By the end of the war, between 40,000 and 60,000 Timorese had died.

Portugal Pulls Out, Indonesia Invades

After WWII the colony reverted to Portuguese rule. After the Carnation Revolution in Portugal on 25 April 1974, Lisbon set about discarding its colonial empire. Within a few weeks political parties had formed in Timor-Leste, and the Timorese Democratic Union (UDT) attempted to seize power in August 1975. A brief but brutal civil war saw UDT's rival Fretilin (previously known as the Association of Timorese Social Democrats) come out on top, and it urgently declared the independent existence of the Democratic Republic of Timor-Leste on 28 November, amidst an undeclared invasion by Indonesia. On 7 December Indonesia finally launched their full-scale attack on Dili after months of incursions (including at Balibo, where five Australia-based journalists were killed).

Anti-communist Indonesia feared an independent Timor-Leste governed by a left-leaning Fretilin would bring communism to its door, and commenced its invasion of Timor-Leste just a day after Henry Kissinger and Gerald Ford departed Jakarta, having tacitly given their assent. (Indeed, the Americans urged the Indonesians to conduct a swift campaign so that the world wouldn't see them using weapons the US had provided). Australia and Britain also sided with Indonesia.

Falintil, the military wing of Fretilin, fought a guerrilla war against Indonesian troops (which numbered 35,000 by 1976) with marked success in the first few years, but weakened considerably thereafter, though the resistance continued. The cost of the takeover to the Timorese was huge; it's estimated that up to 183,000 died in the hostilities, and the ensuing disease and famine.

By 1989 Indonesia had things firmly under control and opened Timor-Leste to limited controlled tourism. On 12 November 1991, Indonesian troops fired on protesters who'd gathered at the Santa Cruz Cemetery in Dili to commemorate the killing of an independence activist. With the event captured on film and aired around the world, the Indonesian government admitted to 19 killings (later increased to more than 50), although it's estimated that over 280 died in the massacre. While Indonesia introduced a civilian administration, the military remained in control. Aided by secret police and civilian pro-Indonesian militia to crush dissent, reports of arrest, torture and murder were commonplace.

Independence

After Indonesia's President Soeharto resigned in May 1998, his replacement BJ Habibie unexpectedly announced a referendum for autonomy in Timor-Leste. January 1999 marked the commencement of attacks by Indonesian military-backed militias who began terrorising the population to coerce them to reject independence.

Attacks peaked in April 1999, just prior to the arrival of the UN Electoral Mission, when, according to a report commissioned by the UN Office of the High Commissioner for Human Rights, up to 60 people were massacred near Liquiçá church. Other attacks occurred in Dili and Maliana while Indonesian authorities watched on. Attacks escalated in the weeks prior to the vote, with thousands seeking refuge in the hills away from the reach of the TNI and militia.

Despite threats, intimidation and brutality, on 30 August 1999, Timor-Leste voted overwhelmingly (78.5%) for independence from, rather than autonomy within, Indonesia. Though the Indonesian government promised to respect the results of the UN-sponsored vote, militias and Indonesian forces went on a rampage, killing people, burning and looting buildings and destroying infrastructure.

While the world watched in horror, the UN was attacked and forced to evacuate, leaving the Timorese defenceless. On 20 September, weeks after the main massacres in Suai, Dili, Maliana and Oecussi, the Australian-led International Force for East Timor (INTERFET) arrived in Dili. The Indonesian forces and their militia supporters left for West Timor, leaving behind an incomprehensible scene of destruction. Half a million people had been displaced, and telecommunications, power installations, bridges, government buildings, shops and houses were destroyed. Today these physical scars remain.

The UN set up a temporary administration during the transition to independence, and aid and foreign workers flooded into the country. As well as physically rebuilding the country, Timor-Leste has had to create a civil service, police, judiciary, education, health system and so on, with staff recruited and trained from scratch.

The UN handed over government to Timor-Leste on 20 May 2002. Falintil leader Xanana Gusmão was elected president of the new nation, and the long-time leader of Fretilin, Mari Alkatiri, who ran the party from exile in Mozambique, was chosen as prime minister.

Birth Pangs

In December 2002, Dili was the scene of riots as years of poverty and frustration proved too much for the nascent democracy. The economy was in a shambles and people were ready for things to start improving – and fast. But without any viable industry or employment potential, Timor-Leste was reliant almost entirely on foreign aid.

Only a small UN contingent remained in Timor-Leste by mid-2005. As the number of outsiders shrank, the challenges of creating a new nation from the ground up became all too apparent. Parliamentary factions squabbled while the enormous needs of the people festered.

The Future

Timor-Leste continues to rely partly on foreign money, and proceeds from its petroleum fields are filtering through.

In 2006 Australia and Timor-Leste signed an agreement that will give US$10 billion in oil revenue to both countries over the next 40 years – though Australia's Howard government was accused of using bullying tactics to deny the struggling and poor country its fair share of the money (initially offering only 20%). Only perseverance on the part of the Timorese saw the Australian government agree on a 50/50 split.

High in the hills outside Dili is another natural resource: coffee. Some 100,000 people work seasonally to produce arabica beans, noted for their cocoa and vanilla character. Shade-grown and organic, Timorese coffee is prized by companies such as Starbucks, and production is increasing.

Timor-Leste's tourism industry has great potential, although there needs to be a perception of stability for numbers to grow beyond the 1500 or so people who visit annually.

The Culture

The National Psyche

Timor-Leste's identity is firmly rooted in its survival of extreme hardship and foreign occupation. As a consequence of the long and difficult struggle for independence, the people of Timor-Leste are profoundly politically aware – not to mention proud and loyal. While there is great respect for elders and church and community leaders, there lurks a residual suspicion surrounding foreign occupiers, most recently in the form of the UN. In a country where Catholicism cloaks animistic beliefs and practices, religious beliefs also greatly inform the national consciousness.

Lifestyle

Most East Timorese lead a subsistence lifestyle: what is farmed (or caught) is eaten. Large families are common (the birth rate is 7.7 children per woman) and infant mortality remains high. According to the World Food Program, food insecurity is widespread – one third of the population regularly experience food shortages. Infrastructure remains limited; only a few towns have 24-hour electricity and running water. Roads are particularly dismal.

Family life exists in simple thatched huts, though rising wages have meant that satellite dishes are appearing beside even the most basic huts, beaming Indonesian TV into homes. NGOs and aid projects have worked to create self-sufficiency, but the ability to rise above poverty seems to be impossible for many as bad roads and drought or floods play havoc. Motorised vehicles remain rare; on weekends, buses are packed with those heading to the family events that form the backbone of Timorese life.

Population

Timor-Leste has at least a dozen indigenous groups, the largest being the Tetun (about 25% of the total population), who live around Suai, Dili and Viqueque. The next largest group (around 10%) is the Mambai, who live in the mountains of Maubisse, Ainaro and Same. Other groups each account for 5% or less of the total population. The Kemak live in the Ermera and Bobonaro districts; the Bunak also live in Bobonaro, and their territory extends into West Timor and the Suai area. The Fataluku people are famous for their high-peaked houses in the area around Lospalos. More groups are scattered among the interior mountains.

Religion

Religion is an integral part of daily life for most Timorese. Recent estimates indicate 98% of Timor-Leste's population is Catholic (underpinned by animist beliefs), 1% is Muslim and 1% Protestant.

Indigenous religions revolve around an earth mother, from whom all humans are born and shall return after death, and her male counterpart, the god of the sky or sun. These are accompanied by a complex web of spirits from ancestors and nature. The *matan d'ok* (medicine man) is the village mediator with the spirits; he can divine the future and cure illness. Many people believe in various forms of black magic and it's not uncommon for people to wish evil spells upon their rivals.

Arts

Music & Dance

The Timorese love a party, and celebrate with *tebe* (dancing) and singing. They're serious about their dancing; weddings often involve all-night three-step sessions. Music has been passed down through the years and changed little during Indonesian times. Traditional trancelike drumming is used in ceremonies, while Timorese rock and hip-hop groups are popular. Country-and-western style is popular, too, and features plenty of guitar use and the usual lovelorn themes.

Textiles

Throughout the country, women weave *tais* using small back-strap looms. Each region has its own style of *tais* and they're usually used as skirts or shawls for men *(tais mane)* or sewn up to form a tube skirt/dress for women *(tais feto)*. Some are made with organic dyes. Some weavers have cottoned on that a *tais* with the words 'Timor-Leste 2012' or similar woven into it makes a good souvenir. For details on where to buy Timorese textiles, see p793.

Environment

The Land

With an area of 15,007 sq km, Timor-Leste consists of the eastern half of the island of Timor, Atauro and Jaco Islands, and the enclave of Oecussi on the north coast, 70km to the west and surrounded by Indonesian West Timor.

Once part of the Australian continental shelf, Timor fully emerged from the ocean only four million years ago, and is therefore composed mainly of marine sediment, principally limestone. Rugged mountains, a product of the collision with the Banda Trench to the north, run the length of the country, the highest of which is Mt Ramelau (2963m).

Wildlife

Timor-Leste is squarely in the area known as Wallacea, a kind of crossover zone between Asian and Australian plants and animals, and one of the most biologically distinctive areas on earth.

Timor-Leste's north coast is a global hot spot of whale and dolphin activity, and its coral reefs are home to a diverse range of marine life. Species spotted include dugongs, blue whales, whale sharks and dolphins. More than 240 species of bird have been recorded in its skies. The Lautem district was declared a national park partly because of its rich bird life: it's home to honeyeaters, critically endangered yellow-crested cockatoos and endangered *wetar* ground-doves. The number of mammals and reptiles in the wild is limited, though crocodiles and snakes make appearances.

Environmental Issues

Timor-Leste's first national park, the Nino Konis Santana National Park, was declared in 2008 – a 123,000-hectare parcel of land (including some tropical forest) and sea at the country's eastern tip, also incorporating Jaco Island and Tutuala. Most of the country, however, is suffering from centuries of deforestation, and erosion is a huge problem. Roads and even villages have been known to slip away.

Food

As an approximate guide, prices for main dishes when eating out are budget ($), under US$5 (a plate of nasi goreng, chicken and rice, or fish and rice; midrange ($$), US$5 to US$15 (pasta, a hamburger, stir-fry, small fish or roast chicken); and top end ($$$), more than US$15 (a starter, an international meal with beef, chicken, pork or seafood, or a large grilled fish, prawns or lobster).

SURVIVAL GUIDE

Directory A–Z

Accommodation

Dili's accommodation is nothing to write home about, expect sit-down loos and air conditioning and, well, little more. Accommodation with adjoining restaurants/bars are a good idea for those who'd prefer not to travel around at night. Elsewhere, don't expect anything swank – if you get a clean room with good mosquito nets and a few hours of electricity for reading and a fan, you're doing well.

In most places you will be able to find some sort of accommodation, even if it is a homestay (offer US$10 a night). Washing facilities are likely to be Indonesian *mandi* style. A *mandi* is a large concrete water tank from where you scoop water to wash yourself. Don't jump in!

The costs per room are indicated in this chapter by the following categories: budget ($), under US$15; midrange ($$), US$15 to US$100; and top end ($$$) more than US$100.

Activities

There are many opportunities for the adventure traveller; think limestone caves, rugged mountain tracks and secret waterfalls. For many activities it will be BYO equipment, or check with Dili's adventure-travel company (p806).

Diving

The diving is sublime in Timor-Leste, and there are three companies that can show you what's out there (see p792). Dive Timor Lorosae has its own boat and takes dive trips out to Atauro Island; FreeFlow is best known for its experienced dive guides and delicious lunches while Compass Charters can take you where you'd like to go. Conditions are best during the dry season (May to November), when visibility is at around 20m to 30m.

Hiking

Serious hikers are popping up in villages around the country (and surprising the locals), and 10-day north-to-south coast hikes are not unheard of. Popular day-long hikes include those to the summit of Mt Ramelau (from where you can see the south and north coasts of Timor-Leste) and to the sacred peak of Mt Matebian. Both mountains have accommodation nearby that can provide guides. There's also hiking in Atauro's interior. Check www.trekkingeasttimor.org for more information.

PRACTICALITIES

» **Currency** The US dollar (US$) and Timor-Leste centavo coins

» **Online East Timor News** www.timornewsnetwork.blogspot.com; www.timornewsline.com; www.timortoday.com

» **Smoking** Common throughout the country and in many hotels and restaurants

Business Hours

In Dili most of the budget and midrange eateries are open from morning until late, with the high-end restaurants only doing lunch (noon to 2pm) and dinner (6pm to 10pm). Expect smaller shops to be open from 9am to 6pm and closed on Sundays. The larger supermarkets are generally open 8am to 8pm everyday. Apart from Dili there are only a handful of places that keep business hours, typically 9am to 6pm Monday to Friday, sometimes with a long lunchtime siesta as a reminder of the old Portuguese influence, and maybe with a few Saturday hours to keep busy.

Exceptions to these hours are noted in individual reviews.

Customs Regulations

You can bring the following into Timor-Leste:

» **Alcohol** 1.5L of any type

» **Cigarettes** 200

» **Money** Limited to the equivalent of US$2000 in foreign currency (non US$) and US$5000 per person. No restrictions on taking cash out of the country.

Dangers & Annoyances

Malaria and dengue are concerns for those staying in Timor-Leste; take precautions (see p943 and p942). Stick to bottled water, avoid tap water and ice, and wipe off water from the tops of beverage cans before drinking. Antibiotics and other pharmaceuticals are easily bought in Dili but are hard to find elsewhere.

Drivers should always be on the lookout for vehicles speeding around corners, roaming children and livestock, potholes, speed humps and landslides. Cases of theft occur most frequently from cars, with mobile phones a prime target. Women should be wary of exercising in isolated spots in Dili, as there have been attacks. Given the regular bouts of political instability in Timor-Leste, check the current situation before you visit (although government travel advisories are usually cautious in the extreme).

Electricity

At hotels you can often plug in Australian flat three-pin plugs, in other places two pin (round) plugs are used. See p927 for details.

Embassies & Consulates

A number of countries have embassies in Dili. Citizens of the UK should contact their embassy in Indonesia (see p305).

Australia (☎332 2111; www.easttimor.embassy.gov.au; Av dos Mártires de Pátria, Dili) They also assist Canadian citizens.

European Commission (☎332 5171; ectimor@mail.timortelecom.tp; Casa Europa, Av Alves Aldeia, Dili)

France (Representative Office) (☎731 4081; frcoopedili@gmail.com; Casa Europa, Av Alves Aldeia, Dili)

Indonesia (☎331 7107; www.kbridili.org; cnr Ruas Marinha & Governador Cesar, Dili)

Ireland (Representative Office) (☎332 4880; www.irishaid.gov.ie; Rua Alferes Duartre Arbiro 12, Dili)

New Zealand (☎331 0087; dili@mfat.govt.nz; Rua Geremias, Dili)

USA (☎332 4684; www.timor-leste.usembassy.gov; Av de Portugal, Dili)

Gay & Lesbian Travellers

There is no organised network for gays and lesbians in Timor-Leste, but it's also unlikely that there will be any overt discrimination. While there is no law against homosexuality it's wise to be less demonstrative in the more conservative rural areas outside of Dili.

Insurance

Travel insurance is vital in Timor-Leste (see p940 for details). Medical facilities outside Dili are limited and any serious cases generally get evacuated from the country to Darwin or Singapore. Accordingly, travellers need to ensure that they have full evacuation coverage.

Worldwide insurance is available at www.lonelyplanet.com/travel_services. You can buy, extend and claim online anytime – even if you're already on the road.

Internet Access

There are plenty of internet cafes, and many hotels in Dili have relatively reliable, albeit slow, access, averaging US$1 an hour. All Timor Telecom offices in the district capitals have access, as do hotels attracting foreigners outside of Dili, such as those in Baucau and Com.

Legal Matters

If you are the victim of a serious crime, go to the nearest police station and notify your embassy. The Timorese police force is only one of a number of national and international groups providing security in the country. If arrested, you have the right to a phone call and legal representation, which your embassy can help locate.

Public Holidays

Timor-Leste has a large list of public holidays. Many special days of commemoration are declared each year. November seems to be the front-runner with five holidays.

New Year's Day 1 January

Good Friday March/April (variable)

World Labour Day 1 May

Restoration of Independence Day 20 May (the day in 2002 when sovereignty was transferred from the UN)

Corpus Christi Day May/June (variable)

Popular Consultation Day 30 August (marks the start of independence in 1999)

Idul Fitri End of Ramadan (variable)

All Saints' Day 1 November

All Souls' Day 2 November

Idul Adha Muslim day of sacrifice (variable)

National Youth Day 12 November (commemorates the Santa Cruz Cemetery massacre)

Proclamation of Independence Day 28 November

National Heroes' Day 7 December

Day of Our Lady of Immaculate Conception and Timor-Leste Patroness 8 December

Christmas Day 25 December

Telephone

International access code ☎0011

International country code ☎670

Landline numbers All start with 3 or 4

International & Local Calls

Can be made from every Timor Telecom office in the country. They can be found in Dili and in every district capital.

Mobile Phones

To get set up with a mobile phone, simply bring an unlocked handset with you to Timor-Leste and buy a **Timor Telecom** (www.timortelecom.tp) SIM card.

Toilets

Hotels and restaurants recommended in this book will have toilet facilities ranging from modern Western flush toilets down to a well-kept hole in the ground with a handy bucket of water.

Tourist Information

Timor-Leste doesn't have a tourist office. However, the expat community is especially generous with information. Drop by any of the popular bars, restaurants or dive shops and soon you'll be hooked into all sorts of info. Language differences aside, locals are also very happy to help.

Visas

Dili International Airport & Dili Seaport arrivals

An entry visa (US$30; up to 30 days) is granted to holders of a valid passport on arrival. Always ask for a 30-day visa, even if you don't plan on staying that long. With valid reason, visas can be extended for US$35 a month. If needing a multiple entry visa or to stay between 30 and 90 days, you can apply for the Visa Application Authorization before arrival.

Land-border arrivals from Indonesia

East Timorese consulates Bali (☎62 2 8133 855 8950; caetanoguterres@hotmail.com; Denpasar); Kupang (☎62 8133 9367 558; caetanoguterres@hotmail.com; Jalan Eltari II, Kupang) All nationalities (other than Indonesian and Portuguese nationals) must apply for a Visa Application Authorisation prior to their arrival at the border – most travellers apply for them at these consulates. Check the Immigration Service's website (http://migracao.gov.tl). You need a photograph and the US$30 fee; it takes 10 working days.

Volunteering

Many organisations take on volunteers to assist in a wide variety of roles. Check the links page at www.etan.org for a voluminous listing.

Alola Foundation (☎332 3855; www.alolafoundation.org; Rua Bispo de Medeiros, Dili)

Australian Volunteers International (☎332 2815; www.australianvolunteers.com; Hotel Central, Av Presidente Nicolau Lobato, Dili)

Women Travellers

Women travellers need to be aware of personal security issues, particularly in Dili. Do not walk or take taxis after dark, unless you're in a group.

Getting There & Away

There are no passenger boat services to Timor-Leste from other countries.

Air

Airports & Airlines

You can fly to Dili from Denpasar (Bali), Jakarta, Darwin and Singapore. Dili's Nicolau Lobato International Airport is a five-minute drive from town. A 24-hour **Airport Shuttle** (Flybus; ☎750 8585; kijoli@bigpond.com; per person one way US$18) can pick you up and drop you off, or catch a taxi for US$10. *Mikrolets* (local buses) charge $US0.25 from the main road into town.

Air North (☎1800 627 474 in Australia; www.airnorth.com.au) Flies twice daily between Darwin and Dili (return fares from US$400, 1½ hours).

Air Timor (☎331 2700; www.air-timor.com) Flies Singapore–Dili return each Tuesday, Thursday and Saturday (return from US$800, 2½ hours).

DEPARTURE TAX

There's an additional departure tax of US$10 when leaving Dili's airport.

Batavia Air (+62 2138 999888 in Indonesia; www.batavia-air.com) Flies Dili–Jakarta four times a week (return fares from US$400, two hours).

Merpati (332 1880; www.merpati.co.id) Flies three times per week (Tuesday, Thursdays & Saturdays) between Denpasar (Bali) and Dili (return fares from US$200, two hours).

Border Crossings

See the boxed text Getting to Indonesia (p798) for details on travelling from Dili to Kupang in West Timor, Indonesia. Overland travellers to Timor-Leste (including Oecussi) need to apply for a visa in advance (see p805) unless they have a multiple entry visa.

Getting Around

Bicycle

New bikes can be purchased in Dili for around US$200. Road conditions away from the north coast can be brutal, which may appeal to mountain bikers.

Boat

Ferry transport is available between Dili and Atauro Island (p795), and Dili and Oecussi (p798). Book in advance. In practice business-class tickets are for foreigners and economy tickets are for locals, but people freely mix across the ship. **Compass Charters** (723 0966; info@compassadventuretours.com; Av dos Mártires de Pátria, next to Tiger Fuel, Dili) runs a daily water-taxi service to Atauro Island (US$30 one way, 90 minutes).

Bus

Mikrolet (small minibuses) operate around Dili and to some towns, often roaming villages looking for passengers. Crowded buses do the main routes from Dili to Lospalos, Viqueque, Maliana and Suai. More rugged routes are covered by *angguna* (tray trucks where passengers, including the odd buffalo or goat, all pile into the back). If *angguna* aren't covering their usual turf you can be assured the road conditions are exceptionally dire.

Car & Motorcycle

There's nothing easy about driving in Timor-Leste; the roads are a minefield of chickens, goats, sleepy dogs and children, and locals congregate on the side of roads in what seems to be a national pastime (moving off the road is optional). Dips, ditches and entire missing sections of road are common, as are very fast UN drivers. There are plenty of blind corners.

While conventional cars can handle Dili, a 4WD is recommended for the roads elsewhere. Better roads include those east to Com (but not to Tutuala) and west to Batugade, and the inland road to Maubisse. Motorcycles can be quite handy, breezing over bumps at a respectable pace.

EDS Car Rentals (723 0880; edsdili@dynamictrade.ch) Offers a good range of high-quality cars, 4WDs, trucks and buses. They also have a team of experienced drivers who know Dili and the back blocks of Timor-Leste. When you are driving toward Dili it is the last right-hand turn before you go over the bridge; follow the river for 1.5km and it is on your left. Rates start at US$75 for 4WDs.

Tiger Fuel (723 0965; Av dos Mártires de Pátria, Comoro) Tiger rents motorcycles from US$30 per day and US$150 per week.

Fuel

Petrol (gasoline) in Portuguese is *besin,* diesel fuel is *solar;* expect to pay around US$1 to US$1.25 per litre.

Hitching

Locals on long walks into towns may ask for a ride. Waiting for a lift may be the only option if you're leaving Oecussi and heading into Kefamenanu in West Timor, and it's likely your payment will be in cigarettes. However, hitchhiking is never entirely safe, so it's not recommended.

Tours

A tour can allow you to visit places not easily accessible by public transport, and a guide can bridge the language barrier. The following agency is based in Dili:

Eco Discovery (332 2454; www.ecodiscovery-easttimor.com; Landmark Plaza, Av dos Mártires de Pátria) Tours range from around Dili to explorations by 4WD and boat.

Vietnam

Includes »

Best Regional Specialities

» White rose (p856)
» Pho (p819)
» Catfish spring rolls (p817)
» Banh xeo (p877)

Best Places for Cultural Connections

» Hiking the highlands (p838)
» Floating lodges (p886)
» Thai stilt-houses (p836)
» Cooking courses (p874)

Why Go?

One of the most intoxicating destinations on planet earth, Vietnam is a kaleidoscope of vivid colours and subtle shades, exotic sights and curious sounds, grand architecture and deeply moving war sites. The nation is a budget traveller's dream, with inexpensive transport, outstanding street food, good-value accommodation and *bia hoi* – perhaps the world's cheapest beer.

Nature has gifted Vietnam with soaring mountains in the north, emerald-green rice paddies in the Mekong Delta and a sensational, curvaceous coastline of ravishing sandy beaches. Travelling here you'll witness children riding buffalo, see the impossibly intricate textiles of hill-tribe communities and hear the buzz of a million motorbikes.

This is a dynamic nation on the move, where life is lived at pace. Prepare yourself for the ride of your life.

When to Go

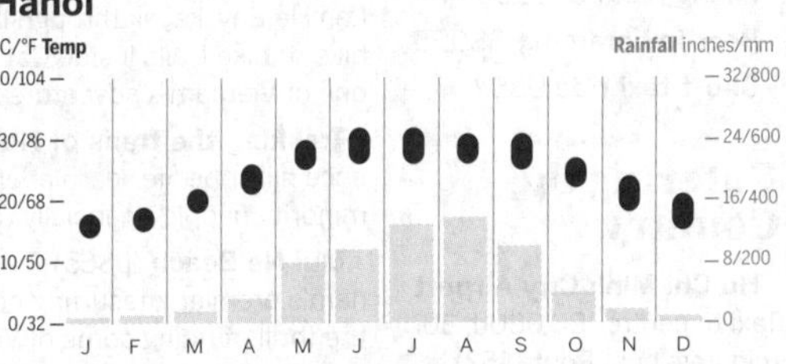

Dec–Mar Expect cool weather north of Hue as the winter monsoon brings cloud, mist and drizzle.

Apr Danang's riverfront explodes with colour and noise during the city's fireworks festival.

Jul–Aug Perfect beach-time on the central coastline, with balmy sea and air temperatures.

AT A GLANCE

- **Currency** Dong
- **Language** Vietnamese
- **Money** ATMs are widespread
- **Visas** Mostly required in advance
- **Mobile phones** Prepay SIM cards available for a few dollars

Fast Facts

- **Area** 329,566 sq km
- **Capital** Hanoi
- **Country code** ☎84
- **Emergency** Police ☎113

Exchange Rates

Australia	A$1	21,650d
Canada	C$1	20,850d
Euro zone	€1	27,500d
Japan	¥100	25,150d
New Zealand	NZ$1	16,900d
UK	£1	33,600d
US	US$1	20,800d

Set Your Budget

- **Budget room** US$8–15
- **Filling meal** US$1.50–4
- **Beer in bar** from US$0.75
- **Short taxi ride** US$2

Entering the Country

- **Ho Chi Minh City Airport** Taxi to centre 100,000d, 30 minutes; bus (Route 152) 4000d, every 15 minutes, 6am-6pm, 40 minutes.
- **Hanoi Airport** Taxi to centre US$14.50, one hour; Vietnam Airlines minibus US$3, every 30 minutes.

Don't Miss

Northern Vietnam comprises one of the world's most impressive limestone landmasses, a vast swath of spectacular scenery that has been eroded into ethereal rock formations. The myriad pinnacle-like islands of **Halong Bay** are one superb example of this spectacular karst scenery, or head to neighbouring **Lan Ha Bay** for less crowds.

Near **Ninh Binh**, the jagged limestone mountains of Tam Coc are a surreal sight, while further south the extraordinary **Phong Nha-Ke Bang National Park** is home to three gargantuan cave systems (including the world's largest cave) set in tropical forest studded with towering peaks.

ITINERARIES

One Week

Begin in Hanoi, immerse yourself in Old Quarter life and tour the capital's sights for a couple of days. Then it's a day-trip to Halong Bay to lap up the surreal karst scenery. Move down to Hue to explore the imperial citadel and then shift to Hoi An for two days of foodie treats, old world ambience and beach time. Finish off with a night in Ho Chi Minh City (Saigon).

Two Weeks

Acclimatise in the capital, see the sights and experience Hanoi's unique streetlife. Tour incomparable Halong Bay, then take in the extraordinary caves and karsts of Phong Nha. Hue, city of pagodas and tombs, beckons next. Then push on to charming Hoi An, where you can rest up. Party in Nha Trang then continue south to idyllic Mui Ne Beach. Round things off Saigon-style in Vietnam' s liveliest metropolis, Ho Chi Minh City.

Essential Outdoor Activities

- **Cat Ba region** (p831) Sail through the idyllic islands of Lan Ha Bay, kayak through lagoons, climb karst walls, and hike or bike trails inside Cat Ba National Park, fast becoming one of Vietnam's adventure-sports epicentres.
- **Trekking the trails of North Vietnam** (p838) Experience hill-tribe life, learn about highland culture and support minority people financially (and get a workout thrown in).
- **Mui Ne Beach** (p865) Feel the rush of the wind at Vietnam's premier kitesurfing hot-spot and, if conditions allow, the thrill of riding some of Vietnam's best waves.

HANOI

☎04 / POP 6.4 MILLION

The grand old dame of the Orient, Hanoi is the most graceful, atmospheric and captivating capital city in the region. Here exotic old Asia blends seamlessly with the dynamic face of the continent, an architectural masterpiece evolving in harmony with its history, rather than bulldozing through it.

A mass of motorbikes swarms through the tangled web of streets that is the Old Quarter, a cauldron of commerce for almost 1000 years and still the best place to check the pulse of this resurgent city. Hanoi has it all: the ancient history, a colonial legacy and a modern outlook. There is no better place to untangle the paradox that is contemporary Vietnam.

Sights

OLD QUARTER & AROUND

This is the Asia we dreamed of from afar. Steeped in history, pulsating with life, bubbling with commerce, buzzing with motorbikes and rich in exotic scents, the Old Quarter is Hanoi's historic heart and soul. Hawkers pound the streets bearing sizzling, smoking baskets that hide a cheap meal. *Pho* (noodle soup) stalls and *bia hoi* (draught beer) dens hug every corner, resonant with the sound of gossip and laughter. Take your time and experience the unique sights, sounds and smells of this chaotic, captivating warren of lanes – this is Asian streetlife at its purist and most atmospheric.

Hoan Kiem Lake LAKE
(Map p814) The liquid heart of the Old Quarter, Hoan Kiem Lake is a good landmark and a great place to catch the pulse of the city. Legend has it that in the mid-15th century, heaven gave Emperor Le Thai To (Le Loi) a magical sword that he used to drive the Chinese out of Vietnam. One day after the war, while out boating, he came upon a giant golden tortoise; the creature grabbed the sword and disappeared into the depths of the lake. Since that time, the lake has been known as Ho Hoan Kiem (Lake of the Restored Sword) because the tortoise returned the sword to its divine owners.

Ngoc Son Temple TEMPLE
(Jade Mountain Temple; Map p816; admission 3000d; ⌚8am-5pm) Founded in the 18th century, this temple occupies an island in the northern part of Hoan Kiem Lake. It's a meditative spot to relax, but also worth checking out for the embalmed remains of a gigantic tortoise. Keep your eyes peeled for Cu Rua (Great Grandfather), a 200kg turtle who still inhabits the lake. This revered reptile was fished out of the lake in April 2011 for medical treatment (precipitated by pollution) before being returned to his watery domain.

Bach Ma Temple TEMPLE
(Map p814; cnr P Hang Buom & P Hang Giay; ⌚8-11.30am & 2.30-5.30pm) One of the oldest temples in Hanoi, Bach Ma was originally built by King Ly Thai To in the 11th century (to honour a white horse that guided him to this site, where he chose to construct his city walls). Pass through the wonderful old wooden doors of the pagoda to see a statue of the legendary white horse, as well as a beautiful red-lacquered funeral palanquin.

St Joseph Cathedral CHURCH
(Map p816; P Nha Tho; ⌚5-7am & 5-7pm) Stepping inside Hanoi's cathedral is like being transported back to medieval Europe. This neo-Gothic cathedral (inaugurated in 1886) is noteworthy for its square belltowers, elaborate altar and stained-glass windows. The main gate is open when Mass is held. At other times you have to enter the compound via a side street, at 40 P Nha Chung. During Sunday Mass (usually at 6pm), the congregation spills out onto the streets, hymns are beamed out, and the devout sit on motorbikes listening intently to the sermon.

Women's Museum MUSEUM
(Bao Tang Phu Nu; off Map p816; www.baotangphunu.org.vn; 36 P Ly Thuong Kiet; admission 30,000d; ⌚8am-4.30pm Tue-Sun) Recently reopened after a long renovation, this excellent museum concentrates on the role of women in Vietnamese society and culture. Superbly laid out and labelled in English and French, it's the memories of the wartime contributions of individual heroic women that are most poignant. There are regular exhibitions held on topics as diverse as human trafficking and street vendors.

Hoa Lo Prison Museum MUSEUM
(Map p816; 1 P Hoa Lo; admission 10,000d; ⌚8am-5pm) The museum is all that remains of the notorious Hoa Lo Prison, ironically nicknamed the 'Hanoi Hilton' by US POWs. Exhibits concentrate on the Vietnamese struggle for independence from France. Other displays focus on American pilots incarcerated here, including Senator John McCain.

Vietnam Highlights

1. Wander the ancient lanes of **Hoi An** (p853), a historic, perfectly preserved port
2. Down a **bia hoi** (p898), Vietnam's uniquely refreshing lager beer
3. Wonder at the thousands of stunning limestone islands in **Halong Bay** (p828)
4. Experience Vietnam's hugely atmospheric capital **Hanoi** (p809) and its captivating sights
5. Explore the colossal caves and outstanding mountainous scenery of **Phong Nha-Ke Bang National Park** (p842)
6. Travel east to the remote, pristine, beach-blessed **Con Dao Islands** (p867)
7. Rave till dawn in **Nha Trang** (p859), a bombastic beach party city
8. Marvel at **Hue** (p842) a majestic former imperial capital of temples, tombs and palaces.
9. Hike and bike **Cat Tien National Park** (p873), which offers terrific wildlife-spotting.
10. Chill in **Mui Ne** (p865), a cosmopolitan beach and watersport resort

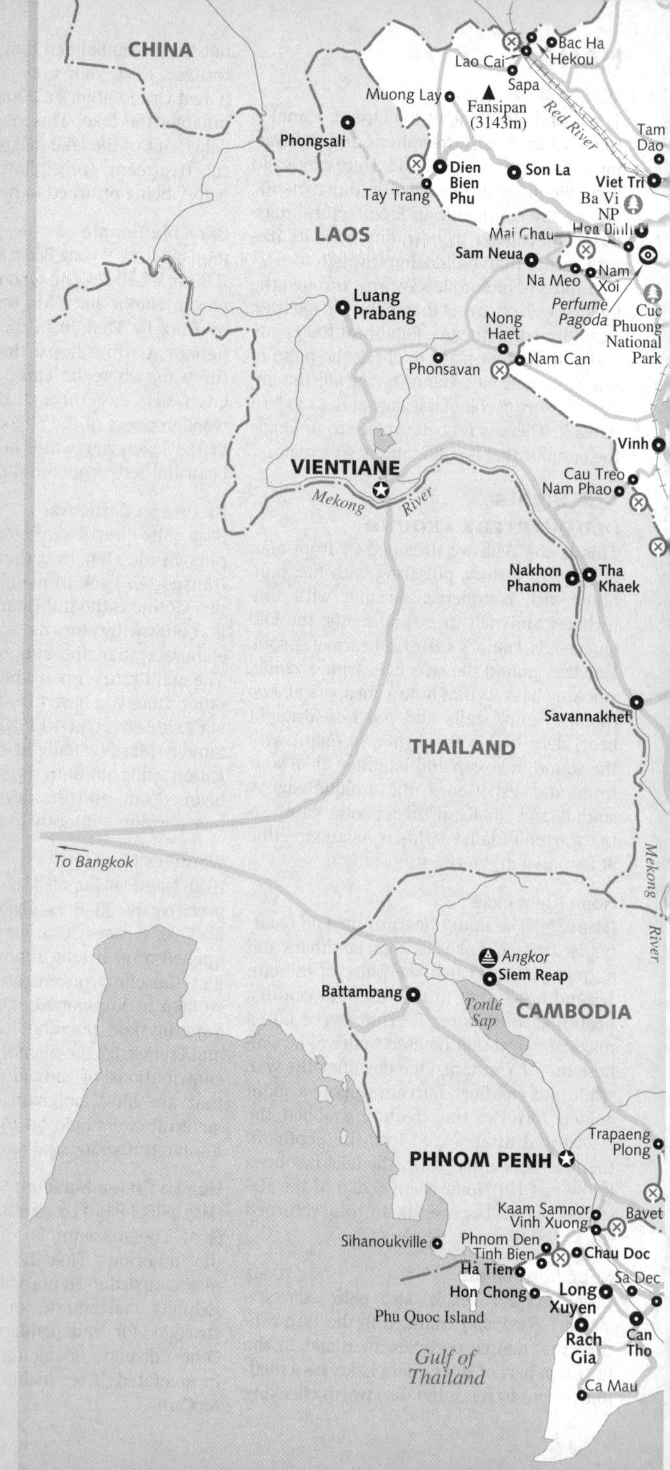

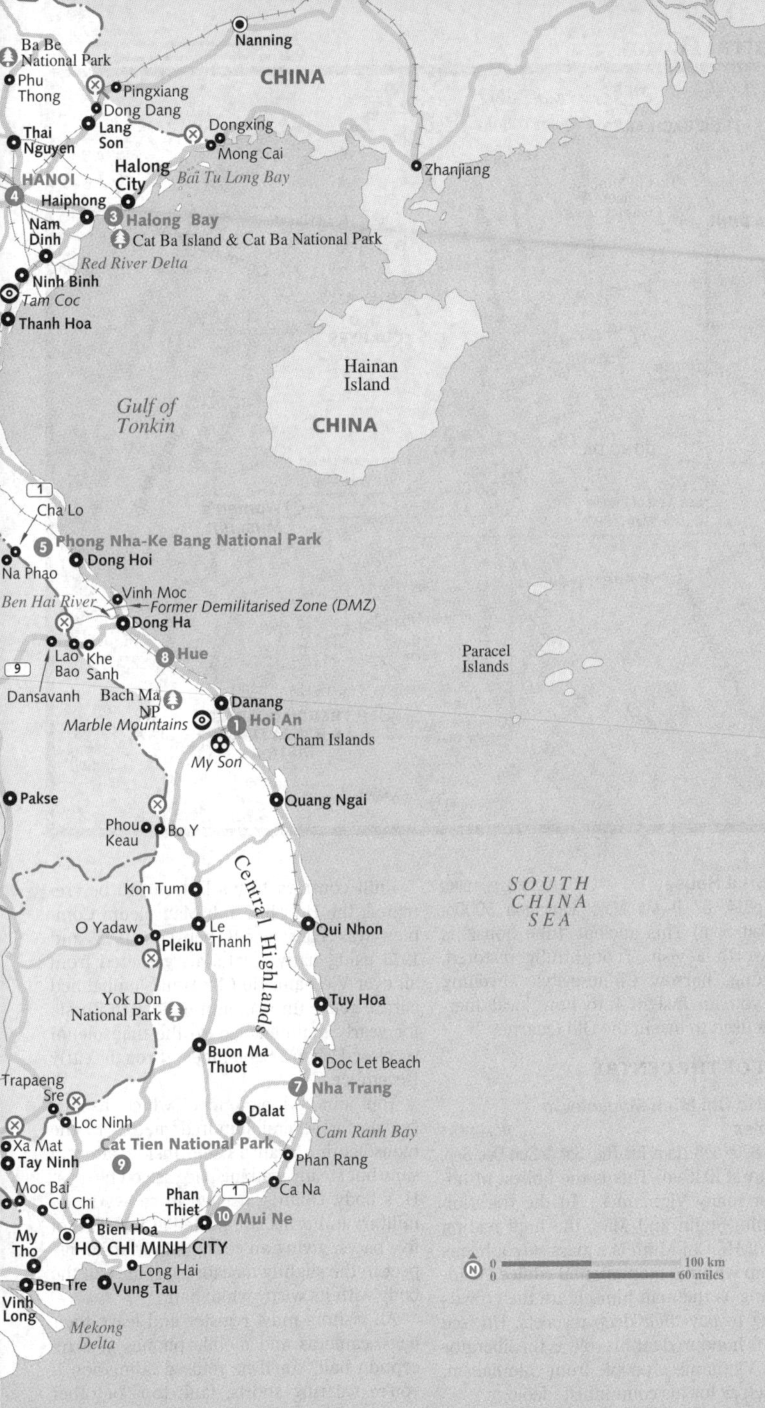

Nanning
CHINA
Ba Be National Park
Phu Thong
Pingxiang
Dong Dang
Thai Nguyen
Lang Son
Dongxing
Mong Cai
Zhanjiang
HANOI
Halong City
Bai Tu Long Bay
4
Haiphong
3 Halong Bay
Nam Dinh
Cat Ba Island & Cat Ba National Park
Red River Delta
Ninh Binh
Tam Coc
Thanh Hoa
Hainan Island
CHINA
Gulf of Tonkin
1
Cha Lo
5 Phong Nha-Ke Bang National Park
Dong Hoi
Na Phao
Vinh Moc
Ben Hai River
Former Demilitarised Zone (DMZ)
Dong Ha
Lao Bao
Khe Sanh
8 Hue
Paracel Islands
9
Dansavanh
Bach Ma NP
Danang
Marble Mountains
1 Hoi An
Cham Islands
My Son
Pakse
Quang Ngai
Phou Keau
Bo Y
Central Highlands
Kon Tum
SOUTH CHINA SEA
O Yadaw
Le Thanh
Qui Nhon
Pleiku
Tuy Hoa
Yok Don National Park
Buon Ma Thuot
Doc Let Beach
Trapaeng Sre
7 Nha Trang
Loc Ninh
Dalat
Xa Mat
Cat Tien National Park
Cam Ranh Bay
Tay Ninh
9
Phan Rang
Moc Bai
1
Ca Na
Cu Chi
Phan Thiet
10 Mui Ne
Bien Hoa
My Tho
HO CHI MINH CITY
Long Hai
Ben Tre
Vung Tau
Vinh Long
Mekong Delta
0 100 km
0 60 miles
6 Con Dao Islands

Central Hanoi

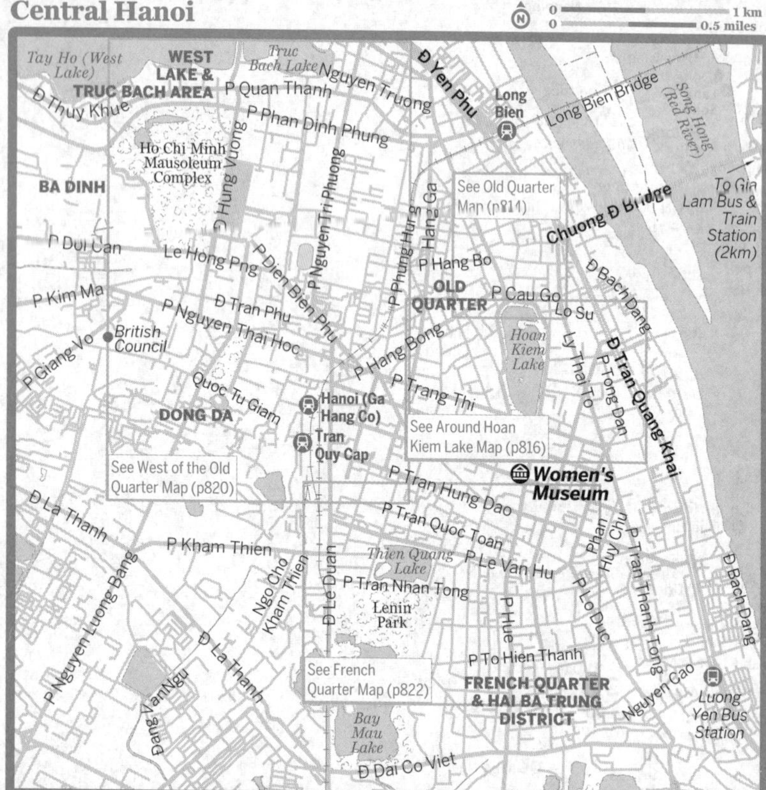

Memorial House HISTORIC BUILDING
(Map p814; 87 P Ma May; admission 5000d; ⏲8.30am-5pm) This ancient 'tube house' is well worth a visit. Thoughtfully restored, this long, narrow Chinese-style dwelling gives you an insight into how local merchants used to live in the Old Quarter.

WEST OF THE CENTRE

FREE Ho Chi Minh Mausoleum Complex MONUMENT
(Map p820; ⏲8-11am Tue-Thu, Sat & Sun Dec-Sep, last entry at 10.15am) This is the holiest of holies for many Vietnamese. In the tradition of Lenin, Stalin and Mao, the final resting place of Ho Chi Minh is a glass sarcophagus set deep within a monumental edifice. As interesting as the man himself are the crowds coming to pay their deep respects. Ho (see p895) is honoured for his role as the liberator of the Vietnamese people from colonialism, as much as for his communist ideology.

Built contrary to his last will to be cremated, the Ho Chi Minh Mausoleum Complex was constructed between 1973 and 1975 using native materials gathered from all over Vietnam. Ho Chi Minh's embalmed corpse gets a three-month holiday to Russia for yearly maintenance, so the mausoleum is closed from September through early December.

You join a long queue, which usually snakes for several hundred metres to the mausoleum entrance itself. Inside, adopt a slow but steady walking pace as you file past Ho's body. Guards, regaled in snowy white military uniforms, are posted at intervals of five paces, giving an eerily authoritarian aspect to the slightly macabre spectacle of the body with its wispy white hair.

All visitors must register and leave their bags, cameras and mobile phones at a reception hall. You'll be refused admission if you're wearing shorts, tank tops or other 'indecent' clothing. Hats must be removed and photography is absolutely prohibited.

After exiting the mausoleum, check out the following nearby sights in the complex.

Ho Chi Minh Museum
(Map p820; www.baotanghochiminh.vn; admission 15,000d; ⌚8-11.30am daily & 2-4.30pm Tue-Thu, Sat & Sun) is a triumphalist monument dedicated to Ho and the onward march of revolutionary socialism. There are Ho mementos and some fascinating photos. Find an English-speaking guide, as some of the symbolism is hard on your own.

Ho Chi Minh's Stilt House
(Map p820; admission 15,000d; ⌚summer 7.30-11am & 2-4pm, winter 8-11am & 1.30-4pm, closed all day Mon & Fri afternoon) Behind the mausoleum, this was supposedly Ho's official residence, on and off, between 1958 and 1969. Its simplicity reinforces his reputation as a man of the people.

One Pillar Pagoda
(Chua Mot Cot; Map p820; admission free) Built by Emperor Ly Thai Tong (reign 1028–54) and designed to represent a lotus blossom, a symbol of purity, rising out of a sea of sorrow.

Presidential Palace
(Map p820) In stark contrast to Ho's stilt house, this imposing restored colonial building was constructed in 1906 as the palace of the Governor General of Indochina. It's not open to the public.

THE 36 STREETS

In the 13th century Hanoi's 36 guilds established themselves here, each taking a different road – hence the area was known at the '36 Streets'. *Hang* means 'merchandise' and is usually followed by the name of the product that was traditionally sold in that street. Thus, P Hang Gai translates as 'Silk Street'.

TOP CHOICE **Temple of Literature** TEMPLE
(Van Mieu; Map p820; P Quoc Tu Giam; admission 10,000d; ⌚8am-5pm) Hanoi's peaceful Temple of Literature was dedicated to Confucius in 1070 by Emperor Ly Thanh Tong, and later established as a university for the education of mandarins. A well-preserved jewel of traditional Vietnamese architecture, with roofed gateways and low-eaved buildings, this temple is an absolute must-see.

Five courtyards are present within the temple grounds. The front gate is inscribed with a request that visitors dismount from their horses before entering. Make sure you do. There's a peaceful reflecting pool in the front courtyard, and don't miss the Khue Van Pavilion at the back of the second courtyard.

SCAM ALERT!

Hanoi is a very safe city on the whole and crimes against tourists are extremely rare. That said, the city certainly has its share of scams.

» **Fake Hotels** The taxi and minibus mafia at the airport take unwitting tourists to the wrong hotel. Invariably, the hotel has appropriated the name of another popular property and will then attempt to swindle as much of your money as possible. Check out a room before you check in. And walk on if you have any suspicions.

» **Hotel Tours** Some budget hotel staff have been verbally aggressive and threatened physical violence towards guests who've declined to book tours through their in-house tour agency. Don't feel pressured, and if it persists, find another place to stay.

» **Women** Walking alone at night is generally safe in the Old Quarter but you should always be aware of your surroundings. Hailing a taxi is a good idea if it's late and you have a long walk home.

» **The Kindness of Strangers** There's a scam going on around Hoan Kiem Lake. A friendly local approaches you, offering to take you out. You end up at a karaoke bar or a restaurant, where the bill is upwards of US$100. Gay men have been targeted in this way. Exercise caution and follow your instincts.

Make sure you report scams to the **Vietnam National Administration of Tourism** (Map p816; ☎3356 0789; www.hanoitourism.gov.vn; 3 Tran Phu), who might well pressure the cowboys into cleaning up their act.

Old Quarter

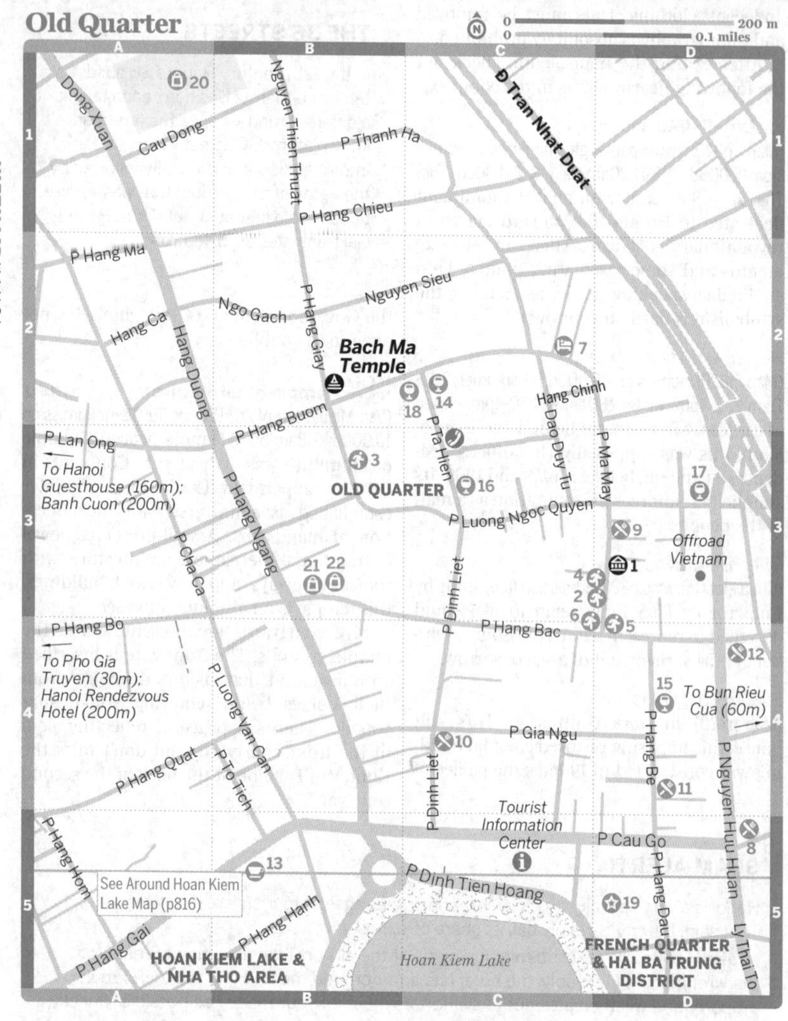

Fine Arts Museum MUSEUM
(Map p820; www.vnfineartsmuseum.org.vn; 66 P Nguyen Thai Hoc; admission 20,000d; ⌚9.15am-5pm Tue-Sun) There are superb textiles, furniture and ceramics in the first building, which also showcases exhibitions. Over in the magnificent main building artistic treasures include ancient Champa stone carvings, astonishing effigies of Guan Yin (the thousand-eyed, thousand-armed Goddess of Compassion) as well as lacquered-wood statues of robed Buddhist monks from the Tay Son dynasty.

OTHER AREAS

TOP CHOICE **Vietnam Museum of Ethnology** MUSEUM
(www.vme.org.vn; Đ Nguyen Van Huyen; admission 25,000d; ⌚8.30am-5.30pm Tue-Sun) This museum features a fascinating collection of art and everyday objects gathered from Vietnam's diverse tribal people. From the making of conical hats to the ritual of a Tay shamanic ceremony, the museum explores Vietnam's cultural diversity.

In the grounds are examples of traditional village houses – a Tay stilt house, an

Old Quarter

Top Sights

Bach Ma Temple B2

Sights

Dong Xuan Market .... (see 20)
1 Memorial House D3

Activities, Courses & Tours

2 Buffalo Tours D3
3 Ethnic Travel B3
Free Wheelin' Tours .... (see 18)
4 Handspan Travel Indochina D3
5 Ocean Tours D4
6 Vega Travel C3

Sleeping

7 Hanoi Backpackers 2 .... C2

Eating

8 Bun Oc Saigon D5
9 Nola D3
10 Quan Bia Minh C4
11 Spot D4
12 Xoi Yen D4

Drinking

13 Café Pho Co B5
14 Cheeky Quarter C2
15 Le Pub D4
16 Mao's Red Lounge C3
17 Roots D3
18 Tet C2

Entertainment

19 Municipal Water Puppet Theatre D5

Shopping

20 Dong Xuan Market A1
21 Hanoi Gallery B3
22 Old Propaganda Posters B3

impressive Bahnar communal structure and a Yao home. Don't miss the soaring, thatched-roofed Giarai tomb, complete with risqué wooden statues.

Displays are labelled in Vietnamese, French and English.

The museum is in Cau Giay District, about 7km northwest of the city centre. A metered taxi here is around 120,000d (one-way); *xe om* (motorbike taxi) about 50,000d. The cheapest way to arrive is to take bus 14 (3000d) from Hoan Kiem Lake and get off at the junction between Đ Hoang Quoc Viet and Đ Nguyen Van Huyen.

Tay Ho (West Lake) LAKE

(Map p812) North of the centre, Tay Ho is the city's largest lake and is ringed by upmarket suburbs. On the south side of the lake, along Đ Thuy Khue, is a string of popular seafood restaurants, and to the east, the Xuan Dieu strip is lined with restaurants, cafes, boutiques and luxury hotels. You'll also find two temples on its shores; the Tay Ho and Tran Quoc pagodas.

A newly installed pathway now circles the lake, making for a great bicycle ride.

Lenin Park PARK

(Map p822; admission 5000d; 4am-9pm) The nearest green lung to the Old Quarter, Lenin Park is about 2km south of Hoan Kiem Lake. It's a great place to escape urban Hanoi (and incorporates Bau Mau Lake) and has a couple of cafes.

Activities

Army Hotel SWIMMING

(33C P Pham Ngu Lao) In central Hanoi, the pool is big enough for laps and open all year.

Courses

Highway 4 COOKING

(3715 0577; www.highway4.com; 3 Hang Tre; classes US$27-50) Incorporates a cyclo ride and market tour, before continuing to Highway 4's Tay Ho restaurant. Also cocktail-making classes (per person US$29) using Son Tinh liquors.

Sleeping

Most budget and midrange visitors make for the Old Quarter or the neighbouring Hoan Kiem Lake area for accommodation.

OLD QUARTER

Hanoi Rendezvous Hotel HOTEL $$

(off Map p814; 3828 5777; www.hanoirendezvous.com; 31 P Hang Dieu; dm/s/d/tr US$7.50/25/30/35;) Aussie-run Hanoi Rendezvous features spacious rooms, good dorms, friendly staff, and well-run tours. Don't miss the reproductions of classic Vietnam-themed movies in the downstairs breakfast bar.

Hanoi Backpackers 2 HOSTEL $

(Map p814; 3935 1890; www.hanoibackpackershostel.com; 9 Ma May; dm US$6-9, tw & d US$40;) Spanking new hostel offering an excellent location, spotless dorms and

Around Hoan Kiem Lake

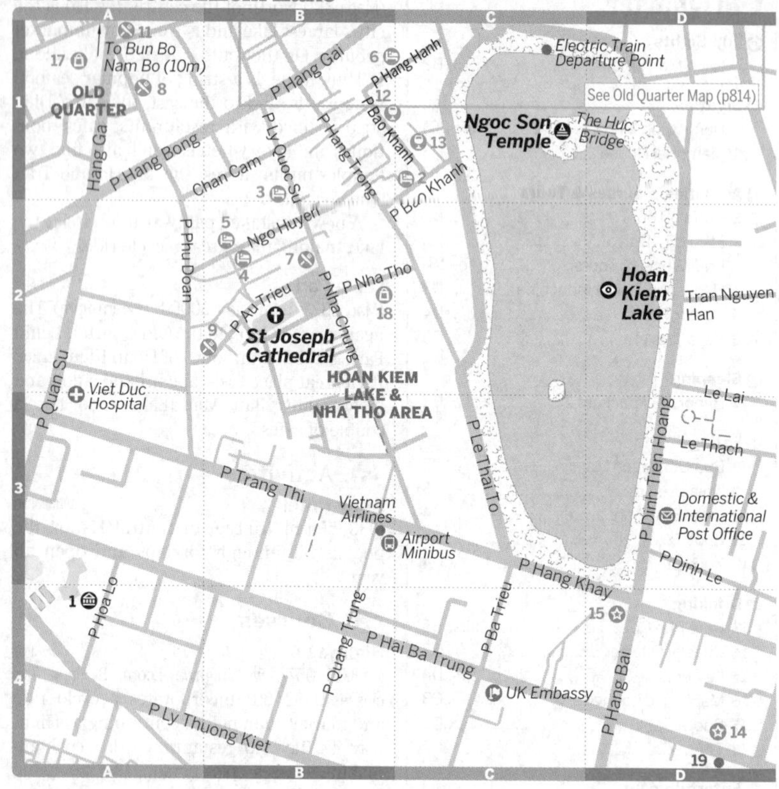

designer doubles. It has a very social restaurant and bar, good travel info and tours too.

Hanoi Guesthouse GUESTHOUSE $
(off Map p814; ☎3824 5732; www.hanoiguesthouse.com; 14 Bat Su; r $20-22; @) A quiet location, eager young English-speaking staff and Hanoi's weekend night market is just a couple of blocks away. Features simple but immaculate rooms.

AROUND HOAN KIEM LAKE

TOP CHOICE **6 on Sixteen** BOUTIQUE HOTEL
(Map p816; ☎6673 6729; www.sixonsixteen.com; 16 Bao Kanh; r US$50-88; @) Decked out in designer textiles and ethnic art, 6 on Sixteen has a warm and welcoming ambience. There are only six rooms, but there's lots of shared areas to encourage guests to mix. Breakfast includes freshly baked pastries and robust Italian coffee.

Madame Moon Guesthouse GUESTHOUSE $
(Map p816; ☎3938 1255; www.madammoonguesthouse.com; 17 P Hang Hanh; r US$22-25; @) Keeping it simple and tasteful, Madame Moon has surprisingly chic rooms and a (relatively) traffic-free location in a street filled with cafes.

Hanoi Backpackers Hostel HOSTEL $
(Map p816; ☎3828 5372; www.hanoibackpackershostel.com; 48 P Ngo Huyen; dm US$6, r US$25-36; @) Impressively organised, perennially popular hostel with custom-built bunk beds and lockers. The dorms all have en-suite bathrooms. It has a rooftop terrace for barbecues and a bar downstairs.

Central Backpackers Hanoi HOSTEL $
(Map p816; ☎3938 1849; www.centralbackpackershostel.com; 16 P Ly Quoc Su; dm US$5; @) Well-run hostel close to good cafes and street eats. It's a pretty social spot, possibly

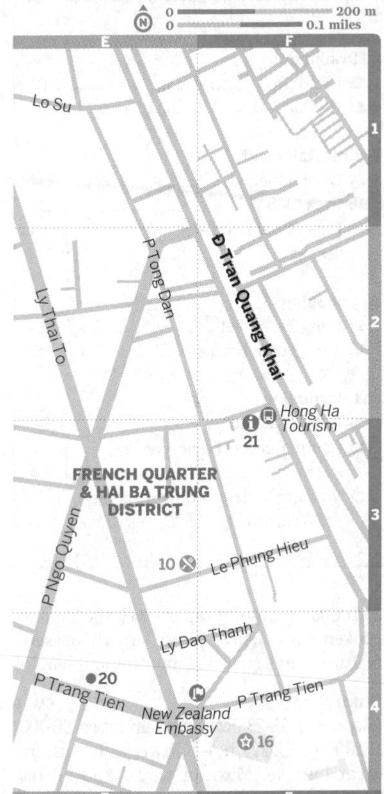

due to the 'Free Beer' (very) happy hour every night from 8pm to 9pm.

Especen Hotel HOTEL $
(Map p816; ☎3824 4401; www.especen.vn; 28 P Tho Xuong; s/d US$17/20; ❄@☁) Spacious, light well-kept rooms and a relatively tranquil location. There are two other branches nearby.

OTHER AREAS

Drift HOSTEL $
(Map p822; ☎3944 8415; www.thedriftbackpackershostel.com; 42 Truong Han Sieu; dm US$6, r US$20-25; ❄@☁) Aussie-run hostel with a social ambience, a free breakfast, a movie room and a cafe specialising in comfort food. It's a 20-minute walk south of the Old Quarter.

Eating

Whatever your budget (or your tastes) it's available here. Get stuck into the local cuisine, which is wonderfully tasty, fragrantly spiced and inexpensive. And don't miss the essential experience of street-food dining.

OLD QUARTER

TOP CHOICE **Highway 4** VIETNAMESE $$
(☎3926 0639; www.highway4.com; 3 P Hang Tre; meals 100,000-200,000d) The original location (inside a tottering old house) of an expanding family of restaurants that specialise in Vietnamese cuisine from the northern mountains. Feast on bite-sized snacks like superb *nem ca xa lo* (catfish spring rolls) and wash it all down with a bottle or two of delicious Son Tinh liquor made from sticky rice. It's on the east side of the Old Quarter, along Hang Bac.

Cha Ca Thang Long VIETNAMESE $$
(off Map p820; 21 P Duong Thanh; cha ca 150,000d; ⏰10am-3pm & 5-10pm) Grill your own succulent fish with a little shrimp paste and plenty of herbs in this place down a small alley. *Cha ca* is an iconic Hanoi fish dish.

Spot INTERNATIONAL $$
(Map p814; P Hang Be; mains 100,000-200,000d) Decorated with propaganda posters, the Spot is good for Western-style grub: salads, grilled tuna and Greek-style salmon sandwiches. There's a decent range of wines by the glass. Occasionally DJs spin tunes later on in the evening.

Quan Bia Minh VIETNAMESE $
(Map p814; 7A P Dinh Liet; meals 80,000-120,000d) A *bia hoi* joint with well-priced Vietnamese food and excellent service. Bag an outdoor table, grab a cold beer and tuck in.

Nola CAFE $
(Map p814; 89 P Ma May; snacks 30,000-60,000d) This fine bar-cafe boasts retro furniture and a boho ambience, so it's coffee and cake in the day and beer after dark. A good place to meet Hanoi's hip young things.

AROUND HOAN KIEM LAKE

TOP CHOICE **Ly Club** GOURMET VIETNAMESE $$
(Map p816; ☎3936 3069; www.lyclub.vn; 4 Le Phung Hieu; meals US$10-15) Set in an elegant French colonial mansion, this restaurant's impressive dining room is a great location for a gourmet meal. The menu excels at both Asian and Vietnamese flavours as well as international dishes. When someone asks, 'So where did you go for your last night in Hanoi?', this is the correct answer.

Around Hoan Kiem Lake

Top Sights
- Hoan Kiem Lake ... D2
- Ngoc Son Temple ... C1
- St Joseph Cathedral ... B2

Sights
- 1 Hoa Lo Prison Museum ... A4

Sleeping
- 2 6 on Sixteen ... C1
- 3 Central Backpackers Hanoi ... B1
- 4 Especen Hotel ... B2
- 5 Hanoi Backpackers Hostel ... B2
- 6 Madame Moon Guesthouse ... B1

Eating
- 7 Banh Ghoi ... B2
- 8 Bun Cha Nem Cua Be Dac Kim ... A1
- 9 Cart ... B2
- 10 Ly Club ... E3
- 11 Mien Xao Luon ... A1

Drinking
- 12 Factory ... B1
- 13 GC Pub ... C1

Entertainment
- 14 Cinematheque ... D4
- 15 Face Club ... D4
- 16 Hanoi Opera House ... F4
- Tunnel ... (see 12)

Shopping
- 17 Hang Da Market ... A1
- 18 Things of Substance ... B2

Information
- 19 American Club ... D4
- 20 Centre Culturel Francaise de Hanoi ... E4
- 21 Vietnam National Administration of Tourism ... F3

Cart CAFE $
(Map p816; www.thecartfood.com; 18 P Au Trieu; baguettes 40,000d; 7.30am-5pm) Superlative pies, interesting baguettes and excellent juices (try the apple, carrot and ginger juice) at this little haven of creative, healthy Western food.

WEST OF THE OLD QUARTER

TOP CHOICE **Quan An Ngon** VIETNAMESE $
(Map p820; 15 P Phan Boi Chau; dishes 35,000-80,000d; 11am-11pm) Incredibly busy, popular place where mini-kitchens turn out terrific street-food-style dishes, including specialities from all over the nation like squid with lemongrass and chilli. Be prepared to wait for a table.

KOTO CAFE $$
(Map p820; www.koto.com.au; 59 P Van Mieu; meals 95,000-140,000d; closed dinner Mon) Stunning four-storey modernist cafe-bar-restaurant near the Temple of Literature. It has daily specials, excellent Vietnamese food and modern Western flavours. KOTO is an extraordinarily successful not-for-profit project that provides career training and guidance to disadvantaged kids.

Southgate FUSION $$
(Map p820; www.southgatehanoi.com; 28 Tong Duy Tan; tapas 90,000-120,000d, mains 130,000-250,000d) Tempting tapas – try the double-cooked pork belly – and superb desserts feature at this stylish restaurant and bar.

Puku CAFE $
(Map p820; 18-28 Tong Duy Tan; mains 60,000-110,000d; 24hr) Kiwi cafe culture: great burgers, Mexican wraps and all day eggy breakfasts.

Net Hue VIETNAMESE $
(Map p820; cnr P Hang Bong & P Cam Chi; mains 30,000-60,000d) Exceptional and well-priced Hue cuisine, including *banh nam* (steamed rice pancake with minced shrimp). Run by a friendly family.

GREATER HANOI

Drinking

Hanoi has sophisticated bars, congenial pubs, grungy clubs and *bia hoi* joints by the barrel-load. Cafes come in every persuasion too: from old school to hip young thing.

Cafes

Coffee meccas include P Trieu Viet Vuong, around 1km south of Hoan Kiem Lake, which has scores of cafes.

Cafe Duy Tri CAFE
(43A P Yen Phu) In the same location since 1936, this caffeine-infused labyrinth is a Hanoi classic. Negotiate the tiny ladders and stairways to

DON'T MISS

THE OLD QUARTER'S TOP STREET FOOD

When in Hanoi, chow down with the masses. Most of these stalls specialise in just one dish and have somewhat flexible opening hours.

» **Bun Cha Nem Cua Be Dac Kim** (Map p816; 67 P Duong Thanh; ⏲11am-3pm) The *bun cha* at this place is a heady combination of grilled pork patties, crab spring rolls, vermicelli noodles and fresh herbs.

» **Banh Cuon** (off Map p814; 14 P Hang Ga; ⏲8am-4pm) Gossamer-light *banh cuon* (steamed rice crepes filled with minced pork, mushrooms and ground shrimp).

» **Pho Gia Truyen** (49 P Bat Dan; ⏲7-10am) Head here for classic *pho* (hearty broth with noodles and tender beef), a breakfast of champions.

» **Banh Ghoi** (Map p816; 52 P Ly Quoc Su; ⏲10am-7pm) Under a banyan tree near St Joseph Cathedral, this stall turns out *banh ghoi*, moreish deep-fried pastries crammed with pork, vermicelli and mushrooms.

» **Bun Oc Saigon** (Map p814; cnr P Nguyen Huu Huan & P Hang Thung; ⏲11am-11pm) Shellfish specials here include *bun oc* (snail noodle soup) with a hearty dash of tart tamarind.

» **Bun Bo Nam Bo** (67 P Hang Dieu; ⏲11am-10pm) *Bu bo nam bo* (dry noodles with beef) is a zingy southern Vietnamese dish mixed with bean sprouts, garlic, lemongrass and green mango.

» **Xoi Yen** (Map p814; cnr P Nguyen Huu Huan & P Hang Mam; ⏲7am-11pm) Specialises in sticky rice topped with goodies including sweet Asian sausage, gooey fried egg and slow-cooked pork.

» **Mien Xao Luon** (Map p816; 87 P Hang Dieu; ⏲7am-2pm) Crunchy fried eels prepared three different ways.

» **Bun Rieu Cua** (off Map p814; 40 P Hang Tre; ⏲7-9am) A Hanoi breakfast classic, *bun rieu cua* (crab noodle soup) is noodle broth laced with fried shallots and garlic, and topped with shrimp paste and chilli.

the 3rd-floor balcony and order the delicious *caphe sua chua* (iced coffee with yoghurt). It's a couple of blocks east of Truc Bach Lake.

Café Pho Co CAFE
(Map p814; 11 P Hang Gai) One of Hanoi's best-kept secrets, this place has plum views over Hoan Kiem Lake. Enter through the silk shop and continue up to the top floor for the mother of all vistas. For something deliciously different try the *caphe trung da*, coffee with a silky-smooth beaten egg white.

Kinh Do Café CAFE
(Map p820; 252 P Hang Bong) Featured in Catherine Deneuve's *Indochine*, this place serves tasty French pastries and feisty coffee.

Cong Caphe CAFE
(Map p822; 152 P Trieu Viet Vuong) The caffeine scene here features eclectic beats and kitsch Communist memorabilia.

Bars

Ha Tien in the Old Quarter has a choice of bars and is a good starting or finishing point for a crawl.

TOP CHOICE **Quan Ly** BAR
(Map p822; 82 Le Van Hu) Traditional *ruou* (Vietnamese liquor) bar complete with ginseng, snake and gecko creations, and you'll also find cheap *bia hoi* and good Vietnamese tucker. Yes, that is the genial owner meeting Ho Chi Minh in the photograph on the wall.

SPLURGE: QUAN HAI SAN NGON

Quan Hai San Ngon (☎3719 3169; 198 Nghi Tam, Tay Ho; mains 150,000-200,000d) is perhaps Hanoi's most atmospheric dining space, arrayed elegantly around giant alfresco reflecting pools, and showcasing excellent Vietnamese seafood – try the briny Halong Bay oysters topped with wasabi. It's a 10-minute-taxi ride from central Hanoi.

West of the Old Quarter

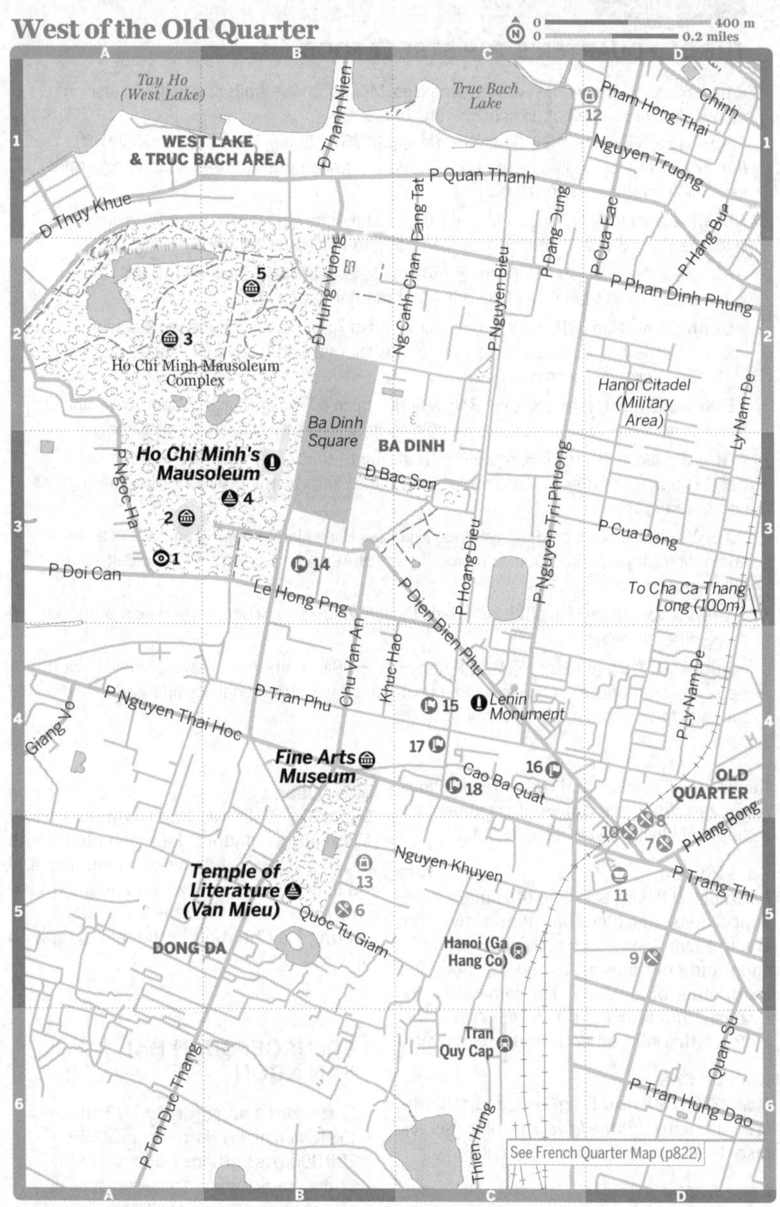

Factory BAR

(Map p816; www.factory.org.vn; 11A P Bao Khanh) Combines a spacious roof terrace with a dramatic interior featuring interesting socialist paintings. There's even a shisha lounge. Regularly hosts music and arts events.

Cheeky Quarter BAR

(Map p814; 1 P Ta Hien; ⌚open late) A tiny, quirky, sociable little bar that has table footy (foosball) and drum 'n' bass or house music.

West of the Old Quarter

Top Sights

	Fine Arts Museum	B4
	Ho Chi Minh's Mausoleum	B3
	Temple of Literature (Van Mieu)	B5
Sights		
1	Ho Chi Minh Mausoleum Complex Entrance	A3
2	Ho Chi Minh Museum	A3
3	Ho Chi Minh's Stilt House	A2
4	One Pillar Pagoda	B3
5	Presidential Palace	B2
Eating		
6	KOTO	B5
7	Net Hue	D5
8	Puku	D5
9	Quan An Ngon	D5
10	Southgate	D5
Drinking		
11	Kinh Do Café	D5
Shopping		
12	Bookworm	D1
13	Craft Link	B5
Information		
14	Canadian Embassy	B3
15	Chinese Embassy	C4
16	German Embassy	C4
17	Singapore Embassy	C4
18	Thailand Embassy	C4

Mao's Red Lounge BAR
(Map p814; 5 P Ta Hien; open late) The most popular place on P Ta Hien, this is jammed with a sociable crowd on weekend nights. It's a classic dive bar with dim lighting and swirling smoke.

Le Pub PUB
(Map p814; 25 P Hang Be) British-style pub with a street-facing terrace popular with travellers and foreign residents. Good comfort grub.

Roots BAR
(Map p814; 2 Luong Ngoc Quyen; 8pm-late) Primarily a reggae bar, this is *the* place for some serious bassline pressure and can be a riot on the right night. Lock-ins have been known.

21N Club BAR
(49 Lang Yen Phu, Tay Ho) A lakeside location spills out onto waterfront seating. There's regular live music and 'Sailor' microbrewed beer.

GC Pub PUB
(Map p816; 7 P Bao Khanh) Looks pretty run down from the street but it gets very lively on weekend nights. Popular with gay Hanoians and has pool tables.

Tet BAR
(Map p814; 2A P Ta Hien) Compact bar that's best *very* late at night when the music is turned up and it morphs into one of Hanoi's smallest clubs.

☆ Entertainment

Cinemas

Megastar Cineplex CINEMA
(Map p822; www.megastarmedia.net/en; 6th fl, Vincom Tower, 191 Ba Trieu) Multiplex with international standards. Tickets from US$2.50.

Cinematheque CINEMA
(Map p816; 22A Hai Ba Trung) A mecca for arthouse film lovers, this is a Hanoi institution.

Clubbing

Hanoi is definitely not the Ibiza of the north, and the often-enforced midnight curfew means dance action is very limited. Also check out the bar-clubs in the Old Quarter.

Face Club CLUB
(Map p816; 6 P Hang Bai) Face Club dishes up lots of lasers, music ranging from hip hop to techno, and a booming sound system. Popular with well-off Hanoians.

Tunnel CLUB
(Map p816; 11B P Bao Khanh) Happy-hour promotions and DJ nights make this a happening multifloor late-night spot.

GAY & LESBIAN HANOI

There are very few gay venues in Hanoi, but plenty of places that are gay-friendly. However official attitudes are still fairly conservative and Hanoi is home to these official attitudes. Police raids in the name of 'social reform' aren't unknown and that tends to ensure gays and lesbians keep a low profile.

The website www.utopia-asia.com has up-to-date information about gay Hanoi. See also the Vietnam information section on www.cambodiaout.com.

Note the warning on p813 regarding possible scams in the area around Hoan Kiem Lake.

French Quarter

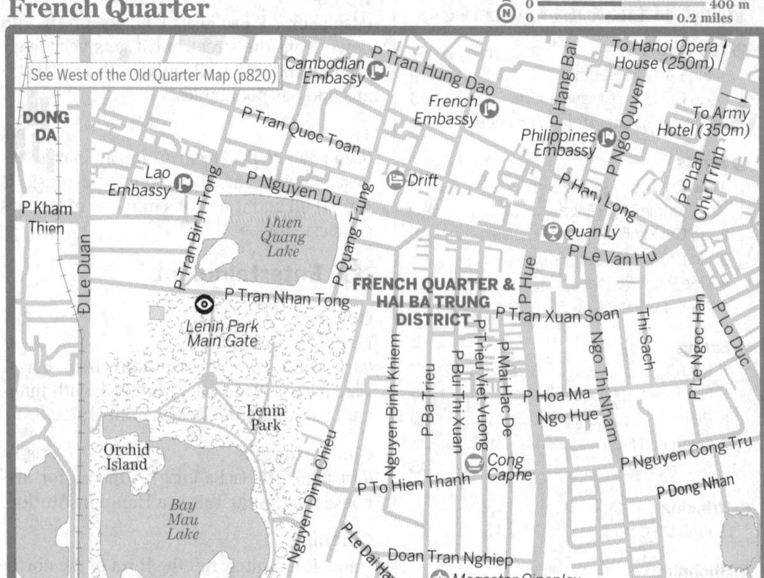

Music

Live traditional music is performed daily at the Temple of Literature.

Hanoi Opera House OPERA
(Map p816; www.hanoioperahouse.org.vn; P Trang Tien) This magnificent 900-seat venue, built in 1911, hosts occasional classical music performances. The atmosphere and acoustics are incredible.

Hanoi Rock City LIVE MUSIC
(www.hanoirockcity.com; 27/52 To Ngoc Van, Tay Ho) A great venue for live music, hip hop, reggae, Hanoi punk and electronica. Located about 7km north of the centre near Tay Ho.

Water Puppetry

Municipal Water Puppet Theatre PUPPETRY
(Roi Nuoc Thang Long; Map p814; www.thanglongwaterpuppet.org; 57B P Dinh Tien Hoang; admission 60,000-100,000d; ⊙performances 2.15pm, 3.30pm, 5pm, 6.30pm, 8pm & 9.15pm) This fascinating art form originated in northern Vietnam, and Hanoi is the best place to catch a show. An absolute must for children.

Shopping

The Old Quarter is brimming with temptations; price labels signal set prices. As you wander around you'll find cosmetics, fake sunglasses, luxury food, T-shirts, musical instruments, herbal medicines, jewellery, spices, propaganda art, fake English Premier League football kits and much, much more.

Art & Handicrafts

For ethnic minority garb and handicrafts P Hang Bac and P To Tich are good hunting grounds.

North and northwest of Hoan Kiem Lake around P Hang Gai, P To Tich, P Hang Khai and P Cau Go are dozens of shops offering handicrafts (lacquerware, mother-of-pearl inlay and ceramics) as well as artwork and antiques.

Private art galleries are concentrated on P Trang Tien, between Hoan Kiem Lake and the Opera House. **Viet Art Centre** (www.vietartcentre.vn; 42 P Yet Kieu) is a fine place to browse contemporary Vietnamese art, photography and sculpture.

Craft Link (Map p820; www.craftlink-vietnam.com; 43 P Van Mieu) sells quality tribal handicrafts and weavings at fair-trade prices.

For Communist propaganda art posters try Hang Bac in the Old Quarter, home to **Hanoi Gallery** (Map p814; 110 P Hang Bac) and **Old Propaganda Posters** (Map p814; 122 P Hang Bac).

Bookshops

Bookworm BOOKS

(Map p820; www.bookwormhanoi.com; 44 Chau Long) Hanoi's best selection of new and used English-language books, including plenty of fiction.

Markets

Dong Xuan Market MARKET

(Map p814) Hundreds of stalls and not touristy. Catch a flavour of Hanoian street life here.

Hang Da Market MARKET

(Map p816; Yen Thai) Small, but good for imported foods, wine, beer and flowers.

Silk Products & Clothing

P Hang Gai, about 100m northwest of Hoan Kiem Lake, and its continuation, P Hang Bong, are good places to look for embroidery and silk (including tailored clothes).

Things of Substance CLOTHING

(Map p816; 5 P Nha Tho) Tailored fashions at moderate prices.

Information

Cultural Centres

American Club (Map p816; ☎3824 1850; 19-21 P Hai Ba Trung)

British Council (☎3728 1922; www.britishcouncil.org/vietnam; 20 Thuy Khue, Tay Ho). Hosts cultural events, exhibitions, workshops and fashion shows.

Centre Culturel Française de Hanoi (Map p816; ☎3936 2164; www.ifhanoi-lespace.com; 24 P Trang Tien) Music and art in the modernist L'Espace building.

Dangers & Annoyances

See p813.

Emergency

Ambulance (☎115)

Fire (☎114)

Police (☎113)

Internet Access

Most budget and midrange hotels offer free internet access as standard, computers in the lobby and wi-fi. You'll find several cybercafes on P Hang Bac in the Old Quarter; rates start at 5000d per hour.

Internet Resources

To get the most out of Hanoi, try the following websites:

Hanoi Grapevine (www.hanoigrapevine.com) A culture vulture's paradise, this site has a useful events calendar.

New Hanoian (www.newhanoian.com) The city's premier online resource, well worth checking out for its up-to-date restaurant, bar and accommodation reviews.

The Word (www.wordhanoi.com) Online version of the excellent, free monthly magazine, *The Word*.

Medical Services

Hanoi Family Medical Practice (☎3843 0748; www.vietnammedicalpractice.com; Van Phuc Diplomatic Compound, 298 P Kim Ma; ⏲24hr) Includes a team of well-respected international physicians and dentists.

L'Hopital Français de Hanoi (☎3577 1100, emergency 3574 1111; www.hfh.com.vn; 1 Phuong Mai; ⏲24hr) Long-established, international-standard hospital with A&E, intensive care, dental clinic and consulting services.

SOS International Clinic (☎3826 4545; www.internationalsos.com; 51 Xuan Dieu; ⏲24hr) English, French, German and Japanese are spoken and there's a dental clinic. It's 5km north of central Hanoi.

Money

Hanoi has many ATMs, and on the main roads around Hoan Kiem Lake are international banks where you can change money and get cash advances on credit cards.

Post

Main post office (Map p816; 75 P Dinh Tien Hoang)

International post office (Map p816; cnr P Dinh Tien Hoang & P Dinh Le)

Telephone

Guesthouses and internet cafes are convenient for local calls. For international services, internet cafes using Skype offer the cheapest rates.

International Call Service (Map p814; 3 P Ta Hien; ⏲7am-10pm) Costs 1500d to 2000d per minute to most countries.

Tourist Information

Even though this is the capital, forget anything really useful like a helpful tourism office that dishes out free information. In the cafes and bars of the Old Quarter look for the excellent local magazine, *The Word*.

Tourist Information Center (Map p814; P Dinh Tien Hoang; ⏲8.30am-9pm) City maps and brochures, but privately run with an emphasis on selling tours. Pick up a copy of the handy pocket-sized *Hanoi City Pass* free book.

Travel Agencies

Hanoi has hundreds of budget travel agencies. It's not advisable to book trips or tickets through guesthouses and hotels. Dealing directly with tour operators gives you a much better idea of

BUSES FROM GIA LAM

DESTINATION	COST (D)	DURATION (HR)	FREQUENCY
(Bai Chay) Halong City	100,000	3½	every 30 min
Haiphong	70,000	2	every 20 min
Lao Cai	250,000	9	1pm & 7pm
Ha Giang	170,000	7	approx hourly
Cao Bang	180,000	8	5 daily

what you'll get for your money; seek out those operators that stick to small groups.

For nationwide operators offering tours of Hanoi and northern Vietnam, see p907. For motorbike tours, see p906.

Successful tour operators often have their names cloned by others looking to trade on their reputation, so check addresses and websites carefully. Consider the following places in the Old Quarter:

Ethnic Travel (Map p814; ☎3926 1951; www.ethnictravel.com.vn; 35 P Hang Giay) Off-the-beaten-track trips across the north in small groups. Some trips are low-impact using public transport and homestays; others are activity based (including hiking, cycling and cooking). Offers Bai Tu Long Bay tours.

Handspan Travel Indochina (Map p814; ☎3926 2828; www.handspan.com; 78 P Ma May) Highly recommended for its wide range of tours: sea-kayaking trips using an ecocamp in Lan Ha Bay, jeep tours, mountain biking, trekking and community-based tourism.

Ocean Tours (Map p814; ☎3926 0463; www.oceantours.com.vn; 22 P Hang Bac) Professional, well-organised tour operator with Halong Bay and Ba Be National Park options, and 4WD road trips around the northeast.

Vega Travel (Map p814; ☎3926 2092; www.vegatravel.vn; cnr P Ma May & 24A P Hang Bac) Well-run tours around the north and throughout Vietnam. Financially supports minority kindergartens and schools around Sapa and Bac Ha.

Getting There & Away

Air

Hanoi has fewer international flights than Ho Chi Minh City (HCMC), but with a change of aircraft in Hong Kong or Bangkok you can get almost anywhere. For more on international flights in and out of Hanoi, see p905.

Vietnam Airlines (Map p816; ☎1900 545 486; www.vietnamair.com.vn; 25 P Trang Thi) Links Hanoi to destinations throughout Vietnam. Popular routes include Hanoi to Dalat, Danang, Dien Bien Phu, HCMC, Hue and Nha Trang, all served daily.

Jetstar Airways (☎1900 1550; www.jetstar.com) Operates low-cost flights to Danang, HCMC and Nha Trang.

Bus

Hanoi has three main long-distance bus stations, each serving a particular area. It's a good idea to arrange your travel the day before you want to leave. The stations are pretty well organised with ticket offices, displayed schedules and fixed prices.

Gia Lam bus station (off Map p812; Đ Ngoc Lam), 3km northeast of the centre on the far bank of the Song Hong (Red River), is the place for buses to points east and northeast of Hanoi.

Loung Yen bus station (Map p812; Tran Quang Khai & Nguyen Khoai), 3km southeast of the Old Quarter, serves destinations to the south and the east, including sleeper buses to Hue, Dalat and Nha Trang and transport to Cat Ba Island.

Note that taxis at Luong Yen are notorious for their dodgy meters. Walk a couple of blocks and hail one off the street.

My Dinh bus station (Đ Pham Hung), 7km west of the city, provides services to the west and the north, including sleeper buses to Dien Bien Phu.

Some buses from Ninh Binh and the south use **Giap Bat bus station** (Đ Giai Phong), it's 7km south of the Hanoi train station.

Tourist-style minibuses can be booked through most hotels and cafes. Popular destinations include Halong Bay and Sapa. Prices are usually about 30% to 40% higher than the regular public bus, but include a hotel pick-up.

Open-tour bus tickets (hop-on hop-off bus services that connect the capital with HCMC) are available in Hanoi for destinations, including Ninh Binh and Hue.

Buses also connect Hanoi with Nanning in China. Two daily services (at 7.30am and 9.30am) to Nanning (450,000d, eight hours) leave from the private terminal of **Hong Ha Tourism** (Map p814; ☎3824 7339; Hong Ha Hotel, 204 Tran Quang Khai). Tickets should be purchased in advance and you may be asked to show your Chinese visa; see p905.

BUSES FROM LOUNG YEN

DESTINATION	COST (D)	DURATION (HR)	FREQUENCY
Dalat	440,000	24	11am & 6pm
Hue	220,000	12	hourly 2-6pm
Danang	240,000	13	hourly from 2-6pm
Ninh Binh	55,000	2½	every 20 min 6am-6pm
Nha Trang	170,000	7	10am & 6pm

Car & Motorcycle

Car hire is best arranged via a travel agency, hotel or tour operator. The roads in the north are in pretty good shape but expect an average speed of 35km to 40km per hour. You'll definitely need a 4WD. Daily rates start at about US$110 a day (including driver and petrol). For more, see p906.

Hanoi is a nightmare to negotiate on a motorbike – we suggest you leave it to the locals. If you're really up for the challenge, try the Hanoi tour operators on p906 for reliable machines.

Train

The main **Hanoi train station** (Ga Hang Co; Map p820; 120 Đ Le Duan; ⏲ticket office 7.30am-12.30pm & 1.30-7.30pm) is at the western end of P Tran Hung Dao. Trains from here go to destinations south.

To the right of the main entrance of the train station is a separate ticket office for northbound trains to Lao Cai (for Sapa) and China (see p905). Note that all northbound trains leave from a separate station (just behind the main station) called **Tran Quy Cap station** (B Station; Map p820; P Tran Qui Cap).

To make things even more complicated, some northbound (Lao Cai and Lang Son included) and eastbound (Haiphong) trains depart from **Gia Lam** (Nguyen Van Cu, Gia Lam District) on the eastern side of the Song Hong (Red River), and **Long Bien** (Map p812) on the western (city) side of the river. Be sure to ask just where you need to go to catch your train.

In theory, **Vietnam Rail** (www.vr.com.vn) has timetables and prices in English, though it's rarely updated; try the rail website www.seat61.com.

It's best to buy tickets at least one day before departure to ensure a seat or sleeper. Travel agents will book train tickets for a commission.

ℹ Getting Around

Bicycle

Many Old Quarter guesthouses and cafes rent bikes for about US$2 per day. Good luck with that traffic.

Bus

Plenty of local buses (fares from 3000d) serve routes around Hanoi but very few tourists bother with them.

Pick up a copy of the *Xe Buyt Hanoi* (Hanoi Bus Map; 5000d) from bookshops if you want to tackle the system.

Cyclo

A few *cyclo* (pedicab) drivers still frequent the Old Quarter. Settle on a price first and watch out for overcharging.

Aim to pay around 25,000d for a shortish journey; night rides are more. Not many *cyclo* drivers speak English, so take a map with you.

TRAINS FROM HANOI

DESTINATION	STATION	COST SOFT SEAT-SLEEPER (D)	DURATION (HR)
Danang	Hanoi	570,000-915,000	15½-21
Haiphong	Long Bien & Gia Lam	47,000-60,000	2-3
HCMC	Hanoi	1,175,000-1,690,000	30-41
Hue	Hanoi	508,000-833,000	12-16
Lao Cai	Tran Quy Cap	210,000-450,000	8½-9½
Nha Trang	Hanoi	1,030,000-1,510,000	19-28

Electric Train

Hanoi's ecofriendly **electric train** (per person 15,000d; ⊙8.30am-10.30pm) is actually a pretty good way to get your bearings. It traverses a network of 14 stops in the Old Quarter and around Hoan Kiem Lake. Catch one at the northern end of Hoan Kiem Lake (p816); a circuit takes around 40 minutes.

Motorcycle

Offers for *xe om* (motorbike taxi) rides are incessant. A short ride should be about 30,000d, about 5km around 70,000d.

Forget getting around Hanoi by motorbike unless you're very familiar with the city – traffic is relentless, road signs are missing, road manners are nonexistent and it's dangerous.

Taxi

Taxis are everywhere. Flag fall is around 15,000d, which takes you 1km or 2km; every kilometre thereafter costs around 10,000d. Some dodgy operators have high-speed meters, so use the following reliable companies:

Mai Linh Taxi (☎3822 2666)
Thanh Nga Taxi (☎3821 5215)
Van Xuan (☎3822 2888)

AROUND HANOI

Perfume Pagoda

The **Perfume Pagoda** (Chua Huong; admission incl return boat trip 55,000d) is a striking complex of pagodas and Buddhist shrines built into the karst cliffs of Huong Tich Mountain. It's mainly a domestic drawcard but the river trip (1½ hours by row boat) is scenic, leaving from My Duc (two hours from Hanoi).

The main pagoda area is about a 4km walk up from where the boat lets you off, or take the cable car (one-way/return 60,000/100,000d).

Hanoi travellers' cafes (see p823) offer day tours to the pagoda from US$10, including transport, guide and lunch.

Handicraft Villages

There are numerous villages surrounding Hanoi that specialise in particular cottage industries. You'll need a good guide to make visits worthwhile.

Bat Trang, 13km southeast of Hanoi is known for the ceramics, vases and other masterpieces fired in its kilns. **So**, 25km southwest of Hanoi, is famed for its delicate noodles, some made from cassava flour. You can see silk cloth being produced on a loom in **Van Phuc**, a village 8km southwest of Hanoi.

Tours of handicraft villages are best arranged in Hanoi; expect to pay around US$40 for a car and driver for the day.

Ninh Binh

☎030 / POP 130,000

The city of Ninh Binh, 93km south of Hanoi, isn't a destination in itself, but it's a good base for exploring some quintessentially Vietnamese karst scenery and bucolic countryside. The town, though industrial, has its pleasant aspects, but the proximity of sights, including the limestone mountains of Tam Coc (p827) and Cuc Phuong National Park (p827), is the real draw.

Sleeping & Eating

Accommodation is excellent value here. All the places listed can arrange tours and hire out motorbikes and bicycles.

Restaurant choices are limited, but while you're here try the local speciality, *de* (goat meat), usually served with fresh herbs and rice paper. There are dozens of places lining the road to Chua Bai Dinh.

TOP CHOICE **Thanhthuy's Guest House & New Hotel** HOTEL $
(☎387 1811; www.hotelthanhthuy.com; 128 Đ Le Hong Phong; guesthouse r US$7-10, hotel r US$15-25; ❄@📶) Probably the best place to mingle with other travellers, this popular hotel is run by a friendly crew, including some very switched-on tour guides. Rooms, all very clean and some with balcony, vary quite a bit in price and comfort level.

Thuy Anh Hotel HOTEL $$
(☎387 1602; www.thuyanhhotel.com; 55A Đ Truong Han Sieu; s/d old wing US$20/25, new wing US$30/45; ❄@📶) A well-run hotel with good-value rooms, particularly the spotless, modern options at the rear. The restaurant serves Western food (including a hearty complimentary breakfast) and Vietnamese dishes.

Thanh Binh Hotel HOTEL $
(☎387 2439; www.thanhbinhhotelnb.com.vn; 31 Đ Luong Van Tuy; s US$10-25, d US$15-30; ❄@📶) Popular with budget travellers – the rooms are good, the owner is friendly and there's a restaurant.

Information

You'll find a cluster of internet cafes on Đ Luong Van Tuy and several ATMs on Đ Tran Hung Dao.

Getting There & Away

Public buses leave very regularly from Giap Bat and Loung Yen bus terminals in Hanoi (55,000d, 2½ hours). The bus station is on the east side of the Van River. Ninh Binh is also a hub on the open-tour bus route.

Ninh Binh is a scheduled stop for some trains travelling between Hanoi and HCMC, but travelling by road is faster.

Around Ninh Binh

TAM COC

Famed for huge limestone rock formations that loom over rice paddies, **Tam Coc** (admission 30,000d, boat 60,000d) boasts breathtaking scenery.

The only way to see Tam Coc is by rowboat on the Ngo Dong River. The boats pass through karst caves on this beautiful two-hour trip. Boats seat two passengers (and have no shade). Arrive before 9am to beat the crowds, as it can be a bit of a circus thanks to the pushy vendors.

Tam Coc is 9km southwest of Ninh Binh. By car or motorbike, follow Hwy 1 south and turn west at the turn-off.

HOA LU

Hoa Lu was the capital of Vietnam under the Dinh (968–80) and Le dynasties (980–1009) due to its proximity to China and the natural protection afforded by the region's craggy mountainous landscape.

The **ancient citadel** (admission 12,000d), most of which, sadly, has been destroyed, once covered an area of about 3 sq km.

There is no public transport to Hoa Lu, which is 12km north of Ninh Binh. Most travellers get here by bicycle, motorbike or car.

CHUA BAI DINH

A vast new Buddhist temple complex, **Chua Bai Dinh** (⏲7am-5.45pm) attracts thousands of Vietnamese visitors.

Cloister-like walkways pass 500 stone *arhats* (statues of enlightened Buddhists). They line the route up to the triple-roofed Phap Chu pagoda, which contains a 10m, 100-tonne bronze Buddha.

An additional 13-storey pagoda and a temple with Vietnam's largest bell are other key attractions at this bombastic sight.

Chua Bai Dinh is 11km northwest of Ninh Binh; you'll pass dozens of goat meat restaurants on the way. Guesthouses in Ninh Binh can arrange transport.

Cuc Phuong National Park

☎030 / ELEV 150-648M

This **national park** (☎384 8006; www.cucphuongtourism.com; admission 20,000d) is one of Vietnam's most important nature preserves, and was declared the nation's first national park in 1963. The hills are laced with grottoes, and the climate is subtropical at the park's lower elevations.

Excellent trekking opportunities abound in the park, including a hike (8km return) to an enormous 1000-year-old tree (*Tetrameles nudiflora,* for botany geeks), and to a Muong village, where you can also go rafting. A guide is mandatory for longer treks.

During the rainy season (July to September) leeches are common; the best time to visit is between December and April.

Be sure to check out the **Endangered Primate Rescue Center** (www.primatecenter.org; ⏲9.30-11.30am & 1.30-4.30pm), which is home to around 150 rare monkeys bred in captivity or confiscated from illegal traders. These gibbons, langurs and lorises are rehabilitated, studied and, whenever possible, released into semi-wild protected areas.

There's also a **Turtle Conservation Center** (⏲9-11.15am & 2-4.45pm), which houses over 1000 turtles, many of them confiscated from smugglers. You'll find excellent information displays, and there are incubation and hatchling viewing areas. The centre successfully breeds and releases turtles of 11 different species, including six native turtles.

Sleeping & Eating

There are three accommodation areas in the park.

At the visitor centre are dark, **basic rooms** (per person US$7) and decent en-suite **guesthouse rooms** (US$23-27), and 2km away you'll find attractive **bungalows** (US$25) overlooking Mac Lake.

The main park centre, 18km from the gate, has simple **rooms** (per person US$7), large **four-bed rooms** (US$20) and a few **bungalows** (r US$28).

There are **restaurants** (meals 25,000-50,000d) at both the park centre and visitor centre. Call ahead and place your order for each meal (except breakfast).

Cuc Phuong can get very busy at weekends and holiday time, when you should make a reservation.

Getting There & Away

Cuc Phuong National Park is 45km west of Ninh Binh, and there are irregular bus connections (18,000d).

NORTHERN VIETNAM

Welcome to the roof of Vietnam, where the mountains of the Tonkinese Alps soar skyward, delivering some of the most spectacular scenery in the country. The attractive old French hill station of Sapa remains the main base in the far north, but nearby Bac Ha is emerging as a less-visited alternative for trekking and exploring hill-tribe villages. South of here, the sublime scenery and idyllic lakes of Ba Be National Park are well worth a diversion.

Bizarre but beautiful, Halong Bay is geology gone wild, with hundreds of limestone pinnacles emerging from the waters. North of Halong Bay is less-visited Bai Tu Long Bay, where nature's spectacular show continues all the way to the Chinese border. Or head to rugged Cat Ba, a verdant island renowned for its hiking, biking, sailing, and world-class rock climbing.

Halong Bay

Majestic and mysterious, inspiring and imperious, Halong Bay's 3000 or more incredible islands rise from the emerald waters of the Gulf of Tonkin. Designated a World Heritage site in 1994, this mystical seascape of limestone islets is a vision of breathtaking beauty.

The islands are dotted with wind- and wave-eroded grottoes, many now illuminated with Technicolor lighting effects. Sadly, litter and trinket-touting vendors are now also part of the experience.

From February through until April, the weather is often cold and drizzly, and the ensuing fog can cause low visibility, although the temperature rarely falls below 10°C. Tropical storms are frequent during the summer months (July to September).

Most visitors sensibly opt for tours that include sleeping on a boat in the bay. Some dodge the humdrum gateway Halong City completely and head independently for Cat Ba Town, from where trips to less-visited, equally alluring Lan Ha Bay are easily set up. See the boxed text, p829, for more on organised trips.

Halong Bay Management Department (☎033-384 6592; http://halong.org.vn; 166 Đ Le Thanh Tong), 2km west of Halong City, regulates independent cruises on the bay. It's easy here to hook up with other people to share a boat with; rates start at about 50,000d an hour.

Halong City

☎033 / POP 193,700

Halong City is the main gateway to Halong Bay. Its seafront is blighted by high-rise hotels but you will fine good budget accommodation here.

An elegant suspension bridge connects the western, touristy side of town (known as Bai Chay) with the much more Vietnamese entity (Hon Gai) to the east.

Sleeping & Eating

The 'hotel alley' of Đ Vuon Dao has more than 50 minihotels, most of them almost identical, with comfortable doubles around US$12. For cheap, filling food there are modest places at the bottom of Đ Vuon Dao with English menus. Seafood lovers should gravitate to the harbourfront Đ Halong.

GETTING TO LAOS: NA MEO TO NAM XOI

Getting to the border This route uses the remote Nam Xoi–Na Meo crossing 175km northwest of Thanh Hoa city and 70km east of Sam Neua (Laos). If at all possible, take a direct bus. There's a daily 8am bus from Thanh Hoa's western bus station (*Ben Xe Mien Tay*) to Sam Neua (275,000d) inside Laos, but expect overcharging.

At the border Na Meo has several basic, serviceable guesthouses. The border crossing is open daily from 7am to 5pm.

Moving on It's best not to get stuck in Nam Xoi, on the Laos side of the border, as transport is extremely irregular and there's no accommodation.

See p345 for information on crossing this border in the other direction.

GETTING TO LAOS: NAM CAN TO NONG HAET

Getting to the border The often mist-shrouded Nam Can–Nong Haet border crossing is 250km northwest of Vinh. Buses between Vinh and Phonsavan cross here, leaving on Wednesday, Friday, Saturday and Sunday (235,000d). For a DIY journey, head to Muong Xen where you'll need a motorbike to take you uphill 25km to the border at Nam Can (around US$7).

At the border Open daily from 8am to 6pm.

Moving on Transport on the Laos side to Nong Haet is erratic, but once you get there, you can pick up a bus to Phonsavan.

See p342 for information on crossing this border in the other direction.

BMC Thang Long Hotel HOTEL $$
(☎384 6458; www.bmcthanglonghotel.com; Đ Halong; r US$25-75; ❄@☜) Large hotel with spacious and recently renovated rooms, some with ocean views. Staff are warm and personal, and the Bai Chay tourist docks are just across the road.

Tung Lam Hotel HOTEL $
(☎364 0743; 29 Đ Vuon Dao; r US$10-12; ❄☜) This minihotel is making a little more effort than most. Rooms all have two beds, TV, minibar and en-suite bathrooms, and those at the front are spacious and include a balcony.

Information

Post office (Đ Halong) Internet access available.
Vietcombank (Đ Halong) Exchange services and ATM.

Getting There & Away

The bus station is 6km south of central Bai Chay, just off Hwy 18.

Cat Ba Island

☎031 / POP 13,500

Rugged, craggy and jungle-clad, Cat Ba is emerging as northern Vietnam's adventure sport and ecotourism mecca. There's a terrific roll-call of activities here – sailing trips, birdwatching, biking, hiking and rock climbing – and some fine tour operators organising them.

Lan Ha Bay, off the southeastern side of the island, is especially scenic and offers numerous beaches to explore. You could spend a year here discovering a different islet every day while swimming and snorkelling the bay's turquoise waters. Cat Ba Island has a few fishing villages, as well as a fast-growing town.

Much of Cat Ba Island was declared a national park in 1986 to protect the island's diverse ecosystems and wildlife, including the endangered golden-headed langur, the world's rarest primate. There are beautiful beaches, numerous lakes, waterfalls and grottoes in the spectacular limestone hills.

DON'T MISS

CRUISING THE KARSTS: TOURS TO HALONG BAY

Budget tours sold out of Hanoi start from a rock-bottom US$35 per person for a dodgy day-trip, rising to around US$150 for two nights on the bay with kayaking. For around US$80 to US$90, you should get a worthwhile overnight cruise.

We get many complaints about poor service, bad food and rats running around boats, but these tend to be on the ultra-budget tours. Spend a little more and enjoy the experience a whole lot more. In February 2011, a budget tour boat sank with the loss of 12 lives. Consequently, new regulations have been introduced to improve safety.

Most tours include transport, meals and, sometimes, island hikes or kayaking. Drinks are extra. Boat tours are sometimes cancelled in bad weather – ascertain in advance what a refund will be.

If you've got more time and want to experience Halong Bay without the crowds, consider heading to Cat Ba Island. From there, tour operators concentrate on Lan Ha Bay, which is relatively untouched and has sublime sandy beaches. See p831.

For a list of reliable Hanoi-based tour outfits operating in Halong Bay, see p823.

BAI TU LONG BAY

The area immediately northeast of Halong Bay is part of **Bai Tu Long National Park** (www.baitulongnationalpark.vn), which is blessed with spectacular limestone islands every bit as beautiful as its famous neighbour. It's definitely a laid-back alternative to the touristy hustle and bustle of Halong Bay.

Charter boats can be arranged to Bai Tu Long Bay from Halong Bay; rates start at around 300,000d per hour, and the trip takes about five hours. A cheaper and more flexible alternative is to travel overland to Cai Rong and visit the outlying islands by boat from there.

Hanoi travel agencies including Ethnic Travel (p824) run trips into the Bai Tu Long area. Another Hanoi contact for Bai Tu Long is **Le Pont Travel** (04-3935 1889; www.letponttravel.com; 102 P Ma May, Old Quarter).

In recent years Cat Ba Town has experienced a hotel boom, and a chain of ugly concrete hotels now frames a once-lovely bay. That said its ugliness is skin deep, as the rest of the island and Lan Ha Bay are so alluring.

Sights

TOP CHOICE Lan Ha Bay — ISLANDS

The 300 or so karst islands of **Lan Ha Bay** (admission 20,000d) are directly south and east of Cat Ba Town. Geologically they are very much an extension of Halong Bay, sharing the same emerald sea and limestone pinnacles, but with the additional attraction of numerous white-sand beaches. Few tourist boats venture here, so the islands have a more isolated, off-the-beaten-track appeal.

Sailing and kayak trips here are best organised in Cat Ba Town. With hundreds of **beaches** to choose from, it's easy to find your own private patch of sand for the day. Camping is permitted on gorgeous **Hai Pie Beach** (also known as Tiger Beach), which is used as a base camp by the Cat Ba adventure -tour operators and even hosts occasional full-moon parties.

Blue Swimmer (p831) offers wonderful sailing excursions in Lan Ha Bay at reasonable rates. The islands also offer superb rock climbing, and are the main destination for trips run by Asia Outdoors (p831).

Cat Ba National Park — NATIONAL PARK

The main habitat of the golden-headed langur (officially the world's most endangered primate, with around 65 remaining), **Cat Ba National Park** (admission 30,000d, guide 60,000-170,000d; dawn-dusk) is a vitally important ecosystem. Macaques, wild boar, deer, civets, several species of squirrel (including the giant black squirrel) and more than 70 species of birds, including hawks, hornbills and cuckoos, are all also present.

There's excellent trekking too, such as a very challenging 18km hike (five to six hours) through the park. You'll need a guide, transport to the trailhead and a boat to return, all of which can be arranged in Cat Ba Town. Proper trekking shoes, rainwear, water and food are recommended. There are shorter trails that are less hardcore.

To reach the national park headquarters at Trung Trang, get a QH public bus (15,000d, 20 minutes) from the hydrofoil docks at Cat Ba Town. Buses leave at 5am, 8.10am, 11.10am and 4pm. Alternatively, a *xe om* costs around 60,000d one-way.

Fort Cannon — WAR MONUMENT

For one of the best views in Vietnam, head to **Fort Cannon** (admission 20,000d; sunrise-sunset). Underground tunnels and gun emplacements were first installed here by the Japanese in WWII.

BUSES FROM HALONG BAY

DESTINATION	COST (D)	DURATION (HR)	FREQUENCY
Hanoi	90,000	3	every 15 min
Haiphong	50,000	1½	every 20 min
Mong Cai	90,000	4	every 30 min
Lang Son	120,000	5½	12.30pm

Well-labelled paths guide visitors. The vistas out to a karst-punctuated sea are quite sublime, and it even has a terrific cafe and juice bar.

The entrance gate is a steep 10-minute walk or a 10,000d *xe om* ride from Cat Ba Town. From the gate, a **tourist train** (40,000d) trundles the last part of the uphill journey, or it's another stiff 20-minute walk.

Hospital Cave WAR MONUMENT

This **cave** (admission 15,000d; ⌚7am-4.30pm) is an intriguing site. It was used as a (bomb-proof) secret hospital during the war in Vietnam and as a safe house for VC leaders. This incredibly well-constructed three-storey feat of engineering was in constant use until 1975. A guide will show you around the 17 rooms, point out the old operating theatre, cinema and small swimming pool. It's about 10km north of Cat Ba Town.

Cat Co Beaches BEACHES

The white-sand Cat Co beaches (called simply Cat Co 1, Cat Co 2 and Cat Co 3) are perfect places to lounge around for the day; however, Cat Co 1 and 3 have been taken over by big resorts. Luckily, Cat Co 2 is the most attractive beach, also offering simple accommodation and camping. The beaches are about 1km from Cat Ba Town.

Activities

Cat Ba is a superb base for adventure sports.

Mountain Biking

Hotels can arrange Chinese mountain bikes (around US$4 per day), and Blue Swimmer rents Trek bikes for US$12 per day.

One possible route traverses the heart of the island, past Hospital Cave down to the west coast's mangroves and crab farms, and then in a loop back to Cat Ba Town past tidal mud flats and deserted beaches.

Rock Climbing

Cat Ba Island and Lan Ha Bay's spectacular limestone cliffs make for world-class rock climbing amid stunning scenery. Asia Outdoors (formerly Slo Pony Adventures), who pioneered climbing in Vietnam, use fully licensed and certified instructors and remain the absolute authorities. Most climbers in Cat Ba are complete novices, but as the instruction is excellent, many leave Cat Ba completely bitten by the bug.

Full-day climbing trips including instruction, transport, lunch and gear start at US$52 per person for Cat Ba Island, or US$75 if you head for Lan Ha Bay. These longer trips by boat incorporate kayaking, beach stops and exploring the amazing karst landscape.

Sailing & Kayaking

Sailing excursions on gorgeous Lan Ha Bay cost US$39 per person. Full-day trips on a Chinese junk to Long Chau lighthouse, built by the French in the 1920s, are also possible.

Plenty of hotels in Cat Ba Town rent kayaks (per half-day around US$8), or rent better kayaks (per day single/double US$12/20) from Blue Swimmer.

Guided overnight kayak tours by Blue Swimmer (per person US$108) include Lan Ha Bay, sea caves and camping on a deserted beach.

Trekking

Most of Cat Ba Island consists of protected tropical forest. For details of trekking routes see Cat Ba National Park. Asia Outdoors and Blue Swimmer both offer a great hike around Cat Ba Island, taking in Butterfly Valley.

☞ Tours

Tours of the island and boat trips around Halong Bay are offered by nearly every hotel in Cat Ba, costing around US$20 for day trips including kayaking and US$70 for two-day, one-night tours.

We have received unfavourable feedback – cramped conditions and dodgy food – about some of these trips. The following adventure-tour operators understand travellers' needs and will steer you to really special areas of Cat Ba, Lan Ha Bay and beyond.

Asia Outdoors ROCK CLIMBING

(☎368 8450; www.slopony.com; Noble House, Đ 1-4) Formerly called Slo Pony, this highly professional company is run by two uber-passionate climbers and explorers. Climbing instruction is their real expertise, but they also offer excellent well-structured sailing, biking and hiking trips. Rock up to their office in Noble House at 6pm every night to see what's planned.

Blue Swimmer SAILING, KAYAKING

(☎369 6079; www.blueswimmersailing.com; 265 Đ Nui Ngoc) A very well-organised, environmentally conscious outfit offering superb sailing and kayaking trips; trekking and biking excursions are also offered.

Cat Ba Ventures BOAT TRIPS, KAYAKING

(☎388 8755, 849 124 67016; www.catbaventures.com; 223 Đ 14) Locally owned and operated

HALONG BAY TO CAT BA ISLAND (WITHOUT THE HASSLE)

Warning! Travelling from Halong City to Cat Ba Island can be fraught with hassles.

Tourist boats (US$8, four hours) depart from Halong Bay around 1pm for Cat Ba Island, but they dock at Gia Luan (40km from Cat Ba Town) and local taxi and *xe om* operators frequently demand up to US$50 for the ride. There *is* actually a local bus (15,000d) – the QH Green Bus – at 5pm, but this usually departs just before the boats arrive. Funny that...

Many boat owners in Halong Bay are part of the scam, so check if onward transport to Cat Ba Town is included. Some operators including **Cat Ba Ventures** (www.catbaventures.com) do include it.

An alternative route is taking the **passenger and vehicle ferry** (per person 40,000d, 1hr; ⏲on the hr 5am-5pm May-Sep & 8am, 11.10am & 3pm Oct-Apr) that travels from the resort island of Tuan Chau to Gia Luan. (A taxi from Halong City to Tuan Chau is around 130,000d, *xe om* 35,000d.) You can then catch a QH Green bus (departures at 6am, 9.30am, 1.10pm, 4pm & 5pm for 15,000d) to Cat Ba Town.

To travel in the other direction, contact **Cat Ba Ventures** (www.catbaventures.com) in Cat Ba Town for the latest information.

company offering excellent boat trips to Halong Bay, kayaking, and hiking.

Sleeping

Most hotels are in Cat Ba Town. Room rates fluctuate greatly between high-season summertime and the slower winter months. The following are low-season prices.

CAT BA TOWN

Duc Tuan Hotel HOTEL $
(☎388 8783; www.catbatravelservice.com; 210 Đ 1-4 178; r US$8-15; ❄📶) Family-owned place with simple, but colourfully furnished rooms; those at the back are quieter, but lack windows. The downstairs restaurant offers seafood *lau* (hotpot) meals.

Cat Ba Dream HOTEL $
(☎388 8274; www.catbadream.com.vn; 226 Đ 1-4; r US$10-15; ❄@📶) A recent addition, this place has perfunctory service, but if you can angle for a seafront room, you'll have a cinematic scroll of Cat Ba action right in front of you.

Vien Dong HOTEL $
(☎388 8555; www.viendong-hotel.com.vn; 225 Đ Nui Ngoc; r US$12-15; ❄@📶) It's a good choice, with sterling views of the bay, well-kept and spacious rooms, and a good grasp of English at reception.

Phong Lan Hotel HOTEL $
(☎388 8605; Đ 1-4; r US$8-12; ❄📶) Request a room at the front of this hotel, which sits right in the middle of the seafront strip and has balconies overlooking the harbour. The English-speaking owner is helpful.

Thu Ha HOTEL $
(☎388 8343; Đ 1-4; r US$8-12; ❄📶) Offering a super-central seafront location, the recently refurbished Thu Ha offers great value. Negotiate hard for a front room with a balcony, and wake up to sea views.

Bungalows BUNGALOWS $
(☎093 447 8156; d 400,000d) On the sandy beach at Cat Co 2, these bungalows are basic, thatched wooden buildings with a fan in an attractive, leafy beachside plot. You'll find a shower block and a cafe for meals (around 70,000d). At the time of writing, a five star resort was planned for Cat Co 2, so this may change.

AROUND CAT BA ISLAND

Whisper of Nature GUESTHOUSE $
(☎265 7678; www.vietbungalow.com; Viet Hai village; dm US$12 & d US$22-28) Located in the hamlet of Viet Hai, these simple concrete-and-thatch bungalows are arrayed around a stream on the edge of the forest. Arrival is an adventure, with the final stage a bike ride through lush scenery. Alternatively, travel via a bamboo boat (200,000d) from Cat Ba Town and then a *xe om* (30,000d). The guesthouse can also arrange transfers from Hanoi.

Eating & Drinking

For a memorable dining experience, try the floating seafood restaurants in Cat Ba or Ben Beo harbours. A rowing boat there and back should cost 100,000d with waiting time; a feast for two will be 200,000d or so. Overcharging is a possibility, so work out meal prices beforehand. All the following places are in Cat Ba Town:

TOP CHOICE **Bamboo Café** VIETNAMESE $

(Đ 1-4; dishes 80,000-120,000d) The best option for a casual bite on the seafront, this enjoyable little place has a small harbour-facing terrace and an intimate bamboo-walled interior. The genial owner is a fluent English speaker and serves up generous portions of Vietnamese and international food. The beer is super-cold and there's wine available by the glass.

Vien Duong VIETNAMESE $$

(12 Đ Nui Ngoc; meals from 100,000d) Of the seafood spots lining Đ Nui Ngoc, Vien Duong is among the most popular. It's often heaving with Vietnamese domestic tourists diving into local crab, squid and steaming seafood hotpots.

Family Bakery BAKERY $

(196 Đ 1-4; dishes 80,000-120,000d; ⏲7am-4pm) Friendly spot that opens early for goodies like Turkish bread and almond pastries. Pop in for a coffee and a croissant.

Thao May VIETNAMESE $

(18 Đ Nui Ngoc; mains 80,000-120,000d) Family-run spot that's recommended by in-the-know expats for authentic local grub and cheap beer.

On the seafront, two good places for a drink are **Good Bar** (Đ 1-4; ⓦ), which is a social HQ for travellers, with pool tables and a lively vibe, and the tiny, Kiwi-owned **Flightless Bird** (Đ 1-4; ⓦ).

Information

Agribank There's branch 1km north of town for changing dollars, and an ATM on the harbourfront.

Internet cafes There are several internet cafes on Cat Ba's seafront.

Main post office (Đ 1-4) Also on the Cat Ba seafront.

Vu Binh Jewellers By the market. Cashes travellers cheques at 3% commission and does credit-card cash advances at 5%.

Getting There & Away

Cat Ba Island is 45km east of Haiphong and 30km south of Halong City. Various boat and bus combinations make the journey, starting in either Hanoi or Haiphong. It's possible to travel by boat from Halong City to Cat Ba Island, but it is a journey often blighted by scams (p832).

To/From Hanoi

The easiest way to/from Hanoi is via the city's Luong Yen bus station (Map p812). Here **Hoang Long** (☎031-268 8008) offer a combined bus-boat-bus ticket (210,000d, 4½ hours) straight through to Cat Ba Town. Buses depart Hanoi at 5.20am, 7.20am, 11.20am and 1.20pm, and return from Cat Ba Town at 7.15am, 9.15am, 1.15pm and 3.15pm.

To/From Haiphong

Fast boats depart Haiphong's Ben Binh harbour to Cat Ba's Cai Vieng harbour at 7am and 10am. From there a bus takes passengers into Cat Ba Town; this boat-bus combo takes around 90 minutes (130,000d). The other way, Haiphong-bound buses depart from the waterfront in Cat Ba Town at 2pm and 4pm.

A second option to/from Haiphong is a bus from Ben Binh harbour in Haiphong to Dinh Vu

ISLAND ESCAPES

These two island resorts are on tiny islands close to Cat Ba Town.

Nam Cat Island Resort

(☎098 955 5773; namcatisland@gmail.com; d US$25-60; ❄) Enjoys a secluded cove location with simple bungalows, plus flasher villas with private facilities. Spend your days swimming and kayaking, and kick back with seafood barbecues and beach bonfires after dark. Cat Ba Ventures uses this as a base on its tours.

Monkey Island Resort

(☎04-3926 0572; www.monkeyislandresort.com; d US$40-60; ❄) There's a nice social vibe at Monkey Island, with a nightly seafood buffet, cool R&B beats and volleyball. Accommodation is in comfortable private bungalows, and there are kayaks for hire. Free transfers from Cat Ba Town are offered. The eponymous primates lurk close by on a karst peak.

port. A fast boat then skips across to Cai Vieng on Cat Ba, and another bus then continues into Cat Ba Town. The journey takes around two hours (150,000d). Buses depart Ben Binh at 6.40am, 8.15am, 9.45am, 1.40pm, 3.10pm & 4.35pm. Return buses from Cat Ba depart at 6.10am, 7.50am, 9.10am, 1.10pm, 2.50pm and 4.10pm.

Getting Around

Rented bicycles are a good way to explore the island.

Motorbike rentals (with or without driver) are available from most of the hotels from US$5 per day. If you're heading to the beaches or national park, pay the fee for guarded parking to ensure your bike isn't stolen.

Haiphong

031 / POP 1.67 MILLION

Vietnam's third-largest city, Haiphong has a graceful air, and its verdant tree-lined boulevards conceal some classic colonial-era structures. It's an important seaport, industrial centre and transport hub, but very few visitors linger long.

Sights & Activities

FREE **Haiphong Museum** MUSEUM
(66 P Dien Bien Phu; 8am-12.30pm & 2-4pm Mon-Fri, 7.30-9.30pm Wed & Sun) In a splendid colonial building, the Haiphong Museum concentrates on the city's history. Some displays have English translations.

Du Hang Pagoda PAGODA
(Chua Du Hang; 121 P Chua Hang; 7-11am & 1.30-5.50pm) Founded three centuries ago and rebuilt several times since, this pagoda has architectural elements that look Khmer.

Sleeping

Monaco Hotel HOTEL $$
(374 6468; monacohotel@vnn.vn; 103 P Dien Bien Phu; r from US$25;) This modern and central hotel has a real polish about it, including the smart lobby. Spacious, spotless rooms come with two double beds, and breakfast is included.

Hoa Viet Hotel HOTEL $
(384 2409; www.hoaviethotel.vn; 50 P Dien Bien Phu; r 250,000-400,000d;) Excellent value in central Haiphong, with simply furnished rooms arranged around a courtyard in a restored colonial building. Rates include breakfast.

Eating & Drinking

Haiphong is noted for fresh seafood; P Quang Trung has point-and-cook tanks as well as *bia hoi* (beer) joints. For more stylish cafes and restaurants, take a wander along P Minh Khai.

GETTING TO CHINA: THE NORTHEAST BORDERS

There are two borders in northeast Vietnam where foreigners can cross into China.

Huu Nghi Quan to Youyi Guan

Getting to the border This is the most popular border crossing. The border post itself is at Huu Nghi Quan (Friendship Gate), 3km north of Dong Dang. Three trains link Hanoi and Lang Son (south of Dong Dang) daily but these are very slow.

A better option is to catch a bus from Hanoi to Dong Dang (130,000d, 3¼ hours) and a *xe om* (20,000d) to the border.

International trains that run direct from Hanoi to Nanning and Beijing also pass through this border, but it's not possible to jump aboard these services in Lang Son or Dong Dang.

For more information on these cross-border trains, see p905.

At the border Open 24 hours. Visas must be arranged in advance.

Moving on On the Chinese side, it's a 20-minute drive from the border to Pingxiang by bus or shared taxi. Pingxiang is connected by train and bus to Nanning.

Mong Cai to Dongxing

Mong Cai and Dongxing straddle the Chinese border in the extreme northeastern corner of Vietnam, but this crossing is rarely used by foreigners. It's about 3km between the border and Mong Cai bus station; aim to pay around 15,000d on a *xe om* or 30,000d in a taxi. The border crossing is open from 7am to 7pm daily and visas must be arranged in advance.

Com Vietnam VIETNAMESE $
(4A P Hoang Van Thu; mains 30,000-80,000d) Diminutive, unpretentious restaurant that hits the spot for its affordable local seafood and Vietnamese specialities.

Phone Box BAR
(79 P Dien Bien Phu; ⊙noon-11.30pm) This tiny bar is run by a musician and is a great place for a relaxed drink, with live music (usually acoustic) on Monday and Friday.

Information

There are internet cafes on P Dien Bien Phu; many cafes have free wi-fi. ATMs dot the city centre.

Haiphong International Hospital (☎395 5888; 124 Nguyen Duc Canh) Newly built and modern, with some English-speaking doctors.

Getting There & Away

Vietnam Airlines (☎381 0890; www.vietnamair.com.vn; 30 P Hoang Van Thu) has flights to HCMC and Danang. **Jetstar Pacific** (www.jetstar.com) has flights to HCMC.

For boat connections to Cat Ba, see p833.

Buses for Hanoi (70,000d, two hours) leave from the **Tam Bac bus station** (P Tam Bac), 4km from the waterfront. Buses heading to points south, including Ninh Binh (90,000d, 3½ hours, every 30 minutes), leave from **Niem Nghia bus station** (Đ Tran Nguyen Han). **Lac Long bus station** (P Cu Chinh Lan) has buses to Halong City (50,000d, 1½ hours).

There are four trains a day to Hanoi (48,000-60,000d, two to three hours) from **Haiphong train station** (Đ Pham Ngu Lao).

Ba Be National Park

☎0281 / ELEV 145M

Boasting mountains high, rivers deep, and waterfalls, lakes and caves, **Ba Be National Park** (☎389 4014; www.babenationalpark.org; admission per person 20,000d) is an incredibly scenic spot. The region is surrounded by steep peaks (up to 1554m) while the park contains tropical rainforest with more than 400 plant species. Wildlife in the forest includes bears, monkeys, bats and lots of butterflies. Surrounding the park are Tay minority villages.

Ba Be (Three Bays) is in fact three linked lakes, with a total length of 8km and a width of about 400m. The Nang River is navigable for 23km between a point 4km above Cho Ra and the **Dau Dang Waterfall** (Thac Dau Dang), which is a series of spectacular cascades between sheer walls of rock. The river cave **Puong Cave** (Hang Puong) is about 30m high and 300m long.

Park staff can organise **tours**, starting at about US$30 per day for solo travellers, less for a group. **Boat trips** (hire around 550,000d) take around seven hours to take in most sights. The departure dock is about 2km from park headquarters.

Other options include dugout-canoe tours or combination cycling, boating and walking possibilities. Longer treks can also be arranged.

An optional guide, worth considering, costs US$12 per day.

Sleeping & Eating

There are two accommodation options not far from the park headquarters.

Park Guesthouse GUESTHOUSE
(☎389 4026) This is fine, if a little overpriced. It includes semi-detached bungalows (350,000d) and rooms (220,000d) that are fairly basic. Meals (from 50,000d) are available here – place your order a few hours ahead.

Stilt house homestays HOMESTAYS
(per person 70,000d) Homestays are available in Pac Ngoi village on the lakeshore; the park office can help organise this. Meals cost 40,000d to 60,000d. Only cash is accepted and the nearest ATM and internet access are in Cho Ra.

Getting There & Around

Ba Be National Park is 240km from Hanoi and 18km from Cho Ra.

Most visitors get here by chartered vehicle from Hanoi (six hours) or on a tour.

By public transport, the most direct route is on a daily bus at noon from the Gia Lam bus station in Hanoi to Cho Ra (150,000d, six hours). Overnight in Cho Ra before continuing on to Ba Be by boat (or motorbike taxi) the following morning.

Mai Chau

☎0218 / POP 47,500

In an idyllic valley, Mai Chau is surrounded by lush paddy fields and the rural soundtrack is defined by gurgling irrigation streams and birdsong.

Dozens of local families have signed up to a highly successful homestay initiative, and for visitors the chance to sleep in a traditional stilt house is a real appeal – though note that the villages are on the tour-group agenda. If you're looking for hardcore exploration, this is not the place, but for biking, hiking and relaxation, Mai Chau fits the bill nicely.

Sights & Activities

You can **walk** past rice fields and **trek** to minority villages. A typical trek further afield covers 7km to 8km; a local guide costs about US$10. Most homestays also rent bikes.

A popular 18km trek is from **Lac village** (Ban Lac) in Mai Chau to the H'mong **Xa Linh village**, near a mountain pass (elevation 1000m) on Hwy 6. This trek takes in a 600m climb in altitude and usually involves an overnight stay.

Many travel agencies in Hanoi run inexpensive trips to Mai Chau.

Sleeping & Eating

Most visitors stay in **Thai stilt houses** (per person incl breakfast around 150,000d) in the villages of Lac or Pom Coong, just a five-minute stroll apart. It's perfectly feasible to just pitch up and find a bed; there's always space. All homestays have electricity, running water, hot showers, mosquito nets and roll-up mattresses.

Most people eat where they stay. Establish the price of meals first as some families charge up to 150,000d for dinner. Warning: cheesy song-and-dance routines follow dinner at some places.

Getting There & Around

Direct buses to Mai Chau leave Hanoi's My Dinh bus station regularly from 6am to 2pm (80,000d, 3¾ hours). Alternatively, catch a regular Son La or Dien Bien Phu bus to Tong Dau junction (80,000d, 3½ hours). From the junction it's another 5km to Mai Chau; *xe om* charge 20,000d.

Lao Cai

020 / POP 46,700

One of the gateways to the north, Lao Cai lies at the end of the train line, 3km from the Chinese border. The town has no sights but is a major hub for travellers journeying between Hanoi, Sapa and the Chinese city of Kunming.

There are ATMs next to the train station, plus internet cafes close by.

With Sapa just up the mountain, there's no need to stay the night, but you'll find plenty of inexpensive hotels around the station. **Terminus Hotel & Restaurant** (383 5470; 342 P Nguyen Hue; r 200,000-300,000d, meals 20,000-45,000d;) is one option, with clean, tidy rooms and filling meals available.

Getting There & Around

Nine daily buses (240,000d, nine hours) ply the Hanoi–Lao Cai route, but virtually everyone prefers the train. Minibuses for Sapa (40,000d,

DON'T MISS

EXPLORING THE FAR NORTH

Motorcycling in Vietnam's wild northern territory is unforgettable. If you're not confident riding a motorbike yourself, it's possible to hire someone to drive you. 4WD trips are also recommended, though the mobility of travelling on two wheels is unrivalled.

One of the most popular routes is the 'Northwest Loop', which follows Hwy 6 through the heart of the Tonkinese Alps. There are many variations, but the standard route involves starting in **Lao Cai**, heading to **Sapa**, the queen of the mountains, then west via a spectacular road to the historic battlefield of **Dien Bien Phu**. Next is a stop in **Son La**, before dropping into the **White Thai villages** around Mai Chau and hitting the highway (to hell) back to Hanoi.

Some companies also specialise in taking bikers right off the trail into the far north of **Ha Giang** or the beautiful northeast province of **Cao Bang** and the nearby lakes of **Ba Be National Park** (p835).

It's certainly possible to organise a motorcycling trip on your own. Northwest Loop roads are almost completely paved, though things can deteriorate in rainy season. Signposts are rare, so bring a good map. The busy, long route north to Lao Cai is not a great ride, so let the train take the strain and load your bike into a goods carriage while you sleep in a berth. Then in Lao Cai, pick it up, fill up, and take off.

Minsks used to be the bike of choice, but many now favour more reliable Japanese bikes. Daily hire rates for a quality bike range from US$20 to US$40 and are best organised in Hanoi. Check out p906 for recommended motorbike tour operators, most of whom offer quality rental bikes too.

GETTING TO CHINA: LAO CAI TO HEKOU

Getting to the border The Lao Cai-Hekou crossing connects northern Vietnam with Yunnan in China. The border is about 3km from Lao Cai train station; *xe om* charge 20,000d.

At the border The border crossing is open from 7am to 10pm. Travellers have reported Chinese officials confiscating Lonely Planet China guides at this border, so you may want to try masking the cover. Visas must be arranged in advance.

Moving on Trains no longer run from Hekou to Kunming, but there are several 'sleeper' buses (Y150). One bus leaves at 7pm and arrives in Kunming around 7am, but there are earlier departures. You'll need to have a pre-arranged visa for China.

one hour) wait by the train station while services to Bac Ha (50,000d, 2½ hours) leave at 6am, 7am, 10am, noon and 3pm from a terminal next to the Red River bridge.

Rail tickets to Hanoi (8½ to 11 hours) start at 110,000d for a hard seat (bad choice) to 450,000d for an air-con soft sleeper, and rise by about 10% at weekends. There are three night trains and two day trains in either direction.

Bac Ha

☎020 / POP 7400

An unhurried and friendly town, Bac Ha makes a relaxed base to explore the northern highlands and hill-tribe villages. The atmosphere is very different from Sapa, and you can walk the streets freely without being accosted by hawkers. The climate here is also noticeably warmer than in Sapa.

Bac Ha has a certain charm, though its stock of traditional old adobe houses is dwindling and being replaced by concrete structures. Wood smoke fills the morning air and chickens and pigs poke around the back lanes. For six days a week Bac Ha slumbers, but its lanes fill up to choking point each Sunday when tourists and Flower H'mong flood in for the weekly market.

Sights

Bac Ha's Sunday market is a riot of colour and commerce. The *ruou* corn hooch produced by the Flower H'mong is so potent it can ignite; there's an entire area devoted to it at the Sunday market.

While you're here, check out the outlandish **Vua Meo** ('Cat King' House; admission free; ⏰8am-5.30pm), a palace constructed in a kind of bizarre 'oriental baroque' architectural style.

Beyond town lie several interesting markets:

Can Cau market One of Vietnam's most exotic, this Saturday market is 20km north of Bac Ha, just 9km south of the Chinese border.

Coc Ly market Takes place on Tuesdays, about 35km from Bac Ha. There's a pretty good road, or you can go by road and river; ask at hotels in Bac Ha.

Lung Phin market Between Can Cau market and Bac Ha, about 12km from the town. It's less busy, and operates on Sundays.

Activities

There's great hiking to hill-tribe villages around Bac Ha. The Flower H'mong village of **Ban Pho** is one of the nearest to town. Other nearby villages include **Trieu Cai**, an 8km return walk, and **Na Ang**, a 6km return walk; it's best to set up a trip with a local guide.

Tour guides in Bac Ha can arrange visits to rural schools as part of a motorbike or trekking day-trip. There's also a **waterfall** near Thai Giang Pho village, about 12km east of Bac Ha, which has a pool big enough for swimming.

Take a peek at the website www.bachatourist.com for inspiration; it's operated by English-speaking **Mr Nghe** (091-200 5952; hoangvutours@hotmail.com), Bac Ha's one-man tourism dynamo. All hotels recommended below offer excursions too.

Sleeping & Eating

Room rates increase on weekends; weekday rates are quoted here.

Hoang Vu Hotel HOTEL $

(☎388 0264; r from US$8) Number one for budget travellers in town. It's nothing fancy, but the large spacious rooms are good value, with TV and fan. Mr Nghe is based here.

FLOWER POWER

Flower H'mong women wear several layers of dazzling clothing. These include an elaborate collar-cum-shawl that's pinned at the neck and an apron-style garment; both are made of tightly woven strips of multicoloured fabric, often with a frilly edge. Highly ornate cuffs and ankle fabrics are also part of their costume, as is a checked headscarf (often electric pink or lime green).

Ngan Nga Gia Huy HOTEL **$$**
(☎388 0231; www.nganngabacha.com; 133 Ngoc Uyen; r US$25-35d; ❄📶) A friendly place above a popular restaurant that does a roaring trade in tasty hotpots. Its new rooms are spotless and quiet, and some are almost ridiculously roomy.

Congfu Hotel HOTEL, RESTAURANT **$$**
(☎388 0254; www.congfuhotel.com; 152 Ngoc Uyen; r US$30; ❄@📶) Boasts attractive rooms demonstrating a notable absence of chintz. All have quality bed linen, and some enjoy floor-to-ceiling windows overlooking Bac Ha market. There's a good restaurant (meals from 40,000d) here too.

Hoang Yen VIETNAMESE, BAR **$**
(mains 40,000-80,000d) Bar-restaurant with a well-priced menu of good breakfast options, tasty rice and noodle dishes, and robust pumpkin soup. Cheap beer and Dalat wine are both available.

ℹ Information

There's no ATM in Bac Ha, but the **Agribank** will cash dollars and the Sao Mai Hotel will change other currencies.

You'll find a **tourist information office** (⏲7.30-11.30am & 1.30-5pm) at the Vua Meo and internet access next to the Hoang Vu Hotel, also home base for the irrepressible Mr Nghe.

ℹ Getting There & Away

Car & Motorbike

Tours to Bac Ha from Sapa cost from US$15 per person; on the way back you can bail out in Lao Cai and catch the train back to Hanoi.

A motorbike/taxi to Lao Cai costs US$20/60, or to Sapa US$25/75.

Sapa

☎020 / POP 36,200 / ELEV 1650M

Perched on a steep slope, Sapa overlooks a plunging valley of cascading rice terraces, with mountains towering above the town on all sides. Founded as a French hill station in 1922, Sapa is the premier tourist destination in northern Vietnam. Views of this epic scenery are often subdued by thick mist rolling across the peaks, but even if it's cloudy, Sapa is still a fascinating place, especially when local hill-tribe people fill the town with colour.

Sapa is known for its cold, foggy winters (down to 0°C). The dry season for Sapa is approximately January to the end of June – afternoon rain showers in the mountains are frequent.

The town's colonial villas fell into disrepair during successive wars, but Sapa has experienced a recent renaissance – the downside of which is a hotel-building boom.

Inherent in this prosperity is cultural change for the hill-tribe people. Many have little formal education but have a good command of several languages, and are canny (and persistent) traders, urging you to buy handicrafts.

👁 Sights & Activities

Surrounding Sapa are the Hoang Lien Mountains, including **Fansipan**, which at 3143m is Vietnam's highest peak. The trek from Sapa to the summit and back can take several days. Some of the better-known sights around Sapa include the epic **Tram Ton Pass**; the pretty **Thac Bac** (Silver Falls); and **Cau May** (Cloud Bridge), which spans the Muong Hoa River.

BUSES FROM BAC HA

DESTINATION	COST (D)	DURATION (HR)	FREQUENCY
Hanoi	400,000	11	8pm
Lao Cai	60,000	2½	6am, 8am, noon, 1pm, 2pm

Treks can be arranged at many guesthouses and travel agencies (see p840); the following are H'mong owned:

Sapa O'Chau HIKING
(☎091-535 1479; www.sapaochau.com) Profits from this tour agency provide training to H'mong children in a learning centre. Excellent day walks, longer homestay treks, and Fanispan hikes are offered. Volunteers are welcome.

Sapa Sisters HIKING
(☎097-621 6140; www.sapasisters.webs.com) Day treks, two- to three-day village homestays, or ascents of Fanispan. Excellent English is spoken, and some French, Spanish and Japanese.

Sleeping

Luong Thuy Family Guesthouse GUESTHOUSE $
(☎387 2310; www.familysapa.com; 028 Đ Muong Hoa; r US$10-15; @) Simple and spotless rooms in a friendly, family-owned guesthouse a short stroll from the hubbub of downtown Sapa. The misty valley view from the front balconies is quite superb.

Cat Cat View Hotel HOTEL $$
(☎387 1946; www.catcathotel.com; 1 Đ Phan Xi Pang; r US$10-90; @) This is a midrange hotel with good pine-trimmed budget rooms that represent great value. Or treat yourself to a splurge.

Pinocchio Hotel HOTEL $
(☎387 1876; www.pinocchiohotel.com; 15 Đ Muong Hoa; r US$15-20; @) The friendly staff who run this excellent guesthouse really make it tick. Rooms have simple but attractive decor, some with impressive views.

Baguette & Chocolat GUESTHOUSE $
(☎387 1766; www.hoasuaschool.com; Đ Thac Bac; r US$22;) Operated by Hoa Sua (a group helping disadvantaged youth), this four-roomed place has style and an excellent French cafe. Rates include a great breakfast.

Sapa Hostel GUESTHOUSE $
(☎387 3073; www.sapahostel.com; 9 & 33 Đ Phan Xi Pang; dm/s/d/tr US$5/12/15/18; @) Spacious rooms in two locations that have a laid-back travellers' vibe.

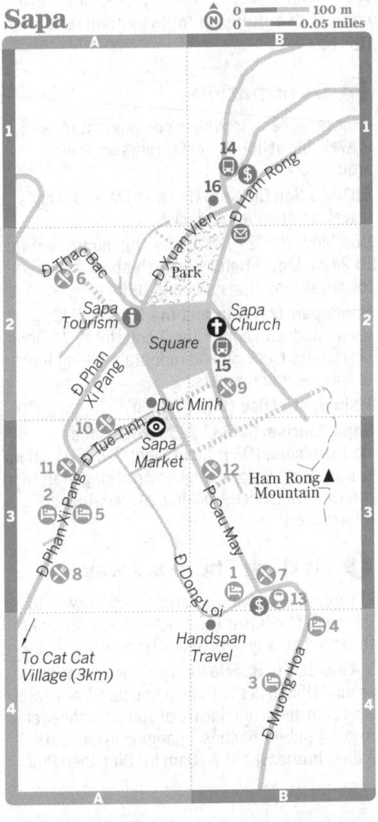

Sapa

Sleeping

- Baguette & Chocolat .... (see 6)
- 1 Casablanca Sapa Hotel B3
- 2 Cat Cat View Hotel A3
- 3 Luong Thuy Family Guesthouse B4
- 4 Pinocchio Hotel B4
- 5 Sapa Hostel A3

Eating

- 6 Baguette & Chocolat A2
- 7 Delta Restaurant B3
- 8 Nature View A3
- 9 Night Market Stalls B2
- 10 Restaurants A3
- 11 Sapa Rooms A3
- 12 Viet Emotion B3

Drinking

- 13 Mountain Bar & Pub B3

Transport

- 14 Bus Station B1
- 15 Minibuses to Lao Cai B2
- 16 Railway Booking Office B1

GETTING TO LAOS: TAY TRANG TO SOP HUN

Getting to the border The Tay Trang-Sop Hun border crossing is 34km from Dien Bien Phu (DBP). Buses (148,000d, seven to eight hours) leave DBP daily at 5.30am for Muang Khua in Laos. Book your ticket the day prior to travelling if you can. The journey can take longer depending on the roads and border formalities. It's possible to hire a *xe om* from DBP to the border at Tay Trang for around 200,000d, but you'll probably then have to walk 5km to the nearest Lao village for transport to Muang May.

At the border Open daily from 7am to 5pm.

Moving on Muang May has basic guesthouses and onward travel options to Muang Khua, but make sure you have cash dollars or Lao kip.

See p339 for information on crossing this border in the other direction.

Casablanca Sapa Hotel HOTEL $
(☎387 2667; www.sapacasablanca.com; Đ Dong Loi; s/d/tr US$17/20/25; 📶) Good-value rooms in a central location. Mr Kien, the attentive owner, speaks fluent English.

Eating

For eating on a tight budget, cheap Vietnamese restaurants huddle below the market, and **night-market stalls** south of the church serve *bun cha* (barbecued pork).

Vietnamese-style hotpot is a very popular local dish; try the area just south of the bus station.

Sapa Rooms CAFE $$
(www.saparooms.com; Đ Phan Xi Pang; snacks 50,000d, meals around 90,000d) A flamboyantly decorated cafe that's great for a snack (think corn fritters or a BLT baguette), meal (try the fish 'n' chips), or just a pot of tea and a piece of cake. Cookery classes are offered too.

Baguette & Chocolat CAFE $
(Đ Thac Bac; cakes from 20,000d, snacks & meals 70,000-160,000d; ✎) Fine breakfasts, *tartines,* baguettes, cakes, salads, pasta and Asian and Vietnamese dishes are served in elegant premises.

Nature View VIETNAMESE $
(Đ Phan Xi Pang; meals from 60,000d) Newish opening offering a good mix of Vietnamese and Western flavours and a great set lunch. Offers some of Sapa's best pizzas and terrific fruit smoothies.

Viet Emotion MEDITERRANEAN $$
(www.vietemotion.com; 27 P Cau May; meals 70,000-150,000d) Stylish bistro that features a cosy fireplace, and, if the weather really sets in there are books, magazines and board games.

Delta Restaurant ITALIAN $$
(P Cau May; mains US$7-12) Renowned for its pizzas, the most authentic in town, plus pretty decent pasta too.

Drinking

Mountain Bar & Pub BAR
(2 Đ Muong Hoa) Dangerously strong cocktails, cold beer, *shisha* (water pipes) and ultra-competitive games of table football feature at this bar.

Information

Internet access, including complimentary wi-fi, is available at hotels, restaurants and cafes around town.

BIDV (Đ Ngu Chi Son) Has an ATM, exchanges travellers cheques and cash.

Duc Minh (☎387 1881; www.ducminhtravel.vn; 10 P Cau May) Friendly English-speaking operator organising transport and treks.

Handspan Travel Indochina (☎387 2110; www.handspan.com; Chau Long Hotel, 24 Dong Loi) Offers trekking and mountain-biking tours to villages and markets.

Main post office (Đ Ham Rong)

Sapa Tourism (☎387 3239; www.sapa-tourism.com; 103 Đ Xuan Vien; ⏲7.30-11.30am & 1.30-5pm) Helpful English-speaking staff offering transport, trekking and weather information.

Getting There & Away

The gateway to Sapa is Lao Cai, 38km away to the west. Minibuses (40,000d, one hour) make the trip regularly until mid-afternoon.

A minibus to Bac Ha for the Sunday market is around US$15 per person; departure from Sapa is at 6am and from Bac Ha at 1pm. It's cheaper to go by public minibus, changing in Lao Cai. A daily bus leaves at 7.30am for Dien Bien Phu

(170,000d, eight hours) and there are regular buses for Lai Chau (70,000d, 6am to 4pm).

There is an official **Railway Booking Office** (Đ Xuan Vien; ⏲7.30-11am & 1.30-4pm), which charges a small commission. For more information on trains to Hanoi, see Lao Cai (p836).

Getting Around

Downtown Sapa can be walked in 20 minutes. For excursions further out, you can hire a motorbike for US$5 to US$10 per day, or take one with a driver from US$12.

Dien Bien Phu

☎0230 / POP 72,700

On 7 May 1954 French colonial forces were defeated by the Viet Minh in a decisive battle at Dien Bien Phu (DBP), and the days of their Indochine empire were numbered.

Previously just a minor settlement, DBP only became a provincial capital in 2004. Boulevards and civic buildings have been constructed and the airport now has daily flights from Hanoi. With the nearby Lao border now open to foreigners, many travellers are passing through the city.

Sights

Dien Bien Phu Museum MUSEUM
(Đ 7-5; admission 5000d; ⏲7-11am & 1.30-5pm) Commemorating the 1954 battle, this well-laid-out museum features an eclectic collection of weaponry and plenty of photographs and documents, some with English translations.

Bunker Headquarters WAR MEMORIAL
(admission 3000d; ⏲7-11am & 1.30-5pm) Across the river, the command bunker of Colonel Christian de Castries has been re-created.

Sleeping & Eating

For a cheap bite, check out the *pho* stalls and simple restaurants opposite the bus station. *Bia hoi* gardens on Đ Hoang Van are ideal for a local brew or two.

Viet Hoang Hotel GUESTHOUSE $
(☎373 5046; 67 Đ Tran Dang Ninh; s/d 100,000/120,000d; ❄@📶) Opposite the bus station, this friendly guesthouse has small, neat rooms. Owner Mr Duc and his family are very hospitable.

Binh Long Hotel GUESTHOUSE $
(☎382 4345; 429 Đ Muong Thanh; d & tw US$10; ❄📶) Another small, friendly family-run place, but on a busy junction. Offers neat, tidy twin rooms and transport info.

Lien Tuoi Restaurant VIETNAMESE $
(Đ Hoang Van Thai; mains 60,000-90,000d) Famous for its filling Vietnamese and Chinese food.

Information

Internet cafes are on Đ Hoang Van Thai.

Agribank (Đ 7-5) ATM and changes US dollars.

Main post office (Đ 7-5)

Getting There & Away

Air

Vietnam Airlines (☎382 4948; www.vietnamairlines.com; Nguyen Huu Tho) Operates two flights daily between DBP and Hanoi. The office is near the airport, about 1.5km from the town centre, along the road to Muong Lay.

Car & Motorbike

The 480km drive from Hanoi to DBP on Hwys 6 and 279 takes around 11 hours.

GETTING TO LAOS: CAU TREO TO NAM PHAO

Getting to the border The Cau Treo–Nam Phao border crossing is 96km west of Vinh and about 30km east of Lak Sao in Laos. This border has a dodgy reputation with travellers, who report chronic overcharging and hassle on local buses (such as bus drivers ejecting foreigners in the middle of nowhere unless they cough up extra bucks).

If you do decide to travel step-by-step, local buses leave Vinh to Tay Son (formerly Trung Tam) regularly from 6am (70,000d, three hours). From Tay Son, it's another 25km to the border. Morning buses to Lak Sao may be available, but if not, *xe om* ask for up to 150,000d for the ride.

At the border The Cau Treo–Nam Phao border crossing is open from 7am to 4.30pm.

Moving on On the Laos side, a jumbo or sǒrngtǎaou between the border and Lak Sao runs to about 45,000 kip (bargain hard).

See p353 for information on crossing this border in the other direction.

BUSES FROM DIEN BIEN PHU

DBP's bus station is on Hwy 12, at the corner of Đ Tran Dang Ninh.

DESTINATION	COST (D)	DURATION (HR)	FREQUENCY
Hanoi	from 300,000d	11½	Frequent until noon
Lai Chau	130,000d	6	5am-2pm
Muong Lay	57,000d	2	5am-2pm
Son La	97,000d	4	Frequent until noon

CENTRAL VIETNAM

With ancient history, compelling culture, incredible food and terrific beaches central Vietnam has real allure. This is an area that packs in the serene city of Hue (Vietnam's former imperial capital), DMZ battle sites, and Hoi An, an exquisite architectural gem that time forgot. Chuck in the ruins of My Son, extraordinary cave systems of Phong Nha and numerous nature reserves and the region's appeal is overwhelming.

Hue

054 / POP 286,400

Hue is the intellectual, cultural and spiritual heart of Vietnam. Palaces and pagodas, tombs and temples, culture and cuisine, history and heartbreak – there's no shortage

PHONG NHA-KE BANG NATIONAL PARK

A Unesco World Heritage Site, the remarkable **Phong Nha-Ke Bang National Park** contains the oldest karst mountains in Asia and is riddled with hundreds of cave systems – many of extraordinary scale and length – including the largest cave in the world. This is nature on a very grand scale indeed.

Above the ground, most of this mountainous national park is near-pristine tropical evergreen jungle, over 90% of which is primary forest.

Until recently access was very tricky. Some sections remain off-limits, but things are gradually opening up.

Sight & Activities

The most popular excursion is the boat trip into 55km-long **Phong Nha Cave** (admission 40,000d, boat 220,000d; 7am-4pm) – though only the first kilometre or so is open to visitors. Boats leave Son Trach and cruise along the Son river past bathing buffalo until you reach the jaws of the cave. Then the engine is cut and you're transported to another world as you're paddled through cavern after cavern – quite a surreal experience. You've also the opportunity to hike up to nearby Tien Son Cave, where there are Cham altars and inscriptions.

Only open to the public since 2011, remote **Paradise Cave** (admission 120,000d; 7.30am-4.30pm) extends for 31km and is said to be the longest dry cave in the world. Once you've climbed the 500-step approach staircase its sheer scale becomes truly apparent, as you enter a cathedral-like space replete with glimmering stalactites of white crystal. The whole experience is a lot less commercial than the Phong Nha Cave trip. Paradise Cave is 18km from Son Trach. Phong Nha Farmstay offer tours (from 900,000d).

A beautiful riverside retreat, **Nuoc Mooc Eco-Trail** (admission 50,000d; 7am-5pm) has paths along the river and is a gorgeous place for a swim. Bring a picnic; it's 12km southwest of Son Trach.

A small, semi-wild **primate reserve** has been set up around a small hill as a breeding centre for critically endangered Ha Tien langurs. You can walk around the perimeter fence via a 1.8km trail. It's 3km from Son Trach.

At the time of research there's no public access to the world's largest cave, **Hang Son Doong**. The sheer scale of the principal cavern (5km long, 150m wide and over 200m of poetic pairings to describe Hue. A World Heritage site, the capital of the Nguyen emperors is where tourists come to see decaying, opulent royal tombs and the grand, crumbling Citadel. Most of these architectural attractions lie along the northern side of the Song Huong (Perfume River). For rest and recreation, plus a little refreshment, the south bank is where it's at.

The city hosts a biennial arts festival, the **Festival of Hue** (www.huefestival.com), every even-numbered year, featuring local and international artists and performers.

Sights & Activities

Citadel HISTORIC SITE

One of Vietnam's treasures, the former imperial city on the northern bank of the Perfume River (Song Huong) is immensely impressive. Though it was heavily bombed by the USA, its scope and beauty still endures, as more and more buildings are being reconstructed.

Emperor Gia Long began building the moated Citadel in 1804. The emperor's official functions were carried out in the **Imperial Enclosure** (Dai Noi, or Hoang Thanh; admission 55,000d; ⌚6.30am-5.30pm Apr-Sep, 7am-5pm Oct-Mar), a 'citadel within the Citadel'. Inside the 6m-high, 2.5km-long wall is a surreal world of deserted gardens, palaces and ceremonial halls.

Within the Imperial Enclosure is the holy-of-the-holy **Forbidden Purple City** (Tu Cam Thanh), which was reserved for the private life of the emperor. The only servants allowed inside were eunuchs. Nowadays, all are welcome. Drop by the beautiful (though crumbling) **Emperor's Reading Room** (Thai Binh Lau) to admire its Gaudiesque roof mosaics.

West of here is the beautifully restored **To Mieu Temple Complex**, which encompasses the three-tiered Hien Lam Pavilion and its nine dynastic urns (*dinh*).

You could spend hours exploring the rest of the Citadel, stumbling across other ruined

high) was only confirmed in 2009. Oxalis offers a great two-day trek (three to four people, US$170) to the mouth of Hang Son Doong, allowing you a glimpse into the abyss – along with lots of pristine jungle on the way.

Sleeping & Eating

There are a dozen or so guesthouses (all 200,000d) and cheap eateries in Son Trach village. Most travellers stay in the nearby **Phong Nha Farmstay** (☎052-367 5135; www.phong-nha-cave.com; dm US$8, r US$25-35; ❄@🛜≋), run by a welcoming Australian-Vietnamese couple. Overlooking rice paddies, this impressive place has a great vibe, a bar, local and Western food (meals 30,000-90,000d), and offers outstanding tours, including kayaking, tubing, biking and hiking. It's in Cu Nam, 13km southeast of Son Trach; pick-ups can be arranged in Dong Hoi.

Practicalities

The coastal city of Dong Hoi, 166km north of Hue on Hwy 1 and on the north-south train line, is the gateway to Phong Nha.

Phong Nha-Ke Bang National Park abuts Son Trach village, which is 50km northwest of Dong Hoi. Local buses (45,000d) offer irregular connections between Dong Hoi and Son Trach. There's also a daily minibus between Phong Nha Farmstay and Danang (200,000d), stopping in Dong Ha and Hue (150,000d) en route.

Information is limited on the ground, and the odd park official can be less than helpful. Doubtless things will improve as organisation gets better. At the time of research travellers were fine entering the national park via Tro Mung ranger post on the Ho Chi Minh Highway, but the officials at the main park entrance gate on Hwy 20 were turning some back.

Organised tours are an excellent way to explore the park – those run by Phong Nha Farmstay are highly recommended and include incredible cultural and historical content; they cost 1,100,000d by motorbike or 900,000d by minibus. **Oxalis** (☎090-337 6776, www.oxalis.co.vn in Vietnamese, Son Trach) is a professional locally owned adventure-tourism outfit offering treks inside the national park.

Hue

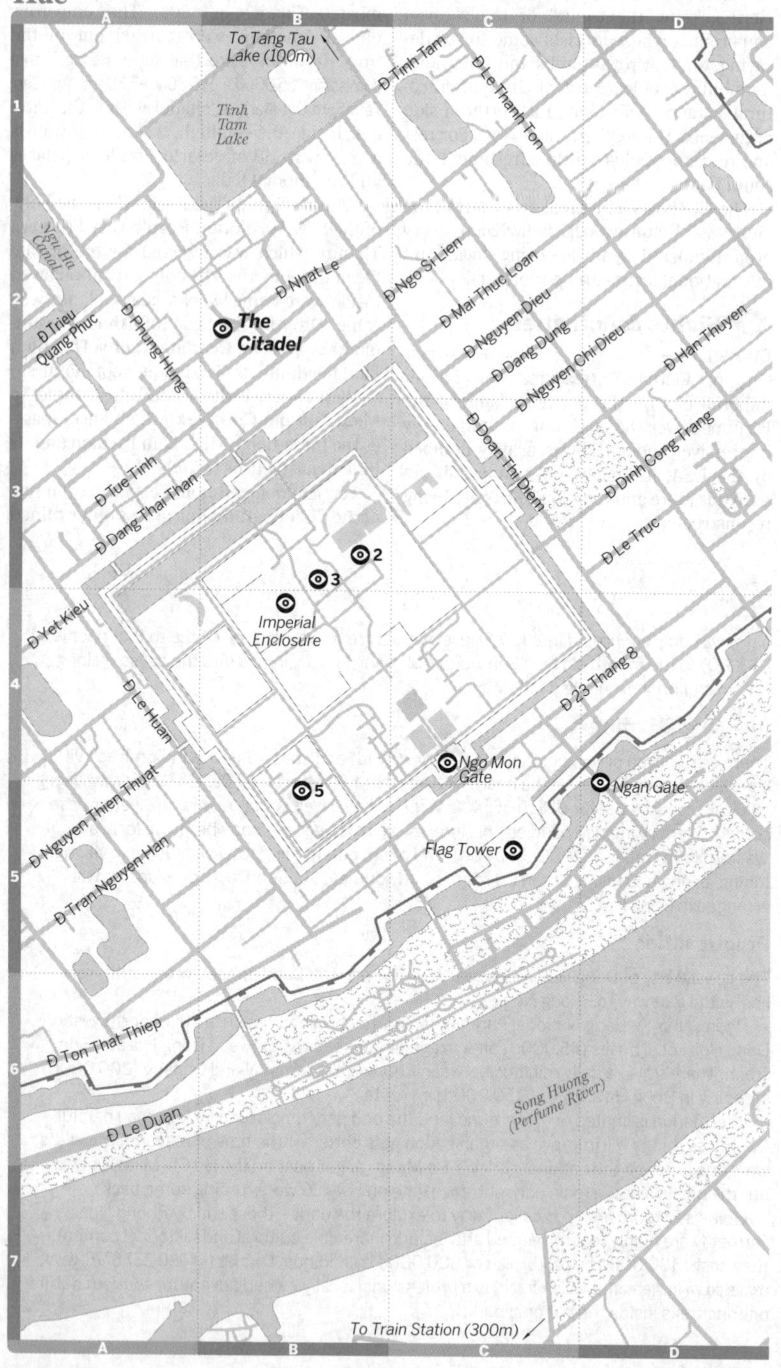

A
B
C
D
To Tang Tau Lake (100m)
Tinh Tam Lake
Đ Tinh Tam
Đ Le Thanh Ton
Ngu Ha Canal
Đ Nhat Le
Đ Ngo Si Lien
Đ Mai Thuc Loan
Đ Trieu Quang Phuc
Đ Phung Hung
The Citadel
Đ Nguyen Dieu
Đ Dang Dung
Đ Nguyen Chi Dieu
Đ Han Thuyen
Đ Doan Thi Diem
Đ Dinh Cong Trang
Đ Tue Tinh
Đ Dang Thai Than
Đ Le Truc
2
3
Imperial Enclosure
Đ Yet Kieu
Đ 23 Thang 8
Đ Le Huan
Ngo Mon Gate
Ngan Gate
5
Đ Nguyen Thien Thuat
Flag Tower
Đ Tran Nguyen Han
Đ Ton That Thiep
Song Huong (Perfume River)
Đ Le Duan
To Train Station (300m)
1
2
3
4
5
6
7

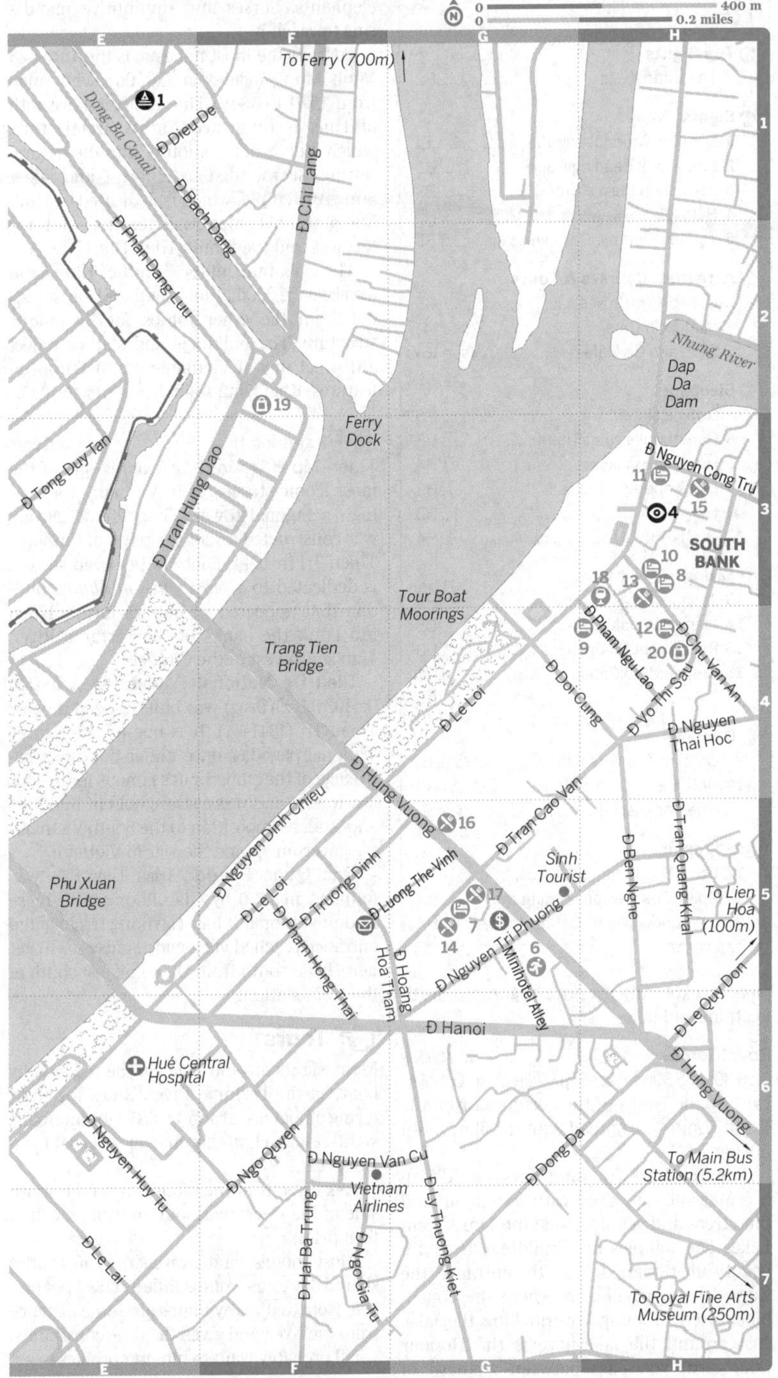

0 400 m
0 0.2 miles
E
F
G
H
1
2
3
4
5
6
7
To Ferry (700m)
Dong Ba Canal
Đ Dieu De
Đ Bach Dang
Đ Chi Lang
Đ Phan Dang Luu
Nhung River
Dap Da Dam
19
Ferry Dock
Đ Tong Duy Tan
Đ Tran Hung Dao
Đ Nguyen Cong Tru
11
15
4
SOUTH BANK
10
8
18
13
Tour Boat Moorings
Trang Tien Bridge
Đ Pham Ngu Lao
12
Đ Chu Van An
9
20
Đ Doi Cung
Đ Vo Thi Sau
Đ Le Loi
Đ Nguyen Thai Hoc
Đ Hung Vuong
Đ Nguyen Dinh Chieu
16
Đ Tran Cao Van
Đ Ben Nghe
Đ Tran Quang Khai
Phu Xuan Bridge
Đ Truong Dinh
Đ Luong The Vinh
Sinh Tourist
17
Đ Le Loi
Đ Pham Hong Thai
7
14
To Lien Hoa (100m)
Đ Nguyen Tri Phuong
6
Minihotel Alley
Đ Hoang Hoa Tham
Đ Le Quy Don
Đ Hanoi
Hué Central Hospital
Đ Hung Vuong
Đ Nguyen Huy Tu
Đ Ngo Quyen
Đ Nguyen Van Cu
Vietnam Airlines
Đ Dong Da
To Main Bus Station (5.2km)
Đ Hai Ba Trung
Đ Ngo Gia Tu
Đ Ly Thuong Kiet
Đ Le Lai
To Royal Fine Arts Museum (250m)

Hue

Top Sights
The Citadel.....B2

Sights
1 Dieu De National Pagoda.....E1
2 Emperor's Reading Room.....B3
3 Forbidden Purple City.....B3
4 Halo.....H3
5 To Mieu Temple Complex.....B5

Activities, Courses & Tours
6 Café on Thu Wheels.....G5
Mandarin Café.....(see 14)
Stop and Go Café.....(see 16)

Sleeping
7 Google Hotel.....G5
8 Guesthouse Nhat Thanh.....H3
9 Hue Backpackers.....H4
10 Hue Thuong.....H3
11 Huenino.....H3
12 Orchid Hotel.....H4

Eating
13 Japanese Restaurant.....H3
14 Mandarin Café.....G5
15 Restaurant Bloom.....H3
16 Stop and Go Café.....G5
17 Take.....G5

Drinking
Café on Thu Wheels.....(see 6)
18 DMZ Bar & Cafe.....H3
Hue Backpackers.....(see 9)

Shopping
19 Dong Ba Market.....F2
20 Spiral Foundation Healing the Wounded Heart Center.....H4

palaces, exploring overgrown gardens, fortifications and lakes.

Royal Tombs MONUMENTS
(6.30am-5.30pm Apr-Sep, 7am-5pm Oct-Mar) Dotting the banks of the Perfume River, the Royal Tombs are spread 2km to 16km south of Hue.

The **Tomb of Tu Duc** (admission 55,000d) is a majestic site, laced with frangipani and pine trees and set alongside the Luu Khiem Lake. The temples and buildings here are beautifully designed. Near the entrance, the Xung Khiem pavilion is where the concubines used to lounge overlooking the lake. Just around the lakeshore is the Honour Courtyard; you pass between a guard of elephants, horses and diminutive mandarins to reach it.

Perhaps the most majestic is the **Tomb of Minh Mang** (admission 55,000d), who ruled from 1820 to 1840. This tomb, 12km south of Hue, is renowned for its architecture, which blends harmoniously into the natural setting, surrounded by a forest and lakes. Sung An Temple, which is dedicated to Minh Mang and his empress, is reached via three terraces and the rebuilt Hien Duc Gate.

The elaborate, hilltop **Tomb of Khai Dinh** (admission 55,000d), 10km south of Hue, stands out from the other tombs for its unique structure. The buildings and statues reflect a distinct mix of Vietnamese and European features. Khai Dinh ruled from 1916 to 1925.

FREE **Pagodas** PAGODAS
Thien Mu Pagoda (Đ Le Duan) is one of the most iconic structures in Vietnam. Its 21m-high octagonal tower, Thap Phuoc Duyen, was constructed under the reign of Emperor Thieu Tri in 1844. Each of the seven storeys is dedicated to a *manushi-buddha* (a Buddha that appeared in human form). Thien Mu is on the banks of the Perfume River, 4km southwest of the Citadel.

Dieu De National Pagoda (Quoc Tu Dieu De; 102 Đ Bach Dang) was built under Emperor Thieu Tri (1841–47). It is one of Hue's three 'national pagodas', once under the direct patronage of the emperor. It's famous for its four low towers and was a stronghold of Buddhist and student opposition to the South Vietnamese government and the war in Vietnam.

Bao Quoc Pagoda (Ham Long Hill) was founded in 1670 by Giac Phong, a Chinese Buddhist monk. It has a striking triple-gated entrance reached via a wide staircase. To get here, head south from Đ Le Loi, just south of the train station.

Tours

Many sights around Hue can be reached by boat via the Perfume River. Rates for chartering a boat are around US$10 for an hour's sightseeing; a half-day charter will cost from US$20.

Ask directly at the moorings on the south side of the river; work out an itinerary then fix a price.

Most hotels and travellers' cafes offer shared day tours from as little as US$3 per person. Note that many tombs are some distance from the river, and given the time constraints, you'll probably want to hire motorbikes to get from the moorings to some tombs. Once the various additional costs have been factored in, many travellers wish they had cycled or arranged a motorbike tour instead.

Motorbike guides from travellers' cafes can do customised day tours of the sights.

Café on Thu Wheels TOURS
(☎383 2241; minhthuhue@yahoo.com; 3/34 Đ Nguyen Tri Phuong) Inexpensive cycling, motorbiking (from US$10pp) and car tours.

Mandarin Café TOURS
(☎382 1281; www.mrcumandarin.com; 24 Đ Tran Cao Van) Boss Mr Cu organises transport and tours.

Stop & Go Café TOURS
(☎382 7051; www.stopandgo-hue.com; 3 Đ Hung Vuong) Personalised motorbike and car tours, including the DMZ.

Sleeping

Google Hotel HOTEL $
(☎383 7468; www.googlehotel-hue.com; 26 Đ Tran Cao Van; d/tr US$15/18; ❄@☎) Offering flashpacker chic at backpacker cheap, the light, spacious rooms here have luxurious beds, huge flat-screen TVs and modish en-suite bathrooms. The large bar-restaurant is a good place to socialise.

Huenino GUESTHOUSE $
(☎625 2171; www.hueninohotel.com; 14 Đ Nguyen Cong Tru; r US$14-22; ❄@☎) The family owners here are super-attentive, and rooms are very attractively presented with artwork, minibar, cable TV and good beds. A generous breakfast is included.

Orchid Hotel HOTEL $$
(☎383 1177; www.orchidhotel.com.vn; 30A Đ Chu Van An; r US$35-60; ❄@☎) Well-run modern hotel offering warm, efficient service and gorgeous accommodation (some rooms have desktop computer and a jacuzzi bath). Your complimentary breakfast is good (eggs are cooked to order).

Hue Backpackers HOSTEL $
(☎382 6567; www.hanoibackpackershostel.com/hue; 10 Đ Pham Ngu Lao; dm/r US$6/20; ❄@☎) With a prime location, eager-to-please staff, good info and a fearsome happy hour, it's easy to why this is a backpacker mecca. Dorms are well designed and have quality mattresses, fans, air-con and lockers.

Hue Thuong HOTEL $
(☎388 3793; 11 Đ Chu Van An; r 250,000d; ❄@☎) Great minihotel, where the newly renovated rooms, though smallish, have a real sparkle.

Guesthouse Nhat Thanh GUESTHOUSE $
(☎393 5589; nhatthanhguesthouse@gmail.com; 17 Đ Chu Van An; r US$13-15; ❄☎) Run by a friendly family. Has light, spacious, well-equipped rooms.

Halo HOTEL $
(☎382 9371; huehalo@yahoo.com; 10A/66 Đ Le Loi; r US$8-15; ❄@☎) Tidy, attractive rooms, many with balcony and a bathtub, right in the heart of backpacker alley.

Eating

We have famed fussy-eater Emperor Tu Duc to thank for the culinary variety of Hue and an imperial cuisine banquet is usually a memorable experience. Royal rice cakes, the most common of which is *banh khoai,* are well worth seeking out.

TOP CHOICE **Lien Hoa** VEGETARIAN $
(3 Le Quy Don; meals 30,000-50,000d; ⏲11am-9.30pm; ✍) Highly authentic Viet veggie restaurant. Eat like an emperor tasting fresh *banh beo* (steamed rice pancakes), noodles dishes and steamboats on a peasant's pay packet.

TOP CHOICE **Take** JAPANESE $
(34 Đ Tran Cao Van; meals 50,000-120,000d; ⏲11.30am-9.30pm) Offering a delightful dining experience, this fine Japanese restaurant has a highly authentic menu. Sample some sushi (around 24,000d for two pieces) or enjoy a yakatori dish (45,000d).

Mandarin Café VIETNAMESE $
(24 Đ Tran Cao Van; mains from 26,000d; ✍) Your host here is photographer Mr Cu, whose inspirational pictures adorn the walls. Offers vegetarian and breakfast choices galore on the varied East-meets-West menu.

GETTING TO LAOS: CHA LO TO NA PHAO

On Monday, Wednesday and Friday bus services pass through the border at Cha Lo–Na Phao (open 7am to 5pm) on the Dong Hoi to Tha Khaek route (260,000d, 11 hours). They return from Tha Khaek the next morning. See p355 for information on crossing this border in the other direction.

GETTING TO LAOS: LAO BAO TO DANSAVANH

Getting to the border The Lao Bao–Dansavanh border is the most popular and least problematic Vietnam–Laos border crossing. It's easy to cross the border on your own; Dong Ha is the gateway. Buses from Dong Ha to Lao Bao bus station (two hours, 85km, 50,000d) leave roughly every 15 minutes. From here *xe om* (motorbike taxi) charge about 12,000d to the border, or it's a 20-minute walk. It's a short walk of a few hundred metres between the Vietnam and Laos border posts.

However, the easiest way of crossing the border is aboard a direct bus. Buses to Savannakhet run from Hue via Dong Ha and Lao Bao. From Hue, there's a 7am air-con bus (280,000d, 9½ hours), on odd days only, that leaves from the Sinh Tourist. This travels via Dong Ha, where it makes a stop at the Sepon Travel office around 8.30am and picks up more passengers (Dong Ha to Savannakhet costs 210,000d) before getting to Savannakhet at 4pm.

At the border The border is open from 7am to 7pm. Laos issues 30-day visas on arrival.

Moving on Entering Laos, *sŏrngtăaou* to Sepon leave fairly regularly.

See p359 for information on crossing this border in the other direction.

Restaurant Bloom CAFE $
(14 Đ Nguyen Cong Tru; snacks from 15,000d; wi-fi) Ideal for a sandwich, baguette, croissant or home-made cake (baked on the premises). This likeable little cafe employs disadvantaged youths.

Stop & Go Café INTERNATIONAL $
(3 Đ Hung Vuong; meals 20,000-60,000d; wi-fi) Casual little place with tasty Vietnamese and backpacker fare, including good rice cakes, pizza and pasta and filling Western breakfasts.

Japanese Restaurant JAPANESE $
(12 Đ Chu Van An; dishes US$1.50-9.00; ⏲6-9pm) Simple place for all your usual Japanese faves. Employs street children and supports a home for them.

Drinking

In the evening, travellers gather over Huda beers in the cafes along Đ Hung Vuong.

Hue Backpackers BAR
(10 Đ Pham Ngu Lao; wi-fi) Party central for backpackers, this hostel bar packs 'em in with its 8pm to 9pm happy hour, infused vodkas and (unashamedly tacky) cocktail list.

Café on Thu Wheels BAR
(10/2 Đ Nguyen Tri Phuong; wi-fi) Hole-in-the-wall with cheap grog, graffiti-splattered walls, a sociable vibe and good info from the feisty owner, Thu.

DMZ Bar & Cafe BAR
(44 Đ Le Loi) As popular as ever, this joint's always abuzz with rocking music, free pool and lively conversation. It serves food till midnight.

Shopping

Hue produces the finest conical hats in Vietnam and is renowned for rice paper and silk paintings. As ever, bargain hard.

Spiral Foundation Healing the Wounded Heart Center BOUTIQUE
(www.hwhshop.com; 23 P Vo Thi Sau) Gorgeous ecofriendly handicrafts and souvenirs (including picture frames from recycled beer cans) made by disabled artisans. Profits aid heart surgery for children in need.

Dong Ba Market MARKET
(Đ Tran Hung Dao; ⏲6.30am-8pm) Anything and everything – clothing, food and coffee – can be bought here.

Information

There are lots of internet cafes on the tourist strips of Đ Hung Vuong and Đ Le Loi.

Café on Thu Wheels (☎383 2241; minhthuhue@yahoo.com; 3/34 Đ Nguyen Tri Phuong) Cycling and motorbiking tours around Hue, overseen by the gregarious and inimitable Thu.

Hue Central Hospital (Benh Vien Trung Uong Hue; ☎382 2325; 16 Đ Le Loi)

Main post office (8 Đ Hoang Hoa Tham)

Mandarin Café (☎382 1281; www.mrcumandarin.com; 24 Đ Tran Cao Van) Reliable information, transport and tours.

Sinh Tourist (☎382 3309; www.thesinhtourist.vn; 7 Đ Nguyen Tri Phuong) Open-tour buses and buses to Laos.

Vietinbank (12 Đ Hung Vuong) An ATM plus exchange services.

Getting There & Away

Air

Vietnam Airlines (☎382 4709; 23 Đ Nguyen Van Cu; ⊙closed Sun) offers three daily flights to both Hanoi and HCMC. **Jetstar** (☎395 5955; Đ 176 Hung Vuong; ⊙closed Sun) also connects Hue with HCMC daily. The office is about 1.5km southeast of the Trang Tien bridge.

Phu Bai airport is 14km south of town. Metered taxis meet all flights and cost about 175,000d to the centre, or use the minibus service for 40,000d. Vietnam Airlines also runs an airport shuttle, which can collect you from your hotel (tickets 55,000d).

Bus

The main bus station is 4km to the southeast of the centre on the continuation of Đ Hung Vuong. **An Hoa bus station** (Hwy 1A), northwest of the Citadel, serves northern destinations, including Dong Ha.

From smaller **Mien Bac bus station**, 7km north of centre, there's also a privately operated minibus to Phong Nha Farmstay (p842) at 1pm (150,000d, 7½ hours).

Hue is also a regular stop on the open-tour bus routes. Mandarin and Stop and Go cafes can arrange bookings for the bus to Savannakhet, Laos.

Train

Hue train station (2 Đ Bui Thi Xuan) is at the southwestern end of Đ Le Loi.

Getting Around

Bicycles (US$1 to US$2), motorbikes (US$4 to US$10) and cars (from US$35 per day) can be hired through hotels all over town. **Mai Linh** (☎389 8989) has air-con taxis with meters. Cyclos and *xe om* will find you when you need them, and when you don't.

Around Hue

DEMILITARISED ZONE (DMZ)

From 1954 until 1975, the Ben Hai River served as the dividing line between South Vietnam and North Vietnam. The DMZ, 90km north of Hue, consisted of the area 5km on either side of the line.

Many of the 'sights' around the DMZ are places where historical events happened, and may not be worthwhile unless you're into war history. To make sense of it all, and to avoid areas where there's still unexploded ordnance, take a guide. Group day tours from Hue cost from US$11 for a budget bus trip to as much as US$100 for a specialised car tour with a Viet vet.

Significant sites:

Vinh Moc Tunnels HISTORIC SITE
(admission 20,000d; ⊙7am-4.30pm) Highly impressive complex of tunnels from the remains of a coastal village that literally went underground in response to unremitting American bombing; 110km from Hue.

Truong Son National Cemetery CEMETERY
(Nghia Trang Liet Si Truong Son) A memorial to the tens of thousands of North Vietnamese soldiers killed along the Ho Chi Minh Trail. Row after row of white tombstones stretch across the hillsides; about 105km from Hue.

Khe Sanh Combat Base HISTORIC SITE
(admission 20,000d; ⊙7am-5pm) The site of the war's most famous siege; about 500 US and 10,000 NVA troops died here in 1968. There's a small museum. About 130km from Hue.

BACH MA NATIONAL PARK

A French-era hill station known for its cool weather, **Bach Ma National Park** (☎054-387 1330; www.bachma.vnn.vn; admission 20,000d) is

TRANSPORT FROM HUE

DESTINATION	CAR/ MOTORBIKE	BUS	TRAIN	AIR
Hanoi	16hr	US$18-27; 13-16hr; 8 daily	US$20-40; 12-17hr; 5 daily	from US$30; 1hr; 3 daily
HCMC	22hr	US$23-37; 19-24hr; 8 daily	US$27-54; 20-22hr; 4 daily	from US$32; 1hr; 4 daily
Danang	2½-4hr	US$3; 3hr; every 20 min	US$3-6; 2½-4hr; 8 daily	N/A
Dong Hoi	3½hr	US$4-7; 3½hr; 12 daily	US$5-10; 3-5½hr; 8 daily	N/A

45km southeast of Hue. There's currently a lot of construction going on inside Bach Ma to upgrade the roads; at the time of research only the lower sections were open. Work is scheduled to finish sometime in 2013.

There's some decent trekking in the lower levels through subtropical forest to villages on the fringes of the park. You can book village and birdwatching tours and English- or French-speaking guides (200,000d per day) at the visitor centre. Unexploded ordnance is still in the area, so stick to the trails.

There's a **guesthouse** (☎054-387 1330; bachmaeco@gmail.com; r with fan/air-con 180,000/270,000d) at the park entrance. When the upper sections reopen, you'll find more accommodation close to the summit.

Danang

☎0511 / POP 788,500

Danang, Vietnam's fifth-biggest city, is on the move. For decades it had a reputation as a slightly mundane provincial backwater, but big changes are brewing. The Han riverfront is resplendent with gleaming new modernist hotels and restaurants. Beachside, five-star hotel developments are emerging on the My Khe strip. And a revamped international airport should open in 2012.

That said, the city itself still has few conventional sightseeing spots except for a decent museum. So for most travellers, a day or two is probably enough.

Sleeping

An excellent selection of new minihotels has opened along the riverside in central Danang, though good budget hotels aren't as easy to find.

CITY CENTRE

TOP CHOICE New Moon Hotel HOTEL $$
(☎382 8488; info@newmoonhotel.vn; 126 Đ Bach Dang; r 300,000-800,000d; ❄@📶) New hotel that offers unrivalled value for money, with a selection of beautifully finished rooms in different price categories, all with flat-screen TV and inviting en-suite marble bathrooms. Book a river-view room for breathtaking vistas.

Rainbow Hotel HOTEL $$
(☎382 2216; rainbowkhachsan@yahoo.com; 220 Đ Bach Dang; r 450,000-600,000d; ❄@📶) A spanking new place with a prime riverfront location, the Rainbow is a hip hotel with a budget price tag. Rooms have contemporary decor and all mod cons.

Winn Hotel HOTEL $
(☎388 8571; ngockhanh_nk@yahoo.com; 36 Đ Hung Vuong; r US$17-20; ❄@📶) Excellent little hotel with 15 modern rooms, painted white and pale pink, all with a good TV and in-room wi-fi. The cheaper options don't have windows.

CHINA BEACH

TOP CHOICE Eena Hotel HOTEL $
(☎222 5123; www.geocities.jp/eenahotel; Khu An Cu 3; s/d/tw US$14/19/24; ❄@📶) Offering astonishing value, this minihotel has immaculately clean, light spacious white rooms, many with views. There's fast wi-fi, friendly English-speaking staff and a good complimentary breakfast too. About 3km west of the centre, just off the beach.

Hoa's Place GUESTHOUSE $
(☎396 9216; 215/14 Đ Huyen Tran Cong Chua; My An Beach; hoasplace@hotmail.com; r U$9) Shabby but not chic, Hoa's is nevertheless a popular backpacker haunt thanks to the fantastic hospitality, food and beachside location. Check it's still open as big resorts are planned nearby. On My An Beach, 6km southwest of Danang.

Eating & Drinking

TOP CHOICE Waterfront INTERNATIONAL, BAR $$
(www.waterfrontdanang.com; 150-152 Đ Bach Dang; meals 90,000-300,000d; ⏲10am-11pm; 📶). Hip new riverfront lounge-cum-restaurant that has really helped put Danang on the map. Gourmet sandwiches (90,000d), light snacks (like salt 'n' pepper calamari) and select mains are offered. Doubles as a bar.

Red Sky INTERNATIONAL $$
(248 Đ Tran Phu; meals 80,000-200,000d; ⏲11.30am-10.30pm; 📶). Casual bar-restaurant that scores highly for Western grub, including good-value steaks, generous salads and Italian food; Vietnamese dishes are also reliable. Beer is very cheap (La Rue is just 15,000d); happy hour is 5pm to 8pm.

Com Nieu VIETNAMESE $
(☎386 7026; 25 Đ Yen Bai; dishes 18,000-140,000d) Very popular with locals, this contemporary restaurant has hearty meals and affable staff. Try the succulent seafood or their claypot rice signature dish.

Bread of Life INTERNATIONAL $$
(www.breadoflifedanang.com; 4 Đ Dong Da; meals 40,000-100,000d; ⊙closed Sun) American-style diner-cum-bakery where the pancakes, burgers, sandwiches, pizza and other comfort foods hit the spot. Run by deaf staff and benefits deaf people.

Le Funk BAR
(166 Đ Bach Dang) Lively riverfront hole-in-the-wall run by a genial French DJ, so expect pumping house tunes.

Chillout Cafe BAR, RESTAURANT
(36 Đ Thai Phien) Hospitable place with Vietnamese and Western owners and a relaxed atmosphere, filling food, quiz nights and great local information.

Tulip Brewery BREWERY
(174 Đ 2/9) Huge Czech-style microbrewery pub 1km south of the centre that draws locals in their hundreds. Also has a menu of Western and Vietnamese dishes.

DON'T MISS

MUSEUM OF CHAM SCULPTURE

Danang's jewel is its famed **Museum of Cham Sculpture** (1 Đ Trung Nu Vuong; admission 30,000d; ⊙7am-5pm). This classic, colonial-era building houses the finest collection of Cham sculpture to be found anywhere on earth. There are more than 300 pieces on display, including altars, *lingas*, garudas, *apsaras*, Ganeshas and images of Shiva, Brahma and Vishnu – all dating from the 5th to 15th centuries. These intricately carved sandstone pieces come from Cham sites all over Vietnam.

Guides hang out at the museum's entrance.

Information

There are internet cafes scattered all over Danang. Consult the website www.indanang.com for reviews and information.

Agribank (202 Đ Nguyen Chi Thanh) ATM and exchange service.

Dana Tours (☎382 5653; 76 Đ Hung Vuong; ⊙Mon-Sat) Offers car hire, boat trips, visa extensions and daytrips.

Danang Family Medical Practice (☎358 2700; www.vietnammedicalpractice.com; 50-52 Đ Nguyen Van Linh) One of Vietnam's most trusted foreign-owned clinics.

Hospital C (Benh Vien C; ☎382 2480; 35 Đ Hai Phong) The most advanced hospital in Danang.

Main post office (☎383 7407; 64 Đ Bach Dang)

Sinh Tourist (☎384 3258; www.thesinhtourist.vn; 154 Đ Bach Dang) Books open-tour buses.

Trong's Real Easy Riders (☎090 359 7971; trongn59@yahoo.com) A branch of the Easy Riders group, which operates out of Danang.

Vietcombank (140 Đ Le Loi) Exchange services and ATM.

Getting There & Away

Air

Danang's only scheduled international connection at the time of research was **Silk Air** (☎356 2708; www.silkair.com; HAGL Plaza Hotel, Đ 1 Nguyen Van Linh) flights (four per week) to Singapore, but expect more routes to open when the new airport terminal opens in 2012 or 2013. For domestic connections, **Jetstar Pacific** (☎358 3538; www.jetstar.com; 307 Đ Phan Chu Trinh) has daily flights from Danang to HCMC and Hanoi while **Vietnam Airlines** (☎382 1130; www.vietnamairlines.com; 35 Đ Tran Phu) operates direct flights to Hanoi, HCMC, Haiphong, Buon Ma Thuot and Nha Trang.

Bus

The **bus station** (Đ Dien Bien Phu) is 3km west of the city centre. Buses run to Hue (64,000d, three hours) and to points up and down the coast all the way to HCMC and Hanoi. For Laos, there are three weekly services to Savannakhet at 8pm (130,000d, 14 hours), crossing the border at Lao Bao. There's also a daily service to Pakse at 6.30am (190,000d, 14 hours). Buses to the Lao Bao border alone are 95,000d (six hours); you may have to change buses at Dong Ha.

Yellow public buses to Hoi An (18,000d, one hour, hourly) travel along Đ Tran Phu in the heart of town.

Travel agencies can also arrange passage on open-tour minibuses running between Danang and both Hoi An and Hue.

Taxis & Motorbikes

A taxi to Hoi An officially costs around 400,000d, but most will drop to 300,000d, while *xe om* charge around 90,000d. Bargain hard if you want to stop at the Marble Mountains or China Beach en route. A ride to the airport is around 55,000d. Call **Mai Linh** (☎356 5656) for a cab.

Train

Danang **train station** is 1.5km from the city centre on Đ Hai Phong at Đ Hoang Hoa Tham.

Danang

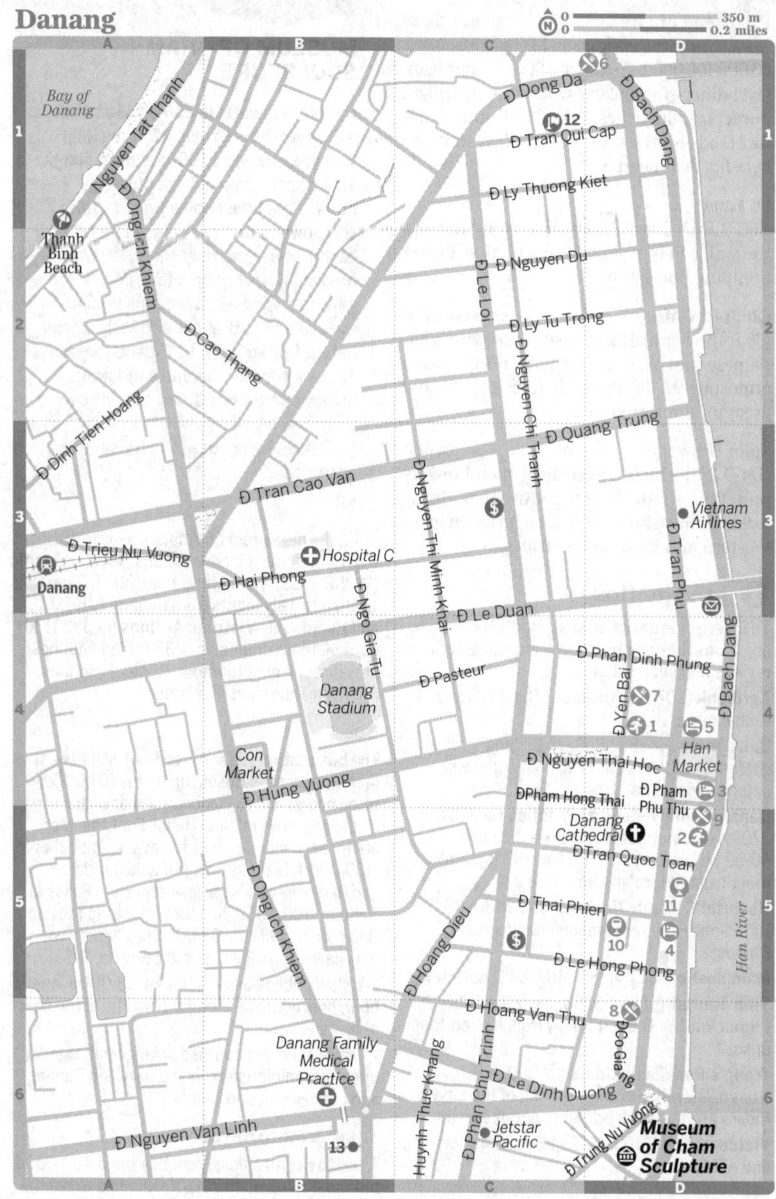

The city is served by all the main north-south trains. Try to take the railway journey up to Hue (from 60,000d, 2½ to four hours, eight daily); it's one of the most beautiful stretches in the country.

Around Danang

About 10km south of Danang are the striking **Marble Mountains** (admission 15,000d; ⏲7am-5pm), which consist of five craggy marble outcrops topped with jungle and

Danang

Top Sights

Museum of Cham Sculpture D6

Activities, Courses & Tours

1 Dana Tours D4
2 Sinh Tourist D5

Sleeping

3 New Moon Hotel D4
4 Rainbow Hotel D5
5 Winn Hotel D4

Eating

6 Bread of Life D1
7 Com Nieu D4
8 Red Sky D6
9 Waterfront D5

Drinking

10 Chillout Cafe D5
11 Le Funk D5

Information

12 Lao Consulate C1

Transport

13 Silk Air B6

pagodas. With natural caves sheltering small Hindu and Buddhist sanctuaries and stunning views of the ocean and surrounding countryside, they're worth taking the time to explore.

China Beach (Bai Non Nuoc), once an R'n'R hang-out for US soldiers during the war, is actually a series of beaches stretching 30km between Hoi An and Danang.

Nearest to central Danang, My Khe Beach is well touristed and accordingly has beachside restaurants and roving vendors. Opposite the Marble Mountains is Non Nuoc Beach, and in between the two are countless spots to spread your beach towel on the sand.

For surfers, China Beach's break gets a decent swell from mid-September to December. The best time for swimming is from May to July, when the sea is at its calmest. There's a mean undertow, so take care.

Buses and minibuses running between Danang and Hoi An can drop you off at the entrance to the Marble Mountains and China Beach, and it's easy to find onward transport.

Hoi An

☎0510 / POP 122,000

Graceful, historic Hoi An is Vietnam's most atmospheric and delightful town. Once a major port, it boasts the grand architecture and beguiling riverside setting that befits its heritage, and the 21st-century curses of traffic and pollution are almost entirely absent.

Hoi An owes its easy-going ambience and remarkably harmonious character more to luck than planning. Had the Thu Bon River not silted up in the late 19th century Hoi An would doubtless be very different today.

The city's allure and importance dwindled until an abrupt revival in fortunes in the 1990s, when a tourism boom transformed the local economy. Today Hoi An is once again a cosmopolitan melting pot, one of the nation's wealthiest towns and a culinary hot spot.

In the Old Town, an incredible legacy of tottering Japanese merchant houses, Chinese temples and ancient tea warehouses has been preserved and converted into stylish restaurants, wine bars and a glut of tailor shops. And yet down by the market and over in neighbouring An Hoi peninsula life has changed little.

Travel a few kilometres further – you'll find some superb bicycle, motorbike and boat trips – and some of central Vietnam's most enticing, bucolic scenery and beaches are within easy reach.

Sights

HOI AN OLD TOWN

A Unesco World Heritage Site, Hoi An Old Town levies an admission fee to most of its historic buildings, which goes towards funding the preservation of the town's architecture. Buying the ticket (admission 90,000d) gives you a choice of five heritage sites to visit – Chinese Assembly Halls, pagodas and temples, historic houses and museums. Booths dotted around the Old Town sell tickets.

The following list of sites is by no means comprehensive.

FREE **Japanese Covered Bridge** BRIDGE

(Đ Tran Phu & Đ Nguyen Thi Minh Khai) Hoi An's iconic bridge was constructed in 1593 and has a roof and a temple built into its northern side. According to one story, the bridge's construction began in the year of the monkey

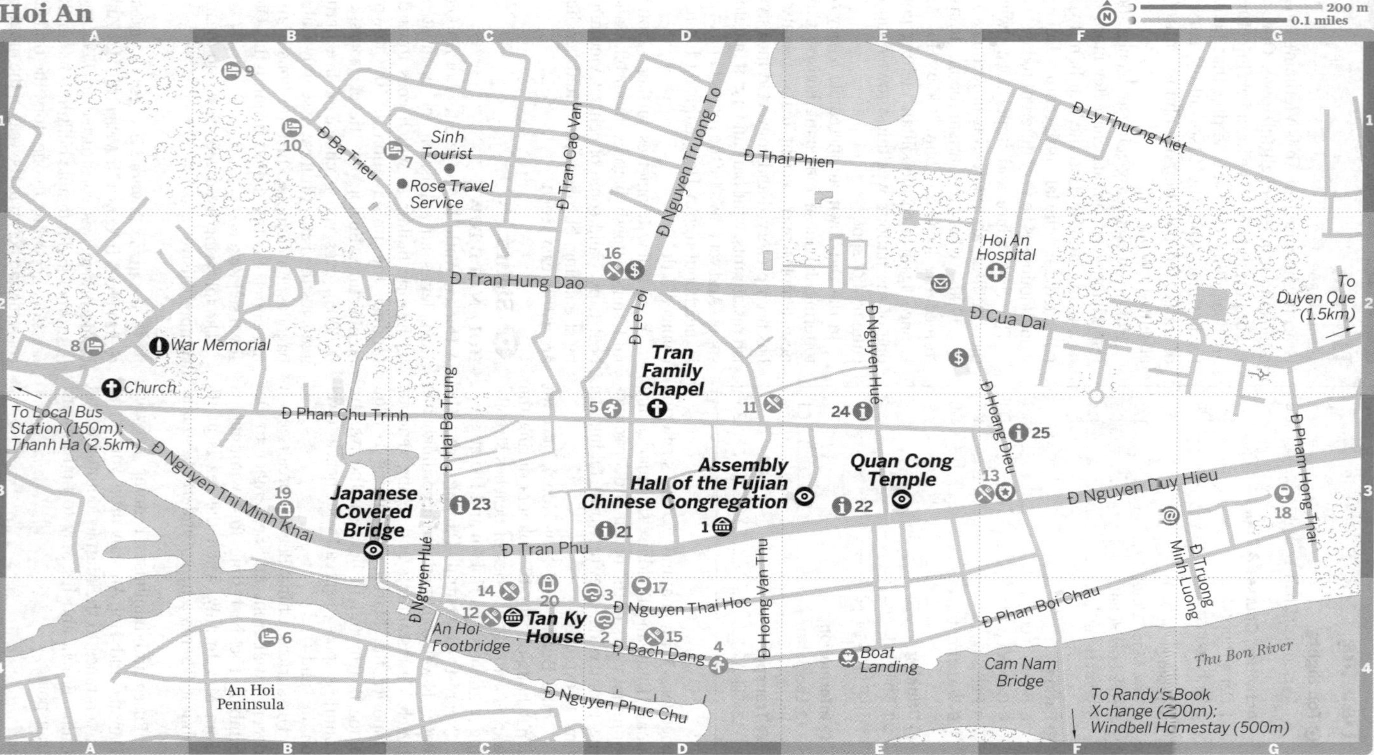
Hoi An
200 m
0.1 miles
Sinh Tourist
Rose Travel Service
Đ Ba Trieu
Đ Tran Cao Van
Đ Nguyen Truong To
Đ Thai Phien
Đ Ly Thuong Kiet
Hoi An Hospital
Đ Tran Hung Dao
Đ Cua Dai
To Duyen Que (1.5km)
War Memorial
Church
To Local Bus Station (150m); Thanh Ha (2.5km)
Đ Phan Chu Trinh
Đ Le Loi
Tran Family Chapel
Đ Nguyen Hué
Đ Hoang Dieu
Đ Hai Ba Trung
Đ Nguyen Thi Minh Khai
Japanese Covered Bridge
Assembly Hall of the Fujian Chinese Congregation
Quan Cong Temple
Đ Nguyen Duy Hieu
Đ Pham Hong Thai
Đ Tran Phu
Đ Hoang Van Thu
Đ Truong Minh Luong
Đ Nguyen Hué
Đ Nguyen Thai Hoc
Tan Ky House
An Hoi Footbridge
Đ Bach Dang
Đ Phan Boi Chau
Boat Landing
Cam Nam Bridge
Thu Bon River
An Hoi Peninsula
Đ Nguyen Phuc Chu
To Randy's Book Xchange (200m); Windbell Homestay (500m)

Hoi An

Top Sights

Assembly Hall of the Fujian Chinese Congregation E3
Japanese Covered Bridge B3
Quan Cong Temple E3
Tan Ky House C4
Tran Family Chapel D3

Sights

1 Museum of Trading Ceramics D3

Activities, Courses & Tours

2 Blue Coral Diving D4
3 Cham Island Diving Center D4
4 Gioan D4
5 Hoi An Motorbike Adventures D3
Morning Glory Cooking School .... (see 14)

Sleeping

6 An Hoi Hotel B4
7 Hoa Binh Hotel C1
8 Hoang Trinh Hotel A2
9 Phuong Dong Hotel B1
10 Thien Nga Hotel B1

Eating

11 Bale Well D3
12 Cargo Club C4
13 Mermaid Restaurant F3
14 Morning Glory Street Food Restaurant C4
15 Phone Café D4
16 Shree Ganesh Indian Restaurant D2

Drinking

17 Before & Now D4
Dive Bar .... (see 3)
18 Why Not? G3

Shopping

19 Art Galleries B3
20 Lotus Jewellery C4
Reaching Out .... (see 12)

Information

21 Hoi An Old Town Booth D3
22 Hoi An Old Town Booth E3
23 Hoi An Old Town Booth C3
24 Hoi An Old Town Booth E3
25 Hoi An Old Town Booth F3

and finished in the year of the dog; thus one entrance is guarded by monkeys, the other by dogs (neither pair will confirm or deny this story).

Assembly Hall of the Fujian Chinese Congregation TEMPLE
(opposite 35 Đ Tran Phu; admission by Old Town ticket; 7am-5.30pm) Founded for community meetings, this hall later became a temple to worship Thien Hau, a deity born in Fujian Province in China. Check out the elaborate mural, the unhealthy skin of the statuary, and the replica of a Chinese boat.

Tan Ky House HISTORIC HOME
(101 Đ Nguyen Thai Hoc; admission by Old Town ticket; 8am-noon & 2-4.30pm) A lovingly preserved house from the 19th century, which once belonged to a Vietnamese merchant. Japanese and Chinese architectural influences are evident throughout. The house is a private home, and has been in the same family for seven generations.

Tran Family Chapel HISTORIC HOME
(21 Đ Le Loi; admission by Old Town ticket; 7.30am-noon & 2-5.30pm) This chapel was built in 1802 for worshipping family ancestors by Tran Tu, who ascended to the rank of mandarin. Its architecture reflects the influence of Chinese (the 'turtle'-style roof), Japanese (triple beam) and vernacular (look out for the bow-and-arrow detailing) styles.

Quan Cong Temple TEMPLE
(Chua Ong; 24 Đ Tran Phu; admission by Old Town ticket) Dedicated to venerated Chinese general Quan Cong, who is worshipped as a symbol of loyalty and justice, this temple has some wonderful papier-mâché and gilt statues. When someone makes an offering to the portly looking Quan Cong, the caretaker solemnly strikes a bronze bowl.

Museum of Trading Ceramics MUSEUM
(80 Đ Tran Phu; admission by Old Town ticket; 7am-5.30pm) Occupies a simply restored wooden house and contains artefacts from all over Asia. The displays are mediocre, but the small exhibition on the restoration of Hoi An's old houses is fascinating.

Arts & Crafts Villages

All those neat fake antiques sold in Hoi An's shops are manufactured in nearby villages. Cross the An Hoi footbridge to reach the **An Hoi Peninsula**, noted for its boat factory and mat-weaving factories. South of the peninsula is **Cam Kim Island**, where people are engaged in woodcarving and boatbuilding. Cross the Cam Nam bridge to **Cam Nam** village, a lovely spot also noted for arts and crafts.

Activities

Diving & Snorkelling

Two reputable dive schools offer trips to the Cham Islands. Both charge exactly the same rates: two fun dives are US$75. The diving is not world class, but can be intriguing, with good macro life – and the day-trip to the Cham islands is superb.

Snorkellers pay US$30 to US$40. Trips only leave between February and September; conditions are best in June, July and August.

Cham Island Diving Center DIVING
(☎391 0782; www.chamislanddiving.com; 88 Đ Nguyen Thai Hoc)

Blue Coral Diving DIVING
(☎627 9297; www.divehoian.com; 77 Đ Nguyen Thai Hoc)

Courses

Informal cooking classes are offered by **Gioan** (☎386 3899; 98B Đ Bach Dang; US$16) and **Phone Café** (80B Đ Bach Dang; US$12).

TOP CHOICE **Morning Glory Cooking School** COOKING COURSE
(☎224 1555; www.restaurant-hoian.com; 106 Đ Nguyen Thai Hoc) Classes are directed by the acclaimed Vy, owner of several restaurants in town, or Lu, her protégé. You'll learn how to tackle local recipes, including *banh khoai* and white rose, plus regional Vietnamese dishes in a professionally organised environment.

Red Bridge Cooking School COOKING COURSE
(☎393 3222; www.visithoian.com) Runs a course that starts with a trip to the market, and is followed by a cruise down the river to its relaxing retreat about 4km from Hoi An. Half day/full day costs US$23/39 per person.

Festivals & Events

Hoi An Legendary Night FESTIVAL
Takes place on the 14th day (full moon) of every lunar month from 5.30pm to 10pm. These festive evenings feature traditional food, song and dance, and games along the lantern-lit streets in the town centre.

Sleeping

Hoi An is awash with excellent accommodation options.

TOP CHOICE **Thien Nga Hotel** HOTEL $$
(☎391 6330; thienngahotel@gmail.com; 52 Đ Ba Trieu; r US$30-35; ❄@🛜🏊) Spacious, light, airy rooms all with balcony and a lovely contemporary feel (though the bathrooms are more prosaic). Book one at the rear for garden views. Staff are smiley and accommodating. The pool is covered by a roof.

Hoang Trinh Hotel HOTEL $
(☎391 6579; www.hoianhoangtrinhhotel.com; 45 Đ Le Quy Don; r US$20-28; ❄@) Well-run place with helpful, friendly service. Rooms here are a little cluttered but spacious and clean, with high ceilings and cable TV. Guests also get a good complimentary breakfast.

Hoa Binh Hotel HOTEL $
(☎391 6838; www.hoianbinhhotel.com; 696 Đ Hai Ba Trung; r US$12-18; ❄@🛜🏊) With a good selection of simple and comfortable modern rooms, all with wi-fi, minibar, cable TV and air-con, this is getting close to budget chic. However, the pool layout (in the lobby!) is bizarre and room rates change according to demand.

Vinh Huy HOTEL $
(☎391 6559; www.vinhhuyhotel.com; 203 Đ Ly Thoung Kiet; r US$10-12; ❄@🛜🏊) All the very cheap, clean well-appointed rooms here represent a great deal and have minibar, fan and cable TV; some have large bathrooms with tubs. It's a 15-minute walk from the Old Town.

Phuong Dong Hotel HOTEL $
(☎391 6477; www.hoianphuongdonghotel.com; 42 Đ Ba Trieu; s/d/tr US$10/12/15; ❄🛜@) Plain, good-value rooms with comfortable mattresses, reading lights, fan and air-con and in-room wi-fi.

An Hoi Hotel HOTEL $
(☎391 1888; www.anhoihotel.com.vn; 69 Đ Nguyen Phuc Chu; r US$20-35; ❄@🛜🏊) Excellent location, with rooms that are a good size, clean and modern. Some on the lower floor lack natural light.

Eating

Hoi An offers a culinary tour de force, including several amazing local specialities. Be sure to try *banh bao* ('white rose'), an incredibly delicate dish of steamed dumpling stuffed with minced shrimp. *Cao lau* – doughy flat noodles mixed with croutons, bean sprouts and greens, topped with pork slices and served in a savoury broth – is also delicious. The other two culinary treats are fried *hoanh thanh* (won ton) and *banh xeo* (crispy savoury pancakes rolled with herbs in fresh rice paper).

TOP CHOICE Morning Glory Street Food Restaurant VIETNAMESE $$
(☎224 1555; www.restaurant-hoian.com; 106 Đ Nguyen Thai Hoc; dishes 42,000-120,000d;) A simply outstanding restaurant, housed in historic premises, that concentrates on street food and traditionally prepared Vietnamese cooking. The exceptional dishes include shrimp mousse on sugarcane skewers, caramelised pork with young bamboo and wonderful salads.

TOP CHOICE Cargo Club INTERNATIONAL $$
(☎391 0489; www.restaurant-hoian.com; 107 Đ Nguyen Thai Hoc; dishes 35,000-105,000d;) For all things Western, from a snack to fine dining, Cargo Club excels: the best breakfasts, delectable *patisserie* selections and mains like grilled seabass and lamb shank rate very highly indeed. Head for the upper terrace for stunning river views.

Shree Ganesh Indian Restaurant INDIAN $$
(www.ganeshindianrestaurant.com; 24 Đ Tran Hung Dao; meals 60,000-120,000d; ⊙noon-10.30pm) Authentic Indian with tantalising thalis, fiery curries and naans freshly baked in a tandoor oven. Prices are reasonable and portions generous.

Mermaid Restaurant VIETNAMESE $$
(www.restaurant-hoian.com; 2 Đ Tran Phu; dishes 35,000-90,000d) One of the original Hoi An eateries (established 1992), this renowned yet simple-looking place serves up wonderful Hoi An specialities and unique family recipes.

Bale Well VIETNAMESE $
(45-51 Đ Tran Cao Van; meals 40,000-75,000d; ⊙11.30am-10pm) Local place that's famous for one dish: delicious barbecued pork, served up satay-style, which you then combine with fresh greens and herbs to create your own fresh spring roll.

Phone Café VIETNAMESE $
(80B Đ Bach Dang; dishes 22,000-62,000d) Phone Café is a humble-looking place that serves the usual faves plus some good claypot specialities.

Drinking

TOP CHOICE Dive Bar BAR
(88 Đ Nguyen Thai Hoc;) Expect a great vibe here thanks to the welcoming service, electronic tunes and party atmosphere. Check out the gorgeous cocktail garden and bar at the rear.

Why Not? BAR
(10B Đ Pham Hong Thai; @) Great late-night hang-out with pool table and YouTube jukebox. Run by a friendly local character who's been in the bar game for decades.

Before & Now BAR
(www.beforennow.com; 51 Đ Le Loi;) Your standard-issue backpackers' bar, complete with (slightly clichéd) pictures of the likes of Che, Marilyn, er...Charles Manson. Expect mainstream pop and rock. Happy hour 6pm to 9pm.

Shopping

Tailor-made clothing is one of Hoi An's best trades, and there are more than 200 tailor shops in town that can whip up an *ao dai* (traditional Vietnamese tunic and trousers), Western suits, shirts and much more. Other hot items include handmade shoes and silk lanterns.

Hoi An also boasts a growing array of interesting art galleries, especially on the west side of the Japanese Covered Bridge.

Reaching Out SOUVENIRS
(www.reachingoutvietnam.com; 103 Đ Nguyen Thai Hoc) This is a fair-trade gift shop is a great place to spend your dong. Profits assist disabled artisans.

Lotus Jewellery JEWELLERY
(www.lotusjewellery-hoian.com; 100 Đ Nguyen Thai Hoc) Very affordable and attractive handcrafted pieces.

Information

For the most part, Hoi An is very safe at any hour. However, late-night bag snatchings in the unlit market have been known, and women should avoid walking home alone late at night.

Most hotels have lobby computers and free wi-fi.

Agribank (Đ Tran Hung Dao) With ATM.

Hoi An Hospital (☎386 1364; 4 Đ Tran Hung Dao) Serious problems should be addressed in Danang.

Hoi An police station (☎386 1204; 84 Đ Hoang Dieu)

Main post office (48 Đ Tran Hung Dao)

Min's Computer (2 Truong Minh Luong; per hr 5000d) You can also print, scan, burn and Skype here.

Randy's Book Xchange (www.randysbookxchange.com; To 5 Khoi Xuyen Trung)

Rose Travel Service (☎391 7567; www.rosetravelservice.com; Đ 111 Ba Trieu) Tours, car rental, bus bookings and boat, jeep and motorbike trips.

Sinh Tourist (☎386 3948; www.sinhtourist.com; 587 Đ Hai Ba Trung) For open-tour buses.

Vietinbank (☎386 1340; 4 Đ Hoang Dieu) Full exchange services, plus ATMs.

Getting There & Away

Most north-south bus services do not stop at Hoi An, but you can head for the town of Vinh Dien (10km to the west) and catch one there. If you're heading for Hue or Nha Trang, open-tour buses, including those run by Sinh Tourist, are easier.

Hoi An bus station (96 Đ Hung Vuong), 1km west of the centre, mainly serves local destinations, including Danang (18,000d, one hour).

The nearest airport and train station are both in Danang.

Getting Around

Metered taxis and motorbike drivers wait for business over the footbridge bridge in An Hoi. Call **Hoi An Taxi** (☎391 9919) or **Mai Linh** (☎392 5925) for a pick-up.

Many hotels offer bicycles/motorbikes for rent from 20,000/100,000d per day.

Around Hoi An

BEACHES

The nearest beach to Hoi An, **Cua Dai** is subject to intense development and the domain of hard-selling beach vendors. There are seafood restaurants here.

Just 3km north of Cua Dai, **An Bang** is fast emerging as one of Vietnam's most happening and enjoyable beaches. It has a wonderful stretch of fine sand and you'll find lots of little cool little beachfront bar-restaurants: **Soul Kitchen** (www.soulkitchen.sitew.com, meals around 90,000d; wi-fi) and **La Plage** (www.laplagehoian.com; meals from 100,000d; wi-fi) both offer terrific European food.

The coastline immediately to the north of An Bang remains pristine, a glorious broad beach lined with casuarina and pandan trees and dotted with the curious coracles of local fisherfolk.

CHAM ISLANDS

☎0510 / POP 2700

A breathtaking cluster of granite islands offshore from Hoi An, the serene **Cham islands** are blissfully undeveloped – for now. Trips to dive or snorkel the reefs and visit the main island of **Hon Lao** make an excellent day out. The Chams are only accessible for about seven months of the year (March to September), as the ocean is usually too rough at other times.

The islands are protected as a marine park and the underwater environment includes 135 species of soft and hard coral and varied macro life.

Bai Lang, Hon Lao's pretty little port, is the only real settlement. Drop by the curious temple **Ong Ngu**, which is dedicated to whales (locals worshipped them as oceanic deities). There are two good, simple guesthouses in town, **Luu Ly** (☎393 0240; r 200,000d) and **Thu Trang** (☎393 0007; r 200,000d), both places serve meals.

A dirt track heads southwest from Hon Lao for 2km past coves to a fine, sheltered beach, home to the excellent **Cham Restaurant** (☎224 1108; meals 50,000-90,000d); call ahead to book your meal.

Getting There & Away

Most visitors arrive on tours (US$25 to US$40) organised by dive schools in Hoi An; see p856. There's also a scheduled daily boat connection from the boat landing on Đ Bach Dang in Hoi An (20,000d, two hours, 7.30am daily), but note foreigners are routinely charged more. Boats do not sail during heavy seas. Bring a copy of your passport and visa.

MY SON

Set under the shadow of Cat's Tooth Mountain are the enigmatic ruins of **My Son** (admission 60,000d; ⏰6.30am-4pm), the most important remains of the ancient Cham empire and a Unesco World Heritage Site. Although Vietnam has better preserved Cham sites, none are as extensive and few have such beautiful surroundings as this, with brooding mountains and clear streams running between the temples.

The ruins are 55km southwest of Hoi An. Day tours to My Son can be arranged in Hoi An for between US$5 and US$7, not including admission, and some trips return to Hoi

An by boat. Independent travellers can hire a motorbike, *xe om* or car. Get here early in order to beat the tour groups, or later in the afternoon.

SOUTH-CENTRAL COAST

Vietnam has an incredibly curvaceous coastline and on this coast it's defined by sweeping sands, towering cliffs and concealed bays.

Nha Trang, Mui Ne and the Con Dao islands are key destinations, but the beach breaks come thick and fast here. If your idea of paradise is reclining in front of turquoise waters, weighing up the merits of a massage or a mojito, then you have come to the right place.

On hand to complement the sedentary delights are activities to set the pulse racing, including scuba diving, snorkelling, surfing, windsurfing and kitesurfing. Action or inaction, this coast bubbles with opportunities.

Nha Trang

☎058 / POP 375,000

Welcome to the beach capital of Vietnam. Visually it's startling, with towering mountains behind the city and a sweeping beach (that forms a fully fledged international resort, complete with high-rise hotels). Offshore islands add to the appeal, offering decadent boat trips and diving in turquoise water.

A party town at heart, people play late here. Yes, the nightlife rocks!

This part of the country has its own microclimate and the rains tend to come from October until December – not the best time for beach bums or scuba divers.

Sights

Nha Trang Coast BEACHES

Coconut palms provide shade for sunbathers and strollers along most of Nha Trang's 6km beachfront. The best beach weather is generally before 1pm, as the afternoon sea breezes can whip up the sand.

Beach chairs are available for rent and vendors peddle food and massages. Head further south and it's still possible to find an empty stretch of sand.

Hon Chong Promontory, 2.5km north of central Nha Trang, is a scenic collection of granite rocks jutting into the South China Sea. The promontory borders a rustic beach cove with island views.

Po Nagar Cham Towers TEMPLE

(Đ 2 Thang 4; admission 16,000d; ⏲6am-6pm) Built between the 7th and 12th centuries on a site used by Hindus for *linga* (phallic symbols) worship, the Po Nagar Cham Towers are 2km north of central Nha Trang. The hill offers blue views of the harbour below.

Originally there were seven or eight towers; four remain. The 28m-high **North Tower** (Thap Chinh), with its terraced pyramidal roof, is a superb example of Cham architecture; it was built in 817.

Cham, ethnic Chinese and Vietnamese Buddhists come to Po Nagar to pray and make offerings.

GETTING TO LAOS: BO Y TO PHOU KEUA

Getting to the border The Bo Y–Phou Keua border connects Kon Tum and Attapeu (Laos). Buses leave Pleiku at 8am daily for Attapeu (240,000d, eight hours, 250km), continuing to Pakse (320,000d, 12 hours, 440km). **Kon Tum Tourist** (☎60 386 3333; www.kontumtourist.com; 2 P Dinh Phung Kontum) can arrange for you to join the bus when it passes through Kon Tum at 9.30am. Mai Linh Express also run daily buses on this route.

Buses also depart Quy Nhon several times a week, passing through Pleiku and Kon Tum en route to Attapeu and Pakse, but as the schedule fluctuates check locally for the latest details.

At the border Lao visas are available on arrival. Crossing the border (open daily 7am to 5pm) is a challenge. On the Vietnam side, the nearest major town is Ngoc Hoi, which can be reached by bus (30,000d, 1½ hours, 60km) from Kon Tum. You'll have to catch a minibus or *xe om* from Ngoc Hoi to cover the 14km to the border.

Moving on On the Laos side, things are even quieter and you'll be at the mercy of passing traffic to hitch a ride onwards. Take a through bus.

See p363 for information on crossing this border in the other direction.

FREE **Long Son Pagoda** PAGODA
(Chua Tinh Hoi Khanh Hoa; Đ 23 Thang 10; ⏲7.30-11.30am & 1.30-8pm) This impressively adorned pagoda is decorated with mosaic dragons covered with glass and ceramic tiles. Founded in the late 19th century, the pagoda still has resident monks. At the top of the hill, behind the pagoda, is the **Giant Seated Buddha**. Around the statue's base are fire-ringed relief busts of Thich Quang Duc and six other Buddhist monks who died in self-immolations in 1963.

Central Nha Trang

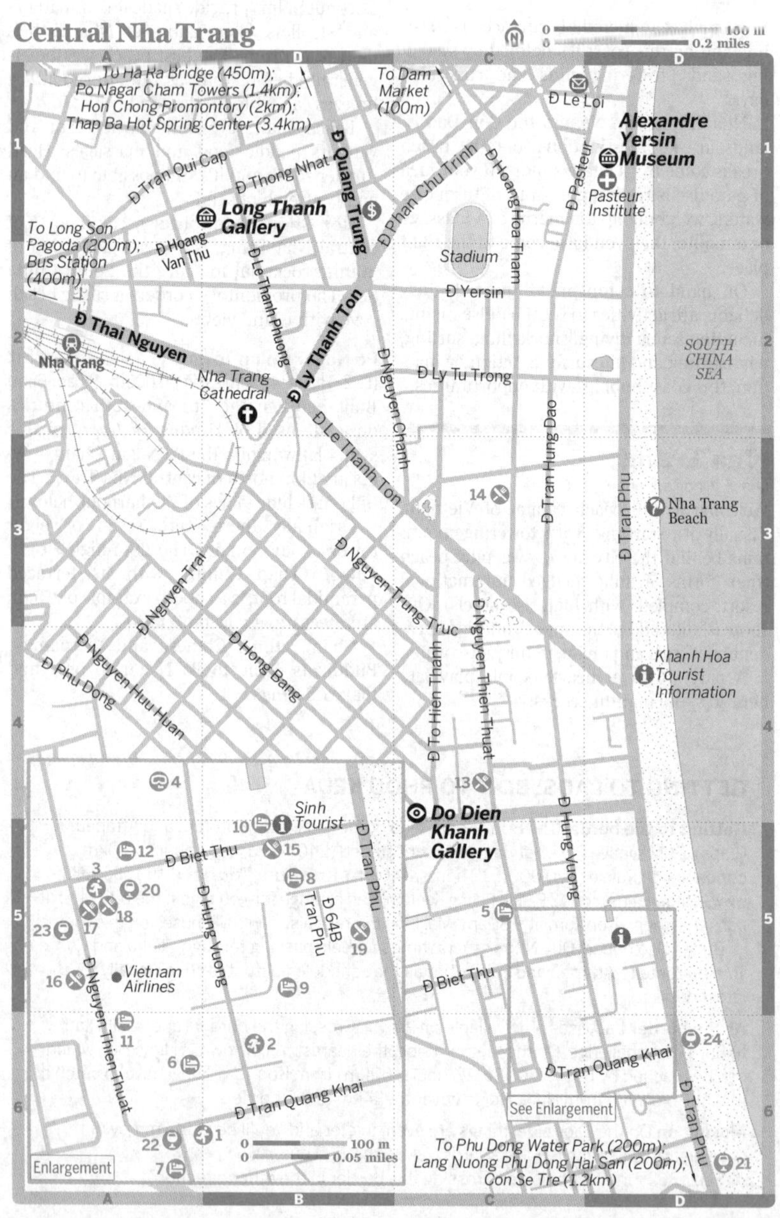

Watch out for scammers claiming to work 'for the monks'. They'll attempt to guide you around the site, then demand a hefty fee.

The pagoda is a 400m west of the train station.

Alexandre Yersin Museum MUSEUM
(10 Đ Tran Phu; admission 26,000d; ⏲7.30-11am & 2-4.30pm Mon-Fri, 8-11am Sat) Dr Alexandre Yersin (1863–1943) founded Nha Trang's Pasteur Institute in 1895. He learned to speak Vietnamese fluently, introduced rubber and quinine-producing trees to Vietnam, and discovered the rat-borne microbe that causes bubonic plague.

Yersin's library and office are now an interesting museum. Tours are in French, English and Vietnamese.

Photographic Galleries ART GALLERIES
The **Long Thanh Gallery** (www.longthanhart.com; 126 Đ Hoang Van Thu; ⏲9am-7pm Mon-Fri) showcases the work of Vietnam's most prominent photographer and his extraordinary black-and-white images of everyday Vietnamese moments. **Do Dien Khanh Gallery** (www.ddk-gallery.com; 126B Đ Hong Bang; ⏲8am-6pm Mon-Fri) has hauntingly beautiful portraits of Cham communities.

Oceanographic Institute MUSEUM
(Vien Nghiem Cuu Bien; 1 Cau Da; admission 15,000d; ⏲6am-6pm) Floating in tanks in the Oceanographic Institute (a French colonial building) are colourful representatives of squirming sea life and 60,000 jars of pickled specimens.

Central Nha Trang

Top Sights

Alexandre Yersin Museum.................D1
Do Dien Khanh Gallery.....................C4
Long Thanh Gallery.........................B1

Activities, Courses & Tours

1 Angel Dive.....................................B6
2 Funky Monkey................................B6
Highland Tours......................(see 23)
3 Mama Linh.....................................A5
4 Rainbow Divers..............................A4
Sailing Club Divers...............(see 24)
Shamrock Adventures.............(see 1)
Waves Watersports................(see 21)

Sleeping

5 AP Hotel..C5
6 Axar Hotel.....................................A6
7 Ha Van Hotel.................................A6
8 Hotel An Hoa.................................B5
9 Mai Huy...B5
10 Perfume Grass Inn.......................B5
11 Sao Mai Hotel...............................A6
12 Violet Hotel..................................A5

Eating

13 Artful Ca Phe.................................C4
14 Au Lac...C3
15 Kirin Restaurant...........................B5
16 Lanterns..A5
Louisiane Brewhouse.............(see 21)
17 Omar's Tandoori...........................A5
18 Truc Linh 2....................................A5
19 Veranda..B5

Drinking

20 Crazy Kim Bar...............................A5
21 Louisiane Brewhouse...................D6
Nghia Bia Hoi.........................(see 9)
22 Oasis...A6
23 Red Apple Club.............................A5
24 Sailing Club..................................D6

Activities

Diving

Nha Trang is Vietnam's most popular diving destination. Visibility averages 15m, but can be as much as 30m, depending on the season (late October to early January are the worst times of year). There are some good drop-offs and small underwater caves to explore and an amazing variety of corals. Among the colourful reef fish, stingrays are occasionally spotted.

A full-day outing, including two dives and lunch, costs between US$40 and US$70. Dive operators also offer a range of courses, recommended centres include the following:

Angel Dive DIVING
(☎352 2461; www.angeldivevietnam.info; 1/33 Đ Tran Quang Khai)

Rainbow Divers DIVING
(☎352 4351; www.divevietnam.com; 90A Đ Hung Vuong)

Sailing Club Divers DIVING
(☎352 2788; www.sailingclubdivers.com; 72-74 Đ Tran Phu)

Other Activities

Waves Watersports WATERSPORTS
(☎090-544 7393; www.waveswatersports.com; Louisiane Brewhouse, 29 Đ Tran Phu) Windsurfing, sea kayaking, wakeboarding, water-skiing, surfing and sailing lessons.

TRIPPING THE BAY BY BOAT

The 71 offshore islands around Nha Trang are renowned for their remarkably clear water. Boat trips (from just 100,000d) to these islands – booze cruises and snorkelling excursions – are wildly popular with young backpackers.

There's a working fish farm on Hon Mieu (Mieu Island) that's also an impressive outdoor **aquarium** (entrance 50,000d). From here, you can rent canoes or hire someone to paddle you out to the nearby islands of Hon Mun (Ebony Island) or Hon Yen (Swallow Island).

Idyllic Hon Tre (Bamboo Island) is the largest island in the area. You can get a boat to Bai Tru (Tru Beach) at the northern end of the island. You'll find great snorkelling and diving off Hon Mun, Hon Tam and Hon Mot.

Virtually every hotel and travel company in town books island-hopping boat tours. Note that the once-notorious hedonistic trips involving free ganja are no more, though others continue the party tradition with cheesy DJs and floating bars.

Con Se Tre (☎381 1163; www.consetre.com.vn; 100/16 Đ Tran Phu) Snorkelling trips from US$13.

Funky Monkey (☎352 2426; www.funkymonkeytour.com.vn; 75A Đ Hung Vuong) Booze cruise (100,000d) with 'live entertainment' from the, er…Funky Monkey boy band.

Mama Linh (☎352 2844; mamalinhvn@yahoo.com; 23C Đ Biet Thu) Still a popular party option.

Khanh Hoa Tourist Information (☎352 8000; khtourism@dng.vnn.vn; Đ Tran Phu) This trip takes in remote and secluded beaches and bays far from the tourist crowd; 349,000d, including lunch. Contact the tourist office for bookings & information.

Whitewater Rafting RAFTING
(☎090-515 0978; www.shamrockadventures.vn; Đ Tran Quang Khai; per person inc lunch from US$35) Rafting tours can be combined with mountain biking.

Thap Ba Hot Spring Center THERMAL BATHS
(☎383 4939; www.thapbahotspring.com.vn; 25 Ngoc Son; from 100,000d; ⏱7am-7.30pm) Get deep down and dirty at these hot thermal mud baths. Also home to hot and cold mineral swimming pools (50,000d).

Phu Dong Water Park SWIMMING
(Đ Tran Phu; admission 40,000d; ⏱9am-5pm) Hydroslides, shallow pools and fountains, right on the beachfront.

Sleeping

TOP CHOICE **Ha Van Hotel** HOTEL $
(☎352 5454; www.in2vietnam.com; 3/2 Đ Tran Quang Khai; r US$22-32; ❄@📶) Under French management, this hotel strives to offer a higher standard of service than the local competition. The rooms are well-appointed and show a welcome decorative flair. It has an inviting rooftop restaurant-bar, and there's an ice-cream counter in reception.

TOP CHOICE **Violet Hotel** HOTEL $$
(☎352 2314; www.violethotelnhatrang.com.vn; 12 Đ Biet Thu; r 450,000-800,000d; ❄@📶🏊) It's hard to beat this new hotel for location and value for money. Rooms are tastefully finished and facilities include a small courtyard swimming pool. Breakfast is also included.

Mai Huy HOTEL $
(☎352 7553; maihuyhotel.vn@gmail.com; 7H Quan Tran, Đ Hung Vuong; r US$7-15; ❄@📶) The family here really make their guests feel at home. Rooms are great value, meticulously clean and include cheaper fan options for those counting the dong.

AP Hotel HOTEL $
(☎352 7545; 34 Đ Nguyen Thien Thuat; r 290,000-450,000d; ❄@📶) Offers excellent facilities, including flat-screen TV, minibar and bathtub. Cheaper rooms have no window, but the VIPs have balconies with distant sea views.

Axar Hotel HOTEL $
(☎352 1655; axarhotel@vnn.vn; 148/10 Đ Hung Vuong; r US$12; ❄@📶) A new hotel tucked away down a side alley. Rooms are spacious and light and the trim is a cut above the competition, making it excellent value.

Perfume Grass Inn HOTEL $$
(☎352 4286; www.perfume-grass.com; 4A Đ Biet Thu; r US$12-30; ❄@📶) Consistently popular, this welcoming inn has rooms with a touch of character, particularly the pricier options with wood panelling. Cheaper fan rooms include satellite TV and hot shower.

Hotel An Hoa HOTEL $
(☎352 4029; www.anhoahotel.com.vn; 64B/6 Đ Tran Phu; r US$8-14; ❄@📶) A reliable, friendly option in budget alley. Has a variety of rooms – some fan-cooled, others larger with air-con.

Sao Mai Hotel HOTEL $
(☎352 6412; saomai2hotel@yahoo.com; 99 Đ Nguyen Thien Thuat; dm US$4, r US$6-12; ❄@📶) Budget crash pad with no-nonsense rooms and a rooftop terrace. Receptionist Mr Mao Loc runs customised photographic tours.

Eating

Nha Trang is a diner's delight, with a diverse mix of international flavours.

For authentic Vietnamese food head away from the main strip; **Dam Market** (Đ Trang Nu Vuong) has good stalls, including veggie options.

Lanterns VIETNAMESE $$
(72 Đ Nguyen Thien Thuat; dishes 35,000-178,000d) Predominantly Vietnamese flavours, such as braised pork in claypot, plus international offerings for anyone who is riced out. Lanterns supports a local orphanage and offers cooking classes (US$18).

TOP CHOICE **Veranda** INTERNATIONAL $$
(66 Đ Tran Phu; mains 40,000-120,000d) This stylish little restaurant offers a small menu of food with flair, blending Vietnamese ingredients and global flavours. Three-course set menus are on offer from just US$5, including a drink.

Louisiane Brewhouse INTERNATIONAL, BREWERY $$
(29 Đ Tran Phu; www.louisianebrewhouse.com.vn; mains 50,000-350,000d; ⏰7am-1am; @🏊) Microbrewery with a pool and an eclectic menu of Thai, Vietnamese and Japanese food. Great cakes and pastries too.

TOP CHOICE **Lac Canh Restaurant** VIETNAMESE $$
(44 Đ Nguyen Binh Khiem; dishes 30,000-150,000d) Locals flock here in numbers to fire up the tabletop barbecues and grill their own meats, squid, prawns, lobsters and more.

Truc Linh 2 VIETNAMESE $$
(www.truclinhrest.vn; 21 Đ Biet Thu; dishes 40,000-190,000d) The Truc Linh empire includes several eateries in the heart of backpackerville. Number 2 has a pretty garden setting and serves authentic dishes at affordable prices.

Lang Nuong Phu Dong Hai San SEAFOOD $
(Đ Tran Phu; dishes 30,000-150,000d; ⏰2pm-3am) It may be plastic chair fantastic, but the seafood is fresh and delicious: choose from scallops, crab, prawns and lobster, all at market prices.

Au Lac VEGETARIAN $
(28C Đ Hoang Hoa Tham; meals from 12,000d; 🖉) A long-running I-can't-believe-it's-not-meat restaurant. Tasty and cheap.

Kirin Restaurant VIETNAMESE $
(1E Đ Biet Thu; dishes 20,000-120,000d) Colonial surrounds and authentic, affordable Vietnamese cuisine.

Omar's Tandoori INDIAN $$
(89B Đ Nguyen Thien Thuat; dishes 40,000-120,000d) Authentic curries plus tandoori specialities.

Artful Ca Phe CAFE $
(20A Đ Nguyen Thien Thuat; mains 20,000-100,000d) Part photography gallery, part cafe, this place is ideal for a coffee, juice or light bite.

Drinking

Oasis BAR
(3 Đ Tran Quang Khai) Popular for cocktail-drinking and shisha-smoking, with happy hours rolling on from 4pm to midnight. The garden terrace is great for sporting events. Stays open until dawn.

Sailing Club BAR
(72-74 Đ Tran Phu; @) Despite gentrification, this remains the definitive Nha Trang night spot. Drinks are more expensive than in other venues, so it takes awhile to fill up. Popular nights attract a cover charge.

Crazy Kim Bar BAR
(www.crazykimbar.com; 19 Đ Biet Thu; @📶) Busy bar that's home to the 'Hands off the Kids!' campaign, which works to prevent paedophilia. Features regular themed party nights, great music and profits go towards the cause. There's a classroom for vulnerable street kids on the premises, and volunteer English teachers are needed.

Louisiane Brewhouse BREWERY
(☎352 1948; 29 Đ Tran Phu; @🏊) Homebrew, Nha Trang-style. Elegant microbrewery with

BUCKET OF WHAT?

There have been a number of reports of dodgy cocktail buckets (laced with moonshine or drugs) doing the rounds in bars and clubs. Keep an eye on what goes into the bucket or avoid them completely – you don't want your night to end in paranoia, illness or robbery.

an inviting swimming pool and a private strip of sand.

Red Apple Club BAR
(54H Đ Nguyen Thien Thuat; @) Backpacker party HQ with cheap beer, flowing shots and indie anthems.

Nghia Bia Hoi BAR
(7G/3 Đ Hung Vuong) Probably the cheapest beer in Nha Trang, including a light lager and a darker brown beer.

Information

Though Nha Trang is generally a safe place, be very careful on the beach during the day (theft) and at night (robbery). Pickpocketing is a perennial problem. Bags with valuables left behind bars for 'safekeeping' are regularly relieved of cash and phones. Drive-by bag snatching is on the rise. And note the warning about cocktail buckets above.

Nha Trang has dozens of internet cafes and most hotels and bars have free wi-fi. ATMs are widespread too.

Highland Tours (☎352 4477; www.highlandtourstravel.com; 54G Nguyen Thien Thuat) Affordable tours to the Central Highlands.

Main post office (4 Đ Le Loi)

Mama Linh's Boat Tours (☎352 2844; 23C Đ Biet Thu) Famed for its raucous boat tours, Mama Linh can also arrange trips around the province and the highlands.

Pasteur Institute (☎382 2355; 10 Đ Tran Phu) Medical consultations and vaccinations.

Sinh Tourist (☎352 2982; www.thesinhtourist.vn; 2A Đ Biet Thu) Cheap local tours and open-tour buses.

Vietcombank (17 Đ Quang Trung; ⊙Mon-Fri) Changes travellers cheques and offers cash advances.

Getting There & Away

Air

Vietnam Airlines (☎352 6768; 91 Đ Nguyen Thien Thuat) connects Nha Trang with HCMC (from 680,000d), Hanoi (from 1,700,000d) and Danang (from 980,000d) daily. **Jetstar** (www.jetstar.com) offers cheaper connections, with Hanoi starting at 775,000d.

Bus

Phia Nam Nha Trang bus station (Đ 23 Thang 10) has buses (via Quy Nhon) to Danang. Regular buses head south to Phan Rang (40,000d, two hours), and HCMC (180,000d, 11 hours), including sleeper buses from 7pm. Buses also run to Dalat (100,000d, five hours) and Buon Ma Thuot (85,000d, four hours).

Open-bus tours are the best option for Mui Ne (four to five hours), these continuing on to HCMC. Open buses also head to Dalat (five hours) and Hoi An (11 hours).

Train

Nha Trang train station (Đ Thai Nguyen; ⊙ticket office 7am-10pm) is in the middle of town.

Getting Around

Nha Trang is now served by Cam Ranh Airport, about 28km south of the city. Shuttle buses (40,000d) ply this route, leaving from the site of the old airport (near 86 Đ Tran Phu) two hours before scheduled departure times, taking about 40 minutes. **Nha Trang Taxi** (☎382 6000) charge 320,000d from the airport to a downtown destination, or only 190,000d in reverse.

Cyclos and *xe oms* cost 20,000d for a shortish ride. Hotels and cafes rent bicycles from 30,000d per day. **Mai Linh** (☎382 2266) taxis are safe and reliable.

TRANSPORT CONNECTIONS WITH NHA TRANG

DESTINATION	CAR/MOTORBIKE	BUS	TRAIN	AIR
HCMC	10hr	US$12/11hr/frequent	US$8-23/12hr/frequent	from US$34/1hr/3 daily
Mui Ne	5hr	US$7/6hr/regular	N/A	N/A
Dalat	4hr	US$6/5hr/regular	N/A	N/A
Danang	11hr	US$12/12hr/regular	US$9-24/15hr/frequent	from US$49/1hr/daily/

Mui Ne

062 / POP 15,000

Once upon a time, Mui Ne was an isolated stretch of sand, but it was too beautiful to be ignored and it's now a string of resorts. Mercifully, most of these are low-rise and set amid pretty gardens by the sea. The area is definitely moving upmarket, as more exclusive resorts open their doors, but there is still a surfer vibe evident.

Mui Ne is the adrenalin capital of southern Vietnam. Surf's up from August to December. Windsurfing and kitesurfing are huge here. It's also the 'Sahara' of Vietnam, with the most dramatic sand dunes in the region looming large.

Sights

Sand Dunes BEACH

Mui Ne is known for its enormous sand dunes, be sure to try the sand-sledding. The Fairy Spring (Suoi Tien) is a stream that flows through a patch of the dunes and rock formations near town. Also nearby are a red stream, a market and a fishing village. Four-wheel-drive tours of the dunes are popular.

Po Shanu Cham Tower TEMPLE

(Km 5; admission 5000d; 7.30-11.30am & 1.30-4.30pm) On Route 706 heading towards Phan Thiet, the small Po Shanu Cham Tower occupies a hill with sweeping views of Phan Thiet, including the boat-filled estuary, and a cemetery filled with candy-like tombstones.

Activities

Jibes KITESURFING, WINDSURFING

(384 7405; www.windsurf-vietnam.com; 90 Đ Nguyen Dinh Chieu) A watersports mecca, offering lessons and renting state-of-the-art gear such as windsurfers, surfboards, kitesurfers and kayaks.

Sankara Kitesurfing Academy KITESURFING

(091-491 0607; www.kiteschoolmuine.com; 78 Đ Nguyen Dinh Chieu) Based at ultra-hip Sankara, this place offers kitesurfing and equipment rentals.

Vietnam Kitesurfing Tours KITESURFING, SURFING

(090-946 9803; www.vietnamkitesurfingtours.com; 117C Đ Nguyen Dinh Chieu) This company takes you to parts others cannot reach. Day trips cost US$80 and two-day trips start at US$180.

Courses

A Taste of Vietnam COOKING

(091-665 5241; atasteofvietnam@gmail.com; Sunshine Beach Resort, 82 Đ Nguyen Dinh Chieu; US$20-25) Learn the secrets of Vietnamese cuisine with a cooking class by the beach.

Sleeping

TOP CHOICE **Mui Ne Backpackers** GUESTHOUSE $

(384 7047; www.muinebackpackers.com; 88 Đ Nguyen Dinh Chieu; dm US$6-10, r US$20-60;) Highly popular, sociable place with hospitable Aussie management. You'll find smart four-bed dorms and fully renovated private rooms.

Indochina Dreams BOUTIQUE HOTEL $$

(384 7271; www.indochinadream.com; 74 Đ Nguyen Dinh Chieu; r US$40-55;) Expanding place in extensive gardens where the newer bungalows are finished in local stone. The swimming pool is a great place to unwind.

Bien Dua Resort GUESTHOUSE $

(Coconut Beach; 384 7241; www.bienduaresort.com; 136 Đ Nguyen Dinh Chieu; r US$10-20;) Intimate, friendly French-run place with bungalow-style rooms that are enticing value for the prime beachfront location. Budget fan-cooled rooms are available too.

Rang Garden Bungalow HOTEL $

(374 3638; 233A Đ Nguyen Dinh Chieu; r US$10-30;) New in 2011, this offers seriously smart rooms around a generously proportioned pool.

Thai Hoa Mui Ne Resort HOTEL $$

(384 7320; www.thaihoaresort.com; 56 Đ Huynh Thuc Khang; r US$20-50;) Popular, attractive bungalows fronting a spacious garden.

Lu Hoang Guesthouse HOTEL $

(350 0060; 106 Đ Nguyen Dinh Chieu; r US$15-20;) Welcoming hosts and lovingly decorated rooms, some with seaviews and breezy balconies.

Eating

Venture beyond the Km 14 mark and there are a host of seafront shacks that serve affordable seafood (mains 30,000d to 80,000d) from sundown.

TOP CHOICE **Lam Tong** VIETNAMESE $

(92 Đ Nguyen Dinh Chieu; dishes 25,000-75,000d) It doesn't look like much but this family-run beachfront restaurant is great value. Fresh

Mui Ne Beach

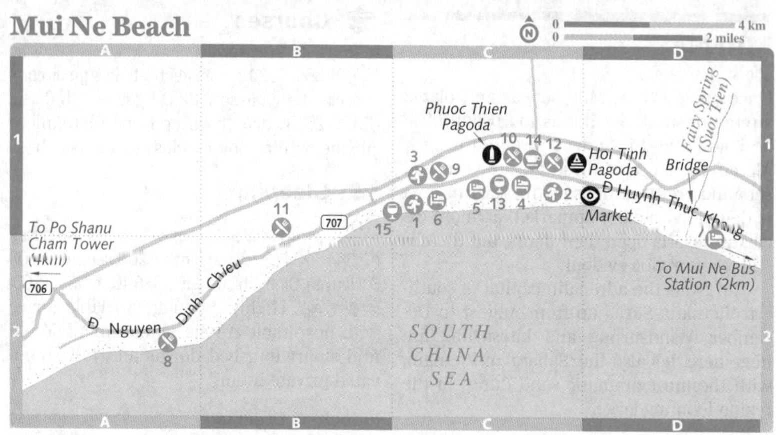

Mui Ne Beach

Activities, Courses & Tours

Jibes ... (see 6)
1 Sankara Kitesurfing Academy ... C1
2 Sinh Tourist ... C1
Taste of Vietnam ... (see 1)
3 Vietnam Kitesurfing Tours ... C1

Sleeping

4 Bien Dua Resort ... C1
Indochina Dreams ... (see 1)
5 Lu Hoang Guesthouse ... C1
6 Mui Ne Backpackers ... C1
Rang Garden Bungalows ... (see 10)
7 Thai Hoa Mui Ne Resort ... D1

Eating

8 Hoa Vien Brauhaus ... A2
9 Hoang Vu ... C1
10 La Taverna ... C1
Lam Tong ... (see 6)
11 Peaceful Family Restaurant ... B1
12 Phat Hamburgers ... C1

Drinking

13 DJ Station ... C1
Fun Key ... (see 13)
14 Info Café ... C1
15 Wax ... C1

seafood is popular and cheap, so the place is always busy with a mix of travellers and locals.

TOP CHOICE **La Taverna** ITALIAN $$
(☎374 3272; 229C Đ Nguyen Dinh Chieu; mains 50,000-150,000d; wi-fi) Around the Km 16 mark, La Taverna has delicious thin-crust pizzas and homemade pastas. Also offers Vietnamese faves, fresh seafood and Italian vino.

TOP CHOICE **Phat Hamburgers** INTERNATIONAL $$
(☎374 3502; 253 Đ Nguyen Dinh Chieu; burgers 50,000-75,000d; wi-fi) Vietnam's finest burgers are available here in a variety of shapes and sizes. Try Phatarella, including cashew-nut pesto and mozzarella cheese.

Peaceful Family Restaurant VIETNAMESE $
(Yen Gia Quan; 53 Đ Nguyen Dinh Chieu; dishes 30,000-70,000d) Traditional Vietnamese cuisine under a breezy thatched roof with reasonable prices and efficient service.

Hoang Vu VIETNAMESE $
(121 Đ Nguyen Dinh Chieu; dishes 40,000-90,000d) The menu is predominantly Asian – with Vietnamese, Chinese and Thai tastes on offer. Expect an atmospheric setting and attentive service.

Hoa Vien Brauhaus INTERNATIONAL $$
(www.hoavien.vn; 2A Đ Nguyen Dinh Chieu; mains 50,000-150,000d; wi-fi) Freshly brewed draft Pilsner Urquell is the big draw, though the huge restaurant offers some Czech and international dishes, as well as a dizzying array of live seafood.

Drinking

DJ Station BAR, CLUB
(120C Đ Nguyen Dinh Chieu; wi-fi) This is the most popular late-night spot in Mui Ne, with a resident DJ and dastardly drink promotions. Gets going after 10pm.

Info Café CAFE $

(241 Đ Nguyen Dinh Chieu; drinks 20,000-50,000d; ⏰7am-10pm; 📶) Travellers are wild about the coffee here, which comes in all styles and flavours. Also a reliable spot for travel info.

Fun Key BAR

(124 Đ Nguyen Dinh Chieu; 📶) New in 2011, this is another 'in' spot, with the backpacker crowd looking for the Ko Pha Ngan experience in Mui Ne.

Wax BAR

(68 Đ Nguyen Dinh Chieu; 📶) Wax has happy hours until midnight, when it lights up the beach bonfire.

Information

A great resource for information on Mui Ne is www.muinebeach.net.

Internet and wi-fi is very wildly available and there are several ATMs.

Main post office (348 Đ Huynh Thuc Khang)

Sinh Tourist (144 Đ Nguyen Dinh Chieu) Operates out of Mui Ne Resort, booking open-tour buses.

Getting There & Around

Mui Ne is connected to Hwy 1 via branch roads to the north and south but few regular buses serve the town.

Open-ticket buses are the best option for Mui Ne, try Sinh Tourist for destinations, including HCMC (90,000d, six hours), Nha Trang (90,000d, five hours) and Dalat (100,000d, five hours). There are also night buses to HCMC (160,000d), Nha Trang (160,000d) and Hoi An (200,000d).

Local buses run from nearby Phan Thiet to Mui Ne, or take a *xe om* (60,000d). **Mai Linh** (☎389 8989) operates metered taxis. *Xe om* charge 20,000d to 40,000d for rides up and down the coast.

Con Dao Islands

☎064 / POP 5500

Isolated from the mainland, the Con Dao Islands are one of the star attractions in Vietnam. Long the prison of political prisoners and undesirables, this place is now turning heads thanks to its striking natural beauty. Con Son, the largest of this chain of 15 islands and islets, is ringed with lovely beaches, coral reefs and scenic bays and remains partially covered in thick forests. Hiking, diving and deserted beaches are all a big draw.

More than three-quarters of the land area in the island chain is part of Con Dao National Park, which protects Vietnam's most important **sea turtle nesting grounds**.

Sights

Your entrance fees for Phu Hai should be valid for the other sights.

Phu Hai Prison HISTORIC BUILDING

(admission 20,000d; ⏰7-11.30am & 1-5pm Mon-Sat) The largest of the 11 jails on the island, this prison dates from 1862. It houses several enormous detention buildings, one with about 100 shackled and emaciated mannequins that are all too lifelike.

The notorious cells dubbed tiger cages were used by the French to incarcerate nearly 2000 political prisoners.

Revolutionary Museum HISTORIC BUILDING

(⏰7-11am & 1.30-5pm Mon-Sat) This museum has exhibits on Vietnamese resistance to the French, communist opposition to the Republic of Vietnam, and the treatment of political prisoners. An impressive-looking new **Con Dao Museum** is located at the eastern end of Đ Nguyen Hue; exhibits from the Revolutionary Museum will be moved here once it opens its doors.

Coastline BEACHES

Bai Dam Trau is arguably the best all-round beach, a secluded cove on the southern end of the island. Other options include tiny **Bai Nhat**, though it's exposed only during low tide. **Bai Loi Voi** is another possibility.

Activities

Con Dao offers the most pristine marine environment in the country. Diving is possible year round, but March to September is best.

Two good dive operators are based here:

Dive! Dive! Dive! DIVING

(☎383 0701; www.dive-condao.com; 36 Đ Ton Duc Thang)

Rainbow Divers DIVING

(☎090 557 7671; www.divevietnam.com; Six Senses Con Dao)

There are lots of treks around forested Con Son Island; it's necessary to take a national park guide (150,000d to 250,000d). Trekking destinations include **Bamboo Lagoon** (Dam Tre), **Ong Dung Bay** and former fruit plantations at **So Ray**.

Sleeping & Eating

Con Dao Camping HOTEL $$
(☎383 1555; condaocamping.com; Đ Nguyen Duc Thuan; r 600,000d; ❄@☁) The curious triangular bungalows may look more holiday camp than heavenly retreat, but they are great value for the beachfront location. Frills (if not thrills) include satellite TV, minibar and showers with a view of the night sky.

Hai Nga Mini Hotel HOTEL $
(☎363 0308; 7 Đ Tran Phu; r 200,000-550,000d; ❄@☁) Small hotel in the heart of town that's run by a friendly family who speak English, French and German. Rooms are basic but good value, including air-con, TV and hot showers.

Thu Tam VIETNAMESE $$
(Đ Nguyen Hue; mains 20,000-100,000d) The plentiful fish and seafood are fresh from bubbling tanks.

Tri Ky VIETNAMESE $$
(7 Đ Nguyen Duc Thuan; mains 40,000-200,000d) Ocean-fresh treats, including squid grilled in five spices and seafood hotpots.

Information

The **National Park HQ** (☎383 0669; www.condaopark.com.vn; 29 Đ Vo Thi Sau; ⏲7-11.30am & 1.30-5pm) has information about excursions and hikes.

There is a branch of **Vietin Bank** (Đ Le Duan) with two ATMs. However, these are notorious for running out of dong, and the bank does not change foreign currency, so bring plenty of cash with you.

Internet access and wi-fi are available at hotels in town.

Getting There & Around

Vasco (☎383 1831; www.vasco.com.vn; 44 Đ Nguyen Hue) offers three flights daily from HCMC from around 900,000d one-way. **Air Mekong** (www.airmekong.info) has daily flights too. The tiny airport is about 15km from the town centre. You can hitch a ride to town on hotel shuttle minibuses for about 60,000d.

Boat trips (2,000,000d to 5,000,000d per day) can be arranged through the national park office. Bicycles (US$2) and motorbikes (from US$7) are available for rent from hotels.

CENTRAL HIGHLANDS

The undulating landscape that once sheltered VC soldiers down the Ho Chi Minh Trail offers an off-the-beaten track destination for travellers. There's a rugged charm to its hill-tribe villages and valleys, waterfalls and winding roads.

Looking for big nature? Check out Cat Tien National Park, where there are gibbons, crocodiles and elusive tigers and rhinos.

Despite a fraught history, the central highlands are safe and easy to travel, and Dalat is a perfect respite from the heat.

Dalat

☎063 / POP 205,000 / ELEV 1475M

Dalat is the alter-ego of lowland Vietnam. The weather is spring-like cool instead of tropical hot. Days are fine, but nights can be chilly. The town is dotted with elegant French-colonial villas, and farms are thick with strawberries and flowers, not rice.

Dalat is small enough to remain charming, and the surrounding countryside is blessed with lakes, waterfalls, evergreen forests and gardens. The town is a big draw for domestic tourists, for whom it's Le Petit Paris, a honeymoon capital and the City of Eternal Spring all rolled into one.

Sights & Activities

Perhaps there's something in the cool mountain air that fosters the distinctly artistic vibe that veers towards cute kitsch in Dalat.

Hang Nga Crazy House NOTABLE BUILDING
(3 Đ Huynh Thuc Khang; admission 30,000d; s US$25-57, d US$35-70) Southeast of central Dalat, this is a funky place that's earned the moniker Crazy House from local residents. It's notable for its *Alice in Wonderland* architecture: you can perch inside a giraffe or get lost in a giant spiderweb.

Crémaillère TRAIN TRIP
(Ga Da Lat; 1 Đ Quang Trung; ⏲6.30am-5pm) The Crémaillère, located 2km east of the centre, is a cog railway that linked Dalat and Thap Cham-Phan Rang from 1928 to 1964. The line is now a tourist attraction. You can ride 8km down the tracks to Trai Mat village, where you can visit the ornate Linh Phuoc Pagoda.

There are five scheduled trains to Trai Mat (return ticket 100,000d, 30 minutes, 8km) every day between 7.45am and 4.05pm.

Bao Dai's Summer Palace PALACE
(off Đ Trieu Viet Vuong; admission 10,000d; ⏲7am-5pm) This art deco-influenced villa was constructed in 1933 and was one of three palaces Bao Dai kept in Dalat. The decor has

EASY DOES IT

For many travellers, the highlight of their trip to the central highlands is an off-the-beaten-track motorcycle tour with an Easy Rider. The flip side to the popularity of the Easy Riders is that now everyone claims to be one. In central Dalat, you can't walk down the street without being invited (sometimes harassed) for a tour.

Rider-guides can be found in hotels and cafes in Dalat. Read testimonials from past clients. Check the bike over. Test-drive a rider first before committing to a longer trip. Then discuss the route in detail – for scenery the new coastal highways that link Dalat to Mui Ne and Nha Trang, plus the old road to the coast via Phan Rang are wonderful. Rates asked are US$20 for a day tour, or US$50 per day for longer journeys.

not changed in decades and retains a quirky appeal.

Bao Dai's Summer Palace is set in a pine grove, 2km southwest of the city centre.

Lam Dong Museum MUSEUM
(4 Đ Hung Vuong; admission 10,000d; 7.30-11.30am & 1.30-4.30pm Mon-Sat) This hillside museum displays ancient artefacts and pottery, as well as costumes and musical instruments of local ethnic minorities. It's located 2.5km east of the centre.

Sleeping

TOP CHOICE Dreams Hotel HOTEL $
(383 3748; dreams@hcm.vnn.vn; 151 Đ Phan Dinh Phung; r US$20-25; @) Quite simply the friendliest and most comfortable place to stay in Dalat. The buffet breakfast spread is legendary. Dreams includes a sauna, steam room and hot tub, free for guests from 4pm to 7pm. There's a second branch at 164B offering more of the same.

Thi Thao Hotel HOTEL $$
(Gardenia Hotel; 383 3333; www.thithaohotel.com; 29 Đ Phan Boi Chau; r from US$25; @) Offers the best-value style in town, rooms are new and spacious with superb bathrooms and a flat-screen TV. All very tasteful.

Hotel Chau Au – Europa HOTEL $
(382 2870; europa@hcm.vnn.vn; 76 Đ Nguyen Chi Thanh; r US$10-20; @) A likable, homely hotel run by a delightful owner. Choose a room at the front with a balcony for views over Dalat.

Trung Cang Hotel HOTEL $
(382 2663; www.thesinhtourist.vn; 4A Đ Bui Thi Xuan; r US$15-25; @) Smart Sinh establishment with tastefully decorated rooms, including local silks, and good tour and transport information.

Le Phuong Hotel HOTEL $
(382 3743; lephuonghotel@gmail.com; 80 Đ Nguyen Chi Thanh; r 250,000-330,000d; @) A new family-run hotel on a busy accommodation strip with large rooms, oversized beds and tasteful bathrooms.

Hoan Hy Hotel HOTEL $
(351 1288; hoanhyhotel@yahoo.com; 16 Đ 3 Thang 2; r US$15; @) New hotel above a bakery where the rooms are serious value for money and well-equipped.

Eating

There are vegetarian food stalls and cheap eats in the market area.

V Cafe INTERNATIONAL $$
(1/1 Đ Bui Thi Xuan; dishes 25,000-79,000d) A travellers' favourite, this friendly restaurant serves a mix of Asian and Western mains, most with sides of mash and fresh vegetables. There's a live duet performing here most nights.

Art Cafe VIETNAMESE $$
(70 Đ Truong Cong Dinh; dishes 25,000-75,000d;) Owned by an artist, this elegant eatery has intimate tables and soft lighting. The menu features Vietnamese dishes with a twist, including plenty of vegetarian options.

Da Quy VIETNAMESE $
(Wild Sunflower; 49 Đ Truong Cong Dinh; dishes 25,000-65,000d) With a sophisticated ambience but unsophisticated prices, this place earns consistently good reviews from travellers of all tastebuds. Try the traditional claypot dishes with fish or shrimp.

An Lac VEGETARIAN $
(71 Đ Phan Dinh Phung; meals from 10,000d;) There's an English menu here, and options range from noodle soups to *banh bao* or steamed rice-flour dumplings stuffed with a savoury filling.

Central Dalat

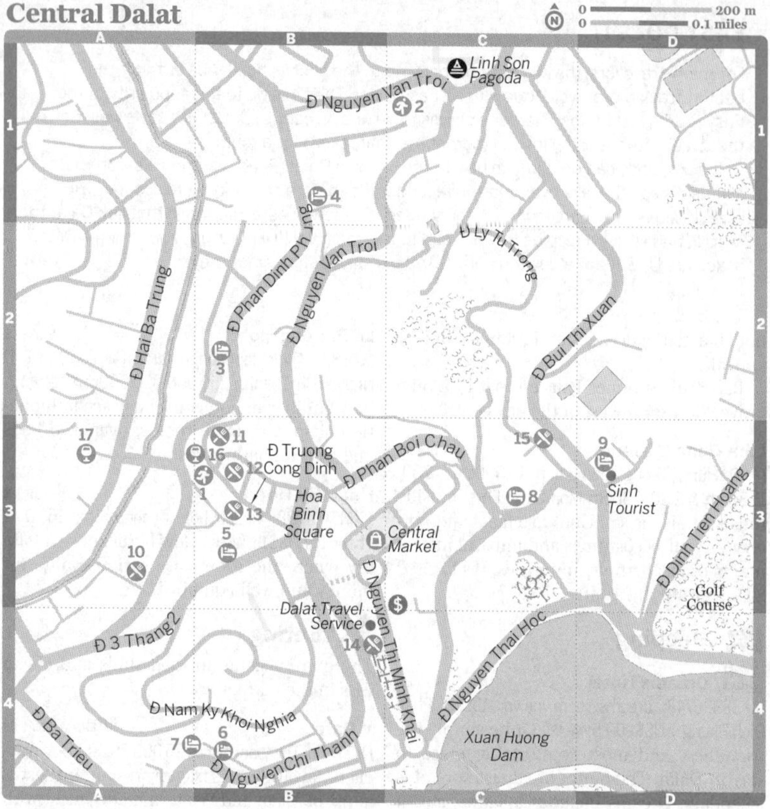

0 200 m
0 0.1 miles

Linh Son Pagoda
Đ Nguyen Van Troi
Đ Phan Dinh Phung
Đ Nguyen Van Troi
Đ Ly Tu Trong
Đ Hai Ba Trung
Đ Bui Thi Xuan
Đ Truong Cong Dinh
Đ Phan Boi Chau
Hoa Binh Square
Central Market
Sinh Tourist
Đ Dinh Tien Hoang
Golf Course
Dalat Travel Service
Đ Nguyen Thi Minh Khai
Đ 3 Thang 2
Đ Nguyen Thai Hoc
Đ Nam Ky Khoi Nghia
Đ Ba Trieu
Đ Nguyen Chi Thanh
Xuan Huong Dam

Chocolate Cafe INTERNATIONAL $
(40A Đ Truong Cong Dinh; dishes 20,000-70,000d) In the busy backpacker strip, this place has affordable pizzas and pastas, well-presented Vietnamese dishes and fine espresso coffee.

Drinking

Hangout DIVE BAR
(71 Đ Truong Cong Dinh) With cheap beers and a pool table, the Hangout acts as an HQ for some of Dalat's Easy Riders, as well as visiting backpackers

Saigon Nite DIVE BAR
(11A Đ Hai Ba Trung) Rundown yet friendly bar where people come for the beer and pool, not for the decor.

Shopping

Hoa Binh Square and the market building adjacent to it are the places to purchase ethnic handicrafts, including Lat rush baskets that roll up when empty. Coffee is another smart purchase.

Information

Dalat has numerous ATMs and internet cafes and wi-fi is widely available.

Dalat Travel Service (☎382 2125; dalattravel service@vnn.vn; D Nguyen Thi Minh Khai) Tours and vehicle rentals.

Groovy Gecko Adventure Tours (☎383 6521; www.groovygeckotours.net; 65 Đ Truong Cong Dinh) Experienced agency offering canyoning, hiking and mountain-biking trips.

Lam Dong Hospital (☎382 1369; 4 Đ Pham Ngoc Thach)

Main post office (14 Đ Tran Phu)

Phat Tire Ventures (☎382 9422; www.ptv-vietnam.com; 109 Đ Nguyen Van Troi) Reputable operator offering adventure sports, including trekking (from US$26) and kayak-

Central Dalat

Activities, Courses & Tours

1 Groovy Gecko Adventure Tours......... B3
2 Phat Tire Ventures C1

Sleeping

3 Dreams Hotel...................................... B2
4 Dreams Hotel (Northern Branch)... B1
5 Hoan Hy Hotel..................................... B3
6 Hotel Chau Au – Europa B4
7 Le Phuong Hotel A4
8 Thi Thao Hotel C3
9 Trung Cang Hotel D3

Eating

10 An Lac.. A3
11 Art Cafe B3
12 Chocolate Cafe B3
13 Da Quy.. B3
14 Food Stalls B4
15 V Cafe C3

Drinking

16 Hangout.. B3
17 Saigon Nite... A3

ing (from US$37). Bike trips include two-day (US$169) rides to Mui Ne.

Sinh Tourist (☎382 2663; www.thesinhtourist.vn; 4A Đ Bui Thi Xuan) Tours and open-tour bus bookings.

Vietcombank (☎351 0586; 6 Đ Nguyen Thi Minh Khai) Exchanges cash and travellers cheques.

Getting There & Around

Vietnam Airlines (☎383 3499; www.vietnamairlines.com; 2 Đ Ho Tung Mau) has daily services to HCMC (680,000d), Danang (980,000d) and Hanoi (1,700,000d). Lien Khuong Airport is 30km south of the city. Vietnam Airlines operates a shuttle bus (35,000d, 30 minutes) timed around flights. Taxis cost about US$12.

Long-distance buses leave from the **station** (Đ 3 Thang 2) about 1km south of the city centre. Services run to HCMC (110,000d to 160,000d, six to seven hours), Nha Trang (70,000d to 100,000d, new road four hours, old road seven hours) and Buon Ma Thuot (from 85,000d, four hours). Open-tour minibuses to Saigon, Mui Ne and Nha Trang can be booked at travellers' cafes.

Full-day tours with motorbike guides (from US$10) are a great way to see the area, as many of the sights lie outside Dalat's centre. Many hotels offer bicycle and motorbike hire. For a taxi call **Mai Linh** (☎352 1111).

Around Dalat

Waterfalls WATERFALLS

Dalat's waterfalls are obviously at their gushing best in the wet season but still flow during the dry. Avoid over-commercialised Prenn and Cam Ly falls.

Datanla Falls (admission 5000d) is 7km southeast of Dalat off Hwy 20. It's a nice walk through the rainforest and a steep hike downhill to the falls. You can also take a **bobsled ride** (return 40,000d) here.

Pongour Falls (admission 6000d), 55km away in the direction of HCMC, are beautiful any time but spectacular in the rainy season when they form a full semicircle.

Dambri Falls (admission 10,000d), 75km from Dalat, are the tallest falls (90m) in the area – you can trek down and take the cable car back up.

You'll need your own wheels to access these waterfalls.

Lang Bian Mountain NATURE RESERVE

(Nui Lam Vien; admission 10,000d) With five volcanic peaks ranging in altitude from 2100m to 2400m, Lang Bian Mountain, 13km north of Dalat, makes a scenic trek (three to four

OFF THE BEATEN TRACK IN THE CENTRAL HIGHLANDS

It's easy to get off the beaten track in the wonderfully scenic highlands. This is a great part of the country to see from the back of a motorbike.

The upgrading of the historic **Ho Chi Minh Trail** has made it easier to visit out-of-the-way places such as **Kon Tum**, one of the friendliest cities in Vietnam.

Buon Ma Thuot is the major city in the region, but the biggest buzz you'll get is from the coffee beans. Nearby **Yok Don National Park** (☎050-378 3049; www.yokdonnationalpark.vn) is home to 38 endangered mammal species, including plenty of elephants and a handful of tigers. Stunning waterfalls in this area include **Gia Long** and **Dray Nur Falls** along the Krong Ana River.

Be sure to also explore **Cat Tien National Park** (see p873), southwest of Dalat.

hours from Lat Village). Views from the top are tremendous.

The nine hill-tribe hamlets of **Lat Village**, about 12km northwest of Dalat, are at the base of Lang Bian Mountain.

HO CHI MINH CITY (SAIGON)

☎08 / POP 7.2 MILLION

Ho Chi Minh City (HCMC) is a metropolis on the move, and we are not just talking about the city's motorbikes. Yes, Saigon is Vietnam at its most dizzying, a high-octane city of commerce and culture that has driven the whole country forward with its limitless energy and booming economy.

Wander through alleys to ancient pagodas or teeming markets, past ramshackle wooden shops selling silk and spices, before fast-forwarding into the future beneath skyscrapers and mammoth malls. The ghosts of the past live on in the churches, temples, former GI hotels and government buildings that one generation ago witnessed a city in turmoil.

Put simply, there's nowhere else quite like it. Saigon has it all.

Sights

CITY CENTRE

War Remnants Museum MUSEUM

(Bao Tang Chung Tich Chien Tranh; Map p875; 28 Đ Vo Van Tan; admission 15,000d; ⏲7.30am-noon & 1.30-5pm) Documenting the atrocities of war, the War Remnants Museum is unique, brutal and an essential stop. On display are retired artillery pieces, a model of the tiger cages used to house VC prisoners, and a heartbreaking array of photographs of the victims of war. The exhibits are labelled in Vietnamese, English and Chinese; they're propagandist but still very powerful.

The **Requiem Exhibition** here is a very powerful collection of war photography.

Ho Chi Minh City

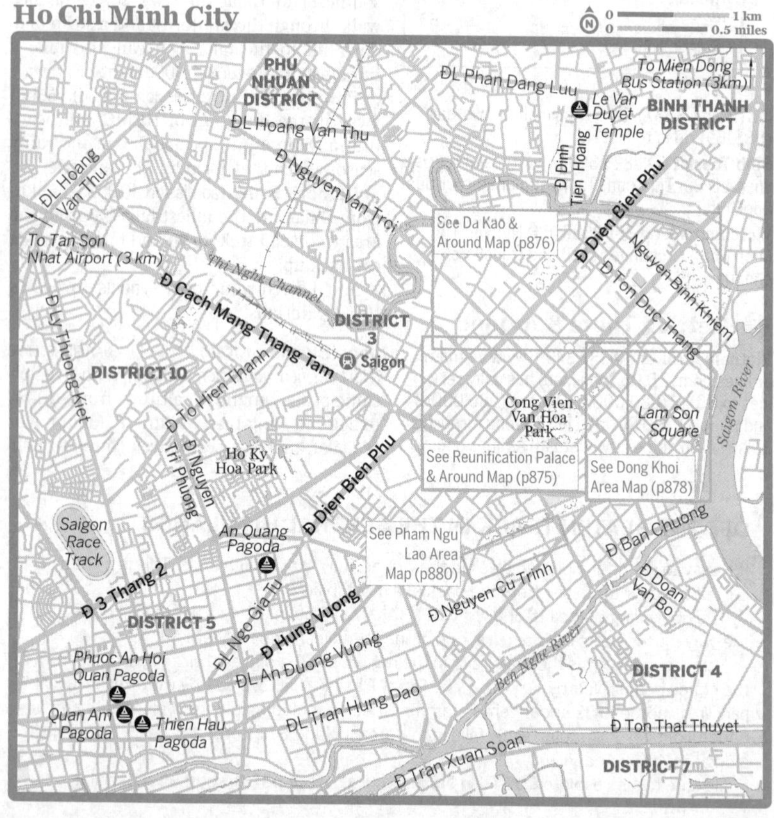

CAT TIEN NATIONAL PARK

One of the outstanding natural spaces in Vietnam, Unesco-listed **Cat Tien National Park** (☎063-366 9228; www.cattiennationalpark.vn; admission 50,000d; ⊙7am-10pm) comprises an amazingly biodiverse area of lowland tropical rainforest. The hiking, mountain biking and birdwatching are outstanding.

Fauna in the park includes 326 bird species, 100 mammals (including elephants) and 79 reptiles. Tiny numbers (as few as eight) of Javan rhinoceros still exist here, and leopards are also believed to be present, though visitors rarely see the larger mammals.

Call ahead for reservations, as the park can accommodate only a limited number of visitors.

Sight & Activities

Cat Tien National Park can be explored on foot, by mountain bike, by 4WD and also by boat along the Dong Nai River. There are many well-established hiking trails in the park, though you'll need a **guide** (from 250,000d), who should be booked in advance.

Trips to the **Crocodile Swamp** (Bau Sau; entry 100,000d, guide fee 300,000d, boat trip 300,000d), taking in a three-hour jungle trek, are popular. **Night safaris** (300,000d) are another option.

Dao Tien Endangered Primate Species Centre (www.go-east.org; entry incl boat ride 150,000d; ⊙8am & 2pm) is located on an island in the Dong Nai River. This rehabilitation centre hosts gibbons, langurs and lorises that have been confiscated as pets or from traffickers; the eventual goal is to release the primates back into the wild.

Wild Gibbon Trek (ecotourism@cattiennationalpark.vn; per person US$60, maximum 4 people) runs daily and involves a 4am start to get out to the gibbons in time for their dawn chorus and a fully guided tour of the Primate Species Centre. Book ahead.

Sleeping & Eating

Avoid weekends and holidays if possible.

Cat Tien National Park (☎063-366 9228; small tent/big tent 200,000/300,000d, bungalow from 500,000d; ❄) offers basic bungalow rooms and tented accommodation close to the park headquarters. There are two small **restaurants** (meals 35,000-200,000d) here.

Practicalities

Cat Tien is 125km north of HCMC and 175km south of Dalat; turn off Hwy 20 at Tan Phu and it's another 25km up a paved access road to the entrance.

Buses between Dalat and HCMC pass the access road; ask for Vuon Quoc Gia Cat Tien. Waiting motorbikes (around 150,000d) will then take you to the park entrance.

We've received mixed reviews about budget tours to Cat Tien. For a reputable customised birdwatching, bike or hiking tour, contact Sinhbalo Adventures (p882).

Bicycles are available for hire in the park, from 20,000d per day.

Reunification Palace HISTORIC BUILDING
(Dinh Thong Nhat; Map p875; Đ Nam Ky Khoi Nghia; admission 30,000d; ⊙7.30-11am & 1-4pm) Built in 1966 to serve as South Vietnam's Presidential Palace, today this 1960s landmark is known as the Reunification Palace. The first communist tanks crashed through the gates of this building on 30 April 1975 when Saigon surrendered to the North. The building is a timewarp, having been left just as it looked on that momentous day.

Jade Emperor Pagoda PAGODA
(Phuoc Hai Tu or Chua Ngoc Hoang; Map p876; 73 Đ Mai Thi Luu) Built in 1909, this a gem among Chinese temples. It's filled with statues of phantasmal divinities and grotesque heroes, and the smoke of burning joss sticks fills the air. The statues represent characters from both the Buddhist and Taoist traditions.

HCMC Museum MUSEUM
(Map p878; www.hcmc-museum.edu.vn; 65 Đ Ly Tu Trong; admission 15,000d; ⊙8am-4pm) A grand,

GETTING TO CAMBODIA: LE THANH TO O YADAW

Getting to the border Remote and rarely used by foreigners the Le Thanh–O Yadaw border crossing links Pleiku with Ban Lung, Cambodia. From Pleiku local buses leave several times a day for Moc Den (30,000d, two hours, 80km), where another bus (20,000d, 15km) heads to the border.

At the border Open 7am to 5pm. Visas are available on arrival in Cambodia.

Moving on After entering Cambodia at O Yadaw, minibuses (30,000r or US$7.50) or motorbikes (US$15) head to Ban Lung. Departing early should make it easier to arrange affordable transport on the Cambodian side.

See p130 for information on crossing this border in the other direction.

neoclassical structure built in 1885, HCMC's city museum is a singularly beautiful and impressive building. It tells the story of the city through archaeological artefacts, ceramics, old city maps and curios.

History Museum MUSEUM
(Bao Tang Lich Su; Map p876; Đ Nguyen Binh Khiem; admission 15,000d; ⏲8-11am & 1.30-4.30pm Tue-Sun) This impressive collection is housed in a stunning Sino-French building constructed in 1929 and displays artefacts from the Dong Son, Funan, Cham and Khmer cultures.

Notre Dame Cathedral CHURCH
(Map p878; Đ Han Thuyen; ⏲Mass 9.30am Sun) Built between 1877 and 1883, this cathedral looks like it's been beamed in directly from Normandy. Romanesque arches and twin 40m-high towers create an imposing facade.

Mariamman Hindu Temple TEMPLE
(Chua Ba Mariamman; Map p875; 45 Đ Truong Dinh; ⏲7.30am-7.30pm) A splash of southern India's colour in Saigon, this temple is dedicated to the Hindu goddess Mariamman.

CHOLON

Cholon, 5km southwest of the centre, forms the city's Chinatown. The district has a wealth of wonderful Chinese temples including **Thien Hau Pagoda** (Ba Mieu or Pho Mieu; 710 Đ Nguyen Trai), dedicated to Thien Hau, the Chinese goddess of the sea, and the fabulously ornamental **Phuoc An Hoi Quan Pagoda** (184 Đ Hung Vuong), built in 1902 by the Fujian Chinese congregation. **Quan Am Pagoda** (12 Đ Lao Tu) has a roof decorated with fantastic scenes, rendered in ceramic, from traditional Chinese plays and stories.

DON'T MISS

SKYHIGH SAIGON

Opened in late 2010, the magnificent Carlos Zapata–designed **Bitexco Financial Tower** (Map p878; 36 Đ Ho Tung Mao; admission 200,000d; ⏲1-9pm Mon-Fri, 10am-10pm Sat & Sun) peaks at 262m and dwarfs all around it. From the Saigon Skydeck, on the 48th floor, the views are extraordinary on a clear day.

Activities

Bach Dang jetty (Map p878)is the place to arrange a boat to tour the Saigon River. Small boats cost around US$10 per hour, larger boats US$15 to US$30.

Vietnamese Traditional Massage Institute MASSAGE
(Map p880; ☎3839 6697; 185 Đ Cong Quynh; per hr 50,000-60,000d) It's not the classiest act in town, but it does offer inexpensive, no-nonsense massages performed by well-trained blind masseurs.

Workers' Club POOL
(Map p875; rear, 55B Đ Nguyen Thi Minh Khai, District 3; admission 14,000d) This swimming pool has colonnades and a degree of art deco charm.

Courses

Saigon Cooking Class COOKING
(Map p878; ☎3825 8485; www.saigoncookingclass.com; 74/7 Hai Ba Trung, District 1; class US$39; ⏲10am & 2pm Tue-Sun) Prepare three mains and one dessert with the chefs from Hoa Tuc. A market visit is optional.

Vietnam Cookery Centre COOKING
(☎3512 7246; www.vietnamcookery.com; 362/8 Đ Ung Van Khiem, Binh Thanh District) Introductory classes and market visits.

Sleeping

Virtually all budget travellers head straight to the Pham Ngu Lao area.

Reunification Palace & Around

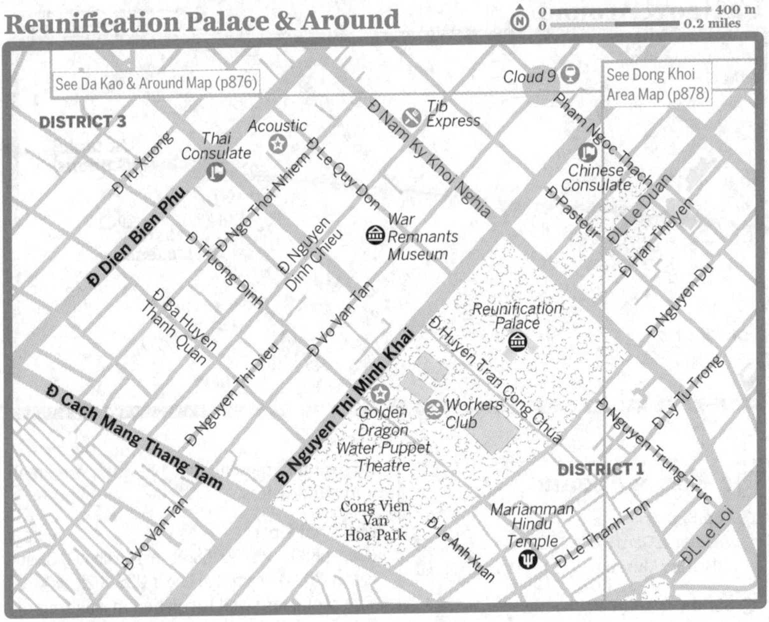

PHAM NGU LAO

Saigon's backpacker precinct has more than 100 places to stay, most between US$10 and US$35, and even the odd dorm. There are also some excellent midrange deals here, with most minihotels priced at US$25 to US$55. Some hotels with D Pham Ngu Lao or D Bui Vien addresses are located in alleys off those main streets.

TOP CHOICE Giang & Son GUESTHOUSE $

(Map p880; 3837 7548; www.giangson.netfirms.com; 283/14 Đ Pham Ngu Lao; r US$16-25;) A clean, comfortable and friendly place on a surprisingly quiet alley. Tall and thin, with three rooms on each floor – the only downer is that there's no elevator. It's worth upgrading to a US$20 room for a window.

TOP CHOICE Hong Han Hotel GUESTHOUSE $

(Map p880; 3836 1927; www.honghan.netfirms.com; 238 Đ Bui Vien; r US$20-25;) Another guesthouse in the tall and skinny mode (seven floors and no lift), Hong Han offers style and comfort. The front rooms have thrilling views to the Bitexco Tower but the smaller rear rooms are quieter and cheaper. Free breakfast too.

Bich Duyen Hotel GUESTHOUSE $

(Map p880; 3837 4588; bichduyenhotel@yahoo.com; 283/4 Đ Pham Ngu Lao; r US$17-25;) This welcoming place on a quiet lane has excellent rooms; pay more for the luxury of a window. Showers are excellent.

Diep Anh GUESTHOUSE $

(Map p880; 3836 7920; diepthеanh@hcm.vnn.vn; 241/31 Đ Pham Ngu Lao; r US$20;) A step above most guesthouses, figuratively and literally (there are endless stairs), Diep Anh's tall and narrow shape makes for light and airy upper rooms. The gracious staff ensure the rooms are kept in good nick.

An An Hotel HOTEL $$

(Map p880; 3837 8087; www.anan.vn; 40 Đ Bui Vien; r US$40-50;) Unassuming, unpretentious and affable, this skinny but smart midrange minihotel has well-proportioned en-suite rooms with safety-deposit boxes and in-room computers.

Beautiful Saigon 2 HOTEL $$

(Map p880; 3920 8929; www.beautifulsaigon2hotel.com; 40/19 Đ Bui Vien; s US$26-37, d $US29-42;) This new minihotel lurks down a back lane. Its deluxe rooms have balconies.

Da Kao & Around

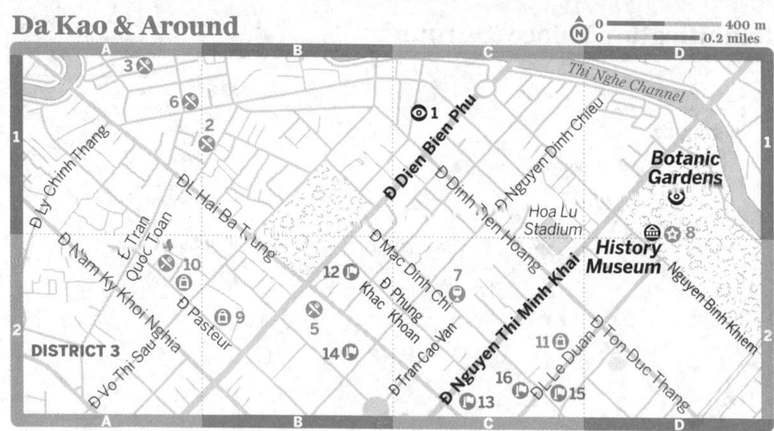

Da Kao & Around

Top Sights

Botanic Gardens D1
History Museum D1

Sights

1 Jade Emperor Pagoda C1

Eating

2 Banh Xeo 46A B1
3 Cuc Gach Quan A1
4 Pho Hoa A2
5 Tib B2
6 Tib Vegetarian A1

Drinking

7 Hoa Vien C2

Entertainment

8 Saigon Water Puppet Theatre D1

Shopping

9 Adidas Puma Factory Shop B2
10 Cham Khanh A2
11 Thu Quan Sinh Vien C2

Information

12 Cambodian Consulate B2
13 French Consulate C2
14 German Consulate B2
15 UK Consulate C2
16 USA Consulate C2

Beautiful Saigon HOTEL $$
(Map p880; ☎3836 4852; www.beautifulsaigonhotel.com; 62 Đ Bui Vien; s US$26-45, d $US29-55;) The original Beautiful Saigon has tidy rooms, the cheaper of which are small and windowless.

Mai Phai Hotel HOTEL $
(Map p880; ☎3836 5868; maiphaihotel@saigonnet.vn; 209 Đ Pham Ngu Lao; r US$18-25;) The rooms are well furnished in this friendly minihotel right on the main strip. It has an elevator.

Nhat Thao GUESTHOUSE $
(Map p880; ☎3836 8117; Nhatthaohotel@yahoo.com; 35/4 Đ Bui Vien; r US$20-22;) Small, clean rooms in this family-run place, set behind a small courtyard. Pay the extra US$2 for a window.

Madame Cuc's 127 GUESTHOUSE $
(Map p880; ☎3836 8761; www.madamcuchotels.com; s US$16-20, d US$25-30; 127 Đ Cong Quynh;) Run by the welcoming Madame Cuc and her friendly staff, this has clean and spacious rooms.

Eating

HCMC is the reigning culinary king of Vietnam. Restaurants here range from dirt-cheap sidewalk stalls to atmospheric villas, each serving a unique interpretation of Vietnam sustenance. Besides brilliant native fare, Saigon offers world cuisine, with Indian, Japanese, Thai, French, Spanish, Korean and Argentinian all on offer.

Good foodie neighbourhoods include the Dong Khoi area, which has many top-quality restaurants, as well as nearby District 3. Pham Ngu Lao's eateries are generally less memorable.

Banh mi – sandwiches with a French look and a very Vietnamese taste – are sold by street vendors. They're fresh baguettes stuffed with something resembling pâté (don't ask), pickled gherkins and various other fillings.

DONG KHOI AREA

Huong Lai VIETNAMESE $$
(Map p878; 38 Đ Ly Tu Trong; mains 40,000-120,000d) Set in the airy loft of an old French-era shop house, this is dining with a difference. All of the staff are from disadvantaged families or are former street children. A must for beautifully presented, traditional, Vietnamese food.

Hoa Tuc VIETNAMESE $$
(Map p878; ☎3825 1676; 74/7 ĐL Hai Ba Trung; mains 50,000-190,000d; ⏰10.30am-10.30pm; 📶) Excellent Vietnamese cuisine in the trendy courtyard of a former opium refinery. Signature dishes include mustard leaves rolled with crispy vegetables and shrimp. Pick up tricks at an in-house cooking class (p874).

DA KAO & AROUND

TOP CHOICE Cuc Gach Quan VIETNAMESE $
(Map p876; ☎3848 0144; http://en.cucgachquan.com; 10 Đ Dang Tat; mains 50,000-200,000d; ⏰9am-midnight) Cleverly renovated old villa with rustic-chic decor and delectable food that balances authentic flavours of the countryside with metropolitan presentation. Despite its tucked-away location in the northernmost reaches of District 1, this is no secret hideaway; book ahead.

TOP CHOICE Pho Hoa VIETNAMESE $
(260C Đ Pasteur; mains 45,000-50,000d; ⏰6am-midnight) A contender for the title of Saigon's best *pho* restaurant, this long-running establishment is more upmarket than most but is definitely the real deal – as evidenced by its popularity with regular Saigonese patrons.

Banh Xeo 46A VIETNAMESE $
(46A Đ Dinh Cong Trang; mains 25,000-50,000d) This renowned spot serves some of the best *banh xeo* in town. These Vietnamese rice-flour pancakes stuffed with bean sprouts, prawns and pork (vegetarian versions available) are the stuff of legend.

Tib VIETNAMESE $$
(www.tibrestaurant.com.vn); Hai Ba Trung (Map p876; ☎3829 7242; 187 Đ Hai Ba Trung; mains 60,000-240,000d; 📶); Express (Map p875; 162 Đ Nguyen Dinh Chieu; mains 28,000-50,000; ✎); Vegetarian (11 Đ Tran Nhat Duat; mains 30,000-40,000; ✎) Justifiably famous, atmospheric old house that showcases imperial Hue cuisine in a wonderful setting. Tib Express and Tib Vegetarian offer a cheaper, more relaxed take on the same.

PHAM NGU LAO AREA

Mumtaz INDIAN $$
(Map p880; www.mumtazrest.com; 226 Đ Bui Vien; mains 45,000-90,000d; ⏰11am-11pm; ✎) Excellent service, pleasant surrounds and succulent vegetarian options, tandoori dishes and the greatest hits of both North and South Indian cuisine. The lunch buffet is a steal.

Dinh Y VEGETARIAN $
(Map p880; 171B Đ Cong Quynh; mains 12,000-40,000d; ✎) Run by a friendly Cao Dai family, this humble eatery is in a very 'local' part of PNL near Thai Binh Market. The food is delicious and cheap, plus there's an English menu.

Mon Hue VIETNAMESE $
(off Map p880; 98 Đ Nguyen Trai; mains 29,000-150,000d; ⏰6am-11pm) Hue's famous cuisine is now available to HCMC's discerning proletariat. This branch offers a good introduction for travellers who don't make it to the old capital.

Sozo CAFE $
(Map p880; www.sozocentre.com; 176 Đ Bui Vien; bagels 40,000d; ⏰7am-10.30pm Mon-Sat; 📶) A classy little cafe ideal for excellent smoothies, doughy cinnamon rolls and other sweet treats. The cafe trains and employs poor, disadvantaged Vietnamese.

Drinking

Wartime Saigon was known for its riotous nightlife. Liberation in 1975 put a real dampener on evening activities, but the bars and clubs have staged a comeback. However, periodic 'crack-down, clean-up' campaigns continue to calm the fun.

Action is concentrated around the Dong Khoi area, with everything from dives to designer bars. However, places in this area generally close around 1am while Pham Ngu Lao rumbles on into the wee hours.

DONG KHOI AREA

Many of Dong Khoi's coolest bars double as restaurants (see Flow and Pacharan) or hover at the top of hotels.

Dong Khoi Area

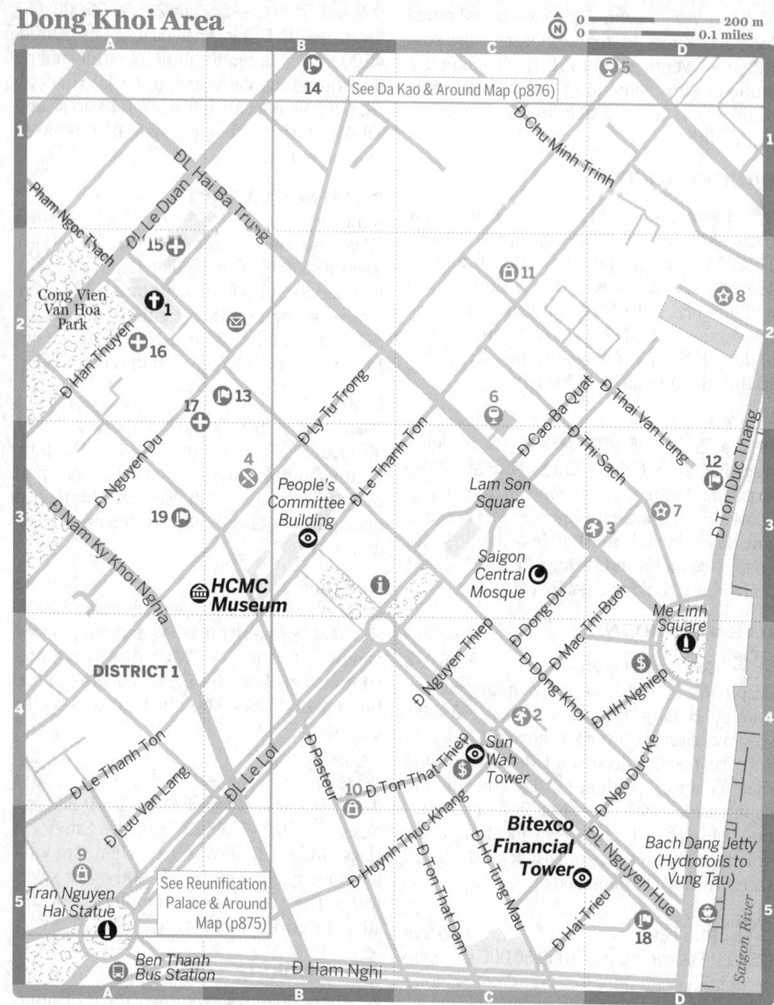

TOP CHOICE **Vasco's** BAR, NIGHTCLUB

(Map p878; www.vascosgroup.com; 74/7D ĐL Hai Ba Trung; ⌚4pm-late; 📶🍴) Vasco's is one of the hippest hang-outs in town. Downstairs is a breezy spot for cocktails and pizza, while upstairs a nightclub-like space regularly hosts DJs and live bands.

Lush BAR, NIGHTCLUB

(Map p878; www.lush.vn; 2 Đ Ly Tu Trong) Once you're done chatting in the garden zone, move to the central bar for serious people-watching and ass-shaking. DJs spin most nights, with Fridays devoted to hip hop.

DA KAO & AROUND

Hoa Vien BREWERY

(Map p876; www.hoavien.vn; 28 Đ Mac Dinh Chi; ⌚8am-midnight; 📶🍴) An unexpected find in the backstreets of HCMC, this Czech restaurant brews up fresh pilsner daily.

REUNIFICATION PALACE & AROUND

Cloud 9 BAR

(Map p875; 6th fl, 2 bis Cong Truong Quoc Te) Fashionable young things flock to the rooftop bar, while dance music pounds in the room below.

Dong Khoi Area

Top Sights
Bitexco Financial Tower......C5
HCMC Museum......A3

Sights
1 Notre Dame Cathedral......A2

Activities, Courses & Tours
2 Buffalo Tours......C4
3 Exotissimo......D3
Saigon Cooking Class......(see 6)

Eating
Hoa Tuc......(see 6)
4 Huong Lai......B3

Drinking
5 Lush......D1
6 Vasco's......C2

Entertainment
7 Apocalypse Now......D3
8 Fuse......D2

Shopping
9 Ben Thanh Market......A5
10 Dogma......B4
11 Vietnam Quilts......C2

Information
12 Australian Consulate......D3
13 Canadian Consulate......B2
14 Dutch Consulate......B1
15 HCMC Family Medical Practice......A2
16 International Medical Centre......A2
17 International SOS......A2
18 Japanese Embassy......D5
19 Lao Consulate......A3
New Zealand Consulate......(see 13)

PHAM NGU LAO AREA

Go2 BAR
(Map p880; 187 Đ De Tham;) There's no better street theatre than watching the crazy goings on from the outside seats of this all-night venue. The music's usually excellent and it has a club upstairs if you feel the need to boogie, and a rooftop bar if you want to cool off.

Le Pub PUB
(Map p880; www.lepub.org; 175/22 Đ Pham Ngu Lao; 7am-late;) Popular with expats and travellers alike, Le Pub has an extensive beer list, nightly promotions, cocktail jugs and tasty pub grub.

Allez Boo BAR
(Map p880; 195 Đ Pham Ngu Lao; 7am-late) Proudly displays its tropical kookiness on a prominent street corner: think bamboo-lined walls and a rattan-shaded bar. A merry-go-round of backpackers and the late-night action upstairs ensures its popularity.

Spotted Cow SPORTS BAR
(Map p880; 111 Đ Bui Vien; 11am-midnight) Aussie-run sports bar with lots of drink specials and a cow-print fetish.

Bobby Brewers CAFE
(Map p880; www.bobbybrewers.com; 45 Đ Bui Vien;) Contemporary cafe set over three floors, offering juices, sandwiches, pastas and salads, plus movies upstairs.

☆ Entertainment

Pick up the *Word HCMC*, *Asialife HCMC* or the *Guide* to find out what's on during your stay in Saigon, or log onto www.anyarena.com or www.thewordhcmc.com.

Clubs

HCMC's hippest club nights include the semi-regular **Everyone's a DJ** (www.everyonesadjvietnam.wordpress.com) loft party, **dOSe** and the **Beats Saigon** (www.thebeats-saigon.com).

Apocalypse Now CLUB
(Map p878; 2C Đ Thi Sach; entry Sat & Sun 150,000d; 7pm-2am) 'Apo' has been around since the early days and remains one of the must-visit clubs. It's quite a circus, with a cast comprising travellers, expats, Vietnamese movers and shakers, plus the odd hooker (some odder than others).

Gossip CLUB
(79 Đ Tran Hung Dao; admission 120,000d; 9.30pm-2.30am) Housed in the Dai Nam Hotel, this long-running club heats up at the weekend with a hard techno soundtrack.

Fuse CLUB
(Map p878; 3A Đ Ton Duc Thang; 7pm-late) Small club, big beats.

Live Music

Acoustic BAR
(Map p875; 6E1 Đ Ngo Thoi Nhiem; 7pm-midnight;) Don't be misled by the name: most of the musicians are fully plugged in and dangerous when they take to the intimate stage of the city's leading live-music venue.

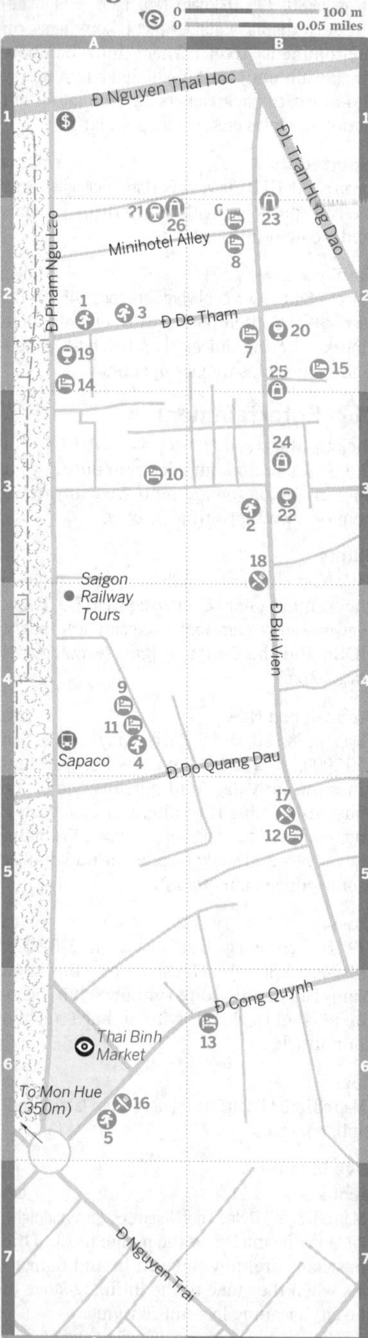

Water Puppets

Golden Dragon Water Puppet Theatre WATER PUPPETS
(Map p875; 55B Nguyen Thi Minh Khai) The main water-puppet venue, with shows starting at 5pm and 6.30pm and lasting about 50 minutes.

Saigon Water Puppet Theatre WATER PUPPETS
(Map p876; History Museum, Đ Nguyen Binh Khiem; entry 40,000d) Within the History Museum, this small theatre has performances at 9am, 10am, 11am, 2pm, 3pm and 4pm, lasting about 20 minutes.

Shopping

Among the tempting wares to be found in Saigon are embroidered silk shoes, min-

Pham Ngu Lao Area

Activities, Courses & Tours
1 Cafe Kim Tourist A2
2 Innoviet B3
3 Sinh Tourist A2
4 Sinhbalo Adventures A4
5 Vietnamese Traditional Massage Institute A6

Sleeping
6 An An Hotel B2
7 Beautiful Saigon B2
8 Beautiful Saigon 2 .... B2
9 Bich Duyen Hotel A4
10 Diep Anh A3
11 Giang & Son A4
12 Hong Han Hotel B5
13 Madame Cuc's 127 .... B6
14 Mai Phai Hotel A2
15 Nhat Thao B2

Eating
16 Dinh Y A6
17 Mumtaz B5
18 Sozo B3

Drinking
19 Allez Boo A2
Bobby Brewers .... (see 25)
20 Go2 .... B2
21 Le Pub A2
22 Spotted Cow B3

Shopping
23 Blue Dragon B2
24 Hanoi Gallery B3
25 Mekong Creations B2
26 SahaBook A2

iature *cyclos,* fake Zippos engraved with GI philosophy and toy helicopters made from beer cans. Boutiques along Đ Le Thanh Ton and Đ Pasteur sell handmade ready-to-wear fashion. In Pham Ngu Lao, shops sell ethnic-minority fabrics, handicrafts, T-shirts and various appealing accessories.

Ben Thanh Market (Cho Ben Thanh; Map p878) is the best place to start. Part of the market is devoted to normal everyday items, but the lucrative tourist trade also has healthy representation. Đ Dong Khoi (Map p878) is one big arts-and-crafts tourist bazaar, but prices can be outrageous – negotiate if no prices are posted.

Check out the following shops around town:

DONG KHOI AREA

Vietnam Quilts HANDICRAFTS

(Map p878; www.mekong-quilts.org; 64 Đ Ngo Duc Ke) The place to buy handmade quilts sewn by the rural poor in support of a sustainable income.

Dogma SOUVENIRS

(Map p878; www.dogmavietnam.com; 1st fl, 43 Đ Ton That Thiep) Reproduction propaganda posters, as well as politically kitsch coffee mugs, coasters and T-shirts.

DA KAO & AROUND

Thu Quan Sinh Vien BOOKSTORE

(Map p876; 2A ĐL Le Duan; 8am-10pm;) Upmarket bookstore that stocks imported books and magazines in English, French and Chinese.

Adidas Puma Factory Shop SHOES, CLOTHING

(Map p876; 232 Đ Pasteur) Authentic trainers/sneakers at a fifth of the price you'll pay back home.

Cham Khanh CLOTHING, TAILOR

(Map p876; 256 Đ Pasteur) One of several *ao dai* (traditional Vietnamese tunic and trousers) shops on this stretch of Đ Pasteur.

PHAM NGU LAO AREA

Mekong Creations HANDICRAFTS

(Map p880; www.mekong-creations.org; 141 Đ Bui Vien) Profits from the sale of bamboo bowls and platters benefit remote Mekong villages.

Hanoi Gallery SOUVENIRS

(Map p880; 79 Đ Bui Vien) Original (or so we're told) and reproduction propaganda posters.

SahaBook BOOKS

(Map p880; www.sahabook.com; 175/24 Đ Pham Ngu Lao) Specialises in guidebooks and travel literature, including genuine Lonely Planet guides.

Blue Dragon HANDICRAFTS

(Map p880; 1B Đ Bui Vien) Popular souvenir store that stocks objets d'art made from recycled motorbike parts, among other things.

OTHER NEIGHBOURHOODS

Mai Handicrafts HANDICRAFTS

(www.maihandicrafts.com; 298 Đ Nguyen Trong Tuyen, Tan Binh District; Mon-Sat) A fair-trade shop dealing in ceramics, ethnic fabrics and other gift items.

Information

For up-to-date information on what's going on in town, check out the **Word HCMC** (www.wordhcmc.com) or **Asialife HCMC** (www.asialifehcmc.com), both quality listings magazines.

Dangers & Annoyances

Be careful in the Dong Khoi area and along the Saigon riverfront, where motorbike 'cowboys' operate and specialise in bag and camera snatching. See the transport section for common taxi and *xe om* scams.

Emergency

Ambulance (115)

Fire (114)

Police (113)

Internet Access

Internet cafes are everywhere in HCMC. Many hotels, cafes, restaurants and bars offer free wi-fi.

Medical Services

HCMC Family Medical Practice (Map p878; 24hr emergency 3822 7848; www.vietnammedicalpractice.com; Diamond Plaza, 34 ĐL Le Duan; 24hr) One of the best places, with prices to match.

International Medical Centre (Map p878; 3827 2366, 24hr emergency 3865 4025; fac@hcm.vnn.vn; 1 Đ Han Thuyen; 24hr) A nonprofit organisation with English-speaking doctors.

International SOS (Map p878; 3929 8424, 24hr emergency 3829 8520; www.internationalsos.com; 65 Đ Nguyen Du; 24hr) Has an international team of doctors speaking English, French and Japanese.

Money

There are ATMs and exchange counters (most offering decent rates) in the airport hallway of arrivals, just after clearing customs.

ANZ Bank (Map p878; 11 Me Linh Sq) With ATM.

Citibank (Map p878; 115 Đ Nguyen Hue) Its ATM allows up to 8,000,000d in one hit.

Sacombank (Map p880; 211 Đ Nguyen Thai Hoc) Conveniently located in the backpacker zone, with ATM.

Post

Main post office (Map p878; 2 Cong Xa Paris) Saigon's striking French-era post office is next to Notre Dame Cathedral.

Tourist Information

Tourist Information Center (Map p878; ☎3822 6033; www.vietnamtourism.com; 4G Le Loi; ⊙8am-8pm) Distributes city maps and brochures and offers limited advice.

Travel Agencies

There are lots of travel agents offering tours of the Mekong Delta and other jaunts beyond HCMC. Some of the better ones include the following:

Sinhbalo Adventures (Map p880; ☎3837 6766; www.sinhbalo.com; 283/20 Đ Pham Ngu Lao; ⊙closed Sat afternoon & Sun) For customised tours, this is one of the best agencies in Vietnam. Specialises in cycling trips, but also arranges special-interest journeys to the Mekong Delta, Central Highlands and further afield.

Handspan Travel Indochina (☎3925 7605; www.handspan.com; 7th fl, Titan Bldg, 18A Đ Nam Quoc Cang, District 1) Known for their innovative, non-generic tours and professional approach.

Exotissimo (Map p878; ☎3827 2911; www.exotissimo.com; 64 Đ Dong Du; ⊙Mon-Sat)

Sinh Tourist (Map p880; ☎3838 9593; www.thesinhtourist.vn; 246 Đ De Tham; ⊙6.30am-10.30pm)

Buffalo Tours (Map p878; ☎3827 9170; www.buffalotours.com; 81 Đ Mac Thi Buoi)

Innoviet (Map p880; ☎6291 5406; www.innoviet.com; 158 Đ Bui Vien)

Cafe Kim Tourist (Map p880; ☎3836 5489; www.thekimtourist.com; 270 Đ De Tham)

Getting There & Away

Air

For more information on international air travel, see p904.

Vietnam Airlines (☎3832 0320; www.vietnamairlines.com) Flies to/from Hanoi, Hai Phong, Dong Hoi, Hue, Danang, Nha Trang, Dalat and Phu Quoc Island.

Air Mekong (☎3846 3666; www.airmekong.com.vn) Flies to/from Hanoi, Dalat, Pleiku, Con Dao Islands and Phu Quoc Island.

Jetstar Pacific Airlines (☎1900 1550; www.jetstar.com) Flies to/from Hanoi, Hai Phong, Vinh, Hue and Danang.

Vietnam Air Service Company (VASCO; ☎3842 2790; www.vasco.com.vn) Flies to/from Chu Lai, Con Dao Islands and Ca Mau.

Bus

Intercity buses operate from three main bus stations around HCMC. Local buses (3000d) travelling to the intercity bus stations leave from the local bus station opposite Ben Thanh Market (Map p878).

An Suong bus station Buses to Tay Ninh and points northeast of HCMC; in District 12, west of the centre. Buses to/from Cu Chi leave from here but tours are far more convenient.

Mien Dong bus station Buses heading north of HCMC; about 5km from downtown on Hwy 13. Express buses depart from the east side of the station, and local buses connect with the west side of the complex.

Mien Tay bus station Serves all the main Mekong Delta towns; located about 10km southwest of Saigon in An Lac.

Open-tour buses depart and arrive in the Pham Ngu Lao area. Destinations include Mui Ne (US$5 to US$10), Nha Trang (US$7 to US$20), Dalat (US$8 to US$15), Hoi An (US$15 to US$37) and Hanoi (US$31 to US$49).

There are plenty of international bus services connecting HCMC and Cambodia, most with departures from the Pham Ngu Lao area. **Sapaco** (Map p880; ☎3920 3623; 309 Pham Ngu Lao)

TRANSPORT FROM HCMC

DESTINATION	AIR	BUS	TRAIN
Dalat	from US$39/50min	US$8-15/7hr	N/A
Nha Trang	from US$44/55min	US$7-20/13hr	US$13-27/6½hr
Hue	from US$37/80min	US$26-37/29hr	US$32-54/18hr
Hanoi	from US$70/2hr	US$31-49/41hr	US$50-79/30hr

has nine direct daily services to Phnom Penh (departing between 6am and 3pm, US$10), as well as one to Siam Riep (US$20).

Car & Motorcycle

Hotels and travellers' cafes can arrange car rentals (from US$35 per day). Pham Ngu Lao is the neighbourhood to look for motorbike rentals (US$5 to US$10 per day).

Train

Trains from **Saigon train station** (Ga Sai Gon; 1 Đ Nguyen Thong, District 3; ticket office ⏲7.15-11am & 1-3pm) head north to destinations including the following:

Nha Trang (272,000d to 550,000d; 6½ to nine hours, eight daily)

Danang (616,000d to 1,019,000d, 15½ to 20¾ hours, six daily)

Hue (655,000d to 1,100,000, 18 to 24½ hours, six daily)

Dong Hoi (759,000d to 1,199,000, 21 to 26 hours, five daily)

In Pham Ngu Lao, purchase tickets from **Saigon Railway Tours** (Map p880; ☎3836 7640; www.railtour.com.vn; 275C Đ Pham Ngu Lao; ⏲7.30am-8pm) or from most travel agents for a small fee.

Getting Around

To/From the Airport

Tan Son Nhat Airport is 7km northwest of central HCMC. Metered taxis are your best bet and cost around 100,000d to/from the centre. English-speaking controllers will shuffle you into a waiting cab and tell the driver your destination. The driver may try to claim your hotel of choice is closed, burned down, is dirty and dangerous, or anything to steer you somewhere else for a commission. Stick to your guns.

Air-conditioned buses (route 152; 4000d, every 15 minutes, 6am to 6pm) also run to and from the airport. These make regular stops along Đ De Tham (Pham Ngu Lao area) and at international hotels along Đ Dong Khoi.

Bicycle

Bicycles are available for hire (US$2) from many budget hotels and cafes. Use parking lots to safeguard against theft.

Car & Motorcycle

HCMC is *not* the place to learn to ride a motorbike. They are nevertheless available for hire around Pham Ngu Lao for US$5 to US$10 per day. Give it a test drive first; you'll be asked to leave your passport as collateral.

Cyclo

Cyclos are an interesting way to get around town, but avoid them at night. They're banned from many streets, so pedal merchants are often forced to take circuitous routes. Overcharging tourists is the norm, so negotiate a price beforehand and have exact change. Short hops around the city centre are 15,000d to 25,000d; District 1 to central Cholon costs about 40,000d.

Taxi

Metered taxis cruise the streets. Flagfall is around 15,000d for the first kilometre and most rides in the city centre cost just two or three bucks. Be wary of dodgy taxi meters that are rigged. These are reliable companies:

Mai Linh (☎3822 6666)

Saigon Taxi (☎3823 2323)

Xe Om

Xe om drivers hang out on parked bikes touting for passengers. The accepted rate is 20,000d for short rides, per hour/day the cost is about US$3/15.

GETTING TO CAMBODIA: MOC BAI TO BAVET

Getting to the border This busy border crossing is the fastest way to get between HCMC and Phnom Penh, travellers' cafes in HCMC sell bus tickets.

At the border Open daily from 6am to 6pm.

Moving on International buses from HCMC run right through to Phnom Penh.

See p79 for information on the remote Vietnam–Cambodia border crossings north of HCMC, beyond Tay Ninh and Binh Long.

AROUND HO CHI MINH CITY

Cu Chi

If the tenacious spirit of the Vietnamese can be symbolised by a place, then Cu Chi could be the one. Its fame is such that it's become a place of pilgrimage for many Vietnamese, and a must-see for travellers.

Sights

Cu Chi Tunnels HISTORIC SITES

(www.cuchitunnel.org.vn; admission 80,000d) The **tunnel network** at Cu Chi was the stuff of legend during the 1960s for its role in facilitating Viet Cong control of a large rural area only 30km from Saigon. At its height, the tunnel system stretched from Saigon to the Cambodian border. In the district of Cu Chi alone, there was more than 200km of tunnels. After ineffective ground operations targeting the tunnels claimed large numbers of casualties, the USA turned its artillery and bombers on the area, transforming it into a moonscape.

Parts of this remarkable tunnel network have been reconstructed and two sites are open to visitors; one near the village of Ben Dinh and the other at Ben Duoc. It's possible to descend into the tunnels themselves. Although some sections have been widened, others remain in their original condition. If you can fit into the narrow passageways, you'll gain an empathetic, if claustrophobic, appreciation for the people who spent weeks underground.

Day tours operated by travellers' cafes charge around US$8 per person (transport only); most include a stop at the Cao Dai Great Temple in Tay Ninh.

Cu Chi Wildlife Rescue Station WILDLIFE CENTRE
(www.wildlifeatrisk.org; admission US$5; ⏲7.30-11.30am & 1-4.30pm) Just a few kilometres down the road from the tunnels of Ben Dinh, this small rescue centre provides protection to wildlife confiscated from illegal traders. Animals here include bears, otters and gibbons. The centre is expanding its enclosures to create more comfortable habitats and there is an informative display on the rather depressing state of wildlife in Vietnam.

It's tough to find the centre, so talk to a travel agent about incorporating it into a Cu Chi Tunnels trip.

Tay Ninh

☎066 / POP 127,000

Tay Ninh town serves as the headquarters of Cao Dai, one of Vietnam's most interesting indigenous religions. The **Cao Dai Great Temple** was built between 1933 and 1955. Victor Hugo is among the Westerners especially revered by the Cao Dai; look for his likeness at the Great Temple.

Tay Ninh is 96km northwest of HCMC. The Cao Dai Holy See complex is 4km east of Tay Ninh. One-day tours from Saigon, including Tay Ninh and the Cu Chi Tunnels, cost around US$8.

Beaches

There are several beach resorts within striking distance of downtown Saigon, although most travellers make for Mui Ne (p865). If time is short and you want a quick fix, consider city-resort Vung Tau, which you can reach by hydrofoil

MEKONG DELTA

The 'rice bowl' of Vietnam, the Mekong Delta is a landscape carpeted in a dizzying variety of greens. It's also a water world where boats, houses, restaurants and even markets float upon the innumerable rivers, canals and streams that flow through like arteries.

Although the area is primarily rural, it is one of the most densely populated regions in Vietnam and nearly every hectare is intensively farmed. Visitors can experience southern charm in riverside cities where few tourists venture, sample fruits traded in the colourful floating markets, or dine on home-cooked delicacies before overnighting as a homestay guest. There are also bird sanctuaries, impressive Khmer pagodas and, inevitably, war memorials.

Those seeking a tropical hideaway will find it on Phu Quoc, an island lined with white-sand beaches and crisscrossed with empty dirt roads.

By far the easiest and cheapest way to see the delta is by taking a tour with a travel agency in Ho Chi Minh City (p882). It's also possible to travel independently, although sometimes time-consuming.

My Tho

☎074 / POP 169,300

Gateway to the Mekong Delta for daytrippers to the region, the slow-paced capital of Tien Giang province is an important market town, but to visit floating markets you'll need to continue on to Can Tho (p886).

On the riverfront, the **My Tho Tourist Boat Station** (8 Đ 30 Thang 4) is home to several tour companies offering cruises to the neighbouring islands and through the maze of small canals. Destinations usually include a coconut-candy workshop, a honey farm (try the banana wine) and an orchid garden. A 2½-hour boat tour costs around 350,000d for one person or 450,000d for two. Prices are significantly better if you can join a group.

Sleeping & Eating

My Tho is well-known for a special vermicelli soup called *hu tieu My Tho,* which is richly garnished with fresh and dried seafood, pork, chicken, offal and fresh herbs.

Song Tien HOTEL **$**
(☎387 2009; www.tiengiangtourist.com; 101 Đ Trung Trac; r from 400,000d; ❄📶) Reliable seven-storey hotel where the rooms include satellite TV, minibars and hot water; 'suites' have fancier furniture.

Quan Oc 283 VIETNAMESE, SEAFOOD **$**
(283 Đ Tet Mau Than; mains 15,000-100,000d) Seafood is the speciality here, including clams, scallops, mussels and snails, or venture behind to the tanks of live fish, crab and shrimp.

Getting There & Around

New bridges and freeways have considerably shortened travel distances to My Tho. The **bus station** (Ben Xe Tien Giang; 42 Đ Ap Bac) is 3km west of the town centre on Đ Ap Bac, the main road to HCMC. Buses head to HCMC's Mien Tay bus station (30,000d, around 75 minutes), Can Tho (50,000d), Cao Lanh (25,000d), Chau Doc (51,000d) and Ca Mau (100,000d).

Ben Tre

☎075 / POP 120,000

Famous for its *keo dua* (coconut candy), Ben Tre's sleepy waterfront is lined with ageing villas and is easy to explore on foot. It's a relatively peaceful city that makes a lovely stop on a Mekong tour.

Ben Tre Tourist (☎382 9618; www.bentretourist.vn; 65 Đ Dong Khoi; ⏰7-11am & 1-5pm) rents out bikes and motor boats (per hour US$10) and arranges excursions, including a motorcart/canal-boat trip to a honey farm and coconut candy workshop (per one/two/three/four people $25/30/42/52) and an 'ecological tour' by bike to coconut, guava and grapefruit groves.

Mekong Delta

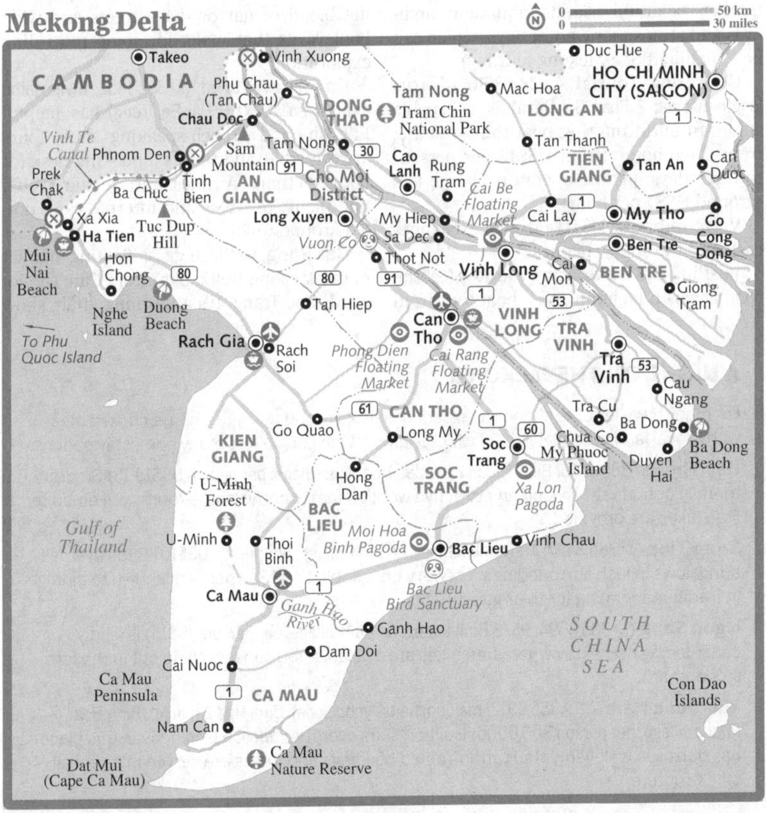

Try the modern **Ham Luong** (☎356 0560; www.hamluongtourist.com.vn; 200 Đ Hung Vuong; r US$18-29; ❄@≋) on the riverfront for nicely furnished rooms. A multistorey barge moored in the river, **Noi Ben Tre** (Đ Hung Vuong; mains 20,000-60,000d) has piquant prawn salads and other local delicacies.

Buses leave regularly from the new bus terminal 5km northeast of town for HCMC (67,000d, last between 1pm and 5pm), Can Tho (55,000d), Ca Mau (103,000d) and Ha Tien (134,000d).

Slow boats can be rented at the public pier near the market for about 70,000d to 90,000d per hour.

Vinh Long

☎070 / POP 130,000

Not a destination in itself, Vinh Long is a noisy, chaotic transit hub. First impressions are not great, but the riverfront has plenty of cafes and restaurants. Close by are several worthwhile sites including Cai Be floating market, beautiful islands, abundant orchards and atmospheric homestays (which can be a highlight of a Mekong journey).

Cuu Long Tourist (☎382 3616; www.cuulongtourist.net; 2 Phan Boi Chau) is a capable state-run outfit offering boat tours ranging from three hours (from US$12 per person) to three days; private operators charge less (around US$7 per hour).

Vietcombank (143 Đ Le Thai To) exchanges cash and travellers cheques.

Bustling **Cai Be floating market** (⏲5am-5pm) is worth including on a boat tour from Vinh Long. It's best to arrive early in the morning. Wholesalers on big boats moor here, each specialising in one or a few types of fruit or vegetable.

We suggest you don't stay in town; instead opt for a homestay; see the boxed text below.

Dong Khanh (49 Đ 2 Thang 9, mains 30,000-50,000d) offers lots of hotpots and rice dishes and has an English-language menu.

Frequent buses go between Vinh Long and HCMC (70,000d, three hours) from the terminal in the middle of town. Buses to other locations, including Can Tho (34,000d), leave from a provincial bus station 3km south of town.

Can Tho

☎071 / POP 1.1 MILLION

Can Tho is the political, economic, cultural and transportation epicentre of the Mekong Delta. It's a buzzing city with a waterfront lined with sculpted gardens and an appealing blend of narrow backstreets and wide boulevards that make for some rewarding exploration.

Can Tho Tourist (☎382 1852; www.canthotourist.com.vn; 50 Đ Hai Ba Trung) has helpful English- and French-speaking staff. Tours are available, and there's a booking desk for both Vietnam Airlines and Jetstar. You'll find plenty of ATMs and internet cafes dotted around town.

Cai Rang is the biggest floating market in the Mekong Delta, 6km from Can Tho towards Soc Trang. It's a morning affair, show

A NIGHT ON THE MEKONG

For many travellers, the chance to experience river life and to share a home-cooked meal with a local family is a highlight of a Mekong visit. Vinh Long offers many homestay options.

Bay Thoi (☎385 9019; Binh Thuan 2 hamlet, Hoa Ninh village; per person US$13-15) Smart, friendly options set around an attractive wooden family home, some rooms are en-suite. Free bikes are provided.

Song Tien (☎385 8487; An Thanh hamlet, An Binh village; per person US$10) Beds in small bungalows in lush surroundings. The very hospitable family owners are known to indulge in traditional singing for their guests.

Ngoc Sang (☎385 8694; 95/8 Binh Luong, An Binh village; per person US$15) Friendly, canal-facing homestay where free bikes are available. You can even help out in the family's orchard.

Mai Quoc Nam 2 (☎385 9912; maiquocnam@yahoo.com; Binh Hoa 2 hamlet, Binh Hoa Phuoc village; per person 300,000d) Built on stilts over the wide Co Chien River, this place has dorms in well-ventilated rattan-roofed buildings and meals are served in a central stilt structure.

up before 9am for the best photo opportunities. You can hire boats (about US$6 per hour) on the river near the Can Tho market. Cai Rang is one hour away by boat, or you can drive to Cau Dau Sau boat landing, where you can get a **rowing boat** (per hr around 80,000d) to the market, 10 minutes away.

Less crowded and less motorised is the **Phong Dien market**, which has more standup rowboats. It's best between 6am and 8am. Twenty kilometres southwest of Can Tho, it's easy to reach by road. You can hire a boat on arrival.

Sleeping & Eating

Kim Lan Hotel HOTEL $$
(☎381 7049; www.kimlancantho.com.vn; 138A Đ Nguyen An Ninh; r US$18-50; ❄@📶) Chic rooms at this solar-powered hotel include artwork and contemporary furnishings in bamboo and wood. Even the small, windowless standard rooms are perfectly adequate.

Xuan Mai Minihotel HOTEL $
(☎382 3578; tcdac@yahoo.com; 17 Đ Dien Bien Phu; r US$12; ❄📶) This place has a real local feel, as it's on a lane that doubles as An Lac Market by day. Offers spacious, clean and surprisingly quiet rooms with TVs, fridges and hot showers.

Hop Pho VIETNAMESE, CAFE $
(6 Đ Ngo Gia Tu; mains 30,000-130,000d; 📶) Serves Vietnamese staples at fair prices and it's a great spot for a coffee or a cocktail, either in air-conditioned comfort inside, or outside in the lush garden.

Mekong VIETNAMESE, PIZZA $
(38 Đ Hai Ba Trung; mains 25,000-105,000d; ⏲8am-2pm & 4-10pm) A travellers' favourite thanks to the good local and international food at very reasonable prices. Doubles as a bar at night.

Xe Loi BAR, CLUB
(Hau Riverside Park; ⏲5pm-late) The most happening nightspot with tables in the large garden, a fake beach on the riverside (yes!) and a full-on club with DJs and regular live music.

Getting There & Around

Air

Can Tho opened a new international airport in early 2011, but at the time of writing the only services were **Vietnam Airlines** (www.vietnamairlines.com) flights to Phu Quoc Island (from 500,000d, daily), the Con Dao islands (from 400,000d, four per week) and Hanoi (from 1,700,000d, daily). The airport is 10km northwest of the city centre.

Boat

Boat services include hydrofoils to Ca Mau (150,000d, three to four hours), passing through Phung Hiep.

Bus

Can Tho's **bus station** (cnr Đ Nguyen Trai & Đ Hung Vuong) is centrally located. Regular buses (75,000d, five hours) and express minibuses (90,000d, four hours) run to HCMC's Mien Tay bus station. Other services include Cao Lanh (30,000d), My Tho (50,000d), Tra Vinh (55,000d), Vinh Long (34,000d), Soc Trang (50,000d), Ca Mau (65,000d) and Ha Tien (83,000d).

Chau Doc

☎076 / POP 112,000

Perched on the banks of the Bassac River, Chau Doc is a charming town near the Cambodian border, with sizeable Chinese, Khmer and Cham communities. Its cultural diversity – apparent in the mosques, temples, churches and nearby pilgrimage sites – makes it a fascinating place to explore.

The popular nearby river crossing (p888) between Vietnam and Cambodia means many travellers pass through. Nearby Sam Mountain is a local beauty spot with terrific views over Cambodia.

War remnants near Chau Doc include Ba Chuc, the site of a Khmer Rouge massacre with a bone pagoda similar to that of Cambodia's Choeung Ek memorial; and Tuc Dup Hill, where an expensive American bombing campaign in 1963 earned it the nickname Two Million Dollar Hill.

It's also possible to visit fish farms set up underneath floating houses on the river.

Mekong Tours (☎386 8222; www.mekongvietnam.com; 14 Đ Nguyen Huu Canh) is a reliable travel agent offering boat or bus transport to Phnom Penh, boat trips on the Mekong, and cars with drivers.

Sleeping & Eating

TOP CHOICE **Trung Nguyen Hotel** HOTEL $
(☎386 6158; trunghotel@yahoo.com; 86 Đ Bach Dang; r US$13-15; ❄@📶) Best of the budget places, with a trim and panache that is decidedly more midrange. Rooms feature balconies overlooking the market. It's on a busy corner site, so pack earplugs.

GETTING TO CAMBODIA: TINH BIEN TO PHNOM DEN

The little-used Tinh Bien–Phnom Den border crossing connects Chau Doc to Takeo in Cambodia. Buses from Chau Doc to Phnom Penh depart at 7.30am and can be booked through Mekong Tours in Chau Doc (US$15 to US$21, five hours). The roads leading to the border are terrible.

See p79 for information on crossing this border in the other direction.

Hai Chau HOTEL $

(☎626 0026; www.haichauhotel.com; 61 Đ Suong Nguyet Anh; r 360,000-560,000d; ❄📶) Sixteen rooms spread over four floors; all are smartly fitted out with dark wooden furniture and good showers.

Good local eateries in Chau Doc include **Bay Bong** (22 Đ Thuong Dang Le; mains from 40,000d) with excellent hotpots and soups, and **Mekong** (41 Đ Le Loi; mains from 35,000), where you could try the *ca kho to* (stewed fish in a clay pot).

Getting There & Around

Buses to Chau Doc depart HCMC's Mien Tay station (120,000d, six hours). For more on the border crossing to Cambodia, see the boxed text below.

Ha Tien

☎077 / POP 93,000

Ha Tien may be part of the Mekong Delta, but lying on the Gulf of Thailand it feels a world away from the ricefields and rivers that typify the region. Dramatic limestone formations define the area, pepper tree plantations dot the hillsides and the town itself has a sleepy tropical charm. Visitor numbers have recently soared thanks to the opening of the border with Cambodia at Xa Xia–Prek Chak and the new fast boat service to Phu Quoc.

The **post office** (3 Đ To Chau) has internet access and **Agribank** (37 Đ Lam Son), one block from the waterfront, has an ATM.

Sleeping

Hai Phuong HOTEL $

(☎385 2240; So 52, Đ Dong Thuy Tram; r 200,000-700,000d; ❄📶) Friendly and family-run, this smart, six-level hotel offers good-value, well-presented rooms, some with excellent river views from their balconies.

Anh Van Hotel HOTEL $

(☎395 9222; So 2, Đ Tran Hau; d/tw/f 200,000/400,000/500,000d; ❄📶) In the new part of town near the bridge, this large hotel has cheap, small windowless rooms brimming with amenities and pricier options with river views.

Eating

It's happy days when shrimp is the cheapest dish on the menu. Local eatery **Xuan Thanh** (20 Đ Tran Hau; mains 30,000-60,000d) has an English menu boasting a range of Vietnamese favourites.

Be sure to try the local coconut, its flesh is mixed with ice and sugar and served in restaurants all over town. For a beer try **Oasis** (www.oasisbarhatien.com; 42 Tuan Phu Dat; ⏰9am-9pm; @) run by an expat and his Vietnamese wife; it's also a great source of impartial travel information.

Getting There & Away

Passenger ferries dock at the ferry terminal, opposite the Ha Tien Hotel. See the Phu Quoc transport section for details of services.

GETTING TO CAMBODIA: VINH XUONG TO KAAM SAMNOR

One of the most enjoyable ways to enter Cambodia is via the Vinh Xuong–Kaam Samnor crossing (open 7am to 6pm) located just northwest of Chau Doc along the Mekong River. Cambodian visas are available at the crossing, but minor overcharging by a dollar or two is common.

Several companies in Chau Doc sell boat journeys from Chau Doc to Phnom Penh via the Vinh Xuong border. **Hang Chau** (☎Chau Doc 076-356 2771; www.hangchautourist.com.vn) has boats departing Chau Doc at 7.30am (US$24, five hours).

The more upmarket **Blue Cruiser** (☎HCMC 08-3926 0253; www.bluecruiser.com) pulls out at 7am (US$55, 4½ hours) from the Victoria Hotel, as do speedboats exclusive to Victoria Hotel guests.

See p79 for information on crossing this border in the other direction.

GETTING TO CAMBODIA: XA XIA TO PREK CHAK

The Xa Xia–Prek Chak crossing (open 7am to 10pm) connects Ha Tien with Kep and Kampot on Cambodia's south coast. Direct buses cross the border twice a day, terminating in Sihanoukville or Phnom Penh. Casinos have sprung up in the no-man's-land between the two border posts.

Direct buses leave Ha Tien for Cambodia at midday and 4pm daily, heading to Kep (US$12, one hour, 47km), Kampot (US$15, 1½ hours, 75km), Sihanoukville (US$20, four hours, 150km) and Phnom Penh (US$18, four hours, 180km). Bookings can be made through Ha Tien Tourism. *Xe om* drivers in Ha Tien will also take you to Kep for around US$15.

See p123 for information on crossing this border in the other direction.

Buses connect HCMC (from 132,000d, 10 hours) and Ha Tien; and also run to destinations including Chau Doc (52,000d), Rach Gia (38,000d) and Can Tho (83,000d). Ha Tien bus station is on the road to Mui Nai Beach and the Cambodian border.

Rach Gia

☎077 / POP 206,000

Rach Gia is something of a boom town, flush with funds from its thriving port and an injection of Viet Kieu (overseas Vietnamese) money. The population here includes significant numbers of ethnic Chinese and ethnic Khmers. Few travellers linger, heading straight to Phu Quoc Island, but the waterfront is lively and the backstreets hide inexpensive seafood restaurants.

Banks, ATMs and internet cafes are scattered around town. **Kien Giang Tourist** (Du Lich Lu Hanh Kien Giang; ☎386 2081; ctycpdulichkg@vnn.vn; 5 Đ Le Loi) is the provincial tourism authority.

Sleeping & Eating

Linda HOTEL $
(☎391 8818; cnr Đ 3 Thang 2 & Nguyen An Ninh; r 180,000-400,000d; ❄📶) New hotel on the emerging seafront strip with some of the smartest rooms in Rach Gia. The priciest are corner suites with two balconies and a massage bath, but the cheapest are a tight squeeze.

Kim Co Hotel HOTEL $
(☎387 9610; www.kimcohotel.com; 141 Đ Nguyen Hung Son; r 300,000d; ❄📶) Centrally located, and the rooms are in good shape, some including decadent bathtubs, making it tempting value. Most face the corridor, so you'll need to pull the shades to get some privacy.

Than Binh VIETNAMESE $
(2 Đ Nguyen Thai Hoc; mains 18,000-35,000d) Humble street-side restaurant jammed with locals slurping fish noodle soup. No menu, so try the point-and-gesture 'I'll have what she's having' approach.

Getting There & Away

Vietnam Airlines flies daily between HCMC (from 500,000d) and Rach Gia, continuing on to Phu Quoc Island (from 500,000d). The airport is about 10km outside town; taxis cost about 160,000d.

For details on getting to Phu Quoc by hydrofoil, see p892. Stop by the **Rach Gia hydrofoil terminal** (☎387 9765) the day before, or phone ahead to book a seat.

There are regular services to Ca Mau (50,000d, three hours), Ha Tien (38,000d, two hours), HCMC (120,000, six to seven hours) and other cities from the **bus station** (Đ Nguyen Binh Khiem), 7km south of Rach Gia.

Phu Quoc Island

☎077 / POP 85,000

Fringed with idyllic beaches and with large tracts still covered in dense, tropical jungle, Phu Quoc is morphing from a sleepy backwater into a favoured escape. Beyond the chain of resorts lining Long Beach, it's still largely undeveloped. Dive the reefs, kayak bays, explore backroads by motorbike – or live the life of a lotus eater by lounging on the beach, indulging in a massage and dining on fresh seafood.

Despite the impending development (of a new international airport, a golf course and a casino), close to 70% of the island is protected as Phu Quoc National Park.

Phu Quoc's rainy season is from July to November; the peak season for tourism is between December and March.

Most beachside accommodation options are at Long Beach, located on the western side of the island, just south of Duong Dong town.

OFF THE BEATEN TRACK IN THE MEKONG DELTA

It's not hard to get off the beaten track in the Mekong Delta, as most tourists are on hit-and-run day trips from HCMC or passing through on their way to or from Cambodia. Here are some lesser-known regional gems:

» Check out some Khmer culture in **Tra Vinh**, home to a significant population of Cambodians and their beautiful temples.

» The Khmer kingdom of Funan once held sway over much of the lower Mekong; its principal port was at **Oc-Eo**, located near Long Xuyen. Archaeologists have found ancient Persian and Roman artefacts here.

» Birdwatching enthusiasts will want to make a diversion to **Tram Chin National Park** near Cao Lanh, a habitat for the rare eastern sarus crane. These huge birds are depicted on the bas-reliefs at Angkor and are only found here and in northwest Cambodia.

» The small and secluded beach resort of **Hon Chong** has the most scenic stretch of coastline on the Mekong Delta mainland. The big attractions here are Chua Hang Grotto, Duong Beach and Nghe Island.

Sights

Deserted white-sand beaches ring Phu Quoc.

Duong Dong NEIGHBOURHOOD

The island's bustling main town is not that exciting, though the excellent night market is filled with delicious food stalls. Take a peek at **Cau Castle** (Dinh Cau; Đ Bach Dang), actually more of a temple-cum-lighthouse, built in 1937 to honour Thien Hau, the Goddess of the Sea.

Phu Quoc is famous for the quality of its fish sauce, and the factory **Nuoc Mam Hung Thanh** (8-11am & 1-5pm), a short walk from the market, exports all over the world.

Long Beach BEACH

(Bai Truong) Aptly named Long Beach stretches from Duong Dong southwards to An Thoi port. The main resort section is concentrated in the northern part, a motorbike or bicycle is necessary to reach some of the remote bays towards the south. You'll find bamboo huts for drinks, and beachside massages are popular.

Phu Quoc National Park FOREST

About 90% of the island is forested and the trees and adjoining marine environment now enjoy official protection. In July 2010, the park was declared a Unesco Biosphere Reserve.

The forest is most dense on the northern half of the island, which forms the Khu Rung Nguyen Sinh reserve. You'll need a motorbike or mountain bike to explore its rough dirt roads; there are no real hiking trails.

An Thoi Islands ISLANDS

Fifteen delightful islets at the southern tip of Phu Quoc, the An Thois can be visited by chartered boat for a wonderful day swimming, snorkelling and fishing. Hon Thom (Pineapple Island) is the largest in the group. As yet, there's no real development on the islands, but expect some movement in the next few years. Trips here can be set up by hotels and resorts on Long Beach and via dive operators.

Vung Bau, Dai & Thom Beaches BEACHES

(Bai Vung Bau, Bai Dai & Bai Thom) Retaining their isolated, tropical charm, these northern beaches are rarely peopled, let alone crowded. The road from Dai to Thom via Ganh Dau is very beautiful, passing through dense forest with tantalising glimpses of the coast below.

Sao, Dam & Vong Beaches BEACHES

(Bai Sao; Bai Dam & Bai Vong) On the east side of the island, Sao and Dam are two beautiful white-sand beaches, just a few kilometres from An Thoi, the main shipping port. North of here is Vong Beach, where the fast boats from the mainland dock. It's also home to Mui Duong Watersports, and you'll find kayaks (60,000d per hour) for rent here.

Activities

Diving & Snorkelling

There's plenty of underwater action around Phu Quoc, but only during the dry months (from November to May). Two fun dives cost from US$40 to US$80; four-day PADI Open Water certification between US$320 and US$360; snorkelling trips are US$20 to US$30. All the following schools are based in the Doung Dong area:

Rainbow Divers DIVING, SNORKELLING
(☎091 340 0964; www.divevietnam.com; 17A Đ Tran Hung Dao) This reputable PADI outfit offers a wide range of diving and snorkelling trips.

Coco Dive Center DIVING, SNORKELLING
(☎398 2100; www.cocodivecenter.com; 58 Đ Tran Hung Dao)

Searama DIVING, SNORKELLING
(☎629 1679; www.searama.com; 50 Đ Tran Hung Dao) French- and English-speaking operators, with new equipment.

Vietnam Explorer DIVING
(☎384 6372; 36 Đ Tran Hung Dao)

Fishing & Boat Trips

Anh Tu's Tours BOAT TRIPS, FISHING
(☎399 6009; anhtupq@yahoo.com) Snorkelling, squid fishing and island tours, plus motorbike rental.

John's Tours BOAT TRIPS, FISHING
(☎091 910 7086; www.johnsislandtours.com; 4 Đ Tran Hung Dao) Snorkelling, island-hopping and fishing trips.

Sleeping

Expect to pay more here than most places in Vietnam and be aware that accommodation prices yo-yo depending on the season.

DUONG DONG

Sea Breeze HOTEL $
(Gio Bien; ☎399 4920; www.seabreezephuquoc.com; 62A Đ Tran Hung Dao; r fan $US15, air-con US$25-40;) New place with smart, contemporary rooms and a breezy rooftop terrace. It's handy for the night markets and beach road.

Hiep Phong Hotel GUESTHOUSE $
(☎384 6057; nguyet_1305@yahoo.com; 17 Đ Nguyen Trai; r 280,000d; @) Very friendly, family-run minihotel in the town centre. The rooms include satellite TV, fridge and hot water.

LONG BEACH

TOP CHOICE **Sea Star Resort** RESORT HOTEL $$
(☎398 2161; www.seastarresort.com; r US$40, bungalow US$50-75; @) A fun and friendly place to stay, the extensive compound includes 37 rooms and bungalows, many fronting a manicured stretch of sand with sea-view balconies.

Beach Club RESORT HOTEL $
(☎398 0998; www.beachclubvietnam.com; r US$25-35;) This chilled retreat, run by an English-Vietnamese couple, has tightly grouped, well-kept, spacious bungalows. Good local info, plus a breezy beachside restaurant for stunning sunsets.

AROUND THE ISLAND

Mango Garden B&B $$
(☎629 1339; mangogarden.inn@gmail.com; r US$35; Sep-Apr; @) Run by a Vietnamese-Canadian, this isolated B&B is surrounded by gorgeous gardens and mango trees. It's reached by a bumpy dirt road (turn left just before Sao Beach). Book ahead, as it has just a handful of rooms.

Freedomland HOMESTAY $$
(☎399 4891; www.freedomlandphuquoc.com; Ong Lang Beach; r US$30-40; @) More like a little hippie commune than a resort, these 11 basic bungalows (with mosquito nets and fans; no hot water) are scattered around a shady plot. The communal vibe and shared meal experience makes it popular with solo travellers.

Eating & Drinking

Most hotels have their own lively cafes or restaurants in-house.

Duong Dong's **night market** (Đ Vo Thi Sau;) is one of the most atmospheric (and affordable) places to dine with a delicious range of Vietnamese seafood, grills and vegetarian options.

The seafood restaurants in the fishing village of Ham Ninh also offer an authentic local experience and taste; try **Kim Cuong I** (mains 30,000-300,000d).

DUONG DONG

Buddy Ice Cream ICE CREAM $
(www.visitphuquoc.info; 26 Đ Nguyen Trai; mains 25,000-130,000d; @) New Zealand ice cream (per scoop 25,000d), plus toasted sandwiches, fish 'n' chips and snacks. Doubles as a tourist information centre and there's free internet too.

Le Giang VIETNAMESE $
(289 Đ Tran Hung Dao; mains 40,000-80,000d) A wide range of Vietnamese favourites in a local-style place with a breeze-catching terrace; try the caramelised-fish claypots.

LONG BEACH

Mondo TAPAS $$
(82 Đ Tran Hung Dao; tapas 50,000-90,000d) Head here for Spanish tapas (chorizo, spicy

meatballs, garlic prawns), Western breakfasts and Asian flavours in a chic setting.

Hop Inn VIETNAMESE $
(Đ Tran Hung Dao; mains 50,000-130,000d) The best Vietnamese food on the Tran Hung Dao strip, including plenty of seafood, as well as sandwiches if you fancy more familiar fare.

Pepper's Pizza & Grill ITALIAN, GERMAN $
(☎384 8773; 89 Đ Tran Hung Dao; mains 65,000-190,000d) Terrific pizzas, and they'll even deliver to your hotel.

AROUND THE ISLAND

My Lan VIETNAMESE, SEAFOOD $$
(mains 55,000-110,000d, Sao Beach) Located on the white sands of Sao Beach, this place has succulent barbecued seafood and fish in claypots.

Information

There are ATMs in Duong Dong and in many resorts on Long Beach. Buddy Ice Cream offers free internet and wi-fi.

Getting There & Away

Air

Demand can be high in peak season, so book ahead. A new international airport should open in early 2012.

Vietnam Airlines (☎399 6677; www.vietnamairlines.com; 122 Đ Nguyen Trung Truc) Flies to/from Rach Gia (from 500,000d, daily), Can Tho (from 500,000d, daily) and HCMC (from 450,000d, 10 daily).

Air Mekong (☎04-3718 8199; www.airmekong.com.vn) Flies to/from HCMC (from 450,000d, four daily) and Hanoi (from 2,230,000d, two daily).

Boat

Hydrofoils to/from the mainland dock at Bai Vong on the east of the island, connecting Phu Quoc to both Ha Tien (1½ hours) and Rach Gia (2½ hours). Phu Quoc travel agents, such as **Green Cruise** (☎397 8111; www.greencruise.com.vn; 14 Đ Tran Hung Dao), have the most up-to-date schedules and can book tickets.

From Ha Tien there are two small boats (departing 8am/1.30pm 180,000/230,000d) and a car ferry (departing 9.30am from Ha Tien and 2.30pm from Phu Quoc; per passenger/motorbike/car 145,000d/100,000d/US$50) departing every day.

Rach Gia has two reputable operators servicing the route:

Savanna Express (☎369 2888; www.savannaexpress.com; 1-way 295,000d) Departs Rach Gia at 8.05am and Phu Quoc at 1.05pm; 2½ hours.

Superdong (☎Rach Gia 077-387 7742, Phu Quoc 077-398 0111; www.superdong.com.vn; 1-way 295,000d) Departs Rach Gia at 8am, 1pm and 1.30pm and Phu Quoc at 8am, 8.30am and 1pm; 2½ hours.

Ferries depart from the pier at Vong Beach (Bai Vong). Buses, timed to meet the ferries, pick up on Đ Tran Hung Dao and Đ 30 Thang 4 (20,000d).

Getting Around

Phu Quoc's airport is in central Duong Dong. Motorbike drivers charge US$1 to US$2 to most places on Long Beach. A metered taxi costs around 90,000d to Long Beach and 250,000d to Ong Lang Beach.

Bicycle rentals are available through most hotels from US$3 per day.

There is a skeletal bus service (every hour or two) between An Thoi and Duong Dong. A bus (20,000d) waits for the ferry at Bai Vong to take passengers to Duong Dong.

Rental motorbikes cost US$7 to US$10 (automatic) per day. Motorbike taxis are everywhere. Short hops cost 20,000d; figure on around 50,000d for about 5km.

Call **Mai Linh** (☎397 9797) for a reliable taxi; Duong Dong to Vong Beach costs about 250,000d.

UNDERSTAND VIETNAM

Vietnam Today

Few places on earth have changed as much as Vietnam in the last few decades. One of the poorest, war-wounded corners of the globe has transformed itself into a stable, prospering nation through industriousness, ingenuity and ambition. The overall standard of living has risen incredibly, and education and healthcare have greatly improved. Blue-chip finance has flooded into a red-flag communist society. Rice paddies have become business parks, and comrades have become entrepreneurs. It's been a breathtaking and largely successful transformation.

And yet... Take a peek beneath those headline-grabbing growth figures and there are concerns. Double-digit growth has faltered as the economy has cooled. Corruption remains systemic: the nation is rated 116 out of 182 on Transparency International's global index. Vietnamese people have to pay backhanders for everything from getting an internet connection to securing a hospital appointment. At the highest level, corrupt politicians have been caught demanding millions of dollars to facilitate infrastructure projects.

The State

Observers argue that this is why Vietnam needs to embrace democracy: to hold those in power accountable for their actions. Such a prospect seems a distant dream; there's no sign that the Communist Party is contemplating relaxing control. The state still controls a vast swath of the economy. More than 100 of the 200 biggest companies in Vietnam are state-owned and the key sectors of oil production, shipbuilding, cement, coal and rubber are government-controlled.

Political dissent remains a no-no; some democracy movement members are sent to prison for spreading 'anti-state propaganda'. Also, the entire nation's internet operates behind a firewall that blocks anything – including Facebook – that might lead to trouble.

Vietnam's Place in the World

In 2000 Bill Clinton became the first US president to visit northern Vietnam. George W Bush followed suit in 2006. Today relations with the USA are politically cordial and economically vibrant (bilateral trade was worth over US$18 billion in 2010). US and Vietnamese militaries hold annual Defense Policy Dialogue talks. Vietnam's suppression of political dissent and issues of freedom of speech and religion remain areas of contention, however. For the Vietnamese, the legacy of Agent Orange and dioxin poisoning remains unresolved – the USA has never paid a cent in compensation to the estimated three million victims of dioxin poisoning resulting from aerial bombing.

Relations with Vietnam's historical enemy China have improved significantly. Trade is booming, borders are hyper-busy and joint cooperation in everything from steel manufacturing to naval patrols continues. Mandarin is the second most popular foreign language studied in Vietnam. The Spratly Islands, rich in oil deposits, remain a potential flash point, however, with both nations claiming sovereignty.

Vietnam counterbalances power politics with China and the USA with active membership of Asean and by fostering important links with India, Russia and former Soviet Bloc countries (from which it buys most of its military hardware).

VIETNAM BY NUMBERS

Population 90.5 million

Life expectancy 69 for men, 75 for women

Infant mortality 21 per 1000 births

GDP US$104.6 billion

Adult literacy rate 94%

Annual rice production 36 million tonnes

Number of mobile phones 98 million plus

Litres of nuoc mam (fish sauce) produced per year 200 million

State of the Nation

Most Vietnamese people have accepted the status quo, for now. They're living in an age of rising prosperity. Times are pretty good, for most, though inflation (running at 22% in September 2011) is a huge concern. The country is stable and tourism is booming, empowering a new generation of young Viets to a better life. Of course, if things turn sour, the tide may turn, but for now the outlook looks decent as long as opportunities remain and the economy prospers.

History

Vietnam has a history as rich and evocative as anywhere on earth. Sure, the war with the USA captured the attention of the West, but centuries before that the Vietnamese were scrapping with the Chinese, the Khmers, the Chams and the Mongols. Vietnamese civilisation is as sophisticated as that of its mighty northern neighbour China, from where it drew many of its influences under a 1000-year occupation. Later came the French and the humbling period of colonialism, from which Vietnam was not to emerge until the second half of the 20th century. The USA was simply the last in a long line of invaders who have come and gone through the centuries and, no matter what was required or how long it took, they too would be vanquished. If only the military planners in Washington had paid a little more attention to the history of this proud nation, the trauma and tragedy of a long war might have been avoided.

VIETNAM IN FILM & LITERATURE

Literature

The Quiet American (Graham Greene) Classic novel set in 1950s

The Sorrow of War (Bao Ninh) The North Vietnamese perspective

Vietnam: Rising Dragon (Bill Hayton) A candid assessment

Catfish & Mandala (Andrew X Pham) Biographical tale of a Vietnamese-American

Film

Apocalypse Now (1979) Director: Francis Ford Coppola

Cyclo (1995) Director: Anh Hung Tran

The Deer Hunter (1978) Director: Michael Cimino

Platoon (1986) Director: Oliver Stone

The Lover (1992) Director: Jean-Jacques Annaud

Early Vietnam

The sophisticated Indianised kingdom of Funan flourished from the 1st to 6th centuries AD in the Mekong Delta area. Archaeological evidence reveals that Funan's busy trading port of Oc-Eo had contact with China, India, Persia and even the Mediterranean. Between the mid-6th century and the 9th century, the Funan empire was absorbed by the pre-Angkorian kingdom of Chenla.

Meanwhile, around present-day Danang, the Hindu kingdom of Champa emerged in the late 2nd century AD. Like Funan, it adopted Sanskrit as a sacred language and borrowed heavily from Indian art and culture. By the 8th century Champa had expanded to include what is now Nha Trang and Phan Rang. The Cham warred constantly with the Vietnamese to the north and the Khmers to the south and ultimately found themselves squeezed between these two great powers.

Chinese Occupation

The Chinese conquered the Red River Delta in the 2nd century BC and over the following centuries attempted to impress a centralised state system on the Vietnamese. There were numerous small-scale rebellions against Chinese rule – which was characterised by tyranny, forced labour and insatiable demands for tribute – between the 3rd and 6th centuries, but all were defeated.

However, the early Viets learned much from the Chinese, including advanced irrigation for rice cultivation and medical knowledge as well as Confucianism, Taoism and Mahayana Buddhism. Much of the 1000-year period of Chinese occupation was typified by both Vietnamese resistance and the adoption of many Chinese cultural traits.

In AD 938 Ngo Quyen destroyed Chinese forces on the Bach Dang river, winning independence and signalling the start of a dynastic tradition. During subsequent centuries the Vietnamese successfully repulsed foreign invaders, including the Monguls, and absorbed the kingdom of Champa in 1471 as they expanded south.

Contact with the West

In 1858 a joint military force from France and the Spanish colony of the Philippines stormed Danang after several missionaries were killed. Early the next year, Saigon was seized. By 1883 the French had imposed a Treaty of Protectorate on Vietnam. French rule often proved cruel and arbitrary. Ultimately, the most successful resistance came from the communists, first organised by Ho Chi Minh in 1925.

During WWII, the only group that significantly resisted the Japanese occupation was the communist-dominated Viet Minh. When WWII ended, Ho Chi Minh – whose Viet Minh forces already controlled large parts of the country – declared Vietnam independent. French efforts to reassert control soon led to violent confrontations and full-scale war. In May 1954, Viet Minh forces overran the French garrison at Dien Bien Phu.

The Geneva Accords of mid-1954 provided for a temporary division of Vietnam at the Ben Hai River. When Ngo Dinh Diem, the anti-communist, Catholic leader of the southern zone, refused to hold the 1956 elections, the Ben Hai line became the border between North and South Vietnam.

The War in Vietnam

Around 1960, the Hanoi government changed its policy of opposition to the Diem regime from one of 'political struggle' to one of 'armed struggle'. The National Liberation Front (NLF), a communist guerrilla group better known as the Viet Cong (VC), was founded to fight against Diem.

An unpopular ruler, Diem was assassinated in 1963 by his own troops. When the Hanoi government ordered North Vietnamese Army (NVA) units to infiltrate the South in 1964, the situation for the Saigon regime became desperate. In 1965 the USA committed its first combat troops, soon joined by soldiers from South Korea, Australia, Thailand and New Zealand in an effort to bring global legitimacy to the conflict.

As Vietnam celebrated the Lunar New Year in 1968, the VC launched a surprise attack, known as the Tet Offensive, marking a crucial turning point in the war. Many Americans, who had for years believed their government's insistence that the USA was winning, started demanding a negotiated end to the war. The Paris Agreements, signed in 1973, provided for a ceasefire, the total withdrawal of US combat forces and the release of American prisoners of war.

Reunification

Saigon surrendered to the NVA on 30 April 1975. Vietnam's reunification by the communists meant liberation from more than a century of colonial oppression, but was soon followed by large-scale internal repression. Hundreds of thousands of southerners fled Vietnam, creating a flood of refugees for the next 15 years.

Vietnam's campaign of repression against the ethnic Chinese, plus its invasion of Cambodia at the end of 1978, prompted China to attack Vietnam in 1979. The war lasted only 17 days, but Chinese-Vietnamese mistrust lasted for well over a decade.

Post-Cold War

After the collapse of the Soviet Union in 1991, Vietnam and Western nations sought rapprochement. The 1990s brought foreign investment and Association of Southeast Asian Nations (Asean) membership. The US established diplomatic relations with Vietnam in 1995, and Bill Clinton and George W Bush visited Hanoi. Vietnam was welcomed into the World Trade Organisation (WTO) in 2007.

Relations have also greatly improved with the historic enemy China, with Vietnam's economic boom catching Beijing's attention.

UNCLE OF THE PEOPLE

Father of the nation, Ho Chi Minh (Bringer of Light) was the son of a fiercely nationalistic scholar-official. Born Nguyen Tat Thanh near Vinh in 1890, he was educated in Hue and adopted many pseudonyms during his momentous life. Many Vietnamese affectionately refer to him as Bac Ho (Uncle Ho) today.

In 1911 he signed up as a cook's apprentice on a French ship, sailing the seas to North America, Africa and Europe. While odd-jobbing in England and France as a gardener, snow sweeper, waiter, photo-retoucher and stoker, his political consciousness developed.

Ho Chi Minh moved to Paris, where he mastered languages including English, French, German and Mandarin and began to promote the issue of Indochinese independence. He was a founding member of the French Communist Party in 1920.

In 1941 Ho Chi Minh returned to Vietnam for the first time in 30 years, and established the Viet Minh (whose goal was independence from France). As Japan prepared to surrender in August 1945, Ho Chi Minh led the August Revolution, and his forces then established control throughout much of Vietnam.

The return of the French compelled the Viet Minh to conduct a guerrilla war, which ultimately lead to victory against the colonists at Dien Bien Phu in 1954. Ho then lead North Vietnam until his death in September 1969 – he never lived to see the North's victory over the South.

Since then the party has worked hard to preserve the image and reputation of Bac Ho. His image dominates contemporary Vietnam. This cult of personality is in stark contrast to the simplicity with which Ho lived his life. For more Ho, check out *Ho Chi Minh*, the excellent biography by William J Duiker.

Trade and tourism is burgeoning across mutual borders.

Culture & People

The Vietnamese are battle-hardened, proud and nationalist, as they have earned their stripes in successive skirmishes with the world's mightiest powers. But that's the older generation, who remember every inch of the territory for which they fought. For the new generation, Vietnam is a place to succeed, a place to ignore the staid structures set in stone by the communists, and a place to go out and have some fun.

As in other parts of Asia, life revolves around the family; there are often several generations living under one roof. Poverty, and the transition from a largely agricultural society to that of a more industrialised nation, sends many people seeking their fortune to the bigger cities, and is changing the structure of the modern family unit. Women make up 52% of the nation's workforce but are not well represented in positions of power.

Vietnam's population is 84% ethnic Vietnamese (Kinh) and 2% ethnic Chinese; the rest is made up of Khmers, Chams and members of more than 50 minority people, who mainly live in highland areas.

Religion

Over the centuries, Confucianism, Taoism and Buddhism have fused with popular Chinese beliefs and ancient Vietnamese animism to form what's collectively known as the Triple Religion (Tam Giao). Most Vietnamese people identify with this belief system, but if asked, they'll usually say they're Buddhist.

Vietnam has a significant percentage of Catholics (8% to 10% of the total population).

Cao Daism is a unique and colourful Vietnamese sect that was founded in the 1920s. It combines secular and religious philosophies of the East and West, and is based on seance messages revealed to the group's founder, Ngo Minh Chieu.

There are also small numbers of Muslims (around 60,000) and Hindus (50,000).

Arts

Contemporary Art & Music

It is possible to catch modern dance, classical ballet and stage plays in Hanoi and Ho Chi Minh City (HCMC).

The work of contemporary painters and photographers covers a wide swath of styles and gives a glimpse into the modern Vietnamese psyche; there are good galleries in Hanoi, HCMC and Hoi An.

Youth culture is most vibrant in HCMC and Hanoi, where there's more freedom for musicians and artists. There are small hip hop, rock and punk (check out Hanoi's Rock City) and DJ scenes. Hot bands include rock band Microwave, metal merchants Black Infinity, the punk band Giao Chi and alt-roots band 6789.

Architecture

The Vietnamese were not great builders like their neighbours the Khmer. Early Vietnamese structures were made of wood and other materials that proved highly vulnerable in the tropical climate. The grand exceptions are the stunning towers built by Vietnam's ancient Cham culture. These are most numerous in central Vietnam. The Cham ruins at My Son (p858) are a major draw.

Sculpture

Vietnamese sculpture has traditionally centred on religious themes and has functioned

THE NORTH–SOUTH DIVIDE

The North–South divide lingers. It's the South that's benefited most from overseas investment as Viet Kieu (overseas Vietnamese, the vast majority of whom are Southerners) have returned and invested in the region. In 2011 HCMC's economy was growing at double the national rate (10.3% compared to 5.5%).

The war may be history, but prejudice is alive and well. For many Southerners the stereotypical Northerner has a 'hard face', is too serious and doesn't know how to have fun. Conversely, for many Northerners the Southerners are too superficial and business-obsessed.

Some older Southerners have never forgiven the North for bulldozing its war cemeteries, imposing communism and blackballing whole families. While some of their peers in the North have never forgiven the South for siding with the USA against its own. Luckily for Vietnam, today's generation seems to have less interest in this harrowing history.

as an adjunct to architecture, especially that of pagodas, temples and tombs.

The Cham civilisation produced exquisite carved sandstone figures for its Hindu and Buddhist sanctuaries. The largest single collection of Cham sculpture is at the Museum of Cham Sculpture (p851) in Danang.

Water Puppetry

Vietnam's ancient art of *roi nuoc* (water puppetry) originated in northern Vietnam at least 1000 years ago. Developed by rice farmers, the wooden puppets were manipulated by puppeteers using water-flooded rice paddies as their stage. Hanoi is the best place to see water-puppetry performances, which are accompanied by music played on traditional instruments.

Politics & Government

Vietnam's political system could not be simpler: the Community Party is the sole source of power. Officially, according to the Vietnamese constitution, the National Assembly (or parliament) is the country's supreme authority, as it selects the President and Prime Minister and manages the legal system. The reality is that National Assembly is a tool of the Party and its carefully controlled elections typify the kind of voting process you'd expect in a one-party state. Currently, 90% of delegates are Community Party members.

Officially, communism is still king, but there can be few party hacks who really believe Vietnam is a Marxist utopia. Market-oriented socialism is the new mantra, although socially responsible capitalism might be nearer the mark. Foreign investment is booming. Capitalism thrives like never before, the dynamic private sector driving the economy. On the street, everyone seems to be out to make a fast buck. Fast.

Economic liberalisation is ongoing, though any meaningful democratic change still seems a long, long way off. Everything is geared to safeguard the Party's grip on power. The media is tightly controlled and critics of the Party are silenced.

Food & Drink

Food

Vietnamese food is one of the world's greatest cuisines; there are said to be nearly 500 traditional dishes. It varies a lot between North, centre and South. Soy sauce, Chinese influence and hearty soups like *pho* typify Northern cuisine. Central Vietnamese food is known for its prodigious use of fresh herbs and intricate flavours; Hue imperial cuisine and Hoi An specialities are key to this area. Southern food is sweet, spicy and tropical – its curries will be familiar to lovers of Thai and Cambodian food. Everywhere you'll find Vietnamese meals are superbly prepared and excellent value.

The range of prices for dining out in this chapter are based on a typical meal, excluding drinks:

Budget ($) under US$5

Midrange ($$) between US$5 and US$15

Top End ($$$) over US$15

Most restaurants trade seven days a week, opening around 7am or 8am and closing around 9pm, often later in the big cities. Where opening hours differ from these, we've provided details in the guide.

A RIGHT ROYAL FOOD CRITIC

Emperor Tu Duc (1848–83) expected 50 dishes to be prepared by 50 cooks to be served by 50 servants at every meal. And his tea had to be made from the dew that accumulated on leaves overnight.

Fruit

Aside from the usual delightful Southeast Asian fruits, Vietnam has its own unique *trai thanh long* (green dragon fruit), a bright fuchsia-coloured fruit with green scales. Grown mainly in the coastal region near Nha Trang, it has white flesh flecked with edible black seeds, and tastes something like a mild kiwifruit.

Meals

Pho is the noodle soup that built a nation and is eaten at all hours of the day, but especially for breakfast. *Com* are rice dishes. You'll see signs saying *pho* and *com* everywhere. Other noodle soups to try are *bun bo Hue* and *hu tieu*.

Spring rolls (*nem* in the North, *cha gio* in the South) are a speciality. These are normally dipped in *nuoc mam* (fish sauce), though many foreigners prefer soy sauce (*xi dau* in the North, *nuoc tuong* in the South).

Because Buddhist monks of the Mahayana tradition are strict vegetarians, *an chay* (vegetarian cooking) is an integral part of Vietnamese cuisine.

Snacks

Street stalls or roaming vendors are everywhere, selling steamed sweet potatoes, rice porridge and ice-cream bars even in the wee hours.

There are also many other Vietnamese nibbles to try including the following:

Bap xao Made from fresh, stir-fried corn, chillies and tiny shrimp.

Bo bia Nearly microscopic shrimp, fresh lettuce and thin slices of Vietnamese sausage rolled up in rice paper and dipped in a spicy-sweet peanut sauce.

Sinh to Shakes made with milk and sugar or yoghurt, and fresh tropical fruit.

Sweets

Many sticky confections are made from sticky rice, like *banh it nhan dau,* which also contains sugar and bean paste and is sold wrapped in banana leaf.

Most foreigners prefer *kem* (ice cream) or *yaourt* (yoghurt), which is generally of good quality.

Try *che,* a cold, refreshing sweet soup made with sweetened black bean, green bean or corn. It's served in a glass with ice and sweet coconut cream on top.

Drink

Alcoholic Drinks

Memorise the words *bia hoi,* which mean 'draught beer'. Probably the cheapest beer in the world, *bia hoi* starts at around 4000d a glass, so anyone can afford a round and you can get 'off yer heed' for just a few bucks.

Places that serve *bia hoi* usually also serve cheap food.

Several foreign labels brewed in Vietnam under licence include Tiger, Carlsberg and Heineken.

National and regional brands include Halida and Hanoi in the north, Huda and Larue in the centre, and BGI and 333 *(ba ba ba)* in the south of the country.

Wine and spirits are available but at higher prices. Local brews are cheaper but not always drinkable.

Nonalcoholic Drinks

Whatever you drink, make sure that it's been boiled or bottled. Ice is generally safe on the tourist trail, but may not be elsewhere.

Vietnamese *cà phê* (coffee) is fine stuff and there is no shortage of cafes in which to sample it.

Foreign soft drinks are widely available in Vietnam. An excellent local treat is *soda chanh* (carbonated mineral water with lemon and sugar) or *nuoc chanh nong* (hot, sweetened lemon juice).

THERE'S SOMETHING FISHY AROUND HERE...

Nuoc mam (fish sauce) is the one ingredient that is quintessentially Vietnamese, and it lends a distinctive character to Vietnamese cooking. The sauce is made by fermenting highly salted fish in large ceramic vats for four to 12 months. Connoisseurs insist high-grade sauce has a much milder aroma than the cheaper variety. Dissenters insist it is a chemical weapon. It's very often used as a dipping sauce, and takes the place occupied by salt on a Western table.

Environment & Wildlife

Environmental consciousness is low in Vietnam. Rapid industrialisation, deforestation and pollution are major problems facing the country.

Unsustainable logging and farming practices, as well as the US's extensive spraying of defoliants during the war in Vietnam, have contributed to deforestation. This has resulted not only in significant loss of biological diversity, but also in a harder existence for many minority people.

The country's rapid economic and population growth over the last decade – demonstrated by the dramatic increase in industrial production, motorbike numbers and helter-skelter construction – has put additional pressure on the already-stressed environment.

The Land

Vietnam stretches more than 1600km along the east coast of the Indochinese peninsula. The country's land area is 329,566 sq km, making it slightly larger than Italy and a bit smaller than Japan.

As the Vietnamese are quick to point out, it resembles a *don ganh,* or the ubiquitous bamboo pole with a basket of rice slung from each end. The baskets represent the

BEWARE YOUR BLEND

Some consider *chon* to be the highest grade of Vietnamese coffee. It is made of beans fed to a certain species of weasel and later collected from its excrement.

main rice-growing regions of the Red River Delta in the north, and the Mekong Delta in the south.

Of several interesting geological features found in Vietnam, the most striking are its spectacular karst formations (limestone peaks with caves and underground streams). The northern half of Vietnam has a spectacular array of karst areas, particularly around Halong Bay (p828), Tam Coc (p827) and Phong Nha (p842)

Wildlife

Because Vietnam has such a wide range of habitats, fauna here is enormously diverse; its forests are estimated to contain 12,000 plant species, only 7000 of which have been identified. Vietnam is home to more than 275 species of mammal, 800 species of bird, 180 species of reptile and 80 species of amphibian. In the 1990s, one species of muntjac (deer) and an ox similar to an oryx were discovered in Vietnam – the only newly identified large mammals in the world in the last 60 years.

Tragically, Vietnam's wildlife is in precipitous decline as forest habitats are destroyed and waterways become polluted. Illegal hunting has also exterminated the local populations of certain animals, in some cases eliminating entire species. Officially, the Vietnamese government recognises 57 mammal species (including several primates) and 64 bird species as endangered.

Many officials still turn a blind eye to the trade in wildlife for export and domestic consumption, though laws are in place to protect the animals. Poachers continue to profit from meeting the demand for exotic animals for pets and traditional medicines. Tragically, one of mainland Asia's few remaining Javan rhino (there are thought to be less than 10) was killed for its horn inside Cat Tien National Park in 2010.

Animal welfare is not yet a priority in Vietnamese culture, evidenced by the appallingly inadequate conditions for caged wildlife found throughout Vietnam.

National Parks

The number of national parks in the country has been rapidly expanding and there are now 30, covering about 3% of Vietnam's total territory. In the north the most interesting and accessible include Cat Ba (p829), Bai Tu Long (see boxed text, p830), Ba Be (p835) and Cuc Phuong (p827). Heading south Phong Nha-Ke Bang (p842), Bach Ma National Park (p849), Yok Don National Park (p871) and Cat Tien National Park (p871) are well worth investigating.

With the help of NGOs, the Vietnamese government is taking steps to expand national-park boundaries, crack down on illegal poaching and educate and employ people living in national-park buffer zones. It's a long process.

Flora and Fauna International produces the excellent *Nature Tourism Map of Vietnam,* which includes detailed coverage of all the national parks in Vietnam. All proceeds from sales of the map go towards supporting primate conservation.

SURVIVAL GUIDE

DIRECTORY A–Z

Accommodation

In general, accommodation in Vietnam offers superb value for money and excellent facilities. In big cities and the main tourism centres you'll find everything from hostel dorm beds to uber-luxe hotels. Cleanliness is generally good and there are very few real dumps.

Most hotels in Vietnam quote prices in Vietnamese dong and/or US dollars. Prices are quoted in dong or dollars throughout this chapter based on the preferred currency of the particular property. The range of prices used in this chapter are as follows:

Budget ($) most rooms cost less than US$25 (525,000d) a night. Dorm-bed prices are given individually.

Midrange ($$) rooms cost between US$25 (525,000d) and US$50 (1,050,000d)

Top End ($$$) over US$50 (1,050,000d)

These reflect high-season rates; discounts are often available at quiet times of year.

Hostel dorm beds (around US$3 to US$6) are usually the cheapest options, but these only exist in a few backpacker centres such as Nha Trang, Ho Chi Minh City, Hue and Hanoi.

Guesthouses are the next level up, rooms here often have private bathrooms and cost from around US$7 to US$20. A class above guesthouses, minihotels typically come with more amenities: satellite TV and free wi-fi.

When it comes to midrange places, flash a bit more cash and three-star touches are available, such as chic decor or access to a swimming pool.

Be aware that some hotels apply a 10% sales tax. Check carefully before taking a room to avoid any unpleasant shocks on departure.

Accommodation is at a premium during Tet (late January or early February), when the whole country is on the move and overseas Vietnamese flood back into the country. Prices can rise by 25% or more. Christmas and New Year represent another high season.

Homestays

Homestays are popular in parts of Vietnam, but it's highly advisable not to just drop into a random tribal village and hope things work out, as there are strict rules about registering foreigners who stay overnight.

Areas that are well set up include the Mekong Delta (p886), the White Thai villages of Mai Chau (p836) and Ba Be (p835).

Business Hours

Offices and other public buildings are usually open from 7am or 8am to 11am or 11.30am and again from 1pm or 2pm to 4pm or 5pm. Banks tend to be open during these hours and until 11.30am on Saturday.

Post offices are generally open from 6.30am to 9pm. Government offices are usually open until noon on Saturday and closed Sunday. Most museums are closed on Monday. Temples are usually open all day, every day.

Many small, privately owned shops, restaurants and street stalls stay open seven days a week, often until late at night.

By law, most bars in Vietnam officially close at midnight and the fun police often enforce this. However, in major centres such as HCMC there are always a few late-night places.

Children

Children get to have a good time in Vietnam. There are some great beaches, but pay close attention to any playtime in the sea, as there are some big riptides.

Kids generally enjoy local cuisine, which is rarely too spicy; the range of fruit is staggering. Comfort food from home (pizzas, pasta, burgers and ice cream) is available in most places too.

Babies & Infants

Baby supplies are available in the major cities. Cot beds are rare, and car safety seats virtually non-existent. Breastfeeding in public is fine.

The main worry throughout Vietnam is keeping an eye on what strange things infants are putting in their mouths: remember dysentery, typhoid and hepatitis are common. Keep their hydration levels up, and slap on the sunscreen.

Customs Regulations

Bear in mind that customs may seize suspected antiques or other 'cultural treasures'. If you do purchase authentic or reproduction antiques get a receipt and customs clearance form from the seller. Duty limits are as follows:

» 200 cigarettes

» 1.5L spirit

» Unlimited foreign currency; large sums (US$7000 and greater) must be declared.

Electricity

Voltage is 220V, 50 cycles. Sockets are two pin, round head. See p927 for details.

Embassies & Consulates

Australia (www.vietnam.embassy.gov.au) Hanoi (☎3774 0100; 8 Đ Dao Tan, Ba Dinh District); HCMC (Map p878; ☎3521 8100; 5th fl, 5B Đ Ton Duc Thang)

Cambodia Hanoi (Map p822; ☎3942 4788; cambocg@hcm.vnn.vn; 71A P Tran Hung Dao); HCMC (Map p876; ☎3829 2751; 41 Đ Phung Khac Khoan)

Canada (www.canadainternational.gc.ca/vietnam) Hanoi (Map p820; ☎3734 5000; 31 Đ Hung Vuong); HCMC (Map p878; ☎3827 9899; 10th fl, 235 Đ Dong Khoi)

China (http://vn.china-embassy.org/chn) Hanoi (Map p820; ☎8845 3736; 46 P Hoang Dieu); HCMC (☎3829 2457; 39 Đ Nguyen Thi Minh Khai)

France (www.ambafrance-vn.org) Hanoi (Map p822; ☎3944 5700; P Tran Hung Dao); HCMC (Map p876; ☎3520 6800; 27 Đ Nguyen Thi Minh Khai)

Germany (www.hanoi.diplo.de) Hanoi (Map p820; ☎3845 3836; 29 Đ Tran Phu); HCMC (Map p876; ☎3829 1967; 126 Đ Nguyen Dinh Chieu)

Japan (www.vn.emb-japan.go.jp) Hanoi (☎3846 3000; 27 P Lieu Giai, Ba Dinh District); HCMC (Map p878; ☎3822 5341; 13-17 ĐL Nguyen Hue)

Laos (www.embalaohanoi.gov.la) Danang (12 Đ Tran Qui Cap); Hanoi (Map p822; ☎3942 4576; 22 P Tran Binh Trong); HCMC (Map p878; ☎3829 7667; 93 Đ Pasteur)

Netherlands (www.netherlands-embassy.org.vn) Hanoi (☎3831 5650; 6th fl, Daeha Office Tower, 360 Kim Ma St, Ba Dinh); HCMC (Map p878; ☎3823 5932; Saigon Tower, 29 ĐL Le Duan)

New Zealand (www.nzembassy.com/viet-nam) Hanoi (Map p816; ☎3824 1481; Level 5, 63 P Ly Thai To); HCMC (Map p878; ☎3827 2745; 8th fl, Metropolitan, 235 Đ Dong Khoi)

Philippines Hanoi (Map p822; ☎3943 7948; hanoi.pe@dfa.gov.ph; 27B P Tran Hung Dao)

Singapore (www.mfa.gov.sg/hanoi) Hanoi (Map p820; ☎3848 9168; 41-43 Đ Tran Phu)

Sweden (www.swedenabroad.com) Hanoi (☎3726 0400; 2 Đ Nui Truc)

Thailand (www.thaiembassy.org) Hanoi (Map p820; ☎3823 5092; 63-65 P Hoang Dieu); HCMC (; ☎3932 7637; 77 Đ Tran Quoc Thao)

UK (http://ukinvietnam.fco.gov.uk) Hanoi (Map p816; ☎3936 0500; Central Bldg, 31 P Hai Ba Trung); HCMC (Map p876; ☎3829 8433; 25 ĐL Le Duan)

USA (http://vietnam.usembassy.gov) Hanoi (☎3850 5000; 7 P Lang Ha, Ba Dinh District); HCMC (Map p876; ☎3822 9433; 4 ĐL Le Duan)

Gay & Lesbian Travellers

Vietnam is pretty hassle-free for gay travellers. There's not much in the way of harassment, nor are there official laws on same-sex relationships. Vietnamese same-sex friends often walk with arms around each other or holding hands, and guesthouse proprietors are very unlikely to question the relationship of same-sex travel companions. But be discreet – public displays of affection are not socially acceptable whatever your sexual orientation.

Check out **Utopia** (www.utopia-asia.com) to obtain contacts and useful travel information.

Insurance

Insurance is a *must* for Vietnam, as the cost of major medical treatment is prohibitive. A travel-insurance policy to cover theft, loss and medical problems is the best bet.

Some insurance policies specifically exclude such 'dangerous activities' as riding motorbikes, diving and even trekking. Check that the policy covers an emergency evacuation in the event of serious injury.

Worldwide travel insurance is available at www.lonelyplanet.com/travel_services. You can buy, extend or claim anytime – even if you're already on the road.

Language Courses

Vietnamese language courses are offered in HCMC, Hanoi and elsewhere. Lessons usually cost from US$5 to US$10 per hour. Decide whether you want to study in northern or southern Vietnam, because the regional dialects are very different.

Legal Matters

If you lose something really valuable such as your passport or visa, you'll need to contact the police. Few foreigners experience much hassle from police, and demands for bribes are rare – it's a different story for the Vietnamese, though...

The Vietnamese government is seriously cracking down on the burgeoning drug trade. You may face imprisonment and/or large fines for drug offences, and drug trafficking can be punishable by death.

Maps

A *must* for its detailed road maps of every province is the *Viet Nam Administrative Atlas,* published by Ban Do. Basic road maps of major cities such as Hanoi, HCMC, Hue and Nha Trang are readily available.

Photography

Memory cards are pretty cheap in Vietnam. Most internet cafes can also burn photos onto a CD or DVD to free up storage space. Photo-processing shops and internet cafes in bigger cities can burn digital photos onto DVDs. Colour print film is widely available; slide film is available in HCMC and Hanoi.

Vietnam's gorgeous scenery and unique character make for memorable photographs. Inspiration will surely strike when you see a row of colourfully dressed hill-tribe women walking to market, but remember to maintain an appropriate level of respect for the people and places you visit. Ask permission before snapping a photo of someone.

Post

International mail from Vietnam is not unreasonably priced when compared with most countries, though parcels mailed from smaller cities and towns may take longer to arrive at their destinations. Be aware that customs inspect the contents before you ship anything other than documents, so don't show up at the post office with a carefully wrapped parcel ready to go. It will be dissected on the table.

Poste restante works in the larger cities but don't count on it elsewhere. All post offices are marked with the words *buu dien*.

Public Holidays

Politics affects everything, including many public holidays, in Vietnam. If a Vietnamese public holiday falls on a weekend, it is observed on the following Monday.

New Year's Day (Tet Duong Lich) 1 January

Vietnamese New Year (Tet) A three-day national holiday; late January or February

Anniversary of the Founding of the Vietnamese Communist Party (Thanh Lap Dang CSVN) 3 February – the date the Party was founded in 1930

Hung Kings Commemorations (Hung Vuong) 10th day of the 3rd lunar month; late March or April

Liberation Day (Saigon Giai Phong) 30 April – the date on which Saigon's surrender is commemorated nationwide as Liberation Day

International Workers' Day (Quoc Te Lao Dong) 1 May

Ho Chi Minh's Birthday (Sinh Nhat Bac Ho) 19 May

Buddha's Birthday (Phat Dan) Eighth day of the fourth moon (usually June)

National Day (Quoc Khanh) 2 September – commemorates Ho Chi Minh's Declaration of Independence in 1945

Safe Travel

All in all, Vietnam is an extremely safe country to travel. Sure, there are scams and hassles in some cities, particularly in Hanoi and Nha Trang, which we've dealt with in relevant sections of the book. But overall the police keep a pretty tight grip on social order and we very rarely receive reports about muggings, armed robberies and sexual assaults.

Watch out for petty theft. Drive-by bag snatchers on motorbikes are not uncommon, and thieves patrol buses, trains and boats. Don't be flash with cameras and jewellery.

Since 1975 many thousands of Vietnamese have been maimed or killed by rockets, artillery shells, mortars, mines and other ordnance left over from the war. Stick to defined paths and *never* touch any suspicious war relic you might come across.

Time

Vietnam is seven hours ahead of Greenwich Mean Time/Universal Time Coordinated (GMT/UTC) and there's no daylight-saving or summer time.

Toilets

Western-style sit-down toilets are the norm but the odd squat bog still survives in some cheap hotels and bus stations. Hotels usually supply a roll, but it's wise to bring your own while on the road.

Tourist Information

Tourist offices in Vietnam have a different philosophy from the majority of tourist offices worldwide. These government-owned enterprises are really travel agencies whose primary interests are booking tours and turning a profit.

Travellers' cafes, travel agencies and your fellow travellers are a much better source of information than most of the so-called 'tourist offices'.

Travellers with Disabilities

Vietnam is not the easiest of places for disabled travellers. Tactical problems include the chaotic traffic, a lack of lifts in smaller hotels and pavements (sidewalks) that are routinely blocked by parked motorbikes and footstalls.

That said, with some careful planning it is possible to enjoy your trip. Find a reliable company to make the travel arrangements. Many hotels in the midrange and above category have elevators, and disabled access is improving. Bus and train travel is tough, but rent a private vehicle with a driver and almost anywhere becomes instantly accessible.

The hazards for blind travellers in Vietnam are pretty acute, with traffic coming at you from all directions, so you'll definitely need a sighted companion.

The Travellers with Disabilities forum on Lonely Planet's **Thorn Tree** (www.lonelyplanet.com) is a good place to seek the advice of other disabled travellers.

You might also try contacting the following organisations:

Accessible Journeys (☎610-521 0339; www.disabilitytravel.com)

Mobility International USA (☎54-1343 1284; www.miusa.org)

Royal Association for Disability and Rehabilitation (Radar; ☎020-7250 3222; www.radar.org.uk)

Society for Accessible Travel & Hospitality (SATH; ☎212-447 7284; www.sath.org)

Visas

Most nationalities have to endure the hassle of pre-arranging a visa (or approval letter) in order to enter Vietnam. Entry and exit points include Hanoi, HCMC and Danang airports or any of the plentiful land borders, shared with Cambodia, China and Laos.

Certain favoured nationalities (see below) qualify for an automatic visa on arrival. Everyone else has to sort out a visa in advance. Arranging the paperwork has become fairly straightforward, but it remains expensive and unnecessarily time-consuming. Processing a tourist-visa application typically takes four or five working days in Western countries.

Tourist visas are valid for a 30-day or 90-day stay (and can be single or multiple entry).

In Asia the best place to pick up a Vietnamese visa is Cambodia, where it costs around US$45 and can be arranged the same day. Bangkok is also a popular place.

If you plan to spend more than a month in Vietnam, or if you plan to exit Vietnam and enter again from Cambodia or Laos, arrange a 90-day multiple-entry visa. These cost around US$95 in Cambodia, but are not available from all Vietnamese embassies.

In our experience personal appearance influences the reception you receive from immigration – if you wear shorts or scruffy clothing, or look dirty or unshaven, you can expect problems. Try your best to look 'respectable'.

Mulitiple-entry Visas

It's possible to enter Cambodia or Laos from Vietnam and then re-enter without having to apply for another visa. However, you must apply for a multiple-entry visa *before* you leave Vietnam.

Multiple-entry visas are easiest to arrange in Hanoi or HCMC, but you will almost certainly have to ask a travel agent to do the paperwork for you. Travel agents charge about US$45; the procedure takes up to seven days.

Visa Extensions

If you've got the dollars, they've got the rubber stamp. Tourist-visa extensions officially cost as little as US$10, but it's advisable to pay more go via a travel agency, as the bureaucracy is deep. The process can take seven days, extensions are 30 to 90 days.

Extensions are best organised in major cities such as HCMC, Hanoi, Danang and Hue.

VIETNAM VISA AGENTS

If you're arriving by air, it's now usually easiest and cheapest to get your visa approved in advance through a visa service company or travel agent. This system does *not* operate at land border crossings.

The company or agent will need passport details, and will then email you an approval document two to three days later, which you need to print and bring with you to the airport. On arrival you need to present the approval document and passport picture then pay a stamping fee (US$25 for single-entry, US$50 for multiple-entry visas).

Recommended companies include **Vietnam Visa Center** (www.vietnamvisacenter.org) and **Visa Vietnam** (www.visatovietnam.org).

VISA ON ARRIVAL

Citizens of the following countries do not have to apply in advance for a Vietnamese visa. Always double check visa requirements before you travel as policies regularly change.

COUNTRY	DAYS
Thailand, Malaysia, Singapore, Indonesia, Laos, Cambodia	30
Philippines	21
Japan, Korea, Russia, Norway, Denmark, Sweden, Finland, Brunei	15
Kyrgyzstan	90

Volunteering

For information on volunteer work opportunities, chase up the full list of non-government organisations (NGOs) at the **NGO Resource Centre** (☎04-3832 8570; www.ngocentre.org.vn; Hotel La Thanh, 218 P Doi Can, Hanoi), which keeps a database of all of the NGOs assisting Vietnam. Projects in need of volunteers include the following:

Koto (www.koto.com.au) Donate your skills, time or money to help give street children career opportunities. Street Voices' primary project is KOTO Restaurant in Hanoi.

Volunteers for Peace (www.vpv.vn) Always looking for volunteers to help in an orphanage on the outskirts of Hanoi.

Work

At least 90% of foreign travellers seeking work in Vietnam end up teaching English, though there is some demand for French teachers too. Pay can be as low as US$5 per hour at a university and up to US$20 per hour at a private academy.

Jobs in the booming private sector or with NGOs are usually organised outside Vietnam before arriving.

Getting There & Away

Most travellers enter Vietnam by plane or bus, but there are also train links from China and boat connections from Cambodia via the Mekong River.

Entering Vietnam

Formalities at Vietnam's international airports are generally smoother than at land borders. That said, crossing overland from Cambodia and China is now relatively stress-free. Crossing the border between Vietnam and Laos can be slow.

Passport

Your passport must be valid for six months upon arrival in Vietnam. Most nationalities need to arrange a visa in advance (see p903).

Air

Airports

There are three established international airports in Vietnam. A fourth major international airport, in Phu Quoc, should become fully operational in 2012.

> Flights, tours rail tickets and other travel services can be booked online at www.lonelyplanet.com/travel_services.

Ho Chi Minh City (SGN; ☎08-3845 6654; www.tsnairport.com) Tan Son Nhat airport is Vietnam's busiest international air hub.

Hanoi (HAN; ☎04 3827 1513; www.hanoiairportonline.com) Noi Bai airport serves the capital.

Danang airport (DAD; ☎051-1383 0339) Only has a few international flights, but a new terminal should result in additional connections.

Airlines

Vietnam Airlines (www.vietnamairlines.com.vn) Hanoi (☎04-3832 0320); HCMC (☎08-3832 0320) is the state-owned flag carrier and has flights to 28 international destinations, mainly in east Asia.

The airline has a modern fleet of Airbuses and Boeings, and has a good recent safety record.

Tickets

From Europe or North America, it's usually more expensive to fly to Vietnam than other Southeast Asian countries. Consider buying a discounted ticket to Bangkok, Singapore or Hong Kong and picking up a flight from there. Air Asia and other low-cost airlines fly to Vietnam.

It's hard to get reservations for flights to/from Vietnam during holidays, especially Tet, which falls between late January and mid-February.

Border Crossings

Vietnam shares land border crossings with Cambodia, China and Laos. Vietnam visas were not available at any land borders at the time of research.

CAMBODIA

Cambodia and Vietnam share a long frontier with seven (and counting) border crossings. One-month Cambodian visas are issued on arrival at all border crossings for US$20, but overcharging is common except at Bavet (the most popular crossing).

There's also a river border crossing between Cambodia and Vietnam at Kaam Samnor–Vinh Xuong on the banks of the Mekong. Regular fast boats ply the route between Phnom Penh in Cambodia and Chau Doc in Vietnam via this border.

Cambodian border crossings are officially open daily between 8am and 8pm.

CHINA

There are currently three border checkpoints where foreigners are permitted to cross between Vietnam and China: Lao Cai (p837), Huu Nghi Quan (the Friendship Pass) and Mong Cai p834).

International trains link China and Vietnam, connecting Hanoi with Nanning (and even on to Beijing!). The train departs Hanoi's Gia Lam station at 9.40pm daily. The journey takes 12 hours and costs 52/76 Swiss Francs per hard sleeper/soft sleeper. Note: you cannot board these international trains in Lang Son or Dong Dang.

Trains are currently not operating on the Chinese side of the Lao Cai–Hekou border. If you're heading for Kunming, you can take sleeper buses from the border.

It is necessary to arrange a Chinese visa in advance.

LAOS

There are seven (and counting) overland crossings between Vietnam and Laos. Thirty-day Lao visas are now available at all borders. Lao Bao–Dansavanh (p848) is the most straightforward route.

Try to use direct city-to-city bus connections between the countries as the potential hassle is greatly reduced – immigration and transport scams are very common on the Vietnamese side of these borders. Bus drivers lie about journey times and some stop in the middle of nowhere and renegotiate the price.

Transport links on both sides of the border can be very hit and miss, so don't use the more remote borders unless you have plenty of time to spare.

Getting Around

Air

Vietnam has good domestic flight connections, and very affordable prices (if you book early). Airlines accept bookings on international credit or debit cards. However, note that cancellations are not unknown.

Vietnam Airlines and Jetstar are the main carriers, while Air Mekong and Vasco provide additional services:

Vietnam Airlines (www.vietnamairlines.com.vn) The leading local carrier with the most comprehensive network and best reliability.

Jetstar Pacific Airlines (www.jetstar.com/vn) This budget airline has very affordable fares, though it only serves the main cities.

Air Mekong (www.airmekong.com.vn) Links HCMC with Phu Quoc, Dalat, Con Dao and Hanoi.

Vasco (www.vasco.com.vn) Flies to the Con Dao islands from HCMC.

Bicycle

Bikes are a great way to get around Vietnam, particularly when you get off the main highways. With the loosening of borders in the Mekong region, more and more people are planning overland trips by bicycle.

The main hazard is the traffic, and it's wise to avoid certain areas (notably Hwy 1). The best cycling is in the northern mountains and the Central Highlands, although you'll have to cope with some big hills. The Mekong Delta is a rewarding option for those who prefer the flat.

Purchasing a good bicycle in Vietnam is hit-and-miss. It's recommended that you bring one from abroad, along with a quality helmet and spare parts.

Bicycles can also be hired locally from guesthouses for about US$2 per day, and are a great way to get to know a new city.

Boat

The extensive network of canals in the Mekong Delta makes getting around by boat feasible in the far south. Travellers to Phu Quoc Island can catch ferries from Ha Tien (p888) or Rach Gia (p889).

In the country's northeast, hydrofoils connect Haiphong with Cat Ba Island (near Halong Bay), and cruises on Halong Bay are extremely popular. Day trips to islands off the coast of Nha Trang, to the Chams off Hoi An and in Lan Ha Bay are also good excursions.

Bus

Vietnam has an extensive network of buses that reach the far-flung corners of the country. Most are painfully slow and seriously uncomfortable local services, but modern buses are now increasingly available on all the main routes.

Whichever class of bus you're on, bus travel in Vietnam is never speedy, reckon on just 50kmh on major routes including Hwy 1.

Bus Stations

Many cities have several bus stations – make sure you get the right one! Bus stations all look chaotic but many now have ticket offices with official prices and departure times displayed.

MOTORBIKE TOURS

Specialised motorbike tours offer an unrivalled way to explore Vietnam's scenic excesses on traffic-light back roads. A little experience helps, but many of the leading companies also offer tuition for first-timers.

Explore Indochina (☎09-1309 3159; www.exploreindochina.com) Excellent tours in the far north on vintage 650 Urals or modified Minsks; US$150-200 per day. Good rental bikes also available.

Free Wheelin' Tours (Map p814; ☎04-3926 2743; www.freewheelin tours.com; 2A P Ta Hien) Trips and custom-made tours utilising the company's own homestays. From US$100 per day (per group of four).

Hoi An Motorbike Adventures (Map p854; ☎0510-391 1930; www.motorbiketours-hoian.com; 54A Phan Chau Trinh) Specialises in short trips (from US$35) in the Hoi An region on well-maintained Minsk bikes.

Offroad Vietnam (☎04-3926 3433; www.offroadvietnam.com) Well-organised tours on Honda road and dirt bikes to remote areas of northern Vietnam for around US$100 per day. Also rents quality Honda road bikes (from US$20).

Voyage Vietnam (☎04-3926 2373; www.voyagevietnam.net) Trips in the north, Mekong Delta and along HCMC highway; from around US$85 per day.

Reservations & Costs

Always buy a ticket from the office, as bus drivers are notorious for overcharging. Reservations aren't usually required for most of the frequent, popular services between towns and cities.

On rural runs foreigners are typically charged anywhere from twice to 10 times the going rate. As a benchmark, a typical 100km ride is between US$2 and US$3.

Bus Types

DELUXE BUSES

On most popular routes, modern air-conditioned Korean and Chinese buses offer comfortable reclining seats or padded flat beds for really long trips. These sleeper buses can be a good alternative to long-distance trains, and costs are comparable.

Deluxe buses are nonsmoking. On the flipside most of them are equipped with TVs and some with dreaded karaoke machines.

OPEN TOURS

Connecting backpacker haunts across the nation open tour buses are wildly popular in Vietnam. These air-con buses use convenient, centrally located departure points and allow you to hop-on, hop-off at any major city along the main north to south route.

Prices are reasonable. A through ticket from Ho Chi Minh City to Hanoi costs around US$45, Nha Trang to Hoi An around US$12.

Travellers' cafes, tour agencies and budget hotels sell tickets. The **Sinh Tourist** (www.thesinhtourist.vn) started the concept and has a good reputation.

LOCAL BUSES

Short-distance buses, most of them pretty decrepit, drop off and pick up as many passengers as possible along their route, so the frequent stops make for a slow journey. Conductors tend to routinely overcharge foreigners on these local services, so they're not popular with travellers.

Car & Motorcycle

Having your own set of wheels gives you maximum flexibility to visit remote regions and stop when and where you please. Car hire always includes a driver. Motorbike hire is good value and this can be self-drive or with a driver.

Driving Licence

In order to drive a car in Vietnam, you need a Vietnamese licence and an International Driving Permit. However, all rental companies only rent out cars with drivers. When it comes to renting motorbikes, it's a case of no licence required.

Fuel

Unleaded gasoline costs 21,000d per litre. Even isolated communities usually have someone selling petrol by the roadside.

Hire

The major considerations are safety, the mechanical condition of the vehicle, the reliability of the rental agency, and your budget.

Car & Minibus

Renting a vehicle with a driver and guide is a realistic option even for budget travellers, providing there are enough people to share the cost.

Costs per day:

Standard model US$40 to US$60
4WD/minibus US$80 to US$115

Motorbike

Motorbikes can be rented from virtually anywhere, including cafes, hotels and travel agencies. Some places will ask to keep your passport as security. Ask for a signed agreement stating what you are renting, how much it costs, the extent of compensation and so on.

It is compulsory to wear a helmet when riding a motorbike in Vietnam, even when travelling as a passenger.

Costs per day:

Moped (semi-auto) US$4-6
Moped (fully auto) US$8-10
Trail and road bikes From US$15-30

Plenty of local drivers will be willing to act as a chauffeur and guide for around US$10 to US$20 per day too.

Insurance

If you are travelling in a tourist vehicle with a driver, then it is almost guaranteed to be insured. When it comes to motorbikes, many rental bikes are not insured, and you will have to sign a contract agreeing to a valuation for the bike if it is stolen.

Road Conditions & Hazards

Road safety is definitely not one of Vietnam's strong points. Vehicles drive on the right-hand side (in theory). Size matters and small vehicles get out of the way of big vehicles. Even Hwy 1 is only a two-lane highway for most of its length and high-speed, head-on collisions are all too common.

In general, the major highways are hard surfaced and reasonably well maintained, but seasonal flooding can be a problem. Non-paved road are best tackled with a 4WD vehicle or motorbike. Mountain roads are particularly dangerous: landslides, falling rocks and runaway vehicles can add an unwelcome edge to your journey.

Local Transport

CYCLOS These are bicycle rickshaws. Drivers hang out in touristy areas and some speak broken English. Bargaining is imperative; settle on a fare before going anywhere. A short ride costs about 10,000d, over 2km about 20,000d.

TAXIS Metered taxis are found in all cities and are very, very cheap by international standards and a safe way to travel around at night. Average tariffs are about 10,000d to 15,000d per kilometre. Only travel with reputable or recommended companies, **Mai Linh** (www.mailinh.vn) is an excellent nationwide firm.

XE OM Motorbike taxis are everywhere. Fares are comparable with those for a *cyclo*. Drivers hang around street corners, markets, hotels and bus stations. They will find you before you find them...

Tours

The following are Vietnam-based travel agencies that offer tours throughout Vietnam:

Buffalo Tours (☎04-3828 0702; www.buffalotours.com; 94 P Ma May, Hanoi)

Exotissimo (☎08-3995 9898; www.exotissimo.com; 80-82 Đ Phan Xich Long, Phu Nhuan District, HCMC)

Handspan Travel Indochina (Map p814; ☎04-3926 2828; www.handspan.com; 78 P Ma May, Hanoi)

TRAIN FARES FROM HANOI

DESTINATION	SOFT SEAT AIR-CON	TOP HARD AIR-CON (6 BERTH)	BOTTOM SOFT AIR-CON (4 BERTH)
Hue	508,000d	785,000d	833,000d
Danang	570,000d	853,000d	915,000d
Nha Trang	1,030,000d	1,340,000d	1,510,000d
HCMC	1,175,000d	1,590,000d	1,690,000d
Lao Cai	210,000d	310,000d	450,000d

Ocean Tours (Map p814; ☎04-3926 0463; www.oceantours.com.vn; 22 P Hang Bac, Hanoi)
Sisters Tours (☎04-3562 2733; www.sisterstoursvietnam.com; 37 Đ Thai Thinh, Hanoi)

Train

The railway system, operated by **Vietnam Railways** (Duong Sat Viet Nam; ☎04-3747 0308; www.vr.com.vn), is an aging, slow but pretty dependable service, and offers a relaxing way to get around the nation. Travelling in an air-con sleeping berth sure beats a hairy overnight bus journey along Hwy 1. And there's spectacular scenery to lap up too.

Routes

The main line connects HCMC with Hanoi. Three rail-spur lines link Hanoi with other parts of northern Vietnam: Haiphong, Lang Son and Lao Cai.

The train journey between Hanoi and HCMC takes from 30 to 41 hours, depending on the train.

Classes & Costs

Trains classified as SE are the smartest and fastest. There are four main ticket classes: hard seat, soft seat, hard sleeper and soft sleeper. These classes are further split according to whether or not they have air-conditioning. Presently, air-con is only available on the faster express trains. Hard-seat class is usually packed, and is tolerable for day travel, but expect plenty of cigarette smoke.

Ticket prices vary depending on the train; the fastest trains are the most expensive.

Reservations

Reservations should be made at least one day in advance, especially for sleeping berths. You'll need to bring your passport when buying train tickets.

Many travel agencies, hotels and cafes sell train tickets for a small commission.

Understand Southeast Asia

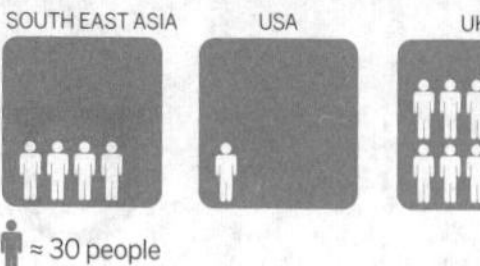

Southeast Asia Today

Surviving the Recession

The Southeast Asian nations waltzed into the end of the millennium's first decade with surprising grace. Their economies remain stable, democracy was restored in Thailand, Myanmar has made promising reforms, and poor nations are getting less poor. Full steam ahead into the Asian century.

Vietnam is one of the world's fastest growing economies and is poised to be among the world's top 20 economies by 2025 according to Goldman Sachs. This expansion is in spite of continued state control on the economy. According to a *New York Times* article, state-owned companies use 40% of the capital invested in Vietnam but contribute only 25% to GDP. Some analysts fear this could derail Vietnam's continued growth but others advise not to underestimate its work ethic and force of will.

Population: 593,000,000

GDP: US$1.486 trillion

GDP per capita: US$2500

Unemployment: 5.7%

Average annual inflation (2011): 5.7%

There is continued economic liberalisation and trade normalisation in Cambodia and Laos. In 2009, both countries were officially removed from the US trade blacklist, an antiquated designation earned during the US involvement in Vietnam in the mid-20th century. With help from South Korea, Laos opened its first stock exchange in 2011, signalling a serious step towards open markets, and Cambodia hopes to follow.

With around nine million overseas Filipino workers, the Philippines is dependent on international remittances. Thus it relies on overseas economies for jobs. Despite the gloomy global environment, remittances have increased every year since the start of the recession, ensuring stability to that 10% sector of the economy. Thanks to high domestic consumption, Indonesia avoided economic contraction and posted 4.6% growth in 2009. Both countries, along with Vietnam, have been tagged as 'Next Eleven' economies by Goldman Sachs, for their growth potential in the next 15 years.

Myanmar's recently elected government has made several reform efforts, inviting democracy leader Aung San Suu Kyi to a presidential

Do & Don'ts

- » Take off your shoes when entering a home, mosque or temple.
- » Respect the region's religions, lest you anger the gods.
- » Smile; it will put people at ease.
- » Don't argue or get visibly angry; you'll cause yourself embarrassment.
- » Dress modestly.
- » Don't sunbathe topless at the beach.
- » Don't expect something for nothing; be reasonable about prices and costs.

economy
(% of GDP)

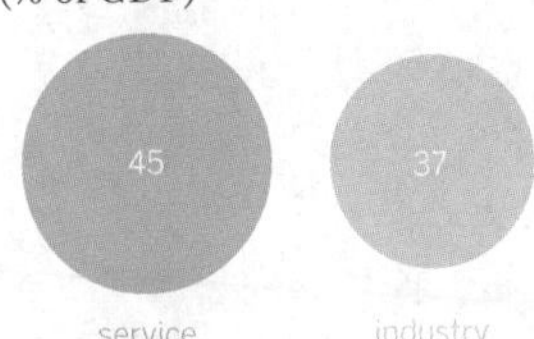

if South East Asia were 100 people

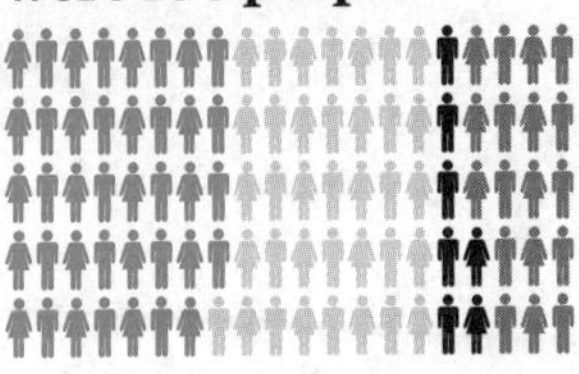

meeting, releasing 200 political prisoners and easing some press restrictions. These steps were recognised by the international community as promising gestures and Myanmar was awarded the rotating chair position of ASEAN, US Secretary of State Hillary Clinton made a landmark diplomatic visit in 2011 and Aung San Suu Kyi was allowed to register as a candidate in the April 2012 parliamentary by-elections.

Looking North

From the 1990s, China resumed its historic role as a trading partner with Southeast Asia. Bilateral trade volume between the region and China reached US$105.9 billion in 2004. China has tapped Laos' rich natural resources for hydroelectric power and resource extraction and has built roads to facilitate trade. China is Cambodia's biggest foreign investor, sinking billions of dollars into garment factories, hydropower, mining and forest concessions. It is Thailand's second biggest investor after Japan. And China and Thailand make up Myanmar's major investors.

Beyond the halls of finance, China represents another opportunity for growth: tourism. ASEAN tourism reports ranked China as the region's third-largest source of visitors, accounting for 3.4 million arrivals. In Thailand, according to Tourism Authority of Thailand statistics, 45% more Chinese tourists (1.2 million in total) visited the kingdom in 2010, on average spending 5000B per day and staying six days.

Southeast Asian tourism bureaus are hoping to remain a home-away-from-home for this expanding market. Proximity and expanding transport networks contribute to a continued relationship. The Asian-Highway Route 3, an old smuggler's route from China to northwest Laos, was completed in 2008, mainly for trade but tourists aren't far behind. And a Chinese-built high-speed passenger train linking Beijing and Kunming to Luang Prabang and Vientiane, Laos, is due for completion in 2014.

Top Noodle Dishes

» *laksa* – Malaysia

» *pho* – Vietnam

» *pad Thai* – Thailand

» *mie goreng* – Indonesia

» *mee kola* – Cambodia

» *lard na* – Laos

» *pancit bihon* – Philippines

» *char kway teow* – Singapore

Top Books

» **Eat, Pray, Love** (2006) Elizabeth Gilbert's book that kindled a love affair with Bali.

» **The Killing Fields** (1984) Based on a real-life tale of the Khmer Rouge takeover.

» **Burmese Days** (1934) George Orwell's classic tale of close-minded colonials living in Burma.

» **A Cook's Tour: In Search of the Perfect Meal** (2001) Anthony Bourdain's culinary adventures through Southeast Asia and beyond.

» **One Crowded Hour** (1987) Tim Bowden's autobiography of Neil Davis, cameraman and war correspondent in Southeast Asia during the tumultuous mid-20th century.

Friend, Foe & Family

Though China is viewed as a friend with deep pockets, Southeast Asian countries are also examining how to compete for manufacturing jobs as Chinese workers demand higher pay. Cambodia, Vietnam and Indonesia all have lower wages, but they lack the infrastructure to mount successful bids for large-scale factory relocation, according to the *Wall Street Journal*.

ASEAN has been working on proposals to create a single economic market to increase the region's competitiveness. Among them is the ASEAN Economic Community (AEC) set for adoption in phases from 2015 to 2020. This will remove restrictions on the movement of goods, services and skilled workers within the member countries and streamline customs. ASEAN has also signed a free-trade agreement with member countries and China; the ASEAN-China agreement created the world's largest population within a free-trade zone. The agreement dismantles tariffs, especially in Indonesia and the Philippines where import duties were highest.

ASEAN's goals differ from the European Union, in that there's no regional central bank, single currency plan or governing body. ASEAN pursues a policy of consensus and non-intervention, especially in regard to members with lacklustre human-rights records (Myanmar) or territorial disputes (Thailand and Cambodia).

Moving towards a Single Visa?

Inspired by Europe's visa system, ASEAN members have been considering a unified system but little progress has been made. Bilateral and sub-regional agreements seem more promising. But for now the nations agree to agree.

Top Films

» **Apocalypse Now** (1979) Set in Vietnam, filmed in the Philippines; it is the classic-rock of war flicks.

» **The Beach** (2000) Beautiful Thai island utopia, based on the book.

» **The Lady** (2011) A French-directed biopic about Myanmar's democracy leader Aung San Suu Kyi.

» **Fable of the Fish** (2011) A Filipino film set in the slums of Manila with a magic-realism plot.

» **Uncle Boonmee Who Can Recall His Past Lives** (2010) Cannes award-winning Thai film about reincarnation.

History

Early Kingdoms

The mainland Southeast Asian countries owe much of their early historical happenings to the more dominant civilisations of China and India. As early as 150 BC, China and India interacted with the scattered Southeast Asian communities for trade and tribute. Vietnam, within short reach of China, was a subject, student and reluctant offspring of its more powerful neighbour for over 1000 years. India, on the other hand, conquered by spiritual means, spreading Hinduism, Buddhism and later Islam across the region, and influencing art and architecture.

Several highly organised states emerged in the region as a result of contact with India. From the 7th to the 9th centuries AD, the Srivijaya empire controlled all shipping through the Java Sea from its capital at Palembang in southeast Sumatra. The Srivijaya capital was also a religious centre for Mahayana Buddhism (Greater Vehicle Buddhism; see p917) and attracted scholars as well as merchants.

But the region's most famous empire emerged in the interior of present-day Cambodia. The Khmer empire ruled the land for four centuries, consuming territory and labour to build unparalleled and enduring Hindu-Buddhist monuments to its god-kings. Eventually the Khmer empire included most of what is now Thailand, Laos and Cambodia. Its economy was based on agriculture, and a sophisticated irrigation system cultivated vast tracts of land around Tonlé Sap (Great Lake). Attacks from emerging city-states on the Thai frontier contributed to the decline of the empire and the abandonment of the Angkor capital.

Ancient Capitals

- Angkor (Cambodia)
- Sukhothai (Thailand)
- Bagan (Myanmar)
- My Son (Vietnam)

The Classical & Colonial Period

As the larger powers withered, Southeast Asia entered an age of cultural definition and international influence. Regional kingdoms created distinctive works of art and literature, and joined the international sphere as

TIMELINE

2800–100 BC

Ancestors of modern Southeast Asians begin to migrate south from China and Tibet, populating river valleys and coastal areas and organising small city-states.

7th century

A Buddhist empire, Srivijaya emerges in present-day Malaysia and Sumatra (Indonesia) as a coastal shipping interest between the Indian–Chinese trade route.

AD 802

King Jayavarman consolidates the Khmer empire in parts of present-day Cambodia, Thailand, Myanmar and Malaysia that supplants the local Funan state.

important ports. The Thais expanded into the dying Khmer empire and exerted control over parts of Cambodia, Laos and Myanmar. Starting around 1331, the Hindu kingdom of Majapahit united the Indonesian archipelago from Sumatra to New Guinea and dominated the trade routes between India and China. The kingdom's reign continued until the advent of Islamic kingdoms and the emergence of the port town of Melaka on the Malay peninsula in 1402. Melaka's prosperity soon attracted European interest, and it fell first to the Portuguese in 1511, then the Dutch and finally the English.

Initially these European nations were only interested in controlling shipping in the region, usually brokering agreements and alliances with local authorities. Centred on Java and Sumatra, the Dutch monopolised European commerce with Asia for 200 years. The Spanish, French and later the English had civilisation and proselytising on their minds. Spain occupied the Philippine archipelago, Britain steadily rolled through India, Myanmar and the Malay peninsula, while the Dutch grasped Indonesia to cement a presence in the region. And France, with a foothold in Vietnam, usurped Cambodia and Laos to form Indochina.

European Hill Stations

- Sapa (Vietnam)
- Cameron Highlands (Malaysia)
- Bokor National Park (Cambodia)

Although its sphere of influence was diminished, Thailand was the only Southeast Asian nation to remain independent. One reason for this was that England and France agreed to leave Thailand as a 'buffer' between their two colonies. Credit is also frequently given to the Thai kings who Westernised the country and played competing European powers against each other.

Independence Movements

The 20th century and WWII signalled an end to European domination in Southeast Asia. As European power receded, the Japanese expanded control throughout the region, invading Thailand, Malaysia and Indonesia. After the war, the power vacuums in formerly colonised countries provided leverage for a region-wide independence movement. Vietnam and Indonesia clamoured most violently for freedom, resulting in long-term wars with their respective colonial powers. For the latter half of the 20th century, Vietnam fought almost uninterrupted conflicts against foreign powers. After the French were defeated by communist nationals, Vietnam faced civil war and the intervention of the USA, which hoped to contain the spread of communism within the region. Cambodia's civil war ended in one of the worst nightmares of modern times, with the ascension of the Khmer Rouge. The revolutionary army evacuated the cities, separated families into labour camps and closed the country off from the rest of the world. An estimated 1.7 million people were killed by the regime during its brief four-year term (1975–79).

Many of the newly liberated countries struggled to unite a land mass that shared only a colonial legacy. Dictatorships in Myanmar, Indonesia

1025

Srivijaya empire is toppled by the Chola kingdom of South India, creating a power vacuum for the rise of smaller regional entities and the introduction of Islam.

13th century

The beginning of the decline of the Khmer empire and rise of powerful states in modern-day Thailand and Vietnam.

» Decorative door lintel on a Khmer building, Thailand

and the Philippines thwarted the populace's hopes for representative governments and civil liberties. Civilian rioters, minority insurgents and communist guerrillas further provoked the unstable governments, and the internal chaos was usually agitated by the major superpowers: China, the Soviet Union and the USA.

Modern Era

Near the turn of the millennium, the region entered a period of unprecedented economic growth. Singapore, along with Hong Kong and South Korea, was classified as an 'Asian Tiger' economy – export-driven countries experiencing as much as 7% annual growth in gross domestic product. Emerging tigers included Thailand, Malaysia, Indonesia and to a lesser extent the Philippines. These countries were quickly industrialising and beginning to dominate sophisticated manufacturing sectors such as automobile, machinery and electronics production.

In 1997, the upward trend was derailed by a currency crisis. Thailand's baht was the first currency to crash (falling from 50B/US$1 to 25B/US$1); neighbouring currencies soon followed. A period of economic retraction and financial austerity restored these developing economies to a more sustainable footing. More than a decade since the economic crash of 1997, many of the former tigers have become house cats, enjoying respectable GDP growth, economic opportunity, foreign investment and an increasingly affluent and educated population.

The formerly cloistered countries of Vietnam, Laos and Cambodia began to open up in the mid- to late 1990s and have experienced various degrees of economic success and industrialisation. Vietnam continues to be the success story of former Indochina with an ever-expanding economy and a youthful optimism that counteracts government inefficiencies.

Born in 1967, the Association of Southeast Asian Nations (ASEAN) is a regional cooperation organisation that includes 10 member countries (excluding Timor-Leste).

BOXING DAY TSUNAMI

One of the deadliest natural disasters ever recorded occurred on 26 December 2004, in Southeast Asia. A massive 9.0 magnitude earthquake struck off the coast of Sumatra (Indonesia) and triggered a tsunami that travelled across the entire Indian Ocean, killing 230,000 people and affecting five Southeast Asian countries (Indonesia, Thailand, Malaysia, Myanmar and Singapore) as well as India, Sri Lanka and countries as far away as the east coast of Africa. The earthquake was so powerful that the entire planet vibrated from its force. Being the closest to the epicentre, the Sumatran province of Aceh suffered the most damage and loss of life. A huge outflow of international humanitarian aid followed in the wave's aftermath and most of the affected regions have rebuilt what was destroyed. Banda Aceh, the provincial capital of Aceh, contains several poignant museums and testaments to this modern calamity.

1511

Melaka falls to the Portuguese and marks the beginning of colonial expansion in the region by such European powers as the Dutch, Spanish, French and British.

1939–45

WWII; Japan occupies much of Southeast Asia using Thailand as a cooperative base and Malaysia and Indonesia as a source of conscripts.

1946–65

Post-war Europe withdraws from the region, ushering in independence movements. First, the Philippines gains independence followed by Myanmar, Indonesia, the countries of Indochina, Malaysia and Singapore.

1955–1975

The US becomes involved in Vietnam's civil war as an anti-communism effort. Laos and Cambodia become peripherally involved. The US withdraws after the fall of Saigon to North Vietnamese troops.

Laos woke up from its backwater slumber to find that China needed it for natural resources and as a trade route to neighbouring markets. Chinese-funded and -built infrastructure projects have included highway and hydroelectric dam construction. Increased infrastructure is helping Laos and its comrade-in-tragedy Cambodia develop a thriving tourism sector that has matured from low-budget adventurers to high-end jet-setters. In addition to tourism, the two countries still depend largely on small-scale agriculture with some industrialisation in the textile industry. Both lag behind their neighbours in terms of economic growth and standard of living and are still classified by the UN as being among the least developed countries in the world.

Indonesia and the Philippines rode the first wave of postcolonial development, stalled during the 1997 economic crisis and then became the region's classic underachievers. Both have incredible natural resource wealth but are hampered by ethnic conflicts, corruption, political instability and vast geography.

Historical Reads

» *Southeast Asia: An Introductory History* (Milton Osborne)

» *In Search of Southeast Asia: A Modern History* (David P Chandler, et al)

» *Southeast Asia: Past and Present* (DR SarDesai)

1999

Timor-Leste votes for independence from Indonesian occupiers. An international peacekeeping force enters the country to prevent violence.

2004

An Indian Ocean earthquake with its epicentre near Sumatra (Indonesia) triggers a giant tsunami that destroys lives and communities in four Southeast Asian countries.

JOHN BORTHWICK / LONELY PLANET IMAGES ©

» Tsunami damage, 2004

2011

Southeast Asia weathers the global economic downturn with positive growth. Massive and historic flooding in Thailand injures its manufacturing sector and Myanmar moves toward democratic reform.

Religion

Religion is a fundamental component of the national and ethnic identities of the people in Southeast Asia. Buddhism and Islam are the region's dominant religions and both have absorbed many of the traditional animistic beliefs of spirit and ancestor worship that predated the region's conversions. Christianity is present in former colonies of Catholic European countries and among missionised ethnic minorities.

Buddhism

Buddhism is the majority religion in most of mainland Southeast Asia and because many of these countries are cultural cousins the religion has a specific regional identity. Outside of the Buddhist majority countries, there are also minority Buddhist populations, mainly ethnic Chinese, in the Philippines, Indonesia, Malaysia and Brunei.

Buddhist Monuments

» Temples of Angkor, Cambodia

» Borobudur, Indonesia

» Bagan, Myanmar

» Sukhothai Historical Park, Thailand

History & Fundamentals of Buddhism

Buddhism begins with the story of an Indian prince named Siddhartha Gautama in the 6th century BC, who left his life of privilege at the age of 29 on a quest to find the truth. After years of experimentation and ascetic practices, he meditated under a bodhi tree for 49 days, reaching final emancipation and breaking the cycle of birth, death and rebirth. He returned as Buddha, the 'Awakened One', to teach the 'middle way' between extremes. Passion, desire, love and hate are regarded as extremes, so Buddhism counsels that constant patience, detachment, and renouncing desire for worldly pleasures and expectations brings peace and liberation from suffering.

The ultimate end of Buddhism is nirvana, which literally means the 'blowing out' or extinction of all grasping and thus of all suffering *(dukkha)*. Effectively, nirvana is also an end to the cycle of rebirths (both moment-to-moment and life-to-life) that is existence.

Conversion to Buddhism

The adoption of Buddhism followed the same route into Southeast Asia as Hinduism – through traders and missionaries from India and Sri Lanka. The Khmer empire's adoption of Buddhism during King Jayavarman's reign in the 12th century marked the beginning of the religion's dominance. The subsequent Thai and Lao kings promoted the religion and were often viewed as divine religious figures as well as national leaders. Most of the monarchies did not survive into the modern era but the religion did with 90% or more of the population in each mainland Southeast Asian country identifying as Buddhist.

Thailand, Cambodia, Laos and Myanmar practise Theravada Buddhism (Teaching of the Elders), which travelled to the region via Sri Lanka. Vietnam adopted Mahayana Buddhism (Greater Vehicle), which took a northern route through Tibet, China and Japan.

One of the major theological differences between the two types of Buddhism lies in the outcome of a devout life. In Theravada, followers strive to obtain nirvana (release from the cycle of existence) over the course of many reincarnations, the final one of which is as a member of the monastic order. The emphasis is on self-enlightenment. But in Mahayana tradition, nirvana can be achieved within a single lifetime and emphasis is on helping other sentient beings become enlightened. With this emphasis on teaching, more attention is given to *bodhisattva* (one who has almost reached nirvana but renounces it in order to help others attain it) than Theravada.

This doctrinal difference and country of origin can be viewed in the two schools' places of worship. Theravada temples typically have one central hall of worship containing a central (Gautama) Buddha image. Hindu elements inherited from South Asia infuse the Theravada religious art and architecture. Mahayana temples conform more to inherited aesthetics from China. Temples contain a hall dedicated to the three Buddhas (including modern incarnations Amitabha and Medicine Buddha) and another hall to the three important bodhisattvas.

Animist beliefs were absorbed into Buddhism and comprise many religious rituals, from tending family altars and spirit houses to consulting monk astrologers.

Islam

Islam in Southeast Asia is characterised by the region's unique cultural, historical and philosophical landscape. For this reason, many Westerners notice a vast difference between the way Islam is practised in Southeast Asia compared with the way it is practised in other parts of the Muslim world (such as the Middle East).

History & Fundamentals of Islam

Islam is a monotheistic religion that originated in Arabia in the 7th century. The religion's primary prophet is Mohammed, who received and promoted the word of God (the *Qur'an,* the holy book of the faith). Islam means 'submission' in Arabic, and it is the duty of every Muslim to submit to Allah (God). This profession of faith is the first of the five pillars of Islam; the other four are to pray five times a day, give alms to the poor, fast during Ramadan and make the pilgrimage to Mecca.

Conversion to Islam

Trade played an important role in the introduction of the religion. Many Southeast Asian communities converted to Islam in order to join a brotherhood of merchants (Muslim Arabs, Indians and Chinese) and to escape the inflexible caste system of the Srivijaya kingdom, a Hindu-Buddhist empire that controlled the Malay peninsula and parts of Indonesia. It is believed that Muslim conversions and settlements first occurred in northern Sumatra's Aceh province and then spread to the port cities, including the important trade and cultural centre of Melaka (Malaysia). Starting around the 12th century, Islam gained in popularity, spreading through Malaysia to southern Thailand, Indonesia and parts of the Philippines.

BUDDHA IMAGES

Buddha images are visual sermons. Elongated earlobes, no evidence of bone or muscle, arms that reach to the knees, a third eye: these non-humanlike elements express Buddha's divine nature. Periods within Buddha's life are also depicted in the figure's 'posture', or pose:

» **reclining** – exact moment of Buddha's enlightenment and death

» **sitting** – Buddha teaching or meditating; if the right hand is pointed towards the earth, Buddha is shown subduing the demons of desire; if the hands are folded in the lap, Buddha is turning the wheel of law

» **standing** – Buddha bestowing blessings or taming evil forces

» **walking** – Buddha after his return to earth from heaven

THE FACE OF MODERN ISLAM

Just going by the numbers, modern Islam is a lot more Asian than Arab. In fact only 15% of the world's Muslims are Arab, while the majority are South and Southeast Asians. If the media were looking for a model citizen, they could choose Indonesia, which has the largest population of Muslims in the world. It is a devout country and sends the largest national delegation of pilgrims to Mecca every year. But it is also a multinational, multi-ethnic and multireligious democratic country – more like Turkey than Saudi Arabia.

The mystical traditions of Sufism are often credited for this widespread adoption of Islam. The Sufis were itinerant holy men ('Suf' is an Arabic word for the 'coarse wool' worn by a religious ascetic) who were believed to have magic abilities and encouraged a personal expression of the religion instead of a strict orthodoxy and adherence to the law. Scholars believe that Sufis helped mould traditional beliefs and folk practices stemming from the region's Hindu-Buddhist past around an Islamic core instead of forcing local communities to abandon pre-Islamic practices. Chanting and drumming remain a component of Southeast Asia's Islamic prayer tradition, shadow puppetry adopted Arabic and Islamic stories as well as the original Hindu myths, the ideas of the annihilation of the ego and of nirvana were tweaked to fit Islamic theology. Women were never cloistered and retained their traditional roles outside the home. In the past, the older generation did not wear headscarves but the younger generation has adopted the practice, much to the concern of non-Muslim observers who fear an increased regional fundamentalism.

Anwar Ibrahim, a Malaysian politician, is a prominent voice for a progressive Islam (pluralistic, democratic and pro-women).

Political Islam

The practice of Islam in Southeast Asia has been characterised by many of the same tensions that have emerged in Muslim communities around the world. Debates continue to rage about the interpretation of various passages in the *Qur'an*, and their implications for legal, social and financial institutions. As the region's colonial era was waning, the reform movement of Wahhabism became a popular political tool. Wahhabism promoted a literal interpretation of the *Qur'an* and intended to purge the religion of its pagan practices. It also emphasised the development of an Islamic political state.

Integral to an Islamic political state is sharia (Islamic law or God's law), which regulates criminal, civil and personal conduct. There are debates within the Muslim world as to the exact extents of sharia and how to overlap contradictory elements within a modern pluralistic state. A few indisputable components are the abstinence from pork products, drinking and gambling as well as modesty in dress, though the latter is also subject to local and generational interpretation.

Within Southeast Asia, only Malaysia maintains a parallel sharia justice system and only Muslim Malays are subject to its rules, though there are censorship rules that often cross over into mainstream film and print media. Indonesia does not have a national sharia system but the national government did allow the province of Aceh to enforce partial sharia under the terms of the 2005 peace deal.

Violent Muslim independence movements exist in southern Thailand and the southern Philippines. These conflicts are considered to be economic and ethnic struggles rather than jihad; typically the movements are in the poorest and most ethnically distinct parts of their respective countries, regions that have been overlooked or misunderstood by the majority government.

Religious Reads

» *Living Faith: Inside the Muslim World of Southeast Asia*, by Steve Raymer

» *Buddhism for Beginners*, by Thubten Chodron

PRINCELY TALES

The literary epic of the *Ramayana* serves as cultural fodder for traditional art, dance and shadow puppetry throughout the region. In this fantastic tale, Prince Rama (an incarnation of the Hindu god Vishnu) falls in love with beautiful Sita and wins her hand in marriage by completing the challenge of stringing a magic bow. Before the couple can live in peace, Rama is banished from his kingdom and his wife is kidnapped by Ravana. With the help of the monkey king, Hanuman, Sita is rescued, but a great battle ensues. Rama and his allies defeat Ravana and restore peace and goodness to the land.

Christianity

Catholicism was introduced to Vietnam by the French, to the Philippines by the Spanish and to Timor-Leste by the Portuguese. Parts of Indonesia are Christian, mainly Protestant, due to the efforts of Western missionary groups. In each of these converted groups there are remnants of the original animistic beliefs and an almost personal emphasis on preferred aspects of the liturgy or the ideology. The local adaptations can often be so pronounced that Westerners of the same faith might still observe the practice as foreign.

Hinduism

Hinduism ruled the spiritual lives of Southeast Asians more than 1500 years ago, and the great Hindu empires of Angkor and Srivijaya built grand monuments to their pantheon of gods. The primary representations of the multiple faces of the one omnipresent god are Brahma, the creator; Vishnu, the preserver; and Shiva, the destroyer or reproducer. All three gods are usually shown with four arms, but Brahma has the added advantage of four heads to represent his all-seeing presence. Although Buddhism and Islam have filtered across the continent, Hinduism has filtered through these mainstream religions and Buddhism regards the Hindi deities with respect. Also, the Hindu island of Bali is a spiritual anomaly in the region. Within the last 100 years, the influx of Indian labourers to Southeast Asia has bolstered the religion's followers.

Trouble Spots

Southeast Asia is a very different place now than it was a generation ago, when post-colonial instability led to civil strife, communist insurgencies and international wars. Today the region is stable enough to be fully integrated into the global marketplace and be the recipient of much overseas investment. There are, however, some isolated spots and ongoing issues of concern: militant religious extremism and ethno-religious separatist movements.

Islamic Militant Groups & Insurgencies

Militant Islamic groups operating in Southeast Asia include Jemaah Islamiyah (JI), which was formed in the 1990s with a mission to establish a pan-Islamic state in the region. The group turned to civilian terror tactics in the 2000s and allegedly orchestrated multiple bombing attacks on government and Western civilian targets in Indonesia and the Philippines during the first half of that decade.

Indonesian counter-terrorism police forces executed a law-enforcement campaign against suspected leaders and masterminds of the attacks, which resulted in 450 arrests followed by court trials – a process that has been lauded by observers for upholding judicial review. Thanks to increased police pressure and mass arrests, the mainstream faction of JI has turned away from Western targets and instead focused on domestic sectarian conflicts, mainly in Sulawesi, with the intentions of establishing a pure Islamic state within the locality, according to seized JI documents. Indonesian police continue to investigate JI activities and to recognise sectarian violence as a potential tool for militant activity.

There is also ongoing insurgency activity in isolated areas of Thailand and the Philippines, where it is believed that separatist groups unaligned with JI are openly hostile to the respective central governments. The violence is largely self-contained in the disputed territories.

Further Reading

- *Jihad in Paradise: Islam and Politics in Southeast Asia* (Mike Millard)
- *A Conspiracy of Silence: The Insurgency in Southern Thailand* (Zachary Abuza)
- *The Next Front: Southeast Asia and the Road to Global Peace with Islam* (Christopher Bond and Lewis M Simons)

Indonesia

Between 2002 and 2005, Indonesia suffered civilian-targeted, allegedly JI-linked bombings on an annual basis. The worst event occurred in October 2002 on the island of Bali, where suicide bombers targeted a crowded nightclub, killing 202 people and injuring 300, mostly Australian, tourists.

Since then, Indonesian security forces have arrested or killed hundreds of JI members. Abu Bakar Bashir, an Indonesian cleric and head of a religious school in Java, was arrested in 2004 and later convicted of conspiracy in connection with the 2002 Bali bombings. Bashir is recognised as the spiritual leader and founder of JI and enjoyed popular support among hardliners. Much to the disappointment of Australian and US governments, Bashir served only 18 months of his 2½-year prison term.

High-profile JI members Noordin Top and Dulmatin, who were linked to Bali and subsequent civilian attacks, were killed in police shoot-outs in 2009 and 2010 respectively. Top was a Malaysian financier and recruiter of suicide bombers who allegedly filled a unique and important role in orchestrating violent attacks.

Dulmatin was an explosives expert and senior member of JI on the USA's most wanted terrorist list. He had formed a splinter group that had set up a training camp in the jungles of Aceh province in northern Sumatra. It was raided by police in early 2010 and Dulmatin was later killed by police forces in south Jakarta. Abu Bakar Bashir was also linked to this training camp and was subsequently convicted and sentenced to 15 years in prison in 2011.

According to Zachary Abuza, an analyst and author on Southeast Asian terrorist groups, terror networks in the region will continue to function, especially with the ongoing unrest in Thailand's and the Philippines' Muslim-majority regions. But, he explained in an article titled 'Indonesian Counter-Terrorism: The Great Leap Forward', Indonesian counter-terrorism efforts have reduced terror activities without jeopardising democratic principles.

DIVERSITY

There are approximately 300 distinct ethnic groups in Indonesia.

Philippines

Insurgency groups active in the Philippines include the Moro Islamic Liberation Front (MILF) and Abu Sayyaf Group (ASG), both of which are Islamic separatist groups operating in the southern island of Mindanao and the Sulu archipelago.

ASG is often described as an insurgent group with gang-style tactics; each year it orchestrates multiple bombings, beheadings and ransom kidnappings on local Filipinos, military personnel and foreign aid workers and missionaries. It allegedly has ties to other global Islamic terror networks and was included on the US government's terrorism watch list. It is believed that JI fugitives, including Dulmatin, escaped to the Sulu archipelago for safe haven prior to returning to Indonesia.

MILF has more of a political nationalist agenda, often perpetrating sectarian or election-related violence. An unprecedented meeting between MILF leadership and the Filipino president considered the option of the Moro region gaining state status, equivalent to US states. But the group has many rogue factions that denounce attempts to negotiate with the national government for anything less than full autonomy. And as of 2011, talks had stalled.

Long considered defunct, the armed guerrilla faction of the Philippine's communist party, known as New People's Army (NPA), has resurfaced with a series of sophisticated attacks on a mining operation in eastern Mindanao, indicating that the group has grown in numbers. Its usual targets have been elected officials, members of the military and suspected spies (though Human Rights Watch charges that NPA-labelled spies are really civilians). Its renewed activity presents an additional roadblock to Mindanao security and potential autonomy status for MILF.

Thailand

Thailand's southernmost provinces – Narathiwat, Pattani, Yala and parts of Songkhla – have been plagued by a bloody insurgency since 2004. This Muslim-majority region was an independent sultanate until 1902 when it was annexed by Siam, but it has long remained ethnically distinct and resentful of the Buddhist-majority government.

Violent attacks include military and civilian targets, monks and teachers who are viewed as agents of cultural assimilation, and seemingly unrelated vendetta killings and beheadings. Sectarian violence within villages often forces out Buddhist residents.

Two army scandals discredited the Thai state in the region and spurred an uptick in violence: the Tak Bai and Krue Sae events of 2004. In the town of Tak Bai, Narathiwat province, the army arrested approximately 80 Muslim protesters and herded them into the cargo hold of a transport vehicle where they suffocated to death. In Pattani province, government troops stormed the Krue Sae mosque and gunned down more than 30 suspected insurgents who were armed with knives and a single gun. The army insists both incidents were accidental.

The insurgency is described by analysts as an ethno-nationalist struggle without a core or central administration. It is believed that insurgents operate independently as a patchwork of village-based cells. Most attacks are confined to the southernmost provinces and show no pattern of attacking Western tourists elsewhere in the country. In the past, there have been attacks in Hat Yai, the south's largest commercial centre, and border-town gambling and prostitution venues frequented by Malaysian tourists. There is also no evidence of cooperation or links with regional or global terror networks.

Political Demonstrations & Violence

Timor-Leste is approaching its first decade as an independent country with high hopes that the 2012 elections will be peaceful. Since its inception, the country has survived several destabilising events: the 2006 civil conflict and the 2008 assassination attempts on the president and prime minister. Aid agencies advise their staff to avoid any political gatherings or demonstrations because of the likelihood of potential violence. Dili has extreme poverty and high unemployment that is often exploited by rival political factions and opportunistic gangs.

Thailand has experienced ongoing political unrest since the 2006 coup. Though democracy was peacefully restored in 2011, there is still the likelihood of political demonstrations, military coups and perhaps even violence if former prime minister Thaksin Shinawatra returns to the country from exile. The country's coups tend to be peaceful but political demonstrations have had a history of violence, such as when the 2010 crackdown on pro-Thaksin supporters in central Bangkok resulted in 91 deaths and US$1.5 billion worth of arson damage. It is important to avoid involvement in political activity and demonstrations, no matter how much fun Thais are apparently having.

In 2006 multiple coordinated bombs exploded in public places leading up to Bangkok's New Year's Eve celebration. No one claimed responsibility and the perpetrators are still unknown today. Some military experts suspected southern insurgents, though others believe the violence was related to the country's 2006 coup and political instability.

Border Conflicts

Since 2008, there have been periodic border conflicts between Cambodian and Thai armies over control of the Angkor ruins of Prasat Preah Vihear (known as Khao Phra Wihan in Thailand). As a result, visa-less cross-border visits from Thailand to the temple have been suspended, though the ruins are accessible from Cambodia. Travellers should inquire about border tensions before making the arduous trip.

TRAVEL WARNING

We advise staying clear of the Muslim-majority provinces of southern Thailand and parts of the Philippines' Sulu archipelago and Mindanao.

Travel Advisory Websites

Travel advisories are often issued by government agencies to update nationals on the latest security situation in any given country. They often focus on the best-practice approach with conservative and overly cautious advice. It is helpful to be aware of official warnings but these shouldn't necessarily be a deterrent to travel.

Australia (www.dfat.gov.au/travel)
Canada (www.voyage.gc.ca/dest/index.asp)
New Zealand (www.mft.govt.nz/travel)
UK (www.fco.gov.uk/travel)
USA (www.travel.state.gov)

Survival Guide

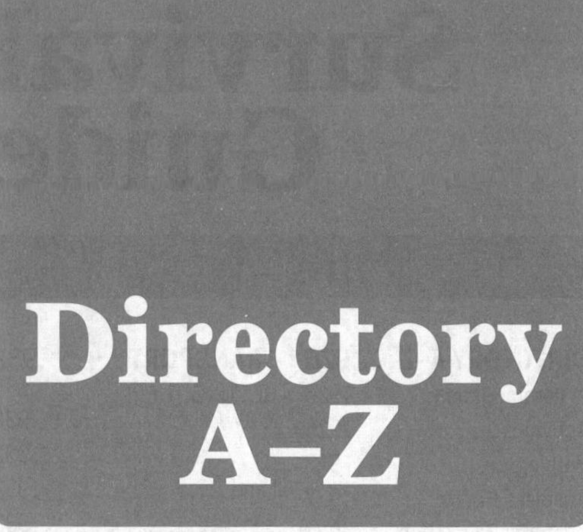

Directory A–Z

This chapter includes general information about Southeast Asia. Specific information for each country is listed in the individual country directories.

Accommodation

The accommodation listed in this guidebook occupies the low end of the price and amenities scale. Rooms typically have four walls, a bed and a fan (handy for keeping mosquitoes at bay). In the cheapest instances, the bathroom is shared. Most places geared to foreigners have Western-style toilets, but hotels that cater to locals usually have Asian squat toilets. Air-con, private bathrooms and well-sealed rooms cost more. Camping is not a widespread option.

Be a smart shopper when looking for a room. Always ask for the price first, then ask to see a room to inspect it for cleanliness, comfort and quiet. Don't feel obligated to take a room just because the place is mentioned in Lonely Planet. Sometimes the quality of a guesthouse plummets after gaining a mention in Lonely Planet, but this can be corrected by diligent travellers who exercise their own judgement.

Other accommodation tips for savvy travellers:

» If the price is too high, ask if they have anything cheaper. We list independent businesses that can alter their prices without notifying us.

» Unless it is the low season, most rates are non-negotiable.

» Once you've paid for a room, there is no chance of a refund, regardless of the size of the rat that scurried across the floor.

» Pay per day rather than upfront.

» Be courteous and pay first thing in the morning to keep staff from resorting to pushiness.

» Settle your bill the night before if you are catching an early bus out of town; most hotels and guesthouses do not staff their desks from midnight to 6am.

» Advance reservations (especially with advance deposits) are generally not necessary.

» If you do make a booking, don't rely on an agent who will charge a commission.

BOOK YOUR STAY ONLINE

For more reviews by Lonely Planet authors, check out http://hotels.lonelyplanet.com. You'll find independent reviews, as well as recommendations on the best places to stay. Best of all, you can book online.

Activities

Ocean sports and jungle trips are the major outdoor activities in Southeast Asia. For casual enthusiasts most tourist businesses hire gear. If you're not a beginner, consider bringing the required gear from home, as equipment here can be substandard.

Diving & Snorkelling

Southeast Asia is a diving and snorkelling paradise with inexpensive dive certificate training and a myriad of undersea environments. Thailand, Malaysia, Indonesia and the Philippines are all famous dive destinations.

Diving and snorkelling put unique pressures on the natural environment. Select reputable and environmentally conscious operators, and see the Responsible Diving boxed text (p39) for additional tips.

Trekking

Trekking in Southeast Asia includes hikes through a diminutive offshoot of the Himalayan range, into soggy rainforests and around smouldering volcanoes. Trekking in Southeast Asia requires a guide, as trails aren't well marked, transport to the trail-head is difficult to arrange, and foreigners are unfamiliar with the region's climate and microclimates. Hiring a guide also provides income for local villagers who regard the natural areas as their own backyards. You should also be aware of local laws, regulations and etiquette about wildlife and the environment.

Be prepared for a trek with proper clothing: long pants, adequate hiking shoes and leech socks (during and after the rainy season). Bring along rain gear (for yourself and your pack) even if the skies are clear. Drink lots of water and pace yourself, as the humidity can make even minimal exercise feel demanding.

Watersports

Surfing and kitesurfing are big draws in Southeast Asia. Indonesia is the region's surfing capital and Vietnam and Thailand have consistent winds for seasonal kitesurfing.

Bathing

In remote corners or basic accommodation, you'll meet the Southeast Asian version of a shower: a large basin that holds water for bathing. Water should be scooped out of the basin with a smaller bowl and poured over the body. Resist the urge to climb in like a bathtub or avoid washing directly over the basin, as this is your source for clean water.

Modern facilities might have a cold-water shower that is a star-rated environmental choice, but it can be difficult to adequately rinse off soap and shampoo. Consider travelling with an easy-to-rinse, biodegradable soap.

More expensive accommodation, large cities and colder regions will offer hot-water showers, usually point-of-use heaters, for an extra charge.

Many rural people bathe in rivers or streams. If you choose to do the same, be aware that public nudity is not acceptable. Do as the locals do and bathe while wearing a sarong.

Business Hours

In the Buddhist countries of Southeast Asia, businesses are typically open seven days a week. In the Muslim countries some businesses close during Friday afternoon prayers. Refer to Business Hours in the individual country directories for details.

Customs Regulations

Customs regulations vary little around the region. Drugs and arms are strictly prohibited – death or a lengthy stay in prison are common sentences. Pornography is also a no-no. Check the Customs sections in the directories of the country chapters for further details.

Discount Cards

The International Student Identity Card (ISIC) is moderately useful in Southeast Asia, with limited success in gaining the holder discounts. Some domestic and international airlines provide discounts to ISIC cardholders, but the cards carry little bargaining power because knock-offs are so readily available.

Discrimination

Skin colour may be a factor in Southeast Asia. White foreigners stand out in a crowd. Children will often point, prices may double and a handful of presumptions may precede your arrival. In general, these will seem either minor nuisances or exotic elements of travel. If you are a Westerner of Asian descent, most Southeast Asians will assume that you are a local until the language barrier proves otherwise. With the colour barrier removed, many Westerners with Asian heritage are treated like family and sometimes get charged local prices. Many Asians might mistake people of African heritage with fairly light complexions for locals or at least distant cousins. People with darker complexions will be regarded to be as foreign as white visitors, but may also be saddled with the extra baggage of Africa's perceived inferior status in the global hierarchy. Mixed Asian and foreign couples may attract some disapproval, especially in Thailand where the existence of a large sex-tourism industry can suggest that the Asian partner is a prostitute.

See also p928 for information for gay and lesbian travellers, and p931 for tips for female travellers.

Driving Licences

Parts of Southeast Asia, including Malaysia, Indonesia and Thailand, are good spots for exploring by car and motorcycle. If you are planning to do any driving, get an International Driving Permit (IDP) from your local automobile association before you leave your home country; IDPs are inexpensive and valid for one year.

Electricity

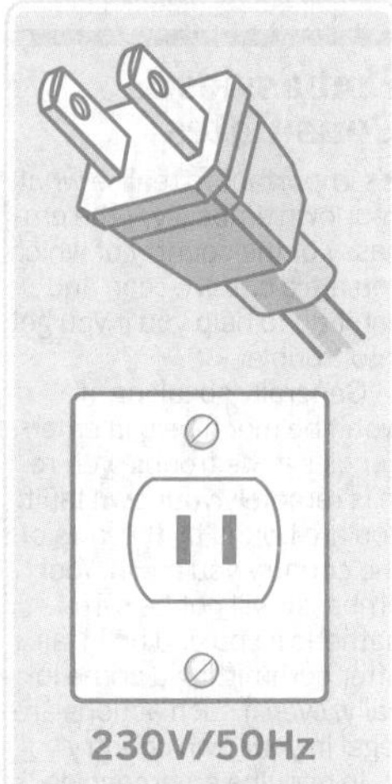

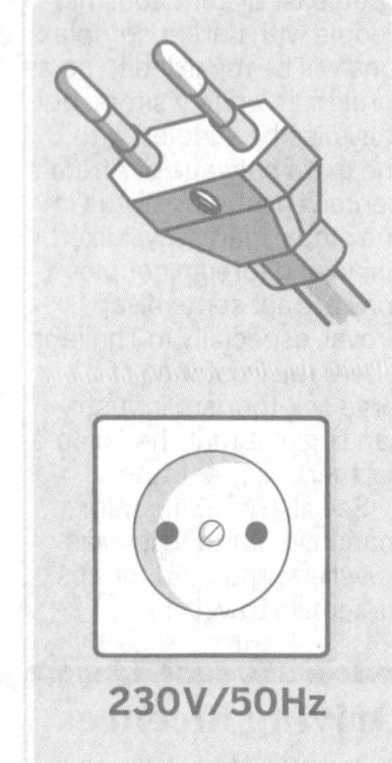

Most countries work on a voltage of 220V to 240V at 50Hz (cycles); note that 240V appliances will happily run on 220V. You should be able to pick up adaptors in electrical shops in most Southeast Asian cities. The plugs shown here are two of the more common types you'll encounter, but note that regional differences do exist. See the individual country chapters for details.

Embassies & Consulates

It's important to realise what your own embassy – the embassy of the country of which you are a citizen – can and can't do to help you if you get into trouble.

Generally speaking, it won't be much help in emergencies if the trouble you're in is remotely your own fault. You are bound by the laws of the country you are in. Your embassy will not be sympathetic if you end up in jail after committing a crime locally, even if such actions are legal in your own country.

In genuine emergencies you might get some assistance if other channels have been exhausted. For example, if you need to get home urgently, a free ticket home is exceedingly unlikely – the embassy would expect you to have insurance. If you have all your money and documents stolen, it might assist with getting a new passport, but a loan for onward travel is out of the question.

Most travellers should have no need to contact their embassy while in Southeast Asia, although if you're travelling in unstable regions or going into unchartered territory, it may be worth letting your embassy know upon departure and return. In this way valuable time, effort and money won't be wasted looking for you while you're relaxing on a beach somewhere.

For details on embassies in Southeast Asia see Embassies & Consulates in the individual country directories.

Gay & Lesbian Travellers

Southeast Asia could easily be ranked as one of the most progressive regions regarding homosexuality outside the Western world. In general most urban centres have gay communities, and attitudes towards same-sex relationships are tolerant, though travellers should still mind the region-wide prescription of refraining from public displays of affection.

Utopia Asian Gay & Lesbian Resources (www.utopia-asia.com) has an excellent profile of each country's record on acceptance, as well as short reviews on gay nightspots and handy travel guides to the various Southeast Asian countries. For more details on gay and lesbian travel, see the specific country directories.

Insurance

A travel-insurance policy to cover theft, loss and medical problems is a necessity. There's a wide variety of policies available, so check the small print. For more information about the ins and outs of travel insurance, contact a travel agent or travel insurer.

Some policies specifically exclude 'dangerous activities', which can include scuba diving, motorcycling and even trekking. A locally acquired motorcycle licence is also not valid under some policies. Check that the policy covers ambulance rides, emergency flights home and, in the case of death, repatriation of a body.

Also see p940 for further information on health insurance, and for info on car and motorcycle insurance, p934.

Internet Access

In metropolitan areas, Southeast Asia is incredibly well wired, with internet cafes, fast connections, cheap prices, Skype headsets and even wi-fi access. Outside the big cities, things start to vary. Good internet connections are usually commensurate with a destination's road system: well-sealed highways usually mean speedy travel through the information superhighway as well.

Censorship of some sites is in effect across the region.

Legal Matters

Be sure to know the national laws so that you don't unwittingly commit a crime. In all of the Southeast Asian countries, using or trafficking drugs carries stiff punishments that are enforced even if you're a foreigner.

If you are a victim of a crime, contact the tourist police, if available; they are usually better trained to deal with foreigners and foreign languages than the regular police force.

Maps

Country-specific maps are usually sold in English bookstores in capital cities. Local tourist offices and guesthouses can also provide maps of smaller cities and towns.

Money

See Need to Know (p16) for advice on availability of ATMs and money exchange. See the individual country chapters for local currencies and check www.xe.com for current exchange rates.

Passports

To enter most countries your passport must be valid for at least six months from your date of entry, even if you're only staying for a few days. It's probably best to have at least a year left on your passport if you are heading off on a trip around Southeast Asia.

Testy border guards may refuse entry if your passport doesn't have enough blank pages available. Before leaving get more pages added to a valid passport (if this is a service offered by your home country). Once on the road, you can apply for a new passport in most major Southeast Asian cities.

Photography

For those travelling with a digital camera, most internet cafes in well-developed areas let customers transfer images from the camera to an online email account or storage site. Flash memory is also widely available and most internet cafes can burn shots on to a DVD. Before leaving home, determine whether your battery charger will require a power adapter by visiting the website of the **World Electric Guide** (www.kropla.com/electric.htm).

The best places to buy camera equipment or have repairs done are Singapore, Bangkok or Kuala Lumpur. Be aware that the more equipment you travel with, the more vulnerable you are to theft.

You should always ask permission before taking a person's photograph. Many hill-tribe villagers seriously object to being photographed, or they may ask for money in exchange; if you want the photo, you should honour the price.

Post

Postal services are generally reliable across the region. There's always an element of risk in sending parcels home by sea, though as a rule they eventually reach their destination. If it's something of value, you're better off mailing home your dirty clothes to make room in your luggage for precious keepsakes. Don't send cash or valuables through government-run postal systems.

Poste restante is widely available throughout the region and is the best way of receiving mail. When getting people to write to you, ask them to leave plenty of time for mail to arrive and to print your name very clearly. Underlining the surname also helps.

Safe Travel

Drugs

The risks associated with recreational drug use and distribution are serious even in places with illicit reputations; just down the road from Kuta Beach in Bali is a jail where travellers are enjoying the tropical climate for much longer than they had intended. In Indonesia you can be jailed because your travel companions had dope and you didn't report them. A spell in a Thai prison can be very grim; in Malaysia and Singapore, possession of certain quantities of dope can lead to hanging. With heightened airport security, customs officials are zealous in their screening of both luggage and passengers.

The death penalty, prison sentences and huge fines are given as liberally to foreigners as to locals; no one has evaded punishment because of ignorance of local laws. In Indonesia in 2005, nine Australians (dubbed the 'Bali Nine') were arrested on charges of heroin possession: seven received life sentences and two were sentenced to death by firing squad.

Recreational drug use is often viewed in the same league as drug trafficking and can result in prison terms. In Thailand, sometimes the drug dealers are in cahoots with the police and use a drug transaction as an opportunity to extract a huge bribe. You also never know what you're really getting. In Cambodia, what is sold as methamphetamine is often a home-made concoction of cheap and toxic chemicals and what is sold as cocaine is heavy-duty heroin that is easily consumed in overdose levels.

Scams & Rip-offs

Every year we get letters and emails from travellers reporting that they've been scammed in Southeast Asia. In most cases, the scams are petty rip-offs, in which a naive traveller pays too much for a ride to the bus station, to exchange money, to buy souvenirs etc. Rip-offs are in full force at border crossings, popular tourist attractions, bus and rail stations and wherever travellers might get confused. See Dangers & Annoyances in the country chapters for how to avoid local scams.

Here are some additional tips for avoiding scams:

» Before arriving in a town check the destination's Getting Around section to figure out how much a ride from the bus station should cost.

» Be suspicious of super-cheap, inclusive transport

packages, which often include extra commission-generating fees.

» Don't accept invitations to play cards or go shopping with a friendly stranger; this is a prelude to a well-rehearsed and expensive scam.

Theft & Violence

Theft in Southeast Asia is usually by stealth rather than by force. Violent theft is rare but usually occurs late at night and after the victim has been drinking. Either way, with just a few sensible precautions, most travellers make their way across the region without incident.

Here are some tips for keeping you and your stuff safe:

» Keep your money and valuables in a money belt worn underneath your clothes.

» Be alert to the presence of snatch thieves, who will whisk a camera or a bag off your shoulder.

» Don't store valuables in easily accessible places such as backpack pockets or packs that are stored in the luggage compartment of buses.

» Don't put valuables in the baskets of a motorcycle or bicycle.

» Be especially careful about belongings when sleeping in dorm rooms.

» Be careful walking alone at night and don't fall asleep in taxis.

» When alcohol is involved, avoid getting into heated exchanges with the locals. What might seem like harmless verbal sparring to you might be regarded as injurious by the local and might provoke extreme retribution.

» Always be diplomatically suspicious of over-friendly locals.

Unexploded Ordnance & Landmines

The legacy of war lingers on in Cambodia, Laos and Vietnam. Laos suffers the fate of being the most heavily bombed country per capita in the world, while all three countries were on the receiving end of more bombs than were dropped by all sides during WWII. There are still many undetonated bombs and explosives out there, so be careful walking off the trail in areas near the Laos–Vietnam border or around the Demilitarised Zone (DMZ). Cambodia suffers the additional affliction of landmines, some four to six million of them according to surveys. Many of these are located in border areas with Thailand in the north and west of the country, but it pays to stick to marked paths anywhere in Cambodia.

Toilets

As tourism continues to grow in the region, Western-style sit-down toilets are increasingly common. However, in rural areas it is another story and squat toilets are widespread.

If you encounter a squat, here's what you should do. Straddle the two footpads and face the door. To flush use the plastic bowl to scoop water out of the adjacent basin and pour into the toilet bowl. Some places supply a small pack of toilet paper available for purchase at the entrance; otherwise bring your own stash or wipe the old-fashioned way with water.

Even in places where sit-down toilets are installed, the septic system may not be designed to take toilet paper. In such cases there will be a waste basket where you're supposed to place used toilet paper and feminine hygiene products.

Tourist Information

Most of the Southeast Asian countries have government-funded tourist offices of varying usefulness. Better information is sometimes available through guesthouses and fellow travellers. See Tourist Information in the individual country chapters for contact information.

Travellers with Disabilities

Travellers with serious disabilities will likely find Southeast Asia to be a challenging place to travel. Even the more modern cities are very difficult to navigate for mobility- or vision-impaired people. Generally speaking, the various countries' infrastructure is often inadequate for those with disabilities.

International organisations that can provide information on mobility-impaired travel include the following:

Mobility International USA (www.miusa.org)

Royal Association for Disability & Rehabilitation (Radar; www.radar.org.uk)

Society for Accessible Travel & Hospitality (SATH; www.sath.org)

Visas

Before arriving in a country (either by air, land or sea), refer to the Visas section in the individual country directories to determine if you need to pre-arrange a visa or if one is available for your nationality upon arrival. Here are some additional visa tips:

» Plan your trip around the length of stay mandated by the visa.

» If you plan on staying longer than the typical allotment, apply for a longer visa from the embassy in your home country or from an embassy in a neighbouring country or investigate the ease of extending a visa within the country.

» Stock up on passport photos, as you'll probably need at least two pictures each time you apply for a visa.

» Dress smartly when you're visiting embassies, consulates and borders; Southeast Asia appreciates appearance.

Women Travellers

While travel in Southeast Asia for women is generally safe, solo women should exercise caution when travelling at night or returning home by themselves from a bar. While physical assault is rare, local men often consider foreign women to be exempt from their own society's rules of conduct. Be especially careful in party towns, especially the Thai islands and Bali, where drunken abandon may be exploited by opportunists.

Travelling in Muslim areas introduces some challenges for women. In conservative Muslim areas, local women rarely go out unaccompanied and are usually modestly dressed. Foreign women doing the exact opposite are observed first as strange and secondly as searching for a local boyfriend. While the region is very friendly, be careful about teaming up with young men who may or may not respect certain boundaries.

Keep in mind that modesty in dress is culturally important right across Southeast Asia. Covering past the shoulders and above the knees helps define you as off limits, while spaghetti-strap singlets inadvertently send the message that you're sexually available.

Finally, you can reduce hassles by travelling with other backpackers. This doesn't necessarily mean bringing a friend from home; you can often pair up with other travellers you meet on the way.

Work

Teaching English is the easiest way to support yourself in Southeast Asia. For short-term gigs, Bangkok, Ho Chi Minh City (Saigon) and Jakarta have language schools and a high turnover of staff. In the Philippines, English speakers are often needed as language trainers for call centres. In Indonesia and Thailand you may be able to find some dive-school work.

Payaway (www.payaway.co.uk) provides a handy online list of language schools and volunteer groups looking for recruits for its Southeast Asian programs.

Transitions Abroad (www.transitionsabroad.com) is a web portal that covers all aspects of overseas life, including landing a job in a variety of fields.

Transport

This chapter gives an overview of the transport options for getting to and around Southeast Asia. For country-specific information, see Getting There & Away and Getting Around sections in each country chapter. For information about crossing international borders within Southeast Asia, see p935.

GETTING THERE & AWAY

Step one is to get to Southeast Asia, and flying is the easiest option. The only overland possibilities from outside the region are from Papua New Guinea into Indonesia – an unlikely scenario – and from China into Vietnam or Laos. Flights, tours and rail tickets can be booked online at lonelyplanet.com/bookings.

Air

The major Asian gateways for cheap flights are Bangkok, Kuala Lumpur, Singapore, Denpasar (Bali) and Manila. Thanks to the proliferation of budget carriers, there are often cheap fares between China and Southeast Asian cities or beach resorts. When pricing flights, compare the cost of flying to an East Asian city, such as Hong Kong, from your home country, and then connecting to a budget carrier to the cost of flying directly to your destination on a long-haul airline. Fares on budget carriers don't usually factor into online search engines and their websites can be awkward to use, but if you have more time than money, may the budget forces be with you.

Also be flexible with travel dates and know when to buy a ticket. Trips longer than two weeks tend to be more expensive. Buying a ticket too early or too late before your departure will affect the price as well. The ticket-purchasing sweet spot is 21 to 15 days before departure. When researching airline fares, dump your computer's cookies, which track your online activity and can sometimes result in a higher fare upon subsequent searches.

The following online resources can help you research bargain airfares:

Attitude Travel (www.attitudetravel.com) A guide to low-cost carriers in Asia, including airlines and destinations.

Lonely Planet (www.lonelyplanet.com) Click on Travel Services to research multi-destination trips.

Round-The-World & Circle Asia Tickets

If Asia is one of many stops on a worldwide tour, consider a round-the world (RTW) ticket, which allows a certain number of stops within a set time period as long as you don't backtrack; for information, talk to a travel agent.

Circle Asia passes are offered by various airline alliances for a circular route originating in the USA, Europe or Australia and travelling to certain destinations in Asia. Use the Air Passes section of www.airtimetable.com to profile the promotional Circle fares offered by several airlines.

Before committing, check the fares offered by the budget regional carriers to see if the Circle pass provides enough of a saving. Contact airlines or a travel agent for more information.

Land

The land borders between Southeast Asia and the rest of Asia include those between Myanmar and India and Bangladesh, and the Chinese border with Myanmar, Laos and Vietnam. Of these, it is possible to travel overland from China into Laos (see p348) and Vietnam (p834). There is also a boat service from Chiang Saen in Thailand to Jinghong in China (see p701).

Another international crossing is between Indonesia and Papua New Guinea, though this isn't a feasible international gateway.

Sea

Ocean approaches to Southeast Asia can be made aboard cargo ships plying routes around the world. Ridiculously expensive and hopelessly romantic, a trip aboard a cargo ship is the perfect chance for you to write that novel that never writes itself. Some freighter ships have space for a few non-crew members, who have their own rooms but eat meals with the crew. Prices vary depending on your departure point, but costs start at around US$150 a day plus additional fees.

GETTING AROUND

Air

Air travel can be a bargain within the region, especially from transit hubs such as Bangkok, Singapore and Kuala Lumpur. No-frills regional carriers have made travelling between capital cities cheaper than taking land transport in some cases. Air routes between Southeast Asian countries are listed in the Getting There & Away sections of each country chapter. Some airports in Southeast Asia charge a departure tax, so make sure you have a bit of local currency left. The following airlines often have affordable fares between cities and capitals:

Air Asia (www.airasia.com)

Cebu Pacific Air (www.cebupacificair.com)

Jetstar/ValueAir (www.jetstar.com)

Tiger Airways (www.tigerairways.com)

Air Passes

National airlines of Southeast Asian countries frequently run promotional deals from select Western cities or for regional travel. Airline alliances also offer regional air passes. You'll have to do a generic web search for 'air passes' to find the most up-to-date information, as monitoring sites aren't always current.

Bicycle

Touring Southeast Asia on a bicycle has long had many supporters. Long-distance cyclists typically start in Thailand and head south through Malaysia to Singapore. Road conditions are good enough for long-haul touring in most places, but mountain bikes are definitely recommended for forays off the beaten track.

Vietnam is a great place to travel by bicycle – you can take bikes on buses, and the entire coastal route is feasible. If flat-land cycling is not your style, then Indonesia might be the challenge you're looking for. Roads here are bad and inclines steep, but the Sumatran jungle is still deep and dark. In Laos and Cambodia, road conditions are improving and the traffic is still light.

Top-quality bicycles and components can be bought in major cities such as Bangkok, but fittings are hard to find. Bicycles can travel by air; check with the airline about charges and specifications.

Biking Asia with Mr Pumpy (www.mrpumpy.net) has route reports and country conditions in Southeast Asia.

Boat

Ferries and boats travel between Singapore and Indonesia, Malaysia and Indonesia, Thailand and Malaysia and the Philippines and Malaysia. You also have the option of crossing the Mekong River from Thailand to Laos and from Cambodia to Vietnam. Guesthouses or travel agents sell tickets and provide travellers with updated departure times. Check visa regulations at port cities; some don't issue visas on arrival.

Bus

In most cases, land borders are crossed via bus, which either travels straight through the two countries with a stop for border formalities or requires a change of buses at the appropriate border towns.

Bus travellers will enjoy a higher standard of luxury in Thailand, the Philippines and Malaysia, where roads are well paved, reliable schedules exist and, sometimes, snacks are distributed. Be aware that theft does occur on some long-distance buses, especially those heading south and north from Bangkok's Th Khao San; keep all valuables on your person, not in a stowed locked bag.

Local buses in Laos, Cambodia and Vietnam are like moving sardine cans, but that is part of their charm.

CLIMATE CHANGE & TRAVEL

Every form of transport that relies on carbon-based fuel generates CO_2, the main cause of human-induced climate change. Modern travel is dependent on aeroplanes which might use less fuel per kilometre per person than most cars but travel much greater distances. The altitude at which aircraft emit gases (including CO_2) and particles also contributes to their climate change impact. Many websites offer 'carbon calculators' that allow people to estimate the carbon emissions generated by their journey and, for those who wish to do so, to offset the impact of the greenhouse gases emitted with contributions to portfolios of climate-friendly initiatives throughout the world. Lonely Planet offsets the carbon footprint of all staff and author travel.

MOTORCYCLE TIP

Most Asians are so adept at riding motorcycles that they can balance the whole family on the front bumper or even take a quick nap as a passenger. Foreigners unaccustomed to motorcycles are not as graceful. If you're riding on the back of a motorcycle, remember to relax. Tall people should keep long legs tucked in as most drivers are used to shorter passengers. Women wearing skirts should collect loose material so it doesn't catch in the wheel or drive chain. On older motorcycles, watch out for the exposed exhaust pipe when riding and disembarking; it gets hot enough to barbecue exposed flesh.

Car & Motorcycle

What is the sound of freedom in Southeast Asia? The 'put-put' noise of a motorcycle. For visitors, motorcycles are convenient for getting around the beaches or touring the countryside. Car hire is also available in most countries and is handy for local sightseeing or long-haul trips. You could hit Thailand and Malaysia by car pretty easily, enjoying well-signposted, well-paved roads. Road conditions in Laos and Cambodia vary, although sealed roads are becoming the norm. Indonesia and the Philippines have roads that vary between islands, but most are in need of repair. Vietnam's major highways are in relatively good health. See the individual countries for driving-license regulations.

Hire

Western car-hire chains camp out at Southeast Asian airports, capitals and major tourist destinations. On many tourist islands, guesthouses and locals will hire motorcycles and cars for an affordable rate, but these fleets are often poorly maintained.

Insurance

Get insurance with a motorcycle if at all possible. The more reputable motorcycle-hire places insure all their motorcycles; some will do it for an extra charge. Without insurance, you're responsible for anything that happens to the bike. To be absolutely clear about your liability, ask for a written estimate of the replacement cost for a similar bike – and take photos as a guarantee. Some agencies will accept only the replacement cost of a new motorcycle. Insurance for a hired car is also necessary. Be sure to ask the car-hire agent about liability and damage coverage.

Road Rules

Drive carefully and defensively; lives are lost at astounding rates on Southeast Asian highways. Remember, too, that smaller vehicles yield to bigger vehicles regardless of circumstances – on the road, might is right. The middle of the road is used as a passing lane, even in oncoming traffic. Your horn notifies other vehicles that you intend to pass.

Safety

Always check a machine thoroughly before you take it out. Look at the tyres for treads, check for oil leaks, test the brakes. You may be held liable for any problems that weren't duly noted before your departure.

Wear protective clothing and a helmet on motorcycles; long pants, long-sleeved shirts and shoes are recommended as sun protection and as a second skin if you fall. If your helmet doesn't have a visor, wear goggles or glasses to keep bugs, dust and other debris out of your eyes.

Hitching

Hitching is never entirely safe and is not recommended. Travellers who hitch should understand that they are taking a small but potentially serious risk. People who do choose to hitch will be safer if they travel in pairs and let someone know where they are planning to go.

Local Transport

Because personal ownership of cars in Southeast Asia is limited, local transport within towns is a roaring business. For the right price, drivers will haul you from the bus station to town, around town, around the corner, or around in circles. The bicycle rickshaw still survives in the region, assuming such aliases as *săhmlór* in Thailand and *cyclo* in Vietnam. Anything motorised is often modified to carry passengers – from Thailand's obnoxious three-wheeled chariot, the túk-túk, to the Philippines' altered US Army jeeps. In large cities, extensive bus systems either travel on fixed routes or do informal loops around the city, picking up passengers on the way. Bangkok, Kuala Lumpur and Singapore boast state-of-the-art light-rail systems that make zipping around town feel like time travel.

Train

The *International Express* train runs from Bangkok all the way through the Malay peninsula, ending its journey in Singapore. Trains also serve Nong Khai, on the Thailand–Cambodia border, and Aranya Prathet, on the Thailand–Laos border. Thailand and Malaysia have the most extensive rail systems, although trains rarely run on time.

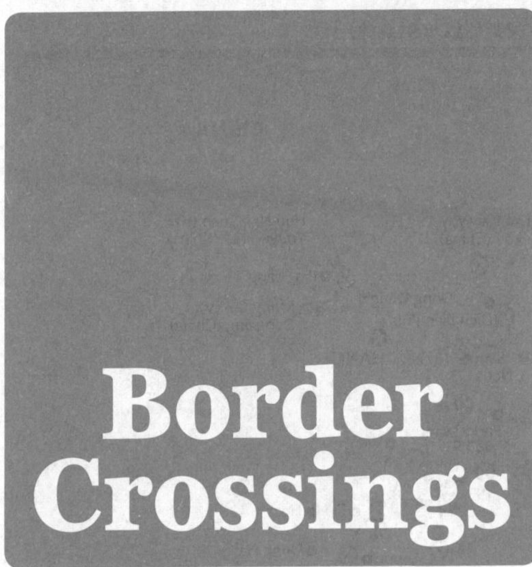

Border Crossings

It is easier than ever to overland (or over water) between neighbouring Southeast Asian countries.

There are some well-trodden routes, especially within mainland Southeast Asia, that have straightforward public transport options and plenty of migrating travellers to share the road with.

In some cases overland travel is the cheapest, though not always the fastest, route between major destinations. However with the increasing affordability of flights, sometimes an airfare is equivalent to a long-distance bus ticket.

Flights have also replaced boat crossings as the primary means of connecting from Malaysia to the Indonesian island of Sumatra, though a few intrepid tourists still follow this old-fashioned path.

Though border relations between most countries have normalised, there is still the possibility of closures, regulation changes and minor scams.

Do be aware that some border crossings are not recommended due to political violence and instability in the region. These areas to avoid include the west coast of Thailand crossing to Malaysia (Sungai Kolok to Rantau Panjang) as well as boat crossings from Malaysian Borneo to the southern Philippines' port of Zamboanga.

Ask around or check the Lonely Planet Thorn Tree (www.lonelyplanet.com/thorntree) for border-crossing trip reports or refer to the border crossing boxes in the country chapters of this book for further information and transport recommendations.

Other considerations when planning the border crossings for your trip include the following:

» Know which borders offer visas on arrival and which ones require prearranged visas.

» When arriving at borders that do issue visas upon arrival, be prepared with two passport photos and enough cash in the required currency to pay the visa fee and complete border formalities.

» Plan your trip so that you arrive at the border during opening hours to avoid being stranded overnight or needing to make last-minute arrangements in a small border town.

» There are few legal money-changing facilities at some border crossings (even at crossings that do not seem remote, such as Cambodia's Poipet crossing with Thailand) so be sure to have some small-denomination US dollars handy.

» The black-market money changers are an option for local currencies, but remember that black marketeers have a well-deserved reputation for short-changing customers and offering unfavourable exchange rates.

» Be aware of border-crossing scams, like dodgy transport schemes and pesky runner boys.

» At some border crossings staff may request or demand extra processing fees, like overtime surcharges or other nonstandard charges, in addition to the legitimate visa-issuing fees. Resisting might result in some savings but it will not make the crossing speedier or smoother. Whatever approach you take, just remember to stay calm and don't get angry.

» Some of the immigration police at land border crossings, especially at the Cambodia, Laos and Vietnam borders, have a reputation for petty extortion.

The following map illustrates the various border crossings within Southeast Asia, the transit towns where you'll need to arrange travel to or from a border and the popular tourist destinations that these crossings link to.

Each border crossing is assigned a map number that is shown on the accompanying table (p938). Refer to the border crossings boxes in the individual country chapters for more information about border formalities and transport options to and from the border, and see the Directory within each country chapter for information about specific visa requirements for that country.

Southeast Asian Border Crossings

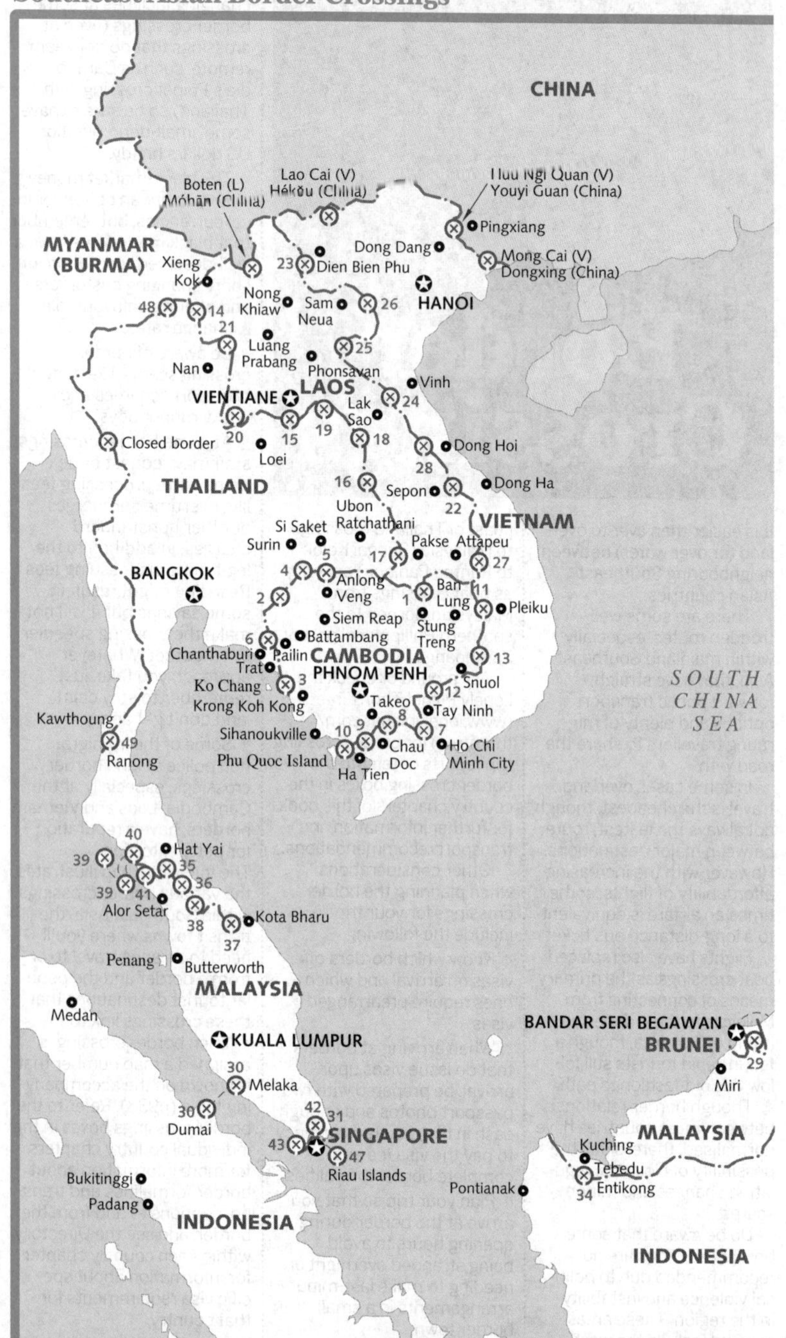

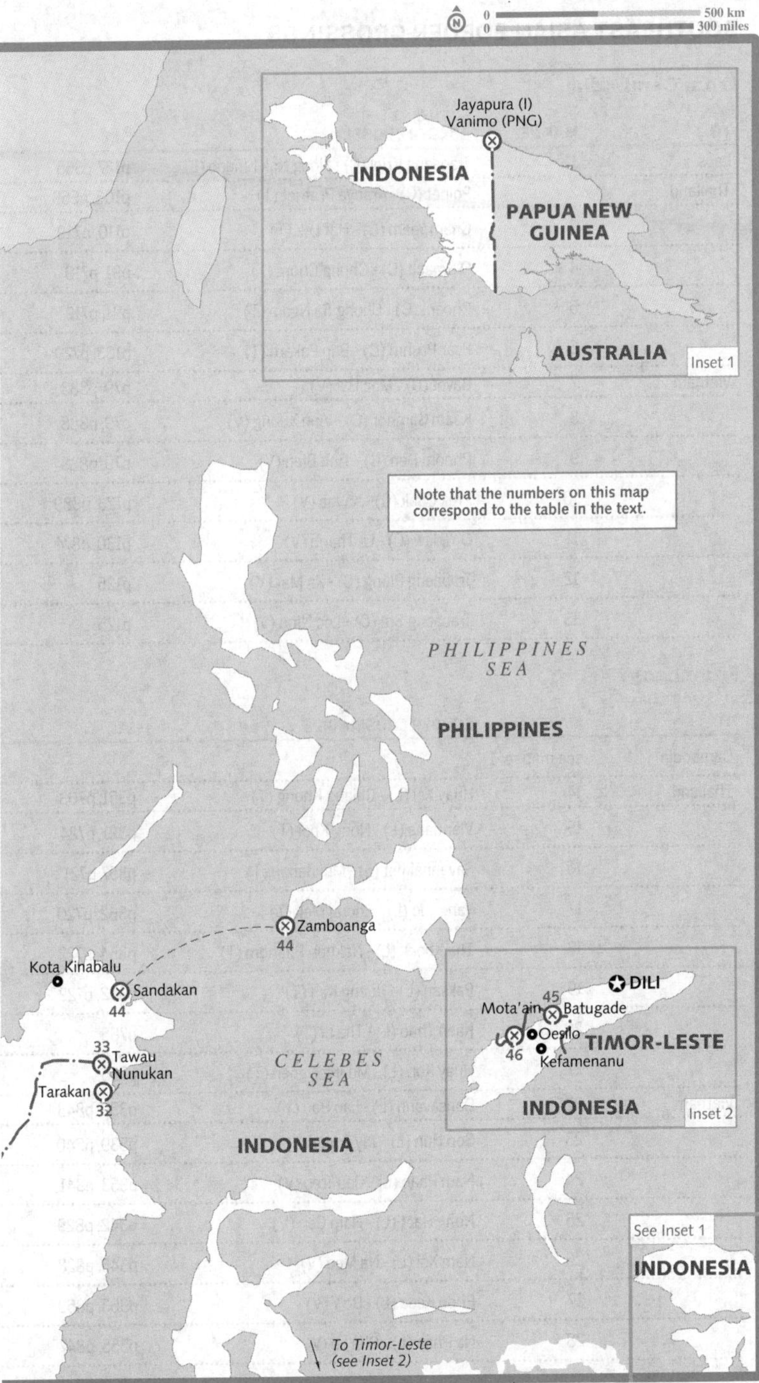
0 500 km
0 300 miles
Jayapura (I)
Vanimo (PNG)
INDONESIA
PAPUA NEW GUINEA
AUSTRALIA
Inset 1
Note that the numbers on this map correspond to the table in the text.
PHILIPPINES SEA
PHILIPPINES
Zamboanga
44
Kota Kinabalu
Sandakan
44
33
Tawau
Nunukan
Tarakan
32
CELEBES SEA
INDONESIA
DILI
45
Mota'ain
Batugade
Oesilo
46
Kefamenanu
TIMOR-LESTE
INDONESIA
Inset 2
See Inset 1
INDONESIA
To Timor-Leste (see Inset 2)

SOUTHEAST ASIAN BORDER CROSSINGS

From Cambodia

TO	MAP REF	BORDER CROSSING	SEE
Laos	1	Trapeang Kriel (C) - Nong Nok Khiene (L)	p127, p365
Thailand	2	Poipet (C) - Aranya Prathet (T)	p105, p669
	3	Cham Yeam (C) - Hat Lek (T)	p110, p729
	4	O Smach (C) - Chong Chom (T)	p91, p719
	5	Choam (C) - Chong Sa Ngam (T)	p91, p719
	6	Psar Pruhm (C) - Ban Pakard (T)	p103, p729
Vietnam	7	Bavet (C) - Moc Bai (V)	p79, p883
	8	Kaam Samnor (C) - Vinh Xuong (V)	p79, p888
	9	Phnom Den (C) - Tinh Bien (V)	p79, p888
	10	Prek Chak (C) - Xa Xia (V)	p123, p889
	11	O Yadaw (C) - Le Thanh (V)	p130, p874
	12	Trapaeng Plong (C) - Xa Mat (V)	p125
	13	Trapaeng Sre (C) - Loc Ninh (V)	p125

From Laos

TO	MAP REF	BORDER CROSSINGS	SEE
Cambodia	see map ref 1		
Thailand	14	Huay Xai (L) - Chiang Khong (T)	p351, p703
	15	Vientiane (L) - Nong Khai (T)	p321, p724
	16	Savannakhet (L) - Mukdahan (T)	p357, p721
	17	Vang Tao (L) - Chong Mek (T)	p362, p720
	18	Tha Khaek (L) - Nakhon Phanom (T)	p354, p722
	19	Paksan (L) - Bueng Kan (T)	p352, p722
	20	Kaen Thao (L) - Tha Li (T)	p785
	21	Huay Kon (L) - Muang Ngoen (T)	p785
Vietnam	22	Dansavanh (L) - Lao Bao (V)	p359, p848
	23	Sop Hun (L) - Tay Trang (V)	p339, p840
	24	Nam Phao (L) - Cau Treo (V)	p353, p841
	25	Nong Haet (L) - Nam Can (V)	p342, p829
	26	Nam Xoi (L) - Na Meo (V)	p345, p828
	27	Phou Keua (L) - Bo Y (V)	p363, p859
	28	Na Phao (L) - Cha Lo (V)	p355, p847

From Malaysia

TO	MAP REF	BORDER CROSSINGS	SEE
Brunei	29	Multiple land & sea routes	p61, p470
Indonesia	30	Melaka (M) - Dumai (I)	p307, p401
	31	Johor Bahru (M) - Riau Islands (I)	p307, p417
	32	Tawau (M) - Tarakan (I)	p447
	33	Tawau (M) - Nunukan (I)	p447
	34	Tebedu (M) - Entikong (I)	p456
Thailand	35	Padang Besar (M) - Kangar (T)	p413, p751
	36	Bukit Kayu Hitam (M) - Sadao (T)	p413, p751
	37	Rantau Panjang (M) - Sungai Kolok	p428
	38	Keroh (M) - Betong (T)	p480
	39	Pulau Langkawi (M) - Ko Lipe (T)	p414, p771
	40	Pulau Langkawi (M) - Satun (T)	p414, p770
	41	Kuala Perlis (M) - Satun (T)	p413, p770
Singapore	42	Johor Bahru (M) - Singapore	p416, p642
	43	Tanjung Kupang (M) - Singapore	p642
Philippines	44	Sandakan (M) - Zamboanga (P)	p444, p596

From Indonesia

TO	MAP REF	BORDER CROSSINGS	SEE
Malaysia	see map refs 30–34		
Timor-Leste	45	Batugade (TL) - Mota'ain (I)	p798, p241
	46	Oesilo (TL) - Kefamanu (I)	p806
Singapore	47	Singapore - Riau Islands (I)	p642, p307

From Thailand

TO	MAP REF	BORDER CROSSINGS	SEE
Cambodia	see map refs 2–6		
Laos	see map refs 14–21		
Malaysia	see map refs 35–41		
Myanmar	48	Tachileik (My) - Mae Sai (T)	p511, p701
	49	Kawthoung (My) - Ranong (T)	p505, p753

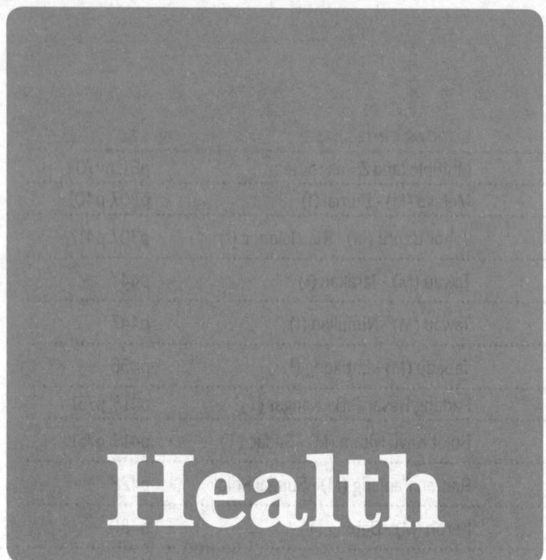

Health

Health issues and the quality of medical facilities vary enormously depending on where you travel in Southeast Asia.

Travellers tend to worry about contracting infectious diseases when in the tropics, but infections are a rare cause of serious illness or death in travellers. Accidental injury (ie traffic accidents) and pre-existing medical conditions account for most life-threatening problems. Becoming ill in some way, however, is relatively common. Fortunately, most common illnesses can be either prevented with some common-sense behaviour or treated easily with a well-stocked traveller's medical kit.

The following advice is a general guide and does not replace the advice of a doctor trained in travel medicine.

BEFORE YOU GO

Pack medications in their original, clearly labelled containers. A signed, dated letter from your physician describing your medical conditions and medications, including generic names, is a good idea. If carrying syringes or needles, have a physician's letter stating their medical necessity. If you have a heart condition, bring a copy of your ECG.

If you take any regular medication, bring a double supply in case of loss or theft. In most Southeast Asian countries, excluding Singapore, you can buy many medications over the counter, but it can be difficult to find some of the newer drugs, particularly the latest antidepressants, blood-pressure medications and contraceptive pills.

Insurance

Even if you are fit and healthy, don't travel without health insurance – accidents do happen. Declare any existing medical conditions. You may require extra cover for adventure activities such as rock climbing. If your health insurance doesn't cover you for medical expenses abroad, consider getting extra insurance that includes emergency evacuation.

Find out in advance if your insurance plan will make payments directly to providers or reimburse you later for overseas health expenditures. (In many countries doctors expect payment in cash.) If you have to claim later, make sure you keep all documentation. Some policies ask you to call (reverse charges) a centre in your home country, where an immediate assessment of your problem is made.

Divers should ensure their insurance covers them for decompression illness – get specialised dive insurance through an organisation such as **Divers Alert Network** (DAN; www.danseap.org). Have a dive medical before you leave your home country; there are certain medical conditions that are incompatible with diving, and economic considerations may override health considerations for some dive operators in Southeast Asia.

Medical Checklist

Recommended items for a personal medical kit:

- ☐ antibacterial cream, eg mupirocin
- ☐ antibiotic for skin infections, eg amoxicillin/clavulanate or cephalexin
- ☐ antibiotics for diarrhoea, such as norfloxacin or ciprofloxacin; azithromycin for bacterial diarrhoea; tinidazole for giardiasis or amoebic dysentery
- ☐ antifungal cream, eg clotrimazole
- ☐ antihistamine, such as cetirizine for daytime and promethazine for night
- ☐ anti-inflammatory such as ibuprofen
- ☐ antiseptic, eg Betadine
- ☐ antispasmodic for stomach cramps, eg Buscopan
- ☐ contraceptives
- ☐ decongestant, eg pseudoephedrine
- ☐ DEET-based insect repellent
- ☐ diarrhoea treatment, including an oral rehydration solution (eg Gastrolyte),

diarrhoea 'stopper' (eg loperamide) and antinausea medication (eg prochlorperazine)

- ☐ first-aid items such as scissors, plasters, bandages, gauze, thermometer (but not one with mercury), sterile needles and syringes, safety pins and tweezers
- ☐ indigestion medication, eg Quick-Eze or Mylanta
- ☐ iodine tablets to purify water
- ☐ laxative, eg Coloxyl
- ☐ paracetamol
- ☐ permethrin to impregnate clothing and mosquito nets
- ☐ steroid cream for allergic or itchy rashes, eg 1% to 2% hydrocortisone
- ☐ sunscreen and hat
- ☐ throat lozenges
- ☐ thrush (vaginal yeast infection) treatment, eg Clotrimazole pessaries or Diflucan tablet
- ☐ Ural or equivalent if you're prone to urine infections
- ☐ Divers and surfers should seek specialised advice stocking medical kits for coral cuts and tropical ear infection treatments.

IN SOUTHEAST ASIA

Availability of Health Care

Most capital cities in Southeast Asia now have clinics that cater specifically to travellers and expats. These clinics are more expensive than local medical facilities but offer a superior standard of care. Additionally, they understand the local system and are aware of the safest local hospitals and best specialists. They can also liaise with insurance companies should you require evacuation. Recommended clinics are listed under Information in the destination sections of country chapters in this book.

It is difficult to find reliable medical care in rural areas. Your embassy and insurance company are good contacts.

Self-treatment may be appropriate if your problem is minor (eg traveller's diarrhoea), you are carrying the appropriate medication and you cannot attend a recommended clinic. If you think you may have a serious disease, especially malaria, travel to the nearest quality facility to receive attention.

The standard of care in Southeast Asia varies from country to country:

Brunei General care is reasonable. There is no local medical university, so expats and foreign-trained locals run the health-care system. Serious or complex cases are better managed in Singapore.

Cambodia There are international clinics in Phnom Penh and Siem Reap and an NGO-run surgical hospital in Battambang that provide primary care and emergency stabilisation. Elsewhere, government hospitals should be avoided. For more serious conditions, including dengue fever, it is advisable to be evacuated to Bangkok.

East Timor No private clinics. The government hospital is basic and should be avoided.

Indonesia Local medical care in general is not yet up to international standards. Foreign doctors are not allowed to work in Indonesia, but some clinics catering to foreigners have 'international advisers'. Almost all Indonesian doctors work at government hospitals during the day and in private practices at night. This means that private hospitals often don't have their best staff available during the day. Serious cases are evacuated to Australia or Singapore.

Laos There are no good facilities in Laos; the nearest acceptable facilities are in northern Thailand. The Australian Embassy Clinic in Vientiane treats citizens of Commonwealth countries.

Malaysia Medical care in the major centres is good, and most problems can be adequately dealt with in Kuala Lumpur.

Myanmar (Burma) Local medical care is dismal and local hospitals should be used only in desperation. There is an international medical clinic in Yangon (Rangoon).

Philippines Good medical care is available in most major cities.

Singapore Excellent medical facilities and referral centre for most of Southeast Asia.

Thailand After Singapore, Bangkok is the city of choice for expats living in Southeast Asia who require specialised care.

Vietnam Government hospitals are overcrowded and basic. In order to treat foreigners, the facility needs to obtain a special licence, and so far only a few have been provided. The private clinics in Hanoi and Ho Chi Minh City should be your first choice.

FURTHER READING

- » **Centers for Disease Control & Prevention** (www.cdc.gov) – country-specific advice.
- » **International Travel & Health** (www.who.int/ith) – health guide published by the WHO.
- » **MD Travel Health** (www.mdtravelhealth.com) – travel-health recommendations for every country.

RECOMMENDED VACCINATIONS

Specialised travel-medicine clinics are your best source of information; they stock all available vaccines and will be able to give recommendations specifically for you and your trip. The doctors will take into account factors such as past vaccination history, the length of your trip, activities you may be undertaking and underlying medical conditions, such as pregnancy. Ask your doctor for an International Certificate of Vaccination (otherwise known as the yellow booklet), which will list all the vaccinations you've received. Some vaccines require multiple injections spaced out over a certain period of time, consult with a medical professional six weeks prior to your trip.

The World Health Organization (WHO) recommends the following vaccinations for travellers to Southeast Asia:

- ☐ Adult diphtheria and tetanus
- ☐ Hepatitis A
- ☐ Hepatitis B
- ☐ Measles, mumps and rubella (MMR)
- ☐ Polio
- ☐ Typhoid
- ☐ Varicella

The following immunisations are recommended for long-term travellers (more than one month) or those at special risk:

- ☐ Japanese B Encephalitis
- ☐ Meningitis
- ☐ Rabies
- ☐ Tuberculosis (TB)

Required Vaccinations

The only vaccine required by international regulations is for yellow fever. Proof of vaccination will be required only if you have visited a country in the yellow-fever zone within the six days before entering Southeast Asia. If you are travelling to Southeast Asia from Africa or South America you should check to see if you require proof of vaccination.

Infectious Diseases

Cutaneous Larva Migrans

Risk areas All countries except Singapore.

This disease, caused by dog hookworm, is particularly common on the beaches of Thailand. The rash starts as a small lump then slowly spreads in a linear fashion. It is intensely itchy, especially at night. It is easily treated with medications and should not be cut out or frozen.

Dengue

Risk areas All countries.

This mosquito-borne disease is becoming increasingly problematic throughout Southeast Asia, especially in the cities. There is no vaccine, only prevention. The mosquito that carries dengue bites day and night, so use insect-avoidance measures at all times. Symptoms include high fever, severe headache and body ache (dengue used to be known as breakbone fever). Some people develop a rash and experience diarrhoea. Thailand's southern islands are particularly high risk. There is no specific treatment, just rest and paracetamol – do not take aspirin as it increases the likelihood of haemorrhaging. See a doctor to be diagnosed and monitored.

Hepatitis A

***Risk areas** All countries.*

A problem throughout the region, this food- and water-borne virus infects the liver, causing jaundice (yellow skin and eyes), nausea and lethargy. There is no specific treatment for hepatitis A; you just need to allow time for the liver to heal. All travellers to Southeast Asia should be vaccinated against hepatitis A.

Hepatitis B

***Risk areas** All countries.*

The only serious sexually transmitted disease that can be prevented by vaccination, hepatitis B is spread by body fluids. In some parts of Southeast Asia, up to 20% of the population carry hepatitis B, and usually are unaware of it. The long-term consequences can include liver cancer and cirrhosis.

Hepatitis E

Risk areas *All countries.*
Hepatitis E is transmitted through contaminated food and water, and has similar symptoms to hepatitis A but is far less common. It is a severe problem in pregnant women, and can result in the death of both mother and baby. There is currently no vaccine, and prevention is by following safe eating and drinking guidelines.

HIV

Risk areas *All countries.*
HIV is now one of the most common causes of death in people under the age of 50 in Thailand. The Southeast Asian countries with the worst and most rapidly increasing HIV problem are Cambodia, Myanmar, Thailand and Vietnam. Heterosexual sex is now the main method of transmission in these countries.

Influenza

Risk areas *All countries.*
Present year-round in the tropics, influenza (flu) symptoms include high fever, muscle aches, runny nose, cough and sore throat. It can be very severe in people over the age of 65, and in those with underlying medical conditions such as heart disease or diabetes; vaccination is recommended for these individuals. There is no specific treatment, just rest and paracetamol.

Leptospirosis

Risk areas *Thailand and Malaysia.*
Leptospirosis is most commonly contracted after river rafting or canyoning. Early symptoms are very similar to the flu, and include headache and fever. The disease can vary from very mild to fatal. Diagnosis is through blood tests and it is easily treated with doxycycline.

Malaria

Risk areas *All countries except Singapore and Brunei.*
Many parts of Southeast Asia, particularly city and resort areas, have minimal to no risk of malaria, and the risk of side effects from the prevention tablets may outweigh the risk of getting the disease. For most rural areas, however, the risk of contracting the disease is increased and malaria can be fatal. Before you travel, seek medical advice on the right medication and dosage.

Malaria is caused by a parasite transmitted by the bite of an infected mosquito. The most important symptom of malaria is fever, but general symptoms such as headache, diarrhoea, cough or chills may also occur. Diagnosis can only be made by taking a blood sample.

Two strategies are combined to prevent malaria – mosquito avoidance and antimalarial medications.

Travellers are advised to prevent mosquito bites by taking the following steps:

» Use an insect repellent containing DEET on exposed skin. Wash this off at night, as long as you are sleeping under a mosquito net. Natural repellents such as citronella can be effective, but must be applied more frequently than products containing DEET.

» Sleep under a mosquito net that is impregnated with permethrin.

» Choose accommodation with screens and fans (if not air-conditioned).

» Impregnate clothing with permethrin when in high-risk areas.

» Wear long sleeves and trousers in light colours.

» Use mosquito coils.

» Spray your room with insect repellent before going out for your evening meal.

Measles

Risk areas *All countries except Singapore and Brunei.*
Measles remains a problem in some parts of Southeast Asia. This highly contagious bacterial infection is spread via coughing and sneezing. Most people born before 1966 are immune as they had the disease during childhood. Measles starts with a high fever and rash, and can be complicated by pneumonia and brain disease. There is no specific treatment.

Rabies

Risk areas *All countries except Singapore and Brunei.*
Still a common problem in most parts of Southeast Asia, this uniformly fatal disease is spread by the bite or lick of an infected animal, most commonly a dog or monkey. You should seek medical advice immediately after any animal bite and commence postexposure treatment. Having a pretravel vaccination means the postbite treatment is greatly simplified. If an animal bites you, gently wash the wound with soap and water, and apply iodine-based antiseptic. If you are not prevaccinated you will need to receive rabies immunoglobulin as soon as possible.

Schistosomiasis

Risk areas *Philippines, Vietnam and Sulawesi (Indonesia).*
Schistosomiasis is a tiny parasite that enters your skin after you've been swimming in contaminated water. Travellers usually only get a light infection and hence develop no symptoms. On rare occasions, travellers may develop 'Katayama fever'. This occurs some weeks after exposure, as the parasite passes through the lungs and causes an allergic reaction; symptoms are coughing and fever. Schistosomiasis is easily treated with medications.

STDs

Risk areas *All countries.*
Sexually transmitted diseases most commonly found in Southeast Asia include herpes, warts, syphilis,

RARE BUT BE AWARE

The following diseases are common in the local population (in all countries except Singapore) but rare in travellers.

» Filariasis – a mosquito-borne disease prevented by mosquito-avoidance measures.

» Typhus – murine typhus is spread by the bite of a flea and scrub typhus is spread via a mite; symptoms include fever, muscle pains and a rash. Prevention is through general insect-avoidance measures or doxycycline.

» Tuberculosis – medical and aid workers and long-term travellers should take precautions and consider pre- and post-travel testing; symptoms are fever, cough, weight loss and tiredness.

» Meliodosis (Thailand only) – an infection contracted by skin contact with soil; symptoms are similar to tuberculosis.

» Japanese B Encephalitis (highest risk areas: Vietnam, Thailand and Indonesia) – a viral disease, transmitted by mosquitoes; most cases occur in rural areas and vaccination is recommended for travellers spending more than one month outside cities.

gonorrhoea and chlamydia. People carrying these diseases often have no signs of infection. Condoms will prevent gonorrhoea and chlamydia but not warts or herpes. If after a sexual encounter you develop any rash, lumps, discharge or pain when passing urine, seek immediate medical attention. If you have been sexually active during your travels, have an STD check on your return home.

Strongyloides

Risk areas *Cambodia, Myanmar and Thailand.*

This parasite, transmitted by skin contact with soil, is common in travellers but rarely affects them. It is characterised by an unusual skin rash called larva currens – a linear rash on the trunk that comes and goes. Most people don't have other symptoms until their immune system becomes severely suppressed, when the parasite can cause an overwhelming infection. It can be treated with medications.

Typhoid

Risk areas *All countries except Singapore.*

This serious bacterial infection is spread via food and water. It gives a high and slowly progressive fever and a headache, and may be accompanied by a dry cough and stomach pain. It is diagnosed by blood tests and treated with antibiotics. Vaccination is recommended for all travellers spending more than a week in Southeast Asia, or travelling outside the major cities. Vaccination is not 100% effective so you must still be careful with what you eat and drink.

Traveller's Diarrhoea

Traveller's diarrhoea is by far the most common problem that affects travellers – between 30% and 50% of people will suffer from it within two weeks of starting their trip. In over 80% of cases, traveller's diarrhoea is caused by bacteria (there are numerous potential culprits), and therefore responds promptly to treatment with antibiotics. Treatment will depend on your situation – how sick you are, how quickly you need to get better etc.

Traveller's diarrhoea is defined as the passage of more than three watery bowel actions within 24 hours, plus at least one other symptom such as fever, cramps, nausea, vomiting or feeling generally unwell.

Treatment consists of staying well hydrated; rehydration solutions such as Gastrolyte are the best for this. Antibiotics such as norfloxacin, ciprofloxacin or azithromycin will kill the bacteria quickly.

Loperamide is just a 'stopper'. It can be helpful if you have to go on a long bus ride. Don't take loperamide if you have a fever, or blood in your stools. Seek medical attention quickly if you do not respond to an appropriate antibiotic.

Amoebic Dysentery

Amoebic dysentery is very rare in travellers but is often misdiagnosed by poor-quality labs in Southeast Asia. Symptoms are similar to bacterial diarrhoea, ie fever, bloody diarrhoea and generally feeling unwell. You should always seek reliable medical care if you have blood in your diarrhoea. Treatment involves two drugs: tinidazole or metronidazole to kill the parasite in your gut, and then a second drug to kill the cysts. If left untreated, complications such as liver or gut abscesses can occur.

Giardiasis

Giardia lamblia is a relatively common parasite in travellers. Symptoms include nausea, bloating, excess gas, fatigue and intermittent diarrhoea. 'Eggy' burps are often attributed solely to giardiasis, but work in Nepal has shown that they are not specific to this infection. The parasite will eventually go away if left untreated but this can take months. The treatment of choice is tinidazole, with metronidazole being a second option.

Environmental Hazards

Heat

Many parts of Southeast Asia are hot and humid throughout the year. For most people it takes at least two weeks to adapt to the hot climate. Swelling of the feet and ankles is common, as are muscle cramps caused by excessive sweating. You can prevent these by avoiding dehydration and excessive activity in the heat; you should also take it easy when you first arrive. Don't eat salt tablets (they aggravate the gut), but drinking rehydration solution or eating salty food helps. Treat cramps by stopping activity, resting, rehydrating with double-strength rehydration solution and gently stretching.

Dehydration is the main contributor to heat exhaustion. Symptoms include weakness, headache, irritability, nausea or vomiting, sweaty skin, a fast pulse, and a normal or slightly elevated body temperature. Treatment involves getting out of the heat, fanning and applying cool wet cloths to the skin, lying flat with legs raised, and rehydrating with water containing a quarter of a teaspoon of salt per litre. Recovery is usually rapid, though it is common to feel weak afterwards.

Heat stroke is a serious medical emergency. Symptoms come on suddenly and include weakness, nausea, a hot dry body with a body temperature of over 41°C, dizziness, confusion, loss of coordination, seizures, and eventually collapse and loss of consciousness. Seek medical help and commence cooling by getting out of the heat, removing clothes, fanning and applying cool wet cloths or ice to the body, especially to the groin and armpits.

Prickly heat is a common skin rash in the tropics caused by sweat being trapped under the skin. The result is an itchy rash of tiny lumps. Treat by moving out of the heat and into an air-conditioned area for a few hours and by having cool showers. Creams and ointments clog the skin so they should be avoided. Locally bought prickly-heat powder can be helpful.

Tropical fatigue is common in long-term expats based in the tropics. It's rarely due to disease and is caused by the climate, inadequate mental rest, excessive alcohol intake and the demands of daily work in a different culture.

Insect Bites & Stings

Bedbugs don't carry disease but their bites are very itchy. They live in the cracks of furniture and walls, and then migrate to the bed at night to feed on you. You can treat the itch with an antihistamine.

Lice inhabit various parts of your body, but most commonly your head and pubic area. Transmission is via close contact with an infected person. Lice can be difficult to treat and you may need numerous applications of an antilice shampoo. Pubic lice are usually contracted from sexual contact.

Ticks are contracted after walking in rural areas. They are commonly found behind the ears, on the belly and in armpits. If you have had a tick bite and experience symptoms such as a rash at the site of the bite or elsewhere, or fever or muscle aches, you should see a doctor. Doxycycline prevents tickborne diseases.

Leeches are found in humid rainforest areas. They do not transmit any disease but their bites are often intensely itchy for weeks afterwards and can easily become infected. Apply an iodine-based antiseptic to any leech bite to help prevent infection.

Bee and wasp stings mainly cause problems for people who are allergic to them. Anyone with a serious bee or wasp allergy should carry an injection of adrenaline (eg an Epipen) for emergency treatment. For others, pain is the main problem – apply ice to the sting and take painkillers.

Most jellyfish in Southeast Asian waters are not dangerous, just irritating. First aid for jellyfish stings involves

FOOD & WATER

Food and water contamination are the biggest risk factor for contracting traveller's diarrhoea. Here are some safety considerations:

» Eat only freshly cooked food and fruit that can be peeled.

» Avoid shellfish and food that has been sitting around for hours.

» Eat in busy restaurants with a high turnover of customers.

» Never drink tap water; opt for bottled or filtered water instead.

» Avoid ice.

» Avoid fresh juices that may have been watered down.

» Boil water or use iodine tablets as a means of purification; pregnant women or those with thyroid problems should avoid iodine use.

pouring vinegar onto the affected area to neutralise the poison. Do not rub sand or water onto the stings. Take painkillers, and if you feel ill in any way after being stung seek medical advice. Take local advice if there are dangerous jellyfish around and keep out of the water.

Parasites

Numerous parasites are common in local populations in Southeast Asia; however, most of these are rare in travellers. The two rules for avoiding parasitic infections are to wear shoes and to avoid eating raw food, especially fish, pork and vegetables. A number of parasites are transmitted via the skin by walking barefoot, including *Strongyloides*, hookworm and cutaneous larva migrans.

Skin Problems

Fungal rashes are common in humid climates. There are two common fungal rashes that tend to affect travellers. The first occurs in moist areas that get less air, such as the groin, armpits and between the toes. It starts as a red patch that slowly spreads and is usually itchy. Treatment involves keeping the skin dry, avoiding chafing and using an antifungal cream such as clotrimazole or Lamisil. *Tinea versicolor* is also common – this fungus causes small, light-coloured patches, most commonly on the back, chest and shoulders. Consult a doctor.

Cuts and scratches become easily infected in humid climates. Take meticulous care of them to prevent complications such as abscesses. Immediately wash all wounds in clean water and apply antiseptic. If you develop signs of infection (increasing pain and redness), see a doctor. Divers and surfers should be particularly careful with coral cuts as they can be easily infected.

Snakes

Southeast Asia is home to many species of both poisonous and harmless snakes. Assume that all snakes are poisonous and never try to catch one. Wear boots and long pants if walking in an area that may have snakes. First aid in the event of a snakebite involves pressure immobilisation using an elastic bandage firmly wrapped around the affected limb, starting at the bite site and working up towards the chest. The bandage should not be so tight that the circulation is cut off, and the fingers or toes should be kept free so the circulation can be checked. Immobilise the limb with a splint and carry the victim to medical attention. Do not use tourniquets or try to suck the venom out. Antivenin is available for most species.

Sunburn

Even on a cloudy day sunburn can occur rapidly. Always use a strong sunscreen (at least factor 30), making sure to reapply after a swim, and always wear a wide-brimmed hat and sunglasses outdoors. Avoid lying in the sun during the hottest part of the day (10am to 2pm). If you become sunburnt, stay out of the sun until you have recovered, apply cool compresses and take painkillers for the discomfort. One per cent hydrocortisone cream applied twice daily is also helpful.

Women's Health

In the urban areas of Southeast Asia, supplies of sanitary products are readily available. Birth-control options may be limited so bring adequate supplies of your own form of contraception. Heat, humidity and antibiotics can all contribute to thrush. Treatment is with antifungal creams and pessaries such as clotrimazole. A practical alternative is a single tablet of fluconazole (Diflucan). Urinary tract infections can be precipitated by dehydration or long bus journeys without toilet stops; bring suitable antibiotics.

Pregnant women should receive specialised advice before travelling. The ideal time to travel is in the second trimester (between 16 and 28 weeks), when the risk of pregnancy-related problems is at its lowest and women generally feel at their best. During the first trimester there is a risk of miscarriage and in the third trimester complications such as premature labour and high blood pressure are possible. It's wise to travel with a companion. Always carry a list of quality medical facilities available at your destination and ensure you continue your standard antenatal care at these facilities. Avoid rural travel in areas with poor transport and medical facilities. Most of all, ensure travel insurance covers all pregnancy-related possibilities.

Malaria is a high-risk disease during pregnancy. WHO recommends that pregnant women do *not* travel to areas with chloroquine-resistant malaria. None of the more effective antimalarial drugs are completely safe in pregnancy.

Traveller's diarrhoea can quickly lead to dehydration and result in inadequate blood flow to the placenta. Many of the drugs used to treat various diarrhoea bugs are not recommended in pregnancy. Azithromycin is considered safe.

Language

WANT MORE?

For in-depth language information and handy phrases, check out Lonely Planet's *Southeast Asia Phrasebook*. You'll find it at **shop.lonelyplanet.com**, or you can buy Lonely Planet's iPhone phrasebooks at the Apple App Store.

This chapter offers basic vocabulary to help you get around Southeast Asia. Read our coloured pronunciation guides as if they were English, and you'll be understood. The stressed syllables are in italics. The polite and informal forms are indicated by the abbreviations 'pol' and 'inf' where needed. The abbreviations 'm' and 'f' indicate masculine and feminine gender respectively.

BURMESE

In Burmese, there's a difference between aspirated consonants (pronounced with a puff of air) and unaspirated ones. These consonants are said with a puff of air after the sound: ch (as in 'church'), k (as in 'kite'), ş (as in 'sick'), t (as in 'talk'); the following ones are pronounced with a puff of air before the sound: hl (as in 'life'), hm (as in 'me'), hn (as in 'not'), hng (as in 'sing'), hny (as in 'canyon'). Note also that the apostrophe (') represents the sound heard between 'uh-oh', th is pronounced as in 'thin' and ţh as in 'their'.

There are three distinct tones in Burmese (the raising and lowering of pitch on certain syllables). They are indicated in our pronunciation guides by the accent mark above the vowel: high creaky tone, as in 'heart' (á), plain high tone, as in 'car' (à), and the low tone (a). Note also that ai is pronounced as in 'aisle', aw as in 'law', and au as in 'brown'.

Basics

Hello.	မင်္ဂလာပါ။	ming·guh·la·ba
Goodbye.	သွားမယ်နော်။	thwà·me·naw
Excuse me.	ဆောရီးနော်။	sàw·rì·naw
Sorry.	ဆောရီးနော်။	sàw·rì·naw
Please.	တဆိတ်လောက်။	duh·şay'·lau'
Thank you.	ကျေးဇူး တင်ပါတယ်။	jày·zù ding·ba·de
Yes.	ဟုတ်ကဲ့။	hoh'·gé
No.	ဟင့်အင်း။	híng·in
Help!	ကယ်ပါ။	ge·ba

What's your name?

နာမည် ဘယ်လို ခေါ်သလဲ။	nang·me be·loh kaw·ţhuh·lè

My name is ...

ကျနော့်/ကျမ နာမည်က --- ပါ။	juh·náw/juh·má nang·me·gá ... ba **(m/f)**

Numbers – Burmese

1	တစ်	di'
2	နှစ်	hni'
3	သုံး	thòhng
4	လေး	lày
5	ငါး	ngà
6	ခြောက်	chau'
7	ခုနစ်	kung·ni'
8	ရှစ်	shi'
9	ကိုး	gòh
10	တစ်ဆယ်	duh·şe

Do you speak English?
အင်္ဂလိပ်လို ပြောတတ်သလား။ — ìng·guh·lay'·loh byàw·da'·thuh·là

I don't understand.
နားမလည်ဘူး။ — nà·muh·le·bòo

How much is it?
ဒါဘယ်လောက်လဲ။ — da be·lau'·lè

Where are the toilets?
အိမ်သာ ဘယ်မှာလဲ။ — ayng·tha be·hma·lè

I'd like the ..., please.	--- ပေးပါ။	... bày·ba
bill	ဘောက်ချာ	bau'·cha
menu	မီးနူး	mì·nù

Call ...	--- ခေါ်ပေးပါ။	... kaw·bày·ba
a doctor	ဆရာဝန်	şuh·ya·wung
the police	ရဲ	yèh

FILIPINO

Filipino is easy to pronounce and most sounds are familiar to English speakers. In addition, the relationship between Filipino sounds and their spelling is straightforward and consistent, meaning that each letter is always pronounced the same way. Note that ai is pronounced as in 'aisle', ay as in 'say', ew like ee with rounded lips, oh as the 'o' in 'go', ow as in 'how' and ooy as the 'wea' in 'tweak'. The r sound is stronger than in English and rolled. The glottal stop, pronounced like the pause between the two syllables in 'uh-oh', is indicated in our pronunciation guides by an apostrophe (').

Basics

Good day.	*Magandáng araw pô.* (pol)	ma·gan·*dang* a·row po'
	Magandáng araw. (inf)	ma·gan·*dang* a·row
Goodbye.	*Paalam na pô.* (pol)	pa·a·lam na po'
	Babay. (inf)	*ba*·bai
Yes.	*Opò.* (pol)	*o*·po'
	Oo. (inf)	*o*·o
No.	*Hindí pô.* (pol)	heen·*dee'* po'
	Hindî. (inf)	heen·*dee'*
Thank you.	*Salamat pô.* (pol)	sa·*la*·mat po'
	Salamat. (inf)	sa·*la*·mat
Help!	*Saklolo!*	sak·*lo*·lo

What's your name?
Anó pô ang pangalan ninyó? — a·*no* po' ang pa·*nga*·lan neen·*yo*

Numbers – Filipino

1	*isá*	ee·*sa*
2	*dalawá*	da·la·*wa*
3	*tatló*	tat·*lo*
4	*apat*	*a*·pat
5	*limá*	lee·*ma*
6	*anim*	*a*·neem
7	*pitó*	pee·*to*
8	*waló*	wa·*lo*
9	*siyám*	see·*yam*
10	*sampû*	sam·*poo'*

My name is ...
Ang pangalan ko pô ay ... — ang pa·*nga*·lan ko po' ai ...

Do you speak English?
Marunong ka ba ng Inglés? — ma·*roo*·nong ka ba nang eeng·*gles*

I don't understand.
Hindí ko náiintindihán. — heen·*dee* ko na·ee·een·teen·dee·*han*

How much is it?
Magkano? — mag·*ka*·no

Where are the toilets?
Násaán ang kubeta? — na·sa·*an* ang koo·*be*·ta

I'd like the menu.
Gustó ko ng menú. — goos·*to* ko nang me·*noo*

Please bring the bill.
Pakidalá ang tsit. — pa·kee·da·*la* ang tseet

Call ...!	*Tumawag ka ng ...!*	too·*ma*·wag ka nang ...
a doctor	*doktór*	dok·*tor*
the police	*pulís*	poo·*lees*

INDONESIAN & MALAY

Indonesian and Malay are very similar, so in this section we've provided translations in both languages – indicated by (I) and (M) respectively – only where the differences are significant enough to cause confusion. Most letters are pronounced more or less the same as their English counterparts, except for the letter *c* which is always pronounced as the 'ch' in 'chair'. Nearly all syllables carry equal emphasis, but a good approximation is to lightly stress the second-last syllable.

Basics

Hello.	*Salam./Helo.* (I/M)
Goodbye.	*Selamat tinggal/jalan.* (by person leaving/staying)

Numbers – Indonesian/Malay

1	*satu*
2	*dua*
3	*tiga*
4	*empat*
5	*lima*
6	*enam*
7	*tujuh*
8	*delapan* (I)
	lapan (M)
9	*sembilan*
10	*sepuluh*

Excuse me.	*Maaf.*
Sorry.	*Maaf.*
Please.	*Silakan.*
Thank you.	*Terima kasih.*
Yes.	*Ya.*
No.	*Tidak.*
Help!	*Tolong!*
What's your name?	*Siapa nama anda/kamu?* (I/M)
My name is ...	*Nama saya ...*
Do you speak English?	*Anda bisa Bahasa Inggris?* (I) *Adakah anda berbahasa Inggeris?* (M)
I don't understand.	*Saya tidak mengerti.* (I) *Saya tidak faham.* (M)
How much is it?	*Berapa harganya?*
Where are the toilets?	*Kamar kecil di mana?* (I) *Tandas di mana?* (M)
I'd like the menu.	*Saya minta daftar makanan.*
Bring the bill, please.	*Tolong bawa kuitansi/bil.* (I/M)
Call a doctor!	*Panggil doktor!*
Call the police!	*Panggil polis!*

KHMER

In our pronunciation guides, vowels and vowel combinations with an h at the end are pronounced hard and aspirated (with a puff of air). The symbols for vowels are read as follows: aa as the 'a' in 'father'; a and ah shorter and harder than aa; i as in 'kit'; uh as the 'u' in 'but'; ii as the 'ee' in 'feet'; eu like 'oo' (with the lips spread flat); euh as eu (short and hard); oh as the 'o' in 'hose' (short and hard); ow as in 'glow'; u as the 'u' in 'flute' (short and hard); uu as the 'oo' in 'zoo'; ua as the 'ou' in 'tour'; uah as ua (short and hard); œ as 'er' in 'her' (more open); ia as the 'ee' in 'beer' (without the 'r'); e as in 'they'; ai as in 'aisle'; ae as the 'a' in 'cat'; ay as ai (slightly more nasal); ey as in 'prey'; o as the 'ow' in 'cow'; av like a nasal ao (without the 'v'); euv like a nasal eu (without the 'v'); ohm as the 'ome' in 'home'; am as the 'um' in 'glum'; ih as the 'ee' in 'teeth' (short and hard); eh as the 'a' in 'date' (short and hard); awh as the 'aw' in 'jaw' (short and hard); and aw as the 'aw' in 'jaw'.

Some consonant combinations in our pronunciation guides are separated with an apostrophe for ease of pronunciation, eg 'j-r' in j'rook and 'ch-ng' in ch'ngain. Also note that k is pronounced as the 'g' in 'go'; kh as the 'k' in 'kind'; p as the final 'p' in 'puppy'; ph as the 'p' in 'pond'; r as in 'rum' but hard and rolling; t as the 't' in 'stand'; and th as the 't' in 'two'.

Basics

Hello.	ជំរាបសួរ	john riab sua
Goodbye.	លាសិនហើយ	lia suhn hao-y
Excuse me.	សុំទោស	sohm toh
Sorry.	សុំទោស	sohm toh
Please.	សូម	sohm
Thank you.	អរគុណ	aw kohn
Yes.	បាទ/ចាស	baat/jaa (m/f)
No.	ទេ	te
Help!	ជួយខ្ញុំផង!	juay kh'nyohm phawng

What's your name?
អ្នកឈ្មោះអី? niak ch'muah ei

My name is ...
ខ្ញុំឈ្មោះ ... kh'nyohm ch'muah ...

Numbers – Khmer

1	មួយ	muy
2	ពីរ	pii
3	បី	bei
4	បួន	buan
5	ប្រាំ	bram
6	ប្រាំមួយ	bram muy
7	ប្រាំពីរ	bram pii
8	ប្រាំបី	bram bei
9	ប្រាំបួន	bram buan
10	ដប់	dawp

Does anyone speak English?
ទីនេះមានអ្នកចេះ ភាសាអង់គ្លេសទេ? — tii nih mian niak jeh phiasaa awngle te

I don't understand.
ខ្ញុំមិនយល់ទេ — kh'nyohm muhn yuhl te

How much is it?
នេះថ្លៃប៉ុន្មាន? — nih th'lay pohnmaan

Where are the toilets?
បង្គន់នៅឯណា? — bawngkohn neuv ai naa

Do you have a menu in English?
មានម៉ឺនុយជាភាសា អង់គ្លេសទេ? — mien menui jea piasaa awnglay te

The bill, please.
សូមគិតលុយ — sohm kuht lui

Call a doctor!
ជួយហៅគ្រូពេទ្យមក! — juay hav kruu paet mao

Call the police!
ជួយហៅប៉ូលីសមក! — juay hav polih mao

LAO

Lao is a tonal language, meaning that many identical sounds are differentiated only by changes in the pitch of a speaker's voice. Pitch variations are relative to the speaker's natural vocal range, so that one person's low tone isn't necessarily the same pitch as another person's. There are six tones in Lao, indicated in our pronunciation guides by accent marks on letters: low tone (eg dįi), high (eg heúa), rising (eg săam), high falling (eg sâo) and low falling (eg khào). Note that no accent mark is used for the mid tone (eg het).

The pronunciation of vowels goes like this: i as in 'it'; ii as in 'feet'; ai as in 'aisle'; aa as the 'a' in 'father'; a as a short aa; ae as the 'a' in 'bad'; eh as the 'a' in 'hate'; oe as the 'u' in 'fur'; eu as the 'i' in 'sir'; u as in 'flute'; uu as in 'food'; ao as in 'now'; aw as in 'jaw'; o as in 'phone'; oh as in 'toe'; ia as in 'lan'; ua as in 'tour'; iu as in 'yew'; and awy as the 'oy' in 'boy'.

Also keep in mind the distinction between the following consonant sounds: k is pronounced as a hard 'k' (a bit like 'g'); kh as the 'k' in 'kite'; p as a hard 'p' (a bit like 'b'); ph as the 'p' in 'put'; t as a hard 't' (a bit like 'd'); and th as the 't' in 'tip'.

Basics

Hello.	ສະບາຍດີ	sábąai-dii
Goodbye.	ສະບາຍດີ	sábąai-dii
Excuse me.	ຂໍໂທດ	khăw thŏht
Sorry.	ຂໍໂທດ	khăw thŏht
Please.	ກະລຸນາ	ga-lú-náa
Thank you.	ຂອບໃຈ	khàwp jąi
Yes.	ແມ່ນ	maan
No.	ບໍ່	baw
Help!	ຊ່ວຍແດ່!	suay dae

Numbers – Lao

1	ນຶ່ງ	neung
2	ສອງ	săwng
3	ສາມ	săam
4	ສີ່	sii
5	ຫາ	hàa
6	ຫົກ	hók
7	ເຈັດ	jét
8	ແປດ	pàet
9	ເກົ້າ	kâo
10	ສິບ	síp

What's your name?
ເຈົ້າຊື່ຫຍັງ — jâo seu nyăng

My name is ...
ຂ້ອຍຊື່ ... — kháwy seu ...

Do you speak English?
ເຈົ້າປາກ ພາສາອັງກິດໄດ້ບໍ່ — jâo pàak pháasăa ąngkít dâi baw

I don't understand.
ບໍ່ເຂົ້າໃຈ — baw khào jąi

How much (for) ...?
... ເທົ່າໃດ? — ... thao dąi

Where are the toilets?
ຫ້ອງສ້ວມຢູ່ໃສ? — hàwng sùam yuu săi

Please bring the ...	ຂໍ ... ແດ່	khăw ... dae
bill	ແຊັກ	saek
menu	ລາຍການ ອາຫານ	láai-kąan ąa-hăan

Call a doctor!

ຊ່ວຍຕາມຫາໝໍ ໃຫ້ແດ່!	suay tąam hăa măw hài dae

Call the police!

ຊ່ວຍເອີ້ນຕຳຫລວດແດ່!	suay ôen tam-lùat dae

TETUN

Tetun pronunciation is pretty straightforward. Letters always have the same sound value, and are generally pronounced just like in English, with the following exceptions: *j* is pronounced as the 's' in 'pleasure' (and sometimes as the 'z' in 'zebra'), *x* is pronounced as the 'sh' in 'ship' (sometimes as the 's' in 'summer'), while *lh* and *nh* are pronounced as the 'ly' in 'million' and the 'ny' in 'canyon' respectively (and outside Dili they are often reduced to *l* and *n* respectively).

Word stress is fairly regular and usually falls on the second-last syllable of a word; if it falls on any other syllable, we've indicated this with an accent mark on the vowel (eg *polísia*).

Basics

Hello.	*Haló./Olá.* (pol/inf)
Goodbye.	*Adeus.*
Excuse me.	*Kolisensa.*
Sorry.	*Disculpa.*
Please.	*Favór ida./Faz favór.*
Thank you.	*Obrigadu/a.* (m/f)
Yes.	*Sin./Diak./Los.*
No.	*Lae.*
Help!	*Ajuda!*
What's your name?	*Ita-nia naran saida?*
My name is ...	*Hau-nia naran ...*
Do you speak English?	*Ita koalia Inglés?*
I don't understand.	*Hau la kompriende.*
How much is it?	*Folin hira?*
Where are the toilets?	*Sintina iha nebé?*
Please bring the menu/bill.	*Favór ida lori hela menu/konta mai.*
Call a doctor!	*Bolu dotór!*
Call the police!	*Bolu polísia!*

Numbers – Tetun

1	*ida*
2	*rua*
3	*tolu*
4	*hat*
5	*lima*
6	*nen*
7	*hitu*
8	*ualu*
9	*sia*
10	*sanulu*

THAI

In Thai the meaning of a syllable may be altered by means of tones. In standard Thai there are five tones: low (eg bàht), mid (eg dee), falling (eg mâi), high (eg máh) and rising (eg săhm). The range of all tones is relative to each speaker's vocal range, so there is no fixed 'pitch' intrinsic to the language.

In our pronunciation guides, the hyphens indicate syllable breaks within words, and for ease of pronunciation some compound vowels are further divided with a dot (eg mêu·a-rai).

The vowel a is pronounced as in 'about', aa as the 'a' in 'bad', ah as the 'a' in 'father', ai as in 'aisle', air as in 'flair' (without the 'r'), eu as the 'er' in 'her' (without the 'r'), ew as in 'new' (with rounded lips), oh as the 'o' in 'toe', or as in 'torn' (without the 'r') and ow as in 'now'.

Note also the pronunciation of the following consonants: b (a hard 'p' sound, almost like a 'b', eg in 'hip-bag'); đ (a hard 't' sound, like a sharp 'd', eg in 'mid-tone'); and r (as in 'run' but flapped; often pronounced like 'l').

Basics

Hello.	สวัสดี	sà-wàt-dee
Goodbye.	ลาก่อน	lah gòrn
Excuse me.	ขออภัย	kŏr à-pai
Sorry.	ขอโทษ	kŏr tôht
Please.	ขอ	kŏr
Thank you.	ขอบคุณ	kòrp kun
Yes.	ใช่	châi
No.	ไม่	mâi
Help!	ช่วยด้วย	chôo·ay dôo·ay

What's your name?

คุณชื่ออะไร	kun chêu à-rai

My name is ...

ผม/ดิฉัน ชื่อ...	pŏm/dì-chăn chêu ... (m/f)

Do you speak English?

คุณพูดภาษา อังกฤษได้ไหม	kun pôot pah-săh ang-grìt dâi măi

Numbers – Thai

1	หนึ่ง	nèung
2	สอง	sŏrng
3	สาม	săhm
4	สี่	sèe
5	ห้า	hâh
6	หก	hòk
7	เจ็ด	jèt
8	แปด	bàat
9	เก้า	gôw
10	สิบ	sìp

I don't understand.
ผม/ดิฉันไม่เข้าใจ — pŏm/dì-chăn mâi kôw jai (m/f)

How much is it?
เท่าไร — tôw-rai

Where are the toilets?
ห้องน้ำอยู่ที่ไหน — hôrng nám yòo têe năi

I'd like the menu, please.
ขอรายการอาหารหน่อย — kŏr rai gahn ah-hăhn nòy

Please bring the bill.
ขอบิลหน่อย — kŏr bin nòy

Call a doctor!
เรียกหมอหน่อย — rêe·ak mŏr nòy

Call the police!
เรียกตำรวจหน่อย — rêe·ak đam·ròo·at nòy

VIETNAMESE

Vietnamese is written in a Latin-based phonetic alphabet, which was declared the official written form in 1910.

In our pronunciation guides, a is pronounced as in 'at', aa as in 'father', aw as in 'law', er as in 'her', oh as in 'doh!', ow as in 'cow', u as in 'book', uh as in 'but' and uhr as in 'fur' (without the 'r'). We've used dots (eg dee·úhng) to separate the combined vowel sounds. Note also that d is pronounced as in 'stop', đ as in 'dog', and ğ as in 'skill'.

Vietnamese uses a system of tones to make distinctions between words – so some vowels are pronounced with a high or low pitch. There are six tones in Vietnamese, indicated in the written language (and in our pronunciation guides) by accent marks on the vowel: mid (ma), low falling (mà), low rising (mả), high broken (mã), high rising (má) and low broken (mạ). The mid tone is flat.

The variation in vocabulary between the Vietnamese of the north and the south is indicated by (N) and (S) respectively.

Basics

Hello.	*Xin chào.*	sin jòw
Goodbye.	*Tạm biệt.*	daạm bee·ụht
Excuse me.	*Xin lỗi.*	sin lõy
Sorry.	*Xin lỗi.*	sin lõy
Please.	*Làm ơn.*	laàm ern
Thank you.	*Cảm ơn.*	ğaảm ern
Yes.	*Vâng./Dạ.* (N/S)	vuhng/ yạ
No.	*Không.*	kawm
Help!	*Cứu tôi!*	ğuhr·oó doy

What's your name?
Tên là gì? — den laà zeè

My name is ...
Tên tôi là ... — den doy laà ...

Do you speak English?
Bạn có nói tiếng Anh không? — baạn ğó nóy dee·úhng aang kawm

I don't understand.
Tôi không hiểu. — doy kawm heẻ·oo

How much is this?
Cái này giá bao nhiêu? — ğaí này zaá bow nyee·oo

Where is the toilet?
Nhà vệ sinh ở đâu? — nyaà vẹ sing ẻr đoh

I'd like the menu.
Tôi muốn thực đơn. — doy moo·úhn tụhrk đern

The bill, please.
Xin tính tiền. — sin díng dee·ùhn

Please call a doctor.
Làm ơn gọi bác sĩ. — laàm ern gọy baák seẽ

Please call the police.
Làm ơn gọi công an. — laàm ern gọy ğawm aan

Numbers – Vietnamese

1	*một*	mạwt
2	*hai*	hai
3	*ba*	baa
4	*bốn*	báwn
5	*năm*	nuhm
6	*sáu*	sóh
7	*bảy*	bảy
8	*tám*	dúhm
9	*chín*	jín
10	*mười*	muhr·eè

GLOSSARY

(m) indicates masculine gender, (f) feminine gender and (pl) plural

ABBREVIATIONS

B – Brunei
C – Cambodia
I – Indonesia
L – Laos
M – Malaysia
My – Myanmar (Burma)
P – Philippines
S – Singapore
T – Thailand
TL – Timor-Leste
V – Vietnam

ABC (M) – Air Batang
adat (B, I, M, S) – customary law
alun alun (I) – main public square of a town
amoc/amok (C) – fish baked in banana leaf
andong (I) – four-wheeled horse-drawn cart
angguna (TL) – tray truck where passengers (including the odd buffalo or goat) all pile into the back
angkot (I) – see *bemo*
ao (T) – bay, gulf
ao dai (V) – traditional Vietnamese tunic and trousers
apsara (C) – dancing girl, celestial nymph
argo (I) – taxi meter; 'luxury' class on trains
Asean – Association of Southeast Asian Nations

bâan (T) – house, village; also written as *ban*
Baba Nonya (M) – descendents of Chinese settlers in the Straits settlements (Melaka, Singapore and Penang) who intermarried with Malays and adopted many Malay customs; also written as 'Baba Nyonya'
bajaj (I) – motorised three-wheeled taxi
Bamar (My) – Burmese ethnic group
bangka (P) – local outrigger, pumpboat
barangay (P) – village
baray (C) – Angkorian reservoir
batik (I, M) – cloth coloured by a waxing and dyeing process
BE (L) – Buddhist Era
becak (I) – bicycle rickshaw
bemo (I) – three-wheeled pick-up truck, often with two rows of seats down the side
benteng (I) – fort
bisnis (I) – business class on buses, trains etc
boeng (C) – lake
BSB (B) – Bandar Seri Begawan
bukit (B, I, M, S) – hill
bumboat (S) – motorised *sampan*
bun (L) – festival
butanding (P) – whale shark
buu dien (V) – post office

Cao Daism (V) – Vietnamese religion
CAT (T) – CAT Telecom Public Company Limited (formerly Communications Authority of Thailand or CAT)
Cham (C,V) – ethnic minority descended from the people of Champa, a Hindu kingdom dating from the 2nd century BC
chedi (T) – see *stupa*
chunchiet (C) – ethno-linguistic minorities
cidomo (I) – horse-drawn cart
colt (I) – see *opelet*
CPP (C) – Cambodian People's Party
CTT (My) – Central Telephone & Telegraph
cyclo (C, V) – pedicab

Đ (V) – abbreviation of *duong*
ĐL (V) – abbreviation of *dai lo*
dai lo (V) – boulevard; abbreviated as 'ĐL'
dangdut (I) – Indonesian dance music with strong Arabic and Hindi influences (I)
datu (P) – traditional local chief, head of village
devaraja (C) – god-king
DMZ (V) – Demilitarised Zone
dokar (I) – two-wheeled horse-drawn cart
DOT (P) – Department of Tourism
duong (V) – road, street; abbreviated as 'Đ'

Ecpat – End Child Prostitution & Trafficking
ekonomi (I, M) – economy class on buses, trains and other transport
eksekutif (I, M) – executive (ie 1st) class on buses, trains and other transport

falang (L) – Western, Westerner; foreigner
faràng (T) – Western, Westerner; foreigner
FEC (My) – Foreign Exchange Certificate

gamelan (I, M) – traditional Javanese and Balinese orchestra with large xylophones and gongs
gang (I) – alley, lane
gopura (C) – sanctuary
gua (I, M) – cave
gunung (I, M) – mountain

hàat (T) – beach; also written as *hat*
habal-habal (P) – motorcycle taxi
HCMC (V) – Ho Chi Minh City
Honda om (V) – see *xe om*
hti (My) – decorated top of a *stupa*

ikat (I) – cloth in which a pattern is produced by dyeing individual threads before the weaving process

istana (B, I, M, S) – palace

jalan (B, TL, I, M, S) – road, street; abbreviated as 'Jl'

JB (M) – Johor Bahru

jeepney (P) – wildly ornamented public transport, originally based on WWII US Army Jeeps

Jl (B, TL, I, M, S) – abbreviation of *jalan*

kaa (My) – city bus

kain songket (M) – fabric woven with gold and/or silver thread

kalesa (P) – two-wheeled horse-drawn cart

kampung (B, I, M, S) – village; also written as *kampong*

karst – limestone region with caves, underground streams, potholes etc

kàter•i (T) – transvestite, transsexual

kedai kopi (M) – coffee shop

khǎo (T) – hill, mountain; also written as *khao*

khlong (T) – canal; also written as *khlawng*

khwǎn (L) – guardian spirits of the body

KK (M) – Kota Kinabalu

KL (M) – Kuala Lumpur

KLIA (M) – Kuala Lumpur International Airport

klotok (I) – motorised canoe

ko (T) – island

koh (C) – island

kongsi (M) – Chinese clan organisations, also known as ritual brotherhoods, heaven-man-earth societies, triads or secret societies; meeting house for Chinese of the same clan

kota (TL, I, M) – fort, city

krama (C) – checked scarf

kraton (I) – palace

kris (I) – traditional dagger

KTM (M) – Keretapi Tanah Melayu; national rail service

kyaung (My) – Buddhist monastery

labuan (M) – port

lí-gair (T) – popular form of folk dance-drama; also written as *likay*

longhouse (I, M, My) – enormous wooden structure on stilts that houses a tribal community under one roof

longyi (My) – wraparound garment worn by women and men

losmen (I) – basic accommodation

LRT (M) – Light Rail Transit

mae nam (T) – river

mandi (TL, I, M) – large concrete basin from which you scoop water to rinse your body and flush the toilet

masjid (M) – mosque; also written as *mesjid*

merdeka (I, M) – independence

mesjid (I) – mosque; also written as *masjid*

mestizo (TL, P) – person of mixed descent

meuang (T) – city

mikrolet (TL, I) – see *opelet*

MILF (P) – Moro Islamic Liberation Front

moto (C) – motorcycle taxi

motodup (C) – motorcycle taxi driver

MRT (S) – Mass Rapid Transit; metro system

MTT (My) – Myanmar Travel & Tours

muay thai (T) – Thai boxing

myint hlei (My) – horse cart

nâam (L, T) – water, river

naga (C, L, T) – mythical serpent being

nákhon (T) – city

nǎng (T) – shadow play

nat (My) – spirit-being with the power to either protect or harm humans; Myanmar's syncretic Buddhism

Negrito (P) – ancient Asian race whose members are distinguished by their black skin, curly hair and short stature

NLD (My) – National League for Democracy

nop (L) – see *wâi*

NPA (L) – National Protected Area

NPA (P) – New People's Army

ojek (I) – motorcycle taxi

opelet (I) – small minibus

Orang Asli (M) – Original People; Malaysian aboriginal people

P (V) – abbreviation of *pho* (street)

padang (M, S) – open grassy area; town square

pantai (B, TL, I, M) – beach

pasar (I, M) – market

pasar malam (I, M) – night market

paya (My) – holy one; often applied to Buddha figures, *zedi* and other religious monuments

Pelni (I) – national shipping line

penginapan (I) – simple lodging house

Peranakan (S) – combination of Malay and Chinese cultures of precolonial Singapore

Ph (C) – abbreviation of *phlauv*

phlauv (C) – road, street; abbreviated as 'Ph'

phleng phêua chii-wít (T) – songs for life; modern Thai folk songs

pho (V) – street; abbreviated as P; also rice-noodle soup

pinisi (I) – fishing boat

polres (I) – local police station

pongyi (My) – Buddhist monk

pousada (TL) – traditional Portuguese lodging

praang (T) – Khmer-style tower structure found on temples; serves the same purpose as a *stupa*

prasat (C, T) – tower, temple

prahoc/prahok (C) – fermented fish sauce

psar (C) – market

pulau (I, M) – island

pwe (My) – show, festival

quan (V) – urban district

raja (B, I, M) – king

Ramakian (T) – Thai version of the *Ramayana*

Ramayana (I, L, M, T) – Indian epic story of Rama's battle with demons

remorque (C) – a kind of motorised rickshaw with a motorcycle-pulled trailer; also called tuk-tuk

roi nuoc (V) – water puppetry

rumah makan (I) – restaurant, food stall

săhmlór (T) – three-wheeled pedicab; also written as *samlor*

samlor (C) – soup

sai-kaa (My) – bicycle rickshaw

sŏrngtăaou (L, T) – small pick-up truck with two benches in the back; also written as săwngthăew

sima (L) – ordination-precinct marker

soi (T) – lane, small street

STB (S) – Singapore Tourism Board, also Sarawak Tourism Board

stung (C) – river

stupa (C, I, L, M, T) – religious monument, often containing Buddha relics

sungai (B, I, M) – river; also written as *sungei*

surat jalan (I) – visitor permit

taman (B, I, M) – park

taman nasional (I) – national park

tambang (M) – double-oared river ferry; small river boat

tamu (B, M) – weekly market

tasik (M) – lake

TAT (T) – Tourism Authority of Thailand

teluk (I, M, S) – bay; also written as *telok*

Tet (V) – lunar New Year

Th (L, T) – abbreviation of *thànŏn*

tâh (T) – ferry, boat pier; also written as *tha*

tâht (L) – Buddhist *stupa*; also written as *that*

thànŏn (L, T) – road, street, avenue; abbreviated as 'Th'

tongkonan (I) – traditional house with roof eaves shaped like buffalo horns

tonlé (C) – river, lake

travel (I) – door-to-door air-con minibus

tukalok (C) – fruit shake made with sweetened condensed milk

túk-túk (L, T) – motorised *săamláw*

tuk-tuk (C) – a kind of motorised rickshaw with a motorcycle-pulled trailer; also called remorque

UXO (C, L, V) – unexploded ordnance

wâi (L, T) – palms-together greeting

wartel (I) – telephone office

warung (I, M) – food stall

wat (C, L, T) – Buddhist temple-monastery

warnet (I) – public internet facility

wayang golek (I) – wooden puppet

wayang kulit (I) – shadow-puppet play enacting tales from the *Ramayana*

wayang orang (I) – dance-drama enacted by masked performers, recounting scenes from the *Ramayana*

wíhăhn (T) – any large hall in a Thai temple, except for the central sanctuary used for official business

wisma (B, I, M, S) – guest house, lodge; office block, shopping centre

xe om (V) – motorbike taxi

yama (C) – Hindu god of death; crystal meth

zedi (My) – see *stupa*

behind the scenes

SEND US YOUR FEEDBACK

We love to hear from travellers – your comments keep us on our toes and help make our books better. Our well-travelled team reads every word on what you loved or loathed about this book. Although we cannot reply individually to postal submissions, we always guarantee that your feedback goes straight to the appropriate authors, in time for the next edition. Each person who sends us information is thanked in the next edition – the most useful submissions are rewarded with a selection of digital PDF chapters.

Visit **lonelyplanet.com/contact** to submit your updates and suggestions or to ask for help. Our award-winning website also features inspirational travel stories, news and discussions.

Note: We may edit, reproduce and incorporate your comments in Lonely Planet products such as guidebooks, websites and digital products, so let us know if you don't want your comments reproduced or your name acknowledged. For a copy of our privacy policy visit lonelyplanet.com/privacy.

OUR READERS

Many thanks to the travellers who used the last edition and wrote to us with helpful hints, useful advice and interesting anecdotes:

Karin Åkerman, Michael Allsopp, Monica Angulo, Benjamin Back, Jacqui Barfoot, Peter Berende, Christian Berker, Gerard Boekel, Travis Bogle, Thomas Cahill, Hannah Carnegie, Felipe Castro, Reynaldo Chialendra, Isabel Coghe, Lucy Crane, Kristin Czernietzki, Miquel Dalmau, Delphine, Martina Dempsey, Rosalinda A Di Stefano, Philipp Drachenberg, Donna-Lee Fancy, Daniel Garcia, Wayne Geerling, Antony Gillingham, Brook Glanville, Dagmar Goehring, Nathaniel Grabman, Andreas Hagan, Gina Haschke, Thomas Jusjong Kull Henriksen, Carlos Hernandez, Andy Herrmann, Damon Horrell, Nicole Jacobson, Joris Jan Voermans, Jeremy Johnson, Simon Jungo, David Kennemer, Justin Klein, Robert Kovacs, M Lambert, Geugje Luik, Michael Magee, Kevin Mannion, Alan Matis, Andrew Mazur, David Menkes, Wouter Meyers, Jason Miller, Katie Miller, John Moloney, Astrid Mrkich, Caroline Murray-Lyon, Kelly Ng, Elisabeth Nielsen, Micheal O'Dea, Viktor Olsson, Denise O'Riordan, Lourie Parel, Elizabeth Pomerantz, Marin Postel, Matt Price, Kimberley Robson, Joseph Ronsyn, Vicki Rothwell, Rebecka Rudström, James Sabin, Daniel Salt, Gunnar Schaefer, Adam Schmidt, Doris Schneidtinger, Ken Silver, Alexander Spivack, Simone Straub, Thibault, Seth Thibault, Morgan Tipper, Amy Tran, Anthony Treadwell, Eline Thijssen, Thijs van den Burg, Alexandra von Muralt, Jim Wallen, David Webb, Sean Wickham, Monica Wilcox, Philipp Winterberg, Inga Wohlleben, Michael Wu, William Wu, Lina Yang, Luis Gutierrez Zapata.

AUTHOR THANKS

China Williams

Thanks ever so much to Nong who was a wonderful second mother to Felix and a good 'wife' to me. Many thanks to Lisa on Ko Chang and Chris and Gae in Hua Hin for showing me around. Felix sends his love to the gals at Seven Hotel (Kan, Goong and Pa too). To Mason and Jane for the brain dump and welcome dinner; Joe and Kong for coffee talk; and Ruengsang for her savoir-faire. And to my husband who survived so long without us; it is good to be home. Final shout-out to Southeast Asia's seasoned co-authors (y'all are beginning to feel like family) and the LP crew.

Greg Bloom

The cumulative knowledge of my *barkada* in Manila was elemental as usual. A special nod to the Edes, Donahue, Fitzpatrick and Blythe clans for putting me up; to Johnny Weekend for tagging along (and researching typhoon travel between Romblon and Batangas); to Glen for the research company on the Boracay-to-PG route; to Peng for the QC bar tour; and to Anna for keeping me sane on the world's worst deadline. Thanks also to her mama for holding down the fort.

Celeste Brash

Thanks to my family for eating so much soup, to Peck Choo Ho and Brandon Tan for durian, Joann Khaw for chicken feet, Eawasian for flat beer and great curry, Emre Sirakaya for shamans, Stephan and Leonie for history, John Wilson for being Irish, Sean Low for hiking fast, Alison and Narelle for style and la famille Ponton for papaya and pictures. Thanks to China and Ilaria for organisation and innovation and to Daniel Robinson for Borneo and baby pics.

Stuart Butler

First and foremost I must thank my wife, Heather, for her patience and understanding on this project and to my baby son Jake for putting up with his daddy going away for so long. Thanks also to my parents for their babysitting skills when my wife joined me on the road and to Gui Girbon for tackling One Palm Point with me. Finally, thank you to all the wonderful Indonesians and to my, equally wonderful, fellow travellers for their advice, tips and just general good company.

Jayne D'Arcy

Thanks to the ever-helpful and cheerful Tracey Morgan, Friends of Suai's Pat Jesson and Friends of Los Palos' Linda Wimetal and Barb Godfrey. Also to Julio Cardoso in Maliana and Tony Armindo in Dili. Thanks again to Sharik Billington and Miles.

Shawn Low

As always thanks to the CE: Ilaria for believing, hiring and being just generally cool. Cheers also to CA: China (yet another one done and dusted!). Thanks to the LP crew who are working on this: eds, cartos, MEs, LDs etc. I've been behind the scenes and know how hard you all work. Big props to co-author Daniel. It was good hanging out. To everyone else I might have forgotten: apologies in advance. Will buy you a round of Tiger if you remind me next time our paths cross. This book will always bear bittersweet memories...

Brandon Presser

As always, a big thank you to the Bambridges for providing the best home-away-from-home on the (lonely) planet. At LP, special thanks to China Williams and Ilaria Walker.

Nick Ray

As always a heartfelt thanks to the people of the Mekong region, whose warmth and humour, stoicism and spirit make it a humbling place to be. Biggest thanks are reserved for my lovely wife Kulikar Sotho and to our young children Julian and Belle for enlivening our lives immeasurably. Thanks to fellow travellers and residents, friends and contacts in the Mekong region who have helped shaped my knowledge and experience in this country. There is no room to thank everyone, but you all know who you are.

Simon Richmond

I was very fortunate on this project to work with a brilliant team of authors and have encouraging support from Ilaria, David, Bruce and the editorial crew at LP HQ. A huge thanks to Scotty Lazar and Michelle St Clair for their hospitality, indefatigable William Myatwunna, his colleague Richard Soe Myint and my driver Chan Ko. I also very much appreciate the time granted and expertise shared by many Burma experts and fellow travellers.

Daniel Robinson

Literally hundreds of people went out of their way to make this a better book, but I'm especially indebted to (in alphabetical order) Al Davies, Captain David (Bennet), Donald & Marina Tan, Eric & Annie Yap, Glenn & Kat van Zutphen, Jessie from the Sibu tourist office, Kelvin Egay, Mrs Lee of Miri, Philip Yong, Rudy Chong and the people of Bario. I dedicate my chapters to my ever-supportive wife Rachel and our beloved son Yair, who's almost one year old.

Adam Skolnick

I'm forever indebted to my good friends in Bali, Nusa Tenggarra and Papua who always make me feel at home. This time around big thanks are owed to Astrid and Grace, Marcus and Harriett, and Simon and Jane on Gili T, Rosa on Gili Air, Church, Paul and the Wicked team in LBJ, my Sumba family at Pantai Oro, and to the great Edwin Lerrick in Kupang. Thanks also to Dex and Mel and the Papua Paradise team in the Raja Ampats, and Kazutaka Fujiwara in Wamena.

Iain Stewart

Many thanks to Ilaria and the Melbourne team for inviting me aboard and China for steering the ship along a steady course. It was great to work with Nick, Peter and Brett in Vietnam. I was greatly aided by kings of the highway Vinh Vu and Mark Wyndham, Ben and Bich in Phong Nha, Tam in Dong Ha, and a great crew in Hoi An including the Dive Bar posse, Ludo, Neil and Caroline and Dzung the tennis ace.

Ryan Ver Berkmoes

This list just seems to grow. Many thanks to friends like Hanafi, Jeremy Allan, Eliot Cohen, Jamie James, Kerry and Milton Turner, Ibu

Cat, Patricia Miklautsch, Pascal & Pika, Neal Harrison, ace filmmaker Dean Allen Tolhurst and the tireless Abba and Michael. At LP, thanks to my buddy Ilaria Walker and the entire publishing and production teams for guidance, understanding and the ability to fix a lot of bad spelling. Co-authors Adam Skolnick and Stuart Butler rock.

Richard Waters

Special thanks to my fiance Ali and kids Finn and Aggie who watch me disappear with a pack on my back at regular intervals. Thanks too to my commissioning ed, Ilaria Walker who sends me to interesting places, mostly involving mosquitoes. In Laos my thanks to Michel Marcel Saada, Matt Verborg, Vong, Somkiad, Derek Beattie, Sousath Travel, WWF, Green Discovery, COPE, MAG and Mark at Apple Regent St who fixed my Mac before this trip.

ACKNOWLEDGMENTS

Climate map data adapted from Peel MC, Finlayson BL & McMahon TA (2007) 'Updated World Map of the Köppen-Geiger Climate Classification', *Hydrology and Earth System Sciences*, 11, 163344.

Illustrations p94 and p95 by Javier Zarracina.

Cover photography: (main) People crossing U Bien's bridge at sunset/Jane Sweeney/ Lonely Planet Images; (inset above) Monks at Shwe Yaunghwe Kyaung temple, Myanmar/ John Elk III/Lonely Planet Images; (inset centre) Longtail boat, Krabi, Thailand/ KKR/Image Broker; (inset below) Túk-túk in Bangkok, Thailand/Jean-Pierre Lescourret/ Lonely Planet Images

Many of the images in this guide are available for licensing from Lonely Planet Images: www.lonelyplanetimages.com.

This Book

This is the 16th edition of *Southeast Asia on a Shoestring*. The 1st edition was written by Tony and Maureen Wheeler in 1975, funded by the cult success of their first guidebook, *Across Asia on the Cheap*, a compilation of journey notes put together back in 1973. As the scope of the book grew, so did the need to share the load: this edition is the work of 14 authors. Coordinating author extraordinaire China Williams led a stellar team: Greg Bloom, Celeste Brash, Stuart Butler, Jayne D'Arcy, Shawn Low, Brandon Presser, Nick Ray, Simon Richmond, Daniel Robinson, Adam Skolnick, Iain Stewart, Ryan Ver Berkmoes and Richard Waters. Original research for Indonesia was provided by Stuart Butler and Adam Skolnick. Original Malaysia research was provided by Celeste Brash, Adam Karlin and Simon Richmond. Original research for Myanmar (Burma) was provided by Austin Bush and Mark Elliott. Original research for the Philippines was provided by Michael Grosberg, Trent Holden and Adam Karlin. Original Thailand research was provided by Mark Beales, Tim Bewer, Celeste Brash, Austin Bush and Alan Murphy. Original research for Timor-Leste was provided by Rodney Cocks. Original research for Vietnam was provided by Brett Atkinson, Peter Dragicevic and Nick Ray. The Health chapter was adapted from an original chapter written by Dr Trish Batchelor. This guidebook was commissioned in Lonely Planet's Melbourne office, and produced by the following:

Commissioning Editor Ilaria Walker

Coordinating Editors Nigel Chin, Catherine Naghten, Martine Power, Kate Whitfield

Coordinating Cartographer Diana Von Holdt

Coordinating Layout Designer Jacqui Saunders

Managing Editor Bruce Evans

Managing Cartographer David Connolly, Amanda Sierp

Managing Layout Designer Jane Hart

Assisting Editors Gordon Farrer, Emma Gilmour, Paul Harding, Kristin Odijk, Alison Ridgway, Ross Taylor, Fionn Twomey, Simon Williamson

Assisting Cartographers Jane Chapman, Valentina Krementchutskaya, Anthony Phelan, Mick Garrett, Sophie Reed, Csanad Csutoros

Cover Research Naomi Parker

Internal Image Research Aude Vauconsant

Language Content Branislava Vladisavljevic, Annelies Mertens

Thanks to Elin Berglund, Laura Crawford, Brigitte Ellemor, Ryan Evans, James Hardy, Evan Jones, Yvonne Kirk, Trent Paton, Laura Stansfeld, Navin Sushil, Gerard Walker

index

000 Map pages
000 Photo pages

F

G

000 Map pages
000 Photo pages

H

I

J

K

L

M

N

O

P

000 Map pages
000 Photo pages

T

000 Map pages
000 Photo pages

U

V

000 Map pages
000 Photo pages

how to use this book

These symbols will help you find the listings you want:

- Sights
- Beaches
- Activities
- Courses
- Tours
- Festivals & Events
- Sleeping
- Eating
- Drinking
- Entertainment
- Shopping
- Information/ Transport

These symbols give you the vital information for each listing:

- Telephone Numbers
- Opening Hours
- Parking
- Nonsmoking
- Air-Conditioning
- Internet Access
- Wi-Fi Access
- Swimming Pool
- Vegetarian Selection
- English-Language Menu
- Family-Friendly
- Pet-Friendly
- Bus
- Ferry
- Metro
- Subway
- Tram
- Train

Reviews are organised by author preference.

Look out for these icons:

- TOP CHOICE — Our author's recommendation
- FREE — No payment required
- A green or sustainable option

Our authors have nominated these places as demonstrating a strong commitment to sustainability – for example by supporting local communities and producers, operating in an environmentally friendly way, or supporting conservation projects.

Map Legend

Sights
- Beach
- Buddhist
- Castle
- Christian
- Hindu
- Islamic
- Jewish
- Monument
- Museum/Gallery
- Ruin
- Winery/Vineyard
- Zoo
- Other Sight

Activities, Courses & Tours
- Diving/Snorkelling
- Canoeing/Kayaking
- Skiing
- Surfing
- Swimming/Pool
- Walking
- Windsurfing
- Other Activity/ Course/Tour

Sleeping
- Sleeping
- Camping

Eating
- Eating

Drinking
- Drinking
- Cafe

Entertainment
- Entertainment

Shopping
- Shopping

Information
- Bank
- Embassy/ Consulate
- Hospital/Medical
- Internet
- Police
- Post Office
- Telephone
- Toilet
- Tourist Information
- Other Information

Transport
- Airport
- Border Crossing
- Bus
- Cable Car/ Funicular
- Cycling
- Ferry
- Metro
- Monorail
- Parking
- Petrol Station
- Taxi
- Train/Railway
- Tram
- Other Transport

Routes
- Tollway
- Freeway
- Primary
- Secondary
- Tertiary
- Lane
- Unsealed Road
- Plaza/Mall
- Steps
- Tunnel
- Pedestrian Overpass
- Walking Tour
- Walking Tour Detour
- Path

Geographic
- Hut/Shelter
- Lighthouse
- Lookout
- Mountain/Volcano
- Oasis
- Park
- Pass
- Picnic Area
- Waterfall

Population
- Capital (National)
- Capital (State/Province)
- City/Large Town
- Town/Village

Boundaries
- International
- State/Province
- Disputed
- Regional/Suburb
- Marine Park
- Cliff
- Wall

Hydrography
- River, Creek
- Intermittent River
- Swamp/Mangrove
- Reef
- Canal
- Water
- Dry/Salt/ Intermittent Lake
- Glacier

Areas
- Beach/Desert
- Cemetery (Christian)
- Cemetery (Other)
- Park/Forest
- Sportsground
- Sight (Building)
- Top Sight (Building)

Iain Stewart

Vietnam Iain Stewart first visited, and was captivated by Vietnam as a traveller in 1991 (armed with a trusty Lonely Planet). He's now a Brighton-based writer, specialising in hot countries a long way from his English seaside abode. For this trip he biked the Ho Chi Minh Highway, sailed to the Chams, drank in Danang and explored the heart of Phong Nha.

Ryan Ver Berkmoes

Indonesia Chapter Coordinator, Bali, Maluku, Sulawesi Ryan Ver Berkmoes first visited Indonesia in 1993. On his visits since he has criss-crossed the archipelago, trying to make a dent in those 17,000 islands. Recent thrills included finally reaching the amazing Banda Islands after 18 years of trying, finding the perfect flat on Bali and being given the seat of honour at a Torajan funeral ceremony (it wasn't his, fortunately). Off-island, Ryan lives in Portland, Oregon and writes about Indonesia, travel and more at ryanverberkmoes.com.

Richard Waters

Laos, Kalimantan A visit to Laos in 1999 as the country was still warming to the west, began a close association with the country that sees Richard returning regularly. His first travels were around Europe as a teenager, then Central America and US by camper van. Writing the Kalimantan chapter was like a journey back in time and a privilege. These days he writes and shoots for *The Sunday Times*, *Independent* and *Observer*. To read more of his work and articles about Laos, visit www.richardwaters.co.uk. He lives with his family in the Cotswolds.